D1294082

The SAGE Handbook of ORGANIZATION STUDIES

second edition

Editorial Board

The SAGE Handbook of
ORGANIZATION
STUDIES second edition

Edited by STEWART R. CLEGG,
CYNTHIA HARDY, THOMAS B. LAWRENCE
and WALTER R. NORD

SAGE Publications
London ● Thousand Oaks ● New Delhi

SAGE Publications Ltd
1 Oliver's Yard
55 City Road
London EC1Y 1SP

SAGE Publications Inc.
2455 Teller Road
Thousand Oaks, California 91320

SAGE Publications India Pvt Ltd
B-42, Panchsheel Enclave
Post Box 4109
New Delhi 110 017

British Library Cataloguing in Publication data

A catalogue record for this book is available from British Library

ISBN-10 0-7619-4996-8
ISBN-13 978-0-7619-4996-1

Library of Congress Control Number: 2005932949

Typeset by C&M Digitals (P) Ltd., Chennai, India
Printed in Great Britain by The Cromwell Press, Ltd., Trowbridge, Wiltshire
Printed on paper from sustainable resources

Contents

Contents

Contributors

Mats Alvesson is a Professor at the Department of Business Administration, Lund University, Sweden. He is interested in critical theory, qualitative method, organizational culture and symbolism, identity, power and leadership. Most of his empirical work has focused on knowledge-intensive organizations. He has published 20 books in these areas, the most recent ones are *Understanding Organizational Culture* (2002, Sage), *Postmodernism and Social Research* (2002, Open University Press) and *Knowledge Work and Knowledge-intensive Firms* (2004, Oxford University Press).

Jay B. Barney is a Professor of Management and holder of the Bank One Chair for Excellence in Corporate Strategy at the Max M. Fisher College of Business, The Ohio State University, USA. He received his undergraduate degree from Brigham Young University and his master's and doctorate from Yale University. Professor Barney taught at the Anderson Graduate School of Management at UCLA and Texas A&M University before joining the faculty at Ohio State in 1994 where he teaches organizational strategy and policy to MBA and PhD students. He also has taught in a variety of executive training programmes at various universities and at several firms, including AEP, SBC, Nationwide and McKinsey & Company. Professor Barney has received teaching awards at UCLA, Texas A&M and Ohio State. He has consulted with a wide variety of public and private organizations, including Hewlett-Packard, Texas Instruments, Tenneco, Arco, Koch Industries Inc., McKinsey and Company, Nationwide Insurance, Columbus Public Schools and others. His consulting focuses on implementing large-scale organizational change and strategic analysis.

Joel A.C. Baum is Canadian National Professor of Strategy and Organization at the Rotman School of Management (with a cross-appointment to the Department of Sociology), University of Toronto, Canada, where he teaches competitive strategy and organization theory. Joel is interested in patterns of competition and co-operation among firms, and their influence on firm behaviour and learning. His recent publications include a series of articles exploring the dynamics of interfirm networks, in particular the evolution of intermediate network structures (e.g. cliques) and the ties connecting them, which are fundamental to 'small world' network phenomena. Joel is a member of the editorial boards of *Administrative Science Quarterly* and *Academy of Management Journal*, editor-in-chief of *Advances in Strategic Management* and founding co-editor of *Strategic Organization*.

Max H. Bazerman is the Jesse Isador Strauss Professor of Business Administration at the Harvard Business School. Max is also formally affiliated with the Kennedy School of Government, the Psychology Department and the Program on Negotiation at Harvard, USA. Max's recent books include *Predictable Surprises* (2004, Harvard Business School Press, with Michael Watkins), *You Can't Enlarge the Pie: The Psychology of Ineffective Government* (2001, Basic Books, with J. Baron and K. Shonk) and *Judgment in Managerial Decision Making* (2006, Wiley, now in its 6th edn). He is a member of the editorial boards of the *Journal of Behavioral Decision Making, American Behavioral Scientist, Journal of Management and Governance, The Journal of Psychology and Financial Markets* and the *International Journal of Conflict Management*, and is a member of the international advisory board of the *Negotiation Journal*. Max's former doctoral students have accepted positions at leading business schools throughout the US, including Kellogg, Duke, Cornell, Carnegie-Mellon, Stanford, Chicago, Notre Dame, Columbia and the Harvard Business School. In 2003, Max received the Everett Mendelsohn Excellence in Mentoring Award from Harvard University's Graduate School of Arts and Sciences.

Suzanne Benn is a Senior Lecturer in the School of Management, University of Technology Sydney (UTS), Australia, where she lectures in corporate sustainability. She is a researcher with the Corporate Sustainability Project at UTS, where she conducts research in organizational change for sustainability, multiple stakeholder arrangements for sustainability and environmental governance. She is a co-author of the text, *Organisational Change for Corporate Sustainability* (2003, Routledge) and of a number of book chapters either currently in press or already published by Palgrave Macmillan, Edward Elgar, Greenleaf Publications and University of British Columbia Press. Her works are also published or in press in journals including *Journal of Risk Research, International Journal for Innovation Research, Policy Analysis and Best Practice, Australian Journal of Political Science, AMBIO, ANZAM* and *Journal of Environmental Management*.

Suzanne Boys is a doctoral candidate at Texas A&M University, USA. Her primary research interest is on organizational communication processes in religious organizations. She is currently researching the priest abuse case in the Catholic Church with a two-fold goal. First, the project foregrounds how stakeholders dialogue about the case through crisis communication, issue management discourse and personal narratives. Secondly, it articulates the implications of engaging a dialogic conceptualization of public relations scholarship. Suzanne's research is situated at the nexus of organizational communication and public relations scholarship.

Alan Bryman is Professor of Organisational and Social Research in the Management Centre, University of Leicester, England. His main research interests lie in research methodology, leadership studies, organizational analysis, the process of Disneyization and theme parks. Currently, he has a specific interest in leadership in higher education. He is author or co-author of many books, including *Quantity and Quality in Social Research* (1988, Routledge), *Social Research Methods* (2001, 2004, Oxford University Press) and *The Disneyization of Society* (2004, Sage). He is co-editor of *The SAGE Encyclopedia of Social Science Research* (2004, Sage) and the *Handbook of Data Analysis* (2004, Sage). He has also contributed to numerous journals.

Marta B. Calás is Associate Professor of Organization Studies and International Management at the Department of Management, Isenberg School of Management, and adjunct professor of Women's Studies, at the Women's Studies Program, University of Massachusetts-Amherst, USA. In her scholarly work, in collaboration with Linda Smircich, she applies perspectives from poststructuralism, cultural studies, feminist postmodernism and postcolonial/transnational theorizing to interrogate and retheorize areas of organizational scholarship such as 'globalization', 'leadership', 'business ethics' and 'information technology'. Through these perspectives she also analyses the logics behind contemporary institutions, such as universities or other work organizations. She is an editor of *Organization: The critical journal of organization, theory & society*.

Stewart R. Clegg is Research Professor at the University of Technology, Sydney, Australia, and Director of ICAN Research (www.ican.uts.edu.au); a Visiting Professor of Organizational Change Management, Maastricht University Faculty of Business; a Visiting Professor at the University of Aston Business School as well as the Vrije University of Amsterdam, where he is Visiting Professor and International Fellow in Discourse and Management Theory, Centre of Comparative Social Studies. He is a prolific publisher in the leading academic journals in management and organization theory and contributor to scholarly collections, where over 200 of his publications may be found, in journals such as *Academy of Management Learning and Education, Administrative Science Quarterly, Organization Science, Organization Studies, Organization, Human Relations, Management Learning* and many others, as well as the author and editor of many books, the most recent of which is *Managing and Organizations* (2005, Sage, with Martin Kornberger and Tyrone Pitsis, Thousand Oaks, CA). He has been an elected Fellow of the Academy of the Social Sciences in Australia since 1988, a Distinguished Fellow of the Australian and New Zealand Academy of Management since 1998 and a Fellow of the Aston Academy since 2005.

Stanley A. Deetz, PhD, is Professor of Communication at the University of Colorado at Boulder, USA. His research primarily focuses on relations of power in work sites and the way these relations are produced and reproduced in everyday interaction. Normatively this work attempts to produce governance structures, decision processes and communicative micropractices that lead to more satisfying work experiences and more inclusive, collaborative and creative decisions. His books include *Leading Organizations through Transitions* (2000, Sage) and *Doing Critical Management Research* (2000, Sage), *Transforming Communication, Transforming Business* (1995, Hampton) and *Democracy in an Age of Corporate Colonization* (1992, SUNY). He has published around 100 essays in scholarly journals and books regarding stakeholder representation, decision-making, culture and communication in corporate organizations and has lectured widely in the US and Europe. He is a Fellow of the International Communication Association serving as its President, 1996–1997, a National Communication Association Distinguished Scholar, and has held many other elected professional positions. He is also an active consultant for companies in the US and Europe. http://comm.colorado.edu/deetz

Marcus W. Dickson is Associate Professor of Industrial/Organizational Psychology at Wayne State University, in Detroit, Michigan, USA. His research has primarily focused on issues of leadership and culture, including culture at the group, organization and societal levels of analysis. He has served as Co-Principal Investigator on the Global Leadership and Organizational Behavior Effectiveness (GLOBE) Research Project (a 62-country study of leadership and culture) and as director of the doctoral programme in I/O Psychology at Wayne State. He is currently working on a book (with Deanne Den Hartog of the University of Amsterdam) on cultural issues in leadership.

Deborah Dougherty received her PhD in Management from M.I.T. She has held academic positions at the Wharton School and McGill University, and is now Professor at Rutgers University, USA. Her scholarship concerns organizing for sustained innovation in complex organizations; new product development; innovation in services; and knowledge management. Currently, she is delving into drug discovery and development in the bio-pharmaceutical sector. She teaches Managing Technology and Innovation, Principles of Management, Managing Strategic Transformation and PhD seminars in Qualitative Methods and Organization Theory. She was elected chair of the Technology and Innovation Management Division of the Academy of Management, is a senior editor for *Organization Science* and has served or is now serving on the editorial boards for *Academy of Management Review, Organization Science, Journal of Business Venturing, Journal of Product Innovation Management, Strategic Organization* and *Organization Studies*.

Jane E. Dutton is the William Russell Kelly Professor of Business Administration at the Stephen M. Ross School of Business at the University of Michigan, USA. She received her PhD from Northwestern and was on the faculty of New York University before joining the University of Michigan. Jane's current research focuses on how organizational conditions enable human thriving. In particular, she focuses on how the quality of connection between people at work affects individual and organizational flourishing. Her research explores compassion and organizations, resilience and organizations, as well as energy and organizations. Her previous work was on the management of strategic change. She is a co-founder of the Center for Positive Organizational Scholarship (see http://www.bus.umich.edu/positive/) and has just become chairperson of the Management and Organizations at the Ross School of Business.

Colin Eden is Professor of Management Science and Strategic Management at the University of Strathclyde Graduate School of Business in Glasgow, Scotland. His most recent books are *The Practice of Making Strategy* (2005, Sage) and *Visible Thinking* (2004, Wiley). He has written over 160 articles for the management science, project management and general management journals. His current particular interests lie in understanding the group processes of strategy making within top management teams and in understanding the failure of complex projects.

Stephen Fineman is Professor of Organizational Behaviour and Head of Research at the School of Management, University of Bath, England. His chapter in this book reflects a long interest in emotion in organizations and with both critical and qualitative approaches to organizational studies. Recent books include *Understanding Emotion at Work* (2003, Sage) and *Emotion in Organizations*, 2nd edn (2000, Sage). He has written a major critique of positive organizational scholarship, published in the *Academy of Management Review* (2006) and co-authored a best-selling introductory text on organizational behaviour, *Organizing and Organization*, 3rd edn (2005, Sage).

Bent Flyvbjerg is Professor of Planning at Aalborg University, Denmark, where he teaches urban policy and planning. He was twice a Visiting Fulbright Scholar to the US, where he did research at UCLA, UC Berkeley and Harvard University. He was a Visiting Fellow with The

European University Institute in Florence. He is the author of numerous publications in 15 languages. His most recent books in English are *Megaprojects and Risk: an Anatomy of Ambition* (2003, Cambridge University Press), *Making Social Science Matter* (2001, Cambridge University Press) and *Rationality and Power* (1998, University of Chicago Press). He is currently doing research on the relationship between truth and lying in policy and planning.

Linda C. Forbes is an Assistant Professor of Organizational Studies at Franklin & Marshall College, Lancaster, PA, USA. Her research interests include cultural studies and symbolism, environmental philosophy and policy and varieties of qualitative inquiry. In a recent project, she researched and interviewed Pete Seeger (music legend, author and storyteller, political and environmental activist and grassroots organizer) on his environmental advocacy, organizing and education in the Hudson River Valley (2004, *Organization & Environment*; republished 2005, *Monthly Review*).

The late **Peter J. Frost** was the Edgar Kaiser Chair of Organizational Behavior at the Sauder School of Business at the University of British Columbia, USA. He was known as an innovative academic who also had managerial and leadership roles during his career. His research and teaching over the past 28 years was mainly on the topic of leadership, organizational culture and emotions in the workplace. He wrote an award-winning book entitled *Toxic Emotions at Work* (2003, Harvard Business School Press) as a result of his experience of emotions in the workplace. Peter wrote about his involvement with this research topic: 'I was thrust into this arena as a result of a personal encounter with melanoma cancer. I had a skin level version of this some 12 years ago. In 1997, specialists at the BC Cancer found that the cancer had metastasized to lymph nodes in my neck that required removal through surgery. This rather traumatic event in my life changed my priorities and my perspective of life and the experiences I had in the hospital ward following surgery opened my eyes to the way compassionate acts can make a difference to people who are suffering. I began to write about compassion and related it to life at work. It is where many of us spend most of our waking hours. And the study of behaviour in organizations is something I do for a living. There seemed, thus, a natural fit between the topics of pain and compassion and the redirection of my research'. Peter founded the 'compassionlab' along with Jane Dutton (see www.compassionlab.com) to advance organizational scholars knowledge about compassion at work. Peter experienced a fatal recurrence of his cancer in 2004. This Handbook chapter was his final piece of academic writing and we are proud to see it published posthumously as a tribute to his dedication to the study of compassion in organizations.

Pasquale Gagliardi is Professor of Sociology of Organization at the Catholic University of Milan, Italy, and Managing Director of ISTUD (Istituto Studi Direzionali, an Italian management institute at Stresa, on Lake Maggiore). Before launching his academic career, he worked as a consultant to many large Italian corporations. During the 1980s he contributed to the foundation and development in Europe of SCOS, the Standing Conference on Organizational Symbolism. His present research focuses on the relationship between culture, aesthetic knowledge and organizational order. He has widely published books and articles on these topics in Italian and English. Among his publications: *Le imprese come culture* (1986, Isedi); *Symbols and Artifacts: Views of the Corporate Landscape* (1990, de Gruyter); *Studies of Organizations in the European Tradition* (1995, Jai Press), co-edited with Sam Bacharach and Bryan Mundell; *Narratives We Organize By* (2003, Benjamins), co-edited with Barbara Czarniawska. Professor

Gagliardi is at present Secretary General of the Giorgio Cini Foundation in Venice. He also serves on the Editorial Boards of *Organization Studies* and *Organization*.

Tiffany Galvin is currently an Assistant Professor of Organization Studies at the Isenberg School of Management at the University of Massachusetts in Amherst, MA, USA. She has also worked at the University of Utah and the University of Texas at Dallas. She received her PhD in Organization Behavior at Northwestern University. Her teaching areas include strategic management, power and politics in organizations, organization theory and research design. Her research interests revolve around understanding the dynamic elements of institutional change processes over time with particular attention given to the role of conflict and contestation frameworks (cognition) at the individual, organization and field level of analysis. Other projects extend on some of these issues, but investigate the role of institutional processes in relation to organizational identity, reputation, legitimacy and image and interorganizational relationships.

Royston Greenwood is the Telus Professor of Strategic Management, and Associate Dean (Research) at the School of Business, University of Alberta, Canada. He is also the Director of the School's inter-disciplinary Centre for Professional Service Firm Management. Professor Greenwood has two primary research interests: organizational change and the emergence of new organizational forms, which he has been studying since the mid-1980s from the perspective of institutional theory; and the organization of professional service firms, which are highly successful yet sadly neglected exemplars of knowledge-intensive organizations. His research into these topics has appeared in the *Academy of Management Journal*, the *Administrative Science Quarterly*, the *Strategic Management Journal*, *Organization Studies*, *Organization Science* and the *Academy of Management Review*. Professor Greenwood received the 2003 JMI Scholar Award from the Western Academy of Management. Currently he serves on the editorial boards of the *Academy of Management Journal*, *Organization Science*, *Organization Studies* and the *Journal of Management Studies*. He is a founding co-editor of *Strategic Organization*. British by birth and education, Professor Greenwood remains bemused by the North American obsession with baseball and is an avid although sorely disappointed fan of Leeds United FC. His ambition is to see Leeds United win the European Cup.

Cynthia Hardy is Professor of Management at the University of Melbourne, Australia, co-director of the International Centre for Research on Organizational Discourse, Strategy & Change and Visiting Professor at the University of Leicester. Her main research interests revolve around the study of power and politics in organizations, organizational discourse theory and critical discourse analysis, and she is particularly interested in how power and politics occur within a larger discursive context. She recently published *Discourse Analysis: Investigating Processes of Social Construction* with Nelson Phillips, as well as co-editing a special issue of *Organization Studies* on organizational discourse and the Sage *Handbook of Organizational Discourse*. In total, she has published 12 books and edited volumes, including the *Handbook of Organization Studies* (1996, Sage), which won the George R. Terry Book Award at the 1997 Academy of Management. She has written over 60 journal articles and book chapters, and her work has appeared in many leading international journals, including the *Academy of Management Journal*, *Academy of Management Review*,

Organization Studies, Journal of Management Studies, Human Relations, Organization Science and *California Management Review*.

William Hesterly is the Zeke Dumke Professor of Management in the David Eccles School of Business at the University of Utah, USA. Along with Jay Barney of Ohio State University, he is the author of *Strategic Management and Competitive Advantage*, which is published by Prentice-Hall. His research on organizational economics, vertical integration, organizational forms and entrepreneurial networks has appeared in top journals including the *Academy of Management Review, Organization Science, Strategic Management Journal, Journal of Management* and the *Journal of Economic Behavior and Organization*. His research on the history of innovation in Major League Baseball recently appeared in *Business History*. He received the Western Academy of Management's Ascendant Scholar Award in 1999. Dr Hesterly serves on the editorial board of *Strategic Organization* and has previously served on the boards of *Organization Science* and the *Journal of Management*. He received his PhD from the University of California, Los Angeles.

C.R. (Bob) Hinings is Professor Emeritus in the Department of Strategic Management and Organization, School of Business, University of Alberta, Canada, and Senior Research Fellow in the Centre for Entrepreneurship and Family Enterprise. He is currently carrying out research on strategic organizational change in professional service firms, healthcare and the Canadian wine industry. He is a Fellow of the Royal Society of Canada, a Fellow of the US Academy of Management and Honorary Member of the European Group for Organizational Studies. He has been a recipient of the Distinguished Scholar Award from the Organization and Management Theory Division of the US Academy of Management.

Chris Huxham is a Senior Fellow of the Advanced Institute of Management Research and Professor of Management and Director of Research in the University of Strathclyde Graduate School of Business. She has led an action research programme spanning more than 16 years that is concerned with the development of practice-oriented theory relating to the management of collaborative ventures. Her book with Siv Vangen, *Managing to Collaborate: the Theory and Practice of Collaborative Advantage* (2005, Routledge, London) draws this work together. She is Vice Chair of the British Academy of Management and was initiating convener of its special interest group on Interorganizational Relations. She regularly works with managers engaged in collaborative initiatives and was a member of the Scottish government task force on Community Planning.

John M. Jermier is Exide Professor of Sustainable Enterprise Research and Professor of Organizational Behavior at the University of South Florida, Tampa, USA. He is co-founding editor (with Paul Shrivastava) and current editor of the Sage journal, *Organization & Environment* (www.coba.usf.edu/jermier/journal.htm). His current interests include critical social theory, the greening of organizations and new forms of leadership.

Jason M. Kanov received his PhD in Organizational Psychology from the University of Michigan, USA, and is currently the Albers Fellow Visiting Assistant Professor of Management at the Albers Business School at Seattle University. His research focuses on feeling and relating at work. In addition to studying compassion, he is particularly interested in exploring the nature and subjective experience of interpersonal disconnection and developing an understanding of how instances of interpersonal disconnection impact the social life of organizations.

Thomas B. Lawrence is the Weyerhaeuser Professor of Change Management at Simon Fraser University in Vancouver, Canada. He received his PhD in organizational analysis from the University of Alberta in 1993. His research focuses on the dynamics of power, change and institutions in organizations and organizational fields. It has appeared in such journals as *Academy of Management Journal, Academy of Management Review, Harvard Business Review, Sloan Management Review, Human Relations, Journal of Management, Journal of Management Studies, Organization Studies, Organization, Journal of Organizational Behavior* and *Journal of Management Inquiry.*

Jacoba M. Lilius is a PhD candidate in the University of Michigan's, USA, Organizational Psychology programme. She received her BS in Psychology from the University of Western Ontario. In addition to her work with the compassionlab, her broad research focus is on how support among work colleagues contributes to organizational functioning. She is currently studying support processes and quality of care in nursing homes.

Steve Maguire is Assistant Professor of Strategy and Organization in the Faculty of Management at McGill University, USA. He received his PhD from HEC-Montreal in 2000, after spending time at the Santa Fe Institute in their Complex Systems Summer School. Interested in formal models of complex systems, he co-edited (with Bill McKelvey) a special issue of *Emergence* devoted to 'Complexity and Management' and has also authored book chapters on the topic. His empirical research focuses on institutional, technological and organizational change resulting when commercial, scientific and political struggles intersect around social or environmental issues. For example, his doctoral dissertation draws lessons from society's experience with the insecticide DDT and was awarded the Academy of Management's 'Organization and Natural Environment (ONE)' Best Doctoral Dissertation Award in 2001. In addition to *Emergence* and the *Academy of Management Journal,* he has published in *Organization Studies, Strategic Organization, Health Care Management Review, Greener Management International* and *Global Governance.*

Sally Maitlis is an Assistant Professor of Organizational Behavior at the Sauder School of Business at the University of British Columbia, Canada. She received her PhD from the University of Sheffield. Alongside her work with the compassionlab, Sally's research examines the role of emotion in individual and organizational sensemaking and decision-making, and social and political aspects of organizational decision-making processes. She is particularly interested in narrative and discursive approaches to the study of emotion in organizations.

Joanne Martin is the Fred H. Merrill Professor of Organizational Behavior at the Graduate School of Business, Stanford University, USA. She holds a BA from Smith College in Fine Arts, a PhD from the Department of Psychology and Social Relations at Harvard University and an Honorary Doctorate in Economics and Business Administration from the Copenhagen Business School and an honorary doctorate in social sciences from the Free

University in Amsterdam. She is a Fellow of the American Psychological Society, the American Psychological Association and the Academy of Management. She received the Distinguished Scholar award from the Organization and Management Theory Division of the Academy of Management and the Distinguished Educator award from the Academy as a whole. She was awarded the Centennial Medal for research-based 'contributions to society' from the Graduate School of Arts and Sciences at Harvard. Her board experience includes: the Board of Governors of the Academy of Management, the Board of Directors of CPP, Inc. (a test and book publisher), the elected, seven-member Faculty Advisory Board at Stanford University, and the Advisory Board of the International Centre for Research in Organizational Discourse, Strategy and Change for the Universities of Melbourne, Sydney, London and McGill. She has published over 60 academic articles and five books including *Cultures in Organizations: Three Perspectives* (1992, Oxford University Press) and *Organizational Culture: Mapping the Terrain* (2002, Sage). Her current research focuses on gender: the subtle ways gender shapes cultures in organizations and why cross-institutional interventions have a greater chance of alleviating gender inequities.

Rita Gunther McGrath joined the faculty of Columbia Business School, USA, in 1993. Prior to life in academia, she was an IT director, worked in the political arena and founded two startups. Her PhD is from the Wharton School, University of Pennsylvania. McGrath's research focuses on innovation, entrepreneurship and growth strategies. She publishes widely in leading academic journals such as the *Strategic Management Journal, Academy of Management Review, Academy of Management Journal* and *Management Science*. She has been recognized by the Strategic Management Society with the McKinsey 'best paper' award in 2001, by the Industrial Research Institute with its Maurice Holland award (2000), by the Academy of Management for the Academy of Management Review 'best paper' award for 'Falling Forward: Real Options Reasoning and Entrepreneurial Failure' (1999) and numerous other entrepreneurship/strategy awards. She is on the editorial boards of the *Academy of Management Review*, the *Strategic Management Journal* and the *Journal of Business Venturing*.

Bill McKelvey, PhD, MIT 1967, is Professor of Strategic Organizing and Complexity Science at the UCLA, England. His book, *Organizational Systematics* (1982, University of California Press) remains the definitive treatment of organizational evolution and taxonomy. He chaired the building committee that produced the $110 000 000 Anderson Complex at UCLA – opened in 1994. In 1997 he became Director of the Center for Rescuing Strategy and Organization Science (SOS). He was a founder of UCLA's Centre for Human Complex Systems & Computational Social Science. Recently, McKelvey co-edited *Variations in Organization Science* (1999, Sage) and a special issue of the journal *Emergence*. A forthcoming book is *Complexity Dynamics in Organizations: Applications of Order-Creation Science* (Cambridge University Press). Recent articles include: 'Postmodernism vs Truth in Management Theory' (in E. Locke (ed.), *Post Modernism and Management*, 2003, Elsevier Science); 'Situated Learning Theory: Adding Rate and Complexity Effects via Kauffman's NK Model' (Y. Yuan (1st author), *Nonlinear Dynamics, Psychology, and Life Sciences*, 2004, 8: 65–101); 'Toward a Complexity Science of Entrepreneurship' (*Journal of Business Venturing*, 2004, 19); 'Toward a 0th Law of Thermodynamics: Order-Creation

Complexity Dynamics from Physics & Biology to Bioeconomics' (*Journal of Bioeconomics*, 2004, 6: 1–31); and 'Complexity Science as Order-Creation Science' (*E:CO*, 2004, 6: 2–28).

Susan J. Miller is Professor of Organizational Behaviour at the University of Hull Business School, England, having previously worked at Durham University for a number of years. Her research interests lie in the area of organizational decision-making, implementation and organizational performance. She is also interested in issues concerning the nature and purpose of management education and critical approaches to pedagogy and practice. Before coming into academia she worked for 9 years in a variety of public and private organizations, including Taylor Woodrow and the BBC.

Laurent Mirabeau is a PhD candidate in the Faculty of Management at McGill University, and an MBA graduate (1997) from the University of Ottawa, Canada, where he currently teaches. Prior to starting his PhD he gained valuable experience in the telecommunications and consulting industries. With a background in mathematics, he was first introduced to complexity science after attending the one-week intensive New England Complex Systems Institute (NECSI) course. His current research focuses on emergent strategy as well as NK fitness landscapes.

Margaret A. Neale is the John G. McCoy-Banc One Corporation Professor of Organizations and Dispute Resolution at the Graduate School of Business at Stanford University, USA. Professor Neale's research interests include bargaining and negotiation, distributed work groups and team composition, learning and performance. She is the author of over 70 articles on these topics and is a co-author of three books: *Organizational Behavior: A Management Challenge*, 3rd edn (2002, Erlbaum Press, with L. Stroh and G. Northcraft), *Cognition and Rationality in Negotiation* (1991, Free Press, with M.H. Bazerman) and *Negotiating Rationally* (1992, Free Press, with M.H. Bazerman) and one research series: *Research on Managing in Groups and Teams* (Elsevier Press, with Elizabeth Mannix). She currently serves as the associated editor of *Organizational Behavior and Human Decision Processes* as well as on the editorial boards of the *Journal of Applied Psychology* and *Human Resource Management Review*.

Stella M. Nkomo is a professor of business leadership at the University of South Africa Graduate School of Business Leadership, South Africa. A former Scholar-in-Residence at the Mary Ingraham Bunting Institute of Radcliffe College and Harvard University, her internationally recognized work on race and gender in organizations and managing diversity appears in numerous academic journals, edited volumes and magazines. She is the past Chair of the Women in Management Division of the Academy of Management.

Walter R. Nord (PhD psychology, Washington University, 1967) is Distinguished University Professor and Professor of Management at the University of South Florida, USA. He received the Distinguished Educator award from the Academy of Management in 2002. Previously he was at Washington University-St. Louis (1967–1989). His current interests centre on developing an agnostic philosophical framework for social science. He has published widely in scholarly journals and edited/authored a number of books. His books include: *The Meanings of Occupational Work* (1990, Lexington Books, with A. Brief),

Implementing Routine and Radical Innovations (1987, Lexington Books, with S. Tucker), *Organizational Reality: Reports from the Firing Line* (1977, Goodyear Publishing) and *Managerial Reality* (1990, Harper Collins, with P. Frost and V. Mitchell), *Resistance and Power in Organizations* (1994, Routledge, with J. Jermier and D. Knights) and *Human Resources Reality: Putting Competence in Context*, 2nd edn (2002, Prentice Hall, with P. Frost and L. Krefting). He is a past book review editor for the *Academy of Management Review* and is currently a member of the editorial boards of *Organization and Environment* and *Organization*. He has served as consultant on organizational development and change for a variety of groups and organizations. He co-edited the *Handbook of Organization Studies* (1996, Sage, with S. Clegg and C. Hardy) that received the 1997 George Terry Award.

Olivia A. O'Neill is an Assistant Professor of Management at the Terry College of Business, University of Georgia, USA. She received her PhD degree (2005) from the Stanford Graduate School of Business and her BS degree in Psychology from the University of Maryland in 2000. She is a recipient of the National Science Foundation Graduation Fellowship (2000–2003). Her research interests include organizational culture, gender and emotions. Her dissertation research introduces a theoretical typology of emotional norms to identify 'masculine organizational cultures' and to quantitatively measure the consequences of organizational culture defined through emotional norms for organizational practices and human resources decision-making. In collaboration with Joanne Martin at the Stanford Graduate School of Business, she conducted qualitative research on gender equality intervention programmes in technology training academies in central Mexico. She is currently conducting a longitudinal, quasi-experimental project on affective culture change in long-term health care facilities in collaboration with Sigal Barsade of the Wharton School at the University of Pennsylvania. Her work with Charles O'Reilly on gender identity and career attainment has appeared in *Fast Company*, *Working Mother Magazine* and *HR Magazine*.

Renato J. Orsato is Senior Research Fellow at the Centre for the Management of Environmental and Social Responsibility (CMER) at INSEAD, Fontainebleau, France. In 2004 he was awarded an International Outgoing Marie Curie Fellowship to conduct research in Australia and New Zealand in the area of Strategic Environmental Management in firms, in partnership with the Innovative Collaborations and Networks (ICAN) Research Centre at University of Technology, Sydney (UTS), and the Centre for Business and Sustainable Development (CBSD) at Massey University, New Zealand. During 1999–2004 Renato co-ordinated the management-related courses within the MSc programme in Environmental Management and Policy at the International Institute for Industrial Environmental Economics (IIIEE) at Lund University, Sweden. His current area of research interest addresses the conditions favouring firms transforming environmental investments into sources of competitive advantage.

Nail Öztas is a member of the Faculty of Management in the Public Administration Department, School of Economics and Administrative Sciences, Gazi University, Ankara, Turkey. He received his MPA (1999) and PhD (2004) in public administration from the University of Southern California. Currently he is working on projects focusing on neighbourhood network structures of social capital, organizational and network learning during disasters and applications of complexity theory to organizations.

Barbara Parker is a Professor in the Albers School of Business and Economics, Seattle University, USA, where she teaches globalization and international management. She conducts research on cross-sectoral partnerships, strategic management of diversity and joint venture management. Her research has appeared in many books and journals including *Human Relations, International Journal of Intercultural Relations, Journal of Business Research, Global Business, Management International Review, Sex Roles, Research in Higher Education* and *Nonprofit and Voluntary Sector Quarterly*. She is the author of three books: *Nonsexist Curriculum Development: Theory into Practice* (1984, University Colorado), *Globalization and business practices: Managing across boundaries* (1998, Sage) and *Introduction to globalization and business: Relationships and responsibilities* (2005, Sage).

Ken W. Parry is Professor of Management at Griffith University in Brisbane, Australia. He was the Founding Director of the Centre for the Study of Leadership at Victoria University of Wellington. His research and executive development interests have always revolved around leadership. His most recent research directions revolve around the Art, Science and Drama of Leadership. His research methods involve grounded theory, quantitative methods generally and hierarchy abstraction modelling. He has published six books and two CDs on these topics, as well as many refereed articles and book chapters. He is on the Management Executive of the Australia and New Zealand Academy of Management and is editor of the *JANZAM* journal. He is a Fellow of the Australian Institute of Management and the Australian Human Resources Institute. He is a regular judge at Prime Minister's and Premier's Awards for Management Excellence, and has addressed the senior executive service of the federal public sector at the National Press Club.

Kelley A. Porter is an Assistant Professor of Strategy and Entrepreneurship at Queen's School of Business at Queen's University in Ontario, Canada. Her research lies at the intersection of entrepreneurship, strategy and organization theory. She is interested in the role that founders' backgrounds play in science-based entrepreneurship, the interplay between multiple types of networks in biotechnology clusters and differences in these strategies across regions and countries. Kelley completed her PhD in Industrial Engineering at Stanford University. She received her MA in Sociology from Stanford and her BA with honours from Wellesley College. Prior to starting at Stanford, Kelley worked as a Research Associate at Harvard Business School, where she wrote cases about the strategic challenges facing high technology firms.

Walter W. Powell is Professor of Education and (by courtesy) Professor of Sociology, Organizational Behavior, and Communication at Stanford University, USA, and an external faculty member of the Santa Fe Institute. His current work focuses on the catalytic role of networks in the emergence and transformation of science-based institutions.

Linda L. Putnam (PhD, University of Minnesota) is George T. and Gladys H. Abell Professor in the Department of Communication at Texas A&M University, USA. Her current research interests include negotiation, organizational conflict and discourse analysis in organizations. She is the co-editor of four books, including *The Sage Handbook of Organizational Discourse* (2004, Sage) and *The New Handbook of Organizational Communication* (2001, Sage). She is a Past President of the International Communication Association and a past Board Member of the Academy of Management. She is a Fellow of the International Communication Association (ICA), the 2005 winner of the Steven H. Chaffee Career Productivity Award, and a Distinguished Scholar of the National Communication Association.

Michael Reed is Professor of Organizational Analysis and Deputy Director (Research), Cardiff Business School, Cardiff University, Wales. His major research interests focus on general theoretical development in organization theory and analysis, new organizational forms, the management of professional and expert workers (with particular reference to public services organizations) and the dynamics of organizational control and governance in contemporary capitalist political economies and societies. He has just finished (after 12 years!) as one of the founding editors of the journal, *Organization*, published by Sage. He has published extensively in major European journals, such as *Organization Studies* and *Journal of Management Studies*. More recently, he is (with colleagues from the Universities of Bath, Bristol and Cardiff) a member of a research team that has secured major funding from the UK's Economic and Social Research Council for a study of 'modernization, leadership and management in contemporary UK public services'. He has also been working on a book on changing forms of organizational control for far too long (as his son never fails to remind him)! He is a current member of the Council of the British Academy of Management (BAM) and the Directors of Research Network (BAM), UK.

Benjamin Schneider is Senior Research Fellow at Valtera Corporation and Professor Emeritus at the University of Maryland, USA, where he had been head of the Industrial and Organizational Psychology programme for many years. Ben has also taught at Michigan State and Yale and for shorter periods of time at Dartmouth, Bar-Ilan University (Israel, on a Fulbright), University of Aix-Marseilles (France) and Peking University (PRC). Ben has published 125 professional journal articles and book chapters, as well as nine books, is listed on Who's Who in America, was awarded the Year 2000 Distinguished Scientific Contributions Award by the Society for Industrial and Organizational Psychology (also a Fellow and Past-President) and is a Fellow of the Academy of Management. Ben's interests concern service quality, organizational climate and culture, personnel selection and the role of personality in organizational life. Ben, over the years, has consulted with numerous companies recently including IBM, Allstate, Giant Eagle, Nextel, Pepsico and Toyota.

Andrew V. Shipilov is an Assistant Professor of Strategy at INSEAD, France. He received his PhD in Strategy and Organization Theory at the Rotman School of Management, University of Toronto. His research interests include economic sociology, strategic organization and, in particular, issues of inter-firm collaboration and inter-personal networks. His articles have been published in such outlets as the *Academy of Management Journal, Administrative Science Quarterly, Strategic Organization, Industrial and Corporate Change, Managerial* and *Decision Economics*. At INSEAD, Andrew teaches courses on Strategy and Strategic Alliances.

John A.A. Sillince teaches at Aston Business School and does research on rhetoric, narrative and discourse in organizations. He writes pieces which seek to reinterpret current organization theories from a rhetorical point of view and which address weaknesses in discourse and organization theory. He is interested in widening the understanding of the relationship between discourse and context. He is currently studying in what way the rhetorics used by strategists vary according to strategic context.

Linda Smircich is Professor of Organization Studies at the Department of Management, Isenberg School of Management, University of Massachusetts-Amherst, USA. She teaches Organizational Behavior and Theory to undergraduates and MBAs and doctoral seminars in Qualitative Research, and Alternative Paradigms in Organizational Analysis. Her earlier scholarly writing centred on organizational culture; she now would describe herself as pursuing a cultural and critical perspective on organization and management. Her research, in collaboration with Marta Calás, applies insights from cultural studies and feminist theorizing to organizational topics such as business ethics, globalization and issues of work and family. She is an editor of *Organization: The critical journal of organization, theory & society*.

D. Brent Smith is an Associate Professor of Management and Psychology at the Jesse H. Jones Graduate School of Management at Rice University and Director of the Rice Center for Organizational Effectiveness Studies. His research interests focus on the intersection of personality psychology and organizational behaviour. He recently co-edited the book *Personality and Organizations* (2004, Lawrence Erlbaum Associates) and is currently editing *The People make the Place*. He has twice won the Scholarly Achievement Award from the HR Division of the Academy of Management and recently was a co-recipient of the Outstanding Publication Award from the OB division of the Academy.

Ralph Stablein is the Academic Director of the DBA programme and a Professor in the Management Department of the Massey University College of Business. He received his BA in psychology and economics from Benedictine University. He has an MA in economics from Western Illinois University. His PhD in organization behaviour with a minor in sociology is from the Kellogg Graduate School of Management at Northwestern University. Ralph has worked at the University of British Columbia, the University of Otago and Massey University. He has been a visiting scholar at Stanford University's Work, Technology & Organization Center, New York University, Benedictine University, South Florida University and the University of Western Sydney. Both his research and teaching focus on inquiry in organization studies. Ralph's publications include contributions on epistemology, methodology and two edited volumes with Peter Frost entitled *Renewing Research Practice* and *Doing Exemplary Research*. Ralph is co-editor of the 'Advances in Organization Studies' series published by Liber/Copenhagen Business School. He is co-editor of the 'Emerging Scholarship' section of the *Organization and Management Journal*. He currently serves on the editorial board of the *Asia Pacific Journal of Human Resources, Journal of Organizational Change Management* and *Organization Studies*. Ralph is a past chair of the Critical Management Studies Interest Group of the Academy of Management.

Marcus M. Stewart is an Assistant Professor of Management at Bentley College, Waltham, MA, USA. Dr Stewart earned his BS and MBA at Bentley College and his PhD in Organizational Behavior at the University of North Carolina at Chapel Hill. His current research examines organizational diversity with a focus on workgroup dynamics and leadership, and social justice with a focus on reactions to affirmative action. His research has been published in the *Journal of Applied Psychology, Personnel Psychology* and several edited volumes.

Roy Suddaby is an Assistant Professor with a joint appointment in the Departments of Accounting & Management Information Systems and Strategic Management and Organization at the School of Business, University of Alberta, Canada. His research focuses on institutional change. His primary empirical context is professions and knowledge intensive firms. Roy's work has appeared in the *Academy of Management Journal*, *Administrative Science Quarterly* and *Human Relations*. He is on the editorial board of *Organization Studies*, *Academy of Management Journal* and *Academy of Management Review*. His current research focuses on post-professional regulation.

Ann E. Tenbrunsel (PhD Northwestern University) is an Associate Professor in the Mendoza College of Business at The University of Notre Dame and is the Arthur F. and Mary J. O'Neil Co-director of the Ethical Institute for Business Worldwide. Her research interests focus on decision-making and negotiations with a particular emphasis in ethics. She is the co-editor of three books on these topics and has published her research in a variety of journals, including *Administrative Science Quarterly*, *Academy of Management Review*, *Academy of Management Journal*, *Organizational Behavior and Human Decision Processes*, *Journal of Applied Psychology* and *Journal of Personality and Social Psychology*.

Stephen P. Turner is Graduate Research Professor of Philosophy at the University of South Florida, USA. His writings include *Sociological Explanation as Translation* (1980, Cambridge), *The Search for a Methodology of Social Science* (1986, Reidel) and *The Social Theory of Practices* (1994, Polity and Chicago). He was editor of the *Cambridge Companion to Weber* (2000, Cambridge) and co-editor of *The Blackwell Guide to the Philosophy of the Social Sciences* (2004, Blackwell) and is presently co-editing the *Handbook of the Philosophy of Anthropology and Sociology* (Elsevier) and *The Handbook of Social Science Methodology* (Sage). He has written extensively on complex organizations, charismatic leadership and the problem of the social organization of expert knowledge. His writings on organizations include *Conflict in Organizations* (1983, Prentice Hall, with Frank Weed), 'Complex Organizations as Savage Tribes', *Journal for the Theory of Social Behavior*, and 'Blau's Theory of Differentiation: Is it Explanatory?', *Sociological Quarterly*.

David C. Wilson is Professor of Strategy and Organization at the University of Warwick Business School, England. He was an original member of the Bradford Research Group studying decision-making in the 1970s and he continues to research the processes and implementation of strategic decisions. His research interests include decision-making, strategy, change, governance, risk and uncertainty. Currently, he is analysing how organizations make decisions about perceived and actual threats from terrorism. His interests are in the private, public and non-profit sectors. He was Editor-in-Chief of the journal *Organization Studies* (1999–2003) and was elected Chair of the European Group for Organization Studies (2003–2006). Prior to that, he was Chair of the British Academy of Management (1996–1999). He is a Fellow of the British Academy of Management.

Monica C. Worline is an Assistant Professor of Organization and Management at the Goizueta Business School at Emory University, USA. She received her PhD from the University of Michigan, where she began her work with the compassionlab. Monica's main topic of study is the way in which organizations enliven their members. In particular, she has written about courage as a primary way in which life is expressed in work organizations.

This book is dedicated to the memory of Peter Frost (30 August 1939–18 October 2004), a comrade in spirit and a fellow traveller whose intellect, wisdom, humour and compassion were an inspiration to us all

Introduction

WALTER R. NORD, THOMAS B. LAWRENCE, CYNTHIA HARDY AND STEWART R. CLEGG

In the first version of this *Handbook* we stated our intentions to provide a map for researchers to navigate their way around organization studies. In so doing, we used various criteria to help us decide which subjects to include in the volume: both old and new, mainstream and peripheral, normal and 'contra' science, and from established authors and relative newcomers. We hoped that the original edition would be a reaffirmation of the dominant streams of thought in organization studies as well as a celebration of some newer modes of inquiry (Clegg and Hardy 1996a). We also wanted to stimulate conversations within and between the different approaches to organization studies. In fact, we conceptualized organization studies as a series of multiple, overlapping conversations that reflect, reproduce and refute earlier conversations:

> Our approach is to conceptualize organization studies as a series of conversations, in particular those of organization studies researchers who help to constitute organizations through terms derived from paradigms, methods and assumptions, themselves derived from earlier conversations (Clegg and Hardy 1996b: 3).

In this regard, our objectives have not changed in this second edition – we still wish to provide an overview of research in organization studies, using the metaphor of conversations to guide our selection of topics and ground our introduction to them.

Our interest in academic conversations is widely shared. Controversy and disagreement have played helpful roles in academic circles for centuries and, while it may not always appear so, such conversations have represented important contributions to the development of organization studies. Recently, however, some researchers have expressed concern that debates in our field have become too heated,

such that people may have stopped listening and, hence, stopped learning from each other. This frustration has led to calls for more measured, respectful conversations, as in the 1999 special issue of the *Journal of Management Inquiry* devoted to theory development, whose subtitle was 'Moving from Shrill Monologues to (Relatively) Tame Dialogues' (Elsbach et al. 1999); in an essay by Calás and Smircich (1999) calling upon their colleagues to write in friendship; and in Weick's (1999) call for reflective conversation. We hope that the contributions to this Handbook reflect these calls, demonstrating respectful and reflective (if not always tame) dialogues.

In this introductory chapter we, therefore, review the conversations that constitute this *Handbook* and reflect on some of the themes that characterize them. In so doing, we provide a way of making sense of the book although, of course, at the outset we must acknowledge that the contents of this book are the product of the judgements of its editors and authors and, as such, they represent partial and personal accounts of the field. Nevertheless, we hope that most scholars in organization studies would agree that this book contains useful insights about important topics that yield interesting information and ideas regarding the nature of organizations and organizing.

The Production and Consumption of Knowledge

This *Handbook* is a text. More specifically, it is a scientific text, and as such it might be seen as an attempt to produce scientific knowledge. The process through which scientific knowledge is produced differs according to the assumptions of the researcher in question. The traditional model – the scientific method – consists of the following:

… observation and description of specific aspects of a phenomenon or group of phenomena (e.g. processes, behaviours) in terms of a general model or theory, the formulation of a hypothesis to predict the existence of other phenomena or to predict quantitatively results of new observations (e.g. a causal or mathematical relation), the performance of experimental study are systematic observation and statistical analyses to rest (sic.) the predictions, and the interpretation of empirical results to confirm, reject, or revise the theory (Cacioppo et al. 2004: 215).

This model involves what Kaplan (1964) termed 'reconstructed logic' – an idealization of scientific practice that is especially significant because it is widely taught to students and is the taken for granted view of how science takes place. The scientific method – or some variation of it – is well recognized within organization and management theory, where many researchers have embarked on building knowledge through objectivist and positivist research. In fact, it was 'actively promoted by mainstream organizational scholars, mostly located in elite business schools, who aimed to build an organization science … [and] develop a standardized approach to organizational analysis' (Lounsbury 2003: 296).

In contrast, a very different view of knowledge production has been inspired by sociological research that developed a set of empirically grounded models of scientific production, and showed more clearly the social and discursive aspects of this knowledge production. Early researchers (e.g. Barnes 1974) argued that scientific knowledge could be understood in the same way as any other area of culture. Subsequent researchers used a variety of means to show the social processes through which scientific problems were closed, how concepts were established, and how methodologies were institutionalized (Latour and Woolgar 1979; Knorr Cetina 1981a, b; Pinch 1985; Callon 1986; Latour 1987; 1988; Woolgar 1988).

The view of knowledge as socially constructed is not new in organization and management theory (e.g. Brown and Duguid 1991; 2001; Tsoukas 1996). Twenty years ago, Astley (1985: 497) argued that the knowledge of administrative science was 'the product of social definition', reinforced by institutional mechanisms that invest it 'with the stamp of scientific authenticity'. Challenging the idea that our knowledge of organizations is the unmediated product of empirical observation, he suggested instead that it results from linguistic conventions – in Wittgenstein's terms, language games (Astley and Zammuto 1992; Mauws and Phillips 1995). In other words, the language used to conduct and report research does not merely describe the phenomena under study, it helps to bring those phenomena into being: researchers 'see the world through the lenses of social theories, and social theories are built borrowing actors' categories and meanings' (Ferraro et al. 2005: 8).

Researchers adhering to this view are more attentive to the institutional, social and political processes that influence the production of knowledge (Calás and Smircich 1999), and the various linguistic and discursive techniques that allow researchers to make knowledge claims (e.g. Knights 1992; Harley and Hardy 2004: Harley et al. 2004). They are also interested in how consumption affects scientific knowledge (Hassard and Keleman 2002): consumption can occur in many different ways – and in shaping how knowledge is received, also shapes what is taken to be knowledge. Without consumption, knowledge does not exist – knowledge is generated 'only when singled out for attention by those who find it "meaningful"' (Hassard and Keleman 2002: 237).

Different chapters in this *Handbook* reflect both models described above, as well as a variety of positions located somewhere between the two; as editors, however, we tend to engage in research more in keeping with the latter. Consequently, we view this *Handbook* as an artifact – a highly institutionalized genre, especially compared to 10 years ago – with which producers and consumers engage to produce 'knowledge' about organizational studies (cf. Hardy et al. 2005). As editors, we are in both the production and the consumption business – having been among the first to read the chapters that constitute the *Handbook* and in writing an introduction that helps to make sense of it for other consumers. Given our empathy for social constructionist views of knowledge, we acknowledge that we use those sense-making devices that will help to direct, encourage or motivate other consumers to make a *particular* kind of sense of the *Handbook*. Accordingly, we focus on providing a guide that emphasizes the *Handbook's* status as both a discursive object and a scientific object: we examine how the chapters produce knowledge by engaging with scientific and other discourses in different ways.

In referring to discourse, we define it as collections of texts and statements that 'provide a language for talking about a topic and a way of producing a particular kind of knowledge about a topic' (du Gay

1996: 43). To the extent that discourses are useful for particular groups, they can be seen as cultural resources (Gergen 2001) that help to bring about particular understandings and practices (Hall 2001). A change in discourse does not just change the way in how people talk about the social world, it also changes the way in which they understand and experience it, as well as who can act upon it and how they can act upon it (Harley and Hardy 2004). Thus, we are interested in the different ways in which the texts that comprise the *Handbook* draw on discourse to make knowledge claims and to promote particular research practices, i.e. the discursive strategies through which the chapters shape the production and consumption of knowledge about organizations.

The Handbook: A Consumer's Guide

This *Handbook* consists of 30 chapters, divided into two sections. The chapters in the first section explore different ways of theorizing the field of organization studies; the chapters in the second sector explore specific issues in the field. Many of the chapters appeared in the first edition of the *Handbook* and have been substantially revised by the original authors. Some chapters are entirely new, as we saw opportunities to present emerging areas of research in this edition. Some chapters and authors that featured in the original version do not appear here for a variety of reasons. Some subjects have been 'spun off' to constitute their own hand-book; some authors had moved on to new ventures and did not wish to revisit their chapters; and some subjects seemed less current than they did 10 years ago. In the remainder of this section, we introduce the chapters, not in the order in which they appear but, in what we hope is an interesting set of categories that describe some of the discursive strategies evident in these texts. Of course, these categories are neither mutually exclusive nor exhaustive and, while we only consider each chapter in relation to a single theme, we acknowledge that chapters might easily be associated with more than one and other scholars, both authors and consumers, might well disagree with our classification.

Discursive Consolidation

The first discursive strategy we discuss is one that focuses on working within a well-defined, convergent scientific discourse to consolidate and enrich concepts, relationships and findings that are already relatively well established. In many ways, this discursive strategy follows in the tradition of what Kuhn (1970) refers to as 'normal science'. This strategy is an important one because the potential for a scientific discourse to influence practice and policy depends on its structure and coherence: the more there is convergence within the discourse and the fewer the alternative discourses, the more powerful the discourse is likely to be (Phillips et al. 2004). As others have shown, drawing on a small number of well established discourses is an effective way to make a text 'stick', by which we mean that they fix meanings so that they appear solid and become taken-for-granted, while alternative meanings are more likely to be viewed with suspicion (Harley and Hardy 2004).

In the *Handbook*, an exemplar of this strategy is described in the chapter by Neale et al. on 'Social Cognition, Behavioural Decision Theory, and the Psychological Links to Micro and Macro Organizational Behaviour', which shows how particular research practices – mainly associated with the discipline of psychology and in the form of carefully controlled laboratory settings – has produced a widely shared view among those conducting research in the area regarding the significance of findings, as well as the particular puzzles which require further research. As a result, while not dismissing the intellectual debates that occur, it can be argued that a substantial body of agreed-upon knowledge on cognition and decision-making has been developed. In this light, it is interesting to note how the authors draw on a relatively small set of discursive resources – journals and topics from within the accepted, dominant discourse. As scholars work with this body of knowledge, not only do appropriate research practices become widely enacted, but the gaps in the body of knowledge become evident to members of the academic community. Thus, science 'progresses' as knowledge gaps are collectively constructed and researchers agree on the ways and means to fill them, e.g. the view that the role of affect or emotions has been ignored has provided the basis for a new sub-topic for inquiry. Thus, as the agreed-upon body of knowledge has become more established, it has been applied to other areas of study, such as organization decision-making, leadership and group decision-making. These new areas remain linked to the original discourse – some discursive 'stretch' may occur to accommodate the new areas, but alternative or incompatible discourses do not emerge. Thus, a relatively convergent discourse is associated with a coherent body of knowledge through a process seemly consistent with that which is commonly referred to as normal science.

Similar consolidation can be seen in the analysis of change advanced by Greenwood and Hinings in their chapter entitled 'Radical Organizational Change'. While these authors do not have the luxury of a powerful discursive resource such as psychology at their disposal, they nonetheless draw together different streams of research on organizational change in a convergent manner, i.e. to demonstrate agreement concerning what we know and do not know about this area. The authors argue that, as recently as the 1970s, change was not considered to be especially problematic. Rather, organizations were presumed to adapt in order to survive. By the middle of the 1980s, however, the environments of organizations had changed so much that change was a central concern and, further, the nature of the change was such that focus shifted from individual organizations to inter-organizational relationships and other aspects of organization environments. By drawing on three well-established theories of change – the punctuated equilibrium model, the neo-institutional approach and work on continuity and change – the authors are able to claim significant progression in the field. In this way, the authors' strategy, by drawing on the change theories summarized in the chapter, helps to consolidate the discourse of organizational change as characterized by broad agreement on such matters as the difficulty of achieving organizational change, key processes involved in the emergence of new organizational forms, the processes by which change unfolds and the importance of field-level processes.

Parry and Bryman's examination of 'Leadership in Organizations' shows how the discourse of leadership in organization studies has progressed through several stages, each associated with a shift in emphasis toward different explanatory factors. They suggest a progression of five stages, beginning with the trait approach that they argue dominated leadership research until the late 1940s, the style approach which was dominant until the late 1960s, the contingency approach (from the late 1960s to the early 1980s), the new leadership approach and, most recently, the post-charismatic approach. Parry and Bryman suggest that it is dynamic conceptualizations and

theories of leadership have highlighted new areas for study. For example, one of the more significant changes highlighted by Parry and Bryman sees a shift from a focus on entities to a focus on processes. The authors demonstrate how this process orientation evolved from the focus on individuals through several stages including a focus on context and now the 'new leadership approach' which treats leadership as being distributed rather than being centred in an individual. This focus on the distributed nature of leadership has, in turn, helped to surface concerns the 'dark' side of leadership which has, in the past, often been ignored. As a result, we see a new discourse of 'post-charismatic' or 'post-transformational' leadership emerging. Despite the changes, these different phases of leadership research remain tightly connected to each other, as the larger discourse of leadership is consolidated by relatively convergent studies. The discourse of leadership in organization studies is highly sedimented, with new theories incorporating concepts and relationships from previous theories, rather than replacing them wholesale.

Borrowing Discourse

A second set of discursive strategies in organizations studies venture further afield and emphasize connecting to different discourses. These strategies explore multiple discourses and the ways these discourses can be connected to each other. Much of what it constitutes as knowledge in organization studies today was, at some earlier point in its history, anchored in research and writing from other disciplines, such as sociology, psychology, economics or political science. This tradition of borrowing continues to be an important source of intellectual resources in modern organization studies. In fact, almost every chapter in this book leverages important ideas from other disciplines, although we have highlighted two particular chapters to show some differences in patterns of borrowing. In some areas of inquiry, the borrowing might be described as relatively distant – concepts originally borrowed from a host discipline have since become fully enmeshed in organization studies. In other cases, we see what we describe as heavy borrowing, where the ideas and assumptions of the parent discipline continue to direct organizational inquiries: the organizational application appears more or less to be a sub-discipline of its parent discipline.

The chapter on 'Organizational Economics: Understanding the Relationship between Organizations and Economic Analysis' is a prime example of this latter case. Barney and Hesterly call their chapter 'organizational economics' rather than something like the economics of organizations. The fact that 'economics' is the noun and 'organizational' is the qualifier seems to suggest that this topic could easily be a sub-topic in economics rather than a part of organization studies. The heaviness of the borrowing is reflected further in the terms and assumptions employed by the theorists. Key elements such as transactions costs, opportunism, as well as the strong reliance on economists in the reference list suggest that economics is playing a hegemonic role in the analysis. In other words, the discourse of economics rivals organizational discourse in dominating this chapter, and economics journals feature heavily in the references, adding legitimacy to knowledge claims.

In contrast, Baum and Shipilov's chapter on 'Ecological Approaches to Organizations' is an example of how borrowed concepts, ideas and metaphors have made a successful transition into the discourse of organization studies. What is especially interesting here is that, for decades, students of organizations had focused on how organizations adapt to different environments, but things changed dramatically when Hannan and Freeman (1977) asked a different question: why are there so many different kinds of organizations? To answer this question they and colleagues turned to an established body of thought from the natural sciences – ecology. Much like economics, this body of thought provided a set of concepts that could be transferred to organization analysis and readily quantified. As a result, sophisticated quantitative tools could be applied to matters of concern to students of organizations. Whereas organization economics continues to draw heavily from the discourse of economics, population ecology has developed its own, largely separate, discourse in organizational studies – the texts on which these authors draw are primarily from organizational journals and by organization scholars, not ecologists – the original discourse is no longer necessary in making knowledge claims.

Comparing Discourses

Despite the differences in the degree of borrowing noted above, both chapters are similar in that they draw on other, highly consistent discourses to reinforce their knowledge claims. A somewhat different inter-discursive strategy involves juxtaposing different discourses that are not normally thought of as compatible. It involves examining two sets of texts and conversations in order to understand each more clearly and to explore the relationship between them. For example in the chapter on 'Complexity Science and Organization Studies', Maguire et al. illustrate how the use of ideas and concepts, which have been developed for other purposes, generate valuable new insights when used to reflect on organizational processes because they offer new ways of talking – and thinking – about familiar objects. Such inter-discursivity creates new knowledge through its potential to develop exciting new ways of understanding the world of organizations as, for example, work on metaphors (Morgan 1986) and reframing (Bolman and Deal 1997) has already shown. It is worth noting that, in the early days of population ecology, the juxtaposition of ecology and organizations was a similar example of positioning two distinct discourses and, over time, a new hybrid discourse – population ecology – evolved. So one question regarding the place of complexity science is whether it has the potential to create a new organizational discourse, as indicated in the chapter on population ecology, or whether it will continue to be subordinated to its origins, as in the case of organizational economics? Interestingly, complexity science found its way into the discourse of organization studies some decades ago with the interest in general systems theory but, at the time, did not appear to 'take'. Given the scope of this chapter, perhaps contemporary complexity science will follow the example of population ecology and create not only new knowledge, but a new discourse.

A new discourse – and associated body of knowledge – is the very aim of the chapter on 'Meso Organizational Behaviour: Comments on the Third Paradigm' by Smith et al. In showing how psychology and sociology have separately emphasized the micro and macro, they provide the detailed histories of how knowledge about the individual and the organizational context has developed. They then review the work of scholars who sought to bridge these two discourses to put the individual in context. For these authors, the proper perspective for organizational studies is a new 'paradigm' – that of the meso-level which bridges micro and macro. By juxtaposing psychology and sociology and carefully comparing them, the authors' discursive strategy shows the overlaps and points out that continued separation comes with costs. Thus, something new is required – neither the contextualization of the individual, nor the individualization of the organizational will do. A new hybrid discourse is required, much like population ecology. At the same time, it is important to note that this inter-discursivity is firmly framed within the parameters of traditional scientific discourse and, when the practices advocated by the authors are explored, there are similarities with the chapter by Neale et al.

A somewhat similar strategy is employed by Alvesson and Deetz in their consideration of the relationship between critical theory and postmodernism in the chapter entitled 'Critical Theory and Postmodernism Approaches to Organizational Studies'. These two approaches have at times been pronounced irreconcilable and at other times confused for each other. Their analysis of both approaches enables them to uncover mutually supporting themes and ideas. The authors tell us that, often, academic debate pushes advocates of different approaches into entrenched camps, making it difficult for them to benefit from each other. In such contexts, it is very easy for members of each camp to not comprehend fully what is going on in the other camp. In the heat of debate, neither side takes the time to do the careful study that would be necessary to understand and benefit from the ideas of the other. Alvesson and Deetz demonstrate how careful scholarship can permit synthesis of such seemingly competing perspectives and thereby contribute to some widely shared goals of all members of the organization studies community such as strengthening marginalized voices. This strategy, as exemplified by Alvesson and Deetz, has a powerful potential to form the foundation for future interdiscursive conversations. In contrast to the previous chapter, the authors do not situate their chapter within scientific discourse. Far from it: they explicitly hope to challenge scientific discourse by showing the advantages of building knowledge based on the dismantlement of boundaries between two alternative discourses – critical theory and postmodernism.

Discourse of Interrogation

This set of chapters adopts a discursive strategy that is focused more explicitly on interrogating the changing nature of theory and research in organization studies. The fact that the discourse of interrogation is present in this *Handbook* will not come as a surprise to readers – genres that focus on reviewing the field are often associated with critique as well as overview. In fact, critique has been a theme promoted heavily in both this and the earlier version of the *Handbook*. The following chapters show how different phases in a field's history and different perspectives to act as lenses to view the achievements – and perhaps more importantly, the deficiencies – of earlier phases of study or alternative approaches. In this regard, interrogation is embedded in the collective – if disjointed – trajectory of research and is an important means whereby knowledge is developed. In contrast to consolidating strategies, which focus to build new knowledge by plugging (agreed upon) gaps and linking developments in a convergent discourse; the discourse of interrogation aims at showing how discursive change and divergence can *expose* gaps that then form a basis for conversation and debate designed to probe those gaps further. Thus, knowledge develops in a far more contested and contestable manner – and, in fact, as result of such contestation.

In 'Organizational Culture: Beyond Struggles for Intellectual Dominance', Martin et al. also employ a discourse of interrogation to show how the treatment of culture in contemporary organization studies was rooted in attempts to comprehend popular and apparently successful organizational practices. When academics initially became involved they, too, were interested in organization culture because of its association with organizational success. However, academic interest developed in the form of particular perspectives which then became subject for interrogation from academics using other perspectives. For example, early research produced an academic literature that emphasized integration. Subsequent interrogation of the integration perspective revealed a series of biases and limitations as the perspective itself became a subject for academic debate and a stimulus for the development of other perspectives – such as differentiation and fragmentation – that in turn became new objects for analysis and debate. As with other topics that have become part of organization studies, this analysis and debate incorporated ideas and perspectives that were popular in the field more generally such as: postmodernism, qualitative vs quantitative methodologies and possible managerial bias. The resulting debates often took on a warlike tone, as diverse academics competed to make their perspective dominant or – using the authors' metaphor – to become 'king of the mountain'. However, at the end of the chapter, the authors propose abandoning the king of the mountain metaphor to one of conversation to avoid repeating the earlier, strident conflicts.

Hardy and Clegg's chapter 'Some Dare Call It Power' also adopts a discourse of interrogation – in two ways. First, they show how different developments and new directions in the work on power have been used to interrogate earlier approaches and the assumptions on which they are based. Secondly, they point out that the study of power itself is a mode of interrogation, particularly of the functionalist orientation of the majority of the management literature. By understanding power, researchers, even those of different denominations, converge in their interest in exploring the often hidden ways in which management and organizational practices dominate and control. In this way, the authors ground their discussion in the work of early theorists such as Karl Marx and Max Weber, showing how each provided contrasting orientations that contribute to tensions in sociological thought that continue today. They discuss the ways in which organizations control individuals, from the strictures of the total institution to the apparently rational nature of hierarchy. They then juxtapose some of the different perspectives that exist within the literature – critical views such of those of labour process theory and in work on the dimensions of power; managerial approaches related to the use of critical resources to defeat conflict and ways of managing meaning; and finally the ideas of disciplinary power and end of sovereignty most commonly associated with Foucault. Different approaches have been used to interrogate each other and Foucault's work, in particular, has laid down a series of challenges to critical theorists and managerial theorists alike. These interrogations and counter-interrogations continue around a series of issues, e.g. agency, resistance and reflexivity. These authors continue to see interrogation and counter-interrogation as a fruitful way to develop knowledge, in contrast to the culture chapter, which calls for the end – or at least a muting – of the discourse of interrogation.

Lawrence and Suddaby interrogate the discourse of institutionalism in organization studies in their chapter on 'Institutions and Institutional Work'. They argue that institutional perspectives focus on the relationships among organizations and the fields in which they operate. Institutional research has produced a huge literature in organization studies that provides robust accounts of the processes through which institutions govern action. Lawrence and Suddaby suggest, however, that institutionalism in organization studies has taken a different turn over the past 10–15 years that emphasizes the role of actors in effecting, transforming and maintaining institutions and fields – practices which the authors refer to as 'institutional work'. Lawrence and Suddaby construct an image of institutional work by drawing on key texts that have highlighted agency in institutional theory and concepts from the sociology of practice. Then, by investigating a relatively small but highly influential body of texts – empirical institutional research in three major journals over the past 15 years – they investigate the degree to which we understand the practices associated with creating, maintaining, disrupting institutions, which together describe a life-cycle of institutional work. In speculating on future research, the authors draw from other discourses to prove a wide range of approaches, including discourse analysis, actor network theory and semiotics. As the authors note, these are more than methodologies since each involves different theoretical and empirical traditions with the potential for developing new knowledge regarding institutions.

Gagliardi's chapter: 'Exploring the Aesthetic Side of Organizational Life' interrogates the tendency to view organizations as 'nothing other than a graphic and summary representation of a set of socioprofessional roles and of relations between these roles'. Instead, he argues that organizations are contexts that cultivate our senses, especially though the artifacts with which contemporary organizations are strewn. Gagliardi first interrogates a history of the field in which the aesthetics have been largely ignored. He then interrogates the idea that artifacts are a secondary and accessory aspect of the cultural system, which was the assumption of much of the research on culture that gave rise to this field of study. He argues that the extent to which the aesthetics of organization is taking shape as a field of inquiry within organizational studies is largely a result of its willingness to challenge these assumptions. He then develops further the idea of the aesthetic to propose conceptual frameworks, language and categories appropriate to the analysis and interpretation of the sensate life of the corporate landscape. In so doing, he makes a case for a new discourse of aesthetics, by interrogating – and ultimately severing links with – the cultural discourse in which it was originally embedded.

The final chapter that employs a strategy of discursive interrogation is Miller and Wilson's review of 'Perspectives on Organizational Decision-Making'. In this chapter, the authors examine the history of the study of decision-making in organizations. Their history of decision-making begins with early approaches that focused on the rationality of decision-making and the degree to which it occurred incrementally or in large strides. Such studies of decision-making were subsequently challenged by the shift in focus to power through the work of organizational scholars such as Pettigrew. A strong processual tradition then emerged, primarily in Britain, which built on both cognitive and political images of organizational decision-making. Most recently, the study of organizational decision-making has been challenged by insights from intellectual currents from outside of management. Drawing on chaos theory, decision-making scholars have examined high-velocity environments (Eisenhardt 1989) and the metaphor of jazz (Hatch 1999); while the sociology of practice, a stream of research has illuminated the practices of 'strategizing' (Wilson and Jarzabkowski 2004). In this way, as with the other chapters in this section, new developments are used to interrogate the existing knowledge. The authors conclude by suggesting that the field of strategy may offer possibilities for theoretical advancement and different ways of making sense of managerial interaction in spite of – or perhaps because of – ontological and epistemological differences.

Investigating Organization Studies as a Discourse

Another discursive strategy is that of investigating organization studies itself as a discourse. Three chapters do so by systematically analysing the field from a historical perspective. Reed's chapter on 'Organizational Theorizing: A Historically Contested Terrain' explores the history of organization studies, arguing its roots extend to 19th century thinkers, such as Saint-Simon, and to the societal transformations that accompanies the industrial revolution. Reed argues that the early roots of organization studies were associated with a celebratory air – modern organizations and organization studies

would bring the victory of rationality and science over irrationality and myth. However, in looking at modern day organization studies, Reed finds not a triumph of rationality but a clash of rationalities. By the late 20th century the meta-narratives of the past that promised collective order and individual freedom from rational organizations had not materialized. In fact, contemporary students of organizations function under conditions where these traditional beliefs have been severely challenged. One result is that fragmentation and discontinuity are the dominant features of the field. Reed argues, in this context, that what is taken as knowledge emerges through the dynamic interaction of social context and ideas. Consequently, modern organization studies are a contested terrain with different languages, approaches and philosophies struggling for recognition and acceptance. Reed adopts a view of theory making as an historically located intellectual activity which is directed at assembling and mobilizing ideational material and institutional resources to legitimate knowledge claims and the political projects that follow from them.

A second chapter that examines organization studies as a discourse is Turner's examination of 'The Philosophy of the Social Sciences in Organization Studies'. In this chapter, Turner, like Reed, adopts an historical perspective on organization studies, but from the perspective of the ongoing relationship between organization studies and the philosophies of science and of social science. A significant benefit of this discursive strategy is that it provides us with a simultaneously broader and deeper view of organization studies. As a discourse, Turner shows the identification of organization studies with a series of dominant metaphors, each with roots in the sciences and the philosophy of science. More than that, however, Turner also shows the interplay of philosophical and scientific ideas with the practical problems and experiences that shaped the political economy of research along the way. As just one example, Turner notes the interaction in the 1930s of the machine and organism metaphors for organization, with the Hawthorne experiments, some major industrial accidents, the money of Standard Oil, and the intellectual climate of Harvard University. The intersection of these various elements led to the emergence of new concepts and relationships – new knowledge – associated with the discourse of organization studies, oriented around the idea of the organization as a large, complex organism which, while not amenable to the straightforward fixes of the machine, was susceptible to therapeutic intervention by managers.

In their chapter on 'Representation and Reflexivity', Clegg and Hardy also take an historical perspective on organization studies, particularly the 10 year history since the first edition of the *Handbook* (Clegg et al. 1996). They are especially interested in what the era of post-9/11, globalization, corporate scandals and virtualization (among others) means for organization studies. They remind us of the status of organizations as empirical objects which have changed in form and substance in recent years, matching that to a renewed interest in research that explores the processual aspects of organizations as they are brought into being, rather than seeing them as reified, solidified structures. They remind us of the various intellectual battles that have characterized the field, such as the paradigm wars, that will never be won, but which carve out intellectual space for alternative approaches; as well as pointing to new battles and new relationships between some of those alternative approaches, such as critical theory and postmodernism. Finally, they remind us of the importance – and difficulties – of reflecting on the field of organization studies. In this way, these authors emphasize the fragility of what passes for knowledge in the organization studies.

Investigating the Discourse of Organization Studies

Whereas the previous set of chapters explored organization studies as a discourse – a structured collection of meaningful texts – the next set explores the discourse of organization studies – the modes of language we employ in our descriptions and theorizing of organizational life. In discourse analytic terms, this approach takes a more micro-orientation, paying attention to particular linguistic practices, rather than the overall structure of the field.

The first chapter that investigates the discourse of organization studies is Sillince's examination of 'The Effect of Rhetoric on Competitive Advantage'. Sillince examines both the discourse of organization studies and the discourse of organization, as he examines the role of rhetoric in the social construction of knowledge as a strategic asset for firms. His analysis highlights important dynamics in the discourse of organization studies by showing the

sharp-edged boundaries still existing between areas such as strategic management and the study of language and rhetoric in organizations. Specifically, Sillince's examination of 'comparative advantage' reveals the consequences of using terms without sensitivity to their entailments. We tend to take for granted that an organization's competitive advantage is a direct function of the resources it controls and the products it produces. Sillince's rhetorical analysis reveals that, by taking this for granted, at least two potentially important questions have often gone unasked. Specifically, we tend not to address either what determines value or what is a resource. Sillince's analysis enables him to bring a new lens to the subject, thereby revealing that the value of the firm's resources is problematic, contestable and socially constructed. Furthermore, this new lens opens our eyes to important processes about value, competitive advantage and resources that students of organizations have often ignored as a result of simply buying into the assumptions of the economists.

The second chapter that takes this approach is Putnam and Boys' 'Revisiting Metaphors of Organizational Communication'. The study of communication in and around organizations is a huge and complex domain that is carried out within a range of institutional homes including business schools, sociology departments and schools of communication studies which, in turn, reflect and contribute to the diversity of terminology, conceptualizations, methodologies and topics of interest that marks the field. Putnam and Boys take on this diversity by examining the metaphors that underpin different sets of research on and theories of organizational communication. This chapter shows that the use of metaphor as a unifying device can organize complex arenas of social inquiry by constructing sets of resonances across what might be seen as disparate studies and theories. At the same time, different metaphors produce different kinds of knowledge through the way in which they frame thinking and practice in the research community. Putnam and Boys propose a number of metaphors to organize and understand research on organizational communication: conduit, information processing, performance, discourse, symbol, voice and contradiction. For each metaphor, Putnam and Boys define its central features and review the organizational communication research that employs it, showing the different types of knowledge that each produces.

Examining the Practice of Organization Studies

Discourses can be understood as 'structured collections of meaningful texts' (Phillips et al. 2004: 636) that bring particular practices into being (Fairclough 1992; Phillips and Hardy 1997). According to this view, organizations are seen as 'locally organized' and 'interactionally achieved' (Boden 1994: 1): and bundles of 'practices and material arrangements' (Schatzki 2005: 474), chains of conversational activity (Collins 1981) or 'bodily expressed reactions' (Shotter 2005: 115). Organization emerges in the interactive exchanges of its members who are recognized as such because they display the practices of its community (Robichaud et al. 2004). Whether a practice is meaningful or not – and whether it has organizational consequences – depends on the larger discourses in which it is situated. Thus, academic organizations comprise the practices that constitute research which, in turn, are given meaning by the discourses in which they are situated. A number of chapters focus their attention on various aspects of academic practices and the way in which they produce knowledge.

The first chapter that focuses on the discursive practices of organization studies is Stablein's examination of 'Data in Organization Studies'. In this chapter, Stablein addresses the thorny issue of what counts as data in organization studies, and the practices through which we produce data. On the subject of what counts as data, Stablein provides a useful and philosophically grounded perspective of data as 'representations' about our ideas about empirical 'reality'. While all data are representation, Stablein warns that not all representations are data. Stablein argues for a 'two-way correspondence' model of data, which suggests that for a representation to count as data it must not only involve the conceptualization of some facet of the empirical world into a symbolic system, but also allow the mapping of that symbolic system to the original empirical phenomenon of interest. Stablein offers a useful set of examples to illustrate this point, and then goes on to discuss several kinds of data in organization studies. Rather than focusing on the well-worn and largely pointless distinction between qualitative and quantitative data, Stablein categorizes data in terms of the practices through which it is collected – surveys, experiments, ethnography, case studies, archival research and the examination of discourse. This typology provides an insightful look into both the data and the data practices of organization studies.

Another chapter that focuses on the practices of organization studies is Eden and Huxham's discussion of 'Researching Organizations Using Action Research'. This chapter provides a set of characteristics that define what they refer to as 'research-oriented action research', and outline its requirements in terms of methods, outputs and validity. As with many other authors in the *Handbook*, Eden and Huxham initially take an historical perspective providing an outline of where action research has come from, how it has developed and the varieties of research practice associated with the term. What connects the different versions of action research, they argue, is that, in contrast to other research approaches, action researchers are directly involved with organizational members on issues of importance to those members and about which they intend to take action. By involvement, Eden and Huxham mean that the researcher is not only observing the process, but is also engaged in practices associated with acting as a facilitator or consultant. Organizational members are, therefore, not only research subjects, but also clients of the action researcher. Thus, action research springs from the intersection of two different domains and involves a conjoining of the discourse and practices of practical action with those of organizational research. This dual status can have drawbacks: the legitimacy of action research is sometimes considered suspect both as practical action and as research. Eden and Huxham provide action researchers with their own discourse in the form of a coherent set of guidelines for judging the status of their practices.

The third chapter that addresses the practices of organization studies can be seen as extending some of the concerns of action research to address the issue of organization studies as a set of practices producing research 'that matters'. Flyvbjerg argues that organizational research needs, if it is to matter, to move away from the aim of emulating the natural sciences and address problems that matter to the communities in which we live, as well as engage in dialogue with those communities regarding the results of our research. To achieve these aims, Flyvbjerg presents a mode of what he refers to as 'phronetic' research, which has as its aim the production of knowledge that is neither universalistic in the sense of epistemic, scientific knowledge, nor artful, as in technique or craft. The term phronetic comes from the Greek, 'phronesis', which translates to something like 'prudence' or 'practical common sense'. A phronetic approach to organizational research, argues Flyvbjerg, would be especially concerned with issues of values and of power, with an approach that emphasizes the concrete, the practical and the ethical. Flyvbjerg's chapter makes an important and, potentially, radical contribution to organization studies. By focusing on organization studies as a set of situated practices, Flyvbjerg is able to construct a coherent and compelling alternative to our dominant modes of inquiry.

Discourses of Instability

Organization studies is an empirical science, intimately connected to the practices, processes, structures and outcomes of the organizational world. As such, an important feature of its discourse is the set of connections made between theories and concepts and the empirical reality to which they point. In developing theories or concepts, therefore, a potentially powerful discursive strategy is to highlight changes that have occurred in the organizational world and to show how they demand new ways of writing about organizations and organizational processes. Consequently, the subject matter of organization studies is closely linked to the affairs of the real world, while many of the concepts that command the attention of organizational researchers have their roots in discussions of everyday lay world affairs. As changes occur in the real world, academic treatment of these imported concepts also changes. As these chapters show, research in organization studies is revised and refocused as real-world conditions change. Thus, the following chapters take their motivation from the changing nature of the empirical world and, by evoking it, authors are able to make sense of the different ways in which knowledge is produced within a field of study.

The first such chapter is Doughtery's chapter on 'Organizing for Innovation in the 21st Century'. As the title suggests, this chapter takes the position that innovation is a dynamic process because of the new problems and environmental challenges faced by organizations. Specifically, Dougherty proposes that innovative organizations of the 21st century must employ simple principles of design, which will be very different from the bureaucratic principles of the past. Although organizations will still need to achieve appropriate levels of differentiation,

integration and control, doing so will require quite different mindsets and approaches. In some ways, Doughtery's observations resemble Langton's (1984) account of the changes in managerial mindset introduced by Wedgewood when he operationalized bureaucracy as an organizational form that far outstripped other organizations of its time in responding to environmental contingencies. Although Wedgwood did it as a practitioner and Dougherty is doing as a theorist, both are demonstrating the need to conceive of organizations in fundamentally new ways to cope with the problems of their respective times. The term 'organization' continues to be applied, but the qualitative features to which it refers are dramatically different.

A second chapter that argues for a changing world and, hence, the need for new concepts and theories is McGrath's chapter, 'Beyond Contingency: From Structure to Structuring in the Design of the Contemporary Organization'. McGrath observes how the concept of organization structure has been at the core of organization theory. Early on, this focus on structure was associated with the idea of finding the one best way to design an organization. However, as organization theory emerged it was agreed that there was no one best way to structure, because the appropriate structure was contingent upon the nature of the organization's environment, technology and so forth. This contingency perspective, while being a major step away from essentializing the organization, tended to view environment as a sort of an entity. Although McGrath recognizes that not all students of organization structure today would agree that we need to move beyond a contingency theory of structure, she points to some important reasons to do so, as a result of recent changes affecting how organizations need to behave. Among other things, we need to think differently about what constitutes 'fit'. Given the variety of responses that organizations need to make, an effective organization will not have just one structure because it needs to be able to change itself into multiple forms – to be ambidextrous. Similarly, conceiving organizations as entities bounded from other organizations and from the environment may be highly misleading: the concept of structure needs to become subordinate to the concept of 'structuring'.

Parker and Clegg's chapter on 'Globalization' reveals another domain in which changing conditions are argued to lead to a reshuffling of academic discussions, debates, concepts and theories. One illustration Parker and Clegg provide is the extraordinary growth in the use of the term 'global' in the academic business press between 1995 and 2004. Drawing on a wide range of sources and perspectives, Parker and Clegg argue that the phenomenon of globalization can be understood as a complex set of interconnections that cut across a series of domains – the natural environment, economics, the political and legal domain, culture and business practices. For each of these domains, Parker and Clegg chart the changes that are occurring and the debates surrounding those changes. Replete with 'real life' business and societal examples, these authors show how the tendency toward oversimplification in the field has led to dichotomies that can have significant effects for individuals around the world. The complexity and instability of globalization demands insights from other disciplines such as international relations, political economy, anthropology, sociology, cultural studies, economic geography and economic history. Expanding on the limited functional knowledge of international business is the only way it can keep up with a changing world.

The final chapter that takes on a discourse of instability is Porter and Powell's examination of 'Networks and Organizations'. These authors argue that, although the concept of social networks can be traced back to the work of Simmel and Merton, the growth in the concept's importance and usage can be linked to certain changes in contemporary society, including the decline of the vertically integrated firm, globalization, the increased importance of extra-organizational resources including knowledge, and the co-ordination requirements that stem from multi-site, geographically dispersed operations. Porter and Powell provide a valuable examination of networks and organizations by considering the role that networks play at different stages of the organizational life cycle. For each of new, growing and mature ventures, they summarize the key impacts of organizational networks, as well as considering what questions are prompted by the relevant research. Thus, differences in how different types of organizations utilize networks and how networks are utilized differently throughout the life cycle of their development creates demands for new knowledge that keeps up with these differences. Further it demands the use of different methodologies, such as ethnographies or longitudinal databases that afford the opportunity to study emergence and

dynamics and how changes over time in network structure can influence both markets and politics.

Discourses of Concern

A number of chapters develop what we refer to as a discourse of concern, by which we mean they approach topics in organization studies from a perspective that highlights both the moral and social dangers associated with organizations, and the potential for organizations and organization studies to improve the well-being of individuals, communities and societies, especially less powerful and marginalized members.

Frost et al.'s chapter 'Seeing Organizations Differently: Three Lenses on Compassion' explores an important new topic in organization studies. Their exploration of compassion not only provides a powerful look at the dynamics of this phenomenon, but also challenges many of taken-for-granted understandings of organizations as social systems. The authors argue that the desire to understand organizations as rational, calculating systems is not only a managerial bias, but also a deeply ingrained aspect of organization studies. Their exploration of suffering and compassion in organizations provides a counter to that desire – this chapter opens the door to what the authors refer to as the 'humane and virtuous aspects of organizational life'. The authors locate the concept of compassion in what for organization studies are non-traditional discourses, such as religion, philosophy and medicine. This provides both a strong underpinning for the concept as an addition to our field, and a bridge to important but overlooked areas for inspiration and intellectual borrowing. While emphasizing a discourse of concern, the authors embed their discussion in three distinct approaches to organization studies – interpersonal work, narrative and organizing – each of which offers important insight into the dynamics of compassion and provides interesting possibilities for research. The authors treat each perspective as a lens on compassion, showing critical aspects of the phenomenon and connecting to important organization studies traditions.

Fineman's chapter on 'Emotion and Organizing' also engages with discourses of concern. Fineman argues that, although emotion-oriented research has become much more prevalent and accepted in organizations studies, emotionality in organizations is still seen as potentially dangerous and so often silenced. This chapter explores many of the twists and turns associated with emotions in organizations and organization studies, the benefits and positive outcomes that can be associated with an appreciation and understanding of emotion, and the potentially painful and depleting consequences of organizational processes and research agendas that might leverage, exploit or suppress the emotions of individuals. Fineman begins the chapter with a discussion of emotional labour and the effects of individuals having to express particular emotions – and suppress others. He points out that emotional *work*, the effort of crafting and negotiating our appearance on different social stages, sustains the emotional hypocrisy that makes social order possible and, at the same time, creates pressures for individuals. He provides a critique of one of the latest areas of interest in this field of research – emotional intelligence. While it has caught the mood of the times, it emphasizes the instrumental control of emotions. It paints a picture of us in control – rather than victims of – our emotions, but it is clear that only certain emotions are acceptable; those that are productive and predominantly productive for organizations rather than individuals. He also examines how some of the major organizational changes that employees are currently experiencing in the outsourced, global, virtual world have emotional consequences, as well as the spectacular orchestration of mass emotions. Throughout the chapter, the emotional experiences of individuals – presented in their own words – are paramount.

The concern of Jermier et al. is the degradation of the natural environment – what they describe as 'one of the most urgent problems of our time'. In 'Beyond the New Corporate Environmentalism: Green Politics and Critical-Reflective Organizational Systems', these authors explore a topic that is driven by concern for the welfare of humanity as well as the rest of the planet's inhabitants. The natural environment and environmentalism are important topics for organization studies: the pollution of the environment is done by organizations (including corporations, but also public and voluntary sector organizations) and by individuals through organized processes in their work and leisure activities. The preservation of the natural environment is also an organizational phenomenon, with environmental NGOs, governmental ministries and corporate departments all involved, as well as large, complex interorganizational

networks connecting many of those players. The authors of this chapter argue that a new ideological framework has recently developed, which stresses the role of businesses as leaders in addressing environmental issues – what the authors refer to as the 'new corporate environmentalism'. In order to examine this ideological development, the authors use the lens of critical theory (see Alvesson and Deetz in this volume). The authors argue that critical theory provides an appropriate and insightful lens because of its ability to highlight the political nature of the new corporate environmentalism, and to provide an intellectual foundation that supports a subversive position on an issue of grave importance.

Nkomo and Stewart's chapter on 'Diverse Identities in Organizations' examines an area of research that is concerned both with human welfare and the instrumental implications of diversity in organizations. The authors show that organization studies has only relatively recently begun to pay attention to issues of diversity, with early assumptions of the field based on an homogeneous, raceless, gender-less workforce. Only with the civil unrest of the 1960s in the US and Europe did organizational researchers begin to seriously incorporate diversity into their research agenda, and even then with an agenda dominated by the process of assimilation. Two early responses from the research community focused on what Nkomo and Stewart refer to as 'prejudice-reduction strategies' and organizational response to equal opportunity legislation. Over time, this orientation was revised. The changes were captured in an early 1990s *Harvard Business Review* article that placed a positive value on diversity. The authors provide an insightful summary of research on diversity from five perspectives: social identity theory; embedded intergroup relations theory; demography; racioethnicity and gender; and postmodern and critical perspectives. For each of these perspectives, they examine how diversity is defined and measured, whose standpoint defined diversity, what level of analysis is employed, and what effects of diversity are highlighted. Through this systematic examination of diversity in organizations, Nkomo and Stewart focus our attention on key research issues and problems that require attention if we are to advance our understanding of this aspect of organizational life.

'From the "Woman's Point of View" Ten Years Later: Towards a Feminist Organization Studies' by Calás and Smircich shows that inquiry in this field originated from an interest in challenging the status quo because of the mistreatment of a particular group of people, i.e. women. Despite stating the chapter is not intended to suggest ways of organizing or managing from feminist perspectives, it opens with a review of conditions of women around the world, and uses stories of Sarah Kelly and Julia Peña throughout to illustrate how theories illuminate – or fail to illuminate – different aspects of gender, especially different forms of subordination of women as a fundamental problem. As the authors state, feminist theoretical perspectives are critical of the status quo and therefore always political, although the degree of critique and the nature of the politics differ. As a result, the impact of different approaches on women and on research may vary widely. Accordingly, the chapter examines a range of theories – from Liberal Feminist Theory to Transnational/(Post)Colonial theories – to show the different knowledges and effects that they produce. As theorizing has developed, new approaches have been employed to uncover limitations in traditional critiques, expose gaps in knowledge, and relate more directly to the concerns of women. Each theoretical tendency gives alternative accounts of gender issues, frames 'problems' differently and proposes different courses of action as solutions. In this regard, the chapter melds discourses of concern and of interrogation. However, at the end of the chapter, the authors return firmly to the discourse of concern when they advocate a version of feminist organization studies that starts from 'a position in which gender relations, and its intersectionalities with other systems of social inequality, is the root organizing principle of contemporary capitalism'. Only in this way, argue Calás and Smircich, can we work towards an equitable and just world.

Conclusion

Reflecting on the process through which we consider the major topics in organization studies today, we can see that both production and consumption play important roles. On the one hand, it is very clear that members of field have been producing – there are many insightful organizations, manuscripts and creative ideas in literature. Interestingly, while we have stated our predilection for challenging the canons and production methods of normal science, we would not deny that this approach has been responsible for generating important knowledge in the field, as much as more constructionist

approaches. In both cases, as these scholars have gone about their work, the consumption process has also played an important role. First, in producing texts, these authors are also consuming other texts and, in addition, reaffirming existing discourse, challenging it or trying to create new discourses. In addition, as editors, we have been among the first consumers of these chapters and have orchestrated them into the production that constitutes this introduction.

It goes without saying that the consumption process is reflected in this book. The contents of the volume reflect the things that we find interesting and meaningful. We have the privilege of embedding our choices in a publication that may influence what others consume. In this regard, this book could be treated as a sort of consumers guide. On the other hand, while cognizant of the fact that the myriad boundaries laid down in and around the *Handbook* – not least in this introduction – will not only constrain and direct consumers, they may frustrate and even enrage them. The important thing, from our point of view, is not whether readers agree or disagree so much as they *engage*. Only in that way can the *Handbook* generate the ongoing conversations that we hope to engender.

References

Astley, W.G. (1985) 'Administrative science as socially constructed truth', *Administrative Science Quarterly*, 30: 497–513.

Astley, W.G. and Zammuto, R.F. (1992) 'Organization science, managers, and language games', *Organization Science*, 3(4): 443–60.

Barnes, B. (1974) *Scientific knowledge and sociological theory*. London: Routledge & Kegan Paul.

Boden, D. (1994) *The business of talk: Organizations in action*. Cambridge: Polity Press.

Bolman, L. and Deal, T. (1997) *Reframing Organizations*, 2nd edn. San Francisco: Jossey Bass.

Brown, J.S. and Duguid, P. (1991) 'Organizational Learning and communities of practice perspective', *Organization Science*, 2(1): 40–57.

Brown, J.S. and Duguid, P. (2001) 'Knowledge and organization: a social-practice perspective', *Organization Science*, 12(2): 198–213.

Cacioppo, J.T., Semin, G.R. and Berntson, G.G. (2004) 'Realism, instrumental, and scientific symbiosis: psychological theory as a search for truth and the discovery of solutions', *American Psychologist*, 59: 214–23.

Calás, M.B. and Smircich, L (1999) 'Past postmodernism? Reflections and tentative directions', *Academy of Management Review*, 24: 649–71.

Callon, M. (1986) 'Some elements of a sociology of translation: domestication of the scallops and the fishermen of St Brieuc Bay', in J. Law (ed.), *Power, action and belief.* London: Routledge and Kegan Paul. pp. 196–223.

Clegg, C. and Hardy, C. (1996a) 'Organizations, organization and organizing', in S.R. Clegg, C. Hardy and W.R. Nord (eds), *Handbook of Organization Studies.* London: Sage. pp. 1–29.

Clegg, S. and Hardy, C. (1996b) 'Representations', in S. Clegg, C. Hardy and W.R. Nord (eds), *Handbook of Organization Studies.* London: Sage. pp. 676–708.

Clegg, S., Hardy, C. and Nord, W.R. (eds) (1996) *Handbook of Organization Studies.* London: Sage Publications.

Collins, R. (1981) 'On the microfoundations of macro-sociology', *American Journal of Sociology*, 86: 984–1013.

Du Gay, P. (1996) *Consumption and identity at work.* London: Sage.

Eisenhardt, K.M. (1989) 'Making fast strategic decisions in 'high-velocity' environments', *Academy of Management Journal*, 32: 543–76.

Elsbach, K.D., Sutton, R.I. and Whetten, D.A. (1999) 'Perspectives on developing management theory, circa 1999: Moving from shrill monologues to (relatively) tame dialogues', *Journal of Management Inquiry*, 8: 627–33.

Fairclough, N. (1992) *Discourse and social change.* Cambridge: Polity Press.

Ferraro, F., Pfeffer, J. and Sutton, T.I. (2005) 'Economics language and assumptions: how theories can become self-fulfilling', *Academy of Management Review*, 30(1): 8–24.

Gergen, K.J. (2001) *Social construction in context.* London: Sage.

Hall, S. (2001) 'Foucault: power, knowledge and discourse', in M. Wetherell, S. Taylor and S.J. Yates (eds), *Discourse theory and practice: A reader.* London: Sage. pp. 72–81.

Hannan, M.T. and Freeman, J.H. (1977) 'The population ecology of organizations', *American Journal of Sociology*, 83: 929–84.

Hardy, C., Grant, D., Oswick, C. and Putnam, L. (2005) 'Diss-ing discourse: a response', *Organization Studies*, 26(5), 799–804.

Harley, B. and Hardy, C. (2004) 'Firing blanks? An analysis of discursive struggle in HRM', *Journal of Management Studies*, 41(3): 377–400.

Harley, B., Hardy, C. and Alvesson, M. (2004) 'Reflecting on reflexivity', in K.M. Weaver (ed.), Conference proceedings, *64th Annual Meeting of the Academy of Management.* New Orleans: Academy of Management.

Hassard, J. and Keleman, M. (2002) 'Production and consumption in organizational knowledge: the case of the paradigms debate', *Organization*, 9: 331–5.

Hatch, M.J. (1999) 'Exploring the empty spaces of organizing: how improvisational jazz helps redescribe organizational structure', *Organization Studies*, 20(1): 75–100.

Kaplan, A. (1964) *The Conduct of Inquiry Methodology for Behavioral Science.* Scranton, PA: Chandler Publishing.

Knights, D. (1992) 'Changing spaces: the disruptive impact of a new epistemological location for the study of management', *Academy of Management Review*, 17: 514–36.

Knorr-Cetina, K. (1981a) *The manufacture of knowledge: An essay on the constructivist and contextual nature of science.* Oxford: Pergamon.

Knorr-Cetina, K. (1981b) 'The micro-sociological challenge of macro-sociology: towards a reconstruction of social theory and methodology', in K. Knorr-Cetina and A.V. Cicourel (eds), *Advances in social theory and methodology.* Boston: Routledge and Kegan Paul. pp. 1–47.

Kuhn, T.S. (1970) *The structure of scientific revolution.* Chicago: University of Chicago Press.

Langton, J. (1984) 'The ecological theory of bureaucracy: the case of Josiah Wedgwood', *Administrative Science Quarterly*, 29: 330–54.

Latour, B. (1987) *Science in action: How to follow scientists and engineers through society.* Cambridge, MA: Harvard University Press.

Latour, B. (1988) *The pasteurization of France.* Cambridge, MA: Harvard University Press.

Latour, B. and Woolgar, S. (1979) *Laboratory life: The construction of scientific facts.* Beverly Hills, CA: Sage.

Lounsbury, M. (2003) 'The death of organization science', *Journal of Management Inquiry*, 12(3): 293–8.

Mauws, M. and Phillips, N. (1995) 'Understanding language games', *Organization Science*, 63: 322–34.

Morgan, G. (1986) *Images of organization.* Newbury Park, CA: Sage.

Phillips, N. and Hardy, C. (1997) 'Managing multiple identities: discourse, legitimacy and resources in the UK refugee system', *Organization*, 4(2): 159–85.

Phillips, N., Lawrence, T. and Hardy, C. (2004) 'Discourse and institutions', *Academy of Management Review*, 29(4): 635–52.

Pinch, T. (1985) 'Towards an analysis of scientific observation: the externality and evidential significance of observational reports in physics', *Social Studies of Science*, 15: 3–36.

Robichaud, D., Girous, H. and Taylor, J.R. (2004) 'The metaconversation: the recursive property of language as a key to organizing', *Academy of Management Review*, 29(4): 617–34.

Schatzki, T.R. (2005) 'The sites of organizations', *Organization Studies*, 26(3): 465–84.

Shotter, J. (2005) 'Inside the moment of managing: Wittgenstein and the everyday dynamics of our expressive-responsive activities', *Organization Studies*, 26(1): 113–35.

Tsoukas, H. (1996) 'The firm as a distributed knowledge system: a constructionist approach', *Strategic Management Journal*, 7: 11–25.

Weick, K.E. (1999) 'Theory construction as disciplined reflexivity: tradeoffs in the 90s', *Academy of Management Review*, 24: 797–807.

Wilson, D.C. and Jarzabkowski, P. (2004) 'Thinking and acting strategically: new challenges for interrogating strategy', *European Management Review*, 1: 14–20.

Woolgar, S. (1988) *Science: The very idea.* Chichester: Ellis Horwood/London and New York: Tavistock.

PART I
Theorizing the Field

1.1 Organizational Theorizing: a Historically Contested Terrain

MICHAEL REED

Organization studies has its proximate historical roots in the socio-political writings of nineteenth century thinkers, such as Saint-Simon, who attempted to anticipate and interpret the nascent structural and ideological transformations wrought by industrial capitalism (Wolin 1960). The economic, social and political changes that capitalist-led modernization brought in its wake created a world that was fundamentally different from the relatively small-scale and simple forms of production and administration which had dominated earlier phases of capitalist development in the eighteenth and early nineteenth centuries (Bendix 1974). The late nineteenth and early twentieth centuries witnessed the growing dominance of large-scale organizational units in economic, social and political life as the complexity and intensity of collective activity moved beyond the administrative capacity of more personal and direct forms of coordination (Waldo 1948). Indeed, the rise of the 'administrative state' symbolized a new mode of governance in which rational, scientific organization transformed human nature:

> The new order would be governed not by men [sic] but by 'scientific principles' based on the 'nature of things' and therefore absolutely independent of human will. In this way, organizational society promised the rule of scientific laws rather than men [sic] and the eventual disappearance of the political element entirely. Organization as power over things – this was the lesson taught by Saint-Simon (Wolin 1960: 338–9).

Thus, the historical roots of organization studies are deeply embedded in a body of writing that gathered momentum from the second half of the nineteenth century onwards. This body of research and writing confidently anticipated the triumph of science over politics and the victory of rationally designed collective order and progress over human recalcitrance and irrationality (Reed 1985).

The growth of an 'organizational society' was synonymous with the inexorable advance of reason, liberation and justice and the eventual eradication of ignorance, coercion and poverty. Organizations were rationally designed to solve permanently the conflict between collective needs and individual wants that had bedeviled social progress since the days of Ancient Greece (Wolin 1960). They guaranteed social order and personal freedom by fusing collective decision-making and individual interest (Storing 1962) through the scientific design, implementation and maintenance of administrative structures that subsumed sectional interests within institutionalized collective goals. The perennial conflict between 'society' and 'individual' would be permanently overcome. Whereas Hegel had relied on the dialectic of history to eradicate social conflict (Plant 1973), organization theorists put their faith in modern organization as the universal solution to the problem of social order.

> The organizationists looked upon society as an order of functions, a utilitarian construct of integrated activity, a means for focusing human energies in combined effort. Where the symbol of community was fraternity, the symbol of organization was power … organization signifies a method of social control, a means for imparting order, structure and regularity to society (Wolin 1960: 325–6).

Viewed from the historical vantage point of the early twenty-first century, however, the practice and study of organization look very different today. The earlier meta-narratives of collective order and individual freedom through rational organization and material progress have fragmented and frayed into a cacophony of querulous 'voices' totally lacking in general moral force and analytical coherence (Reed

1992). The once seemingly cast-iron guarantee of material and social progress through sustained technological advance, modern organization and scientific administration now looks increasingly threadbare. Both the technical effectiveness and moral virtue of 'formal' or 'complex' organization are called into question by institutional and intellectual transformations that push inexorably towards social fragmentation, political disintegration and ethical relativism. Who amongst us can afford to ignore Bauman's (1989: 75) argument that 'the typically modern, technological-bureaucratic patterns of action and the mentality they institutionalize, generate, sustain and reproduce' were the sociopsychological foundations of and organizational preconditions for the Holocaust?

In short, contemporary students of organization find themselves at a historical juncture and in a social context where all the old ideological 'certainties' and technical 'fixes' that once underpinned their 'discipline' are fundamentally being called into question. Over the last two decades, a meta-theoretical debate over the nature of organization and the intellectual means most appropriate to its understanding has been underway. This has badly shaken, if not totally undermined, the philosophical foundations of and substantive rationale for contemporary organizational analysis (Burrell and Morgan 1979; Powell and DiMaggio 1991; Reed and Hughes 1992; Casey 2002; Tsoukas and Knudsen 2003; Westwood and Clegg 2003). Underlying assumptions about the inherently rational and ethical quality of modern organization are challenged by alternative voices that radically undermine the 'taken-for-granted' objectivity and integrity of corporate agency (Cooper and Burrell 1988; Burrell 1997; 2003). Key texts published in the 1950s and early 1960s bridled with self-confidence concerning their 'discipline's' intellectual identity and rationale, as well as its critical policy significance (see Haire 1960; Blau and Scott 1963; Argyris 1964). However, this self-confidence simply drained away in the 1980s and 1990s, to be replaced by uncertain, complex and confused expectations concerning the nature and merits of an organization studies increasingly racked by philosophical self-doubt, theoretical fragmentation and ideological polarization.

In Kuhnian terms, we still seem to be in a phase of 'revolutionary' rather than 'normal' science (Kuhn 1970). Normal science is dominated by puzzle-solving activity and incremental research programmes carried out with generally accepted and strongly institutionalized theoretical frameworks (Lakatos and Musgrave 1970). Revolutionary science occurs when 'domain assumptions' about subject matter, interpretative frameworks and knowledge are exposed to continuous critique, reevaluation and redesign (Gouldner 1971). Research and analysis are shaped by the search for anomalies and contradictions within prevailing theoretical frameworks, generating an internal intellectual dynamic of theoretical struggle. It signifies a discipline racked by internal conflict and dissension over ideological and epistemological fundamentals whose various supporters occupy and represent different paradigmatic 'worlds' between which communication, much less mediation, becomes impossible (Kuhn 1970; Hassard 1990). Fragmentation and discontinuity become the dominant features of a field's identity and rationale, rather than the relative stability and cohesion characteristic of 'normal science' (Willmott 1993; Van Maanen 1995; Clark 2000; Hancock and Tyler 2001; Casey 2002).

One, very potent, response to the divisive impact of the break with the functionalist/positivist orthodoxy is the retreat into a nostalgic yearning for past certainties and the communal comfort they once provided (Donaldson 1985; McKelvey 2003). This 'conservative' reaction may also demand an enforced and tightly policed philosophical and political consensus within the field to repair intellectual tissue scarred by decades of theoretical infighting and to re-establish the theoretical hegemony of a particular research paradigm (Pfeffer 1993; 1997). Both 'nostalgic' and 'political' forms of conservatism aim to resist the centripetal trends set in motion by intellectual struggle and to return to ideological and theoretical orthodoxy. A robust combination of 'back to basics' and 'paradigm enforcement' can be a very attractive option for those unsettled by the intellectual fermentation routinely occurring in contemporary organization studies.

Rather than 'paradigm enforcement', others look towards 'paradigm proliferation' through the separate intellectual development and nurturing of distinctive approaches within different domains, uncontaminated by contact with competing, and often more entrenched, perspectives (Morgan 1986; Jackson and Carter 2000; Hassard and Keleman 2002). This response to intellectual upheaval provides sustenance for a 'serious playfulness' in organization studies where postmodern irony and humility replace the sanctimonious platitudes typical of a rational modernism that is incapable of seeing that 'objective truth is not the only game in town' (Gergen 1992).

If neither conservatism nor relativism appeals, a third option is to retell organization theory's history in ways that rediscover the analytical narratives and ethical discourses that shaped its development and legitimated its character (Reed 1992; Willmott 1993; Shenhav 2003; Starbuck 2003). Such approaches question both a return to fundamentals and an unrestrained celebration of discontinuity and diversity: neither intellectual surfing or free riding on the rising tide of relativism, nor retreating into the cave of orthodoxy, are attractive futures for the study of organization. The former promises unrestrained intellectual freedom, but at the price of isolationism and fragmentation. The latter falls back on a worn and outmoded consensus, sustained through continuous intellectual surveillance and control.

This chapter adopts the third response. It attempts to reconstruct the history of organization theory's intellectual development in a way that balances social context with theoretical ideas, and structural conditions with conceptual innovation. It offers the prospect of rediscovering and renewing a sense of historical vision and contextual sensitivity that gives both 'society' and 'ideas' their just desserts. Neither the history of organization studies nor the way in which that history is told can be regarded as neutral representations of past achievements. Indeed, any telling of history to support reconstructions of the present and visions of the future is a controversial and contested interpretation that is always open to challenge and refutation. Thus, the purpose of this chapter is to map organizational theory as a historically contested terrain within which different languages, approaches and philosophies struggle for recognition and acceptance.

The next section examines theory making and development in organization studies as an intellectual activity that is necessarily implicated in the social and historical context in which it is made and remade. The chapter then examines seven interpretative frameworks that have structured the fields' development over the last century or so and the socio-historical contexts in which they attained a degree of, always contested, intellectual pre-eminence. The penultimate section considers the most significant exclusions or silences that are evident in these major narrative traditions. The chapter

concludes with an evaluation of potential future intellectual developments in organization studies, set within the wider intellectual context provided by the narratives outlined earlier.

Theorizing Organization

This conception of organizational theorizing is based on Gouldner's (1980: 9) view that both the process and the product of theorizing should be seen as a 'doing and a making by persons caught up in some specific historical era'. The theoretically informed analysis of and debate about organizations and organizing are outcomes of a precarious combination of individual vision and technical production located within a dynamic socio-historical context and the diverse intellectual inheritance that it offers to contemporary generations. As such, theory making is always liable to subvert institutionalized conventions that have petrified into unreflectively accepted orthodoxies that can never be contained completely within established cognitive frames and conceptual parameters. However, the probability of specific theoretical initiatives metamorphosing into much more significant conceptual 'paradigm shifts' is largely dependent on their cumulative impact on the particular intellectual communities and traditions through which they are mediated and received (Willmott 1993; Tsoukas and Knudsen 2003). Thus, while theory making is always potentially subversive of the intellectual status quo, its actual impact is always refracted through existing knowledge/power relationships and the 'contextual receptiveness' of particular socio-historical conditions and structures to specific intellectual developments (Toulmin 1972).

In short, theory making is a historically located intellectual practice directed at assembling and mobilizing ideational, material and institutional resources to legitimate certain knowledge claims and the political projects which flow from them. The intellectual and social contexts in which theoretical debate is embedded have a crucial bearing on the form and content of particular conceptual innovations as they struggle to attain a degree of support within the wider community (Clegg 1994; Thompson and McHugh 2002; Westwood and Clegg 2003). As Bendix (1974: xx) maintains, 'A study of ideas as weapons in the management of organizations could afford a better understanding of the relations between ideas and actions'.

Table 1.1.1 Analytical narratives in organization analysis

Meta-narrative interpretative framework	Major problematic	Illustrative/exemplary/perspectives	Contextual transitions
Rationality	Order	Classical OT, scientific management, decision theory, Taylor, Fayol, Simon	from nighwatchman state to industrial state
Integration	Consensus	Human relations, neo-HR, functionalism, contingency/systems theory, corporate culture, Durkheim, Barnard, Mayo, Parsons	from entrepreneurial capitalism to welfare capitalism
Market	Liberty	Theory of firm, institutional economics, transaction costs, agency theory, resource dependency, population ecology, liberal OT	from managerial capitalism to neo-liberal capitalism
Power	Domination	Neo-radical Weberians, critical/structural Marxism, labour process, institutional theory Weber, Marx	from liberal collectivism to bargained corporatism
Knowledge	Control	Ethnomethod, organizational culture/symbol, poststructuralist, post-industrial, post-Fordist/modern, Foucault, Garfinkel, actor-network theory	from industrialism/ modernity to post-industrialism/ postmodernity
Justice	Participation	Business ethics, morality and OB, industrial democracy, participation theory, critical theory, Habermas	from repressive to participatory democracy
Network	Complexity	Post-Bur/network theory, Castells, Beck Giddens, Lash and Urry	from post-indust to network society

It does not mean, however, that no recognized, collective basis exists on which contradictory knowledge claims can be evaluated. At any point in time, organization studies is constituted through shared lines of debate and dialogue which establish intellectual constraints and opportunities within which new contributions are assessed. Negotiated rules and norms are generated through which collective judgements concerning new and old work are made and a vocabulary and a grammar of organizational analysis emerge. This 'grounded rationality' (Reed 1993) may lack the universality associated, however mistakenly (Putnam 1978), with the 'hard' sciences, but it nonetheless establishes an identifiable framework of procedures and practices 'that

provide for their own relevant discourse about proof' (Thompson 1978: 205–6). Thus, organization theory is subject to shared, although necessarily revisable, methodological procedures by means of which reasoned evaluations of competing analytical narratives and explanatory theories are negotiated and debated. The interaction and contestation of rival intellectual traditions imply the existence of negotiated, historicized and contextualized understandings that make rational argumentation possible (Reed 1993; 2003).

The interpretative frameworks in Table 1.1.1 constitute the historically contested intellectual terrain on which organization analysis developed. They constitute a terrain that must be mapped and traversed in relation to the interplay between the procedural and contextual factors that shape the debates around and through which 'the field' has emerged and been structured (Morgan and Stanley 1993). These frameworks have shaped the emergence and subsequent development of organization studies as a recognizable intellectual field over a century or more. They provide a grammar and a context through which analytically structured narratives can be built and communicated; symbolic and technical resources through which the nature of organization can be debated; and a communal store of texts and discourses that mediate these debates for both specialist and lay audiences alike. They develop in a dialectical relationship with historical and social processes as loosely structured and contested ways of conceptualizing and debating key features of organization. Each is defined in relation to the central problematic around which it developed and the socio-historical context in which it was articulated. The discussion, thus, provides a grounded appreciation of the strategic analytical narratives through which the field of organization studies is constituted as a dynamic intellectual practice, permeated by theoretical controversies and ideological conflicts concerning the ways in which 'organization' can and ought to be.

Rationalism Triumphant

As Stretton (1969: 406) argued, 'we take in rationality with our mother's milk'. Yet, this belief in the naturalness of calculated ratiocination has definite historical and ideological roots. Saint Simon (1958) has a very strong claim to being the first 'theorist of organization'. He

> was probably the first to note the rise of modern organizational patterns, identify some of their distinctive features, and insist on their prime significance for the emerging society … the ground rules of modern society had been deeply altered and the deliberately conceived and planned organization was to play a new role in the world (Gouldner 1959: 400–1).

The belief that modern society is dominated by a 'logic of organization' recurs throughout the history of organization studies, promoting a principle of social organization in which rationally assigned technical function defines the socio-economic location,

authority and behaviour of every individual, group and class. According to Saint Simon, it provides a cast-iron defense against social conflict and political uncertainty by establishing a new structure of power based on technical expertise and its pivotal contribution to the smooth functioning of society. Social order is to be based upon 'organization' rather than on randomly allocated or 'anarchic' market advantages or birth privileges.

The conception of organization as a rationally constructed artifice directed to the solution of collective problems of social order and administrative management is reflected in the writings of Taylor (1912), Fayol (1949), Urwick and Brech (1947) and Brech (1948). Such work advocates that the theory of organization 'has to do with the structure of coordination imposed upon the work division units of an enterprise … Work division is the foundation of organization; indeed, the reason for organization' (Gulick and Urwick 1937: 3). It legitimates the idea that society and its constituent organizational units will be managed through scientific laws of administration from which human emotions and values can be totally excluded (Waldo 1948). Epistemological principles and administrative techniques translate highly contestable, normative precepts into universal, objective, immutable and, hence, unchallengeable scientific laws. The 'rational individual is, and must be, an organized and institutionalized individual' (Simon 1957: 1012). Human beings became the 'raw material' to be transformed by modern organizational technologies into well-ordered, productive members of society unlikely to interfere with the long-term plans of ruling classes and elites. Thus, social, political and moral problems could be transformed into engineering tasks amenable to technical solutions (Gouldner 1971). Modern organizations heralded the triumph of rational knowledge and technique over seemingly intractable human emotion and prejudice.

This model insinuated itself into the ideological core and theoretical fabric of organization studies in such a pervasive and natural manner that its identity and influence were virtually impossible to ascertain, much less question. As Gouldner (1959) argued, it prescribed a 'blueprint' for an authority structure where individuals and groups were required to follow certain laws. Principles of efficient and effective functioning were promulgated as an axiom to direct all forms of organizational practice and analysis. It provided a universal characterization of the 'reality' of formal organization, irrespective of time, place and situation. Once this blueprint was accepted, it legitimated a view of organizations as autonomous and independent social units, above and beyond the purview of moral evaluation and political debate (Gouldner 1971).

Although the 'age of organization' demanded a new professional hierarchy to meet the needs of a developing industrial society, superseding the claims of both moribund aristocracy and reactionary entrepreneurs, this view was profoundly anti-democratic and anti-egalitarian. A technically and administratively determined conception of hierarchy, subordination and authority had no truck with rising socio-political agitation based on notions of universal suffrage in either workplace or polity (Wolin 1960; Mouzelis 1967; Clegg and Dunkerley 1980). Rational bureaucratic organization was socially and morally legitimated as an indispensable form of organized power, based on objective technical functions that were necessary for the efficient and effective functioning of a social order founded on rational-legal authority (Presthus 1975; Frug 1984).

These principles are deeply embedded in the epistemological and theoretical foundations of those analytical perspectives that constitute the conceptual core of organization studies. Taylor's 'scientific management' is directed towards a permanent monopolization of organizational knowledge through the rationalization of work performance and job design. It is the first modern attempt to design and impose a form of 'knowledge management' that will universally subject work behaviour and relations to rational surveillance and control (Burawoy 1979; Sewell 2001; Alvesson 2004). As Merkle (1990: 62) argues:

> Evolving beyond its technical and national origins, Taylorism became an important component of the philosophical outlook of modern industrial civilization, defining virtue as efficiency, establishing a new role for experts in production, and setting parameters for new patterns of social distribution.

As both ideology and practice, Taylorism was extremely hostile towards entrepreneurial theories of organization that focused on the political and technical needs of a small ownership elite (Bendix 1974; Rose 1975; Clegg and Dunkerley 1980). As Bendix (1974: 9) stresses, 'the managerial ideologies

of today are distinguished from the entrepreneurial ideologies of the past in that managerial ideologies are thought to aid employers or their agents in controlling and directing the activities of workers'.

Fayol's principles of organization, although modified by a perceptive awareness of the need for contextual adaptation and compromise, were driven by the need to construct an architecture of coordination and control to contain the inevitable disruption and conflict caused by 'informal behaviour'. Classical organization theory is founded on the underlying belief that organization provides a principle of structural design and a practice of operational control that can be rationally determined and formalized in advance of actual performance. Indeed, it assumed that work performance automatically follows the design rationale and control instrumentation entailed in the organization's formal structure (Massie 1965).

Simon's (1945) concept of 'bounded rationality' and theory of 'administrative behaviour' flow from a penetrating critique of the excessive rationalism and formalism of classical management and organization theory. However, his ideas are framed within an approach that sees rational choice between clearly delineated options as the basis of all social action (March 1988). It reduces the vital 'interpretative work', performed by individual agents and corporate actors, to a purely cognitive process dominated by standardized rules and operating programmes. Politics, culture, morality and history are significant by their absence from this model of 'bounded rationality'. Treated as random, extraneous variables beyond the influence, much less control, of rational cognitive processes and organizational procedures, they become analytically marginalized, left outside the conceptual parameters of Simon's preferred model.

Rationalism exerted a profound influence over the historical and conceptual development of organization analysis. It established a cognitive frame and research agenda that could not be ignored, even by those who wished to take a radically different line (Perrow 1986). It also generated a powerful discursive resonance and elective ideological affinity with the development of political institutions and economic structures during the early and mid-twentieth century, rendering the corporation and political state 'knowable' (Rose 1999). Finally, it provided a representation of emerging organizational forms that legitimated their increasing power and influence as inevitable features of a long-term historical trajectory through discourses of rational technocratic administration and management (Ellul 1964; Child 1969; Gouldner 1976). This legitimation strategy 'lifted' the theory and practice of organizational management from an intuitive craft into a codified and analysable body of knowledge that traded on the immensely powerful cultural capital and symbolism of 'science'. In due course, it would come to provide the intellectual and ideological bedrock of a theory of 'managerialism' that would dominate much of twentieth century thought and practice in the domain of work organization and management (MacIntyre 1981; Anthony 1986; Locke 1989; Enteman 1993; Townley 1994).

Rationalism underpinned a conception of organization theory and analysis as a portmanteau intellectual technology. It's geared to the provision of a 'mechanism for rendering reality amenable to certain kinds of action [and] it involves inscribing reality into the calculations of government through a range of material and rather mundane techniques' (Miller and Rose 1990: 7). The 'organization' becomes a tool or instrument for the authorization and realization of collective goals through the design and management of structures directed to the administration and manipulation of organizational behaviour (Donaldson 1985). Organizational decision-making rests on a rational analysis of all the options available, based on certified expert knowledge and deliberately oriented to the established legal apparatus. This 'logic of organization' became the guarantor of material advance, social progress and political order in modern industrial societies as they converged around a pattern of institutional development and governance through which the 'invisible hand of the market' was gradually replaced by the 'visible hand of organization'.

Despite the primary position of the rational framework in the development of organization theory, its ideological and intellectual dominance was never complete. It is always open to challenge by alternative narratives. Challengers often shared its ideological and political 'project' of discovering a new source of authority and control within the processes and structures of modern organization, but used different discourses and practices to achieve it. In particular, many saw the rational framework's inability to deal with the dynamism and instability of complex organizations as a major intellectual and operational failure. This growing

sense of its conceptual and practical limitations and the utopian nature of the political project which it supported provided organicist thought with an intellectual and institutional space where it could prosper in a field of study previously held in the sway of mechanistic forms of discourse.

The Rediscovery of Community

The substantive issue that most perplexed critics, from the 1930s and 1940s onwards, was the failure of rationalistic organization theory to address the problem of social integration and the implications for the maintenance of social order in a more unstable and uncertain world. This approach remained blind to the criticism that authority is ineffective without 'spontaneous or willing co-operation' (Bendix 1974). Critics, uneasy about the highly mechanistic and deterministic character of rationalism, emphasized both a practical and a theoretical need for an alternative foundation of contemporary managerial power and authority to that provided by formal organization design. Organicist thinking was also concerned with how modern organizations combine authority with a feeling of community and collective identity among their members:

> The mission of the organization is not only to supply goods and services, but fellowship as well. The confidence of the modern writer in the power of organization stems from a larger faith that the organization is man's [sic] rejoinder to his own mortality ... In community and in organization modern man has fashioned substitute love-objects for the political. The quest for community has sought refuge from the notion of man [sic] as a political animal; the adoration of organization has been partially inspired by the hope of finding a new form of civility (Wolin 1960: 369).

This issue is at the forefront of the emergence of a human relations perspective in organization analysis that sets itself apart, in terms of solutions if not problems, from the rational model.

The *Management and the Worker* monograph (Roethlisberger and Dickson 1939) and the writings of Mayo (1933; 1945) thus accuse the rational tradition of ignoring the natural and evolutionary qualities of the new social forms which industrialization generated. The whole thrust of the human relations perspective and project is a view of social isolation and conflict as a symptom of social pathology and disease. The 'good society' and the effective organization are defined in relation to their capacity to facilitate and sustain the socio-psychological reality of spontaneous cooperation and social stability in the face of economic, political and technological changes that threaten the integration of the individual and group within the wider community.

Over time, this conception of organization – as the intermediate social unit that integrates individuals into modern industrial civilization, under the tutelage of a benevolent and socially skilled management – became institutionalized in such a way that it began to displace the dominant position held by exponents of the rational model (Child 1969; Nichols 1969; Bartell 1976; Thompson and McHugh 2002). It converged in more abstract and sociologically-oriented theories of organization that held an elective affinity with the naturalistic and evolutionary predilections of the human relations school (Merton 1949; Selznick 1949; Blau 1955; 1974; Parsons 1956; Blau and Schoenherr 1971). Thus, the origins of organicist thought in organization studies lay in a belief that rationalism provided an extremely limited and often misleading vision of the 'realities' of organizational life (Gouldner 1959; Mouzelis 1967; Silverman 1970). It stressed mechanically imposed order and control instead of integration, interdependence and balance in organically developing social systems, each with a history and dynamic of its own. 'Interference' by external agents, such as the planned design of organizational structures, threatens the system's survival.

The organization as a social system facilitates the integration of individuals into the wider society and the adaptation of the latter to changing, and often highly volatile, sociotechnical conditions. This view is theoretically anticipated, in embryonic form, by Roethlisberger and Dickson (1939: 567). They see the industrial organization as a functioning social system striving for equilibrium with a dynamic environment. This conception draws on Pareto's (1935) theory of equilibrating social systems in which disparities in the rates of socio-technical change and the imbalances which they generate in social organisms are automatically counteracted by internal responses that, over time, re-establish system equilibrium.

Organizational structures are viewed as spontaneously and homeostatically maintained. Structural change is accounted for as the cumulative and unintended outcome of unplanned, adaptive responses to, actual and potential, threats to the equilibrium of the system as a whole. Responses to problems are thought of as taking the form of organically developed defense mechanisms and being importantly shaped by shared values that are deeply internalized in the members. The empirical focus is thus directed to the spontaneously emergent and normatively sanctioned structures in the organization (Gouldner 1959: 405–6).

In this way, emergent processes, rather than planned structures, ensure long-term system stability and survival.

By the late 1940s and early 1950s, this conception of organizations as social systems geared to the integrative and survival 'needs' of the larger societal orders of which they were constituent elements established itself as the dominant theoretical framework within organization analysis (Stinchcombe 1965). It converged with theoretical movements in 'general systems theory', as originally developed in biology and physics (von Bertalanffy 1950; 1956), which provided considerable conceptual inspiration for the subsequent development of socio-technical systems theory (Miller and Rice 1967) and 'soft system' methodologies (Checkland 1994). It was, however, the structural-functionalist interpretation of the systems approach which assumed the intellectual 'pole position' within organization analysis and which was to dominate theoretical development and empirical research within the field between the 1950s and 1970s (Silverman 1970; Clegg and Dunkerley 1980; Reed 1985; Casey 2002). Structural functionalism and its progeny, systems theory, provided an 'internalist' focus on organizational design with an 'externalist' concern with environmental uncertainty (Thompson 1967). The former highlighted the need for a minimum degree of stability and security in long-term system survival; the latter exposed the underlying indeterminacy of organizational action in the face of environmental demands and threats beyond the organization's control. The key research issue that emerges from this synthesis of structural and environmental concerns is to establish those combinations of internal designs and external conditions that will facilitate long-term organizational stability and growth (Donaldson 1985).

Structural functionalism and systems theory also effectively 'de-politicized' the decision-making processes through which the appropriate functional fit between organization and environment was achieved. Certain 'functional imperatives', such as the need for long-term system equilibrium for survival, were assumed to impose themselves on all organizational actors, determining the design outcomes that their decision-making produced (Crozier 1964; Child 1972; 1973; Crozier and Friedberg 1980). This theoretical sleight of hand consigns political processes to the margins of organization analysis. In keeping with the wider ideological resonance of systems theory, it converts conflicts over valued means and ends into technical issues which can be 'solved' through effective system design and management. As Boguslaw (1965) indicates this conversion relies on a theoretical facade, not to say utopia, of value homogeneity in which the political realities of organizational change, and the strains and stresses they inevitably cause, are glossed as frictional elements in an otherwise perfectly functioning system. It also gels with the ideological and practical needs of a rising group of systems designers and managers who aspire to overall control within an increasingly differentiated and complex society that reaches its apogee in Bell's (1973) model of a 'post-industrial society'.

Thus, the general enthusiasm with which systems theory was received by the organization studies community in the 1950s and 1960s reflected a wider renaissance of utopian thinking which presumed that the functional analysis of social systems would provide the intellectual foundations for a new science of society (Kumar 1978). The process of socio-organizational differentiation, perhaps with a helping hand from expert social engineers, would solve the problem of social order through naturally evolving structures capable of handling endemic, escalating tensions between institutional demands and individual interests. The conceit that society itself would solve the problem of social order depended on a 'domain assumption' that 'the whole of human history has a unique form, pattern, logic or meaning underlying the multitude of seemingly haphazard and unconnected events' (Sztompka 1993: 107). Functional systems analysis provided the theoretical key to unlock the mysteries of this socio-historical development, enabling social and organizational scientists to predict, explain and control both its internal dynamics and its institutional consequences. This view traded on a form of socio-organizational evolutionism and functionalism that had its roots in the writings of Comte, Saint-Simon

and Durkheim (Weinberg 1969; Clegg and Dunkerley 1980; Smart 1992). The latter reached its first intellectual high water-mark in the work of those social scientists who contributed to the development of the convergence theory of industrial society in the 1950s and 1960s (Kerr et al. 1960) and who displayed little, if any, of the historical circumspection and political sensitivity of their academic predecessors. It would rise even further in the rash of post-industrial theorizing that spread like a virus in the 1970s and early 1980s.

Consequently, the functionalist/systems orthodoxy which came to dominate, or at least structure, the intellectual practice and development of organization analysis between the 1940s and 1960s was merely one part of a much broader movement that resurrected the evolutionary form of the nineteenth century (Kumar 1978: 179–90). In organization theory, it reached its theoretical consummation in the development of 'contingency theory' between the late 1960s and early 1970s (Lawrence and Lorsch 1967; Thompson 1967; Woodward 1970; Pugh and Hickson 1976; Donaldson 1985; 1995). This approach exhibited all the intellectual virtues and vices of the larger theoretical tradition on which it drew for ideological and methodological inspiration. It also reinforced a managerialist ethic that presumed to solve, through expert social engineering and flexible organizational design (Gellner 1964; Giddens 1984), the fundamental institutional and political problems of modern industrial societies (Bell 1960; Lipset 1960; Galbraith 1969).

Yet, as the 1960s progressed the virtues of organicist thought were eclipsed by a growing appreciation of its vices, especially as social, economic and political realities refused to conform to the explanatory theories promulgated by this narrative. In time, alternative interpretative frameworks, grounded in very different historical and intellectual traditions, would emerge to challenge functionalism. Before we can consider these perspectives, however, we need to take stock of market-based theories of organization.

Enter the Market

Market-based theories of organization seem a contradiction in terms; if markets operate in the way specified by neo-classical economic theory, as perfectly functioning 'clearing mechanisms' balancing price and cost, there is no conceptual role or technical need for 'organization'. As Coase (1937) realized in his classic paper, if markets are perfect, then firms (and organizations) should not develop in perfectly regulated market transactions based on voluntary exchange of information between equal economic agents. Coase was, however, forced to recognize the reality of firms as collective economic agents, accounting for them as 'solutions' to market failure or breakdown. As mechanisms for 'internalizing' recurring economic exchanges, firms reduce the cost of individual transactions through standardization and routinization. They increase the efficiency of resource allocation within the market system as a whole by minimizing transaction costs between economic agents who are naturally distrustful and suspicious of their partners.

Coase unintentionally borrows a great deal from the rational framework in assuming that behaviour is primarily motivated by the goal of minimizing market costs and maximizing market returns. Both rationalistic and economistic traditions in organization analysis rest on a conception of 'bounded rationality' to explain and predict individual and social action. They jointly subscribe to theories that account for organization in terms of efficiency and effectiveness and pay collective intellectual homage to the organic framework by emphasizing the 'natural' evolution of organizational forms that optimize returns within environments whose competitive pressures restrict strategic options. Economic theories of organization also trade on elements of the organicist tradition in focusing on organizations as an evolutionary and semi-rational product of spontaneous and unintended consequences (Hayek 1978; Fleetwood 1995; Lawson 1997). Organizations are an automatic response to (and a reasonable price to pay for) the need for formally free and equal economic agents to negotiate and monitor contracts in complex market transactions that cannot be accommodated in existing institutional arrangements.

Such economic theories of organization emerged in response to the inherent analytical and explanatory limitations of classical and neoclassical theories of the firm (Cyert and March 1963). They demand that a more serious consideration be accorded to resource allocation as a primary determinant of organizational behaviour and design (Williamson and Winter 1991). This focus on the 'micro-economics of organization' (Donaldson 1990; Williamson 1990) and a theory of firm behaviour that is more sensitive to the institutional constraints within which

economic transactions are conducted encouraged the formulation of a research agenda emphasizing corporate governance structures and their link to organizational functions (Williamson 1990). This framework also draws intellectual inspiration from Barnard's (1938: 4) conception of organization as cooperation 'which is conscious, deliberate and purposeful', and which can only be explained as the outcome of a complex interaction between formal and substantive rationality or technical requirements and moral order (Williamson 1990). Barnard's original attempt to provide a conceptual synthesis of 'rational' and 'natural' systems conceptions of organization provides the foundations of market-based theories of organization which flourished in the 1970s and 1980s, such as transaction cost analysis (Williamson 1975; Francis 1983) and population ecology (Aldrich 1979; 1992; 1999; Hannan and Freeman 1989).

There are significant theoretical differences between these approaches, particularly in relation to the form and degree of environmental determinism in which they engage (Morgan 1990). Yet, both subscribe to a set of domain assumptions that unify internal administrative forms and external market conditions by means of an evolutionary logic which subordinates collective and individual action to efficiency and survival imperatives largely beyond human influence (Swedberg 2003). Transaction cost theory concerns itself with the adaptive adjustments that organizations need to make in the face of pressures for maximizing efficiency in their internal and external transactions. Population ecology highlights the role of competitive pressures in selecting certain organizational forms over others. Both perspectives are based on a model of organization in which its design, functioning and development are treated as the direct outcomes of universal and immanent forces that cannot be influenced or changed through strategic action.

What is conspicuous by its absence in the market framework is any sustained interest or concern with social power and human agency. Neither the markets/hierarchies approach nor population ecology nor, indeed, Donaldson's (1990; 1994) 'liberal theory of organization' take much interest in how organizational change is structured by power struggles between social actors and the forms of domination which they legitimate (Francis 1983; Perrow 1986; Thompson and McHugh 2002). These approaches treat 'organization' as constituting a unitary social and moral order in which individual and group interests and values are simply derived from overarching 'system interests and values' uncontaminated by sectional conflict and power struggles (Willman 1983). Once this unitary conception is taken for granted as an 'accepted', 'natural', and virtually invisible feature of organization, power, conflict and domination can be safely ignored as being 'outside' the framework's field of analytical vision and empirical concern.

This unitary conception of organization is entirely in keeping with a wider ideological and political context dominated by neo-liberal theories of organizational and societal governance. The latter raise 'impersonal market forces' to the analytical status of ontological universals determining the chances of individual and collective survival (Silver 1987; Miller and Rose 1990; Rose 1992). From neo-liberal or Darwinian ideologies in the last century (Bendix 1974) to more recent doctrines emphasizing the 'survival of the fittest' (Hodgson 1999), such ideologies and theories advocate the unrestrained expansion of the market, private enterprise and economic rationality. This is advocated at the expense of increasingly residual and marginalized conceptions of community, public service and social concern. Through globalization, nations and enterprises engage in an expanding economic struggle which will be won by those organizations and economies that single-mindedly adapt themselves to market demands (Du Gay and Salaman 1992; Du Gay 1993). In this respect, market-based theories of organization trade on cyclical movements within the encompassing socio-economic, political and ideological context of which they are a part (Barley and Kunda 1992). Nevertheless, they remain consistently silent on the power structures and struggles in and through which organizations respond to putatively 'objective' and 'neutral' economic pressures.

Faces of Power

Power remains the most overused and least understood concept in organization analysis. It provides the ideological foundations and epistemological scaffolding for a theory of organization that stands in sharp contrast to the analytical narratives and interpretative frameworks previously discussed. It proffers a logic of organization and organizing analytically rooted in strategic conceptions of social power and human agency which are sensitive to the dialectical interplay between structural constraint and social action as it shapes the institutional forms reproduced and transformed through social practice (Giddens 1984; 1985; 1990; DuGay 1992; Layder 1994; 1997). It rejects the environmental determinism inherent in market-based theorizations of organization with their unremitting emphasis on the efficiency and effectiveness imperatives that secure the long-term survival of certain organizational forms rather than others. It also calls into question the unitary assumptions that underpin the rational, organic and market frameworks by conceptualizing the organization as an arena of conflicting interests and values constituted through power struggle.

The power framework in organization analysis is grounded in Weber's sociology of domination and the analysis of bureaucracy and bureaucratization that flows from it (Weber 1978; Ray and Reed 1994). More recently, this Weberian tradition has been complemented by theorizations of power that draw their inspiration from Machiavelli's interest in the micro-politics of organizational power and its contemporary expression in the work of Foucault (Clegg 1989; 1994). Weberian-based analyses emphasized the relational character of power as a differentially distributed capacity or resource that, if deployed with the appropriate degree of strategic and tactical skill by social actors, produces and reproduces hierarchically-structured relationships of autonomy and dependence (Wrong 1978; Clegg 1989). This tends to prioritize the structural forms and mechanisms through which power is struggled over and institutionalized in systems of imperative coordination and domination that achieve temporal continuity and spatial sustainability. The 'emphasis is on wider constraints and the determinants of behaviour – principally the forms of power derived from structures of class and ownership, but also the impact of markets and occupations, and of increasing interest lately the normative structures of gender' (Fincham 1992: 742). Thus, Weber's analysis of the dynamics and forms of bureaucratic power in modern society highlights the complex interaction between societal and organizational rationalization as it reproduces institutionalized structures controlled by 'experts' or 'specialists' (Silberman 1993).

This structural or institutional conception of organizational power has been complemented by a more concentrated focus on the micro-political processes through which power is attained and mobilized in opposition or in parallel to established regimes and the domination structures through which they rule. This approach resonates very strongly with Foucault's (2003) work on the mosaic of cross-cutting coalitions and alliances mobilizing particular disciplinary regimes (Lyon 1994) which provides a 'bottom-up' or capillary, rather than a 'top-down' or hierarchical, analytical perspective on the detailed organizational practices through which power 'over others' can be temporarily secured. This processual conception of organizational power tends to concentrate on the detailed tactical maneouvrings that generate a shifting balance of advantage between contending socio-political interests (Fincham 1992). However, it is less convincing when attempting to explain the broadly-based organizational mechanisms which become institutionalized as accepted authority structures and discursive regimes legitimating more permanent and taken-for-granted 'imperatively coordinated associations'. Thus, the more recent research focus on the interaction order (Layder 1997) or 'micro-politics' through which power relationships are temporarily sedimented into relatively more permanent and stable authority structures deflects attention away from the 'hierarchical mechanisms that sustain the reproduction of power' (Fincham 1992: 742).

This dialogue between Weberian/institutional and Machiavellian/processual conceptions of power led to a much more sophisticated understanding of the multi-faceted nature of power relations/ processes and their implications for the structuring of organizational forms. Lukes' (1974) analysis of the multiple 'faces of power' has become the major reference point for contemporary research on the dynamics and outcomes of organizational power. His differentiation between three faces or dimensions of power, between the 'episodic', 'manipulative' and 'hegemonic' conceptions of power (Clegg 1989), results in a considerable broadening of the research agenda for the study of organizational power and the theoretical frameworks through which it is approached.

The 'episodic' conception of power concentrates on observable conflicts of interest between identifiable social actors with opposing objectives in particular decision-making situations. The 'manipulative' view concentrates on the 'behind the scenes' activities through which already powerful groups manipulate the decision-making agenda to screen out issues that have the potential to disturb, if not threaten,

their domination and control. The 'hegemonic' interpretation emphasizes the strategic role of existing ideological and social structures in constituting and, thus, selectively limiting, the interests and values – and hence action options – available to social actors in any particular decision arena. As we move from the 'episodic' through the 'manipulative' to the 'hegemonic' conceptions of power, there is a progressive analytical and normative shift occurring. This moves from the role of human agency in constituting power relations to that of structural and ideological mechanisms in determining the forms of domination and control through which the latter are institutionalized (Clegg 1989: 86–128). There is also an increasing explanatory emphasis on the macro-level structures and mechanisms that determine the organizational designs through which micro-political power struggles are mediated and a corresponding downgrading of the organizationally specific practices that produce and reproduce institutional forms.

Researchers (e.g. Knights and Willmott 1989; Fincham 1992; Clegg 1994) attempted to overcome this potential split between institutional/structural and processual/agency conceptions by focusing on the general but 'localized' organizational practices through which patterns of domination and control are sustained. They attempted to synthesize a Weberian-based concern with the institutional reproduction of domination structures and a Foucauldian interest in the micro-practices generating changing forms of disciplinary power. The focal point, both analytically and empirically, is the 'expert' discourses and practices through which particular patterns of organizational structuring and control are established in different societies or sectors (Larson 1979; 1990; Abbott 1988; Miller and O'Leary 1989; Powell and DiMaggio 1991; Alvesson and Willmott 1992; Reed and Anthony 1992; Dean 1999; Rose 1999; Alvesson and Karreman 2000). These discourses and practices create specific types of disciplinary regimes (at an organizational and institutional level) that mediate between strategic governmental policies formulated by centralized agencies and their tactical implementation within localized domains (Miller and Rose 1990; Johnson 1993; also see some of the recent work on labour process theory, e.g. Burawoy 1985; Thompson 1989; Littler 1990; and total quality management, e.g. Kirkpatrick and Martinez 1995; Reed 1995; Knights and McCabe 2003).

This research programme accounts for the decay and breakdown of 'corporatist' structures (within the political economies and organizational practices of advanced industrial societies) by focusing on their internal contradictions and failure to respond to external ideological and political initiatives led by a resurgent neo-liberal right (Alford and Friedland 1985; Cerny 1990; Miller and Rose 1990; Johnson 1993). It also raises questions about the analytical coherence and explanatory range of a power framework with limited capacity to deal with the material, cultural and political complexities of organizational change.

Knowledge is Power

The knowledge-based framework is deeply suspicious of the institutional and structural bias characterizing the analytical frameworks previously reviewed. It rejects their various forms of theoretical and methodological determinism and the 'totalizing' logic of explanation on which they trade. Instead, this approach treats all forms of institutionalized or structured social action as the temporary patterning of a mosaic of tactical interactions and alliances which form relatively unstable and shifting networks of power always prone to internal decay and dissolution. It explains the development of modern 'systems' of organizational discipline and governmental control in terms of highly contingent and negotiated power mechanisms and relationships whose institutional roots lie in 'the capacity to exert effective management of the means of production of new forms of power itself' (Cerny 1990: 7).

In this context, the cultural and technical mechanisms through which particular fields of human behaviour, such as health, education, crime and business, are colonized as the preserves of certain specialist or expert groups emerge as the strategic focus of analysis. These mechanisms take on a far greater explanatory significance than sovereign political and economic powers such as the 'state' or 'class'. Knowledge, and the power that it potentially confers, assume a central explanatory role. It provides the key cognitive and representational resource for the application of a set of techniques from which disciplinary regimes, however temporary and unstable, can be constructed (Clegg 1994; Scarbrough 2001). Highly specialized and seemingly esoteric knowledge, which can potentially be accessed and controlled by any individual or group with the required training and skill (Blackler 1993; Amin and Cohendet 2003; Alvesson 2004), provides the strategic resource from which the appropriation of time, space and consciousness can be realized. Thus, the production, codification, storage and usage of knowledge relevant to the regulation of social behaviour become strategic considerations in the mobilization and institutionalization of a form of organized power that facilitates 'control at a distance' (Cooper 1992).

Reworked within this problematic, 'organization' becomes a portable carrier of the sociotechnical knowledge and skills through which particular patterns of social relationships emerge and reproduce themselves in specific material and social circumstances (Law 1994a). It has neither inherent ontological status nor explanatory significance as a generalizable, monolithic structure or entity. Contingency, rather than universality, reigns – both in the localized and constrained knowledge that makes organizing possible and in the power relationships they generate. The research focus is directed to the 'interaction order' that produces 'organization' and the locally embedded stocks of knowledge through which agents engage in the situational practices constitutive of the structures through which 'organization' is reproduced (Goffman 1983; Layder 1994; 1997).

A number of specific theoretical approaches draw on this general orientation to develop a research agenda for organization analysis that takes the knowledge production processes through which 'organization' is reproduced as its strategic research interest. Ethnomethodology (Boden 1994), postmodernist approaches to organization culture and symbolism (Calas and Smircich 1991; Martin 1992; 2002), neo-rationalist decision-making theory (March and Olsen 1986; March 1988), actor-network theory (Law 1991; Hassard 1993; 1994b; Amin and Cohendet 2003) and post-structuralist/modernist theory (Kondo 1990; Cooper 1992; Gane and Johnson 1993; Clegg 1994; Perry 1994; Kilduff and Mehra 1997; Linstead 2004) have collectively contributed to a substantial shift of analytical focus and explanatory concern. This moves us away from macro-level formalization or institutionalization and towards micro-level social ordering or 'heterogeneous engineering'. These approaches (many of which are represented in this book) radically re-define and re-locate the study of organization away from its intellectual roots in rationalist/functionalist ontologies and positivist epistemologies. The organization is transformed from a materially determined mechanism for functional coordination and control into a socially constructed and sustained 'order' necessarily grounded in the localized stocks of knowledge, practical work routines and technical devices mobilized by communities of social actors in their everyday interaction and discourse.

Taken as a whole, contemporary studies of the knowledge/power discourses through which organizational members engage in organizational ordering to generate dynamic and ambiguous relational networks reinforce a view of organizations as 'the condensation of local cultures of values, power, rules, discretion and paradox' (Clegg 1994: 172). They resonate with the images and prejudices of a 'post-industrial' or 'postmodern' Zeitgeist in which organization is deconstructed into 'localized, decentred, on-the-spot decision-making ... transformations and innovation in organizations occur at the intersection of information and interaction' (Boden 1994: 210). In many respects, this in keeping with general theories of post-industrial society (Bell 1973; 1999), flexible specialization (Piore and Sabel 1984; Sabel 1991) and disorganized or informational capitalism (Lash and Urry 1987; 1994; Webster 2002). Within these, more macro-level, theories, the axial institutional forms or structures once deemed constitutive of modern 'political economy' dissolve, or more appropriately implode, into fragmented information flows and networks. These theories will, again in time, provide the intellectual and empirical foundations for the development of another analytical narrative around the leitmotif of 'network' that will come to re-orient much social and organizational analysis in the late twentieth and early twenty-first centuries (Clark 2003).

There is, however, a lingering doubt as to what is lost in this 'localization' of organization analysis, and its seeming obsession with micro-level processes and practices, which makes these approaches seem strangely disengaged from the wider issues of justice, equality, democracy and rationality. What of the classical sociological concern with the macrostructural features of modernity (Layder 1994; 1997) and their implications for how we 'ought' to lead our organizational lives?

Scales of Justice

The analytical retreat into the local aspects of organizational life takes the study of organizations a long way, theoretically and epistemologically, from the normative themes and structural issues that shaped its historical development and intellectual rationale. At the very least, it radically re-defines the 'intellectual mission' away from ethical universals and conceptual abstractions towards cultural relativities and interpretative schema that are inherently resistant to historical and theoretical generalization. Yet, the turn towards 'the local' in organization analysis and the disinclination to engage with wider ideological and structural issues have not gone unnoticed. A number of commentators have attempted to redirect the study of organizations back towards institutional forms and the analytical and normative questions they raise.

One relatively obvious example of this development is to be found in 'neo-institutionalism' (Meyer and Rowan 1977; Powell and DiMaggio 1991; Meyer and Scott 1992; Perry 1992; Whitley 1992; Scott 1995; Greenwood and Hinings 1996; Barley and Tolbert 1997; Lounsbury and Ventrescu 2003). Another can be seen in the resurgence of interest in the political economy of organization and its implications for the extension, in a complex range of institutional practices and forms, of bureaucratic surveillance and control in 'late modernity' (Alford and Friedland 1985; Giddens 1985; 1990; 1994; Wolin 1988; Cerny 1990; Dandeker 1990; DuGay 1993; Silberman 1993; Thompson 1993; 2003b; Courpasson 2000). Finally, debates about the immediate and longer-term prospects for organizational democracy and participation within the corporate governance structures which developed in political economies dominated by neo-liberal ideologies and policies during the 1980s and 1990s (Lammers and Szell 1989; Fulk and Steinfield 1990; Morgan 1990; Hirst 1993; Putnam 1994; McLaughlin et al. 2002) have re-awakened interest in the 'global' issues which organization analysis must address.

Each of these bodies of literature raises fundamental questions about the types of corporate governance and control prevailing in contemporary organizations and their grounding in moral and political judgements concerning justice and fairness, as measured against certain preferred interests and values. They also re-assert the centrality of issues relating to the institutionalized distribution of economic, political and cultural power in developed and developing societies that tend to be marginalized in postmodernist and post-structuralist discourses centred on local representational and interpretative practices. These approaches re-vivify a conception of the organization as an institutionalized structure of power and authority over and above the localized micro-practices of organizational members.

DiMaggio and Powell (1991: 8) argued that 'new institutionalism' necessarily entailed a:

> rejection of rational-actor models, an interest in institutions as independent variables, a turn towards cognitive and cultural explanations, and an interest in properties of supra-individual units of analysis that cannot be reduced to aggregations or direct consequences of individuals' attributes or motives.

They argued for a sustained focus on organizational structures and practices found across different institutional sectors, the 'rationality myths' which legitimate and routinize prevailing arrangements, and 'the ways in which action is structured and order made possible by shared systems of rules that both constrain the inclination and capacity of actors to optimize as well as privilege some groups whose interests are secured by prevailing rewards and sanctions' (DiMaggio and Powell 1991: 11). Their emphasis on practices which penetrate organizational structures and processes, such as the state, social class, professions and industry/sector recipes, reveals the strategic role played by power struggles between institutional actors over 'the formation and reformation of rule systems that guide political and economic action' (DiMaggio and Powell 1991: 28).

While recognizing that the generation and implementation of institutional forms and practices 'are rife with conflict, contradiction and ambiguity' (DiMaggio and Powell 1991: 28), neo-institutional theory takes its central concern to be the cultural and political processes through which actors and their interests/values are institutionally constructed and mobilized in support of certain 'organizing logics' rather than others. In this way, the macro-level contexts that indelibly shape organizational behaviour and design assume explanatory primacy. They are constituted by and through 'supra-organizational patterns of activity through which human beings conduct their material life in time and space, and symbolic systems through which they categorize that activity and infuse it with meaning' (Friedland and Alford 1991: 232). As institutionalized forms of social practice, organizations are seen as 'structures

in which powerful people are committed to some value or interest' and that 'power has a great deal to do with the historical preservation of patterns of values' (Stinchcombe 1968: 107). Thus, the historical, structural and contextual positioning of collective actors' values and interests, rather than their local (re)production through micro-level practices, emerges as the analytical and explanatory priority for neo-institutional theory.

Over the last decade or so, neo-institutional theory has oscillated between this primary explanatory focus on the strategic role of macro-level institutional structures and cultures in determining situated organizational forms and practices and, a somewhat under-developed, concern with the complex and overlapping organizational discourses in which 'institutionalization' is practically grounded and precariously realized (Tolbert and Zuker 1996; Phillips and Hardy 2002). This underlying ontological and analytical tension between 'structure' and 'agency' has tended to be resolved in favour of the former. However, it continues to frame much of the ongoing research and debate within neo-institutionalism, as it does within other theoretical communities and research programmes in contemporary organizational studies.

The sustained explanatory focus on the historical development and structural contextualization of organizations characteristic of the 'new institutionalism' is reflected in recent work on the changing 'surveillance and control' capacities of modern organizations which, as Giddens suggests, takes the theme of 'institutional reflexivity' (Beck 1992) as its strategic concern. This is regarded as:

> institutionalization of an investigative and calculative attitude towards generalized conditions of system reproduction; it both stimulates and reflects a decline in traditional ways of doing things. It is also associated with the generation of power (understood as transformative capacity). The expansion of institutional reflexivity stands behind the proliferation of organizations in circumstances of modernity, including organizations of global scope (Giddens 1994: 6).

The rise of modern organizational forms and practices is seen to be intimately tied to the growing sophistication, scope and variety of bureaucratic systems of surveillance and control that can be adapted to very different socio-historical circumstances (Dandeker 1990). The emergence and institutional sedimentation of the nation state and professional administrative structures play a crucial role in advancing the material and social conditions in which organizational surveillance and control can be extended in ways that facilitate in much more self-reflexive social engineering regime to emerge (Cerny 1990; Silberman 1993). Relatively new technological, cultural and political changes encouraged the creation and diffusion of more unobtrusive surveillance systems that are much less dependent on direct supervision and control (Zuboff 1988; Lyon 1994; 2001; Reed 1999; Rosenberg 2000). The growing technical sophistication and social penetration of more highly interdependent control systems also serve to reassert the continuing relevance of Weber's concern about the long-term prospects for meaningful individual involvement in a social and organizational order that seems increasingly close to, yet remote from, everyday lives (Ray and Reed 1994; Reed 1999; Rosenberg 2000).

Organization analysis seems, then, to have come full circle, both ideologically and theoretically. The perceived threat to freedom and liberty presented by 'modern', bureaucratic organizational forms at the beginning of the twentieth century is echoed in debates over the prospects for meaningful participation and democracy in the much more technologically sophisticated and socio-politically unobtrusive 'surveillance and control regimes' emerging at the end of the century (Webster and Robins 1993; Rosenberg 2000; Lyon 2001). In so far as the 'postmodern' or 'post-bureaucratic' organization becomes a highly dispersed, dynamic and de-centred mechanism of socio-cultural control (Clegg 1990; Heckscher and Donnellon 1994) that is virtually impossible to detect, much less resist, questions relating to political responsibility and citizenship are as important now as they were a hundred years ago. As Wolin (1961: 434) so elegantly argued, organizational and political theory 'must once again be viewed as that form of knowledge that deals with what is general and integrative to man [sic]; a life of common involvements'.

This aspiration to retrieve an 'institutional vision' in organization analysis that speaks to the relationship between the citizen, organization, community and state in modern societies (Etzioni 1975; 1993; Arhne 1994; Feldman 2002) is a potent theme. Research on organizational authority, democracy and participation suggests that efforts to develop more open, participative and egalitarian organizational designs, grounded in sustainable traditions of collective ethical and political engagement, have had an extremely difficult time over the last fifteen years or so (Lammers and Szell 1989). Long-term prospects for democracy seem equally pessimistic in an increasingly globalized and fragmented world that destabilizes, if not destroys, established socio-political traditions and coherent cultural identities, corroding the ideological certainty and cognitive security they once bestowed (Cable 1994; Feldman 2002).

The combination of neo-libertarian policies and sophisticated surveillance that has exerted such a corrosive, not to say destructive, impact on communal social capital and collective political action (Putnam 1990) has not succeeded, however, in eradicating a continuing challenge to unobtrusive and self-reinforcing forms of organizational discipline and control (Lyon 1994). As Cerny (1990: 35–6) argued in relation to institutional changes at the turn of the twentieth century:

> Individuals and groups must define themselves strategically and maneuvre tactically in the context of the logic of the state, whether conforming to legal rules, competing for resources distributed or regulated by the state, or attempting to resist or avoid the influence of control of other state and non-state actors … the state itself is constituted by a range of middle-level and micro-level games, which are also characterized by contrasting logics, interstitial spaces, structural dynamics and ongoing tensions.

Within these overlapping, and often contradictory, political games (Parker 2000), new organizing principles and practices are emerging that require a fundamental reconsideration of the rapidly changing relationship between the individual and the community in a socio-political context where the 'agenda for identity politics' has become much more diverse, unstable, fragmented and contested (Cable 1994: 38–40). Lyon's (1994) survey of the social movements, interest groups and political coalitions challenging centralized and undemocratic regimes of surveillance and control indicates that there are options available other than 'postmodern paranoia' and the extreme political pessimism that it seems to encourage. Similarly, writers such as Hirst (1993) and Arhne (1994; 1996) re-discovered civil society and the diverse range of 'associative' forms of social and economic governance that it continues to generate and support, even in the teeth of socio-technical pressures for enhanced centralized power and control.

Thus, this narrative demands that we re-connect, analytically and politically, the local with the global; organizationally situated practices and processes with institutional rationalities and structures; negotiated order with strategic power and control. In short, we must address the fact that:

> We live in a massively but unevenly, unequally, interconnected and interdependent world, where 'organization' (and disorganization), and particular kinds of organizations, represent fundamental 'nodes', conceptually, practically, but where a dominant big business vision, for example, can only be blinkered and imperialistic, conceptually, practically. Seeking to understand and analyse such complex intersections and their ramifications must, it seems to me, represent a key component for the future development of the field if it is to meet the intellectual and practical challenges posed by such (Jones 1994: 208).

Thus, the analytical structured narrative of organizational justice and democracy seeks to reconnect the study of locally contextualized discourses and practices with institutionalized orders of power, authority and control that possess a societal rationale and historical dynamic that cannot be understood, much less explained, through a limited focus on 'everyday' interaction and events (Layder 1994). It forces us to re-discover the vital link between the practical demands and intellectual needs of the study of organizations, the 'points of intersection' between the normative and the analytical, that must be realigned if organization studies is to retain its relevance and vitality in a world where long established structures are under extreme pressure to change, indeed metamorphose, into very different institutional forms.

The Rise of Network Society

The theme and concept of 'network' has come to exert a powerful intellectual influence within organization studies over the last decade or so. It constitutes the seventh, and final, interpretative framework/analytically structured narrative reviewed in this opening chapter.

The theme/concept of 'network' is by no means radically new or original in organization studies – having figured prominently, if implicitly, in a wide range of work concerned with intra-organizational

behaviour/design and inter-organizational relations from the 1950/1960s onwards. However, it has come to attain something close to an iconic theoretical status and political significance far beyond these, relatively humble, intellectual beginnings (Nohria and Eccles 1992). This is not to say that its ontological status and explanatory significance is unchallenged or unchallengeable (Reed 2005a). However, it has begun to shape and direct much of our understanding of the complex interpenetration of strategic global change and local organizational restructuring within a geo-political context characterized by increasingly polarized 'power blocs' and the much more fragmented, but deep-seated, ideological, cultural and political conflicts this has generated (Harvey 2003). This is largely due to the theoretically diverse ways in which the theme/concept of 'network' has been developed and extended over the last two decades or so to describe and explain many of the most significant, not to say putatively 'transformational' or 'revolutionary', changes occurring in OECD societies and organizations at the turn of the century. Indeed, the theme/concept of 'network' has come to symbolize and signify momentous changes in the global, societal, institutional and organizational forms and logics that collectively define an epochal 'paradigm shift' in the dynamics, form and content of 'modernity' as it came to be identified and debated in twentieth century social science (Kumar 1995). Thus, the forms of theorizing and research that have emerged out of the network framework/narrative are less significant in relation to what they may have to say about any particular phenomena or changes to those phenomena than what they have to say about putative system-wide transformations at all levels of social organization and analysis. Network theory and analysis has generated new and important insights into phenomena as diverse as corporate structures, inter-organizational exchange relations, industrial networks, communication systems, supply chains, incentive systems, expert groups and communities, bureaucratic control systems, comparative business systems, governance systems and information technologies. However, it is the 'big story' that it has to tell about the emergence, development and impact of 'discontinuous or disjunctive change' (Unger 1987a; b; Blackler 1993; 1995) that signifies its crucial importance for organizational analysis now and in the foreseeable future. This larger and more inclusive analytical narrative speaks to wide-ranging and subterranean structural and ideological changes that are fundamental to our understanding of the contemporary world and the various developmental trajectories along which it may travel over the coming decades. These include the putative emergence of new forms of globalized and 'informationalized' capitalism; a new mode of socio-technical innovation driven by integrated information and communication technologies; systems of knowledge generation, production and diffusion that overcome temporal and spatial barriers to global transformation in political economies and cultural systems; and new forms of collective cognition, action and governance that dissolve conventional distinctions between the individual and society. Considered in these terms, the emergence of network theory and analysis (as the 'leading-edge' intellectual framework and agenda in organization studies at the present time) can be interpreted as a collective response to the perception of escalating levels of endemic complexity, ambiguity and uncertainty that seem to defy the rationalist/functionalist/positivist verities in which the field became embedded from the second-half of the nineteenth century onwards. Such a response also radically calls into question whether or not 'organization' can be sustained as a general theoretical category and practical device generating the kind of intellectual resources and institutional forms necessary to maintain social order in the twenty-first century. If 'organization' – as a materially-anchored, cognitively-ordered, socially-structured and rationally-managed entity or reality – doesn't exist anymore (assuming it ever did?), then what is the point of maintaining a commitment to an intellectual and ideological edifice that is well-past its ontological and epistemological 'sell-by date'?

A number of overlapping but sometimes contradictory clusters of literature constitute the body of knowledge associated with the network framework/narrative at this juncture. First, extremely wide-ranging and broadly focused studies that attempt to develop general theories of network-based organization and management on a global scale. Most of these works are pitched at the level of international/comparative political economy and socio-technical/cultural systems, while having their roots in the post-Fordist/postmodernist debates that dominated social scientific research and analysis in the West for much of the 1980s and 1990s. Secondly, a more narrowly focused, 'middle-range'

rather than 'macro-level', body of work that uses network-based theories, concepts and models to understand the dynamics and outcomes of change within and between specific institutional fields or sectors. Thirdly, a more micro-level, situated and contextually-specific body of research and writing that attempts to identify, map and describe the highly complex networking activities and relations that 'lie beneath' the surface level of institutionalized orders and regimes. Each of these bodies of work and literature draw on a highly diverse and extremely rich matrix of intellectual resources to do their respective 'thing'. However, taken as a complete, if loosely tied, package, they seem to signify a very distinctive 'turn' towards a configuration of issues and a set of theoretical practices and discourses that break with much of the inherited intellectual capital that previous generations of organization theorists have bequeathed to their successors.

As 'grand theory', the network framework/narrative has played a pivotal role in fundamentally re-shaping our understanding of the intersecting material, structural and cultural transformations that are re-defining globalized systems of economic, social and symbolic exchange. Seminal contributions from Giddens (1990; 2000), Castells (1989; 1996; 2000), Harvey (1989; 1996; 2001; 2003), Beck (1992; 1997; 2000), Beck et al. (1994), Bauman (1992; 1995; 1997), Fukuyama (1992; 1995) and Lash and Urry (1987; 1994) have set a new agenda concerning the underlying dynamics that are driving structural transformation on a global scale and their long-term implications for social action and organization. Of course, there are fundamental intellectual and ideological differences between each of these authors in relation to the theoretical resources they draw on, the ways in which these are deployed and its implications for the diagnoses and prognoses that they proffer to their respective readerships. In particular, there is an underlying tension between those who continue to rely on neo-Marxist political economy (Harvey/Castells) to provide a basic understanding of the structural dynamics that continue to drive global capitalism and those who are much more reliant on postmodernism and post-structuralism to provide theoretical insight into the 'culture of globalization'. Nevertheless, there is sufficient analytical and substantive consistency in this body of work as it tracks, dissects and projects the emergence of a new phase in the restructuring of contemporary capitalism on a global scale (Whitley

1999). They are all agreed that networks constitute the fundamental texture of social structuration at all levels of social organization. They also indelibly shape the socio-technical circuits (of information, knowledge, power and control) through which new, network-based organizational forms are reproduced and sustained (Clark 2003). In short, that the social architecture of global capitalism is strategically dependent on spatio-temporal flows (of money, symbols, ideas, people and technologies) that have to pass through highly complex relational networks and the modes of collective action that they sustain (Thrift 2004). These network configurations have become pervasive within the vertical and horizontal chains of interaction and exchange through which global capitalism and transnational corporations go about their business of capital accumulation and profit maximization. They are the critical levers of power and control that are struggled over by individual actors and corporate agents within the new divisions of labour and allocations of authority and governance emerging in global capitalism.

Middle-range research and analysis within the network framework/narrative has been more concerned to identify and explain the specific organizational forms that are taking shape within the network morphology characteristic of global capitalism and the 'new political economy' that it reproduces (Sabel 1982; 1991; Heckscher and Donnellon 1994; Harrison 1997; Castells 2000; Clark 2000; 2003; Adler 2001; Child and McGrath 2001; DiMaggio 2001; Leicht and Fennel 2001; Ackroyd 2002; Jessop 2002; Hudson 2003; Thompson 2003a; Thrift 2004). A plethora of descriptive labels have been developed to try and highlight the major structural and cultural features of these new organizational forms such as 'mobius strip organization', 'virtual corporation', 'post-bureaucratic organization', 'horizontal firm', 'network enterprise', 'knowledge-intensive organization' and 'the neo-entrepreneurial workplace'. Again, there is a considerable range of theoretical and empirical variation in the type of conceptual modelling and sectoral location through and in which these ideas have been developed and applied. However, there is a shared explanatory focus on the more complex corporate forms and flexible organization structures that have emerged in response to the network morphology that now dominates both the political economy and socio-technical infrastructure of contemporary capitalism

on a world-wide scale. Thus, the shift from vertically integrated, centrally managed, bureaucratically administered and task-continuous corporate structures (that dominated the Fordist era of national/international capitalist development between the mid-1940s and late 1970s) to horizontally dispersed, team managed, knowledge-driven and continuously innovating networked enterprises constitutes the central explanatory problem for this 'middle range' body of research and writing. There is a considerable degree of caution regarding the speed, scale, depth and range of this putative general movement to network enterprise. However, there is broad agreement that most Western transnational corporations are re-structuring themselves into much more complex inter-firm and intra-firm networks under the new conditions generated by the shift from a 'materials-based' to an 'information-based' economy (Powell 1990; Gulati et al. 2000; Child and McGrath 2001). Yet, these very same capitalist corporations are also seen as retaining selected, but strategic, elements of the multi-divisional form and the organizational norms and routines associated with it (Pettigrew and Fenton 2000; Whittington and Meyer 2000; Marchington et al. 2005). Within this 'hybridized' context, the business project, enacted by and through a network, emerges as the basic operating unit, and project management becomes the major coordinating and controlling mechanism counteracting endemic tendencies towards excessive differentiation and consequent fragmentation. Thus, the rise of network enterprise seems to signal a dramatic shift in corporate strategy and management away from 'system reproduction' by means of bureaucratic mechanisms of hierarchical command and control and towards 'system transformation' by means of network mechanisms that compress and stretch time-space resources and relations combining rapid global mobility and flexible local diversity (Clark 2003).

The third stream of writing and research developed within the network framework/narrative has been concerned to unpack the micro-level or workplace implications of network-based restructuring at a global and corporate level. Its primary explanatory focus has been directed towards the longer-term impact of global/corporate restructuring on the dynamics of workplace re-organization and the struggles for power and control within and between different occupational groups and cultures caught up in the socio-political upheavals that globalization has produced. A broad range of research issues have emerged to frame a new research agenda for the sociology of workplace behaviour and organization. These encompass high risk/low trust work environments and cultures, shifting occupational and organizational identities, more extensive and intensive technologies of surveillance and control (Scarbrough and Corbett 1992), and hybridized regimes of enterprise/workplace governance in which the search for 'continuous innovation' and 'high performance' are the major drivers of change. Much of the research and analysis conducted in this area has been focused around the discursive technologies through which organizational identities are reconstructed in post-Fordist/postmodern economies and societies (Kondo 1990; Townley 1994; Casey 1995; DuGay 1996; Jacques 1996; Grant et al. 1998; McKinlay and Starkey 1998; Barker 1999; Whetten 1999; Sewell 2001; Alvesson and Willmott 2002; Knights and McCabe 2003). Professional service business and 'knowledge-intensive organizations' have provided particularly fruitful research sites in which the complex dynamics of discursive innovation and change and their longer-term impact on the emergence of new 'professional' and 'managerial' identities can be explored (Cohen et al. 2002; Dent and Whitehead 2002; Newell et al. 2002; Alvesson 2004; Karreman and Alvesson 2004). The underlying thrust of this work indicates that *hybridized* control strategies and regimes, in which elements of bureaucratic control are selectively combined with elements of concertive control (Barker 1999), are becoming the dominant governance form in high value-added, service sector organizations. Within the latter, the re-engineering of corporate culture and the fabrication of new organizational subjectivities/identities – better aligned with the incessant demands and endemic uncertainties of globalized competition – emerges as the primary focus for managerial action.

Considered in these terms, hybridization is a mutil-level, systemic process that simultaneously responds to and generates increased complexity in organizational forms, relations and practices. Hybrids combine and contain cultures and roles based on contradictory norms and principles by providing mechanisms for loosely-coupling competing 'logics of collective action' that are required in more unstable, uncertain and competitive environments. They tend to facilitate horizontal, rather than vertical, decision-making processes because they have to absorb and cope with much higher

levels of contradiction, tension and conflict than would normally be the case in simpler forms of organizing and managing. Thus, Courpasson (2000: 154) refers to 'soft bureaucracy' as entailing 'the expansion of liberal management based on decentralization and "marketization" of organization and autonomy hand in hand with the development of highly centralized and authoritarian forms of government'.

However, in the more standardized and mass customized 'low value-added' segment of service sector employment, a rather different story emerges of highly individualized and routinized work cultures and relations in which cultural re-engineering and identity management is a somewhat less pressing concern for management teams locked into a 'pile it high, sell it cheap' ethos (Korczynski et al. 2000; Korczynski 2002; 2003). Indeed, within this segment of the service sector the emergence of a neo-Taylorist control strategy (Webster and Robins 1993), in which new information and computer technologies are combined with cultural engineering programmes geared to more indirect forms of work intensification, surveillance and discipline, is the dominant reality (Bunting 2004). Rationalization, through simplification, standardization and intensification, seems to be the order of the day, rather than the enhanced complexity, flexibility and individuality associated with hybrid organizational forms.

Overall, research, analysis and debate around the network theme/narrative have re-shaped the field of organization studies over the last decade or so. They have re-defined the philosophical, theoretical and political terrain on which contemporary organizational studies has developed and challenged the cognitive, intellectual and ideological resources through which that terrain can be mapped, traversed and re-shaped. By mounting a frontal attack on the underlying domain assumptions that have informed the emergence and evolution of the field since the second half of the nineteenth century, network theory and analysis have challenged the compulsory points of departure – the neo-Weberian model of bureaucracy (DuGay 2005), empiricist/objectivist ontology, rationalist/positivist epistemology, social engineering philosophy and managerialist ideology – from which those who wished to traverse the terrain necessarily had to begin their journey. Once these, seemingly fixed and immutable, points of departure have been removed, then all sorts of intellectual possibilities and institutional potentialities are opened up that were previously denied or at least hidden from view. In turn, these might lead to very different kinds of ideological and practical destinations than those envisaged in more orthodox approaches based on outmoded assumptions of long-run continuity, stability and order.

Nevertheless, considerable scepticism remains as to whether the 'world we have lost' and the 'world we have gained' are as fundamentally and irreconcilably opposed as many network theorists and analysts seem to suggest (Child and McGrath 2001; Jessop 2002; Hudson 2003; Thompson 2003b; Courpasson and Reed 2004; Reed 2005a). For all the academic talk and media hype around highly decentralized networks and dispersed self-managing teams embedded in complex flows of collectively distributed resources, effective strategic power and control remain highly centralized and remote from local needs and aspirations. The academic discourse that has crystallized around 'networks' belies a brute reality in which institutionalized hierarchical power structures stubbornly refuse to conform to their allotted role as social dinosaurs on the verge of extinction in a 'brave new world' of unprecedented spatial mobilities and temporal mutations (Urry 2000). Corporate power and control may be forced to adapt to new conditions of 'high velocity change' and the endemic risks and uncertainties that it generates. This may indeed call for more streamlined organizational flows and more flexible routines and structures in which communities of 'knowledge workers' enjoy levels of work autonomy and socio-economic reward only dreamt of by their counterparts in the 'low value added' service sector. However, these new, network-based organizational forms and cultures remain embedded in power structures and control regimes that are there to protect and legitimate the material, social and political interests of dominant classes and elites. Thus, the rather inflated claims made for the radical impact of network-based forms of organizing on governance structures and control regimes need to be tempered by the realization that:

> One might well question this celebration of the miracle of ICT-enabled global networking in the light of the continued importance of vertical divisions of economic power and authority as well as horizontal divisions of labour in economic networks and the network state ... we have yet to see the state dissolve itself into a series of free-floating, self-organizing networks with no overarching co-ordination and

preservation of the right to re-centralize control if the operation and/or results of networks do not fulfill the expectations of state managers, affected interests or public opinion (Jessop 2002: 237).

Points of Intersection

A number of interconnected themes provide the 'analytical spine' around which the seven narrative frames reviewed in this chapter can be interpreted as historically contested attempts to represent and control our understanding of such a strategic institutionalized social practice as 'organization'. As with the discourse of political theory, the discourse of organization theory must be considered as a contestable and contested network of concepts and theories which are engaged in a struggle to impose certain meanings rather than others on our shared understanding of organizational life in late modernity. As Connolly (1993: 225–31) puts it:

> To say that a particular network of concepts is contestable is to say that the standards and criteria of judgement it expresses are open to contestation. To say that such a network is essentially contestable is to contend that universal criteria of reason, as we now understand them, do not suffice to settle these contests definitely. The proponent of essentially contestable concepts charges those who construe the standards operative in their own way of life to be fully expressive of God's will or reason or nature with transcendental provincialism; they treat the standards with which they are intimately familiar as universal criteria against which all other theories, practices and ideals are assessed. They use universalist rhetoric to protect provincial practices ... The phrase 'essentially contestable concepts', properly interpreted, calls attention to the internal connection between conceptual debates and debates over the form of the good life, to the reasonable grounds we now have to believe that rational space. For such contestation will persist into the future, to the values of keeping such contests alive even in settings where a determinate orientation to action is required, and to the incumbent task for those who accept the first three themes to expose conceptual closure where it has been imposed artificially.

Connolly (1993: 213–47) develops this argument to sustain a critique of the 'rational universalism' and 'radical relativism' that dominates political analysis in the arenas of Anglo-American analytic philosophy and continental postmodernism. He is particularly critical of the artificial and unwarranted 'conceptual closure' of Foucauldian accounts of knowledge/power discourses that construe social actors as artifacts, rather than agents, of power. According to this view, the 'thesis of essential contestation gives way to the practice of total deconstruction' (Connolly 1993: 233). Thus, Connolly conceives of political theory as an essentially contested domain or space in which rival interpretations of political life can be analytically identified and rationally debated by responsible agents without recourse to the 'transcendental provincialism' characteristic of either epistemological universalism or cultural relativism. Such a conception can be used to survey the underlying themes that emerge from the historical account of organization theory provided in this chapter.

These themes can be summarized as follows: a meta-theoretical debate between positivism, constructionism and realism about social ontology and its implications for the nature and status of the knowledge that organization theorists produce; a theoretical debate concerning the rival explanatory claims of the concepts of 'agency' and 'structure' as they are deployed to account for key features of organization; an analytical debate between the relative priority to be attached to the 'local' as opposed to the 'global' level of analysis in organization studies; a normative debate between 'individualism' and 'collectivism' as competing ideological conceptions of the 'good life' in late modern societies. Each of the seven narratives contributes to and participates within the contested intellectual spaces that these debates open up.

The Ontology/Epistemology Debate

Meta-theoretical debates over the constitution of social reality and its implications for the ways in which we attempt to generate and evaluate knowledge claims in the study of organizations have played a much more strategic role in the development of organization studies over the last decade or so (Reed 2005b). For much of the 1980s and 1990s, this meta-theoretical debate revolved around the rival claims of positivism and constructionism to provide all-inclusive philosophical paradigms that defined the nature of the social reality in which

'organization' was necessarily embedded and the methodological principles and tools through which it could be explained (Donaldson 1985; 1996; Hassard 1990; 1993; Reed and Hughes 1992; Willmott 1993; Tsoukas and Knudsen 2003; Westwood and Clegg 2003). The rationalist, organicist/integrationist and market narratives developed on the basis of a strong commitment to a positivist epistemology and an empiricist ontology (in which individual sense-experience and theory-free observational data are regarded as the only firm foundations for scientific knowledge). In turn, positivism severely restricts the range of 'knowledge claims' allowable in organization studies to those who pass a rigorous 'trail by method' and the law-like generalizations that it sanctions.

In direct contrast, the power, knowledge and justice traditions have been more favourably disposed towards a constructionist ontology and epistemology in which actors' interpretations and discourses play a much more central explanatory role. Thus, the first three narratives treat 'organization' as an object or entity existing in its own right that be defined and explained in terms of the general principles or laws governing its operation that can be uncovered through the application of 'positive science'. However, the social constructionist leanings of the second group of three narratives promote a conception of 'organization' as a social constructed and dependent artifact that can only be understood in terms of sets of highly restricted and localized methodological conventions that are open to infinite revision and change (Westwood and Clegg 2003; Linstead 2004). Constructionism also takes a much more liberal, not to say permissive, relativistic stance and falls back on the, necessarily restricted and localized, communal norms and practices associated with specific research communities as they develop over time (Reed 1993; 2005b). Various attempts have been made to follow a middle course between these opposed philosophical paradigms (Bernstein 1983), but the contested ontological and epistemological terrain mapped out by positivism and constructionism continued to shape theoretical development in organization studies for much of the 1980s and 1990s.

More recently, a third meta-theoretical paradigm or framework has emerged in organization studies to challenge the ontological assumptions and epistemological principles on which both positivism and constructionism traded to legitimate their respective philosophical and methodological positions. Realism (Putnam 1990) – or more precisely 'critical realism' – has emerged as a radical meta-theoretical alternative to both positivism and constructionism (Reed 1997; 2001; 2003; 2005b; Fleetwood 1999; Ackroyd and Fleetwood 2000; Clark 2000; 2003; Lopez and Potter 2001; Danermark et al. 2002; Fleetwood and Ackroyd 2004). It maintains that 'organization' is necessarily embedded in pre-existing material and social reality that fundamentally shapes the structures and processes through which it is generated, reproduced and transformed. This means that the epistemological principles and theoretical practices through which we attempt to understand and explain 'organization' must focus on the underlying 'real or generative' structures and mechanisms through which the interrelated entities and processes that constitute it are generated, sustained and changed. By rejecting the material determinism inherent in positivism and the cultural relativism endemic to constructionism, critical realism provides a meta-theoretical framework in which explanatory theories and models of historical and structural change in organizational forms and processes can be developed. The theories and models give full recognition to the complex interplay between pre-existing constraints and contemporary possibilities generated through forms of corporate agency, such as 'organization'.

Indeed, the seventh narrative of 'network' has become a contemporary theoretical and empirical battleground in which the respective philosophical and explanatory claims of positivism, constructionism and realism are fought out. Those who are most sceptical of the 'miracle' of global transformation through ICT-generated networks and their unrivaled capacity to deconstruct, indeed destroy, governance structures based on vertical command and control through hierarchical power and domination – such as Harvey, Jessop, Webster, Rosenberg and Clark – have been much closer to a critical realistic 'take' on social ontology and its explanatory implications. For them, political economy, rather than global culture, is central to any understanding, much less explanation, of the major structural changes occurring now and likely to emerge in the future. In direct contrast, those who have most enthusiastically embraced the doctrine of an ICT-led neo-liberal global transformation and its revolutionary impact on everything from consumption patterns to belief systems and life styles – such as

Giddens, Beck, Lash and Urry – have been much closer to a social constructionist ontology and a postmodernist epistemology. For them, radical transformations in globalized cultural and symbolic frameworks and the discursive formations through which these are represented and interpreted, rather than underlying continuities in capitalist political economies, are the major focus for analysis and debate. Those who remain closest to policy-making and implementing elites in the dominant OECD countries – such as Fukuyama, Sabel and Pfeffer – are committed to some variant of the positivist paradigm and the legitimacy that it provides for globalized neo-liberalism and market populism (Frank 2000). All the signs currently indicate that this underlying philosophical and theoretical struggle between positivism, constructionism and realism will continue to shape the emerging research agenda that the network narrative has engendered over the last decade.

The Agency/Structure Debate

Layder (1994: 4) argues that the 'agency/structure' debate in social theory 'concentrates on the question of how creativity and constraint are related through social activity –how can we explain their co-existence?' Those who emphasize agency focus on an understanding of social and organizational order that stresses the social practices through which human beings create and reproduce institutions. Those located on the 'structure' side highlight the importance of the objectified external relations and patterns that determine and constrain social interaction within specific institutional forms (Reed 1988).

Within these generic narrative frames, a theoretical fault line has emerged between two fundamental conceptions of 'organization'. On the one side of this line, a conception of organization has appeared that refers to determinate structures which condition individual and collective behaviour. On the other side stands a conception of organization that is a theoretical shorthand for consciously fabricated action networks through which such structures are generated and reproduced as temporary and constantly shifting ordering mechanisms or devices. The rational, integrationist and market narratives come down firmly in support of the structural conception of organization; while researchers working within the power, knowledge and justice traditions support the agency conception of organization.

Much effort has been expended in trying to overcome, or at least reconcile, this theoretical duality through approaches which emphasize the mutually consti-tuted and constituting nature of agency and structure in the reproduction of organization (e.g. Giddens 1984; 1993; Smith 1993; Boden 1994; Willmott 1994). However, the underlying conflict between competing explanatory logics remains a source of creative tension within organization studies and will do for the fore-seeable future (Reed 2003; 2005b).

There is always the danger that agency-oriented conceptions will detach the organization from its sur-rounding societal context and be unable to deal with major shifts in dominant institutional forms. On the other hand, structure-oriented views tend towards a more deterministic explanatory logic in which society can crush agency through monolithic force (Whittington 1994: 64). Whittington's (1994: 71) conclusion is that organization analysis needs a 'theory of strategic choice adequate to the impor-tance of managerial agency in our society'. His rejec-tion of the theoretical extremes of individualistic reductionism and collectivist determinism is well taken. The need to develop explanatory theories in which 'agency derives from the simultaneously enabling and contradictory nature of the structural principles by which people act' (Whittington 1994: 72) constitutes one of the central issues on the research agenda for organization analysis. Again, organization theorists and analysts working within the critical realist meta-theoretical paradigm referred to earlier have focused on the 'agency/structure' debate as a, indeed *the*, major analytical and theoret-ical issue confronting the field of organization stud-ies. They have argued that the ontological premises and explanatory principles on which critical realism rests can provide exactly the kind of approach that meets Whittington's demand for a non-deterministic theory of collective or corporate agency that fully rec-ognizes the crucial importance of the complex inter-play between structural constraint and pro-active agency (Reed 1997; 2003; 2005b).

The Local/Global Debate

The agency/structure debate raises fundamental questions about the logics of explanation that orga-nization analysts should follow and the construc-tivism/positivism debate highlights deep-seated controversy and contestation over the representa-tional forms through which the knowledge should

be developed, evaluated and legitimated. The localism/ globalism debate that emerges from the narratives focuses on questions relating to the level of analysis at which organizational research and analysis should be pitched. As Layder (1994) maintains, questions relating to levels of analysis crystallize around different models of social reality and the analytic properties of entities or objects located at different levels within those models. Thus, the 'micro/ macro' debate relates to whether the empha-sis should be on 'intimate and detailed aspects of face-to-face conduct [or] more impersonal and large-scale phenomena' (Layder 1994: 6).

A range of theoretical approaches developed under the auspices of the power, knowledge and justice frameworks tend to favour a focus on local/micro-organizational processes and prac-tices; while the rational, integrationist and market narratives take a more global/macro conception of the 'reality of organization' as their starting point. Ethnomethodological and post-structuralist approaches take the local focus the furthest; while population ecology, neo-institutionalism and theo-retical approaches (such as labour process theory and analysis) based on critical realist principles have a more well-developed global level of analysis. Approaches fixated with the local/micro-level of analysis in organization studies run the risk of basing their research on 'flat ontologies' which makes it very difficult, if not impossible, to go beyond everyday practices in which members are engaged (Layder 1994: 218–29; Archer 1995; 2000). As a result, their theoretical capability to perceive, much less explain, the intricate and complex inter-meshing of local practices – in all their variability and contingency – and institutionalized structures is severely compromised (Smith 1988). The corre-sponding danger with 'stratified ontologies' is that they may underestimate the explanatory signifi-cance of the dialectic between and mutual consti-tuting of social structures and social practices.

The prevailing tendency in organization analysis to shift the analytical focus so far towards the local/micro-level risks losing sight of the wider structural constraints and resources which shape the process of organizational (re)production or 'ordering'. Some studies, however, manage to keep the highly intricate, but absolutely vital, intermesh-ing of the local and the global, agency and structure, construction and constraint, constantly in view. Indeed, examples of the most significant recent research in the study of organizations is to be found in Zuboff's (1988) work on information technology, Jackall's (1988) analysis of the 'moral mazes' to be discovered in large American business corporations, Kondo's (1990) research on the 'crafting of selves' in Japanese work organizations, Zukin's (1993) work on the transformation of urban landscapes and organizational forms and Sennett's (1998) critique of the corrosion of moral character engendered by globalized capitalism. These studies re-discover and renew the mutual constituting of situated practices and structural forms that lies at the core of any type of organization analysis which reaches beyond the boundaries of everyday understanding to connect with the historical, social and organizational dynamics which frame trajectories of long-term socio-economic development.

The Individualism/Collectivism Debate

The final analytical vertebra constituting the theoretical backbone of this brief history of organization studies is the ideological debate between individualistic and collectivist visions of organizational order. Individualistic theories of organization are grounded in an analytical and normative outlook that sees organizational order as an aggregated outcome of individual actions and reactions that are always potentially reducible to their component parts. Thus, market-based theories of organization, and the rich vein of decision-making theorizing that is woven around this individualistic perspective (Whittington 1994), deny that collective concepts, such as 'organization', have any ontological or methodological status beyond shorthand code for the performances of individual actors. The ideological justification for this ontological/methodological precept lies in the belief that forms of social organization that go beyond direct interpersonal association can only be justified in terms of their positive contribution to the protection of individual freedom and autonomy.

Collectivism lies at the opposite end of the ideological/methodological spectrum in that it refuses to recognize individual actors as constituent components of formal organization; they simply become ciphers for the cognitive, emotional and political programming provided by larger structures. If individualism offers a vision of organization as the unintended creation of individual actors

following the dictates of their particular instrumental and political objectives, then collectivism treats organization as an objective entity that imposes itself on actors with such force that they have little or no choice but to obey its commands (Whittington 1989; 1994; Reed 2003). The integrationist narrative relies on this view most strongly insofar as it identifies a logic of organizational functioning and development which goes on 'behind the backs' of individuals and tightly constrains the decision-making options available to the latter virtually to the point of extinction. While it has become much less fashionable of late, such collectivism continues to offer a conception of organization and organization analysis that directly challenges the dominance of analytical perspectives which are grounded in an individualist/reductionist programme.

Narrating Theoretical Futures

Law (1994b: 248–9) has suggested that, over the last two decades, organization studies has gone through a 'bonfire of the certainties' in relation to its ontological foundations, theoretical commitments, methodological conventions and ideological predilections. Domain assumptions relating to the analytical dominance of 'order' over 'disorder', 'structure' over 'process', 'internalities' over 'externalities', 'boundaries' over 'ecologies' and 'rationality' over 'emotion' have been put to the flames in a coruscating critique of innate theoretical hubris and methodological pretentiousness. He outlines two possible responses to this situation: 'carry on regardless' or 'let a thousand flowers bloom'. The first option suggests a retreat back into, appropriately refurbished, intellectual fortifications that offer protection against the radically destabilizing effects of continuing critique and deconstruction. It supports a general regrouping around an accepted theoretical paradigm and core research programme that counteracts the fragmentary dynamic let loose by approaches that have broken with orthodoxy. The second calls for a further proliferation of 'more questions and uncertainties and … more narratives that generate questions' (Law 1994b: 249). It need not necessarily result in organization studies slipping into a vortex of anarchic and uncontrollable relativism, Law (1994b: 249) argues, because it sensitizes us to the need to preserve and build on the intellectual pluralism that critique has made possible and to reveal 'the processes by which story-telling and ordering produce themselves'.

As has already been intimated in earlier sections of this chapter, the urge to retreat and re-group back into reheated intellectual orthodoxy is a powerful tendency within the field at the present time. In their different ways, Donaldson (1985; 1988; 1989; 1994; 2003) and Pfeffer (1993) attempt to revive the narrative of organization studies as a scientific enterprise that speaks directly to the technical needs and political interests of policy-making elites, an aspiration and leitmotiv which has dominated the field's development since the early decades of this century. Their call for paradigmatic consensus and pragmatic discipline around a dominant theoretical and methodological orthodoxy to deliver, cumulatively, codified bodies of knowledge that are 'user-friendly' to policy-making elites resonates with the current desire to re-establish intellectual order and control in an increasingly fragmented and uncertain world. They are intellectual and ideological heirs to the technocratic scientism that pervades the rational, integrationist and market narrative traditions reviewed earlier. Their call for intellectual closure around a refurbished theoretical paradigm and ideological consensus over the restrictive technocratic needs that organization analysis should serve rests on the assumption that a return to orthodoxy is a viable political project.

The alter ego of the 'return to orthodoxy' vision is the 'incommensurability thesis' into which new intellectual life has been pumped by the growing influence of post-structuralist and postmodernist approaches as represented in Foucauldian-inspired discourse theory and actor-network theory (Jackson and Carter 2000). Supporters of the 'incommensurability thesis' luxuriate in epistemological, theoretical and cultural relativism. They reject the possibility of shared discourse between conflicting paradigmatic positions in favour of an unqualified relativism that completely politicizes intellectual debate and adjudication between rival traditions. Relations of mutual exclusivity between paradigms offer polarized visions of organization and languages of organization analysis that cannot be reconciled. Thus, the rival narratives that constitute 'our' field are locked into a struggle for intellectual power with no hope of mediation. A transcendental Nietzschean 'will to power' and a geopolitical

Darwinian 'survival of the fittest' impose intellectual and institutional parameters within which this struggle has to be fought. There is no question of sustaining a narrative through argument, logic and evidence; there is simply the power of a dominant paradigm and the disciplinary practices that it generates and legitimates. There is no recognition of negotiated ground rules within which contestation can rationally proceed (Connolly 1993: 233–4), or of a shared interest in mediating mutual suspicion and rivalry. The conception of organization studies as an historically contested and contextually mediated terrain thus gives way to the practice of total deconstruction and the unqualified relativism on which it rests (Linstead 2004).

This 'Hobson's choice' between re-vamped orthodoxy and radical relativism is not the only option: greater sensitivity to the socio-historical context and political dynamics of theory development need not degenerate into unreflective and total deconstruction as the only viable alternative to a resurgent orthodoxy. Willmott's (1993) reworking of Kuhn's approach to the process of theoretical development within natural and social science offers a way out of the intellectual cul-de-sac in which both orthodoxy and relativism terminate. His focus on the communal processes and practices of critical reflection required to identify anomalies within existing theories offers a more attractive alternative to both the hubris of 'carry on regardless' and the despondency of 'anything goes'. Willmott (1993) resists the dogma of paradigm incommensurability, while highlighting the crucial role of institutionalized academic politics in determining access to the resources and infrastructure (appointments, grants, journals, publishers, etc.) that shape the conditions under which different paradigms of knowledge production are legitimated. However, this sensitivity to the 'production practices' that facilitate the acceptance of certain theories of organization and marginalize or exclude others does not go far enough. Willmott's analysis reveals little awareness of the ways in which these production practices mesh with *adjudicatory practices*, built up over a protracted period of intellectual development, to form the negotiated rules through which competing approaches and traditions can be evaluated. We need to develop greater awareness of the subtle and intricate ways in which material conditions and intellectual practices intermesh to generate and sustain the inherently dynamic narrative traditions and research programmes that constitute the field of organization studies over time.

'Institutional reflexivity' (Giddens 1993; 1994) is not only the defining feature of the phenomena to which organizational researchers attend; it is also a constitutive feature of the intellectual trade they practice. The study of organization is both progenitor of and heir to this institutionalized reflexivity in that it necessarily depends on and systematically cultivates a critical and questioning attitude to its concerns, as mediated through a dynamic interaction within and between the narrative traditions that constitute its intellectual inheritance. Students of organization cannot avoid this inheritance: it sets the background assumptions and moral context that informs the decisions that researchers make concerning ideology, epistemology and theory. These choices are made within an inheritance that is not simply 'handed down', but is constantly revisited, re-evaluated and renewed as it passes through the critical debate and reflection which is the intellectual life-blood of organization studies.

Reflexivity and criticality are institutionalized within the intellectual practices that constitute the study of organization. The specific criteria through which these 'generalized mandates' are defined and the particular socio-economic and political conditions under which they are activated vary across time and space. The material and symbolic power mobilized by different academic communities clearly affects the survival of rival narrative traditions. Nevertheless, the indelible link between practical reasoning, within and between competing analytically structured narratives, and theory development in a dynamic socio-historical context, can be erased by neither conservative orthodoxy nor radical relativism. It is the confrontation between rival narrative traditions, particularly when their internal tensions and contradictions or anomalies are most clearly and cruelly exposed, that provides the essential intellectual dynamism through which the study of organization re-discovers and renews itself. As Perry (1992: 98) argues, 'we cannot escape from either history or the game of culture. All theorizing is therefore partial; all theorizing is selective'. However, this is not a rationalization for a forced paradigmatic consensus or for unrestrained paradigm proliferation. Instead, it calls for a more sensitive appreciation of the complex interaction between a changing set of institutional conditions

and intellectual forms as they combine to reproduce the reflexivity and criticality that is the hallmark of contemporary organization studies.

The underlying thrust of the chapter is to suggest that organization theorists have developed, and will continue to develop, a network of critical debates within and between narrative traditions that will indelibly shape their field's evolution. Three debates seem particularly intense and potentially productive at the present time. The first is the perceived need to develop a 'theory of the subject' (Casey 2002) that does not degenerate into the simplicities of reductionism or the absurdities of determinism (Reed 2003). More recent work on the discursive practices and formations through which new organizational cultures and identities are fashioned and re-fashioned is central to this area of concern (Grant et al. 2004). The second is a general desire to construct a 'theory of organization' that analytically and methodologically mediates between the restrictions of localism and the blandishments of globalism (Calas 1994). This becomes particularly important at a time and within an era in which the 'hybridization' of organizational forms generated by global shifts in contemporary capitalist political economies, and the highly complex macro-, meso- and micro-level networks through which it occurs, necessitates more sophisticated understandings of and explanations for the dynamics of change at a multiplicity of interrelated levels of analysis. Work on the new political economy of globalized capitalism (Clark 2003) and the global 'service or knowledge class' through which it is maintained (Reed 1996; Sklair 2001; Alvesson 2004) is central to this key theme of changing organizational forms and the long-term development of organization theory as a 'critical science' (Willmott 2003). The third key area of contemporary debate is the imperative of nurturing a 'theory of (intellectual) development' that resists the constrictions of conservatism and the distortions of relativism.

The philosophical and theoretical resources through which contemporary organization theory might be most appropriately developed as a 'critical science' remain the subject of continuing intellectual controversy and political struggle. Some look to social constructionism and post-structuralism as a major source of intellectual inspiration for developing understanding and critique of the discursive practices and formations through which unaccountable concentrations of power and control are generated and sustained (Deetz 1992; Flyvbjerg 2001; Alvesson and Willmott 2002; Hatch and Yanov 2003; Tsoukas and Knudsen 2003; Willmott 2003). Others, while rejecting the search for invariant 'laws or principles of organization' typical of positivist organization theory (Donaldson 1996; 2003), argue that a critical science of organization must consistently retain core philosophical principles and theoretical practices if it is to develop forms of scientific knowledge that simultaneously facilitate 'good explanation' and the efficacious practical action that can flow from it (Clark 2000; 2003; Reed 2003; 2005b; Fleetwood and Ackroyd 2004).

Thus, the intellectual and ideological pluralism that has characterized modern organization theory and analysis as it emerged from the second industrial revolution that gathered momentum and pace from the second half of the nineteenth century onwards seem set to remain with us well into the twenty-first century. This should not be seen as providing a justification for a retreat into an intellectual orthodoxy in which all the uncertainties, ambiguities, tensions and conflicts released by the breakdown of the post-1945 'orthodox consensus' in social and organization theory are either unceremoniously 'swept under the carpet' or selectively edited out of their past, present and future. Neither does it justify a celebration of cognitive, linguistic, cultural and ideological 'incommensurability' (Jackson and Carter 1991) in which groups of organization theorists literally inhabit separate worlds and the radical ontological idealism and epistemological relativism that it legitimates. If we are to develop theorizations of organization and organizing that facilitate adequate explanations of the way the world is and efficacious practical political interventions that may flow from them, then we have to engage with our history and the rich intellectual inheritance that it bequeaths to us. Only in this way can we hope to continue our journey across the contested intellectual terrain that defines organization studies as a field of study that has been, and still is, in the making over the last two centuries.

References

Abbott, A. (1988) *The System of Professions*. Chicago: University of Chicago Press.

Ackroyd, S. (2002) *The Organization of Business*. Oxford: Oxford University Press.

Ackroyd, S. and Fleetwood, S. (2000) *Realist Perspectives on Management and Organizations*. London: Routledge.

Adler, P. (2001) 'Market, hierarchy and trust: the knowledge economy and the future of capitalism', *Organization Science*, 12(2): 215–34.

Aldrich, H. (1979) *Organizations and Environments*. Englewood-Cliffs, NJ: Prentice Hall.

Aldrich H. (1992) 'Incommensurable paradigms?: vital signs from three perspectives', in M. Reed and M. Hughes (eds), *Rethinking Organizations: New Directions in Organization Theory and Analysis*. London: Sage. pp. 17–45.

Aldrich, H. (1999) *Organizations Evolving*. London: Sage.

Alford, R. and Freidland, R. (1985) *Powers of Theory: Capitalism, the State and Democracy*. Cambridge: Cambridge University Press.

Alvesson, M. (2004) *Knowledge Work and Knowledge-Intensive Firms*. Oxford: Oxford University Press.

Alvesson, M. and Karreman, D. (2000) 'Varities of discourse: on the study of organizations through discourse', *Human Relations*, 53(9): 1125–49.

Alvesson, M. and Willmott, H. (1992) *Critical Management Studies*. London: Sage.

Alvesson, M. and Willmott, H. (2002) 'Identity regulation as organizational control: producing the appropriate individual', *Journal of Management Studies*, 39(5): 620–44.

Amin, A. and Cohendet, P. (2003) *Architecture of Knowledge: Firms, Capabilities and Communities*. Oxford: Oxford University Press.

Anthony, P. (1986) *Foundations of Management*. London: Tavistock.

Archer, M. (1995) *Realist Social Theory: the Morphogenetic Approach*. Cambridge: Cambridge University Press.

Archer, M. (2000) *Being Human: the Problem of Agency*. Cambridge: Cambridge University Press.

Argyris, C. (1964) *Integrating the Individual and the Organization*. New York: Wiley.

Arhne, G. (1994) *Social Organizations*. London: Sage.

Arhne, G. (1996) 'Civil society and civil organizations', *Organization*, 3(1): 109–20.

Barker, J.R. (1999) *The Discipline of Teamwork*. Thousand Oaks, CA: Sage.

Barley, S.R. and Kunda, G. (1992) 'Design and devotion: surges of rational and normative ideologies of control in managerial discourse', *Administrative Science Quarterly*, 37(3): 363–99.

Barley, S.R. and Tolbert, P. (1997) 'Institutionalization and structuration: studying the links between action and structure', *Organization Studies*, 18(1): 93–117.

Barnard, C. (1938) *Functions of the Executive*. Cambridge, MA: Harvard University Press.

Bartell, T. (1976) 'The human relations ideology', *Human Relations*, 29(8): 737–49.

Bauman, Z. (1989) *Modernity and the Holocaust*. Cambridge: Polity Press.

Bauman, Z. (1992) *Intimations of Postmodernity*. London: Routledge.

Bauman, Z. (1995) *Life in Fragments*. Oxford: Blackwell.

Bauman, Z. (1997) *Postmodernity and its Discontents*. New York: New York University Press.

Beck, U. (1992) *The Risk Society: Towards a New Modernity*. London: Sage.

Beck, U. (1997) *The Re-invention of Politics: Rethinking Modernity in the Global Social Order*. Cambridge: Polity Press.

Beck, U. (2000) *The Brave New World of Work*. Cambridge: Polity Press.

Beck, U., Giddens, A. and Lash, S. (1994) *Reflexive Modernization: Rethinking Modernity in the Global Social Order*. Cambridge: Polity Press.

Bell, D. (1960) *The End of Ideology*. New York: Collier Macmillan.

Bell, D. (1973) *The Coming of Post-Industrial Society*. New York: Basic Books.

Bell, D. (1999) *The Coming of Post-Industrial Society (Special Anniversary Edition)*. New York: Basic Books.

Bendix, R. (1974) *Work and Authority in Industry*. California: University of California Press.

Bernstein, B. (1983) *Beyond Objectivism and Relativism*. Oxford: Blackwell.

Blackler, F. (1993) 'Knowledge and the theory of organizations: organizations as activity systems and the reframing of management', *Journal of Management Studies*, 30: 863–84.

Blackler, F. (1995) 'Knowledge, knowledge work and organizations: an overview and interpretation', Organization Studies, 16(6): 1021–46.

Blau, P. (1955) *The Dynamics of Bureaucracy*. Chicago: University of Chicago Press.

Blau, P. (1974) *On the Nature of Organizations*. New York: Wiley.

Blau, P. and Schoenherr, R.A. (1971) *The Structure of Organizations*. New York: Basic Books.

Blau, P. and Scott, W.R. (1963) *Formal Organizations: a Comparative Approach*. London: Routledge.

Boden, D. (1994) *The Business of Talk: Organizations in Action*. Cambridge: Polity Press.

Boguslaw, R. (1965) *The New Utopians: the Study of System Design and Social Change*. Englewood Cliffs, NJ: Prentice Hall.

Brech, E. (1948) *Organization: the Framework of Management*. New York: Collier Macmillan.

Bunting, M. (2004) *Willing Slaves: How the Overwork Culture is Ruling Our Lives*. London: Harper Collins.

Burawoy, M. (1979) *Manufacturing Consent*. Chicago: University of Chicago Press.

Burawoy, M. (1985) *The Politics of Production*. London: Verso.

Burrell, G. (1997) *Pandemonium: Towards a Retro-Organization Theory*. London: Sage.

Burrell, G. (2003) 'The future of organization theory: prospects and limitations', in H. Tsoukas and C. Knudsen (eds), *The Oxford Handbook of Organization Theory: Meta- Theoretical Perspectives*. Oxford: Oxford University Press. pp. 525–35.

Burrell, G. and Morgan, G. (1979) *Sociological Paradigms and Organizational Analysis*. London: Heinemann.

Cable, V. (1994) *The World's New Fissures*. London: Demos.

Calas, M. (1994) 'Minerva's owl?: introduction to a thematic section on globalization', *Organization*, 1(2): 243–8.

Calas, M. and Smircich, L. (1991) 'Voicing seduction to silence leadership', *Organization Studies*, 12(4): 567–601.

Casey, C. (1995) *Work, Self and Society: After Industrialism*. London: Routledge.

Casey, C. (2002) *Critical Analysis of Organizations: Theory, Practice, Revitalization*. London: Sage.

Castells, M. (1989) *The Informational City: Information Technology, Economic Restructuring and the Urban-Regional Process*. Oxford: Blackwell.

Castells, M. (1996) *The Rise of the Network Society*. Oxford: Blackwell.

Castells, M. (2000) *The Rise of the Network Society, Second Edition*. Oxford: Blackwell.

Cerny, P. (1990) *The Changing Architecture of Politics*. London: Sage.

Checkland, P. (1994) 'Conventional wisdom and conventional ignorance: the revolution organization theory missed', *Organization*, 1(1): 29–34.

Child, J. (1969) *British Management Thought*. London: Allen and Unwin.

Child, J. (1972) 'Organization structure, environment and performance: the role of strategic choice', *Sociology*, 6(1): 163–77.

Child, J. (1973) 'Organization: a choice for man', in J. Child (ed.), *Man and Organization*. London: Allen and Unwin. pp. 234–57.

Child, J. and McGrath, R. (2001) 'Organizations unfettered: organizational form in an information-intensive economy', *Academy of Management Journal*, 44(6): 1135–48.

Clark, P.A. (2000) *Organizations in Action: Competition between Contexts*. London: Routledge.

Clark, P.A. (2003) *Organizational Innovations*. London: Sage.

Clegg, S. (1989) *Frameworks of Power*. London: Sage.

Clegg, S. (1990) *Modern Organizations: Organization Studies in the Postmodern World*. London: Sage.

Clegg, S. (1994) 'Weber and Foucault: social theory for the study of organizations', *Organization*, 1(1): 149–178.

Clegg, S. and Dunkerley, D. (1980) *Organization, Class and Control*. London: Routledge.

Coase, R. (1937) 'The nature of the firm', *Economica*, new series, 386–405.

Cohen, L., Finn, A., Wilkinson, A. and Arnold, J. (2002) 'Professional work and management', *International Studies of Organization and Management*, 32(2): 3–24.

Connolly, W. (1993) *The Terms of Political Discourse*, 3rd edn. Oxford: Blackwell.

Cooper, R. (1992) 'Formal organization as representation: remote control, displacement and abbreviation', in M. Reed and M. Hughes (eds), *Rethinking Organization: New Directions in Organization Theory and Analysis*. London: Sage. pp. 254–72.

Cooper, R. and Burrell, G. (1988) 'Modernism, postmodernism and organizational analysis: an introduction', *Organization Studies*, 9(1): 91–112.

Courpasson, D. (2000) 'Managerial strategies of domination: power in soft bureaucracies', *Organization Studies*, 21(1): 141–62.

Courpasson, D. and Reed, M. (2004) 'Introduction to special issue: Bureaucracy in the age of enterprise', *Organization*, 11(1): 5–12.

Crozier, M. (1964) *The Bureaucratic Phenomenon*. Chicago: University of Chicago Press.

Crozier, M. and Friedberg, M. (1980) *Actors and Systems: The Politics of Collective Action*. Chicago: University of Chicago Press.

Cyert, R. and March, J. (1963) *A Behavioural Theory of the Firm*. Englewood Cliffs, NJ: Prentice Hall.

Dandeker, C. (1990) *Surveillance, Power and Modernity*. Cambridge: Polity Press.

Danermark, B., Ekstrom, M., Jakobsen, L. and Karlsson, J.C. (2002) *Explaining Society: Critical Realism in the Social Sciences*. London: Routledge.

Dean, M. (1999) *Governmentality: Power and Rule in Modern Society*. London: Sage.

Deetz, S. (1992) *Democracy in an Age of Corporate Colonization: Developments in Communication and the Politics of Everyday Life*. New York: State University of New York Press.

Dent, M. and Whitehead, S. (2002) *Managing Professional Identities*. London: Routledge.

DiMaggio, P.J. (ed.) (2001) *The Twenty-First-Century-Firm: Changing Economic Organization in International Perspective*. Princeton: Princeton University Press.

DiMaggio, P.J. and Powell, W.W. (1991) 'Introduction', in W.W. Powell and P.J. DiMaggio (eds), *The New Institutionalism in Organizational Analysis*. Chicago: University of Chicago Press. pp. 1–38.

Donaldson, L. (1985) *In Defence of Organization Theory: A Response to the Critics*. Cambridge: Cambridge University Press.

Donaldson, L. (1988) 'In successful defence of organization theory: a routing of the critics', *Organization Studies*, 9(1): 28–32.

Donaldson, L. (1989) 'Review article: Redirections in organizational analysis by Michael Reed', *Australian Journal of Management*, 14(2): 243–54.

Donaldson, L. (1990) 'The ethereal hand: organization economics and management theory', *Academy of Management Review*, 15: 369–81.

Donaldson, L. (1994) 'The liberal revolution and organization theory', in J. Hassard and M. Parker (eds), *Towards a New Theory of Organizations*. London: Routledge. pp. 190–208.

Donaldson, L. (1995) *Anti-American Theories of Organization*. Cambridge: Cambridge University Press.

Donaldson, L. (1996) *For Positivist Organization Theory*. London: Sage.

Donaldson, L. (2003) 'Position statement for positivism', in R. Westwood and S. Clegg (eds), *Debating Organization: Point-Counterpoint in Organization Studies*. Oxford: Blackwell. pp. 116–27.

DuGay, P. (1992) 'Colossal immodesties and hopeful monsters: pluralism and organizational conduct', *Organization*, 1(1): 125–48.

DuGay, P. (1993) *Consumption and Identity at Work*. London: Sage.

DuGay, P. (1996) *In Praise of Bureaucracy*. London: Sage.

DuGay, P. (2005) *The Values of Bureaucracy*. Oxford: Oxford University Press.

DuGay, P. and Salaman, G. (1992) 'The cult[ure] of the customer', *Journal of Management Studies*, 29(5): 615–34.

Ellul, J. (1964) *The Technological Society*. New York: Vintage Books.

Enteman, W. (1993) *Managerialism: the Emergence of a New Ideology*. Wisconsin: University of Wisconsin Press.

Etzioni, A. (1975) *A Comparative Analysis of Complex Organizations*. New York: Free Press.

Etzioni, A. (1993) *The Spirit of Community*. Chicago: University of Chicago Press.

Fayol, H. (1949) *General and Industrial Management*. London: Pitman.

Feldman, S.P. (2002) *Memory as Moral Decision: The Role of Ethics in Organizational Culture*. New Brunswick: Transaction Publishers.

Fincham, R. (1992) 'Perspectives on power: processual, institutional and 'internal' forms of organizational power', *Journal of Management Studies*, 26(9): 741–59.

Fleetwood, S. (1995) *Hayek's Political Economy: The Socio-Economics of Political Order*. London: Routledge.

Fleetwood, S. (1999) *Critical Realism in Economics: Development and Debate*. London: Routledge.

Fleetwood, S. and Ackroyd, S. (2004) *Critical Realist Applications in Organization and Management Studies*. London: Routledge.

Flyvbjerg, B (2001) *Making Social Science Matter*. Cambridge: Cambridge University Press.

Foucault, M. (2003) *Society Must be Defended*. London: Allen Lane, Penguin Press.

Francis, A. (1983) 'Markets and hierarchies: efficiency or domination?', in A. Francis, J. Turk and P. Willman (eds), *Power, Efficiency and Institutions*. London: Heinemann. pp. 105–16.

Frank, T. (2000) *One Market Under God: Extreme Capitalism, Market Populism and the End of Economic Democracy*. New York: Secker and Warburg.

Friedland, R. and Alford, R. (1991) 'Bringing society back in: symbols, practices and institutional contradictions', in W.W. Powell and P.J. DiMaggio (eds), *The New Institutionalism in Organizational Analysis*. Chicago: University of Chicago Press. pp. 232–66.

Frug, G.E. (1984) 'The ideology of bureaucracy in American law', *Harvard Law Review*, 97(6): 1276–388.

Fukuyama, F. (1992) *The End of History and the Last Man*. New York: Free Press.

Fukuyama, F. (1995) *Trust: The Social Virtues and the Creation of Prosperity*. London: Penguin Books.

Fulk, J. and Steinfield, C. (1990) *Organizations and Communications Technology*. California: Sage.

Galbraith, J.K. (1969) *The New Industrial State*. Harmondsworth: Penguin.

Gane, M. and Johnson, T. (1993) *Foucault's New Domains*. London: Routledge.

Gellner, E. (1964) *Thought and Change*. London: Weidenfeld and Nicholson.

Gergen, K. (1992) 'Organization theory in the postmodern era', in M. Reed and M. Hughes (eds), *Rethinking Organization: New Directions in Organization Theory and Analysis*. London: Sage. pp. 207–26.

Giddens, A. (1984) *The Constitution of Society*. Cambridge: Polity Press.

Giddens, A. (1985) *The Nation State and Violence*. Cambridge: Polity Press.

Giddens, A. (1990) *The Consequences of Modernity*. Cambridge: Polity Press.

Giddens, A. (1993) *New Rules of the Sociological Method*, 2nd edn. Cambridge: Polity Press.

Giddens, A. (1994) 'Living in a post-traditional society', in U. Beck, A. Giddens and S. Lash (eds), *Reflexive Modernization: Politics, Tradition and Aesthetics in the Modern Social Order*. Cambridge: Polity Press. pp. 56–109.

Giddens, A. (2000) *The Third Way and its Critics*. Cambridge: Polity Press.

Goffman, E. (1983) 'The interaction order', *American Sociological Review*, 48: 1–17.

Gouldner, A. (1959) 'Organizational analysis', in R. Merton, L. Broom and L. Cottrell (eds), *Sociology Today: Problems and Prospects*. New York: Basic Books. pp. 400–28.

Gouldner, A. (1971) *The Coming Crisis of Western Sociology*. London: Heinemann.

Gouldner, A. (1976) *The Dialectic of Ideology and Technology*. London: Macmillan.

Gouldner, A. (1980) *The Two Marxisms*. London: Macmillan.

Grant, D., Hardy, C., Oswick, C. and Putnam, L. (2004), *The Sage Handbook of Organizational Discourse*. London: Sage.

Grant, D., Keenoy, T. and Oswick, C. (eds) (1998) *Discourse and Organization*. London: Sage.

Greenwood, R and Hinings, C.R. (1996) 'Understanding radical organizational change: bringing together the old and new institutionalism', *Academy of Management Review*, 21: 1022–54.

Gulati, R., Nohria, N. and Akbar, Z. (2000) 'Guest editors' introduction to the special issue: strategic networks', *Strategic Management Journal*, 21(3): 302–15.

Gulick, L. and Urwick, L. (1937) *Papers on the Science of Administration*. New York: Columbia University.

Haire, M. (1960) *Modern Organization Theory*. New York: Free Press.

Hancock, P. and Tyler, M. (2001) *Work, Postmodernism and Organization*. London: Sage.

Hannan, M. and Freeman, J. (1989) *Organizational Ecology*. Cambridge, MA: Harvard University Press.

Harrison, B. (1997) *Lean and Mean: Why Large Corporations Will Continue to Dominate the Global Economy*. New York: The Guilford Press.

Harvey, D. (1989) *The Condition of Postmodernity*. Oxford: Oxford University Press.

Harvey, D. (1996) *Justice, Nature and the Geography of Distance*. Oxford: Blackwell.

Harvey, D. (2001) *Spaces of Capital: Towards a Critical Geography*. London: Routledge.

Harvey, D. (2003) *The New Imperialism*. Oxford: Oxford University Press.

Hassard, J. (1990) 'An alternative to paradigm incommensurbility in organization theory', in J. Hassard and D. Pym (eds), *The Theory and Philosophy of Organizations: Critical Issues and New Perspcetives*. London: Routledge. pp. 219–30.

Hassard, J. (1993) *Sociology and Organization Theory: Positivism, Paradigms and Post-modernity*. Cambridge: Cambridge University Press.

Hassard, J. and Kelemen, M. (2002) 'Production and consumption in organizational knowledge: the case of the paradigms debate', *Organization*, 9(2): 331–56.

Hatch, M.J. and Yanov, D. (2003) 'Organization theory as an interpretive science', in H. Tsoukas and C. Knudsen (eds), *The Oxford Handbook of Organization Theory: Meta-Theoretical Perspectives*. Oxford: Oxford University Press. pp. 63–112.

Hayek, F. (1978) *The Road to Serfdom*. London: Routledge.

Heckscher, C. and Donnellon, A. (1994) *The Post-Bureaucratic Organization; New Perspectives on Organizational Change*. Thousand Oaks, CA: Sage.

Hirst, P. (1993) *Associative Democracy: New Forms of Economic and Social Governance*. Cambridge: Polity Press.

Hodgson, G. (1999) *Economics and Utopia: Why the Learning Economy is not the End of History*. London: Routledge.

Hudson, R. (2003) *Producing Places*. New York: Guilford Press.

Jackall, R. (1988) *Moral Mazes: the World of Corporate Managers.* Oxford: Oxford University Press.

Jackson, N. and Carter, P. (1991) 'In defence of paradigm incommensurability', *Organization Studies*, 12(1): 190–207.

Jackson, N. and Carter, P. (2000) *Rethinking Organizational Behaviour.* Harlow: Financial Times/Prentice Hall.

Jacques, R. (1996) *Manufacturing the Employee: Management Knowledge for the 19th to 21st Centuries.* London: Sage.

Jessop, R. (2002) *The Future of the Capitalist State.* Cambridge: Polity.

Johnson, T. (1993) 'Expertise and the state', in M. Gane and T. Johnson (eds), *Foucault's New Domains.* London: Routledge. pp. 139–52.

Jones, S. (1994) 'Many worlds – or, La ne sont pas de morts', *Organization*, 1(1): 203–17.

Karreman, D. and Alvesson, M. (2004) 'Cages in tandem: management control, social identity, and identification in a knowledge-intensive-firm', *Organization*, 11(1): 149–75.

Kerr, C., Dunlop, J., Harbison, F.H. and Mayers, C.A. (1960) *Industrialism and Industrial Man.* Cambridge, MA: Harvard University Press.

Kilduff, M. and Mehra, A. (1997) 'Postmodernism and organizational research', *Academy of Management Review*, 22: 453–81.

Kirpatrick, I. and Martinez, M. (1995) *The Politics of Quality Management.* London: Routledge.

Knights, D. and McCabe, D. (2003) *Organization and Innovation: Gurur Schemes and American Dreams.* London: Sage.

Knights, D. and Willmott, H. (1989) 'Power and subjectivity at work: from degradation to subjugation in social relations', *Sociology*, 23(4): 535–58.

Kondo, D. (1990) *Crafting Selves: Power, Gender and Discourses of Identity in a Japanese Workplace.* Chicago: University of Chicago Press.

Korczynski, M. (2002) *Human Resource Management in Service Work.* London: Macmillan/Palgrave.

Korczynski, M. (2003) 'Communities of coping: collective emotional labour in service work', *Organization*, 10(1): 55–79.

Korczynski, M., Shire, K., Frenkel, S. and Tam, M. (2000) 'Service work in consumer capitalism: customers, control and contradictions', *Work, Employment and Society*, 14(4): 669–87.

Kuhn, T. (1970) *The Structure of Scientific Revolutions*, 2nd edn. Chicago: University of Chicago Press.

Kumar, K. (1978) *Prophecy and Progress: The Sociology of Industrial and Post-Industrial Society.* London: Allen Lane.

Kumar, K. (1995) *From Post-Industrial to Post-Modern Society.* Oxford: Blackwell.

Lakatos, I. and Musgrave, A. (1970) *Criticism and the Growth of Knowledge.* Cambridge: Cambridge University Press.

Lammers, C. and Szell, G. (1989) *International Handbook of Participation in Organizations.* Oxford: Oxford University Press.

Larson, M.S. (1979) *The Rise of Professionalism; a Sociological Analysis.* Berkeley: University of California Press.

Larson, M.S. (1990) 'In the matter of experts and professionals'. in R. Torstendahl and M. Burrage (eds), *The Formation of Professions.* London: Sage. pp. 24–50.

Lash, S. and Urry, J. (1987) *The End of Organized Capitalism.* Cambridge: Polity Press.

Lash, S. and Urry, J. (1994) *Economies of Signs and Space.* London: Sage.

Law, J. (1991) *A Sociology of Monsters: Essays on Power, Technology and Domination.* London: Routledge.

Law, J. (1994a) *Organizing Modernity.* Oxford: Blackwell.

Law, J. (1994b) 'Organization, narrative and strategy', in J. Hassard and M. Parker (eds), *Toward a New Theory of Organization.* London: Routledge. pp. 248–68.

Lawrence, P. and Lorsch, J. (1967) *Organization and Environment.* Cambridge, MA: Harvard University Press.

Lawson, T. (1997) *Economics and Reality.* London: Routledge.

Layder, D. (1994) *Understanding Social Theory.* London: Sage.

Layder, D. (1997) *Modern Social Theory.* London: UCL Press.

Leicht, K. and Fennel, M. (2001) *Professional Work: A Sociological Approach.* Oxford: Blackwell.

Linstead, S. (2004) *Organization Theory and Postmodern Thought.* London: Sage.

Lipset, S.M. (1960) *Political Man.* London: Macmillan.

Littler, C. (1990) 'The labour process debate: a theoretical review', in D. Knights and H. Willmott (eds), *Labour Process Theory.* London: Macmillan. pp. 45–68..

Locke, R. (1989) *Management and Higher Education Since 1940.* Cambridge: Cambridge University Press.

Lopez, J. and Potter, G. (2001) *After Postmodernism: An Introduction to Critical Realism.* London: The Athlone Press.

Lounsbury, M. and Ventrescu, M. (2003) 'The new structuralism in organizational theory', *Organization*, 10(3): 457–80.

Lukes, S. (1974) *Power: a Radical View.* London: Macmillan.

Lyon, D. (1994) *The Electronic Eye: the Rise of Surveillance Society.* Cambridge: Polity Press.

Lyon, D. (2001) *Surveillance Society.* Buckinghamshire: Open University Press.

MacIntyre, A. (1981) *After Virtue: A Study in Moral Theory.* London: Duckworth.

March, J.G. (1988) *Decisions and Organizations.* Oxford: Blackwell.

March, J.G. and Olsen, J.P. (1986) *Ambiguity and Choice in Organizations.* Bergen: Universitetsforlaget.

Marchington, M., Grimshaw, D., Rubery, J. and Willmott, H. (eds) (2005) *Fragmenting Work: Blurring Organizational Boundaries and Disordering Hierarchies.* Oxford: Oxford University Press.

Martin, J. (1992) *Culture in Organizations: Three Perspective.* New York: Oxford University Press.

Martin, J. (2002) *Organizational Culture: Mapping the Terrain.* Thousand Oaks, CA: Sage.

Massie, J. (1965) 'Management theory', in J.G. March (ed.), *Handbook of Organizations,* New York: Rand McNally. pp 387–422.

Mayo, E. (1933) *The Human Problems of an Industrial Civilization.* London: Routledge.

Mayo, E. (1945) *The Social Problems of an Industrial Civilization.* London: Routledge.

McKelvey, W. (2003) 'From fields to science: can organization studies make the transition?', in R Westwood and S Clegg (eds), *Debating Organization: Point-Counterpoint in Organization Studies.* Oxford: Blackwell. pp. 47–73.

McKinlay, A. and Starkey, K. (1998) *Foucault, Management and Organization Theory.* London: Sage.

McLaughlin, K., Osborne, S.P. and Ferlie, E. (2002) *New Public Management: Current Trends and Future Prospects.* London: Routledge.

Merkle, J. (1990) *Management and Ideology.* Berkeley: University of California Press.

Merton, R.K. (1949) *Social Theory and Social Structure.* New York: Collier Macmillan.

Meyer, J.W. and Rowan, B. (1977) 'Institutionalized organizations: formal structures as myth and ceremony', *American Journal of Sociology,* 83: 340–63.

Meyer, J.W. and Scott, E.R. (1992) *Organizational Environments: Ritual and Rationality.* Thousand Oaks, CA: Sage.

Miller, E.J. and Rice, A.K. (1967) *Systems of Organizations.* London: Tavistock.

Miller, P. and O'Leary, T. (1989) 'Hierarchies and the American ideals, 1900–1940', *Academy of Management Review,* 14(2): 250–65.

Miller, P. and Rose, N. (1990) 'Governing economic life', *Economy and Society,* 19: 1–31.

Morgan, D. and Stanley, L. (1993) *Debates in Sociology.* Manchester: Manchester University Press.

Morgan, G. (1986) *Images of Organization.* London: Sage.

Morgan, G. (1990) *Organizations in Society.* London: Macmillan.

Mouzelis, N. (1967) *Organization and Bureaucracy.* London: Routledge.

Newell, S., Robertson, M., Scarbrough, H. and Swan, J. (2002) *Managing Knowledge Work.* London: Palgrave.

Nichols, T. (1969) *Ownership, Control and Ideology.* London: Allen and Unwin.

Nohria, N. and Eccles, R.G. (1992) *Networks and Organizations.* Cambridge, MA: Harvard Business School Press.

Pareto, V. (1935) *The Mind and Society.* Cambridge, MA: Harvard University Press.

Parker, M. (2000) *Organizational Culture and Identity.* London: Sage.

Parsons, T. (1956) 'Suggestions for a sociological approach to the theory of organizations 1 and 11', *Administrative Science Quarterly,* 1(1/2):63–85, 225–39.

Perrow, C. (1986) *Complex Organizations: A Critical Essay,* 3rd edn. New York: Random House.

Perry, N. (1992) 'Putting theory in its place: the social organization of organizational theorizing', in M. Reed and M. Hughes (eds), *Rethinking Organization: New Directions in Organization Theory and Analysis.* London: Sage. pp. 85–101.

Perry, N. (1994) 'Travelling theory/nomadic theorizing', *Organization,* 2(1): 35–54.

Pettigrew, A.M. and Fenton, E.M. (eds) (2000) *The Innovating Organization.* London: Sage.

Pfeffer, J. (1993) 'Barriers to the advance of organizational science: paradigm development as a dependent variable', *Academy of Management Review,* 18(4): 599–620.

Pfeffer, J. (1997) *New Directions for Organization Theory: Problems and Prospects.* New York: Oxford University Press.

Phillips, N. and Hardy, C. (2002) *Discourse Analysis: Investigating Processes of Social Construction.* Newbury Park, CA: Sage.

Piore, M. and Sabel, C. (1984) *The Second Industrial Divide.* New York: Basic Books.

Plant, G. (1973) *Hegel.* London: Allen and Unwin.

Powell, W.W. (1990) 'Neither markets or hierarchy: network forms of organization', *Research in Organizational Behaviour,* 12: 295–336.

Powell, W.W. and DiMaggio, P. (1991) *The New Institutionalism in Organizational Analysis.* Chicago: University of Chicago Press.

Presthus, R. (1975) *The Organizational Society,* 2nd edn. New York: Random House.

Pugh, D. and Hickson, D. (1976) *Organizational Structure in its Context: the Aston Programme 1.* Farnborough, Hants: Saxon House.

Putnam, H. (1978) *Meaning and the Moral Sciences.* London: Routledge.

Putnam, H. (1990) *Realism with a Human Face.* Cambridge, MA: Harvard University Press.

Putnam, R. (1994) *Bowling Alone: Democracy at the End of the Twentieth Century.* Princeton: Princeton University Press.

Ray, L. and Reed, M. (1994) 'Max Weber and the dilemmas of modernity', in L. Ray and M. Reed (eds), *Organizing Modernity: Neo-Weberian Perspectives on Work, Organization and Society.* London: Routledge. pp. 158–97.

Reed, M. (1985) *Redirections in Organizational Analysis.* London: Tavistock.

Reed, M. (1988) 'The problem of human agency in organizational analysis'. *Organization Studies,* 9(1): 33–46.

Reed, M. (1992) *The Sociology of Organizations: Themes, Perspectives and Prospects*. Hemel Hempstead: Harvester Press.

Reed, M. (1993) 'Organizations and modernity: continuity and discontinuity in organization theory', in J. Hassard and M. Parker (eds), *Postmodernism and Organizations*. London: Sage. pp. 163–82.

Reed, M. (1995) 'Managing quality and organizational politics: total quality management as a governmental technology', in I. Kirkpatrick and M. Martinez (eds), *The Politics of Quality Management*. London: Routledge. pp. 44–64.

Reed, M. (1996) 'Expert power and control in late modernity: an empirical review and theoretical synthesis', *Organization Studies*, 17(4): 573–97.

Reed, M. (1997) 'In praise of duality and dualism: rethinking agency and structure in organizational analysis', *Organization Studies*, 18(1): 21–42.

Reed, M. (1999) 'From the cage to the gaze?: the dynamics of organizational control in late modernity', in G. Morgan and L. Engwall (eds), *Regulation and Organizations: International Perspectives*. London: Routledge. pp. 17–49.

Reed, M. (2001) 'Organization, trust and control: a realist analysis'. *Organization Studies*, 22(2): 201–23.

Reed, M. (2003) 'The agency/structure dilemma in organization theory: open doors and brick walls', in H. Tsoukas and C. Knudsen (eds), *The Oxford Handbook of Organization Theory: Meta-Theoretical Perspectives*. Oxford: Oxford University Press, pp. 289–309.

Reed, M. (2005a) 'Beyond the iron cage?: bureaucracy and democracy in the knowledge economy and society', in P. DuGay (ed.), *The Values of Bureaucracy*. Oxford: Oxford University Press. pp. 116–40.

Reed, M. (2005b) 'Reflections on the realist turn in organization and management studies', *Journal of Management Studies*, 42(8): 1621–44.

Reed, M. and Anthony, P.D. (1992) 'Professionalizing management and managing professionalization: British management in the 1980s', *Journal of Management Studies*, 29(5): 591–614.

Reed, M. and Hughes. M. (1992) *Rethinking Organization: New Directions in Organization Theory and Analysis*. London: Sage.

Roethlisberger, F.J. and Dickson, W.J. (1939) *Management and the Worke*. Cambridge MA: Harvard University Press.

Rose, M. (1975) *Industrial Behaviour: Theoretical Developments since Taylor*. London: Allen and Lane.

Rose, N. (1992) *Governing the Soul*. London: Routledge.

Rose, N. (1999) *Powers of Freedom: Reframing Political Thought*. Cambridge: Cambridge University Press.

Rosenberg, J. (2000) *The Follies of Globalization Theory*. London: Verso.

Sabel, C. (1982) *Work and Politics and the Division of Labour in Industry*. Cambridge: Cambridge University Press.

Sabel, C. (1991) 'Mobius strip organizations and open labour markets: some consequences of the re-integration of conception and execution in a volatile economy', in J. Coleman and P. Bordieu (eds), *Social Theory for a Changing Society*. Boulder, CO: Westview Press. pp. 23–54.

Saint-Simon, H. (1958) *Social Organization, the Science of Man, and other Writings*. New York: Harper Torch.

Scarbrough, H. (2001) *The Management of Expertise*. London: Macmillan.

Scarbrough, H. and Corbett, M.J. (1992) *Technology and Organization*. London: Routledge.

Scott, W.R. (1995) *Institutions and Organizations*. Thousand Oaks, CA: Sage.

Selznick, P. (1949) *The TVA and the Grass Roots*. New York: Harper and Row.

Sennett, R. (1998) *The Corrosion of Character: The Personal Consequences of Work in the New Capitalism*. London: Norton and Company.

Sewell, G. (2001) 'The prison-house of language: the penitential discourse of organizational power', in R. Westwood and S. Linstead (eds), *The Language of Organization*. London: Sage. pp. 176–98.

Shenhav, Y. (2003) 'The historical and epistemological foundations of organization theory: fusing sociological theory and engineering discourse', in H. Tsoukas and C. Knudsen (eds), *The Oxford Handbook of Organization Theory: Meta-Theoretical Perspectives*. Oxford: Oxford University Press. pp. 183–99.

Silberman, B.S. (1993) *Cages of Reason: the Rise of the Rational State in France, Japan, the Unites States and Great Britain*. Chicago: University of Chicago Press.

Silver, J. (1987) 'The ideology of excellence: management and neo-conservatism', *Studies in Political Economy*, 24(August): 105–29.

Silverman, D. (1970) *The Theory of Organizations*. London: Heinemann.

Simon, H. (1945) *Administrative Behaviour*. New York: Macmillan.

Simon, H. (1957) *The New Science of Management Decision*. New York: Harper.

Sklair, L. (2001) *The Transnational Capitalist Class*, Oxford: Blackwell.

Smart, B. (1992) *Modern Conditions: Postmodern Contoversies*. London: Routledge.

Smith, D. (1988) *The Everyday World as Problematic*. Milton Keynes: Open University Press.

Smith, D. (1993) *The Rise of Historical Sociology*. Cambridge: Polity Press.

Starbuck, W.H. (2003) 'The origins of organization theory', in H. Tsoukas and C. Knudsen (eds), *The Oxford Handbook of Organization Theory: Meta-Theoretical*

Perspectives. Oxford: Oxford University Press. pp. 143–82.

Stinchcombe, A.L. (1965) 'Social structure and organizations', in J.G. March (ed.), *Handbook of Organizations*. Chicago: Rand McNally. pp. 142–93.

Stinchcombe, A.L. (1968) *Constructing Social Theories*. New York: Harcourt Brace.

Storing, H. (1962) 'The science of administration', in H. Storing (ed.), *Essays on the Scientific Study of Politics*. New York: Holt, Reinhart and Winston. pp. 38–57.

Stretton, H. (1969) *The Political Sciences*. London: Routledge.

Swedberg, R. (2003) 'Economic versus sociological approaches to organization theory', in H. Tsoukas and C. Knudsen (eds), *The Oxford Handbook of Organization Theory: Meta-Theoretical Perspectives*. Oxford: Oxford University Press. pp. 373–91.

Sztompka, P. (1993) *The Sociology of Social Change*. Oxford: Blackwell.

Taylor, F.W. (1912) *Principles of Scientific Management*. New York: Harper.

Thompson, E.P. (1978) *The Poverty of Theory and Other Essays*. London: Merlin.

Thompson, G. (2003a) *Between Hierarchies and Markets: The Logic and Limits of Network Forms of Organization*. Oxford: Oxford University Press.

Thompson, J.D. (1967) *Organizations in Action*. New York: McGraw-Hill.

Thompson, P. (1989) *The Nature of Work*, 2nd edn. London: Macmillan.

Thompson, P. (1993) 'Postmodernism: fatal distraction', in J. Hassard and M. Parker (eds), *Towards a New Theory of Organizations*. London: Routledge. pp. 183–203.

Thompson, P. (2003b) 'Disconnected capitalism or why employers can't keep their side of the bargain', *Work, Employment and Society*, 17(2): 359–78.

Thompson, P. and McHugh, D. (2002) *Organizations: A Critical Introduction*, 3rd edn. London: Palgrave.

Thrift, N. (2004) *Knowing Capitalism*. London: Sage.

Tolbert, P. and Zuker, L. (1996) 'The institutionalization of institutional theory', in S. Clegg, C. Hardy and W. Nord (eds), *Handbook of Organization Studies*. London: Sage. pp. 169–84.

Toulmin, S. (1972) *Human Understanding*, Vol 1. Princeton: Princeton University Press.

Townley, B. (1994) *Reframing Human Resource Management*. London: Sage.

Tsoukas, H. and Knudsen, C. (2003) *The Oxford Handbook of Organization Theory: Meta-Theoretical Perspectives*. Oxford: Oxford University Press.

Unger, R.M. (1987a) *Social Theory: its Situation and its Task: A Critical Introduction to Politics: A Work in Constructive Social Theory*. Cambridge: Cambridge University Press.

Unger, R.M. (1987b) *False Necessity: Anti-Necessitarian Social Theory in the Service of Radical Democracy*. Cambridge: Cambridge University Press.

Urry, J. (2000) *Sociology Beyond Society*. London: Routledge.

Urwick, L. and Brech, E. (1947) *The Making of Scientific Management*. London: Pitman.

Van Maanen, J. (1995) 'Fear and loathing in organization studies', *Organization Science*, 6: 687–92.

von Bertalanffy, L. (1950) 'The theory of open systems', *Science*, 3: 55–68.

von Bertalanffy, L. (1956) 'General systems theory', *General Systems*, 1: 1–10.

Waldo, D. (1948) *The Administrative State*. New York: Knopf.

Weber, M. (1978) *Economy and Society: an Outline of Interpretative Sociology*, Vols 1 and 2. Berkeley: University of California Press.

Webster, F. (2002) *Theories of the Information Society*, 2nd edn. London: Routledge.

Webster, F. and Robins, K. (1993) 'I'll be Watching you: comment on Sewell and Wilkinson', *Sociology*, 27(2): 243–52.

Weinberg, I. (1969) 'The problem of convergence of industrial societies: a critical look at the state of a theory', *Comparative Studies in Society and History*, 11(1): 1–15.

Westwood, R. and Clegg, S. (2003) *Debating Organization: Point-Counterpoint in Organization Studies*. Oxford: Blackwell.

Whetten, D. (1999) *Organizations and Identity*. Thousand Oaks, CA: Sage.

Whitley, R. (1992) *European Business Systems*. London: Sage.

Whitley, R. (1999) *Varieties of Capitalism*. Oxford: Oxford University Press.

Whittington, R. (1989) *Corporate Strategies in Recovery and Recession: Social Structure and Strategic Choice*. London: Unwin Hyman.

Whittington, R. (1994) 'Sociological pluralism, institutions and managerial agency', in J. Hassard and M. Parker (eds), *Towards a New Theory of Organizations*. London: Routledge. pp. 53–74.

Whittington, R. and Meyer, C. (2000) *The European Corporation*. Oxford; Oxford University Press.

Williamson, O.E. (1975) *Markets and Hierarchies: Analysis and Antitrust Implications*. New York: Free Press.

Williamson, O.E. (1990) *Organization Theory: From Chester Barnard to the Present and Beyond*. New York: Oxford University Press.

Williamson, O.E. and Winter, S.G. (1991) *The Nature of the Firm*. New York: Oxford University Press.

Willman, P. (1983) 'The organizational failures framework and industrial sociology', in A. Francis, J. Turk and P. Willman (eds), *Power, Efficiency and Institutions*. London: Heinemann. pp. 117–36.

Willmott, H. (1993) 'Breaking the paradigm mentality', *Organization Studies*, 14(5): 681–719.

Willmott, H. (1994) 'Bringing agency (back) into organizational analysis: responding to the crisis of postmodernity', in J. Hassard and D. Pym (eds), *Towards a New Theory of Organizations*. London: Routledge. pp. 87–130.

Willmott, H. (2003) 'Organization theory as a critical science?: Forms of analysis and new organizational forms', in H. Tsoukas and C. Knudsen (eds), *The Oxford Handbook of Organization Theory: Meta-Theoretical Perspectives*. Oxford: Oxford University Press. pp. 88–112.

Wolin, S. (1960) *Politics and Vision*. Princeton: Princeton University Press (expanded edition 2004).

Wolin, S. (1988) 'On the theory and practice of power', in J. Arac (ed.), *After Foucault: Humanistic Knowledge, Postmodern Challenges*. New Brunswick, NJ: Rutgers University Press. pp. 179–201.

Woodward, J. (1970) *Industrial Organization: Behaviour and Control*. Oxford: Oxford University Press.

Wrong, D. (1978) *Power: its Forms, Bases and Uses*. Oxford: Blackwell.

Zuboff, S. (1988) *In the Age of the Smart Machine*. London: Heinemann.

Zukin, S. (1993) *Landscapes of Power: from Detroit to Disney World*. Berkeley: University of California Press.

1.2 Ecological Approaches to Organizations

JOEL A. C. BAUM AND ANDREW V. SHIPILOV

Introduction: What Organizational Ecology Is and Isn't

Until the mid-1970s, the prominent approach in organization and management theory emphasized adaptive change in organizations. In this view, as environments change, leaders or dominant coalitions in organizations alter appropriate organizational features to realign their fit to environmental demands (e.g. Lawrence and Lorsch 1967; Thompson 1967; Child 1972; Chandler 1977; Pfeffer and Salancik 1978; Porter 1980; Rumelt 1986). Since then, an approach to studying organizational change that places more emphasis on environmental selection processes, introduced at about that time (Aldrich and Pfeffer 1976; Hannan and Freeman 1977; Aldrich 1979; McKelvey 1982), has become increasingly influential. The stream of research on ecological perspectives of organizational change has generated tremendous excitement, controversy and debate in the community of organization and management theory scholars.

Inspired by the question, *Why are there so many kinds of organizations?* (Hannan and Freeman 1977: 936), organizational ecologists seek to explain how social, economic and political conditions affect the relative abundance and diversity of organizations and attempt to account for their changing composition over time. Organizational ecologists are very empirically oriented – that is, driven by the cumulative research findings of an international community of scholars that attempts to replicate and extend empirical generalizations derived from theoretical expectations. Although differences exist among individual investigators, ecological research typically begins with three basic observations: (1) diversity is a property of aggregates of organizations that has no analogue at the level of the individual organization, (2) organizations often have difficulty devising and

executing changes fast enough to meet the demands of uncertain, changing environments, and (3) the community of organizations is rarely stable – organizations arise and disappear continually. Given these observations, organizational ecologists pursue explanations for the diversity of organizations at higher levels of analysis of the organizational population and community and focus on rates of organizational founding and failure and rates of creation and death of organizational populations as sources of increasing and decreasing diversity.

Organizations, populations and communities of organizations constitute the basic elements of an ecological analysis of organizations (Hannan and Freeman 1977; 1989). A set of organizations engaged in similar activities and with similar patterns of resource utilization constitutes a population (Hannan and Freeman 1977; 1989). Populations form as a result of processes that isolate or segregate one set of organizations from another, including technological incompatibilities, institutional actions such as government regulations and imprinting effects (Stinchcombe 1965; McKelvey 1982; Hannan and Freeman 1989; Baum and Singh 1994a). Populations themselves develop relationships with other populations engaged in other activities that bind them into organizational communities (Astley 1985; Fombrun 1986; Hannan and Freeman 1989). Organizational communities are functionally integrated systems of interacting populations. In an organizational community, the outcomes for organizations in any one population are fundamentally intertwined with those of organizations in other populations that belong to the same community system.

Although organizational ecology has been a prominent subfield in organization studies for nearly three decades, numerous critics and skeptics remain. *Why?* The debate centres primarily on assumptions about the relative influences of organizational history, environment and strategic choice on patterns of organizational change advanced by structural inertia theory (Hannan and Freeman 1977; 1984). Structural inertia theory asserts that existing organizations frequently have difficulty changing strategy and structure quickly enough to keep pace with the demands of uncertain, changing environments and emphasizes that major organizational innovations often occur early in the life-histories of organizations and populations. Organizational change and variability are thus regarded to reflect primarily relatively inert (i.e. inflexible) organizations replacing each other over time. To organizational ecology's critics and skeptics this means environmental determinism and loss of human agency (e.g. Astley and Van de Ven 1983; Perrow 1986).

Do ecological approaches imply that the actions of particular individuals do not matter for organizations? The answer is no, of course. One part of the confusion about organizational ecology is that *determinism* is mistakenly contrasted with *voluntarism* rather than with *probabilism* (Hannan and Freeman 1989; Singh and Lumsden 1990). Leaving aside whether their actions are intelligent or foolish, carefully planned or seat-of-the-pants, individuals can clearly influence their organization's future – but under conditions of uncertainty and ambiguity there are severe constraints on the ability of individuals to conceive and implement correctly changes that improve organizational success and survival chances reliably in the face of competition. Thus, 'in a world of high uncertainty, adaptive efforts … turn out to be essentially random with respect to future value' (Hannan and Freeman 1984: 150). A second part of the confusion has to do with the level of analysis. The actions of individuals matter more to their organization than they do to their organization's population as a whole. The actions of particular individuals may thus not explain much of the diversity in organizational populations.

Changes in organizational populations reflect the operation of four basic processes: *variation*, *selection*, *retention* and *competition* (Campbell 1965; Aldrich 1979; McKelvey 1982). Variations are human behaviours. Any kind of change, intentional or blind, is variation. Individuals produce variations in, for example, technical and management competencies constantly in their efforts to adjust their organization's relationship to the environment. Organizational variations provide the raw material from which selection can be made. Some variations

prove more beneficial to organizations than others in acquiring resources in a competitive environment and are thus selected positively – not by *the environment*, but by managers inside organizations and investors, customers and government regulators in the resource environment (Burgelman 1991; Burgelman and Mittman 1994; McKelvey 1994; Meyer 1994; Miner 1994).

When successful variations are known, or when environmental trends are identifiable, individuals can attempt to copy and implement these successful variations in their own organization, or they can attempt to forecast, anticipate, plan and implement policies in the context of the predictable trends (Nelson and Winter 1982; DiMaggio and Powell 1983; McKelvey 1994). However, when successful variations are unknown, because, for example, the behaviour of consumers and competitors is unpredictable, the probability of choosing the correct variation and implementing it successfully is very low. Even when effective variations are identifiable, ambiguity in the *causes* of success may frustrate attempts at imitation. Under such conditions, variations can be viewed as experimental trials, some of which are consciously planned and some of which are accidental, some of which succeed and some of which fail (McKelvey 1994; Miner 1994). Whether or not they are known, over time, successful variations are retained as surviving organizations come to be characterized by them.

If the survival odds are low for organizations with a particular variant, it does not mean that these organizations are destined to fail. Rather, it means the capacity of individuals to change their organizations successfully is of great importance (Hannan and Freeman 1989). However, there are strong constraints on the capacity of individuals to change existing organizations successfully, including established practices, norms and incentives, scarcity of resources, competition and limits to individual rationality. Nevertheless, the existence of these constraints does not mean that individuals are irrelevant to processes of organizational change – only that there are limits on the influence of individuals' actions on variability in organizational properties.

Ecological theory does not remove individuals from responsibility for or control (influence, at least) over their organization's success and survival – *individuals do matter*. Ecological theory does, however, assume that individuals cannot always (or often) determine in advance which variations will succeed.

Ecological theory also stresses that individuals have difficulty changing existing organizations' strategies and structures quickly enough to keep pace with the demands of uncertain, changing environments.

Because the success of particular variations is often unknown in advance and because there are strong constraints on the ability of individuals to change their organizations, ecological analysis formulates issues of organizational change and variability at the population level. It attempts to estimate the odds of success for any particular variation by studying the survival chances of organizations with the variation and the rate at which organizations adopt the variation. Consequently, in contrast to adaptation approaches, which explain changes in organizational diversity exclusively in terms of the cumulative strategic choices and changes of existing organizations, ecological approaches also highlight the creation of new organizations and the demise of old ones in addition.

Also in contrast to most organizational research, which concentrates on the largest and most successful organizations at a particular point in time, ecological research examines entire organizational populations, from the largest and longest-lived, to the smallest and shortest-lived members, over extended periods of time. Why? Because it is often not possible to learn about the processes that create success and failure by examining only current successes. The problem is that comparison between success and failure is implicit. Successful organizations in an industry may have certain strategies and structures – but without information on failures we cannot be certain poor performers didn't have the very same ones. Moreover, if success and failure depend on the environment, winners and losers may change as conditions change. The success of a strategy in an industry at one point in time doesn't mean success next year under different conditions. Thus, concentrating on organizations that succeed at a particular point in time can result in misleading inferences about the factors that produced the success. These are examples of the methodological problem of sample-selection bias (Heckman 1979; Berk 1983). For these reasons, organizational ecologists undertake exhaustive data collection efforts to identify all organizations in a population or community (Hannan and Freeman 1989).

Current ecological theory and research takes four distinct levels (Carroll 1984a; Hannan and Freeman 1989; Baum and Singh 1994a). Research at level one investigates *intraorganizational ecology*. Research at this level focuses on variation, selection and retention processes within organizations. Intraorganizational ecology models seek to describe how organizations' internal contexts and individuals' purposeful and accidental use of variation, selection and retention processes in organizations influence rates of creation, transformation and death of organizational routines and strategies. Research at level two focuses on the *demography of organizations*. Research at this level considers variations in vital rates (i.e. rates of organizational founding, change and failure) for organizational populations. It examines variations in these rates over time and among populations. It seeks to identify empirical regularities in these rates and specify their relations to organizational characteristics. Research at level three concerns the *population ecology of organizations*. At this level, research concentrates on growth and decline of individual populations. Population ecology models seek to describe how vital rates of one population are influenced by processes endogenous to that population as well as interactions with other populations. It also seeks to specify how these rates are shaped by patterns of environmental change. Research at level four concerns the *community ecology of organizations*. Community ecology research investigates the evolution of community structures and examines how the links binding a set of populations into a community affect the likelihood of persistence and stability of the community as a whole. Community ecology research also emphasizes processes of creation and demise of populations of organizational forms.

To date, ecological theory and research has focused primarily on demographic and population ecology analyses of rates of organizational founding, failure and change and to a much less (but increasing) extent on intraorganizational and community ecology (for recent reviews see Galunic and Weeks 2002; Rao 2002; Baum and Rao 2004). Organizational founding and failure figure prominently in organizational ecology because they affect the relative abundance and diversity of organizations. Ecological theory stresses the difficulty individuals have changing existing organizations' strategies and structures to keep pace with the demands of uncertain, changing environments. Consequently, for organizational ecologists, the rates at which new and diverse organizations are created and the rates at which organizations of various types disappear are central to the dynamics of organizational demography.

The focus of ecological research is changing rapidly, however, as researchers turn their attention to processes of organization-level change and tests of structural inertia theory (e.g. Barnett and Carroll 1995). As Hannan and Freeman (1977: 930) point out, a full treatment of organization–environment relations must cover both adaptation and selection. Researchers have embarked on development of a combined perspective that sees processes of adaptation and selection as complementary and interacting. The emerging view takes seriously the occurrence of selection processes and combines it with the systematic study of organization-level changes that may, under certain conditions, be adaptive. And, consequently, that organizational change can best be studied by examining how social and environmental conditions and interactions within and among populations influence the rates at which new organizations and new populations are created, existing organizations and populations die out and individual organizations change (Singh and Lumsden 1990; Baum and Singh 1994a).

Chapter Aims and Overview

Our goal is to assess and consolidate the current state-of-the-art in organizational ecology. To accomplish this we review major theoretical statements, empirical studies and arguments that are now being made. Although we attempt to survey ecological approaches to organizations comprehensively, because ecological research now constitutes a very large body of work, and because other extensive reviews are available (Singh and Lumsden 1990; Aldrich and Wiedenmayer 1993; Barnett and Carroll 1995; Baum 1996; Baum and Amburgey 2002; Carroll et al. 2002; Galunic and Weeks 2002; Rao 2002; Baum and Rao 2004), we emphasize recent work that challenges and extends established theory and highlight new and emerging directions for future research that appear promising. Our appraisal focuses on two main themes – demographic processes and ecological processes – the main research areas in each is summarized in Table 1.2.1.

Demographic Processes

Ecological approaches to founding and failure constitute a radical departure from traditional approaches to founding and entrepreneurship and business failure, which focus on individual initiative, skills and abilities (Carroll 1984a; Romanelli 1991; Aldrich and Wiedenmayer 1993). The traditional *traits* approach to founding and entrepreneurship assumes that there is something about an individual's background or personality that leads him or her to found an organization. Gartner's (1989) review of traits studies suggests that they have hit a dead end: most are based on small, cross-sectional samples, drawn from unknown populations whose generality is not clear, and typically do not use multivariate analytical techniques, raising doubts about the significance of occasionally significant 'trait' variables. Similarly, traditional business policy research typically attributes organizational failure to managerial inexperience, incompetence, or inadequate financing (e.g. Dun and Bradstreet 1978). By concentrating on the 'traits' of entrepreneurs and managers, traditional approaches to organizational founding and failure deflected attention away from the volatile nature of organizational populations and communities (Aldrich and Wiedenmayer 1993). Ecological approaches to organizational founding and failure, by comparison, emphasize contextual or environmental causes – social, economic and political – that produce variations in organizational founding and failure rates over time by influencing opportunity structures that confront potential organizational founders and resource constraints that face existing organizations.

Because existing organizations have histories and structures that influence their rates of failure and change, studying organizational failure and change is complicated by the need to consider processes at both organizational and population levels. Although founding processes have typically been conceived in ecological research as attributes of a population, since no organization exists prior to founding, recently founding processes too are increasingly seen as occurring at both organizational and population levels. Demographic analysis examines the effects of organizational characteristics on rates of organizational founding, failure and change.

Organizational Founding

Although organizational founding is an important theme in ecological research, in large part, foundings have been treated as identical additions to homogenous populations: the characteristics of new

Table 1.2.1 Major ecological approaches to organizational founding, failure and change

Key topics	Key variables	Key predictions	Key references
Demographic processes			
Organizational founding	Spatial heterogeneity	Variation in social, institutional and economic conditions across regions produce unobservable region-specific proneness to experiencing the founding of particular organizational forms	Lomi (1995); Stuart and Sorenson (2003a, b)
	Entrant's similarity to incumbents	Avoidance of direct competition pushes entrants away from similar organizations, while complementary differences pull them together; agglomeration economies pull entrants toward competitors	Baum and Haveman (1997)
Age dependence	Organizational age	Liability of newness: failure rates decline with age as roles and routines are mastered and links with external constituents established	Freeman et al. (1983); Henderson (1999)
		Liability of adolescence: failure rates rise with age until initial buffering resource endowments are depleted, then decline with further increases in age	Bruderl and Schussler (1990); Fichman and Levinthal (1991)
		Liability of obsolescence: failure rates increase with age as their original fit with the environment erodes	Baum (1989); Ingram (1993)
		Liability of senescence: failure rates increase with age as internal friction, precedent and political pacts accumulate, impeding action and reliable performance	Barron et al. (1994); Ranger-Moore (1997)
Size dependence	Organizational size	Liability of smallness: failure rates decline with size, which buffers organizations from threats to survival	Freeman et al. (1983); Mitchell (1994)
Structural inertia	Organizational change	Change: structural inertia increases as organizations age and grow, lowering rates of organizational change Failure: the failure rate increases after a 'core' change, but then declines with the passage of time; the disruptive effects of change increase (decrease) with organizational age (size)	Hannan and Freeman (1984); Amburgey et al. (1993); Baum and Singh (1996); Dobrev et al. (2001; 2003)
Organizational momentum	Cumulative organizational change	The rate of an organizational change of the same type increases with the number of prior changes of the same type, but then declines with the passage of time since the last change of the same type.	Amburgey and Miner (1992); Amburgey et al. (1993); Greve and Taylor (2000)
Organizational learning	Organizational operating experience	Initial increases in operating experience lower failure rates as organizations move down learning curves for their routines, but further increases reduce responsiveness to changing environmental demands, raising failure rates	Baum and Ingram (1998); Ingram and Baum (1997a)
	Organizational competitive experience	The greater an organization's historical exposure to competition, the lower its failure rate	Barnett (1997)

(Continued)

Table 1.2.1 *(Continued)*

Key topics	Key variables	Key predictions	Key references
Ecological processes			
Niche width dynamics	Specialist strategy	Exploit a narrow range of resources and are favoured in fine-grained and concentrated environments	Freeman and Hannan (1983; 1987); Carroll (1985); Carroll et al. (2002)
Population dynamics	Generalist strategy	Tolerate widely varying environmental conditions and are favoured in coarse-grained, high variability environments	
	Prior foundings	Initial increases in prior foundings signal opportunity, stimulating new foundings, but further increases create competition, suppressing new foundings	Carroll and Delacroix (1982); Delacroix and Carroll (1983); Delacroix et al. (1989)
	Prior failures	Initial increases in prior deaths free up resources, stimulating new foundings, but further increases signal a hostile environment suppressing new foundings	
Density dependence	Population density	Initial increases in density increase the institutional legitimacy of a population, increasing foundings and lowering failures, but further increases produce competition, suppressing foundings and increasing failures	Hannan and Freeman (1987; 1988; 1989); Hannan and Carroll (1992); Hannan et al. (1995)
Population-level learning	Population operating experience	An organization's failure rate declines as a function of the operating experience of its population at the time of its entry and of the population's increasing operating experience after the organization's founding	Baum and Ingram (1998); Ingram and Baum (1997a)
	Population competitive experience	An organization's failure rate declines as a function of its population's history of competitive outcomes (e.g. failures) at the time of its entry and of the population's increasing competitive experience after the organization's founding	Ingram and Baum (1997a)

organizations, which define their domains, have not been of central interest. The absence of organization-specific factors in studies of founding stands in sharp contrast to ecological studies of failure and change, in which issues of organizational demography have long been conspicuous. Studying heterogeneity in founding is more complicated than studying heterogeneity in failure or change: organizational attributes cannot be used as explanatory variables in analyses of founding because they cannot be observed for organizations that do not yet exist (Delacroix and Carroll 1983). As a result, the organization itself cannot be the focal point of study.

Ecological researchers initially sidestepped this complication by considering the population itself as the unit experiencing the events. The problem with this approach is that variations in social and economic conditions across a population's environment will produce differences in founding rates. If not properly accounted for, this heterogeneity will result in specification bias. Some progress on this problem has been made by researchers using differences among foundings within populations to specify more fine-grained population substructures into which organizations are differentially founded. A variety of criteria have be used for this purpose including legal form (Ranger-Moore et al. 1991; Rao and Neilsen 1992; Baum and Oliver 1996), core technology (Barnett 1990), customer base (Baum and Singh 1994a), strategy (Brittain 1994) and geographical location (Barnett and Carroll 1987; Carroll and Wade 1991; Swaminathan and Wiedenmayer 1991; Cattani et al. 2003). In this approach, studying founding involves first specifying potential organizational subpopulations and then examining differences in the rate at which these subpopulations receive new entrants.

Unfortunately, this approach suffers operational problems (e.g. artificial, arbitrary and large numbers of organizational niches, ambiguous risk-set definition) that can undermine efforts to operationalize the approach empirically. Consequently, subpopulation entry studies typically provide descriptive accounts of organizational niches that were actually filled. Three alternative approaches have recently appeared that make it possible to examine how differentiation within populations and variation in their environments affect the founding process.

The first begins with the observation that organizational environments have spatial components – geographical barriers, localized resource environments – that affect the dynamics of organizational populations. Variation in social and economic conditions across regions or local differences in a population's institutional history can produce differences in intrinsic founding rates, or in unobservable region-specific proneness to experiencing the founding of particular organizational forms. If different segments of an organizational environment cannot be considered equally at risk of experiencing foundings of organizations of a given type, then we should expect location dependence and unobserved heterogeneity in organizational founding rates.

To address these problems empirically, Lomi (1995) proposes a model of location dependence in organizational founding rates. In contrast to other work, Lomi's approach does not require subdivision of organizational populations on the basis of abstract *a priori* categories; instead empirical corrections for unobserved heterogeneity are estimated directly from data. His analysis of founding rates of Italian cooperative banks based on the model indicates that models neglecting unobserved heterogeneity across geographic regions tend to overestimate the effects of ecological processes on founding rates. The analysis revealed the existence of two distinct segments within the population; when the founding rate was allowed to vary within segments, evidence of heterogeneous response to general population processes was found. Lomi's study contributes to a growing literature showing that organizational populations are internally differentiated and that vital rates vary systematically across heterogeneous segments of the population. Bringing the role of spatial factors to the forefront of ecological analyses enriches our understanding of organizational founding processes.

Sorenson and colleagues (Barnett and Sorenson 2002; Stuart and Sorenson 2003a, b) recently pioneered a second approach to dealing with geographic heterogeneity in founding rates. Like Lomi's, their approach does not require arbitrary subdivision of the population. Unlike Lomi's, however, it makes use of continuous measures of the distance between fine-grained geographic units (i.e. single zip codes) at risk of founding and variables of theoretical interest, rather than estimating corrections from the data. This permits effects of particular variations in social and economic conditions on the founding rate to be estimated directly. Sorenson et al. have used the approach to examine whether location-specific founding rates of biotechnology firms depend on geographic proximity to other biotechnology firms, lead inventors of patented biotechnologies, venture capital firms, or universities with leading biotechnology labs (Stuart and Sorenson 2003a), as well as biotechnology firms that have recently made an initial public offering or that have been acquired (Stuart and Sorenson 2003b). Their findings provide substantial evidence of spatial heterogeneity, suggesting that the spatial distribution of resources materially affects entrepreneurs' ability and propensity to create new organizations.

A third approach, introduced by Baum and Haveman (1997), complements traditional ecological analyses that ask when a founding will occur – by any kind of organization within a population, in any location in that population's niche – by taking organizational foundings as given and asking *what kind* of organization is founded and *where*. Like Sorenson et al.'s, their approach is relational, focusing on organizations' positions relative to each other in the resource space, and so does not require any specification of subpopulations where foundings can occur. They are concerned with new organizations' similarity to (or difference from) incumbent organizations. Given that a new organization appears, they examine how similar it is to neighbouring organizations. They investigate key entrepreneurial decisions, namely how close new organizations should locate in product and geographic space to incumbent organizations in their industry. Baum and Haveman thus go beyond geographic heterogeneity to consider product heterogeneity as well. Their analysis of the roles of size, price and location similarity on Manhattan hotel foundings finds evidence of both avoidance of direct competition pushing similar hotels apart and pulling complementary hotels together (e.g. Hawley 1950; White 1981), as well as of agglomeration economies and institutional forces pulling similar hotels together (e.g. Hotelling 1929; DiMaggio and Powell 1983). The 'hotel districts' resulting from these processes help reduce consumer search costs regarding hotels' locations (e.g. proximity to points of tourist interest or business activity) and class (i.e. economy or luxury).

Together, these studies refocus organizational ecologists' emphasis on temporal heterogeneity and time dependence in organizational founding to less studied issues of spatial heterogeneity and location dependence. The approaches to the dynamics of location choice they advance make it possible to subject theoretical predictions from spatial economics and organizational sociology to empirical testing, improving our knowledge of key entrepreneurial decisions and processes, and the tendency for firms to cluster (or not) in product and geographic space.

Age and Size Dependence

A central line of inquiry in ecological research has been the effect of organizational ageing on failure. Until recently, the predominant view was the *liability of newness* (Stinchcombe 1965: 148–9), the propensity of young organizations to have higher failure rates. Underlying Stinchcombe's (1965) liability of newness is the assumption that young organizations are more vulnerable because they have to learn new roles as social actors and create organizational roles and routines at a time when organizational resources are stretched to the limit. New organizations are also assumed to typically lack broad bases of influence and endorsement, stable relationships with important external constituents and the legitimacy that years of experience in providing particular products or services confer on older organizations. In a complementary viewpoint, Hannan and Freeman (1984) suggest that selection pressures favour organizations capable of demonstrating their reliability and accountability. Reliability and accountability require organizations to be highly reproducible. This reproducibility, and the structural inertia that it generates, are expected to increase as organizations age. Since selection processes favour highly reproducible structures, older organizations are predicted to be less likely to fail than young organizations.

A second important line of research examines how organizational size influences failure rates. Larger organizations are thought to be less likely to fail for a variety of reasons. Since inertial tendencies in organizations increase with size, and since selection pressures favour structurally inert organizations for their reliability, large organizations are expected to be less vulnerable to the risk of failure (Hannan and Freeman 1984). The propensity of small organizations to fail is also argued to result from several *liabilities of smallness*, including problems of raising capital, recruiting and training a workforce, meeting higher interest payments and handling the administrative costs of compliance with government regulations (Aldrich and Auster 1986).

Large size also tends to legitimate organizations to the extent that stakeholders interpret organizational size as an outcome of prior success and an indicator of future dependability.

One major reason the liability of smallness is studied is related to the liability of newness. Since new organizations tend to be small, if, as the liability of smallness predicts, small organizations have higher failure rates, then liabilities of newness and smallness are confounded and must be separated empirically (Freeman et al. 1983). For example, Levinthal (1991a) shows that a simple simulation model in which change in organizational assets over time is represented as a random walk replicates the liability of newness in organizational mortality rates. Thus, if organizational size increases with age and failure decreases with size, then what appears as a liability of newness may be an artifact of unmeasured size. This is one example of the well-known problem of unobserved heterogeneity, which can result in spurious negative age dependence in failure rates (e.g. Tuma and Hannan 1984; Petersen and Koput 1991).

Notably, although early ecological studies supported the liability of newness hypothesis consistently (e.g. Carroll and Delacroix 1982; Carroll 1983; Freeman et al. 1983), as Table 1.2.2 shows, later studies find that, after controlling for contemporaneous organizational size, failure rates do not generally decline with age. Since much of the original support for the liability of newness comes from studies in which organizational size is not controlled, the early supportive findings may simply reflect this. On the other hand, with few exceptions, studies in Table 1.2.2 support the liability of smallness prediction that organizational failure rates decline with increased size.

Bigger may be Better, but is Older Wiser?

These empirical findings have prompted two alternative theoretical perspectives on age dependence that question the basic liability of newness argument. The first alternative, the *liability of adolescence hypothesis* (Bruderl and Schussler 1990; Fichman and Levinthal 1991), predicts an inverted U-shaped relationship between age and failure. This model observes that new organizations start with an initial stock of assets (e.g. goodwill, psychological commitment, financial investment) that buffers them from failure during a honeymoon period – even when early outcomes are unfavourable. The larger an organization's initial stock of assets, the longer the expected duration the organization is buffered. As this original stock is depleted, however, organizations face a liability of adolescence and those unable to generate needed resource flows because, for example, they were unable to establish necessary roles and routines or develop stable relationships with important external constituents, fail. After adolescence, the future probability of failure declines, since surviving organizations are those able to acquire sufficient ongoing resources.

Liability of newness and adolescence arguments provide divergent accounts of age dependence for young organizations, but agree that failure rates decline monotonically for older organizations. Notably, processes underlying these models (e.g. learning and creating new roles and routines, establishing relations with external constituents, depleting initial endowments) occur early in the organizational life cycle. These arguments thus have little to say about organizations that are not new or adolescent. The *liability of ageing hypothesis* identifies processes that become important later in the organizational life cycle and predicts an increasing rate of failure for older organizations as a result of these processes (Aldrich and Auster 1986; Baum 1989; Ingram 1993; Barron et al. 1994; Ranger-Moore 1997). Thus, the liability of ageing hypothesis complements and extends liability of newness and adolescence hypotheses (Baum 1989).

The liability of ageing argument begins with another insight from Stinchcombe's (1965: 153) essay: '... the organizational inventions that can be made at a time in history depend on the social technology available at that time'. Organizations thus reflect the environment at the time of their founding. The initial fit between organizations and their environments erodes, however, as incomplete information, bounded rationality, and inertial tendencies make it difficult, if not impossible, for individuals to keep their organizations aligned with rapidly changing and unpredictable environmental demands. Environmental change also creates opportunities for new organizations to enter and undermine the competitive positions of established organizations (e.g. Tushman and Anderson 1986). Thus, encountering a series of environmental changes that decreases the alignment between organizations and environments exposes ageing organizations to an increased risk of

Table 1.2.2   Age and size dependence failure studies, 1983–2003

Population	Age[a]	Size[a]	Size variable	References
US Labor Unions, 1836–1985[b]	–	+	Membership at founding	Freeman et al. (1983); Hannan and Freeman (1989); Carroll and Hannan (1989a, b); Carroll and Wade (1991); Hannan and Carroll (1992)
US Brewers, 1633–1988	–	na		
Argentina Newspapers, 1800–1900	–	na		
Ireland Newspapers, 1800–1975	–	na		
San Francisco Newspapers, 1800–1975	–	na		
Little Rock Newspapers, 1815–1975	–	na		
Springfield Newspapers, 1835–1975	–	na		
Shreveport Newspapers, 1840–1975	–	na		
Elmira Newspapers, 1815–1975	–	na		
Lubbock Newspapers, 1890–1975	–	na		
Lafayette Newspapers, 1835–1975	–	na		
California Wineries, 1940–1985	0	–	Storage capacity	Delacroix et al. (1989); Delacroix and Swaminathan (1991)
Iowa Telephone Companies, 1900–1929	0	0	Subscribers	Barnett (1990); Barnett and Amburgey (1990)
Pennsylvania Telephone Companies, 1879–1934	–	0		Barnett (1997)
West German Business Organizations, 1980–1989	+/–	–	Employees at founding	Bruderl and Schussler (1990)
Bavarian Brewers, 1900–1981	0	–	Small firm dummy	Swaminathan and Wiedenmayer (1991)
Toronto Day Care Centers, 1971–1989	+	–	Licensed capacity	Baum and Oliver (1991; 1992); Baum and Singh (1994b)
Toronto Nursery Schools, 1971–1987	–	–	Licensed capacity	Olzak and West (1991)
US Immigrant Newspapers, 1877–1914	–	na		
African-American Newspapers, 1877–1914	–	na		
Manhattan Banks, 1840–1976	0	–	Assets	Banaszak-Holl (1992; 1993)
Manhattan Hotels, 1898–1990	+	–	Number of rooms	Baum and Mezias (1992)
California S&Ls, 1970–1987	0	0	Assets	Haveman (1992; 1993c)
US Mutual S&Ls, 1960–1987	+/–	0	Assets	Rao and Neilsen (1992)
US Stock S&Ls, 1960–1987	+/–	0	Assets	
US Cement Producers, 1888–1982	0/–	na		Anderson and Tushman (1992)
US Minicomputer Manufacturers, 1958–1982	+/–	na		
US Group HMOs, 1976–1991	0	–	Enrolment	Wholey et al. (1992)

(Continued)

Table 1.2.2 *(Continued)*

Population	Age[a]	Size[a]	Size variable	References
US Independent Practice Assn. HMOs, 1976–1991	+	–	Enrolment	Amburgey et al. (1993)
Finish Newspapers, 1771–1963	–	na		Carroll et al. (1993)
US Brewers, 1878–1988	+	–	Production in 1878 and 1879	
US Microcomputer Manufacturers, 1975–1986	+	–	Units sold	Ingram (1993)
US Integrated Circuit Manufacturers, 1971–1981	0	–	Employees	Loree (1993)
Medical Diagnostic Imaging Firms, 1953–1989	+/–	0	Corporate sales	Mitchell and Singh (1993)
US Trade Associations, 1901–1990	0/–	–	Membership	Aldrich et al. (1994)
US Credit Unions, 1980–1989[c]	+	–/+/–	Assets	Amburgey et al. (1994)
US Hotel Chains, 1896–1980	0	–	Number of hotels	Ingram (1994)
New York City Credit Unions, 1914–1990	+	–	Log real total assets	Barron et al. (1994)
Medical Equipment Manufacturers, 1950–1990	–	–	Sales	Mitchell (1994)
New York State Life Insurance & Assessment Companies, 1881–1931	–	–	Number of policies sold	Lehrman (1994)
New York State Life Insurance Fraternal Societies, 1881–1931	–	+	Number of policies sold	Carroll et al. (1996)
US Automobile Producers, 1885–1981	–	–	Production capacity	Ingram and Inman (1996)
Niagara Falls Hotels, 1885–1991	0	–	Number of rooms	Ranger-Moore (1997)
NY State Life Insurance Companies, 1813–1935	+/0	–	Assets	Reuf (1997)
California Hospitals, 1980–1990	0	–	Log number of beds	Singh (1997)
US Hospital Systems Software Firms, 1961–1991	na	–	Log sales	Ingram and Baum (1997a)
US Hotel Chains, 1896–1990	+	0	Log number of components	Reuf and Scott (1998)
San Francisco Hospitals, 1945–1990	0	0	Log number of beds	Wade et al. (1998)
US Breweries, 1845–1918	–	na		
Proprietary Strategists, US Personal Computer Industry, 1975–1992	+	–	Log sales	Henderson (1999)

(Continued)

Table 1.2.2 (Continued)

Population	Age[a]	Size[a]	Size variable	References
Standards Strategists, US Personal Computer Industry, 1975–1992	+/−	−	Log sales	
New York Credit Unions, 1914–1990	+	−	Assets	Barron (1999)
Ontario Independent Nursing Homes, 1971–1996	0	−	Log number of beds	Baum (1999)
Ontario Chain Nursing Homes, 1971–1996	+	0		
US Breweries, 1938–1997	0	−	Production capacity	Carroll and Swaminathan (2000)
US Bicycle Industry, 1880–1916	−	na	na	Dowell and Swaminathan (2000)
Israeli Worker Cooperatives, 1920–1992	0	na	Cooperatives absorbed	Ingram and Simons (2000)
US Wineries, 1941–1990	na	−/+	Acres of vineyard owned	Swaminathan (2001)
	na	−	Log gallons of installed capacity	
French Auto Manufacturers, 1885–1981[d]	−	−	Log production	Dobrev et al. (2001); Dobrev and Carroll (2003)
German Auto Manufacturers, 1885–1981[d]	−	−	Log production	
British Auto Manufacturers, 1885–1981[d]	−	−	Log production	Phillips (2001; 2002)
Law Firms/Attorneys in Silicon Valley, 1945–1996	0	−	Number of partners	
	0	−	Number of associates	
MIT Start-Ups, 1980–1994	−	0	Log of cumulative revenues	Shane and Stuart (2002)
US Auto Manufacturers, 1885–1981	−	−	Log production	Dobrev and Carroll (2003); Dobrev et al. (2003)
Canadian Biotechnology Firms, 1991–2000	0	−	Log R&D employees	Baum and Silverman (2004)

[a] X/Y gives the signs of significant ($p < 0.05$) linear and squared terms, respectively, when estimated. X gives the sign of the effect of initial increases in age, Y gives the sign of the effect for later increases.

[b] See Hannan and Freeman (1989: 257–9) for an interpretation of this positive size effect.

[c] Amburgey et al. (1994) test a cubic effect of size to examine the failure risk of mid-sized organizations.

[d] Results differ somewhat in the two studies; Dobrev and Carroll (2003) exclude the smallest firms from their sample.

obsolescence and, concomitantly, failure. Ageing may also bring about *senescence*: an accumulation of internal friction, precedent and political pacts that impede action and reliable performance. Notably, obsolescence does not require inertia to increase with organizational age – even if inertia is constant over time there will be a liability of obsolescence. Obsolescence and senescence thus pose separate risks: senescence is a direct effect of ageing; obsolescence a result of environmental change.

Available empirical evidence regarding age-dependence is equivocal. Among studies in Table 1.2.2 that control for contemporaneous organizational size, 12 populations exhibited a liability of newness, 11 a liability of ageing, six a liability of adolescence and 15 no age dependence. Several explanations may help account for the varied findings.

Two sample-selection problems may bias results away from a liability of newness. First, the new organizations studied may be old new organizations, that is organizations late in the process of emergence (Katz and Gartner 1988). If researchers were able to obtain data on organizations earlier in the founding process (e.g. prior to formal incorporation – see, for example, Rao 2001), liability of newness findings might be stronger. Secondly, in several studies, left-censored organizations, that is organizations founded before the start of the observation period with known founding dates are included in the analysis. Because they are already survivors, left-censored organizations tend to be low-risk cases; treating these cases as standard subjects can lead to an underestimation of failure rates at shorter durations (Guo 1993).

It may also be that support for the liability of ageing is overstated. If organizational age coincides with the amount of environmental change experienced by an organization, and if the risk of failure increases with cumulative environmental change, then the probability of failure will increase, spuriously, with age if accumulated environmental change is uncontrolled (Carroll 1983: 313) – and it typically is not. Thus, in the same way that negative age dependence can result spuriously from uncontrolled size, positive age dependence (after controlling for size) may result spuriously from uncontrolled organizational exposure to environmental change. Notably, this implies that, after controlling for size and environmental change, *no* age dependence should be observed unless there is a liability of senescence.

The more limited support for the liability of adolescence hypothesis may have a benign explanation: Because most researchers examine only monotonic age dependence specifications, tests of the liability of adolescence hypothesis are infrequent. Notably, however, six of the eight studies in Table 1.2.2 that permit non-monotonic age dependence and control for size find a liability of adolescence.

Hannan et al. (1998a, b) recently suggested that divergent age dependence results might reflect non-proportionality in age effects, combined with heterogeneity in the size distributions of populations studied. And, although they find evidence that patterns of age dependence vary for small and large automobile producers in four European countries, no systematic pattern emerges from their results. More generally, divergent age dependence results might reflect variation in age dependence across populations or subpopulations (Baum 1996). Henderson (1999), for example, hypothesized contingent age dependence effects based on an organization's technology strategy – proprietary or standards-based. Henderson's analysis of sales growth and failure among US personal computer manufacturers during 1975–92 provided strong support for his contingency view, demonstrating how multiple patterns of age dependence can operate simultaneously in a single population. His study also revealed important trade-offs between growth and the risk of failure resulting from the joint effects of age and strategy.

To advance our understanding of these issues, research on age dependence must move beyond the use of age as a surrogate for all constructs underlying the various age dependence models and begin to test the models' assumptions directly. Although there has been much debate concerning the underlying source of the hazards facing new firms, most of the research in this debate implicitly assumes that new entrants are typified by a lack of stable relationships and sufficient resources. For example, the liability of newness hypothesis assumes that a lack of social approval, stability and sufficient resources typifies recent entrants and that these shortcomings increase their risk of failure, but organizational variation in these factors is rarely measured directly. Yet, newly founded organizations display considerable variation in their access to resources and stable relationships. Among US biotechnology firms, for example, Barley et al. (1992) showed that startups exhibited greater variability in alliances than established firms, and Kogut et al. (1993) showed that startups were more likely to develop alliances than incumbents. To date, only a few studies other than Henderson's (1999) have explored the potential for variation in liability of newness and smallness effects. Singh et al. (1986b) found that external legitimacy – measured as inclusion in community directories or charitable registration – decreased the liability of newness among voluntary social service organizations. Reinforcing and extending these results, Baum and Oliver (1991) showed that institutional linkages with municipal government and community agencies moderated both liabilities of newness and smallness for day care centres and nursery schools. These studies, along with Henderson's, support the idea that the liability of newness is attributable to the absence of stable relationships to important institutional actors and suggest that if young organizations obtain early legitimacy and access to resources through the formation of institutional attachments to community and public constituents, a liability of newness may not be observed.

A further benefit of taking this approach is that liabilities of newness, adolescence and obsolescence can be treated as *complementary* rather than as competing organizational processes. Thus, although we still know very little about *how* ageing affects organizational failure, or the *conditions* under which one, the other or some combination of these models will predominate, several recent studies offer promise for future progress.

Structural Inertia Theory

Structural inertia theory depicts organizations as relatively inert entities for which adaptive response is not only difficult and infrequent, but hazardous as well. Consequently, change in individual organizations is viewed as contributing considerably less to population-level change than organizational founding and failure. Given the centrality of this theoretical position to ecological approaches, it is not surprising that organizational ecologists have amassed a wealth of studies on the influence of organizational and environmental factors on rates of organizational change, as well as the survival consequences of different kinds of changes.

Organization theory focuses frequently on the relative advantages of alternative configurations of organizational features. Consequently, a great deal of research on organizational change has concentrated on the *content of organizational change*. A change to a more advantageous configuration is considered as adaptive, while a switch to a less advantageous configuration is considered detrimental (Miller and Friesen 1980; Amburgey et al. 1993). Complementing this focus, Hannan and Freeman's (1984) structural inertia theory offers a model of the *process of organizational change* that considers both internal and external constraints on change. Structural inertia theory addresses two main questions: (1) How changeable are organizations? and (2) is change beneficial for organizations? Figure 1.2.1 summarizes structural inertia theory.

How Changeable are Organizations?

Hannan and Freeman (1977) pointed out that organizations face both internal and external constraints on their capacity for change and that, given these constraints, selection processes are important to explaining change in organizational populations. Building on this idea, Hannan and Freeman (1984) adopt a somewhat different approach that takes seriously the potential for organizational change by viewing inertia as a *consequence of* rather than *antecedent to* selection processes. Although some kinds of organizational changes occur frequently in organizations and sometimes these can even be radical changes, the nature of selection processes is such that organizations with inert features are more likely to survive (Hannan and Freeman 1984: 149).

The *structure* in structural inertia theory refers to some, but not all, features of organizations. Hannan and Freeman (1984: 156) emphasize *core* features of organizations, which are related to '… the claims used to mobilize resources for beginning an organization and the strategies and structures used to maintain flows of scarce resources'. Core features include, the goals, forms of authority, core technology and market strategy of organizations. *Peripheral* features protect an organization's core from uncertainty by buffering it and by broadening the organization's connections to its environment. Peripheral features include number and size of subunits, number of hierarchical levels, spans of control, communication patterns and buffering mechanisms.

Hannan and Freeman (1984: 156) argue that core features have higher levels of inertia than peripheral features. Thus, in comparison to the probability of change in peripheral features, the probability of

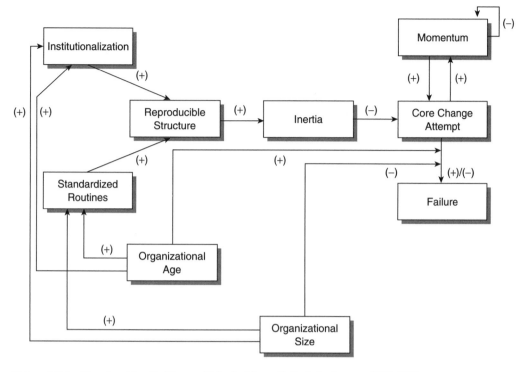

Figure 1.2.1   Structural Inertia Theory (Adapted from Kelly & Amburgey 1991: 593)

change in core features is very low (p. 157). However, they do not claim that organizations never change. Instead, they define inertia relative to environmental change: 'Structures of organizations have high inertia when the speed of reorganization [change in core features] is much lower than the rate at which environmental conditions change' (Hannan and Freeman 1984: 151). This formulation poses some rather difficult measurement problems – how can rates of organizational and environmental change be matched? Consequently, most studies reviewed here examine absolute rates of organizational change and report tests of structural inertia theory, but not relative inertia theory (an exception is Ruef 1997).

In addition to varying by facet of organizational structure, Hannan and Freeman (1984) also propose that inertial pressures vary with organizational age and size. Because older organizations have had time to more thoroughly formalize internal relationships, standardize routines and institutionalize leadership and power distributions, as well as

develop rich networks of dependencies and commitments with other social actors, reproducibility of structure and inertia should increase with age (Hannan and Freeman 1977; Pfeffer and Salancik 1978; Nelson and Winter 1982; Granovetter 1985; Aldrich and Auster 1986). Thus, older organizations should be most limited in their ability to adapt to changing environmental demands, and so the probability of attempting change in core features to decline with age (Hannan and Freeman 1984: 157). Organizational size is also associated with resistance to change. As organizations increase in size, they emphasize predictability, formalized roles and control systems and organizational behaviour becomes predictable, rigid and inflexible, increasing the level of structural inertia (Downs 1967; Aldrich and Auster 1986). Moreover, by buffering organizations from failure, large size may reduce the impetus for change (Levinthal 1994; Barnett 1997). Consequently, the probability of attempting change in core features declines with size (Hannan and Freeman 1984: 159).

Age and Size Dependence in Rates of Organizational Change

Tests of age and size dependence in rates of organizational change, presented in Table 1.2.3, are mixed and, overall, appear to offer little support for structural inertia theory's predictions. In their 1990 review, Singh and Lumsden used Hannan and Freeman's (1984) core-periphery distinction to interpret the mixed findings available to them. They speculated that rates of core feature change decrease with age, while rates of peripheral feature change increase with age. Does this distinction help account for the mixed age (and size) dependence findings available now? It appears not. For example, diversification – the development of new products or services, often for new clients and frequently requiring implementation of new administrative, production or distribution technologies – is one core change studied across multiple populations. Inspection of Table 1.2.3 reveals little evidence that diversification is related negatively to either age or size. What might account for the findings? Below, we examine several possibilities.

Fluidity of Age and Size

In contrast to structural inertia arguments, some theoretical views suggest that organizations become more fluid with age (Singh et al. 1988). Although selection processes favour organizations that are fit with their environment, the match between organizations and their environments is constantly eroding as managerial bounded rationality, informational constraints and inertial pressures prevent organizations from keeping pace with constantly changing environments. Thus, '… through a cumulative history of having been alive, the stresses and strains of living through multiple environmental changes cumulate in organizations, increasing the pressure on organizations to change' (Singh et al. 1988: 6). This implies a discontinuous rather than incremental pattern of organizational change (Miller and Friesen 1980; Tushman and Romanelli 1985).

Some theoretical views also support the idea that larger organizations are more fluid. Internal complexity, differentiation, specialization and decentralization, all features of large organizations, have each been associated with the adoption of innovations (Haveman 1993a). The slack resources available to larger organizations may both enable them to initiate change in response to environmental change

(Cyert and March 1963; Thompson 1967). Greater size relative to other actors also increases market power, lowering barriers to entry stemming from scale economies (Bain 1956; Scherer and Ross 1990) and reducing external political considerations (Pfeffer and Salancik 1978; Aldrich and Auster 1986).

Age and size estimates in Table 1.2.3 support fluidity and inertia predictions with approximately equal frequency. Although Singh et al.'s (1988) original study did not include left-censored organizations, many subsequent studies that find evidence of fluidity did. Because left-censored organizations, founded before the observation period begins, are not observed when they are youngest and smallest, including these organizations in analyses without appropriate corrections, can lead to an underestimation of rates of change at younger ages and smaller sizes (Guo 1993). Moreover, if large organizations are buffered by their resources from the risks of change (Hannan and Freeman 1989), support for the fluidity of size may reflect sample selection bias resulting from right censoring: Small organizations are not observed responding to changing environments because they fail prior to the realization of such efforts. Once again, sample selection problems may account, in part, for the mixed findings.

Repetitive Momentum

Although Hannan and Freeman (1984) do not include prior changes in their theoretical model, Amburgey and colleagues (Amburgey and Kelly 1985; Kelly and Amburgey 1991; Amburgey and Miner 1992; Amburgey et al. 1993) suggest that a complete understanding of organizational change requires consideration of an organization's *history of change*. From an organizational learning perspective, making a change furnishes an organization with the opportunity to routinize the change (Nelson and Winter 1982; Levitt and March 1988). Each time an organization engages in a particular kind of change, it increases its competency at that change. The more experienced an organization becomes with a particular change, the more likely it is to repeat the change. If a particular change becomes causally linked with success in the minds of organizational decision-makers – irrespective of whether such a link actually exists – reinforcement effects will make repetition even more likely. Thus, once change is initiated, the change process itself may become routinized and subject to inertial

Table 1.2.3 Rate of organizational change studies, 1985–2003

Population	Type of change	Age[a]	Size	# Prior	Dynamic	Reference
US Business Periodicals, 1774–1865	Ownership	−	0	+	na	Amburgey and Kelly (1985)
	Editor	−	0	+	na	
	Name	−	0	0	na	
	Layout	−	0	+	na	
	Content	0	0	0	na	
Voluntary Social Service Organizations, 1970–1982	Name	+	+	na	na	Singh et al. (1988; 1991); Tucker et al. (1990a, b)
	Sponsor	0	0	na	na	
	Location	+	0	na	na	
	Service area	+	0	na	na	
	Goals	+	0	na	na	
	Client groups	0	0	na	na	
	Service conditions	0	0	na	na	
	Chief executive	+	+	na	na	
	Structure	+	0	na	na	
Silicon Valley Semiconductor Producers[b]	Change in initial strategy	+	na	na	na	Boeker (1989)
US Medical Diagnostic Imaging Firms, 1959–1988	Entry to emerging subfield	na	0	na	na	Mitchell (1989)
Toronto Day Care Centres, 1971–1987	Specialist to generalist	+	−	na	na	Baum (1990a)
	Generalist to specialist	+/−	0	na	na	
US Health Maintenance Organizations[b]	For-profit to non-profit	+	0	na	na	Ginsberg and Buchholtz (1990)
US Airlines, 1962–1985	Business-level specialism	−	0	+	na	Kelly and Amburgey (1991; see also, Kelly 1988)
	Business-level generalism	0	−	+	na	
	Corporate-level specialism	0	0	+	na	
	Corporate-level generalism	0	−	+	na	
Edmonton Gasoline Stations, 1959–1988	Domain enlargement	0	na	na	0	Usher (1991); Usher and Evans (1996)
	Domain contraction	0	na	na	+	
	Niche migration	+/−	na	na	na	
California Wineries, 1946–1984	Brand portfolio	0	−	+	−	Delacroix and Swaminathan (1991)
	Product line	0	0	0	0	
	Land ownership status	0	0	+	0	

Table 1.2.3 *(Continued)*

Population	Type of change	Age[a]	Size	# Prior	Dynamic	Reference
Fortune 500 Companies, 1949–1977	Product-extension mergers	na	–	+	na	Amburgey and Miner (1992); Amburgey and Dacin (1994)
	Conglomerate mergers	na	0	+	na	
	Horizontal mergers	na	0	+	na	
	Vertical integration	na	0	+	na	
	Product market diversification	na	0	–	0	
	Structural decentralization	na	–	0	–	
Finnish Newspapers, 1771–1963	Content	–	na	+	–	Amburgey et al. (1993); Miner et al. (1990)
	Publication frequency	–	na	+	–	Halliday et al. (1993)
State Bar Associations, 1918–1950	Unification attempt	+	–	na	na	Zajac and Kraatz (1993)
US Private Liberal Arts Colleges, 1972–1986	Change to coed	+	0	na	na	
	Add graduate programme	–	+	na	na	
	Add business programme	0	+	na	na	
US Bank Holding Companies, 1956–1988	Related acquisition	–	na	+	–	Ginsberg and Baum (1994)
	Unrelated acquisition	0	na	+	0	
California S&Ls, 1977–1987	Real estate (entry rates)	0	+	na	na	Haveman (1994; see also, Haveman 1992; 1993a, b)
	Non-residential mortgages	0	0	na	na	
	Mortgage-backed securities	0	0	na	na	
	Consumer lending	0	0	na	na	
	Commercial lending	0	0	na	na	
	Service companies	+	0	na	na	
US Trade Associations, 1900–1980	Change in organizing domain or goals	0/0	0	na	na	Aldrich et al. (1994)
US Airlines, 1979–1986	Tactical competitive actions	0	0	+	na	Miller and Chen (1994)
	Strategic competitive actions	0	+	0	na	
US Radio Stations, 1984–1993	Abandon format	na	–	na	na	Greve (1995)
	Abandon format and re-enter	na	0	na	na	
US Airlines, 1985–1986	Propensity for action	na	–	na	na	Chen and Hambrick (1995)
	Action execution speed	na	–	na	na	
	Action visibility	na	+	na	na	
	Responsiveness	na	+	na	na	
	Response announcement speed	na	0	na	na	
	Response execution speed	na	+	na	na	
	Response visibility	na	–	na	na	

(Continued)

Table 1.2.3 *(Continued)*

Population	Type of change	Age[a]	Size	# Prior	Dynamic	Reference
Toronto Day Care Centres, 1971–1989	Market entry	+	–	–	+	Baum and Singh (1996)
	Market exit	0	0	0	0	
California Airlines, 1979–1984	Route entry	+	–	na	na	Baum and Korn (1996)
	Route exit	–	+	na	na	
US Radio Stations, 1984–1992	Innovative changes	na	0	0	0	Greve (1996; 1998);
	Format changes	na	–	0	0	Greve and Taylor (2000)
	Satellite entry	na	0	+	+	
	Production changes	na	0	0	0	
California Hospitals, 1980–1990	Market change	+	+	na	na	Ruef (1997)
US Semiconductor Producers, 1978–1992	Change in diversification	0	+	na	na	Boeker (1997)
US Liberal Arts Colleges, 1971–1986	Adoption of new professional programme	0	+	na	na	Kraatz (1998)
Russian Construction Companies, 1989–1993	Spin-off of state-owned units into independent companies	na	na	+	na	Suhomlinova (1999)
US Voluntary Associations, 1955–1986	Protest to advocacy	0	0	+	0	Minkoff (1999)
	Advocacy to protest	0	0	+	0	
	Advocacy to service	+	+	+	–	
	Service to advocacy	+	+	+	–	
US Rural Hospitals, 1984–1991	Change in provided services	0	–	na	na	D'Aunno et al. (2000)
Ontario Nursing Homes, 1971–1996	Acquisition	na	na	na	+	Baum et al. (2000)
California Hospitals, 1978–1991	Domain enlargement	0	+	na	na	Haveman et al. (2001)
	CEO	+	–	na	na	
500 Public US Corporations, 1963–1968	Diversifying acquisitions	na	+	+	na	Palmer and Barber (2001)
Largest Dutch Firms, 1966–1994	Acquisition	na	+	na	na	Vermeulen and Barkema (2001)
French Auto Manufacturers, 1885–1981	Change in niche width	0	0	+	na	Dobrev et al. (2001)
German Auto Manufacturers, 1885–1981	Change in niche width	0	0	+	na	
British Auto Manufacturers, 1885–1981	Change in niche width	+	+	+	na	
US Auto Manufacturers, 1885–1981	Change in niche width	–	+	+	na	Dobrev et al. (2003)

[a] X/Y gives the signs of significant ($p < 0.05$) linear and squared terms, respectively, when estimated.
[b] Observation period dates not given.

forces. This creates *repetitive momentum*, that is the tendency to maintain direction and emphasis of prior actions in current behaviour (Miller and Friesen 1980). Experience with change of a particular type is thus predicted to increase the likelihood that the change will be repeated in the future (Amburgey and Miner 1992).

To reconcile the idea that organizational change is propelled by repetitive momentum with evidence that organizations move from periods of change to periods of stability (e.g. Miller and Friesen 1980; Tushman and Romanelli 1985), Amburgey et al. (1993) advance a dynamic effect of prior change. Since organizational search processes begin with recently utilized routines (Cyert and March 1963), the likelihood of repeating a particular change should be highest immediately after its occurrence, but decline as time since the change was last made increases. Combined, the main and dynamic effects of prior change imply that the likelihood of repeating a particular change jumps immediately after a change of that type, the size of the jump increasing after each additional change, but declines with increases in the time since that type of change last occurred.

Support for repetitive momentum in organizational change is strong: Among the estimates in Table 1.2.3, rates of change increase with the number of prior changes of the same type in 29 of 40 empirical tests. Estimates for the dynamic effect are weak, however, with only seven of 22 tests supporting this idea. Notably, studies that control for one or both prior change effects account for most of the support for age-dependent structural inertia – eight of 12 negative age coefficients occur in these studies. Support for fluidity of ageing may thus reflect a specification bias: Older organizations may be more likely to change not because they are older, but because they have accumulated experience with change that is not accounted for. Overall, these findings suggest strongly the merit of a broader view of inertial forces in organizations – one that includes momentum in the change process as well as inertia.

Although addressing left-censoring, right-censoring and specification bias issues can improve our understanding of organization-level change processes incrementally, larger gains may be made by testing the underlying arguments directly. Because, as noted earlier, age and size coefficients reveal little about the underlying organizational processes of interest, we still know very little about *how* age and size affect rates of change, or the *conditions* under which fluidity, inertia or momentum will predominate. To learn what is really going on, studies using more direct measures of the underlying organizational processes are needed. Fluidity and inertia arguments are not necessarily competing. Indeed, fluidity of ageing arguments rely on inertia to create a gap between organizations and environments. They may thus be complementary ideas, and the underlying relationships they predict potentially operate simultaneously.

Is Change Beneficial?

Perhaps the most striking aspect of structural inertia theory is the relationship hypothesized between change in core features and the liability of newness (Stinchcombe 1965). Hannan and Freeman (1984: 160) propose that attempting core change produces a renewed liability of newness by robbing an organization's history of survival value. Attempting change in core features lowers an organization's performance reliability and accountability back to that of a new organization by destroying or rendering obsolete established roles and routines, and by disrupting relations with important external actors. Attempting core change may also undermine an organization's acquired legitimacy by modifying its visible mission. Since stakeholders favour organizations that exhibit reliable performance and accountability for their actions, Hannan and Freeman (1984: 160) conclude that, frequently, attempts to change core features to promote survival – even those that might ultimately reduce the risk of failure by better aligning the organization with its environment – expose organizations to an increased short-run risk of failure. Thus, structural inertia theory predicts that organizations may often fail precisely as a result of their attempts to survive.

In addition to their effects on reproducibility and inertia, organizational age and size also both affect the likelihood of surviving the short-run shock of a core change attempt. Because their internal structures and routines are more institutionalized and their external linkages are more established, older organizations are particularly likely to experience disruption as a result of core change (Hannan and Freeman 1984: 157). In contrast, larger organizations, although less likely to attempt core changes in the first place, are less likely to die during a core change attempt (p. 159). Large size can buffer organizations from the disruptive effects of core change by, for example, helping to maintain both old and new ways of doing things during the transition period or to overcome short-term deprivations and competitive challenges that accompany the change attempt.

If an organization manages to survive the short-run shock of a core change, Hannan and Freeman (1984: 161) predict the risk of failure to decline over time as performance reliability is re-established, external relationships are restabilized and organizational legitimacy is reaffirmed. The rate of decline in the failure rate after a core change is not specified by the structural inertia model, however. If the rate of decline in the failure rate continues at the same rate as before the change, the organization will face the short-term risk of change without any long-term benefit. If the rate of decline is slower than before, the organization will increase both its short- and long-term risk of failure. If, however, the rate of decline is faster than before the change, the organization will benefit in the long-run from taking on the short-term risks of change. Thus, although structural inertia theory views core change as disruptive in the short-run, it may, ultimately, be adaptive in the long-run if the organization manages to overcome the hazards associated with the initial disruption.

Thus, structural inertia theory frames the question of whether organizational change occurs at the population level (through founding and failure) or at the level of individual organizations as an issue of the rate of change of organizations relative to the rate of change in the environment. Organizations may be unable to respond to environmental change either because they are unwilling or unable to change or because they fail prior to the realization of their change efforts.

Organizational Change and Failure

Table 4 presents findings for studies examining the survival consequences of organizational change. As the table shows, organizations in the study populations do not necessarily fail as a result of their efforts to change – but they do not necessarily improve their organizational survival chances either. Do organizations operate in a world so uncertain that adaptive efforts turn out to be essentially random with respect to future value (Hannan and Freeman 1984: 150)? Thirteen of the studies in Table 1.2.4 separate the short- and long-run effects of change, but only six of these

also test for age variation, one for size variation and one for both age and size variation in the disruptive effects of change. Thus, despite the relatively large number of studies, any conclusions drawn at this point would be premature.

In addition to the need for future research on the adaptiveness of organizational change that specifies structural inertia theory predictions fully, future research may also benefit by considering several additional issues.

Left-censored organizations, founded before the start of the observation period, are not observed when they are youngest and smallest and, according to structural inertia theory, when they are both most likely to change and most vulnerable to the hazards of change. Including these organizations in the analysis can lead to under-estimation of the overall hazard of change as well as variation in the hazard for organizations of different ages and sizes. Moreover, if core organizational change is as perilous in the short-term as structural inertia arguments assert, unless data are fine-grained, core changes may frequently not be observed, because these deadliest of changes will not be detected in the yearly data typically available. This right censoring problem lowers estimates of the hazardousness of change because the most hazardous changes are not included in the analysis.

Although poor and superior performing organizations are likely to experience different risks of failure as well as rates and kinds of change (e.g. Hambrick and D'Aveni 1988; Haveman 1992; 1993a, b; 1994; Greve 1998), ecological analyses of the effects of organizational change on failure do not typically include measures of ongoing organizational performance (Haveman et al. 2001). This results in two potential problems. Firstly, cause and effect logic is blurred because some changes or types of change are symptoms of organizational decline rather than causes of organizational death. Secondly, model estimates are prone to specification bias: If rates of organizational change and failure are both influenced by recent performance, a spurious relationship between change and failure will be observed if prior performance is not controlled. Although organization-specific indicators of performance are difficult to obtain for entire populations over time, one option is to use organizational growth and decline as a proxy performance measure (Baum 1990a; Scott 1992: 342–62; Haveman 1993c; Baum and Singh 1996). Others include focusing on shorter time periods of interest (Haveman et al.

Table 1.2.4 Organizational change and failure studies, 1984–2003

Population	Type of change	Change*	Dynamic	x Age	x Size	Reference
US Newspapers, 1800–1975	Editor	+	0	na	na	Carroll (1984b)
US Business Periodicals, 1774–1865	Ownership	+	na	na	na	Amburgey and Kelly (1985)
	Editor	0	na	na	na	
	Name	0	na	na	na	
	Layout	0	na	na	na	
	Content	0	na	na	na	
Voluntary Social Service Organizations, 1970–1982	Sponsor	+	na	na	na	Singh et al. (1986a)
	Location	–	na	na	na	
	Service area	+	na	na	na	
	Goals	0	na	na	na	
	Client groups	+	na	na	na	
	Chief executive	–	na	na	na	
	Structure	0	na	na	na	
US Airlines, 1962–1985	Business-level specialism	0	na	na	na	Kelly and Amburgey (1991; see also Kelly 1988)
	Business-level generalism	0	na	na	na	
	Corporate-level specialism	0	na	na	na	
	Corporate-level generalism	0	na	na	na	
	Peripheral change	0	na	na	na	
Edmonton Gasoline Stations, 1959–1988	Domain enlargement or contraction	0	+	na	na	Usher (1991); Usher and Evans (1996)
California Wineries, 1946–1984	Brand portfolio increase	0	0	na	na	Delacroix and Swaminathan (1991; see also Swaminathan and Delacroix 1991)
	Brand portfolio decrease	0	0	na	na	
	Product line increase	–	0	na	na	
	Product line decrease	0	0	na	na	
	Land acquisition	–	0	na	na	
	Land divestment	0	0	na	na	
Finnish Newspapers, 1774–1963	Content	+	–	+	na	Amburgey et al. (1990; 1993)
	Frequency	+	–	+	na	
	Layout	0	–	+	na	
	Location	0	–	+	na	
	Name	+	–	+	na	
California S&Ls, 1977–1987	Residential mortgages	–	na	na	na	Haveman (1992)
	Real estate (+ invest)	0	na	na	na	

(Continued)

Table 1.2.4 *(Continued)*

Population	Type of change	Change*	Dynamic	x Age	x Size	Reference
	Non-residential mortgages	–	na	na	na	
	Mortgage-backed securities	0	na	na	na	
	Cash and investment securities	–	na	na	na	
	Consumer lending	0	na	na	na	
	Commercial lending	0	na	na	na	
	Service companies	0	na	na	na	
Iowa Telephone Companies, 1900–1917	Presidential succession	+	–	0	na	Haveman (1993c)
	Managerial succession	+	–	0	na	
US Medical Diagnostic Imaging Firms, 1954–1989	Expand and survive in new subfield	+	na	na	na	Mitchell and Singh (1993)
	Expand and exit subfield	–	na	na	na	
Toronto Day Care Centres, 1971–1989	Market entry	0	0	–	+	Baum and Singh (1996)
	Market exit	+	–	+	–	
US Liberal Arts Colleges, 1971–1986	Addition of a new programme	0	na	na	na	Kraatz and Zajak (1996)
California Hospitals, 1980–1990	Market change	+	na	na	na	Ruef (1997)
US Voluntary Associations, 1955–1986	Protest to advocacy	0	na	na	na	Minkoff (1999)
	Advocacy to protest	0	na	na	na	
	Advocacy to service	+	0	na	na	
	Service to advocacy	+	0	na	na	
US Computer Manufacturers, 1975–1992	Change from proprietary to standards strategy	–	+	na	na	Henderson (1999)
US Bicycle Industry, 1880–1916	New product introduction	+	0	0	na	Dowell and Swaminathan (2000)
French Auto Manufacturers, 1885–1981	Niche expansion	0	0	0	na	Dobrev et al. (2001)
	Niche contraction	0	0	0	na	
	Change in relative market position	0	0	na	na	
	Change in absolute market position	+	0	0	na	
German Auto Manufacturers, 1885–1981	Niche expansion	0	0	0	na	
	Niche contraction	0	0	0	na	
	Change in relative market position	–	0	na	na	
	Change in absolute market position	+	0	0	na	
British Auto Manufacturers, 1885–1981	Niche expansion	–	0	0	na	
	Niche contraction	–	0	0	na	
	Change in relative market position	0	0	na	na	
	Change in absolute market position	+	0	0	na	
US Auto Manufacturers, 1885–1981	Change in niche width	–	0	na	–	Dobrev et al. (2003)

* X gives the signs of significant ($p < 0.05$) coefficients.

2001) or modelling the effects of organizational change directly on observable performance indicators such as market share (Greve 1998; 1999).

A closely related issue is that all organizations are assumed to be equally susceptible to the effects of change on failure. Hannan and Freeman (1984) have identified age and size as factors that alter the exposure of organizations to the liabilities of change. However, as noted above, to date, few studies have accounted for this variability (see Table 1.2.4). Institutional linkages (i.e. ties to important state and community institutions) may also provide a buffer against change by conferring resources and legitimacy on organizations (Miner et al. 1990; Baum and Oliver 1991; Baum and Mezias 1993). Like unmeasured performance, unmeasured variation in organizational susceptibility to the risks of change can bias in model estimates.

A final issue is that, although researchers do differentiate broad categories of changes, variation in the ecological consequences of the changes is not considered; rather, all instances of a particular category of change are considered equivalent. For many kinds of change, however, there may be significant within-type differences with substantial survival implications. One such difference is within-type variation in the effect of changes on the intensity of competition. For example, depending on how an organization's specific actions alter the size of its domain relative to the number of organizations competing over its domain, the organization's diversification activities can increase, decrease or leave unchanged the intensity of competition the organization faces. Baum and Singh (1996), for example, found that the effects of market domain changes (both expansion and contraction) on the failure rate in a population of day care centres depended on how the changes affected the intensity of competition: Changes that lowered the intensity of competition improved organizational survival chances, while those that increased the intensity of competition lowered survival chances. Such within-type variation may help account for some earlier mixed results in studies examining the adaptive consequences of organizational change.

Reconciling Adaptation and Selection

Although adaptationist and ecological views are frequently presented as mutually exclusive alternatives

with very different implications for organization studies, these views are not fundamentally incompatible. While ecological theory emphasizes the predominance of selection over adaptation, the complementarity of adaptive and ecological effects is clearly reflected in the research reviewed here. Research in Tables 1.2.3 and 1.2.4 does not support strong ecological arguments: organizations appear to change frequently in response to environmental changes, and often without any harmful effects. Moreover, rates of change are often not constrained by age and size as predicted by structural inertia theory.

At the same time, however, in contrast to a strong adaptation view, survival consequences of change appear more consistent with random groping or imitation than calculated strategic action (Delacroix and Swaminathan 1991; Baum and Singh 1996; Ruef 1997; Baum and Korn 1999; Dobrev et al. 2001). In his study of California hospitals, for example, Ruef (1997) found little correspondence between organizational change and ecological conditions. Hospitals did not experience improved fitness as a result of their own adaptive efforts, but rather as a result of their withdrawal from unsuitable market niches, wariness of competitors to enter incumbents' markets and ecological drift associated with competitors' differentiation strategies. Consequently, while studies provide clear evidence of organizations' adaptive potential, they offer little systematic support for a belief in the fundamental adaptability of organizations.

Taken together, empirical evidence indicates that the evolution of organizational populations is shaped jointly by processes of selection and adaptation and their interaction: Because organizational change can affect organizational failure, the population-level result of combined adaptation and selection is not the simple aggregate of each process separately.

One interpretation for the absence of systematic effects of organizational change on survival chances may be anchored in the bounded rationality of decision-makers in organizations (March and Simon 1958). Consider, for example, the case of market niche change, one of the most frequently studied organizational changes (see Table 1.2.4). It seems plausible that decision-makers are more knowledgeable about the environment they face in their current market niches from past experience than they are about the environments of other markets. And expanding their markets would expose them to a different environment. Thus, intentionally rational expansions into new markets may sometimes have the surprising consequence of exposing the organization to unanticipated environmental conditions (e.g. greater competition). Of course, at other times, expansion into new markets may prove beneficial *ex post*. However, on average, there would be no effect. The problem for organizations, then, is not that adaptive changes are impossible (or even rare), it is that organizational decision-makers are not, on average, able to distinguish between beneficial and detrimental organizational changes in advance. This suggests that organizations more experienced with a particular kind of change may be more likely to benefit from it.

Another explanation is that *non*-bureaucratic organizations make most of the changes (Baum and Singh 1996). In the realm of adaptiveness, the absence of bureaucracy can be viewed as both an advantage (change is relatively easy) and a disadvantage (the ability to collect information on the environment is weak). The combination of reduced information gathering ability with a relatively organic organizational structure could account for such findings – a good deal of change, but not systematically effective change. Contained in this interpretation is a paradox: Organizations that can collect a lot of information often have organizational structures that are difficult to change, while those that can change the fastest often have trouble collecting relevant information to guide changes. Thus, although simplicity might lead one to expect organizations to possess a high potential for developing *adaptive* actions, in fact, it may lead them only to be active. More generally, whether changes in response to environments have adaptive consequences may depend upon the nature of learning processes in organizations (Levinthal 1991b).

Organizational Learning

Complementing the growing interest in organizational change and its consequences is an emerging stream of ecological research that explores the effects of organizations' *experiential learning* on their survival chances. Experience is one of the fundamental mechanisms facilitating organizational learning (Cyert and March 1963; Huber 1991). Organizations adjust their behaviour based on their goals and past performance. Such 'learning by doing' is widely held to be a critical source of

organizational knowledge, capabilities and improved organizational performance (Argote et al. 1990). In addition to advancing our understanding of how experiential processes shape organizational survival, this research contributes to an answer to the question of how ageing influences organizational failure by modelling more directly experiential learning constructs invoked by the liability of newness and ageing hypotheses.

Organizations' Operating and Competitive Experience

Organizations' learning from their operating experience has been advanced as a source of production efficiencies and through improved efficiency, a source of sustainable competitive advantage (Yelle 1979; Argote 1999). There is substantial evidence that organizations become more efficient at doing something by repeatedly doing it. The learning curve for operations has been demonstrated in many manufacturing (Yelle 1979) and service organizations (Darr et al. 1995). Although learning theorists recognize that experience may ultimately influence organizational failure (e.g. Huber 1991), the existing empirical literature typically uses efficiency as the dependent variable (Yelle 1979; Darr et al. 1995). Efficiency is linked to failure, with more efficient organizations being less likely to fail, but care must be taken in relating learning curve research to organizational failure; operating experience is not a cure-all for organizations. Learning from its own experience can constrain an organization by leading it into *competency traps*, where it focuses on perfecting routines that are ultimately rendered obsolete by changing environmental demands (Levinthal and March 1993).

Organizations must allocate energy between the exploration of new routines and the exploitation of old ones (March 1991). An organization that engages in too much exploration will not harvest the value of its current competencies; one that engages in too much exploitation can stagnate. Typically, short run rewards of exploitation drive out exploration, since each increase in competence at an activity increases the likelihood of benefiting from that activity, while returns from exploration are less certain. Given initial success with a routine, organizations tend to continue using it because they know how to, and because it is less risky than exploring alternatives (Amburgey et al. 1993).

Consequently, organizational routines tend to be determined more by initial conditions, experiences and actions than by information gained from later learning situations (Stinchcombe 1965; Levitt and March 1988).

In the face of ambiguity and uncertainty, an emphasis on exploitation can prevent organizations from adjusting their routines too quickly in response to idiosyncratic events and from engaging in costly explorations (Levinthal 1991b). In the face of production pressures and the need for reliability and consistency of action, exploitive learning may enhance performance by reducing variability in the quality or efficiency of task performance (Yelle 1979; Hannan and Freeman 1984). Exploitation can become harmful, however, if the criteria for organizational success and survival change *after* an organization has learned. Then the organization may perform poorly and even fail when doing well what it learned in the past (Levitt and March 1988).

The notion of a competency trap suggests that organizations may reduce their exploratory activity prematurely and, in the case of a changing environment, not renew exploratory search and learning activities, despite the fact that new opportunities and threats are present. In this way, organizations' experience contributes to the inertia that binds them to routines of the past, leading them to employ routines well beyond their point of usefulness and ultimately resulting in their failure (Starbuck 1983; Henderson and Clark 1990; Miller 1990; Baum et al. 1995).

The idea that own experience improves efficiency, which is strongly supported by empirical evidence, is not inconsistent with the possibility that, simultaneously, overall organizational effectiveness decreases if the organization does not adjust to new demands (Baum and Ingram 1998). Based on these arguments, Baum and Ingram (1998) predicted a non-monotonic effect of an organization's operating experience on its failure rate. Initially, the rate of failure decreases with operating experience as the organization moves down the learning curve for its favoured set of routines. Eventually, however, accumulating experience causes the organization to become less able to adapt and, as the demands of the environment change, more likely to fail. Supporting this prediction, they found that the failure rates of Manhattan hotels first fell and then increased with increases in their own operating experience, measured in terms of accumulated room-operating

years, discounted for possible decay in the value of operating experience over time due to forgetting and antiquation (Argote et al. 1990).

Ingram and Baum (1997b) replicated this finding for US hotel chains, where operating experience was computed as the (discounted) number of hotel-years a hotel chain had accumulated between the time it was founded and the current year. Notably, in neither study did incorporating operating experience in the empirical model alter the pattern of age dependence, suggesting that the liability of newness is due to external endorsement (not internal routinization), and that the liability of ageing is due to obsolescence (not senescence). This suggests that it is organization-environment processes and not intraorganizational phenomena that account for liabilities of newness and obsolescence.

Most studies of organizational learning operationalize organizational experience based on historical operations, corresponding to operating experience. When it involves interactions with competitors, however, experience may also contribute to the external capability of organizations by helping to improve their models of markets and competitive interaction, which contribute critically to effective strategizing and success. Organizations thus face both internal and external strategic demands (Saloner 1994). *Operational* and *competitive* organizational experiences correspond, respectively, to the internal and external differentiation of strategic demands, and together contribute to satisfying all of the strategic and competitive demands faced by an organization. Two recent studies advance measures of organizations' competitive experience to test the idea that organizations become more adept competitors by observing the competitive actions and outcomes of other organizations.

Barnett et al. (1994) consider the average historical number of competitors a retail bank has faced in its past (see also Barnett 1997). They found opposing effects of competitive experience accumulated before and after bank deregulation on Illinois banks' return on assets. Before deregulation, competitive experience was negatively related to the performance of single unit banks; afterward it was positively related to single unit banks' performance. Performance of multi-unit banks was not affected by the average historical number of competitors either before or after deregulation. Barnett et al. (1994) interpret their findings as suggesting that simpler organizational forms are more able and likely to learn from their competitive experience than more complex forms.

Elaborating this approach, Barnett and Hansen (1996) modelled competitive organizational experience as the aggregate number of years that an organization had been exposed to competition from rival organizations. They also differentiate between an organization's recent and distant competitive experience, expecting that recent competitive experience (accumulated within the past 10 years) would be beneficial, while older competitive experience (accumulated more than 10 years earlier) would be detrimental. Moreover, they consider not only an organization's own competitive experience, but also the competitive experience accumulated by its competitors. The latter is a sum of the competitors' exposure to their own rivals (both recent and distant). Again using data on Illinois banks, they find support for their ideas – a bank's recent competitive experience reduced its failure rate, while its distant competitive experience increases it; and, moreover, a bank's competitors' recent competitive experience increased the bank's failure rate while its competitors' distant competitive experience lowered it. Barnett and Hansen view their results as supporting the existence of a 'Red Queen' effect in which competing organizations search for ways to improve their performance, increasing their competitive strength, triggering a further cycle of learning (and so on), and, as a result, success and survival become increasingly difficult.

Recent ecological studies of organizational learning have advanced our understanding of the role of experiential processes in organizational adaptation and selection. Experiential learning is a double-edged sword – it can enhance organizational survival chances while at the same time hindering adaptation; it can strengthen competitive abilities while at the same time making competition harder. To shine additional light on the complexities and tradeoffs associated with organizational learning, future research is needed to refine and link typologies of organizational learning – exploration vs exploitation, local vs non-local, recent vs distal, operational vs competitive – and to identify the types of experiences that are most likely to trigger learning.

Between-organization differences in learning also deserve examination. Organizations likely vary in their capacities for experiential learning, and so, while organizations with superior capacities can improve their survival chances, the fates of other weaker learners may be either unaffected (or even harmed) by their efforts to learn. Differences in internal information processing capabilities, for example, may generate learning advantages (Cyert et al. 1993). Incorporating heterogeneity in organizational learning into the approaches outlined here would extend them in an important way.

Ecological Processes

Niche Width Dynamics

Niche width theory (Hannan and Freeman 1977) focuses on two aspects of environmental variability to explain differential survival of *specialists*, which possess few slack resources and concentrate exploiting a narrow range of customers, and *generalists*, which appeal to the mass market and exhibit tolerance for more varied environments. *Variability* refers to environmental fluctuations about the mean over time. *Grain* refers to the patchiness of these fluctuations with frequent variations termed *fine-grained* and periodic termed *coarse-grained*.

Niche width theory builds on the idea that a specialist well designed for a particular environmental condition will always outperform a generalist in that same condition, because the generalist must carry extra capacity that sustains its ability to perform in other environmental conditions. Thus, the specialist 'maximizes its exploitation of the environment and accepts the risk of having that environment change' while the generalist 'accepts a lower level of exploitation in return for greater security' (Hannan and Freeman 1977: 948).

Niche width theory predicts that specialists perform better in stable or certain environments and in fine grained environments. In contrast, when environmental variability is high and coarse grained, specialists have trouble outlasting the long unfavourable periods and the generalist strategy conveys advantage. The key prediction is that, in fine-grained environments with large magnitude variations relative to organizational tolerances, specialists out-compete generalists regardless of environmental uncertainty. Specialists ride out the fluctuations; generalists are unable to respond quickly enough to operate efficiently. Thus, niche-width theory challenges the classical contingency theory prediction that uncertain environments always favour generalists that spread their risk.

In contrast to niche width theory, which predicts that for a given population one optimal strategy exists, Carroll (1985) proposes that, in environments characterized by economies of scale, competition among generalists to occupy the centre of the market where resources are most abundant frees peripheral resources that are most likely to be used by specialists. He refers to the process generating this outcome as *resource partitioning*. His model implies that, in concentrated markets with a few generalists, specialists can exploit more of the available resources without engaging in direct competition with generalists. It also implies that economies of scale and scope may be sufficiently large that they overwhelm any costs of sustaining extra capacity to maintain a broad niche, thus giving advantage to generalists. Based on these ideas, resource partitioning theory yields the novel prediction that increasing market concentration increases the failure rate of generalists operating in the centre of the market and lowers the failure rate of specialists operating at its periphery.

Resource-partitioning theory has been supported in studies of newspapers (Carroll 1985; 1987; Dobrev 2000; Boone et al. 2002), American breweries and microbreweries (Carroll and Swaminathan 1992; 2000), Rural Cooperative Banks in Italy (Freeman and Lomi 1994), US farm wineries (Swaminathan 1995), Dutch auditing firms (Boone et al. 2000), US feature film producers and distributors (Mezias and Mezias 2000) and US and European automobile producers (Dobrev et al. 2001; 2002). Each of these studies provides at least partial support for the theory. For example, in a study of founding rates of specialist farm wineries over a 50-year period starting shortly after the end of Prohibition, Swaminathan (1995) found that farm winery foundings were lower in states with more generalist mass-production wineries, suggesting localized competition between these two organizational forms. Consistent with resource partitioning theory, however, increasing concentration of mass-producers increased the farm winery founding rate.

Although the specialist-generalist distinction is common in ecological research, tests of niche-width theory's predictions are scarce, and studies of resource-partitioning theory do not typically explicitly contrast niche-width and resource-partitioning predictions. Yet, a tension exists between these two theories of niche width dynamics. They define specialism and generalism differently and make different claims regarding the tradeoff between organizational fitness and niche width. The theories also focus on different kinds of niches (Carroll et al. 2002). Niche width theory emphasizes *fundamental niches*, that is, the set of environments in which an organization can survive in the absence of competition from other entities. Resource partitioning theory's focus is on an organization's resource location relative to other organizations. As such, it emphasizes *realized niches* – the subset of the fundamental niche in which an organization can survive in the presence of competitors. This difference is important because the absence of overlap between realized niches takes on a very different meaning depending on whether or not the underlying fundamental niches overlap.

Given these differences, it is an open question whether the two theories differ fundamentally or whether they can be integrated into a unified theory. However, the recent flurry of theoretical efforts (Hannan et al. 2003a; b), empirical work on resource partitioning (for a review, see Carroll et al. 2002) and initial efforts to link the two theories (Dobrev et al. 2001) provide a foundation for a potential integration that would see niche width theory's emphasis on environmental dynamics joined with resource partitioning's emphasis on scale advantages.

Population Dynamics and Density Dependence

Research on founding and failure in organizational ecology has paid considerable attention to population-level processes of *population dynamics*, the number of prior foundings and failures in a population, and *population density*, the number of organizations in a population. Although related, these perspectives are not identical – population dynamics focuses on how current founding and failure rates are more related to *changes* in density, while density dependence focuses on levels of density itself (Tucker et al. 1988).

Density-dependent explanations for founding and failure are broadly similar, though not identical. Initial increases in population density can increase the institutional legitimacy of a population. The capacity of a population's members to acquire resources increases greatly when those controlling resources take the organizational form for granted.

However, as a population continues to grow, the nature of interdependence among a population's members becomes competitive. When there are few organizations in a population, competition with others for scarce common resources can easily be avoided. However, as the number of potential competitors grows, avoidance becomes more difficult. Combined, the mutualistic effects of initial increases in density and the competitive effects of further increases suggest curvilinear effects of density on founding and failure rates in organizational populations (Hannan and Freeman 1989; Hannan and Carroll 1992).

Hannan and Freeman (1989), Hannan and Carroll (1992) and others provide substantial empirical support for the curvilinear relationships predicted by the density dependence model in a variety of organizational populations. By comparison, although often significant, population dynamics findings are mixed (for reviews, see Singh and Lumsden 1990; Aldrich and Wiedenmayer 1993). Moreover, as illustrated in Table 1.2.5, when population dynamics and population density are modelled together, with few exceptions (e.g. Tucker et al. 1988; Delacroix et al. 1989), recent studies find population dynamics effects are generally weaker and less robust (for a review of earlier work, see Singh and Lumsden 1990). Even Delacroix and Carroll's (1983) original Argentina and Ireland newspaper population findings do not hold up when density is introduced in a re-analysis of their data (Carroll and Hannan 1989b).

There are several possible explanations for the apparent dominance of density dependence processes over population dynamics processes. One is the more systematic character of density relative to the transitory nature of changes in density that result from ongoing foundings and failures. A related explanation is that the effects of foundings and failures on resource availability are more transitory than the yearly data that is typically available are able to detect. For example, if foundings and failures keep pace with each other *during* a year, density will remain stable, but population dynamics will vary throughout the year (Aldrich and Wiedenmayer 1993). A third explanation is the much greater sensitivity of estimates for quadratic specifications of prior foundings and failures to outliers. This is especially true for prior foundings, which are usually Poisson distributed (Hannan and Freeman 1989). These issues need to be researched more thoroughly before population dynamics

effects are abandoned, which has been the trend in recent research (e.g. Baum and Mezias 1992; Rao and Neilsen 1992; Amburgey et al. 1993).

Elaborations of the Density Dependence Model

Although support for density dependence theory is quite strong, it has not been without its critics. Density dependence theory has received some critical attention for its proposed integration of ecological and institutional perspectives (e.g. Zucker 1989; Delacroix and Rao 1994; Baum and Powell 1995). Some authors have questioned the implicit assumption that each organization in a population influences and is influenced by competition equally (e.g. Singh and Lumsden 1990; Winter 1990; Baum and Mezias 1992). In a methodological critique, Petersen and Koput (1991) argue that the negative effect of initial increases in population density on the failure rate may result from unobserved heterogeneity in the population (for a reply on this point, see Hannan et al. 1991). Singh (1993) observes that some of the debate about density dependence stems from the model's main strength, its generality, which has been achieved at the expense of precision of measurement and realism of context. Singh (1993: 471) concludes that 'we have ample general supportive evidence for density dependence, we may do well to sacrifice some generality, provided it moves the research toward greater precision and realism'. Density effects are clear empirically, but the specific conditions that generate legitimacy and competition are more ambiguous – defined by outcomes rather than by substance. Thus, the precise interpretation of the extensive density dependence findings needs to be explored further.

Elaborations, respecifications and new measures have been advanced to address questions raised by the initial density dependence formulation. Although Hannan and Carroll (1992: 38–9, 71–4) have questioned some of these developments, they appear to hold real promise for improving the precision and realism of the density dependence model with respect to both legitimation and competition. Additionally, the focus of several approaches on organization-level differences within populations may provide a bridge between organizational ecologists and researchers who focus primarily on the organizational level of analysis. These developments, summarized in Table 1.2.6, are reviewed below.

Table 1.2.5   Population dynamics and density dependence studies, 1986–2003*

Population	Found	Fail	Density	Event	References
US Labor Unions, 1836–1985	+/-	na	+/-	Founding	Hannan (1986); Hannan and Freeman (1989);
	na	0	-/+	Failure	Carroll and Hannan (1989a, b); Carroll and Swaminathan (1991); Hannan and Carroll (1992)
US Brewers, 1633–1988	+/-	0	+/-	Founding	
	+	-	-/+	Failure	
San Francisco Newspapers, 1800–1975	0/0	-/+	+/-	Founding	
	0/0	+/-	-/+	Failure	
Argentina Newspapers, 1800–1900	-/+	0/-	+/-	Founding	
	0/0	+/0	-/+	Failure	
Ireland Newspapers, 1800–1975	+/-	0/0	+/-	Founding	
	0/0	+/-	-/+	Failure	
Little Rock Newspapers, 1815–1975	0/0	0/+	+/-	Founding	
	+/-	0/0	0/0	Failure	
Springfield Newspapers, 1835–1975	0/+	0/+	+/-	Founding	
	0/0	0/0	0/+	Failure	
Shreveport Newspapers, 1840–1975	0/0	0/0	+/-	Founding	
	0/0	0/0	0/0	Failure	
Elmira Newspapers, 1815–1975	+/0	0/0	+/0	Founding	
	+/0	0/0	0/0	Failure	
Lubbock Newspapers, 1890–1975	0/0	0	0/0	Founding	
	0/0	0	0/-	Failure	
Lafayette Newspapers, 1835–1975	na	0	0/0	Founding	
	0/0	0	0/0	Failure	
California Wineries, 1940–1985	-	-	0/0	Failure	Delacroix et al. (1989)
Pennsylvania Telephone Cos., 1879–1934	+	-	-/+	Founding	Barnett and Amburgey (1990)
	-/+	+/	-/+	Failure	
US semiconductor firms	+	0	+/-	Founding	Freeman (1990)
	0	-	-/+	Failure	
Metro Toronto Day Care Centres, 1971–1989	+/-	na	+/-	Founding	Baum and Oliver (1992)
	+/0	-	-/+	Failure	
US State Life Insurance Cos., 1759–1937	+/-	na	+/-	Founding	Ranger-Moore et al. (1991)
Manhattan Banks, 1840–1976	+/0	na	+/-	Founding	Banaszak-Holl (1992; 1993)
NY State Life Insurance Cos., 1842–1904	-	-	0/+	Founding	Budros (1993; 1994)
German Breweries, 1861–1988	-/0	na	+/-	Founding	Carroll et al. (1993)
US Trade Associations, 1901–1990	0/0	0/0	+/-	Founding	Aldrich et al. (1994)
	+	-	-/+	Failure	

(Continued)

Table 1.2.5 *(Continued)*

Population	Found	Fail	Density	Event	References
US Medical Equipment Manufacturers, 1950–1990	+	na	–/+	Failure	Mitchell (1994)
Manhattan Fax Transmission Cos., 1965–1992	–/+	0	+/–	Founding	Baum et al. (1995)
Pre-dominant design cohort	–	–	+/0	Failure	
Post dominant design cohort	–/+	0	+/–	Founding	
	0	0	–/+	Failure	West (1995)
All US Immigrant Newspapers, 1877–1914	0	–	+/–	Founding	
Polish US Immigrant Newspapers, 1877–1914	–	–	+/+	Founding	
Swedish US Immigrant Newspapers, 1877–1914	0	0	+/–	Founding	
Italian US Immigrant Newspapers, 1877–1914	–	0	+/–	Founding	
Belgian Automobile Manufacturers, 1885–1981	+/0	na	+/–	Founding	Hannan et al. (1995);
British Automobile Manufacturers, 1885–1981	+/0	na	+/–	Founding	Dobrev et al. (2001)
	0	na	–/0	Failure	
French Automobile Manufacturers, 1885–1981	+/0	na	+/–	Founding	
	0	na	–/+	Failure	
German Automobile Manufacturers, 1885–1981	0/0	na	+/–	Founding	
	0	na	0/+	Failure	
Italian Automobile Manufacturers, 1885–1981	+/0	na	+/–	Founding	Ingram and Inman (1996)
Niagara Falls Hotels, 1885–1991	na	0/0	–/+	Failure	
Massachusetts Railroads, 1826–1922	+	0	+/–	Founding	Dobbin and Dowd (1997)
Finnish Newspapers, 1771–1963	+	na	+/–	Founding	Dacin (1997)
New York State Life Insurance Companies, 1813–1985	+	na	0/0	Failure	Ranger-Moore (1997)
US Breweries, 1845–1918	+	–	0/–	Founding	Wade et al. (1998)
	+	–	–/+	Failure	
Dutch Accounting Firms, 1880–1990	0	+	0	Failure	Pennings et al. (1998)
Egyptian Investment Firms, 1974–1989	+/0	0	0	Founding	Messalam (1998)
US Computer Manufacturers, 1975–1992	–	na	0	Failure	Henderson (1999)
New York City Credit Unions, 1914–1990	0	na	0/+	Failure	Barron (1999)
US Specialist Feature Film Producers, 1912–1929	+/–	na	–/+	Founding	Mezias and Mezias (2000)
US Specialist Feature Film Distributors, 1912–1929	0	na	–/+	Founding	
US Wineries, 1941–1990	+	na	–/+	Failure	Swaminathan (2001)
Bulgarian Newspapers, 1846–1992	+/–	na	+/–	Founding	Dobrev (2001)
Illinois Banks, 1900–1993	–	+	+/–	Founding	Barnett and Sorenson (2002)

* Includes only analyses that estimate both population dynamics and density dependence effects; many additional studies estimate density dependence effects alone. X/Y gives the signs of significant ($p < 0.05$) linear and squared terms, respectively.

Table 1.2.6 Elaborations of the density dependence model, 1989–2003

Model	Key variables	Nature of elaboration	References
Institutional processes			
Density delay	Population density at founding	Adds an imprinting effect of density at founding to the original formulation. Helps explain the commonly observed decline in population density in older populations	Carroll and Hannan (1989a); Hannan and Carroll (1992)
Institutional embeddedness	Relational density (number of linkages between a population and the institutional environment)	Attempts to explain the legitimation of an organizational form in terms of endorsements by powerful actors and organizations	Baum and Oliver (1992); Hybels et al. (1994)
Non-density-based measures of legitimacy	Certification contests and media-based content measures	Models legitimation effects with non-density-based measures of institutionalization	Rao (1994); Hybels (1994); Lamertz and Baum (1998); Deeds et al. (2004)
Competitive processes			
Level of analysis	City density; state density; regional density; national density (population density at various levels of geographic aggregation)	Attempts to uncover the appropriate level of analysis to study density-dependent processes by comparing patterns of density dependence across multiple levels of analysis	Carroll and Wade (1991); Swaminathan and Wiedenmayer (1991); Hannan et al. (1995)
Localized competition	Size similarity; price similarity; location similarity (population density weighted by the size of differences in various organizational features)	Re-specifies competition effect of population density by allowing more similar organizations to compete at a greater level of intensely	Hannan et al. (1990); Baum and Mezias (1992); Ranger-Moore et al. (1995); Baum and Haveman (1997)
Organizational niche overlap	Overlap density; non-overlap density (population density weighted by (non)overlap in resource needs of organizations)	Re-specifies population density by disaggregating it into competitive and mutualistic components using information on the overlap and non-overlap of resource requirement of population members	Baum and Singh (1994b, c); Baum and Oliver (1996)
Accounting for concentration			
Mass dependence	Population mass (population density weighted by organizational size)	Re-specifies competition effect of population density by allowing larger organizations to generate stronger competition. Helps explain the tendency toward concentration in organizational populations	Barnett and Amburgey (1990)

(Continued)

Table 1.2.6 *(Continued)*

Model	Key variables	Nature of elaboration	References
Changing basis of competition	Population age × population density[2], population mass, size similarity and concentration	As the basis of competition in a population evolves from r-selection to K-selection to differentiation, the strength of density-dependent competition declines, and the strength of mass-dependent, size-localized and concentration-based competition increase	Baum (1995)
Competitive intensity	Organizational age × size; average historical density	Organizations exposed to greater competition over their lifetimes generate the strongest competition	Barnett et al. (1994); Barnett (1997)
Coupled clocks	Population age × population density and density[2]	As a population matures, its density becomes decoupled from legitimacy and competition	Hannan (1997); Hannan et al. (1998a, b); Dobrev et al. (2001)
Dynamic selection	Mean of the log size distribution; organizational size × population density	As a population's density approaches its carrying capacity, large organizations are better able to face the more intense competition, increasing their survival chances. The founding rate declines as a population's size distribution shifts right and incumbents establish reputations, customer loyalties and staff expertise	Barron (1999)
Scale-based selection	Aggregate distance of an organization to all larger organizations in the population	An organization's competitive (dis) advantage is a function of its position in the size distribution of its population	Dobrev and Carroll (2003)

Density and Institutional Processes

Drawing on the neo-institutional literature (Meyer and Rowan 1977; Zucker 1977; DiMaggio and Powell 1983), organizational ecologists draw a distinction between cognitive and sociopolitical legitimacy (Aldrich and Fiol 1994). Zucker (1977) treats institutionalization as a process, emphasizing that legitimacy is a cognitive phenomenon reflected in taken-for-granted assumptions. Meyer and Rowan (1977) and DiMaggio and Powell (1983) stress that legitimacy is embedded in relational networks and normative codes of conduct. Thus, they viewed institutionalization as both a sociopolitical process through which certain organizational forms come to be regarded as obligatory, and as a state in which organizational forms are butressed by legal mandate or by widely shared cultural, professional and political norms and values. From a cognitive legitimacy perspective, an organizational form is legitimated 'when there is little question in the minds of actors that it serves as the natural way to effect some kind of collective action' (Hannan and Carroll 1992: 34).

The sociopolitical approach emphasizes how embeddedness in relational and normative contexts influences an organizational form's legitimacy by signalling its conformity to social and institutional expectations. Although institutionalists view these two facets of legitimation as complementary and fundamentally interrelated, density dependence theory emphasizes *only* cognitive legitimacy. Although cognitive legitimacy may be achieved without sociopolitical approval, sociopolitical legitimacy is considered a vital source of, or impediment to, cognitive legitimacy. Indeed, since contemporary organizational populations rarely operate in isolation from the state, the professions and broader societal influences sociopolitical legitimacy cannot be ignored (Baum and Oliver 1992; Baum and Powell 1995).

Hannan and colleagues defend their exclusive focus on population density with a series of interrelated arguments. The first claim is that legitimacy defies measurement. '[R]econstructing the exact details of changing levels of legitimation ... over the history of any one population demands attention to all of the unique features of that population' (Hannan and Carroll 1992: 37). Indeed, '[a] direct measure of legitimation as we define it requires learning what fraction of relevant individuals take a particular organizational form for granted' (Hannan and Carroll 1992: 38–9), thus severely limiting the historical scope of analysis. This assertion leads them to argue '... that theories of legitimation and competition can be studied systematically and comparatively *only* by testing their implications for the relationships between other observables' (Hannan and Carroll 1992: 39). Consequently, it makes sense to study variables that can be easily observed and compared across populations and over long periods of time, such as density and vital rates. This indirect measurement approach has generated criticism because conforming findings cannot be interpreted precisely; density coefficients reveal little about the theoretical explanations designed to account for them (Singh 1993).

Critics question the legitimacy interpretation of density effects, suggesting that legitimation is invoked ex-post and that density estimates are proxies for a wide range of other possible effects. In her provocative commentary, Zucker (1989) takes Hannan and colleagues to task for invoking the concept of legitimation ex-post to explain the effects of density on founding and failure rates, and suggests that density estimates are proxies for other effects (see also Petersen and Koput 1991; Miner 1993). She advocates the use of more direct and precise measures of the underlying institutional processes. Building on Zucker's critique, Baum and Powell (1995) argue that the point is not that legitimacy must be measured *directly*, but rather that it should be gauged using *different observables* from organizational density. Of course, there are sound methodological reasons for multiple measures. In their essay, Delacroix and Rao (1994) provide a more general critique that suggests that the density-dependence conception of legitimation bundles together at least three kinds of externalities – reputational, vicarious learning, and infrastructural – only one of which is related to legitimation.

These critiques appear to have led to the density-as-process argument, in which legitimation is no longer a variable to be measured, but a process that relates density to founding and failure. Thus, Hannan and Carroll (1992: 69) make the strong claim that 'growth in density *controls* ... [legitimation] processes – it does not reflect them'. These competing proxy and process views suggest different effects of adding covariates. According to Hannan and Carroll (1992: 70–1), if density is an indirect indicator, measuring legitimation more directly and precisely would dampen the first-order effects of density or lead them to disappear altogether. However, from the density-as-process view, the inclusion of such covariates implies a sharpening and strengthening of density's legitimation effects.

Institutional Embeddedness and Sociopolitical Legitimacy

Baum and Oliver (1992) address exactly this question (see also Singh 1993: 471). They argue that an important limitation of the density dependence model is that it focuses exclusively on cognitive legitimacy and interdependencies among organizations within populations and neglects the evolution of a population's interdependencies with surrounding organizations and institutions. However, where relations with community and government are dense, these institutional actors may exert considerable influence over the conditions that regulate competition for scarce resources and legitimacy in the population. Baum and Oliver (1992) propose an alternative hypothesis in which legitimation is explained in terms of the institutional embeddedness of a population in its institutional environment influences the population's sociopolitical legitimacy by signalling its conformity to social and institutional expectations (Meyer and Rowan 1977; Aldrich and Fiol 1994). Institutional embeddedness refers to interconnections between a population and its institutional environment (DiMaggio and Powell 1983; Fombrun 1986; 1988).

According to institutional theory, conformity to the norms and social expectations of the institutional environment improves an organization's survival chances significantly (Meyer and Rowan 1977; Scott and Meyer 1983; Oliver 1991). When organizations establish ties to reputable societal institutions, they typically obtain benefits that contribute to their likelihood of survival. These benefits include greater legitimacy and status (Scott and Meyer 1983; Singh et al. 1986b; Baum and Oliver 1991), and enhanced resource access and predictability (Pfeffer and Salancik 1978; Aldrich and Auster 1986; Miner et al. 1990). Thus, the endorsement of an organization's practices by a community or state agency increases the organization's legitimacy and enhances the organization's ability to attract clients and resources (Wiewel and Hunter 1985).

Organizational population growth is typically accompanied by increasing institutional embeddedness (DiMaggio and Powell 1983; Zucker 1989). As a population grows and its social or public impact becomes more widely recognized, community advocacy groups, government agencies, professional associations and other social actors take an increasingly active role in monitoring population members' activities, distributing endorsements and rewards and shaping the rules and standards about what are legitimate activities and outputs for the population. Institutional theorists predict that this increasing interconnectedness between a population and its institutional environment enhances the growth and survival of the population over time (Scott and Meyer 1983). For example, Meyer and Rowan (1977: 352) suggest that 'the long-run survival prospects of organizations increase as state structures elaborate and as organizations respond to institutionalized rules … schools, hospitals and welfare organizations show considerable ability to survive, precisely because they are … almost absorbed by their institutional environments'.

Baum and Oliver model institutional embeddedness with *relational density*, defined as the number of formal relations between the members of a population and key institutions in the population's environment. Key institutions refer to government agencies and community organizations in a population's environment. Although initial estimates in their study of Metropolitan Toronto day care centres support the curvilinear density dependence predictions for both founding and failure rates, legitimation effects of initial increases in organizational density disappear after inclusion of relational density and the relationship between density and founding and failure rates became purely competitive. Relational density, in contrast, exhibited either predicted curvilinear effects or purely mutualistic effects.

Baum and Oliver thus test the proxy-vs-process prediction, and their results support the proxy view. However, as Baum and Oliver (1992: 556) point out, their results also support ecological explanations of the underlying institutional processes. Since organizational populations rarely operate in isolation from state and community institutions, future research incorporating both population and relational densities may provide further clarification of the role of institutional processes in population dynamics. Baum and Oliver's findings were replicated in Hybels et al.'s (1994) study of founding of US biotechnology firms in which vertical (input and output) strategic alliances are used to measure industry embeddedness in relational and institutional contexts. These studies suggest that the initial density-as-proxy formulation of legitimacy was more accurate and, in addition, that organizational density may be a proxy for relational as well as (or instead of) cognitive legitimacy.

Non-Density-Based Measures of Legitimacy

Density dependence theory's exclusive emphasis on one facet of legitimation misses its multidimensional nature (Baum and Powell 1995). Researchers have, however, begun to measure other aspects of legitimation and examine how diverse social processes combine with organizational density to contribute to the legitimacy of organizational forms, and several promising non-density-based alternatives to studying legitimation have recently been examined.

In many industries, special purpose organizations institute certification contests to evaluate products or firms and rank-order participants according to their performance on preset criteria. Certification contests offer a common social test of products and organizations that serve as a social diffusion mechanism. Rao (1994) argues that cumulative victories in such certification contests enhance organizational reputations in the eyes of risk-averse consumers and financiers, improving their access to resources and their survival chances. Moreover, Rao argues that, by increasing opportunities for certification and diffusing knowledge about organizations and their products, these contests establish the identity and legitimacy of a product and its producers, lowering the risk of producer failure. His analysis of the early American automobile industry supports these ideas, demonstrating that winning heavily publicized road races improved the survival chances of individual automobile manufacturers and, in addition, that the cumulative prevalence of contests lowers the aggregate failure rate. In addition to certification contests, a wide range of accreditation, certification and credentialing activities signal reliability, raising the sociopolitical legitimacy of organizational forms, as well as contributing to their cognitive legitimacy by spreading knowledge about them (Baum and Powell 1995).

Another basic source of information diffusion about the activities of an organizational form are the print media. Detailed archives of media coverage exist for many industries and content analyses of these public records offer a potentially powerful technique for operationalizing legitimation. Measurement of this kind is used widely in social movement research (e.g. Olzak 1992; Tilly 1993). Content-based measures promise high comparability across settings covered by the business press as well as temporal comparability within a given context. Hybels (1994) successfully employed media-based measures of legitimacy in an analysis of US biotechnology firm foundings, as have Pollock and Rindova (2003) and Deeds et al. (2004) in studies of US biotechnology firm initial public offerings. In a related study, Lamertz and Baum (1998) used media accounts to track the legitimation of management downsizing in Canada.

Density and Competitive Processes

Density dependence theory assumes that the intensity of competition depends on the number of organizations in a population. Some researchers, however, question the assumption implicit in this approach that all members of a population are equivalent, with each member assumed to compete for the same scarce resources and to contribute to and experience competition equally (e.g. Winter 1990: 286). Although research demonstrates that this assumption may be a reasonable starting approximation, theory in organizational ecology suggests that the intensity of competition between organizations in a population is largely a function of their similarity in resource requirements: the more similar the resource requirements, the greater the potential for intense competition (e.g. Hannan and Freeman 1977; 1989; McPherson 1983).[1] If all organizations in a population are not equal competitors, then population density may not provide the most precise measure of the competition faced by different organizations in a population.

Building on this logic, three elaborations of the density dependence model – localized competition, levels of analysis and organizational niche overlap – that incorporate organizational differences explicitly to specify competitive processes within organizational populations more precisely have been advanced. Each of these refinements to the original model enriches the ecological approach to competition by integrating ideas on population microstructures into density dependence research.

Localized Competition

Following a long tradition in organizational sociology, Hannan and Freeman (1977: 945–6) propose that organizations of different sizes use different strategies and structures. And, as a result, they propose that, although organizations of different sizes are engaged in similar activities, large and small-sized organizations depend on different mixes of resources. This implies that organizations compete most intensely with similarly-sized organizations. For example, if large and small organizations depend on different resources (e.g. large hotels depend on conventions while small hotels depend on individual travellers), then patterns of resource use will be specialized to segments of the size distribution. Consequently, competition between large and small organizations will be less intense than competition among large or small organizations. Large organizations may, however, pose a threat to medium-sized organizations. Whatever strategy medium-sized organizations adopt to compete with large organizations will make them more vulnerable to competition from small organizations and vice versa. Therefore, the emergence of large organizations should be accompanied by a decline in the number of medium-sized organizations, while small ones flourish as their most intense competitors are removed from the environment. Thus, size-localized competition may also play a role in the consolidation of organizational populations over time.

Although size-localized competition did not receive empirical attention initially (Hannan et al. 1990), studies of Manhattan banks (Banaszak-Holl 1992), Manhattan hotels (Baum and Mezias 1992), US health maintenance organizations (Wholey et al. 1992) and Niagara Falls hotels (Ingram and Inman 1996) now provide empirical evidence of that size-localized competition raises organizational failure rates. Ranger-Moore et al. (1995) have also demonstrated that size-localized competition dampens organizational growth rates in the New York State life insurance industry. These findings demonstrate that the intensity of competition faced by organizations in a population depends not only on the number (i.e. density) of other organizations in the population, but on their relative sizes as well. Baum and Mezias (1992) generalize the size-localized model to other organizational dimensions and show that, in addition to similar-sized organizations, competition within a population can be more intense for organizations that are geographically proximate and charge similar prices, lowering their survival prospects. Baum and Haveman (1997) showed that localized competitive processes also shape key entrepreneurial decisions at the time of founding, namely how near new organizations should locate in product and geographic space to other firms in their industry.

Future research on localized competition can offer direct insights into the dynamics of organizational diversity. Localized competition models imply a pattern of disruptive or segregating selection (Baum 1990b; 2006; Amburgey et al. 1994; Baum and Haveman 1997) in which competition between like entities for finite resources leads eventually to differentiation (see also, Durkheim 1933; Hawley 1950: 201–3). This mode of selection, which has not been emphasized in the ecological literature, tends to increase organizational differentiation by producing gaps rather than smooth, continuous variation in the distribution of the members of a population along some organizational dimension.

Level of Analysis

Recurrent patterns of organizational concentration in space across different industries and national contexts suggests that location may be a general factor shaping the evolution of organizational populations. If forces exist that give advantages to organizations located near other organizations or in specific geographical areas, then the internal structure of organizational populations cannot be considered homogeneous and organizational birth and death rates will vary systematically across locations. It is essential, therefore, to select the appropriate level of analysis to examine the dynamics of populations, since different levels of spatial aggregation imply different assumptions about how general processes of legitimation and competition unfold.

Although density dependence theory assumes implicitly that geographically distant members of an organizational population compete with each other at intensity equal to neighbouring organizations, several studies have refined this assumption by disaggregating population density according to geographic proximity to explore the geographic boundaries on competitive (and institutional) processes. For example, Hannan and Carroll (1992), Carroll and Wade (1991) and Swaminathan and Wiedenmayer (1991) analysed density dependence in founding and failure rates of US and German Breweries at a variety of level of geographic aggregation (e.g. city, state, nation). These studies estimated the density dependence model separately for each level of analysis and then compared coefficients across levels. In their analysis of the US brewing industry, Carroll and Wade (1991) found support for density dependence at the state and regional levels but not city level, while Hannan and Carroll (1992) found that founding rates of newspaper organizations depend on density in a manner consistent with theory only in small metropolitan areas. Although these studies vary in their support for the density dependence model, estimates consistently reveal stronger competitive effects among breweries for populations defined at more local geographic levels than for national populations as a whole, while local and national legitimation effects were similar in magnitude.

Taken together, these studies, along with other research examining effects of geographic levels (e.g. Rao and Neilsen 1992; Budros 1993; 1994; Baum and Singh 1994b, c; Lomi 1995; Cattani et al. 2003) robustly support Zucker's (1989: 543) speculation that 'smaller geographic areas should theoretically involve more intense competition since they are more tightly bounded resource areas'. Competitive processes in organizational populations may thus often be heterogeneous, operating most strongly in local competitive arenas, and therefore may generally be modelled more precisely specified at a local geographic level. And, it seems likely that the greater the geographic segmentation of a population's environment, the more geographically localized competitive processes in the population will be (Carroll and Huo 1986).

Geographic segmentation of organizational environments occurs for a variety of reasons. Institutional and political constraints may limit the geographic scope of organizational activities, leading to distinct geographic markets in which organizations can compete for resources (Hannan et al. 1995). The nature of a population's activities can also affect where potential consumers come from when, for example, organizations provide services on their premises (e.g. nursing homes, banks); when transportation costs are high (e.g. brewers, automobile manufacturers); when products are made for specific locales (e.g. newspapers); or when

the demand for organizations' products or services is depends on location (e.g. hotels). Among recent studies the level of analysis at which competition is most intense appears to vary directly with the degree of geographic segmentation: among Manhattan hotels competition is most intense within a few city blocks segmented by proximity to particular business and tourist activities (Baum and Mezias 1992; Baum and Haveman 1997), among bank branches within city wards (Greve 2002), among newspapers within metropolitan areas (Hannan and Carroll 1992), among Dutch auditing firms within province (Catttani et al. 2003), and among European automobile producers within countries segmented by political boundaries (Hannan et al. 1995).

Level of analysis issues are also relevant to institutional processes. Singh (1993: 467–8) speculates that, while a local level of analysis may often be more appropriate for analysing competition, it may not be so for legitimation processes, which are likely to require much broader boundaries. Hannan et al. (1995) estimated models of organizational founding in the European automobile industry in which density-dependent legitimation and competition were measured at *different* levels of analysis. Supporting Singh's (1993) speculation, they found stronger density-dependent competition at the country level, and some evidence (support for two of five countries) of stronger density-dependent legitimation at the European level. Thus, Hannan et al.'s (1995) findings provide some support for the idea that, in contrast to competitive processes, institutional processes in organizational populations operate relatively homogeneously, and at a broad geographic level serving to contextualize competitive processes (Scott 1992; Tucker et al. 1992; but see Lomi 2000; Cattani et al. 2003). This conclusion is less well established, however, and may depend on the type of institutional process.

Organizational Niche Overlap

Baum and Singh (1994b, c) advance and test a resource overlap model in which the potential for competition between any two organizations is directly proportional to the overlap of their targeted resource bases, or *organizational niches*. Following McPherson (1983), Baum and Singh conceive each member of a population as occupying a potentially unique organizational niche that delineates its location in a multidimensional resource space. The organizational niche, which is defined by the intersection of resource requirements and productive capabilities at the organization level, depends on where the organization is located and what it does (e.g. the clients it has the capacity to target, how it responds to the environment). The organizational niche is a result, not a cause, of organizational adaptation – it is 'carved out'. Thus, the organizational niche is a dynamic concept. Depending on the particular organizational niches they target, organizations encounter different competitive landscapes. Attending to the internal structure of population niches, and in particular the resource overlaps of multiple organizational niches comprising a population, provides a simple way to isolate competitive and non-competitive forces within a population.

Baum and Singh view the potential for competition between organizations in any two organizational niches as directly proportional to the extent of the overlap in their resource requirements. Potential competition for each organization is measured using *overlap density*, the aggregate overlap of an organization's resource requirements with those of all others in the population (i.e. population density weighted by the overlap in resource requirements). Overlap density has a complementary property, *non-overlap density*. Whereas overlap density captures the potential for competition by aggregating resource overlaps, non-overlap density aggregates the resource non-overlaps. Non-overlap density estimates the number of organizations whose resource requirements do not overlap with those of the focal organization. Together, overlap and non-overlap densities disaggregate competitive and non-competitive forces for each organization in a population with respect to the underlying resources.

Entrepreneurs are predicted to be unlikely to target or to be capable of founding organizations in parts of the resource space where overlap density is high. Organizations operating in high overlap density conditions are also predicted to be less sustainable. Conversely, entrepreneurs are predicted to be likely to target and be capable of founding organizations in parts of the resource space where non-overlap density is high because of the absence of direct competition for resources and the potential for complementary demand enhancement. For these reasons, high non-overlap density is also expected to lower failure rates.

Baum and Singh (1994a, b) found support for these predictions in a population of day care centres

in Metropolitan Toronto for which resource requirements were defined in terms of the ages of the children they had the capacity to enrol. These studies indicate that organizations have different likelihoods of being established and endure different survival fates after founding as a function of the locations they target in a multidimensional resource space. If generalized to other populations, the disaggregation of population density into overlap and non-overlap densities may help clarify the role of population heterogeneity in interpretations of the non-monotonic density dependence findings (Hannan et al. 1991; Petersen and Koput 1991).

Overlap and non-overlap densities capture the *absolute* presence and absence of resource overlaps but fail to consider the situation in which organizations are competitive and non-competitive at the same time. Baum and Oliver (1996) extended the organizational niche overlap framework to consider the *relative* influence of organizational niche overlap and non-overlap with *non-overlap intensity*, which aggregates the ratio of an organization's niche non-overlap to overlap with other organizations in the population. While low non-overlap intensity suggests competitive effects between organizations because they share common resource needs, recognizing their potential for competition, organizations occupying partially overlapping niches, and thus relatively high non-overlap intensity, may be more inclined to cooperate. Baum and Oliver (1996) found relative as well as absolute effects of overlap and non-overlap densities on organizational founding, and, in particular, that interorganizational cooperation is strengthened when it is combined with an element of competition.

Although measures of organizational niche overlap are now quite common (e.g. Podolny et al. 1996; Dobrev et al. 2001; 2003) and results generally supportive, measures of non-overlap and non-overlap intensity have not been replicated, largely because of the difficulty of obtaining information on the distribution of production in the various niches. Taking on questions about how interorganizational competition and coexistence interact in a multidimensional resource space represents an important direction for future research.

Accounting for Concentration

The growth trajectories of diverse organizational populations appear to follow a common path: The number of organizations grows slowly initially, then increases rapidly to a peak. Once this maximum is reached, there is a decline in the number of population members and increased concentration. In organizational ecology, the density dependence model is used to account for the shape of the growth trajectory to its peak (Hannan and Carroll 1992). Since no organization or small group of organizations is allowed to dominate (each organization in a population is assumed to contribute to and experience competition equally), the density dependence model predicts logistic growth in numbers to an equilibrium level. However, it does not account for the later decline in numbers and increase in concentration (Carroll and Hannan 1989a; Hannan and Carroll 1992). This limitation of the original density-dependence model formulation has received considerable attention with five elaborations specifically advanced to address this particular question.

Density Delay

In the density dependence model it is *contemporaneous* population density – density at particular historical times – that is the focus. Carroll and Hannan (1989a) propose a refinement of the model to include an additional, *delayed* population density effect that helps explain the decline of populations from their peak density. Carroll and Hannan (1989a) suggest that organizations' survival chances are sensitive to population density levels at the time of their founding. Specifically, they argue that organizations founded in high-density conditions experience persistently higher failure rates. High density at founding creates a *liability of resource scarcity* that prevents organizations from moving quickly from organizing to full-scale operation. High density also results in *tight niche packing*, forcing newly founded organizations, which cannot compete head-to-head with established organizations, to use inferior or marginal resources. These founding conditions imprint themselves on organizations, affecting their viability throughout their existence. Carroll and Hannan show that population density at the time of organizational founding is positively related to failure rates in six of the seven populations they analyse (Carroll and Hannan 1989a; Hannan and Carroll 1992). This means that organizations entering populations in high-density conditions have persistently elevated failure rates, contributing to an explanation for the decline in population density

from its peak. This finding has been replicated in several studies (e.g. Carroll et al. 1996; Ingram and Inman 1996), however, several others have failed to do so (e.g. Wholey et al. 1992; Aldrich et al. 1994). Moreover, the *density delay* effect appears to produce an oscillating equilibrium, not a definite, singular downturn (Hannan and Carroll 1992: 183). It also does not permit the competitive strengths of organizations to vary.

Mass Dependence

Barnett and Amburgey (1990) point out that various perspectives in organization and management theory suggest that larger organizations generate stronger competition than their smaller rivals as a result of their superior access to resources, greater market power and economies of scale and scope (e.g. Edwards 1955; Bain 1956; Starbuck 1965; Thompson 1967; Caves and Porter 1977; Pfeffer and Salancik 1978; Aldrich and Auster 1986; Scherer and Ross 1990; Winter 1990). If large organizations generate stronger competition, then ecological models of population dynamics should reflect their greater significance. Barnett and Amburgey (1990) advance an elaboration of the density dependence model that incorporates this possibility. They do this by modelling the effects of *population mass*, the sum of the sizes of all organizations in the population, or, in other words, population density weighted by organizational size. If large organizations generate stronger competition, then, after controlling for population density, increases in population mass should have a competitive effect, slowing the founding rate and increasing the failure rate of smaller organizations.

By permitting the competitive strengths of organizations to vary as a function of their size, the mass dependence model permits larger organizations in a population to dominate by generating stronger competition than smaller organizations, displacing their population's size in numbers. Mass-dependent competition may thus help account for populations' later declines in number and increases in concentration. Large organizations may therefore play a central role in organizational ecology, not because they are affected individually by selection pressures, but because they have a disproportionate influence on population dynamics (Barnett and Amburgey 1990). Unfortunately, mass dependence findings are mixed. Some studies find the predicted competitive effects (e.g. Banaszak-Holl 1992; 1993; Baum and

Mezias 1992). Others find either no or mixed effects (e.g. Hannan and Carroll 1992) or mutualistic effects (e.g. Barnett and Amburgey 1990).

Although contradictory findings appear to be attributable to data limitations (Hannan and Carroll 1992: 130–1) or significant features of the study population (Barnett and Amburgey 1990: 98–9), a more general explanation may be that the ability of organizations to differentiate themselves from one another varies from population to population (Baum and House 1990). When a population's members do not possess the capacity for differentiation, the competitive strength of larger organizations is felt throughout the population, causing the population to become increasingly concentrated. However, when meaningful differentiation is possible, population density may remain relatively high as differentiated specialists that do not compete directly either with each other or the large organizations in the population flourish (e.g. Carroll 1985). A related explanation may be found in strategic groups theory (e.g. Caves and Porter 1977), which suggests that industry-wide inferences of market power cannot be made when strategic groups characterize competition, since mobility barriers differentially protect strategic groups. Future research examining the effects of organizational differentiation and mobility barriers on competitive dynamics may therefore improve our understanding of concentration processes in organizational populations.

Competitive Intensity

Barnett (1997: 135) suggests that mixed evidence for mass-dependence results from a 'failure to think about organizational size in an evolutionary way'. His interpretation is that, while large organizations may be less likely to fail, as much evidence shows (see Table 1.2.2), this does not necessarily mean that they are stronger competitors. If they are not, then increasing mass does not necessarily increase the intensity of competition experienced by the members of the population. Barnett's (1997) argument is that the 'fitness' of large organizations is equal to the average of the fitness of their subunits. Since, protected by their membership in a large organization, subunits with low fitness will be less likely to fail than their independent counterparts, the average fitness of large organizations will tend to be lower than that of small organizations. Consequently, smaller, not larger, organizations will provide the stiffest competition.

Barnett (1997: 139) operationalizes the relative weakness of large organizations by 'allowing each organization's competitive intensity to develop over time depending on its size'. This implies an interaction between an organization's size and its age, reducing the competitive strength of a large organization as it grows. To test his idea, Barnett models the effects of the sum of the ages of all organizations in the population (i.e. population age), the sum of the sizes of all organizations in the population (i.e. population mass) and *competitive intensity*, the sum of the age × size interaction for all population members. Since Barnett's model predicts greater competition as organizations become older and as population mass increases, population age and mass should both lower the rate of founding and increase the rate of failure, but since competitive intensity is expected to decline as organizations grow it should be positively related to the rate of founding and negatively related to the failure rate. Barnett finds support for his model in analyses of founding and failure among Pennsylvania telephone companies and US breweries.

Although Barnett's approach to explaining the common concave pattern of population growth is theoretically intriguing and holds promise as an explanation for population concentration, there appears to be little support for the model's basic premise, that older organizations generate stronger competition. Stinchcombe's (1965) liability of newness hypothesis suggests that new organizations have higher failure rates than other organizations, not that older organizations have lower failure rates than younger organizations. Organizational and environmental change can reset the fitness of older organizations, muddling the relationship between age and fitness. Even in the absence of such change, Levinthal's (1991a) finding that previously accumulated capital can account for the liability of newness suggests that the survivability of older organizations may have little to do with their ageing. Mounting empirical evidence that, after controlling for organizational size, organizational failure rates increase with age reinforces this point. The fitness of older organizations may thus have little to do with their age.

Changing Basis of Competition

While Barnett's competitive intensity model focuses on heterogeneous competitive abilities among organizations to explain the concentration of organizational populations, several other approaches emphasize a population-wide shift in the basis of competition.

In the original statement of the density dependence model in organization theory, Brittain and Freeman (1980) described how organizational populations undergo a competitive transition from 'r-selection' to 'K-selection' as increasing population density alters the basis of competition from first-mover advantage to efficiency. The distinction between these two bases of competition is grounded in the Lotka Volterra growth model from bioecology:

$$\frac{dN}{dt} = rN \frac{K-N}{K} \qquad (1)$$

where K is the carrying capacity of the population's environment, r is the natural growth rate of the population, N is population density and t is a time interval. In this equation, when population density is initially low, the natural growth term r dominates and organizations enter at a slow but exponentially increasing rate. As population density increases, the carrying capacity term K becomes dominant and the rate of growth slows. Growth stops when population density equals the carrying capacity.

In an emerging population, no organization or small group of organizations is dominant and new entrants are typically similar in size to established organizations. Competition is dominated by r-selection, which favours small organizations capable of moving quickly to exploit new resource opportunities in the resource-rich but dispersed and uncertain environments that characterize low-density conditions. As the population continues to grow, its markets become connected, demand becomes more predictable and some organizations begin making broad appeals to all customers to expand their market shares. Along with the increased potential for competition that accompanies increasing population size (relative to the abundance of resources), this begins to orient competition among the population's members toward cost and price reduction, favouring larger population members capable of achieving efficiency advantages.

When a population reaches the carrying capacity, the resources available to its members are exploited fully and competitive pressures shift to K-selection, which favours larger organizations competing on the basis of efficiency. The economic and competitive advantages of the population's large members

enable them to out-compete their smaller rivals, which are crowded out by the asymmetric competition. This 'shakeout' decreases the number of organizations in the population, raises the level of market concentration and creates a log-normal or bimodal size distribution in which a few large organizations tend to dominate many smaller ones (Hannan and Freeman 1977; Ijiri and Simon 1977).

Ultimately, however, increasing market concentration forces large organizations to compete increasingly with one another for central markets capable of sustaining their large-scale operations (Carroll 1985). This specializes resource use to particular segments of the size distribution and creates pockets of demand that smaller, more specialized members of the population may be able to exploit without engaging in direct competition with the larger generalists. Thus, resource partitioning localizes the competitive effects of organizations – even large ones – to their particular segments of operations.

Competition at carrying capacity also initiates a more general process of functional and territorial differentiation within the population as competition pushes entrepreneurs to seek out distinct functions in which they hold a competitive advantage (Hawley 1950). This creates organizational sub-groupings that fulfill complementary roles in which they are dependent on, but non-competitive with, each other and lowers the potential for competition by reducing the number of direct competitors each population member confronts.

The foregoing characterization of the evolution of organizational populations suggests that the basis of competition changes over the population life cycle (Baum 1995). And, in particular, that the influence of density-dependent competition weakens over a population's history and that the effects of size-based competitive process (e.g. mass dependence, size-localized competition) become increasingly influential as efficiency-based advantages grow and resource partitioning proceeds. Baum finds evidence of such a shift in the basis of competition over time in the Manhattan hotel industry. Although, to date, no research has attempted to replicate his findings, two related approaches have appeared, supporting similar arguments and model specifications.

Coupled Clocks

Hannan (1997) advanced a related model in which density becomes 'decoupled' from legitimacy and competition as a population matures. Early in a population's history, density has a powerful effect on the legitimacy of an organizational form. However, as the population grows older, density plays a less important role in determining the extent to which an organizational form is viewed as legitimate. The mere fact of a population having been in existence for some time is likely to play a role in its being 'taken-for-granted'. In addition, organizations develop durable network ties with other kinds of actors over time. '… as an organizational population ages, its taken-for-grantedness presumably comes to depend upon its network position' (Hannan et al. 1998b: 305). Therefore, legitimacy is relatively stable and not easily eroded, even if the population density declines.

Competition also becomes decoupled as organizations become more fixed into networks of alliances, develop specializations and so on. In other words, the population becomes more 'structured' as it gets more mature. 'As diverse forms of structure develop, competition can shift from diffuse ecological competition to focused, direct rivalry between organizations with similar positions in the industry…' (Hannan et al. 1998b: 305). These arguments imply that the effect of density on legitimation and competition weaken as an industry ages, which Hannan operationalizes as an interaction effect involving population density, population density squared and population age, and finds support for his ideas among European automobile producers.

Dynamic Selection and Scale-Based Competition

Barron (1999) has also proposed a variant of the changing basis of competition model that emphasizes the organizational size distribution of a population. In Barron's version, as organizations grow in scale they may be able to take deliberate steps to prevent the formation of new competitors. And, even if they do not, the fact that they already have well-established exchange networks, reputations, customer loyalties and staff expertise makes it more difficult for new entrants. Therefore, as the size distribution of a population shifts to the right, Barron predicts that the founding rate will decline. He tests this prediction using the mean of the log size distribution, which is approximately symmetric.

For failure, Barron's argument is somewhat different. In the early years of a population, when density is low, the failure rate is high because the legitimacy of the organizational form is also low. However, competition is also weak. Under early low-density conditions, therefore, he proposes that failures are distributed randomly, with no organizations heavily disadvantaged relative to any other. As density increases further, however, competition increases and organizations best able to withstand the more intense competition should have an increasing advantage in terms of survival chances. Barron's argument implies an interaction between the intensity of competition experienced by the members of a population and some factor that confers a survival advantage, the size of the advantage increasing as competition intensifies. Thus, the gap in survival chances of robust and frail organizations should widen as the density increases. Barron uses size to differentiate robust and frail organizations and thus predicts that, as the number of organizations in a population increase, the survival benefits of large size should increase. He tests his hypothesis by interacting population density and the log of organizational size. Barron tested and corroborated the model in an analysis of founding and failure of New York State credit unions during 1914–90.

Dobrev and Carroll (2003) have recently advanced a related model, measuring what they term 'scale-based competition' as the aggregate distance of an organization from its larger competitors. Their model is based on the idea that the aggregate distance of an organization from its larger competitors captures the extent to which it can capitalize on potential competitive advantages derived from its scale of operations. Their analysis of European automobile producer failure in four countries supports the model. Like Barron's model, they emphasize an organization's location in the size distribution, but distinct from it posit that the benefits of size are a function of positional differences with larger, rather than all other organizations.

Future research comparing the ability of these models to explain the historical growth trajectories of diverse organizational populations is needed to refine or integrate these models into a more unified theoretical and empirical approach. Baum and Hannan, for example, share a common emphasis on temporal variation in population density effects and agree that density becomes increasingly decoupled from population dynamics over a population's history. Hannan, however, does not specify what population dynamics become coupled to, while

Baum identifies the increasing influence of size-based competitive processes. Baum and Barron both highlight how a shift toward efficiency-based competition gives larger organizations a competitive advantage over smaller organizations, leading them to displace their population's size in numbers, but Barron's empirical specification, which ties large organizations' competitive advantage to population density, conflicts with the idea that population density becomes decoupled from competition over a population's history. Dobrev and Carroll's approach relies on the population's evolving size distribution to capture the increasing significance of scale-based competition, but does not permit the strength of the process to vary over time.

Connecting these models to Barnett's competitive intensity model is also important given that the different models emphasize different processes – heterogeneous competitive abilities among organizations vs population-wide shifts in the basis of competition. Future research is needed to determine the relative significance of these two basic competitive processes in accounting for concentration and to identify their distinct roles in population evolution.

Population-Level Learning

In addition to organization-level experiential learning, collective experiences of organizations at the population level lay the foundation for *population-level learning*. Although individual organizations may tend to engage in too much exploitation, populations of organizations may still engage in substantial exploration and generate new knowledge that individual organizations may acquire for themselves. At the population level, a lack of cohesion (i.e. diverse goals and incentives) and authority structures may allow the proliferation of new ideas and routines (Miner and Haunschild 1995). Even recklessly innovative organizations that quickly fail can generate new knowledge that adds to the experience of the population (Ingram and Baum 1997a). Although learning in established organizations tends to focus on exploiting old routines rather than on developing new ones, these organizations may, at a relatively low cost, be able to exploit new routines produced by the ongoing explorations and advances of other organizations in their population. So, 'the best strategy for any individual organization is often to emphasize the exploitation of successful explorations of others' (Levinthal and March 1993: 104).

By observing their population, organizations can potentially learn a multiplicity of strategies, practices and technologies employed by other organizations. Thus, an organization's own experience is not the only opportunity for learning; organizations may also learn from *population experience* – the operating and competitive experience of others in their population.

Population Operating and Competitive Experience

The operating experience of other organizations in the same population may contribute to internal efficiency in a similar way to an organization's own operating experience. An organization may be able to use other organizations' operating experience to improve its efficiency at providing service and managing employees and assets. By observing the internal operations of other organizations; reading about them in trade journals; listening to lectures about them; or by hiring the employees of other organizations, an organization can gain ideas about how to efficiently manage its own operations. The contribution of population operating experience to the organization's external capabilities, however, is probably more important (Ingram and Baum 1997a). Industry operating experience provides additional evidence about the consumers' preferences. Just as an organization can observe consumers' responses to it, it can observe (perhaps less accurately) consumers' responses to another organization. Every organization in a population provides information about consumers' preferences (White 1981).

Population experience has several advantages over own experience for learning. Any one organization is limited in how much it can learn from its own experience. The constraint on experimenting is not just an organization's resources, but also limits on how much variance the organization's internal systems can handle and external constituents will accept (Hannan and Freeman 1984). Unlike an organization, a population can encompass a great deal of variety without violating internal or external standards of consistency and reliability, and therefore more varied in their experience than individual organizations. Populations may thus engage in exploration, even while the organizations comprising them engage in exploitation of old routines.

For US hotel chains, Ingram and Baum (1997a) operationalize population operating experience as the operating experience (total chain units operated) other US hotel chains had accumulated since a given hotel chain was founded. They also operationalize population experience at founding as the operating experience other hotel chains had accumulated at the time the hotel chain was founded. To account for a possible decay in the value of population operating experience over time due to forgetting and antiquation, they discounted these variables using weights that depreciated experience as various functions of its age. Controlling for organizational operating experience, both population experience at entry and accumulated since entry had significant negative effects on hotel chain failure rates. Baum and Ingram (1998) attempted to replicate these findings for Manhattan hotels, measuring population operating experience at founding and since founding based on the operating experience (total rooms operated) other Manhattan hotels had accumulated since a given hotel was founded. Controlling for organizational operating experience, population operating experience at founding had a significant negative effect on the hotel failure rate; population operating experience accumulated since a hotel's founding did not.

Because organizational outcomes are also dependent on the actions of competitors, organizations also need a model of competitors. Operating experience can generate part of what is necessary for a model of competitors by locating them in multi-dimensional attribute space (White 1981). However, with competition, an organization's success is interdependent with other organizations' competitive moves. How should a competitor's moves be interpreted? How will the competitor respond to the organization's moves? What will it take to drive the competitor from a market position or cause it to fail? To answer these questions it is necessary to observe competitive outcomes.

Ingram and Baum (1997a) suggest measuring population competitive experience based on organizational failures in a population. At the level of the organization, Sitkin (1992) argues that small failures can enhance long-term performance by facilitating learning. This applies also at the population level. As organizations fail, the population has an opportunity to learn. Even organizations that break radically from standards of effective practice and quickly fail contribute to the experience of the population. Indeed, since the failing organization disappears, it is only the population that can learn from its

experience. Past failures are promising as a measure of population competitive experience for at least two reasons. First, organizational failures are usually salient and well publicized events. Managers naturally attend to failures and, unlike other sources of population experience, since the failing organization is no longer trying to protect a competitive future the details of its experience are more accessible. People who participated in the failed organization facilitate dissemination of its experience when they join other organizations. Secondly, failures are rich in information that matters for competitive strategy: what kills other organizations? By examining a failed organization's successful rivals other organizations can learn what competitive moves are effective at driving others from the market.

Ingram and Baum (1997a) operationalized population competitive experience based on the number of failures observed by US hotel chains both at the time of their founding and accumulated thereafter, discounted to account for possible decay in the value of the experience. Controlling for organizational and population operating experience, they found that population competitive experience since chain entry was negatively related to its failure; whereas, population competitive experience at the time of entry had no effect on chain failure.

These studies highlight the often neglected fact that organizational forms are not homogenous across time, providing evidence that successive cohorts of new organizations are improved as a function of the experience of the population (see also Sorenson 2000). In population level learning, variation and selective retention of bundles of organizational routines as well as organizations are important forces for population-level change. By emphasizing both organizations' learning of routines and organizational selection (i.e. founding and failure) as mechanisms for population-level change, population level learning admits both adaptation and selection. That new organizations benefit from the experience of their population suggests, for example, that entrepreneurs are not strangers to the populations they enter; they recognize the unexploited potential of the organizations they challenge. Thus population level learning complements and extends traditional ecological analyses of organizational founding and failure, which emphasize that organizational change and variability reflect primarily inert organizations replacing each other but do not typically explore the implications of entrepreneurs and ongoing organizations engaging in vicarious selective learning of new routines.

Existing research would be complemented by attention to processes within organizations that can affect the capacity of organizations to learn from their populations. Cyert et al. (1993), for example, suggest that differences in internal information processing capabilities can generate sustainable competitive advantages. Cohen and Levinthal (1990) argue that past preparation makes learning effectiveness path dependent. Additionally, the implications of organizations' efforts to protect their own operating experience as a source of competitive advantage (e.g. Barney 1991; Peteraf 1993) for their population as a whole – the tension between individual and collective benefits from experience – would appear to be an important topic for future research.

Conclusion: Progress, Problems and Future Directions

As we have shown, organizational ecology is a vital subfield within organization studies, its research agenda expanding and methodological sophistication increasing constantly. *However, what does organizational ecology contribute to progress in organization studies?* One way to answer this question is to examine the problems organizational ecology solves (Lauden 1984; Tucker 1994). According to Lauden (1984: 15), scientific theories must solve two kinds of problems: *empirical problems*, which are substantive questions about the objects that constitute the domain of inquiry, and *conceptual problems*, which include questions about internal logical consistency and conceptual ambiguity of theories advanced to solve empirical problems, as well as the methodological soundness of tests of theoretical arguments. From this perspective, organizational ecology's contribution to progress can be defined in terms of its capacity to accumulate *solved* empirical problems while minimizing the scope of unsolved empirical problems and conceptual problems.

As revealed in this review, the primary emphasis of organizational ecology is the development of theoretical explanations for specific empirical problems (e.g. age, size and density dependence in organizational failure). Although organizational ecology has advanced knowledge about a wide range of empirical problems, few (if any) of these can be considered solved conclusively. Of course, other organization studies subdisciplines have not solved these problems either. From a conceptual standpoint, while examples of internal logical inconsistencies are uncommon in ecological theory, and those that are identified being tackled directly (see for example, Péli 1997; Hannan 1998; Hannan et al. 2003a, b), instances of conceptual ambiguities are more prevalent. Questions about the meaning of central concepts such as population, founding, failure and legitimacy have been raised frequently (e.g. McKelvey 1982; Carroll 1984a; Astley 1985; Delacroix and Rao 1994; Rao 2001). To be fair, such ambiguities are not unique to organizational ecology, but seem endemic to organization studies.

One persistent source of conceptual problems is the methodological soundness of tests of theoretical arguments. One area of frequent debate is the appropriateness of inferring underlying processes of legitimation from population density estimates instead of measuring the underlying construct directly (Zucker 1989; Baum and Oliver 1992; Hannan and Carroll 1992; Miner 1993). Inferring processes of learning from cumulative organizational and industry experience estimates is subject to similar concerns (Baum and Ingram 1998). In part, this problem stems from organizational ecology's use of large-scale, historical databases in which, by necessity, measures are frequently removed from concepts. Research on age dependence and, to a lesser degree, research on size dependence, also suffer from this problem (Henderson 1999).

Although unsolved empirical problems and conceptual problems are not uncommon in emerging areas of scientific inquiry, the longer these problems remain unresolved, the greater their importance becomes in debates about the veracity of the theories that generated them (Lauden 1984: 64–6). What produces organizational ecology's problems? Although organizational ecologists would like their theories to maximize generality across organizational populations, realism of context and precision in measurement of variables, in fact, no theory can be general, precise and realistic all at the same time (McGrath 1982; Puccia and Levins 1985). Theories must sacrifice on some dimensions to maximize others. For example, realistic theories may apply to only a limited domain, while general theories may be inaccurate or misleading for specific applications.

Historically, organizational ecologists appear to have favoured a trade-off of precision and realism for generality in their theories (Singh 1993). For example, precision and realism are clearly sacrificed for generality in the original formulations of density dependence and structural inertia theories. On the one hand, this research strategy produces organizational ecology's main strength: A wealth of comparable empirical evidence from diverse organizational settings on a range of empirical problems unparalleled in organization studies. On the other hand, it also creates a major weakness: The large pool of coefficients for indirect measures such as age, size, population density and population experience reveals little about underlying theoretical explanations designed to account for the empirical problems of interest. This creates conceptual problems by fostering skepticism regarding the veracity of inferred underlying processes because conforming findings cannot be interpreted precisely, and creates unsolved empirical problems by making it difficult to account for non-conforming findings on theoretical grounds.

The sacrifice of contextual realism and measurement precision for generality thus underlies several key problems in organizational ecology. By sacrificing some generality for more precision and realism, however, organizational ecologists have begun to address this. Over the past decade, ecological theory and analysis has become increasingly sensitive to the need for more fine-grained theory and measurement that captures in a more nuanced and direct manner the underlying processes of interest. Ecological research adopting this problem-solving strategy has already contributed to the literature in several important ways. Perhaps most notable are elaborations of the original density dependence model (see Table 1.2.6) help increase precision by measuring underlying processes of competition and legitimation more directly (Baum and Oliver 1992; 1996; Baum and Singh 1994b, c; Deeds et al. 2004). They also enhance contextual realism by incorporating additional features of population such as organizational size distributions (Barnett and Amburgey 1990; Barron 1999; Dobrev and Carroll 2003), market niche structures (Baum and Singh 1994b, c) and competitive heterogeneity into the model (Baum 1995; Barnett 1997). The result is a more compelling and less problematic account of the ecological dynamics of organizational populations. At the demographic level, research emphasizing greater measurement precision has shed new light on the underlying causes of structural inertia and age and size dependence in organizational change and failure (e.g. Greve 1999; Henderson

1999). More robust organization-level measures are necessary to establish the micro-foundations of ecological theory.

Organizational ecology is making good progress on its problems. Continued emphasis on increasing precision and realism in theory and research is essential to enhancing the impact and influence of ecological approaches to organizations. Getting closer to research problems will reveal important aspects of phenomena that more distanced researchers cannot detect. Understanding anomalies – results that are inconsistent with each other, theory or observation – is crucial to specifying contingent predictions and increasing precision. Letting research problems drive the choice of research design and methodology (rather than vice versa) will yield study designs best suited to answering the questions posed. These shifts in the ecological research orientation will foster new kinds of questions that enhance links with other research streams in organization theory and related subfields such as strategy. In turn, these linkages will help realize more of the great potential of ecological approaches to contribute to theory and research in organization studies, as well as to practice in public policy, management and entrepreneurship.

Note

1. Strategic and economic models make the same prediction (e.g. Porter 1980; Tirole 1988; Scherer and Ross 1990).

References

Aldrich, H.E. (1979) *Organizations and Environments*. Englewood Cliffs, NJ: Prentice-Hall.

Aldrich, H.E. and Auster, E.R. (1986) 'Even Dwarfs started small: Liabilities of age and size and their strategic implications', *Research in Organizational Behavior*, 8: 165–98.

Aldrich, H.E. and Fiol, C.M. (1994) 'Fools rush in? The institutional context of industry creation', *Academy of Management Review*, 19: 645–70.

Aldrich, H.E. and Pfeffer, J. (1976) 'Environments of organizations', *Annual Review of Sociology*, 2: 79–105.

Aldrich, H.E. and Wiedenmayer, G. (1993) 'From traits to rates: an ecological perspective on organizational foundings', *Advances in Entrepreneurship, Firm Emergence, and Growth*, 1: 145–95.

Aldrich, H.E., Zimmer, C., Staber, U. and Beggs, J. (1994) 'Minimalism, mutualism, and maturity: The evolution of the American trade association population in the 20th century', in J.A.C. Baum and J.V. Singh (eds), *Evolutionary Dynamics of Organizations.* New York: Oxford University Press. pp. 223–39.

Amburgey, T.L. and Dacin, T. (1994) 'As the left foot follows the right? The dynamics of strategic and structural change', *Academy of Management Journal,* 37: 1427–52.

Amburgey, T.L. and Kelly, D. (1985) 'Adaptation and selection in organizational populations: A competing risk models', *Paper presented at the Academy of Management meetings,* San Diego, CA.

Amburgey, T.L. and Miner, A.S. (1992) 'Strategic momentum: The effects of repetitive, positional, and contextual momentum on merger activity', *Strategic Management Journal,* 13: 335–48.

Amburgey, T.L., Dacin, T. and Kelly, D. (1994) 'Disruptive selection and population segmentation: Interpopulation competition as a segregating process', in J.A.C. Baum and J.V. Singh (eds), *Evolutionary Dynamics of Organizations.* New York: Oxford University Press. pp. 240–54.

Amburgey, T.L., Kelly, D. and Barnett, W.P. (1990) 'Resetting the clock: The dynamics of organizational change and failure', in J.L. Wall and L.R. Jauch (eds), *Academy of Management Proceedings.* San Francisco, CA: Academy of Management. pp. 160–4.

Amburgey, T.L., Kelly, D. and Barnett, W.P. (1993) 'Resetting the clock: The dynamics of organizational change and failure', *Administrative Science Quarterly,* 38: 51–73.

Anderson, P. and Tushman, M.L. (1992) 'Technological, ecological and economic determinants of industry exit: A longitudinal study of the American cement (1888–1980) and minicomputer (1958–1982) industries'. Unpublished manuscript, Johnson Graduate School of Management, Cornell University.

Argote, L. (1999) *Organizational Learning: Creating, Retaining and Transferring Knowledge.* Boston: Kluwer.

Argote, L., Beckman, S.L. and Epple, D. (1990) 'The persistence and transfer of learning in industrial settings', *Management Science,* 36: 140–54.

Astley, W.G. (1985) 'The two ecologies: Population and community perspectives on organizational evolution', *Administrative Science Quarterly,* 30: 224–41.

Astley, W.G. and Van De Ven, A.H. (1983) 'Central perspectives and debates in organizational theory', *Administrative Science Quarterly,* 28: 245–73.

Bain, J.S. (1956) *Barriers to New Competition.* Cambridge, MA: Harvard University Press.

Banaszak-Holl, J. (1992) 'Historical trends in rates of Manhattan bank mergers, acquisitions, and failures'. Unpublished manuscript, Center for Health Care Research, Brown University.

Banaszak-Holl, J. (1993) 'Avoiding failure when times get tough: Changes in organizations' responses to competitive pressures'. Unpublished manuscript, Center for Health Care Research, Brown University.

Barley, S.R., Freeman, J. and Hybels, R.C. (1992) 'Strategic alliances in commercial biotechnology', in N. Nohria and R. Eccles (eds), *Networks and Organizations: Structure, Form, and Action.* Boston: Harvard Business School Press. pp. 311–47.

Barnett, W.P. (1990) 'The organizational ecology of a technological system', *Administrative Science Quarterly,* 35: 31–60.

Barnett, W.P. (1997) 'The dynamics of competitive intensity', *Administrative Science Quarterly,* 42: 128–60.

Barnett, W.P. and Amburgey, T.L. (1990) 'Do larger organizations generate stronger competition?', in J.V. Singh (ed.), *Organizational Evolution: New Directions.* Newbury Park, CA: Sage. pp. 78–102.

Barnett, W.P. and Carroll, G.R. (1987) 'Competition and mutualism among early telephone companies', *Administrative Science Quarterly,* 32: 400–21.

Barnett, W.P. and Carroll, G.R. (1995) 'Modeling internal organizational change', *Annual Review of Sociology,* 21: 217–36.

Barnett, W.P. and Hansen, M. (1996) 'The red queen in organizational evolution', *Strategic Management Journal,* 17(S): 139–57.

Barnett, W.P. and Sorenson, O. (2002) 'The red queen in organizational creation and development', *Industrial and Corporate Change,* 11: 289–325.

Barnett, W.P., Greve, H.R. and Park, D.Y. (1994) 'An evolutionary model of organizational performance', *Strategic Management Journal,* 15: 11–28.

Barney, J. (1991) 'Firm resources and sustained competitive advantage', *Journal of Management,* 17(1): 99–120.

Barron, D.N. (1999) 'The structuring of organizational populations', *American Sociological Review,* 64: 421–45.

Barron, D.N., West, E. and Hannan, M.T. (1994) 'A time to grow and a time to die: Growth and mortality of credit unions in New York City, 1914–1990', *American Journal of Sociology,* 100: 381–421.

Baum, J.A.C. (1989) 'Liabilities of newness, adolescence, and obsolescence: Exploring age dependence in the dissolution of organizational relationships and organizations', *Proceedings of the Administrative Sciences Association of Canada,* 10(5): 1–10.

Baum, J.A.C. (1990a) 'Inertial and adaptive patterns in the dynamics of organizational change', in J.L. Wall and L.R. Jauch (eds), *Academy of Management Proceedings.* San Francisco, CA: Academy of Management. pp. 165–9.

Baum, J.A.C. (1990b) 'Why are there so many (few) kinds of organizations? A study of organizational diversity', in C. Kirchmeyer (ed.), *Proceedings of the Administrative Sciences Association of Canada,* 11(5): 1–10.

Baum, J.A.C., (1995) 'The changing basis of competition in organizational populations: The Manhattan hotel industry, 1898–1990', *Social Forces,* 74: 177–204.

Baum, J.A.C. (1996) 'Organizational Ecology', in S.R. Clegg, C. Hardy and W.R. Nord (eds) *Handbook of Organization Studies.* London: Sage. pp. 77–114.

Baum, J.A.C. (1999) 'The rise of nursing home chains in Ontario, 1971–1996', *Social Forces*, 78: 543–84.

Baum, J.A.C. (2006) 'Competitive and institutional isomorphism in organizational populations', in W.W. Powell and D.L. Jones (eds), *Bending the Bars of the iron Cage: Institutional Dynamics and Processes*. Chicago: University of Chicago Press. In press.

Baum, J.A.C. and Amburgey, T.L. (2002) 'Organizational ecology', in J.A.C. Baum (ed.), *Companion to Organizations*. Oxford, UK: Blackwell. pp. 304–26.

Baum, J.A.C. and Haveman, H.A. (1997) 'Love thy neighbor? Differentiation and agglomeration in the Manhattan hotel industry', *Administrative Science Quarterly*, 42: 304–38.

Baum, J.A.C. and House, R.J. (1990) 'On the maturation and aging of organizational populations', in J.V. Singh (ed.), *Organizational Evolution: New Directions*. Newbury Park, CA: Sage. pp. 129–42.

Baum, J.A.C. and Ingram, P. (1998) 'Survival-enhancing learning in the Manhattan hotel industry, 1898–1980', *Management Science*, 44(7): 996–1016.

Baum, J.A.C. and Korn, H. (1999) 'Dynamics of dyadic competition', *Strategic Management Journal*, 20: 251–78.

Baum, J.A.C. and Mezias, S.J. (1992) 'Localized competition and organizational failure in the Manhattan hotel industry, 1898–1990', *Administrative Science Quarterly*, 37: 580–604.

Baum, J.A.C. and Mezias, S.J. (1993) 'Competition, institutional linkages and organizational growth', *Social Science Research*, 22: 131–64.

Baum, J.A.C. and Oliver, C. (1991) 'Institutional linkages and organizational mortality', *Administrative Science Quarterly*, 36: 187–218.

Baum, J.A.C. and Oliver, C. (1992) 'Institutional embeddedness and the dynamics of organizational populations', *American Sociological Review*, 57: 540–59.

Baum, J.A.C. and Oliver, C. (1996) 'Toward an institutional ecology of organizational founding', *Academy of Management Journal*, 39: 1378–427.

Baum, J.A.C. and Powell, W.W. (1995) 'Cultivating an institutional ecology of organizations: Comment on Hannan, Carroll, Dundon, and Torres', *American Sociological Review*, 60: 529–38.

Baum, J.A.C. and Rao, H. (2004) 'Dynamics of organizational populations and communities', in M.S. Poole and A.H. Van de Ven (eds), *Handbook of Organizational Change and Innovation*. New York: Oxford University Press. pp. 212–58.

Baum, J.A.C. and Silverman, B.S. (2004) 'Picking winners or building them? Alliance, intellectual, and human capital as selection criteria in venture financing and performance of biotechnology startups', *Journal of Business Venturing*, 19: 411–36.

Baum, J.A.C. and Singh, J.V. (1994a) 'Organizational hierarchies and evolutionary processes: Some reflections on a theory of organizational evolution', in J.A.C. Baum and J.V. Singh (eds), *Evolutionary Dynamics of Organizations*. New York: Oxford University Press. pp. 3–22.

Baum, J.A.C. and Singh, J.V. (1994b) 'Organizational niche overlap and the dynamics of organizational founding', *Organization Science*, 5: 483–501.

Baum, J.A.C. and Singh, J.V. (1994c) 'Organizational niche overlap and the dynamics of organizational mortality', *American Journal of Sociology*, 100: 346–80.

Baum, J.A.C. and Singh, J.V. (1996) 'Dynamics of organizational responses to competition', *Social Forces*, 74: 1261–97.

Baum, J.A.C., Korn, H.J. and Kotha, S. (1995) 'Dominant designs and population dynamics in telecommunications services: Founding and failure of facsimile service organizations, 1969–1992', *Social Science Research*, 24: 97–135.

Baum, JA.C., Li, S.X. and Usher, J.M. (2000) 'Making the next move: How experiential and vicarious learning shape the locations of chains' acquisition', *Administrative Science Quarterly*, 45(4): 766–801.

Berk, R.A. (1983) 'An introduction to sample selection bias in sociological data', *American Sociological Review*, 48: 386–98.

Boeker, W. (1989) 'Strategic change: The effects of founding and history', *Academy of Management Journal*, 32: 489–515.

Boeker, W. (1997) 'Strategic change: The influence of managerial characteristics and organizational growth', *Academy of Management Journal*, 40: 152–70.

Boone, C., Brocheler, V. and Carroll, G. (2000) 'Custom service: Application and tests of resource-partitioning theory among Dutch auditing firms for 1896 to 1992', *Organization Studies*, 21: 355–81.

Boone, C., Carroll, G.R. and van Witteloostuijin, A. (2002) 'Environmental resource distributions and market partitioning: Dutch daily newspaper organizations from 1968 to 1994', *American Sociological Review*, 67: 408–31.

Brittain, J.W. (1994) 'Density-independent selection and community evolution', in J.A.C. Baum and J.V. Singh (eds), *Evolutionary Dynamics of Organizations*. New York: Oxford University Press. pp. 355–78.

Brittain, J.W. and Freeman, J.H. (1980) 'Organizational proliferation and density dependent selection', in J. Kimberly and R. Miles (eds), *The Organizational Life Cycle*. San Francisco, CA: Jossey-Bass. pp. 291–338.

Bruderl, J. and Schussler, R. (1990) 'Organizational mortality: The liabilities of newness and adolescence', *Administrative Science Quarterly*, 35: 530–47.

Budros, A. (1993) An analysis of organizational birth types: Organizational start-up and entry in the nineteenth-century life insurance industry', *Social Forces*, 70: 1013–30.

Budros, A. (1994) 'Analyzing unexpected density dependence effects on organizational births in New York's life insurance industry, 1842–1904', *Organization Science*, 5: 541–53.

Burgelman, R.A. (1991) 'Intraorganizational ecology of strategy-making and organizational adaptation: Theory and field research', *Organization Science*, 2: 239–62.

Burgelman, R.A. and Mittman, B.S. (1994) 'An intraorganizational ecological perspective on managerial risk behavior, performance, and survival: Individual, organizational, and environmental effects', in J.A.C. Baum and J.V. Singh (eds), *Evolutionary Dynamics of Organizations*. New York: Oxford University Press. pp. 53–74.

Campbell, D.T. (1965) 'Variation and selective retention in socio-cultural evolution', in H.R. Barringer, G.I. Blanksten and R.W. Mack (eds), *Social Change in Developing Areas: A Reinterpretation of Evolutionary Theory*. Cambridge, MA: Schenkman. pp. 19–48.

Carroll, G.R. (1983) 'A stochastic model of organizational mortality: Review and reanalysis', *Social Science Research*, 12: 303–29.

Carroll, G.R. (1984a) 'Organizational ecology', *Annual Review of Sociology*, 10: 71–93.

Carroll, G.R. (1984b) 'Dynamics of publisher succession in newspaper organizations', *Administrative Science Quarterly*, 29: 93–113.

Carroll, G.R. (1985) 'Concentration and specialization: Dynamics of niche width in populations of organizations', *American Journal of Sociology*, 90: 1262–83.

Carroll, G.R. (1987) *Publish and Perish: The Organizational Ecology of Newspaper Industries*. Greenwich CT: JAI Press.

Carroll, G.R. and Delacroix, J. (1982) 'Organizational mortality in the newspaper industries of Argentina and Ireland: An ecological approach', *Administrative Science Quarterly*, 27: 169–98.

Carroll, G.R. and Hannan, M.T. (1989a) 'Density delay in the evolution of organizational population: A model and five empirical tests', *Administrative Science Quarterly*, 34: 411–30.

Carroll, G.R. and Hannan, M.T. (1989b) 'Density dependence in the evolution of newspapers organizations', *American Sociological Review*, 54: 524–41.

Carroll, G.R. and Huo, Y.P. (1986) 'Organizational task and institutional environments in ecological perspective: Findings from the local newspaper industry', *American Journal of Sociology*, 91: 838–73.

Carroll, G.R. and Swaminathan, A. (1991) 'Density dependent organizational evolution in the American brewing industry from 1633–1988', *Acta Sociologica*, 34: 155–76.

Carroll, G.R. and Swaminathan, A. (1992) 'The organizational ecology of strategic groups in the American brewing industry from 1975–1990', *Corporate and Industrial Change*, 1: 65–97.

Carroll, G.R. and Swaminathan, A. (2000) 'Why the microbrewery movement? Organizational dynamics of resource partitioning in the U.S. brewing industry', *American Journal of Sociology*, 106: 715–62.

Carroll, G.R. and Wade, J.B. (1991) 'Density dependence in the evolution of the American brewing industry across different levels of analysis', *Social Science Research*, 20: 271–302.

Carroll, G.R., Bigelow, L., Seidel, M.-D. and Tsai, L. (1996) 'The fates of de novo and de alio producers in the American automobile industry, 1885–1981', *Strategic Management Journal*, 17: 117–38.

Carroll, G.R., Dobrev, S.D. and Swaminathan, A. (2002) 'Organizational processes of resource partitioning', in R. Kramer and B. Staw (eds), *Research in Organizational Behavior*, 24. Oxford, UK: JAI/Elsevier. pp. 1–40.

Carroll, G.R., Preisendoerfer, P., Swaminathan, A. and Wiedenmayer, G. (1993) 'Brewery and Braueri: The organizational ecology of brewing', *Organization Studies*, 14: 155–88.

Cattani, G., Pennings, J.M. and Wezel, F.C. (2003) 'Spatial and temporal heterogeneity in founding patterns', *Organization Science*, 14: 670–85.

Caves, R.E. and Porter, M.E. (1977) 'From entry barriers to mobility barriers', *Quarterly Journal of Economics*, 90: 241–61.

Chandler, A. (1977) *The Visible Hand*. Cambridge, MA: Belknap.

Chen, M.-J. and Hambrick, D.D. (1995) 'Speed, stealth, and selective attack: How small firms differ from large firms in competitive behavior', *Academy of Management Journal*, 38(2): 453–82.

Child, J. (1972) 'Organization structure, environment and performance: The role of strategic choice', *Sociology*, 6: 1–22.

Cohen, W.M. and Levinthal, D.A. (1990) 'Absorptive capacity: A new perspective on learning and innovation', *Administrative Science Quarterly*, 35: 128–52.

Cyert, R.M. and March, J.G. (1963) *A Behavioral Theory of the Firm*. Englewood Cliffs, NJ: Prentice-Hall.

Cyert, R.M., Kumar, P. and Williams, J.R. (1993) 'Information, market imperfections and strategy', *Strategic Management Journal*, 14(Winter Special Issue): 47–58.

Dacin, M.T. (1997) 'Isomorphism in context: The power and prescription of institutional norms', *Academy of Management Journal*, 40: 46–81.

D'Aunno, T., Succi, M. and Alexander, J. (2000) 'The role of institutional and market forces in divergent organizational change', *Administrative Science Quarterly*, 45: 679–703.

Darr, E.D., Argote, L. and Epple, D. (1995) 'The acquisition, transfer, and depreciation of knowledge in service organizations: Productivity in franchises', *Management Science*, 42: 1750–62.

Deeds, D.L., Mang, P.Y. and Frandsen, M.L. (2004) 'The impact of industry and firm legitimacy on the flow of capital into high technology ventures', *Strategic Organization*, 2: 9–34.

Delacroix, J. and Carroll, G.R. (1983) 'Organizational foundings: An ecological study of the newspaper industries of Argentina and Ireland', *Administrative Science Quarterly*, 28: 274–91.

Delacroix, J. and Rao, H. (1994) 'Externalities and ecological theory: Unbundling density dependence', in J.A.C. Baum and J.V. Singh (eds), *Evolutionary Dynamics of Organizations*. New York: Oxford University Press. pp. 255–68.

Delacroix, J. and Swaminathan, A. (1991) 'Cosmetic, speculative, and adaptive organizational change in the wine industry: A longitudinal study', *Administrative Science Quarterly*, 36: 631–61.

Delacroix, J., Swaminathan, A. and Solt, M.E. (1989) 'Density dependence versus population dynamics: An ecological study of failings in the California wine industry', *American Sociological Review*, 54: 245–62.

DiMaggio, P.J. and Powell, W.W. (1983) 'The iron cage revisited: Institutional isomorphism and collective rationality in organizational fields', *American Sociological Review*, 48: 147–60.

Dobbin, F. and Dowd, T. (1997) 'How policy shapes competition: Early railroad foundings in Massachusetts', *Administrative Science Quarterly*, 42: 501–29.

Dobrev, S.D. (2000) Decreasing concentration and reversibility of the resource partitioning process: Supply shortages and deregulation in the Bulgarian newspaper industry, 1987–1992. *Organization Studies*, 21: 383–404.

Dobrev, S.D. (2001) 'Revisiting organizational legitimation: Cognitive diffusion and sociopolitical factors in the evolution of Bulgarian newspaper enterprises, 1846–1992', *Organization Studies*, 22: 355–81.

Dobrev, S.D. and Carroll, G.R. (2003) 'Size (and competition) among organizations: Modeling scale-based selection among automobile producers in four major countries', *Strategic Management Journal*, 24: 541–58.

Dobrev, S.D., Kim, T.-Y. and Carroll, G.R. (2002) 'The evolution of organizational niches', *Administrative Science Quarterly*, 47: 233–64.

Dobrev, S.D., Kim, T.-Y. and Carroll, G. (2003) 'Shifting gears, shifting niches: Organizational inertia and change in the evolution of the U.S. automobile industry, 1885–1981', *Organization Science*, 14: 264–82.

Dobrev, S.D., Kim, T.-Y. and Hannan, M. (2001) 'Dynamics of niche width and resource partitioning', *American Journal of Sociology*, 106: 1299–338.

Dowell, G. and Swaminathan, A. (2000) 'Racing and back-pedalling into the future: New product introduction and organizational mortality in the US bicycle industry, 1880–1918', *Organization Studies*, 21: 405–31.

Downs, A. (1967) *Inside Bureaucracy*. Boston: Little, Brown.

Dun and Bradstreet (1978) *The Failure Record*. New York: Dun & Bradstreet Inc.

Durkheim, E. (1893) (1933 tr.) *The Division of Labor in Society*. Glencoe, IL: Free Press.

Edwards, C.D. (1955) 'Conglomerate bigness as a source of power', in National Bureau of Economic Research, *Business Concentration and Public Power*. Princeton, NJ: Princeton University Press. pp. 331–59.

Fichman, M. and Levinthal, D.A. (1991) 'Honeymoons and the liability of adolescence: A new perspective on duration dependence in social and organizational relationships', *Academy of Management Review*, 16: 442–68.

Fombrun, C.J. (1986) 'Structural dynamics within and between organizations', *Administrative Science Quarterly*, 31: 403–21.

Fombrun, C.J. (1988) 'Crafting an institutionally informed ecology of organizations', in G.R. Carroll (ed.), *Ecological Models of Organizations*. Cambridge, MA: Ballinger. pp. 223–39.

Freeman, J. (1990) 'Ecological analysis of semiconductor firm mortality', in J.V. Singh (ed.), *Organizational Evolution: New Directions*. Newbury Park, CA: Sage. pp. 53–77.

Freeman, J.H. and Hannan, M.T. (1983) 'Niche width and the dynamics of organizational populations', *American Journal of Sociology*, 88: 1116–45.

Freeman, J.H. and Hannan, M.T. (1987) 'The ecology of restaurants revisited', *American Journal of Sociology*, 92: 1214–20.

Freeman, J. and Lomi, A. (1994) 'Resource partitioning and foundings of banking cooperative in Italy', in J.A.C. Baum and J.V. Singh (eds), *Evolutionary Dynamics of Organizations*. New York: Oxford University Press. pp. 269–93.

Freeman, J.H., Carroll, G.R. and Hannan, M.T. (1983) 'The liability of newness: Age dependence in organizational death rates', *American Sociological Review*, 48: 692–710.

Galunic, C. and Weeks, J.R. (2002) 'Intraorganizational ecology', in J.A.C. Baum (ed.), *Companion to Organizations*. Oxford, UK: Blackwell. pp. 75–97.

Gartner, W.B. (1989) 'Some suggestions for research on entrepreneurial traits and characteristics', *Entrepreneurship: Theory and Practice*, 14: 27–37.

Ginsberg, A. and Baum, J.A.C. (1994) 'Evolutionary processes and patterns of core business change', in J.A.C. Baum and J.V. Singh (eds), *Evolutionary Dynamics of Organizations*. New York: Oxford University Press. pp. 127–51.

Ginsberg, A. and Buchholtz, A. (1990) 'Converting to for-profit status: Corporate responsiveness to radical change', *Academy of Management Journal*, 33: 447–77.

Granovetter, M. (1985) 'Economic action and social structure: the problem of embeddedness', *American Journal of Sociology*, 91: 481–510.

Greve, H.R. (1995) 'Jumping ship: The diffusion of strategy abandonment', *Administrative Science Quarterly*, 40(September): 444–73.

Greve, H.R. (1996) 'Patterns of competition: The diffusion of a market position in radio broadcasting', *Administrative Science Quarterly*, 41: 29–60.

Greve, H.R. (1998) 'Performance, aspirations and risky organizational change', *Administrative Science Quarterly*, 43: 58–86.

Greve, H.R. (1999) 'The effect of core change on performance: Inertia and regression toward the mean', *Administrative Science Quarterly*, 44: 590–614.

Greve, H.R. (2002) 'An ecological theory of spatial evolution: Local density dependence in Tokyo Banking, 1894–1936', *Social Forces*, 80: 847–79.

Greve, H.R. and Taylor, A. (2000) 'Innovations as catalysts for organizational change: Shifts in organizational cognition and search', *Administrative Science Quarterly*, 45: 54–83.

Guo, G. (1993) 'Event history analysis for left-truncated data', *Sociological Methodology*, 23: 217–44.

Halliday, T., Powell, M.J. and Granfors, M.W. (1993) 'After minimalism: Transformations of state bar associations, 1918–1950', *American Sociological Review*, 58: 515–35.

Hambrick, D.C. and D'Aveni, R.A. (1988) 'Large corporate failures as downward spirals', *Administrative Science Quarterly*, 33: 1–23.

Hannan, M.T. (1986) 'A model of competitive and institutional processes in organizational ecology', Technical Report 86-13, Department of Sociology, Cornell University.

Hannan, M.T. (1997) 'Inertia, density and the structure of organizational populations: Entries in European automobile industries, 1886–1981', *Organization Studies*, 18: 193–228.

Hannan, M.T. (1998) 'Rethinking age dependence in organizational mortality: Logical formalizations', *American Journal of Sociology*, 104: 126–64.

Hannan, M.T. and Carroll, G.R. (1992) *Dynamics of Organizational Populations: Density, competition, and legitimation*. New York: Oxford University Press.

Hannan, M.T. and Freeman, J.H. (1977) 'The population ecology of organizations', *American Journal of Sociology*, 83: 929–84.

Hannan, M.T. and Freeman, J.H. (1984) 'Structural inertia and organizational change', *American Sociological Review*, 49: 149–64.

Hannan, M.T. and Freeman, J.H. (1987) 'The ecology of organizational founding: American labor unions, 1836–1985', *American Journal of Sociology*, 92: 910–43.

Hannan, M.T. and Freeman, J.H. (1988) 'The ecology of organizational mortality: American labor unions, 1836–1985', *American Journal of Sociology*, 94: 25–52.

Hannan, M.T. and Freeman, J.H. (1989) *Organizational Ecology*. Cambridge, MA: Harvard University Press.

Hannan, M.T., Barron, D. and Carroll, G.R. (1991) 'On the interpretation of density dependence in rates of organizational mortality: A reply to Peterson and Koput', *American Sociology Review*, 56: 410–5.

Hannan, M.T., Carroll, G.R., Dobrev, S.D., Han, J. and Torres, J.C. (1998a) 'Organizational mortality in European and American automobile industries, Part I: Revising age dependence', *European Sociological Review*, 14: 279–302.

Hannan, M.T., Carroll, G.R., Dobrev, S.D., Han, J. and Torres, J.C. (1998b) 'Organizational mortality in European and American automobile industries, Part II: Coupled clocks', *European Sociological Review*, 14: 303–13.

Hannan, M.T., Carroll, G.R., Dundon, E. and Torres, J.C. (1995) 'Organizational evolution in a multinational context: Entries of automobile manufacturers in Belgium, Britain, France, Germany, and Italy', *American Sociological Review*, 60: 509–28.

Hannan, M.T., Carroll, G.R. and Pólos, L. (2003a) 'The organizational niche', *Sociological Theory*, 21: 309–40.

Hannan, M.T., Carroll, G.R. and Pólos, L. (2003b) A formal theory of resource partitioning, Working Paper, Graduate School of Business, Stanford University.

Hannan, M.T., Ranger-Moore, J. and Banaszak-Holl, J. (1990) 'Competition and the evolution of organizational size distributions', in J.V. Singh (ed.), *Organizational Evolution: New Directions*. Newbury Park, CA: Sage. pp. 246–68.

Haveman, H.A. (1992) 'Between a rock and a hard place: Organizational change and performance under conditions of fundamental environmental transformation', *Administrative Science Quarterly*, 37: 48–75.

Haveman, H.A. (1993a) 'Organizational size and change: Diversification in the savings and loan industry after deregulation', *Administrative Science Quarterly*, 38: 20–50.

Haveman, H.A. (1993b) 'Follow the leader: Mimetic isomorphism and entry into new markets', *Administrative Science Quarterly*, 38: 593–627.

Haveman, H.A. (1993c) 'Ghosts of managers past: Managerial succession and organizational mortality', *Academy of Management Journal*, 36: 864–81.

Haveman, H.A. (1994) 'The ecological dynamics of organizational change: Density and mass dependence in rates of entry into new markets', in J.A.C. Baum and J.V. Singh (eds), *Evolutionary Dynamics of Organizations*. New York: Oxford University Press. pp. 152–66.

Haveman, H.A., Russo, M.V. and Meyer, A.D. (2001) 'Organizational environments in flux: The impact of regulatory punctuations on organizational domains, CEO succession and Performance', *Organization Science*, 12: 253–73.

Hawley, A.H. (1950) *Human Ecology: A Theory of Community Structure*. New York: Ronald.

Heckman, J.J. (1979) 'Sample selection bias as a specification error', *Econometrica*, 47: 153–61.

Henderson, A. (1999) 'Firm strategy and age dependence: A contingent view of the liabilities of newness, adolescence, and obsolescence', *Administrative Science Quarterly*, 44: 281–324.

Henderson, R.M. and Clark, K.B. (1990) 'Architectural innovation: The reconfiguration of existing product technologies and the failure of established firms', *Administrative Science Quarterly*, 35: 9–30.

Hotelling, H. (1929) 'Stability in competition', *Economic Journal*, 39: 41–57.

Huber, G.P. (1991) 'Organizational learning: The contributing processes and the literatures', *Organization Science*, 2: 88–115.

Hybels, R.C. (1994) Legitimation, population density, and founding rates: The institutionalization of commercial biotechnology in the U.S., 1971–1989. Unpublished PhD dissertation, Cornell University.

Hybels, R.C., Ryan, A.R. and Barley, S.R. (1994) 'Alliances, legitimation, and founding rates in the U.S. Biotechnology field, 1971–1989'. Paper presented at the Academy of Management national meetings, Dallas, TX.

Ijiri, Y. and Simon, H.A. (1977) *Skew Distributions and the sizes of Business Firms*. Amsterdam: North Holland.

Ingram, P. (1993) 'Old, tired, and ready to die: The age dependence of organizational mortality reconsidered'. Paper presented at the Academy of Management meetings, Atlanta, GA.

Ingram, P. (1994) Endogenizing environmental change: The evolution of hotel chains, 1896–1980. Unpublished manuscript, Johnson Graduate School of Management, Cornell University.

Ingram, P. and Baum, J.A.C. (1997a) 'Opportunity and constraint: Organizations' learning from the operating and competitive experience of industries', *Strategic Management Journal*, 18: 75–98 (Summer Special Issue).

Ingram, P. and Baum, J.A.C. (1997b) 'Chain affiliation and the failure of Manhattan hotels, 1898–1980', *Administrative Science Quarterly*, 42: 68–102.

Ingram, P. and Inman, C. (1996) 'Institutions, intergroup competition, and the evolution of hotel populations around Niagara Falls', *Administrative Science Quarterly*, 41: 629–58.

Ingram, P. and Simons, T. (2000) 'State formation, ideological competition, and the ecology of Israeli workers cooperatives, 1920–1992', *Administrative Science Quarterly*, 45: 25–53.

Katz, J. and Gartner, W.B. (1988) 'Properties of emerging organizations', *Academy of Management Review*, 13: 429–41.

Kelly, D. (1988) 'Organizational transformation and failure in the U.S. airline industry, 1962–1985. Unpublished PhD dissertation, Graduate School of Business, Northwestern University.

Kelly, D. and Amburgey, T.L. (1991) 'Organizational inertia and momentum: A dynamic model of strategic change', *Academy of Management Journal*, 34: 591–612.

Kogut, B., Shan, W., and Walker, G. (1993) 'Knowledge in the network and the network as knowledge: The structure of new industries', in G. Grabher (ed.), *The Embedded Firm: On the Social Economics of Industrial Networks*, London: Routledge. pp. 67–94.

Kraatz, M. (1998) 'Learning by association? Interorganizational networks and adaptation to environmental change', *Academy of Management Journal*, 41: 29–60.

Kraatz, M. and Zajac, E. (1996) 'Exploring the limits of the new institutionalism: The causes and consequences of illegitimate organizational change', *American Sociological Review*, 61: 812–36.

Lamertz, K. and Baum, J.A.C. (1998) 'The legitimacy of organizational downsizing in Canada: An analysis of media accounts, 1988–1995', *Canadian Journal of Administrative Sciences*, 15: 93–107.

Lauden, L. (1984) *Progress and its Problems*. Berkeley, CA: University of California Press.

Lawrence, P.R. and Lorsch, J.W. (1967) *Organizations and Environments: Managing Differentiation and Integration*. Boston, MA: Harvard Business School Press.

Lehrman, W. (1994) 'Diversity in decline: Institutional environment and organizational failure in the American life insurance industry', *Social Forces*, 73: 605–35.

Levinthal, D.A. (1991a) 'Random walks and organizational mortality', *Administrative Science Quarterly*, 36: 397–420.

Levinthal, D.A. (1991b) 'Organizational adaptation and environmental selection–Interrelated processes of change', *Organization Science*, 2: 140–5.

Levinthal, D.A. (1994) 'Surviving Schumpeterian environments: An evolutionary perspective', In J.A.C. Baum and J.V. Singh (eds), *Evolutionary Dynamics of Organizations*. New York: Oxford University Press. pp. 167–78.

Levinthal, D.A. and March, J.G. (1993) 'The myopia of learning', *Strategic Management Journal*, 14: 95–112.

Levitt, B. and March, J.G. (1988) 'Organizational learning', *Annual Review of Sociology*, 14: 319–40.

Lomi, A. (1995) 'The population ecology of organizational founding: Location dependence and unobserved heterogeneity', *Administrative Science Quarterly*, 40: 111–44.

Lomi, A. (2000) Density dependence and spatial duality in organizational founding rates: Danish commercial banks, 1846–1989', *Organization Studies*, 21: 433–61.

Loree, D.W. (1993) 'Organizational mortality: The price paid for institutional linkages in the semiconductor industry', Paper presented at the Academy of Management meetings, Atlanta GA.

March, J.G. (1991) 'Exploration and exploitation in organizational learning', *Organization Science*, 2: 71–87.

March, J.G. and Simon, H.A. (1958) *Organizations*. New York: Wiley.

McGrath, J.E. (1982) 'Dilemmatics: The study of research choices and dilemmas', in J.E. McGrath, J. Martin and R.A. Kulka (eds), *Judgement Calls in Research*. Beverly Hills, CA: Sage. pp. 69–102.

McKelvey, B. (1982) *Organizational Systematics*. Berkeley, CA: University of California Press.

McKelvey, B. (1994) 'Evolution and organizational science', in J.A.C. Baum and J.V. Singh (eds), *Evolutionary Dynamics of Organizations*. New York: Oxford University Press. pp. 314–26.

McPherson, J.M. (1983) 'An ecology of affiliation', *American Sociological Review*, 48: 519–32.

Messalam, A. (1998) 'The organizational ecology of investment firms in Egypt: Organizational founding', *Organization Studies*, 19: 23–46.

Meyer, J.W. and Rowan, B. (1977) 'Institutionalized organizations: Formal structure as myth and ceremony', *American Journal of Sociology*, 83: 340–63.

Meyer, M.W. (1994) 'Turning evolution inside the organization', in J.A.C. Baum and J.V. Singh (eds), *Evolutionary Dynamics of Organizations*. New York: Oxford University Press. pp. 109–16.

Mezias, J.M. and Mezias, S.J. (2000) 'Resource partitioning, the founding of specialist firms, and innovation: The American feature film industry, 1912–1929', *Organization Science*, 11: 306–22.

Miller, D. (1990) *The Icarus Paradox: How Exceptional Companies Bring about Their Own Downfall*. New York: Harper Collins.

Miller, D. and Chen, M.-J. (1994) 'Sources and conseqences of competitive inertia: A study of the U.S. airline industry', *Administrative Science Quarterly*, 39: 1–23.

Miller, D. and Friesen, P.H. (1980) 'Momentum and revolution in organizational adaptation', *Academy of Management Journal*, 22: 591–614.

Miner, A.S. (1993) 'Review of *Dynamics of Organizational Populations: Density, competition, and legitimation*, by Michael T. Hannan and Glenn R. Carroll', *Academy of Management Review*, 18: 355–67.

Miner, A.S. (1994) 'Seeking adaptive advantage: Evolutionary theory and managerial action', in J.A.C. Baum and J.V. Singh (eds), *Evolutionary Dynamics of Organizations*. New York: Oxford University Press. pp. 76–89.

Miner, A.S. and Haunschild, P.R. (1995) 'Population level learning', in L.L. Cummings and B.M. Staw (eds), *Research in Organizational Behavior*, 17. Greenwich CT: JAI Press. pp. 115–66.

Miner, A.S., Amburgey, T.L. and Stearns, T. (1990) 'Interorganizational linkages and population dynamics: Buffering and transformational shields', *Administrative Science Quarterly*, 35: 689–713.

Minkoff, D. (1999) 'Bending with the wind: Strategic change and adaptation by women's and racial minority organizations', *American Journal of Sociology*, 104: 1666–703.

Mitchell, W. (1989) 'Whether and when? Probability and timing of entry into emerging industrial subfields', *Administrative Science Quarterly*, 34: 208–30.

Mitchell, W. (1994) 'The dynamics of evolving markets: The effects of business sales and age on dissolutions and divestitures', *Administrative Science Quarterly*, 39(4): 575–99.

Mitchell, W. and Singh, K. (1993) 'Death of the lethargic: Effects of expansion into new technical subfields on performance in a firm's base business', *Organization Science*, 4: 152–80.

Nelson R.R. and Winter, S.G. (1982) *An Evolutionary Theory of Economic Change*. Cambridge, MA: Harvard University Press.

Oliver, C. (1991) 'Strategic responses to institutional processes', *Academy of Management Review*, 16: 145–79.

Olzak, S. (1992) *Dynamics of Ethnic Competition and Conflict*. Stanford, CA: Stanford University Press.

Olzak, S. and West, E. (1991) 'Ethnic conflict and the rise and fall of ethnic newspapers', *American Sociological Review*, 56: 458–74.

Palmer, D. and Barber, B. (2001) 'Challengers, elites, and owning families: A social class theory of corporate acquisitions in the 1960s', *Administrative Science Quarterly*, 46: 87–122.

Péli, G. (1997) 'The niche hiker's guide to population ecology: A logical reconstruction of organizational ecology's niche theory', *Sociological Methodology*, 27: 1–46.

Pennings, J., Lee, K. and van Witteloostuijn, A. (1998) 'Human capital, social capital, and firm dissolution', *Academy of Management Journal*, 41: 425–40.

Perrow, C. (1986) *Complex Organizations: A Critical Essay*, 3rd edn. New York: Random House.

Peteraf, M.A. (1993) 'The cornerstones of competitive advantage: A resource-based view', *Strategic Management Journal*, 14: 179–91.

Petersen, T. and Koput, K.W. (1991) 'Density dependence in organizational mortality: Legitimacy or unobserved heterogeneity', *American Sociological Review*, 56: 399–409.

Pfeffer, J. and Salancik, G.R. (1978) *The External Control of Organizations*. New York: Harper and Row.

Phillips, D. (2001) 'The promotion paradox: Organizational mortality and employee promotion chances in Silicon Valley law firms, 1946–1996', *American Journal of Sociology*, 106: 1058–98.

Phillips, D. (2002) 'A genealogical approach to organizational life chances: The parent-progeny transfer among Silicon Valley law firms, 1946–1996', *Administrative Science Quarterly*, 47: 474–506.

Podolny, J.M., Stuart, T.E. and Hannan, M.T. (1996) 'Networks, knowledge, and niches: Competition in the worldwide semiconductor industry, 1984–1991', *American Journal of Sociology*, 102: 659–89.

Pollock, T.G. and Rindova, V. (2003) 'Media legitimation effects in the market for initial public offerings', *Academy of Management Journal*, 46: 631–42.

Porter, M.E. (1980) *Competitive Strategy*. New York: The Free Press.

Puccia, C.J. and Levins, R. (1985) *Qualitative Modeling of Complex Systems*. Cambridge, MA: Harvard University Press.

Ranger-Moore, J. (1997) 'Bigger may be better, but is older wiser? Organizational age and size in the New York life insurance industry', *American Sociological Review*, 62: 903–20.

Ranger-Moore, J., Banaszak-Holl, J.J. and Hannan, M.T. (1991) 'Density-dependent dynamics in regulated industries: Founding rates of banks and life insurance companies', *Administrative Science Quarterly*, 36: 36–65.

Ranger-Moore, J., Breckenridge, R.S. and Jones, D.L. (1995) 'Patterns of growth and size-localized competition in the New York State life insurance industry, 1860–1985', *Social Forces*, 73: 1027–49.

Rao, H. (1994) 'The social construction of reputation: Certification contests, legitimation and the survival of organizations in the American automobile industry; 1895–1912', *Strategic Management Journal*, 15(Special Issue): 29–44.

Rao, H. (2001) 'The power of public competition: Promoting cognitive legitimacy through certification contests', in C. Schoonhoven and E. Romanelli (eds), *The Entrepreneurship Dynamic*. Stanford CA: Stanford University Press. pp. 262–86.

Rao, H. (2002) 'Interorganizational ecology', in J.A.C. Baum (ed.), *Companion to Organizations*. Oxford, UK: Blackwell. pp. 541–56.

Rao, H. and Neilsen, E.H. (1992) 'An ecology of agency arrangements: Mortality of savings and loan associations, 1960–1987', *Administrative Science Quarterly*, 37: 448–70.

Romanelli, E. (1991) 'The evolution of new organizational forms', *Annual Review of Sociology*, 17: 79–103.

Ruef, M. (1997) 'Assessing organizational fitness on a dynamic landscape: An empirical test of the relative inertia thesis', *Strategic Management Journal*, 18: 837–53.

Ruef, M. and Scott, W.R. (1998) 'A multidimensional model of organizational legitimacy: Hospital survival in changing institutional environments', *Administrative Science Quarterly*, 43: 877–904.

Rumelt, R. (1986) *Strategy, Structure, and Economic Performance*. Boston, MA: Harvard Business School Press.

Saloner, G. (1994) 'Game theory and strategic management: Contributions, applications and limitations', in R.P. Rumelt, D.E. Schendel and D.J. Teece (eds), *Fundamental Issues in Strategic Management*. Boston MA: Harvard Business School Press. pp. 155–94.

Scherer, F.M. and Ross, D. (1990) *Industrial Market Structure and Economic Performance*, 3rd edn. Boston: Haughton Mifflin.

Scott, W.R. (1992) *Organizations: Rational, Natural, and Open Systems*, 3rd edn. Englewood Cliffs, NJ: Prentice-Hall.

Scott, W.R. and Meyer, J.W. (1983) 'The organization of societal sectors', in J.W. Meyer and W.R. Scott (eds), *Organizational Environments: Ritual and Rationality*. Beverly Hills, CA: Sage. pp. 1–16.

Shane, S. and Stuart, T. (2002) 'Organizational endowments and the performance of university start-ups', *Management Science*, 48: 154–70.

Singh, J.V. (1993) 'Review essay: Density dependence theory—Current issues, future promise', *American Journal of Sociology*, 99: 464–73.

Singh, J.V. and Lumsden, C.J. (1990) 'Theory and research in organizational ecology', *Annual Review of Sociology*, 16: 161–95.

Singh, J.V., House, R.J. and Tucker, D.J. (1986a) 'Organizational change and organizational mortality', *Administrative Science Quarterly*, 31: 587–611.

Singh, J.V., Tucker, D.J. and House, R.J. (1986b) 'Organizational legitimacy and the liability of newness', *Administrative Science Quarterly*, 31: 171–93.

Singh, J.V., Tucker, D.J. and Meinhard, A.G. (1988) 'Are voluntary social service organizations structurally inert? Exploring an assumption in organizational ecology', Academy of Management Meeting, Anaheim, CA.

Singh, J.V., Tucker, D.J. and Meinhard, A.G. (1991) 'Institutional change and ecological dynamics', in W.W. Powell and P.J. DiMaggio (eds), *The New Institutionalism in Organizational Analysis*. Chicago, IL: University of Chicago Press. pp. 390–422.

Singh, K. (1997) 'The impact of technological complexity and interfirm cooperation on business survival', *Academy of Management Journal*, 40: 339–67.

Sitkin, S.B. (1992) 'Learning through failure: The strategy of small losses', in B.M. Staw and L.L. Cummings (eds), *Research in Organizational Behavior*, 14. Greenwich, CT: JAI Press. pp. 231–66.

Sorenson, O. (2000) 'The effect of population level learning on market entry: The American automobile industry', *Social Science Research*, 29: 307–26.

Starbuck, W.H. (1965) 'Organizational growth and development', in J.G. March (ed.), *Handbook of Organizations*. Chicago: Rand-McNally. pp. 451–533.

Starbuck, W.H. (1983) 'Organizations as action generators', *American Sociological Review*, 48: 91–102.

Stinchcombe, A.L. (1965) 'Social structure and organizations', in J.G. March (ed.), *Handbook of Organizations*. Chicago, IL: Rand McNally. pp. 153–93.

Stuart, T.E. and Sorenson, O. (2003a) 'The geography of opportunity: Spatial heterogeneity in founding rates and the performance of biotechnology firms', *Research Policy*, 32: 229–53.

Stuart, T.E. and Sorenson, O. (2003b) 'Liquidity events and the geographic distribution of entrepreneurial activity', *Administrative Science Quarterly*, 48: 175–201.

Suhomlinova, O. (1999) 'Constructive destruction: Transformation of Russian state-owned construction enterprises during market transition', *Organization Studies*, 20: 451–83.

Swaminathan, A. (1995) 'The proliferation of specialist organizations in the American wine industry: 1941–1990', *Administrative Science Quarterly*, 40: 653–80.

Swaminathan, A. (2001) 'Resource partitioning and the evolution of specialist organizations: The role of location and identity in the U.S. wine industry', *Academy of Management Journal*, 44: 1169–85.

Swaminathan, A. and Delacroix, J. (1991) 'Differentiation within an organizational population: Additional evidence from the wine industry', *Academy of Management Journal*, 34: 679–92.

Swaminathan, A. and Wiedenmayer, G. (1991) 'Does the pattern of density dependence in organizational mortality rates vary across levels of analysis? Evidence from the German brewing industry', *Social Science Research*, 20: 45–73.

Thompson, J.D. (1967) *Organizations in Action*. New York: Academic Press.

Tilly, C. (1993) *European Revolutions, 1492–1992*. Cambridge, MA: Blackwell.

Tirole, J. (1988) *The Theory of Industrial Organization*. Cambridge, MA: MIT Press.

Tucker, D.J. (1994) 'Progress and problems in population ecology', in J.A.C. Baum and J.V. Singh (eds), *Evolutionary Dynamics of Organizations*. New York: Oxford University Press. pp. 327–36.

Tucker, D.J., Baum, J.A.C. and Singh, J.V. (1992) 'The institutional ecology of human service organizations', in Y. Hasenfeld (ed.), *Human Service Organizations*. Newbury Park, CA: Sage. pp. 47–72.

Tucker, D.J., Singh, J.V. and Meinhard, A.G. (1990a) 'Organizational form, population dynamics, and institutional change: The founding patterns of voluntary organizations', *Academy of Management Journal*, 33: 151–78.

Tucker, D.J., Singh, J.V. and Meinhard, A.G. (1990b) 'Founding characteristics, imprinting, and organizational change', in J.V. Singh (ed.), *Organizational Evolution: New Directions*. Newbury Park CA: Sage. pp. 182–200.

Tucker, D.J., Singh, J.V., Meinhard, A.G. and House, R.J. (1988) 'Ecological and institutional sources of change in organizational populations', in G.R. Carroll (ed.), *Ecological Models of Organizations*. Cambridge, MA: Ballinger. pp. 127–51.

Tuma, N.B. and Hannan, M.T. (1984) *Social Dynamics: Models and Methods*. New York: Academic Press.

Tushman, M.L. and Anderson, P. (1986) 'Technological discontinuities and organizational environments', *Administrative Science Quarterly*, 31: 439–65.

Tushman, M.L. and Romanelli, E. (1985) 'Organizational evolution: A metamorphosis model of convergence and reorientation', *Research in Organizational Behavior*, 7: 171–222.

Usher, J.M. (1991) 'Exploring the effects of niche crowding on rates of organizational change and failure'. Unpublished manuscript, Faculty of Business, University of Alberta.

Usher, J.M. and Evans, M.G. (1996) 'Life and death along gasoline alley: Darwinian and Lamarckian processes in a differentiating population', *Academy of Management Journal*, 39: 1428–66.

Vermeulen, F. and Barkema, H. (2001) 'Learning through acquisitions', *Academy of Management Journal*, 44: 457–76.

Wade, J.B., Swaminathan, A. and Saxon, M.S. (1998) 'Normative and resource flow consequences of local regulations in the American brewing industry, 1845–1918', *Administrative Science Quarterly*, 43: 905–35.

West, E. (1995) 'Organization building in the wake of ethnic conflict: A comparison of three ethnic groups', *Social Forces*, 73: 1333–63.

White, H.C. (1981) 'Where do markets come from?', *American Journal of Sociology*, 87: 517–47.

Wholey, D.R., Christianson, J.B. and Sanchez, S.M. (1992) 'Organizational size and failure among health maintenance organizations', *American Sociological Review*, 57: 829–42.

Wiewel, W. and Hunter, A. (1985) 'The interorganizational network as a resource', *Administrative Science Quarterly*, 30: 482–96.

Winter, S.G. (1990) 'Survival, selection, and inheritance in evolutionary theories of organization', in J.V. Singh (ed.), *Organizational Evolution: New Directions*. Newbury Park CA: Sage. pp. 269–97.

Yelle, L.E. (1979) 'The learning curve: Historical review and comprehensive survey', *Decision Sciences*, 10: 302–28.

Zajac, E.J. and Kraatz, M.S. (1993) 'A diametric forces model of strategic change: Assessing the antecedents and consequences of restructuring in the higher education industry', *Strategic Management Journal*, 14(S): 83–102.

Zucker, L.G. (1977) 'The role of institutionalization in cultural persistence', *American Sociological Review*, 42: 726–43.

Zucker, L.G. (1989) 'Combining institutional theory and population ecology: No legitimacy, no history', *American Sociological Review*, 54: 542–5.

1.3 Organizational Economics: Understanding the Relationship between Organizations and Economic Analysis

JAY B. BARNEY AND WILLIAM HESTERLY

The field of organizational economics can be defined in a variety of ways. Some have argued that organizational economics is distinguished from other types of organizational analysis by its reliance on equilibrium analysis, assumptions of profit maximizing managers and the use of abstract assumptions and models. In fact, some organizational economists do engage in these kinds of analyses and build models of organizations using these kinds of tools. However, not all organizational economists apply all the tools, all the time. For example, both evolutionary economic theory (Nelson and Winter 1982) and Austrian economics (Jacobson 1992) are explicitly non-equilibrium in nature. Models of risk shifting (Arrow 1985), decision-making (March and Simon 1958) and transaction economics (Williamson 1975) do not assume perfect rationality. Agency theory (Jensen and Meckling 1976) and theories of tacit collusion (Tirole 1989) and strategic alliances (Kogut 1988) do not assume that all managers, all the time, adopt profit maximizing objectives in their decision-making. Finally, a great deal of organizational economics is neither very mathematical nor highly technical, although questions of how abstract a model is are usually matters of taste.

Indeed, the diversity of perspectives subsumed under organizational economics seem to have only two things in common in their approach to organizational analysis. The first is an abiding interest in organizations or firms (as economists usually call organizations). Unlike most economists, who are interested in the structure, functioning and implications of markets, organizational economists are interested in the structure, functioning and implications of firms.

Secondly, most organizational economists have an unflagging interest in the relationship between competition and organizations. Even organizational economists who study organizations under conditions of monopoly (where, presumably, there is relatively little competition) tend to focus on competitive processes that increase competition for monopolists over time (see the discussion of 'contestable market theory' below). For organizational economists, organizations exist in 'seething caldrons' of competition, where other firms, individuals, institutions and governments are all seeking to obtain some part of the success that a particular firm may enjoy.

It is interesting to note that other forms of organizational analysis share this interest in organizations and competition. For example, the population ecology model (Hannan and Freeman 1977), in organization theory, has a well developed notion of competition, although (some might argue) a somewhat under-developed appreciation for the complexity of modern firms. Resource dependence theory discusses organizational responses to more or less munificent environments (Pfeffer and Salancik 1978). Even institutional theory (DiMaggio and Powell 1983) discusses the importance of legitimacy for an organization's survival. The probability of organizational survival is also of major interest in organizational economics. Organizational economics is hardly divorced from this broader organizational literature.

Incidentally, the focus on competition in organizational economics does not preclude discussions of co-operation within and between firms. As will be discussed later, intra-firm co-operation is one of the core issues in agency theory and inter-firm co-operation (in the form of tacit collusion or strategic alliances) is an important topic in organizational economics as well. However, the role of co-operation in the

Organizational Economic models is generally to enable a firm to more effectively respond to its competitive threats (Kogut 1988).

This twin focus on organizations, their origins and consequences and on competition has generated a very large and ever growing literature. This huge literature can be conveniently divided into four major streams, each stream focusing on a slightly different, though related, central research question. These four research streams and their associated research questions are: (1) transactions cost economics (why do organizations exist?), (2) agency theory (do those associated with a firm agree about how it should be managed?), (3) strategic management theory (why do some organizations outperform others?), and (4) co-operative organizational economics (how can organizations co-operate?). These four research streams, and their associated research questions, are discussed in subsequent sections of this chapter.

Why do Organizations Exist?

This question is, in many ways, the most central to organizational economics, in particular, and to organizational analysis more generally (Weingast and Marshall 1988; Moe 1991). To many, the question 'why do organizations exist?' may sound odd. After all, it is pretty obvious that organizations do exist. Why go to such great effort to explain the existence of such a common phenomenon? However, this question becomes important in the context of neoclassical microeconomic theory.

Classical and neo-classical theory, beginning with Adam Smith, point to the amazing ability of markets to co-ordinate economic production and exchange at very low cost and without government planning. Simply stated, Smith's fundamental proposition was that an economy could be co-ordinated by a decentralized system of prices (the 'invisible hand'). Indeed, much of economics since the publication of *The Wealth of Nations* has involved formalizing this proposition, identifying the necessary conditions for the effective use of the invisible hand, and designing changes in those settings where the conditions are lacking (Demsetz 1990: 145). In most economics textbooks, this work is called the theory of the firm – although the theory actually focuses exclusively on the structure and operation of markets and is unable to explain the existence of firms. Given that markets are so effective in co-ordinating economic exchanges

it has always been a bit of a mystery why not all exchanges are managed through market, i.e. why economic exchanges would ever be managed through firms (Coase 1937).

Remarkably, the answer to the question 'why do organizations exist?' was formulated by Ronald Coase while he was a 21-year-old student at the London School of Economics. It was Coase's great insight – published in his 1937 article 'The nature of the firm' – that the reason organizations exist is that, sometimes, the cost of managing economic exchanges across markets is greater than the cost of managing economic exchanges within the boundaries of an organization. The cost of using the price system involves such activities as discovering what prices are, negotiating contracts, renegotiating contracts, inspections and settling disputes. The most lasting contribution of Coase's (1937) article was to place transaction costs at the centre of analysis of the questions of why firm exist and to suggest that markets and organizations are alternatives for managing the same transactions. However, by Coase's (1972: 63) own admission, 'The nature of the firm' was 'much cited and little used'. This early lack of influence stems largely from Coase's failure to operationalize his approach and his lack of precision about which transactions will be left to the market and which will be internalized within firms. Later theorists addressed these deficiencies by developing a more complete model of the costs of using a market to manage economic exchanges. This work has come to be known as transaction cost economics (TCE).

The Alchian-Demsetz Approach

The first influential extension of Coase's reasoning emphasized measurement or metering problems as the reason firms exist (Alchian and Demsetz 1972). Measurement problems occur as a result of team production. Team production typically involves gains from co-operation when complex production processes are involved. The members of the team can produce more working co-operatively with one another than separately. Thus, they have an incentive to co-operate. This incentive to co-operate, however, declines as the potential for shirking among team members increases. Shirking includes behaviours that range from outright cheating to merely giving less than one's best effort. While the interdependence between team members yields potentially greater production, it also makes it more difficult to assess the contribution of each individual member. With no mechanism to monitor or measure each team member's efforts, the team cannot reward members based on individual productivity. If team members know that their individual efforts are only imperfectly connected to their individual rewards, then they have an incentive to work less diligently. The team may seek another way to reward members for their efforts.

One alternative is to split the income generated by the team equally among members. However, this equal sharing arrangement does not remove the incentive of team members to shirk. This incentive occurs because individuals know that the costs of any additional efforts on their part will be theirs alone, while the rewards that come from these efforts will be split among the team. Since each team member has this same incentive to shirk, team production will fall. Indeed, the possibility of shirking also may discourage high-output individuals from joining the team in the first place. When high-output individuals do join the team, they may become shirkers once they become members.

The firm emerges to meet the need to monitor the efforts of those individuals that make up a team. Monitoring each individual reduces the likelihood of shirking. As individuals are assigned to monitoring roles, a hierarchy emerges. Shirking is not completely eliminated by the hierarchy, however. Because monitoring is costly, it is efficient to monitor only to the point where the marginal benefits from reduced shirking equal the marginal costs of monitoring. It is typically neither reasonable nor efficient to completely remove shirking, even when technically possible to fully monitor the efforts of team members (Zenger and Marshall 2000).

Assigning someone the task of monitoring the performance of individuals on a team creates yet another problem. Specifically, who will monitor the monitor? As with other team members, the monitor has an incentive to shirk unless contrary incentives exist. Alchian and Demsetz's (1972) solution to this problem is to have the monitor bear the cost of her shirking by giving this person the right to negotiate contracts with all team members, to monitor their productive efforts and (most importantly) to claim any residual value created by a team, after team members receive their expected compensation. The monitor then pays team members based on their individual productivity and keeps the remaining portion as income. This arrangement leaves the monitor with a strong incentive to monitor the

efforts of each team member. The results are reduced incentives for shirking and increased team productivity that is shared between the team members and the monitor. In the modern corporation, this ultimate 'monitor of monitors' is a firm's stockholders. Just as Alchian and Demsetz expect, stockholders have a claim on a firms residual profits, i.e. profits that remain after all other legitimate claims on a firm have been satisfied.

Williamson's Formulation of Transaction Cost Economics

The Alchian-Demsetz approach to explaining the existence of organizations has several strengths. For example, it does explain the existence of managerial hierarchies and the existence of stockholders as a firm's residual claimants. However, many organizational economists have found that Alchian and Demsetz's exclusive focus on team production obscures some important issues associated with understanding the nature of the firm. The most highly developed alternative to the Alchian and Demsetz approach can be found in the work of Oliver Williamson. Indeed, it can be said that Williamson's answers to why organizations exist are now considered to be the core of transaction cost economics.

A basic assertion of Williamson's TCE is that markets and hierarchies are alternative instruments for completing a set of transactions (Williamson 1975: 8). As instruments for completing a set of transactions, markets and hierarchies are often also called 'governance mechanisms'. In general, market forms of governance rely on prices, competition and contracts to keep all parties to an exchange informed of their rights and responsibilities. Hierarchical forms of governance, on the other hand, bring parties to an exchange under the direct control of a third party (typically called 'the boss'). This authoritative third party then attempts to keep all parties to an exchange informed of their rights and responsibilities. Moreover, this third party has the right to directly resolve any conflicts that might emerge in an exchange. Williamson calls the exercise of this right 'managerial fiat'.

Behavioural Assumptions

TCE rests on two essential assumptions about economic actors (be they individuals or firms) engaged in transactions: bounded rationality and opportunism. Bounded rationality means that those who engage in economic transactions are 'intendedly rational, but only limitedly so' (Simon 1947: xxiv). Within economics, this assumption is an important departure from the traditional omniscient hyper-rationality of *homo economicus* (Simon 1947; Hesterly and Zenger 1993). Without cognitive limits, all exchange could be conducted through planning (Williamson 1985). People could write contracts of unlimited complexity that would specify all possible contingencies in an economic exchange (Williamson 1975). However, given bounded rationality, complex contracting breaks down in the face of uncertainty. Economic actors simply cannot foresee all possible outcomes in an exchange relationship or formulate contractual or other responses to those (unforeseeable) eventualities.

Opportunism is also a departure from the behavioural assumptions used in mainstream economics.[1] While traditional economics assumes simply that economic actors behave out of self-interest, TCE assumes the possibility of self-interest seeking with guile (Williamson 1975: 26). For Williamson (1985: 47), opportunism includes lying, stealing and cheating, but it more generally 'refers to the incomplete or distorted disclosure of information, especially to calculated efforts to mislead, distort, disguise. obfuscate or otherwise confuse' partners in an exchange. TCE does not assume that all economic actors are always opportunistic. Rather, all it assumes is that some of these actors may behave opportunistically and that it is costly to distinguish those who are prone to opportunism from those who are not. The threat of opportunism is important because, in a world without opportunism, all economic exchange could be done on the basis of promise. Parties in such a transaction would simply pledge at the outset to perform their part of an exchange fairly (Williamson 1985: 31). Given, however, that some are prone to opportunism, people and firms must design safeguards so they will not be victimized by others.

The Choice of Governance

The governance decision, as characterized in TCE, is straightforward. Economic actors will choose that form of governance (market or hierarchy) that reduces any potential exchange problems created by bounded rationality, on the one hand, and by the threat of opportunism, on the other, at the lowest cost (Masten et al. 1991). The governance of economic

transactions is costly. However, as suggested by Adam Smith and many others, markets have lower fixed costs compared to hierarchical forms of governance. If a market form of governance enables parties to an exchange to reduce potential exchange problems created by bounded rationality and the tendency towards opportunism, then a market form of governance will be preferred over a hierarchical form of governance. However, if market governance does not solve these exchange problems, then more costly forms of hierarchical governance may have to be employed.

Put differently, if all economic actors had to worry about was minimizing the effects of bounded rationality and opportunism on their exchanges, then they would always choose hierarchical forms of governance. In hierarchical governance, there is always a third party whose sole responsibility is to manage an exchange in ways that minimize problems created by bounded rationality and opportunism. Of course, economic actors need to be concerned both about the problems created by bounded rationality and opportunism *and* about the cost of governing economic exchanges.

When Will Bounded Rationality and Opportunism Create Exchange Problems?

Given this characterization of the governance decisions facing economic actors, it is important to understand the attributes of transactions that will make bounded rationality and opportunism problematic. While this aspect of TCE has evolved some over the years, two attributes of transactions are now widely seen as creating the most problems for economic actors in transactions: uncertainty and transaction specific investment.

Without uncertainty, bounded rationality is irrelevant. If parties to a transaction could anticipate precisely how a transaction will evolve over time, and how rights and responsibilities in a transaction will evolve, then managing that transaction over time is very simple. All that has to be done is for parties to an exchange to write a contract that specifies all current and future states in an exchange, and the rights and responsibilities of all actors in those future states. Of course, under conditions of uncertainty, this is not possible. In general, the greater the level of uncertainty in a transaction, the more difficult it will be to use contracts and other forms of market governance to manage that transaction, and the more likely that hierarchical forms of governance will be adopted. Under hierarchical governance, a third party can decide how unanticipated problems in a transaction can be resolved. Moreover, parties in a transaction need not anticipate what these problems might be (they cannot do so), nor do they need to anticipate what the third party will do in response to these problems (they cannot do so). Rather, all they need to do is agree that, if such problems arise in the future, a third party will mediate and solve those problems.

As important as uncertainty in a transaction is for exchange partners to choose hierarchical forms of governance, the level of transaction specific investment in a transaction is generally seen as being even more important. It is often the case that parties in a transaction will need to make investments in that transaction in order to facilitate its completion. These investments can take many forms. For example, parties to a transaction may need to modify some of their physical technology to expedite the exchange (e.g. a firm may have to change the height of its loading docks to accommodate another firm's trucks). In many transactions, parties may need to modify some of their operating policies and procedures to expedite the exchange (e.g. a firm may have to simplify its order entry procedures to ensure more timely delivery of critical supplies). In other transactions, individuals involved may learn the special language, the informal working style and the business practices of transaction partners, all to facilitate a transaction.

All these investments have value in the particular transaction where they were originally made. Some of these investments may have value in other transactions as well. For example, a sales person may need to learn a new word processing language in order to efficiently interact with a group of new customers who already use this language in their work. However, this word processing language may also be used by numerous other potential customers. Thus, the investment in this new language is valuable in the transaction between the sales person and her new set of customers, but it may also be valuable in possible transactions between this sales person and another set of potential customers.

On the other hand, certain investments in a transaction are only valuable in that particular transaction and have little or no value in any other transaction. Such investments are transaction specific. Formally,

transaction specific investments are investments that are much more valuable in a particular transaction compared to other possible transactions. The greater the difference in value between an investment's first best use (in the current transaction) and the second best use (in some other transaction), the more specific the investment.

The existence of transaction specific investments increases the threat of opportunism. For example, suppose that a firm A is a supplier to firm B. Also, suppose that firm A has totally revised its manufacturing, sales and distribution processes to fit firm B's needs, that firm B's needs are completely unique, and that firm A has not had to make any special investments in firm B. Also, suppose firm A has several alternative suppliers, besides firm B. In this situation, firm A has made significant transaction specific investments in its relationship with firm B. It may be the case that firm B decides to exploit firm A by, say, insisting on a lower price for firm A's supplies than what had been agreed to in the original supply contract. What can firm A do? If firm A refuses to give in to firm B's demand, it loses the economic value of its investment in A. As long as the price reductions demanded by firm B are not as costly as entirely abandoning its investment in firm B, firm A will acquiesce to firm B's demands. The specific investment made by firm A creates an opportunity for firm B to behave opportunistically.

The greater the level of transaction specific investment in an exchange, the greater the threat of opportunism. The greater the threat of opportunism, the less likely that market governance will effectively reduce this threat and the more likely that hierarchical forms of governance will be chosen – despite their additional costs. In the simple example discussed above, hierarchical governance would imply that firm A and firm B would be brought together into a single corporation and that a corporate manager ('the boss') would mediate the relationship between what would then be division A and division B. With this mediator in place, division A could make the transaction specific investments it needs to facilitate its supply relationship with division B, relying on the mediator to make sure that division B did not take unfair advantage of these specific investments.

In short, Williamson's answer to the question 'why do organizations exist?' is that hierarchy arises to resolve the problems of market governance with transaction specific investments under conditions of uncertainty. Once under common ownership, the two parties in the exchange have less incentive to seek advantage over each other. Disputes are less likely to occur because the hierarchy is able to establish joint goals which lead to convergent expectations between those in a transaction. Additionally, hierarchy facilitates the development of codes and language that are unique to a firm which allow for more accurate and efficient communication (Arrow 1974; Williamson 1975).

While hierarchy provides a resolution to the problem of transaction specific investments under uncertainty, there are, however, limits to using hierarchy. Firms are prone to important incentive and bureaucratic disabilities that limit their size. The high-powered incentives of the market are not easily duplicated within firms, particularly large ones.

Applications of Transaction Cost Economics

Vertical Integration

The most researched application of TCE, vertical integration, is the most direct examination of the question 'why do organizations exist?' (see Joskow 1988; Mahoney 1992; Shelanski and Klein 1995; David and Han 2004 for reviews). TCE studies approach vertical integration differently than much of the previous work in economics (see Blair and Kaserman 1983 for review). Instead of viewing vertical integration as an aggregate measure of value added for an entire firm, TCE scholars typically use the transaction as their level of analysis (MacMillan et al. 1986; Caves and Bradburn 1988). This research, which examines what in mundane terms is labelled make or buy decisions, finds consistent support for the proposition that transaction specific investment increases the likelihood that a transaction will be internalized (Armour and Teece 1980; Walker and Weber 1984; 1987; Levy 1985; John and Weitz 1988).

The Multidivisional Form

Another important extension of TCE to internal organization focuses on the multidivisional (M-form) firm, which Williamson (1985: 279) regards as the 'most significant organizational innovation of the twentieth century'. Chandler's (1962) historical study of strategy and structure in large American firms documented the rise of the M-form. Superimposing transaction costs logic over Chandler's findings, Williamson sees bounded rationality and opportunism at the root of the M-form's broad diffusion

among US firms. He argues that, as functionally organized firms (U-forms) expand in size and diversity, it becomes increasingly difficult for the top managers to deal with the myriad of operating problems faced by the company. Moreover, combining greater diversity with the interdependence between functional units makes it difficult to assign responsibility for successes and failures for a product or line of business. Thus, the complexity of the enterprise overwhelms the information processing capacity – or, in TCE terms, the bounded rationality – of top managers. Additionally, increased complexity makes it more difficult to tie the goals of functional units to the goals of the firm as a whole. This inability to operationalize functional goals causes managers to pursue functional subgoals in sales, manufacturing, etc., often at the expense of firm performance – or in TCE terms, the problem of opportunism.

The M-form resolves these difficulties by organizing firms into either product or geographic divisions where operational decisions and accountability for performance are placed on a division manager. A typical M-form structure is presented in Figure 1.3.1. Ideally, this structure separates strategic and operational decisions. Strategic decisions are limited to senior managers in the corporate office. Operational decisions are delegated to senior managers within operating divisions. By limiting their responsibility to strategic decision-making, the M-form reduces the bounded rationality problem faced by top managers in the corporate office. Dividing the firm into quasi-autonomous divisions facilitates clearer performance goals at lower levels of the organization. Responsibility for the performance of a business line is fixed upon a single divisional manager.

Ultimately, the M-form structure also allows the firm to function as a miniature capital market where the corporate office monitors division performance, assigns cash flows to their highest yield uses, and engages in diversification, acquisition and divestiture activities (Williamson 1970; 1975; 1985). From the TCE perspective, the M-form possesses important advantages over the external capital market: (1) it has access to more accurate information about divisions; (2) it can manipulate incentives and replace poorly performing managers more easily; and (3) it can exercise control over the strategies pursued by divisions.

Empirical evidence tends to support Williamson's contention that the M-form outperforms the functional structure in large, diversified firms (see

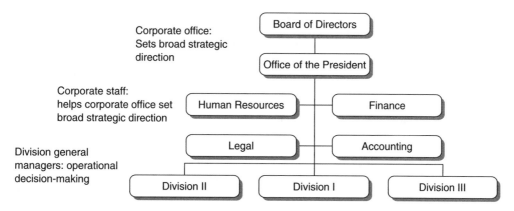

Figure 1.3.1 Typical multidivisional (M-form) structure

Hoskisson et al. 1993 for review). In their seminal study of M-form adoption in the oil industry, Armour and Teece (1978) found that early adopters enjoyed performance advantages over the rest of the industry. As expected, though, these performance advantages disappeared as other firms adopted the M-form structure. Several other studies offer at least some support for the M-form hypothesis (Steer and Cable 1978; Grinyer et al. 1980; Teece 1981; Thompson 1981; Hall 1983; Harris 1983; Hill 1985; Hoskisson and Galbraith 1985; Hoskisson et al. 1991; Ollinger 1993). A few studies of non-US firms found no evidence that firms with an M-form structure enjoyed superior performance (Cable and Dirrheimer 1983; Cable and Yasuki 1985; Hill 1985; 1988). Reliance upon archival data sources suggests, however, that many of these studies may not have accurately classified M-form structures (Hill 1988). Thus, some debate remains as to what can be learned from these empirical tests (Hoskisson et al. 1993).

Criticisms of the M-form tend to focus on its effectiveness as an internal capital market (Bhagat et al. 1990). The emergence of more powerful, concentrated, institutional investors in recent years has greatly reduced the advantages enjoyed by top managers over external investors. Arguably, the informational asymmetries between managers and outside investors has been reduced. Anecdotal accounts also suggest that external investors are much more effective at displacing top executives and even influencing strategy than in the past. Assuming these changes are true, the governance advantages of the M-form over

the external capital market have eroded. Thus, according to this reasoning, the M-form hypothesis may have been true when it was formulated, but it is likely outdated (Bettis 1991: 315–6; Bartlett and Ghoshal 1993). This criticism, however, remains to be tested (Hoskisson et al. 1993: 275).

Other criticisms of the M-form are based on the notion that it does not adequately align the interests of top managers with those of shareholders. In short, it assumes away the agency problem (Hoskisson and Turk 1990, and the discussion below). While the M-form assumes strong incentives on the part of divisional managers to maximize performance, there is no explicit mechanism that motivates top managers to do the same for the firm. Thus, top managers are able to pursue inefficient diversification. The M-form, with its decomposed structure of quasi-firms, only facilitates this excessive diversification. Incentive problems at the divisional level are not completely eliminated either. With the M-form's emphasis on financial evaluation, division managers may choose to focus on risk averse, short-term profit maximization while sacrificing activities such as R&D investment that are critical to long-term success. Research supporting these criticisms is somewhat equivocal, however, since it typically fails to disentangle the effects of strategy (diversification) from structure (the M-form) (Hoskisson and Johnson 1992).

Markets, Bureaucracies and Clans

Ouchi (1979; 1980) extended the transactions cost framework to explain alternative ways of co-ordinating activities within firms. He argued that firms rely on three basic forms of control: markets, bureaucracies and clans. Markets co-ordinate through prices, bureaucracies co-ordinate through authority and rules, and clans combine authority with shared values and beliefs to effect co-operation. As with Williamson's general formulation of TCE, the efficiency of these mechanisms varies depending on the conditions of the exchange. In these conditions of exchange, however, Ouchi departs from Williamson by emphasizing goal incongruence and performance ambiguity as the crucial dimensions of exchanges. Transaction costs in Ouchi's (1980: 130) framework arise from a demand for equity and include 'any activity which is engaged in to satisfy each party to an exchange that the value given and received is in accord with his or her expectations'.

For Ouchi (1980), markets are efficient when goal incongruence is high and performance ambiguity is low. Prices adequately convey the information necessary to co-ordinate activity and the parties need not share congruent goals. As performance becomes more ambiguous and the need for congruent goals increases, firms will find bureaucratic governance more efficient than market exchange. Bureaucracy uses authority and rules which allow the firm to resolve performance ambiguity problems through monitoring employees and constrains goal incongruence through rules and other operating procedures (Ouchi 1979). When performance ambiguity reaches very high levels, then neither the measurement of market mechanisms nor bureaucratic monitoring can insure that employees' efforts will be directed towards the organization's goals. Under these circumstances, clan governance is most efficient. Clan governance requires intensive people processing (Ouchi 1979) or socialization (Ouchi 1980) and long-term associations within the firm to serve as an effective means of control. These activities are more costly than market and bureaucratic control, however. Thus, an investment in clan control is not warranted when performance ambiguity is low or moderate (Murphy et al. 1999). Ouchi's theory of markets, bureaucracies and, particularly, clans was influential in stimulating interest in the topic of organizational culture.

The Multinational Enterprise

TCE perhaps found its earliest and most complete acceptance among international business and economics scholars. The internalization school (Buckley and Casson 1976; Rugman 1981; Hennart 1982) applied TCE to understanding where multinational enterprises (MNEs) would internalize transactions within the firm and where they would rely upon market exchange. The explanation for MNEs centred around market imperfections. Markets for different assets, particularly some types of knowledge (Buckley and Casson 1976: 39), are subject to market imperfections. The main conclusion of this early work was that markets will tend to be more efficient when there are a large number of buyers and sellers. Transactions characterized by high uncertainty and complex, heterogeneous products between a small number of buyers and traders, on the other hand, favour internalization (Buckley and Casson 1976: 167–8).

Teece (1986) extended Casson and Buckley's reasoning on the role of knowledge in determining firm boundaries. He argued that when knowledge is difficult to trade – either because doing so would give away that knowledge or because the necessary infrastructure of capabilities, communication codes or culture is absent – firms will internalize those transactions. Empirical evidence (see Teece 1986 for review) supports the transaction cost economics of the MNE. Although fairly distinct literatures on vertical integration and MNEs have emerged, there is little in the TCE theory of the MNE that is distinctly international. The MNE from a TCE perspective is largely a special case of the vertical integration problem. In essence, this literature is a simple restatement of the question 'why do organizations exist?' to become 'why do MNEs exist?'

Organizational Forms

Early TCE focused on the polar opposites of markets and hierarchies for organizing economic activity. Alternatives to markets other than hierarchies were acknowledged, but how these intermediate forms are viewed has shifted over time. Initially, Williamson (1975) saw them as unstable, then later acknowledged that they might occur as often as markets and hierarchies (Williamson 1985). TCE labels these intermediate forms hybrids. Hybrids include governance structures that are neither hierarchy nor market. Research on hybrids has focused on long-term contracting (Joskow 1985), joint ventures (Hennart 1991) and franchises (Brickley and Dark 1987; Brickley et al. 1991; Fladmoe-Lindquist and

Jacque 1995). More recently, network organizations – production among a set of firms with continuing ties – have received much attention (Thorelli 1986; Powell 1987). Scholars have observed such networks in areas as diverse as the US film industry (Baker and Faulkner 1991), publishing (Powell 1987), construction (Eccles 1981), Italian textiles (Mariotti and Cairnarca 1986), the Japanese auto industry (Fruin 1992; Nishiguchi 1994) and Silicon Valley (Saxenian 1994). More recently, the focus on hybrids has been extended to the governance properties of interfirm networks (Jones et al. 1997) and 'molecular' units that co-ordinate their efforts either within or between firms (Zenger and Hesterly 1997; Brusoni et al. 2001).

The existence of hybrids extends Coase's original question: 'Why do hybrids exist?' The most general answer is that hybrids have stronger incentives and adaptive capabilities than hierarchies while offering more administrative control than markets (Williamson 1991a: 281). Thus, for transactions that require a mix of incentives, adaptation and control, hybrids are well-suited (Williamson 1991a).

Debate remains, however, about whether hybrid governance structures are discrete mechanisms or consist of a continuum of forms ranging from pure market to pure hierarchy (Bradach and Eccles 1989). On the one hand, Williamson (1991c: 165, 176) argues that the impossibility of selective intervention (i.e. the problem of infusing market attributes into hierarchies and hierarchical features into markets) precludes a continuum of governance forms. According to this logic, differences in contract law also drive governance towards discrete forms (Masten 1988; Williamson 1991c). Conversely, others view hybrid governance structures as a continuum of plural forms that combine the features of hierarchy and market (Bradach and Eccles 1989; Hennart 1993). This question has not been resolved with any finality with some suggesting that the inability of top management to credibly commit to not intervene in decentralized decision-making makes selective intervention unstable (Foss 2003). Others, notably Zenger and Hesterly (1997), take the more optimistic view that, given organizational units that are decomposable and measurable, information technology and performance measurement innovations have facilitated selective infusions of market governance into hierarchies and hierarchical governance into markets. Nickerson and Zenger (2004) argue that the

decomposability of problems that organizations seek to solve strongly affects governance choices.

Criticisms of Transaction Cost Economics

Transaction cost economics has attracted its share of critics (see, for example, Putterman 1984; Perrow 1986; Robins 1987; Demsetz 1988). Of the many criticisms directed at TCE, three are particularly central: (1) TCE focuses on cost minimization; (2) it understates the cost of organizing; (3) it neglects the role of social relationships in economic transactions; and (4) the emphasis on opportunism is harmful when employed by managers.

TCE focuses on cost minimization as the organizational imperative. Or, as Williamson (1991b: 76) argues, 'economizing is more fundamental than strategizing – or, put differently, *economy is the best strategy*'. Resource-based theory (discussed below), particularly, takes exception to this emphasis. As we shall see, resource-based logic suggests that creating and exploiting transaction specific investments under conditions of uncertainty is essential if firms are to gain long-term success (Conner 1991; Kogut and Zander 1992). Avoiding opportunism and minimizing governance costs are a secondary consideration. Minimizing transaction costs is of relatively little benefit if a firm has no transaction specific assets (including knowledge) that are highly valued by the market.

A second criticism of TCE is that it tends to understate the costs of organizing transactions within the firm (Jones and Hill 1988). The use of authority is assumed to resolve internal disputes more efficiently than the market. Clearly, this is not always the case. Lengthy and costly haggling may often be more severe within a firm than between firms, as Eccles's (1985) study of transfer pricing shows. Indeed, internal organization is often susceptible to costly bargaining and influence behaviour (Dow 1985; Milgrom and Roberts 1988). Even where authority may efficiently resolve some disputes, it also may be abused opportunistically (Dow 1987).

Another criticism of TCE is that it understates the role of social and cultural forces in economic activity (Granovetter 1985). While TCE seeks to adopt realistic assumptions of human nature, it does take a decidedly calculative view (Williamson 1993a) of humans that discounts the impact of social relationships and culture. Granovetter pointed out that, contrary to this atomistic view of economic exchange, transactions are embedded within networks of social relationships. These transactions are influenced by expectations that are formed by the history of the relationship. Abstract transaction dimensions such as asset specificity and uncertainty do not alone determine the governance arrangements that we observe. Close friends, for example, may trade co-specialized assets without hierarchy, a formal contract or other tangible credible commitments because they trust one another. Although certainly under-appreciated in earlier work, TCE scholars are focusing more attention to understanding social forces such as trust on economic exchange (Ring and Van de Ven 1992; Williamson 1993a). While work by social network theorists such as Granovetter (1985) and Uzzi (1997) strongly suggests that relationships and networks serve as substitutes for formal safeguards such as contracts. Recent empirical work has shown that social forces and economic calculation can be complementary rather than antithetical (Dyer 1996; Poppo and Zenger 1998; Mayer and Argyres 2004).

A final major criticism of TCE is that the emphasis on opportunism is bad for practice (Ghoshal and Moran 1996). Critics suggest that the emphasis on opportunism in TCE leads to two fundamental problems. First, an emphasis on opportunism may lead managers to adopt practices that, while intended to prevent opportunism, may have the opposite effect. The suggestion is that close supervision and other safeguards designed to minimize slacking, cheating and other questionable behaviour may produce alienation that will make such behaviour more likely to occur (Ghoshal and Moran 1996). In essence, they argue that the opportunism assumption leads to a self-fulfilling prophecy. Ferraro et al. (2005) argue more generally that, as economic theories become institutionalized, people tend to conform their behaviour to economic predictions. While it seems reasonable to suggest that people will try to behave consistent with widely accepted prescriptions, researchers have yet to show that the specific predictions of TCE (and other perspectives in organizational economics) have become institutionalized among managers. Indeed, the findings of TCE and these other perspectives have meaning only because researchers have consistently observed significant variation in practice. Simply stated, empirical observation shows that many managers do not conform to economic prescriptions of how they should behave. Moreover,

observed performance differences between firms that align transactions and governance and those that do not also suggest that more than self-fulfilling prophecy is at work (Silverman et al. 1997; Poppo and Zenger 1998; Nickerson and Silverman 2003). The second problem with assuming opportunism according to Ghoshal and Moran is that making such an assumption ignores the positive co-ordinative benefits of organizations that are independent of transaction costs. Most notably, organizations may foster the creation and development of valuable firm-specific knowledge (Kogut and Zander 1992; Conner and Prahalad 1996).

Despite these criticisms, TCE's answer to the fundamental question of why firms exist has been undeniably influential. Historically, economic theory viewed the organization as irrelevant and unworthy of economic science (Stiglitz 1991: 15) while organization theory took the existence of organization for granted. TCE has provided an approach that provoked economists to look inside the black box of the firm at the same time that it opened up a new approach for organization theorists.

Do Those Associated with the Firm Agree about How it Should be Managed?

Given that traditional neo-classical economics did not look inside the firm, it is not surprising that it did not address the possibility of intra-firm conflict over the way a firm should be managed. Neo-classical economics assumed a monolithic goal for the firm: profit maximization. Firms that behaved contrary to this assumption were thought to have little chance of survival. Thus, there was little need to look inside the firm, since once one could explain why a firm was created, what happened inside a firm's boundaries did not really aid in scientific prediction (Stiglitz 1991). In neglecting conflict within organizations, economics ran parallel to early organization theory, which also long neglected the topic (Mintzberg 1983; Perrow 1986).

Early Departures from the Neo-Classical Firm

The neglect of intra-firm conflict ended, to some extent, with the research of a multidisciplinary group of scholars at Carnegie-Mellon University (March and Simon 1958; Cyert and March 1963; Simon 1964). Their work was an important departure for both economics and organization theory in looking more explicitly at conflicts over goals and means within organizations. Cyert and March's (1963) book *A Behavioral Theory of the Firm* addressed most directly the problems with the neo-classical theory of the firm. They rejected basic components of the neo-classical firm such as profit maximization and perfect information. In place of a single actor focused exclusively on maximizing profits (in many ways, analogous to Alehian and Demsetz's monitors), Cyert and March saw goals within the firm emerging and changing over time as coalitions formed and shifted among organizational members. Ironically, this and related work (e.g. March and Simon 1958; Simon 1964) was much more influential in organization theory than in economics. This was ironic, since many of those associated with the Carnegie-Mellon research group were economists. A few economists focused on potentially conflicting goals within the firm and argued that managers may pursue objectives other than profit maximization (e.g. they may pursue growth (Marris 1964): they may pursue discretion and perquisites (Williamson 1964)). Nevertheless, the traditional view of the firm remained the mainstream perspective.

Transactions cost theory is of surprisingly little help in analysing conflicting goals of those associated with a firm. TCE explains why organizations exist; but it fails to address how or if those affiliated with the firm agree on its goals. The implicit assumption in TCE is that agreement on how the firm should be managed is non-problematic. However, just because economic exchange partners find it in their mutual self-interest to form an organization does not mean that differences in interests, tastes and preferences cease. Indeed, Williamson seems to argue that the problems of opportunism and bounded rationality that so plague transactions across markets almost magically disappear when transactions are internalized into an organization (Grossman and Hart 1986). This assertion seems unrealistic, at best, and is particularly ironic given Williamson's (1964) early work that examined managers' propensity to pursue their own goals at the expense of corporate profits. This lack of appreciation for the variety and complexity within organizations highlights the

acknowledged incompleteness of TCE (Williamson 1985: 392, 402).

Agency Theory

A literature in organization economics, agency theory, seeks to understand the causes and consequences for organizations of these goal disagreements. It draws heavily from the property rights literature (Alchian and Demsetz 1972) and to a lesser extent from transaction cost. Like TCE, agency theory assumes that humans are boundedly rational, self-interested and prone to opportunism (Eisenhardt 1989). The theories are also similar in their emphasis on information asymmetry problems in contracting and on efficiency as the engine that drives the governance of economic transactions (Barney and Ouchi 1986; Eisenhardt 1989). Agency theory, however, differs from TCE in its emphasis on the risk attitudes of principals and agents (Eisenhardt 1989: 64).

As it originally developed, agency theory research focused on the relationship between managers and stockholders (Jensen and Meckling 1976). In this form, the theory has been used to analyse corporate governance, including issues such as the role of boards of directors and the role of top management compensation. More recently, agency theory has been applied to relationships between many stakeholders in a firm such as those between different managers within the same firm, between employees and customers (Grinblatt and Titman 1987) and between employees and different groups of stockholders and debt holders (Copeland and Weston 1983). All these conflicts have important effects on a variety of attributes of organizations, including corporate governance, compensation and organizational structure.

Agency relationships occur whenever one partner in a transaction (the principal) delegates authority to another (the agent) and the welfare of the principal is affected by the choices of the agent (Arrow 1985). An obvious example is the relationship between outside investors in a firm and its managers. The investors delegate management authority to managers who may or may not have any equity ownership in the firm. The delegation of decision-making authority from principal to agent is problematic in that: (1) the interests of principal and agent will typically diverge; (2) the principal cannot perfectly and costlessly monitor the actions of the agent; and (3) the principal cannot perfectly and costlessly monitor and acquire the information available to or possessed by the agent. Taken together, these conditions constitute the agency problem – the possibility of opportunistic behaviour on the agent's part that works against the welfare of the principal. Jensen and Meckling (1976: 309) view the agency problem as central to both economics in general and to organization theory specifically:

> It is worthwhile to point out the generality of the agency problem. The problem of inducing an 'agent' to behave as if he were maximizing the 'principal's' welfare is quite general. It exists in all organizations and in all cooperative efforts – at every level of management in firms. ... The development of theories to explain the form which agency costs take in each of these situations (where the contractual relations differ significantly), and how and why they are born will lead to a rich theory of organizations which is now lacking in economics and the social sciences generally.

To protect the principal's interests, attempts must be made to reduce the possibility that agents will misbehave. In this attempt, costs are incurred. These costs are called agency costs. Total agency costs are the monitoring expenditures by principals, the bonding expenditures by agents, and the residual loss of the principal. The residual loss acknowledges that in many situations it will simply be too costly for principals to completely monitor agents and too costly for agents to completely assure principals that interests do not diverge (Jensen and Meckling 1976).

Assuming that agency costs exist, it is clear that principals have a strong incentive to minimize these costs (i.e. to minimize the sum of monitoring, bonding and residual agency costs). However, agents also have an incentive to minimize these costs. Where significant savings in agency costs are possible, these benefits may be shared between agents and principals. Thus, the principal and agent have common interests in defining a monitoring and incentive structure that produces outcomes as close as possible to what would be the case if information exchange was costless (Pratt and Zeckhauser 1985).

Arrow (1985) notes two essential sources of agency problems: moral hazard, which he equates to hidden actions, and adverse selection, which he equates to hidden information. Moral hazard involves situations in which much of the agent's actions are either hidden from the principal or are costly to observe. Thus, it is either impossible or costly for the principal to fully monitor the agent's actions. Stockholders or even directors, for example, might find it prohibitively costly to fully monitor the behaviour of their top management team. Indeed, the employment relation in general is one in which effort and ability are difficult to observe.

Agency problems may also involve adverse selection. In adverse selection, the agent possesses information that is, for the principal, unobservable or costly to obtain. Consequently, principals cannot fully ascertain whether or not their interests are best served by agents' decisions. For example, a lower-level manager may submit proposals to the CEO (in this instance, the principal) even though, based on information possessed by the manager and not the CEO, these proposals are unlikely to generate economic value. By doing so, the lower-level manager may be able to gain some private benefits (e.g. broader experience that may be useful in other firms). Obviously, the CEO is at an informational disadvantage. This disadvantage is only exacerbated as the number of agents with similar incentives and advantages multiplies.

At the most general level, principals and agents resolve agency problems through monitoring and bonding. Monitoring involves observing the behaviour and/or the performance of agents. Bonding refers to arrangements that penalize agents for acting in ways that violate the interests of principals or reward them for achieving principals' goals. The contracts between agents and principals specify the monitoring and bonding arrangements. Indeed, contracts are central in agency theory. Jensen and Meckling (1976: 310) argue that most 'organizations are simply legal fictions which serve as a nexus for a set of contracting relationships among individuals'. Within this nexus, however, firms adopt rules about monitoring and bonding.

Given this general description of agency problems and their costly solutions, three important questions come to mind. First, why do principals delegate authority to agents, when they know that such delegation of authority will inevitably lead to agency problems? Secondly, what specific monitoring mechanisms can principals put in place to minimize these agency problems? Finally, what specific bonding mechanisms can agents use to reassure principals? Each of these questions is discussed in subsequent sections.

Delegating Authority

Given agency costs, principals will not delegate authority to agents unless they find compelling reasons to do so. Sometimes there are no compelling reasons and single economic actors engage in a full range of economic activities. For small firms with relatively simple operations, a single individual may be quite effective in accomplishing the numerous tasks of the enterprise. In such settings, there will be no delegation of authority to agents and thus no agency costs. However, the situation facing larger, more complex business enterprises is not so simple. In these settings, a single individual may be unable to engage in all these business activities in a timely and effective way. This inability does not reflect, necessarily, a lack of will to accomplish all these tasks. Rather, individual bounded rationality and real constraints on time and energy may make it impossible to conduct business without significant delegation of authority. Such delegation always implies agency costs.

Fama and Jensen (1983) observe that the process of making most business decisions can be divided into two large categories: (1) decision management (i.e. how a decision possibility is originally initiated and how that decision is implemented) and (2) decision control (i.e. how a decision is ratified and how performance relative to a decision is monitored). As suggested above, it may not be necessary to assign decision management and decision control responsibilities to different agents in relatively less complex business settings. However, in more complex settings, Fama and Jensen (1983) argue that delegating decision management to one group and decision control to a second group may, on average, lead to higher-quality decisions. The management group's task is simplified, and they are able to focus on questions concerning the initiation and implementation of decisions. The control group's task is also simplified, and they are able to focus on questions concerning the ratification and monitoring of decisions. Put differently, in settings where the decision-making situation is likely to overwhelm the cognitive capacity of a single individual, assigning different groups different parts of the decision-making process is likely to improve the quality of decisions. Of course, this delegation also implies the existence of agency costs.

Monitoring

Given the existence of agency costs, principals will find it in their self-interest to try to monitor agents

(Eisenhardt 1985). One way that principals can try to monitor agents is by collecting relatively complete information about an agent's decisions and actions – an agent's behaviour. From this behavioural information, principals can then form judgements about the underlying goals and objectives of agents. In particular, principals can attempt to judge how similar their agent's goals and objectives are to their own goals and objectives.

Of course, monitoring agent behaviour will rarely generate perfect information about an agent's decisions and actions, let alone about an agent's goals and objectives. This is especially unlikely if agents are engaging in relatively complex, highly unstructured tasks. For example, suppose that it was possible for a principal to directly observe the behaviour of a group of research scientists she hired to conduct research for new products. It may well be the case that this principal would observe her scientists spending at least part of their day sitting in comfortable chairs, staring out a window. What can the principal conclude from this behaviour – that the scientists are shirking? Perhaps. On the other hand, the scientists may also be thinking about some fundamental research problem, the solution to which will generate a string of very valuable products. Given this behaviour, by itself, it is not possible to deduce the scientists' goals and objectives.

This limitation of behavioural monitoring is not limited to just scientists. Managerial behaviour at the top levels of an organization, for example, is notoriously difficult to monitor and even more difficult to interpret. This does not mean that behavioural monitoring does not, or should not, take place at these high levels in an organization. Institutional investors monitor critical strategic decisions made by senior managers; boards of directors monitor major policy changes implemented by senior management teams; and corporate management teams monitor the decisions and strategic plans of division general managers. However, these efforts at monitoring the behaviour of agents can only imperfectly reduce agency costs.

As an alternative (or supplement) to monitoring agent behaviour, principals can also monitor the consequences of (only partially observed) agent behaviour. Thus, instead of monitoring actions and decisions, principals may elect to monitor the performance implications of those actions and decisions. In general, monitoring performance (or output) is more efficient when tasks are not highly programmable (Eisenhardt

1985; Mahoney 1992). Output measurement, however, is not without problems. It becomes more problematic where team production is involved (Alchian and Demsetz 1972). Interdependence between agents creates ambiguity about how much each agent contributed to the final output. Thus, measuring the output of different agents is imprecise at best.

A large segment of the agency theory literature examines the abilities of owners (stockholders) to monitor shareholders (Hill and Snell 1989). Since large shareholders have a greater incentive and more resources to monitor management behaviour and performance, the information asymmetries between investors and firms' managers are reduced. Thus, with the increasing presence of institutional shareholders and large shareholders, we should see less evidence of certain types of agency problems. Firms with more concentrated ownership are less likely to engage in wealth-destroying activities such as inefficient diversification (Hill and Snell 1989) but are more likely to undertake wealth-enhancing actions such as restructuring (Bethel and Liebeskind 1993).

Another mechanism that agency theory prescribes for monitoring managerial behaviour and performance is the use of independent directors on corporate boards. The independent board members provide objectivity as the board ratifies and monitors the decisions of management.

A number of studies have examined the occurrence of firm policies that are thought to have negative consequences for the shareholders of a firm, including such anti-takeover amendments as greenmail and poison pills. These studies have yielded mixed support of agency theory (Kosnik 1987; Weisbach 1988; Mallette and Fowler 1992). However, recent studies suggest that the adoption of these policies may, in fact, not always signal agency problems in a firm (Mahoney and Mahoney 1993; Brickley et al. 1994; Coles and Hesterly 2000). Instead, this more recent work suggests that these policies, while they can often entrench managers to the detriment of shareholders, may also increase the bargaining power of the target firm in takeover contests. The existence of outside directors has been shown to be the primary determinant of whether these policies are used to hurt or help a firm's shareholders.

Bonding and Incentives

The existence of agency costs suggests that principals have an incentive to monitor agents. However,

agents also have an incentive to assure principals that they are behaving in ways consistent with the principals' interests. Recall that, in many situations, principals and agents both absorb some agency costs associated with the delegation of authority. In general, principals can use bonding mechanisms to reassure principals. Frequently, bonding mechanisms take the form of incentives that agents create for themselves – incentives that make it in their self-interest to behave in ways consistent with the interests of principals.

Perhaps the most common form of incentive bonding focuses on the compensation package of agents. If agent compensation depends, to a significant extent, upon behaving and performing in ways consistent with a principal's interests, then – assuming that agents value financial rewards – they will behave in ways consistent with those interests. Put differently, the willingness of an agent to accept this form of compensation can be understood as a bond, a bond that reassures principals that their interests will be considered when decisions are made.

A large part of the agency theory literature examines the incentives firms use to induce agents to work in the best interests of principals. Ideally, principals would prefer an incentive scheme that fully penalizes agents for shirking and opportunism. This, however, is extremely difficult to achieve without exposing agents to risks they will find unacceptably high. Often these risks are tied to conditions beyond the agents' control. On the other hand, policies that allow agents to be compensated in ways that are independent of the principals' interests insure that an agent's earnings will not fluctuate with conditions outside of the agent's control, but provide weak inducements against opportunism. Thus, though principals prefer schemes that emphasize incentives, they must design compensation systems in ways that sometimes compromise between pure incentives and fixed compensation plans (Winship and Rosen 1988).

Research in agency theory has examined a variety of compensation plans, including bonuses and stock options for executives (Murphy 1986; 2003; Carter and Lynch 2001), salary versus commissions (Eisenhardt 1985; 1988), the effect of incentive pay on turnover (Zenger 1992), the impact of firm size on incentive intensity (Zenger and Marshall 2000), choices between piece rates and time rates (Lazear 1986) and promotion contests (McLaughlin 1988). Other studies examine managerial ownership in the firm (see Eisenhardt 1989; Dalton et al. 2003 for reviews). Some studies, for example, indicate that managers with a significant ownership interest in their firm are less likely to engage in conglomerate diversification (Amihud and Lev 1981; 1999; Argawal and Mandelker 1987; Denis et al. 1999), resist takeover bids (Walking and Long 1984) and use golden parachutes to the benefit of shareholders (Singh and Harianto 1989).

Rewards other than financial compensation also serve to link the welfare of principals and agents. Managers may receive promotions or other forms of recognition which may enhance their reputations and the probability of increased future income. Even if firms do not explicitly tie performance to rewards, market forces may work to reduce agency problems (Fama 1980). The managerial labour market, for instance, views the previous associations of managers with success and failure as information about their talents (Fama 1980: 292). Managers in more successful firms may not receive any immediate gain in wages, but the success of their firm may increase their value in the managerial labour market. In contrast, the managers of failing firms may not see a reduction in wages, but will be disciplined as the managerial labour market attaches less value to their services.

The Role of Market Discipline

Market discipline plays an important role in determining the arrangements and outcomes predicted by agency theory (Ravenscraft and Scherer 1987). Such a focus pre-supposes that markets, particularly capital markets, are efficient. Indeed, agency theory adopts at least a semi-strong form assumption of capital market efficiency (Fama 1970). Semi-strong capital market efficiency maintains that the value of a firm's assets mirrors completely and immediately all public information concerning the value of those assets (Barney and Ouchi 1986). This differs from the strong-form assumption which asserts that asset prices reflect all information regardless of whether it is public or private. It also varies from weak-form capital market efficiency which avers that asset prices reflect only the historically available information about the firm's assets.

Perhaps the most obvious example of market discipline as it is used in agency theory is the market for corporate control (Shleifer and Vishny 1991). Generally, this market is assumed to be semi-strong efficient, i.e. the value of a firm in the market for

corporate control reflects all publicly available information about the value of that firm. If the agents (managers) of a firm take actions that are viewed by the market as adversely affecting the value of the firm's assets, then the price of these assets (i.e. the stock price) will likely drop. Managers in other firms, believing that they can more profitably manage the assets of the under-performing firm, may engage in a contest for control of the firm and a takeover battle may ensue. Barring outside interference, the troubled firm's management will eventually lose control of the firm, and old high agency cost managers will be replaced by new low agency cost managers.

In other instances, market discipline may take more subtle forms. Managerial labour markets, for example, will attach less value to the services of managers in less successful firms (Fama 1980). Or, boards of directors may replace high agency cost managers with others hired from outside the firm (Faith et al. 1984).

Empirical evidence on the wealth effects of takeovers is largely consistent with the market discipline argument in agency theory. The shareholders of takeover targets receive, on average, significant wealth gains (Jensen and Ruback 1983; Jarrell et al. 1988; Ruback 1988; Andrade et al. 2001; Holmstrom and Kaplan 2001). These wealth gains reflect, at least in part, reductions in agency costs thought likely to occur after an acquisition is completed.

While economics was slow to recognize conflicts within the firm, and between the firm and its numerous stakeholders, the influence of agency theory in organization economics is difficult to overstate. It has spawned literally hundreds of empirical studies. While these studies examine a vast array of topics, the underlying question is the same: how do organizations deal with conflicting goals between those who delegate authority and those to whom authority has been delegated? The theory addresses this question in only a few fundamental propositions.

Criticisms of Agency Theory

Agency theory has clearly become the dominant theory of corporate governance and executive compensation among economics and strategy scholars. Much of the empirical evidence is clearly supportive of agency theory, although some have suggested that the empirical results are mixed (see Dalton et al. 1998; 2003; Daily et al. 2003). Important fundamental questions have also been raised about agency theory. Foremost among these is that agency theory seems to adopt an unrealistic view of humans and organizations (Hirsch et al. 1990). In agency theory, humans are primarily motivated by financial gain. Much of the early research, particularly, ignored the other behavioural sciences. Studies combining agency theory with ideas from other disciplines such as institutional theory (Eisenhardt 1988), equity theory (Zenger 1992) and social influence (Wade et al. 1990; Davis 1991) have yielded additional insights and questions about the theory. Besides taking an unrealistic view of humans, others fault agency theory for not dealing with the real processes of governance. Pettigrew (1992: 171), for example, takes agency theory to task for black box theorizing where, 'Great inferential leaps are made from input variables such as board composition to output variables such as board performance with no direct evidence on the processes and mechanisms which presumably link the inputs and the outputs'. Related to concerns about agency theory's realism are concerns about its generality. Implicit in much of the recent research on agency theory is the implicit question of whether agency theory predictions are valid for large US corporations or do they apply to a wider set of firms in different geographic contexts. Several studies examine agency theory in various international contexts (Roth and O'Donnell 1996; Sanders and Carpenter 1998; Gedajlovic and Shapiro 2002; Chang 2003; Lee and O'Neil 2003; Tihanyi et al. 2003) and find at least mixed support for its tenets. Other scholars have extended agency theory applications to diverse organizational contexts such as family firms (Schulze et al. 2001; 2003), entrepreneurial enterprises (Mosakowski 1998) and high technology firms (Balkin et al. 2000).

A final criticism of agency theory is more philosophical. Perrow and others (Hirsch et al. 1990) argue that agency theory has an inherent investor focus. This criticism is true of most research in the area, but may not be inherent in the theory. The framework of agency theory is, in itself, neutral. It could just as well be used to examine issues that focus on the concerns of agents (Hesterly et al. 1990). This is essentially what Shleifer and Summers (1988) have done in their review of much of the corporate control research. They argue that much of the gains to shareholders from merger and acquisition activity result from redistributing wealth from other stakeholders such as employees to owners.

Why do Some Organizations Outperform Others?

Taken together, transaction cost economics and agency theory constitute a powerful theory of the firm. Transaction cost economics explains the conditions under which economic exchanges can be most efficiently managed using hierarchical forms of governance. If a firm is, in essence, a bundle of interrelated transactions managed through hierarchical forms of governance, then transactions cost economics is a theory of the firm. Agency theory extends this theory of the firm by enabling a researcher to examine, in more detail, linkages among these different transactions. It does this by focusing attention on the effects of compensation, corporate governance, capital structure and other attributes of firm governance on agency problems within the firm, and between a firm and its external stakeholders.

While transaction cost economics and agency theory can be used to explain why firms exist, they cannot be used to explain why some firms might outperform others. These models both assume that firms are essentially homogeneous in their transaction and agency governance skills. Put differently, these models assume that two or more firms, facing similar kinds of economic exchanges, will develop similar governance solutions. When a group of competing firms all choose similar approaches to solving similar transactions cost and agency theory problems, these common approaches cannot be sources of competitive advantage or superior performance for any one firm. To explain why some firms might outperform other firms, substantially greater levels of heterogeneity must be introduced into the analysis.

Of course, transaction cost economics and agency theory are not alone in being unable to explain why some firms are able to outperform others. Indeed, a major implication of neoclassical microeconomic theory is that, barring artificial barriers to competition (e.g. government regulations that limit competition), the performance of firms in an industry will converge to a common level. This level of firm performance is called 'normal economic performance' (Tirole 1989). Normal economic performance is a level of performance just large enough to enable a firm to pay all of its suppliers, including suppliers of capital, labour and technology, the return they expect. Firms that earn normal economic performance are able to survive, although they will not prosper. In neoclassical theory, firms earning above normal economic performance must be protected by artificial barriers to competition. Any superior firm performance that is not attributable to such barriers is difficult to explain using neo-classical theory.

None of this would be problematic if the performance of firms was not very heterogeneous. However, both casual observation and empirical research suggest that it is: some firms, in fact, do outperform others (Jacobson 1988). For example, while most firms in the US airline industry have struggled to break even, Southwest Airlines has made substantial economic profits (Hallowell and Heskett 1993). Some firms in the discount retail industry have been unable to survive. Others have just been able to survive, by earning normal economic profits. However, WalMart has been massively successful, generating over $3 billion in wealth for its founder, Sam Walton (Ghemawat 1986). Also, while virtually every integrated steel company in the world has experienced losses in economic value over the last 30 years, Nucor Steel has seen its economic value consistently increase (Ghemawat and Stander 1993). Transaction cost economics, agency theory and neo-classical microeconomics cannot explain this level of performance heterogeneity.

Understanding why some firms outperform others is the primary research topic of strategic management (Rumelt et al. 1991). As this field of inquiry has evolved, two basic explanations of the performance heterogeneity of firms have been proposed. The first builds on what has come to be known as the structure-conduct-performance (SCP) paradigm in industrial organization economics, and focuses on the structure of the industries within which a firm operates to explain heterogeneity in firm performance. The second builds on a variety of research traditions in economics and organization theory, including Penrosian economics (Penrose 1959), Austrian economics (Jacobson 1992) and the evolutionary theory of the firm (Nelson and Winter 1982), and focuses on attributes of firms to explain heterogeneity in performance. This second approach has come to be known as the resource-based view of the firm (Wernerfelt 1984; Barney 1991). These two approaches to explaining why some firms outperform others are reviewed below.

The SCP Paradigm and Firm Performance

Original work on the SCP paradigm can be traced to Mason (1959) and Bain (1956). The original purpose of this framework was to assist government regulators in identifying industries that were less than perfectly competitive, and thus where firms were earning greater than normal economic performance. Traditionally, it was thought that when firms in an industry were earning above normal economic performance, customers were paying too high prices for the goods and services they purchased, the level of innovation was below what it should have been, and the quality of goods or services was less than it should have been – in short, that social welfare was not being maximized (Bain 1956). Once these non-competitive industries were discovered, regulators could then implement a variety of remedies to increase the level of competition in them, and thereby increase social welfare.

Industry Structure and Firm Performance

As suggested earlier, the primary explanation of heterogeneity in firm performance in the SCP paradigm is industry structure. The critical performance-enhancing attributes of industry structure, isolated by SCP theorists, are: (1) industry concentration, (2) level of product differentiation, and (3) barriers to entry. Industry concentration was thought to enhance performance in one of two ways. First, in highly concentrated industries, a relatively small number of firms could collude – either explicitly or tacitly – and reduce industry output below a competitive level, and thus prices above the competitive level (Tirole 1989). As long as the cost of this collusion was less than the economic profits it created, firms that operated in highly concentrated and collusive industries would outperform firms that operated in less highly concentrated and thus not collusive industries.

The implicit assumption in these assertions is that the difficulty of implementing tacit collusion strategies increases as the number of firms in an industry increases (Scherer 1980). This assumption will be discussed in more detail in later sections of this chapter.

Industry concentration can also lead to performance heterogeneity through the operation of economies of scale. Economies of scale exist when there is a close relationship between a firm's economic costs and its volume of production. In concentrated industries, where economies of scale are operating, only relatively few firms will be able to take full advantage of these economies. These few firms will, all things being equal, have lower economic costs than smaller firms in the industry, thus leading to performance heterogeneity (Scherer 1980).

Product differentiation can also enable some firms to gain above normal performance in an industry. As first discussed by Chamberlain (1933) and Robinson (1933), firms that implement product differentiation strategies are able to enhance the perceived value of the products or services they sell. In effect, these firms become monopolists for those consumers who are attracted to a firm's differentiated products. Indeed, Chamberlain first described competition in industries with product differentiation as 'monopolistic competition'. Like all monopolists (Tirole 1989), these firms are able to charge greater than the fully competitive price for their products or services. Assuming the cost of differentiating their products is less than the extra revenue created by charging greater than the competitive price, product differentiation can also be a source of above normal economic profits.

By themselves, industry concentration and product differentiation should be sources of only the very briefest above normal economic profits. The SCP paradigm suggests that any profits earned by firms in an industry will instantly lead to entry, (either by new firms coming into an industry or by firms already in that industry) modifying their strategies to duplicate the strategies of profitable firms (Bain 1956). Entry will continue until all profits in an industry are competed away. If entry into an industry, or entry into new industry segments, is costless, then there will be no performance heterogeneity in an industry.

A particularly strong form of this entry argument has been developed by Baumol et al. (1982), called 'contestable market theory'. These authors argue that actual entry is not required to ensure that firms do not make above normal profits. Indeed, all that is required to ensure that firms in an industry will not earn above normal profits is the *threat* of low-cost entry.

Of course, if entry into an industry is not free, then profit reducing entry may not occur. In general, if the cost of entry is greater than or equal to the value that a firm will obtain from entry, entry will not occur. The value that a firm will obtain from entry depends on the structure within that industry, i.e. the higher the level of concentration and the greater the product differentiation, the greater the potential economic value of entry. On

the other hand, the cost of entry depends on the existence of barriers to entry; the more significant the barriers to entry, the more costly (and thus the less likely) that entry will actually occur (Bain 1956).

Several barriers to entry have been identified by SCP researchers, including: (1) economies of scale, (2) product differentiation, (3) cost advantages independent of scale, (4) contrived deterrence, and (5) government imposed restrictions on entry (Porter 1980). The way that each of these barriers to entry acts to deter entry is discussed, in detail, elsewhere (Bain 1956; Barney 1995).

Strategic Management and the SCP Paradigm

Strategic management researchers have turned the original intent of the SCP paradigm upside-down (Porter 1981; Barney 1986a). Where traditional SCP research was designed to help government regulators to increase competition in an industry, strategic management researchers have used SCP insights to suggest strategies firms can implement that have the effect of reducing competition in an industry, and thus enabling firms in an industry to earn above normal profits.

While several people have contributed to the SCP-based strategic management research, no one has been more influential than Michael Porter. In a series of books (Porter 1980; 1985; 1990) and articles (Porter 1974; 1979a, b), Porter and his colleagues have developed a powerful model firms can use to choose and implement strategies that will generate above normal economic performance. Among the frameworks and tools Porter has developed out of the SCP tradition are: (1) the five-forces model of environmental threats, (2) a model of generic industry structure and environmental opportunities, and (3) the strategic groups concept.

The five-forces model of environmental threats, as developed by Porter, is presented in Figure 1.3.2. Based on earlier SCP research, Porter isolated five sets of threats to the profits of a firm in an industry: the threat of rivalry, the threat of entry, the threat of substitutes, the threat of suppliers and the threat of buyers. All these threats act to either reduce a firm's revenues (rivalry, entry, substitutes and buyers) or increase a firm's economic costs (suppliers) until a firm earns only normal economic performance. Porter (1980) describes, in detail, the attributes of

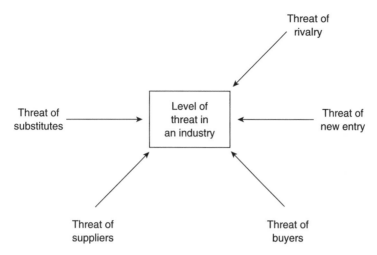

Figure 1.3.2   The five-forces model of environmental threats (Porter 1980)

industries that reduce the level of each of these threats. Most of these industry attributes are completely consistent with earlier SCP research, e.g. to reduce the threat of entry, firms should implement barriers to entry. They implement barriers to entry (1) by exploiting economies of scale, (2) by differentiating their products, (3) by exploiting cost advantages independent of scale, (4) by implementing contrived deterrence strategies, or (5) by encouraging the government to impose barriers to entry.

Porter's model of generic industry structures and opportunity identified five types of industries and the opportunities typically associated with them. These five industry types and associated opportunities are: (1) emerging industries (first mover advantages), (2) fragmented industries (consolidation), (3) mature industries (emphasis on service, process innovation), (4) declining industries (lead, niche, harvest, divest), and (5) global industries (multinational organization, global integrated organization). Detailed definitions of these industry types, of the opportunities associated with them and examples of each are presented in Table 1.3.1.

As suggested earlier, firm profits can motivate entry from at least two sources: from firms entering an industry from the outside, or from firms that are already in an industry entering into a new segment of that industry. This second form of entry led Porter, in co-operation with Richard Caves, to develop the concept of 'strategic groups' (Caves and Porter 1977). A strategic group is a set of firms in an industry pursuing similar strategies. Strategic groups may, or may not, be protected from entry by firms already in an industry by what Caves and Porter call 'mobility barriers'. Mobility barriers are like barriers to entry, except they are applied to strategic groups of firms within an industry, not to an industry as a whole. Thus, entry into an industry is deterred by barriers to entry; entry into a strategic group is deterred by mobility barriers.

This SCP-based approach to understanding heterogeneity in firm performance has numerous important research and managerial implications. A great deal of research has been conducted testing the SCP foundations of this model of firm performance (see Scherer 1980 for an extensive review). Additional research has also been conducted examining the empirical implications of the strategic management versions of this SCP framework. Some of this work supports the theories and frameworks developed by Porter and his colleagues. For example, the five-forces model has been shown to be a reasonably accurate predictor of the overall competitiveness of an industry. On the other hand, some of the other parts of the Porter framework have not fared as well, empirically. For example, while extensive research has been conducted on the existence and performance implications of strategic groups in industries, some have argued that most of this work

Table 1.3.1 Industry structure and opportunities

Industry type	Definition	Opportunities	Examples of firms exploiting these opportunities
Emerging industries	Recent changes in demand or technology; new industry standard operating procedures have yet to develop	First mover advantages	Intel in microprocessors
Fragmented industries	Large numbers of firms of approximately equal size	Consolidation	McDonald's in fast food
Mature industries	Slow increases in demand, numerous repeat customers, limited product innovation	Emphasis on service and process innovation	GE in light bulbs
Declining industries	Consistent reduction in industry demand	Leadership, niche, harvest, divest	General dynamics in defense
Global industries	Significant international sales	Multinational, global	Nestlé; Ciba-Geigy

has been badly flawed, and that the essential elements of this concept remain untested (Barney and Hoskisson 1989). Interest in strategic group research has waned significantly, although some impressively creative strategic group research continues (e.g. Reger and Huff 1993).

Criticisms of the SCP Paradigm in Strategic Management

While research continues on the theory underlying SCP-based models of firm performance, albeit at a slower pace, at least two important questions have arisen concerning the managerial implications of these models. The first of these questions revolves around the appropriateness of the unit of analyses in these models – the industry or the strategy group. These models assert that the primary determinant of firm performance is the industry (or strategic group) within which a firm operate. However, research has shown that there is often more heterogeneity in the performance of firms within a single industry than there is heterogeneity in the performance of firms across industries (Rumelt 1991; McGahan and Porter 1997; see Bowman and Helfat 2001 for review). Indeed, each of the examples of heterogeneous firm performance cited previously focused on performance heterogeneity of firms within an industry, i.e. Southwest Airlines in the airline industry, WalMart in the discount retail industry, and Nucor Steel in the steel industry. By

adopting the industry (strategic group) as the unit of analysis, SCP-based models cannot explain intra-industry (intra-group) heterogeneity in performance.

Put differently, SCP explanations of heterogeneous firm performance continue to assume that firms within an industry or within a strategic group are homogeneous. In this framework, only differences between industry groups can explain differences in firm performance. While there is more heterogeneity in these SCP models than in transaction cost, agency theory or neo-classical theory, many have argued that there still is not enough heterogeneity in these SCP models, i.e. that the appropriate unit of analysis for the study of heterogeneous firm performance is the firm (Barney and Hoskisson 1989).

The limitations of the industry/group focus are brought into relief by examining their managerial implications. SCP logic suggests that firms seeking to earn above normal economic performance should enter and operate only in 'attractive' industries. An attractive industry is one characterized by low levels of threat, and high levels of opportunity, as defined by Porter (1980). However, the attractiveness of an industry cannot be evaluated independently of the unique skills and abilities that a firm brings to that industry (Barney 1994). Thus, while the airline industry has been unattractive for many airlines, it has been quite attractive for Southwest Airlines; while the discount retail industry has been unattractive for many firms, it has been quite attractive for WalMart; while the steel industry has been unattractive for many firms, it has been quite attractive for Nucor Steel. While the level of threat and opportunity in an industry is obviously an important component of any model of firm performance, a more complete model of performance must necessarily also include some discussion of a firm's unique resources and capabilities.

A second question about the managerial implications of SCP-based models of firm performance concerns the social welfare implications of these models. Recall that the original purpose of the SCP paradigm was to isolate industries that were not maximizing social welfare and to correct this problem. Strategy researchers have turned this objective upside down, by trying to help firms discover settings that are less than fully competitive. By implication, this suggests that firms that implement SCP-based strategies will reduce competition below the socially optimal level. Many academics find research that may have the effect of reducing overall social welfare morally unacceptable.

The Resource-Based View of the Firm and Firm Performance

Several authors have recognized the limitations of SCP-based models of firm performance and have developed a complementary approach. This approach builds on other traditions in economics, rather than on the SCP framework, including work by Penrose (1959), Schumpeter (1934) and Michael Ricardo (Scherer 1980), among others, and is known as the resource-based view of the firm. Work on the resource-based view of the firm in strategic management began with the publication of three articles, one each by Rumelt (1984). Wernerfelt (1984) and Barney (1986b). Other early resource-based work in strategic management includes Teece (1982) and Prahalad and Bettis (1986).

The Unit of Analysis, and Basic Assumptions of Resource-Based Logic

Unlike SCP-based models of firm performance, the resource-based view of the firm adopts, as its primary unit of analysis, the resources and capabilities controlled by a firm. A firm's resources and capabilities include all those attributes of a firm that enable it to conceive of and implement strategies. A firm's

resources and capabilities can conveniently be divided into four types: financial resources (e.g. equity capital. debt capital, retained earnings, etc.), physical resources (e.g. the machines, factories and other tangibles used by a firm), human resources (e.g. the experience, intelligence, training, judgement and wisdom of individuals associated with a firm) and organizational resources (e.g. the teamwork, trust, friendship and reputation of groups of individuals associated with a firm) (Barney 1991).

The resource-based view of the firm builds on two basic assumptions about a firm's resources and capabilities: (1) that resources and capabilities can vary significantly across firms (the assumption of firm heterogeneity), and (2) that these differences can be stable (the assumption of resource immobility). These assumptions differ significantly from neo-classical economic assumptions, where firms within an industry are assumed to be essentially identical, and where any differences that do emerge are quickly destroyed as firms without certain resources and capabilities move quickly to acquire or develop them (Scherer 1980). These assumptions also differ significantly from the assumptions adopted in the SCP paradigm. In this paradigm, it is assumed that firm resources and capabilities may vary across industries (or strategic groups) and that these differences can only be sustained if important barriers to entry (or mobility barriers) are in place. In resource-based logic, not all firms are assumed to be heterogeneous with respect to their resources and capabilities, nor is it assumed that all these differences will be sustained over time. Rather, it is only assumed that resources and capabilities *can* be heterogeneously distributed over time, and that heterogeneity can last, not simply because of barriers to entry, but because of the essential attributes of some of a firm's resources and capabilities.

Firms' Resources and Sustained Competitive Advantage

To turn these assumptions into testable propositions, Barney (1991) has suggested that, in order for a firm's resources and capabilities to be sources of superior performance they must be (1) valuable (in the sense of enabling a firm to exploit its environmental opportunities and/or neutralize its threats), (2) rare among its current or potential competitors, (3) costly to imitate, and (4) without close strategic substitutes. One resource or capability is a strategic substitute of another resource or capability if they both address approximately the same environmental opportunities and threats in about the same way and at about the same cost.

Imitability is an important component of the resource-based view of the firm. If other firms can acquire or develop the same, or substitute, resources as a firm that already possesses these resources, and can do so at approximately the same cost as the firm that already possesses them, then they cannot be a source of competitive advantage for any firm. Several researchers have suggested reasons why a firm's resources and capabilities may be costly to imitate (Dierickx and Cool 1989; Peteraf 1993). Barney (1991) divides these sources of costly imitation into three categories: the role of history, the role of causal ambiguity, and the role of socially complex resources and capabilities.

Sometimes, firms are able to acquire certain resources or capabilities at low cost because of their unique path through history. Dierickx and Cool (1989) suggest that these types of resources and capabilities have 'time compression diseconomies'. Arthur et al. (1987) suggest that these types of resources and capabilities accrue in a 'path dependent' way, i.e. their development depends upon a unique series of events in a firm's history. Of course, firms that have not passed through these same historical circumstances will face a significant cost disadvantage in developing or acquiring these resources, compared to firms that have passed through these circumstances. History is a linear process. Once it endows a few firms with special resources and capabilities, firms without these resources and capabilities face high cost imitation.

Sometimes it is not clear exactly why a firm with superior performance enjoys that performance advantage. This can happen whenever two or more competing hypotheses about the determinants of a firm's performance exist and when these hypotheses cannot be tested. Both Lippman and Rumelt (1982) and Reed and DeFillippi (1990) emphasize the importance of this 'causal ambiguity' in increasing the cost of imitation. When competing firms cannot know, with certainty, what enables a particular firm to enjoy its superior performance, these firms cannot know, with certainty, which of that firm's resources and capabilities it should imitate. This uncertainty effectively increases the cost of imitation.

Finally, sometimes the resources and capabilities that enable a firm to gain superior performance are socially complex. Examples of these types of resources include a firm's culture, teamwork among its employees, its reputation with suppliers and customers, and so forth. In this context, there may be little or no uncertainty about why a firm is able to enjoy high levels of performance, and imitation can still not occur. While managers can describe these socially complex resources, their ability to manage and change them rapidly are limited (Barney 1986c). Knowledge and capabilities that are embedded within the social fabric of a firm have received special attention from scholars employing resource-based logic. Indeed, for many, knowledge – and its synonymous terms such as competences and dynamic capabilities – has become *the* resource (Teece et al. 1997; Eisenhardt and Martin 2000; see also Felin and Hesterly, forthcoming for review). The importance of these socially complex resources as potential sources of sustained competitive advantage has led several resource-based theorists to call for increased co-operation between strategic management researchers and those who study organizational behaviour. In an important sense, the dependent variables of organizational behaviour and organization theory are potentially important independent variables in resource-based models of firm performance.

The empirical implications of the resource-based view of the firm have been extensively examined in the last decade. Most results are consistent with resource-based expectations in a wide variety of industrial settings and for diverse types of resources. For example, several studies point to the importance of intangible resources such as culture, knowledge and reputation (Hansen and Wernerfelt 1989; Hall 1993; Miller and Shamsie 1996; Knott et al. 2003; Hatch and Dyer 2004). A particularly important stream of empirical findings establishes the importance of knowledge and capabilities in determining firm performance (Henderson and Cockburn 1994; Pisano 1994; Silverman 1999; Afuah 2000). Studies also show the predicted effects for resources for a wide array of phenomena such as diversification (Silverman 1999; Miller 2004), market share (Makadok 1999), first-mover advantages (Lieberman and Montgomery 1998; Carow et al. 2004), mergers and acquisitions (Capron 1999), divestitures (Chang and Singh 2001), information technology (Powell and Dent-Micallef 1997), co-operative ventures (Madhok and Tallman 1998) and firm boundaries (Schilling and Steensma 2002; Leiblein 2003; Leiblein and Miller

2003). Taken together, a plethora of studies support the fundamental prediction of the resource-based view that the unique attributes of a firm are more important determinants of its performance than the industry within which it operates.

Managerial Implications

The managerial implications of the resource-based view of the firm stand in marked contrast to more traditional SCP-based strategic management models. In particular, where the SCP-based models would have managers choose to enter and conduct businesses in 'attractive' industries, resource-based logic suggests that firms should look inward, discover their own valuable, rare and costly to imitate resources and capabilities, and then discover markets where those resources could be exploited. While a particular industry may be very unattractive based on SCP criteria, it may be very attractive to a firm with just the right set of valuable, rare and costly to imitate resources and capabilities (Barney 1991).

The social welfare implications of resource-based strategies are also very different from the social welfare implications of SCP-based strategies. SCP-based strategies are designed to reduce competition below the competitive level and thus reduce the level of general social welfare in favour of a few firms earning above normal profits. Resource-based strategies suggest that firms should discover those business activities for which they are uniquely well suited. Exploiting a firm's special resources and capabilities can, in this sense, enhance social welfare. Put differently, superior firm performance in the SCP framework suggests that firms have effectively protected themselves from competition. Superior firm performance of firms in the resource-based framework suggests that firms have discovered those business activities that they can conduct more efficiently than any current or potentially competing firms.

How can Firms Co-Operate?

All the organizational economic models discussed so far assume that firms can be analysed as if they were independent economic entities. The picture painted, in most of these models, is of individual firms making transactions-cost vertical integration and boundary choices, solving their important agency problems, and competing against other independent firms for competitive advantage. And, indeed, there are many times when this 'independent firm' approach to economic analysis is appropriate.

However, over the last several years, scholars have come to recognize the importance of sets of co-operating firms as major players in competitive settings (Tirole 1989). Competition is still important in these settings. However, more and more frequently, competition seems to manifest itself between groups of co-operating firms rather than simply between firms.

Organizational economic models of co-operation between firms have a common form and structure (Barney 1995). First, these models examine the economic incentives, otherwise independent firms have to co-operate in some way. It can be shown that firms have such incentives in a wide variety of settings. Once these co-operative incentives are understood, these economic models of co-operation then examine the incentives that co-operating firms have to 'cheat' on their co-operative agreements. It is, perhaps, ironic, but each of the economically valuable reasons that firms can find to co-operate generally imply economically valuable ways that firms can cheat on those co-operative agreements. Finally, these models focus on activities that firms can engage in to monitor potential cheating in their co-operative relationships. If this monitoring is done well, then the incentives to cheat on co-operative agreements can be reduced and co-operation can continue. This form of analysis has been applied to two major forms of co-operation in organizational economics: tacit collusion and strategic alliances.

Tacit Collusion as Co-Operation

Traditional economics has long recognized the importance of co-operation among firms in an industry (Scherer 1980). The most common way this co-operation has been analysed is as collusion, either explicit or tacit. A set of firms is said to be colluding when they co-operate to reduce the total output of products or services in an industry below what would be the case if they were competing in that industry (Tirole 1989). Of course, assuming that demand for an industry's products remains relatively stable, these reductions in supply will be reflected in increased prices. These increased prices can generate levels of performance much greater than what would be expected in a more competitive industry.

Incentives to Co-Operate

Consider, for example, a hypothetical industry with six firms. Imagine, for simplicity, that these firms sell undifferentiated products, and that the cost of manufacturing these products is $3 per unit. Also, imagine that total demand for these products is fixed, equal to 10 000 units, but that these six firms have agreed to restrict output below this level. Again, for simplicity, suppose that each of these firms has agreed to restrict output to only 1000 units. Since demand (10 000 units) is much greater than supply (6000), there are a large number of customers chasing after a relatively small number of products, and prices will rise. In a fully competitive industry, these firms would only be able to charge about $3 per unit. However, in this collusive industry, they may be able to charge as much as $10 per unit. Whereas in the competitive case, these firms would all about 'break even', in the colluding case they could each earn substantial economic profits of $7000 (($10 × 1000) – ($3 × 1000)). That $7000 economic profit is the economic incentive for these firms to co-operate in the form of collusion.

However, whenever there is an incentive to co-operate, there is also an incentive to cheat on those co-operative agreements. This incentive can be seen by what happens to the profits of one of our hypothetical firms if it violates the agreement to sell 1000 units at $10, and instead sells 3000 units at $9. In this situation, the five firms that stick with the collusive agreement still earn their $7000 profit, but the cheating firm earns a much larger profit of $18 000 (($9 × 3000) – ($3 × 3000)). The $11 000 difference between the $7000 that is earned if collusion is maintained, and the $18 000 the one firm earns if it cheats on this collusive agreement is the economic incentive to cheat on collusion.

Cheating on these collusive agreements usually spreads rapidly. Once other firms discover that a particular firm is cheating on a collusive agreement, they may begin cheating on this agreement, and collusive co-operation in this industry will cease (Scherer 1980). This can be seen in the simple case depicted in Figure 1.3.3. In this case, there are just two firms in the industry (I and II), who have agreed to collude, restrict output and set a price equal to P^*. P^* is greater than the price these firms could

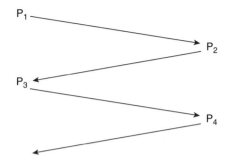

Figure 1.3.3 Cheating on collusive alliances

charge in a non-collusive setting. Also, to simplify this example, assume that the products or services these two firms sell are undifferentiated, and that customers face no costs switching back and forth from Firm I to Firm II (this roughly approximates competition between, say, two gas stations across the street from each other).

Now suppose Firm I decides to cheat on this collusive agreement and charge a price $P_1 < P^*$. As soon as this happens, all those customers who had been purchasing products from Firm II will instantly switch to Firm I for the lower price. Firm II will have to respond by lowering its price to P_2. P_2 must be less than P_1 or customers would have no incentive to shift back from Firm I to Firm II. When Firm II sets its price at P_2, all of Firm I's customers will instantly switch to Firm II, and Firm I will have to readjust its price to P_3. P_3 must be less than P_2, and so forth. This competition will continue until the prices these Firms charge exactly equal their economic costs, at which time any superior performance that could have been obtained from collusion will have been competed away.

Much of what has come to be known as game theory is dedicated to understanding interactions like those depicted in Figure 1.3.3. This particular game was originally studied by Bertrand (1883) and examines what happens when colluding firms cheat on their agreements by lowering their prices. It can be easily demonstrated that such 'Bertrand cheating' will lead firms to earn rates of return equal to that of firms in perfectly competitive markets (Tirole 1989). Another early, and very influential, game of this sort was studied by Cournot (1897). Cournot analysed what will happen to prices and performance if firms cheat on their collusive agreements by increasing their output beyond agreed levels. Such 'Cournot cheating' will lead to performance somewhere between that which fully colluding firms could have earned and what firms in a perfectly competitive market will earn (Tirole 1989). Hundreds of other game theoretic models examine different types of interactions between firms and the implications of such interactions on the performance of firms in an industry (Scherer 1980; Tirole 1989). The conclusion of many of these models is that the economic incentives to cheat on collusive arrangements, despite the increased competition such cheating almost always creates, is often larger than the economic incentives firms have to maintain their collusive arrangements.

Of course, much of this problem with cheating on collusive arrangements could be resolved if managers in colluding firms could sit down together, face-to-face, and work out their problems. However, such direct, face-to-face negotiations about the level of output in an industry and prices is, in most developed economies, illegal. Such explicit collusion can lead to very real negative consequences for managers and firms, including large fines and time in prison. Most governments actively discourage explicit collusion because the lower levels of production and the higher prices it creates, while they may improve the profits of colluding firms, are generally very bad for consumers, and for society as a whole (Scherer 1980). Indeed, as was suggested earlier, the effort to eliminate collusion was one of the primary policy objectives of the SCP framework.

Given the risks associated with explicit collusion, firms seeking to engage in this form of co-operation must use, instead, tacit collusion. In tacit collusion, there again is an agreement to reduce output below, and prices above, the competitive level. However, these agreements are not directly negotiated. Rather, firms seeking to implement tacit collusion must interpret the intent of other firms to collude through the behaviours and signals these other firms send out (Spence 1974). Such interpretation of intentions to collude can be difficult. For example, suppose a firm that has been able to reduce its economic costs does not pass these lower costs along to customers in the form of lower prices. Does this mean that this firm is interested in developing some collusive relationships, or does it mean that this firm believes that demand for its highly differentiated product is sufficient to increase sales without price reductions?

One tactic suggested for sustaining tacit collusion is to punish those that either raise their output level or reduce their prices. For example, Axelrod (1984) suggests that tit-for-tat strategies where such non-co-operative behaviour is immediately punished through some sort of retaliation (in this case increased output and price reductions) by competitors will discourage such behaviour in the future. The effectiveness of tit-for-tat strategies in assuring collusion, however, depends upon the ability of those involved to perceive one another's moves with a high degree of certainty. As Axelrod (1984) found in his simulations, co-operative outcomes are more difficult to sustain when there is uncertainty about the moves made by players in a game. Moreover, tit-for-tat can lead to an escalation in competition as has been the case in price wars among US airlines.

Industry Structure and the Ability to Collude

The ability to interpret intentions to collude varies with several important attributes of industries and of the firms in those industries. For example, in general, tacit collusion is easier when there are relatively few firms in an industry (Scherer 1980). In such industries, firms need only receive and interpret signals of intentions to collude from a small number of firms, rather than from a large number of firms. Also, tacit collusion is typically easier in industries where all firms have about the same economic costs and sell undifferentiated products. When firms have about the same economic costs, they have about the same optimal level of production (Scherer 1980). If collusion reduces production below this optimal level, all these firms will absorb about the same extra production costs. They will also all earn about the same level of economic profits. In this setting, no one firm has a strong incentive to cheat on collusion, since no one firm is obtaining a disproportionately smaller level of benefit from colluding. The lack of product differentiation helps maintain collusion by limiting the ways that firms can cheat on collusive arrangements. If firms can differentiate their products, they can increase demand for their own products in ways that are less obvious than by simply lowering their prices. However, if product differentiation is difficult to do, then any cheating on collusive agreements will be reflected in a firm's prices. Prices are relatively easy to monitor, and thus cheating on prices will typically lead to quick retaliation against the cheating firm. Quick retaliation, in turn, reduces the time period during which a cheating firm will be able to earn extra economic performance from cheating, and thus reduces the incentives to cheat (Scherer 1980).

Scherer (1980) describes several other industry attributes that tend to enhance the ability of firms to interpret signals of intention to collude, and thus enhance the ability of tacit collusion to emerge and remain. However, none of these other industry attributes is more important than high barriers to entry. As suggested earlier, barriers to entry increase the cost of entry into an industry. Firms that are successfully implementing tacit collusion will be earning substantial economic profits. Such profits, other things being equal, should motivate entry into an industry. New entrants, in turn, are less likely to be part of the collusive agreements in an industry and thus more likely to 'cheat' on these agreements. Such cheating will almost always have the effect of increasing competition in an industry and reducing the probability that tacit collusion agreements can be maintained. Thus, in order for colluding firms to continue in their colluding ways, they must be protected from new entry by substantial barriers to entry. These barriers to entry were discussed previously in the context of the SCP-based approach to understanding heterogeneity in firm performance.

In general, those attributes of firms and industries that have an effect on the ability of firms to interpret signals of intentions to collude can be thought of as part of the monitoring process firms engage in to reduce the probability of cheating in this form of co-operation. As suggested earlier, while there are often substantial incentives to co-operate, there are also substantial incentives to cheat on these co-operative agreements. By monitoring the behaviour of their partners in collusion, the probability of cheating can be reduced, and the extra economic performance promised by collusion can be realized. The easier it is to monitor a colluding firm's behaviour, the less likely cheating will occur, and the more likely that collusion will continue.

Strategic Alliances and Co-Operation

Previous work suggests that tacit collusion, as a form of co-operation, is possible. However, given the difficulties associated with interpreting signals of intent to collude, most organizational economists expect this form of collusion to be relatively rare. Strategic alliances, as a form of co-operation, are, on the other hand, much more common than tacit collusion. Indeed, the number of international strategic alliances entered into by US firms has grown dramatically over the last several years (Harrigan 1986; Kogut 1988). Firms like IBM, AT&T and Corning have, literally, hundreds of strategic alliances (Kogut 1988). One of Corning's alliances, with Dow Chemical (Dow Corning), is, itself, a *Fortune* 500 company. Thus, strategic alliances are a much more common, and economically important, form of co-operation than tacit collusion (Barney 1995). Moreover, strategic alliances usually have none of the social welfare reducing side effects of collusion (Kogut 1988).

Types of Alliances

There are multiple ways to classify alliances (see, for example, Doz and Hamel 1998; Noteboom 1999) but, in general, there are two broad classes of strategic alliances: contractual alliances and joint ventures (Hennart 1988). A contractual alliance is any form of co-operative relationship between two or more firms, the purpose of which is to develop, design, manufacture, market or distribute products or services, and where a separate firm is *not* created to manage this relationship. Rather, this relationship is managed through some sort of contract. Notice that, unlike tacit collusion, the effect of contractual strategic alliances is to increase economic activity, not to reduce economic activity below the competitive level. Common examples of contractual strategic alliances include: long-term supply relationships, licensing arrangements, distribution agreements, and so forth.

Joint ventures are also co-operative relationships between two or more firms with the purpose of developing, designing, manufacturing, marketing or distributing products or services. However, unlike contractual alliances, joint ventures always involve the creation of a separate firm (the joint venture) to manage this relationship. Partners in this joint venture provide capital and other resources to this separate firm, which is typically managed by its own management team reporting to a board of directors consisting of representatives of the joint venture partners. Partners in this joint venture are compensated for their investment from the profits that are generated by this firm. Financial interests may be equally distributed across joint venture partners, or some partners may have larger financial interest in a joint venture than other partners. For example, Dow and Corning each own 50% of the Dow Corning joint venture; Corning owns over 60% of its television glass joint venture with Asahi (Nanda and Bartlett 1990).

Incentives to Co-Operate in Alliances

The primary economic incentive for engaging in strategic alliances is to exploit resource complementarity (Hennart 1988; Kogut 1988). The resources controlled by two or more firms are complementary when their economic value combined is greater than their economic value separately. Obviously, when firms have complementary resources, an important economic synergy among these firms exists. A strategic alliance is one way that synergy can be realized.

While economic complementarity is a general requirement for firms to pursue strategic alliances, this complementarity can come from numerous different sources. Some of the most important of these sources of complementarities between firms are listed in Table 1.3.2. For example, firms may engage in an alliance to realize economies of scale that cannot be realized by each firm on its own (Kogut 1988). In the aluminium industry, the minimum efficient scale of bauxite mining is much greater than the maximum efficient scale of aluminium smelting. Individual smelting companies, on their own, could never operate an efficient bauxite mining operation. Any smelting operation large enough to absorb all the bauxite mined in an efficient mine would be terribly inefficient and lead to high smelting costs; a mine small enough to supply just an efficient smelting operation would also be terribly inefficient and lead to high mining costs. One solution to this problem would be for a single firm to operate an efficient (i.e. very large) mine and an efficient (i.e. relatively small) smelting operation, and then to sell excess bauxite on the open market. Unfortunately, bauxite is not a homogeneous ore, and refining bauxite purchased from a large mine would require a smelting firm to make enormous transaction specific investments in that mine. Such investments put these firms at risk of opportunistic behaviour (see the discussion of transaction cost economics earlier), and thus these refiners would prefer not to have to purchase an independent efficient mining firm's excess bauxite (Hennart 1988). Thus, to

Table 1.3.2	Motivations for entering strategic alliances

1. Exploit economies of scale
2. Low-cost entry into new markets
3. Low-cost entry into new industry segments and new industries
4. Learning from competition
5. Managing strategic uncertainty
6. Managing costs and sharing risks
7. To facilitate tacit collusion

simultaneously exploit the economies of scale associated with a large mining operation, while maintaining relatively small and efficient aluminium smelting operations, and not requiring smelting firms to make high levels of transaction specific investments across market exchanges, most bauxite mines are owned by joint ventures, where joint venture partners are smelting firms (Scherer 1980; Stuckey 1983).

Another important economic motivation for entering into a strategic alliance is to reduce the cost of entry into a new market (Kogut 1988). In a global economy, many firms are beginning to recognize the importance of selling their products and services in markets around the world. However, entry into these markets can be costly and difficult. New market entrants often have to build costly new distribution networks. Moreover, new market entrants often do not have the local expertise they need to respond to customer needs in these new markets. In this setting, co-operating with a firm in a local market can be a very effective way to enter that market. Instead of building a new distribution network, market entrants can exploit the already existing distribution networks of their partner in that new market. That partner is also more likely to have the local expertise that will be necessary to be successful in that new market. On the other hand, the local partner may gain access to valuable new products and technologies that it can distribute in its traditional market. For these reasons, low-cost entry into new markets is, perhaps, one of the most common motivations behind strategic alliances (Harrigan 1986).

Alliances can also facilitate low-cost entry into new industries, or new segments of an industry (Kogut 1988). For example, Dow Chemical believed that it had some resources and capabilities that might be valuable in the electronics industry. However, as a chemical firm, they had relatively little experience in this industry. Rather than trying to enter on their own, Dow formed a strategic alliance with Philips Electronics. This alliance uses Dow's chemical expertise, and Philips' electronics expertise, to manufacture compact disks for sale in North America. It was almost certainly less costly for Dow to enter into this segment of the electronics industry with Philips as a partner than it would have been for Dow to enter into this industry by itself (Barney 1995).

Alliances can also be used to learn from competitors (Kogut 1988). Since the early 1980s, General Motors has consistently lost market share in the US automobile industry. Much of this share loss can be traced to poor quality manufacturing, especially among GM's small car lines. GM has been trying to learn how to manufacture high-quality automobiles, especially high-quality small automobiles, while still making a profit. In 1983, GM formed a strategic alliance with Toyota. Called NUMMI, this Fremont, CA, assembly operation has given GM an opportunity to directly observe how Toyota builds high-quality small cars at a profit. GM has transferred much of the knowledge they gained from NUMMI, and other of their strategic alliances, to its Saturn division – a division that has been very successful at manufacturing high-quality cars (although still not at a profit).

Alliances can also be used by firms to manage strategic uncertainty (Kogut 1991). Sometimes, a firm may have several strategic options, but be unable to choose which of those options promises the most economic success. For example, after the US federal government broke up AT&T, AT&T was not completely sure what its long-term strategy should be. To be sure, it had numerous options and substantial financial and other resources at its disposal, but the best path forward was not obvious. In this context, AT&T invested in a very large number (almost 400 at one time) of strategic alliances (Kogut 1991). Each of these alliances gave AT&T some insight into the competitive and economic potential of a different business activity. In financial terms, these numerous alliances can be thought of as real options (Kogut 1991). Once the actual economic potential of different strategies becomes clear (i.e. once uncertainty is reduced), a firm can either divest itself of an option (by backing out of the alliance) or exercise an option (by, say, purchasing its alliance partner, and thus entering into an industry). In this uncertain context, multiple alliances

can be thought of as a way a firm keeps its 'options open'. Once AT&T decided that the telecommunications industry and the computer industry were likely to come together in an economically valuable way, AT&T exercised some of its earlier strategic alliance options by purchasing several computer firms, including NCR.

Alliances can also be used by firms to reduce their costs and manage their risk (Barney 1995). Some potentially valuable investments are so large, or so risky, that individual firms would literally 'bet the company' if they made these investments on their own. In this case, an alliance of some sort can help a firm reduce the costs it bears from an investment, thereby reducing the risks of this investment. This is one reason why most deep water drilling platforms (typically, very risky investments) are owned by alliances of oil and gas companies and not just a single firm (Scherer 1980; Kogut 1988).

A final reason that firms may enter into strategic alliances is to facilitate the development of tacit (or even explicit) collusion (Kogut 1988). Indeed, for many years, the development of tacit collusion was seen as one of the primary motivators of strategic alliances. After all, firms that are able to directly communicate through a strategic alliance may be able to transfer this relationship to other of their businesses, where collusion may be forthcoming. For this reason, the alliance between GM and Toyota was subjected to intense regulatory scrutiny, to ensure that GM and Toyota would not use this alliance to develop collusion in the automobile industry. While alliances may, in principle, help facilitate the development of tacit collusion, most organizational economists now believe that, given the enormous economic potential of alliances from other sources, the development of tacit collusion is a relatively unimportant motivation for the creation of most alliances (Kogut 1988).

In all of the above incentives to enter into strategic alliances, resource complementarity is the central motivation for firms entering into an alliance. However, the institutional context also affects the feasibility of alliances (Williamson 1993b). It may either facilitate or inhibit the formation of alliances. In Italy, for example, one argument for the reliance on extensive networks of small firms in some industries is that labour laws provide an incentive for firms to stay small and rely on extensive co-operation. Another example of the impact of institutional conditions is Japanese subcontracting (Williamson 1985; Fruin 1992). Multiple factors – such as cross-ownership, the legal system, and culture – contribute to a greater willingness to enter into alliances than was historically the case in some countries. Cross-ownership patterns contribute to ease in entering into alliances. Firms often hold a mutual equity interest in one another which leads to a perception that they have a 'common destiny' (Williamson 1985: 121). Culture may also contribute to alliance patterns. In Japan, greater importance is attached to maintaining harmony than in some other cultures. Such a focus on harmony likely engenders less risk in entering into alliances with others who share that focus. Although institutional context clearly makes it either more or less difficult to successfully enter into alliances, organizational economics nevertheless views this as secondary to resource complementarity in explaining strategic alliances. In all of the above examples, firms also have clear resource complementarity reasons for entering into alliances and, indeed, it is potential complementarities that discriminate between firms that are potential alliance partners and those that are not.

Incentives to Cheat in Alliances

While there are significant economic incentives for firms to co-operate in strategic alliances, there are also significant economic incentives to cheat on those alliances once they are formed. Such cheating can take at least three forms: adverse selection cheating, moral hazard cheating, and hold-up cheating (Barney and Ouchi 1986). Each of these types of cheating in alliances can be thought of as specific examples of opportunistic behaviour – of the sort described in transaction cost economics and agency theory. Indeed, adverse selection and moral hazard have already been discussed as problems in agency relationships; hold-up, as a function of transaction specific investments, has already been discussed as a problem in transaction cost economics.

Adverse selection exists when an alliance partner misrepresents the resources and capabilities they can bring to an alliance (Barney and Hansen 1995). For example, suppose firm I needs political contacts in a particular country in order to facilitate entry into a new market. If firm II informs Firm I that it possesses these contacts, when it really does not possess them, Firm II has engaged in adverse selection. In this case, Firm II will be able to appropriate whatever resources and capabilities Firm I makes available to the alliance, without providing any of its own resources and capabilities to the alliance.

Moral hazard exists when an alliance partner really does possess the resources and capabilities it says it possesses, but simply does not make them available to the alliance (Barney and Hansen 1995). For example, suppose that Firm I and Firm II are co-operating in a joint research and development effort. Also, suppose that, as part of this agreement, both firms promise to assign only their best engineering talent to this alliance. Firm I may, in fact, fulfil its part of the agreement and send top-level engineering talent to the alliance. Firm II, on the other hand, may decide to keep its best engineering talent in the parent company, where it can be used in other development projects. Rather than sending the best engineering talent, Firm II might send engineers who are just well-enough-trained to learn everything that Firm I's engineers can teach them, but not sufficiently well-trained to actually contribute to the alliance. In this case, Firm II has engaged in moral hazard. It has been able to gain significant value from the alliance (it has learned a great deal from Firm I's engineers), and it has been able to do so at very low cost (it retained its best engineers to continue working on its own development projects).

Hold-up exists when an alliance is characterized by high levels of transaction specific investment, and where those that have made these investments are exploited by those who have not made them. In the discussion of transaction cost economics, it was suggested that high levels of transaction specific investment can subject a firm to significant threats of opportunistic behaviour and may motivate vertical integration (Williamson 1975). This argument holds in the case of alliances as well: alliances characterized by high levels of specific investment may not be stable, and may have to be replaced by vertically integrated exchanges (Kogut 1988).

Reducing the Threat of Cheating

Just as different industry and firm attributes can facilitate the monitoring of cheating by partners in collusive arrangements, firms in strategic alliances can engage in activities designed to reduce the probability of adverse selection, moral hazard and hold-up. These monitoring devices fall into two broad categories: governance and trust.

The role of governance in strategic alliances precisely parallels the role of governance in transaction cost economics. In general, the greater the value of cheating in a strategic alliance, the greater the threat of cheating. The greater the threat of cheating, the more elaborate the governance that will be required to manage an alliance. When the threat of cheating is small, simple market forms of governance (e.g. simple contracts) can reduce the threat of cheating and do so at low cost. As the threat of cheating increases, more elaborate – and costly – forms of governance will have to be implemented (e.g. contractual alliances). At even higher levels of threat, joint ventures may have to be used to manage a co-operative relationship. By creating a joint venture, parties in an alliance create a new firm to manage a relationship. Since compensation for investing in this firm depends entirely on its profits, parties in this form of alliance have incentives to not behave opportunistically when creating the joint venture. However, sometimes even joint ventures cannot efficiently reduce the threat of cheating in an exchange, and that exchange will have to be integrated into a single firm, to be managed through hierarchical forms of governance (Hennart 1988; Kogut 1988). In general, firms will prefer that form of governance that minimizes the probability of opportunism, but does so at the lowest governance cost possible (Williamson 1975).

A second approach to managing cheating in alliances builds on the trust that can develop between parties to an alliance (Madhok 1995). Over a period of time, parties to an alliance may discover that they can all be trusted to not behave opportunistically in this relationship. With this trust in place, normal governance mechanisms can be dismantled. In this sense, trust among alliance partners may be a low-cost substitute for costly governance (Barney and Hansen 1995).

However, not only can trust be a low-cost substitute for governance, but firms that trust each other may be able to explore exchange opportunities that are not available to firms that cannot trust each other. If, as transactions cost theorists suggest, governance is costly, there may well be potentially valuable economic exchanges whose value cannot be realized. This can happen in at least two ways. First, the potential gains from these exchanges may only be modest, but the threat of opportunism sufficient, such that the cost of governance is greater than the gains from trade. Secondly, the potential gains from these trades may be enormous. However, the threat of opportunism in these exchanges may be so large that no cost effective governance mechanism can be created. Even vertical integration may not be able to solve all the

problems of opportunism that might plague these exchanges (Grossman and Hart 1986). In the absence of efficient governance, the exchanges will not occur – despite their economic potential. However, if parties in an alliance trust each other, these firms will be able to explore these exchange opportunities and, perhaps, realize their economic potential. Moreover, if relatively few sets of alliance partners trust one another in this manner, and if this trust is costly for other sets of firms to imitate, then the resource-based view of the firm suggests that firms that are able to trust each other may be able to gain sustained competitive advantages from their co-operative efforts. Indeed, trust surfaces as the 'magic ingredient' in much alliance research (Koza and Lewin 1998: 261) as evidenced by the large number of studies devoted to the topic (see, for example, Madhok 1995; Zaheer et al. 1998; Inkpen and Currall 2004).

Conclusion

Organization economics has been, and will continue to be, an important set of theoretical tools for the analysis of organizations and organizational phenomena. It addresses some of the most fundamental issues in all of organizational research, including the four questions around which this chapter is organized. Progress in answering these questions, both theoretically and empirically, has been impressive although, clearly, much work remains.

Of course, organization economics is not alone in addressing these and related, fundamental questions of organizational analysis. Both organizational behaviour and organization theory are also concerned with understanding why organizations exist, the implications of interest conflicts among those associated with an organization, why some organizations outperform others, and how organizations can co-operate with one another. Given this overlapping set of interests, one might expect that these three literatures should build on each other, should inform work done in these different research streams – in short, that a theoretical integration of organizational economics, organizational behaviour and organization theory should be emerging.

Most observers would agree, however, that, despite the potential for integration and cross-fertilization, relatively little of this integrative work has occurred. At best, cross-disciplinary work of this sort takes the form of public debates about the assumptions of economics, the quality of behavioural research and so forth (e.g. Hirsch et al. 1990 versus Hesterly and Zenger 1993; Donaldson 1990 versus Barney 1990; Williamson and Ouchi 1981a, b versus Perrow 1981). At worst, these sets of disciplines ignore each other.

There is little doubt that both organizational economists, on the one hand, and organizational behaviour and theory scholars, on the other, bear responsibility for the limited integration that has developed between these fields so far. More behaviourally oriented scholars have often adopted an overly simplistic view of organizational economics, asserting that organizational economists all assume perfect rationality (which they don't), perfect information (which they don't) and equilibrium (which they don't). Economically oriented scholars criticize the 'fuzzy' and 'ill-defined' assumptions of behavioural research, despite applying many of those same assumptions (e.g. imperfect information, bounded rationality) in their own research.

One can only hope that discourse among these organizational scholars will continue, and that the real opportunities for bringing behavioural research into organizational economics, and an economic orientation into organizational behaviour and organization theory, will be fully realized.

Note

1. The assumption of opportunism may be new to economics, but, as Douglas (1990) notes, it is more familiar to organization theorists. Indeed, notions of opportunism are central to resource dependence theory in particular and to power theories in general.

References

Afuah, A. (2000) 'How much do your competitors' capabilities matter in the face of a technological change?', *Strategic Management Journal*, 21: 387–404.

Alchian, A.A. and Demsetz, H. (1972) 'Production, information costs, and economic organization', *American Economic Review*, 62: 777–95.

Amihud, Y. and Lev, B. (1981) 'Risk reduction as managerial motive for conglomerate mergers', *Bell Journal of Economics*, 12: 605–16.

Amihud, Y. and Lev, B. (1999) 'Does corporate ownership structure affect its strategy towards diversification?', *Strategic Management Journal*, 20: 1063–9.

Anderson, E. (1985) 'The salesperson as outside agent or employee', 4: 234–54.

Anderson, E. and Schmittlein, D. (1984) 'Integration of the sales force: an empirical examination', *Rand Journal of Economics*, 15(3): 385–95.

Andrade, G. Mitchell, M. and Stafford, E. (2001) 'New evidence and perspectives on mergers', *Journal of Economic Perspectives*, 15: 103–20.

Argawal, A. and Mandelker, G. (1987) 'Managerial incentives and corporate investment and financing decisions', *Journal of Finance*, 42: 823–37.

Armour, H.O. and Teece, D.J. (1978) 'Organizational structure and economic performance', *Bell Journal of Economics*, 9: 106–22.

Armour, H.O. and Teece, D.J. (1980) 'Vertical integration and technological innovation', *Review of Economics and Statistics*, 60: 470–4.

Arrow, K.J. (1974) *The Limits of Organization.* New York: W.W. Norton.

Arrow, K.J. (1985) 'The economics of agency', in J.W. Pratt and R.J. Zeckhauser (eds), *Principals and Agents: the Structure of American Business.* Boston: Harvard Business School Press. pp. 37–51.

Arthur, W., Ermolieve, U. and Kaniovsky, Y. (1987) 'Path dependent processes and the emergence of macro structure', *European Journal of Operations Research*, 30: 294–303.

Axelrod, R. (1984) *Tine Evolution of Cooperation.* New York: Basic Books.

Bain, J.S. (1956) *Barriers to New Competition.* Cambridge, MA: Harvard University Press.

Baker, W.E. and Faulkner, R.R. (1991) 'Role as resource in the Hollywood film industry', *American Journal of Sociology*, 97: 279–309.

Balkin, D.B., Markman, G.D. and Gomez-Mejia, L.R. (2000) 'Is CEO pay in high-technology firms related to innovation?', *Academy of Management Journal*, 43: 1118–29.

Barney. J.B. (1986a) 'Types of competition and the theory of strategy', *Academy of Management Review*, II: 791–800.

Barney, J.B. (1986b) 'Strategic factor markets: expectations, luck, and business strategy', *Management Science*, 42: 1231–41.

Barney, J.B. (1986c) 'Organizational culture: can it be a source of sustained competitive advantage?', *Academy of Management Review*, 11: 656–65.

Barney, J.B. (1990) 'The debate between traditional management theory and organizational economics: substantive differences or inter-group conflict?', *Academy of Management Review*, 15: 382–93.

Barney, J.B. (1991) 'Firm resources and sustained competitive advantage', *Journal of Management*, 17: 99–120.

Barney, J.B. (1994) 'What is an attractive industry?', *Praktisk Økonomi og Ledelse*, 71–81.

Barney, J.B. (1995) *Advanced Strategic Management.* Reading, MA: Addison-Wesley.

Barney, J.B. and Hansen, M. (1995) 'Trustworthiness source of competitive advantage', *Strategic Management Journal*, 15: 175–90.

Barney, J.B. and Hoskisson, R.E. (1989) 'Strategic groups: untested assertions and research proposals', *Managerial and Decision Economics*, 11: 187–98.

Barney, J.B. and Ouchi, W.G. (1986) *Organizational Economics: Toward a New Paradigm for Understanding and Studying Organizations*. San Francisco: Jossey-Bass.

Bartlett, C.A. and Ghoshal, S. (1993) 'Beyond the M-form: toward a managerial theory of the firm', *Strategic Management Journal*, 14(S2): 23–46.

Baumol, W.J., Panzar, J.C. and Willig, R.P. (1982) *Contestable Markets and the Theory of Industry Structure*. San Diego, CA: Harcourt Brace Jovanovich.

Bertrand, J. (1883) 'Theorie mathematique de la richesse sociale', *Journal des Savants*, 499–508.

Bethel, J.E. and Liebeskind, 1. (1993) 'The effects of ownership structure on corporate restructuring', *Strategic Management Journal*, 14: 15–32.

Bettis, R.A. (1991) 'Strategic management and the straightjacket: an editorial essay', *Organization Science*, 2: 315–9.

Bhagat, S., Shleifer, A. and Vishny, R. (1990) 'Hostile takeovers in the 1980s: the return to corporate specialization', *The Brookings Papers on Economic Activity: Microeconomics*, 1–84.

Blair, R.D. and Kaserman, D.L. (1983) *Law and Economics of Vertical Integration and Control*. New York: Academic Press.

Bowman, E.H. and Helfat, C.E. (2001) 'Does Corporate Strategy Matter?', *Strategic Management Journal*, 22: 1–23.

Bradach, J.L. and Eccles, R.G. (1989) 'Price, authority. and trust: from ideal types to plural forms', *Annual Review of Sociology*, 15: 97–118.

Brickley, J.A. and Dark, F. (1987) 'The choice of organizational form: the case of franchising', *Journal of Financial Economics*, 18: 401–20.

Brickley, J.A., Coles, J.L. and Terry, R.L. (1994) 'The board of directors and the enactment of poison pills', *Journal of Financial Economics*, 35: 371–90.

Brickley, J.A., Dark, F. and Weisbach, M. (1991) 'The economic effects of franchise termination laws', *Journal of Law and Economics*, 34: 101–32.

Brusoni, S., Prencipe, A. and Pavitt, K. (2001) 'Knowledge specialization, organizational coupling, and the boundaries of the firm: why do firms know more than they make?', *Administrative Science Quarterly*, 46: 597–621.

Buckley, P.J. and Casson, M. (1976) *The Future of the Multinational Enterprise*. London: Longman.

Cable, J. and Dirrheimer, M.J. (1983) 'Hierarchies and markets: an empirical test of the multidivisional hypothesis in West Germany', *International Journal of Industrial Organization*, 1: 43–62.

Cable, J. and Yasuki, H. (1985) 'Internal organization, business groups and corporate performance: an empirical test of the multidivisional hypothesis in Japan', *International Journal of Industrial Organization*, 3: 401–20.

Capron, L. (1999) 'The long-term performance of horizontal acquisitions', *Strategic Management Journal*, 20: 987–1018.

Carow, K.A., Heron, R. and Saxton, T. (2004) 'Do early birds get the returns? An empirical investigation of early-mover advantages with acquisitions', *Strategic Management Journal*, 25: 563–85.

Carter, M.E. and Lynch, L.J. (2001) 'An examination of executive stock option repricing', *Journal of Financial Economics*, 61: 207–25.

Caves, R.E. and Bradburd, R.M. (1988) 'The empirical determinants of vertical integration', *Journal of Economic Behavior and Organization*, 9: 265–79.

Caves, R.E. and Porter, M.E. (1977) 'From entry barriers to mobility barriers: conjectural decisions and contrived deterrence to new competition', *Quarterly Journal of Economics*, 91: 241–62.

Chamberlain, E.H. (1933) *The Theory of Monopolistic Competition*. Cambridge, MA: Harvard University Press.

Chandler, A.D. (1962) *Strategy and Structure: Chapters in the History of the American Industrial Enterprise*. Cambridge, MA: MIT Press.

Chang, S.J. (2003) 'Ownership structure, expropriation, and economic performance of group-affiliated companies in Korea', *Academy of Management Journal*, 46: 238–53.

Coase, R.H. (1937) 'The nature of the firm', *Economica*, 4: 386–405.

Coase, R.H. (1972) 'Industrial organization: a proposal for research', in V. R. Fuchs (ed.), *Policy Issues and Research Opportunities in Industrial Organization*, New York: National Bureau of Economic Research. pp. 59–73.

Coles, J.W. and Hesterly, W.S. (2000) 'Independence of the chairman and board composition: firm choices and shareholder value' (with J.W. Coles), *Journal of Management*, 26: 195–214.

Conner, K. and Prahalad, C.K. (1996) 'A resource-based theory of the firm: knowledge versus opportunism', *Organizational Science*, 7: 477–501.

Conner, K.R. (1991) 'A historical comparison of resource-based theory and five schools of thought within industrial organization economics: do we have a new theory of the firm?', *Journal of Management*, 17: 121–54.

Copeland, T.E. and Weston, J.F. (1983) *Financial Theory and Corporate Policy*. Reading, MA: Addison-Wesley.

Cournot, A. (1897) *Research into the Mathematical Principles of the Theory of Wealth*. New York: Macmillan.

Cyert, R.M. and March, J.G. (1963) *A Behavioral Theory of the Firm*. Englewood Cliffs, NJ: Prentice-Hall.

Daily, C.M., Dalton, D.R. and Canella, A.A. (2003) 'Corporate governance: decades of dialogues and data', *Academy of Management Review*, 28: 371–382.

Dalton, D.R., Daily, C.M., Certo, S.T. and Roengpitya, R. (2003) 'Meta-analysis of financial performance and equity: fusion or confusion?', *Academy of Management Journal*, 46: 13–26.

Dalton, D.R., Daily, C.M., Ellstrand, A.E. and Johnson, J.L. (1998) 'Meta-analytic reviews of board composition, leadership structure, and financial performance', *Strategic Management Journal*, 19: 269–90.

David, R.J. and Han, S.K. (2004) 'A systematic assessment of the empirical support for transaction cost economics', *Strategic Management Journal*, 25(1): 39–58.

Davis, G.F. (1991) 'Agents without principles? The spread of the poison pill through the intercorporate network', *Administrative Science Quarterly*, 36: 583–613.

Demsetz, H. (1988) 'The theory of the firm revisited', *Journal of Law, Economics, and Organization*, 4: 141–62.

Demsetz, H. (1990) *Ownership, Control, and the Firm.* Oxford: Basil Blackwell.

Denis, D.J., Denis, D.K. and Sarin, A. (1999) 'Agency theory and the influence of equity ownership structure on corporate diversification strategies', *Strategic Management Journal*, 20: 1071–6.

Dierickx, I. and Cool, K. (1989) 'Asset stock accumulation and sustainability of competitive advantage', *Management Science*, 35: 1504–11.

DiMaggio, P. and Powell, W. (1983) 'The iron cage revisited: institutional isomorphism and collective rationality in organizational fields', *American Sociological Review*, 48: 147–60.

Donaldson, L. (1990) 'The ethereal hand: organizational economics and management theory', *Academy of Management Review*, 15: 369–81.

Douglas, M. (1990) 'Converging on autonomy: anthropology and institutional economics', in O. Williamson (ed.), *Organization Theory: From Chester Barnard to the Present and Beyond.* Oxford: Oxford University Press.

Dow, G.K. (1985) 'Internal bargaining and strategic innovation in the theory of the firm', *Journal of Economic Behavior and Organization*, 6: 301–20.

Dow, G.K. (1987) 'The function of authority in transaction cost economics', *Journal of Economic Behavior and Organization*, 8: 13–38.

Doz, Y. and Hamel, G. (1998) *Alliance advantage: The art of creating value through partnering.* Boston: Harvard Business School Press.

Dyer, J.H. (1996) 'Specialized supplier networks as a source of competitive advantage: evidence from the auto industry', *Strategic Management Journal*, 17(4): 271–92.

Eccles, R.G. (1981) 'The quasifirm in the construction industry', *Journal of Economic Behavior and Organization*, 2: 335–58.

Eccks, R.G. (1985) *The Transfer Pricing Problem.* Lexington, MA: Lexington Books.

Eisenhardt, K.M. (1985) 'Control: organizational and economic approaches', *Management Science*, 31: 134–49.

Eisenhardt, K.M. (1988) 'Agency and institutional theory explanations: the case of retail sales compensation', *Academy of Management Journal*, 31: 488–511.

Eisenhardt, K.M. (1989) 'Agency theory: as assessment and review', *Academy of Management Review*, 14: 57–74.

Eisenhardt, KM and Martin, JA (2000) 'Dynamic capabilities: what are they?', *Strategic Management Journal*, 21: 1105–21.

Faith, R.L., Higgins, R.S. and Tollison, R.D. (1984) 'Managerial rents and outside recruitment in the Coasian firm', *American Economic Review*, 74: 660–72.

Fama, E.F. (1970) 'Efficient capital markets: a review of theory and empirical work', *Journal of Finance*, 25: 383–417.

Fama, E.F. (1980) 'Agency problems and the theory of the firm', *Journal of Political Economy*, 88: 288–307.

Fama, E.F. and Jensen, M.C. (1983) 'Separation of ownership and control', *Journal of Law and Economics*, 26: 301–26.

Felin, T. and Hesterly, W.S. (forthcoming) 'The knowledge-based view and the individual: philosophical considerations on the locus of knowledge', *Academy of Management Review*.

Ferraro, F., Pfeffer, J. and Sutton, R.I. (2005) 'Economics language and assumptions: how theories can become self-fulfilling', *Academy of Management Review*, 30: 8–24.

Fladmoe-Lindquist, K. and Jacque, L. (1995) 'Control modes in international service operations: the propensity to franchise', *Management Science*, 41: 1–12.

Foss, N.J. (2003) 'Selective intervention and internal hybrids: interpreting and learning from the rise and decline of the oticon spaghetti organization', *Organizational Science*, 14: 331–49.

Fruin, W.M. (1992) *The Japanese Enterprise System: Competitive Strategies and Cooperative Structures.* Oxford: Oxford University Press.

Gedajlovic, E. and Shapiro, D.M. (2002) 'Ownership structure and firm profitability in Japan', *Academy of Management Journal*, 45: 565–75.

Ghemawat, P. (1986) 'WalMart Stores' discount operations'. Harvard Business School Case no. 9–387–018.

Ghemawat, P. and Stander, H. (1993) 'Nucor at a crossroads'. Harvard Business School Case no. 9–793–039.

Ghoshal, S. and Moran, P. (1996). 'Bad for practice: a critique of the transaction cost theory', *Academy of Management Review*, 21: 13–47.

Granovetter, M. (1985) 'Economic action and social structure', *American Journal of Sociology*, 91: 481–510.

Grinblatt, M. and Titman, S. (1987) 'How clients can win the gaming game', *Journal of Portfolio Management*, 13: 14–20.

Grinyer, P.H., Yassai-Ardekani, M. and Al-Bazza, S. (1980) 'Strategy, structure, the environment, and financial performance in 48 United Kingdom companies', *Academy of Management Journal*, 23: 193–220.

Grossman, S. and Hart, O. (1986) 'The costs and benefits of ownership: a theory of vertical and lateral integration', *Journal of Political Economy*, 94: 691–719.

Hall, P. (1983) 'Discretionary behaviour and the M-form hypothesis in large UK firms'. Paper presented at the annual conference of the European Association for Research in Industrial Economics, Bergen, Norway.

Hall, R. (1993) 'A framework linking intangible resources and capabilities to sustainable competitive advantage', *Strategic Management Journal*, 14: 607–18.

Hallowell, R. and Heskett, J. (1993) 'Southwest Airlines'. Harvard Business School Case no. 9–694–023.

Hannan, M. and Freeman, J. (1977) 'The population ecology of organizations', *American Journal of Sociology*, 82: 929–64.

Hansen, G.S. and Wernerfelt, B. (1989) 'Determinants of firm performance: the relative importance of economic and organizational factors', *Strategic Management Journal*, 10: 399–411.

Harrigan, K. (1986) *Money for Joint Venture Success*. Lexington. MA: Lexington Books.

Harris, B.C. (1983) *Organization: the Effect of Large Corporations*. Ann Arbor, Ml: University of Michigan Press.

Hatch, N.W. and Dyer, J.H. (2004) 'Human capital and learning as a source of sustainable competitive advantage', *Strategic Management Journal*, 25: 1155–78.

Henderson, R. and Cockburn, I. (1994) 'Measuring competence? Exploring firm effects in pharmaceutical research', *Strategic Management Journal*, 15: 63–84.

Hennart, J.-F. (1982) *A Theory of Multinational Enterprise*. Ann Arbor, Ml: University of Michigan Press.

Hennart, J.-F. (1988) 'A transactions cost theory of equity joint ventures', *Strategic Management Journal*, 9: 361–74.

Hennart, J.-F. (1991) 'The transaction cost theory of joint ventures: an empirical study of Japanese subsidiaries in the United States', *Management Science*, 37: 483–97.

Hennart, J.-F. (1993) 'Explaining the swollen middle: why most transactions are a mix of "Market" and "Hierarchy"', *Organization Science*, 4: 529–47.

Hesterly, W.S. and Zenger, T.R. (1993) 'The myth of a monolithic economics: fundamental assumptions and the use of economic models in policy and strategy research', *Organization Science*, 4: 496–510.

Hesterly, W.S., Liebeskind, J. and Zenger, T.R. (1990) 'Organizational economics: an impending revolution in organization theory', *Academy of Management Review*, 15: 402–20.

Hill, C.W.L. (1985) 'Internal organization and enterprise performance', *Managerial and Decision Economics*, 6: 210–6.

Hill, C.W.L. (1988) 'Internal capital market controls and financial performance in multidivisional firms', *Journal of Industrial Economics*, 37: 67–83.

Hill, C.W.L. and Snell, S.A. (1989) 'Effects of ownership structure and control on corporate productivity', *Academy of Management Journal*, 32: 25–46.

Hirsch, P.M., Friedman, R. and Koza, M.P. (1990) 'Collaboration or paradigm shift? *Caveat emptor* and the risk of romance with economic models for strategy and policy research', *Organization Science*, 1: 87–98.

Holmstrom, B. and Kaplan, S.N. (2001) 'Corporate governance and merger activity in the United States: making sense of the 1980s and 1990s', *Journal of Economic Perspectives*, 15(Spring): 121–144.

Hoskisson, R.E. and Galbraith, C.S. (1985) 'The effect of quantum versus incremental M-form reorganization: a time series exploration of intervention dynamics', *Journal of Management*, 11: 55–70.

Hoskisson, R.E. and Johnson, R.E. (1992) 'Corporate restructuring and strategic change: the effect of diversification strategy and R&D intensity', *Strategic Management Journal*, 13: 625–34.

Hoskisson, R.E. and Turk, T.A. (1990) 'Corporate restructuring: governance and control limits of the internal market', *Academy of Management Review*, 15: 459–77.

Hoskisson, R.E., Harrison, J.S. and Dubosky, D.A. (1991) 'Capital market evaluation of M-form implementation and diversification strategy', *Strategic Management Journal*, 12: 271–9.

Hoskisson, RE., Hill, C.W.L. and Kim, H. (1993) 'The multidivisional structure: organizational fossil or source of value?', *Journal of Management*, 19: 269–98.

Inkpen, A.C. and Currall, S.C. (2004) 'The coevolution of trust, control, and learning on joint ventures', *Organization Science*, 15: 586–99.

Jacobson, R. (1988) 'The persistence of abnormal returns', *Strategic Management Journal*, 9: 415–30.

Jacobson, R. (1992) 'The "Austrian" school of strategy', *Academy of Management Review*, 17: 782–807.

Jarrell, G.A., Brickley, J.A. and Netter, J.M. (1988) 'The market for corporate control: the empirical evidence since 1980', *Journal of Economic Perspectives*, 2: 49–68.

Jensen, M.C. and Meckling, W.H. (1976) 'Theory of the firm: managerial behavior, agency costs and ownership structure', *Journal of Financial Economics*, 3: 305–60.

Jensen, M.C. and Ruback, R.S. (1983) 'The market for corporate control: the scientific evidence', *Journal of Financial Economics*, 11: 5–50.

John, G. and Weitz, B.A. (1988) 'Forward integration into distribution: an empirical test of the transaction cost analysis', *Journal of Law, Economics, and Organization*, 4: 337–55.

Jones, C., Hesterly, W.S. and Borgatti, S.P. (1997) 'A general theory of network governance: exchange conditions and social mechanisms', *Academy of Management Review*, 22: 911–45.

Jones, G.P. and Hill, C.W.L. (1988) 'Transaction cost analysis of strategy-structure choice', *Strategic Management Journal*, 9: 159–72.

Joskow, P.L. (1985) 'Vertical integration and long term contracts: the case of coal-burning electric generating plants', *Journal of Law, Economics, and Organization*, 1: 33–80.

Joskow, P.L. (1988) 'Asset specificity and the structure of vertical relationships', *Journal of Law, Economics, and Organization*, 4: 95–117.

Knott, A.M., Bryce, D. and Posen, H. (2003) 'On strategic accumulation of intangible assets', *Organization Science*, 14: 192– 207.

Kogut, B. (1988) 'Joint ventures: theoretical and empirical perspectives', *Strategic Management Journal*, 9: 319–32.

Kogut, B. (1991) 'Joint ventures and the option to expand and acquire', *Management Science*, 37: 19–33.

Kogut, B. and Zander, U. (1992) 'Knowledge of the firm, combinative capabilities, and the replication of technology', *Organization Science*, 3: 383–97.

Kosnik, R.D. (1987) 'Greenmail: a study of hoard performance in corporate governance', *Administrative Science Quarterly*, 32: 163–85.

Koza, M.P. and Lewin, A.Y. (1998) 'The co-evolution of strategic alliances', *Organization Science*, 9: 255–64.

Lazear, E.P. (1986) 'Salaries and piece rates', *Journal of Business*, 59: 405–31.

Lee, P.M. and O'Neil, H.M. (2003) 'Ownership structures and R&D investments of U.S. and Japanese firms: agency and stewardship perspectives', *Academy of Management Journal*, 46: 212–25.

Leiblein, M.J. (2003) 'The choice of organizational governance form and firm performance: predictions from transaction cost, resource-based, and real options theories', *Journal of Management*, 29: 937–62.

Leiblein, M.J. and Miller, D.J. (2003) 'An empirical examination of transaction- and firm-level influences on the vertical boundaries of the firm', *Strategic Management Journal*, 24: 839–59.

Levy, D.T. (1985) 'The transactions cost approach to vertical integration: an empirical investigation', *Review of Economics and Statistics*, 67: 438–45.

Lieberman, M.B. and Montgomery, D.B. (1998) 'First-mover (dis)advantages: retrospective and link with the resource-based view', *Strategic Management Journal*, 19: 1111–25.

Lippman, S. and Rumelt, R. (1982) 'Uncertain imitability: an analysis of interfirm differences in efficiency under competition', *Bell Journal of Economics*, 13: 418–38.

MacDonald, J.M. (1985) 'Market exchange or vertical integration: an empirical analysis', *Review of Economics and Statistics*, 67: 327–31.

MacMillan, I., Hambrick, D.C. and Pennings, J.M. (1986) 'Uncertainty reduction and the threat of supplier retaliation: two views of the backward integration decision', *Organization Studies*, 7: 263–78.

Madhok, A. (1995) 'Revisiting multinational firms' tolerance for joint ventures: a trust-based approach', *Journal of International Business Studies*, 26: 117–38.

Madhok, A. and Tallman, S. (1998) 'Resources, transactions and rents: managing value in interfirm collaborative relationships', *Organization Science*, 9: 326–39.

Mahoney, J.M. and Mahoney, J.T. (1993) 'An empirical investigation of the effect of corporate charter antitakeover amendments on stockholder wealth', *Strategic Management Journal*, 14: 17–31.

Mahoney, J.T. (1992) 'The choice of organizational form: vertical financial ownership versus other methods of vertical integration', *Strategic Management Journal*, 13: 559–84.

Makadok. R. (1999) 'Interfirm differences in scale economies and the evolution of market shares', *Strategic Management Journal*, 20: 935–52.

Mallette, P. and Fowler, K. (1992) 'Effects of board composition and stock ownership on the adoption of poison pills', *Academy of Management Journal*, 35: 1010–35.

March, J.G. and Simon, H.A. (1958) *Organizations*. New York: Wiley.

Mariotti, S. and Cairnarca, G.C. (1986) 'The evolution of transaction governance in the textile clothing industry', *Journal of Economic Behavior and Organization*, 7: 351–74.

Marris, R. (1964) *The Economic Theory of Managerial Capitalism*,. Glencoc, IL: Free Press.

Mason, E.S. (1959) *The Corporation in Modern Society*. Cambridge, MA: Harvard University Press.

Masten, S.E. (1988) 'A legal basis of the firm', *Journal of Law, Economics, and Organization*, 4: 181–98.

Masten, S.E., Meehan, J.W. and Snyder, E.A. (1991) 'The costs of organization', *Journal of Law, Economics, and Organization*, 7: 1–25.

Mayer, K.J. and Argyres, N. (2004), 'Learning to contract: evidence from the personal computer industry', *Organization Science*, 15: 394–410.

McGahan, A.M. and Porter, M.E. (1997). How much does industry matter, really? *Strategic Management Journal*, 18: 15–30.

McLaughlin, K.J. (1988) 'Aspects of tournament models: a survey', in R.G. Ehrenberg (ed.), *Research in Labor Economics*. Greenwich, CT: JAI Press.

Milgrom, P. and Roberts, J. (1988) 'An economic approach to influence activities in organizations', *American Journal of Sociology*, 94(Supplement): 8154–79.

Miller, D. and Shamsie, J. (1996) 'The resource-based view of the firm in two environments: the Hollywood film studios from 1936 to 1965', *Academy of Management Journal*, 39: 519–43.

Miller, D.J. (2004) 'Firms' technological resources and the performance effects of diversification: a longitudinal study', *Strategic Management Journal*, 25: 1097–119.

Mintzberg, H. (1983) *Power in and around Organizations*. Englewood Cliffs, NJ: Prentice-Hall.

Moe, T.M. (1991) 'Politics and the theory of organization', *Journal of Law, Economics, and Organization*, 7:106–30.

Mosakowski, E. (1998) 'Entrepreneurial resources, organizational choices, and competitive outcomes', *Organization Science*, 9: 625–43.

Murphy, K.J. (1986) 'Incentives, learning, and compensation: a theoretical and empirical investigation of managerial labor contracts', *Rand Journal of Economics*, 17: 59–76.

Murphy, K.J. (2003) 'Stock-based pay in new economy firms', *Journal of Accounting and Economics*, 34: 129–47.

Murphy, K.J., Baker, G. and Gibbons, R. (1999) 'Informal authority in organizations', *Journal of Law, Economics, and Organizations*, 15: 56–73.

Nanda, A. and Bartlett, C. (1990) 'Corning incorporated: a network of alliances'. Harvard Business School Case no. 9–391–102.

Nelson, R.R. and Winter, S.G. (1982) *The Evolutionary Theory of the Firm*. Cambridge, MA: Harvard University Press.

Nickerson, J.A. and Silverman, B.S. (2003) 'Why firms want to organize efficiently and what keeps them from doing so: inappropriate governance, performance, and adaptation in a deregulated industry', *Administrative Science Quarterly*, 48: 433–65.

Nickerson, J.A. and Zenger, T.R. (2004) 'A knowledge-based theory of the firm – the problem-solving perspective', *Organization Science*, 15: 617–32.

Nishiguchi, T. (1994) *Strategic Industrial Sourcing: the Japanese Advantage*. Oxford: Oxford University Press.

Noteboom, B. (1999) *Inter-firm alliances: Analysis and design*. London: Routledge.

Ollinger, M. (1993) *Organizational Form and Business Strategy in the US, Petroleum Industry*. Lanham: University Press of America.

Ouchi, W.G. (1979) 'A conceptual framework for the design of organizational control mechanisms', *Management Science*, 25: 838–48.

Ouchi, W.G. (1980) 'Markets, bureaucracies, and clans', *Administrative Science Quarterly*, 25: 129–41.

Penrose, E. (1959) *The Theory of the Growth of the Firm*. Oxford: Basil Blackwell.

Perrow, C. (1981) 'Markets, hierarchies, and hegemony: a critique of Chandler and Williamson', in A. Van de Ven and J. Joyce (eds), *Perspectives on Organization Design and Behavior*. New York: Wiley. pp. 347–70.

Perrow, C. (1986) *Complex Organizations: A Critical Essay*. New York: Random House.

Peteraf, M.A. (1993) 'The cornerstones of competitive advantage: a resource-based view', *Strategic Management Journal*, 14: 179–92.

Pettigrew, A. (1992) 'On studying managerial elites', *Strategic Management Journal*, 13: 163–82.

Pfeffer, J. and Salancik, G. (1978) *The External Control of Organizations*. New York: Harper and Row.

Poppo, L. and Zenger, T. (1998) 'Testing alternative theories of the firm: transaction cost, knowledge-based, and measurement explanations for make-or-buy decisions in information services', *Strategic Management Journal*, 19: 853–77.

Porter, M.E. (1974) 'Note on the structural analysis of industries'. Harvard Business School Case no. 9–376–054.

Porter, M.E. (1979a) 'How competitive forces shape strategy', *Harvard Business Review*, 57: 137–56.

Porter, M.E. (1979b) 'The structure within industries and companies' performance', *Review of Economics and Statistics*, 61: 214–27.

Porter, M.E. (1980) *Competitive Strategy*. New York: Free Press.

Porter, M.E. (1981) 'The contributions of industrial organization to strategic management', *Academy of Management Review*, 6: 609–20.

Porter, M.E. (1985) *Competitive Advantage*. New York: Free Press.

Porter, M.E. (1990) *The Competitive Advantage of Nations*. New York: Free Press.

Powell, T.C. and Dent-Micallef, A. (1997) 'Information technology as competitive advantage', *Strategic Mangement Journal*, 18(5): 375–405.

Powell, W.W. (1987) 'Hybrid organizational arrangements', *California Management Review*, 30(Fall): 67–87.

Prahalad, C.K. and Bettis, R.A. (1986) 'The dominant logic: a new linkage between diversity and performance', *Strategic Management Journal*, 7: 484–502.

Pratt, J.W. and Zeckhauser, R.J. (1985) 'Principals and agents: an overview', in J.W. Pratt and R.J. Zeckhauser (eds), *Principals and Agents: the Structure of American Business*. Boston: Harvard Business School Press. pp. 1–36.

Putterman, L. (1984) 'On recent explanations of why capital hires labor', *Economic Inquiry*, 22: 171–87.

Ravenscraft, D.M. and Scherer, F.M. (1987) *Mergers, Sell-offs, and Economic Efficiency*. Washington, DC: Brookings Institution.

Reed, R. and DeFillippi, R. (1990) 'Causal ambiguity, barriers to imitation, and sustainable competitive advantage', *Academy of Management Review*, 15: 88–102.

Reger, R. and Huff, A. (1993) 'Strategic groups: a cognitive perspective', *Strategic Management Journal*, 14: 103–24.

Ring, P.S. and Van de Ven, A.H. (1992) 'Structuring cooperative relationships between organizations', *Strategic Management Journal*, 13: 483–98.

Robins, J.A. (1987) 'Organizational economics: notes on the use of transaction-cost theory in the study of organizations', *Administrative Science Quarterly*, 32: 68–86.

Robinson, J. (1933) *Economics of Imperfect Competition*. London: Macmillan.

Roth, K. and O'Donnell, S. (1996) 'Foreign subsidiary compensation strategy: an agency theory perspective', *Sharon. Academy of Management Journal*, 39: 678–703.

Ruback, R.S. (1988) 'An overview of takeover defenses', in A. A. Auerbach (ed.), *Mergers and Acquisitions*. Chicago: University of Chicago Press. pp. 49–68.

Rugman, A.M. (1981) *Inside the Multinational*. London: Croom Helm.

Rumelt, R.P. (1984) 'Toward a strategic theory of the firm', in R. Lamb (ed.), *Competitive Strategic Management*. Englewood Cliffs, NJ: Prentice-Hall. pp. 556–70.

Rumelt, R.P. (1991) 'How much does industry matter?', *Strategic Management Journal*, 12: 167–86.

Rumelt, R.P., Schendel, D. and Teece, D. (1991) 'Strategic management and economics', *Strategic Management Journal*, 12: 5–29.

Sanders, W.G. and Carpenter, M.A. (1998) 'Internationalization and firm governance: the roles of CEO compensation, top team composition, and board structure', *Academy of Management Journal*, 41: 158–78.

Saxenian, A. (1994) *Regional Advantage*. Cambridge. MA: Harvard University Press.

Scherer, F.M. (1980) *Industrial Market Structure and Economic Performance*. Boston: Houghton Mifflin.

Schilling, M. and Steensma, K. (2002) 'Disentangling theories on firm boundaries', *Organization Science*, 13: 387–401.

Schulze, W.S., Lubatkin, M.H., Dino, R.N. and Buchholtz, A.K. (2001) 'Agency relationships in family firms: theory and evidence', *Organization Science*, 12: 99–116.

Schulze, W.S., Lubatkin, M.H. and Dino, R.N. (2003) 'Exploring the agency consequences of ownership dispersion among the directors of private family firms', *Academy of Management Journal*, 46: 179–94.

Schumpeter, J. (1934) *The Theory of Economic Development*. Cambridge, MA: Harvard University Press.

Shelanski, H. and Klein, P. (1995) 'Empirical research in transaction cost economics: a review and assessment', *Journal of Law, Economics, and Organization*, 11: 335–61.

Shleifer, A. and Summers, L.H. (1988) 'Breach of trust in hostile takeovers', in A.J. Auerbach (ed.), *Corporate Takeovers: Causes and Consequences*. Chicago: University of Chicago Press. pp. 533–61.

Shleifer, A. and Vishny, R.W. (1991) 'Takeovers in the 60's and the 80's: evidence and implications', *Strategic Management Journal*, 12: 51–9.

Silverman, B.S. (1999) 'Technological resources and the direction of corporate diversification: toward an integration of the resource-based view and transaction cost economics', *Organization Science*, 10: 1109–24.

Silverman, B.S., Nickerson, J.A. and Freeman, J. (1997) 'Profitability, transactional alignment and organizational mobility in the U.S. trucking industry', *Strategic Management Journal*, 18: 31–52.

Simon, H.A. (1947) *Administrative Behavior*. New York: Free Press.

Simon, H.A. (1964) 'On the concept of organizational goal', *Administrative Science Quarterly*, 9: 1–22.

Singh, H. and Chang, S.J. (2001) 'Reconfiguring multibusiness corporations: linking modes of entry and exit', *Strategic Management Journal*, 22.

Singh, H. and Harianto, F. (1989) 'Management–board relationships, takeover risk and the adoption of golden parachutes: an empirical investigation', *Academy of Management Journal*, 32: 7–24.

Spence, M. (1974) 'Competitive and optimal responses to signals', *Journal of Economic Theory*, 7: 298–315.

Steer, P. and Cable, J. (1978) 'Internal organization and profit: an empirical analysis of large U.K. companies', *Journal of Industrial Economics*, 27: 13–30.

Stiglitz, J. (1991) 'Symposium on organizations and economics', *Journal of Economic Perspectives*, 5: 15–24.

Stuckey, J. (1983) *Vertical Integration and Joint Ventures in the Aluminum Industry*. Cambridge, MA: Harvard University Press.

Teece, D.J. (1981) 'Internal organization and economic performance: an empirical analysis of the profitability of principal firms', *Journal of Industrial Economics*, 30: 173–99.

Teece, D.J. (1982) 'Towards an economic theory of the multiproduct firm', *Journal of Economic Behavior and Organization*, 3: 39–63.

Teece, D.J. (1986) 'Transaction cost economics and the multinational enterprise: an assessment', *Journal of Economic Behavior and Organization*, 7: 21–45.

Teece, D., Pisano, G. and Shuen, A. (1997) 'Dynamic capabilities and strategic management', *Strategic Management Journal*, 18: 509–33.

Thompson, R.S. (1981) 'Internal organization and profit: a note', *Journal of Industrial Economics*, 30: 201–11.

Thorelli, H.B. (1986) 'Networks, between markets and hierarchies', *Strategic Management Journal*, 7: 37–51.

Tihanyi, L., Johnson, R.A., Hoskisson, R.E. and Hitt, M.A. (2003) 'Institutional ownership differences and international diversification: the effects of boards of directors and technological opportunity', *Academy of Management Journal*, 46: 195–211.

Tirole, J. (1989) *The Theory of Industrial Organization*. Cambridge, MA: MIT Press.

Uzzi, B. (1997) 'Social structure and competition in interfirm networks: the paradox of embeddedness', *Administrative Science Quarterly*, 42: 35–67.

Wade, J., O'Reilly, C.A. and Chandratat, L. (1990) 'Golden parachutes: CEOs and the exercise of social influence', *Administrative Science Quarterly*, 35: 587–603.

Walker, G. and Weber, D. (1984) 'A transaction cost approach to make-or-buy decisions', *Administrative Science Quarterly*, 29: 373–91.

Walker, G. and Weber, D. (1987) 'Supplier competition, uncertainty, and make-or-buy decisions', *Academy of Management Journal*, 30: 589–96.

Walking, R. and Long, M. (1984) 'Agency theory, managerial welfare, and takeover bid resistance', *Rand Journal of Economics*, 15: 54–68.

Weingast, B.R. and Marshall, W. (1988) 'The industrial organization of congress', *Journal of Political Economy*, 96: 132–63.

Weisbach, M.S. (1988) 'Outside directors and CEO turnover', *Journal of Financial Economics*, 20: 431–60.

Wernerfelt, B. (1984) 'A resource-based view of the firm', *Strategic Management Journal*, 5: 171–80.

Williamson, O.E. (1964) *The Economics of Discretionary Behavior: Managerial Objectives in a Theory of the Firm*. Englewood Cliffs, NJ: Prentice-Hall.

Williamson, O.E. (1970) *Corporate Control and Business Behavior*. Englewood Cliffs, NJ: Prentice-Hall.

Williamson, O.E. (1975) *Markets and Hierarchies: Analysis and Antitrust Implications*. New York: Free Press.

Williamson, O.E. (1985) *The Economic Institutions of Capitalism: Firms, Markets, Relational Contracting*. New York: Free Press.

Williamson, O.E. (1991a) 'Comparative economic organization: the analysis of discrete structural alternatives', *Administrative Science Quarterly*, 36: 269–96.

Williamson, O.E. (1991b) 'Strategizing, economizing, and economic organization', *Strategic Management Journal*, 12(Special Winter): 75–94.

Williamson, O.E. (1991c) 'Economic institutions: spontaneous and intentional governance', *Journal of Law, Economics, and Organization*, 7: 159–87.

Williamson, O.E. (1993a) 'Calculativeness, trust, and economic organization', 36: 453–86.

Williamson, O.E. (1993b) 'Transaction cost economics and organization theory', *Industrial and Corporate Change*, 2: 107–56.

Williamson, O.E. and Ouchi, W. (198la) 'The markets and hierarchies program of research: origins, implications, prospects', in A. Van de Yen and J. Joyce (eds),

Perspectives on Organization Design and Behavior. New York: Wiley.

Williamson, O.E. and Ouchi, W. (1981b) 'A rejoinder', in A. Van de Yen and J. Joyce (eds), *Perspectives on Organization Design and Behavior.* New York: Wiley.

Winship, C. and Rosen, S. (1988) 'Introduction: sociological and economic approaches to the analysis of social structure', *American Journal of Sociology*, 94: S1–16.

Zaheer, A., McEvily, B. and Perrone, V. (1998) 'Does trust matter? Exploring the effects of interorganizational and interpersonal trust on performance', *Organization Science*, 9: 141–59.

Zenger, T.R. (1992) 'Why do employers only reward extreme performance? Examining the relationships among performance, pay, and turnover', *Administrative Science Quarterly*, 37: 198–219.

Zenger, T.R. (1994) 'Understanding organizational diseconomies of scale: the allocation of engineering talent, ideas, and effort by firm size', *Management Science*, 40:

Zenger, T.R. and Hesterly, W.S. (1997) 'The disaggregation of corporations: selective intervention, high-powered incentives, and molecular units', *Organization Science*, 8: 209–22.

Zenger, T.R. and Marshall, C.R. (2000) 'The determinants of incentive intensity in group-based rewards', *Academy of Management Journal*, 43: 149–63.

1.4 Meso Organizational Behaviour: Comments on the Third Paradigm

D. BRENT SMITH, BENJAMIN SCHNEIDER AND MARCUS W. DICKSON

Introduction

[t]he causal arrows neatly point in one direction although common sense and research make all of us aware that everything interacts with everything else (Huber 1991: 6).

In this quotation from her introduction to *Macro-Micro Linkages in Sociology*, Huber notes that which is implicitly understood by most organizational researchers – our models are simplifications of dynamic and interactive processes that are usually much more complex than we make them out to be. Whether it be the result of pragmatics or scientific purity, organizational research rarely models the richness of organizational processes. Recently, this observation that everything interacts with everything else has been a consistent theme in reviews of the organizational behaviour (OB) literature. Beginning with Cummings' (1982) *Annual Review of Psychology* chapter on the state of OB research, several commentators have suggested that the most significant impediment to the advancement of OB knowledge has been the failure to simultaneously incorporate individual and organizational influences interacting across levels of analysis.

The problem is that what has been called the micro–macro distinction has been institutionalized in OB with two parallel yet largely non-overlapping literatures (and some might argue journals) serving the separate disciplines (Staw and Sutton 1992; Schneider et al. 1995). Cappelli and Sherer (1991) argue that it is impossible to develop a common paradigm for organizational behaviour without incorporating multiple levels of analysis in our research. Who could disagree? Cappelli and Sherer (1991), Rousseau and House (1994) and House et al. (1995)

offered the meso (literally meaning 'between') paradigm as a means to integrate micro and macro research and foster a common thematic focus. The focus of meso theory and research is the incorporation of multi-level and cross-level influences in research on and in organizations. We will show that this seeming institutionalization of the separation of the micro and the macro foci in OB is more apparent than real and that significant advances have been made, both conceptually and methodologically, to deal with at least some of the cross-level complexity that characterizes organizational life. While it is clearly not time to be sanguine, our review suggests that some progress has been made – and for a considerable period of time – in consciously entangling the micro and the macro. We suspect this would be truer if we were able to decide what meso is!

In preparation for this chapter, we conducted a very informal survey of a few colleagues (who would likely classify themselves as micro or macro and were both psychologists and sociologists) regarding the meaning of the term 'meso', specifically as it refers to organizational behaviour research. Our review of the literature had led us to anticipate there to be no clear consensus regarding the definition of 'meso' or those characteristics that delineate meso research, and our informal survey did not disappoint us. There were as many definitions of meso as there were colleagues asked, and there was little overlap in the defining characteristics mentioned.

In addition to the ambiguity surrounding the term meso, we noted a curious disjuncture in our colleagues' accompanying responses. That is, in addition to responding to the specific question about the meaning of 'meso' for organizational research, our colleagues made several observations about the current state of that research and these responses clearly fell into two categories. Some colleagues noted the relative absence of context in organizational behaviour research ('the focus is so much on individuals'), while others noted the disappearance of the individual ('the focus is so situational'). What, we asked, was left?

Interestingly, our review of the literature on meso OB also illuminated this disjuncture. Take for instance the review of Cappelli and Sherer (1991) regarding the lack of context in organizational research. They were quite adamant in their suggestion that the failure to unify OB under the meso rubric was due to the decontextual nature of micro OB. However, Nord and Fox (1996) filed what they called a 'missing persons report' regarding the disappearance of individual constructs and behaviour in organizational research. Are we losing context or are we losing person?

In this chapter, we hope to provide some clarity to the state of the 'third paradigm' of organizational research, the meso paradigm; and if not clarity, we at least will show the current state of affairs. We will show that, while there is considerable ambiguity over the terms micro and macro, as well as the newer concept meso, there is considerable agreement present regarding the necessity to simultaneously conceptualize and assess issues across and between levels of analysis, as well as to include additional issues such as a time frame of reference and the reciprocal nature of effects across different levels of analysis.

We begin by describing our view of the current status of the concepts of micro, macro and meso from psychological, sociological and organizational behaviour perspectives. We focus on the basic disciplines of psychology and sociology as well as OB because the history of OB is built on paradigms endemic to psychology on the one hand and sociology on the other. OB is a hybrid discipline and, we hope to show, has the potential vitality of a hybrid because of its current and future capacity to both profit from its parent frameworks and become its own autonomous discipline. Finally, we offer several comments on the present and future state of meso research in OB.

On Micro, Macro and Meso: A Brief Review

How one defines the domains of micro, macro and meso is likely to differ depending on academic province. In our review of the literature from psychology, sociology and OB research, we amassed quite a list of definitions, too many to catalogue here. However, we do think it is instructive to emphasize some of the critical differences between definitions of micro and macro. We have discovered that it is agreed that micro refers to something small and macro to something large; the agreement appears to stop there! Indeed, what defines 'small' and 'large' is quite relative – one of us was surprised recently when talking with a colleague in the field of organizational strategy to hear him refer to 'micro concepts like organizational culture'. When prodded on this point, he responded that 'macro refers to the web of interactions between organizations or industries – things like supply chains, for example'. Clearly, there is a great deal of ambiguity in the definitions ascribed to these terms, though it appears that there is often great certainty that the definition most common within one's own sub-discipline is seen as the 'right' way to think about them.

Staw and Sutton (1993: 351) noted that the micro–macro distinction alternatively 'refers to the unit of analysis in which behaviour is explained or to the discipline from which the explanatory concepts are derived'. Staw and Sutton were writing from an implicitly psychological vantage point where micro tends to refer to the individual as the unit of analysis in predictors and outcomes and macro refers to aggregates and/or structural properties (of jobs, of hierarchies) in research. Rousseau and House (1994) equated micro-organizational behaviour with psychological research and macro organizational behaviour with sociological research. Similarly, Kozlowski and Klein (2000) placed the origins of the micro and macro perspectives with psychology and sociology, respectively. However, Staw and Sutton (1993) suggested that distinguishing micro from macro organizational behaviour on the basis of disciplinary labels is inappropriate. Psychology should have no more valid a claim to the study of individual behaviour than Sociology has to the study of groups, populations or structures.[1] In what follows it will be seen that these distinctions merely begin to tap into the issue of what is micro and what is macro – much less issues surrounding the definition of meso.

Psychological Inquiry

Psychology is all about understanding and predicting human behaviour. The micro–macro distinction has not been as explicit in psychology as it has been in sociology, yet the distinctions within psychology between a focus on person variables and a focus on contextual variables has characterized the discipline since its beginnings. Of course, psychology has always had a predilection for the prediction and understanding of individual behaviour. The very earliest research in psychology was designed to explore the ways by which humans experience their physical world. Studies of light, sound, touch and taste were essentially studies of the human as a sensor of external stimuli; they were not designed to be studies of the internal world of feelings or emotions of the human doing the experiencing. Very early in the history of psychology, however, a group of psychologists began to study the internal experiential world of people, and it is this form of psychology, the world of experiences and emotions, that most people associate with the science.

However, this was not the form of the science that dominated early experimental research. Early experimental research in psychology was focused on two parallel tracks. While the first track focused on individual differences attributes (personality, ability, attitudes), the second track focused on situational contingencies (rewards, punishments) as the determinants of individual differences in behaviour. In psychology, the former scholars were members of the school of Functionalism. Their emphasis was on individual differences in humans and the functionality of those differences; they had their greatest influence on educational and industrial psychology. For all intents this group could be called the micro group in psychology, though they would not have known themselves by that label.

What we might now call the macro group in psychology focused on context for the explanation and prediction of behaviour. Dominated by the school of psychology called behaviourism, first Watson (1919) and then Hull (1943) and Skinner (1938) showed that the appropriate configuration of the context was all one needed in order to predict behaviour. And the focus was clearly on behaviour and not on intervening variables or hypothetical constructs like cognition, motivation or feelings and emotions. In this regard it is interesting to note that the titles of each of these scholars' major work contains the word behaviour or behaviourist: Watson (1919; *Psychology from the Standpoint of a Behaviorist*); Skinner (1938; *The Behavior of Organisms*); and Hull (1943; *Principles of Behavior*).

So, it is clear that psychology did emphasize both person and context in the description of individual behaviour. In this regard, Cappelli and Sherer (1991) have erroneously suggested that the lack of context in most micro-organizational behaviour research was a function of the field's psychological lineage. While we would agree that psychology focuses on the individual as the unit of theory and analysis, it is also the case that psychology has had a long appreciation for context. Further, we believe that the current recognition of context in psychology is, in part, a function of the resolution of the person-situation debate in psychology and the shift to person-situation (interactional) explanations of behaviour (Bowers 1973; Pervin 1989).

The person-situation debate in psychology was equivalent in many ways to the micro–macro distinction in OB, except that in psychology it concerned the degree to which individual attributes of people or the context of their behaviour predicted their behaviour. In what follows, we provide an overview of this debate because it so closely parallels contemporary debates in OB regarding micro, macro and meso thinking. Space does not afford a comprehensive review of the literature here and our choices have been, admittedly, idiosyncratic.

The most significant example of 'meso thinking' in the history of psychology was Lewin's field theory of personality. Lewin (1946: 919) proposed his now famous dictum when he noted that 'to understand and predict behavior, the person and his environment have to be considered as *one* constellation of interdependent factors. We call the totality of these factors the life space (LSp) of that individual, and write B = F(P,E)'. Lewin recognized, as did the Gestalt psychologists before him, that 'forces' both within and outside the individual determined behaviour. Lewin believed that these forces existed as an interactive whole (a gestalt) – the environment was as much dependent on the person as the person was dependent on the environment (Monte 1977). It is not simply the interactive independent effects of person and environment that determine behaviour. Rather, the characteristics of people and environments are reciprocally and inextricably linked. The environment cannot be understood without first understanding the people who comprise it, nor can people be understood without examination of the environments in which they are embedded. Lewin's thesis was a major step in founding what has come to be called interactional psychology (Endler and Magnusson 1978; Pervin 1978). It is very important to note that Lewin and what follows as interactional psychology was concerned with the behaviour of individuals, regardless of the level of analysis of the causes of that individual behaviour.

The richness of Lewin's description of interactional psychology was lost during the exchanges between Mischel (1968), Bowers (1973) and others during what has come to be known as the person-situation debate. Mischel (1968) conducted a highly selective review of research on personality traits and concluded that traits explain little variance in human behaviour. He suggested, therefore, that situational influences (or context) were the primary determinants of action. Mischel (1968) espoused a situational determinism that was reminiscent of Skinnerian psychology. The debate that ensued (into the mid-1980s) nearly exhausted the subdiscipline of personality psychology – although it now seems to be acknowledged that people again have personalities (Schneider and Smith 2004a)!

Ultimately a compromise was reached. This compromise was that the behaviour of individuals is a function of both person characteristics and situation characteristics in interaction – had we only listened to Lewin 30 years before. Interactional psychology is now the dominant perspective regarding the causes of individual behaviour. Pervin (1989: 352) noted 'most psychologists are now interactionists'. Even Mischel (cf. Mischel et al. 2002) embraced interactional models in his later writings on the issue of person behavioural consistency across situations.

Our point is simply that meso thinking with regard to individual behaviour and the joint exploration of context and individual attributes are central components of modern psychology. We believe that Cappelli and Sherer's (1991) suggestion that micro-OB is decontextual because of the need to remain consistent with psychology neglects this fundamental shift to an interactional model in psychology that occurred during the 1970s and beyond (Schneider 1983a, b).

Sociological Inquiry

From the sociological literature, we uncovered a number of alternative definitions of micro and macro; the distinction is more salient in sociology than in psychology where the unit of theory and the unit of data has consistently (although not

exclusively) been the individual. In psychology, as summarized earlier, the debate has been on person vs situation in understanding the behaviour of individuals, not micro vs macro in the unit of analysis. Some interpretive sociologists defined micro sociological research as quantitative and macro sociological research as qualitative (for reasons that are unclear to us). Collins (1981) suggested that micro and macro refers to continuous variation along the dimensions of time, space and number. In this view, the focus of macro research is events or structures that are relatively durable and longer lasting, including larger groupings of people occupying larger spatial entities. Blau (1977) presents a conceptualization that is more in keeping with contemporary literature in OB: micro research focuses on social processes engendering relations among individuals and macro research refers to the structure of positions in a population and their constraints on interaction.

By necessity, the micro–macro linkage has been central to the intellectual heritage of sociological inquiry, much more so than it has been for psychological inquiry. This is perhaps a function of the discrepancy between the unit of analysis/observation for sociologists and the unit of theory. Sociologists most typically begin with the individual as the unit of analysis/observation and then must move to the collective or aggregate of those individuals to make meaningful statements regarding relationships between structural properties and those aggregates. As a result, sociologists have been debating the micro–macro distinction for decades – and this is true also of cross-level or meso thinking.

Thus, it is interesting to note (in historical context) that meso thinking was alive and well in sociology at least dating back to Weber. Take for instance Weber's seminal work, *The Protestant Ethic and the Spirit of Capitalism*, in which he proposed that Protestantism gave rise to conditions conducive to the emergence of capitalism. If we dissect Weber's argument further (here we borrow from Coleman 1987), his thesis leads to three general propositions that outline a multi-level theory of the relation between a social construct (religion), individual constructs (values and economic behaviour) and economic constructs (capitalism). First, Protestantism imputes certain values (ethics) in its adherents. Secondly, these values determine the nature of individual economic behaviour. Thirdly, this orientation towards certain types of economic behaviour provides the context in which capitalism flourishes. So, Weber hypothesized structural determinants of individual characteristics and individual determinants of structural characteristics. Likely, in the parlance of modern social science, Weber would have suggested a reciprocal determinism between individual and society in creating the conditions for the emergence and propagation of capitalism.

Parsons provides another example of meso thinking in traditional sociology. Parsons objected to the lack of a micro-theory (a social psychology) to explain Durkheim's notion of collective order. Durkheim's notion of a collective consciousness assumes that order occurs in the heads of people, but he had no means of explaining the individual cognitions. Parsons applied Freud's notion of internalization, central to psychoanalytic theory, as the means by which collective order is represented in the minds of individual actors. He, therefore, linked individual and society by 'sociologizing psychoanalytic theory' (Alexander and Giesen 1987).

Alexander and Giesen (1987) noted that between the early 1960s and the mid 1980s, sociology regressed from Parsons' attempts to link macro-structural processes with micro-individual processes. Although many factors surely played a role in the dichotomization of sociology, we consider two to be extremely influential. First, Homans' (1963) presidential address to the American Sociological Association (published in 1964) called for a theoretical and methodological individualism based on a reduction to social behaviourism. Homans completely rejected the collectivistic tradition in sociology, arguing that there is nothing beyond individual action. This radical departure represented a significant shift in emphasis to a more micro sociology.[2]

Secondly, Merton (1973), reacting to Parsonian functionalism, proposed that sociology must find a middle ground between 'grand theorizing' and 'abstracted empiricism'. By doing so, he suggested sociology had not yet advanced to the stage of natural sciences and, therefore, was ill-prepared for attempts at unified theory. Further, however, Merton espoused a philosophy of science that emphasized the importance of pluralism for the advancement of knowledge, i.e. that micro-sociology and macro-sociology could co-exist, in fact should co-exist, if we wish to advance knowledge. In his view, attempts at unified theories should be replaced by a focus on the 'middle range'. Recently, there has been a renewed emphasis in elaborating these

middle range linkages between macro and micro sociology (see Huber 1991; Udehn 2002).

Our point is that within sociology, the micro–macro distinction has a long history, and so too does meso-theory with its emphasis on cross-level and reciprocal determinism. The recent calls for meso-organizational behaviour, we believe are epiphenomena of the trends that have developed in the disciplines supplying organizational behaviour with its intellectual heritage. In psychology, the current state of thinking emerging out of the person–situation debates clearly requires simultaneous (if not reciprocal) thinking about the causes and correlates of individual behaviour. In sociology, Merton's (1973) call for middle range theories has a very similar flavour, though here again the notion of reciprocity across levels is sometimes difficult to identify (but recall Weber's theory). It is safe, however, to conclude that the intellectual heritage associated with the emerging field of organizational behaviour (developing from meso-thinking in sociology and psychology) was well in place when the field began and has accompanied the development of OB as well.

In summary, if we were forced to distill some consensus from the issues we have reviewed to this point, we believe it is most applicable to consider micro research as that which focuses on individuals and the personal and contextual factors that are determinants of individual behaviour, while macro research focuses on the collective and the determinants of the behaviour of the collective. Meso thinking can be both micro and macro as a function of the level of analysis of the behaviour to be predicted and understood. Micro–meso research focuses on individual and contextual attributes in combination as correlates of individual behaviour; macro-meso research focuses on individual and contextual attributes in the prediction and understanding of aggregate and collective behaviour. We admit that these definitions are, in part, a convenience for organizational behaviour researchers and we now turn to an overview of micro, macro and meso thinking in OB.

Organizational Behaviour Inquiry

The year 1960 marks the advent of the paradigm shift from individual differences to the group and organization as a focus for study in understanding human behaviour in the work place. While there had been earlier work on the influence of context on behaviour (e.g. the Hawthorne studies), the almost simultaneous publication of works by Argyris (1957; 1960), McGregor (1960) and Likert (1961) signalled the end of the dominance of what Nord and Fox (1996) have called the 'essentialist individual' model for understanding human behaviour in the work place. What Argyris, McGregor and Likert accomplished was specification of psychologically based frameworks for understanding human behaviour *in the aggregate* in groups and organizations. The concept of individual differences in behaviour and/or the prediction and understanding of individual behaviour was, for most purposes, non-existent in their thinking; organizational behaviour, literally, was the outcome of interest. Organizational behaviour was the outcome of interest and the proximate cause of that behaviour concerned specific ways of organizing for the management of people. The principles and practices of organizing and management identified rested firmly on ways psychologists conceptualized contextual effects on behaviour.

Until that time, the study of behaviour in the work place had been dominated by the field of industrial psychology, a field that rested on a foundation of individual differences – the person focus in psychology discussed earlier (e.g. Ghiselli and Brown 1955; Tiffin and McCormick 1960). Indeed, Viteles (1932: 29, emphasis in original), in his early summary of the field of industrial psychology, put it this way: 'Industrial psychology is based on the study of *individual differences* – of human variability …'.

In contrast, Argyris's (1957) book, *Personality and Organization,* focused not on individual differences in personality but on identifying how the implicit theories management holds about workers (in the aggregate) results in particular management tactics that infantilizes them. (It should be noted here that Argyris was perhaps the first organizational scientist to identify the importance of simultaneously conceptualizing and studying work issues across levels of analysis, from the individual to the group and organization and even the larger culture (Argyris 1958; 1960).) Similar to Argyris, McGregor (1960) proposed that managerial cosmology (managers' philosophies about the psychology of workers) yields a view of them as an aggregate that denies the possibility that they might have aspirations for self-actualization. In McGregor's famous Theory Y, three

of the basic six assumptions about people that characterize the Theory Y cosmology contain the words 'average human being' (McGregor 1960: 47–8). For McGregor, then, the application of Maslow's (1954) theory of personality in the work place was to assume that the average human being can achieve self-actualization if the contexts in which they work are managed and created by managers who believe in Theory Y. It is instructive that Maslow (1954: 106) said essentially this in his book *Motivation and Personality*: 'The good or healthy society would then be defined as one that permitted man's highest purposes to emerge by satisfying all his basic needs'. McGregor substituted the words 'work place' for 'society' and the rest, as they say, is history.

Likert (1961) presented an integrated total systems theory of the role of leadership and management in organizational performance. His work emerged from research that was ongoing at the University of Michigan and elsewhere (e.g. the Ohio State leadership studies; cf. Fleishman 1953) that was psychologically based but organizationally framed (also see Bass 1960). The point cannot be over-emphasized here that what these scholars did was to (a) focus on organizations as human systems of co-ordinated human action rather than on the structural attributes of those organizations, and (b) emphasize the idea that how humans behave in business organizations is related to the effectiveness of those businesses. The prediction and understanding of individual behaviour in organizations was not of interest; the prediction and understanding of organizational effectiveness based on an understanding of the human component of organizations was the focus.

It is important to frame this paradigm shift of 1960 because, at that time, the aforementioned field in psychology called, then, industrial psychology, dominated the study of behaviour in the work place. In 1960 there was no 'organizational' psychology (Schein's book called *Organizational Psychology* and Bass's book including these same words in the title did not appear until 1965), much less a field called organizational behaviour (and there is considerable debate over who first used this latter term; see Bass 1960). In 1960, few business schools even offered courses in human behaviour beyond what was then called personnel administration. McGregor's influence at MIT (in the Sloan School of Management with a young Ed Schein), Argyris' influence at Yale (in the Department of Administrative Sciences) and Likert's collaboration with others at the University of Michigan's Institute for Social Research (including Katz and Kahn (1966) and the Center for Group Dynamics of Cartwright and Zander (1953)) formed the nexus of what is now called organizational behaviour.[3]

It is difficult to pinpoint the causes of the *zeitgeist* that yielded this shift in paradigms from locating the causes and consequences of behaviour in individual differences to locating the causes and consequences of behaviour in the external world. Likert (1961: 1) speculates that these new forms of management (his book is called *New Patterns in Management*) were due to changes ongoing in society at the time:

> Supervisors and managers report in interviews that people are less willing to accept pressure and close supervision than was the case a decade or two ago. The trend in America, generally, in our schools, in our homes, and in our communities, is toward giving the individual greater freedom and initiative. There are fewer direct unexplained orders in schools and homes and youngsters are participating increasingly in decisions that affect them.

As with most change, however, it is noticed after a critical mass is achieved – the critical mass is an outcome of a more long-term process and this was true for what appeared to happen in 1960, too. For example, Lewin and his colleagues had been studying the influence of leadership and the group on individual behaviour since he had left Germany in the late 1930s (cf. Lewin et al. 1939). The aforementioned Hawthorne studies were begun in 1927 and, by 1928, what has come to be called the 'Hawthorne effect' had already been observed and documented (Homans 1941). McGregor (1960), who applied Maslow's concept of self-actualization to 'the average human being', actually had been writing for more than a decade on new ideas for leadership in organizations (e.g. McGregor 1944). As just one other example, Stogdill (1948) and his colleagues had the programme of research on leadership at Ohio State well underway by the late 1940s.

It seems important to note that most of these research programmes developed either immediately prior to or in the immediate aftermath of World War II, when as Bennis (1993: 21) notes 'social scientists … myself included, tended to view all authority with deep-seated skepticism, if not suspicion'. Milgram's (1963) classic work on compliance to authority, which largely originated with his attempts to understand why during the war ordinary German citizens obeyed orders to decimate the German Jewish population, similarly takes a view of external/environmental causation (thus supporting an aggregated approach), rather than placing the focus on internal individual differences. In other words, much of the work of this time was focused on placing the 'blame' for behaviours of individuals on external circumstances, largely circumstances created by authority figures.

The confluence of these research programmes and others (e.g. the important research on small groups; cf. Hare et al. 1955) in which people are conceptualized and analysed in larger aggregates, began to dominate theory and practice in what has come recently to be called organization science and was just then being called organizational behaviour. Industrial psychology moved partially into business schools and became organizational behaviours (and later added human resources management) – and is now called Industrial and Organizational Psychology in Psychology departments.

The movement of industrial psychologists into business schools, however, was accompanied by a phenomenon that we will call the microizing of OB. That is, while Argyris, McGregor and Likert conceptualized business performance based on psychological theories of people, industrial psychologists proceeded to study these theories using their individual differences paradigms with a focus on individual behaviour and performance. For example, the idea that participation in decision-making might enhance morale and organizational functioning was translated by industrial psychologists into a study of individuals' perceptions of participation in decision making as a correlate of individual job satisfaction or individual performance. In other words, the idea that the environments created for humans might be reflected in group and organizational behaviour was invisible to the individual differences level of analysis through which most industrial psychologists viewed the causes and correlates of behaviour – individual behaviour.

Naturally, this is an over-generalization of what transpired because, even in the early days of OB in business schools, there was concern for the idea that individual and context were both responsible for the behaviour and attitudes of interest – but the behaviour and attitudes of interest were individual attitudes and individual behaviour. Thus, while there were hundreds or even thousands (Locke 1976) of studies of the relationship between individual job satisfaction and individual turnover or between individual job satisfaction and individual performance (Brayfield and Crockett 1955), there were also early studies of the joint effects of person variables and contextual variables on behaviour – still, of course, individual behaviour. For example, Hackman and Lawler (1971) conceptualized and studied the effects of job characteristics on individual employee job satisfaction and this research eventuated in the programme of research by Hackman and Oldham (1975; 1980) in which the higher order need strength of individual employees was studied jointly with the characteristics of jobs in an understanding of individual employee work motivation and job satisfaction. In today's world this would be meso level research; in our terms micro–meso research because the focus was on individual behaviour and individual outcomes.

In the study of leadership, Fiedler (1967) proposed, tested and found some support for contingency ideas regarding the joint use of a personal variable (the Least Preferred Co-Worker or LPC measure) and attributes of the situation for understanding leadership effectiveness. Since Fiedler's research studied the joint effects of person and situation on behaviour, it is appropriately called meso level research; because the criterion of interest was group behaviour we would call it macro–meso research. Similarly, in the Management Progress Study at AT&T (Bray et al. 1974), early analyses of the data by Berlew and Hall (1966) revealed that both individual attributes (intelligence, personality) and context (job challenge) jointly predicted the success of the managers involved in the study. We would term this a micro–meso study because the outcome of interest was the level in the hierarchy and salary level achieved by individual managers compared to their cohort.

Our perception is that most of the early meso level research in OB was of the form we call micro–meso – individual behaviour is the unit of theory and the unit of data in the dependent variable. This concern for individual behaviour and a conceptualization of human systems primarily with an internal organizational frame of reference on individuals resulted, we believe, in increased use of sociological constructs and methods designed to understand *aggregate* behaviour, resulting in the field now called Organizational Theory or OT. OT was a later arrival than OB to business schools and is more associated with sociology than psychology (see Perrow 1973) especially in the US (e.g. Pelz and Andrews 1966; Turner and Lawrence 1967). In the UK there was earlier attention to psychosocial issues integrated with organizational variables (especially technology; e.g. Trist and Bamforth 1951).

The relative persistence of micro and micro–meso research in OB, of course, has come at some costs to the field. Schneider (1996) argues that the continued focus on individual behaviour both in OB and I/O has marginalized those who study personnel selection both in academic research and in the business world. While personnel selection focuses on the attributes of people and the effect of these attributes on individual performance, the growing trend is to focus on human resources practices as organizational systems and these systems as predictors of differences in organizational performance (Dobbins et al. 1991; Huselid 1995; Jackson and Schuler 1995), thus explicitly denying the potential role of individual behaviour in such models.

It is clear from Cappelli and Sherer's (1991) review that they consider meso research in OB to be cross-level research in which both context and individual characteristics are determinants of individual behaviour – our micro–meso. However, Mowday and Sutton (1993) noted that, additionally, meso research should incorporate processes by which individuals affect the contexts they inhabit. In this view environments are, themselves, created and maintained by the people in them (Schneider et al. 1995; 1998; Weick 1995; Giberson et al. 2005). We here add the idea that meso research should be macro–meso and address person and context as correlates of group and organizational behaviour. Schneider et al.'s (2000; see also Schneider and Smith 2004b) model of the multilevel framework of links between individual and organizational attributes, and individual and organizational performance, is an example of such a macro–meso approach.

Klein et al. (1994) provided a useful framework for categorizing the various types of multilevel or meso-research. They suggest that meso-research occurs in one of four forms: (1) cross-level models, (2) mixed effects models, (3) mixed determinants models, and (4) multilevel models. Cross-level models specify the relationship between independent and dependent variables at different levels of analyses. For example, a model that hypothesizes a group level determinant of an individual behavioural or outcome variable would be a cross-level model. A mixed effects model posits that a single intervention (determinant) may have an effect at multiple levels. For example, implementing an incentive based pay system may increase employee job satisfaction while decreasing group cohesion. Mixed determinants models suggest that predictors from many levels of analysis affect a particular outcome of interest. The mixed determinants model is consistent with the methodological framework of hierarchical linear modelling (HLM) which cumulates data at multiple levels of analysis in an attempt to explain individual behaviour as the dependent variable. Finally, multi-level models specify the nature of the relationships between predictor and outcomes across levels (for example isomorphisms, discontinuities, etc.). We believe that these four models represent the majority of the possibilities for meso-research, although they do not explicitly incorporate the concept of time.

Rousseau and House (1994), however, noted that meso-OB should also be emergent. That is, it should move beyond the constraints of micro and macro variables. In other words, meso-OB should investigate the processes by which organizations (groups or context) are constructed by interpersonal and social dynamics. A characteristic of much of the meso research (and OB research in general) is its static nature. Yet we are aware in our daily lives of the continuing development and evolution of both ourselves and the contexts in which we find ourselves. The inclination for organisms to seek homeostasis and to resist change, the processes by which people and contexts merge and emerge over time, and the implications of different processes for the attainment of alternative outcomes are rarely studied – whether at one level or in any one of the meso models identified in Klein et al. (1994).

Using recent history as our guide, it appears to us that the critical reviews of Cummings (1982), O'Reilly (1991), Cappelli and Sherer (1991), Mowday and Sutton (1993) and House et al. (1995) may now be somewhat misplaced. The field is advancing in a decidedly meso direction – a direction consistent with the shift in psychology to the interactionist framework and the re-examination of micro–macro linkages in sociology. Interest and activity in the realm of multilevel research now abounds. For example, a simple search online shows that the recent book entitled *Multi-level theory, research, and methods in organizations*, edited

by Klein and Kozlowski (2000), has been widely adopted in part or in whole in I/O and OB research methods and statistics courses. Even more telling is that Rousseau's (1997) *Annual Review of Psychology* chapter on organizational behaviour made no mention of levels issues; given her historical connection to such issues (e.g. Roberts et al. 1978; Rousseau 1985; House et al. 1995) this silence to our ears makes a loud statement.

However, we are far from sanguine about the future of theory and research for a meso OB. We see reasons for concern over the direction that meso OB thinking and research may take, some of which are caused by the ease with which data may be analysed and others by a failure to think reciprocally, as suggested by the Huber (1991) quotation at the start of this chapter. In what follows, we address some of our concerns with meso-organizational research and provide some direction for future thinking.

Concerns for the Future of Meso OB

Methodological Ease

Currently, the dominant methodological approach to meso research is based on what Klein et al. (1994) called the mixed determinants model. In this model both context and person variables are hypothesized to affect an outcome variable at the individual level of analysis. This model responds to Cappelli and Sherer's (1991) suggestion that we contextualize micro-organizational behaviour; i.e. contextualize the prediction and understanding of individual behaviour. However, it is important to remember that the 'individuals nested within organizations' model implicitly recommended by Cappelli and Sherer is not the only model in which we might be interested – depending on our theoretical framework, it might also be appropriate to look at organizations within and across industries, or across societies, etc.

Analysis of mixed determinants models are easily performed using hierarchical linear modelling (HLM) (Bryk and Raudenbush 1987; Hofmann 1997). HLM can be conceptualized as a two-step procedure. In step 1, simple regressions are performed in each lower level unit. This yields an intercept and a slope for each lower level unit. In step 2, the intercepts and slopes serve as dependent variables predicted by a higher-level variable. Slope models are similar to moderator variable analysis, while intercept models ask if group means differ as a function of a higher-level variable. Similar procedures have been developed in structural equation modelling to handle multiple level models.

Our concern is that the ease and availability of HLM may create a methodological hegemony and dictate the type of multilevel research that we perform, in effect constraining the questions that we ask. (We remember quite clearly our simultaneous excitement and worry when we first encountered software that relied on a pictorial representation rather than coding of structural models, and subsequently of hierarchical models – excitement based on the new possibilities this presaged for the further emergence of the meso approach in organizational research, and worry because we fully expected it to lead to less coherent and detailed thinking about levels issues. Why think through the issues when one need only draw a model of boxes and arrows?)

Indeed, our review suggests that the majority of multilevel organizational research now falls in the mixed determinants category and HLM is the dominant analytical tool. We do not wish to suggest that HLM is detrimental to multilevel research. Rather, it should not be viewed as the panacea. At this stage, multilevel research requires creativity, and it is important that we not allow a technique of data analysis to become a constraining analytical framework. For example, HLM research in OB almost exclusively has focused on individual level outcomes, even when contextual variables are included, making it micro–meso in focus.

Additionally, we are just beginning to answer some of the critical questions regarding HLM as an analytical procedure. For instance, what are the sample size requirements at each level of analysis to achieve acceptable power levels? What are the implications of violating normality assumptions, and so on? Some of these questions are beginning to be answered, of course, and some of the strengths of HLM for meso research are becoming clearer. For example, Davison et al.'s (2002) article on person by organization interactions compares HLM to moderated multiple regression (MMR) and shows that HLM can better handle large numbers of organizations, which should enhance power, though it does not necessarily answer the power question mentioned above (i.e. sample size requirements at each level of analysis).

However, it is not the methodological issues that should be driving meso-level research, but the

conceptual ones. Our point again is that techniques such as HLM which focus on individual outcomes should not depress research that simultaneously considers multiple levels of analysis with aggregate or organizational level outcomes. Ployhart and Schneider (2002) note, for example, that relationships at a given level of analysis are conceptually likely to be more strongly related than are relationships across levels of analysis due to the potential impact of mediating variables on the latter relationships. So, one would hypothesize that individual differences in ability are more strongly related to individual performance than are contextual variables and that contextual variables are more strongly related to group effectiveness than are individual variables. However, individual variables are related to group effectiveness in the aggregate, too, and consideration of both individual differences in the aggregate and contextual variables (e.g. management practices) likely will improve understanding and prediction of group performance.

The Nature of Error

One of the implicit distinctions between researchers who have generally focused at individual levels of analysis and those who have focused at aggregated levels of analysis has been the question of within-unit agreement, and how to conceptualize degrees of agreement. For many of those focused on organizational climate, for example, climate is conceived of as a shared phenomenon, and the degree to which an individual varies from that climate mean is simply considered error that will randomize away. For example, it has become a 'rule of thumb' that if there is sufficient agreement on a topic within a group to yield an r_{wg} of 0.70, then aggregation is justified (e.g. Cohen et al. 2001), and further consideration of individual variability is typically abandoned at that point. Many organizational climate researchers seem to have bought into that assumption, largely (we believe) because the methodological tools available allowed little other consideration. Several approaches emerged with which to determine whether there was in fact sufficient agreement among unit members to justify aggregation to a group mean (see Bliese (2000), for an excellent review of issues surrounding data aggregation).

However, recent research in several streams is much more oriented towards a meso model in which variation at each level of analysis is meaningful. For example, using a sample of bank tellers in branches, Schneider et al. (2002) elucidated the construct of 'climate strength' defined as the degree of agreement within a branch on the climate for service there. They demonstrated that degree of agreement moderated the relationship between climate means and customer satisfaction such that climate related to customer satisfaction significantly more strongly when agreement (strength) was high. Dickson and Resick (in press) recently demonstrated that there is greater agreement among organization members about the environment in which they work when the environment is more extremely mechanistic or organic, with lesser agreement among organization members when the mean of descriptions about the environment was less extreme.

In a related vein, an entire line of research is emerging on the societal cultural dimension of tightness/looseness, which is the degree to which a society tolerates deviation from societal norms (Chan et al. 1996). Dickson et al. (2000) have argued that, on dimensions that are particularly salient in a given society or organization, small individual deviations from expected group norms are likely to be highly salient (i.e. the 'just noticeable difference' is quite small but the effect is large), while on other dimensions that are less central, deviation of greater objective magnitude are likely to be less attended to (i.e. the 'just noticeable difference' will be larger with small effects).

In other words, there is plenty of reason to abandon the proposition that individual level variation is meaningless error when aggregating to a higher level of analysis, even if the aggregation indices justify aggregation. Indeed, recent work on the GLOBE Project (e.g. Hanges et al. 2004) presents an example of an analytical model (using multi-level confirmatory HLM) in which individuals are nested within organizations, which are nested within societies, with an industry factor that crosses societies, with meaningful and interpretable variation emerging at each level. In short, we believe that it is important to explicitly recognize that the act of aggregation does not magically make trivial the variation at lower levels of analysis.

The Importance of Reciprocity

As we have noted, HLM and other multi-level data analytic techniques have promise in moving our disciplines towards a more meso approach to research and theory. However, these techniques are still limited in their ability to adequately test the wide range of theoretical models that emerge from a meso view. One particularly unfortunate downfall of HLM as an analytic technique is that it cannot achieve what we think of as a critical task of meso organizational research – modelling dynamic and reciprocal causation across levels of analysis. The HLM is limited to determinants of outcome variables at lower levels of analysis. Currently, there is no analytical framework that allows modelling lower level determinants of higher-level variables. This is critical for the reciprocal interactionism that is implied by most meso thinking.[4]

We do see as a positive sign the scholarly attention that has been received by Meyer et al.'s (1993) exploration of several examples of moving beyond the mixed determinants model, presented in their special research forum on configurational approaches to organization (from the *Academy of Management Journal*). Although not all of the studies claiming to build from their recommendations actually do so, in the past few years several researchers have published research using meso approaches (but not a mixed determinants model) at various levels of analysis (e.g. Koh and Yer 2000; Child 2002; Dwyer et al. 2003).

Our enumeration of the limitations of HLM fails to address the need to develop models and frameworks that identify the reciprocal nature of many important organizational phenomena. For example, Kohn and Schooler (1983), a psychologist and a sociologist, have conceptualized and studied reciprocal interaction since 1964 showing how the attributes of jobs change people and how people attributes change the nature of jobs, including how the attributes of jobs affect the intellectual choices people make for their leisure activities!

Schein (1992) and Schneider et al. (2000) conceptualize the work place as one in which the attributes of people and settings continuously reinforce each other; both place great emphasis on the founders of organizations for the creation and maintenance of organizational culture. Schneider and Smith (2004b) have focused on the reciprocal relationships between personality (and aggregated personality) and organizational culture, noting that culture is clearly a reflection of the people in the organization, but that 'it is also obviously reasonable to conceptualize organizational culture as the cause of personality, and, indeed, organizational performance as a cause of organizational culture – or, for that matter, individual performance as a cause of personality' (p. 351). Their argument is that these variables likely have reciprocal relationships over time, and that the nature of these relationships is worthy of attention (despite the fact that to date it has received so little).

Indeed, Schneider et al. (2000) propose that the Lewinian concept of person and environment being inextricably entwined provides a useful heuristic for understanding the selection and retention of people in organizations and the subsequent understanding of how organizations come to have the culture they display to observers.

Note here that 'context' in the form of 'culture' now takes on meaning consistent with the sociological and psychological conceptualizations of the terms referring not to the physical world only (in the form of structures and hierarchies and division of labour), but in terms of the meaning the contexts have for people. The fact that those in the context frequently share these meanings makes them certainly as 'real' as those assessed through measurement tools of the physical sciences (Martin 2002). Integrations across levels of analysis with the outcome being the emerging nature of the cultures as contexts based on the collective individual attributes and behaviour of those there are consistent with the kind of directions we see possible in a meso OB (Schneider 1987; Schneider et al. 2000).

Expanding the Meaning of Meso

Rousseau and House (1994) suggested that multi-level research is similarly impeded by a limiting definition of context or level. They note that we need to expand the units of study beyond the traditional focus on individuals, groups and organizations to a study of events, routines and activities. Rousseau and House argue that we have reified structures in organizations that serve as the focus of study. These structures, albeit convenient, may fail to advance the linkages because they artificially demarcate micro and macro levels. Instead, we should be examining systems of interdependent action in the form of crises, routines, co-ordinated decision-making, etc. In other words, our units of analysis should be those features of organization where linkages between macro and micro naturally occur.

In a clear case of doing what one encourages others to do, Rousseau, as editor of *Journal of Organizational*

Behavior (JOB), has established a new policy for that journal. Wherever possible, manuscripts submitted to that journal are supposed to address issues of context (e.g. the organizational environment and dynamics at the time of data collection that might affect the individual functioning reported in the manuscript, or the industrial environment and pressures that might affect the organizational functioning reported in the manuscript, etc.). While JOB does not require articles it publishes to contain multi-level analyses or to be meso studies *per se*, there is a distinct emphasis on recognizing contextual issues that could affect the interpretation of results, and we see this as a significant step forward in the field. Such an emphasis can only serve to remind researchers of the need to attend to the issue of the organization in its context, rather than assume generalizability as so often happens.

Multilevel Construct Validity

Chan (1998), following Roberts et al. (1978) and Rousseau (1985) called for greater attention to the development and articulation of composition theories to explain the functional relationship between similar constructs across levels of analysis. The development of composition models and a framework or typology of composition theories aids in the validation of constructs across levels of analysis. Klein et al. (1994) appropriately criticized much multilevel research for its failure to adequately specify the nature of the construct as it moves across levels of analysis. This is tantamount to asking if the meaning of the construct changes or remains constant as we move across levels of analysis. Chan (1998) developed a typology of composition theories to aid in this classification, and we believe researchers need to pay close attention to the specification of the variables in their models. The frequency with which the Chan (1998) article has been cited suggests that the tide may be beginning to turn. However, we still believe that too little effort is typically placed on construct validation of aggregated measures.

On Pluralism and Unified Theory

Some years ago, Pfeffer (1993) suggested that the lack of a common OB paradigm was a significant barrier to the advancement of knowledge about organizations. One could conclude from Pfeffer's view that to advance organizational science we must be intolerant of diverse approaches, theories and methods of research (Canella and Paetzold 1994). In fact, Pfeffer stopped just short of proposing an elite guard of journal editors whose task was to guide organizational research down a more narrowly defined path. It is not our intent to rekindle the debate regarding philosophical pluralism, and we have noted throughout this chapter evidence that progress is being made. However, we agree with Merton and with Canella and Paetzold that at this stage of organizational behaviour as a science, diversity of thought and opinion are necessary to advance knowledge. It is misplaced to assume that organizational behaviour has reached the status of a natural science, nor indeed whether it would be useful to do so, and we should not be searching for a unified theory.

organizations. At the same time, our field is just beginning to embrace the notion that the theories and tools we use fall short of reflecting the richness and complexity of organizational life. Our concern in this chapter was with a more complete understanding of the varieties of ways micro, macro and meso are currently understood. Our conclusion is that this variety, as in most interesting arenas, is, indeed, the spice of life. This variety to our way of thinking symbolizes the vigour being brought to bear on important features of organizational life and life in organizations. Life exists at many levels of analysis simultaneously and it will take variety in conceptual and methodological approaches to adequately explore it. Hybrids have the vigour needed and we should do nothing to attempt to oversimplify the complexity that exists.

Conclusions

Our intent with this chapter was to suggest that the call for a 'third paradigm' had been heard. In fact, we believe that significant contributions are now being made to the understanding of the cross-level and reciprocal effects that characterize real life in real organizations. Further, we believe that the call for meso-research, the third paradigm, reflected the particular direction that psychology and sociology were taking throughout the 1970s and 1980s. Although there is an enormous amount of work to be done, we see that a fundamental shift in the intellectual focus and direction of OB has occurred: (a) it is increasingly multi-level in the independent variables being studied; (b) it is increasingly multi-level in the dependent variables being studied; (c) it is increasingly compositional in the nature of the multi-level theory being proposed and tested; (d) it is increasingly reciprocal, iterative and dynamic in specification of the mutual and cross-level effects that occur over time; and (e) it is increasingly accepting of alternative conceptual and methodological paradigms.

While our efforts at the explication of micro, macro and meso research has been somewhat abstract, we felt it important to make clear that the disciplinary heritages on which the meso models can be built provide a strong conceptual foundation for the newer theories and research paradigms required for the understanding and study of the particular phenomena that exist in and of work

Notes

1. Sociologists have, for example, been essential researchers of such individual phenomena as self-esteem (c.f. Rosenberg 1979, *Conceiving the Self*) and psychologists have demonstrated equal clarity of thinking with regard to behaviour in the aggregate (c.f. Barker 1968, *Ecological Psychology*).

2. Of course, Homans didn't reach this position without prior influence. Udehn (2002) argues that Homans' position is reflective of a clear influence by John Stuart Mill (1843/1974), who argued that causal explanations of large-scale social phenomenon are possible, but require *a priori* the existence of psychological laws.

3. Page limitations do not permit an elaboration of the many individual scholars who contributed to the early history of OB; as noted several times, the choices here are quite idiosyncratic. It is important, however, to note that simultaneous with the more 'macro' foci identified here in the persons of Argyris, McGregor and Likert there were also significant advances in theory and research focused on the individual level of theory and data. Examples here would include Vroom's (1964), Porter and Lawler's (1968) and Herzberg's (1966) contributions in understanding work motivation as well as continual efforts to understand the role of leadership in the prediction and understanding of individual employee behaviour (Stogdill 1974). One last note here: Argyris and McGregor both studied with Lewin, and Lewin founded the Institute for Group Dynamics at the University of Michigan where Likert worked and Vroom obtained his PhD; not just coincidence, we think.

4. We should note that some attempts have been made by Griffin (1997) to model multilevel reciprocal interactions

using the HLM model, though to date very little topic-focused research has incorporated this approach (though Mason and Griffin (2002) do provide one counter-example).

References

Alexander, J.C. and Giesen, B. (1987) 'From reduction to linkage: the long view of the micro-macro link', in J.C. Alexander, B. Giesen, R. Munch and N.J. Smelser (eds), *The micro-macro link.* Berkeley, CA: University of California Press. pp. 153–76.

Argyris, C. (1957) *Personality and organization.* New York: Harper.

Argyris, C. (1958) 'Some problems in conceptualizing organizational climate', *Administrative Science Quarterly,* 2: 501–20.

Argyris, C. (1960) *Understanding organizational behavior.* New York: Harper.

Barker, R.G. (1968) *Ecological psychology: Concepts and methods for studying the environment of human behavior.* Stanford: Stanford University Press.

Bass, B.M. (1960) *Leadership, psychology and organizational behavior.* New York: Harper.

Bennis W.G. (1993) *An invented life.* London: Century.

Berlew, D.E. and Hall, D.T. (1966) 'The socialization of managers: effects of expectations on performance', *Administrative Science Quarterly,* 11: 207–24.

Blau, P. (1977) *Inequality and heterogeneity.* New York: Free Press.

Bliese, P.D. (2000) 'Within-group agreement, non-independence, and reliability: Implications for data aggregation and analyses', in K.J. Klein and S.W.J. Kozlowski (eds), *Multilevel theory, research, and methods in organizations: Foundations, extensions, and new directions).* San Francisco: Jossey-Bass. pp. 349–81.

Bowers, K.S. (1973) 'Situationism in psychology: an analysis and critique', *Psychological Review,* 80: 307–36.

Bray, D.W., Campbell, R.J. and Grant, D.L. (1974) *Formative years in business: A long-term AT&T study of managerial lives.* New York: Wiley.

Brayfield, A.H. and Crockett, W.H. (1955) 'Employee attitudes and performance', *Psychological Bulletin,* 52: 396–428.

Bryk A. and Raudenbush, S. (1987) 'Application of hierarchical linear models to assessing change', *Psychological Bulletin,* 101: 147–58.

Canella, A. and Paetzold, R. (1994) 'Pfeffer's barriers to the advance of organizational science: a rejoinder', *Academy of Management Review,* 19: 331–41.

Cappelli, P. and Sherer, P.D. (1991) 'The missing role of context in OB: the need for a meso-level approach', *Research in Organizational Behavior,* 13: 55–110.

Cartwright, D. and Zander, A. (1953) *Group dynamics: Research and theory.* New York: Row, Peterson.

Chan, D. (1998) 'Functional relations among constructs in the same content domain at different levels of analysis: a typology of composition models', *Journal of Applied Psychology,* 83: 234–46.

Chan, D.K.S., Gelfand, M.J., Triandis, H.C. and Tzeng, O. (1996) 'Tightness-looseness revisited: a systematic examination in Japan and the United States', *International Journal of Psychology,* 31: 1–12.

Child, J. (2002) 'A configurational analysis of international joint ventures', *Organization Studies,* 23: 781–815.

Cohen, A., Doveh, E. and Eick, U. (2001) 'Statistical properties of the $r_{wg(j)}$ index of agreement', *Psychological Methods,* 6: 297–310.

Coleman, J.S. (1987) 'Microfoundations and macrosocial behavior', in J.C. Alexander, B. Giesen, R. Munch and N.J. Smelser (eds), *The micro-macro link.* Berkeley, CA: University of California Press. pp. 153–76.

Collins, R. (1981) 'The micro-foundations of macro-sociology', *American Journal of Sociology,* 86: 984–1014.

Cummings, L.L. (1982) 'Organizational behavior', *Annual Review of Psychology,* 33: 541–79.

Davison, M.L., Kwak, N., Seo, Y.S. and Choi, J. (2002) 'Using hierarchical linear models to examine moderator effects: Person-by-organization interactions', *Organizational Research Methods,* 5: 231–54.

Dickson, M.W. and Resick, C.J. (under revision) 'When organizational climate is unambiguous, it is also strong', *Journal of Applied Psychology.*

Dickson, M.W., Aditya, R.N. and Chhokar, J.S. (2000) 'Definition and interpretation in cross-cultural organizational culture research: some pointers from the GLOBE research program', in N. Ashkanasy, C. Wilderom and M. Petersen (eds), *Handbook of Organizational Culture and Climate.* Thousand Oaks, CA: Sage. pp. 447–64.

Dobbins, G.H., Cardy, R.L. and Carson, K.P. (1991) 'Examining fundamental assumptions: a contrast of person and system approaches to human resource management', in G.R. Ferris and K.W. Rowland (eds), *Research in personnel and human resources management,* Vol. 9. Greenwich, CT: JAI Press. pp. 1–38.

Dwyer, S., Richard, O.C. and Chadwick, K. (2003) 'Gender diversity in management and firm performance: the influence of growth orientation and organizational culture', *Journal of Business Research,* 56: 1009–19.

Endler, N.S. and Magnusson, D. (1976) 'Toward an interactional psychology of personality', *Psychological Bulletin,* 83: 956–79.

Fiedler, F.E. (1967) *A theory of leadership effectiveness.* New York: McGraw-Hill.

Fleishman, E.A. (1953) 'The description of supervisory behavior', *Journal of Applied Psychology,* 37: 1–6.

Ghiselli, E.E. and Brown, C. (1955) *Personnel and industrial psychology.* New York: McGraw-Hill.

Giberson, T.R., Resick, C.J. and Dickson, M.W. (2005) 'Embedding leader characteristics: An examination of homogeneity of personality and values in organizations', *Journal of Applied Psychology*, 90(5): 1002–10.

Griffin, M.A. (1997) 'Interaction between individuals and situations: using HLM procedures to estimate reciprocal relationships', *Journal of Management*, 23: 759–73.

Hackman, J.R. and Lawler, E.E., III. (1971) 'Employee reactions to job characteristics', *Journal of Applied Psychology Monograph*, 55: 259–86.

Hackman, J.R. and Oldham, G.R. (1975) 'Development of the job diagnostic survey', *Journal of Applied Psychology*, 60: 159–70.

Hackman, J.R. and Oldham, G.R. (1980) *Work redesign.* Reading, MA: Addison-Wesley.

Hanges, P.J., Dickson, M.W. and Sipe, M.S. (2004) 'Rationale for GLOBE statistical analyses: scaling of societies and testing of hypotheses', in R.J. House, P.J. Hanges, M. Javidan, P.W. Dorfman, V. Gupta and GLOBE Associates (eds), *Leadership, culture, and organizations: The GLOBE study of 62 societies.* Thousand Oaks, CA: Sage. pp. 219–33.

Hare, A.P., Borgotta, E.F. and Bales, R.F. (eds) (1955) *Small groups: Studies in social interaction.* New York: Knopf.

Herzberg, F.I. (1966) *Working and the nature of man.* New York: Crowell.

Hofmann, D.A. (1997) An overview of the logic and rationale of hierarchical linear models. *Journal of Management*, 23: 723–44.

Homans, G.C. (1941) 'The Western electric researchers', *Fatigue of Workers.* Reinhold Press. pp. 56–65.

Homans, G.C. (1964) 'Bringing men back in', *American Sociological Review*, 29(5): 809–18.

House, R.J., Rousseau, D.M. and Thomas-Hunt, M. (1995) 'The meso paradigm: a framework for the integration of micro and macro organizational behavior', *Research in Organizational Behavior*, 17: 71–114.

Huber, J. (1991) *Macro-micro linkages in Sociology.* Newbury Park, CA: Sage Publications.

Hull, C.L. (1943) *Principles of behavior.* New York: Appleton-Century-Crofts.

Huselid, M.A. (1995) 'The impact of human resources management practices on turnover, productivity, and corporate financial performance', *Academy of Management Journal*, 38: 635–72.

Jackson, S.E. and Schuler, R.S. (1995) 'Understanding human resource management in the context of organizations and their environments', *Annual Review of Psychology*, 46: 237–64.

Katz, D. and Kahn, R.L. (1966) *The social psychology of organizations.* New York: Wiley.

Klein, K.J. and Kozlowski, S.W.J. (2000) 'A multilevel approach to theory and research in organizations: contextual, temporal, and emergent processes', in K.J. Klein and S.W.J. Kozlowski (eds), *Multilevel theory, research, and methods in organizations: Foundations, extensions, and new directions.* San Francisco: Jossey-Bass. pp. 3–90.

Klein, K.J., Dansereau, F. and Hall, R.J. (1994) 'Levels issues in theory development, data collection, and analysis', *Academy of Management Review*, 19: 195–229.

Koh, W.L. and Yer, L.K. (2000) 'The impact of the employee-organization relationship on temporary employees' performance and attitude: testing a Singaporean sample', *International Journal of Human Resource Management*, 11: 366–87.

Kohn M.L. and Schooler, C. (1983) *Work and personality: An inquiry into the impact of social stratification.* Norwood, NJ: Ablex Publishing Corp.

Lewin, K. (1946) 'Behavior and development as a function of the total situation', in L. Carmichael (ed.), *Manual of child psychology.* New York: John Wiley.

Lewin, K., Lippitt, R. and White, R.K. (1939) 'Patterns of aggressive behavior in experimentally created social climates', *Journal of Social Psychology*, 10: 271–301.

Likert, R. (1961) *New patterns of management.* New York: McGraw-Hill.

Locke, E.A. (1976) 'The nature and causes of job satisfaction', in M.D. Dunnette (ed.), *Handbook of industrial and organizational psychology.* Chicago: Rand McNally. pp. 1297–343.

Martin, J. (2002) *Organizational culture: Mapping the terrain.* Thousand Oaks, CA: Sage Publishing.

Maslow, A. (1954) *Motivation and personality.* New York: Harper

Mason, C.M. and Griffin, M.A. (2002) 'Group task satisfaction – applying the construct of job satisfaction to groups', *Small Group Research*, 33: 271–312.

McGregor, D.M. (1944) 'Conditions of effective leadership in the industrial organization', *Journal of Consulting Psychology*, 8: 55–63.

McGregor, D.M. (1960) *The human side of enterprise.* New York: McGraw-Hill.

Merton, R.K. (1973) *The sociology of science.* Chicago, IL: The University of Chicago Press.

Meyer, A.D., Tsui, A.S. and Hinings, C.R. (1993) 'Configurational approaches to organizational analysis', *Academy of Management Journal*, 36: 1175–95.

Milgram, S. (1963) 'Behavioral study of obedience', *Journal of Abnormal and Social Psychology*, 67: 371–8.

Mill, J.S. (1843–1872/1974) *A System of logic: Ratiocinative and inductive. Collected Works*, Vols VII–VIII. Toronto: University of Toronto Press.

Mischel, W. (1968) *Personality and assessment.* New York: John Wiley.

Mischel, W., Shoda, Y. and Mendoza-Denton, R. (2002) 'Situation-behavior profiles as a locus of consistency in personality', *Current Directions in Psychological Science*, 11: 50–4.

Monte, C.F. (1977) *Beneath the mask: An introduction to theories of personality.* New York: Praeger.

Mowday, R.T. and Sutton, R.I. (1993) 'Organizational behavior: linking individuals and groups to organizational contexts', *Annual Review of Psychology*, 44: 195–229.

Nord, W. and Fox, S. (1996) 'The individual in organizational studies: the great disappearing act?', in S.R. Clegg, C. Hardy and W. Nord (eds), *Handbook of organization studies*. London: Sage. pp. 148–74.

O'Reilly, C. (1991) 'Organizational behavior: where we've been, where we're going', *Annual Review of Psychology*, 42: 427–58.

Pelz, D.C. and Andrews, F.M. (1966) *Scientists in organizations*. New York: John Wiley & Sons.

Perrow, C. (1973) 'The short and glorious history of organizational theory', *Organizational Dynamics*, 2: 2–15.

Pervin, L. (1978) 'The relations of situations to behavior', in D. Magnusson (ed.), *The situation: An interactional perspective*. Hillsdale, NJ: Lawrence Earlbaum Associates. pp. 343–60.

Pervin, L. (1989) 'Persons, situations, and interactions: the history of a controversy and discussion of theoretical models', *Academy of Management Review*, 14: 350–60.

Pfeffer, J. (1993) 'Barriers to the advance of organizational science: paradigm development as a dependent variable', *Academy of Management Review*, 18: 599–620.

Ployhart, R.E. and Schneider, B. (2002) 'A multi-level perspective on personnel selection research and practice: implications for selection system design, assessment and construct validation', in F.J. Yammarino and F. Dansereau (eds), Research in multi-level issues, Vol. 1. Oxford, UK: JAI. pp. 95–140

Porter, L.W. and Lawler, E.E., III. (1968) *Managerial attitudes and performance*. Homewood, IL: Irwin-Dorsey.

Roberts, K.H., Hulin, C.L. and Rousseau, D.M. (1978) *Developing an interdisciplinary science of organizations*. San Francisco: Jossey-Bass.

Rosenberg, M. (1979) *Conceiving the self*. New York: Basic Books.

Rousseau, D.M. (1985) 'Issues of level in organizational research: multi-level and cross-level perspectives', in B.M. Staw and L.L. Cummings (eds), *Research in organizational behavior*, Vol. 7. Greenwich, CT: JAI. pp. 1–37.

Rousseau, D.M. (1997) 'Organizational behavior in the new organizational era', *Annual Review of Psychology*, 48: 514–46.

Rousseau, D. and House, R.J. (1994) 'MESO organizational behavior: avoiding three fundamental biases', in C.L. Cooper and D.M. Rousseau (eds), *Trends in organizational behavior*, Vol. 1. London: Wiley. pp. 13–30.

Schein, E.A. (1992) *Organizational culture and leadership*, 2nd edn. San Francisco: Jossey-Bass.

Schneider, B. (1983a) 'An interactionist perspective on organizational effectiveness', in K.S. Cameron and D.A. Whetten (eds), *Organizational effectiveness: A comparison of multiple models*. New York: Academic Press. pp. 27–70.

Schneider, B. (1983b) 'Interactional psychology and organizational behavior', in B.M. Staw and L.L. Cummings (eds), *Research in organizational behavior*. Greenwich, CT: JAI. pp. 1–32.

Schneider, B. (1987) 'The people make the place', *Personnel Psychology*, 40: 437–53.

Schneider, B. (1996) 'When individual differences aren't', in K.R. Murphy (ed.), *Individual differences and behavior in organizations*. San Francisco: Jossey-Bass. pp. 548–71.

Schneider, B. and Smith, D.B. (eds) (2004a) *Personality and organizations*. Mahwah, NJ: Lawrence Erlbaum Associates.

Schneider, B. and Smith, D.B. (2004b) 'Personality and organizational culture', in B. Schneider and D.B. Smith (eds.), *Personality and organizations*. Mahwah, NJ: Lawrence Erlbaum Associates. pp. 347–70.

Schneider, B., Goldstein, H. and Smith, D.B. (1995) 'The ASA framework: an update', *Personnel Psychology*, 48: 747–73.

Schneider, B., Salvaggio, A.N. and Subirats, M. (2002) 'Climate strength: A new direction for climate research', *Journal of Applied Psychology*, 87(2): 220–9.

Schneider, B., Smith, D.B. and Goldstein, H.W. (2000) 'Attraction-selection-attrition: toward a person-environment psychology of organizations', in W.B. Walsh, K.H. Craik and R.H. Price (eds), *Person-environment psychology,: New directions and perspectives*. Mahwah, NJ: Lawrence Erlbaum Associates. pp. 61–86.

Schneider, B., Smith, D.B., Taylor, S. and Fleenor, J. (1998) 'Personality and organization: a test of the homogeneity of personality hypothesis', *Journal of Applied Psychology*, 83: 462–70.

Skinner, B.F. (1938) *The behavior of organisms*. East Norwalk, CT: Appleton and Lange.

Staw, B.M. and Sutton, R.I. (1993) 'Macro organizational psychology', in K.J. Murninghan (ed.), *Social psychology of organizations: Advances in theory and research*. Englewood Cliffs, NJ: Prentice-Hall. pp. 350–384.

Stogdill, R.M. (1948) 'Personal factors associated with the study of leadership: a survey of the literature', *Journal of Psychology*, 25: 35–71.

Stogdill, R.M. (1974) *Handbook of leadership*. New York: Free Press.

Tiffin, J. and McCormick, E.M. (1960) *Industrial psychology*, 2nd edn. Englewood Cliffs, NJ: Prentice-Hall.

Trist, E.L. and Bamforth, K.W. (1951) 'Some social and psychological consequences of the longwall method of goal getting', *Human Relations*, 4: 3–38.

Turner, A.N. and Lawrence, P.R. (1967) *Industrial jobs and the worker*. Boston: Harvard University, Graduate School of Business Administration.

Udehn, L. (2002) 'The changing face of methodological individualism', *Annual Review of Sociology*, 28: 479–507.

Viteles, M.S. (1932) *Industrial psychology*. New York: Norton.

Vroom, V.H. (1964) *Work and motivation*. New York: Wiley.

Watson, J.B. (1919) *Psychology from the standpoint of a behaviorist*. Philadelphia: Lippencott.

Weick, K.E. (1995) *Sensemaking in organizations*. Thousand Oaks, CA: Sage Publishing.

1.5 Complexity Science and Organization Studies

STEVE MAGUIRE, BILL MCKELVEY, LAURENT MIRABEAU AND NAIL ÖZTAS

The application of complexity science to questions interesting to organizational scholars has grown dramatically over the past two decades: books have been written; special issues of journals have been published; new organizational complexity journals have been created; and articles applying complexity science are increasingly appearing in top journals. In this chapter, we review and bring order to this diverse literature. In so doing, we have kept in mind a dual audience – researchers new to complexity science as well as the existing community of organizational complexity scholars. It is our hope that the chapter can serve as a convenient and useful reference for both, and we have written and structured it accordingly.

We begin by introducing complexity science, noting its disciplinary foundations, defining key terms and contrasting European and North American approaches. We then describe different measures of complexity along with related epistemological issues concerning representation, prediction and interpretation. Next, we narrow our focus to organization studies, noting early work addressing complexity and systems thinking before tracing the outlines of the movement of complexity science into the discipline. Our map of the field is then presented. It serves to organize the review portion of the chapter in which we juxtapose different strands of research and summarize contributions. We identify four broad clusters of work that we term Introductions, Foundations, Applications and Reflections.

Both objectivist and interpretivist perspectives appear in the organizational complexity literature, and this is reflected in our map of the field. These two approaches may be usefully conceptualized, respectively, as *reduction* and *absorption* strategies for handling complexity (Boisot and Child 1999); objectivists are complexity-reducers while interpretivists are complexity-absorbers. The former favour models while the latter explore meanings and are more likely to advocate metaphoric treatments, although the distinction is not as sharp as one might think. As regards the large volume of metaphorical writing, we distinguish work that is reflexive and thus sensitive to epistemological issues from work that is not. While the latter is faddish and prone to unsupportable claims, the former rests on firmer foundations (Maguire and McKelvey 1999).

Although agent-based models (ABMs)[1] and computational approaches to organizations are central to our review, the chapter should not be considered exhaustive as regards these methods. And whereas other reviews address complexity and computation together as a single topic (see Baum 2002), our view of the field is broader and more inclusive. Our chapter highlights how, despite its association with ontologies emphasizing information-processing and ABM methods, complexity science has also been enthusiastically embraced by researchers using ontologies emphasizing interpretation and narrative methods.

The chapter concludes with suggestions for future research using a three-pronged approach: (1) continuing the most promising conversations within the community of organizational complexity scholars to extend and refine the extant knowledge base; (2) initiating new intra-community conversations to reconcile and leverage different approaches but recognizing that full reconciliation may be neither possible nor desirable; and (3) initiating new inter-community conversations with other groups of organizational scholars to better anchor and integrate complexity science with traditional organizational research. If strengthened and connected more seamlessly to mainstream research, complexity science could very well transform organization studies.

Complexity Science

Complex systems have received increased attention from numerous scientific disciplines recently, and from this has emerged a broad ranging interdisciplinary science of complexity (see Anderson et al. 1988; Nicolis and Prigogine 1989; Lewin 1992; Waldrop 1992; Kauffman 1993; Mainzer 1994; Casti 1994; Bar-Yam 1997). Several authors define key features of complex systems (Holland 1988; Bar Yam 1997; Anderson 1999), including Cilliers (1998), whose comprehensive and accessible list is shown in Table 1.5.1.

Features of Complex Systems

A complex system is a whole comprised of a large number of parts, each of which behaves according to some rule or force that relates it interactively to other parts. In responding in parallel to their own local contexts, the parts can, without explicit inter-part co-ordination or any one of them having a global view, cause the system as a whole to display emergent patterns at the global level – the emergence of orderly phenomena and properties of the whole that cannot be predicted from properties of parts. Interactions are usually but not necessarily local and very rich. That is, although parts typically interact with neighbouring parts, this does not preclude long-range influence nor self-regulatory loops of negative feedback, loops of positive feedback causing vicious or virtuous cycles or some combination of these as near-range interactions cascade forward in time.

Interactions among parts can be material/energetic or informational and may be characterized by non-linearity, which means that small causes are associated with disproportionately large effects in a system's state variables – the variables of interest to observers and used to characterize the system. Thus, complex systems display sensitivity to initial conditions, sometimes referred to as the 'butterfly effect' after meteorologist Lorenz's (1963) claim that the flap of a butterfly's wings in one region of the world could affect weather patterns in others. Significantly, history matters in complex systems: their evolution over time is one of path dependence and irreversibility. Thus, in some important sense, the past co-produces present and future system states; change in a complex system follows what Eddington (1930) called the 'arrow of time'.

Table 1.5.1   Features of complex systems*

1. Complex systems consist of a large number of elements.
2. These elements interact dynamically.
3. Interactions are rich; any element in the system can influence or be influenced by any other.
4. Interactions are non-linear.
5. Interactions are typically short-range.
6. There are positive and negative feedback loops of interactions.
7. Complex systems are open systems.
8. Complex systems operate under conditions far from equilibrium.
9. Complex systems have histories.
10. Individual elements are typically ignorant of the behaviour of the whole system in which they are embedded.

* from Cilliers (1998).

Complex systems are open systems operating under conditions described as far-from-equilibrium; ongoing interaction of their parts is maintained by the import of energy-matter and information from the environment. Because of this openness and exchange, distinguishing a complex system from its environment is not always straightforward. Ultimately, delimiting the boundary of a complex system is an analytic choice, determined by the position, perspective and purpose of those who seek to describe it.

The language of complex systems is useful for describing any system that has these features, such as an immune system, an ecosystem or an economy. In some complex systems, the constituent parts are not themselves complex systems and so act as 'agents'[2] governed by unchanging rules. In other complex systems, parts can themselves be complex systems capable of learning, which simply means that they are governed by rules that themselves evolve. Here it is common to refer to the parts as adaptive agents guided by internal models or schemata, with their interactions giving rise to a whole referred to as a complex adaptive system[3] (Holland 1995). In these systems, it is possible for a mutually consistent ecology of parts, along with the rules guiding them, to emerge from what is effectively a decentralized, bottom-up process of co-design. Thus, system level processes of adaptation, learning and evolution may equally be described at the level of parts with a terminology of co-adaptation, co-learning and co-evolution.

Complexity arises when emergent system-level phenomena are characterized by patterns in time or a given state space that have neither too much nor too little form. Neither in stasis nor changing randomly, these emergent phenomena are interesting, due to the coupling of individual and global behaviours as well as the difficulties they pose for prediction. Broad patterns of system behaviour may be predictable, but the system's specific path through a space of possible states is not. In stable, highly structured things, like crystals for instance, nothing new can emerge. However, conversely, overly random media like gases are formless. If our socio-economic system was like a crystal (i.e. the perfect equilibria of neoclassical economics or the iron institutional cages of structuralist sociology) or like a gas (i.e. a Hobbesian anarchy), then there would be little need for complexity science within social science.

In summary, complexity science[4] is the study of complex systems and of the phenomena of complexity and emergence to which they give rise. Like systems theory to which some of its roots can be traced, complexity science offers organizational researchers a set of concepts at a level of abstraction almost mathematical in its flexibility and diversity of applications. For example, a 'whole' organization might be conceptualized as being made up of, and thus decomposable into, different interdependent 'parts', including: business units; departments; individuals; value chain activities; or, more abstractly, decisions. Work at different levels of analysis is afforded as well. For example, the economy can be conceptualized as a complex system decomposable into nation-states or sectors or organizations. Or technology writ large can be conceptualized as a complex system made up of individual technological artifacts. The possibilities are numerous.

European and North American Approaches to Complexity

Complexity science has origins in many disciplines, but two broad scientific programmes, increasingly overlapping, anchor its development. A European School of complexity began with the work of Prigogine, Haken, Allen, Nicolis, Cramer and Mainzer, among many others (see Table 1.5.2). They emphasize far-from-equilibrium conditions and, specifically, how unorganized entities in a given system subjected to an externally imposed energy source seemingly organize themselves into structures that sustain or reproduce themselves as long as the energy difference is maintained. For example, increasing the heat under water molecules in a vessel exposed to colder air above leads to geometric patterns of hotter and colder water – order and organization appear. Prigogine (1955) termed such order a '*dissipative structure*' because, in maintaining itself it dissipated the concentration of energy. Absent the energy source (or if closed to the environment), natural entropic processes would cause the system to equilibrate and to remain without order or organization, in accordance with the 2nd Law of Thermodynamics – e.g. there would be no discernable patterns and water temperature would be homogeneous throughout. This work, drawing from the physical sciences, using mathematical models and emphasizing critical values and phase transitions (e.g. the amount of heating and series of events necessary to trigger the appearance of patterns in the water) focuses on 'self-organization' as the emergence of order from disorder due to small perturbations – 'order through fluctuations' (Nicolis and Prigogine 1977) or 'order out of chaos' (Prigogine and Stengers 1984).

In contrast, the North American School is rooted in the work of Mandelbrot, Lorenz, Anderson, Kauffman, Kaye, Holland, Arthur, Wolfram, Casti and Bak, among others (see Table 1.5.2), and is associated with the Santa Fe Institute (SFI), a private, not-for-profit, multidisciplinary research and education centre founded in 1984 and devoted to the study of complex systems and 'the sciences of complexity' (Pines 1988). Drawing from the life sciences and making extensive use of computational approaches and agent-based models, they emphasize the spontaneous coevolution of entities (i.e. agents) in a complex system. Agents restructure themselves continuously, leading to new forms of emergent order consisting of patterns of evolved agent attributes and hierarchical structures displaying both upward and downward causal influences. At the point of '*self-organized criticality*' (Bak 1996) towards which it has been hypothesized that complex systems naturally evolve, the size and frequency of restructuring events observed in the system are related by an inverse power law.

McKelvey (2001a), using thermodynamic theory and building on Cramer (1993), focuses attention on a complex system's 1st and 2nd '*critical values*'. These demark phase transitions and thus define upper and lower bounds of a region of emergent

Table 1.5.2 Disciplinary origins of complexity science

Reference	Discipline	Key concepts
European School		
Poincaré (1890)	Mathematics	Non-predictability of non-linear dynamic systems; three-body problem
Bénard (1901)	Fluid dynamics	Bénard cells
Prigogine (1955; 1962; 1980)	Thermodynamics	Non-linear thermodynamics; non-equilibrium, dynamical statistical mechanics
Popper (1959)	Philosophy	Irreversible processes in physics
Allen (1975; 1976; 1988; 1993a, b)	Physics	Complexity, evolutionary adaptation modeled via stochastic systems dynamics
Haken (1977; 1983)	Synergetics	Synergetics; order and control parameters
Eigen and Schuster (1979)	Biology	Self-optimization; quasi-species
Prigogine and Stengers (1984)	Thermodynamics	New worldview implied by self-organization
Favre et al. (1988)	Fluid dynamics	Transitions of systems from turbulence to order; multidisciplinary perspective
Cramer (1993)	Molecular biology	Dissipative structures; chaos; multidisciplinary perspective
Cohen and Stewart (1994)	Biology; mathematics	Emergence of simplicity from the interaction of chaos and complexity
Mainzer (1994)	Philosophy	Order creation, from quantum physics and biology to the econosphere
Prigogine (with Stengers) (1997)	Thermodynamics	Arguments against reversibility of time, Einstein's determinism and pure chance
North American School		
Mandelbrot (1961; 1963; 1975)	Mathematics	Fractal geometry; chaos; rank/frequency power laws
Lorenz (1963; 1972)	Atmospheric science	Strange attractors; sensitivity to initial conditions
Kauffman (1969; 1993; 2000)	Medicine	Spontaneous origins of biological order; fitness landscape models
Holland (1975; 1988; 1995; 1998)	Engineering	Genetic algorithms; emergence and co-evolving agents; bottom-up science
Thom (1975)	Mathematics	Catastrophe theory
Arthur (1983; 1988)	Economics	Self-reinforcing positive feedback processes in firms and economies
Wolfram (1983)	Computer science	Computational modelling of emergent structures
Bak et al. (1987)	Physics	Self-organized criticality
Gleick (1987)	Multidisciplinary	Chaos theory
Pines (1988)	Multidisciplinary	SFI founding; Gell Mann's 'surface complexity arising out of deep simplicity'
Anderson et al. (1988)	Economics	Complexity applications to economics
Kaye (1989; 1993)	Physics	Fractal geometry
Langton (1989)	Biology	Artificial life
Lewin (1992)	Multidisciplinary	Personalized account of the origins of complexity science at SFI
Waldrop (1992)	Multidisciplinary	History of the origins of complexity science at SFI
Salthe (1993)	Evolutionary biology	Self-organization in biology
Casti (1994)	Mathematics	Counterintuitive non-linear surprises in all kinds of phenomena
Depew and Weber (1995)	Evolutionary biology	Evolution of evolutionary thinking from Darwin to self-organization biology

complexity. Whereas the European School emphasizes *system–environment processes* resulting in the emergence of complex order at the 1st critical value, and in particular the imposed energy differential or contextual tension necessary to trigger this phase transition, the American school emphasizes *intra-system processes* resulting in emergent complexity and, in particular, the co-evolution of parts to a state of self-organized criticality as a complex system approaches its 2nd critical value – the so-called edge of chaos[5] beyond which order disappears as disorder overwhelms the system (Lichtenstein and McKelvey 2004). A full explanation of emergent phenomena in complex systems requires reference to concepts from both schools.

Distinguishing Complexity, Chaos and Catastrophe

Complexity, chaos and catastrophe theory are commonly associated, so it is helpful to relate but distinguish these fundamentally different concepts.

Whereas the complexity science expressions 'order out of chaos' and 'edge of chaos' employ the term chaos in its vernacular usage as synonymous for disorder or randomness (i.e. stochastic chaos), chaos theory, a branch of dynamical systems theory within mathematics, addresses something else: a precisely and mathematically defined phenomenon in a given system's time series data called deterministic chaos that appears as, but is definitely not, randomness. To understand the distinction between deterministic and stochastic chaos, Dooley and Van de Ven's (1999) typology is helpful. It distinguishes different types of complex dynamics commonly observed in time series data for dependent variables of interest in organization studies, based on (1) the underlying causal system's dimensionality (i.e. low vs high degrees of freedom: the number of variables whose initial conditions are required to uniquely specify the system's trajectory) and (2) causal variable interactions (no or linear vs non-linear interactions).

If systems generate time series data characterized by obvious order, i.e. equilibria (the system is drawn to a single state called a 'point attractor') or recognizable cycles of change (the system oscillates between states collectively referred to as a 'periodic attractor'), then researchers should consider deterministic causal theories in which only a few factors interact linearly or not at all. On the other hand, time series data characterized by disorder, i.e. what

appears to be randomness, require researchers to consider different forms of causal theories; not only does randomness come in different 'colours', but what appears on the surface as stochastic behaviour may actually be 'deterministic chaos'. Statistical tests are available to distinguish between different observed dynamics and thus to guide researchers in developing appropriate causal theories.

Systems in which many independent causal factors contribute to observed dynamics are characterized by complete randomness called 'white noise', while systems in which many causal factors interact non-linearly give rise to 'constrained randomness' called 'pink noise'. The latter are especially important for complexity researchers because it has been suggested that complex systems naturally evolve towards a state of self-organized criticality governed by inverse power laws: 'small events happen often, events of moderate size happen sometimes, and events of enormous size happen rarely' (Dooley and Van de Ven 1999: 362), as with earthquakes.

Chaos theory is a branch of dynamical system theory addressing deterministic chaos (Ott 1993). Chaotic system behaviour arises from just a few causal factors which interact interdependently and in a non-linear fashion. Although accurate prediction of chaotic system's path through a space of possible states is very difficult because of sensitivity to initial conditions, clear overall patterns are nevertheless observable because the system's trajectory is constrained by what is called a 'strange attractor' – the system's path bounces about but does not visit every point as it would if governed by truly random processes. Despite the fact that chaos and complexity are often linked and sometimes confused, the two are distinct; chaotic systems are in fact closer, in an ontological sense, to linear systems because both are deterministic (Dooley and Van de Ven 1999).

Catastrophe theory is also a branch of dynamical systems theory. It offers precise mathematical tools for studying and classifying sudden discontinuous shifts in behaviour resulting from small changes to continuous variables of a system called control parameters (Thom 1975; Poston and Stewart 1978; Brown 1995). Catastrophes – discontinuous and significant changes brought on by incremental causes – occur as the system moves from the influence of one attractor to another, at points of bifurcation. Catastrophe theory is used to mathematically locate these points where a system equivocates between different attractors and thus trajectories.

In summary, complexity, chaos and catastrophe theory are related but distinct approaches to understanding the dynamics of systems. The wisdom of adopting one approach over another depends upon the specific system being studied.

Defining and Measuring Complexity

In part because the field has attracted a diverse set of researchers from different disciplines, but more importantly, because defining and measuring complexity is intimately tied up with difficult questions of ontology and epistemology, there is no consensus about how to define or measure complexity. Some lists of distinct definitions include more than 30 entries (Horgan 1995), although these can generally be grouped into two clusters – information and resource measures. Most fundamentally, a key question is whether complexity is ontological or epistemological: is it a property of a system, its parts and their interactions; or is it a property of a given interpretation, representation or simulation of a system? The emerging consensus is that it is both.

One view of complexity is that it is an objective system property that correlates with a system's structural intricacy (Moldoveanu 2005). The complexity of a system thus increases with the number of parts and with the density and variability of interconnections or relations among them. Alternatively, complexity can be seen more subjectively as correlating with the difficulty of representing and making valid or accurate predictions about a system (Moldoveanu 2005), making it essentially an epistemological phenomenon. For human systems, Boisot and Child (1999) label the former relational complexity and the latter cognitive complexity.

Intuitively, we might expect that these two would be related – that structurally simple systems would be easy to represent and predict, and that structurally complex systems would be more difficult to represent and predict – but this is not always the case. Chaos theory shows how structurally simple systems may behave in unpredictable ways (Ott 1993), while the fact that many structurally intricate systems behave simply and predictably is the basis of all modular design. In other words, the complexity of wholes cannot be inferred from knowledge of parts and their relations; both emergent complexity *and* emergent simplicity are counterintuitive system-level possibilities (Bar-Yam 1997).

Although there is no consensus on a single definition or measure of complexity, there is consensus on the following: before assessing the complexity of a system, the level of coarse graining and scale of observation must be determined; a certain amount of previous knowledge and understanding about the world must be assumed; and the language used in descriptions of the system under consideration must be agreed upon (Gell-Mann 1995; Bar-Yam 1997). Drawing from computer science but seeking more generality, Gell-Mann (1994: 34) defines 'crude complexity' as 'the length of the shortest message that will describe a system, at a given level of coarse graining, to someone at a distance, employing language, knowledge and understanding that both parties share (and know they share) beforehand'. Related measures include 'effective complexity', which is the length of the shortest description of a system's regularities only, and 'computational complexity', which is a measure of the resources required to manipulate representations of a system for prediction.

Thus, unavoidably, defining and understanding what constitutes complexity involves defining and understanding what constitutes information within and about a system. That observers play such a key role in constituting complexity is non-trivial. Gell-Mann (1995: 17) points to an important challenge – one likely to be even more difficult to surmount in the study of social as compared to natural systems – when, in his description of effective complexity, he concludes that 'since it is impossible to find all regularities of an entity, the question arises as to who or what determines the class of regularities to be identified'. In other words, it raises the question of whose perspective, ontology and assumptions get to dominate, an obviously political matter when it comes to generating representations of and within social systems. Even natural scientists cannot escape interpretive issues: the challenge of selecting an appropriate scale of observation opens the door for competing appreciations that differ in terms of coarseness of grain and therefore, given emergent phenomena, ontology.

Natural scientists commonly sidestep issues of interpretation by introducing the notion of intersubjective validity to replace objectivity; wherever subjectivity and interpretation are unavoidable, they simply assume intersubjective agreement and get on with the task of building formal models. Such a maneouvre is perhaps acceptable in disciplines where (1) the difficulty of reaching intersubjective agreement pales in comparison to that of representing and making predictions about a given system, and (2) the achievement of intersubjective agreement is conceived of as an apolitical act. However, the situation is different for social systems where, in addition to its overtly political nature, reaching intersubjective agreement is often where the most difficulty – and, dare we say, complexity – resides.

Thus, in addition to difficulties in compressing data from and thus *representing* a system (i.e. crude or effective complexity) and then subsequently *generating predictions* about the system (i.e. computational complexity), the difficulty associated with *achieving intersubjective agreement on fundamentally interpretive issues* prior to these activities points to yet another way of defining complexity – one associated with ambiguities, diverse views and competing appreciations. Such 'interpretive complexity' (Lopez-Garay and Contreras 2003) is also suggested by natural scientists. For example, Casti (1994: 276, 269, emphasis in original) argues that 'the complexity of the system N *as seen by the observer* is directly proportional to the number of such [inequivalent] descriptions', and advocates defining complexity as 'a joint property of the system *and* its interaction with another system, most often an observer and/or controller'. In other words, complexity comes into existence as particular representational frames are brought to bear on specific phenomena, a conclusion that recalls postmodernists' dissolution of the ontology-epistemology distinction.

As we will see, different groups of organizational scholars emphasize different aspects and definitions of complexity.

Complexity Science and Organization Studies

Complexity and Systems Approaches in Early Organization Studies

Neither complexity nor systems approaches are new in organization theory. Formal theorizing about complex systems from the emerging trans-disciplinary science of complexity can be related to an important heritage within the organizational literature.

Historically, complexity was used as a structural variable to characterize organizations and their environments (Hall et al. 1967; Anderson 1999), and figured prominently in the development of structural contingency theory (Carley 2002a). Researchers typically addressed relational complexity (i.e. complexity as a structural property of a real-world system) and viewed it, implicitly, as an objective feature, yet sometimes confounded this with more subjective notions of cognitive complexity (i.e. complexity as a property of a representation or of a prediction of a real-world system), ignoring emergent complexity or emergent simplicity as possibilities. For instance, Simon's (1962) groundbreaking work on the 'architecture of complexity' is a classic work even among complexity scientists, and he characterizes a complex system as one with many parts interacting richly and interdependently so as to make knowledge and predictions of system-level behaviour difficult to derive from knowledge about the behaviour of parts, thus introducing an observer into his definition (Moldoveanu 2005). Thompson's (1967) open systems view of organizations, although focusing more attention on complex systems' interdependence with their environments, addresses complexity in a similar manner.

Structural measures of complexity commonly build upon these approaches: 'in many empirical studies, the complexity of the organization is measured in terms of perceived coupling among subgroups, tasks or procedures, the length of the process needed to go through to make a decision, or the number of people, resources or constraints involved' (Carley 2002a: 212). For example, looking internally, Daft (1992) views organizational complexity as proportional to the number of organizational subsystems and recommends measuring it using three dimensions: vertical, capturing the number of hierarchical levels; horizontal, capturing the number of units; and geographic, capturing the number of distinct sites. Similarly, looking externally, Scott (2002) recommends measuring environmental complexity by the number of different entities to which an organization must pay attention.

Systems approaches also have a long history in organization studies. Historically, it was common to conceptualize organizations in their environments as systems, and organizational theorists today still view organizations as 'rational, natural and open systems' (Scott 2002). Indeed, some claim that systems theorists dominated organizational analysis from the 1930s until the 1970s when they began to lose their grip on the field (Reed 1985).

Functionalism, the dominant paradigm (Burrell and Morgan 1979) and approach to theory-building in organization studies (Gioia and Pitre 1990), is premised upon implicit systems principles, taking as given the existence of social systems with functional needs met through appropriate organizing (Parsons 1961). In terms of early theorizing of organizations, Barnard (1938) not only referred to organizations as co-operative systems, but made implicit reference to the notion of emergence when he argued that, as a result of co-operation and co-ordination of behaviour, something qualitatively new is created. Subsequent research based on systems thinking includes von Bertalanffy's (1950; 1968), Boulding's (1956) and Miller's (1978) elaborations of general systems theory; Simon's (1962) work on information-processing and decision-making in complex organizations; Ashby's (1956) articulation of his 'Law of Requisite Variety'; open systems theory of Katz and Kahn (1966); and Thompson's (1967) argument that the more significant drama of administrative action arises because of anomalies occurring when managers attempt to govern natural system dynamics by 'norms of rationality'. Forrester's (1971) exploration of the counterintuitive behaviour of social systems, along with the entire systems dynamics movement, also made a significant contribution to 'hard' systems thinking.

In contrast and more recent is 'soft' systems thinking. Checkland (1994), a key advocate, finds early evidence of the nascent divide between 'hard' informational and softer interpretivist views in Silverman's (1970) review of organization theory. There, Silverman distinguishes between the orthodox systems view of organizations and the increasingly popular 'action frame of reference' – organization theories in which the analytical focus is centred on organizational members' actions and, in particular, on the meanings attributed to these that are both causes and consequences of actions. Building upon and extending Vickers' (1965) notion of an appreciative system, Checkland's (1981) presentation of soft systems thinking and methodologies exemplifies the interpretivist systems perspective: actors' interpretations of their problem situations, *in situ*, are an important – indeed, integral – part of the system under study and thus the focus of research.

Daft and Weick's (1984: 284) characterization of organizations as 'interpretation systems' is a good example of how the two views can generate insights from juxtaposition if not reconciliation; beginning with the hard systems premise 'that organizations are open systems that process information from the environment', they introduce the soft systems ideas that the environment may not be analysable (which suggests crude, effective and computational complexity) and that it may be intruded upon, shaped and ultimately enacted (which suggests interpretive complexity). In other words, researchers who adopt systems thinking have moved towards the conclusion that systems and their interpretations – including those of researchers – interpenetrate each other.

The foregoing helps put our tracing of the movement of formal complexity science into organization studies in context. There is little doubt the popularization of 'new sciences' (Wheatley 1992) influenced the timing and pace of adoption of chaos and complexity science concepts into organization studies. Indeed, the appearance of books accessible to a wide audience – Jantsch's (1980) depiction of the 'self-organizing universe'; Prigogine and Stenger's (1984) introduction of 'order out of chaos' and dissipative structures; Gleick's (1987) description of deterministic chaos; Lewin's (1992) presentation of complexity 'at the edge of chaos', and Waldrop's (1992) story of how complexity science emerged – more or less parallels the movement of key ideas into the organizational literature. Our review found a similarly sequenced pattern of interest in different topics: first came self-organization, dissipative structures and order out of stochastic chaos; next appeared deterministic chaos; and then, more recently, complexity science.

One of the earliest organizational applications of a framework now associated with complexity science is Gemmill and Smith's (1985) dissipative structure model of organizational transformation. Similarly, Goldstein (1988) elaborated a far-from-equilibrium approach for understanding resistance to change. A key assumption of this early work was that organizations could usefully be viewed and studied systematically as processes that were far from, rather than at, equilibrium. This view is also one of Morgan's (1986) celebrated '*Images of Organization*'.

Associated with orderly dissipative structures was the disorderly chaos out of which they emerged, leading organizational researchers to posit a positive role for chaos in its vernacular sense of disorder (i.e. stochastic chaos). For example, Quinn (1985) suggests 'controlled chaos' as a strategy for managing innovation; Weick (1987) suggests that, analogous to Ashby's (1956) *Law of Requisite Variety*, organizations may need to match their environment's chaotic nature and become adaptive through 'chaotic acts' rather than 'orderly idleness'; Peters (1987) argues that organizations should be 'thriving on chaos'; and Nonaka (1988a: 72) maintains that 'the self-renewal strategy of an organization lies in its ability to manage the continuous dissolution and creation of organizational order'. Key insights from this work include the constructive role of disorder and even crisis in organizations, as well as the merits of management relinquishing and distributing control to a more autonomous workforce. Interestingly, this early work tends to adopt an interpretive rather than information-processing approach, emphasizing the critical role played by meaning, interpretation and sense making in organizations. For example, Nonaka (1988b) explicitly advocates a view of organizations and their members as sense-making and meaning-making actors – 'information creators' – rather than simply as information processors.

Early pioneers explicitly translating 'new sciences' for an organizational audience include Allen (1976), Stacey (1992), Wheatley (1992), Goldstein (1994) and Merry (1995), among others. In addition to decrying the historical managerial emphasis on equilibrium and certainty, these early works also reinforce ideas from the empowerment movement – that managers' obsession with tight, top-down control is misplaced and in the long-term dysfunctional to their organizations. For example, Stacey (1992; 1993) turns on its head conventional wisdom that managers should establish and maintain organizational stability and harmony, by pointing out how successful organizations embraced instability and benefited from tension and conflict. He proposed that strategy be seen as 'order emerging from chaos' (Stacey 1993). Wheatley (1992) popularizes three so-called 'new sciences' – quantum physics, self-organizing systems and chaos theory – for a wide audience arguing that they provide insights into leadership. Goldstein (1994) demonstrates that only through self-organization can enduring change occur, counselling managers to allow and even to amplify unpredicted deviations rather than seeking to abolish or control them. Similarly, Merry (1995) advises 'coping with uncertainty' and embracing its transformational possibilities rather than seeking to eliminate it.

Following this came a veritable flood of books aimed at managers, many of which are reviewed in a special issue[6] of *Emergence*, the first journal devoted to complexity science and organization studies, appearing in 1999 and reconstituted recently as *Emergence: Complexity and Organization (E:CO)*. Among books highly recommended therein are Brown and Eisenhardt (1998), Zimmerman et al. (1998), Kelly and Allison (1999) and Marion (1999). The reviewers also conclude that much practitioner-targeted work is highly metaphorical and suffers from an absence of reflexivity about this quality. In the worst cases, metaphors are used but not acknowledged as such, resulting in some bizarre organizational ontologies. As a result, a common criticism of complexity science in organization studies is that it is overly metaphorical.

Accompanying this activity was the incorporation of computational approaches into organization studies – the journal *Computational and Mathematical Organization Theory (CMOT)* first appeared in 1995 and often features work applying methods associated with complex systems – as well as special issues of several management journals[7]. Each furthered the movement of complexity science into organization studies.

Complexity Science and Contemporary Organization Studies: Mapping the Field

In this section, we conceptualize and map the field emerging at the intersection of complexity science and organization studies. We develop categories for classifying work and relate these, as shown in Figure 1.5.1, to organize our discussion.

One of our aims in developing Figure 1.5.1 was to do justice to the diversity of work in the literature. As compared to earlier reviews (Carley 2002a; Eisenhardt and Bhatia 2002; Sorenson 2002), we focus more attention on philosophy-driven foundational work as well as interpretivist research. Unfortunately, space limitations preclude an extended discussion of all of the exciting lines of inquiry opened up by researchers. Our goal, rather, is to provide an overview that summarizes these, places them in context and highlights important contributions. To this end, we employ a series of summary tables to complement Figure 1.5.1.

We conducted our literature review as follows. To identify articles in management and organization journals, we extracted articles from the database

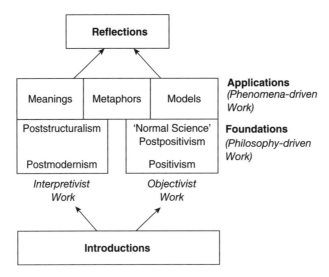

Figure 1.5.1   A map of the field of complexity science and organization studies

ABI/INFORM using keywords such as 'complexity', 'complexity science', 'complexity theory', 'self-organization' and 'chaos theory', then eliminated those from social science disciplines other than organization studies. Journals focusing on complexity (e.g. *Complexity, Interjournal*) were also searched using keywords such as 'organization' and 'management'. Articles appearing in *Emergence* were also included. In addition, we drew upon reviews by Maguire and McKelvey (1999), Contractor (1999), Levy (2000), Richardson and Cilliers (2001), Carley (2002a), Eisenhardt and Bhatia (2002) and Sorenson (2002). These sources were supplemented with suggestions from colleagues[8].

Figure 1.5.1 should be read from bottom to top. Much of the early complexity-inspired organizational literature is devoted to Introductions – articles that introduce complexity and related sciences to organizational scholars, assert their applicability and utility, and spell out implications for some field of study. Next is a body of work that distinguishes itself by its concern with exploring and establishing the Foundations of complexity science in organization studies. This comprises work that is 'Philosophy-driven' in that it addresses, directly and explicitly, issues of ontology, epistemology and methodology. Classed as Applications, on the other hand, is a body of work that is 'Phenomena-driven' in that it draws upon complexity science concepts and

formal models of complex systems to investigate and to explain specific organizational phenomena. Of note, the list of different focal phenomena to which researchers have applied complexity science is long and varied. We have placed Applications atop Foundations in Figure 1.5.1 to indicate how the latter supports the former. The final category, Reflections, includes a handful of articles and book chapters that review the field. Given the field's emerging nature, it is perhaps not surprising to see much more work classed as Introductions as compared to Reflections.

To further characterize the core of the complexity science and organization studies literature – our Foundations and Applications clusters – we find it useful to distinguish work based on the explicit or implicit epistemological stance informing it – objectivist or interpretivist[9] – thus yielding the depiction shown in Figure 1.5.1. In terms of the philosophy of science which underpins it, objectivist work tends towards positivism or those strands of post-positivism described as 'normal science' (Suppe 1977; Curd and Cover 1998; McKelvey 2002b). It adopts an information-based ontology and an epistemology premised on the existence and accessibility of objective information about a given system (or, less strongly, information that is inter-subjectively agreed upon and valid). It employs a view of organizations and their members as information-processing systems or as adaptive systems coming to grips with some objective environment about which information that could help them to adapt can be ascertained. This work also tends towards quantitative research, mathematical formalism and agent-based computational modelling. It also commonly considers representation as an apolitical act and scientific representations in particular as neutral. On the other hand, interpretivist work tends towards postmodernism or post-structuralism. It adopts a meaning-based ontology and epistemology, and is premised on the impossibility of identifying any information as objective. Rather, it views organizations and their members as interpretive, sense-making systems. More qualitative, this work is typically also more sensitive to the politics of representation as well as to the limits and provisional nature of knowledge about complex systems.

Interestingly, these two approaches mirror two recognized strategies for dealing with complexity – 'complexity reduction' and 'complexity absorption' (Boisot and Child 1999). We argue that objectivists can be usefully viewed as implementing the former and interpretivists the latter. This is because objectivists aim to 'elicit the most appropriate single representation' of the variety associated with complex organizational phenomena, while interpretivists 'can hold multiple and sometimes conflicting representations' (Boisot and Child 1999: 238). The aim of the former is convergence, while that of the latter is often explicitly divergent – 'to generate new insights, and thus contribute to expanding the possibilities for thought and action' (Tsoukas and Hatch 2001: 981).

As regards the generation of new insights, the metaphorical deployment of complexity science concepts to do so has been very popular, and Figure 1.5.1 shows that this is the case with objectivist as well as interpretivist research. Some claim that the provision of new metaphors is perhaps complexity science's most valuable contribution to organization studies (Stacey 1996), while others criticize this emphasis and call for more rigorous use of complexity science models and methods (Sorenson 2002). Others seek out middle ground; they are 'willing to deal in metaphor, recognizing the importance of metaphors – from "nexus of contracts" to "garbage can" to "iron cage" – within organization theory' and 'try to advance complexity theory by beginning to ground the metaphor in rough constructs and propositions, which can be explored with a variety of research methods including computation' (Eisenhardt and Bhatia 2002: 461). We

concur: metaphorical applications can lead to insights, contribute to sense-making and advance science (Tsoukas 1991) but, equally, can obscure and confuse. Some researchers are more reflexive and self-conscious than others when it comes to metaphors, recognizing their potentially beneficial role but also limitations, and we include this epistemologically sensitive work in our review. It stands in contrast to the large volume of metaphorical writing, depicted in Figure 1.5.1 by the unsupported middle section of Applications, which does not rest on firm philosophical foundations.

Introductions

A surprisingly large amount of the scholarly literature is devoted to introducing the 'new sciences' of complexity and chaos, drawing inferences and making claims about their implications for some area of organization studies. This portion of the literature is summarized in Table 1.5.3.

In works we have classified as Introductions, authors commonly propose a complexity or chaos view of 'X' or an introduction to complexity and its implications for 'X', where 'X' is some relevant area of organization studies. Besides complexity science's terminology, basic premises and stylized facts, several articles also introduce the mathematical and computational methods associated with formal models of complex systems (e.g. Anderson 1999). Relevant area of study ranges from very wide (e.g. all of social science) to more narrow foci (e.g. total quality management), and the list of relevant areas of study, as Table 1.5.3 shows, is quite long. The vast majority of this work is enthusiastic and optimistic about the potential offered by complexity science to organization studies; the overall message is that complexity science has something to offer almost everyone. Some writers, however, are skeptical or agnostically cautionary, underlining limitations in addition to promise (e.g. Johnson and Burton 1994, Cohen 1999).

Most works classed as Introductions are descriptive; they describe complexity or a related science and relate it to some relevant area of study, but rarely develop formal theories or models, although notable exceptions include Drazin and Sandelands (1992), Levy (1994), Stacey (1995), Thietart and Forgues (1995) and Morel and Ramanujam (1999). In addition, although real world examples are frequently invoked illustratively – to point out similarities

Table 1.5.3 Introductions of complexity science and related topics

Reference	Introduction of ...	Implications drawn for ...
Kiel (1989)	Non-equilibrium theory	Public administration
Priesmeyer and Baik (1989)	Chaos	Planning
Daneke (1990)	Advanced systems theory	Public administration
Zuijderhoudt (1990)	Chaos and self-organization	Organizational structure
Kiel (1991)	Non-linear paradigm of dissipative structures	Social sciences
Smilor and Feeser (1991)	Chaos	Entrepreneurial processes
Reed and Harvey (1992)	Complexity; new science	Realist social science
Drazin and Sandelands (1992)	Autogenesis; self-organizing systems theory	Organizing
Gregersen and Sailer (1993)	Chaos theory	Social science research
Begun (1994)	Chaos and complexity theory	Organization science
Johnson and Burton (1994)	Chaos and complexity theory	Management
Levy (1994)	Chaos theory	Strategy
Dooley et al. (1995)	Chaos and complexity	Total quality management
Smith (1995)	Chaos	Social science
Stacey (1995)	Complexity	Strategic change processes
Stumpf (1995)	New science theories	Leadership development
Thietart and Forgues (1995)	Chaos theory	Organization
Glass (1996)	Chaos; non-linear systems	Day-to-day management
Overman (1996)	Chaos and quantum theory	Administration
Wheatley and Kellner-Rogers (1996)	Chaos and complexity	Organizations
Lissack (1997b)	Chaos and complexity	Management
McDaniel (1997)	Chaos and quantum theory	Strategic leadership
Mendenhall et al. (1998)	Non-linear dynamics	International human resources management
Anderson (1999)	Complexity theory	Organization science
Cohen (1999)	Complex systems theories	Study of organization
Morel and Ramanujam (1999)	Complex systems theory	Organization theory
Mathews et al. (1999)	Complexity sciences	Social sciences
Duffy (2000)	Chaos theory	Career-plateaued worker
Arndt and Bigelow (2000)	Chaos and complexity theory	Health services management
Colbert (2004)	Complexity (with resource-based view)	Strategic human resource management

between organizational phenomena and features of other complex systems, typically, using resemblance thinking or argument by analogy – this work is by and large not empirical. In addition to introducing chaos and complexity, these works also commonly contain a set of arguments aimed at justifying the importation of terminology, theories and models from natural to social and organization science. We summarize here reasons offered for incorporating complexity science into organization studies (primarily from Gregersen and Sailer 1993; Begun 1994; Epstein and Axtell 1996; Cohen 1999; Mathews et al. 1999):

- Limited success of traditional science, as evidenced by poor analytical and statistical results, and inapplicability of findings to managerial action;

- Recognition of the iterative or recursive nature of social phenomena, rarity of linear relations and equilibria, pervasiveness of dynamical (non-linear) phenomena, changes to organizational environments that favour adaptability and increasing rates of change in organizations;

- Increased appreciation of dynamical formal models and the advantages of agent-based computational simulations and experiments;

- Focus on scientific realist methods and explanation instead of (only) traditional logical positivist reductionism and instrumental predictive measures;

- Emerging shift from force-based science rooted in physics and with assumptions of independence of units of analysis to bottom-up agent-based or rule-based science in which attention focuses on changes to the interdependent agents or to the rules governing their behaviour; and

- Growing appreciation of the need for qualitative, process and holistic types of research along with a re-awakening of the systems-theory precursors to complexity science.

Limitations of complexity science methods are also recognized (Johnston and Burton 1994; Cohen 1999):

- Difficulties in ascertaining appropriate variables, equations and agent rules pertaining to human cognitive and social behaviour;
- Modelling problems arising from interaction-based co-evolution and consequent changing variables and structural equations;
- Challenges of evaluating computational models (validation, empirical corroboration and model replication or docking problems) and making them intelligible to the wider research community;
- Definitional and measurement problems; and
- Use of insufficient time-series data, with data collection intervals determined by convenience rather than theory.

Foundations

Our Foundations cluster includes 'Philosophy-driven' works that explicitly explore issues of ontology, epistemology and methods. We distinguish work advocating an objectivist stance from that arguing for interpretivist approaches.

Philosophy-driven Objectivist Work

We begin with studies that draw heavily from modernized updates of traditional natural science epistemology. We find four sub-clusters of work focusing on: emergence as a construct; the status of complexity science as postmodern or not; complexity science as the basis for a 'new' normal and model-centred science; and the limits to knowledge about complex systems. Significant works are summarized in Table 1.5.4.

Construct of emergence. One sub-cluster of work centres on the construct of emergence and, specifically, its history within science and it implications from an epistemological perspective. Goldstein (1999) explains how emergence is an alternative to the functioning of parts for explaining behaviour of some whole, thus avoiding the perils of both reductionism and holism. The construct thus contributes to non-reductionist accounts wherein higher level properties are dependent upon, but cannot be explained totally with reference to, lower

level units (Hodgson 2000). The notion of emergence can obfuscate as much as it enlightens, however, claims Goldstein (1999; 2000) who elaborates on the metaphysical, empirical and normative issues associated with the construct. For example, debates about the ontological and epistemological status of 'emergence' parallel those about 'complexity' outlined above, and also lead quickly to the difficult issue of causality across different levels or scales of analysis. Questions of inter-level causality, upward (i.e. agents produce emergent structures) and downward (i.e. emergent structures constrain agent action), can become questions of self-causality, thus linking complex systems with the enduring philosophical puzzle of reflexivity.

Status of complexity science as postmodern or not. Whether complexity science is postmodern or not has generated another cluster of work. Byrne (1998: 7), for instance, argues that the ontological and epistemological implications of complexity 'make it essentially part of the realist programme of scientific understanding and inquiry' such that it challenges 'in the most fundamental way the postmodernist view'. Phelan (2001) and Morcol (2001) also conclude that complexity science is not postmodern. Phelan (2001) advocates an empiricist and historicist approach to defining science; he argues that the research agenda of most non-organizational complexity scientists is positivist. He thus laments that most complexity-inspired organizational research is 'pseudo-science' based on mere resemblance thinking – be it in a sophisticated form of noting qualitative similarities of computational model behaviour and real world systems, or in a less sophisticated form of 'inappropriate metaphors'. He recommends using 'complexity theory' or 'complexity studies' rather than 'complexity science' as more inclusive terms that better describe complexity-inspired organizational research, as does McKelvey (2003b). Morcol (2001) draws a similar conclusion re postmodernism, but concludes that complexity science is post-positivist after comparing the ontology, epistemology and methodology of Newtonian science with those of complexity science and of postmodernism.

Complexity science as a new normal and model-centred science. Whereas the foregoing authors tend to treat postmodernism as monolithic and irreconcilable with complexity science, other objectivists distinguish among different strands of postmodernism – skeptical and affirmative (Rosenau 1992; Kilduff and Mehra 1997) – and see connections between complexity science and the latter. McKelvey,

Table 1.5.4 Foundations I – Philosophy-driven objectivist works

Reference	Topic	Contribution
Construct of emergence		
Goldstein (1999)	Describes history of 'emergence' as a construct in science	'Emergence' is appealed to with, not instead of, appeals to functioning of parts to explain system behaviour. In organizations, self-organized hierarchical structures represent 'emergent leadership'; self-organized participative structures represent 'emergent networks'
Goldstein (2000)	Deconstructs 'emergence' to identify associated metaphysical, empirical and normative issues	'Emergence' obfuscates as much as enlightens; researchers should be aware of inherent issues and use term carefully issues and use term carefully
Hodgson (2000)	Describes history of 'emergence' as a construct in social science	'Emergence' affords non-reductionist accounts of phenomena wherein higher level properties are dependent upon, but cannot be explained totally with reference to, lower level units
Status of complexity science as post-modern or not		
Byrne (1998; 2001)	From critical realist perspective, outlines a chaos/complexity-inspired quantitative programme for sociology; criticizes reductionism and post-modernism	Computational models can play important role in describing possible futures within a complexity-based social engineering science not of absolute prediction but rather in which rational knowledge informs but does not determine social action
Phelan (2001)	Reviews different philosophies of science and places complexity science in context	Complexity science is positivist rather than post-positivist; much organizational complexity research is pseudo-science meriting a label of 'complexity studies' not 'complexity science'
Morcol (2001)	Reviews ontology, epistemology and methodology of Newtonian science, complexity science and post-modernism; critiques post-modernism	Complexity science is consistent with realist ontology and post-positivist epistemology
Complexity science as a new normal and model-centred science		
McKelvey (1997)	Develops 'quasi-natural organization science'	The epistemological and methodological foundations for a more legitimate and effective organization science are developed; such a science focuses on top-down and bottom-up emergent causal influences and emphasizes complexity and rate dynamics
McKelvey (1999d)	Develops a post-positivist Campbellian scientific realism	A modernized basis for a more legitimate organization science is developed by drawing upon the positivist legacy, realism, as well as evolutionary and semantic conception epistemologies

(Continued)

Table 1.5.4 (Continued)

Reference	Topic	Contribution
McKelvey (2002b)	Argues for a model-centred organization science	Bottom-up agent-based models are best means of developing a model-centred organization science; probabilistic truth rests jointly on analytical & onto-logical adequacy (i.e. theory ⇔ model ⇔ phenomena links)
McKelvey (2003c)	Defines complexity science as a new normal science; rejects skeptical and anti-science strands of post-modernism	The integration of normal science epistemology with post-structuralist ontological perspectives is possible; agent-based computational models figure prominently in new normal science
McKelvey (2004b)	Develops an order-creation science by building from Mainzer (1994), physics, biology and thermodynamics	A 0th law of thermodynamics addressing order creation is developed, and implications are drawn for practice: by managing *adaptive tension*, emergence of order within organizations can be influenced by managers
Limits to knowledge about complex systems		
White et al. (1997)	Describes contemporary empirical evolutionary science and relates it to complexity science; addresses question of determinism vs free will	Strategic choice vs selection can be reconciled; neither fully explains organizational success or failure
Dooley and Van de Ven (1999)	Develops typology and describes dynamics of four classes of observed dynamics in systems	Dimensionality of causal system and nature of interactions among causal factors determine observed dynamics; researchers should be observed dynamics; researchers should be sensitive to this when constructing models
Allen (2000)	Reviews limits of knowledge for different types of system	Evolution in human systems is process of continual, imperfect learning rarely resulting in complete understanding

arguing from a Campbellian realist perspective (McKelvey 1999b), advocates a 'quasi-natural' (McKelvey 1997) and 'model-centred' organization science (McKelvey 1999b; 2002b). His 'programme' aims to make the study of organizations an 'effective' science; he points out that such sciences gain legitimacy by developing and adhering to their justification logic for claiming 'truth'; offering practical value to user constituencies; and viewing phenomena as dynamic rather than static (McKelvey 2003b). He rejects skeptical postmodernism as radically relativist, ontologically nihilist and anti-science, but accepts affirmative postmodernism, drawing principally on Cilliers' (1998) presentation of post-structuralism (Derrida 1978; Baudrillard 1983a; Lyotard 1984) as the 'responsible core' of postmodernism. They offer, in his view, an accurate view of organizational ontology. McKelvey also emphasizes four 'normal science' post-positivisms in current philosophy of science – the legacy of positivism; scientific realism; selectionist evolutionary epistemology; and the Semantic Conception of theory – to define a new epistemology consistent with complexity science and agent-based modelling. By integrating the two, his 'model-centred organization science' creates a justification logic legitimated by 'new' normal science yet is based on postmodernists' ontological perspectives. McKelvey thus provides epistemological and methodological foundations for a realist, predictive and generalizable science of organizations based on idealized models emphasizing rate dynamics and focusing on background laws rather than contingent details.

Limits to knowledge about complex systems. In addition to debates over the nature of knowledge about complex systems, complexity science has also prompted consideration of the limits of knowledge. For example, Allen (2000; 2001) reminds us that all knowledge is a reduction of reality of some kind, and shows systematically how assumptions associated with 'complexity reduction' strategies necessarily concern: (1) system boundaries, in terms of excluding what is less relevant; (2) reduction of full heterogeneity to a typology of constituent elements; (3) individual elements of an average type; and (4) processes that run at their average rate. If all four assumptions can be made, then deterministic differential equations may be used to model the system; with the first three assumptions, stochastic differential equations may be used. However, to capture adaptive evolutionary change, only the first two

assumptions are justified. He highlights limits to knowledge for different classes of systems, arguing that evolution in human systems is a continual, imperfect learning process driven by differences between expectations and experience that rarely provides complete understanding. Ignorance is thus, in some important sense, the consequence *and* cause of complexity, the outcome but also motor of evolution in complex systems (Allen 1993a, b).

Philosophy-driven Interpretivist Work

Within the body of 'Philosophy-driven' interpretivist work, we identify sub-clusters of research addressing the status of complexity science as postmodern or not as well as the related question of limits to knowledge about complex systems; action theory and phenomenal complexity; and the role of narrative methods in organizational complexity research. We summarize significant works in Table 1.5.5.

Status of complexity science as postmodern or not. Just as McKelvey bridges towards interpretivists from an objectivist position, Cilliers' (1998; 2000b, c; 2002) view of complexity and postmodernism is anchored firmly in post-structuralism, yet engages with objectivist understandings of complex systems. Explicitly dissociating himself from 'those postmodern approaches that may be interpreted as relativistic', Cilliers' (1998: 21) work affords conceptual linkages of 'new normal' complexity science with a post-structuralist view of social ontology as connectionist, localized and emergent (McKelvey 2003c). With the aim of reconciling, rather than casting as dual or mutually exclusive, scientific and narrative knowledge, Cilliers (1998) introduces complexity science and demonstrates how it can be related to post-structuralism. Emphasizing relationality and connectionism, he links post-structuralist views of language to the workings of complex systems as they adapt to their environments, arguing that post-structuralist theories of representation – i.e. distributed and relational – are relevant to complexity science and, in particular, modelling. This theme is also addressed in Cilliers' (2000b) discussion of how complex systems are constituted, in which he contrasts rule-based and relationship-based descriptions and argues that, while complicated things can be assembled and described by rules, complex things are constituted by relationships. Because generating a description of a complex system implies a selection of constitutive rules rather than relationships,

Table 1.5.5 Foundations II – Philosophy-driven interpretivist works

Reference	Topic	Contribution
Status of complexity science as post-modern or not, and limits to knowledge about complex systems		
Cilliers (1998)	Relates complexity science to post-structuralism to reconcile, rather than cast as dual or mutually exclusive, scientific and narrative knowledge	Even hard science must face the impossibility of objectivity; no single, exclusive description can capture what is relevant about complex systems; post-structuralist theories of representation are relevant to modelling
Cilliers (2000a)	Summarizes what can be learned from complexity science as well as what cannot; highlights nature and limits of knowledge about complex systems	Calculation and computation are useful but never sufficient in understanding complex systems; the need to reflect critically on nature and limits of knowledge is indispensable to the study of complexity
Cilliers (2000b)	Contrasts rule-based and relationship-based descriptions; argues that while complicated things can be assembled and described by rules, complex things consist of relationships	The constitutive framework of a complex system is not naturally determinable; descriptions of complex systems imply a *selection* of constitutive rules; rule-based models will not provide general and accurate descriptions of complex systems
Richardson et al. (2001)	Develops the notion of complexity thinking as epistemology; complexity-based epistemology implies reflexivity and multiple perspectives	Complexity science highlights impossibility of supporting claims with appeals to objectivity and thus inevitability of ethical concerns as systems are determined by our choices which cannot be backed up scientifically
Cilliers (2002)	Explores ontological-epistemological distinctions and argues that they cannot be maintained	Knowledge of complex systems is unavoidably limited, incomplete
Action theory and phenomenal complexity		
Juarrero (1999; 2000)	Employs complexity as a theory-constitutive metaphor for rethinking causality appropriate to history- and context-bound processes, and thus human action	Meaningful intentions constraining behaviour are emergent phenomena; hermeneutics and interpretive narrative models of explanation are appropriate for human action; a renewed emphasis on Aristotle's multiple causes rather than solely *efficient* cause is required
Letiche (2000a)	Drawing on Bergson (1912), introduces and argues for 'phenomenal complexity theory' which seeks to include the experiencing subject in its epistemology	Understanding complex systems requires acceptance of multiple valid perspectives and an appreciation of 'phenomenal truth' emerging from a process of *différence* as perspectives imply, support, criticize, complement and deny one another
Letiche (2000b)	Rejects ontological approaches to complexity and emergence as prior to lived awareness; argues for an ontic approach where these are time and space bound	Self-organization, understood as actors making things happen, requires a re-complexified neo-Aristotelian concept of causation rather than an emphasis on *efficient* cause; this in turn implies an acceptance of multiple perspectives
Letiche and Boje (2001)	Argues that any social science basing itself on one basic truth or a single theoretical ground becomes unable to deal with unavoidable fundamental dialogical relationships	Phenomenal complexity theory entails making three choices: prioritizing experience and consciousness; choosing dialogic complexity rather than dualistic cause and effect; being willing to link the experiential to the complex
Narrative methods		
Tsoukas and Hatch (2001)	Argues that narrative epistemology and methods are appropriate for complex systems	Complexity arises from how knowledge is organized (i.e. second order complexity) as well as pre-existing relations (first order complexity); narrative mode of thinking complements logico-scientific one, dealing effectively with contextuality, reflexivity, purpose and temporality
Luhman and Boje (2001)	Argues that organizational discourse is a complex system and relates complexity science to organization studies	A complexity science of organizations involves understanding contextualized, emergent discourse as individual members interpret and negotiate within a spatial/temporal intersection

he argues, rule-based models will never provide general and accurate descriptions of complex systems; the constitutive framework of a complex system is, in his view, not naturally determinable.

Limits to knowledge about complex systems. Cilliers' work, like Allen's (2000; 2001), also displays a sensitivity to the limits of knowledge. His view is that, because no theory of complexity or complex systems can ignore contingency, no single description can capture all that is relevant about complex systems. Knowledge about a complex system is thus inevitably and unavoidably incomplete, and we ignore or downplay this epistemological reality to our peril. The epistemological challenges of complexity lead, in particular, to ethical challenges that even the harder sciences cannot escape. Indeed, coming to grips with the impossibility of a single objectivity means foregrounding and wrestling with the ethical and political implications of representation, scientific or other (Cilliers 1998; 2000a). He reminds us that ongoing critical reflection on the nature and limits of knowledge is indispensable to the study of complexity. Richardson et al. (2001) explore this link between epistemological and ethical issues by developing the notion of complexity thinking – a middle ground between soft complexity metaphors and hard computational models (Richardson and Cilliers 2001) – as epistemology. They argue that an epistemology based upon and appropriate to complexity implies (1) *reflexivity* (i.e. a 'weak' *intra*-perspective exploration of alternative representations), and (2) *multiple perspectives* (i.e. a 'strong' *inter*-perspective exploration of alternative representations). By acknowledging limits of, and alternatives to, a particular representation, researchers are more likely to be sensitive to the ethical and political consequences of privileging it.

Action theory and phenomenal complexity. Another sub-cluster of interpretivist philosophy-driven research has emerged around an action perspective to organizational knowledge and the exploration of phenomenal complexity. Letiche (2000a, b) and Letiche and Boje (2001) develop 'phenomenal complexity theory' which, in the tradition of Bergson (1912), includes the experiencing subject in its epistemology and aims to avoid being one-sidedly rationalist or subjectivist. Like Cilliers, these authors claim that complexity cannot be approached solely from the objectivist position if it is to be understood in a meaningful way. They argue that any social science that tries to base itself on the assumption of one basic truth or a single theoretical

ground is unable to deal with the dialogical relationships between: researchers and research subjects; the subjective and objective; the world and consciousness. Rather, phenomenal complexity theory entails making three choices: prioritizing experience and consciousness above outcomes of the 'natural bent'; choosing dialogic complexity rather than a logic of dualistic cause and effect; and linking the experiential to the complex.

Philosopher of mind, Juarrero (1999; 2000) uses complexity science to reformulate action theory, summarized as understanding the difference between a wink and a blink. Like other scholars working on foundational questions, she too criticizes the traditional philosophical emphasis on Aristotle's *efficient* cause only, rather than in combination with his other three causes – *final*, *formal* and *material* – and the resulting inability to deal with self-causality. She draws upon complexity science as a 'theory-constitutive metaphor' for rethinking causality and explanations appropriate to history and context bound processes, especially human action. Using information theory, she links intentions and actions; meaningful intentions, that purposively constrain subsequent behaviour, are emergent she argues. To explain and understand intentional action, she argues, hermeneutics and interpretive narrative models of explanation are most appropriate. In essence, Juarrero distinguishes between knowledge developed from the perspective of participants in a complex system and knowledge developed from a God's eye view; objectivists tend towards the latter and interpretivists the former (Hendrickx 1999).

Like Juarrero, Letiche (2000b) argues that complexity science can be used to develop an action theory, and he too believes researchers need to re-complexify their concept of causation away from an obsession with Aristotle's *efficient* cause and towards self-organization. However, he disagrees with Juarrero's ontological approach and her emphasis on causal analysis in favour of an ontic approach where emergence is not prior to lived experience but, rather, is a process of becoming that is time and space bound. He argues that emergence has to be understood as a form of action theory – as occurrence, event and process – and in terms of lived, not scientific, time. Foregrounding agency – multiple agencies, in fact – he argues that self-organization, understood as actors making things happen, requires a recomplexified neo-Aristotelian concept of causation and that this, in turn, implies an acceptance of multiple, valid perspectives.

Letiche (2000a) advocates ethnographic studies that use the phenomenon and concept of emergence to focus attention on change, experience and consciousness in order to illuminate the experiential, narrative and story-telling aspects of organizing.

Narrative methods. The final sub-cluster concerns methods and therein authors make the case for narrative approaches to complexity (Luhman and Boje 2001; Tsoukas and Hatch 2001). Tsoukas and Hatch (2001) draw upon complexity science, and specifically the ontological-epistemological debates surrounding notions and measures of complexity, to argue that complexity, besides being a feature of the systems that organizational scholars study (i.e. 'first-order' complexity in their terms or 'relational' complexity from above), also arises from the way in which scholars organize their thinking (i.e. 'second-order' or 'cognitive' complexity). Their second-order complexity construct comprises *both* information-processing (i.e. difficulty of representing and predicting) *and* interpretive (i.e. difficulty of reaching intersubjective agreement) considerations: 'entering the domain of second-order complexity – the domain of the thinker thinking about complexity – raises issues of interpretation (and ... narration) that have heretofore been ignored by complexity theorists' (Tsoukas and Hatch 2001: 980). Narrative approaches can thus compensate for limitations of traditional hard science research and be used to generate new insights into complexity that address, in particular, contextuality, reflexivity, purpose and temporality.

Applications

Our Applications cluster includes 'Phenomena-driven' work that applies complexity science constructs and methods to investigate, explain and generate usable knowledge of particular organizational phenomena. As with the Foundations upon which this work builds, we distinguish work advocating an objectivist stance from that arguing for interpretivist approaches. As we show, organizational complexity scholars have applied complexity science to a wide range of phenomena of interest to strategists and managers.

Phenomena-driven Objectivist Work

Applications of complexity science to questions of interest to management theorists and practitioners – and done from an objectivist epistemological position – comprise the most voluminous category of research in our typology. In fact, other reviews of organizational complexity science (e.g. Baum 2002) focus almost exclusively on this type of work. One of the hallmarks of the North American School is the use of ABMs to simulate phenomena, which Casti (1997) claims will ultimately be an important part of SFI's legacy. Continuing the positivist normal science tradition of building models and conducting experiments – what McKelvey (2002b) calls model-centred science – complexity researchers use ABMs to simulate real-world behaviour and, then, having baseline simulations, carry out computational experiments. The many ABMs used to study organizational phenomena classify into two primary categories: those using Kauffman's *NK* model and others. A significant amount of qualitative research complements this computational work.

Kauffman's Fitness Landscape Models. Originating in theoretical biology, fitness landscape models have been enthusiastically adopted by organizational scholars. One reason is that the notion of organizational fitness is well accepted (Hannan and Freeman 1977). Significant organizational works using the fitness landscape framework are summarized in Table 1.5.6.

Within biology, a formalized notion of fitness landscapes over a space of discrete objects has long been used (see Wright 1931). Biologists frequently characterize adaptive evolution as the search of a combinatorial space of all possible genotypes for points that map to higher fitness, and use mathematical and computational models of combinatorial optimization to simulate evolutionary processes, the most celebrated of which is Kauffman's (1993) *NK* model.[10] Genotypes are modelled as strings of genes, with each gene able to take on one of a finite number of states: if there are N genes or parts for each of which there are A possible states, this gives rise to a space of A^N possible genotypes or wholes, each of which will be associated with a particular fitness. Kauffman uses a cellular automata (CA)[11] model with $A = 2$ to facilitate binary representation; he assigns fitness values randomly to different genotypes to generate a random fitness function. When combined with the notion of neighbouring points, the fitness function becomes a fitness landscape. K represents the number of interdependencies among parts (i.e. whether and how much a particular gene in a specific state contributes to fitness depends on the state of other genes). Random fitness landscapes vary in their ruggedness, and this is reflected in the number of peaks present (a peak

Table 1.5.6   Applications I – Phenomena-driven objectivist works: Fitness landscape models

Reference	Topic and key concepts	Contribution
Kauffman (1993; 1995a, b)	Tunable fitness landscapes, complexity catastrophe, increasing network complexity	Complexity triggers self-organization (order for free); catastrophe effect; life emerges as a phase transition
Kauffman and Macready (1995)	Adaptive evolution, fitness peaks, fitness landscapes	For a firm seeking technological improvements, early search can give rise to dramatic improvements via significant alterations found far away; later search closer to home yields finer and finer focus on details
Levinthal (1997a, b)	Strategy as design, selection pressure, internal interdependence among organization routines	Interdependence affects diversity and survival; a high level of interdependence yields many successful strategies while the lack of synergies promotes the emergence of a dominant firm
Sorenson (1997; 2003)	Vertical integration, learning, complexity catastrophe	Interdependence from vertical integration limits an organization's ability to learn in stable environments, but facilitates it in volatile environments
Baum (1999)	Levels, pace of co-evolution, strategies	Faster lower level co-evolution dynamics undermine the emergence of co-ordinated higher-level strategies
Levinthal and Warglien (1999)	Landscape design, coupled landscapes	Reducing interdependencies leads to stability; interdependence leads to greater exploration at the expense of co-ordination difficulties; co-operative behaviour creates a positive, reinforcing dynamic
Maguire (1999)	Search strategies appropriate for different landscapes; configuration school of strategy	Empirically demonstrated archetypal configurations of strategy, structure and environment are explained by conceptualizing firms as evolving solutions to complex technological design problems
McKelvey (1999a, c)	Catastrophe, melting zone, co-evolution, value chain and competitive advantage	A firm's internal complexity should match the environment's complexity; co-evolving firms focusing on improving a moderate number of competencies are more likely to achieve success
Gavetti and Levinthal (2000)	Policy choices, cognitive vs experiential based logic	Cognitive representation plays an important role in experiential learning; mental models help map the landscape, although imperfectly, while experiential learning enables validation of mental maps
Rivkin (2000)	Catastrophe effect, strategic advantage, sensitivity to initial conditions	Strategy as design leads to uniqueness in case of moderate complexity by creating barriers to entry for new firms; in cases of high complexity it can preclude firms from replicating their own success

(Continued)

Table 1.5.6 *(Continued)*

Reference	Topic and key concepts	Contribution
Fleming and Sorenson (2001)	Catastrophe effect, invention as recombination over technology landscape	Inventors may face a complexity catastrophe when they attempt to combine highly interdependent technologies; the process of invention differs in important ways from biological evolution
Rivkin (2001)	Moderate complexity, strategic interdependence	Moderate complexity allows firms to replicate their advantage in new markets while still preventing rival firms to imitate; the gap between replicability and imitability is greatest at moderate complexity
Levitan et al. (2002)	NKC model; group size, external connections, performance	For tasks of short duration, larger groups having fewer external connections perform better; over longer time horizons advantage goes to smaller groups having more external connections
Rivkin and Siggelkow (2002)	Local peaks vs sticking points, delegation, interdependencies, local-global incentives	Organizations can get stuck on sticking points that are not local Nash equilibria because of delegation, interdependencies among decision makers, and local vs global incentives
Siggelkow and Levinthal (2003)	Centralization, decentralization, exploration, exploitation, performance	Modelling of three structural designs: unchanging centralization, unchanging decentralization and 'temporary decentralization with subsequent reintegration' – termed 're-integrator firms'
Rivkin and Siggelkow (2003)	Search and stability, organization design, decision processing, performance	Models interaction of managerial decision processing with interdependencies of organization design elements such as hierarchy, incentives and departmentalization
Yuan and McKelvey (2004)	Rate vs amount of group learning	Catastrophe curve is a function of rate and amount of learning; minimizes the use of graphics for presenting modelling results and instead substitutes standard statistical methods – t-tests, longitudinal regressions
Garrido (2004)	K, interaction, co-ordination, evolution	Attempts to simplify problems of co-ordination, over time, leads to agents using many different strategies
Moldoveanu and Bauer (2004)	Computational complexity, production functions	Theoretical argument linking computational complexity to production functions of firms, then relating different classes of computational problems to organizational structuration and task partitioning
Siggelkow and Levinthal (2005)	Sticking points, competency traps, structurally constrained search, structural change	Because organizational structures constrain search and are associated with different 'sticking points', structural change can be functional even in stable environments as a means to escape competency traps

is a point where all neighbours are of lower fitness; rugged landscapes have more peaks than smooth ones) as well as the relative fitness of neighbouring points (on more rugged landscapes neighbouring points can be associated with dramatically increased or decreased fitness). Increasing the ruggedness of a landscape (i.e. the parameter K) is roughly equivalent to increasing the complexity of the optimization problem facing the agents who must adapt – i.e. seek out points of higher fitness – on it. Co-evolution can be captured by adding yet another parameter, C, which represents the number of external interdependencies among parts, thus extending Kauffman's NK model to his NKC model. Thus, biologists conceptualize the challenge facing species as a problem of combinatorial optimization – of navigating the landscape in search of higher peaks by sampling points in the space, ascertaining the associated fitness, and moving – then theorize about adaptation, competition and co-evolution using computational experiments. Agents, thus, try to climb toward fitness peaks, but run the risk of getting trapped on suboptimal ones. Kauffman argues that complexity alters the landscape by lowering the height of peaks (i.e. their adaptive advantage). He calls this *tuning the landscape*. At the limit, increased complexity flattens peaks to the point where they offer meaningless adaptive advantage. This, he calls *complexity catastrophe*. If this happens, even though Darwinian selection still prevails, little advantage results. Consequently, biological order is not really due to selection but, instead, to complexity effects. Given this, he proposes a complexity-based theory of spontaneous order creation.

Recently, the fitness landscape framework has been used to explain a number of important organizational phenomena: learning curves, dominant designs and eras of ferment in technology evolution (Kauffman 1995b; Kauffman and Macready 1995); organizational adaptation (Levinthal 1997a, b; Levinthal and Warglien 1999); the likelihood of selection processes optimizing outcomes in an industry and the potential for complexity catastrophes given the interdependencies of firms' value chains (Sorenson 1997; McKelvey 1999a, c); the appropriate level of firm complexity to render imitation by others more difficult and less profitable than self-replication (Rivkin 2000); whole-part competition within organizations (Baum 1999) and the fit of different archetypal configurations of organizational structure, strategy and leadership with different industry

environments (Maguire 1999). In these models, a firm is characterized abstractly as a string of specific decisions regarding strategy or technology or routines or value chain components.

Applying the NK model to organizations and specifically to the technological design choices they make, Kauffman and Macready (1995) demonstrate the perils of error-free local search and logical incrementalism as these lead to getting trapped on poor local optima. As complexity – i.e. K or the ruggedness of the landscape – increases, the introduction of noise in fitness comparisons, representing human errors and subjectivity, is shown to help the agent reach higher fitness levels thus demonstrating the functionality of error-making (Kauffman and Macready 1995; Maguire 1999). Another parameter, search distance, is introduced to show how, as complexity increases from low to moderate levels, it becomes increasingly advantageous to search far away in the combinatorial space. This suggests the need to link landscape complexity with exploration strategies as well as differential payoffs to incremental vs radical innovation. Finally, searching far away is best done early in the process (Kaufman and Macready 1995). Maguire (1999) connects these findings to the Configuration school of strategy (Miller 1986; Mintzberg 1990), demonstrating how they provide a theoretical basis for explaining empirical findings that machine bureaucracies outperform adhocracies in stable environments and later in an industry's life cycle, as well as other archetypal patterns of strategy, structure and environment.

McKelvey uses the NKC fitness landscapes to model value chain and inter-firm interdependencies. N describes the components of the value chain of the firm, K their interdependence and C the linkages with rival's value chains. He shows how firms focusing on improving a challenging but manageable number of value chain competencies are more likely to achieve success than those working on too few or too many. Successful firms match their internal complexity with external complexity (McKelvey 1999a). Rivkin (2000; 2001) addresses the imitation and replication of strategies, demonstrating how moderate complexity in the set of strategic decisions facing firms presents firms with opportunities for finding positions with both high payoff and high inimitability. However, too much complexity, although it may yield a position that is difficult to imitate, may also result in a position that is difficult for the same firm to replicate as it grows. Arriving at a similar conclusion, Levinthal (1997a, b) and Levinthal and Warglien (1999) model the firm as a set of organizational routines to show how interdependence (i.e. more rugged landscapes) enables many successful strategies to co-exist while more simple landscapes lead to the emergence of a single dominant design. These models afford a fresh look into an old dilemma of *exploration vs exploitation* (March 1991) by relating this dilemma facing firms to the degree of interdependence of routines.

Unfortunately, few scholars have endeavoured to corroborate fitness landscape model findings against real world data (Sorenson 2002). An exception is Sorenson (1997; 2003), who uses data from the American computer workstation industry. Vertical integration serves as a proxy for the degree of interdependence while environmental volatility is studied by looking at technological volatility (diversity of standards) and market volatility (changing consumer preferences). Using these data, he corroborates findings from *NK* model experiments that non-integrated firms outperform integrated ones in stable environments, while the contrary becomes true for unstable environments. In yet another empirical corroboration, Fleming and Sorenson (2001) use patent data to show that patents recombining highly interdependent components receive fewer citations. This type of empirical corroboration goes a long way in establishing fitness landscape models as a valid approach to conducting organizational science based on model-centred epistemology (McKelvey 2002b).

Other Agent-based Models. ABM[12] usage dates back at least to Cohen et al. (1972), with renewed interest in the early 1990s (see Carley 1991; March 1991). Such models seek to model aspects of complex systems by simulating self-organization, order creation and emergence of structures or cultures. These variables and processes are often related to a measure of performance or fitness such that, over time, learning and adaptation can also be simulated. Lichtenstein and McKelvey (2004) document over 300 ABMs relevant to organization studies. We highlight some here and summarize a broader set in Table 1.5.7. Our groupings have considerable overlap, as one might expect given the variables studied.

Decision-making and learning. Using a CA, Cohen et al. (1972) model organized anarchies such as universities with their 'garbage can model', one of the organizational literature's most famous explanations of decision-making. They view agents as providing solutions and searching for problems to which to apply these solutions. Their simulation provides a means for understanding how organizational problems are solved in an organization plagued with goal ambiguity and conflict. March (1991) uses a simple CA model that features learning and socialization of agents who hold beliefs that are modified by an organization's norms, which in turn adapts its norms to the group's beliefs. The simulation shows a distinct advantage to retaining a mix of fast and slow learners to balance the trade-offs from exploration vs exploitation dynamics. Learning processes are shown to reduce the variability of performance rather than increase it. Bruderer and Singh (1996) use a genetic algorithm (GA)[13] to model organization creation, learning and death. The model is built around three organizational processes of variation, adaptation and selection of routines. They demonstrate how environmental selection influences adaptation, which in turn influences the selection process. The results confirm empirical findings that organizational evolution happens along three distinct phases: (1) experimentation which characterizes new organizations; (2) revolution from which a dominant design emerges; and (3) incremental improvement.

Group formation and stability. Carley (1991) examines the structural and cultural bases of group stability. She uses a model that features three main processes: action, adaptation and motivation. Action describes the agents' interaction and information exchange, adaptation accounts for the individual learning, while motivation guides the choices of with whom agents prefer to interact. Her model articulates how groups that are the most stable in the short-run may not have the greatest reconstructive capabilities in the long-run. Indeed, groups with less complex structures are more reconstructive in the long run. Epstein and Axtell (1996) use a CA model to study emergent economy, culture and structure. They show how collective behaviours such as group formation, cultural transmission, combat and trade emerge from the interaction of individual agents. Carley and Hill (2001) use the CONSTRUCT-O model to study the rapid formation of subgroups and the emergence of culture. The model shows how structural learning and experiential learning affect the stability of the organization.

Restructuring and adaptation. Carley and Svoboda (1996) use a hierarchical model, ORGAHEAD,

Table 1.5.7 Applications II – Phenomena-driven objectivist works: Other agent-based models

Reference	Model type: Topic and key concepts	Contribution
Cohen et al. (1972)	CA: Organizational decision making; problems vs solutions	Garbage-can model: problems require attention and solutions have a life of their own, carried by organizational members who look for decision opportunities and come and go as decision participants. Stands in contrast to rational and bounded rational models of decision-making
March (1991)	CA: Organizational learning; exploration vs exploitation	There is an advantage to having a mix of fast and slow learners in an organization; learning processes reduce the variability of performance rather than increase it
Carley (1991)	Construct: Group dynamics; group stability; culture and information	Groups that are the most stable in the short-run may not have the greatest reconstructive capabilities in the long-run
Carley and Svoboda (1996)	Orgahead: Organizational restructuring, learning and adaptation; simulated annealing	Individual learning is superior to organizational learning. Simple agent rules about organization restructuring lead to a wide range of emergent organizational structures that improve organization-level problem-solving. Organizations can locate designs associated with high performance regardless of agents' intelligence; however, emergent designs depend on agent and organizational task performance
Epstein and Axtell (1996)	CA: 'Bottom-up' social science; emergent structures of economic, political and cultural activity	Collective behaviours such as group formation, cultural transmission, combat and trade emerge from the interaction of individual agents
Bruderer and Singh (1996)	GA: Organization creation, learning, death; adaptation and selection	Environmental selection influences adaptation and adaptation, in turn, influences the selection process in a Darwinian model of evolution
Crowston (1996)	GA: Organizational evolution and novel forms; fitness	GA model finds organizational forms optimal for intermediate conditions where theory makes conflicting predictions; GAs can identify factors contributing to the performance of an organizational form
Paul et al. (1996)	GA: Organizational learning and adaptability; resource allocation	The ability of a GA model to learn has more impact on model performance than the initial endowments and/or configurations of active agents
Carley and Lee (1998)	Orgahead: Organizational adaptation; meta-learning	Meta-learning involves not just acquiring the appropriate attributes but also developing the right change strategies; organizations need to learn strategies for when and how to change and when to take risks
Carley (1999)	Orgahead: Individual and organizational learning	Organization and population level performance improvements, mis-learning and shakeouts emerge from the on-going processes of change at the individual level. Links micro- and macro-level organizational phenomena
Carley and Hill (2001)	Construct-O: Structural change and learning	Interactions between structural change and learning and experiential learning affect the stability of an organization at the structural and cultural level
Cartier (2004)	GA: Darwinian vs Lamarckian evolution	Darwinian and Lamarckian evolution are not contradictory; using environmental complexity as a variable, emergence of dominant innovations is modelled; results compared with data from automobile firms

which features interacting agents led by an executive team that develops firm-level strategies. It examines restructuring, learning and adaptation. The simulation shows that, under certain conditions, individual adaptation is superior to structural learning. Using the same model, Carley and Lee (1998) show that meta-learning involves not only acquiring appropriate attributes but also developing appropriate strategies for changing these; organizations need to learn when and how to change along with when to take risks. The model links micro- and macro-level organizational phenomena by showing how performance improvements, mis-learning and shakeouts emerge from on-going processes of change at the individual level (Carley 1999). Paul et al. (1996) use a GA to model organizational adaptation and resource allocation. They conclude that the ability to adapt has more impact on performance than the initial configuration of active agents. Crowston (1996) also uses a GA to study organizational structure. In his model, agents may co-ordinate tasks to expedite their completion, yet there is a cost to such co-ordination that reduces total time allotment to perform the task. Incorporating upward and downward causality and co-evolution effects, he shows that the model successfully identifies factors that contribute to the performance of an organizational form. So and Durfee (1996) examine the role of structure in predicting performance of a distributed information gathering task in computer network environments. The issues of organizational self-redesign by agents, span of control and asynchronous communications are addressed. They conclude that the optimal span of control in an organization is dependent on the nature of the task-environment (task size and granularity) and a performance measure (response time).

Qualitative Research. Not all work using formal models of complex systems draws on or develops computational or mathematical models. Much objectivist work is, in fact, qualitative and aimed at building theory to serve as a basis for subsequent hypothesis testing or computational modelling. Eisenhardt (1989) and Yin (2003) argue that qualitative, case-style research may be designed and conducted so as to yield *objective* depictions from thick descriptions (Geertz 1973) of real-world organizational phenomena. Our analysis reveals several sub-clusters of objectivist qualitative work addressing organizations: as systems at the edge of chaos; as dissipative or self-organizing systems; as parts of an

ecosystem undergoing cycles of change; and as adaptive systems in an institutional information space (I-space). Objectivist qualitative research is summarized in Table 1.5.8.

Edge of chaos. Brown and Eisenhardt (1997; 1998) link empirical organizational phenomena with formal models of complex systems using the notion of the 'edge of chaos'. They use ideas about how complex systems adapt – and specifically, ideas about which structural and processual features of a complex system make it most adaptive – to address the question of how firms engage in continuous innovation and change, especially in high-velocity industries. Building theory from case studies of six firms in the computer industry, Brown and Eisenhardt (1997) identify three properties of firms enjoying success at multi-product innovation and change: (1) semi-structures that combine limited structure with extensive interaction and thus balance order and disorder; (2) links in time that focus attention on different time scales, such as experimental products, reports of futurists and strategic alliances and thus balance planning and a completely reactive stance; and (3) sequenced steps that choreograph transition processes from old to new projects in a predictable, time-paced manner. In other words, successful firms combine improvization in the present with probes into the future, carefully and systematically managing evolution from the former to the latter. In other work, the authors elucidate the related notions of time pacing and patching (Eisenhardt and Brown 1998; 1999). Pascale (1999: 91) picks up on the theme of tuning the degree of structure and stress to which the firm is subjected when reporting on 'design for emergence' experiments at Royal Dutch Shell: 'two determinants – (1) a precise tension between amplifying and damping feedback, and (2) [unique to humans] … the application of mindfulness and intention – are akin to rudder and sail when surfing near the edge of chaos' (see also Pascale et al. 1999).

Dissipative structures and self-organization. The idea that groups spontaneously self-organize in a manner analogous to Prigogine's dissipative structures has a relatively long history. Gemmill and Smith (1985) introduce Prigogine's far-from-equilibrium thermodynamic arguments and draw parallels with the sense-making work of Weick (1969; 1977) as well as with the organizational learning literature (Argyris and Schön 1978; Argyris 1982). Leifer (1989)

Table 1.5.8 Applications III – Phenomena-driven objectivist work: Qualitative studies

Reference	Topic	Contribution
Edge of chaos		
Dubinskas (1994)	Turbulence in organizations; chaos theory vs bio-evolutionary models	Homeostatic equilibria are far rarer than punctuated equilibria in organizations; internal and external forces cause turbulence, but self-organization processes enable projects to be completed successfully
Brown and Eisenhardt (1997; 1998)	Innovation in computer industry, with organizations cast as complex systems	Successful firms have: (1) *Semistructures* operating at the edge of chaos; (2) *links in time* such as experimental products, futurist and strategic alliances; (3) *sequenced steps* with time-paced transition processes
Eisenhardt and Brown (1998; 1999)	Strategies for competing in fast-paced, unpredictable environments; time-pacing; patching	In fast-paced, unpredictable environments, successful firms (1) systematically 'time-pace' the creation of new products or services, launching of new businesses or entering of new markets; and (2) continually remap business units via splitting, recombining, etc. to focus on opportunities and to re-size while balancing agility and efficiency
Pascale (1999)	Implications for strategy of viewing organizations as complex systems	Equilibrium means death for organizations; firms are better viewed as self-organizing systems far-from-equilibrium and drawn towards the edge of chaos; as such, firms can be influenced but not directed or completely controlled
Dissipative structures and self-organization		
Gemmill and Smith (1985)	Far-from-equilibrium theory of organizational transformation	Change via emergence of dissipative structure stems from four elements: disequilibrium; symmetry breaking of relationships and patterns; experimentation; and reformulation around one of many possible new configurations
Goldstein (1988)	Theory of organizational change with resistance conceived as autopoiesis	Conceives of resistance to change as autopoiesis; combines difference questioning from family therapy with far-from-equilibrium systems models to suggest strategies for working with, not against, resistance
Leifer (1989)	Far-from equilibrium theory of organizational transformation	New order is created via non-equilibrium conditions; model focuses on: points of singularity; transformation utilizing radical strategies; inefficient acting and experimentation; and re-synthesis (emergent macro order)
Smith and Gemmill (1991)	Dynamics of groups under near chaos conditions	Group effectiveness in complex, turbulent environments requires self-organization, tolerance for error and deviation, breaking of existing relationships, creative processes of boundary reparation and movement to new configurations
Svyantek and DeShon (1993)	Attractors as buffers to fundamental change in systems	A chaos theory about why cultural efforts often fail; attractor is a two-part system – an adaptive part where the organization seeks to continue by competing economically; and a conformational part maintaining existing culture

(Continued)

Table 1.5.8 *(Continued)*

Reference	Topic	Contribution
Romme (1995)	Self-organizing processes in top management teams	Self-organization implies: (1) research should focus on the interplay of deep and manifest levels of structure; (2) relationships between partially closed (deep) system and its environment is reversed
MacIntosh and MacLean (1999)	Emergence via *dissipative structures*; change, transformation, learning	Conditioned emergence via: (1) conditioning (articulating and reconfiguring rules of underpinning deep structure); (2) crisis (ensuring far-from-equilibrium); and (3) strategic change (managing positive and negative feedback loops)
Lichtenstein (2000a)	Self-organization; managing transitions with complexity principles	Transformation is a system-wide process that is dynamic and non-linear with the following three qualities: high self-reference, increased capacity and interdependent organizing; offers managers a new method of distributed control
Lichtenstein (2000b)	Change via self-organization in complex systems	Four assumptions explaining emergence of order in organizations are: (1) change is constant; (2) emergent systems are not reducible to their parts; (3) mutual dependence; and (4) complex systems behave in non-proportional ways
Lichtenstein (2000c)	Self-organization; reviews D. Schön's work	Second order learning is a non-linear, discontinuous process, and self-organization is an excellent framework for understanding the nature of generative knowledge
Chiles et al. (2004)	Self-organization; emergence of new organizational collectives	Organizational collectives emerge from spontaneous fluctuations initiating new order that is amplified by positive feedback and stabilized by co-ordinating mechanisms; re-combinations of resources add variety and renew social order
Resilience		
Hurst and Zimmerman (1994)	Eco-cycle theory; organizational resilience and collapse	Organizational success can reduce resilience; organizations evolve through four stages: birth, growth, creative destruction and renewal; organizational collapse need not always be viewed negatively
I-space		
Boisot and Child (1999)	Relational and cognitive complexity; network vs market capitalism	Mix of cognitive and relational complexity affects effectiveness of reduction vs absorption strategies; bureaucracies, markets, fiefs and clans are different ways of organizing transactions to cope with differently complex environments
Boisot (2000)	Relationship between environmental complexity and organizing activities	As incompressible complexity increases, firms move from bureaucratic structures to those best characterized as markets, clans and fiefdoms; differently complex environments call for different managerial approaches

also relates the dissipative structure model of organizational transformation to other paradigms of organizational change. Smith and Gemmill (1991) liken change in small groups to change in dissipative structures and draw on parallels in the organizational literature to support their argument that group effectiveness in complex and turbulent environments require 'the key elements of self-organization': an ongoing tolerance for error and deviation, the breaking of existing relationships so that new ones can emerge, a reflective self-referencing mode of thought and action, a creative process of boundary maintenance and repair, and movement into new configurations. Building on this, Smith and Comer (1994) show empirical findings from quasi-experimental research indicating that the presence of self-organizing features contributes to group effectiveness under turbulent conditions.

Working at the organizational rather than group level of analysis, MacIntosh and MacLean (1999) advocate a dissipative structure model of change, but one over which management may indeed have some control through prior setting of process parameters or 'conditioning'. This involves managing the organization's 'deep structure' – the simple rules invoked, usually implicitly, during decision-making. Using two illustrative case examples, they introduce the notion of 'conditioned emergence' and describe it as a three-step process: (1) conditioning (articulating and reconfiguring the rules underpinning an organization's deep structure); (2) crisis (ensuring far-from-equilibrium conditions); and (3) strategic change (managing the loops of positive and negative feedback so as to move the organization towards improved forms).

Goldstein (1988; 1994) also works at the organizational level but focuses on possible negative consequences of emergence by using thinking about far-from-equilibrium systems to reconsider resistance to change, which he conceptualizes as autopoiesis – resistance can be seen as a system self-organizing and maintaining itself even in the face of managerial fiats and interventions aimed at changing it. He combines difference questioning from family therapy with far-from-equilibrium systems models to suggest several strategies for working with, rather than against, resistance. Similarly, Svyantek and DeShon (1993) address failed change efforts and posit that organizational culture – the set of deeply held and, in most cases, tacit or implicit values – functions as an attractor that frustrates change efforts that don't take this force into consideration.

Lichtenstein (2000a, b, c) applies complexity science to the question of how to manage organizations through archetypal transitions like those encountered by new ventures as they grow. Using a comparative case study method, Lichtenstein (2000a) finds three qualities that increase the level of self-organizing activity in organizations: self-referencing; increasing their capacity to attain goals; and interdependent organizing that balances structure and flexibility, much like Brown and Eisenhardt (1997). His view of self-organization as leading to positive outcomes leads him to suggest that managers 'give control to the system' to let emergence happen, but only after seeding it with core values – a guiding vision and set of simple rules or essential principles that managers may apply locally to solve problems.

Resilience. Hurst and Zimmerman (1994) draw on models of complex ecological systems to explain how small, young entrepreneurial firms grow to become large, mature bureaucratic organizations that even though institutionalized, are nonetheless vulnerable to sudden collapse. They use 'ecocycle' theory and the concept of 'resilience' (Holling 1986) to make sense of organizations' emergence, expansion, maintenance and dissolution. In contrast to a life cycle model, dissolution is not analogous to death, but rather renewal, and can be seen positively as the creative destruction pre-requisite for the emergence of new organizations.

I-Space. Boisot and Child (1999) categorize information in organizational environments as more or less codified, more or less abstract and more or less diffused to develop their three-dimensional 'I-space'. They then relate types of complexity – relational and cognitive – as well as ways of organizing transactions – bureaucracies, markets, fiefs and clans – to different regions within this I-space. Using an institutional analysis of China's modernization, they show how cultural differences for tolerating and coping with complexity affect organizing. Western firms, comfortable with 'market capitalism', prefer to *reduce* complexity by transacting in markets and bureaucracies of standard procedures with which they are familiar. Alternatively, they can *absorb* complexity by engaging directly with China's 'network capitalism' through partnerships with local firms and the clans of which they are part. They conclude that, in organizing, there is a tradeoff between the complexity of relations and the complexity of what can be transacted through these.

Table 1.5.9 Applications IV – Phenomena-driven interpretivist works

Reference	Topic	Contribution
Metaphors as tools		
Dubinskas (1994)	Examination of why chaos theory better explains drastic organizational change than biological and evolutionary models	Internal and external forces cause turbulence in organizations yet self-organization in a turbulent context can enable project success
Polley (1997)	Theoretical argument about role of metaphors; describes non-linear dynamic systems and two promising metaphors: *bifurcation* and *chaos*	Integration of complexity metaphors with process research; practical implications for managing turbulence; theoretical implications for building process models
Lissack (1997a)	Investigation of role of complexity metaphors, and description of practical applications of several key metaphors	Complexity metaphors are of more value in units where investments in knowledge are required as opposed to investments in infrastructure
Lissack (1999)	Theoretical argument about reality-constituting role of language and especially metaphors	Complexity metaphors foreground processes rather than reified constructs and can lead managers to manage uncertainty rather than seeking to eliminate it
Knowledge management (KM)		
Lissack (2000)	Theoretical argument linking KM with view of individuals and organizations as interpretive systems seeking coherence	KM is about creating contexts that facilitate (inter)actions by individuals that respect identities; domain of corporate anthropologists rather than IT specialists
Snowden (2000)	Theoretical argument, supported by reports from empirical projects, linking KM with storytelling	Storytelling is effective means of surfacing, mapping and embedding knowledge in organizations; insights and knowledge are *emergent* from interactions
Stacey (2000; 2001)	Theoretical argument linking KM with phenomenon of emergence	Knowledge cannot be made explicit and stored; it is emergent from interactions of organizational members; its existence is endemic to relationships
Cilliers (2000c)	Theoretical argument linking KM with complexity science that affords getting beyond the objectivist-subjectivist divide	Knowledge is the interpretation of data by some agent yet latter are not atomistic entities but rather constituted through interactions; no substitute for experience
Coherence		
Lissack and Letiche (2002)	Theoretical argument linking coherence with experienced complexity and highlighting need for managers to embrace emergence of meaning	Coherence as socially tested awareness; groups find ways for parts of their narration to fit together meaningfully; coherence implies resilience
Phenomenal complexity		
Boje (2000)	Application of phenomenal complexity theory to interactions of an organization and interest groups seeking to influence its behaviour, each with their own experiential truth	As interaction density increases, organizations are drawn to 'edge of chaos'; they cannot act in response to another without generating 2nd order responses from others; result is emergent, combined effect greater than sum of individual effects

Phenomena-driven Interpretivist Work

Within our Applications cluster, we identify four sub-clusters of interpretivist applications of complexity science: the reflexive use of metaphors as management tools; knowledge management; coherence; and applied phenomenal complexity theory. We summarize these works in Table 1.5.9.

Metaphors as tools. The first sub-cluster of work self-consciously addresses the use of – rather than merely asserts the applicability of – complexity metaphors. For instance, Polley (1997) begins with a theoretical argument about the role of metaphors in science and in organization studies specifically, highlighting possible benefits and risks of employing them, then moves to a description of non-linear dynamical systems and two metaphors it has generated – bifurcation and chaos. Paying particular attention to the mathematical meaning and implications of the terms, he integrates them into different families of organizational process research (Van de Ven and Poole 1995), showing their practical implications for managing turbulence in organizations and their theoretical implications for constructing organizational process models. Lissack (1999) writes theoretically about the reality-constituting role of language and, especially, metaphors, underlining how complexity metaphors focus attention on relations and processes rather than reified constructs. In so doing, they lead managers to embrace the acceptance and management of uncertainty rather than the control or elimination of it. However, metaphors must be understood and applied contextually, thus complexity-inspired metaphors are more appropriate in certain contexts and less so in others. Lissack (1997a) argues that complexity metaphors are of more value in units where investments in knowledge are required (i.e. a domain of increasing returns) as opposed to investments in infrastructure (i.e. a domain of decreasing returns).

Knowledge management. Another sub-cluster of applied work with an interpretivist flavour can be found around the topic of knowledge management (KM), with researchers viewing knowledge as an emergent outcome of interactions by agents within a complex system. For instance, Stacey (2000; 2001) explicitly links knowledge and its management to emergence, with human interaction analogous to agent interaction in models of complex systems. Knowledge cannot be made explicit and stored,

he argues, as it is emergent from interactions of organizational members and is thus destroyed and/or created along with relationships and interactions. Cilliers (2000c) argues that complexity science gets beyond the unhelpful objectivist-subjectivist divide because it highlights the dialectic relationship between knowledge and the system in which it is constituted, reminding us that knowledge is the interpretation of data by some subject. Because subjects are not atomistic entities but are, rather, constituted through interactions and relations, a deeper understanding of knowledge implies a better understanding of subjects. The implications are not trivial: in many settings, there is simply no substitute for *experience*.

Snowden (2000) too argues that insights and knowledge are emergent from interactions in organizations. He reinforces the importance and practical utility of narrative approaches to knowledge in complex systems by demonstrating that storytelling is a highly effective means of surfacing, mapping and embedding knowledge in organizations, drawing upon reports from empirical projects. Lissack (2000) argues that the practice of knowledge management would benefit from explicitly viewing individuals and organizations as nested, sense-making, interpretive systems seeking coherence at multiple levels. He claims that knowledge management is about creating an organizational context that facilitates interactions by individuals and that respects their identities, making the case that it should be the domain of corporate anthropologists and not simply that of information technology specialists as has been the trend (see also Benbya and McKelvey 2005).

Coherence. In a related argument about the emergence of meaning, Lissack and Letiche (2002) link coherent knowledge with lived experience. They view coherence as socially tested awareness of a situation in which group members find ways for the parts of their narration to fit together meaningfully. For them, the value of complex systems models and complexity thinking comes not from providing purported answers to important organization science questions but rather from evoking questions and narratives told in response to them.

Phenomenal complexity. Finally, Boje (2000) applies phenomenal complexity theory in an empirical, qualitative case study of the interactions of Disney and interest groups, each with their own experiential 'truth'. He demonstrates how, as the density of interorganizational interactions increases, organizations can be drawn beyond the edge of

Table 1.5.10 Reflections on the field of complexity science and organization studies

Reference	Focus	Topics reviewed
Maguire and McKelvey (1999)	Complexity and management	Adaptive tension; fitness landscapes; information-processing vs interpretive approaches to complexity; linkages between complexity and post-modernism
Contractor (1999)	Self-organizing systems research in the social sciences	Benefits and limitations of using self-organizing systems as (1) metaphors; and (2) models
Levy (2000)	Complexity theory in organization theory and strategy	Applications and limitations of chaos and complexity theories; NK models; fitness landscapes
Richardson and Cilliers (2001)	What is complexity science?	Three strands of complexity-inspired work: hard reductionism; soft metaphorical; authors put *complexity thinking* between hard and soft perspectives
Carley (2002a)	Intraorganizational complexity and computation	Complex systems; agents; decision-making and problem-solving; networks; information technology; algorithmic complexity; computational theorizing
Eisenhardt and Bhatia (2002)	Organizational complexity and computation	Complex systems; loose coupling; NK models; edge of chaos; simple rules and complex behaviour; emergence; recombination and evolution
Sorenson (2002)	Interorganizational complexity and computation	Complex systems; interdependence; micro-behaviour and macro-structure; sensitivity to initial conditions; path dependence; NK models; CA models

chaos; they cannot act in response to one actor without generating a second order response from another, an emergent, combined effect that is greater than the sum of individual effects.

Reflections

We have labelled our final cluster of work Reflections to highlight their common feature of *reviewing* and *reflecting* upon work in the field of complexity science and organization studies. We summarize these overviews and review works in Table 1.5.10.

Maguire and McKelvey's (1999) early reflection on the field highlights the emerging tension between hard information-processing and soft interpretive approaches to complexity, as well as the linkages between complexity science and postmodernism. Although the authors are skeptical about skeptical postmodernism, they affirm postmodernism's affirmative strand, suggesting that the postmodern sensibility of appreciating competing appreciations – of grappling with the multiple idiosyncratic truths of agents *in situ* – is indeed very relevant to managers over short time scales. They argue that a useful distinction can be drawn between 'soft' or 'embedded' complexity and 'hard' or 'abstracted' complexity, with the former characterizing systems subject to conflicting *appreciations* (Checkland 1994) by actors with different beliefs, values, goals and interests. Knowledge developed from participants' view *inside* the system may be more relevant for coping with embedded complexity than that developed from a God's eye view; no matter how sophisticated and advanced formal models become for *problem-solving* or *navigating* complex situations, this still leaves managers with the social and political task of *problem-defining* or *negotiating* them. In other words, from managers' perspective the interpretive challenges of complexity are often prior to its information-processing challenges; interpretive complexity must be addressed before crude or computational complexity become relevant. In the absence of intersubjective agreements required to 'reduce' complexity, managers and other participants in complex systems may have no choice but to 'absorb' it.

Contractor (1999) discusses the benefits and limitations of using self-organizing systems as metaphors or as models, and he too addresses the dilemma of the relative utility of knowledge developed from

God's- as opposed to an agent's-eye view. He criticizes metaphorical approaches for the imprecise and unclear meanings they proliferate. He also proffers seven indictments of computational models associated with complexity science; unfortunately, they are often: (1) not logically consistent; (2) not theoretically grounded; (3) not sufficiently complex; (4) based on simulation environments that do not have good user interfaces and are not sufficiently documented; (5) not easily replicable by a third party using a different simulation environment; (6) not comprehensible to scholars interested in the substantive domain but unfamiliar with computational modelling; and (7) not substantiated by empirical data from the field or experiments, thus raising questions of validity.

Richardson and Cilliers (2001) are also sensitive to the benefits and limitations of soft and hard approaches and advocate a third way – 'complexity thinking', which they describe as a revised philosophic stance that implies methodological pluralism and explicit recognition of limits to our knowledge about complex phenomena. They remind us that *both* narrative and computational or mathematical descriptions contribute to our understanding complex systems. Neither, alone, is sufficient.

Finally, the reviews in Baum (2002), organized around three levels of analysis (intraorganizational, organizational and interorganizational), are excellent resources for scholars interested in: computational approaches (Carley 2002a); edge of chaos phenomena (Eisenhardt and Bhatia 2002); and fitness landscape or cellular automata models (Sorenson 2002).

Future Directions

As is apparent from our review, the field emerging at the intersection of complexity science and organization studies is an exciting one where diverse researchers and approaches come together. Not only are we witnessing, increasingly, the application of complexity science theories, models and methods to study and generate knowledge about a wide range of organizational phenomena (Tables 6–9), there is also a renewed focus on important philosophical questions of epistemology and methods, the very foundations of organizational knowledge (Tables 4 and 5). Combined with numerous articles that introduce complexity and discuss its potential within organization studies (Table 3), and reviews of the field that are beginning to appear (Table 10), future organizational scholarship has much to build upon. Indeed, we see possibilities for transforming a significant part of organization studies, currently a conglomerate of what Kuhn (1962) called fields, into a somewhat more monoparadigmatic organization science (McKelvey 2003b).

It is important to appreciate the radical shifts in perspective inherent in complexity science: (1) from an equilibrium-focused worldview to one focused on disequilibrium processes; as well as (2) from an *energy-force-based* science drawing on mathematical formalism to an *agent-rule-based* science drawing on computational methodologies. Coming with the legitimacy of long established natural sciences, complexity science is a '*new*' normal science upon which organizational researchers can draw. Importantly, it shifts ontological assumptions and epistemological standards away from those rooted in planetary physics and thermodynamics, which were developed for understanding physical systems in which equilibrating forces govern dynamics. Complexity science, on the other hand, offers approaches more appropriate to studying organizational phenomena where what is fundamental in the near term is the creation of new order (e.g. processes, behaviour, structure, strategy, etc.), not an inevitable trend toward equilibrium. Further, the shift from elegant mathematical representations of idealized processes to agent-based computational models also allows organizational researchers to pursue the epistemological advantages of models and experiments without having to assume away important – or, as some would say, essential – features of organizational reality simply to make the mathematics tractable. These include idiosyncratic heterogeneity among individuals or firms, commonly eliminated by assuming homogeneity; interdependence among agents, commonly eliminated by assuming independence; and the emergent outcomes of agent interactions, commonly ignored because equations necessarily focus on relations among variables at a single level of analysis, treating fast variables as insignificant noise and slow variables as unchanging constants.

These important changes in perspective and methods mean that organizational researchers may now approach phenomena using a science well described as '*bottom-up*' (Epstein and Axtell 1996). So, instead of conceptualizing and studying the world as made up of independent homogeneous agents responding as automatons to equilibrating forces – seemingly without choice or, equivalently, with omnisciently rational choice – bottom-up science offers a more realistic alternative. As we show in our review, complexity science allows for conceptualizations that capture the interactions of interdependent (i.e. semi-autonomous) heterogeneous agents with specific rules governing their behaviour *and* the emergent structure and order that may arise from this.

Our chapter documents how organizational researchers are beginning to harness these conceptual, epistemological and methodological advances stemming from complexity science. This should continue in future work, as these advances synthesize diverse sub-fields of organization studies into an organization science that is more coherent and legitimate in the eyes of important constituencies (McKelvey 2003b, c). In order to fully realize this potential, we now make some suggestions for future work. We organize our discussion of future research directions around three related thrusts: (1) extending and refining existing lines of inquiry that bring complexity science to bear on organizational phenomena; (2) reconciling disparate perspectives within the community of organizational complexity scholars; and (3) integrating and anchoring complexity science even more solidly within organization studies by broadening the range of phenomena addressed.

Continuing Promising Intra-Community Conversations

To realize the potential of complexity science in organization studies, the community of organizational complexity scholars must continue the most promising intra-community conversations about epistemological and methodological Foundations of their field as well as about Applications of complexity science to the range of organizational phenomena addressed. This is equally the case if one considers the broader community of complexity researchers; an ongoing exchange of insights between natural scientists and organizational researchers must be maintained. Thus, lines of inquiry discussed above need to be extended and refined. The diversity of these lines of inquiry, combined with space limitations, make a discussion of the future directions of all of them impossible. We would like to suggest, however, how the field would benefit in particular (1) from more works aimed at building theories of emergence, and (2) from complementing this with increased and improved efforts to model emergence.

Theorizing Emergence: Order-Creation, Fractals and Power Laws

Those lines of inquiry that directly address the phenomenon of emergence merit more attention. Theory building here could advance our understanding of related organizational phenomena which researchers have begun to address and discussed above, including: organizational change and adaptation; inertia and resistance to change; organizational learning and unlearning; self-organization; co-evolution; and emergent strategy. To more effectively understand emergence processes, organizational scholars need to exploit the findings of natural scientists regarding the creation of order, and then translate these to the particularities of organizations.

Order creation. The traditional view of order creation in organizations is a top down one of managers deciding what to do and then organizing. This often results in the oppositional rise of informal organizations (Roethlisberger and Dixon 1939; Homans 1950). Instead, we advocate a view of organizations as '*entangled*' bottom-up *and* top-down hierarchies (Thomas et al. 2006) or '*circular*' (Romme 1999). McKelvey (1997) refers to organization structures resulting from the joint effects of prepensive managerial design and the bottom-up formation of structures as '*quasi-natural*'. Absent managerial designs, how order emerges from the possibly random interactions of agents is a question already studied by prominent natural scientists. Rather than start from scratch, we believe there is much that organization theorists may learn from several approaches to order creation, although extension and refinement of these to fit organizational contexts is required:

1. Bénard's externally imposed energy differential, R, that fuels the *process* of emergence (and which organizational researchers can translate into contextual tensions such as demand, competitor actions, environmental resources and constraints, etc.) along with his *1st and 2nd critical values* that define the *region* of emergence, are key parameters that, in appropriate combinations, result in the creation of pockets of order as *cells*. McKelvey (2004b) summarizes key elements of this view, proposing a

0th law of thermodynamics that is applicable to human organization as well. Future work should investigate the nature and sources of adaptive tension, the nature of organizational critical values, as well as the underlying mechanisms relating these.

2. Some insights into these questions and upon which organizational researchers can draw come from Haken (1983) who takes a close look at the important transition at the 1st critical value. His work focuses on how a large number of different kinds of contextual tensions are reduced down to a few driving forces termed order parameters, and demonstrates how most external imposing effects are randomized and thus enslaved to a few other tensions that dictate system behaviour. McKelvey (2003a) extends this discussion to organizations, but more work is required.

3. Complementing this is the North American School's work focusing on internal dynamics – how agents react interdependently to tensions to yield structure and order. Holland's (1988; 1995) work is a good example of the analysis of intra-system order creation: a set of heterogeneous agents exist inside a system and, triggered by some event, begin to co-evolve. While some co-evolution of behaviours diminishes and halts because of negative feedback processes, his work highlights how positive feedback may occur, resulting in the emergence of new order. Organizational researchers could fruitfully bring work on vicious and virtuous circles in organizations (Masuch 1985) together with this theorizing.

We realize, of course, that human agents at any level in an organization have sophisticated cognitive processing capabilities and that these alone may lead to new order. We emphasize the natural science theories here, however, because they show how the interaction of agents (governed by simple rules, but without much human capital capability), co-evolutionary dynamics (i.e. social capital) and contextual dynamics work to produce new order absent explicit top-down, prepensive, managerial attempts to produce it or absent authorizing mandates.

Fractals and power law phenomena. In addition to positive feedback and co-evolution, fractals, scalability, scale-free theory and power laws are also hallmarks of the North American School. The structure of a cauliflower illustrates all of the latter (Andriani and McKelvey 2005a), as does a Romanesque broccoli (Strogatz 2005). It is composed of branches that have smaller branches that have even smaller branches and so on down to those one can't even see. The branches look the same no matter what size ruler is used or from what distance we look – this is *scalability*. They look and behave the same at each level – their design is *fractal*. Their adaptive functioning – and the theory used to explain it – is the same at each level – that is, it is *scale-free*. Finally, if one plots the branches by size and number on double log paper, their rank-size distribution will approximate a straight line – a plot indicating a *power law* effect. By way of proof-of-existence, Andriani and McKelvey (2005a) list 68 power law discoveries, half in social science. They also give a preliminary description of several prevailing scale-free theories explaining why the power law effect occurs. These theories all focus on interdependencies and positive feedback as causes of emergent power laws and fractal structures.

All of the foregoing phenomena are likely to apply to organizations. Why? Because organizations are comprised of interdependent parts. From these, positive feedback may give rise to new structures such as the vicious and virtuous circles analysed by Masuch (1985). First attempts at developing scale-free and power law theories to explain emergent multi-level structure in organizations appear in Andriani's (2003) rank/size analysis of Italian industrial districts and in Lichtenstein and McKelvey's (2004) connection of power laws to their stage theory of emergent structures in organizations – agents, then networks, then groups, then hierarchies, then complex co-ordination structures, and so on.

Scale-free theories explain why many networks – e.g. the Internet, commercial airplane flights, co-authorships – show power law formations, as well as how new entities form, including mass explosions (or extinctions) of biodiversity by studying the unlikely, but possible joint occurrence of ecological elements all helping (or hindering) speciation and adaptation. Applicable to organizations as well as natural phenomena, we list seven 1st Principles of the emergence, maintenance and development of complex structures (drawn from Andriani and McKelvey (2005b)):

- *Adaptive Tension*: Environmentally imposed tensions (energy differentials) stimulate adaptive order creation – Prigogine's (1955) *dissipative structures* theory.
- *Requisite Variety*: Adaptive order creation occurs if internal complexity exceeds external complexity – Ashby' (1956) *Law of Requisite Variety*.
- *Change Rate*: Higher internal rates of change offer adaptive advantage in a changing environment – Fisher's (1930) *genetic variance* theorem.

- *Modular Design*: Nearly autonomous subunits increase complexity and rate of adaptive response – Simon's (1962) *near decomposability* principle.
- *Positive Feedback*: Insignificant instigating events among agents or modules may result in significant order creation – Maruyama's (1963) *deviation amplification* theory.
- *Causal Intricacy*: Complexity requires advantageously coping with multiple causes: bottom-up, top-down, horizontal, diagonal, intermittent and Aristotelian – Lindblom's (1959) *science of muddling through*.
- *Causal Rhythms*: Rhythmic alternation of causal dominance offers more functional adaptive response than balance – Dumont's (1966) *entangled hierarchy* theory.

Given organization studies' multiple levels of analysis and its roots in several disciplines, there are many perspectives and, consequently, a resulting complication of independent and/or conflicting theories. This has led to the well-discussed challenge of multiple paradigms (Pfeffer 1993; McKelvey 2003b). Where power law effects are demonstrated, the development of scale-free theory may offer a focal point for reconciling multiple paradigms.

Modelling Emergence: Agent-based Models (ABMs)

Earlier we cited Casti's (1997) suggestion that one of SFI's most memorable contributions to complexity science will be computational agent-based modelling. As we have seen, although very early in their development within organization studies, ABMs nonetheless demonstrate much promise, but also have drawbacks. Future work using ABMs must address these. Carley (2002a) makes a point of calling for more attention to the degree to which internal model elements represent real-world phenomena. In addition, agents in models need to become much more sophisticated with respect to learning, memory, cognitive abilities and emotions, she notes. In most current models emergence occurs, but with little attention to how and when agents become activated, why emergence occurs here rather than there, how changes in agent capabilities (learning, cognition, memory, etc.) affect emergence, nor how other organizational contingencies, which might be tasks, human capital, network configuration, information flows, markets and technology and the like, affect emergence.

Another challenge involves temporal dimensions. Sorenson (2002) observes that in current models agents all update according to a single time clock. E and Engquist (2003) suggest multiscale modelling as a preferred approach. Thus, the main model (or equation) runs by the primary clock, but sub-elements run on their own clocks and, then at various times, results from these models feed up into the main model. Simon (1999) notes that across most phenomena, dynamics at lower levels run at frequencies faster than at higher levels. In addition, at this time, as Sorenson notes, model agents contribute more or less equally to emergent outcomes. Yet, in real human systems, agents act and contribute differentially. Not all participate all the time or act consistently in the same ways and some are better interconnected than others – conditions that affect the onset of positive feedback spirals. For instance, Yuan and McKelvey (2004) compare Kauffman's *NK* model under conditions of all links the same vs networks composed of well-connected stars and poorly-connected loners. Although McKelvey (1999a) observes that the basis for the *NK* model is discipline-free, and thus the model is applicable to organizations as it is to biology or statistical physics, there is reason to expect that, in principle, agent sophistication will have to be much higher in social rather than in natural science.

There is also a need to address the question of whether computational models do what their coders claim. Axtell et al. (1996) describe 'docking' as a way to test models – one model is docked against another by testing whether they produce the same results. A recent model-to-model conference suggests that dockings are usually not successful – mostly because of different interpretations of theory in writing up the code rather than coding mistakes (Edmonds and Hales 2003; Rouchier 2003). Getting models matched up against real-world phenomena is not easy either. Contractor et al. (2000) use agent rules based on stylized facts they draw from underlying bodies of research. They, as does Carley (1996), also test their results against a real-world organizational quasi-experiment; we would like to see more such work. Sorenson (1997) tests the *NK* model against data from the computer workstation industry and patent data, with confirmatory results (see also Fleming and Sorenson 2001), and Rivkin (2000) is exemplary in his attention to robustness. Despite these efforts, however, most models are not yet as well validated against real-world phenomena as they should be.

Finally, we would like to see more models starting with built-in structure rather than randomly

positioned or linked agents. Thus, a model would start with a t_1 structure of agent positioning, attributes and connectedness. Given this structure and its imposing context, a relevant theory about how the target network might be transformed from its t_1 configuration to some other pattern at time t_x could then be translated into agent rules.

Initiating New Intra-Community Conversations

In addition to pursuing existing lines of inquiry, the field would also benefit from reconciling different approaches where possible, and we encourage organizational complexity scholars to initiate new intra-community conversations to this end. Both philosophy-driven and phenomena-driven research would benefit and, in our view, existing work suggests opportunities for synthesis and reconciliation. In particular, we see opportunities to advance our understanding of organizations by studying processes of emergence in ways that combine (1) objectivist epistemology with interpretivist ontology, in research seeking to establish the foundations of complexity science in organization studies; (2) agent-based models with qualitative research, in applications of complexity science to particular organizational phenomena; and (3) an emphasis on the internal complexity of organizations with one on the external complexity of their environments when studying organizations.

Studying Emergence: Objectivist Epistemology with Interpretivist Ontology

At this juncture, the objectivists and interpretivists in organization studies are quite obviously paradigmatically disconnected. Objectivists cannot study the co-evolving richness of organizational ontologies reported on by interpretivist researchers, and tend to hold to mid-20th century normal science epistemological standards, the basis of legitimized truth claims (McKelvey 2003c). Interpretivists, on the other hand, tend to hold to the view that objectivists assume away most of what is important so as to make the math, econometrics and statistics work. Their work, in some instances, can take on an anti-science tone, with the result that the two approaches are sharply differentiated, as noted by writers such as Holton (1993) and Koertge (1998). In organization studies, as Pfeffer

(1993) noted a decade ago, ongoing paradigmatic struggles reduce our field's legitimacy in the eyes of important constituencies and maintain the field in a state of Kuhn's 'prescience' (McKelvey 2003b).

This need not, however, remain a permanent impasse, as the philosophy-driven foundational work addressing complexity science and organization studies suggests at least some degree of reconciliation is possible. McKelvey (2003c) uses the work of Cilliers (1998) to metaphorically marry complexity's new normal science epistemology to post-structuralist ontology. Cilliers draws principally from post-structuralists (Derrida 1978; Baudrillard 1983b; Lyotard 1984), and interprets their work from a connectionist perspective, much like a modeller of neural networks, emphasizing connections among agents rather than attributes of the agents themselves. This perspective comes from modern conceptions of how brains and (distributed) intelligence function (Fuster 1995). In the connectionist perspective, co-ordinated functioning that maintains order, or intelligence, is neither in the neurons, nor 'in the network', but rather 'is the network' (Fuster 1995: 11). Distributed intelligence also characterizes firms and many other social systems (McKelvey 2001b). Cilliers (1998: 37) makes his foundational argument as follows:

- 'Complexity is best characterized as arising through large-scale, non-linear interaction.
- Since it is based on a system of relationships, the post-structural inquiry into the nature of language helps us to theorize about the dynamics of the interaction in complex systems. In other words, the dynamics that generate meaning in language can be used to describe the dynamics of complex systems in general.
- Connectionist networks share the characteristics of complex systems, including those aspects described by a post-structural theory of language. It should therefore be possible to use them (or other distributed modelling techniques with similar capabilities) as general models for complex systems. These models can be physically implemented or simulated computationally'.

These points link post-structuralism and complexity science by virtue of their common focus on connectionism and relationality among entities in a system. This work suggests that some strands of post-structuralism can be bridged with those portions of post-positivism described as 'new normal science'.

Studying Emergence: Agent-based Models with Qualitative Research

Given the foregoing, it appears the time has come for a rapprochement between qualitative case-based work and computational modelling. Narrative studies are assuredly rich descriptions, a la Geertz (1973). They are the best representations of organizational ontology and emergent complexities therein. However, they are typically difficult to generalize beyond a specific time and place or, indeed, a single observer. Ideally, computational models should start with baseline models that attempt to *simulate* as many elements of a specific narrative description of emergence as possible. This would include starting models with built-in structures as opposed to the current practice of starting with no structure followed by random draws, as discussed earlier. This would enhance the empirical validation of the model. Having agent rules that, in addition, appear as stylized facts rooted in bodies of research would also help robustness (see Contractor et al. (2000) for a good example). Given this baseline simulation model, computational *experiments* can follow that unlock the time/place/observer limitations of case-based research. With models, ambiguities in the narrative can be unravelled, restrictive conditions can be relaxed and time spans set up to let starting conditions progress into emergent non-linearities. Following this method, we see a rapprochement of interpretivist and objectivist research while at the same time following the path of model-centred science (McKelvey 2002b).

Ideally, agent-based models (ABMs) would bring experimental corroboration and elaboration to findings from narrative studies. ABMs could offer tests for broadening generality and for studying dynamics. ABMs also allow the juxtaposition of variables from different disciplines. Thus, narrative studies could be more multidisciplinary. Narrative researchers can also help to develop better ABMs by offering clearer data for the purpose of validating baseline models. Thus, ABMs would simulate the narrative findings first, and then advance into experimental manipulations. Qualitative researchers should also design studies to enlighten or challenge model-centred findings. For example, Carley and Svoboda (1996) find that individual learning is far more important in adaptation than organizational learning. Here is an example of a striking finding from computational modelling that deserves follow-on qualitative research to confirm, reject, elaborate, specify the domain of generalizability, and so on.

Studying Emergence: Internal Complexity with External Complexity via Ashby's Law

European and North American approaches to complexity would benefit from reconciliation, and organization studies presents opportunities for doing so. Whereas the former emphasize adaptive tension, critical values, order parameters and mathematics, the latter stress interacting agents governed by rules, resulting self-organization and, especially, the evolution of complex systems to states of self-organized criticality. It is hard to imagine one without the other. In Churchman and Ackoff's (1950) terms, they are co-producers.

Such a reconciliation within organization studies may benefit by exploring the implications of Boisot and McKelvey's (2006) modernization of Ashby's Law of Requisite Variety that states firms need to develop internal complexity in the same measure as the imposing external complexity with which they are coping. Following Allen's (2001) extension of Ashby's Law to develop the Law of Excess Variety [Complexity], only excess internal complexity can destroy external complexity. In other words, given that some number of the internal degrees of freedom will be inappropriate, coping with environmental complexity requires some probabilistic quantity of degrees of freedom accumulated *in advance* of the time they are actually needed. Thus, more work needs to be done with the notion of strategic fit (Andrews 1971), as it is evident that for organizations that successfully maintain and sustain themselves, external and internal degrees of freedom come into balance recursively. An appreciation of the recursive nature of organizing, and thus managing *both* internal and external degrees of freedom, is required (Boisot and McKelvey 2006). There are obvious connections between this line of work and that on sense making and the enactment of organizational environments (Weick 2001). Instead of passively studying complexity dynamics like physicists and biologists, organizational scholars need to worry about helping managers to intervene into and work with external and internal complexity dynamics to capitalize upon the reality of Ashby's Law. Here is where organization studies scholars need to take leave of their natural

science counterparts to chart a new course. Positive feedback, co-evolution, emergence, fractals and power law outcomes are not simply spontaneous natural phenomena – they can be managed. A start down this path appears in McKelvey (2002a).

Initiating New Inter-Community Conversations

In addition to new *intra*-community conversations, future work should also initiate new *inter*-community conversations. As we have shown, organizational scholars are applying complexity science to a wide range of organizational phenomena. More effort must be put into translating and disseminating findings to other researchers, outside of the community of organizational complexity scholars, but researching the same phenomena. In addition, the list of phenomena to which complexity science may fruitfully be applied is hardly exhausted. Three lines of inquiry showing promise involve reconceptualizing fundamental management phenomena: (1) entrepreneurship, viewed as creating emergent order; (2) leadership, viewed as fostering or enabling emergence inside organizations; and (3) strategy, viewed as the outcome of managing emergence strategically to ensure content and process appropriate to the far-from-equilibrium economy in which firms today operate.

Creating Emergence: Entrepreneurship

Schumpeter (1942) built Austrian economics from the basic idea of phase transitions – fundamental to new order creation in the European School – although he called it 'creative destruction'. With complexity science, organizational scholars now have new concepts and tools to understand this important phenomenon, and several researchers have begun to apply these to generate insights into entrepreneurial firms, and especially archetypal transition points in the growth of entrepreneurial firms (see Brown and Eisenhardt 1997; Lichtenstein 2000c; Lichtenstein and Brush 2001; Lichtenstein et al. 2006). McKelvey (2004c) links aspects of complexity science epistemology to entrepreneurial research. He also details some of the complexity dynamics entrepreneurs must marshal so as to enable the kind of entrepreneurial activities that figure so prominently in the self-organizing associated with the emergence of new firms. Along this line, Miles et al. (1999) point to holding companies comprised of smaller entrepreneurial firms as examples of the '*cellular networks*' they argue are critical to organizational viability in 21st century economies (see also Marion and Uhl-Bien 2001; 2002). Drawing on Boisot and McKelvey's (2006) modernization of Ashby's Law, a preliminary lesson for entrepreneurs from complexity science is that they need to be mindful of the recursive dynamics between external and internal complexity as they create new relations among members internally and initiate new interorganizational relations externally. A complexity science-based approach to entrepreneurial success and failure shows promise.

Leading Emergence: Leadership

A cursory review of two recent volumes edited by Dansereau and Yammarino (1998a, b) shows that much work on leadership focuses on leaders of groups of production workers, an emphasis perhaps inappropriate for the contemporary economy in which knowledge work figures so prominently (McKelvey forthcoming). It is argued that good leaders are visionary and charismatic (Bryman 1996) and the top-down control they exercise produces a group culture of cohesion and homogeneity (Waldman and Yammarino 1999) because followers are incentivized to implement the vision of the leader (Bennis 1996). Marion and Uhl-Bien (2001; 2002) give detailed critiques of leadership theory from a complexity-based perspective, including a critique of the more recent transformational leadership theory by Avolio and Bass (1998). McKelvey (2001b; 2004a; forthcoming), Marion and Uhl-Bien (2001; 2002) and Uhl-Bien et al. (2004) take the first steps in developing the notion of *complexity leadership*. Mackey et al. (2005) reduce leadership to 12 simple rules about how leaders at the top – validated against Jack Welch's leadership approach – can use complexity dynamics to enable the bottom-up formation of effective emergent structures. There is no doubt that they offer a very different perspective on leadership for the 21st century. Needless to say, much work needs to be done, both empirically and with agent-based modelling approaches.

Strategically Managing Emergence: Strategy

A number of writers have begun integrating strategy thinking with complexity science. Stacey (1991;

1992) is perhaps the earliest, with Thiétart and Forgues (1995) following. Both highlight the role of externally imposed tension for setting order-creation dynamics in motion. Inasmuch as much of the foundational work in strategy stems from industrial organization economics, we note that recent work in economics attempts to move that discipline away from its roots in the equilibrium dynamics and mathematical models of classical physics and draws upon complexity science to do so: Arthur (1988; 1990; 2000) emphasizes positive feedback processes; Ormerod (1994; 1998) shows how much the classical physics-based of assumptions of economists' general equilibrium theory do not hold, demonstrating the empirical validity of non-equilibrium dynamics, changing attractors and aperiodic behaviour; and Rosser (1999; 2001) also discusses complex economic dynamics. Using agent-based computational modelling, Epstein and Axtell (1996) demonstrate that economies can emerge given just one simple rule for the constituents. Anderson et al. (1988) and Arthur et al. (1997) offer edited volumes that point to non-linear emergent aspects of economies rather than the imagined equilibrium tendencies of the neoclassical economists, highlighting the utility of viewing the economy as a complex evolving system. McCain (2000) shows that economic dynamics between developed and developing countries are mutually causal and driven by positive feedback rather than equilibrium processes. Since much strategy content research is rooted in neoclassical economic thinking, the field of strategy appears primed for updating. Strategy research would benefit significantly by viewing the economy as a complex system and applying complexity science concepts and tools to generate new knowledge (Colander 2000). Given that its underpinning discipline is being challenged and changed by complexity science, we recommend that organizational scholars seize this opportunity to lead, not follow, this transformation.

Conclusion

The future is promising for the field emerging at the intersection of complexity science and organization studies. As we have shown, complexity science not only (1) builds on an important heritage of studying complexity and applying systems thinking in organization studies; (2) offers researchers a set of abstract concepts and principles applicable to a wide range of organizational phenomena; (3) comes with powerful modern agent-based computational methods appropriate for studying the processes of emergence and order creation by interdependent (not independent), heterogeneous (not homogeneous) rule-governed actors interacting under far-from-equilibrium (not equilibrium) conditions that characterize organizations and economies; but also (4) challenges accepted notions of causality that emphasize Aristotle's efficient cause only; and (5) provides a fresh perspective on longstanding debates as to the merits of objectivist and interpretivist approaches, quantitative and qualitative methods, and whether organizations and individuals are best viewed as interpreters of their worlds or information-processors. Our chapter makes clear that complexity is ontological *and* epistemological, relational *and* cognitive, first-order *and* second-order.

The study of complex systems can serve as form of inquiry for bridging between post-positivism in the tradition of 'normal science' and those 'affirmative' strands of postmodernism and post-structuralism that are not anti-science. In addition, complexity challenges scholars to think not only about knowledge – its nature, how to generate it, etc. – but also its limits, as no representation of a complex system can be complete. Thus, sensitivity to alternative representations is required, i.e. reflexivity and appreciation of multiple perspectives. And, as concerns human systems, researchers should not forget that choosing among alternative representations is always an act with political and ethical implications. This means that, in social systems like those studied by organizational scholars, the difficulties associated with achieving intersubjective agreement (i.e. interpretive complexity) compound those with which natural scientists must also cope, i.e. difficulties associated with representing a system (i.e. crude or effective complexity) and with subsequently generating predictions (i.e. computational complexity). Organizational complexity scholars can fruitfully import models and methods from natural sciences, but in so doing they must be careful to think through the assumptions underlying them, assess the appropriateness of applying them to social systems, adapt them when necessary and recognize their limits. Organizational complexity scholars should also not be afraid of developing new models and methods, of boldly charting their own path within the broader programme that is complexity science.

Notes

1. In agent-based computational models (ABMs) a population of 'agents' co-evolve, which means that their individual states are updated (i.e. recomputed) during successive time periods as the simulation progresses. Agents' behaviours – transitions from one state to another – are governed by rules. In cellular automata models (CA), agents often follow a few simple rules. CA simulations usually create a two-dimensional grid which limits the dimensionality of the simulated world and constrains the maximum number of immediate neighbours. In genetic algorithms (GA), agents may have many rules while the dimensionality of the simulated world is often significantly greater than two and is only limited by our current computing capabilities. Rules are designed to simulate various real world cause–effect relations and capture such things as individual behaviours, interactions between agents, environmental effects and the acquisition or loss of attributes and/or endowments such as fitness. Models may be simple for analytical purposes or more complicated for veridicality purposes (Carley 2002b).

2. 'Agent' is a general term used to designate the semi-autonomous entities which comprise a complex system, which may be such things as atoms, molecules, biomolecules, organelles, organs, organisms, species, processes, individuals, groups, firms, industries, and so on.

3. One must be careful with terminology: Holland's (1995) 'adaptive agents', 'internal models' and 'complex adaptive systems' are Gell-Mann's (1994; 1995) 'complex adaptive systems', 'schema' and 'composite complex adaptive systems'.

4. The term 'complexity theory' is a popular one that, in most uses, can be used interchangeably with 'complexity science'. We prefer and use the latter term because (1) there is no single unified theory of the phenomenon of complexity, and (2) 'science' is a broader term that encompasses 'theory' but also ontological constructs, epistemology, methods, models, etc., and our focus is on the broader 'science'. We sometimes use 'complexity theory' however when describing research in which that terminology is explicitly invoked by authors to frame or title their works.

5. There has been a long running debate over the meaningfulness of 'the edge of chaos' since the concept was introduced (see story in Lewin 1992). On the one hand, Mitchell et al. (1993) present computational experimental evidence that does not replicate the original experiments, finding no clear evidence of a phase transition. On the other hand, Kauffman (1993) and others (see review in McKelvey 1999c) do show a 'melting zone' dividing the region of emergent complexity from stochastic chaos. Cramer (1993) argues that moving a complex system across its 1st and 2nd critical values of R (a measure of externally imposed energy) results in phase transitions: there is a stable simple order

below the 1st, stochastic chaos above the 2nd, and a region of emergent complex order in between. Given this, the focus of organizational researchers on 'the edge' appears valid.

6. 1999, vol. 1.2.

7. *Human Systems Management* (1990, vol. 9.4) on 'Chaos and Self-organization in Companies'; *Journal of Management Inquiry* (1994, vol. 3.4) on 'Chaos and Complexity'; *Organization Science* (1999, vol. 10.3) on 'Applications of Complexity Theory to Organization Science'; *Management Communication Quarterly* (1999, vol. 13.1) on 'Dialogues of Self-organizing'; *Health Care Management Review* (2000, vol. 25.1) on 'Chaos and Complexity Theory for Health Care Management'; *Journal of Organizational Change Management* (2000, vol. 13.6) on 'Change, Emergence and Complexity Theory'; *Research Policy* (2000, vol. 29.7–8) on 'Complexity and Innovation'; *The Learning Organization* (2003, vol. 10.6; 2004, vol. 11.6) on 'Chaos, Complexity and Organizational Learning'.

8. Length restrictions forbid us from giving each article, book chapter and book the mention and/or discussion it might merit, and we undoubtedly make editorial decisions different from what others might. Our editorial decisions aim toward producing a chapter that serves as a good introduction and overview, as well as being comprehensive and inclusive. In achieving these latter qualities, whereas length restrictions prevent us from doing so in terms of individual works, we believe we succeed in terms of perspectives and major foci of research.

9. We classify work as interpretive if (1) authors explicitly acknowledge their work as such, or (2) the work implicitly rejects a view of knowledge as valid and meaningful only if general and universal. The idea is not to pigeonhole researchers or works but, rather, not to burden the text with qualified labels such as 'more interpretivist' or 'more objectivist'. We proceed without such qualifications but they should be understood.

10. Because McKelvey (1999a) offers a detailed description of the *NK[C]* model as well as how and why it may be validly applied to organization studies, we limit ourselves to short discussion here.

11. Cellular automata (CAs) were first introduced by von Neumann (1951) and entail agents (i.e. cells) modifying their states according to simple rules based on their local interaction with neighbouring agents. Often modelled in a two-dimensional grid, CAs are used to study how the following local rules by each agent can lead to the emergence of global patterns observed at the level of the grid as a whole.

12. For space reasons, we omit the few organizational complexity-relevant models that are *not* ABMs; see for example: Cheng and Van de Ven (1996), and Frank and Fahrbach (1999). In pioneering work, Allen (e.g. 1975; 1976; 1988; 1993a, b) uses systems dynamics models composed of 'noisy differential equations' – meaning that stochasticity is introduced. Although not agent-based

models, they produce outputs and allow analytical conclusions not unlike those from ABMs.

13. Genetic algorithms (GAs) were first developed by Holland (1975) and imply defining an optimization challenge, a search space and a heuristic function. Agents, usually represented by binary strings, are subject to the heuristic function in search of fitter solutions. With GAs, the search process finds better solutions by mimicking biological processes of genetic reproduction including random mutations, recombinations of sections of the string and natural selection.

References

Allen, P.M. (1975) 'Darwinian evolution and a predator-prey ecology', *Bulletin of Mathematical Biology*, 37: 389–405.

Allen, P.M. (1976) 'Evolution, population dynamics and stability', *Proceedings of the National Academy of Sciences (USA)*, 73(3): 665–8.

Allen, P.M. (1988) 'Evolution: why the whole is greater than the sum of its parts', in W. Wolff, C.J. Soeder and F.R. Drepper (eds), *Ecodynamics*. Berlin: Springer-Verlag. pp. 2–30.

Allen, P.M. (1993a) 'Evolution: persistent ignorance from continual learning', in R.H. Day and P. Chen (eds), *Nonlinear Dynamics & Evolutionary Economics*. Oxford: Oxford University Press, Chapter III, 8. pp. 101–12.

Allen, P.M. (1993b) 'Policy in a world of evolutionary learning and ignorance', in K.B. de Greene (ed.), *A Systems-based Approach to Policy Making*. Dordrecht: Kluwer Academic Publishers. pp. 43–64.

Allen, P.M. (2000) 'Knowledge, ignorance, and learning', *Emergence*, 2(4): 78–103.

Allen, P.M. (2001) 'What is complexity science? Knowledge of the limits to knowledge', *Emergence*, 3(1): 24–42.

Anderson, P. (1999) 'Complexity theory and organization science', *Organization Science*, 10(3): 216–32.

Anderson, P.W., Arrow, K.J. and Pines, D. (eds) (1988) *The Economy as an Evolving Complex System*. Proceedings of the Santa Fe Institute – Volume V, Redwood: Addison-Wesley.

Andrews, K.R. (1971) *The Concept of Corporate Strategy*. Homewood: Dow Jones-Irwin.

Andriani, P. (2003) 'The emergence of self-organisation in social systems: the case of the geographic industrial clusters'. Unpublished PhD thesis, Durham Business School, University of Durham.

Andriani, P. and McKelvey, B. (2005a) 'Beyond averages: extending organization science to extreme events and power laws'. Presented at the *21st EGOS Colloquium*, Berlin, Germany.

Andriani, P. and McKelvey, B. (2005b) 'If power law phenomena in organizations: where is the scale-free theory?', Working paper, Durham, Durham Business School, University of Durham.

Argyris, C. (1982) *Reasoning, Learning, and Action: Individual and Organizational.* San Francisco: Jossey-Bass.

Argyris, C. and Schön, D.A. (1978) *Organizational Learning: A Theory of Action Perspective.* Reading: Addison Wesley.

Arndt, M. and Bigelow, B. (2000) 'Commentary: the potential of chaos theory and complexity theory for health services management', *Health Care Management Review*, 25(1): 35–8.

Arthur, W.B. (1983) 'Competing technologies and lock-in by historical events: the dynamics of allocation under increasing returns', I.I.A.S.A. paper WP-83-90. Laxenburg, Austria. [Revised as C.E.P.R. Paper 43, Stanford University.]

Arthur, W.B. (1988) 'Self-reinforcing mechanisms in economics', in P.W. Anderson, K.J. Arrow and D. Pines (eds), *The Economy as an Evolving Complex System.* Reading: Addison-Wesley. pp. 9–32.

Arthur, W.B. (1990) 'Positive feedback in the economy', *Scientific American*, 262(2): 92–9.

Arthur, W.B. (2000) 'Complexity and the economy', in D. Colander (ed.), *The Complexity Vision and the Teaching of Economics.* Cheltenham: Edward Elgar. pp. 19–28.

Arthur, W.B., Durlauf, S.N. and Lane, D.A. (eds) (1997) *The Economy as an Evolving Complex System II.* Proceedings of the Santa Fe Institute – Volume XXVII. Reading: Addison-Wesley.

Ashby, W.R. (1956) *An Introduction to Cybernetics.* London: Chapman & Hall.

Avolio, B.J. and Bass, B.M. (1998) 'Individual consideration viewed at multiple levels of analysis: a multi-level framework for examining the diffusion of transformational leadership', in F. Dansereau and F.J. Yammarino (eds), *Leadership: Multiple-Level Approaches: Contemporary and Alternative.* Stamford: JAI Press. pp. 53–74.

Axtell, R., Axelrod, R., Epstein, J. and Cohen, M. (1996) 'Aligning simulation models: A case study and results', *Computational and Mathematical Organization Theory*, 1(2): 123–41.

Bak, P. (1996) *How Nature Works: The Science of Self-organized Criticality.* New York: Copernicus.

Bak, P., Tang, C. and Wiesenfeld, K. (1987) 'Self-organized criticality: An explanation of $1/f$ noise', *Physical Review Letters*, 59(4): 381–4.

Barnard, C.I. (1938) *The Functions of the Executive.* Cambridge: Harvard University Press.

Bar-Yam, Y. (1997) *Dynamics of Complex Systems.* Reading: Addison-Wesley.

Baudrillard, J. (1983a) *In the Shadow of the Silent Majorities, or, the End of the Social and Other Essays.* New York: Semiotext(e).

Baudrillard, J. (1983b) *Simulations.* New York: Semiotext(e).

Baum, J.A.C. (1999) 'Whole-part coevolutionary competition in organizations', in J.A.C. Baum and B. McKelvey (eds), *Variations in Organization Science:*

in honor of Donald T. Campbell. Thousand Oaks: Sage. pp. 113–35.

Baum, J.A.C. (ed.) (2002) *The Blackwell Companion to Organizations.* Oxford: Blackwell.

Begun, J.W. (1994) 'Chaos and complexity frontiers of organization science', *Journal of Management Inquiry*, 3(4): 329–35.

Bénard, H. (1901) 'Les tourbillons cellulaires dans une nappe liquide transportant de la chaleur par convection en régime permanent', *Annales de Chimie et de Physique*, 23: 62–144.

Benbya, H. and McKelvey, B. (2005) 'Toward a complexity theory of information systems development'. Working paper, Anderson School, UCLA.

Bennis, W.G. (1996) 'Becoming a leader of leaders', in R. Gibson (ed.), *Rethinking the Future.* London: Brealey. pp. 148–63.

Bergson H. (1912) *An Introduction to Metaphysics.* New York: G. P. Putnam's.

Boisot, M. (2000) 'Is there a complexity beyond the reach of strategy', *Emergence*, 2(1): 114–34.

Boisot, M. and Child, J. (1999) 'Organizations as adaptive systems in complex environments: the case of China', *Organization Science*, 10(3): 237–52.

Boisot, M. and McKelvey, B. (2006) 'Speeding up strategic foresight in a dangerous, complex world: a complexity approach', in G.G.S. Suder (ed.), *Corporate Strategies under International Terrorism and Adversity.* Cheltenham, UK: Edward Elgar. In press.

Boje, D.M. (2000) 'Phenomenal complexity theory and change at Disney: response to Letiche', *Journal of Organizational Change Management*, 13(6): 558–66.

Boulding, K.E. (1956) 'General systems theory: the skeleton of a science', *Management Science*, 2(3): 197–208.

Brown, C. (1995) *Chaos and Catastrophe Theories.* Thousand Oaks: Sage.

Brown, S.L. and Eisenhardt, K.M. (1997) 'The art of continuous change: linking complexity theory and time-paced evolution in relentlessly shifting organizations', *Administrative Science Quarterly*, 42(1): 1–34.

Brown, S.L. and Eisenhardt, K.M. (1998) *Competing on the Edge: Strategy as Structured Chaos.* Boston: Harvard Business School Press.

Bruderer, E. and Singh, J.V. (1996) 'Organizational evolution, learning, and selection: a genetic-algorithm-based model', *Academy of Management Journal*, 39(5): 1322–49.

Bryman, A. (1996) 'Leadership in organizations', in S.R. Clegg, C. Hardy and W.R. Nord (eds), *Handbook of Organization Studies.* Thousand Oaks: Sage. pp. 276–92.

Burrell, G. and Morgan G. (1979) *Sociological Paradigms and Organisational Analysis.* London: Heinemann.

Byrne, D.S. (1998) *Complexity Theory and the Social Sciences: An Introduction.* New York: Routledge.

Byrne, D.S. (2001) 'What is complexity science? Thinking as a realist about measurement and cities and arguing for natural history', *Emergence*, 3(1): 61–76.

Carley, K.M. (1991) 'A theory of group stability', *American Sociological Review*, 56(3): 331–54.

Carley, K.M. (1996) 'A comparison of artificial and human organizations', *Journal of Economic Behavior and Organization*, 31(2): 175–91.

Carley, K.M. (1999) 'Learning within and among organizations', in P.C. Anderson, J.A.C. Baum and A.S. Miner (eds), *Advances in strategic management*. New York: Elsevier. pp. 33–56.

Carley, K.M. (2002a) 'Intra-organizational complexity and computation', in J.A.C. Baum (ed.), *The Blackwell Companion to Organizations*. Oxford: Blackwell. pp. 208–32.

Carley, K.M. (2002b) 'Simulating society: The tension between transparency and veridicality', *Proceedings of Agent 2002*. University of Chicago, Chicago, IL.

Carley, K.M. and Hill, V. (2001) 'Structural change and learning within organizations', in A. Lomi and E.R. Larsen (eds), *Dynamics of Organizational Societies*. Cambridge: MIT Press/AAAI Press/Live Oak. pp. 63–92.

Carley, K.M. and Lee, J.S. (1998) 'Dynamic organizations: organizational adaptation in a changing environment', in J.A.C. Baum (ed.), *Advances in Strategic Management, Disciplinary Roots of Strategic Management Research*, Vol 15. New York: Elsevier. pp. 267–95.

Carley, K.M. and Svoboda, D.M. (1996) 'Modeling organizational adaptation as a simulated annealing process', *Sociological Methods and Research*, 25(1): 138–68.

Cartier, M. (2004) 'An agent-based model of innovation emergence in organizations: Renault and Ford through the lens of evolutionism', *Computational and Mathematical Organization Theory*, 10(2): 147–53.

Casti, J.L. (1994) *Complexification: Explaining a Paradoxical World Through the Science of Surprise*. New York: HarperPerennial.

Casti, J.L. (1997) *Would-be Worlds: How Simulation is Changing the Frontiers of Science*. New York: John Wiley and Sons.

Checkland, P. (1981) *Systems Thinking, Systems Practice*. Chichester: John Wiley and Sons.

Checkland, P. (1994) 'Systems theory and management thinking', *American Behavioral Scientist*, 38(1): 75–91.

Cheng, Y.T. and Van de Ven, A.H. (1996) 'Learning the innovation journey: order out of chaos?', *Organization Science*, 7(6): 593–614.

Chiles, T.H., Meyer, A.D. and Hench, T.J. (2004) 'Organizational emergence: the origin and transformation of Branson, Missouri's Musical Theaters', *Organization Science*, 15(5): 499–519.

Churchman, C.W. and Ackoff, R.L. (1950) 'Purposive behavior and cybernetics', *Social Forces*, 29(1): 32–9.

Cilliers, P. (1998) *Complexity and Postmodernism: Understanding Complex Systems*. London: Routledge.

Cilliers, P. (2000a) 'What can we learn from a theory of complexity', *Emergence*, 2(1): 23–33.

Cilliers, P. (2000b) 'Rules and complex systems', *Emergence*, 2(3): 40–50.

Cilliers, P. (2000c) 'Knowledge, complexity, and understanding', *Emergence*, 2(4): 7–13.

Cilliers, P. (2002) 'Why we cannot know complex things completely', *Emergence*, 4(1/2): 77–84.

Cohen, J. and Stewart, I. (1994) *The Collapse of Chaos: Discovering Simplicity in a Complex World*. New York: Viking.

Cohen, M.D. (1999) 'Commentary on the organization science special issue on complexity', *Organization Science*, 10(3): 373–6.

Cohen, M.D., March, J.G. and Olsen, J.P. (1972) 'A garbage can model of organizational choice', *Administrative Science Quarterly*, 17(1): 1–25.

Colander, D. (ed.) (2000) *The Complexity Vision and the Teaching of Economics*. Cheltenham, UK: Edward Elgar.

Colbert, B.A. (2004) 'The complex resource-based view: implications for theory and practice in strategic human resource management', *Academy of Management Review*, 29(3): 341–58.

Contractor, N.S. (1999) 'Self-organizing systems research in the social sciences: reconciling the metaphors and the models', *Management Communication Quarterly*, 13(1): 154–66.

Contractor, N.S., Whitbred, R., Fonti, F., Hyatt, A., O'Keefe B. and Jones, P. (2000) 'Structuration theory and self-organizing networks', Presented at the *Organization Science Winter Conference*, Keystone, CO.

Cramer, F. (1993) *Chaos and Order: The Complex Structure of Living Things* (translated by D. L. Loewus). New York: VCH.

Crowston, K. (1996) 'An approach to evolving novel organizational forms', *Computational and Mathematical Organization Theory*, 2(1): 29–47.

Curd, M. and Cover, J.A. (1998) *Philosophy of Science: The Central Issues*. New York: Norton.

Daft, R.L. (1992) *Organization Theory and Design*. Saint Paul: West.

Daft, R.L. and Weick, K.E. (1984) 'Toward a model of organizations as interpretation systems', *Academy of Management Review*, 9(2): 284–95.

Daneke, G.A. (1990) 'A science of public administration?', *Public Administration Review*, 50(3): 383–92.

Dansereau, F. and Yammarino, F.J. (eds) (1998a) *Leadership: Multiple-Level Approaches: Classical and New Wave*. Stamford: JAI Press.

Dansereau, F. and Yammarino, F.J. (eds) (1998b) *Leadership: Multiple-Level Approaches: Contemporary and Alternative*. Stamford: JAI Press.

Depew, D.J. and Weber, B.H. (1995) *Darwinism Evolving: Systems Dynamics and the Genealogy of Natural Selection*. Cambridge: MIT Press.

Derrida, J. (1978) *Writing and Difference*. Chicago: University of Chicago Press.

Dooley, K.J. and Van de Ven, A.H. (1999) 'Explaining complex organizational dynamics', *Organization Science*, 10(3): 358–72.

Dooley, K.J., Johnson, T.L. and Bush, D.H. (1995) 'TQM, chaos and complexity', *Human Systems Management*, 14(4): 287–303.

Drazin, R. and Sandelands, L. (1992) 'Autogenesis: A perspective on the process of organizing', *Organization Science*, 3(2): 230–49.

Dubinskas, F.A. (1994) 'On the edge of chaos: A metaphor for transformative change', *Journal of Management Inquiry*, 3(4): 355–66.

Duffy, J.A. (2000) 'The application of chaos theory to the career-plateaued worker', *Journal of Employment Counseling*, 37(4): 229–36.

Dumont, L. (1966) *Homo Hiérarchicus Essai Sur le Système des Castes*. Paris: Bibliothèque des Sciences Humaines, Paris: Editions Gallimard.

E, W. and Engquist, B. (2003) 'Multiscale modeling and computation', *Notices of the American Mathematical Society*, 50(9): 1062–70.

Eddington, A.S., Sir (1930) *The Nature of the Physical World*. London: Macmillan

Edmonds, B. and Hales, D. (2003) 'Replication, replication and replication: some hard lessons from model alignment', *Journal of Artificial Societies and Social Simulation*, 6(4): <http://jasss.soc.surrey.ac.uk/6/4/11.html>.

Eigen. M. and Schuster, P. (1979) *The Hypercycle: A Principle of Natural Self-Organization*. New York: Springer-Verlag.

Eisenhardt, K.M. (1989) 'Building theories from case study research', *Academy of Management Review*, 14(4): 532–50.

Eisenhardt, K.M. and Bhatia, M.M. (2002) 'Organizational complexity and computation', in J.A.C. Baum (ed.), *The Blackwell Companion to Organizations*. Oxford: Blackwell. pp. 442–66.

Eisenhardt, K.M. and Brown, S.L. (1998) 'Time pacing: competing in markets that won't stand still', *Harvard Business Review*, 76(2): 59–69.

Eisenhardt, K.M. and Brown, S.L. (1999) 'Patching: restitching business portfolios in dynamics markets', *Harvard Business Review*, 77(3): 72–82.

Epstein, J.M. and Axtell, R. (1996) *Growing Artificial Societies: Social Science from the Bottom Up*. Cambridge: MIT Press.

Favre, A., Guitton, H., Guitton, J., Lichnerowicz, A. and Wolff, E. (eds) (1988) *De la Causalité à la Finalité: A Propos de la Turbulence*. [Reprinted in English as *Chaos and Determinism* (trans. B. E. Schwarzbach). Baltimore, MD: Johns Hopkins University Press, 1995.]

Fisher, R.A., Sir (1930) *The Genetical Theory of Natural Selection*. Oxford, UK: Clarendon.

Fleming, L. and Sorenson, O. (2001) 'Technology as a complex adaptive system: evidence from patent data', *Research Policy*, 30(7): 1019–39.

Forrester, J.W. (1971) 'Counterintuitive behavior of social systems', *Technology Review*, 73(3): 53–68.

Frank, K.A. and Fahrbach, K. (1999) 'Organization culture as a complex system: balance and information in models of influence and selection', *Organization Science*, 10(3): 253–77.

Fuster, J.M. (1995) *Memory in the Cerebral Cortex: An Empirical Approach to Neural Networks in the Human and Nonhuman Primate*. Cambridge: MIT Press.

Garrido, N. (2004) 'The desirable organizational structure for evolutionary firms in static landscapes', *Metroeconomica*, 55(2–3): 318–31.

Gavetti, G. and Levinthal, D. (2000) 'Looking forward and looking backward: cognitive and experiential search', *Administrative Science Quarterly*, 45(1): 113–37.

Geertz, C. (1973) *The Interpretation of Cultures*. New York: Basic Books.

Gell-Mann, M. (1994) *The Quark and the Jaguar: Adventures in the simple and the complex*. New York: W.H. Freeman.

Gell-Mann, M. (1995) 'What is complexity?', *Complexity*, 1(1): 16–19.

Gemmill, G. and Smith, C. (1985) 'A dissipative structure model of organization transformation', *Human Relations*, 38(8): 751–66.

Gioia, D.A. and Pitre, E. (1990) 'Multiparadigm perspectives in theory building', *Academy of Management Review*, 15(4): 584–602.

Glass, N. (1996) 'Chaos, non-linear systems and day-to-day management', *European Management Journal*, 14(1): 98–106.

Gleick, J. (1987) *Chaos: Making a New Science*. New York: Penguin.

Goldstein, J.A. (1988) 'A far-from-equilibrium systems approach to resistance to change', *Organizational Dynamics*, 17(2): 16–26.

Goldstein, J.A. (1994) *The Unshackled Organization: Facing the challenge of unpredictability through spontaneous reorganization*. Portland: Productivity Press.

Goldstein, J.A. (1999) 'Emergence as a construct: history and issues', *Emergence*, 1(1): 49–72.

Goldstein, J.A. (2000) 'Emergence: a construct amid a thicket of conceptual snares', *Emergence*, 2(1): 5–22.

Gregersen, H. and Sailer, L. (1993) 'Chaos theory and its implications for social science research', *Human Relations*, 46(7): 777–802.

Haken, H. (1977) *Synergetics, An Introduction: Non-Equilibrium Phase Transitions and Self-Organization in Physics, Chemistry, and Biology*. Berlin: Springer-Verlag.

Haken, H. (1983) *Synergetics, An Introduction: Non-Equilibrium Phase Transitions and Self-Organization in Physics, Chemistry, and Biology (Third edition)*. Berlin: Springer-Verlag.

Hall, R.H., Haas, J.E. and Johnson, N.J. (1967) 'Organizational size, complexity, and formalization', *American Sociological Review*, 32(6): 903–12.

Hannan, M.T. and Freeman, J. (1977) 'The population ecology of organizations', *American Journal of Sociology*, 82(5): 929–64.

Hendrickx, M. (1999) 'What can management researchers learn from Donald T. Campbell, the philosopher:

an exercise in hermeneutics', in J.A.C. Baum and B. McKelvey (eds), *Variations in Organization Science: In Honor of Donald T. Campbell*. Thousand Oaks: Sage. pp. 339–82.

Hodgson, G.M. (2000) 'The concept of emergence in social science: its history and importance', *Emergence*, 2(4): 65–77.

Holland, J.H. (1975) *Adaptation in Natural and Artificial Systems: An introductory analysis with applications to biology, control, and artificial intelligence*. Ann Arbor: University of Michigan Press.

Holland, J.H. (1988) 'The global economy as an adaptive system', in P.W. Anderson, K.J. Arrow and D. Pines, (eds), *The Economy as an Evolving Complex System*, Vol 5. Proceedings of the Santa Fe Institute – Volume V, Reading: Addison-Wesley. pp. 117–24.

Holland, J.H. (1995) *Hidden Order: How adaptation builds complexity*. Reading: Addison-Wesley.

Holland, J.H. (1998) *Emergence: From Chaos to Order*. Cambridge: Perseus.

Holling, C.S. (1986) 'The resilience of terrestrial ecosystems: local surprise and global change', in W.M. Clark and R.E. Munn (eds), *Sustainable Development in the Biosphere*. Cambridge: Cambridge University Press. pp. 292–320.

Holton, G.J. (1993) *Science and Anti-science*. Cambridge: Harvard University Press.

Homans, G.C. (1950) *The Human Group*. New York: Harcourt.

Horgan, J. (1995) 'From complexity to perplexity', *Scientific American*, 272(6): 104–9.

Hurst, D.K. and Zimmerman, B.J. (1994) 'From life cycle to ecocycle: a new perspective on the growth, maturity, destruction, and renewal of complex systems', *Journal of Management Inquiry*, 3(4): 339–54.

Jantsch, E. (1980) *The Self-Organizing Universe: Scientific and human implications of the emerging paradigm of evolution*. New York: Pergamon.

Johnson, J.L. and Burton, B.K. (1994) 'Chaos and complexity theory for management: caveat emptor', *Journal of Management Inquiry*, 3(4): 320–8.

Juarrero, A. (1999) *Dynamics in Action: Intentional Behavior as a Complex System*. Cambridge: MIT Press.

Juarrero, A. (2000) 'Dynamics in action: intentional behavior as a complex system', *Emergence*, 2(2): 24–57.

Katz, D. and Kahn, R.L. (1966) *The Social Psychology of Organizations*. New York: Wiley.

Kauffman, S.A. (1969) 'Metabolic stability and epigenesis in randomly constructed nets', *Journal of Theoretical Biology*, 22(3): 437–67.

Kauffman, S.A. (1993) *The Origins of Order: Self-Organization and Selection in Evolution*. New York: Oxford University Press.

Kauffman, S.A. (1995a) *At Home in the Universe: The Search for the Laws of Self-Organization and Complexity*. New York: Oxford University Press.

Kauffman, S.A. (1995b) 'Escaping the red queen effect', *The McKinsey Quarterly*, 1: 119–29.

Kauffman, S.A. (2000) *Investigations*. New York: Oxford University Press.

Kauffman, S.A. and Macready, W. (1995) 'Technological evolution and adaptive organizations', *Complexity*, 1(2): 26–43.

Kaye, B.H. (1989) *A Random Walk through Fractal Dimensions*. Weinheim: VCH.

Kaye, B.H. (1993) *Chaos & Complexity: Discovering the surprising patterns of science and technology*. New York: VCH.

Kelly, S. and Allison, M. A. (1999) *The Complexity Advantage: How the science of complexity can help your business achieve peak performance*. New York: McGraw-Hill.

Kiel, L.D. (1989) 'Nonequilibrium theory and its implications for public administration', *Public Administration Review*, 49(6): 544–51.

Kiel, L.D. (1991) 'Lessons from the nonlinear paradigm: applications of the theory of dissipative structures in social sciences', *Social Science Quarterly*, 72(3): 431–42.

Kilduff, M. and Mehra, A. (1997) 'Postmodernism and organizational research', *Academy of Management Review*, 22(2): 453–81.

Koertge, N. (1998) *A House Built on Sand: Exposing Postmodernist Myths about Science*. New York: Oxford University Press.

Kuhn, T.S. (1962) *The Structure of Scientific Revolutions*. Chicago: University of Chicago Press.

Langton, C.G. (ed.) (1989) *Artificial Life*. Reading: Addison-Wesley.

Leifer, R. (1989) 'Understanding organizational transformation using a dissipative structure model', *Human Relations*, 42(10): 899–916.

Letiche, H. (2000a) 'Phenomenal complexity theory as informed by Bergson', *Journal of Organizational Change Management*, 13(6): 545–57.

Letiche, H. (2000b) 'Self-organization, action theory, and entrainment', *Emergence*, 2(2): 58–71.

Letiche, H. and Boje, D.M. (2001) 'Phenomenal complexity theory and the politics of organization', *Emergence*, 3(4): 5–31.

Levinthal, D.A. (1997a) 'Adaptation on rugged landscapes', *Management Science*, 43(7): 934–50.

Levinthal, D.A. (1997b) 'The slow pace of rapid technological change: gradualism and punctuation in technological change'. Working paper, The Wharton School, University of Pennsylvania.

Levinthal, D.A. and Warglien, M. (1999) 'Landscape design: designing for local action in complex worlds', *Organization Science*, 10(3): 342–57.

Levitan, B., Lobo, J., Schuler, R. and Kauffman, S.A. (2002) 'Evolution of organizational performance and stability in a stochastic environment', *Computational and Mathematical Organization Theory*, 8(4): 281–313.

Levy, D.L. (1994) 'Chaos theory and strategy: theory, application, and managerial implications', *Strategic Management Journal*, 15(Summer): 167–78.

Levy, D.L. (2000) 'Applications and limitations of complexity theory in organization theory and strategy', in J. Rabin, G.J. Miller and W.B. Hildreth (eds), *Handbook of Strategic Management*, 2nd edn. New York: Marcel Dekker. pp. 67–87.

Lewin, R. (1992) *Complexity: Life at the Edge of Chaos*. Chicago: University of Chicago Press.

Lichtenstein, B.M. (2000a) 'Self-organized transitions: a pattern amid the chaos of transformative change', *The Academy of Management Executive*, 14(4): 128–41.

Lichtenstein, B.M. (2000b) 'Emergence as a process of self-organizing: new assumptions and insights from the study of non-dynamic systems', *Journal of Organizational Change Management*, 13(6): 526–44.

Lichtenstein, B.M. (2000c) 'Generative knowledge and self-organized learning: reflecting on Don Schon's research', *Journal of Management Inquiry*, 9(1): 47–54.

Lichtenstein, B.M. and Brush, C.G. (2001) 'How do 'resource bundles' develop and change in new ventures? A dynamic model and longitudinal exploration', *Entrepreneurship Theory and Practice*, 25(3): 37–58.

Lichtenstein, B.M. and McKelvey, B. (2004) 'Complexity science and computational models of emergent order: what's there? What's missing?', Presented at the *Academy of Management Annual Meeting*, 6–11 August, New Orleans, LA.

Lichtenstein, B.M. Dooley, K.J. and Lumpkin, G.T. (2006) 'Measuring emergence in the dynamics of new venture creation'. *Journal of Business Venturing*, 21(2): 153–75.

Lindblom, C.E. (1959) 'The science of "Muddling Through"', *Public Administration Review* 19(2): 79–88.

Lissack, M.R. (1997a) 'Mind your metaphors: lessons from complexity science', *Long Range Planning*, 30(2): 294–8.

Lissack, M.R. (1997b) 'Of chaos and complexity: managerial insights from a new science', *Management Decision*, 35(3): 205–18.

Lissack, M.R. (1999) 'Complexity: the science, its vocabulary, and its relation to organizations', *Emergence*, 1(1): 110–26.

Lissack, M.R. (2000) 'Knowledge management redux: reframing a consulting fad into a practical tool', *Emergence*, 2(3): 78–89.

Lissack, M.R. and Letiche, H. (2002) 'Complexity, emergence, resilience, and coherence: gaining perspective on organizations and their study', *Emergence*, 4(3): 72–94.

Lopez-Garay, H. and Contreras, J. (2003) 'Dealing with complex human systems from an interpretive systemic perspective', in Y. Bar-Yam and A.A. Minai (eds), *Unifying Themes in Complex Systems (Volume II): Proceedings of the Second International Conference on Complex Systems*. Boulder: Westview Press. pp. 331–9.

Lorenz, E.N. (1963) 'Deterministic nonperiodic flow', *Journal of the Atmospheric Sciences*, 20(2): 130–41.

Lorenz, E.N. (1972) 'Predictability: does the flap of a butterfly's wings in Brazil set off a tornado in Texas?' Paper presented at the 1972 meeting of the *American Association for the Advancement of Science*. Washington, DC.

Luhman, T.J. and Boje, D.M. (2001) 'What is complexity science? A possible answer from narrative research', *Emergence*, 3(1): 158–68.

Lyotard, J.F. (1984) *The Postmodern Condition: A Report on Knowledge*. Manchester: Manchester University Press.

MacIntosh, R. and MacLean, D. (1999) 'Conditioned emergence: a dissipative structures approach to transformation', *Strategic Management Journal*, 20(4): 297–316.

Mackey, A., McKelvey, B. and Kiousis, P.K. (2005) 'What causes economy-wide CEO turnover? Leadership failure? Board failure? Complex new age economies?', Working paper, Fisher College of Business, The Ohio State University.

Maguire, S. (1999) 'Strategy as design: A fitness landscape framework', in M.R. Lissack and H.P. Gunz (eds), *Managing Complexity in Organizations: A View in Many Directions*. Westport: Quorum Books. pp. 67–104.

Maguire, S. and McKelvey, B. (1999) 'Complexity and management: moving from fad to firm foundations', *Emergence*, 1(2): 19–61.

Mainzer, K. (1994) *Thinking in Complexity: The Complex Dynamics of Matter, Mind, and Mankind*. New York: Springer-Verlag. [Much enlarged 4th edn published in 2004.]

Mandelbrot, B.B. (1961) 'Stable Paretian random functions and the multiplicative variation of income', *Econometrica*, 29(4): 517–43.

Mandelbrot, B.B. (1963) 'The variation of certain speculative prices', *Journal of Business*, 36(4): 394–419.

Mandelbrot, B.B. (1975) *Les Objets Fractals: Forme, Hasard et Dimension*. Paris: Flammarion. [Reprinted in English as *Fractals, Form, Chance and Dimension*. San Francisco, CA: Freeman, 1977.]

March, J.G. (1991) 'Exploration and exploitation in organizational learning', *Organization Science*, 2(1): 71–87.

Marion, R. (1999) *The Edge of Organization: Chaos and Complexity Theories of Formal Social Systems*. Thousand Oaks: Sage.

Marion, R. and Uhl-Bien, M. (2001) 'Leadership in complex organizations', *Leadership Quarterly*, 12(4): 389–418.

Marion, R. and Uhl-Bien, M. (2002) 'Complexity v. transformation: the new leadership revisited'. Presented at the *Managing the Complex IV Conference on Complex Systems and the Management of Organizations*, Ft. Meyers, FL.

Maruyama, M. (1963) 'The second cybernetics: Deviation-amplifying mutual causal processes', *American Scientist*, 51(2): 164–79. [Reprinted in W.F. Buckley (ed.), *Modern Systems Research for the Behavioral Scientist*, Chicago: Aldine, 1968, pp. 304–13.]

Masuch, M. (1985) 'Vicious circles in organizations', *Administrative Science Quarterly*, 30(1): 14–33.

Mathews, K.M., White, M.C. and Long, R.G. (1999) 'Why study the complexity sciences in the social sciences?', *Human Relations*, 52(4): 439–62.

McCain, R.A. (2000) *Agent-Based Computer Simulation of Dichotomous Economic Growth*. Boston: Kluwer.

McDaniel, R.R., Jr. (1997) 'Strategic leadership: a view from quantum and chaos theories', *Health Care Management Review*, 22(1): 21–37.

McKelvey, B. (1997) 'Quasi-natural organization science', *Organization Science*, 8(4): 352–80.

McKelvey, B. (1999a) 'Avoiding complexity catastrophe in coevolutionary pockets: strategies for rugged landscapes', *Organization Science*, 10(3): 294–321.

McKelvey, B. (1999b) 'Complexity theory in organization science: seizing the promise or becoming a fad?', *Emergence*, 1(1): 5–32.

McKelvey, B. (1999c) 'Self-organization, complexity catastrophe, and microstate models at the edge of chaos', in J.A.C. Baum and B. McKelvey (eds.), *Variations in Organization Science: In Honor of Donald T. Campbell*. Thousand Oaks: Sage. pp. 279–307.

McKelvey, B. (1999d) 'Toward a Campbellian realist organization science', in J.A.C. Baum and B. McKelvey (eds), *Variations in Organization Science: In Honor of Donald T. Campbell*. Thousand Oaks: Sage. pp. 383–411.

McKelvey, B. (2001a) 'What is complexity science? It is really order-creation science', *Emergence*, 3(1): 137–57.

McKelvey, B. (2001b) 'Energizing order-creating networks of distributed intelligence', *International Journal of Innovation Management*, 5: 181–212.

McKelvey, B. (2002a) 'Managing coevolutionary dynamics: some leverage points', Presented at the *18th EGOS Conference*, 4–6 July, Barcelona, Spain.

McKelvey, B. (2002b) 'Model-centered organization science epistemology', in J.A.C. Baum (ed.), *The Blackwell Companion to Organizations*. Oxford: Blackwell. pp. 752–80.

McKelvey, B. (2003a) 'Emergent order in firms: complexity science vs. the entanglement trap', in E. Mitleton-Kelly (ed.), *Complex Systems and Evolutionary Perspectives on Organisations: The Application of Complexity Theory to Organisations*. Amsterdam: Elsevier Science. pp. 99–125.

McKelvey, B. (2003b) 'From fields to science: can organization studies make the transition?', in R. Westwood and S. Clegg (eds), *Debating Organization: Point/Counterpoint in Organization Studies*. Oxford: Blackwell. pp. 47–72.

McKelvey, B. (2003c) 'Postmodernism vs. truth in management theory', in E. Locke (ed.), *Post Modernism and Management: Pros, Cons, and the Alternative, Research in the Sociology of Organizations*, Vol 21. Amsterdam: Elsevier. pp. 113–68.

McKelvey, B. (2004a) '"Simple rules" for improving corporate IQ: basic lessons from complexity science', in P. Andriani and G. Passiante (eds), *Complexity Theory and the Management of Networks: Proceedings of the workshop on organisational networks as distributed systems of knowledge*. London: Imperial College Press. pp. 39–52.

McKelvey, B. (2004b) 'Toward a 0th law of thermodynamics: order creation complexity dynamics from physics and biology to bioeconomics', *Journal of Bioeconomics*, 6(1): 65–96.

McKelvey, B. (2004c) 'Toward a complexity science of entrepreneurship', *Journal of Business Venturing*, 19(3): 313–41.

McKelvey, B. (forthcoming) 'Microstrategy from macroleadership: distributed intelligence via new science', in A.Y. Lewin and H.W. Volberda (eds), *Mobilizing the Self-renewing Organization: The Coevolution Advantage*. New York: Palgrave Macmillan.

Mendenhall, M.E., Macomber, J.H., Gregersen, H. and Cutright, M. (1998) 'Nonlinear dynamics: a new perspective on IHRM research and practice in the 21st century', *Human Resource Management Review*, 8(1): 5–22.

Merry, U. (1995) *Coping with Uncertainty: Insights from the New Sciences of Chaos, Self-Organization, and Complexity*. Westport: Praeger.

Miles, R., Snow, C.C., Matthews, J.A. and Miles, G. (1999) 'Cellular-network organizations', in W.E. Halal and K.B. Taylor (eds), *Twenty-First Century Economics: Perspectives of socioeconomics for a changing world*. New York: Macmillan. pp. 155–73.

Miller, D. (1986) 'Configurations of strategy and structure: towards a synthesis', *Strategic Management Journal*, 7(3): 233–49.

Miller, J.G. (1978) *Living Systems*. New York: McGraw-Hill.

Mintzberg, H. (1990) 'Strategy formation: schools of thought', in J.W. Frederickson (ed.), *Perspectives on Strategic Management*. New York: Harper. pp. 105–235.

Mitchell, M., Hraber, P.T. and Crutchfield, J.P. (1993) 'Revisiting the edge of chaos: evolving cellular automata to perform computations', *Complex Systems*, 7: 89–130.

Moldoveanu, M.C. (2005) 'An inter-subjective measure of complexity grounds: a new approach to the study of organizational complexity', in K.A. Richardson (ed.), *Managing Organizational Complexity: Philosophy, Theory, and Application*. Greenwich: Information Age Publishing. pp. 225–86.

Moldoveanu, M.C. and Bauer, R.M. (2004) 'On the relationship between organizational complexity and organizational structuration', *Organization Science*, 15(1): 98–118.

Morçöl, G. (2001) 'What is complexity science? Postmodernist or postpositivist?', *Emergence*, 3(1): 104–19.

Morel, B. and Ramanujam, R. (1999) 'Through the looking glass of complexity: the dynamics of organizations as adaptive and evolving systems', *Organization Science*, 10(3): 278–93.

Morgan, G. (1986) *Images of Organization*. Thousand Oaks: Sage.

Nicolis, G. and Prigogine, I. (1977) *Self-Organization in Nonequilibrium Systems*. New York: John Wiley and Sons.

Nicolis, G. and Prigogine, I. (1989) *Exploring Complexity: An Introduction*. New York: W.H. Freeman.

Nonaka, I. (1988a) 'Creating organizational order out of chaos: self-renewal in Japanese firms', *California Management Review*, 30(3): 57–73.

Nonaka, I. (1988b) 'Toward middle-up-down management: accelerating information creation', *Sloan Management Review*, 29(3): 9–18.

Ormerod, P. (1994) *The Death of Economics*, New York: John Wiley and Sons.

Ormerod, P. (1998) *Butterfly Economics: A New General Theory of Social and Economic Behavior*. New York: Pantheon.

Ott, E. (1993) *Chaos in Dynamical Systems*. New York: Cambridge University Press.

Overman, E.S. (1996) 'The new sciences of administration: chaos and quantum theory', *Public Administration Review*, 56(5): 487–91.

Parsons, T. (1961) 'An outline of the social system', in T. Parsons, E. Shils, K.D. Naegele and J.R. Pitts (eds), *Theories of Society: Foundations of modern sociological theory*. New York: Free Press of Glencoe. pp. 30–79.

Pascale, R.T. (1999) 'Surfing the edge of chaos', *Sloan Management Review*, 40(3): 83–94.

Pascale, R.T., Millemann, M. and Gioja, L. (1999) *Surfing the edge of chaos: The laws of nature and the new laws of business*. New York: Three Rivers Press.

Paul, D.L., Butler, J.C., Pearlson, K.E. and Whinston A.B. (1996) 'Computationally modeling organizational learning and adaptability as resource allocation: an artificial adaptive systems approach', *Computational and Mathematical Organization Theory*, 2(4): 301–24.

Peters, T.J. (1987) *Thriving on Chaos: Handbook for a management revolution*. New York: Knopf.

Pfeffer, J. (1993) 'Barriers to the advancement of organizational science: paradigm development as a dependent variable', *Academy of Management Review*, 18(4): 599–620.

Phelan, S.E. (2001) 'What is complexity science, really?', *Emergence*, 3(1): 120–36.

Pines, D. (ed.) (1988) *Emerging Syntheses in Science: Proceedings of the Founding Workshops of the Santa Fe Institute (Volume I)*. Reading: Addison-Wesley.

Poincaré, H. (1890) 'Sur le problème des trios corps et les équations de la dynamique', *Acta Mathematica*, 13: 1–270.

Polley, D. (1997) 'Turbulence in organizations: new metaphors for organizational research', *Organization Science*, 8(5): 445–57.

Popper, K.R. (1959) *The Logic of Scientific Discovery*. London: Hutchinson.

Poston, T. and Stewart, I. (1978) *Catastrophe theory and its applications*. London: Pitman

Priesmeyer, H.R. and Baik, K. (1989) 'Discovering the patterns of chaos: a potential new planning tool', *Planning Review*, 17(6): 14–23.

Prigogine, I. (1955) *An Introduction to Thermodynamics of Irreversible Processes*. Springfield: Thomas.

Prigogine, I. (1962) *Non-Equilibrium Statistical Mechanics*. New York: Wiley-Interscience.

Prigogine, I. (1980) *From Being to Becoming: Time and complexity in the physical sciences*. San Francisco: Freeman.

Prigogine, I. (with Stengers, I.) (1997) *The End of Certainty: Time, Chaos, and the New Laws of Nature*. New York: Free Press.

Prigogine, I. and Stengers, I. (1984) *Order Out of Chaos: Man's New Dialogue with Nature*. New York: Bantam.

Quinn, J.B. (1985). 'Managing innovation: controlled chaos', *Harvard Business Review*, 63(3): 73–84.

Reed, M.I. (1985) *Redirections in Organizational Analysis*. London: Tavistock.

Reed, M. and Harvey, D. (1992) 'The new science and the old: complexity and realism in the social sciences', *Journal for the Theory of Social Behavior*, 22(4): 353–80.

Richardson, K. and Cilliers, P. (2001) 'What is complexity science? A view from different directions', *Emergence*, 3(1): 5–23.

Richardson, K.A., Cilliers, P. and Lissack, M. (2001) 'Complexity science: a "gray" science for the "stuff in between"', *Emergence*, 3(2): 6–18.

Rivkin, J.W. (2000) 'Imitation of complex strategies', *Management Science*, 46(6): 824–44.

Rivkin, J.W. (2001) 'Reproducing knowledge: replication without imitation at moderate complexity', *Organization Science*, 12(3): 274–93.

Rivkin, J.W. and Siggelkow, N. (2002) 'Organizational sticking points on *NK* landscapes', *Complexity*, 7(5): 31–43.

Rivkin, J.W. and Siggelkow, N. (2003) 'Balancing search and stability: interdependencies among elements of organizational design', *Management Science*, 49(3): 290–311.

Roethlisberger, F.J. and Dixon, W.J. (1939) *Management and the Worker: An account of a research program conducted by the Western electric company, Hawthorne works, Chicago*. Cambridge: Harvard University Press.

Romme, G.L. (1995) 'Self-organizing processes in top management teams: a boolean comparative approach', *Journal of Business Research*, 34(1): 11–34.

Romme, G.L. (1999) 'Domination, self-determination and circular organizing', *Organization Studies*, 20(5): 801–32.

Rosenau, P.M. (1992) *Post-Modernism and the Social Sciences: Insights, Inroads, and Intrusions*. Princeton: Princeton University Press.

Rosser, J.B., Jr. (1999) 'On the complexities of complex economic dynamics', *Journal of Economic Perspectives*, 13(4): 169–92.

Rosser, J.B., Jr. (2001) 'Complex ecologic-economic dynamics and environmental policy', *Ecological Economics*, 37(1): 23–37.

Rouchier, J. (2003) 'Re-implementation of a multi-agent model aimed at sustaining experimental economic research: the case of simulations with emerging specu-lation', *Journal of Artificial Societies and Social Simulation*, 6(4): <http://jasss.soc.surrey.ac.uk/6/4/7.html>.

Salthe, S.N. (1993) *Development and Evolution: Complexity and Change in Biology*. Cambridge: MIT Press.

Schumpeter, J.A. (1942) *Capitalism, Socialism, and Democracy*. New York: Harper & Brothers.

Scott, W.R. (2002) *Organizations: Rational, Natural and Open Systems*, 5th edn. Englewood Cliffs: Prentice-Hall.

Siggelkow, N. and Levinthal, D.A. (2003) 'Temporarily divide to conquer: centralized, decentralized, and rein-tegrated organizational approaches to exploration and adaptation', *Organization Science*, 14(6): 650–69.

Siggelkow, N. and Levinthal, D.A. (2005) 'Escaping real (non-benign) competency traps: linking the dynamics of organizational structure to the dynamics of search', *Strategic Organization*, 3(1): 85–115.

Silverman, D. (1970) *The Theory of Organisations: A Sociological Framework*. London: Heinemann.

Simon, H.A. (1962) 'The architecture of complexity', *Proceedings of the American Philosophical Society*, 106(6): 467–82.

Simon, H.A. (1999) 'Coping with complexity', in Groupe de Recherche sur l'Adaptation la Systémique et la Complexité Economique GRASCE) (ed.), *Entre Systémique et Complexité Chemin Faisant… Mélanges en l'honneur du professeur Jean-Louis Le Moigne*. Paris: Presses Universitaires de France. pp. 233–40.

Smilor, R.W. and Feeser, H.R. (1991) 'Chaos and the entre-preneurial process: patterns and policy implications for technology entrepreneurship', *Journal of Business Venturing*, 6(3): 165–72.

Smith, C. and Comer, D. (1994) 'Self-organization in small groups: a study of group effectiveness within non-equilibrium conditions', *Human Relations*, 47(5): 553–81.

Smith, C. and Gemmill, G. (1991) 'Change in the small group: a dissipative structure perspective', *Human Relations*, 44(7): 697–716.

Smith, R.D. (1995) 'The inapplicability principle: what chaos means for social science', *Behavioral Science*, 40(1): 22–40.

Snowden, D.J. (2000) 'New wine in old wineskins: from organic to complex knowledge management through the use of story', *Emergence*, 2(4): 50–64.

So, Y. and Durfee E.H. (1996) 'Designing tree-structured organizations for computational agents', *Computational and Mathematical Organization Theory*, 2(3): 219–45.

Sorenson, O. (1997) 'The complexity catastrophe in the evolution in the computer industry: interdependence and adaptability in organizational evolution'. Unpublished PhD thesis, Department of Sociology, Stanford University

Sorenson, O. (2002) 'Interorganizational complexity and com-putation', in J.A.C. Baum (ed.), *The Blackwell Companion to Organizations*. Oxford: Blackwell. pp. 664–85.

Sorenson, O. (2003) 'Interdependence and adaptability: organizational learning and the long-term effect of integration', *Management Science*, 49(4):446–63.

Stacey, R.D. (1991) *The Chaos Frontier: Creative Strate-gic Control for Business*. Oxford: Butterworth-Heinemann.

Stacey, R.D. (1992) *Managing the unknowable: Strategic boundaries between order and chaos in organizations*. San Francisco: Jossey-Bass.

Stacey, R.D. (1993) 'Strategy as order emerging from chaos', *Long Range Planning*, 26(1): 10–17.

Stacey, R.D. (1995) 'The science of complexity: an alterna-tive perspective for strategic change processes', *Strategic Management Journal*, 16(6): 477–95.

Stacey, R.D. (1996) *Complexity and Creativity in Organizations*. San Francisco: Berrett-Koehler.

Stacey R.D. (2000) 'The emergence of knowledge in orga-nizations', *Emergence*, 2(4): 23–39.

Stacey, R.D. (2001) *Complex Responsive Processes in Organizations: Learning and Knowledge Creation*. London: Routledge.

Strogatz, S.H. (2005) 'Complex systems: romanesque net-works', *Nature*, 433: 365–6.

Stumpf, S.A. (1995) 'Applying new science theories in lead-ership development activities', *The Journal of Management Development*, 14(5): 39–49.

Suppe, F. (ed.) (1977) *The Structure of Scientific Theories*, 2nd edn. Urbana: University of Illinois Press.

Svyantek, D.J. and DeShon, R.P. (1993) 'Organizational attractors: a chaos theory explanation of why cultural change efforts often fail', *Public Administration Quarterly*, 17(3): 339–55.

Thietart, R.A. and Forgues, B, (1995) 'Chaos theory and organization', *Organization Science*, 6(1): 19–31.

Thom, R. (1975) *Structural Stability and Morphogenesis: An outline of a general theory of models*. Reading: Benjamin/Cummings.

Thomas, C., Kaminska-Labbé, R. and McKelvey, B. (2006) 'Managing the MNC and exploitation/exploration dilemma: from static balance to dynamic oscillation', in G. Szulanski, Y. Doz and J. Porac (eds), *Advances in Strategic Management: Expanding Perspectives on the Strategy Process*, Vol 22. London: Elsevier. pp. 213–47.

Thompson, J.D. (1967) *Organizations in Action: Social science bases of administrative theory*. New York: McGraw-Hill.

Tsoukas, H. (1991) 'The missing link: a transformational view of metaphors in organizational science', *Academy of Management Review*, 16(3): 566–85.

Tsoukas, H. and Hatch, M.J. (2001) 'Complex thinking, complex practice: the case for a narrative approach to organizational complexity', *Human Relations*, 54(8): 979–1013.

Uhl-Bien, M., Marion, R. and McKelvey, B. (2004) 'Complex leadership: shifting leadership from the industrial age to the knowledge era', presented at the

Academy of Management Annual Meeting, 6–11 August, New Orleans, LA.

Van de Ven, A.H. and Poole, M.S. (1995) 'Explaining development and change in organizations', *Academy of Management Review*, 20(3): 510–40.

Vickers, G., Sir (1965) *The Art of Judgment: A Study of Policy Making*. London: Chapman and Hall.

von Bertalanffy, L. (1950) 'An outline of general system theory', *British Journal for the Philosophy of Science*, 1(2): 134–65.

von Bertalanffy, L. (1968) *General System Theory: Foundations, development, applications*. New York: George Braziller.

von Neumann, J. (1951) 'The general and logical theory of automata', in L.A. Jeffress (ed.), *Cerebral Mechanisms in Behavior: The Hixon Symposium*. New York: John Wiley. pp. 1–41.

Waldman D.A. and Yammarino, F.J. (1999) 'CEO charismatic leadership: levels-of-management and levels-of-analysis effects', *Academy of Management Review*, 24(2): 266–85.

Waldrop, M.M. (1992) *Complexity: The Emerging Science at the Edge of Order and Chaos*. New York: Simon and Schuster.

Weick, K.E. (1969) *The Social Psychology of Organizing*. Reading: Addison-Wesley.

Weick, K.E. (1977) 'Organization design: organizations as self-designing systems', *Organizational Dynamics*, 6(2): 31–46.

Weick, K.E. (1987) 'Substitutes for strategy', in D. Teece (ed.), *The Competitive Challenge: Strategies for indus-*

trial innovation and renewal. New York: Harper and Row. pp. 221–33.

Weick, K.E. (2001) *Making Sense of the Organization*. Oxford: Blackwell.

Wheatley, M.J. (1992) *Leadership and the New Science: Learning About Organization from an Orderly Universe*. San Francisco: Berrett-Koehler

Wheatley, M.J. and Kellner-Rogers, M. (1996) 'Self-organization: the irresistible future of organizing', *Strategy & Leadership*, 24(4): 18–24.

White, M.C., Marin, D.B., Brazeal, D.V. and Friedman, W.H. (1997) 'The evolution of organizations: suggestions from complexity theory about the interplay between natural selection and adaptation', *Human Relations*, 50(11): 1383–401.

Wolfram, S. (1983) 'Statistical mechanics of cellular automata', *Reviews of Modern Physics*, 55(3): 601–44.

Wright, S. (1931) 'Evolution in mendelian populations', *Genetics*, 16(2): 97–159.

Yin, R.K. (2003) *Case Study Research: Design and Methods*, 3rd edn. Thousand Oaks: Sage.

Yuan, Y. and McKelvey, W. (2004) 'Situated learning theory: adding rate and complexity effects via Kauffman's NK model', *Nonlinear Dynamics, Psychology, and Life Sciences*, 8(1): 65–101.

Zimmerman, B., Lindberg, C. and Plsek, P. (1998) *Edgeware: Insights from Complexity Science for Health Care Leaders*. Irving: VHA

Zuijderhoudt, R.W.L. (1990) 'Chaos and the dynamics of self-organization', *Human Systems Management*, 9(4): 225–38.

1.6 Institutions and Institutional Work

THOMAS B. LAWRENCE AND ROY SUDDABY

Introduction

Institutional approaches to organization studies focus attention on the relationships among organizations and the fields in which they operate, highlighting in particular the role of rational formal structures in enabling and constraining organizational behaviour. A key contribution of institutional studies has been the development of strong accounts of the processes through which institutions govern action. This has been accomplished in part through theoretical statements which have delineated key sets of concepts and relationships that tie institutional structures and logics to organizational forms and conduct (Meyer and Rowan 1977; DiMaggio and Powell 1983; Greenwood and Hinings 1996). Also key in the development of institutional understandings of organizational action has been the large set of empirical studies that have documented the connections among institutions, fields and organizations. These studies have catalogued the impact of institutional forces in a wide variety of sectors and geographic contexts, and at varying levels of analysis including intra-organizational (Zilber 2002), interorganizational (Leblebici et al. 1991) and international (Keohane 1989; Meyer et al. 1997). Finally, there has emerged an influential set of reviews of institutionalism in organization studies that have summarized and synthesized the major work in the area into coherent frameworks (DiMaggio and Powell 1991; Tolbert and Zucker 1996; Scott 2001; Schneiberg and Clemens 2006).

Although the traditional emphasis of institutional approaches to organization studies has been on the explanation of organizational similarity based on institutional conditions, there has over the past 10–15 years emerged a new emphasis in institutional studies on understanding the role of actors in effecting, transforming and maintaining institutions and fields. The role of actors in creating new institutions has been examined primarily under the rubric of institutional entrepreneurship (Eisenstadt 1980; DiMaggio 1988). DiMaggio (1988: 14) argues that institutional entrepreneurs are central to institutional processes, since 'new institutions arise when organized actors with sufficient resources (institutional entrepreneurs) see in them an opportunity to realize interests that they value highly'. The concept of institutional entrepreneurship is important because it focuses attention on the manner in which interested actors work to influence their institutional contexts through such strategies as technical and market leadership, lobbying for regulatory change and discursive action (Suchman 1995; Fligstein 1997; Hoffman 1999; Garud et al. 2002; Maguire et al. 2004). The role of actors in the transformation of existing institutions and fields has also risen in prominence within institutional research. Institutional studies have documented the ability of actors, particularly those with some key strategic resources or other forms of power, to have significant impacts on the evolution of institutions and fields (Clemens 1993; Holm 1995; Oakes et al. 1998; Greenwood et al. 2002), including both institutional transformation and deinstitutionalization (Oliver 1992; Ahmadjian and Robinson 2001). Finally, a more modest amount of research has begun to examine the role of actors in maintaining institutions: although definitions of institution emphasize their enduring nature (Hughes 1936), institutions rely on the action of individuals and organizations for their reproduction over time (Berger and Luckmann 1966; Giddens 1984).

In this chapter, we aim to provide a summary and synthesis of research on what we refer to as 'institutional work' – the purposive action of individuals and organizations aimed at creating, maintaining and disrupting institutions. Thus far, research on institutional work has been largely unconnected as such – literatures on institutional entrepreneurship and deinstitutionalization have emerged as semi-coherent research streams, but the overall focus has remained largely unarticulated. Thus, a key contribution of this chapter will be the provision of a framework that connects previously disparate studies of institutional work and the articulation of a research agenda for the area. By focusing on empirical work that has occurred in the past 15 years and mapping it in terms of the forms of institutional work that it has examined, we are able to both provide a first cataloguing of forms of institutional work and point to issues and areas that have been under-examined.

The structure of the chapter is as follows: (1) a definition and discussion of the concept of institutional work; (2) a map of empirical studies of institutional work; and (3) a discussion of emerging and illustrative approaches to the study of institutional work.

The Concept of Institutional Work

The concept of an institution is at the heart of all institutional approaches to organizational research: central to both theoretical and empirical examinations of organizational phenomena that adopt an institutionalist perspective is the idea that there are enduring elements in social life – institutions – that have a profound effect on the thoughts, feelings and behaviour of individual and collective actors. The literature is replete with definitions of institutions. Scott (2001: 48) describes institutions as consisting of 'cultured-cognitive, normative and regulative elements that … provide stability and meaning to social life … Institutions are transmitted by various types of carriers, including symbolic systems, relational systems, routines and artifacts' and they 'operate at multiple levels of jurisdiction'. Fligstein (2001: 108) echoes Scott's emphasis on regulation and human cognition in defining institutions as 'rules and shared meanings … that define social relationships, help define who occupies what position in those relationships and guide interaction by giving actors cognitive frames or sets of meanings to interpret the behaviour of others'. The neo-institutional view of institutions has been criticized for privileging the role of cognition in conceptualizing

institutional action (Greenwood and Hinings 1996; Hirsch 1997; Hirsch and Lounsbury 1997). Institutional economists, by contrast, emphasize the role of human agency in devising institutions. North (1990: 97), for example, describes institutions as 'humanly devised constraints that structure political, economic and social interaction. They consist of both informal constraints (sanctions, taboos, customs, traditions and codes of conduct) and formal rules (constitutions, laws and property rights)'. Jepperson's (1991: 143–5) definition comes closest to the position we adopt here; that institutions are the product (intentional or otherwise) of purposive action. Institutions, he argues, are 'an organized, established procedure' that reflect a set of 'standardized interaction sequences'. In contrast to previous definitions of institutions, which view them as the relatively passive construction of meaning by participants, Jepperson points toward the possibility of viewing institutions as patterns of sequenced interaction supported by specific mechanisms of control. Institutions, in this view, are the product of specific actions taken to reproduce, alter and destroy them.

Jepperson's approach points to an emerging focus within institutional studies. Along with understanding the processes through which institutions affect organizational action, research has become increasingly concerned with the effects of individual and organizational action on institutions. This concern seems to us to represent an important part of the future of institutional studies in management and organization theory. In this section, we introduce the concept of 'institutional work' to represent the broad category of purposive action aimed at creating, maintaining and disrupting institutions. We do so by discussing two sets of writing, one that articulated the core elements of the study of institutional work and motivated organizational researchers to pursue this direction, and a second that has the potential to provide a robust theoretical foundation for the concept of institutional work.

Agency in Institutional Studies

Our conception of institutional work is rooted in a small set of articles that articulate a broad theoretical outline for the study of institutional work, parallel to the way in which the articles by Meyer and Rowan (1977) and DiMaggio and Powell (1983) provided the underpinnings for the new institutionalism in organization studies. The first of these articles is

DiMaggio's (1988) essay on 'Interest and agency in institutional theory'. Here, DiMaggio describes the concept of institutional entrepreneurship as a means of understanding how new institutions arise. This essay not only re-introduced strategy and power into neo-institutional explanations (Eisenstadt 1980; DiMaggio 1988), but also provided the foundation for a shift in the attention of institutional researchers toward the effects of actors and agency on institutions. The concept of institutional entrepreneurship focuses attention on the manner in which interested actors work to influence their institutional contexts through such strategies as technical and market leadership or lobbying for regulatory change (Fligstein 1997; Hoffman 1999; Rao et al. 2000; Maguire et al. 2004). Thus, it highlights the importance of the practices of individuals and organizations in the creation of new institutions. We believe, however, that such practices go well beyond those of institutional entrepreneurs – the creation of new institutions requires institutional work on the part of a wide range of actors, both those with the resources and skills to act as entrepreneurs and those whose role is supportive or facilitative of the entrepreneur's endeavours (Leblebici et al. 1991).

The other major articles in which agency was first recognized as central in the new institutional theory were Oliver's (1991) discussion of strategic responses to institutional processes, and her (Oliver 1992) account of deinstitutionalization. In the first of these articles, Oliver (1991) presented a framework for understanding the range of responses available to organizations facing institutional pressures, and the contexts under which these different responses would be most likely to occur. Oliver (1991: 145) argued that what the institutional literature was lacking to that point was 'explicit attention to the strategic behaviours that organizations employ in direct response to the institutional processes that affect them'. In response to this gap in the literature, Oliver proposed a five-part typology of such strategic responses that varied in the degree to which they involved 'active agency' on the part of the organization: from most to least passive, the five responses are acquiescence, compromise, avoidance, defiance and manipulation. While the potential for actors to respond to institutional processes and pressures in a variety of ways had been recognized in early institutional theory (Selznick 1949), Oliver (1991) represented the first systematic attempt at

articulating the range of potential responses. This article has since provided the theoretical foundation for numerous empirical studies and theoretical extensions (Rao et al. 2001; Seo and Creed 2002; Thornton 2002; Zilber 2002; Lawrence 2004; Washington and Zajac 2005; Greenwood and Suddaby 2006).

The second key article by Oliver examined the antecedents of deinstitutionalization. Oliver (1992: 564) argued that deinstitutionalization represents 'the delegitimation of an established organizational practice or procedure as a result of organizational challenges to or the failure of organizations to reproduce previously legitimated or taken-for-granted organizational actions'. Although not explicitly focused on action, Oliver's discussion of deinstitutionalization highlights two important categories of institutional work. First, the notion of deinstitutionalization points to the potential for organizational actors to actively engage in the disruption of institutions – to engage in institutional work aimed not at creating or supporting institution but at tearing them down or rendering them ineffectual. Oliver (1992: 567) describes this work as the 'rejection' of an institution: a 'direct assault on the validity of a long-standing tradition or established activity'. As an example, Oliver (1992: 567) points to the example of 'direct challenges to the appropriateness of traditional job classifications on the basis of stereotypical gender roles [which] have led to the deinstitutionalization of this practice in many organizations'.

The second category of institutional work pointed to by Oliver's discussion of deinstitutionalization is the work done by individuals and organizations in order to maintain existing institutions. Oliver (1992: 564) highlights this form of institutional work indirectly when she mentions 'the failure of organizations to reproduce previously legitimated or taken-for-granted organizational actions'. Thus, the reproduction and continuation of institutions cannot be taken for granted, even the most highly institutionalized technologies, structures, practices and rules require the active involvement of individuals and organizations in order to maintain them over time (Lawrence et al. 2001). Zucker (1988) argues that even among institutions, entropy is a natural tendency that needs to be overcome by organized action. Despite the potential importance of this category of institutional work, it has gained relatively little attention. As Scott (2001: 110) notes, 'most institutional scholars accord little attention to the issue of institutional persistence, and those who do disagree over what mechanisms underlie stability'.

Of course, the articles by DiMaggio (1988) and Oliver (1991; 1992) are by no means the only ones that deal with institutional work. Each of these articles has themselves spawned a host of articles and book chapters in which the empirical dynamics and theoretical implications of their ideas has been explored, and that have consequently added considerably to our understanding of institutional work. There have also been a number of attempts to provide more general descriptions of the relationship between action and institutions (DiMaggio and Powell 1991; Beckert 1999; Lawrence 1999; Fligstein 2001). DiMaggio and Powell (1991), for instance, describe a model of 'practical action' in which they emphasize a number of shifts which have occurred between the old and new institutionalisms:

> from object-relations to cognitive theory, from cathexis to ontological anxiety, from discursive to practical reason, from internalization to imitation, from commitment to ethnomethodological trust, from sanctioning to ad hocing, from norms to scripts and schemas, from values to accounts, from consistency and integration to loose coupling, and from roles to routines (DiMaggio and Powell 1991: 26–7).

Together, these shifts lead to an image of action as dependent on cognitive (rather than affective) processes and structures, and thus suggests an approach to the study of institutional work that focuses on understanding how actors accomplish the social construction of rules, scripts, schemas and cultural accounts.

Beckert (1999) extends this emphasis on the cognitive links between action and institutions, arguing that institutional rules and 'strategic agency' both act as co-ordinating mechanisms in market situations where actors are attempting to pursue (perhaps institutionalized) goals of profit or competitive advantage. Beckert argues that institutions can provide actors with the ability to act when the 'complexity of the situation and the informational constraints do not allow them to assign probabilities to the possible consequences of choices'; at the same time, however, institutions 'come under pressure from agents who recognize their constraining qualities for more efficient outcomes' (Beckert 1999: 779).

Consistent with this general approach is Lawrence's (1999) concept of institutional strategy, which he describes as: 'patterns of organizational action concerned with the formation and transformation of institutions, fields and the rules and standards that control those structures'. The concept of institutional strategy describes the manipulation of symbolic resources, particularly membership access and the definition of standards, which are key aspects of the type of work necessary in the early stages of an institutionalization project. Fligstein (2001), in a related fashion, uses the construct of 'social skill' to describe the various tactics that social actors use to gain the co-operation of others. Fligstein (2001: 106) further observes that the social skills used to reproduce fields are different from those used in conditions of crisis or change. These latter skills are used by entrepreneurs who 'find ways to get disparate groups to co-operate precisely by putting themselves into the positions of others and creating meanings that appeal to a large number of actors'.

We believe that the theoretical pieces by DiMaggio (1988) and Oliver (1991; 1992) represent a signal shift in the attention of institutional researchers toward the impact of individual and collective actors on the institutions that regulate the fields in which they operate. From these early works has emerged an important tradition within institutional theory that explores theoretically and empirically the ways in which actors are able to create, maintain and disrupt institutions.

Sociology of Practice

The second major foundation for the concept of institutional work comes from research in the tradition of and inspired by the sociology of practice (Bourdieu 1977; 1993; de Certeau 1984; Giddens 1984; Lave and Wenger 1991). This tradition understands practices as 'embodied, materially mediated arrays of human activity centrally organized around shared practical understanding' (Schatzki et al. 2001: 2). Thus, studies of practice focus on the situated actions of individuals and groups as they cope with and attempt to respond to the demands of their everyday lives (de Certeau 1984). Practice theory and research are most easily understood in contrast to process-oriented studies: as Brown and Duguid (2000: 95) argue, to focus on practice is to focus on the 'internal life of process'. Whereas a process-oriented theory articulates a sequence of events that leads to some outcome, a practice theory describes the intelligent activities of individuals and organizations who are working to effect those events and achieve that outcome.[1]

In organizational research, an interest in practice has begun to be seen in a variety of domains, including organizational learning (Brown and Duguid 1991; Lave and Wenger 1991), strategy (Whittington 2003; Whittington et al. 2003), technology management (Orlikowski 2000), accounting (Hopwood and Miller 1994; Miller 2001), organization theory (Pentland 1992; Dutton et al. 2001) and time in organizations (Orlikowski and Yates 2002). In all of these areas, researchers have begun to examine organizational actors as knowledgeable and practical in their affairs (Giddens 1984). The central tenets of practice theory are consistent with and have the potential to contribute substantially to institutional research. As in institutional theory, the practice perspective locates the concept of a 'field' as central to all things social. Summarizing this issue, Schatzki et al. (2001: 3) argue that 'practice approaches promulgate a distinct social ontology: the social is a field of embodied, materially interwoven practices centrally organized around shared practical understandings'.

Our concept of institutional work follows in this practice tradition: we view institutional work as intelligent, situated institutional action. A practice perspective on institutional work is made clearer in its contrast with a process perspective on institutions. The focus of processual descriptions of institutionalization (e.g. Greenwood and Hinings 1996; Tolbert and Zucker 1996) has been on the institutions: what happens to them; how they are transformed; what states they take on and in what order. In contrast, a practice orientation focuses on the world inside the processes (Brown and Duguid 2000; Whittington 2003) – the work of actors as they attempt to shape those processes, as they work to create, maintain and disrupt institutions. This does not mean that the study of institutional work is intended to move back to an understanding of actors as independent, autonomous agents capable of fully realizing their interests through strategic action; instead, a practice perspective highlights the creative and knowledgeable work of actors which may or may not achieve its desired ends and which interacts with existing social and technological structures in unintended and unexpected ways. As

Orlikowski (2000: 407) argues with respect to technology, for example, a practice perspective:

> acknowledges that while users can and do use technologies as they were designed, they also can and do circumvent inscribed ways of using the technologies – either ignoring certain properties of the technology, working around them, or inventing new ones that may go beyond or even contradict designers' expectations and inscriptions.

Thus, adopting a practice perspective on institutions points research and theory toward understanding the knowledgeable, creative and practical work of individual and collective actors aimed at creating, maintaining and transforming institutions.

Key Elements of the Study of Institutional Work

We believe that bringing together the interest in agency within institutional theory spawned by DiMaggio (1988) and Oliver (1991; 1992) with the practice turn in social theory provides a solid conceptual foundation for the emerging study of institutional work. Together, they suggest an approach to the study of institutional work with three key elements.

First, the study of institutional work would highlight the awareness, skill and reflexivity of individual and collective actors. Some versions of institutional theory strongly emphasize the 'taken-for-grantedness' of institutions, and thus have the potential to construct actors as cultural dopes (Hirsch and Lounsbury 1997). In contrast, the concept of institutional work suggests culturally competent actors with strong practical skills and sensibility who creatively navigate within their organizational fields. This is not to suggest, however, a return to the rational actor model. Rather, we draw on an understanding of actors as rational in the sense that they are able to work with institutionally-defined logics of effect or appropriateness (March 1994), and that doing so requires culturally-defined forms of competence and knowledge, as well as the creativity to adapt to conditions that are both demanding and dynamic (Giddens 1984; Cassell 1993).

The second element is an understanding of institutions as constituted in the more and less conscious action of individual and collective actors. In an essay exploring the ontological status of macrosociological phenomena, including institutions,

Barnes (2001) argues that, from a practice perspective, these phenomena are located in the sets of practices people engage in as a part of those macro-phenomena, rather than, for instance, emerging from those practices and existing at some other 'level'. Democracy, for instance, resides in the acts of polling, campaigning and related activities that people do as citizens of a democratic society, rather than describing some emergent property of the society that is separate from those practices. This leads us to suggest that the study of institutional work be centrally concerned with understanding both the sets of practices in which institutional actors engage that maintain institutions, and the practices that are associated with the creation of new institutions and the disruption of existing ones.

Finally, a practice perspective on institutional work suggests that we cannot step outside of action as practice – even action which is aimed at changing the institutional order of an organizational field occurs within sets of institutionalized rules. Giddens (1984: 21) describes rules as 'techniques or generalizable procedures applied in the enactment/reproduction of social practices' – to this we would add that there are techniques and generalizable procedures that are applied in the disruption/transformation of social practices. This in no way suggests a lack of potential innovation in institutional fields, but merely that the practices which might lead to institutional innovations are themselves institutionally embedded and so rely on sets of resources and skills that are specific to the field or fields in which they occur. In the remainder of this chapter, we work from this perspective to begin to outline the terrain of institutional work – the sets of practices through which individual and collective actors create, maintain and disrupt the institutions of organizational fields.

Institutional Work in Organizations

In this section, we examine empirically-based institutional research in order to provide an overview of what we do and do not understand about institutional work. In order to do this, we draw primarily from empirical research published since 1990 in three major organizational journals in which institutional research appears – *Administrative Science Quarterly, Academy of Management Journal* and *Organization Studies*. Our intention here is not to conduct an exhaustive overview, nor to provide a definitive schema of institutional work. Rather, our objective is to reveal and illustrate the sediment of institutional work in the existing literature and, thereby, outline the terrain of an emerging object of institutional inquiry. Although relatively few articles within the now voluminous body of empirical research in neo-institutional theory focus solely on institutional work, a significant number of them provide descriptions of institutional work, some directly as they examine the rise and fall of various institutional arrangements, and others in the context of background empirical material intended to aid understanding of institutional processes. Together these studies reveal considerable insight into the often overlooked constituent elements of institutional work.

We organize our analysis around three broad categories of institutional work – creating, maintaining and disrupting institutions. Together these categories describe a rough life-cycle of institutional work that parallels the life-cycle of institutions described by Scott (2001) and Tolbert and Zucker (1996). Our review suggests a set of insights into creating, maintaining and disrupting institutions with which we end each discussion.

Creating Institutions

Of the three broad categories of institutional work we examine, the work aimed at creating institutions has received the most attention by organizational scholars. Building particularly on the notion of institutional entrepreneurship (Eisenstadt 1980; DiMaggio 1988), significant efforts have been undertaken to describe and explain the role of interested actors in the formation of institutions (Dacin et al. 2002). The primary focus of much of this research, however, has been to elaborate the characteristics of, and the conditions that produce, institutional entrepreneurs. Somewhat less evident in these accounts are detailed descriptions of precisely what it is that institutional entrepreneurs do.

In the empirical research we reviewed, we observed ten distinct sets of practices through which actors engaged in actions that resulted in the creation of new institutions. While we do not suggest that the practices we identify provide an exhaustive list of the kind of institutional work used to create institutions, we observe that they reflect three broader categories of activities. The first three types of institutional work, 'vesting', 'defining' and

Table 1.6.1 Creating Institutions

Forms of institutional work	Definition	Key references for empirical examples
Advocacy	The mobilization of political and regulatory support through direct and deliberate techniques of social suasion	Elsbach and Sutton (1992); Galvin (2002)
Defining	The construction of rule systems that confer status or identity, define boundaries of membership or create status hierarchies within a field	Fox-Wolfgramm et al. (1998)
Vesting	The creation of rule structures that confer property rights	Russo (2001)
Constructing identities	Defining the relationship between an actor and the field in which that actor operates	Lounsbury (2001); Oakes et al. (1998)
Changing normative associations	Re-making the connections between sets of practices and the moral and cultural foundations for those practices	Townley (1997); Zilber (2002)
Constructing normative networks	Constructing of interorganizational connections through which practices become normatively sanctioned and which form the relevant peer group with respect to compliance, monitoring and evaluation	Lawrence et al. (2002); Orssatto et al. (2002)
Mimicry	Associating new practices with existing sets of taken-for-granted practices, technologies and rules in order to ease adoption	Hargadon and Douglas (2001); Jones (2001)
Theorizing	The development and specification of abstract categories and the elaboration of chains of cause and effect	Kitchener (2002); Orssatto et al. (2002)
Educating	The educating of actors in skills and knowledge necessary to support the new institution	Lounsbury (2001); Woywode (2002)

'advocacy', reflect overtly political work in which actors reconstruct rules, property rights and boundaries that define access to material resources. The second set of practices, 'constructing identities', 'changing norms' and 'constructing networks', emphasize actions in which actors' belief systems are reconfigured. The final group of actions, 'mimicry', 'theorizing' and 'educating', involve actions designed to alter abstract categorizations in which the boundaries of meaning systems are altered. We discuss and illustrate each of these in turn. See Table 1.6.1 for a summary of the forms of institutional work associated with creating institutions.

Advocacy

The first type of work important for the creation of institutions is *advocacy* – the mobilization of political and regulatory support through direct and deliberate techniques of social suasion. Holm (1995) provides an excellent illustration of the importance of advocacy work in his description of the way in

which the collective action of fisherman and their mobilization of state power behind their institutional project was key to the ultimate success of the fisherman. Holm (1995: 405–6) observes that it was '[b]ecause of the close ties between the Fisherman's Association and the Labour party' that the Herring Act was ultimately successful in preserving the fishermen's interests in the impending re-engineering of the Norwegian fishing industry. Advocacy is an important component of the institutional work of interest associations or organizations 'that are formally established to make claims for – to represent – important constituencies in an organizational field' (Galvin 2002: 673). One form of advocacy work identified by Galvin involves deliberate and direct representation of the interests of specific actors. This work entails lobbying for resources, promoting agendas and proposing new or attacking existing legislation. It is similar to the forms of institutional work accomplished by political regimes (Carroll et al. 1988) or by social movements (Clemens 1993). The object of such institutional work is to redefine the allocation of material resources or social and political capital needed to create new institutional structures and practices.

We identify advocacy as a form of institutional work associated with the creating of institutions because it is a key element by which marginal actors initially acquire the legitimacy they may need to effect new institutions. Suchman (1995) observes that different forms of advocacy, such as lobbying, advertising and litigation, allow less powerful institutional actors to actively shape their institutional environment and, ultimately, acquire cognitive legitimacy. Elsbach and Sutton (1992) identify extreme examples of how advocacy offers marginalized actors the opportunity to create institutions by manipulating cognitive legitimacy. The authors demonstrate how two social movements, Earth First and the AIDS Coalition to Unleash Power, employed controversial forms of advocacy, including coercion and illegitimate activities, to gain legitimacy by first violating existing norms and then articulating awareness of their marginalized position. Advocacy, thus, is a powerful form of institutional work that permits actors to influence when and how institutional norms are perceived. Used effectively, advocacy can determine which norms are followed and which may be violated, both of which are key elements in the cognitive legitimacy of new institutions.

Defining

A second form of institutional work involves activity directed toward *defining*: the construction of rule systems that confer status or identity, define boundaries of membership or create status hierarchies within a field. At the societal level, an illustration of this process is the way in which citizenship rules and procedures confer status and membership (Meyer et al. 1997). More generally, Lawrence (1999) describes the defining of membership rules and practice standards as the two broad categories of institutional strategy.

A rich example of defining comes from Fox-Wolfgramm et al.'s (1998) analysis of institutional change in a sample of banks. Here, a key element of institutional work involved the formalization of rule systems, by bank examiners, to construct definitional categories of compliance. The examiners constructed 12 criteria for categorizing banks as outstanding, satisfactory, need to improve or substantial non-compliance; formal categories that would, ultimately, determine differential access to

resources. Definitional work, thus, extends to formal accreditation processes, the creation of standards and the certification of actors within a field. Certification was the primary form of definitional work identified by Guler et al. (2002) in the emergence and diffusion of ISO practices globally. Russo (2001), similarly, points to the formalization of contract standards and the definition of standard exchange rates between utilities by the federal government as a key component of the success of the emerging independent power industry. Advocates of the new industry were clearly reliant upon the ability of the state to impose standardized cost definitions and contract terms on industry participants.

From the empirical research we examined, it seems that most defining work focuses actors on the creation of 'constitutive rules' (Scott 2001) or rules that enable rather than constrain institutional action. In contrast to the prohibitive nature of most regulatory activity, defining is directed more often toward establishing the parameters of future or potential institutional structures and practices. Rules of membership, accreditation and citizenship engage actors in processes directed toward defining (and re-defining) boundaries and frameworks within which new institutions can be formed.

Vesting

Vesting refers to institutional work directed toward the creation of rule structures that confer property rights (Roy 1981; Russo 2001). Vesting occurs when government authority is used to reallocate property rights, such as occurred in the fledgling independent power-production industry (Russo 2001). The industry was created by US federal mandate that large established utilities had to purchase electricity from independent producers. Previously, large power producers held state enforced monopolies over the generation of electricity. Such monopolies were an historical artifact of the large risks and capital costs required to build and maintain massive hydroelectric projects. To counterbalance the monopolistic power of utilities, state governments conferred the right to set prices on public utility commissions. In this early example of vesting, thus, the government simultaneously divided two elements of exchange (production and pricing) between two distinct sets of actors (utilities and utility commissions). Although this division of vested rights and interests worked well for a time, the oil crisis of the 1970s focused attention on the need to develop alternative sources of electricity. A second round of vesting legislation, therefore, created a new set of actors and redefined the exchange relations between them. A comprehensive energy plan introduced by President Jimmy Carter required large utilities to purchase power from qualifying independent producers. By changing the pricing formula for energy, the legislation gave immediate status and legitimacy to small power producers that, previously, were shut out of the industry by established energy corporations. Vesting, as illustrated in this case, refers to the micro-processes of creating new actors and new field dynamics by changing the rules of market relations.

A common element of vesting is the negotiation of a 'regulative bargain' between the state or another coercive authority and some other interested actor. This was particularly evident in the 'compact' that developed between large utilities and public utility commissions described by Russo (2001). The vesting process 'yoked' these two sets of actors together in an implicit contract that required one to produce power and the other to set prices that would cover costs and generate a reasonable rate of return. The introduction of independent power producers in this relationship required the creation of a new implicit contract in which exchange relationship was based on the avoidance of risk, rather than assumptions of reasonable returns.

Such regulative bargains also commonly occur in professional fields, where the state, in exchange for the grant of an economic monopoly over a particular jurisdiction, expects the profession to support its own project of state-building (Abbott 1988; Cooper et al. 1994). While vesting is most apparent in the 'public duty' obligations of established professions such as law and auditing, it has also been demonstrated in less established professions such as personnel professionals (Baron et al. 1986) and finance (Lounsbury 2002). Ultimately, the process of vesting involves some degree of sharing of coercive or regulatory authority.

Several general observations can be made regarding these first three forms of institutional work. First, they appear to potentially constitute a mutually reinforcing cycle. Advocacy work is an important precursor to the defining of rules that confer status and privilege, which in turn provide the foundation for vesting work; vesting, in turn, constrains and constitutes those actors with preferential ability

to advocate. Secondly, the forms of institutional change that result from this type of institutional work often involve the dramatic, wholesale reconstruction of institutions or institutional structures and practices – revolutionary rather than evolutionary institutional change (Greenwood and Hinings 1996). Thirdly, while the preceding discussion clearly privileges the role of the state in this form of institutional work, the state is not the only actor with coercive or regulatory authority. Thornton (2002; 2004) describes the work of exogenous actors in the college textbook publishing industry where coercion was expressed financially rather than through regulatory authority. Fligstein (1990: 19), similarly, describes the ability of the emerging field of large industrial multinationals to construct their own coercive mechanisms of governance, albeit 'as a result of strategic interaction between actors in the state and actors in firms'.

Constructing Identities

The construction of identities as a form of institutional work is central to the creating of institutions because identities describe the relationship between an actor and the field in which that actor operates (Bourdieu and Wacquant 1992). A powerful example of this form of work comes from Oakes et al.'s (1998) study of institutional change in the field of Alberta historical museums. In this case, the government department responsible for museums worked to reorient the identities of museum employees:

> people in the organizations [were] encouraged to see themselves, perhaps for the first time, as working in businesses rather than working in museums that are run in a businesslike manner. The desirable positional identity [was] no longer solely curator, researcher, interpreter, or educator. It [was] also entrepreneur, often described as being 'realistic' and becoming 'change-agents' and 'risk-takers' (Oakes et al. 1998: 279–80).

The institutional work of providing new identities is not, however, an unproblematic accomplishment: as Oakes et al. (1998: 277) describe it,

> some people to try to remake themselves, while others may stop contributing or withdraw completely. Some, particularly those with curatorial backgrounds, felt uncomfortable and tended to

become less involved as they no longer understood the rules of the game; others not only embraced the new field but helped give it shape.

In institutional theory, the construction of identities as a form of institutional work has been primarily associated with the development of professions, as illustrated in studies of both the emergence of new professions and the transformation of existing ones (Covaleski et al. 1998; Brock et al. 1999). In the literature we reviewed for this chapter, the construction of professional identities was engaged in both from outside of the professional groups in questions (Oakes et al. 1998) and by the groups themselves, as in Lounsbury's (2001) examination of recyclers. This latter study highlights the importance of collective action in accomplishing the construction of identities as a form of normative institutional work:

> status-creation recyclers began to forge a new and distinct occupational identity that was connected to the ideals of the broader environmental movement. In the early 1990s, status-creation recyclers began to identify each other through their joint participation in the National Recycling Coalition (NRC) ... In 1993, a group of full-time recycling co-ordinators formed the College and University Recycling Co-ordinators (CURC) occupational association [which] ... established procedures to elect officials and developed committees to study measurement standards, 'buy recycled' campaigns, co-operation between university operations and academics, and other issues related to the construction of campus recycling programmes (Lounsbury 2001: 33).

Changing Normative Associations

A different form of work aimed at creating new institutions involved the reformulating of normative associations: re-making the connections between sets of practices and the moral and cultural foundations for those practices. This form of institutional work often led to new institutions which were parallel or complementary to existing institutions and did not directly challenge the pre-existing institutions but, rather, simultaneously supported and led actors to question them. An interesting example of such work comes from Zilber's (2002) institutional account of a rape crisis centre in Israel. Zilber provides a detailed analysis of the means by which founding practices, based upon feminist

logics and assumptions, were maintained but reinterpreted from an alternative normative perspective – that of therapeutic professionalism. While training routines and rotation procedures were kept more or less intact 20 years after the centre's founding, members no longer remembered the feminist origins and readily accepted the extension of meaning of these practices to incorporate a new ideological understanding of the institution. Practices such as consensus decision-making and rotation of speakers, which were originally adopted by feminists to 'avoid domination and promote an open, respectful dialogue' (Zilber 2002: 243) were extended by therapeutic professionals to promote the re-creation of the centre as a medical rather than a political institution. Feminist practices of consensus decision-making and speaker rotation were relatively easily extended to promote psychotherapeutic practices of open or closed group counselling or interventions.

One version of this form of institutional work that has been observed across a wide variety of domains is the substitution of generalized private-sector, for-profit norms for field-specific norms that focus on such issues as human welfare or professional autonomy (Townley 1997; Hinings and Greenwood 1988; Kitchener 2002; Amis et al. 2004). Townley (1997), for instance, documents the institutional work of university administrators and government agencies as they attempted to institute a private-sector approach to HR in UK universities. A critical piece of work in this regard was the 'Report of the Steering Committee for Efficiency Studies in Universities (Jarratt)': 'For Jarratt, the key to more dynamic and efficient universities lay in the practices and policies associated with private sector organizations, the latter commanding ideological overtones of efficiency and effectiveness' (Townley 1997: 265). Kitchener (2002: 401) describes similar forms of institutional work in the field of US healthcare in the 1980s: in that arena, a group of 'political reformers' wrote a series of policy papers that 'renewed calls for healthcare organizations to adopt "business-like" structures and managerial practices'.

Constructing Normative Networks

Another form of work aimed at creating institutions involves the construction of what we refer to here as 'normative networks', which are the interorganizational connections through which practices become normatively sanctioned and which form the relevant peer group with respect to normative compliance, monitoring and evaluation. A detailed illustration of this process comes from Lawrence et al.'s (2002) description of how a 'proto-institution' emerged in the field of child nutrition in Palestine from the construction of a normative network including CARE, the University of Oslo, the Australian embassy, a government agency and others. Although each actor had independent motivations and interests, the emerging 'proto-institution' became a repository for each actor's pre-existing institutionalized practices for addressing issues of malnutrition. Thus, the new structure or proto-institution was established in parallel with existing institutional structures, including those of the Ministry of Health, CARE and other organizations, designed to address the same problem.

A number of other studies provide similar accounts of how groups of actors construct normative networks that provide the basis for new institutions. Leblebici et al. (1991) describe the role played by patent pooling arrangements in the early stages of radio, in which networks of prominent and powerful actors such as General Electric, AT&T and others, created a new institutional structure (RCA) that effectively separated the manufacturing and broadcasting activities of the industry. Guler et al. (2002) analyse the diffusion of ISO 9000 practices, and document the early diffusion of ISO 9000 in manufacturing occurring through the work of engineers and production managers in creating a normative network aimed at promoting manufacturing standards and practices. Orssatto et al. (2002: 6748) describe the way in which the institutionalization of recycling in the European auto industry depended upon 'industry groups, such as Renault, the PSA Group and CFF' who believed that 'industry-wide co-operation, collective liability, and commercial relations between the various parties involved, were better principles from which to solve the waste problem of shredder residues'.

The key observation in these accounts is that formerly loose coalitions of somewhat diverse actors construct normative networks which effect new institutions, often alongside pre-existing institutional activities and structures. In some cases, the newly formed institution mimics regulatory activities that one might expect would be performed by the state, such as in the separation of industry activities or the creation of manufacturing and process standards. In other cases, as in the formation of a proto-institution, the new institutional structure simply supplements and supports activities that were once performed by the state (and by other actors).

The three forms of institutional work identified above share the common attribute of focusing on the normative structure of institutions. That is, they each attend to the roles, values and norms that underpin institutions. The types of institutional work differ, however, in the contextual relationships that define the normative structure of institutions. *Constructing identities*, for example, is a form of institutional work that concentrates attention on the relationship between an actor and the institutional field or fields in which they function. *Changing normative associations*, by contrast, involve work that manipulates the relationship between norms and the institutional field in which they are produced. Finally, *constructing normative networks* describes a form of institutional work that alters the relationship between actors in a field by changing the normative assumptions that connect them. We, thus, observe three different types of interactions (actor-field; norm-field; actor-actor) that provide the foundation for new institutional formation. More significant, perhaps, is the observed need for greater analytic attention to be paid by future research to the ways in which actors work to make these interactions cohere into a consistent and enduring institutional structure.

Mimicry

Actors attempting to create new institutions have the potential to leverage existing sets of taken-for-granted practices, technologies and rules, if they are able to associate the new with the old in some way that eases adoption. One way in which this is done is through mimicry. In Hargadon and Douglas' (2001: 479) rich historical account of Edison's efforts to institutionalize electric light, they argue that, '[b]y designing the incandescent light around many of the concrete features of the already-familiar gas system, Edison drew on the public's pre-existing understandings of the technology, its value, and its uses'. Despite the many practical and technical advantages of electric light, '[Edison] deliberately designed his electric lighting to be all but indistinguishable from the existing system, lessening rather than emphasizing the gaps between the old institutions and his new innovation' (Hargadon and

Douglas 2001: 489). This mimicry was accomplished, in part, through the clever use of skeumorphs – design elements that symbolically connected previous and current technologies – such as bulbs that mimic the shape of flames in gas lamps. Edison engaged in this mimicry to the extent that he intentionally undermined the practical effectiveness of electric light in order to make it more similar to gas: gas jets produced light equivalent to a 12-watt bulb; Edison's designed his bulbs to produce 13 watts, despite having early prototypes that would produce two or three times this amount of light. Similarly, Edison mimicked the gas companies' underground pipes, despite the fact than 'when buried, the bare copper wires leaked electricity and blew out entire circuits' (Hargadon and Douglas 2001: 490).

Mimicry was also an important form of institutional work in the development of the early American motion picture industry, where one group of entrepreneurs, referred to as 'immigrant content entrepreneurs' by Jones (2001: 925), 'imitated high culture symbols and formats of Broadway theatres to evoke accepted cognitive heuristics from consumers, such as providing uniformed ushers, plush chairs, 2-hour shows, and elaborate buildings'. This strategy was in contrast to those entrepreneurs who relied primarily on technical and regulatory strategies, and whose films were primarily short pieces shown in nickelodeons. In order to establish the feature film as an institution in this emerging industry, these entrepreneurs, including Adolph Zuckor and Jesse Lasky, who later formed Famous Players Lasky, the forerunner of Paramount Studio, 'specialized in filming established Broadway plays or novels with prominent Broadway actors' (Jones 2001: 925).

Part of the success of mimicry in creating new institutional structures is that the juxtaposition of old and new templates can simultaneously make the new structure understandable and accessible, while pointing to potential problems or shortcomings of past practices. This was the observation by Townley (2002) on changes in Alberta cultural organizations. Layering new business techniques, such as budgeting or performance measurement, on traditional professional practices, actors developed an acute awareness of how past routines became problematized when viewed through the lens of business rationality. Townley (2002: 173) notes that the technique of demonstrating problems of efficiency by juxtaposing old and new templates of organizing,

ultimately, succeeded as actors succumbed, cognitively, to conformity:

> The 'causes' of the introduction of these measures, the appeal to efficiency, and hence the legitimacy of government, were not questioned, nor was the legitimacy of the government in making these changes ... Limited attempts at protecting or decoupling internal work activities from formal structures, although initially successful, were inhibited as business planning and performance measures had to be introduced at the increasingly lower unit levels of the division and the sites, and eventually at the individual level.

Theorizing

Theorizing is 'the development and specification of abstract categories, and the elaboration of chains of cause and effect' (Greenwood et al. 2002: 60). An important aspect of theorizing is the naming of new concepts and practices so that they might become a part of the cognitive map of the field. In their study of business planning in Alberta historical museums, for instance, Oakes et al. (1998: 276–7) describe the importance and difficulty associated with such work:

> The meaning of everyday words like 'goals' and 'objectives' became precarious. The difficulty in remembering a new language and all its categories – goals, objectives, measures, etc. – was expressed several times. ... Some departments presented their completed business plans to the Legislature only to be told that what they described as objectives were really goals and that what they defined as outcomes were really processes or outputs.

Naming represents a critical first step that provides the foundation for further theorizing, as described by Orssatto et al. (2002: 646) in their study of the evolution of recycling in the European auto industry. A critical naming was by 'VDA', the German automobile industry, which in October 1990 coined the notion a 'concept for the future processing of end-of-life vehicles'. This naming allowed both the communication of the concept and its elaboration through further theorizing: 'the car manufacturers elaborated further on the "VDA concept", communicated it to the BMU and the general public, and engaged in technical and market research to prepare for its implementation'. Naming and theorizing does not, however, necessarily indicate agreement: in this case, Orssatto et al. (2002: 646–7) argue that the 'common concept should be seen more as a political stake than a technical document, since all auto-makers endorsed the proposal, despite their preferences for different solutions at the technical level'.

Similarly, Kitchener's (2002: 402) study of healthcare mergers describes the way in which naming and theorizing can have an impact on an entire sector.

> members of the Jackson Hole group helped to translate the ideology of market-managerialism into US health policy. In the early 1970s, they coined the term health maintenance organization (HMO), labelled its organizational characteristics, and successfully lobbied the Nixon administration to endorse it as a means of encouraging savings (by managers) as opposed to spending (by professionals).

Kitchener's study also highlights the narrative component of theorizing (Bruner 1987) in which actors articulate the causal and consequently temporal relationships among institutional elements. Kitchener describes the way in which a variety of actors engaged in storying in support of the adoption of mergers by healthcare organizations: 'the popular business press (e.g. the Wall Street Journal, Fortune, Business Week and Forbes) conveys tales of industrialists who merge organizations to achieve spectacular turnarounds'; 'standard economics and management texts … propose mergers as a rational strategic response to increasingly competitive market conditions'; and the 'management consultancy industry … added advice on mergers to the list of services that it offers to health executives' (Kitchener 2002: 403).

Educating

The final instance of institutional work we found that was aimed at creating institutions involved the educating of actors in skills and knowledge necessary to support the new institution. This was an important form of cognitive work because the creating of new institutions often involves the development of novel practices as well as connecting those practices to control mechanisms. This form of cognitive work was evidenced in several studies, including Hargadon and Douglas' (2001) discussion

of Edison's electric light, which demanded the development of significant new skills on the part of workers:

> To wire a building for electricity, Edison had to pull up floors and snake wires around doorways, a skill at that time known only, and incompletely, to installers of burglar alarms … over the first few years, Edison lobbied local schools to develop training programmes in electrical engineering and, when that initiative fell short, started his own training programme (Hargadon and Douglas 2001: 487).

Similarly, the institutionalization of recycling programmes in American universities demanded a new set of skills and knowledge on the part of a large population. Consequently, a key role of the SEAC was as an educator: As Lounsbury (2001: 36–7) describes, 'It sponsors annual student conferences and maintains an elaborate network of experienced student organizers who travel to campuses and hold workshops, provide training and support work on activities such as campus solid waste audits'.

One key strategy employed by the SEAC to educate a large population of students and universities was to create templates – frameworks that provided other actors with an outline, or template, for action. The SEAC facilitated the institutionalization of recycling by providing 'access to key information such as case studies of other socially similar schools that helped student environmental organizations shape their arguments to administrators' (Lounsbury 2001: 37). Moreover, the SEAC 'provided student groups with evidence from comparable schools … [which] was communicated in formal documents created by student environmental groups that were presented to school administrators in support of their claims' (Lounsbury 2001: 50).

Templating also includes work done less directly. One important such case involved the creation of a template that helped foster the global quality movement. Woywode (2002: 506–7) examines the introduction of working groups as a formal structural component in the European auto industry, and concludes that:

> The decision to introduce working groups coincided more or less with the date of publication of the MIT study by Womack et al. in 1990, which praised the Japanese method of production. This book, *The Machine that Changed the World,* of which, according to the co-author Daniel T. Jones, more

than 500,000 copies were sold, as of June 2000, has been translated into 11 different languages. … Several interviewees from French as well as from German plants explicitly stated that top managers or production specialists of their car companies had gone to visit Japanese car manufacturing plants prior to the decision to introduce the working-group concept in their home country, and had made repeated visits thereafter. … Two companies even hired Japanese consulting firms to help them introduce the original Toyota production concept in their company.

These final three forms of institutional work aimed at creating institutions focus primarily on the cognitive side of institutions – the beliefs, assumptions and frames that inform action by providing meaningful and understandable interaction patterns to be followed. *Mimicry* draws on existing patterns of action in order to articulate and legitimate new practices and structures; *theorizing* develops concepts and beliefs that can support new institutions; *educating* provides actors with the knowledge necessary to engage in new practices or interact with new structures. Each form of institutional work supports the creating of new institutions by leveraging the costs that actors might bear if they seek to engage in new practices or develop new structures on their own; mimicry, theorizing and educating provide actors with alternatives to the effort and risk associated with isolated innovation.

Insights into Creating Institutions

The existing literature on institutional change provides some useful insights into the institutional work necessary to create institutions. In enumerating these forms of institutional work, our intention here is not to suggest that we have uncovered any exhaustive list, but rather to sketch the terrain associated with the creating of institutions by interested actors. As with all of our observations in this section, we draw our insights regarding institutional work associated with the creating of institutions from a small sample of research, primarily case studies, and have been unable to gauge their generalizability.

The concept of institutional work highlights the effortful and skillful practices of interested actors, and so our sketch provides several insights regarding the actors involved in the creation of institutions, the skills and resources on which they draw in order to create institutions, and the institutional dynamics associated with each form of work. Key to creating institutions is the ability to establish rules and construct rewards and sanctions that enforce those rules. Only some actors in any given field will have that ability tied directly to their position; in many fields, such a role is restricted to the state or a delegate of the state, such as a professional body. That ability can however be gained through political and economic processes in which an actor establishes a superior position in the field. This position might be based either on the resource dependence of other actors (Pfeffer and Salancik 1978). It might also reflect a specialized identity relative to an issue, and thus emerge out of the normative work described above in terms of constructing identities.

An important insight with respect to the differences between forms of institutional work that focus on rules (i.e. vesting, defining and advocacy) and forms of institutional work that effect changes in norms and belief systems (i.e. constructing identities, changing norms and constructing normative networks), in terms of creating institutions, is the far greater potential for rules-based work to lead to the *de novo* construction of new institutions. Unlike the remaining types of institutional work, work that focuses on rule systems is much more likely to be associated with the relatively wholesale construction of new institutions: vesting and defining, in particular, can lead to the relatively immediate institutionalization of practices, technologies and rules, so long as the putative agent has the authority to enforce those institutions.

In contrast, work that focuses on changing norms or belief systems is more often associated with creating of institutionalized rules, practices and technologies that parallel or complement existing institutions. This may be because this type of work is the most 'co-operative' of the three approaches to creating institutions. Unlike rules-based work, which depends on the ability of some actor to enforce compliance, normative work relies on cultural and moral force, which is embedded in communities of practice. Consequently, the forms of normative work all depend significantly on the co-operation of those communities to make real the intended new institutions. The clearest example of this is the forming of normative networks which are crucial to lending an institution some cultural or moral force; these networks are by their nature a co-operative enterprise and so creating them involves a form of institutional work that depends heavily on the ability of actors to establish and maintain co-operative ties. This does not mean that normative institutional work can not be highly conflictual as competing communities vie for legitimacy and influence with respect to a particular issue (Zietsma et al. 2002). The constructing of identities as a type of institutional work, for instance, is also often a highly co-operative endeavour since the actor whose identity is being constructed will often depend on others to sanction, formally or informally, that identity. Along with the social connections that co-operation requires, normative work is also facilitated by discursive legitimacy (Hardy and Phillips 1998), a perceived 'right' to speak on a particular issue; this is in contrast to the authority and material resources that make possible rule-oriented institutional work.

From our review of the empirical literature, it seems that creating institutions through work that changes abstract categories of meaning (i.e. mimicry, theorizing and educating) may involve well-established actors in a field, but at the same time hold the greatest potential for institutional entrepreneurship on the part of relatively small, peripheral or isolated actors. Less powerful actors are particularly associated with this type of work which involves associating new practices with existing institutions. Mimicry can provide a powerful means for new entrants into a domain to legitimate and institutionalize new practices, rules and technologies employ: Edison's imitation of gas lighting; the cultural mimicry of Zuckor and Lasky as they entered the motion picture industry. Theorizing and educating, on the other hand, seem to be associated primarily with larger, central actors in a field – those actors with the resources and legitimacy to articulate cause and effect relations provide peripheral actors with templates for action and educate whatever publics are relevant to an institution. While marginal actors do, on occasion, mobilize the resources and social capital necessary to engage in theorizing, templating and educating, this can only occur when they act collectively, in the form of a social movement, thereby elevating their position from atomistic marginal players to a unified and central actor (Clemens 1993; Lounsbury et al. 2003). Templating, theorizing and educating forms of institutional work, in contrast to work that focuses on reconstructing rule systems, are associated more strongly with the extension and elaboration of institutions than with the creating of

strikingly new institutions; as Edison's example illustrates, even when a new technology represents a breakthrough advance, reliance on cognitive work to institutionalize may mean highlighting its continuities with the past as much as its distinctiveness. Templating and theorizing, in particular, appear to incorporate elements of *bricolage*, or the 'makeshift, improvisatory and creative' (Gabriel 2002) capacity of entrepreneurs to use existing social material to reconfigure structures and institutions (Clemens and Cook 1999).

Maintaining Institutions

The issue of how institutions are maintained by actors in organizational fields has received significantly less attention than how institutions are created (Scott 2001: 110). Nevertheless, the question of what forms of institutional work are associated with maintaining institutions is an important one: although institutions are associated with automatic mechanisms of social control that lead to institutions being relatively self-reproducing (Jepperson 1991), relatively few institutions have such powerful reproductive mechanisms that no ongoing maintenance is necessary. As an example, consider the institution of 'democracy'. Jepperson (1991) argues that democracy is highly institutionalized in the US and relatively less institutionalized in some other countries: taking the recent example of the 2004 national election in Afghanistan (the country's first), the low level of institutionalization was evidenced by the large amount of work necessary by a range of governmental and non-governmental actors in order to mount the election. In contrast, Jepperson (1991) argues, democratic elections in the US are not exceptions but rather taken-for-granted parts of contemporary life. However, this does not mean that the maintenance of democracy, or even of democratic elections, goes on without significant institutional work. One example of such work is the organizing of voter registration drives, which are an important example of institutional work aimed not at creating or disrupting institutions, but at ensuring that elections remain democratic processes. Voter registration drives have been a historically important form of institutional work toward maintaining democracy in the US, with the 1964 'Freedom Summer' campaign being among the most famous. Voter registration drives are not, however, simply a remnant of a less democratic time in

Table 1.6.2   Maintaining Institutions

Forms of institutional work	Definition	Key references for empirical examples
Enabling work	The creation of rules that facilitate, supplement and support institutions, such as the creation of authorizing agents or diverting resources	Leblebici et al. (1991)
Policing	Ensuring compliance through enforcement, auditing and monitoring	Fox-Wolfgramm et al. (1998); Schuler (1996)
Deterring	Establishing coercive barriers to institutional change	Holm (1995); Townley (2002)
Valourizing and demonizing	Providing for public consumption positive and negative examples that illustrates the normative foundations of an institution	Angus (1993)
Mythologizing	Preserving the normative underpinnings of an institution by creating and sustaining myths regarding its history	Angus (1993)
Embedding and routinizing	Actively infusing the normative foundations of an institution into the participants' day to day routines and organizational practices	Townley (1997); Zilber (2002)

the US: as we wrote this chapter, the US was preparing for a presidential election in the fall of 2004, with voter registration drives being organized by a wide variety of organizations, from the League of Women Voters of Monroe Township (Harvie 2004) to local chapters of the NAACP (Campbell 2004). These drives remain an important means through which individual and collective actors are able to bolster the institution of democracy, and more importantly represent just one of a wide range of forms of institutional work that are necessary to maintain democracy as an institution in any democratic state, including technical work that ensures the validity of vote collecting and counting, etc. Thus, a large amount of institutional work is needed to maintain even highly institutionalized phenomena such as democratic elections in the US and other Western democracies. Considering the sorts of institutions that are typically examined in organizational research, we expect that even greater amounts of institutional work are necessary for their maintenance.

In general, institutional work aimed at maintaining institutions involves supporting, repairing or recreating the social mechanisms that ensure compliance. Thus, in reviewing the empirical institutional literature for instances of such work, we searched for any concrete description of an actor engaged in some activity that was intended to maintain the controls which underpinned an institution. As with our review of the descriptions of creating institutions, the descriptions we found of maintaining institutions

were often located as often in the sections providing background and context for an empirical study as in the 'results' sections. Overall, we identify six types of institutional work devoted to maintaining institutions. The first three, 'enabling', 'policing' and 'deterring', primarily address the maintenance of institutions through ensuring adherence to rule systems. The latter three, 'valourizing/demonizing', 'mythologizing' and 'embedding and routinizing', focus efforts to maintain institutions on reproducing existing norms and belief systems. Each of these types are elaborated below. See Table 1.6.2 for a summary of the forms of institutional work associated with maintaining institutions.

Enabling Work

Enabling work refers to the creation of rules that facilitate, supplement and support institutions. This may include the creation of authorizing agents or new roles needed to carry on institutional routines or diverting resources (i.e. taxation) required to ensure institutional survival. Examples of enabling work come from Leblebici et al.'s (1991) study of the radio industry and Guler et al.'s (2002) study of the international diffusion of ISO 9000. A key set of institutions in the field of radio transmission involves the legitimate use of the radio spectrum: in order to maintain the legislated institutional framework that governs the spectrum, the US federal government has, since 1925, created regulatory agencies with the power 'to control the allocation, use, and transfer of spectrum rights' (Leblebici et al. 1991: 341). Similarly, the ISO authorizes various organizations to act as 'registrars', including 'government laboratories, private testing organizations, firms that were early adopters of ISO, industry trade groups, and accounting firms': these organizations are 'qualified to conduct audits and award certificates' with respect to ISO 9000 compliance. These examples illustrate the importance of distributed authority and responsibility for maintaining institutions in large or geographically dispersed fields. Enabling work also maintains institutions by introducing certainty into institutional arrangements which allows actors to avoid intra-institutional conflict. Professional associations often engage in this type of work with the 'construction and maintenance of intraprofessional agreement over boundaries, membership and behaviour' (Greenwood et al. 2002). By introducing constitutive rules (of membership, standards or identity), associations 'function in a primarily regulatory capacity ... as they enable the formation, dissemination and reproduction of shared meanings and understandings in an organizational arena' (Galvin 2002: 677).

Policing

A second category of work aimed at maintaining institutions involves ensuring compliance through enforcement, auditing and monitoring. We term this form of institutional work 'policing'. Policing can involve the use of both sanctions and inducements (Scott 1994; Russo 2001), often simultaneously and by the same agents, as illustrated by the US government's attempts to stabilize labour during the war effort (Baron et al. 1986), and the state's use of both penalties and incentives in maintaining common economic institutions such as property rights, corporate status and control over economic production (Campbell and Lindbergh 1991). An example of a non-state actor engaged in policing work comes from the early years of the American film industry, when key technologies were institutionalized through patents and copyrights, many of which were held by Thomas Edison: as a means of enforcing compliance, Edison 'initiated 33 suits on patent rights and copyrights at federal level between 1897 and 1905' (Jones 2001: 933). This use of state apparatus by a non-state actor to police an institution is similar to what Schuler (1996) describes in

his analysis of political strategies in the carbon steel industry: an important strategy of these firms for maintaining institutions was the launching of petitions to international trade bodies appealing to have a regulation or agreement enforced. In a very different context, managers of a coal mine in Newfoundland enforced institutionalized but unsafe work practices by punishing those who refused to comply: one worker who 'refused to work in these types of unsafe conditions ... [was] assigned more denigrating tasks such as working on the roof or at the coal-face'; another was 'suspended for refusing to stay in the mine because his colleagues were using torches in unsafe conditions' (Wicks 2001: 672).

Less overtly conflictual enforcement strategies for maintaining institutions have also been described, particularly in professionalized fields where auditing and monitoring are often enough to ensure compliance. Fox-Wolfgramm et al. (1998), for instance, describe the role of auditing in the field of banking when new regulation was established to ensure non-discriminatory lending procedures:

In mid-1987, the bank was given an official [regulatory] compliance examination, due to its holding company starting the process of acquiring another bank in the Southwest. ... A full crew was sent to the bank, and several weeks were spent assessing compliance. The bank was found 'below average' in [regulatory] compliance and was prohibited from further branching until compliance was shown' (Fox-Wolfgramm et al. 1998: 107–8).

Similarly, Guler et al.'s (2002) study of ISO 9000 diffusion documents the importance of regular monitoring as a means of maintaining institutionalized practices: the ISO 9000 'certificate is typically awarded for a period of 3 years', with regular audits 'conducted after awarding a certificate to make sure that the firm is in compliance with the standards' (Guler et al. 2002: 209–10). As well as periodic auditing, actors working to maintain institutions may demand ongoing disclosure of information on the part of those participating in the institution: in response to the concerns of record producers, recording agents and artists that records played on the radio would hurt their record sales, 'the Secretary of Commerce sanctioned large stations for using records and required stations to disclose whether their programmes were transcribed' (Leblebici et al. 1991: 347).

Deterrence

A final category of work aimed at maintaining institutions by compliance with rules focuses on establishing coercive barriers to institutional change. We call this category of institutional work 'deterrence', which involves the threat of coercion to inculcate the conscious obedience of institutional actors. The best example of this category comes from Hargadon and Douglas' (2001: 485) study of Edison's introduction of electric lighting, and the responses by politicians who were interested in maintaining the institutionalized lighting system based on natural gas:

> When Edison first applied for an operating license, the mayor of New York flatly opposed even granting the company an operating franchise. When that opposition failed … the Board of Aldermen proposed Edison pay $1000 per mile of wiring and 3% of the gross receipts … Gas companies, by comparison, were permitted to lay their mains for free and paid only property tax to the city.

Another example of such tactics comes from Holm's (1995) study of the Norwegian fisheries, in which the Fisherman's Association was able to subvert the government's attempt to industrialize the industry, and hence maintain the institutions of system of small-scale fishermen and coastal communities.

Effective deterrence is highly dependent upon the legitimate authority of the coercive agent. Townley (2002: 173) describes the effective deterrence work of the Alberta government in ensuring compliance of actors in provincial cultural institutions:

> Formally, there was acquiescence or compliance with the requests to introduce strategic performance measurement systems. This took the form of conscious obedience rather than incorporation of norms of the institutional requirements. Although the planning exercise was of some use in clarifying organizational goals, performance measures were rejected as being valuable in evaluating the outcomes of organizations … Although there was compliance with coercive isomorphism, there was resistance to mimetic isomorphism.

Deterrence may also derive from the threat of economic coercion. Thornton (2002: 87) describes the policing work of parent corporations in the college textbook publishing industry in which policing was primarily accomplished through accounting practices. Annual profits of the college divisions were closely monitored and each year's profits had to 'be better than the previous year'.

Looking across the categories of rules-based work that maintains institutions, we see that such work is concerned with preserving the mechanisms through which rewards and sanctions were associated with institutional compliance on the part of actors in a field. Enabling work, policing and deterrence act together to make real the coercive underpinnings of an institution: without such work, the coercive foundations for institutions are likely to crumble, becoming empty threats or promises rather than self-activating means of institutional control. Notably, the coercive work used to maintain institutions is more visible and apparent than cognitive or normative equivalents. Those actors who engage in such work, as well as the actors that comply, are conscious of the effects of such work and its purpose in maintaining and preserving institutions.

Valourizing and Demonizing

This work maintains institutions by providing for public consumption especially positive and especially negative examples that illustrates the normative foundations of an institution. Good examples of this category come from Angus' (1993) study of a Christian Brothers College in Australia – a boy's school in which competition, machismo and violence were key institutions. An important way in which the 'Brothers' – the ordained teachers who dominated the school – maintained these institutions was through public demonstrations of what was right and what was wrong. Successes in athletic competition, for instance, 'were publicly recognized at CBC and formed a large part of the agenda for school assemblies' (Angus 1993: 241); this public recognition provided a clear indication to all participants of what it meant to be a proper CBC boy. In contrast, students who failed to live up to the competitive and macho ethic of the school were widely demonized: 'The greatest insult a pupil could deliver to another was to doubt his masculinity by referring to him as a "poofter" or as a "girl". At all year levels there was continual joking about "poofters", both inside and outside classrooms, by male teachers as well as by boys' (Angus 1993: 242). Valourizing and demonizing represent institutional work in which actors identify and evaluate the moral status of participants in the field, both as an enactment of institutionalized beliefs and as a way of maintaining the power of those beliefs.

Mythologizing

A related category of institutional work focuses on the past, rather than the present: a key way in which actors work to preserve the normative underpinnings of institutions is by mythologizing their history. Again, key examples of this category of work come from Angus' (1993) study of the Christian Brothers School. To create and sustain a myth, one needs a story and an occasion to tell it: Brother Cas Manion

> in his editorial to the hundredth issue of the Christian Brothers' journal, *Studies*, in which he reflects upon the Brothers' schools of the 1930s: 'The objective of the school was to hand on the Faith intact and ready to fight; to raise the working class boy to a level of prestige in Public Service or Profession; and to attain high levels of examination success in open competition' (Angus 1993: 242).

This mythologizing work provides to all those concerned with the school a normative understanding of why competition is and should be such a central facet of the school's culture. Similarly, Angus (1993) describes the ways in which teachers in the school mythologized the school's principals: 'one soon became aware of legends of "great men" who have been principals of Brothers' schools – tireless, dedicated and inspiring leaders who have followed in the footsteps of the Irish founder of the Order' (Angus 1993: 251–2).

Embedding and Routinizing

Whereas, valourizing, demonizing and mythologizing provide discursive resources, this category of institutional work involves actively infusing the normative foundations of an institution into the participants' day-to-day routines and organizational practices. Institutions, thus, are maintained and reproduced through the stabilizing influence of embedded routines and repetitive practices such as training, education, hiring and certification routines and ceremonies of celebration. In Townley's (1997) study of the implementation of performance appraisal in UK universities, for example, the institutionalized myth of appraisal and accountability was maintained by the universities, particularly in their formal, documented rhetoric, as in this university document:

> The university has a general responsibility to the community for the provision of high quality teaching and research within the funds allocated from the public purse. ... By considering the achievements and needs of each of its staff on an individual basis it can build up at department, faculty and university levels an assessment of what steps are needed to motivate and retain staff of high quality (University document, quoted in Townley (1997: 270).

More active forms of embedding and routinizing were evidenced in Angus' (1993) study of the Christian Brothers School:

> It was not unusual for the feast of Immaculate Conception, March 25, to be a day on which boys in various cases received instruction about sex, manners and appropriate relationships with girls, and the 'mysteries' of female biology. The general message conveyed was that girls and women are 'special' people deserving special care and respect (Angus 1993: 243).

While this example illustrates explicit education as a means of normative maintenance, vivid though implicit examples were also used in the school to maintain normative understandings of gender: 'At an assembly of Years 7 and 8 students ... a number of boys who had committed various offences were lined up and strapped by Brother Sterling. ... [The] group of women who taught Years 7 and 9 ... [were] asked to leave the scene of public humiliation before the strapping could proceed'. This incident 'emphasized the stereotypical division of male toughness and female delicateness and sensibility', 'women's lack of belonging in the mail domain of the school, and marked them out as not being real teachers' (Angus 1993: 247).

Institutional work can also maintain institutions by routinizing the reproduction of shared frameworks of members, through recruitment practices. Zilber (2002: 242) describes how feminist norms were maintained in a rape-crisis centre by routinely recruiting from a close-knit network:

> [V]olunteers highlighted the atmosphere of friendship and warmth. The importance of friendly, positive and equal relations among volunteers, staff and board members, and between these groups, was perceived as part of the feminist struggle against domination. The centre aimed at being a 'woman's space', where not only the victims of sexual assault, but the volunteers as well, would feel empathy and acceptance. As recruitment was based on social networks-that is, spreading the word in closed

circles of feminist supporters (at demonstrations, rallies and other political activities) – members felt affinity with each other. Many were friends, both in their daily life and in the general feminist sense of 'sisterhood'.

Other practices, such as talking in rotation and making decisions by consensus, were also routinized in the centre. By embedding these practices in routines, the practices continued to be ritually reproduced long after the original purpose or intent had been forgotten. The routines, however, provided comfort and assurance to members. As one volunteer noted

> Someone, at the beginning, there were [feminist] women here, and they decided how we would do certain things … [these procedures] take care of us. I think [that they] guard us, without our knowing … Some of us don't know where it came from or what is its meaning, or whether its feminist (Zilber 2002: 242).

Insights into Maintaining Institutions

Echoing Scott (2001: 122), we observe that, while institutional research has been attentive to the mechanisms of institutional diffusion, the work required to maintain institutions remains a relatively unstudied phenomenon. We clearly need to focus more attention on the ways in which institutions reproduce themselves. Indeed, this may be a more fundamental question for institutional research, in many respects, than the question of how institutions are created. While institutional entrepreneurs are interesting because of the scale and scope of the product of their actions, the real mystery of institutions is how social structures can be made to be self-replicating and persist beyond the life-span of their creators.

In our review of the empirical literature describing the ways in which actors maintain institutions, we found a range of strategies. One of the immediate observations that can be made based on this review is that the range of institutional work used to maintain institutions can be ordered on a continuum of 'comprehensibility'. Clearly, the work used to maintain rule systems (enabling, policing and deterring) is distinguished by its high degree comprehensibility in the sense that the actors engaged in, and subject to, this type of work are aware of its purpose and influence. On the other end of the spectrum, maintenance of institutions through reproduction of norms and belief systems (valourizing/demonizing, mythologizing and embedding/ routinizing) is generally less comprehensible; the actors engaged in the routines and rituals of reproduction appear to be largely unaware of the original purpose, or the ultimate outcome, of their actions. A useful line of inquiry, thus, would be to examine the processes by which institutional participants 'forget' or lose the comprehensibility of their actions.

A second important observation based on the research reviewed above concerns the relationship between institutional maintenance and change. From our review, it seems that the maintaining of institutions must be distinguished from simple stability or the absence of change: rather, institutional work that maintains institutions involves considerable effort, and often occurs as a consequence of change in the organization or its environment. That is, in order to maintain institutions, actors must cope with the entrance of new members into the organization or the field, the evolution of the field in new and unexpected directions, and changes in pan-institutional factors such as technology and demographics. Consequently, actors need to develop specialized techniques by which new members are engaged and socialized, and new norms, demographic patterns and changes in the external environment incorporated into pre-existing routines and patterns. Understanding how institutions maintain themselves, thus, must focus on understanding how actors are able to effect processes of persistence and stability in the context of upheaval and change.

Disrupting Institutions

Although institutional research and theory did for a period of time emphasize the processes and forces that led to the diffusion and endurance of organizational structures, practices and technologies, the possibility of institutions being disrupted by the work of individual or collective actors has been highlighted in institutional theory both in the early work of Selznick and in more recent research that has focused on institutional change in fields and organizations (Holm 1995; Greenwood and Hinings 1996; Scott et al. 2000; Greenwood et al. 2002; Maguire et al. 2004; Suddaby and Greenwood 2005).

More broadly, research on the dynamics of organizational fields suggests that there will very often be actors whose interests are not served by existing

Table 1.6.3 Disrupting Institutions

Forms of institutional work	Definition	Key references for empirical examples
Disconnecting sanctions	Working through state apparatus to disconnect rewards and sanctions from some set of practices, technologies or rules	Jones (2001); Leblebici et al. (1991)
Disassociating moral foundations	Disassociating the practice, rule or technology from its moral foundation as appropriate within a specific cultural context	Ahmadjian and Robinson (2001)
Undermining assumptions and beliefs	Decreasing the perceived risks of innovation and differentiation by undermining core assumptions and beliefs	Leblebici et al. (1991); Wicks (2001)

institutional arrangements, and who will consequently work when possible to disrupt the extant set of institutions (Abbott 1988; DiMaggio 1991; Bourdieu and Wacquant 1992; Bourdieu 1993). As Bourdieu (1993) argues, the differential allocation of capital based on institutional structures embeds conflict in organizational fields: actors will compete to gain privileged positions or disrupt the institutions which restrict their access to capital. Abbott's (1988) analysis of professional fields highlights this dynamic in the form of inter-jurisdictional conflicts in which professional groups compete for the right to engage in particular forms of activity (Dezalay and Garth 1995; Covaleski et al. 2003). See Table 1.6.3 for a summary of the forms of institutional work associated with disrupting institutions.

Institutional work aimed at disrupting institutions involves attacking or undermining the mechanisms that lead members to comply with institutions. In order to catalogue these forms of institutional work in the recent empirical institutional literature, we searched for concrete descriptions of actors engaged in activities intended to disrupt the controls which underpin institutions. Although Oliver (1992) established the importance of deinstitutionalization as a process, and several studies allude to the dynamics associated with institutions being disrupted, concrete descriptions of the institutional work that actors must engage in to make this happen are relatively rare in the empirical literature we examined. Where institutional change is examined, the emphasis is primarily on the creation and emergence of new institutions, rather than the work that is done to disrupt existing ones. Although it may be the case that an important way

in which existing institutions are disrupted is through the development of new ones, we believe that this is not the only, or even the dominant process through which the disruption of institutions occurs. Oliver (1992) argues that deinstitutionalization is a distinct process with its own antecedents; we similarly believe that the disruption of institutions involves institutional work that is distinct from that associated with the creation of new institutions. Although few in number, the descriptions of such work in the empirical literature are consistent with this belief.

Disconnecting Sanctions/Rewards

Most of the institutional work aimed at disrupting institutions that we found involved work in which state and non-state actors worked through state apparatus to disconnect rewards and sanctions from some set of practices, technologies or rules. The most direct manner in which this occurs is through the judiciary, which is capable of directly invalidating previously powerful institutions. In Jones' (2001) study of the early American film industry, for instance, the courts played an important role in disrupting key institutions: Edison and the Trust had worked hard to create and maintain technical institutions that provided their firms with a competitive advantage, but these institutions were disrupted by the courts invalidating their foundation in a series of decisions: 'In 1902, Judge Wallace of the Court of Appeals declared: "It is obvious that Mr Edison was not a pioneer ... He dismissed Edison's patent right and legitimacy claims"' (Jones 2001: 924); in reaction to an FTC anti-trust complaint, 'Judge Dickson ... ruled that the Trust had violated the Sherman Anti-Trust Act' (Jones 2001: 927). these rulings effectively razed the institutional basis for Edison's and the Trust's competitive advantage, eliminating their ability to control the use of key technologies.

Along with this kind of direct disruption, the state can also be an important lever for actors to work to disrupt institutions by undermining the technical definitions and assumptions on which they were founded. In the early American radio industry, for example, an important institution was the set of technical standards for local radio stations, which effectively restricted small markets to a single station. Following World War II, Congress pressured and veterans' groups lobbied the FCC to relax these standards, challenging 'the long-held belief that numerous local stations would create interference' which led to 'the allowable ranges for local stations [being] reduced, enabling growth in small markets' (Leblebici et al. 1991: 354). A similar dynamic occurred in the Norwegian fisheries (Holm 1995: 414), when the government adopted an approach to fisheries regulation based on 'science-based recommendations of a total allowable catch (TAC) for each of the most important commercial fish stocks': this undermined both the Main Agreement, the dominant regulative institution, as well as the MSO system through which fishermen dominated the sector, while at the same time freeing processors and exporters from 'the fine-meshed system of regulations in which they were entangled'. Thus, a redefinition of the basis on which the permitted catch was calculated disrupted the regulative basis of the institutional arrangements of the sector.

From looking at these few examples, it seems that an important aspect of coercive work aimed at disrupting institutions involves defining and redefining sets of concepts (Suchman 1995) in ways that reconstitute actors and reconfigure relationships between actors. This definitional work seems to often effect large-scale, revolutionary change (Greenwood and Hinings 1996; Lawrence and Phillips 2004). Consequently, this type of work may be easier to accomplish in contexts in which significant social upheaval is perceived as necessary by important stakeholders. War is one such context (Baron et al. 1986). Imminent economic failure, as occurred in the Depression, is another (Lounsbury

2001). In either context, the conditions are such that actors are willing to accept the massive mobilization of power necessary to produce radical new boundaries, new actors and new rules for the distribution of resources.

Although both the state and professions are likely to be involved in disrupting institutions, their relationship is quite different from that associated with their work in maintaining institutions. Whereas the state and the professions often work together to maintain institutions, this is not necessarily the case when one of them is working to disrupt institutions. When professional groups or bodies work to disrupt institutions, they are often observed to do so by challenging the prevailing regulatory structure (Abbott 1988), as was the case when professional curators worked to disrupt the existing templates for US art museums (DiMaggio 1991). Dezalay and Garth (1995) similarly describe the work of multiple professions to dislodge control over commercial disputes from state judicial systems when they created the field of international commercial arbitration. On the other hand, the state may also work against professions as it redefines and re-regulates, as observed in Holm's (1995) Norwegian fisheries study.

Disassociating Moral Foundations

Institutional work has the potential to disrupt institutions by disassociating the practice, rule or technology from its moral foundation as appropriate within a specific cultural context. Although the empirical literature that we reviewed contains relatively few concrete descriptions of such work, those that we found were consistent in their description of such work as being focused on the gradual undermining of the moral foundations of institutions, rather than their wholesale turnover.

One of the most detailed examinations of the disruption of an institution is Ahmadjian and Robinson's (2001) study of the deinstitutionalization of permanent employment in Japan. In this study, they found that institutional factors shaped the pace and process of the spread of downsizing, a practice that was completely antithetical to the institution of permanent employment. Ahmadjian and Robinson (2001: 622) argue that normative factors affected which firms downsized sooner and later: 'Large, old, wholly domestically owned, and high-reputation Japanese firms were resistant to downsizing at first, as were firms with high levels of human capital, as reflected by high wages, but these social and institutional pressures diminished as downsizing spread across the population'. This description represents the institutional process, but the practices associated with downsizing were much more fine-grained and subtle, slowly undermining the normative basis of permanent employment:

> Along the path to layoffs, firms also resorted to hiring freezes. While employers may have viewed hiring cuts as a means to protect the jobs of existing employees, hiring freezes were nevertheless threats to the permanent employment system in several ways. Since the permanent employment system depended on successive cohorts of new employees entering each year, a hiring freeze meant a gaping hole in a firm's age and promotion hierarchy (Ahmadjian and Robinson 2001: 625).

Thus, what we see from this study is the way in which the normative foundations of an institution are disrupted by indirect sets of practices which go around and undermine, rather than directly attack, those foundations.

The actors most likely to adopt disassociative techniques to disrupt institutional practices are elites. This was the observation of Greenwood and Suddaby (2006), who identified the largest firms and professional associations as actors most likely to disrupt institutional practices. Sherer and Lee (2002: 115), similarly, observe that it was the elite law firms that first adopted the Cravath system of human resources management in the legal profession. They observe that 'these initial innovators were particularly adept at using their prestige to develop and disseminate technical rationales that justified being different'. Notably, while elites first adopted new practices on the basis of technical reasons, Sherer and Lee (2002: 116) observe that 'late adopters appear to have faced moral coercion to reform'.

Undermining Assumptions and Beliefs

The final category of institutional work we consider here is the work done to disrupt institutions by undermining core assumptions and beliefs. Institutions are kept in place by the costs associated with actors moving away from taken-for-granted patterns of practice, technologies and rules (Scott 2001): these costs include the effort associated with innovation and the risks of differentiation. Thus,

work aimed at disrupting institutions is effective when it removes those costs in some way, facilitating new ways of acting that replace existing templates, or decreasing the perceived risks of innovation and differentiation. In the institutional research we examined, there was little documentation of institutional work of this type. Two kinds of such work, however, did emerge: innovation that broke existing, institutional assumptions, and gradual undermining through contrary practice.

In Leblebici et al.'s (1991) study of the American radio industry, small independent radio stations disrupted taken-for-granted templates of how radio was financed through their production of alternative forms of radio content:

> independent stations, like WOR (Newark, New Jersey), WLW (Cincinnati), and WMAQ (Chicago), evolved the practice of spot advertising. Spots were advertising announcements inserted between programmes. They offered an alternative to national and regional advertisers who could not afford the expense of sponsoring the production of an entire programme. These independent stations also began to produce their own local shows to draw listeners from the networks in their area. But lacking the enormous resources of the networks, they violated some precepts of the industry, producing cheap quiz shows and using recorded music (Leblebici et al. 1991: 352).

Thus, located outside of the positions that benefited from the financing templates of the industry, independent stations were able to disrupt existing institutions.

An example of the gradual undermining of an institution comes from Wicks' (2001) study of the Westray coal mining disaster. This example is interesting because the institutional work done focused on assumptions or beliefs to undermine an institution that was previously supported primarily by regulative means. The institution in this case was the set of safety rules that were meant to control the level of coal dust that accumulated in the mine (the greater the amount, the more likely an explosion might occur):

> A situation had resulted in which although a regulatory system was in place, it had failed to accomplish its health and safety objectives. Over time, these repeated violations of rules became the norm, with the rules being in place only to the extent that they created the veneer of legitimacy

necessary to avoid sanctions from government regulators. The coal-dust accumulation became commonplace and was only dealt with when inspection visits were anticipated (Wicks 2001: 675).

Insights into Disrupting Institutions

The first insight from this section is that we simply do not know much about the work done by actors to disrupt institutions. Despite the prominence of Oliver's (1992) discussion of deinstitutionalization as a process, very little research has documented the practices through which actors purposively engage in the disrupting of institutions. What we do know comes mainly from studies that are focused on the creating of new institutions, and which only incidentally discuss the disruptive institutional work done by actors in the same domain. We see that institutional work aimed at disrupting institutions focuses primarily on the relationship between an institution and the social controls that perpetuate it: disconnecting rewards and sanctions, disassociating moral foundations and undermining assumptions and beliefs all disrupt institutions by lowering in some way the impact of those social controls on non-compliance. This set of categories, however, only describes a small subset of the potential strategies available to actors intent on disrupting institutions.

A substantive insight that we can take from this review of the institutional work associated with disrupting institutions concerns the relative influence of institutional pressures on different types of actors. Some institutional research has characterized institutions as 'totalizing' structures that hold their subject actors captive to unremitting coercive, normative and cognitive pressures for conformity. Our review, however, suggests that institutional pressures are less 'totalizing' for some actors and in some contexts. For instance, the ability to disconnect rewards and sanctions from behaviours is most directly associated with the state and the judiciary, as well as with those professions and elites that have the financial and intellectual resources to harness the capacity of the state and the judiciary to disrupt institutions that de-privilege them in some way. This suggests that state actors and some other elites may operate with a heightened awareness and potential for strategic response to societal rewards and sanctions. From the instances we observed of institutional work that disrupts institutions by disassociating behaviours from their moral foundations, it is difficult to associate such work clearly with any particular actor, but we can make some general observations. The ability of an actor to engage in practices that exist just outside of the normative boundaries of an institution reflects a high level of cultural competence; thus, normative work of this sort is mostly likely to be accomplished by members of a field or organization with sophisticated understanding of the cultural boundaries and meanings of institutions. We are similarly constrained regarding any generalizations about actors who disrupt institutions by undermining beliefs or assumptions, but the empirical literature, along with our own conjecture, suggests another sort of actor – not a powerful or culturally sophisticated actor, but one capable of working in highly original and potentially counter-cultural ways. Thus, the different forms of institutional work demand different categories of actor, ones that are immune or somehow less affected by the governance mechanisms of their institutional environment. This issue suggests a rich basis for research into why and how these actors gain such immunity.

A second observation from this category of institutional work is that the activities that these actors engage in to disrupt institutional structures are largely discursive and relate to what Lamont and Molnar (2002) have described as 'boundary work'. Lamont and Molnar make a distinction between social and symbolic boundaries. Social boundaries would include those that refer to economic, physical and political location. Symbolic boundaries include moral boundaries, socioeconomic boundaries and cultural boundaries. In the work we have described, both types of boundaries are the focus of institutional work. Actors appear to disrupt institutions primarily by redefining, recategorizing, reconfiguring, abstracting, problematizing and, generally, manipulating the social and symbolic boundaries that constitute institutions.

Studying Institutional Work

In this last section of the chapter, we turn to the issue of studying institutional work – the research approaches we might use to document, analyse and understand the practices through which actors create, maintain and disrupt institutions. We believe a wide range of approaches are potentially well suited to the study of institutional work, ranging from traditional qualitative methods such as ethnography and oral history, to quantitative approaches including the statistical analyses of event histories and social networks. Along with a new focus within institutional studies, there may also be the emergence of new forms of institutional research. In this section, we highlight three approaches which have only begun to be applied to institutional research, but which represent important potential sources of insight into the dynamics of institutional work: discourse analysis, actor-network theory and semiotics. Each of these domains represents far more than a methodology; each is associated with a significant theoretical and empirical tradition, a review of which is well beyond the scope of this chapter. The aim of this section, therefore, is to provide an overview of some of the key ideas from each approach, examine how the approach might be applied to the study of institutional work, and illustrate some of the benefits that might stem from such an application.

Discourse Analysis and the Study of Institutional Work

One of the observations we have made is that institutional work is often language-centred – many forms of institutional work we have identified involve practices of speaking and writing that are aimed at affecting the institutional context within which those practices occur. We reviewed institutional work that included composing legislation, telling stories, writing histories, making jokes and insults, writing memos and letters, writing legal opinions, writing and making speeches and making announcements, among other discursive acts. Thus, we argue one approach to the study of institutional work that holds significant promise is discourse analysis.

Discourse analysis describes a wide range of methods and approaches to organizational analysis, the common element among which involves a focus on 'organizational discourse', which Grant et al. (2004: 3) define as

> structured collections of texts embodied in the practices of talking and writing (as well as a wide variety of visual representations and cultural artifacts) that bring organizationally related objects into being as these texts are produced, disseminated and consumed.

By organizationally related objects, Grant et al. (2004) are referring to the range of discursive

elements that constitute the linguistic and symbolic life of organizations – concepts, ideas, names, roles, strategies, products, plans, stories, places, people, things (or at least their discursive representation). These objects from a discourse analytic perspective are constructed in and through discursive practices that create new texts and connect them to existing texts (Grant et al. 2004). Objects become institutions when they are associated with sets of social controls that ensure the object's ongoing reproduction (Phillips et al. 2004). Thus, discourse analysis fits neatly with our interest in institutional work: it provides methods and theories to aid in understanding how linguistic and symbolic practices create new objects and associate those objects with social controls that institutionalize them.

Discourse analysis is a highly heterogeneous intellectual domain which points to several forms of organizational discourse, each of which might highlight particular categories of institutional work. Here we consider just three forms of organizational discourse identified by Grant et al. (2004): rhetoric, narrative and dialogue.

Rhetoric

One important form of discourse in organizations is rhetoric, which refers to 'the use of symbols to persuade others to change their attitudes, beliefs, values or actions' (Cheney et al. 2004: 79). Suddaby and Greenwood (2005) argue that, in contrast to other forms of language-centred analysis which tend to focus on the content of discourse, rhetorical analysis analyses the effectiveness of specific linguistic moves by contrasting the interplay of emotional impact (pathos), character (ethos) and logical content (logos). A focus on rhetoric shares the broader interest of discourse analysis in the role of language in structuring social action, but is distinguished by a very specific focus on suasion and influence. Rhetorical analysis 'restricts its focus to explicitly political or interest laden discourse and seeks to identify recurrent patterns of interests, goals and shared assumptions that become embedded in persuasive texts' (Suddaby and Greenwood 2005: 8).

The importance of persuasion as a form of institutional work has been highlighted in a range of studies (Heracleous and Barrett 2001; Greenwood et al. 2002; Suddaby and Greenwood 2005). Suddaby and Greenwood (2005) identify two elements of the role of rhetoric in a contest over the legitimacy of a new organizational form in the professions. First, actors adopted 'institutional vocabularies' or clusters of identifying words and referential texts that were used to expose contradictions in institutional logics embedded in historical understandings of professionalism. Secondly, actors employed recurring 'rhetorical strategies' designed to connect the innovation to broad templates or scenarios of change. Heracleous and Barrett's (2001) study of the role of language in promoting the adoption of electronic communication in the London Insurance Market focused similarly on identifying enthymemes or 'arguments in use' by competing stakeholders at different stages of a change effort.

Applying rhetorical analysis to the domain of institutional work would involve an examination of the forms of argument associated with creating, maintaining and disrupting institutions. An analysis of the rhetoric associated with various attempts at advocacy, for instance, might help to illuminate why some attempts to gain political or regulatory support are successful while others fail. In a situation described by Holm (1995: 405–7), the Norwegian fishermen and fish exporters each attempted to persuade the Norwegian government of the cause of and potential solution to economic problems in the industry. The fishermen argued that the problem was with the 'free market', that it 'was the fundamental problem' and should be replaced by 'a system of centralized fish export under government control'. In contrast,

> [t]he fish exporters opposed this vehemently. The problem, they claimed, was international in character. There simply was no internal Norwegian cause for or solution to the crisis. In the absence of international agreements, government intervention in Norwegian fish exports could only magnify the problems. Any restraints on the Norwegian fish exporters would advantage their foreign competitors (Norway, Director of Fisheries, 1928).

Holm's (1995) analysis highlights the importance of several facets of rhetoric in the creating of new institutions. The outcome of this rhetorical battle was a win for the fish exporters – they were not put under government control, but gained the government's protection. Holm (1995: 406) explains this result in terms of 'the class bias of Norwegian politics at the time', with the fish exporters being 'core constituents of the ruling liberal-conservative coalition', while fishermen, peasants and workers were but marginal

groups within the Norwegian polity. This analysis points to an important aspect of rhetoric – the role of social position, or ethos, clearly plays an important role in the institutional dynamics described by Holm. The analysis might have benefited from a deeper incorporation of a broader set of rhetorical tools, bringing out the roles of reason (logos) and emotion (pathos) more fully in explaining this result. While an analysis of social position is often critical to understanding institutional outcomes, the force of such positions usually needs to be channelled through persuasive arguments based on both reason and emotion in order to effect institutional change. This channelling is the institutional work that we are interested in studying – how actors leverage their positions through the construction of persuasive arguments is a central question for this domain of research.

Narrative

The analysis of narrative has emerged as an important feature of discourse-oriented organization studies (Czarniawska 1997; Phillips and Hardy 2002). Narratives constitute a particular form of discourse characterized not by its intent, as with rhetoric, but by its structure: 'narratives involve temporal *chains* of interrelated events or actions, undertaken by characters' (Grant et al. 2004: 63). The analysis of narratives can involve a wide range of techniques from formal analyses of narrative structure, to interpretive analyses which emphasize the cultural meanings and locations of a narrative (Czarniawska 2000). As we have seen in our review of institutional work, actors interested in creating, maintaining and disrupting institutions often rely on narrative devices to do so (Angus 1993; Kitchener 2002). Thus, research on institutional work could utilize narrative analysis, for instance to investigate the relationship between narrative structures or cultural associations and their effectiveness as institutional devices.

Some forms of institutional work that are obvious candidates for narrative analysis include advocacy, constructing identities, theorizing, educating, valourizing and demonizing, mythologizing and undermining; each of these forms of institutional work is likely to rely at times on persuasive or compelling stories which lead actors to support the creation, maintenance or disruption of some institution. In our examination of 'mythologizing', for instance, we discussed the way in which a Brother in the Christian Brothers School relied on narrative to provide a compelling foundation for the school's institutionalized devotion to competition. This example illustrates both the use of narrative to support and maintain institutions, and the work required to establish an enduring, stable narrative: as Czarniawska (2000: 14) argues, 'the "petrification" of narratives is not the result of the myopia of the researcher, but of intensive stabilizing work by the narrators'. From our perspective, this stabilization of narrative is an important form of institutional work; if narratives are to underpin institutions, then those narratives themselves must be stabilized, either through the employment of some enduring media or through a nested process of institutional work in which the narrative itself is institutionalized.

Narrative analysis can, therefore, help to illuminate the processes through which actors are able to fashion, communicate and embed stories that support the creating, maintaining or disrupting of institutions. Kitchener's (2002) study of institutional change in healthcare, for instance, highlights the ways in which the popular business press, academic textbook writers and consultants all engaged in the production of narratives that helped to institutionalize the merger as a solution to organizational problems of competitiveness and efficiency. Understanding the nature of this institutional work might be furthered through a more systematic analysis of the narratives produced by these actors. One interesting and useful form of narrative analysis might focus on the tropes or 'stock narratives' (Washbourne and Dicke 2001) from which these new narratives are fashioned. All narratives are constructed from existing stocks of discursive objects, so this form of analysis might help illuminate the narrative strategies employed by institutional actors as they work to create a new institution, as well as the connections between this 'new' institution and existing institutions.

Dialogue

Dialogue is distinguished from other forms of discourse by its collective accomplishment: unlike rhetoric or narrative, which can be attributed to a single actor, dialogue is always constructed by multiple actors (Gergen et al. 2004). Investigations of dialogue range from highly technical forms of

conversation analysis (Sacks 1992) to studies of appreciative inquiry (Cooperrider and Srivastva 1987). What is of interest to the study of institutional work is the generative potential of dialogue (Weick 1995; Taylor and Van Every 2000). As Gergen et al. (2004: 45) explain, a focus on generative dialogue illuminates 'those kinds of dialogic moves that may bring realities and ethics into being and bind them to particular patterns of action'. From our perspective, generative dialogue is a potentially powerful form of institutional work, creating mechanisms of social control and associating them with sets of interaction sequences to effect institutions. Although dialogical processes have not been a central feature of institutional research, a number of studies have highlighted the degree to which dialogue can be a central element in the creating, maintaining and disrupting of institutions (Sharfman et al. 1991; Lawrence et al. 2002; Everett and Jamal 2004; Mahalingam and Levitt 2004). Of the forms of institutional work we have examined in this chapter, several are likely to include dialogue and thus may be open to a dialogical analysis: these include constructing identities, constructing normative networks, educating, enabling, disconnecting and disassociating.

Gergen et al. (2004) suggest four key components of dialogue that contribute to its taking on a generative quality, and consequently provide a foundation for understanding the relationship between dialogue and institutional work: affirmation, which they argue 'may stand as the key building block to creating conjoint realities' (Gergen et al. 2004: 45); the construction of productive differences, which extend, bridge, amplify and illustrate previous statements in the dialogue; the creation of coherence through statements which 'enable preceding expressions to create a singular, ordered world about which to organize' (Gergen et al. 2004: 47); and narrative and temporal integration, which involves the use of past accounts to 'fortify the present, fill out its contours, add to its dimensions, and/or ratify its value' (Gergen et al. 2004: 48). These four aspects of generative dialogue provide an analytical basis for investigating the potential for actors to engage in institutional work through dialogue: they suggest describe the practices in which actors need to engage in order to utilize dialogue as a means of creating, maintaining or disrupting institutions. A fruitful approach to studying institutional work through dialogue, therefore, would involve the detailed analysis of a dialogical process over time. Such a study might be done through real-time observation of an interorganizational collaboration, an archival analysis of the dialogues associated with a public issue, or an ethnography of intra-organizational dialogues. In any case, the focus would be on the practices through which participants accomplish (or fail to accomplish) the production of generative dialogue aimed at creating, maintaining or disrupting institutions.

Actor Network Theory (ANT) and the Study of Institutional Work

Actor Network Theory holds considerable promise for extending our understanding of institutional work. Derived from efforts to understand the ways in which scientific ideas emerge out of interactions embedded in social networks (Callon 1986; Latour 1987), ANT offers a combined theory and method based on the observation that social structure 'is not a noun but a verb' (Law 1992: 5). ANT focused on social processes, rather than structures, and thus offers support for a renewed focus on the social practices associated with institutionalization, rather than institutions as reified social structures (Tolbert and Zucker 1996). ANT is distinguished by its analytic focus which emphasizes the micro-interactions of both human and non-human 'actants', including technologies, media and any object that mediates social interaction (Callon 1987; Lee and Hassard 1999). From this perspective, actants vie to construct networks of social support in an ongoing competition; networks of support emerge and grow as key actants mobilize support for their position and, simultaneously, for their network of supporters. Over time, the object of interaction and the network become indistinguishable (Lee and Hassard 1999) or, in neo-institutional terms, become taken-for-granted.

ANT offers a fresh perspective for neo-institutionalists interested in understanding how institutions are created, maintained and disrupted, in several respects. First it draws attention away from the reified elements of institutions and focuses on the struggles and contests that generate and reproduce them. From an ANT perspective, the stable and enduring elements of institutions are a 'relational effect' (Law 1992) that mask an ongoing and dynamic internal struggle between competing actor-networks. Instead of studying the ephemeral outcome of institutions

(i.e. norms), an ANT perspective suggests that we might instead focus on the interactions that produce and contest those outcomes. So, for example, rather than tracking the diffusion of a managerial practice through time and space (Abrahamson 1991), institutional researchers adopting an ANT perspective would focus on exploring the processes of interaction through which the adoption of similar practices can support and reinforce coalitions and alliances between distinct networks of actants with different objectives or goals.

In this respect, ANT offers a means of addressing a particularly thorny issue for institutional research, in general, and institutional work, specifically. The agency that underlies institutional work is most visible and accessible during times of profound institutional change – when institutions are being created or destroyed. It is during those moments that the institutional fabric of taken-for-grantedness is torn and the inner workings of institutions and the intentions of actors are made available for all to see. However, it is the long periods of apparent institutional stasis, during which institutions are routinely and habitually reproduced, that present a problem for traditional empirical investigation. The epistemological issue faced by neo-institutional research is, 'how can a traditionally trained empiricist investigate a phenomenon that has become reified and is, therefore, unavailable to conscious perception?'[2] The way forward, offered by ANT, is to avoid being distracted by outcomes of institutional processes and focus, instead on how distinct networks develop around conflicting definitions and interpretations that produce those outcomes. In this respect, ANT offers a useful research strategy or methodology that is well suited to extending our understanding of institutional work by problematizing the common view of institutions as concrete and enduring social structures and reminding researchers that institutions and organizations are fictions actively created and re-created by actants.

ANT's concept of 'translation' offers a second avenue for research into institutional work. A key construct within ANT, translation refers to the process by which actants within a network mobilize support by making a unified whole from different interpretations, meanings and motivations. As Law (1992: 6) describes it:

[Translation] is the core of the actor-network approach: a concern with how actors and organizations mobilize, juxtapose and hold together the bits and pieces out of which they are composed; how they are sometimes able to prevent those bits and pieces from following their own inclinations and making off and how they manage, as a result, to conceal for a time the process of translation itself and so turn a network from a heterogeneous set of bits and pieces each with its own inclinations, into something that passes as a punctualized actor.

A key observation is that the translator-actant, itself, becomes an object of translation as the network congeals and becomes taken-for-granted. Through this process, the power structure that generates a network becomes hidden or masked through the process of translation, in much the same way that agency structures in institutions become masked as the institutions that surround them become cognitively legitimated (DiMaggio 1988; Fligstein 2001).

Translation offers both a conceptual and methodological way forward for researchers interested in moving beyond the totalizing view of institutions and institutional outcomes. Most traditional research on institutions, for example, has focused on processes of diffusion, or the ways in which organizations become isomorphic through the transmission of common templates (DiMaggio and Powell 1983) or practices (Abrahamson 1991). So, for example, researchers have traced the movement of common personnel systems (Baron et al. 1986), poison pills and golden parachutes (Davis 1991) and market entry patterns (Haveman 1993) across time and space. An ANT perspective, however, would accept that common organizational practices have diffused, but would be more attentive to local variations in motivations for adopting similar practices and would also look for local variations in the use and outcome of adopting isomorphic practices. The key distinction here is in avoiding the assumption that all actants within an emerging network behave the same way for the same reasons.

Some institutional researchers have already adopted a version of translation to avoid an oversimplified view of diffusion (Rovik 1996; Sahlin-Andersson 1996). Sahlin-Andersson (1996: 69) adeptly identifies the weakness of traditional notions of diffusion in ignoring the role of actants:

The impression is that new organization models spread almost automatically; organizations are regarded as passive entities which simply react and adapt to the latest trends. If we acknowledge that

organizations consist of thinking and acting persons, and that each change in organizational practice or organizational form requires that people act, we will find that the mechanical explanations leave unanswered most of the questions about why organizations adopt new trends.

Sahlin-Andersson reminds us that, not only do different actants adopt similar forms or practices for different reasons, in the process of adopting they also introduce subtle changes to them. That is, the process of translation means that actants adopt similar institutional practices based on different meanings, and, in the process, introduce the potential for future institutional change. A key distinction between diffusion and translation is that, while the former connotes the movement of a physical object through time and space, the latter emphasizes the changes that occur in meanings and interpretations as a physical or social object moves through a network (Czarniawska and Sevon 1996).

A third contribution ANT offers for the study of institutional work is to re-conceptualize power in processes of institutional creation, reproduction and demise. Power is less a property and more a diffuse product of network interactions in ANT (Callon and Latour 1981). That is, power is referential and distributed amongst actors within a network and it is the collective interaction that produces the power (of an idea, a position or an institution) rather than any individual actant within the network. Viewing power as a distributed process within a system (rather than a property possessed by some and not others) changes the way in which we perceive institutional change. Rather than seeking the locus of change (i.e. core or periphery) or the agents of change (i.e. institutional entrepreneurs), research should focus on the manner in which actor networks grow in size, complexity and influence. ANT theorists describe this process as four moments of translation (Denis et al. 2004: 7):

'problematization' in which translators attempt to define an issue and offer an 'obligatory passage point' drawing an initial set of actors together to solve it; 'interessement' in which translators determine and fix the interests of key actors so that they are willing to stay with an emerging project; 'enrolment' in which representatives of main groups of actors are assigned 'roles' and drawn together to build an alliance; 'mobilization' in which the actor-network is extended beyond an initial group.

These terms draw attention away from power used to mobilize resources within an institutional field, and focus attention on the social practices and skills needed to mobilize competing frames or interpretations that, in turn, define the resources and actants that comprise the field. ANT, in this respect, offers a political perspective of power in which institutions appear as powerful and stable social structures, not because of their intrinsic or material nature, but only because the network of actors that produced them see them as such. Power and agency, thus, are products of a capacity to stabilize networks and researchers interested in understanding institutional work ought, therefore, to attend to the 'social skills' (Fligstein 2001) used by actants to form associations, construct normative meaning systems and advocate new rule structures.

Semiotics and the Study of Institutional Work

The final approach to the study of institutional work that we consider is semiotics. Most simply, semiotics is the study of signs (Deely 1990; Cobley and Janz 2004). More broadly, semiotics focuses on ways in which meaning is constructed (Sebeok 1976), and so is connected to though distinct from discourse analysis. A 'sign' is the dyadic relationship between 'signifier' and 'signified', where the signifier is some material manifestation (i.e. the vocalization or writing of a word) and the signified is the abstract idea or mental concept it represents (Saussure 1974). A key idea in semiotics is that signs are arbitrary or social constructs: there are no necessary or 'natural' relationships between the sounds/images of a signifier and those things signified. Instead, signs reflect meaning by accepted understandings of how systems of signs fit together. Individual speech acts gain meaning by virtue of how they fit with or differ from other speech acts.

An important extension of semiotics that bridges with existing approaches to neo-institutional research is the shared interest in mythologies. Barthes (1972), in particular, observed that sign systems become aggregated in myths. He demonstrated how the denotative content of signs in popular culture was built on connotations drawn from larger sign systems of mythologies; cultural understandings that underpin not only societal conventions, but also the means by which individuals come to understand and experience the world they inhabit.

Mythologies, similarly, occupy a central place in neo-institutional theory, with Meyer and Rowan (1977) having identified myths about rationality as the primary context within which institutions exert social control. Such myths reflect subject positions that confer legitimacy (and thus material resources) on actors, and provide the meaning system by which actors interpret and adopt practices and structures that reflect assumptions about 'rationality'. A more recent extension of this central concept is a growing awareness of other, subsidiary or possibly competing mythologies within organizational fields. These have been variously described as 'institutional logics' (Friedland and Alford 1991), 'institutional myths' (Townley 2002); 'interpretive schemes' (Ranson et al. 1980) or 'legitimating accounts' (Creed et al. 2002).

Although recent research on processes of institutional change has advanced our understanding of the importance and diversity of mythologies in creating and dismantling institutions, we still lack a detailed understanding of precisely how mythologies communicate to actors and how skilled actors can appropriate and manipulate myths during processes of institutional stasis and change. Semiotics offers some important opportunities to address these issues. According to Barthes, mythologies communicate to actors in three ways. First, they offer a 'linguistic message' – the overt meaning communicated, for example, by the text in a magazine advertisement. Secondly, they offer a 'coded iconic message' embedded in the images that surround the text. The meaning from the coded iconic message must be deconstructed by relating the specific images in the advertisement to the overall sign system in the social field that produced the ad. Finally, mythologies present 'non-coded iconic messages' or the literal denotation of the images contained in the ad that are independent of the meta-societal code or sign system.

Some neo-institutional research has adopted elements of semiotic analysis to understand the ways in which myths are used to construct legitimacy. Zilber (2006), for example, used newspaper articles and advertisements to track the ways in which broader societal myths of Israeli culture were appropriated and manipulated to legitimate actions in the burgeoning high-technology industry. Zilber identifies four distinct myths (the individual, the state, information and the 'enchantment of technology') each of which echo pre-existing myths of Israeli culture, but were skillfully modified by different sub-communities to appropriate the legitimacy of technology for their own purposes. More interesting, perhaps, is her meticulous analysis of how these underlying myths change over time and in reaction to changes in the marketplace (described as 'moments of translation'). The key observation offered by this research is that the signs and symbols that comprise rational myths are connotatively related to broader social and cultural myths and these relationships form and contribute significantly to a toolkit of institutional work.

A related application of mythologies to institutional work occurs in Suddaby and Greenwood's (2005) analysis of the emergence of multidisciplinary practices (MDPs) in the professions. Proponents and opponents of MDPs drew on common mythologies of 'professionalism' to advocate their position for change or stasis. Those opposing the new form drew on the accepted and dominant myth of professionalism as a public service or a form of 'trusteeship'. Opponents, by contrast, offered an emerging myth of 'professional expertise' in which commercial interests were viewed to support, rather than detract from, the public interest. Suddaby and Greenwood (2005) conclude that institutional change is predicated on actors' skill in exploiting the contradictions inherent in the myths that underpin institutions.

Semiotics offers both a methodology and a language for describing and understanding mythologies. Mythologies, in turn, offer a key point of access for enriching our understanding of institutional logics, interpretive schemes and other constructs that have been identified as key to creating, maintaining and disrupting institutions. While current research has paid attention to describing the characteristics of institutional logics and demonstrating their spread through organizational fields, considerably less attention has been focused on the social practices by which actors identify and respond to the appropriate symbolic trappings of rational structure among the myriad of signs and signifiers available to them. Research on institutional work could draw on semiotics to attend to the denotative and connotative elements of rational myths, and the social and cultural practices which erect and maintain those myths.

The semiotic approach offered by Charles Saunders Peirce differs from that of Saussure by its more 'realist' assumptions about the origins of signs.

That is, unlike Saussure, Peirce thought that the sign was a 'real' object independent of the linguistic process required to encode or decode it. Two significant bridges may be built from a structuralist approach to semiotics and our understanding of institutional work. The first is the potential for the inclusion of non-linguistic matter in the semiotic analysis of institutional work. Physical symbols, object and artifacts form an important but relatively unexplored element in the chains of activities that constitute institutional work (Mitroff and Kilmann 1976; Morgan et al. 1983). Physical symbols have long been understood as an important method of understanding relationships between individuals and organizations: dress codes (Rafaeli and Pratt 1993; Pratt and Rafaeli 2001), office arrangement and design (Elsbach 2004) and even contracts (Kaghan and Lounsbury 2006) have been identified as important indicia of power structures and cultural interactions within organizations. All of these physical objects represent potential sites of institutional work, as they are designed, crafted, modified and destroyed in relation to sets of institutions that give them meaning and power (Pratt and Rafaeli 2001). Semiotic analyses could help to unpack the relationships between these physical artifacts (signifiers), their institutional meanings (signified) and the institutional work that establishes these connections.

A second contribution of semiotics to the study of institutional work stems from Peirce's structuralist orientation to meaning systems. Implicit in Peirce's complex and formal semiotic system is an assumption that meaning structures are both formal and logical. That is, the patterns of relations between signs within a larger sign system exist objectively and can be accessed empirically. As such, researchers ought to be able to capture and compare the cultural meaning systems embedded in various semiotic codes. As Mohr (1998: 345) has argued, researchers adopting a strong structuralist perspective of semiotics ought to be able to measure the meanings 'that are embedded within institutions, practices and cultural artifacts'. Applying diverse relational methods such as lattice and correspondence analysis (the former was first developed by C.S. Peirce) to textual data, Mohr has developed a unique methodology and body of work that measures and maps the basic structures of meanings within discourse communities (Mohr 1994; 1998; Mohr and Duquenne 1997). While clearly acknowledging the risks and dangers of reducing meaning systems inappropriately, Mohr's body of work offers a useful impetus to formally quantify semiotic technique and make the comparison of discursive relationships more systematic and transparent. More significantly, Mohr's work demonstrates the refreshing absence of 'methodological dogmatism' (Mick 1986) within semiotic approaches.

A third contribution of semiotics to the study of institutional work is the focus on meaning. Although researchers have analysed the role of the symbolic in institutional processes, such research has often been based on relatively dismissive assumptions about the role of symbols in opposition to the technical or material environment that produces them. In such research, symbolic action is described as an empty gesture that decouples ceremony from function, as when companies adopt long-term incentives plans but do not actually use them (Westphal and Zajac 1998). Rather than dismissing such action as 'merely symbolic', however, semiotics reminds us of the value of making symbolic aspects of experience primary in our analyses. It is insufficient to show that a managerial practice is adopted ceremonially. We need to know what message this action communicates, to which audiences it is intended, and why this 'signal' was selected from the entire strata of symbolic material available. Elevating the empirical status of symbols and signs, in turn, creates many new research sites and questions for researchers interested in how meaning can be manipulated to effect institutional change or maintain institutional arrangements. The work associated with such symbolic phenomena as corporate logos, board meetings, product design, corporate architecture and corporate art collections can be interrogated to provide useful data on how sign systems construct meaning and maintain or alter institutional understandings. Adopting semiotic approaches to institutional work can, therefore, draw attention to 'the quotidian and most institutionalized behaviours' and 'the replication of symbolic orders' which, as Friedland and Alford (1991: 250) observe, underpins the way that institutions are reproduced and changed.

Other Approaches

By focusing on discourse analysis, actor-network theory and semiotics as approaches to the study of institutional work, our aim has been to open up the analytical space of institutional theory. We are not suggesting that these represent any kind of exhaustive set of methodologies or analytic frames, or that they are incompatible with the data collection and analysis techniques familiar to most institutional scholars. Indeed, we believe most research on institutional work will tend to 'look' very much like traditional institutional research, relying on archival analyses, qualitative field-work, ethnographic observation and hopefully incorporating quantitative techniques such as social network analysis and correspondence analysis. What discourse analysis, actor-network theory and semiotics offer is an additional set of lenses for institutional scholars to try on in order to more clearly see and describe the dynamics of institutional work, which have only begun to be revealed using our traditional frames.

Conclusion

In this chapter, we have begun to document a new direction in institutional research – the study of institutional work. We have argued that this direction stems significantly from a small set of articles by DiMaggio (1988) and Oliver (1991; 1992) which highlighted the important influence of actors on institutions – purposefully creating, maintaining and disrupting them. We further argued that the emergence of practice theory provides a theoretical foundation for understanding institutional work. In reviewing the empirical institutional research in three major journals over the past 15 years, we found that scholars have indeed been paying attention to institutional work; instances of each category of institutional work – creating, maintaining, disrupting – were in evidence. Thus, we were able in this chapter to develop a preliminary taxonomy of institutional work which outlines specific forms of work undertaken to create, maintain and disrupt institutions. In doing so, this chapter provides a foundation for future research into the active agency and specific tasks undertaken by actors in institutional contexts. Our review also points out, however, that our understanding of institutional work is formative at best. Large gaps exist in our ability to describe institutional work, let alone explain it. The study of institutional work has the potential to provide organizational scholars with a fascinating and important arena for theoretical and empirical work for many years. To conclude the chapter, we discuss a set of issues that are illustrative of the potential that the study of institutional work has to reinvigorate institutional research and theory.

Opening up the Black Box of Diffusion

The concept of diffusion is central to institutional theory, and particularly to the empirical research that makes up the central core of this tradition. A range of institutional writings have located diffusion as a central dynamic in the institutionalization of a structure or practice (Zucker 1987; Tolbert and Zucker 1996; Greenwood et al. 2002). The pattern of events and relationships among them that define the process of institutionalization involves an object first being recognized, then accepted by relatively few actors, and then widely diffused and broadly accepted within a field (Stinchcombe 1965; Meyer and Rowan 1977; Zucker 1987; Leblebici et al. 1991). For many years, an archetypal form of institutional research has been based on this model, examining the diffusion of some organizational structure or practice, and attempting to explain the factors that led organizations to take on that structure or practice (Tolbert and Zucker 1983; Baron et al. 1986; Hinings and Greenwood 1988; Davis 1991; Haveman 1993). In their study of the diffusion of civil service reform, for example, Tolbert and Zucker (1983) found that this pattern of diffusion involved two sets of mechanisms, with early adopters basing their decisions on technical grounds and later adopters responding primarily to legitimacy pressures.

What these discussions of diffusion tend to gloss over, however, is the practical, creative work necessary to make diffusion happen: organizations rarely take on the structures and practices of other organizations wholesale, without conflict and without effort. Rather, the diffusion of innovation throughout a field involves substantial institutional work on the part of organizational actors who must persuade others in their organizations of the merits of the innovation, experiment with the innovation in an effort to understand it and how it might apply to their own situations, modify it in order to gain internal legitimacy, and forge practical connections for the new structure or practice. These forms of work are especially important when diffusion involves the translation of institutions across domains, such as from work to non-work life, or from market-based fields of activity to previously non-market arenas, such as healthcare, education or social welfare.

Institutional Work as a Critical Approach

A second set of issues that are raised by attending to institutional work concern the power dynamics in fields and organizations. One of the important facets of the 'old institutionalism' that has largely been lost with the shift in emphasis associated with the 'new institutionalism' is the highlighting of power relations and their relationship to institutions in organizations and societies (Selznick 1949; Gouldner 1954). This move away from power has mirrored a more general move away from considerations of power in organization theory following the demise of Marxist and neo-Marxist analyses that were prominent in the 1970s. Neo-Marxist perspectives lent to organization theory a political perspective from which critiques of organizational structures and practices could be launched (Clegg and Dunkerley 1980). Absent from this perspective, institutional studies since the 1980s have tended to remain apolitical in their analyses of power in social life (Hinings and Greenwood 2002).

The concept of institutional work provides an opportunity for the re-injection of political critique into institutional research and theory. The focus of institutional work on the micro-practices of actors in relation to organizational and societal institutions is consistent with the broader shift in social theories of power: the work of such scholars as Foucault (1979) and Bourdieu (1977; 1993) has prompted scholars from across a range of disciplines to examine the micro-level routines, practices and habits of power. A critical approach to institutional work could examine a number of issues in relation to the role of power and politics in creating, maintaining and disrupting institutions. At a most basic level, all of the practices we described above as institutional work require resources, which are available to some actors and not others. A critical view of institutional work could begin to examine how those resources are distributed and controlled, and by whom. Although we argue that institutional life incorporates the work of many actors, we do not imagine it does so in anything but a highly structured and hierarchical manner – many of the forms of institutional work we have highlighted, such as vesting and policing, for instance, often require the involvement of the state or other elite agencies with the capacity to rely on force or domination to effect institutional ends (Lawrence et al. 2001).

A second level of critical analysis might begin to look at the relationship between institutional work and the contradictions (Seo and Creed 2002) that are inherent in organizational fields. Seo and Creed (2002: 225) argue that 'multilevel processes produce a complex array of interrelated but often mutually incompatible institutional arrangements' which together 'provide a continuous source of tensions and conflicts within and across institutions'. Seo and Creed link these institutional contradictions to the potential for transformational action, but another equally likely possibility is that institutional contradictions will engender a host of practices aimed not at institutional transformation, but at repairing or concealing those contradictions. Since all institutional arrangements privilege some actors, it will be in the interest of those actors to try to maintain such arrangements even, or especially, when they recognize the contradictions constituted by the overlapping institutions and fields which effect their own situations. A critical analysis of institutional work could highlight that repairing and concealing work, who is doing it and why, what resources are being drawn on, which actors are suffering because of it, and what conditions might change should those contradictions be more widely exposed, discussed and potentially addressed.

In sum, adopting a critical perspective of institutional work should reacquaint theorists with the primary research question of political economy – 'who benefits from existing institutional arrangements?' Unlike traditional approaches of political economy, however, a critical approach to institutional work concentrates attention on the act of production, rather than the product itself. That is, a critical view is premised on the assumption that no institutional outcome is to be regarded as material, stable or enduring. Rather, institutional work must be conceived of as the production of unity and attention must be paid to the means by which such unity is achieved. A critical methodology should seek to strip away the 'naturalizing' effects of taken-for-grantedness away from institutional research and address the core problem of how man-made products and events come to perceived and represented as natural social orders.

Bridging Levels of Analysis

The third direction for research on institutional work that we want to address here stems from the status of institutions as nested systems (Holm 1995). A nested systems perspective is completely consistent with the notion of institutional work: as Holm (1995: 400) explains, from a 'nested-systems perspective, a distinction is made between action guided by institutions, on the one hand, and action aimed explicitly at manipulating institutional parameters, on the other'. If we take a broad view of institutions, then we see that they exist in nested systems across many levels, from micro-level institutions in groups and organizations that regulate forms of interaction among members, to field-level institutions such as those associated with professions or industries, to societal institutions concerned with the role of family, the nature of gender and the status of religion. The study of institutional work provides a distinctive way of understanding and examining the relationship between institutions at these different levels. From an institutional perspective, levels are not 'aggregate' phenomena. Fields are no more a collection of organizations than organizations are a collection of individuals; rather, higher-order social collectives are accomplishments of their members, socially constructed and discursively maintained. The nested relationship between institutions at different levels, therefore, involves particular forms of institutional work – translation, interpretation, modification, accommodation – that connects institutions across levels, potentially drawing one level to create new institutions at another level.

Adopting a nested view of institutional work means that researchers will have to become accustomed to viewing institutional phenomena as a homologous microcosm of broader social structures (Bourdieu and Wacquant 1992). So, for example, if we are to know anything about the institutional logic of a particular organizational field, we cannot understand that logic without exploring and gaining insight into the logics of the social fields that surround it. Similarly, researchers must shed the unfortunate structural assumption that an actor engages only in a single organizational field. Rather, actors occupy simultaneous (and Bourdieu would add, homologous) positions in multiple fields and it is really the intersection and contestation of multiple logics within nested fields that provide actors the resources to engage in activities of contestation and reconceptualization that we refer to here as 'institutional work'. Institutions, thus, are to be viewed as the ongoing product of a series of integrated and semi-autonomous social fields, each of which has a distinct history, logic and structure. While such fields are somewhat distinct, they are best described as open systems whose boundaries are always in dispute. Research on institutional work must attend specifically to the conflict that exists between contested fields and the ways in which boundaries are maintained in fields where the conflict is less overt.

To conclude, we suggest that the concept of institutional work provides a new way of seeing institutions. We urge researchers to focus on the interstitial elements of institutions: the gap between structure and action, the moment that separates agency from unintended consequences or the frenetic production of meaning that generates the illusion of stasis and permanence in institutions. Most emphatically, we want to break the dramatic spell of institutions and draw attention behind the scenes, to the actors, writers and stage-hands that produce them. In this sense our call to attend to institutional work draws a distinctly political approach to institutions in which our core puzzle is to understand the ways in which disparate sets of actors, each pursuing their own vision, can become co-ordinated in a common project. By paying attention to institutional work, theorists can avoid the subjective illusion of institutional outcomes and begin to unpack the relational and interactive moments of institutional production.

Acknowledgements

We would like to thank Petter Holm, Woody Powell, Mike Lounsbury, Christine Oliver, Charlene Zietsma and Cynthia Hardy for their insightful comments on earlier drafts of this chapter.

Notes

1. There is a variant of practice theory employed by more structuralist neo-institutionalists (see, for example, Mohr 1998; Lounsbury and Ventresca 2003). This strand of practice theory involves a shift of traditional structuralist approaches toward richer conceptualizations of social structure and process that occur at the intersection of the sociology of culture, stratification, politics and institutional analysis. This work often draws on network methods and draws inspiration from Bourdieu's 'field' construct.

2. The extent of this empirical problem is reflected in the relatively high number of instances of institutional work we were able to identify in the literature for creating new institutions as compared to the low number of observed instances of maintaining or disrupting institutions.

References

Abbott, A. (1988) *The system of professions.* Chicago: University of Chicago Press.

Abrahamson, E. (1991) 'Managerial fads and fashions: the diffusion and rejection of an innovation', *Academy of Management Review*, 16(3): 586–612.

Ahmadjian, C.L. and Robinson, P. (2001) 'Safety in numbers: downsizing and the deinstitutionalization of permanent employment in Japan', *Administrative Science Quarterly*, 46: 622–54.

Amis, J., Slack, T. and Hinings, C.R. (2004) 'The pace, sequence and linearity of radical change', *Academy of Management Journal*, 47(1): 15–39.

Angus, L.B. (1993) 'Masculinity and women teachers at Christian Brothers College', *Organization Studies*, 14(2): 235–60.

Barnes, B. (2001) 'Practice as collective action', in T.R. Schatzki, K.K. Cetina and E. von Savigny (eds), *The practice turn in contemporary theory*. London: Routledge. pp. 17–28.

Baron, J.N., Dobbin, F.R. and Jennings, P.D. (1986) 'War and peace: the evolution of modern personnel administration in U.S. industry', *American Journal of Sociology*, 92: 350–83.

Barthes, R. (1972) *Mythologies.* London: Paladin.

Beckert, J. (1999) 'Agency, entrepreneurs, and institutional change: the role of strategic choice and institutionalized practices in organizations', *Organization Studies*, 20(5): 777–99.

Berger, P.L. and Luckmann, T. (1966) *The social construction of reality: A treatise in the sociology of knowledge.* Hammondsworth: Penguin Books.

Bourdieu, P. (1977) *Outline of a theory of practice.* Cambridge: Cambridge University Press.

Bourdieu, P. (1993) *Sociology in question.* London: Sage.

Bourdieu, P. and Wacquant, L.J.D. (1992) *An invitation to reflexive sociology.* Chicago: University of Chicago.

Brock, D.M., Powell, M.J. and Hinings, C.R. (eds) (1999) *Restructuring the professional organization: accounting, healthcare and law.* London: Routledge.

Brown, J.S. and Duguid, P. (1991) 'Organizational learning and communities of practice: toward a unified view of working, learning, and innovation', *Organizational Science*, 2: 40–57.

Brown, J.S. and Duguid, P. (2000) *The social life of information.* Cambridge, MA: Harvard Business School Press.

Bruner, J. (1987) 'Life as narrative', *Social Research*, 54: 11–32.

Callon, M. (1986) 'Some elements of a sociology of translation: domestication of the scallops and the fisherman of St. Brieuc Bay', in J. Law (ed.), *Power, action and belief. A new sociology of knowledge?*. London: Routledge & Kegan Paul. pp. 196–223.

Callon, M. (1987) 'Society in the making: the study of technology as a tool for sociological analysis', in W.E. Bijker, T.P. Hughes and T.J. Pinch (eds), *The social construction of technological systems*. Cambridge, MA: MIT Press. pp. 83–103.

Callon, M. and Latour, B. (1981) 'Unscrewing the big Leviathan: how actors macrostructure reality and how sociologists help them to do so', in K.D. Knorr-Cetina and A.V. Cicourel (eds), *Advances in social theory and methodology: Toward an Integration of micro- and macro-sociologies*. Boston, MA: Routledge and Kegan Paul. pp. 277–303.

Campbell, C. (2004) 'NAACP promoting voter registration', *Washington Observer-Reporter*. Available online at: http://www.observer-reporter.com/282357491796160.bsp. Accessed 13 August 2004.

Campbell, J.L. and Lindbergh, L.N. (1991) 'The evolution of governance regimes', in J.L. Campbell, J.R. Hollingsworth and L.N. Lindbergh (eds), *Governance of the American Economy*. Cambridge, UK: Cambridge University Press. pp. 319–55.

Carroll, G.R., Delacroix, J. and Goodstein, J. (1988) 'The political environments of organizations: an ecological view', in B.M. Staw and L.L. Cummings (eds), *Research in Organizational Behavior (Vol. 10)*. Greenwich, CT: JAI Press. pp. 359–92.

Cassell, P. (1993) *The Giddens reader*. Stanford, CA: Stanford University Press.

Cheney, G., Christensen, L.T., Conrad, C. and Lair, D.J. (2004), 'Corporate rhetoric in organizational discourse', in D. Grant, C. Hardy, C. Oswick and L. Putnam (eds), *The Sage handbook of organizational discourse*. London: Sage. pp. 79–103.

Clegg, S.R. and Dunkerley, D. (1980) *Organization, class and control*. London: Routledge.

Clemens, E.S. (1993) 'Organizational repertoires and institutional change: women's groups and the transformation of US politics, 1890–1920', *American Journal of Sociology*, 98: 755–98.

Clemens, E.S. and Cook, J.M. (1999) 'Politics and institutionalism: explaining durability and change', *Annual Review of Sociology*, 25: 441–66.

Cobley, P. and Janz, L. (2004) *Introducing semiotics*. Royston, UK: Icon Books.

Cooper, D.J., Puxty, T., Robson, K. and Willmott, H. (1994) 'Regulating accountancy in the UK: episodes in a changing relationship between the state and the profession', in A. Hopwood and P. Miller (eds), *Accounting as a social and institutional practice*. Cambridge, UK: Cambridge University Press. pp. 270–99.

Cooperrider, D.L. and Srivastva, S. (1987) 'Appreciative inquiry in organizational life', in W. Pasmore and R. Woodman (eds), *Research in organizational change and development, Vol. 1*. Greenwich, CT: JAI Press. pp. 129–69.

Covaleski, M.A., Dirsmith, M.W., Heian, J.B. and Samuel, S. (1998) 'The calculated and the avowed: techniques of discipline and struggle over identity in Big Six public accounting firms', *Administrative Science Quarterly*, 43: 293–327.

Covaleski, M.A., Dirsmith, M.W. and Rittenberg, L. (2003) 'Jurisdictional disputes over professional work: the institutionalization of the global knowledge expert', *Accounting, Organizations and Society*, 28: 323–55.

Creed, W.E.D., Scully, M.A. and Austin, J.R. (2002) 'Clothes make the person? The tailoring of legitimating accounts and the social construction of identity', *Organization Science*, 13(5): 475–96.

Czarniawska, B. (1997) *Narrating the organization: Dramas of institutional identity*. Chicago: University of Chicago Press.

Czarniawska, B. (2000) *The uses of narrative in organization research*. Göteborg: Gothenburg Research Institute.

Czarniawska, B. and Sevon, G. (1996) 'Introduction', in B. Czarniawska and G. Sevon (eds), *Translating organizational change*. Berlin: Walter de Gruyer. pp. 1–12.

Dacin, M.T., Goodstein, J. and Scott, W.R. (2002) 'Institutional theory and institutional change: introduction to the special research forum', *Academy of Management Journal*, 45: 45–56.

Davis, G.F. (1991) 'Agents without principles? The spread of the poison pill through the intercorporate network', *Administrative Science Quarterly*, 36: 583–613.

de Certeau, M. (1984) *The practice of everyday life* (S. Rendell, Trans.). Berkeley, CA: University of California Press.

Deely, J.N. (1990) *Basics of semiotics*. Bloomington, IN: Indiana University Press.

Denis, J.L., Langley. A. and Rouleau, L. (2004) 'Studying strategizing in pluralistic contexts: a methodological agenda'. Working Paper, Universite de Montreal and HEC, Montreal.

Dezalay, Y. and Garth, B. (1995) 'Merchants of law as moral entrepreneurs: constructing international justice from the competition for transnational business disputes', *Law and Society Review*, 29(1): 12–27.

DiMaggio, P.J. (1988) 'Interest and agency in institutional theory', in L.G. Zucker (ed.), *Institutional patterns and organizations: Culture and environment*. Cambridge, MA: Ballinger. pp. 3–22.

DiMaggio, P.J. (1991) 'Constructing an organizational field as a professional project: U.S. art museums, 1920–1940', in W.W. Powell and P.J. DiMaggio (eds), *The new institutionalism in organizational analysis*. Chicago: University of Chicago Press. pp. 267–92.

DiMaggio, P.J. and Powell, W.W. (1983) 'The iron cage revisited: institutional isomorphism and collective rationality in organizational fields', *American Sociological Review*, 48: 147–60.

DiMaggio, P.J. and Powell, W.W. (1991) 'Introduction', in W.W. Powell and P.J. DiMaggio (eds), *The new institutionalism in organizational analysis*. Chicago: University of Chicago Press. pp. 1–38.

Dutton, J.E., Ashford, S.J., O'Neill, R.M. and Lawrence, K.A. (2001) 'Moves that matter: issue selling and organizational change', *Academy of Management Journal*, 44: 716–36.

Eisenstadt, S.N. (1980) 'Cultural orientations, institutional entrepreneurs, and social change: comparative analysis of traditional civilizations', *American Journal of Sociology*, 85: 840–69.

Elsbach, K.D. (2004) 'Relating physical environment to self categorizations: a study of identity threat and affirmation in a non-territorial office space', *Administrative Science Quarterly*, 48: 622–44.

Elsbach, K.D. and Sutton, R.I. (1992) 'Acquiring organizational legitimacy through illegitimate actions: a marriage of institutional and impression management theories', *Academy of Management Journal*, 35(4): 699–738.

Everett, J. and Jamal, T.B. (2004) 'Multistakeholder collaboration as symbolic marketplace and pedagogic practice', *Journal of Management Inquiry*, 13(1): 57–78.

Fligstein, N. (1990) *The Transformation of corporate control*. Cambridge, MA: Harvard University Press.

Fligstein, N. (1997) 'Social skill and institutional theory', *American Behavioral Scientist*, 40: 397–405.

Fligstein, N. (2001) 'Social skill and the theory of fields', *Sociological Theory*, 19: 105–25.

Foucault, M. (1979) *Discipline and punish: The birth of the prison* (A. M. Sheridan-Smith trans). Harmondsworth: Penguin.

Fox-Wolfgramm, S., Boal, K. and Hunt, J. (1998) 'Organizational adaptation to institutional change: a comparative study of first-order change in prospector and defender banks', *Administrative Science Quarterly*, 43: 87–126.

Friedland, R. and Alford, R.R. (1991) 'Bringing society back in: symbols, practices, and institutional contradictions', in W.W. Powell and P.J. DiMaggio (eds), *The new institutionalism in organizational analysis*. Chicago: University of Chicago Press. pp. 232–63.

Gabriel, Y. (2002) 'Essai: on paradigmatic uses of organization theory – a provocation', *Organization Studies*, 23(1): 133–51.

Galvin, T. (2002) 'Examining institutional change: evidence from the founding dynamics of U.S. health care interest associations', *Academy of Management Journal*, 45(4): 673–96.

Garud, R., Jain, S. and Kumaraswamy, A. (2002) 'Institutional entrepreneurship in the sponsorship of common technological standards: the case of Sun Microsystems and Java', *Academy of Management Journal*, 45(1): 196–214.

Gergen, K.J., Gergen, M.M. and Barrett, F.J. (2004) 'Dialogue: life and death of the organization', in D. Grant, C. Hardy, C. Oswick and L. Putnam (eds), *The Sage handbook of organizational discourse*. London: Sage. pp. 39–59.

Giddens, A. (1984) *The constitution of society: Outline of a theory of structuration*. Cambridge, UK: Polity Press.

Gouldner, A.W. (1954) *Patterns of industrial bureaucracy*. New York: Free Press.

Grant, D., Hardy, C., Oswick, C. and Putnam, L. (2004) *The handbook of organizational discourse*. London: Sage.

Greenwood, R. and Hinings, C.R. (1996) 'Understanding radical organizational change: bringing together the old and the new institutionalism', *Academy of Management Review*, 21: 1022–54.

Greenwood, R. and Suddaby, R. (2006) 'Institutional entrepreneurship in mature fields: the Big Five accounting firms', *Academy of Management Journal*, 49(1): 29–49.

Greenwood, R., Suddaby, R. and Hinings, C.R. (2002) 'Theorizing change: the role of professional associations in the transformation of institutionalized fields', *Academy of Management Journal*, 45: 58–80.

Guler, I., Guillen, M.F. and MacPherson, J.M. (2002) 'Global competition, institutions and the diffusion of organizational practices: the international spread of ISO 9000 quality certificates', *Administrative Science Quarterly*, 47: 207–33.

Hardy, C. and Phillips, N. (1998) 'Strategies of engagement: lessons from the critical examination of collaboration and conflict in an interorganizational domain', *Organization Science*, 9: 217–30.

Hargadon, A. and Douglas, Y. (2001) 'When innovations meet institutions: Edison and the design of the electric light', *Administrative Science Quarterly*, 46: 476–501.

Harvie, J. (2004) 'Oct 4 deadline set for registration', *The Cranbury Press*. Available online at: http://www.zwire.com. Accessed 13 August 2004.

Haveman, H.A. (1993) 'Follow the leader: mimetic isomorphism and entry into new markets', *Administrative Science Quarterly*, 38: 593–627.

Heracleous, L. and Barrett, M. (2001) 'Organizational change as discourse: communicative actions and deep structures in the context of information technology implementation', *Academy of Management Journal*, 44: 755–78.

Hinings, C.R. and Greenwood, R. (1988) 'The normative prescription of organizations', in L. Zucker (ed.), *Institutional patterns and organizations: Culture and environment*. Cambridge, MA.: Balinger. pp. 53–70.

Hinings, C.R. and Greenwood, R. (2002) 'Disconnects and consequences in organization theory', *Administrative Science Quarterly*, 47: 411–21.

Hirsch, P. (1997) 'Sociology without structure: neoinstitutional theory meets brave new world', *American Journal of Sociology*, 102: 1702–23.

Hirsch, P. and Lounsbury, M. (1997) 'Ending the family quarrel: toward a reconciliation of 'old' and 'new' institutionalisms', *American Behavioral Scientist*, 40: 406–18.

Hoffman, A.J. (1999) 'Institutional evolution and change: environmentalism and the US chemical industry', *Academy of Management Journal*, 42: 351–71.

Holm, P. (1995) 'The dynamics of institutionalization: transformation processes in Norwegian fisheries', *Administrative Science Quarterly*, 40: 398–422.

Hopwood, A.G. and Miller, P. (1994) *Accounting as social and institutional practice*. Cambridge, UK: Cambridge University Press.

Hughes, E.C. (1936) 'The ecological aspect of institutions', *American Sociological Review*, 1: 180–9.

Jepperson, R.L. (1991) 'Institutions, institutional effects, and institutionalism', in W.W. Powell and P.J. DiMaggio (eds), *The new institutionalism in organizational analysis*. Chicago: University of Chicago Press. pp. 143–63.

Jones, C. (2001) 'Co-evolution of entrepreneurial careers, institutional rules and competitive dynamics in American film, 1895–1920', *Organization Studies*, 22(6): 911–44.

Kaghan, W.N. and Lounsbury, M. (2006) 'Artifacts, articulation work and institutional residue', in A. Rafaeli and M. Pratt (eds), *Artifacts and Organizations*. New York: Lawrence Earlbaum. Forthcoming.

Keohane, R.O. (1989) *International institutions and state power: Essays in international relations theory*. Boulder, CO: Westview.

Kitchener, M. (2002) 'Mobilizing the logic of managerialism in professional fields: the case of academic health centre mergers', *Organization Studies*, 23(3): 391–420.

Lamont, M. and Molnar, V. (2002) 'The study of boundaries in the social sciences', *Annual Review of Sociology*, 28: 167–95.

Latour, B. (1987) *Science in action: How to follow scientists and engineers through society*. Cambridge, MA: Harvard University Press.

Lave, J. and Wenger, E. (1991) *Situated Learning. Legitimate peripheral participation*. Cambridge, UK: University of Cambridge Press.

Law, J. (1992) *Notes on the theory of the actor network: Ordering, strategy and heterogeneity*. Available online at: http://www.comp.lancs.ac.uk/sociology/papers/Law-Notes-on-ANT.pdf, accessed 15 December 2005. Lancaster, UK: Lancaster University, Centre for Science Studies.

Lawrence, T.B. (1999) 'Institutional strategy', *Journal of Management*, 25: 161–87.

Lawrence, T.B. (2004) 'Rituals and resistance: membership dynamics in professional fields', *Human Relations*, 57: 115–43.

Lawrence, T.B. and Phillips, N. (2004) 'From Moby Dick to Free Willy: macro-cultural discourse and institutional entrepreneurship in emerging institutional fields', *Organization*, 11(5): 689–711.

Lawrence, T.B., Hardy, C. and Phillips, N. (2002) 'Institutional effects of interorganizational collaboration: the emergence of proto-institutions', *Academy of Management Journal*, 45: 281–90.

Lawrence, T.B., Winn, M.I. and Jennings, P.D. (2001) 'The temporal dynamics of institutionalization', *Academy of Management Review*, 26: 624–44.

Leblebici, H., Salancik, G.R., Copay, A. and King, T. (1991) 'Institutional change and the transformation of interorganizational fields: an organizational history of the U.S. radio broadcasting industry', *Administrative Science Quarterly*, 36: 333–63.

Lee, N. and Hassard, J. (1999) 'Organization unbound: actor-network theory, research strategy and institutional flexibility', *Organization*, 6(3): 391–404.

Lounsbury, M. (2001) 'Institutional sources of practice variation: staffing university and college recycling programs', *Administrative Science Quarterly*, 46: 29–56.

Lounsbury, M. (2002) 'Institutional transformation and status mobility: the professionalization of the field of finance', *Academy of Management Journal*, 45(1): 255–66.

Lounsbury, M. and Ventresca, M. (2003) 'The new structuralism in organization theory', *Organization*, 10: 457–80.

Lounsbury, M., Ventresca, M. and Hirsch, P. (2003) 'Social movements, field frames and industry emergence: a cultural political perspective on US recycling', *Socio-Economic Review*, 1: 71–104.

Maguire, S., Hardy, C. and Lawrence, T.B. (2004) 'Institutional entrepreneurship in emerging fields: HIV/AIDS treatment advocacy in Canada', *Academy of Management Journal*, 47: 657–79.

Mahalingam, A. and Levitt, R.E. (2004) *Challenges on global projects: An institutional perspective*. International Symposium of the CIB W92 on Procurement Systems. Chennai, India.

March, J.G. (1994) *A primer on decision making*. New York: Free Press.

Meyer, J.W. and Rowan, B. (1977) 'Institutionalized organizations: formal structure as myth and ceremony', *American Journal of Sociology*, 83: 340–63.

Meyer, J.W., Boli, J., Thomas, G.M. and Ramirez, F.O. (1997) 'World society and the nation-state', *American Journal of Sociology*, 103(1): 144–81.

Mick, D.G. (1986) 'Consumer research and semiotics: exploring the morphology of signs, symbols and significance', *Journal of Consumer Research*, 13(2): 196–214.

Miller, P. (2001) 'Governing by numbers: why calculative practices matter', *Social Research*, 68: 379–96.

Mitroff, I. and Kilmann, R.H. (1976) 'On organization stories: an approach to the design and analysis of organizations through myths and stories', in R. H. Kilmann, L.R. Pondy and D.P. Slevin (eds), *The management of organization design*. New York: Elsevier North Holland. pp. 189–207.

Mohr, J. (1994) 'Soldiers, mothers, tramps and others: discourse roles in the 1907 New York City Charity Directory', *Poetics: Journal of Empirical Research on literature, the Media and the Arts*, 22: 327–57.

Mohr, J. (1998) 'Measuring meaning structures', *Annual Review of Sociology*, 24: 345–70.

Mohr, J. and Duquenne, V. (1997) 'The duality of culture and practice: poverty relief in New York City, 1888–1917', *Theory and Society*, 26: 305–56.

Morgan, G., Frost, P.J. and Pondy, L.R. (1983) 'Organizational symbolism', in L.R. Pondy, P.J. Frost, G. Morgan and T. Dandridge (eds), *Organizational symbolism*. Greenwich, CT: JAI Press. pp. 3–35.

North, D.C. (1990) *Institutions, Institutional change and economic performance.* Cambridge, UK: Cambridge University Press.

Oakes, L., Townley, B. and Cooper, D.J. (1998) 'Business planning as pedagogy: language and control in a changing institutional field', *Administrative Science Quarterly*, 43: 257–92.

Oliver, C. (1991) 'Strategic responses to institutional processes', *Academy of Management Review*, 16: 145–79.

Oliver, C. (1992) 'The antecedents of deinstitutionalization', *Organization Studies*, 13: 563–88.

Orlikowski, W.J. (2000) 'Using technology and constituting structures: a practice lens for studying technology in organizations', *Organization Science*, 11(4): 404–28.

Orlikowski, W.J. and Yates, J. (2002) 'It's about time: temporal structuring in organizations', *Organization Science*, 13(6): 684–99.

Orssatto, R.J., den Hond, F. and Clegg, S.R. (2002) 'The political ecology of automobile recycling in Europe', *Organization Studies*, 23(4): 639–65.

Pentland, B.T. (1992) 'Organizing moves in software support hot lines', *Administrative Science Quarterly*, 37(4): 527–48.

Pfeffer, J. and Salancik, G.R. (1978) *The external control of organizations: A resource dependence perspective.* New York: Harper & Row.

Phillips, N. and Hardy, C. (2002) *Discourse analysis: Investigating processes of social construction.* Thousand Oaks, CA: Sage.

Phillips, N. Lawrence, T.B. and Hardy, C. (2004) 'Discourse and institutions', *Academy of Management Review*, 29: 635–52.

Pratt, M.G. and Rafaeli, A. (2001) 'Symbols as a language of organizational relationships', *Research in Organizational Behavior*, 23: 93–103.

Rafaeli, A. and Pratt, M.G. (1997) 'Organizational dress as a symbol of multilayered social identities', *Academy of Management Journal*, 40: 862–98.

Ranson, S., Hinings, C.R. and Greenwood, R. (1980) 'The structuring of organizational structures', *Administrative Science Quarterly*, 25: 1–7.

Rao, H., Greve, H.R. and Davis, G.F. (2001) 'Fool's gold: social proof in the initiation and abandonment of coverage by Wall Street analysts', *Administrative Science Quarterly*, 46: 502–26.

Rao, H., Morrill, C. and Zald, M.N. (2000) 'Power plays: how social movements and collective action create new organizational forms', *Research in Organizational Behavior*, 22: 239–82.

Rovik, K.A. (1996) 'Deinstitutionalization and the logic of fashion', in B. Czarniawska and G. Sevon (eds), *Translating organizational change.* Berlin: Walter de Gruyer. pp. 139–72.

Roy, W.G. (1981) 'The vesting of interests and the determinants of political power: size, network structure and mobilization of American industries, 1886–1905', *American Journal of Sociology*, 86: 1287–310.

Russo, M.V. (2001a) 'Institutions, exchange relations and the emergence of new fields: regulatory policies and independent power production in America, 1978–1992', *Administrative Science Quarterly*, 46: 57–86.

Russo, M.V. (2001b) 'Institutions, exchange relations, and the emergence of new fields: regulatory policies and independent power production in America, 1978–1992', *Administrative Science Quarterly*, 46: 57–86.

Sacks, H. (1992) *Lectures on conversation.* Oxford: Basil Blackwell.

Sahlin-Andersson, K. (1996) 'Imitating by editing success: the construction of organizational fields', in B. Czarniawska and G. Sevon (eds), *Translating organizational change.* Berlin: Walter de Gruyer. pp. 69–92.

Saussure, F. (1974) *Course in general linguistics.* London: Fontana.

Schatzki, T.R., Knorr Cetina, K. and Von Savigny, E. (2001) *The practice turn in contemporary theory.* London: Routledge.

Schneiberg, M. and Clemens, E. (2006) 'The typical tools for the job: research strategies in institutional analysis', in W.W. Powell and D.L. Jones (eds), *How institutions change.* Chicago: University of Chicago Press. Forthcoming.

Schuler, D.A. (1996) 'Corporate political strategy and foreign competition: the case of the steel industry', *Academy of Management Journal*, 39(3): 720–37.

Scott, W.R. (1994) 'Conceptualizing organizational fields: Linking organizations and societal systems', in H.-U. Derlien, U. Gerhardt and F.W. Scharpf (eds), *Systemrationalitat und partialinteresse* [Systems rationality and partial interests]. Baden-Baden: NomosVerlagsgesellschaft. pp. 203–221.

Scott, W.R. (2001) *Institutions and organizations,* 2nd edn. Thousand Oaks, CA: Sage.

Scott, W.R., Ruef, M., Mendel, P. and Caronna, C. (2000) *Institutional change and healthcare organizations.* Chicago: University of Chicago Press.

Sebeok, T.A. (1976) *Contributions to the doctrine of signs.* Bloomington, IN: University of Indiana press.

Selznick, P. (1949) *TVA and the grass roots.* Berkeley: University of California Press.

Seo, M. and Creed, W.E.D. (2002) 'Institutional contradictions, praxis, and institutional change: a dialectical perspective', *Academy of Management Review*, 27: 222–47.

Sharfman, M.P., Gray, B. and Yan, A. (1991) 'The context of interorganizational collaboration in the garment industry: an institutional perspective', *Journal of Applied Behavioral Science*, 27(2): 181–208.

Sherer, P.D. and Lee, K. (2002) 'Institutional change in large law firms: a resource dependency and institutional perspective', *Academy of Management Journal*, 45: 102–19.

Stinchcombe, A. (1965) 'Social structure and organizations', in J.G. March (ed.), *Handbook of organizations*. Chicago: Rand-McNally. pp. 142–93.

Suchman, M.C. (1995) 'Managing legitimacy: strategic and institutional approaches', *Academy of Management Review*, 20: 571–611.

Suddaby, R. and Greenwood, R. (2005) 'Rhetorical strategies of legitimacy', *Administrative Science Quarterly*, 50: 35–67.

Taylor, J.R. and Van Every, E.J. (2000) *The emergent organization: Communication as its site and surface*. Mahwah, NJ: Lawrence Erlbaum.

Thornton, P.H. (2002) 'The rise of the corporation in a craft industry: conflict and conformity in institutional logics', *Academy of Management Journal*, 45: 81–101.

Thornton, P.H. (2004) *Markets from culture*. Palo Alto, CA: Stanford University Press.

Tolbert, P. and Zucker, L.G. (1996) 'The institutionalization of institutional theory', in S.R. Clegg, C. Hardy and W.R. Nord (eds), *The Handbook of Organization Studies*. London: Sage. pp. 175–90.

Tolbert, P.S. and Zucker, L.G. (1983) 'Institutional sources of change in the formal structure of organizations: the diffusion of civil service reform, 1880–1935', *Administrative Science Quarterly*, 28: 22–39.

Townley, B. (1997) 'The institutional logics of performance appraisal', *Organization Studies*, 18(2): 261–85.

Townley, B. (2002) 'The role of competing rationalities in institutional change', *Academy of Management Journal*, 45: 163–79.

Washbourne, N. and Dicke, W. (2001) 'Dissolving organization theory? A narrative analysis of water management', *International Studies of Management and Organization*, 31(3): 91-112.

Washington, M. and Zajac, E. (2005) 'Status evolution and competition: theory and evidence', *Academy of Management Journal*, 48(2): 281–96.

Weick, K.E. (1995) *Sensemaking in organizations*. Thousand Oaks, CA: Sage.

Westphal, J.D. and Zajac, E.J. (1998) 'The symbolic management of stockholders: corporate governance reforms and shareholder reactions', *Administrative Science Quarterly*, 43: 127–53.

Whittington, R. (2003) 'The work of strategizing and organizing: for a practice perspective', *Strategic Organization*, 1(1): 55–65.

Whittington, R., Jarzabkowski, P., Mayer, M., Mounoud, E., Nahapiet, J. and Rouleau, L. (2003) 'Taking strategy seriously: responsibility and reform for an important social practice', *Journal of Management Inquiry*, 12(4): 396–409.

Wicks, D. (2001) 'Institutionalized mindsets of invulnerability: differentiated institutional fields and the antecedents of organizational crisis', *Organization Studies*, 22(4): 659–92.

Woywode, M. (2002) 'Global management concepts and local adaptations: working groups in the French and German car manufacturing industry', *Organization Studies*, 23(4): 497–524.

Zietsma, C., Winn, M., Branzei, O. and Vertinsky, I. (2002) 'The war of the woods: facilitators and impediments of organizational learning processes', *British Journal of Management*, 13(Special Issue): S61–74.

Zilber, T. (2002) 'Institutionalization as an interplay between actions, meanings and actors: the case of a rape crisis center in Israel', *Academy of Management Journal*, 45: 234–54.

Zilber, T. (2006) 'The work of the symbolic in institutional processes: translations of rationalized myths in Israeli hi tech', *Academy of Management Journal*. Forthcoming.

Zucker, L.G. (1987) 'Institutional theories of organization', *Annual Review of Sociology*, 13: 443–64.

Zucker, L.G. (1988) 'Where do institutional patterns come from? Organizations as actors in social systems', in L.G. Zucker (ed.), *Institutional patterns and organizations*. Cambridge, MA: Ballinger. pp. 23–52.

1.7 Critical Theory and Postmodernism Approaches to Organizational Studies

MATS ALVESSON AND STANLEY A. DEETZ

Providing a short, understandable and useful overview of critical theory and postmodernism in organization studies is not easy. Each label refers to a massive body of sophisticated literature. Some researchers draw on both traditions while others argue for irreconcilable differences between them (see, for example, the separated treatment in the *Oxford Handbook of Organization Theory*, Chia 2003; Willmott 2003). The differences and conflicts within and between these two traditions have filled many pages both in and outside of organization studies. Interest in the relationship between the two is increasing, as can be seen in the recent development of Critical Management Studies (CMS) Conferences in 1999 and the establishment of Critical Management Studies as an interest group within the Academy of Management in 1998 (see Fournier and Grey (2000) and Grey (2004) for overviews of these developments). The label CMS often refers to a combination of Frankfurt School/radical humanism and critical postmodernism oriented research. It might well be argued that nothing that is concomitantly fair, coherent and brief can be written on this topic. Many proponents of postmodernism argue that this is the case of any topic, but the point may be especially relevant when applied to efforts to produce a representation of postmodernism itself – or rather the heterogeneous mixture of ideas, authors and texts loosely coupled together as postmodernism. However, striving to understand these literatures is important and it makes sense to be pragmatic about the project.

We are also pragmatic about our emphasis on the focused versions of critical organization studies: Frankfurt School/radical humanism and critically oriented postmodernism. We acknowledge that there are many other important and valuable critical streams that we on the whole do not address, including more objectivist and structural forms of critique, e.g. labour process theory.

Both critical theory and postmodernism provide unique and important ways to understand organizations and their management. Each provide enriched conceptions of power, demonstrate the value of including the representation of diverse interests and bring to the surface suppressed conflict for the sake of reconsideration. Critical and postmodern studies have shown how managerial values embedded in language systems, social practices and decision routines have lessened the quality of organizational decisions and reduced the capacity to meet important human needs. These contributions will be expanded and detailed in the development of the essay.

Initially we will consider the social and historical context giving rise to these approaches and why the themes they address are becoming increasingly important to organization studies. We will then demonstrate how postmodern and critical theories of organizations are different from other approaches to organization studies as well as different from (and within) each other. As the chapter develops, we will consider different ways of doing postmodern and critical work. In addition to reviewing and discussing existing work, we will sketch some fruitful lines of development between and within these two approaches. At the end we will spend some time discussing methodology for critical studies reflecting on the prospect of expanded empirical work. While there are obvious overlaps between gender and both critical theory and postmodernism (Martin 2003; Ashcraft and Mumby 2004), we will only marginally treat gender issues since this volume has a chapter devoted to feminist approaches (see Calás and Smircich, in this volume).

Both critical theory and postmodernism surfaced in organizational studies in the latter part of the 20th century; critical theory emerged in the late

1970s and beginning of the 1980s (for example, Benson 1977; Burrell and Morgan 1979; Frost 1980; Deetz and Kersten 1983; Fischer and Sirianni 1984) and postmodernism emerged in the late 1980s (for example, Smircich and Calás 1987; Cooper and Burrell 1988). Part of the reason both critical theory and postmodern writings found fertile ground in management studies is the decline of and disillusionment with what is broadly referred to as modernist assumptions by organizational theorists and practitioners. The attack on the modernist tradition is central to both critical and postmodern studies.

Management in a modernist discourse works on the basis of control: the progressive rationalization and colonization of nature and people, whether workers, potential consumers or society as a whole. However, there are structural limits to control. The costs of integration and control systems often exceed the value added by management within the corporation. The shift from manufacturing to service industries as the most typical economic form in the Western world also has implications for control forms. As the cost of control grows and the means/end chains grow longer, strategy and instrumental reasoning are strained. Objects for management control are decreasingly labour power and behaviour and increasingly the mind-power and subjectivities of employees.

Even though it is important not to exaggerate these, bureaucracy is still a dominating organizational form, social changes increase the relevance of postmodern and critical theory work in organization studies (consider the amount of critical theory work on organizational culture; see Alvesson (2002a) and Willmott (1993) for overviews) but have little to do with their formation. These rather indicate the new social conditions to which critical theory and postmodern writing have provided innovative and instructive analyses. While these new conditions have provided opportunity for organizational changes, we think little is gained by proclaiming a new postmodern period, or talking about postmodern organizations (Alvesson 1995). We are only interested in postmodernism and critical theory as theoretical approaches and what they offer to organization studies. Therefore, while acknowledging that there is a material basis for the rapid expansion of interest in critical theory and postmodernism in organization theory, we are not interested in claims of organizations as postmodern.

What is then included under the umbrella concepts of critical theory and postmodernism? Sometimes critical theory is given a broad meaning and includes all work taking a basically critical or radical stance on contemporary society with an orientation toward investigating exploitation, repression, unfairness, asymmetrical power relations (generated from class, gender, race or position), distorted communication and false consciousness. We, however, use the term here with a more restricted meaning, referring to organization studies drawing concepts primarily, though not exclusively, from the Frankfurt School (Adorno, Horkheimer, Marcuse and Habermas). See Burrell and Morgan's (1979) radical humanism paradigm and Morgan's (1997) images of domination and neuroses for summaries of this work.

Postmodernism is in many ways much harder to delimit. In the social sciences, the term has been used to describe a social mood, a historical period filled with major social and organizational changes, and a set of philosophical approaches to organizational and other studies (Featherstone 1988; Kellner 1988; Parker 1992b; Hassard and Parker 1993; Alvesson 2002b). We will focus on this last designation, emphasizing the more socially and politically relevant writings and the use of conceptions of fragmentation, textuality and resistance in organization studies. These philosophically-based approaches to organization studies have largely emerged out of works of Derrida and Foucault and also, to a lesser degree, those of Baudrillard, Deleuze and Guattari, and Laclau and Mouffe.

Much more so than critical theory, postmodernism includes a wide group of writers with quite different research agendas. Still their work shares features and moves that can be highlighted in treating them together. Postmodern themes focus on the constructed nature of people and reality, emphasize language as a system of distinctions which are central to the construction process, and argue against grand narratives and large-scale theoretical systems such as Marxism or functionalism. They also emphasize the power/ knowledge connection and the role of claims of expertise in systems of domination, emphasizing the fluid and hyper-real nature of the contemporary world and the role of mass media and information technologies and stressing narrative/fiction/rhetoric as central to the research process.

We emphasize the critical edge of postmodernism. We see it as part of a broader critical tradition which challenges the status quo and supports silenced or marginalized voices. This is a common emphasis, but by no means the only one. Many postmodernist ideas have been utilized for different political purposes. The critique of foundations and utopian ideals has been understood by some as leaving a distinctly a-political, socially irrelevant or even neo-conservative stance (Sarup 1988; Margolis 1989). The absence of a political stance grounded in a systematic philosophy has been a source of complaint, but this does not mean that a different, more 'local' and 'responsive', political stance is absent (see Waltzer 1986). Sometimes people distinguish between 'reactionary postmodernism' and a 'postmodernism of resistance' (Foster 1983; Smircich and Calás 1987). Some advocates are 'neutral' in the sense that they emphasize the processual, fragile and discursively constituted character of social phenomena without taking any political stance (e.g. Cooper 1989; Chia 2000; 2003).

The Development of Critical Theory and Postmodernism

Every historical period has probably had its particular equivalences of traditionalists, modernists, critical theorists and postmodernists – those who lament the passing of a purer time, those instrumentally building a future, those concerned with disadvantaged segments and the direction of the future, and those seeing fragmentation and decay mixed with radical potential. In transitional periods, as compared to relatively stable periods, the mix of these figures is probably different. Remembering this situates the historical account of critical theory and postmodernism in the history of ideas. Let us be clear at the start that all such social histories are types of fiction. They often serve current social purposes rather than record the past. They are reconstructions that give us a particular way to think about the present. The history is nonetheless interesting for these productive capacities. The developmental accounts of critical theory and postmodernism are no exceptions.

Theoretical Sources of Inspiration and Distinction

Both critical theory and postmodern writers often position their work in regard to four specific

developments in Western thought. The way in which they engage with them accounts for many of the differences between and within postmodernism and critical theory. These are (a) the power/knowledge relation arising with Nietzsche's perspectivalism, (b) a non-dualistic constructionist account of experience and language arising from phenomenological hermeneutics and structural linguistics, (c) a historically-based social conflict theory arising from Marx, and (d) a complex human subject arising from Freud. The first posed a challenge to any possible foundations for knowledge: all knowledge claims primarily reference social communities filled with specific power relations rather than an essential world or knowing subjects. The second situated all perspectives within specific social/historical/linguistic contexts: intersubjectivity precedes any subjectivity or objectivity in specifiable ways. The third removed the innocence of social/historical/linguistic perspectives by positioning them within materially-produced social divisions and denied any smooth unitary historical development. The fourth provided for a complex, conflict ridden and often mistaken *subject* in place of a knowing, unitary, autonomous *person*, thereby challenging any claim to simple rationality and a clear and fixed identity. Together people, realities and social relations become non-essential constructions, constructed under specific conditions of power and contestation, and filled with opacities, contradictions and conflict suppression. These different concepts provide the historically-specific tools for encountering the dominant discourses of the time.

These shared intellectual heritages should not prevent us from emphasizing the differences in how critical theory and postmodernism draw upon them. Postmodernism typically, for example, uses Freud much more unconventionally than critical theory, and merges psychoanalytic ideas with language philosophy in efforts to deconstruct and show the fragmentation of the subject. Other important sources of inspiration that are clearly different for postmodernism and critical theory include structuralist language theory (Saussure), which postmodernism draws heavily upon, and Weberian notions of the rationalization process of modern society, which is central for critical theory. In addition, critical theory is inspired by German moral philosophy and its faith in autonomy and reason (Hegel, Kant).

Embedded in these choices are long-term oppositions between French and German cultural contexts.

If it were not for this historical context some of the differences would not be as clear. For example, Horkheimer and Adorno's (1979) cultural criticism of administratively-induced control as contingent upon the conception of progress in the Enlightenment can be read as sounding as close to Foucault as to Habermas' later writings. However, few would think of them in that way, despite the fact that Foucault, when he became acquainted with the Frankfurt School toward the end of his life, expressed himself very positively, almost over generously, about it:

> ... if I had been familiar with the Frankfurt School ... I would not have said a number of stupid things that I did say and I would avoided many of the detours which I made while trying to pursue my own humble path – when, meanwhile, avenues had been opened up by the Frankfurt School (Foucault 1983: 200).

Despite this affinity between Foucault and the Frankfurt School, most early commentators have been most interested in debating the positions of Habermas and Foucault (see e.g. the contributions in Hoy (1986) and Kelly (1995)). This may be seen as indicating the distance between the two influential thinkers, but also – and perhaps primarily – the interest of critically-minded people in both of them. Today, we see more willingness to draw on both works and, while some people point to the dangers of a project drawing upon both critical theory and postmodernism, we maintain that there are some similarities – more pronounced in the case of Foucault than, for example, Derrida – and emphasize the potential for productive tensions of this overall project (Deetz 1992; 2005).

Critical Theory and Postmodernism Respond to Modernism

Since both postmodernism and critical theory writings are filled with attempts to distinguish themselves in comparison to the modernist project, a brief rendition of it may be helpful. Kant described the enlightenment as the escape from self-inflicted tutelage. In pre-enlightenment communities, personal identities, knowledge, social order and dominant historical narratives were carried and legitimized by tradition, although individuals

actively 'inflicted' the tradition upon themselves. The enlightenment promised an autonomous subject progressively emancipated by knowledge acquired through scientific methods. It noted the rise of reason over authority and traditional values. It proclaimed a transparent language (freed from the baggage of traditional ideology) and representational truth. Positivity and optimism in acquisition of cumulative understanding would lead to the progressive enhancement of the quality of life. The enlightenment's enemy was darkness, ideology, irrationality, ignorance and tradition-based authority.

Each of these themes of the enlightenment are deeply embedded in modernist management theory. 'Modernist' is used here to draw attention to the instrumentalization of people and nature through the use of scientific-technical knowledge (modelled after positivism and other 'rational' ways of developing safe, robust knowledge) to accomplish predictable results measured by productivity and technical problem-solving. This, in turn, leads to a 'good' economic and social life, primarily defined by the accumulation of wealth by investors and greater consumption by consumers. Modernism initially represented emancipation over myth, authority and traditional values through knowledge, reason and opportunities based on heightened capacity. Early 20th century organization studies were organized around the development of modernist over traditional discourses. For example, Taylor's and Weber's treatment of rationalization and bureaucratization showed the corporation as a site of the development of modernist logic and instrumental reasoning.

While writings in human relations, quality of work life and, later, cultural studies would continue to claim a place for traditional values and norms with their particular logics, each would be 'strategized' to aid further rationalization of work for the sake of convenience, efficiency and direction of the work effort. 'Performativity' would come to be valued over any earlier enlightenment narrative of emancipation or human values (Lyotard 1984). In fact, one could even be emancipated from the body's emotions and spirit, and faith could be brought under rational control with the rise of self-surveillance and bio-power as control systems (Foucault 1977; 1978; 1980; 1988).

Both critical theory and postmodernism see their work as responding to specific social conditions. Contemporary society, as a result of science, industrialization and communication/information technologies, has developed positive capacities but also dangerous forms of domination. Both critical theory and postmodernism describe Western development as one where a progressive, instrumental modernism gradually eclipsed traditional society with fairly clear payoffs but also great costs. Both agree that something fundamental has gone awry and that more technical, instrumental 'solutions' will not fix it. While their diagnoses are similar, they differ in their treatment. Critical theorists see the dominant version of the modernist's project as misguided, but see hope for recovery by redirecting the future. Postmodernists pronounce its end and question its most basic themes.

Critical theorists, especially Habermas (1984; 1987), focus on the incompletion of the positive potentialities of the enlightenment. Different forces have utilized their power and advantages to force new forms of tutelage, often *consentful* in character. As we will discuss in regard to organizational studies, critical theorists have focused on the skewing and closure of the historical discourse through naturalization of social order, universalization of managerial interests, domination of instrumental reasoning and production of consent. In different ways, critical theorists hope to recover a rational process through understanding social/historical/political constructionism, a broader conception of rationality, inclusion of more groups in social determination and overcoming systematically distorted communication. Central to this is the critique of domination and the ways those subjugated actively participate in their own subjugation. The politically astute intellectual is given an active role in the production of an enlightened understanding. The hope is to provide forums so that different segments of society and different human interests can be part of a better, more moral historical dialogue, so that each may equally contribute to the choices in producing a future for all.

Postmodernists also focus on the dark side of the enlightenment, its destruction of the environment and native peoples, its exclusions and the concealed effects of reason and progress, but postmodernists, in contrast, see the entire project as wrong. The problem is not who or what participates in it: The project is inherently problematic. They seek to find the 'non-enlightened' voices, the human possibilities that the enlightenment itself suppresses.

This discourse is filled with the pronouncement of the end of the historical discourse of progress and emancipation and its endless deferral of the social

promise that more technology, knowledge and rationality will somehow accomplish it. Man (the humanist subject as a coherent entity with natural rights and potential autonomy) is pronounced dead and in *his* place is the decentred, fragmented, gendered, classed subject. The grand narratives of theory and history are replaced by disjoined and fragmented local narratives. Metaphysics with its philosophies of presence and essence loses to the celebration of multiple perspectives and a carnival of positions and structurings. The future is endlessly deferred and without positive direction, although life can be made more interesting through deconstruction and the recovery of suppressed conflicts and marginalized groups. The intellectual has no privileged position or special knowledge, but can only act in situational, local ways like all others. Since there can be no theory of history or projection into the future, resistance and alternative readings rather than reform or revolution become the primary political posture.

Critical Theory and Organizational Research

The central goal of critical theory in organizational studies has been to create societies and work places which are free from domination, where all members have an equal opportunity to contribute to the production of systems that meet human needs and lead to the progressive development of all. Studies have focused externally on the relation of organizations to the wider society, emphasizing the possible social effects of colonization of other institutions and the domination or destruction of the public sphere. Internally they have explored the domination by instrumental reasoning, discursive closures and consent processes within the workplace. As indicated, critical researchers tend to conduct their studies with a full set of theoretical commitments that aid them analytically to ferret out situations of domination and distortion. Organizations are largely seen as political sites, thus general social theories and especially theories of decision-making in the public sphere are seen as appropriate (see Deetz 1992; 1995).

Key Themes of Critical Theory in Organizational Studies

Critical theorists sometimes have a clear political agenda focused on the interests of specific identifiable groups such as women, workers or people of colour, but they usually address general issues of goals, values, forms of consciousness and communicative distortions within corporations. Increasingly important to critical studies is the enrichment of the knowledge base, improvement of decision process and increases in 'learning' and adaptation (Willmott 2003). Their interest in ideologies considers the difficulties of disadvantaged groups in understanding their own political interest, but is more often addressed to limitations on people in general, challenging technocracy, consumerism, careerism and exclusive concern with economic growth. Most of the work has focused on ideology critique which shows how specific interests fail to be realized owing partly to the inability of people to understand or act on these interests.

In the context of management and organization studies, it should be emphasized that critical theory, compared to Marxism, is not anti-management *per se*, even though one tends to treat management as institutionalized and ideologies and practices of management as expressions of contemporary forms of domination. Critical theory can offer much to management and managers. Contributions include input to reflection on career choices, intellectual resources for counteracting totalitarian tendencies in managerially controlled corporate socialization, anti-dotes to falling prey for fashionable ideas and isomorphism (tendencies to uncritically imitate the examples of others) and stimulation for incorporating a broader set of criteria and consideration in decision-making – especially in cases where profit and growth do not clearly compete with other ends or where uncertainty exists regarding the profit outcomes of various alternative means and strategies (Alvesson and Willmott 1996: ch 8; Deetz 2003a). Two principle types of critical studies can be identified in organization studies: ideology critique and communicative action.

Ideology Critique

Ideology critique shows how specific interests fail to be realized, owing partly to the inability of people to understand or act on these interests. Critical theorists' interest in ideologies considers the difficulties of disadvantaged groups in understanding their own political interest, but is more often addressed to limitations on people in general, challenging technocracy, consumerism, careerism and exclusive

concern with economic growth. The earliest ideological critiques of the workplace were offered by Marx. In his analysis of work processes, he focused primarily on practices of economic exploitation through direct coercion and structural differences in work relations between the owners of capital and the owners of their own labour. However, Marx also describes the manner in which the exploitative relation is disguised and made to appear legitimate. This is the origin of ideology critique. Economic conditions and class structure still were central to the analysis, whether this misrecognition of interests was a result of the domination of ruling class's ideas (Marx [1844] 1964) or the dull compulsions of economic relations (Marx [1867] 1967).

The themes of domination and exploitation by owners and later by managers has been central to ideology critique of the workplace in this century by Marxist-inspired organization theorists (see, for example, Braverman 1974; Lukes 1974; Edwards 1979; Clegg and Dunkerley 1980; Salaman 1981). Analysts from the left focused on ideology, since workers often seemed to fail to recognize this exploitation and their class-based revolutionary potential in industrial countries. Later analyses became less concerned with coercion, class and economic explanations as their focus changed to examine why coercion was so rarely necessary and how systemic processes produced active consent. As a result, 'workers' self-understanding of experience' became more central (for example, Gramsci [1929–35] 1971; Burawoy 1979).

Accordingly, recent studies broaden the picture and study how cultural-ideological control operates in relationship to all employees, including levels of management (Hodge et al. 1979; Czarniawska-Joerges 1988; Jackall 1988; Deetz and Mumby 1990; Kunda 1992; Alvesson 2002a). Ideology produced in the workplace stands alongside that present in the media and the growth of the consumer culture and welfare state as accounting for worker's failure to act on their own interests (DuGay 1997). Ideology accounts for professionals and managers' failure to achieve autonomy in relationship to needs and wants and the conformist pressure to standardize paths for satisfying these (conspicuous consumption, careerism and self-commodification, see Heckscher 1995).

Four themes re-occur in the numerous and varied writings about organizations that stem from the perspective of ideology critique: (a) the naturalization of social order; (b) the universalization of managerial interests and suppression of conflicting interests; (c) domination of instrumental reasoning processes; and (d) the production of consent.

Naturalization of Social Order

In naturalization, a social formation is abstracted from the historical conflictual site of its origin and treated as a concrete, relatively fixed, entity. As such, the reification becomes the reality rather than life processes. Through obscuring the construction process, institutional arrangements are no longer seen as choices but as natural and self-evident. The illusion that organizations and their processes are 'natural' objects and functional responses to 'needs' protects them from examination as produced under specific historical conditions (which are potentially passing) and out of specific power relations. In organization studies, organismic and mechanistic metaphors dominate, leading research away from considering the legitimacy of control and political relations in organizations (Morgan 1997). Examining the naturalization of the present and the reifications of social processes help display the structural interrelation of institutional forces, the processes by which they are sustained and changed, and the processes by which their arbitrary nature is concealed and hence closed to discussion.

Ideology critique reclaims organizations as social-historical constructions and investigates how they are formed, sustained and transformed by processes both internal and external to them (see Lukács 1971; Benson 1977; Giddens 1979; Frost 1980; 1987; Thompson 1984; Alvesson and Willmott 1992; 1996). The self-evident nature of an organizational society, basic distinctions and division of labour between management and workers, men and women, and so forth are called into question by ideology critique (Jacques 1996). In so doing, ideology critique demonstrates the arbitrary nature of these phenomena and the power relations that result and sustain these forms for the sake of discovering the remaining places of possible choice.

Universalization of Managerial Interests

Lukács (1971), among many others (see Giddens 1979), has shown that particular sectional interests are often universalized and treated as if they were

everyone's interests. In contemporary corporate practices, managerial groups are privileged in decision-making and research. Management is ascribed a superior position in terms of defining the interests and interest realizations of the corporation and thereby of wide segments of the population. The interests of the corporation are frequently equated with specific managerial self-interests. For example, worker, supplier or host community interests can be interpreted in terms of their effect on corporate – i.e. universalized managerial – interests. As such they are exercised only occasionally (and usually reactively) and are often represented as simply economic commodities or 'costs' – for example, the price the 'corporation' must pay for labour, supplies or environmental clean-up (Deetz 1995; 2003a).

Central to the universalization of managerial interest is the reduction of the multiple claims of ownership to financial ownership. The investments made by other stakeholders are minimized while capital investment is made central. One could here note that critical theorists seldom consider the possible divergent interests and conflicts between owners and managers. Management by virtue of its fiduciary responsibility (limited to monetary investors) speaks for (and is often conceptually equated with) the corporation (Storey 1983). In ideological critique managerial advantages can be seen as historically produced and actively reproduced through ideological practices in society and in corporations (see Knights and Willmott 1985; Tompkins and Cheney 1985; Deetz 1992; Lazega 1992). Critical studies explore how interest articulation is distorted through the dominating role of money as a simple and powerful media (Deetz in press; Deetz and Kuhn in press) and confront productivity and consumption with suppressed values such as autonomy, creativity and pleasure as objectives for the organization of work (Burrell and Morgan 1979; Willmott and Knights 1982; Alvesson 1987; Burrell 1994; Willmott 2003).

Domination of Instrumental Reasoning Processes

Habermas (1971; 1975; 1984; 1987) traced the social/historical emergence of technical rationality over competing forms of reason. He described *technical reasoning* as instrumental, governed by the theoretical and hypothetical, and focusing on control through the development of means-ends chains. The natural opposite is *practical interest*. Practical reasoning focuses on the process of understanding and mutual determination of the ends to be sought, rather than control and development of means of goal accomplishment (Apel 1979). Studies informed by ideology critique show how 'the understanding of meaning is directed in its very structure toward the attainment of possible consensus among actors in the framework of a self-understanding derived from tradition' (Habermas 1971: 310). In a balanced system, these two forms of reasoning become natural complements. However, the social constitution of expertise aligns with organizational structures to produce the domination of technical reasoning (see Stablein and Nord 1985; Mumby 1988; Fischer 1990; Alvesson and Willmott 1996; 2003).

To the extent that technical reasoning dominates, it lays claim to the entire concept of rationality which causes alternative forms of reason to appear irrational. Even the 'human' side of organizations (climate, job enrichment, quality of work life, worker participation programmes and culture) has been transformed from alternative ends into new means to be brought under technical control for extending the dominant interests of the corporation (Alvesson 1987). Sievers (1986: 338), for example, suggests that

> motivation only became an issue – for management and organization theorists as well as for the organization of work itself – when meaning either disappeared or was lost from work; that the loss of meaning is immediately connected with the way work has been, and still is organized in the majority of our Western enterprises.

These studies show how productive tension between technical control and humanistic aspects becomes submerged to the efficient accomplishment of often unknown but surely 'rational' and 'legitimate' corporate goals.

Production of Consent

Although Gramsci's ([1929–35] 1971) analysis and development of hegemony aimed at a general theory of society and social change, with the workplace as one component, his conceptions have been widely used as a foundation for examining the workplace itself (for example, Burawoy 1979; Clegg 1989; 1990) as well as broader organizational issues like strategic management (Levy et al. 2003). Hegemony in the workplace is supported by economic arrangements enforced by contracts and reward systems, cultural arrangements enforced by advocacy of specific values

and visions, and command arrangements enforced by rules and policies. These are situated within the larger society with its supporting economic arrangements, civil society and governmental laws.

The conception of hegemony suggests the presence of multiple dominant groups with different interests and the presence of power and activity even in dominated groups (Mumby 1997). The integration of these arrangements, however, favours dominant groups, and the activity of both dominant and dominated groups is best characterized as a type of manufactured 'consent'. The hegemonic system works through pervading common sense and becoming part of the ordinary way of seeing the world, understanding one's self and experiencing needs (see Angus 1992). Such a situation always makes possible a gap between that inscribed by the dominant order and that which a dominated group would have preferred. A number of studies of organizations have investigated a variety of 'consent' processes (for example, Burawoy 1979; Kunda 1992; Vallas 1993). Several studies have shown how employees 'strategize their own subordination', achieving marginal gains for themselves through subordination but also perpetuating dominant systems which preclude their autonomy and ability to act on their own wider interests (see Burawoy 1985; Willmott 1993; Deetz 1995; 1998).

In particular, studies of culture in the 1980s and 1990s pointed towards hegemony (Jermier 1985; Rosen 1985; Knights and Willmott 1987; Mumby 1988; Alvesson and Willmott 1996; Alvesson 2002a). Willmott (1993: 534), for example, explored how 'corporate culture programmes are designed to deny or frustrate the development of conditions in which critical reflection is fostered. They commend the homogenization of norms and values within organizations … Cultural diversity is dissolved in the acid bath of the core corporate values'. In practice, as Willmott and other critical theorists point out, management control strategies are seldom fully successful. Resistance and subversive behaviour normally prevail (Prasad and Prasad 1998; Ackroyd and Thompson 1999). So does typically some level of cultural diversity (Parker 2000; Martin 2002). The role of critical theory, but even more so postmodernism, can be seen as trying to preserve and reinforce this diversity.

A Critique of Ideology Critique

Ideology work has itself been critiqued from within critical theory (e.g. Abercrombie et al. 1980). However, as we will demonstrate, postmodern writings provide a more damning critique showing that a centred agent-subject is as central to ideology critique as it is to dominant groups and the systems that advantage them. The hope for a rational and reflective agent who is capable of acting autonomously and coherently may in itself be a worthy target of ideology critique. The modern corporation's legitimacy is based on both the assumption of the existence of such an individual and its ability to foster that individual's development. Ideology critique does not, on the whole, question this basic notion of the individual. In response, critical theorists have (a) advocated research that empirically investigates expressions of dominating systems of thought, in particular communicative situations rather than explains outcomes (for example, Rosen 1985; Knights and Willmott 1987; Rosen 1988; Ashcraft 1998); (b) refrained from directive statements regarding what people should do (revolt, liberate) but while emphasizing the problematization of dominating beliefs and values (Deetz 1992); (c) recognized pluralistic qualities, while still insisting that there are strong asymmetries between various interests and perspectives; and (d) treated ideologies as dominating without seeing them as a simple instrument or in the interest of an elite group, thus showing that elites may have internalized and may suffer from the effects of dominating sets of ideas and related practices (such as pollution, moral conflict or stressful work (Jackall 1988; Heckscher 1995)).

Another response to the problems of ideology critique is the development of a communicative perspective within critical theory. It represents a development from a focus on socially repressive ideas and institutions to the explorations of the communicative processes through which ideas are produced, reproduced and critically examined (especially in decision-making contexts). As a result, while the concept of ideology still has its place in critical theory, critical work today focuses more on the ways discourse shapes understandings and reproduces specific values and understandings. This is part of the continuing development of the 'linguistic turn' which directs our attention to social interaction and language and de-emphasizes more cognitive and psychological ways of thinking (Deetz 2003b). We discuss this in more detail below.

Communicative Action

Habermas' work since the late 1970s has reduced the significance of traditional ideology critique and has concentrated instead on building a systematic philosophy in which theory and communicative action are of pivotal importance (Habermas 1984; 1987). This project retains many of the features of ideology critique, including the ideal of sorting out constraining social ideas from those grounded in reason, but it envisages procedural ideas rather than substantive critique and thus becomes quite different from traditional ideology critique. It also introduces an affirmative agenda, not based on a utopia, but still a hope of how we might reform institutions along the lines of morally driven discourse in situations approximating an ideal speech situation (Habermas 1979; Deetz 1992; 1999).

Habermas separates two historical learning processes and forms of rationality, the technological-scientific-strategic, associated with the system world, and the communicative-political-ethical, associated with the lifeworld, and tries to contribute to the latter. He argues for the systematic improvement of the lifeworld through an expanded conception of rationality focusing on the creation and re-creation of patterns of meaning. The lifeworld can be regarded as potentially fully rational – rather than instrumentalized or strategized – to the extent that it permits interactions that are guided by communicatively achieved understanding rather than by imperatives from the system world – such as those contingent upon the money code or formal power – or by the unreflective reproduction of traditional cultural values (Habermas 1984).

Communicatively achieved understanding is dependent on undistorted communication: the presence of free discussion based on good will, argumentation and dialogue. On the basis of undistorted, rational discussion he assumes that consensus can be reached regarding both present and desirable states. He maintains that in language itself and the way it is used there are certain conditions for achieving this ideal: the expectation and the wish to be understood and believed, and the hope that others will accept our arguments and other statements (see Thompson 1984; Deetz 1992: ch 6 and 7). Undistorted communication provides the basis for the 'highest' (or perhaps the widest, most reflective) form of rationality, namely communicative rationality. Here it is not power, status, prestige, ideology, manipulation, the rule of experts, fear, insecurity, misunderstanding or any other form of mischief that furnishes a base for evolving ideas; instead, decision-making is based on the strength of well-grounded arguments provided in an open forum.

This concept of communicative rationality carries with it connotations based ultimately on the central experience of the unconstrained, unifying, consensus-bringing force of argumentative speech, in which different participants overcome their merely subjective views and, owing to the mutuality of rationality motivated conviction, assure themselves of both the unity of the objective world and the intersubjectivity of their lifeworld (Habermas 1984: 10).

Communicative rationality denotes a way of responding to (questioning, testing and, possibly, accepting) the validity of different claims. Communicative action allows for the exploration of every statement on a basis of the following (universal) validity criteria: comprehensibility, sincerity, truthfulness and legitimacy. Communicative action is therefore an important aspect of social interaction in society, social institutions and daily life. The ideal speech situation, which enables communicative rationality and is in turn pervaded by it, exists under the following conditions, 'the structure of communication itself produces no constraints if and only if, for all possible participants, there is a symmetrical distribution of chances to choose and to apply speech-acts' (Habermas, cited by Thompson and Held 1982: 123). Of course, the ideal speech situation is not a quality of ordinary communication. Rather, the conditions necessary for the ideal speech situation are an ideal or counterfactual anticipation. The idealized anticipation is evoked when we seek mutual understanding and try to accomplish free and open argumentation. The ideal required steping out of the flow of everyday action to investigate the process of producing mutual understanding. Such an ideal, when used as an analytic frame in organization studies, can provide much guidance to restructuring discussions and decision-making in organizations (for example, Lyytinen and Hirschheim 1988; Power et al. 2003; Deetz in press).

We will not here repeat the critique of Habermas' theory (see Thompson and Held 1982; Fraser 1987; 1997; Benhabib 1992; Burrell 1994), except to mention that it stresses the possibility of rationality as well as the value of consensus (Deetz 1992), and puts too much weight on the clarity possible in language and human interaction. To some extent, it relies on a model of the individual as potentially autonomous and clarified, but this assumption plays a less central role compared to earlier critical theory, as the focus is not on consciousness, but on the structure of communicative interaction as the carrier of rationality. However, still Habermas can

be criticized for his 'benign and benevolent view of human kind' (Vattimo 1992) which relies on knowledge and argumentation to change thought and action, a position about which postmodernists are highly skeptical.

The Contribution of Critical Theory in Organization Studies

Critical studies in organization theory has developed these themes and illustrated their relevance for understanding modern organizations, corporations in particular. Studies draw attention to the role of management expertise leading to passivity on the behalf of other organizational participants, how ambiguity and contradictions are masked, how the engineering of values and definitions of reality tend to weaken low-level and other marginal groups in the negotiation of workplace reality and, respectively, how the codes of money and formal power exercise a close to hegemonic position over workplace experiences and articulated values and priorities. Two basic foci can be identified: one content-oriented, emphasizing sources of constraints and one process-oriented, emphasizing variation in communicative action in organizations.

First, critical theory draws attention to the narrow thinking associated with the domination of instrumental reason and the money code. Potentially, when wisely applied, instrumental reason is a productive form of thinking and acting. However, in the absence of practical reason (aiming at political-ethically informed judgement), it's highly specialized, means-fixated and unreflective character makes it strongly inclined to also contribute to the objectification of people and nature and thus to various forms of destruction. Most salient are (a) constrained work conditions where intrinsic work qualities (creativity, variation, development, meaningfulness) are ignored or subordinated to instrumental values (Sievers 1986; Alvesson 1987); (b) the development and reinforcement of asymmetrical social relations between experts (including management elites) and non-experts (Hollway 1984; Fischer 1990; Alvesson and Willmott 1996); (c) discursive closures whereby contestation cannot occur in potentially important negotiations of personal identities, knowledge and values (Deetz 1992; Thackaberry 2004; Deetz et al. in press); (4) gender bias in terms of styles of reasoning, asymmetrical social relations and political priorities (Ferguson 1984;

Hearn and Parkin 1987; Calás and Smircich 1992a, b; Mumby and Putnam 1992; Alvesson and Billing 1997; Ashcraft and Mumby 2004); (e) extensive control of employee mindsets and a freezing of their social reality (Deetz and Kersten 1983; Frost 1987; Mumby 1987); (f) far reaching control of employees, consumers and the general political-ethical agenda in society through mass media and lobbying that advocates consumerism and the priority of the money code as a yardstick for values and individual and collective political decision-making (Deetz 1992; Alvesson and Willmott 1996; Klein 2000); (g) destruction of the natural environment through waste and pollution (Stead and Stead 1992; Jermier and Forbes 2003); and (h) the constraints and narrow channelling of ethical issues in business and work and an emphasis on image-management producing a look-good-ethics discoupled from operations (Jackall 1988; Parker 2003; Roberts 2003).

In the guise of technocracy, instrumental rationality has pretenses to neutrality and freedom from the value-laden realms of self-interest and politics. It celebrates and 'hides' behind techniques and the false appearance of objectivity and impartiality of institutionalized sets of knowledge, bureaucracy and formal mandates. Not surprisingly, technocracy is promoted by management 'specialists' as they claim monopolies of expertise in their respective domains. Human resource specialists, for example, advance and defend their position by elaborating a battery of 'objective' techniques for managing the selection and promotion of employees (Hollway 1984; Steffy and Grimes 1992; Deetz 2003c). Strategic management institutionalizes a particular way of exercising domination through legitimizing and privileging the 'management' of the organization-environment interface, producing some actors as 'strategists' and reducing others as troops whose role is to subordinate themselves and to implement corporate strategies (Shrivastava 1986; Levy et al. 2003). The concept of technocracy draws attention to some of the darker and more disturbing aspects of so-called 'professional management'. It points to a restricted understanding of human and organizational goals: those that are identified and validated by experts. By associating management with technocracy and its instrumentalization of reason, the domination of a narrow conception of reason is at once exposed and questioned.

The domination of groups, ideas and institutions producing and drawing upon the idea of technocracy

leads to a technocratic consciousness (Habermas 1970; Alvesson 1987). Here basic conflicts between different ideals and principles are seen as dissolving as a consequence of the development of more and more rational methods. In work organizations, conflicts between practical reason – emphasizing the removal of repression – and instrumental reason – focused on the maximization of output – are portrayed as avoidable through the use of optimal management methods, such as job enrichment, QWL, TQM, corporate culture and so forth, that simultaneously produce human well-being and development as well as high quality and productivity. Basic political issues are then transformed into technical problem-solving.

Secondly, Habermas' ideas may also be used in a pragmatic way, more suitable for social science and organization studies than the original philosophical-theoretical version. With the communicative turn in Habermas' work, there follow possibilities for a more applied and empirical development in the use of critical theory. This means, as Forester (1993: 3, emphasis added) argued, 'putting *ideal* speech aside' and expanding the exploration of 'the *actual* social and political conditions of "checking", of political voice, and thus too of possible autonomy'. Forester (1983; 1985; 1989; 2003) has developed a 'critical pragmatism' based on an independent and creative reading of Habermas. Forester's work is particularly interesting as it combines theoretical sophistication with an empirical and applied orientation and can serve as an example here of what critical can look like in practice. To Forester (1993: 2), an empirically-oriented critical theory should '(1) empirically sound and descriptively meaningful; (2) interpretively plausible and phenomenologically meaningful; and yet (3) critically pitched, ethically insightful, as well'.

Postmodernism and Organizational Research

Much has been made of the multiple uses of the term postmodern and the different versions of it (Thompson 1993; Alvesson 1995; Chia 2003). We will not here deny the variation within the body of work. Nevertheless, in contexts such as the present one, it can be helpful to produce common themes in which variation in key authors' agendas are downplayed and commonalities are highlighted.

Key Themes of Postmodernism in Organizational Studies

In postmodernism as a philosophically-based research perspective, which is our major concern in this chapter, the following, on the whole interrelated, set of ideas are often emphasized: (a) the centrality of discourse, (b) fragmented identities, (c) the critique of the philosophy of presence, (d) the loss of foundations and master narratives, (e) the power/knowledge connection and (f) hyperreality. Let us consider each briefly.

The Centrality of Discourse

Postmodernism grew out of French structuralism by taking seriously the linguistic turn in philosophy. In this sense, postmodernists in the French tradition made a move on structuralist thought similar to the one Habermas made on ideological critique in the German tradition. As systematically distorted communication replaces false consciousness in critical theory, textual/discursive fields replace the structure of the unconscious in postmodern thought. Both were used to fight a two-front war on objectivists, on the one hand, with their science aimed at predicting/controlling nature and people, and humanists, on the other, who privileged the individual's reported experience and unique human rights, advancing a naïve version of human freedom. Focusing on language allowed a constructionism that denied the objectivist claim of certainty and truth, as well as the humanists' reliance on essential claims that ignored the social/linguistic politics of experience. The linguistic turn enabled a postmodern rejection of objectivism through a critique of the philosophy of presence and representation and a rejection of humanism through a critique of autonomy and unitary identities (Weedon 1997; Deetz 2003a,c).

To note the primacy of discourse is to suggest that each person is born into ongoing discourses that have a material and continuing presence. The experience of the world is structured through the ways in which discourses lead one to attend to the world and provide particular unities and divisions. As a person learns to speak these discourses, they more properly speak him or her in that available discourses position the person in the world in a particular way prior to the individual having any sense of choice. As discourses structure the world, at the same time they structure the person's subjectivity providing him/her with a particular social identity and way of being in the world. The person, contra humanism, is always social first and only mistakenly claims the personal self as the origin of experience (Broadfoot et al. 2004).

There are two major versions of this theme. One emphasizes discourses in a special linguistic sense, where language in use is intrinsically related to meaning and perception. Perception is never of a preformed object with specific characteristics. Rather, the object is constituted in a specific way in a 'seeing as'. The indeterminate 'stuff' of the world may be constituted as many different objects, thus there is a fundamental 'signifying' or 'language' part of object constitution. The distinctions historically carried in language enable a reproduction of specific 'seeing as' relations. Different discourses are always possible – although they may be more or less powerful or marginal. This version focuses more on the act of object production and less on institutionalized practices that provide stability (Weedon 1997). The second, a Foucauldian version, views discourses as systems of thought that are contingent upon and inform material practices not only linguistically, but also practically through particular power techniques (clearly visible in prisons, psychiatric hospitals, schools, factories and so forth), which produce particular forms of subjectivity (Foucault 1977; 1980). In both versions, human subjectivity can be relatively open or closed. Discursive closure according to the first version is temporary, though often continually reproduced, while Foucault tends to emphasize a more systematic fixation of subjectivity as a result of the network of power relations in operation (Kondo 1990).

Organizational discourse is a popular area and there is variety of work using this label (Grant et al. 2004). Of the more critical organizational researchers most have followed Foucault. For example, Knights and Morgan (1991: 260) address the construction of person and world in the discourse of corporate strategy. They argue that 'strategic discourses engage individuals in practices through which they discover the very "truth" of what they are – viz. "a strategic actor"'. They point to a number of power effects of corporate strategy discourse, including the sustaining and enhancement of the prerogatives of management, the generation of a sense of personal security for managers, the expression of a gendered masculinity for (male) management, and the facilitation and legitimization of the exercise of power. Covaleski et al. (1998) demonstrated how professionals in public accounting firms became 'disciplined' and 'self-disciplined' as their language and lifestyles came to reflect the imperative of the organization, as well as how the language and discourse of professional autonomy provided a grounds for resistance and struggle.

Fragmented Identities

The position of the 'person' follows directly from the conception of discourse. Postmodernism rejects the notion of the autonomous, self-determining individual with a secure unitary identity as the centre of the social universe. There are two versions of this critique. The first suggests that the Western conception of *man* has always been a myth. It represents a rather ethnocentric idea. Freud's work on tensions and conflicts as central for the human psyche is used to show the growing awareness in Western thought of the fundamental inner fragmentation and inconsistency, although postmodernists go further in their deconstruction of the Western self-image. The conception of a unitary self is considered a fiction used to suppress those conflicts and to privilege masculinity, rationality, vision and control. To the extent that dominant discourses speak the person (and produce the person as the origin of thought), the person gains a secure identity while participating in the reproduction of domination and marginalizing other parts of the self, as well as other groups. The sense of autonomy serves to cover this subservience and give conflict a negative connotation.

The other version suggests that the view of the individual as coherent, integrated and (potentially) autonomous has become untenable in the contemporary historical and cultural situation. If identity is a social production, identity may be relatively stable in homogeneous and stable societies with few dominant discourses; but in contemporary, heterogeneous, global, teleconnected societies, the available discourses expand greatly. They also change rapidly. The individual comes to be spoken by so many discourses that fragmentation is inevitable (Gergen 1991; Thomas and Linstead 2002). As society becomes more hyper-real or virtual (discourse is disconnected from any reference images), identity-stabilizing forces are lost. Such a position suggests the possibility of tremendous freedom and opportunity for marginalized groups and self to enter the discourse, however insecurities lead to normalization

strategies in which people 'voluntarily' cling themselves to consumer identities offered by commercial forces (Klein 2000) or to organizational selves provided by the orchestration of corporate cultures (Willmott 1994; Deetz 1995). This loose self is very susceptible to manipulation, leading not to ecstasy but domination without any dominant group, as in Baudrillard's (1983; 1988) conception of simulation. These two versions are often a matter of emphasis (see Gergen 1991; 1992) and variations may occur in different local contexts.[1] This view of the human subject creates difficulties in developing political action. Flax (1990), for example, shows the awkward position it leaves women in. If gender is treated as a social construction and dominant discourse produces marginality and a sense of women as being 'other' – taking all the negative terms in the linguistic system and discourse – then ridding society of strong gender ascriptions (making gender irrelevant in many situations) seems a good idea. One should simply stop talking about 'men' and 'women', and stop reproducing this pervasive and powerful distinction. However, to accomplish such a move requires subjects (primarily – but not exclusively – women) to organize and show that gender is a problematic issue. However, if women's experience arises out of an essential difference (bodily and/or socially produced), it cannot be denied as important and should be taken into account; however, to make the essentialist argument denies social constructionism and can easily be used to stigmatize women in a society where, to formulate the matter in distinctly non-postmodernist terms, men have more resources.

Such theoretical tensions are not easily escaped (see Fraser and Nicholson 1988; Alvesson and Billing 1997). Ironically, however, this type of deep tension and inability to develop a single coherent position appears to weaken postmodern work and at the same time give it its reason for being. Such tensions have also led some researchers to borrow from critical theory to strengthen this political programme (see Martin 2003), while others focus on more local forms of resistance (see Calás and Smircich 1993).

Important implications for organizational analyses follow from the destabilization of human actors and their organizing processes. Linstead (1993: 60) suggests that 'organization then is continuously emergent, constituted and constituting, produced and consumed by subjects ...' and argues for investigations that move 'towards those processes which *shape* subjectivity rather than the process by which individual subjects act upon the word'. Knights and Willmott (1989) have provided such work demonstrating the way being subjected leads to particular forms of subjugation. Pringle (1988) has shown how the identity of 'secretary' becomes constructed and reproduced. Jacques (1996) carefully details the genealogy of the employee as a certain feature of contemporary organizational life. Deetz (1998) has shown how the nature of 'knowledge-intensive' work situates the production of specific work identities.

In a similar way, Townley (1993) applied Foucault's analysis to the discourse of human resource management. In this work, Townley argued that the basic unit of analysis in understanding human resources management was 'the nature of exchange embodied in the employment relation'. Since this relation in itself is indeterminant, the exchange relation is organized through imposing order on the inherently undecidable. The construction of knowledge in human resource management 'operates through rules of classification, ordering, and distribution; definition of activities; fixing of scales; and rules of procedure, which lead to the emergence of a distinct HRM discourse' (Townley 1993: 541).

This body of knowledge operates to objectify (determine) the person, thus both constraining and subordinating the person's fuller social and personal character (Holmer-Nadesan 1996a,b). In these studies, the subjects become produced in a rather effective manner, leading to stabilized outcomes. Other researchers have raised some doubts on the 'muscularity' of discourse (Alvesson and Kärreman 2000), partly on empirical grounds. Alvesson and Sveningsson (2003) argue that a discourse on 'leadership' – emphasizing visions, values, directives and support – lead to managers struggling to live up to its normalizing standards, expressing a disjointed, tension-ridden work situation in which operative matters and inability to integrate leadership talk and practice are salient features. Thomas and Linstead (2002) also suggest that the identities of middle managers are best portrayed as fluid, diverse and fragmented.

The Critique of the Philosophy of Presence

Normative social science as well as most of us in everyday life treat the presence of objects as unproblematic and believe that the primary function of

language is to re-present them. When asked what something is we try to define it and list its essential attributes. Postmodernists find such a position to be illusionary in the same way as the conception of identity. The *stuff* of the world only becomes an *object* in specific relation to a being for whom it can be such an object. Linguistic and non-linguistic practices thus are central to object production. A discourse approach 'examines how language constructs phenomena, not how it reflects and reveals it' (Phillips and Hardy 2002: 6). Such a position has been familiar for some time in works as varied as Mead, Wittgenstein and Heidegger, but postmodernists tend to radicalize this position. It has often been seen as a claim of relativism and there are versions of postmodernism that invite such critique. The position is not, however, necessarily relativistic in any loose or subjective way. Some postmodernists reject the idea of being 'anti-science'. Knowledge is more 'relational' than relative (Deetz 2000). Those making the charge sometimes misunderstand the conception of objects or the strength of the conception of discourse. Most postmodernists are less concerned with the relativist label than with the apparent stability of objects and the difficulty of unpacking the full range of activities that produce particular objects and sustain them.

Postmodernists differ in the extent to which they describe discourse in textual vs a more extended form. On the whole, however, they start with Saussure's emphasis on the importance of the value-laden nature of the system of distinctions in language and the fact that the linguistic and non-linguistic practices quickly interrelate. Let us use a brief example. A 'worker' is an object (as well as a subject) in the world, but neither God nor nature made a 'worker'. Two things are required for a 'worker' to exist, a language and set of practices that makes possible distinctions between people, and something to which those distinctions can be applied. A worker is a product of the linguistic and non-linguistic practices that make this something into an object. To have a worker already implies a division of labour, the presence of management ('non-workers'). The 'essence' of worker is not the properties the 'object' contains but sets of relational systems including the division of labour. The focus should not be on the object and the object's properties but on the relational systems which are a human understanding of the world and are discursive or textual (Holmer-Nadesan 1996a,b; Deetz 2000).

The meaning of 'worker' is not evident and present (contained there) but deferred to the sets of oppositions and junctures, the relations that make it like and unlike other things, postmodernists would argue.

Discourse emphasizes the 'process of differentiating, fixing, labelling, classifying and relating – all intrinsic processes of discursive organization – that social reality is systematically constructed' (Chia 2000: 513). In Jacques' (1996) historical account of the emergence of the 'employee', we see the complex ways that various discourses come to institutionalize a specific sense of identity. Since any something in the world may be constructed/expressed as many different objects, limited only by human creativity and readers of traces of past understandings, meaning can never be final, it is always incomplete and indeterminant. The appearance of completeness and closure leads us to both overlook the politics in and of construction and the possibilities for understanding that are hidden behind the obvious. Language is thus central to the production of objects in that it provides the social/historical distinctions that provide unity and difference. Language cannot mirror the reality 'out there' or people's mental states (Shotter and Gergen 1989; 1994). Language is figural, metaphorical, full of contradictions and inconsistencies (Cooper and Burrell 1988; Brown 1990). Meaning is not universal and fixed, but precarious, fragmented and local (Linstead and Grafton-Small 1992; Shotter 1993).

Organizational researchers have used these conceptions to deconstruct objects of organizational life including the bounded concept of an organization itself. Perhaps among the most productive have been those studying accounting practices. The bottom line, profit and loss, expenses and so forth have no reality without specific practices creating them (Montagna 1986; Hopwood 1987; Power et al. 2003). Others have looked at knowledge and information (Boland 1987), and others yet reporting practices (Sless 1988), categories of people (Epstein 1988) and spatiality (Fleming and Spicer 2004). Each of these shows the conditions necessary for objects to exist in organizational life. Any attempt at representation is thus always partial (one-sided and favouring a side). The making of distinction through language use is both a necessary condition of life with others, and yet inevitably limiting in that it hides important alternative distinctions (see Bourdieu 1984; 1991).

The Loss of Foundations and Master Narratives

The power of any position has been traditionally gathered from its grounding: a metaphysical foundation (such as an external world in empiricism, mental structures in rationalism or human nature in humanism) or a narrative, a story of history (such as Marxism's class struggle, social Darwinism's survival of the fittest or market economy's invisible hand). With such groundings, positions are made to seem secure and inevitable rather than opportunistic or driven by advantage. Certainly much organizational theory has been based on such appeals – even critical theory in its morally guided communicative action.

Again, postmodernists take two different but not incompatible stances, one categorical and one interested in recent historical trends. The first position asserts that foundations and legitimating narratives have always been a hoax. They have been used (usually unknowingly) to support a dominant view of the world and its order. Feminists, for example, have argued that the historical narrative has always been *his*tory. Empiricists' appeal to the nature of the external world covered the force of their own concepts and methods in constructing that world.

Other postmodernists note growing social incredulity toward narratives and foundational moves. For example, Lyotard (1984) showed the decline of grand narratives of 'spirit' and 'emancipation'. The proliferation of options and growing political cynicism (or astuteness) of the public leads to a suspicion of legitimating moves. This conception is not far from Habermas' (1975) idea of legitimation crises in late-capitalistic society. For Lyotard, however, all that is left are local narratives. Such a position has led to sensitive treatments of how stories in organizations connect to grand narratives while also having a more local, situational character (see Martin 1990). Others have used this opening to display the false certainty in the master narratives in management (Jehenson 1984; Ingersoll and Adams 1986; Carter and Jackson 1987; Calás and Smircich 1991).

Not all postmodernists see this as necessarily positive. Certainly the decline of foundations and grand narratives takes away a primary prop of a dominant group's offer of security and certainty as a trade for subordination. However, the replacement is not necessarily freedom and political possibility on the part of marginalized groups. Lyotard demonstrated the rise of 'performativity' where measures of means toward social ends become ends in themselves (see also Power 1994). Access to computers and information – contingent less upon knowledge integrated in the person ('scholarship') than upon financial resources – have become a significant source of knowledge and power. Along with this come new forms of control not directed by a vision of society and social good but simply more production and consumption.

The loss of grand integrative narratives has not however been missed by management groups. One could say that corporate 'visions' and 'cultures' are strategic local narrative constructions to provide the integration and motivation in a pluralistic society, formerly provided by wider social narratives. On the other hand, one could say that these forms of management control represent large-scale systematic efforts which resemble grand narratives, though at a corporate level. Management control and performativity can be seen as corporate grand narratives taking over some of the functions of political programs. The decline of vision, hope and community in politics have paved the way for management ideologies and practices that may fill parts of the vacuum (Deetz 1992). Through the massive promotion of consumerist ideals, business colonizes more and more sectors of society and culture and thus aspirations for the good life, in which identity for many becomes a matter of the consumption of the most heavily promoted brand (Klein 2000).

The difficulty in postmodernism with this (as with the concept of fragmented identities) is how to generate a political stance in regard to these developments. If one rejects an essentialist foundation and believes that more than local resistance is needed, some kind of combination between postmodernism and critical theory may well provide the best remaining option. We will come back to this.

The Knowledge/Power Connection

Foucault has been the most significant influence on this topic (Foucault 1977; 1980; see Clegg 1994). The power that is of interest is not that which one possesses or acquires. Such appearances of power are the outcome of more fundamental power relations. Power resides in the discursive formation itself – the combination of a set of linguistic distinctions, ways of reasoning and material practices that together organize social institutions and

produce particular forms of subjects. For example, the discourse that produces a 'manager' both empowers and disempowers the group of individuals formed as that object. It simultaneously provides solidarity and interests and sets into play conflicts, material and symbolic resources and self-understandings.

Power thus resides in the demarcations and the systems of discourse that sustain them, including material arrangements – for example, recruitment and selection procedures, office arrangements, reward and control structures, inclusion/exclusion in significant meetings and so forth. One of the most useful terms entering into organizational studies has been Foucault's (1977) concept of discipline. The demarcations provide forms of normative behaviour supported by claims of knowledge. Training, work routines, self-surveillance and experts are discipline in that they provide resources for normalization. Normative experts in particular and the knowledge they create provide a cover for the arbitrary and advantaging discursive practices and facilitate normalization (Hollway 1984; 1991). Townley (1993) showed how the development of the human resource expert and human resource knowledge was used as a way to 'determine' and subordinate employees. Such knowledge can also be utilized by employees to engage in self-surveillance and self-correction of attitudes and behaviours toward norms and expectations established by others (Deetz 1994, 1998; Holmer-Nadesan 1996a,b). The concept of disciplinary power has enabled a number of studies that show the complex relations between enablement and constraint in organizational processes (Papa et al. 1995). Other researchers have been able to conduct sophisticated analyses of new forms of control and resistance (Tretheway 1997; 2001; Covaleski et al. 1998; Murphy 1998; Prasad and Prasad 1998; Meriläinen et al. 2004).

Hyperreality

Postmodern writings vary in terms of how they handle the relation of language to the non-linguistic realm of people and world. A strict linguistic focus and a critique of the philosophy of presence leave little interest in references to a pre-formed and relatively constant extra-textual reality. Most postmodernists treat the external as a kind of excess or 'otherness' that serves as a resource for formations. The indeterminate quality of the outside can be used to question the certainty and naturalness of any determination made of it. Thus, the ability to return to the outside prevents language systems from becoming closed and purely imaginary (Roberts 2003). While the referent has no specific character it always exceeds the objects made of it and thus reminds one of the limited nature of all systems of representation and their fundamental indeterminacy (Cooper 1989). The presence of 'otherness' in the indeterminacy provides a moment to show the domination present in any system, to open it up and to break the sealed self-referentiality of some textual systems.

Many existing linguistic or representational systems are thus shown to be self-referential by postmodernists. Such systems are neither anchored in a socially produced (objective) world nor do they respect the excess of an outside. They produce the very same world that they appear to accurately represent. For example, contemporary media and information systems have the capacity to rapidly construct images that replace, rather than represent, an outside world. Such systems can dominate the scene with an array of reproduced imaginary worlds. The referent disappears as anything more than another sign, thus signs only reference other signs; images are images of images.

Such systems can become purely self-referential or what Baudrillard calls *simulations*. In such a world, signs reach the structural limit of representation by referencing only themselves with little relation to any exterior or interior. Baudrillard (1975: 127–8) expresses this relation as follows:

> The form-sign [present in a monopolistic code] describes an entirely different organization: the signified and the referent are now abolished to the sole profit of the play of signifiers, of a generalized formalization in which the code no longer refers back to any subjective or objective 'reality', but to its own logic. ... The sign no longer designates anything at all. It approaches its true structural limit which is to refer back only to other signs. All reality then becomes the place of semi-urgical manipulation, of a structural simulation.

The world as understood is not really a fiction in this situation since there is no 'real' outside to portray falsely or otherwise. It is properly imaginary; it has no opposite, no outside. Baudrillard (1983: 5) used the example of the difference between feigning and simulating an illness to show the character of this postmodern representation: 'feigning or dissimulation leaves the reality principle intact; the difference is always clear, it is only masked; whereas simulation threatens the difference between "true" and "false", between "real" and "imaginary". Since the simulator produces "true" symptoms, is he ill or not? He cannot be treated objectively either as ill, or not ill'. These ideas have inspired some organization studies emphasizing the imaginary character of modern organizations (Berg 1989; Alvesson 1990; Deetz 1995).

The Contribution of Postmodern Organizational Studies

The role of postmodern research is very different from more traditional roles assigned to social science. It primarily serves to open up the indeterminacy that modern social science, everyday conceptions, routines and practices have closed off. The expected outcome is to produce dissensus rather than a new consensus (Deetz 1996). The result is a kind of anti-positive knowledge (Knights 1992). The primary methods are deconstruction, resistance readings and genealogy. These terms have been used in many different ways and in the short space here we can do little beyond a sketch.

Deconstruction works primarily to critique the philosophy of presence by recalling the suppressed terms (the deferred term) which provides the system and thus which allows the positive terms to appear to stand for an existing object. When the suppressed term is given value both the dependency of the positive term on the negative is shown and a third term is recovered which shows a way of world making that is not dependent on the opposition of the first two (see Cooper 1989; Martin 1990; Calás and Smircich 1991; Mumby and Putnam 1992; Hardy and Phillips 1999).

Resistance readings both demonstrate the construction activity and recover the indeterminacy of the world by reclaiming the possibility of multiple determinacies and the excess of the world over any subjective relation to it. The positive and the polar construction are both displayed as acts of domination, subjectivity doing violence to the world and limiting itself in the process. In this move, conflicts that were suppressed by the positive are brought into view and the conflictual field out of which objects are formed is recovered for creative redetermination – constant dedifferentiation and redifferentiation. Given the power of closure and the way it enters common sense and routines, such rereadings require a particular form of rigour and imagination.

They are formed out of a keen sense of irony, a serious playfulness and often guided by the pleasure one has in being freed from the dull compulsions of a world made too easy and too violent.

A good example is Calás and Smircich's (1988) account of a mainstream positivist journal article – where they start with the question 'why should we believe in this author?' and then point at the rhetorical tricks involved in order to persuade the reader. Another interesting example is Sangren's (1992) critical review of Clifford and Marcus (1986) 'Writing Culture'. Sangren, drawing upon Bourdieu (1979), uses their points about the politics of representation – intended to indicate the problems of ethnographies in mirroring cultures and exemplified through important anthropological works – against themselves, showing how representations of Clifford, Marcus and co-authors of earlier work can be seen in terms of politics. Particular kinds of representations are used that create the impression that earlier works are flawed and that there is a large and open space for novel contributions (and the career options) of the new heterodoxi (Clifford, Marcus, et al.) and what they claim to be their more informed view on the politics of representation.

The point of social science is not to get it right but to challenge guiding assumption, fixed meanings and relations, and reopen the formative capacity of human beings in relation to others and the world, qualities that Gergen (1978) and Astley (1985) displayed as vital to any important theory. As Sangren (1992) illustrates, the challenge of dogma, fixed ideas and reopenings surely implies new dogmas, fixations and closures, leading to the type of elitism criticized in critical work. Wray-Bliss (2003), for example, uses Foucault's five 'methodological precautions' to show how well intended researchers may inadvertently construct a superior subject position for themselves in contrast to those available to the researched subject. Wray-Bliss's careful attention to the ethnographic interview demonstrates the possibilities of open meaning formation with sensitivity to moments of resistance and subtly of power relations.

One outcome of the themes reviewed above is a strong current interest in experimenting with different writing styles. This is prominent in anthropology (Clifford and Marcus 1986; Marcus and Fisher 1986; Geertz 1988; Van Maanen 1988; Rose 1990), but also in organization theory (for example, Linstead and Grafton-Small 1990; Calás and Smircich 1991;

1999; Jeffcutt 1993; Blaug 1999; Bougen and Young 2000; Fouray and Stork 2002). Typically, 'realist' ways of writing are superseded or complemented by other styles, for example, ironic, self-ironic or impressionistic ones. In an investigation of texts in organizational culture and symbolism, Jeffcutt (1993: 32) shows how it is 'distinguished by heroic quests for closure; being dominated by authors adopting representational styles that privilege epic and romantic narratives over tragic and ironic forms. These representational strategies expose an overriding search for unity and harmony that suppresses division and conflict'. One would imagine that the inspiration to develop new ways of writing could be one of the most powerful and interesting contributions of postmodernism, but so far the produced texts have not fully lived up to expectations. Experimenting with texts is difficult (Wolf 1992).

Relating Critical Theory and Postmodernism

Critical theory and postmodernism, as has been shown, are both alike and different. Some people see the difference as a matter of mutual exclusion – you either sympathize with one or the other. We recognize the tensions but don't share this view, in particular as we focus on the more critical versions of postmodernism, which tend to be politically and ethically committed and avoid the stronger versions of relativism, and on the less objectivist and rationalist versions of critical theory. We think that each has much to contribute to organizational studies, and we believe that they have a contribution to make together. We also think that relating the two will facilitate empirical work and make it more likely that some powerful idea within an overall critical theory/postmodernism framework will have a bearing on empirical material and ensure that a single idea will not pre-structure the interpretations and outcomes. Without considering postmodern themes, critical theory easily becomes unreflective in regard to cultural elitism and modern conditions of power; without incorporating some measure of critical theory thought (or something similar that provides direction and social relevance), postmodernism simply becomes esoteric.

Both draw attention to the social/historical/political construction of knowledge, people and social relations, including how each of these appears in contemporary organizations. And they share a view that domination is aided, and both people and organizations lose much, if we overlook these construction activities by treating the existing world as natural, rational and neutral. Both streams emphasize how ideologies and discourses tend to freeze social institutions and identities through the operations of power and share a commitment to destabilize frozen social forms. In critical theory's language, the concern is reification; in postmodernism, the concern is the philosophy of presence. Based on this naturalization and freezing of contemporary social reality, important potential conflicts – options for reconsiderations and questioning – are lost and different groups of people as well as vital values are marginalized and disadvantaged. Both see organizations and the social sciences that support them as relying increasingly on a form of instrumental reasoning privileging means over ends and aiding the dominant groups' ability to invisibly accomplish their ends. Habermas describes this in terms of 'instrumental technical reasoning' and Lyotard in 'performativity'.

The differences are also important. Critical theory sees the response in terms of an expanded form of morally-guided communicative reasoning leading to individual autonomy and better social choices. Through reflections on the ways ideology enters into person/world/knowledge construction and by providing more open forums of expression and a type of discourse aimed at mutual understanding there is hope for the production of social consensus and social agreements that better fulfil human needs. The grand narrative of the enlightenment might, according to critical theory, yet be advanced. Even though the somewhat grandiose term emancipation is less frequently used today, it still signals some of the ambitions of critical theory.

However, postmodernism rejects such reflection and consensus and the ideal of emancipation, suspecting the replacement of old illusions with new ones and the creation of new elites and new forms of marginalization. The ambition is limited to the inspiration of resistance. Critical theory replies: without reflection and the striving for consensus and rationality, there is no politics, no agenda for a constructive alternative. Postmodernism counters: politics are by necessity local and situational – responsiveness is more important than systematic planning. Critical theory responds: local politics is too weak to confront system-wide gender and class dominations as well as global poverty and environmental problems. Postmodernism maintains: organizing against domination both props up and solidifies dominant groups – it creates its own forms of domination. The difference is in a sense the same as between a push and pull theory. Critical theory wants us to act and provides direction and orchestration; postmodernism believes that such a move will be limited by the force of our own subjective domination and encourages us to get out of the way and allow the world to pull us to feelings and thought here-to-fore unknown; but critical theory does not have enough faith to let go. And so on.

There are also ways to think of them both at once, though not necessarily through some new synthesis. We have a need for both conflict and consensus, for resistance and plans. The issue is not which but the balance, and choosing the right moments (Deetz 1992; 1996). To say that consensus implies domination does not mean we should not make the best decisions we can together, but that we need to continue to look for domination and be ready to move on. To say that resistance lacks a clear politics does not mean that it is not doing something important and ultimately may be the only way we can see through the forms of domination that we like or that benefit *and* limit us.

One option is thus to work with unresolved tensions within a text where one follows different themes of postmodernism and critical theory without attempting synthesis – working with the tensions and contrastive images. Examples of this include work by Martin (1990; 1995), Knights and Willmott (1989) and Deetz (1998). Another version is to allow space for various discrete voices in texts by organizing them around conversations between various theoretical perspectives or interest groups (Alvesson and Willmott 1996: ch 7) or to conduct multiple interpretations of the same phenomenon (Alvesson 1996; Morgan 1997), such as interpreting a phenomenon from both critical theory and postmodernist (and perhaps other) positions.

Another way of combining insights from critical theory and postmodernism is to see both as metatheories useful as inspiration for reflexivity rather than as theories directly relevant for guiding and interpreting studies of substantive matters (Alvesson and Sköldberg 2000). Still another option is to restrict the approach to the careful study of language use and communicative practices in 'real' social settings, which is done by discourse and conversation analysis (Potter and Wetherell 1987;

Parker 1992a) and constructivists (Steier 1991; Shotter and Gergen 1994). Such studies can be used to sensitize us to the powerful effects of language and ground Habermasian and postmodernist ideas in portions of organizational reality (Forester 2003). This is also the route suggested by critical discourse analysis (Fairclough 1993). Such a language focus avoids the philosophy of presence but maintains an empirical context.

A reoccurring criticism of critical theory and even more so postmodernism is the lack of clear empirical studies. Part of the criticism arises from a narrow view of the notion of 'empirical' but researchers can still be faulted for doing many conceptual essays without extended field experience and reports and for failing to bring Foucault 'fully' into fieldwork. Critical theory and postmodernism's strong critique of empiric*ism* and their emphasis on data as constructions open for a multitude of interpretations does not mean that reflective empirical work is not worth doing (Alvesson 2002b). Some texts have limited feelings for organizational contexts and the lives of real people. However, as we have shown, the amount of empirical work is growing. Much more of this work is finely textured showing much 'feel' for the complexities of organizational life and enabling organizational participants to 'say something' that is not immediately domesticated by theories locating the all too predictable 'bureaucracy', 'patriarchy', 'capitalism', 'managerialism' and 'disciplinary power' (Ashcraft 2001). A balance between being too critical and too utopian is certainly emerging (Jermier 1998). In the following section we explore how organizational scholars might achieve this balance of relating critical and postmodern theoretical perspectives in their empirical work.

Methodology for Critical Theory and Postmodernist Studies

Critical theory and postmodernist approaches to organization studies have been most distinct in theoretical work, but the body of empirical work continues to grow. Some empirical works have focused on limited chunks of text, for example, an advertisement or a talk (e.g. Martin 1990; Fairclough 1993; Alvesson 1996). Others have looked at particular organizations or even industries by beginning with 'qualitative' and 'interpretive' data and using some inspiration from

Frankfurt School, Habermasian, Foucauldian or other postmodernist versions to guide the analysis and interpretations. The special issue of *Administrative Science Quarterly* (June 1998) focused on critical perspectives of organizational control and provided a broad array of critical theory, postmodern inspired work but also more generally critical work. Similar empirical work appears in *Organization, Organization Studies* and *Management Communication Quarterly*. There is also a wealth of critical empirical work on the dark side and negative byproducts of modern organizations, for example, environmental pollution, corporate crimes, sexual harassment, racial discrimination, effects of manipulation of customers and other more or less obvious illegitimate effects.

Most versions of the critical theory and postmodernist research addressed in this chapter, however, are oriented toward investigating themes that are more hidden, that do not materialize so easily, or that are not fully registered or experienced by the subjects involved (Sotorin and Gottfried 1999; Martin 2001). A high degree of theoretical sophistication must inform critical sensitivity in organization research in order to study cultural 'depth structures', how common-sense categories and dominating vocabularies carry hidden meanings that pre-structure and constrain choices and space for action. There is a real challenge in developing critical studies that (a) use the powerful theoretical frameworks discussed here and (b) are open to learning experiences through empirical encounters not pre-determined by these frameworks. The insight that no knowledge is neutral, innocent or simply good call for reflexivity. Knowledge about organizations cannot be separated from broader social struggles. Both these struggles and the concrete life experiences of organization members must be brought into relation with each other. Jermier (1998) expressed these relations well:

> Contemporary critical theorists prefer to refrain from speaking for their informants ... but, instead, listen and interpret carefully as their informants speak for themselves. ... The critical theorist's agenda is not identical to that of a conventional ethnographer, however, for, in addition to portraying the informants' world view, critical theorists also aim to reveal socioeconomic conditions that produce and reinforce asymmetrical structures of control. ... A hallmark of critical research is the blending of informants' words, impressions, and activities with an analysis of the historical and

structural forces that shape the social world under investigation.

How should we design and conduct research that is sensitive to both postmodernism and critical theory? In Alvesson and Deetz (2000), we proposed a critical methodology structured in three moments: interpretation producing insights, critique exploring domination and repression, and transformative re-definition indicating alternative ways of imagining and relating to what exists. The first move points at hidden or at the least obvious aspects and meanings of a chunk of social reality; the second shows the problematic nature of these meanings (and the material arrangements and social orders these indicate); and the third undermines their seeming robustness by encouraging alternative ways of constructing this reality. Critical research calls for at least the first two elements. The third may be included in a more or less ambitious version.

In research practice, the three (or two) moments may not be easily distinguishable. Researchers may immediately apply a critical framework that means that the interpretations and insights do 'immediately' express critique. We believe that there are some advantages by postponing critique: interpretive work becomes more systematic and the steps may be thought through more clearly, more aspects may be explicitly considered before moving further with the critical project and the reader may follow the logic more clearly.

A particularly important element in critical research is to turn the self-evident and familiar social world into something less obvious, natural, rational and well-ordered. To conceptualize and interpret contemporary organizations as rather strange places can counteract the effects of ideology and normalization. Research then becomes a matter of de-familiarization, of observing and interpreting social phenomena in novel, even shocking, ways compared to culturally dominant categories and distinctions. The works of Horkheimer and Adorno and Foucault are very inspiring in this respect. De-familiarization means that we see things not as self-evident or rational but as exotic and arbitrary, not as functional and helpful but as constraining and repressive. It becomes an expression of action and thinking within frozen, conformist patterns (Marcus and Fischer 1986; Alvesson and Deetz 2000).

Creating cultural/framework distance, working with negations and drawing upon specific versions of critical theories and metaphors are possible means for de-familiarization. Being strongly inspired by a particular critical theory may, however, in certain ways reduce the chance of producing interesting breakdowns of understandings or surprises that typically are a key element in de-familiarization: at worst a particular theory may lead to the routine and predictable slotting in of findings in this theory and the sense-making machinery it fuels.

Technocratic consciousness (Habermas), male domination (feminism) or prison-like organizational arrangements (Foucault) may be the interpretation searching for empirical material to respond to. An effort to accomplish some de-familiarization not only from conventional frameworks (dominant social constructions), but also from the conventions that, over time, critical theorists and postmodernists may embrace, is therefore called for. Theory should be used in a self-critical way, providing space also for de-familiarizations in other terms than those of the favoured vocabulary. Creativity, imagination and a flexible mind are necessary in order to learn from empirical studies. This is more easily preached than practiced. We think that ambitious empirical studies, in which critical theories are drawn upon and empirical material is allowed to kick back at the frameworks, may be helpful here. Sometimes one has the impression that critical theorists are too respectful of their points of departures. A few empirical studies discussing Foucault indicate that the grip of the discourses of strategy, leadership and HRM are less clear-cut (Newton 1998; Alvesson and Sveningsson 2003) than readings of more textbook approaches (e.g. Knights and Morgan 1991; Townley 1993) to which these themes sometimes imply.

By combining elements of distance creation, working with negations and reflectively working with theoretical frameworks and metaphors (and doing so under the guideline of critical imagination), empirical accounts, interpretations and critical/transformative 'results' may involve de-familiarization as a key methodological principle as well as an outcome of the study. Developments of critical and reflexive methodologies may be helpful here (Hardy and Clegg 1997; Alvesson and Deetz 2000; Alvesson and Sköldberg 2000).

Developing critical sensitivity is hardly accomplished without losses and sacrifices. It is here important to consider a real danger in critical theory research: a sensitivity that is too strongly biased toward power, domination and social imperfections may lead to negativity and hyper-critique. It may mean that a fine-tuned feeling for the operations of power and ideology is developed at the expense of the capacity to appreciate the positive or not-so-bad features of management and corporate life. A strong belief in the importance of questioning conventional beliefs and assumptions – a major task of academic knowledge that is seriously under-represented in the majority of management studies – does not prevent us from recognizing a tendency to one-sidedness in many critical projects (including some of our own works).

A related problem is the marginalization and perceived irrelevance of critical research in management – the host discipline of most organization studies. Some postmodernist authors of a critical bend also risk this fallacy. Some advocates of postmodernism argue that it 'calls for management research to be brought down from the ivory tower to speak of the concerns of those present in the city square, the factory, the boardroom and the village street' (Kilduff and Kelemen 2003: 96). There is nevertheless frequently a privileging of discourse, fluidity and indeterminancy and/or a determination to deconstruct that make the outcomes of knowledge projects less unpredictable than a reader with somewhat different preferences may have hoped for. This one-sidedness parallels, in some respect, the one-dimensional technicism that dominates conventional management theory (Alvesson and Willmott 1992; 1996). The negativity of much critical research creates problems, both in terms of how the objects and subjects of critique are represented, and in terms of demonstrating the relevance of its concerns (Hardy and Clegg 1997). Wray-Bliss (2003: 307–8) remarks that the critical researcher is 'critiquing and commenting upon, rather than co-constructing and contributing to, the lives of the researched'. The exercise of power through knowledge highlighted by postmodernists, in particular, but also other critical theorists may also be a key element in critical research favouring the discursively constituted and normalized subject and/or the victim of capitalist or managerialist ideologies, Wray-Bliss argues. This is partly an ethical issue.

Critical research thus must be careful about hyper-critique, i.e. a one-sided and intolerant approach, in which only what are seen as imperfections of the corporate world are highlighted. As shown by in-depth studies of socially and ethically ambitious organizations, trying to live up to feminist and other ideals negating those that critical theorists portray

as oppressive forms is difficult; these also typically contain elements of bureaucracy, hierarchy and contradictions between ideal and practice (e.g. Ashcraft 2001). Critical work may benefit from being somewhat more generous and tolerant about the imperfections of organizational life. However, acknowledging this often means a watering down of the theoretical edge of critical theory and postmodernism: there is no easy way out.

We suggest a broadening of the capacity for making interpretations as a partial 'solution' to this problem. This calls for going outside the critical approaches discussed here and also considering issues from an organizational participant's point of view, including appreciating the legitimacy of managerial viewpoints. To fully use the tensions of critical theory and postmodernism this must appear as a vital element in order to create a strong but not too fixed framework for empirical work (Alvesson and Sköldberg 2000).

Conclusion

Critical theory and postmodernist work both contribute to a complex interrelated set of critical projects composed of many other groups, including cultural, feminist, race, labour process and postcolonial scholars. They do not have an independent trajectory. This work will shape and be shaped by others.

Critical and postmodern studies are important in many ways. First, they can provide useful and interesting ways for people to attend to and think about their historically situated dissatisfactions in and suspicions about contemporary social institutions. These dissatisfactions and suspicions arise from strains in the work experience itself, the quality of organizational decision, and the relation of organization life to the development and sustaining of a rather singularly-directed consumption-based social value system. Secondly, gradually, critical and postmodern work is engaging more traditional concerns in organization studies. This work can help make productive already present tensions internal to organizations, for example, such as that between profitability and social good and the differing values of different stakeholders. Thirdly, as studies of specific organizations continue to become more detailed and empirical, they can stimulate development of research methods suited to deeper, more inclusive research, including theoretically informed ethnographies, critical discourse analysis and participatory action research (Fairclough 1993; Alvesson and Deetz 2000; Broadfoot et al. 2004; Mumby 2004). Future work can (a) detail the nature of resistance and change more carefully; (b) move beyond studies based in assumed class or other groupings' differences and pay greater attention to how groupings are formed, how they intersect and the complexities and varieties in and amongst groups; and (c) look more to communicative processes of dissensus and consensus production, and identify more carefully forms of discursive closure and conflict suppression (Thackaberry 2004). And, finally, the work can provide important future direction. While contemporary work still primarily engages in critique without doing much to propose positive alternatives and put them in place, looking at relations of stakeholder involvement and organizational governance or communication in participation processes provides the possibility of pilot programmes and positive change efforts to compete with those that are managerially directed. Together these provide an important alternative future for organizational theory and research.

Note

1. Some authors (e.g. Sennett 1998) emphasize the fragmentation of identity as a response of destructive social forces in contemporary society putting up a clear picture of a more integrated and coherent identity, claimed to be historically grounded. This is based on critical theory thinking and quite antagonistic to the radical de-centring of postmodernism.

References

Abercrombie, N., Hill, S. and Turner, B.S. (1980) *The Dominant Ideology Thesis.* London: Allen and Unwin.

Ackroyd, S. and Thompson, P. (1999) *Organizational Misbehaviour.* London: Sage.

Alvesson, M. (1987) *Organization Theory and Technocratic Consciousness: Rationality, Ideology, and Quality of Work.* Berlin, New York: de Gruyter.

Alvesson, M. (1990) 'Organization: from substance to image?', *Organization Studies*, 11: 373–94.

Alvesson, M. (1995) 'The meaning and meaninglessness of postmodernism: some ironic remarks', *Organization Studies*, 15: 1049–77.

Alvesson, M. (1996) *Communication, Power and Organization.* Berlin/New York: de Gruyter.

Alvesson, M. (2002a) *Understanding Organizational Culture.* London: Sage.

Alvesson, M. (2002b) *Postmodernism and Social Research.* Buckingham: Open University Press.

Alvesson, M. and Billing, Y. (1997) *Understanding Gender and Organization.* London: Sage.

Alvesson, M. and Deetz, S, (2000) *Doing Critical Management Research.* London: Sage.

Alvesson, M., and Kärreman, D. (2000) 'Varieties of discourse: on the study of organizations through discourse analysis', *Human Relations*, 53: 1125–49.

Alvessson, M. and Sköldberg, K. (2000) *Reflexive Methodology.* London: Sage.

Alvesson, M. and Sveningsson, S. (2003) 'The good visions, the bad micro-management and the ugly ambiguity: contradictions of (non-)leadership in a knowledge-intensive company', *Organization Studies*, 24(6): 961–88.

Alvesson, M. and Willmott, H. (eds) (1992) *Critical Management Studies.* London: Sage.

Alvesson, M. and Willmott, H. (1996) *Making Sense of Management: A Critical Analysis.* London: Sage.

Alvesson, M. and Willmott, H. (eds) (2003) *Studying Management Critically.* London: Sage.

Angus, I. (1992) 'The politics of common sense: articulation theory and critical communication studies', in S. Deetz (ed.), *Communication Yearbook 15.* Newbury Park, CA: Sage. pp. 535–70.

Apel, K.-O. (1979) *Toward a Transformation of Philosophy.* Translated by G. Adey and D. Frisby. London: Routledge and Kegan Paul.

Ashcraft, K.L. (1998) '"I wouldn't say I'm a feminist, but …": organizational micropractice and gender identity', *Management Communication Quarterly*, 11: 587–97.

Ashcraft, K.L. (2001) 'Organized dissonance: feminist bureaucracy as hybrid organization', *Academy of Management Journal*, 44: 1301–22.

Ashcraft, K.L. and Mumby, D.K. (2004) *Reworking Gender: A Feminist Communicology of Organization.* Thousand Oaks, CA: Sage.

Astley, G. (1985) 'Administrative science as socially constructed truth', *Administrative Science Quarterly*, 30: 497–513.

Baudrillard, J. (1975) *The Mirror of Production.* St. Louis: Telos Press.

Baudrillard, J. (1983) *Simulations.* New York: Semiotext(e).

Baudrillard, J. (1988) 'Simulacra and simulations', in M. Poster (ed.), *Jean Baudrillard: Selected Writings.* Stanford: Stanford University Press. pp. 166–84.

Benhabib, S. (1992) *Situating the Self: Gender, Community and Postmodernism in Contemporary Ethics.* New York: Routledge.

Benson, J.K. (1977) 'Organizations: a dialectical view', *Administrative Science Quarterly*, 22: 1–21.

Berg, P.O. (1989) 'Postmodern management? From facts to fiction in theory and practice', *Scandinavian Journal of Management*, 5: 201–17.

Blaug, R. (1999) 'The tyranny of the visible: problems in the evaluation of the anti-institutional radicalism', *Organization*, 6(1): 33–56.

Boland, R. (1987) 'The in-formation of information systems', in R. Boland and R. Hirschheim (eds), *Critical Issues in Information Systems Research*. New York: Wiley. pp. 363–79.

Bougen, P.D. and Young, J.J. (2000) 'Organizing and regulating as rhozomatic lines: bank fraud and auditing', *Organization*, 7(3): 403–26.

Bourdieu, P. (1979) *Outline of a Theory of Practice*. Cambridge: Cambridge University Press.

Bourdieu, P. (1984) *Distinctions: A Social Critique of the Judgement of Taste*. Cambridge: Cambridge University Press.

Bourdieu, P. (1991) *Language and Symbolic Power*. Cambridge: Harvard University Press.

Braverman, H. (1974) *Labor and Monopoly Capital*. New York: Monthly Review Press.

Broadfoot, K., Deetz, S. and Anderson, D. (2004) 'Integrated approaches to the study of discourse', in D. Grant, C. Hardy, C. Oswick and L. Putnam (eds), *The Handbook of Organizational Discourse*. London: Sage. pp. 193–212.

Brown, R.H. (1990) 'Rhetoric, textuality, and the postmodern turn in sociological theory', *Sociological Theory*, 8: 188–97.

Burawoy, M. (1979) *Manufacturing Consent*. Chicago: University of Chicago Press.

Burawoy, M. (1985) *The politics of production: Factory regimes under capitalism and socialism*. London: Verso.

Burrell, G. (1994) 'Modernism, postmodernism and organisational analysis 4: the contribution of Jürgen Habermas', *Organization Studies*, 15: 1–19.

Burrell, G. and Morgan, G. (1979) *Sociological Paradigms and Organizational Analysis*. Aldershot: Gower.

Calás, M. and Smircich, L. (1988) 'Reading leadership as a form of cultural analysis', in J.G. Hunt, B.R. Baliga, H.P. Dachler and C. Schriesheim (eds), *Emerging Leadership Vistas*. Lexington, MA: Lexington Books. pp. 201–6.

Calás, M. and Smircich, L. (1991) 'Voicing seduction to silence leadership', *Organization Studies*, 12: 567–602.

Calás, M. and Smircich, L. (1992a) 'Using the "F" word: feminist theories and the social consequences of organizational research', in A. Mills and P. Tancred (eds), *Gendering Organizational Analysis*. London: Sage. pp. 222–34.

Calás, M. and Smircich, L. (1992b) 'Re-writing gender into organizational theorizing: directions from feminist perspectives', in M. Reed and M. Hughes (eds), *Rethinking Organization: New Directions in Organizational Theory and Analysis*. London: Sage. pp. 227–53.

Calás, M. and Smircich, L. (1993) 'Dangerous liaisons: the 'feminine-in-management' meets 'globalization' – female-oriented approach to globalization', *Business Horizons*, 36(2): 73–83.

Calás, M. and Smircich, L. (1999) 'Past postmodernism? Reflections and tentative directions', *Academy of Management Review*, 24(4): 649–71.

Carter, P. and Jackson, N. (1987) 'Management, myth, and metatheory – from scarcity to postscarcity', *International Studies of Management and Organization*, 17(3): 64–89.

Chia, R. (2000) 'Discourse analysis as organizational analysis', *Organization*, 7(3): 513–8.

Chia, R. (2003) 'Organization theory as a postmodern science', in H. Tsoukas and C. Knudsen (eds), *The Oxford Handbook of Organizational Theory*. Oxford: Oxford University Press. pp. 113–40.

Clegg, S. (1989) *Frameworks of Power*. London: Sage.

Clegg, S. (1990) *Modern Organization: Organization Studies in the Postmodern World*. London: Sage.

Clegg, S. (1994) 'Weber and Foucault: social theory for the study of organizations', *Organization*, 1: 149–78.

Clegg, S. and Dunkerly, D. (1980) *Organization, Class and Control*. London: Routledge and Kegan Paul.

Clifford, J. and Marcus, G.E. (eds) (1986) *Writing Culture*. Berkeley: University of California Press.

Cooper, R. (1989) 'Modernism, postmodernism and organisational analysis 3: the contribution of Jacques Derrida', *Organisation Studies*, 10: 479–502.

Cooper, R. and Burrell, G. (1988) 'Modernism, postmodernism and organisational analysis: an introduction', *Organisation Studies*, 9: 91–112.

Covaleski, M., Dirsmith, M., Heian, J. and Samuel, S. (1998) 'The calculated and the avowed: techniques of discipline and struggles over identity in the big six public accounting firms', *Administrative Science Quarterly*, 43: 293–327.

Czarniawska-Joerges, B. (1988) *Ideological Control in Nonideological Organizations*. New York: Praeger.

Deetz, S. (1992) *Democracy in the Age of Corporate Colonization: Developments in Communication and the Politics of Everyday Life*. Albany: State University of New York Press.

Deetz, S. (1994) 'The micro-politics of identity formation in the workplace: the case of a knowledge intensive firm', *Human Studies*, 17: 23–44.

Deetz, S. (1995) *Transforming Communication, Transforming Business: Building Responsible and Responsive Workplaces*. Cresskill, NJ: Hampton Press.

Deetz, S. (1996) 'Describing differences in approaches to organizational science: rethinking Burrell and Morgan and their legacy', *Organization Science*, 7: 191–207.

Deetz, S. (1998) 'Discursive formations, strategized subordination, and self-surveillance: an empirical case', in A. McKinlay and K. Starkey (eds), *Foucault, management and organizational theory*. London: Sage. pp. 151–72.

Deetz, S. (1999) 'Multiple stakeholders and social responsibility in the international business context: A critical perspective', in P. Salem (ed.), *Organization communication and change: Challenges in the next century*. Cresskill, NJ: Hampton Press. pp. 289–319.

Deetz, S. (2000) 'Putting the community into organizational science: exploring the construction of knowledge claims', *Organization Science*, 11: 732–8.

Deetz, S. (2003a) 'Corporate governance, communication, and getting social values into the decisional chain', *Management Communication Quarterly*, 16: 606–11.

Deetz, S. (2003b) 'Taking the "linguistic turn" seriously', *Organization*, 10: 421–9.

Deetz, S. (2003c) 'Disciplinary power, conflict suppression and human resource management', in M. Alvesson and H. Willmott (eds), *Studying Management Critically*. London: Sage. pp. 23–45.

Deetz, S. (2005) 'Critical theory', in S. May and D. Mumby (eds), *Engaging Organizational Communication Theory: Multiple Perpectives*. Thousand Oaks, CA: Sage. pp. 85–111.

Deetz, S. (in press) 'Corporate governance, communication and CRS', in S. May, G. Cheney and J. Roper (eds), *The Debate Over Corporate Social Responsibility*. Oxford: Oxford University Press.

Deetz, S. and Kersten, A. (1983) 'Critical models of interpretive research', in L. Putnam and M. Pacanowsky (eds), *Communication and organizations: An interpretive approach*. Beverly Hills: Sage. pp. 147–71.

Deetz, S. and Kuhn, T. (in press) 'A critical management theory view on corporate social responsibility', in A. Crane, A. McWilliams, D. Matten, J. Moon and D. Siegel (eds), The *Oxford Handbook of Corporate Social Responsibility*. Oxford: Oxford University Press.

Deetz, S. and Mumby, D. (1990) 'Power, discourse, and the workplace: reclaiming the critical tradition in communication studies in organizations', in J. Anderson (ed.), *Communication Yearbook 13*. Newbury Park: Sage. pp. 18–47.

Deetz, S., MacDonald, J. and Heath, R. (in press) 'On talking to not make decisions: models of bridge and fish markets', in F. Cooren (ed.), *Interacting and organizing: Analysis of a board meeting*. Mahwah, NJ: Lawrence Erlbaum.

DuGay, P. (1997) *Production of Culture, Culture of Production*. London: Sage.

Edwards, R. (1979) *Contested Terrain: The Transformation of the Workplace in the Twentieth Century*. New York: Basic Books.

Epstein, C. (1988) *Deceptive Distinctions*. New Haven: Yale University Press.

Fairclough, N. (1993) 'Critical discourse analysis and the marketization of public discourse', *Discourse and Society*, 4: 133–59.

Featherstone, M. (ed.) (1988) *Postmodernism*. Newbury Park: Sage.

Ferguson, K. (1984) *The Feminist Case Against Bureaucracy*. Philadelphia: Temple University Press.

Fischer, F. (1990) *Technocracy and the Politics of Expertise*. Newbury Park, CA: Sage.

Fischer, F. and Sirianni, C. (eds) (1984) *Critical Studies in Organization and Bureaucracy*. Philadelphia: Temple University Press.

Flax, J. (1990) *Thinking Fragments: Psychoanalysis, Feminism and Postmodernism in the Contemporary West*. Berkeley: University of California Press.

Fleming, P. and Spicer, A. (2004) '"You can checkout anytime, but you can never leave": spatial boundaries in a high commitment organization', *Human Relations*, 57(1): 75–94.

Forester, J. (1983) 'Critical theory and organizational analysis', in G. Morgan (ed.), *Beyond Method*. Beverly Hills: Sage. pp. 234–46.

Forester, J. (ed.) (1985) *Critical Theory and Public Life*. Cambridge: MIT Press.

Forester, J. (1989) *Planning in the Face of Power*. Berkeley, CA: University of California Press.

Forester, J. (1993) *Critical Theory, Public Policy, and Planning Practice*. Albany: State University of New York Press.

Forester, J. (2003) 'On fieldwork in a Habermasian way: critical ethnography and the extra-ordinary character of ordinary professional work', in M. Alvesson and H. Willmott (eds), *Studying Management Critically*. London: Sage. pp. 1–20.

Foster, H. (1983) *Postmodern Culture*. London: Pluto.

Foucault, M. (1977) *Discipline and Punish: The Birth of the Prison*. New York: Random House.

Foucault, M. (1978) *The History of Sexuality*. New York: Random House.

Foucault, M. (1980) *Power/Knowledge*. New York: Pantheon.

Foucault, M. (1983) 'Structuralism and post-structuralism: an interview with Michel Foucault, by G. Raulet', *Telos*, 55: 195–211.

Foucault, M. (1988) 'Technologies of the self', in L. Martin, H. Gutman and P. Hutton (eds), *Technologies of the Self*. Amherst: University of Massachusetts Press. pp. 16–49.

Fouray, J.M and Stork, D. (2002) 'All for one: a parable of spirituality and organization', *Organization*, 9(3): 497–509.

Fournier, V. and Grey, C. (2000) 'At the critical moment: conditions and prospects for critical management studies', *Human Relations*, 53(1): 5–32.

Fraser, N. (1987) 'What's critical about critical theory? The case of Habermas and gender', in S. Benhabib and D. Cornell (eds), *Feminism as Critique*. Cambridge: Polity Press. pp. 31–55.

Fraser, N. (1997) *Justice Interruptus: Critical Reflections on the 'Postsocialist' Condition*. New York: Routledge.

Fraser, N. and Nicholson, L. (1988) 'Social criticism without philosophy: an encounter between feminism and postmodernism', *Theory, Culture and Society*, 5: 373–94.

Frost, P.J. (1980) 'Toward a radical framework for practicing organizational science', *Academy of Management Review*, 5: 501–7.

Frost, P.J. (1987) 'Power, politics, and influence', in F. Jablin, L. Putnam, K. Roberts and L. Porter (eds), *Handbook of Organizational Communication*. Newbury Park: Sage. pp. 503–548.

Geertz, C. (1988) *Work and Lives: The Anthropologist as Author*. Cambridge: Polity Press.

Gergen, K. (1978) 'Toward generative theory', *Journal of Personality and Social Psychology,* 31: 1344–60.

Gergen, K. (1991) *The Saturated Self: Dilemmas of Identity in Contemporary Life.* New York: Basic Books.

Gergen, K. (1992) 'Organization theory in the postmodern era', in M. Reed and M. Hughes (eds), *Rethinking Organizations.* London: Sage. pp. 207–26.

Giddens, A. (1979) *Central Problems in Social Theory.* London: MacMillan.

Gramsci, A. (1971) *Selections from the Prison Notebooks.* Translated by Q. Hoare and G.N. Smith. New York: International.

Grant, D., Hardy, C., Oswick C. and Putnam, L. (eds) (2004) *Handbook of Organizational Discourse.* London: Sage.

Grey, C. (2004) 'Reinventing business schools: the contribution of critical management education', *Academy of Management Learning and Education,* 3: 178–86.

Habermas, J. (1970) *Toward a Rational Society.* London: Heinemann.

Habermas, J. (1971) *Knowledge and Human Interests.* Translated by J. Shapiro. London: Heinemann.

Habermas, J. (1975) *Legitimation Crisis.* Translated by T. McCarthy. Boston: Beacon Press.

Habermas, J. (1979) *Communication and the Evolution of Society.* Translated by T. McCarthy. Boston: Beacon.

Habermas, J. (1984) *The Theory of Communicative Action, volume 1: Reason and the Rationalization of Society.* Boston: Beacon.

Habermas, J. (1987) *The Theory of Communicative Action, volume 2: Lifeworld and System.* Boston: Beacon Press.

Hardy, C. and Clegg, S. (1997) 'Relativity without relativism: reflexivity in post-paradigm organization studies', *British Journal of Management,* 8: S5–17.

Hardy, C. and Phillips, N. (1999) 'No joking matter: discursive struggle in the Canadian refugee system', *Organization Studies,* 20: 1–24.

Hassard, J. and Parker, M. (eds) (1993) *Postmodernism and Organizations.* London: Sage.

Hearn, J. and Parkin, W. (1987) *'Sex' at 'Work'. The Power and Paradox of Organisation Sexuality.* Brighton: Wheatsheaf Books Ltd.

Heckscher, C. (1995) *White-Collar Blues: Management Loyalties in an Age of Corporate Restructuring.* New York: BasicBooks.

Hodge, H., Kress, G. and Jones, G. (1979) 'The ideology of middle management', in R. Fowler, H. Hodge, G. Kress and T. Trew (eds), *Language and Control.* London: Routledge and Kegan Paul. pp. 81–93.

Hollway, W. (1984) 'Fitting work: psychological assessment in organizations', in J. Henriques, W. Hallway, C. Urwin, C. Venn and V. Walkerdine (eds), *Changing the Subject.* New York: Methuen. pp. 26–59.

Hollway, W. (1991) *Work Psychology and Organizational Behavior.* London: Sage.

Holmer-Nadesan, M. (1996a) 'Constructing paper dolls: the discourse of personality testing in organizational practice', *Communication Theory,* 7: 189–218.

Holmer-Nadesan, M. (1996b) 'Organizational identity and space of action', *Organization Studies,* 17: 49–81.

Hopwood, A. (1987) 'The archaeology of accounting systems', *Accounting, Organizations and Society,* 12: 207–34.

Horkheimer, M. and Adorno, T. (1979 [1947]) *The Dialectics of Enlightenment.* London: Verso.

Hoy, D. (1986) 'Power, repression, progress: Foucault, Lukes, and the Frankfurt school', in D. Hoy (ed.), *Foucault: A critical reader.* Oxford: Blackwell. pp. 123–48.

Ingersoll, V. and Adams, G. (1986) 'Beyond organizational boundaries: exploring the managerial myth', *Administration and Society,* 18: 360–81.

Jackall, R. (1988) *Moral Mazes.* New York: Oxford University Press.

Jacques, R. (1996) *Manufacturing the Employee: Management Knowledge from the 19th to 21st Centuries.* Thousand Oaks, CA: Sage.

Jehenson, R. (1984) 'Effectiveness, expertise and excellence as ideological fictions: a contribution to a critical phenomenology of the formal organization', *Human Studies,* 7: 3–21.

Jeffcutt, P. (1993) 'From interpretation to representation', in J. Hassard and M. Parker (eds), *Postmodernism and Organizations.* London: Sage. pp. 25–48.

Jermier, J. (1985) '"When the sleeper wakes": a short story extending themes in radical organization theory', *Journal of Management,* 11(2): 67–80.

Jermier, J. (1998) 'Introduction: critical perspectives on organizational control', *Administrative Science Quarterly,* 43: 235–56.

Jermier, J. and Forbes, L. (2003) 'Greening organizations: critical issues', in M. Alvesson and H. Willmott (eds), *Studying Management Critically.* London: Sage. pp. 157–76.

Kellner, D. (1988) 'Postmodernism as social theory: some challenges and problems', *Theory, Culture and Society,* 5(2–3): 239–69.

Kelly, M. (ed.) (1995) *Critique and Power.* Cambridge: MIT Press.

Klein, N. (2000) *No Logo.* London: Flamingo.

Knights, D. (1992) 'Changing spaces: the disruptive impact of a new epistemological location for the study of management', *Academy of Management Review,* 17: 514–36.

Knights, D. and Morgan, G. (1991) 'Corporate strategy, organizations, and subjectivity: a critique', *Organization Studies,* 12: 251–73.

Knights, D. and Willmott, H. (1985) 'Power and identity in theory and practice', *The Sociological Review,* 33: 22–46.

Knights, D. and Willmott, H. (1987) 'Organisational culture as management strategy', *International Studies of Management and Organization,* 17(3): 40–63.

Knights, D. and Willmott, H. (1989) 'Power and subjectivity at work: from degradation to subjugation in social relation', *Sociology*, 23: 535–58.

Kondo, D.K. (1990) *Crafting Selves: Power, Gender, and Discourses of Identity in a Japanese Workplace*. Chicago: University of Chicago Press.

Kunda, G. (1992) *Engineering Culture: Control and Commitment in a High-Tech Corporation*. Philadelphia: Temple University Press.

Lazega, E. (1992) *Micropolitics of Knowledge: Communication and Indirect Control in Workgroups*. New York: Aldine de Gruyter.

Levy, D., Alvesson, M. and Willmott, H. (2003) 'Critical approaches to strategic management', in M. Alvesson and H. Willmott (eds), *Studying Management Critically*. London: Sage. pp. 92–110.

Linstead, S. (1993) 'Deconstruction in the study of organizations', in J. Hassard and M. Parker (eds), *Postmodernism and Organizations*. London: Sage. pp. 49–70.

Linstead, S. and Grafton-Small, R. (1990) 'Theory as artefact: artefact as theory', in P. Gagliardi (ed.), *Symbols and Artifacts: Views of the Corporate Landscape*. Berlin/New York: de Gruyter. pp. 387–419.

Linstead, S. and Grafton-Small, R. (1992) 'On reading organizational culture', *Organization Studies*, 13: 331–55.

Lukács, G. (1971) *History and Class Consciousness*. Cambridge: MIT Press.

Lukes, S. (1974) *Power: A Radical View*. London: Macmillan.

Lyotard, J.-F. (1984) *The Postmodern Condition: A Report on Knowledge*. Minneapolis: University of Minnesota Press.

Lyytinen, K. and Hirschheim, R. (1988) 'Information systems as rational discourse: an application of Habermas's theory of communicative action', *Scandinavian Journal of Management*, 4: 19–30.

Marcus, G. and Fischer, M. (1986) *Anthropology as Cultural Critique*. Chicago: University of Chicago Press.

Margolis, S. (1989) 'Postscript on modernism and postmodernism: both', *Theory, Culture and Society*, 6: 5–30.

Martin, J. (1990) 'Deconstructing organizational taboos: the suppression of gender conflict in organizations', *Organization Science*, 11: 339–59.

Martin, J. (1995) 'The organization of exclusion: the institutionalization of sex inequality, gendered faculty jobs, and gendered knowledge in organizational theory and research', *Organization*, 1: 401–31.

Martin, J. (2002) *Organizational Culture*. Thousand Oakes: Sage.

Martin, J. (2003) 'Feminist theory and critical theory: unexplored synergies', in M. Alvesson and H. Willmott (eds), *Studying Management Critically*. London: Sage. pp. 66–91.

Martin, P.Y. (2001) '"Mobilizing masculinities": women's experiences of men at work', *Organization*, 8(4): 587–618.

Marx, K. (1964 [1844]) *Economic and Political Manuscripts of 1844*. Translated by M. Miligan. New York: International.

Marx, K. (1967 [1867]) *Das Kapital. Bd 1*. Berlin: Dietz.

Meriläinen, S., Tienari, J., Thomas, R. and Davies, A. (2004) 'Management consultant talk: a cross-cultural comparison of normalizing discourse and resistance', *Organization*, 11(4): 539–64.

Montagna, P. (1986) 'Accounting rationality and financial legitimation', *Theory and Society*, 15: 103–38.

Morgan, G. (1997) *Images of Organization*, 2nd edn. Thousand Oaks, CA: Sage.

Mumby, D.K. (1987) 'The political function of narrative in organizations', *Communication Monographs*, 54: 113–27.

Mumby, D. (1988) *Communication and Power in Organizations: Discourse, Ideology, and Domination*. Norwood, NJ: Ablex.

Mumby, D.K. (1997) 'The problem of hegemony: rereading Gramsci for organizational communication studies', *Western Journal of Communication*, 61: 343–75.

Mumby, D. (2004) 'Discourse, power and ideology: Unpacking the critical approach', in D. Grant, C. Hardy, C. Oswick and L. Putnam (eds), *The Handbook of Organizational Discourse*. London: Sage. pp. 237–58.

Mumby, D. and Putnam, L. (1992) 'The politics of emotion: a feminist reading of bounded rationality', *Academy of Management Review*, 17: 465–86.

Murphy, A.G. (1998) 'Hidden transcripts of flight attendant resistance', *Management Communication Quarterly*, 11: 499–535.

Newton, T. (1998). 'Theorizing subjectivity in organizations: the failure of Foucauldian studies', *Organization Studies*, 19(3): 415–47.

Papa, M.J., Auwal, M.A. and Singhal, A. (1995) 'Dialectic of control and emancipation in organizing for social change: a multitheoretic study of the Grameen Bank in Bangladesh', *Communication Theory*, 5: 189–223.

Parker, I. (1992a) *Discourse Dynamics*. London; Routledge.

Parker, M. (1992b) 'Post-modern organizations or postmodern organization theory?', *Organization Studies*, 13: 1–17.

Parker, M. (2000) *Organizational Culture and Identity*. London: Sage.

Parker, M. (2003) 'Business, ethics and business ethics: critical theory and negative dialectics', in M. Alvesson and H. Willmott (eds), *Studying Management Critically*. London: Sage. pp. 197–219.

Phillips, N. and Hardy, C. (2002) *Discourse analysis: Investigating processes of social construction*. Newbury Park, CA: Sage

Potter, J. and Wetherell, M. (1987) *Discourse and Social psychology. Beyond Attitudes and Behaviour*. London: Sage.

Power, M. (1994) 'The audit society', in A. Hopwood and P. Miller (eds), *Accounting as social and institutional practice*. Cambridge: Cambridge University Press. pp. 299–316.

Power, M., Laughlin, R. and Cooper, D. (2003) 'Accounting and critical theory', in M. Alvesson and H. Willmott (eds), *Studying Management Critically*. London: Sage. pp. 113–35.

Prasad, P. and Prasad, A. (1998) 'Everyday struggles at the workplace', *Research in the Sociology of Organizations*, 15: 225–57.

Pringle, R. (1988) *Secretaries Talk: Sexuality, Power and Work*. London: Verso.

Roberts, J. (2003) 'The manufacture of corporate social responsibility', *Organization*, 10: 249–66.

Rose, D. (1990) *Living the Ethnographic Life*. Newbury Park: Sage.

Rosen, M. (1985) 'Breakfirst at Spiro's: dramaturgy and dominance', *Journal of Management*, 11(2): 31–48.

Rosen, M. (1988) 'You asked for it: christmas at the bosses' expense', *Journal of Management Studies*, 25(5): 463–80.

Salaman, G. (1981) *Class and the Corporation*. Glasgow: Fontana.

Sangren, S. (1992) 'Rhetoric and the authority of ethnography', *Current Anthropology*, 33(Supplement): 277–96.

Sarup, M. (1988) *An Introductory Guide to Post-structuralism and Post-modernism*. Hemel Hempstead: Harvester Wheatsheaf.

Sennett, R. (1998) *The Corrosion of Character*. New York: Norton.

Shotter, J. (1993) *Conversational Realities: The Construction of Life through Language*. Newbury Park, CA: Sage.

Shotter, J. and Gergen, K. (eds) (1989) *Texts of Identity*. London: Sage.

Shotter, J. and Gergen, K. (1994) 'Social construction: knowledge, self, others, and continuing the conversation', in S. Deetz (ed.), *Communication Yearbook 17*. Newbury Park: Sage. pp. 3–33.

Shrivastava, P. (1986) 'Is strategic management ideological?', *Journal of Management*, 12(3): 363–77

Sievers, B. (1986) 'Beyond the surrogate of motivation', *Organization Studies*, 7: 335–52.

Sless, D. (1988) 'Forms of control', *Australian Journal of Communication*, 14: 57–69.

Smircich, L. and Calás, M. (1987) 'Organizational culture: a critical assessment', in F. Jablin, L. Putnam, K. Roberts and L. Porter (eds), *Handbook of Organizational Communication*. Newbury Park: Sage. pp. 228–63.

Sotorin, P. and Gottfried, H. (1999) 'The ambivalent dynamics of secretarial 'bitching': control, resistance, and the construction of identity', *Organization*, 6(1): 57–80.

Stablein, R. and Nord, W. (1985) 'Practical and emancipatory interests in organizational symbolism', *Journal of Management*, 11(2): 13–28.

Stead, W.E. and Stead, J.G. (1992). *Management for a Small Planet*. Newbury Park: Sage.

Steffy, B. and Grimes, A. (1992) 'Personnel/organizational psychology: a critique of the discipline', in M. Alvesson and H. Willmott (eds), *Critical Management Studies*. London: Sage. pp. 181–201.

Steier, F. (1991) 'Reflexivity and methodology: an ecological constructionism', in F. Steier (ed.), *Research and Reflexivity*. London: Sage. pp. 163–85.

Storey, J. (1983) *Managerial Prerogative and the Question of Control*. London: Routledge and Kegan Paul.

Thackaberry, J.A. (2004) 'Discursive opening and closing in organizational self study: culture as the culprit for safety problems in wildland firefighting', *Management Communication Quarterly*, 17: 319–59.

Thomas, R. and Linstead, S. (2002) 'Losing the plot? Middle managers and identity', *Organization*, 9(1): 71–93.

Thompson, J. (1984) *Studies in the Theory of Ideology*. Berkeley: University of California Press.

Thompson, J.B. and Held, D. (eds) (1982) *Habermas. Critical Debates*. London: Macmillan.

Thompson, P. (1993) 'Post-modernism: fatal distraction', in J. Hassard and M. Parker (eds), *Postmodernism and Organizations*. London: Sage. pp. 183–203.

Tompkins, P. and Cheney, G. (1985) 'Communication and unobtrusive control in contemporary organizations', in R. McPhee and P. Tompkins (eds), *Organizational Communication: Traditional Themes and New Directions*. Newbury Park, CA: Sage. pp. 179–210.

Townley, B. (1993) 'Foucault, power/knowledge, and its relevance for human resource management', *Academy of Management Review*, 18: 518–45.

Tretheway, A. (1997) 'Resistance, identity, and empowerment: a postmodern feminist analysis of clients in a human service organization', *Communication Monographs*, 64: 281–301.

Tretheway, A. (2001) 'Reproducing and resisting the master narrative of decline: midlife professional women's experiences of aging', *Management Communication Quarterly*, 15: 183–226.

Vallas, S. (1993) *Power in the Workplace: The Politics of Production at ATandT*. Albany: State University of New York Press.

Van Maanen, J. (1988) *Tales of the Field*. Chicago: University of Chicago Press.

Vattimo, G. (1992) *The Transparent Society*. Baltimore: John Hopkins University Press.

Waltzer, M. (1986) 'The politics of Foucault', in D. Hoy (ed.), *Foucault: A Reader*. Oxford: Basil Blackwell. pp. 151–68.

Weedon, C. (1997) *Feminist Practice and Poststructuralist Theory*, 2nd edn. Oxford: Basil Blackwell.

Willmott, H. (1993) 'Strength is ignorance; slavery is freedom: managing culture in modern organizations', *Journal of Management Studies*, 30(4): 515–52.

Willmott, H. (1994) 'Bringing agency (back) into organizational analysis: responding to the crises of (post)modernity', in J. Hassard and M. Parker (eds),

Towards a New Theory of Organizations. London: Routledge. pp. 87–130.

Willmott, H. (2003) 'Organizational theory as a critical science', in H. Tsoukas and C. Knudsen (eds), *The Oxford Handbook of Organizational Theory*. Oxford: Oxford University Press. pp. 88–112.

Willmott, H. and Knights, D. (1982) 'The problem of freedom: Fromm's contribution to a critical theory of work organization', *Praxis International*, 2: 204–25.

Wolf, M. (1992) *A Thrice-Told Tale. Feminism, Postmodernism and Ethnographic Representation*. Stanford: Stanford University Press.

Wray-Bliss, E. (2003) 'Research subjects/research subjections: exploring the ethics and politics of critical research', *Organization*, 10: 307–25.

1.8 From the 'Woman's Point of View' Ten Years Later: Towards a Feminist Organization Studies

MARTA B. CALÁS AND LINDA SMIRCICH

During the last 30 years, the 'women's liberation' movement achieved profound social, political, and economic gains, improving the situation of many women. At the same time, feminist movements have contributed strongly to contemporary cultural analyses and, in universities all over the world, women's studies programmes have helped foster energetic cross-disciplinary scholarship and a plurality of feminist 'theories' aimed at rethinking the grounds of knowledge. Despite these gains, however, the sex segregation of occupations and organizations persists world wide, as does pay inequity between women and men (Calás and Smircich 1996: 218).

We started our chapter for the first edition of this handbook with these words, attempting to capture the impact of feminist theorizing on organization studies. We wrote convinced there was much more feminist theorizing could contribute to our field. Our task was articulating, at least in part, such possibilities. Now, we have to consider: What difference has 10 years made? Have conditions changed enough so that writing a chapter like this is no longer necessary? Have organizational practices and organizational theories become more 'gender-mindful'? Should gender continue to be an important category of analysis in organization studies?

Today we believe that bringing gender into organization studies, as a central analytical category, is as important as ever. Our conviction stems not only from recognizing the important contributions that feminist theorizing can make – and in fact has already made – to our field.[1] It stems from observing, as well, its limited impact toward changing the conditions that prompted its earlier expression. In the following pages we build on our 1996 work, revisiting our earlier insights and adding to them.

Over the years numerous arguments have been forwarded to forecast that women's equality may be around the corner, but the only prediction of which one might be certain is that more and more explanations are being and will continue to be produced to explain why equality and equity elude women (e.g. van de Vliert and van der Vegt 2004). Regardless of how many statistical contortions are made (e.g. Gastelaars 2002) or sociological, psychological and economic explanations are marshalled (e.g. Jacobs 1999a), to date no single indicator shows that the economic conditions of women in the world, as a whole, are at parity with the conditions of men. In the last 10 years the percentage of women employed worldwide has risen slightly to just above 40%; yet in its recent report on global employment trends the International Labor Organization observes that 'improved equality in terms of quantity of male and female workers has yet to result in real socioeconomic empowerment for women, an equitable distribution of household responsibilities, equal pay for work of equal value, and gender balance across all occupations' (ILO March 2004: 1). Further, women are still the larger proportion – 60% – of the world's working poor, i.e. those people who work but who do not earn enough to lift themselves and their families above the poverty line (ILO 2004).

These are general trends worldwide, but country conditions vary. In the US, despite some appearances to the contrary, society is generally not changing in the direction of gender equity. Not only has the tipping phenomenon continued, where traditionally male high paying occupations lose earning power once women dominate them (Strober 1984), but even more startling, the opposite has also been the case: As men have entered traditionally female occupations wage disparity persists, with men obtaining higher salaries than women (ILO 2004). In 2000, women in the US working full time year round earned 74 cents for every dollar earned by men – a marginal to non-existent improvement over the past 20 years (GAO 2003).

Some argued the solution to pay inequality rests with eliminating the sex segregation of occupations, for if women enter higher paid male-dominated occupations their wages would increase (e.g. Reskin 1984). Others claimed the problem of women earning less was due to their crowding in lower earning occupations, which made women cheaper to hire than men (e.g. Gibson et al. 1998; Boraas and Rodgers 2003). At the end, these may be circular arguments. The fact continues to be that women are more likely to earn less than men for the same type of work, even in traditionally female occupations, and thus traditional economic explanations leave much unexplained.

Conditions are not much different in the European Union, where women's earnings average 86% of men's earnings in 2001 if private and public sector are measured, but go down to 75% if only the private sector is measured. The EU has approached this situation as primarily a sociological problem by attempting to mainstream gender issues in all sectors. Gender mainstreaming, approved as part of the platform of the 1995 UN World Conference on Women in Beijing, is based on principles of gender equality through the transformation of gender relations pervading all social institutions, and through integrating a gender perspective into all analyses, procedures, policies and organizational practices (Hafner-Burton and Pollack 2002; True 2003; Woodward 2003). Concurrently, the pay gap is addressed through legislation as well as initiatives in the public, private and labour sectors.

In most industrialized countries the numbers of women engaged in paid employment and increasing numbers of dual earner couples results in competing demands of work and family, and has become a highly visible social concern (e.g. Leira 2002; OECD 2003; Pocock 2005). Global economic conditions – among them new emphasis on flexibility often resulting in downsizing of careers to temporary employment and technological developments instigating a '24/7' work philosophy – place work force members, women and men, under pressure in their lives. Yet, women and men are not affected equally by these conditions: '... persisting gender inequality continues to place women at a disadvantage.

Women shoulder more responsibility for domestic work, and they also face larger obstacles at the workplace ...' (Jacobs and Gerson 2004: 114). In the US context this is accompanied by what researchers document as a motherhood wage penalty, while for men fatherhood is a career asset (Budig and England 2001; Anderson et al. 2003). And, as more and more women enter employment, concerns are voiced more generally about a 'care deficit' in society (Folbre 2001; Rianne 2002).

Yet, countries also vary in their approaches and policies for addressing work/family conflicts. Cross-national research indicates that in countries such as the Netherlands and Sweden, with strong institutional supports for achieving work family balance, the associated price is that women's more frequent use of part time work results in less gender equity in the workplace. While in countries such as Finland and the US, where the model of full-time work prevails and couples put in long work weeks, greater equity in the workplace is achieved at the cost of a time squeeze on families (Jacobs et al. 2004).

All these trends are well represented in the most recent World Economic Forum study ranking 58 countries on gender equality, in which the US came in 17th – behind Latvia, Lithuania, Estonia and Ireland, among others (Lopez-Claros and Zahidi 2005). While in the US a higher-than-average percentage of women are in the work force, hold political positions and obtain college degrees, women fare less well in health care and opportunity for advancement, for economic advancement is linked to policies of paid maternity leave and government-provided child-care, mostly lacking in this country. Echoing previous studies, this report concluded:

> the reality is that no country in the world, no matter how advanced, has achieved true gender equality, as measured by comparable decision-making power, equal opportunity for education and advancement, and equal participation and status in all walks of human endeavour. Gender disparities exist, even in countries without glaring male-domination ... (Lopez-Claros and Zahidi: 2005: 2).

Our purpose in portraying these conditions is not to offer a comparative analysis but to highlight that sex/gender inequality in the context of pay, work and family issues continues to exist the world over. In particular, in the industrialized world and in countries where democracy and capitalism reign supreme, inequality is sometimes more marked than in other regions (e.g. Kucera and Milberg 2000). How is this industrialized world organized – a world that wants to set the example for 'global development' – such that it has not been able to eliminate sex/gender inequality, as well as poverty? What assumptions support the taken for granted in our ways of organizing and what function does gender play, materially and symbolically, in maintaining these conditions?

As we will discuss, a growing body of multidisciplinary feminist theorizing addresses these issues and many others that lie underneath gender and other forms of social inequality. Meanwhile, we observe that the terms 'feminism', 'feminist theory' and even 'gender' are less in evidence in scholarly work in US-based management academic publications and on the US Academy of Management programmes. Yet in other places where critical work is more typical, feminist theorizing for organizational analysis has accelerated since our original chapter in 1996. For example, *Gender, Work & Organization*, published in the UK since 1994, has become a well-established academic journal dedicating its pages to important organization scholarship inspired by diverse feminist approaches. In a neighbouring discipline, *Feminist Economics* also began at this time. Recent scholarly books in organizational communication are also explicitly feminist (e.g. Buzzanell 2000; Ashcraft and Mumby 2004). There are indeed synergies between feminist and gender analyses and other critical perspectives on organization and management studies, calling attention to needed scrutiny of the politics of knowledge in these fields (e.g. P.Y. Martin and Collinson 2002; Gherardi 2003; Martin 2003a; Ashcraft 2004; Calás and Smircich 2004a).

In the following pages we hope to make a contribution to this conversation by forwarding possibilities for a *feminist organization studies*, where the accent is on *studies*. To be clear, our project is an epistemological one. We are not intending to suggest ways of organizing or managing from feminist perspectives. Rather, our intent is to foster feminist theories as conceptual lenses to enact a more relevant 'organization studies'; an organization studies which will bring 'into the picture' the concerns of many others, not only women, who are often made invisible in/through organizational processes. In

bringing together reviews of literature from a variety of feminist theoretical tendencies and the now substantive body of work in organization and management scholarship that draws from these tendencies, we signal the existence and strengths of possibilities already opened, and wish to inspire many more. As our chapter progresses, we also expect to show that, in the context of contemporary global social and economic conditions, a feminist organization study is also a contribution to feminist theorizing more generally.

Feminist Analyses and Organizational Studies

The chapter reviews liberal, radical, psychoanalytic, socialist, poststructuralist/postmodern, transnational/(post)colonial feminist theorizing. Despite their diversity, most feminist theoretical tendencies share certain assumptions, notably the recognition of gendered dominance in social arrangements, and a desire for changes from this form of domination (e.g. Flax 1987; Chafetz 1997; Fraser and Naples 2004). More generally, feminist theoretical perspectives are *critical* discourse in that feminist theory is a critique of the status quo and therefore *always political*. Yet, the degree of critique and the nature of the politics vary, leading to agendas that, when applied to organization studies, range from reforming organizations; to transforming organizations *and* society; to transforming our prior understandings of what constitutes knowledge/ theory/ practice in organization studies.

Each theoretical tendency gives alternative accounts for gender issues, frames 'problems' differently and proposes different courses of action as 'solutions'. As we illustrate, feminist analyses, shown in their different instances, elucidate the very different assumptions that are being made about the nature of humanity, the concept of gender and the nature of society, and how those assumptions define different understandings of gendered social and economic issues, as well as how they are researched, and the implications of such research articulated. Those differences also account for how research results are translated into institutional practices and public policy, and how issues of social inequality are confronted more broadly.

A key conceptual distinction among feminist theories is the way *gender* is understood. Earliest theories of liberal feminism were concerned with inequality between 'the sexes', i.e. between two categories of persons ('males' and 'females') denoted by biological characteristics. Later, theorizing made a distinction between biologically-based 'sex' and 'gender' as a product of socialization and experience. Even here, though, feminist theorizing differs over what aspects of experience are most important in constituting gender. For instance, liberal feminism would focus on socialization into sex/gender roles; radical feminism would address cultural practices that value men's experiences over women's; black 'womanists' would question which 'women's experiences' are constitutive of 'gender'; while psychoanalytic feminism would be concerned with experiences acquired in early developmental relations with parents.

The notion of *gender* becomes more distanced from 'personal experience' when socialist feminists consider gender(ing) a process embedded in power relations and particular historical material conditions, including practices of masculinity as well as identities formed in the intersectionalities of gender, race, class, sexuality and other categories of social oppression. Both poststructuralists and transnational/(post)colonial approaches and several other approaches to gender that have emerged in the wake of various 'posts', such as 'queer theory', problematize the whole notion of 'experience'. They critique investing 'sex' and 'gender' with a certain stability as analytical categories, noting that subjectivity and identity are constructed linguistically, historically and politically, and is therefore flexible and multiple. Thus, *gender* is a term still 'in the making' (Scott 1986) and often contested (e.g. Hawkesworth (1997) and comments that followed), that both reflects and constitutes the variety and vibrancy of feminist theorizing (Ahmed 2000).

In the rest of the chapter, we describe how each theoretical tendency in feminist thought connects with organizational research and theorizing, and discuss their actual and potential contributions to organization studies. We show how each feminist theoretical strand highlights certain organizational issues while ignoring others. As we discuss these various approaches, the issues addressed and the questions raised shift, as does the vocabulary, from concerns about women (their access to organizations and their performance in organizations), to concerns about gender and organization (the notion of gendered organizational practices), to concerns about the very stability of such categories as 'gender', 'masculinity', 'femininity' and 'organization'.

We present these theoretical tendencies in sequence, although this is somewhat misleading for they have developed and changed in conversation with one another. While they may look discrete and unified the lines are blurry and blurring. Thus, we have tried to highlight their historical and intellectual relationships by organizing our discussion into two main sections, the first centred on 'women' and the second centred on 'gendering'. Altogether, our goal is not to judge which of these tendencies is 'best', but to recognize that each offers an important contribution. The need for brevity here means a less detailed and nuanced exposition than we would prefer, but we hope our limited words will inspire further reading into *feminist theorizing* and an *explicit* recognition of the *feminist theorists* whose works have made, and continue to make, a difference in organization studies.

Several key feminist philosophical frameworks shape our staging of these arguments (Jaggar 1983; Tuana and Tong 1995; Weedon 1997; Jaggar and Young 1998; Tong 1998; Kourany et al. 1999; Kolmar and Bartkowski 2000; Holmstrom 2002; Mohanty 2003) and discussions of gender epistemology and analysis (Harding and Hintikka 1983; Harding 1986; 1991; 1998; 2004a; Code 1991; Haraway 1997; Hesse-Biber et al. 1999; Walby 2001). In 1996, vignettes about the 'glass ceiling' were guideposts for illustrating how different analytical approaches from feminist theorizing can enrich organization and management scholarship. This time 'work-family' concerns will light the way, as discussions on this topic are of interest to multiple sectors in various societies. Specifically, the story of Sarah Kelly, a figure drawn from an assemblage of media accounts portraying the struggles of working mothers (e.g. Belkin 2003; Douglas and Michaels 2004; O'Kelly 2004; Wallis 2004), provides a starting point for our feminist analyses. To be sure, 'the glass-ceiling' has not gone away. Rather, our original glass-ceiling vignettes read in relationship to our current work-family stories become a strong way to remark that 'gender issues' in societies and organizations are persistent, and the question of women's place in society still under debate.

A Work/Family Story

Sarah Kelly, 37, has just said goodnight to her nanny, Julia Peña. It is 7 pm and Sarah looks in at her 3 year old daughter, Becky, and her 2 year old son, Will, who have been put to bed by Julia. Sarah is feeling tired, she is 6 months pregnant and the day has been a busy one at the law firm where she works. This morning started badly, with Will scratching Becky, so that Sarah found herself doing six things at once; soothing her daughter, making sure that Will's swimming bag was ready for his weekly baby-swim classes and that Julia had enough money to go grocery shopping later on. Sarah remained calm as usual though. She has learnt to deal with this 'morning madness' alone. Her husband Michael, 41, left for work at 6 am. He is a director of an architect's firm and, although he regrets missing out on this part of family life, he needs to be in the office by 7.30 am and must leave early to beat the rush hour traffic. Sarah left the apartment at 8.00 am. Every morning she goes into 'action mode' to make sure that she has enough time to get the toddlers up and ready for the day, and to get herself out of the house in time to catch the bus and make her morning meeting at 9 am.

While Sarah is at work as a lawyer, she makes sure to find a moment to call Julia around lunchtime to check up on the kids. Now Sarah sits down to eat her evening meal, she will not wait for Michael who is still at work. At the same time she checks the messages on her cell phone to see if work has called and she also looks over some notes from a meeting that day. Sarah likes to do this every evening, and feels guilty if she doesn't.

Sarah loves her job and considers it her 'vocation'. She earns a good salary and is on track for promotion. However, she has decided that once the new baby arrives she will leave work for a couple of years to concentrate on her family. This has been a tough decision for Sarah but she feels that it is 'the right thing to do'.

Finally, we do not write as 'detached' observers: as authors we have our favoured positions in between the 'post' discourses and thereafter (e.g. Calás and Smircich 1999). That is, *we are writing from the perspective of third wave feminist theorizing* 'incorporating multiple definitions from equity to gender feminism, and strategically combining elements of poststructuralist feminism, black feminism, women of colour feminism, working-class feminism, prosex feminism, and so on' (Braithwaite 2002: 342; also Heywood and Drake 1997; Hawkesworth 2004). Writing as feminist organizational academics in the US, we note also our situatedness to mark the situatedness of all other scholarship in our field, in particular that which passes itself as neutral and which pretends to perform the 'God trick' (Haraway 1989). Thus, this chapter is also written attempting to illustrate such scholarly positioning.

The Woman's Condition: Same or Different?

Here we review liberal, radical and psychoanalytic feminist theoretical tendencies. While their epistemological assumptions for understanding women's oppression vary, and thus the solutions they propose are different, they share a fundamental ontological assumption: that women's oppression is located in the condition of *women*. That is, while different in appearance, these tendencies hold in common traces of a view that posits a transcultural and transhistorical 'woman', and thus their emphasis is on addressing what is unique to this universally sexualized human being that may account for her subordination to her other, 'man'. Most arguments therefore become centred on issues of her 'equality', 'similarity' or 'difference', expecting to resolve how the two sexes, and even their sexualities, may come to share common or separate spaces in society but without oppression or subordination. They are united in a politics concerned with 'reforming' organizations and institutions, even though there are fundamental differences on what that means. Assumptions supporting these perspectives underpin much of what is thought of as 'women's issues', and even 'feminism' in US organization studies, and in US and other societies more generally. Table 1.8.1 summarizes the perspectives discussed in this section.

Liberal Feminist Theory

Liberal feminism initially articulated the notions of 'equality' and 'equity' usually associated with 'women's issues' in the popular domain. Today, it can be viewed as the historical starting point for all other contemporary feminist theorizing as well as a

Table 1.8.1 The woman's condition: same or different?

School of thought	Liberal	Radical	Psychoanalytic
Intellectual roots	Evolved from 18th and 19th century liberal political theory	Generated in the women's liberation movements of the late 1960s	Evolved from Freudian and other psychoanalytic theories, in particular object-relations theories
Conception of human nature	Individual are autonomous beings capable of rationality (mind/body dualism and abstract individualism)	Human beings are fundamentally embodied sexed beings	Human nature develops biologically and psychosexually
Conception of sex/gender	Sex is part of essential biological endowment, a binary variable. Gender is socialized onto sexed human beings for appropriate behaviour, e.g. gender roles	'Sex class' is the condition of women as an oppressed class. Gender is a social construction that ensures women's subordination to men	Individuals become sexually-identified as part of their psychosexual development. Gender structures a social system of male domination which influences psychosexual development
Conception of 'the good society'	The 'good society' is a just society that allows individuals to exercise autonomy and to fulfil themselves through a system of individual rights	The 'good society' is a gender/sex-free society (or perhaps a matriarchy)	The 'good society' has no gender structuring. Children develop valuing equally both 'the feminine' and 'the masculine'
Epistemological positions	Positivist, gender-neutral objectivity	Holistic female-centred knowledge is possible outside of patriarchal structures	Women's way of knowledge is different from men's because of different psychosexual development
Some favoured methodologies	Positivist social science; laboratory experiments; mostly quantitative	Consciousness-raising groups and case studies	Clinical case studies, focus on context-specific social relations and developmental processes; life histories
Conceptualization of sex/gender and organization	Organizations are gender-neutral institutions established to maintain the rational social order	Organizations are mostly institutions of the patriarchal order, created to maintain gender segregation and discrimination in the public domain and sexual oppression in the private domain	Organizations reproduce patriarchal psycho-sexual development. The sexuality of organizations maintain the dominant system of gender relations and domination
Needed organizational change	Sex/gender imbalances can be corrected through human development and/or structural/legal interventions	Sex/gender oppression could be eradicated only through separatist institutions: e.g. feminist organizations; women's empowering	Understanding psycho-sexual dynamics in organizations would contribute to establishing organizations where feminine values are also appreciated
Some favoured interventions	Integrationist approaches; gender mainstreaming	Externalization of feminine private values into public domain, e.g. in areas of sexuality and reproduction; health	Articulation of feminine and masculine values to create more balanced, androgynous organizational cultures

much contested theoretical perspective for its inability to move gender issues beyond a conversation about 'women being as good as men', despite some later trends toward positing 'women's difference' as valuable for changing the social order (e.g. Friedan 1981).

This perspective has its roots in the liberal political tradition developed in the 17th and 18th century, when feudalistic, church-dominated rule was giving way to capitalistic, civil society, and when aspirations for equality, liberty and fraternity were supplanting the monarchical order (Cockburn 1991). A new vision of persons and society was emerging, allowed by two key assumptions about human nature: *normative dualism* (mind/body dualism) where rationality is conceived as mental capacity, separated from embodiment, and *abstract individualism*, where human action is conceived of in abstraction from any social circumstances (Jaggar 1983). Further, individuals were assumed to inhabit a world of scarcity, and to be motivated by the desire to secure as large an individual share as possible of the available resources. Thus, for liberal political theorists, a 'good' or 'just' society allowed individuals to exercise autonomy and to fulfil themselves through a system of individual rights.

Where did women stand in this society? Women were unable to vote, own property in their own names, and, with the transition from a home-centred form of economic production to an industrial economy, became increasingly economically dependent and isolated. Early liberal political theorists in England, Wollstonecraft (1792), Mill (1851) and Mill (1869), considered that women's true potential went unfulfilled because of their exclusion from the academy, the forum and the marketplace: they were 'non-persons' in the public world (Tong 1998).

Strongly influenced by these ideas, in the US, the women's rights movement of the 19th century overlapped with the abolitionist movement. However, the women's rights issues introduced at the time, and articulated by white, middle class, educated women such as Lucretia Mott and Elizabeth Cady Stanton, seldom addressed the interests of less privileged women or people of colour (Davis 1981). A notable exception was the black feminist and abolitionist Sojourner Truth (e.g. 1851; 1867); her impassioned appeal on behalf of *all women's* rights brought together issues of women's equality and slavery. Nonetheless, early liberal theorists were reformists rather than revolutionaries: white male

was the paradigm of human nature; thus, their concern was to demonstrate that women and non-whites were as fully human as white men (Jaggar 1983) and aimed, for instance, to attain *universal* suffrage as a basic *human* right.

In the 1960s, in the US the Second Wave women's movement followed these ideas in aiming for equal access and equal representation in public life for women without stressing sex differences. Acknowledging differences was seen to be reactionary and harmful to the 'cause' (e.g. Friedan 1963). However, by the 1980s, Friedan (1981), among others, began to question this reasoning, arguing it treated women as 'male clones', when 'there has to be a concept of equality that takes into account that women are the ones who have the babies' (Friedan, in Tong 1998: 30). Liberal feminism thus made a transition from themes of equality, in the 1960s and 1970s, to themes of difference in the 1980s and 1990s, noting that sex, a matter of chromosomes and anatomy, has been conflated with gender, cultural constructs about what are appropriately 'masculine' or 'feminine' traits and behaviour. An overriding goal became sexual equity or 'gender justice' (Evans 1995; Tong 1998).

Regardless of view, whether of equality or difference, liberal feminist research favours positivist epistemologies, which are assumed to be gender-neutral (Jaggar 1983). Further, it adheres to an ideal, ahistorical, universal humanity toward which both men and women should aspire (Parvikko 1990). How closely individuals approximate that ideal humanity determines their level of benefit and reward; yet, this research seldom acknowledged that the 'ideal humanity' and the 'ideal society' were modelled after Eurocentric, elite, masculinist ideals.

Black feminists have shown, however, that Liberal feminism, as manifested in the second wave American women's movement, represented only the interests of white, middle class, heterosexual women under the guise of representing all women. They pointed to the irony that both the first and second wave American women's liberation movements emerged from the strength of race liberation movements: the anti-slavery and civil rights movements. They specified that it is impossible to address issues of 'gender justice' without taking race into account, for together they constitute particular forms of oppression and discrimination (e.g. Combahee River Collective 1977; Lewis 1977; hooks 1981; Joseph and Lewis 1981; Hull et al. 1982; Dill 1983; Giddings 1984).

Liberal Feminist Theory and the Women-in-Management Literature

Organizational scholarship has been, primarily, a literature written by men, for men and about men: how to gain the co-operation of men to achieve organizational ends through rationality: how to man/age (e.g. Schein et al. 1996; Wajcman 1998; Maier 1999; Deem 2003). Despite the fact that women occupied organizational jobs from early industrialization, and women were organizational researchers soon after the turn of the century (e.g. Mary Parker Follett; Lillian Gilbreth), most writers addressed women in organizations as *anomalies* if in managerial positions (e.g. *Fortune*, August 1935; September 1935; Alpern 1993); or *normalized* them in subordinate roles (e.g. Barnard 1938; Roethliesberger and Dickson 1939).

Most of the 'gender and organization' literature since the 1960s falls under the category of women-in-management, and is consistent with liberal political theory's assumptions about human nature: abstract individualism; mind/body dualism; the separation of the private and the public sphere in social life; the right to ownership of private property; and a notion of rationality whereby self-interested individuals would see to it that scarce resources are distributed according to universal rules of fairness and moral judgement. There is no acknowledgement that in its original formulation the ideal humanity, *the people* of liberal political theory, was coded as 'propertied white male'. For example, in l965, a *Harvard Business Review* article, based on a survey of business people, asked 'Are Women Executives People?'

> When women act like people, ask no special privileges, and display no undue temperament, they are more likely to be treated like people. Conversely, when women are treated like people on a case-by-case basis rather than as a category, they are more likely to think of themselves as managers, not women, and to behave naturally in a work situation (Bowman et al. 1965: 174).

Male respondents 'overwhelmingly' agreed that '*only the exceptional*, indeed the overqualified, *woman can hope to succeed in management*. They see little, if any, chance for the woman of only average ability' (Bowman et al. 1965: 176, emphasis in original).

It may seem unkind to say that the majority of the women-in-management literature is still trying to demonstrate that women are people too. Yet, consistent with liberal political theory, insofar as this literature conceives of organizations as made up of rational, autonomous actors, whose ultimate goal is to make organizations efficient, effective and fair, it is difficult to imagine how it would be otherwise. For instance, women-in-management research is highly oriented toward comparative analyses of men and women in managerial positions but has tended to ignore how notions of 'managerial positions' came to be/are still defined. While often voicing concerns about gender stereotypes, such concerns assume a fundamental humanity 'underneath it all', and do not question the gendered images already embedded in such 'fundamental humanity'.

In that sense, most of this literature takes for granted the early premises of second wave feminism concerning women's equality rather than its later trend towards recognizing women's differences. The pursuit of *equity* (i.e. maintaining a just institutional system for the exercise of all people's individual rights) is a consistent goal, rather than the elimination of *inequality* (i.e. acknowledging fundamental problems in the premises that support the institutions which disadvantage particular groups). That is, organizations and management, as institutions of liberal political and economic systems, are assumed to be by definition sex/gender neutral, where all individuals have equal access insofar as they are equally meritorious. Assuring the good functioning of a meritocratic system within these neutral institutions is the central aim. A good functioning system of this kind cannot produce systemic inequality and thus, if such were the case, remedies are likely to focus on improving the system such that disparities, if they ever occur, would only need to be addressed *one person at a time*.

Women in management research, taken as a whole, mostly documents the persistence of sex segregation in organizations, looking for explanations as to why it continues within what is assumed to be fundamentally a just system, trying to enumerate the causes through measurable constructs. Its epistemological premises show a marked functionalist/positivist orientation, favouring quantitative methodologies but sometimes also using qualitative research (e.g. Cianni and Romberger 1997; Mason 1997). In the majority of these studies, sex/gender is a *variable* (i.e. defined as women and/or men), not an analytical framework (Smircich 1985; Alvesson and Billing 1997).

Consistent with the tenets of liberal political thought, the research is premised on assumptions about the gender neutrality and universality of organization and management theory. As such, it assumes that the causes of barriers for women's equality in organizations lie in individual limitations and structural errors, rather than in problematic assumptions behind theories and concepts (e.g. Appold et al. 1998). This research argues, for instance, that attitudes, traditions and cultural norms still represent barriers to women's access to higher status and higher paying positions in the workplace despite legal sanctions against sex discrimination. Whether hierarchical organizational and management practices (i.e. normal 'meritocratic' practices) may be producers/reproducers, rather than neutral contexts, of such happenings is seldom a question.

Early women-in-management research placed strong emphasis on *psychological* variables that accounted for discrimination. Later, there has been an increasing interest in structural explanations as the emphasis shifted to *sociological*-based research. A third approach goes beyond legal remedies to address the connections of *organization and the broader social system*. Below, we briefly discuss representative themes in this literature (also see Powell 1999; Powell and Graves 2003).

Psychological and Individual Level Research

This stream of research is strongly influenced by experimental and behaviourist psychology. The topics and research approaches tend to follow that disciplinary line as part of organizational behaviour and human resources scholarship, and because there is an implicit assumption about the *neutrality of the theories*, it is difficult to find any gender-specific theoretical development among these works. That is, the questions asked, and the research approaches that followed mimic those developed and utilized in research that does not address gender.

An overriding concern in this literature is to determine if there are sex/gender differences in behaviours assessed through traditional organizational concepts such as *leadership* (e.g. Eagly and Johannesen-Schmidt 2001; Eagly and Karau 2002); *uses of power* (e.g. Ragins 1997; Cole 2004); *job stress*

(e.g. Doyle and Hind 1998; Yang 1998; Reitman and Schneer 2003); *job satisfaction* (e.g. Burke 2001; Cron 2001) and *organizational commitment* (e.g. Singh and Vinnicombe 2000). Further, in this research sex/gender-specific concepts such as *gender stereotypes* (e.g. Heilman 2001; Powell et al. 2002; Bird 2003) and *androgyny* (e.g. McGregor and Tweed 2001) seem to be of interest mostly for corrective purposes: the possibility of eliminating notions of sex/gender differences from conventional organizational practices. That is, throughout these approaches there is a reaffirmation of the gender neutrality of organizational concepts and practices as such.

There is also considerable work focusing on *human resource management* topics that could be impacted by sex/gender differences in *recruitment* (Drentea 1998; Freeman 2003); *selection* (Chapman and Rowe 2001; Guthrie et al. 2003); *performance appraisal* (Igbaria and Shayo 1997; Varma and Stroh 2001); and *pay* (Armstrong and Cornish 1997; Whitehouse et al. 2001), but also, more recently, about the acquisition of *human capital* by women (Metz and Tharenou 2001; Chênevert and Tremblay 2002) and about new work arrangement involving *technology*, such as telework, women's participation in them, and issues raised for traditional HRM systems (Zauchner et al. 2000; Perez Perez et al. 2002).

Sociological and Structural Research

Because of its more macro-structural focus, this literature can be considered organizational sociology or organization theory, but some research, such as the literature on teams, tries to integrate both structural and behavioural issues (e.g. Fenwick and Neal 2001; Anderson 2003). The majority of this work appeared after the mid-1980s, much of it inspired by Kanter (1977) and Bartol (1978). Central to these writings is a concern around the sex structuring of organizations and its consequences for traditional organizational activities and expectations. Among representative topics are the *glass-ceiling* (Ragins et al. 1998; Lyness and Thompson 2000; Meyerson and Fletcher 2000; Cotter et al. 2001; Powell and Butterfield 2002; Tharenou 2005); *organizational demography* (Kossek et al. 2003); *careers* (Linehan and Walsh 1999; Evetts 2000; Bailyn 2003; Hurley et al. 2003; Ranson 2003; Brown and Jones 2004) including some new career topics such as the effects of part time work (Warren and Walters 1998; Jacobs

1999b; Lane 2000; Caputo and Cianni 2001); and *social networks* (Ibarra 1997). Nonetheless, we could consider most research within this structural strand as *glass ceiling* research, for examining conditions that contribute to women's fair access to managerial positions has been its overriding objective.

The Organization and the Broader Social System

Within this strand is research that addresses topics of general social and legal concerns and their relationship to organizational issues. Among these are *equal opportunity, affirmative action and discrimination* (Liff and Cameron 1997; Woodall et al. 1997; Ashford et al. 1998; Cunningham et al. 1999; Duncan and Loretto 2004); *sexual harassment* (Hughes and Tadic 1998; Firestone and Harris 2003) and *work/family* issues (Lewis 1997; Kirchmeyer 1998; Milliken et al. 1998; Walters et al. 1998; Greenhaus and Parasuraman 1999; Bardoel 2003; Perrons 2003).

The academic literature on work/family issues has grown dramatically since the 1980s (e.g. Kossek and Lambert 2005; Pitt-Catsouphes et al. 2006). The topic of work/family in the women-in-management literature overlaps with old topics, such as careers (e.g. Schwartz 1996) and commitment (e.g. Osterman 1995) and newer ones, such as changing types of work, jobs and organization (e.g. Hill et al. 1998; Valcour and Tolbert 2003). Much of the research tries to specify the precise nature of interdependence between work and family domains, often asking whether work-family conflict helps or hinders organizational and/or individual outcomes or, more recently, whether family experiences may enrich work and organizations (e.g. Friedman and Greenhaus 2000; Rothbard 2001; Nordenmark 2002).

The type of problems addressed by this research and ways they are conceptualized is summed up in the situation facing Sarah Kelly. Her response, portrayed in Inset 1, that 'it's the right thing' to stay at home, is consistent with liberal political thought as it highlights 'freedom of choice', a belief which pervades US society. Yet, as a *liberal feminist* Sarah Kelly would surely agitate for reforms – reforms not frequently called for by the women-in-management literature (see Inset 2 – Sarah Kelly: a liberal feminist). The women in management literature, while often sharing the philosophical premises of liberal feminist theory, is less likely to address 'gender justice' policy implications. As we go on to discuss other feminist theories, Sarah Kelly will become our guide: as her feminist 'consciousness' changes so does the concept of work/family, its meaning and its importance, and therefore its connotation for theory and research in organization studies.

Sarah Kelly: A Liberal Feminist

As she reflects on the interview she recently gave to a journalist for an article on working moms who decide to stay home, Sarah is having second thoughts. She doubts 'it's the right thing'. Of course she believes in a woman's right to choose her life path, but why should she abandon her career to stay home with the children? After all, she obtained an excellent education and worked hard. Clearly she's making an important contribution to her community with her work. Her predecessors in the women's movement fought for the opportunities she has taken for granted. She's grateful that her rights to education and employment are no longer in question, as well as her freedom of choice to take time out from the workplace. But she also thinks that now it's her turn to continue the movement and to agitate for reforms that will make it unnecessary for women to have to choose between the work and the people they love. What's needed are some adjustments on the corporate and public policy side – Job sharing? Working from home? On site childcare? Or maybe family policies similar to those in Scandinavia that don't force women to choose between work and family. She's ready to shift gears to become an activist. After all, she's already a labour lawyer experienced in negotiation!

Radical Feminist Theory

Feminism of 'equality' in the US liberal tradition eventually spawned several types of feminisms of 'difference'. The most notable of these is radical feminism, which grew out of women's dissatisfaction with the sexism of the supposedly liberatory movements of New Left politics, the civil rights and the anti-Vietnam war movement, as well as what was considered the conservative or elitist trends in liberal feminism (Willis 1975; Gilmore 2003). It takes the subordination of women as its fundamental problematic: gender is a system of male domination, a fundamental organizing principle of patriarchal society, at the root of all other systems of oppression (Jaggar 1983). What are seen by liberal feminists as essentially personal problems within a gender-neutral system, such as failing to get a promotion, being sexually harassed or being unable to achieve orgasm, are seen here as a more general condition of the social system, as the consequence of male gender privilege in a society where the male and the masculine define the norm (Jaggar 1983).

From its 1960s roots, radical feminism developed into a wide ranging and fluid perspective, calling for the transformation not only of the legal and political structures of patriarchy, but of social and cultural institutions, such as the family, the church, the academy and even language (Daly 1978). Radical feminism's stance marked an epistemological position in which there is no distinction between 'political' and 'personal' realms: every area of life is the sphere of 'sexual politics' (Jaggar 1983: 101) and worthy of political analysis. 'Consciousness raising' developed as a method located in practice, whereby women could interrogate their experiences in light of systemic male domination. Research, from this perspective, is always 'interested'. It is a political activity, locating the origins of women's oppression in patriarchy and trying to find ways to overcome it.

Two distinct strands of thought exist within radical feminism: *libertarian* and *cultural* (Tong 1998). *Radical-libertarian feminism* developed earlier and emphasized the view that the patriarchal sex/gender system is the fundamental cause of women's oppression and should be transcended by separating notions of sex from notions of gender. They believe that the notion of 'femininity', including women's reproductive and sexual roles, is at the centre of women's oppression as they limit women's full human development. Representative scholars in this strand include Rubin (1976), Millett (1970) and Firestone (1970).

For example, Firestone (1970) argued that while women's subordination rests in biological reproductive processes, biological imperatives are overlaid by social institutions, particularly sexual and child-rearing practices, reinforcing male dominance. New and developing technology make it possible to free women from their historical reproductive roles, permitting development of a society no longer dependent upon the sexual division of labour and its

biological base. Other scholars proposed androgyny as an answer, suggesting the dualism: masculinity/ femininity could be eradicated (Ferguson 1977). A biological male or female would be culturally 'androgynous', both masculine and feminine.

Radical-cultural feminists downplayed androgyny by affirming women's essential 'femaleness'. They emphasized values often associated with women such as absence of hierarchy, nature, the body, peace, connection, emotion and so on, while rejecting values often associated with men, such as autonomy, domination, war, rationality, etc. Specifically, radical-cultural feminists took the traditional association of woman with nature (in contrast to man with culture) and found within it a source of strength and power. Because of their closer connection to nature, they claimed, women have a different way of knowing the world: emotional, non-verbal, spiritual; in contrast to patriarchal ways of knowing, relying on reason and logic (Jaggar 1983). They suggest it is possible for women to regain a sense of wholeness and connectedness to the 'authentic feminine' outside of patriarchy through a female counter culture: a cultural feminism (Echols 1983; Eisenstein 1983). Representative scholars in this strand include Daly (1978) and Rich (1979).

More generally, radical feminism is 'radical' because it is 'women centred', envisioning a new social order where women are not subordinated to men. For this purpose, it focuses on the interconnections of sexuality and power relations (Weedon 1997). It proposes alternative, often separatist, social, political, economic and cultural arrangements that challenge the values of a male-dominated culture (Koedt et al. 1973), including the values of alternative sexualities (e.g. lesbianism) as life and work organizing principles. By stressing all women's values, radical-cultural feminism has also provided a space for women of colour as well as lesbians to articulate, not unproblematically, their differences, personal and political, from white heterosexual women (e.g. Frye 1983; Lorde 1983; Moraga and Anzaldúa 1983). Yet, the radical views of women of colour tend to emphasize more fluid and flexible subjectivities than the strong essentialist positions of the radical-cultural perspectives (e.g. Alcoff 1988).

Radical Feminist Theory and Alternative Organizations

Starting in the late 1960s, radical feminists discovered and put into practice organizational forms reflecting feminist values, such as equality, community, participation and an integration of form and content (Brown 1992; Ferree and Martin 1995). In the early days of the women's liberation movement, this implied negation of leadership and negation of structure (Joreen 1973; Koen 1984). They were thus reactive in nature, seeking to reject elements associated with male forms of power.

Radical feminism focused on creating a 'woman-space' through alternative institutions and organizations to fulfil women's needs: putting medical care into women's own hands, and creating women's health centres; creating battered women's shelters and rape crisis centres as ways to address troubling violence against women; providing skills often associated with men which women traditionally lacked, such as auto mechanics and carpentry; as well as establishing cultural organizations such as bookstores, art galleries, film, music festivals, to nurture women's cultural expression. These spaces were needed to support, nurture and revalue what is devalued in 'malestream' culture.

Consciousness raising groups, forums for the collective analysis of women's oppression, were referred to as 'leaderless' and 'structureless'. Such groups sought to institutionalize equality, participation and skill development of the members (Koen 1984). While such organizational forms proved excellent for creating communities for learning, they were less effective at sustaining political action: as their energy dissipated and fragmented, groups began to dissolve. Consequently, groups began to experiment with organizational forms that were egalitarian and non-oppressive, but that also acknowledged a role for certain types of 'structure' and 'leadership' (Brown 1992).

Numerous case studies have detailed feminist organizational practices (e.g. Leidner 1991b; Hyde 1992; Farrell 1994; Reinelt 1994; Riger 1994; Ferree and Martin 1995; Balka 1997; Baines and Wheelock 2000; Colgan and Ledwith 2000; McBride 2001). Many of these organizations embrace the goals and values of radical feminism combined with attention to issues of hierarchy and organization structure similar to that found in theories of anarchy and in collectivist organizations (Iannello 1992) and several have an explicit agenda to invert the values of capitalist masculinist organization (Martin 1990b; 1993). Yet, the literature on this topic has also been criticized for a lack of structural analysis of the social conditions that promote such values (e.g. Munro 2001).

In attempting to invent feminist business and organizational practices, women confront the practical dilemma of trying to actualize equality in concrete activities. For instance, Cholmeley (1991: 228) describes her feminist business in a capitalist world as a 'living case study of a major theoretical problem of the women's liberation movement'. Struggles are documented where 'the rhetoric of equality, the collective decision-making structure, and the explicit goals of women's and community empowerment' confront differences in work styles and class, race and ethnicity conflicts (Morgen 1994: 681; also Ostrander 1999). How can equality be enacted in the face of differences of class, race, sexuality, education, skills, dependents, financial resources? The identification of a shared set of core values informing organizing activity in the women's movement does not mean that their enactment is unproblematic or uncontentious (Brown 1992), as illustrated for instance by Zilber's (2002) study of competing ideologies, feminist and professional-therapeutic, in a rape crisis centre in Israel.

Other women-centred organizations, such as the 'learning set' created by a group of women managers as a space for exploring the relationships between their experiences as women and as senior managers, may have explicitly distanced themselves from the principles of radical feminism, but their espoused values and practices mirrored the features of the earlier consciousness raising groups, as well as shared many of the dilemmas of radical feminist organizations (Fournier and Kelemen 2001). As with the other organizations discussed above, evaluating their 'success' cannot be based solely in terms of long-term survival, but on their impact on their participants' lives over time (Staggenborg 1995).

Feminist values in action are documented as challenges to the impersonality of bureaucracies, by blurring the distinction between the personal and the organizational and focusing on situations that are emotionally charged (e.g. Martin et al. 1998; Ashcraft 2001), but some contemporary studies of early feminist organizations also document that in order to survive over the years several of these organizations have developed organizational forms which combine traditional Weberian bureaucracy with various feminist values (e.g. Thomas 1999).

It may seem surprising that there is seldom any work/family organizational literature inspired by this feminist theoretical tendency, however one must recall some of the original premises of radical feminism to understand such absence (for exceptions, see Dunne (1998) and Sullivan and Lewis (2001)). Perhaps one of the most contested arguments in radical feminism is the question of 'mothering'. While radical-libertarians would consider that 'mothering' under patriarchy was part and parcel of the sex/gender system of oppression (e.g. Oakley 1974), radical-culturalist would emphasize a women's culture where mothering is valued but the patriarchal family is indicted and

replaced by feminist child-rearing. (e.g. Rich 1979). Thus, as illustrated by Sarah Kelly, one could conceive of the 'feminist organization' literature as a 'workfamily' literature (no separation between these terms), for these organizations themselves might have been intended to function as alternatives to the patriarchal family, allowing as well for 'parenting' in more ways than what might be exclusively determined by biology.

Sarah Kelly: A Radical Feminist

As she reflects on the interview she recently gave to a journalist for an article on working moms who decide to stay home, Sarah is having second thoughts. She doubts 'it's the right thing'. Thanks to her consciousness-raising group she's gained a very different perspective. And now she's full of questions. Isn't her 'personal' situation just one manifestation of the sex/gender system known as patriarchy? Why is she the one to stay home? Why not Michael? Does her biological capability to give birth make her naturally a better caretaker? Or is her situation merely a reflection of male power? She should get out of the competitive rat race into a more holistic, harmonious existence, join a women-centred organization, one expressing the emotional ways of being she is so comfortable with, maybe a legal services organization defending other women in need, and maybe bring her children to work … But, what about Michael?

Psychoanalytic Feminist Theorizing

Freud's theories of sexuality, and its application to women's *problems* in psychoanalytic practice, became objects of critique by liberal and radical feminists during the late 1960s and early 1970s. Friedan (1974) criticized Freud's biological determinism, which depicted women as defective men and encouraged their passivity. Firestone (1970) argued that women's passivity was recreated in the therapeutic encounter, which encouraged women to 'fit' into the patriarchal order represented by the nuclear family. Millett (1970) critiqued, as well, the psychoanalytic establishment for maintaining the patriarchal order as naturally determined, despite the possibility that much Freudian interpretation (e.g. the issue of women's hysteria) reflected a lack of recognition of women's very real social oppression.

Psychoanalytic feminist theorizing during the 1970s went beyond these critiques. It engaged with Freudian psychoanalysis but as a correction of its misogynist biases, or as a basis for a female-centered psychoanalytic interpretation (Mitchell 1974; Tong 1998). It also built on the groundwork laid during

the 1920s and 1930s by European feminist psychoanalysts such as Karen Horney and Melanie Klein, who engaged directly with Freud's views of femininity at the time (e.g. Garrison 1981).

Specifically, Freud proposed that to develop as normal adults, children must pass through several stages of psychosexual development. In early infancy, children, regardless of biological sex, are 'polymorphously perverse', deriving sexual pleasure from several forms of bodily stimulation. They move from this multiple and perverse sexuality toward normal heterosexual genital sexuality when they pass, successfully, through specific developmental stages. The most critical passage resides in the resolution of the Oedipus complex, i.e. the mother as object of love and desire, which appears when they are about 3 or 4 years old. For boys, the resolution of the Oedipus complex resides in their ability to transfer their love for mother into fear of father. The fear of castration by the father makes them renounce their desire for the mother and submit to the father's authority, thus developing a strong superego and eventually becoming one of the fathers. Girls resolve their Oedipal drama differently. When they realize they don't have a penis but boys do, they assume they have been castrated and start envying the superiority of the boy's (non-castrated) anatomy. Because of this, girls start rejecting their mothers and transfer their love to the (superior) father. Eventually the desire for the father is transcended by their desire to have a baby.

According to Freud, females have more difficulties attaining the mature, balanced post-Oedipal stage and in developing a normal adult sexuality. His writings are explicit about different neuroses and limitations in their psychosexual development, including references to their inferior ethical sense (Tong 1998). Women never attain men's strong superegos; they lack men's strong sense of justice; are less likely to obey authority, are more influenced by feelings rather reason. Thus, early feminist psychoanalysts criticized Freudian theory as an insensitive and inaccurate view of women's psychological make-up or rejected Freudian biological determinism and re-interpret psychoanalytic theory in terms of cultural influences, which affect women's gender identity (e.g. Adler 1927; Thompson 1964; Horney 1967).

Currently, two strands are identified within this feminist theoretical approach: the original *psychoanalytic* (Freudian) feminism and *gender-cultural* feminism. In a still influential example of *psychoanalytic feminism*, Dinnerstein (1977) focuses on the pre-Oedipal stage, and the relations between mother and child following Klein's (1948) object-relations theory. Dinnerstein argues that children learn to blame the women/mother for all that goes wrong in life because of early encounters with mothers as the basic source of their pain and pleasure. In turn, this leads to a set of gender arrangements that produces the subordination of women. Yet, critics object to the lack of differentiation in Dinnerstein's work regarding context-specific influences, and call into question what she proposes as an almost universal human condition: that women are the first parent (Flax 2002).

Meanwhile, Chodorow (1978), inspired by Winnicott's (1975) object-relations theory, emphasizes the reproduction of mothering. Boys see their mothers as different from themselves, as 'other', and eventually, during the Oedipal stage, cease to identify with them. Girls, however, never really break the connection to their mothers, whom they see as an extension of self. While girls distance themselves from their mothers during the Oedipal stage – mostly a test of the possibility of a separate identity symbolized by the father – the separation is never complete. For this reason, women find their most

solid emotional relations with other women, despite the fact that most girls develop into heterosexual women. Girls tend to have an overdeveloped capacity for relatedness in contrast to boys, but a balance is attained when girls and boys are brought up experiencing both their parents as loving and autonomous beings. Thus, changes in parenting arrangements are a way toward a less male-dominated society.

Today, the feminist revisionist impetus directed at Freudian psychoanalysis and its implications has declined. The clinical practice of psychoanalysis is receding due, among other reasons, to the impact of managed care in mental health practice. As observed by Flax (2004: 906) '[o]ne is more likely to find a serious course in psychoanalytic theory taught by a feminist literature professor than a psychologist'. This seems to be the culmination of an earlier trend in psychoanalytic feminism that regarded psychosexual development and the emergence of different notions of gendered self and identity not only a problem to be resolved by socialization, but also an epistemological problem regarding whose self-knowledge is valued and whose is devalued (e.g. Flax 1983; Braidotti 1989).

In contrast to psychoanalytic feminism, *gender-cultural feminism* does not emphasize psychosexual development, focusing instead on psychomoral development. According to Tong (1998: 154), gender-cultural feminists argue that 'boys and girls grow up into men and women with gender-specific values and virtues that (1) reflect the importance of separateness in men's lives and of connectedness in women's lives and (2) serve to empower men and disempower women in a patriarchal society'. Gender-cultural feminists speak to these issues in several ways.

Gilligan's (1982) work challenges the masculinist epistemological bases of traditional psychological research as, for instance, in Freud's contention that women did not develop a strong sense of justice. Her studies of solutions to moral dilemmas challenged Kohlberg's moral development scale by pointing out that it had been designed and normed through men's method of moral reasoning. Gilligan argued, and demonstrated empirically, that women and men have *different* concepts of justice and morality, both reasonable and well developed. She described 'male' morality as an *ethics of justice*, while 'female' morality supports an *ethics of care*.

Noddings (1984) further emphasized a feminine ethics of care, positing it as not just different, but also better than a masculine ethics of justice. She articulates the ethics of care as a form of relationship requiring an active encounter with specific individuals to care for and be cared by, similar to the mother–child relationship. In her views, developing this kind of moral caring attitude, which emerges out of natural caring memories, can be attained through education.

Aside from the ethics of care, two other themes: relational development (Miller 1976) and women's way of knowing (Goldberger et al. 1996; Belenky et al. 1997/1986) are also well known within the gender-cultural literature. As a psychoanalyst, Miller inaugurated a therapy model built on developing a connected relationship between therapist and client. This model worked toward fully developing the self as a self-in-relationship. She viewed this form of human development as a better representation of women's psychology and also as a correction to typical masculinist bias in psychotherapy. The original project on women's way of knowing (Belenky et al. 1986), on the other hand, was based on field research focusing on the way women think. Drawing from case studies, the researchers developed a theory encompassing five types of knowledge through which, they argue, women perceive themselves and approach the world. Similar to Noddings', this work focused on creating educational approaches towards realizing such forms of knowledge.[2]

In general, and consistent with its intellectual roots, psychoanalytic feminist research favours clinical approaches that connect the mind-world of individuals with their developmental experiences. While a variety of methods are used, all share an emphasis in understanding the whole person and her mode of relating to her world, for feminists within this theoretical tendency believe that 'the fundamental explanation for women's way of acting is rooted deep in women's psyche, specifically, in women's way of thinking' (Tong 1998: 131).

Not surprisingly, charges of essentialism, whether social or biological, have often been levelled at psychoanalytic and, in particular, at gender-cultural feminism, but both strands deny the biological determinism embedded in traditional psychoanalytic interpretations of gender and sexuality. Rather, they consider specific social arrangements (e.g. the patriarchal family) as leading to distinctions in male and female psychological development, which can be changed by changing the structural conditions that produce unequal gender development (Flax 1990; Tong 1998).

Others are critical of psychoanalytic feminism's representations of the 'norm(al) gendered humanity', including claims that Chodorow's analyses represent the same white, middle class, heterosexual nuclear family in capitalist societies that was at the centre of Freud's psychoanalysis (e.g. Spelman 1988; Brennan 1998). However, some have seen in Chodorow's object-relations approach a good starting point for articulating alternative identities that develop within differential conditions of race and class (e.g. Abel 1990; Flax 1990). In fact, interrogating who is the 'subject of psychoanalysis' is one of the areas where feminist psychoanalytic theorizing has made its major recent contributions, including works focusing on race, class, sexualities, ethnicities and colonialism in the formation of subjectivities that interrogate psychoanalysis (Abel et al. 1997; Cheng 2001; Nair 2002; Flax 2004; Wyatt 2004).

Psychoanalytic Feminist Theories and Women's Ways of Managing

Early 'applications' of psychoanalytic theory to women in management research focused on feminine character traits to explain women's subordinate economic status (Blum and Smith 1988). For instance, Horner (1970; 1972) posited that women's 'fear of success' stemmed from a 'basic inconsistency' between femininity and achievement that derived from their sex-role socialization. Hennig and Jardim's (1977) *The Managerial Woman* examined how early socialization experiences of males and females, and their differing resolutions of the Oedipal complex, carried over into their managerial behaviour. Most women are socialized to be passive, to see themselves as victims rather than agents, are ambivalent toward career, and lack the drive for mastery men have. Successful women managers, it was argued, have atypical relationships with their fathers.

Thus, most women fall short in the corporate culture, because the rules, norms, ethos of modern business reflect the male developmental experience (Blum and Smith 1988: 531). For women to succeed they must change themselves but, unlike the liberal feminist literature which emphasized an 'instant re-making' of women through 'dressing-for-success' or through assertiveness-training, this literature sees psychosexual development as *both* a personal and a societal issue, with cultural and historical roots (e.g. Lowe et al. 2002).

Other popularized organizational research has combined 'women's difference' arguments from feminist psychologists and psychoanalysts including Dinnerstein and Chorodow, with arguments from gender-cultural feminism, including Gilligan, Miller and Belenky, et al., and arguments from radical-cultural and from second stage liberal 'difference' feminisms. In these works, women's differences are not seen as a problem but as beneficial for both organizations and women themselves. For instance, it has been claimed that women's unique sex-role socialization, and different character traits, including an ethics of care, were not deficiencies, but *advantages* for corporate effectiveness (Helgesen 1990; Rosener 1990; Liedtka 1999).

Women's ways of knowing and leading have been studied and advocated (e.g. Freeman 1990; Rosener 1995; Amos-Wilson 2000; Mavin 2001). Women's relational skills, capacity for empathy and interpersonal sensitivity became critical human resources skills and women's 'interactive leadership' was cited as 'the management style of choice for many organizations … as the work force increasingly demands participation and the economic environment increasingly requires rapid change …' (Rosener 1990: 125). The successful union organizing drive among technical and clerical workers at Harvard University was attributed, at least in part, to the relational-practice approach of its female leadership (Hoerr 1997).

One should not forget that some 'women's' approaches to organizational structuring' favouring images of circle and web, over pyramid and chain, also suited the demands of the information economy and the team approach (Helgesen 1990). Women became, as well, a non-traditional but increasingly valuable and skillful resource for global competition (Jelinek and Adler 1988; Peters 1990; Rosener 1995). Thus, the rush towards valuing 'women's differences' occurred (co-incidentally?) at a difficult time in corporate America, concerned with leading in the global marketplace (Calás and Smircich 1993; 2004b).

Nonetheless, even from within this literature some have questioned whether 'the focus on the female advantage actually "advantages" females' (Fletcher 1994: 74) or further entrenches gender stereotypes (Rutherford 2001). The women's ways perspective has been positioned as an 'enlightened' correction to liberal-inspired research, but also criticized as in service to the instrumental ends of organizations that objectify women (Fletcher 1994; Fondas 1997; Billing and Alvesson 2000; Vieira da Cunha and Pina e Cunha 2002). Yet, several feminist organizational scholars also find within this perspective a way to challenge the status quo by emphasizing the power of relational activities (Calvert and Ramsey 1992; 1994; Jacques 1993; Marshall 1995; Fletcher 1998; 2001; Fletcher and Jacques 1998).

Today, while perhaps in a less celebratory tone, 'women's ways' influences are still present in the literature (e.g. Hughes 2000; Eagly and Carli 2003), including in debates over the possibility of a feminine ethics (e.g. Wicks 1996; Larson and Freeman 1997; White 1999; Adam and Ofori-Amanfo 2000; Lampe 2001), of an African American women's leadership approach (Parker and Ogilvie 1996) and of relational practices that would transform organizations (Buttner 2001), or that could account for women's different, 'kaleidoscope', careers (Mainiero and Sullivan 2005).

Finally, concerning work/family, some recent research questions the devaluation of 'caring work' (Rasmussen 2001; McKie et al. 2002), while others address the place of maternity in modern organizations (e.g. Ashcraft 1999). Starting from women-centred approaches, most of these works resist incorporation by the mainstream management discourse, seeking more fundamental organizational transformations rather than celebrating or essentializing 'women's way'. Hence, this is how Sarah Kelly will make it happen.

Sarah Kelly: A Psychoanalytic Feminist

As she reflects on the interview she recently gave to a journalist for an article on working moms who decide to stay home, Sarah is having second thoughts. She doubts 'it's the right thing'. Sarah realizes her thoughts reflect the child-rearing practices, parenting patterns and socialization of earlier decades. She, as well as her husband and their friends, might be trapped in a mode of thinking about what mothers and fathers should do. If she's the one who stays home with the children, won't she just be reproducing and perpetuating these patterns? Maybe she and her husband will commit to dual and equal parenting. Together they'll forge new patterns of relating that will erode the patriarchal patterns to which they've contributed. On the other hand, maybe her feminine values: love, trust, authenticity – so important to raising children – should be what pervades not only the home, but the workplace and the world as well. Time for the women's way of managing to be valued and for Dads to stay at home.

In Summary: The Woman's Condition: Same or Different?

The three feminist theoretical tendencies examined in this section, liberal, radical and psychoanalytic, have been, in each case, preoccupied with the status of women in society. The signs are visible that equality for women in a male-dominated society is still a distant goal, which leads to the continued examination of this problem, and to different approaches for its understanding and resolution.

Liberal 'difference' feminism shares with radical and psychoanalytic theories a conviction that there is something specific about women in society that could account for their difficulties and serve as the basis for needed resolutions. It is not surprising, therefore, that each of these theoretical tendencies has been charged with 'essentialism', in particular the charge that in privileging a 'woman's difference' they are also recreating conditions for their continued discrimination (e.g. Elshtain 1981). In that sense, traditional liberal 'sameness' feminism, while less likely to examine the gender norms to which it aspires – i.e. that to be 'equal' is to occupy the position of dominant members of society, usually privileged white men – is also less likely to fall into essentialist debates, making it easier to advocate 'women's equal rights' in agendas for social and institutional changes.

However, as demonstrated by Scott (1988) an equality/difference debate is a fallacy, for these are not opposite notions but rather functional terms that describe legal rights (equality) and socio/cultural conditions (difference). Arguing for both equality *and* difference may be a more appropriate way to address women's current inequalities. All these tendencies, whether addressing sameness or differences, have also been criticized for foregrounding a 'woman' who is usually white, Euro-American, middle class, heterosexual and, therefore, that the theories do not always address and sometimes even deny the validity of other women's experiences, their oppressions and discrimination.

Significantly, in the organizational and management literature most women-in-management research, despite its volume and apparent variety, fails to recognize that there are strong political implications even in liberal feminism. Attaining basic feminist goals of equality might imply very fundamental organizational changes, not small corrections in what is taken to be, ultimately, a rational

and just system and a desired state of affairs (i.e. organizational rationality, its goals and values). Moreover, this literature, as its name illustrates, is explicitly elitist in the sense that it is skewed towards managerial women rather than addressing the conditions of *all* women in organizations, as would be a goal of liberal feminism.

There are exceptions, including research addressing race and gender, which tend to be more critical of both traditional organizational goals and conditions, and traditional organizational research (e.g. Betters-Reed and Moore 1991; Bell et al. 1993; Maume 1999; Bell 2000; Combs 2003; Holvino 2003). Further, much of the European literature on 'women in organizations' inspired by the equality tenets of liberalism exhibits a 'social issues' sensibility when addressing topics such as discrimination by sexual orientation (Busby and Middlemiss 2001), gendered leadership (Højgaard 2002) and sex segregation in careers (Tienari 1999).

Other organizational scholars, mostly under the inspiration of liberal 'difference' feminism, have been willing to incorporate insights from radical and psychoanalytic theories and revise approaches and practices of organizational research and theorizing. Starting from 'women centred theorizing', theorizing from the lives and experiences of women, including Black women, a number of scholars have been re-visioning organizational concepts such as career, personality, leadership, the glass ceiling, negotiation and so on (e.g. Marshall 1984; 1995; Martin 1993; Gray 1994; Tancred 1995; Boucher 1997; Putnam and Kolb 2000; Aaltio-Marjosola and Kovalainen 2001; Bell and Nkomo 2001; Liff and Ward 2001; Wilson and Thompson 2001; Bailyn 2004; Marshall and Witz 2004).

Yet, the most important 'women's difference' argument in each feminist theory discussed above deals with the question of *women as bearers and rearers of children, and the valuing/devaluing in society of mothering experiences and activities*. Thus, it is ironic that despite the ongoing increase in research addressing work/family issues, the organizational literature has barely examined this topic through 'women's centred theorizing'.

As forwarded by Martin (1990a) and documented, for instance, by Rudin and Byrd (2003), work/family literature, in particular the US research, is strongly oriented towards benefiting organizations (i.e. the *work* side of work/family). The 'family' side of work/family is, more often than not, a code term that functions to make 'mothers' invisible because it avoids focusing on the value of reproduction and caring activities at home from which organizations receive 'free benefits'. This literature ignores, for instance, the extra burden on families from changing working conditions (e.g. Powell 1998). This emphasis has not gone without acknowledging that policies that benefit families can also benefit organizations (Bailyn et al. 1997; Rapoport et al. 2002). However, what have not been called into question are problems inherent in the concept of work/family. A 'workfamily' literature true to 'women's difference' feminist theorizing would put women's work at the centre of analysis, in particular women's work as mothers, placing family and the value of parenting more generally on equal footing with all other value-creating institutions in society, including business organizations.

In short, while women-in-management research inspired by liberal feminism provides much needed documentation regarding inequalities between men and women in organizations, in taking a 'how to succeed' perspective it tends to be uncritical of the gendered (male) nature of organizations – including the organization of organizational research and theorizing. Organization studies research, if further inspired by radical and psychoanalytic feminisms, would put the perspectives and practices of women at the centre of analyses. As observed by Ferguson (1994: 90), it would privilege 'the world as seen from this set of vantage-points, thus problematizing the conventional equation of men with humanity'. What this means for organizational researchers is well articulated by Segal (1996: 75), in that it would convey 'the importance of organizational experiences in shaping their identities, specifically in relationship to their awareness of gender, and conversely how their identities in turn affect the way the research approaches and makes sense of their lives inside and beyond organizations'.

Gendering: Power Relations, Identities, Discourses, Subjectivities, Without Borders

In this section we discuss socialist, poststructuralist/ postmodern and transnational/(post)colonial feminist theoretical tendencies, and contemporary trends emerging from their blending and interweaving. It would be simplistic to claim easy commonalities among these perspectives, but they do share an aim to complicate notions of 'gender' as primarily referring to specifically sexed bodies. As they see it, gender(ing) as *social(ly) system(ic)* is a process, produced and reproduced through relations of power among differently positioned members of society, including relations emerging from historical processes, dominant discourses and institutions and dominant epistemological conceptualizations, all of which become naturalized as 'the way it is'.

In their contemporary modes, these feminist tendencies regard social and economic structuring, subjectivities and sexualities and transnational processes as simultaneously implicated in systems of knowledge and knowledge production. They are critically focused on analysing the dynamics that articulate relations of oppression and subordination for many, not only women, within the complexities of gendered/racialized/classist/homophobic/Eurocentric/knowledge systems, historically and at present, to denaturalize their sustaining assumptions through varieties of analytical engagements.

These tendencies consider insufficient feminist projects attempting to address 'the women's condition' for their focus on women's oppression and discrimination leaves unattended how these conditions are effects of multiply related processes contributing to their reproduction. Critique and rethinking for changing conditions should start from the complex structuring of social, economic, cultural and knowledge relations, as relations of power, in which gendered (and other) identities and subjectivities are thus formed. Table 1.8.2 summarizes the perspectives discussed in this section.

Socialist Feminist Theorizing

Socialist feminism is a confluence of Marxist, radical and psychoanalytic feminism resulting from Marxist feminists' dissatisfaction during the 1970s with the gender-blind character of Marxist thought and the tendency of traditional Marxism to dismiss women's oppression as not nearly as important as workers' oppression (Ferguson 1998; Holmstrom 2002). Marxist feminists, concerned with women's double oppression of both class and sex, *added* gender to the analytical interests of Marxism to 'correct for' its inattention to gender dynamics. Following traditional Marxist theory, a class struggle between labour and capital was at the centre of analysis; yet, Marxist feminists analysed as well the ongoing productive and

Table 1.8.2 Gendering: power relations, identities, discourses, subjectivities, without borders

School of thought	Socialist	Poststructuralist/Postmodern	Transnational/(Post)colonial
Intellectual roots	Emerged in the 1970s as part of women's liberation movements' attempt to synthesize Marxist, psychoanalytic and radical feminisms	Located in contemporary French poststructuralist critiques of 'knowledge', 'identity' and 'subjectivity'	Emerging from intersections of gendered critiques of Western feminisms and postcolonial critiques of Western epistemologies
Conception of human nature	Human nature is created historically and culturally through dialectical interrelations between human biology, society and human labour	Decentring of the rational, self-same subject of humanism. 'Subjectivity' and 'consciousness' are discursive effects	Analysed as a Western construct that emerged by making its 'other' invisible or 'almost human'. Also 'strategic essentialism'; 'hybrid subjectivities'
Conception of sex/gender	Gender is processual and socially constituted through several intersections of sex, race, sexuality, ideology and experiences of oppression under patriarchy-capitalism	Sex/gender are discursive practices and social performances that constitute specific subjectivities through power, resistance and the materiality of human bodies	Considers the constitution of complex subjectivities beyond Western conceptions of sex/gender focusing on gendered aspects of globalization and transnational processes
Conception of 'the good society'	The 'good society' has eliminated all systems of private/public oppression based on sex, gender, race, class, etc. and thus, transformed social relations	The 'good society' requires ongoing deconstruction and denaturalization of discourses and practices that constitute it	The 'good society' is a Western ideology produced through colonial relationships and through contemporary neoliberal policies. Other social relations are possible
Epistemological positions	Feminist standpoints represent a particular historical condition of oppression that is more adequate for understanding contemporary society	'Epistemology' is problematized by the heterogeneity of subject positions and social identities – i.e. there is no 'subject of knowledge' to sustain it	'Knowledge' is a system of power relations deployed by the 'West' on 'the rest'. Other's knowledges/subjectivities are possible

(Continued)

Table 1.8.2 (Continued)

School of thought	Socialist	Poststructuralist/Postmodern	Transnational/(Post)colonial
Some favoured methodologies	Case studies, institutional ethnographies, ethnomethodology focus on micro-social activities and practices as they connect to macro-social processes	Textual analyses, deconstruction, Foucauldian genealogies, queering institutions	Textual analyses, post-colonial deconstructions/reconstructions, testimonial writings, hybrid representations
Conceptualization of sex/gender in/and organization	Organizations are systems of gender/race/class power relations and practices emerging through intersections of, or patriarchy-capitalism. Organizations produce and reproduce this system	'Organizations' as primary signifiers in the general text of our society. 'Gender' and other discourses and discursive practices constitute organizations' conditions of possibility and subject positions	'Organizations' as institutions of the colonizer; exist in historical relations to other people of the world. Transnational corporations/organizations are primary actors in the perpetuation of race/gender/sex relations of modernities
Needed organizational change	Because organizations are relational systems, change must start by understanding them as processes, their production and reproduction	Discourses of 'organization' (i.e. theory and practice) should be denaturalized. 'Gender/race/class/sexualities' as other's subject position	To address intersections of gender-sex/racio-ethnicities, with questions of 'the nation', 'the state' and their complicity with transnational institutions. To articulate the other's knowledge
Some favoured interventions	Analysis of intersections of capitalism/gender stratification	Deconstructive, genealogical analyses in sites of 'pedagogy'; queering organizations through performance that expose the norm	Analysis of intersections of capitalism/imperialism/global-economy Deconstructing 'development' and other modernization activities; 'following hybrid networks'

reproductive gender dynamics of patriarchal, capitalist organization of economy-society, highlighting that though a hierarchy exists among men through a system of class, men as a group dominate and control women as a group, through a system of gender. As such, gender inequality persists and will not change without major structural changes (Jaggar 1983; Delphy 1984; Lorber 1994).

Consistent with Marxist theory's views on human nature, socialist feminist perspectives conceptualize gender and gender identity as structural, historical and material, and analyse how identities are constructed through social practices such as work, observing that power and sexuality are interwoven in work relations. Gender is theorized dynamically in processual and material ways – more than a socially constructed, binary identity – as 'a constitutive element of social relationships based on perceived differences between the sexes, and [...] a primary way of signifying relationships of power' (Scott 1986: 1067).

These perspectives claim to incorporate several positive insights of psychoanalytic and radical feminist theories while overcoming most of their limitations. In particular, socialist feminists critique radical and psychoanalytic feminism because they exhibit universalizing tendencies, assuming (western) patriarchal conditions as a normative phenomenon with limited regard for culture or historical circumstances. Further, radical feminism is criticized as naïve for suggesting that there could be a separate 'women's culture' under patriarchy *and* capitalism, while liberal feminism is seen as totally inadequate for explaining the subordinate position of women in the economy. The capitalist economy is *not* best described through such concepts as market forces, exchange patterns, supply and demand, as liberal/classic economic theory posits; rather, capitalist economy should be analysed by focusing on *relations of inequality and power*.

In this sense, then, work organizations and the family are important sites for analysing the ongoing reproduction of sex/gender inequality for they expose the relationships between patriarchy *and* capitalism. Socialist feminists employed two main approaches for analysing this: dual-systems theory and unified-systems theory. Dual systems consider capitalism and patriarchy as separate, but related to one another dialectically. Capitalism is seen as a material, historically rooted mode of production, but patriarchy is considered either as a material or

an ideological structure. For example, Mitchell (1974) takes inspiration from feminist psychoanalytic theory and observes that a woman's status and function in a patriarchal system are ideologically determined by her role in production, reproduction, the socialization of children and sexuality. Hartmann (1981a, b), by contrast, considers patriarchy as a material structure and argues that a Marxist analysis of capitalism needs to be complemented with a feminist analysis of patriarchy: the different forms of men's interest in the domination of women. Thus the 'family wage' is negotiated by men to maintain wives' servitude and subordination at home; the 'dual income family' has not really changed the patriarchal situation: women in the workforce remain underpaid and overworked as they bear the major responsibilities for housework and family nurturance.

Dual-systems theories have not been without their critics (e.g. Young 1980; Folbre 1987). In particular, Young's unified-system approach sees materialist accounts of patriarchy as promoting a separate-spheres model of family and economy that does not question when and how the public/private split came about and is maintained. She also argues that patriarchy as a psychological construct could be falsely regarded as being less oppressive to women than capitalist economic oppression. What is needed is a single theory that explains gender-biased capitalist patriarchy, the concept of *gendered division of labour*. Through this concept, Young highlights how capitalism developed historically and continues to be reproduced through the marginalization of women as a secondary labour force.

Importantly, socialist feminist theorists have been concerned with epistemological issues: not only what is to be known but also how knowledge is constituted and for what purposes. Theoretical developments such as *standpoint theory* (e.g. Smith 1979; Hartsock 1983; Code 1998, Harding 2004a, b), *institutional ethnography* (Smith 1987) and analyses of *intersectionalities* (Moraga and Anzaldúa 1983; Anzaldúa 1987; 1990; Crenshaw 1989; 1991; King 1988) stand out among these.

Standpoint theory has a long trajectory of debate and often confusing understandings (e.g. Hekman 1997, and comments that followed; also Harding 2004a). In Code's (1998: 180) words:

[a] feminist standpoint is not to be confused with a 'women's standpoint', which would be theirs just by

virtue of their femaleness; nor it is merely an interchangeable perspective which anyone could occupy just by deciding to do so. On the contrary, it is a hard-won product of consciousness-raising and social-political engagement that exposes the false presuppositions upon which patterns of domination and subordination are built and sustained.

Harding (2004b) emphasizes the aims of standpoint projects to engage epistemologically, to advance the growth of knowledge in the social *and* the natural sciences. Yet, in order to do so, standpoint projects 'require both science and politics' (Harding 2004b: 30) for addressing institutionalized knowledge systems that may deny legitimacy to other knowledges. 'Standpoint theory shifts the question from how to eliminate politics from science to two different questions: which politics advance and which obstruct the growth of knowledge; and, for whom (for which groups) does such politics advance or obstruct knowledge?' (Harding 2004b: 30–1). Thus, consistent with its Marxist theory roots, *standpoint* is both the formation of a subject(ivity) *and* a form of knowledge which function strategically such that oppressed groups are able to survive their subordination within a social order and, at the same time, gain the means for undermining that order through other forms of knowledge.

An early proponent of standpoint theory, Smith (1979), developed the notion of institutional ethnography as a sociological approach *for* women (rather than *of* women). Starting from a women's standpoint as a *point of entry* into the everyday world, institutional ethnography focuses on encounters and relations between 'the everyday' and the institutions that produce conceptual practices and activities as extra-local, objectified *relations of ruling* (Smith 1987). Analysis proceeds from the experiences of women in their everyday/everynight lives and the organizational practices outside their experiences that define, nonetheless, how their life should be lived. Institutional ethnography has provided important epistemological and methodological insights for critical feminist research and activism (e.g. Campbell 2002; Coffield 2002; DeVault and McCoy 2002), including focusing on racial and ethnic aspects of research that may otherwise go unnoticed (e.g. DeVault 1995).

Feminists of colour have further articulated theoretical constructs such as *intersectionality* to refer to the simultaneity and linkages of oppressions in the intersections of race, class, gender, sexuality, etc., aiming to understand these *as processes and outcomes* in the context of social structuring (e.g. Collins 1986; 1998; Hurtado 1989; Essed 1991; Crenshaw 1995; Glenn 1999; Williams 2004). Sometimes, though, these arguments have been confused with other notions of 'intersection', articulated in more functionalist terms, that end up 'ranking' different oppressions, or forwarding an additive model that reduces possibilities for dynamic representations (West and Fenstermaker 1995a, b; McCall 2005).

To be clear, *intersectionality* is an analytical approach that affirms the importance of multiple categories of oppression *emphasizing their simultaneity and fluidity*, and thus going beyond their mere intersections. The focus is on what is produced (i.e. racing, classing, sexualizing, etc.) at these intersections, unveiling how power clusters around them and how other forms of oppression may appear. It is also from intersectionalities that agency and political projects would emerge, for example by reconceptualizing *race* as a coalition between men and women of colour or between straight and gay people of colour. Crenshaw (1991/1995: 375) indicates that 'intersectionality might be [...] broadly useful as a way of mediating the tension between assertions of multiple identities and the ongoing necessity of group politics'. Further critical analytics of race include explicit considerations of *whiteness* as a racialized identity (Frankenberg 1993; Cuomo and Hall 1999).

Socialist feminist theoretical tendencies are also implicated in what Hearn (2004) calls critical studies of men, a range of studies that critically address men in the context of gendered power relations. Many would associate this view with notions of *masculinity* and, in particular, *hegemonic masculinity*, widely used in the gender literature (e.g. Connell 1987; 1995; 2005; Hearn 1996; Nye 2005). Recently, however, Hearn (2004: 49, emphasis in original) proposes a move 'from masculinity to men, to focus on "the hegemony of men"' noticing 'the double complexity that men are both a *social category formed by the gender system* and [...] *often dominant collective and individual agents, of social practices*' (2004: 49, emphasis in original).

In general, research inspired by socialist feminism favours case studies, ethnomethodological and ethnographic methods, that make visible the informal and invisible processes of segregation, inaccessible to those who favour survey research. Empirical work shows how gendered assumptions are embedded in societal expectations and how they interact with institutional rules and practices. It reveals the micro-processes and practices constitutive of macro-social and economic structural arrangements (West and Zimmerman 1987; Acker 1990; Greene et al. 2002). Under these premises, socialist feminists have highlighted the importance of analytical integration of social structure and human agency in explaining the persistence of gender segregation and gendered and other oppressions (e.g. Wharton 1991), with the ultimate aim of social critique and social transfomation.

Socialist Feminist Theorizing and the Gendering of Organizing

Historically, the transition from agrarian to industrial modes of production created the separation of workplace and home, and produced a gendered structure where women and men work in different jobs, in different industries and in different organization levels (Crompton and Sanderson 1990; Alpern 1993; Crompton 1999). The unequal and persistent sex-based patterns in employment, observable across multiple industries and situations, are referred to variously as the *gendered division of labour*, the *sexual division of labour*, the *sex structuring* of *organizations* and *occupational sex segregation* (Acker and Van Houten 1974; Game and Pringle 1984; Reskin and Roos 1990; Reskin 2000) and is the focus of much organizational research under this feminist perspective. According to this view, the sexual division of labour is a basic characteristic of capitalist society (Jaggar 1983), which affects men as well as women.

Acker's (1990; 1992; 1994; 1998; 2004) formulation of the interrelation of gendered practices with a gender substructure of organization has been enormously influential in the last decade, serving as a theoretical foundation for much contemporary 'gendered organization' scholarship (Britton 2000; Martin and Collinson 2002), and stimulating much empirical research. Together, studies taking a 'gendered organization perspective' begin to illuminate how changing organizations is much more than a matter of bringing in more female/other bodies.

As conceptualized by Acker, persistent structuring of organizations along gender lines is reproduced in a number of ways. One is through

ordinary, daily procedures and decisions that segregate, manage, control and construct hierarchies in which gender, class and race are involved (e.g. Tolich and Briar 1999). The 'vicious circles of job segregation' are played out in recruiting and promoting practices (Collinson et al. 1990; Rubin 1997; Wajcman 1998; Healy 1999; Wallace 1999) and work restructuring (Khan 1999; Stanworth 2000; Rasmussen 2001; Jenkins et al. 2002). When firms hire part-time workers, they tend to be women, thereby increasing the proportion of women at the lowest levels of the organization (Blackwell 2001); but this also affects the notion of 'flexible work' in which women are over-represented (Brewer 2000; Fagan 2001; Jenkins 2004; Sheridan 2004).

Gendering, racing, sexualizing of organizations also occurs through symbols, images, ideologies that legitimate inequalities and differences (Acker 1990; 1992; Gherardi 1994; 1995; Bell and Nkomo 2001; Ward 2004), including intersections of race and gender in the labour market (Browne and Misra 2003). Symbolic processes are also associated with work activities leading to gendered jobs. They constitute the gendered 'opportunity structures' (Kanter 1977) through which sexed bodies get allocated, for example in academia (e.g. Martin 1994b; Goode and Bagilhole 1998; Katila and Meriläinen 1999; 2002; Knights and Richards 2003) or when entrepreneurship (Mirchandani 1999; Bruni et al. 2004), insurance sales (Leidner 1991a) and temporary work (Gottfried 2003) are constituted as gendered. Gender structuring persists through wage setting practices and job evaluation schemes with embedded gender assumptions, resulting in the undervaluing of the interpersonal dimensions of work, such as nurturing, listening, empathizing. 'Caring work' is 'women's work' and caring work pays less (e.g. Folbre 2001).

Gender structuring, embodiment and embeddedness are also produced through social interactions that enact dominance and submission (Acker 1990; 1992; Cockburn 1991; Hall 1993; Halford et al. 1997; Rantalaiho and Heiskanen 1997; Martin 2003b). Analysis of conversations shows how gender differences in interruptions, turn-taking and setting the topic of discussion recreate gender inequality in the flow of ordinary talk (West and Zimmerman 1987), so that organization itself is shown to be a gendered communication act (Mills and Chiaramonte 1991; Buzzanell 1995). Identity making processes, for example, the choice of appropriate work, use of language, style of clothing and the presentation of self as a gendered member of an organization also contribute to structuring along gendered lines (Acker 1990; Korvajärvi 1998; Trethewey 2000; Kang 2003).

Images of the ideal organization member, the top manager and the organizational hero tend to be those of forceful masculinity (e.g. Benschop and Doorewaard 1998a, b ; Prokos and Padavic 2002) or 'machismo' (Stobbe 2005). Other work references masculinity/ies in terms of intrapersonal dimensions (e.g. including an individual's view of self and of success) and interpersonal dimensions of corporate masculinity (e.g. approaches to conflict) (Maier 1999). Researchers' attentions are also being drawn to 'men' as a social category, with examination of masculinities, management and organization (e.g. Collinson and Hearn 1994; 1996).

Martin (2001) further differentiates between individual men's 'doing of masculinities' and collectivities of men 'mobilizing masculinity', by which she refers to practices where two or more men concertedly bring into play masculinity/ies. This distinction is important for exploring the social consequences for women of men's relational work with men and for patterns that come to constitute organizational cultures. Of course, masculinity is not only practiced by men, as shown in Forbes' (2002) study of black women managers, centred on the ways in which internalized masculinity is manifested in their actions and self-understandings. Thus, women, as well as men, are active participants in the re-production of masculinity in organizations.

An interesting aspect of this process occurs when men enter 'women's jobs' (Cross and Bagilhole 2002) and women enter 'men's jobs' (Miller 2004). Cross and Bagilhole's interviews with men as a minority working in various 'caring' jobs revealed how they either attempted to maintain a traditional masculinity by distancing themselves from female colleagues, and/or partially reconstructed a different masculinity by identifying with feminine features of their non-traditional occupations. Yet, either way, these worked to maintain their dominance. Miller's study of women engineers in the oil industry, by contrast, details the 'dense cultural web of masculinities' created through everyday interactions, the values and beliefs of engineering as an occupation, and the powerful symbols of the frontier myth. As women develop coping strategies within this context, their efforts have a double-edge quality: while

achieving some measure of individual gain, little is done to disrupt the powerfully masculine culture.

Much of the empirical work in this area looks at masculinity practices within specific contexts, e.g. in relation to gendered organizational cultures in the airlines (e.g. Mills 1998; Ashcraft and Mumby 2004), in mining (Eveline and Booth 2002), in managerial discourse and practices such as business process engineering (Knights and McCabe 2001); in academic settings (e.g. Sinclair 1995; Roper 1996; Katila and Merilainen 1999); in the tourism and leisure industry (Guerrier and Adib 2004); or in nightclub security work (Monaghan 2002).

In short, 'doing organization' and 'management', whether practicing or theorizing organization, implies 'doing gender' (West and Zimmerman 1987; Brooks and MacDonald 2000; Roper 2001; Benschop and Brouns 2003; Kovalainen 2004). This is well illustrated in one of the few organizational change projects undertaken with socialist feminist theory as a guiding framework (Coleman and Rippin 2000; Ely and Meyerson 2000; Meyerson and Kolb 2000). With a view of gender as both an organizing principle and an axis of power, the researcher/consultants conceived change strategies with manufacturing workers and corporate executives, aiming to advance gender equity while also seeking to increase organizational effectiveness.

In their self-critical analysis, the researchers acknowledge that the project ultimately failed because of contradictions in trying to advance a 'dual agenda' (gender equity and organizational effectiveness). In this process, they 'lost gender'. Hearn (2000: 620), in his comments on the project, indicates, 'it suggests that there is a strong case for examining the simultaneous and mutually reinforcing occurrence of gendering and organizing', while Acker (2000: 631), also commenting on this project, observes 'their experience tells us a great deal about how power in organizing processes perpetuates gender inequity'.

Finally, the persistent structuring of organizations along gender lines is supported and sustained by the gendered substructure of organizations, for example, the practices related to the 'extra-organizational reproduction of members' (Acker 1994: 118). Women are the 'hidden providers' in the economy (Stoller 1993: 153), for the physical and social reproduction of employees happens outside the workplace and is done primarily, but not always by women (e.g. Brandth and Kvande 2002), most of it as unpaid work (Gibson 1992; Folbre 1994).

Smith's institutional ethnography is especially well-positioned for analysis of the gendered sub-structure of organizations. For example, Griffith and Smith's (1987; 2005) research with mothers of school children shows how the 'labour of mothering' is hooked into the requirements of 'a school day', the work of the teacher and the functioning of the school system. Suggestions for how 'parents' (read mothers) could promote reading skills, for instance, presuppose resources of time, effort and skills on the part of the parent, as well as physical materials and space. As Griffith and Smith's research demonstrates, teachers routinely transfer some of the work of schooling to mothers without cost to the school, and this 'free good' of 'donated' labour supports the school's functioning.

What accounts for mother's willingness to contribute in this way? In their interviews with women with school-age children, Griffith and Smith came upon what they called 'the mothering discourse', related to the earlier 'discourse of domesticity' that arose in North America in the earlier 20th century, associated to the rise of the new middle class organized around education, credentials and career-structured occupations and the professions (e.g. Williams 2000). As this research helps us see, the educational system exercises leverage over mothers, in particular, as they have been inculcated with an understanding of themselves and their responsibilities as part of the educational system. This example can be easily extrapolated to other unpaid work happening in the 'local' family context as a matter of course, done to fulfil the often invisible 'requirements' of an 'extra-local' institution (e.g. a business organization) who is the ultimate beneficiary.

As Sarah Kelly's socialist feminist standpoint now reveals, the private sphere cannot be separated from the public one; organizations, families and societies are mutually constituted through gender, race, class and so on, relations of domination and subordination (e.g. Gibson, 1992; Procter and Padfield 1999). Her 'personal' situation needs to be understood historically, culturally and ideologically, as part of 'domesticity', a gender system organizing market and family work and providing the gender norms that reproduce such organization.

Sarah Kelly: A Socialist Feminist

As she reflects on the interview she recently gave to a journalist for an article on working moms who decide to stay home, Sarah is having second thoughts. She doubts 'it's the right thing'. The situation she faces is not really a matter of 'choice', but of constraint. Despite their equal years of education and employment, her husband earns more money than she, so it's 'reasonable' for her to be the one to stay at home. Thanks to her study of standpoint theory, Sarah realizes that her situation reflects the gendered division of labour under patriarchy *and* capitalism. Her unpaid labour at home will support its continuation. Beyond that Sarah notes that she and her husband as well educated, white middle class, heterosexuals with professional jobs can afford for her take some time out from work; but many others aren't so privileged. Her nanny Julia Peña has just learned she's pregnant with twins and she's really worried about how she'll cope. Over a cup of tea the two women and their friends, of different class backgrounds, races and ethnicities, talk with increasing intensity about their alienation and frustration. Globalization, downsizing, the 24/7 economy – it's not only outside in the workplace but inside the homespace. What's needed they realize is not simply individual action, but a total re-organization of the modes of production and re-production in today's society. No small goal, but one that their foremothers in the late 19th and early 20th century who sought to overcome the split between domestic life and public life created by industrial capitalism, would surely recognize.

Poststructuralist/Postmodern Feminist Theorizing

Feminist poststructuralist and postmodern approaches were recognized as such during the 1980s, becoming more clearly articulated, as well as contested, during the 1990s. Their influence continues with reformulated notions and in conversation with contemporary concerns in philosophy and social theory, including questioning the ontological status of the body and the subject, and debating the subsequent implications for agency and politics (e.g. Alcoff 2000; Braidotti 2002; Butler 2004; Salih and Butler 2004).

The move towards poststructuralist/postmodern theorizing in the humanities and the social sciences is captured by the phrase the 'linguistic turn', due to its usual association with de Saussure's (1974) structural linguistics. A core insight is that the relationship between signifier and signified is contingent – i.e. the sign we use to signify anything is only meaningful because we are able to *differentiate* it from another sign rather than because it *names* any essential object or concept. The priority of language over thought is thus established, for language as a system of differences is *constitutive* of the things we can think/know rather than simply *representative* of them.

This view reveals the instability of language as a representational form: language is malleable insofar as it is not located in any 'essential character' of its representation. Such an insight fostered poststructuralist views on language as a *system of signification* that is not only malleable, but also ambiguous and excessive: a single term can signify a multiplicity of things and ideas. Thus, the possibility of universal and generalizable knowledge based on fixed and stable language, which grounded much of the Enlightenment (i.e. modern) epistemologies, was called into question.

On one hand, 'knowledge' is given to us only as a representation: for example, we learn as we read about something assumed to exist outside of the text, but we have immediate knowledge only of the textual representation. On the other hand, that which is represented in language has never been outside of language: it is through language that researchers constitute the subject of their investigations (what is to be researched, paid attention to, ignored) and their own subjectivities. It is through language that we can 'tell' who we 'are'. In this argument, 'knowledge' ends up being nothing but the difference from that which is 'not knowledge'; a representation that depends on an often devalued, invisible 'other' for its legitimization.

The interrogation of modern knowledge by poststructuralist/postmodern theorizing brought further moments of reflexivity to feminist theorizing. Specifically, while liberal and Marxist theories provided positive but alternative groundings for feminist knowledge, poststructuralist approaches questioned 'positive knowledge' as we know it, and in so doing 'periodized' the Enlightenment's (i.e. modern) philosophical and scientific traditions, including the existence of transcendental reason, and the possibility of objective knowledge. These approaches, in scrutinizing the ontological and epistemological claims of modern theories, their foundationalism, essentialism and universalism, questioned as well the claims of many feminist theories in so far as they articulated a 'privileged knowing subject' (e.g. women's experience; women's standpoint), an 'essential feminine' and a general representation of 'woman'.

Some feminist theorists expressed ambivalence toward postmodern/poststructuralist approaches, considering it risky for women to abandon modern projects concerning knowing the 'good', the 'true' and the 'beautiful', as women rarely had the opportunity to contribute to their theorization (Nicholson 1990). Others claimed that postmodern relativism denied core values that would otherwise legitimate theories of knowledge (e.g. Harding 1990) and morality (e.g. Benhabib 1984), based on women's standpoints and needs. Concerns were voiced that feminist politics was not yet strong enough to withstand a de-centred politics that would preclude women from speaking from a unified subject position (Di Stefano 1988); and that postmodernism's abandoning of universal categories would imply abandoning the category 'gender' in favour of endless difference attached to human bodies, rendering a coherent theory and politics impossible (e.g. Bordo 1990).

Yet advocates asserted that 'postmodern-feminist theory would replace unitary notions of woman and feminine gender identity with plural and complexly constructed conceptions of social identity, treating gender as one relevant strand among others, attending also to class, race, ethnicity, age, …' (Fraser and Nicholson 1988: 393). By recognizing the heterogeneity within the apparently unitary category 'gender', political engagement was possible to the extent women were willing to make up 'a patchwork of overlapping alliances, not one circumscribable by an essential definition' (Fraser and Nicholson 1988: 394). Flax (1987) articulated a politics of heterogeneity, arguing that partiality and difference are the reality of everyday social relations. Any view that conceives the world to be otherwise mystifies and disempowers alternative political engagements.

Feminist theories would then engage directly in demonstrating the unstable, complex and ambiguous 'nature' of social reality (e.g. de Lauretis 1984; 1987). For example, Alcoff (1988) proposed the notion of positionality for locating 'woman' as a relative identity, both flexible and agential. Ferguson

(1993: 183) considered the possibility of mobile subjectivities 'prepared to accept the partiality of any set of solutions to public problems and the necessity of continued political struggle', which, similar to Haraway's (1985: 73) cyborg imagery, offered 'affinity, not identity'. More recently, discussions about possibilities for feminist methodologies 'after' postmodernism have also appeared (e.g. St. Pierre and Pillow 2000; Villenas 2000; Lather 2001; Schneider 2002; Fonow and Cook 2005).

Meanwhile, questions of race have also been raised. For instance, hooks (1990) finds in postmodernism the space where the racialized 'other' could be multiply rearticulated, but Collins (2000a) is troubled by what she sees as the contradictory nature of postmodernism. Its rarefied language, while able to undermine the language of the oppressor, lacks actual political effectiveness if intended as the means for political struggle against racism outside the academy. However she does see it as a powerful analytical tool for legitimating black women and other intellectuals of colour, whose struggles take place in the academic domain. Interestingly, some poststructuralist analyses show how whiteness is complicit in the creation of 'otherness' beyond sex and gender (Chow 1999; Winnubst 2003).

None of these debates have come to a resolution, but there is no doubt that encounters between feminist and postmodern theorizing have been and continue to be productive as they have continued the conversation. Below we briefly discuss some of these works, identifying the general theoretical tendencies from which they draw and addressing their specific contributions.

'Postmodern feminism' comprises a collection of eclectic approaches, drawing from diverse sources but sharing concerns regarding the consequences of the postmodern incredulity towards metanarratives (Lyotard 1984) and the limits of representation for a 'politics of feminism' (e.g. Butler 1992; Butler and Scott 1992; Ahmed 1996; Bartky 1998; Chanter 1998; Nicholson 1998; McNay 2003). While much poststructuralist feminist theorizing has drawn from the works of Derrida, Foucault, Lacan and more recently Deleuze and Guattari (Goulimari 1999), they have rearticulated these works and often contested them through feminist insights.

For instance, Derrida's deconstructions emphasize the multiplicity of 'the other' as a condition that always defers the fixity of meaning accorded to the primary term (what is claimed as 'knowledge'). In Derrida's work the focus is on the impossibility of attaining a way of saying that does not contradict itself, for in language we always proliferate other meanings as we further refer to what we want to say. French feminist Irigaray (1985a, b) engaged deconstruction as a question in Derrida's representation of 'woman' as that which cannot be named, as always deferred. Irigaray's deconstructive writings reclaimed 'woman' in her essential sexual difference to claim her own representation. In so doing she called into question the possibility of deconstruction as a critique of Western philosophy that could be written in a feminine key (Whitford 1991; Armour 1997).

The influences of psychoanalysis, especially Lacan's work, are also evident with French feminist writers, including Irigaray, Cixous and Kristeva. Linguistic arguments in the constitution of the 'self' are considered in Lacan's reinterpretation of Freudian theories about the Oedipal/Pre-Oedipal stages, emphasizing the importance of children's entrance into the domain of language. Lacan argues that splitting occurs as the child enters the Symbolic (linguistic) stage and loses the sense of wholeness and completion of the Imaginary (pre-linguistic stage). Thus, the self that is possible within the Symbolic order is always a lacking, desiring self, wanting to be whole again – which is impossible for language is never complete. Lacan's notion of *jouissance* – an impossibility of total joy and meaning for the lacking subject – is rearticulated by these feminist writers. Each considers that women's difference within the Imaginary and the Symbolic allows them to make sense differently of *jouissance* in a space not of lack but of plenitude, which is not defined by the Law of the Father.

In summary, each of these writers focused her arguments around the relationship between language and 'being woman', extending deconstructive and psychoanalytic insights to consider the space the linguistic figure of 'woman' occupies as that which is 'other' to the dominant (phallogocentric) language, system of rules and concepts of knowledge in modernity. For these authors, tenuously inspired by Simone de Beauvoir, 'women's otherness' needed to be both reclaimed and problematized (Braidotti 1998; Weedon 1998; Moi 2004).

Much Anglo-American feminist poststructuralist theory has drawn from Foucault's genealogies and concepts of power/knowledge (Diamond and Quinby 1988; Sawicki 1991; Hekman 1996; Weedon

1998). Foucault's genealogical work emphasizes the power/knowledge relations and discursive practices constituting our 'selves' and defining our subjectivities. The human body becomes a locus that legitimates and normalizes certain discourses and practices throughout the historical emergence, for instance, of medical, psychoanalytic, educational and other institutionalized forms of 'knowledge'. Foucault's influence in feminist theory is not surprising if one considers the more immediate political appeal of his arguments around power, and his departure from traditional theories of the subject that privilege dominant (patriarchal) views about knowledge and knowing (Diamond and Quinby 1988). His work has also been particularly influential in contemporary feminist theorizations of the body.

The body has been central to feminist theorizing at least since radical feminism articulated its political force both in its materiality and its symbolism – i.e. the personal is political. It has been, as well, a place for epistemological debate regarding Cartesian dualisms that privileged mind over body in the knowing subject. Questioning associations of mind/reason/culture with masculine 'same/identity', vs body/emotion/nature with feminine 'other/difference', became important epistemological pursuits in feminist theorizing (Code 1991; Collins 1991; Harding 1991; Lloyd 1993).

Fonow and Cook (2005) observe that in addition to epistemological arguments regarding *the nature of embodied knowing*, contemporary feminist scholarship addresses the body in at least three other modalities: *the body as object of inquiry, the body as a category of analysis* and *the body in relationship to the material*. The body as object of inquiry reflects early feminist works, including radical feminism, showing that control over women's bodies, from medicine to sexuality, violence to media representations and so on, might be at the core of women's oppression but that the body is also the most immediate space from which women's liberation must emerge. As a category of analysis, 'the body's' ontological status is highlighted as historically, culturally and discursively inscribed. Works such Bordo's (1989; 1993; 1998), focusing on the historical inscription of 'the feminine' over women's bodies as, for instance, hysterical, agoraphobic and more recently, anorexic, and those of Martin (1994a), addressing contemporary representations of the body as 'flexible' from medicine to corporate training, show the influence of Foucault's genealogical approaches.

Scholarship on the body in relationship to the material or 'corporeal feminism' has become most visible recently (Bray and Colebrook 1998). Writings on corporeal feminism often take as a reference point Irigaray's (1993) meditations on the notion of 'sexual difference', but also draw from writings by Deleuze and Guattari (e.g. Jardine 1985; Braidotti 1991; Grosz 1994; 1995; 2000; Gatens 1996; 1998). In general, Deleuze and Guattari privilege 'notions of mobility, movement and becoming over conceptions of being, essence or stable subjectivity' (Wuthnow 2002: 184). Such conceptualizations as 'rhizomes', 'nomadic subjectivity', 'body without organs', among many others, interrogate ontological premises and question the possibility of the unitary subject not only from a psychoanalytic perspective but also reconsidering representations of 'the body' as socio-historical constructs.

Deleuze and Guattari focus on psychoanalytic conceptions of the self, including Lacan's, in which processes of Oedipalization are social inscriptions requiring understanding one's body as a predetermined functional unity. Such understanding, they argue, is not only produced by the discourse of psychoanalysis but is, as well, located in the historical conditions of possibility that underscore capitalist development. Through concepts such as 'deterritorialization' and 'reterritorialization', they forward the body as 'assemblage' ('agençment' in French, which is both 'arranging' and the 'arrangements' which result from that action) which allows for thinking about the possibility of different social arrangements where bodies could instead be conceived as 'collections of disparate flows, materials, impulses, intensities and practices, which congeal under particular and specific conditions, in complex relations with the flows and intensities of surrounding objects, to produce transitory but functional assemblages' (Currier 2003: 326).

Radical potentialities for conceptualizing gendered subjectivities emerge from such ideas. Both Deleuzian and feminist poststructuralism aim to move beyond Cartesian dualisms, which devalue the materiality of the body in the thinking subject; however, for feminism it is also important to address the postmodern critique of essentialism without losing the possibilities of a feminist politics of difference (e.g. Ahmed 1996). Irigaray's articulation of 'sexual difference' seems to fulfil these possibilities, but Deleuzian conceptualizations of fluid bodily arrangements also contribute to maintaining a degree of indeterminacy for the subject.

Handbook of Organization Studies

Specifically, some scholars forward 'sexual difference' as the inception in feminist theorizing of an irreducible feminine difference that escapes Cartesian dualisms. As Braidotti argues, '[s]exual difference theory [...] stresses the positivity of difference, while opposing the automatic counter-affirmation of oppositional identities ... Irigaray pleads for a feminist reappropriation of the imaginary ... the images and representations that structure one's relation to subjectivity' (Braidotti 1998: 302). Butler, however, reads Irigaray's 'sexual difference' somewhat differently in that she sees this claim rather as 'a question for our times' (Butler 2004: 177). In Butler's view, reading from Irigaray's (1993) later work, sexual difference 'is not a given, not a premise, not a basis on which to build a feminism; ... rather, as *a question* that prompts a feminist inquiry, it is something that cannot be quite stated ... and that remains, more or less permanently, to interrogate' (Butler 2004: 178).

Juxtaposing these two views on 'sexual difference' brings to the fore key contemporary debates on the meaning of 'the body' for a politics of feminism and feminist theorizing more generally. First, there is the question of gender. In Braidotti's (1994; 2002) readings 'sexual difference' is located in the body of 'woman', even if re-read through various multiplicities for becoming Woman. Her readings correct Deleuzian corporeal excessiveness through Lacanian symbolic limits, but the basic materiality of the sexed body is the point of reference. In Butler's reading, 'sexual difference' brings up, instead, the issue of 'materialization'. In this sense, bodies are always becoming embodied in reference to that which is stated as the norm, and it is there that her theoretical preoccupations are perhaps best known.

Butler's analyses are strongly influenced by Foucault's questioning of the conditions of possibility for a subject embedded in a power/knowledge matrix which normalizes categories of identification and, in that sense, her work connects with Deleuze's via Foucault. Yet Butler's extensive writings are informed by a much longer list of philosophical, psychoanalytic, feminist and literary arguments, from Hegel to Freud, Lacan, Wittig, Kristeva, Irigaray, Derrida and so on, including her notion of 'melancholic sexuality' from Freud and 'the abject' from Kristeva. Her celebrated notion of 'performative gender' includes Austin's speech act theory, but also Derrida's critique of this theory and Nietzsche's argument that there is no 'being' behind any doing,

for the doing is everything while the subject is its effect (e.g. Butler 1990; Salih and Butler 2004).

It is from these latter perspectives that Butler collapses sex and gender, where gender is the effect of assigning it to a sexed body (i.e. at the moment of birth). Such effect continues to be produced and naturalized in its repetition by every-body over time. Following Althusser's notion of interpellation, Butler (1993) also problematizes the possibility of sex as prior to gender, for at the moment of birth every one is 'hailed' (i.e. called into) a sex. Thus, naming as well as performing one sex/gender is part of a power/knowledge system that maintains such distinctions institutionally and discursively.

Performative gender theory is cited frequently, but there seems to be much misunderstanding about its meanings and implications, and Butler (e.g. 1999; 2004) has been intent in providing clarifications. Performativity *is not* a social constructionist account of what gender is or may be (i.e. its basic insight is not 'doing gender'); rather, it is an analytical approach for problematizing such 'doing'. Performativity is a mode of describing what makes gender intelligible – i.e. its conditions of possibility within a context – as well as a mode of addressing the norms of gender in such context. A central preoccupation is how these norms delimit acceptable and unacceptable expressions of gender, including desire and sexuality. In other words, Butler's ultimate concern is not how gender is 'done' but examining the conditions of possibility for, and the consequences of such 'doings'. She also addresses questions of race regarding performativity by reiterating that her argument is not whether a theory of performativity is transposable into race, but rather what happens to the theory when it tries to function on questions of race (Butler 1999). Some answers to this question can be found in Bettie's (2003) reflexive ethnography on high school girls, race and identity.

An important aspect of Butler's works is in her contribution to queer studies and queer theory. Lesbian and gay studies emerged during the 1980s and were distinguished from women's studies by the emphasis on sexuality rather than gender, but followed a parallel trend with women's studies, going from a radical movement to an institutionalized field of study. Queer studies emerged more recently and adopted insights from gay and lesbian studies that regard sexuality and gender as fundamental in ordering social and political norms in most societies. Yet queer studies also questioned assumptions about the meaning of both sexuality and gender, avoiding categorization by sexual practice, and contesting social norms by appropriating a pejorative term – i.e. 'queer' (Auslander 1997).

Influenced by poststructuralism, using the term 'queer' signals rejection of the fixity of sexual identity, refusing both normative heterosexuality and homosexuality and questioning instead what is presented as 'normal'. Its emphasis on 'practice' rather than categories of identification is related to Foucaldian genealogical analytics of sexuality discourse and power/knowledge. This emphasis also attempts to undermine the logic of the social order by questioning conventional categorizations based on binary opposites – i.e. hetero/homosexual – and showing their mutual implication. At the same time, the notion of 'queer' is very directly linked to contemporary mobilization for social change, including recognizing the danger of abiding by the dominant heteronormative discourse in the context of the AIDS epidemic (Spargo 1999).

Beyond analyses and critiques of heteronormativity, Butler's work forwarded queerness as a space where marginal social practices such as gender parody and drag can contribute to destabilizing the norms of heterosexuality, while recognizing that there are intrinsic difficulties when claiming parody or drag as subversive social practice. No matter how much recited or recontextualized such practices might be, as with any other discursive practice they are implicated in that which they oppose. Similar to Sedgwick's (1990) analysis of the 'closet', where both the discourse of being 'in' or 'out' performs heterosexuality as the norm, there is a question of whether drag is a contestation or a reiteration of heterosexual hegemony. Further, Butler is clear that practices of 'resignification' associated with her work, which appropriate and deploy the norm under new premises – i.e. other genders such as those of transgenders – could be appropriated and deployed by radical and conservatives alike. However, the force of these practices enter the political field 'not only by making us question what is real, or what has to be, but by showing us how contemporary notions of reality can be questioned and new modes of reality instituted' (Butler 2004: 217).

In summary, corporeal feminism, including Butler's contributions to feminist and queer theory, as much as other contemporary arguments regarding the body, sexuality and sexual difference such as Braidotti's, reconsider rather than resolve possibilities

for political practice and social change via the agency of a feminist subject. They also reconsider possibilities for the ontological constitution of a subject outside Cartesian dualism, often articulated through Spinoza's monism – i.e. that the human mind is the idea of an actually existing human body (Gatens 1998).

These issues, central to feminist theorizing more generally, continue to be rethought in evaluations of feminist poststructuralism. Innovative conceptualizations of the body and the subject brought about by corporeal feminism inform, for example, analyses of science-fiction films (Stacey 2005) as well as disability studies, biology and medicine (Fausto-Sterling 2005), but they are also criticized, Butler's in particular, as too extreme in their rejection of the modernist subject (Hekman 2000) or as coming from a negative discursive paradigm that constrains subject formation and is unable to provide a determinate account of agency (McNay 2003).

Thus, the matter of 'agency' continues to haunt poststructuralist feminism and, for that reason, it has also contributed to advancing other important contemporary conceptualizations, such as those in encounters of feminist theorizing and science and technology studies (e.g. Lykke and Braidotti 1996; Haraway 1997; Harcourt 1999; Hawthorne and Klein 1999). Perhaps more notably, Barad (2003) offers the concept of 'agential realism' which denies the existence of independent agency emerging from distinct entities, and recasts notions of 'matter' (i.e. materiality) and 'discourse' (i.e. meaning) as mutually articulating. Her work brings together considerations from Butler, Foucault, Haraway and the physicist Niels Bohr, among others, provoking an unusual encounter between science studies and poststructuralist feminism. Like Haraway, she uses a model of diffraction to reiterate the indefinite nature of boundaries. Diffraction allows one to 'sharpen the theoretical tool of performativity for science studies and feminist and queer theory endeavors alike, and to promote their mutual consideration' (Barad 2003: 803). Her elaboration of 'performativity' is materialist, naturalist and posthumanist, giving no primacy to either of those terms and remarking, instead, the importance of actual 'matter' as not outside but as activity within (intra-activity) the world's becoming.

It is in this context that 'agency' is rethought. Agency is not human intentionality or subjectivity; rather 'it is an enactment of iterative changes to particular practices through the dynamics of intra-activity' (Barad 2003: 827) in a world that is always becoming. Furthermore, by denying the separability of ontology and epistemology, forwarding instead 'onto-epistemology' – the study of practices of knowing in being – where 'knowing is a matter of part of the world making itself intelligible to another part' (Barad 2003: 829), she moderates the privilege of the thinking human subject to its being part of the world rather than over it. Altogether, Barad's conceptualizations call for a fundamental metatheoretical rethinking of current formulations in corporeal feminisms, questioning the underlying basis of many of these debates as still located within a humanist paradigm, which limits the possibility to account for human finitude.

Poststructuralist/Postmodern Feminist Theorizing and Organizational Analysis

As with scholarship inspired by socialist feminism, applications of feminist poststructuralism to organization studies have proliferated since our 1996 chapter, while at the same time debate continued over its value and implications (e.g. Calás and Smirch 1999; 2003; 2004a). 'Applications' revolve around exploration of several closely interrelated themes: the ontological and epistemological bases of modern organization knowledge including the practices of organizing and managing and the practices of theorizing about them; the dualisms through which knowing and practicing gender and organizing occurs; the power/knowledge relations and discursive practices that constitute 'identities' 'selves' and define gendered subjectivities; the meanings and potentiality of the body, and its conditions of possibility and intelligibility. As Ashcraft and Mumby (2004: 108) remark, postmodern feminist organization studies is developing a significant body of work exploring relationships among 'discourse, gendered identities, power relations and organizing'. To clarify, here we are discussing work on discourse as understood under poststructuralist premises and that also addresses gender. Not every work in organization studies using notions of discourse is poststructuralist, and not every poststructuralist analysis of organizational discourse address gender.

One strand of inquiry articulates an epistemological concern – to show how organizational knowledge is underpinned with masculine imagery and connotations, how masculinity is the unstated but present norm in knowledge construction, and to offer suggestions for how such knowledge could be re-written (e.g. Gray 1994; Wilson 2001; Krefting 2003; Casey 2004; Ross-Smith and Kornberger 2004). Other poststructuralist feminist applications have scrutinized with unsettling effect traditional concepts, theories and practices, including those on leadership (Calás and Smirch 1991; Calás 1993), rationality (Mumby and Putnam 1992), theory-building (Jacques 1992), self-actualization (Cullen 1997), globalization (Calás and Smirch 1993; 2004b), bureaucracy (Martin and Knopoff 1997), business ethics (Calás and Smirch 1997), stress and burnout (Meyerson 1998), teamwork (Metcalfe and Linstead 2003) and work-family discourse (Martin 1990a; Runté and Mills 2004).

Collectively this form of inquiry is demonstrating how the texts/language producing 'organizational knowledge' are not naïve or innocent, but rather engaged in a politics of representation that can gender organizations. The works cited above, more generally, while not all strictly 'deconstructive', share an interest in complicating the claims of such 'knowledge' by pointing at the contradictions in their representations. By attending to the rhetorical nature of texts such writings work to cast suspicion on the proclaimed objectivity and universality of organizational knowledge and to assert the possibility of other voices to demonstrate how it might be otherwise.

For example, Kark and Waismel-Manor (2005) critically reread and rethink the gendered assumptions underlying 'organizational citizenship behaviour', a widely investigated topic in US psychologically informed research, where questions are usually framed in the manner: do men and women differ in their display of OCB? The authors use two reading strategies to examine the OCB construct as an instance of gendered constitution of knowledge and to explore the potential differential consequences of this mode of conceptualization for women and men. Although the concept of OCB held promise for enabling the rethinking of traditional notions of work by suggesting the importance of practices usually regarded as outside the bounds of standard job performance and often associated with women, the paper demonstrates how OCB is, after all, grounded in masculinist assumptions. The authors unveil the 'darker side' of OCB for women and men in that 'extra role' behaviours that define the 'good citizen' at work are likely to become expected, incorporated into the normal scope of the job as the intensification of work occurs. The authors ask whether being a good citizen at work makes for being a good citizen in the community? Or a good family member at home?

Closely related explorations, also epistemic in concern, are undertaken by scholars trying to challenge dualistic thinking. They sometimes invoke notions of sexual difference, but often proceed to deconstruct them. For example, Oseen (1997) invokes the work of Irigary as a source of promise of how to loosen the bonds of domination and subordination which confine the leader and leadership theory. She argues that the notion of the 'not-yet' woman help with the creation of new ways of thinking about leadership. Höpfl (2000), offers a meditation on Kristeva's writings, emphasizing that there is no parallel term to emasculate – effeminate isn't parallel, thus there is no term to describe the taking away of female power, and that has implications for how sex is written in organizational texts.

Several other articles try to break away from stereotypical dualistic conceptions of gender via narratives of empirical work that intervene in such dualisms, and conceptualizations that challenge 'dualism' as such. Among these, Johansson (1998) offers three gender constructs not as a suggestion for a new stereotypical way of looking at gender, but rather to play with existing limitations, making them more obvious; while Pini (2005) argues that women leaders in agriculture in Australia constitute a third sex. Her interviews demonstrate that the subject position 'women leader in agriculture' requires the simultaneous assertion and subjugation of gender. Further, Baxter and Hughes (2004) explore the difficulties in going beyond dualistic thinking, presenting a case for the retention of the binary by recognizing the embeddedness of dualism in organizational life; but also refusing dualism, as learned, to create new frames of meaning and new ways of being to express the fluidity of gendered identities.

An increasing body of work uses notions of discourse, mostly Foucaldian, to examine the discursive formations of gendered organizational subjectivities and subject positions, as well as discourses of resistances to these formations. Several articles consider these issues in recently emerging organizational lexicon. Among these, Marks (1997) explores 'caring discourses' which may function not

as expressive qualities emanating from emotional and subjective feelings of a woman, but as part of the political economy of power/knowledge within organizations; Thomas and Davies (2002) examine the discourse of 'new public management', specific to the British context and pertaining to marketization and managerialism in higher education, which influences the professional identities of women academics, but also might activate resistances and offer a site of political struggle for these women; while Rees and Garnsey (2003) show that a 'competence approach' is not a gender-neutral approach to assessment but functions as a form of 'self-management' that disadvantage women's normative behaviours. Through textual analyses, Ahl (2004) further reiterates how discourse, in this case in academic writings about 'women's entrepreneurship', reproduces gender inequality under the guise of 'scientific knowledge'.

Others examine the 'history of the present' in gendered organizational practices and discourses of knowledge. An excellent example is Brewis (2001), who contests the assumption that knowledge about sexual harassment works against sexual exploitation. She challenges this notion by arguing that the way this is written, thought and spoken about may reproduce the subject positions of harasser and recipient. In her view, 'harassment knowledge' is an historical artifact emerging under specific conditions, and not some enduring truth about organizational life. Similarly, Hatcher (2003) looks at the contemporary notion that managers have to be 'passionate' about work in contrast to the historical masculinity credentials required of such positions. This new 'regime of truth' about what it means to be a successful manager emerged from feminist movements aiming to distinguish women's contribution to social life but attained, instead, a reshaping of the traditional masculine/feminine hierarchy of logic/emotion.

Other works, still inspired by Foucaldian analyses, focus on the production of masculinities in organizations as practices of the 'self'. For example, Hodgson (2003) draws on Foucault's writing on discipline and the self and examines the strategies of control employed in the highly gendered environment of financial services. Certain masculinist notions of identity are implicated in modes of resistance/subversion appearing in these contexts. In another example, Knights and McCabe (2001) explore business processes re-engineering as informed by a masculine discourse emphasizing competition, control and conquest while simultaneously asking for care, trust, creativity in teamwork. These contradictions are reflected in the language and practice of management.

Among the literature that examines the gendering of professional identities as discursive positioning, Sotirin and Gottfried (1999) analyse the 'bitching' of secretaries as an ambivalent communicative practice that maintained gendered attributes and destabilized the proper secretarial identity. These were seen as an interplay of control and resistance in gendered workplaces. By contrast, Jorgenson (2002) explored the narrative construction of professional identities among women engineers, suggesting that they adopt a variety of distinct and sometimes contradictory positionings to present themselves as qualified professionals.

A few works are considering the meaning and potentiality of the body as a focus of analysis. Among these, Sinclair (2005) celebrates particular body performances at the site of management pedagogy, seeing her own bodily experiences as freeing, but also as obstacle and as site of new possibilities. Others explore the body in the context of technology, such as Ball (2005) who, based on Gatens, and Deleuze and Guattari, examines possibilities for resistance to biometric surveillance practices; and Gustavsson and Czarniawska (2004), who focus on the appearance of virtual females as electronic-mediated customer assistants on the Web. More recently, Ellehave's (2005) innovative dissertation draws from Butler and Barad to study the performance of 'practices of gender' into 'differences that matter' in two workplaces.

There is also increasing interest in the value of queer theorizing for organizational analysis. In an early work, Gibson-Graham (1996) queers capitalist organization by decoupling the familiar association of 'capitalism' with comodification and 'the market'. This strategy asks for reimagining the body of capitalism as open and permeable and full of orifices, rather than as hard and impervious to penetration. This resignification opens space to observe the possibilities for non-capitalist organization. Parker (2002) makes connections between 'queer' theory and contemporary thinking about management and organization. The discussion, based on the work of Butler and Sedgwick, looks into the potential implications of queering for managers, managerial practices and the science of management. Meanwhile, Bowring (2004) argues that gender and leadership are caught within what Butler calls the heterosexual matrix. Using a character from Star Trek to guide the analysis, she forwards ways to move towards fluidity in the theorizing and practice of both gender and leadership. Finally, Skidmore (2004) claims that sexuality/organization, organization/sexuality, needs to be interpreted in the context of a heteronormative society. The heteronormative axis around which work is constructed, organized and managed needs to be exposed and revealed in order to develop an understanding of how scripts of gender and sexuality are embedded into the workplace.

Can work/family be subject to feminist deconstruction? Martin's (1990a) might function as the paradigmatic text to answer that question. Her C-section story is a powerful argument to show the fictional boundaries between private and public domains by deconstructing the pregnant body as an 'organizational taboo'; but on noticing the limits of deconstruction, she calls as well for a fundamental realignment of government policies concerning both the family and the marketplace. More recently, Runté and Mills (2004) deconstruct the discourse of 'work–family conflict' to show, again, the fiction of two separate spheres of life. Rather, the demands on time-effort balance in the workplace make home life an appendage of the workplace. Would Sarah Kelly be able to deconstruct this discourse any further?

Sarah Kelly: A Poststructuralist/Postmodern Feminist

Sarah sits reading the newly arrived news magazine, the one featuring her in its cover story. She reflects ruefully on that encompassing identity – 'stay at home Mom' – soon to be hers, with considerable ambivalence. She finds herself flooded with a sense of well being, knowing she'll be seen by many as a 'good parent'. But just as quickly, the moment passes, and she finds a tide of anger rising up. There are so many other 'kinds of Moms' she could be, to say nothing of the many other 'kinds of persons' she could be. How is it possible that the complexity of her life boils down to this one simple label? Why must it?

Yet, thanks to her background in Critical Legal Studies, Sarah is able to understand that she is in fact the subject of competing discourses in society. Her conflicting feelings are the products of those competing discourses, with their norms of acceptability about gender and sexuality. There she is in magazine, performing as a woman within the norms of what defines a livable life in her society. And it's not only her, there is Michael, the 'dutiful husband and father,' and Julia, the 'faithful servant.' A pretty picture, indeed.

She imagines that later on, she and Michael and Julia will have a good laugh together when they all have another look at the magazine. It's not *really* them in the story, after all!

Or, is it?

If it were not … would the magazine have been interested in doing a story about them?

Transnational/(Post)Colonial Feminist Theorizations

In revisiting her 'Under Western Eyes' 16 years after its publication, Mohanty (2003: 230) affirms that her original article 'sought to make the operations of discursive power visible, to draw attention to what was left out of feminist theorizing, namely the material complexity, reality and agency of Third World women's bodies and lives'. This is exactly the analytical strategy that she now uses 'to draw attention to what is unseen, undertheorized and left out in the production of knowledge about globalization … [because] … I believe capital as it functions now depends on and exacerbates racist, patriarchal and heterosexist relations of rule' (Mohanty 2003: 231).

This declaration captures well the general tendencies and changes in what our 1996 chapter identified as Third World/(Post)Colonial theorizations. A shorthand would be to say that if the influence of poststructuralism had then marked the '(post)colonial', there was also more than a trace of materialism turning up in such arguments. At present the materialist accent signified by global capitalism comes through strongly and, thus, another signifier to reiterate these changes – transnational – is added to the title of this section. As Mohanty is keen to remark, she was all along less of a poststructuralist than readers of her work conceded during the boom-times of academic postmodernism; her writings were always explicit on the need for materialist analyses. In fact, our own renditions of these topics in 1996 were written and read with a 'post' accent, and thus serve now as a point of reference for the distinctions we have just made.

Transnational/(post)colonial feminisms, while not monolithic, include several critics who challenge Western feminist theorizations of gender and gender relations as furthering the images and social experiences of mostly privileged women (and men) in the 'First World'. These arguments go beyond those raised by black and other race theorists who questioned the white, middle class, heterosexist, representations of gender in feminist theorizing, and interrogate, for instance, the function of 'the nation' in gendering and racializing 'others' through specific, patriarchal, heterosexist, political projects between and within different countries (e.g. Alexander 1997; Monhanram 1998; Collins 2000b). They also promote notions such as transversal politics instead of identity politics to address both the heterogeneity of citizenship in its current global dimensions, within and between nations, and the possibility of feminist projects cutting across differences without assimilation (e.g. Yuval-Davis 1997). Some historical analyses demonstrate, as well, the material involvement of Western white women as perpetrators rather than merely marginal actors in histories of colonization (e.g. Jayarwardena 1995).

While (post)colonial feminist analyses hold in common with poststructuralism a fundamental suspicion of 'gender' as a stable and sufficient analytical lens to be applied unproblematically across cultures and histories, they have extended the insights of postmodern and poststructuralist theorizations to their logical consequences: if Western knowledge has been constituted in difference from 'others', by rendering them invisible, what would happen if those 'others' were to speak back? What if they were to show how they are constituted as others? What if these others were to reclaim their own specificities, away from the dualisms (e.g. male/female) embedded in Western (including feminist) discourses of knowledge? (e.g. Mohanty 1991a; El Guindi 1999 on the veil as resistance, part of Islamic feminism).

Issues of representation loom large in these analyses, but so do questions of power and identity, justice and ethics in practices of globalization (e.g. Spivak 1999). For instance, Mohanty's (1991a, b) original arguments make the case that 'Third World women' have often been constituted as 'others' of 'First World women' by representing them as underdeveloped, oppressed, illiterate, poor, contributing to overpopulation, etc. These representations reaffirm Western 'knowledge' by highlighting 'indicators' such as life expectancy, sex-ratio, nutrition, fertility, education and income-generating activities, which homogenize and freeze non-Western women, denying the fluid, historical and dynamic nature of their lives. That is, these apparently neutral categories construct 'third world peoples' (not just women), as backward, ignorant and passive recipients of Western 'knowledge', obliterating other representations that articulate their agency, capabilities, involvement in struggles and strategies for survival. In so doing, they universalize a Eurocentric version of 'knowledge' as if were 'truth' (e.g. Harding 1996; 1998).

Calling for a rewriting of history based on the specific locations and histories of struggle of (post)colonial peoples, Mohanty reaffirmed the need to voice 'other knowledges' which would illuminate the simultaneity of oppressions as fundamental for grounding a feminist politics in the histories of racism and imperialism, the significance of memory and writing in the creation of oppositional agency, and the differences, conflicts and contradictions internal to third world women's organizations and communities (Mohanty 1991b). Transnational/(post)colonial analyses, thus, go beyond the deconstruction of Western texts. They show the production of knowledge at the (Western) centre to be a form of self-fashioning, widely implicated in the constitution and legitimation of imperialism and colonialism (e.g. Said 1978; 1985; Minh-ha 1989; Prakash 1995; Narayan 1997; Kaplan et al. 1999).

Such works articulate the existence of complex subjectivities and heterogeneous subject positions and relations, produced by intersections of gender, race, class, ethnicity, sexualities and so on, in the context of specific First-World/Third-World historical and contemporary relationships. As such, possibilities for a transnational feminism in the context of globalization soon appear, for these complex subjectivities contribute to rethinking solidarity within and across borders, not in the old homogenizing and apparently benign model of 'global sisterhood' but in contemporary encounters, moments and spaces 'dedicated to praxis rooted in postcolonial critiques of racism, ethnocentrism, sexism and heteronormativity and committed to the subversion of multiple oppressions' (Mendoza 2002: 310).

One way to read these arguments is that the more materialist focus on transnationalism and globalization may have displaced the philosophical concerns of the 'post' regarding language and representation, however the latter are as much key issues as the former. For example, Mohanty's (1991b) work deploys a series of notions elaborated in US women-of-colour feminist theorizing from Alarcón (1990), Hurtado (1989) and Sandoval (1991), to emphasize the interconnectedness of different people's exploitation at present – no matter where they are located – as produced within the political economy of globalization. Her recent analyses include the notion of 'One-Third/Two-Thirds Worlds' (Mohanty 2003: 226–7) from Esteva and Prakash (1998), instead of the more common 'First-/Third World'. She has chosen this language not only to dispel assumptions of homogeneous rich/poor, North/South people, but also because it draws attention to the continuities and discontinuities between the majority of people in the world and a minority who controls the images of consumer culture as if it were the 'good life' for all. In so doing, she also reiterates that the boundaries between the haves and the haves-not exist as much within nations as between nations and indigenous communities, highlighting 'the fluidity and power of global forces that situate communities of people as social majorities/minorities in disparate forms' (Mohanty 2003: 226).

There is now sufficient scholarship demonstrating that it is not a matter of either representation or materialism but rather how to deploy the best analyses – i.e. both/and – afforded by multiple disciplinary conceptualizations (e.g. Ong 1999; *Signs* 2001). Kaplan and Grewal (1999) express this well as they acknowledge that at present it is necessary to work in the interlocking fields of postcolonial discourse, international feminist theory and literary and cultural production because what is needed is 'a feminist analysis that refuses to choose among economic, cultural and political concerns' and instead engages in critical practices linking 'our understanding of postmodernity, global economic structures, problematics of nationalism, issues of race and imperialism, critiques of global feminism, and emergent patriarchies' (Kaplan and Grewal 1999: 358).

To be clear, concerns remain regarding whose language and theories are used by the 'rest/Two-Thirds' to engage the 'West/One-Third'. Some argue that the theoretical tools in (post)colonial analyses are those of the oppressors but others demonstrate how the colonized always re-appropriate the texts of the colonizer and redeploy them into other images, contesting the seamless appearance of colonial authority (e.g. Bhabha 1985; Parry 1995). Dilemmas continue to exist, nonetheless, regarding how to portray (post)colonial subjectivities without depicting them either as a romanticized 'native other' or existing only in relationship to their oppressors (e.g. Lal 1999). Moreover, others such as McClintock (1995a: 13), consider that the 'post' in 'the postcolonial' should not be used analytically or otherwise, for it re-inscribes a teleology that assumes, wrongly, that colonialism no longer is. Further, the use of 'postcolonial' contributes to ignoring other areas in the world that were never subjects in the history of colonization but are now subject to the continuities of imperial power through military, economic, political, cultural, 'imperialism-without-colonies'.

These may seem to be esoteric and inconsequential academic arguments, but very concrete imperatives fuel them. In the face of disintegrating community and identity under forces of globalization, what possibilities exist for collective action and the articulation of common interests? Is it, as Mohanty (2003) observes, that the subject of globalization is the 'private citizen-consumer' and therefore only wealth determines citizenship and representation (i.e. in the market)? Or, as Ang (1997: 62) remarks, that the issue is the necessity to create conditions for negotiating life with the 'apparently impossible simultaneity of incommensurable realities'? One way or another, are there possibilities for social movements and solidarity among and between those in the Two-Third Worlds?

Several responses to these concerns have been offered. A very well known example is 'strategic essentialism' (e.g. Said 1988; Spivak 1988), describing 'a strategic use of positivist essentialism in a scrupulously visible political interest' (Spivak 1988: 13) to demonstrate the possibility for engaging in seemingly contradictory political struggles, while mobilizing support for and from groups that might otherwise appear to stand on different agendas. Yet,

Radhakrishnan (1994) views strategic essentialism as another instance of redeploying the 'master's tools' (Lorde 1983) through a reversal of its metropolitan tactics, while Butler (in Salih and Butler 2004: 331) argues that Spivak eventually reneged on this notion because, as any other notion, its semantic life exceeds 'the intention of the strategist ... as it travels though discourse ... tak[ing] on new ontological meanings'.

More recently, other important conceptualizations have been offered. Moya (1997) reassesses Moraga's 'theory in the flesh' to suggest a 'realist' account of identity that goes beyond essentialism by showing connections between social location, experience, cultural identity and knowledge, while Saldivar-Hull (1999) proposes Cisneros' work regarding a transnational, 'transfronteriza' practice, 'feminismo popular', as border-crossing to identify emergent types of movements across geopolitical boundaries. Further, Ferguson (1996) submits 'bridge identity politics' for a reconstitution of identities into affinity networks and practices. The goal here is to achieve the ethico-political goal of egalitarian and reciprocal relations between differently situated actors, who share common political demands.

Finally, 'hybrid identities' and 'hybridization' have become very important concepts in these debates, for they can be read both as ways of resisting the forces of assimilation into a dominant culture, and as representing new subjectivities that simultaneously integrate and disintegrate modernity and tradition all over the world (e.g. Bhabha 1988; García-Canclini 1990; Escobar 1995). In Felski's (1997: 12) words: 'Metaphors of hybridity and the like not only recognize difference within the subject, fracturing and complicating holistic notions of identity, but also address connections between subjects by recognizing affiliations, cross-pollinations, echoes and repetitions [...] such metaphors allows us to conceive of multiple interconnecting axes of affiliation and differentiation'.

Theoretical conceptualizations as those proposed above are clear on the implications of 'theory' for possibilities to articulate transnational collective action and resistance to oppression and exploitation within the circuits of capital, in particular for Two-Thirds World women. These implications are also present in several methodological considerations. For instance, Latin American 'testimonios' suggest opportunities for inquiry of strong political force, portraying very different gender configurations through women 'from below' who speak up, initiate action, fight in all kinds of struggles, while resisting any easy classification within First World images of 'woman' or 'feminism' (e.g. Franco 1992; Sommer 1995; Gugelberger 1996; Beverly 2000). Others such as Visweswaran (1994) and Lal (1999) propose ethnographic approaches that foreground, reflexively *and* proactively, the relationship of the researcher and the research subject – i.e. 'knowledge' and 'the other' – as they both are multiply traversed by institutional, political and economic interests and power relations.

More recently, Khan (2005) suggests 'reconfiguring the native informant'; that is, to no longer consider as 'the informant' only those who provide a narrative for the researcher, but also the researcher herself who narrates another story for western audiences as well as the reader who further interprets these stories in the context of dominant societies. Such reconfiguration makes 'native informing' a complex process that can better articulate linkages between specific local conditions of oppression and forces of globalization, that otherwise may go unexamined. Further, the need for more concrete researcher's interventions are brought to the fore in reconsiderations of action research which, despite poststructuralist critiques, revalourize researcher's participation at a transnational scale to empower those who are most vulnerable (Kesby 2005). In contrast, Mohanty (2003) continues to reiterate the importance for research of older theoretical and methodological developments such as the notion of 'relations of ruling' in the institutional ethnographies of Smith. She endorsed this notion in her earlier work (Mohanty 1991b) because it encourages the necessary relational analyses to foreground multiple intersections of structures of power, identities, forms of knowledge and organized practices and institutions in exploitation of Third World women.

Altogether, whether newer or older, transnational/(post)colonial feminist research approaches portray and emphasize the agency of 'the other', and articulate the multiple relationships between the 'local' and the 'global'. More importantly, they also make visible how *transnational practices of research* can further empower or exploit those who they claim to represent.

In summary, what constitutes transnational/(post)colonial feminist scholarship? It would be misleading to narrow these feminist theoretical tendencies to the few conceptualizations and arguments discussed above, for scholarship on these topics continues to grow while cutting across disciplines and territories, including theory, method and practice; and most of these newer works are as significant for cultural concerns as they are for concerns in political economy. Moreover, in principle, and while not always successful, a good amount of this scholarship is intended to cross over the boundaries of the academy and to contribute to actual political action 'in the world'. Thus, without intending to be exhaustive, we highlight below a few recent examples to illustrate the possible variety of contemporary research 'between gender and nation'.

The functions and possibilities of *textual and other representations* continue to be an important theme in these writings, from literature to cultural studies (e.g. Nagy-Zekmi 2003; Darling-Wolf 2004). A good example is Fernandes (1999), who juxtaposes a testimonial text and a film depicting the life of a lower caste Indian woman accused of killing several upper caste landowners who had allegedly raped her. Her analysis focuses on the contexts in which these representations circulate and conclude that a 'trans/national feminist perspective' would pay attention to how multinational cultural products from the Third World may be commodities for First World consumption, but they also intervene in complex ways in the context of their own local production.

Within feminist theory more generally, debates ensue regarding *postcolonial theoretical conceptualizations vis-a-vis poststructuralist conceptualizations.* For example, on the one hand, Wuthnow (2002) examines the implications of the Deleuzian concept of 'nomad thought' in the context of postcoloniality and indigenous politics. In her view, this concept diminishes the possibility of effective indigenous agency because it displaces any 'politics of location'. As a counterpoint to Deleuze she recuperates, in a non-essentialist manner, concepts such as 'experience' and 'local knowledge' via feminist postcolonial writers. Gedalof (2000), on the other hand, considers the cyborg and the nomad as two important identity concepts from white western feminism that can function side-by-side with concepts from diasporic and postcolonial feminism.

Issues of *sexuality* are not new in postcolonial feminist analyses (e.g. McClintock 1995b), and the notion of *global sex workers* is now part of the transnational feminist lexicon (e.g. Wardlow 2004), but contemporary queer theory and Butler's notions of performativity as well as the concept of intersectionalities have provided additional approaches and analytical lenses to address these issues (e.g. Gamson and Moon 2004). The range of examples in this case extends from transnational feminist analyses of queer tourism (e.g. Puar 2001; 2002) to disruptions of masculine and feminine identities as performative understandings in contemporary travel writing (Lisle 1999), to understanding the body as a site of inscription, struggle and performance in the context of globalization (Underhill-Sem 2003).

Of course, processes of *globalization* are central focus of attention and multiply articulated through various analytical frames and themes. For example, Bergeron (2001) questions conventional representations of globalization in the political economy literatures and addresses the implications of these representations for imagining feminist subjectivities within and in resistance to global capital. In contrast, Vargas (2003) considers, concretely, the World Social Forum as a space for new tendencies and new ways of existence for feminisms in the collective constructions of alternatives to dominant notions of globalization. Further, Kuumba (1999) examines contemporary population policy directed toward women of African descent on the African continent as well as African diaspora as 'reproductive imperialism'. This work draws attention to the relationship between population control and increasing international economic polarization, for global population policies simultaneously facilitate racial inequality, class exploitation and gender subordination.

Meanwhile, scholarship on *transnational feminism* proper is mindful of the tenuous and possibly ambiguous nature of this notion but also hopeful for the analytical and practical possibilities that it unlocks. For instance, Mendoza (2002) interrogates transnational feminisms as a concept and as a practice. She suggests that transnational feminists and feminist postcolonial theorists see themselves as committed to intersectional analysis and transversal politics, but their theoretical tactics do not attain their expected practical outcomes. Further, Hemment (2004) and Ghodsee (2004) show the complicated relationships that develop between western NGOs and local women's movements in Russia and other Postsocialist countries in Europe. Thayer (2001), however, offers a more optimistic picture. In her fieldwork with rural Brazilian women she found that these women willingly appropriate and transform transnational feminist discourses, drawing on resources of their own to create meaning and action in a transnational web of political/cultural relations.

Throughout these writings, one concern reappearing often is the possibility of *new subjectivities in the context of transnationalism*. What would this mean concretely? While the theoretical arguments discussed above articulate several possible conceptualizations, current practices of 'transmigration' appear as a promising avenue for observing transnational subjectivities and hybrid identity formation as ongoing processes in practice. The transmigration phenomenon, as part of globalization flows, goes beyond earlier notions of transnational migration, where immigrants were seen as becoming settled in the countries to which they migrate, often in diasporic communities as 'home away from home'. By contrast, transmigrants continuously traverse national boundaries often in response to global demands for labour, while straddling social, political, geographic and cultural borders, linking 'home' and 'host' countries. In these flows, identity, behaviours and values are renegotiated and not limited by location (e.g. Dijkstra et al. 2001; Lam and Yeoh 2004), or class for these can also be seen emerging within the circuits of capital and the elite, and examined through notions such as 'flexible citizenship' (Ong 1999).

Several studies highlight the centrality of gender in the transformative as well as political aspects of these processes. For instance, Gerholm (2003) demonstrates the importance of masculinity and sexuality in the negotiation of new identities for a community of Arab Muslim male transmigrants in Stockholm, while Aranda (2003), in a study of transmigration of Puerto Rican professionals, underscores how gender, cultural and geopolitical factors mediate the split between professional success and emotional fulfillment, contributing to permanently unsettled identities.

To sum up, how to speak (knowledge) as 'other' may still be a central problematic in the scramble for signification in the global economy, however subjugation, oppression and exploitation of the 'Two-Third Worlds', women in particular, have acquired an urgent and concrete centrality in the specificity of the everyday life of people the world over. Today, it is impossible to negate the implications of global capitalism in these processes, and transnational/(post)colonial feminist arguments offer a much needed discursive space for engaging with these 'new colonialisms' of globalization and the market.

Transnational/(Post)Colonial Feminist Theorizations and Organization Studies

Considering the increasing importance of transnationalism and globalization in the world and in contemporary organization literatures and, concurrently, the steady production of gender and organization scholarship, one would expect to see these topics taken up through *feminist* transnational/(post)colonial analyses. However, our literature review found few works in our field representing intersections of these themes. While the postcolonial as analytical lens has been increasingly deployed, the appearance in this literature of feminist analyses, and even gender issues, is limited (e.g. Calás 1992; Calás and Smircich 1993; 2003; 2004b; Banerjee and Linstead 2001). These are issues still waiting to become apparent in contemporary organizational literature, not to 'save the women and children' through an old humanist patriarchal gesture, but as a matter of feminist analysis of much that lies invisible behind the 'value-creation processes' of globalization.

In 1996 we drew primarily from the 'women/gender and development' literatures to illustrate parallels with feminist literature in organization studies, from liberal to poststructuralist, and to remark the inroads that postcolonial feminist analyses, still in the more discursive mode, were then making into development scholarship. This was a move intended to illustrate lacunas as well as greater possibilities for our field. Today, 'development' in the context of globalization has been well deconstructed through varieties of feminist analyses (e.g. McEwan 2001; Müller 2003; *Signs* 2004), but there is much more that needs to be done in organization studies.

Perhaps we were naïve in expecting to see feminist organizational analyses of these topics emerging rather quickly, in particular because they would have been an explicit critique of our field's most taken-for-granted and unexamined truths, increasingly supporting so much of what we see around us: *that capitalism in its contemporary form, in particular globalized capitalism, is/must be good, necessary, and inevitable the world over, and that gender has little to do with it.* Indeed, from the vantage point of

the mid-1990s, during more reflexive scholarly times, a critique of such truths suggested through our development examples seemed possible, but today we appreciate much better how difficult it is to achieve such critical analyses in organization studies.

Thus, similar to our chapter in 1996, we move somewhat beyond our field to find pertinent illustrations. This time, however, rather than merely suggest we want to bring to visibility more pointed critiques of these unspoken truths, inspired by Acker's (2004) articulation of three interrelated areas for analysis where gender, capitalism and globalization appear to be uniquely intertwined: masculinities in globalizing capital; the gendered construction of a division between capitalist production and human reproduction; and gender as a resource for globalizing capital.

'Gendering' globalization, according to Acker, will expose the discontinuities between the realities of women's and men's lives in local arenas, as well as expose the discontinuities of those realities with mainstream scholarly work about global processes. To be clear, gender in these analyses does not simply pertain to sexed bodies; rather 'gendering' analyses examine subjectivities and subject positions and institutions over time and space as relational products and producers of transnational and global processes. Gendering (and the race, ethnic, class, sexualities and other subjectivation processes with which gendering intersects) should produce a better understanding of current global processes at the specific sites where they appear. We explicitly present these analytical directions and the examples that follow as an agenda for analytical changes in organization studies.

Analyse Masculinities in Globalizing Capital

As identified by Acker, this topic offers an important dimension of analysis for organization studies: Who makes the decisions that define 'globalization', in theory and in practice? There are both material and symbolic arguments to be made here. First, there is no doubt that certain groups of men occupy most top decision-making positions in business and other organizations, including transnational institutions fostering globalization policies, *and* academic domains creating theories about them (e.g. business management and organization; economics). At the same time, images of top decision-makers in organizations involved in global processes already promote particular notions of how such individuals should act, look and so on (e.g. Benería 1999). These images carry both historical and cultural baggage, but at the most basic level they are gendered (and raced and sexed) in particular ways.

Connell, cited by Acker (2004: 14), describes the existence of a 'trans-national business masculinity' that is egocentric, whose loyalties are conditional, showing a declining sense of responsibility for others. Arrogance, a passion to control, ruthlessness and aggression are also part of this identity, which is not easy to ignore if we consider the 'texts of management', including media and academic, that pervade our societies. Observe, for instance, that these images are difficult to counter with other, 'softer' images of masculinity of recent vintage, such as 'the caring father' in a dual career family. If we think about images of decision-makers at the global level, the 'caring father', a less powerful, i.e. classed, even feminized, entity in the corporate and social landscape is not among the people making these decisions. As Connell (2005) argues more recently, these images are also fuelled by global media interest and conservative political, religious and economic agendas in several countries, often reinscribing a gender order that promotes 'essential inequalities' between men and women as well as within groups of men and women the world over.

Said differently, global decision-making is coded 'masculine' in specific ways and the men, but also the few women, who make decisions under this code, are immediate beneficiaries of most of the wealth and power thus produced. At the same time these decisions produce cultural and economic dislocations affecting gender/race/class relations, both in particular local arenas and at global levels, between and within most other actual men and women. These dislocations may, in fact, perpetuate several forms of patriarchal subordination but also provoke resistances to them in emerging forms of masculinities and femininities (e.g. Schild 1997; Freeman 2001). Thus, the varieties and complexities of globalized masculinities in business and other organizations, *and in the organization* of management and economic theorizing, need to be recognized and their fissures and foibles exposed.

For example, Kondo (1997) shows the complicity of marketing campaigns and globalization theorists through various forms of masculinity deployed in a transnational fashion industry from Japan, while Saunders (1996) addresses how neoliberal economic theory limits understanding and policy-making

which might remedy African-American men's earning inequalities. Fernández-Kelly's (1994) work in the maquiladora industry in Mexico is a very good illustration of how increasing male employment in this industry, and apparent greater equality between the sexes, may be the result of deteriorating conditions for men's wages and not solely the effects of gains by women's earnings. More recently, Salzinger (2004) documents the complicated gender relations that continue to develop in maquiladoras within ongoing globalization processes. In general, these examples demonstrate that there are contradictions and fragility behind notions of global capitalist masculinity and, as Hearn (1996) reminds us in his outline to 'deconstruct the dominant', it is possible and necessary to bring these contradictions to visibility.

Analyse the Gendered Construction of a Division Between Capitalist Production and Human Reproduction

We focus here on a specific point drawn from Acker's more extensive analysis, to illustrate the following argument: that corporate practices, at local and global levels, claim non-responsibility for the reproduction of human life, creating a distinction between production as monetary economy and reproduction as non-monetary. These practices may create first, at the local level, a gendered system supported by the unpaid reproductive work of women (caring work, household work) as well as by the lower paid women's work in the for-profit economy. Here one can easily imagine how the work/family literature under the aegis of women-in-management scholarship is broadly implicated in furthering these practices. Non-responsibility at the local level in the name of capitalist accumulation becomes naturalized as a globalization process when production is continuously moved from location to location in search of the cheapest labour, which is often women's labour.

These global processes, however, must be nuanced with local specificities. For instance, relationships between households, families and communities, as well as the conditions of women in different societies, cannot be interpreted only from the perspective of the gendering effects of these processes in Western societies. Thus, while the flows of global capital may move in certain directions, their effects, as well as resistances must be considered both relationally, and also in their differential local effects and implications (e.g. Battacharjee

1997; Dallalfar and Movahedi 1996; Méndez and Wolff 2001; Acker 2004; Ong and Collier 2005).

An example of this type of work is Mohanty's (1997), where she examined the category of analysis 'women's work' in global capitalism, to show how this apparently neutral category naturalizes gender and race hierarchies while obscuring historical specificities in different areas of the world. Focusing on women's work as a particular form of Third-World women's exploitation in the contemporary economy she foregrounds not only historical differences but commonalities between Third- and First-world women within 'the logic and operation of capital in the contemporary global arena' (Mohanty 1997: 28). In 2003, Mohanty further reiterates these arguments: 'particular kinds of women – poor, Third and Two-Thirds World, working-class and immigrant/migrant women – are the preferred workers in these global, "flexible", temporary job markets' (Mohanty 2003: 245–6). Yet, her analyses also highlight conditions of possibility for global social movements, in solidarity and resistance to global capitalist exploitation.

Feminist economists have provided, as well, detailed analyses of how capital operates through these processes at the macro- and micro-levels, including the ways in which neoliberal economic assumptions and extreme faith in the neutrality of markets are in fact gendered in their premises and their effects (e.g. Benería et al. 2000). Following these analyses, it would be possible to demonstrate relationships between gender and poverty the world over as partial effects of global corporate processes, in contrast to the conventional argument that over time 'economic liberalization' will bring wealth to all.

Analyse Gender as a Resource for Globalizing Capital

This third area of analysis shows further interconnections between different forms of transnational economies, not just through the mobility of capital but also through the mobility of bodies. That women in the 'Third World' have been a central resource to capitalist production, as discussed above, is amply documented in the transnational feminist literatures, yet, as Acker (2004) notices, the relations of capitalist production and globalization today prosper in more complex ways than simply moving production to a 'low wage country', be it physically or through virtual offshoring of services.

In particular and as already discussed, patterns of immigration and transmigration from Third-World and other less affluent regions to rich Euro-American countries and other affluent areas, such as those exemplified by 'global cities' (e.g. Singapore) create newer transnational relations between labour and capital (e.g. Yeoh et al. 2000). These relations, still mediated by gender, race, class and so on, often occur as members of the One-Third World, both men and women often subject to work intensification, require services from members of the Two-Third Worlds (housework, cleaning work, caring work) so that they can go on about their businesses.

While these patterns can easily be explained by the existence of a transnational labour market, the specificity of new social, political and economic relations formed under these conditions are important to consider. In particular, there are complicated questions regarding the effects of these service providers on wages in the lower paid sectors of the affluent regions, the possible exploitation of many immigrants, and often the appearance of newer forms of discrimination, as well as new forms of identity formation in relationship to the state (e.g. Chio 1996; Parreñas 2001; Lutz 2002; Adib and Guerrier 2003). Further, these services contribute to the naturalization of work intensification but also to further privatization of economies, as public services for families and workers continue to recede, as a matter of course, under neoliberal state policies (e.g. Pocock 2005). What does Julia Peña (Sarah Kelly's nanny) have to say on these matters?

Julia Peña: A Transnational/(Post)colonial Feminist

Julia Peña sits reading the newly arrived news magazine, the one featuring her boss in its cover story. She reflects on what she is reading. So, Sarah has decided to stay home with this new baby. What does that imply for Julia? Will she be fired? Will Sarah ask her to stay on working, but ask her to take a cut in pay because of the family's reduced income? Though with a new baby there's bound to be more work.

It's difficult enough to make ends meet now – Julia considers ruefully – supporting her children here and sending money back home to the family as she does. A pay cut, or lost working time looking for new employment, could be devastating. There has to be a way to achieve more security and better income in this line of work. Now looks like the right time to let Sarah know of her activities on behalf of the Union de Trabajadoras Domésticas, the U.T.D., organizing the nannies in the city. Who knows, as a lawyer, perhaps Sarah can be convinced to do pro bono work for the newly forming union. She'll try to be optimistic, to appeal to her sense of solidarity (after all they are both women who work long hours), but, if things don't go well in her negotiations with Sarah, she can always take recourse in her community, with their own version of 'feminismo popular'. What may be the best way to organize a transnational strike of 'global domestic workers'?

A Coda on Gendering: Materialism, Materiality, Materialization

The three theoretical perspectives in this section, socialist, poststructuralist/postmodern and transnational/(post)colonial feminist tendencies exist, at present, in profound conversation with one another. While the materialism of early socialist feminism was subject to much critique for its economic reductionism, the move toward more cultural analyses, eventually culminating in varieties of postmodern feminisms, has now been rendered suspect as extreme in its focus on language and signification, and unable to engage in effective critique by separating the cultural from the material (e.g. Fraser 1998; Ebert 1999).

Some have tried to reconcile the arguments, offering a model of subversive subjectivity that draws from corporeal feminism and standpoint theory (e.g. Weeks 1998), but others ask for a return to a materialist feminism after postmodernism, based on social reproduction, which pulls together the subjective, the affective and the sexual into the realm of the material, without forfeiting economic explanations (Ferguson 1991; 1999). Significantly, Holmstrom's (2002) recent anthology, *The Socialist Feminist Project*, demonstrates the vibrancy and urgency of contemporary feminist materialist analyses. She writes: 'the time is ripe for a positive reappraisal of the socialist-feminist perspective. The brutal economic realities of globalization make it impossible to ignore class, and feminists are now asking on a global level the kind of big questions they asked at a societal level in the 1970s' (Holmstrom 2002: 8).

It seems that today there is indeed a broader positive reassessment of the material for feminist theorizing (Acker 2006). Hearn's (2004) call for an analytical shift from 'hegemonic masculinity to the hegemony of men' can be included in this trend, as well as Smith's (1987; 1990a, b; 1999) use of 'materialism' to conceptualize gendered structures and power relations in their everyday meanings, interactions and practices that constitute gendered lived experience. Meanwhile, Rahman and Witz (2003) argue there is value in recuperating the concepts of materiality and materialization, as deployed by Butler (1993), for the purposes of a better integration of material and symbolic gendered practices today. They agree with Butler that the materiality of bodies, as given, should be problematized insofar as processes of materialization are concurrently recognized. Their focus is thus on the socially materializing effects of cultural and discursive processes. Further, Stone (2004) celebrates the active corporeality of the body in Irigaray's recent works, seeing in them an important move towards much needed realist essentialism for feminist political projects.

These debates, as may have already been gleaned, come to a degree of resolution in much of the transnational feminist literature, for processes of globalization are indeed material in their effects and much of these affect particular people in the world in ways that require the availability of strong political spaces where 'bodies' matter. As advised by Kaplan and Grewal (1999: 358) we must refuse to choose among economic, cultural and political concerns and instead link our 'understanding of postmodernity, global economic structures, problematics of nationalism, issues of race and imperialism, critiques of global feminism, and emergent patriarchies'.

However, it would be ironic if we simply left these as merely 'academic arguments'. How can these arguments become no longer 'academic'? Mohanty (2003) emphasizes the importance of the site of pedagogy as a space of critical engagement. She also warns us about the loss of such space if we do not interrogate current reconfigurations of universities, transnationally, as the domain of private interests. And, thus, even if we want to evade economic reductionism, it is surely time to see ourselves as workers/owners (of intellectual capital) rather than as intellectual elites in complicity with the dominant. As organizational scholars, it is time to reclaim ownership of our institutional spaces, engaging ourselves in solidarity with others in the world for whom our work may truly matter.

Towards a Transnational Feminist Organization Studies

How to give voice to these issues in such a way that organizations studies, as a field of study and as an academic practice of research and teaching, becomes altogether 'gendered', reflecting its contemporary mode of existence in the context of transnationalism and globalization? Our work to this point brought forward several analytical possibilities and now we are proposing several strategies for engaging in the constitution of a different kind of organization studies, *transnational and feminist*, which would require, no doubt, much rewriting of our current field.

First, *issues of representation* cannot go without attention. Acker (2004) continues to point out that gendered images and ideologies of femininity and masculinity matter in the symbolic construction of desirable workers, the stereotyping of jobs and occupations, and images of successful professionals and managers used in various sectors of international capital, and thus reproduce particular gender/race/class/sexuality relations with very material consequences. Similarly, Fernández-Kelly and Wolff (2001) reiterate the necessity of representing multivocality and acknowledging the role of power in the construction of globalization narratives. Some of these approaches have been used in organization studies already, but there is much more to be done (e.g. Henry and Pringle 1996; Holvino 1996; Mir et al. 1999; Chio 2005).

Secondly, *articulate other forms of academic organization*. For instance, Peterson (2002) suggests creating integrative scholarship, beyond disciplinary divides, which in her case would confound political and economic theories. Her analytical frame deploys a Foucauldian economics that denies separation of culture and economy and offers a multidimensional and cross-disciplinary analysis of reproduction, production and virtual economies in relation to globalization dynamics.

These two strategies must be considered together for a real intervention. While at the most 'local' level of research and teaching, *within discipline*, issues of writing, discourse and representation are important starting points, these would achieve little by themselves beyond (another) celebratory (and liberally tolerated) moment of faddish intellectual prowess. Notice that our suggestions in the paragraph above engage with more 'global' levels, *beyond discipline*, starting from institutional change. Transgressing disciplinary boundaries is indeed an important intervention, for it facilitates learning and articulating arguments that might otherwise be shaded by the interests and limits of one's own discipline. It also contributes to the formation of networks among those with similar interests who might otherwise never realize their commonalities. Notice, however that there is nothing extraordinary to be said about these strategies, which could be easily folded into the rubric of 'good contemporary scholarship' unless we reiterate that these are *feminist interventions*, intended to produce fundamental *organizational change in the knowledge we produce, how we produce it and for whom we do so.*

Our third strategy helps to further formulate this: *Legitimizing transnational feminist networks as new organizational forms* in our teaching and our research. For example, Moghadam (2000) considers these transnational networks as a new form of women's collective action in an era of globalization. She argues that these should be understood not only in terms of their local manifestations but also as a global phenomenon, with supra-national constituencies, objectives, strategies and organizations. Such recognition promotes envisioning a crisscrossing of boundaries that extends from questioning the sanctioned 'organizational forms' from within our discipline, to acknowledging the power of women of different races, classes, sexualities, able to come together, in global forum, to further their common interests.

One may argue that these are not any different from the transnational networks formed through the circuits of capital among elite masculinities. The latter, however, are the only ones recognized as transnational networks in our field, supported by our own disciplinary notions of what an organizational network is, including the practices that we deploy among ourselves through academic conferences. The difference that our strategy can make lies in the power granted to these alternatives if we legitimate them as feasible and important in the context of our disciplines (e.g. the World Social Forum vis-à-vis the World Economic Forum), for 'networks' are indeed the dominant discourse in the contemporary organizational lexicon. In so doing we will be clearly articulating not only that all organizational forms are fundamentally systems of power relations, but that such should be the starting point of organizational analysis, recognizing power differentials thus deployed and their differential effects on *all people in the world*, as well as the strategies and resistances that may emerge from them.

Our fourth and last strategy reiterates *the increasing importance of electronic networks and cyberspace* in our field. Who gets to engage in what forum and in which ways is today a fundamental point (Knorr-Cetina and Bruegger 2002). Questions of access continue to be important; however, questions of empowerment are not limited only to access but to institutional context in the global arena of 'distance learning', where corporate interests impinge upon what *accredited knowledge* is, and how and for whom it should be deployed. For example, Gajjala (2003) discusses theoretical and applied concerns in attempts to design and produce cyberfeminist e-spaces, which negotiate diasporic and nationalist gender, class and caste identity formations in online corporate and academic cultures, situated in an increasingly global economy.

We think it unnecessary to remark any further on the complicity of our universities, and our disciplines in particular, in the interests promoting these 'knowledge networks', as universities become further privatized the world over and accelerate the production of MBAs as 'cash cows' in the global economy. Thus, the challenge would be, of necessity, to start by interrogating ourselves about the ways we might be supporting and condoning these processes in how and what we teach, and where and for whom we do so. From where we stand, the most urgent questions that a *transnational feminist organization studies* must now be able to address is: Who '*knows*' in the world, and for whom is this 'knowledge' good?

Conclusions: It's Not Only About 'Gender' Anymore

As the Third World/(Post)colonial arguments make obvious, what we have written so far in this chapter comes from a very specific time period and place in the world. As such, we don't believe anything we write today will 'withstand the test of time' or perhaps even endure until the next handbook of organization studies. After all, we don't believe in ahistorical, acultural, universals. But from where we do stand today we want to underscore that we consider feminist approaches to organization studies one of the few spaces left for reflecting upon and criticizing the excesses and violence of contemporary global capitalism, as it impacts many people all over the world.

With those words we started our concluding comments in 1996. Now, as we hope we have shown throughout the chapter, we are even more convinced they were the right words. However, before we close, and by way of summary, we reflect on several points forwarded through our narrative.

Firstly, recent trends in feminist theorizing are strongly influenced by intersections of insights from socialist, poststructuralist and transnational feminisms. These include an emphasis on subjectivity and identity with particular focus on the body and power relations, addressing both the discursive constructions of our understanding of the self as well as the materiality of the social and economic systems in which such constructions become embedded. Important literatures here also include influences from queer theory and masculinity studies, insofar as they emphasize connections and disruptions between sex and gender in the context of normative social formations.

Secondly, this work includes a more immediate focus on the empirical world, where the social conditions of existence of multiple populations intersect with global flows of capital and newer formations in capitalist development. Important literature here includes analysis of gender and globalization as well as of the gender division of labour, with particular attention to intersectionalities of gender, race, class, ethnicities as analytical lenses.

Thirdly, liberal feminism lives on as a pragmatic engagement between theorizing and policy making – i.e. it could be seen as the language of 'the dominant' if not 'the dominant language' in encounters between the One-Third and the Two-Thirds Worlds, but also within each world as westernization proceeds and liberal political thought becomes 'lingua franca' through neoliberal economics. However, pragmatics should not be confused with an absence of critique. Rather, the language of liberal feminism can be the starting place for re-launching critique about issues such as poverty and health as part of global conditions of inequality, for it allows for more immediate ways of addressing neoliberal regimes.

What value do these points hold for organization studies? Feminist theorizing opens views to a world of many other subject positions. This is of central importance because it tells us that the subjects and objects of our concepts and theories can no longer be that which benefits mostly the dominant, the elite and the organizational. To this effect, as well, feminist theorizing, more generally, has always engaged with the world from which its theories emerge with the intention of offering possibilities for fundamental change against oppressions and discriminations. In that sense, feminist theories are always becoming (a point that has been more forcefully stated in recent re-articulations of feminist theorizing), not in search of universal 'knowledge' but as a way to continue critical engagement in a world that evolves in multiple directions maintaining, or even exacerbating, conditions of inequality. In that sense, 'a woman's work is never done', including the work of theorizing newer social formations.

Further, one cannot engage with a world of gender and other forms of oppression from insular disciplinary languages, positions, frameworks or forms of knowledge production, and for that reason feminist theorizing has been interdisciplinary from its inception. Interdisciplinarity is not only about learning from different disciplines for a more complex engagement with the problems of the day; it is also a way for keeping in view the need for change in frames of thinking and understanding, as those problems evolve partially as a result of prior ways of understanding and acting upon them. Complexity rather than simplification is the aim, as much as change rather than stability is.

What is then, in our view, truly relevant for organization studies today? In emphasizing, perhaps more than in the past, the very material conditions of inequality continuing to be produced by gender and other power relations the world over, we are also attempting to advance the possibility of a different kind of organization studies. Our version, *feminist*

organization studies, starts from a position in which gender relations and its intersectionalities with other systems of social inequality, is the root organizing principle of contemporary capitalism. Emerging from this perspective, *a transnational feminist organization studies* would obtain very different disciplinary lenses, and see to it that organizational knowledge-production would work ever more forcefully towards an equitable and just world. Once again, we need a disciplinary field that allows us to ask: What prevents change? Who keeps the gates closed? Whose knowledge is allowed? What kind of politics are the politics of knowledge in our field?

Notes

1. Our conviction owes much to Ann Ferguson, dear colleague in Women's Studies at UMass. We thank her for many years of inspiration, support for our work and generosity in teaching us much about feminist theorizing.
2. Gender-cultural feminism may be sometimes confused with radical-cultural feminism, but a key difference resides in their different notions of 'connection'. *Gender-cultural feminists*, '[v]alourizing the traits and behaviours traditionally associated with women, praise women's capacities for sharing, nurturing, giving, sympathizing, empathizing and especially, connection ... relationships are so important to women that they view separation from others as the quintessential harm' (Tong 1998: 296–7). *Radical-cultural feminists* agree that 'connection' is a fundamental reality for women, but see this also as a curse, for 'connections set women up for exploitation and misery' (Tong 1998: 297) within a patriarchal order, which helps explain why radical-cultural feminists may valourize a separate women's culture.

References

Aaltio-Marjosola, I. and Kovalainen, A. (2001) 'Personality', in E. Wilson (ed.), *Organizational Behavior Reassessed*. London: Sage. pp. 17–36.
Abel, E. (1990) 'Race, class, and psychoanalysis? Opening questions', in M. Hirsch and E. Fox Keller (eds), *Conflicts in Feminism*. New York: Routledge. pp. 184–204.
Abel, E., Christian, B. and Moglen, H. (eds) (1997) *Female Subjects in Black and White: Race, Psychoanalysis, Feminism*. Berkeley: University of California Press.
Acker, J. (1990) 'Hierarchies, jobs, bodies: a theory of gendered organizations', *Gender & Society*, 4(2): 139–58.
Acker, J. (1992) 'Gendering organizational theory', in A.J. Mills and P. Tancred (eds), *Gendering Organizational Analysis*. Newbury Park CA: Sage. pp. 248–60.

Acker, J. (1994) 'The gender regime of Swedish banks', *Scandinavian Journal of Management*, 10(2): 117–30.

Acker, J. (1998) 'The future of 'gender and organizations': connections and boundaries', *Gender, Work and Organization*, 5(4): 195–206.

Acker, J. (2000) 'Gendered contradictions in organizational equity projects', *Organization*, 7(4): 625–32.

Acker J. (2004) 'Gender, capitalism and globalization', *Critical Sociology*, 30(1): 17–41.

Acker, J. (2006) *Class Questions: Feminist Answers*. Lanham: Rowman & Littlefield Publishers.

Acker, J. and Van Houten, D.R. (1974) 'Differential recruitment and control: the sex structuring of organizations', *Administrative Science Quarterly*, 19(2): 152–63.

Adam, A. and Ofori-Amanfo, J. (2000) 'Does gender matter in computer ethics?', *Ethics and Information Technology*, 2(1): 37–47.

Adib, A. and Guerrier, Y. (2003) 'The interlocking of gender with nationality, race, ethnicity and class: the narratives of women in hotel work', *Gender, Work & Organization*, 10(4): 413–32.

Adler, A. (1927) *Understanding Human Nature*. New York: Greenberg.

Ahl, H.J. (2004) *The Scientific Reproduction of Gender Inequality: A Discourse Analysis of Research Texts on Women's Entrepreneurship*. Copenhagen: Copenhagen Business School.

Ahmed, S. (1996) 'Beyond humanism and postmodernism: theorizing a feminist practice', *Hypatia*, 11(2): 71–93.

Ahmed, S. (2000) 'Whose counting?', *Feminist Theory*, 1(1): 97–103.

Alarcón, N. (1990) 'The theoretical subject(s) in This Bridge Called My Back and Anglo-American Feminism', in G. Anzaldúa (ed.), *Making Face, Making Soul/Haciendo Caras*. San Francisco: Spinsters/Aunt Lute. pp. 356–69.

Alcoff, L. (1988) 'Cultural feminism versus post structuralism: the identity crisis in feminist theory', *Signs*, 13(3): 405–36.

Alcoff, L.M. (2000) 'Philosophy matters: a review of recent work in feminist philosophy', *Signs*, 25(3): 841.

Alexander, M.J. (1997) 'Erotic autonomy as a politics of decolonization: an anatomy of feminist and state practice in the Bahamas tourist economy', in J. Alexander and C.T. Mohanty (eds), *Feminist Genealogies, Colonial Legacies, Democratic Futures*. New York: Routledge. pp. 63–100.

Alpern, S. (1993) 'In the beginning: a history of women in management', in E. Fagenson (ed.), *Women in Management: Trends, Issues and Challenges in Managerial Diversity*. Newbury Park, CA: Sage. pp. 19–51.

Alvesson, M. and Billing, D.Y. (1997) *Understanding Gender and Organizations*. London: Sage.

Amos-Wilson, P. (2000) 'Women Civil Servants and transformational leadership in Bangladesh', *Equal Opportunities International*, 19(5): 23–31.

Anderson, D. (2003) 'The integration of gender and political behavior into Hambrick and Mason's upper echelons model of organizations', *Journal of American Academy of Business*, 3(1/2): 29.

Anderson, D.J., Binder, M. and Krause, K. (2003) 'The motherhood wage penalty revisited: experience, heterogeneity, work effort, and work-schedule flexibility', *Industrial and Labor Relations Review*, 56: 273–95.

Ang, I. (1997). 'Comment on Felski's 'The Doxa of Difference': the uses of incommensurability', *Signs*, 23(1): 57–64.

Anzaldúa, G. (1987) *Borderlands/ La Frontera: The New Mestiza*. San Francisco: Aunt Lute.

Anzaldúa, G. (ed.) (1990) *Making Face, Making Soul: Haciendo Caras*. San Francisco: Aunt Lute.

Appold, S.J., Siengthai, S. and Kasarda, J.D. (1998) 'The employment of women managers and professionals in an emerging economy: gender inequality as an organizational practice', *Administrative Science Quarterly*, 43(3): 538–65.

Aranda E.M. (2003) 'Global care work and gendered constraints: the case of Puerto Rican transmigrants', *Gender & Society*, 17(4): 609–26.

Armour, E.T. (1997) 'Crossing the boundaries between deconstruction, feminism, and religion', in N.J. Holland (ed.), *Feminist Interpretations of Jacques Derrida*. University Park: Pennsylvania State University Press. pp. 193–214.

Armstrong, P. and Cornish, M. (1997) 'Restructuring pay equity for a restructured work force: Canadian perspectives', *Gender Work and Organization*, 4(2): 67–86.

Ashcraft, K.L (1999) 'Managing maternity leave: a qualitative analysis of temporary executive succession', *Administrative Science Quarterly*, 44: 40–80.

Ashcraft, K.L. (2001) 'Organized dissonance: feminist bureaucracy as hybrid form', *Academy of Management Journal*, 44(6): 1301–22.

Ashcraft, K.L. (2004) 'Gender, discourse, and organization: framing a shifting relationship', in D. Grant, C. Hardy, C. Oswick, N. Phillips and L. Putnam (eds), *The Sage Handbook of Organizational Discourse*. London: Sage. pp. 275–98.

Ashcraft, K.L. and Mumby, D. (2004) *Reworking Gender: A Feminist Communicology of Organization*. Thousand Oaks: Sage.

Ashford, S.J., Rothbard, N.P., Piderit, S.K. and Dutton, J.E. (1998) 'Out on a limb: the role of context and impression management in selling gender-equity issues', *Administrative Science Quarterly*, 43(1): 23–57.

Auslander, L. (1997) 'Do women's + feminist + men's + lesbian and gay + queer studies = gender studies?', *differences: A Journal of Feminist Cultural Studies*, 9(3): 1–29.

Bailyn, L. (2003) 'Academic careers and gender equity: lessons learned from MIT', *Gender, Work & Organization*, 10(2): 137–53.

Bailyn, L. (2004) 'Time in careers – careers in time', *Human Relations*, 57(12): 1507–21.

Bailyn, L., Fletcher, J.K. and Kolb, D. (1997) 'Unexpected connections: considering employees' personal lives can revitalize your business', *Sloan Management Review*, 38(4): 11–19.

Baines, S. and Wheelock, J. (2000) 'Work and employment in small business: perpetuating and challenging gender traditions', *Gender, Work & Organizations*, 7(1): 45–56.

Balka, E. (1997) 'Participatory design in women's organizations: the social world of organizational structure and the gendered nature of experience', *Gender, Work & Organization*, 4(2): 99–115.

Ball, K. (2005) 'Organization, surveillance and the body: towards a politics of resistance', *Organization*, 12(1): 89–108

Banerjee, S.B. and Linstead, S. (2001) 'Globalizaton, multiculturalism and other fictions: colonialism for the new millennium?', *Organization*, 8(4): 683–722.

Barad, K. (2003) 'Posthumanist performativity: toward an understanding of how matter comes to matter', *Signs*, 28(3): 801–31.

Bardoel, E.A. (2003) 'The provision of formal and informal work-family practices: The relative importance of institutional and resource dependent explanations versus managerial explanations', *Women In Management Review*, 18(1/2): 7–19.

Barnard, C.I. (1938) *The Functions of the Executive*. Cambridge, MA: Harvard University Press.

Bartky, S.L. (1998) 'Body politics', in A.M. Jaggar and I.M. Young (eds), *A Companion to Feminist Philosophy*. Malden: Blackwell. pp. 321–9.

Bartol, K.M. (1978) 'The sex structuring of organizations: a search for possible causes', *Academy of Management Review*, 3(4): 805–15.

Battacharjee, A. (1997) 'The public/private mirage: mapping home and undomesticating violence work in the South Asian immigrant community', in J. Alexander and C.T. Mohanty (eds), *Feminist Genealogies, Colonial Legacies, Democratic Futures*. New York: Routledge. pp. 308–29.

Baxter, L. and Hughes, C. (2004) 'Tongue sandwiches and bagel days: sex, food and mind/body dualism', *Gender, Work & Organization*, 11(4): 363–80.

Belenky, M.F., Clinchy, B.M., Goldberger, N.R. and Tarule, J.M. (eds) (1997/86) *Women's Ways of Knowing: The Development of Self, Voice and Mind*, 10th anniversary edn. New York: Basic Books.

Belkin, L. (2003) 'The opt-out revolution', *New York Times Magazine*. Available online at: http://www.nytimes.com/2003/10/26/magazine/26WOMEN.html, accessed 26 October 2005.

Bell, E.L.J. (2000) 'What does it mean to be an intellectual woman? A comparative essay', *Journal of Management Inquiry*, 9(2): 200–6.

Bell, E.L.J. and Nkomo, S.M. (2001) *Our Separate Ways: Black and White Women and the Struggle for Professional Identity*. Boston: Harvard Business School Press.

Bell, E.L., Denton, T.C. and Nkomo, S. (1993) 'Women of color: toward an inclusive analysis', in E.A. Fagenson (ed.), *Women in Management: Trends, Issues and Challenges in Managerial Diversity*. Newbury Park, CA: Sage. pp. 105–30.

Benería L. (1999) 'Globalization, gender and the Davos Man', *Feminist Economics*, 5(3): 61–83.

Benería L., Floro M., Grown C. and MacDonald, M. (2000) 'Globalization and gender', *Feminist Economics*, 6(3): 7–18.

Benhabib, S. (1984) 'Epistemologies of postmodernism: a rejoinder to Jean-Francois Lyotard', *New German Critique*, 33: 103–26.

Benschop, Y. and Brouns, M. (2003) 'Crumbling ivory towers: academic organizing and its gender effects', *Gender, Work & Organization*, 10(2): 194–212.

Benschop, Y. and Doorewaard, H. (1998a) 'Six of one and half a dozen of the other: the gender subtext of Taylorism and team-based work', *Gender, Work & Organization*, 5(1): 5–18.

Benschop, Y. and Doorewaard, H. (1998b) 'Covered by equality: the gender subtext of organizations', *Organization Studies*, 19(5): 787.

Bergeron, S. (2001) 'Political economy discourses of globalization and feminist politics', *Signs*, 26(4): 983–1006.

Betters-Reed, B. and Moore, L.L. (1991) 'Managing diversity: focusing on women and the whitewash dilemma', in U. Sekaran and F. Leong (eds), *Womanpower: Managing in Times of Demographic Turbulence*. Newbury Park, CA: Sage.

Bettie, J. (2003) *Women Without Class*. Berkeley: University of California Press.

Beverly, J. (2000) 'Testimonio, subalternity, and narrative authority', in N.K. Denzin and Y.S. Lincoln (eds), *Handbook of Qualitative Research*, 2nd edn. Thousands Oaks, CA: Sage. pp. 555–65.

Bhabha, H. (1985) 'Signs taken for wonders: questions of ambivalence and authority under a tree outside Delhi, May 1817', *Critical Inquiry*, 12(1): 144–65.

Bhabha, H. (1988) 'The commitment to theory', *New Formations*, 5: 5–23.

Billing, Y.D. and Alvesson, M. (2000) 'Questioning the notion of feminine leadership: a critical perspective on the gender labeling of leadership', *Gender, Work & Organization*, 7(3): 144–57.

Bird, S.R. (2003) 'Sex composition, masculinity stereotype dissimilarity and the quality of men's workplace social relations', *Gender, Work & Organization*, 10(5): 579–604.

Blackwell, L. (2001) 'Occupational sex segregation and part-time work in modern Britain', *Gender, Work & Organization*, 8(2): 146–63.

Blum, L. and Smith, V. (1988) 'Women's mobility in the corporation: a critique of the politics of optimism', *Signs*, 13(3): 528–45.

Boraas, S. and Rodgers, W.M. III. (2003) 'How does gender play a role in the earnings gap? An update', *Monthly Labor Review*, 126(3): 9–15.

Bordo, S.R. (1989) 'The body and the reproduction of femininity: a feminist appropriation of Foucault', in S.R. Bordo and A.M. Jaggar (eds), *Gender/Body/Knowledge: Feminist Reconstructions of Being and Knowing*. New Brunswick: Rutgers University Press. pp. 13–33.

Bordo, S. (1990) 'Feminism, postmodernism, and gender-scepticism', in L.J. Nicholson (ed.), *Feminism/Postmodernism*. London: Routledge. pp. 133–56.

Bordo, S. (1993) *Unbearable Weight: Feminism, Western Culture and the Body*. Berkeley, CA: University of California Press.

Bordo, S. (1998) 'Bringing body to theory', in D. Welton (ed.), *Body and Flesh: A Philosophical Reader*. Oxford: Blackwell. pp. 84–97.

Boucher, C. (1997) 'How women socially construct leadership in organizations: a study using memory work', *Gender, Work & Organization*, 4(3): 149–58.

Bowman, G.W., Worthy, N.B. and Greyser, S.A. (1965) 'Are women executives people?', *Harvard Business Review*, 43(July–August): 14–178 (not continuous).

Bowring, M.A. (2004) 'Resistance is not futile: liberating Captain Janeway from the masculine-feminine dualism of leadership', *Gender, Work & Organization*, 11(4): 381–405.

Braidotti, R. (1989) 'The politics of ontological difference', in T. Brennan (ed.), *Between Feminism and Psychoanalysis*. London: Roultedge. p. 97.

Braidotti, R. (1991) *Patterns of Dissonance*. Cambridge: Polity Press.

Braidotti, R. (1994) *Nomadic Subjects: Embodiment and Sexual Difference in Contemporary Feminist Theory*. New York: Columbia University Press.

Braidotti, R. (1998) 'Sexual difference theory', in A.M. Jaggar and I.M. Young (eds), *A Companion to Feminist Philosophy*. Malden: Blackwell. pp. 298–306.

Braidotti, R. (2002) *Metamorphoses: Towards a Materialist Theory of Becoming*. Cambridge: Polity Press.

Braithwaite, A. (2002) 'The personal, the political, third-wave and postfeminisms', *Feminist Theory*, 3(3): 335–44.

Brandth, B. and Kvande, E. (2002) 'Reflexive fathers: negotiating parental leave and working life', *Gender, Work & Organization*, 9(2): 186–203.

Bray, A. and Colebrook C. (1998) 'The haunted flesh: corporeal feminism and the politics of (dis)embodiment', *Signs*, 24(11): 35–67.

Brennan, T. (1998) 'Psychoanalytic feminism', in A.M. Jaggar and I.M. Young (eds), *A Companion to Feminist Philosophy*. Malden: Blackwell. pp. 272–9.

Brewer, A.M. (2000) 'Work design for flexible work scheduling: barriers and gender implications', *Gender, Work & Organization*, 7(1): 33–44.

Brewis, J. (2001) 'Foucault, politics and organizations: (re)-constructing sexual harassment', *Gender, Work & Organization*, 8(1): 37–60.

Britton, D.M. (2000) 'The epistemology of the gendered organization', *Gender & Society*, 14(3): 418–34.

Brooks, I. and MacDonald, S. (2000) '"Doing life": gender relations in a night nursing sub-culture', *Gender, Work & Organization*, 7(4): 221–9.

Brown, C. and Jones, L. (2004) 'The gender structure of the nursing hierarchy: the role of human capital', *Gender, Work & Organization*, 11(1): 1–25.

Brown, H. (1992) *Women Organizing*. London: Routledge.

Browne, I and Misra, J. (2003) 'The intersection of gender and race in the labor market', *Annual Review of Sociology*, 29: 487–513.

Bruni, A., Gherardi, G. and Poggio, B. (2004) 'Doing gender, doing entrepreneurship: an ethnographic account of intertwined practices', *Gender, Work & Organization*, 11(4): 406–29.

Budig, M.J. and England, P. (2001) 'The wage penalty for motherhood', *American Sociological Review*, 66: 204.

Burke, R.J. (2001) 'Managerial women's career experiences, satisfaction and well-being: a five country study', *Cross Cultural Management*, 8(3/4): 117–33.

Busby, N. and Middlemiss, S. (2001) 'The equality deficit: protection against discrimination on the grounds of sexual orientation in employment', *Gender, Work & Organization*, 8(4): 387–410.

Butler, J. (1990) *Gender Trouble: Feminism and the Subversion of Identity*. New York: Routledge.

Butler J. (1992) 'Gender entry', in E. Wright (ed.), *Feminism and Psychoanalysis: A Critical Dictionary*. Oxford: Blackwell. pp. 140–5.

Butler, J. (1993) *Bodies That Matter: On the Discursive Limits of 'Sex'*. New York: Routledge.

Butler, J. (1999) 'Preface from *Gender Trouble* anniversary edition. Reproduced in S. Salih (ed.), with J. Butler (2004) *The Judith Butler Reader*. Malden: Blackwell Publishing. pp. 94–103.

Butler, J. (2004) *Undoing Gender*. New York: Routledge.

Butler, J. and Scott, J.W. (1992) *Feminists Theorize the Political*. New York: Routledge

Buttner, E.H. (2001) 'Examining female entrepreneurs' management style: an application of a relational frame', *Journal of Business Ethics*, 29(3): 253–69.

Buzzanell, P.M. (1995) 'Reframing the glass ceiling as a socially constructed process: implications for understanding and change', *Communication Monographs*, 62(4): 327–54.

Buzzanell, P.M. (ed.) (2000) *Rethinking Organizational and Managerial Communication from Feminist Perspectives*. Thousand Oaks, CA: Sage.

Calás, M.B. (1992) 'An/other silent voice? Representing 'Hispanic woman' in organizational texts', in A.J. Mills and P. Tancred (eds), *Gendering Organizational Analysis*. Newbury Park, CA: Sage. pp. 201–21.

Calás, M.B. (1993) 'Deconstructing charismatic leadership: re-reading Weber from the darker side', *Leadership Quarterly*, 4(3/4): 305–28.

Calás M.B. and Smircich, L. (1991) 'Voicing seduction to silence leadership', *Organization Studies*, 12(4): 567–602.

Calás, M. and Smircich, L. (1993) 'Dangerous liaisons: the 'feminine-in-management' meets globalization', *Business-Horizons*, 36(2): 71–81.

Calás, M.B. and Smircich, L. (1996) 'From "the woman's point of view": feminist approaches to organization studies', in S. Clegg, C. Hardy and W. Nord (eds), *Handbook of Organization Studies*. London: Sage. pp. 218–57.

Calás, M.B. and Smircich, L. (1997) 'Predicando la moral en calzoncillos? Feminist inquiries into business ethics', in A.L. Larson and R.E. Freeman (eds), *Women's Studies and Business Ethics*. New York: Oxford University Press. pp. 50–79.

Calás, M.B. and Smircich, L. (1999) 'Past postmodernism? Reflections and tentative directions', *Academy of Management Review*, 24(4): 649–71.

Calás, M.B. and Smircich, L. (2003) 'At home from Mars to Somalia: recounting organization studies', in H. Tsoukas and C. Knudsen (eds), *The Oxford Handbook of Organization Theory*. Oxford: Oxford University Press. pp. 596–606.

Calás, M.B. and Smircich, L. (2004a) 'To be done with progress and other heretical thoughts for organization and management studies', in E. Locke (ed.), *Postmodernism and management: Pros, cons and the alternative*. Research in the Sociology of Organizations volume 21. Amsterdam: JAI. pp. 29–56.

Calás, M.B. and Smircich, L. (2004b) 'Revisiting 'dangerous liaisons' or does the 'feminine-in-management' still meet 'globalization'?', in P.J. Frost, W.R. Nord and L.A. Krefting (eds), *Managerial and Organizational Reality*. Upper Saddle River, NJ: Pearson Prentice Hall. pp. 467–81.

Calvert, L.M. and Ramsey, V.J. (1992) 'Bringing women's voice to research on women in management: a feminist perspective', *Journal of Management-Inquiry*, 1(1): 79–88.

Calvert, L.M. and Ramsey, V.J. (1994) 'Speaking as female and white', *Organization*, 3(4): 468–85.

Campbell, M.L. (2002) 'Research for activism and institutional ethnography: understanding social organization from inside it', Presented at: *Sociology for Changing the World: Political Activist Ethnography Conference*. Laurentian University, Sudbury, 8–10 November.

Caputo, R.K. and Cianni, M. (2001) 'Correlates of voluntary vs. involuntary part-time employment among US women', *Gender, Work & Organization*, 8(3): 311–25.

Casey, C. (2004) 'Contested rationalities, contested organizations: feminist and postmodernist visions', *Journal of Organizational Change Management*. 17(3): 302.

Chafetz, J.S. (1997) 'Feminist theory and sociology: underutilized contributions for mainstream theory', *Annual Review of Sociology*, 23: 97–120.

Chanter, T. (1998) 'Postmodern subjectivity', in A.M. Jaggar and I.M. Young (eds), *A Companion to Feminist Philosophy*. Malden: Blackwell. pp. 263–71.

Chapman D.S. and Rowe, P.M. (2001) 'The impact of videoconference technology, interview structure, and interviewer gender on interviewer evaluations in the employment interview: a field experiment', *Journal of Occupational and Organizational Psychology*, 74(3): 279–98.

Chênevert, D. and Tremblay, M. (2002) 'Managerial career success in Canadian organizations: is gender a determinant?', *International Journal of Human Resource Management*, 13(6): 920–41.

Cheng, A.A. (2001) *The Melancholy of Race*. New York: Oxford University Press.

Chio, V.C.M. (1996) 'Boundaries and visibilities: anthropologizing women and work in the international economic arena', *Organization*, 3(4): 627–40.

Chio, V.C.M. (2005) *Malaysia and the Development Process: Globalization, Knowledge Transfers and Postcolonial Dilemmas*. New York: Routledge.

Chodorow, N. (1978) *The Reproduction of Mothering*. Berkeley: University of California Press.

Cholmeley, J. (1991) 'A feminist business in a capitalist world', in N. Redclift and M.T. Sinclair (eds), *Working Women, International Perspectives on Labour and Gender Ideology*. London: Routledge. pp. 213–32.

Chow, R. (1999) 'When whiteness feminizes …: some consequences of a supplementary logic. *Differences: A Journal of Feminist Cultural Studies*, 11(3): 137.

Cianni, M. and Romberger, B. (1997) 'Life in the corporation: a multi-method study of the experiences of male and female Asian, Black, Hispanic and White employees', *Gender, Work & Organization*, 4(2): 116–29.

Cockburn, C. (1991) *In the Way of Women*. Ithaca: ILR Press.

Code, L. (1991) *What Can She Know? Feminist Theory and the Construction of Knowledge*. Ithaca: Cornell.

Code, L. (1998) 'Epistemology', in A. Jaggar and I.M. Young (eds), *A Companion to Feminist Philosophy*. Oxford: Blackwell. pp. 173–84.

Coffield, C.D. (2002) 'Welfare reform in Indiana: the political economy of restricting access to education and training', *Journal of Family and Economic Issues*, 23(3): 261–84.

Cole, N. (2004) 'Gender differences in perceived disciplinary fairness', *Gender, Work & Organization*, 11(3): 254–79.

Coleman, G. and Rippin, A. (2000) 'Putting feminist theory to work: collaboration as a means towards organizational change', *Organization*, 7(4): 573–88.

Colgan, F. and Ledwith, S. (2000) Diversity, identities and strategies of women trade union activists. *Gender, Work & Organization*, 7(4): 242–57.

Collins, P.H. (1986) 'Learning from the outsider within: the sociological significance of Black feminist thought', *Social Problems*, 33(6): S14–32.

Collins, P.H. (1991) *Black Feminist Thought: Knowledge, Consciousness and the Politics of Empowerment*. New York: Routledge.

Collins, P.H. (1998) 'It's all in the family: intersections of gender, race, and nation', *Hypatia*, 13(3): 62–82.

Collins, P.H. (2000a) 'What's going on? Black feminist thought and the politics of postmodernism', in E.A. St.Pierre and W.S. Pillow (eds), *Working the Ruins: Feminist Poststructural Theory and Methods in Education*. New York: Routledge. pp. 41–73.

Collins, P.H. (2000b) 'It's all in the family: intersections of gender, race, and nation', in U. Narayan and S. Harding (eds), *Decentering the Center: Philosophy for a Multicultural, Postcolonial, and Feminist world*. Bloomington: Indiana University Press. pp. 156–76.

Collinson, D. and Hearn, J. (1994) 'Naming men as men: implications for work, organization and management', *Gender, Work & Organization*, 1(1): 2–22.

Collinson, D. and Hearn, J. (1996) *Men as managers, managers as men: Critical perspectives on men, masculinities, and management*. Thousand Oaks, CA: Sage.

Collinson, D., Knights, D. and Collinson, M. (1990) *Managing to Discriminate*. London: Routledge.

Combahee River Collective (1977) 'A black feminist statement', in W. Kolmar and F. Bartkowski (eds), *Feminist Theory: A Reader*. Mountainview, CA: Mayfield. pp. 272–7.

Combs, G.M. (2003) 'The duality of race and gender for managerial African American women: implications of informal social networks on career advancement', *Human Resource Development Review*, 2(4): 385–405.

Connell, R.W. (1987) *Gender and Power*. Cambridge: Polity.

Connell, R.W. (1995) *Masculinities*. Berkeley: University of California Press.

Connell, R.W. (2005) 'Change among the gatekeepers: men, masculinities, and gender equality in the global arena', *Signs*, 30(3): 1801–26.

Cotter, D.A., Hermsen, J.M., Ovadia, S. and Vanneman, R. (2001) 'The glass ceiling effect', *Social Forces*, 80(2): 655–81.

Crenshaw, K. (1989) 'Demarginalizing the intersection of race and sex: a Black feminist critique of antidiscrimination doctrine, feminist theory, and antiracist politics', *University of Chicago Legal Forum*, 5: 139–67.

Crenshaw, K. (1991/1995) 'Mapping the margins: intersectionality, identity politics, and violence against women of color', *Stanford Law Review*, 43(6): 1241–70. Reprinted in K. Cresnshaw, N. Gotanda, G. Peller and K. Thomas. *Critical Race Theory*. New York: The New Press. pp. 357–83.

Crompton, R. (ed.) (1999) *Restructuring Gender Relations and Employment*. Oxford: Oxford University Press.

Crompton, R. and Sanderson, K. (1990) *Gendered Jobs and Social Change*. London: Unwin Hyman.

Cron, E.A. (2001) 'Job satisfaction in dual-career women at three family life cycle stages', *Journal of Career Development*, 28(1): 17.

Cross, S. and Bagilhole, B. (2002) 'Girls jobs for the boys? Men, masculinity and non-traditional occupations', *Gender, Work & Organization*, 9(2) : 204–26.

Cullen, D. (1997) 'Maslow, monkeys and motivation theory', *Organization*, 4(3): 355–73.

Cunningham, R., Lord, A. and Delaney, L. (1999) "Next steps' for equality: the impact of organizational change on opportunities for women in the civil service', *Gender, Work & Organization*, 6(2): 67–78.

Cuomo, C.J. and Hall, K.Q. (eds) (1999) *Whiteness: Feminist Philosophical Reflections*. Boulder: Rowman and Littlefield.

Currier, D. (2003) 'Feminist technological futures: Deleuze and body/technology assemblages', *Feminist Theory*, 4(3): 321–38.

Dallalfar, A. and Movahedi, S. (1996) 'Women in multinational corporations: old myths, new constructions and some deconstructions', *Organization*, 3(4): 546–62.

Daly, M. (1978) *Gyn/Ecology*. Boston: Beacon.

Darling-Wolf, F. (2004) 'Sites of attractiveness: Japanese women and westernized representations of feminine beauty', *Critical Studies in Media Communication*, 21(4): 325–45.

Davis, A.Y. (1981) *Women, Race and Class*. New York: Random House.

De Lauretis, T. (1984) *Alice Doesn't: Feminism, Semiotics and Cinema*. Bloomington: University of Indiana Press.

De Lauretis, T. (1987) *Technologies of Gender*. Bloomington: Indiana University Press.

De Saussure, F. (1974) *Course in General Linguistics*. London: Fontana.

Deem, R. (2003) 'Gender, organizational cultures and the practices of manager-academics in UK universities', *Gender, Work & Organization*, 10(2): 239–59.

Delphy, C. (1984) *Close to Home: A Materialist Analysis of Women's Oppression*. Amherst: University of Massachusetts Press.

DeVault, M.L. (1995) 'Ethnicity and expertise: racial-ethnic knowledge in sociological research', *Gender & Society*, 9(5): 612–31.

DeVault, M.L. and McCoy, L. (2002) 'Institutional ethnography: using interviews to investigate ruling relations', in J.F. Gabrium and J.A. Holstein (eds), *Handbook of Interview Research*. Thousand Oaks: Sage. pp. 751–75.

Di Stefano, C. (1988) 'Dilemmas of difference: feminism, modernity, and postmodernism', *Women and Politics*, 8(3/4): 1–24.

Diamond, I. and Quinby, L. (eds) (1988) *Feminism & Foucault*. Boston: Northeastern University Press.

Dijkstra S., Geuijen K. and de Ruijter A. (2001) 'Multiculturalism and social integration in Europe', *International Political Science Review*, 22(1): 55–84.

Dill, B.T. (1983) 'Race, class, and gender: prospects for all-inclusive sisterhood', *Feminist Studies*, 9: 131–50.

Dinnerstein, D. (1977) *The Mermaid and the Minotaur: Sexual Arrangements and Human Malaise.* New York: Harper.

Douglas, S.J. and Michaels, M.W. (2004) *The Mommy Myth.* New York: Free Press.

Doyle, C. and Hind, P. (1998) 'Occupational stress, burnout and job status in female academics', *Gender, Work and Organization,* 5(2): 67–82.

Drentea, P. (1998) 'Consequences of women's formal and informal job search methods for employment in female-dominated jobs', *Gender and Society,* 12(3): 321–38.

Duncan, C. and Loretto, W. (2004) 'Never the right age? Gender and age-based discrimination in employment', *Gender, Work & Organization,* 11(1): 95–115.

Dunne, G.A. (ed.) (1998) *Living 'Difference': Lesbian Perspectives on Work and Family Life.* New York: Haworth.

Eagly, A.H. and Carli, L.L. (2003) 'The female leadership advantage: an evaluation of the evidence', *Leadership Quarterly,* 14(6): 807.

Eagly, A.H. and. Johannesen-Schmidt, M.C. (2001) 'The leadership style of men and women', *Journal of Social Issues,* 57(4): 781–97.

Eagly, A.H. and Karau, S.J. (2002) 'Role congruity theory of prejudice toward female leaders', *Psychological Review,* 109(3): 573–98.

Ebert, T.L. (1999) *Ludic Feminism and After: Postmodernism, Desire and Labor in Late Capitalism.* Ann Arbor: University of Michigan Press.

Echols, A. (1983) 'The new feminism of yin and yang', in A. Snitow, C. Stansell and S. Thompson (eds), *Powers of Desire: The Politics of Sexuality.* New York: Monthly Review Press. pp. 430–59.

Eisenstein, H. (1983) *Contemporary Feminist Thought.* Boston: G.K. Hall.

El Guindi, F. (1999) 'Veiling resistance', *Fashion Theory,* 3(1): 51–80.

Ellehave, C.F. (2005) *Differences that Matter: An Analysis of Practices of Gender and Organizing in Contemporary Workplaces.* Copenhagen: Copenhagen Business School.

Elshtain, J.B. (1981) *Public Man, Private Woman.* Princeton, NJ: Princeton University Press.

Ely, R.J. and Meyerson, D.E. (2000) 'Advancing gender equity in organizations: the challenge and importance of maintaining a gender narrative', *Organization,* 7(4): 589–608.

Escobar, A. (1995) *Encountering Development.* Princeton: Princeton University Press.

Essed, P. (1991) *Understanding Everyday Racism: An Interdisciplinary Theory.* Newbury Park, CA: Sage.

Esteva, G. and Prakash, M.S. (1998) *Grassroots Postmodernism: Remaking the Soil of Cultures.* London: Zed Press.

Evans, J. (1995) *Feminist Theory Today.* London: Sage.

Eveline, J. and Booth, M. (2002) 'Gender and sexuality in discourses of managerial control', *Gender, Work & Organization,* 9(5): 556–78.

Evetts, J. (2000) 'Analysing change in women's careers: culture, structure and action dimensions', *Gender, Work & Organization,* 7(1): 57–67.

Fagan, D. (2001) 'Time, money and the gender order: work orientations and working-time preferences in Britain', *Gender, Work & Organization,* 8(3): 239–66.

Farrell, A.E. (1994) 'A social experiment in publishing: *Ms.* magazine, 1972–1989', *Human Relations,* 47(6): 707–30.

Fausto-Sterling, A. (2005) 'The bare bones of sex: part 1 – sex and gender', *Signs,* 30(2): 1491–527.

Felski, R. (1997) 'The doxa of difference', *Signs,* 23(1): 1–21.

Fenwick, G.D. and Neal, D.J. (2001) 'Effect of gender composition on group performance', *Gender, Work & Organization,* 8(2): 205–25.

Ferguson, A. (1977) 'Androgyny as an ideal for human development', in M. Vetterling-Braggin, F. Elliston and J. English (eds), *Feminism and Philosophy.* Totowa, NJ: Littlefield, Adams. pp. 45–69.

Ferguson, A. (1991) *Sexual Democracy: Women, Oppression and Revolution.* Boulder: Westview Press.

Ferguson, A. (1996) 'Bridge identity politics: an integrative feminist ethics of international development', *Organization,* 3(4): 571–87.

Ferguson, A. (1998) 'Socialism', in A. Jaggar and I.M. Young (eds), *A Companion to Feminist Philosophy.* Malden, MA: Blackwell. pp. 520–9.

Ferguson, K.E. (1993) *The Man Question: Visions of Subjectivity in Feminist Theory.* Berkeley, CA: University of California Press.

Ferguson, K.E. (1994) 'On bringing more theory, more voices and more politics to the study of organization', *Organization,* 1(1): 81–99.

Ferguson, S. (1999) 'Building on the strengths of the socialist feminist tradition', *New Politics,* 7(2). Available online at: http://www.wpunj.edu/~newpol/issue26/fergus26.htm.

Fernandes, L. (1999) 'Reading 'India's Bandit Queen': a trans/national feminist perspective on the discrepancies of representation', *Signs,* 25(1): 123–52.

Fernández-Kelly, M.P. (1994) 'Making sense of gender in the world economy', *Organization,* 1(2): 249–75.

Fernández-Kelly, M.P. and Wolff, D.L. (2001) 'A dialogue on globalization', *Signs,* 26(4): 1243–9.

Ferree, M.M. and Martin, P.Y. (eds) (1995) *Feminist Organizations: Harvest of the New Women's Movement.* Philadelphia: Temple University Press.

Firestone, J.M. and Harris, R.J. (2003) 'Perceptions of effectiveness of responses to sexual harassment in the US military, 1988 and 1995', *Gender, Work & Organization,* 10(1): 42–64.

Firestone, S. (1970) *The Dialectic of Sex.* New York: Morrow.

Flax, J. (1983) 'Political philosophy and the patriarchal unconscious: a psychoanalytic perspective on epistemology and metaphysics', in S. Harding and

M. Hintikka (eds), *Discovering Reality: Feminist Perspectives on Epistemology, Metaphysics, Methodology, and Philosophy of Science.* Dordrecht, Holland: D. Reidel Publishing. pp. 245–81.

Flax, J. (1987) 'Postmodern and gender relations in feminist theory', *Signs*, 16(2): 621–43.

Flax, J. (1990) *Thinking Fragments: Psychoanalysis, Feminism, and Postmodernism in the Contemporary West.* Berkeley, CA: University of California Press.

Flax, J. (2002) 'Reentering the labyrinth: revisiting Dorothy Dinnerstein's *The Mermaid and the Minotaur*', *Signs*, 27(4): 1037–55.

Flax, J. (2004) 'What is the subject? Review essay on psychoanalysis and feminism in postcolonial time', *Signs*, 29(3): 905–24.

Fletcher, J.K. (1994) 'Castrating the female advantage: feminist standpoint research and management science', *Journal of Management Inquiry*, 3(1): 74–82.

Fletcher, J.K. (1998) 'Relational practice: a feminist reconstruction of work', *Journal of Management Inquiry*, 7(2): 163–86.

Fletcher, J.K. (2001) *Disappearing Acts: Gender, Power, and Relational Practice at Work.* Cambridge: MIT Press.

Fletcher, J.K. and Jacques, R. (1998) 'Relational practice: an emerging stream of theorizing and its significance for organizational studies', *Simmons Graduate School of Management*, Center for Gender and Organizational Effectiveness, Boston, MA, working paper #3.

Folbre, N. (1987) 'Patriarchy as a mode of production', in R. Albelda, C. Gunn and W. Walker (eds), *Alternatives to Economic Orthodoxy.* New York: ME Sharpe. pp. 323–38.

Folbre, N. (1994) *Who Pays for the Kids?: Gender and the Structures of Constraint.* London: Routledge.

Folbre, N. (2001) *The Invisible Heart: Economics and Family Values.* New York: The New Press.

Fondas, N. (1997) 'Feminization unveiled: management qualities in contemporary writings', *Academy of Management Review*, 22(1): 257–82.

Fonow, M.M. and Cook, J.A. (2005) 'Feminist methodology: new applications in the academy and public policy', *Signs*, 30(4): 2211–36.

Forbes, D.A. (2002) 'Internalized masculinity and women's discourse: a critical analyses of the (re)production of masculinity in organizations', *Communication Quarterly*, Summer–Fall: 269–92.

Fortune (August 1935) 'Women in business: II being a commentary upon the great American office and the distinction between the girl who works to marry and the girl who marries to work'. pp. 50–86.

Fortune (September 1935) 'Women in business: III sixteen exceptions to prove the rule that woman's place is not in the executive's chair'. pp. 81–91.

Fournier, V. and Kelemen, M. (2001) The crafting of community: recoupling discourses of management and womanhood', *Gender, Work & Organization*, 8(3): 267–90.

Franco, J. (1992) 'Going public: reinhabiting the private', in G. Yudice, J. Franco and J. Flores (eds), *On Edge: The Crisis of Contemporary Latin American Culture.* Minneapolis: University of Minnesota Press. pp. 65–83.

Frankenberg, R. (1993) *White Women, Race Matters: The Social Construction of Whiteness.* Minneapolis: University of Minnesota Press.

Fraser, N. (1998) 'Heterosexism, misrecognition and capitalism: a response to Judith Butler', *New Left Review*, 228: 140–50.

Fraser, N. and Naples, N.A. (2004) 'To interpret the world and to change it: an interview with Nancy Fraser', *Signs*, 29(4): 1103–24.

Fraser, N. and Nicholson, L. (1988) 'Social criticism without philosophy: an encounter between feminism and postmodernism', *Theory, Culture and Society*, 5(2&3): 373–94.

Freeman, C. (2003) 'Recruiting for diversity', *Women in Management Review*, 18(1/2): 68–76.

Freeman, S. (2001) 'Is local:global as feminine:masculine? Rethinking the gender of globalization', *Signs*, 26(4): 1005–37.

Freeman, S.J.M. (1990) *Managing Lives: Corporate Women and Social Change.* Amherst, MA: University of Massachusetts Press.

Friedan, B. (1963) *The Feminine Mystique.* New York: Dell.

Friedan B. (1974) *The Feminine Mystique.* New York: Dell.

Friedan, B. (1981) *The Second Stage.* New York: Summit Books.

Friedman, S.D. and Greenhaus, J.H. (2000) *Work and Family – Allies or Enemies?* New York: Oxford University Press.

Frye, M. (1983) *The Politics of Reality.* Freedom, CA: Crossing Press.

Gajjala R. (2003) 'South Asian digital diasporas and cyberfeminist webs: negotiating globalization, nation, gender and information technology design', *Contemporary South Asia*, 12(1): 41–56.

Game, A. and Pringle, R. (1984) *Gender at Work.* London: Pluto.

Gamson, J. and Moon, D. (2004) 'The sociology of sexualities: queer and beyond', *Annual Review of Sociology*, 30: 47–64.

GAO (October 2003) *Women's Earnings: Work Patterns Partially Explain Difference Between Men's And Women's Earnings.* Washington, DC: US General Accounting Office.

García-Canclini, N. (1990) *Culturas Hibridas: Estrategias para Entrar y Salir de las Modernidad.* Mexico: Grijalbo.

Garrison, D. (1981) 'Karen Horney and feminism', *Signs*, 6(4): 672–91.

Gastelaars, M. (2002) 'How do statistical aggregates work? About the individual and organizational effects of general classifications', in B. Czarniawska and H. Höpfl (eds), *Casting the Other: The Production and Maintenance of Inequalities in Work Organizations.* London: Routledge. pp. 7–22.

Gatens, M. (1996) *Imaginary Bodies: Ethics, Power and Corporeality*. London: Routledge.

Gatens, M. (1998) 'Modern rationalism', in A.M. Jaggar and I.M. Young (eds), *A Companion to Feminist Philosophy*. Malden: Blackwell. pp. 21–9.

Gedalof, I. (2000) 'Identity in transit: nomads, cyborgs and women', *The European Journal of Women's Studies*, 7(3): 337–54.

Gerholm L. (2003) 'Overcoming temptation: on masculinity and sexuality among Muslims in Stockholm', *Global Networks: A Journal of Transnational Affairs*, 3(3): 401–16.

Gherardi, S. (1994) 'The gender we think, the gender we do in our everyday organizational lives', *Human Relations*, 47(6): 591–610.

Gherardi, S. (1995) *Gender, Symbolism and Organizational Culture*. London: Sage.

Gherardi, S. (2003) 'Feminist theory and organization theory: a dialogue on new bases', in H. Tsoukas and C. Knudsen (eds), *The Oxford Handbook of Organizational Theory: Meta-Theoretical Perspectives*. Oxford: Oxford University Press. pp. 210–36.

Ghodsee, K. (2004) 'Feminism-by-design: emerging capitalisms, cultural feminism, and women's nongovernmental organizations in postsocialist Eastern Europe', *Signs*, 29(3): 728–53.

Gibson, K. (1992) 'Hewers of cake and drawers of tea: women, industrial restructuring, and class processes on the coalfields of Central Queensland', *Rethinking Marxism*, 5(4): 29–56.

Gibson, K.J., Darity, W.A. Jr. and Myers, S.L. Jr. (1998) 'Revisiting occupational crowding in the United States: a preliminary study', *Feminist Economics*, 4(3): 73–95.

Gibson-Graham, J.K. (1996) 'Queer(y)ing capitalist organization', *Organization*, 3(4): 541–5.

Giddings, P. (1984) *When and Where I Enter: The Impact of Black women on Race and Sex in America*. New York: Bantam.

Gilligan, C. (1982) *In a Different Voice*. Cambridge, MA: Harvard University Press.

Gilmore, S. (2003) 'The dynamics of second-wave feminist activism in Memphis, 1971–1982: rethinking the liberal/radical divide', *NWSA Journal*, 15(1): 94–117.

Glenn, E.N. (1999) 'The social construction and institutionalization of gender and race: an integrative framework', in M.M. Ferree, J. Lorber and B.B. Hess (eds), *Revisioning Gender*. Thousand Oaks: Sage.

Goldberger, N.R., Tarule, J.M., Clinchy, B.M. and Belenky, M.F. (eds) (1996) *Knowledge, Difference, and Power: Essays Inspired by Women's ways of knowing*. New York: Basic Books.

Goode, J. and Bagilhole, B. (1998) 'Gendering the management of change in higher education: a case study', *Gender, Work & Organization*, 5(3): 148–64.

Gottfried, H. (2003) 'Temp(ting) bodies: shaping gender at work in Japan', *Sociology*, 37(2): 257–76.

Goulimari, P. (1999) 'A minoritarian feminism? Things to do with Deleuze and Guattari', *Hypatia*, 14(2): 97.

Gray, B. (1994) 'The gender-based foundations of negotiation theory', in R.J. Lewicki, B.H. Sheppard and R. Bies (eds), *Research on Negotiation in Organizations* (v. 4). Greenwich, CT: JAI. pp. 3–36.

Greene, A., Ackers, P. and Black, J. (2002) 'Going against the historical grain: perspectives on gendered occupational identity and resistance to the breakdown of occupational segregation in two manufacturing firms', *Gender, Work & Organization*, 9(3): 266–85.

Greenhaus, J.H. and Parasuraman, S. (1999) 'Research on work, family and gender', in G.N. Powell (ed.), *Handbook of Gender & Work*. Thousand Oaks: Sage. pp. 391–412.

Griffith, A. and Smith, D.E. (1987) 'Constructing cultural knowledge: mothering as discourse', in J. Gaskell and A. McLaren (eds), *Women and Education: A Canadian Perspective*. Calgary: Detselig.

Griffith, A. and Smith, D.E. (2005) *Mothering for Schooling*. New York: Routledge.

Grosz, E. (1994) *Volatile Bodies: Towards a Corporeal Feminism*. Bloomington: Indiana University Press.

Grosz, E. (1995) *Space, Time, and Perversion: Essays on the Politics of Bodies*. New York: Routledge.

Grosz, E. (2000) 'Deleuze's Bergson: duration, the virtual and a politics of the future', in I. Buchanan and C. Colebrook (eds), *Deleuze and Feminism*. Edinburgh: Edinburgh University Press. pp. 214–34.

Guerrier, Y. and Adib, A. (2004) 'Gendered identities in the work of overseas tour reps', *Gender, Work & Organization*, 11(3): 334–50.

Gugelberger, G.M. (1996) *The Real Thing: Testimonial Discourse and Latin America*. Durham: Duke University Press.

Gustavsson, E. and Czarniawska, B. (2004) 'Web woman: the on-line construction of corporate and gender images',. *Organization*, 11(5): 651–70.

Guthrie, J.P., Ash, R.A. and Stevens, C.D. (2003) 'Are women 'better' than men? Personality differences and expatriate selection', *Journal of Managerial Psychology*, 18(3): 229–43.

Hafner-Burton, E. and Pollack, M.A. (2002) 'Mainstreaming gender in global governance', *European Journal of International Relations*, 8(3): 339–73.

Halford, S., Savage, M. and Witz, A. (1997) *Gender, Careers and Organisations*. London: Macmillan.

Hall, E.J. (1993) 'Smiling, deferring, and flirting: doing gender by giving 'good service'', *Work and Occupations*, 20(4): 452–71.

Haraway, D. (1985) 'A manifesto for cyborgs: science, technology, and socialist feminism in the 1980s', *Socialist Review*, 80: 65–107.

Haraway, D. (1989) *Primate visions: Gender, race, and nature in the world of modern science*. New York: Routledge.

Haraway, D.J. (1997) *Modest_Witness@Second_ Millennium. FemaleMan_Meets_OncoMouse.* New York: Routledge.

Harcourt, W. (ed.) (1999) *Women @Internet.* London: Zed.

Harding, S. (1986) *The Science Question in Feminism.* Ithaca, NY: Cornell University Press.

Harding, S. (1990) 'Feminism, science, and the anti-Enlightenment critiques', in L.J. Nicholson (ed.), *Feminism/Postmodernism.* London: Routledge. pp. 83–106.

Harding, S. (1991) *Whose Science? Whose Knowledge?* Ithaca, NY: Cornell University Press.

Harding, S. (1996) 'European expansion and the organization of modern science: isolated or linked historical project?', *Organization,* 3(4): 497–509.

Harding, S. (1998) *Is Science Multicultural? Postcolonialisms, Feminisms, and Epistemologies.* Bloomington: Indiana University Press.

Harding, S. (ed.) (2004a) *The Feminist Standpoint Reader.* New York: Routledge.

Harding, S. (2004b) 'A socially relevant philosophy of science? Resources from standpoint theory's controversiality', *Hypatia,* 19(1): 25–47.

Harding, S. and Hintikka, M. (eds) (1983) *Discovering Reality: Feminist Perspectives on Epistemology, Metaphysics, Methodology, and Philosophy of Science.* Dordrecht, Holland: D Reidel.

Hartmann, H. (1981a) 'The family as the locus of gender, class, and political struggle: the example of housework', *Signs,* 6(3): 366–94.

Hartmann, H. (1981b) 'The unhappy marriage of Marxism and feminism: towards a more progressive union', in L. Sargent (ed.), *Women and Revolution.* Boston: South End Press. pp. 1–41.

Hartsock, N. (1983) 'The feminist standpoint: developing the ground for a specifically feminist historical materialism', in S. Harding and M.B. Hintikka (eds), *Discovering Reality.* Dordrecht, Holland: D. Reidel Publishing Co. pp. 283–310.

Hatcher, C. (2003) 'Refashioning a passionate manager: gender at work', *Gender, Work & Organization,* 10(4): 391–412

Hawkesworth, M. (1997) 'Confounding gender', *Signs,* 22(3): 649–85. And comments that follow by McKenna and Kessler, S.G. Smith, J.W. Scott, R.W. Connell, and reply by Hawkesworth. pp. 686–713.

Hawkesworth, M. (2004) 'The semiotics of premature burial: feminism in a postfeminist age', *Signs,* 29(4): 961–85.

Hawthorne, S. and Klein, R. (1999) *Cyberfeminism.* N. Melbourne: Spinifex.

Healy, G. (1999) 'Structuring commitments in interrupted careers: career breaks, commitment and the life cycle in teaching', *Gender, Work & Organization,* 6(4): 185–201.

Hearn, J. (1996) 'Deconstructing the dominant: making the one(s) the other(s)', *Organization,* 3(4): 611–26.

Hearn, J. (2000) 'On the complexity of feminist intervention in organizations', *Organization,* 7(4): 609–24.

Hearn, J. (2004) 'From hegemonic masculinity to the hegemony of men', *Feminist Theory,* 5(1): 49–72.

Heilman, M. (2001) 'Description and prescription: how gender stereotypes prevent women's ascent up the organizational ladder', *Journal of Social Issues,* 57(4): 657–74.

Hekman, S. (1996) *Feminist Interpretations of Michel Foucault.* University Park: Pennsylvania State University Press.

Hekman, S. (1997) 'Truth and method: feminist standpoint theory revisited', *Signs,* 22(2): 341–65. And comments that followed by N.C.M. Hartsock, P.H. Collins, S. Harding, D.E. Smith and reply by Hekman. pp. 367–402.

Hekman, S. (2000) 'Beyond identity: feminism, identity and identity politics', *Feminist Theory,* 1(3): 289–308.

Helgesen, S. (1990) *The Female Advantage: Women's Ways of Leadership.* New York: Doubleday.

Hemment, J. (2004) 'Global civil society and the local cost of belonging: defining violence against women in Russia', *Signs,* 29(3): 815–40.

Hennig, M. and Jardim, A. (1977) *The Managerial Woman.* Garden City, NY: Anchor Press/Doubleday.

Henry, E. and Pringle, J. (1996) 'Making voices, being heard in Aotearoa/New Zealand', *Organization,* 3(4): 534–40.

Hesse-Biber, S., Gilmartin, C. and Lyndenberg, R. (1999) *Feminist Approaches to Theory and Methodology.* New York: Oxford University Press.

Heywood, L. and Drake, J. (eds) (1997) *Third Wave Agenda: Being Feminist, Doing Feminism.* Minneapolis: University of Minnesota Press.

Hill, E.J., Miller, B.C., Weiner, S.P. and Colihan, J. (1998) 'Influences of the virtual office on aspects of work and work/life balance', *Personnel Psychology,* 51(3): 667–83.

Hodgson, D. (2003) '"Taking it like a man": masculinity, subjection and resistance in the selling of life assurance', *Gender, Work, & Organization,* 10(1): 1–21.

Hoerr, J. (1997) *We Can't Eat Prestige: The Women Who Organized Harvard.* Philadelphia: Temple University Press.

Højgaard, L. (2002) 'Tracing differentiation in gendered leadership: an analysis of differences in gender composition in top management in business, politics and the civil service', *Gender, Work & Organization,* 9(1): 15–38.

Holmstrom, N. (ed.) (2002) *The Socialist Feminist Project: A Contemporary Reader in Theory and Politics.* New York: Monthly Review Press.

Holvino, E. (1996) 'Reading organizational development from the margins: outsider within', *Organization,* 3: 520–33.

Holvino, E. (2003) 'Complicating gender: the simultaneity of race, gender, and class in organization change(ing)', in R. Ely, E.G. Foldy, M.A. Scully and the Center for Gender in Organizations Simmons School of

Management (eds), *Reader in Gender, Work, and Organization*. London: Blackwell. pp. 87–98.

hooks, b. (1981) *Ain't I a Woman*. Boston: South End Press.

hooks, b. (1990) 'Postmodern blackness (chapter 3)' in b. hooks (ed.), *Yearnings: Race, Gender and Cultural Politics*. Boston: South End Press. pp. 23–31.

Höpfl, H. (2000) 'The suffering mother and the miserable son: organizing women and organizing women's writing', *Gender, Work & Organization*, 7(2): 98–105.

Horner, M. (1970) 'Femininity and successful achievement – a basic inconsistency', in J. Bardwick, E. Douvan, M. Horner and D. Gutmann (eds), *Feminine Personality and Conflict*. Belmont, CA: Brooks-Cole.

Horner, M. (1972) 'Toward an understanding of achieve- ment- related conflicts in women', *Journal of Social Issues*, 28(2): 157–76.

Horney, K. (1967) *Feminine Psychology*. New York: W.W. Norton.

Hughes C. (2000) 'Painting new (feminist) pictures of human resource development (and) identifying research issues for political change', *Management Learning*, 31(1): 51–65.

Hughes, K.D. and Tadic, V. (1998) "Something to deal with': customer sexual harassment and women's retail service work in Canada', *Gender Work and Organization*, 5(4): 207–19.

Hull, G.T., Scott, P.D. and Smith. B. (eds) (1982) *But Some of Us Are Brave*. Old Westbury, NY: Feminist Press.

Hurley, A.E., Wally, S., Segrest, S.L., Scandura, T. and Sonnenfeld, J.A. (2003) 'An examination of the effects of early and late entry on career attainment: the clean slate effect?' *Personnel Review*, 32(1/2): 133–50.

Hurtado, A. (1989) 'Relating to privilege: seduction and rejection in the subordination of white women and women of color', *Signs*, 14(4): 833–55.

Hyde, C. (1992) 'The ideational system of social movement agencies: an examination of feminist health centers', in Y. Hasenfeld (ed.), *Human Services as Complex Organizations*. London: Sage. pp. 121–44.

Iannello, K. (1992) *Decisions without Hierarchy: Feminist Interventions in Organization Theory and Practice*. London: Routledge.

Ibarra, H. (1997) 'Paving an alternative route: gender dif- ferences in managerial networks', *Social Psychology Quarterly*, 60(1): 91–102.

Igbaria, M. and Shayo, C. (1997) 'The impact of race and gender difference on job performance evaluations and career success', *Equal Opportunities Interna- tional*, 16(8): 12–23.

International Labor Organization (2004) *Global Employment Trends for Women (March)*. Geneva: ILO.

Irigaray, L. (l985a/74) *Speculum of the Other Woman*, translated by Gillian C. Gill. Ithaca, NY: Cornell University Press.

Irigaray, L. (l985b/77) *This Sex Which Is Not One*, trans- lated by Catherine Porter. Ithaca, NY: Cornell University Press.

Irigaray. L. (1993) *An Ethics of Sexual Difference*. Ithaca: Cornell University Press.

Jacobs, J.A. (1999a) 'The sex segregation of occupations: prospects for the 21st century', in G.N. Powell (ed.), *Handbook of Gender and Work*. Thousand Oaks: Sage. pp. 125–39.

Jacobs, J.A. and Gerson, K. (2004) *The Time Divide: Work, Family and Gender Inequality*. Cambridge, MA: Harvard University Press.

Jacobs, J.A., Gerson, K. and Gornick, J.C. (2004) 'American workers in cross-national perspective. Chapter 6, in J.A. Jacobs and K. Gerson (eds), *The Time Divide*. Cambridge, MA: Harvard University Press. pp. 119–47.

Jacobs, S. (1999b) 'Trends in women's career patterns and in gender occupational mobility in Britain', *Gender, Work & Organization*, 6(1): 32–46.

Jacques, R. (1992) 'Critique and theory building: Producing knowledge from the kitchen', *Academy of Management of Review*, 17(3): 582–606.

Jacques, R. (1993) 'Untheorized dimensions of caring work: caring as a structural practice and caring as a way of see- ing', *Nursing Administration Quarterly*, 17(2): 1–10.

Jaggar, A.M. (1983) *Feminist Politics and Human Nature*. Totowa, NJ: Rowman & Allanheld.

Jaggar, A.M. and Young, I.M. (eds) (1998) *A Companion to Feminist Philosophy*. Oxford: Blackwell.

Jardine, A.A. (1985) *Gynesis*. Ithaca, NY: Cornell University Press.

Jayawardena, K. (1995) *The White Woman's Other Burden: Western Women and South Asia During British Rule*. London: Routledge.

Jelinek, M. and Alder, N.J. (1988) 'Women: world class managers for global competition', *Academy of Management Executive*, 2(1): 11–19.

Jenkins, S. (2004) 'Restructuring flexibility: case studies of part-time female workers in six workplaces', *Gender, Work & Organization*, 11(3): 306–33.

Jenkins, S., Lucio M.M. and Noon, M. (2002) 'Return to gender: an analysis of women's disadvantage in postal work', *Gender, Work & Organization*, 9(1): 81–104.

Johansson, U. (1998) 'The transformation of gendered work: dualistic stereotypes and paradoxical reality', *Gender, Work & Organization*, 5(1): 43–58.

Joreen (1973) 'The tyranny of structurelessness', in A. Koedt, E. Levine and A. Rapone (eds), *Radical Feminism*. New York: Quadrangle Books. pp. 285–99.

Jorgenson, J. (2002) 'Engineering selves', *Management Communication Quarterly*, 15(3): 350–81.

Joseph, G. and Lewis, J. (1981) *Common Differences: Conflicts in Black and White Feminist Perspectives*. New York: Anchor.

Kang, M. (2003) 'The managed hand: the commercializa- tion of bodies and emotions in Korean immigrant- owned nail salons', *Gender & Society*, 20(10): 1–20.

Kanter, R.M. (1977) *Men and Women of the Corporation*. New York: Basic Books.

Kaplan, C. and Grewal, I. (1999) 'Transnational feminist cultural studies: beyond the Marxism/poststructuralism/feminism divides', in C. Kaplan, N. Alarcón and M. Moallem (eds), *Between Woman and Nation: Nationalisms, Transnational Feminisms and the State*. Durham: Duke University Press. pp. 349–63.

Kaplan, C., Alarcón, N. and Moallem, M. (eds) (1999) *Between Woman and Nation: Nationalisms, Transnational Feminisms and the State*. Durham: Duke University Press.

Kark, R. and Waismel-Manor, R. (2005) 'Organizational citizenship behavior: what's gender got to do with it?' *Organization*, 12 (6): 889-917.

Katila, S. and Merilainen, S. (1999) 'A serious researcher or just antoher nice girl? Doing gender in a male-dominated scientific community', *Gender, Work & Organization*, 6(3): 163–73.

Katila, S. and Merilainen, S. (2002) 'Metamorphosis: from 'nice girls' to 'nice bitches': resisting patriarchal articulations of professional identity', *Gender, Work & Organization*, 9(3): 336–54.

Kesby, M. (2005) 'Retheorizing empowerment-through-participation as a performance in space: beyond tyranny to transformation', *Signs*, 30(4): 29.

Khan, P. (1999) 'Gender and employment restructuring in British National Health Service manual work', *Gender, Work & Organization*, 6(4): 202–12.

Khan, S. (2005) 'Reconfiguring the native informant: positionality in the global age', *Signs*, 30(4): working draft 20 pages.

King, D. (1988) 'Multiple jeopardy, multiple consciousness: the context of a Black feminist ideology', *Signs*, 14: 42–72.

Kirchmeyer, C. (1998) 'Determinants of managerial career success: evidence and explanation of male/female differences', *Journal of Management*, 24(6): 673.

Klein, M. (1948) *Contributions to Psychoanalysis 1921–1945*. London: Hogarth Press.

Knights, D. and McCabe, D. (2001) "A different world': shifting masculinities in the transition to call centres', *Organization*, 8(4): 619–46.

Knights, D. and Richards, W. (2003) 'Sex discrimination in UK academia', *Gender, Work & Organization*, 10(2): 213–38.

Knorr-Cetina, K. and Bruegger, U. (2002) 'Global microstructures: the virtual societies of financial markets', *American Journal of Sociology*, 107(4): 905–51.

Koedt, A., Levine, E. and Rapone, A. (eds) (1973) *Radical Feminism*. New York: Quadrangle Books.

Koen, S. (1984) Feminist workplaces: alternative models for the organization of work. PhD dissertation, Union for Experimenting Colleges, University of Michigan Dissertation Information Service.

Kolmar, W. and Bartkowski, F. (2000) *Feminist Theory: A Reader*. Mountainview, CA: Mayfield Publishing.

Kondo, D. (1997) 'Fabricating masculinity: gender, race and nation in the transnational circuit', in D. Kondo (ed.), *About Face*. New York: Routledge. pp. 157–86.

Korvajärvi, P. (1998) 'Reproducing gendered hierarchies in everyday work: contradictions in an employment office', *Gender, Work & Organization*, 5(1): 19–30.

Kossek, E.E. and Lambert, S.J. (2005) *Work and Life Integration*. Mahwah, NJ: Lawrence Erlbaum.

Kossek, E.E., Markel, K.S. and HcHugh, P.P. (2003) 'Increasing diversity as an HRM change strategy', *Journal of Organizational Change Management*, 16(3): 328–52.

Kourany, J., Sterba, J.P. and Tong, R. (eds) (1999) *Feminist Philosophies*. Upper Saddle River: Prentice Hall.

Kovalainen, A. (2004) 'Rethinking the revival of social capital and trust in social theory: possibilities for feminist analysis', in B.L. Marshall and A. Witz (eds), *Engendering the Social: Feminist Encounters with Sociological Theory*. Berkshire, UK: Open University Press. pp. 155–70.

Krefting, L. (2003) 'Intertwined discourses of merit and gender: evidence from academic employment in the USA', *Gender, Work & Organization*, 10(2): 260–78.

Kristeva, J. (1980) *Desire in Language*. New York: Columbia University Press.

Kucera, D. and Milberg, W. (2000) 'Gender segregation and gender bias in manufacturing trade expansion: revisiting the 'Wood Asymmetry '', *World Development*, 28(7): 1191–210.

Kuumba M.B. (1999) 'A cross-cultural race/class/gender critique of contemporary population policy: the impact of globalization', *Sociological Forum*, 14(3): 447–63.

Lal, J. (1999) 'Situating locations: the politics of self, identity and 'other' in living and writing the text', in S. Hesse-Biber, C. Gilmartin and R. Lyndenberg (eds), *Feminist Approaches to Theory and Methodology*. New York: Oxford University Press. pp. 100–37.

Lam, T. and Yeoh, B.S.A. (2004) 'Negotiating 'home' and 'national identity': Chinese-Malaysian transmigrants in Singapore', *Asia Pacific Viewpoint*, 45(2): 141–64.

Lampe, M. (2001) 'Mediation as an ethical adjunct of stakeholder theory', *Journal of Business Ethics*, 31(2): 165–73.

Lane, N. (2000) 'The low status of female part-time NHS nurses: a bed-pan ceiling', *Gender, Work & Organization*, 7(4): 269–81.

Larson, A.L. and Freeman, R.E. (1997) *Women's Studies and Business Ethics*. Oxford: Oxford University Press.

Lather, P. (2001) 'Postbook: working the ruins of feminist ethnography', *Signs*, 27: 199.

Leidner, R. (1991a) 'Serving hamburgers and selling insurance: gender, work, and identity in interactive service jobs', *Gender & Society*, 5(2): 154–77.

Leidner, R. (1991b) 'Stretching the boundaries of liberalism: democratic innovation in a feminist organization', *Signs*, 16(2): 263–89.

Leira, A. (2002) *Working Parents and the Welfare State. Family Change and Policy Reform in Scandanavia*. Cambridge: Cambridge University Press.

Lewis, D. (1977) 'A response to inequality: black women, racism, sexism', *Signs*, 3: 339–61.

Lewis, S. (1997) "Family friendly' employment policies: a route to changing organizational culture or playing about at the margins?', *Gender, Work & Organization*, 4(1): 13–23.

Liedtka, J. (1999) 'Linking competitive advantage with communities of practice', *Journal of Management Inquiry*, 8(1): 5–16.

Liff, S. and Cameron, I. (1997) 'Changing equality cultures to move beyond 'women's problems'', *Gender, Work & Organization*, 4(1): 35–46.

Liff, S. and Ward, K. (2001) 'Distorted views through the glass ceiling: the construction of women's understandings of promotion and senior management positions', *Gender, Work & Organization*, 8(1): 19–36.

Linehan, M. and Walsh, J.S. (1999) 'Mentoring relationships and the female managerial career', *Career Development International*, 4(7): 348–52.

Lisle, D. (1999) 'Gender at a distance', *International Feminist Journal of Politics*, 1(1): 66–88.

Lloyd, G. (1993) *The Man of Reason: 'Male' and 'Female' in Western Philosophy*. Minneapolis: University of Minnesota Press.

Lopez-Claros, A. and Zahidi, S. (2005) 'Women's empowerment: measuring the global gender gap'. World Economic Forum. Available online at: http://www.weforum.org/pdf/Global_Competitiveness_Reports/Reports/gender_gap.pdf, accessed 19 May 2005.

Lorber, J. (1994) *Paradoxes of Gender*. New Haven: Yale University Press.

Lorde, A. (1983) 'The master's tools will never dismantle the master's house', in C. Moraga and G. Anzaldua (eds), *This Bridge Called My Back*. New York: Kitchen Table Press. pp. 98–101.

Lowe L., Mills, A. and Mullen, J. (2002) 'Gendering the silences: psychoanalysis, gender and organization studies', *Journal of Managerial Psychology*, 17(5): 422–34.

Lutz, H. (2002) 'At your service madam! The globalization of domestic service', *Feminist Review*, 70(1): 89–104.

Lykke, N. and Braidotti, R. (1996) *Between Monsters, Goddesses and Cyborgs*. London: Zed.

Lyness, K.S. and Thompson, D.E. (2000) 'Climbing the corporate ladder: do male and female executives follow the same route?', *Journal of Applied Psychology*, 85(1): 86–101.

Lyotard, J.F. (1984) *The Postmodern Condition: A Report on Knowledge*. Minneapolis: University of Minnesota Press.

Maier, M. (1999) 'On the gendered substructure of organization: dimensions and dilemmas of corporate masculinity', in G.N. Powell (ed.), *The Handbook of Gender & Work*. Thousand Oaks: Sage. pp. 69–93.

Mainiero, L.A. and Sullivan, S. (eds) (2005) 'Kaleidoscope careers: an alternate explanation for the opt-out revolution', *Academy of Management Executive*, 19(1): 106–23.

Marks, D. (1997) 'The crafting of care: Rationality, gender and social relations in educational decisionmaking', *Gender, Work and Organization*, 4(2): 87–97.

Marshall, B.L. and Witz, A. (2004) *Engendering the Social: Feminist Encounters with Sociological Theory*. Berkshire, UK: Open University Press.

Marshall, J. (1984) *Women Managers: Travelers in a Male World*. London: Wiley.

Marshall, J. (1995) *Women Managers Moving On*. London: Routledge.

Martin, E. (1994a) *Flexible Bodies: The role of immunity in American culture from the days of polio to the age of AIDS*. Beacon: Beacon Press.

Martin, J. (1990a) 'Deconstructing organizational taboos: the suppression of gender conflict in organizations', *Organization Science*, 1(4): 339–59.

Martin, J. (1994b) 'The organization of exclusion: institutionalization of sex inequality, gendered faculty jobs and gendered knowledge in organizational theory research', *Organization*, 1(2): 401–31.

Martin, J. (2003a) 'Feminist theory and critical theory: unexplored synergies', in M. Alvesson and H. Willmott (eds), *Studying Management Critically*. London: Sage. pp. 67–91.

Martin, J. and Knopoff, K. (1997) 'The gendered implications of apparently gender-neutral theory: re-reading Max Weber', in A.L. Larson and R.E. Freeman (eds), *Women's Studies and Business Ethics*. New York: Oxford University Press. pp. 30–49.

Martin, J., Knopoff, K. and Beckman, C. (1998) 'An alternative to bureaucratic impersonality and emotional labor: bounded emotionality at The Body Shop', *Administrative Science Quarterly*, 43(2): 429–69.

Martin, P.Y. (1990b) 'Rethinking feminist organization', *Gender and Society*, 4(2): 182–206.

Martin, P.Y. (1993) 'Feminism and management', in E. Fagenson (ed.), *Women in Management: Trends, Perspectives and Challenges*. Newbury Park, CA: Sage. pp. 274–96.

Martin, P.Y. (2001) "Mobilizing masculinities': women's experiences of men at work', *Organization*, 8(4): 587–618.

Martin, P.Y. (2003b) "Said and done' versus 'saying and doing': gendering practices, practicing gender at work', *Gender & Society*, 17(3): 342–66.

Martin, P.Y. and Collinson, D. (2002) "Over the pond and across the water': developing the field of 'gendered organizations'', *Gender, Work & Organization*, 9: 244–65.

Mason, E.S. (1997) 'A case study of gender differences in job satisfaction subsequent to implementation of an employment equity programme', *British Journal of Management*, 8(2): 163–73.

Maume, D.J. (1999) 'Glass ceilings and glass escalators', *Work and Occupations*, 26(4): 483–509.

Mavin, S. (2001) 'Women's career in theory and practice: time for change?', *Women in Management Review*, 16(4): 183–92.

McBride, A. (2001) 'Making it work: supporting group representation in a liberal democratic organization', *Gender, Work and Organization*, 8(4): 411–29.

McCall, L. (2005) 'The complexity of intersectionality', *Signs*, 30(3): 1771–800.

McClintock, A. (1995a) 'Postcolonialism and the angel of progress. Introduction', in A. McClintock (ed.), *Imperial Leather: Race, Gender and Sexuality in the Colonial Context*. London: Routledge. pp. 1–17.

McClintock, A. (1995b) *Imperial Leather: Race, Gender and Sexuality in the Colonial Context*. London: Routledge.

McEwan, C. (2001) 'Postcolonialism, feminism and development: Intersections and dilemmas', *Progress in Development Studies*, 1(2): 93–111.

McGregor, J. and Tweed, D. (2001) 'Gender and managerial competence: support for theories of androgyny?', *Women In Management Review*, 16(5/6): 279–86.

McKie, L., Gregory, S. and Bowlby, S. (2002) 'Shadow times: the temporal and spatial frameworks and experiences of caring and working', *Sociology: the Journal of the British Sociological Association*, 36(4): 897.

McNay, L. (2003) 'Agency, anticipation and indeterminacy in feminist theory', *Feminist Theory*, 4(2): 139–48.

Méndez, J.B. and Wolff, D.L. (2001) 'Where feminist theory meets feminist practice: border-crossing in a transnational academic feminist organization', *Organization*, 8(4): 723–50.

Mendoza, B. (2002) 'Transnational feminisms in question', *Feminist Theory*, 3(3): 295–314.

Metcalfe, B. and Linstead, A. (2003) 'Gendering teamwork: re-writing the feminine', *Gender, Work & Organization*, 10(1): 94–119.

Metz, I. and Tharenou, P. (2001) 'Women's career advancement: the relative contribution of human and social capital', *Group and Organization Management*, 26(3): 312–42.

Meyerson, D.E. (1998) 'Feeling stressed and burned out: a feminist reading and re-visioning of stress-based emotions within medicine and organization science', *Organization Science*, 9(1): 103.

Meyerson D.E. and Fletcher, J.K. (2000) 'A modest manifesto for shattering the glass ceiling', *Harvard Business Review*, 78(1): 127.

Meyerson, D.E. and Kolb, D.M. (2000) 'Moving out of the 'armchair': developing a framework to bridge the gap between feminist theory and practice', *Organization*, 7(4): 553–72.

Mill, H.T. (1851/69a) 'Enfranchisement of women', in J.S. Mill and H. Taylor Mill (eds), *Essays on Sex Equality*, edited by A.S. Rossi. Chicago: University of Chicago Press. 1970. pp. 89–122.

Mill, J.S. (1851/69b) 'The subjection of women', in J.S. Mill and H. Taylor Mill (eds), *Essays on Sex Equality*, edited by A.S. Rossi. Chicago: University of Chicago Press. 1970. pp. 123–242.

Miller, G.E. (2004) 'Frontier masculinity in the oil industry: the experience of women engineers', *Gender, Work & Organization*, 11(1): 47–73.

Miller, J.B. (1976) *Toward a New Psychology of Women*. Boston: Beacon.

Millet, K. (1970) *Sexual Politics*. Garden City, NY: Doubleday.

Milliken, F.J., Martins, L.L. and Morgan, H. (1998) 'Explaining organizational responsiveness to work-family issues: the role of human resource executives as issue interpreters', *Academy of Management Journal*, 41(5): 580–92.

Mills, A.J. (1998) 'Cockpit, hangars, boys and galleys: corporate masculinities and the development of British Airways', *Gender, Work & Organization*, 5(3): 172–88.

Mills, A.J. and Chiaramonte, P. (1991) 'Organization as gendered communication act', *Canadian Journal of Communication*, 16: 381–98.

Minh-ha, T.T. (1989) *Woman, native, other: Writing Postcoloniality and Feminism*. Bloomington: Indiana University Press.

Mir, R., Calás, M.B. and Smircich, L. (1999) 'Global technoscapes and silent voices: challenges to theorizing global cooperation', in D.L. Cooperrider and J.E. Dutton (eds), *Organizational Dimensions of Global Change: No Limits to Cooperation*. Thousand Oaks: Sage, pp. 270–90.

Mirchandani, K. (1999) 'Feminist insight on gendered work: new directions in research on women and entrepreneurship', *Gender, Work & Organization*, 6(4): 224–35.

Mitchell, J. (1974) *Psychoanalysis and Feminism*. New York: Vintage Books.

Moghadam V.M. (2000) 'Transnational feminist networks: collective action in an era of globalization', *International Sociology*, 15(1): 57–85.

Mohanty, C.T. (1991a) 'Under western eyes: feminist scholarship and colonial discourses', in C.T. Mohanty, A. Russo and L. Torres (eds), *Third World Women and the Politics of Feminism*. Bloomington: Indiana University Press. pp. 51–80.

Mohanty, C.T. (1991b) 'Cartographies of struggle: third world women and the politics of feminism', in C.T. Mohanty, A. Russo and L. Torres (eds), *Third World Women and the Politics of Feminism*. Bloomington: Indiana University Press. pp. 1–47.

Mohanty, C.T. (1997) 'Women workers and capitalist scripts: ideologies of domination, common interests, and the politics of solidarity', in J. Alexander and C.T. Mohanty (eds), *Feminist Genealogies, Colonial Legacies, Democratic Futures*. New York: Routledge. pp. 3–29.

Mohanty, C.T. (2003) *Feminism Without Borders: Decolonizing Theory, Practicing Solidarity*. Durham: Duke University Press.

Moi, T. (2004) 'From femininity to finitude: Freud, Lacan and feminism, again', *Signs*, 29(3): 841–78.

Monaghan, L.F. (2002) 'Embodying gender, work and organization: solidarity, cool loyalties and contested hierarchy in a masculinist occupation', *Gender, Work & Organization*, 9(5): 504–36.

Monhanram, R. (1998) '(In)visible bodies? Immigrant bodies and constructions of nationhood in Aotearoa/New Zealand', in R. Du Plessis and L. Alice (eds),

Feminist Thought in Aotearoa/New Zealand: Connections and Differences. Auckland: Oxford University Press. pp. 21–8.

Moraga, C. and Anzaldúa, G. (1983) *This Bridge Called My Back.* New York: Kitchen Table Press.

Morgen, S. (1994) 'Personalizing personnel decisions in feminist organizational theory and practice', *Human Relations,* 47(6): 665–83.

Moya, P.M.L. (1997) 'Postmodernism, 'realism' and the politics of identity: Cherríe Moraga and Chicana feminism', in J. Alexander and C.T. Mohanty (eds), *Feminist Genealogies, Colonial Legacies, Democratic Futures.* New York: Routledge. pp. 125–50.

Müller, C. (2003) 'Knowledge between globalization and localization: the dynamics of female spaces in Ghana', *Current Sociology,* 51(3/4): 329–46.

Mumby, D.K. and Putnam, L.L. (1992) 'The politics of emotion: a feminist reading of bounded rationality', *Academy of Management Review,* 17(3): 465–86.

Munro, A. (2001) 'A feminist trade union agenda? The continued significance of class, gender and race', *Gender, Work and Organization,* 8(4): 454–71.

Nagy-Zekmi, S. (2003) 'Images of Sheherazade 1: representations of the postcolonial female subject', *Journal of Gender Studies,* 12(3): 171–80.

Nair, R.B. (2002) *Lying on the Postcolonial Couch: The Idea of Indifference.* Minneapolis: University of Minnesota Press.

Narayan, U. (1997) *Dislocating Cultures: Identities, Traditions, and Third-World Feminism.* New York: Routledge.

Nicholson, L.J. (ed.) (1990) *Feminism/Postmodernism.* New York: Routledge.

Nicholson, L. (1998) 'Gender', in A.M. Jaggar and I.M. Young (eds), *A Companion to Feminist Philosophy.* Malden: Blackwell. pp. 289–97.

Noddings, N. (1984) *Caring: A Feminine Approach to Ethics and Moral Education.* Berkeley: University of California Press.

Nordenmark, M. (2002) 'Multiple social roles – a resource or a burden: is it possible for men and women to combine paid work with family life in a satisfactory way?', *Gender, Work & Organization,* 9(2): 125–45.

Nye, R.A. (2005) 'Locating masculinity: some recent work on men', *Signs,* 30(3): 1937–62.

Oakley, A. (1974) *Woman's work: The housewife, past and present.* New York: Pantheon Books.

OECD (2003) *Babies and Bosses: Reconciling Work and Family Life in Austria, Ireland and Japan,* vol 2. Paris: OECD.

O'Kelly, L. (2004) 'It beats working', *Guardian,* 6 June, also obtained from the website: http://www.guardian.co.uk/gender/story/0,,1232242,00.html

Ong, A. (1999) *Flexible Citizenship: The Cultural Logics of Transnationality.* Durham: Duke University Press.

Ong, A. and Collier, S.J. (2005) *Global Assemblages.* London: Blackwell.

Oseen, C. (1997) 'Luce Irigaray, sexual difference, and theorizing leaders and leadership', *Gender, Work & Organization,* 4(3): 170–84.

Osterman, P. (1995) 'Work family programs and the employment relationship', *Administrative Science Quarterly,* 40(4): 681–700.

Ostrander, S.A. (1999) 'Gender and race in a pro-feminist, progressive, mixed-gender, mixed race organization', *Gender & Society,* 13(5): 628–42.

Parker, M. (2002) 'Queering management and organization', *Gender, Work & Organization,* 9(2): 146–66.

Parker, P.S. and Ogilvie, D.T. (1996) 'Gender, culture, and leadership: toward a culturally distinct model of African-American women executives' leadership strategies', *Leadership Quarterly,* 7(2): 189–214.

Parreñas, R.S. (2001) 'Transgressing the nation-state. The partial citizenship and 'imagined (global) community' of migrant Filipina domestic workers', *Signs,* 26(4): 1129–54.

Parry, B. (1995) 'Problems in current theories of colonial discourse', in B. Ashcroft, G. Griffiths and H. Tiffin (eds), *The Post-Colonial Studies Reader.* London: Routledge. pp. 36–44.

Parvikko, T. (1990) 'Conceptions of gender equality: similarity and difference', in M. Keranen (ed.), *Finnish 'Undemocracy': Essays on Gender and Politics.* Jyvaskyla: Finnish Political Science Association, Gummerus Printing. pp. 89–111.

Perez Perez, M., de Luis Carnicer, M.P. and Martinez Sanchez, A. (2002) 'Differential effects of gender on perceptions of teleworking by human resources managers', *Women in Management Review,* 17(5/6): 262–75.

Perrons, D. (2003) 'The new economy and the work-life balance: conceptual explorations and a case study of new media', *Gender, Work & Organization,* 10(1): 65–93.

Peters, T. (1990) 'The best new managers will listen, motivate, support: isn't that just like a woman?', *Working Woman,* Sept: 216–7.

Peterson V.S. (2002) 'Rewriting (global) political economy as reproductive, productive, and virtual (foucauldian) economies international', *Feminist Journal of Politics,* 4(1): 1–30.

Pini, B. (2005) 'The third sex: women leaders in Australian agriculture', *Gender, Work & Organization,* 12(1): 73–88.

Pitt-Catsouphes, M., Kossek, E., and Sweet, S. (eds.) (2006). *Work and family handbook: Multi-disciplinary perspectives.* Mahwah, NJ: Erlbaum Publishers.

Pocock, B. (2005) 'Work/care regimes: institutions, culture and behaviour and the Australian case', *Gender, Work and Organization,* 12(1): 32–49.

Powell, G.A. and Butterfield, D.A. (2002) 'Exploring the influence of decision makers' race and gender on actual promotions to top management', *Personnel Psychology,* 55: 397–428.

Powell, G.N. (1998) 'The abusive organization', *The Academy of Management Executive,* 12(2): 95–7.

Powell, G.N. (ed.) (1999) *The Handbook of Gender and Work.* Thousand Oaks, CA: Sage.

Powell, G.N. and Graves, L.M. (2003) *Women and Men in Management*. Thousand Oaks, CA: Sage.

Powell, G.N., Butterfield, D.A. and Parent, J. (2002) 'Gender and managerial stereotypes: have the times changed?', *Journal of Management*, 28: 177–93.

Prakash, G. (1995) After Colonialism: Imperial Histories and Postcolonial Displacements. Princeton, NJ: Princeton University Press.

Procter, I. and Padfield, M. (1999) 'Work orientations and women's work: a critique of Hakim's theory of the heterogeneity of women', *Gender, Work & Organization*, 6(3): 152–62.

Prokos, A. and Padavic, I. (2002) "There oughtta be a law against bitches': masculinity lessons in police academy training', *Gender, Work & Organization*, 9(4): 439–59.

Puar, J.K. (2001) 'Global circuits: transnational sexualities and Trinidad', *Signs*, 26(4): 1039–65.

Puar, J.K. (2002) 'A transnational feminist critique of queer tourism', *Antipode*, 34(5): 935–46.

Putnam, L. and Kolb, D. (2000) 'Rethinking negotiation', in P. Buzzanell (ed.), *Rethinking Organizational & Managerial Communication from Feminist Perspectives*. Thousand Oaks, CA: Sage. pp. 76–104.

Radhakrishnan, R. (1994) 'Postmodernism and the rest of the world', *Organization*, 1(2): 305–40.

Ragins, B.R. (1997) 'Diversified mentoring relationships in organizations: a power perspective', *The Academy of Management Review*, 22(2): 482–521.

Ragins, B.R., Townsend, B. and Mattis, M. (1998) 'Gender gap in the executive suite: CEOs and female executives report on breaking the glass ceiling', *The Academy of Management Executive*, 12(1): 28.

Rahman, M. and Witz, A. (2003) 'What really matters? The elusive quality of the material in feminist thought', *Feminist Theory*, 4(3): 243–61.

Ranson, G. (2003) 'Beyond 'gender differences': a Canadian study of women's and men's careers in engineering', *Gender, Work & Organization*, 10(1): 22–41.

Rantalaiho, L. and Heiskanen, T. (eds) (1997) *Gendered Practices in Working Life*. London: Macmillan.

Rapoport, R., Bailyn, L., Fletcher, J.K. and Pruitt, B.H. (2002) *Beyond Work-Family Balance: Advancing Gender Equity and Workplace Performance*. San Francisco: Jossey-Bass.

Rasmussen, B. (2001) 'Corporate strategy and gendered professional identities: reorganization and the struggle for recognition and positions', *Gender, Work & Organization*, 8(3): 291–310.

Rees, B. and Garnsey, E. (2003) 'Analysing competence: gender and identity at work', *Gender, Work & Organization*, 10(5): 551–78.

Reinelt, C. (1994) 'Fostering empowerment, building community: the challenge for state-funded feminist organizations', *Human Relations*, 47(6): 685–705.

Reitman, F. and Schneer, J.A. (2003) 'The promised path: A longitudinal study of managerial careers', *Journal of Managerial Psychology*, 18(1/2): 60–75.

Reskin, B.F. (1984) *Sex segregation in the workplace: Trends, explanations, remedies*. Washington, DC: National Academy Press.

Reskin, B.F. (2000) 'Getting it right: sex and race inequality in work organizations', *Annual Review of Sociology*, 26: 707–9.

Reskin, B.F and Roos, P.A. (1990) *Job queues, gender queues: Explaining women's inroads into male occupations*. Philadelphia: Temple University Press.

Rianne, M. (2002) 'Child care: toward what kind of 'social Europe'?', *Social Politics*, 9(3): 343–79.

Rich, A. (1979) *Of Woman Born*. New York: Norton.

Riger, S. (1994) 'Challenges of success: stages of growth in feminist organizations', *Feminist Studies*, 20(2): 275–300.

Roethliesberger, F.J. and Dickson, W. (1939) *Management and the Worker*. Cambridge: Harvard University Press.

Roper, M. (1996) *Masculinity and the British Organization Man Since 1945*. Oxford: Oxford University Press.

Roper, M. (2001) 'Masculinity and the biographical meanings of management theory: Lyndall Urwick and the making of scientific management in inter-war Britain', *Gender, Work & Organization*, 8(2): 182–204.

Rosener, J.B. (1990) 'Ways women lead', *Harvard Business Review*, 68(November–December): 119–25.

Rosener, J.B. (1995) *America's Competitive Secret: Utilizing Women as a Management Strategy*. New York: Oxford University Press.

Ross-Smith, A. and Kornberger, M. (2004) 'Gendered rationality? A genealogical exploration of the philosophical and sociological conceptions of rationality, masculinity and organization', *Gender, Work & Organization*, 11(3): 280–305.

Rothbard, N. (2001) 'Enriching or depleting? The dynamics of engagement in work and family roles', *Administrative Science Quarterly*, 46: 655–84.

Rubin, G. (1976) 'The traffic in women', in R. Rapp (ed.), *Toward an anthropology of women*. New York: Monthly Review Press. pp. 157–210.

Rubin, J. (1997) 'Gender, equality and the culture of organizational assessment', *Gender, Work & Organization*, 4(1): 24–34.

Rudin, J.P. and Byrd, K. (2003) 'U.S. pay equity legislation: sheep in wolves clothing', *Employee Responsibilities and Rights Journal*, 15(4): 183–90.

Runté, M. and Mills, A.J. (2004) 'Paying the toll: a feminist post-structural critique of the discourse bridging work and family', *Culture and Organization*, 10(3): 237.

Rutherford, S. (2001) 'Any difference? An analysis of gender and divisional management styles in a large airline', *Gender, Work & Organization*, 8(3): 326–45.

Said, E. (1978) *Orientalism*. Harmondsworth: Penguin.

Said, E. (1985) 'Orientalism reconsidered', *Race and Class*, 27(2): 1–15.

Said, E. (1988) 'Representing the colonized: anthropology's interlocutors', *Critical Inquiry*, 15: 205–25.

Saldivar-Hull, S. (1999) 'Women hollering transfronteriza feminisms', *Cultural Studies*, 13(2): 251–62.

Salih, S. and Butler, J. (eds) (2004) *The Judith Butler Reader*. Oxford: Blackwell.

Salzinger L. (2004) 'From gender as object to gender as verb: rethinking how global restructuring happens', *Critical Sociology*, 30(1): 43–62.

Sandoval, C. (1991) 'U.S. Third World: the theory and method of oppositional consciousness in the postmodern world', *Genders*, 10(spring): 1–24.

Saunders, L. (1996) 'Why do African-American men earn less?', *Organization*, 3(4): 510–9.

Sawicki, J. (1991) *Disciplining Foucault*. London: Routledge.

Schein, V.E., Mueller, R., Lituchy, T. and Liu, J. (1996) 'Think manager – think male: a global phenomenon', *Journal of Organizational Behavior*, 17(1): 33–41.

Schild, V. (1997) 'New subjects of rights? Gendered citizenship and the contradictory legacies of social movements in Latin America', *Organization*, 4(4): 604–19.

Schneider, J. (2002) 'Reflexive/diffractive ethnography', *Culture Studies Critical Methodologies*, 2(4): 460.

Schwartz, D.B. (1996) 'The impact of work-family policies on women's career development: boon or bust?', *Women in Management Review*, 11(1): 5–19.

Scott, J.W. (1986) 'Gender: a useful category of historical analysis', *American Historical Review*, 91: 1053–75.

Scott, J.W. (1988) 'Deconstructing equality-versus-difference: or, the uses of poststructuralist theory for feminism', *Feminist Studies*, 14(2): 32–51.

Sedgwick, E.K. (1990) *Epistemology of the Closet*. Berkeley: University of California Press

Segal, A. (1996) 'Flowering feminism: consciousness raising at work', *Journal of Organizational Change Management*, 9(5): 75–90.

Sheridan, A. (2004) 'Chronic presenteeism: the multiple dimensions to men's absence from part-time work', *Gender, Work & Organization*, 11(2): 207–25.

Signs (2001) 'Special issue on globalization and gender', A. Basu, I. Grewal, C. Kaplan and L. Malkki (special issue eds), *Signs*, 26(4).

Signs (2004) 'Special issue on development cultures: new environments, new realities, new strategies', F. Lionnet, O. Nnaemeka, S.H. Perry and C. Schenck (special issue eds), 29(2).

Sinclair, A. (1995) 'Sex and the MBA', *Organization*, 2(2): 295–317.

Sinclair, A. (2005) 'Body and management pedagogy', *Gender, Work & Organization*, 12(1): 89–104.

Singh, V. and Vinnicombe, S. (2000) 'Gendered meanings of commitment from high technology engineering managers in the United Kingdom and Sweden', *Gender, Work and Organizations*, 7(1): 1–19.

Skidmore, P. (2004) 'A legal perspective on sexuality and organization lesbian and gay case study', *Gender, Work & Organization*, 11(3): 229–53.

Smircich, L. (1985) 'Toward a woman centered organization theory', Paper presented at the Annual Meetings of the Academy of Management, San Diego, CA, August.

Smith, D.E. (1979) 'A sociology for women', in J. Sherman and F. Beck (eds), *The Prism of Sex: Essays in the Sociology of Knowledge*. Madison, WI: University of Wisconsin Press.

Smith, D.E. (1987) *The Everyday World as Problematic: A Feminist Sociology*. Toronto: University of Toronto Press.

Smith, D.E. (1990a) *Texts, Facts, and Femininity: Exploring Exploring the Relations of Ruling*. London: Routledge & Kegan Paul.

Smith, D.E. (1990b) *The Conceptual Practices of Power*. Boston: Northeastern University Press.

Smith, D.E. (1999) *Writing the Social: Critique, Theory and Investigations*. Toronto: University of Toronto Press.

Sommer, D. (1995) 'Taking a life: hot pursuit and cold rewards in a Mexican testimonial novel', *Signs*, 20(4): 913–40.

Sotirin, P. and Gottfried, H. (1999) 'The ambivalent dynamics of secretarial 'bitching': control, resistance, and the construction of identity', *Organization*, 6(1): 57–80.

Spargo, T. (1999) *Foucault and Queer Theory*. New York: Totem Books.

Spelman, E.V. (1988) *Inessential Woman: Problems of Exclusion in Feminist Thought*. Boston: Beacon Press.

Spivak, G.C. (1988) 'Can the subaltern speak?', in C. Nelson and L. Grossberg (eds), *Marxism and the Interpretation of Culture*. Chicago: University of Illinois Press. pp. 271–313.

Spivak, G.C. (1999) *A Critique of Postcolonial Reason: Toward a History of the Vanishing Present*. Cambridge: Harvard University Press.

Stacey, J. (2005) 'Masculinity, masquerade, and genetic impersonation: *Gattaca*'s queer visions', *Signs*, 30(3): 1851–77.

Staggenborg, S. (1995) 'Can feminist organizations be effective?', in M. Ferree and P.Y. Martin (eds), *Feminist Organizations: Harvest of the New Women's Movement*. Philadelphia: Temple University Press. pp. 145–64.

Stanworth, C. (2000) 'Women and work in the information age', *Gender, Work & Organization*, 7(1): 20–32.

Stobbe, L. (2005) 'Doing machismo: legitimating speech acts as a selection discourse', *Gender, Work & Organization*, 12(2): 105–23.

Stoller, E.P. (1993) 'Gender and the organization of lay health care: a socialist-feminist perspective', *Journal of Aging Studies*, 7(2): 151–70.

Stone, A. (2004) 'From political to realist essentialism: rereading Luce Irigaray', *Feminist Theory*, 5(1): 5–23.

St. Pierre, E.A. and Pillow, W.S. (2000) *Working the Ruins: Feminist Poststructural Theory and Methods in Education*. New York: Routledge.

Strober, M. (1984) 'Toward a general theory of occupational sex segregation: the case of public school teaching', in B.F. Reskin (ed.), *Sex Segregation in the Workplace*. Washington, DC: National Academy Press. pp. 144–56.

Sullivan, C. and Lewis, S. (2001) 'Home based telework, gender and the synchronization of work-family', *Gender, Work & Organization*, 8(2): 123–45.

Tancred, P. (1995) 'Women's work: a challenge to the sociology of work', *Gender, Work & Organization*, 2(1): 11–20.

Tharenou, P. (2005) 'Women's advancement in management', in R.J. Burke and M.C. Mattis (eds), *Supporting Women's Career Advancement*. Cheltenham, USA: Edgar Elgar Publishing. pp. 31–57.

Thayer, M. (2001) 'Transnational feminism: reading Joan Scott in the Brazilian sertao', *Ethnography*, 2(2): 243–71.

Thomas, J.E. (1999) "Everything about us is feminist': the significance of ideology in organizational change', *Gender & Society*, 13(1): 101–19.

Thomas, R. and Davies, A. (2002) 'Gender and the new public management: reconstituting academic subjectivities', *Gender, Work & Organization*, 9(4): 372–97.

Thompson, C. (1964) Interpersonal Psychoanalysis: The Selected papers of Clara Thompson, M.P. Green (ed.). New York: Basic Books.

Tienari, J. (1999) 'The first wave washed up on shore: reform, feminization and gender resegregation', *Gender, Work & Organization*, 6(1): 1–19.

Tolich, M. and Briar, C. (1999) 'Just checking it out: exploring the significance of informal gender divisions amongst American supermarket employees', *Gender, Work & Organization*, 6(3): 129–33.

Tong, R.P. (1998) *Feminist Thought: A More Comprehensive Introduction*. Boulder, CO: Westview.

Trethewey, A. (2000) 'Revisioning control: a feminist critique of disciplined bodies', in P.M. Buzzanell (ed.), *Rethinking Organizational and Managerial Communication from Feminist Perspectives*. Thousand Oaks, CA: Sage. pp. 107–27.

True, J. (2003) 'Mainstreaming gender in global public policy', *International Feminist Journal of Politics*, 5(3): 368–96.

Truth, S. (1851) 'Ain't I a woman?', in W. Kolmar and F. Bartkowski (eds), *Feminist Theory: A Reader*. Mountainview, CA: Mayfield. p. 66.

Truth, S. (1867) 'Keeping the thing going while things are stirring', in W. Kolmar and F. Bartkowski (eds), *Feminist Theory: A Reader*. Mountainview, CA: Mayfield. pp. 66–7.

Tuana, N. and Tong, R. (eds) (1995) *Feminism and Philosophy*. Boulder, CO: Westview.

Underhill-Sem, Y. (2003) Marked bodies in marginalized places: understanding rationalities in global discourses. *Development*, 46(2): 13–17.

Valcour, P.M. and Tolbert, P. (2003) 'Gender, family and career in the era of boundarylessness: determinants and effects of intra- and inter-organizational mobility', *International Journal of Human Resource Management*, 14(5): 768–87.

van de Vliert, E. and van der Vegt, G.S. (2004) 'Women and wages worldwide: how the national proportion of working women brings underpayment into the organization', *Organization Studies*, 25: 969–86.

Vargas, V. (2003) 'Feminism, globalization and the global justice and solidarity movement', *Cultural Studies*, 17(6): 905–20.

Varma, A. and Stroh, L.K. (2001) 'The impact of same-sex LMX dyads on performance evaluations', *Human Resource Management*, 40(4): 309–20.

Vieira da Cunha, J. and Pina e Cunha, M. (2002) 'Reading between the lines: unveiling masculinity in feminine management practices', *Women in Management Review*, 17(1): 5–11.

Villenas, S. (2000) 'This ethnography called my back: writings of the exotic gaze, 'othering' Latina, and recuperating Xicanisma', in E.A. St. Pierre and W.S. Pillow (eds), *Working in the Ruins: Feminist Poststructural Theory and Methods*. New York: Routledge. pp. 74–95.

Visweswaran, K. (1994) *Fictions of Feminist Ethnography*. Minneapolis: University of Minnesota Press.

Wajcman, J. (1998) *Managing Like a Man*. University Park: Penn State Press.

Walby, S. (2001) 'Against epistemological chasms: the science question in feminism revisited', *Signs*, 26(2): 485.

Wallace, T. (1999) "It's a man's world!': restructuring gender imbalance in the Volvo truck company?', *Gender, Work & Organization*, 6(1): 20–31.

Wallis, C. (2004) 'The case for staying home', *Time*, 22 March: 51–9.

Walters, V., Eyles, J., Lenton, R., French, S. and Beardwood, B. (1998) 'Work and health: a study of the occupational and domestic roles of women registered nurses and registered practical nurses in Ontario, Canada', *Gender, Work & Organization*, 5(4): 230–44.

Ward J. (2004) 'Not all differences are created equal: Multiple jeopardy in a gendered organization', *Gender & Society*, 18(1): 82–102.

Wardlow, H. (2004) 'Anger, economy, and female agency: problematizing 'prostitution'' and 'sex work' among the Huli of Papua New Guinea', *Signs*, 29(4): 1017–40.

Warren, T. and Walters, P. (1998) 'Appraising dichotomy: a review of 'part-time/full-time' in the study of women's employment in Britain', *Gender, Work and Organization*, 5(2): 102–18.

Weedon, C. (1997) *Feminist Practice & Poststructuralist Theory*. Oxford: Blackwell.

Weedon, C. (1998) 'Postmodernism', in A.M. Jaggar and I.M. Young (eds), *A Companion to Feminist Philosophy*. Malden: Blackwell. pp. 75–84.

Weeks, K. (1998) *Constituting Feminist Subjects*. Ithaca: Cornell University Press.

West, C. and Fenstermaker, S. (1995a) 'Doing difference', *Gender & Society*, 9(1): 8–37.

West, C. and Fenstermaker, S. (1995b) 'Reply: (re)doing difference', *Gender & Society*, 9(4): 506–13.

West, C. and Zimmerman, D.H. (1987) 'Doing gender', *Gender & Society*, 1(2): 125–51.

Wharton, A.S. (1991) 'Structure and agency in socialist-feminist theory', *Gender & Society*, 5(3): 373–89.

White, R.D. Jr. (1999) 'Are women more ethical? Recent findings on the effects of gender upon moral development', *Journal of Public Administration Research and Theory*, 9(3): 459–71.

Whitehouse, G., Zetlin, D. and Earnshaw, J. (2001) 'Prosecuting pay equity: evolving strategies in Britain and Australia', *Gender, Work and Organization*, 8(4): 365–86.

Whitford, M. (1991) *Luce Irigaray: Philosophy in the Feminine.* London: Routledge.

Wicks, A.C. (1996) 'Reflections on the practical relevance of feminist thought to business', *Business Ethics Quarterly*, 6(4): 523–31.

Williams, C.C. (2004) 'Race (and gender and class) and child custody: theorizing intersections in two Canadian court cases', *NWSA Journal*, 16(2): 46–69.

Williams, J. (2000) *Unbending Gender: Why Family and Work Conflict and What to Do About It.* New York: Oxford University Press.

Willis, E. (1975) 'The conservatism of *Ms*', in Redstockings (ed.), *Feminist Revolution.* New York: Random House. pp. 170–1.

Wilson, E. (2001) *Organizational Behaviour Reassessed: The Impact of Gender.* London: Sage.

Wilson, F. and Thompson, P. (2001) 'Sexual harassment as an exercise of power', *Gender, Work & Organization*, 8(1): 61–83.

Winnicott, D.W. (1975) *Through Paediatrics to Psychoanalysis.* New York: Basic Books.

Winnubst, S. (2003) 'Vampires, anxieties, and dreams: race and sex in the contemporary United States', *Hypatia*, 18(3): 1–20.

Wollstonecraft, M. (1792) *A Vindication of the Rights of Woman*, edited by C. Poston. New York: W.W. Norton.

Woodall, J., Edwards, C. and Welchman, R. (1997) 'Organizational restructuring and the achievement of an equal opportunity culture', *Gender, Work & Organization*, 4(1): 2–12.

Woodward A. (2003) 'European gender mainstreaming: promises and pitfalls of transformative policy', *Review of Public Policy Research*, 20(1): 65–88.

Wuthnow, J. (2002) 'Deleuze in the postcolonial: on nomads and indigenous politics', *Feminist Theory*, 3(2): 183–200.

Wyatt, J. (2004) 'Toward cross-race dialogue: Identification, misrecognition and difference in feminist multicultural community', *Signs*, 29(3): 879–903.

Yang, N. (1998) 'An international perspective on socioeconomic changes and their effects on life stress and career success of working women', *SAM Advanced Management Journal*, 63(3): 15–20.

Yeoh, B., Huang, S. and Willis, K. (2000) 'Global cities, transnational flows and gender dimensions: the view from Singapore', *Tijdschrift voor Economische en Sociale Geografie*, 91(2): 147–58.

Young, I.M. (1980) 'Socialist feminism and the limits of dual systems theory', *Socialist Review*, 10(2–3): 169–88.

Yuval-Davis, N. (1997) *Gender and Nation.* London: Sage Publications.

Zauchner, S., Korunka, C., Weiss, A. and Kafka-Lutzow, A. (2000) 'Gender-related effects of information technology implementation', *Gender, Work & Organization*, 7(2): 119–32.

Zilber, T. (2002) Institutionalization as an interplay between actions, meanings, and actors: the cape of a rape crisis center in Israel', *Academy of Management Journal*, 45(1): 234.

1.9   Data in Organization Studies

RALPH STABLEIN

Organization studies (OS) is about understanding the social world we organization students inhabit. Because it is not a closed system of study like logic or mathematics, there is little room for deductive science. OS is necessarily an empirical study, exploring attitudes, behaviours, desires, practices, experiences, artefacts, symbols, documents, texts, feelings, judgements, beliefs, meanings, measures, facts and figures. Even the armchair/conceptual theorists must muse on empirical data.

However, what is to count as data of organizational life? There is no clear consensus on an answer among the community (or is it communities?) of scholars who study organizations. Some organizational students run well-controlled experiments to produce data which others claim 'have little or nothing to say about the realities of organizational behaviour' (Lawler 1985: 4). Some spend months in the field reporting their data as ethnographic tales that others dismiss as mere anecdotes (Martin 1990). Some ask hundreds and thousands of people to answer carefully chosen questions producing data which others disparage as simplistic, distorted reflections of the respondents' organizational reality, unrelated to their organizational behaviour.

Can we reconcile these paradigm-laden positions and arrive at an acceptable definition of data for OS? The advantages of a common position are clear. If the field can establish a common paradigm, resources will flow more freely, and research will accumulate more 'successfully' (Pfeffer 1993). We could all use the money! However, will the accumulation of knowledge reflect the variety and complexity of organizational reality? Many argue that accumulation is an illusion; the debate goes on (Jaros 1994; Pfeffer 1995; Van Maanen 1995a, b; Moldoveanu and Baum 2002).

A more recent and enduring challenge comes from postmodern and poststructural theorizing in the humanities (Zald 1996; Chia 2003). Early advocates, Cooper (Cooper and Burrell 1988; Cooper 1989) and Burrell (1988) wrote extensively on the implications of postmodernism for organizational studies. Hassard and Parker (1993), Calas and Smircich (1997) and Linstead (2004) provide samplers of views on the utility and significance of postmodernism for organization studies. Postmodern theorizing challenges the very notion of a common ground. In particular, OS postmodernists warn against any totalizing narrative (e.g. Jeffcut 1994b; Kilduff and Mehra 1997; Calas and Smircich 1999), i.e. an attempt to provide an all encompassing explanation. They would argue that any attempt to develop a universal definition of data for OS is doomed. Yet, as these ideas have gained greater currency in OS (Tsoukas and Knudsen 2003) the very suggestion that a universal approach could be possible and beneficial may be generative (Jones 2003).

Thus, my strategy in this review will be to offer such a definition of data in organization studies. However, I make no claim to absolute truth in doing so. Instead, I offer this grand narrative, bracketed as a heuristic for OS. I believe we can self-consciously use modernist writing techniques to forge temporary consensus, to create the shared explicit and tacit knowledge and assumptions required to do OS. Thus, I do not write in opposition to the postmodern. As Deetz has noted in discussing competing research programmes, they can be seen not as 'alternative routes to truth, but as specific discourses which, if freed from their claims of universality and/or completeness, could provide important moments in a larger dialogue about organizational life' (Deetz 1996: 195). Although I cannot promise the beauty of *Kubla Khan*, I join Coleridge in asking you, the reader, for the suspension of your disbelief.

The Universal Narrative

If one abstracts highly enough, the differences between entrenched research practices blur, revealing the contours of the research landscape. From this height, we can describe the universal characteristics of all OS research. Three features stand out: researcher purpose, audience and data.

Purpose

Organizational research is a purposeful human activity. These purposes can be described broadly by Habermas's (1971) typology of human interests. OS researchers may work for a technical interest in control and prediction, for a practical interest in achieving mutual action-oriented understanding and/or for an emancipatory interest in extending human autonomy and responsibility (Stablein and Nord 1985; Willmott 2003b). More local framing of a particular study specify these more general purposes, e.g. 'resolving a debate in the literature', 'being concerned for the welfare of the group', 'solving a morale problem', 'developing an understanding of …', 'legitimating resistance in a workplace'. The purpose of a research project or programme is often called the research question, but this expression is too suggestive of traditional hypothesis testing to cover the varieties of contemporary organization studies.

Note that purpose is research-specific. More basic human motivations such as 'to get tenure' or 'to help humankind' must be funnelled through a particular research endeavour. Each research project or research stream has a purpose or purposes.

Like all people, OS researchers are complex. They are limitedly rational and more than rational. Their purposes may be multiple, changing, emergent, even conflicting. All OS is 'on purpose'.

Audience

The second feature of OS is audience. Organization studies, like all knowledge production, is a social business (Frost and Stablein 1992; Stablein and Frost 2004). Although we may toil individually, we always work on common problems. Kuhn (1970) described most natural science as 'puzzle solving' with paradigm-defined problems and boundaries. The description holds for OS. The very structure of OS journal articles, opening with introduction and literature review,

illustrates the social nature of our activity. The ritualistic, even cynical, nature of these paeans in no way reduces their function of linking individual projects to a larger community of understanding. Czarniawska (1998) describes the ways our referencing practices fulfil the same function. Even paradigm-making research defines itself in relation to existing puzzles and solutions (Gersick 1992).

Of course, an individual may have a personal understanding of organization that he or she does not or cannot share. While it remains an idiosyncratic insight, OS is not enriched or changed. Our studies are incomplete until we communicate our results to others who study organization.

Usually this communication is written: working paper, journal article, consulting report, book chapter. The postmodernists emphasize the role of the audience. They remind us that these papers are not just written, they are read as well (Rhodes 2001). The failure of authors to acknowledge diverse audiences and the expectation of readers that all reports are written for them has created unnecessary and irresolvable debates, such as that over the relevance of OS (Rynes et al. 2001). Once we acknowledge the audience, it is no surprise that the elegant technical jargon of the journal article intended for other initiates of the researcher cult is nearly indecipherable for the novice student or stressed-out manager or employee.

Five key audiences can be identified for OS. Most important to the organizational scholar is the audience of his or her peers, other organizational researchers. If we limit our count to active researchers, i.e. those who publish in English language researcher-oriented journals, the total would not exceed a few thousand world-wide. Academic book authors and chapter contributors would add a few more. The audience for a particular manuscript in a sub-field is a good deal smaller. If we limit the circle of active researchers to those whose work is cited, the estimate of their numbers falls to the hundreds. The majority of publishing organizational scholars received their PhDs from, and are employed in, a relatively small number of 'elite' North American and British universities.

Those who primarily teach organizational studies comprise the next largest group, numbering in the tens of thousands. Most have earned research degrees. They read the research literature. It is these scholar teachers who pay the bills for research publications by maintaining professional association memberships and seeing that their libraries order the books and journals. Some of these teachers will be employed in tertiary institutions with an explicit teaching mission. A growing number are itinerant adjunct faculty who receive no support for research work. Some teaching-oriented scholars in the US and elsewhere work in institutions that espouse research values. However, the empirical reality is that many employed in these institutions will publish infrequently over their career.

For students, we write textbooks, in which we try to provide uncomplicated summaries of research. Most texts also include attempts to create proxy organizational experiences. We may even try to make OS interesting.

Participants in organizations, in their millions, include almost everyone in the world, but organizational researchers show interest in reaching but a few. As critical scholars are fond of reminding us (Alvesson and Willmott 1992), managers benefit most from the vast bulk of participant-oriented writing efforts. Their dollars for practice-oriented journals, executive education and consultancy provide welcome additions to the researcher's personal bank balance and the university's drooping bottom line. Arguably, managerial framing can dominate the way we think about, do and write up organizational research (Barley et al. 1988).

The final audience to consider is the external monitor: the Research Assessment Exercise in the UK, the Performance Based Research Fund in New Zealand, US News Rankings in the US, etc. These accountability exercises accelerate the shift in the meaning of research publication away from research communication within the community of scholars. More and more publication is simply evidence for resource allocation and for personal career advancement (Prichard and Willmott 1997; Willmott 2003a; Harley et al. 2004).

Data

The third universal feature of organization studies, data, links the researcher's purpose and the audience. More specifically, all organization students select and interpret data for their audience in the attempt to achieve their purposes. I choose the phrase 'interpret data' quite carefully over alternatives such as 'present data' or 'summarize data'. These phrases suggest a mechanical process of recording and playing back, i.e. that the data speak

for themselves. This does not do justice to the effort and creativity required of researchers in data collection, analysis and reporting (Hackman 1992; Meyer et al. 1992; Alvesson 2003: 14). This language also hides the researcher in a haze of objectivity that is unwarranted in reports of quantitative (Gephart 1988) or qualitative studies (Van Maanen 1988).

In another modernist move, I will draw a boundary around my aims for this text. I will attempt to focus my attention on the data of OS, i.e. data collection as opposed to data analysis. I leave discussion of the various data analytic techniques to others (Pedhazur and Schmelkin 1991; Miles and Huberman 1994; Hardy and Bryman 2003; Silverman 2004).

So, What are Data?

All data are representations. Respondents' questionnaire answers, experimental subjects' behaviours, employee records, financial records, boardroom conversations, production records, shopfloor humour, corporate balance sheets, informants' expressions, participant or non-participant observations and emotional reactions, annual reports, acetycoline blood levels and pulse rates, photos, videos, corporate architecture and the products of earlier research may all be used by organization students to represent aspects of organizational reality.

However, not all representations are data. For example, one might estimate the morale of assembly line workers by speaking to the firm's public relations officer. The polished response is a representation, but it is unlikely to be data. It will do little to inform our understanding of shopfloor attitudes. At the extreme, one could use a random number generator to represent respondents' ages. Not very smart, not data, but it is a representation. We need to identify what kinds of representations are to count as data.

As representations, data imply things that are represented, and a process of representing. Both characteristics must be examined to separate data from other sorts of representations.

The 'Thing' Represented

Traditionally, scientists understood the empirical world, the thing measured, as the 'real thing', out there waiting to be discovered (Lakatos 1970). That view of science has been thoroughly revised. Philosophers of science have undermined the logical foundations of deduction, induction and falsification (see Chalmers (1999) for an accessible account). Historians of science (e.g. Kuhn 1970) and sociologists of scientific knowledge (see Ashmore (1989) for a review) have studied historical and contemporary scientific practice. They have discovered that the traditional account bears little resemblance to the practices of working scientists. Mitroff and Kilmann (1978), Burrell and Morgan (1979), Astley (1985) and others have applied and extended these views to OS.

Today most scholars would conclude that we invent rather than discover the empirical world. Any appeal to scientific evidence regarding the 'true' nature of the world is suspect and subject to revision as science evolves and changes (Kuhn 1970). The 'thing' that our data represent is not a concrete object or experience. Instead it is a human conception, constituted by the interactive sensemaking of scientists. This view is broadly consistent with most postmodern and post-structural understandings, as well, explicitly avoiding any debates about crises of representation.

The impact of this conclusion for OS is sometimes misunderstood. Some would conclude that 'anything goes', that each individual scientist is free to proceed as they prefer. However, it is strikingly clear that this is not the case. Science is never an isolated individual activity. It is a social practice. In the words of Vidich and Lyman (1994: 42):

> Although it is true that at some level all research is a uniquely individual enterprise – not part of a sacrosanct body of accumulating knowledge – it is also true that it is always guided by values that are not unique to the investigator: we are all creatures of our own social and cultural pasts. However, in order to be meaningful to others, the uniqueness of our own research experience gains significance when it is related to the theories of our predecessors and the research of our contemporaries.

For a study to be *personally* meaningful (Sandelands 1993), an organizational scholar may hold a realist metaphysical belief, e.g. how can I accept that there is no underlying structure to the world? Doing organization studies does not require revision of such a belief. Nor are such ontological commitments necessary to do organizational studies, contrary to the claims of some critical realists (Reed 2003). The

analytic strategies of the realist may be adopted without the metaphysical baggage. Similarly, the ontological commitment of an individual postmodernist to language as the only reality is acceptable, but irrelevant to organization studies.

The empirical world that we represent is what we, as a human scholarly community, understand it to be. It amounts to the ideas and conceptions we use to understand: the constructs and relations of our theories. The 'we' is important. Individuals may claim anything they like about organizations but a claim does not become organizational reality until it is socially accepted. Dissertation advisers, examiners, editors, reviewers, readers and conference participants must see the reality, too.

As a social practice, OS is not only an intellectual enterprise. It is an economic, political and moral enterprise as well (Stablein and Frost 2004).

As the title of this *Handbook* suggests, there is no *one* study of organization. There is not a single community of organizational scholars. This opens the possibility of multiple organizational realities. Some aspects of organizational reality are universally perceived by organization researchers, e.g. workers and managers. Other aspects are contested, e.g. whether the organization or the individual is a reification or a legitimate social actor. Still other organizational phenomena are perceived by some groups of organization students but not others, e.g. class.

Discussions of this issue in OS have been framed as discussions of paradigm incommensurability (Burrell and Morgan 1979). Groups holding diverse paradigms see different worlds and set different questions. My position is in line with Weaver and Gioia (1994), Martin (1990), Hassard (1990) and others who argue that complete incommensurability is rare, if not impossible. Advocates of this position argue for an end to paradigm wars (Martin and Frost 1996). Today, paradigm differences must be taken seriously, not ignored or granted 'separate but equal' status (Reed 1996). Paradigm wars should be replaced by less antagonistic conversations (Czarniawska 2003). Studying different organizational realities will yield different questions and answers which are more, or less, insightful for the various paradigms represented within OS. (See the dialogue between Stewart Clegg and John Jermier for a thoughtful discussion of the relationship between empirical research and theory (Jermier 1994).)

In summary, if data are representations, they must represent empirical things. The 'things' are our ideas about empirical 'reality'. Organizational students attempt to represent aspects of empirical organizational reality. Different groups of scholars will have different ideas about different empirical realities. Thus, each will try to represent a different organizational reality. Successful data require that other scholars understand the reality a researcher's data are trying to represent. The starting point of any data-producing effort must be participation in a shared understanding of the empirical organizational phenomena to be represented.

The Process of Representing

Representing a shared organizational reality requires systematic activity undertaken by the researcher. Often, this activity goes unnoticed or unreported in OS. It is part of the background, taken-for-granted assumptions that lie behind our organizational explorations. A successful representation process provides data that organizational scholars can interpret and analyse in ways that increase their shared understanding of what is treated as an empirical reality. Such data are characterized by a two-way *correspondence* between the data and the organizational reality the data represent.

The term comes from a well-established tradition in mathematical psychology that approaches the measurement of psychological attitudes as a representational problem (Coombs et al. 1970). I will develop their ideas in defining data for organization studies. Remembering that the empirical world is a shared system of concepts, representation is achieved when one maps the 'thing' that we have conceptualized into a symbol system, what Dawes (1972) would call a 'one-way correspondence' between the empirical world and the symbolic system. However, for the representations to produce data, there is a stronger requirement, a two-way correspondence. The mapping must be into a symbolic system which allows one to map back from the symbolic system to the original empirical system of interest. An example should help make sense of this rather awkward criterion.

I use a ruler to independently measure the height of Jena in one room, then Sal in another room. I am using the ruler to map a one-way correspondence between an empirical quality (our concept of height) and a symbolic system (the real numbers – a ratio scale). Relying solely on the relations of this symbolic system, I am able to determine that Jena is taller than Sal, i.e. two way correspondence. I have used properties of the symbolic system to make true inferences about the empirical world. If this conclusion holds when I bring Jena and Sal together and see them standing side-by-side, then we have evidence that two-way correspondence has been achieved. We will trust rulers as height measuring instruments. In this example, the real number system property of magnitude or order allows me to determine who is taller without reference to the empirical world. Six is bigger than five, therefore Jena is taller than Sal. If I apply my ruler to lots of people, I might use additional properties of the real number system (addition and division to calculate a mean) to confirm that, for example, basketball players are generally taller than football players. For both examples, a mapping from the empirical world into a symbolic system, symbolic manipulation within the rules of that system, then mapping back on to the empirical world, provides insight. The data are successful in representing an empirical world in a way that produces shared understandings.

By way of counterexample, a Māori activist in New Zealand recently adopted the name 'Te Ureturoa', which means 'mighty warrior'. A newspaper reported his name to mean 'the long penis'. This embarrassing mistake occurred when a newspaper reporter used a Māori-English dictionary (the ruler which the journalist used to map the world of Māori words into the symbol system of the English language) to map a one-way correspondence between the activist's name and an English language representation. The reporter presumed that the literal translation would provide English speaking readers with data on the reality of Māoridom. However, the one-way representation did not provide data about the Māori world. Two-way correspondence, i.e. a meaningful understanding of the activist's name, is not achieved. The literal translation, in this case, is not data. As is often the case, literal translation was not an effective representational strategy. A more sophisticated strategy, taking into account context and utilizing back-translation, would be required to produce successful data.

The representational measurement theorists are especially interested in representing psychological attributes using the properties of various formal number systems to produce measuring scales (e.g. nominal, ordinal, interval and ratio). They warn us that just because one assigns numerals to an empirical phenomenon (one-way correspondence), it does not follow that these numerals are from the real number system. The manner of assigning the numerals must reflect the relations of the empirical world and match the real number system relations (i.e. equal intervals relative to an absolute zero). Because parametric statistics are derived from the properties of the real number system, representational measurement theorists are wary of the extensive use of statistics in empirical research. (For reviews of the issues and subsequent controversies, see Michell (1997; 2002).) Some commentators have argued that Item Response Theory (IRT) avoids the problem (Muniz 1998; Borsboom and Mellenbergh 2004). However, IRT has had little uptake in OS (Austin et al. 2004).

If one measures several persons' preferences for participation in two groups on a Likert scale where 1 equals strong agreement to the statement, 'I like to work in a participative group', one-way correspondence is achieved. However, the numerals 1, 2, 3, 4 and 5 represent real numbers only if the psychological distances represented by these reports are equal relative to an absolute zero point of no preference for participation. Can one calculate a mean using real number properties to determine if the two groups are equivalent in their preferences? Lord (1953) suggests that the numbers don't know where they come from. Indeed the computer will churn out a t-ratio. However, as MacRae (1988) and others have correctly observed, the researcher does know where the numbers come from!

Therefore, representational measurement theorists insist on a representation theorem. For a particular measuring strategy, the representational theorem is an explicit statement of the assumptions required to justify the claim that data, i.e. two-way correspondence, have been produced. In the case of measurement of preferences on a ratio scale, the representational theorem is that transitivity (i.e. if a is preferred to b, and b is preferred to c, then a is preferred to c) applies to the preferences (Coombs et al. 1970: 13). Because of their exclusive interest in numerical symbol systems, the representation theorem consists of a mathematical proof. This requirement limits the representational theorist to a small number of alternative symbol systems. Even within the scope of numerical systems, only a few types are considered, usually counting, ratio, interval, ordinal or nominal. OS scholars tend to be less orthodox. For the participation item above, most would agree that the measuring strategy fails to map into a ratio

or even an interval scale. But if the response is on an ordinal scale, the representational measurement theorist would argue that any monotonic transformation (i.e. order preserving) of the respondents' answers would yield the same information about the respondents' attitudes. However, I suspect most OS researchers would be very surprised if people gave the same responses when the alternatives offered were 1, 2, 3, 4 and 500.

Thus, most psychologically-oriented scholars implicitly consider Likert scale responses to roughly map the empirical world called respondent opinion onto a mixed ordinal and interval numerical system, which can be manipulated statistically to produce roughly valid inferences about the respondents' psychological states.

The representational assumptions for Likert style research might include:

- Respondents will be willing to respond. Unfortunately, a recent review notes that 'falling response rates is perhaps the greatest threat survey researchers have faced in the past 10 years' (Tourangeau 2004: 781).
- Respondents are willing to respond truthfully, e.g. no socially desirable responding (Zerbe and Paulhus 1987; Sloan et al. 2004). If this assumption is untenable, then we might consider unobtrusive, non-reactive measures (Webb et al. 1966).
- Respondents understand the item as the researchers intended it to be understood, including such issues as respondent literacy, shared dialect and framing (Clark and Schrober 1992; Tourangeau 2000).
- Respondents can make the judgement the item requires, e.g. memory retrieval and information processing capacities are adequate (Ericsson and Simon 1980; Schaeffer and Presser 2003). Recent research shows that apparently minor variations in the formatting of response alternatives can affect judgements (Tourangeau et al. 2004).
- Respondents can report the judgement, e.g. translate it into the metric of the response format. This is not as simple as it sounds. For example, describing autobiographical events can change autobiographical memory (Skowronski and Walker 2004).

Another general challenge to the statistical research practices of OS comes on the basis that the thing represented is the *wrong thing*. The statistics that we have inherited and developed from agricultural research focus on the central tendency (the mean, the average) in a context where the cases of the phenomenon are independent and distributed normally. But some authors have argued that the important thing is not the mean or the typical. Goffman (1959) argues that extreme cases are more informative. Starbuck (2004) makes a similar point in his study of an exceptionally successful law firm. McKelvey and Andriani (2005) extend the logic to a critique of most organizational strategy research that is based on this Gaussian statistical model.

However, in OS, we are not limited to numerical symbol systems. Much of our data utilize natural language or various technical languages as the symbol systems which represent the empirical world. Then, we manipulate these symbols to make inferences about the organizational world. Van Maanen's (1979) elegant title to his preface of the landmark *Administrative Science Quarterly (ASQ)* special issue on qualitative methodology expresses my sentiment: 'The territory is not the map'. The tape recordings and field notes of the fieldworker are not the culture of the group. They are the symbols which are analysed to present, we hope, an insightful description of the culture.

For a non-quantitative example of representational assumptions consider Spradley (1979a), which provides an introduction to semantic ethnography. He begins from the observation that the researcher and the researched speak different languages or dialects. As an ethnographer, I must map the meaning of the native speaker into my language, such that a two-way correspondence is achieved. That is, the inferred meanings must also allow me to use the phrase correctly in new situations and settings. If I am able to operate successfully in novel situations then true measurement or understanding has occurred. A researcher who can demonstrate this level of cultural understanding will be taken seriously by other ethnosemanticists.

Data in OS should be representations which maintain a two-way correspondence between the empirical world and the symbol system. The rule for evaluating the criterion is the adequacy of the representational process. The representational process is essentially a theory of data production. Like all theories, measurement theories cannot be proven correct. However, if we make our representational process explicit, we can examine the representational assumptions and actively consider evidence relevant to them. Consider again the introductory example of the ruler and height. As an everyday practice, we measure away with no concern for the validity of the ruler. However, if we consciously

attend to the rationale for ruler use, we can develop demonstrations that are socially accepted evidence in favour of this representational process. The same is true for representational processes in OS. We can, for example, develop scales to detect socially desirable responding or compare the reports of various informants to increase our confidence that we have achieved two-way correspondence.

I cannot overestimate the importance of taking our representational assumptions seriously. At the most basic level, if respondents don't know the answers to our questions, then their answers will not inform us. We rarely address these issues explicitly. It is not just a theoretical point. For example, in an increasingly convincing set of studies Mezias and Starbuck seriously question the ability of managers to report accurately on important aspects of their work (Starbuck and Mezias 1996; Mezias and Starbuck 2003a, b, c).

A Definition of Data

Data in OS are representations which maintain a two-way correspondence between an empirical reality and a symbol system

An empirical reality is the set of ideas constituted, developed and sustained by a subcommunity of organizational scholars. Data are produced by a representing process that is documented by representational assumptions. Data are then manipulated within the symbol system, yielding results that increase our understanding of an organizational reality.

Applying an explicit and defensible representational process to a well-known portion of empirical reality yields good organizational data. Poor data result from an inadequate representational process and/or an inadequate understanding of the organizational phenomenon represented. If the phenomenon is understood and the representational strategy is flawed, the data are usually found wanting, the article rejected (Schwab 1985). If the underlying empirical phenomenon is not well understood, messier data are acceptable. As our understanding increases, we generally insist on better data.

The development of organizational culture and qualitative methodology provides an example. Early organizational research defines the concept of culture very broadly. The same term (culture) is used by different authors to indicate different empirical phenomena (Smircich 1983). With the contributions of many scholars these differences have been identified and several different traditions of cultural research have developed (Martin 2002; 2003). Alongside the conceptual developments, the representational practices have developed. Previously, vague qualitative methods were uneasily described in opposition to the quantitative orthodoxy, but often using the terms and criteria of quantitative methods. Reviewers were not impressed, but editors recognized the need to create a space for this new work in a series of special issues. Today, organizational culture researchers can articulately describe their methods and the interpretive traditions from which they arise (Hatch and Yanow 2003; Prasad 2005).

Kinds of Data

We have arrived at a general definition of data in organizational studies. Now it is time to return from the heights of generalization to the diversity of data produced in organizational researches. The heart of the postmodern and poststructural challenge is the challenge to *one* answer, *one* empirical reality, *one* representational strategy. At the local sites of organizational studies, differences in culture, moral ethic, intellectual history, academic discipline, etc., have yielded different subcommunities of organizational scholars who produce different sorts of data. Thus, for example, we observe differences between North American, Australasian and European scholarship, between organizational psychology, organizational sociology, organizational economics, and organizational anthropology, between managerial studies, critical studies, feminist studies and postcolonial studies.

Different kinds of data result from the intersection of the nature of the empirical reality each subcommunity is attempting to understand, and the representational processes each uses to represent aspects of that organizational world. Each combination is institutionalized as the research practice that each subcommunity develops, teaches and enforces. It would be neat and tidy if these various data could be logically connected in a two-dimensional space of shared organizational reality and representational practice. Alas, my perception of the organizational studies landscape is not so simple. Descending from the conceptual heights of a data

definition to represent the data-using reality of OS, I do not find consistent groupings. Rather than attempt to force the variety of organizational data into a clean typology, I will try to do justice to the diversity of OS research.

Abandoning the Quantitative/Qualitative Divide

Often, a high level distinction is drawn between quantitative and qualitative data. I do not use the distinction. Instead, I attempt to reposition this key distinction in the organizational sciences. The quantitative/qualitative distinction is a binary opposition that hides a set of more complex, non-dichotomous and non-hierarchical distinctions.

The popular quant-qual distinction is rooted in the separation of numerical representations from non-numerical representations. Usually numerical representations are uncritically taken as real numbers. However, as we have seen above, numerical representations are not members of a single class. The Arabic numerals 1, 2, 3, etc. may represent counting, positions on the real number line, equally spaced intervals, ordered magnitudes on an ordinal scale, labels in a nominal classification system or some hybrid of these systems. Frequently, the numerals represent non-numbers, e.g. the sentence: 'I strongly agree with the statement'. Thus, I find the distinction hazy and not very informative on the numerical side of the divide.

In practice, the quant/qual distinction condemns 'everything else' to the non-numerical, subordinate side of the divide. Along with the subordinate status, non-numerical methods are treated as a single class. Yet, the 'everything else' includes a diverse set of target organizational realities and representational practices (Van Maanen et al. 1982: 15). Thus, attempts to arrive at a unifying definition of 'qualitative' data are hopeless. Prasad (2005) tackles the problem by making an initial distinction between positivist and postpositivist qualitative traditions. The remainder of the book is dedicated to the identification and explication of the postpositivist traditions. She describes the very different empirical realities posited by the interpretive, structural, critical and 'post' traditions. Then within each of these meta-traditions, she describes the varied representational practices associated with the sub-traditions, for example, symbolic interaction, hermeneutics, dramaturgy, ethnomethodology and ethnography within the interpretive tradition.

In the following sections, I will briefly characterize the natures of the empirical realities and the types of representational processes utilized in the production of various kinds of organizational data. In most instances, I adopt conventional terms: survey data, experimental data, case data, secondary data. Together these provide an overview of data used in contemporary organization studies.

One conventional category of organizational data, interviewing, does not constitute a type of data in the framework proposed here. The term is used so loosely that the only commonality across uses is simply talking. The term is too broad. It does not stand as a symbol system oriented to the representation of an organizational reality. Several communities of organizational scholars who do not share an understanding of organizational reality engage in the apparently shared practice of talking with people. I recommend Alvesson's (2003) exploration of this problem. He unravels some of the complexities of the interview, describing eight metaphors for this research practice. To become a distinct sort of data the interview requires an adjective, such as in ethnographic interviewing (Spradley 1979a) or behaviour description interviewing (Janz et al. 1986).

Survey Data

The paper-and-pencil questionnaire is probably the most frequently used method of data production in organization studies. Podsakoff and Dalton (1987) have provided one estimate of usage. They surveyed the 193 empirical research articles published in the 1985 volumes of *Academy of Management Journal (AMJ)*, *ASQ*, *Journal of Applied Psychology (JAP)*, *Journal of Management (JOM)* and *Organizational Behaviour and Human Decision Processes (OB&HDP)*. The authors of over a third (36%) of the articles primarily employed the questionnaire. Scandura and Williams (2000) compare articles published in 1985–1987 against those published in 1995–1997 from *AMJ*, *ASQ* and *JOM*. Their categories are not the same, but it would appear that the uses of questionnaires are about the same in more recent years.

The organizational reality of the questionnaire user is a nomological net of causal relationships between constructs. The nomological relations hypothesized by the researcher constitute middle range theories intended to explain a portion of organizational reality (Pinder and Moore 1980), e.g.

employee turnover. The terminology of middle range theory is Merton's (1968). He developed the term to contrast his 'modest' approach with that of comprehensive (i.e. grand) social theories such as those of Parsons and Marxist scholars. Middle range theory is an analytic approach to understanding organization. The researcher simplifies the complexity of organizational life by specifying a subset of relations that can be extracted and explored with relative independence from the rest by asking respondents questions.

The basic organizational phenomenon is the construct. For organization studies, an annual chapter by Schwab (1980) has emerged as a foundational statement for this approach to data. Schwab (1980: 5) defines the construct as 'a conceptual variable', i.e. an 'entity capable of assuming two or more values which is of a mental nature'. Thus, a construct is an idea, a researcher's idea, related to other ideas in a theory of organizational behaviour, belief, etc. As the construct only exists in the head of the individual researcher and the collective head of the community as revealed by the 'literature', only indirect assessment of organizational reality is possible. To study organizational life, the construct must be represented by a concrete operation.

The first step in the representational process for survey data is careful definition of the construct, its psychometric properties and the relationship between the construct and other constructs in the researcher's theory. Next, questions which are intended to represent (measure) the construct are developed. Individual respondents are asked to answer the questions. These answers are data.

The method for demonstrating the two-way correspondence of the data is called construct validation. The construct validity of the data is defined as 'the correspondence between a construct and the operational procedure to measure or manipulate that construct' (Schwab 1980: 6). The correspondence can never be directly demonstrated. However, several procedures can provide falsifying or confirming evidence regarding the degree of construct validity of a data-producing operation.

Description of the representational process is the most important way to demonstrate the correspondence of construct and measure. The ability to do so relies on clear definition of the construct. The Job in General scale (Ironson et al. 1989; Russell et al. 2004) provides an example in the measurement of job satisfaction.

Ironson et al. (1989) carefully distinguish between the constructs of overall (general) job satisfaction, job facet satisfactions (e.g. with pay, co-workers, etc.) and facet composites (e.g. averaging pay and co-worker satisfaction). Only in the light of these distinctions does the fancy number crunching that follows make sense as evidence of validity.

Having achieved clear definition of the construct, current practice requires developing multiple questions to represent all but the most straightforward of constructs (e.g. self-reported sex, age, etc.). Multiple items allow estimation of internal consistency reliability, i.e. the degree to which the multiple items that are intended to measure the same construct actually are interrelated. Other types of reliability may also be estimated, in particular, reliability over time (stability or test–retest reliability).

Again, note the importance of defining the construct when conducting reliability analyses. Some constructs, such as personality states, are expected to be stable over time. Thus, high test–retest reliability estimates for the measure would provide evidence of construct validity. Other constructs, e.g. mood, are not expected to be stable: thus high reliability could provide evidence of construct invalidity.

It is a truism among questionnaire data users that appropriate demonstration of reliability is a necessary but not a sufficient condition for judging the data to be construct valid. Reliability evidence establishes that respondents view the multiple items (a scale) in a common way, but it does not establish that the respondents view the items in the way that the researcher intended. The appropriate evidence would show that the scale is related to other scales that are construct valid measures of the same construct (convergent validity) and relate less strongly to construct valid measures of related, but not identical, constructs (differential or discriminant validity). For example, a questionnaire measure of global work satisfaction should relate more closely to other general work satisfaction scales than to measures of specific facets of job satisfaction (Ironson et al. 1989). Schwab (1980) is especially keen to encourage the demonstration of differential construct validity.

Research practice does not always live up to prescription. Relying on the Podsakoff and Dalton (1987) survey, about two-thirds of published articles reported reliability evidence. A paltry 4.48 per cent of authors provided validity evidence. Hinkin's

(1995) review of 277 measures used in 75 articles published in *JAP, OB&HDP, Human Relations, JOM, AMJ and Personnel Psychology* from 1989 to 1994 concluded that there were significant problems in measure development, particularly in item generation and evidence of construct validity. More recent evidence from the mid-90s reveals a *decrease* in the construct validity of research published in the top management journals (Scandura & Williams, 2000). The failure to provide validity evidence is extremely important if one accepts the definition of data proposed here. The failure to provide validity evidence is a failure to document two-way correspondence. The representational assumptions underlying survey data require construct validation evidence. Substantive findings from surveys assume that the inferences are based on construct valid measures. Schwab (1980: 4) argues that our failure to provide for adequate construct validation of our measures means that 'our knowledge of substantive relationships is not as great as is often believed, and (more speculatively) not as great as would be true if the idea of construct validity received greater attention'.

Should researchers choose to demonstrate reliability and validity, a variety of methods are available. Hinkin (1998) provides a clear, concise tutorial. Increasingly, the measurement model is estimated by treating the latent variables calculated with confirmatory factor analysis as estimates of the constructs (Scandura and Williams 2000).

Sometimes experimental data are produced to support the construct validity of a measure. For example, Breaugh and Becker (1987) report three studies as part of a larger research programme to provide construct validity evidence for the three facets of the work autonomy scale (Breaugh 1985; 1999). One of these studies is an experiment in which the authors created high and low autonomy working conditions for experimental subjects. The subjects were then asked to complete the questionnaire. The answers varied from high to low, as predicted. The authors interpret these data as evidence of construct validity.

This tradition of data production is associated with researchers in the areas of industrial/organizational (I/O) psychology and organization behaviour. Its roots in psychological testing and classical test theory have been traced in a recent history (Austin et al. 2004). I/O psychologists and mainstream OB researchers will find the language of this section familiar. Other OSers who use questionnaires may find the language alien, but the essential view of organizational reality and the survey representational process should still hold. For example, Schwab (1980) points out the similarity of his construct validation position and Blalock's (1968) discussions of questionnaires in sociological research.

Experimental Data

In an earlier handbook review, Weick (1965) observed that the experiment was an infrequent, but useful, way to generate organizational data. The Podsakoff and Dalton (1987) data from 1985 is a bit ambiguous, but it would appear that about 30% of the articles reviewed used experimental procedures in either the laboratory or the field. In 2000, the proportion is about the same in the psychologically oriented *JAP* (Austin et al. 2004). However, in the management journals the proportion of laboratory experiements has fallen significantly from nearly 11% in 1985–1987 to nearly 5% in 1995–1997 (Scandura and Williams 2000). Just over 2% of the studies are field experiments in the later period. Taylor et al. (2003), Greenberg and Tomlinson (2004) and others have argued for more experimental data in OS.

The empirical reality of the organizational experimentalist is essentially the same as that of the survey user. Both test middle range theories which posit causal relations among constructs. They differ on one important point. The experimentalists are far less optimistic about the ability to isolate the set of causal relations of interest from the rest of organizational reality. Experimentalists are convinced that the world is a densely inter-related net of constructs with subtle, complex and powerful effects on each other. They have shown that seemingly minor factors can destroy the two-way correspondence of a representational process (Rosenthal and Rosnow 1969). For example, if the experimenter is aware of the hypotheses under study, his or her expectations can influence the responses of experimental subjects.

Two-way correspondence for experimental data is achieved by demonstrating *internal validity*. To do so, the experimental representational strategy follows the traditional natural scientific method (Boring 1969). A hypothesized cause (independent variable) is varied by the experimenter. The effect or dependent variable is observed. If the dependent variable varies more than could be expected by chance alone, a causal relation is inferred. Because the world is causally dense, other possible causes (alternative explanations) of any effect must be discounted to produce experimental data. This sort of experimental design is said to possess internal validity. It yields interpretable data.

There are three strategies for eliminating alternative explanations (Caporaso 1973). First, the experimenter can control other possible causes, seeing to it that they do not vary. Secondly, potential causes that cannot be held stable may be measured and accounted for in the statistical analysis of the effect. Thirdly, protection against the effects of causes that can be neither controlled nor measured is gained through random assignment of subjects to the different states of the hypothesized cause. This strategy is the least desirable because it increases the total variation of the dependent variable, making it harder to detect the co-variation of the hypothesized cause and effect. However, randomization has the strength of protecting against unanticipated causes. Taken together, these strategies can produce an experimental situation which generates two-way correspondence. When there is adequate control for the effects of alternative explanations, experimental data can be informative.

The organizational experimentalists appear to rely on the behaviourist tradition in psychology for their version of this model of data production. Individual subjects (rats, people) are placed in simplified environments to control other causes. The researcher manipulates an aspect of the environment, the hypothesized cause (reinforcement schedule, pay plan), called the stimulus, operation, manipulation, condition or treatment. The effect, the subjects' 'behaviour' (bar pressing, widgets produced), is recorded. This is called the response.

The cognitive revolution in psychology has left the behaviourists behind (Bruner 1990), but their influence on representational strategy remains (see Landy (1986) for a discussion of this point with respect to testing). For example, the behaviourist assumptions are betrayed in the experimentalist's treatment of behavioural vs verbal data. Behavioural data are counted and treated as unproblematic. Verbal data are treated with suspicion (Nisbet and Wilson 1977) and require elaborate defences (Ericsson and Simon 1980), though recently there has been an increase in the use of self-report measures. In contrast, other subcommunities within OS, e.g. ethnographers, tend to privilege the verbal and worry about the meaning of the behavioural.

Field experiments play an important role in organization studies. Just how important is an issue of perennial debate (Locke 1986; Greenberg and Tomlinson 2004). The foundational guidance for organizational field experimentation is provided by Campbell and Stanley (1966) in their discussions of how to design experiments that produce valid data. Subsequent updates with other colleagues expand their discussion of threats to validity (Cook and Campbell 1979; Shadish et al. 2002). Limiting the threats to validity increases the likelihood that the experiment will produce good data, i.e. that two-way correspondence is achieved.

Where the surveyor measures constructs, the experimentalist manipulates constructs. Where the surveyor emphasizes the measurement of each construct, the experimentalist is more concerned about representing the relationships between constructs.

Ethno-Data

Ethno-data are data that researchers claim represent the native experience. Ethno-data emerge from a variety of representational strategies, but are united in their commitment to representing the empirical reality as it is experienced by the organizational participants. Many terms could be used to describe this sort of data. Evered and Reis (1981) describe ethnoresearch as 'inquiry from the inside' as opposed to 'from the outside'. Their catalogue of synonyms includes: antipositivistic, phenomenological, ethnomethodological, experiential, existential, ideographic, participative, anthropological, qualitative, dialectic, pragmatic, subjective, intensive, soft and high context. Morey and Luthans (1984) draw on the emic-etic distinction from anthropology for a label.

The defining characteristic of this sort of organizational data is the nature of the empirical reality that the researcher is attempting to represent. Ethno-researchers are intent on discovering and communicating an organizational reality as it is experienced by the inhabitants of that reality. The 'ethno-' prefix has come to be associated specifically with this view. The phrase 'ethno-data' is intended to be broad enough to encompass a variety of research practices and traditions that aim to produce data that represent insiders' lived experiences.

The organizational reality studied by the ethno-researcher is different from that of the experimenter or survey researcher. In contrast to their researcher-designed organizational reality of constructs to be measured or manipulated, the ethno-researcher's organizational world is full of constructs to be discovered. The participants of this world make their own meanings and weave their own patterns. The ethno-researcher is a visitor, a voyeur, a stranger on a journey of discovery (Agar 1996).

The quality of ethno-data, i.e. the degree to which two-way correspondence has been achieved, is equivalent to the fidelity with which representation matches the native viewpoint. There is strong agreement on the organizational reality to be represented, but much less consensus on the representational strategies which yield two-way correspondence. Some ethno-researchers discuss this in terms of reliability and validity, as defined above (Becker 1970). Kunkel and McGrath (1972) argue that there is a necessary trade-off between the two. Others explicitly deny the applicability of these criteria. As substitutes, Lincoln and Guba (1985) propose the criteria of credibility, transferability, dependability and confirmability. Golden-Biddle and Locke (1993) identify authenticity, plausibility and criticality in their analysis of three exemplary ethno-research reports. The Denzin and Lincoln (Denzin and Lincoln 1994; 2000; 2005) handbooks devote several chapters to the discussion of criteria (Altheide and Johnson 1994; Denzin 1994; Smith and Hodkinson 2005).

Achieving two-way correspondence for the ethno-researcher usually involves 'firsthand involvement in the social world' (Filstead 1970: title) as a participant observer. Participant observers listen, learn, take notes, converse, interview, ask questions, test preliminary understandings, watch, read, count and anything else that seems to help them understand the meanings of the world they are exploring. Participant observation is best characterized as immersion in the field setting. Participant observation is a multi-method representational enterprise. Participant observation in organizations almost always includes: casual and systematic interviewing, casual and systematic observation and collection of substantial documentary materials.

There has been an emphasis on learning how to do 'fieldwork' (a synonym for participant observation) by actually going out and doing it. The 'do-it-yourself' tradition is giving way to more regularized specifications of representational practice. Methodological appendices (Whyte 1955; Mills 1959; Willis 1977; Kunda 1992) and collections of war stories (Hammond 1964) are being replaced or complemented by textbooks. Some ethnodata representational processes are very systematic, for example ethnosemantics. Spradley's (1979a, b) manuals lay out step-by-step protocols for ethno-semantic investigations.

Note that ethno-data need not be produced by participant observation techniques. Gersick (1988) provides an example of non-participant observation of work groups. Sometimes, the ethno-researcher may interpret artefacts from the field. For example, Barley et al. (1988) develop a sophisticated content analysis technique to represent the insider's under-standing of organizational culture. They argue that the symbolic and conceptual view of organizational culture held by academic and practitioner subcul-tures can be derived from analyses of the pragmat-ics of written communications in each subculture's journals. The paper provides an excellent exposition of their theoretical rationale, and of the representa-tional process they designed. Stablein (2002) pro-vides a theoretical rationale and detailed description of an existential phenomenological approach. The *Handbook of Qualitative Research* describes a variety of representational processes, many of which could be used to produce ethno-data for organization studies (Denzin and Lincoln 1994; 2000; 2005).

Ethno-data were brought into the consciousness of OS in a big way by the explosion of organiza-tional culture research in the early 1980s (docu-mented by Barley et al. 1988) and the discussion of alternative paradigms (Van Maanen 1979; Burrell and Morgan 1979; Morgan 1983; Lincoln and Guba 1985). Corners of OS have been long aware of this sort of data, e.g. occupations and professions folks could not avoid the Chicago School sociology of the 1920s onward (e.g. Roy 1952).

Conferences and subsequent publications have served to support the use of ethno-data in the study of organizations. Key conferences have included those held in Illinois (Pondy et al. 1983); Vancouver (Frost et al. 1985) and a series of small conferences on interpretative approaches held at Alta. Of partic-ular note is the biennial meeting sponsored by the mainly European Standing Conference on Organi-zational Symbolism (SCOS). European OS has shown a greater affinity for ethno-data. Until recently, research using ethno-data has had limited access to the mainstream journals of OS, with the exception of special issues (*ASQ*, Van Maanen 1979; *JOM*, Frost 1981; *ASQ*, Jelinek et al. 1983). The Podsakoff and Dalton (1987) survey of 1985 jour-nals classified only two studies that may have been

based on ethno-data. Although on the increase, journal articles utilising ethno-data are still rare. There have been a number of calls for more ethno-data, even in the psychologically-oriented side of OS (Lee et al. 1999).

Ethno-data is often reported in books. The amount of data produced, the wordiness of the symbolic system and the subsequent analyses often require more pages than the journals allow (Nelsen and Barley 1997 is an exemplary exception). The classics books in this tradition include Whyte's (1955) *Street Corner Society,* Dalton's (1966) *Men Who Manage* and Becker et al.'s (1961) *Boys in White.* Prichard (2005) has identified the most frequently cited recent OS ethnographies: Kunda's (1992) *Engineering Culture,* Collinson's (1992) *Managing the Shopfloor,* Jackall's (1988) *Moral Mazes,* Law's (1994) *Organizing Modernity,* Watson's (1994) *In search of management.* Orr's (1996) *Talk-ing about Machines* is worth a look, too. Hodson (2004) provides the most complete list of workplace ethnographies along with a number of variables that he has coded for each ethnography.

Case Data

In the early days case studies were an important type of data. Daft (1980) documents the dominance of case reports in *ASQ* in 1959. The foundational works in organizational sociology are cases (Gouldner 1954; Blau 1955). Cases undergirded the theory and practice of the Tavistock Institute (e.g. Trist and Bamforth 1951; Rice 1958). By the late 1960s there is evidence of a decline in the reliance on cases in *ASQ* (Daft 1980) and in sociology (Hamel 1993). However, there is evidence of increased interest in case studies in the 1980s and 1990s in the US and Europe (Ragin and Becker 1992; Bartunek et al. 1993; Hamel 1993).

The case study method is a well-used term that has many meanings. Ragin and Becker (1992) dis-cuss these at length. Gummesson (2000) offers an interesting discussion of case varieties from a Scan-dinavian point of view. The various types of cases share the focus on one, complex organizational unit. The various types of cases share a common representational process of multi-method immer-sion. However, they differ in important aspects of the organizational reality that is studied. Here I will make a distinction between two main styles of case study: 'theory-generating' cases; and 'exemplar' cases. Stake (2005) provides an overview of case study in the interpretive tradition.

Theory generating cases are oriented to generalizable theoretical propositions. Thus, the organizational reality of this sort of case writer is the world of researcher-defined constructs. Unlike the world of the questionnaire researcher, the organizational world is a complex and tangled world where cutting the Gordian knot is not as simple as asking the right questions. Experimentation is not an available strategy because the case researcher's issues are more sociological and there are insufficient independent units for a field experiment. Case research in this tradition generally involves the same multiple method immersion of the ethnograhers, but researcher views are the starting point. The classic cases of industrial sociology fit this mould. For example, in *Patterns of Industry Bureaucracy*, Gouldner (1954) attempts to discover and describe the ways Weber's ideal bureaucracy is found in an American factory and mine. *The Dynamics of Bureaucracy* by Blau (1955) tackles a similar project in two government agencies.

Kanter's (1977) case study of *Men and Women of the Corporation* is frequently cited as a masterpiece of this genre of case research. In her methodological appendix, she clearly states: 'This study represents primarily a search for explanation and theory rather than just a report of an empirical research' (Kanter 1977: 291). Justifying the representational strategy of case immersion, she quotes another pioneer of organizational studies:

Crozier, who framed the methodological problems inherent in studies of large-scale organizations well: 'Comprehensive studies of human relations problems at the management level are usually hampered by two sets of difficulties. First, the complexity of the role structure in modem organizations causes much ambiguity and overlapping, making it impossible to match really comparable cases and to use rigorous methods meaningfully. Second, the general emphasis on status and promotions gives a crucial importance to the human relations game, thus preventing the researcher from obtaining reliable data on the central problem of power relationships' (Crozier 1964: 112). Thus, a combination of methods such as used in the classical sociological field studies emerges as the most valid and reliable way to develop understanding of such a complex social reality as the corporation (Kanter 1977: 297).

The contemporary champion for this positivist approach is Eisenhardt (1989; 1991). The most popular case method text largely follows in the theory generating tradition (Yin 2002). Snook's (2002) multi-level examination of a friendly fire incident provides a recent book-length example.

Exemplar case data is amongst the most influential data in OS. Exemplary case data are influential because they are often presented to organizational participants and students in OS classrooms. Often, such presentations are oriented to action. The audience comprises powerful organizational participants who can follow the template provided by an exemplar to intervene in their own organizations. For students, these vivid cases provide ersatz organizational experiences against which they test other data and ideas.

The organizational reality of the exemplar based researcher consists of nearly universal problems, processes or solutions relevant to most organizations. The lessons drawn from studying individual leaders, events or organizations are taken to be informative for most organizational behaviour. At its worst this involves unreflective generalization and cheerleading.

The representational strategy for the exemplary case varies on an important dimension from that of other cases. For the types of data that we have discussed, the representational strategies are sensitive to issues of bias, authenticity and validity using a variety of techniques such as reliability, experimental control, triangulation, multiple informants, etc. The researcher, as data generator, has taken a critical stance in their work. The exemplary case researcher tends to be less concerned about this aspect of the representational process. Sometimes, the reporter is a key organizational participant and clear partisan, e.g. Jack Welsh or the CEO of Johnsonville Sausage. Sometimes, the researcher is ideologically committed, e.g. Walton (1977) at Topeka Pet Food, or maybe acting as a paid consultant.

Exemplary case data make a bigger break with the traditional views of scientific work that linger in OS approaches. Thus, other OS researchers have tended to ignore or attack exemplary case data. I argue that this reflects an outdated view of science. The impetus of the approach suggested in this chapter is to be more open-minded in considering OS data. When identifying the organizational reality and representational strategy of the exemplary case researcher, other researchers can more carefully develop their views regarding a particular exemplar and take from the case report what may be of value.

Yes, the lack of criticality may be taken as a disadvantage for OS purposes and audiences. However, there may be offsetting advantages, beginning with the availability of the data. The access and resources of top consultants and powerful organizational participants are beyond the reach of most OS researchers. The particular bias of exemplary data is not *a priori* worse than the bias of a critical or cynical view.

Secondary and Archival Data

Data interpreted by an organizational scholar that were originally collected for another purpose are called secondary or archival data. The data could be employment records, annual reports, government censuses, production figures, regulatory reports, meeting minutes, websites, call centre records, etc. Secondary data could have been collected for another research project, but, usually, have been collected for non-research purposes, such as meeting compliance requirements.

The use of secondary and archival data is increasing in OS (Scandura and Williams 2000; Ventresca and Mohr 2002). Ventresca and Mohr (2002) claim population ecology, a renewed interest in history and OS, and what they term the new archival tradition account for the increase. The empirical reality of the new archivalists is 'the shared forms of meaning that underlie social organizational processes' (Ventresca and Mohr 2002: 810). Relations rather than objects or attributes of organizations are considered central. They review a range of representational processes including network analysis and content analysis.

It is difficult to meet the criteria for good data using secondary data. The secondary data user has the task of demonstrating that the data represent the organizational reality of interest in the second research project. This reality may be the same as that of the original data collector, or it may not be. The researcher cannot assume that the original collector was trying to represent the same organizational reality. The burden of proof is on the secondary data user to demonstrate that the data work for the new use. Stewart and Kamins (1993) provide many colourful examples of the misuse of secondary data and an introduction to their proper use. Recent research develops and illustrates a method for validating

archival measures that would be applicable in some situations (Payne et al. 2003; Tremble et al. 2003).

Difficulty is often encountered when organizational researchers use performance data in studies of employee behaviour. Sometimes explicitly, sometimes implicitly, organizational indices collected for technical or management reasons are used as measures of employee controlled outcomes. When these numbers, which may be excellent data for production planning, are used in models of employee behaviour, two-way correspondence can break down.

Sutton and Rafaeli (1988; 1992) discovered the problem in their attempt to use a convenience store's sales figures to represent the effectiveness of employee friendliness. When they found a negative relationship between friendliness and sales, they did not advise store owners to hire gruff sales clerks. Instead they accepted that two-way correspondence had broken down. The data did not inform them about organizational reality. Next, they generated ethno-data in a variety of field settings. With a richer understanding of organizational reality in this particular retail setting, they realized that sales represented how busy a store was, i.e. store pace. Sales did not represent the original dependent variable (clerk performance) that the authors thought clerk friendliness would influence. A slow pace, reflected in low sales, provides both the opportunity and the motivation for otherwise bored sales clerks to be friendly.

The secondary data user cannot design a representational process that will yield the desired two-way correspondence. Nor can the researcher assume that the original data collector did. Thus, the researcher must demonstrate that the existing data do represent the empirical reality of interest.

Discourse as Data

The linguistic turn in social science has been embraced by many scholars in OS. For those who understand language to be central to (or constitutive of) organizational reality, discourse is the primary data. However, there is no single consensus on the definition of discourse. Several commentators have attempted to map the variety of uses (Alvesson and Karreman 2000; Prichard et al. 2004). Using the frame presented in this chapter, I will divide discourse analysis into two groupings according to the nature of the organizational reality that the scholars are trying to understand.

The first group is primarily oriented to understanding meaning. These scholars follow the interpretive tradition. The representational practice is to examine texts (writ broadly to include documents, interviews, work practices, etc). Recently published resources provide a series of examples in this tradition (Wetherell et al. 2001; Grant et al. 2004). Under-utilized in this branch of OS discourse analysis is the oldest interpretive tradition, that of hermeneutics. Prasad (2002) surveys the developments in this tradition, particularly as they relate to the contributions of Gadamer, Habermas and Ricoeur. He goes on to develop the methodological implications for OS with a brief illustration from his research on the oil industry.

The second group consists of scholars who are trying to understand the knowledges that constitute organizational reality. These authors have been strongly influenced by Derrida (Jones 2004) and Foucault (Knights 1992; 2004). Some neo-institutional theorists share this interest in the taken-for-granteds that constrain and enable organizational participants and action, for example, Tolbert and Zucker's (1996) concept of sedimentation.

Following Derrida, some scholars treat the texts authored by organizational scholars as the data. They are not interested in the organizational reality that the original authors try to expose, understand, predict, etc. The original writer presents the text as a report of his or her interpretation of the data, yielding greater understanding of organizational reality. Instead, the postmodernist treats the text as the empirical reality to be studied. As presented by the original author the text constitutes a reality. For the poststructural researcher the text is data that represent and constitute multiple realities. However, the representational process of *deconstruction* is required to reveal these realities. The deconstructive process involves overturning and displacing the intended meanings of the text (Cooper 1990). It is not simply a dialectical process of antithesis and synthesis. Deconstruction has been associated with revealing patriarchal, capitalist and racial oppression but, much to the dismay of some feminists, critical theorists and colonial theorists, it does not directly privilege the cause of the previously oppressed or hidden. Nor does it deny the validity of the intended meanings of the powerful. It does not simply reverse the ordering or priority of meaning. A good deconstruction represents and constitutes multiple realities without refreezing the potential meaning of the text.

Two-way correspondence for textual data means unsettling, discomforting and disturbing our taken-for-granted knowledge of reality.

Therefore, not every text provides data for the deconstructionist. Texts which are considered significant and influential in forming our knowledge of organization are the appropriate raw data. It is foundational texts that constitute our well-accepted, comfortable empirical reality. Thus, Kilduff (1993) chose March and Simon's *Organizations*, and Calas and Smirch (1991) chose Mintzberg's *oeuvre*, as organizational texts to deconstruct.

A related interest of OS scholars interested in knowledge is in the ways that authors construct texts which readers accept as authentic and credible accounts. For example, Jeffcut (1994a) treats organizational ethnographies as data. He identifies the epic structure of the ethnographic account as crucial to the effectiveness of these accounts. Locke and Golden-Biddle (1997) study how OS authors construct the opportunities for contribution that their articles fulfil. Thus, in this sense, postmodern analyses can be meta-analyses: analyses of the products of other organizational scholars.

Knowledge as data need not lead to studies of existing OS scholarship. I will close this section with two book length investigations with very similar understandings of the empirical reality, which lean heavily on Foucault. Yet, the authors use very different representational strategies. Kondo (1990) relies on a period of long-term participant observation in a Japanese pastry factory for the data in *Crafting Selves*. Her Japanese physical appearance clashes radically with her American cultural upbringing allowing a particular insight into how cultural, gender and work identities are constructed. In contrast, Jacques' (1996) *Manufacturing the Employee* examines the construction of the employee identity in America using a wide array of management and self-development texts as data.

Discussion and Future Directions

In my attempt to survey the breadth and depth of OS data, much has been lost. I have violated the integrity of the organizational research I describe. I have torn data from their analyses. I have largely ignored the content that the symbols have represented and the insight that subsequent analyses have generated. Fortunately, other chapters in this volume do summarize and review the substantive gains of various data users in their endeavours to understand organization.

What do I offer in defence of this exercise? First, I present a definition of data in OS that takes account of contemporary views on the nature of organizational studies as a human enterprise. In summary, a subcommunity of organizational studies shares a view of an empirical, organizational reality. Members of that community attempt to represent that empirical reality in ways that allow the development of that view and the generation of deeper understanding. Two-way correspondence between the reality and the symbol system used to represent it will yield success in the attempt. By thinking about data in this way, we can be clearer about what we are doing. This will benefit the development of research within subcommunities, and communication across subcommunity boundaries.

Secondly, I present a survey of the kinds of data in use in OS. The definition offers a different perspective on what we do, and invites different sorts of comparisons. It is not a comprehensive, a complete, or a final survey. I hope the definition offered here invites new categories and comparisons. Too often we focus on critique of the other research traditions.

Statistics are often contrived and misleading. Ethnography has at times aided colonization. The social and physical sciences have at times produced bad theories and been put to very negative uses. Some early postmodernist theorists, Christians and scientists were Nazis, and elements of each of their fundamental conceptions could be co-opted to support this particular form of barbarism. This potential utilization, however, does not lead for me to a blanket condemnation of postmodernism, science, ethnography, religion or statistics. Devotees of each have used their special understandings to fight tyranny. Both postmodernism and science also draw on fundamental conceptions that are productive, enable open choices and help us see through the masters and ideologies of a particular time and place. I am less interested in blame than on finding what each can contribute. I look to an ongoing community discussion that helps us to do the best we can to sort out the good from the bad (Deetz 2000: 732).

My closing hope is that this chapter (1) contributes to the understanding and development of our research practices and thus to our insights, and (2) increases our appreciation of OS research outside our comfort zone and thus reduces the forces of fragmentation, while denying the need for unification in OS.

References

Agar, M. (1996) *The professional stranger: an informal introduction to ethnography*, 2nd edn. San Diego: Academic Press.

Altheide, D.L. and Johnson, J.M. (1994) 'Criteria for assessing interpretive validity in qualitative research', in N.K. Denzin and Y.S. Lincoln (eds), *Handbook of qualitative research*. Thousand Oaks: Sage Publications. pp. 485–99.

Alvesson, M. (2003) 'Beyond neopositivists, romantics, and localists: a reflexive approach to interviews in organizational research', *Academy of Management Review*, 28(1): 13–33.

Alvesson, M. and Karreman, D. (2000) 'Varieties of discourse: on the study of organizations through discourse analysis', *Human Relations*, 53(9): 1125–49.

Alvesson, M. and Willmott, H. (eds) (1992) *Critical management studies*. London; Newbury Park: Sage.

Ashmore, M. (1989) *The reflexive thesis: wrighting sociology of scientific knowledge*. Chicago: University of Chicago Press.

Astley, W.G. (1985) 'Administrative science as socially constructed truth' *Administrative Science Quarterly*, 30(4): 497–513.

Austin, J.T., Scherbaum, C.A. and Mahlman, R.A. (2004) 'History of research methods in industrial and organizational psychology: measurement, design, analysis', in S.G. Rogelberg (ed.), *Handbook of research methods in industrial and organizational psychology*. Oxford: Blackwell. pp. 3–33.

Barley, S.R., Meyer, G.W. and Gash, D.C. (1988) 'Cultures of culture – academics, practitioners and the pragmatics of normative control', *Administrative Science Quarterly*, 33(1): 24–60.

Bartunek, J.M., Bobko, P. and Venkatraman, N. (1993) 'Toward innovation and diversity in management research methods', *Academy of Management Journal*, 36(6): 1362–73.

Becker, H.S. (1970) 'Problems of inference and proof in participant observation', in W.J. Filstead (ed.), *Qualitative methodology: first and involvement with the social world*. Chicago: Markham. pp. 189–201.

Becker, H.S., Geer, B., Hughes, E.C. and Strauss, A. (1961) *Boys in white: student culture in medical school*. New Brunswick, NJ: Transaction Books.

Blalock, H.M. (1968) 'The measurement problem: the gap between the languages of theory and research', in H.M. Blalock and A.B. Blalock (eds), *Methodology in social research*. New York, McGraw-Hill. pp. 5–27.

Blau, P.M. (1955) *The dynamics of bureaucracy*, Rev. 2nd edn. Chicago: University of Chicago Press.

Boring, E.G. (1969) 'Perspective: artifact and control', in R. Rosenthal and R.L. Rosnow (eds), *Artifact in behavioral research*. New York: Academic Press. pp. 1–11.

Borsboom, D. and Mellenbergh, G.J. (2004) 'Why psychometrics is not pathological – a comment on Michell'. *Theory & Psychology*, 14(1): 105–20.

Breaugh, J.A. (1985) 'The measurement of work autonomy'. *Human Relations*, 38(6): 551–70.

Breaugh, J.A. (1999) 'Further investigation of the work autonomy scales: two studies', *Journal of Business & Psychology*, 13(3): 357–73.

Breaugh, J.A. and Becker, A.S. (1987) 'Further examination of the Work Autonomy Scales: three studies', *Human Relations*, 40(6): 381–400.

Bruner, J.S. (1990) *Acts of meaning*. Cambridge, MA: Harvard University Press.

Burrell, G. (1988) 'Modernism, post modernism and organizational analysis. 2. The contribution of Foucault, Michel', *Organization Studies*, 9(2): 221–35.

Burrell, G. and Morgan, G. (1979) *Sociological paradigms and organisational analysis: elements of the sociology of corporate life*. London: Heinemann.

Calas, M.B. and Smircich, L. (1991) 'Voicing seduction to silence leadership', *Organization Studies*, 12(4): 567–601.

Calas, M.B. and Smircich, L. (eds) (1997) *Postmodern Management Theory*. Aldershot: Ashgate.

Calas, M.B. and Smircich, L. (1999) 'Past postmodernism? Reflections and tentative directions', *Academy of Management Review*, 24(4): 649–71.

Campbell, D.T. and Stanley, J.C. (1966) *Experimental and quasi-experimental designs for research*. Chicago: R. McNally.

Caporaso, J.E. (1973) 'Quasi-experimental approaches and social science', in J.E. Caporaso (ed.), *Quasi-experimental approaches: testing theory and evaluating policy*. Evanston, Illinois: Northwestern University Press. pp. 3–38.

Chalmers, A.F. (1999) *What is this thing called science?* Buckingham: Open University Press.

Chia, R. (2003) 'Organization theory as a postmodern science', in H. Tsoukas and C. Knudson (eds), *The Oxford handbook of organization theory*. New York: Oxford University Press. pp. 113–40.

Clark, H.H. and Schrober, M.F. (1992) 'Asking questions and influencing answers', in J.M. Tanur (ed.), *Questions about questions: inquiries into the cognitive bases of surveys*. New York: Russell Sage Foundation. pp. 15–48.

Collinson, D. (1992) *Managing the shopfloor: subjectivity, masculinity, and workplace culture*. Berlin, New York: W. de Gruyter.

Cook, T.D. and Campbell, D.T. (1979) *Quasi-experimentation: design & analysis issues for field settings*. Boston: Houghton Mifflin.

Coombs, C.H., Dawes, R.M. and Tversky, A. (1970) *Mathematical psychology*. Englewood Cliffs, NJ: Prentice-Hall.

Cooper, R. (1989) 'Modernism, post modernism and organizational analysis. 3. – The contribution of Derrida, Jacques', *Organization Studies*, 10(4): 479–502.

Cooper, R. (1990) 'Organization/disorganization', in J. Hassard and D. Pym (eds), *The theory and philosophy of organizations: critical issues and new perspectives*. London; New York: Routledge. pp. 167–97.

Cooper, R. and Burrell, G. (1988) 'Modernism, postmodernism and organizational analysis – an introduction', *Organization Studies*, 9(1): 91–112.

Czarniawska, B. (1998) *A narrative approach to organization studies*. Thousand Oaks, CA: Sage Publications.

Czarniawska, B. (2003) 'Styles of organization theory', in H. Tsoukas and C. Knudsen (eds),. *The Oxford handbook of organization theory*. New York: Oxford University Press. pp. 235–61.

Daft, R.L. (1980) 'The evolution of organization analysis in ASQ, 1959–1979', *Administrative Science Quarterly*, 25(4): 623–36.

Dalton, M. (1966) *Men Who Manage*. New York: John Wiley.

Dawes, R.M. (1972) *Fundamentals of attitude measurement*. New York: Wiley.

Deetz, S. (1996) 'Describing differences in approaches to organization science: rethinking Burrell and Morgan and their legacy', *Organization Science*, 7(2): 191–207.

Deetz, S. (2000) 'Putting the community into organizational science: exploring the construction of knowledge claims', *Organization Science*, 11(6): 732–8.

Denzin, N.K. (1994) 'The art and politics of interpretation', in N.K. Denzin and Y.S. Lincoln (eds), *Handbook of qualitative research*. Thousand Oaks, CA: Sage Publications. pp. 500–15.

Denzin, N.K. and Lincoln, Y.S. (eds) (1994) *Handbook of qualitative research*. Thousand Oaks, CA: Sage Publications.

Denzin, N.K. and Lincoln, Y.S. (eds) (2000) *Handbook of qualitative research*. Thousand Oaks, CA: Sage Publications.

Denzin, N.K. and Lincoln, Y.S. (eds) (2005) *The SAGE handbook of qualitative research*. Thousand Oaks, CA: Sage Publications.

Eisenhardt, K.M. (1989) 'Building theories from case study research', *Academy of Management Review*, 14(4): 532–50.

Eisenhardt, K.M. (1991) 'Better stories and better constructs: the case for rigor in comparative logic', *Academy of Management Review*, 16(3): 620–7.

Ericsson, K.A. and Simon, H.A. (1980) 'Verbal reports as data', *Psychological Review*, 87(3): 215–51.

Evered, R. and Reis, M. (1981) 'Alternative perspectives in the organizational sciences: 'inquiry from the inside' and 'inquiry from the outside'', *Academy of Management Review*, 6(3): 385–95.

Filstead, W.J. (ed.) (1970) *Qualitative methodology: first and involvement with the social world*. Chicago: Markham.

Frost, P.J. (1981) 'Special issue on organizational symbolism', *Journal of Management*, 11(2): 5–136.

Frost, P.J. and Stablein, R.E. (eds) (1992) *Doing exemplary research*. Newbury Park, CA: Sage Publications.

Frost, P.J., Moore, L.F., Louis, M.R., Lundberg, C.C. and Martin, J. (eds) (1985) *Organizational culture*. Beverly Hills: Sage Publications.

Gephart, R.P. (1988) *Ethnostatistics: qualitative foundations for quantitative research*. Newbury Park, CA: Sage Publications.

Gersick, C.J.G. (1988) 'Time and transition in work teams: toward a new model of group development', *Academy of Management Journal*, 31(1): 9–41.

Gersick, C.J.G. (1992) 'Time in transition in my work in teams: looking back on a new model of group development', in P.J. Frost and R.E. Stablein (eds), *Doing exemplary research*. Thousand Oaks, CA: Sage Publications. pp. 52–64.

Goffman, E. (1959) *The presentation of self in everyday life*. Garden City, NY: Doubleday.

Golden-Biddle, K. and Locke, K. (1993) 'Appealing work: an investigation of how ethnographic texts convince', *Organization Science*, 4(4): 595–616.

Gouldner, A.W. (1954) *Patterns of industrial bureaucracy*. New York: Free Press.

Grant, D., Hardy, C., Oswick, C. and Putnam, L. (eds) (2004) *The Sage handbook of organizational discourse*. London: Sage.

Greenberg, J. and Tomlinson, E.C. (2004) 'Situated experiments in organizations: transplanting the lab to the field', *Journal of Management*, 30(5): 703–24.

Gummesson, E. (2000) *Qualitative methods in management research*, 2nd edn. Thousand Oaks, CA: Sage Publications.

Habermas, J. (1971) *Knowledge and human interests*, Translated by Jeremy J. Shapiro. Boston: Beacon Press.

Hackman, J.R. (1992) 'Time and transitions', in P.J. Frost and R.E. Stabein (eds), *Doing exemplary research*. Newbury Park, CA: Sage Publications. pp. 73–8.

Hamel, J. (1993) *Case study methods*. Newbury Park, CA: Sage Publications.

Hammond, P.E. (ed.) (1964) *Sociologists at work*. New York: Basic Books.

Hardy, M. and Bryman, A. (eds) (2003) *Handbook of data analysis*. London: Sage.

Harley, S., Muller-Camen, M. and Collin, A. (2004) 'From academic communities to managed organisations: the implications for academic careers in UK and German universities', *Journal of Vocational Behavior*, 64(2): 329–45.

Hassard, J. (1990) 'An alternative to paradigm incommensurability in organization theory', in J. Hassard and D. Pym (eds), *The theory and philosophy of organizations:* critical issues and new perspectives. London; New York: Routledge. pp. 219–30.

Hassard, J. and Parker, M. (eds) (1993) *Postmodernism and organizations*. London, Newbury Park, CA: Sage Publications.

Hatch, M.J. and Yanow, D. (2003) 'Organization theory as an interpretive science', in H. Tsoukas and C. Knudsen (eds), *The Oxford handbook of organization theory*. New York: Oxford University Press. pp. 63–87.

Hinkin, T.R. (1995) 'A review of scale development practices in the study of organizations', *Journal of Management*, 21(5): 967–88.

Hinkin, T.R. (1998) 'A review of scale development practices in the study of organizations', *Organization Research Methods*, 1(1): 104–21.

Hodson, M. (2004) *Work ethnography project* [Online]. Available online at: http://www.sociology.ohio-state.edu/rdh/Workplace-Ethnography-Project.html, accessed 2 February 2006.

Ironson, G.H., Smith, P.C., Brannick, M.T., Gibson, W.M. and Paul, K.B. (1989) 'Construction of a job in general scale: a comparison of global, composite, and specific measures', *Journal of Applied Psychology*, 74(2): 193–200.

Jackall, R. (1988) *Moral mazes: the world of corporate managers*. New York: Oxford University Press.

Jacques, R. (1996) *Manufacturing the employee: management knowledge from the 19th to 21st centuries*. London, Thousand Oaks, CA: Sage Publications.

Janz, T., Hellervick, L. and Gilmore, D.C. (1986) *Behavioral description interviewing*. Boston: Allyn & Bacon.

Jaros, S.J. (1994) 'Reconciling knowledge accumulation and resource acquisition: issues in organizational science', *Academy of Management Review*, 19(4): 643–4.

Jeffcutt, P. (1994a) 'From interpretation to representation in organizational analysis: postmodernism, ethnography and organizational symbolism', *Organization Studies*, 15(2): 241–74.

Jeffcutt, P. (1994b) 'The interpretation of organization: contemporary analysis and critique', *Journal of Management Studies*, 31(2): 225–50.

Jelinek, M., Smircich, L. and Hirsch, P. (1983) 'Introduction: a code of many colors', *Administrative Science Quarterly*, 28(3): 331–8.

Jermier, J.M. (1994) 'Critical issues in organization science', *Organization Science*, 5(1): 1–13.

Jones, C. (2003) 'Theory after the postmodern condition', *Organization*, 10(3): 503–25.

Jones, C. (2004) 'Jacques Derrida', in S. Linstead (ed.), *Organization theory and postmodern thought*. London: Sage. pp. 34–63.

Kanter, R.M. (1977) *Men and women of the corporation*. New York: Basic Books.

Kilduff, M. (1993) 'Deconstructing organizations', *Academy of Management Review*, 18(1): 13–31.

Kilduff, M. and Mehra, A. (1997) 'Postmodernism and organizational research', *Academy of Management Review*, 22(2): 453–81.

Knights, D. (1992) 'Changing spaces – the disruptive impact of a new epistemological location for the study of management', *Academy of Management Review*, 17(3): 514–36.

Knights, D. (2004) 'Michel Foucault', in S. Linstead (ed.), *Organization theory and postmodern thought*. London: Sage Publications. pp. 14–33.

Kondo, D.K. (1990) *Crafting selves: power, gender, and discourses of identity in a Japanese workplace*. Chicago: University of Chicago Press.

Kuhn, T.S. (1970) *The structure of scientific revolutions*. Chicago: University of Chicago Press.

Kunda, G. (1992) *Engineering culture: control and commitment in a high-tech corporation*. Philadelphia: Temple University Press.

Kunkel, P.J. and McGrath, J.E. (1972) *Research in human behavior*. New York: Holt, Rinehart and Winston.

Lakatos, I. (1970) 'Falsification and the methodology of scientific research programmes', in I. Lakatos and A. Musgrave (eds), *Criticism and the growth of knowledge*. Cambridge: Cambridge University Press. pp. 91–196.

Landy, F.J. (1986) 'Stamp collecting versus science – validation as hypothesis-testing', *American Psychologist*, 41(11): 1183–92.

Law, J. (1994) *Organizing modernity*. Oxford, Cambridge, MA: Blackwell.

Lawler III, E.E. (1985) 'Challenge traditional research assumptions', in E.E. Lawler III, A.M. Mohrman, S.A. Mohrman, G. Ledford Jr, T.G. Cummings and associates (eds), *Doing research that is useful for theory and practice*. San Francisco: Jossey-Bass. pp. 1–17.

Lee, T.W., Mitchell, T.R. and Sablynski, C.J. (1999) 'Qualitative research in organizational and vocational psychology, 1979–1999', *Journal of Vocational Behavior*, 55(2): 161–87.

Lincoln, Y.S. and Guba, E.G. (1985) *Naturalistic inquiry*. Beverly Hills, CA: Sage.

Linstead, S. (ed.) (2004) *Organization theory and postmodern thought*. London: Sage.

Locke, E.A. (ed.) (1986) *Generalizing from laboratory to field settings: research findings from industrial organizational psychology, organizational behavior and human resource management*. Lexington, MA: Lexington Books.

Locke, K. and Golden-Biddle, K. (1997) 'Constructing opportunities for contribution: structuring intertextual coherence and 'problematizing' in organizational studies', *Academy of Management Journal*, 40(5): 1023–62.

Lord, F.M. (1953) 'On the statistical treatment of football numbers', *American Psychologist*, 8: 750–1.

MacRae, G. (1988) 'Measurement scales on statistics: what can significance tests tell us about the world?', *British Journal of Psychology*, 79(2): 161–71.

Martin, J. (1990) 'Breaking up the mono-method monopolies in organizational analysis', in J. Hassard and D. Pym (eds), *The theory and philosophy of organizations: critical issues and new perspectives*. London; New York: Routledge. pp. 30–43.

Martin, J. (2002) *Organizational culture: mapping the terrain*. Thousand Oaks: Sage Publications.

Martin, J. (2003) 'Meta-theoretical controversies in studying organizational culture', in H. Tsoukas and C. Knudsen (eds), *The Oxford handbook of organization theory*. New York: Oxford University Press. pp. 392–419.

Martin, J. and Frost, P.J. (1996) 'The organizational culture war games: a struggle for intellectual dominance', in S.R. Clegg, C. Hardy and W.R. Nord (eds), *Handbook of organization studies*. London; Thousand Oaks: Sage Publications. pp. 599–621.

McKelvey, B. and Andriani, P. (2005) 'Why Gaussian statistics are mostly wrong for strategic organization', *Strategic Organization*, 3(2): 219–28.

Merton, R.K. (1968) *Social theory and social structure*. New York: Free Press.

Meyer, G.W., Barley, S.R. and Gash, D.C. (1992) 'Obsession and naïveté in upstate New York: a tale of research', in P.J. Frost and R.E. Stablein (eds), *Doing exemplary research*. Newbury Park, CA: Sage Publications. pp. 22–35.

Mezias, J.M. and Starbuck, W.H. (2003a) 'The odyssey continues', *British Journal of Management*, 14(1): 45–7.

Mezias, J.M. and Starbuck, W.H. (2003b) 'Studying the accuracy of managers' perceptions: a research odyssey', *British Journal of Management*, 14(1): 3–17.

Mezias, J.M. and Starbuck, W.H. (2003c) 'What do managers know, anyway?', *Harvard Business Review*, 81(5): 16–17.

Michell, J. (1997) 'Quantitative science and the definition of measurement in psychology', *British Journal of Psychology*, 88(3): 355–83.

Michell, J. (2002) 'Stevens's theory of scales of measurement and its place in modern psychology', *Australian Journal of Psychology*, 54(2): 99–104.

Miles, M.B. and Huberman, A.M. (1994) *Qualitative data analysis: an expanded sourcebook*. Thousand Oaks, CA: Sage Publications.

Mills, C.W. (1959) *The sociological imagination*. New York: Oxford University Press.

Mitroff, I.I. and Kilmann, R.H. (1978) *Methodological approaches to social science*. San Francisco: Jossey-Bass.

Moldoveanu, M.C. and Baum, J.A.C. (2002) 'Contemporary debates in organizational epistemology', in J.A.C. Baum (ed.), *The Blackwell companion to Organizations*. Malden, MA: Blackwell. pp. 733–51.

Morey, N.C. and Luthans, F. (1984) 'An emic perspective and ethnoscience methods for organizational research', *Academy of Management Review*, 9(1): 27–36.

Morgan, G. (1983) *Beyond method: strategies for social research*. Beverly Hills, CA: Sage Publications.

Muniz, J. (1998) 'Psychological measurement', *Psicothema*, 10(1): 1–21.

Nelsen, B.J. and Barley, S.R. (1997) 'For love or money? Commodification and the construction of an occupational mandate', *Administrative Science Quarterly*, 42(4): 619–53.

Nisbet, R.E. and Wilson, T.D. (1977) 'Telling more than we can know: verbal reports on mental processes', *Psychological Review*, 84(3): 231–59.

Orr, J.E. (1996) *Talking about machines: an ethnography of a modern job*. Ithaca, NY: ILR Press.

Payne, S.C., Finch, J.F. and Tremble, T.R. (2003) 'Validating surrogate measures of psychological constructs: the application of construct equivalence to archival data', *Organizational Research Methods*, 6(3): 363–82.

Pedhazur, E.J. and Schmelkin, L.P. (1991) *Measurement, design, and analysis: an integrated approach*. Hillsdale, NJ: Lawrence Erlbaum Associates.

Pfeffer, J. (1993) 'Barriers to the advance of organizational science – paradigm development as a dependent variable', *Academy of Management Review*, 18(4): 599–620.

Pfeffer, J. (1995) 'Mortality, reproducibility, and the persistence of styles of theory', *Organization Science*, 6(6): 680–6.

Pinder, C.C. and Moore, L.F. (eds) (1980) *Middle range research and the study of organizations*. Boston: Martinus Nijhoff.

Podsakoff, P.M. and Dalton, D.R. (1987) 'Research methodology in organizational studies', *Journal of Management*, 13(2): 419–41.

Pondy, L.R., Frost, P.J., Morgan, G. and Dandridge, T.C. (eds) (1983) *Organizational symbolism*. Greenwich, CN: JAI Press.

Prasad, A. (2002) 'The contest over meaning: hermeneutics as an interpretive methodology for understanding texts', *Organizational Research Methods*, 5(1): 12–33.

Prasad, P. (2005) *Crafting qualitative research: working in the postpositivist traditions*. Armonk, NY: M.E. Sharpe.

Prichard, C. (2005) 'The contribution of discourse to organizational studies: the case of Law and Watson ethnographies', Working paper, Palmerston North, NZ: Massey University.

Prichard, C. and Willmott, H. (1997) 'Just how managed is the McUniversity?', *Organization Studies*, 18(2): 287–316.

Prichard, C., Jones, D. and Stablein, R.E. (2004) 'Doing research on organizational discourse: the importance of researcher context', in D. Grant, C. Hardy, C. Oswick and L. Putnam (eds), *The Sage handbook of organizational discourse*. London: Sage Publications. pp. 213–36.

Ragin, C.C. and Becker, H.S. (eds) (1992) *What is a case? exploring the foundations of social inquiry*. Cambridge, New York: Cambridge University Press.

Reed, M. (1996) 'Organizational theorizing: a historically contested terrain', in S.R. Clegg, C. Hardy and W.R. Nord (eds), *Handbook of Organization Studies*. London, Thousand Oaks: Sage Publications. pp. 31–56.

Reed, M. (2003) 'The agency/structure dilemma in organization theory: open doors and brick walls', in H. Tsoukas and C. Knudsen (eds), *The Oxford handbook*

organization theory. New York: Oxford University Press. pp. 289–309.

Rhodes, C. (2001) *Writing organization: (re)presentation and control in narratives at work*. Amsterdam; Philadelphia: J. Benjamins.

Rice, A.K. (1958) *Productivity and social organization: the Ahmedabad experiment: technical innovation, work organization and management*. London: Tavistock.

Rosenthal, R. and Rosnow, R.L. (eds) (1969) *Artifact in behavioral research*. New York: Academic Press.

Roy, D. (1952) 'Quota restriction and goldbricking in a machine shop', *American Journal of Sociology*, 57(5): 427–42.

Russell, S.S., Spitzmuller, C.T., Lin, L.F., Stanton, J.M., Smith, P.C. and Ironson, G.H. (2004) 'Shorter can also be better: the abridged Job in General scale', *Educational & Psychological Measurement*, 64(5): 878–93.

Rynes, S.L., Bartunek, J.M. and Daft, R.L. (2001) 'Across the great divide: knowledge creation and transfer between practitioners and academics', *Academy of Management Journal*, 44(2): 340–55.

Sandelands, L. (1993) 'Review of *Doing Exemplary Research*', *Academy of Management Review*, 18(2): 377–80.

Scandura, T.A. and Williams, E.A. (2000) 'Research methodology in management: current practices, trends, and implications for future research', *Academy of Management Journal*, 43(6): 1248–64.

Schaeffer, N.C. and Presser, S. (2003) 'The science of asking questions', *Annual Review of Sociology*, 29: 65–88.

Schwab, D. (1985) 'Reviewing empirically based manuscripts: perspectives on process', in L.L. Cummings and P.J. Frost (eds), *Publishing in the organizational sciences*. Homewood, IL: Irwin. pp. 171–81.

Schwab, D.P. (1980) 'Construct validity in organizational behavior', *Research in Organizational Behavior*, 2: 3–43.

Shadish, W.R., Cook, T.D. and Campbell, D.T. (2002) *Experimental and quasi-experimental designs for generalized causal inference*. Boston: Houghton Mifflin.

Silverman, D. (2004) *Doing qualitative research: a practical handbook*. London: Sage.

Skowronski, J.J. and Walker, W.R. (2004) 'How describing autobiographical events can affect autobiographical memories', *Social Cognition*, 22(5): 555–90.

Sloan, J.J., Bodapati, M.R. and Tucker, T.A. (2004) 'Respondent misreporting of drug use in self-reports: social desirability and other correlates', *Journal of Drug Issues*, 34(2): 269–92.

Smircich, L. (1983) 'Concepts of culture and organizational analysis', *Administrative Science Quarterly*, 28(3): 339–58.

Smith, J.K. and Hodkinson, P. (2005) 'Relativism, criteria, and politics', in N.K. Denzin and Y.S. Lincoln (eds), *The SAGE handbook of qualitative research*, 3rd edn. Thousand Oaks: Sage Publications. pp. 915–32.

Snook, S.A. (2002) *Friendly fire: the accidental shootdown of U.S. Black Hawks over northern Iraq*. Princeton, NJ, Chichester: Princeton University Press.

Spradley, J.P. (1979a) *The ethnographic interview*. New York: Holt Rinehart and Winston.

Spradley, J.P. (1979b) *Participant observation*. New York: Holt Rinehart and Winston.

Stablein, R.E. (2002) 'Using existential-phenomenology to study a work team: research on managing groups and teams', in H. Sondak (ed.), *Toward phenomenology of groups and group membership*. Greenwich, CN: JAI. pp. 1–26.

Stablein, R.E. and Frost, P.J. (eds) (2004) *Renewing research practice*. Stanford, CA: Stanford Business Books.

Stablein, R.E. and Nord, W. (1985) 'Practical and emancipatory interests in organizational symbolism: a review and evaluation', *Journal of Management*, 11(2): 13–28.

Stake, R.E. (2005) 'Qualitative case studies', in N.K. Denzin and Y.S. Lincoln (eds), *The SAGE handbook of qualitative research*, 3rd edn. Thousand Oaks: Sage Publications. pp. 443–66.

Starbuck, W.H. (2004) 'Why I stopped trying to understand the real world', *Organization Studies*, 25(7): 1233–54.

Starbuck, W.H. and Mezias, J.M. (1996) 'Opening Pandora's box: studying the accuracy of managers' perceptions', *Journal of Organizational Behavior*, 17(2): 99–117.

Stewart, D.W. and Kamins, M.A. (1993) *Secondary research: information sources and methods*. Thousand Oaks, CA: Sage Publications.

Sutton, R.I. and Rafaeli, A. (1988) 'Untangling the relationship between displayed emotions and organizational sales – the case of convenience stores', *Academy of Management Journal*, 31(3): 461–87.

Sutton, R.I. and Rafaeli, A. (1992) 'How we untangled the relationship between displayed emotion and organizational sales: a tale of bickering and optimism', in P.J. Frost and R.E. Stablein (eds), *Doing exemplary research*. Thousand Oaks, CA: Sage Publications. pp. 115–29.

Taylor, L.A., Goodwin, V.L. and Cosier, R.A. (2003) 'Method myopia – real or imagined?', *Journal of Management Inquiry*, 12(3): 255–63.

Tolbert, P.S. and Zucker, L.G. (1996) 'The institutionalization of institutional theory', in S.R. Clegg, C. Hardy and W.R. Nord (eds), *Handbook of organization studies*. London, Thousand Oaks, CA: Sage Publications. pp. 175–90.

Tourangeau, R. (2000) *The psychology of survey response*. New York: Cambridge University Press.

Tourangeau, R. (2004) 'Survey research and societal change', *Annual Review of Psychology*, 55: 775–801.

Tourangeau, R., Couper, M.P. and Conrad, F. (2004) 'Spacing, position, and order – interpretive heuristics for visual features of survey questions', *Public Opinion Quarterly*, 68(3): 368–93.

Tremble, T.R., Payne, S.C., Finch, J.F. and Bullis, R.C. (2003) 'Opening organizational archives to research: analog measures of organizational commitment', *Military Psychology*, 15(3): 167–90.

Trist, E.A. and Bamforth, K.W. (1951) 'Some social and psychological consequences of the long wall method of coal getting', *Human Relations*, 4(1): 3–38.

Tsoukas, H. and Knudsen, C. (eds) (2003) *The Oxford handbook of organization theory*. New York: Oxford University Press.

Van Maanen, J. (1979) 'Reclaiming qualitative methods of organizational research: a preface', *Administrative Science Quarterly*, 24(4): 520–6.

Van Maanen, J. (1988) *Tales of the field: on writing ethnography*. Chicago: University of Chicago Press.

Van Maanen, J. (1995a) 'Fear and loathing in organization studies', *Organization Science*, 6(6): 687–92.

Van Maanen, J. (1995b) 'Style as theory', *Organization Science*, 6(1): 132–43.

Van Maanen, J., Dabb, J.M. Jr. and Faulkner, R.R. (eds) (1982) *Varieties of qualitative research*. Beverly Hills, CA: Sage Publications.

Ventresca, M.J. and Mohr, J.W. (2002) 'Archival research methods', in J.A.C. Baum (ed.), *The Blackwell companion to organizations*. Malden, MA: Blackwell Publishers. pp. 805–28.

Vidich, A.J. and Lyman, S.M. (1994) 'Qualitative methods: their history in sociology and anthropology', in N.K. Denzin and Y.S. Lincoln (eds), *Handbook of qualitative research*. Thousand Oaks: Sage Publications. pp. 23–59.

Walton, R.E. (1977) 'Work innovations at Topeka – after 6 Years', *Journal of Applied Behavioral Science*, 13(3): 422–33.

Watson, T.J. (1994) *In search of management: culture, chaos and control in managerial work*. London, New York: Routledge.

Weaver, G.R. and Gioia, D.A. (1994) 'Paradigms lost: incommensurability vs structurationist inquiry', *Organization Studies*, 15(4): 565–90.

Webb, E.J., Campbell, D.T., Schwartz, R.D. and Sechrest, L. (1966) *Unobtrusive measures: Nonreactive research in the social sciences*. Chicago: Rand McNally.

Weick, K.E. (1965) 'Laboratory experimentation with organizations', in J.G. March (ed.), *Handbook of organizations*. Chicago: Rand McNally. pp. 194–260.

Wetherell, M., Taylor, S. and Yates, S.J. (eds) (2001) *Discourse as data: a guide for analysis*. London: Sage Publications.

Whyte, W.F. (1955) *Street corner society*. Chicago: University of Chicago Press.

Willis, P.E. (1977) *Learning to labour: how working class kids get working class jobs*. Farnborough: Saxon House.

Willmott, H. (2003a) 'Commercialising higher education in the UK: the state, industry and peer review', *Studies in Higher Education*, 28(2): 129–41.

Willmott, H. (2003b) 'Organization theory as a critical science? Forms of analysis and 'new organizational forms", in H. Tsoukas and C. Knudsen (eds), *The Oxford Handbook of Organization Theory.* New York: Oxford University Press. pp. 88–112.

Yin, R.K. (2002) *Case study research: design and methods.* Thousand Oaks, CA: Sage Publications.

Zald, M.N. (1996) 'More fragmentation? Unfinished business in linking the social sciences and the humanities', *Administrative Science Quarterly*, 41(2): 251–61.

Zerbe, W.J. and Paulhus, D.L. (1987) 'Socially desirable responding in organizational-behavior – a reconception', *Academy of Management Review*, 12(2): 250–64.

1.10 Making Organization Research Matter: Power, Values and Phronesis

BENT FLYVBJERG

If we want to empower and re-enchant organization research, we need to do three things. First, we must drop all pretence, however indirect, at emulating the success of the natural sciences in producing cumulative and predictive theory, for their approach simply does not work in organization research or any of the social sciences (for the full argument, see Flyvbjerg 2001). Second, we must address problems that matter to groups in the local, national, and global communities in which we live, and we must do it in ways that matter; we must focus on issues of context, values, and power, as advocated by great social scientists from Aristotle and Machiavelli to Max Weber and Pierre Bourdieu. Finally, we must effectively and dialogically communicate the results of our research to our fellow citizens and carefully listen to their feedback. If we do this – focus on specific values and interests in the context of particular power relations – we may successfully transform organization research into an activity performed in public for organizational publics, sometimes to clarify, sometimes to intervene, sometimes to generate new perspectives, and always to serve as eyes and ears in ongoing efforts to understand the present and to deliberate about the future. We may, in short, arrive at organization research that matters.

What I describe below as 'phronetic organization research' is an attempt to arrive at such organization research. I would like to emphasize at the outset, however, that this effort should be considered as one among many possible, as a first approximation that will undoubtedly require further theoretical and methodological refinement, just as it will need to be developed through further practical employment in actual organizational studies. Despite such qualifications, I hope the reader will agree that given what is at stake – organization research that matters – the attempt at reforming such research is worthwhile.

What is Phronetic Organization Research?

Phronetic organization research is an approach to the study of organizations based on a contemporary interpretation of the classical Greek concept *phronesis*. Following this approach, phronetic organization researchers study organizations and organizing with an emphasis on values and power. In this paper I will first clarify what *phronesis* and phronetic organization research is. Second, I will attempt to tease out the methodological implications of this research approach.[1]

Aristotle is the philosopher of *phronesis* par excellence. In Aristotle's words *phronesis* is an intellectual virtue that is 'reasoned, and capable of action with regard to things that are good or bad for man' (Aristotle, *The Nicomachean Ethics*, hereafter abbreviated as *N.E.*, 1976: 1140a24–b12, 1144b33–1145a11). *Phronesis* concerns values and goes beyond analytical, scientific knowledge (*episteme*) and technical knowledge or know how (*techne*) and it involves judgements and decisions made in the manner of a virtuoso social actor. I will argue that *phronesis* is commonly involved in practices of organization and, therefore, that any attempts to reduce organization research to *episteme* or *techne* or to comprehend them in those terms are misguided.

Aristotle was explicit in his regard of *phronesis* as the most important of the three intellectual virtues: *episteme, techne,* and *phronesis. Phronesis* is most important because it is that activity by which instrumental rationality is balanced by value-rationality, to use the terms of German sociologist Max Weber; and because, according to Aristotle and Weber, such balancing is crucial to the viability of any organization, from the family to the state. A curious fact can be observed, however. Whereas *episteme* is found in the modern words 'epistemology' and 'epistemic', and *techne* in 'technology' and 'technical', it is indicative of the degree to which scientific and instrumental rationality dominate modern thinking and language that we no longer have a word for the one intellectual virtue, *phronesis*, which Aristotle and other founders of the Western tradition saw as a necessary condition of successful social organization, and the most important prerequisite to such organization.

Aristotle on *Episteme, Techne* and *Phronesis*

The term 'epistemic science' derives from the intellectual virtue that Aristotle calls *episteme*, and which is generally translated as 'science' or 'scientific knowledge'.[2] Aristotle defines *episteme* in this manner:

[S]cientific knowledge is a demonstrative state, (i.e. a state of mind capable of demonstrating what it knows) ... i.e. a person has scientific knowledge when his belief is conditioned in a certain way, and the first principles are known to him; because if they are not better known to him than the conclusion drawn from them, he will have knowledge only incidentally – this may serve as a description of scientific knowledge (*N.E.*: 1139b18–36).

Episteme concerns universals and the production of knowledge that is invariable in time and space and achieved with the aid of analytical rationality. *Episteme* corresponds to the modern scientific ideal as expressed in natural science. In Socrates and Plato, and subsequently in the Enlightenment tradition, this scientific ideal became dominant. The ideal has come close to being the only legitimate view of what constitutes genuine science, such that even intellectual activities like organization research and other social sciences, which are not and probably never can be scientific in the epistemic sense, have found themselves compelled to strive for and legitimate themselves in terms of this Enlightenment ideal.[3] Epistemic organization research claims universality and searches for generic truths about organization and organizing. Epistemic organization research is the mainstream of organization research.

Whereas *episteme* resembles our ideal modern scientific project, *techne* and *phronesis* denote two contrasting roles of intellectual work. *Techne* can be translated into English as 'art' in the sense of 'craft';

a craftsperson is also an *arti*san. For Aristotle, both *techne* and *phronesis* are connected with the concept of truth, as is *episteme*. Aristotle says the following regarding *techne*:

[S]ince (e.g.) building is an art [*techne*] and is essentially a reasoned productive state, and since there is no art that is not a state of this kind, and no state of this kind that is not an art, it follows that art is the same as a productive state that is truly reasoned. Every art is concerned with bringing something into being, and the practice of an art is the study of how to bring into being something that is capable either of being or of not being ... For it is not with things that are or come to be *of necessity* that art is concerned [this is the domain of *episteme*] nor with natural objects (because these have their origin in themselves) ... Art ... operate[s] in the sphere of the variable (*N.E.*: 1140a1–23).

Techne is thus craft and art, and as an activity it is concrete, variable, and context-dependent. The objective of *techne* is application of technical knowledge and skills according to a pragmatic instrumental rationality, what Foucault calls 'a practical rationality governed by a conscious goal' (Foucault 1984b: 255). Organization research practiced as *techne* would be a type of consulting aimed at better running organizations by means of instrumental rationality, where 'better' is defined in terms of the values and goals of those who employ the consultants, sometimes in negotiation with the latter.

Whereas *episteme* concerns theoretical *know why* and *techne* denotes technical *know how*, *phronesis* emphasizes practical knowledge and practical ethics. *Phronesis* is often translated as 'prudence' or 'practical common sense'. Let us again examine what Aristotle has to say:

We may grasp the nature of prudence [*phronesis*] if we consider what sort of people we call prudent. Well, it is thought to be the mark of a prudent man to be able to deliberate rightly about what is good and advantageous ... But nobody deliberates about things that are invariable ... So ... prudence cannot be a science or art; not science [*episteme*] because what can be done is a variable (it may be done in different ways, or not done at all), and not art [*techne*] because action and production are generically different. For production aims at an end other than itself; but this is impossible in the case of action, because the end is merely doing *well*. What remains, then, is that it is a true state, reasoned, and capable of action with regard to things that are good or bad for man ... We consider that this quality belongs to those who understand the management of households or states (*N.E.*: 1140a24–b12; emphasis in original).

Please note that the word 'management' is not mine, but that of the original English translator of Aristotle's text. The person possessing practical wisdom *(phronimos)* has knowledge of how to manage in each particular circumstance that can never be equated with or reduced to knowledge of general truths about managing. *Phronesis* is a sense or a tacit skill for doing the ethically practical rather than a kind of science. For Plato, rational humans are moved by the cosmic order; for Aristotle they are moved by a sense of the proper order among the ends we pursue. This sense cannot be articulated in terms of theoretical axioms, but is grasped by *phronesis* (Taylor 1989: 125, 148).

One might get the impression in Aristotle's original description of *phronesis* that *phronesis* and the choices it involves in concrete management are always good. This is not necessarily the case. Choices must be deemed good or bad in relation to certain values and interests in order for good and bad to have meaning. Phronetic organization research is concerned with deliberation about values and interests.

In sum, the three intellectual virtues *episteme*, *techne* and *phronesis* can be characterized as follows:

- *Episteme* Scientific knowledge. Universal, invariable, context-independent. Based on general analytical rationality. The original concept is known today by the terms 'epistemology' and 'epistemic'. Organization research practiced as *episteme* is concerned with uncovering universal truths about organization and organizing.
- *Techne* Craft/art. Pragmatic, variable, context-dependent. Oriented toward production. Based on practical instrumental rationality governed by a conscious goal. The original concept appears today in terms such as 'technique', 'technical', and 'technology'. Organization research practiced as *techne* is consulting aimed at running organizations better by means of instrumental rationality, where 'better' is defined in terms of the values and goals of those who employ the consultants, sometimes in negotiation with the latter.
- *Phronesis* Ethics. Deliberation about values with reference to praxis. Pragmatic, variable, context-dependent. Oriented toward action. Based on practical value-rationality. The original concept has no analogous contemporary term. Organization research practiced as *phronesis* is concerned with deliberation about (including questioning of) values and interests.

The Priority of the Particular

Phronesis concerns the analysis of values – 'things that are good or bad for man' – as a point of departure for managed action. *Phronesis* is that intellectual activity most relevant to praxis. It focuses on what is variable, on that which cannot be encapsulated by universal rules, on specific cases. *Phronesis* requires an interaction between the general and the concrete; it requires consideration, judgement, and choice.[4] More than anything else, *phronesis* requires *experience*. About the importance of specific experience Aristotle says:

> [P]rudence [*phronesis*] is not concerned with universals only; it must also take cognizance of particulars, because it is concerned with conduct, and conduct has its sphere in particular circumstances. That is why some people who do not possess theoretical knowledge are more effective in action (especially if they are experienced) than others who do possess it. For example, suppose that someone knows that light flesh foods are digestible and wholesome, but does not know what kinds are light; he will be less likely to produce health than one who knows that chicken is wholesome. But prudence is practical, and therefore it must have both kinds of knowledge, or especially the latter (*N.E.*: 1141b8–27).

Here, again, Aristotle is stressing that in practical management (in this case the management of health, which was a central concern for the ancient Greeks), knowledge of the rules ('light flesh foods are digestible and wholesome') is inferior to knowledge of the real cases ('chicken is wholesome'). Some of the best management schools, such as Harvard Business School, have understood the importance of cases over rules and emphasize case-based and practical teaching. Such management schools may be called Aristotelian; whereas schools stressing theory and rules may be called Platonic.

Some interpretations of Aristotle's intellectual virtues leave doubt as to whether *phronesis* and *techne* are distinct categories, or whether *phronesis* is just a higher form of *techne* or know-how.[5] Aristotle is clear on this point, however. Even if both *phronesis* and *techne* involve skill and judgement, one type of intellectual virtue cannot be reduced to the other; *phronesis* is about value judgement, not about producing things.

Similarly, in other parts of the literature one finds attempts at conflating *phronesis* and *episteme* in the sense of making *phronesis* epistemic. But insofar as *phronesis* operates via a practical rationality based on judgement and experience, it can only be made scientific in an epistemic sense through the development of a theory of judgement and experience. In fact Alessandro Ferrara has called for the 'elaboration of a theory of judgement' as one of 'the unaccomplished tasks of critical theory' (Ferrara 1989: 319). In line with Jürgen Habermas, Ferrara says that a theory of judgement is necessary in order to avoid contextualism, although he also notes that such a theory 'unfortunately is not yet in sight' (Ferrara 1989: 316; see also Ferrara 1999). What Ferrara apparently does not consider is that a theory of judgement and experience is not in sight because judgement and experience cannot be brought into a theoretical formula. Aristotle warns us directly against the type of reductionism that conflates *phronesis* and *episteme*.

With his thoughts on the intellectual virtues, Aristotle emphasizes properties of intellectual work, which are central to the production of knowledge in the study of organizations and other social phenomena. The particular and the situationally dependent are emphasized over the universal and over rules. The concrete and the practical are emphasized over the theoretical. It is what Martha Nussbaum calls the 'priority of the particular' in Aristotle's thinking (Nussbaum 1990: 66; see also Devereux 1986). Aristotle practices what he preaches by providing a specific example of his argument, viz. light flesh foods vs chicken. He understands the 'power of example'. The example concerns the management of human health and has as its point of departure something both concrete and fundamental concerning human functioning. Both aspects are typical of many Classical philosophers.

We will return to these points later. At this stage we simply conclude that despite their importance, the concrete, the practical, and the ethical have been neglected by modern science. Today one would be open to ridicule if one sought to support an argument using an example like that of Aristotle's chicken. The sciences are supposed to concern themselves precisely with the explication of universals, and even if it is wrong the conventional wisdom is that one cannot generalize from a particular case.[6] Moreover, the ultimate goal of scientific activity is supposedly the production of theory. Aristotle is here clearly anti-Socratic and anti-Platonic. And if modern theoretical science is built upon any body of thought, it is that of Socrates and Plato. We are dealing with a profound disagreement here.

Below, we will look at specific examples of phronetic organization research. More generally, in contemporary social science, Pierre Bourdieu's 'fieldwork in philosophy' and Robert Bellah's 'social science as public philosophy' are examples of intellectual pursuits that involve elements of *phronesis* (Bellah et al. 1985: especially the Methodological Appendix, 297; Bourdieu 1990: 28). Bourdieu explicitly recognizes Aristotle as the originator of the habitus concept, which is so centrally placed in Bourdieu's work, and he sees the practical knowledge that habitus procures as being analogous to Aristotle's *phronesis* (Bourdieu and Wacquant 1992: 128). In philosophy Richard Bernstein's and Stephen Toulmin's 'practical philosophy' and Richard Rorty's philosophical pragmatism are also phronetic in their orientation, as are Foucault's genealogies (Bernstein 1985: 40; Toulmin 1988: 337; Rorty 1991b; 1995: 94–5). As pointed out by Rorty, 'philosophy' in this interpretation is precisely what a culture – including organizational cultures – becomes capable of when it ceases to define itself in terms of explicit rules, and becomes sufficiently leisured and civilized to rely on inarticulate know-how, to 'substitute *phronesis* for codification' (Rorty 1991a: 25). Aristotle found that every well-functioning organization and society was dependent on the effective functioning of all three intellectual virtues – *episteme, techne,* and *phronesis.* At the same time, however, Aristotle emphasized the crucial importance of *phronesis,* 'for the possession of the single virtue of prudence [*phronesis*] will carry with it the possession of them all'.[7] *Phronesis* is most important, from an Aristotelian point of view, because it is that intellectual virtue that may ensure the ethical employment of science (*episteme*) and technology (*techne*). Because *phronesis* today is marginalized in the intellectual scheme of things, scientific and technological development take place without the ethical checks and balances that Aristotle saw as all-important. This is a major management problem in its own right.

Organization Research and 'Real' Science

Regardless of the lack of a term for *phronesis* in our modern vocabulary, the principal objective for organization research with a phronetic approach is to perform analyses and derive interpretations of the status of values and interests in organizations aimed at organizational change. The point of departure for classical phronetic research can be summarized in the following three value-rational questions:

(1) Where are we going?
(2) Is this development desirable?
(3) What, if anything, should we do about it?

   The 'we', here consists of those organization researchers asking the questions and those who share the concerns of the researchers, including people in the organization under study. Later, when I have discussed the implications of power for *phronesis*, I will add a fourth question:

(4) Who gains and who loses, and by which mechanisms of power?

Organization researchers who ask and provide answers to these questions, use their studies not merely as a mirror for organizations to reflect on their values, but also as the nose, eyes, and ears of organizations, in order to sense where things may be going next and what, if anything, to do about it. The questions are asked with the realization that there is no general and unified 'we' in relation to which the questions can be given a final, objective answer. What is a 'gain' and a 'loss' often depend on the perspective taken, and one person's gain may be another's loss. Phronetic organization researchers are highly aware of the importance of perspective, and see no neutral ground, no 'view from nowhere', for their work.

It should be stressed that no one has enough wisdom and experience to give complete answers to the four questions, whatever those answers might be. Such wisdom and experience should not be expected from organization researchers, who are on average no more astute or ethical than anyone else. What should be expected, however, is attempts from phronetic organization researchers to develop their partial answers to the questions. Such answers would be input to the ongoing dialogue about the problems, possibilities, and risks that organizations face and how things may be done differently.

A first step in achieving this kind of perspective in organization research is for researchers to explicate the different roles of research as *episteme*, *techne*, and *phronesis*. Today's researchers seldom clarify which of these three roles they are practicing. The entire enterprise is simply called 'research' or 'science', even though we are dealing with quite different activities. It is often the case that these activities are rationalized as *episteme*, even though they are actually *techne* or *phronesis*. As argued previously, it is not in their role of *episteme* that one can argue for the value of organization research and other social sciences. In the domain in which the natural sciences have been strongest – the production of theories that can explain and accurately predict – the social sciences, including organization research, have been weakest. Nevertheless, by emphasizing the three roles, and especially by reintroducing *phronesis*, we see there are other possibilities for organization research and other social sciences. The oft-seen image of impotent social sciences vs potent natural sciences derives from their being compared in terms of their epistemic qualities. Yet such a comparison is misleading, for the two types of science have their respective strengths and weaknesses along fundamentally different dimensions. As mentioned previously, the social sciences, in their role as *phronesis*, are strongest where the natural sciences are weakest.

It is also as *phronesis* that organization research and other social sciences can provide a counterweight to tendencies toward relativism and nihilism. The importance of *phronesis* renders the attempts of organization research and social science to become 'real' theoretical science doubly unfortunate; such efforts draw attention and resources away from those areas where they could make an impact and into areas where they do not obtain, never have obtained, and probably never will obtain any significance as genuinely normal and predictive sciences.

Methodological Guidelines for Phronetic Organization Research

What, then, might a set of methodological guidelines for phronetic organization research look like? This question will be the focus of the remainder of the chapter. I would like to stress immediately that the methodological guidelines summarized below should not be seen as imperatives; at most they are cautionary indicators of direction. Let me also mention that undoubtedly there are ways of practising phronetic organization research other than those outlined here. The most important issue is not the individual methodology involved, even if methodological questions may have some significance. It is more important to get the result right – to arrive at organization research that effectively deals with deliberation, judgement, and praxis in relation to the four value-rational questions mentioned above, rather than being stranded with organization research that vainly attempts to emulate natural science.

As mentioned earlier, few scholars seem to have reflected explicitly on the comparative strengths and weaknesses of research practised as either *episteme*, *techne*, or *phronesis*. Even fewer are actually conducting research on the basis of such reflection, and fewer still have articulated the methodological considerations and guidelines for *phronesis*-based research. In fact, it seems that researchers doing *phronesis*-like work have a sound instinct for proceeding with their research and not involving themselves in methodology. Nonetheless, given the interpretation of the actual and potential role of organization research as outlined above, it is essential for the development of such research that methodological guidelines be elaborated.

The main point of departure for explicating methodological guidelines for phronetic organization research is a reading of Aristotle and Michel Foucault,[8] supplemented with readings of other thinkers – mainly Pierre Bourdieu, Clifford Geertz, Alasdair MacIntyre and Richard Rorty – who emphasize phronetic before epistemic knowledge in the study of organizations and society, despite important differences in other domains.[9]

Focusing on Values

By definition, phronetic organization researchers focus on values and, especially, evaluative judgements; for example, by taking their point of departure in the classic value-rational questions: 'Where are we going?' 'Is it desirable?' 'What should be done?' The objective is to balance instrumental rationality with value-rationality and increase the capacity of employees and managers to think and act in value-rational terms. Asking value-rational questions does not imply a belief in linearity and continuous progress. The phronetic organization researcher knows enough about power to understand that progress is often complex, ephemeral, and hard-won, and that set-backs are an inevitable part of organizational life (on power, see below).

Focusing on values, phronetic organization researchers are forced to face questions of foundationalism vs relativism – that is, the view that there are central values that can be rationally and universally grounded, vs the view that one set of values is as good as another. Phronetic organization researchers reject both of these 'isms' and replace them with contextualism or situational ethics. Distancing themselves from foundationalism does not leave phronetic organization researchers normless, however. They take their point of departure in their attitude to the situation in the organization and society being studied. They seek to ensure that such an attitude is not based on idiosyncratic morality or personal preferences, but on a common view among a specific reference group to which the organization researchers refer. For phronetic organization researchers, the socially and historically conditioned context – and not the universal grounding that is desired but not yet achieved by certain scholars, constitutes the most effective bulwark against relativism and nihilism.[10] Phronetic organization researchers realize that our sociality and history is the only foundation we have, the only solid ground under our feet; and that this sociohistorical foundation is fully adequate for our work as organization researchers.

As regards validity, phronetic organization research is based on interpretation and is open for testing in relation to other interpretations and other research. But one interpretation is not as good as any other, which would be the case for relativism. Every interpretation must be built upon claims of validity, and the procedures ensuring validity are as demanding for phronetic organization research as for any other activity in the social sciences. Phronetic organization researchers also oppose the view that any one among a number of interpretations lacks value because it is 'merely' an interpretation. As emphasized by Alexander Nehamas, the key point is the establishment of a *better* option, where 'better' is defined according to sets of validity claims (Nehamas 1985: 63). If a new interpretation appears to better explain a given phenomenon, that new interpretation will replace the old one – until it, too, is replaced by a new and yet better interpretation. This is typically a continuing process, not one that terminates with 'the right answer'. Such is the procedure that a community of organization researchers would follow in working together to put certain interpretations of organizational life ahead of others (see also the section on 'dialogue' below). The procedure does not describe an interpretive or relativistic approach. Rather, it sets forth the basic ground rules for any social inquiry, inasmuch as social science and philosophy have not yet identified criteria by which an ultimate interpretation and a final grounding of values and facts can be made.

Placing Power at the Core of Analysis

Aristotle, the philosopher of *phronesis* par excellence, never elaborated his conception of *phronesis* to include explicit considerations of power. Hans-Georg Gadamer's authoritative and contemporary conception of *phronesis* also overlooks issues of power (Gadamer 1975). Yet, as Richard Bernstein points out, if we are to think about what can be done to the problems, possibilities, and risks of our time, we must advance from the original conception of *phronesis* to one explicitly including power (Bernstein 1989: 217). Unfortunately, Bernstein himself has not integrated his work on *phronesis* with issues of power. Elsewhere I have argued that conflict and power have evolved into phenomena constitutive of organizational inquiry. Modern organizational inquiry can only be complete if it deals with issues of power. I have therefore made an attempt to develop the classic concept of *phronesis* to a more contemporary one, which accounts for power (Flyvbjerg 2001: chapters 7 and 8).

Besides focusing on the three value-rational questions mentioned above, which are the classical Aristotelian questions, a contemporary reading of *phronesis* also poses questions about power and outcomes: 'Who gains, and who loses?' 'Through what kinds of power relations?' 'What possibilities are available to change existing power relations?' 'And is it desirable to do so?' 'What are the power relations among those who ask the questions?' Phronetic organization research poses these questions with the intention of avoiding the voluntarism and idealism typical of so much ethical thinking. The main question is not only the Weberian: 'Who governs?' posed by Robert Dahl and most other students of power. It is also the Nietzschean question: What 'governmental rationalities' are at work when those who govern govern? (See also Clegg 1989; 1997; Hardy and Clegg 1996). With these questions and with the focus on value-rationality, phronetic organization researchers relate explicitly to a primary context of

values and power. Combining the best of a Nietzschean–Foucauldian interpretation of power with the best of a Weberian–Dahlian one, the analysis of power is guided by a conception of power that can be characterized by six features:

(1) Power is seen as productive and positive, and not only as restrictive and negative.
(2) Power is viewed as a dense net of omnipresent relations, and not only as being localized in 'centers', organizations, and institutions, or as an entity one can 'possess'.
(3) The concept of power is seen as ultradynamic; power is not merely something one appropriates, it is also something one reappropriates and exercises in a constant back-and-forth movement within the relationships of strength, tactics, and strategies inside of which one exists.
(4) Knowledge and power, truth and power, rationality and power are analytically inseparable from each other; power produces knowledge, and knowledge produces power.
(5) The central question is *how* power is exercised, and not merely *who* has power, and *why* they have it; the focus is on process in addition to structure.
(6) Power is studied with a point of departure in small questions, 'flat and empirical', not only, nor even primarily, with a point of departure in 'big questions' (Foucault 1982: 217).

Analyses of organizational power following this format cannot be equated with a general analytics of every possible power relation in organizations. Other approaches and other interpretations are possible. They can, however, serve as a possible and productive point of departure for dealing with questions of power in doing *phronesis*.

Getting Close to Reality

Campbell, Lindblom and others have noted that the development of organization and other social research is inhibited by the fact that researchers tend to work with problems in which the answer to the question: 'If you are wrong about this, who will notice?' is usually: 'Nobody' (Campbell 1986: 128–9; see also Lindblom and Cohen 1979: 84; Lindblom 1990). Mary Timney Bailey calls the outcome of such research '"so what" results' (Bailey 1992: 50). Phronetic organization researchers seek to transcend this problem of relevance by anchoring their research in the context studied and thereby ensuring what Gadamer called a hermeneutic 'fusion of horizons'. This applies both to contemporary and historical organization studies. For contemporary studies researchers get close to the organization, phenomenon, or group that they study during data collection, and remain close during the phases of data analysis, feedback, and publication of results. Combined with the above-mentioned focus on relations of values and power, this strategy typically creates interest in the research by parties outside the research community. These parties will test and evaluate the research in various ways. Phronetic organization researchers will consciously expose themselves to positive and negative reactions from their surroundings, and are likely to derive benefit from the learning effect, which is built into this strategy. In this way, the phronetic organization researcher becomes a part of the phenomenon studied, without necessarily 'going native' or the project becoming simple action research. Action researchers and anthropologists who have gone native typically identify with the people they are studying; they adopt the perspective and goals of those studied and use research results in an effort to achieve these goals. This is not necessarily the case for phronetic organization researchers who at all times, in the service of truth, retain the classic academic freedom to problematize and be critical of what they see.

Phronetic organization researchers performing historical studies conduct much of their work in those locales where the relevant historical materials are placed, and they typically probe deeply into archives, annals, and individual documents. To the attentive researcher archives will reveal a knowledge whose visible body 'is neither theoretical or scientific discourse nor literature, but a regular, daily practice' (Foucault 1969: 4–5; here quoted from Eribon 1991: 215). In historical studies, as in contemporary ones, the objective is to get close to reality. *Wirkliche Historie* (real history), says Foucault, 'shortens its vision to those things nearest to it' (Foucault 1984a: 89). Christensen, arguably one of the fathers of the case method at Harvard University, expresses a similar attitude about his research by invoking Miller to describe the approach taken by case researchers: 'My whole work has come to resemble a terrain of which I have made a thorough, geodetic survey, not from a desk with pen and ruler, but by touch, by getting down on all fours, on my stomach, and crawling over the ground inch by inch, and this over an endless period of time in all conditions of weather' (Miller 1941: 27; quoted in

slightly different form in Christensen with Hansen 1987: 18).

Emphasizing Little Things

Phronetic organization researchers begin their work by phenomenologically asking 'little questions' and focusing on what Geertz, with a term borrowed from Ryle, calls 'thick description' (Geertz 1973: 6; 1983). This procedure may often seem tedious and trivial. Nietzsche and Foucault emphasize that it requires 'patience and a knowledge of details', and it depends on a 'vast accumulation of source material' (Foucault 1984a: 76). Geertz explicates the dilemma involved in skipping minutiae. The problem with an approach that extracts the general from the particular and then sets the particular aside as detail, illustration, background, or qualification, is, as Geertz says, that 'it leaves us helpless in the face of the very difference we need to explore…[it] does indeed simplify matters. It is less certain that it clarifies them' (Geertz 1995a: 40; see also Geertz 1990b; 1995). Nietzsche, who advocates 'patience and seriousness in the smallest things' (Nietzsche 1968a: 182 (§59)) expresses a similar, though more radical, point regarding the importance of detail when he says that '[a]ll the problems of politics, of social organization, and of education have been falsified through and through … because one learned to despise 'little' things, which means the basic concerns of life itself' (Nietzsche 1969a: 256 (§10)).

The focus on minutiae, which directly opposes much conventional wisdom about the need to focus on 'important problems' and 'big questions', has its background in the fundamental phenomenological experience of small questions often leading to big answers. In this sense, phronetic organization research is decentered in its approach, taking its point of departure in organizational micropractices, searching for the Great within the Small and vice versa. 'God is in the detail', the proverb says. 'So is the Devil', the phronetic organization researcher would add, doing work that is at the same time as detailed and as general as possible.

Looking at Practice Before Discourse

Through words and concepts we are continually tempted to think of things as being simpler than they are, says Nietzsche: 'there is a philosophical mythology concealed in *language*' (emphasis in original) (Nietzsche 1968a: 191 (Appendix C)). Michel Serres puts the matter even more succinctly, saying that: 'Language has a disgust for things'. Phronetic organization research attempts to get beyond this problem. Thus, organizational practice or what people do in organizations is seen as more fundamental than either discourse or theory – what people say. Goethe's phrase from *Faust*, 'Am Anfang war die Tat' (in the beginning was the deed), could be the motto for phronetic organization research. It is echoed by Foucault who says, 'discourse is not life'; regular, daily practice is life.[11] Phronetic organization research does not accept the maxim that there is nothing outside the text or outside discourse. Such an approach is too easy, giving its practitioners limitless sovereignty by allowing them to restate the text indefinitely (Foucault 1979: 27). Textual analysis must be disciplined by analysis of practices. Here, again, the position is not relativism but contextualism. The context of practices disciplines interpretation.

Phronetic organization research focuses on practical activity and practical knowledge in everyday situations in organizations. It *may* mean, but is certainly not limited to, a focus on known sociological, ethnographic, and historical phenomena such as 'everyday life' and 'everyday people', with their focus on the so-called 'common'. What it *always* means, however, is a focus on the actual daily practices – common or highly specialized or rarefied – which constitute a given organizational field of interest, regardless of whether these practices constitute a stock exchange, a grassroots organization, a neighbourhood, a multinational corporation, an emergency ward, or a local school board.

At the outset, organizational practices are recorded and described simply as events. 'The question which I ask', says Foucault, 'is not about codes but about events ... I try to answer this question without referring to the consciousness ... the will intention' (Foucault 1991: 59; 1981: 6–7). The phronetic organization researcher records what happened 'on such a day, in such a place, in such circumstances' (Foucault 1972: 15; here quoted from Miller 1993: 191). In *The Will to Power*, in describing his 'principles of a new evaluation', Nietzsche similarly says that when evaluating human action one should 'take doing *something*, the 'aim', the 'intention', the 'purpose', back into the deed after having artificially removed all this and thus

emptied the deed' (emphasis in original) (Nietzsche 1968b: 356 (§675)). Events and phenomena are presented together with their connections with other events and phenomena (for more on eventualization, see Abbott 1992). Discontinuities and changes in the meaning of concepts and discourses are documented. The hermeneutic horizon is isolated and its arbitrariness elaborated. At first, the organization researcher takes no position regarding the truth-value and significance ascribed by participants to the organizational practices studied. No practice is seen as more valuable than another. The horizon of meaning is initially that of the single organizational practice. The researcher then attempts to understand the roles played by single practices studied in the total system of organizational and contextual relations. If it is established, for example, that a certain organizational practice is seen as rational according to its self-understanding – that is, by those practicing it, but not when viewed in the context of other horizons of meaning – the researcher then asks what role this 'dubious' rationality plays in a further context, historically, organizationally, and politically, and what the consequences might be.

In addition to the Nietzschean removal of the doer from the deed, the focus on organizational practices as events also involves a self-removal on the part of the organization researchers to allow them to disinterestedly inspect the *wirkliche Historie* of organizations. This distancing enables the researcher to master a subject matter even when it is hideous, and when there is a 'brutality of fact' involved in the approach. This approach may, in turn, offend people who mistake the researcher's willingness to uncover and face the morally unacceptable for immorality. There may also be intensity and optimism, however, in facing even the pessimistic and depressing sides of power and human action in organizations. The description of practices as events endures and gains its strength from detecting the forces that make life in the organization work. And if the researcher uncovers an organizational reality that is ugly or even terrifying when judged by the moral standards, which, we like to believe, apply in modern organizations, this reality may also demonstrate something deeply human that may have to be faced squarely by people in the organization, by organization researchers, and by the general public, if this reality is to be changed. Nietzsche acutely named this approach to research 'The Gay [*fröhliche*] Science', and he called those practising the approach 'free spirits', describing them as 'curious to a vice, investigators to the point of cruelty, with uninhibited fingers for the unfathomable, with teeth and stomachs for the most indigestible … collectors from morning till late, misers of our riches and our crammed drawers' (Nietzsche 1966: 55). We need more 'free spirits' in organization research and this depiction of what they would be like may serve as a description of phronetic organization researchers.

Studying Cases and Contexts

We have seen that Aristotle explicitly identifies knowledge of 'particular circumstances' as a main ingredient of *phronesis* (*N.E.*: 1141b8–1141b27). Foucault similarly worked according to the dictum 'never lose sight of reference to a concrete example' (Foucault 1969: 7; quoted in Eribon 1991: 216). Phronetic organization research thus benefits from focusing on case studies, precedents, and exemplars. *Phronesis* functions on the basis of practical rationality and judgement. As I have argued elsewhere, practical organizational rationality and judgment evolve and operate primarily by virtue of in-depth case experiences (Flyvbjerg 1989; see also MacIntyre 1977). Practical rationality, therefore, is best understood through cases – whether experienced or narrated – just as judgement is best cultivated and communicated via the exposition of cases. The significance of this point can hardly be overstated, which is why Richard Rorty, in responding to Max Weber's thesis regarding the modern 'disenchantment of the world', invokes John Dewey to say: 'the way to re-enchant the world ... is to stick to the concrete' (Rorty 1985: 173).

Context is important to case studies in organizations. What has been called the 'primacy of context' follows from the observation that in the history of science, human action has shown itself to be irreducible to predefined elements and rules unconnected to interpretation (Rabinow and Sullivan 1987: 8; see also Henderson 1994). Therefore, it has been impossible to derive praxis from first principles and theory. Praxis has always been contingent on context-dependent judgement, on situational ethics. It would require a major transformation of current philosophy and science if this view were to change, and such a transformation does not seem to be on the horizon. What Pierre Bourdieu calls the 'feel for the game' (a.k.a. *Fingerspitzengefühl*) is

central to all human action of any complexity, including organizational action, and it enables an infinite number of 'moves' to be made, adapted to the infinite number of possible situations, which no rule-maker, however complex the rule, can foresee (Bourdieu 1990: 9). Therefore, the judgement, which is central to *phronesis* and praxis, is always context dependent. The minutiae, practices, and concrete cases that lie at the heart of phronetic organization research must be seen in their proper contexts; both the small, local context, which gives phenomena their immediate meaning, and the larger, international and global context in which phenomena can be appreciated for their general and conceptual significance. (For more on context, see Fenno, Jr 1986; Shannon 1990: 157–66; Calhoun 1994; Andler 1998; Engel 1999). Given the role of context in phronetic organization research, insofar as such research is practised as applied ethics, it is situational ethics. The focus is on *Sittlichkeit* (ethics) rather than *Moralität* (morality).

Asking 'How?' Doing Narrative

Phronetic organization research focuses on the dynamic question, 'How?' in addition to the more structural 'Why?' It is concerned with both *Verstehen* (understanding) and *Erklären* (explanation). Outcomes of organizational phenomena are investigated and interpreted in relation to organizational processes. In the study of relationships of power in organizations, we already emphasized with Foucault the how-question, 'the little question ... flat and empirical', as being particularly important. Foucault stressed that our understanding will suffer if we do not start our analyses with a 'How?'

Asking 'How?' and conducting narrative analysis are closely interlinked activities. Earlier we saw that a central question for *phronesis* is: What should we do? To this Alasdair MacIntyre answers: 'I can only answer the question 'What am I to do?' if I can answer the prior question 'Of what story or stories do I find myself a part?' (MacIntyre 1984: 216). Thus Nietzsche and Foucault see history as being fundamental to social science and philosophy, and criticize social scientists and philosophers for their lack of 'historical sense' (Nietzsche 1968c: 35 (§1)). The same may be said about organization research and researchers. History is central to phronetic organization research in both senses of the word – that is, *both* as narrative containing specific actors and events, in what Clifford

Geertz calls a story with a scientific plot; *and* as the recording of a historical development (Geertz 1988: 114; see also Geertz 1990, 'History and Anthropology', with responses by Rosaldo and Lerner 1997). Narratology, understood as the question of 'how best to get an honest story honestly told', is more important than epistemology and ontology (Geertz 1988: 9; in organization research, see Van Maanen 1988; Czarniawska 1997; 1998).

Several observers have noted that narrative is an ancient method and perhaps our most fundamental form for making sense of experience (Novak 1975: 175; Mattingly 1991: 237; see also Arendt 1958; MacIntyre 1984; Ricoeur 1984; Carr 1986; Abbott 1992; Fehn et al. 1992; Rasmussen 1995; Bal 1997). To MacIntyre, the human being is a 'story-telling animal', and the notion of a history is as fundamental a notion as is the notion of an action (MacIntyre 1984: 214, 216). In a similar vein, Mattingly points out that narratives not only give meaningful form to our experiences. They also provide us with a forward glance, helping us to anticipate situations even before we encounter them, allowing us to envision alternative futures (Mattingly 1991: 237). Narrative inquiries into organizations do not – indeed, cannot – start from explicit theoretical assumptions. Instead, they begin with an interest in a particular organizational phenomenon that is best understood narratively. Narrative inquiries then develop descriptions and interpretations of the phenomenon from the perspective of participants, stakeholders, researchers, and others. In historical organizational analysis, both event and conjuncture are crucial, just as practices are studied in the context of several centuries, akin to what Fernand Braudel calls *longue durée*. The century-long view is employed in order to allow for the influence on current organizational practices of traditions with long historical roots, an influence that is often substantially more significant than is assumed in mainstream organization research. (For examples of the influence on current organizational practices of traditions with long historical roots, see Putnam et al. 1993; Flyvbjerg 1998: chapter 8, 'The *Longue Durée* of Power').

Moving Beyond Agency and Structure

In an attempt to transcend the dualisms of agency/structure, hermeneutics/structuralism, and voluntarism/determinism, phronetic organization

research focuses on both actors and structures, and on the relationship between the two.[12] Organizational actors and their practices are analysed in relation to the structures of the organization. And structures are analysed in terms of agency – not for the two to stand in a dualistic, external relationship, but so structures can be part of, can be internalized in actors, and so actors can be part of, can be internalized in, structures. Understanding from 'within' the organization and from 'without' are both accorded emphasis, which is what Bourdieu, in adapting the Aristotelian and Thomist concept of 'habitus' – a highly relevant concept for phronetic organization research – calls 'the internalization of externality and the externalization of internality' (Bourdieu 1977: 72). Elsewhere, Bourdieu explicitly states that the use of the notion of habitus can be understood as a way of escaping the choice between 'a structuralism without a subject and the philosophy of the subject' (Bourdieu 1990: 10).

As anyone who has tried it can testify, it is a demanding task to account simultaneously for the structural influences that shape the development of a given organizational phenomenon while crafting a clear, penetrating narrative or microanalysis of that phenomenon (see also Vaughan 1992: 183). As Vaughan has said, theorizing about actors and structures remains bifurcated (Vaughan 1992: 183). Researchers generally tend to generate either macro-level or micro-level explanations, ignoring the critical connections. Empirical work follows the same pattern. Instead of research that attempts to link macro-level factors and actors' choices in a specific organizational or social phenomenon, scholars tend to dichotomize. Structural analyses and studies of actors each receive their share of attention, but in separate projects, by separate researchers. Those who join structure and actor in empirical work most often do so by theoretical inference: data at one level of analysis are coupled with theoretical speculation about the other. Although issues of actor and structure combine with particular emphasis in organizations and institutions, classic social-science research methodology is less developed for studying organizations and institutions than for studying individuals and aggregate patterns (Bellah et al. 1991: 302). Organization research carries the burden of this fact. Therefore, many organization researchers may not be convinced that there is an escape from the duality of structural and individual analysis. They may believe there is no middle ground, for the very recalcitrance of the problem seems to attest to its intractableness.

There is mounting evidence, however, that the actor/structure connection is not an insurmountable problem. In fact, it may not be a problem at all, says Vaughan, but simply an artifact of data availability and graduate training (Vaughan 1992: 182). And we now have excellent examples from other areas of the social sciences showing us how to integrate and move beyond the simple dichotomy of actors and structures. Geertz's classic description of the Balinese cockfight progressively incorporates practices, institutions, and symbols from the larger Balinese social and cultural world in order to help the reader understand the seemingly localized event of the cockfight (Geertz 1973, 1977). Putnam and his associates similarly combine individual and structural analysis – as well as contemporary history and the history of the *longue durée* – in their attempt to explain the performance of modern, democratic institutions in Italy (Putnam et al. 1993). Ferguson demonstrates how local, intentional development plans in Lesotho interact with larger, unacknowledged structures to produce unintended effects that are instrumental to the organization of 'development' and development agencies (Ferguson 1990). Herzfeld throws new light on bureaucratic organization by studying what appears to be peculiar administrative practices in relation to structural explanations of the nation state (Herzfeld 1992). And, Tillyard works from the basis of personal histories and family dynamics to incorporate the larger socioeconomic and political scene of the entire Hanoverian Age (Tillyard 1994). Like these scholars, phronetic organization researchers deliberately seek information that will answer questions about the intermeshing of actors and structures in actual settings, in ways that dissolve any rigid and preconceived conceptual distinction between the two. (For more on the actor/structure issue, see Collins 1980; Giddens 1984; Coleman 1985; Bourdieu 1988; Fine 1988; Harrison 1989; Rosen 1989; Lévi-Strauss and Eribon 1991: 102–4; Sewell 1992).

Dialoguing with a Polyphony of Voices

Phronetic organization research is dialogical in the sense that it incorporates, and, if successful, is itself incorporated into, a polyphony of voices, with no one voice, including that of the researcher, claiming final authority. The goal of phronetic organization research is to produce input to the ongoing dialogue and praxis in relation to organizations, rather than to generate ultimate, unequivocally verified knowledge about the nature of organizations. This goal accords with Aristotle's maxim that in questions of praxis, one ought to trust more in the public sphere than in science. (For more on the relationship between the public sphere and science, see Bellah 1993). Dialogue is not limited to the relationship between researchers and the people they study in the field, however. The relevant dialogue for a particular piece of research typically involves more than these two parties – in principle anyone interested in and affected by the subject under study. Such parties may be dialoguing independently of researchers until the latter make a successful attempt at entering into the dialogue with their research. In other instances there may be no ongoing dialogue initially, the dialogue being sparked by the work of phronetic researchers. In *Habits of the Heart*, Bellah and his co-authors expressed their hope that 'the reader will test what we say against his or her own experience, will argue with us when what we say does not fit, and, best of all, will join the public discussion by offering interpretations superior to ours that can then receive further discussion' (Bellah et al. 1985: 307). This hope is as fine an expression of the phronetic dialogical attitude as we will find for a specific piece of research. *Habits of the Heart* was ultimately successful in achieving its aims of entering into and intensifying debate in USA about US values. (For an interpretation of *Habits of the Heart* as phronetic social science, see Flyvbjerg 2001: 62–5).

Thus, phronetic organization research explicitly sees itself as not having a privileged position from which the final truth can be told and further discussion arrested. We cannot think of an 'eye turned in no particular direction', as Nietzsche says. 'There is *only* a perspective seeing, *only* a perspective 'knowing'; and the *more* affects we allow to speak about one thing, the *more* eyes, different eyes, we can use to observe one thing, the more complete will our 'concept' of this thing, our 'objectivity', be' (emphasis in original) (Nietzsche 1969b: 119 (§3.12)). Hence, 'objectivity' in phronetic organization research is not 'contemplation without interest' but employment of 'a *variety* of perspectives and affective interpretations in the service of knowledge' (emphasis in original). (Nietzsche 1969b; see also Nietzsche 1968b: 287 (§530): 'There are no isolated judgements! An isolated judgment is never 'true', never knowledge; only in the connection and relation of many judgments is there any surety').

The significance of any given interpretation in a dialogue will depend on the extent to which the validity claims of the interpreter are accepted, and this acceptance typically occurs in competition with other validity claims and other interpretations. The discourses in which the results of phronetic organization research are used have, in this sense, no special status, but are subordinated to the same conditions as any other dialogical discourse. If and when the arguments of researchers carry special weight it would likely derive not from researchers having access to a special type of validity claim, but from researchers having spent more time on and being better trained at establishing validity than have other organizational actors. We are talking about a difference in degree, not in kind. To the phronetic researcher, this is the reality of organization research, although some organization researchers act as if validity claims can and should be given final grounding. The burden of proof is on them. By substituting *phronesis* for *episteme*, phronetic organization researchers avoid this burden, impossible as it seems to lift.

Some people may fear that the dialogue at the center of phronetic organization research, rather than evolving into the desired polyphony of voices, will all too easily degenerate into a shouting match, a cacophony of voices, in which the loudest carries the day. In phronetic organization research, the means of prevention is no different from that of other research: only to the extent that the validity claims of phronetic organization researchers are accepted will the results of their research be accepted in the dialogue. Phronetic organization researchers thus recognize a human privilege and a basic condition: meaningful dialogue in context. 'Dialogue' comes from the Greek *dialogos*, where *dia* means 'between' and *logos* means 'reason'. In contrast to the analytical and instrumental rationality, which lie at the cores of both *episteme* and *techne*, the practical rationality of *phronesis* is based on a socially conditioned, intersubjective 'between-reason'.

Examples of Phronetic Organization Research

The result of phronetic organization research is a pragmatically governed interpretation of the studied organizational practices. The interpretation does not require the researcher to agree with the actors' everyday understanding; nor does it require the discovery of some deep, inner meaning of the practices. Phronetic organization research is in this way interpretive, but it is neither everyday nor deep hermeneutics. Phronetic organization research is also not about, nor does it try to develop, theory or universal method. Thus, phronetic organization research is an analytical project, but not a theoretical or methodological one.

The following examples serve as brief representations of examples in an emerging body of organization research that contains elements of Aristotelian–Foucauldian *phronesis* as interpreted above. It must be stressed again, however, that phronetic organization research may be practised in ways other than those described here, as long as they effectively deal with deliberation, judgement, and praxis in relation to values and power, and as long as they answer the four value-rational questions mentioned above. In the organization of the firm and of accounting, the work of Miller must be mentioned (Miller 1994: 239–264; 2003). In the organization of science and technology there is the work of Latour and Rabinow (Latour 1996; 1999; Rabinow 1996; 1999). And in the organization of government there is Mitchell Dean's work (Dean 1999). The work of Clegg has already been mentioned.

Examples also exist from more specialized fields of research such as the organization of consumption (Miller and Rose 1997: 1–36), insurance and risk (Ewald 1986; 1996), space and architecture (Rabinow 1989; Crush 1994: 301–24), policing (Donzelot 1979; Harcourt 2001), poverty and welfare (Dean 1991; Procacci 1993), sexual politics (Bartky 1990; Minson 1993), and psychology (Rose 1985; 1996). Specifically in Scandinavia, the work of Brytting, Johansson, and Leijon, on ethics, responsibility, and the organization of labour and municipalities, may serve as examples of phronetic organization research (Leijon 1993; 1996; Brytting et al. 1997; Johansson 1998; Brytting 2001). My own attempts at developing phronetic research have been aimed at the organization of democracy and its institutions, public and private (Flyvbjerg 1998; 2001; Flyvbjerg et al. 2003. For more examples of relevant research, see Dean 1999: 3–5; Flyvbjerg 2001: 162–5).

One task of organization research practised on the basis of the methodological guidelines presented here, is to provide concrete examples and detailed narratives of the ways in which power and values work in organizations and with what consequences, and to suggest how power and values could be changed to work with other consequences. Insofar as organizational situations become clear, they are clarified by detailed stories of who is doing what to whom. Such clarification is a principal concern for phronetic organization research and provides the main link to praxis.

Phronetic organization research explores current practices and historic circumstances to find avenues to praxis. The task of phronetic organization research is to clarify and deliberate about the problems, possibilities, and risks that organizations face, and to outline how things could be done differently – all in full knowledge that we cannot find ultimate answers to these questions or even to a single version of what the questions are.

Notes

1. For an example of the practical implementation of phronetic organization research in actual studies of public and private organizations, I refer the reader to Flyvbjerg (1998). See also shorter examples in the main text of this chapter.

2. In the short space of this chapter, it is not possible to provide a full account of Aristotle's considerations about the intellectual virtues of *episteme*, *techne*, and *phronesis*. Instead, I have focused upon the bare essentials, based on a reading of the original texts. A complete account would further elaborate the relations between *episteme*, *techne*, and *phronesis*, and the relationship of all three to *empeiria*. It would also expand on the relationship of phronetic judgements to rules, on what it means to succeed or to fail in the exercise of *phronesis,* and on the conditions that must be fulfilled if *phronesis* is to be acquired. For further discussion of these questions and of the implications of Aristotle's thinking for contemporary social science, see my discussion with Hubert and Stuart Dreyfus (Dreyfus and Stuart 1991: 101). See also MacIntyre (1984); Bernstein (1985); Heller (1990); Lord and O'Connor (1991); and Taylor (1995).

3. For the full argument that organization research and other social science can probably never be scientific in the epistemic sense, see Flyvbjerg (2001: chapters 3 and 4).

4. On the relationship between judgement and *phronesis*, see Ruderman (1997).

5. For such an interpretation, with an unclear distinction between *phronesis* and *techne*, see Hubert and Stuart Dreyfus (1990). See also my discussion of this issue with the Dreyfus brothers in Flyvbjerg (1991: 102–7).

6. Regarding ways of generalizing from a single case, see Flyvbjerg (2004).

7. *N.E.*, 1144b33–1145all. For Aristotle, man [*sic*] has a double identity. For the 'human person', that is, man in politics and ethics, *phronesis* is the most important intellectual virtue. Insofar as man can transcend the purely human, contemplation assumes the highest place. *N.E.*, 1145a6 ff. and 1177a12 ff.

8. For an interpretation of Foucault as a practitioner of *phronesis*, see Flyvbjerg (2001: chapter 8, 'Empowering Aristotle').

9. It should be mentioned that MacIntyre's Aristotle is substantially more Platonic than the Aristotle depicted by the others, and more Platonic than the interpretation given here. MacIntyre explicitly understands Aristotle 'as engaged in trying to complete Plato's work, and to correct it precisely insofar as that was necessary in order to complete it'. See MacIntyre (1988: 94) and (1990).

10. Nihilism is a theory promoting the state of believing in nothing or of having no allegiances and no purposes.

11. After Ludwig Wittgenstein had abandoned any possibility of constructing a philosophical theory, he suggested that Goethe's phrase from *Faust*, quoted in the main text, might serve as a motto for the whole of his later philosophy. See Monk (1990: 305–6). The Foucault quote is from Foucault (1991: 72). On the primacy of practices in Foucault's work, see also Foucault (1981: 5); and Foucault quoted in Eribon (1991: 214–6).

12. For a discussion of the problems incurred in moving beyond these dualisms, see Dreyfus and Rabinow (1982), and McCarthy's considerations on hermeneutics and structural analysis in his introduction to Habermas's *The Theory of Communicative Action*, Vol. 1 (1984: xxvi–vii). See other works of interest on this problem, which, in my view, is one of the more challenging in phronetic organization research: Giddens (1982); Seung (1982); Schmidt (1985).

References

Abbott, A. (1992) 'What do cases do? Some notes on activity in sociological analysis', in C.C. Ragin and H.S. Becker (eds), *What is a case? Exploring the foundations of social inquiry*. Cambridge: Cambridge University Press. pp. 53–82.

Andler, D. (1998) 'The normativity of context'. Unpublished paper, Université Paris X, Nanterre.

Arendt, H. (1958) *The human condition*. Chicago, IL: University of Chicago Press.

Aristotle (1976) *The Nicomachean ethics* (abbreviated as *N.E.*), translated by J.A.K. Thomson, revised with notes and appendices by Hugh Tredennick, introduction and bibliography by Jonathan Barnes. Harmondsworth: Penguin.

Bailey, M.T. (1992) 'Do physicists use case studies? Thoughts on public administration research', *Public Administration Review*, 52: 47–54.

Bal, M. (1997) *Narratology: Introduction to the theory of narrative*. Toronto: University of Toronto Press.

Bartky, S.L. (1990) *Femininity and domination: Studies in the phenomenology of oppression*. New York, NY: Routledge.

Bellah, R. (1993) 'Professionalism and citizenship: Are they compatible?' *Symposium on redefining leadership: New visions of work and community*, Wake Forest University, Winston-Salem, North Carolina, 21 May.

Bellah, R.N., Madsen, R., Sullivan, W.M., Swidler, A., and Tipton, S.M. (1985) *Habits of the heart: Individualism and commitment in American life*. New York: Harper and Row.

Bellah, R.N., Madsen, R., Sullivan, W.M., Swidler, A., and Tipton, S.M. (1991) *The good society*. New York: Alfred A. Knopf.

Bernstein, R. (1985) *Beyond objectivism and relativism: Science, hermeneutics, and praxis*. Philadelphia: University of Pennsylvania Press.

Bernstein, R. (1989) 'Interpretation and solidarity', an interview by Dunja Melcic, *Praxis International*, 9: 201–19.

Bourdieu, P. (1977) *Outline of a theory of practice*. Cambridge: Cambridge University Press.

Bourdieu, P. (1988) *Homo academicus*. Stanford, CA: Stanford University Press.

Bourdieu, P. (1990) *In other words: Essays towards a reflexive sociology*. Cambridge: Polity Press.

Bourdieu, P. and Wacquant, L.J.D. (1992) *An invitation to reflexive sociology*. Chicago: The University of Chicago Press.

Brytting, T. (2001) *Att vara som gud? Moralisk kompetens i arbetslivet*. Malmö: Liber AB.

Brytting, T., De Geer, H. and Silfverberg, G. (1997) *Moral i verksamhet: Ett etiskt perspektiv på företag och arbete*. Stockholm: Natur och Kultur.

Calhoun, C. (1994) 'E. P. Thompson and the discipline of historical context', *Social Research*, 61: 233–43.

Campbell, D.T. (1986) 'Science's social system of validity-enhancing collective belief change and the problems of the social sciences', in Donald W. Fiske and Richard A. Shweder (eds), *Metatheory in social science: Pluralisms and subjectivities*. Chicago, IL: University of Chicago Press. pp. 108–35.

Carr, D. (1986) *Time, narrative, and history*. Bloomington, IN: Indiana University Press.

Christensen, C.R. with Hansen, A.J. (1987) 'Teaching with cases at the Harvard Business School', in C.R. Christensen and A.J. Hansen (eds), *Teaching and the case method*. Boston, MA: Harvard Business School Press. pp. 16–49.

Clegg, S. (1989) *Frameworks of power*. Newbury Park, CA: Sage.

Clegg, S. (1997) 'Foucault, power and organizations', in A. McKinlay and K. Starkey (eds), *Foucault, management and organization theory: From panopticon to technologies of self*. London: Sage. pp. 29–48.

Coleman, J. (1985) 'Social theory, social research, and a theory of action', *American Journal of Sociology*, 91: 1309–35.

Collins, R. (1980) 'On the microfoundations of macrosociology', *American Journal of Sociology*, 86: 984–1014.

Crush, J. (1994) 'Scripting the compound: Power and space in the South African mining industry', *Environment and Planning D: Society and Space*, 12: 301–24.

Czarniawska, B. (1997) *Narrating the organization: Dramas of institutional identity*. Chicago, IL: University of Chicago Press.

Czarniawska, B. (1998) *A narrative approach to organization studies*. Thousand Oaks, CA: Sage.

Dean, M. (1991) *The constitution of poverty: Toward a genealogy of liberal governance*. London: Routledge.

Dean, M. (1999) *Governmentality: Power and rule in modern society*. Thousand Oaks, CA: Sage.

Devereux, D.T. (1986) 'Particular and universal in Aristotle's conception of practical knowledge', *Review of Metaphysics*, 39: 483–504.

Donzelot, J. (1979) *The policing of families*. New York: Pantheon.

Dreyfus, H. and S. (1990) 'What is morality: a phenomenological account of the development of expertise', in D. Rasmussened, *Universalism vs communitarianism*. Cambridge, MA: MIT Press. pp. 237–64.

Dreyfus, H. and Rabinow, P. (1982) *Michel Foucault: Beyond structuralism and hermeneutics*. Brighton: Harvester Press.

Dreyfus, H. and Stuart, S. (1991) 'Sustaining non-rationalized practices: Body-mind, power, and situational ethics', *Praxis International*, 11: 93–113.

Engel, S. (1999) *Context is everything: the nature of memory*. New York: W. H. Freeman.

Eribon, D. (1991) *Michel Foucault*. Cambridge, MA: Harvard University Press.

Ewald, F. (1986) *L'etat providence*. Paris: B. Grasset.

Ewald, F. (1996) *Histoire de l'etat providence: Les origines de la solidarite*. Paris: Grasset.

Fehn, A., Hoesterey, I., and Tatar, M. (eds) (1992) *Neverending stories: Toward a critical narratology*. Princeton: Princeton University Press.

Fenno, R.F. Jr (1986) 'Observation, context, and sequence in the study of politics', *American Political Science Review*, 80: 3–15.

Ferguson, J. (1990) *The anti-politics machine: 'Development', depoliticization, and bureaucratic power in Lesotho*. Cambridge: Cambridge University Press.

Ferrara, A. (1989) 'Critical theory and its discontents: On Wellmer's critique of Habermas', *Praxis International*, 8: 305–20.

Ferrara, A. (1999) *Justice and judgement: The rise and the prospect of the judgement model in contemporary political philosophy.* Thousand Oaks, CA: Sage.

Fine, G.A. (1988) 'On the macrofoundations of microsociology: Constraint and the exterior reality of structure', paper presented at the annual meetings of the American Sociological Association, Atlanta.

Flyvbjerg, B. (1989) 'Socrates didn't like the case method, why should you?' in Hans E. Klein (ed), *Case method research and application: New vistas.* Needham, MA: World Association for Case Method Research and Application. pp. 33–42.

Flyvbjerg, B. (1998) *Rationality and power: Democracy in practice.* Chicago: University of Chicago Press.

Flyvbjerg, B. (2001) *Making social science matter: Why social inquiry fails and how it can succeed again.* Cambridge: Cambridge University Press.

Flyvbjerg, B. (2004) 'Five misunderstandings about case study research', in C. Seale, G. Gobo, J.F. Gubrium and D. Silverman (eds), *Qualitative Research Practice.* London and Thousand Oaks, CA: Sage. pp. 420–34.

Flyvbjerg, B., Bruzelius, N., and Rothengatter, W. (2003) *Megaprojects and risk: An anatomy of ambition.* Cambridge: Cambridge University Press.

Foucault, M. (1969) *Titres et travaux.* Pamphlet printed in fulfillment of requirements for candidacy at the Collège de France. Paris: privately printed.

Foucault, M. (1972) 'Le discours de toul', *Le Nouvel Observateur*, 372: 15.

Foucault, M. (1979) 'My body, this paper, this fire', *Oxford Literary Review*, 4: 9–28.

Foucault, M. (1981) 'Questions of method: An interview', *I&C*, 8: 3–14.

Foucault, M. (1982) 'The subject and power', in Hubert Dreyfus and Paul Rabinow, *Michel Foucault: Beyond structuralism and hermeneutics.* Brighton: Harvester Press. pp. 214–32.

Foucault, M. (1984a) 'Nietzsche, genealogy, history', in Paul Rabinow (ed.), *The Foucault reader*, New York: Pantheon. pp. 76–100.

Foucault, M. (1984b) 'Space, knowledge, and power', interview with Paul Rabinow, in Paul Rabinow (ed.), *The Foucault reader*, New York: Pantheon. pp. 239–56.

Foucault, M. (1991) 'Politics and the study of discourse', in G. Burchell, C. Gordon and P. Miller (eds), *The Foucault effect: Studies in governmentality*, Chicago, IL: University of Chicago Press. pp. 53–72.

Gadamer, H.-G. (1975) *Truth and method.* London: Sheed and Ward.

Geertz, C. (1973) *The interpretation of cultures.* New York: Basic Books.

Geertz, C. (1977) 'Deep play: Notes on the Balinese cockfight', in C. Geertz, *The interpretation of cultures: Selected essays,.* New York: Basic Books. pp. 412–53.

Geertz, C. (1983) *Local knowledge: Further essays in interpretive anthropology.* New York: Basic Books.

Geertz, C. (1988) *Works and lives: The anthropologist as author.* Stanford, CA: Stanford University Press.

Geertz, C. (1995a) *After the fact: Two countries, four decades, one anthropologist.* Cambridge, MA: Harvard University Press.

Geertz, C. (1995b) 'Disciplines', *Raritan*, 14: 65–102.

Geertz, C. (1995c) 'History and anthropology', *New Literary History*, 21: 321–35.

Giddens, A. (1982) 'Hermeneutics and social theory', in *Profiles and critiques in social theory*, Berkeley, CA: University of California Press. pp. 1–17.

Giddens, A. (1984) *The constitution of society: Outline of the theory of structuration.* Cambridge: Polity Press.

Habermas, J. (1984) *The Theory of Communicative Action.* Boston, MA: Beacon Press (volume 1).

Harcourt, B.E. (2001) *Illusion of order: The false promise of broken windows policing.* Cambridge, MA: Harvard University Press.

Hardy, C. and Clegg, S. (1996) 'Some dare call it power', in S. Clegg, C. Hardy and W.R. Nord (eds), *Handbook of organization studies.* London: Sage. pp. 622–41.

Harrison, P.R. (1989) 'Narrativity and interpretation: On hermeneutical and structuralist approaches to culture', *Thesis Eleven*, 22: 61–78.

Heller, A. (1990) *Can modernity survive?* Berkeley: University of California Press.

Henderson, D.K. (1994) 'Epistemic competence and contextualist epistemology: Why contextualism is not just the poor person's coherentism', *The Journal of Philosophy*, 91: 627–49.

Herzfeld, M. (1992) *The social production of indifference: Exploring the symbolic roots of western bureaucracy.* Chicago: University of Chicago Press.

Johansson, U. (1998) *Om ansvar: Ansvarföreställningar och deras betydelse för den organisatoriska verkligheten.* Lund: Lund University.

Latour, B. (1996) *Aramis, or the love of technology.* Cambridge, MA: Harvard University Press.

Latour, B. (1999) *Pandora's hope: Essays on the reality of science studies.* Cambridge, MA: Harvard University Press.

Leijon, S. (ed) (1993) *God kommunal organisation: Lyssning, tolkning och handling.* Kfi-rapport 22. Göteborg: Kfi.

Leijon, S. (1996) *Arbete i brytningstid: Tankar om tillvarons dualiteter.* BAS, Göteborg.

Lerner, G. (1997) *Why history matters.* Oxford: Oxford University Press.

Lévi-Strauss, C. and Eribon, D. (1991) *Conversations with Claude Lévi-Strauss.* Chicago: University of Chicago Press.

Lindblom, C.E. (1990) *Inquiry and change: The troubled attempt to understand and shape society.* New Haven: Yale University Press.

Lindblom, C.E. and Cohen, D.K. (1979) *Usable knowledge: Social science and social problem solving.* New Haven, CT: Yale University Press.

Lord, C. and O'Connor, D.K. (eds) (1991) *Essays on the foundations of Aristotelian political science.* Berkeley: University of California Press.

MacIntyre, A. (1977) 'Epistemological crises, dramatic narrative, and the philosophy of science', *Monist,* 60: 453–72.

MacIntyre, A. (1984) *After virtue: A study in moral theory.* Notre Dame: University of Notre Dame Press.

MacIntyre, A. (1988) *Whose justice? Which rationality?* Notre Dame, IN: University of Notre Dame Press.

MacIntyre, A. (1990) *Three rival versions of moral enquiry: Encyclopaedia, genealogy, and tradition.* London: Duckworth.

Mattingly, C. (1991) 'Narrative reflections on practical actions: Two learning experiments in reflective story-telling', in D.A. Schön (ed.), *The reflective turn: Case studies in and on educational practice.* New York: Teachers College Press. pp. 235–57.

Miller, H. (1941) 'Reflections on writing', in H. Miller, *The wisdom of the heart.* New York: New Directions. pp. 19–30.

Miller, J. (1993) *The passion of Michel Foucault.* New York: Simon and Schuster.

Miller, P. (1994) Accounting and objectivity: The invention of calculating selves and calculable spaces, in A. Megill (ed.), *Rethinking objectivity.* Durham: Duke University Press. pp. 239–64.

Miller, P. (2003) 'Management and accounting', in T.M. Porter and D. Ross (eds), *The Cambridge History of Science,* vol. 7, *The Modern Social Sciences.* Cambridge: Cambridge University Press. pp. 565–76.

Miller, P. and Rose, N. (1997) 'Mobilising the consumer: Assembling the subject of consumption', *Theory, Culture and Society,* 14: 1–36.

Minson, J. (1993) *Questions of conduct: Sexual harrassment, citizenship and government.* London: Macmillan.

Monk, R. (1990) *Ludwig Wittgenstein: The duty of genius.* New York: Free Press.

Nehamas, A. (1985) *Nietzsche: Life as literature.* Cambridge, MA: Harvard University Press.

Nietzsche, F. (1966) *Beyond good and evil.* New York: Vintage Books.

Nietzsche, F. (1968a) *The anti-christ.* Harmondsworth: Penguin.

Nietzsche, F. (1968b) *The will to power.* New York: Vintage Books.

Nietzsche, F. (1968c) *Twilight of the idols.* Harmondsworth: Penguin.

Nietzsche, F. (1969a) *Ecce homo.* New York: Vintage Books.

Nietzsche, F. (1969b) *On the genealogy of morals.* New York: Vintage Books.

Novak, M. (1975) '"Story" and Experience', in J.B. Wiggins (ed.) *Religion as story.* Lanham, MD: University Press of America. pp. 175–97.

Nussbaum, M.C. (1990) 'The discernment of perception: An Aristotelian conception of private and public rationality', in *Love's knowledge: Essays on philosophy and literature.* Oxford: Oxford University Press. pp. 54–105.

Procacci, G. (1993) *Gouverner la misère: La question sociale en France (1789–1848).* Paris: Éditions du Seuil.

Putnam, R.D. with Leonardi, Robert and Nanetti, Raffaella Y. (1993) *Making democracy work: Civic traditions in modern Italy.* Princeton, NJ: Princeton University Press.

Rabinow, P. (1989) *French modern: Norms and forms of the social environment.* Cambridge, MA: MIT Press.

Rabinow, P. (1996) *Making PCR: A story of biotechnology.* Chicago: The University of Chicago Press.

Rabinow, P. (1999) *French DNA: Trouble in purgatory.* Chicago: The University of Chicago Press.

Rabinow, P. and Sullivan, W.M. (1987) 'The interpretive turn: A second look', in P. Rabinow and W.M. Sullivan (eds) *Interpretive social science: A second look.* Berkeley, CA: University of California Press. pp. 1–30.

Rasmussen, D. (1995) 'Rethinking subjectivity: Narrative identity and the self', *Philosophy and Social Criticism,* 21: 159–72.

Ricoeur, P. (1984) *Time and narrative.* Chicago, IL: University of Chicago Press.

Rorty, R. (1985) 'Habermas and Lyotard on postmodernity', in R.J. Bernstein (ed.) *Habermas and modernity.* Cambridge, MA: MIT Press. pp. 161–75.

Rorty, R. (1991a) 'Solidarity or objectivity?' in *Philosophical Papers,* volume 1. Cambridge: Cambridge University Press. pp. 21–34.

Rorty, R. (1991b) *Philosophical papers.* Cambridge: Cambridge University Press.

Rorty, R. (1995) 'Response to James Gouinlock', in Herman J. Saatkamp, Jr (ed.), *Rorty and pragmatism: The philosopher responds to his critics.* Nashville: Vanderbilt University Press. pp. 91–9.

Rose, N. (1985) *The psychological complex: Psychology, politics and society in England, 1869–1939.* London: Routledge and Kogan Paul.

Rose, N. (1996) *Inventing our selves: Psychology, power and personhood.* Cambridge: Cambridge University Press.

Rosen, L. (1989) *The anthropology of justice: Law as culture in Islamic society.* Cambridge: Cambridge University Press.

Ruderman, R.S. (1997) 'Aristotle and the recovery of political judgment', *American Political Science Review,* 91: 409–20.

Schmidt, J. (1985) *Maurice Merleau-Ponty: Between phenomenology and structuralism.* New York: St. Martin's Press.

Seung, T. K. (1982) *Structuralism and hermeneutics.* New York: Columbia University Press.

Sewell, W.H. Jr (1992) 'A theory of structure: Duality, agency, and transformation', *American Journal of Sociology,* 98: 1–29.

Shannon, B. (1990) 'What is context?' *Journal for the Theory of Social Behaviour,* 20: 157–66.

Taylor, C.C.W. (1995) 'Politics', in Jonathan Barnes (ed.), *The Cambridge companion to Aristotle*. Cambridge: Cambridge University Press. pp. 233–58.

Taylor, C. (1989) *Sources of the self: The making of the modern identity*. Cambridge, MA: Harvard University Press.

Tillyard, S. (1994) *Aristocrats*. New York: Farrar, Straus, and Giroux.

Toulmin, S. (1988) 'The recovery of practical philosophy', *The American Scholar*, 57: 337–52.

Van Maanen, J. (1988) *Tales of the field: On writing ethnography*. Chicago, IL: University of Chicago Press.

Vaughan, D. (1992) 'Theory elaboration: The heuristics of case analysis', in C.C. Ragin and H.S. Becker (eds) *What is a case?* Cambridge: Cambridge University Press. pp. 173–202.

1.11 Researching Organizations Using Action Research

COLIN EDEN AND CHRIS HUXHAM

Introduction

Since its inception in the middle of the 20th century, *action research* has gradually gained in prominence. In the last few years, however, there has been an explosion of interest and a concurrent abundance of articles and books about it and using it. The term is used to describe a range of approaches involving interventions in organizations that have the purpose of bringing about practical transformation and advancing knowledge.

A myriad of terms and approaches are used in connection with action research. These include collaborative and participatory research, co-operative, collaborative, appreciative and clinical inquiry and process consultation, process management and soft systems methodology. The field is confused and, despite the numerous attempts to differentiate the approaches (see for example, Argyris and Schon 1991; Elden and Chisholm 1993a; Schein 1995; Raelin 1997), precise interpretations of each seem largely to depend on the user or author and the audience they are playing to.

In this chapter we will be presenting a particular view of action research as a phenomenological methodology for *researching organizational processes and practices*. From this perspective it naturally sits alongside ethnography (Thomas 1993; Tedlock 2000), case study research (Stake 1995; Yin 2002) and the development of grounded theory (Glaser 1992; Strauss and Corbin 1998; O'Connor et al. 2003). The distinguishing feature of this type of action research, as compared to these other research approaches, is an involvement by the researcher with members of organizations over matters that are of genuine concern to them and over which they intend to take action. By 'involvement' we mean taking a role such as facilitator or consultant to a client or clients (or being an employee), having some influence on choices and accepting the accountability and responsibility that this implies. In contrast to most research approaches, which presume the researcher takes a 'fly-on-the-wall' perspective, action research presumes that behavioural and/or organizational changes *will* result from the researcher's involvement. Nevertheless, as with the other research approaches, there is a primary commitment by the researcher to advance a field of knowledge in a manner that has some general implications.

Interventions of this kind will necessarily be 'one-off's', so action research has frequently been criticized for its lack of repeatability, and, hence, lack of rigour. These criticisms are countered by the arguments that the involvement with practitioners over things that actually matter to them provides a richness of insight *that could not be gained in other ways* (Whyte 1991). In addition, because the output derives from close interactions with practitioners it is likely to be of practical value. It, therefore, broadly, at least, fulfils the criteria for the 'Mode 2' (i.e. practice-oriented) type of research that has been called for by some organizational researchers (Gibbons et al. 1994; Hodgkinson 2001).

We are especially interested in exploring the particular nature of research rigour and value in situations in which the researcher intentionally is a part of the action. As we suggest above, we distinguish *action research as a methodology for researching organizational practice* in a number of ways: firstly, from organizational intervention projects that do not satisfy characteristics of *rigorous research*; secondly, from research within an organization that does not satisfy characteristics of *action orientation*; and, thirdly, from forms of action research that do not have research output as their primary *raison d'être*. We shall call this type of action research 'research oriented action research' (*RO-AR*). In making such distinctions, we are not intending to imply that the research approach that we will delineate is better than other forms of research or other forms of action research, but merely that it is a different approach and leads to different outputs.

We shall begin by delving into the history and range of current interpretations of 'action research' and other approaches that are often regarded as a part of the same family. Our exploration will continue with the development of characteristics that are required if action research is to satisfy the criterion of being *both* action-oriented and research-oriented. The characteristics, when taken together, will act as a summary of the important aspects of action research and of the features that distinguish it both from pure consultancy-type interventions and from other forms of organizational research. The chapter concludes with a discussion of some of the issues concerned with the reporting of action research.

Some History and Recent Developments

Our purposes in exploring the way action research has developed are two-fold and these are in some senses opposites. On the one hand the history may be of general interest and it provides important antecedents for the approach we shall be characterizing, from which some of our arguments will be drawn. On the other hand, however, we need to clarify the alternative approaches to action research as a precursor to distinguishing our focus from theirs (as indicated in the previous section). We hope that this will provide helpful structure for categorizing further reading in the field. The literature on action research and related approaches – including articles and books both about it and using it – is very extensive and there is no possibility of covering it all in this chapter. However, we hope to give a flavour of the main strands.

There is general agreement that action research had its naissance in the US in the mid-1940s. Chein (1948), Coch and French (1948), Collier (1945) and Curle (1949) have all been cited as early pioneers, but it is Lewin (1943; 1946; 1947) who is generally regarded as the father of action research. Lewin (1946: 36) argued that research for social practice needs to take an integrated approach across social science disciplines and should be concerned with

'two rather different types of questions, namely the study of general laws … and the diagnosis of a specific situation'. His approach was to design hypothesis-testing experiments into workshops which he had been asked to run for delegates who were concerned, for example, to design ways of tackling race relations issues. He emphasized that the research data (in his case, concerned with understanding the kinds of change the workshops had produced) would be complex and difficult to keep hold of. The need to design methods for recording ill-structured data was, therefore, seen as important, as was a focus on the relationship between perception and action – an interpretist approach to research.

Lewin's work on encouraging the use of meat entrails in everyday cooking is one of the first applications of social science knowledge that was to be labelled 'action research' (Lewin 1943). In some ways, this was more akin to the traditional controlled experimentation of the physical sciences (Clark 1972), but it did have the explicit aim of changing behaviour and recording the outcomes of the attempts to do so. The crucial difference between this work and others was the recognition that the researcher was visible and was expected to have an impact on the experiment. Lewin's work produced a great deal of mistrust about the research conclusions because of the difficulties in measuring outcomes and controlling contextual variables.

The emphasis on hypothesis testing is still prevalent among some groups of action researchers (for example, Alderfer 1993). However, as action research has gained credence, the early notions have been used, extended or recreated by others. This process has led to the development of various action research and related approaches.

Soon after the pioneering work in the US, the Tavistock Institute in the UK began a programme of research in the coal mining industry which gradually led to an exposition of the relationship between investigatory research and its implications for action (Trist and Bamforth 1951). This work was to lead to the development of the socio-technical systems approach to thinking about organizational interventions (Emery and Trist 1963). The work was strongly aimed at conducting research and undertaking associated theory development alongside attempting to make significant changes in organizations. Socio-technical thinking was to dominate action research across the globe, and the work of the Tavistock Institute continued to act as a reference point for others wishing to undertake action research (see Clark 1975). Collaboration between UK and Norwegian researchers led to Scandinavia enjoying a long association with the development of action research (for example, Emery and Thorsrud 1969; Thorsrud 1970; Elden 1979; Elden and Levin 1991; Ottosson 2003). Notably, significant institutional support was provided for the extensive work in Sweden on the democratization of the work place. All of this early work focused upon understanding organizations and organizational change.

As the term 'action research' gradually became embedded in the language of organization studies and spread worldwide, a range of related terms and approaches also emerged. Action *learning* was promoted by Revans (1977; 1978; 1982) and the term has been widely taken up and is (mis)used to cover a multitude of formal learning arrangements. Those who adhere to its original principle of learning from others in the workplace, however, see it as a process of collaborative transformation involving participative reflection-in-action (Zuber-Skerrit 2002). Torbert's (1976; 1991; 2000) notion of action *inquiry* has some similarity with this. He refers to 'consciousness in the midst of action' (Torbert 1991: 221) and a process of taking actions consciously and then reflecting on them.

In partial contrast to the above, Argyris et al. (1985) proposed action *science*. They described it as a process in which '... clients are participants in a process of public reflection that attempts both to comprehend the concrete details of particular cases and to discover and test propositions of a general theory' (Argyris et al. 1985: 4). A key concern is to use these to facilitate an '... internal critique of (one's) own practical reasoning ...' (Putnam 1999: 81) and hence to challenge organizational defensive routines and so encourage 'double loop learning' (Argyris 1995). Bate's (2000) more recent notion of action *ethnography* or action *anthropology* in which anthropological data and concepts are fed back to the parties to help them bring about change could be argued to be in a similar vein.

Finally, *participatory* action research (PAR) (Whyte 1991) has as its distinguishing feature a requirement for members of the organization being studied to participate actively in the design and analysis of the research. The same acronym (PAR) has also been used by Ottosson (2003) to stand for *participation* action research in which it is the researcher that participates fully in the organizational life.

Although all of the above approaches are concerned with the use of careful methodologies for the 'research', 'learning', 'science', 'inquiry' or 'ethnography', the predominant focus in most recent writing on these topics is on the use of this to inform action and transformation *in the local organizational setting* where the research is taking place. For one group of scholars the main concern is with the use of some of the principles of action research as a method for developing effective professional practice (for example, Stringer 1999; Marshall 2000; Blenkin and Kelly 2001; Brown and Jones 2001). The focus of this form of action research is the *individual* practitioner, who undertakes research on their own personal practice, in their own practical context, and seeks to use the research for their own personal benefit. This kind of action research is thus a form of self-development: '... a systematic form of enquiry undertaken by practitioners into their attempts to improve the quality of *their own* practice' (Whitehead 1994: 138, our emphasis). Action research of this sort has been extensively used by professionals in education and health (for example, Kember 2000; Winter and Munn Goddings 2001; Stringer and Genat 2003; Tomal 2003). Indeed the work of Corey (1953) on improving school practices is another early example of action research.

Another dominant perspective considers action research as a form of *organizational* development (OD) (for example, Elden and Chisholm 1993b). Indeed, Bate (2000) claims that action research was *the* foundation stone of OD. Some action researchers use the terms action research and organizational development as if they were synonymous and seem to imply that action research is *solely* about creating organizational change (Alderfer 1993). A particular slant on this is when the action research is done in 'your own' organization (Coghlan and Bannick 2001). Others extend this OD perspective in the other direction arguing for action research to be focused on large-scale social changes that involve networks of organizations (Chisholm 1998; Bonnet and Cristallini 2003).

The focuses on individual, organization or network development are neither distinct nor mutually exclusive (for example, Dickens and Watkins 1999; Fisher 2003). A number of themes run through the literature that focuses on these action research perspectives. There is a dominant concern with participation of organizational members in the research. Many authors argue that action research is necessarily of this type (for example, Peters and Robinson 1984) although some (like ourselves) see this as a matter of choice (for example, Dick 2002). For many action researchers, the emphasis on participation is linked to deeper ideological issues. For example, participatory action research developed largely within the context of social research concerned with issues such as worker participation in organizational decision-making or community participation in public decision-making and is often driven by concerns for the emancipation and empowering of groups and individuals (for example, Kemmis and McTaggart 1988; Elden and Levin 1991; Zuber-Skerritt 1992; Bhatt and Tandon 2000). In this case, '... the values researchers hold and the ideological perspectives that guide them exert a powerful influence on choices they make in the course of inquiry' (Brown and Tandon 1983: 281). In practice this has often meant being interested in helping under-privileged groups and being concerned with the kind of social change which seriously questions the dominant values within society (for example, Bryden-Miller 1997; Greenwood and Levin 1998).

Others concentrate on different issues: 'one important difference between classical action research and participatory action research is that, in addition to solving practical problems and contributing to general theory, contemporary forms of action research also aim at making change and learning a self-generating and self-maintaining process in the systems in which action researchers work' (Elden and Chisholm 1993a: 125). The breadth of outlooks that are encompassed by those who see action research as fundamentally concerned with ideological issues is perhaps encapsulated in the declared 'What do we hope for?' statement of the Action Learning, Action Research and Process Management group that runs a World Congress every 2 years: 'Our vision is that action learning and action research processes are widely used and publicly shared by individuals and groups creating local and global change for the achievement of a more equitable, just, joyful, productive, peaceful and sustainable society'. There is, however, a question about the extent to which this is actually achieved. One argument is that in practice PAR interventionists do not necessarily take the side of the underdog but unconsciously may take the side of the agencies funding the research (David 2002). Another is that action research tends to be marginalized precisely because it threatens social change (Greenwood and Levin 1998).

Throughout the history of these action-oriented approaches to research and learning, whichever tradition has been followed, there has been a consistent defensiveness on the part of those attached to it. In 1972, Clark argued that the distinctive features tend to be neglected and slighted, albeit unintentionally, and that much academic commentary is little more than negative criticism (Clark 1972). However, in the late 1970s and early 1980s a number of attempts were made to argue positively not just that action research was valid, but that in a number of respects it was better than the alternatives. In the US, a paper by Susman and Evered (1978) sought to legitimize action research within the context of a system of research accreditation in North American academia that has been – some would argue still is – driven by positivism. Notably a book brought together writers from many of the traditions mentioned above and argued for the legitimacy of a 'new paradigm' of research based upon co-operative and collaborative research. The *Handbook of Action Research* may be seen as a recent encapsulation of the same objectives. Striving for legitimacy continues. For example, Greenwood and Levin (1998) have put forward a carefully constructed argument that, when compared to physics and chemistry, action research is more scientific than orthodox science. By contrast, Brown and Jones (2001) have sought to locate the argument in postmodernism. McTaggart (1998) provides an extensive tour de force on the issue of validity in PAR. The prevalence of books, journal articles, journal special editions and even journals centred on action research and related approaches in recent years suggests that they are gaining in acceptance.

Our own view is that action research can be good science, though not in a way which depends necessarily upon meeting all the tenets of traditional scientific method. However, this requires a clear understanding of what is needed to achieve 'good quality research'. The main thrust of this chapter is, thus, an exploration of the nature and boundaries of action research as a rigorous methodology for researching organizational processes and practice.

Locating Research-Oriented Action Research (*RO-AR*)

Despite the concerns with validity, the preoccupation in much of the writing in the traditions referred to above appears to be with using this to inform or justify social action in the particular situations being studied. More generally applicable theoretical advances, if conceived as relevant at all, are often regarded as something that will emerge over a number of action research projects (Marsick et al. 2003) and it is rare to find authors explicitly discussing how this may happen.

There are, of course, exceptions to the above perspectives. For example, Ayas (2003: 28) argues that action research can overcome some of the problematic issues, such as the effect of prior knowledge of success or failure on interview data, and discusses issues in 'maintaining the balance between action and research'. Ottosson (2003) similarly sees his *participation* action research as a way for a researcher to get reliable, detailed and subtle data. Dick's (2002) focus on action research in postgraduate programmes is a clear exposition of design issues for research rigour.

The perspective of this article is broadly in line with these latter accounts. Our central focus is on *RO-AR* as a research methodology and, like Checkland and Holwell (1998: 17), we are concerned with the 'recoverability' of results for the transfer to other situations. From this perspective, the action intervention or interventions into organizations by the researcher are an essential part of the research process that must be carried out professionally, but the primary raison d'être for intervening is the research. *Action ethnography* is, in many respects, an attractive descriptor of this type of action research because it takes from ethnography the notion of building theory from naturally occurring data but emphasizes that the data follows from action-oriented interventions. Like case study research, it is concerned with building general theory from a single or relatively small number of data gathering situations.

Our approach is distinguished from most others in a number of ways. The form of the intervention is not restricted to action science or action inquiry types of processes and the considerations of emancipation and social change that so often inspire action researchers are not seen as a necessary condition of appropriateness. Rather, in agreeing to work with organization members as 'clients' for the intervention, the researcher would normally accept their dominant ideology. Research results are often derived from many intervention settings and so cannot, by definition, help action in the specific situations in which data is being collected. Indeed, the action agenda and the research agenda are conceived as interdependent but separate. The research agenda is dependent on the genuine-ness of the action agenda but the action agenda can be independent from the interests of the research. For example, it would be possible to intervene as (that is, be seen by clients as) a consultant with expertise in the particular industry but have a research agenda concerned with organizational change. However, interventions will usually be informed, at least at a general level, by output from the research to date. Finally, as we shall discuss in the following section, our approach is concerned with a grounded approach to theory building and not with rigidly testable hypotheses or propositions.

Although the above discussion has sought to distinguish action research aimed at organizational research from other varieties, action researchers of all sorts pay a great deal of attention to the intricacies of research data and argue that traditional positivist research methods trivialize data collection. It is commonplace for those engrossed in all the related endeavours of action learning, action inquiry, action science, action research and participatory action research to be concerned, at least, with the validity of research data. There is a concern to collect more subtle and significant data than that which is easily accessed through traditional research methods. Those writing under these headings do offer important comment on data collection that is highly relevant to action research as we describe it. They also, similarly, have much of relevance to say about issues such as analysis or synthesis of data and about the presentation of results. Since many of these issues are of concern to all action-oriented researchers, this chapter will draw selectively from all of the traditions, when to do so is consistent with its outlook.

We do not formulate a definition of *RO-AR* here because we believe that to do so is likely to narrow its application as well as encourage wasteful definitional debate. Instead, we aim to capture its essence through an interlocking set of characteristics. Inevitably many of the characteristics of *RO-AR* apply equally to other research methods. Many of these characteristics are often ignored in the context of other varieties of action research, because they are seen either as not relevant or taken to be not attainable. Indeed, some are actually counter to the tenets of other forms of action research.

We indicated, in the first paragraph of the chapter, our starting point for an exploration of the nature and boundaries of action research. We asserted that the distinguishing feature of action research is the involvement by the researcher with members of organizations over matters that are of genuine concern to them and over which they intend to take action together with is a primary commitment by the researcher to advance a field of knowledge in a manner that has some general implications. The underlying argument of the chapter is that, while the above attributes are clearly important to action research, they do not alone give sufficient guidance about its nature. The chapter will, thus, both narrow down this initial description and elaborate on the detail of it.

Research-Oriented Action Research Characterized

The purpose of the previous sections was to build up a picture of the kind of action research with which we are concerned, by placing it in the context of its historical development and of other contemporarily-related approaches. With that as background, we now continue to enhance the picture by exploring its important characteristics in much greater depth.

We have divided our discussion of the characteristics of RO-AR for researching organizations into four sections. In this preliminary section we will discuss just one characteristic: the key feature that distinguishes action research from other forms of management research. The next two sections focus on RO-AR *outcomes* and *processes*. We focus on the features that distinguish it from studies of organizational processes and practices, and distinguish it from other forms of action research. The fourth section focuses on the nature of reporting in RO-AR.

We are seeking to identify a set of characteristics that can inform practically the research process. Ultimately, we shall re-group the characteristics so that we are able to commend the final grouped list of 15 characteristics as a checklist to guide thinking about the design and validity of RO-AR. However, we regard the discussion leading to the derivation of each characteristic as crucial to a proper understanding of its use in this way.

The characteristics presented are demanding for researchers, and each of them represents an ideal view of RO-AR. It is unlikely that any researcher will satisfactorily meet the requirements implied by the characteristics. Nevertheless, they are presented as important goals.

The Action Focus of Research-Oriented Action Research

Our first characteristic is encapsulated in our opening statement:

(i) *RO-AR* requires *both* an involvement by the researcher with members of organizations over matters that are of genuine concern to them and over which they intend to take action, *and* most importantly, a primary commitment of the researcher to advance a field of knowledge in a manner that has some general implications.

This is saying two things of importance: a declaration of intent to change creates organizational tensions that will reveal a particular form of data; and the researcher will use analysis of this data to both inform action and develop knowledge.

The Characteristics of Action Research Outcomes

Generality of the Contributions to Knowledge

In common with Lewin, many authors on action research stress the importance of the work being useful to the client. For example, Reason (1988: 12), when discussing knowledge in action, argues 'that knowledge is formed *in and for action* rather than in and for reflection' (emphasis added). Other authors stress that the development of 'local theory' – theory which applies in the specific context of the research – is a central feature of the approach (Elden 1979). The recently introduced journal – *Action Research* – reinforces this view of action research through its editorial statement: 'The aim of the journal is to offer a viable alternative to dominant "disinterested" models of social science, one that is relevant to people in the conduct of their lives, their organizations and their communities'. Many critics of action research reasonably take from the above authors the view that results can only be bounded tightly by context. We see RO-AR as an approach that can build and extend theoretical conceptualizations of more general use than implied above. We are not, of course, arguing for a level of generality that is devoid of context. Rather, we are arguing that the theoretical conceptualizations derived from *RO-AR* must be applicable significantly beyond the specific situation.

As suggested earlier, while most proponents of action research support its role for enhancing action, they tend to ignore the role of research for a wider audience. For the research-oriented practitioner there can be significant benefits that go beyond the moment of action towards some generality that is related to their expectation of implications for future situations. This circumstance provides the opportunity for collaborative or participatory research. For researchers, the generality will go even beyond this by having something to say about other contexts than that within which this specific practitioner operates. This may be through a recognition that the analysis of multiple cases can lead to more general (less local) theory (Huxham 2003; Marsick et al. 2003), but it may also be through consideration of how the results *could* apply to other situations.

Following from this discussion, our second characteristic expands the first and is:

(ii) *RO-AR* must have some *implications beyond those required for action or generation of knowledge in the domain of the project.* It must be possible to envisage talking about the theories developed in relation to other situations. Thus, it must be clear that the results *could* inform other contexts, at least in the sense of suggesting areas for consideration.

This means that the research process must permit the outcomes of the research to be couched in other than situation-specific terms. Thus, 'the name you choose [for a category] … must be a more abstract concept than the one it denotes' (Strauss and Corbin 1990: 67). It is important to avoid abstractness being meaningless and simply generating more unnecessary jargon and obfuscating the power of the research. The ability of the researcher to characterize or conceptualize the particular experience in ways that make the research *meaningful to others* is crucial. This usually means that the researchers must translate the reported research so that others can envisage it applied to different circumstances. It is this careful reporting process that may promote interest from other practitioners in how to understand situations they expect to find themselves in, and from researchers by informing their own theory development.

The Nature of the Contribution to Knowledge

It is the careful *characterization* of experiences that creates the theoretical constructs. This amounts to the theoretical conceptualization that may be carefully drawn out of *RO-AR*. Our third characteristic elaborates aspects of the second, and is thus that:

(iii) As well as being relevant to everyday life, *RO-AR* demands valuing theory, with the *elaboration and development* of theoretical constructs as an explicit concern of the research process.

This may appear to suggest a dichotomy between research aims and intervention aims, but in *RO-AR* these must, and can, be integrated (see, for example, Guba and Lincoln 1989). There is no reason why the two need to be seen as mutually exclusive. It is possible to fulfil the requirements of the client and at the same time consider the more theoretical implications, though it should be recognized that addressing these dual aims often means that more effort has to be put into achieving research results than would be the case with more conventional research paradigms. Research output can often be the direct converse of what is required for a client, where situation-specific terminology may be key to gaining ownership of the results. A client report that is different from the research output is often required.

The research output will also tend to be different from the immediate concerns of professional interventionists (that is, consultants) even though, as we suggested above, the latter may have an interest in generally transferable aspects of their interventions in order to enhance their professional expertise. Our fourth characteristic, below, relies on exploring this point further.

Interventionists who earn their primary living from doing so are inevitably engaged by immediate and incremental development of practice – 'how will I do better, work more effectively and efficiently, on my next project?'. Among other things, they will be interested in a transfer of tools, techniques, models and methods from one specific situation to another. This does demand the need to generalize from the specific, but this is most likely to be an incremental transfer from one specific context to another specific context. By contrast, observations about the specific situation will, *for the researcher*, raise broader questions that are of interest to a wider community who will work in a wider variety of contexts.

Researchers *qua* interventionists, as distinct from interventionists *qua* researchers, address themselves to a different primary audience. The 'interventionist as researcher' seeks to uncover general principles with implications for practice that can be shared between practitioners. The 'researcher as interventionist' seeks to talk to other researchers, and then, in addition, to other interventionists. Notably, both reflect a practical orientation and both are focusing on the generality of the ideas expressed (that is, they are extending them beyond the setting in which they were designed) but they are meeting different needs and (in the first instance) satisfying different audiences. There is a distinction here between concern with direct practice and the concern of *RO-AR* to *develop theoretical conceptualizations to inform a more reliable and robust development of practice*. Lewin's (1945: 129) much quoted, 'there's nothing so practical as a good theory' should be the action researcher's motto.

Despite this we consider the development of tools, techniques, models or methods as important expressions of the outcome of *RO-AR*. These can be excellent outcomes providing they embody a clear expression of a coherent and consistent set of theoretical constructs (that may draw upon and draw together theoretical constructs already well established through traditional research). Unfortunately, the embodiment is often implicit, if it exists at all. In such cases tools and techniques are devised as if they were products to be subjected to the 'hard sell' of claims that it 'works in practice' rather than as practical expressions of a set of theoretical conceptualizations. *RO-AR* demands that the research output explain the link between the specific experience of the intervention and the design of the tool or method – it is this *explanation which is a part of extending theory*. Thus:

(iv) If the generality drawn out of the *RO-AR* is to be expressed through the design of tools, techniques, models and method then this, alone, is not enough – the basis for their design must be explicit and shown to be related to the theoretical conceptualizations which inform the design and which, in turn, are supported or developed through *RO-AR*.

Theory Development from Research-Oriented Action Research

What kind of theoretical conceptualizations then are appropriate outputs of *RO-AR*? The notion of *drawing out* conceptualizations is important for *RO-AR* and suggests an approach to theory development which recognizes that, while the researcher always brings a pre-understanding (Gummesson 1991) – a starting position – to the situation, it is important to defer serious reflection on the role of this until the later stages of the project. This contrasts with most other research approaches, which are committed to establishing and setting out in advance the biases of the researcher.

In *RO-AR* the researcher needs to be committed to *opening up the frame* within which the research situation and data related to it is explored. To do so requires the researcher to have a commitment to the temporary suppression of pre-understanding. This decreases the likelihood of the researcher's theoretical stance closing off new and alternative ways of understanding the data and so extending theory. In addition, suppression of pre-understanding encourages generation of a holistic and complex body of theory, concepts and experience. By contrast, being explicit about pre-understanding tends to result in a neatly bounded and 'chunked' list of biases that inevitably, even if unintentionally, takes on the form of separable theoretical constructs.

Thus, for *RO-AR* it is important to move towards reflecting upon the role of pre-understanding *only as the theoretical conceptualizations begin to emerge*, rather than in advance of the research. This is a matter of emphasis and timing not a question about whether the researcher's own theoretical stance is influential and will need to be made explicit. This *is* influential and it *must* be made explicit, but its influence will be less constraining if made explicit later rather than earlier. It is important to note that this is neither the position taken by Glaser (1992), who argues for the complete suppression of pre-understanding, or, at the other extreme, of the approaches which assume a hypothesis testing approach for action research (Alderfer 1993).

By its very nature, *RO-AR* does not lend itself to repeatable experimentation; each intervention, or series of interventions, will be different from the last. Over time, it is possible to try out emerging theoretical constructs over and over again, but each

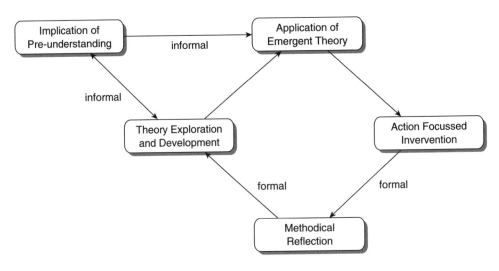

Figure 1.11.1   The cyclical process of research-oriented action research

context will be slightly different, so each time it will be necessary to adjust the interpretation of the theoretical constructs to the circumstances. *RO-AR* is, therefore, not a good vehicle for rigorous and detailed *testing* of theoretical constructs (at least in the traditional sense where explicit awareness of a theoretical pre-understanding is crucial).

On the other hand, interventions in organizations provide ideal opportunities for loose experimentation in the sense that they provide opportunities to try out complex and inter-linked conceptual *frameworks* that cannot be pulled apart for controlled evaluation of individual constructs. This is important in management and organization studies research where it is often the systemic nature of a uniquely interlocking set of theoretical constructs from many disciplines that makes *the body of* constructs powerful and useful. RO-AR is, at its best, therefore, importantly concerned with such *systemic relationships*, rather than with single theoretical constructs; the aim is to understand conceptual *frameworks* where each construct must be understood in the context of other related constructs.

Intervention settings can also provide rich data about what people do and say when faced with a genuine need to take action. These settings are, thus, likely to provide both new and often unexpected insights. They are settings that are much more

amenable to extending theoretical conceptualizations than to theory testing.

It would be unusual for *RO-AR* to deliver fundamentally new theories. Rather, the research insights are likely to link with, and so elaborate, the work of others. The areas in which research-oriented action researchers choose to work will often be influenced by their interest in the kinds of theoretical ideas that already exist (or do not exist) in the area. So each intervention provides an opportunity to revisit these ideas and develop them further. The overall process of extending knowledge is a *continuous cyclic process.* The combination of the developing conceptualizations from the research and implicit pre-understanding informs action. In turn, reflection upon the action informs the theory development.

There will be a close interconnection between what may emerge from the data (and indeed what data is used), and what will emerge from the implicit, and explicit, use of emerging theoretical constructs for driving the intervention (Figure 1.11.1).

Thus:

(v)   *RO-AR* is concerned with a system of *emergent theoretical conceptualizations,* in which theoretical constructs develop from a synthesis of that which emerges from the data and that which emerges from the use in practice of the body of theoretical constructs which informed the intervention and research intent.

And:

(vi) Theory building, as a result of *RO-AR*, is incremental, moving through a cycle of 'extending theory-to-action-to-critical reflection-to-developing theory' from the particular to the general in small steps. This cyclical process allows convergence over time to knowledge that is increasingly more useful for both action and understanding.

This contrasts with Lewin's argument for hypotheses to be empirically testable. The very richness of the insights and the relative complexity of the conceptual framework which *RO-AR* should produce suggest that it will usually be difficult to design experimental situations in which we could be clear about confirmation or disconfirmation (Sandford 1981; Eden 1995; 2000). We are not arguing that hypothesis testing is impossible or improper, but rather that the alternative presented here is likely to be more productive for organizational research when using action research.

The differentiating value of *RO-AR* can, therefore, be seen to be in the *development and elaboration of theoretical conceptualizations from practice by exploring emergent and continuously changing theoretical constructs*. As an aside, developing 'grounded theory' (Glaser and Strauss 1967; Glaser 1992; Strauss and Corbin 1998) is a well recognized, but only one of many, example of emergent theory building (Eisenhardt 1989; Stake 1995; Ladkin 2004). Whereas much management research demands the advanced identification of a precise research question, *RO-AR* demands a fuzzy research question that is changed and elaborated through the action research cycle – sometimes called the 'hermeneutic cycle' (Gummesson 1991).

The Pragmatic Focus of Research-Oriented Action Research

Most of the often referred to writers on action research, including Lewin, demand that action research be pragmatic. This is not a criterion that distinguishes *RO-AR* from consultancy, but one that justifies the use and value of *RO-AR* rather than other forms of research.

If the practicality criterion is taken seriously, this might be interpreted as suggesting that prescriptive theory is more appropriate than descriptive theory. This is a false dichotomy. Descriptive theory can, and does, seriously influence the actions of the consumer of the research because it does (not necessarily intentionally) highlight the important factors the consumer should be concerned about. For example, descriptive insights about why things go wrong are suggestive of actions that might be taken to avoid problems in similar situations. By implication, descriptive theory also draws attention away from those aspects of the situation that are not included in the description. It is thus, by implication, prescribing one way of accounting for a situation rather than another (Allison 1971). However, if descriptive theory is to be the output of *RO-AR* it is important that its practical implications be recognized even if these are presented implicitly. This means that the researcher must recognize that the language, metaphors and value orientation used to present the theory will seriously influence the understanding of the theory in relation to the future thinking and actions of the consumer of the research.

Thus, our seventh characteristic is that:

(vii) What is important for *RO-AR* is not a (false) dichotomy between prescription and description, but a recognition that description will be prescription, even if implicitly so. Thus, presenters of *RO-AR* should be clear about what they expect the consumer to take from it and present it with a form and style appropriate to this aim.

The Characteristics of Research-Oriented Action Research Processes

Designing Research-Oriented Action Research

In order to be effective in *RO-AR*, it is clearly important to be credible as an interventionist. A researcher thus needs to pay attention to developing a competent intervention style and process. However, while consultancy and facilitation skills are an important part of the *RO-AR* toolkit, they do not, in themselves, justify the activity as *research*. Much more fundamental *is the need to be aware of what must be included in the process of consulting to achieve the research aims*. This, of course, implies being aware of the research aims themselves – which we have argued will be fuzzy.

This demand is, thus, not intended to imply that the researcher should have a precise idea – or pre-understanding – of the nature of the research outcome at the start of any intervention, but rather, a strategic intent for the research project. Indeed, since we are almost always concerned with inductive theory-extending research, the really valuable insights are often those that emerge from the consultancy process in ways that cannot be foreseen. Whilst it is legitimate for an action researcher to enter a consultancy interaction with no expectation about what the specific research output will be, it is crucial that an *appropriate degree of reflection* by the researcher is built into the process, and reflection has to be guided by a research intent. This process must include some means of recording both the reflection itself and the method for reflecting.

RO-AR, therefore, demands a high degree of *self-awareness* or *reflexivity* (Alvesson and Sköldberg 2000) in knitting together the role of the consultant with that of researcher. In addition, researchers must recognize that they not only have the roles of researcher and interventionist, but – because of their role as interventionists – are also a part of the situation that is being researched. For sociologists this role is more akin to what Adler and Adler (1987) present as a 'complete member researcher' in contrast to the lesser involved roles of an 'active member researcher' or 'peripheral member researcher'. For them, however, complete membership means 'going native' in a manner that does not match the role of an action researcher as facilitator/consultant. It is also important to consider the role that the client or other participants play in the generation and extension of the theoretical conceptualizations. There are many different levels at which they may be involved, ranging from 'pure subjects' whose aim is to get the benefits of the intervention but have no involvement with the research, to 'full collaborating partners' in the research. Exactly how the roles of the action researcher and the practitioners are played out at any level of involvement can vary, but they need to be thought about and understood.

A consciousness of the roles to be played by the researcher and the participants and a process of reflection and data collection should be designed into any RO-AR programme. This is a separate activity from – though often connected to – the intervention itself (Figure 1.11.1). At the least, this demands that extensive amounts of time away from the intervention setting and the 'hands-on' problems are devoted to reflecting critically about

process and data in relation to research issues. Glaser and Strauss (1967) suggest an appropriate approach to this process of methodical reflection in the context of their Grounded Theory methodology. However, for our purposes, the exact nature of the reflection is relatively immaterial (though we may debate the validity of any particular one); what is crucial is that the process exists explicitly. An extended discussion of some alternative design choices for data collection and their implications for reflection and for the range of validity of the results can be found in Huxham and Vangen (2003).

Thus, our eighth characteristic is that:

(viii) *RO-AR* requires a high degree of systematic method, orderliness and reflexivity in reflecting critically about, and holding on to, the research data and the emergent theoretical outcomes of each episode or cycle of involvement in the organization.

Furthermore, and our ninth characteristic,

(ix) For *RO-AR*, the processes of exploration of the data – rather than collection of the data – in the detecting of emergent theoretical constructs and the development of existing theoretical constructs, must either be replicable or, at least, capable of being explained to others.

Thus, the outcome of data exploration cannot be defended by the role of intuitive understanding alone; any intuition must be informed by a *method of exploration*. Put simply, this means that compared to 'everyman' as researcher, researchers who expect to earn a living from their research must adhere to explicit standards that are accepted by at least a part of the research community.

Towards the closing stages of a project, the design of *RO-AR* must also acknowledge an important extension of the cycle depicted in Figure 1.11.1. This is concerned with the process of explication about pre-understanding and the role of writing about research outcomes in a formal manner for theory development (see Figure 1.11.2). Writing about research outcomes is a 'way of "knowing" – a method of discovery and analysis' (Richardson 2000: 923). It is a *formal process* of integrating the records of methodical reflection, prior theory development and the explication of pre-understanding. At this stage the use of pre-understanding is more formal than the reciprocal influence between the (deliberately suppressed) implicit pre-understanding and theory exploration and development that has been occurring throughout the project (Figure 1.11.1). This

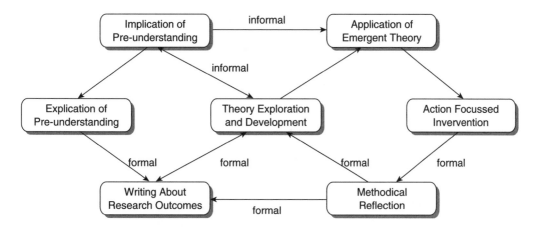

Figure 1.11.2   The latter stages of an action research project

writing process continues to inform theory exploration and implicit pre-understanding. Also, in this way, action researchers use this cycle to acknowledge to themselves and the consumers of the research that the research process and outcomes were influenced by the researcher's particular pre-understanding.

(x)   The full process of *RO-AR* involves a series of interconnected cycles, where writing about research outcomes at the latter stages of an *RO-AR* project is an important aspect of the exploration and development of new and existing theoretical constructs. The process combines the processes of explicating pre-understanding and methodical reflection to explore and develop theoretical conceptualizations formally.

The Validity of Research-Oriented Action Research

Adhering to Action Research as a Coherent Paradigm

We have argued above that action research as intervention does not lend itself to repeatable experimentation; indeed its distinctive role is played when such experiments are inappropriate. The results of action research, thus, lie open to criticism if their validity is judged *solely* by the traditional criteria of positivist social science. Under these circumstances it is likely to fail.

Reliable research into management and organizations may be less valid when the traditional tests of validity are applied. There often may be a trade-off between validity and reliability (Kirk and Miller 1986). This is because reliable data about organizational life is predominantly qualitative, situational and is collected as the opportunity arises. Traditional tests of validity, therefore, cannot be used when data is collected in this manner. Thus, systematic method, as well as critical reflection and triangulation, becomes particularly important.

Action researchers, therefore, need to be keenly aware of the key issues in the validity of *RO-AR* and that a designed action research process must address these issues. In this section, we consider what we see as the most important of these.

Adhering to the ten characteristics above is a necessary *but not sufficient* condition for the validity of *RO-AR*. Without attention to each of these characteristics, an intervention cannot be considered as research at all. These characteristics may thus be thought of as concerned with the *internal validity* of the research *as RO-AR*. By contrast, the remaining topics that we discuss are concerned with *external validity*. That is, they are concerned with the degree to which the results may both be *justified as representative* of the situation in which they were generated and have *claims to generality*.

(xi)   The dependability of *RO-AR* is a function of both internal validity of the research *as RO-AR* (as encapsulated in characteristics (i)–(x)) and external validity of the research in terms of the knowledge claims it makes.

Theory in Use

Much of action research's validity comes from the theoretical constructs developed being not simply 'grounded in the data' in Glaser and Strauss's (1967) sense, but also being *grounded in action*. One of the most persuasive reasons for using *RO-AR* is that, when practitioners do not have to commit to real action and to creating a future that they will inhabit, any data gained from them is inherently unreliable.

The role of the past, of history and of the significance of established patterns of social relationships and of 'negotiated order' (Strauss and Schatzman 1963; Eden and Ackermann 1998) in determining organizational behaviour cannot be over-estimated (Vickers 1983). *Reliable* data, and hence theories, about both past and future aspects that influence the way in which people change a situation are much more likely to emerge from a research process which is geared to action than from more traditional approaches. This is because it is possible to track what participants actually say and do *in circumstances that really matter to them*, as compared with what they might say hypothetically, or do in controlled circumstances (as for example in the use of students as research subjects acting as if participants in an organization) (Alvesson 2003). Using Argyris and Schon's (1974) terms, an action research setting increases the chances of getting at participants' 'theories-in use' rather than their 'espoused theorie'. The change process provides a forum in which the articulation of complex or normally hidden factors is likely to emerge.

However, it is important to recognize that there will be forces pushing against, as well as in favour of, the articulation of theories-in-use in action research settings. Most obviously, most interventions are designed to create organizational change and so will challenge the *status quo* and thus generate a political dynamic. Inevitably some people will anticipate being disadvantaged by the proposed changes and it is unlikely that the interventionist will gain full trust from all parties (Argyris and Schon 1991). *The politics of organizational change are thus a force acting against getting straightforward (in the sense of being simple to interpret) data from all concerned.* The case example of *RO-AR* in Huxham and Vangen (2003) illustrates this point. Here it became very difficult to disentangle data about the politics of the innate situation from data about the usefulness of new tools for managing collaboration, which was the intended focus of the research.

Yet there are other arguments, not directly linked to the reliability issue, in favour of the action orientation. An important one is the notion that the best way of learning about an organization is by attempting to change it. The very process of change is likely to reveal factors which would not have been unearthed in a stable environment. *The process of change forces a dialectic – a contrast – which helps articulation.* For example, Fineman's (1983) research on unemployed executives probably provided more useful data about the nature of employment than it did about unemployment. It was the dialectical experience of unemployment that enabled an understanding and so articulation about the role employment played in the lives of the research subjects.

In summary, we are arguing that while there may be some forces acting against easily getting reliable data through action research, *the method is likely to produce insights which cannot be gleaned in any other way*. This means – as with any kind of research – that it is important to consider explicitly where the kinds of weaknesses and strengths discussed above are likely to occur in any particular research situation. However, it also means that:

(xii) It is difficult to justify the use of *RO-AR* when the same aims can be satisfied using approaches (such as controlled experimentation or surveys) that can demonstrate the link between data and outcomes more transparently. Thus in *RO-AR*, the reflection and data collection process – and hence the emergent theoretical constructs – are most valuably focused on the aspects that cannot be captured by other approaches.

This, in turn, suggests that having the knowledge about, and skills to apply, method and analysis procedures for collecting and exploring rich data is essential. A detailed introduction to methods for the analysis of rich data is beyond the scope of this chapter, but in Huxham (2003) we have outlined in detail one approach which uses the causal mapping software, *Decision Explorer*. *Decision Explorer* provides a powerful tool for 'playing' with the structure and content of qualitative research data (Bryson et al. 2004). It is particularly useful because of its ability to link directly to content analysis using *NVivo* (see also http://caqdas.soc.surrey.ac.uk/ for additional information on software for the analysis of quantitative data). The added advantage of using computer software of this sort is that it can provide a continuous record of the process of play and exploration and so of the emerging theoretical construct development. Other forms of analysis have been extensively outlined by others. For example, the kinds of approaches suggested by Miles and Huberman (1994), Strauss and Corbin (1990), Glaser (1992) and Symon and Cassell (2004) fulfil most of the requirements for a systematic and methodical exploration of data. None of these methods are easy to use; they all require craft skills both in applying the analysis to the data and, in drawing out valuable insights and conceptualizations. As with all craft skills, they are developed as much through experience as through training.

Triangulation

In the course of the preceding discussion, we have highlighted some concerns about getting at 'truths' of situations, rather than 'the truth'. Argyris et al. (1985) also emphasize the difficulty of ensuring that the theories identified by the research process are thoroughly developed or the only theories that could have been developed. Our third topic, therefore, focuses on *triangulation*.

Triangulation of research data refers to the method of checking its validity by approaching the research question from as many different methodological, data, investigator and theoretical angles as possible (Denzin 1989). Triangulation is always important in understanding uncertainty in interpretation or measurement. In part, this is an argument for a multi-method approach to research (Brewer 1989; Brannen 1992). Denzin (1978a, b) and Fielding and Fielding (1986) provide a comprehensive argument for the use of multiple studies where each study acts as a cross-check on others, and so the process of developing reliable conclusions is enhanced.

Triangulation to check the validity of data is as important in *RO-AR* as in other forms of research. However, action research provides *also* a uniquely different interpretation of the concept of triangulation. Typically different understandings in action research arise from different settings for data collection. For example, reactions to change provided in the formal setting of the office are not the same as those provided over lunch or after work. These different perspectives are not competing but provide alternative meanings to the data that nevertheless need to be triangulated with respect to emerging insights. Exceptionally, therefore, action research provides an opportunity to seek out triangulation

between (i) *observation* of events and social processes, (ii) the *accounts* each participant offers in different settings, and (iii) the changes in these accounts and interpretation of events *as time passes* (Haré and Secord 1976). From *these* three perspectives *the data are not expected to triangulate* (agree). Indeed we may be more surprised if they do agree than if they do not given the deliberate attempts at discovering multiple views. This procedure 'underlines the possibilities of multiple, competing perspectives on how organizations are and might be' (Jones 1987: 45). Importantly, a lack of triangulation acts as an effective dialectic for the generation of new concepts. The focus is, therefore, on building richer conceptualizations about 'what could be' rather than on checking out 'what is'.

Thus, triangulation has a different significance for action research compared with using triangulation only as a cross-checking method. Similarly, action research provides the opportunity for *cyclical* data collection through exploiting more continuous and varied opportunities than is occasioned by more controlled research. The chaos and the changing pace and focus of action research are used as a virtue. Thus:

(xiii) In RO-AR, the opportunities for triangulation, including those that do not offer themselves with other methods, act as a dialectical device that powerfully facilitates the incremental development of theoretical constructs should be exploited fully and reported.

The Role of History and Context

The previous two topics have been largely about external validity in the specific project context. The fourth topic focuses on the issues of generalizing beyond that. It concerns the need to understand and project the role of history and context in deriving research outcomes (Pettigrew 1985; 1990). Given that action research generally deals with a single or small number of intervention settings (and hence incurs all the issues inherent in case study research (Stake 1995):

(xiv) The history and context for the intervention(s) must be taken as critical to the interpretation of the likely range of validity and applicability of the results of RO-AR. Where theoretical constructs develop over many cases and often many years the range of validity will be extended.

Identification of the crucial variables that determine the particularity of the context is non-trivial and it is likely that individuals with different experiences and aims would focus in different areas. Discovering history and its relevance is, in any case, problematic. History, and context, are differently defined by different actors in the situation and by different observers; historians have always recognized the contribution of bias, selectivity and interpretation. Nevertheless, even given these difficulties, *a concern* to understand *the role of* context, and the different interpretations of it, is a most important requirement of *RO-AR*. Indeed, working with *the selective nature of different accounts* of how a history of the organization, of the individuals and their relationships with one another, and of the wider context within which the research took place, is as important as paying attention to their role.

The Nature of Reporting in Research-Oriented Action Research

In addressing issues in doing *RO-AR* we have highlighted the role of writing about research outcomes on a number of occasions. In particular, characteristic (x) emphasizes that this is an integral part of the research process: '... an important aspect of the exploration and development of new and existing theoretical constructs'. Comments about the nature and content of that writing are embedded in five of the other characteristics:

- 'It must be possible to envisage talking about the theories developed in relation to other situations' (characteristic (ii));
- 'The design of tools, techniques, models and method must be explicit and shown to be related to the theoretical conceptualizations which inform the design' (characteristic (iv));
- 'Presenters of *RO-AR* should be clear about what [prescriptively] they expect the consumer to take from it and present it with a form and style appropriate to this aim' (characteristic (vii));
- 'The processes of exploration of the data ... must ... be at least, *capable of being explained to others*' (characteristic (ix)); and
- 'The history and context for the intervention(s) [are] critical to the interpretation of the likely range of validity and applicability of the results of *RO-AR*' (characteristic (xiv)).

These suggest issues that should be addressed in any rigorous reporting of the research output from *RO-AR*. However, they do not represent the whole of the writing task. What matters also is that the style in which the output is couched reflects the nature and boundaries of the validity that is claimed. For example, action research data can generally only support a 'what could be' rather than a 'what is' conceptualization (Elden and Chisholm 1993b) so the phraseology used should suggest this. It is easy to fall into the trap of making claims framed in language that is over ambitiously assertive relative to the data on which they are based.

Our final characteristic thus is:

(xv) Reporting outcomes from *RO-AR* requires a style of expression that implies a generality of relevance but which reflects the nature and boundaries of validity that can reasonably be claimed. Reporting generally should include discussion of at least: the research design including the data analysis process, the history and context and the implied prescriptions.

The demands we have set out in the first 14 characteristics mean that it is unlikely that *RO-AR* can be written about fully in anything shorter than a book type format, although, aspects of the research can be adequately captured through articles. Indeed, many of the examples given in this chapter have been reduced to articles by ignoring full reports on the action research process. Relative to 'straightforward' positivist research there will always be more to say about: the incremental nature of the theory development; research method in overall terms as well as the detail of data exploration method; history and context; and implications of theory for practice. This is more material than can be contained easily within the confines of an article. It is not sufficient simply to state that the research was undertaken using an action research methodology. As we have sought to illustrate above, there are so many different interpretations of action research that such a statement is meaningless.

In 1994/5, when we were drafting this chapter for the first edition of the book, we were interested in the difficulty we were having in finding written exemplars of *RO-AR* that explicitly acknowledged action research. It appeared as though most *RO-AR* was published indirectly or not explicitly. Typical examples included presentation of methods, tools and techniques without explanation of the action research process that produced them (for example, Checkland 1981; Eden et al. 1983; Nutt and Backoff 1992; Bryson 2004; Ackermann et al. 2005) and the presentation of carefully argued theoretical constructs with the action research data used as examples to illustrate these but no acknowledgement of the role of the data in deriving the constructs (for example, Mangham 1979). A particularly interesting example for indirectly reporting the outcomes of action research was used in the book called 'The Carpetmakers' by Jones and Lakin (1978). Here one of the authors was an interventionist and the other author was one of the managers in the client organization – that made carpets. The book is written and presented as if it were a novel, and the content makes no reference to the roles played by the authors. And yet the authors conducted a form of action research that enabled them to develop a theory of the 'four orders of administration' that is exposed in the middle section of the book. The reader is given no indication of the nature of the method and nature of the research; indeed it is never clear whether the story is of a real case, even though it is clear that the theory derives from the story. The use of journalism – and 'faction', to report research is not necessarily misplaced – it provides an entertaining and engaging way of learning about research outcomes.

None of these examples meet fully the demands set out above in the 15th characteristic. Nevertheless, we know from personal contact with the authors, that the published outcomes are the result of well-constructed RO-AR. Since writing the early version of this chapter, we have deliberately set out to meet the requirements discussed above when writing about the outcomes of our own research. On some occasions a direct imposition of these has proven to be possible and appropriate (for example, Huxham and Vangen 2000; Vangen and Huxham 2003). On other occasions we have judged that the best form of expression for exemplifying the relationship between the development of theory and practice has been to use another calculated device to reflect the requirements. This involved cross-linked accounts of an inter-disciplinary conceptual framework, many 'real' vignettes and methods and tools (Eden and Ackermann 1998).

Comment

This chapter has sought to describe, and set in context, a form of research-oriented action research

that is appropriate for research in organizational studies. The standards we have set for this to be considered as rigorous research are far from simple to achieve. RO-AR is an imprecise, uncertain and sometimes unstable activity compared to many other approaches to research so understanding the methodological issues involved in RO-AR in practice is difficult and must be expected to take time and experience. Enacting the standards in practice demands holistic attention to all of the issues. Given the complexity and pressure of the real world RO-AR setting, this provides a major challenge. As we suggested at the beginning of this chapter, *it is probably not an achievable challenge*, though we hope this will not deter researchers either from using RO-AR or from trying to achieve the standards. We know that our own research never fully satisfies the standards we have set. What matters is having a sense of the standards that make for good RO-AR and evaluating the research in relation to them.

Action research, of the type we present here, is also challenging for two further reasons: (i) the uncertainty and lack of control creates anxiety for anyone other than confident and experienced researchers; and (ii) doing the action in RO-AR demands experience and understanding of methods for consultancy and intervention. For these reasons, we generally advise new researchers not to use RO-AR unless they are already experienced consultants or managers.

We have set out a framework for undertaking research through 15 characteristics. We have argued that each of them is an important aspect of good RO-AR. Each of these represents, in effect, a test against which RO-AR may be judged. We have presented them so that the arguments to support them follow naturally and gradually build up one another. However, in now representing them as a whole we have set them out into the following clusters so that users of this type of action research can identify with a 'check-list' relating the key tasks (see Figure 1.11.3):

- those that establish some differentiation from other types of research and are, therefore, almost *definitional*;
- those that imply directly or indirectly the *method* of RO-AR;
- those that discuss the nature of RO-AR *output*; and
- those that relate to issues of *validity*.

The clusters are not mutually exclusive, and the relevant parts of the characteristic have been italicized.

Relating to DEFINITION (differentiation from other research)

(i) *RO-AR* requires both *an involvement by the researcher with members of organizations over matters that are of genuine concern to them and over which they intend to take action*, and most importantly, a primary commitment of the researcher to advance a field of knowledge in a manner that has some general implications.

(v) *RO-AR* is concerned with a system of *emergent theoretical conceptualizations*, in which theoretical constructs develop from a synthesis of that which emerges from the data and that which emerges from the use in practice of the body of theoretical constructs which informed the intervention and research intent.

Relating to METHOD

(i) *RO-AR* requires both an involvement by the researcher with members of organizations over matters that are of genuine concern to them and over which they intend to take action, and most importantly, a primary commitment of the researcher to *advance a field of knowledge in a manner that has some general implications.*

(iii) As well as being relevant to everyday life, *RO-AR* demands valuing theory, with *the elaboration and development of theoretical constructs as an explicit concern of the research process.*

(v) *RO-AR* is concerned with a system of emergent theoretical conceptualizations, in which theoretical constructs develop from a synthesis of that which emerges from the data and that which emerges from the use in practice of the body of *theoretical constructs which informed the intervention and research intent.*

(vi) Theory building, as a result of *RO-AR*, is incremental, *moving through a cycle of <extending theory-to-action-to-critical reflection-to-developing theory> from the particular to the general in small steps.* This cyclical process allows convergence over time to knowledge that is increasingly more useful for both action and understanding.

(viii) *RO-AR* requires a *high degree of systematic method, orderliness and reflexivity* in reflecting critically about, and holding on to, the research data and the emergent theoretical outcomes of each episode or cycle of involvement in the organization.

(x) The full process of *RO-AR* involves *a series of interconnected cycles, where writing about research outcomes at the latter stages of an RO-AR project is an important aspect of the exploration and development of new and existing theoretical constructs.* The process combines the processes of explicating pre-understanding and methodical reflection to explore and develop theoretical conceptualizations formally.

(xiii) In *RO-AR*, the *opportunities for triangulation, including those that do not offer themselves with other methods, act as a dialectical device* that powerfully facilitates the incremental development of theoretical constructs should be exploited fully and reported.

Relating to OUTPUT

(ii) *RO-AR* must have some implications beyond those required for action or generation of knowledge in the domain of the project. *It must be possible to envisage talking about the theories developed in relation to other situations.* Thus, it must *be clear that the results could inform other contexts*, at least in the sense of suggesting areas for consideration.

(iv) If the generality drawn out of the *RO-AR* is to be expressed through the design of tools, techniques, models and method then this, alone, is not enough – *the basis for their design must be explicit and shown to be related to the theoretical conceptualizations which inform the design* and which, in turn, are supported or developed through *RO-AR*.

(vii) What is important for *RO-AR* is not a (false) dichotomy between prescription and description, but *a recognition that description will be prescription, even if implicitly so.* Thus, *presenters of RO-AR should be clear about what they expect the consumer to take from it and present it with a form and style appropriate to this aim.*

(xiv) *The history and context for the intervention(s) must be taken as critical to the interpretation of the likely range of validity and applicability of the results of RO-AR.* Where theoretical constructs develop over many cases and often many years the range of validity will be extended.

(xv) Reporting outcomes from *RO-AR* requires *a style of expression that implies a generality of relevance but which reflects the nature and boundaries of validity that can reasonably be claimed.* Reporting generally should include discussion of at least: the research design including the data analysis process, the history and context and the implied prescriptions.

Relating to VALIDITY

(ix) For *RO-AR, the processes of exploration of the data* – rather than collection of the data – in the detecting of emergent theoretical constructs and the development of existing theoretical constructs, *must either be replicable or, at least, capable of being explained to others.*

(xi) The dependability of *RO-AR* is a function of both internal validity of the research *as RO-AR* (as encapsulated in characteristics (i)–(x)) and external validity of the research in terms of the knowledge claims it makes.

(xii) It is difficult to justify the use of *RO-AR* when the same aims can be satisfied using approaches (such as controlled experimentation or surveys) that can demonstrate the link between data and outcomes more transparently. Thus, in *RO-AR, the reflection and data collection process – and hence the emergent theoretical constructs – are most valuably focused on the aspects that cannot be captured by other approaches.*

(xiii) In *RO-AR, the opportunities for triangulation, including those that do not offer themselves with other methods, act as a dialectical device* that powerfully facilitates the incremental development of theoretical constructs should be exploited fully and reported.

Figure 1.11.3   The Fifteen Characteristics in Four Clusters: definition, method, output, and validity

This chapter is an attempt to reinforce the value of action research as a legitimate and rigorous research method, and to suggest standards which will encourage 'careful analytical researchers' who are also concerned with intervention and action.

References

Ackermann, F., Eden, C. and Brown, I. (2005) *The Practice of Making Strategy.* London: Sage.

Adler, P.A. and Adler, P. (1987) *Membership roles in field research.* Newbury Park, CA: Sage Publications.

Alderfer, C. (1993) 'Emerging developments in action research', *Journal of Applied Behavioural Science,* 29: 389–492.

Allison, G.T. (1971) *Essence of Decision: explaining the Cuban missile crisis.* Boston: Little Brown.

Alvesson, M. (2003) 'Beyond neopositivists, romantics and localists: A reflexive approach to interviews in organizational research', *Academy of Management Review,* 28: 13–33.

Alvesson, M. and Sköldberg, K. (2000) *Reflexive Methodology New Vistas for Qualitative Research.* London: Sage.

Argyris, C. (1995) 'Action science and organizational learning', *Journal of Managerial Psychology,* 10: 20–6.

Argyris, C. and Schon, D.A. (1974) *Theories in Practice.* San Francisco: Jossey Bass.

Argyris, C. and Schon, D.A. (1991) 'Participatory action research and action science compared: A commentary', in W.F. Whyte (ed.), *Participatory action research.* London: Sage. pp. 85–96.

Argyris, C., Putnam, R. and Smith, D.M. (1985) *Action Science.* San Francisco: Jossey-Bass.

Ayas, K. (2003) 'Managing action research for rigour and relevance', *Human Resource Planning,* 26: 19–29.

Bate, P. (2000) 'Synthesizing research and practice: Using action research approach in health care settings', *Social Policy and Administration,* 34: 478–93.

Bhatt, Y. and Tandon, R. (2000) 'Citizen participation in natural resource management', in P. Reason and H. Bradbury (eds), *Handbook of action research.* London: Sage. pp. 301–6

Blenkin, G.M. and Kelly, A.V. (2001) *Action research for professional development.* London: Paul Chapman.

Bonnet, M. and Cristallini, V. (2003) 'Enhancing the efficiency of networks in an urban area through socio-economic interventions', *Journal of Organizational Change Management*, 16: 72–83.

Brannen, J. (1992) *Mixing Methods: Qualitative and Quantitative Research*. Aldershot: Avebury.

Brewer, J. (1989) *Multimethod research: a synthesis of styles*. Newbury Park: Sage.

Brown, D. and Tandon, R. (1983) 'Ideology and political economy in inquiry', *Journal of Applied Behavioural Science*, 19: 277–94.

Brown, T. and Jones, L. (2001) *Action research and postmodernism*. Buckingham: Open University press.

Bryden-Miller, M. (1997) 'Participatory action research: Psychology and social change', *Journal of Social Issues*, 53: 657–66.

Bryson, J. (2004) *Strategic Planning for Public and Nonprofit Organizations*, 3rd edn. San Francisco: Jossey-Bass.

Bryson, J., Ackermann, F., Eden, C. and Finn, C. (2004) *Visible Thinking: Unlocking Causal Mapping for Practical Business Results*. Chichester: Wiley.

Checkland, P. (1981) *Systems Thinking, Systems Practice*. Chichester: Wiley.

Checkland, P. and Holwell, S. (1998) 'Action research: its nature and validity', *Systems Practice*, 11: 9–21.

Chein, J. (1948) 'The field of action research', *The American Psychologist*, 3: 43–50.

Chisholm, R. (1998) *Developing network organizations: Learning from practice and theory*. Reading, MA: Addison-Wesley.

Clark, A.W. (1975) *Experimenting with organizational life*. New York: Plenum.

Clark, P.A. (1972) *Action research and organizational change*. London: Harper & Row.

Coch, L. and French, J.R.P.J. (1948) 'On overcoming resistance to change', *Human Relations*, 1: 512–33.

Coghlan, D. and Bannick, T. (2001) *Doing Action Research in Your Own Organization*. London: Sage.

Collier, J. (1945) 'United States Indian administration as a laboratory of ethnic relations', *Social Research*, 12: 275–6.

Corey, S. (1953) *Action research to improve school practices*. New York: Bureau of Publications, Columbia University.

Curle, A. (1949) 'A theoretical approach to action research', *Human Relations*, 2: 269–80.

David, M. (2002) 'Problems of participation: The limits to action research', *Journal of Social Research Methodology*, 5: 11–18.

Denzin, N. (1978a) *The Research Act: a theoretical introduction to sociological methods*. New York: McGraw-Hill.

Denzin, N. (1978b) *Sociological Methods: a source book*, 2nd edn. New York: McGraw-Hill.

Denzin, N.K. (1989) *The Research Act*, 3rd edn. Englewood Cliffs, NJ: Prentice Hall.

Dick, B. (2002) 'Postgraduate programs using action research', *The Learning Organization*, 9: 159–70.

Dickens, L. and Watkins, K. (1999) 'Action research: Rethinking Lewin', *Management Learning*, 30: 127–40.

Eden, C. (1995) 'On evaluating the performance of 'wideband' GDSS's', *European Journal of Operational Research*, 81: 302–11.

Eden, C. (2000) 'On evaluating the performance of GSS: furthering the debate', *European Journal of Operational Research*, 120: 218–22.

Eden, C. and Ackermann, F. (1998) *Making Strategy: the journey of strategic management*. London: Sage.

Eden, C., Jones, S. and Sims, D. (1983) *Messing About in Problems*. Oxford: Pergamon.

Eisenhardt, K.M. (1989) 'Building theories from case study research', *Academy of Management Review*, 14: 532–50.

Elden, M. (1979) 'Three generations of work democracy experiments in Norway', in C. Cooper E. Mumford (eds), *The quality of work in eastern and western Europe*. London: Associated Business Press. pp. 226–57.

Elden, M. and Chisholm, R. (1993a) 'Emerging varieties of action research: Introduction to the special issue', *Human Relations*, 46: 121–42.

Elden, M. and Chisholm, R. (1993b) 'Special issue on action research', *Human Relations*, 46: 121–298.

Elden, M. and Levin, M. (1991) 'Cogenerative learning: bringing participation into action research', in W.F. Whyte (ed.), *Participatory action research*. Newbury Park, CA: Sage. pp. 127–42.

Emery, F. and Thorsrud, E. (1969) *Democracy at work*. Leiden: Martinus Nijhoff.

Emery, F.E. and Trist, E.L. (1963) 'Sociotechnical systems', in C.W. Churchman (ed.), *Management science: Models and techniques*. Vol. 2. London: Pergamon. pp. 83–97.

Fielding, N.G. and Fielding, J.L. (1986) *Linking data: The articulation of qualitative and quantitative methods in social research*. Beverly Hills, CA: Sage.

Fineman, S. (1983) *White Collar Unemployment: impact and stress*. London: Wiley.

Fisher, D. (2003) *Personal and organisational transformations through action inquiry*. Lydney, Gloucestershire: Harthill group.

Gibbons, M., Limoges, C., Nowotny, H., Schwartzman, S., Scott, P. and Trow, M. (1994) *The New Production of Knowledge: the dynamics of science and research in contemporary societies*. London: Sage.

Glaser, B.G. (1992) *Basics of Grounded Theory*. Mill Valley, CA: Sociology Press.

Glaser, B.G. and Strauss, A.L. (1967) *The Discovery of Grounded Theory*. Chicago: Aldine.

Greenwood, D.J. and Levin, M. (1998) 'Action research, science and the co-optation of social research', *Studies in Cultures, Organizations and Societies*, 4: 237–61.

Guba, E.G. and Lincoln, Y.S. (1989) *Fourth generation evaluation*/Newbury Park, CA: Sage.

Gummesson, E. (1991) *Qualitative methods in management research*. Newbury Park, CA: Sage.

Haré, R. and Secord, P.F. (1976) *The Explanation of Social Behaviour*. Oxford: Blackwell.

Hodgkinson, G. (2001) 'Facing the future: the nature and purpose of management research re-assessed', *British Journal of Management*, 12: S1–80.

Huxham, C. (2003) 'Action research as a methodology for theory development', *Policy and Politics*, 31: 239–48.

Huxham, C. and Vangen, S. (2000) 'Leadership in the shaping and implementation of collaboration agendas: how things happen in a (not quite) joined up world', *Academy of Management Journal*, 43: 1159–75.

Huxham, C. and Vangen, S. (2003) 'Researching organizational practice through action research', *Organizational Research Methods*, 6: 383–403.

Jones, R. and Lakin, C. (1978) *The Carpetmakers*. London: McGraw-Hill.

Jones, S. (1987) 'Choosing action research', in I.L. Mangham (ed.), *Organisation Analysis and Development: a social construction of organisational behaviour*. London: Wiley. pp. 23–46.

Kember, D. (2000) *Action learning and action research: Improving the quality of teaching and learning*. London: Kogan Page.

Kemmis, S. and McTaggart, R.E. (1988) *The action research planner*. Victoria: Deakin University.

Kirk, J. and Miller, M.L. (1986) *Reliability and validity in qualitative research*. Beverly Hills, CA: Sage.

Ladkin, D. (2004) 'Action research', in C. Seale, G. Gobo, J.F. Gubrium and D. Silverman (eds), *Qualitative Research Practice*. London: Sage. pp. 537–48.

Lewin, K. (1943) 'Forces behind food habits and methods of change', *Bulletin of the National Research Council*, CVIII: 35–65.

Lewin, K. (1945) 'The Research Center For Group Dynamics at Massachusetts Institute of Technology', *Sociometry*, 8: 126–13.

Lewin, K. (1946) 'Action research and minority problems', *Journal of Social Issues*, 2: 34–46.

Lewin, K. (1947) 'Frontiers in group dynamics: channel of group life: social planning and action research', *Human Relations*, 1: 143–53.

Mangham, I.L. (1979) *The Politics of Organizational Change*. London: Associated Business Press.

Marshall, J. (2000) 'Self reflective inquiry practices', in P. Reason and H. Bradbury (eds), *Handbook of Action Research*. London: Sage. pp. 433–9.

Marsick, V.J., Gephart, M.A. and Huber, J.M. (2003) 'Action research: Building the capacity for learning and change', *Human Resource Planning*, 26: 13–18.

McTaggart, R. (1998) 'Is validity really an issue for participatory action research?', *Studies in Cultures, Organizations and Societies*, 4: 211–36.

Miles, M.B. and Huberman, A.M. (1994) *Qualitative Data Analysis: an expanded sourcebook*, 2nd edn. Thousand Oaks: Sage Publications.

Nutt, P.C. and Backoff, R. (1992) *Strategic Management of Public and Third Sector Organizations*. San Francisco: Jossey-Bass.

O'Connor, G.C., Rice, M.P., Peters, L., and Veryzer, R.W. (2003) 'Managing interdisciplinary, longitudinal research teams: Extending grounded theory-building methodologies', *Organization Science*, 14: 353–73.

Ottosson, S. (2003) 'Participation action research: A key to improved knowledge of management', *Technovation*, 23: 87–94.

Peters, M. and Robinson, V. (1984) 'The origins and status of action research', *Journal of Applied Behavioural Science*, 20: 113–24.

Pettigrew, A.M. (1985) *The Awakening Giant*. Oxford: Blackwell.

Pettigrew, A.M. (1990) 'Longitudinal field research on change theory and practice', *Organization Science*, 1: 267–92.

Putnam, W. (1999) 'Transforming social practice: An action science perspective', *Management Learning*, 30: 177–87.

Raelin, J. (1997) 'Action learning and action science: Are they different?', *Organizational Dynamics*, 25: 21–35.

Reason, P. (ed.) (1988) *Human Inquiry in Action*. London: Sage.

Revans, R.W. (1977) 'Action learning and the nature of knowledge/learning', *Education and Training*, 19: 318–20.

Revans, R.W. (1978) 'Action learning and the nature of knowledge/learning', *Education and Training*, 20: 8–11.

Revans, R.W. (1982) *The Origins and Growth of Action Learning*. Bickley, Kent: Chartwell-Bratt.

Richardson, L. (2000) 'Writing: A way of knowing', in N.K. Denzin and Y.S. Lincoln (eds), *Handbook of Qualitative Research*, 2nd edn. Thousand Oaks, CA: Sage. pp. 923–48.

Sandford, N. (1981) 'A model for action research', in P. Reason and R. Rowan (eds), *Human Inquiry. A Sourcebook of New Paradigm Research*. Chichester: Wiley. pp. 173–82.

Schein, E. (1995) 'Process consultation, action research and clinical inquiry: Are they the same?' *Journal of Managerial Psychology*, 10: 14–19.

Stake, R.E. (1995) *The Art of Case Study Research*. London: Sage.

Strauss, A. and Corbin, J. (1990) *Basics of Qualitative Research*. London: Sage.

Strauss, A. and Corbin, J. (1998) *Basics of Qualitative Research*, 2nd edn. London: Sage.

Strauss, A. and Schatzman, L. (1963) 'The hospital and its negotiated order', in E. Friedson (ed.), *The Hospital in Modern Society*. New York: Macmillan. pp. 147–69.

Stringer, E.T. (1999) *Action Research*. Thousand Oaks, CA: Sage.

Stringer, E.T. and Genat, W.J. (2003) *Action Research in Health*. Englewood Cliffs, NJ: Prentice Hall.

Susman, G. and Evered, R. (1978) 'An assesment of the scientific merits of action research', *Administrative Science Quarterly*, 23: 582–603.

Symon, G. and Cassell, C. (2004) *Essential guide to qualitative methods in organizational research.* London: Sage.

Tedlock, B. (2000) 'Ethnography and ethnographic representation', in N. Denzin and Y. Lincoln (eds), *Handbook of qualitative research.* Thousand Oaks, CA: Sage. pp. 455–86.

Thomas, J. (1993) *Doing critical ethnography.* Newbury Park, CA: Sage.

Thorsrud, E. (1970) 'A strategy for research and social change in industry: a report on the industrial democracy project in Norway', *Social Science Information,* (October): 65–90.

Tomal, D.R. (2003) *Action research for educators.* Lanham, MD: Scarecrow Press.

Torbert, W.R. (1976) *Creating a community of inquiry: conflict, collaboration, transformation.* New York: Wiley.

Torbert, W.R. (1991) *The Power of Balance: transforming self, society, and scientific inquiry.* Newbury Park, CA: Sage.

Torbert, W.R. (2000) *Transforming social inquiry, transforming social action.* Amsterdam: Kluwer.

Trist, E. and Bamforth, K.W. (1951) 'Some social and psychological consequences of the Longwall method of coal getting', *Human Relations,* 4: 3–38.

Vangen, S. and Huxham, C. (2003) 'Enacting leadership for collaborative advantage: Dilemmas of ideology and pragmatism in the activities of partnership managers', *British Journal of Management,* 14: S61–76.

Vickers, G. (1983) *The Art of Judgement.* London: Harper and Row.

Whitehead, J. (1994) 'How do I improve the quality of my management?', *Management Learning,* 25: 137–53.

Whyte, W.F. (1991) *Participatory Action Research.* Newbury Park, CA: Sage.

Winter, R. and Munn Goddings, C.E. (2001) *Handbook for Action Research in Health and Social Care.* London: Routledge.

Yin, R.K. (2002) *Case study research: design and methods,* 3rd edn. Thousand Oaks, CA: Sage Publications.

Zuber-Skerrit, O. (2002) 'The concept of action learning', *The Learning Organization,* 9: 114–24.

Zuber-Skerritt, O. (1992) *Action research in higher education: examples and reflections.* London: Kogan Page.

1.12 The Philosophy of the Social Sciences in Organizational Studies

STEPHEN P. TURNER

The philosophy of science, the philosophy of social science, and organizational studies have a long and complex history of interaction. Some of this interaction has been direct, between philosophical conceptions of science and organizational thinkers, some mediated through sociology and those metatheoretical debates that have influenced the sociology of organizations. Several key figures in the history of organizational theory, notably Churchman and Schon, were philosophers by training who carried their philosophical concerns into their thinking about organizations. In what follows, I will give an overview, necessarily very incomplete, of the main phases in this history, and draw some conclusions about themes that reappear in the history.

The Science of the Social and the Engineering Metaphor

The origin of the philosophy of the social sciences itself is to be found in a series of closely related problems that became particularly salient in the period after the French Revolution. The Enlightenment's critique of tradition and ambitious account of rationality and the rationality of social institutions contain elements that proved to be less than fully compatible. One was the ideal of what we might now speak of as social engineering by recourse to reason alone, which Mill later ridiculed as the application of the geometric method to politics. The events following the French Revolution deeply damaged this idea of a new social order grounded in reason which all citizens would acknowledge. When 'reason' was put into practice what ensued were revolutionary tribunals, a ruling Directory in which the revolutionaries sent one another to the guillotine for disagreements which they characterized as betrayals of the revolution and

ultimately Bonapartism and restoration. The sheer violence of the terror served to discredit the program of the rational grounding of society, the notion of human malleability, and the idea that society was merely a system of irrational customs which could be rearranged at will, or that politics could be replaced by some sort of calculus of consent (Manuel 1962; Manuel and Manuel 1966).

One reaction to the French Revolution took the form of recognition that however artificial the institutions of society might appear, they were better understood as parts of a natural object with hidden and unknown elements that resisted intervention and coercive change. The new preferred metaphor was the organism, and with this the characteristic problems of the philosophy of social science emerged. What sort of object is society? How is it like an organism? Does it have its own vital purpose or emergent properties, or are those properties totally dependent on the property of the individuals who compose it? What are the best and most basic data relevant to an understanding of society? What is the significance of statistical regularities and the stability of statistics such as suicide rates? Are there laws or fundamental social factors that cause societies to have particular properties? Are there natural categories of society, such as particular forms of society at particular stages of development or particular types of society? What is the motive force for social development? What sorts of interventions in society can be justified and will produce predictable progressive results, if any? What is the relevance of the self-understanding of individuals, their subjectivity, and their beliefs about their own actions and the world they inhabit? Is the world causally impervious to their beliefs, as the natural world is or is it in some sense the product or partial product of their beliefs and intentions?

In a peculiar way the history of organizational studies is a kind of re-enactment of this primal situation. 'Scientific management' was 'scientific' in the specific sense that had a great deal in common with many reform movements of the early twentieth century in that the ideal model of science was engineering (Nelson 1980). The engineering metaphor was not used by the French revolutionaries themselves, but oddly enough, in the aftermath of the revolution not only did the idea of engineering become a cultural touchstone with the emergence of steam power (Serres 1982), the utopian social projects of thinkers like Saint-Simon that emerged out of the wreckage of the French revolution seized on this metaphor. The utopians were not only technophilic, but closely associated with the prominent engineering schools of the day. Saint-Simon's followers were pivotal in the construction of railways in Egypt and the like early in the first half of the nineteenth century, and it was the scientifically oriented mill owner and reformer Owen who established the New Harmony community in Indiana, turned from technology innovation in his mills to social innovation, and became known as the father of cooperation. He converted Holyoake, the son of an engineer (who was fond of the term 'system') who pioneered the first success at co-operativism at Rochdale.

There is a complex but interesting line of descent from the socialist schemes of the early nineteenth century to scientific management, and also to the critics of scientific management. In the middle part of the century, especially in the period after the American civil war, a variety of industrial schemes involving 'cooperation' and profit-sharing were proposed, each of which was premised on the idea that sufficiently well designed incentives would lead to greater productivity and more profits for the workers to share, thus having the best of the competitive system without the evils. The movement of the 1870s to establish labour statistics bureaus was closely associated with this cooperative movement, and avidly reported on cooperative industrial experiments such as the Rochdale plan (which in 1844 made the breakthrough of dividing profits in proportion to purchases made from the cooperative [cf. Giddings 1886]), and profit-sharing schemes. Many other experiments followed. Scientific Management, devised by Taylor as an attempt to improve productivity so as to achieve labour peace through plenty, was one of them.

The engineering achievements of the nineteenth century such as the conversion from sail to steam, construction of railroads, building of the great bridges of steel, and so forth, only enhanced the power of the engineering metaphor. The theory that extended engineering into the human realm followed from the idea that the things of the social world, such as cities and work organizations, were themselves artifacts, things made by men, and therefore, as one social reformer, Kellogg, put it, open to being properly engineered and designed (1912: 4). These ideas were known to later theorists. In an interesting note Simon pointed out that the idea of society as artificial is present in Ward, who concluded that the idea is therefore inevitably 'ethical'. Simon accepted 'artificial' but denied that the study of society required ethical assumptions ([1945]1959: 251).

Engineering had developed largely independently of the advances of science in the nineteenth century, and, as a consequence, contemporary conceptions of the relation of science and engineering characteristically stressed the idea that enough was known to perform tasks of engineering without further advances in science. This idea was carried over into the social realm: it was believed by social reformers that 'standards', a common engineering concept, already were understood sufficiently to be applied in the design of social institutions. Of course, engineering standards have a history largely rooted in practical experience. Standard practice in the construction of elevators, for example, involved doubling the size of the elevator cable for the sake of safety. The development of the steam engine was the major engineering problem of the early nineteenth century. The devices were prone to explosion, and this produced a practical problem of identifying and adhering to standards of thickness and quality of the walls of the boilers in their manufacturing.

With this background, it is not at all surprising that Taylor, the creator of scientific management and thus modern organizational theory, should have been an engineer, presented his ideas to engineers, and presented them in terms of ideas about standards, limits, the capacities of the human body, and so forth. Organization-making and boiler-making thus came to be seen as analogous processes, involving an analogous kind of empirical inquiry in which the goal was the setting of standards for the various stressed elements of an assembly. Understanding work processes and the designing of work processes, symbolized and epitomized by the assembly line itself, represented an important conceptual breakthrough.[1] But the idea of organizations as fundamentally cooperative persisted: in the first half of Barnard's *Functions of the Executive* of 1938, which I will discuss shortly, he uses the term cooperation and cooperative system as the basic characterizing concept.

From Fatigue to the Hawthorne Experiments

The thread running through early 'scientific' studies of organization was fatigue. Fatigue was a key engineering concept, in effect the limit of productive capacity, a limit not unlike, in its significance for early organizational studies, the bursting of boilers for the engineering of steam engines. Understanding fatigue and limiting fatigue but maximizing output in the face of the limits of fatigue were central problems of early organizational analysis, not only in Taylorism, whose time and motion studies were a practical engineering model for dealing with the problem of fatigue, but among the new psychologists whose origins in biology and the experimental tradition attuned them to fatigue as the 'natural' element of the work process and the one with the greatest effects on output, as well the one which is easiest to measure and easiest to experiment on.[2]

Harvard University, in its psychology department in particular, which was dominated by such figures as the introspectionist James, was involved with studies of fatigue, led by Münsterberg (1913) who brought the Germanic experimentally based style of psychology to the psychology department. Oddly enough, experimentally based psychology too was based on introspection or at least self-reporting, and fatigue, though it could be measured very indirectly through output, was viewed as a physiological factor which, like other psychophysical attributes, was directly accessible only through self-reports. This too was central to the German psychological tradition, which took psychologizing and the Weber-Fechner law as its paradigmatic achievement.

The 'philosophy of science' that went along with this tradition emphasized both the experimental, the measurable, and the subjective or self-reported aspects of natural phenomena, and saw its goal as fitting curves to experimental data to produce laws. The method of experiment was claimed to be a significant advance over the method of surveys of workers that had preceded this work. As Münsterberg (1913: 239) said of one of these surveys:

a few careful experimental investigations could lead further than the heaping up of material from men who are untrained in self-observation and in accurate reports, and above all are accessible to any kind of suggestion and preconceived idea.

The paradigm changed in the 1920s with the advent of behaviourism. Behaviourism in the form advanced by Watson (Danziger 1990) was a multifaceted programme, but the key doctrine was his rejection of mental entities and even mental processes that could not reasonably be directly associated with measurable behavioural inputs and outputs. This represented an attack on the subjective elements of the fatigue tradition in that fatigue as an explanation of outputs was merely another problematic mental variable which could be got rid of in favour of behavioural and material inputs and measurable behavioural outputs.

The indirect influence of behaviourism on organizational studies was substantial. It shifted the focus from the natural but subjectively experienced variables of fatigue to measurable inputs and outputs, and in a sense liberated the psychologists to consider all inputs and outputs whether or not they could be plausibly related to such subjective phenomena as fatigue. But the behaviourist paradigm also puts a much higher emphasis on prediction. If the subjective, experimental variable of fatigue was no longer the object of analysis, and the object was behavioural inputs and outputs, the only way a variable could earn credibility was through its capacity to predict. Prediction became an independent standard, and in a sense also an obstacle to understanding organizational processes, since the variables in the behavioural paradigm that could be successfully employed to predict were removed from any subjective experience of either workers or managers, and were also difficult to connect with the interventions available to managers. The effect of removing even the limited aspect of the subjective experience of fatigue had the consequence of omitting the subjective experience of workers entirely and relegating such concepts as morale to the scrapheap of the immeasurable. We will see the consequences of this change in Simon's aptly named *Administrative Behavior* of [1945]1959, which incorporated the behaviourist suspicion of lived experience, but expanded this suspicion to organizational processes themselves, which he attempted to reduce to regularities that could be accounted for by 'mechanisms'.

The behaviourist paradigm had its enemies within psychology, and they were particularly strong in the setting of organization studies. Mayo was the leading intellectual figure in this group. He was committed to a model in which morale and productivity depended on what he called human relations, which is to say the aspects of the work experience which neither behaviourism nor the fatigue tradition had attempted to assess. In *The Human Problems of an Industrial Civilization*, he developed a critique of the 'fatigue' and 'monotony' traditions ([1933]1960: 1–52) based largely on the Hawthorne experiments.

The Hawthorne experiments, which were nominally engaged with a 'boiler-making' problem, namely the limitation of fatigue through the careful manipulation of such variables as lighting, involved essentially the same paradigmatic conception of scientific proof and evidence. The quantities being measured were all, or to the extent that they could be, natural, and this included blood pressure and vascular skin reaction measures. The curve fitting involved 'work-curves' of actual productivity. There was extensive interviewing, however, and differences between what was reported and what was actually done (Roethlisberger and Dixon [1939]1961: 426–28) proved to be a clue to the social processes of output control. Mayo concluded that the idea that understanding organizations entirely as machines, machines made either of biological, fatigue ridden parts or of behaviourally manipulable individuals, was fundamentally mistaken; the mistake was a matter of seeing organizations as entirely artificial or machine-like.

Human relations, morale, and so forth were qualities of social groups, located somewhere beyond the individual and beyond the individual's performances of particular specified tasks, but this supraindividual domain needed to be theorized, and this meant it needed to be understood in terms of existing scientific exemplars or models of something other than machines. Mayo (1960: 140), and as it happens a larger group of Harvard thinkers, found the concept of 'organism' a model for talking about these things. Mayo (1960: 116) employed the Durkheimian language of anomie and Pareto's idea that, as Mayo puts it,

> Human collaboration in work ... has always depended for its perpetuation on the evolution of a non-logical social code which regulates the relations between persons and their attitudes to one another. Insistence on a merely economic logic of production – especially if the logic is frequently changed – interferes with the development of such a code ... and the formation of a social code at a lower level and in opposition to the economic logic.

L. J. Henderson and Homeostasis

As a result of the Bayway refinery (Elizabeth, NJ) industrial accident of 1924 (Gibb and Knowlton 1956: 541–2), Standard Oil of New Jersey granted an immense amount of money to Harvard University to study industrial accidents (Buxton and Turner 1992). The biologist Henderson was one of the leading participants in this grant, and he was much influenced by one of the dominant ideas in 1930s Harvard science, namely the idea of homeostasis and systems, as well as by the sociological writings of Pareto, whose expression 'non-logical', as we have seen, appears in Mayo. Whereas Mayo was not a 'scientifically' oriented thinker, Henderson was, and he supplied a developed methodological defense of this approach. Cannon (1939) was the influential local exemplar on homeostasis and his work was eagerly taken up by social scientists who were funded by the Industrial Hazards Project, such as the young Talcott Parsons, who participated in a circle led by Henderson which studied the work of Pareto (cf. Henderson 1927). Cannon and Pareto were made to provide a solution to the theoretical problems that had been thrown up by the Hawthorne experiment, the human relations approach, and so forth. The lessons from the failures of scientific management, behaviourism, and the fatigue school were that organizations were not entirely artificial, that the subjective, especially the social experiences of workers and managers, could not be ignored, and that productivity was closely related to what traditionally had been understood as morale. The lesson of Münsterberg was that workers couldn't be trusted to report on themselves, their motivations, and emotions. The phenomena of anomie and resistance arose from a level deeper than immediate subjective experience. Pareto supplied the missing link in this analysis. Pareto's conception of society was at once mentalistic and organic. He was, despite being an eminent economist, an anti-rationalist in his social theory, arguing that the rationalizations that people offer for their behaviour were deeply misleading about their actual motivations, which were for the most part the result of stable emotional reactions which could be understood only socially, that is to say in terms of the particular social settings in which they were manifested, or as Mayo put it, the social code.

For Pareto, social life was relatively impervious to manipulation and was, moreover, reactive, so that attempts at manipulation typically produced protective responses. This could be understood organically, in terms of the homeostasis of the social organism, but more important, it made sense of the phenomena that the Hawthorne experiment had identified, such as the resistance, beyond certain limits, to attempts at improving productivity and the evident connection between both resistance and morale to the social solidarity of groups, especially work groups.

The idea that complex organizations were vast organisms in which managers could at best intervene therapeutically was strongly suggested by this new way of thinking, and Henderson's most important managerial disciple, Barnard, took up these lessons enthusiastically. Barnard was an executive in New Jersey Bell and brought to his writings a wealth of personal experience as well as quite strong views on management and management research. He had a collection of telling anecdotes, such as one in which the operator of a telephone exchange who could see through the window that her home was burning followed her New Jersey Bell training to the letter and did not leave her post in order to save her home, thus illustrating the intensively strong pull of the code of telephone operators, a pull that could only be understood organically and in terms of powerful sentiments rather than mechanically.

Henderson was not a methodologist or philosopher of social sciences, but he *had* a philosophy of social science, which was important to the development of these ideas. Central to it was the notion of 'conceptual schemes'. He emphasized the idea that science necessarily went beyond the data and needed organizing ideas, but that these ideas or conceptual schemes were to be evaluated on the basis of their utility. He said of Hippocrates, 'his conceptual scheme worked for a long time and worked well. This is, in fact, the test of a conceptual scheme and the only test: it must work well enough for the purpose of the moment' (Henderson 1970: 76). And he warned against believing in the 'truth' of conceptual

schemes, against premature systematization, and indeed about an excessive concern with methodology and philosophy of science (Barber 1970: 13).

Henderson admired men of affairs who could bridge theory and practice – the basis of his esteem for Barnard (Barber 1970: 16). And Henderson was enamoured of ideas about equilibria, which were central to his approach to the problem of the complexity of the social sciences, which he characterized by comparison to the work of the American mathematical physicist Gibbs. Gibbs had cut through the complexities of chemical situations involving heterogeneity and equilibria by focusing on the major thermodynamic factors, deriving key relationships, then adding terms to deal with particular chemical differences, thus bringing a whole domain of phenomena under the laws of thermodynamics for the first time. Henderson believed that Pareto had done the same thing in his social theory by focusing on the persistent, the resistive, and the equilibria-producing facts of sentiment, and by ignoring the surface rationalizations that made up the subjective experience of participants. Pareto was, in this respect, similar to Freud, as Henderson himself noted ([1935]1967: 21). The image of organizations this equilibrium concept served to support made the non-artificial aspects of the organization, the informal structure, more important than the artificial formal arrangements, and broadened the concept of organization to that of an organism. This was the source of later functionalist organizational sociology, and one can see works like Gouldner's *Wildcat Strike* (1954) as its heirs. The lines of succession were tangled, but there were many. Parsons was turned into a sociologist by his contact with the Henderson circle, as was Homans, and the publication of Parsons's own first attempt at constructing a conceptual scheme was subsidized by the industrial hazards grant.

Positivism and Behavioural Science

The idea of system and associated ideas of function, which appear both in Barnard's title *The Functions of the Executive* (1938) and in the anthropology and sociology of the period, square neither with the model of deductive theory nor with the idea of rigorous experimental and survey empirical inquiry based on measurement that took hold in the behavioural sciences during this period. Henderson had nothing against quantification or the idea of theoretical social science. But Pareto's sentiment or 'residues' were not susceptible to the kind of mathematical formulation that Gibbs was able to produce.

There were, however, many ways forward, and some of them were about to get a boost from new forms of funding, the arrival of Logical Positivism on the American academic scene, and especially from World War II, which created a new set of research organizations with new relationships, leading to both postwar 'behavioural science' and to operations research as a model for abstract thinking that held the promise of mathematization. The war itself led to funding of a substantial amount of research on morale as a wartime exigency. The Likert scale, which provided a highly generic and simple technique for generating numbers about attitudes of all kinds, was a product of this. And, especially in the bombing survey done under military auspices at the end of World War II and the American soldier (Stouffer et al. 1949), large scale interdisciplinary behavioural science research, complete with a complex division of labour, emerged. In the postwar period a significant expansion of the behavioural sciences occurred based in part on these wartime innovations (Converse 1987).

The vast investment in the behavioural sciences in the postwar period by the Carnegie and Ford Foundations focused on a new idea of 'behavioural science' which was to be anchored primarily by experimental social psychology, and which established the social psychology experiment and survey research involving measurement of attitude as the standard models of non-economic social science. These models as well as the image of science as a collection of established findings, found its way into the business school setting very quickly.

The increased need for teaching materials, especially during the expansion of universities in the 1960s led to the construction of a textbook conception of organizations, which in turn strongly influenced subsequent research. It also led to a new relation between theory and practice. McGregor formulated Theory X and Theory Y (McGregor 1960), theory (X) being that managers operate by threat and individuals are motivated by reward and punishment and a second theory (Y) that they are motivated in accordance with Maslow's hierarchy of needs, and used this distinction to understand these theories as elements of the manager's tool kit rather than final

truths that scientific inquiry could decide between. Berelson and Steiner's compendium of research findings, *Human Behavior* (1964), which was published while Steiner was a professor of psychology at the Business School of the University of Chicago, presented the behavioural sciences in a similar way.

The philosophy of science, which had been, up to World War II, only sporadically taught and institutionalized within philosophy departments now came into its own as a subdiscipline of philosophy, and it indeed became its dominant subdiscipline. Its pronouncements were taken seriously by writers in and across the behavioural sciences. Philosophy of science of the postwar period was itself a product of a process of intellectual consolidation and the creation of a standard view. Works that had been circulated as notes or manuscripts for many years were gradually published, but more importantly an important series of textbooks, such as Braithwaite's *Scientific Explanation* (1953) and seminal articles such as Hempel and Oppenheim's (1948) paper on explanation ([1948]1965) were widely read outside of philosophy and to a considerable extent set the bar for management science as well as the central disciplines of behavioural science. The later writings of the positivists, especially Braithwaite (1953: 319–41), but also Nagel (1961: 520–35), who participated in an influential cross-disciplinary seminar on the methodology of the social sciences with Lazarsfeld and Merton at Columbia, accommodated, within their own framework, functional explanations, and even Hempel (1965) attempted to provide an analytic restatement of functional explanations which had the effect of legitimating these kinds of explanations as 'scientific' and thus retrospectively legitimating the tradition in management theory which treated the organization as an organism, particularly an organism devoted to its self-protection. The next step was to make these ideas digestible and useful to managers.

Operations research was the most unusual, and in the view of some recent commentators (Mirowski 2004), most consequential product of the war. The approach originated as a way of improving weapons systems by breaking them into processes which could be abstractly modelled by mathematical formulae, which allowed the consequences of decisions (for example, to use fewer aircraft to search for submarines) to be predicted and strategies to be revised. In the United States, most of the few mathematical logicians (who were also involved in philosophy of science and later in social science) were employed by the Rand Corporation to work on these kinds of analytic problems, as well as larger human systems problems. Operations research did not depend on traditional social science 'data', measurement, or substantive research. Statistical regularities in the form of inputs and outputs were identified, and then the mechanisms were modelled as stochastic equations. There was little interest in the 'truth' of these formulae. They were simply predictive devices. The idea was that highly abstract models based on little data and little knowledge of the connecting mechanisms were as good or better as predictors than descriptively rich theory and data, and perhaps even better, because in a mathematically defined 'system' one could much more readily predict the effects of changes in one system state on the other outputs of the system simply by virtue of the mathematical character of the linkages.

One of the central figures in both operations research and the philosophy of science was Churchman. Churchman was a cofounder of the journal *Philosophy of Science*. He had been trained philosophically as a student of Singer, whose 'experimental' philosophy of science Churchman had earlier attempted to apply to topics such as municipal planning. In 1958 he was appointed Professor of Business Administration at the University of California Berkeley, where he wrote influential books on the systems approach. As the systems idea expanded to corporate notions like 'open system' (Katz and Kahn [1966]1978) these ideas came to be seen as a vindication or fulfillment of the insufficiently 'scientific' functionalism of the 1950s and the functionalist idea of the nature of organizations. But the new model of the organization that was salvaged was, implicitly, based on the core implication of operations research – that if organizational processes could be predicted and manipulated without paying attention to such things as informal organization, these things effectively did not exist, or were not important. This was an implication that Herbert Simon, who was deeply influenced by his own experience with operations research, drew in *Administrative Behavior* ([1945]1959).

Enter Kuhn

Nagel's *Structure of Science* (1961), was the apogee of the Logical Positivist movement, its best and last significant textbook. Kuhn's *The Structure of Scientific Revolutions* was published in 1962, in a book series controlled by logical positivists. In a few years *The Structure of Scientific Revolutions* had effectively ended logical positivism as a philosophical movement and dramatically undermined its influence in behavioural sciences. It also produced a language for understanding the sometimes violent generational conflict between the enemies of the behavioural science path to science and the advocates of a wide variety of other approaches.

Kuhn's basic idea was drawn, through Kuhn's mentor James Bryant Conant, straight from the Harvard tradition of talking about conceptual schemes. But where Conant, and Henderson before him, had understood the history of science as a succession of conceptual schemes that were replaced when they no longer were useful or no longer fit the data and the problems of a science, Kuhn, more radically, held that the data and problems of a science were themselves relative to paradigms. What counted as data, in short, was a matter of one's paradigm. So was what counted as measurement.

What Kuhn called 'normal science' was puzzle-solving within a paradigm, a term which was understood to refer to an amalgam of conceptual scheme, exemplary experiments, background assumptions about what sorts of evidence counts most heavily, what sorts of inferences from data are admissible, and so forth. When a 'revolution' occurs, and a new paradigm replaces the old, all of this changes. But because the very standards of evaluation and the conceptual language of science are part of the paradigm, there can be no 'rational' or external evaluation of the conflict between paradigms. Indeed, strictly speaking, they are not comparable with respect to truth – they are 'incommensurable'. The concepts they use, even if they appear to be the same, are not the same – 'motion' in Aristotle and Newton refers to differently conceived things. Thus the replacement of one paradigm by another is not a matter of calm rationality. It is a situation of revolutionary confusion, failure of communication, and generational conflict.

What happened to 'reality' in all this? In a word, it became 'internal' to paradigms. What was 'real' was something that could be determined within a paradigm, but not outside it. And in this, Kuhn was a legitimate successor of logical positivism, which had long missed the concept of reality as metaphysical. The dismissal of realism and the traditional opponent of realism, namely sense data theory, by the logical positivists occurred in a famous paper by

Carnap in 1930 in which he argued that there was no actual scientific question that could be verifiably settled with respect to the preferability of what he called an 'object' language over a 'sense data' language (Carnap 1967), meaning that when observation sentences in the form of object claims were used to support theories in science, the same support could be given by observational sentences which involved only sense data. If there was no reason in principle to prefer the one to the other, the question of whether the world was 'real' apart from sense data was metaphysical, uninteresting, and insoluble. The implication of Kuhnianism that the sciences were based fundamentally on *a priori* commitments that could not be justified had the effect of extending this argument to the facts of science themselves: whether atoms are real now became a matter of an apparently arbitrary choice not of sense data or object language but of a paradigm.

For many philosophers, this was one step too far, and in the 1970s a reaction set in, especially around the question of how does science succeed? Putnam, in a series of papers (1976), argued that the success of science could be understood as essentially analogous to the success of a scientific experiment. The success of science is a fact that needs to be explained, and the only plausible explanation of its success (and its continuing and increasing success) was that science was in accordance with reality. Realism in a sense that is related to this became important again in philosophy of science as a result of these considerations. But the 'explaining success' argument was a double-edged sword that cut in a different direction for the social sciences, which could not boast a dramatic record of increasing success. Instead, organization studies and management theory looked, in the light of Kuhn, like a collection of paradigm-like movements, none of which had any realistic hope of becoming dominant. And the explosion of approaches in sociology in the 1960s meant that new approaches – culture, network analysis, phenomenology, feminism, and so on – were available to be applied to organizations. Each of these was paradigm-like. So there was a strong motivation to understand this new situation, and if possible to resolve it.

From Krupp to Burrell and Morgan

Management theorists had begun to respond to these issues very early. An important influence on

Kuhn was one of the early critics of logical positivism, Hanson (1958), whose *Patterns of Discovery* (1958) had been an attack on the logical positivist notion of data and on the theory-observation distinction. This was taken up by Krupp in his *Pattern in Organization Analysis* (1964[1961]), which drew from Hanson the lesson that 'what an organization is' depends on what one sees an organization as, and that there was no stable reality to organizational life apart from the theories and perspectives that had been developed about them. He provided a critical history of organization theory making this point.

The critique of positivism in organizational studies, although it had many targets, was primarily a critique of the kind of organizational analysis that was dominant in the 1960s, which had allied itself with (and justified itself by appealing to) logical positivism. This included such thinkers as Pugh and sociologists of organizations such as Blau. Blau had flirted with various sociological perspectives, such as 'exchange' and functionalism, but by the 1970s was talking about 'laws' of organizations. He focused on quantifiable dimensions of organizations, such as 'differentiation', which he supposed could be the subject of predictive scientific laws (Blau 1970; cf. Turner 1977; Donaldson 1985). Because positivism of this sort accepted the perspective of management, typically defining organizations in terms of efficiency or of function, and 'measured' what were the artificial creations of management, such as standards of control and the dimensions of organization charts, and correlated these measures with one another, it was caught up in the problematic of the artificial and the natural. Artifactual features of the organization, creations of management, were treated as though they were natural facts governed by natural laws.

This was vulnerable to a critique which insisted on the dependence of organizations on the beliefs and ideas of individuals. The critics brought arguments derived from Krupp and Kuhn together with a different philosophical tradition, phenomenology. One of the important philosophical sources for phenomenological critics of the managerial organizational conception was a body of writings on 'typification' in the 1950s and 1960s. The literature was the result of an attempt by Natanson (1963) to confront positivism with the phenomenological critique in the form of a debate over categories or types. The question of the status of typologies was marginal to both phenomenology and positivism, but proved to be a fruitful point of contact. The positivists located the problem of types in the general context of concept formation in relation to scientific theories, stressing the idea that typifications were subordinate to larger tasks of prediction and control, and were the business of the analysts or scientists, and had a claim to our respect as being valid that rested on their theoretical and predictive utility. Schutz, the protagonist of phenomenology, located the process of typification in interactions between individuals and in their own attempts to make sense of the world and one another: in the course of making sense of one another, individuals came to share typifications (Schutz [1954] 1963). This meant that social categories, the categories in terms of which social interaction and societal life occurred, and which were meaningful to the individuals involved, were constructed by the agents themselves, and accessible through an analysis of their phenomenological experience of the world. Types were thus in a strict sense subjective or intersubjective in character.

This had a natural application to organizational life, which was after all conducted in terms of categories of an obviously artificial kind in terms of which meaning was conferred on actions, particularly the actions of managers and subordinates. From the point of view of phenomenology, organizations seemed to be no more than the sum total of these typifications, and the organization itself was not an organism-like being, but a socially constructed typification in terms of which people interacted. The decade of the 1960s thus began with Krupp's perspectivism, in which different theories of organization constructed their object in different ways, and ended with an important book by Silverman (1970), who argued that the work of constructing done by organizational participants themselves was the source of the object-like character of organizations. The subject of organization studies, the organization, was disappearing.

The Reaction

Two developments in organization studies responded to this state of affairs. One was 'realism', which attempted to recapture the idea of organizations as real objects. The other was an attempt to make sense of organization studies as a multi-paradigm discipline, destined to a state of permanent perspectivalism. In Britain, the term 'realism' was associated with Critical Realism, a movement of thinkers whose first concern was the social sciences and who were primarily Marxist in orientation. Their basic intuition was that positivist research methodology stayed on the surface of social reality and failed to adequately depict and theorize the underlying social reality which determined the surface relationships that could be accessed through ordinary statistical investigation. The more acerbic critics of this sort of realism suggested that realism was a refuge for purists who wished to preserve their theory even if all of the predictions, in the case of Marxism the prediction of the proletarian revolution, had failed to be borne out by events. Nevertheless, quite robust traditions of realist writings developed especially in sociology in Britain which has had a more direct influence on organizational studies than realism in traditional philosophy of science has had.

The philosophical side of this form of realism in many ways presaged the writings of Hacking, to whom I will turn in the next section, and the movement developed over time in parallel to other discussions of realism, but without much interaction. Like Hacking, Bhaskar objected to placing the focus of the discussions of realism on the problem of the reality of theoretical entities. He argued that practical activity presupposed the reality of its objects, and accordingly proposed what he called transcendental realism, by which he meant a realism that was a 'condition of the possibility' of experiments and applications of scientific knowledge that act independently of the activities of science. The thought was that we are different kinds of realists about such things than we are about such things as neutrinos, which are never a part of experience other than in the context of scientific activity. He also argued that invariant successions were rare outside of the context of experiment, so that the appropriate focus for realism was causal laws or mechanisms that took the form of tendencies and capacities rather than Humean causation.

This reasoning allowed Critical Realism to take a distinctive approach to the problem of multiple perspectives. If 'perspectives' are largely theoretical ways of framing reality, they can each share a common reality at the level of entities with causal properties. So Critical Realism is not required to suppose that one perspective alone will prove to be closest to reality. And thinking about the reality of objects separately from considerations of theoretical truth allowed for greater openness to the kinds of objects that could be granted some sense of reality.

Realism in the British tradition was concerned particularly with the reality of social structures, and represented a response to the idea that the reality of social institutions depended on the beliefs of agents, something that is central to the tradition represented by Weber, for whom collective concepts were unacceptable. Under the influence of the formulation of the structure-agency problem by Giddens, much of the discussion was concerned with the claim that there were identifiable mechanisms at the social level which needed to be treated as more or less autonomously real. Organizations fell into this category.[3] The feature of Critical Realism that made it most appealing to organizational theorists was its openness to different kinds and levels of 'real' social and organizational structures and mechanisms, and the fact that Critical Realism had the effect of lowering the standard for what was to count as real, and allowing the entities of many perspectives to be seen as real.

One peculiarity of Critical Realism in comparison to the realism of Hacking resulted from its origin in 'transcendental realism', the idea that theories presupposed the reality of the objects of the theories. Although Bhaskar also held that the transtheoretical reality of these objects, that is to say their appearance in applications, was important, he argued that the 'reality' in question in these cases was transcendental as well, that is to say was a matter of presupposing the reality of something in order to act on it (Bhaskar 2003). One consequence of this focus was that claims about real structures often were closely allied to the theories that presupposed them, to the point that the claim that the objects of the theories were 'real' was largely indistinguishable from the theories themselves. Not surprisingly, the problem of 'perspectives' continued to dominate discussion, and Critical Realism reemerged in these discussions as a meta-theoretical perspective alongside positivism and hermeneutics (cf. Outhwaite 1987).

The central attempt to make sense of organizational analysis in terms of paradigms was Burrell and Morgan's *Sociological Paradigms and Organizational Analysis* (1979), and its more methodologically oriented counterpart, *Beyond Method*, in which Critical Realism appears precisely as a perspective (Outhwaite 1983), along with a large number of other perspectives, such as feminism. It is probably the case that no work in the history of organizational analysis had so many index entries under 'ontology' as *Sociological Paradigms and Organizational Analysis*: 31. The book was a painstaking survey of approaches to what their subtitle termed 'the sociology of corporate life' that left no doubt that, as the book began, 'all theories of organization are based upon a philosophy of science and a theory of society' (1979: 1), and that, as the book concluded, the future held even more diversity. Morgan was troubled about this state of affairs, and wanted to find some way to systematically relate, if not synthesize, the approaches to organizational life. *Beyond Method* (1983) was the result of a conference that brought together representatives of 20 different approaches to organization analysis in an attempt to see where dialogue would lead. Morgan concluded the book with a call for reflective conversation between practitioners, and for openness (1983: 406).

The idea that diversity could be handled in this way was swept away by a new set of ideas from sociologists, under the name of 'constructionism', which derived from both the sociology of knowledge and from an influential book of the 1960s, Berger and Luckman's *The Social Construction of Reality* (1966). The tradition of sociology of knowledge, and indeed Burger and Luckman's book, exempted ordinary scientific knowledge from their analyses. Traditional sociology of knowledge analysed social doctrines as ideologies; Berger and Luckman considered the categories of everyday life. Both were contrasted with scientific truths. The argument was that the apparent realities of social life were fundamentally ideological or ideational in character, and that what we took to be real was the product of our shared structures of thinking (as Mannheim put it in a book on conservatism [1982]), or, in Berger and Luckman, the continuous product of phenomenological processes of interaction which produced shared typifications. In the radicalized form which this line of argument took in the sociology of science in the 1970s and 1980s, not only social knowledge but scientific knowledge came to be seen as the product of shared and constructed typifications in categories just as ordinary social life was.

The idea that science was a social phenomena came to be understood as the idea that the processes of knowledge, especially the processes of making something taken for granted or factual, were social in the sense that they were fundamentally matters of agreement about such things as what counts as evidence, what counts as fact, and so forth. The lesson of Kuhnianism was that these agreements were temporary, revisable, ungrounded, that is to say ungrounded in deeper facts or deeper realities. So the 'sociology of scientific knowledge', as it styled itself, took on board and radicalized the *a priorism* implicit in Kuhn's account of scientific paradigms and made it 'social' in the sense that the *a priori* elements, the 'counting as' elements, were fundamentally a matter of what was accepted in or soon to be accepted in particular groups, in this case groups of scientists.

The reply of social constructionism to realism was that the facts of science and also the realities of science come to be counted as realities through a social process of accounting that involved, and necessarily involved, not the direct confrontation of theories with reality but a confrontation controlled by a large collection of *a priori* socially accepted accounting devices (or in the older phenomenological terminology, typifications) which enabled their users to construct, or count something as a fact or as admissible to the category of 'real'. Science was an activity in which the objective character of things resulted from a social process in which this character came to be taken for granted.

The focus on the taken-for-granted was telling here, in part because it pointed back to the phenomenological tradition but also because it pointed to the phenomena well known to Kuhn and also to the figures who influenced him, such as Polanyi and Kuhn's mentor, Conant. Science, especially physics, in the late nineteenth century seemed even to its most prominent practitioners to be essentially final and complete and any advances they expected would consist largely of adding a few more decimals of precision to observations and formulae. The quantum revolution showed very dramatically that the taken-for-granted world even of the scientists was insecure. As young men Polanyi and Conant had lived through the quantum revolution and were acutely aware, on a personal level, of the fact that the scientists' taken-for-granted world, despite its apparent solidity and its rootedness in accepted techniques, technologies, and standards, was in fact open to fundamental and unexpected transformation. For them this meant that the sense that realists had of increasing mastery of the realities of the world was essentially an illusion, and that no one could predict, as realism seemed to predict, the continuity between our picture of the world and future pictures of the world. This had been the germ of Kuhn's ideas. Constructionism posed the same challenge to normal science. The apparent solidity and

natural character of our favourite distinctions and categories, they argued, was sustained by the interconnections that the social institution of science established; it was a social achievement, rather than a matter of nature. As Bloor (1976) and Barnes pointed out (1974), if one is to explain scientific change, one cannot appeal to 'reality', for reality presumably did not change. What changed were the social conditions of belief and the conditions for sustaining of a sense of the naturalness, solidity, and reality of the distinctions, categories, and through which we construct 'reality'.

Constructivism in the sociology of scientific knowledge was rooted in an empirical tradition of case studies which depicted the processes of fact-making. But the idea of social construction had a quite different and quite radically extended trajectory in the hands of activist groups and various academic movements, which used these notions to challenge educational and bureaucratic practices of various kinds. Perhaps the most famous formulation of the radical extension of these ideas was in the context of sex roles and the assertion of Butler (1993) that everyone is in drag, meaning that all gender is as artificially 'constructed' as the drag queen's manifestly fake construction of himself as a woman. This reasoning has the effect of breaking down the distinction between the natural and the artificial by collapsing the supposedly natural into the artificial.

Constructivism in this sense has an undeniable applicability to many of the central practices of the production of organizational 'realities', particularly in connection with accounting, which could be seen as representing the hardest of hard facts, the 'bottom line' being a conventional cultural characterization of the factual stripped of the elements of rhetoric and decoration. But the facts of accounting that go into the 'bottom line' are manifestly facts by convention, and the processes by which these conventions have been constructed in the first place could be deconstructed by careful historical analysis, and this led to a constructionist literature in accounting itself (Ritson 2001).

Hacking and Intervention: Beyond Realism vs Relativism

Although by this point the development of the philosophy of science and the development of management science in organizational studies had begun to diverge so that little in the way of development in the philosophy of science was to have any impact on management science, a major textbook in the philosophy of science was published the same year as Morgan's *Beyond Method*, Hacking's *Representing and Intervening* (1983) that pointed to a different way of dealing with the problem of 'reality'. Although this work had very minimal direct impact on organizational studies or practical management science, it had an important effect on the philosophical community.

Hacking's main concern in his book was to supply an alternative vocabulary for the understanding of science, which salvages the bench scientist's sense of the reality of the entities which experiments probe – a self-consciously less 'theory-centered' view of science. The positivist view had been that the aim of science was the construction of general theories containing exceptionless laws which could be arranged in deductive structures so that higher level laws could explain lower level laws. This structure provided an account of the relationship between theoretical domains as well, such as reduction, or explaining one discipline's theories using another discipline's theory, which proceeded by accounting for the phenomena of a particular field, such as biology, by showing that the laws of biology could be explained by more fundamental or general laws. With experiment, the idea was that experiments served as confirmatory evidence of the general character or generality of an empirical hypothesis, and enabled scientists to determine the scope of the applicability as well as the validity of a generalization. A variant of this idea was Popper's influential notion of falsification, which gave a significant role in scientific development to the construction of falsifying instances which at the same time served to overthrow a generalization and to provide the additional data which a new theory or conjecture needed to account for.

Kuhn's account of paradigms conflicted with both Popper and the positivists about negative instances. He argued that in normal science the focus was on the extension of the existing paradigm through puzzle-solving activities within the paradigm. Experiment played a subordinate role to paradigms: paradigms determined the form, method, and exemplary cases of experiment, which the researcher applied to new cases as long as the paradigm kept working. Disconfirming results had no special role. The conservativism of scientists, their interest in preserving their paradigm, and the fact that adjustments could always be made to other parts of the theory or its associated theories which removed the inconsistency (a fact which led to holism about theories), meant that negative results were made to conform to the existing theories, or, when they could not be made to conform, were treated as anomalies which were of limited interest. They became of interest only when a sufficient number of these anomalies had accumulated so that the paradigm could be challenged by critics and the anomalies used in the creation of a new paradigm.

Hacking argued that the process of interaction between theory and research could be understood, as his title suggested, as an ongoing activity of representing and intervening, rather than an enterprise of matching a theory to external reality. Intervening was intervening in the causal processes of the world in order to understand them. Representing was the activity of understanding or depicting the interventions and their results, but *not* formulating them in sentences or theories. The basic idea of representation was that of a model, such as a clay likeness (1983: 135). 'Reality' is, for Hacking, an *attribute* of representation – the answer to the question 'is representation realistic?' And, because there are several ways to represent the same facts, we need criteria for choosing between representations (1983: 143). Interventions provided a kind of test of the representation but at the same time produced new data which needed additional representation when the new data did not fit the original representation and thus required revisions in the representation. This apparently simple idea had radical consequences for the way in which the dominant problem of the 1950s and 1960s and early 1970s, namely the problem of the relationship between theory and data, had been conceived. Data were no longer understood as the Latin meaning of the term implied as 'the given' or as sensory, but instead were necessarily partly, one might say, artificial, the product of intervention by the scientist. Representing could no longer be thought of as the perfect depiction of the given but as part of a continuing dynamic process of performing interventions based on one's representations and revising these representations as a result of the unanticipated consequences of these interventions.

One particularly interesting and relevant consequence of the representing and intervening picture for organizational studies is that it has the effect of collapsing both the natural/artificial distinction and the inquiry/practice distinctions. Intervening is an act of art based on the intervener's ideas or way of representing the domain in question which produces consequences which are not artificial but are real, but real in a somewhat different sense than the image of the real as the orderly world of nature that the scientist unveils or discovers. Because the model of what is real is no longer theory-centered, but is centered on the daily activities of the bench scientist working with things to understand their causal powers, typically through manipulating them (1983: 274), Hacking's image of it suggests a different approach to thinking about organizational interventions – as a means of revealing the causal powers and properties of organizations. Both reality and science that lends itself to the idea of more or less indefinite change and revision as well as a kind of objectivity which no longer consists in defining the proper transparent relationship between subject and object, researcher and data, and this too fits organizational studies. Organizational actors engage in interventions and organizational phenomena are the product of them.

Diversity and Application

The paradoxical consequence of Kuhnianism and the concept of paradigm, as they played out in the social sciences, was that they produced the exact opposite of what Kuhn described in the natural sciences. Instead of providing a recipe for 'becoming scientific' by creating a highly consensual body of exemplars, standard techniques, standard terms, and so forth, and using this 'paradigm' as the basis of a claim to be scientific, the concept of paradigm legitimated every perspective. It did not produce what Kuhn called normal science, but made permanent a situation of revolutionary science in which different potential paradigms competed with one another, created their own basic ideas, exemplars, terminology, and so forth, free from the threat of delegitimation by a standard method, set of definitions, and so on. This situation, had it occurred in connection with the applications of a conventional scientific field, in which standard practice is grounded by standard science, would have been catastrophic. No one would have been able to claim to possess the basic principles of the field of application – instead of engineering one

would have had magic. In fact, the opposite occurred. The practical side of management science, especially the consulting business as it was institutionalized in the practice of training within corporations, operated in a mode that served to reinforce diversity of perspectives in a way that compensated for the ineffectiveness of the techniques themselves. Organizational consultants came to be known, not entirely jokingly, as witch doctors. Practical solutions to organizational problems were marketed in training packages, which either represented some sort of simplified form of a fashionable academic theory or idea such as organizational culture, or represented its own novel but readily understandable theory or representation of an organizational phenomenon, and of course involved an intervention which promised results.

The competitive consulting market had the effect of reinforcing diversity. Consultants and trainers exploited whatever market niches they could identify. This meant that there was demand for theoretical ideas about particular problems for which training markets could be found, such as organizational communication, leadership, conflict, and so forth. The fact that the perspectives had to be tailored to demands of these markets and customers meant that they had to be communicable to non-academic audiences who would need to find them credible and useful. These were powerful constraints that produced a wide range of distinctive intellectual creations, and, although few of these had any significant impact on academic organizational theory, the successes of consultants established the reality of particular organizational facts by showing that they were manipulable. When Ford Motor Company made systematic efforts to change the organizational culture with respect to production quality, for example, and visibly did so by firing senior managers who failed to conform to the new culture, the story was front page in the *Wall Street Journal*. One could scarcely ignore something like organizational culture, for example, when it was a concept actively deployed as part of the management strategy of major organizations. In this way, what was initially merely a minor perspective on organizational life was now a permanent part of management practice, a phenomenon that was subject to managerial intervention, a part of management training curricula, and a part of the academic training of future managers in business schools. This example is especially illustrative of the problem of the natural and the artificial in organizational studies. Organizational culture had been initially thought of, as it was still thought by Barnard, as one of the organic or natural aspects of the organization as distinct from the artificial or formal system of command and control, something that constrained managers and led to resistance to change, but resistive rather than manipulable. Its new form invited the creation of interventions, which themselves were a kind of a test of the theory that did more to validate the phenomena and the approach than any traditional behavioural science methodology could have.

Artificial and Natural

With this we come to the great irony of organizational theory, an irony which the long historical account of the interaction between the philosophy of science and organizational theory I have given here will make unsurprising. The general distinction between the artificial and the natural aspects of organizations is the organization theorist's analogue to the subject-object distinction in philosophy: it is intrinsic to the subject. Organizations are, as the engineering conception correctly supposed, human creations. The theme of human creation, which continues on through Krupp and to the later phenomenological and constructionist conceptions of organizations, contains something that is absolutely critical to an understanding of the methodological problems of organizational study. Organizations are human creations; the naturalness of organizations or their 'reality' is an illusion. Organizations are historical realities which depend on subjects: the manager, the employees, and all those who recognize and respond to organizational realities. Ironically, organizations are real and stable precisely because the actual purposes and the institutional concepts of managers, employees, the law, and so forth are themselves stable. The naturalistic conception of organization, from Elton Mayo to the realists of the present contains its own truth, namely that the world that is open to causal manipulation contains more than is contained in any of these perspectives, concepts, and constitutive principles, whether of participants or theorists. What is engineered and artificial is not the whole story, and even to understand organizations in terms of the goals of engineering, such as efficiency, organizational effectiveness, and so forth requires us to

theorize about and take cognizance of a great deal more. Organizations are not perfect machines and the rules of organizations are not perfect blueprints. The things beyond the blueprints that need to be taken into account, such as the human relations of managers, are incompletely theorizable in terms of the particular perspective that the theorists of these natural aspects or organizations provide. And no correction produces 'completion'. There is always something more. In the case of the Hawthorne studies, the 'more', at least in the central case of the bank wiring room, seems to have been the enforcement of a rationally chosen level of productivity, productivity restricted so as to preserve the jobs of the workers, that proved recalcitrant both to the efforts of managers and to the perspectives of theorists. But theorizing this particular additional element in turn is not sufficient. It may work very well for the particular case in question, but in the next case to which the perspective is applied it may not. Then the recalcitrance of the real requires us to construct it, represent it, and theorize about it in novel ways.

The aims of securing profit, efficiency, and effectiveness through division of labour and cooperation, together with authority and discipline, are relatively stable. What distinguishes organization studies is the specificity of the constitutive motives which give the object of its study their apparent fixity, their object-like character, and so forth, characteristics that make it initially plausible to be a realist or empiricist about them. The purposes and beliefs of agents who do the object-making work here are impermanent and multiform. They are historical: the indirect products of past interventions and representations of the facts and traditions of organizational practice. Organizations are what they are because people have thought of them, thought about them, and acted on these thoughts. They can only be temporarily 'detached' from these thoughts for the purpose of analysis. They are real in Hacking's sense, not in the sense of traditional realism.

Notes

1. Of course it had deep roots. Weber discusses the organization of work and the Swiss watchmaking houses of the sixteenth and seventeenth centuries and the workers' monastic-like work discipline and refined specialization in the performance of manufacturing tasks (Weber [1927]1961). Weber himself did fatigue studies of the

workers in his family's linen factories in Oerlinghausen (Schluchter 2000: 59–61).

2. There is an interesting and under-utilized study, *Manufacturing Rationality*, of the extension of the systems idea from engineering to management by Shenhav, which deals with the progressive era and later (1999). A more popular historical study, full of interesting items, is *Machine Age Ideology* (Jordan 1994).

3. The long history of the application of Critical Realism in organizations would take us beyond the range of this overview, but particularly good explications include Reed (1997), which presents a reconsideration of the agency/structure problem and points to such works as Casey (1995) as exemplifying the realist approach by conceiving of the organization as a mediating mechanism 'connecting macro-level structuring with local re-ordering' (Reed 1997: 36). Introductions to Critical Realism include Outhwaite (1987) and Collier (1994).

References

Barber, B. (1970) 'Introduction', in L.J. Henderson (ed.), *L. J. Henderson on the Social System*. Chicago: The University of Chicago Press. pp. 1–53.

Barnard, C.I. (1938) *The Functions of the Executive*. Cambridge, MA: Harvard University Press.

Barnes, B. (1974) *Scientific Knowledge and Sociological Theory*. London: Routledge & Kegan Paul.

Berger, P.L. and Luckman, T. (1966) *The Social Construction of Reality: A Treatise in the Sociology of Knowledge*. Garden City, NY: Doubleday.

Berelson, B. and Steiner, G.A. (1964) *Human Behavior: An Inventory of Scientific Findings*. New York: Harcourt, Brace & World, Inc.

Bhaskar, R. (2003) 'Realism', in W. Outhwaite (ed.), *The Blackwell Dictionary of Modern Social Thought*, 2nd edn. Malden, MA: Blackwell Publishers. pp. 558–60.

Blau, P. (1970) 'A formal theory of differentiation in organizations', *American Sociological Review*, 35: 201–18.

Bloor, D. (1976) *Knowledge and Social Imagery*. London: Routledge and Kegan Paul.

Braithwaite, R.B. (1953) *Scientific Explanation: A Study of the Function of Theory, Probability, and Law in Science*. Cambridge: Cambridge University Press.

Burrell, G. and Morgan, G. (1979) *Sociological Paradigms and Organizational Analysis: Elements of the Sociology of Corporate Life*. London: Heinemann.

Butler, J. (1993) *Bodies that Matter: On the Discursive Limits of 'Sex'*. New York: Routledge.

Buxton, W. and Turner, S. (1992) 'Education and Expertise: Sociology as a "Profession"', in T.C. Halliday and M. Janowitz (eds), *Sociology and Its Publics*. Chicago: University of Chicago Press. pp. 373–407.

Cannon, W.B. (1939) *The Wisdom of the Body*. New York: W. W. Norton & Company, Inc.

Carnap, R. (1967) 'On the character of philosophical problems', in R. Rorty (ed.), *The Linguistic Turn: Recent Essays in Philosophical Method*. Chicago: University of Chicago Press. pp. 54–62.

Casey, C. (1995) *Work, Self, and Society after Industrialization*. London: Routledge.

Collier, A. (1994) *Critical Realism: An Introduction to Roy Bhaskar's Philosophy*. London: Verso.

Converse, J.M. (1987) *Survey Research in the United States: Roots and Emergence, 1890–1960*. Berkeley: University of California Press.

Danziger, K. (1990) *Constructing the Subject: Historical Origins of Psychological Research*. Cambridge: Cambridge University Press.

Donaldson, L. (1985) *In Defence of Organization Theory: A Reply to the Critics*. Cambridge: Cambridge University Press.

Gibb, G.S. and Knowlton, E. (1956) *History of Standard Oil Company (New Jersey): The Resurgent Years 1911–1927*. New York: Harper and Brothers.

Giddings, F.W. (1886) 'Co-operation', in G.E. McNeill (ed.), *The Labor Movement: The Problem of Today*. Boston MA: A.M. Bridgman & Co. pp. 508–31.

Gouldner, A. (1954) *Wildcat Strike*. Yellow Springs, OH: Antioch Press.

Hacking, I. (1983) *Representing and Intervening: Introductory Topics in the Philosophy of Natural Science*. Cambridge: Cambridge University Press.

Hanson, N.R. (1958) *Patterns of Discovery: An Inquiry into the Conceptual Foundations of Science*. Cambridge: Cambridge University Press.

Hempel, C.G., and Oppenheim, P. (1948) 'Studies in the logic of explanation', *Philosophy of Science*, 15: 135–175. Reprinted (1965) with a Postscript in *Aspects of Scientific Explanation and Other Essays*. New York: The Free Press. pp. 245–95.

Hempel, C. (1965) *Aspects of Scientific Explanation, and Other Essays in the Philosophy of Science*. New York: Free Press.

Henderson, L.J. (1927) The science of human conduct: An estimate of Pareto and one of his greatest works', *The Independent*, 119: 575–7, 585.

Henderson, L.J. ([1935]1967) *Pareto's General Sociology: A Physiologist's Interpretation*. New York: Russell and Russell.

Henderson, L.J. (1970) 'Sociology 23 lectures' in B. Barber (ed.), *L. J. Henderson on the Social System*. Chicago: The University of Chicago Press. pp. 57–148.

Jordan, J.M. (1994) *Machine-Age Ideology: Social Engineering and American Liberalism, 1911–1939*. Chapel Hill, NC: University of North Carolina Press.

Katz, D. and Kahn, R.L. ([1966]1978) *The Social Psychology of Organizations*, 2nd edn. New York: John Wiley.

Kellogg, P.U. (1912) 'The spread of the survey idea', in P. Kellogg, S.M. Harrison and G.T. Palmer (eds), *The Social Survey*, 2nd edn. New York: The Russell Sage

Foundation. Reprinted from *The Proceedings of the Academy of Political Science,* 2 July.

Krupp, S. ([1961]1964) *Pattern in Organization Analysis: A Critical Examination.* New York: Holt, Rhinehart and Winston.

Kuhn, T. ([1962]1996) *The Structure of Scientific Revolutions,* 3rd edn. Chicago: The University of Chicago Press.

Mannheim, K., Kettler, D., Meja, V. and Stehr, N. (1982) *Structures of Thinking,* trans. J.J. Shapiro and S.W. Nicholsen. Boston: Routledge and Kegan Paul.

Manuel, F.E. and Manuel, F.P. (1966) *French Utopias: An Anthology of Ideal Societies.* New York: Free Press.

Manuel, F.E. (1962) *The Prophets of Paris.* Cambridge, MA: Harvard University Press.

Mayo, E. ([1933]1960) *The Human Problems of an Industrial Civilization.* New York: Viking Press.

McGregor, D. (1960) *The Human Side of Enterprise.* New York: McGraw-Hill.

Merton, R. ([1910]1957) *Social theory and Social Structure,* Rev. and Enl. Glencoe, IL: Free Press.

Mirowski, P. (2004) 'The scientific dimensions of social knowledge and their distant echoes in 20th century American philosophy of science', *Studies in the History of the Philosophy of Science,* 35: 283–326

Morgan, G. (ed.) (1983) *Beyond Method: Strategies for Social Research.* Beverly Hills, CA: Sage Publications.

Münsterberg, H. (1913) *Psychology and Industrial Efficiency.* Boston: Mifflin.

Nagel, E. (1961) *The Structure of Science: Problems in the Logic of Scientific Explanation.* New York: Harcourt, Brace & World, Inc.

Natanson, M. (ed.) (1963) *Philosophy of the Social Sciences: A Reader.* New York: Random House.

Nelson, D. (1980) *Frederick W. Taylor and the Rise of Scientific Management.* Madison, WI: University of Wisconsin Press.

Outhwaite, W. (1983) 'Toward a realist perspective', in G. Morgan (ed.), *Beyond Method: Strategies for Social Research.* Beverly Hills: Sage Publications. pp. 321–30.

Outhwaite, W. (1987) *New Philosophies of Social Science: Realism, Hermeneutics and Critical Theory.* London: MacMillan.

Putnam, H. (1976) 'Realism and reason', in H. Putnam (ed.), *Meaning and the Moral Sciences.* London: Rutledge and Kegan Paul. pp. 123–38.

Reed, M.I. (1997) 'In praise of duality and dualism: rethinking agency and structure to organizational analysis', *Organization Studies,* 18: 21–42.

Ritson, P. (2001) 'Social constructionism in three accounting journals', paper given at the Asian Pacific Inter-disciplinary Research in Accounting Conference, University of Adelaide. Available online at: http://www.commerce.adelaide.edu.au/apira/papers/Ritson186.pdf, accessed March 2004.

Roethlisberger, F. J. and Dixon, W.J. ([1939]1961) *Management and the Worker: An Account of a Research Program Conducted by the Western Electric Company, Hawthorne Works, Chicago.* Cambridge, MA: Harvard University Press.

Schluchter, W. (2000) 'Psychophysics and culture', in S.P. Turner (ed.), *The Cambridge Companion to Weber,* Cambridge: Cambridge University Press. pp. 59–82.

Schutz, A. (1954) 'Concept and theory formation in the social sciences', *Journal of Philosophy,* 51: 257–72. Reprinted (1963) in *Philosophy of the Social Sciences: A Reader,* M. Natanson (ed.). New York: Random House. pp. 231–49, and (1964) *Collected Papers II: Studies in Social Theory,* A. Brodersen (ed.). The Hague: Martinus Nijhoff. pp. 48–66.

Serres, M. (1982) *Hermes: Literature, Science, Philosophy,* V. Harari and D. F. Bell (eds). Baltimore, MD: Johns Hopkins University Press.

Shenhav, Y. (1999) *Manufacturing Rationality: The Engineering Foundations of the Managerial Revolution.* Oxford: Oxford University Press.

Silverman, D. (1970) *The Theory of Organizations: A Sociological Framework.* London: Heinemann Educational.

Simon, H. ([1945]1959) *Administrative Behavior: A Study of Decision-Making Processes in Administrative Organization,* 2nd edn. New York: The Macmillan Company.

Simon, H. ([1969]1996) *The Sciences of the Artificial,* 3rd edn. Cambridge, MA: The MIT Press.

Stouffer, S.A., Suchman, E.A., DeVinney, L.C., Lumsdaine, A.A., Lumsdaine, M.H., Williams, R.M., Jr., Smith, M.B., Janis, I.L., Star, S.A. and Cottrell, L.S., Jr. (1949) *The American Soldier.* Princeton, NJ: Princeton University Press.

Turner, S.P. (1977) 'Blau's theory of differentiation: is it explanatory?', *The Sociological Quarterly,* 18: 17–31.

Weber, M. ([1927]1961) *General Economic History,* trans. F.H. Knight. New York: Collier Books; 1981, New Brunswick, NJ: Transaction.

1.13 Representation and Reflexivity

STEWART CLEGG AND CYNTHIA HARDY

When we wrote the original handbook in 1996, we asked: What is the world like today? How has it changed? What does it mean for the study of organizations? At the time, we cast our minds back to the mid 1960s, when *The Handbook of Organizations* edited by James G. March (1965) was published. We remembered that the Vietnam War had been starting to heat up during this period, while the Cold War was still frigid. In Europe the Berlin Wall had only recently gone up, while in Asia and the Caribbean, the dominoes were threatening to come down; in the USA, the civil rights movement was in full swing and the Berkeley Free Speech Movement was gaining momentum; in Asia, Mao's 'Cultural Revolution' was imminent; India and Pakistan were at war; in Africa, Rhodesia's 'Unilateral Declaration of Independence' broke colonial ranks, while to the south, Nelson Mandela had just started a prison sentence that would last a quarter of a century.

So much for the big picture history; in terms of organizations most were premised on instruction and surveillance through personal, written or verbal communication, and relied on professional discretion to monitor the less routine areas of organization life; hierarchies were the norm; personal computers had not been invented; the only mode of instantaneous communication was the telephone, and the new technologies that were to challenge accepted organization designs were largely unheard of.

In the intervening 30 years, communism imploded, neo-conservatism exploded, apartheid disappeared, feminism appeared, and organizations – and organization studies – continued to change. We noted that those 30 years had produced new approaches and concepts for the study of organizations. The 'orthodox consensus' (Atkinson 1971), premised on assumptions concerning the unitary and orderly nature of organizations, had been challenged and complemented by a panoply of other theoretical approaches drawing on both normal and 'contra' social science (Marsden and Townley 1996), a pluralism which many of the contributors to the original *Handbook* supported.

Changing and Questioning

The question for us now to consider is: What has changed in the last 10 years? And what do these changes mean for organizations and organization studies? What implications do changing conceptions of security and risk in the post-9/11 era have for how power shapes organizational space and access? In the wake of the many recent corporate collapses and scandals, will the ethic of success shift to one of responsibility? Will the heightened interest in identity lead to the rise of more identity-centered practices as organizations try to claim the hearts and souls of their employees, as some observers of change programs (Hardy and Clegg 2004) have noted? What role do emotions and compassion play in the 'postmodern' organization? Is dematerialization and virtualization leading to a re-enchantment of organization – a new *gemeinschaft*, as some commentators on Japanese organizations suggest (Kono and Clegg 2001)? Does the immediacy of time, where everything is always already present in a virtual world, mean the intensification of time – management at the speed of light, perhaps? Is the increased power *of* organizations leading to increasingly concentrated power *in* organizations? In a world where people think of themselves as team members or associates, rather than as solidaristic individuals defined in class terms, do the dynamics of power and resistance still mean the same? Can we speak of struggle in the old ways? Where boundaries of organizations, markets, customers, environments are dissolving, is the traditional conception of the organization as a clear locus of ownership and internal control also dissolving? In an era of knowledge management, will we see the emergence of new power/knowledge relations or will the normalization of management knowledge and its widespread distribution through organizational ranks simply produce greater conformity (Clegg et al. 2004)? These are some – but certainly not all – of the questions that we think will shape the research agenda for the next generation.

Changing Organizations: Questioning Organization

Organizations are empirical objects, such that we 'see' something when we see an organization, but each of us may see something different, see that thing seen differently, and see different things at different times, not just because of material or representational change over time in the thing seen but also, of course, in ways of seeing. Indeed, that which is known as such-and-such a thing cannot be so other than through institutionalized ways of seeing. For a long time, the theme of bureaucracy dominated organization studies. Weber (1978) systematized the concept of bureaucracy as a form of organization characterized by centralization, hierarchy, authority, discipline, rules, career, division of labour, and tenure. It was the staple of the typological studies of the 1950s (see Clegg and Dunkerley 1980); it represented one of the most common archetypes of organization design (e.g. Chandler 1962; Mintzberg 1979); and it was the site of key case material for subsequent critiques (Silverman 1970; Reed 1985). In more recent years, new forms of organization have emerged: external boundaries that formerly circumscribed the organization have been breaking down as individual entities have merged and blurred in 'chains', 'clusters', 'networks' and 'strategic alliances', questioning the relevance of an 'organizational' focus; internal boundaries that once delineated the bureaucracy have lost shape as a result of empowered, flat, cross-functional, flexible post-Fordist structures. For some writers at least, these new organizational forms were sufficiently different from the bureaucratic features of modern organization to suggest the appellation of 'postmodern' (e.g. Clegg 1990). They were seen as the key to radical innovation, competitive advantage, organizational learning, and knowledge management among other holy grails.

Competitive pressures, total quality management, the trend towards knowledge work, and time based

competition are all business forces that create a need for decision making and staff support to be closer to customers and products ... businesses have to move from single profit centres to multiple profit-measurable units. In business units, general management decisions have to move to teams with direct product, project, or customer contact. As decision power moves to teams, the teams need additional knowledge, information and rewards that are tied to the businesses they manage. Finally, in work units employee involvement must move decisions to work teams. In all cases, faster decision making, control of quality at the point of origin, and delivery of service at the point of customer contact require that decisions be moved to lower levels, which in turn leads to focus on new, more distributed organizations, and the decline of hierarchy (Galbraith et al. 1993: 285–6).

Whereas the old-style modern organization was centralized at corporate headquarters, the postmodern organization is distributed around an internal network of divisions or units, linked through electronic forms of communication. Leadership is no longer hierarchical but team based, requiring skills in team building, conflict resolution and problem solving. Communication is extensive and information distributed and shared, rather than hoarded. Organizations are characterized by openness, trust, empowerment and commitment; open decision-making eliminates the inefficiency of traditional hierarchical styles of secrecy, sycophancy and sabotage. Decisions are based upon expertise, openly elicited and listened to throughout increasingly polyphonic organizations (Clegg 1990; Dodgson 1993; Fairtlough 1994; Kornberger et al. 2005). The result is a very different organization compared to the bureaucracy and even to the matrix organization (Galbraith 1973) and adhocracy (Mintzberg 1979).

In the last ten years, the preoccupation with new organizational forms has continued and new terminology exploded on to the scene, including 'intelligent, chaotic, improvisational, boundaryless, collaborative, empowered, horizontal, self-designed and minimalist organizations; clusters, shamrocks, spider's webs, starbursts and consortia; circular, front/back, cyclical, and modular organizations; spherical, stable, internal and dynamic networks; organizations that are spun out, intersected, infinitely flat, inverted, fuzzy, fractal federalist and virtual organizations' (Palmer and Hardy 2000: 11–3). They continue to be characterized by flat structures, empowered teams and permeable boundaries.

Despite some changes and the exponential growth in epithets, bureaucracies remain a factor in contemporary organizations. While some have claimed that the notion of hierarchy is as 'archaic as the medieval belief in the divine right of kings' (Halal 1994: 69), others are less optimistic (or pessimistic) about the demise of the bureaucracy.

> Hierarchies are necessary, inevitable, and desired fixtures for organizational life. As long as organizations have limited resources and contain multiple perspectives, there will be a need for some people to be leaders and make decisions for others (Ashkenas et al. 1995: 33).

Other researchers argue that new forms – such as alliances and cross-functional teams – do not replace bureaucracy but are grafted on to more traditional hierarchies (Palmer and Dunford 1997; Palmer and Hardy 2000). In other words, it appears that the concept of bureaucracy remains a relevant and useful concept for organization theorists (Walton 2005).

While bureaucracy may still be relevant, it is not to say that organizations have not changed. About the time that we were writing the first incarnation of this chapter, Peter Drucker (1994) was heralding the rise of knowledge workers, a term he had coined in 1959, who would occupy more jobs than manufacturing workers ever had (except in war time), and have more opportunities and earn more money to boot. The knowledge worker, knowledge intensive firm, and knowledge society have been the subject of considerable interest – and debate – over the last 10 years. Idealized views of this 'brave new world' present a picture of greater job discretion and worker autonomy, with more worker involvement which allows them to draw on their specialized knowledge to solve problems, while critics argue that the changes reinforce managerial control, erode informal work cultures, and reduce the power of unions (see Powell and Snellman 2004). As a result, managing knowledge, knowledge workers, and knowledge intensive firms continues to attract considerable attention (e.g. Blackler 1995; Nonaka and Takeuchi 1995; Grant and Oswick 1996; Von Krogh 1998; Thompson and Walsham 2004; Reich 2005). Despite optimistic predictions of growth in 'high end', autonomous, high status, highly paid knowledge work, the outcome is more mixed: more complex patterns of employment growth in 'low end', routine, repetitive and highly controlled jobs is also occurring (Fleming et al. 2004).

The knowledge society is associated with the spectacular growth of the Internet and other information technologies. When we wrote the first version of this chapter, there were only 25 million Internet users in the world, seven years later there were 500 million; today, there are over 800 million (Wellman and Haythornthwaite 2002; www. InternetWorldStats. com). The digital divide notwithstanding, organizations make use of ICT to a degree and in ways unanticipated by most employees (and most organizational theorists) ten years ago. The electronic era has been associated with changes to organizational structures and management practices (Dewett and Jones 2001), as managers struggle with the relatively new phenomena of teleworking and virtual teams. These challenges have, not surprisingly, attracted considerable interest (e.g. special issue *of Organization Science*, 10(6), 1999; Cascio 2000; Kirkman et al. 2002) although, as O'Leary et al. (2002) point out, managing distance is a problem so old that it was an issue for the Roman Empire. In examining the management practices that Canada's largest retailer, the Hudson's Bay Company, used over three centuries ago, they found that many management solutions, such as building trust, socializing, monitoring and reporting, were fundamentally the same as today even if they did manifest themselves in different ways.

A related area of debate has been the impact of these changes on workers and, especially, the intensification of work and the implications for surveillance. For example, studies of teleworking considered the extension of surveillance into the home, as well as addressing the impact of home-workers being distanced from work colleagues but more vulnerable to their professional and personal lives coming into conflict or collision with each other (Brocklehurst 2001). Similarly, call centres have attracted considerable interest (e.g. Knights and McCabe 1998; Taylor and Bain 1999, Taylor et al. 2002) because they involve novel and extensive forms of control that, on the one hand, are clearly technologically advanced and yet, at the same time, remind us of the enduring influence of scientific management (Taylor and Bain 2003). In addition, call centres, with repetitive tasks and a lack of discretion, are excellent examples of work intensification – the less glamorous side of knowledge work. Some have referred to them as 'electronic panopticons' where surveillance is so complete that it cannot be resisted; although others challenge these assertions and point to a variety of forms of resistance (e.g. Bain and Taylor 2000; Taylor and Bain 2003).

These organizational changes are complex: bureaucracy seems to be both more and less relevant; knowledge work may be liberating or oppressive; new organizational forms are substantively different from the predecessors, or more a question of rhetorical difference. Despite debates about the nature, extent and effects of change in organizational structures and practices, it appears that, at the very least, they are providing interesting new research sites and, in some cases, generating very different research questions to those that informed and stimulated past theoretical practices. One such area concerns the need for researchers to overcome the longstanding tradition that emphasizes stability and order and to see organizations as in a constant state of change (Weick 1998, Pettigrew et al. 2001). Tsoukas and Chia (2002: 567) argue that organizations take the form of an emerging pattern and are also the outcome of it: 'organization aims at stemming change but in the process of doing so it is generated by it'. There has been a growing realization that many of our current theories and our empirical research do not adequately capture the emergent and changeable nature of organizational phenomena (Weick and Quinn 1999; Kornberger et al. 2005). The response to this challenge has been a growing interest in process research (e.g. Dooley and Van de Ven 1999; Langley 1999).

There are, broadly speaking, two approaches to process research: synoptic and performative (Tsoukas and Chia 2002) or episodic and continuous (Weick and Quinn 1999). The former views 'change as an accomplished event whose key features and variations, and causal antecedences and consequences, need to be explored and described' (Tsoukas and Chia 2002: 570). It explores change from the outside and examines 'states' of change that exist at different points in time, between which there are occasional episodes of revolutionary change. Performative accounts of continuous change focus on 'situated human agency unfolding in time' and offer insights into the actual accomplishment of change (Tsoukas and Chia 2002: 572). The first perspective appears dominant in much of organizational and social scientific research, and tends to be pragmatic, empirically grounded, and analytical in orientation. The latter faces considerable ontological and epistemological challenges (Weick 1998) as researchers must adopt more micro, qualitative, longitudinal and

ethnographic methods. Such an approach has been found in work using a practice lens (e.g. Orlikowski 2000), which sees organizations as 'locally organized' and 'interactionally achieved' (Boden 1994: 1); and bundles of 'practices and material arrangements' (Schatzi 2005: 474), chains of conversational activity (Collins, 1981) or 'bodily expressed reactions' (Shotter 2005: 115). Thus the interest in 'process' appears to be giving rise to a methodological and empirical interest in 'practice' as researchers struggle to challenge the longstanding dominance of organization and explore the tenuous and complex processes of organizing.

To conclude, as researchers, we choose those aspects of organizations – new or old, bureaucratic or fluid, processual or static – that we wish to focus on. We make empirical sense of them by deciding how we wish to represent them in our work. Representation, by any device, always involves a choice concerning what aspects of the 'organization' we wish to represent and how we will represent them. For example, some see organizations as characterized by dimensions like formalization, standardization and routinization; others as exhibiting variation, selection, retention and competition; or incurring transaction costs; or distinguished by institutionalized cultures, or whatever. We would say that to the extent that organizations achieve representation in particular terms, they always do so as an effect of theoretical privileges afforded by certain ways of seeing, certain terms of discourse, and their conversational enactment. (Some ways of seeing are certainly more privileged within the academic communities that constitute organizational studies.) At the same time, these terms of representation are already ways of not seeing, ways of not addressing other conversational enactments, and hence, ways of not acknowledging other possible attributes of organizations. Organizations are thus sites of situated social action more or less open both to explicitly organized and formal disciplinary knowledge, such as marketing, production, and so on, and also to conversational practices embedded in the broad social fabric. These practices might include gender, ethnic, and other culturally defined social relations, which are themselves potentially the subjects of formally organized disciplinary knowledge, such as anthropology, sociology, or even organization studies. Choices are to be made concerning the methodological resources available; some face greater challenges because resources are not available or are not legitimate but, in making our choices of how to represent the organization, none provides a more 'correct' analysis than any other – they offer different possibilities. Like any good conversation, the dialectic is reflexive, interlocutive and oriented not to ultimate agreement but to the possibilities of understanding of action, and creation of action, within these contested terrains.

Changing and Questioning in Organization Studies

An aim of the original *Handbook* was to support changes that had been taking place in organization studies in the form of new approaches that provided alternatives to orthodox perspectives. In this regard, we were trying to continue a tradition that had started much earlier. In the British context, the publication of David Silverman's (1970) *The Theory of Organisations* had provided an important early counterpoint to the functionalist view. It opened a Pandora's Box, releasing actors as opposed to systems; social construction as opposed to social determinism; interpretative understanding opposed to causal explanation; plural definitions of situations rather than a singular definition articulated around organizational goals. In the USA, Karl Weick's (1969) book *The Social Psychology of Organizing* provided another impetus for alternative work by focusing attention on the processes of organizing, rather than those entities called organizations, using similar phenomenological resources to Silverman (1970). The publication of Braverman's (1974) study of 'the labour process' brought the concerns of Marxist thinking on to the organization studies agenda, reinforcing concerns with conflict, power and resistance (Clegg and Dunkerley 1980; Littler 1982; Burawoy 1979; Knights and Willmott 1990).

Elsewhere, in the broader realms of social theory, changes were taking place under the rubric of 'postmodernism' (Laclau 1988). While resistant to definition (Jencks 1989), postmodernism has typically been marked by discontinuity, indeterminacy and immanence (Hassan 1985). Building on the pioneering work of intellectuals like Lyotard (1984), postmodern critiques coalesced around an antipathy to 'modernist' tendencies emphasizing grand narrative, the notion of totality, and essentialism. The early target was Marxism, a master narrative *par excellence*: the sweep of class struggle was

supposed to deliver a teleological 'end of history' in communist society. Few categories could be more 'totalizing' than the notion of the 'mode of production', which was the key to explaining all social change everywhere. At the core of this theoretical project was 'class struggle', the essential fulcrum on which social and economic development occurred; individuals were visible only in so far as they were bearers of identities that their class position either ascribed, in which case their consciousness was 'authentic', or denied, in the case of 'false' consciousness. Postmodernism challenged each one of these assumptions: no grand narrative marked the unfolding of human histories. They are histories, not a history: one must attend to local, fragmented specificities, the narratives of everyday lives. Any pattern that is constituted can only be a series of assumptions framed in and by a historical context. The great totalities such as 'the economy' are merely theoretical artefacts. In addition, the 'individual' – no longer acknowledged as a stable constellation of essential characteristics, but as a socially constituted, socially recognized, category of analysis – ceased to occupy the centre of the social, psychological, economic, and moral universe.

One important resource in the journey away from orthodoxy was the publication of *Sociological Paradigms and Organizational Analysis* (Burrell and Morgan 1979). It was a first step in promoting the idea that organization studies should comprise a parallel set of different conversations, and became part of an extremely influential debate during the 1980s. At the time, the framework, which classified research on organizations according to functionalist, interpretative, radical humanist and radical structuralist paradigms, may have seemed just a relatively straightforward way to catalogue a limited number of available options for the study of organizations. But *Paradigms* was not proposed merely as a theory of knowledge: it was a means to carve out a protected niche where 'alternative' researchers could do their thing, protected from the criticisms of functionalists, free from what they saw as the necessity of having to try to explain their work to them. The key to this strategy resided in the 'incommensurability' of the paradigms and the language differences that precluded communication among them.

For those who see in functionalist science an exercise in intellectual imperialism, dominating organization studies both epistemologically and politically, the paradigmatic understanding of organization theory offers a way of legitimating approaches whose probity would be denied by functionalism … What it [incommensurability] implies is that each paradigm must, logically, develop separately, pursuing its own problematic and ignoring those of other paradigms as paradigmatically invalid and that different claims about organizations, in an ideal world, be resolved in the light of their implications for social praxis (Jackson and Carter 1991: 110).

Paradigms thus issued a Janus-headed challenge: *could* one bridge the language 'problem' to allow paradigms to communicate; and on the other, *should* it be bridged or would, doing so, allow imperialists to invade and dominate the weaker territories?

The result was a frenzy of discussion on the subject in a three-cornered debate. One group of supporters of alternative paradigms felt the relativism of incommensurability too hard to bear. Academics trained in rational debate and the search for truth sought solutions to the incommensurability 'problem' through the use of sophisticated philosophical and linguistic discourse (e.g. Reed 1985; Hassard 1988; 1991; Gioia and Pitre 1990; Parker and McHugh 1991; Marsden 1993; Willmott 1993a; 1993b). A second group, including its creators (Burrell and Morgan 1979; also Jackson and Carter 1991), maintained a hard line on any bridge between the paradigms. The third group in the paradigm wars were the defenders of the 'orthodox' faith of functionalism and normal science (e.g. Donaldson 1985; Aldrich 1988). Polemics flourished between defenders and detractors (e.g. Clegg 1990; also see the debate in *Organization Studies* 1988). Most debate, both incisive and accusatory, occurred between members of the 'alternative' paradigms. Despite sharing a discontent with the imperialistic tendencies of the dominant 'orthodoxy', these protagonists engaged each other with such energy that they appeared less like different voices in one broad community separated by minor spats about doctrine, such as Catholics and Protestants debating the rite of communion, and more like Catholics and Protestants during the Protestant Reformation when heretics, Catholic and Protestant alike, were tortured, killed and consumed by fire. An extreme example, perhaps, but as Burrell (1996) pointed in the original *Handbook*, the issue was not one of epistemology, logic or linguistic theory; it was one of politics. Those defending incommensurability believed it to be the

best way to protect alternative approaches from the continuing onslaught of mainstream approaches in their various and evolving forms, while many others attacked it as counterproductive.

Regardless of which side of the commensurability divide they happened to be on, these paradigm warriors were trying to carve out new space for alternative approaches; a strategy that we supported as a way to enhance our understanding of how organization studies are constituted, both empirically and normatively. It is in the struggle between different approaches – from the diversity and ambiguity of meaning – that we learn (Zald 1994); not through the recitation of a presumed uniformity, consensus, and unity, given in a way that requires unquestioning acceptance. Many of the more fascinating debates have arisen around the textual meaning of writers notoriously difficult to interpret: for example divergent readings of Weberian writings from functionalist and interpretive perspectives; discussions that follow from what Foucault may or may not have said. Fragmentation creates a space for weaker voices (Hardy 1994) who would otherwise be marginalized by institutionalization, centralization and concentration.

Ten years ago, we noted that it was unlikely that a 'solution' to the 'problem' of paradigm incommensurability would ever be found. As theories became ever more sophisticated in attempts to bridge the yawning chasm between the paradigms, the very basis of the theorizing became more vulnerable to criticism. For example, as Burrell pointed out in 1996, Kuhn used the term 'paradigm' in at least twenty different ways; writers debated whether critiques of *Paradigms* should draw on Kuhn at all, since the authors had not intended to use a Kuhnian version of 'paradigm' (e.g. Jackson and Carter 1993; critiquing Willmott 1993a); still others levelled charges of misrepresenting or misunderstanding Kuhn (e.g. Cannella and Paetzold 1994 with respect to Pfeffer 1993) and pointed to differences between the earlier and later Kuhn. Given that the emphasis on language games as barrier or bridge draws on Wittgenstein and Derrida, the possibilities for reinterpretation are endless. These are theoretical resources conducive not to definitive resolution, but to sophisticated debate; a 'speech conversation' (Habermas 1979) whose ideal is not closure but an infinite horizon of possibilities. Even if a 'solution' was to be found, it is unlikely it would be accepted, not if it let down the defences that some individuals believed necessary to protect 'alternative' work. So, for these reasons we did not believe that the paradigm debate could be resolved and we noted that, in fact, it may well had run its course. Perhaps it was time to move on. It seems that we were accurate in that regard. The paradigm wars, which were so important to the emergence of alternative approaches, now seem a part – an important part – of our history. They have shaped our thinking and led to countless illuminating – and obscure – conversations, but they no longer appear to be a major part of organization studies' version of a *lingua franca*.

These paradigm wars were never part of the language used by adherents of the orthodoxy, who appeared mainly to ignore the alternative approaches they brought into relief (Aldrich 1988). When the notion of paradigm was taken up in the US, it had little to do with the struggles described above. Instead, Pfeffer (1993) made a plea for paradigm consensus which, he argued, was necessary to protect organization studies from 'hostile takeover' (1995: 618), the threat of which came primarily from Economics. Pfeffer's protectionism was interpreted by many as a deliberately political strategy to define organization studies by investing the old elite with the necessary power to screen out undesirable elements.

> Pfeffer requires blind faith and unquestioning adherence to a dogma decreed to be 'true' by the elites of organization studies … [Pfeffer's solution] … doubtless would increase the comfort level of those who are already established … [but] it will increase the costs of entry for new scholars and restrict innovative results on the output side (Cannella and Paetzold 1994: 337–8).

Pfeffer ignored most of the original paradigm warriors (Clegg and Hardy 1996b) and, in this regard, was not atypical of the broader intellectual establishment in the US, where the rationalist, quantitative, normative approaches associated with functionalism and normal science had their strongest foothold. A comparison of the different citation patterns found in *Organization Studies* and *Administrative Science Quarterly* for a matched period of coterminous publication found that the only European amongst 103 sources that received three or more citations in *ASQ* was Max Weber, who has been dead for most of the twentieth century. The European-based journal, *Organization Studies,* on the other hand, was found to be far more catholic, with cites of scholars based both in North America and elsewhere (Üsdiken and Pasadeos 1995). Aldrich's (1998) finding that critical theorists

had made a minimal impact on leading North America journals was interpreted as an unwillingness of parts of the United States intellectual 'establishment' in organization theory to welcome new, contradictory, and challenging ideas (Marsden, 1993), especially when written by 'alien' scholars.

Counter-attacks were made, however, including John Van Maanen's condemnation of the tyranny of the 'Pfeffer-digm' at the subsequent Academy of Management meeting (also see Van Maanen 1995). Van Maanen (1979) had edited a special issue of *Administrative Science Quarterly* on qualitative methodologies as early as 1979. Karl Weick and Steve Barley had been editors of *Administrative Science Quarterly*, neither of whom can be called practitioners of 'orthodoxy'. Qualitative articles started to appear in the quantitative sanctum of the *Academy of Management Journal* (e.g. Dutton and Dukerich 1991; Elsbach and Sutton 1992); a special issue of which (36(6), 1993) included such exotica as hermeneutics (Phillips and Brown 1993), symbolic interactionism (Prasad 1993) and textual deconstructionism (Gephart 1993). The winner of the Annual Conference of the Academy of Management's best paper award in 1994 was an ethnomethodological piece with a distinctly critical edge (Barker 1993). The *Academy of Management Review* published a special issue (17(3), 1992) on new intellectual currents in organization and management theory; *Administrative Science Quarterly* (43(2)) followed in 1998 with a special issue on critical perspectives on organizational control. In 1997, the first edition of the *Handbook of Organization Studies* won the Academy of Management's George F. Terry Award for the book judged to have made the most outstanding contribution to the advancement of management knowledge in the previous year. Critical Management Studies (CMS) appeared in the pre-conference portion of the 1998 Academy of Management meetings to provide a forum for researchers interested in critical approaches and, in 2003, became a fully fledged interest group, while in the UK, the first CMS conference was launched in 1999 and afterwards held biennially. In 1999, the Academy of Management declared itself as taking a journey into a 'pluralist world', although as one observer noted, it was not clear that it necessarily wanted to stay there (Hardy 2002). The first section of the 2003 *Oxford Handbook of Organization Theory* edited by Haridimos Tsoukas and Christian Knudsen covered positivism, interpretivism, critical theory and postmodernism. In 2004, the *Academy of Management Review* published a special issue (29(4)) on language and organization: the doing of discourse. As a result, while it cannot be said that normal science is an endangered species (or even a singular species), new ways of doing and thinking about research are clearly emerging and, increasingly, receiving some degree of blessing from bastions of orthodoxy, such as the Academy of Management. There have been significant responses from other conceptions of the field as well; for instance, Joel C. Baum's (2002) edited *Blackwell Companion to Organizations*, in which a collection of authors, largely from the US, divided the field into different levels: the intraorganizational, organizational and interorganizational, together with a discussion of organizational epistemology and research methods. It is a useful collection, despite the somewhat arbitrary definition of 'levels' (Collins, 1998), but somewhat less pluralistic than the present collection.

Of course, over the last ten years, alternative approaches have themselves changed. Purist forms of postmodernism seem to have retreated from view and, to a certain extent there has been a melding of ideas from postmodernism and critical theory (Fournier and Grey 2000), although not without some dissent (Thompson 2004). As critical work has become more institutionalized, it has become more sympathetic towards management (Alvesson and Willmott 1996; 2003; Fournier and Grey 2000; Adler 2002; Clegg et al. 2004). In the past, many critical theorists were unwilling to engage with managers for fear of transforming CMS into 'just another "tool kit" for managers, who, equipped with their better understanding of power relations in organizations … [can] further their domination' (Fournier and Grey 2000: 25). However, more recently, critical perspectives have engaged with management practice (Anthony 1998; Fournier and Grey 2000; Clegg et al. forthcoming). Critical work is even promoted for its potential benefits for managers (e.g. Carson et al 2000), as well as other stakeholders, such as politicians, policymakers, regulators, and the general public (Zald 2002a). The institutionalization of critical work also appears to be producing a debate about what it means to be critical (Adler 2002; Grey and Willmott 2002; Nord 2002; Walsh and Weber 2002; Zald 2002a; Alvesson and Willmott 2003; Clegg et al. forthcoming). For example, different writers have argued that critical work should: take the interests of 'society' into account rather than emphasizing a concern with

profit; recognize the existence of divergent interests; provide a voice for those who are traditionally marginalized; produce more equitable and ethical outcomes; denaturalize commonly taken-for-granted understandings; appreciate the centrality of language to understanding; and promote fundamental reflection on the part of managers and academics (Alvesson and Willmott 1996; 2003; Fournier and Grey 2000; Adler 2002; Grey 2002; Grey and Willmott 2002).

In other words neither the orthodox nor the unorthodox are fixed: through 'an ongoing, gradual and subtle diversification of research practice away from a reliance on positivist practices, space [in the mainstream] has been formed for a repertoire of discursive, critical and post structural approaches' (Hardy et al. 2005: 803). Some are concerned that the result may be cooptation (e.g. Rhodes 2005) but, rather than seeing this as problematic for alternative approaches, we feel it reflects changes in research and publishing practices. Mainstream theorization is being required, at best, to rethink its position or, at the very least, to accept the existence of other positions. What this engagement raises is the question of the form that theorizing of this future 'identity work' will assume in order to maintain an alternative status.

Theorizing

Theorizing, as any other representational practice, is nothing less, nothing more, and nothing other than its practices of representation. Now, this is not to surrender the field to relativism. Any representation can be related to other, earlier, later, alternative representations, especially when ostensibly of the same thing. The fact is, as we shall argue, there are no *objective* grounds that exist from which to criticize any one genre of representation from another. We need to abandon those oppositions that insist that, on the one hand, the objective is privileged because it stands free of all phenomenology and exists as it is, in its magnificent facticity and, on the other hand, the view that privileges subjectivity as the authentic and natural locus of real experience.

Metaphysically, objectivity is the recognition that objects and events are independent of one's perceptions of them, or one's personal feelings, opinions and beliefs. While we have no problem with recognizing the objectivity of organizations as phenomena that exist independently of those more or less theorized representations that we have of them, simultaneously, we know them only through such representations. And our penchant for particular forms of practice is such that feelings, opinions and beliefs do enter into the judgements that we make of the epistemic adequacy of representations. It could not be otherwise, at least, not according to the insights of embodied realism, which start from the well-grounded premise that, contra Cartesianism, the mind is inherently embodied; much of its thought is unconscious and, where it is accomplished through abstract concepts, these are largely metaphorical (Lakoff and Johnson 1999: 3). If knowledge is metaphorical, this locates it in an uneasy space for both literal realists and literal constructionists, because our metaphors are determined neither by the nature of things nor do they determine the things of nature. The relation between words and the world is far more contingent and, because it is contingent, there are elements of historical, contextual and cultural specificity in the knowledge that we produce.

Lakoff and Johnson (1999: 7) note of metaphorical thought, '[it] is the principal tool that makes philosophical insight possible and that constrains the forms that philosophy can take'. When we construct concepts of organization theory, or anything else, we do so out of metaphors, not out of literal relations. The argument that an increase in organization size will lead to its becoming more bureaucratic depends on a complex set of metaphorical equations. These equations do have some primary literalness – such as being bigger or smaller – but, in scientific terms, they will always depend on the metaphors we use to enact them. For instance, organizations grow larger through the contracts of employment they write because this determines the number of people contractually embedded within them. But this is a metaphorical choice: it was made at a time when it seemed as if this was the only way that organizations might grow, before outsourcing contracts were common and networks extended capabilities. Today, the metaphor of size, to be literal, to be consistent with our experience of the changing world of organizations, would have to be more complex – and we have to devise some way of reconciling calculations and comparisons made in terms of the different instrumentalities that the different literalities might suggest. The aptness of the size metaphor premised on employment contracts

has declined with ontological changes in the ways in which organizations are constituted. That which is being represented is no more unchanging than a shoreline or a reef remains the same: they change organically and so do organizations. While reefs and shorelines change as a result of unanticipated consequences of myriad small acts of nature and intervention by various agencies, not least those that are human, organizations change as a result of acts conceived autopoietically, as an extension of human intersubjectivities. Organizations change according to reflexive acts of organizing as well as a result of non-cognitive phenomena.

All extensions of human intersubjectivities, such as organizations, create phenomena that exist independently of the understanding that any observers or participants might have of them. The university in which these words are being written is not merely an effect of the understandings that its members and significant others have of it. But the nature of the university as a phenomenon is not such that it has a being that constitutes the concepts that we have of it, or that somehow tell us which concepts are right and which are wrong – there are no absolute truths – but this does not entail that there is no apt knowledge.

Interesting scientific theories have inferences about multiple subject matters, as Lakoff and Johnson (1999: 91) note; for instance, in organization studies we might draw inferences from discourse analysis, business histories, ethnographic studies, as well as cross-sectional survey data. At present our theories tend to be representationally embedded in each of these different forms of activity; in each one we will find assumptions that both predetermine the results of inquiry before data is collected, as well as assumptions that already circumscribe what is to count as data, thus these assumptions are obstacles to building scientific knowledge. For instance, when discourse theory uses methods derived from conversational analysis, the analysts will concentrate on discursively available and recordable data. On the other hand, phenomena that are not discursively available will not feature any more than would discursively available but unrecordable data. Contingency theorists using tried and tested instruments to collect their data already subscribe to a specific ontology of organizations before they cross any organization's threshold because they assume, a priori, that the size of the organization is a function of its employment contracts. They may not know the outcome of any data specific act of collection – but what data collection will occur is already prefigured by the assumptions that have been constituted in its instruments. It is therefore becoming increasingly evident that researchers need to draw on the rich pluralities available in organization studies to review reflexively the methods they do choose and what they imply, by which we mean not so much an engagement with the confirmation of deductive logic, but an engagement that questions its auspices through reflections on other methods, approaches, and assumptions.

Reflexivity also means questioning whether or not social sciences can establish general knowledge claims, as Flyvbjerg (2006) does in this volume. He believes research in the social sciences should rely on the study of particular cases rather than generalized theory. His methodology is 'contextual' in that it considers the particular and context-dependent over the universal; the concrete and practical over the theoretical; and regards most phenomena of significance as relational. This *phronesis* raises questions concerning values, power, closeness, minutiae, practices, concrete case studies, context, how-questions, narrative/ history, actor/structure, and dialogue. It questions the strict object/subject divisions that have riddled conventional accounts of science. This division only admits two solutions: objects determine what subjects objectively should think and the trick is to unravel nature's message; or subjects determine the nature of objects through intersubjective agreement. The subject/object split is mistaken: objects only exist in as much as subjects perceive them to be, a perception which describes and categorizes them as being what they are taken to be. Organizations do not exist apart from the actions of people: those who are their subjects, other interested parties, and those upon whom their effects are registered as objects. How such subjects, parties and objects articulate their experience of organizations through their own metaphors and categorizations is then translated through the filter of additional metaphors and categorizations that organization theorists use to make sense of their studies.

Methodological assumptions are, therefore, inescapable but they do not have to be hermetically sealed. To the extent that the metaphors and categorizations that we use fail to connect with the embodied experiences of those in organizations, they will lack realistic content. And of course, as complex stratified

entities, there is a plurality of experiences with which to connect – or not connect. An embodied realism demands conversation with the subjects of its science and help us understand what our metaphors have missed. Conversations also help us see the figures in the landscape, moving through it, retreating to its margins, filling it with their voices, their anxieties, their emotions, their feelings, their beauty, and the ghosts that haunt them; their ancestors, both literal and real, affording a 'physical engagement with an environment in an ongoing series of interactions' (Lakoff and Johnson 1999: 90). The broader these interactions are, ethnographically, and the deeper they are historically, the more reflexive they will be. Reflexivity thus points to the limits of inquiry and pervades all concerns with theory, epistemology, methodology, and ontology, which are always bound up with any and every instance of practical research. Bonner (2001) argues that the way in which one makes sense of any given sense-making phenomena, such as organizations, will be oriented to the very same environment that the phenomena constitutes. Organization members are reflexive insofar as their action is oriented by taking into account the behaviour of others; this members' reflexivity thus has to be taken into account by the theorist whose task it is to interpret this action; thus, one needs to reflect both on the members' reflexivity and on one's own reflexivity.

Reflexivity opens up a vortex. In looking at the assumptions of inquiry one has to deal with 'problems of community and authority as against just theory and empiricism' (Bonner 2001: 270). Mostly, organization theory has preferred just theory and empiricism. By this we mean that it has been easier for theorists to work from their theoretical communities, relatively untroubled by their principles of construction, inclusion and exclusion. Doing so they allow either the empiricism of their subjects (the constructs, phenomena and data that they construct), or their own empiricism (the theoretical sense made of these constructs), to dominate. Excluding from examination the way that organization members' structure how a phenomenon is recognized in the first place means unreflectively adopting the taken-for-granted assumptions of these members precisely at the point where these are what need to be examined. It is to fail to ask the basic question – how is this phenomenon possible? And how is our understanding of this phenomenon as *that* phenomenon possible? After post-structuralism, the answer to these questions is that all understandings – both lay and expert – exist as a form of moral community, even though such an idea violates scientific moral communities' self-understanding as neutral and detached.

Method, theory and values are deeply tangled up. It might seem comforting if these problems could be solved by expertise – the organization scientist making pronouncements as the truth and falsity of certain representations – but it should be equally evident that there are no privileged grounds from which to do so. The growth of 'postmodern' work obliterated the privileged 'individual' – that stable constellation of essential characteristics at the centre of the social, psychological, economic, and moral universe – in favour of the 'subject' – a decentred, relative, socially constituted, and socially recognized category of analysis. As the status of the subject became challenged so, too, was that of the researcher.

Reflecting

No longer all-knowing, all-seeing, objective and omnipotent, the researcher has been forced to re-examine his or her relation to the research process, and is now acutely aware of the social and historical positioning of all subjects and the particular intellectual frameworks through which they are rendered visible, the researcher could now only produce knowledge already embedded in the power of those very frameworks. No privileged position remained from which analysis could arbitrate (Denzin and Lincoln 1994). As these ideas gained currency, more researchers began to engage in 'reflexivity', which can be broadly defined to mean an understanding of the knowledge-making enterprise and, particularly, a consideration of the institutional, social and political processes whereby research is conducted and knowledge is produced (Calás and Smircich 1999). Normative work was deemed to completely ignore such issues (Hardy and Clegg 1997). The majority of interpretive work in organization studies also fell short of reflexivity because of the tendency to focus on cultural engineering (see chapter by Martin et al. (2006)), which left little space for problematizing the research process (Hardy and Clegg 1997). It was, as a result, left largely to postmodern and critical researchers to tackle these issues.

Postmodernist writers responded to these challenges by directly targeting the privileged position of the researcher and critically examining the assumptions that underpinned the holy trinity of 'author', 'text' and 'reader'. 'The notion of an expert writing from within an institution in social scientific language is one that cannot be sustained if postmodernism is accepted' (Parker 1992: 12).

However, critics charged that, in focusing on the text, postmodernist researchers distanced themselves from those who experienced and consumed the phenomena around which they constructed their academic endeavours, especially as Marsden and Townley (1996) pointed out at the time, not much empirical research was being conducted (Hardy and Clegg 1997). Instead, scholars were urged to spend their time with other scholars. For example, Burrell (1994) asked us to be less like social science researchers (carrying out empirical work) and more like philosophers.

> To confront a professional philosopher is to confront one's own ignorance. Nevertheless, the embarrassment must be endured. As social scientists, we need to be more like philosophers; as people locked into empiricism we should be more excited by the transcendental; as pursuers of practice we should be more utopian in what we advocate (Burrell 1994: 15).

Recognition of the impossibility of theory-neutral observation appeared to undermine confidence in empirical work, lest it be tainted with empiricism, and encouraged a retreat into the relative safety of theory. The world was not a stage, 'but a text to be read and interpreted' (Marsden and Townley 1996: 670). The pollution of everyday life was kept at textual length; reducing opportunities for listening to, never mind learning from, the subject.

> The problems of (fictional) individuals in (mythical) organizations are safely placed behind philosophical double-glazing and their cries are treated as interesting examples of discourse (Parker 1992: 11).

It seemed that postmodernist writers had retreated to the safety of a relativist position, which enabled them to speak primarily to other researchers and academics, rather than acknowledge the subjects being 'studied'.

Critical theorists came in for similar censure (Denzin 1994; Hardy and Clegg 1997). Under the rubric of 'false consciousness' and 'real interests', they presumed to judge what their research subjects' best interests were. Subjects were told what to feel and how to act; subjects who did not act in this way were translated as a cultural idiot who has fallen prey to false consciousness. Other subjects, such as managers, were not allowed to feel, speak or act at all (Nord and Jermier 1992). In this way, critical work, despite its emancipatory ideals, was distanced from the subjects it purported to serve. For example, in contrasting Freire's (1992) philosophy and teaching method, Taylor (1993) found the latter undermined the former by being anti-dialogic and manipulative, partly as a result of the practical and logistical difficulties involved in translating a thought into action in a way that was consistent with the underpinning philosophy. It is, it appeared, one thing to write a coherent critical position, and another to act in its terms, especially when the use of esoteric theoretical terminology offered little illumination or practical help (Nord and Doherty 1994).

> You can write ... in a literature mode because the subjects do not read your work any more. You are not worried about your audience, which is purely academic (Zald quoted in O'Connor et al. 1995: 125).

Again, the distance between researcher and subject, combined with the lack of empirical work, resulted in a lack of reflexivity.

Researchers were 'developing' their understanding of the research process and, yet, they seemed to become further removed from it and, especially, the research subjects who populated it. As Burrell (1996: 645) pointed out, analysis 'requires the death or at least the mutilation of that which is analysed'. Normal scientists issued edicts and predictions about appropriate behaviour, as measured by highly sophisticated, quantitative analyses and experimental paraphernalia, from the safety of their laboratories. Subjects to them were like rats in a maze. The theoreticians who populated much of the critical and postmodernist genres preferred the haven of the library. Everyone ignored someone: the functionalists ignored workers; critical theorists ignored managers; the philosophers ignored everyone. Even ethnographers seemed distanced as they returned with 'stories about strange people' (Denzin and Lincoln 1994a: 7) and misrepresented 'deviants as heroes' (Denzin and Lincoln 1994a: 9). Being reflexive, it seemed, was not easy!

In the last 10 years, reflexivity has hit its stride, leading Weick (1999: 803; also see Weick 2002) to argue that theory construction has become largely an 'exercise in disciplined reflexivity' as it has captured the

interest of not only critical and postmodern theorists, but also positivists and interpretivists (e.g. Alvesson and Willmott 1996; Calás and Smircich 1999; Easterby-Smith and Malina 1999; Barge and Oliver 2003). As a result, a number of different reflexive practices may be noted in the literature (Harley et al. 2004).

One set of practices is associated with attempts to 'reveal' the authorial identity of the field worker through measures developed in anthropology (Harley et al. 2004). According to this view, researchers are subjects just like any other (Olesen 2000), constructed in and through the research project. It therefore behoves them to declare the authorial personality and to divulge the steps taken in order to present their work as respectable research (e.g. Boje and Rosile 1994; Jeffcutt 1994; Reinharz 1997). Such practices force the researcher to ask questions about the relationship between the author and the 'Other' – the research subject (Gergen and Gergen 2000). In so doing, the privileged power position of the researcher in relation to the research subject is reduced (Marcus 1994), and the reader is given a more active role in interpreting meaning (Jermier 1985). Such practices provide ways for the reflexive researcher to 'decenter authors as authority figures; and to involve participants, readers and audiences in the production of research' (Putnam 1996: 386). However, as some writers have noted (Hardy and Clegg 1997), attempts to let the (research) subject speak in this way often had the opposite effect:

> Though I clearly empathized with, sought to empower, and indeed suffered for my support of the disadvantaged in the setting, my summative account was staged as a dramatized monologue. The voices of other indigenous participants in the setting, that I so carefully recorded and transcribed, were indeed extensively presented 'verbatim' in the text. However, the presence of these indigenous voices, though apparently dialogic, was in actuality dramatic, in which their contributions had been selected and staged as typifications of a culture to be represented, the emotional intensity of the melodrama, as well as the staging of authority and credibility in the quest for persuasion, were inextricably linked to the author's need to successfully withstand the ordeal of an academic rite of passage (i.e. the achievement of completing a doctorate) (Jeffcutt 1994: 251–2).

Ironically, by problematizing the researcher in this way, we draw all the attention to her, especially as researchers have engaged increasingly in forms of experimental writing to achieve reflexivity through such means as fiction, narratives of the self, performance science, polyvocal texts, responsive readings, aphorisms, comedy and satire, visual presentations, auto-enthnographies and mixed genres (see Richardson 1994).

Another approach to reflexivity owes much to the writings of Derrida (1974; 1982) and Foucault (1979; 1980). Operating from the premise that all knowledge projects are dangerous, insofar that any version of truth carries with it a particular configuration of political privileges, knowledge claims need to be closely interrogated. Consequently, Foucauldian insights have been used to work on strategy (Knights and Morgan 1991; Knights 1992), TQM (Knights and McCabe 2002) and HRM (Townley 1993). Calás and Smircich (1991), Kilduff (1993) and Mumby and Putnam (1992) use the ideas of Derrida (Linstead 1993) to deconstruct classic organizational texts. Such an approach to reflexivity tends to highlight the lack of reflexivity on the part of others and, unlike the work above, is rarely directed towards itself. Self-reflexivity is not applied to enrich ones own research, but to point out the shortcomings of others (Harley et al. 2004).

A third set of reflexive practices is associated with the use of multiple perspectives (Harley et al. 2004), including paradigms, metaphors, vocabularies, theories, interpretations and frames (e.g. Hassard 1991; Martin 1992; Willmott 1993a, b; Alvesson 1996; 2003; Schultz and Hatch 1996; Alvesson and Sköldberg 2000; Knights and McCabe 2002). Researchers use tensions among different perspectives to open up new ways of thinking. For example, Knights and McCabe (2002: 235) use rational managerialist, critical control, and processual interpretations 'to build on earlier approaches [to TQM] in the anticipation we might move beyond our present understanding'. These practices help to counter the foundational claim of any single perspective that it offers a better understanding of reality, by helping researchers to ask: What are the different ways in which a phenomenon can be understood and how do they produce different knowledge(s)? Constructive rather than deconstructive, epistemological problems nonetheless exist concerning the choice of particular perspectives and moving among them (Harley et al. 2004).

A fourth set of practices acknowledges that social processes shape knowledge through controls embedded in the research process (Harley et al.

2004), meaning that the researcher can construct 'knowledge' only in the context of a particular research community and society (e.g. Alvesson and Sköldberg 2000; Hardy et al. 2001). Building on work in the sociology of scientific knowledge and science and technology studies, this approach helps to identify the political and rhetorical processes by which knowledge claims are accepted as true or false in a particular institutional setting (Shapin 1995). It is thus the social institutions of academia and society that shape research processes and outcomes as context, power, and historical circumstances combine to produce knowledge (Deetz 1996; Putnam 1996), although some researchers can skilfully negotiate them through the judicious use of power (Putnam 1996), artful deployment of rhetorical maneuvers (Shapin 1995), and knowing the rules of the game (Mauws and Phillips 1995). As a result, this approach tends to return us to a view of the heroic researcher, elevating the status of the author once again (Harley et al. 2004).

Reflexivity has, indeed, come to occupy a more prominent place in the last 10 years – as Reed points out in this volume – it is a hallmark of contemporary work in organization studies, although, as Weick (1999) has pointed out, reflexivity can also lead to narcissism, self-indulgence, and paralysis, when the injunction to be reflexive is enacted in terms of the thinking ego rather than the auspices of those traditions through which any subject in question thinks. Nonetheless there has been considerable effort made over the last 10 years to conduct empirical work that tries to put these ideas into practice in forms of self-reflexivity (see Phillips and Hardy 2002 on reflexivity as part of the empirical work using discourse analysis). Despite the challenges posed by reflexive research – and the fact that it is not and cannot be perfect – we maintain our commitment, voiced 10 years ago, to reflexivity. We consider reflexive theoretical positions to be those best able to account for their own theorizing, as well as whatever it is they theorize about. It is not the alleged 'disinterestedness' of a position that makes it worthwhile, but the degree of reflexivity that it exhibits in relation to the conditions of its own existence. Severing the conversational elements that nurtured the theory in the first place and which link it to practice makes it harder to attain this reflexivity. Thus we argue for the grounding of theoretical claims in local and specific circumstances, rather than their radical and rapid translation out of them.

This makes most sense in an organizational world that is part of the social, and inscribed with the materiality of words and the indeterminacy of meaning. Nor should we overlook the fact that the researcher is just another subject, subjected to and resistant against the controls embedded in the research process, of which she or he is a part.

Concluding

Our perspective differs from Popperian conceptions of what a science should be, which suggest that it consists of 'objective' knowledge that is neutral about – and separate from – what it studies. We suggest instead that 'objective' knowledge is knowledge better able to account for its own production, and the production of the phenomena to which it attends. Objectivity inheres in the degree of reflexivity that knowledge exhibits in relation to the conditions of its own existence. So, for instance, we find the work of Callon (1986) compelling in its objectivity, not because it is disinterestedly Popperian in its methodology, aping a normative science model, but because it seeks to be reflexive. It addresses the conditions of its own existence as theory; it addresses the conditions of existence of other interests touched by this theory, and it addresses the conditions of existence as they are theorized by these other interests, both as 'science' and as 'lay practice'.

Theoretical positions can be judged according to three criteria. The first criteria of differentiation relates to the ways in which theories separate themselves from the practices of 'individual(s)' in the 'organization(s)' that sustain them. How does the epistemology of a theoretical position translate into the practical knowledge of those researching and those being researched? Is this knowledge mediated, and, if so, on whose terms? For instance, Barley et al (1988) demonstrate how organization theorists' accounts of culture have been progressively interpellated on terms determined by an agenda of consultancy rather than research, even in research work. In this respect, the differentiation of 'culture' from 'practice' has diminished, to the detriment of theorization that is able to account for itself reflexively. Instead, empirically grounded knowledge has given way to research agendas shaped increasingly by prescriptive and normative conceptions of practice; not, please note, by practice itself, but by 'normative' accounts of it that fail to differentiate research and practice.

Differentiation means being able to acknowledge the interplay between them by being able to tell the difference between them: research never escapes practice but it is not the same as practice.

The second criteria refers to the ways in which theory knows itself to be the type of theory that it is, and it is not; the reference images it uses in fixing its identity. How does the theory recognize itself, and achieve its epistemological self-recognition? Is the identity of the theory fixed in reference to other theories, or is it the outcome of a deliberate process of ritualized self-reference? For instance, Donaldson (1985) defines the Aston Studies as incorrigible because no other theory has used the protocols and rituals of the Aston Studies to prove otherwise. Of course, to do so would mean that the 'other' theory would already have lost its identity and been enrolled into a project whose rituals would make its truths indubitable (an argument addressed at greater length in Clegg 1990). We advocate theorizing that adopts a broad discourse. Not patterns of self-citation within discursive communities (e.g. population ecology citing population ecology) but recognition, negative and positive, of and from theoretical 'others'. Theorizing that is nomadic, that ranges across territories of intellectual life is, we believe, more valuable and more interesting than theory which sticks tight to its own knitting, secure within its own conventions and boundaries. Better boundary spanning and extension than boundary maintenance.

Third, theoretical communities that are pluralistic, whose members engage in debate among and between themselves are more reflective than those who conform to the conventional wisdom, who ignore dissidents, who reveal theoretical group think. Better the paradigm 'warriors' (e.g. Burrell and Morgan 1979; Donaldson 1985; Reed 1985; Hassard 1988; 1991; Organization Studies 1988; Clegg 1990; Gioia and Pitre 1990; Jackson and Carter 1991; 1993; Parker and McHugh 1991; Marsden 1993; Willmott 1993a, b), like-minded academics in terms of their disdain for the orthodox consensus, who cite, engage, struggle, argue with each other, at times vigorously and incisively, more than the self-contained Pfefferdigm (Pfeffer 1993). It is in the struggle that we learn (see Zald 1994): from the diversity and ambiguity of meaning, not through the recitation of a presumed uniformity, consensus, and unity, given in a way that requires unquestioning acceptance.

Forms of theoretical representation that cannot address criteria such as these are unreflexive about their existence, a lack of reflexivity that augurs ill for their 'knowledge' in and of the organizational world. Theories which differentiate between themselves and the practices that sustain them; whose identity is formed with reference to other positions; which recognizes and engages in dialogue and debate is most likely to be reflexive. Self-regarding behaviour in the absence of recognition by and from others is of no value in itself. On these criteria, it is not the alleged 'disinterestedness' of positions that makes them worthwhile, but the degree of reflexivity that they exhibit in relation to the conditions of their own existence.

References

Adler, P. (2002) 'Critical in the name of whom and what?', *Organization*, 9: 387–95.

Aldrich, H. (1988) 'Paradigm warriors: Donaldson versus the critics of organization theory', *Organization Studies*, 9(I): 19–25.

Alvesson, M. (1996) *Communication, Power and Organization*. Berlin/New York: de Gruyter.

Alvesson, M. (2003) 'Beyond neopositivists, romantics and localists: A reflexive approach to interviews in organisational research', *Academy of Management Review*, 28: 13–33.

Alvesson, M. and Sköldberg, K. (2000) *Reflexive Methodology: New Vistas for Qualitative Research*. London: Sage.

Alvesson, M. and Willmott, H. (1996) *Making Sense of Management: A Critical Introduction*. London: Sage.

Alvesson, M., and Willmott, H. (2003) *Studying Management Critically*. Sage: London.

Anthony, P. (1998) 'Management education: Ethics versus morality', in M. Parker (ed.), *Ethics and Organization*. London: Sage. pp. 269–81.

Ashkenas, R., Ulrich, D., Jick, T. and Kerr, S. (1995) *The Boundaryless Organization: Breaking the Chains of Organizational Structure*. San Francisco: Jossey-Bass.

Atkinson, M. (1971) *Orthodox Consensus and Radical Alternative: A Study in Sociological Theory*. London: Heinemann.

Bain, P. and Taylor, P. (2000) 'Entraped by the 'electronic panopticon'? Worker resistance in the call centre', *New Technology, Work and Employment*, 15(1): 2–18.

Barge, J. and Oliver, C. (2003) 'Working with appreciation in managerial practice', *Academy of Management Review*, 28: 124–39.

Barker, J. R. (1993) 'Tightening the iron cage: Concertive control in self-management teams', *Administrative Science Quarterly*, 38: 408–37.

Barley, S., Meyer, G. and Gash, D. (1988) 'Cultures of cultures: Academics, practitioners and the pragmatics of normative control', *Administrative Science Quarterly*, 33: 24–60.

Baum, J. (ed.) (2002) *The Blackwell Companion to Organizations*. Oxford: Blackwell.

Blackler, F. (1995) 'Knowledge, knowledge work and organizations: An overview and interpretation', *Organization Studies*, 16(6): 1021–46.

Boden, D. (1994) *The Business of Talk: Organizations in Action*. Cambridge: Polity Press.

Boje, D. and Rosile, G. (1994) 'Diversities, differences and authors' voices', *Journal of Organisational Change Management*, 7: 8–17.

Bonner, K.M. (2001) 'Reflexivity and interpretive sociology: the case of analysis and the problem of nihilism', *Human Studies*, 24: 267–92.

Braverman, H. (1974) *Labour and Monopoly Capital*. Chicago: University of Chicago Press.

Brocklehurst, M. (2001) 'Power, identity and new technology homework: Implications for 'new forms' of organizing', *Organization Studies*, 22(3): 445–66.

Burawoy, M. (1979) *Manufacturing Consent*. Chicago: Chicago University Press.

Burrell, G. and Morgan, G. (1979) *Sociological Paradigms and Organizational Analysis Elements of the Sociology of Corporate Life*. London: Heinemann.

Burrell, G. (1994) 'Modernism, postmodernism and organizational analysis 4: The contribution of Jurgen Habermas', *Organization Studies*, 15(1): 1–19.

Burrell, G. (1996) 'Normal science, paradigms, metaphors, discourses and genealogies of analysis', in S.R. Clegg, C. Hardy and W.R. Nord (eds), *Handbook of organization studies*. London: Sage. pp. 642–58.

Calás, M. and Smircich, L. (1991) 'Voicing seduction to silence leadership', *Organization Studies*, 12: 567–602.

Calás, M.B. and Smircich, L. (1999) 'Past postmodernism? Reflections and tentative directions', *Academy of Management Review*, 24: 649–71.

Callon, M. (1986) 'Some elements of a sociology of translation: Domestication of the scallops and the fishermen of St Briene Bay', in J. Law (ed.), *Power Action and Belief: a Sociology of Knowledge? Sociological Review Monograph*, 32. London: Routledge. pp. 132–61.

Cannella, A.A. and Paetzold, R.L. (1994) 'Pfeffer's barriers to the advance of organization science: a rejoinder', *Academy of Management Review*, 19: 331–41.

Carson, P., Lanier, P., Carson, D. and Guidry, B. (2000) 'Clearing a path through the management fashion jungle: Some preliminary trailblazing', *Academy of Management Journal*, 43: 1146–58.

Cascio, W.F. (2000) 'Managing a virtual workplace', *The Academy of Management Executive*, 14: 81–90.

Chandler, A.D. (1962) *Strategy and Structure: Chapters in the History of the American Industrial Enterprise*. Cambridge, MA: MIT Press.

Clegg, S.R. (1990) *Modern Organizations: Organization Studies in the Postmodern World*. London: Sage.

Clegg, S.R. and Dunkerley, D. (1980) *Organization, Class and Control*. London and Boston: Routledge and Kegan Paul.

Clegg, S.R. and Hardy, C. (1996) 'Representations', in S.R. Clegg, C. Hardy and W. Nord (eds), *Handbook of Organization Studies*. London: Sage. pp. 676–708.

Clegg, S.R, Kornberger, M. Carter, C. and Rhodes, C. (forthcoming) 'For management?', *Management Learning*.

Clegg, S.R., Kornberger, M. and Rhodes, C. (2004) 'Noise, parasites and translation', *Management Learning*, 35(1): 31–44.

Collins, R. (1981) 'On the microfoundations of macrosociology', *American Journal of Sociology*, 86: 984–1013.

Collins, R. (1998) *The Sociology of Philosophies: A Global Theory of Intellectual Change*. Cambridge: Harvard University Press.

Deetz, S. (1996) 'Describing differences in approaches to organization science: Rethinking Burrell and Morgan and their legacy', *Organization Science*, 7: 191–207.

Denzin, N.K. (1994) 'The art and politics of interpretation', in N.K. Denzin and Y.S. Lincoln (eds), *Handbook of Qualitative Research*. London: Sage. pp. 500–15.

Denzin, N.K. and Lincoln, Y.S. (1994) 'Entering the field of qualitative research', in N.K. Denzin and Y.S. Lincoln (eds.) *Handbook of Qualitative Research*. London: Sage. pp. 1–18.

Derrida, J. (1974) *Of Grammatology*. Baltimore: The Johns Hopkins University Press.

Derrida, J. (1982) *Margins of Philosophy*. Chicago: University of Chicago Press.

Dewett, T. and Jones, G.R. (2001) 'The role of information technology in the organization: A review, model, and assessment', *Journal of Management*, 27: 313–46.

Dodgson, M. (1993) 'Organisational learning: A review of some lieratures', *Organization Studies*, 14(3): 375–94.

Donaldson, L. (1985) *In Defence of Organization Theory: A Reply to the Critics*. Cambridge: Cambridge University Press.

Dooley, K.J. and Van de Ven, A.H. (1999) 'Explaining complex organizational dynamics', *Organization Science*, 10(3): 358–72.

Drucker, P. (1994) 'The age of social transformation', *The Atlantic Monthly*, November, 53–78.

Dutton, J. and Dukerich, J. (1991) 'Keeping an eye on the mirror: Image and identity in organizational adaptation', *Academy of Management*, 34(3): 517–54.

Easterby-Smith, M. and Malina, D. (1999) 'Cross-cultural collaborative research: Toward reflexivity', *Academy of Management Journal*, 42: 76–86.

Elsbach, K.D. and Sutton, R.I. (1992) 'Acquiring organizational legitimacy through illegitimate actions: A marriage of institutional and impression management theories', *Academy of Management*, 35: 699–738.

Fairtlough, G. (1994) *Creative Compartments: A Design for Future Organisation*. London: Adamantine.

Fleming, P., Harley, B. and Sewell, G. (2004) 'A little knowledge is a dangerous thing: Getting below the surface of growth of 'knowledge work' in Australia', *Work, Employment & Society*, 18(4): 725–47.

Flyvbjerg, B. (2006) 'Making organization research matter: power, values and *phronesis*', in S.R. Clegg, C. Hardy, W.R. Nord and T. Lawrence (eds) *Handbook of Organization Studies*. London: Sage. pp. 370–87.

Foucault, M. (1979) *Discipline and Punish: The Birth of the Prison*. New York: Vintage/Random House.

Foucault, M. (1980) *Power/knowledge*. New York: Pantheon.

Fournier, V. and Grey, C. (2000) 'At the critical moment: Conditions and prospects for critical management studies', *Human Relations*, 53: 7–32.

Freire, P. (1992) Pedagogy of the Oppressed. New York: Continuum.

Galbraith, J.R. (1973) *Designing Complex Organizations*. Reading, MA: Addison Wesley.

Galbraith, J.R., Lawler, E.E.III and Associates (1993) *Organizing for the Future*. San Francisco: Jossey-Bass.

Gephart, R.P. (1993) 'The textual approach: Risk and blame in disaster sensemaking', *Academy of Management Journal*, 36(6): 1465–514.

Gergen, M. and Gergen, K. (2000) 'Qualitative inquiry: Tensions and transformations', in N. Denzin and Y. Lincoln (eds), *Handbook of Qualitative Research*, 2nd edn. Thousand Oaks, CA: Sage. pp. 1025–46.

Gioia, D.A. and Pitre, E. (1990) 'Multi-paradigm perspectives in theory building', *Academy of Management Review*, 15(4): 584–602.

Grant, D. and Oswick, C. (eds) (1996) *Metaphor and Organizations*. London: Sage.

Grey, C. (2002) 'What are business schools for? On silence and voice in management education', *Journal of Management Education*, 26(5): 496–511.

Grey, C. and Willmott, H. (2002) 'Contexts of CMS', *Organization*, 9: 411–8.

Habermas, J. (1979) *Communication and the Evolution of Society*. Toronto: Beacon Press.

Halal, W.E. (1994) 'From hierarchy to enterprise: Internal markets are the new foundation of management', *Academy of Management Executive*, 8(4): 69–83.

Hardy, C. (1994) 'Understanding interorganizational domains: The Case of the refugee system', *Journal of Applied Behavioral Science*, 30(3): 278–96.

Hardy, C. (2002) 'On the edge of a Pluralistic World', *Journal of Management Inquiry*, 11(1): 16–8.

Hardy, C. and Clegg, S. (1997) 'Relativity without relativism: reflexivity in post-paradigm organization studies', *British Journal of Management*, 8: S5–17.

Hardy, C. and Clegg, S.R. (2004) 'Power and change: A critical reflection', in J.J. Boonstra (ed.) *Dynamics of Organizational Change and Learning*. London: Wiley. pp. 343–56.

Harley, B., Hardy, C. and Alvesson, M. (2004) 'Reflecting on reflexivity', in K.M. Weaver (ed.) Conference

Proceedings, *64th Annual Meeting of the Academy of Management*. New Orleans: Academy of Management.

Hassan, I. (1985) 'The culture of postmodernism', *Theory, Culture and Society*, 2(3): 119–32.

Jackson, N. and Carter, P. (1991) 'In defence of paradigm incommensurability', *Organization Studies*, 12(1): 109–27.

Jeffcutt, P. (1994) 'From interpretation to representation in organizational analysis: postmodernism, ethnography and organizational symbolism', *Organization Studies*, 15(2): 241–74.

Jencks, C. (1989) *What is Post-Modernism*, 3rd edn. New York: Academy Editions, St Martin's Press.

Jermier, J. (1985) 'When the sleeper wakes: A short story extending themes in radical organization theory', *Journal of Management*, 11(2), 67–80.

Kilduff, M. (1993) 'Deconstructing organizations', *Academy of Management Review*, 18: 3–31.

Kirkman, B.L. et al. (2002) 'Five challenges to virtual team success: Lessons from Sabre, Inc.', *Academy of Management Executive*, 16(3): 67–79.

Knights, D. (1992) 'Changing spaces: The disruptive impact of a new epistemological location for the study of management', *Academy of Management Review*, 17: 514–36.

Knights, D. and McCabe, D. (1998) 'What happens when the phone goes wild? Staff, stress and spaces for escape in a BPR telephone banking work regime', *Journal of Management Studies*, 35(2): 163–94.

Knights, D. and McCabe, D. (2002) 'A road less travelled: Beyond managerialist, critical and processual approaches to total quality management', *Journal of Organisational Change Management*, 15: 235–54.

Knights, D. and Morgan, G. (1991) 'Strategic discourse and subjectivity: Towards a critical analysis of corporate strategy in organisations', *Organization Studies*, 12: 251–73.

Knights, D. and Willmott, H. (1990) *Labour Process Theory*. London: Macmillan.

Kono, T. and Clegg, S. R. (2001) *Trends in Japanese Management*. London: Palgrave.

Kornberger, M, Clegg, S.R. and Rhodes, C. (2005) 'Learning/becoming/organizing', *Organization*, 12(2): 147–67.

Kuhn, T.S. (1996) *The Structure of Scientific Revolutions*. Chicago: University of Chicago Press.

Laclau, E. (1988) 'Politics and the limits of modernity', in A. Ross (ed.), *Universal Abandon: The Politics of Postmodernism*. Minneapolis: University of Minnesota Press. pp. 63–82.

Lakoff, G. and Johnson, M. (1999) *Philosophy in the Flesh: The Embodied Mind and its Challenge to Western Thought*. New York: Basic Books.

Langley, A. (1999) 'Strategies for theorizing from process data', *Academy of Management Review*, 24(4).

Linstead, S. (1993) 'From postmodern anthropology to deconstructive ethnography', *Human Relations*, 46: 97–120.

Littler, C.R. (1982) *The Development of the Labour Process in Capitalist Societies*. London: Heinemann.

Lyotard, J. (1984) *The Postmodern Condition*. Minneapolis: University of Minnesota Press.

March, J.G. (1965) (ed.) *Handbook of Organizations*. Chicago: Rand McNally.

Marcus, G.E. (1994) 'What comes (just) after "post"? The case of ethnography', in N.K. Denzin and Y.S. Lincoln (eds), *Handbook of Qualitative Research*. London: Sage. pp. 563–74.

Marsden, R. (1993) 'The politics of organizational analysis', *Organization Studies*, 14(1): 92–124.

Marsden, R. and Townley, B. (1996) 'The Owl of Minerva: reflections on theory in practice', in S.R. Clegg, C. Hardy and W.R. Nord (eds), *Handbook of Organization Studies*. London: Sage. pp. 659–76.

Martin, J. (1992) *The Culture of Organizations: Three Perspectives*. New York: Oxford University.

Martin, J., Frost, P.J. and O'Neill, O.A. (2006) 'Organizational culture: beyond struggles for intellectual dominance', in S.R. Clegg, C. Hardy, W.R. Nord and T. Lawrence (eds) *Handbook of Organization Studies*. London: Sage. pp. 725–53.

Mauws, M. and Phillips, N. (1995) 'Understanding language games', *Organization Science*, 63: 322–34.

Mintzberg, H. (1979) *The Structuring of Organizations*. Englewood Cliffs, New Jersey: Prentice-Hall.

Mumby, D. and Putnam, L. (1992) 'The politics of emotion: A feminist reading of bounded rationality', *Academy of Management Review*, 17: 465–86.

Nonaka, I. and Takeuchi, H. (1995) *The Knowledge Creating Company*. New York, NY: Oxford University Press.

Nord, W. (2002) 'Spinning disciplines with Mayer Zald: Some further thoughts on critical management studies and management education', *Organization*, 9(3): 437–46.

Nord, W.R. and Doherty, E.M. (1994) Towards an assertion perspective for empowerment: Blending employee rights and labor process theories, unpublished paper. College of Business Administration, University of South Florida.

Nord, W.R. and Jermier, J.M. (1992) 'Critical social science for managers? Promising and perverse possibilities', in M. Alvesson and H. Willmott (eds), *Critical Management Studies*. London: Sage. pp. 202–22.

O'Leary, M., Orlikowski, W. and Yates, J. (2002) 'Distributed work over the centuries: Trust and control in the Hudson's Bay Company, 1670–1826', in P. Hinds and S. Kiesler (eds), *Distributed Work*. Cambridge, Mass: MIT Press. pp. 27–53.

Olesen, V. (2000) 'Feminisms and qualitative research at and into the millennium', in N. Denzin and Y. Lincoln (eds), *Handbook of Qualitative Research*, 2nd edn. Thousand Oaks, CA: Sage. pp. 563–74.

Orlikowski, W. J. (2000) 'Using technology and constituting structures: A practice lens for studying technology in organizations', *Organization Science*, 11(4): 404–28.

Palmer, I. and Dunford, R. (1997) 'Organising for hyper-competition: New organisational forms for a new age?', *New Zealand Strategic Management*, 2(4): 38–45.

Palmer, I. and Hardy, C. (2000) *Thinking about Management: Implications of Organizational Debates*. London: Sage.

Parker, M. (1992) 'Post-modern organisations or post-modern organisation theory?', *Organization Studies*, 13: 1–13.

Parker, M. and McHugh, G. (1991) 'Five texts in search of an author: a response to John Hassard's "Multiple paradigms and organizational analysis"', *Organizational studies*, 12(3): 451–6.

Pettigrew, A.M., Woodman, R.W. and Cameron, K.S. (2001) 'Studying organizational change and development: Challenges for future research', *Academy of Management Journal*, 44(4): 697–714.

Pfeffer, J. (1993) 'Barriers to the advance of organizational science: paradigm development as a dependent variable', *Academy of Management Review*, 18(4): 599–620.

Phillips, J.J.H. and Brown, J.C. (1993) 'Book review – Guide to the sun', *The Observatory*, 113: 148.

Phillips, N. and Hardy, C. (2002) *Discourse Analysis: Investigating processes of social construction*. Newbury Park, CA: Sage.

Powell, W.W. and Snellman, K. (2004) 'The knowledge economy', *Annual Review of Sociology*, 30: 199–220.

Prasad, P. (1993) 'Symbolic processes in the implementation of technological change: a symbolic interactionist study of work computerization', *Academy of Management Journal*, 36: 1400–29.

Putnam, L. (1996) 'Situating the author and text', *Journal of Management Inquiry*, 5: 382–6.

Reed, M. (1985) *Redirections in Organisational Analysis*. London: Tavistock.

Reich, R. (2005) 'Plenty of knowledge to go around', *Harvard Business Review*, 83(4): 17.

Reinharz, S. (1997) 'Who am I? The need for a variety of selves in fieldwork', in R. Hertz (ed.), *Reflexivity and Voice*. Thousand Oaks, CA: Sage. pp. 3–20.

Rhodes, C. (2005) 'Review of handbook of organizational discourse', in D. Grant, C. Hardy, C. Oswick and L. Putnam (eds), *Organization Studies*, 26(5): 793–804.

Richardson, L. (1994) 'Writing: A method of inquiry', in N.K. Denzin and Y.S. Lincoln (eds), *Handbook of Qualitative Research*. London: Sage. pp. 516–29.

Schultz, M. and Hatch, M.J. (1996) 'Living with multiple paradigms: The case of paradigm interplay in organizational culture studies', *Academy of Management Review*, 21(2): 529–57.

Shapin, S. (1995) 'Here and everywhere: Sociology of scientific knowledge', *Annual Review of Sociology*, 21: 289–321.

Shotter, J. (2005) 'Inside the moment of managing: Wittgenstein and the everyday dynamics of our expressive-responsive activities', *Organization Studies*, 26(1): 113–35.

Silverman, D. (1970) *The Theory of Organizations*. London: Heinemann.

Taylor, P.V. (1993) *The Texts of Paulo Freire*. Milton Keynes: Open University Press.

Taylor, P. and Bain, P. (1999) 'An assembly line in the head: Work and employee relations in the call centre', *Industrial Relations Journal*, 30(2): 101–17.

Taylor, P. and Bain, P. (2003) 'Subterranean worksick blues: Humour as subversion in two call centres', *Organization Studies*, 24(9): 1487–509.

Taylor, P., Hyman, J., Mulvey, G. and Bain, P. (2002) 'Work organization, control and the experience of work in call centres', *Work, Employment & Society*, 16(1): 133–50.

Thompson, M.P.A. and Walsham, G. (2004) 'Placing knowledge management in context', *Journal of Management Studies*, 41(5): 725–47.

Thompson, P. (2004) 'Brands, boundaries and bandwagons: A critical reflection on critical management studies', in S. Fleetwood and S. Ackroyd (eds), *Critical Realist Applications in Organisation and Management Studies*. London: Routledge.

Townley, B. (1993) 'Foucault, power/knowledge and its relevance for human resource management', *Academy of Management Review*, 18: 518–45.

Tsoukas, H. and Chia, R. (2002) 'On organizational becoming: Rethinking organizational change', *Organization Science*, 13(5): 567–82.

Tsoukas, H. and Knudsen, C. (eds) (2003) *The Oxford Handbook of Organization Theory*. Oxford: Oxford University Press.

Van Maanen, J. (1979) 'Reclaiming qualitative methods for organizational research: A preface', *Administrative Science Quarterly*, 24(4): 520–6.

Van Maanen, J. (1995) 'Style as theory', *Organizational Science*, 6: 133–43.

Von Krogh, G. (1998) Care in knowledge creation, *California Management Review*, 40(3): 133–53.

Walsh, J.P. and Weber, K. (2002) 'The prospects for critical management studies in the American Academy of Management', *Organization*, 9(3): 402–10.

Walton, E.J. (2005) 'The persistence of bureaucracy: A meta-analysis of Weber's model of bureaucratic control', *Organization Studies*, 26(4): 569–600.

Weber, M. (1978) *Economy and Society*. Berkeley, CA: University of California Press.

Weick, K. (1969) *The Social Psychology of Organizing*. Reading, MA: Addison Wesley.

Weick, K. (1999) 'Theory construction as disciplined reflexivity: Tradeoffs in the 90s', *Academy of Management Review*, 24: 797–806.

Weick, K. (2002) 'Real-time reflexivity: Prods to reflection', *Organisation Studies*, 3: 893–99.

Weick, K.E. (1998) 'Improvisation as a mindset for organizational analysis', *Organization Science*, 9: 543–55.

Weick, K.E. and Quinn, R.E. (1999) 'Organizational change and development', *Annual Review of Psychology*, 50: 361–86.

Wellman, E. and Haythornthwaite, C. (eds) (2002) *The Internet in Everyday Life*. Oxford: Blackwell.

Willmott, H. (1993a) 'Breaking the paradigm mentality', *Organization Studies*, 14(5): 682–719.

Willmott, H. (1993b) 'Paradigm gridlock: a reply', *Organization Studies*, 14(5): 727–30.

Zald, M.N. (1994) 'Organization studies as a scientific and humanistic enterprise: toward a reconceptualization of the foundations of the field', *Organization Science*, 4(4): 513–28.

Zald, M.N. (2002a) 'Spinning disciplines: Critical management studies in the context of the transformation of management education', *Organization*, 9: 365–85.

Zald, M. (2002b) 'Afterword', *Organization*, 9(3): 453–7.

PART 2
Exploring the Issues

2.1 Leadership in Organizations

KEN W. PARRY AND ALAN BRYMAN

Leadership has long been a major area of interest among social scientists and in particular organizational and political psychologists. The notion of leadership is one that continues to attract generations of writers, in large part because we tend to view leadership as an important feature of everyday and organizational affairs.

Leadership is still not an easy concept to define. Its widespread currency and use in everyday life as an explanation affects the way it is defined and indeed probably makes it more difficult to define than a concept that is invented as an abstraction *ab initio*. Most definitions of leadership have tended to coalesce around a number of elements which can be discerned in the following definition by a researcher whose work had a profound impact on one of the stages of theory and research to be encountered below:

Leadership may be considered as the process (act) of influencing the activities of an organized group in its efforts toward goal setting and goal achievement (Stogdill 1950: 3).

Three elements can be discerned in this definition that are common to many definitions: influence, group and goal. First, leadership is viewed as a process of influence whereby the leader has an impact on others by inducing them to behave in a certain way. Second, that influence process is conceptualized as taking place in a group context. Group members are invariably taken to be the leader's subordinates, although that is by no means obligatory. This focus on the leader in relation to a definable group is invariably translated into research in which supervisors and their work groups constitute the focus of analysis. However, leadership need not come from the person in charge. Leadership, being a process of influence, can come from anyone in the group. Third, a leader influences the behaviour of group members in the direction of goals with which the group is faced. Effective leadership – the holy grail of leadership theory and research – will be that which accomplishes the group's goal(s).

This definition applies best to theory and research that was conducted up to the mid-1980s. While it by no means fell into disuse, later definitions, insofar as they were specifically articulated, tended to dwell on the leader as a *manager of meaning* – a term employed by Smircich and Morgan (1982). In a similar fashion, Pfeffer (1981) and Weick (1995) write about leadership as symbolic action, by which they mean that leaders engage in 'sense-making' on behalf of others and develop a social consensus around the resulting meanings. In both cases, leadership is seen as a process whereby the leader identifies for subordinates a sense of what is important – defining organizational reality for others. The leader gives a sense of direction and of purpose through the articulation of a compelling worldview. The phrase 'manager of meaning' (and the complementary notion of 'symbolic leadership') is meant to draw attention to the defining characteristic of true leadership as the active promotion of values, which provide shared meanings about the nature of the organization. The years either side of the turn of the century saw the process of leadership become more of a social as well as a psychological process of influence. In effect, more effort was put into determining the nature of the leadership processes that were manifest in organizational settings.

Perhaps because of the vast amounts of effort that have been expended on uncovering the factors associated with effective leadership in organizations, there has sometimes been pessimism about the fruits of this labour because of the many different approaches and frequently contradictory findings (Miner 1975), although the field is less imbued with a sense of negativity nowadays.

The history of leadership research can be broken down into five main stages, which are the focus of the next section.

Five Stages of Leadership Theory and Research

Each of the five approaches to the study of leadership covered in this section is generally associated with a particular time period. The *trait approach* dominated the scene up to the late 1940s; the *style approach* held sway from then until the late 1960s; the heyday of the *contingency approach* was from the late 1960s to the early 1980s; and the *New Leadership approach* was the major influence on leadership research from the early 1980s. The *post-charismatic and post-transformational* leadership approach (Storey 2004) emerged through the late 1990s. Each of these stages signals a change of emphasis rather than the demise of the previous approach(es). Transformational leadership research, for example, is still very much alive in the 2000s: the point is that each of the time periods is associated with a change of prominence.

The Trait Approach

The trait approach seeks to determine the personal qualities and characteristics of leaders. This orientation implies a belief that leaders are born rather than made – nature is more important than nurture. Research tended to be concerned with the qualities that distinguished leaders from non-leaders or followers. For many writers concerned with leadership in organizations the findings of such research had implications for their area of interest because of a belief that the traits of leaders would distinguish effective from less effective leaders, although relatively few trait studies examined this specific issue. In general, the simplicity of the trait theory has reduced its attractiveness for scholars and from the 1940s, a more persuasive trend shifted to the examination of leadership style, although a reorientation in thinking about leadership traits and a reconsideration of research associated with the approach have resulted in a renaissance for the approach in recent years (House and Aditya 1997: 411–8).

The Style Approach

The emphasis on leadership style from the late 1940s signalled a change of focus from the personal characteristics of leaders to their behaviour as leaders. As much as a change in what was to be studied, this shift denoted an alteration in the practical

implications of leadership research. The trait approach drew attention to the kinds of people who become leaders and in the process had great potential for supplying organizations with information about what should be looked for when *selecting* individuals for present or future positions of leadership. By contrast, since leader behaviour is capable of being changed, the focus on the behaviour of leaders carried with it an emphasis on *training* rather than selecting leaders.

There are a number of possible exemplars of the style approach but arguably the best known is the stream of investigations associated with an approach generated by a group of researchers at the Ohio State University, one of whose main figures was Stogdill. Not only did the Ohio State researchers generate a large number of studies, but, the concepts and methods that they employed were widely used well beyond the confines of the Ohio group, an influence that was still felt through the 1990s. The two main components of leader behaviour that Ohio State researchers tended to focus upon were dubbed *consideration* and *initiating structure*. The former denotes a leadership style in which leaders are concerned about their subordinates as people, are trusted by subordinates, are responsive to them, and promote camaraderie. Initiating structure refers to a style in which the leader defines closely and clearly what subordinates are supposed to do and how, and actively schedules work for them. Later research often suggested that high levels of both consideration and initiating structure were the best leadership style. Consideration is conceptually similar to other terms such as concern for people, employee-centered leadership, supportive, and relationship-oriented leadership. Initiating structure is conceptually similar to terms such as concern for production, production-centered leadership, directive and task-oriented leadership.

At quite an early stage in the development of the Ohio Studies, it was noted by Korman (1966) that they were plagued by inconsistent results. He noted also that insufficient attention was paid to the possibility that the effectiveness of the two types of leader behaviour is situationally contingent; in other words, what works well in some situations may not work well in others. Later research in the Ohio tradition reflected a greater sensitivity to this possibility (e.g. Kerr et al. 1974), a trend that was consistent with the growing adherence to a contingency approach that marked the 1970s (see below).

Studies using experimental and longitudinal research designs often found the leader-causes-outcome inference to be highly questionable (e.g. Lowin and Craig 1968; Greene 1975). Second, informal leadership processes were rarely investigated, and such processes have been the focus of researchers in recent years. Intra-group differences were not considered. Recognition of the impact of people's 'implicit leadership theories' on how they rated the behaviour of leaders was very damaging to the Ohio researchers. Rush et al. (1977), for example, showed that when rating the behaviour of an imaginary leader, people generated ratings that were very similar to those pertaining to real leaders in Ohio investigations. In other words, Ohio research might merely be tapping people's generalized perceptions of the behaviour of leaders. The theoretical implications of such research have become an area of interest in its own right (Lord and Maher 1991). The main drift from the late 1960s was toward contingency models of leadership.

Contingency Approach

Proponents of contingency approaches place situational factors towards the centre of any understanding of leadership. Typically, they seek to specify the situational variables that will moderate the effectiveness of different leadership approaches. This development parallels the drift away from universalistic theories of organization in the 1960s and the gradual adoption of a more particularistic framework which reflected an 'it all depends' style of thinking (e.g. Lawrence and Lorsch 1967).

Arguably, one of the best-known exemplars of contingency thinking is Fiedler's Contingency Model of leadership effectiveness (Fiedler 1967, 1993; Fiedler and Garcia 1987). Fiedler's approach has undergone a number of revisions and changes of emphasis over the years. At its heart is a measurement instrument known as the Least Preferred Coworker (LPC) scale, which purports to measure the leadership orientation of the person completing it. If their orientation is relationship-oriented, they are primarily concerned with fostering good relationships with subordinates, and are considerate. If they are task-motivated, they are preoccupied with task accomplishment. In spite of an apparent similarity with the Ohio consideration and initiating structure pairing, it should be appreciated that for Fiedler there is a key difference between his and other conceptualizations like that of the Ohio researchers. Whereas for the latter there was a focus on consideration and initiating structure as contrasting styles of leadership, for Fiedler relationship- and task-motivation are *personality* attributes, a conceptualization which ties his work much more with earlier trait approaches. As leaders, subjects would be either relationship- or task-motivated. Fiedler's work commenced a trend that lasted through the 1990s in which organizational leadership was seen more as a psychological process than as a social process.

From results relating to numerous studies conducted in a variety of work and non-work settings, Fiedler found that the effectiveness of relationship- and task-motivated leaders varied according to how favourable the situation was to the leader. More recently, this notion of situational favourableness has been dubbed 'situational control'. This idea has three components: leader-member relations; task structure; and position power. Fiedler's accumulated evidence led him to propose that task-oriented leaders are most effective in high control and low control situations; relationship-oriented leaders perform best in moderate control situations. The practical implication of Fiedler's work was that since a person's personality is not readily subject to change, it is necessary to change the work situation to fit the leader rather than the other way around.

Fiedler's model has been the subject of a great deal of controversy and debate. Much of this has centred upon the LPC scale, with many writers and researchers unconvinced by the link that is made between a person's LPC score and their approach to leadership. There has also been considerable unease over the conceptualization of situational control or favourableness. Many students of leadership asked why situational control was the only situational factor that was the object of attention and why the three components previously mentioned were the only crucial elements in situational control. Fiedler has responded to some extent to this kind of criticism by including stress within the model's purview in more recent years (Fiedler and Garcia 1987; Fiedler 1993). But probably most damaging of all is that there has been widespread disagreement over the model's validity, that is, whether results really are consistent with the model. Fiedler's contingency approach shares with the Ohio studies a tendency to emphasize formally designated leaders to the virtual exclusion of informal leadership processes.

In the end, contingency approaches like Fiedler's probably became less popular because of inconsistent results that were often generated by research conducted within their frameworks and problems with the measurement of key variables. The idea of a contingency approach still has considerable support, although research sometimes suggests that situational factors are not always as important as might be expected. By the early 1980s, there was considerable disillusionment with contingency theories. Much of this disillusionment was as a result of controversy about the reliability and meaning of Fiedler's LPC measure. Vecchio (1983) and Peters et al. (1985) are examples of this debate. It appeared there were too many contingencies for this approach to grasp adequately. Further, the approach was beset with somewhat inconsistent findings (e.g. Hosking 1981).

In addition to specific problems with each of the contingency approaches (such as those outlined in the previous paragraph in relation to Fiedler's approach), some general deficiencies were identified. Bryman (1986: 158–9) identified several general problems. First, other contingency approaches shared with Fiedler's model the tendency for findings to be inconsistent in terms of their support. Secondly, it was frequently not clear why some situational factors were the focus of attention rather than other possible candidates. Thirdly, there was growing evidence in the 1980s that leader behaviours are not always situationally contingent (e.g. Podsakoff et al. 1984). Fourthly, the identification of leader behaviours had not moved on significantly from the era of the style approach with its emphasis on person- and task-orientation and participation. Fifthly, Bryman noted Korman's (1973) argument that there were problems of knowing in advance what critical values of a situational variable are relevant to any leadership style-outcome relationship. Sixthly, there were concerns about identifying causal patterns among variables gleaned from the typical cross-sectional design that pervaded most research. Finally, it was observed that there was little guidance in any of the theories regarding how leaders might deal with conflicting situational factors, that is, when one factor suggested a particular form of leader behaviour but another factor suggested a different form.

The New Leadership Approach

The term 'New Leadership' has been used to describe and categorize a number of approaches to leadership

which emerged in the 1980s that seemed to exhibit common or at least similar themes, although there were undoubtedly differences between them (Bryman 1992). Together these different approaches seemed to signal a new way of conceptualizing and researching leadership. Writers employed a variety of terms to describe the new kinds of leadership with which they were concerned: transformational leadership (Bass 1985; Tichy and Devanna 1986), charismatic leadership (House 1977; Conger 1989), visionary leadership (Sashkin 1988; Westley and Mintzberg 1989), and, simply leadership (Bennis and Nanus 1985; Kotter 1990; Kouzes and Posner 1998). Together these labels revealed a conception of the leader as someone who defines organizational reality through the articulation of a vision, which is a reflection of how he or she defines an organization's mission, and the values that will support it. Thus, the New Leadership approach is underpinned by a depiction of leaders as managers of meaning rather than in terms of an influence process.

While many of the ideas associated with the New Leadership were presaged by some earlier writers like Selznick (1957) and Zaleznik (1977), its intellectual impetus derives in large part from the publication of Burns's study of political leadership in 1978. In this work, Burns proposed that political leaders could be distinguished in terms of a dichotomy of transactional and transforming leadership. Transactional leadership comprises an exchange between leader and follower in which the former offers rewards, perhaps in the form of prestige or money, for compliance with his or her wishes. In Burns's view, such leadership is not ineffective but its effectiveness is limited to the implicit contract between leaders and their followers. They are not bound together 'in a mutual and continuing pursuit of a higher purpose' (1978: 20). The transforming leader raises the aspirations of his or her followers such that the leader's and the follower's aspirations are fused. Burns's distinction was popularized in Peters and Waterman's (1982) hugely successful book *In Search of Excellence*, where they asserted that a transforming leader had influenced almost all of the highly successful companies that they studied at some stage in their development. The link between transforming leadership and vision was forged by a number of writers at around the same time and can be seen in the work of Bass (1985), Bennis and Nanus (1985), Tichy and Devanna (1986), and more latterly Kouzes and Posner (1998) and Alimo-Metcalfe and Alban-Metcalfe (2001).

In the process, the nomenclature changed so that transform*ing* became transform*ational* leadership.

Bennis and Nanus (1985) and Tichy and Devanna (1986) adopted a similar approach of interviewing successful chief executives to determine the nature of their approaches to leadership. Bennis and Nanus are somewhat different in that they also tracked a number of their subjects. They also viewed their chief executives as leaders rather than as managers, suggesting a parallel between transactional/transforming and manager/leader. Kouzes and Posner conducted survey work across thousands of organizations worldwide. In all cases, the importance of articulating a vision was found to be a central element of leadership, which invariably involved the transformation of followers and often of organizations in correspondence with their vision. Each pair of writers recognized that the vision must be communicated and made intelligible and relevant to the leader's followers.

Much of the research into charismatic leadership has centered on community or political leadership (the sociological, psychoanalytic and political approaches), rather than leadership in organizations. The approaches, which have involved organizational leadership, include the behavioural approach (House 1977; Bass 1985; Conger 1989), the attribution approach (Shamir 1992; Conger and Kanungo 1998; Shamir and Howell 1999) and the follower self-concept approach (Shamir et al. 1993). Whereas most work on charismatic leadership has focused on the leader behaviours and follower effects as independent and dependent variables, Shamir has added to the debate by positing an explanation for the intervening variable which links leadership and effect. He suggests that charismatic leadership has its effect by heightening the self-concept of followers. In particular, charismatic leadership generates heightened self-esteem and self-worth, increased self-efficacy and collective efficacy, personal identification with the leader, identification with a prestigious and distinctive social group, and internalization of the values of the leader.

These various writings on the New Leadership can, then, be viewed as signalling a change of orientation toward the leader as a manager of meaning and the pivotal role of vision in that process. However, two other ingredients stand out. First, in the New Leadership most research is conducted on very senior leaders, often chief executive officers, rather than low- to middle-level leaders such as supervisors, sergeants, middle managers, foremen,

and sports coaches, as in the Ohio and Fiedler research. Second, unlike the three earlier stages of leadership research, substantial use is made of qualitative case studies. Some writers, like Bennis and Nanus (1985) and Tichy and Devanna (1986), employed informal, semi-structured interviews as their chief source of data, others like Westley and Mintzberg (1989) employed documentary evidence. The use of such methods represents a substantial methodological shift from the quantitative studies that were typical of earlier phases of leadership research. However, a stream of highly influential research inaugurated by Bass (1985) and Kouzes and Posner (1993) includes leaders at lower levels and uses a quantitative approach in the manner of much leadership style and contingency research.

Bass's Research on Transactional and Transformational Leadership

Bass's approach (Bass 1985; Bass and Avolio 1990) draws heavily on Burns's (1978) work for its basic ideas, but goes much further in two respects. First, rather than opposite ends of a continuum, Bass views transactional and transformational leadership as separate dimensions. Indeed, for Bass, the ideal approach exhibits both forms of leadership (Bass 1998). Second, in contrast to Burns's broad-brush style of discussing the two types of leadership, Bass has specified their basic components and has developed a battery of quantitative indicators for each component. His specification of these components has varied somewhat as his model has undergone development. According to Avolio et al. (1999), the leadership factors are:

- *Transformational leadership*

  - *Charisma/Inspiration* – developing a vision, engendering pride, respect and trust; creating high expectations, modeling appropriate behaviour.
  - *Intellectual stimulation* – continually challenging followers with new ideas and approaches; using symbols to focus efforts.

- *Developmental exchange*

  - *Individualized consideration* – giving personal attention to followers, giving them respect and responsibility.
  - *Contingent reward* – rewarding followers for conformity with performance targets.

- *Corrective avoidant*

  - *Management-by-exception (Active)* – looking for mistakes or exceptions to expected behaviour and then taking corrective action.
  - *Passive avoidant* – waiting for mistakes to occur before intervening, abdicating leadership responsibility.

Each of these components is measured in a manner similar to the Ohio approach, in that followers complete questionnaires that specify types of leader behaviour each of which relates to one of these components, through the use of the Multifactor Leadership Questionnaire (MLQ). The research, which has been conducted on a host of different levels of leader in a variety of settings, typically shows transformational leadership and developmental exchange to be the components of leader behaviour that are most strongly associated with desirable outcomes such as performance of subordinates. Management-by-exception produces inconsistent results in that in some studies it is positively and in others negatively related to desirable outcomes. Programmes for the selection and training of leaders, which draw on this conceptualization and measurement of transactional and transformational leadership have been developed (Bass and Avolio 1990). Podsakoff et al. (1984; 1990) also developed a questionnaire to test for six factors of transformational leadership and four factors representing contingent and non-contingent reward, and contingent and non-contingent punishment. Podsakoff's six transformational leadership factors are: articulates vision, provides appropriate role model, fosters the acceptance of goals, communicates high performance expectations, provides individualized support, and intellectual stimulation. Like Bass's original operationalization of transformational and transactional leadership, these are pitched very much at the individual level of analysis. Alimo-Metcalfe and Alban-Metcalfe (2001) also developed a Transformational Leadership Questionnaire (TLQ). This questionnaire measures nine factors, once again at the individual level of analysis and measuring 'close' or 'nearby' leadership, as opposed to 'distant' leadership.

Those nine transformational leadership factors are:

- genuine concern for others
- empowers and develops potential
- integrity, trustworthy, honest and open
- accessibility and approachability
- clarifies boundaries, involves others in decisions
- encourages critical and strategic thinking
- inspirational networker and promoter
- decisiveness, determination, self-confidence
- political sensitivity and skills.

Once again, they have been adapted for the selection and training of leaders. Importantly, Bass's and Podsakoff's measure of leadership contain a transactional component as well as transformational. Kouzes and Posner's and Alimo-Metcalfe and Alban-Metcalfe's measures do not. Waldman et al. (1990) drew attention to the importance of the augmentation effect of transformational leadership over and above the effect of transactional leadership. This finding has been supported by den Hartog et al. (1997) with questionnaire analysis. These theoretical findings that transactional leadership by itself is necessary but not sufficient for optimal organizational performance support the conceptual conclusions of Kotter (1990) and others that 'leadership' without 'management' is insufficient for optimal organizational performance.

The notion of transformational leadership has generated an impressive set of findings and has made a great impact on the study of leadership. Some reflections about the New Leadership approach can be found in the following overview.

Limitations of the New Leadership Approach

The New Leadership offers a distinctive approach that ties in with the great appetite for stories about heroic chief executives which was referred to above and with the growing self-awareness of many organizations about their missions. The New Leadership is at once cause, symptom and consequence of this self-reflection that can be seen in the widespread reference to visions and missions in newspaper advertisements and company reports.

With the exception of the research stemming directly or indirectly from Bass's work, the New Leadership approach can be accused of concentrating excessively on top leaders. While a switch toward the examination of the leadership *of*, rather than *in*, organizations is an antidote to the small-scale, group-level studies of earlier eras, it could legitimately be argued that the change in focus has gone too far and risks having little to say to the majority of leaders. Second, as with earlier phases of research, the New Leadership has little to say about informal leadership processes, though the qualitative case studies that have grown in popularity have great potential in this regard. On the other hand, quantitative approaches like the work of Bass, Podsakoff, Alimo-Metcalfe and Alban-Metcalfe and Kouzes and Posner, are likely to replicate the tendency to focus on formally designated leaders. Third, there has been little situational analysis. Much effort was exerted in the late 1990s to testing the situational validity of the New Leadership, transformational leadership in particular. Keller (1992) reports the results of a study of research and development (R&D) groups which use Bass's measures and which show that transformational leadership was a stronger predictor of project quality for research than for development projects. Bryman et al. (1996) show from a multiple case study of specialized transportation organizations in England how such factors as pre-existing levels of trust and resource constraint can have a pronounced impact on the prospects of transformational leadership. Similarly, Leavy and Wilson conclude from their investigation of four private and public sector Irish organizations that their leaders were 'tenants of time and context' (1994: 113). In so doing they draw attention to a wide range of contextual factors that can limit the room for maneouvre of prospective transformational leaders. The contextual factors that they identified were: technology; industry structure; the international trading environment; national public policy; and social and cultural transformation. Pawar and Eastman (1997) have proposed several factors that may influence the receptiveness of organizations to transformational leadership, such as an adaptation rather than an efficiency orientation and the nature of an organization's structural form and its mode of governance. Variables such as these may influence the nature of the relationship between transformational leadership and various outcome variables. Therefore, there is growing evidence that situational constraints may be much more important in restricting the transformational leader's room for maneuver than is generally appreciated. On the other hand, Bass (1997) is insistent that transformational leadership works in almost any situation, except that the way in which it works very definitely is situationally contingent. Fourth, Bass's research approach probably suffers from some of the technical problems identified in relation to the Ohio research, such as problems of direction of causality and of implicit

leadership theories (for a discussion of such issues, see Bass and Avolio 1989 and Bryman 1992). Fifth, there is a tendency for New Leadership writers to emphasize the exploits of successful leaders, and insufficient examination of the reasons for the loss of charisma. This can generate a distorted impression since there may be important lessons to be learned from failed transformational leaders.

Apart from these concerns, Yukl (1999) provided an evaluation of the conceptual weaknesses in the transformational leadership theories. One weakness is the omission of the specification of important behaviours, and ambiguity about other transformational behaviours. In part, this criticism has led to the development of Alimo-Metcalfe and Alban-Metcalfe's transformational leadership questionnaire, with a broader range of leadership behaviours and interactions with followers. Another weakness was insufficient identification of the negative effects of transformational leadership. This shortfall has in part been rectified by Bass and Steidlmeier's (1999) examination of authentic and inauthentic transformational leadership, and also by discussion by Maccoby (2000) and Kets de Vries and Miller (1985) and others on the problems of narcissism with people in senior leadership positions. A third weakness was ambiguity about the underlying influence processes associated with transformational leadership. It is expected that the greater use of qualitative methods to research leadership will remedy this perceived weakness over time. A final weakness identified by Yukl (1999) was an overemphasis on dyadic processes of transformational leadership. Once again, the greater use of qualitative methods to research leadership, as a social process found generally within organizations, should move researchers toward a resolution of this problem.

In spite of such problems, the New Leadership provided a 'shot in the arm' for leadership researchers, by providing an approach which enjoyed a broad swathe of support among both leadership researchers (and many writers of popular works on management) and which broke with many aspects of earlier phases of the field. It is possible to exaggerate the differences. Like its predecessors, much if not most New Leadership writing is wedded to a rational model of organizational behaviour. However, Bass and Steidlmeier (1999) have acknowledged the differences between authentic and pseudo-transformational leadership. They argue that authentic transformational leadership is more than just behaving in a transformational way. They argue that it is grounded upon moral and virtuous foundations. Whereas an authentic transformational leader will focus on universal values, the pseudo-transformational leader might highlight 'our' values against 'their' values. Whereas an authentic transformational leader will sound the alarm when real threats arise, the pseudo-transformational leader might manufacture crises where none exist. Whereas an authentic transformational leader will develop followers into leaders, the pseudo-transformational leader might develop submissive disciples. Both leaders will achieve these very different outcomes by *behaving* in essentially the *same* way. Also Post (1986), Kets de Vries and Miller (1985) and Maccoby (2000) have discussed the impact of personality aberrations such as narcissism upon the performance of people in senior leadership roles. Craig and Gustafson (1998) developed an instrument to assess the perceived integrity of leaders. Parry and Proctor-Thomson (2002) utilized a modified version of that scale to test the relationship between transformational leadership and perceived integrity. They found a generally positive relationship, but that six per cent of leaders in New Zealand organizations were found to be above average in the display of leadership yet below average in perceived integrity. These figures resonate with Gustafson and Ritzer's (1995) and Babiak's (1996) finding that approximately one in 20 managers are aberrant self-promoters, a mild form of organizational psychopath. The implication is that some people are enacting all the right transformational behaviours, yet what is in their heart is not as honorable as they would like their followers to believe.

Distributed Leadership

A separate tradition which focuses on 'distributed' or 'dispersed' leadership seems to be emerging to offset these tendencies. Five strands in recent writing illustrate this development. First, Manz and Sims (1991) and Sims and Lorenzi (1992) have developed an approach, which specifies the advantages of a type of leadership that is expected to supersede the 'visionary hero' image that is a feature of the perception of leaders in the New Leadership tradition. They develop the idea of SuperLeadership, which is 'the leadership culture of the future, the new leadership paradigm' (Sims and Lorenzi 1992: 296). A keynote feature of SuperLeadership is the emphasis that is placed on

'leading others to lead themselves' (1992: 295), so that followers are stimulated to become leaders themselves, a theme that was in fact a feature of Burns's (1978) perspective on transforming leadership. Second, Kouzes and Posner (1998) argue that credible leaders develop capacity in others, and have the capacity to turn their 'constituents' into leaders. For Kouzes and Posner, the issue is not one of handing down leadership to others, but of liberating them so that they can use their abilities to lead themselves and others. These three strands signal a change of focus away from heroic leaders, from the upper echelons, and towards a focus on teams as sites of leadership (see also, Reich 1987).

The third expression of an emergent dispersed leadership tradition can be seen in the suggestion that there should be much greater attention paid to leadership processes and skills, which may or may not reside in formally designated leaders. Hosking (1988; 1991) conceptualizes leadership in terms of an 'organizing' activity and spells out some of the distinctive features of leadership in terms of such a perspective. For example, she identifies 'networking' as a particularly notable organizing skill among leaders, in which the cultivation and exercise of wider social influence is a key ingredient. But such a skill is not the exclusive preserve of formally appointed leaders; it is the activity and its effects that are critical to understanding the distinctiveness of leadership. In like fashion, Knights and Willmott (1992) advocate greater attention to what they call the 'practices' of leadership. This emphasis means looking at how leadership is constituted in organizations, so that in their study of a series of verbal exchanges at a meeting in a British financial services company, they show how the chief executive's definition of the situation is made to predominate. Unfortunately, the distinctiveness of this research and Hosking's (1991) investigation of Australian chief executives is marred somewhat by a focus on designated leaders. As a result, it is difficult to disentangle leadership as skill or activity from leadership as position. However, the potential implication of these ideas is to project an image of leadership as much more diffuse and dispersed within organizations than would be evident from the tendency for leadership to be viewed as the preserve of very few leaders, as in many versions of the New Leadership approach.

A fourth expression of distributed leadership is Gordon's (2002) distinction between dispersed and traditional leadership discourse. By using observation and discourse analysis within an organizational setting, Gordon asserts that the deep power structures of organizations serve to maintain traditional notions of differentiation between leader and follower with low levels of sharing of power and information. This high differentiation adversely affects the behaviour of team members. Further, Gordon asserts that organizations frequently have surface level, or espoused empowerment, but serve to maintain domination at the deep structure levels. The surface level empowerment includes the discourse of empowerment, the flattening of hierarchy and the act of delegation. However, the deep power structures are represented by seating arrangements, intimidating language, deference, implied threat, offensive humour, the allocation of rewards and the like. By so doing, the deep power structures serve to reinforce pre-existing leadership relativities in spite of the rhetoric and discourse of the distribution of power that those in senior positions would have followers believe. By contrast, Collins (2001) asserts that Level 5 leadership, a combination of humility and fierce resolve, will enhance leader credibility and achieve genuine empowerment and the motivation of followers to achieve optimum performance.

A fifth expression of distributed leadership is leadership within the context of e-commerce (Brown and Gioia 2002) or an advanced information technology environment (Avolio et al. 2001). The technology associated with e-commerce and with advanced technology systems, also called Group Support Systems (GSS; Sosik et al. 1997) provides particular challenges for leadership. On the one hand, leaders are able to get information to large groups of followers quickly and in large volume. On the other hand, group members can access large amounts of information independently of their leaders. In effect, leaders lose much control over information flow and the power that goes with it. Avolio et al. (2001) conclude that in some settings, people can observe and model from others how they should interact. By so doing, technology becomes part of the social transformation in the organization, and in turn, part of the leadership process. In other settings, other leaders may view the technology as a cost-effective way of controlling employee behaviour through constant monitoring of deviations from standards. This latter style of leadership is likely to generate a very different social system from the former. Brown and Gioia (2002) found that the e-commerce environment was

characterized by speed, ambiguity and complexity. They agree with Avolio et al. (2001) that not only is leadership influenced by this context, but also integrated with and even defined by it. To Brown and Gioia, leadership is not solely a set of characteristics possessed by an individual, but an emergent property of a social system, in which 'leaders' and 'followers' share in the process of enacting leadership. The notion here is very clear that effective leadership depends upon multiple leaders for decision-making and action-taking. 'Collective effort' with 'mental and organizational agility' would describe their interactions and leadership style.

In these five sets of writings, we can see an alternative perspective that emphasizes the importance of recognizing the need for leadership to be viewed as a widely dispersed activity which is not necessarily lodged in formally designated leaders, especially the heroic leader who is a feature of much New Leadership writing.

Post-charismatic and Post-transformational Leadership

Storey (2004) has posited that transformational and charismatic leadership were very much constructs of the late twentieth century. The technology of the time and the prevailing management orthodoxies were very much those of the heroic or capable individual leader being able to transform corporations and transform the perceptions and motivations of people within those corporations. The increasingly distributed nature of leadership, combined with concerns about narcissistic and pseudo-transformational leaders and the shadow or 'dark' side of charisma has led to a more recent conceptualization of leadership for organizations. Fullan (2001) bases this new and implicit model of 'post-charismatic' or 'post-transformational' leadership around embedded learning, truly distributed leadership in teams, and learning from experience and failure. Leadership practice is more consciously made public and open to challenge and testing. Some major failures of corporate leadership at the turn of the century have provided fertile ground for the uptake of these ideas. By examining the life and achievements of Benjamin Franklin, Mumford and Van Doorn (2001) proposed a theory of pragmatic leadership, which would help to meet the shortfalls of the transformational, transactional and charismatic approaches. Transformational and charismatic leadership rely overly upon communication of values and ideals while transactional leadership relies overly upon control and the exercise of power. Mumford and Van Doorn argue that pragmatic leaders exercise influence by identifying and communicating solutions to significant social problems, meeting the practical needs of followers, working through elites in solution generation, creating structures to support solution implementation, and demonstrating the feasibility of these solutions. These tactics are just as valid in modern organizational settings as they are in public leadership. This pragmatic or utilitarian notion helps to bring more conventional management theory into the function of leadership in organizations, the absence of which has been a shortfall of leadership theory for some time.

Spirituality of Leadership

The movement away from the behaviours and styles of the transformational or charismatic leader has also led to an interest in the spirituality of leadership. Conversations about the dark side of charisma, narcissism and pseudo-transformational leadership have led inevitably to theoretical discussion about the 'right' and 'wrong' of leadership, rather than just the utilitarian effectiveness of organizational leadership. After all, Bass's original (1985) notion of transformational leadership included the role of enabling followers to transcend their interests above the day-to-day transactional concerns and to take inspiration from emotional appeals to a higher spiritual level of interest. The notion is not new, but the interest in it is escalating as the twenty-first century unfolds.

While much of the discussion at the turn of the century has a theological angle to it, authors such as Hicks (2002) are at pains to differentiate leadership from religious or theological canons. As Hicks notes, there are a number of characteristics of leadership that resonate in the mainstream literature, which have a spiritual tone to them. These characteristics include self-actualization and self-consciousness, authenticity, balance, the management of meaning, emotion and passion, intrinsic motivation, wisdom, discernment, courage, transcendence, and interconnectedness; as well as morality, integrity, values, honesty and justice. However, it is unwise simply to conclude that leadership is about living a good life and being a good Christian or Muslim or Hindu, or whatever. Rather, to avoid eschewing 50 years of leadership research, any theory of spiritual leadership should demonstrate its utility through its ability

to impact favourably upon organizational performance (Sass 2000) as well as its ability to discern right from wrong and to morally uplift leader and follower alike.

Fry's (2003) theory of spiritual leadership posits that leader values, attitudes and behaviours, which essentially are covered comprehensively within the New Leadership literature, will generate organizational outcomes via the intrinsic motivation of followers. Further, it posits that intrinsic motivation is a factor of followers' needs for spiritual survival. Those needs are met through being understood and appreciated, and by a feeling that life has meaning for them and that they can make a difference. In one sense, it could be argued that followers' needs for spiritual survival are merely a reiteration of Shamir's self-concept theory of motivation blended with Smircich's sense-making and the management of meaning theory. On the other hand, more realistically, Fry's theory is a more comprehensive examination of how these more recent leadership concepts come to have their ultimate impact upon organizational performance. The spiritual leadership literature is also an effective and persuasive way to integrate and make sense of concepts as disparate as altruistic love, honesty and integrity on the one hand and narcissism and pseudo-transformational leadership on the other. In a sense, the literature on spirituality is about the spirituality of leadership rather than a new theory of spiritual leadership. The latter reads like a new type of leadership, which the literature is not suggesting. Instead, the spirituality literature attempts to make better sense of the extant leadership literature.

The Art of Leadership

Another trend in the literature is to examine leadership more as an art than as a science. Grint (2000) looked at leadership through the lenses of:

- the performing arts – the deployment of persuasive communication
- the martial arts – the choice of organizational tactics
- the philosophical arts – the invention of common identity
- the fine arts – the formulation and transmission of a strategic vision.

Grint argues that the extant knowledge about leadership can be viewed through these four lenses, and all existing dimensions of leadership are represented in virtually every leadership challenge in organizations. Rosener (1997) and Calás and Smircich (1997) looked at leadership through the lens of gender stereotyping and concluded that mainstream leadership literature has traditionally been couched in masculine terms and that leadership can be interpreted as seduction. The use of dramatic performance as the metaphor for leadership is discussed later in this chapter. However, the artistic or aesthetic approach to leadership involves more than merely using art or acting as metaphors for leadership. Ropo and Eriksson (1997) and Ropo and Parviainen (2001) brought an aesthetic perspective to the study of leadership when they examined leadership as 'bodily' knowledge within the context of the performing arts industry. They asserted that a result of organizational leadership could be bodily knowledge, as distinct from cognitive knowledge or affective influence. Bodily knowledge is a type of tacit knowledge, derived from demonstration and learning-by-doing, and is conceptually similar to the 'sixth sense'. Just as the conductor of an orchestra might have a 'feel' for the music, the leader within an organization will have a 'feel' for what other employees are sensing and feeling. As far back as 1938 Chester Barnard (cited in Ottensmeyer 1996) cited terms pertinent to the executive process of management as being 'feeling', 'judgment', 'sense', 'proportion', 'balance' and 'appropriateness'. The appreciation of the art of leadership is not new. In researching R&D intensive knowledge work, Alvesson and Sveningsson (2003) found an inherent ambiguity of senior management work in that this work was found to be characterized by incoherence, contradiction, confusion and fragmentation, instead of the coherence, pattern and predictability which many years of leadership literature have led us to expect will result from visions, values and strategies. This ambiguity was reflected in the discourse, which emerged from the leaders of the organization. The ideals that are reflected in the leadership discourse were found to be contradicted by the discourse of 'micro-management' that leaders must engage in. This ambiguous muddle presents an 'ugly' or 'un-aesthetic' and therefore unappealing side to organizational leadership. Another example of research into the aesthetics of leadership is the study of the photography and portraiture of chief executive officers by Guthey (2001) and within organizational life more generally by Strati (2000). These works have illuminated the intended and unintended impact of leadership within large organizations.

Clearly, the aesthetics of organizational life have always been relevant to leadership, but leadership research had been dominated by cognitive science for many years. This aesthetic perspective on management emerged through the 1980s, but took until the late 1990s to have an impact on leadership research and scholarship.

Leadership and Organizational Culture

There is an affinity in many scholarly discussions between leadership and organizational culture. This tendency can be seen in the advantages that were seen as stemming from an organization's possession of a 'strong culture' (for example, Peters and Waterman 1982) or a 'transformational culture' (Bass and Avolio 1993). Such cultures were seen as providing organizational members with a sense of their distinctiveness, a sense of purpose and the 'glue' that binds people together. Companies became increasingly self-conscious and forthcoming about their values and traditions. Moreover, the visions of leaders were seen by many writers as making a distinctive contribution to cultures. The notion of leadership as having culture creation as a core (if not *the* core) element can be discerned in a number of writings, other than that of Peters and Waterman. Schein, for example, asserted that the unique and essential function of leadership is the manipulation of culture (1992). In Bass's model, changing organizational culture is an outcome of transformational leadership, which in turn has an impact on the follower's level of effort and performance.

Changing vis-à-vis Creating Culture

The connection between leadership and organizational culture is especially noticeable in the case of the founders of new organizations whose values and preoccupations often leave a distinctive imprint on their creations (Schein 1992). Leaders who follow in the founder's footsteps often see their role as that of maintaining and reinforcing the early culture. At a later stage in their development the distinctive cultures that were created might come to be seen as liabilities, as environmental realities change. Trice and Beyer (1990; 1993) helpfully distinguish between the maintenance and innovation aspects of 'cultural leadership'. Innovation takes place as the founder creates a new culture or when a new leader replaces an existing culture. Much of the New Leadership writing tended to concentrate on situations in which the leader is confronted with a culture that is in need of change because it is out of tune with current realities or because the culture is a barrier to a change of strategic direction. Such a view is exemplified by an investigation of Jaguar and Hill Samuel in the UK, which concluded that a transformation of the organization's culture was a prerequisite for radical strategic change (Whipp et al. 1989). Similarly, Kotter and Heskett's (1992) quantitative study of the links between organizational culture and firms' performance led them to conclude that the really critical factor is that a culture is adaptive, that is, it seeks to anticipate and adapt to environmental change. Leadership becomes a particular consideration for Kotter and Heskett in that it is needed to change cultures so that they are more adaptive. Here too, then, is a depiction of leaders as having a responsibility for culture creation.

It is striking that this perspective on leadership as culture management ties the study of leadership to 'value engineering' – the leader comes to be seen as someone who moulds how members are to think about the organization and their roles within it. In this way, leadership theory and research become implicated in the drift in the study of organizational culture from essentially academic discussions towards more normative, managerial approaches (Barley et al. 1988). Willmott (1993) argues that in these managerial discussions, culture is little more than an extension of management control in which the aim is to colonize the minds of members of the organization. Therefore, the wider political and ethical ramifications of cultural manipulation tend to be marginalized. Equally, the predominant paradigm for examining leadership in relation to culture is imbued with what Martin (1992) refers to as an 'integration' perspective. Martin distinguishes this approach from two others – a differentiation and a fragmentation perspective.

Integration Perspective

In the integration perspective, there is consistency between the various components of culture and there is fairly widespread agreement and understanding of the culture's precepts. Leadership is about creating, maintaining or changing cultures along the lines that have just been encountered in the writings of Schein et al. and Trice and Beyer. Alvesson (1992) provides an alternative position within an integration perspective, which views leaders as transmitters of culture within organizations. He shows how subsidiary managers in a Swedish computer consultancy firm have a social integrative function in that they transmit the organization's culture to combat the potential for the firm to splinter due to the highly decentralized and heterogeneous nature of the work of consultants. In this case, leaders transmit rather than mould culture.

Differentiation Perspective

In the differentiation perspective, leadership occupies a quite different position. Culture is seen as pervaded by lack of consensus across the organization. The perspective particularly draws attention to subcultural diversity and the resulting enclaves of consensus that form within the wider organization. Martin suggests that when investigators have explored leadership within a differentiation perspective, they have typically examined leadership exercised by groups. Such a perspective brings into play informal leadership processes that have invariably been absent in organizational research. However, it is difficult to believe that individual leaders, albeit informal ones, do not exercise leadership to promote or express subcultural positions. The notion of a collective arrogation of leadership by a group is feasible, but it is hard to believe that individual leaders are not instrumental in the process. Indeed, Martin cites the illustration from her own research (Martin and Siehl 1983) of the way in which John DeLorean formed a contraculture in his division at General Motors. He employed alternative dress codes, physical arrangements, and formal practices to promote an oppositional culture within the company. It may be that leadership by individuals has a greater role to play in the fostering of contracultures than of subcultures, but studies of informal organization have frequently pointed to the important role played by leaders in the context of subcultures (Homans 1950). The issue of how senior organizational leaders deal with subcultural variety within organizations also needs greater attention than it has been given so far, but the main contribution of the differentiation perspective is that it departs from the naive view of consensus within organizations and of leaders as sources of that integration.

Fragmentation Perspective

Martin distinguishes a third approach to reading organizational cultures – the fragmentation perspective. This approach seems almost to decentre if not eliminate the role of leadership in organizational cultures. The fragmentation perspective characterizes organizational cultures as suffused with ambiguity and confusion. The meaning of cultural artifacts and their relationships to each other are unclear and confusing to members of the organization. The sheer complexity and heterogeneity of modern organizations tends to engender cultures whose elements lack the capacity to provide 'sense-making' that was often attributed to them by earlier generations of culture researchers in the early 1980s and by the exponents of the integration perspective in particular. The decentring of leadership in the fragmentation perspective can be discerned though a number of themes in Martin's (1992) writing, though it is not confronted in a direct way. She argues that the perspective offers very few guidelines to those individuals (presumably mainly senior executives) who might wish to implement cultural change. Indeed, from the fragmentation perspective the attempt to impose a coherent culture by dint of one's organizational vision is futile and dishonest because it fails to acknowledge the diversity, ambiguity and fluidity of modern cultures. However, the fragmentation perspective need not marginalize leadership as much as Martin's analysis implies.

An important feature of leadership within the fragmentation perspective is that leaders, far from being the sources of a coherent world-view as in the integration perspective, may come to be sources of ambiguity themselves, an observation that is consistent with Alvesson and Sveningsson's (2003) previously mentioned research. Tierney (1989) notes how the presidents of 32 higher education establishments in which he conducted his research frequently sent out symbols, which were inconsistent with other cultural elements or with other symbols in which they dealt.

In another investigation, an ethnographic study of a catholic liberal arts college in crisis, Tierney (1987) shows how others consistently misunderstood the new leader's symbols and messages. The new president,

Sister Vera, attempted to change the organization's culture from a family orientation to a more professional one. She introduced an Executive Committee as a forum for the discussion of important decisions and to broaden the constituency of staff involved in decision-making. For Sister Vera, the Executive Committee was meant to symbolize a shift away from autocracy and towards a team approach to decision-making, but instead of signifying 'open communication and more team involvement' it actually signified the opposite (1987: 242). When she decided that the committee's agenda should be published as a further sign of her commitment to openness, this too was widely interpreted as the opposite of what was intended. Even her 'open door' policy was interpreted, not as a symbol of openness, but as indicative of a failure of communication. In large part, this misinterpretation (though within a fragmentation perspective it is questionable whether the notion of misinterpretation has any meaning) arose because of the clash between the open door and other signs and symbols that she emitted that indicated otherwise, such as her practice of not going into staff members' rooms to chat to them.

This case and the fragmentation perspective more generally may provide a lesson, which shows that leaders' signs and symbols may be inherently more tenuous and equivocal than has typically been appreciated. Equally, the case demonstrates how matters of leadership can have a significant role within the purview of the fragmentation perspective, but perhaps their chief frame of reference is not so much leadership as the management of meaning as the transmission of equivocality. The former is intentional and is indicated by attempt to impose clear-cut meanings on others; the second is often an unintended consequence of the management of meaning in that the resulting messages may be more ambiguous to the listener than is typically appreciated by writers within the integration perspective and leaders themselves.

Imaginative Consumption of Culture

In support of the fragmentation perspective is the notion of the imaginative consumption of culture. This notion receives reinforcement from an emerging emphasis within organizational culture research on how culture is received. Linstead and Grafton-Small argue for greater understanding 'through the examination of users' meanings and the practice of *bricolage*' of the creativity that is involved in culture *consumption* (1992: 332). This orientation shifts attention away from examinations of culture production, which is the main interest of New Leadership, culture management and integration perspective writers, towards the investigation of the imaginative consumption of cultural messages. In the process the role of leadership in culture production shifts from the centre to the periphery of the empirical agenda. This kind of position can be discerned in Hatch's (1993) reworking of an ethnographic investigation of strategic change by the new president at a large US university who employed a 'symbolic vision' to propel the change (Gioia and Chittipeddi 1991). Hatch notes that the president's actions underwent modifications and were even resisted by many organizational members. She argues that:

> Although the president was a major player in the initiation of strategic change, his influence depended heavily on the ways in which others symbolized and interpreted his efforts. The outcome of the president's influence ultimately rested with others' interpretations and the effect these interpretations had on cultural assumptions and expectations. In this light, it is worthwhile questioning whether the president was as central to the initiation effort, or the organizational culture, as he first appeared to be. (Hatch 1993: 681–2)

The implication which can be derived from Linstead and Grafton-Small (1992) and Hatch (1993), as well as from the foregoing discussion of leadership within a fragmentation perspective, is that organizational members are not passive receptacles, but *imaginative consumers*, of leaders' visions and of manipulated cultural artifacts. Similarly, Martin et al. (1998) conducted research on a leader-led culture change programme in a British local authority and found considerable skepticism about the programme, as well as apparent misinterpretations of its main tenets. Research such as this reminds us that organizational participants interpret and react to the cultural messages that leaders purvey and as such do not react as automata. They forge their own meanings of cultural messages and symbols.

There is much that is attractive about this view of organizational members as imaginative consumers of culture. There is a kind of optimism in the view that people are able to carve out spheres of interpretative autonomy which distance them from the mind-games of leaders who attempt to control what others think and feel. It countervails the tendency for studies of organizational culture to adopt the managerialist, normative stance with an emphasis on the control that was identified by Barley et al. (1988). It also has affinities with the interpretative stance with which much culture research is imbued (for example, Louis 1991), but as Linstead and Grafton-Small (1992) recognize, it is inconsistent with the emphasis on shared meanings that is a feature of much interpretative thinking. Also, it is congruent with and probably requires the kind of in-depth ethnographic approach to which many culture researchers are drawn.

Control of the Cultural Agenda

However, the implicit optimism of the imaginative consumer account of organizational culture and of the roles of leaders in relation to it requires an element of caution. It must not be forgotten that visions and the cultures, which may spring from them, are attempts to frame people's ways of thinking. This is not to suggest that organizational members passively absorb cultural messages, but that these messages set limits and boundaries on how people are supposed to think and respond. The very language within which visions and cultures are couched and the intentional privileging of some themes and issues over others frame how people think about organizational issues, even if it means that some people reject the message or react with cynicism. The rejection of the messages takes place within the frame of those messages. Organizational members can only respond to the messages that are transmitted. They cannot be imaginative consumers of cultural messages that are absent. Those messages, which are transmitted, will have been designed with certain effects (such as control, performance enhancement, or reorientation) at their core. They may have a greater impact on how members think about organizational issues than the emphasis on imaginative consumption implies, since senior leaders' control over the cultural agenda means that many potential themes do not surface. Organizational members cannot be imaginative consumers of willfully omitted messages and symbols and therefore the impact of cultural manipulation and of the part played by leaders in moulding organizational members' thinking should not be under-estimated. Instead, there should be direct examination of the extent to which leaders' attempts to manage culture are subverted in the act of consumption by others. This would involve attention being paid to the significance of leaders' control over the cultural agenda as well as to how the messages and symbols are consumed. A balance is needed in empirical investigation, which assumes that people are neither cultural dopes who passively imbibe cultural messages emanating from leaders, nor that the manipulation of organizational culture is constantly being undermined through imaginative consumption on the part of organizational members. The former position also invites us to question the seeming omnipotence with which leaders are often imbued by New Leadership writers, whereby the capacity of leaders to effect fundamental change is barely questioned.

Opportunities for Research

The examination of leadership in relation to organizational culture has been a fertile area for theory and research. After an initially rather naive view in which leaders were viewed as builders of cultures, which in turn had an impact on the thinking and behaviour of members of the organization, the role of leaders and the implications of culture were problematized. Leadership seemed to be marginalized as a focus for analysis. It is being suggested here that the processes whereby leaders frame the ways in which members conceptualize organizational concerns and how the ensuing culture closes down alternative discourses and modes of thinking should be major issues in their own right. When issues such as these have been touched on, it has been shown that even when a culture and the vision that maintains it is treated with considerable skepticism, the culture nonetheless has considerable implications for how people apprehend organizational matters (e.g. Smircich and Morgan 1982; Smircich 1983). Interestingly, there is an affinity between the fragmentation perspective and the emerging focus on distributed leadership in that both emphasize the diffusion of power. Also culture can be instrumental (or not) in conditioning people's responsiveness to such things as self-leadership. However, a fragmentation analysis invites us to question whether the symbols of a cultural emphasis on dispersed leadership will be unambiguously understood and whether it might sometimes be viewed as a political maneuver for securing greater effort from employees under the guise of handing over greater responsibility and empowerment.

Gender and Leadership

There is no consensus in the literature about gender differences in leadership styles. For example, only weak evidence exists suggesting that women display more transformational leadership than men (e.g. Eagly and Johnson 1990; Bass and Avolio 1994; Bass 1998). Eagly et al.'s (2003) meta-analysis of transformational leadership research revealed a slight but significantly more frequent display of transformational leadership by women over men. Some studies point to gender differences in particular behaviours. For example, Astin and Leland (1992, cited in Tucker et al. 1999) found that women believe more so than men that listening to and empowering followers is important, and are more likely to use conferences and networks to achieve results. Burke and McKeen (1992) suggest that such differences occur because men and women view the world differently, and consequently male leaders seek autonomy and control over their followers, while women favour connection and relatedness.

Furthermore, people do have stereotypical beliefs about 'natural' leadership gender styles (Cann and Siegfried 1990), and these might influence actual behaviours within the work place. Eagly's (1987) social role theory suggests that to avoid criticism and to achieve praise, people behave consistent with society's expectations of their gender. Therefore, as leaders women will strive to be nurturing and caring, while men will be more task-focused, ambitious and competitive. In a large-scale meta-analysis of organizational, laboratory and assessment studies, Eagly and Johnson (1990) reported small, but reliable gender differences in leadership style. Female leaders were found to emphasize both interpersonal relations and task accomplishment more than men. However, these differences reduced considerably among organizational leaders vis-à-vis leaders at lower levels. These findings suggest that women might engage in more social processes by establishing more interpersonal relations as well as clarifying task objectives and resolving uncertainties.

Eagly and Johnson's (1990) findings suggest that leadership processes might vary according to the gender composition of the workplace as much as the gender dominance of the industry. Chatman and O'Reilly (2004) found that women expressed greater commitment, positive affect and perceptions of cooperation when they worked in all-female groups. Walker et al. (1996) found that in mixed sex groups, men were much more likely to exercise opinion leadership than women.

Gardiner and Tiggemann (1999) found that women and men in male-dominated industries did not differ in their interpersonal leadership orientation, however women in female-dominated industries were more interpersonally oriented than men. Furthermore, women exhibiting an interpersonal oriented leadership style in male-dominated industries reported worse levels of mental health. This finding suggests that both the gender of leader as well as the gender ratio of the industry in general affects leadership styles, although the findings are inconclusive overall. Clearly, one future direction for research is to assess the impact on leadership of gender domination in the workplace and within the industry generally.

Methodological and Epistemological Issues in the Study of Leadership

There can be little doubt that the bulk of leadership research has been conducted within the tradition of quantitative research in which leadership variables are related to various outcomes. That domination is enduring. Qualitative research has had increasing influence on the field, but the change in trend has been slow in emerging. The drift towards the New Leadership approach in the 1980s and the growing interest in organizational culture and post-transformational perspectives resulted in greater use of qualitative research. Within the New Leadership approach, there has been greater emphasis on the leader as a manager of meaning. This emphasis has led to an awareness that the ways in which this process occurs requires in-depth understanding of particular cases and detailed probing among both leaders and subordinates of aims and impacts. To such ends, a methodological strategy seems to be required which involves observation, in-depth interviewing and the detailed examination of documents, all of which are closely associated with qualitative research. Another strategy is dramaturgical analysis of the discourse associated with leadership (Gardner 1992; Starratt 1993; Gardner and Avolio 1998; Harvey 2001; Clark and Mangham 2004).

Gardner and Avolio examined charismatic leadership from the perspective of it being a performance, with a script, plot, audience, stage, and emotional and cognitive impact upon the intended audience.

The role that is typically given to qualitative research by quantitative researchers is as preparation; in other words, if it has a role at all, qualitative research has often been reduced to a source of hypotheses to be taken up by quantitative researchers for subsequent verification. Such a division of labour keeps quantitative research very much in the methodological driver's seat. However, in the social sciences at large there is a growing recognition of the contribution that qualitative studies can make. In the process of generating such recognition, it has been necessary to discard some of the baggage of epistemological debate that has sometimes held back discussions of quantitative and qualitative research. For some writers, quantitative research is ineluctably tied to the label of positivism, while qualitative research is similarly enjoined with phenomenology. As a result of such associations, quantitative and qualitative research is deemed to be irreconcilable paradigms because of their incompatible epistemological underpinnings (e.g. Smith and Heshusius 1986). An alternative view is to recognize that quantitative and qualitative research are simply different approaches to the research process, and as such can be mutually informative and illuminating about an area like leadership, and can even be combined (Bryman 1988; Conger 1998; Bryman and Bell 2003; Kan and Parry 2004).

There can be little doubt that quantitative research on leadership offers huge advantages to the researcher who wants clear-cut specification of causal connections between different types of leader behaviour and various outcomes (like subordinate job satisfaction and performance) under specific conditions. The very fact that the New Leadership has been dominated by a quantitative research approach is a testament to these strengths, which can be seen in the stream of research deriving from Bass's work, as well as that of alternative quantitative research approaches such as those of Podsakoff et al. (1990), Kouzes and Posner (1998), Graen and Uhl-Bien (1995) and Schriesheim et al. (1995). On the other hand, qualitative research brings to the study of leadership an approach that sees leadership through the eyes of leaders and followers. In the process, the very notion of leadership is problematized by depicting the variety of meanings associated with 'leadership' or of 'good leadership' among leaders and followers (e.g. Mumford and Van Doorn 2001).

Qualitative research is also acutely sensitive to the contexts of leadership. Through the use of a single case over time or the judicious comparison of cases, the qualitative researcher is able to highlight specific features of context and how they impinge on leaders (Bryman 2004). In the multiple case study by Bryman et al. (1988) of three construction projects in England, the specific circumstances of such projects and the variations in those circumstances proved to be important factors which influenced the styles of construction project leaders. Also, qualitative research can be especially instructive when it comes to the examination of processes of leadership. By 'process' is here meant how leadership is accomplished and how leadership impacts occur over time. In detailed case studies, both features of a processual investigation may be in evidence. Examples include the basic social processes that emerge from grounded theory analysis of leadership phenomena. The social processes of 'resolving uncertainty' and 'enhancing adaptability' emerged from Parry's (1999) examination of the leadership processes at work in a local government amalgamation. Irurita's (1994) process of 'optimizing' emerged from her examination of nursing leadership in an Australian city. Kan's theory of 'identifying paradox' (Kan and Parry 2004) emerged from her research into leadership within a major hospital in New Zealand. All these processes emerged as the essence of the leadership process being enacted in each setting.

Equally, as in the social sciences generally, quantitative and qualitative studies can usefully be combined (Bryman 1988; Bryman and Bell 2003, chapter 22) and conducted concurrently as readily as they can be conducted consecutively. The use of quantitative and qualitative research in tandem is still quite unusual in leadership studies. One major example is House et al.'s (2004) GLOBE study of leadership around the world. It combined a range of methodologies to research organizational leadership within the context of the culture of the society within which that leadership was embedded. Kirby et al. (1992) employed a combined approach in the context of an investigation of school leaders and found a slight difference between the two sets of findings. When they employed Bass's framework and measures, their findings were extremely similar to those typically found by researchers using this approach. By contrast, their analysis of narrative

descriptions of 'extraordinary leaders' found that the capacity of leaders to provide opportunities for professional development was more prominent than the kinds of leadership orientation identified by Bass. Kan and Parry (2004) found conflicting results between qualitative data and quantitative data. The quantitative questionnaire data, using Bass and Avolio's MLQ, suggested that there was considerable leadership being displayed. The qualitative data, mainly from observation and interview, suggested that leadership was not being realized within that particular organizational context. Further theoretical coding analysis of the questionnaire data and of new and existing qualitative data provided a resolution of this apparent paradox. The managers who were the subject of the questionnaire were attempting to display leadership, rather than successfully displaying it, because of the characteristics of the culture of the workforce and the deep power structures underlying the working environment. Either data set, by itself, would have provided an inaccurate perspective on the leadership processes that were in operation. Together, and analyzed qualitatively, they provided a richer and more accurate and insightful interpretation of the phenomenon. Egri and Herman (2000) also used qualitative and quantitative data as well as both types of analysis in their examination of leadership in the environmental sector. Once again, the impact of context upon leadership could be determined, along with other psychological variables such as personal values, need for achievement and the like.

It is easy to view these differences within a framework of 'triangulation' (Jick 1979; Webb et al. 1966) and to ask which is right. However, a much more promising avenue is to ask why the different contexts of questioning produce contrasting results and to see them as having gained access to different levels of cognition about leadership – general behaviours in the case of the quantitative study and more specific behaviours in the qualitative one – and to recognize that the research question needs to be linked to the appropriate kind of research design and instruments.

The injection of qualitative research into the study of leadership has great potential for the field. More particularly, the *concurrent* use of multiple sources of data and multiple methods of analysis seem to have greatest potential. It can allow a different set of questions to be addressed and can address issues that are not readily accessible to a quantitative approach. For example, informal leadership has typically been neglected by quantitative researchers but may be more accessible to qualitative research. One of the reasons quantitative researchers concentrate on leaders is that they provide a ready-made focus for the administration of questionnaires. If acts of leadership are indeed dispersed, an important issue for researchers is that of identifying leadership and the acts and skills associated with it. Qualitative research is much more likely to provide the open-endedness that such a stance requires.

There continues to be great optimism about the field of leadership in organizations. In shifting towards a range of post-transformational approaches to the phenomenon of leadership, and in recognizing the potential of a greater range of research styles, the subject is well placed as a major area within the field of organization studies.

Overview

There is clearly much greater optimism about the field of leadership in organizations than in the early 1980s. In shifting towards a view of leadership as the management of meaning and in recognising the potential of a greater range of research styles, the subject is well placed as a major area within the field of organization studies. Here we want to suggest two issues that are of particular significance. Firstly, leadership theory and research has been remarkably and surprisingly uncoupled from organization theory more generally, in spite of the fact that the two fields clearly have implications for each other. Thus, for example, one of the more influential theories in the field since the late 1970s has been the population ecology perspective (Hannan and Freeman 1984). This approach represents something of an implicit critique of leadership theory and research, but has hardly been acknowledged as such by those working within the leadership field. Population ecology proposes that the environments within which populations of organizations operate have a limited carrying capacity and that as a result some organizations are 'selected out' and die. This perspective suggests that human agency is of limited help in effecting the survival of organizations. The implications for the study of leadership are considerable because population ecology seems to reduce the importance of leadership greatly. The specific issue of whether leadership can make a difference to organizational survival is an important one for students of leadership and cannot be ignored.

Secondly, one feature that leadership theory and research of recent years shares with organization theory (and indeed the social sciences more generally) is the growing influence of research methods and research designs that lie outside the field's dominant methodological paradigm. As we have shown in this chapter, studies of leadership involving qualitative research and case studies, for example, have become much more commonly seen in the journals than in the past, although the majority of research in this area continues to involve experimental or questionnaire studies (Lowe and Gardner 2000). However, the growing influence of methodological approaches that lie outside the conventional paradigm is significant in at least two respects. First, it has resulted in a greater sense of eclecticism in the field. Second, a considerable number of researchers who have employed alternative methodological approaches have been from outside North America. As House and Aditya (1997: 409) have observed, the main theories of leadership and around 98 per cent of the empirical evidence 'are distinctly American in character'. While some writers have employed qualitative research to illuminate aspects of leadership that are associated with the conventional ways of approaching leadership, others have employed it to explore areas that are not typically emphasized (for example, the discursive aspects of leading or the aesthetics of leadership). Thus, the growing use of qualitative research is associated with a wider variety of aspects of leadership being the focus of attention and the greater impact of non-American writers and ways of approaching the field.

Perhaps for these reasons, one senses less pessimism about the field than when writers summarized developments in theory and research in the 1970s through the early 1990s. Avolio et al. (2003: 277) have remarked that part of the way through many conferences on leadership someone intones: 'Never has a construct been studied so much that we know so little about.' These authors argue that this remark is both obsolete and wrong, and indeed we have a sense that such a remark is unlikely to be heard nowadays. The growing infusion of new approaches, methodologies, and writers from outside the North American orbit has almost certainly contributed to a greater degree of optimism about the field, such that calls like Miner's (1975) for the leadership concept to be abandoned are both far less likely to be heard and less credible when viewed in relation to the exciting and productive field that leadership has become.

References

Alvesson, M. (1990) 'Organization: from substance to image?', *Organization Studies*, 11: 373–94.

Alvesson, M. (1992) 'Leadership as social integrative action: a study of a computer consultancy company', *Organization Studies*, 13: 185–209.

Alvesson, M. and Sveningsson, S. (2003) 'Good visions, bad micro-management and ugly ambiguity: contradictions of (non-)leadership in a knowledge-intensive organization', *Organization Studies*, 24(6): 961–988.

Alimo-Metcalfe, B. and Alban-Metcalfe, R.J. (2001) 'The development of a new Transformational Leadership Questionnaire', *Journal of Occupational and Organizational Psychology*, 74: 1–28.

Astin, H.S. and Leland, C. (1992) *Women of Influence, Women of Vision: A Cross-Generational Study of Leaders and Social Change*. San Francisco: Jossey-Bass.

Avolio, B.J., Bass, B.M. and Jung, D.I. (1999) 'Re-examining the components of transformational and transactional leadership using the multifactor leadership questionnaire', *Journal of Occupational and Organizational Psychology*, 72: 441–62.

Avolio, B.J., Kahai, S. and Dodge, G.E. (2001) 'E-Leadership: Implications for theory, research, and practice', *The Leadership Quarterly*, 11(4): 615–68.

Avolio, B.J., Sosik, J.J., Jung, D.I. and Berson, Y. (2003) 'Leadership models, methods and application', in W.C. Borman, D.R. Ilgen, and R.J. Klimoski (eds), *Handbook of Psychology, Volume 12: Industrial and Organizational Psychology*. New York: Wiley, pp. 277-307.

Babiak, P. (1996). 'Psychopathic manipulation in organizations: Pawns, patrons, and patsies', in D.J. Cooke, A.E. Forth, J.P. Newman and R.D. Hare (eds), *Issues in Criminological and Legal Psychology: No. 24, International Perspectives on Psychopathy*. Leicester, UK: British Psychological Society. pp. 12–7.

Barley, S.R., Meyer, G.W. and Gash, D.C. (1988) 'Cultures of culture: academics, practitioners and the pragmatics of normative control', *Administrative Science Quarterly*, 33: 24–60.

Bass, B.M. (1985) *Leadership and Performance Beyond Expectations*. New York: Free Press.

Bass, B.M. (1997) 'Does the transactional and transformational leadership paradigm transcend organisational and national boundaries?', *American Psychologist*, 52(2): 130–9.

Bass, B.M. (1998) *Transformational Leadership: Industrial, Military and Educational Impact*. Mahwah, NJ: Lawrence Erlbaum.

Bass, B.M. and Avolio, B.J. (1989) 'Potential biases in leadership measures: how prototypes, leniency, and general satisfaction relate to ratings and rankings of transformational and transactional leadership constructs', *Educational and Psychological Measurement*, 49: 509–27.

Bass, B.M. and Avolio, B.J. (1990) 'The implications of transactional and transformational leadership for individual, team, and organizational development', *Research in Organizational Change and Development*, 4: 231–72.

Bass, B.M and Avolio, B.J. (1993) 'Transformational leadership and the organizational culture', *Public Administration Quarterly*, 17: 112–22.

Bass, B.M. and Avolio, B.J. (1994) 'Shatter the glass ceiling: women may make better managers', *Human Resource Management*, 33: 549–60.

Bass, B.M. and Steidlmeier, P. (1999) 'Ethics, character, and authentic transformational leadership behaviour', *The Leadership Quarterly*, 10(2): 181–217.

Bennis, W.G. and Nanus, B. (1985) *Leaders: the Strategies for Taking Charge*. New York: Harper & Row.

Brown, M.E. and Gioia, D.A. (2002) 'Making things click: Distributive leadership in an online division of an offline organization', *The Leadership Quarterly*, 13(4): 397–419.

Bryman, A. (1986) *Leadership and Organizations*. London: Routledge and Kegan Paul.

Bryman, A. (1988) *Quantity and Quality in Social Research*. London: Routledge.

Bryman, A. (1992) *Charisma and Leadership of Organizations*. London: Sage.

Bryman, A. (2004) Qualitative research on leadership: a critical but appreciative review. *The Leadership Quarterly*, 15(6): 729-770.

Bryman, A. and Bell, E. (2003) *Business Research Methods*. Oxford: Oxford University Press.

Bryman, A., Bresnen, M., Beardsworth, A. and Keil, T. (1988) 'Qualitative research and the study of leadership', *Human Relations*, 41: 13–30.

Bryman, A., Gillingwater, D., and McGuinness, I. (1996) 'Leadership and organizational transformation', *International Journal of Public Administration*, 19: 849–72.

Burke, R.J. and McKeen, C.A. (1992) 'Women in management', *International Review of Industrial and Organizational Psychology*, 7: 245–84.

Burns, J.M. (1978) *Leadership*. New York: Harper & Row.

Calas, M.B. and Smircich, L. (1997) 'Voicing seduction to silence leadership', in K. Grint (ed.), *Leadership: Classical, Contemporary and Critical Approaches*. Oxford: Oxford University Press.

Cann, A. and Siegfried, W.D. (1990) Gender stereotypes and dimensions of effective leader behaviour, *Sex Roles*, 23: 413–9.

Chatman, J.A. and O'Reilly, C.A. (2004) 'Asymmetric reactions to work group sex diversity among men and women', *Academy of Management Journal*, 47(2): 193–208.

Clark, T. and Mangham, I. (2004) 'From dramaturgy to theatre as technology: the case of corporate theatre', *Journal of Management Studies*, 41(1): 37–59.

Collins, J. (2001) 'Level 5 leadership: the triumph of humility and fierce resolve', *Harvard Business Review*, 79(1): 67–76.

Conger, J.A. (1989) *The Charismatic Leader: Behind the Mystique of Exceptional Leadership*. San Francisco: Jossey-Bass.

Conger, J. (1998) 'Qualitative research in the understanding leadership', *The Leadership Quarterly*, 9(1): 107–21

Conger, J.A. and Kanungo, R.N. (1998) *Charismatic Leadership in Organizations*. Thousand Oaks: CA. Sage.

Craig, S.B. and Gustafson, S.B. (1998) 'Perceived leader integrity scale: An instrument for assessing employee perceptions of leader integrity', *The Leadership Quarterly*, 9(2): 127–45.

den Hartog, D.N., Van Muijen, J.J. and Koopman, P.L. (1997) 'Transactional versus transformational leadership: an analysis of the MLQ', *Journal of Occupational and Organizational Psychology*, 70(1): 19.

Eagly, A.H. (1987) *Sex Differences in Social Behaviour: A Social-Role Interaction*. Hillsdale: Erlbaum.

Eagly, A.H. and Johnson, B. (1990) 'Gender and leadership: A meta-analysis', *Psychological Bulletin*, 108: 233–56.

Eagly, A.H., Johannesen-Schmidt, M.C. and van Engen, M. (2003) 'Transformational, transactional and laissez-faire leadership styles: A meta-analysis comparing women and men', *Psychological Bulletin*, 95: 569–91.

Egri, C.P. and Herman, S. (2000) 'Leadership in the environmental sector: Values, leadership styles and contexts of environmental leaders and their organizations', *Academy of Management Journal*, 43(4): 571–604.

Fiedler, F.E. (1967) *A Theory of Leadership Effectiveness*. New York: McGraw-Hill.

Fiedler, F.E. (1993) 'The leadership situation and the black box in contingency theories', in M.M. Chemers and R. Ayman (eds), *Leadership Theory and Research: Perspectives and Directions*. New York: Academic Press.

Fiedler, F.E. and Garcia, J.E. (1987) *Improving Leadership Effectiveness: Cognitive Resources and Organizational Performance*. New York: Wiley.

Fry, L.W. (2003) 'Toward a theory of spiritual leadership', *The Leadership Quarterly*, 14: 693–727.

Fullan, M. (2001) *Leading in a Culture of Change*. San Francisco: Jossey Bass.

Gardiner, M. and Tiggemann, M. (1999) Gender differences in leadership style, job stress and mental health in male and female-dominated industries, *Journal of Occupational and Organizational Psychology*, 72: 301–15.

Gardner, W.L. (1992) 'Lessons in organizational dramaturgy: The art of impression management', *Organizational Dynamics*, 21(1): 33–41.

Gardner, W.L. and Avolio, B.J. (1998) 'The charismatic relationship: A dramaturgical perspective', *Academy of Management Review*, 23: 32–58.

Gioia, D.A. and Chittipeddi, K. (1991) 'Sensemaking and sensegiving in strategic change initiation', *Strategic Management Journal*, 12: 433–48.

Gordon, R. (2002) 'Viewing the dispersion of leadership through a power lens: Exposing unobtrusive tensions and problematic processes', in K.W. Parry and J. Meindl (eds), *Grounding Leadership Theory and Research: Issues, Perspectives, and Methods*. Connecticut, USA: Information Age Publishing. pp. 39–56.

Graen, G.B. and Uhl-Bien, M. (1995) 'Development of leader-member exchange (LMX) theory of leadership over 25 years: Applying a multi-level domain perspective', *The Leadership Quarterly*, 6: 219–47.

Greene, C.N. (1975) 'The reciprocal nature of influence between leader and subordinate', *Journal of Applied Psychology*, 60: 187–93.

Grint, K. (2000) *The Arts of Leadership*. New York: Oxford University Press.

Gustafson, S.B. and Ritzer, D.R. (1995) 'The dark side of normal: A psychopathy-linked pattern called aberrant self-promotion', *European Journal of Personality*, 9: 147–83.

Guthey, E. (2001) 'Ted Turner's corporate cross-dressing and the shifting images of American business leadership', *Enterprise and Society*, 2(1): 111–42.

Hannan, M. and Freeman, J. (1984) 'Structural inertia and organizational change: Liability of inertia', *American Sociological Review*, 49: 149–164.

Harvey, A. (2001) 'A dramaturgical analysis of charismatic leader discourse', *Journal of Organizational Change Management*, 14(3): 253–65.

Hatch, M.J. (1993) 'The dynamics of organizational culture', *Academy of Management Review*, 18: 657–93.

Hicks, D. A. (2002) 'Spiritual and religious diversity at the workplace: Implications for leadership', *The Leadership Quarterly*, 13: 379–96.

Homans, G.C. (1950) *The Human Group*. New York: Harcourt, Brace.

Hosking, D.M. (1981) 'A critical evaluation of Fiedler's contingency hypothesis', in G.M. Stephenson and J.M. Davis (eds), *Progress in Applied Social Psychology, Volume 1*. New York: Wiley.

Hosking, D.M. (1988) 'Organizing, leadership and skilful process', *Journal of Management Studies*, 25: 147–66.

Hosking, D.M. (1991) 'Chief executives, organising processes, and skill', *European Journal of Applied Psychology*, 41: 95–103.

House, R.J. (1977) 'A 1976 theory of charismatic leadership', in J.G. Hunt and L.L. Larson (eds), *Leadership: the Cutting Edge*. Carbondale, IL: Southern Illinois University Press.

House, R.J. and Aditya, R. (1997) 'The social scientific study of leadership: *Quo Vadis?*', *Journal of Management*, 23: 409–73.

House, R.J., Hanges, P.J., Javidan, M., Dorfman, P.W. and Gupta, V. (eds) (2004) *Culture, Leadership, and Organizations: The GLOBE Study of 62 Societies*. London: Sage.

Irurita, V.F. (1994) 'Optimism, values, and commitment as forces in leadership', *Journal of Nursing Administration (JONA)*, 24(9): 61–71.

Jick, T.D. (1979) 'Mixing qualitative and quantitative methods: Triangulation in action', *Administrative Science Quarterly*, 24(4): 602–11.

Kan, M. and Parry, K.W. (2004) 'Identifying paradox: A grounded theory of leadership in overcoming resistance to change', *The Leadership Quarterly*, 15(4): 467–91.

Keller, R.T. (1992) 'Transformational leadership and the performance of research and development project groups', *Journal of Management*, 18: 489–501.

Kerr, S., Schriesheim, C.A., Murphy, C.J. and Stogdill, R.M. (1974) 'Toward a contingency theory of leadership based upon the consideration and initiating structure literature', *Organizational Behaviour and Human Performance*, 12: 62–82.

Kets de Vries, M.F.R. and Miller, D. (1985) 'Narcissism and leadership: an object relations perspective', *Human Relations*, 38(6): 583–601.

Kirby, P.C., King, M.I. and Paradise, L.V. (1992) 'Extraordinary leaders in education: understanding transformational leadership', *Journal of Educational Research*, 85: 303–11.

Knights, D. and Willmott, H. (1992) 'Conceptualizing leadership processes: a study of senior managers in a financial services company', *Journal of Management Studies*, 29: 761–82.

Korman, A.K. (1966) '"Consideration", "initiating structure", and organizational criteria – a review', *Personnel Psychology*, 19: 349–61.

Korman, A.K. (1973) 'On the development of contingency theories of leadership: some methodological considerations and a possible alternative', *Journal of Applied Psychology*, 21: 84–7.

Kotter, J.P. (1990) *A Force for Change: How Leadership Differs from Management*. New York: Free Press.

Kotter, J.P. and Heskett, J.L. (1992) *Corporate Culture and Performance*. New York: Free Press.

Kouzes, J.M. and Posner, B.Z. (1993) *Credibility: How Leaders Gain and Lose It, Why People Demand It*. San Francisco: Jossey-Bass.

Kouzes, J.M. and Posner, B.Z. (1998) *Encouraging the Heart*. San Francisco, Jossey-Bass.

Lawrence, P.R. and Lorsch, J. (1967) *Organization and Environment*. Cambridge, Mass.: Harvard University Press.

Leavy, B. and Wilson, D. (1994) *Strategy and Leadership*. London: Routledge.

Linstead, S. and Grafton-Small, R. (1992) 'On reading organizational culture', *Organization Studies*, 13: 331–55.

Lord, R.G. and Maher, K.J. (1991) *Leadership and Information Processing: Linking Perceptions and Performance*. Cambridge, Mass.: Unwin Hyman.

Louis, M.R. (1991) 'Reflections on an interpretive way of life', in P.J. Frost et al. (eds), *Reframing Organizational Culture*. Newbury Park: Sage.

Lowe, K. B. and Gardner, W. L. (2000) 'Ten years of *The Leadership Quarterly*: contributions and challenges for the future', *The Leadership Quarterly*, 11: 459–514.

Lowin, A. and Craig, C.R. (1968) 'The influence of performance on managerial style: an experimental object lesson in the ambiguity of correlational data', *Organizational Behaviour and Human Performance*, 3: 440–58.

Maccoby, M. (2000) 'Narcissistic leaders: The incredible pros, the inevitable cons', *Harvard Business Review*, 78(1): 68–77.

Manz, C.C. and Sims, H.P. (1991) 'SuperLeadership: beyond the myth of heroic leadership', *Organizational Dynamics*, 19: 18–35.

Martin, G., Beaumont, P., and Staines, H. (1998) 'Changing corporate culture: paradoxes and tensions in a local authority', in C. Mabey, D. Skinner, and T. Clark (eds), *Experiencing Human Resource Management*, London: Sage.

Martin, J. (1992) *Cultures in Organizations: Three Perspectives*. New York: Oxford University Press.

Martin, J. and Siehl, C. (1983) 'Organizational culture and counterculture: an uneasy symbiosis', *Organizational Dynamics*, 12: 52–64.

Miner, J.B. (1975) 'The uncertain future of the leadership concept: an overview', in J. G. Hunt and L.L. Larson (eds), *Leadership Frontiers*. Kent, Ohio: Kent State University Press.

Mumford, M.D. and Van Doorn, J. (2001) 'The leadership of pragmatism: reconsidering Franklin in the age of charisma', *The Leadership Quarterly*, 12: 279–310.

Ottensmeyer, E. (1996) 'Too strong to stop, too sweet to lose; Aesthetics as a way to know organizations', *Organization*, 3(2): 189–94.

Parry, K.W. (1999) 'Enhancing adaptability: leadership strategies to accommodate change in local government settings', *Journal of Organizational Change Management*, 12(2): 134–56.

Parry, K.W. and Proctor-Thomson, S.B. (2002) 'Perceived integrity of transformational leaders in organisational settings', *Journal of Business Ethics*, 35(2): 75–96.

Pawar, B.S. and Eastman, K.K. (1997) 'The nature and implications of contextual influences on transformational leadership: a conceptual examination', *Academy of Management Review*, 22(1): 80–109.

Peters, L.H., Hartke, D.D. and Pohlmann, J.T. (1985) 'Fiedler's contingency theory of leadership: an application of the meta-analysis procedures of Schmidt and Hunter', *Psychological Bulletin*, 97: 274–85.

Peters, T. and Waterman, R.H. (1982) *In Search of Excellence: Lessons from America's Best-Run Companies*. New York: Harper & Row.

Pfeffer, J. (1981) 'Management as symbolic action: the creation and maintenance of organizational paradigms', *Research in Organizational Behaviour*, 3: 1–52.

Podsakoff, P.M., MacKenzie, S.B., Moorman, R.H. and Fetter, R. (1990) 'Transformational leader behaviours and their effects on followers' trust in leader, satisfaction, and organizational citizenship behaviours', *The Leadership Quarterly*, 1: 107–42.

Podsakoff, P., Todor, W., Grover, R. and Huber, V. (1984) 'Situational moderators of leader reward and punishment behaviour: fact or fiction?', *Organizational Behaviour and Human Performance*, 34: 21–63.

Post, J.M. (1986) 'Narcissism and the charismatic leader-follower relationship', *Political Psychology*, 7(4): 675–87.

Reich, R.B. (1987) 'Entrepreneurship reconsidered: the team as hero', *Harvard Business Review*, 65: 77–83.

Ropo, A. and Eriksson, M. (1997) 'Managing a theatre production: Conflict, communication, and competence', in M. Fitzgibbon and A. Kelly (eds), *From Maestro to Manager: Critical Issues in Arts and Culture Management*. Dublin: Oak Tree Press.

Ropo, A. and Parviainen, J. (2001) 'Leadership and bodily knowledge in expert organizations: An epistemological rethinking', *Scandinavian Journal of Management*, 17: 1–18.

Rosener, J.B. (1997) 'Sexual static', in K. Grint (ed.), *Leadership: Classical, contemporary and critical approaches*. Oxford: Oxford University Press, pp. 211–233.

Rush, M.C., Thomas, J.C. and Lord, R.T. (1977) 'Implicit leadership theory: A potential threat to the internal validity of leader behaviour questionnaires', *Organizational Behaviour and Human Performance*, 20: 93–110.

Sashkin, M. (1988) 'The visionary leader', in J.A. Conger and R.N. Kanungo (eds), *Charismatic Leadership: the Elusive Factor in Organizational Effectiveness*. San Francisco: Jossey-Bass, pp. 122–160.

Sass, J.S. (2000) 'Characterizing organizational spirituality: An organizational communication culture approach', *Communication Studies*, 51: 195–207.

Schein, E.H. (1992) *Organizational Culture and Leadership*, 2nd edn. San Francisco: Jossey Bass.

Schriesheim, C.A., Cogliser, C.C. and Neider, L.L. (1995) 'Is it 'trustworthy?': a multiple-levels-of-analysis reexamination of an Ohio state leadership study, with implications for future research', *The Leadership Quarterly*, 6(2): 111–45.

Selznick, P. (1957) *Leadership in Administration*. New York: Harper and Row.

Shamir, B. (1992) 'Attribution of influence and charisma to the leader: the romance of leadership revisited', *Journal of Applied Social Psychology*, 22: 386–407.

Shamir, B. and Howell, J.M. (1999) 'Organisational and contextual influences on the emergence and effectiveness of charismatic leadership', *The Leadership Quarterly*, 10(2): 257–83.

Shamir, B., House, R.J. and Arthur, M.B. (1993) 'The motivational effects of charismatic leadership: A self-concept based theory', *Organisation Science*, 4(4): 577–94.

Sims, H.P. and Lorenzi, P. (1992) *The New Leadership Paradigm*. Newbury Park: Sage.

Smircich, L. (1983) 'Leadership as shared meanings', in L. Pondy, P. Frost, G. Morgan, and T. Dandridge (eds), *Organizational Symbolism*. Greenwich, CT: JAI Press.

Smircich. L. and Morgan, G. (1982) 'Leadership: the management of meaning', *Journal of Applied Behavioural Science*, 18: 257–73.

Smith, J.K. and Heshusius, L. (1986) 'Closing down the conversation: the end of the quantitative-qualitative debate among educational inquirers', *Educational Researcher*, 15: 4–12.

Sosik, J., Avolio, B. and Kahai, S. (1997) 'Effects of leadership style and anonymity on group potency and effectiveness in a group decision support system environment', *Journal of Applied Psychology*, 82(1): 89–103.

Starratt, R.J. (1993) *The Drama of Leadership*. London: The Falmer Press.

Stogdill, R.M. (1950) 'Leadership, membership and organization', *Psychological Bulletin*, 47: 1–14.

Storey, J. (ed.) (2004) *Leadership in Organizations: Current Issues and Key Trends*. London: Routledge.

Strati, A. (2000) 'Putting people in the picture: art and aesthetics in photography and in understanding organisational life', *Organization Studies*, 21: 53–69.

Tichy, N.M. and Devanna, M.A. (1986) *The Transformational Leader*. New York: Wiley.

Tierney, W.G. (1987) 'The semiotic aspects of leadership: an ethnographic perspective', *American Journal of Semiotics*, 5: 233–50.

Tierney, W.G. (1989) 'Symbolism and presidential perceptions of leadership', *Review of Higher Education*, 12: 153–66.

Trice, H.M. and Beyer, J.M. (1990) 'Cultural leadership in organizations', *Organizational Science*, 2: 149–69.

Trice, H.M. and Beyer, J.M. (1993) *The Cultures of Work Organizations*. Englewood Cliffs, NJ: Prentice Hall.

Vecchio, R.P. (1983) 'Assessing the validity of Fiedler's contingency model of leadership effectiveness', *Psychological Bulletin*, 93: 404–8.

Waldman, D.A., Bass, B.M. and Yammarino, F.J. (1990) 'Adding to contingent reward behaviour: The augmenting effect of charismatic leadership', *Group and Organization Studies*, 15(4): 381–94.

Walker, H., Ilardi, B., McMahon, A. and Fennell, M. (1996) 'Gender, interaction, and leadership', *Social Psychology Quarterly*, 59: 255–72.

Webb, E.J., Campbell, D.T., Schwartz, R.D. and Sechrest, L. (1966) *Unobtrusive Measures*. Chicago: Rand McNally.

Weick, K.E. (1995) *Sensemaking in Organizations*. Thousand Oaks, CA: Sage.

Westley, F.R. and Mintzberg, H. (1989) 'Visionary leadership and strategic management', *Strategic Management Journal*, 10: 17–32.

Whipp, R., Rosenfeld, R. and Pettigrew, A. (1989) 'Culture and competitiveness: evidence from two mature UK industries', *Journal of Management Studies*, 26: 561–85.

Willmott, H. (1993) 'Strength is ignorance; slavery is freedom: managing culture in modern organizations', *Journal of Management Studies*, 30: 515–52.

Yukl, G.A. (1999) 'An evaluation of conceptual weaknesses in transformational and charismatic leadership theories', *The Leadership Quarterly*, 10(2): 285–305.

Yukl, G. A. (2002) *Leadership in Organizations*, 5th edn. Englewood Cliffs, NJ: Prentice Hall.

Zaleznik, A. (1977) 'Managers and leaders: are they different?', *Harvard Business Review*, 55: 67–78.

2.2 Perspectives on Organizational Decision-Making

SUSAN J. MILLER AND DAVID C. WILSON

Introduction

The study of organizational decision-making has a long history encompassing a variety of perspectives, philosophical positions and prescriptions. As with most areas of organization theory, and management research generally, it is not without controversy. There has been much debate over the years about the possibilities and practices of 'effective' decision-making, the import of decision-making for other aspects of organizational functioning, the links with power in organizational settings, and even whether the concept of 'decision' has any utility.

This chapter will chart the development of decision-making as an arena of discourse and managerial practice. It will begin by highlighting the key ideas, research studies and debates that have characterized the field before moving on to examine how it interfaces with topics of current interest in related areas within business and management.

Early Perspectives on Strategic Decision-Making: Rational and Incremental Approaches

As Hendry (2000: 957) notes, the earliest perspectives of strategic decision-making provide us with a picture of decisions as being conceptually unchallenging, ontologically unproblematic and shaped by managerial intention. This is a view grounded in notions of *rationality*. A decision is a rational choice based on logical connections between cause and effect where the decision-maker identifies a problem, searches for alternative potential solutions, prioritizes preferences according to identified criteria and arrives at an optimizing choice. Neo-classical economic assumptions underpin such perspectives.

Individuals are maximizing entrepreneurs arriving at decisions through a sequential process that is both logical and linear.

The economic perspective aggregates the behaviour of individuals and groups without compunction. Since individual managers make rational decisions, then decisions made by groups within organizations are equally rational. This view of organizations and decision-making represents a mainstay of functionalist thinking; however, the limitations of the approach have long been recognized by theorists from within, and outside, the paradigm.

Simon (1945) was one of the earliest authors to provide a comprehensive critique of the limitations of this 'rational actor' model. Constrained by the complexity of modern organizations and by their own limited cognitive capacities, Simon asserted that decision-makers were simply unable to operate under conditions of perfect rationality. The issue for decision is likely to be unclear or open to varying interpretation, information about alternatives may be unavailable, incomplete or misrepresented, and criteria by which potential solutions are to be evaluated are often uncertain or unagreed. In addition, the time and energy available to decision-makers to pursue a maximizing outcome is both limited and finite. Searching for better choices can simply take too long. The net result of these constraints is that the outcome is likely to be a 'satisficing' rather than optimising choice; one which satisfies and suffices in the circumstances.

Thus, managers operate within a *'bounded rationality'*. They are intendedly rational, and indeed their behaviour is reasoned, not *irrational*, which is an important distinction, but it is unrealistic to expect them to meet the stringent requirements of strictly rational behaviour. Human frailties and contextual demands from both within and outside the organization bound the degree of rationality that can be employed.

Even so, Simon makes the important observation that different types of decisions can be processed in different ways. Some decision processes may approximate to rational prescriptions, others may not. Decisions that occur more frequently, which are familiar, almost routine, may be made in a relatively straightforward fashion. These decisions are comprehensible to managers and there usually exist tried and tested protocols, formulae or procedures for making them. They are 'programmed' (Simon 1960), in the sense that they can be made by reference to existing rubrics. Programmed decisions are often made lower down in the organizational hierarchy, they are the operational decisions that can be safely left to subordinates. It is likely that these decisions can be made in a way that parallels more closely the prescripts of rational choice models. In fact, there may be little in the way of formal deciding to be done (Butler 1990).

In contrast, 'non-programmed' decisions are those that are unfamiliar, they have not been encountered in quite the same way before; they are to some extent novel, unusual. The topic for decision may be complex, making definition problematic, information may be needed that is both difficult to collect and categorize, potential solutions may be hard to recognize and may in turn create new problems. They therefore present a challenge to managers, for there are no obvious well-trodden paths to follow. To make matters more challenging, these decisions are usually about the more significant areas of organizational activities involving the commitment of significant resources (Papadakis and Barwise 1998). They will have consequential repercussions, are often hard to reverse (Wilson et al. 1996; 1999; Papadakis and Barwise 1998) and will set precedents for other decisions which follow. Since decisions are intended to shape actions for the future and since the future is inherently uncertain, the potential consequences of non-programmed, or *strategic*, decisions have worrying implications for managers. Because of their consequentiality, these decisions are usually sanctioned or authorized by the most senior executives in the elite. Since there is less likely to be an existing template to shape the process by which they are made, what happens may differ considerably from what might be fully rational. It is not easy to follow a step-by-step, smoothly escalating, sequential process under such conditions. 'Problemistic search' may occur, where activity is spurred by the immediate

problems, rather than being an orderly collection of information prompted by foresight (Cyert and March 1963).

This continuum of decisions along a programmed/non-programmed dimension represents an early but significant step in distinguishing the characteristics of decisions and associating them with types of process.

The empirical studies of Lindblom (1959) and Braybrooke and Lindblom (1963) in the US public sector and Quinn (1978; 1980) in the private sector provide an alternative to the linear, sequential process of traditional approaches. Decisions here were made in a halting 'incremental' way with periods of re-cycling, iteration and reformulation. The process was both dynamic and non-linear.

So, instead of final choices being arrived at after the full rational process of search and evaluation is completed, small adjustments are made to ongoing strategies. The full range of alternative solutions is not considered, only ones that do not differ markedly from the status quo. Decisions proceed by a series of small steps, rather than implementing the complete solution in one large stride. For Lindblom the advantages of this approach are clear. Because each step, in itself, is not too dissimilar from what is already being done, it does not disturb too many stakeholders. Unthreatened by radical change, they may be more willing to give commitment. The repercussions from changes which, initially at least, are relatively minor, are likely to be less serious and more predictable. Most importantly, the decision has more chance of being 'undone' if necessary – it is more reversible. Once each small step has been taken it gives a clearer picture of what has to be done and the future becomes more focused. If the chosen path now seems unlikely to lead to the desired destination, or if changing circumstances make the destination less appropriate, a small step can be retraced with less difficulty than a larger one.

Lindblom argues that this is not only a description of what is done in organizations but also what ought to be done, given the inherent unpredictability of the context in which most decision-makers work. The incrementalist model is therefore both normative and prescriptive, as Smith and May (1980) have commented.

Some have suggested that incrementalism, or 'muddling through' as Lindblom has referred to it, is less a recipe for change, more likely a formula for inertia. It has been argued that small decisions which are only marginally different from the status quo are fine – if the current position is acceptable. However, if change needs to be immediate and substantial, for example if the organization is in crisis, then incrementalism is not enough. Lindblom has countered that radical change can be equally swift whether it is effected by a series of small frequent steps or one large one. In fact, smaller steps may be quicker since they may encounter less delaying opposition.

When Mintzberg et al. (1976) studied 25 strategic decisions in a variety of Canadian organizations they found even clearer evidence of cycling and re-cycling of information and alternatives, again showing that the making of this level of decision is likely to require constant adjustment and re-appraisal. Their study distinguished seven kinds of process: simple impasse, political design, basic search, modified search, basic design, blocked design and dynamic design processes. Most of these experience delays and interruptions and repeated reconsideration. Nutt's (1984) work analysed 73 decisions in health-related organizations in the US and noticed some similar patterns occurring in search processes.

On the other hand, Heller et al. (1988) were prepared to assume common sequential phases across decision processes in British, Dutch and (former) Yugoslav organizations. They examined 217 cases of medium- and long-term decisions in each of these three countries: 80 cases in the UK, 55 in the Netherlands and 82 in former Yugoslavia (in addition to lower-level operational decision-making, which is not relevant for our purposes here). Four distinct phases were identified, namely: start-up, development (which includes the search for alternatives); finalization; and implementation. Not everything may be circuitous. Indeed, it is claimed that in periods of crisis decisions can be made in a relatively speedy and straightforward way (Dutton 1986; Rosenthal 1986; Miller 1997). When organizations are in trouble and urgent action is required, those in authority can be given great freedom to act, even by subordinates whose jobs may be affected, particularly if they are perceived to have the necessary grasp of the situation and are likely to be able to do something to help.

Decision-Making and Power

In Simon's definition of the term, 'bounded rationality' is largely the result of human and organizational

constraints. It can be argued that this view underplays the role of power and political behaviour in setting those constraints. Many writers have pointed out that decision-making may be seen more accurately as a game of power in which competing interest groups vie with each other for the control of scarce resources.

Power is an ever-present feature of organizational life, indeed all areas of life (Foucault 1977), though 'rational-legal' power (Weber 1947) is allocated on the basis of authority positions in the hierarchy. This ostensibly regularizes access to the decision-making process. Those with the requisite authority can participate in what occurs. Some can both discuss decisions and authorize them. The contribution of others is relegated to the providing or cataloguing of data or the recording of outcomes. Others do not take part at all, and in the majority of organizations they are the great majority.

However, the use of power legitimately is not the only way influence is exercised. Power-holders may choose to behave in ways that further their own, or others', interests. They may frame the matter for decision in ways that suit their own ends or block the objectives of others. They push for preferred alternatives, whether or not these will lead to decisions that are of general benefit. They manipulate information, withhold it and ignore some or all of it. They negotiate for support and suppress opposition. This applies not only to those who are directly engaged in the process, but also those who, although only indirectly involved, still have the power to influence the process in some way – such as by having access to those who are involved or by providing information for the process. Since all interest groups may be engaging in similar behaviour the final choice may be characterized by various forms of bargaining, negotiation and compromise that may lead to outcomes which are less than optimum for all parties. So, although it might seem rational for each to pursue their own sectional interests in this way, from the perspective of neo-classical theory this can lead to outcomes which for the whole are less than rational. Thus, the *means* by which decisions are made may be rational while the *ends* may not be.

Some writers have long considered power to be the key factor in explaining how decisions are made. Pettigrew's (1973) longitudinal analysis of a British retail business reached that conclusion. A similarly vivid example of politics at work has been described by Wilson (1982) in his account of a chemical manufacturer where a decision about electricity generation turned into an intense and sometimes bitter career struggle between two senior executives.

One way of explaining this kind of power play is to see it as the inevitable outcome of the way we organize. The intrinsic nature of organizations as entities which are driven by the imperatives of specialization and the division of labour leads inexorably to fragmentation. Differentiation, which is required to maintain efficiency and cope with turbulent, unpredictable environments, also creates sectional interests, each with their own needs and priorities. A functionalist paradigm, though recognizing the beneficial 'constraining power' of work for the individual (Foucault 2003), has difficulty with the notion of goal dissensus, even though it appears that once organizational groups are given different tasks they also begin to formulate their own sets of norms and goals, reinterpreting objectives or constructing personal goals that serve their own interests.

This notion of differentiation is at the heart of the resource dependence perspective (Pfeffer and Salancik 1978). This explores how some parts of the organization gain power as a result of their ability to control access to resources. Power accrues to those parts of the organization that can control the flow of resources, especially if these are scarce and critical for organizational functioning.

It is expertise, rather than resources that underlies the strategic contingencies theory enunciated by Hickson et al. (1971) in their explanation of why some subunits within organizations exert more influence than others. They showed (Hinings et al. 1974) that if the differential allocation of tasks confronts a subunit in its specialist area with an uncertainty that is critical for its organization, and it copes in such a way as to buffer other subunits from any resulting instability, then it can widely influence even beyond its own competence. This influence is conditional upon it being sufficiently central and non-substitutable for the others to be dependent upon it. It is this *coping with uncertainty* that confers power.

Hence, organizations can be seen as *ensemble des jeux* (Crozier and Friedberg 1980) where individuals and groups jockey for position in a hierarchy which is mediated by on-going negotiation and bargaining. There are shifting, multiple coalitions of interests and thus only 'quasi-resolution of conflict' as interests seek to impose their own 'local rationalities' on any given decision (Cyert and March 1963).

Particular decisions will enfold particular subsections, drawn in to the game by the nature of what is being decided. The matter for decision therefore shapes the interests which become involved and the way the game is played. In this way power positions are formed and transformed depending on what is on the agenda.

This acknowledges the increased political complexity of decisions made in organizational settings. Allison (1971) explores this by showing how both organizational interests and government influence can shape events. He also shows how different assumptions and ways of viewing the world provide different interpretations of, and explanations for, these events. Using as an example the Cuban missile crisis (when the US and the Soviet Union, as it was then, teetered on the brink of war), Allison offers three alternative models for viewing what happened; the rational actor model (which views the situation as an outcome of logical and rational decisions), the organizational process model (which takes into account the complicating effects of the organizational context from which the events arose), and the governmental politics model (which focuses on the various bargaining games played out on the larger scale between actors at the level of government). The model produces alternative views of reality that sometimes complement one another, but often conflict. So ways of seeing produce ways of understanding, which has penetrating implications for the ways in which research is done.

Pluralist positions are predicated upon the notion of unequal but shifting power relations among elites, under the auspices of a largely neutral set of institutional arrangements. Here, Schattsneider's (1960: 71) statement begins to have resonance: 'All forms of political organization have a bias in favour of some kinds of conflict and the suppressions of others because organization is the mobilization of bias. Some issues are organized into politics while others are organized out'. This suggests that something else is happening 'behind the scenes' of even the pluralists' complex scenario – that the action is not all that it might seem at first glance. This is turn implies that to gain a deeper picture of power in organizations we need to look beyond what is readily observable. Attending solely to manifest conflict reveals only the most easily discernible 'face' of power. Ideally, what is going on underneath the surface also needs to be fully understood: the less explicit, more covert, subtle and insidious exercise of power which is used to suppress conflict in the first place. Conflict can be kept quiet; it is not allowed to surface into open debate and so does not become an item for discussion. This means that some decisions do not get onto the agenda. This is the 'second face' of power which Bachrach and Baratz (1962) argue has such import for organizational decision-making. This is the sphere of 'non-decisions'.

What then are non-decisions and do they have a place in the study of decision-making? Bachrach and Baratz maintain that non-decisions are equally if not more important than the decisions which are overtly made. Non-decisions are the covert issues about which a decision has effectively been taken that they will not be decided. They are the controversial topics which go against the interests of powerful stakeholders, they do not engender support, they are not considered acceptable for discussion, so they are quietly side-stepped or suppressed or dropped. A knowledge of what these issues are is likely to be as revealing, or more so, as knowledge of what is overtly being discussed. They are what is really going on, not just on the surface but underneath it. The decisions being discussed by executives and managers in the boardroom, or in meetings, represent the tip of the iceberg, according to this view. The really key issues and problems are only partially apparent from studies of topics which are being decided.

Bachrach and Baratz's (1962; 1970) ideas have been the spur to a broadening of debate about power and decisions. However, they have come under criticism from those who ask questions about how the existence of non-decisions can be investigated. If even decision-making itself is a fairly ephemeral, intangible activity (how do you spot a decision, where are decisions made?) then the epistemological and methodological problems associated with the discovery and analysis of non-decisions are yet more difficult. Bachrach and Baratz maintain that non-decisions are rooted in observable behaviour, that is pre-existing conflict which leads to action to close off areas of decision-making, but those attempting to carry out empirical research in organizations have so far found this a difficult lead to follow.

Going beyond this position, Lukes (1974) developed a third dimension, or 'face' of power. He maintains that the weakness of Bachrach and Baratz's approach is that the second face of power is still primarily concerned with what should be intrinsically observable behaviour and conflict, even though it is

so difficult to detect. Surely a more sinister, insidious and yet ultimately more effective way of exercising power would be to prevent any awareness of conflict in the first place? One way of achieving this would be to shape views and beliefs in such a way that one's own interests are not recognized. If all interests are perceived to be shared then conflict does not occur. This Orwellian view of the world echoes Marx's concept of 'false consciousness', whereby the hearts and minds of the proletariat are so manipulated by dominant institutions of state (abetted by the hegemony of religious institutions) that they only see things as others wish them to be seen. It also echoes Giddens' (1990) and Beck's (1992) view of society overall as 'unreflexive'. That is, the current state of affairs is left unquestioned. Firms can implement decisions that are hazardous, risky and detrimental to the environment. Yet, such corporate actions are, according to Giddens, largely taken for granted and left unquestioned. Awareness that such actions might be in conflict with large sections of society is suppressed and rarely open to question.

The analysis of power can be developed by reference to Foucauldian interpretations that suggest that power is relational, an inescapable feature of all areas of life. Not simply rooted in structural constraints, it is diffused through discourses and multiple, all-pervading, processes of panoptical surveillance and control (Foucault 1977). Power operates through taken-for-granted routines in the activities of daily life. In this way individuals create their own networks of power through their ongoing interactions and relationships, and their acceptance of prevailing codes of normalcy that shape such interactions. Thus power defines reality, but since all individuals possess countervailing power outcomes may be unexpected and unpredictable. In this interpretation, rationality is context-dependent, though the greater the power, the less likely the rationality (Flyvbjerg 1998); a conclusion that has obvious import for organizational decision-making.

Power and knowledge are intimately related. Administrative and technical knowledge are one of a number of power resources (Hales 2001, others are physical, economic and normative) and, since decisions require both information and expertise, knowledge is a particularly important resource. However, if knowledge is power, then power is also knowledge (Flyvbjerg 1998) in that power shapes the social construction of knowledge, defining what counts as knowledge and rationality. In fact 'knowledge and power, truth and power, rationality and power are analytically inseparable from each other; power produces knowledge, and knowledge produces power' (Flyvbjerg 2003: 369).

The implications for decision-making are onto-logically and epistemologically profound, having consequences for theorists and practitioners alike. Such an analysis presents decision-making as far removed from the coolly logical appraisal and selec-tion of alternatives. Rather it is at the centre of a web of political machinations, and dynamic power exchanges, the true nature of which is not fully recognized, even by those involved.

So, although some may see conflict as an endemic, but controllable, part of organizational life, created by the dysfunctions of a functional drive for efficiency, others explain conflict as arising from inherently inequitable and fluctuating, power rela-tionships in wider society. In the former view, the context for decision-making is the ongoing power play between interest groups, in which situations of disharmony are an expected but usually reconcilable by-product of organizational structure. In the latter view, decisions are shaped in ways which are not always obvious, by unseen influential power-holders playing within a larger arena.

This has spurred some writers to press for a more critical approach to the study of organizations which explores the nature of economic relations in a capitalist system where management serves the exploitative, sectional, interests of capital. A critical approach to management, recognizing that ortho-dox approaches are 'locked into an acceptance of managerially defined problems' (Burrell and Morgan 1993: 366) urges organization theorists to challenge the 'performative' intent (Lyotard 1984; Fournier and Grey 2000) of managerial praxis. The view of management as a 'morally and politically neutral technical activity' (Grey and Mitev 1995: 74) requires questioning, indeed replacing, by a criti-cally reflexive stance (Reynolds 1998; 1999) whose teleological purpose is emancipation. In this view, traditional perspectives are blind to the true causes of organizational conflict. In contrast, critical approaches compel an examination of the relations between organizational participants and the societal context in which management is 'performed'.

The implication of the above is that decision-making theory should therefore critically assess the notion of decisions and decision-making in organizations. This will be explored in greater detail in due course, but first we examine the empirical chal-lenges thrown up by the issue of power in decision-making. How is power to be conceptualized and how is it to be studied? If much of power is employed covertly, how can it be reached? The fact that it is all-pervading does not help to make it any more tangible. Recognizing that political behaviour does shape decisional processes, what other factors besides power might be important?

For empirical researchers these are some of the issues with which they have to grapple. The follow-ing section looks at studies that try to understand the way power is enacted in the making and imple-menting of decisions.

Processual Aspects of Deciding and Implementing

Deciding

The 'Bradford Studies' research (Hickson et al. 1986; Cray et al. 1988; 1991) set out to try and answer these questions. The Bradford team investigated the making of 150 decisions in 30 organizations (five decisions in each), covering manufacturing and service industries in both public and private sectors. Examples included glass and engineering manufac-turers, brewers, electricity and water utilities, insur-ance companies and financial institutions, universities and local government. Using face-to-face interviews with senior executives as well as a number of case studies with a range of informants, the research built up a detailed picture of decision-making from initiation to authorization. That is, from '... the first recalled deliberate action which begins movement towards a decision (when, for example, the matter is discussed in a meeting, or a report is called for)', to a point '... when the decision and its implementation are authorized'. A further development of the research, discussed later in this chapter, focuses on the implementation and out-comes of a subset of 55 of these decisions.

As the researchers recognize, decision start and end points are not easy to identify. The beginnings and endings of organizational processes commingle and it is no simple matter to carve out a slice of time for detailed inspection. Nevertheless, the limits of time and attention that constrains all organizational research necessitates selection. Given this caution an interesting statistic emerges from the Bradford work. The mean time that it takes to make a strategic decision is just over 12 months. An unexpectedly short time perhaps? The range, however, is from 1 month to 4 years. Immediately then, a wide variation along this dimension – duration – emerges. How else did decision-making differ and why?

Three kinds of processes were found, labelled *sporadic, fluid* and *constricted*. The sample of cases divided almost evenly between each cluster, so about a third of all decisions studied were made in sporadic ways, a third were made in a fluid manner while a third follow a constricted path.

Sporadic processes are subject to more disrupting delays than either fluid or constricted processes. The information used will be uneven in quality, some good, some bad, and come from a wide range of sources, and there will be scope for negotiation. This kind of process is 'informally spasmodic and protracted' (Hickson et al. 1986: 118). The tale of electricity generation already referred to in this chapter (Wilson 1982) is a colourful example.

Fluid processes are almost the opposite of sporadic ones. There is much less informal interaction and the process flows more through formal meetings with fewer impediments and delays. These processes are rather faster and the decision is likely to be made in months, rather than years. In short, a fluid process is 'steadily paced, formally channelled and speedy' (Hickson et al. 1986: 120).

Lastly, constricted processes share some of the characteristics of each of the other two but have features distinctive from both. They are less fluid than the fluids and less sporadic than the sporadics, but constrained in a way that neither of the others is. They tend to revolve around a central figure such as a finance or production director who draws on a wide range of expertise in other departments before arriving at a decision. In short, they are 'narrowly channelled' (Hickson et al. 1986: 122).

Although public sector organizations and manufacturing firms each show some bias towards sporadic processes, each process is found in every type of organization. So the managements of organizations in any sector of type of business, making strategic decisions about any aspect of their products or services, may go through any of the three kinds of process, sporadic, fluid or constricted. The type of organization is not the strongest determinant of process. So what is? The

Bradford team found that the primary and 'dual' explanation is the degree of *politicality* and *complexity* inherent in the matter for decision itself.

In other words, it is the political and complex nature of what is being decided which is all important. With regard to politicality, all decisions draw in a specific 'decision-set' of interests: those who have a stake in the outcome. They are drawn from inside and outside the organization: individuals, departments, divisions, owners, suppliers, government agencies and so on. However, not all interests are equally influential and not every decision draws in the same number or configuration of them. Some decisions attract less attention, they are less controversial perhaps, or require work to be done by relatively fewer people. Others are a whirl of interested activity. So every decision is shaped to some degree by the influence of the decision set. Politicality refers to the degree of influence which is brought to bear on a decision and how this influence is distributed within and across the organization.

Complexity refers to the problems which making the decision encompasses. The reasons for complexity are varied. Some decisions are more unusual than others; they may require information to be garnered from more diverse sources, they may have more serious or widespread consequences, or set more fundamental precedents for the future. Since each decision process is made up of various problems – some of which are more complex than others – decisions will vary in terms of how comprehensible they are. Some will be relatively straightforward while others will be more problematic, depending on the nature of the issues involved.

Together, these concepts of politicality and complexity are the primary explanation of why strategic decisions follow the processes they do. The strength and distribution of influence, coupled with the complexity of what is being decided, shape the process which ensues. As the authors put it, in accounting for what happens 'the matter for decision matters most' (Hickson et al. 1986: 248).

By their comprehensive mapping of decision processes, the Bradford team demonstrate that not all decision-making is politically tumultuous. Far from it. Sporadic processes are most inclined that way, perhaps a third of all decisions at most. The greater proportion of decisions is less contentious.

Yet below what was reached empirically must have lain the concealed second and third faces of power. Were there no signs of what lay beneath? The research did show that in at least a third of all decisions the outcome was a foregone conclusion. The results were known before the process of deciding was completed, indeed often before it began. The Bradford team call this 'quasi-decision making' (Hickson et al. 1986: 52). Sometimes this occurred because there was only one realistic alternative, but on other occasions quasi-decision making must have been the result of prior manoeuvres by powerful parties involved. This strongly suggests that overt, aware decision-making frequently does 'go through the motions' within limits set by pre-existent positions.

A great deal of influence is exercised overtly, of course, and this research also has much to say about who has it and who does not. Generally, trade unions do not influence decisions, neither does the personnel function nor the purchasing department, nor government in most cases. The most influential interests (apart from the CEO) come from production (or the equivalent), sales and marketing and accounting. This core triad of 'heavyweights' functions is involved more often and exert most influence whatever the type of organization. Although external power holders do take part in the game, the balance of power is held internally. And this remains true throughout the process, for these same interests hold sway over implementation (Miller and Wilson 2004).

Building on the Bradford Studies, Butler et al. (1993) studied 17 cases of a specific decision topic – strategic investment decisions. Reflecting Thompson and Tuden (1976), they argued that four elements were important in realizing effective investment decisions, namely computation, judgement, negotiation and inspiration. They found that inspiration alone was not a recipe for effectiveness, since decision-making not only had to have accurately analysed the complexity of the situation (judgement and computation), but also had to steer a course through the political reality of persuading others of the inspiration idea (negotiation).

However, does what happens in the process leading to the formal decision have any effect on the subsequent outcomes? What factors lead to success during implementation and beyond?

Implementation and Outcomes

Getting things done in an organizational setting is not always straightforward and many writers have drawn attention to the problems of 'collective action' (Pressman and Wildavsky 1973). Several authors have looked at the way in which implementation is carried out. It has been suggested (Nutt 1986; 1987; 1989) that managers choose from a repertoire of implementation tactics. These are the ways managers get others to action decisions. According to Nutt, they comprise *intervention*, where key executives justify the need for change by introducing new norms to identify performance inadequacies; *participation*, where task forces are set up to develop implementation and identify stakeholders; *persuasion*, when implementation strategies are delegated to technical staff or experts who then 'sell' their ideas back to the decision-makers; and finally, *edict*, where decisions-makers use control and personal power while avoiding any form of participation (Nutt 1986: 249). In Nutt's American sample, persuasion has been shown to be the most popular form of implementation tactic (it was used in 42% of the cases), followed by edict (23%), then intervention (19%), and least of all participation (17%). However, if the measure of success is taken as being whether decisions are fully 'adopted' (that is, implemented) at the end of this process, then intervention with a 100% success rate is clearly the most successful tactic. Persuasion and participation were moderately successful and edict was the least successful with a success rate of 43%. One conclusion from this work is that managers only rarely hit on implementation strategies which are likely to lead to success.

The Bradford Studies work has been extended to explore the issue of implementation (Hickson et al. 2003; Miller et al. 2004), by covering what happened when the decisions were put into effect during the years following the original fieldwork. As already mentioned, a subset of 55 decisions was chosen to search for any factors that might have affected the success of what was done. Success in implementing is assessed primarily by performance in terms of what was intended by the decision-makers, that is 'achievement' over time, a concept that builds on Miller's (1997) definition of success and mirrors the measure of decision effectiveness used by Dean and Sharfman (1996).

The study identified two ways of managing implementation (Hickson et al. 2003), labelled the Experience-based and Readiness-based approaches, so-called because of the originating conditions that give rise to each. As its name suggests, the

Experience-based approach is grounded in prior experience, or *familiarity* with what has to be implemented. Understanding enough of what has to be done, or realizing that sufficient experience is lacking and so buying it in from new staff, or consultants, or outsourcing, means that the objectives can be better *assessed*, tasks clearly *specified* and *resources* allocated. This approach, the more planned of the two ways of managing implementation (Miller et al. 2004) does not of itself lead to success, but instead to an acceptance within the organization that makes it more likely that the decision will progress towards a successful outcome.

The other method of implementation, the Readiness-based approach, may be taken when management is much less sure of what it is doing and therefore is less able to plan (Miller et al. 2004). Its originating condition is *receptivity* – having a receptive context in which to launch implementation. This facilitates the allocation of appropriate responsibilities and roles (*structural facilitation*) and ensures implementation is made a *priority*, leading again to greater chance of a successful outcome.

As with the original study of decision-making (Hickson et al. 1986) this subsequent study of implementation found that type of organization, sector or topic made little difference to the way that decisions were implemented. Public and private sector firms in either manufacturing or service industries show little preference for a particular approach to implementation, no matter what is being implemented. The reasons why management opt for one approach rather than the other relates to how far they know what they are doing, or how far others are receptive to it (Hickson et al. 2003: 1822). The first way relies on planning, the second provides an alternative way of managing when 'plan-ability' is low (Miller et al. 2004).

Although each approach enhances the chance of success; the most advantageous position is to follow both approaches together, although it is relatively rare. In the sample of 55 cases only six (11%) followed both processes simultaneously and comprehensively. However, these six enjoyed the highest level of success in the sample (scoring a mean of 5.0 on a 6-point achievement scale, where 6 was the highest scale point). So a high level of success is very likely. This suggests that managers need to be skilled at managing both approaches, having a versatile repertoire of implementation strategies to hand.

Linking Decision-Making and Implementation

Studies of decision-making are now fairly numerous, but there are relatively fewer accounts of implementation. Work that focuses on what links the deciding and doing is rarer still. This is perhaps unsurprising since 'research from the traditional perspective assumes a rational and linear relationship between decisions and actions that is not empirically proven and so pre-empts discussion as to how decisions and actions might in fact be related' (Hendry 2000: 959).

Some intriguing findings emerge when both phases of the Bradford Studies are brought together. Three forms of what is called 'connectedness' are identified that appear to link deciding and implementing. These are termed continuous, causal and anticipatory connectedness (Miller and Wilson 2004) and are elaborated below.

The first, *continuous* connectedness, refers to the interest units who take part in the processes of making and enacting decisions. Overall, there are many more interests involved in deciding than in actioning strategic decisions. In the 55 cases of implementation on which these findings are based, 426 interests were mentioned by informants as having been involved in the making of decisions, whereas only 263 were mentioned as being involved in implementation. Decision-making draws in many interests, not all of whom stay to effect it. Of those who do, a few key interests appear to hold sway over the entire process, from deciding through implementation, being involved and influential throughout. These are a triumvirate of production, finance, and marketing. They appear more frequently, and most consistently, in both deciding and implementing, following a decision through to its conclusion and providing the essential stability that holds the process together. In *continuous* connectedness these three interests preserve the 'identity' of the decision as it gets put into effect.

They also retain the memory (Cohen and Levinthal 1990; Moorman and Miner 1997; 1998) of the processes that led to the decision. This is important; for the research suggests that the tenor and import of those discussions are remembered by those involved and prefigure the context for what happens subsequently (Miller and Wilson 2004). So what goes on during the deciding influences implementation; there is a *causal* connectedness. The research indicates that three aspects of deciding: *contention of objectives, seriousness of consequences* and *endurance of consequences* (abbreviated to *contention, seriousness* and *endurance*, respectively) each shape what follows.

Contention is an indicator of how far the interest units involved in deciding either pulled together or in opposite directions, and has a generally negative effect on implementation. Firstly, high contention reduces *familiarity*, the key originating condition for the Experience-based approach, probably because it distracts from making the most of available experience or realizing the need to buy it in. Secondly, prior contention during decision-making may well diminish *receptivity* towards implementation, the key originating condition for the other, Readiness-based approach. Conflicting aims produce an unstable foundation for change whichever approach is followed.

Surprisingly though, contention appears to reduce the time it takes to implement the decision. In the 55 cases under discussion the most protracted implementation lasted 16 years while the shortest just a few months. The mean is 2 years; prior contention making it more likely that an implementation will be towards the lower end of this range. This unexpected finding nevertheless provides some confirmation of Dooley et al.'s (2000) equally puzzling, 'reverse' finding that *consensus* improved *commitment* which tended to lengthen implementation. As these authors wonder, it may simply be that 'it takes longer to do something well' (Dooley et al. 2000: 1251), which conversely would mean that if there is contention beforehand things may be hurried through badly.

While the effects of contention seem to be largely negative, the effects of the second decision-making variable, *seriousness*, are wholly positive. Seriousness is the import of what is being decided. It indicates decision-makers' perception of the gravity of the problem if things were to go wrong. Would the consequences be containable or disastrous? Again, it links to both ways of implementing. In the Experience-based approach a decision considered to be more serious at the time of deciding seems to lead to a higher level of *specificity* during implementation. Put another way, the more a decision is thought to have significant repercussions, the more it is likely that great care will be taken to set out the steps to be taken to action it. The other association with *priority* in the Readiness-based approach also

makes intuitive sense. Serious decisions are more likely to get higher priority, ensuring that implementation stays at the top of the agenda even though specific directives are fewer. This is crucial to success, meaning that implementation receives managerial attention ahead of other competing demands. The more serious the likely impact of the decision, the more it demands such priority, so that it is given a head-start.

Finally, there is an association between the third decision-making feature, *endurance* – an indication of how long the consequences of the decision were expected to last – and *acceptability*, the crucial underpinning of the more planned Experience-based approach. *Acceptability* is the degree to which those affected were in accordance with what was done. It is crucial because assessing and specifying what has to be done and resourcing it, though key components of this approach, do not in themselves lead directly to a successful outcome, but rather to a state of accord with how the decision is being carried out. It is this latent function of planning upon attitudes that enhances the chances of success as much as the plans themselves (Hickson et al. 2003). The connection between *endurance* and *acceptability* shows that if a decision is thought to have long-lasting consequences, managers should take greater care in carrying others with them in going along with what is to come.

An implication of the continuous connectedness of production, finance and marketing, discussed above, is now clear. Should a very serious decision with long-term consequences occur, over which they take opposing positions and are in contention, then putting anything at all into effect will be difficult. If implementation does get going, it will have limited support, be of uncertain priority and dubious acceptability. In consequence the chances of success are much diminished. However, *contention, seriousness* and *endurance* do not intercorrelate, so even among 55 cases there is no example of this, although it is a probabilistic possibility that this could occur.

The final form of connectedness, *anticipatory* connectedness, also relates to associations between deciding and implementing, but in a particular sense, in reverse. It is where thinking ahead to implementation influences what happens at the deciding. It is their anticipation of what may happen in the future that influences those involved in decision-making. The thought of what is likely to be faced later affects the way in which the decision is perceived and dealt with before this stage is reached. This is manifested in the strong positive relationship between the complex nature of implementation and how long it takes to decide. The study suggests that the more implementation is *intricate*, that is, comprising multiple different tasks that require bringing together, the longer decisions take to make. Since it is difficult to argue that a longer decision-making process makes subsequent implementation into a more intricate set of tasks, the postulated causation points the other way. Intricacy of implementation lengthens decision-making. However, the decision-making largely happened first, before the intricacy was encountered. So it must be the *anticipation* of intricacy to come which lengthens the deciding. There is more to think about, more to plan, more to discuss than when a simpler implementation is expected, and all of this takes time. It took a mean 22.8 months to make the 15 decisions with the most intricate implementations compared to 7.5 months for the 15 with the least intricate implementation. So the concept of anticipatory connectedness provides at least part of the explanation why some decisions take so much longer than others, which is intriguing since the earlier study of decision-making (Hickson et al. 1986) could find no explanation at all.

These three concepts – continuous, causal and anticipatory connectedness – help to account for some of the explanation as to how decision-making and implementation may be linked. However, some have argued that there are circumstances in which such links are tenuous, and may even break down. We turn now to some alternative reflections on decision-making which, though drawing on a variety of perspectives, all to some extent question the portrayal of decision-making as a coherent and purposeful activity, instead emphasizing the apparent chaotic nature of organizational processes and the key role of interpretation and flexible improvisation.

Chaos and Interpretative Approaches

In traditional decision theory, a decision is taken to be indicative of a corresponding action that will occur in the future, or at least the decision is assumed to increase the probability of such an action. In practice there are not always strong connections among talk, decisions, and actions: People talk, decide, and act on separate occasions and in different contexts. … It is possible to act without making a decision or talking about it, and it is possible to talk and decide without actually acting on it. So there is reason to suspect that there will often be discrepancies among what is said, what is decided, and what is done (Brunsson 2003: 202).

However much power and political behaviour may shape organizational processes, however muddled and multifarious the links between deciding and implementing, much of the research discussed hitherto assumes at least minimal coherence between means and ends.

Yet one of the most imaginative, coherent and penetrating perspectives is that of the evocatively named 'garbage can' model (Cohen et al. 1972; March and Olsen 1976), where the depiction of decision-making turns much of what we have previously discussed on its head. Garbage cans are found predominantly in 'organized anarchies', complex organizations whose internal processes are not really understood, even by people working in them. In these situations the means and ends of decisions become 'uncoupled' (Weick 1976) so that actions do not lead to expected outcomes, but are high-jacked along the way by other decisions and other actions. The main components of decisions – problems, solutions, participants and choice situations, pour into the organizational garbage can in a seemingly haphazard way, a stream of demands for the fluid attention and energy of decision-makers. If a problem, solution, participant and choice situation happen to collide, then a decision occurs. It may not be foreseen. It may not be one which actually solves the problem to which it has been attached. For not only are the means and ends of decisional processes disconnected but solutions to problems are in existence before the problems themselves are recognized.

All the while participants move in and out of decision-making processes since 'every entrance is an exit somewhere else' (Cohen et al. 1972: 3), which creates discontinuity. Perversely, actors jostle for the right to get involved and then appear uninterested either in exercising it, or in whether decisions are carried out (which may account for the finding that the number of interests declines markedly from decision-making to implementation (Miller and Wilson 2004)). The conventionally accepted order of things is transformed, put back to front, jumbled beyond recognition. The picture is one of seeming chaos, of disorder. And yet there are some patterns under the confusion and these can be modelled once the parameters are known. The process is not truly random and can be predicted to some extent, although it can feel like chaos to participants. Decisions do get made, although the process is about as far removed from rational choice prescriptions as it is possible to get.

Outside direct research into decision-making in organizations, chaos theories have received increasing attention in recent years. Beginning with iconoclastic revelations in the natural and physical sciences, their provocative and rather disturbing conclusions have thrown many orthodox assumptions into turmoil. With the basic postulate that small changes can, by means of complex feedback cycles, result in ever more complex, dynamic changes of unpredictable and epic proportions, it asks fundamental questions about the nature of cause and effect mechanisms.

One of the implications of such increasingly turbulent and unpredictable 'high-velocity' environments (Eisenhardt 1989) is that decision-makers may need to adopt more flexible, adaptive and innovative practices to cope in such circumstances. Recently some authors have developed the metaphor of jazz to suggest new forms of praxis that utilize sense-making (Weick 1995) and improvization (Weick 1998; Hatch 1999; Zack 2000; Kamoche and Pina e Cunha 2001; Eisenhardt 2003) to manage in conditions of ambiguity and indeterminacy. This stance reinforces and develops Allison's (1971) emphasis on interpretation. Although interpretation is essentially individual, as with jazz musicians, organizational actors may generate new meanings that can be 'shared' through on-going interactions as they create their 'performance'. In essence, order and control are breached (Weick 1998) and a new order is created.

As Eisenhardt (2003: 225) notes:

> ... an improvisational view assumes that strategic choice is conducted by a small group of decision-makers. Like musicians, these executives are skilled individuals, often with a particular expertise. However, instead of expertise with particular musical instruments, the expertise centres on functional areas such as finance, geographic location, or some other source of expertise. Moreover, while these decision-makers are individuals, their task is collective. That is, their task is to make effective strategic choices that blend adaptiveness and execution.

Weick (1998: 544) suggests that improvisation lies on a continuum that ranges from 'interpretation', through 'embellishment' and 'variation' ending in 'improvisation', noting that full scale improvisation might be rare in time-pressured conditions but, if achieved, could be a significant source of competitive advantage.

While the jazz metaphor is seductive, it raises questions. How far does a significant amount of 're-working' actually take place – how far do managers stray into realms that are genuinely new and innovative, or how far do they cling to tried and tested themes? Since each improviser determines to what extent they will improvise – do they choose to improvise within existing forms, or outside them (Zack 2000: 230)? In addition, what is being spontaneously 'composed', and who decides which interpretation will be heard. In organizations, as in orchestras, some players have more powerful voices and can overwhelm the rest of the ensemble. The jazz metaphor in much of its development has little to say about the relations of power that may induce silence rather than voice.

Yet, if used as re-description (Hatch 1999) rather than simple analogy, the idea of improvisation can provide a vivid and penetrating understanding of the dynamic imprecision of much of organizational 'action'. Its ontological status hints at postmodernist notions of 'becoming', rather than 'being' (Weick 1998: 551), where fragmentation, flux, fluidity and transformation shape versions of reality that are continually reinterpreted and revised. This perspective focuses attention on the micro-processes (Weick 1998) that give rise to 'ordering' (Law 1994), a temporal, transient and shifting arrangement resulting from the interweaving of interdependent actors (Newton 2002) that never quite settles into order. From this perspective 'chaos, disorder, multiplicity and noise are not in opposition to, but are the precondition of, organization' (Clegg et al. 2004b: 34).

This call to attend to the micro-processes of organizational life has found echoing answers in the field of strategic management, an area which some claim is currently facing its own crisis of legitimation, and which can be argued to have important connections to the field of strategic decision-making.

Strategic Decisions and Strategy

Although it might appear obvious that strategic decisions and strategic management are connected, each is largely the subject of a separate discourse. Each has developed largely independently and with relatively limited points of crossover (Maritan and Schendel 1998). As Hendry (2000: 968) notes: 'researchers have tended either to see decision-making as central to the strategy process or to ignore it altogether, but not to ask how decisions might fit into the broader discourses accompanying strategic change'.

However, any benefits of attempting to develop links between decisions and strategy are called into question by those who suggest the concept of decision 'gets in the way' (Mintzberg and Waters 1990) of understanding strategic processes. This view re-visits the argument that although decisions imply a commitment to action, there are situations where actions are taken without decisions having been made, so traditional positions may 'privilege activity over passivity, the conscious over the unconscious and the explicit over the implicit' (Chia 1994: 789). Hence, traditional emphases on decision-*making* may over-concretize the rather ambiguous, uncertain processes of change and underplay the continual re-definition, re-shaping and re-formulation through which strategies arise.

However, what is strategy? There is conceptual imprecision here too. One definition suggests it is 'pattern in a stream of actions' (Mintzberg and Waters 1985), pointing out that strategies may *emerge* rather than being deliberately decided in advance, arising from the combined effects of various actions which may or may not be directly connected. Over time, and with hindsight, these may be sufficiently consistent as to be viewed as forming some kind of pattern. In this case it is possible to talk of the organization having a strategy, although it may not have been intentional.

Although this view has been linked with chaos perspectives of strategy (for example, Stacey 1993), echoing garbage can 'logics of organizational disorder' (Warglien and Masuch 1996), others have countered (Butler 1990) that to discard the concept of a decision altogether goes too far. As Hendry comments: 'the fundamental point underlying the Mintzberg and Waters critique is not that deciding in unimportant but that organizational decisions as commonly understood are rarely decisive' (Hendry 2000: 960).

Definitional points aside, the field of strategic management itself has been undergoing a period of sustained critique, as some authors have begun to critically re-examine its status and relevance to practice. The notion of 'strategy' is problematic. As indicated, there is a conceptual dichotomy between strategy as deliberate intention and strategy as emergent action; the concept is grounded in an unproblematized holistic view of the corporation; and the word 'strategy' is culturally bounded, having different meanings in different cultures (Bower 1998: 27).

Notwithstanding the above, strategy research and theorising have grown apace. One of the more recent perspectives, the resource-based approach, though also beset by definitional challenges, at least suggests what the role of strategic decisions should be. It views firms as bundles of assets or resources, both tangible and intangible, which require managerial action in order to maintain, build and utilize organizational capabilities (Maritan and Schendel 1998). From this perspective, therefore, strategic decisions are concerned with leveraging these capabilities to create and sustain competitive advantage.

Yet, we know little of the micro-processes by which managers effect this transformation. Traditional research into the 'content' of strategy has centred on factors within macro-competitive environments and, while yielding some important insights, the criticism is that it has now 'trapped itself into a cul-se-sac of high abstraction, broad categories and lifeless concepts' (Johnson et al. 2003: 6).

Summarizing the tensions in strategy as symptomatic of a Cartesian dualism, Clegg et al. (2004a: 23) submit that this results in seven fallacies of strategic management. These are constituted in terms of gaps between: managerial fantasy and organizational capabilities; actual, clear goals and possible, unpredictable futures; planning and implementation; planned change and emerging evolution; means and ends; a planning head (management) and a planned body (organization); and, finally, between order and disorder.

Since managers manage strategy, it has been argued that one potentially fruitful way forward is to re-focus attention on what goes on inside organizations, 'to investigate what is actually done and by whom' (Johnson et al. 2003: 5). To facilitate this understanding, it may be helpful to explore how strategists *think* and *act strategically* (Wilson and Jarzabkowski 2004). In other words, we need to better understand how individuals map complex ideas so that they can be understood, communicated and debated (*thinking strategically*), and how resources are mobilized so that a strategic journey can be envisioned (*acting strategically*). As with postmodernist interpretations, the emphasis is on *strategizing*, rather than strategy – a process of becoming that is forever on-going and incomplete.

Regnér's (2003) detailed longitudinal case analysis involving four multinational companies is an attempt to develop this 'strategy-as-practice' agenda. He found fundamentally different strategic activities in the *periphery* of the firm (comprising those groups that are remote from the hierarchy and from the dominant practices and beliefs) and the *centre* (the corporate and divisional management), and that each used markedly different approaches to develop strategy, to learn about it, and to interpret clues and patterns. Essentially strategy making was more inductive in the periphery, being developed through externally oriented activities involving trial and error, informal contacts, experiments and heuristics (Regnér 2003: 77). In the centre it was more deductive, concentrating on planning, analysis, formal reports, intelligence and routines.

This focus on the micro-activities of managers within the strategy-as-practice agenda holds promise, but ontological and epistemological challenges remain. As Chia (2004: 29) queries, 'Are these visible practices really strategy-shaping? Or are they in fact the mere manifestations of an underlying unconscious pattern of dispositions that provides consistency to managerial actions …?' As with the old tautology that arises in the study of managerial work that 'management is what managers do' – is strategy what strategists do? Or is it simply that we choose to see it as 'strategic'?

What is the importance of all this for the study of decision-making? Although requiring much more in the way of theoretical development, these recent deliberations in the field of strategy may offer possibilities for theoretical advancement which is mutually beneficial both for the study of strategy and for decision-making. If organizational action can usefully be understood in terms of the (strategic) processes in which managers engage, perhaps it is time to bring decisions within the ambit of this debate. This is not to suggest an unequivocal correspondence with intended actions or outcomes, nor to gloss over issues of their ontological and epistemological status, but to recognize their place in managerial praxis, and the fact that they may provide a sense-making framework for understanding managerial interaction. At the very least, the field of organizational decision-making could usefully take account of strategizing to become more self-reflexively aware of the fluidity of organizational processes, while the field of strategy might find that strategic decisions

have something to offer as a micro-unit of analysis. It remains to be seen to what extent any latent potentiality can be realized.

References

Allison, G.T. (1971) *Essence of Decision: Explaining the Cuban Missile Crisis.* Boston: Little Brown.
Bachrach, P. and Baratz, M.S. (1962) 'The two faces of power', *American Political Science Review*, 56: 947–52.
Bachrach, P. and Baratz, M.S. (1970) *Power and Poverty: Theory and Practice.* London: Oxford University Press.
Beck, V. (1992) *The Risk Society, Series in Theory, Culture and Society.* London: Sage.
Bower, J.L. (1998) 'Process research on strategic decisions: a personal perspective', in V. Papadakis and P. Barwise (eds), *Strategic Decisions.* Dordrecht: Kluwer Academic Publishers. pp. 17–33.
Braybrooke, D. and Lindblom, C.E. (1963) *A Strategy of Decision.* New York: Free Press.
Brunsson, N. (2003) 'Organized hypocrisy', in T. Berlings Skogs (ed.), *The Northern Lights: Organizational Theory in Scandinavia*, Oxfordshire: Marston Book Services. pp. 201–22.
Burrell, G. and Morgan, G. (1993) *Sociological Paradigms and Organisational Analysis: Elements of the Sociology of Corporate Life.* Hants: Ashgate Publishing.
Butler, R. (1990) 'Studying deciding: an exchange of views between Mintzberg and Waters, Pettigrew, and Butler', *Organization Studies*, 11(1): 2–16.
Butler, R.J., Davies, L., Pike, R. and Sharp, J. (1993) *Strategic Investment Decisions.* London: Routledge.
Chia, R. (1994) 'The concept of decision: a deconstructive analysis', *Journal of Management Studies*, 31(6): 781–806.
Chia, R. (2004) 'Strategy-as-practice: reflections on the research agenda', *European Management Review*, 1: 29–34.
Clegg, S.R., Carter, C. and Kornberger, M. (2004a) 'Get up, I feel like being a strategy machine', *European Management Review*, 1(1): 21–8.
Clegg, S.R., Kornberger, M. and Rhodes, C. (2004b) 'Noise parasites and translation: theory and practice in management consulting', *Management Learning*, 35(1): 31–44.
Cohen, M.D., March, J.G. and Olsen, J.P. (1972) 'The garbage can model of organizational choice', *Administrative Science Quarterly*, 17: 1–25.
Cohen, W.M. and Levinthal, D. (1990) 'Absorptive capacity: a new perspective on learning and innovation', *Administrative Science Quarterly*, 35: 128–52.
Cray, D., Mallory, G.R., Butler, R.J., Hickson, D.J. and Wilson, D.C. (1988) 'Sporadic, fluid and constricted processes: three types of strategic decision-making in organizations', *Journal of Management Studies*, 25(1): 13–39.
Cray, D., Mallory, G.R., Butler, R.J., Hickson, D.J. and Wilson, D.C. (1991) 'Explaining decision processes', *Journal of Management Studies*, 28(3): 227–51.

Crozier, M. and Friedberg, E. (1980) *Actors and Systems*. Chicago: University of Chicago press (published in French in 1977 by Editions du Seuil).

Cyert, R. and March, J.G. (1963) *A Behavioural Theory of the Firm*. Englewood Cliffs, NJ: Prentice-Hall.

Dean, J.W. Jr and Sharfman, M.P. (1996) 'Does decision process matter? A study of strategic decision-making effectiveness', *Academy of Management Journal*, 39(2): 368–96.

Dooley, R.S., Fryxell, G.E. and Judge, W.Q. (2000) 'Belaboring the not-so-obvious: consensus, commitment and strategy implementation speed and success', *Journal of Management*, 26(6): 1237–57.

Dutton, J.E. (1986) 'The processing of crisis and non-crisis strategic issues', *Journal of Management Studies*, 23(5): 501–17.

Eisenhardt, K.M. (1989) 'Making fast strategic decisions in high-velocity environments', *Academy of Management Journal*, 32: 543–76.

Eisenhardt, K.M. (2003) 'Strategic decision making as improvisation', in T. Berlings Skogs (ed.), *The Northern Lights: Organizational Theory in Scandinavia*. Oxfordshire: Marston Book Services. pp. 251–7.

Flyvbjerg, B. (1998) *Rationality and Power: Democracy in Practice*. Chicago: University of Chicago Press.

Flyvbjerg, B. (2003) 'Making organization research matter: power, values and phronesis', in T. Berlings Skogs (eds), *The Northern Lights: Organizational Theory in Scandinavia*. Oxfordshire: Marston Book Services. pp. 357–80.

Foucault, M. (1977) *Discipline and Punish: the Birth of the Prison*. London: Allen Lane.

Foucault, M. (2003) *Madness and Civilization*. London: Routledge.

Fournier, V. and Grey, C. (2000) 'At the critical moment: conditions and prospects for critical management studies,' *Human Relations*, 53(1): 7–32.

Giddens, A. (1990) *The consequences of modernity*. Cambridge: Polity Press.

Grey, C. and Mitev, N. (1995) 'Management education – a polemic', *Management Learning*, 26(1): 73–90.

Hales, C. (2001) *Managing Through Organisation*. London: Thompson.

Hatch, M.J. (1999) 'Exploring the empty spaces of organizing: how improvisational jazz helps redescribe organizational structure', *Organization Studies*, 20(1): 75–100.

Heller, F., Drenth, P., Koopman, P. and Rus, V. (1988) *Decisions in organizations – a three country comparative study*. London: Sage.

Hendry, J. (2000) 'Strategic decision making, discourse, and strategy as social practice', *Journal of Management Studies*, 37(7): 955–77.

Hickson, D.J., Butler, R.J., Cray, D., Mallory, G.R. and Wilson, D.C. (1986) *Top Decisions: Strategic Decision-making in Organizations*. Oxford: Basil Blackwell. San Francisco: Jossey-Bass.

Hickson, D.J., Hinings, C.R., Lee, C.A., Schneck, R.C. and Pennings, J.M. (1971) 'A strategic contingencies theory of intra-organizational power', *Administrative Science Quarterly*, 16(2): 216–29.

Hickson, D.J., Miller, S.J. and Wilson, D.C. (2003) 'Planned or prioritized? Two options in managing the implementation of strategic decisions', *Journal of Management Studies*, 40(7): 1803–36.

Hinings C.R., Hickson, D.J., Pennings, J.M. and Schneck, R.E. (1974) 'Structural conditions of intraorganizational power', *Administrative Science Quarterly*, 19(2): 21–44.

Johnson, G., Melin, L. and Whittington, R. (2003) 'Micro strategy and strategizing: towards an activity-based view', *Journal of Management Studies*, 40(1): 3–22.

Kamoche, K. and Pina e Cunha, M. (2001) 'Minimal structures: from jazz improvisation to product innovation', *Organizational Studies*, 22(5): 733–64.

Law, J. (1994) *Organizing Modernity*. Oxford: Blackwell.

Lindblom, C.E. (1959) 'The science of 'muddling through'', *Public Administration Review*, 19(2): 79–88.

Lukes, S. (1974) *Power: a Radical View*. London: Macmillan.

Lyotard, J.-F. (1984) *The Postmodern Condition: A Report on Knowledge*. Manchester: Manchester University Press.

March, J.G. and Olsen, J.P. (1976) *Ambiguity and Choice in Organizations*. Bergen, Oslo and Tromso: Universitets-forlaget.

Maritan, C.A. and Schendel, D.E. (1998) 'Strategy and decision processes: what is the linkage?', in V. Papadakis and P. Barwise (eds), *Strategic Decisions*. Dordrecht: Kluwer Academic Publishers. pp. 259–66.

Miller, S. (1997) 'Implementing strategic decisions: four key success factors', *Organization Studies*, 18(4): 577–602.

Miller S. and Wilson D.C. (2004) 'Actioning strategic decisions: connecting deciding and implementing', Paper presented at the Academy of Management conference, New Orleans.

Miller, S., Wilson D. and Hickson, C. (2004) 'Beyond planning: strategies for successfully implementing strategic decisions', *Long Range Planning*, 37(3): 201–18.

Mintzberg, H. and Waters, J.A. (1985) 'Of strategies, deliberate and emergent', *Strategic Management Journal*, 6: 257–72.

Mintzberg, H. and Waters, J.A. (1990) 'Studying deciding: an exchange of views between Mintzberg and Waters, Pettigrew, and Butler', *Organization Studies*, 11(1): 2–16.

Mintzberg, H., Raisinghani, D. and Theoret, A. (1976) 'The structure of 'unstructured' decision processes', *Administrative Science Quarterly*, 21: 246–75.

Moorman, C. and Miner, A.S. (1997) 'The impact of organizational memory on new product performance and creativity', *Journal of Marketing Research*, 34: 91–107.

Moorman, C. and Miner, A.S. (1998) 'Organizational improvisation and organizational memory', *Academy of Management Review*, 23(4): 698–724.

Newton, T.J. (2002) 'Creating the new ecological order? Elias and Actor-Network Theory', *Academy of Management Review*, 27(4): 523–40.

Nutt, P.C. (1984) 'Types of organizational decision processes', *Administrative Science Quarterly*, 29(3): 414–50.

Nutt, P.C. (1986) 'Tactics of implementation', *Academy of Management Journal*, 29(2): 230–61.

Nutt, P.C. (1987) 'Identifying and appraising how managers install strategy', *Strategic Management Journal*, 8: 1–14.

Nutt, P.C. (1989) 'Selecting tactics to implement strategic plans', *Strategic Management Journal*, 10: 145–61.

Papadakis, V. and Barwise, P. (1998) *Strategic Decisions*. Dordrecht: Kluwer Academic Publishers.

Pettigrew, A.M. (1973) *The Politics of Organizational Decision-making*. London: Tavistock.

Pfeffer, J. and Salancik, G.R. (1978) *The External Control of Organizations: A Resolute Dependence Perspective*. London: Harper and Row.

Pressman, J.L. and Wildavsky, A. (1973) *Implementation*. Berkeley: University of California.

Quinn, J.B. (1978) 'Strategic change: logical incrementalism', *Sloan Management Review*, 20(Fall): 7–21.

Quinn, J.B. (1980) *Strategies for change: logical incrementalism*. Homewood, IL: Irwin.

Regnér, P. (2003) 'Strategy creation in the periphery: inductive versus deductive strategy making', *Journal of Management Studies*, 40(1): 57–82.

Reynolds, M. (1998) 'Reflection and critical reflection in management learning', *Management Learning*, 29(2): 183–200.

Reynolds, M. (1999) 'Grasping the nettle: possibilities and pitfalls of a critical management pedagogy', *British Journal of Management*, 9: 171–84.

Rosenthal, U. (1986) 'Crisis decision-making in the Netherlands', *The Netherlands Journal of Sociology*, 22(2): 103–29.

Schattsneider, E. (1960) *Semi-sovereign People: A realist's view of Democracy in America*. New York: Holt, Rinehart and Winston, quoted in A.G. McGrew and M.J. Wilson (eds) (1982) *Decision-making: Approaches and Analysis*. Manchester: Manchester University Press. p. 321.

Simon, H.A. (1945) *Administrative Behaviour*, 2nd edn. New York: Free Press.

Simon, H.A. (1960) *The New Science of Management Decision*. New York: Harper & Row.

Smith, G. and May, D. (1980) 'The artificial debate between rationalist and incrementalist models of decision-making', in A.G. McGrew and M.J. Wilson (eds), *Decision Making: approaches and analysis*. Manchester: Manchester University Press. pp. 116–24.

Stacey, R. (1993) 'Strategy as order emerging from chaos', *Long Range Planning*, 26(1): 10–17.

Thompson, J.D. and Tuden, A. (1976) 'Strategies, structures and processes of organizational decision', in W.A. Rushing and M.N. Zald (eds), *Organizations and Beyond: Selected essays of James D. Thompson*. Boston, MA: Lexington Books, D.C. Heath and Co. Ch. 5,

Warglien, M. and Masuch, M. (eds) (1996) *The Logic of Organizational Disorder*. Berlin: de Gruyter.

Weber, M. (1947) *The Theory of Social and Economic Organization*, translated by A. Henderson and T. Parsons. Glencoe, IL: Free Press.

Weick, K.E. (1976) 'Educational organizations as loosely coupled systems', *Administrative Science Quarterly*, 21(1): 1–19.

Weick, K.E. (1995) *Sensemaking in organizations*. Newbury Park, CA: Sage.

Weick, K.E. (1998) 'Improvisation as a mindset for organizational analysis', *Organization Science*, 9(5): 543–55.

Wilson, D.C. (1982) 'Electricity and resistance: a case study of innovation and politics', *Organization Studies*, 3(2): 119–40.

Wilson, D.C. and Jarzabkowski, P. (2004) 'Thinking and acting strategically: new challenges for interrogating strategy', *European Management Review*, 1: 14–20.

Wilson, D.C., Hickson, D.J. and Miller, S. (1996) 'How organizations can overbalance: decision overreach as a reason for failure', *American Behavioral Scientist*, 39(8): 995–1010.

Wilson, D.C., Hickson, D.J. and Miller, S.J. (1999) 'Failing the unusual way: commonplace failures versus over-reach in managerial decision-making', in H.K. Anheier (ed.), *When things go wrong: organizational failures and breakdowns*. California: Sage Publications. pp. 35–49.

Zack, M.H. (2000) 'Jazz improvisation and organizing: once more from the top', *Organization Science*, 11(2): 227–34.

2.3 A Decision Perspective on Organizations: Social Cognition, Behavioural Decision Theory and the Psychological Links to Micro- and Macro-Organizational Behaviour

MARGARET A. NEALE, ANN E. TENBRUNSEL, TIFFANY GALVIN AND MAX H. BAZERMAN

Over the last two decades, the study of organizational behaviour (OB) has witnessed a dramatic shift away from a variety of traditional topics and toward a more cognitive and social–cognitive perspective. This change in perspective has influenced both research and application in the field, and, more recently, has redefined topics typically viewed under the heading of OB. Over the years, OB, particularly that segment of OB that is based on the study of the individual, has been chastised for lacking a central set of theories, for offering limited theoretical development of the theories it imports from psychology, and for covering topics that lack connection to issues of interest to practitioners (O'Reilly 1991). One remedy for these problems has been to expand the boundaries of the field to include the study of psychological issues that are relevant to understanding behaviour in organizations. Incorporating the lens of social cognitive psychology and theories of behavioural decision theory has, in the last two decades, dramatically expanded the perspectives available to OB scholars, and revitalized the field of OB.

In the 1988 *Annual Review of Psychology*, Ilgen and Klein wrote about what Markus and Zajonc (1985) term 'a shift of near revolutionary proportions in the behaviour sciences: the cognitive perspective'. Ilgen and Klein documented the ways in which many traditional topics in OB were being influenced by this cognitive revolution. While their review is important, we believe that the cognitive revolution and, subsequent, evolution of the social cognitive perspectives has created even more dramatic changes in OB by specifically incorporating the decision making process as a primary focus of

research. The journal *Organizational Behaviour and Human Performance* reflected this evolution by changing its name to *Organizational Behaviour and Human Decision Processes*, emphasizing the increasing importance of decision behaviour to the study of OB. Indicative of the change taking place in the field, decision processes emerged as a mainstream topic within OB, with researchers focusing on how decisions influence managerial behaviour (Gioia and Sims, 1986; Bazerman 2001). In addition, negotiations emerged as a central topic of OB, and have been dominated by a cognitive orientation (Neale and Bazerman 1991; Bazerman et al. 2000). As evidence of these changes, negotiation has become the most commonly published topic in *Organizational Behaviour and Human Decision Processes*, and both decision processes and negotiation have been institutionalized as part of the field by the creation of new divisions within the *Academy of Management* that specifically address these topics.

We believe that these developments reflect the tension between research and practice in business and management schools for research that provides managers with more levers for change. The structure of the situation is often given. Characteristics of the parties involved are not readily changeable. However, organizational members can have significant influence in their environment and on their organizations through their decisions. Thus, from this perspective, the traditional debates between situationists and personalogists (Davis–Blake and Pfeffer 1989; Staw et al. 1986) have obfuscated more important determinants of behaviour in organizations – the decisions and the cognitive processing that leads to these decisions – by organizational members.

The purpose of this chapter is to provide the background for readers to appreciate psychological research that has provided the base for the cognitive revolution in OB, to see its advantages, and to motivate future research. While the term cognition has been used in a variety of ways in the organizational field, we will limit our attention to theories, models, and studies of cognition that have their root in the psychology of how people make decisions. The areas of social cognition and behavioural decision theory will provide the over-arching theoretical structures. This chapter is a revision of the chapter that appeared in the first edition of the *Handbook of Organizational Studies* (1996). While we have updated many parts of this chapter as well as added new sections, the structure of the chapter remains largely consistent with the earlier version. Because of space limitations, we will refer the reader, at times to the original chapter for more extensive discussion of certain topics.

In this chapter, we examine the cognitive processes involved as organizational actors respond to their social world, and identify the systematic errors that limit the effectiveness of decision making among individuals and groups in organizations. The social cognitive psychology literature is the basis for the former task, while behavioural decision theory is the basis for the latter task.

We begin by discussing our underlying research values that bias the material that is reviewed and the conclusions that we reach. Next, we examine the psychological foundations for a cognitive perspective to organizations; specifically, we overview the development of the areas of social cognition and behavioural decision theory (BDT). We then examine and evaluate the contributions of this cognitive perspective to specific micro and macro OB topics. Finally, we conclude with an overall evaluation of the application of the cognitive perspective to organizations and discuss an agenda for future research possibilities.

Values and Assumptions that Undergird Our Cognitive Perspective

Much of our own research, and that of other cognitive researchers in OB, is affected by a series of underlying values and assumptions (Bazerman 1993). We choose to be explicit about these values and assumptions since we believe that they distinguish cognitive from non–cognitive work in OB and motivate much of the cognitively based research in OB.

Research should attempt to understand the world as it is, not as we would like it to be or think that it should be. The assumption of rationality or utility maximization on the part of human actors is a hallmark of economics, but also is ubiquitous among organizational theories and researchers. The rationality assumption characterizes many micro–level OB theories, including virtually all of expectancy theory research (Lawler 1971) and the path–goal theory of leadership (House 1971). This assumption is also extended to the more macro–level rationality of organizational selection in population ecology (Hannan and Freeman 1989). Further, many behavioural researchers offer advice that is based on their assumptions rather than on the empirical realities of the organizations. For example, the field of OB has long conveyed the importance of participation, cooperation, collectivism, and empowerment before sufficient empirical support for these notions exists. Indeed, much of OB has been based on the way we think the world should be. In contrast, we believe that the field should be based on more accurate understandings of human behaviour as it is observed. Our assumption of human behaviour is consistent with the work of Simon (1957) who envisioned individuals trying to maximize their utility, but bounded by a variety of cognitive limitations. Research that is reviewed in this chapter clarifies a variety of these limitations, and specifies an alternative view of human decision-making.

Descriptive research is strengthened by comparisons to prescriptive benchmarks. The descriptive nature (the study of what we actually do) of the OB literature is a natural extension of the descriptive orientation of the disciplines, social psychology and sociology, from which such literature is traditionally drawn. This predisposition toward a descriptive orientation is exacerbated by organization scholars who view prescription/application as being of lesser value, often associated with instrumental pursuits, rather than scientific values. Yet, many of these same scholars will offer prescriptions when they change from the role of researcher to that of teacher or consultant. Rather than foster such dualistic thinking or sacrifice one component for another, we believe there should be a more direct connection between the empirical and theoretical literature of OB and the prescriptive base we offer. We will return to this value in the behavioural decision research section, and outline what this interaction would look like. For now, we simply note that the tension between these two perspectives may increase our ability to communicate with other disciplines (e.g. economics), improve the theoretical base of organizational research, and help create a defensible, empirically based position from which to inform practitioners.

Descriptive research can provide important adaptations to normative prescriptions. Just as prescriptive models serve to direct improvements in descriptive models, descriptive research can enhance the quality of normative models. If one assumes that actors are not typically rational utility maximizers, then the predictive quality of the normative models are enhanced by knowledge of the way in which individuals deviate from rationality. This argument is central to Raiffa's (1982) argument that prescriptive models need to better incorporate descriptive models of human behaviour.

Decisions and decision-making are core activities for both understanding and changing individual behaviour in organizations. Historically, behavioural researchers have debated whether the person or the situation is more influential in the particular behavioural responses of individuals. This debate has led to the proposal that the way in which the individual perceives, filters, and conceptualizes information is critical to how he or she responds to situations; these responses in turn change the nature of their interaction and enact their perceptions of the environment (Weick 1992). This view emphasizes the importance of developing better models of decision-making and cognition to understand behaviour in organizations.

The values described above underlie many of the judgements that we will make throughout the chapter. We will return to these values when we evaluate the cognitive perspective of OB near the end of this chapter.

Psychological Foundations of Cognitive Research in Organizations

Two primary research areas of psychology – social cognition and behavioural decision theory – have served to inform organizational researchers in their attempts to understand the influence of human cognitions on OB. While there may be overlap

between these two perspectives, there are also some sharp differences in orientation. Social cognition research is a purely descriptive field that tries to explain how people make sense of the world. Behavioural decision research, while also being a descriptive field, uses normative models as a base by which to identify and, subsequently explain the systematic imperfections in human decision processes. Where the broader interpretive process is the focus of the social cognition area, the decision is the key unit of action in BDT. Our review of these two areas will highlight some of the key differences between BDT and social cognition in terms of their influence on OB. As our goal is to provide a sufficient appreciation of the backgrounds of these basic literatures to evaluate the developments that have occurred within OB, we will not provide comprehensive reviews of these two fields. However, we will suggest where such reviews can be found.

Social Cognition

Social cognition has been defined as the study of how people make sense of other people and themselves, and how cognitive processes influence social behaviour (Fiske and Taylor 1991). The social cognition approach attempts to understand the storage of social behaviour in our cognition, the aspects or dimensions of stored social knowledge that affect our information processing, inferences, judgements, decisions, and actions, and the factors that influence changes in stored social information or knowledge (Sherman et al. 1989). Traditionally, this line of study has been associated with the proposition that people perceive and think about the social world differently than what would be expected based solely on stimulus information and principles of formal logic (Higgins and Bargh 1987).

Social cognition has become the dominant perspective in social psychology (Schneider 1991). Within this domain, social cognition have been applied to several phenomena including oneself, others, imaginary persons, interpersonal relationships, groups, and memory of social information (cf. Leyens and Codol 1988). Despite the breadth of applicability that the field offers, several limitations to its approach should be noted. As Schneider (1991) pointed out, the research is often driven more by model testing than by traditional social psychological efforts to explain social phenomena. In addition, there is often the argument that the 'social' aspect of social cognition is missing. Many critics share Schneider's complaint that 'at less than its best, however, social cognition research can be more concerned with the latest fashions from cognitive psychology than with social phenomena' (1991: 553). The implication is that social cognition researchers borrow cognitive psychology models originally developed for nonsocial objects and test their generalisability to social objects (Levine et al. 1993). In defence of these limitations and weaknesses, Higgins (1992) argues that there have been several cognitive models originated by social psychologists, such as the study of attribution processes, which have in turn been imparted into the field of cognition.

Research in the field of social cognition has developed in a diverse set of directions. The three areas that have most profoundly affected OB include: (1) attribution theories; (2) knowledge structures: schemas, person perception, categorization, and stereotyping; and (3) implicit attitudes and stereotyping. We review each of these areas below.

Attribution Theories

Many scholars categorize attribution theory as the core of social cognitive psychology. Attribution theory is concerned with the way that people associate behaviour to discrete causes, and thus focuses on the everyday, common-sense explanations that individuals construct for social events or actions of others. Theories in this field examine how the social perceiver gathers, combines and uses information to arrive at causal explanations for events (Fiske and Taylor 1991). While work in this area dates back to the mid-1940s, current research continues to be undertaken in quantity. There are three main theories that are considered to be the defining contributions to attribution theory. These theories stem from the works of Heider (1944), Jones and Davis (1965) and Kelley (1967). Combined, their work and resulting theories share a concern with common-sense explanations and answers to the question 'why', while attempting to formalize the rules people might be using to make causal attributions.

Heider's (1944) work on naive psychology treated the layperson as a naive scientist who linked observable behaviour to unobservable causes. Naive psychology maintained that the natural language people use to characterize causal action could form the basis for a theory of causal inference. Heider's

major contribution to attribution theory was the division of potential sources of action into internal (personal) and external (environmental) types. Heider asserted that social perception research must consider attributes of the target person and the perceiver as well as the context and manner in which the perception occurs. The perceiver was proposed to decide whether an action results from something within the person who is performing the action or from some external source.

A second main contribution to attribution theory involves Jones and Davis' (1965) correspondent inference theory. This theory maintains that the goal of the causal attribution process is to infer that the observed behaviour and the intention that produced it correspond to stable, underlying attributes of individuals, and thus explain their behaviour across situations. There are two major stages in the process of inferring personal dispositions: the attribution of intention and the attribution of dispositions. A noncommon effects principle is also at work, which maintains that a perceiver makes a correspondent inference by identifying the distinctive (non-common) consequences of an actor's chosen course of action. The fewer the distinctive consequences, the more confident the perceiver is of the inference about the causal attribution. According to the theory, the perceiver processes information backwards from effects, through action to inferences about knowledge and ability. Behaviours/actions that are believed (by the perceiver) to be unconstrained, freely chosen, out of character/role, socially undesirable, violating prior expectations, and producing distinctive consequences are expected to reveal underlying attributes.

The third main cornerstone of attribution theory involves Kelley's (1967) theories about the process of ascribing causes. His covariation model explores how individuals form causal inferences when they have access to multiple instances of similar events. To attribute the outcome to a stable cause or pattern of causes, individuals employ a covariation principle to determine how the outcome in question varies across entities, time, and people. However, if the perceiver is faced with only a single observation, then he/she must take account of the plausible causes of the observed effect, employing what are known as causal schemata. These schemata are ready-made beliefs, preconceptions, and theories, formed by experience, that help an individual ascertain how certain kinds of causes interact to produce a specific effect. Thus, for a given attribution, the perceiver may have to interpret information and events by comparison and integration of schema.

Outside of the three theories mentioned, there have been other lines of work that influenced early attribution formulations. For example, Weiner's (1986) work on attribution theory developed dimensions of attributional experience, integrates attributions with emotional processes, and enlightened the attributional and affective experience that underlies concrete domains of experience (see Fiske and Taylor 1991 for a more detailed discussion of other perspectives in attribution theory).

Attribution research has been extensive and varied and represents one of social cognition's most popular exports to other fields (see Harvey et al. 1976; 1978; 1981; Kelley and Michela 1980; Ross and Fletcher 1985; Fiske and Taylor 1991 for more extensive reviews of the attribution field). Hundreds of empirical studies were prompted by the theories previously discussed and various other social phenomena have been analysed within a causal attribution framework. Tests of attribution theory have uncovered various biases that people employ during the attribution process (e.g. fundamental attribution error, use of consensus information, and the self-serving attributional bias (see cf. Harvey et al. 1976; 1978; 1981; Ross 1977; Zuckerman 1979; Marks and Miller 1987 for further discussion). The empirical research that has been conducted has been used as a basis for many attributional theories that analyse a variety of social and personal issues.

Knowledge Structures: Schemas, Person Perception, Categories and Stereotyping

Social objects, when they are targets of perception and cognition, are distinct from natural objects in a number of ways that influence the processing of information about them (Markus and Zajonc 1985). A major assumption of classic social cognition is that because our information–processing apparatus is resource-limited, we develop highly abstract knowledge structures (Schneider 1991). One such knowledge structure is a schema, which may be defined as a cognitive structure that represents knowledge about a concept or type of stimulus, including its attributes and the relations among those attributes (Fiske and Taylor 1991). Categories

and schemas refer to people's expectations about themselves, other people, the situations they encounter, and the effects of these expectations. People have available to them a repertoire of schemata representing situations as well as a catalog of actors or personality types (person schema) which encompass our organized knowledge (or knowledge structures) of other people (Bazerman and Carroll 1987). The basic premise of schema research has been that individuals simplify reality by storing knowledge at a broader, inclusive level rather than acquiring specific experiences and incorporating these on an individual basis.

The schema concept originated in person perception research with Asch's (1946) configural model of impression formation and Heider's (1958) balance theory of relationship. Their work focused on people's tendency to form unified overall impressions from discrete social elements (Fiske and Taylor 1991). Person schemas were proposed to constitute a knowledge structure which, when evoked, influences social judgements, behaviour, and responses to that individual (as dictated in part by the characteristics of the person-schema). Person schemas are believed to represent classifications that contain a great deal of information about traits, preferences, and goals that enable the perceiver to understand exhibited behaviour, predict future behaviour, and develop appropriate responses (Bazerman and Carroll 1987). The field of person perception has been built around the assumption that information about others includes both instances and abstractions, and that these abstract judgements in impression formation can either be an overall evaluation of the target derived from trait attributes or from behaviours performed by the target (Sherman et al. 1989). Research in this area continues to explore the role of information processing and the storage of information during schema-formation and person perception. The role of schemas in organizations has also been the focus of recent research. One such application of this area is that of gender-based schemas, which have been used to investigate gender-based selection in the workplace (Perry et al. 1994). Cognitive schemas have also been utilized in understanding how employee dress influences employees' comprehension and behaviour (Rafaeli et al. 1997).

Before schematic prior knowledge can be applied to social perception, the person or situation has to be classified into a category (Fiske and Taylor 1991).

Categories are useful in distinguishing among people, interpreting information, and evaluating others and thus play an important role in providing meaning for social perceivers (Fiske 1993). While schema research is more concerned with the application of organized, generic prior knowledge to the understanding of new information, the domain of categorization research is more concerned with the classification of instances (Fiske and Taylor 1991). Categorization does not merely serve cognitive purposes; it also operates within a social and motivational context and can have important evaluative implications (Fiske 1993). Categorization research is abundant (cf. Hamilton and Sherman 1993), and has focused on a variety of areas, including an exploration of the information basis of knowledge structures, the cognitive representation of categories, the processing of category relevant information, the choice of categories, an understanding of the categorization process and how can it be controlled, and the relation of categorization to other processes such as attributions (cf. Schneider 1991). The resulting research has explored models of social categorization, identified core categories used by people to portray other people, and, in contrast, identified the use of concrete representation, exemplars, and target cases instead of person schemas (or stereotypes) (cf. Fiske 1993).

Implicit Attitudes and Stereotyping

A major focus of social cognition research is in the areas of stereotyping and prejudice (Markus and Zajonc 1985). Tajfel (1969) proposed that stereotypes are a special case of categorization that accentuates similarities within groups and differences between groups. Models of stereotyping focus on the pragmatic implications for perceivers who use the stereotypes as a rich resource for making sense of their world (Fiske 1993). People use stereotypes when they seem to have explanatory value, give information, provide motivation, or comply with social norms. The effects of stereotyping have been a major concern, particularly with the attribution of characteristics to in-group/out-groups, inter-individual and inter-group relationships and conflict, and work on illusory correlation (see reviews, e.g. Hamilton and Sherman 1989; Messick and Mackie 1989; Mullen and Johnson 1990).

Through the end of the last millennium, stereotyping and prejudicial behaviour was generally viewed as revealing explicit attitudes toward various groups. Over the last decade, the core of research on attitudes has made a dramatic shift to viewing stereotypes and prejudice as existing largely below the threshold of conscious awareness (Banaji and Greenwald 1995; Devine 1989). The apparent ubiquity of these implicit attitudes led Banaji (2001) to go as far as to refer to negative attitudes toward certain groups as ordinary prejudice, and connects these ideas to behavioural decision research world through the concept of bounded ethicality (Banaji and Bhaskar 2000). Banaji and Bhaskar (2000) argue that stereotyping is linked to the limitations of human cognition.

Research on implicit attitudes argues that most fair-minded people strive to judge others according to their merits, but cannot consciously overcome their 'implicit prejudices'. Implicit attitudes researchers believe that implicit prejudice is rooted in the fundamental ways that we learn to associate things that commonly go together and expect them to inevitably coexist; thunder and rain, for instance, or old age and disability (Neely 1977; Fazio et al. 1995; Banaji et al. 2003). But, these cognitive associations are only approximations of the truth – rain doesn't always accompany thunder, and the elderly are often alert. However, because we automatically make these associations, we grow to trust them, and they can blind us to those instances in which the associations are inaccurate (Banaji et al. 2003). Moreover, because these associations may exist below the threshold of consciousness, developing conscious distrust may not be sufficient to eliminate their potentially pernicious effects (Bargh 1999).

Implicit attitudes are defined as the cognitive associations between social groups and either particular concepts (e.g. intelligence or violence) or evaluations (i.e. good or bad). Measures of implicit attitudes are designed to assess the strength of these associations. The most common method for doing this entails measuring the extent to which exemplars of a social group facilitate responses to stereotypic compared to non-stereotypic information (Perdue and Gurtman 1990; Fazio et al. 1995; Greenwald et al. 1995). Currently, the most common measure of implicit attitudes is the Implicit Association Test (IAT; Greenwald et al. 1995). The IAT is typically conducted on a computer, and assesses the difference in how quickly people can do stereotypic as compared to non-stereotypic categorizations. For example, in a test of implicit racial attitudes participants classify black and white faces and good and bad words in two different configurations. In the stereotypic configuration participants make black-bad and white-good pairings by pressing one key if a word is bad or the face is black, and a different key if the word is good and the face is white. In the non-stereotypic configuration participants make black-good and white-bad pairings by pressing one key if the word is bad and the face is white, and a different key if the word is good and the face is black. Measuring the difference in how quickly people can complete stereotypic as compared to non-stereotypic association then creates an implicit bias score. These measures often show that even when people honestly believe that they have no negative feelings toward black Americans, they have an easier time with the stereotypic than counter-stereotypic associations. Greenwald et al. (2003) put the IAT online (www.implicit.harvard.edu) and people from around the world have taken over 2.5 million tests. The results confirm that implicit biases are strong and pervasive.

Interestingly, although implicit and explicit attitudes have only a moderate association, implicit attitudes explain unique variation in a variety of outcomes (see Greenwald and Nosek 2001; Fazio and Olson 2003, for reviews). Rudman and Glick (2001) show how implicit biases lead people to exclude qualified people from certain roles. Pro-social behaviour toward Blacks is negatively related to implicit prejudice assessed by the IAT (McConnell and Leibold 2001; Rudman and Lee 2002; Sinclair et al. 2005). Discriminating against female job applicants is predicted by implicit stereotypes (Rudman and Glick 2001).

More recently, Chugh et al. (2004) found that MBA students have an implicit stereotype that women are better 'value creators' in negotiation and that men are better 'value claimers'. This research also shows that similarity between negotiators' implicit biases is positively related to the ability to create joint value. Collectively, the emerging evidence supports implicit attitudes as a source of unique variation in important outcomes, and demonstrates that these biases have consequences for equal opportunity (Dasgupta 2004).

Despite the growing number of findings relating implicit attitudes to behaviour, it is still unclear exactly what behaviours respond to implicit attitudes and which are immune. Preliminary evidence suggests that explicit attitudes predict consciously controlled behaviour, but implicit attitudes are better predictors of non-verbal behaviours that are difficult to consciously monitor or control (Dovidio et al. 1997; 2002). An application of this possibility is that it may be easier to observe the effect of implicit attitudes in others than in us. Consistent with this formulation, there is evidence that in white-black interactions white participants' experience of the interaction is best predicted by their explicit attitudes, but black participants' reports of the interaction are best predicted by their partners' implicit attitudes (cf. Fazio et al. 1995; Dovidio et al. 2002). These results suggest that in addition to subtle effects on behaviour, implicit prejudice can create conscious misunderstandings of shared experiences.

An emerging body of research suggests that implicit attitudes are much more malleable than initially believed. They are quite responsive to a range of situational factors, mental strategies, and social motives (for a review see Blair 2002). The majority of this work focuses on three means of influencing automatic attitudes: changing the representatives of the group or the context in which the representatives are presented (Blair et al. 2001; Dasgupta and Greenwald 2001; Wittenbrink et al. 2001; Livingston and Brewer 2002), being motivated to control one's prejudice (Moskowitz et al. 2000; Devine et al. 2002), and social motives not directly related to prejudice (Lowery et al. 2001; Richeson and Ambady 2003; Sinclair et al. in press).

Of the three means of altering implicit attitudes, the focus on social motives may offer the most promise for those interested in engineering changes in others' implicit attitudes. These studies suggest that implicit attitudes respond to changing social pressures without explicit mention of prejudice. For example, when motivated to get along with a person that projects non-prejudiced attitudes, individuals express less negative implicit ethnic attitudes than when interacting with a person that does not indicate their ethnic attitudes (Lowery et al. 2001; Sinclair et al. in press). Similarly, individuals express less automatic prejudice when interacting with a Black superior than a Black subordinate (Richeson and Ambady 2003). Thus, although a number of impediments make the direct conscious control of automatic attitudes difficult, evidence that situational variables affect these attitudes suggest that the problems they represent are not insurmountable.

At a basic level, automaticity can be considered a form of behaviour in which people attempt to gain control over their thoughts. Exploration about the varying kinds and degrees of mental control continues to spark research, and extends itself to studies on thought suppression and willpower in social and personality psychology (Schneider 1991).

Automaticity is seen as increasingly relevant in the domain of stereotyping. The application of subjective essentialism (Medin 1989) to the process of social categorization suggests that particular social categories (such as race and gender) represent basic, ingrained divisions. These divisions are perceived to be the result of biological processes and hence are seen as basic, fundamental components of decision-making.

Cognitive Influence of Affect

Research on affect has historically focused on the organizational impact of affective states. For example, Isen and Baron (1991) reviewed the impact of positive affect on work attitudes and behaviour. George and Brief (1992) examined the relationship between individual affect and extra-role behaviour such as organizational citizenship, while Weiss and Cropanzano (1996) attempted to distinguish between affect-driven and judgement-driven behaviours. From their perspective, one of the main differences is the immediacy of the resulting behaviour. Other researchers have explored the impact on affect on judgement, focusing particularly on the judgement of individual performance (e.g. Saavedra and Early 1991; Brief et al. 1995; Fried et al. 1999). Further research has illustrated the positive relationship of positive affect to a number of valued organizational outcomes including problem solving (Isen 1990), creativity, and pro-social behaviours (George 1990; George and Bettenhausen 1990).

However, a growing body of research in social psychology was examining the effects of emotions, moods, and affect on information processing and judgement. These researchers suggested that people engage in more systematic processing when in a negative emotional state and people in positive emotional states engage in more heuristic processing (Bless et al. 1990; Schwarz 1990; Mackie and Worth 1991; Schwarz et al. 1991; Sinclair and Mark 1992; Staw and Barsade 1993). Explanations for these results claim that differences in information processing were typically associated with the valence of the emotional state. Although there have been several different mechanisms which have been used

to explain this effect, namely capacity, motivation, and information mechanisms, they all typically argue that it is the valence of the emotional state (its positiveness or its negativeness) that is responsible for the effects of emotion on cognitive processing.

In contrast to a valence perspective, appraisal theorists have suggested that emotions can also be grouped along a dimension of certainty-uncertainty (Roseman 1984; Smith 1989; Smith and Lazarus 1993). Some emotions are characterized by the expresser feeling uncertain, not understanding what is currently happening, and not knowing what will happen next, whereas other emotions are experienced by the expresser as feelings of certainty, an understanding of the current situation, and an predictability of what is to come (Smith and Ellsworth 1985). In addition to being associated with specific emotional states, certainty has been linked to information processing. Researchers have suggested that feelings of certainty act as cues that one's assessments are already accurate and, therefore, further processing is unnecessary (Chaiken et al. 1989). For example, findings by Martin et al. (1993) support the idea that positive emotional states result in more heuristic (rather than systematic) processing because they convey a feeling of certainty.

Tiedens and Linton (2001) extended this reasoning to suggest that emotions associated with feelings of certainty promotes heuristic processing and emotions associated with feelings of uncertainty should lead to more systematic processing, regardless of valence. In their research, they induced participants to feel either positive or negative emotions that were associated with certainty or uncertainty and then measured the participants' degree of heuristic or systematic information processing on subsequent tasks. They consistently found that certainty-associated emotions resulted in more heuristic processing than did uncertainty-associated emotions that resulted in systematic processing.

In their 1993 review of organizational behaviour, Mowday and Sutton (1993) lament organizational behaviour's pre-occupation with cognitive processes, suggesting that 'organizational members (are portrayed) as cognitive stick figures whose behaviour is unaffected by emotions' (p. 197). Clearly one cannot focus solely on pure cognition to try to understand the behaviour of organizational actors. Yet, neither does it appear to be the case that cognition and affect exist independently. Rather, it may be that there is a recursive relationship between how we feel and how we think, that each influences the other. Interestingly, ten years after Mowday and Sutton's piece, the research landscape is much more hospitable to the exploration of the interdependence of cognition and affect as evidenced by Brief and Weiss' (2002) review of organizational behaviour that describes the last decade (the 1990s) as the era when organization researchers rediscovered affect and emotions, brought on, in part, by the intense interest that social cognitive researchers evidenced in studying the interstitial space between cognition and emotion.

Social cognition is a rich and broad perspective represented in various fields and disciplines, particularly within social and cognitive psychology. Because of the blend of various issues and methodologies used throughout research in the field, many of the concepts and developments are easily applicable to understanding the cognitions and behaviour of people in structured social contexts such as organizations. We will return to the relevance of these theories when we consider their application to OB later in the chapter.

Behavioural Decision Theory

The standard of economic rationality has long been the cornerstone of the formal study of decision making. Individuals were assumed to act in accord with their self-interest and make choices that were consistent with the predictions of maximizing this self-interest. The tenets of rational action, however, have not proved particularly useful in describing the actual choice or decision behaviour of individuals, nor were they particularly useful in prescribing or predicting actual choice behaviour. Real decision makers typically behaved in ways that deviated from the predictions of economic models, made decisions that were not Pareto efficient, and were inconsistent in their choices or made decisions based on normatively irrelevant factors (Bazerman 2001). From the perspective of economic rationality, these errors were assumed to be the result of ignorance, lack of correct incentives, or unrevealed preferences.

What was presumed to be a result of inattention, ignorance, or error by those subscribing to the notion of rational decision making was viewed by another group of researchers as systematic variations that were, in their own right, deserving of attention. The systematic study of choice, especially in the behavioural sciences, had as its roots in the

publication, almost 40 years ago, of Nobel-prize winner Herbert Simon (1957; March and Simon 1958). The work on bounded rationality suggested that if economists were to understand real decision behaviour, they had to focus on the perceptual, psychological, and cognitive factors that caused human beings to make decisions that deviated systematically from the predictions of the 'rational actor'.

The discrepancies between the formal prescriptions of economists and the descriptive observations of Simon's bounded rationality result, according to Simon, from our inability to evaluate decision alternatives simultaneously (rather than sequentially), from failing to choose the optimal alternative (preferring, instead, to select an alternative that is 'good enough' – to satisfice), and from using simplifying rules or heuristics to reduce the cognitive demand of decision making. Thus, Simon's (1957) concept of bounded rationality highlighted the differences between what normative models predict and what people actually do. As suggested by Bell et al. (1988), behaviour decision theory's primary focus encompasses the normative, descriptive and prescriptive perspectives of decision making, with a somewhat greater emphasis on the latter two. That is, BDT research seems more concerned with the empirical validity of descriptive models and the pragmatic value of prescriptive models than with the development of normative models.

A central question in the area of behavioural decision research, then, is how decision makers actually go about making decisions, using as a comparison the benchmark of optimal (i.e. rational) performance. Juxtaposing the standard of rationality against actual behaviour, several researchers in the decision arena began mapping the systematic deviations from rationality that they observed. Behavioural decision researchers focus on these systematic inconsistencies in the decision making process that prevents humans from making fully rational decisions. Kahneman and Tversky (1979; Tversky and Kahneman 1974) have provided critical information about specific systematic biases that influence judgement. This work has elucidated our modern understanding of judgement. The importance of this perspective has, with the awarding of the 2002 Nobel Prize in Economics to Danny Kahneman, received considerable validation both for economic and psychology scholars.

When making decisions, people rely on a number of simplifying strategies, or rules of thumb called heuristics. Although heuristics often prevent us from finding the optimal decision by eliminating the best choice, they do have some benefits: the expected time saved by using them could outweigh any potential loss resulting from a full search strategy. By providing people with a simple way of dealing with a complex world, heuristics produce correct or partially correct judgements more often than not. In addition, it may be inevitable that humans will adopt some way of simplifying decisions. The only drawback is that individuals frequently adopt these heuristics without being aware of them. The misapplication of heuristics to inappropriate situations, unfortunately, often leads people astray.

The three most important heuristics are the availability heuristic, the representativeness heuristic, and anchoring and adjustment. Decision makers assess the frequency, probability or likely causes of an event by the degree to which instances or occurrences of that event are readily 'available' in memory (Tversky and Kahneman 1973). To the extent that an event evokes emotions and is vivid, easily imagined, and specific, it will be more 'available' from memory than equally occurring events which are unemotional in nature, bland, difficult to imagine, or vague. For example, the subordinate in close proximity to the manager's office will receive a more critical performance evaluation at year-end, since the manager is more aware of this subordinate's errors (Bazerman 2001).

People also assess the likelihood of an event's occurrence by the similarity of that occurrence to their stereotypes of similar occurrences. As Nisbett and Ross (1980) note, 'A botanist assigns a plant to one species rather than another by using this judgement strategy. The plant is categorized as belonging to the species that its principle features most clearly resemble' (pg. 7). In this case, the degree to which the unknown plant is representative of a known species of plant is the best information available to the botanist.

People also make assessments by 'anchoring' on an initial value and adjusting to yield a final decision. The initial value, or starting point, may be suggested from historical precedent, the way in which a problem is presented, or random information. For example, managers make salary decisions by adjusting from an employee's past year's salary. In ambiguous situations, a trivial factor can have a profound effect on our decision if it serves as a starting point from which we make adjustments (Dawes 1988). Frequently, people will realize the unreasonableness

of the anchor (e.g. 'the other firm was only paying her $22,000 a year'), yet their adjustment will often remain irrationally close to this anchor.

Unfortunately, heuristics lead to predictable biases. A number of the predominant biases described in this literature were reviewed in the original version of this chapter. The interested reader is directly not only to that version of this chapter but also to a research summary that has been provided in Bazerman (2001). During the 1980s and 1990s, these biases have had a profound influence on the field of OB. They have been used to help organizational members better understand their limitations, and have been extended to the organizational level of analysis to help account for the systematic errors of organizations.

However, it should be noted that BDT is not without its critics. Garb (1989) and Kagel and Levin (1986) suggest that experience may eliminate or at least attenuate decision bias as performance feedback can correct the inappropriate use of information and decision heuristics. These researchers see these well-replicated effects as the artificial creation of one-shot experiments. While much of the seminal work in the area of BDT was conducted in the relatively context-free environment of the laboratory, it is not so clear that real-world experience would provide decision makers with superior information or useful feedback. As Tversky and Kahneman (1986) suggest, responsive learning requires accurate and immediate feedback which is rarely available because: (1) outcomes are commonly delayed and not easily attributable to a particular action; (2) variability in the environment degrades the reliability of the feedback; (3) there is often no information about what the outcome would have been if another decision had been made; and (4) most important decisions are unique and therefore provide little opportunity for learning: 'Any claim that a particular error will be eliminated by experience must be supported by demonstrating that the conditions for effective learning are satisfied' (see Einhorn and Hogarth 1978, pp. 274–75).

In fact, recent research has shown that most of the effects described above occur with real managers, with multiple trials available for learning, and with rewards for successful performance (Neale and Northcraft 1990). In virtually all cases, these biases are robust to the tests that critics have provided (Bazerman 2001).

Other researchers have argued that our decision heuristics are adaptive (Gigerenzer 1991), and that researchers have tricked participants in ways that are not ecologically valid (Gigerenzer 1991). Despite these criticisms, it would be hard to identify any sophisticated decision researchers or practitioners who would want these biases to affect their most important decisions. More importantly, we see the tools of behavioural decision researchers increasingly used on Wall Street, in medical education, and in legal education, where the value of the decisions being made is considerable, whether in financial, social or humanitarian terms.

The research in social cognition and BDT is theoretically and empirically rich. The two fields have both unique and overlapping topic areas. Together, these two literatures will provide the basic structure for reviewing and evaluating the development of a cognitive perspective within OB.

Cognitive Perspectives in Micro-Organizational Behaviour

Social Cognition in Micro-Organizational Behaviour

Social cognition can be characterized as the application of cognitive research methods to social contexts, with the organization being one of these contexts (Brewer and Kramer 1985). Micro-organizational research, a central component of organizational research, has been criticized in the past for the relatively passive role it affords to individuals (Brief and Aldag 1981). In response to this charge, it has been argued that this research could be enhanced if the interaction among employee behaviour, cognitions and the environment was addressed (Brief and Aldag 1981). Indeed, Cummings (1982) went so far as to state that 'the work on cognitive processing of stimuli comes as close as organizational behaviour has come to date in understanding the processes which underlie so many of the functional relationships central to the discipline'. In the next section, we will focus on a particular topic – leadership – and examine the impact that various social cognitive theories have had on our understanding of this important organizational role.

Leadership

Leadership is an old topic in OB, yet our review shows the area to be alive in producing new empirical research, with social cognition playing an active role. Social cognition has been applied to the study of leadership in a number of ways. An attributional perspective on leadership has been hailed as one of the most important cognitive applications (Cummings 1982). In addition, the simultaneous study of attitudes and leadership has been the focus of numerous studies. Finally, memory, self-concepts and stereotyping have also been linked, albeit to a lesser degree, to the study of leadership.

Attributional studies of leadership have incorporated leadership attributions, subordinate attributions, or some combination of these two. Heneman et al. (1989) found that internal, but not external, attributions were significantly related to critical performance incidents and leader–member exchange. An effort (versus ability) attribution has been shown to influence the variance in performance evaluations (Knowlton and Mitchell 1980).

In addition to influencing evaluations, attributions made by the leader also influence actions taken by that leader. Green and Mitchell (1979) proposed an attributional model of leader behaviour that suggested that leaders' attributions influenced their subsequent actions. Evidence suggests that the belief about the cause of a subordinate's performance affects the choice of supervisory actions (Tjosvold 1985) and the extent to which organizational policy is implemented (Green and Liden 1980). This relationship has been influenced by the type of situation (James and White 1983), the gender compatibility between the leader and the subordinate (Dobbins et al. 1983), and the nature of the relationship (Heneman et al. 1989).

An attributional perspective has also been used to address attributions made by subordinates about their leader. Meindl et al. (1985) propose that leadership is a romantic concept that individuals utilize to make causal attributions about organizational outcomes. Meindl and Ehrlich (1987) provide support for this proposition in their findings that performance evaluations of leaders were better when the cause was attributed to leadership rather than non-leadership factors.

There has been recognition that both leader and member attributions may have important implications for organizational research. Integrating these two concepts, Martinko and Gardner (1987) proposed a model that combines the attributions of members and leaders. The simultaneous study of self-serving biases in both leader and member decision making processes suggested that leaders attributed poor performance to internal subordinate factors while subordinates attributed poor performance to internal leader factors (Dobbins and Russell 1986).

Attitudinal research has also enhanced leadership research. Wexley and Pulakos (1983) found that the more aware a subordinate was of their manager's work-related attitudes, the more favourable they were in evaluating the leader. In addition, attitudes, such as intrinsic job satisfaction, have been proposed as substitutes for leadership behaviour, thus negating the leader's ability to influence the subordinate (Kerr and Jermier 1978). Leadership styles and employee attitudes have also been used together as independent variables. For example, work group effectiveness has been found to be positively associated with the match between leadership style and the member's attitude toward the leader's style (White and Bassford 1978).

Memory and self-concept have also been integrated with leadership research. Specifically, the attitudes ascribed to leader behaviour have been studied from a memory perspective. Phillips (1984) found that leader behaviour that was consistent with the initial leadership labels of subordinates influenced the frequency with which subordinates assigned a particular behaviour to a leader. Memory (selective encoding specifically) has also been proposed as a mediator of the performance-leader ratings relationship (Larson et al. 1984). The notion of a self-concept has been used to enhance leadership theory. The idea of self-concept has been used to separate leaders from non-leaders (Peppers and Ryan 1986). The mutual influence of leader and follower on self-concepts has also been investigated, examining the impact that followers have on the leader's self-schema and, at the same time, the effect that the leader has on the employee working self-concept (Lord et al. 1999). Self-concepts have also formed the foundation for understanding the influence of charismatic leadership (Shamir et al. 1993) and both liking and leader-member exchange (Engle and Lord 1997).

Finally, we examine recent research on the social cognitive aspects of power as it influences the behaviour of the powerful. While these individuals may be powerful with respect to their immediate social environment, the recent studies in this area shed considerable light on the cognition and behaviour of leaders in power as well as that of their subordinates in less powerful roles. In the last decade social cognitive researchers have explored the impact of how power influences the cognitive processes of the powerful in terms of stereotyping and social reasoning for example.

One of the more interesting and provocative perspectives in this area is represented by the recent work of Keltner et al. (2003). They suggest that power has its impact in that the experience of power catalyses a tendency to approach social situations while the experience of powerlessness, the tendency to inhibit. With respect to leaders who are typically in a powerful position relative to their followers, they show that power is disinhibiting because it reduces concerns for the social consequences of one's actions and, thus, strengthens the link between the leader's goals and his or her goal-directed behaviours. Their research has found that power leads to an action orientation, especially in competitive situations (Galinsky et al. 2003); increases in the probability that powerful leaders will act in ways that defy social norms (Kelter et al. 2003); increases in single-mindedness (Gruenfeld and Kim 2003); and a reduced tendency to take another's perspective (Gruenfeld et al. 2003).

Consistent with this perspective, Lee and Tiedens (2001) provide evidence that when people are in position of high status (e.g. leadership positions), they are more likely to have independent self-construals. They view themselves as separate and independent from others. In contrast, those in low power or subordinate positions focus much more on their relationships, connections and interdependencies. That is, low power or low status individual are more likely to evidence an interdependent self-construal. This perspective and the associated research results stand in sharp contrast to the finding of researchers studying networks as well as the skills in reading social contexts relationship building. For example, network researchers find that high power individuals are typically at the nexus of series of relations and connections while low power individuals are those with many fewer connections and relationships (Burt 1992; Misrucki 1993; Ibarra 1995). High power parties are often found to have greater awareness of and attention to social cues (Chen and Ybarra 2000). While there has been little resolution of this controversy to date, Lee and Tiedens (2001) have proposed that high power parties may, simultaneously, hold independent self-contruals and interdependent relationship structures. Thus, power and its impact on social cognition may have at least two dimensions: the independence of the social construal (i.e. the subjective nature of power) interacting with the necessary relational structure (e.g. the objective nature of power) that creates stable social power.

This line of inquiry is particularly thought provoking, given the recent organizational and political examples of the destructive power of leaders in modern society. Leaders shape the culture of groups, organizations, and countries; and because of their power, leaders are more likely to show less complex styles of reasoning with a more direct connection between their thoughts and subsequent actions (Keltner et al. 2003). Thus, the evidence is quite consistent that the experience of power – or the lack thereof – directly influences the social cognition and decision-making propensities of individuals (Lee and Tiedens 2001).

Behavioural Decision Theory in Micro-Organizational Behaviour

Behavioural decision theory has developed into a recognized topic of the field of OB. This can be seen in the existence of OB textbook chapters on the topic (Stroh et al. 2001), a mainstream OB journal that focuses much attention on the topic (*Organizational Behaviour and Human Decision Processes*), and faculty and courses in OB departments devoted to BDT at many leading management schools (e.g. MIT, Cornell, Duke, Northwestern and Chicago). From a theoretical and empirical standpoint, BDT has been used as a basic component in the development of the literatures on negotiation and group decision-making. As such, this perspective has now taken on a richness that extends beyond its early roots of heuristics and biases. A review of each of these application areas is provided below.

Negotiation

The last decade has seen a proliferation of interest in the topic of negotiation by OB researchers. Many scholars outside the BDT area have argued that the central negotiation perspective by OB researchers has been Neale and Bazerman's (1991) BDT perspective that focuses on the decisions made by negotiators (Greenhalgh 1993).

The development of this descriptive literature, which accounts for the limitations in negotiator decision-making, is closely connected to the leading prescriptive work on negotiation (Raiffa 1982; Raiffa et al. 2002). Raiffa argues for an asymmetrically prescriptive/descriptive approach. This approach suggests that the decision analyst should asymmetrically (to only one of actors) provide prescriptions to the negotiator based on the best possible description of the likely behaviour of the opponent. In contrast to mainstream economic and game theoretic approaches, Raiffa explicitly acknowledges that the actual behaviour of the opponent may fall far short of rationality.

Raiffa's work was a key turning point in negotiation research for a number of reasons. First, in the context of developing a prescriptive model, he explicitly realizes the importance of forming accurate descriptions of the opponent rather than assuming them to be fully rational. Second, his realization that negotiators need advice implicitly acknowledges that negotiators do not intuitively follow purely rational strategies. Most importantly, he initiated the ground for dialogue between prescriptive and descriptive researchers. His work utilizes descriptive models that allow the focal negotiator to anticipate the likely behaviour of the opponent. In addition, we argue that a central focus of the decision analyst should be to realize that the focal negotiator might have decision biases that limit his/her ability to follow such advice.

Our research has addressed some of the questions that Raiffa raised. For example, if negotiators do not act rationally, what systematic departures from rationality can be predicted? Initial research has addressed some of the questions and has provided a set of empirical studies that integrate the value of existing descriptive and prescriptive research in creating a decision perspective of negotiation.

Building on BDT, a number of deviations from rationality that can be expected in negotiations have been identified. Specifically, research on two-party negotiations suggests that negotiators tend to: (1) be inappropriately affected by the frame in which risks are viewed (Bazerman et al. 1985; Neale and Bazerman 1985; Huber et al. 1987); (2) anchor their judgements in negotiation based on rationally irrelevant information (Tversky and Kahneman 1974; Huber and Neale 1986; Northcraft and Neale 1987); (3) overweight readily available information (Neale 1984); (4) be overconfident (Bazerman and Neale 1982; Neale and Bazerman 1985); (5) nonrationally assume that negotiation tasks are fixed-sum, and thus miss opportunities for mutually beneficial trade-offs

(Bazerman et al. 1985); (6) nonrationally escalate commitment to a previously selected course of action (Bazerman and Neale 1983; Northcraft and Neale 1986); (7) ignore the valuable information that is available by considering the cognitions of others (Samuelson and Bazerman 1985; Bazerman and Carroll 1987); (8) devalue any concession that is made by the other side – reactive devaluation (Curhan et al. 2004); (9) erroneously assume that the opponent's interests are completely opposed to those of their own, when in fact, negotiators' interests are perfectly compatible with those of the other party (Thompson and Hastie 1990); and (10) egocentrically interpret what would be fair in a negotiated agreement (Thompson and Loewenstein 1992; Loewenstein et al. 1993).

While the behavioural decision perspective had a significant influence on the field of negotiation, many authors have criticized this perspective for ignoring too many factors that were obviously important in negotiation (Greenhalgh and Chapman 1998; Bazerman et al. 2000). In response, research in the last decade has emerged that adds social psychological variables within the behavioural decision research perspective. The social factors argued to be missing from earlier research on decision-making have become specific topics of study. This new social psychology of negotiations accepts some of the features of the BDT perspective, including the backdrop of rationality (Murnighan 1994; Thompson 1998).

One important set of variables that has been studied deal with the importance of relationships in negotiation (for reviews, see Valley et al. 1995; Greenhalgh and Chapman 1999). The study of relationships and negotiation can be divided into three basic levels, focusing on the individual, the dyad, and the network. At the individual level, an example of this work is Loewenstein et al.'s (1989) study, which found that disputants' reported preferences for monetary payoffs were greatly influenced by payoffs to and relationships with their hypothetical counterparts. At the dyadic level, Valley et al. (1998) demonstrated that certain behaviours that appear irrational from the individual perspective might be rational from the perspective of the dyad. This work shows that, given the opportunity to communicate freely, negotiators often appear irrational in their individual decision making, yet reach dyadic outcomes that outperform game theoretic models (Valley et al. 1998). At the network level, Tenbrunsel

et al. (1996) examine the implications of relationships on the selection of a negotiation partner. Essentially, they argued that people 'satisfice' (March and Simon 1958) by matching with other people they already know rather than seeking out new partners (Tenbrunsel et al. 1996) at a cost to finding better-fitting matches.

Another stream of research argues that fairness judgements in negotiation are not purely objective. Instead, parties tend to overweight the views that favour themselves – which is referred to as egocentric judgements of fairness (Babcock and Loewenstein 1997; Diekmann et al. 1997) in addition to the cognitively based biases reviewed earlier. Bazerman and Neale (1983) and Thompson and Loewenstein (1992) found negotiators to be egocentric, and that the more egocentric the parties were, the more difficulty they had coming to agreement. This pattern has been replicated both in studies that used financial incentives for performance and across negotiation contexts (Camerer and Loewenstein 1993; Loewenstein et al. 1993; Babcock et al. 1995). Furthermore, Thompson and Loewenstein (1992) found that the provision of more (neutral) information increases egocentrism. Those participants who received this additional neutral information tended to make more extreme estimates of a fair outcome. Participants also showed self-serving recall bias, remembering better those facts that favoured themselves.

Another set of biases in negotiation comes from the desire to view oneself, the world, and the future in a considerably more positive light than reality can sustain (Taylor and Brown 1988; Taylor 1989). Humans perceive themselves as being better than others on desirable attributes (Messick et al. 1985) and have unrealistically positive self-evaluations. In the negotiations domain, Kramer et al. (1993) found that 68 percent of the MBA students in a negotiation class predicted that their bargaining outcomes would fall in the upper 25 percent of the class.

Finally, researchers have begun to explore the role of emotion on the rationality of decisions. Anger makes negotiators more self-centered in their preferences (Loewenstein et al. 1989) and increases the likelihood that they will reject profitable offers in ultimatum games (Pillutla and Murnighan 1996). While some researchers have found little advantage for the expression of anger in negotiations (Allred et al. 1997), other researchers have found a consistent benefit primarily associated with anger for value claiming, especially for the more powerful party

(Sinaceur and Tiedens in press). Extending the work of cognitive appraisal theorists into a negotiation context, Anderson and Neale (2004) found that angry but uncertain negotiators not only were able to claim more value when compared to a control condition but also were able to create more value than either negotiators in a control condition or negotiators who were angry, but certain.

Other research shows a conflict between what people think they should do (cognitive) versus what they want to do (emotional). The results of a series of studies indicates that it is the 'want' self that dominates at the moment of negotiator action, resulting in a behavioural preference for self-destructive choices (Bazerman et al. 1998; O'Connor et al. 2002). These results have had a strong influence on research and teaching in negotiation; BDT-influenced negotiation research is now commonly seen in OB journals and negotiation has been the fastest new topic of courses in OB courses during the 1980s and 1990s. Many of these courses try to provide students with useful prescriptions based on descriptive models rooted in BDT.

Group Decision-Making

As characterized in the description of BDT, individuals often use heuristics to make decisions. Often, these heuristics are incorrectly used, resulting in biased decision making. While early work in this area focused on extending the concept of biases in individual decision making to the group context, more recent research has broadened the research questions to include examining the systematic ways in which the multi-party setting of groups and teams influences the decision processes that goes on within these groups. Specifically, BDT research has influenced the questions raised by scholars studying group decision making in three ways: (1) the application of 'individual' biases to a group context; (2) the identification of group–specific heuristics and biases; and (3) systematic influences of heuristic thinking at the group level.

One of the individual biases that has been applied to group research is the framing bias. In an attempt to explain Stoner's (1961) finding that groups are more risk-seeking, Bazerman (1994) offered framing as an alternative interpretation which focused on group discussion as a mechanism for mitigating any one individual's frame. Following this line of reasoning, Bazerman predicted that a positive frame would mitigate risk-averse behaviour displayed by individuals, thus creating an apparent risk-seeking tendency on the part of groups. Likewise, a negative frame in a group context would appear to create risk-averse behaviour for groups when they were compared to individuals. Neale et al. (1986) find support for this prediction.

The tendency to adhere to the representativeness heuristic has also been studied in groups. Argote et al. (1986) found that this heuristic was used by both individuals and groups, with groups exhibiting an even greater biasing effect than individuals. This result was later clarified in a paper by Argote et al. (1990), who tested subjects' ability to judge the probabilities that an individual belonged to a certain category. They found that groups tend to judge primarily by representativeness when individuating information is informative, but were less affected by this heuristic when descriptions were not representative of categories. Overconfidence is also characteristic of both groups and individuals. Specifically, Sniezek and Henry (1989) found that groups, while perhaps more accurate in their judgements regarding uncertain ends, fell prey to the overconfidence bias just as often as individuals. Egocentrism appears to occur at both the individual and the group level, with group-serving biases having even a greater effect than self-serving biases (Taylor and Doria 1981).

Bazerman et al. (1984) discovered that groups exhibited a similar tendency of nonrational escalation to a course of action as individuals. Whyte (1991), however, found that when responsibility was varied, groups in a group-responsibility condition actually exhibited a decrease in the escalation of commitment as compared to individuals in a responsibility condition. The explanation for this effect centers on the ability of members of a group to diffuse responsibility for a decision that is not a possibility in individual decision-making.

The formation, maintenance and interaction of coalitions have also been informed by BDT research. Mannix and White (1992) found that the anchoring and adjustment heuristic characterized the distribution of resources within a coalition. In particular, in the absence of a distribution rule, past performance information served as an anchor for distributive outcomes. Bazerman (1984) suggests that coalitions may also be influenced by other biases. For example, Bazerman asserts that the reemergence of successful coalitions may be because of a reliance on the availability heuristic. In addition, the escalation of commitment bias and the positive framing effect imply that individuals may stay in a coalition longer than they should. Furthermore, individuals may be overconfident in their ability to form a new coalition.

Janis' work on groupthink (1972) suggested that groups may also exhibit biases unique to a group context. The eight symptoms of groupthink (illusion of invulnerability, collective rationalization, a belief in the group's inherent morality, stereotypes of outgroups, direct pressure on dissenters, self-censorship, illusion of unanimity and the use of self-appointed mind guards) are believed to lead to deficiencies in the decision-making process of groups, including an incomplete survey of alternatives and objectives, a failure to examine the risks of choices and reappraise initially rejected alternatives, poor information search, biased processing of information, and a failure to work out contingency plans (Janis and Mann 1977). Thus, groupthink can be thought of as a heuristic within highly cohesive groups that interferes with rational decision-making (Bazerman 2001).

Research on negotiation and group decision-making connect when more than two parties are making a decision together and do not have the same preferences. One interesting bias that emerges is a group form of egocentrism. Members of groups, MBA teams, co-authors, fishers, and others often reason egocentrically, believing that they contributed more work than they objectively deserve (Wade-Benzoni et al. 1996; Caruso et al. in press). Caruso et al (in press) have found, in two experiments involving real groups of journal authors and MBA students, leading participants to think about (or 'unpack') their collaborators as individuals reduced strong egocentric biases in responsibility allocation. Surprisingly, however, unpacking other group members also decreased interest in continued collaboration among those who believed they contributed more than others.

Were the BDT perspective to limit itself to the discovery and cataloging of biases in human judgement, it would rapidly devolve into a focus on increasingly more microscopic and, subsequently, less useful prescriptions for managers. Rather, as we suggested earlier, the BDT perspective is concerned primarily with the descriptive and prescriptive aspects of decision-making. Moving beyond the study of the presence or absence of cognitive biases in groups and teams, researchers have also been exploring factors that influence information exchange and subsequent decision making in groups. The general finding of this stream of research as that information exchange in groups typically focus on (i.e. present, repeat, emphasize) shared, rather than unshared information in their interactions (see, for a review, Wittenbaum and Stasser 1996; Argote et al. 2000). Using a hidden profile task (Stasser and Titus 1987; Stasser et al. 1989), task-relevant information is distributed to participants in such a way that the shared information among group members supports a sub-optimal alternative while the unshared information possessed by each group member (if fully explored) leads to a different, optimal alternative. While most of the research in this area has typically focused on the framing of the task and what members know, more recent research has explored the impact of opinion and social subgroups on the information processing and decisions of the team as a whole. Gruenfeld et al. (1996) compared the information exchange and decision-making of three person teams composed of familiars, strangers or two familiars and one stranger faced with a hidden profile or common information task. They found that groups composed of familiars outperformed stranger groups in hidden profile tasks but groups composed of strangers outperformed familiar groups when information was common to all members. Because the mixed (2 familiar and 1 stranger) groups did not behave consistently as either of the two pure groups, Phillips et al. (2004) explicitly considered the impact of the congruence of the social and information ties on the decision behaviour of these diverse groups. Congruence occurred when group members who are socially-tied also shared the same information while a stranger (no social ties) had unique information. In contrast, incongruence occurred when one of the familiars had the same information as the stranger, but (by nature of their familiarity) shared a relationship tie (but not information) with a familiar other. They found that the three-person groups with congruent social and knowledge ties utilized information more effectively, reported more effective group processes, and outperformed groups with incongruent ties. Interestingly, when they used four-person groups and compared the impact of congruence with either a single minority information holder or two equal–sized subgroups they found that congruent groups outperformed incongruent groups, but only when groups had a minority information holder.

Phillips (2003) extended this research to show that, regardless of the task-relevance of salient differences, individuals responded most favourably when categorical and opinion differences are congruent. Specifically, the results of her studies suggested that out-group minority opinion holders may be more influential in diverse group decision-making settings than in-group minority opinion holders.

In all of these studies, the focus was on the influence of the social and information ties among group members on the willingness of some to share their unique information and the capability of others to incorporate that unique information into their decision making processes. The story gets a bit more complicated when one adds differential status – above and beyond the status that accrues as a result of in-group membership – to the mix. For example, Thomas-Hunt et al. (2003) found that while perceived expertise did not increase the individual's emphasis on own unique knowledge, perceived experts were more likely than non-experts to emphasize shared knowledge and other member's unique knowledge contributions. However, recent work by Sinaceur et al. (2004) illustrate that status (in this case perceived expertise) can influence the private decision processes of minority and majority members. This research finds that perceived expertise makes minorities more likely to enhance the quality of majority members' private decisions, but not of the group's public decision. Specifically, majority members are more likely to change their opinions from inaccurate to accurate after discussion in groups whose minorities are seen as expert. Perceived expertise not only impacts majorities' but also minorities' cognitive flexibility. While majority members are more willing to change, minority members are less willing to change, their private opinions. Further, when the minority possesses perceived expertise, minority members are less reserved in stating their opinions, and a livelier debate takes place within the group. In fact, groups whose minorities are seen as expert experience more conflict and diversity of opinions than do groups whose minorities are not seen as such.

An Evaluation of Cognition Perspectives in Micro-Organizational Behaviour

We concur with Ilgen and Klein's (1988) conclusion about the important and now, continuing role of cognitive perspectives in OB. In general, we consider our review of the social cognition area to be extremely consistent with the perspectives of Ilgen and Klein. Both regard social cognitive research as critical to the continued development of individual, dyadic, and multiparty research in OB. Our review of BDT research in the micro OB literature suggests that in addition to helping with the advancement of traditional OB areas (e.g. group decision making), BDT has also been instrumental in creating new topics in the field of OB, namely, decision making and negotiation. Both are now common topics of leading OB journals, textbooks, and courses. This was not true two decades ago.

We believe that the success of BDT in creating new topics is tied to the values and assumptions that we offered at the beginning of this chapter. We argued that research should understand the world as it is, not as we would like it to be. We also argued that descriptive research is strengthened by comparison to a normative benchmark. This is an important lever of the BDT approach that highlights areas in which we can see limitations in behaviour in organizations. We further argued that descriptive research could inform prescriptive frameworks. We believe that this aspect of BDT has been critical to its level of influence in the negotiation area. People want to know how to negotiate better, and BDT provides useful insights. Finally, we argued that decision-making is a core activity in organizations. This perspective is critical to the emergence of decision making as a topic of inquiry by OB scholars.

Collectively, we see both social cognition and BDT as playing a crucial role in contemporary micro OB. What the future is likely to hold for these two perspectives is a greater alignment between them. For example, there is an increasing interest in examining decision maker and negotiator cognitions through the lens of social comparisons. Issues of fairness (Bies et al. 1993; Kahneman et al. 1986), relationships (Valley et al. 1995), and justice concerns are becoming more salient considerations in the lexicon of BDT researchers (Kahneman 1992). In understanding the biases that impact strategic decision making, it has been argued that both individual and organizational influences on information gathering and alternative generation must be considered (Corner et al. 1994). Time constraints are yet another more recently identified contextual influence on decision maker cognition, impacting the extent and degree to which cognitive tasks are performed (Ordonez and Benson 1997). In fact, recent research by Blount and her colleagues suggests the importance of dyads and teams members being 'in-synch' or 'in-pace' with each other (Blount and Janicik 2001).

Research on ethical decision-making in particular is making important strides, in part because it has focused on the integration of cognitions and the social context. Messick and Tenbrunsel (1996) highlighted the importance of considering the contributions that psychology and behavioural economics could make for the field of business ethics, both in identifying the contextual influences on unethical decision-making and the cognitions that underlie such decisions. Situational variables such as the incentive to behave unethically, through the influence on the decision maker's temptation, have been found to bias perceptions of the opponent's unethical behaviour and increase the likelihood of unethical behaviour (Tenbrunsel 1998). One promising area that links contextual influences to unethical behaviour is the notion of decision frames, which has been asserted to impact perceptions, norms, and behaviours (Messick 1999). Situational variables are seen as influencing the type of decision (i.e. an ethical versus a business decision) with which a decision maker perceives that they are faced, in turn impacting the perceptions of others' unethical behaviour and the likelihood of engaging in unethical behaviour and perceptions of others. The presence of a surveillance or monitoring system is one such contextual factor, decreasing both the likelihood that a decision is perceived to be ethical and the degree of cooperative behaviour (Tenbrunsel and Messick 1999). Schminke et al. (1997) also demonstrate the importance of understanding the ethical perspective of the decision maker, demonstrating that the ethical framework of a decision maker (i.e. ethical formalists versus ethical utilitarians) influenced perceptions of organizational justice.

Understanding the cognitions of negotiators, and the contextual influences on such cognitions, has also received considerable attention. Negotiators conceptualization of utility – as an objective attribute, subjective preference, or as a function of the interpersonal relationship – is seen as essential in understanding negotiators' cognitive maps, which in turn influence their assumptions and motivation (Simons 1993). Negotiator frame – viewing outcomes as gains or losses – and the congruency between the negotiator and her opponent's

frame are important influences in concession patterns, demands, and perceptions of the opponent (Pinkley and Northcraft 1994). Negotiator cognitions are not seen as static, however, but rather influenced by the social context. For example, the influence of reference points, which can serve as powerful cognitive anchors in negotiations (Blount et al. 1995), depend on aspects of the interaction (i.e. social cognitions) that are present in the negotiation. White and Neale (1994) provide evidence that initial offers influence perceptions of an opponent's reservation price and the negotiation bargaining zone, which in turn are linked to attributions of unfairness and greediness. Culture has also been identified as an important contextual influence on judgement biases in negotiation, with, for instance, individualistic cultures more prone to the fixed pie bias than collectivist cultures (Gelfand and Christakopoulou 1999; Gelfand and Brett 2003).

As these examples suggest, understanding the influence that cognitions have on behaviour, one must also place this behaviour in the context of social interactions and, thus, social cognitions. Doing so allows for a more informed and more complete understanding of the decisions and social interactions that exist at the micro–level of organizations. As we turn now to a more macro–level perspective, we see an equally important influence of cognitions.

Cognitive Perspectives in Macro-Organizational Research

The last two decades have also witnessed a growing influence of cognitive perspectives and theories on macro-organizational research. There are several research streams that focus on using psychological and cognitive theories to explain the behaviour of organizations and whole sets of organizations (i.e. industries, fields, or societies) such as macro-organizational psychology (e.g. Staw and Sutton 1992), strategic or organizational decision–making (e.g. Schwenk 1988; Zajac and Bazerman 1991), strategy formulation (Bateman and Zeithaml 1989), organizational memory and learning (e.g. Senge 1990; Walsh and Ungson 1991), and organization-environment relations, industry or field-level belief systems (Lant 2002; Porac et al. 2002). In particular, most recent approaches that focus on inter-organizational relationships highlight the processes around strategic choice and interactions as well as the conceptualization of collective cognitive structures to explain organizational and competitive actions and outcomes (Porac et al. 2002).

Efforts to apply psychological theories and cognitive perspectives to organization-level behaviour can be traced back to the work of Dill (1958), March and Simon (1958), Cyert and March (1963), Katz and Kahn (1966; 1978), Lawrence and Lorsch (1967), Weick (1969; 1979a; 1979b), Pondy and Mitroff (1979), and Daft and Weick (1984). Two primary perspectives evolved from this body of work that addressed how organizations obtain information about their environments and prior experiences and how this information is used to make decisions and take action (Lant 2002). One perspective views organizations as information processing systems consisting of embedded routines through which information is stored and enacted (March and Simon 1958; Cyert and March 1963; Lant and Shapira 2000). In this view, attention is directed towards the limited information processing abilities of individuals, and thus organizations, extending into research streams investigating how interpretations of information differ across organizations, what organizations pay attention to and how they interpret the information that is gathered, and the role of managers and leaders as key information processors in organizations (Lant 2002). As a result, from the 1980s through the early 1990s, issues of environmental scanning and search, subjective perceptions, and interpretations became the dominant focus of cognitive research at the macro level (e.g. Kiesler and Sproull 1982; Meyer 1982; Jackson and Dutton 1988; Walsh 1988; Milliken 1990; Thomas and McDaniel 1990; Thomas et al. 1993).

By drawing on the theoretical assumptions of work emphasizing organizations as quasi-rational information processing systems, another cognitive perspective emerged that emphasizes organizations as 'enacting bodies' or 'interpretation systems' (Daft and Weick 1984), emphasizing the importance of language and symbols in the social construction of reality in organizations (Berger and Luckman 1967). In this view, organizations then began to be viewed as systems of patterned or structured activity in which participants attempt to develop causal explanations and rationalizations for these patterns of activity (Pfeffer 1981; Smircich and Stubbart 1985). These explanations and rationalizations are seen as a part of the 'management of meaning'

process within organizations that can be examined through a more cognitive approach (e.g. Bartunek 1984; Donnellon et al. 1986; Weick and Roberts 1993; Fiol 1994; Gioia et al. 1994). Weick (1979a) pointed out that organizations can be viewed as bodies of thought and, as such, described as recurrent schemata, causal textures, and sets of reference levels or in terms of dominant rules for combining cognitions, routine utterances, mixtures of habituation and reflection, and preferences for simplification (Schwenk 1986; 1988; Walsh 1988). These arguments established the groundwork for general cognitive concepts to be adapted to the descriptions of organizations, their actions, and to the diagnosis of organizational properties and problems.

One line of subsequent research has examined how the organizational context can be influenced by individual behaviours. One argument is that organizational actions are merely reflections of individual behaviours such that autonomous individuals are seen as posing or 'dressing up' as organizations (Staw 1991; Staw and Sutton 1992), taking actions that reflect their own preferences, and yet disguising them as actions reflecting organizational policies and/or procedures (Staw 1991). As such, psychological theories are useful for explaining the behaviour of organizations. Cognitive, or more specifically social cognitive areas, are equally applicable for developing a greater understanding of organizational action and would likely provide valid research leads. As of yet, however, such concepts have not been explicitly studied (Mowday and Sutton 1993). However, there has been related research focusing on the influence that certain key individuals (such as founders, CEOs, and managers) exert on organizations and thus act as more than just agents of organizations. While leaders of organizations are not completely powerful in scope, there is evidence that they have at least a modest influence on organizations, particularly on small and young firms (Pfeffer and Davis-Blake 1986; Thomas 1988; Bass 1990). There are numerous ways that leaders and other key individuals can influence organizations, including shaping thoughts, feelings, perceptions, and actions of people inside and outside the organization and making decisions that affect the organization (Mowday and Sutton 1993). In addition to shaping the set of members who make up the organization, leaders also create conditions that influence member's emotion, behaviours, and cognitions (Staw and Sutton 1992; Lord et al. 1999).

Closely related to our cognitive focus is the stream of literature that focuses on understanding the nature of a leader's influence relative to the cognitions of follower's as well as the larger social context. In 1975, Eden and Leviathan (1975) proposed the idea that 'leadership factors are in the mind of the respondent...' (p. 741) which catalysed a cognitive revolution in leadership research. As a result, cognition has been accorded a central place in current models of leadership that establish how leadership factors reside not only in the minds of followers but also in the minds of leaders, in leaders' behaviour and attitudes, and in the social context in which leaders and their followers interact (Lord and Emrich 2001). In their review of ten years of leadership research, Lord and Emrich (2001) highlight how prominent the information processing viewpoint has been in leadership studies, reflecting on the central role of knowledge structures and schema as well, in accordance with work by Walsh (1995) and Hall and Lord (1995). Fruitful research agendas, in this vein, are aimed at developing understandings around dynamic leadership processes, the interplay between individual cognitions and social/contextual factors, and the relation of intervening and outcome processes.

Other work on leadership and cognition focuses on the leader's role of providing explanations, legitimization, and rationales for organizational activities (symbolic management as proposed by Pfeffer 1981). In this vein research, like that of Gioia et al. (1994), Nutt (1998), Westphal and Zajac (1998), Arndt and Bigelow (2000) and Seeger and Ulmer (2002) explores the role of symbolic corporate actions in framing organizational problems, introducing radical solutions, crises, and in perpetuating power imbalances in organizations. Several studies have related concepts of attribution theories to leadership, including an examination of how leaders shape membership attitudes and expectations and how explanations provided by CEOs are shaped in regards to corporate performance (Bettman and Weitz 1983; Staw et al. 1983; Salancik and Meindl 1984; Simons 2002; Alvesson and Sveningsson 2003). These studies suggest that self-serving attributions used by managers and CEOs (as well as other impression management behaviours) help to position the work and activities of the individuals themselves, as well as the firm, affecting impressions of control, shareholder perceptions, and even stock prices. Self-serving behaviour and attributions are relevant to a wide variety of organizational

phenomena at several levels, including performance appraisal, escalation of commitment, unethical behaviour, intergroup conflict, institutional processes, and agency problems (Johns 1999).

Another way in which powerful people influence organizations is through the decisions that they make. Strategy formulation is often treated as a process in which decisions are incremental, interdependent, and shaped by a variety of contextual and psychological influences (see Bateman and Zeithaml 1989; Sparrow 1999). The study of strategists' cognition provides information about the workings of these informed brains and therefore, the factors which contribute to the successes and failures of organizations (Schwenk 1988). This stream of research tends to focus more on cognitive structures and processes that may be shared by multiple strategists than on individuals and their differences in cognition. It calls for more detailed descriptions of the ways that individual-level cognitions and orientations contribute to organization-level strategies. For example, the stream of literature known as upper echelons research has examined how top managers' cognitive orientations influence the decision making processes that are related to firm-level outcomes (e.g. Hambrick and Mason 1984; Jackson and Dutton 1988; Starbuck and Milliken 1988; Isabella 1990). In particular, numerous studies have established a link between the cognitive orientation of decision makers, particularly based on personal characteristics or prior experience, to the strategic adaptation of the firm to its environment (Hitt et al. 1982; Gupta 1984; Chaganti and Sambharya 1987; Walsh 1988; Govindarajan 1989; Bigley and Wiersma 2002). In this view, extending from earlier arguments about variance in individual interpretations of environments and social information (Daft and Wieck 1984; Fiske and Taylor 1984), the different career paths and personal backgrounds that result in different cognitive orientations, impacting strategic decisions are explored (e.g. Hambrick and Mason 1984; Tushman et al. 1985; Lyles and Schwenk 1992; Wiersma and Bantel 1992; Ocasio 1994; Boeker 1997).

Drawing from the literature on social cognitive influences, there has been a stream of articles relating organizational decision-making to cognitive structures and processes. This research addresses such topics as a decision-maker's frame of reference (e.g. Mason and Mitroff 1981; Shrivastava and Mitroff 1983; 1984; Shrivastava and Schneider 1984;

El Sawy and Pauchant 1988), strategic assumptions (e.g. Schwenk 1988; King and Zeithaml 2003), knowledge structures (Prahalad and Bettis 1986; Lyles and Schwenk 1992; Walsh 1995), categorization (Dutton and Jackson 1987; Day and Lord 1992; Papadakis and Kaloghirou 1999), and the concepts of scripts, cognitive maps, schemas, organizational learning, and interpretive systems (cf. Lyles and Schwenk 1992; Walsh 1995). Specific examples of the application of social cognitive concepts include Dutton and Jackson's (1987) model that integrates interpretive views of organizational decision making with categorization theory. It attempts to explain why organizations in the same industry respond differently to the same environmental trends and events. Prahalad and Bettis (1986) and Lyles and Schwenk (1992) suggest that the shared perspectives of organization members create knowledge structures for environmental events and organization capabilities. These structures can store a shared dominant general management logic that influences strategic actions and organization learning within the firm. Analysis of executives' strategic schemata is thought to aid in explanations of strategic choices in response to environmental and industry forces (Schwenk 1988).

Other research concentrates on the cognitive shortcomings that can affect the decisions made by top managers, which in turn affect the organization (e.g. Tyler and Steensma 1998; Das and Bing-Sheng 1999; Hodgkinson and Bown 1999; Hodgkinson et al. 2002; Wright and Goodman 2002). This research stems directly from BDT literature and the notion that decision heuristics – including representativeness, framing, availability, anchoring, the hindsight bias, and overconfidence – influence managerial behaviour (Bazerman 2001). As Schwenk (1988) supports, decisional biases found in many laboratory contexts can also affect strategic decision-making. He lists applicable biases, such as those previously mentioned along with selective perception bias, illusory correlation, conservatism, the law of small numbers, regression bias, illusion of control, logical reconstruction and wishful thinking that interact and reinforce each other; consequently, researchers are attempting to describe the ways that individual biases interact to affect such decisions. Zajac and Bazerman (1991) integrated theory concerning cognitive shortcomings with insights from the strategy literature to develop hypotheses about why and how decision makers in competitive

situations make nonrational judgements. Duhaime and Schwenk (1985) supports this work with their theory that business decision makers may use cognitive simplifying processes in defining ill-structured problems such as acquisition and divestment decisions. Other examples include Staw et al.'s (1981) work on the threat-rigidity model which suggests that distress can hinder the cognitive processes of leaders and cause them to make poor decisions. Most current work revolves around addressing ways to eliminate cognitive shortcomings through other cognitive tools and decision-making processes, such as cognitive mapping (Hodgkinson and Bown 1999; Hodgkinson et al. 2002; Wright and Goodwin 2002). Further work in strategic decision making agendas include more integration of psychological and cognitive research through the exploration of which heuristics are most relevant to which kinds of strategic decision makers, how they work, why they work, and when they are most appropriate (Eisenhardt and Zbaracki 1992; Busenitz and Barney 1997; Krabuanrat and Phelps 1998; Das and Bing-Sheng 1999; Kogut and Kulatilaka 2001; Regner 2003). It is argued that such heuristics allow organizational experts to make sense of strategic issues quickly and respond in an efficient and effective manner (Day and Lord 1992).

In addition to the influence of individual members on organizational actions, there also exists the argument that organizations are influenced by the aggregation of individual attributes, thoughts, feelings, and behaviours (Staw and Sutton 1992; Mowday and Sutton 1993). However, more recent work recognizes that collective or shared cognition is neither created nor housed in the mind of a single individual but instead reflective of a socially constructed understanding of the world derived from social exchanges and interactions among multiple individuals in a group or organizations, and, as such, is more than a simple aggregation of individual cognitions to the group, individual, organizational, or group level (Thompson and Fine 1999; Lord and Emrich 2001; Fiol 2002; Lant 2002; Porac et al. 2002). Work on organizational learning, memory, and sensemaking (e.g. Senge 1990; Weick 1990; Walsh and Ungson 1991), for example, draws parallels between individual processes and organizational processes. Implicit in these perspectives is a mediating concept called organizational intelligence through which an organizational entity learns, remembers, and processes information effectively

(Glynn 1996). As Staw and Sutton (1992) note, the classic work of March and Simon (1958) illustrates this analogy through its treatment of organizational information processing as synonymous with individual information processing. Another example is present in Walsh and Ungson's (1991) review and integration of the literature on organizational memory. They suggest that an organization's memory is an individual-level phenomenon since it is determined partly by the aggregation of individuals' remembered information and records. Walsh and Ungson (1991) note that individuals '… largely determine what information will be acquired and then retrieved from other memory stores' present in the organization, and contribute to the source of retained information of the organization. Extensions from these arguments have been fostered in work examining organizational innovation as a fundamentally cognitive process (Glynn 1996). As such authors have hinted at the role of cognition in fostering innovation, as well as change processes, as it is related to learning and memory processes at the organizational level (Cohen and Levinthal 1990; Mezias and Glynn 1993).

Lastly, newer cognitive perspectives at the macro level concentrate on larger collectivities of meaning that dictate or influence activities, behaviours, and forms present within a system of organizations (from strategic groups and industries to organizational fields and societies). As discussed earlier, the correctness of a decision is dependent on the point of view being used to evaluate it, thus is it largely interpretative depending on the perception of the 'communities of believers' with individual interpretive stances (Daft and Weick 1994; Weick 1995; Porac et al. 1996). These 'local' interpretations or rationalities are embedded in larger systems of meaning (from collective cognitions to industry-level belief systems). These wider belief systems have been linked to theories on knowledge structures and mental models, yet they have been expanded to include a variety of terms including attentional fields, belief structures, causal or cognitive maps, dominant logics, distilled ideologies, frame of references, schemas, mindsets, and world views (Sparrow 1999) as well as macro level cognitive representations termed as industry macrocultures (Abrahamson and Fombrun 1994), mindsets (Phillips 1994), recipes (Spender 1989), collective strategic concepts (Huff 1982), conceptions of control (Fligstein 1991) and institutional logics (Friedland and Alford 1991). In particular,

recent work in this vein emphasizes how these wider cognitions or logics as constellations of meanings, values, and organizational practices have implications for specifying appropriate actors, solutions and technologies, as well as shaping tangible structures and strategies within a field of activity (Thornton and Ocasio 1999; Galvin 2002; Thornton 2002; Thornton and Ventresca 2002; Lounsbury et al. 2003). These bodies of research focuses on actors within industries and organizational field that work with varied mental models of the industry or field define relevant actors, practices, and forms, define competition, and hence ground strategic action in socially-shared systems of belief (Porac et al. 2002). This area remains ripe for investigation as a substantial body of literature exists on the emergence of management logics and managerial schemas within organizations as collectivities of meaning (see Walsh 1995), yet the relationship between managerial schemas and broader or 'grand' themes at the industry or societal level is a much newer concern (Barley and Kunda 1992; Abrahamson 1997; Eastman and Bailey 1998; Dijksterhuis et al. 1999; Porac et al. 2002).

An Evaluation of Cognition Perspectives in Macro-Organizational Behaviour

In summary, the topic of cognition has reached the agendas of several macro-organization behaviour researchers, from streams in strategic management, organizational theory, and entrepreneurship to more interdisciplinary areas focusing the states and traits of individuals (e.g. leadership) as explanations of collective behaviour. The extension of applicable findings within the areas of BDT and social cognition provides more than alternative explanations; in many contexts, it is possible that it brings a more axiomatic interpretation of organizational action than traditional sociological approaches. Cognitive-based theories can add theoretical substance to existing macro models by supplying missing mechanisms to explain the behaviour of organizations through a focus on micro-level processes (Staw and Sutton 1992). At the other end of the perspective, applying cognitive perspectives allows for the establishment of new theories expanding on the role of cognitive processes at the collective level (e.g. organizational learning or industry belief systems). More importantly, the integration of non-traditional disciplines in the development of theoretical ideas in macro OB is not only useful but also helps to make the existing lines between micro and macro-organization behaviour a little less obvious. This represents a realm for future research as well as a renewal of ideas within the field of organization theory and behaviour.

The Future of Cognition in Organizations

As is evident in our review, social cognition and BDT have had a significant influence on micro and macro-organizational research. We see this influence as coming from several directions, including additional theoretical and empirical research in topic areas previously mentioned in this paper, in the identification of additional topics that are important to the field, and in the integration of concepts from social cognition and BDT.

As previously discussed, memory and self-concept have been identified as important factors in the topic of leadership. This research is still in the recognition phase, with many propositions offered but little empirical evidence presented. Further theoretical clarification and additional empirical research will enhance our understanding of these areas and in turn present useful recommendations to organizations. For example, additional research on the role of memory in the evaluation of leaders promises to identify sources of errors in these processes that in turn may indicate potential areas for improvement. Similarly, an understanding of self-concept differences in leaders versus non–leaders can result in the development of propositions and suggestions aimed at self-concept improvement, which will in turn enhance leadership and productivity in organizations.

One of the primary contributions of BDT research has been the identification of biases that lead to a decrement in decision performance. The identification of new biases will continue, albeit at a diminishing rate. Increased attention is expected to be directed at how this information can be used to increase the decision-making ability of individuals, dyads, and teams. Heuristics are helpful shortcuts only when they are appropriately applied; identification of the factors that result in misapplication will enhance the usefulness of this research.

A consideration of the integration of BDT and social cognition theories raises several questions, the answers to which could further augment micro-organizational research. For example, there is an increasing emphasis among researchers who study affect and emotion to explore the impact of emotion on how individuals process information, particularly the factors that lead to more systematic or more heuristic information processing (Tiedens and Litton 2001).

At the group level, there seems to be considerable interest in examining how teams process and store information. Recent research on transactive memory has only just begun to explore how team members learn who knows what in their groups – and the reliability of that information (e.g. Argote and Moreland 2003). In addition, recent advances in technology have opened up the study of virtual teams – teams that have no direct, face-to-face contact (Griffith and Neale 2001; Griffith et al. 2003). How does their decision making process differ from teams who are able to conduct their work within the same physical setting.

Another relatively untouched but nonetheless important question centers around the influence of attitudes on the prevalence of biases – are some attitudes influential in promoting the inappropriate use of heuristics? What role does anchoring and adjustment play in the attribution process? What is the connection between memory and the representativeness heuristic?

One of the most important topics to emerge in the new millennium is managerial ethics. Ethics have played a minor role in education up until the scandals that have rocked Wall Street, starting with the fall of Enron. Ethics is typically treated as an issue that can be dealt with through incentives and moral persuasion. Recent evidence suggests that ethics may be more of an issue of self-serving biasing affecting the judgement of honest people (Messick and Bazerman 1996). Earlier in this chapter, we discuss the likelihood of stereotypes operating without the awareness of the decision maker. This is an issue for psychology, more than an issue for economics or the philosophy. Undoubtedly, there are some 'bad apples'. But, should that be the focus of managerial education? We believe that this is a mistake. Rather, we believe that far more can be learned by examining the unethical behaviour of typically ethical people: the kind that we run into in our universities and businesses on a regular basis. We need to better understand favouritism toward an in-group (Dasgupta 2004). We need to also understand why humans have a propensity to overclaim credit (Epley and Caruso 2004), and how we are so affected by conflicts of interests, while being sure that conflicts of interest affect other people – rather than affecting us (Moore et al. 2005).

A related application of decision research in organization behaviour has been to the area of environmental behaviours. Decisions are central to the environmental destruction created by consumers, engineers, builders, executives, and policy decision makers, among others. Selfishness may be a partial cause. Some may degrade the earth because they are unconcerned with future generations. But, growing evidence suggests poor quality decisions made by individuals with no intention of being a parasitic influence on the environment is also a cause. The documented errors include over-discounting the future (Daly and Cobb 1994; Wade-Benzoni et al. 1996), egocentrism is assessments of what people, organizations or nations should make the sacrifices needed (Wade-Benzoni et al. 1996), the mythical fixed-pie preventing wise trades between the environment and the economy (Bazerman et al. 1999; Bazerman and Hoffman 1999), and perceptions that some issues are not tradable, even when the trades could make all parties better off (Tetlock et al. 1996; Thompson and Gonzalez 1997).

In agreement with March (1999), our discussion of cognitive perspectives in macro-organizational research highlight how organizations will always face both the dilemma of ignorance (a problem of computation requiring information and predictions) and the dilemma of ambiguity (a problem of interpretation played up in a social and contextual domain). It is difficult to separate the work on organizational cognition from that of individual level cognition and inter-organizational or field level cognition. It is arguable that making these distinctions are not where fruitful avenues of research are headed since all levels of organizational cognition and decision-making are affected by issues that arise from the nature of the human mind, the way in which the mind is embedded in and shaped by social context, and the nature of collective action and beliefs (Lant 2002; Porac et al. 2002). It is evident that the extension of individual information processing and social cognitive processes to the organizational and industry level are not straightforward because managerial and collective cognitions are complex and highly influenced by context (Walsh 1995; Lant 2002). Thus, the relationships among cognition, organizational action, and performance appear substantial while findings are still tentative and, unfortunately, disparate among the research streams of decision-making, organizational

behaviour, organizational theory, and strategic management.

As such, both BDT and social cognition will continue to be influential in the development of new research paradigms. As evident by recent surges in theories aimed at understanding cognition among 'collectivities', new avenues for research as well as theoretical models are developing among macro level areas focusing on organizational learning and industry or field level meaning systems. Lessons learned about knowledge structures and mental models at the psychological level will be particularly relevant for these broader applications of mental models and organizational activity. Similarly, understanding how organizational leaders and key actors make use heuristics and attributions in enabling or inhibiting organizational change, as well as responding to organizational events and crises is particularly applicable given more recent events and scandals that impact whole industries and society.

In conclusion, a new definition of OB that encompasses both social cognition and BDT addresses many of the criticisms aimed at this field. As evident in both past research and potential future research, these perspectives give new light to old issues and open up new doors to additional topics. Incorporating the theories of social cognition and BDT into the OB domain will ensure that OB remains a field that is alive and here to stay.

References

Abrahamson, E. (1997) 'The Emergence and Prevalence of Employee Management Rhetorics: The Effect of Long Waves, Labor Unions, and Turnover, 1875 to 1992.' *Academy of Management Journal*, 40: 491–533.

Abrahamson, E. and Fombrun, C. (1994) 'Macrocultures: Determinants and consequences', *Academy of Management Review*, 19: 728–55.

Allred, K.G., Mallozzi, J.S., Matsui, F. and Raia, C.P. (1997) 'The influence of anger and compassion on negotiation performance', *Organizational Behaviour and Human Decision Processes*, 70: 175–87.

Alvesson M. and Sveningsson S. (2003) 'The great disappearing act: difficulties in doing leadership', *Leadership Quarterly*, 14: 359–81.

Anderson, N. and Neale, M.A. (2004) 'All fired up, but who to blame? The benefit of anger and uncertainty in negotiation', working paper, Department of Psychology, Stanford University, Stanford, CA.

Argote, L., Devadas, R. and Melone, N. (1990) 'The base-rate fallacy: Contrasting processes and outcomes of group and individual judgment.', *Organizational Behaviour and Human Decision Processes*, 46: 296–310.

Argote, L., Gruenfeld, D.H. and Naquin, C. (2000) 'Group learning in organizations.' In M.E. Turner (ed.), *Groups at Work: Advances in Theory and Research*. Hillsdale, NJ: Lawrence Erlbaum and Associates, pp. 369–411.

Argote, L. and Moreland R. (2003) 'Transactive memory in dynamic organizations.' in R. Peterson and E. Mannix (ed.), Understanding the dynamic organization, pp. 135–162, Lawrence Eribaum Associates, Mahwah, NJ.

Argote, L., Seabright, M.A. and Dyer, L. (1986) 'Individual versus group: Use of base–rate and individuating information', *Organizational Behaviour and Human Decision Processes*, 38: 65–75.

Asch, S.E. (1946) 'Forming impressions of personality', *Journal of Abnormal and Social Psychology*, 41: 1230–40.

Arndt, M. and Bigelow, B. (2000) 'Presenting structural innovation in an institutional environment: hospitals' use of impression management', *Administrative Science Quarterly*, 45: 494–522.

Babcock L. and Loewenstein G. (1997) 'Explaining bargaining impasse: The role of self–serving biases', *Journal of Economic Perspectives*, 11: 109–26.

Babcock L, Loewenstein G, Issacharoff S and Camerer C. (1995) 'Biased judgments of fairness in bargaining', *American Economic Review*, 85: 1337–43.

Banaji, M.R. (2001) 'Ordinary prejudice. Psychological Science Agenda', *American Psychological Association*, 14: 8–11.

Banaji, M.R. and Greenwald, A.G. (1995) 'Implicit gender stereotyping in judgments of fame', *Journal of Personality and Social Psychology*, 68: 181–98.

Banaji, M.R. and Bhaskar, R. (2000) 'Implicit stereotypes and memory: the bounded rationality of social beliefs', in Schacter, D.L. and Scarry E. (eds), *Memory, Brain, and Belief*. Cambridge, Massachusetts: Harvard University Press. pp. 139–75).

Banaji, M.R., Bazerman, M.H. and Chugh. D. (2003) 'How (un)ethical are you?', *Harvard Business Review*, December, 56–64.

Bargh, J.A. (1999) 'The cognitive monster: The case against the controllability of automatic stereotype effects', in S. Chaiken and Y. Trope (eds), *Dual–process Theories in Social Psychology*. New York: Guilford Press. pp. 361–82.

Barley, S. and Kunda, G. (1992) 'Design and devotion: Surges of rational and normative ideologies of control in managerial discourse', *Administrative Science Quarterly*, 37: 363–99.

Bartunek, J. (1984) 'Changing interpretive schemes and organizational restructuring: the example of a religious order', *Administrative Science Quarterly*, 29: 355–72.

Bass, B.M. (1990) *Bass and Stogdill's Handbook of Leadership*. New York: Free Press.

Bateman, T.S. and Zeithaml, C.P. (1989) 'The psychological context of strategic decisions: A test of relevance to practitioners', *Strategic Management Journal*, 10: 587–92.

Bazerman, M.H. (1984) 'The relevance of Kahneman and Tversky's concept of framing to organization behaviour', *Journal of Management*, 10: 333–43.

Bazerman, M.H. (1993) 'Fairness, social comparison, and irrationality', in J.K. Murnighan (ed.), *Social Psychology in Organizations: Advances in Theory and Research*. New jersey: Prentice Hall.

Bazerman, M.H. (2001) '*Judgment in managerial decision making*', fifth edition. New York: John Wiley and Sons.

Bazerman, M.H. and Carroll, J.S. (1987) 'Negotiator cognition', *Research in Organizational Behaviour*, 9: 247–88.

Bazerman, M.H. and Hoffman, A.J. (1999) 'Environmental destruction: individual, organizational, and institutional explanations', in R.I. Sutton and B.M. Staw (eds), *Research in Organizational Behaviour*, pp. 39–71, JAI Press, Volume 21.

Bazerman M.H. and Neale M.A. (1982) 'Improving negotiation effectiveness under final offer arbitration: The role of selection and training', *Journal of Applied Psychology* 67: 543–8.

Bazerman, M.H. and Neale, M.A. (1983) 'Heuristics in negotiation: Limitations to dispute resolution effectiveness', in M.H. Bazerman and R.J. Lewicki (eds), *Negotiating in Organizations*. Beverly Hills: Sage Publications, Inc.

Bazerman M.H., Curhan J.R. and Moore D.A. (2000) 'The death and rebirth of the social psychology of negotiation', in M. Clark and G. Fletcher (eds), *Blackwell Handbook of Social Psychology*. 279–369 Cambridge, MA: Blackwell.

Bazerman, M.H., Gillespie, J. and Moore, D. (1999) 'Our mind as a barrier to wiser agreements', *American Behavioural Scientist*, 42: 1254–76.

Bazerman, M.H., Giuliano, T. and Appelman, A. (1984) 'Escalation in individual and group decision making', *Organizational Behaviour and Human Performance*, 33: 141–52.

Bazerman, M.H., Loewenstein, G. and Moore, D.A. (2000), Why good accountants do bad audits, *Harvard Business Review*, November, 1–6.

Bazerman, M.H., Magliozzi, T. and Neale, M.A. (1985) 'The acquisition of an integrative response in a competitive market', *Organizational Behaviour and Human Performance*, 34, 294–313.

Bazerman M.H., Tenbrunsel A.E. and Wade-Benzoni K.A. (1998) 'Negotiating with yourself and losing: Understanding and managing competing internal preferences', *Academy of Management* Review, 23: 225–41.

Bell, D.E., Raiffa, H. and Tversky, A. (1988) *Decision Making: Descriptive, Normative, and Prescriptive Interactions*. Cambridge: Cambridge University Press.

Bettman, J.R. and Weitz, B.A. (1983) 'Attributions in the board room: Causal reasoning in corporate annual reports', *Administrative Science Quarterly*, 28: 165–83.

Berger, P. and Luckman, T. (1967) *The Social Construction of Reality*. New York: Doubleday.

Bies, R. J., Tripp, T. M., and Neale, M. A. (1993) 'Procedural fairness, framing and profit seeking: Perceived legitimacy of market exploitation.' *Journal of Behavioral Decision Making*, 6, 243–256.

Bigley, G. and Wiersma, M. (2002) 'New CEOs and corporate strategic refocusing: How experience as heir apparent influences the use of power', *Administrative Science Quarterly*, 47: 707–27.

Blair, I. (2002) 'The malleability of automatic stereotyping and prejudice', *Personality and Social Psychology Review*, 6: 242–61.

Blair, I., Ma, J. and Lenton, A. (2001) 'Imagining stereotypes away: The moderation of automatic stereotypes through mental imagery', *Journal of Personality and Social Psychology*, 81: 828–41.

Bless, H., Bohner, G., Schwarz, N. and Strack, F. (1990) 'Mood and persuasion: A cognitive response analysis', *Personality and Social Psychology Bulletin*, 16: 311–45.

Blount, S., Bazerman, M.H. and Neale, M.A. (1995) 'Alternative models of negotiated outcomes and the nontraditional utility concerns that limit their predictability', *Research on Negotiation in Organizations*, 5: 95–116.

Blount, S. and Janicik, G. (2001) 'When plans change: Examining how people evaluate timing changes in work organizations.' *Academy of Management Review*, 26: 566–585.

Boeker, W. (1997) 'Strategic change: The influence of management characteristics and organizational growth', *Academy of Management Journal*, 40: 152–70.

Brewer, M.B. and Kramer, R.D. (1985) 'The psychology of intergroup attitudes and behaviour', *Annual Review of Psychology*, 36: 219–43.

Brief, A.P. and Aldag, R.J. (1981) 'The self in work organizations: A conceptual review', *Academy of Management Review*, 6: 75–88.

Brief, A. and Weiss, H. (2002) 'Organizational behaviour: Affect in the workplace', *Annual Review of Psychology*, 53: 279–307.

Brief, A.P., Butcher, A.H. and Roberson, L. (1995) 'Cookies, disposition, and job attitudes: The effects of positive mood-inducing events and negative affectivity on job satisfaction in a field experiment', *Organizational Behaviour and Human Decision Processes*, 62: 55–62.

Burt, R. (1992) *Structural Holes: The Social Structure of Competition.* Cambridge, MA: Harvard Press.

Busenitz, L. and Barney, J. (1997) 'Differences between entrepreneurs and managers in large organizations: Biases and heuristics in strategic decision-making', *Journal of Business Venturing*, 12: 9–30.

Camerer C. and Loewenstein G. (1993) 'Information, fairness, and efficiency in bargaining. In psychological perspectives on justice', in B.A. Mellers, J. Baron (eds) Boston: Cambridge Univ. Press. pp. 155–81.

Caruso, E.M., Epley, N. and Bazerman, M. (in press) 'The good, the bad, and the ugly of perspective taking in groups', in E Mannix, M.A Neale and A.E Tenbrunsel (eds), *Research on Managing Groups and Teams, Vol. 9.* London: Elsevier.

Chaganti, R. and Sambharya, R. (1987) 'Strategic orientation and characteristics of upper management', *Strategic Management Journal*, 8: 393–401.

Chaiken, S., Liberman, A., and Eagly, A.H. (1989) 'Heuristic and systematic information processing within and beyond the persuasion context', in J. Uleman and J. Bargh (eds), *Unintended Thought.* New York: Guilford. pp. 212–52.

Cohen, W. and Levinthal, D. (1990) 'Absorptive capacity: A new perspective on learning and innovation', *Administrative Science Quarterly*, 35: 128–52.

Chen, S. and Ybarra, O. (2000) 'Power and person perception', unpublished data, University of Michigan.

Chugh, D., Lane, K. and Banaji, M. (2004) Implicit attitudes and negotiations, ongoing data collection, Harvard Business School, Cambridge, MA.

Corner, P.D., Kinicki, A.J. and Keats, B.W. (1994) 'Integrating organizational and individual information processing perspectives on choice', *Organizational Science*, 5: 294–308.

Cummings, L.L. (1982) 'Organizational behaviour', *Annual Review of Psychology*, 33: 541–79.

Curhan, J.R., Gerber, L., Neale, M.A. and Ross, L. (2004) 'Dynamic valuation: Preference change in the context of face-to-face negotiations', *Journal of Experimental Social Psychology*, 40: 142–51.

Cyert, R. and March, J. (1963) *A Behavioural Theory of the Firm.* Englewood, CA: Prentice-Hall.

Daft, R.L. and Weick, K.E. (1984) 'Toward a model of organizations as interpretation systems', *Academy of Management Review*, 9: 284–95.

Daly, H. and Cobb, J. (1994) *For the Common Good.* Boston: Beacon Press.

Das, T.K., and Teng, Bing-Sheng. (1999) 'Managing risks in strategic alliances.' *The Academy of Management Executive*, November: 50–62.

Dasgupta, B. (2004) 'Implicit ingroup favouritism, outgroup favouritism, and their behavioural manifestations', *Social Justice Research*, 17: 143–169.

Dasgupta, N. and Greenwald, A.G. (2001) 'On the malleability of automatic attitudes: Combating automatic prejudice with images of admired and disliked individuals', *Journal of Personality and Social Psychology*, 81: 800–14.

Dawes, R.M. (1988) *Rational Choice in an Uncertain World.* New York: Harcourt, Brace and Jovanovich.

Day, D.V. and Lord, R.G. (1992) 'Expertise and problem categorization: The role of expert processing in organizational sense-making,' *Journal of Management Studies*, 29: 35–47.

Devine, P.G. (1989) 'Stereotypes and prejudice: Their automatic and controlled components', *Journal of Personality and Social Psychology*, 56: 1–13.

Devine, P.G., Plant, E.A., Amodio, D.M., Harmon-Jones, E. and Vance, S.L. (2002) 'Exploring the relationship between implicit and explicit race bias: The role of motivations to respond without prejudice', *Journal of Personality and Social Psychology*, 82: 835–848.

Diekmann K.A., Samuels S.M., Ross L., Bazerman M.H. (1997) 'Self-interest and fairness in problems of resource allocation: Allocators versus recipients', *Journal of Personality and Social Psychology*, 72: 1061–74.

Dijksterhuis, M., Van den Bosch, F. and Volberda, H. (1999) 'Where do new organizational forms come from?' Management logics as a source of coevolution, *Organization Science*, 10: 569–82.

Dill, W. (1958) 'Environment as an influence on managerial activity', *Administrative Science Quarterly*, 2: 409–43.

Dobbins, G.H. and Russell, J.M. (1986) 'Self-serving biases in leadership: A laboratory experiment', *Journal of Management*, 12: 475–83.

Dobbins, G.H., Pence, E.C., Orban, J.A. and Sgro, J.A. (1983) 'The effects of sex on the leader and sex of the subordinate on the use of organizational control policy', *Organizational Behaviour and Human Performance*, 32: 325–43.

Donnellon, A., Gray, B. and Bougon, M. (1986) 'Communication, meaning, and organized action', *Administrative Science Quarterly*, 31: 43–55.

Dovidio, J., Kawakami, K. and Gaernter, S. (2002) 'Implicit and explicit prejudice and interracial interactions', *Journal of Personality and Social Psychology*, 82: 62–8.

Dovidio, J., Kawakami, K., Johnson, C., Johnson, B. and Howard, A. (1997) 'On the nature of prejudice: Automatic and controlled processes', *Journal of Experimental Social Psychology*, 33: 510–40.

Duhaime, I.D. and Schwenk, C.R. (1985) 'Conjectures on cognitive simplification in acquisition and divestment decision making', *Academy of Management Review*, 10: 287–95.

Dutton, J.E. and Jackson, S.E. (1987) 'Categorizing strategic issues: Links to organizational action', *Academy of Management Review*, 12: 76–90.

Eastman, W. and Bailey, J. (1998) 'Mediating the fact–value antimony: Patterns in managerial and legal rhetoric, 1890–1900', *Organization Science*, 9: 232–45.

Eden, D. and Levitan, U. (1975) 'Implicit leadership theory as a determinant of the factor structure underlying supervisory behaviour scales', *Journal of Applied Psychology*, 60: 736–41.

Einhorn, H.J. and Hogarth, R.M. (1978) 'Confidence in judgment: Persistence illusion of validity', *Psychological Review*, 85: 395–416.

Eisenhardt, K.M. and Zbaracki, M.J. (1992) 'Strategic decision making', *Strategic Management Journal*, 13: 17–37.

El Sawy, O. and Pauchant, T. (1988) 'Triggers, templates, and twitches in the tracking of emerging strategic issues', *Strategic Management Journal*, 9: 455–74.

Engle, E.M. and Lord, R.G. (1997) 'Implicit theories, self–schemas, and leader–member exchange', *Academy of Management Journal*, 40: 988–1010.

Epley, N. and Caruso, E. (2004) *Egocentric Ethics. Social Justice Research*, 17: 171–187.

Fazio, R.H. and Olson, M.A. (2003) 'Implicit measures in social cognition research: Their meaning and use', *Annual Review of Psychology*, 54: 297–327.

Fazio, R.H., Jackson, J.R., Dunton, B.C. and Williams, C.J. (1995) 'Variability in automatic activation as an unobtrusive measure of racial attitudes: A bona fide pipeline?', *Journal of Personality and Social Psychology*, 69: 1013–27.

Fiol, M. (1994) 'Consensus, diversity, and learning in organizations', *Organization Science*, 5: 403–20.

Fiol, M. (2002) 'Intraorganizational cognition and interpretation', in J. Baum (ed.), *Companion to Organizations*. Oxford, UK: Blackwell. pp. 119–37.

Fiske, S.T. (1993) 'Social cognition and social perception', *Annual Review of Psychology*, 44: 155–94.

Fiske, S.T. and Taylor, S.F. (1991) *Social Cognition*, 2nd edition. New York: McGraw-Hill, Inc.

Fligstein, N. (1991) 'The structural transformation of American industry: An institutional account of the causes of diversification in the largest firms', in W. Powell and P. DiMaggio (ed.), *The New Institutionalism*. Chicago: University of Chicago Press. pp. 311–36.

Fried, Y., Levi, A.S., Ben David, H.A. and Tiegs, R.B. (1999) 'Inflation of subordinates performance ratings: main and interactive effects of rater negative affectivity, documentation of work behaviour and appraisal visibility', *Journal of Organizational Behaviour*, 20: 431–44.

Friedland R. and Alford, R. (1991) 'Bringing society back in: Symbols, practices, and institutional contradictions', in W. Powell and P. DiMaggio (eds), *The New Institutionalism in Organizational Analysis*. Chicago: University of Chicago Press pp. 232–263.

Galinsky, A., Gruenfeld, D.H. and Magee, J. (2003) 'From power to action', *Journal of Personality and Social Psychology*, 85: 453–66.

Galvin, T. (2002) 'Examining institutional change: Evidence from the founding dynamics of US health care interest associations', *Academy of Management Journal*, 45: 673–96.

Garb, H.N. (1989) 'Clinical judgment, clinical training, and professional experience', *Psychological Bulletin*, 105: 387–96.

Gelfand, M. and Brett, J. (2003) *Negotiation and culture: Integrative perspectives for theory and research*, Palo Alto: Stanford University Press.

Gelfand, M.J. and Christakopoulou, S. (1999) 'Culture and negotiator vognition: Judgment accuracy and negotiation processes in individualistic and collectivist cultures', *Organizational Behaviour and Human Decision Processes*, 79: 248–69.

George, J.M. (1990) 'Personality, affect, and behaviour in groups', *Journal of Applied Psychology*, 76: 107–16.

George, J.M. and Bettenhausen, K. (1990) 'Understanding prosocial behaviour, sales performance and turnover: A group-level analysis in a service context', *Journal of Applied Psychology*, 75: 698–709.

George, J.M. and Brief, A.P. (1992) 'Personality and work related distress', in B. Schneider and B. Smith (eds), *Personality and Organizations*. Mahwah, NJ: Erlbaum.

Gigerenzer, G. (1991) 'From tools to theories: A heuristic of discovery in cognitive psychology', *Psychological Review*, 103: 650–64.

Gioia, D.A. and Sims, H.P. (1986) 'Cognition-behaviour connections: Attribution and verbal behaviour in leader-subordinate interactions', *Organizational Behaviour and Human Decision Processes*, 37: 197–229.

Gioia, D., Thomas, J., Clark, S. and Chittipeddi, K. (1994) 'Symbolism and strategic change in academia: The dynamics of sensemaking and influence', *Organization Science*, 5: 363–83.

Glynn, M. (1996) 'Innovative genius: A framework for relating individual and organizational intelligences to innovation', *Academy of Management Review*, 21(4): 1081–100.

Govindarajan, V. (1989) 'Implementing competitive strategies at the business unit level: Implications of matching managers to strategies', *Strategic Management Journal*, 10: 251–70.

Green, S.G. and Liden, R.C. (1980) 'Contextual and attributional influences on control decisions', *Journal of Applied Psychology*, 65: 453–58.

Green, S.G. and Mitchell, T.R. (1979) 'Attributional processes of leaders in leader-member interactions', *Organizational Behaviour and Human Performance*, 23: 429–58.

Greenhalgh, L. (1993) Discussant remarks, negotiating in organizations, Research in Negotiation Conference, Georgetown University, Washington, D.C.

Greenhalgh L. and Chapman D.I. (1995) 'Joint decision making: The inseparability of relationships and negotiation', in R.M. Kramer and D.M. Messick (eds), *Negotiation as a Social Process*. Thousand Oaks, CA: Sage.

Greenhalgh L. and Chapman D.I. (1998) Negotiator relationships: Construct measurement, and demonstration of their impact on the process and outcomes of negotiations. *Group Decision and Negotiation*, 7:465–489.

Greenwald, A. G., Klinger, M. R., & Schuh, E. S. (1995). 'Activation by marginally perceptible ("subliminal") stimuli: Dissociation of unconscious from conscious cognition.' *Journal of Experimental Psychology: General*, 124: 22–42.

Greenwald, A.G.and Nosek, B.A. (2001) 'Health of the implicit association test at age 3', Zeitschrift Fuer Experimentelle Psychologie, 48: 85–93.

Greenwald, A.G., Nosek, B.A. and Banaji, M.R. (2003) 'Understanding and using the Implicit Association Test: An improved scoring algorithm', *Journal of Personality and Social Psychology*. 85: 197–216.

Griffith, T.A., and Neale, M.A. (2001) Information processing in traditional, hybrid, and virtual teams: From nascent knowledge to transactive memory. In Staw, B.M. & Sutton, R. (eds). *Research in Organizational Behavior*, 23 Greenwich, CT: JAI Press, pp. 379–421.

Griffith, Terri, Sawyer, John E., and Neale, Margaret A. (2003). Information technology as a jealous mistress: Competition for knowledge between individuals and organizations, *Management Information System Quarterly*, 27: 265–287.

Gruenfeld, D.H. and Kim, P.H. (2003) Dissent and decision making on the US Supreme Court, working paper, Stanford University.

Gruenfeld, D.H, Galinsky, A., Magee, J. and Inesa, E. (2003) Power and perspective taking, working paper, Stanford University.

Gruenfeld, D.H., Mannix, E.A., Williams, K.Y. and Neale, M.A. (1996) 'Group composition and decision making: How member familiarity and information distribution affect process and performance', *Organizational Behaviour and Human Decision Processes*, 67: 1–15.

Gupta, A. (1984) 'Contingency linkages between strategy and general manager characteristics: a conceptual examination', *Academy of Management Review*, 9: 399–412.

Hall, R. and Lord, R. (1995) 'Multi-level information-processing explanations of followers' leadership perceptions', *Leadership Quarterly*, 6: 265–87.

Hambrick, D. and Mason, P. (1984) 'Upper echelons: The organization as a reflections of the top managers', *Academy of Management Review*, 9: 193–206.

Hamilton, D.L. and Sherman, J.W. (1993) 'Stereotypes', in R.S. Wyer, Jr. and K. Srull (eds), *Handbook of Social Cognition*, 2nd edition. Hillsdale, N.J.: Erlbaum.

Hamilton, D.L. and Sherman, S.J. (1989) 'Illusory correlations: Implications for stereotype theory and research', in D. Bar-Tal, C.F. Graumann, A.W. Kruglanski and W. Stroebe (eds), *Stereotypes and Prejudice: Changing Conceptions*. New York: Springer–Verlag.

Hannan, M.T. and Freeman, J. (1989) *Organizational Ecology*. Cambridge, MA: Harvard University Press.

Harvey, J.H., Ickes, W.J. and Kidd, R.F. (eds) (1976) *New Directions in Attribution Research*, vol. 1. New Jersey: Erlbaum.

Harvey, J.H., Ickes, W.J. and Kidd, R.F. (eds) (1978) *New Directions in Attribution Research*, vol. 2. New Jersey: Erlbaum.

Harvey, J.H., Ickes, W.J. and Kidd, R.F. (eds) (1981) *New Directions in Attribution Research*, vol. 3. New Jersey: Erlbaum.

Heider, F. (1944) 'Social perception and phenomenal causality', *Psychological Review*, 51: 358–74.

Heider, F. (1958) *The Psychology of Interpersonal Relations*. New York: Wiley.

Heneman, R.L., Greenberger, D.B. and Anonyuo, C. (1989) 'Attributions and exchanges: The effects of interpersonal factors on the diagnosis of employee performance', *Academy of Management Journal*, 32: 466–76.

Higgins, E.T. (1992) 'Social cognition as a social science: How social action creates meaning', in D.N. Ruble, P.R. Costanzo and M.E. Oliveri (eds) *The Social Psychology of Mental Health*. New York: The Guilford Press.

Higgins, E.T. and Bargh, J.A. (1987) 'Social cognition and social perception', *Annual Review of Psychology*, 38: 369–425.

Hitt, M., Ireland, R. and Palia, K. (1982) 'Industrial firms' grand strategy and functional importance: Moderating effects of technological uncertainty', *Academy of Management Journal*, 25: 265–98.

Hodgkinson, G. and Bown, N. (1999) 'Breaking the frame: An analysis of strategic cognition and decision making under uncertainty', *Strategic Management Journal*, 20: 977–85.

Hodgkinson, G., Maule, J., Bown, N., Pearman, A. and Glaister, K. (2002) 'Further reflections on the elimination of framing bias in strategic decision making', *Strategic Management Journal*, 23: 1069–76.

House, R.J. (1971) 'A path-goal theory of leadership', *Administrative Science Quarterly*, 16: 321–38.

Huber, V.L. and Neale, M.A. (1986) 'Effects of cognitive heuristics and goals on negotiator performance and subsequent goal setting', *Organizational Behaviour and Human Decision Processes*, 38: 342–65.

Huber, V.L., Neale, M.A. and Northcraft, G.B. (1987) 'Decision bias in personnel selection decisions', *Organizational Behaviour and Human Decision Processes*, 40: 136–47.

Huff, A. (1982) 'Industry Influences on strategy reformulation', *Strategic Management Journal*, 3: 119–31.

Ibarra, H. (1995) 'Race, opportunity, and diversity of social circles in managerial networks', *Academy of Management Journal*, 38: 673–703.

Ilgen, D.R. and Klein, H.J. (1988) 'Organization behaviour', *Annual Review of Psychology*, 40: 327–51.

Isabella, L. (1990) 'Evolving interpretations as a change unfolds: how managers construe key organizational events', *Academy of Management Journal*, 33: 7–41.

Isen, A. M. (1990). The influence of positive and negative affect on cognitive organization: Some implications for development. In N. Stein, B. Leventhal, & J. Trabasso (Eds.), *Psychological and biological approaches to emotion* (pp. 75–94). Hillsdale NJ: Lawrence Erlbaum Associates Inc.

Isen, A. and Baron, R. (1991) 'Positive affect as a factor in organizational behaviour', in B. Staw and L.L. Cummings (eds), *Research in Organizational Behaviour*, Volume 14. Greenwich, CT: JAI Press. pp. 1–53.

Jackson, S.E. & Dutton, J.E. (1988) 'Discerning threats and opportunities.' *Administrative Science Quarterly*, 33: 370–387.

James, L.R. and White, J.F. (1983) 'Cross-situational specificity in managers' perceptions of subordinate

performance, attributions, and leader behaviours', *Personnel Psychology*, 36: 809–56.

Janis, I.L. (1972) *Victims of Groupthink*. Boston: Houghton Mifflin.

Janis, I.L. and Mann, L. (1977) *Decision Making*. New York: Free Press.

Johns, G. (1999) 'A multi-level theory of self-serving behaviour in and by organizations', *Research In Organizational Behaviour*, 21: 1–38.

Jones, E.E. and Davis, K.E. (1965) 'From acts to dispositions: The attribution process in person perception', in L. Berkowitz (ed.), *Advances in Experimental Social Psychology*, vol 2. New York: Academic Press.

Kagel, J.H. and Levine, D. (1986) 'The winner's curse and public information in common value auctions', *American Economic Review*, 76: 894–920.

Kahneman, D. (1992) 'Concession points, anchors, norms, and mixed feelings', *Organizational Behaviour and Human Decision Processes*, 51: 296–312.

Kahneman, D. and Tversky, A. (1979) 'Prospect theory: An analysis of decision unrisk', Econometrica, 47: 263–91.

Kahneman, D., Knetsch, J., & Thaler, R. (1986) 'Fairness as a constraint on profit seeking: Entitlements in the market.' *American Economic Review*, 76: 728–41.

Katz, D. and Kahn, R.L. (1966) *The Social Psychology of Organizations*. New York: John Wiley.

Katz, D. and Kahn, R.L. (1978) *The Social Psychology of Organizations*, 2nd ed. New York: John Wiley.

Kelley, H.H. (1967) Attribution theory in social psychology, in D. Levine (ed.), *Nebraska Symposium on Motivation*, 15. Nebraska: University of Nebraska Press. pp. 192–240.

Kelley, H.H. and Michela, J.L. (1980) 'Attribution theory and research', *Annual Review of Psychology*, 31: 457–501.

Keltner, D., Gruenfeld, D.H. and Anderson, C. (2003) 'Power, approach and inhibition', *Psychological Review*, 110: 265–284.

Kerr, S. and Jermier, J.M. (1978) 'Substitutes for leadership: Their meaning and measurement', *Organizational Behaviour and Human Performance*, 22: 375–403.

Kiesler, S. and Sproull, L. (1982) 'Managerial responses to changing environments: Perspectives on problem sensing from social cognition', *Administrative Science Quarterly*, 27: 548–70.

King, A. and Zeithaml, C. (2003) 'Measuring organizational knowledge: A conceptual and methodological framework', *Strategic Management Journal*, 24: 763–72.

Knowlton, W.A. and Mitchell, T.R. (1980) 'Effects of causal attributions on a supervisor's evaluation of subordinate performance', *Journal of Applied Psychology*, 65: 459–66.

Kogut, B. and Kulatilaka, N. (2001) 'Capabilities as real options', *Organization Science*, 12(6): 744–58.

Kramer, R.M., Newton, E, Pommerenke, P.L. (1993) 'Self-enhancement biases and negotiator judgment: Effects of self-esteem and mood', *Organizational Behaviour and Human Decision Processes*, 56: 110–33.

Krabuanrat, K. and Phelps, R. (1998) 'Heuristics and rationality in strategic decision making: An exploratory study', *Journal Of Business Research*, 41: 83–93.

Lant, T. and Shapira, Z. (2000) *Organizational Cognition: Computation and Interpretation*. Mahwah, NJ: Lawrence Erlbaum Associates.

Lant, T. (2002) 'Organizational cognition and interpretation', in Joel Baum (ed.), *Companion to Organizations*. Oxford, UK: Blackwell. pp. 344–62.

Larson, J.R., Lingle, J.H. and Scerbo, M.M. (1984) 'The impact of performance cues on leader–behaviour ratings: The role of selective information availability and probabilistic response bias', *Organizational Behaviour and Human Performance*, 33: 323–49.

Lawler, E.E. (1971) *Pay and Organizational Effectiveness: A Psychological View*. New York: McGraw-Hill.

Lawrence, P.R. and Lorsch, J.W. (1967) *Organization and Environment: Managing Differentiation and Integration*. Boston: Graduate School of Business Administration, Harvard University.

Lee, F. and Tiedens, L.Z. (2001) 'Is it lonely at the top? The independence and interdependence of power holders', in Staw, B.M. and R.I. Sutton (eds), *Research in Organizational Behaviour*, 23. JAI: Amsterdam. pp. 43–92.

Levine, J.M., Resnick, L.B. and Higgins, E.T. (1993) 'Social foundations of cognition', *Annual Review of Psychology*, 44: 585–612.

Leyens, J.P. and Codol, J.P. (1988) Social cognition, in M. Hewstone, W. Stroebe, J.P. Codol, and G. Stephenson (eds), *Introduction to Social Psychology: A European Perspective*. Oxford, UK: Basil Blackwell Ltd.

Livingston, R. and Brewer, M. (2002) 'What are we really priming? Cue-based versus category-based processing of facial stimuli', *Journal of Personality and Social Psychology*, 82: 5–18.

Loewenstein, G., Issacharoff, S., Camerer, C. and Babcock, L. (1993) 'Self-serving assessments of fairness and pretrial bargaining', *Journal of Legal Studies*, 23: 135–59.

Lord, R. and Emrich, C. (2001) 'Thinking outside the box by looking inside the box: Extending the cognitive revolution in leadership research', *Leadership Quarterly*, 11: 551–79.

Lord, R.G., Brown, D.J. and Freiberg, S.J. (1999) 'Understanding the dynamics of leadership: The role of follower self-concepts in the leader/follower relationship', *Organizational Behaviour and Human Decision Processes*, 78: 167–203.

Lounsbury, M., Ventresca, M. and Hirsch, P. (2003) 'Social movements, field frames, and industry emergence: A cultural–political perspective on US recycling', *Socio-Economic Review*, 1: 71–104.

Lowery, B. S., Hardin, C. D. and Sinclair, S. (2001) 'Social influence effects on automatic racial prejudice', *Journal of Personality and Social Psychology*, 81: 842–55.

Lyles, M. and Schwenk, C. (1992) 'Top management, strategy, and organization knowledge structures', *Journal of Management Studies*, 29: 155–74.

Mackie, D.M. and Worth, L.T. (1991) 'Feeling good, but not thinking straight: The impact of positive mood on persuasion', in J.P. Forgas (ed.), *Emotion and Social Judgments*. New York: Wiley. pp. 201–20.

Mannix, E.A. and White, S.B. (1992) 'The impact of distributive uncertainty on coalition formation in organizations', *Organizational Behaviour and Human Decision Processes*, 51: 198–219.

March, J.G. (1999). *The pursuit of organizational intelligence*. Blackwell: London.

March, J.G. and Simon, H.A. (1958) *Organizations*. New York: Wiley.

Marks, G. and Miller, N. (1987) 'Ten years of research on the false-consensus effect: An empirical and theoretical review', *Psychological Bulletin*, 102: 72–90.

Markus, H. and Zajonc, R.B. (1985) 'The cognitive perspective in social psychology', in G. Lindzey and E. Aronson (eds), *The Handbook of Social Psychology*. New York: Random House.

Martin, L.L., Ward, D.W., Achee, J.W. and Wyer, R.S. (1993) 'Mood as input: People have to interpret the motivational implications of their moods', *Journal of Personality and Social Psychology*, 64: 317–26.

Martinko, M.J. and Gardner, W.L. (1987) 'The leader/member attribution process', *Academy of Management Review*, 12: 235–49.

Mason, R.O. and Mitroff, I.I. (1981) *Challenging Strategic Planning Assumptions*. New York: Wiley.

McConnell, A. R., and Leibold, J. M. (2001) 'Relations among the Implicit Association Test, explicit attitudes, and discriminatory behaviour', *Journal of Experimental Social Psychology*, 37: 435–42.

Medin, D.L. (1989) 'Concepts and conceptual structure', *American Psychologist*, 44: 1469–81.

Meindl, J.R. and Ehrlich, S.B. (1987) 'The romance of leadership and the evaluation of organizational performance', *Academy of Management Journal*, 30: 91–109.

Meindl, J.R., Ehrlich, S.B. and Dukerich, J.M. (1985) 'The romance of leadership', *Administrative Science Quarterly*, 30: 78–102.

Messick, D.M. (1999) 'Alternative logics for decision making in social settings', *Journal of Economic Behaviour and Organization*, 38: 11–28.

Messick, D.M. and Bazerman, M.H. (1996) 'Ethics for the 21st Century: A decision making approach', *Sloan Management Review*, 37: 9–22.

Messick, D.M. and Mackie, D.M. (1989) 'Intergroup relations', *Annual Review of Psychology*, 40: 45–81.

Messick, D.M. and Tenbrunsel, A.E. (eds) (1996) *Codes of Conduct: Behavioural Research into Business Ethics*. New York: Russell Sage.

Messick, D.M., Bloom, S., Boldizar, J.P. and Samuelson, C.D. (1985) 'Why we are fairer than others', *Journal of Experimental Social Psychology*, 21: 480–500.

Meyer, A. (1982) 'Adapting to environmental jolts', *Administrative Science Quarterly*, 27: 515–37.

Mezias, S. and Glynn, M. (1993) 'The three faces of corporate renewal: Institution, revolution, and evolution', *Strategic Management Journal*, 14: 77–101.

Milliken, F. (1990) 'Perceiving and interpreting environmental change: An examination of college administrators' interpretations of changing demographic', *Academy of Management Journal*, 33: 42–63.

Moore, D., G. Loewenstein, D. Cain, and M. H. Bazerman, eds. *Conflicts of Interest.* Cambridge University Press, 2005.

Moskowitz, G.B., Salomon, A.R. and Taylor, C.M. (2000) 'Preconsciously controlling stereotyping: Automatically activated egalitarian goals prevent the activation of stereotypes', *Social Cognition*, 18: 151–77.

Mowday, R.T. and Sutton, R.I. (1993) 'Organizational behaviour: Linking individuals and groups to organizational contexts', *Annual Review of Psychology*, 44: 195–229.

Mullen, B. and Johnson, C. (1990) 'Distinctiveness-based illusory correlations and stereotyping: A meta-analytical integration', *British Journal of Social Psychology*, 29: 11–28.

Murnighan, J.K. (1994) 'Game theory and organizational behaviour', in B.M. Staw and L.L. Cummings (eds), *Research in Organizational Behaviour*, vol. 16. Greenwich, CT: JAI. pp. 83–123.

Neale, M.A. (1984) 'The effect of negotiation and arbitration cost salience on bargainer behaviour: The role of arbitrator and constituency in negotiator judgment', *Organizational Behaviour and Human Performance*, 34: 97–111.

Neale, M.A. and Bazerman, M.H. (1985) 'The effects of framing and negotiator overconfidence on bargainer behaviour', *Academy of Management Journal*, 28: 34–49.

Neale, M.A. and Bazerman, M.H. (1991) *Cognition and Rationality in Negotiation.* Free Press: New York, NY.

Neale, M.A. and Northcraft, G.B. (1990) 'Experience, expertise, and decision bias in negotiation: The role of strategic conceptualization', in B. Sheppard, M. Bazerman, and R. Lewicki (eds), *Research in Bargaining and Negotiating in Organizations*, volume 2. Greenwich, CT: JAI Press.

Neely, J.H. (1977) 'Semantic priming and retrieval from lexical memory: Roles of inhibitionless spreading activation and limited–capacity attention', *Journal of Experimental Psychology: General*, 106: 226–54.

Nisbett, R. and Ross, L. (1980) *Human Inference: Strategies and Shortcomings of Social Judgment.* New Jersey: Prentice-Hall, Inc.

Northcraft, G.B. and Neale, M.A. (1986) 'Opportunity costs and the framing of resource allocation decisions', *Organizational Behaviour and Human Decision Processes*, 37: 348–56.

Northcraft, G.B. and Neale, M.A. (1987) 'Expert, amateurs, and real estate: An anchoring-and-adjustment perspective on property pricing decisions', *Organizational Behaviour and Human Decision Processes*, 39: 228–41.

Nutt, P. (1998) 'Framing strategic decisions', *Organization Science*, 9: 195–216.

Ocasio, W. (1994) 'Political dynamics and the circulation of power: CEO succession in US industrial corporations, 1960–1990', *Administrative Science Quarterly*, 39: 285–312.

O'Connor, K.M., deDreu, C.K.W., Schroth, H., Barry, B., Lituchy, T. and Bazerman, M.H. (2002) 'What we want to do versus what we think we should do', *Journal of Behavioural Decision Making*, 15: 403–18.

Ordonez, L. and Benson, L. (1997) 'Decisions under time pressure: How time constraint affects risky decision making', *Organizational Behaviour and Human Decision Processes*, 72: 121–40.

O'Reilly, C.A. (1991) *Organizational Behaviour: Where We Have Been, Where We're Going. Annual Review of Psychology.* Palo Alto, CA: Annual Reviews, Inc.

Papadakis, V. and Kaloghirou, Y. (1999) 'Strategic decision making: From crises to opportunity', *Business Strategy Review*, 10: 29–37.

Peppers, L. and Ryan, J. (1986) 'Discrepancies between actual and aspired self: A comparison of leaders and nonleaders', *Group and Organization Studies*, 11: 220–8.

Perdue, C. W., Gurtman, M. B. (1990). Evidence for the automaticity of ageism. *Journal of Experimental Social Psychology*, 26: 199–216.

Perry, E.L., Davis-Blake, A. and Kulik, C.T. (1994) 'Explaining gender-based selection: A synthesis of contextual and cognitive approaches', *Academy of Management Review*, 19: 786–820.

Pfeffer, J. (1981) 'Management as symbolic action: The creation and maintenance of organizational paradigms', *Research in Organizational Behaviour*, 3: 1–52.

Pfeffer, J. and Davis-Blake, A. (1986) 'Administrative succession and organizational performance. How administrator experience mediates the succession effect', *Academy of Management Journal*, 29: 72–83.

Phillips, J.S. (1984) 'The accuracy of leadership ratings: A cognitive categorization perspective', *Organizational Behaviour and Human Performance*, 33: 125–38.

Phillips, M. (1994) 'Industry mindsets: Exploring the cultures of two macro–organizational settings', *Organization Science*, 5: 384–402.

Phillips, K. W. (2003) 'The effects of categorically based expectations on minority influence: The importance of congruence', *Personality and Social Psychology Bulletin*, 29: 3–13.

Phillips, K.W., Mannix, E.A., Neale, M.A. and Gruenfeld, D.H. (2004) 'Diverse groups and information sharing: The effect of congruent ties', *Journal of Experimental Social Psychology*, 40: 497–510.

Pillutla, M.M. and Murnighan, J.K. (1996) 'Unfairness, anger, and spite: Emotional rejections of ultimatum offers', *Organizational Behaviour and Human Decision Processes*, 68: 208–24.

Pinkley, R.L. and Northcraft, G.B. (1994) 'Conflict frames of reference: Implications for dispute processes and outcomes', *Academy of Management Journal*, 37: 193–205.

Pondy, L.R. and Mitroff, I.I. (1979) 'Beyond open system models of organizations', *Research in Organizational Behaviour*, 1: 3–39.

Porac, J., Meindl, J. and Stubbart, C. (1996) 'Introduction', in J. Meindl, C. Stubbart and J. Porac (eds), *Cognition Within and Between Organizations*. London: Sage. pp. 1–14.

Porac, J., Ventresca, M. and Mishina, Y. (2002) 'Interorganizational cognition and interpretation', in J. Baum (ed.), *Companion to Organizations*. Oxford, UK: Blackwell. pp. 579–98.

Prahalad, C.K. and Bettis, R.A. (1986) 'The dominant logic: A new linkage between diversity and performance', *Strategic Management Journal*, 7: 485–501.

Rafaeli, A., Dutton, J., Harquail, C.V. and Mackie-Lewis, S. (1997) 'Navigating by attire: The use of dress by female administrative employees', *Academy of Management Journal*, 40: 9–45.

Raiffa, H. (1982) *The Art and Science of Negotiation*. Cambridge, MA: Belknap.

Raiffa, H., Richardson, J. and Metcalfe, D. (2002) *Negotiation Analysis*. Belknap Press, Cambridge, MA.

Regner, P. (2003) 'Strategy creation in the periphery: Inductive versus deductive strategy making', *Journal of Management Studies*, 40: 57–82.

Richeson, J. and Ambady, N. (2003) 'Effects of situational power on automatic racial prejudice', *Journal of Experimental Social Psychology*, 39: 177–83.

Roseman, I.J. (1984) 'Cognitive determinants of emotion: A structural theory', *Review of Personality and Social Psychology*, 5: 11–36.

Ross, L. (1977) 'The intuitive psychologist and his shortcomings: Distortions in the attribution process', in L. Berkowitz (ed.), *Advances in Experimental Social Psychology*, 35: 485–94.

Ross, M. and Fletcher, G.J.O. (1985) 'Attribution and social perception', in G. Lindzey and A. Aronson (eds), *The Handbook of Social Psychology*, 3rd ed. Reading MA: Addison-Wesley.

Rudman, L.A. and Glick, P. (2001) 'Prescriptive gender stereotypes and backlash toward agentic women', *Journal of Social Issues*, 57: 743–62.

Rudman, L. A. and Lee, M. R. (2002) 'Implicit and explicit consequences of exposure to violent and misogynous rap music', *Group Processes and Intergroup Relations*, 5, 133–50.

Salancik, G.R. and Meindl, J.R. (1984) 'Corporate attributions as strategic illusions of management control', *Administrative Science Quarterly*, 29: 238–54.

Samuelson, W.F. and Bazerman, M.H. (1985) 'The winner's curse in bilateral negotiations', in V. Smith (ed.), *Research in Experimental Economics*, 3. Greenwich, CT: JAI Press. pp. 105–37.

Schminke, M., Ambrose, M.L. and Noel, T.W. (1997) 'The effect of ethical frameworks on perceptions of organizational justice', *The Academy of Management Journal*, 40: 1190–207.

Schneider, D.J. (1991) 'Social cognition', *Annual Review of Psychology*, 42: 527–61.

Schwarz, N. (1990) 'Feelings as information: Information and motivational function of affective states', in E.T. Higgins and R.M. Sorrentino (eds), *Handbook of Motivation and Cognition*, vol. 2. New York: Guilford. pp. 527–61.

Schwarz, N., Bless, H. and Bohner, G. (1991) 'Mood and persuasion: Affective states influence the processing of persuasive communications', in M.P. Zanna (ed.), *Advances in Experimental Social Psychology*, 24. Orlando, FL: Academic Press. pp. 161–99.

Schwenk, C. (1986) 'Information, cognitive biases, and commitment to a course of action', *Academy of Management Review*, 11: 298–310.

Schwenk, C. (1988) 'The cognitive perspective on strategic decision-making', *Journal of Management Studies*, 25: 41–55.

Seeger, M. and Ulmer, R. (2002) 'A post-crisis discourse of renewal: The cases of Malden Mills and Cole Hardwoods', *Journal of Applied Communication Research*, 30: 126–42.

Senge, P. (1990) *The Fifth Discipline: The Art and Practice of the Learning Organization*. New York: Doubleday.

Shrivastava, P. and Mitroff, I.I. (1983) 'Frames of reference managers use: A study in applied sociology of knowledge', in R. Lamb (ed.), *Advances in Strategic Management*, vol 1. Connecticut: JAI Press.

Shrivastava, P. and Mitroff, I.I. (1984) 'Enhancing organizational research utilization: The role of decision makers' assumptions', *Academy of Management Review*, 9: 18–26.

Shrivastava, P. and Schneider, S. (1984) 'Organizational frames of reference', *Human Relations*, 37: 795–809.

Shamir, B., House, R.J. and Arthur, M.B. (1993) 'The motivational effects of charismatic leadership: A self-concept based theory', *Organization Science*, 4: 577–94.

Sherman, S.J., Judd, C.M. and Park, B. (1989) 'Social cognition', *Annual Review of Psychology*, 40: 281–326.

Simon, H. A. (1957) *Models of Man*. New York: Wiley.

Simons, T. (1993) 'Speech patterns and the concept of utility in cognitive maps: The case of integrative bargaining', *Academy of Management Journal*, 36: 139–56.

Simons, T. (2002) 'Behavioural integrity: The perceived alignment between managers' words and deeds as a research focus', *Organization Science*, 13: 18–35.

Sinaceur, M. and Tiedens, L. Z. (in press) 'Get mad and get more than even: The benefits of anger expressions in negotiations', *Journal of Experimental Social Psychology*.

Sinaceur, M., Thomas-Hunt, M., Neale, M. and O'Neill, O.A. (2004) 'Catalyzing individual accuracy in group decisions: The differential effect of minority members' perceived expertise on private vs public decision', working paper, Graduate School of Business, Stanford University.

Sinclair, R.C. and Mark, M.M. (1992) 'The influence of mood state on judgment and action: Effects on persuasion, categorization, social justice, person perception, and judgmental accuracy', in L.L. Martin and A. Tesser (eds), *The Construction of Social Judgments.* Hillsdale, NJ: Erlbaum. pp. 165–93.

Sinclair, S., Dunn, E., Lowery, B.S. and Colangelo, A. (2005) 'The relationship between parental racial attitudes and children's automatic prejudice', *Journal of Experimental Social Psychology*, 283–289.

Sinclair, S., Lowery, B. and Hardin, C. (in press) 'Social tuning of automatic ethnic attitudes: The role of relationship motivation', *Journal of Personality and Social Psychology.*

Smircich, L. and Stubbart, C. (1985) 'Strategic management in an enacted world', *Academy of Management Review*, 10: 724–36.

Smith, C.A. (1989) 'Dimensions of appraisal and physiological response in emotion', *Journal of Personality and Social Psychology*, 48: 813–838.

Smith, C.A. and Ellsworth, P.C. (1985) 'Patterns of cognitive appraisal in emotion', *Journal of Personality and Social Psychology*, 48: 813–38.

Smith, C.A. and Lazarus, R.S. (1993) 'Appraisal components, core relational themes, and the emotions', *Cognition and Emotion*, 7: 233–69.

Sniezek, J.A. and Henry, R.A. (1989) 'Accuracy and confidences in group judgment', *Organizational Behaviour and Human Decision Processes*, 43: 1–28.

Sparrow, P. (1999) 'Strategy and cognition: Understanding the role of management knowledge structures, organizational memory and information overload', *Creativity and Innovation Management*, 8(2): 140–8.

Spender, J. (1989) *Industry Recipes: An enquiry into the nature and sources of managerial judgment.* New York: Blackwell.

Starbuck, W. and Milliken, F. (1988) 'Challenger: Fine-tuning the odds until something breaks', *Journal of Management Studies*, 25: 319–40.

Stasser, G. and Titus, W. (1987) 'Effects of information load ad percentage of shared information on the dissemination of unshared information during group discussion', *Journal of Personality and Social Psychology*, 53: 81–93.

Stasser, G., Taylor, L. A. and Hanna, C. (1989) 'Information sampling in structured and unstructured discussion of three-and six-person groups', *Journal of Personality and Social Psychology*, 57: 67–78.

Staw, B.M. (1991) 'Dressing up like an organization: When psychological theories can explain organizational action', *Journal of Management*, 17: 805–19.

Staw, B.M. and Barsade, S. (1993) 'Affect and managerial performance: A test of the sadder-but-wiser vs. happier-and-smarter hypotheses', *Administrative Science Quarterly*, 38: 304–31.

Staw, B.M. and Sutton, R.I. (1992) 'Macro organizational psychology', in J.K. Murnighan (ed.), *Social Psychology in Organizations: Advances in Theory and Research.* New Jersey: Prentice Hall.

Staw, B.M., Bell, N.E. and Clausen, J.A. (1986) 'The dispositional approach to job attitudes: A lifetime longitudinal test', *Administrative Science Quarterly*, 31: 56–77.

Staw, B.M., McKechnie, P.I. and Puffer, S.M. (1983) 'The justification of organizational performance', *Administrative Science Quarterly*, 28: 582–600.

Staw, B.M., Sandelands, L.E. and Dutton, J.E. (1981) 'Threat-rigidity effects in organizational behaviour: A multilevel analysis', *Administrative Science Quarterly*, 26: 501–24.

Stroh, L. Northcraft, G. and Neale, M. (2001) *Organizational Behaviour: The Managerial Challenge.* Hillsdale, NJ: Erlbaum.

Tajfel, H. (1969) 'Cognitive aspects of prejudice', *Journal of Social Issues*, 25: 79–97.

Taylor, D.M. and Doria, J.R. (1981) 'Self-serving and group-serving bias in attribution', *Journal of Social Psychology*, 113: 201–11.

Taylor, S. E. (1989) *Positive Illusions.* New York: Basic Books.

Taylor, S. E. and Brown, J.D. (1988) 'Illusion and well-being: a social psychological perspective on mental health', *Psychological Bulletin.* 103: 193–210.

Tenbrunsel, A.E. (1998) 'Misrepresentation and expectations of misrepresentation in an ethical dilemma: The role of incentives and temptation', *Academy of Management Journal*, 41: 330–9.

Tenbrunsel, A.E. and Messick, D.M. (1999) 'Sanctioning systems, decision frames, and cooperation', *Administrative Science Quarterly*, 44: 684–707.

Tenbrunsel, A. E, Wade-Benzoni, K.A, Moag, J. and Bazerman, M.H. (1999) 'When is a friend not a friend? A look at relationships and partner selection in negotiations', *Organizational Behaviour and Human Decision Processes*, 252–83.

Tetlock P.E., Peterson R.S. and Lerner J.S. (1996) 'Revising the value pluralism model: Incorporating social content and context postulates', in C. Seligman, J. Olson, M. Zanna (eds), *Values: Eighth Annual Ontario Symposium on Personality and Social Psychology.* Hillsdale, NJ: Erlbaum.

Thomas, A.B. (1988) 'Does leadership make a difference to organizational performance?', *Administrative Science Quarterly*, 33: 338–400.

Thomas, J. and McDaniel, R. (1990) 'Interpreting strategic issues: Effects of strategy and information processing structure of top management teams', *Academy of Management Journal*, 3: 386–406.

Thomas, J., Clark, S. and Gioia, D. (1993) 'Strategic sense-making and organizational performance: Linkages among scanning, interpretation, action, and outcomes', *Academy of Management Journal*, 36: 239–70.

Thomas-Hunt, M.C., Ogden, T.Y. and Neale, M.A. (2003) 'Who's really sharing? Effect of social and expert status on knowledge exchange within groups', *Management Science*, 49: 464–77.

Thompson L. (1998) *The Mind and Heart of the Negotiator.* Upper Saddle River, NJ: Prentice Hall.

Thompson, L. and Fine, G. (1999) 'Socially shared cognition, affect, and behaviour: A review and integration', *Personality and Social Psychology Review*, 3: 278–302.

Thompson L.L. and Gonzalez, R. (1997) 'Environmental disputes: Competition for scarce resources and clashing of values', in M.H. Bazerman, D.M. Messick, A.E. Tenbrunsel and K.A. Wade-Benzoni (eds), *Environment, Ethics, and Behaviour*. San Francisco: New Lexington. pp. 75–104.

Thompson, L.L. and Hastie, R. (1990) 'Negotiator's perceptions of the negotiation process', in B.H. Sheppard, M.H. Bazerman and R.J. Lewicki (eds), *Research in Negotiation in Organizations*, vol 2. Greenwich, Conn: JAI Press.

Thompson, L.L. and Loewenstein, G.F. (1992) 'Egocentric interpretations of fairness and interpersonal conflict', *Organizational Behaviour and Human Decision Processes*, 51: 176–97.

Thornton, P. (2002) 'The rise of the corporation in a craft industry: Conflict and conformity in institutional logics', *Academy of Management Journal*, 45: 81–101.

Thornton, P. and Ocasio, W. (1999) 'Institutional logics and the historical contingency of power in organizations: Executive succession in the higher education publishing industry, 1958–1990', *American Journal of Sociology*, 105: 801–44.

Thornton, P. and Ventresca, M. (2002) 'Entrepreneurial strategies and boundary redefinition in organizations, markets, and industries: An actor–based method to study institutional change', in M. Ventresca and J. Porac (eds), *Constructing Industries and Markets*. UK: Elsevier Science.

Tiedens, L.Z. and Linton, S. (2001) 'Judgment under emotional certainty and uncertainty: The effects of specific emotions on information processing', *Journal of Personality and Social Psychology*, 81: 973–88.

Tjosvold, D. (1985) 'The effects of attribution and social context on superior's influence and interaction with low performing subordinates', *Personnel Psychology*, 38: 361–76.

Tushman, M., Virany, B. and Romanelli, E. (1985) 'Executive succession, strategic reorientations, and organizational evolution', *Technology in Society*, 7: 297–313.

Tversky, A. and Kahneman, D. (1973) 'Availability: A heuristic for judging frequency and probability', *Cognitive Psychology*, 5: 207–32.

Tversky, A. and Kahneman, D. (1974) 'Judgment under uncertainty: Heuristics and biases', *Science*, 185: 1124–31.

Tversky, A. and Kahneman, D. (1983) 'Extensional versus intuitive reasoning: The conjunction fallacy in probability judgment', *Psychological Review*, 90: 293–315.

Tversky, A. and Kahneman, D. (1986) 'Rational choice and the framing of decisions', *Journal of Business*, 59: 251–84.

Tyler, B. and Steensma, K. (1998) 'The effects of executives' experiences and perceptions on their assessment of potential', *Strategic Management Journal*, 19: 939–65.

Valley, K., Neale, M.A. and Mannix, E.A. (1995) 'Relationships in negotiations: The role of reputation, the shadow of the future, and interpersonal knowledge on the process and outcome of negotiations', in R.J. Bies, R. Lewicki and B. Sheppard (eds), *Research in Bargaining and Negotiation in Organizations*, vol 5. Greenwich, CT: JAI Press.

Valley, K.L., Moag, J. and Bazerman, M.H. (1998) 'A matter of trust: Effects of communication on the efficiency and distribution of outcomes', *Journal of Economic Behaviour in Organizations*, 34: 211–38.

Wade-Benzoni, K., Tenbrunsel, A. and Bazerman, M. (1996) 'Egocentric interpretations of fairness of asymmetric, environmental social dilemmas: Explaining harvesting behaviour and the role of communication', *Organizational Behaviour and Human Decision Processes*, 67: 111–26.

Walsh, J. (1988) 'Selectivity and selective perception: An investigation of managers' belief structures and information processing', *Academy of Management Review*, 31: 873–96.

Walsh, J. (1995) 'Managerial and organizational cognition: Notes from a trip down memory lane', *Organization Science*, 6: 280–321.

Walsh, J.P. and Ungson, G.R. (1991) 'Organizational memory', *Academy of Management Review*, 16: 57–91.

Weick, K. (1990) 'Cognitive processes in organizations', in L.L. Cummings and B. Staw (eds), *Information and Cognition in Organizations*. Greenwich, CT: JAI Press, pp. 287–320.

Weick, K. (1995) *Sensemaking in Organizations*. London: Sage.

Weick, K. and Roberts, K. (1993) 'Collective mind in organizations: Heedful interrelating on flight decks', *Administrative Science Quarterly*, 38: 357–81.

Weick, K.E. (1969) *The Social Psychology of Organizing*. Massachusetts: Addison-Wesley.

Weick, K.E. (1979a) 'Cognitive processes in organizations', *Research in Organizational Behaviour*, 1: 41–74.

Weick, K.E. (1979b) *The Social Psychology of Organizing*. Massachusetts: Addison-Wesley.

Weick, K.E. (1992) 'Sensemaking in organizations: Small structures with large consequences', in J.K. Murnighan (ed.), *Social Psychology in Organizations: Advances in Theory and Research*. Englewood Cliffs, N.J.: Prentice-Hall, Inc.

Weiner, B. (1986) *An Attributional Theory of Motivation and Emotion*. New York: Springer-Verlag.

Westphal, J.D. and Zajac E.J. (1998) 'The symbolic management of stockholders: Corporate governance reforms and shareholder reactions.' *Administrative Science Quarterly*, 43: 127–153.

Wexley, K.N. and Pulakos, E.D. (1983) 'The effects of perceptual congruence and sex on subordinates' performance appraisals of their managers', *Academy of Management Journal*, 26: 666–76.

White, H.C. and Bassford, G.L. (1978) Achieving results: leadership style and small-group effectiveness. Medical Recorrd News, 49, 87–88 and 90–92.

White, S.B and Neale, M.A. (1994) 'The role of negotiator aspiration and settlement expectancies on bargaining outcomes', *Organizational Behaviour and Human Decision Processes*, 57: 303–17.

Whyte, G. (1991) 'Diffusion of responsibility: Effects on the escalation tendency', *Journal of Applied Psychology*, 76: 408–15.

Wiersma, M. and Bantel, K. (1992) 'Top management team demography and corporate strategic change', *Academy of Management Journal*, 35: 91–121.

Wittenbaum, G. M. and Stasser, G. (1996) 'Management of information in small groups', in J.L. Nye and A.M. Brower (eds), *What's Social About Social Cognition? Social Cognition Research in Small Groups*. Thousand Oaks, CA: Sage Publications.

Wittenbrink, B., Judd, C. M. and Park, B. (2001) 'Spontaneous prejudice in context: Variability in automatically activated attitudes', *Journal of Personality and Social Psychology*, 81: 815–27.

Wright, G. and Goodwin, P. (2002) 'Eliminating a framing bias by using simple instructions to 'think harder' and respondents with managerial experience: Comment on 'breaking the frame'', *Strategic Management Journal*, 23(11): 1059–67.

Zajac, E.J. and Bazerman, M.H. (1991) 'Blind spots in industry and competitor analysis: Implications of inter-firm (mis)perceptions for strategic decisions', *Academy of Management Review*, 16: 37–56.

Zuckerman, M. (1979) 'Attribution of success and failure revisited, or: The motivational bias is alive and well in attribution theory', *Journal of Personality*, 47: 245–87.

2.4 Diverse Identities in Organizations

STELLA M. NKOMO AND MARCUS M. STEWART

Introduction

When the first edition of this handbook was written, diversity was a nascent topic in organization studies. Most attention had come from practitioners interested in how to 'manage diversity' in light of the forecasted changes in the demographic composition of the US workforce (Johnston and Packer 1987; Thomas 1989; Johnston 1991; Loden and Rosener 1991; Morrison 1992). At the time, scholarly attention to diversity was rather sparse (Jackson et al. 1992; Cox 1993; Watson et al. 1993). In the first edition of this handbook, Nkomo and Cox (1996) pointed out six ways in which the study of diversity could be advanced. The good news is that a substantial body of academic research on diversity has appeared since the first edition of this handbook. At the same time, the interest in diversity has spread beyond US borders to other areas of the world (e.g. D'Netto and Sohal 1999; Glastra 2000; Lorbiecki and Jack 2000; Nyambegera 2002). In Europe, the influx of immigrant workers coupled with falling birth rates of native populations have resulted in employers defining managing diversity as a significant challenge (Point and Singh 2003).

The bad news is that, while some of the issues identified by Nkomo and Cox (1996) have been addressed, there is still much to do about diversity, despite efforts to extend existing frameworks and the emergence of post-modern and critical theory perspectives on diversity. The increased volume of work has not brought agreement on the very meaning of diversity. All of this makes the task of reviewing the field cumbersome. As Ragins and Gonzalez (2003) note, any attempt to summarize the field places one on a slippery slope. However, it is somewhat clear that diversity refers to identities based on membership in social and demographic groups and how differences in identities affect social relations in organizations. We define diversity as a mixture of people with different group identities within the same social system. Thus, our treatment of diversity in this chapter is grounded in the notion of diverse group identities and their meaning within the context of organizations.

Faced with the challenge of writing about a construct that is presented as appearing out of nowhere, we begin by tracing the evolution and history of the concept within the broader frame of modernist approaches to organization and contemporary post-modernist projects (Clegg 1990; Martin 1992; Smircich and Calás 1999). This history sheds light on when and why the topic has become important as well as illuminating why diversity research has taken its particular direction. Next, we review the literature on diversity in organizations with particular attention to understanding what happens when groups with different identities come together in an organization. For each theory/body of work, we used the following five questions as a lens for our review: How is diversity defined? How is diversity measured? From whose standpoint is diversity defined? What is the level of analysis? What are the effects of diversity in organizations? We conclude with a number of dilemmas and problematic issues that remain despite the increased scholarly attention to diversity in organizations.

History of the Study of Diversity in Organizations

The term 'diversity' has a rather short history if we merely focus on its recent emergence in the organization studies literature. However, a closer reading of the organization studies literature and related sociological texts reveal many of the issues subsumed under diversity have been previously addressed in one form or another. The obvious beginning point for tracing the evolution of 'diversity' is to examine dominant assumptions and theories during the early development of management thought. In the early conceptualizations of organizations found in the work of Fayol, Taylor, Barnard, Mayo and others, the notion of diversity is evident by its omission. The universalizing tendencies of these approaches ignored the idea of diverse group identities. Organizations and employees were void of race, ethnicity, gender, age, sexuality and other social identities (Martin 1992; Burrell 1994). These modernist projects were about the elimination of difference and the rationalization out of existence of less rational forms of life (Clegg 1990: 29).

The influence of the classical tradition of sociology is evident in early ideas about organizations. At the beginning of the 20th century, it was quite common to regard the social system as a machine with its members interacting with one another in defined ways (Morgan 1986). Early management proponents advocated bureaucratization as the ideal form of organization. Social relations were depersonalized as organizations were constructed in ways that would eliminate difference.

While Mayo, Follett and other proponents of the human relations school of management recognized that workers were social beings, diversity in the identities of these social beings in terms of race, gender, ethnicity, age or sexual orientation were not part of that realization. While data relevant to gender, age and ethnicity were reported throughout the famous Hawthorne research, their effects did not enter into the final conceptual analysis (Roethlisberger and Dickson 1939). The pioneering work of sociologists like Dollard (1937) and Hughes (1946) on issues of race, ethnic and class differences dating back almost to when the discipline gained prominence in the US also did not find its way into the conceptualization of social relations in organizations. For example, Hughes' (1946) small-scale study of race relations in industry demonstrated how race affected individual and group dynamics on the factory floor. Hughes showed how race and gender affected patterns of established labour-management relations, informal seniority among employees, and group control of individual productivity (Banton 1998). For instance, he found that black female workers were not admitted to the friendship cliques of white women workers. And because they were not fully accepted into the group, they were not subjected to the same level of 'group pressure'. Hence, their productivity patterns did not conform to established output norms. Ironically, Hughes work led to the 'race problem' being perceived as a problem of group conflict (Banton 1998).

Large-scale attention to issues of diversity (e.g. race and gender) in organizations had its origins in the passage of legislation requiring equal opportunity for women and racial minorities that grew out of the upheavals of the 1960s in the US and certain parts of Western Europe. When organization theorists turned their attention to these issues, in particular racial and ethnic diversity, much of the research relied upon work growing out of a structural-functionalist framework dominated by the process of assimilation of those perceived as different (Nkomo 1992). The research took two trajectories. One trajectory focused on prejudice-reduction strategies. The other centred on responses to the requirements of equal employment opportunity. One of the major strategies of diversity work today, prejudice-reduction training or diversity awareness training has its genesis in this first trajectory. The roots of this training which was known as Race Awareness Training or RAT began in the late 1960s in the US after the famous Kerner Commission Report defined racism in the US as a white problem institutionalized in major societal institutions. Forms of this type of training cropped up in other countries including Britain after the passage of 1976 Race Relations Act (Katz 1978; Sivanandan 1985). Within the management field efforts emerged from human relations training and appeared under the rubric of intergroup or minority group relations (e.g. Blalock 1967; Fromkin and Sherwood 1976).

The second trajectory focused on organizational responses to equal employment legislation. Organizational responses were centred upon creating equal employment opportunities for groups excluded on the basis of race, ethnicity, gender, national origin and age. Emphasis was on recruitment and the development of affirmative action plans that would facilitate legal compliance. Research on issues relevant to diversity during this period was dominated by a search for objective evidence of discrimination in various human resource management and organizational processes or in documenting differences between majority group members and minority group members and differences between men and women.

Scholars like Litvin (2000), Lorbiecki and Jack (2000) and Kelly and Dobbin (1998) argue that what is today known as 'diversity management' is a repackaging of equal employment opportunity to make it more acceptable to white males. Litvin (2000) points out how diversity management in its attempt to make equal employment opportunity more palatable to white males may not actually deliver change as the social structures which perpetuate long-standing inequities are left intact. During the period of equal employment emphasis through Title VII in the US, diversity was mainly a legal imposition to deal with inequality and was not framed as a competitive, strategic issue for organizations as it is positioned today. In the early 1980s, the Reagan Administration curtailed enforcement of Title VII and Affirmative Action. However, according to Kelly and Dobbin (1998), EEO/AA specialists primarily in the US retheorized anti-discrimination and affirmative action practices as diversity management. Using Selznick's (1957) institutional theory, they demonstrate how EEO/AA managers downplayed legal compliance and emphasized the goal of increasing profits by expanding diversity in the workforce and customer base.[1] An article by Thomas (1990) published in *Harvard Business Review* frames this transition from affirmative action to affirming diversity as the need to move 'beyond race and gender'. Indeed much of the positivist research on diversity in organizations today focuses on demonstrating the business case for diversity and its benefits to work group functioning and the bottom line (e.g. Richard 2000; Richard et al. 2004).

Literature Review

Given the review of the history of diversity, we turn now to the extant research and theory on diversity in organizations. Social identity theory, embedded intergroup theory, organization demography and the research on racioethnicity[2] and gender have been the dominant theoretical paradigms utilized by organizational scholars to understand diversity in organizations. However, postmodern and critical theory views of diversity have emerged that present a very different conceptualization and approach to diversity in organizations.

Social Identity Theory

We defined diversity as a mixture of people with different group identities within the same social system. As noted in the first edition of the handbook,

one of the most prominent intergroup theories informing us about group identities in organizations has been social identity theory (SIT) (Ashforth and Mael 1989). Today, SIT continues to be one of the theories scholars utilize to examine diversity in organizations. SIT is a cognitive theory which holds that individuals tend to classify themselves and others into social categories and that these classifications have a significant effect on human interactions. Principally, Tajfel and Turner did the foundational work on SIT in the field of social psychology (Tajfel 1972; Turner 1975; Tajfel and Turner 1979). A number of issues pointed out in the earlier chapter are now being addressed in the current research. Nkomo and Cox (1996) identified an apparent disconnect between the definition of the process of social identification, 'the process of locating oneself or another person within a system of social categorizations' (Turner 1982: 18) and social identity, the sum total of the social identifications a person uses to define him or herself. The first definition acknowledges the categorization of a focal person by other people, while the latter does not. SIT theorists have advanced the conceptualization of identity to: (1) identify specific contextual influences on identification processes (evoking salience and content); (2) identify the influence of two-way or reciprocal identification processes between organizational/workgroup members; and (3) address more fully the notion that members of any given social group or category vary in the extent to which identity group membership is a central and salient aspect of their overall self concept.

In her model of communicative interactions in culturally diverse workgroups, Larkey (1996) utilized Cox's (1991) continuum of organizational types, from monolithic organizations, which are homogeneous with few minority employees, and where formal policy alone is utilized to incorporate diversity, to multicultural organizations, where the integration of minority employees and perspectives is ideal. Larkey (1996) predicted categorization or specification (individuating) processes as a function of the organizational culture within which workgroups were embedded. For example, monolithic organizational and workgroup types were theorized to make salient identity group boundaries, with negative and divisive norms resulting among workgroup members. Multicultural workgroup orientations were theorized to produce specification, where individual group members are perceived and assessed based on their personal attributes and characteristics, rather than stereotypes generally attributed to their relevant social groups (e.g. race, gender). Specification and its influence on group and organization culture were to result in more inclusive norms among workgroup members.

Garcia-Prieto et al. (2003) recently utilized SIT to propose a dynamic model of diversity, conflict and emotion in teams. Garcia-Prieto et al. (2003: 420) emphasize the 'subjectivity and flexibility of team members' multiple social identities', and expand upon the notion of diversity being experienced as multiple social identities when in workgroups. Diversity is considered not only as objective and stable differences between group members, but also as idiosyncratic within each team member as a function of his/her multiple social identities, with identity salience driven by the context and issue at hand. The resulting model addresses motivational and contextual conditions that enhance social identity salience. Individuals' social identification and influence of others' reactions and expectations of the target are included in the model, as are contextual factors such as intergroup competition, faultlines and ongoing within-group interaction. The authors provide a comprehensive discussion of SIT processes from identity salience to resulting appraisals of group issues, through resulting emotions and subjective experiences of conflict theorized to drive behaviour in workgroup contexts. A significant contribution of their framework is the clear explication of the 'link between the diversity of people's group membership and their cognitive appraisals of an issue' (Garcia-Prieto et al. 2003: 433), which indicates whether diversity may be beneficial or detrimental to team outcomes.

Hogg and Terry (2000) provided an integration of SIT and its extension, self-categorization theory. Self-categorization theory is used to explicitly describe the process by which aspects of one's self-concept (i.e. social identities) translate into context-related cognition and behaviour. These authors provide a comprehensive discussion of identity, categorization and specific outcomes of interest to organizations including cohesion, deviance and leadership. The basis for Hogg and Terry's (2000: 123) conceptualization of identification processes is the depersonalization of the self and the internalizing of group prototypes – 'fuzzy sets that capture the context-dependent features of group membership, often in the forms of exemplary members'. To the

extent that they identify with, value or want to be accepted by the group, individuals internalize and attempt to conform to these prototypes. These prototypes also serve to maximize similarities within and differences between groups satisfying individuals' identity-based needs for self-enhancement and uncertainty reduction. Mutual influence between majority and minority group members was theorized to be a function of the extent to which individuals fit organizational and workgroup prototypes. Accordingly, minority members can potentially face difficulty because of the lack of fit between their identity group memberships and organizational prototypes for roles such as leadership, which are often white and male.

Much of the research reviewed above follows the traditional notion in diversity research conducted via SIT, suggesting that diverse identities give rise to the salience of group boundaries. Thus, the predominant solution to overcome resulting dysfunctional workgroup dynamics is the re-establishing of these group boundaries to incorporate larger, superordinate groups. The ameliorating process in this theory and practice is the reduction of personal or 'non-work' related identities, and the replacement of these identities with collective identities or prototypes deemed more organizationally relevant or functional. Ironically, this suppression of perhaps valued aspects of group members' identities may result in dysfunctional outcomes such as a loss of the diversity in perspective that is theorized to be the primary value added aspect of group and organizational diversity. In addition, minority members may experience a lack of perceived value and thus decreased organizational or workgroup attachment because important aspects of the self-concept (social group identities) are perceived as not welcome or accepted. A perhaps more optimistic and progressive line of theorizing is emerging in SIT research suggesting that, in fact, the expressing of individuals' unique qualities, including aspects of themselves directly related to diverse identities such as race and gender, may lead to increased acceptance by workgroup members, and increased satisfaction and contributions on the part of both minority and majority members.

For example, building on the work of Brewer and Gardner (1996), and incorporating consideration of the nature of organizational factors (policies, task structure) on identification processes, Brickson (2000) extended SIT's traditional consideration of personal (individual) and collective (group) identities to include a third conceptualization, relational identity. While personal and collective identities are associated with the primary motivation to enhance an individual's own or group well being, a relational orientation or identity is associated with the motivation to enhance the well being of one's relationship partner. Brickson argues that efforts to design work that enhances or facilitates relational efforts via task and reward structure, wherein individuals' focus or motivation is the 'other's benefit', can overcome the inherent limitations in both personal and collective identities. This is important where personal and/or group boundaries persist and elicit competitive or in-group/out-group conceptualizations and behaviour. Examples of relation-oriented task and reward structures include mentoring and providing emotional and professional support for the development of colleagues. Brickson theorizes that, because meaningful relationships are particularly powerful at improving intergroup relations under the particular condition that sub-group (e.g., minority) identities do remain visible, for both majority and minority organizational members, the social cognitive complexity afforded by a relational orientation means individuals' valued identities can remain evident without becoming the cognitive focus of interaction. Brickson (2000: 90) states 'Although diversity in and of itself typically enhances organizational inputs, organizations will not truly benefit from a diverse membership unless sufficient communication, trust and openness enable minority individuals to feel comfortable expressing their unique opinions and perspectives'.

This aspect of Brickson's theorizing is in contrast to other treatments of SIT, where individuating and perhaps valued personal identities are to be suppressed in favour of superordinate group or collective identities. Indeed, Brickson draws parallels with relational identification processes and Thomas and Ely's (1996; cf. Ely and Thomas 2001) organizational diversity perspective, the learning and integration paradigm.

Despite Brickson's attempts to bring a macro perspective to SIT, the diversity research using SIT theory is still overwhelmingly dominated by a micro perspective (Ragins and Gonzalez 2003; cf. Garcia-Prieto et al. 2003, for an exception). While social identity offers ways to gain a broad understanding of diversity effects, it does not thoroughly address

the question of the specific content of socially marked identity categories. It also does not address the organization structures and systems. Social identity theory cannot fully account for the saturated significance of race, gender, class and sexual orientation so deeply rooted in history and social experience in the US and other countries as well. SIT assumes that groups categorized by socially marked differences will experience similar effects as nominally constituted groups. Therefore, empirical research examining the influence of SIT in organizations as it relates cultural diversity (e.g. race, gender) has lagged behind theory, though some research has emerged. For example, Davidson and Friedman (1998) examined black and white managers' reactions to a scenario in which a black employee appears to be taken advantage of (his idea stolen) by his white manager. A race main effect was observed such that black managers perceived greater injustice in the scenario than white managers. Davidson and Friedman also observed a 'persistent injustice' effect, such that among black managers, those with relatively high racial identity persisted in their conclusions of injustice even as additional information (a social account) designed to ameliorate the concerns of mistreatment was provided, whereas those with relatively low racial identity perceived less injustice when provided with additional information (a social account). In another study, Kim and Gelfand (2003) found that, regardless of race (black or white), individuals with higher levels of ethnic identity made more positive inferences about organizations and had greater job pursuit intentions when recruited with a brochure that made specific reference to organizational diversity initiatives. Via SIT, Lewis and Sherman (2003) found more complex implications of identity group membership and patterns of in- and out-group favouritism and denigration in the context of hiring decisions.

Embedded Intergroup Relations Theory

Like SIT, embedded intergroup relations theory falls under the general rubric of intergroup perspectives. However, Alderfer and Smith (1982) proposed a theory of embedded intergroup relations for organizations, which explicitly integrates identity-group membership and group membership resulting from organizational categorization. Their theory posits that two types of groups exist within organizations: identity groups – groups whose members share some common biological characteristic (e.g. sex), equivalent historical experiences, are subjected to similar social forces, and thus have relatively consonant world views; and organization groups – groups whose members share common organizational positions and participate in equivalent work experiences, resulting in relatively consonant world views. While there is little choice about physical membership in identity groups, members may feel more or less identified (psychologically attached) with their various identity groups.

Although identity group membership precedes organization group membership, identity and organization group memberships are frequently highly related. Certain organization groups tend to be populated by members of particular identity groups. For example, executive management in organizations in the US and other industrialized countries tend to be concentrated with older white males. According to embedded intergroup relations theory, individuals and organizations are constantly attempting to manage potential conflicts arising from the interface between identity groups and organizational group membership. How tensions are managed depends on several factors, the most important of which is how the groups are embedded within the organization. Embeddedness can be congruent, wherein power relations among groups at one level are reinforced by power relations at the suprasystem and subsystem level, or incongruent, where power relations are not consistent with suprasystem dynamics (Alderfer 1987).

Alderfer and his colleagues (Alderfer et al. 1980; Alderfer and Smith 1982; Alderfer 1987) used embedded intergroup theory primarily to study white women and racial minorities in predominantly white male organizations. Organizational diversity researchers have recently extended Alderfer and colleagues' seminal work in this area (cf. Brief et al. 2005; Sacco and Schmitt 2005). In a qualitative study of three large service-oriented organizations, Ely and Thomas (2001: cf. Thomas and Ely 1996) considered the embedded nature of workgroups in organizations as they sought to determine the conditions under which workgroup diversity yielded positive, negative or neutral outcomes. Their research identified three primary organization and workgroup orientations or 'diversity paradigms' toward diversity, each with different implications

for organizational and workgroup functioning. While all three paradigms served to diversify organizations, the paradigm adopted had significant implications for sustained effective integration and utilization of diverse identities and perspectives. The 'discrimination and fairness' paradigm is based primarily on creating diversity and equality among organizational members via human resources policies such as affirmative action, sensitivity training and formal mentoring programmes. Under this paradigm, minority members are expected to assimilate and organizational members are trained and encouraged to take a 'colour-blind' perspective to establish the principle that demographic differences do not matter.

In contrast, organizations operating under the 'access and legitimacy' paradigm seek explicitly to draw on or exploit the nature of employees' demographic differences to gain access and legitimacy with diverse markets. This is also commonly referred to as the business case for diversity. Organizational structures that typify this paradigm include special divisions or business units largely comprised of female or minority employees dedicated to the service of emerging niche/minority markets. Finally, organizations operating under the 'integration and learning' paradigm seek to incorporate diversity throughout the organization, vertically and horizontally, inclusive of the nature of the organizations' approach to processes, strategy and work. The model that emerged from Ely and Thomas' study clearly specified organizations' or workgroups' diversity paradigm as a moderator of the relationship between workgroup diversity and outcomes. The nature of decision-making power and reciprocal influence not only between minority and majority members, but also between workgroups and the suprasystem within which they are embedded (diversity paradigm), were theorized to be key mechanisms in determining the success of organizations in effectively managing diversity to achieve sustained competitive advantage.

The Diversity Research Network (DRN) has also contributed to embedded intergroup relations theory with empirical studies of several large multinational corporations (Kochan et al. 2003; Jackson and Joshi 2003). These studies explicitly set out to identify and measure contextual factors such as organizational culture, business strategy, human resources policies and practices, workforce stability, task structure and organizational resources and constraints that moderate the influence of diversity on performance. In a partial test of this model with the DRN, Ely and Thomas (Kochan et al. 2003; study 2) found empirical support for the positive influence of the 'learning and fairness' paradigm. Also via the DRN, Jackson and Joshi (2003) examined the interactive effects between demographic diversity (age, sex and tenure) at multiple organizational levels. Their results clearly indicate that the effects of workgroup composition become weaker as additional elements of the social context (i.e. demographic make up of local management, demographic make up of regional/district management) are included as predictors of team performance, emphasizing the influence of the organizational/social context in which workgroups are embedded.

The significance of embedded intergroup theory for understanding identity is its attention to the effects of diverse identities within a larger organizational context. The identity of individuals in organizations is said to be determined not only by organizational categorization but also by identity group membership. It recognizes that individuals don't leave their racial, gender or ethnic identities at the door when they enter an organization. Embedded intergroup theory also suggests that identity group categorization will always be relevant in an organization context.

Demography

Demography research refers to the study of 'the causes and consequences of the composition or distribution of specific demographic attributes of employees in an organization' (Tsui et al. 1995: 4). Research in demography has extended from the initial work on organizational demography, which focused on the macro level of analysis (cf. Pfeffer 1983; Tsui et al. 1995), to include the group and relational levels of analyses. Group demography research examines group processes and outcomes as a function of group composition along various dimensions of diversity, including demographics and non-visible characteristics such as personality. Relational demography research focuses on individuals' demographic similarity to a given group, assessing each members' similarity by taking into account the demographic characteristics of others in the group. Riordan (2000: 134) suggests this 'cross-level theory' aspect of relational demography, wherein the individual is examined within the context of the group 'differentiates it from other types of compositional demography research'. Even though organization demography has been used as a theoretical base for diversity research, some proponents view it as being different from the study of diversity. Tsui and Gutek (1999) argue that demography research focuses on the effect of demographic distributions on everyone, not only on minorities, which is the focus of diversity research. They further argue that diversity research has a policy and practice orientation while demography scholars emphasize understanding and explanation. Nevertheless, it is one of the paradigms used to study diversity. Demography research increasingly discusses dimensions of diversity in terms of 'visible' or 'surface-level' variables, such as race, gender, age and other readily identifiable traits, and 'non-visible' or 'deep-level' variables such as attitudes and personality, which are typically only recognized over time (e.g. Pelled 1996; Harrison et al. 1998).

Group and relational demography have emerged as perhaps the dominant paradigm for the empirical study of group and organizational diversity in recent years. Our study of this work also suggests that, despite a relatively small number of studies that have considered characteristics such as personality and skill (e.g. Boone et al. 2005; Van der Vegt and Van de Vliert 2005) group identity is generally treated as a nominal scale variable which signifies social categories based on physical or work history characteristics, rather than a function of the meaning and significance individuals place on a given identity (Cox 1993). Thus, a limitation of demography research is the predominant measurement of social identity as a nominal rather than continuous variable (cf. Jackson et al. 2003).

Some research in relational and group demography is moving toward more socially constructed operationalizations of identity, however. Riordan's (2000) analyses of extant demography research pointed out that theoretical arguments drawn from SIT and similarity attraction theory that comprise much of the foundation of demography research refer specifically to perceptions of, not actual, demographic (dis) similarity as the primary mechanism driving individuals' reactions to diversity in workgroups. Riordan's review of empirical results found that the amount of variance accounted for by studies assessing actual demographic (dis) similarity was relatively small (range of $R^2 = 0.01–0.19$). Research utilizing both actual and perceived measures of demographic (dis) similarity increased the amount of variance accounted for significantly (e.g. from 0.01–0.58). Harrison et al.'s (2002) study of the changing effects of surface and deep level diversity over time on group functioning is a recent example of this theoretical argument. Harrison et al.'s study utilized concurrent measurement of actual and perceived (dis) similarity (cf. Maurer et al. 2003). In addition to the potential increase in the variance explained in empirical studies, perceptual measures of relative demographic status are more consistent with and representative of the notion of diverse identities as socially constructed, and may represent significant potential for advancing future research in group and organizational demography.

Demography researchers have established that minority and majority status in diverse workgroups is not experienced equivalently across sex, race or age, among other dimensions of diversity. Both Chattopadhyay (1999) and Riordan (2000) observed that there is strong theoretical and empirical support for the need to incorporate asymmetrical predictions for the effects of relative demographic similarity in demography research. Early demography work by Tsui et al. (1992) also supports this contention. They found that white male employees reported adverse reactions to increasing minority representation in workgroups, while women and racial minorities did not. Chattopadhyay (1999) reasoned that organization-specific power dynamics, and expectations with regard to the make-up of the most favourably perceived (powerful) workgroups drive these effects. In organizations where males comprise the most powerful or prestigious positions such as executive management, organizational members likely perceive workgroups predominantly composed of males more favourably. Therefore, women who are placed in these groups may likely perceive these assignments positively from a career and organization-specific perspective.

However, in this same organization, males placed in groups comprised largely of women, or in groups where female representation is increasing, likely perceive these groups as lacking in power and status. Their placement in these groups is taken as a signal they are not on track to achieve greater power within the organization. Empirical tests of asymmetrical predictions have been mixed. For example, Chattopadhyay (1999) found support for asymmetrical hypotheses along the dimensions of race, and age, but not sex.

An advance in demography research tangentially related to the notion of asymmetrical dynamics, but that should similarly inform context-specific hypotheses, is the notion of group faultlines – which divide a workgroup's members on the basis of one or more attributes – developed by Lau and Murnighan (1998; 2005). For example, sex faultlines divide groups into relatively male and female subgroups. Group faultlines increase in strength as more attributes are highly correlated, reducing the number and increasing the homogeneity of the resulting subgroups. For example, a group composed of three young, white, male entry level auditors who had worked for a company for less than 1 year and three middle-aged, black female vice presidents who had been with the company for 20 years or more would have a strong faultline because all of the listed characteristics are perfectly correlated. Such perfect correlation facilitates social identification processes, which reinforce in-group and out-group boundary formation. According to Lau and Murnighan's (1998: 328) analyses, this should result in an increased likelihood of conflict over a wide array of issues with 'highly predictable memberships in two subgroups'. When potential subgroup members are similar in one attribute (i.e. race) but differ in others (i.e. age and sex), group members are less likely to expect similarity in attitudes, expectations and behavioural scripts, leading to weaker faultlines or subgroups. Several empirical studies have established analytical techniques and initial support for the faultline theory of group functioning (e.g. Thatcher et al. 2003; Shaw 2004; Lau and Murnighan 2005; Sawyer et al. 2006). Phillips and her colleagues (e.g., Phillips and Loyd forthcoming; Phillips et al. forthcoming) have similarly extended demography research to consider the interactive effects of both 'surface' level group membership diversity (e.g., ethnicity) and 'deep' level characteristics such as information or opinion diversity.

Recent demography research has followed calls to undertake a conscientious effort to examine intervening variables in demography models and empirical studies to lend increased explanatory power to, or open the 'black box' of, this field of research (e.g. Bacharach et al. 2005; Chatman and Spataro 2005; cf. Lawrence 1997). Among the process variables receiving theoretical and empirical attention have been norms such as conflict (e.g. Jehn et al. 1999; Pelled et al. 1999), co-operation (e.g. Chatman and

Flynn 2001), cohesion (e.g. Harrison et al. 1998), team empowerment (e.g. Kirkman et al. 2003) and task structure/orientation (e.g. Karakowsky and Siegel 1999). Other research has extended demography research to include the impact of time or group tenure on group norms such as cohesion and social integration (e.g. Harrison et al. 1998; 2002; Chatman and Flynn 2001). Focus on process variables should likely continue, as results have been equivocal, and demography research drawing on the groups literature (cf. Chatman and Flynn 2001) asserts that much of the influence of group diversity on performance outcomes is manifest through the types of norms that emerge in these groups.

In addition to process variables, the intervening influence of person variables on outcomes has also been examined in diverse groups (Roberts 2005). For example, Flynn et al. (2001) reasoned that impression formation efforts on the part of minority group members should influence the extent to which they were satisfied, socially integrated and ultimately performed in diverse groups. Results indeed demonstrated that the negative effect of being demographically different disappeared when impression formation, which was driven by extraversion and self-monitoring on the part of minority group members, was considered. Also arguing that reciprocal influence between group members drives outcomes in diverse workgroups, Polzer, Swann and colleagues (Polzer et al. 2001; Swann et al. 2004; cf. Roberts 2005) have extended research in group demography by establishing two important dynamics. Firstly, as per Flynn et al. (2001), group members are not passive in determining fellow group members' appraisals of them. Secondly, by achieving 'interpersonal congruence' – the degree to which group members see others in the group as others see themselves – group members can achieve harmonious and effective work processes and outcomes by expressing, rather than suppressing, the characteristics or identities that make them unique. This represents a departure from traditional notions of diversity management via the suppression of individual differences.

Commensurate with the proliferation of empirical research conducted under the demography paradigm, several reviews of the theoretical and empirical research on organizational demography have been published over the last 10 years (e.g. Tsui et al. 1995; Williams and O'Reilly 1998; Riordan 2000; Webber and Donahue 2001; cf. Ragins and Gonzalez 2003). Each of these reviews discusses the conflicting and confounding positive and negative effects of diversity

on work outcomes of interest to practitioners, sometimes referred to as the 'double-edged sword' of diversity (cf. Milliken and Martins 1996; Ragins and Gonzalez 2003). Heterogeneity (as compared to homogeneity in groups) has been found to reduce intra-group cohesiveness, psychological attachment or commitment to the workgroup, and member satisfaction (at least among white group members in US organizational contexts), and to increase turnover, while heterogeneity in certain contexts has been associated with increased workgroup creativity, decision-making quality and innovation (cf. Williams and O'Reilly 1998; Riordan 2000).

In general, based on recent empirical demography research, it appears that organizational majority members (i.e. whites in a predominantly white organization) exhibit aversive reactions to increasing group diversity, while minority members may not exhibit these negative reactions (e.g. Chattopadhyay 1999). However, minority members often still suffer from negative group norms such as exclusion from processes and discriminatory behaviour on the part of majority group members (cf. Larkey 1996; Riordan et al. 2005). Research also has established that over time, 'surface' level diversity such as age and race can become less influential with regard to some workgroup processes, while 'deeper' or attitudinal/personality-related forms of diversity can become more influential (e.g. Harrison et al. 1998; 2002; Chatman and Flynn 2001).

Research on Racioethnicity and Gender

The body of literature reviewed in this section does not constitute a theory per se, but research that has looked at two specific identity categories: race and gender. We review these two together, despite the fact that scholars have typically studied them independently of one another ignoring calls for recognizing the simultaneity of race, gender and class (Ferdman 1999; Bell and Nkomo 2001). Prior to the 1960s, little attention was paid to the study of race and gender in organizations. It is only after the passage of equal employment and anti-discrimination legislation in many countries that scholars turned their attention to these issues in organizations. The focus of much of this research has been to document differential treatment in organizations based on race and gender.

Less attention has been paid to age, religion, sexual orientation and physical ability. However, there is an emerging body of research on sexual orientation in organizations. This work has focused on discrimination in recruitment and selection processes, and on perceptions of discrimination and disclosure of sexuality among coworkers (e.g. Van Hoye and Lievens 2003; DeSouza and Solberg 2004). For example, Griffith and Hebl (2002) examined the influence of social-psychological variables such as self-acceptance and social identification in conjunction with contextual variables such as coworker reactions on disclosure behaviours. House (2004) also considered sexual orientation in the context of mainstream theoretical models of identity and career development such as Super's (1990) Archway Model. This qualitative study found that issues of identity and concerns for self-expression (e.g. questions such as 'In what career can I be myself?' p. 253) significantly influenced career choices and development among the women in the sample. Ragins and Cornwell (2001) found that perceived workplace discrimination partly mediated relationships between relevant employment legislation, organizational policies and perceived coworker/supervisor sexual orientation and employee disclosure, in addition to outcomes such as turnover intentions, organizational and career commitment and job satisfaction. Ragins et al. (2003) recently examined the influence of multiple group memeberships and relational demography on the organizational experiences of over 500 gay employees, 162 of whom were racial minorities. Results indicated that race and gender were unrelated to heterosexism. Lesbians and gay men were equally lilkely to disclose their sexuality at work, but gay employees of colour were less likely to disclose than whites. Relational demography was also found to intervene on heterosexism and employee experiences. Additional research on sexual orientation and other stigmas can be found in the work of Harris (1994); Maurer et al. (2003); Sanchez and Brock (1996); Shore et al. (2003); and Stone et al. (1992).

The bulk of research on racioethnicity in the US, in particular, has been on comparing blacks and whites. Scholars have also treated race and gender as objective, fixed properties of individuals that can be operationalized into measurable levels (e.g. 1 = white and 2 = black; 1 = male and 2 = female). Attention to racial identity, ethnic identity and/or gender identity are only now gaining a foothold in the literature (e.g. Ely 1995; Bell and Nkomo 2001; Kim and Gelfand 2003).

Researchers continue to focus their attention on two strands of research. One strand focuses on uncovering objective, quantifiable evidence of race and gender discrimination in organizational practices. Although results of these studies are mixed, taken as a whole they suggest that racial minorities and women face both access and treatment discrimination in organizations (e.g. Bowes-Sperry and O'Leary-Kelly 2005; Brett and Stroh 1997; Elvira and Zatzick 2002; Heilman and Chen 2005; Heilman and Haynes 2005; Stauffer and Buckley 2005; Ziegert and Hanges 2005; cf. Williams and O'Reilly 1998; Roth et al. 2002; 2003; Ragins and Gonzalez 2003). Emerging research has begun to examine organizationally relevant employee attitudes and reactions toward organizational and management practices designed to ameliorate discrimination including affirmative action (e.g. Parker et al. 1997; Slaughter et al. 2002). In one of the few direct comparisons of white and black individuals' responses to affirmative action selection procedures, Stewart and Shapiro (2000) found fundamental differences across race, with black individuals generally failing to exhibit anticipated negative responses (e.g. lowered self-esteem, decreased desire to lead, etc.) to affirmative action procedures.

A second strand focuses on racial and gender differences in a host of traditional organizational behaviour topics including job satisfaction, job attitudes and performance (e.g. Avery 2003). Despite a sizable quantity of work, the results are largely inconsistent, with little evidence of systematic differences between blacks and whites and men and women in behaviour. However, recent meta-analyses conducted by Roth et al. (2003) identified larger standardized ethnic group differences in performance than anticipated (cf. Kraiger and Ford 1985), and among objective measures more so than subjective measures across several indicators. These analyses also revealed that Hispanic-white standardized differences were generally smaller than black–white differences in several categories.

Despite a persistent gender wage gap, research has failed to find consistent evidence of performance differences (e.g. Roos and Gatta 1999; Tomaskovic-Devey and Skaggs 1999). Some research has found differences across sex, such as LePine and Van Dyne's (1998) finding that men engaged in more voice behaviour – constructive challenges to the status quo – than women, and consistent evidence of differences in tendencies to find Pygmalion and Galatea effects across sex (e.g. Eden 2003). Other research has failed to find differences across sex, including attitudes such as organizational commitment or propensity to quit between men and women (Bielby and Bielby 1998; Lyness and Judiesch 2001; cf. Stroh and Reilly 1999). However, evidence of the continued prevalence of negative outcomes associated with sex in organizations was reported by Ostroff and Atwater (2003: 734), who found that workgroups characterized by a majority of women depressed wages for those workgroups' managers, 'regardless of occupational or functional area or the gender of the manager'. There is also a significant body of work that has raised the question of whether women managers have different leadership styles compared to men (Butterfield and Grinnell 1999; Eagly and Carli 2003). Some researchers have suggested that women do not use hierarchical transactional styles but more transformational, participative styles (Bass and Avolio 1994). A recent meta analysis of the research on gender differences in transformational leadership behaviour suggests that the female advantage is statistically quite small (Eagly and Carli 2003). Despite a proliferation of studies focusing on gender differences, cumulatively it is difficult to make blanket statements about what systematically differentiates female managers from male managers in attitudes toward work, personality and behaviour.

The final strand of research (e.g. Greenhaus et al. 1990; Thomas 1990; 1993; Thomas and Gabarro 1999; Moving Forward 2000; Bell and Nkomo 2001; Burke and Nelson 2002; Gvozdeva and Gerchikov 2002) has focused on documenting the organizational and career experiences of black managers and women managers as a group. The literature is replete with studies documenting negative effects on the careers of racial minorities and white women, including tokenism; differential access to mentoring (Ragins and Cotton 1999; Thomas 2001); exclusion from organizational networks (Ibarra 1993); glass ceilings (Powell 1999; Wirth 2001); and other forms of restricted career mobility (Thomas and Gabarro 1999; Bell and Nkomo 2001).

In sum, this body of literature suggests that racioethnicity and gender are important forms of social differentiation shaping the way individuals experience organizations. Both bodies of research have suffered from narrow conceptualizations of these constructs, however. For the most part, the study of gender has equalled a focus on women and race has equaled the study of racial minorities.

Postmodern and Critical Perspectives on Diversity

The work discussed previously fits squarely within a positivist paradigm. Postmodern and critical theories

depart drastically from the ideas and notions about diverse identities previously discussed. Both postmodern and critical theory approaches are oriented, albeit in different ways, to questioning dominating practices, discourses and ideologies (Alvesson and Wilmot 1992; Alvesson and Deetz 2000). One of the common themes running through postmodern and critical theory perspectives on diversity is skepticism that it will produce real change in organizations. Postmodernist analyses of diversity begin with questioning the origins and basic assumptions of diversity (Cavanaugh 1997; Litvin 1997; 2000; Prasad et al. 1997). Attention is focused on the discourse of diversity, positioning it essentially as a generalized re-writing project to maintain the status quo and not as an effort to truly value diverse identities (Litvin 2000). Drawing upon institutional theory and critical theory, Cavanaugh (1997) argues that diversity management as it is presently conceptualized and practiced ends up affirming and reproducing social divisions in organizations with the aim of maintaining white male superiority and control of organizations. He argues that diversity side-steps issues of inequality, affirmative action and discrimination. Instead diversity discourse proposes a happy solution to resolving the messy problem of 'otherness' and heterogeneity in the labour force.

Postmodern and critical theories also question the tendency to essentialize gender, race and other categories of identity. For instance, there is a small but growing body of theoretical and empirical work in organizational studies challenging the idea of gender as an objective property of individuals (e.g. Cockburn 1991; Acker 1992; Mills and Tancred 1992; Wharton 1992; Calas and Smircich 1996; Alvesson and Biling 1997; Benschop 1998; Karakowsky and Siegel 1999; Maier 1999; Forbes 2002). Interest is on the subjective social and organizational meaning of gender. These scholars argue the reification of gender as 'women' has resulted in a general neglect of understanding gender relations and power in organizations. They argue that because gender has been largely treated as an objective property, little attention has been paid to the gendered nature of organizations or in understanding the social construction of gender. Mills and Tancred (1992) argue for a theoretical stance that recognizes that organizations are not spaces into which people enter but, rather, networks of relationships that are deeply gendered. This body of work suggests that the study of gender requires attention to meta-organizational understandings – organizational discourses – that shape the very gendered ways we conceive of organizations (Ely and

Meyerson 2000; Fletcher 2001). For example, Fletcher (2001) in a study of female engineers shows that emotional intelligence and relational behaviour, even when they are in line with stated organizational goals, are often viewed as inappropriate because they collide with powerful, gender linked images of good workers and successful organizations. Maier (1999: 71) explains that gendered processes and practices both 'reflect and reinforce prevailing conceptions of masculinity and femininity'.

Work by Collinson and Hearn (1996) and Cheng (1996) explicates the nature and practices of masculinity. Cheng (1996) uses the concept of hegemonic masculinity to describe the masculinist ethos that privileges what have traditionally been seen as natural male traits. Masculinity is not about males, however. According to Cheng (1996: xii), 'writing about masculinities need not be about the male sex. Masculinity can be and is performed by women. Women who are successful managers perform hegemonic masculinity'. For example, executive level women have reported that developing an interpersonal style 'comfortable for men', accepting more risky assignments, and meeting higher than normal performance expectations were critical to their success (Nelson and Burke 2000), indicating the gendered and masculine nature of their organizations, and the necessity of explicit recognition of this dynamic in order to succeed. Another example is Whitehead's (2001) study of women managers' ontological investment in the secure systems of a masculinist organizational culture. The recognition of the hegemonic masculinity of organizations raises the question of just how much 'diversity' can really flourish in organizations.

In a similar vein, Kersten (2000) argues that in spite of the dialogic and inclusive claims made by diversity management, its basic framework and methods serve to limit and repress productive dialogue on race rather than produce effective organizational change. In her analysis, diversity management fails to critically examine the racialized nature of organizations. Race is treated as something possessed by racial minorities and not a feature of organizations. Grimes (2001), along with other scholars (e.g. Ramsey 1994), suggests one way to unmask the racialized nature of organizations is to interrogate whiteness. According to Grimes (2001: 135) 'interrogating whiteness refers to an activity that involves critical reflection about whiteness and privilege and the implications of living in a race-centred society'. Interrogating whiteness in organizations means attending to the discourse, images and actions that institutionalize white privilege and domination. A consideration of whiteness challenges the hidden assumption that whites in organizations are raceless.

Other scholars demonstrate how racism is a regular feature of organizational practices and discourse. Van Djik (1987) offers an analysis of informal discourse about ethnic minorities and the way racism is reproduced through everyday talk. Essed's (1991) research on *everyday racism* illustrates the ways in which racialized practices are part of the fabric of daily organizational life. Recent studies report evidence that blacks experience everyday racism in US organizations (Bell and Nkomo 2001; Deitch et al. 2003). Bell and Nkomo (2001) found that everyday incidents of racism were so pervasive that the black women in their study talked of it as 'your normal kind', suggesting it is a regular feature of many organizations. Deitch et al. (2003) reported everyday racism was negatively associated with job satisfaction and physical well-being for blacks.

Finally, postmodernism takes a very different view of identity. It is conceptualized as a complex, multifaceted and transient construct. Identity cannot be measured nominally as an objective property of an individual. Hall (1992) emphasizes that identity is not stable or fixed but socially and historically constructed and subject to contradictions, revisions and change. The emphasis is on the contingent, fluid and uncertain character of identity. A postmodern understanding of identity in organizations focuses on the processes and experiences of identity rather than viewing it as a static and absolute position.

Still Much to Do About Diversity

As our literature review demonstrates, scholars have relied on multiple theoretical and research perspectives to understand diversity in organizations. Despite a proliferation of academic research in the last few years, we argue there is still much to do about diversity. While our review acknowledges the advances made since the first review, a number of dilemmas and contradictions still remain. This is not to say that all contradictions in a discipline must be resolved before it can move forward. We do believe, however, they are worth revisiting. Postmodern and critical theory perspectives offer fuel for greater reflection and provide a platform for raising the sobering question of: Where to from here?

First, scholars need to pay greater attention to understanding the origins of diversity and whether a distinction should be made between research on 'diversity' versus research on issues of race, gender, inequality and/or equal employment opportunity. Many of these issues are in danger of being subsumed by diversity or marginalized further as legitimate research issues (Linnehan and Konrad 1999). Another sign pointing to the need to carefully examine its origins is that managing diversity, deeply embedded in cultural assumptions of the US is fast becoming a globalizing vocabulary of difference. The construct is being applied in European, Australian and African contexts (e.g. Nyambegera 2002; Point and Singh 2003) despite scholarly work questioning its universalism. For example, Jones et al. (2000), using the example of Aotearoa/New Zealand, show that a diversity based on the demographics and dominant cultural assumptions of the US fails to address and may in fact obscure key local 'diversity issues'. They point to the inadequacy of demography-driven arguments for managing diversity in New Zealand, a country with a very different political and social history to the US.

What does diversity really address in organizations? is another way of thinking about this dilemma. The fact that diversity management exists along side inequality pushes us back to the ontological nature of diversity. The slippery slope for scholars doing diversity work is researching 'diversity', while simultaneously challenging its ontological status. Research demonstrating continued inequality and problems of racism, sexism, heterosexism and ageism in organizations raises the issue of whether diversity management is achieving its stated aim of valuing difference. Ironically, under the rubric of celebrating or valuing differences, diversity management often reproduces the very discourse that guarantees the status quo. A case in point is what occurred at Texaco, Inc. in the US. Texaco executives were making racist and discriminatory remarks and talking of obstructing the progress of a discrimination lawsuit even as the company had a 'model' diversity management programme in place. In an uncanny way, the Texaco incident makes the point that diversity management has nothing to do with discrimination or race and gender as some diversity proponents argue. Lorbiecki and Jack (2000) point to a similar incident in London. In response to a charge of institutionalized racism within the south London police force, police officials pointed to a diversity management programme

everyone had undergone. Critics of the police saw this as an indication that the diversity management programme had no discernible impact on the attitudes or racist practices of the police.

Secondly, we need to attend the labels we use in our work. Corollary to the points above is the categorization of diversity into primary and secondary dimensions or recently, deep-level diversity and surface-level diversity characteristics (e.g. Harrison et al. 1998). Race and gender are placed within the surface-level category whereas personality traits and values fall within deep-level diversity. The hypothesis is that over time deep-level diversity may be more important to team dynamics than surface-level diversity. Some scholars go so far as to extol the attention to deep level diversity 'as marking the start of a new time in research on work team diversity' (Harrison et al. 2002: 1029). There is real danger in reducing diversity to benign differences among people or reifying a form of modern racism and a discourse of colour blindness (Dovidio and Gaertner 1986; Dovidio et al. 1989). This is not to say that personality traits of team members should not be studied. People do have multiple identities and the recognition thereof is important. However, to imply one type of diversity is 'surface' while another is 'deep' overlooks the role of conflict, power, dominance and the history of how race, gender and other socially marked categories have been created and maintained. Positioning race and gender as surface diversity can also end up reducing them to biological constructs without any social meaning. Zanoni and Janssens (2003) interviewed 25 Flemish HR managers from a critical discourse analysis and rhetorical perspective. Their findings illustrate how power enters HR managers' local discourse of diversity. Zanoni and Janssens (2003) argue for the development of a non-essentialist reconceptualization of diversity that acknowledges power.

When diversity is seen as a condition of existence, the effects of practices of exclusion and discrimination that define some people and groups as different from what is taken to be the norm are overlooked. Organizational researchers seeking to extend our understanding of discrimination and attitudes toward various ameliorative organizational policies may draw on emerging research in social and political psychology using social dominance orientation (SDO), derived from social dominance theory. Social dominance orientation is 'the degree to which individuals desire and support a group-based hierarchy and the domination of "inferior" groups by "superior" groups' (Sidanius and Pratto 1999: 48). Specifically, SDO shows promise to inform organizational researchers interested in workplace discrimination and prejudice. Considerable research has associated high scores in SDO with greater prejudice and political conservatism, including opposition to affirmative action, while lower scores have been associated with more favourable attitudes towards women's and gay rights, and social programmes in general (Pratto et al. 1994; Jost and Thompson 2000; Federico and Sidanius 2002). A recent study by Aquino et al. (2005) found evidence that SDO was associated with negative stereotyping of a Black/African-American affirmative action beneficiary, and that these stereotypes determined performance perceptions.

More analysis is needed of the complex power relations in which gender and race are embedded. A case in point is the work of Collinson et al. (1990). In their study of 45 companies in five industries in the UK, they show how sex discrimination can be reproduced, rationalized and resisted by those in positions of domination and subordination within the recruitment and selection processes of the organization. Essed's (1991) work on everyday racism cited earlier also illuminates how organizational practices and policies produce and reproduce diverse identities, valuing some and devaluing others. At the same time, scholars need to recognize the intersectionality of race, gender and class in understanding inequality and exclusion in organizations. Despite calls for this type of analysis (e.g. Ferdman 1999; Bell and Nkomo 2001), there is a tendency to study gender or race, rarely both or both with class. The concept of intersectionality offered by black feminist theory underscores the point that everyone in organizations has race, gender and class (hooks 1984; Hill-Collins 1990; Glenn 1999). Black feminists also suggest that people are oppressed and social hierarchy is maintained by a number of other bases besides these three – including ethnicity, sexual orientation, age and physical ability. Categories of domination are relational concepts and gain meaning in relation to one another. Hence, differences among groups in organizations must be viewed as systematically related. Glenn (1999) proposes an integrative framework in which race and gender are defined as socially constructed relational concepts whose construction involves representation, micro-interaction and social structural processes in which power is a constitutive element. She argues that racialization and engendering take place at multiple levels in all social organizations. Scholars might also benefit from examining work in the field of critical race theory and postcolonial studies (e.g. Delgado 1995; Prasad 1997).

Thirdly, if identity in organizations is viewed as fluid rather than fixed, constantly in the process of being constructed and deconstructed as the social-political context changes, then greater attention should be paid to the processes of identification. Hall (1992) argues for seeing identity in the process of becoming rather than a state of being. He points out that identities are not pre-given but come into being within representation. This would suggest more work focusing on representation of diverse identities in organizations, specifying how representations create and sustain inequality in organizations. The study of representation requires attending to the symbols, language, rhetoric and images in organizations that convey racialized gender meanings and how these representations help to not only create inequality and exclusion but to maintain them (Glenn 1999). A simple example is the accepted use of the term 'women and minorities' in organizations. Although not explicitly stated, it has come to represent white women and all men and women who are non-white, even though the word 'white' does not appear as a prefix to women, and gender is not explicitly included in the minorities part of the phrase. This representation says a lot about how race and gender groups are constructed in organizations. Foremost, race and gender are positioned as mutually exclusive categories. Additionally, white males are a familiar group and therefore do not have to be labelled. They are neither racialized nor gendered. White men are not represented as a group but as individuals. It is those who do not fit the familiar representation of 'manager' who must be labelled. A similar analysis can be performed for sexual orientation and other socially marked categories.

Finally, the study of diversity is largely positioned as a normative project. The focus is on demonstrating why diversity is good for organizations or how diversity can be managed to eliminate the conflict that diversity brings. In other words, there is much focus on normalizing diversity. If diversity is a complex phenomenon, then perhaps we must live with multiple and contradictory effects in our research. The search for general laws for understanding diverse identities in organizations may be a difficult if not impossible task. We also need to explore the tension points between diversity and other areas of organization studies. For example, calls for valuing diversity clashes with prescriptions from work on organization culture that calls for universal values and norms as a way of building strong cultures to support attainment of competitive advantage. Wilmott (1993: 534) suggests 'cultural diversity is dissolved in the acid bath of corporate values'.

Conclusion

We have attempted to map the theoretical terrain for examining diverse identities in organizations. Our review suggests that understanding diverse identities in organizations has been pursued through a meta-theoretical approach. The present discussion is in line with other recent reviews of diversity that recognize its complexity and multiple orientations (Prasad et al. 2006). We have also tried to point to some of the continuing dilemmas. Perhaps it will be frustrating to some that we do not offer a single passageway out of these dilemmas. Instead, we feel at this juncture in the study of diversity that we pause to reflect upon the slippery slope of how we conceptualize and research diverse identities in organizations (Ragins and Gonzalez 2003). We also feel it is important that we reflect upon the strategies for change emanating from the perspectives that we use to study diversity. Perspectives rooted in social identity and demography largely suggest strategies of increasing contact between people with different identities (premised upon the contact hypothesis), manipulating demographic composition (e.g. cross-cutting job assignments) and changing cognitions. There is an overwhelming predilection for experimental control and highly generalizable theory, which we argue poses a barrier to research that might illuminate structural change strategies at the organizational level. Is micro-level change the aim? On the other hand, postmodern and critical theory perspectives imply far more radical approaches to changing organizations from structures of exclusion to inclusion. While both perspectives are highly skeptical about change emanating from positivist prescriptions, critical theorists see hope in attending to the social, historical and political context of diversity as a means of achieving inclusion and equality (Alvesson and Deetz 2000; Kersten 2000). However, postmodernists would be more comfortable with the very death of diversity, constantly destablizing and deconstructing its meaning (Alvesson and Deetz 2000).

Notes

1. Institutional theory (see Selznick 1957) posits that practices and routines become institutionalized when they are 'infused with value beyond the technical requirements at hand'. In his research, Selznick discovered that structures and practices survived even when they no longer achieved the goals for which they had been designed. Instead of changing their structures, organizations adopt new goals suited to existing structures.

2. We use the term 'racioethnicity' suggested by Cox (1990). He suggests that distinct classification of groups as racial or ethnic is often inappropriate because they imply a group is either phenotypically or culturally distinct from another, whereas it generally is both. The term racioethnic is used to indicate that groupings can be based on phenotype and/or culture.

References

Acker, J. (1992) 'Gendering organizational theory', in A. Mills and P. Tancred (eds), *Gendering organizational analysis*. Newbury Park, CA: Sage. pp. 248–60.

Alderfer, C.P. (1987) 'An intergroup perspective on group dynamics', in J. Lorsch (ed.), *Handbook of organizational behavior*. Englewood Cliffs, NJ: Prentice-Hall. pp 190–222.

Alderfer, C.P. and Smith, K.K. (1982) 'Studying intergroup relations embedded in organizations', *Administrative Science Quarterly*, 27: 35–65.

Alderfer, C.P., Alderfer, C.J., Tucker, L. and Tucker, R. (1980) 'Diagnosing race relations in management', *Journal of Applied Psychology*, 16: 135–66.

Alvesson, M. and Billing, Y.D. (1997) *Understanding gender and organization*. London: Sage.

Alvesson, M. and Deetz, S. (2000) *Doing critical management research*. London: Sage Publications.

Alvesson, M. and Wilmot, H. (1992) *Critical management studies*. London: Sage Publications.

Aquino, K., Stewart, M.M. and Reed II, A. (2005) 'How social dominance orientation and job status influence perceptions of African-American affirmative action beneficiaries', *Personnel Psychology*, 58: 703–44.

Ashforth, B.E. and Mael, F. (1989) 'Social identity theory and the organization', *Academy of Management Review*, 14: 20–39.

Avery, D.R. (2003) 'Reactions to diversity in recruitment advertising – are differences black and white?', *Journal of Applied Psychology*, 88(4): 672–79.

Bacharach, S.B., Bamberger, P.A. and Vashdi, D. (2005) 'Diversity and homophily at work: Supportive relations among White and African-American peers', *Academy of Management Journal*, 48: 619–44.

Banton, M. (1998) *Racial theories*. Cambridge: Cambridge University Press.

Bass, B.M. and Avolio, B.R. (1994) 'Shatter the glass ceiling: women may make better managers', *Human Resource Management*, 33: 549–60.

Bell, E. and Nkomo, S.M. (2001) *Our separate ways: Black and white women and the struggle for professional identity*. Boston: Harvard University Press.

Benschop, Y. (1998) 'Covered by equality: the gender subtext of organizations', *Organization Studies*, 19(5): 787–805.

Bielby, D. and Bielby, W. (1998) 'She works hard for the money: household responsibilities and the allocation of work effort', *American Journal of Sociology*, 93: 1031–59.

Blalock, H.M. (1967) *Toward a theory of minority group relations*. New York: Wiley.

Boone, C., Van Olffen, W. and van Witteloostuijn, A. (2005) 'Team locus-of-control composition, leadership structure, information acquisition, and financial performance: A business simulation study', *Academy of Management Journal*, 48: 889–909.

Bowes-Sperry, L. and O'Leary-Kelly, A.M. (2005) 'To act or not to act: The dilemma faced by sexual harassment observers', *Academy of Management Review*, 30: 288–306.

Brewer, M.B. and Gardner, W. (1996) 'Who is this "we"?: levels of collective identity and self-representations', *Journal of Personality and Social Psychology*, 71: 83–93.

Brickson, S. (2000) 'The impact of identity orientation on individual and organizational outcomes in diverse settings', *Academy of Management Review*, 25: 82–101.

Brief, A.P., Umphress, E.E., Dietz, J., Burrows, J.W., Butz, R.M. and Scholten, L. (2005) 'Community matters: Realistic group conflict theory and the impact of diversity', *Academy of Management Journal*, 48: 830–44.

Burke, R.J. and Nelson, D.L. (2002) *Advancing women's careers*. London: Blackwell Publishers.

Burrell, G. (1994) 'Modernism, postmodernism and organizational analysis 4: the contribution of Jurgen Habermas', *Organization Studies*, 15: 1–9.

Butterfield, D.A. and Grinnell, J.P. (1999) 'Re-viewing gender, leadership, and managerial behavior: do three decades of research tell us anything?', in G.N. Powell (ed.), *Handbook of gender and work*. Thousand Oaks, CA: Sage. pp. 224–38.

Calás, M. and Smircich, L. (1996) 'From "the woman's" point of view: feminist approaches to organization studies', in S. Clegg, C. Hardy and W. Nord (eds), *Handbook of Organization Studies*. London: Sage. pp. 218–59.

Cavanaugh, M.J. (1997) '(In)corporating the other? Managing the politics of workplace difference', in P. Prasad and A. Mills (eds), *Managing the organizational melting pot: dilemmas of workplace diversity*. Newbury: Sage. pp. 31–53.

Chatman, J.A. and Flynn, F.J. (2001) 'The influence of demographic heterogeneity on the emergence and consequences of cooperative norms in work teams', *Academy of Management Journal*, 44(5): 956–74.

Chatman, J.A. and Spataro, S.E. (2005) 'Using self-categorization theory to understand relational demography-based variations in people's responsiveness to organizational culture', *Academy of Management Journal*, 48: 321–31.

Chattopadhyay, P. (1999) 'Beyond direct and symmetrical effects: the influence of demographic dissimilarity on organizational citizenship behavior', *Academy of Management Journal*, 42(3): 273–87.

Cheng, C. (ed.) (1996) *Masculinites in organizations*. Newbury Park, CA: Sage.

Clegg, S. (1990) *Modern organization: Organization studies in the postmodern world*. London: Sage.

Cockburn C. (1991) *In the way of women: Men's resistance to sex equality in organizations*. Ithaca, NY: ILR Press.

Collinson, D.L. and Hearn, K.J. (eds) (1996) *Men as managers, managers as men: Critical perspectives on men, masculinities, and managements*. Thousand Oaks, CA: Sage Publications.

Collinson, D.L., Knights, D. and Collinson, M. (1990) *Managing to Discriminate*. London: Routledge.

Cox, T. Jr. (1990) 'Problems with doing research on race and ethnicity', *Journal of Applied Behavioral Science*, 26(1): 5–24.

Cox, T. (1991) 'The multicultural organization', *Academy of Management Executive*, 5: 34–47.

Cox, T. Jr. (1993) *Cultural Diversity in Organizations: Theory, Research, and Practice*. San Francisco, CA: Berrett-Koehler.

Davidson, M. and Friedman, R. (1998) 'When excuses don't work: the persistent injustice effect among Black managers', *Administrative Science Quarterly*, 43: 154–83.

DeSouza, E. and Solberg, J. (2004) 'Women's and men's reactions to man-to-man sexual harassment: does the sexual orientation of the victim matter?', *Sex Roles*, 50: 623–40.

Deitch, E.A., Barsky, A., Butz, R.M., Brief, A.P., Chan, S. and Bradey, J.C. (2003) 'Subtle yet significant: the existence and impact of everyday racial discrimination in the workplace', Unpublished manuscript.

Delgado, R. (ed.) (1995) *Critical race theory. The cutting edge*. Philadelphia, PA: Temple University Press.

D'Netto, B. and Sohal, A.S. (1999) 'Human resource practices and workforce diversity: an empirical assessment', *International Journal of Manpower*, 20: 530–48.

Dollard, J. (1937) *Caste and class in a southern town*. New York: Doubleday.

Dovidio, J.F. and Gaertner, S.L. (eds) (1986) *Prejudice, discrimination and racism*. San Diego, CA: Academic Press.

Dovidio, J.F., Mann, J.A. and Gaertner, S.L. (1989) 'Resistance to affirmative action: the implication of aversive racism', in F.A. Blanchard and F.J. Crosby (eds), *Affirmative action in Perspective*. New York: Springer-Verlag. pp. 83–102.

Eagly, A.H. and Carli, L.L. (2003) 'The female leadership advantage: an evaluation of the evidence', *Leadership Quarterly*, 14: 807–34.

Eden, D. (2003) 'Self-fulfilling prophecies in organizations', in J. Greenberg (ed.), *Organizational behavior: The state of the science*. Mahway, NJ: Lawrence Erlbaum Associates. p. 529.

Elvira, M.M. and Zatzick, C.D. (2002) 'Who's displaced first? The role of race in layoff decisions', *Industrial Relations*, 41: 329–61.

Ely, R.J. (1996) 'The power in demography: women's social constructions of gender identity at work', *Academy of Management Journal*, 38: 589–634.

Ely, R. and Meyerson, D. (2000) 'Advancing gender equity in organizations: the challenge and importance of maintaining a gender narrative', *Organization*, 7: 589–608.

Ely, R.J. and Thomas, D.A. (2001) 'Cultural diversity at work: the effects of diversity perspectives of work group processes and outcomes', *Administrative Science Quarterly*, 46: 229–73.

Essed, P. (1991) *Everyday Racism*. Thousand Oaks, CA: Sage.

Federico, C.M. and Sidanius, J. (2002) 'Racism, ideology, and affirmative action revisited: the antecedents and consequences of "principled objections" to affirmative action', *Journal of Personality and Social Psychology*, 82: 488–502.

Ferdman, B. (1999) 'The color and culture of gender in organizations: attending to race and ethnicity', in G. Powell (ed.), *Handbook of Gender & Work*. Thousand Oaks, CA: Sage Publications. pp. 17–36.

Fletcher, J.K. (2001) *Disappearing acts: Gender, power, and relational practice at work*. Cambridge, MA: MIT Press.

Flynn, F.J., Chatman, J.A. and Spataro, S.E. (2001) 'Getting to know you: the influence of personality on impressions and performance of demographically different people in organizations', *Administrative Science Quarterly*, 46: 414–42.

Forbes, D. (2002) 'Internalized masculinity and women's discourse: a critical analysis of the (re) production of masculinity in organizations', *Communication Quarterly*, 50: 269–91.

Fromkin, H.L. and Sherwood, J.J. (1976) *Intergroup and minority Relations: An Experiential Handbook*. La Jolla, CA: University Associates.

Garcia-Prieto, P., Bellard, E. and Schneider, S.C. (2003) 'Experiencing diversity, conflict, and emotions in teams', *Applied Psychology: An International Review*, 52: 413–40.

Glastra, F. (2000) 'Broadening the scope of diversity management', *Industrial Relations (Quebec)*, 55: 698–732.

Glenn, E.N. (1999) 'The social construction and institutionalization of gender and race: an integrative framework', in M. Ferree, J. Lorber and B. Hess (eds), *Revisioning Gender*. Thousand Oaks, CA: Sage. pp. 3–43.

Greenhaus, J.H., Parasuraman, S. and Wormley, W.M. (1990) 'Effects on race on organizational experiences, job performance evaluations, and career outcomes', *Academy of Management Journal*, 33: 64–86.

Griffith, K.H. and Hebl, M.R. (2002) 'The disclosure dilemma for gay men and lesbians: 'Coming out' at work', *Journal of Applied Psychology*, 87: 1191–9.

Grimes, D. (2001) 'Putting our own house in order: whiteness, change and organization studies', *Journal of Organizational Change Management*, 14: 132–49.

Gvozdeva, E. and Gerchikov, V. (2002) 'Sketches for a portrait of women managers', *Russian Social Science Review*, 43(4): 72–86.

Hall, S. (1992) 'The question of cultural identity', in S. Hall, D. Held and T. McGrew (eds), *Modernity and its Futures*. Cambridge: Polity. pp. 273–316.

Harris, C. (1994) 'Acknowledging lesbians in the workplace: confronting the heterosexuality of organizations', *Paper presented at the 1994 Academy of Management Meeting*, Dallas.

Harrison, D.A., Price, K.H. and Bell, M.P. (1998) 'Beyond relational demography: time and the effects of surface- and deep-level diversity on work group cohesion', *Academy of Management Journal*, 41(1): 96–107.

Harrison, D.A., Price, K.H., Gavin, J.H. and Florey, A.T. (2002) 'Time, teams and task performance: changing effects of surface- and deep-level diversity on group functioning', *Academy of Management Journal*, 45(5): 1029–45.

Heilman, M.E. and Chen, J.J. (2005) 'Same behavior, different consequences: Reactions to men's and women's altruistic citizenship behavior', *Journal of Applied Psychology*, 90: 431–41.

Heilman, M.E. and Haynes, M.C. (2005) 'No credit where credit is due: Attributional rationalization of women's success in male-female teams', *Journal of Applied Psychology*, 90: 905–16.

Hill-Collins, P. (1990) *Black Feminist Thought: Knowledge, Consciousness, and the Politics of Empowerment*. New York: Routledge.

Hogg, M.A. and Terry, D.J. (2000) 'Social identity and self-categorisation processes in organizational contexts', *Academy of Management Review*, 25: 121–40.

hooks, b. (1984) *Feminist theory: From center to margin*. Boston: South End Press.

House, C.J.C. (2004) 'Integrating barriers to Caucasian lesbians' career development and Super's life-span, life-space approach', *Career Development Quarterly*, 52: 246–55.

Hughes, E.C. (1946) 'The knitting of racial groups in industry', *American Sociological Review*, 11: 512–9.

Ibarra, H. (1993) 'Personal networks of women and minorities in management: a conceptual framework', *Academy of Management Review*, 18: 56–87.

Jackson, S.E. and Joshi, A. (2003) 'Diversity in social context: A multi-attribute, multi-level analysis of team diversity and performance in a sales organization', Working paper, Rutgers University.

Jackson, S.E., Joshi, A. and Erhardt, N.L. (2003) 'Recent research on team and organizational diversity: SWOT analysis and implications', *Journal of Management*, 29: 801–30.

Jackson, S.E. and Associates (1992) *Diversity in the Workplace: Human Resource Initiatives*. New York: Guilford Press.

Jehn, K.A., Northcraft, G.B. and Neale, M.A. (1999) 'Why differences make a difference: a field study of diversity, conflict and performance in work groups', *Administrative Science Quarterly*, 44: 741–63.

Johnston, W. (1991) 'Global workforce 2000: the new world labor market', *Harvard Business Review*, 69: 115–27.

Johnston, W. and Packer, A. (1987) *Workforce 2000: Work and Workers for the 21st Century*. Indianapolis: Hudson Institute.

Jones, D., Pringle, J. and Shepherd, D. (2000) 'Managing diversity meets Aotearoa/New Zealand', *Personnel Review*, 29(3): 364–80.

Jost, J.T. and Thompson, E.P. (2000) 'Group-based dominance and opposition to equality as independent predictors of self-esteem, ethnocentrism, and social policy attitudes among African Americans and European Americans', *Journal of Experimental Social Psychology*, 36: 209–32.

Karakowsky, L. and Siegel, J.P. (1999) 'The effects of proportional representation and gender orientation of the task on emergent leadership behavior in mixed-gender work groups', *Journal of Applied Psychology*, 84: 620–31.

Katz J.H. (1978) *White awareness: Handbook for anti-racism training*. Oklahoma: University of Oklahoma Press.

Kelly, E. and Dobbin, F. (1998) 'How affirmative action became diversity management', *American Behavioral Scientist*, 41: 960–85.

Kersten, A. (2000) 'Diversity management: dialogue, dialectics and diversion', *Journal of Organizational Change Management*, 13(3): 235–48.

Kim, S.S. and Gelfand, M.J. (2003) 'The influence of ethnic identity on perceptions of organizational commitment', *Journal of Vocational Behavior*, 63: 396–416.

Kirkman, B.L., Tesluk, P.E. and Rosen, B. (2003) 'The impact of demographic heterogeneity and team leader-team member demographic fit on team empowerment and effectiveness', *Group and Organization Management*,: 1–34.

Kochan, T., Bezrukova, K., Ely, R., Jackson, S., Joshi, A., Jehn, K., Leonard, J., Levine, D. and Thomas, D. (2003) 'The effects of diversity on business performance: report of the diversity research network', *Human Resource Management*, 42: 3–21.

Kraiger, K. and Ford, J.K. (1985) 'A meta-analysis of rate race effects in performance ratings', *Journal of Applied Psychology*, 70: 56–65.

Larkey, L.K. (1996) 'Toward a theory of communicative interactions in culturally diverse workgroups', *Academy of Management Review*, 21: 463–91.

Lau, D.C. and Murnighan, J.K. (1998) 'Demographic diversity and fault lines: the compositional dynamics of organizational groups', *Academy of Management Review*, 23: 325–40.

Lau, D.C. and Murnighan, J.K. (2005) 'Interactions within groups and subgroups: The effects of demographic faultlines', *Academy of Management Journal*, 48: 645–60.

Lawrence, B. (1997) 'The black box of organizational demography', *Organization Science*, 8: 1–22.

LePine, J.A. and Van Dyne, L. (1998) 'Predicting voice behavior in work groups', *Journal of Applied Psychology*, 83: 853–68.

Lewis, A.C. and Sherman, S.J. (2003) 'Hiring you makes me look bad: social-identity based reversals of the ingroup favouritism effect', *Organizational Behavior and Human Decision Processes*, 90: 262–76.

Linnehan, F. and Konrad, A. (1999) 'Diluting diversity: implications for intergroup inequality in organizations', *Journal of Management Inquiry*, 8: 399–414.

Litvin, D.R. (1997) 'The discourse of diversity: From biology to management', *Organization*, 4: 187–210.

Litvin, D.R. (2000) 'The business case for diversity and the 'iron cage'', *The 16th EGOS Colloquium*, Helsinki.

Loden, M. and Rosener, J. (1991) *Workforce America! Managing Employee Diversity as a Vital Resource*. Homewood, IL: Business One Irwin.

Lorbiecki, A. and Jack, G. (2000) 'Critical turns in the evolution of diversity management', *British Journal of Management*, 11: 17–31.

Lyness, K.S. and Judiesch, M.K. (2001) 'Are female managers quitters? The relationships of gender, promotions, and family leaves of absence to voluntary turnover', *Journal of Applied Psychology*, 86: 1167–78.

Maier, M. (1999) 'On the gendered substructure of organization: dimensions and dilemmas of corporate masculinity', in G. Powell (ed.), *Handbook of Gender*. Thousand Oaks, CA: Sage Publications. pp. 69–94.

Martin, J. (1992) *Organization culture: Three perspectives*. New York: Oxford University Press.

Maurer, T.J., Weiss, E.M. and Barbeite, F.G. (2003) 'A model of involvement in work-related learning and development activity: the effects of individual, situational, motivational, and age variables', *Journal of Applied Psychology*, 88: 707–24.

Milliken, F.J. and Martins, L.L. (1996) 'Searching for common threads: understanding the multiple effects of diversity in organizational groups', *Academy of Management Review*, 21: 402–33.

Mills, A. and Tancred P. (eds) (1992) *Gendering organizational analysis*. Newbury Park, CA: Sage.

Morgan, G. (1986) *Images of organization*. Newbury Park: Sage.

Morrison, A.M. (1992). *The New Leaders: Guidelines on Leadership Diversity in America*. San Francisco: Jossey-Bass.

Moving Forward (2000) *The experiences and attitudes of executive women in Canada*. Toronto: Pollara.

Nelson, D.L. and Burke, R.J. (2000) 'Women executives: health, stress and success', *Academy of Management Executive*, 14(2): 107–22.

Nkomo, S.M. (1992) 'The emperor has no clothes: rewriting race into the study of organizations', *Academy of Management Review*, 17: 487–513.

Nkomo, S.M. and Cox, T. (1996) 'Diverse identities in organizations', in S.R. Clegg, C. Hardy and W.R. Nord (eds), *Handbook of Organization Studies*. London: Sage. pp. 338–56.

Nyambegera, S.M. (2002) 'Ethnicity and human resource management practice in sub-Saharan Africa: the relevance of the managing diversity discourse', *International Journal of Human Resource Management*, 13: 7.

Ostroff, C. and Atwater, L.E. (2003) 'Does whom you work with matter? Effects of referent group gender and age composition on managers' compensation', *Journal of Applied Psychology*, 88: 725–40.

Parker, C.P., Baltes, B.B. and Christiansen, N.D. (1997) 'Support for affirmative action, justice perceptions, and work attitudes: a study of gender and racial-ethnic group differences', *Journal of Applied Psychology*, 82: 376–89.

Pelled, L.H. (1996) 'Demographic diversity, conflict, and work group outcomes: an intervening process theory', Organization *Science*, 7: 615–31.

Pelled, L.H., Eisenhardt, K.M. and Xin, K.R. (1999) 'Exploring the black box: an analysis of work group diversity, conflict, and performance', *Administrative Science Quarterly*, 44: 1–28.

Pfeffer, J. (1983) 'Organizational demography', in L.L. Cummings and B.M. Staw (eds), *Research in organizational behavior*, 5. Greenwich, CT: JAI Press. pp. 299–357.

Phillips, K.W. and Loyd, D.L. (forthcoming) 'When surface and deep-level diversity collide: The effects of dissenting group members', *Organizational Behavior and Human Decision Processes*.

Phillips, K.W., Northcraft, G. and Neale, M. (forthcoming) 'Surfact-level diversity and information sharing: When does deep-level similarity help?', *Group Processes and Intergroup Relations*.

Point, S. and Singh, V. (2003) 'Defining and dimensionalising diversity: evidence from corporate websites across Europe', *European Management Journal*, 2(6): 750–61.

Polzer, J.T., Milton, L.P. and Swan, W.B. (2001) 'Capitalizing on diversity: interpersonal congruence in small work groups', *Administrative Science Quarterly*, 47: 296–324.

Powell, G.N. (1999) *Handbook of Gender and Work*. Thousand Oaks, CA: Sage Publications.

Prasad, A. (1997) 'The colonizing consciousness and representations of the other: a postcolonial critique of the discourse of oil', in P. Parsad, A. Mills, M. Elmes and A. Prasad (eds), *Managing the Organizational Melting Pot: Dilemmas of Workplace Diversity*. Newbury: Sage. pp. 285–311.

Prasad, P., Mills, A.J., Elmes, M. and Prasad, A. (eds) (1997) *Managing the organizational melting pot: Dilemmas of workplace diversity*. Newbury: Sage.

Prasad, P., Pringle, J. and Konrad, A. (2006) 'Examining the contours of workplace diversity: Concepts, contexts and challenges', in P. Prasad, J.K. Pringle and A.M. Konrad (eds), *Handbook of Workplace Diversity*. Thousand Oaks, CA: Sage. pp. 1–21.

Pratto, F., Sidanius, J., Stallworth, L.M. and Malle, B.F. (1994) 'Social dominance orientation: a personality variable predicting social and political attitudes', *Journal of Personality and Social Psychology*, 67: 741–63.

Ragins, B.R. and Cornwell, J.M. (2001) 'Pink triangles: antecedents and consequences of perceived workplace discrimination against gay and lesbian employees', *Journal of Applied Psychology*, 86: 1244–61.

Ragins, B.R. and Cotton, J.L. (1999) 'Mentor functions and outcomes: a comparison of men and women in formal and informal mentor relationships', *Journal of Applied Psychology*, 84(4), 529.

Ragins, B.R. and Gonzalez, J.A. (2003) 'Understanding diversity in organizations: getting a grip on a slippery construct', in J. Greenberg (ed.), *Organizational behavior: The state of the science*, 2nd edn. Mahway, NJ: Lawrence Erlbaum Associates. pp. 125–63.

Ragins, B.R., Cornwell, J.M. and Miller, J.S. (2003) 'Heterosexism in the workplace: do race and gender matter?', *Group and Organization Management*, 28(1): 45–74.

Ramsey, V. (1994) 'A different way of making a difference: learning through feelings', *Journal of Organizational Change Management*, 7: 59–71.

Richard, O.C. (2000) 'Racial diversity, business strategy, and firm performance', *Academy of Management Journal*, 43(2): 164–77.

Richard, O.C., Barnett, T., Dwyer, S. and Chadwick, K. (2004) 'Cultural diversity in management, firm performance, and the moderating role of entrepreneurial orientation dimensions', *Academy of Management Journal*, 47(2): 255–66.

Riordan, C.M. (2000) 'Relational demography within groups: past developments, contradictions, and new directions', Research *in Personnel and Human Resources Management*, 19: 131–73.

Riordan, C.M., Schaffer, B.S. and Stewart, M.M. (2005) 'Relational demography within groups: through the lens of discrimination', in R. Dipboye and A. Collela, (eds), *Frontiers in Discrimination*. Mahwah, NJ: Lawrence Erlbaum Associates. pp. 37–61.

Roberts, L.M. (2005) 'Changing faces: Professional image construction in diverse organizational settings', *Academy of Management Review*, 30: 685–711.

Roethlisberger, F.J. and Dickson, W. (1939) *Management and the worker*. Cambridge, MA: Harvard University Press.

Roos, P.A. and Gatta, M.L. (1999) 'The gender gap in earnings: trends, explanations, and prospects', in G. Powell (ed.), *Handbook of Gender and Work*. Sage Publications.

Roth, P.L., Huffcutt, A.I. and Bobko, P. (2003) 'Ethnic group differences in measures of job performance: a new meta-analysis', *Journal of Applied Psychology*, 88(4): 694–706.

Roth, P.L., Van Iddekinger, C.H., Huffcutt, A.I., Eidson, C.E. and Bobko, P. (2002) 'Corrections for range restriction in structured interview ethnic group differences: the values may be larger than researchers thought', *Journal of Applied Psychology*, 82(1): 369–76.

Sacco, J.M. and Schmitt, N. (2005) 'A dynamic multilevel model of demographic diversity and misfit effects', *Journal of Applied Psychology*, 90: 203–31.

Sanchez, J. I. and Brock, P. (1996) 'Outcomes of perceived discrimination among hispanic employees: is diversity management a luxury or necessity', *Academy of Management Journal*, 3: 704–19.

Sawyer, J.E., Houlette, M.A. and Yeagley, E.L. (2006) 'Decision performance and diversity structure: Comparing faultlines in convergent, crosscut, and racially homogeneous groups', *Organizational Behavior and Human Decision Processes*, 99: 1–15.

Selznick P. (1957) *Leadership in Administration*. New York: Harper & Row.

Shaw, J.B. (2004) 'The development and analysis of a measure of group faultlines', *Organizational Research Methods*, 7: 66–100.

Shore, L.M., Cleveland, J.N. and Goldberg, C.B. (2003) 'Work attitudes and decisions as a function of manager age and employee age', *Journal of Applied Psychology*, 88: 529–37.

Sidanius, J. and Pratto, F. (1999) *Social dominance: An intergroup theory of social hierarchy and oppression*. New York: Cambridge University Press.

Sivanandan, A. (1985) 'RAT and the degradation of the black struggle', *Race and Class*, 26: 1–34.

Slaughter, J.E., Sinar, E.F. and Bachiochi, P.D. (2002) 'Black applicants' reactions to affirmative action plans: effects of plan content and previous experience with discrimination', *Journal of Applied Psychology*, 87(2): 333–4.

Smircich, L. and Calás, M. (1999) 'Past postmodernism? Reflection and tentative directions', *Academy of Management Review*, 24: 549–671.

Stauffer, J.M. and Buckley, M.R. (2005) 'The existence and nature of racial bias in supervisory ratings', *Journal of Applied Psychology*, 90: 586–91.

Stewart, M.M. and Shapiro, D.L. (2000) 'Selection based on merit versus demography: implications across race and gender lines', *Journal of Applied Psychology*, 85: 219–31.

Stone, E.F., Stone, D.L. and Dipboye, R.L. (1992) 'Stigmas in organizations: race, handicaps, and physical attractiveness', in E. Kelley (ed.), *Issues, Theory and Research in Industrial/Organizational Psychology*. Amsterdam: North Holland. pp. 385–457.

Stroh, L.K. and Reilly, A.H. (1999) 'Gender and careers: present experiences and emerging trends', in G. Powell (ed.), *Handbook of Gender and Work*. Sage. p. 529.

Super, D.E. (1990) 'A life-span, life-space approach to career development', in D. Brown, L. Brooks and associates (eds), *Career choice and development*, 2nd edn. San Francisco: Jossey-Bass. pp. 197–261.

Swann, W.B., Polzer, J.T., Seyle, D.C. and Ko, S.J. (2004) 'Finding value in diversity: verification of personal and social self-views in diverse groups', *Academy of Management Review*, 29: 9–27.

Tajfel, H. (1972) 'Social categorization', English version of 'La categorisation sociale', in S. Moscovici (ed.), *Introduction a la psychologie sociale*, vol. I. Paris: Larousse. pp. 272–302.

Tajfel, H. and Turner, J.C. (1979) 'An integrative theory of intergroup conflict', in W.G. Austin and S. Worchel (eds), *The Social Psychology of Intergroup Relations*. Monterey, CA: Brooks/Cole. pp. 33–47.

Thatcher, S.M.B., Jehn, K.A. and Zanutto, E. (2003) 'Cracks in diversity research: The effects of diversity faultlines on conflict and performance', *Group Decision and Negotiation*, 12: 217–41.

Thomas, D.A. (1990) 'The impact of race on managers' experiences of developmental relationships: an intraorganizational study', *Journal of Organizational Behavior*, 11: 479–92.

Thomas, D.A. (1993) 'Racial dynamics in cross-race developmental relationships', *Administrative Science Quarterly*, 38: 169–94.

Thomas, D.A. (2001) 'The truth about mentoring minorities: race matters', *Harvard Business Review*, 79: 98–107.

Thomas, D.A. and Ely, R.D. (1996) 'Making differences matter: a new paradigm for managing diversity', *Harvard Business Review*, 74(Sept–Oct): 79–90.

Thomas, D.A. and Gabarro, J.J. (1999) *Breaking through: The making of minority executives in corporate America*. Boston, MA: Harvard Business School Press.

Thomas, R.R. (1989) 'From affirmative action to affirming diversity', *Harvard Business Review*, 68: 107–19.

Tomaskovic-Devey, D. and Skaggs, S. (1999) 'An establishment-level test of the statistical discrimination hypothesis', *Work and Occupations*, 26: 422–45.

Tsui, A.S. and Gutek, B. (1999) *Demographic differences in organizations: current research and future directions*. Lanham, MD: Lexington Books.

Tsui, A.S., Egan, T.D. and O'Reilly, C.A. (1992) 'Being different: relational demography and organizational attachment', *Administrative Science Quarterly*, 37: 547–79.

Tsui, A.S., Egan, T.D. and Xin, K.R. (1995) 'Diversity in organizations: Lessons from demography research', in M. Chemers, S. Oskamp and M. Costanzo (eds), *Diversity in the workplace*. Thousand Oaks, CA: Sage. pp. 37–61.

Turner, J.C. (1975) 'Social comparison and social identity: some prospects for intergroup behaviour', *European Journal of Social Psychology*, 5: 5–34.

Turner, J.C. (1982) 'Towards a cognitive redefinition of social group', in H. Tajfel (ed.), *Social identity and intergroup relations*. New York: Cambridge University Press. pp. 15–40.

Van der Vegt, G.S. and Van de Vliert, E. (2005) 'Effects of perceived skill dissimilarity and task interdependence on helping in work teams', *Journal of Management*, 31: 73–89.

Van Djik, T.A. (1987) *Communicating racism*. Beverly Hills, CA: Sage Publications.

Van Hoye, G. and Lievens, F. (2003) 'The effects of sexual orientation on hirability ratings: an experimental study', *Journal of Business and Psychology*, 28: 15–30.

Watson, E.E., Kumar, K. and Michaelson, L.K. (1993) 'Cultural diversity's impact on interaction processes and performance: comparing homogeneous and diverse task groups', *Academy of Management Journal*, 36: 590–602.

Webber, S.S. and Donahue, L.M. (2001) 'Impact of highly and less job-related diversity on work group cohesion and performance: A meta-analysis', *Journal of Management*, 27: 141–62.

Wharton, A.S. (1992) 'The social construction of gender and race in organizations: a social identity and group mobilization perspective', *Research in the Sociology of Organizations*, 10: 55–84.

Whitehead, S. (2001) 'Woman as manager: a seductive ontology', *Gender, Work and Organisation*, 8(1): 84–107.

Williams, K.Y. and O'Reilly, C.A. (1998) 'Demography and diversity in organizations: a review of 40 years of research', *Research in Organizational Behavior*, 20: 77–140.

Wilmott, H. (1993) 'Strength is ignorance; slavery is freedom: managing culture in modern organizations', *Journal of Management Studies*, 30(4): 515–52.

Wirth, L. (2001). *Breaking through the glass ceiling: Women in management.* Geneva: ILO.

Wu, F.H. (2002) *Yellow: Race in America Beyond Black and White.* New York: Basic Books.

Xin, K.R. (2004) 'Asian American managers: An impression gap? An investigation of impression management and supervisor-subordinate relationships', *The Journal of Applied Behavioral Science*, 40: 160–81.

Zanoni, P. and Janssens, M. (2003) 'Deconstructing difference: The rhetoric of human resources managers' diversity discourses', *Organization Studies*, 25(1): 55–74.

Ziegert, J.C. and Hanges, P.J. (2005) 'Employment discrimination: The role of implicit attitudes, motivation, and a climate for racial bias', *Journal of Applied Psychology*, 90: 553–62.

2.5 Revisiting Metaphors of Organizational Communication

LINDA L. PUTNAM AND SUZANNE BOYS

Organizational communication research has mushroomed in the past decade. This growth is evident in the shear volume of work – well over 200 articles published in communication and management journals; multiple research-based books, texts on theoretical perspectives and paradigm development (Corman and Poole 2000; Taylor and Van Every 2000; May and Mumby 2005), and two *Handbooks* that survey different aspects of the field (Jablin and Putnam 2001; Grant et al. 2004). In comparing state-of-the-art reviews published in the 1980s (Putnam and Cheney 1985; Redding and Tompkins 1988) with the current research, Mumby (in press) concludes that the field has not only grown, it has experienced 'its own Copernican revolution'. Other scholars echo this theme and agree that the field has made a major paradigm shift (Krone 2005).

This shift moves the study of communication from linear transmission within organizations to the way that social interaction, discursive processes and symbolic meanings constitute organizations (Taylor et al. 2001; Mumby 2006). This shift is also apparent in discussions of the reflexive relationships among key constructs, such as action-structure (Conrad and Hayes 2001; Taylor et al. 2001), permeable and fixed organizational boundaries (Mumby and Stohl 1996); and organizational control and resistance (Mumby 2005). These changes in research direction may stem from the field's interdisciplinary connections or its reliance on diverse epistemologies (Krone 2005).

However, some scholars contend that organizational communication's eclectic past and endorsements of multiple perspectives create false dichotomies that locate research arenas in isolated philosophical camps (Clair 1999). Although scholars agree that finding common ground among perspectives is not the goal (Corman and Poole 2000), researchers differ as to whether diverse perspectives infuse each other, privilege some approaches over others, or contribute to making organizations a more humane place.

This updated state-of-the art review of organizational communication aims to assess whether different perspectives remain isolated from each other and, if so, to what extent. As with the 1996 chapter, it does so by reviewing studies that espouse different metaphorical assumptions about communication and organization, based on what assumptions underlie each. Thus, similar to the original chapter, communication emerges as figure and the organization as ground in this metaphorical analysis. This chapter also follows the original one in identifying ways that metaphors chain with each other, thus forming a basis to assess the isolation or integration of research perspectives. Unlike the original chapter, this review will not focus on the organization–communication relationship or the ontology of organizations. For discussions of these issues, readers can consult essays on organizations as discursive constructions (Taylor and Van Every 2000; Fairhurst and Putnam 2004; Putnam and Cooren 2004).

In keeping with the original chapter, a metaphor is defined as a way to link abstract concepts to concrete things (Ortony 1979) or to tie the familiar to the unknown (Hawkes 1972). Originally, we identified seven metaphors that depicted different approaches to organizational communication – the conduit, the lens, linkage, performance, symbol, voice and discourse. This chapter reorganizes these seven, makes some shifts in metaphor labels, and develops one additional metaphor that was not covered in the 1996 chapter. Our project also differs from Morgan's (1986; 1997) *Images of Organizations* by centring on organizational communication rather than on organizational theory as the impetus for these metaphors. Similar to Morgan's work, however, we use metaphors to reveal the assumptive ground of different research programmes and to cut across different levels of analysis and theoretical domains.

This chapter, then, poses the following general questions: (1) How have the metaphors in organizational communication changed in the past decade? (2) To what extent do they highlight new arenas of research, reveal new clusters, chain together differently, and/or exclude important metaphor entailments? (3) Based on the relationships among metaphors, to what extent are research perspectives isolated or connected with each other?

We begin with an overview of the way metaphor analysis can inform theory building. Then we provide a brief description of the metaphor clusters that frame this chapter and indicate how they differ from the original seven metaphors. Then we define each metaphor, describe the role of organizational communication in each, review current research, discuss metaphor chains and clusters, and critique each one through exploring deep-level associations and metaphor entailments. The discussion portion of this chapter compares and contrasts the metaphors from the original chapter and addresses the issues of chaining and isolation of perspectives.

Similar to the original version, this chapter is not an exhaustive review of organizational communication, as it appears in Jablin and Putnam (2001), Jones et al. (2004) and Taylor et al. (2001). Instead, this chapter casts a broad stroke to illustrate various metaphors. Thus, it reviews and integrates a complex body of organizational communication literature published between 1996–2005, not only to show the relevance of this work to organization studies, but also to explore how different metaphors depict theory development in the field.

Metaphors and Organizational Theory Building

A metaphor is a way of seeing a thing as if it were something else (Lakeoff and Johnson 1980); thus, it provides a cognitive bridge between two domains. Although originally examined as a literary trope, metaphors are more than ornaments that decorate language and more than typologies or classification systems. Metaphors facilitate the construction of social reality by forming insights about one thing in light of another.

Metaphors make meaning through resonance; that is, they establish figure–ground relationships

through comparing and contrasting similarities between a source and a target. Focusing on similarities, however, diverts attention away from dissimilarities (Oswick et al. 2004). For example, to treat organizational mergers as 'ambushes and shootouts' highlights the surprise attack, hostile takeover, winners and losers, and hired guns who orchestrate these deals (Hirsch and Andrews 1983). This imagery, however, conceals the wooing, match-making and compatibility elements that a courtship metaphor might reveal.

Metaphor analysis has received considerable attention in organizational theory building. Scholars use metaphors to generate new theories, decentre old ones and unpack nuances of different perspectives (Clegg and Gray 1996; Cazel and Inns 1998; Inns 2002). Metaphors also reveal the assumptive ground of organizational constructs and chart new directions for research in human resource management (Dunn 1990), organizational change (Marshak 1996) and socialization (Smith and Turner 1995).

The use of metaphors to facilitate theory building, however, has not gone without criticism. Although some essays stand outside the constructivist base of this work (Tinker 1986), other critiques note three shortcomings that merit close attention. First, by highlighting only similarities, metaphors may crystallize partial views of organizations (Tinker 1986). One way to minimize this problem is to form chains of interlocking components through linking related images. Chains of relationships introduce continual reflexivity into the analysis by casting the figure in one metaphor as the ground for the next image (Smith and Turner 1995). This approach works against freezing or crystallizing metaphor categories.

A second concern is that metaphors are too imprecise, promote 'sloppy thinking' and lack rigour (Carr and Leivesley 1995). This imprecision can also lead to confounding metaphors with other figures of speech, such as metonymies and synecdoche, thus reducing precision (Morcol 1997). The issue of not confusing metaphors with other resonance tropes may not be as important as adding rigour to this work. One approach for doing this is to focus on both surface and deep relationships in metaphor analyses (Oswick et al. 2004).

Specifically, Tsoukas (1993) identifies four types of relationships – *abstractions*, based on relational similarities, e.g. the organization is like a brain;

analogies, based on the links between sets of characteristics and structures of the source and target, e.g. the organization is to culture as societies are to communities; *literal similarities*, which transfer characteristics from the source to the target, e.g. organizations are bureaucratic institutions; and *mere appearances*, that transfer some specific attributes, but not the entire relationship between the source and the target, e.g. the organization is like a psychic prison in which members are subject to a variety of oppressive tactics. *Literal similarities* parallel Lakeoff and Johnson's (1980) notion of dormant or dead metaphors that are deeply ingrained and operate only on a surface level while *mere appearances* function like embellishments with only a modicum of commonality between target and source (Boland and Greenberg 1988). Unpacking these relationships could add rigour to metaphorical analyses.

A third criticism is that metaphors trap discourse in ideological images that promote pseudo knowledge and maintain status quo power relationships (Tinker 1986; Carr and Leivesley 1995); thus scholars should recognize that metaphors can produce distortions, obfuscate social struggles and perpetuate false consciousness. Theorizing from a wide array of research that embraces the scope and breadth of a field works against the tendency to ignore social struggles. Focusing on metaphor entailments and second-order resemblances that frame or inform other metaphors, also unpacks the ideological assumptions that underlie metaphors (Alvesson 1993; Oswick et al. 2004: 110). Second-order metaphors stem from subsets of related metaphors that are linked to deep-level frameworks. For example, rather than simply depicting an organization as a family, a scholar might explore related and less obvious images, such as in-law relationships, family feuds and sibling rivalry (Oswick et al. 2004).

This chapter applies these steps to metaphor analysis. As with the original chapter, we develop metaphor clusters or groups of submetaphors that form distinct but interrelated categories. To avoid locking categories into fixed meanings, we explore ways that figure-ground relationships shift, form chains with other metaphors, and emerge as new clusters. To sharpen the rigour of our analysis, we explore the relationships embodied in metaphor clusters and entailments. That is, we acknowledge the deep-level assumptions and ideological roots of each metaphor and show how efforts to explore

metaphor entailments can add missing elements to research.

Metaphors of Communication and Organization

In the 1996 chapter, we identified seven metaphors that guided research programmes in organizational communication – the conduit, lens, linkage, performance, symbol, voice and discourse. Although these metaphors continue to encompass major bodies of research, this chapter makes three changes. First, information processing has replaced the lens metaphor as research now focuses on information search and exchange rather than filtering and gatekeeping. Secondly, the discourse metaphor has grown dramatically and infused the performance, symbol and voice metaphors. Hence, this chapter reorganizes these metaphors and sub-metaphors to reflect this shift. Thirdly, we have added a new metaphor – contradiction – that emerges from combining aspects of the voice and discourse metaphors. Thus, this chapter focuses on eight metaphors – the conduit, information processing, linkage, performance, discourse, symbol, voice and contradiction views of communication.

This chapter defines the central features of each metaphor and reviews the findings of studies that fall into these eight clusters and their sub-metaphors. Each section concludes with a discussion of the types of metaphor associations and concepts that emerge from second-order alignments. As with the original chapter, this list of metaphors is neither exhaustive nor mutually exclusive; that is, they continue to represent 'blurred genres' (Geertz 1973) and mutations (Weick 1979) that overlap and thread together to form spin-off relationships.

The *conduit* metaphor treats communication as a *channel* that transmits messages. In this metaphor, an organization surfaces as a *container* in which channels reside. This metaphor forms two clusters – communication as a *tool* and communication as *transmission*. The tool cluster includes studies that cast communication as media for transmission or as a skill for performing instrumental goals. The second sub-metaphor – communication as transmission – encompasses work that focuses on the adequacy or amount of communication sent and received.

In this chapter, the lens metaphor becomes *information processing* by focusing on the *nature and flow of information,* particularly targets of information exchange, types of feedback, and patterns of seeking and receiving information. An organization in this metaphor functions as a *map or a trajectory* for routing, targeting and processing information flow. Organizational circumstances, such as assimilation of new members, change or turnover, impact the target and routing of information. Metaphor clusters include feedback, information exchange and information flow.

The *linkage* metaphor treats organizations as *networks* of relationships in which communication *connects* individuals, groups and institutions. Organizational linkages arise from similarities among members, physical proximity, diffusion of attitudes and meanings, activity processes and collective actions. Research within this metaphor focuses on the adoption of new technologies, social support systems, public goods and communities of practice. Metaphor clusters in this category include contact systems, knowledge structures and relational bonds.

The next group of metaphors moves away from the transmission roots of communication to focus on social interaction, meaning and discourse. Grounded in social construction approaches, the metaphor of *performance* cast communication as *social interaction,* as evident in studies of organizations as self-referential systems, enactment and sensemaking, interaction analysis and structuration. In this metaphor, organizations as *co-ordinated actions* enact their own rules, structures and environments through dynamic processes that have no clear beginning and ending. Metaphors clusters include co-constructing, sequential patterns and evolving actions.

In the last 10 years, the *discourse* metaphor has become a large-scale umbrella that encompasses the symbol, voice and contradiction metaphors; that is, the study of discursive practices infuses the other metaphors. The discourse metaphor in this chapter takes a narrow focus through treating communication as *language* in use, that is words and signifiers that constitute an organization as *inter-relationships among texts.* This metaphor includes studies that fall into the areas of conversational analysis, emotional expressions, ambiguity and rhetorical strategies. Metaphor clusters for discourse include semantics, linguistics, written and oral texts and expression.

The metaphor of *symbol* draws from literary forms to cast communication as *sensemaking* through rituals and narratives. These symbols serve as vehicles of contestation to negotiate social identities and develop understandings of organization life. The diversity of studies on organizational narratives breaks into five sub-metaphors: cultural stories; life stories; storytelling; narrative schemas; and embedded, multivocal stories. Thus, the organization emerges as a *literary text or a novel,* jointly authored by organizational members as they create and interpret a range of symbolic activities. Metaphor clusters include semiotics, folklore and artistic forms.

The metaphor of *voice* is broader than it was in the initial chapter. Communication in this metaphor is both *suppression* and *expression.* Similar to the original chapter, two sub-metaphors – distorted voices and dominant voices – focus on the practices that prevent individuals from fully engaging in organizational life, but this chapter also reviews the literature on silence as a response to suppression. Expression extends beyond speaking to encompass the ability to act, construct knowledge and exert power; thus three sub-metaphors, dissent, in a different voice, and access to voice, explore social and political processes that have the potential to instantiate voice. Clusters included in this metaphor include concertive control, discursive closure, muted voices, silence, dissent and empowerment.

Finally, the metaphor of *contradiction* treats communication as the *opposing forces* or binary relationships between contradictory messages. An organization in this metaphor becomes the *ongoing struggle or the tensions* between oppositions. Contradiction subsumes research in four sub-clusters: dialectic of control, dialectical tensions, paradox, and dialogue. Metaphor clusters include dualities, Janusian thinking, incongruities, incompatibilities and bi-polar extremes.

These eight metaphors serve as frames for reviewing the organizational communication literature published in the past decade. As diverse perspectives, they shed light on the multifaceted nature of the field. This chapter, then, reveals the changes that have occurred and the new directions in the field. It admonishes researchers to become aware of their unconscious assumptions and the limitations of each metaphor. This chapter, then, builds on the original one, in positing ways to conceptualize and think about the nature of organizational communication.

The Conduit Metaphor

As previously defined, a *conduit* is a channel through which something is conveyed, such as a tube, cable or cylinder (Axley 1984). In this metaphor, communication becomes a *tool* for accomplishing organizational goals through *transmitting messages*. Organizations appear as *containers* or *passageways* for the conduit. Early research treated the conduit as a literal metaphor, one that was deeply ingrained in phrases like 'convey' and 'transfer' and one that was isomorphic with communication itself. Adopting a sender bias, researchers presumed that communication sent parallelled messages received.

In the past decade, very few studies have embraced the conduit as a literal metaphor. Scholars continue to use both transmission and tool models of communication, but they function as abstractions in which relational similarities are drawn between communication as transmission and media as channel. Unlike early studies, current research treats senders and receivers as active agents who are engaged in two-way message flows.

Two clusters characterize the conduit metaphor – communication as a tool and communication as transmission. A *tool* is an instrument, a device or a means for accomplishing goals. Communication acts as a tool in this metaphor by serving as *media* for transmitting messages or by functioning as a *skill* or a particular competency. Research that compares communication media reveals that mass-mediated channels have greater influence on goal consensus than do interpersonal channels (Collins-Jarvis 1997), but small informal discussions work more effectively in disseminating information during a planned organizational change (Lewis 1999). Rated more important than the telephone, email users oppose the implementation of regulatory policies and remain concerned about privacy issues (Hacker et al. 1998).

Media richness theory also examines comparisons among different media. This theory purports that managers select particular media to match task characteristics, particularly the ambiguity of the task. Richer media, such as face-to-face communication, telephone and teleconferencing have more potential for immediate feedback and provide multiple cues (Daft and Lengel 1986). Support for media richness theory continues to be mixed. Recent studies reveal that the choice of media depends on the formality of department structure and types of issues under consideration (Whitfield et al. 1996), the variety and analysability of managerial tasks (Donabedian et al. 1998), interaction goals and message complexity (Christensen and Bailey 1997), and the degree of mindlessness or mindfulness of the choice (Timmerman 2003). Managers prefer rich media for responding to messages from the external environment, conveying positive information, working on novel tasks and pursuing relational goals while they prefer lean media, especially written communication, to undertake complex tasks, reduce distortion and transmit routine decisions (Sheer and Chen 2004). Overall, the choice of media often contradicts media richness predictions by depending on the complexity and variety of tasks.

Another type of tool that falls within the conduit metaphor is communication as a *skill*, which focuses on the communication competencies of organizational members. Employees judged as competent communicators express control over their jobs and workplace relationships (Avtgis and Kassing 2001), exhibit strong listening skills (Cooper et al. 1997), and demonstrate high self-efficacy (Chiles and Zorn 1995). Competent supervisors embody a communication style characterized by reciprocity (McCroskey and Richmond 2000), collaborative approaches to conflict management (Weider-Hatfield and Hatfield 1996), and effective impression management (Gardner and Cleavenger 1998; Dillard et al. 2000). Competent communicators, then, are employees who are confident, responsive to others, and manage impressions well.

The second cluster in the conduit metaphor, communication as *transmission*, focuses on the amount or adequacy of communication. Grounded in diffusion theory, this work examines adequacy as it relates to targets of exchange and organizational changes, such as downsizing and mergers. Specifically, employees who receive an adequate amount of information place higher trust in top management than those who are uninformed about company events (Ellis and Shockley-Zalabak 2001). However, field and office personnel differ in the messages that they need about company objectives and policies (Rosenfeld et al. 2004). Receiving high levels of information during a merger increases employee anxiety (Zhu et al. 2004) but leads to high satisfaction during downsizing (Tourish et al. 2004). Thus, the adequacy of information varies across organizational circumstances with more data needed during downsizings than mergers. Adequacy, however, may account for only a portion of employee communication needs since the design and delivery of information also impacts on feelings of satisfaction.

The conduit metaphor, while clearly prevalent in current research, treats communication as a *tool* or a way of *transmitting* messages. Research continues to focus on comparisons among different communication channels, factors that affect media choice, the skills and competencies of organizational members, and the amount of information employees need. The conduit metaphor depicts an organization as a *container* or a hollow object that houses communication and information processing. Clusters subsumed within the conduit metaphor include media, channel, skill and information flow.

Of importance to theory building, research within the conduit metaphor embraces assumptions that differ from the 1970s to mid-1990s. Communication flow becomes a two-way exchange in which more communication is not necessarily better. In addition, the conduit metaphor has shifted from literal similarity to an abstraction in that researchers draw relational similarities among tools, transmission and communication rather than equating them.

At a deep level, the conduit metaphor espouses a functionalist ideology linked to organizational effectiveness, employee satisfaction and managerial goals. These outcomes stem from focusing on managerial preferences for media, subordinates' satisfaction with supervisors' communication, and tying communication adequacy to organizational goals. Scholars may lack awareness that a conduit protects information, functions as a means to an end, and becomes an instrument of production.

The Information Processing Metaphor

The *information processing* metaphor is closely related to the conduit approach. Current research departs from the screening and distorting functions of the previous lens metaphor. This chapter instead centres on information processing; that is on the targets of information exchange and patterns of seeking and receiving information. Information processing draws from conduit notions of transmission, but it includes targets, content and patterns of information flow. In the information processing metaphor, the *organization becomes a map or a trajectory;* that is, organizational circumstances such as

socialization, turnover or innovation affect the nature and routing of information.

Research within this metaphor focuses on *positive and negative feedback.* Specifically, message style affects the nature of positive and negative performance feedback (Geddes and Lineham 1996), with male supervisors employing direct, specific information and female managers using indirect and mutual problem definition (Lizzio et al. 2003). Subordinate reactions to feedback relate directly to the type and delivery of information. When negative feedback is considerate in tone, timely and constructive, it is less likely to evoke feelings of anger (Geddes and Baron 1997).

Two areas of this metaphor encompass a large number of studies – *information seeking* in organizational assimilation and communication during planned organizational change. For newcomers in an organization, information seeking serves to reduce uncertainty primarily through using unobtrusive approaches, such as disguised conversations, observing co-workers and third party inquiries (Casey et al. 1997; Kramer 1999; 2004; Kramer and Noland 1999). From this search process, newcomers form scripts and schemas to process information about organizational tasks and roles (Teboul 1997; Sias and Wyers 2001; Cooper-Thomas and Anderson 2002; Kramer 2004). Insufficient information during assimilation is one of the strongest predictors of intent to leave or voluntary turnover (Johnson et al. 1996; Scott et al. 1999).

Communication in planned organizational change focuses on the way that changes are announced and how stakeholders provide feedback to these changes (Lewis and Seibold 1998). Choosing an information-sharing model hinges on communication efficiency and the need for consensus building among stakeholders (Lewis et al. 2001), specifically, whether information should be shared with all stakeholders, revealed selectively or marketed to specific groups. In mergers and acquisitions, communication reduces uncertainty, but this reduction does not necessarily lead to positive attitudes toward organizational changes (Kramer et al. 2004).

A basic assumption of this metaphor is that attaining and processing information are critical prerequisites to organizational effectiveness. Information in this metaphor takes on a material quality with particular characteristics, like completeness, relevancy and directness. Metaphor clusters include feedback, targets, dimensions of exchange and direction of information flow. An organization in this metaphor becomes a map or trajectory for guiding choices about the patterns and nature of information flow. Even though the map varies with organizational circumstances, such as mergers or assimilation, the organization has self-contained boundaries. In this type of association, information processing combines literal similarity with mere appearances; that is, some scholars treat information processing as communication itself and others view the types and targets of information exchange as symptoms of communication.

Examining this metaphor at a deeper level calls into question the ownership of information and its bias for processing of data. Studies within this metaphor treat information as if it were neutral without concern for who has power and who seeks it. Current approaches to knowledge management challenge this assumption and the neutrality of information. In addition, this metaphor holds a bias for movement or information flow throughout the organization. Few scholars question whether information processing is necessarily advantageous or whether the critical issues in information flow centre on dissemination or on meanings that employees construct about data.

The Linkage Metaphor

The *linkage* metaphor shifts the focus of communication from transmission and information processing to *connection*; thus, communication is the link that ties people together and forms organizations as *networks* of relationships. Linkages define network roles, create patterns and structures, determine the strength or weakness of ties and shape interorganizational relationships. In the linkage metaphor, organizations are patterns of relationships that cross time and space rather than entities with fixed structures and boundaries. Unlike the 1996 chapter, this metaphor centres on emergent linkages rather than comparing informal networks with formal organizational structures (Monge and Contractor 2004). Although some research within this metaphor relies on a transmission view of communication, the linkage metaphor is very broad with ties to the discourse and performance metaphors. This review organizes studies according to four major theories or contributors to network formation: homophily-proximity, contagion, cognitive, and public goods (Monge and Contractor 2001; 2004).

Theories of homophily and proximity posit that similarities and physical closeness foster communication linkages. Three types of similarities appear in the literature: network roles, electronic proximity, and social support. Specifically, individuals who share centrality in a network develop dense linkages, exhibit less role conflict and have lower turnover rates than do individuals who are not central (Feeley 2000; LaFrance et al. 2003). Moreover, newcomers who have large, dense organizational networks develop a better understanding of how to fit into organizations than do employees with small and dispersed networks (Morrison 2002).

Other studies suggest that physical closeness increases the formation of organizational linkages (Van den Bulte and Moenaert 1998). In an investigation of employees who assist with IT problems, however, organizational proximity did not predict help networks (Rice et al. 1999). New media, however, can bridge geographic distance and substitute for physical closeness (Monge and Contractor 2004). The effects of electronic proximity, though, are complex and recursive, often yielding contradictory findings about the way new media and subsequent networks are appropriated (Jackson et al. 2002).

Grounded in homophily, social support networks aid in reducing stress and offering emotional encouragement. Supervisors who have legal worries and family problems often rely on informal support from their managers (Hopkins 2001). Organizational approval of these types of networks facilitates employee participation, particularly for Hispanic employees (Amason et al. 1999). These networks lead to improved job satisfaction, but they can also result in job burnout for individuals who provide the support.

Contagion theories focus on the spread of attitudes and beliefs through social learning networks. At the dyadic level, coworkers and supervisors directly influence an employee's job satisfaction (Pollock et al. 2000), use of email systems (Fulk et al. 1995), workplace attitudes (Heald et al. 1998), and beliefs about new technologies (Contractor et al. 1996). Linkages formed through structural equivalence or similarity in personal relationship patterns, accounts for media choice (Chang and Johnson 2001), opinions about one's job (Johanson 2000), and the intent to leave (Feeley and Barnett 1996).

A variation of contagion theories examines similarities in interpretations through semantic networks and knowledge structures. In particular, linkages form around shared interpretations of mission statements, especially for employees who have organizational longevity (Monge and Contractor 2004). The density of a network and the homogeneity of a group also contribute to the time it takes for members to converge on similar meanings (Contractor and Grant 1996). Another type of cognitive approach treats knowledge as a dynamic property of linkages rather than an area of individual expertise (Contractor and Monge 2002). Using a discourse-based technique, Kuhn and Corman (2003) report that organizational knowledge structures become heterogeneous over time during a planned change, even though core clusters of meanings converged at each time period.

Interestingly, membership in these core clusters varies over time; thus, knowledge networks evolve out of *collective action* as well as similarity in meanings (Iverson and McPhee 2002), particularly through computer support systems that function as knowledge workers (Holsapple et al. 1996; Orlikowski 2002). Three features influence the formation of collective action and networks of practice – relationships among members, interdependence between local and global goals, and attaining resources needed at the local level (Vaast 2004). Through disseminating texts, knowledge is generated collaboratively, not as a product of networks, but as both tacit and explicit communication practices (Heaton and Taylor 2002). Tacit knowledge then is produced by and enables collaborative task accomplishment. In a like manner, an organization as a 'firm' becomes an emergent or generative process in which linkages transform discursive practices into organizational identities (Kuhn and Ashcraft 2003).

At the macro level, communication researchers investigate how organizations contribute to the jointly-owned public domain through connectivity and shared information (Fulk et al. 1996). Organizations create public goods through participatory federations that form interorganizational linkages (Flanagin et al. 2001). CEOs of smaller organizations have the interest and resources to create the federations that in turn provide them with information. Sharing information, though, can lead to a dilemma when the organization's need for it contradicts an individual's self-interest to share it (Kalman et al. 2002). These social dilemmas are often resolved through transforming individual self-interest into public goods.

In the linkage metaphor, organizations consist of multiple, overlapping networks that negotiate both stable and fluid boundaries. Clusters subsumed under this metaphor include connections, contact systems, knowledge structures and relational bonds. Members are interlocked in a variety of relationships that 'transcend physical walls' through new technologies, new organizational forms and global networks. Organizational linkages arise from similarities among members, physical proximity, diffusion of attitudes and meanings and collective actions.

The general assumption underlying the linkage metaphor is that networks form through social contacts that disseminate information among individuals; linkages, in turn, create emergent organizational structures from dynamic patterns of relationships. As a type of metaphor, linkage is analogous to communication; that is, linkage is to networks as communication is to organizing. However, networks are literal similarities in that many new organizational forms, such as alliances, partnerships and virtual teams become networks that co-ordinate actions across space and time (Monge and Fulk 1999). Thus, linkage functions as an analogy of communication and network as a literal similarity for an organization.

At the surface level, networks often appear ideologically neutral. However, closer examination of second-order entailments suggests that alliances grow out of networks to form what critical theorists call 'dominant coalitions'. Traditional network studies seem devoid of work on the ideology of linkages, and the literature on dominant coalitions ignores the potential that network analysis offers for tracking the emergence and shifting of alliances. An integration of the linkage and the voice metaphors might address this vacuum and challenge the neutral ideology implicit in this metaphor.

The Metaphor of Performance

The next five metaphors differ from the previous three in focusing on interaction and meaning. In the *performance* metaphor, *social interaction* becomes the focal point for organizational communication research. Performance refers to the process of enacting organizing, rather than to an organization's productivity or output. Performance combines Turner's (1980) view of accomplishment with Weick's (1979) notion of enactment. In this metaphor, 'organizational reality is brought to life in communicative performances' (Pacanowsky and O'Donnell-Trujillo 1983: 131).

Social interaction arises from the sequences, patterns and meanings embedded in verbal and non-verbal messages; hence, the performance metaphor chains out of the discourse perspective. The key features that distinguish social interaction from the conduit and information processing metaphors are ongoing, dynamic processes, interlocking behaviours, reflexivity and sensemaking (Fisher 1978). Communication becomes part of an ongoing series of actions that has no clear beginning and ending. In the performance metaphor, organizations are *co-ordinated actions* derived from the rules, structures and social environments that members enact. Performance, though, serves as an umbrella for very diverse perspectives, including cybernetic theory, structuration and speech acts. Research in this metaphor falls into five categories: self-referential systems (Luhmann 1990), interaction analysis (Fairhurst 2004), structuration (Giddens 1979), enactment and sensemaking (Weick 1979; 1995), and text-conversation relationships (Cooren 2000; Taylor and Van Every 2000).

Unlike the linkage metaphor, *self-referential systems* cast communication as a reflexive performance (Contractor 1994; 1999; Hawes 1999). Popularized by management gurus, models of chaos and complexity posit that structures emerge at the edge of chaos or on the border between order and disorder (Miller 1998). In this approach, organizations are dynamic, chaotic and non-linear systems in which communication acts recursively to produce and reproduce the system. The application of self-referential or auto-communication systems to organizations provides new insights into the ways that organizations define markets as images of their own evolving identities (Cheney and Christensen 2001). Scholars also use chaos theory to explain why organizational change efforts fail, how health care delivery systems create stress and anxiety for nurses (Miller 1998), and how groups self-organize through the use of computer decision support systems (Contractor and Seibold 1993). These models, as scholars note, presuppose a cybernetic system in which human actors reside outside of organizing; thus, the role of agency in this metaphor is problematic (Miller 1998; Hawes 1999; Houston 1999).

Unlike self-referential systems, *interaction analysis* draws from the discourse metaphor, particularly for studies that focus on types and sequences of talk (Putnam and Fairhurst 2001). Studies of interactional analyses, however, assume that talk is patterned, has

a sense of progression or becomes structured into predefined or emergent functions over time (Fairhurst 2004). Current studies that employ this approach analyse types of troublesome work situations (Fritz 2002), patterns of differential treatments among co-workers, especially between newcomers and temporary workers (Sias 1996; Sias et al. 1997), face support in messages that regulate volunteers (Adams and Shepherd 1996), and interactions about work-family policies (Kirby and Krone 2002).

The performance metaphor also guides research on social interaction in negotiation. In particular, exchanging information about priorities, introducing multiple rather than single issues, avoiding reciprocal argumentative cycles, and integrating competitive with co-operative processes are patterns that foster reaching settlements, often with high joint gains (Weingart et al. 1999; Olekalns and Smith 2000). Critics of social interaction analyses chide scholars for relying on thin descriptions, using *a priori* coding systems, and removing agency from the process (Firth 1995), but defendants of it claim that interaction analysis broadens the notion of structures-in-action and shows how organizational processes become patterned and recurrent over time (Fairhurst 2004).

Structuration research often relies on interaction analysis to investigate actions and structures, particularly the way that structural forces simultaneously shape and constrain actions while they reproduce and transform them (Conrad and Hayes 2001). Adaptive structuration theory centres on group member interactions that appropriate and make sense of new organizational technologies (Poole and DeSanctis 1992; DeSanctis and Poole 1994). The effects of new technologies on group decision-making depends on the spirit or intent of the media as well as on sensemaking about media use. Similarly, Bastien et al. (1995) show how climate becomes a recursively-constructed structure that changes regularly in reproducing an organization's culture. Communicative acts are ways that organizational members socially construct their individual and organizational identities through making their multiple selves salient during particular events (Scott et al. 1998). Thus, in contrast to interaction analysis, structuration researchers infer actor's intentions and extend their analyses to the macro level.

Interaction patterns also characterize research on *enactment and sensemaking* as types of organizational performances that emerge from bracketing ongoing experiences and making sense of them. For example, enactment depicts how organizational members perform time (e.g. tight deadlines, flexible hours) and task co-ordination (Ballard and Seibold 2000; 2003), and develop their roles through negotiating daily interactions (Apker 2001). In a study of nurses, communication both facilitates uncertainty reduction and increases role ambiguity as nurses cope with a constantly changing health care environment (Miller et al. 2000). In like manner, the enactment of social support in a drug rehabilitation youth service organization functions as both comforting and discomforting as individuals negotiate the meanings of their painful experiences (Sass and Mattson 1999). Role negotiations between superiors and subordinates occur through direct requests during information interactions and through improvisations that serve as role elaborations and concessions (Meiners and Miller 2004). Women employees negotiate work–family conflicts through modifying daily routines, improvising requests and restructuring incompatible goals (Medved 2004).

Text–conversation approaches challenge traditional views of enactment through integrating language structures with action and sensemaking. Two different schools of thought, activity theory and speech act schematics, embrace notions of conversations as performances, discourse as co-orientation and texts as discursive processes of sensemaking (Cooren 2004; Taylor and Robichaud 2004). In *activity theory*, the locus of organizing resides in connecting patterns of talk and action to collective action systems (Engestrom 1999). Discourse, then, constructs texts as manifestations of sensemaking that are both produced and drawn upon in conversation as members relate to each other about organizational objects of concern (Cooren and Taylor 1997; Robichaud et al. 2004). Conversations perform organizing through routine patterns of language use that becomes layered or laminated in texts that are open to endless negotiations, interpretations, and inscriptions as they develop staying power that transcends particular interaction episodes (Taylor and Cooren 1997; Taylor and Van Every 2000; Robichaud 2001). For example, conversations among individuals on a drug rehabilitation board develop staying power as they become co-produced, amended and jointly interpreted in a series of textual blocks that constitute the group's collective intelligence (Cooren 2004).

Similar processes occur in *speech act schematics* in which the classic speech acts enable conversations

and texts to perform organizing (Cooren 2000). That is, action words, such as informatives, directives, commissives, declaratives and expressives, constitute organizing through performing by giving content, enacting orders and promises, transferring authority and performing sanctions, respectively. Co-ordination occurs through the energy that comes from integrating emotion into these speech acts and conversations (Quinn and Dutton 2005). In this approach, even material or objective texts assume an agency role of performing through leaving memory traces, issuing work orders and signalling actions over time and space (Cooren 2004). In essence, activity theory and speech act schematics alters the foundations of the performance metaphor by adding the organizing properties of language and texts to social interaction and co-ordination.

These five diverse but related threads of the performance metaphor treat communication as ongoing, dynamic, reflexive and an interconnected process. Clusters in the performance metaphor include co-constructing, sequential patterns and co-orientation. Organizations emerge from *co-ordinated actions* that surface through reflexive systems, negotiated orders, layered conversations and laminated texts. As a type of metaphor, performance functions as an abstraction in which the relational similarities of process, pattern and evolution are mapped onto communication and structured into co-ordinated actions.

Although unified through a social interaction focus, schools within this metaphor differ markedly as to the roles of agency and structure. At a deep level, interaction analysis and self-referential systems downplay agency, locating it in an evolving system. Text–conversations locate agency in the connection among talk, action and objects of organizing. Enactment studies and interaction analyses privilege order and reduce uncertainty, while self-referential systems capitalize on ambiguity and disorder. Structuration research introduces power into the metaphor while the other approaches typically treat power as an outcome of organizing. Text–conversation perspectives problematize discursive properties of interaction while the other schools centre on the functions of social interaction in producing organizations. Performance, then, is a loosely formed metaphor that treats social interaction as the generative mechanism for organizing, but one that is in transition through its ties to the discourse and voice metaphors.

The Discourse Metaphor

The *discourse* metaphor, in the original chapter, sub-sumed a potpourri of literature linked to micro and macro aspects of language and discursive practices. In the past several years, the growth of research in this area is evident in a *Handbook of Organizational Discourse* (Hardy et al. 2004), special issues of journals (Boje et al. 2004; Grant et al. 2004; Hardy et al. 2004; Putnam and Cooren 2004), and multiple state-of-the-art reviews (Grant et al. 2001; 2004; Putnam and Fairhurst 2001; Fairhurst and Putnam 2004; Grant and Hardy 2004). Discourse, as broadly defined, not only infuses the performance metaphor through work on interaction analysis and text-conversations, but it serves as an umbrella for work in the symbol, voice and contradiction metaphors. In this chapter, we treat discourse as a separate metaphor to highlight research that employs traditional linguistic and rhetorical approaches.

In this metaphor, *language*, that is words and signifiers, becomes the essence of communication. This metaphor includes studies that focus on the structure and function of words, use of words in talk and text, and the meanings of discursive practices (Putnam and Fairhurst 2001). This metaphor encompasses studies that employ discourse with a little 'd' or that examine talk and text in specific organizational practices (Alvesson and Karreman 2000). Also known as language-in-use, this metaphor includes studies that fall into the domains of conversational analysis, postmodern language analyses and organizational rhetoric.

An organization in the discourse metaphor refers to *the layering of texts* that enact organizing through a wide array of forms, including speeches, written materials, meetings, ongoing conversations, technical documents and emails (Hardy et al. 2005). The practices of producing and disseminating texts bring organizations into being, particularly through the ways that discourse interacts with historical, political and economic contexts. Texts, then, embody the discursive practices and associated meanings that constitute organizations. Research in the discourse metaphor clusters into: (1) conversational analysis, (2) emotional expressions, (3) ambiguity and (4) rhetorical strategies.

Conversational analysis focuses on talk turns, interruptions, topic managements, openings and closings of talk and questions/answers in interaction (Fairhurst and Cooren 2004). Organizational researchers use conversational analysis to study face management by examining how dispatchers in 911 emergency calls inadvertently threaten the caller's face through challenging their trustworthiness, intelligence or good character (Tracy 2002); the way physicians interact with patients in medical interviews to manage the face of interns (Pomerantz et al. 1997), and how flight attendants use unexpected voice stress and non-junctures in public announcements to negotiate the tensions between work requirements and their identities (Banks 1994).

Discourse practices of face management are intertwined with emotional reactions in conversations. *Emotional expression* centres on the way that feelings are manifested in the workplace. Since Chapter 3.3 in this volume addresses emotions and organizing, this review focuses only on the nature of emotional expressions and compassionate work. Drawn from interactionist models, the expression of emotions is a social, reciprocal and contagious discursive act (Callahan 2004). Emotions also function as symbolic performances in that they rely on rules for front and backstage displays, masking or faking emotions and collective sensemaking (Tracy 2000; Bodtker and Jameson 2001); hence, research on emotional expressions overlaps with both the performance and the symbol metaphors.

Recent research in this area examines the appropriateness of organizational display rules and their links to workplace contexts. Using content analysis and ethnographic studies, scholars report that appropriate displays entail the masking of both positive and negative emotions (Fiebig and Kramer 1998; Kramer and Hess 2002) that influence stress and burnout (Kruml and Geddes 2000), identity formation, and managerial control (Tracy 2000; Guerrier and Adib 2003). Thus, display rules work within social contexts to produce emotional fatigue and numbing as well as exhilaration (Clair and Dufresne 2004).

Managing emotions in the workplace is ultimately a struggle with dualities, namely balancing rationality and emotionality and compassion and dispassion. Cultures and circumstances that unite rationality and emotionality produce different display rules and patterns of emotional expressions than do cultures that keep them distinct (Krone et al. 1997; Miller 2002). The research on compassion in the workplace responds to this plea by demonstrating how organizations can become places of healing and caring as well as arenas for task accomplishment (Frost et al. 2000, Frost 2003; Kanov et al. 2004).

Tensions between these dualities also produce *ambiguity,* not through the failure to be precise in the meaning of a word, but through the way discursive situations introduce interpretive flexibility. Ambiguity then is often intentional and strategic and used to unify diverse goals, gloss over differences and legitimate plausible deniability (Eisenberg 1984). For example, imperative statements in technical documents produce ambiguity through homogenizing divergent views and making the group seem uniform (Irons 1998). Similarly, faculty members in a curriculum committee negotiate a vague definition of diversity to preserve strategic ambiguity and reach an agreement on a controversial policy (Castor 2005). Strategic ambiguity may also emerge in metapatterns of shared cultures to legitimate withholding information about initiatives and to appeal to the special interests of stakeholders (Brown 1995; Myers 2002).

Strategic ambiguity also surfaces in studies of organizational rhetoric that uses language to persuade internal and external publics (Cheney et al. 2004). Research on *rhetorical strategies* treats discourse as argumentation and persuasive appeals for research on: (1) corporate advocacy, (2) issue management and (3) rhetorical apologia. Studies of *corporate advocacy* examine how organizational speakers tailor their messages and adapt to different audiences through public presentations, newsletters, advertising and promotional materials. In newsletters managers use common ground language and the discourse of recognition to foster organizational identification (DiSanza and Bullis 1999), legitimate changes and ignore financial and political concerns (Mueller et al. 2004). Similarly, in public announcements about corporate earnings, organizational speakers conceal their persuasive appeals; thus blurring receiver, text and context in the guise of informational messages (Rogers 2000). Ironically, both management and labour use similar types of persuasive appeals in a union organizing campaign with labour relying on sarcasm, polarization and solidification and management employing appeals to company unity (Brimeyer et al. 2004). In addition to persuasive messages, corporate advocacy encompasses image branding to build relationships between organizations and customers. Image branding shields the corporation from ethical scrutiny through rhetorical strategies that convey the inevitable, evoke the American mythos, and turn the individual buyer into a product (Lair et al. 2005).

Issue management is a type of corporate advocacy that aligns an organization's public image with its policies through developing strategic plans that anticipate social changes and engaging in crisis prevention (Kuhn 1997). Organizations draft mission and vision statements (Fairhurst et al. 1997) and engage in crisis planning (Ulmer 2001) to buffer employees and the public from unforeseen events that might threaten them. These messages typically ignore social responsibility, bifurcate public/private audiences and fail to capture the complex roles of multi-stakeholder membership (Boyd 2001). Thus, corporate rhetoric acts to preserve free market fundamentalism, often elevating private financial gain over the concerns of stakeholders and obscuring executive accountability, as evident in the 2002 corporate meltdowns (Conrad 2003; Seeger and Ulmer 2003).

Despite efforts to prepare for unforeseen events, crises occur and organizations turn to *corporate apologia* to respond to these situations. Apologia is a type of genre aimed at restoring organizational images and legitimacy (Huxman and Bruce 1995). Scholars examine the way corporations label a crisis (whether an accident, faux pas or transgression), attribute blame to internal or external sources, make promises for corrective actions, or respond with strategic ambiguity (Coombs 1995; Tyler 1997; Ulmer and Sellnow 1997; Campbell et al. 1998; Brinson and Benoit 1999; Metzler 2001). Effective responses to crises entail taking responsibility for problems and initiating corrective actions (Sellnow et al. 1998). Since crisis situations are complex, however, organizations often match their responses to the level of responsibility the public assigns them for the situation (Coombs and Holladay 2002). The restoration of social legitimacy necessary for organizational recovery, however, may hinge on meeting expectations of the larger community through value-based actions as well as the rhetoric of apologia (Hearit 1995).

The discourse metaphor focuses on language-in-use or the structure, function and meaning of words. Research within this metaphor illustrates how conversations enact face management and the nature, type and level of emotional expressions. It illustrates how ambiguity functions to narrow decisions, unify diverse viewpoints and enforce implicit rules. It encompasses research on the way that organizations target messages to internal and external audiences, project corporate images, manage the legitimacy of issues and respond to social crises.

The discourse metaphor includes clusters on argument, language-in-use, semantics, linguistics and written and oral texts. In its narrow definition, this perspective highlights the structure and functions of language. Structural elements are central to the role that conversations play in face management and in the implicit rules that govern emotional displays. Ambiguity embraces both structure and function through norms that shape language specificity and define strategic ambiguity. Message functions play a dominant role in research on rhetorical strategies. Attention to the structure and function of language, however, presents a limited view of both discourse and audiences. Scholars need to challenge presumptions about senders and receivers and to probe more deeply to understand the levels of conversation, text and intertextuality (Heracleous and Marshak 2004; Hardy et al. 2005).

In this type of metaphor, discourse functions as literal similarity in that it transfers characteristics from discourse to communication. Because of its widespread use, this metaphor borders on becoming dead or dormant as it infuses other metaphors and spins off into different sub-clusters. Some theorists claim that discourse is used to cover muddled thinking and is in danger of standing for everything and almost nothing (Alvesson and Karreman 2000). In the future, 'discourse' may lose its metaphorical image and operate only at a surface level. An organization as layered texts, however, functions as an analogy in this metaphor; that is, discourse is to communication as texts are to organizations.

The Symbol Metaphor

Discourse chains into the *symbol* metaphor, particularly for such literary forms as narratives and storytelling; but the symbol metaphor privileges meaning rather than language as the locus of communication. A symbol is something that represents or stands for something else through association or convention (de Saussure 1983). Organizational actors use symbols to produce meanings through cultural, historical and/or political interpretations.

Symbols encompass a broad array of forms including architecture (Berg and Kreiner 1990) and cultural knowledge (Lyon 2004), as well as literary and rhetorical devices. In this metaphor, communication functions as *sensemaking* through the production, maintenance and interpretation of symbols, and organizations surface as *novels or literary texts*. Life in organizations becomes the making of novels, fiction and theatre in which members enact and negotiate the meanings for the symbols that they inscribe on their organizational landscapes. Research on organizational symbols has mushroomed in the past decade. Because of its scope and complexity, this review focuses on only two particular literary forms: rituals and narratives. Other chapters provide extensive reviews of metaphors, irony and rhetorical tropes in organizational studies (Oswick et al. 2004).

Rituals are routine observable practices expressed through symbolic interactions (Trice and Beyer 1984). As such, they encompass both formal public events like ceremonies and less scripted activities like staff meetings. Most studies centre on how the enactment of rituals maintains power relationships, normalizes atypical situations and legitimates organizational members. For example, on airplanes, rituals such as serving food, using euphemistic announcements and watching movies neutralize the dangers of flying and reinforce a status hierarchy among personnel (Murphy 2002). Just as rituals bind passengers together, participants in Alcoholics Anonymous unite through tales of personal experiences, friendship cocoons, birthday litanies and dress codes to celebrate sobriety and create a spiritual atmosphere for recovery (Witmer 1997). Old timers in AA often 'discipline' newcomers when stories deviate from these rituals of reformed alcoholics (Kitchell et al. 2000). These organizations engage in rehearsals that convert unpleasant routines to 'fun' and scapegoat delinquent members (Scheibel et al. 2002). They also reveal how different types of rituals produce multiple meanings for different stakeholders, for instance the baseball park as simultaneously a capitalistic division of labour, community family reunion and social drama (Trujillo 1992). For the most part, studies shows how rituals reaffirm status quo power relations and accent organizational reality.

Stories and narratives, in contrast, serve as vehicles of contestation as well as vessels for conveying corporate meanings. Narratives are temporal chains of interrelated events that involve symbolic meanings (Brown 1998; Gabriel 2004). For some theorists, stories differ from narratives in that they entail a poetic license that involves complex plots, colourful characters, intense emotions and ambiguity (Gabriel 2000; 2004). Other scholars treat stories as fragments or pieces of full-fledged narratives

(Brown 1990), while others view the two concepts as interchangeable (Eisenberg and Riley 2001). Scholars also differ regarding the aesthetic quality of stories, their fidelity (coherence) and verisimilitude (believability), their links to knowledge, and the roles of tellers and listeners (Czarniawska-Joerges 1995; Gabriel 2000; Boje 2001). These differences are evident in five diverse clusters of organizational narrative research: (1) cultural stories, (2) life stories, (3) storytelling, (4) narrative schema, and (5) embedded and multi-vocal stories.

Narratives that reflect organizational *cultures* serve as 'shock observers' during socialization, organizational changes and conflicts (Gabriel 2000). Through dramatizing actions, they display values (Meyer 1995), influence sensemaking (Sass 2000) and legitimate changes (Vaughn 1995). Stories told by human resource practitioners often centre on their needs to take action; however, they cast themselves as victims who are constrained by uncontrollable forces (Hansen et al. 1994). Stories about organizational change differ across levels and between profit and non-profit sectors. Specifically, senior managers tell epic stories of rescuing the organization from destruction while subordinates construct tragedies in which lower level employees are victims of flawed managerial strategies (Brown and Humphreys 2003). In constructing stories of excellence, managers in the non-profit sector centre their stories on external relationships while profit-based managers focus on internal aspects of the organization (Barge and Hackett 2003). Cultural stories serve a myriad of organizational functions, including socializing newcomers, identifying subcultures and affirming power relationships (Kramer and Berman 2001).

Life stories differ from cultural narratives by focusing on the lives and occupations of organizational members. Rooted in identity work, 'storying' serves to organize experiences and make sense of one's life. That is, through telling and retelling stories, individuals constitute their individual and organizational identities (Ainsworth and Hardy 2004). Individuals engage in discursive positioning in which their language and stories confirm their identities, for example, women engineers tell life stories about being career-oriented professionals to disassociate themselves from the 'chit-chatty' or 'ditzy' females in the workplace (Jorgenson 2002). Life stories also reveal the tensions between farming and family values in the agribusiness (Morgan et al.

2004), the double binds of middle managers who must please different audiences (Sims 2003), the trials of a mining community that socializes its young people to embrace a sense of pride and inner determination characteristic of the occupation (Lucas and Buzzanell 2004), and the difficulties of building camaraderie with peers, supervisors and family in an organizational wellness programme (Farrell and Geist-Martin 2005). Research on personal narratives grasps the emotional aspect of workers' lives and illustrates how life stories break the boundaries that separate work, family and community.

Storytelling refers to the process by which tellers and listeners co-construct narratives in conversations and collective experiences. Thus, storytelling chains with the performance metaphor through the way that social interaction weaves the collective telling of plots and action scenes. In Boje's (2001) view, storytelling emerges as an ante-narrative or bottom-up process of sharing terse stories that lack poetic qualities and complete form. These fragments evolve from the non-linear flows of experience and incoherent accounts that compete for meaning. Ante refers to making a wager or a bid that a particular story line will become a sensemaking account. Managers trained in systematic story making develop skills in introducing story fragments into conversations, following and developing them, and weaving them into the narratives of other employees (Barge 2004a).

Research on storytelling occurs at both micro and macro organizational levels. At the micro-level, storytelling about organizational change shows that over time middle managers become skeptical of changes and then senior managers modify their story lines to blame external agents for the new initiatives (Currie and Brown 2003). Retelling stories affirms that sensemaking is a shared experience (Weick 1995). For example, members of an academic department respond with disbelief and disdain in retelling stories of an outsider's sexual inappropriateness with three women instructors. Through humour, they create a culture that simultaneously supports the victims while denying that the outsider's actions were actually sexual harassment (Dougherty and Smythe 2004). Storytelling then serves ironic outcomes as it does for the staff members of a Roman Catholic parish who enact egalitarianism in sharing tales while reaffirming hierarchical power relations in the content of their stories (Coopman and Meidlinger 2000). Storytelling can also reaffirm the status quo by pre-serving symbolic oppositions, as evident in the ten-sions between honest horsemen and drug users and men and women trainers and groomers at a harness racetrack (Helmer 1993).

At the macro-level, storytelling functions differ-ently for internal and external audiences. For exam-ple, narratives about corporate bamboozling function as curative acts when directed outwardly to customers, but as embarrassing moments when shared with fellow employees (Scheibel 2002). In a study of media production, Smith and Keyton (2001) show how the process of scripting serves as an allegory for an organizational conflict, one that has different meanings for external audiences vs internal actors. Studies of corporate giants, like the Nike Corporation and Enron, reveal how the founder's narratives intersect with employees' sto-ries to compete for local and public sensemaking (Boje et al. 1999). Comparing narrative forms, Boje and Rosile (2003) demonstrate how reporters, regu-lators and analysts close off dramatic action in the Enron crisis through telling tragic rather than epic tales. Epic stories, in contrast, can open up action through tracking historical periods, incorporating lesser characters and producing different remedies for these social problems.

Another approach to narrative draws on Greimas's (1987) semio-narrative theory or *narrative schema* (Cooren 2000). This approach focuses on how dis-cursive acts structure narratives around a request for a desired goal or objective. A narrative schema con-sists of initiating the story, pursuing a mission, mobi-lizing others to help, fulfilling the quest and exercising praise or blame for the outcome. Narrative schemas become embedded in each other and create a social structure through a series of actions. Coalitions form through linking one narrative schema into the interests of another, thus making agendas compatible, as occurred in the alliances that supported policy actions in the Great White Whale case (Cooren 2001). Narrativity also develops in managerial sensemaking through the embedded sets of schemas that connect conversations of public administrators (Taylor and Lerner 1996).

Embedded and plurivocal narratives refer to the layering of stories in texts, contexts and audiences that lead to ongoing and unending construction of meaning. Organizational actors often strive to cen-tralize the production of meaning through unifying stories, resolving incompatible interpretations and excluding other realities. Plurivocal narratives, how-ever, expose the polyphony of simultaneous and sequentially occurring tales. Integrating narrative with intertextuality reveals fragmented images in which multiple voices surface and stories shift through alternating literary forms. For example, organizational changes in public administration can lead to multi-vocal tales; namely, a tragedy that results from increased regulation, a romantic com-edy of simultaneously decentralizing while central-izing, and a fragmented satire as the gaps between problems and solutions increase (Skoldberg 1994). These inconsistencies occur, in part, because narra-tives become embedded in historical contexts in which the past surfaces as an incongruent resource for present and future dilemmas (O'Connor 2000).

Narratives also become plurivocal through the ways that organizational stories are crafted for dif-ferent audiences, often revealing conflicting values and cultures (Allen and Tompkins 1996; Brown 1998; Stutts and Barker 1999). Plurivocality occurs when stories splinter, thus transforming the meta-narratives of top management (O'Connor 1997; Brown 1998). Researchers also introduce multi-vocal reads of narratives by casting the same study through different interpretive lenses, for example, integrative, differentiated and fragmented cultures (Eisenberg et al. 1998; Hylmo and Buzzanell 2002; Martin 2002) or functional, romantic and critical interpretations of organizational change (Zorn et al. 2000). Treating strategy as narrative reduces its authoritative role, increases it reflexivity and reveals multiple conflict-ing views (Barry and Elmes 1997).

The metaphor of symbol casts communication as representation and sensemaking. Studies within this metaphor, such as rituals and narratives, constitute organizations as novels and literary works that shape organizational practices. Metaphor clusters include semiotics, folklore and literary and artistic forms that enact changes as well as develop 'staying power' over time. Research examines how rituals naturalize recur-ring practices and legitimate power relationships. Narrative studies show how members constitute cultures, develop personal and organizational identi-ties, break institutional boundaries, and enact compet-ing views of social reality. Research in this metaphor crosses ontological perspectives (including post-positivism, interpretive studies, critical scholarship and postmodernism) and represents a transformation from its early roots as cultural artifacts.

The versatility of this metaphor makes it difficult to decipher its type and entailments. For many organizational scholars, sensemaking has literally become communication in both a cognitive and interactional way (Weick 1995). Some scholars who view organizations as literary texts treat this metaphor as a mere appearance or embellishment (Boland and Greenberg 1988), while other researchers view it as an abstraction for teasing multiple 'truths' out of organizational fiction (Gabriel 2000; Boje 2001). Deep-level analyses and metaphor entailments raise issues regarding audiences and storytelling as persuasive maneouvres as well as concerns about artistic and ethical features of good and bad narratives.

The Metaphor of Voice

The metaphor of voice has become very prominent in organizational communication studies. In some research, voice refers to altering the structures and practices that keep organizational members from speaking, being heard and making choices in organizational life. In other studies, voice is not simply having a say, but the ability to act, to construct knowledge and to exert power (Deetz 1992). This metaphor then focuses on communication as the *expression* or *suppression* of voice in organizational life, not simply as a property of speaking, but through the social and political processes that produce and reproduce meanings, identities and power relationships. Thus, the metaphor of voice includes engagement as well as the processes that marginalize individuals, silence groups and prohibit expression. An organization within the voice metaphor becomes a *dialogic process of social formation* or a *radical engagement* in the process of constituting organizational life.

In the past decade, voice has become a sub-metaphor within the larger rubric of discourse. Studies within this metaphor employ Foucauldian analyses of power and knowledge, critical discourse analysis (Phillips and Hardy 2002) or critical linguistics (Fairclough 1992; Fairclough and Wodak 1997). Some research incorporates micro-discourse analyses, but the majority of publications employ a meso approach that is sensitive to language in use but centres on broad patterns linked to local and global contexts (Alvesson and Karreman 2000). A number of projects embrace Discourse with a big 'D'; that is, studies of the general and enduring

systems of texts or the culturally standardized constellations that constitute organizations and individuals in particular ways (Foucault 1976; 1980). Thus, research within the voice metaphor subsumes work that examines the micro-practices of language, centres on the big 'D' of discourse, and focuses on intertextuality or the relationships among texts. All studies within this metaphor, however, share a concern for exposing power relationships and reducing inequalities of organizational life.

Similar to the original chapter, the voice metaphor clusters into the subcategories of distortion and domination, different voices and access to voice. This chapter, however, adds new subcategories that have become prevalent in research – silence and dissent. This review begins with distorted and dominated voices as acts of suppression and then reviews research on silence and dissent as complex responses to suppressed voices. Then we examine communicative research on a different voice and access to voice. The next metaphor, contradiction, also embodies voice, but it focuses on the symbolic struggles between oppositional tensions.

In *distorted voices*, preferred ways of organizing go unchallenged because they seem natural, neutral and legitimate (Deetz 1992; 1995). Suppression of conflict produces communication distortion amidst the absence of challenges to the clarity, truthfulness or appropriateness of particular claims. Specifically, the discourse of wellness at a plant's recreation centre links healthiness to individual lifestyles, such as diet and exercise, in ways that neutralize and suppress concerns about occupational safety hazards, job injuries and chemical exposures (Zoller 2003). In like manner, working arrangements for temporary employees normalize detachment and inadequate feedback in ways that distort and privilege full-time, in-house employees (Gossett 2002).

Discursive closure can also occur when organizational members rely on cultural routines that seem normal and natural, as occurred with a US Forest Service self-study of firefighter safety. Rather than encouraging firefighters to make decisions at the moment, participants distorted a change process by relying on management's safety rules (Thackaberry 2004). Voices of diversity are often distorted as human resource managers depict differences as a group- rather than an individual-level phenomenon that fosters comparisons between races and genders and reaffirms existing biases (Zanomi and Janssens 2003) and as corporate websites that marginalize stay-at-home-mothers as caregivers in domestic labour (Medved and Kirby 2005). Organizations instantiate these hegemonic processes through discourses rooted in instrumental goals, workforce availability and norms of compliance.

At the macro-level, organizations rely on controlling issues in the public sphere to normalize and legitimate their agendas. The 'public' becomes a concern in healthcare systems as stakeholders use symbolic meanings to normalize power relationships and legitimate decisions (Contandriopoulos et al. 2004). The public plays a role in private organizations like Nike, who legitimate widespread abuses of labour in a consumerist caste system through marketing discourses of social responsibility (Stabile 2000). Discourses of consumerism also promote a new educational mission and legitimate funding from private sources in transformations of the modern university (Fairclough 1993; McMillian and Cheney 1996).

Discourses of technology and spirituality function covertly to shape organizational identities in narcissistic and self-absorbing ways (Ganesh 2003) and to produce therapeutic practices that neutralize subjects as autonomous agents while obscuring corporate power (Nadesan 1999). Distortion also occurs in the midst of public disputes; for example, when a manufacturing corporation dissolves a coalition between labour and community ministers through relegating union interests to the private sphere and isolating the coalition from public debates (McClure 1996) and when a global alliance between business and government publicly champions a pseudo dialogue to stifle expression of voices and control self-interested definitions of trade policies (Zoller 2004).

Research on concertive control represents another approach to distorted voices (Barker 1993). In concertive control, management typically delegates power to groups who engage in highly interactive, semi-autonomous activities while internalizing managerial premises that fit their own values and experiences; thus, workplace decisions appear natural and inevitable rather than as instruments of control (DiSanza and Bullis 1999). In a team-based programme, workers in an international bank discipline fellow employees, identify strongly with the bank, and engage in a consensus paradox that closes off challenges to organizational policies (Papa et al. 1997).

Concertive control, as distorted communication, is also evident in electronic surveillance that decreases privacy and increases covert practices (Botan 1996). Performance monitoring is less controlling if managers involve employees in the system design and include two-way supportive feedback (Adler and Tompkins 1997). The pervasive discourses of organizational change also exert concertive control through the way ambiguous terms like *quality, customer service* and *efficiency* become symbolic umbrellas to reshape practices with managerial biases (Zorn et al. 2000).

Similar to distorted voices, *voices of domination* focus on power relations, particularly the way hegemony and control mystifies voice. Hegemony refers to the ways that subjects participate in their own subordination through socially constructing their identities, knowledge and institutions. Specifically, research norms of scientists and investigators shape the production of knowledge through constructing data and reports that privilege dominant groups (Kinsella 1999; Schneider 2001). Similarly, the discourses of environmental sustainability operate within the power-knowledge dynamics of corporate social reporting that support the ideology of market competition while appearing to promote social justice (Livesey 2002).

In studies of gender and hegemony, women in an office supply firm, especially ones who share tales of female jealousy, cattiness and backstabbing, enact discursive practices that reinforce gender stereotypes and contribute to their own oppression (Ashcraft and Pacanowsky 1996). In like manner, black women managers, who value being one of the boys, select masculine company names and navigate the organization with 'a hunting knife in their teeth', thus reinforcing patriarchy and their own subordination (Forbes 2002). Feminist organizations, however, also rely on suppressing conflicts and silencing dissent to preserve their own ideology and values (Edley 2000). Even men privilege particular definitions of masculinity through their roles as subjects who accrue power reflexively through taken-for-granted practices (Mumby 1998). Thus, voices of domination extend beyond a particular gender to shape how organizational ideology exerts control and preserves the status quo.

One response to domination is *silence*. Silence is typically viewed as the opposite of voice in that it evokes acquiescence, resignation and disengagement (Morrison and Milliken 2000). Cultures of silence often surface from organizational climates that stifle diversity of beliefs and ideas (Morrison and Milliken 2000); engender fears through employee mistreatment and systematic abuse (Lutgen-Sandvik 2003; Meares et al. 2004); and put down others through ridicule, homophobia and racism (Houston and Kramarae 1991). Silence, however, is not simply withholding voice; it is sometimes a proactive form of dissent and resistance (Van Dyne et al. 2003). Silence, as both an individual and collective reaction to power, orchestrates new realities through conveying defensiveness and self-protection (Clair 1998). Silence, then, constitutes the suppression of voice, as evident when homosexual employees struggle with remaining silent about their sexual orientations or going public (Spradlin 1998; Bowen and Blackmon 2003; Ward and Winstanley 2003).

Silence can also become a form of dissent through refusing to collaborate with majority discourses, serving as a rhetorical mask to hide assertive actions, or surfacing as small steps toward change through tempered radicalism (Meyerson 2001; Creed 2003). Thus, paradoxically, silence invokes the dichotomy of absence-presence that merges positive talk with negative space (Mumby and Stohl 1991; Ward and Winstanley 2003). That is, discursive meanings arise from both the absence and the presence of discussions on key organizational topics.

Specifically, ignoring talk about family and private life in interactions with gay and lesbian colleagues function as self-censorship or absence, even in organizations that have positive and supportive diversity policies (Ward and Winstanley 2003). 'Coming out', as a form of voice, then makes employees visible, but it rarely alters power relationships or heterosexual workplace norms. Research shows that open and supportive climates for sharing opinions in an inclusive symbolic context can facilitate genuine dialogue on practices of presence/absence (Bowen and Blackmon 2003; Creed 2003; Milliken and Morrison 2003). Silence then can assume multiple meanings and be a powerful presence in 'walking the talk'. Voice and silence are not necessarily opposite concepts; rather they depend on and interact with each other in constituting organizational life.

The sub-metaphor of *dissent* is a particular form of organizational resistance, one that focuses on disagreements, criticisms and contradictory opinions about organizational policies and practices (Kassing 1997). Dissent as a form of protest differs from resistance in its use of active-constructive efforts to alter dissatisfactory conditions within current organizational practices; thus it parallels voice, loyalty and exit (Hirschman 1970). It differs from whistleblowing by complaining directly to the source rather than going to the media or public audiences (King and Hermodson 2000; Kassing 2001). Employees who object to organizational policies confront manager by using direct-factual arguments, repetition of concerns, solution presentations and threats to resign. They also complain about ethical practices and potential harms to workers primarily to friends and family members (Kassing 1998; 2002; Kassing and Armstrong 2002). Willingness to engage in dissent depends on freedom of speech in the workplace, the quality of supervisory relationships, an employee's status and his or her personal influence in the company (Kassing and Avtgis 1999; Kassing 2001).

The metaphor of voice finds its most direct and common usage in feminist organizational studies, an area that has experienced extensive growth in the past decade (Buzzanell 2000; Ashcraft and Mumby 2004; Buzzanell et al. 2004). This work highlights the fact that some people speak *in a different voice* through their values, ethics of care and notions of empowerment. Because their voices are unique, they are often ignored, silenced or misunderstood. Organizational communication scholars explore ways to reconceptualize the public sphere, ethics, leadership and socialization from feminist perspectives (Buzzanell 2000).

Research on speaking in a different voice falls into three main arenas – feminist organizing, studies of sexual harassment and the racial dynamics of organizations. The first arena draws from critiques of patriarchy and privileges women's ways of organizing (Buzzanell 1994). Focusing on discipline and job loss, Mattson and Buzzanell (1999) contrast feminist approaches that privilege fairness and dialogue with traditional ones that centre on making individuals the source of problems. This approach to an ethics of care makes it possible to deliberate across differences rather than to reify masculine values (Hallstein 1999).

Studies of feminist organizations aim to empower organizational members through promoting consciousness about oppression and fostering mutually influential relationships (Ashcraft 2001b). In a study of leadership change, a founder's maternity leave empowers organizational members to increase their autonomy and revise the founder's role (Ashcraft 1999). Ironically, the enactment of an ideal form of feminist organizing often privileges a rational voice, as seen in a battered women's shelter when members adopt a code of conduct that silenced employees and created a paradox of empowering while simultaneously controlling actions (Ashcraft 2000; 2001a, b). Empowerment is also contingent on an employee's temporal investment in an organization. For volunteer workers, it means freedom from responsibility, but for paid workers, it signifies participation in decision-making (Ashcraft and Kedrowicz 2002).

A second way in which a different voice guides research is the study of sexual harassment. Current scholars treat sexual harassment as a discursive process in which women and men may differ in their views about sexual overtures, touching and explicit messages in the workplace (Solomon and Williams 1997a, b; Keyton and Rhodes 1999; Lee and Guerrero 2001). Employees see greater threats of sexual harassment from co-workers than supervisors and in work climates in which zero tolerance policies exist, but are not enforced (Keyton et al. 2001). Sharing stories about sexual harassment may create space for resisting sexual advances, but it also highlights the hegemonic belief that no response to it really works to prevent it (Dougherty and Smythe 2004). Sexual harassment is clearly embedded in structures of power and coercion that seem absent from many of these investigations.

This notion of a different voice extends to issues of race and ethnicity in organizations (Allen 2004; Parker 2005). From a feminist standpoint, race is a constitutive element of organizing, one in which the voices of African-American women emerge from sharing lived experiences (Allen 1996). Finding voice in organizational assimilation entails efforts to subvert or transform power plays, to deflect and reframe patronizing comments, to build informal power relationships and to dispel stereotypes (Allen 2000; Parker 2002). Fundamentally, race is about interrogating whiteness; that is, the subtle ways that race pervades our language in such phrases as 'the dark side of downsizing'; and becomes masked through depicting minorities as 'protected groups' and 'disadvantaged' (Grimes 2001). The absence of race in organizational communication studies stems from treating it as a separate category of research, linking it conceptually to diversity and locating discriminatory practices in personal bias (Ashcraft and Allen 2003). Researchers need to treat race as theoretically inscribed in organizational life by integrating it with other organizational constructs and developing alternatives that avoid essentializing colour.

Empowerment issues that feminist scholars raise overlap with *access to voice*. Research in this arena focuses on workplace democracy (Cheney 1995). Defined as a system of governance rooted in participatory processes, democracy is most likely to emerge when communication is pivotal to an organization's goals. Communication scholars investigate alternative organizations, especially collectives that foster and maintain shared workplace control, such as a kibbutz, a religious order or the Mondragon cooperatives (Russell 1997; Cheney 1999; Hoffman 2002). To provide access to voice, organizations need to encourage authentic participation, avoid mission drift, manage size through committees and representatives, maintain a self-reflective communication system, and learn to use dialogue effectively (Cheney 1995; Cheney et al. 1998; Hoffman 2002). Even though most workplace democracy studies focus on internal communication, organizations must eventually respond to market pressures and function in a public sphere (Metzler 1997; Cheney 1999).

The metaphor cluster of voice brings together different orientations to the notion of speaking as a way of exerting power in organizational life. The cluster within the voice metaphor includes such concepts as concertive control, discursive closure, muted voices and empowerment. The voice metaphor centres on the factors that shape communication, namely the way that power becomes neutralized and normalized to distort voices, the role of concertive control in legitimating voices, the way hegemony and ideology function to suppress voices, silence as both compliance with and resistance from power, and the role of dissent in registering disagreements and criticism. Studies of feminist organizing and race/ethnicity advocate a different voice to challenge patriarchy, masculinity and whiteness. In a like manner, research on workplace democracy sets forth alternative models of organizing that employ the metaphor of dialogue and radical engagement to express voice.

For many scholars, the metaphor of voice exhibits literal similarity to communication; that is, suppression or expression of voice equals communication. Other researchers treat voice as an abstraction for the presence or absence of power and domination, one that parallels communication, but is not isomorphic with symbolic meaning. The voice metaphor embodies second-order alignments, as evident in research on silence as absence/presence and voice as suppression and expression. Perhaps more than other metaphors scholars overtly challenge the ideology and hegemony of voice itself, particularly the goals for relationships between voice and communication. For some scholars, organizational research aims to emancipate suppressed and distorted voices, interrogate dominant voices and privilege pluivocal expressions. Other researchers aim to disentangle voices by understanding, comparing, questioning and qualifying them based on particular values for organizations in society (Gabriel 2004). Another group of scholars believe that the metaphor of voice obscures economic laws of capitalism and the material bases of power (Reed 2000; Cloud 2005). Hence, future work within the voice metaphor needs to recognize the presence of these ideological struggles and incorporate them in research designs.

As these arenas suggest, voice is more than different people speaking or participating in a liberal democracy. Rather it is a way that meanings are constructed and disguised through social and political processes (Deetz 2003). Use of this metaphor, then, needs to incorporate the structural, economic and coercive aspects of voice; preserve the contradictions between and within multiple voices, and explore the dialogic processes of social formations.

The Metaphor of Contradiction

A spin-off of the voice metaphor extends the work on power and resistance to oppositional struggles. *Contradiction* refers to messages and actions that are diametrically opposed to each other (Putnam 1986). This metaphor purports that tensions and contradictions underlie human social systems. Even though the term *contradictory* often carries negative connotations, contradiction forms the building blocks of organizational life; that is, it underlies such arenas as role conflict and ambiguity, organizational change, participation programmes, control systems and leadership (Putnam 1986; Stohl and Cheney 2001). Thus, contradictions and workplace dilemmas are natural occurrences in ever-changing complex organizations.

In this metaphor, communication as *contradiction* highlights the interaction between oppositional forces that are situated in bi-polar relationships; hence, the *ongoing struggle or tensions* between these forces constitutes the *organization* in this metaphor. This struggle is a dynamic process in that one phase of a negotiated relationship often sets the stage for the next one (Baxter and Montgomery 1996). For some scholars, resolution of dualities and contradiction involves a grand synthesis or transcendent knowledge (Marx 1961; Hegel 1968). Others cast it as a constant exploration and struggle that maintains tension, one that should be kept in constant play and should open space for critical reflection and practice (Adorno 1973; Bakhtin 1981). Contradiction serves as a metaphor for four subcategories: (1) dialectic of control, (2) dialectical tensions, (3) paradox, and (4) dialogue.

In Gidden's (1984) *dialectic of control*, the enactment of rules and resources presumes the presence of opposites that undermine initial actions. For instance, in a study of corporate downsizings, the primary contradiction of people vs profits produces a set of secondary contradictions (for example, short-term vs long-term solutions and targeted vs across the board layoffs) that result in unintended consequences of lower profits from the layoffs (Fairhurst et al. 2002). Similarly, in a corporate merger, the profit vs people contradiction produces tensions between empowerment vs powerlessness and identification vs estrangement in ways that inhibit change and freeze ideological positions (Howard and Geist 1995). A similar dialectic between control and emancipation in a Grameen Bank draws from paternalistic dependency to teach employees about self-sufficiency (Papa et al. 1995). Thus, the dialectic of control focuses on the ways that primary and secondary contradictions constrain and enable the nature of organizing.

Similar to the dialectic of control, *paradoxes* stem from contradictions, but paradoxes often bankrupt choice – leading to feelings of paralysis or producing double binds that trap organizational members between non-existent options (Abeles 1976; Putnam 1986; Stohl and Cheney 2001; Tracy 2004). Paradoxes stem from messages that invoke mutually exclusive injunctions; pragmatic situations in which goals, actions and practices are incompatible; and vicious cycles that are hard to break (Hylmo and Buzzanell 2002). Thus, paradoxes, if managed in particular ways, often lead to detrimental organizational outcomes.

Paradoxes arise from changes that produce inconsistencies in organizational actions. Specifically, they pervade workplace democracy programmes when the top of the company orders the bottom to participate, when employees become empowered by giving up individual rights, when a high frequency of meetings leads to an absence of communication, and when self-discipline in a team becomes more oppressive than supervisory control (O'Conner 1995; Wendt 1998; Stohl and Cheney 2001; Carroll and Arneson 2003). Paradoxes also arise from ambiguous communication when managers give equivocal messages, engage in emotional outbursts and create a climate of fear that suppresses inquiries and stifles productivity (Markham 1996).

Reactions to contradictions are the keys to managing paradoxes effectively (Lewis 2000; Lewis and Dehler 2000). Specially, separation, vacillation and splitting choices are common ways to deal with paradoxes by selecting one end of the pole and adhering to it, vacillating between contradictory choices, or prioritizing among the incompatible options. These actions often result in organizational withdrawal and burnout, as occurred in a study of prison correctional officers who viewed paradoxes as mutually exclusive options (Tracy 2004). Humour, as a reframing mechanism, aids women in managing organizational paradoxes of power and agency (Martin 2004). By reframing paradoxes as complementary dialectics, employees can engage in creative thinking, transform oppositions and introduce metacommunication to talk about the structures and practices that lead to paranoia and paralysis (Tracy 2004).

In contrast, the sub-category of *dialectical tensions* centres on the unity of opposites as organizational members struggle to embrace the *both-and* of bi-polar pairs. This unity occurs because the dualities are essential interdependent parts of a social system or because one concept has meaning only through its opposite; for example, certainty has meaning only through comparison with uncertainty (Baxter and Montgomery 1996). A postmodern approach to organizational dialectics treats change as evolving from a continual interplay of three types of opposing forces: autonomy vs connection, stability vs change and resistance vs compliance.

For example, dialectical struggles between *autonomy and connectedness* surface as political tensions between nurses and anaesthesiologists regarding issues of supervision and educational training (Jameson 2004). Tensions between autonomy and connection are also evident in simultaneously embracing control and yielding in developing tacit norms during a teacher–administrator negotiation (Putnam 2003) and in constructing solidarity and division within a symphony company through negotiating the identities of musicians, board members and administrators (Rudd 1995; 2000). This dialect also arises in negotiations between a parent company and its Thai subsidiary as the two cultures struggle to define independence–dependence and equitable–inequitable practices (Stage 1999) and in staff–client interactions in a battered women's shelter as clients struggle for emancipation amidst asymmetrical roles and contrasting experiences (Vaughn and Stamp 2003).

The dialectic of *stability vs change* is particularly prevalent in non-traditional organizations. Leaders of co-operatives struggle with absorbing environmental changes while protecting their core ideologies (Harter and Krone 2001) and resisting bureaucratic structures (Buzzanell et al. 1997). Similarly, the discourse of business process re-engineering simultaneously supplants and replaces masculinity in reacting to uncertainty and stability in a planned change programme. Thus, dialectical tensions form the process of change as organizational members decide what to do and how to react to new organizational developments (Kellett 1999).

Closely related to change are the dialectical tensions that underlie *compliance and resistance*. Resistance is a process through which organizational members struggle to keep meanings open and contingent (Prasad and Prasad 1998). Drawing on the tensions between resistance and compliance, research in this area shows how control is never absolute; that is, employees typically find ways to evade, subvert and alter organizational processes (Ackroyd and Thompson 1999).

Resistance surfaces through overt and covert practices, formal and informal interactions, and in diffuse and targeted ways (Ashforth and Mael 1998). Covert processes embodied in cynicism, irony, parody, gossip and bitching serve as hidden transcripts to resist gender hierarchy and managerial surveillance through simultaneously granting compliance while engaging in resistant acts (Murphy 1998; Sotirin and Gottfried 1999; Fleming and Spicer 2002; Hafen 2004). With a goal of creating discursive spaces, organizational members employ ambiguous accommodations, subtle subversions and being unreasonably reasonable to resist managerial encroachments on worker autonomy and identity (Prasad and Prasad 2000; Ezzamel et al. 2001; Fleming and Sewell 2002).

Thus, examining the struggle between compliance and resistance enables organizational members to redefine identities while simultaneously adhering to organizational practices that objectify them (Trethewey 1997; 1999; Tracy 2000). For instance, the discourse of entrepreneurism allows mid-career professional women to resist loss and decline within the master narrative of ageing (Trethewey 2001). Discursive practices that neutralize sexual harassment, with such phrases as 'unwanted sexual advances', allow victims to regain subject positions while accepting and struggling against sexual representations in academic life (Townsley and Geist 2000).

Resistance is also overt, as evident in the corporate merger between Ozark and TWA when Ozark pilots struggled to retain their identities through wearing their old company pins and using Ozark flying standards while complying with TWA's management strategy (Pierce and Dougherty 2002). Similarly, resistance in a splinter group of a pilot's union surfaced in a campaign as they struggled to defeat a proposed contract and comply with management prerogatives (Real and Putnam 2005). It was also apparent in the way that union members conducted a discursive campaign in a 2-year lock out that led to violence and victimization of workers (Cloud 2005). These dialectical struggles between resistance and compliance, however, raise questions about the goals of resistance and its role in helping workers shift identities, gain voice or increase their power (Cloud 2005). Clearly more work is needed on the interface between material conditions and the discursive struggles between compliance and resistance.

One way to keep dialectical tensions in play is to engage in *dialogue*. Dialogue is a discursive medium in which participants rely on dialectical tensions in conversations with each other to reveal presumed opposites and to develop a third space that might embrace both poles of the dichotomy (Baxter and Montgomery 1996; Hawes 1999). Intertwined with organizational learning (Isaacs 1999), dialogue typically arises through a structured, facilitated intervention like reflective practice or appreciative inquiry (Kellett 1999; Barge and Oliver 2003; Barge 2004b). For example, facilitators use dialogue to confront diversity conflicts, to raise questions about organizational mission statements (Kellett 1999)

and to develop a reflexive mentoring programme (Bokeno and Gantt 2000).

Drawn from actor–network theory, reflective practice refers to a type of conversation that introduces multiple voices, circularity and invitational rhetoric (Barge 2004b). Through creating an inclusive and safe environment, managers use life scripts, stakeholder maps and speech acts to get organizational members to share diverse stories. Managers and subordinates can also engage in reflexive practice through incorporating each other's words and meanings, affirming and connecting to each other, and highlighting situated judgements rather than expert opinions. Appreciative inquiry, then, is a conversational structure in which managers introduce multiple perspectives and privilege the role of listeners and learners (Barge and Oliver 2003). Through unblocking feelings of paralysis, reflexive practices of dialogue aim to provide opportunities for employees to transform their experiences (Hawes 1999; Barge 2004b).

In the contradiction metaphor, communication focuses on mutually exclusive relationships and antithetical messages. Organizations are ongoing struggles between forces in opposition and communication mediates this struggle by holding these forces in tension with one another. This metaphor cluster includes related concepts of dialectics and dualities, Janusian thinking, incongruities and bi-polar extremes. Research within this metaphor focuses on four types of contractions: *dialectics of control* as the way that primary contradictions underlie secondary enactments of rules and resources; *paradoxes* as reflexive contradictions that lead to vicious or virtuous cycles, feelings of entrapment or double binds; *dialectical tensions* that arise from the unity of opposites or embracing both autonomy and connection, stability and change, and compliance and resistance; and *dialogue* as discourse that engages opposites in conversation with each other.

Research within this metaphor presumes that contradictions are natural – an inevitable outgrowth of the complexity and ever-changing process of organizing. Management of these tensions, through denial, selection of only one side and oscillating back and forth between poles, may lead to inaction and entrapment that prevents organizational members from moving forward. Embracing both poles simultaneously through dialogue and reflexive practice exposes the tensions and fosters options for creative transformation.

An analysis of metaphor entailments reveals a strong reliance on discourse and related families of irony and dissonance. Unpacking the linkages among contradiction and ironical or unintended consequences might be a direction for future research. Contradiction in this metaphor functions as mere appearance in that it relies on only part of the relationship between source and target. It operates at both the deep and surface levels to explore tensions and incompatibilities, but it excludes consensus and consistency from its purview. Dissonance introduces the emotive aspect of struggles between opposing forces and calls for connections between contradiction and the emotional expression sub-metaphor of discourse. At the deep level of analysis, contradiction relies heavily on discursive practices that typically ignore the material and economic foundation of these relationships. Introducing this element through retaining the postmodern orientation of this metaphor presents an important challenge for future research.

Discussion and Conclusions

The field of organizational communication has experienced dramatic changes in the past decade. These changes are evident in the sheer volume of research as well as in shifts from linear transmission to discourse, symbol and voice models of communication. Although the seven original metaphors serve as perspectives for building knowledge, sub-metaphors under these seven have dramatically changed. Moreover, new areas are beginning to surface, such as the contradiction metaphor. These areas emerge as researchers draw from the original seven in creative ways to form new domains of organizational communication research. This discussion section reviews the types of changes noted in the seven original metaphors, types of chains between the metaphors and new cluster areas. It concludes by commenting on what these changes say about the field, the degree to which different perspectives infuse each other and the way metaphor entailments point to future research directions.

In general, scholars have moved away from the *conduit metaphor* as the primary lens for studying organizational communication; however, this image is clearly alive and well in interdisciplinary research, particularly among scholars who treat communication as a tool for achieving organizational goals.

Studies of communication competencies as well as research on media choice are particularly prevalent in this metaphor. The conduit metaphor also chains into information processing and linkage metaphors through a focus on information flow that treats communication as a social contact system.

Unlike the conduit metaphor, major shifts have occurred in the treatment of communication as a filter for information flow. Basically, research within the *information processing* metaphor draws from the conduit and performance approaches to focus on information seeking and types of message exchange. The organization within this metaphor becomes a map or trajectory for routing different types of information rather than an eye that scans and filters information flow, as evident in the lens metaphor. Even though the two metaphors are similar, their figure–ground relationships differ. Some research within this metaphor chains into the performance approach through examining uncertainty reduction and focusing on the enactment of feedback. In both the conduit and the information processing metaphors, however, scholars continue to view organizations as containers with physical, objective boundaries.

Research that adopts a *linkage* metaphor often employs conduit and information processing views of transmission and information flow; yet, the communication focus of this metaphor centres on connections or the formation of organizations as networks. In the linkage metaphor, organizations are contact systems of relationships that span time and space; thus, moving away from the fixed boundaries of organizations. The major shift in this metaphor is the focus on emergent linkages and theoretical explanations for network formations. Research continues to centre on such topics as electronic communication, social support, knowledge structures and macro networks. The linkage metaphor also chains into the performance, discourse and symbol metaphors through studies of role enactment and semantic networks.

The *performance* metaphor shifts communication away from transmission and contact systems to social interactions and meaning. In this metaphor, organizations become accomplishments through the way that social interaction coordinates actions. Scholars who embrace this metaphor focus on enactment and sensemaking, but they also draw from the linkage metaphor through studies of self-referential systems and from the discourse metaphor for research on interaction analysis, structuration and text–conversation research. Thus, domains of research formerly included in the discourse metaphor now appear as performances through examining action-structures and the organizing properties of language.

Growth in the *discourse* metaphor in the past decade has led to splintering it into other metaphors based on the figure–ground role of discourse in these studies. Organizations in this metaphor consist of the layering of texts. Discourse, however, has become a generic metaphor to encompass a large array of research, but in this chapter, the discourse metaphor centres primarily on studies of language in use, the functions of talk and texts and the meanings of discursive practices. This metaphor incorporates conversational analyses, emotional expressions, ambiguity and rhetorical strategies. Organizational rhetoric studies parallel macro analyses through examining the persuasive functions of image formation, branding and apologia as targeted to different audiences. The discourse metaphor also includes communication research on emotional expression, an arena that is beginning to develop into its own separate metaphor. Because of its scope and breadth, the discourse metaphor, as broadly defined, interfaces with the symbol and voice metaphors.

The *symbol* metaphor privileges meaning and the interpretive functions of discourse, especially through such symbolic forms as rituals and narratives. Communication in this metaphor refers to sensemaking and the organization becomes a literary text or novel. The volume and type of research in this metaphor has mushroomed in the past decade, necessitating a narrow focus for this chapter. Research on organizational narratives clusters into the categories of culture, life stories, storytelling, narrative schema and plurivocal narratives. Overall, these studies present a more complex understanding of symbols in organizational life – ones that integrate cultural, political and historical issues into organizational processes. Research in the symbol metaphor also chains into the discourse, voice and contradiction metaphors, as evident with the work on paradoxes in the contradiction metaphor of this chapter.

The metaphor that has expanded the most from the 1996 volume is *voice*. Although it continues to focus on suppression and expression, voice also means the ability to construct knowledge and exert power in addition to speaking out. This metaphor also incorporates studies of distorted and dominant voices, different voices and access to voice. This chapter, however, unlike the original one, examines metaphor alignments of voice, namely silence, presence–absence and dissent. An organization within this metaphor is more than a chorus of voices, as depicted in the original chapter. Rather organizations consist of participants who speak out, promote radical engagement or engage in dialogue to reveal suppressed conflicts that foster power shifts. The voice metaphor chains into the discourse and symbol approaches and also spills into the contradiction metaphor.

In response to the tensions in organizational life, communication as *contradiction* focuses on the messages, actions and structures that stand in opposition to each other. In this metaphor, organizational change evolves from the dynamic, ongoing struggles among opposing forces and surface through the ways that these tensions are managed. The sub-metaphors in this cluster cast communication as a dialectic of control, paradoxical interactions, dialectical tensions and dialogue. Research also examines ways that organizational members engender creativity and critical reflection through keeping oppositional forces in constant play. The contradiction metaphor bridges with the voice, discourse and symbol metaphors, particularly in studies of presence–absence, irony and dissonant symbols.

As communication has evolved through different perspectives, the nature of organizations has also shifted. This chapter highlights how studies within the original seven metaphors have changed in the past decade, becoming more integrated and less isolated than in the original chapter. This integration is evident in the tight links between the discourse, symbol and voice metaphors and their connections to the study of contradictions. It also surfaces in the performance metaphor, as studies of organizational roles have become constitutive and action-oriented rather than static structures.

Studies of socialization span an array of metaphors and illustrate how a concept develops over time, moving from its original managerial roots to research on uncertainty reduction in information processing to ambiguity in discourse and to the life experiences of black feminists. Our assessment of the current literature in the field suggests that these eight research perspectives infuse each other rather than exist in isolated camps. Our discussion of the metaphorical chains throughout this chapter supports this position. Even though these perspectives are not isolated from each other, they clearly have different preferential positions in the extant literature. The exponential growth of studies in the latter four metaphors indicates that interpretive, critical and postmodern studies have become widely prevalent in organizational communication research.

If organizational reality is determined, in part, by the perspectives that we take rather than the phenomena we observe (Bergquist 1993), then this chapter responds to the plea for new perspectives and alternative metaphors of organizing.

References

Abeles, G. (1976) 'Researching the unresearchable: experimentation on the double bind', in C. Sluzki and D. Ransom (eds), *Double Bind: The Foundation of the Communication Approach to the Family*. New York: Grune and Stratton. pp. 113–50.

Ackroyd, S. and Thompson, P. (1999) *Organization Misbehavior*. London: Sage.

Adams, C.H. and Shepherd, G.J. (1996) 'Managing volunteer performance: face support and situational features as predictors of volunteers' evaluations of regulative messages', *Management Communication Quarterly*, 9(4): 363–88.

Adler, G.S. and Tompkins, P.K. (1997) 'Electronic performance monitoring: an organizational justice and concertive control perspective', *Management Communication Quarterly*, 10(3): 259–88.

Adorno, T. (1973) *Negative dialectics*, translated by E.B. Ashton. New York: Continuum.

Ainsworth, S. and Hardy, C. (2004) 'Discourse and identities', in D. Grant, C. Hardy, C. Oswick and L. Putnam (eds), *The Sage Handbook of Organizational Discourse*. London: Sage. pp. 153–73.

Allen, B.J. (1996) 'Feminist standpoint theory: a black woman's (re)view of organizational socialization', *Communication Studies*, 47: 257–71.

Allen, B.J. (2000) 'Learning the ropes: a black feminist standpoint analysis', in P.M. Buzzanell (ed.), *Rethinking Organizational and Managerial Communication From Feminist Perspectives*. Thousand Oaks, CA: Sage. pp. 177–208.

Allen, B.J. (2004) *Difference Matters: Communicating Social Identity*. Long Grove, IL: Waveland Press, Inc.

Allen, B. and Tompkins, P. (1996) 'Vocabularies of motives in a crisis of academic leadership', *Southern Communication Journal*, 61(4): 322–31.

Alvesson, M. (1993) *Cultural Perspectives on Organizations*. Cambridge: Cambridge University Press.

Alvesson, M. and Karreman, D. (2000) 'Varieties of discourse: on the study of organizations through discourse analysis', *Human Relations*, 53: 1125–49.

Amason, P., Allen, M.W. and Holmes, S.A. (1999) 'Social support and acculturative stress in the multicultural workplace', *Journal of Applied Communication Research*, 27: 310–34.

Apker, J. (2001) 'Role development in the managed care era: a case of hospital-based nursing', *Journal of Applied Communication Research*, 29(2): 117–36.

Ashcraft, K.L. (1999) 'Managing maternity leave: a qualitative analysis of temporary executive succession', *Administrative Science Quarterly*, 44: 240–80.

Ashcraft, K.L. (2000) 'Empowering 'professional' relationships: organizational communication meets feminist practice', *Management Communication Quarterly*, 13(3): 347–92.

Ashcraft, K.L. (2001a) 'Feminist organizing and the construction of 'alternative' community', in G.J. Shepherd and E.W. Rothenbuhler (eds), *Communication and Community*. Mahwah, NJ: Lawrence Earlbaum Associates Publishers. pp. 79–110.

Ashcraft, K.L. (2001b) 'Organized dissonance: feminist bureaucracy as hybrid form', *Academy of Management Journal*, 44(6): 1301–22.

Ashcraft, K.L. and Allen, B.J. (2003) 'The racial foundation of organizational communication', *Communication Theory*, 13(1): 5–38.

Ashcraft, K.L. and Kedrowicz, A. (2002) 'Self-direction or social support? Nonprofit empowerment and the tacit employment contract of organizational communication studies', *Communication Monographs*, 69(1): 88–110.

Ashcraft, K.L. and Mumby, D.K. (2004) *Reworking Gender: A Feminist Communicology of Organization*. Thousand Oaks, CA: Sage.

Ashcraft, K.L. and Pacanowsky, M.E. (1996). ''A woman's worst enemy': reflections on a narrative of organizational life and female identity', *Journal of Applied Communication Research*, 24: 217–39.

Ashforth, B.E. and Mael, F.A. (1998) 'The power of resistance: Sustained value identities', in R.M. Kramer and M.A. Neale (eds), *Power and Influence in Organizations*. Thousand Oaks, CA: Sage Publications. pp. 89–119.

Avtgis, T.A. and Kassing, J. (2001) 'Elucidating influences on superior-subordinate communication: attributional confidence and organizational control expectancies', *Communication Research Reports*, 18: 255–63.

Axley, S. (1984) 'Managerial and organizational communication in terms of the conduit metaphor', *Academy of Management Review*, 9: 428–37.

Bakhtin, M. (1981) *The Dialogic Imagination*, translated by C. Emerson and M. Holquist. Austin, TX: University of Texas Press.

Ballard, D.I. and Seibold, D.R. (2000) 'Time orientation and temporal variation across work groups: implications for group and organizational communication', *Western Journal of Communication*, 64: 218–42.

Ballard, D. and Seibold, D.R. (2003) 'Communicating and organizing in time: a meso-level model of organizational temporality', *Management Communication Quarterly*, 16(3): 380–415.

Banks, S.P. (1994) 'Performing public announcements: the case of flight attendants' work discourse', *Text and Performance Quarterly*, 14: 253–67.

Barge, J.K. (2004a) 'Antenarrative and managerial practice', *Communication Studies*, 55(1): 106–27.

Barge, J.K. (2004b) 'Reflexivity and managerial practice', *Communication Monographs*, 7(1): 27–53.

Barge, J.K. and Oliver, C. (2003) 'Working with appreciation in managerial practice', *Academy of Management Review*, 29(1): 124–42.

Barge, K. and Hackett, S. (2003) 'The intersection of cultural and professional identity in nonprofit management', *Communication Research Reports*, 20(1): 34–44.

Barker, J. (1993) 'Tightening the iron cage: concertive control in self-managing teams', *Administrative Science Quarterly*, 38: 408–37.

Barry, D. and Elmes, M. (1997) 'Strategy retold: toward a narrative view of strategic discourse', *Academy of Management Review*, 22(2): 429–52.

Bastien, D.T., McPhee, R.D. and Bouton, K.A. (1995) 'A study and extended theory of the structuration of climate', *Communication Monographs*, 62: 87–109.

Baxter, L.A. and Montgomery, B.M. (1996) *Relating: Dialogues & Dialectics*. New York: Guildford Press.

Berg, P.O. and Kreiner, K. (1990) 'Corporate architecture: Turning physical settings into symbolic resources', in P. Gagliardi (ed.), *Symbols and Artifacts: Views of the Corporate Landscape*. New York: Walter de Gruyter. pp. 41–67.

Bergquist, W. (1993) *The Postmodern Organization: Mastering the Art of Irreversible Change*. San Francisco, CA: Jossey-Bass.

Bodtker, A.M. and Jameson, J.K. (2001) 'Emotion in conflict formation and its transformation: application to organizational conflict management', *The International Journal of Conflict Management*, 12(3): 259–75.

Boje, D.M. (2001) *Narrative Methods for Organizational & Communication Research*. London: Sage.

Boje, D.M. and Rosile, G.A. (2003) 'Life imitates art: Enron's epic and tragic narration', *Management Communication Quarterly*, 17(1): 85–125.

Boje, D.M., Luhman, J.T. and Baack, D.E. (1999) 'Stories and encounters between storytelling organizations', *Journal of Management Inquiry*, 8(4): 340–60.

Boje, D.M., Oswick, C. and Ford, J.D. (2004) 'Introduction to special topic forum – language and organization: the doing of discourse', *Academy of Management Review*, 29(4): 571–7.

Bokeno, R.M. and Gantt, V.W. (2000) 'Dialogic mentoring: core relationships for organizational learning', *Management Communication Quarterly*, 14(2): 237–70.

Boland, R.J. and Greenberg, R.H. (1988) 'Metaphorical structuring of organizational ambiguity', in L.R. Pondy, R.J. Boland Jr. and H. Thomas (eds), *Managing ambiguity and change*. New York: John Wiley & Sons. pp. 17–36.

Botan, C. (1996) 'Communication work and electronic surveillance: a model for predicting panoptic effects', *Communication Monographs*, 63: 293–313.

Bowen, F. and Blackmon, K. (2003) 'Spirals of silence: the dynamic effects of diversity on organizational voice', *Journal of Management Studies*, 40(6): 1393–418.

Boyd, J. (2001) 'Corporate rhetoric participates in public dialogue: a solution to the public/private conundrum', *Southern Communication Journal*, 66(4): 279–92.

Brimeyer, T.M., Eaker, A.V., Clair, R.P. (2004) 'Rhetorical strategies in union organizing: a case of labor versus management', *Management Communication Quarterly*, 18(1): 45–75.

Brinson, S.L. and Benoit, W.L. (1999) 'The tarnished star: restoring Texaco's damaged public image', *Management Communication Quarterly*, 12(4): 483–510.

Brown, A.D. (1995) 'Managing understandings: politics, symbolism, niche marketing and the quest for legitimacy in IT implementation', *Organization Studies*, 16(6): 951–69.

Brown, A.D. (1998) 'Narrative, politics and legitimacy in an IT implementation', *Journal of Management Studies*, 35(1): 35–58.

Brown, A.D. and Humphreys, M. (2003) 'Epic and tragic tales: making sense of change', *Journal of Applied Behavioral Science*, 39(2): 121–44.

Brown, M.H. (1990) 'Defining stories in organizations: characteristics and functions', in J.A. Anderson (ed.), *Communication Yearbook 13*. Newbury Park, CA: Sage. pp. 162–90.

Buzzanell, P. (1994) 'Gaining a voice: feminist organizational communication theorizing', *Management Communication Quarterly*, 7(4): 339–83.

Buzzanell, P., Ellingson, L., Silvio, C., Pasch, V., Dale, B., Mauro, G., Smith, E., Weir, N. and Martin, C. (1997) 'Leadership processes in alternative organizations: invitational and dramaturgical leadership', *Communication Studies*, 48: 285–310.

Buzzanell, P.M. (ed.) (2000) *Rethinking Organizational and Managerial Communication from Feminist Perspectives*. Thousand Oaks, CA: Sage Publications.

Buzzanell, P.M., Sterk, H. and Turner, L.H. (eds) (2004) *Gender in Applied Communication Contexts*. Thousand Oaks, CA: Sage Publications.

Callahan, J.L. (2004) 'Reversing a conspicuous absence: mindful inclusion of emotion in structuration theory', *Human Relations*, 57(11): 1427–48.

Campbell, K.S., Follender, S.I. and Shane, G. (1998) 'Preferred strategies for responding to hostile questions in environmental public meetings', *Management Communication Quarterly*, 11(3): 401–21.

Carr, A. and Leivesley, R. (1995) 'Metaphors in organizational studies: a retreat to obscurantism or ideology in drag?', *Administrative Theory and Praxis*, 17(1): 55–66.

Carroll, L.A. and Arneson, P. (2003) 'Communication in a shared governance hospital: managing emergent paradoxes', *Communication Studies*, 54(1): 35–55.

Casey, M.K., Miller, V.D. and Johnson, J.R. (1997) 'Survivor's information seeking following a reduction in workforce', *Communication Research*, 24: 755–81.

Castor, T.R. (2005) 'Constructing social reality in organizational decision making: account vocabularies in a diversity discussion', *Management Communication Quarterly*, 18(4): 479–508.

Cazal, D. and Inns, D. (1998) 'Metaphor, language, and meaning', in D. Grant, T. Keenoy and C. Oswick (eds), *Discourse and Organization*. London: Sage. pp. 177–92.

Chang, H. and Johnson, J. (2001) 'Communication networks as predictors of organizational members' media choices', *Western Journal of Communication*, 65(4): 349–69.

Cheney, G. (1995) 'Democracy in the workplace: theory and practice from the perspective of communication', *Journal of Applied Communication Research*, 23: 167–200.

Cheney, G. (1999) *Values at Work: Employee Participation Meets Market Pressure at Mondragón*. London: ILR Press.

Cheney, G. and Chrisensen, L. (2001) 'Organizational identity: linkages between internal and external communication', in F.M. Jablin and L.L. Putnam (eds), *The New Handbook of Organizational Communication*. Thousand Oaks, CA: Sage. pp. 231–69.

Cheney, G., Christensen, L.T., Conrad, C. and Lair, D.J. (2004) 'Corporate rhetoric as organizational discourse', in D. Grant, C. Hardy, C. Oswick and L. Putnam (eds), *The Sage Handbook of Organizational Discourse*. London: Sage. pp. 79–103.

Cheney, G., Straub, J., Speirs-Glebe, L., Stohl, C., De Gooyer, Jr., D., Whalen, S., Garvin-Doxas, K. and Carlone, D. (1998) 'Democracy, participation, and communication at work: a multidisciplinary review', in M.E. Roloff (ed.), *Communication Yearbook 21*. Thousand Oaks, CA: Sage. pp. 35–91.

Chiles, A. and Zorn, T. (1995) 'Empowerment in organizations: employees' perceptions of the influences on empowerment', *Journal of Applied Communication Research*, 23: 1–25.

Christensen, E.W. and Bailey, J.R. (1997) 'A source accessibility effect on media selection', *Management Communication Quarterly*, 10(3): 373–87.

Clair, R.P. (1998) *Organizing Silence: A World of Possibilities*. Albany, NY: State University of New York Press.

Clair, R.P. (1999) 'Standing still in an ancient field: a contemporary look at the organizational communication discipline', *Management Communication Quarterly*, 13: 283–93.

Clair, J.A. and Dufresne, R.L. (2004) 'Playing the grim reaper: how employees experience carrying out a down sizing', *Human Relations*, 57(12): 1597–625.

Clegg, S. and Gray, J. (1996) 'Metaphors in organizational research: of embedded embryos, paradigms and powerful people', in D. Grant and C. Oswick (eds), *Organization and Metaphor*. London: Sage. pp. 74–93.

Cloud, D.L. (2005) 'Fighting words: labor and the limits of communication at Stanley, 1993 to 1996', *Management Communication Quarterly*, 18(4): 509–42.

Collins-Jarvis, L. (1997) 'Participation and consensus in collective action organizations: the influence of interpersonal versus mass-mediated channels', *Journal of Applied Communication Research*, 25: 1–16.

Conrad, C. (2003) 'Setting the stage: introduction to the special issue on the 'corporate meltdown'', *Management Communication Quarterly*, 17(1): 5–19.

Conrad, C. and Hayes, J. (2001) 'Development of key constructs' in F.M. Jablin and L.L. Putnam (eds), *The New Handbook of Organizational Communication*. Thousand Oaks, CA: Sage. pp. 47–77.

Contandriopoulos, D., Denis, J.-L. and Langley, A. (2004) 'Defining the 'public' in a public healthcare system', *Human Relations*, 57(12): 1573–96.

Contractor, N.S. (1994) 'Self-organizing systems perspective in the study of organizational communication', in B. Kovacic (ed.), *New Approaches to Organizational Communication*. Albany, NY: State University of New York. pp. 39–66.

Contractor, N.S. (1999) 'Self-organizing systems research in the social sciences: reconciling the metaphors and the models', *Management Communication Quarterly*, 13(1): 154–66.

Contractor, N.S. and Grant, S. (1996) 'The emergence of shared interpretations in organizations: a self-organizing systems perspective', in J. Watt and A. Van Lear (eds), *Cycles and Dynamic Processes in Communication Processes*. Newbury Park, CA: Sage. pp. 216–30.

Contractor, N.S. and Monge, P.R. (2002) 'Managing knowledge networks', *Management Communication Quarterly*, 16: 249–58.

Contractor, N.S. and Seibold, D.R. (1993) 'Theoretical frameworks for the study of structuring processes in group decision support systems: adaptive structuration theory and self-organizing systems theory', *Human Communication Research*, 19: 528–63.

Contractor, N.S., Seibold, D.R. and Heller, M.A. (1996) 'Interactional influence in the structuring of media use in groups: Influence of members' perceptions of group decision support system use', *Human Communication Research*, 22: 451–81.

Coombs, W.T. (1995) 'Choosing the right words: the development of guidelines for the selection of the 'appropriate' crisis-response strategies', *Management Communication Quarterly*, 8: 447–76.

Coombs, W.T. and Holladay, S.J. (2002) 'Helping crisis managers protect reputational assets: initial tests of the situational crisis communication theory', *Management Communication Quarterly*, 16(2): 165–86.

Cooper, L., Siebold, D. and Suchner, R. (1997) 'Listening in organizations: an analysis of error structures in models of listening competency', *Communication Research Reports*, 14(3): 312–20.

Cooper-Thomas, H. and Anderson, N. (2002) 'Newcomer adjustment: the relationship between organizational socialization tactics, information acquisition and attitudes', *Journal of Occupational and Organizational Psychology*, 75: 423–37.

Coopman, S.J. and Meidlinger, K.B. (2000) 'Power, hierarchy, and change: the stories of a Catholic parish staff', *Management Communication Quarterly*, 13(4): 567–625.

Cooren, F. (2000) *The Organizing Property of Communication*. Amsterdam and Philadelphia: John Benjamins.

Cooren, F. (2001) 'Translation and articulation in the organization of coalitions: the Great Whale River case', *Communication Theory*, 11(2): 178–200.

Cooren, F. (2004) 'The communicative achievement of collective minding: analysis of board meeting excerpts', *Management Communication Quarterly*, 17(4): 517–51.

Cooren, F. and Taylor, J.R. (1997) 'Organization as an effect of mediation: redefining the link between organization and communication', *Communication Theory*, 11: 178–200.

Corman, S.R. and Poole, M.S. (2000) *Perspectives on Organizational Communication: Finding Common Ground*. New York: The Guilford Press.

Creed, W.E.D. (2003) 'Voice lessons: tempered radicalism and the use of voice and silence', *Journal of Management Studies*, 40(6): 1503–36.

Currie, G. and Brown, A.D. (2003) 'A narratological approach to understanding processes of organizing in a UK hospital', *Human Relations*, 56(5): 563–86.

Czarniawska-Joerges, B. (1995) 'Narration or science? Collapsing the division in organization studies', *Organization*, 2(1): 11–33.

Daft, R.L. and Lengel, R.H. (1986) 'Organizational information requirements, media richness, and structural design', *Management Science*, 32: 554–71.

Deetz, S.A. (1992) *Democracy in an Age of Corporate Colonization*. Albany, NY: State University of New York Press.

Deetz, S. (1995) *Transforming Communication, Transforming Business: Building Responsive and Responsible Workplaces*. Cresskill, NJ: Hampton Press.

Deetz, S. (2003) 'Reclaiming the legacy of the linguistic turn', *Organization*, 10: 421–9.

DeSanctis, G. and Poole, M.S. (1994) 'Capturing the complexity in advanced technology use: adaptive structuration theory', *Organizational Science*, 5: 121–47.

de Saussure, F. (1983) *Course in General Linguistics*. La Salle, IL: Open Court.

Dillard, C., Browning, L.D., Sitkin, S.B. and Sutcliffe, K.M. (2000) 'Impression management and the use of procedures at the Ritz-Carlton: moral standards and dramaturgical discipline', *Communication Studies*, 51(4): 404–14.

DiSanza, J.R. and Bullis, C. (1999) ''Everybody identifies with Smokey the Bear': employee responses to newsletter identification inducements at the U.S. Forest Service', *Management Communication Quarterly*, 12(3): 347–99.

Donabedian, B., McKinnon, S.M. and Bruns, W.J. Jr. (1998) 'Task characteristics, managerial socialization, and media selection', *Management Communication Quarterly*, 11(3): 372–400.

Dougherty, D.S. and Smythe, M.J. (2004) 'Sensemaking, organizational culture, and sexual harassment', *Journal of Applied Communication Research*, 32(4): 293–317.

Dunn, S. (1990) 'Root metaphor in the old and new industrial relations', *British Journal of Industrial Relations*, 28: 1–31.

Edley, P.P. (2000) 'Discursive essentializing in a woman-owned business: gendered-stereotypes and strategic subordination', *Management Communication Quarterly*, 14(2): 271–306.

Eisenberg, E.M. (1984) 'Ambiguity as strategy in organizational communication', *Communication Monographs*, 51: 227–42.

Eisenberg, E.M. and Riley, P. (2001) 'Organizational culture', in F.M. Jablin and L.L. Putnam (eds), *New Handbook of Organizational Communication*. Newbury Park, CA: Sage. pp. 291–322.

Eisenberg, E.M., Murphy, A. and Andrews, L. (1998) 'Openness and decision making in the search for a university provost', *Communication Monographs*, 65: 1–23.

Ellis, K. and Shockley-Zalabak, P. (2001) 'Trust in top management and immediate supervisor: the relationship to satisfaction, perceived organizational effectiveness, and information receiving', *Communication Quarterly*, 49(4): 382–98.

Engestrom, Y. (1999) 'Communication, discourse and activity', *The Communication Review*, 3(1–2): 165–85.

Ezzamel, M., Willmott, H. and Worthington, F. (2001) 'Power, control and resistance in the factory that time forgot', *Journal of Management Studies*, 38: 1053–78.

Fairclough, N. (1992) *Discourse and Social Change*. Cambridge: Polity Press.

Fairclough, N. (1993) 'Critical discourse analysis and the marketization of public discourse: the universities', *Discourse and Society*, 4(2): 133–68.

Fairclough, N. and Wodak, R. (1997) 'Critical discourse analysis', in T. van Dijk (ed.), *Discourse as Social Interaction*. London: Sage. pp. 258–84.

Fairhurst, G.T. (2004) 'Textuality and agency in interaction analysis', *Organization*, 11(3): 335–53.

Fairhurst, G.T. and Cooren, F. (2004) 'Organizational language in use: interaction analysis, conversational analysis and speech act schematics', in D. Grant, C. Hardy, C. Oswick and L. Putnam (eds), *The Sage Handbook of Organizational Discourse*. Thousand Oaks, CA: Sage. pp. 131–52.

Fairhurst, G.T. and Putnam, L.L. (2004) 'Organizations as discursive constructions', *Communication Theory*, 14(1): 5–26.

Fairhurst, G.T., Cooren, F. and Cahill, D.J. (2002) 'Discursiveness, contradiction, and unintended consequences in successive downsizings', *Management Communication Quarterly*, 15(4): 501–40.

Fairhurst, G.T., Jordan, J. and Neuwirth, K. (1997) 'Why are we here? Managing the meaning of an organizational mission statement', *Journal of Applied Communication Research*, 25: 243–63.

Farrell, A. and Geist-Martin, P. (2005) 'Communicating social health: perceptions of wellness at work', *Management Communication Quarterly*, 18(4): 543–92.

Feeley, T. (2000) 'Testing a communication network model of employee turnover based on centrality', *Journal of Applied Communication Research*, 28(3): 262–77.

Feeley, T.H. and Barnett, G.A. (1996) 'Predicting employee turnover from communication networks', *Human Communication Research*, 23: 370–87.

Fiebig, G.V. and Kramer, M.W. (1998) 'A framework for the study of emotions in organizational contexts', *Management Communication Quarterly*, 11(4): 536–72.

Firth, A. (1995) 'Introduction and overview', in A. Firth (ed.), *The Discourse of Negotiation: Studies of Language in the Workplace*. Oxford: Pergamon. pp. 3–39.

Fisher, B.A. (1978) *Perspectives on Human Communication*. New York: Macmillan.

Flanagin, A.J., Monge, P. and Fulk, J. (2001) 'The value of formative investment in organizational federations', *Human Communication Research*, 27(1): 69–93.

Fleming, P. and Sewell, G. (2002) 'Looking for the good soldier, svejk: alternative modalities of resistance in the contemporary workplace', *Sociology*, 36: 857–73.

Fleming, P. and Spicer, A. (2002) 'Workers' playtime? Unravelling the paradox of covert resistance in organizations', in S. Clegg (ed.), *Management and organizational paradoxes*. Amsterdam: John Benjamins. pp. 65–85.

Forbes, D.A. (2002) 'Internalized masculinity and women's discourse: a critical analysis of the (re)production of masculinity in organizations', *Communication Quarterly*, 50(3 and 4): 269–91.

Foucault, M. (1976) *The History of Sexuality: Volume 1*. New York: Pantheon.

Foucault, M. (1980) *Power/Knowledge: Selected Interviews and Other Writings, 1972–1977*. New York: Pantheon.

Fritz, J.M.H. (2002) 'How do I dislike thee? Let me count the ways: constructing impressions of troublesome others at work', *Management Communication Quarterly*, 15(3): 410–38.

Frost, P.J. (2003) *Toxic Emotions at Work: How Compassionate Managers Handle Pain and Conflict*. Boston, MA: Harvard Business School Press.

Frost, P.J., Dutton, J.E., Worline, M.C. and Wilson, A. (2000) 'Narratives of compassion in organizations', in S. Fineman (ed.), *Emotion in Organizations*. Thousand Oaks, CA: Sage. pp. 25–45.

Fulk, J., Flanagin, A.J., Kalman, M.E., Monge, P.R. and Ryan, T. (1996). 'Connective and communal public goods in interactive communication systems', *Communication Theory*, 6: 60–87.

Fulk, J., Schmitz, J. and Ryu, D. (1995) 'Cognitive elements in the social construction of communication technology', *Management Communication Quarterly*, 8: 259–88.

Gabriel, Y. (2000) *Storytelling in Organizations, Facts, Fictions, and Fantasies*. New York: Oxford University Press.

Gabriel, Y. (2004) 'Narratives, stories and texts', in D. Grant, C. Hardy, C. Oswick and L. Putnam (eds), *The Sage Handbook of Organizational Discourse*. Thousand Oaks, CA: Sage. pp. 61–77.

Ganesh, S. (2003) 'Organizational narcissism: technology, legitimacy, and identity in an Indian NGO', *Management Communication Quarterly*, 16(4): 558–94.

Gardner, W.L. and Cleavenger, D. (1998) 'The impression management strategies associated with transformational leadership at the world-class level', *Management Communication Quarterly*, 12(1): 3–41.

Geddes, D. and Baron, R.A. (1997) 'Workplace aggression as a consequence of negative performance feedback', *Management Communication Quarterly*, 10(4): 433–54.

Geddes, D. and Lineham, F. (1996) 'Exploring the dimensionality of positive and negative feedback performance', *Communication Quarterly*, 44: 326–44.

Geertz, C. (1973) *The Interpretation of Cultures*. New York: Basic Books.

Giddens, A. (1979) *Central Problems in Social Theory: Action, Structure and Contradiction in Social Analysis*. Berkeley, CA: University of California Press.

Giddens, A. (1984) *The Constitution of Society: Outline of the Theory of Structure*. Berkeley, CA: University of California Press.

Gossett, L. (2002) 'Kept at arm's length: questioning the organizational desirability of member identification', *Communication Monographs*, 69(4): 385–404.

Grant, D. and Hardy, C. (2004) 'Struggles with organizational discourse', *Organization Studies*, 25(1): 5–14.

Grant, D., Hardy, C., Oswick, C. and Putnam, L. (eds) (2004) *The Sage Handbook of Organizational Discourse*. London: Sage.

Grant, D., Keenoy, T. and Oswick, C. (2001) 'Organizational discourse: key contributions and challenges', *International Studies of Management and Organization*, 31(3): 5–24.

Greimas, A.J. (1987) *On Meaning: Selected Writings in Semiotic Theory*. Trans. P.J. Perron and F.H. Collins. London: Frances Pinter.

Grimes, D. (2001) 'Putting our own house in order: whiteness, change and organization studies', *Journal of Organizational Change*, 14(2): 132–49.

Guerrier, Y. and Adib, A. (2003) 'Work at leisure and leisure at work: a study of the emotional labour of tour reps', *Human Relations*, 56(11): 1399–417.

Hacker, K.L. Goss, B., Townley, C. and Horton, V.J. (1998) 'Employee attitudes regarding electronic mail policies: a case study', *Management Communication Quarterly*, 11(3): 422–52.

Hafen, S. (2004) 'Organizational gossip: a revolving door of regulation and resistance', *Southern Communication Journal*, 69(3): 223–40.

Hallstein, D.L.O. (1999) 'A postmodern caring: feminist standpoint theories, revisioned caring, and communication ethics', *Western Journal of Communication*, 63(1): 32–56.

Hansen, C., Kahnweiler, W. and Wilensky, A. (1994) 'Human resource development as an occupational culture through organizational stories', *Human Resource Development Quarterly*, 5: 253–67.

Hardy, C., Grant, D., Keenoy, T., Oswick, C. and Phillips, N. (2004) 'Introduction: struggles with organizational discourse', *Organization Studies*, 25(1): 5–13.

Hardy, C., Lawrence, T.B. and Grant, D. (2005) 'Discourse and collaboration: the role of conversations and collective identity', *Academy of Management Review*, 30(1): 58–77.

Harter, L. and Krone, K. (2001) 'The boundary-spanning role of a cooperative support organization: managing the paradox of stability and change in non-traditional organizations', *Journal of Applied Communication Research*, 29(3): 248–77.

Hawes, L.C. (1999) 'Dialogics, posthumanistic theory, and self-organizing systems', *Management Communication Quarterly*, 13(1): 146–53.

Hawkes, D.F. (1972). *Metaphor*. London: Methuen.

Heald, M.R., Contractor, N.S., Koehly, L.M. and Wasserman, S. (1998) 'Formal and emergent predictors of coworkers' perceptual congruence on an organization's social structure', *Human Communication Research*, 24(4): 536–63.

Hearit, K. (1995) 'Mistakes were made: organizations, apologia, and crises of social legitimacy', *Communication Studies*, 46: 1–17.

Heaton, L. and Taylor, J.R. (2002) 'Knowledge management and professional work: a communication perspective on the knowledge-based organization', *Management Communication Quarterly*, 16(2): 210–36.

Hegel, G.W.F. (1968) *Lectures on the History of Philosophy* (Vol. 1). London: Routledge & Kegan Paul.

Helmer, J. (1993) 'Storytelling in the creation and maintenance of organizational tension and stratification', *Southern Communication Journal*, 59: 34–44.

Heracleous, L. and Marshak, R.J. (2004) 'Conceptual organizational discourse as situated symbolic action', *Human Relations*, 57(10): 1285–312.

Hirsch, P.M. and Andrews, J.A.Y. (1983) 'Ambushes, shootouts, and knights of the roundtable: the language of corporate takeovers', in L.R. Pondy, P.J. Frost, G. Morgan and T.C. Dandridge (eds), *Organizational Symbolism*. Greenwich, CT: JAI Press. pp. 145–55.

Hirschman, A. (1970) *Exit, Voice and Loyalty: Responses to Decline in Firms, Organizations and States*. Cambridge, MA: Harvard University Press.

Hoffman, M. (2002) ''Do all things with counsel': Benedictine women and organizational democracy', *Communication Studies*, 53(3): 203–18.

Holsapple, C.W., Johnson, L.E. and Waldron, V.R. (1996) 'A formal model for the study of communication support systems', *Human Communication Research*, 22(3): 422–47.

Hopkins, K. (2001) 'Manager intervention with troubled supervisors: help and support start at the top', *Management Communication Quarterly*, 15(1): 83–99.

Howard, L.A. and Geist, P. (1995) 'Ideological positioning in organizational change: the dialectic of control in a merging organization', *Communication Monographs*, 62(2): 110–31.

Houston, M. and Kramarae, C. (1991) 'Speaking from silence: methods of silencing and of resistance', *Discourse and Society*, 2(4): 387–99.

Houston, R. (1999) 'Self-organizing systems theory: historical challenges to new sciences', *Management Communication Quarterly*, 13(1): 119–34.

Huxman, S. and Bruce, D. (1995) 'Toward a dynamic generic framework of apologia: a case study of Dow Chemical, Vietnam, and the napalm controversy', *Communication Studies*, 46: 57–72.

Hylmö, A. and Buzzanell, P. (2002) 'Telecommuting as viewed through cultural lenses: an empirical investigation of the discourses of utopia, identity, and mystery', *Communication Monographs*, 69(4): 329–56.

Inns, D. (2002) 'Metaphor in the literature of organizational analysis: a preliminary taxonomy and a glimpse at a humanities-based perspective', *Organization*, 9(2): 305–30.

Irons, L.R. (1998) 'Organizational and technical communication: terminological ambiguity in representing work', *Management Communication Quarterly*, 12(1): 42–71.

Isaacs, W.N. (1999) *Dialogue and the Art of Thinking Together*. New York: Currency.

Iverson, J.O. and McPhee, R.D. (2002) 'Knowledge management in communities of practice: being true to the communicative character of knowledge', *Management Communication Quarterly*, 16(2): 259–66.

Jablin, F.M. and Putnam, L.L. (eds) (2001) *The New Handbook of Organizational Communication: Advances in Theory, Research, and Methods*. Thousand Oaks, CA: Sage.

Jackson, M., Poole, M.S. and Kuhn, T. (2002) 'The social construction of technologies in studies of the workplace', in L. Lievrouw and S. Livingstone (eds), *Handbook of New Media*. London: Sage. pp. 236–53.

Jameson, J.K. (2004) 'Negotiating autonomy and connection through politeness: a dialectical approach to organizational conflict management', *Western Journal of Communication*, 68(3): 257–77.

Johanson, J.-E. (2000) 'Intraorganizational influence: theoretical clarification and empirical assessment of intraorganizational social influence', *Management Communication Quarterly*, 13(3): 393–425.

Johnson, J.R., Bernhagen, M.J., Miller, V. and Allen, M. (1996) 'The role of communication in managing reductions in work force', *Journal of Applied Communication Research*, 24: 139–64.

Jones, E., Watson, B. and Gallois, C. (2004) 'Organizational communication: challenges for the new century', *Journal of Communication*, 54(4): 722–50.

Jorgenson, J. (2002) 'Engineering selves: negotiating gender and identity in technical work', *Management Communication Quarterly*, 15(3): 350–80.

Kalman, M.E., Monge, P.R., Fulk, J. and Heino, R. (2002) 'Resolving communication dilemmas in database-mediated collaboration', *Communication Research*, 29: 125–54.

Kanov, J., Maitlis, S., Worline, M.C., Dutton, J.E., Frost, P.J. and Lilius, J.M. (2004) 'Compassion in organizational life', *American Behavioral Scientist*, 47(6): 808–27.

Kassing, J.W. (1997) 'Articulating, antagonizing, and displacing: a model of employee dissent', *Communication Studies*, 48: 311–32.

Kassing, J.W. (1998) 'Development and validation of the organizational dissent scale', *Management Communication Quarterly*, 12(2), 183–229.

Kassing, J.W. (2001) 'From the looks of things: assessing perceptions of organizational dissenters', *Management Communication Quarterly*, 14(3): 442–70.

Kassing, J.W. (2002) 'Speaking up: identifying employees' upward dissent strategies', *Management Communication Quarterly*, 16(2): 187–209.

Kassing, J.W. and Armstrong, T.A. (2002) 'Someone's going to hear about this: examining the association between dissent-triggering events and employees' dissent expression', *Management Communication Quarterly*, 16(1): 39–65.

Kassing, J.W. and Avtgis, T.A. (1999) 'Examining the relationship between organizational dissent and aggressive communication', *Management Communication Quarterly*, 13(1): 100–15.

Kellett, P. (1999) 'Dialogue and dialectics in managing organizational change: the case of a mission-based transformation', *Southern Communication Journal*, 64: 211–31.

Keyton, J. and Rhodes, S.C. (1999) 'Organizational sexual harassment: translating research into application', *Journal of Applied Communication Research*, 27: 158–73.

Keyton, J., Ferguson, P. and Rhodes, S.C. (2001) 'Cultural indicators of sexual harassment', *Southern Communication Journal*, 67(1): 33–50.

King, G. and Hermodson, A. (2000) 'Peer reporting of coworker wrongdoing: a qualitative analysis of observer attitudes in the decision to report versus not report unethical behavior', *Journal of Applied Communication Research*, 28(4): 309–29.

Kinsella, W.J. (1999) 'Discourse, power, and knowledge in the management of 'big science': the production of consensus in a nuclear fusion research laboratory', *Management Communication Quarterly*, 13(2): 171–208.

Kirby, E.L. and Krone, K.J. (2002) 'The policy exists but you can't use it: negotiating tensions in work-family policy', *Journal of Applied Communication Research*, 30: 50–77.

Kitchell, A., Hannan, E. and Kempton, W. (2000) 'Identity through stories: story structure and functions in two environmental groups', *Human Organizations*, 59: 96–105.

Kramer, M.W. (1999) 'Motivation to reduce uncertainty: reconceptualizing uncertainty reduction theory', *Management Communication Quarterly*, 13: 305–16.

Kramer, M.W. (2004) *Managing Uncertainty in Organizational Communication*. Mahwah, NJ: Lawrence Erlbaum Associates.

Kramer, M.W. and Berman, J.E. (2001) 'Making sense of a university's culture: an examination of undergraduate students' stories', *Southern Communication Journal*, 66(4): 297–311.

Kramer, M.W. and Hess, J.A. (2002) 'Communication rules for the display of emotions in organizational settings', *Management Communication Quarterly*, 16(1): 66–80.

Kramer, M.W. and Noland, T. (1999) 'Communication during job promotions: a case of ongoing assimilation', *Journal of Applied Communication Research*, 27: 335–55.

Kramer, M.W., Dougherty, D.S. and Pierce, T.A. (2004) 'Managing uncertainty during a corporate acquisition: a longitudinal study of communication during an airline acquisition', *Human Communication Research*, 30(1): 71–101.

Krone, K. (2005) 'Trends in organizational communication research: sustaining the discipline, sustaining ourselves', *Communication Studies*, 56: 95–105.

Krone, K.J., Chen, L., Sloan, D.K. and Gallant, L.M. (1997) 'Managerial emotionality in Chinese factories', *Management Communication Quarterly*, 11(1): 6–50.

Kruml, S.M. and Geddes, D. (2000) 'Exploring the dimensions of emotional labor: the heart of Hochschild's work', *Management Communication Quarterly*, 14(1): 8–49.

Kuhn, T. (1997) 'The discourse of issues management: a genre of organizational communication', *Communication Quarterly*, 45(3): 188–210.

Kuhn, T. and Ashcraft, K.L. (2003) 'Corporate scandal and the theory of the firm: formulating the contributions of organizational communication', *Management Communication Quarterly*, 17(1): 20–57.

Kuhn, T. and Corman, S. (2003) 'The emergence of homogeneity and heterogeneity in knowledge structures during a planned organizational change', *Communication Monographs*, 70(3): 198–229.

La France, B.H., Boster, F.J. and Darrow, S. (2003) 'An analysis of role conflict and role ambiguity within the cancer information service's communication network', *Communication Studies*, 54(4): 420–37.

Lair, D.J., Sullivan, K. and Cheney, G. (2005) 'Marketization and the recasting of the professional self: the rhetoric and ethics of personal branding', *Management Communication Quarterly*, 18(3): 307–43.

Lakeoff, G. and Johnson, M. (1980) *Metaphors We Live By*. Chicago: University of Chicago Press.

Lee, J.W. and Guerrero, L.K. (2001) 'Types of touch in cross-sex relationships between co-workers: perceptions of relational and emotional messages, inappropriateness, and sexual harassment', *Journal of Applied Communication Research*, 29(3): 197–220.

Lewis, L.K. (1999) 'Disseminating information and soliciting input during planned organizational change: Implementers' targets, sources, and channels of communication', *Management Communication Quarterly*, 13: 43–75.

Lewis, L.K. and Seibold, D.R. (1998) 'Reconceptualizing organizational change implementation as a communication problem: a review of literature and research agenda', in M.E. Roloff (ed.), *Communication Yearbook 21*. Thousand Oaks, CA: Sage. pp. 93–151.

Lewis, L.K., Hamel, S.A. and Richardson, B.K. (2001) 'Communicating change to nonprofit stakeholders: models and predictors of implementers' approaches', *Management Communication Quarterly*, 15(1): 5–41.

Lewis, M.W. (2000) 'Exploring paradox: toward a more comprehensive guide', *Academy of Management Review*, 25(4): 760–76.

Lewis, M.W. and Dehler, G.E. (2000) 'Learning through paradox: a pedagogical strategy for exploring contradictions and complexity', *Journal of Management Education*, 24: 708–25.

Livesey, S.M. (2002) 'The discourse of the middle ground: citizen Shell commits to sustainable development', *Management Communication Quarterly*, 15(3): 313–49.

Lizzio, A., Wilson, K.L., Gilchrist, J. and Gallois, C. (2003) 'The role of gender in the construction and evaluation of feedback effectiveness', *Management Communication Quarterly*, 16(3): 341–79.

Lucas, K. and Buzzanell, P.M. (2004) 'Blue-collar work, career, and success: occupational narratives of Sisu', *Journal of Applied Communication Research*, 32(4): 273–92.

Luhmann, N. (1990) *Essays on Self-Reference*. New York: Columbia University Press.

Lutgen-Sandvik, P. (2003) 'The communicative cycle of employee emotional abuse: generation and regeneration of workplace mistreatment', *Management Communication Quarterly*, 16(4): 471–501.

Lyon, A. (2004) 'Participants' use of cultural knowledge as cultural capital in a dot-com start-up organization',

Management Communication Quarterly, 18(2): 175–203.

Markham, A. (1996) 'Designing discourse: a critical analysis of strategic ambiguity and workplace control', *Management Communication Quarterly*, 9(4): 389–421.

Marshak, R.J. (1996) 'Metaphors, metaphoric fields and organizational change', in D. Grant and C. Oswick (eds), *Metaphors and Organizations*. Thousand Oaks, CA: Sage. pp. 147–65.

Martin, J. (2002) *Organizational Culture: Mapping the Terrain*. Thousand Oaks, CA: Sage.

Martin, D.M. (2004) 'Humor in middle management: women negotiating the paradoxes of organizational life', *Journal of Applied Communication Research*, 32(2): 147–70.

Marx, K. (1961) *Capital* (Vol. 1). Moscow: Foreign Languages Publishing House.

Mattson, M. and Buzzanell, P.M. (1999) 'Traditional and feminist organizational communication ethical analyses of messages and issues surrounding an actual job loss case', *Journal of Applied Communication Research*, 27: 49–72.

May, S. and Mumby, D.K. (eds) (2005) *Engaging Organizational Communication Theory and Research: Multiple Perspectives*. Thousand Oaks, CA: Sage.

McClure, K. (1996) 'The institutional subordination of contested issues: the case of Pittsburgh's steelworkers and ministers', *Communication Quarterly*, 44(4): 487–501.

McCroskey, J. and Richmond, V. (2000) 'Applying reciprocity and accommodation theories to supervisor/subordinate communication', *Journal of Applied Communication Research*, 28(3): 278–89.

McMillan, J.J. and Cheney, G. (1996) 'The student as consumer: the implications and limitations of a metaphor', *Communication Education*, 45: 1–14.

Meares, M.M., Oetzel, J.G., Torres, A., Derkacs, D. and Ginossar, T. (2004) 'Employee mistreatment and muted voices in the culturally diverse workplace', *Journal of Applied Communication Research*, 32(1): 4–27.

Medved, C.E. (2004) 'The everyday accomplishment of work and family: accounting for practical actions and commonsense rules in daily routines', *Communication Studies*, 55: 128–54.

Medved, C.E. and Kirby, E.L. (2005) 'Family CEOs: a feminist analysis of corporate mothering discourses', *Management Communication Quarterly*, 18(4): 435–78.

Meiners, E.B. and Miller, V.D. (2004) 'The effect of formality and relational tone on supervisor/subordinate negotiation episodes', *Western Journal of Communication*, 68(3): 302–21.

Metzler, M. (1997) 'Organizations, democracy, and the public sphere: the implications of democratic (r)evolution at a nuclear weapons facility', *Communication Studies*, 48: 333–58.

Metzler, M. (2001) 'Responding to the legitimacy problems of big tobacco: an analysis of the 'people of Philip Morris' image advertising campaign', *Communication Quarterly*, 49(4): 336–81.

Meyer, J.C. (1995) 'Tell me a story: eliciting organizational values from narratives', *Communication Quarterly*, 43(2): 210–24.

Meyerson, D.E. (2001) *Tempered Radicals: How People Use Difference to Inspire Change at Work*. Boston: Harvard Business School Press.

Miller, K. (1998) 'Nurses at the edge of chaos: the application of 'new science' concepts to organizational systems', *Management Communication Quarterly*, 12(1): 112–27.

Miller, K. (2002) 'The experience of emotion in the workplace: professing in the midst of tragedy', *Management Communication Quarterly*, 15(4): 571–600.

Miller, K., Joseph, L. and Apker, J. (2000) 'Strategic ambiguity in the role development process', *Journal of Applied Communication Research*, 28(3): 193–214.

Milliken, F.J. and Morrison, E.W. (2003) 'Shades of silence: emerging themes and future directions for research on silence in organizations', *Journal of Management Studies*, 40(6): 1563–68.

Monge, P.R. and Contractor, N.S. (2001) 'Emergence of communication networks', in F.M. Jablin and L.L. Putnam (eds), *The New Handbook of Organizational Communication*. Thousand Oaks, CA: Sage. pp. 440–502.

Monge, P.R. and Contractor, N.S. (2004) *Theories of Communication Networks*. New York: Oxford University Press.

Monge, P.R. and Fulk, J. (1999) 'Communication technology for global network organizations' in G. DeSanctis and J. Fulk (eds), *Shaping Organizational Form: Communication, Connection, Community*. Thousand Oaks, CA: Sage. pp. 71–100.

Morçöl, G. (1997) 'A meno paradox for public administration: have we acquired a radically new knowledge from the 'new sciences'?', *Administrative Theory and Praxis*, 19(3): 305–17.

Morgan, G. (1986) *Images of Organizations*. Beverly Hills, CA: Sage.

Morgan, G. (1997) *Images of Organizations*, 2nd edn. Thousand Oaks, CA: Sage.

Morgan, J.M., Reynolds, C.M., Nelson, T.J., Johanningmeier, A.R., Griffin, M. and Andrade, P. (2004) 'Tales from the fields: sources of employee identification in agribusiness', *Management Communication Quarterly*, 17(3): 360–85.

Morrison, E. (2002) 'Newcomers' relationships: the role of social network ties during socialization', *Academy of Management Journal*, 45(6): 1149–60.

Morrison, E.W. and Milliken, F.J. (2000) 'Organizational silence: a barrier to change and development in a pluralistic world', *Academy of Management Review*, 25(4): 706–31.

Mueller, F., Sillince, J., Harvey, C. and Howorth, C. (2004) 'A rounded picture is what we need': rhetorical strategies, arguments, and the negotiation of change in a UK hospital trust', *Organization Studies*, 25(1): 75–93.

Mumby, D.K. (1998) 'Organizing men: power and discourse and the social construction of masculinity(s) in the workplace', *Communication Theory*, 8(2): 164–82.

Mumby, D. (2005) 'Theorizing resistance in organization studies: a dialectical approach', *Management Communication Quarterly*, 19(1): 19–44.

Mumby, D.K. (in press) 'Organizational communication', in G. Ritzer (ed.), *Encyclopedia of Sociology*. New York: Blackwell Publishers.

Mumby, D.K. and Stohl, C. (1991) 'Power and discourse in organization studies: absence and the dialectic of control', *Discourse and Society*, 2(3): 313–32.

Mumby, D.K. and Stohl, C. (1996) 'Disciplining organizational communication studies', *Management Communication Quarterly*, 10: 50–72.

Murphy, A.G. (1998) 'Hidden transcripts of flight attendants' resistance', *Management Communication Quarterly*, 11(4): 499–535.

Murphy, A.G. (2002) 'Organizational politics of place and space: the perpetual liminoid performance of commercial flight', *Text and Performance Quarterly*, 22(4): 297–316.

Myers, P. (2002) 'Customers, boardrooms and gossip: theme repetition and metapatterns in the texture of organizing', *Human Relations*, 55(6): 669–90.

Nadesan, M.H. (1999) 'The discourses of corporate spiritualism and evangelical capitalism', *Management Communication Quarterly*, 13(1): 3–42.

O'Connor, E.S. (1995) 'Paradoxes of participation: textual analysis and organizational change', *Organization Studies*, 16(5): 769–803.

O'Connor, E. (1997) 'Discourse at our disposal: stories in and around the garbage can', *Management Communication Quarterly*, 10(4): 395–432.

O'Connor, E. (2000) 'Plotting the organization: the embedded narrative as a construct for studying change', *Journal of Applied Behavioral Science*, 36(2): 174–92.

Olekalns, M. and Smith, P.L. (2000) 'Negotiating optimal outcomes: the role of strategic sequences in competitive negotiations', *Human Communication Research*, 24: 528–60.

Orlikowski, W.J. (2002) 'Knowing in practice: enacting a collective capability in distributed organizing', *Organizational Science*, 13(3): 249–73.

Ortony, A. (ed.) (1979) *Metaphor and Thought*. Cambridge: Cambridge University Press.

Oswick, C., Putnam, L.L. and Keenoy, T. (2004) 'Tropes, discourse and organizing', in D. Grant, C. Hardy, C. Oswick and L. Putnam (eds), *The Sage Handbook of Organizational Discourse*. Thousand Oaks, CA: Sage. pp. 105–27.

Pacanowsky, M.E. and O'Donnell-Trujillo, N. (1983) 'Organizational communication as cultural performance', *Communication Monographs*, 50: 126–47.

Papa, M.J., Auwal, M.A. and Singhal, A. (1995) 'Dialectic of control and emancipation in organizing for social change: a multitheoretic study of the Grameen Bank in Bangladesh', *Communication Theory*, 5(3): 189–223.

Papa, M.J., Auwal, M.A. and Singhal, A. (1997) 'Organizing for social change within concertive control systems: member identification, empowerment, and the masking of discipline', *Communication Monographs*, 64: 219–49.

Parker, P.S. (2002) 'Negotiating identity in raced and gendered workplace interactions: the use of strategic communication by African American women senior executives within dominant culture organizations', *Communication Quarterly*, 50(3 and 4): 251–68.

Parker, P.S. (2005) *Race, Gender, and Leadership: Revisioning Organizational Leadership from the Perspectives of African American Women Executives*. Mahwah, NJ: Lawrence Erlbaum Associates.

Phillips, N. and Hardy, C. (2002) *Discourse Analysis: Investigating Processes of Social Construction*. Thousand Oaks, CA: Sage.

Pierce, T. and Dougherty, D.S. (2002) 'The construction, enactment, and maintenance of power-as-domination through an acquisition: the case of TWA and Ozark Airlines', *Management Communication Quarterly*, 16(2): 129–64.

Pollock, T., Whitbred, R.A. and Contractor, N. (2000) 'Social information processing and job characteristics: a simultaneous test of two theories with implications for job satisfaction', *Human Communication Research*, 26: 292–330.

Pomerantz, A., Fehr, B.J. and Ende, J. (1997) 'When supervising physicians see patients: strategies used in difficult situations', *Human Communication Research*, 23(4): 589–615.

Poole, M.S. and DeSanctis, G. (1992) 'Microlevel structuration in computer-supported group decision-making', *Human Communication Research*, 19: 5–49.

Prasad, A. and Prasad, P. (1998) 'Everyday struggles at the workplace: the nature and implications of routine resistance in contemporary organizations', in P.A. Bamberger and W.J. Sonnenstuhl (eds), *Research in the Sociology of Organizations, 15: Deviance in and of Organizations*. Stanford, CT: JAI Press. pp. 225–57.

Prasad, P. and Prasad, A. (2000) 'Stretching the iron cage: the constitution and implications of routine workplace resistance', *Organizational Science*, 11(4): 387–403.

Putnam, L.L. (1986) 'Contradictions and paradoxes in organizations', in L. Thayer (ed.), *Organizational Communication: Emerging Perspectives I*. Norwood, NJ: Ablex. pp. 151–67.

Putnam, L.L. (2003) 'Dialectical tensions and rhetorical tropes in negotiations', *Organizational Studies*, 25(1): 35–53.

Putnam, L.L. and Cheney, G. (1985) 'Organizational communication: historical development and future directions', in T.W. Benson (ed.), *Speech Communication in the Twentieth Century*. Carbondale, IL: Southern University Press. pp. 130–56.

Putnam, L.L. and Cooren, F. (2004) 'Special issue on text and agency: alternative perspectives on the role of text and agency in constituting organizations', *Organization*, 11(3): 323–33.

Putnam, L.L. and Fairhurst, G.T. (2001) 'Language and discourse in organizations', in F.M. Jablin and L.L. Putnam (eds), *The New Handbook of Organizational Communication*. Thousand Oaks, CA: Sage. pp. 78–136.

Quinn, R.W. and Dutton, J.E. (2005) 'Coordination as energy-in-conversation', *Academy of Management Review*, 30(1): 36–57.

Real, K. and Putnam, L.L. (2005) 'Ironies in the discursive struggle of pilots defending the profession', *Management Communication Quarterly*, 19(1): 91–119.

Redding, W.C. and Tompkins, P.K. (1988) 'Organizational communication – past and present tenses', in G.M. Goldhaber and G.A. Barnett (eds), *Handbook of Organizational Communication*. Norwood, NJ: Ablex. pp. 5–33.

Reed, M. (2000) 'The limits of discourse analysis in organizational analysis', *Organization*, 7(3): 524–30.

Rice, R.E., Collins-Jarvis, L. and Zydney-Walker, S. (1999) 'Individual and structural influences on information technology helping relationships', *Journal of Applied Communication Research*, 27: 285–309.

Robichaud, D. (2001) 'Interaction as a text: a semiotic look at an organizing process', *American Journal of Semiotics*, 17(1): 141–61.

Robichaud, D., Giroux, H. and Taylor, J.R. (2004) 'The meta-conversation: the recursive property of language as a key to organizing', *Academy of Management Review*, 29(4): 617–34.

Rogers, P.S. (2000) 'CEO presentations in conjunction with earning announcements', *Management Communication Quarterly*, 13(3): 426–85.

Rosenfeld, L.B., Richman, J.M. and May, S.K. (2004) 'Information adequacy, job satisfaction and organizational culture in a dispersed-network organization', *Journal of Applied Communication Research*, 32(1): 28–54.

Rudd, G. (1995) 'The symbolic construction of organizational identities and community in a regional symphony', *Communication Studies*, 46: 201–21.

Rudd, G. (2000) 'The symphony: organizational discourse and the symbolic tensions between artistic and business ideologies', *Journal of Applied Communication Research*, 28(2): 117–43.

Russell, R. (1997) 'Workplace democracy and organizational communication', *Communication Studies*, 48: 280–84.

Saas, J.S. and Mattson, M. (1999) 'When social support is uncomfortable: the communicative accomplishment of support as a cultural term in a youth intervention program', *Management Communication Quarterly*, 12(4): 511–43.

Sass, J. (2000) 'Characterizing organizational spirituality: an organizational communication culture approach', *Communication Studies*, 51(3): 195–217.

Scheibel, D. (2002) 'The cat with the 'strat' comes back: a Burkeian-Weickian primer for organizing narrative', *Southern Communication Journal*, 67(4): 303–18.

Scheibel, D., Gibson, K. and Anderson, C. (2002) 'Practicing 'sorority rush': mockery and the dramatistic rehearsing of organizational conversations', *Communication Studies*, 53(3): 219–33.

Schneider, B. (2001) 'Constructing knowledge in an organization: the role of interview notes', *Management Communication Quarterly*, 15(2): 227–55.

Scott, C.R., Connaughton, S.L., Diaz-Saenz, H.R., Maguire, K., Ramirez, R., Richardson, B., Shaw, S.P. and Morgan, D. (1999) 'The impacts of communication and multiple identifications on intent to leave: a multimethodological exploration', *Management Communication Quarterly*, 12(3): 400–35.

Scott, C.R., Corman, S.R. and Cheney, G. (1998) 'Development of a structurational model of identification in the organization', *Communication Theory*, 8: 298–336.

Seeger, M.W. and Ulmer, R.R. (2003) 'Explaining Enron: communication and responsible leadership', *Management Communication Quarterly*, 17(1): 58–84.

Sellnow, T.L., Ulmer, R.R. and Snider, M. (1998) 'The compatibility of corrective action in organizational crisis communication', *Communication Quarterly*, 46(1): 60–74.

Sheer, V.C. and Chen, L. (2004) 'Improving media richness theory: a study of interaction goals, message valence, and task complexity in manager-subordinate communication', *Management Communication Quarterly*, 18(1): 76–93.

Sias, P. (1996) 'Constructing perceptions of differential treatment: an analysis of coworker discourse', *Communication Monographs*, 63: 172–87.

Sias, P.M. and Wyers, T.D. (2001) 'Employee uncertainty and information-seeking in newly formed expansion organizations', *Management Communication Quarterly*, 14(4): 549–73.

Sias, P.M., Kramer, M.W. and Jenkins, E. (1997) 'A comparison of the communication behaviors of temporary employees and new hires', *Communication Research*, 24: 731–54.

Sims, D. (2003) 'Between the millstones: a narrative account of the vulnerability of middle managers' storying', *Human Relations*, 56(10): 1195–211.

Skoldberg, K. (1994) 'Tales of change: public administration reform and narrative mode', *Organizational Science*, 5(2): 219–38.

Smith, F.L. and Keyton, J. (2001) 'Organizational storytelling: metaphors for relational power and identity struggles', *Management Communication Quarterly*, 15(2): 149–82.

Smith, R.C. and Turner, P. (1995) 'A social constructionist reconfiguration of metaphor analysis: an application of 'ACMA' to organizational socialization theorizing', *Communication Monographs*, 62: 152–81.

Solomon, D.H. and Williams, M.L.M. (1997a) 'Perceptions of social-sexual communication at work: the effects of message, situation, and observer characteristics on judgments of sexual harassment', *Journal of Applied Communication Research*, 25: 196–216.

Solomon, D.H. and Williams, M.L.M. (1997b) 'Perceptions of social-sexual communication at work as sexual harassment', *Management Communication Quarterly*, 11(2): 147–84.

Sotirin, P. and Gottfried, H. (1999) 'The ambivalent dynamics of secretarial 'bitching': control, resistance, and the construction of identity', *Organization*, 6(1): 57–80.

Spradlin, A.L. (1998) 'The price of 'passing': a lesbian perspective on authenticity in organizations', *Management Communication Quarterly*, 11(4): 598–605.

Stabile, C. (2000) 'Nike, social responsibility, and the hidden abode of production', *Critical Studies in Media Communication*, 17(2): 186–204.

Stage, C.W. (1999) 'Negotiating organizational communication cultures in American subsidiaries doing business in Thailand', *Management Communication Quarterly*, 13(2): 245–80.

Stohl, C. and Cheney, G. (2001) 'Participatory processes/paradoxical practices: communication and the dilemmas of organizational democracy', *Management Communication Quarterly*, 14(3): 349–407.

Stutts, N.B. and Barker, R.T. (1999) 'The use of narrative paradigm theory in assessing audience value conflict in image advertising', *Management Communication Quarterly*, 13(2): 209–44.

Taylor, J.R. and Cooren, F. (1997) 'What makes communication 'organizational'? How the many voices of a collectivity become the one voice of an organization', *Journal of Pragmatics*, 27: 409–38.

Taylor, J.R. and Lerner, L. (1996) 'Making sense of sensemaking: how managers construct their organization through their talk', *Studies in Cultures, Organizations and Societies*, 2: 257–86.

Taylor, J.R. and Robichaud, D. (2004) 'Finding the organization in the communication: discourse as action and sensemaking', *Organization*, 11(3): 395–413.

Taylor, J.R. and Van Every, E.J. (2000) *The Emergent Organization: Communication as Its Site and Surface*. Mahwah, NJ: Lawrence Erlbaum Associates, Publishers.

Taylor, J.R., Flanagin, A.J., Cheney, G. and Siebold, D.R. (2001) 'Organization communication research: key moments, central concerns, and future challenges', in W.B. Gudykunst (ed.), *Communication Yearbook 24*. Thousand Oaks, CA: Sage. pp. 99–137.

Teboul, J. (1997) ''Scripting' the organization: new hire learning during organizational encounter', *Communication Research Reports*, 14(1): 33–57.

Thackaberry, J.A. (2004) 'Discursive opening and closing in an organizational self-study', *Management Communication Quarterly*, 17(3): 319–59.

Timmerman, C.E. (2003) 'Media selection during the implementation of planned organizational change', *Management Communication Quarterly*, 16(3): 301–40.

Tinker, T. (1986) 'Metaphor or reification: are radical humanists really libertarian anarchists?', *Journal of Management Studies*, 25: 363–84.

Tourish, D., Paulsen, N., Hobman, E. and Bordia, P. (2004) 'The downsides of downsizing: communication processes and information needs in the aftermath of a workforce reduction strategy', *Management Communication Quarterly*, 17(4): 485–516.

Townsley, N.C. and Geist, P. (2000) 'The discursive enactment of hegemony: sexual harassment and academic organizing', *Western Journal of Communication*, 64(2): 190–217.

Tracy, S.J. (2000) 'Becoming a character for commerce', *Management Communication Quarterly*, 14(1): 90–128.

Tracy, S.J. (2002) 'When questioning turns to face threat: an interactional sensitivity in 911 call-taking', *Western Journal of Communication*, 66(2): 129–57.

Tracy, S.J. (2004) 'Dialectic, contradiction, or double bind? Analyzing and theorizing employee reactions to organizational tension', *Journal of Applied Communication Research*, 32(2): 119–46.

Trethewey, A. (1997) 'Resistance, identity, and empowerment: a postmodern feminist analysis of clients in a human service organization', *Communication Monographs*, 64: 281–301.

Trethewey, A. (1999) 'Isn't it ironic: using irony to explore the contradictions of organizational life', *Western Journal of Communication*, 63(2): 140–67.

Trethewey, A. (2001) 'Reproducing and resisting the master narrative of decline', *Management Communication Quarterly*, 15(2): 183–226.

Trice, H.M. and Beyer, J.M. (1984) 'Studying organizational culture through rites and ceremonies', *Academy of Management Review*, 9: 653–69.

Trujillo, N. (1992) 'Interpreting (the work and talk of) baseball: perspectives on ballpark culture', *Western Journal of Communication*, 56: 350–71.

Tsoukas, H. (1993) 'Analogical reasoning and knowledge generation in organization theory', *Organization Studies*, 14: 323–46.

Turner, V. (1980) 'Social dramas and stories about them', *Critical Inquiry*, 7: 141–68.

Tyler, L. (1997) 'Liability means never being able to say you're sorry: corporate guilt, legal constraints, and defensiveness in corporate communication', *Management Communication Quarterly*, 11(1): 51–73.

Ulmer, R.R. (2001) 'Effective crisis management through established stakeholder relationships: Malden Mills as a case study', *Management Communication Quarterly*, 14(4): 590–615.

Ulmer, R. and Sellnow, T. (1997) 'Strategic ambiguity and the ethic of significant choice in the tobacco industry's crisis communication', *Communication Studies*, 48: 215–33.

Vaast, E. (2004) 'O brother, where art thou? From communities to networks of practice through intranet use', *Management Communication Quarterly*, 18(1): 5–44.

Van den Bulte, C. and Moenaert, R.K. (1998) 'The effects of R&D team collocation on communication patterns among R&D marketing and manufacturing', *Management Science*, 44: S1–18.

Van Dyne, L., Ang, S. and Botero, I.C. (2003) 'Conceptualizing employee silence and employee voice as multidimensional constructs', *Journal of Management Studies*, 40(6): 1359–92.

Vaughn, M. (1995) 'Organizational symbols: an analysis of their types and functions in a reborn organization', *Management Communication Quarterly*, 9: 219–50.

Vaughn, M. and Stamp, G.H. (2003) 'The empowerment dilemma: the dialectic of emancipation and control in staff/client interaction at shelters for battered women', *Communication Studies*, 54(2): 154–68.

Ward, J. and Winstanley, D. (2003) 'The absent presence: negative space within discourse and the construction of minority sexual identity in the workplace', *Human Relations*, 56(10): 1255–80.

Weick, K.E. (1979) *The Social Psychology of Organizing* (1969). Reading, MA: Addison-Wesley.

Weick, K.E. (1995) *Sensemaking in Organizations*. Thousand Oaks, CA: Sage Publications.

Weider-Hatfield, D. and Hatfield, J.D. (1996) ''Superiors' conflict management strategies and subordinate outcomes', *Management Communication Quarterly*, 10(2): 189–208.

Weingart, L.R., Prietula, M.J., Hyder, E. and Genovese, C. (1999) 'Knowledge and the sequential processes of negotiation: a Markov chain analysis of response-in-kind', *Journal of Experimental Social Psychology*, 35: 366–93.

Wendt, R.F. (1998) 'The sound of one hand clapping: conterintuitive lessons extracted from paradoxes and double binds in participative organizations', *Management Communication Quarterly*, 11(3): 323–71.

Whitfield, J.M., Lamont, B.T. and Sambamurthy, V. (1996) 'The effects of organization design on media richness in multinational enterprises', *Management Communication Quarterly*, 10(2): 209–26.

Witmer, D.F. (1997) 'Communication and recovery: structuration as an ontological approach to organizational culture', *Communication Monographs*, 64: 324–49.

Zanoni, P. and Janssens, M. (2003) 'Deconstructing difference: the rhetoric of human resource managers' diversity discourses', *Organization Studies*, 25(1): 55–74.

Zhu, Y., May, S.K. and Rosenfeld, L.B. (2004) 'Information adequacy and job satisfaction during a merger and acquisition', *Management Communication Quarterly*, 18(2): 241–70.

Zoller, H.M. (2003) 'Working out: managerialism in workplace health promotion', *Management Communication Quarterly*, 17(2): 171–205.

Zoller, H.M. (2004) 'Dialogue as global issue management: legitimizing corporate influence in the transatlantic business dialogue', *Management Communication Quarterly*, 18(2): 204–40.

Zorn, T.E., Page, D.J. and Cheney, G. (2000) 'Nuts about change: multiple perspectives on change-oriented communication in a public sector organization', *Management Communication Quarterly*, 13(4): 515–66.

2.6 Beyond Contingency: From Structure to Structuring in the Design of the Contemporary Organization

RITA GUNTHER McGRATH

Introduction

On 7 February 2005, the Hewlett Packard company is reported by an external observer to be 'imprisoned in its structure' (Loomis 2005: 60). Within weeks of this observation, HP's CEO was fired by the Board, who cited ineffectiveness at operational leadership as a key reason.

On 19 July 2005, the board of Charles Schwab and company fired its long-time leader, David Pottruck, angered by an acquisition gone dreadfully wrong and a perception that Schwab was 'caught in the middle' in the industry it helped to create (Morris 2005: 94).

In Japan, the Boards of poorly-performing companies have brought in teams of Western CEOs, including Carlos Ghosn at Nissan Motor Corp., Thierry Porte at Shinsei Bank and Howard Stringer for SONY. Observers cited the 'wrenching contraction of the 1990s' as a key factor behind the adoption of foreign management practices (Dawson 2005).

These stories, and many more like them, can be found in a casual perusal of any business publication. What interested me about them is that, unlike tales of business flops involving ill-conceived strategies, in these cases the blame was cast squarely on organizational structure. After literally decades of grappling with issues of strategy and structure, we would hope that the scholarly community would have a lot to say about how tomorrow's CEOs might avoid a similar write-up. In this chapter, I hope to provide some evidence of what we have learned, as well as identify challenges that remain.

As a point of departure, it is worth noting that in both practice and scholarship, the challenges of effective co-ordination of the complex organization have somewhat eclipsed the more analytical concepts long favoured in the strategy tradition. One indicator is the popularity of execution-focused tomes such as Bossidy and Charan's (2002) *Execution: The discipline of getting things done.* The book hit the best-seller lists for months on end as executives pored over guidelines such as 'make sure you get the right people in the right place' and 'link strategy to operations'. While academics might scoff at the simplicity of such prescriptions, the enthusiasm with which the commonsense advice has been received suggests that there is a substantial hunger for better understanding the 'how' of creating an effective organization, a hunger that perhaps we have not done a good job in addressing.

The essential task I hope to achieve here is to provide some evidence with respect to the progress made in our understanding of organizational structure since the first *Handbook* in 1996, but also to suggest where more insight is sorely needed. Among the significant changes since 1996 is an increased velocity and frequency of substantial structural changes, such as reorganizations (Brown and Eisenhardt 1997). We have moved away from a concept of structure as the primary tool for co-ordinating efforts to execute strategy. Instead, we can trace a shift in focus from structure to structuring; from hierarchical relationships to lateral ones; and from contained organizational entities to unbounded networks of semi-tied activities.

I'll start with a core concept that informed the 1996 *Handbook* chapter on structure, that of contingency. We'll have a look at how the contingency argument has evolved since the publication of the first *Handbook*, assess the relevance of the idea to newer forms of organization, particularly as our understanding of the nature of information-intensive environments matures, and suggest new directions for understanding the intersection of organizational design and firm level strategy (Child and McGrath 2001).

Contingency: Then and Now

Contingency Then

Structure as the Key Factor for Co-Ordinating Strategy

There have been few ideas with respect to the design of organizational forms that have been as influential or enduring within organization studies as the notion of contingency (Donaldson 1995; 1996). In a nutshell, the contingency hypothesis maintains that organizations with forms that 'fit' their environmental context will out-perform organizations with forms that do not. In his 1996 review, Donaldson suggests that contingency theory offers, in effect, a conceptual infrastructure on which to hang the analysis of organizational forms that has progressed, cumulatively, along a normal science paradigm.

A key task for the management of organizations has thus been viewed as conceiving and implementing organizational forms that permit organizations to achieve fitness, which we will here refer to as the challenge of organizational design. Not only must leaders figure out how to do this, but they must do so repeatedly as environments change or they put the organization at risk. Students of structure typically look at how activities are grouped or separated, how differing hierarchical levels relate to one another and how key processes are carried out across internal groupings (Galbraith 1973; Burton and Obel 1995; Volberda 1998; Van den Bosch et al. 1999).

Chandler (1962: 14) was highly influential in proposing the primary of structure for fitness. He proposed that structure can be thought of as:

> ... the design of organization through which the enterprise is administered. This design, whether formally or informally defined, has two aspects. It includes first, the lines of authority and communication between the different administrative offices and officers and second the information and data that flow through these lines of communication and authority. Such lines and such data are essential to assure the effective coordination, appraisal and planning is necessary in carrying out the basic goals and policies and in knitting together the total resources of the enterprise.

Chandler's work typifies the assumption that hierarchical structure is the primary mechanism through which the implementation of strategy is co-ordinated. His work was echoed in subsequent studies that looked at different forms of hierarchical organization, such as the multidivisional firm (or M-form), as organizations attempted to diversify and operate in increasingly complex environments (Hoskisson 1987; Gomez-Mejia 1992; Bartlett and Ghoshal 1993).

Unlike Chandler, who presumed that once the choice of strategy was settled, the right structure would be implemented in a well-run organization, other scholars, operating mostly with case data and in the field, suggested a more contingent view of structural choice. Burns and Stalker (1995 originally 1961), for example, made a famous distinction between what they termed 'mechanistic' and 'organic' forms of organization. They suggested that the former structure was more appropriate to conditions of relative stability, while the latter better suited rapidly changing conditions. Lawrence and Lorsch (1967) argued that the internal structures of organizations needed to accommodate both the need for integration across units and differentiation of unit functions.

Like Lawrence and Lorsch, Thompson saw the need for different structures to serve different purposes within a single organization (Thompson 1967). He distinguished among those parts of the organization which could be open to external influence and those which should be buffered (what he termed the 'technical core'). An assumption that drove Thompson's thinking was that of a tradeoff between efficiency and flexibility. The core idea is that structures appropriate for efficient production within a given external environment tended to also introduce rigidity in the system. This reduces the flexibility an organization might require to change structures and respond to a changing environment. Thompson's notion of a tradeoff continues to exert a powerful influence upon today's scholars, who have elaborated the conditions under which efficiency-oriented processes, such as re-engineering or six-sigma quality, might have a negative impact on innovation or change processes (Benner and Tushman 2002; 2003).

Emergence of the Quantification of Structural Attributes

Beginning in the 1960s, with the powerful new analytic tools made possible by advances in computing, it became possible to deploy statistical methods to the study of organizational forms. Early empirical work on the relationship between structural characteristics and other organizational attributes initially focused on relatively easy-to-measure contingent factors, such as organizational size and age (Dewar and Hage 1978). A major contribution of such early work was to demonstrate that empirical analysis could be brought to bear on matters that had frequently been considered suitable primarily for multiple case comparisons using qualitative methodologies (Sorge 2001).

One of the most influential streams of research in this early tradition came to be known as the Aston Programme (Pugh 1998). Over the course of some 30 years, researchers associated with the Aston school essentially tested the Weberian thesis that organizations of increasing size and complexity required increasingly bureaucratic management structures to be able to sustain their growth and co-ordinated development (Weber 1947; Gerth and Mills 1958). Although relatively few of these papers attempted to link structural attributes directly with firm performance, they measured and tested multivariate relationships among constructs drawn from Weber's bureaucratic model.

Weber was explicit in his view that structure provides the primary vehicle for co-ordination of efforts to execute strategy. Among the central concepts in his theory were the primacy of rules, the importance of top-down authority to setting goals and transmitting information, specialized roles within the organization to most efficiently get work done, documented patterns of information exchange, and tight linkages between formal authority and control over significant organizational resources. This meant that personal quirks and individual idiosyncrasies would be subordinate to impersonal policies, rendering the administrative activities of organizational office-holders consistent, and reducing the scope for inconsistent individual action. Individual discretion became increasingly limited as one descended the organizational hierarchy. Among the implications for structure were that, as an organization became more complex, for instance by adopting a multidivisional structure, there was a need for 'more specialist staff, procedures and written documents to permit effective co-ordination and control from the central or general office ...' (Grinyer and Yasai-Ardekani 1980: 406).

Building on Weber's ideas, the Aston team set about attempting to identify and predict the relations among various dimensions of organizational structure (Pugh et al. 1968). Among the constructs they examined were specialization, both of functions and of roles; standardization of policies and rules; formalization by documentation; centralization of authority to make key decisions and structural configuration which often included variables such as managerial span of control or number of hierarchical levels (Child 1972). Over the vast body of work in the Aston tradition, debates have involved the extent to which one type of structural form might substitute for others (for instance, whether bureaucracy offers a sophisticated form of control over essentially decentralized decision-making).

Despite the foundational contributions of these studies, two significant open issues remain. The first, as was identified in a compendium of Aston work (Pugh 1998), is that causal relationships among the constructs assessed in the Aston studies could never be unambiguously established. Indeed, despite studies that sought to establish clear independent variable to dependent variable causal linkages among constructs, at the end of the day there appeared to be interdependence between structure, behaviour, performance and context, implying that the ultimate goal of a contingent perspective (to find the 'best' fit) had not yet been realized. Instead, we have obtained a better portrayal of the landscape of possible structural alternatives and some insights into potentially important boundary conditions, as well as significant progress in the quantitative study of organizational attributes.

Structure and Performance?

The Aston researchers traced their intellectual heritage to Weber, within a (broadly speaking) sociological tradition. Another view of contingency, with a strong emphasis on performance outcomes, was emerging in what was gradually becoming known as the field of strategic management, which traced many of its founding insights to industrial organization economics. As with the sociological work, the economists emphasized that the 'essence of formulating a competition strategy is relating a firm to its environment' (Teece 1984: 96).

Their work tended to emphasize specific practices of firms, such as pricing policies, inter-firm cooperation and coordination, investment in R&D and investment in production, rather than structural attributes such as dispersion or centralization of authority. Another difference in the industrial economics tradition was that the outcome for a firm was seen only partially as a consequence of a firm's decision-making. Rather, the behaviour of other firms had a significant role to play, introducing the idea that competitive environments were to some extent shaped by the actions of the contenders within them (Schelling 1980).

Bain (1959) and Mason (1949) developed the basic concepts behind what came to be known as the structure-conduct-performance paradigm, creating central premises that scholars built upon for the structural analysis of industries. Confusingly, when writers in this tradition refer to 'structure', they don't mean organizational attributes. Rather, they are referring to the more-or-less stable patterns of industry competition, such as the incidence of rivalry and price-taking, the relative power of trading parties and the availability of substitutes for a firm's offerings. In a shift from the original goal of the Bain/Mason frameworks to best develop institutional structures to increase welfare, strategists turned the problem on its head. The strategists' goal, according to Porter (1980; 1983), would instead be to shield the firm from competition to develop a position of sustainable competitive advantage.

Indeed, a considerable amount of research throughout the 1980s and into the 1990s in strategic management focused on the efficacy of various forms of 'conduct' with respect to performance outcomes (Woo and Cooper 1981; Ramanujan and Venkatraman 1984; Miller and Friesen 1986). This research, however, largely omitted questions of organization design, focusing instead on problems of organizational activity.

At the extremes, it was not uncommon for research in the economics tradition to treat questions of organizational form and design as more or less irrelevant (Williamson 1996). Thus, the 'how' questions relevant to managers and the causal relationships between structure and outcomes that were not clear in the Aston School were also not dealt with in much of industrial organization economics. Where this line of thought did provide key insights, however, were in identifying key activity patterns associated with firm-level performance.

Structure and Economizing

Elsewhere in economics, a different group of scholars was pursuing the structural question with fervor (Teece 1984). Drawing their inspiration from Coase (1937), these scholars came up with another powerful contingency argument that would dictate how

best to organize activity. This research stream, which came to be known as 'transaction cost economics', contrasted two alternative ways of coordinating transactions. A transaction could be consummated using arms-length market contracting in which one party would buy from another in a competitive market, or they could be coordinated within the boundaries of a single firm, as when a vertically integrated firm handles both raw-materials acquisition and manufacturing. The major insight with respect to structure was that the choice of form should depend on which co-ordination type would consummate the transaction with the greatest efficiency. The underlying structural assumption was that in competitive markets, managers should choose structures that economize on costs, particularly transaction costs (Williamson 1992).

Transaction cost economics has been used to explain why some firms prefer vertical integration to diversification or specialization and why certain structural practices within firms are utilized (Klein et al. 1978; Ouchi 1980; Walker and Weber 1984). Among the topics that interested these researchers were whether firms faced limitations on the size or scope of their operations as their capacity to coordinate complex transactions internally was challenged. Of particular concern to scholars such as Williamson (1991; 1992) were the conditions under which a firm would tend to house a transaction internally, which he argued would occur when there was significant potential for opportunism, when numbers of transactions are small, when assets are specific to a particular type of transaction and when information is imperfect.

Note that in transaction cost economics, as with other research developing the contingency perspective, choice of structure was seen as the primary vehicle for coordinating strategic activities. Unlike other schools, however, transaction cost economics introduced the notion that alternative organizational forms could accomplish similar purposes, introducing a new nuance to the contingency perspective. While providing more guidance to structural decision-making, the perspective has been criticized for too narrow a concept of when a practice will be internalized.

The Role of the Strategist

A different thread of strategic management research, meanwhile, emphasized the constraints on structural choice that emerge from an organization's past history. Beginning with Selznick's (1957) concept of 'distinctive competence', scholars in this tradition suggested that a key leadership task is to fit together the internal capabilities an organization had developed with the external challenges necessary for its survival. This idea became an intellectual centre-piece of some research and even more teaching in the strategy arena (Christensen et al. 1982).

The core idea is that effective strategy-making followed a consistent set of analytical steps, beginning with the formulation challenge and concluding with implementation, of which organizational design was a part. In this framework, executives would begin with external and internal analysis, identify potential opportunities and threats, tie these together with organizational strengths and weaknesses (the SWOT framework still very much in use in strategic analysis today), formulate a strategy, select the right organizational structures to implement that strategy, and repeat. Unlike Chandler's emphasis on structure as the essential companion to strategy, structure in this discussion was lumped together with other issues of implementation (Hrebiniak and Joyce 1984).

This approach to strategy was well-entrenched in practice, though not as broadly represented in research as either industrial economics or transaction cost economics. Moreover, despite a strongly normative bent, few conclusions on the efficacy of a given set of leadership practices *ex ante* emerged from research in this tradition, a point that did not escape notice by critics (Stinchcombe 2000). Towards the end of the decade, an approach now widely known as the 'resource-based' view of the firm (Wernerfelt 1984) once again took up the idea that competitive advantage was in part a function of idiosyncratic firm-based resource combinations and that heterogeneity of resources, rather than choice of competitive position, explained differential performance (Barney 1991; Peteraf 1993; Teece et al. 1997).

Unlike earlier contingency views of the structural choices, resource-based perspectives placed significant emphasis on the path-dependent and sticky nature of critical firm resources and the difficulty of replicating even successful combinations elsewhere (Dierickx and Cool 1989; Zander and Kogut 1995; Szulanski 1996; Helfat and Raubitschek 2000). Thus, it was no longer enough to identify key external contingencies and select the best structure to

'fit'; instead, organizational designers were seen as significantly constrained by the assets and routines in place within their organizations and with the difficulty of coordinating the deployment of specific combinations. Although the resource-based view has been influential, scholars have struggled with how to define general operating guidelines derived from it, and with distinguishing it from other concepts, such as that of 'emergent strategy' (Mintzberg and Waters 1985).

Current Perspectives on Contingency

Empirical support for the classic contingency arguments was typically mixed, due perhaps to difficulties in establishing the locus of 'fitness' and measuring it independently from other organizational factors (Schoonhoven 1981; Drazin and Van de Ven 1985; Courtright et al. 1989). Nonetheless, scholars have been diligent in introducing evermore contingencies which organization designers need to take into account.

Scholars interested in punctuated equilibrium models of environmental change have emphasized the extent to which particular structures are appropriate for different product or industry life-cycle stages (Romanelli and Tushman 1994; Tushman and O'Reilly 1996). A slightly different distinction was made by Christensen and Bower (1996), who stressed that a key design issue involved the extent to which particular innovations sustained a firm's technological trajectory or disrupted it. They also suggest that the extent to which a change is disruptive should dictate the form of organization (see also Christensen 1997; Christensen and Raynor 2003a).

In a highly influential article, March (1991) introduced learning as a key contingent variable. He argued that the extent to which an organization was engaging in exploring new domains versus exploiting a presence in established domains should strongly influence its structure. One reason March's article has attracted considerable attention was that he proposed that rather than a dominant contingency affecting much of the organization, instead a key challenge for organizational design was establishing the correct balance between structures intended to facilitate exploratory learning vs exploitative learning. Although not inconsistent with previous notions of contingency, March's thinking placed significant emphasis on the importance of choosing an organizational form that facilitated both forms of learning, and emphasized that intra-firm structures were as important as firm-level structures.

Rather than depicting a more-or-less stable dominant contingency, March's article suggested that the correct or best organizational form changes. Further, that within a given firm both structures that facilitate order, coherence and productivity and structures that facilitate creativity, play and (to use March's word) 'foolishness' should be permitted – even encouraged – to exist. Perhaps because March was quite careful in developing the exploration and exploitation constructs, a virtual explosion of research has by now built on this distinction. Subsequent empirical work has sought to shed light on the mechanisms through which the choice of form operates, and with what consequences (Levinthal and March 1993; Benner and Tushman 2002; Garcia et al. 2003; Nerkar 2003; He and Wong 2004; Holmqvist 2004).

The work on exploration and exploitation represents a substantial advance in the characterization of contingencies by scholars in two ways. First, scholars recognized that critical contingencies operate at the sub-firm level, not at the level of the firm. Secondly, they now observed that part of the design challenge facing managers lies in creating contexts in which inconsistent structural forms can be accommodated, a substantial nod to the implementation of the requisite variety construct (Ashby 1956). Moreover, the emphasis on learning in these later models suggests significant dynamism in the choice of organizational form.

The notion of multiple contingencies that change frequently has led to a different interpretation of what fitness implies for organizations and to different research questions than were framed in the classic work. Among the dilemmas it has created is a sort of Heisenberg principle for organizational design. As soon as an executive learns enough about the environment in which the organization is operating to make the right decision with respect to structure, the appropriate organizational form will change due to imitation and environmental response (March and Sutton 1997).

The concept of contingency, thus, has had a certain utility for organizational scholars. It is intuitively sensible. It had the advantage of departing from the 'one best way' view of structures that preceded it (Sloan 1963; Spender and Kijne 1996). It suggests important boundary conditions. It makes key assumptions explicit so that work can accumulate and build upon what came before. Nonetheless, it is worthwhile at this juncture to consider how contingency ideas might need, themselves, to evolve as the environment confronting organizations does. Among contingencies' critics are those that observe that very little empirical research built on the concept addresses the complexity or ambiguity of actual design activities (Gerwin 1979; Gresov 1989).

Contingency Now?

As Victor and Stephens (1994) have observed, questions of appropriate organizational design have moved in the last decade or so from a relatively peripheral line of inquiry in organization studies to a central, hotly-debated topic. On the scholarly side, considerable energy has gone into describing what new forms of organization might look like. Terms such as post-industrial, post-bureaucratic, network, virtual, co-evolved, modular and the like, have been minted to try to capture key aspects of such new forms (Huber 1984; Burns and Wholey 1993; Nohria and Ghoshal 1997; Lewin and Volberda 1999; Child and McGrath 2001; Galunic and Eisenhardt 2001). On the more practical side, bewildered managers have sought guidance as to appropriate organizational design offered by a large number of books and articles, each arguing that selecting the right design would enhance the prospects for strategic success (Hammer and Champy 1993; Champy 1995; Slywotzky and Morrison 1997). In neither the academic nor the scholarly worlds has a definitive consensus emerged on what structural principles should prevail.

Current research has de-emphasized a core premise of all of the preceding contingency views; namely the idea of clear-cut connections between structural attributes within a firm, its boundaries, and the environments in which it must function. I shall briefly highlight four ideas that challenge these premises: complementarity, equifinality, networks and co-evolution.

Complementarity

Milgrom and Roberts (1995) found, in an economic analysis, that complementarities had significant performance consequences for firms. The basic intuition behind complementarity is that a design should leverage interdependencies between organizational elements, meaning that configurations, rather than individual elements, are the appropriate level of analysis to determine fitness. In their analysis of manufacturing systems, for instance, they found that the successful introduction of one type of innovation depended on the simultaneous introduction of other relevant innovations (Liker et al. 1987; Milgrom and Roberts 1990).

The complementarity idea builds upon earlier assumptions about organizational design – namely that certain configurations should be treated as wholes, rather than being understood through dis-aggregation into parts (Ackoff and Emery 1972). The design challenge is thus to create entire self-reinforcing structural systems that are aligned with the strategy of the organization (Galbraith 1973). The most direct assertions about the performance effects of such configurations can be found in a variety of typologies that seek to establish a linkage between different strategic postures of firms (for instance, an emphasis on innovation or on low-cost) and different configurations (Miles and Snow 1978; Hambrick 1983). Even Porter's typology of alternative strategies (niche, differentiation or low-cost) carries with it structural implications (Porter 1980).

In their discussion of the implications of complementarities and configurational approaches for organizational structure, Whittington et al. (1999) point out two major challenges to traditional notions of contingency. First is the idea that, even if managers attempt to move an organization toward a new configuration, partial implementation is likely to diminish performance even more than had the organization been left well enough alone. This suggests that the transition from configuration to configuration is far more complex than a carefully defined effort to generate greater 'fitness'.

Downsizing, for instance, has proved a popular and widely used approach for restructuring organizations on a massive scale. In an article published in the late 1990s, Appelbaum et al. (1999) reported that over 85% of *Fortune* 500 companies have engaged in downsizing, and that virtually all of them intended to adopt the practice in their current strategies. Although sources vary, estimates of the numbers of individuals affected range as high as two million per year for the years 2003 and 2004 (DeMeuse et al. 2004).

Astonishingly, given the considerable impact that a significant downsizing can have, the efficacy of the practice has yet to be demonstrated conclusively.

Indeed, considerable evidence suggests that downsizing can have extremely negative effects, ranging from a negative impact on a firm's innovative capacity (Dougherty and Bowman 1995) to devastating loss of 'organizational memory' (Cameron et al. 1987) to damaging consequences for morale (Brockner et al. 1988). When it is effective, some studies suggest, it is because downsizing is but one element of a host of reconfiguration practices that include changes to leadership behaviour, communication practices, measurements, budgeting, information systems and training activities, reinforcing the interdependent nature of design considerations. One clear implication is that reconfiguring an organization's structure requires reconfiguration of processes and lateral, as well as horizontal, structural changes.

A second challenge is that, since the performance consequences of different elements in a configuration are interdependent, it becomes extraordinarily difficult to pin down the dis-aggregated effects of individual practices. One implication is that it is relatively uninteresting for scholars to study individual practices in isolation – what matters in comprehending the relationship between structure and performance in the modern organization, is the adeptness of management at fostering system-wide changes in parallel.

Equifinality

If the study of individual practices is either not interesting or misleading, what would make sense to study instead? One suggestion, offered by Gresov and Drazin (1997), is to incorporate concepts of equifinality into the study of organizational design. Equifinality was originally developed in systems theory to describe how open systems can proceed from different initial conditions to arrive at a similar, often steady, end state (von Bertalanffy 1968). As the vernacular phrase suggests, equifinality acknowledges that there's more than one way to skin a cat or, more specifically, to design an effective organization. Moreover, organizations facing more or less the same contingent conditions might develop different responses to those conditions that produce equivalent levels of 'fitness'. Thus, an organization facing a threatened performance decline might respond in a number of ways: by redoubling efforts in its existing business, by expanding to alternative markets and seeking to capture demand there, by retrenching or by otherwise re-organizing.

Gresov and Drazin provide some guidance for a perspective that both allows for equifinality, but is still possible to research. This first requires abandoning some cherished assumptions in the conventional contingency studies, namely that a given organizational structural element is responsible for handling one (and only one) critical organizational function. One might, for example, argue that a formal computerized tracking system is primarily an element used for controlling the behaviour of far-flung employees, and conclude that the presence of such tracking systems will generate higher performance in an environment in which consistent performance creates value for a firm. Merton (1967), however, argued that this view of structural elements is erroneous.

Instead, he suggested that scholars consider the concept of functional equivalence, in which the structural artifact and the outcome it creates are distinguished from one another. Thus, the tracking system could allow the organization to perform other functions (such as improved insight into specific customer requirements or an ability to troubleshoot remotely), while the function of consistent behaviour could be the result of the combination of several structural elements (such as training, monitoring, supervision and teamwork, in addition to the computerized system). The main insight from making the distinction, as Gresov and Drazin (1997: 407) argue, is that 'The environment (or any other contingency, such as technology or stage of life cycle) determines the function(s) the organization must perform, but not its specific structures'. Thus, organizations might be required by their environments to respond to similar challenges, but may organize and structure differently to meet those challenges.

The prospect of equifinality suggests that scholars interested in organizational design need to shift their emphasis from what are essentially inputs to the organization's level of functioning (such as structural artifacts), to outputs reflecting its effectiveness at producing the required functionality. Thus, an organization might meet an information-processing demand by implementing an enterprise resource system such as SAP, engaging in horizontal structures, adding communication resources or investing in boundary-spanning skills among individuals. The real test of the skill of its designers is in how effectively it was able to produce the necessary level of information processing. Such research would also view design as a process rather than a steady state, and place emphasis on the cognitive and informational conditions that suggest to designers what choices are best under what circumstances.

A second clear implication of the equifinality concept is that horizontal, as well as vertical mechanisms to produce organizational cohesion, need to be considered if understanding functionality is the desired outcome. Ghoshal and Gratton (2002) offer a description of what such mechanisms, for what they term 'horizontal integration' operate. They specifically identify four practices that produce the end functionality of consistent behaviour: (1) standardization of technological infrastructure to integrate operations; (2) sharing of knowledge to integrate intellectual capacity; (3) peer-to-peer performance assessment and challenge to integrate motivation; and (4) sharing of identity, meaning and values to create emotional integration. Note that, although structure (in this case a transition from vertical to horizontal structures) is a factor in their analysis, it is the joint operation of many structural elements that produces the functionality of co-ordination and cohesion in the firms they studied.

Networks

Just as equifinality suggests that more than one structural element might be involved in producing a given result, network analysis observes that more than one kind of organizational relationship produces different results. Network research offers the insight that because modern organizations are embedded in inter-firm relationships of many kinds, the design problem needs to take network ties into account (Kogut et al. 1993; Uzzi 1996; Andersson et al. 2001). Among the conclusions scholars studying networks have come to is that firms often cope with environmental contingencies, not by adapting their internal structures, but by creating extra-firm linkages. Some scholars have gone so far as to argue that any view of organizational design would be incomplete absent a serious consideration of the network relationships within which an organization operates (Dyer and Singh 1998).

Co-operative arrangements often exhibit a powerful geographic influence, linking current studies of organization design more closely to traditional examinations of the industrial district or co-operative network of firms. The issue is that the relevant organizational units that are involved in a given design configuration are not within the control of any individual designer. Thus, firms within economic clusters and industrial districts are depicted as working together in a co-operative way even though technically no one is 'in charge', which certainly violates some of the core assumptions in conventional contingency theory (Saxenian 1994; Lorenzoni and Lipparini 1999). Here, too, we see the switch in emphasis from vertical structures to horizontal structures, where other forms of coordination than managerial fiat are used to produce consistent behaviour by actors.

Cooperation can even extend to firms taking differing roles within clusters, sometimes differentiating their structures internally, while drawing upon the variety in their networks to cope with challenges from the environment (Garud and Kumaraswamy 1993). Sometimes, an entire organizational type is comprised of and dependent on linkages between the different parties (Tushman and Anderson 1986). The dark side of depending on a clustered form of organization is that, since no one entity directs its development, the entire cluster can fail to respond effectively to a significant environmental shift, particularly what some scholars have termed 'architectural' shifts in production (Glasmeier 1991; Tripsas 1997).

The key point here from the perspective of contingency theory is that if the organizational design extends beyond the boundaries of a firm, designers are in fact relying on repeated interactions with other firms to establish the design, not creating the design as a function of individual choice. Thus, the contingency to which a particular organization is responding is conflated with the choices of other organizations, making it very difficult to untangle what is in fact the relevant external contingency to which a design should respond.

Co-Evolution

Finally, we come to the problem that, in conventional contingency theorizing, the environment is perceived as exogenous to the firm. Organizations are not characterized as having the capacity to change their environments (with the exception of the emphasis on changes to regulatory regimes in the structure-conduct-performance school). In other words, the environment creates challenges,

and the firm responds more or less effectively. What then of the co-evolutionary idea that as organizations act, they precipitate change in their environments? Organizations and environments co-evolve.

Instead of being selected in or out of a particular context, organizations influence their selection environments and redefine the trajectory along which they, their institutions and the environment develops (Lewin et al. 1999). Scholars examining co-evolution have concluded, among other things, that an alternative to developing a more suitable organizational design for the context is to change the context in which a firm competes (Romo and Schwartz 1995). Thus, a firm whose structure puts it at a disadvantage from a regulatory or technological point of view might, rather than engage in organizational change, act instead to change aspects of their environment.

This is not armchair theorizing. Consider the case of Citigroup. When confronted with strict bans on the interest rates it could charge for consumer credit in its home state of New York, its lawyers negotiated a more favourable arrangement with the state of South Dakota and simply moved its entire operation there. Threatened with losing jobs in its core financial services industry, the New York legislature (and that of many other states) responded by changing their regulatory regimes, in effect relaxing an environmental constraint that set the stage for the rapid growth of the American credit card system (Barrett 2001).

Co-evolutionary ideas challenge the concept of contingency as a design principle in several ways. If one abandons the idea of designing to cope with relatively stable contingencies, contingency thinking offers little guidance, because the boundary condition is highly subject to change – the contingency, in other words, doesn't stay put long enough for design to cope with it. Further, a core idea in co-evolutionary thinking is that of self-correcting feedback loops. The existence of such loops suggests that, even if a design were to emerge that offered advantages to a particular unit or firm, responses on the part of the system in which the unit is operating will adjust in such a way that the advantage is eroded (March and Sutton 1997). This phenomenon has been observed in many natural and organizational phenomena, resulting in both the standards of performance and the measurements used to assess performance to lose variance (Gould 1996). Once variance is gone, the utility of design based on a particular contingency is suspect.

A New Paradigm?

One could probably identify even more ways in which current organizational scholarship has gone beyond the basic contingency idea. For our purposes, it suffices to note that challenges to the basic notion of contingency (define an environmental challenge and design to cope with it) have, at their core, a fundamental shift in the organization of production in more advanced economies. As Victor and Stephens (1994: 480) point out, it is no longer 'science fiction' to observe that 'full-time industrial employment of the majority of adults [has become] obsolescent'.

The boundary conditions that informed notions of contingency have changed radically, because the constraints to which designers attempted to respond have also changed radically. It made sense to buffer what Thompson (1967) called the 'technical core' when that core was capital-intensive, slow to change and extraordinarily difficult to replace. It makes little sense to invest in such buffering capacity when the 'core', such as it is, may be distributed across time and space, be relatively easy to reconfigure and replace and consist not of physical assets with the capital intensity that these imply, but of digital processes.

In the next section, I will consider the implications of the replacement of industrial production with information-based production for our assumptions with respect to organizational structure.

Why the Information Economy Really Does Matter to Organizational Design

Although it was fashionable a few years ago to identify the Internet as a primary culprit in changing our fundamental understanding of how things work in our economy, the emergence of service-based 'intangible' business models has been in progress for some time (Bazen and Thirlwell 1987; Quinn et al. 1990; Quinn 1992). Unfortunately, perhaps, the bursting of the Internet bubble doesn't allow us to return to industrial-age theorizing, because fundamental economic and social transitions are already well advanced. The transition from a largely industrial mode of production to one in which services or intangibles constitute a firm's offerings have important implications for our theories of organizational structure (Boisot and Child 1999).

Challenges to Taken For Granted Assumptions

Consider some taken-for-granted assumptions in extant theorizing with respect to the constraints within which organizational design operates. Without an attempt to be exhaustive, some of the most important of these involve: (1) the nature of productive assets; (2) the stability of the relationship between a firm and its owners; (3) new agency issues; (4) the ability to hoard information; (5) ambiguity with respect to the creation and capture of value; and (6) the nature and locations of ties between workers.

The Nature of Productive Assets

In industrial economies, factors of production include physical assets, such as operating plant and equipment. When a firm's competitive well-being depends on how these assets are deployed, the design assumptions with respect to the critical contingencies facing that firm relate directly to the effective use of those assets. Capital is presumed to be scarce. Because the assets are difficult or expensive to acquire and require substantial investment, maintaining them in peak operating mode becomes the most significant operational challenge for the organization. When such productive assets are replaced by service or information goods, however, these assumptions no longer apply.

In information-intensive situations, meaning, not capacity, becomes a key scarce resource (Boisot 1995b) because people that can more rapidly make sense out of signals can act to capitalize on their insights faster than rivals without equivalent sense-making capability. When one doesn't need to construct a plant to capitalize on an insight, the people with the insight and ability to move quickly become scarce; the equipment they use to do this becomes commoditized. The design implication is that structures need to facilitate sensemaking across boundaries, not buffer internal operations from external influence (Weick 1995). In fact, appropriate structures in an information-intensive economy might almost amplify signals from the external environment in order to help the organization respond quickly. The idea that organizations exist as interpretation systems becomes critical to design (Daft and Weick 1984). So, too, do structures that facilitate the creation of collective capacity to create meaning (Weick and Roberts 1993).

One implication of these ideas is that, in information-intensive settings, the design of horizontal issue management processes becomes every bit as important as the vertical design of physical production processes. Marshalling attention, creating focus and developing meaning in decision-making groups within the firm become competitively important activities. Unfortunately, current research suggests that the state-of-the-art in intelligently doing these things is at a fairly low standard (Werner 2004). Clearly, what I will call the problem of agenda management – how management time and attention are allocated – has become a critically important issue about which relatively little has been done. How are the leaders of a firm to decide quite literally what goes on the agenda? How can they allocate limited sense-making capacity? How do they choose among the increasing number of design options this chapter suggests they have?

The Stability of the Corporate Ownership Relationship

The assumption that there is a relatively stable relationship between the owners of an organization and the activities of an organization is deeply rooted, not only in organization studies but in other areas of social science (such as economics). Derivative assumptions from this primary one include the idea that shareholders base investment decisions on the expected performance of the firm (thus the widespread use of stock price as a dependent variable in organization studies); that firms that are performing well will be rewarded by an appreciation in their market capitalization and that stable, reliable performance is desired by a firm's owners. The organizational structures one might design based on these assumptions would be those that promote long-term organizational effectiveness. In information-intensive, international settings, however, it becomes more and more difficult to suppress volatility in stock movement and volatility in firm-level performance (Hassler 1999; Henry and Vickers 2003).

One consequence of increased volatility, combined with dramatically lower transaction costs, is that shareholders have become increasingly fickle (Byrne 1999). Thus, any shift in the public perception of a firm's prospects can be instantly translated into a buy or sell action. This has two effects: first, making the value of publicly traded firms far more sensitive to new information; and secondly, promoting a roving disloyalty among owners of firms. In

combination, these factors create a condition in which the management of external perceptions about internal activities is absolutely core to the real market value of a firm.

From an organizational design perspective, this situation actually creates a need for new information buffering mechanisms, in this case between a firm and its owners. The challenge is how to ethically and transparently communicate what is going on, while at the same time inhibiting the damage that can be done by owners with little interest in a firm, save the money that can be made by capitalizing on movements in its stock price.

New Agency Issues

Like transaction cost economics (with which it bears some theoretical resemblance), agency perspectives on organizations make the assumption that one goal of organizational design is to ensure that those managing firms act in the best interest of those who own the firm. In the case of large public corporations, this generally means that governance structures are intended to make sure that managers do not enrich themselves at the expense of their shareholders (Child and Rodrigues 2003). Processes for managing such agency issues, however, have clearly fallen short of this ambition, with scandal, incredibly high levels of executive pay, and greater potential to influence the stock price of a firm competing with efforts to strengthen oversight (such as the passage of the Sarbanes-Oxley act intended to make financial reporting transparent and senior executives accountable).

An area that begs for deeper understanding is the relationship between provisions for executive compensation and the structural and other choices made by executives affected. This is particularly acute in light of recent research that suggests that the market capitalization of a firm needs to be understood in quite a different light than its usual positioning as a dependent variable.

Practically, executives today speak of 'managing' the stock price of their firms, belying the idea that they do their jobs as best they can to generate profits in product markets, and investors judge their effectiveness by increasing or decreasing the value of their firm's shares. Recent inquiries into the finances of Vivendi Universal and insurer AIG are simply two instances in which managers in firms took deliberate actions to influence their share prices. Such behaviour challenges the conventional wisdom in academic research that the stock price is an outcome variable. Indeed, recent research suggests that because organizations respond to changes in the stock price by taking actions to improve it (such as committing to stock buybacks), it is actually an independent variable (Kock 2004). The insight that under many conditions stock price is an input variable, not an output variable, calls into question considerable amounts of research in finance and economics that operate on the assumption that all relevant information is incorporated into the stock price, and that managers can do relatively little to influence it.

Further, the assumption that leaders tie their fates to their company's well-being doesn't seem to hold either. On the one hand, we can now observe organizations that are not created to become enduring enterprises. Instead, they are 'built to flip' – created to demonstrate just enough viability or demand to be of interest to a potential purchaser, or even to go through an IPO (Hammonds et al. 2002). Even for large, established corporations, stability in the leadership ranks is becoming increasingly rare. Turnover at the top is widespread, and by many accounts the tenure of CEO's is declining (Lucier and Schuyt 2002). This then challenges the idea of the CEO as chief long-term strategist, and calls into question where the locus of design decisions needs to be.

The Ability to Hoard Information

As Boisot has often pointed out, a fundamental assumption in economic reasoning is that value is a joint product of utility combined with scarcity (Walras 1984; Boisot 1998). A derivative assumption with relevance to organizational design is that firms should endeavour, where they can, to hoard information that might reduce the scarcity value of their offerings. Thus, a substantial literature on knowledge spillovers, for instance, presumes that when a firm's knowledge 'leaks out' to other firms, the originating firm loses out because it cannot capture the gains to its investment in creating that knowledge (Griliches 1984; Mansfield 1985). Among the implications for organizational design are that designs should facilitate the preservation, internally, of valuable knowledge, while preventing such knowledge from crossing firm boundaries and leaking out to others.

Whether or not it is good in general for a firm to hoard information, it seems pretty clear that successfully doing so is becoming increasingly more difficult, to the point that in some industries, such as software development, taking out patents is seen as virtually useless, because the action of trying to protect your knowledge alerts competitors to its existence. Widespread adoption of media that allow increasingly rich communication for a given investment of time or money exacerbates the speed at which information can travel from organization to organization (Evans and Wurster 1997). Moreover, some spillovers are in all likelihood healthy, because they facilitate inter-firm learning and development of a technological trajectory that benefits all participants (Allen 1983; Baumol 2002).

The implications for organizational design are ambiguous. On the one hand, designs should perhaps separate people with key organizational knowledge from contact with those who might appropriate that knowledge to their benefit. On the other, considerable evidence suggests that this would be a mistake. For one thing, contact with customers, suppliers and even competitors are vital sources of innovative ideas (von Hippel 1987). For another, firms that cannot absorb information from other organizations are likely to be at a disadvantage relative to rivals that have developed such an ability (Cohen and Levinthal 1990; Van den Bosch et al. 1999). One general principle, articulated by Boisot (1995a), is that, if it is difficult to hoard information, it becomes imperative to generate new, valuable information ever more rapidly. The structures that facilitate this activity are likely to be different from those that facilitate stable hoarding of valuable information.

Ambiguity With Respect to the Creation and Capture of Value

It was never presumed to be easy for firms to capture returns for their investments in creating valuable assets. As those assets more often take the form of an intangible product or a service, the complexity of not only creating value but benefiting from it increases exponentially. One dilemma is that often the good is co-produced: thus, the value created by the provision of a service is in part a function of the effort made by both the service provider and the service recipient. It is ambiguous who gets to appropriate any rents that might ensue. This type of ambiguity has focused attention on property rights as a core issue in the design of products and services and, consequently, on the design of organizations (Arora 1995).

Another dilemma is that with intangible or digital offerings, the offering may be more or less costlessly copied. This insight is familiar (Arrow 1974). What is less familiar is the dilemma that often facilitating offerings that make others possible or that leverage complementary offerings do not generate returns for their inventors. The widespread dissemination of email applications might be a case in point – although demand for email certainly increases the utility of a wide range of other applications and the hardware that goes with them, the inventor of email would find it rather difficult to capture the value created by the offering.

With respect to organizational design, ambiguity about where value is created and what vehicles contain it suggests that design also needs to take into account the actions and intentions of competitors. A competitor motivated to sell hardware, for instance, might be perfectly comfortable giving away the software that would make this hardware more valuable. A firm designed to develop and distribute software on a standalone basis might find itself at a significant disadvantage, save some vehicle by which the scarcity value of the software might be preserved.

The Nature and Locations of Ties Between Workers

One of the most prevalent assumptions in organizational design is that organizations consist of groups of people who are linked together in some way: through sharing of common space and assets, within a stable, well-understood boundary that defines the limit of who is in the organization and who is not (Aldrich 1999). Conventionally, geography has had an enormous influence on people who have created and joined organizations. Most founders start their businesses in locations in which they already have ties or roots (Reynolds and White 1997; Schoonhoven and Romanelli 2001), and most employees of new firms come from the same area or come strongly recommended by someone the founder trusts. Likewise, most new employees entering established organizations have been found to do so as a function of referrals from existing organization members (Granovetter 1974). Thus, the emergence of important knowledge-containing structures that Aldrich has termed a 'community of practice' is facilitated. Aldrich (1999: 141) defines such a community as 'the patterned social interaction between members that sustains organizational knowledge and facilitates its reproduction'.

What happens to such communities, however, when membership 'in' and 'out' of the organizational

boundary is not easy to establish? Even worse, when boundaries extend across geographic space and different time zones? As organizations experiment with various forms of boundarylessness and virtuality, it seems clear that the emergence of a community of practice will follow a different process than in relatively bounded, geographically co-located entities. Further, given that it is fairly well established that greater effort is required to convey information over distance (Allen 1977), it seems to make sense that greater effort will be necessary to create and sustain such communities. Here, however, organizations face a conundrum.

In the interest of streamlining information flows, reducing decision layers and becoming more responsive to their environments, organizations have de-layered, downsized and slashed away at the ranks of middle management (Freeman and Cameron 1993; Dougherty and Bowman 1995). Yet at the same time, the effort required to create and sustain communities of practice, communicate within and across boundaries and create coherent, bounded structures (which Aldrich asserts are essential for the fundamental work of sustaining an organization) is very likely to have increased, rapid communication by electronic media notwithstanding. This conundrum raises the possibility that the task of creating organizational coherence is one that is quite often given short-shrift or neglected altogether, because the human capacity to do this critical, yet largely unrecognized, work is extremely limited.

New Questions

I have described the impact of new technologies on our theories of organizational design primarily in terms of the challenges to design assumptions articulated in previous research. These challenges present an intriguing set of questions for the designers of tomorrow's organizational structures.

The first cluster of questions devolves around property rights and the structure of ownership for intangible assets. When the most important assets in an organization leave for home every night, the entire infrastructure of ownership assumptions that have underpinned our understanding of organizational structure and associated metrics is challenged. Moreover, such assets create the real probability that organizations can create enormous value and fail to profit at all from this creation. As a case in point, consider the challenges faced simply in accounting for intangible assets (Bryant 1989). One strong implication for future research is that organizational design cannot be considered separately from issues of value appropriation – a linkage that is currently not made with any force.

A second set of questions concerns the relevance of the classic 'industry' construct for understanding how organizations operate. While it is not a new observation that in rapidly changing markets the notion of industry is not necessarily useful (Aldrich and Fiol 1994), this insight is not widely applied to mainstream theorizing. Yet, the assumption of who one is competing with, and for what, surely influences structural choices. For instance, clearly, automobile makers compete with one another to sell automobiles. Yet, if the primary value added in the car stems from the information assets embedded in its design and functionality, the quest for capturing superior value may involve technologies and industry conceptions that are quite distinct from car-making's mass-manufacturing roots.

A third set of questions concerns the nature of the institution–organization interaction. Conventionally, the institutions of an organization's home country and those in which it is physically present, have been seen as most relevant to its structural choices. For instance, in examining governance or innovation systems, the relevant boundary used by most scholars is the national or regional one. Electronic connections pose intriguing new challenges to defining boundaries. For example, if one set of firms operates in a laissez-faire institutional context, but are connected electronically to a strict institutional context de-facto, the stricter context will likely set a global standard. Three examples come to mind: in privacy restrictions, use of genetically modified food, and regulations with respect to single-use packaging, European standards are stricter than those elsewhere. Companies (and countries) wishing to sell in Europe are thus put in a position in which they must respond to the stricter standard or yield the market – in a sense, yielding to an alternative institutional regime in their strategic decisions.

Conclusion: Whither The Pragmatics of Organizational Design?

Although it would be misleading to conclude at this juncture that scholars have established a consensus on what one might think of as a post-contingency theory of organizational structure, I hope to have identified some clear points of departure for working on such a theory. Clearly, such a theory would accommodate different assumptions about organizations and the constraints under which they operate, particularly with respect to relevant organizational boundaries. Such a theory would incorporate strategy – where by strategy I mean the choices made by organizational leaders in an effort to pursue good performance. And in such a theory, analysis of change, rather than analysis of state conditions, assumes centre stage (Whittington et al. 1999).

From Structural Artifacts to Functions

A clear implication of work that has taken place since the publication of the original *Handbook* is that we need to modify what we mean by 'fitness'. Today, it is fairly clear that the design challenge is complex, in the sense that many alternative choices are both possible and viable. The concept of 'structure' thus becomes subordinate to the concept of 'structuring' as an ongoing, central activity in the management of modern organizations, with the ultimate goal of the activity being the creation of new forms of functional capacity (Whittington 2004).

While this shift does unfortunately relegate a good deal of work that came before to the past, it does open up some fascinating new areas of inquiry. The bad news for researchers is that if the process of structuring is more important than the specific outcome of structuring, cross-sectional, single period studies are unlikely to yield much insight. The good news is that the change in perspective opens up new points of departure, some of which might be quite straightforward, to research. For instance, if we accept the idea that management of agenda and issue processing are core to the interpretation of environmental signals that lead to organizational changes, such a process could be studied by the activities managers use to set agendas, who is engaged in those activities and what streams of decisions and actions emerge from them that affect organizational processes (Mankins 2004). It would also be beneficial if researchers could define constructs that are recognizable by practitioners as issues they can influence (such as the preparation of a management agenda or the specific design of a common horizontal information technology platform).

Another interesting set of questions involves tradeoffs. For example, scholars are now beginning to more closely examine how organizations accommodate traditional tradeoffs in design – for instance, the tradeoff between flexibility and efficiency. One emergent theme includes work that is being done on modularity as a design principle (Baldwin and Clark 2000; Galunic and Eisenhardt 2001; Schilling and Steensma 2001). In theories of modular structures, the assumption is made that creating the capacity to restructure is of greater value than identifying the 'best' structure for the moment. Some authors have gone so far as to argue that creating and maintaining the capacity to restructure is the real core of organizational design (Sanchez and Mahoney 1996).

Another set of themes emerging in more recent examinations of structure have to do with organizational 'software'. Discussions of human resource practices, culture, communication processes, knowledge management, procedural justice, identity and leadership are only a few of the process themes emerging in more recent work on structure and restructuring (Whittington et al. 1999). Such processes suggest an expanded definition of the domain of organizational design, beyond the conventional concept of structure in terms of activities, hierarchy (reporting relationships) and linking processes. Indeed, there is far greater awareness that structure is far from the only mechanism to promote co-ordination and coherence in organizational functioning. Horizontal and process views are today seen as equally important.

From Effectiveness to Requisite Variety

One fairly robust conclusion from recent work on structure is that preserving variety within the organization has value, even if at first glance such variety would appear to be wasteful. Levinthal's (1997) work on rugged competitive landscapes, for example, suggests that entities that optimize for one set of conditions without simultaneously preserving some capacity to rapidly adapt to different conditions will be at a long-run disadvantage. Unlike the distinction in the exploration/exploitation literature, the variety that is useful to preserve within an organization is not necessarily aligned along these two dimensions. It might instead reside in peripheral capabilities or peripheral activities that are not perceived as core to the main mission of the organization, regardless of their novelty. Organizational lore is replete with examples of companies that turned, in desperation, to a relatively neglected, non-strategic, non-core activity for their subsequent survival – consider Nokia with telecommunications, Intel with microprocessors and 3M with Post-It notes, to name but three popular examples.

An implication for structure is that it will be easier to maintain variety to the extent that resources and decision structures are relatively dispersed. The downside, of course, is that in the short run such structures are 'dissipative' (Cheng and Van de Ven 1996). It's harder to control distributed structures and to hold them accountable for near-term performance results. It's harder to promote change in a federation than in a hierarchy (Child and McGrath 2001). Moreover, it is hard to know what those results ought to be in order to justify their continuance.

Options reasoning, borrowed originally from the field of finance and now growing in influence in the strategy field, is relevant here. The emerging theory of real options attempts to place a value on choices made by organizations in the present that create the right, but not the obligation, to take subsequent actions in the future (Bowman and Hurry 1993). In so doing, options create a financial and performance justification for maintaining organizational variety that is consistent also with a combinatorial view of organizational structures (McGrath and Boisot 2003). Most scholars agree on this point. They disagree on whether the variety-preserving and enhancing effects of options are positive or negative (Chatterjee et al. 1999; Adner and Levinthal 2004; McGrath et al. 2004).

The Routinization of Innovation

The usual suspects that make managing today's organizations challenging include shorter competitive cycles, global competition, increasingly rich and rapid flows of information and the like. What these phenomena have at their core is a recognition that increasingly, competition in the modern enterprise (at least in free-market systems) is dependent on innovation in disequilibrium conditions rather than price-maneouvring in equilibrium conditions (Baumol 2002). As noted by Stiglitz (2004), recognition of information asymmetries and the normalcy of disquilibria have the potential to represent a paradigm change in economics, and in related fields such as strategy, that draw on economic modeling.

The primacy of innovation as a force in competition suggests that students of organizational structure are likely to find themselves with interests in common with students of technology, innovation and entrepreneurship. Indeed, a growing literature reflects this intersection (Eisenhardt and Tabrizi 1995; Brown and Eisenhardt 1997; Brown and Eisenhardt 1998). A practitioner-oriented example of this intersection can be seen in Christensen and Raynor's (2003a) recent book, *The Innovator's Solution*. A significant chunk of the text is devoted to issues of organization design, with chapters on business scope, organizational capabilities, the strategy process and senior executives as chief organization designers. In both the academic and the practitioner-oriented streams of thought, a key message for organizational design is that, in innovative regimes, it is extremely easy for past capabilities to become tomorrow's liabilities (a point made also by Leonard-Barton (1992)). The design challenge is thus increasingly one of managing continuous change.

And Now?

We began this effort in an attempt to catalogue how thinking in organization studies with respect to structure has developed since the publication of the original *Handbook of Organizations* in 1996. Hopefully, the chapter has done justice to a considerable body of work touching on structural questions. As I draw the chapter to a close, however, it is daunting to realize how much we still have to learn.

One concern that this review has suggested to me is that scholars are doing a lot of hard work; but it is work that is not necessarily directed at the questions most pressing to executives. What would we have told Carly Fiorina or David Pottruck or the departed Japanese executives we opened the chapter with? Executives are concerned with 'how' questions; while scholars tend to excel at documenting 'what' constructs. Moreover, constructs that scholars find compelling are not necessarily those that executives believe they can act upon. To generate work with appeal to both an executive and an academic constituency, both 'how' issues and 'what' issues would be of value.

A second observation is that the process of structuring, restructuring or reorganizing is not a rare or unusual event, and it is one that occupies a considerable amount of managerial effort. Indeed, such activities have become something of a way of life in

many companies attempting to compete with high-velocity environments. Molloy and Whittington (2005) note that the rate at which companies are undergoing massive reorganizations appears to be accelerating. An implication is that research capable of capturing the dimensions of frequency, impact and magnitude of an organization has more potential for generating insight than research that either treats all major changes as though they were similar, or that captures only a few of these constructs.

Finally, there is hope for the intellectual descendants of contingency arguments in developing a set of boundary conditions for the appropriate action with respect to structure. These could create both very interesting research questions and significant contributions to better theory (Christensen and Raynor 2003b). For instance, take innovation. It is clear that there are occasions when innovative activities are best developed when there are frequent flows of information and personnel exchange with established business units. It is equally clear that there are occasions when this is not the case.

Scholars interested in the structural challenges facing the modern organization might use the insights from its rich past to move forward and tackle such questions. What do we need to learn? Ideally, some insights about what causes what in the structuring–performance relationship. We need to go beyond simple contingencies to better understand boundary conditions. We need to make sure our constructs are not simply used because we can operationalize them, but are used because they promise to shed light on poorly understood relationships. And 5 years from now, wouldn't it be remarkable if solid research helped managers figure out where to start and how to proceed in their structuring tasks?

Acknowledgements

I am extremely grateful for the helpful comments on this chapter from Schon Beechler, Tom Lawrence, Henk Volberda and Richard Whittington, as well as input from the editors of the revised *Handbook*.

References

Ackoff, R. and Emery, F. (1972) *On Purposeful Systems.* Seaside, CA: Intersystems Publications.

Adner, R. and Levinthal, D. (2004) 'What is NOT a real option? Considering boundaries for the application of real options to business strategy', *Academy of Management Review*, 29(1): 74–85.

Aldrich, H. (1999) *Organizations Evolving*. Thousand Oaks, CA: Sage Publications.

Aldrich, H.E. and Fiol, C.M. (1994) 'Fools rush in? The institutional context of industry creation', *Academy of Management Review*, 19(4): 645–70.

Allen, R.C. (1983) 'Collective invention', *Journal of Economic Behavior and Organization*, 4(1): 1–24.

Allen, T.J. (1977) *Managing the flow of technology: technology transfer and the dissemination of technological information within the R&D organization*. Cambridge, MA: MIT Press.

Andersson, U., Forsgren, M. and Holm, U. (2001) 'Subsidiary embeddedness and competence development in MNCs – a multi-level analysis', *Organization Studies*, 22(6): 1013.

Appelbaum, S.H., Henson, D. and Knee, K. (1999) 'Downsizing failures: an examination of convergence/reorientation and antecedents – processes – outcomes', *Management Decision*, 37(6): 473.

Arora, A. (1995) Licensing tacit knowledge: intellectual property rights and the market for know-how', *Economics of Innovation and New Technology*, 4: 41–59.

Arrow, K.J. (1974) 'Limited knowledge and economic analysis', *American Economic Review*, 64(1): 1–10.

Ashby, W.R. (1956) *An Introduction to Cybernetics*. London: Chapman and Hall, Ltd.

Bain, J.S. (1959) *Industrial Organization*. New York: Wiley.

Baldwin, C.Y. and Clark, K.B. (2000) *Design rules the power of modularity, volume 1*. Cambridge, MA: MIT Press.

Barney, J.B. (1991) 'Firm resources and sustained competitive advantage', *Journal of Management*, 17(1): 99–120.

Barrett, S. (2001) 'Give South Dakota credit for its savvy; finance: law ending cap on interest rates drew Citibank charge-card center that now employs 3,750', *Los Angeles Times*, 4 March: C.9.

Bartlett, C. and Ghoshal, S. (1993) 'Beyond the M-Form: toward a managerial theory of the firm', *Strategic Management Journal*, 14: 23–46.

Baumol, W.J. (2002) *The Free-Market Innovation Machine: Analyzing the Growth Miracle of capitalism*. Princeton, NJ: Princeton University Press.

Bazen, S. and Thirlwell, T. (1987) *Deindustrialization (Studies in the U.K. Economy)*. Oxford: Heinemann.

Benner, M.J. and Tushman, M. (2002) 'Process management and technological innovation: a longitudinal study of the photography and paint industries', *Administrative Science Quarterly*, 47(4): 676.

Benner, M.J. and Tushman, M.L. (2003) 'Exploitation, exploration, and process management: the productivity dilemma revisited', *Academy of Management. The Academy of Management Review*, 28(2): 238.

Boisot, M. (1995a) 'Is your firm a creative destroyer? Competitive learning and knowledge flows in the technological strategies of firms', *Research Policy*, 24(4): 489–506.

Boisot, M. (1995b) *Information Space: A framework for learning in organizations, institutions and culture*. London, New York: Routledge.

Boisot, M. (1998) *Knowledge Assets: Securing Competitive Advantage in the Information Economy*. Oxford: Oxford University Press.

Boisot, M. and Child, J. (1999) 'Organizations as adaptive systems in complex environments: the case of China', *Organization Science*, 10(3): 237.

Bossidy, L. and Charan, R. (2002) *Execution: The discipline of getting things done*. New York: Crown Business.

Bowman, E.H. and Hurry, D. (1993) 'Strategy through the option lens: an integrated view of resource investments and the incremental-choice process', *Academy of Management Review*, 18(4): 760–82.

Brockner, J., Grover, S.L. and Blonder, M. (1988) 'Predictors of survivors' job involvement following layoffs: a field study', *Journal of Applied Psychology*, 73(3): 436–42.

Brown, S. and Eisenhardt, K. (1998) *Competing on the Edge: Strategy as Structured Chaos*. Boston: Harvard Business School Press.

Brown, S.L. and Eisenhardt, K.M. (1997) 'The art of continuous change: linking complexity theory and time-paced evolution in relentlessly shifting organizations', *Administrative Science Quarterly*, 42: 1–34.

Bryant, R. (1989) The value of separable intangibles. *Accountancy*, 103(1147): 106–10.

Burns, L.R. and Wholey, D.R. (1993) 'Adoption and abandonment of matrix management programs: effects of organizational characteristics and interorganizational networks', *Academy of Management Journal*, 36: 106–38.

Burns, T. and Stalker, G.M. (1995) *The Management of Innovation*, 3rd edn (originally 1961).

Burton, R.M. and Obel, B. (1995) *Strategic Organizational Diagnosis and Design*. Boston: Kluwer Academic Publishers.

Byrne, J. (1999) 'When capital gets antsy', *Business Week*, 13 September: 72–76.

Cameron, K.S., Whetten, D.A. and Kim, M.U. (1987) 'Organizational dysfunctions of decline', *Academy of Management Journal*, 30(1): 126–38.

Champy, J. (1995) *Reengineering Management: The mandate for new leadership*. London: HarperCollins.

Chandler, A. (1962) *Strategy and Structure: Chapters in the History of the Industrial Enterprise* (18th Printing, 1993 ed.). Cambridge, MA: The MIT Press.

Chatterjee, S., Lubatkin, M. and Schulze, W.S. (1999) 'Toward a strategic theory of risk premium: moving beyond CAPM', *Academy of Management Review*, 24(3): 556–72.

Cheng, Y. and Van de Ven, A.H. (1996) 'Learning the innovation journey: order out of chaos?', *Organization Science*, 7(6): 593–614.

Child, J. (1972) 'Organization structure and strategies of control: a replication of the Aston study', *Administrative Science Quarterly*, 17: 163–73.

Child, J. and McGrath, R.G. (2001) 'Organizations unfettered: organizational form in an information-intensive economy', *Academy of Management Journal*, 44(6): 1135–48.

Child, J. and Rodrigues, S.B. (2003) 'Corporate governance and new organizational forms: issues of double and multiple agency', *Journal of Management & Governance*, 7(4): 337.

Christensen, C. and Bower, J. (1996) 'Customer power, strategic investment, and the failure of leading firms', *Strategic Management Journal*, 17(3): 197–219.

Christensen, C.M. (1997) *The innovator's dilemma: when new technologies cause great firms to fail*. Boston, MA: Harvard Business School Press.

Christensen, C.M. and Raynor, M.E. (2003a) *The innovator's solution: creating and sustaining successful growth*. Boston, MA: Harvard Business School.

Christensen, C.M. and Raynor, M.E. (2003b) 'Why hard-nosed executives should care about management theory', *Harvard Business Review*, 81(9): 66–74.

Christensen, C.R., Andrews, K.R., Bower, J.L., Hamermesh, R.G. and Porter, M.E. (1982) *Business Policy: Text and Cases*. Homewood, IL: Irwin.

Coase, R.H. (1937) 'The nature of the firm', *Economica*, 4(November): 386–405.

Cohen, W.M. and Levinthal, D.A. (1990) 'Absorptive capacity: a new perspective on learning and innovation', *Administrative Science Quarterly*, 35: 128–52.

Courtright, J.A., Fairhurst, G.T. and Rogers, L.E. (1989) 'Interaction patterns in organic and mechanistic systems', *Academy of Management Journal*, 32(4): 773–802.

Daft, R.L. and Weick, K.E. (1984) 'Toward a model of organizations as interpretation systems', *Academy of Management Review*, 9(2): 284–95.

Dawson, C. (2005) 'The wild, wild, East: Japanese companies are benefiting from a dose of Western Capitalism', *BusinessWeek*, 21 March: 33.

DeMeuse, K.P., Bergmann, T.J., Vanderheiden, P.A. and Roraff, C.E. (2004) 'New evidence regarding organizational downsizing and a firm's financial performance: a long-term analysis'. *Journal of Managerial Issues*, 16(2): 155.

Dewar, R. and Hage, J. (1978) 'Size, technology, complexity and structural differentiation: toward a theoretical synthesis', *Administrative Science Quarterly*, 23: 111–24.

Dierickx, I. and Cool, K. (1989) 'Asset stock accumulation and sustainability of competitive advantage', *Management Science*, 35(12): 1504–13.

Donaldson, L. (ed.) (1995) *Contingency Theory*. Brookfield, VT: Dartmouth Publishing.

Donaldson, L. (1996) 'The normal science of structural contingency theory', in S.R. Glegg, C. Hardy and W.R. Nord (eds), *Handbook of Organization Studies*. Thousand Oaks, CA: Sage Publications. pp. 57–76.

Dougherty, D. and Bowman, E.H. (1995) 'The effects of organizational downsizing on product innovation', *California Management Review*, 37(4): 28.

Drazin, R. and Van de Ven, A. (1985) 'Alternative forms of fit in contingency theory', *Administrative Science Quarterly*, 30: 514–39.

Dyer, J.H. and Singh, H. (1998) 'The relational view: cooperative strategy and sources of interorganizational competitive advantage', *Academy of Management Review*, 23(4): 660–79.

Eisenhardt, K. and Tabrizi, B. (1995) 'Accelerating adaptive processes: product innovation in the global computer industry', *Administrative Science Quarterly*, 40: 84–110.

Evans, P.B. and Wurster, T.S. (1997) 'Strategy and the new economics of information', *Harvard Business Review*, 75: 71–82.

Freeman, S.J. and Cameron, K.S. (1993) 'Organizational downsizing: convergence and reorientation framework', *Organization Science*, 4(1): 10–29.

Galbraith, J.R. (1973) *Designing complex organizations*. Reading, MA: Addison-Wesley Pub. Co.

Galunic, D.C. and Eisenhardt, K.L. (2001) 'Architectural innovation and modular organizational forms', *Academy of Management Journal Special Research Forum on New and Evolving Organizational Forms*, 44(6): 1229–49.

Garcia, R., Calantone, R. and Levine, R. (2003) 'The role of knowledge in resource allocation to exploration versus exploitation in technologically oriented organizations', *Decision Sciences*, 34(2): 323.

Garud, R. and Kumaraswamy, A. (1993) 'Changing competitive dynamics in network industries: an exploration of Sun Microsystems' open systems strategy', *Strategic Management Journal*, 14(5): 351–69.

Gerth, H.H. and Mills, C.W. (eds) (1958) *From Max Weber – Essays in Sociology*. New York: Galaxy Books.

Gerwin, D. (1979) 'The comparative analysis of structure and technology: a critical appraisal', *Academy of Management. The Academy of Management Review (pre-1986)*, 4(000001): 41.

Ghoshal, S. and Gratton, L. (2002) 'Integrating the enterprise', *Sloan Management Review*, 44(1): 31–8.

Glasmeier, A. (1991) 'Technological discontinuities and flexible production networks: the case of Switzerland and the world watch industry', *Research Policy*, 20: 469–485.

Gomez-Mejia, L.R. (1992) 'Structure and process of diversification, compensation strategy, and firm performance', *Strategic Management Journal*, 13: 381–97.

Gould, S.J. (1996) *Full house: the spread of excellence from Plato to Darwin*, 1st edn. New York: Harmony Books.

Granovetter, M. (1974) *Getting a Job: A Study of Contacts and Careers*. Cambridge: Harvard University Press.

Gresov, C. (1989) 'Exploring fit and misfit with multiple contingencies', *Administrative Science Quarterly*, 34(3): 431.

Gresov, C. and Drazin, R. (1997) 'Equifinality: functional equivalence in organization design', *Academy of Management. The Academy of Management Review*, 22(2): 403.

Griliches, Z. (1984) *R&D, patents and productivity*. Chicago: University of Chicago Press.

Grinyer, P. and Yasai-Ardekani, M. (1980) 'Dimensions of organizational structure: a critical replication', *Academy of Management Journal*, 23: 405–21.

Hambrick, D.C. (1983) 'Some tests of the effectiveness and functional attributes of miles and snow's strategic types', *Academy of Management Journal (pre-1986)*, 26(000001): 5.

Hammer, M. and Champy, J. (1993) *Reengineering the Corporation: A Manifesto for Business Revolution*. London: Nicholas Brealy.

Hammonds, K.H., Collins, J., Levine, E. and Pink, D.H. (2002) 'The secret life of the CEO', *Fast Company*, 63(October): 81.

Hassler, J. (1999) 'Does increased international influence cause higher stock market volatility?', *The Scandinavian Journal of Economics*, 101(1): 1–9.

He, Z.-L. and Wong, P.-K. (2004) 'Exploration vs. exploitation: an empirical test of the ambidexterity hypothesis', *Organization Science*, 15(4): 481.

Helfat, C. and Raubitschek, R.S. (2000) 'Product sequencing: co-evolution of knowledge, capabilities and products', *Strategic Management Journal*, 21(10–11): 961–80.

Henry, D, and Vickers, M. (2003) 'Whipsawed by Wall Street', *Business Week*, 10 March: 55–61.

Holmqvist, M. (2004) 'Experiential learning processes of exploitation and exploration within and between organizations: an empirical study of product development', *Organization Science*, 15(1): 70.

Hoskisson, R.E. (1987) 'Multidivisional structure and performance: the contingency of diversification strategy', *Academy of Management Journal*, 30(4): 625.

Hrebiniak, L. and Joyce, W. (1984) *Implementing Strategy*. New York: MacMillan.

Huber, G. (1984) 'The Nature and design of post-industrial organization', *Management Science*, 30(8): 928–51.

Kock, K. (2004) *The Impact of Financial Markets on Firm Behavior and Industry Evolution*. Philadelphia, PA: University of Pennsylvania, The Wharton School.

Kogut, B., Shan, W. and Walker, G. (1993) *The Embedded Firm: On the Socio-Economics of Industrial Networks*. London: Routledge.

Lawrence, P.R. and Lorsch, J.W. (1967) *Organization and Environment: Managing Differentiation and Integration*. Homewood, IL: R.D. Irwin.

Leonard-Barton, D. (1992) 'Core capabilities and core rigidities: a paradox in managing new product development', *Strategic Management Journal*, 13: 111–26.

Levinthal, D. (1997) 'Adaptation on rugged landscapes', *Management Science*, 43(7): 934–50.

Levinthal, D. and March, J.G. (1993) 'The myopia of learning', *Strategic Management Journal*, 14: 95–112.

Lewin, A. and Volberda, H. (1999) 'Prolegomena on coevolution: a framework for research on strategy and new organizational forms', *Organization Science*, 10(5): 519–34.

Lewin, A.Y., Long, C.P. and Carroll, T.N. (1999) 'The coevolution of new organizational forms', *Organization Science*, 10(5): 535.

Liker, J.K., Roitman, D.B. and Roskies, E. (1987) 'Changing everything all at once: work life and technological change', *Sloan Management Review*, 28: 29–47.

Loomis, C.J. (2005) 'Why Carly's big bet is failing', *Fortune*, 7 February: 50–64.

Lorenzoni, G. and Lipparini, A. (1999) 'The leveraging of interfirm relationships as a distinctive organizational capability: a longitudinal study', *Strategic Management Journal*, 20(4): 317–38.

Lucier, C.S., Schuyt, E.R. (2002) 'Why CEO's fail: the causes and consequences of turnover at the top', *Strategy + Business 28 Special Report*. Available online from Booz/Allen/Hamilton at: www.bah.com.

Mankins, M.C. (2004) 'Stop wasting valuable time', *Harvard Business Review*, 82(9): 58.

Mansfield, E. (1985) 'How rapidly does new technology leak out?', *Journal of Industrial Economics*, 34: 217–23.

March, J. and Sutton, R. (1997) 'Organizational performance as a dependent variable', *Organization Science*, 8(6): 698–706.

March, J.G. (1991) 'Exploration and exploitation in organizational learning', *Organization Science*, 2(1): 71–87.

Mason, E. (1949) 'The current state of the monopoly problem in the US', *Harvard Law Review*, 62: 1265–85.

McGrath, R.G. and Boisot, M. (2003) 'Real options reasoning and the dynamic organization: strategic insights from the biological analogy. Chapter 10', in R. Peterson and E. Mannix (eds), *Leading and Managing People in the Dynamic Organization*. New Jersey: Lawrence Erlbaum Associates Press. pp. 201–26.

McGrath, R.G., Ferrier, W. and Mendelow, A. (2004) 'Real options as engines of choice and heterogeneity', *Academy of Management Review*, 29(1): 86–101.

Merton, R.K. (1967) *On Theoretical Sociology*. New York: The Free Press.

Miles, R.E. and Snow, C.C. (1978) *Organizational strategy, structure and process*. New York: McGraw-Hill.

Milgrom, P. and Roberts, J. (1990) 'The economics of modern manufacturing', *American Economic Review*, 80: 511–28.

Milgrom, P. and Roberts, J. (1995) 'Complementarities and fit: strategy, structure and organizational change in manufacturing', *Journal of Accounting and Economics*, 19(2/3): 179–208.

Miller, D. and Friesen, P.H. (1986) 'Porter's (1980) generic strategies and performance: an empirical examination with American data. Part I: testing Porter', *Organization Studies*, 7(1): 37.

Mintzberg, H. and Waters, J.A. (1985) 'Of strategies, deliberate and emergent', *Strategic Management Journal*, 6: 257–72.

Molloy, E. and Whittington, R. (2005) 'Practices of organizing: inside and outside the processes of change', in Y. Doz, J.F. Porac and G. Szulanski (eds), *Advances in Strategic Management, 2005*.

Morris, B. (2005) 'Charles Schwab's big challenge', *Fortune*, 30 May: 89–99.

Nerkar, A. (2003) 'Old is gold? The value of temporal exploration in the creation of new knowledge', *Management Science*, 49(2): 211.

Nohria, N. and Ghoshal, S. (1997) *The Differentiated Network: Organizing Multinational Corporations for Value Creation*. San Francisco: Jossey-Bass.

Ouchi, W.G. (1980) 'Markets, bureaucracies and clans', *Administrative Science Quarterly*, 25: 129–41.

Peteraf, M.A. (1993) 'The cornerstones of competitive advantage: a resource-based view', *Strategic Management Journal*, 14(3): 179–92.

Porter, M. (1980) *Competitive Strategy: Techniques for Analyzing Industries and Competitors*. New York: The Free Press.

Porter, M.E. (1983) 'Industrial organization and the evolution of concepts for strategic planning: the new learning', *Managerial and Decision Economics (pre-1986)*, 4(3): 172.

Pugh, D. (ed.) (1998) *The Aston Programme, Vols I–III. The Aston Study and its developments*. Singapore and Sydney: Ashgate.

Pugh, D.S., Hickson, D.J., Hinings, C.R. and Turner, C. (1968) 'Dimensions of organization structure', *Administrative Science Quarterly*, 13: 65–95.

Quinn, J.B. (1992) *Intelligent Enterprise: A Knowledge and Service Based Paradigm for Industry*. New York: The Free Press.

Quinn, J.B., Doorley, T.L. and Paquette, P.C. (1990) 'Beyond products: services-based strategy', *Harvard Business Review*, 68: 58–65.

Ramanujan, V. and Venkatraman, N. (1984) 'An inventory and critique of strategy research using the PIMS database', *Academy of Management Review*, 9(1): 138–51.

Reynolds, P. and White, S.B. (1997) *The Entrepreneurial Process: Economic Growth, Men, Women and Minorities*. Westport, CT: Quorum Books.

Romanelli, E. and Tushman, M.L. (1994) 'Organizational transformation as punctuated equilibrium: an empirical test', *Academy of Management Journal*, 37(5): 1141–66.

Romo, F.P. and Schwartz, M. (1995) 'The structural embeddedness of business decisions to migrate', *American Sociological Review*, 60(6): 874–907.

Sanchez, R. and Mahoney, J.T. (1996) 'Modularity, flexibility, and knowledge management in product and organizational design', *Strategic Management Journal*, 17: 63–76.

Saxenian, A. (1994) *Regional advantage: culture and competition in Silicon Valley and Route 128*. Cambridge, MA: Harvard University Press.

Schelling, T.C. (1980) *The Strategy of Conflict*, 2nd edn. Cambridge, MA: Harvard University Press.

Schilling, M.A. and Steensma, H.K. (2001) 'The use of modular organization forms: an industry level analysis', *Academy of Management Journal Special Research Forum on New and Evolving Organizational Forms*, 44(6): 1149–68.

Schoonhoven, C.B. (1981) 'Problems with contingency theory: testing assumptions hidden within the language of contingency "theory"', *Administrative Science Quarterly*, 26: 349–77.

Schoonhoven, C.B. and Romanelli, R. (2001) *The entrepreneurship dynamic: Origins of entrepreneurship and the evolution of industries*. Stanford, CA: Stanford University Press.

Selznick, P. (1957) *Leadership in Administration: A Sociological Interpretation*. New York: Harper and Row.

Sloan, A.P. (1963) *My Years with General Motors*. New York: Doubleday.

Slywotzky, A.J. and Morrison, D.J. (1997) *The Profit Zone: How strategic business design will lead you to tomorrow's profits*. New York: Random House.

Sorge, A. (2001) 'Derek S Pugh (ed.), The Aston Programme, Vols. I–III. The Aston Study and its developments', *Organization Studies*, 22(4): 717.

Spender, J.C. and Kijne, H. (1996) *Scientific Management: Frederick Winslow Taylor's Gift to the World?* Boston: Kluwer Academic.

Stiglitz, J.E. (2004) 'Information and the change in the paradigm in economics, Part 2', *American Economist*, 48(1): 17–49.

Stinchcombe, A.L. (2000) 'Social structure and organizations: a comment', in J. Baum and F. Dobbin (eds), *Economics Meets Sociology in Strategic Management: Advances in Strategic Management*. Greenwich, CT: JAI Press.

Szulanski, G. (1996) 'Exploring internal stickiness: impediments to the transfer of best practices within the firm', *Strategic Management Journal*, 17: 17–43.

Teece, D.J. (1984) 'Economic analysis and strategic management', *California Management Review*, XXVI(3): 87–110.

Teece, D.J., Pisano, G. and Shuen, A. (1997) 'Dynamic capabilities and strategic management', *Strategic Management Journal*, 18(7): 509–33.

Thompson, J. (1967) *Organizations in Action: Social Science Bases of Administrative Theory*. New York: McGraw-Hill.

Tripsas, M. (1997) 'Unraveling the process of creative destruction: complementary assets and incumbent survival in the typesetter industry', *Strategic Management Journal*, 18(special issue): 119–42.

Tushman, M. and Anderson, P. (1986) 'Technological discontinuities and organizational environments', *Administrative Science Quarterly*, 31: 439–65.

Tushman, M.L. and O'Reilly, C.A.I. (1996) 'Ambidextrous organizations: managing evolutionary and revolutionary change', *California Management Review*, 38(4): 8.

Uzzi, B. (1996) 'The sources and consequences of embeddedness for the economic performance of organizations: the network effect', *American Sociological Review*, 61: 674–98.

Van den Bosch, F.A., Volberda, H.W. and de Boer, M. (1999) 'Coevolution of firm absorptive capacity and knowledge environment: organizational forms and combinative capabilities', *Organization Science*, 10(5): 551.

Victor, B. and Stephens, C. (1994) 'The dark side of the new organizational forms: an editorial essay', *Organizational Science*, 5(4): 479–82.

Volberda, H. (1998) *Building the Flexible Firm: How to Remain Competitive.* Oxford: Oxford University Press.

von Bertalanffy, L. (1968) *General system theory.* New York: Braziller.

von Hippel, E. (1987) 'Cooperation between rivals: informal know-how trading', *Research Policy*, 16: 291–302.

Walker, G. and Weber, D. (1984) 'A transaction cost approach to make-or-buy decisions', *Administrative Science Quarterly*, 29(3): 373.

Walras, L. (1984) *Elements of Pure Economics or the Theory of Social Wealth* (W. Jaffe, Trans.). Philadelphia, PA: Orion Editions.

Weber, M. (1947) *The Theory of Social and Economic Organization.* Glencoe, IL: The Free Press.

Weick, C. (1995) *Sensemaking in Organizations.* Thousand Oaks, CA: Sage Publications, Inc.

Weick, K.E. and Roberts, K.H. (1993) 'Collective mind in organizations: heedful interrelating on flight decks', *Administrative Science Quarterly*, 38: 357–81.

Werner, U. (2004) 'Innovation and execution: how to achieve both', *Paper presented at The Strategic Management Society 24th Annual Conference*, San Juan, Puerto Rico.

Wernerfelt, B. (1984) 'A resource-based view of the firm', *Strategic Management Journal*, 5: 171–80.

Whittington, R. (2004) Personal communication. San Juan, Puerto Rico.

Whittington, R., Pettigrew, A., Peck, S., Fenton, E. and Conyon, M. (1999) 'Change and complementarities in the new competitive landscape: a European panel study 1992–1996', *Organization Science*, 10(5): 583–600.

Williamson, O.E. (1991) 'Comparative economic organization: the analysis of discrete structural alternatives', *Administrative Science Quarterly*, 36: 269–96.

Williamson, O.E. (1992) 'Strategizing, economizing and economic organization', *Strategic Management Journal*, 12: 75–94.

Williamson, O.E. (1996) 'Economics and organization: a primer', *California Management Review*, 38(2): 131.

Woo, C.Y. and Cooper, A.C. (1981) 'Strategies of effective low share businesses', *Strategic Management Journal*, 2: 301–18.

Zander, U. and Kogut, B. (1995) 'Knowledge and the speed of the transfer and imitation of organizational capabilities: an empirical test', *Organization Science*, 6(1): 1–17.

2.7 Organizing for Innovation in the 21st Century

DEBORAH DOUGHERTY

Product innovation is a primary means to adapt to changing markets, technologies and competition. Product innovation concerns bringing new products and services into use, and encompasses the whole process of conceptualizing, developing, designing, manufacturing and distributing new products (Schon 1967). Innovative organizations are more profitable, grow faster, create more jobs and are more productive than their non-innovative competitors, even in mature industries (Franko 1989; Capon et al. 1992; Baldwin and Da Pont 1993). The ability to generate streams of new products or services over time is therefore vital to many organizations. Organizational design plays a significant role in this ability, so understanding how to organize for innovation is a central problem in innovation management (Galbraith 1995; Tushman and O'Reilly 1997; Dougherty 2001). The most recent Product Development Management Association survey finds that organizing is the 'last frontier' in innovativeness (Adams 2004). Previous PDMA surveys found that innovative companies used more 'best practices', especially strategic systems. The 2003 survey found that the most innovative organizations used practices selectively, moulded the ones they did use to fit particular situations, and implemented them more effectively. Moreover, innovative organizations managed the entire organization to support innovation by ensuring that resources flowed smoothly to innovation teams, that structures, processes and other organizational mechanisms supported innovation, and that long-term investments in supporting technologies were made. Innovation thus involves explicit managing of organization design and practices.

The purpose of this chapter is to develop four principles of organizational design that synthesize current ideas into a new understanding of what is involved in organizing for innovation. I focus on the principles for defining jobs, grouping jobs into work units (aka differentiation), integrating the differentiated units, and controlling the whole system over time. These are the principles that are often discussed in textbooks (e.g. Robbins and Coulter 1999; Dessler 2002) and by theorists (Blau and Meyer 1987; Mintzberg 1991; Galbraith 1995). The argument developed in this chapter is that the essence of organizing for innovation depends on how these four principles are understood and enacted, not on how more manifest structures are deployed (e.g. centralization vs decentralization of R&D, organizing businesses on products vs markets, use of portfolio strategies and other processes and techniques). These four principles constitute the core structuring upon which systems, processes, procedures, routines and techniques are built. I propose new approaches for each principle that enable sustained product innovation in general, and suggest contingencies that may require different configurations among the principles.

These new principles of innovative organizational design are both empirically and theoretically grounded. Regarding the first, in all my fieldwork on innovation (more than 350 interviews since 1985 with people working on new products or services in 33 different organizations), the organization's design always had a strong presence – it was a significant part of people's stories. Even in the 'early days' when product innovation was fairly rare in established firms, most people who worked on new products understood that it was necessary to involve different functions, to work with customers, and that good teamwork and project management mattered. Most people understood the importance of these practices for basic new product development, but were prevented from following these practices by how their company was organized (Dougherty 1990; Dougherty and Heller 1994; Dougherty and

Hardy 1996). The organization of work in many of these firms straightforwardly inhibited teamwork, knowledge creation and recombination and creativity. Many of the people interviewed were *very* frustrated. However, much of the scholarly and managerial attention was focused at the individual level – sending people off to creativity training or encouraging renegade 'champions', or at the project level – facilitating gatekeepers, team meetings or fixing the 'market-technology' interface locally.

The insight that 'it's the organization, stupid!' was also grounded in theory. Indeed, the importance of organization design to a firm's ability to innovate is hardly new, but it is continually rediscovered. Burns and Stalker (1961), Schon (1963; 1967), Kanter (1983), Nord and Tucker (1987), Jelinek and Schoonhoven (1990) and Brown and Eisenhardt (1997) discovered essentially the same thing: people working on successful innovation know what their jobs are, who they work with and how, to whom they report, what the priorities are, and how their activities fit with those of the enterprise as a whole. In other words, the work of innovation is *organized*, as any complex set of activities would have to be. All these studies also rediscover the fact that organizing for innovation is qualitatively different from organizing for efficiency via the familiar bureaucracy. However, many describe the innovative design in terms of its deviance from the bureaucratic model: as something that occurs in a parallel place (Kanter 1983), or as 'quasi-formal' (Jelinek and Schoonhoven 1990), 'semi-structured' (Brown and Eisenhardt 1997) or *not* bureaucracy (e.g. *de*-centralized, *in*-formal, *de*-layered).

To develop my argument, I build on four basic premises. The first premise is that the innovative organization needs to be defined in its own terms, not in terms of its deviation from a 20th century bureaucratic model. The second premise is that, to fit with the first premise, theory must be based on the actual practices that are being organized. While many theories break away from the bureaucratic model, they differ greatly about what it is that is being organized. Alternate models include the postmodern and postbureaucratic (Clegg 2002), heterarchical (Hedlund 1986), boundaryless (Devanna and Tichy 1990), hyptertext (Nonaka and Takeuchi 1995), ambidextrous (Tushman and O'Reilly 1997), horizontal (Ofstroff 1999), 'edge-of-chaos' (Brown and Eisenhardt 1998), transnational (Bartlett and Ghoshal 1989), 'front-back' (Galbraith 1995),

shamrock (Handy 1989) and adhocracy (Mintzberg and McHugh 1985), to mention but a few. Sustained product innovation refers to generating streams of new products continually over time. A focus on sustained rather than one-off product innovation limits the generality of the implications, but affords a thorough treatment of the particular activities that underlie this important kind of innovation. The third premise is that organizing for innovation has to be the 'default option' for many organizations, not bureaucracy. The reason is simple: high volume and low cost are subsets of innovation management that also include radical, breakthrough, platform and derivative products. Effectively innovative organizations like Intel, Sony or 3M all produce products with high volumes at low cost as well as new and breakthrough products. They are capable of these economies of scope because they organize around innovativeness, not around efficiency. Being innovative is not incommensurate with being efficient, although limits can be explored empirically. I argue in the next section that using the bureaucratic model to organize around the central idea of efficiency is, however, incommensurate with innovativeness. I will show that the bureaucracy is not a monolithic institution of modern life, but a particular kind of organizing, one with particular principles of design that happen to preclude innovation. Innovation is not more costly, more risky or more difficult to do *per se*, but it is all three if attempted from within the bureaucracy.

The final premise is that the underlying principles of organization design helps to put the 'T' and the 'O' back into OT (organization theory). Organization design was the 'meat and potatoes' of organization theory at the outset of this field (Nystrom and Starbuck 1981; Tushman 2004). While still central for managers, organization design has all but fallen off the OT table for two reasons. First, organization design has been given over to consultants, in part because 'design' is understood in a-theoretical terms, as the use of tools and techniques that are based more on fads than on scholarship (e.g. process re-engineering, total quality, stage-gate). Bringing the 'T' back into organization design will build in a theoretical foundation for when, why and how to use these tools. Secondly, OT has shifted to inter-organizational issues such as the causes and effects of institutional pressures, industry emergence and evolution or networks. Inter-organizational issues are important, since value creation and even specific innovations are conceived, developed and launched by a community of organizations, not simply by 'the firm'. However, the 'O' of OT is either a blackbox, or a series of poorly defined 'umbrella concepts' such as routines, dynamic capabilities, organizational capacities, cognitions, culture, slack, effectiveness and identity (Hirsch and Levin 1999). These ideas are used so broadly that each often encompasses the others. Rethinking the essence of organization design relieves these other constructs of the burden of explaining work roles and relationships, and pushes for more thoughtful conceptualization of them.

This chapter has three main sections. The first section lays the foundation for new principles of organizing by explaining four paradoxical practices that comprise organization-wide product innovation. These practices reflect the inherent tensions of innovation by capturing both the activities of product innovation and the challenges of organizing them. To justify the need for new principles of organizing, I explain why the bureaucratic principles for job definition, differentiation, integration and control cannot handle the inherent tensions of product innovation, and thus cannot organize these activities. In the second section, I review current theories of organizing for innovation and derive from them four new principles of organizing that do effectively embrace these tensions, and thus are able to organize innovation. I also suggest how various best practices for innovation and for organizing fit with each new principle. In the final section, I clarify the implications of this new theory of organizing for innovation, and suggest ways to test, refute or elaborate it.

What Is to Be Organized and Why Bureaucratic Principles Cannot Work

First, it is necessary to define the practices of innovation that are to be organized. There are many processes, techniques and procedures for managing innovation teams and projects, building and shaping technology and manufacturing for innovation, assessing user needs and strategic opportunities – indeed the PDMA study mentioned in the first paragraph asked respondents about their use of more than 70 specific techniques. I focus on four higher level practices that cut across functions,

levels and locations but still represent particular challenges of sustained product innovation, as outlined in Table 2.7.1 (second column). These are presented as 'paradoxical practices' to reflect the fact that innovation embodies inherent, complex tensions that must be balanced in some way rather than ignored or split up (see Clegg 2002; Clegg et al. 2002, on paradoxes). Innovation researchers have always pointed out that product innovation involves true tensions (Pelz and Andrews 1966; Lawrence and Lorsch 1967; Jelinek and Schoonhoven 1990; Weick and Westley 1996). While other tensions are also involved, research suggests that these four relate to innovation success (Kohler 2003). As argued in Dougherty (1996), thinking of the organizing challenges of innovation as inherent tensions emphasizes the dialectical nature of ongoing innovation, where the organization and new products mutually constitute each other.

The first column in Table 2.7.1 connects each paradoxical practice with a particular principle of design. There is no strict one-to-one correspondence between practices and principles, but I organize the discussion row by row in Table 2.7.1 for ease of exposition. The third and fourth columns explain that the familiar bureaucratic version of these principles cannot organize the paradoxical practices of innovation, which is why a new set of principles is necessary.

Enabling Motivation and Commitment to Balance Freedom vs Responsibility

The first paradoxical practice concerns motivating employees to engage in, and be committed to accomplishing, the very complicated, confusing and ambiguous work of sustained innovation. People must work in multi-functional teams because people from different specialties have unique insights (Dougherty 1992b), but orchestrating teamwork is always difficult. In addition, the teams inevitably encounter unanticipated problems as they design and develop a new product, which means that they often must rethink the very problem they are solving – what will the product do for whom and how – as they proceed. They continually 'set' their problem, defined by Schon (1983) as the artful competence of finding the problem by defining the decisions to be made, the ends to be achieved, and the means that may be chosen.

Table 2.7.1   What is to be Organized for Innovation and Why the Bureaucracy Cannot do it

Generic principles of organizational design	Paradoxical practices of work of innovation, organization-wide	Bureaucratic version of principles	Why bureaucratic principles cannot organize innovation
Define jobs, work rights, obligations, roles, relationships, dignity	Balancing freedom vs responsibility to enable commitment; ambiguous, problem-setting, in parallel, be mindful of whole	By precisely specified duties, clear and individual accountability, contract	Work cannot be precisely defined; induces chronic anxiety. Big Q: how to define work so people are energized, reliable, competent?
Group jobs (differentiation) simplifies, gives familiarity, self-designing within boundaries	Balancing new vs old for creative problem-solving; many interdependent problems, actions, products, etc. leveraged or woven in	By function or solution, add product, market, region; chops of flow of activity into separate parts	Eliminates problem (can't be seen), induces dynamic conservatism (fixation on old): Big Q: how to define related sets of activities that makes work 'simple' but whole?
Integrate separate groupings quality of state of collaboration …	Balancing inside vs outside, for market-technology linking; mutual adjustment and mutual adaptation	By hierarchy, snap together decomposed units	Prevents continual market-technology linking, mutual adaptation; drives inward focus. Big Q: how to enable MA and MA?
Control so right things are done at right time	Balancing emergence vs determination for monitoring and evaluation processes, means, not ends; situated judgement	By *a priori* standards, direct supervision	Ignores emergence, so innovation out of control; focus on ends and ignores means, removes situatedness, judgement. Big Q: what to control?

Innovators also actively solve that problem, but must proceed in parallel, with horizontal flows of activities that continually interrelate: people push forward issues in their own area (e.g. prioritizing customer needs, planning advertising for the launch, developing the production process) in sync with others' activities, but they also must shift their attention quickly to problems that affect all functions (e.g. a part cannot be made reliably after all, which affects the price, or the launch time, or the target market –Yang and Dougherty 1993).

To work collectively in parallel on such ambiguous tasks, innovators must anticipate problems in other functions and appreciate others' constraints as they work (Clark and Fujimoto 1991). They need 'T'-shaped skills, or both a deep understanding of a specialty and an intimate understanding of the potential systemic impacts of their specialty (Iansiti 1993). People must shape their specialized knowledge to fit the problem at hand rather than insist that the problem appear in a certain way (Leonard 1998). These are *very* sophisticated skills that can be enacted only if others also enact them, which means that developing these skills is not simply a matter of hiring the right people!

Motivating employees to do the work of innovation invokes the tension between freedom and responsibility. People are expected to be free to do what is necessary, and to be creative and proactive, yet also to be responsible about the use of firm resources, and to co-ordinate their actions with others carefully. People must rely on their peers to achieve what they personally are held accountable for, yet they have little control over their peers. The design principle most associated with the tension between freedom and responsibility is defining 'jobs' in the first place, which clarifies people's roles and responsibilities. The question is how to construct sensible but motivating jobs and also invoke responsible, principled action?

Bureaucratic rules produce autonomous, precisely defined jobs (Weber 1946; Blau and Meyer 1987). One rule is that 'the office' comprises clearly defined set of solutions that 'the officer' applies. Problem-setting occurs only occasionally and only by officers and work is split into autonomous specialities. The second rule is hierarchy: the officer has control over what people reporting to him or her do and how they do it. Managers think and employees do as they are told which focuses attention on vertical information processing rather than on parallel or horizontal flows of activities. The third rule is individual accountability, which means that jobs must be precisely defined ahead of time. Work in a bureaucracy is understood as static slices of specialized labour, whose pre-defined activities can be executed without ambiguity (Schon 1983; Brown and Duguid 1991; Barley 1996). Bureaucratic jobs eliminate the tension between freedom and responsibility by specifying responsibility and removing freedom from all below the officers.

The challenge is to re-conceive work *at all levels*, so that people can take on a fuzzier set of responsibilities without feeling overwhelmed, and that managers can 'manage' the work without being 'officers' and thus micromanaging, or making all the choices and decisions. Redefining work touches on many complex issues in human relations (e.g. justice, creativity, identity), but this challenge can be sorted out in part by the next three design principles.

Creative Problem-Solving to Balance Old vs New

The second paradoxical practice is creative problem-solving. Conceptualizing, designing, developing, manufacturing and launching a new product requires that innovators solve a variety of complex problems, many of which arise unexpectedly as new alternatives are tried out or as unfamiliar customers are addressed. A large organization will have scores of new product teams creatively solving unique problems while drawing on common R&D, manufacturing, distribution or selling capabilities, for example, so creative problem-solving goes on across the organization, at all levels. Functional managers oversee how well their people contribute to the new product teams and how carefully the teams take functional constraints into account (e.g. limited plant capacity); business managers incorporate new products in their business models and portfolio plans, and corporate managers make the necessary investments in capabilities to support all the teams, functions and businesses. Together, these people combine resources in new ways, fit new products into existing families and businesses, and transform businesses to adapt to shifting market opportunities (Helfat and Raubitschek 2000).

All this creative problem-solving invokes the tension between old and new, for three reasons. First, organizations cannot abandon existing assets as they create new products. Even high technology firms must leverage the significant investments in production facilities and the knowledge that is embedded in them (Jelinek and Schoonhoven 1990). A very new firm might use only new assets for their first new product, but their second product necessarily invokes the tension of old vs new, since the two products now must share resources. Secondly, path dependencies exist since knowledge builds up over time based on choices that are made and on opportunities that are selected ; thus, history matters (Dosi 1982). Thirdly, there is a large empirical record of rigidity, local search and becoming stuck in old ways even in high technology firms (Kanter 1983; Henderson and Clark 1990). Any theory must explain how organizations can overcome pressures to favour old over new.

The organizational design principle most associated with creating problem-solving practices is *differentiation*, or the grouping of work and workers around related activities. Differentiation is essential in complex organizations because it simplifies work in three key ways. First, differentiation helps to define what people are to do on a regular basis. People can come to the 'office', the 'lab' or the sales route every day with a good idea already in their minds about what to do with whom and how. Without differentiation, people would have to be assigned to specific jobs everyday, like day labourers. Secondly, the specialization inherent in differentiation enables continued learning and development since what to know is bounded into a coherent system. Thirdly, differentiation enables self-designed work. As Galbraith (1995) suggests, if work is differentiated appropriately, people will interact, communicate and make sense of everyday work fairly automatically and naturally with others in their unit, so work is self-designing within those boundaries.

The bureaucracy differentiates work by functional specialty that decomposes the value creation process into separate parts, or steps. Differentiation by function cannot organize the practice of creative problem-solving because it precludes the collective definition of problems in the first place. The problem that people are working on is already set or defined, so there is no 'new' to weave together with 'old'. Only people at the very top understand the problem in its entirety. As well, functions are solutions, not problems, so organizing by function further inhibits problem-setting, which precludes creative problem-solving. People can create new solutions within their functions, but that increases conflicts because there is no way to assure that one function's new ideas fit with another's. Expanding bureaucratic differentiation to include product line, geographical location, national locality, market place and business increases conflict further, since many more lines of authority are involved in each solution, and all these lines have to be checked and perhaps rewired every time something changes.

A fundamentally new principle for differentiating work is necessary for innovation. The question is how does one identify those related activities that would provide the simplicity and familiarity, yet also enable people to creatively solve all the problems of innovation? What core sets of related activities can connect so many old ways, processes and so forth with so many new ones?

Market-Technology Linking to Balance Inside with Outside

The third paradoxical practice of innovation is linking technologies with markets, which invokes the tension of inside vs outside in the broad sense, because usually we think of technology as inside and the market as outside. A new product is a package of features and benefits, each of which must be articulated and designed. To create value, this package must address core customer needs and wants in a way that leverages the organization's unique technology capability. Market-technology linking connects insides and outsides across multiple boundaries. Firstly, market-technology linking is multi-functional because all functions have unique insights for a given product design (Dougherty 1992b). Engineers, marketers and manufacturing all must reach beyond their boundaries to absorb others' insights, while also making their own specialized insights sensible to others. Secondly, products rarely stand alone. The necessary integrity of each product (cf. Clark and Fujimoto 1991) must be

balanced with how well it fits into product families and platforms. And the integrity of product families and platforms must be balanced with firm-wide resources that must be collectively leveraged, and perhaps with a common brand or image that presents a common face to 'the marketplace'. Thirdly, inside functions and businesses are linked outside in a variety of alliances, partnerships and associations (R&D, distribution, supply chain). In most industries value is created and delivered by a network of players who provide complementary assets, components, basic R&D and so on (Chesbrough 2003; Miller and Floricel 2003).

The design principle most associated with the tension of inside vs outside is *integration*, defined by Lawrence and Lorsch (1967: 11) as '... the quality of the state of collaboration that exists among departments that are required to achieve unity of effort by the demands of the environment'. The 'state' of collaboration is far more complex in 21st century innovative organizations, since the organization is not only integrating functional departments, but also product families, platforms, opportunities, alliance partners, newly acquired units, geographical foci – many more 'insides' need to integrate with many 'outsides'. While there are numerous specific techniques for integration (e.g. standards, direct supervision, liaison people and common values), there are also two general aspects: mutual adjustment (Thompson 1967; Mintzberg 1991) and mutual adaptation (Leonard 1998).

Mutual adjustment refers to the continuous adjustment of actions by one specialist to the actions of others on a team, as people literally figure out what to do and how to do it as they do the work. To work in parallel, people must interrelate heedfully – carefully, critically, willfully and purposefully rather than habitually. According to Weick and Roberts (1993) if interrelations are heedful, people are more mindful of the big picture to which they contribute, can comprehend unexpected events, and can share ideas and experiences more quickly. To interrelate heedfully, people must envisage a system of joint action, construct their own contribution to fit that collective representation, and relate their contribution to the system that is envisaged.

Dougherty and Takacs (2004) argue that a very new kind of boundary is necessary if scores of new product teams that exist at any one time in a large organization are to work interdependently, or heedfully. Rather than the imaginary line that signifies a limit, they propose a new metaphor based on 'team play'. People involved in team play easily engage in heedful yet improvised action, provided there is a clear game with a few simple rules. They propose that 'team play' is a metaphor for ongoing mutual adjustment by heedful interrelating, because play enables 'adaptive variability' (Sutton-Smith 2001), other oriented roles and a sharp focus on the means, or the processes and manner in which activities are carried out. Team play, however, requires a very different strategic context to enable multiple teams to work together at once: senior managers must actively define the business, customers and goals to create a 'game' in the first place, and they must develop capabilities and resources to support all the team play. People cannot readily join projects over time, and scores of teams cannot play at once, without resources, facilities, shared rules and of course a clear game (albeit one that emerges over time).

Mutual adaptation refers to the reinvention of one system such as manufacturing to conform to a new strategy, and the simultaneous reinvention of the organization to conform to the new system; this involves moving back 'up' the design hierarchy (Clark 1985), to rethink prior choices among alternatives, because new technologies now make previously rejected options feasible, or changes in customer needs now highlight different kinds of performance, and thus involves revisiting prior decision points, reopening issues that had been resolved, and unfreezing organizational routines (Leonard 1998).

Bureaucratic integration is based on pre-set standards that standardize action rather than facilitate the interweaving of improvised plays. Bureaucratic integration therefore presumes pre-programmed co-ordination (sequential and pooled rather than reciprocal), and focuses primarily on the inside (efficiency). Bureaucracies accommodate mutual adjustment as a very costly add-on (e.g. in a venture unit or special department), not because mutual adjustment is inherently costly but because it does not fit. Thompson (1967), for example, argued that mutual adjustment should be used sparingly, and only in task forces that are bracketed off from the rest of the organization. Bureaucratic organizing cannot accommodate mutual adaptation at all, since managerial attention is focused on small cycles of change and cannot detect when large spirals of change are necessary. Organizing for innovation requires a fundamentally new principle for integration that enables mutual adjustment and mutual adaptation across

so many insides and outsides, or so many market-technology linkages.

Monitoring and Evaluation to Balance Emergence vs Determination

The fourth paradoxical practice is monitoring the work, which invokes the tension of emergence vs determination. Innovations always involve surprises since customers, needs and technologies are often new and untried, and actually emerge through trial and error. However, innovation also makes it easy to squander huge amounts of resources, so resources must be channelled, processes must be monitored, and activities occurring at different levels must be kept in sync somehow. The fact that many new products still fail, even when they are relatively incremental efforts, is testimony to the need to monitor and evaluate the activity. The design principle most associated with the tension of emergence vs determination is control, or assuring that the right activities are carried out at the right time with the right resources. Indeed, many 'best practices' for innovation are formal approaches for establishing priorities, milestones and objectives, which highlights the utter necessity of control in innovation work (Bacon et al. 1994). Controlling innovation involves two thrusts: focusing on the processes or activities through which people accomplish their work to keep means and ends connected, and enabling situated judgement (Dougherty 1996) on the part of innovators. Each complements the other, so both are necessary. Firstly, the ends or outcomes of innovation take a long time to be achieved and may change in any case, so innovation cannot be controlled by measuring achievement of objectives alone, especially not in the short-term. Managers must also control the processes of innovation by monitoring such things as cycle time, yields, percentage of usable components, platform efficiency, share of industry value and market shares and changes. These process measures help to both surface problems and prevent capability traps that can arise if people shift attention from process improvements to defects. Jelinek and Schoonhoven (1990) describe weekly operational reviews that are focused on providing individuals with useful information about their status, burn rates and so on. Clark and Fujimoto (1991) outline an alternate paradigm for prototyping and plant ramp-up that helps to surface potential design and

Table 2.7.2   New Principles for Organizing Innovation

Design	Proposed principle of organization design for innovative organizing	Contingencies
Define jobs, define work so people are energized, reliable, competent	Define 'work' as practice, like professional practice	All jobs are practice? Need a frame for practice (I propose value creation); enables alliancing and outsourcing of professional jobs
Differentiate: define related sets of activities that makes work 'simple' but whole?	By core problems of innovation, with communities of practice around each: strategy, business, capability (technology, manufacturing, IT), project: highlights problems and horizontal flows of work	Relative emphasis, which dominates, why, when or gets stuck; R&D as capability solves decent/cent problems; context may intervene, prevent
Integrate, enable MA and MA	Strategic articulation across four communities (each with own strategy); lines of sight into future	Requires clear articulation and strategic abilities (rare); regulations, etc. may reduce reach and sight; ask how well connected externally
Control processes, not just ends; judgement	Human process controls, rules and resources: explore potential, knowledge matters, take responsibility for whole cycle; resources are access to: options and control of choices; knowledge; and time, attention.	Most best practices are process controls, so select and apply to context; relative emphasis of rules, resources?

manufacturing problems rather than to show proof of concept. The purpose of the process controls is to enable people to surface (or set) and to solve problems, and to revise processes themselves as necessary. Secondly, innovation is inherently unpredictable so the organization must rely on people to make the right call as they monitor emergent flows of activities. The control system must enable both situated judgement, and the continued situating of the process controls outline above, to keep them grounded in everyday reality, and continually refreshed. Benner (2003) refers to a similar term, the 'clinical judgement' that practitioners such as nurses, teachers, architects, technicians and other knowledge workers must rely on to do their work. As Dougherty (1996) explained, 'situated' refers to being engaged in the details of the innovation and its emergence, because these are complex, often tacit issues that must be 'visceralized' to be understood, to use a phrase developed by Schon (1985). 'Judgement' refers to the capability to use insights and heuristics developed from experience, and to 'appreciation', which Vickers (1965) uses to refer to sizing-up unstructured situations and judging the significance of various facts – much like the reflection-in-action that Schon (1983) argues is central to work as a

professional. Situated judgement implies occupational control (Barley 1996), which is based on the authority of expertise rather than of the position.

The bureaucratic principle for control specifically excludes processes, situatedness and judgement (except by officers), and therefore cannot organize innovation. First, bureaucratic control rests on premises of rationality that separate means from ends (Schon 1983; Benner 2003) and concentrates on the accomplishment of ends. Processes are monitored to detect deviance or variance from prescribed standards, not to surface problems with the process. Once they have been scientifically measured, processes are given. Standards are generalized to fit across contexts, so situational issues are noise, not important data. And judgement by workers is illegitimate: knowledge workers must use judgement to do their work but that fact is not recognized by the managerial system (Brown and Duguid 1991; Barley 1996; Benner 2004).

In the next section, I develop an alternate approach for each of these design principles that can embody the tensions of innovation, by contrasting some current thinking on these aspects of innovation. Table 2.7.2 outlines the overall argument, and Table 2.7.3 provides details for each section.

Table 2.7.3 Details for Differentiation, Integration and Control for Each Community of Practice

The core problems of innovation that communities of practice differentiate by	Integration by strategic articulation	Control by processes, everyday rules (explore potential; honour knowledge; take responsibility for whole project) and resources (time, authority, options)
Strategic community and problem to be set and solved: problem of strategic articulation, investments, building organizational systems; make investments; network with other CEOs, competitors, governments	Integrate businesses, capabilities into strategic path (link corporate vision with business models, capabilities); juxtapose bus, tech enactments vs strategy to keep strategic directions refreshed; select kinds of opportunities; track evolution of performance and functionality	Define general value to be created by firm, where it is going. Control resources for exploration to communities; provide common frameworks, practices and procedures; create selection rules for setting and solving problems. Process controls: managerial and reward systems, control and movement of charters, strategic planning, probing and learning, six sigma
Business management problem: making money over time by matching bundles of resources with market opportunities, filling in product for life cycle of business	Integrate products with business opportunities (link business models with product ideas and portfolios); juxtapose products vs strategic standards (attributes, value that are basis of competition): select new products; manage product portfolios; probe new opportunities	Define business model for achieving value over time; provide business expertise to others; pace evolution within businesses via platforms and portfolios Processes: patching, probing and learning, market share growth, new product contributions, customer satisfaction
Capabilities problem – includes technology, manufacturing, marketing, supply chain: developing deep expertise and capabilities for long-term value creation	Integrate technology with products and businesses (link tech strategy with projects and business models); select kinds of technologies needed to produce functionality, performance; select new functionality for new opportunities	Define, create knowledge sets and expertise for innovation, keep it viable and emerging over time; control technology trajectories and monitor alternates; oversee how well people contribute to projects, businesses. Processes: concurrent engineering, QFD, TQ, technology mapping, market value measures
New product development problem: defining and fleshing out product concepts, pulling new product together from firm resources to fit specific market needs	Integrate market and technology possibilities in new products. Link product concepts with actual needs and tech options; select, apply technologies to achieve particular functionality of project; interpret specific user needs	Provide expertise in project management, integrate across projects, move new insights around projects, Control how criteria for performance are understood, implemented; processes: phase reviews, project management, VOC,

New Principles for Organizing the Practices of Innovation

Commitment, Freedom and Responsibility

The first challenge outlined above is to develop a new principle for defining work, so that jobs encompass: (1) problem-setting and problem-solving rather than the application of predetermined solutions, (2) working in parallel with other experts rather than apart from them, and (3) being mindful of the systemic impact of one's activities rather than ignoring it. Innovation researchers do not directly address the principle of defining work, but they do propose that a variety of special roles be added to the organization to enable innovation. For example, the 'gatekeeper' (Allen 1977) connects a research team with external sources of knowledge and filters out unnecessary noise; 'ambassadors' obtain resources and legitimacy, 'scouts' and 'co-ordinators' manage dependence on other functions, and 'guards' control outward information flow (Ancona and Caldwell 1990); 'hunters' and 'gatherers' search for new opportunities (Delbecq and Mills 1985); the 'product champion' forces new activities through the organization (Schon 1963); senior sponsors enable champions (Maidique 1980; Day 1994); and the 'heavy weight' project leader possesses the necessary clout to complete a project successfully (Clark and Fujimoto 1991); see Knowledge work researchers, however, do emphasize an alternate understanding of work, that of *practice* (Schon 1983; Brown and Duguid 1991; Dougherty 1992a; Barley 1996; Orlikowski 2002). Since creating new products is about creating, combining and recombining knowledge about markets and technologies, I propose that everyone's jobs, from front line workers to senior managers, be based on the principle of *work as practice*. All jobs are understood as a professional practice or occupation, which involves hands-on, active participation in innovating. Defining work as practice means that jobs embody the means and the ends of work, the practical wisdom people rely on, and the '… rich, socially embedded clinical know-how that encompasses perceptual skills, transitional understandings across time, and understanding of the particular in relation to the general' (Benner 2003: 5). 'Practice' highlights the spontaneous, inventive and improvisational ways through which people get things done (Schon 1983; Brown and Duguid 2000). According to Brown and Duguid (2000), practice

concerns 'knowing how', defined as the ability to put know-what into practice.

Work as practice is based on two very different rules than is work as a bureaucratic functionary. First, instead of 'the office', the rule for practice is that each person takes responsibility for the whole task and for one's contribution to that task. In professional communities such as medicine, equipment repair and technicians (Brown and Duguid 1991; Barley 1996), people understand themselves to be responsible for the practice and for contributing their own expertise effectively to it, which helps them understand their work in terms of its contribution to the larger whole. Secondly, instead of the rule of top-down authority where senior people think and lower levels do, practice requires that everyone be a knowledgeable expert. The rule for work as practice, therefore, is that knowledge is central, and that people actively create new knowledge as they practice innovation. Dougherty et al. (2004) suggest that, as part of the rule that knowledge is central, people are skilled at articulating their own knowledge in a way that is sensible to people with different expertise, which keeps all the knowledge flowing.

While it is different to being a cog in a big machine, working as a professional practitioner is not entirely unfamiliar. For example, scholars have always emphasized the importance of extensive hands-on involvement on the part of senior managers in innovation (Quinn 1980; Jelinek and Schoonhoven 1990). Maidique and Hayes (1984) argue that senior management involvement in innovation provides them with an in-depth appreciation of how the technology works and how their organization works, so they can better understand strategic possibilities. Hands-on involvement such as this reflects work as practice. Scientists, engineers, market researchers, technicians and even shop floor workers work as practitioners rather than as bureaucrats. However, I suspect that the design principle of work as practice cannot be implemented without transforming the other three principles of organizational design as well, since differentiation helps to define work, integration lays out pathways for collective action, and control keeps attention focused on the practices and channels resources to the right places.

Differentiation by Communities of Practice Focused on Innovation Problems

The second organizing challenge is how to differentiate the work of innovation in a way that makes the necessary creative problem-solving sensible, doable and reasonably simple. Innovation researchers focus considerable attention on defining work boundaries, and on differentiating activities into ambidextrous units that focus on different kinds of innovation (e.g., era of ferment, incremental, discontinuous – see Tushman and O'Reilly 1997), or into various product families (Brown and Eisenhardt 1998) and shifting charters among units (Helfat and Raubitschek 2000), or setting up special 'hubs' for radical innovation (Liefer et al. 2000). These theorists recognize the need to balance the tension between old and new in creative problem-solving for innovation, acknowledge (at least implicitly) the centrality of differentiation in this balancing, and emphasize horizontal organizing around activities that flow over time.

However, the theorists differ over whether or not 'old' practices, markets, technologies and perspectives dominate new ones, whether that imbalance is inherent in organizing, and how the balancing is done. This difference arises from the kinds of industries and scopes of activities that the theorists focus on: the corporate wide strategic and business challenges of innovation in established organizations that become stuck in existing markets, vs the R&D and project challenges of innovation in high technology firms that can emerge effectively over time.

I combine both perspectives to suggest that all four sets of innovation challenges – working on the strategic, business, R&D and other capabilities and project-level problems of innovation – are the core sets of related activities around which work is differentiated for all innovative organizations (Dougherty 1996; 2001). I propose that the innovation practitioners be differentiated into four communities of practice that focus on setting and solving each of these kinds of innovation problems (Lave and Wenger 1991). A community is not a tightly knit group, but an identifiable, recognizable group of people who do that set of work. They know who they are and others know who they are, which means that none of the problems are addressed on an ad hoc basis. Each problem area is a horizontal slice of activities that unfold in time, thus embracing old and new as they flow together. Each of these problems is also a simple set of related activities that can be separated from the others, provided the other problems are being addressed competently. Work is self-designing within each community of practice, where people set and solve specific problems

autonomously within strategic guidelines, choose among alternatives, access resources and apply their expertise as they see fit.

For example, new product projects and R&D capabilities communities both work on technology. However, the latter develops basic physics for a certain use of optics, for example, while the former builds a piece of equipment that applies those basic principles of physics in a way that can be produced at a certain cost. The business unit matches bundles of products to specific markets to make a profit, while the strategic managers look for new opportunities. These are very different problems that should be managed in their own way. This principle of differentiation makes these four activities the most central ones for the innovative organization.

Tushman and O'Reilly (1997) and Christensen (1997) emphasize the strategic and business problems of innovation. The strategic problem involves looking where the marketplace might be going and for emerging customers and technologies, articulating the corporate direction for value creation and making it sensible to people, and making long-term investments in competencies. The business problem involves making a profit by bundling organizational resources to fit with particular market, technology and competitive trends over the life cycle of a business, and tracking changes in marketplaces. When organizations fail to address these two problems effectively, they become trapped by 'the tyranny of success', according to Tushman and O'Reilly (1997) and fixate on current products or customers (Christensen 1997). Units tend to develop a tight configuration of structure, strategy and culture that limits activities. As well, business units cannot evolve on their own from one configuration to another, because new technologies are discontinuous. A big gap exists between one technology and the next, like a step function, and requires a big 'leap' to cross it. These authors argue that senior managers must make this leap by creating new business units and differentiating them from old ones.

Other theorists focus on projects and R&D management, and tend to emphasize continued incorporation of new activities. Leonard (1998), for example, suggests that projects drive daily business as teams dissolve and regroup according to the dictates of the business needs. At the project level, people define product concepts within strategic guidelines, determine customer needs in priority order, and jointly solve problems in the design, manufacture and marketing of the new product. All these projects give the organization considerable fluidity, because managers can shift business charters from one unit to another, and people can move along product lines (Galunic and Eisenhardt 1996; Helfat and Raubitschek 2000; Helfat and Eisenhardt 2004). As well, these theorists argue that technology discontinuities are not so drastic when managers concentrate on the activities that create the underlying technical knowledge and make small checks on position, direction and proximity to competitors (Leonard 1998). If technology, manufacturing, IT and marketing are managed as capabilities, then practitioners can develop deep expertise in these knowledge bases for long-term value creation, and actively keep these capabilities connected to projects and businesses (Dougherty 2001).

Differentiating the practice of innovation into four communities of practice organized around distinct problems of innovation management captures these alternate views. Table 2.7.3 outlines each community's practice. This principle of differentiation makes each of the four problems in innovation management salient, and centres the organizing on these core processes of work – highlighting the practices of doing rather than only outcomes.

My theory is that all four communities of practice are necessary in all organizations, because it is only by actively working on these very different problems that people maintain and enact the requisite hands-on, situated knowledge of each of these issues. However, the horizontal communities and their flows of action must now be integrated, since each is dependent on the other. I turn next to a new principle for integration that would allow people to work with a common understanding of the same problem, so they can readily interact, make sense of unexpected issues, and absorb market and technology knowledge across the organization.

Integration by Strategic Articulation

The third principle of organizing for innovation must integrate the differentiated communities of practice to link up markets and technologies and to balance the tension between inside vs outside. The horizontal communities of practice facilitate market-technology linking within each, since each encompasses user issues with technological ones. As well, each community is a network that extends beyond the organization's boundaries. For example, managing the R&D capability includes participation on standards boards and various partnerships with others to develop technology, while managing the business embraces supply chains and customer partnerships. Mutual adjustment within each community is important but can be managed straightforwardly with various techniques (committees, task forces, product family and portfolio management, regular meetings).

The major strategic challenge for integration that remains is mutual adaptation among the four horizontal communities of practice, to keep them in synchronization. Innovation theorists agree that the organization's strategy is the primary source of integration, but disagree over how tightly integrated the insides are with their outsides, and whether strategy is mostly imposed or mostly enacted. Tushman and O'Reilly (1997) highlight limited strategic choices for businesses, arguing that each business must take a particular position along the technology trajectory, and that senior managers keep the organization connected with its market by making experiments and selecting among them. Strategic meaning is largely imposed.

Others argue that strategy will not be meaningful unless innovators continuously enact it, so managers cannot impose the strategy. Brown and Eisenhardt (1997) suggest that innovative organizations operate at the edge of chaos, and continuously balance present and future (and inside with outside) with such techniques as patching (mapping modular activities onto marketplaces), probing (experimental products, future oriented alliances) and pacing (setting rhythms for change). Leonard (1998) argues that a focus on technology draws attention outward to connections with universities, alliance partners, sourcing mechanisms such as licensing and acquisitions, which keeps people attuned to the outside rather than primarily inward. The more fluid strategies are not imposed but rather directed and shaped by managers.

Organizational sensemaking captures the insights of both these alternate views (Tsoukas 1996; Dougherty et al. 2000). I propose that the communities of practice are integrated by ongoing sensemaking of the strategy across communities of practice. Organizational sensemaking balances generically sensible understandings, such as an articulated strategy, with intersubjective understandings that are enacted in the situation (Weick

1995). Sensemaking emerges from continuous processes of renegotiating and reconciling understandings. Integration by strategic sensemaking juxtaposes the articulated strategy of one community of practice with the unarticulated and thus inter-subjective strategic insights of another, which refreshes the meaning of the articulated strategy by drawing out insights from the emerging insights.

To understand how this sensemaking works, first, research shows that each of the four communities requires a strategic framework to do its work: a strategic path, a competitive strategy, a technology strategy and a product concept (Wheelwright and Clark 1992; Khurana and Rosenthal 1997; Cooper 1998). These strategies need to be articulated, which refers to lifting them out of the tacit, private, complex activity to make them explicit, simpler, ordered and relevant to the situation (Obstfeld 2005). Articulation is vital since without it complex frames like innovation strategies tend to fall into the background and become taken for granted (Suchman 1996). Moreover, the articulated strategy integrates markets and technologies for its level, and connects a different scope of inside with outside.

As outlined in Table 2.7.3, the strategic community integrates the various businesses with capabilities into a strategic path that defines what the company as a whole will do for what kinds of customers. The business community integrates products with business opportunities and with the life cycle of a business as it emerges over time to generate profit. The capabilities communities integrate businesses and projects into functionalities and performance levels that the organization can provide. And the product development community integrates specific technology designs with specific customer needs into product concepts.

In any kind of complex work, however, the press of continual challenges draws attention to the minutia of everyday life, so these articulated strategies must be continually articulated and re-articulated to keep them salient, and to refresh and update them as new experiences become relevant. And the articulation of the strategy in one community enables the re-articulation of strategies in the others. For example, in the product development community, teams create their product concepts by drawing on strategic thrusts and available resources from businesses and capabilities. The product concept articulates a particular value to be produced for customers, and provides a blue print for how the team will create

that value. However, the collection of product concepts developed by the teams across the organization embodies new insights into market and technology trends, and can inform the ongoing directions of businesses and capabilities. As well, people also continually enact the strategy as they do their work, so the strategy takes on new meanings. People make sense of new or tacit knowledge (such as 'sticky' customer needs, new strategic paths) by interacting face-to-face to communicate interpretations of these, to sort out possible attributes of them, and to explore different takes on them. The organization can build up new manufacturing and technology capabilities based on what works and does not work.

The theory suggests that each community of practice needs strategic sensemaking, and that the articulation of each depends on interactions with activities in other communities. A business strategy will become stuck if there are no product trials to explore options and no technological alternatives to think about. Technology development will become limited or esoteric if the businesses become static. The theory also says that the firm's strategy has to be clear and vivid, which may limit in the scope of innovation activities that any organization can undertake.

Part of integration is acceptance of the apparent looseness within and among the four domains of innovative action. Integration is enacted in the practice. The looseness is not a loosening of standards, but rather a recognition that a common space of work, based on a deeper understanding of shared appreciation of the joint activity that people are collectively engaged in, is necessary. In the bureaucratic model, such looseness implies out of control, but now, looseness is necessary for survival, and so is necessary for control. It is thus necessary to redefine control as well, to focus on controlling the terrain of the looseness.

Control by Generative Rules and Resources

Finally, I argued above that the principle of control for the work of innovation must combine a focus on the processes of value creation with situated judgement. Most theorists agree that the kind of control that is needed for innovation is cultural, not mechanical, because people must continually make sense of what they need to do and how they need to do it when they do innovation work. However, theorists differ on how culture affects everyday actions – is culture a set of meanings, or a medium for enacting meanings?

Some suggest that culture itself conveys meanings that people must share, and that senior managers impose these meanings by promoting particular norms and values. According to Tushman and O'Reilly (1997: 102): 'Culture is a system of shared values and norms that define appropriate attitudes and behaviours for its members'. A problem with this perspective is that the list of possible norms and values can be quite large (e.g. change-oriented, focused on customers, entrepreneurial, risk-taking, valuing failure, proactive). Others draw on complexity theory at least metaphorically, and propose a few simple rules such as sharply defined priorities, extensive communication, especially across projects, where people stay abreast of what everyone else is doing with weekly formal meetings, and time-pacing (Brown and Eisenhardt 1998). A problem with this perspective is identifying what are these few simple rules.

I propose to resolve this theoretical conflict by bringing good old, instrumental process controls back in. However these process controls focus on human rather than physical processes. I also propose to drop control by 'culture' and build instead on structuration theory (Giddens 1982): that a few particular rules and resources structure everyday work by providing the common ground upon which people can work together. First, all three new principles are based on processes that emerge over time. These processes include objectives to be achieved, but emphasize how those objectives come to be, how they emerge continually over time, and how they are interpreted. Rather than abstracted, objectified and simplified physical flows that can be represented mathematically (e.g. by OR), the processes to be controlled are human processes that are socially enacted, interpreted, negotiated and renegotiated over time. The process controls therefore must foster these human activities of interpretation and sensemaking.

Control by controlling the human processes keeps these practices of work out in the open, to be evaluated, monitored and reconceived as necessary. These process controls therefore keep the practices themselves rich, sensible and visceral, therefore enabling 'reflection-in-action' or situated judgement. I have already noted that many of the best practices, procedures, processes, tools and techniques for managing innovation are process controls, in the sense that they map out possible pathways and frame shorter-term activities. I theorize that these best practices will not work unless the organization is based on control by keeping the human practices as processes out in the open and revising them as necessary.

If this design principle is incorporated, then managers have any number of systems, milestones and devices to pace the flows in each community of practice over time. Examples would be aggregate product plans combines product concepts with technology and manufacturing strategies; measuring cycle times, yield rates, percentage of which sets of experts are over-subscribed or not, capacity utilization, product quality, capacity for variety, customer satisfaction, delivery times, market share or profit margins may help keep the projects, businesses and strategies in sync; measuring effectiveness of alliances for bringing new products to market, for developing new technologies that have certain potential, for absorbing and leveraging acquisitions (e.g. how many people were retained), and how well platforms deliver over time keeps organizational capabilities in sync with businesses – see Leonard (1998); Meyer and deTore (2001); Wheelwright and Clark (1992); and Cooper (1998).

Paralysis by analysis (Langley 1989) is still possible, perhaps more so now because processes are much more sensible, and because scholars and consultants alike seem to *really like* all these tools, techniques, tactics and 'best practices' (e.g. everything from concurrent engineering to phase reviews, to QFD, to aggregate product planning … the list is almost endless). The organization therefore must also foster situated judgement, as argued above, so that people can make selective and judicious use of the many 'best practices'. Situated judgement perhaps can be fostered or even instituted by a certain kind of culture. All innovative organizations may well share a certain universal culture in the sense that they all have certain values or norms – this is an empirical question.

Rather than culture as broadly defined, it is more to the point to focus on what people do, on enabling certain actions, and on fostering a common experience people can draw on to make sense of their work. Managing what people think is difficult even in closed or total institutions (Goffman 1959), and the innovative organization is inherently open. Managers cannot make people think certain things easily, but they can enable and foster particular activities.

The process controls outlined above would be enabled if managers fostered certain kinds of social rules and resources (Wesley 1990; Kogut 2000). Structuration theory explains the duality of emergence and determination with the insight that they are part of each other. Emergence needs something that is already determined, since people cannot improvise easily or meaningfully without some pre-existing rules. However, determination needs emergence, because social structures do not exist other than if they are enacted. And since they are always enacted in particular contexts, their reality is always situated. In structuration, 'structure' refers to the set of rules and resources that are instantiated in recurrent practice.

The innovative organization, I propose, is controlled by three particular rules and three particular kinds of resources. The first two rules have already been discussed as the basis for work as practice: take responsibility for the whole task rather than just your part, and value knowledge for its own sake, so you make what you know accessible to others. The third rule concerns how people approach the problem of value creation that they are working on – as exploring potential (Dougherty et al. 2004). The opposite is to move quickly to a solution or to eliminate problems – which is the rule in most non-innovative organizations I have studied. This third rule frames and helps define the problems that the four communities of practice set and solve, and helps control the nature of these problems. If people define all problems in terms of *what we can do*, and what the customers will do or can do, then searching for alternatives and options and exploring new opportunities becomes normal and natural (Dougherty et al. 2004).

With this rule for defining problems as exploring potential, people look for longer-term possibilities and actively search for opportunities rather than fixate on the current product. A given product might not embody new ideas, but the ideas would be considered so that possibilities for the next iteration or the next generation are on the table (Garud and Kumaraswamy 1995). This rule for work enables people to consider a variety of possibilities at once in their decision-making for strategic directions, building manufacturing capability or designing a product, and also to quickly weed out alternatives (cf. Iansiti 1993). Dealing with the inevitable challenges, glitches and slips of innovation by looking for alternatives and exploring

potential in fact makes the work easier to do. The rule fosters stepping away from the immediate, so people can consider a wide variety of options. If everyone follows this rule, there would be a variety of viable options ready at hand.

Resources are central elements of structuring as well, because they provide the capabilities of achieving outcomes (Giddens 1982). Resources are the medium through which power is exercised, and through which 'structures of domination' are reproduced. 'Structures of domination' refer to who dominates and how, and brings to the fore the fact that large organizations can be dominated by a managerial elite through a 'command and control' structure (Perrow 1986). Innovation scholars have always emphasized the importance of power. For example, Clark and Fujimoto (1991) find that 'heavy weight' project managers have enough clout to push new products through the system. Dougherty and Hardy (1996) find that successful innovators had the power to make their projects meaningful, while Kanter (1988) points to the need to 'empower' innovators. However, most studies take the existing structure of domination as given, rather than question it.

I propose that all innovators have control over three kinds of resources that are necessary to achieving their outcomes, the setting and solving of problems: access to other people's time and attention, control over how one's own work will contribute to the entire task (e.g. participatory control over the product concept or technology direction), and control over the specific choices that are made to solve situated problems. These are the most central resources in an organization, so everyday control over them assures that the necessary resources are available to innovators. These resources go hand-in-hand with the three rules. If everyone takes responsibility for the entire task, then each person working on that task has access to the time and attention of other people. Each knows that the others will do their part. If everyone makes their knowledge accessible to others, everyone has the resource of being in the know, and of control over their expertise, how their knowledge will be used. If everyone is exploring potential and pushing for options, then whenever anyone encounters a problem some options are already available. Together, these resources comprise a qualitatively different structure of domination.

Managers control the processes and the procedures that enable these rules and resources. Plus they control over their own processes. With these basic rules and resources for control, entrepreneurial, attentive, energized people are the outcome – no magic culture or mystical capabilities are needed since these arise from the structuring of everyday work.

Synthesis, Contingencies and Empirical Questions

I have proposed four new principles of organization design that together define the innovative organization in its own terms rather than as a deviation from the bureaucracy. These are simple principles of design, but also very different from the familiar bureaucratic principles, in fact almost inside out. Instead of generalizing, they situate work in actual, hands-on activities that are carried out by everyone, not just by labourers. Instead of breaking work down by an established technique, they weave work together around knowing and learning. Instead of static efficiency, they highlight evolving processes of work. Instead of standardizing action, they activate emergent standards that are negotiated and reconciled as the work proceeds. These principles organize the four paradoxical practices of innovation, and they are grounded specifically in doing this kind of work. These are high-level principles through which people collectively generate and regenerate the work of innovation. The principles produce the context for innovation, and can be complemented by specific structuring techniques to further shape that context for particular industry, strategic and cultural conditions.

Established organizations with a history of bureaucracy will have considerable difficulty transforming, unless they can implement all four principles, because the familiar bureaucratic principles are waiting in the wings. Burns and Stalker (1961) found that many organizations did not become more innovative because people who began to work in more organic ways experienced 'chronic anxiety' about what they were to do with whom and how. The organic form did not induce chronic anxiety, but it was induced by the failure to define people's new roles and relationships – the new organizing scheme was not articulated. So people slipped back into their defined, comfortable bureaucratic work roles. Given the continued prevalence of 'the bureaucracy' as an institution of modern life, organizations that need only occasional new products may be better off

managing innovation the old fashioned way – as an exception to regular work that is located outside the normal organization.

For organizations that must continually update, rethink and occasionally transform products and product categories, I propose that all four new principles are necessary. My theory is that these principles are universal, in the sense that all innovative organizations need them. However, the principles are underlying rules that can be enacted in many different ways, depending on how each one is carried out, on the balancing among them, and on the variety of best practices and other structuring devices that are used. I review each principle and the contingencies and implications it raises. Not all implications are positive, in the sense of creating a glorious, free work life for all.

Work as practice highlights the knowing competence of workers, and raises two types of issues for further research. One, instituting work as practice, will be difficult without a legitimate frame or schema for 'the practice'. Professions and occupations have a frame that provides members with a sense of identity, but work in organizations does not (except for particular occupations). Focusing on services, I have proposed that organizational practices must be defined vividly by articulating the kind of value the practitioners are creating for customers (Dougherty 2004). I also proposed that activities of designing and using the service be built into every job, so that practitioners had an active, experiential sense of the whole problem-setting and – solving process. That is, the work must be hands-on, situated and real rather than conceptual, generalized and abstracted from the context – aka bureaucratic. The second issue is that work as practice opens the organization to partnering with external parties, as well as outsourcing. If all partners were oriented to practice, co-ordinating joint work and sharing knowledge should be fairly easy. However, practice also makes it easy to outsource professional work, and to rely on temporary professionals rather than employees (Barley and Kunda 2004).

Differentiating work into four communities organized around distinct problems of innovation reinforces the principle of practice. This principle of differentiation also reduces, if not eliminates, two of the factors that Morison (1966), in his 'Gunfire at Sea' example, suggested prevented innovation – severely limited identification with just a part rather than the whole, and a fixation on a specific product rather than on the process. I would expect to find all four communities in all innovative organizations, but how each is organized would vary considerably. In a small organization, the strategic community of practice may be a board of directors or a committee of managers who come together regularly to work on this set of problems, while in a large multinational, this community may be comprised of all business and functional heads who come together quarterly. The relative balance within and among the communities would vary by industry as well. Technology dominates in some industries, while businesses dominate in others. When the 'shelf life' of new products or technologies is short, projects and technologies dominate, as Brown and Eisenhardt (1997) suggest.

Turning vertical functions into horizontal flows of capabilities is a noteworthy part of this principle. The specialized labour that is the hallmark of the bureaucracy is still here, but managed as capabilities to support continuous streams of new products, businesses and opportunities. For example, if R&D is organized as a horizontal flow of capability rather than a vertical function, specialized centres of excellence are much less likely to become fixated on suboptimal goals. Whether or not the capabilities have authority over all practitioners in their specialty is contingent upon the industry and dynamics of knowledge. In some industries it may be necessary for R&D to supervise all scientists, engineers and/or technicians to assure that people stay up to date, while in others a career process that rotates experts among projects over time may be all that is necessary. However, the theory is that the managers of the capabilities are held responsible for how well their people contribute to the projects and businesses.

Imbalances among communities can also arise, which if severe can lead to the failure to attend to the four key problems, which returns the organizing system back to a bureaucracy. If the businesses dominate then short-term ROI is the focus, and adaptation to new business models would be difficult (as Christensen predicts). One biotech company I know seems to ignore strategic problems – or perhaps the striking complexity of this industry precludes strategic problem-setting and -solving. The upshot, however, is that they appear to be drifting from one relatively short-term income source to another. A variety of empirical questions can be raised to explore the differences among existing theories that were outlined in the second section

above. For example, the strict separation of new from old businesses proposed by Tushman and O'Reilly (1997) may be necessary when established organizations must begin to change, but less necessary once the transformation has occurred.

The principle of integration by strategic articulation across communities of practice emphasizes a much more fluid mutual adaptation among the four communities of practice. However, this form of integration works only if the strategies of each community are regularly articulated and juxtaposed – something that apparently is very hard to do, based on the fact that it does not occur often (cf. Tushman and O'Reilly 1997). This principle of integration may also require a more focused kind of strategy, a clear, crisp understanding of the value the corporation as a whole creates, and a clear connection among the businesses. Such limitations are empirical questions, and management teams may possess unique competencies for strategic sensemaking. As well, in some industries, the possibilities for innovation may be constrained by regulations, by the capital intensity (e.g. oil and gas) or by preferences of customers. Such constraints would limit the spiralling of adaptation, and may cause the organizing to revert, once again, to a static bureaucracy. One can also ask how tightly or loosely synchronized the communities of problem-setting and -solving need to be, how various approaches to time-pacing can help, and how more manifest integrating tactics and techniques fit in. Finally, a number of people would be participants in two or more communities (e.g. business level technology directors link technologies to their business and link their concerns to the technology capability community). How these linkages work to reinforce the principle of integration requires study.

Finally, the new principle of control transforms the structure of domination. The process controls include many of the best practices for innovation, and serve to channel attention to the processes themselves, not only to abstracted outcomes. This new principle of control supports reflection-in-action, and helps define the problems that all the practitioners are working on. These necessary controls will not work, however, unless the practitioners have control over the everyday resources of time and attention, access to knowledge and the ability to make their own choices from among the options and alternatives that have been generated. The new principle of control brings us full circle, because it requires the new understanding of work roles and relationships – work as practice – that focuses people's attention on how they can contribute to the overall task, and how they can make their special knowledge accessible to others. It requires work differentiation into coherent yet sensible practices of problem-setting and -solving. And it requires strategic articulation, since that shapes the process controls. Contingencies involve which rules and resources are more or less dominant in different industries, how they are enacted, and the number and types of procedures that can be used effectively, based on the underlying rules and resources that make them usable.

In conclusion, organizing for innovation is not mystical, weird or visionary. It requires reasonably straightforward approaches to defining jobs, grouping those jobs into sensible units, co-ordinating the units and controlling it all over time. These are ordinary, everyday processes of managing and organizing. However, rather than ignore the work to be done, I focused explicitly on the actual work of innovation, which leads me to develop new principles of organizing. The challenge of organizing for innovation in the 21st century is to develop experience with these new principles, so that this new kind of organizing becomes obvious, simple and sensible, just like the bureaucracy became for the 20th century.

References

Adams, M. (2004) 'Comparative performance assessment study findings', presentation at the *Comparative performance assessment conference*, PDMA Foundation, March.

Allen, T. (1977) *Managing the Flow of Technology*. Cambridge, MA: MIT Press.

Ancona, D. and Caldwell, D. (1990) 'Beyond boundary spanning: managing external dependence in product development teams', *Journal of High Technology Management Research*, 1(2): 119–35.

Bacon, G., Beckman, S., Mowery, D. and Wilson, E. (1994) 'Managing product definition in high-technology industries: a pilot study', *California Management Review*, 36: 34–56.

Baldwin, J. and DaPont, M. (1993) 'Innovation in Canadian enterprises: survey of innovation and advanced technology', *Statistics Canada*, 88, 513–XPB.

Barley, S. (1996) 'Technicians in the workplace: ethnographic evidence for bringing work into organization studies', *Administrative Science Quarterly*, 41: 404–41.

Barley, S. and Kunda, G. (2004) *Gurus, Hired Guns, and Warm Bodies*. Princeton, NJ: Princeton University Press.

Bartlett, C. and Ghoshal, S. (1989) *Managing Across Borders: The Transnational Solution*. Boston, MA: Harvard Business School press.

Benner, P. (2003) 'Situated action and practice', working draft, School of Nursing, UC San Francisco.

Benner, P. (2004) 'Articulating knowledge, skills, and meanings embedded in nursing practice: confronting over-simplification, leveling, and the limits of formalism in formal classification systems', working draft, School of Nursing, UC San Francisco.

Blau, P. and Meyer, M. (1987) *Bureaucracy in Modern Society*, 3rd edn. New York: Random House.

Brown, J.S. and Duguid, P. (1991) 'Organizational learning and communities of practice: toward a unified view of working, learning, and innovation', *Organization Science*, 2: 40–57.

Brown, J.S. and Duguid, P. (2000) 'Balancing act: how to capture knowledge without killing it', *Harvard Business Review*, May–June: 73–80.

Brown, S. and Eisenhardt, K. (1997) 'The art of continuous change: linking complexity theory and time-paced evolution in relentlessly shifting organizations', *Administrative Science Quarterly*, 42: 1–35.

Brown, S. and Eisenhardt, K. (1998) *Competing on the Edge*. Boston, MA: Harvard Business School Press.

Burns, T. and Stalker, G.M. (1994: originally 1961) *The Management of Innovation*. Cambridge: Oxford University Press.

Capon, N, Farley, J., Lehmann, D. and Hulbert, J. (1992) 'Profiles of product innovators among large US manufacturers', *Management Science*, 38(2): 157–69.

Chesbrough, H. (2003) 'The era of open research', *Sloan Management Review*, 44(3): 35–41.

Christensen, C. (1997) *The Innovator's Dilemma*. Boston: Harvard Business School Press.

Clark, K. (1985) 'The interaction of design hierarchies and market concepts in technological evolution', *Research Policy*, 14: 235–51.

Clark, K. and Fujimoto, T. (1991) *Product Development Performance*. Boston: Harvard Business School Press.

Clegg, S.R. (ed.) (2002) *Paradoxes of Management and Organizations*. Amsterdam: Benjamins.

Clegg, S.R., da Cunha, J.V. and e Cunha, M.P. (2002) 'Management paradoxes: a relational view', *Human Relations*, 55(5): 483–504.

Cooper, R. (1998) *Product Leadership: Creating and Launching Superior New Products*. Reading, MA: Perseus Books.

Day, D. (1994) 'Raising radicals: different processes for championing innovative corporate ventures', *Organization Science*, 5(2): 148–72.

Delbecq, A. and Mills, P. (1985) 'Managerial practices that enhance innovation', *Organization Dynamics*, 14(1): 24–34.

Dessler, G. (2002) *A Framework for Management*. Upper Saddle River, NJ: Prentice Hall.

Devanna, M and Tichy, N. (1990) 'Creating the competitive organization of the 21st century: the boundaryless corporation', *Human Resource Management*, 29(4): 455–71.

Dosi, G. (1982) 'Technological paradigms and technological trajectories', *Research Policy*, 11: 147–62.

Dougherty, D. (1990) 'Understanding new markets for new products', *Strategic Management Journal*, 11: 59–79.

Dougherty, D. (1992a) 'A practice-centered model of organizational renewal through product innovation', *Strategic Management Journal*, 13: 77–92.

Dougherty, D. (1992b) 'Interpretive barriers to successful product innovation in large firms', *Organization Science*, 3: 179–203.

Dougherty, D. (1996) 'Organizing for innovation', in S. Clegg, C. Hardy and W. Nord (eds), *Handbook of Organization Studies*. London: Sage. pp. 424–39.

Dougherty, D. (2001) 'Re-imagining the differentiation and integration of work for sustained product innovation', *Organization Science*, 12(5): 612–31.

Dougherty, D. (2004) 'Organizing practice in services to capture knowledge for innovation', *Strategic Organization*, 2(1): 35–64.

Dougherty, D. and Hardy, C. (1996) 'Sustained product innovation in large, mature organizations: overcoming innovation-to-organization problems', *Academy of Management Journal*, 39(5): 1120–53.

Dougherty, D. and Heller, T. (1994) 'The illegitimacy of successful new products in large firms', *Organization Science*, 5(2): 200–18..

Dougherty, D. and Takacs, C.H. (2004) 'Interrelating in innovative organizations: team play as the boundary for work and strategy', *Long Range Planning*, special issue on boundaries and innovation, 37: 569–90.

Dougherty, D., Barnard, H. and Dunne, D. (2005) 'The rules and resources that generate the dynamic capability for sustained product innovation', *Qualitative Organizational Research, best papers from the Davis Conference on Qualitative Research*, K. Elsbach, Ed. Greenwich, CN: Information Age Publishing, pp. 37–74.

Dougherty, D., Borrelli, L., Munir, K. and O'Sullivan, A. (2000) 'Systems of organizational sensemaking for sustained product innovation', *Journal of Engineering and Technology Management*, 17: 321–55.

Dougherty, D., Munir, K. and Subramaniam, M. (2004) 'Technology flows in practice: managing the human side of organizational technology', *Proceedings of the Academy of Management* meeting, August 2002.

Franko, L. (1989) 'Global corporate competition: who's winning, who's losing, and the R&D factor as one reason why', *Strategic Management Journal*, 10: 449–74.

Galbraith, J. (1995) *Designing Organizations*. San Francisco: Jossey-Bass.

Galunic, C. and Eisenhardt, K. (1996) 'The evolution if intracorporate domains: divisional charter losses in high-technology, multi-divisional corporations', *Organization Science*, 7(3): 255–82.

Garud, R. and Kumaraswamy, A. (1995) 'Technological and organizational designs for realizing economies of substitution', *Strategic Management Journal*, 16: 93–111.

Giddens, A. (1982) *Profiles and Critiques in Social Theory*. Berkeley, CA: University of California Press.

Goffman, E. (1959) *The Presentation of Self in Everyday Life*. Garden City, NY: Doubleday.

Handy, C. (1989) *The Age of Unreason*. Boston, MA: Harvard Business School press.

Hedlund, G. (1986) 'The hypermodern mnc – a heterarchy?', *Human Resource Management*, 25(1): 9–35.

Helfat, C. and Eisenhardt, K. (2004) 'Inter-temporal economies of scope, organizational modularity, and the dynamics of diversification', *Strategic Management Journal*, 25(13): 1217–1232.

Helfat, C. and Raubitschek, R. (2000) 'Product sequencing: co-evolution of knowledge, capabilities, and products', *Strategic Management Journal*, 21(10–11): 961–80.

Henderson, R. and Clark, K. (1990) 'Architectural innovation: the reconfiguration of existing product technologies and the failure of established firms', *Administrative Science Quarterly*, 35: 9–30.

Hirsch, P. and Levin, D. (1999) 'Umbrella advocates versus the validity police', *Organization Science*, 10(2): 199–212.

Iansiti, M. (1993) 'Real world R&D: jumping the product generation gap', *Harvard Business Review*, May–June: 138–47.

Jelinek, M. and Schoonhoven, C. (1990) *The Innovation Marathon: Lessons From High Technology Firms*. Oxford: Basil Blackwell.

Kanter, R. (1983) *The Change Masters*. New York: Simon and Schuster.

Kanter, R. (1988) 'When a thousand flowers bloom', in *Research in Organization Behavior*, Greenwich, CT: JAI Press. pp. 168–211.

Khurana, A. and Rosenthal, S. (1997) 'Integrating the fuzzy front end of new product development', *Sloan Management Review*, Winter.

Kogut, B. (2000) 'The network as knowledge: generative rules and the emergence of structure', *Strategic Management Journal*, 21: 405–25.

Kohler, T. (2003) 'Logistics innovation management: evidence from two longitudinal studies', DBA project, Cranfield U.

Langley, A. (1989) 'In search of rationality: the purposes behind the use of formal analysis in organizations', *Administrative Science Quarterly*, 34: 598–631.

Lave, J. and Wenger, S. (1991) *Situated Learning*. Cambridge, UK: Cambridge University Press.

Lawrence, P. and Lorsch, J. (1967) *Organization and Environment*. Boston: Harvard School of Business Administration Press.

Leonard, D. (1998) *Well-Springs of Knowledge: Building and Sustaining the Sources of Innovation*, 2nd edn. Boston: Harvard Business School Press.

Liefer, R., McDermott, C., O'Connor, G., Peters, L., Rice, M. and Veryzer, R. (2000) *Radical Innovation: How*

Mature Companies Can Outsmart Upstarts. Boston: Harvard Business School Press.

Maidique, M. (1980) 'Entrepreneurs, champions, and technological innovation', *Sloan Management Review*, 21: 59–76.

Maidique, M. and Hayes, R. (1984) 'The art of high technology management', *Sloan Management Review*, 24: 18–31.

Meyer, M. and deTore, A. (2001) 'Creating a platform-based approach for developing new services', *Journal of Product Innovation Management*, 18(3): 188–204.

Miller, R. and Floricel, S. (2003) 'An exploratory comparison of the management of innovation in the new and old economies', *R&D Management*, 35(5): 501–25.

Mintzberg, H. (1991) 'The structuring of organizations', in H. Mintzberg and J. Quinn (eds), *The Strategy Process*. Englewood Cliffs, NJ: Prentice Hall. pp. 330–50.

Mintzberg, H. and McHugh, A. (1985) 'Strategy formulation in an adhocracy', *Administrative Science Quarterly*, 30: 160–97.

Morison, E. (1966) *Men, Machines, and Modern Times*. Cambridge, MA: MIT Press.

Nonaka, I and Takeuchi, H. (1995) The Knowledge Creating Company. Oxford: Oxford University Press.

Nord, W. and Tucker, S. (1987) *Implementing Routine and Radical Innovations*. Lexington, MA: Lexington Books.

Nystrom, P. and Starbuck, W. (1981) *Handbook of Organization Design*. Oxford: Oxford University Press.

Obsfeld, D. (2005) 'Social networks, the tertius lungens orientation, and involvement in innovation', Adminstrative Science Quarterly, 50(1): 100–130.

Orlikowski, W. (2002) 'Knowing in practice: enacting a collective capability in distributed organizing', *Organization Science*, 13(3): 249–73.

Ostroff, F. (1999) *The Horizontal Organization*. New York: Oxford University Press.

Pelz, D. and Andrews, F. (1966) *Scientists in Organizations*. New York: Wiley.

Perrow, C. (1986) *Complex Organizations: A Critical Essay*, 3rd edn. New York: Random House.

Quinn, J.B. (1980) *Strategies for Change: Logical Incrementalism*. Homewood, IL: Richard D. Irwin.

Robbins, S. and Coulter, M. (1999) *Management*. Upper Saddle River, NJ: Prentice Hall.

Schon, D. (1963) 'Champions for radical new inventions', *Harvard Business Review*, 41(2): 77–86.

Schon, D. (1967) *Technology and Change*. Oxford: Oxford University Press.

Schon, D. (1983) *The Reflective Practitioner: How Professionals Think in Action*. New York: Basic Books.

Schon, D. (1985) 'Keynote Address: Marrying science, artistry, the humanities, and professional practice', Cornell University.

Suchman, L. (1996) 'Supporting articulation work', in R. Kling (ed.), *Computerization and Controversy: Value Conflicts and Social Choices*, 2nd edn. San Diego: Academic Press. pp. 407–23.

Sutton-Smith, B. (2001) *The Ambiguity of Play*. Boston: Harvard University Press.

Thompson, J. (1967) *Organizations in Action*. New York: McGraw Hill.

Tsoukas, H. (1996) 'The firm as a distributed knowledge system: a constructionist approach', *Strategic Management Journal*, 17: 11–25.

Tushman, M (2004) Presentation given at University of Maryland, January.

Tushman, M. and O'Reilly, C. (1997) *Winning Through Innovation*. Boston: Harvard Business School Press.

Vickers, G. (1965) *The Art of Judgment*. New York: Basic Books.

Weber, M. (1946) *From Max Weber: Essays in Sociology*, edited by H.H. Gerth, C.W. Mills. New York: Oxford University Press.

Weick, K. (1995) *Sensemaking in Organizations*. Thousand Oaks, CA: Sage.

Weick, K. and Roberts, K. (1993) 'Collective mind in organizations: Heedful interrelating on flight decks', *Administrative Science Quarterly*, 38(3): 357–81.

Weick, K. and Westley, F. (1996) 'Organizational learning: affirming an oxymoron', in S.R. Clegg, C. Handy and W.R. Nord (eds) *Handbook of Organization Studies*. London: Sage. pp. 440–58.

Westley, F. (1990) 'Middle managers and strategy: microdynamics of inclusion', *Strategic Management Journal*, 11: 337–51.

Wheelwright, S. and Clark, K. (1992) *Revolutionizing Product Development*. New York: The Free Press.

Yang, E. and Dougherty, D. (1993) 'Product innovation management: more than just making a new product', *Creativity and Innovation Management*, 2: 137–55.

2.8 The New Corporate Environmentalism and Green Politics

JOHN M. JERMIER, LINDA C. FORBES, SUZANNE BENN AND RENATO J. ORSATO

Introduction

In focusing this chapter on the natural environment, we invite organizational studies scholars and other readers to think critically about what many believe is one of the most urgent practical problems of our time – a problem compounded in its gravity by the apparently insurmountable political barriers to any real solutions. Ours, as Brown (2003) aptly put it, is a planet under stress wherein systemic degradation is exceeding the earth's regenerative capacity. Given the severity of many environmental problems and their anthropogenic character, you might expect to find concerned, responsible citizenries engaged in public discussions about these issues. Serious green political movements and other forms of green politics would be expected to emerge from these public activities. The activities might be expected to resemble Habermas' (1989) image of the vibrant public sphere, an arena that joins all interested citizens in educative, rational debate under conditions of high trust, mutual respect, openness to difference and consensus building norms. The green public sphere would influence environmental policy making through both formal politics and more informally through diffusion of environmental discourse and the vocabulary of the environment (see Torgerson 2000).

This idealized scenario of *democratic environmentalism* has some applicability in the current circumstances, but increasingly corporations and other business organizations are being urged to take the major responsibility for halting environmental degradation or have come to the realization on their own that they should play the key leadership role in addressing and abating environmental problems. The result has been ambitious campaigns to 'green' business and other organizations and institutions,

campaigns that have become so popular that they have been described as a management fashion (Fineman 2001; Rhee and Lee 2003).

In this chapter, we examine this trend as a form of green politics. We refer to it as the *new corporate environmentalism (NCE)* – defined as *rhetoric* concerning the central role of business in achieving both economic growth and ecological rationality and as a *guide* for management that emphasizes voluntary, proactive control of environmental impacts in ways that exceed or go beyond environmental laws and regulatory compliance. The NCE is most directly relevant to business organizations but, to some degree, it puts pressure on all contemporary organizations and their leaders.

Taken at face value, the NCE seems like a positive development, one certain to contribute to environmental protection and restoration. Not everyone, however, sees this as a uniformly positive trend. Some analysts contend that much of the greening of business and other organizations can be dismissed as greenwashing – all style and no substance (Greer and Bruno 1996; Tokar 1997; Beder 2002). Due to the pervasiveness of NCE campaigns, others have questioned whether business interests have co-opted or hijacked the broader environmental movement (e.g. Welford 1997; Bruno and Karliner 2002). The position we take in this chapter is that the voluntary greening of organizations is too important to green politics to dismiss, and green politics are too important to the establishment of peace, security, social justice, ecological welfare and other vital ends to settle for a one-dimensional public sphere controlled by limited business interests. The main purpose of this chapter is to critically review and analyse the NCE discourse, principally the academic research on this phenomenon. Aspects of the NCE have received some critical attention but further systematic scrutiny and critical analyses are warranted. By locating the NCE in the broader context of green politics, we open it up for further useful critique and evaluation. Based on our assessment of the NCE literature, in particular the absence of linkages between the workplace and the broader public sphere, we outline a need for new models of corporate and organizational greening and propose a direction for developing new models.

Calls for research that brings the natural environment into the centre of the field of organizational studies are over a decade old (e.g. Gladwin 1993; Shrivastava 1994; 1995; Egri and Pinfield 1996). These calls have been fruitful, providing scholars with extensive evidence that green issues matter in theory development work and in practical situations in organizations. We hope this chapter will serve as a useful bridge to some of the promising work in this area and as a stimulus for integrating the NCE with both key concepts in organizational studies (such as technology, structure, learning, communication, culture and change) and with broader discussions in green political thought.

Critical Theory and the New Corporate Environmentalism

To achieve the purpose of critically reviewing and analysing the NCE discourse, we use the lens of critical theory, an approach to organizational studies that advocates systematic critical reflection and evaluation, and the development of emancipatory alternatives (see Alvesson and Deetz 1996; Jermier 1998; Fournier and Grey 2000; Calas and Smircich 2002; Alvesson and Willmott 2003; Hancock and Tyler 2004). Critical theory is sometimes miscast as an approach to social and political analysis that lacks nuance. It is seen as subversive of capitalism and sympathetic to totalitarian political regimes. While such blanket mischaracterizations are less typical today, it is true that critical theorists strive to promote subversive thinking. This may seem extreme to some readers, but there is a scholarly tradition in epistemology that provides instruction on the most appropriate way to approach theory and politics. Max Horkheimer and his Frankfurt School colleagues distinguished between traditional and critical theory based on the theory's political content – whether the theory assists in the process of social reproduction or is subversive of the established order (Therborn 1970). They argued that theory should be critical and

that theorists should strive to contribute to positive economic and social change.

Of course the field of ecology itself is sometimes viewed as a subversive subject (or science) because it advances fundamentally crucial challenges concerning humanity's 'right' to degrade the environment. Shepard (1969: 9) put it this way:

> The ideological status of ecology is that of a resistance movement. Its Rachel Carsons and Aldo Leopolds are subversive (as Sears recently called ecology itself). They challenge the public or private right to pollute the environment, to systematically destroy predatory animals, to spread chemical pesticides indiscriminately, to meddle chemically with food and water, to appropriate without hindrance space and surface for technological and military ends ...

Those who are not familiar with critical theory approaches may wonder how an emphasis on political factors can contribute to a better understanding of organizations and the natural environment and may think scientific investigators in all fields should avoid partisan interests. One response critical theorists make to this concern is the assertion that, because power is exercised everywhere, in all directions, politics cannot be avoided. There are no politically impartial social forces because every experience, action and event serves either to reinforce or undermine existing relations of power. The fact that we are not always aware of the political consequences of our actions does not mean that we can avoid being engaged in struggles that affect the world. In a wide variety of ways, we make political statements continuously that can be read by astute observers. Even in activities in which we strive to be unbiased, such as scientific work, critical theorists tend to believe there are at least political overtones. They believe it is more effective to be aware of interests and biases so that they can be considered when making and interpreting knowledge or truth claims. Through action and inaction, in all facets of our professional and personal lives, we exercise power and are (at least partially) the subjects of the forces of power in our midst. Therefore, we cannot avoid being engaged in politics and political neutrality is not possible.

For organization and management studies scholars, 'overtly' employing critical perspectives acknowledges the political content of organizations and organizational research. Grey (2004: 179) illustrated this point by stating: 'To engage in management, or to research management, is to commit to some kind of stance on political and moral values, such as the desirability of efficiency or of productivity or of profitability or, even, of employee satisfaction and well-being'. In this chapter, we invite organizational studies scholars to think politically about the natural environment and about the discourse on the NCE. Through the lens of critical theory and in the time-honored tradition of subversive work in the field of ecology, we will explore this new discourse and raise some fundamental questions about its relationship with the rest of green politics.

In the next section of the chapter, we review current authoritative assessments of the state of the environment and discuss one specific environmental problem – toxins – that is seen as emblematic of the environmental crisis tendencies facing humanity and the broader ecosystem. In the fourth section, we discuss several segments of the contemporary environmental movement, segments that are highly varied in how they respond to the environmental crisis. They provide a broader context for understanding the role of the NCE. In the fifth section, we focus specifically on the NCE and on some practical, organizational manifestations of it that are described in the burgeoning body of academic research devoted to understanding it. In this section, we elaborate the concept of the NCE, examine it from a meta-theoretical point of view, map the academic research on it, and critique it using concepts from critical theory. In the sixth section of the chapter, we argue that there is great potential to develop new models of organizational greening that go beyond the NCE and that have the capacity to address the institutional deficiencies and perverse politics underpinning the environmental crisis. The approach we suggest draws on Jurgen Habermas' theory of communicative rationality and the neo-Habermasian literature that extends the theory of communicative rationality to the natural environment. We close the chapter with a perspective on the contemporary environmental movement and the challenges facing organizational studies scholars who are interested in the NCE.

A Looming Global Environmental Crisis

We the undersigned, senior members of the world's scientific community, hereby warn all humanity of what lies ahead. A great change in our stewardship of the Earth and the life on it is required if vast human misery is to be avoided and our global home on this planet is not to be irretrievably mutilated (World Scientists 1996: 244).

'The World Scientists' Warning to Humanity', a document signed by 1575 scientists, including more than half of all living scientists awarded the Nobel Prize, contains some alarming language. Nearly a decade later, similar forebodings continue to be raised by numerous experts and groups from both the public and private sectors. In a recent, authoritative report offering a comprehensive picture of the health of the planet and reflecting the considered opinions of 1300 leading scientists from 95 countries, it is asserted that approximately two-thirds of the earth's ecosystems studied have been degraded significantly as a result of human activities (Millenium Ecosystem Assessment 2005). The report, praised by Secretary-General of the United Nations Kofi Annan as 'an unprecedented contribution to our global mission for development, sustainability and peace', (www.islandpress.org/books/detail.html), identifies several 'tipping points' that could abruptly lead to total environmental collapse and raises serious doubts about the earth's ability to continue to provide services essential to human survival and well-being. The Millenium Ecosystem Assessment report echoes similar, far-reaching concerns expressed by Secretary-General Annan on the 30th anniversary of the United Nations Conference on the Human Environment when he warned of 'the perilous state of the Earth and its resources' (Annan 2002: xiv). Annan (2002: xiv) also commented on the lack of progress in moving towards environmental health and sustainability:

Since the conference in 1972, the natural environment has borne the stresses imposed by a four-fold increase in human numbers and an 18-fold growth in world economic output. Despite the wealth of technologies, human resources, policy options and technical and scientific information at our disposal humankind has yet to break decisively with unsustainable and environmentally unsound policies and practices.

Outlining numerous human factors that are stressing the planet, Brown (2003: 3), founder and president of the Earth Policy Institute (and founder and past president of the Worldwatch Institute, a highly respected source of analytical information on the environment – see Wallis (1997)) recently wrote:

We are cutting trees faster than they can regenerate, overgrazing rangelands and converting them into deserts, over pumping aquifers, and draining rivers dry. On our cropland, soil erosion exceeds new soil formation, slowly depriving the soil of its inherent fertility. We are taking fish from the ocean faster than they can reproduce.

We are releasing carbon dioxide (CO_2) into the atmosphere faster than nature can absorb it, creating a greenhouse effect. As atmospheric CO_2 levels rise, so does the earth's temperature. Habitat destruction and climate change are destroying plant and animal species far faster than new species can evolve, launching the first mass extinction since the one that eradicated the dinosaurs 65 million years ago.

Voices from business organizations are also focusing on the impact of industry on the natural environment. For instance, Ray Anderson, chairman of Interface, Inc., the world's leading commercial carpet manufacturer and a leading advocate for sustainable industry, declared himself a 'plunderer of the Earth' after reading Hawken's (1993) *Ecology of Commerce*. Anderson was moved to do more than comply with the law. He was convicted to change the way his company does business:

One needs only to take the long view – the truly long view of evolutionary time – to know that the present take-make-waste linear system, driven by fossil fuels, wasteful and abusive of a finite biosphere, simply cannot go on and on and on (Anderson 2003: 18).

Not all scientists, policy analysts and other experts agree that the earth is, as one commentator put it (Connor 2005), on the 'brink of disaster'. However, given the complexity and fragility of nature's systems and the tendency for many negative environmental trends to 'spike' in unprecedented ways – simultaneously and in combinations – there is certainly reason for serious concern (Bright 2000). To the extent these negative synergistic forces present even greater dangers than most people realize, credence is added to the hypothesis of a looming, global environmental crisis.

Toxic Chemicals as Exemplar: Poison and Perverse Politics

If we are going to live so intimately with these chemicals – eating and drinking them – taking

them into the very marrow of our bones – we better know something about their nature and their power (Carson 1962: 25).

We are conducting a vast toxicologic experiment, and we are using our children as the experimental animals (Landrigan 2001).

What the General Public Still Does Not Know: Poison and Unbounded Risk

It can be reasonably argued that environmental degradation today, in its scope and severity, is unique in the history of human inhabitation of the planet. However, it would be easy to over-state the level of public awareness of the threats this poses. Some dimensions of environmental deterioration (such as global warming, depletion of the ozone layer and species extinction) regularly make news headlines and correspond well with various widely circulated, doomsday scenarios. Other negative trends seem to be less noticeable and do not alarm people as much despite their profoundly destructive impact on the ecosystem and human health. To illustrate, consider the deleterious environmental effects of synthetic chemicals. While some chemicals are thought to be a relatively benign and beneficial part of the 'chemical economy', one of the world's largest and most diverse industrial sectors, a vast number are not (McGinn 2002: 77–80). What causes greatest concern among experts is the thorough assimilation of synthetic chemicals into daily life in the absence of evidence to support their safety. In fact, the immediate and cumulative environmental impacts of synthetic chemicals are not fully known. Yet, their proliferation continues. Even seemingly innocuous industries produce chemicals that can harm human beings and the broader ecosystem. For example, most people are not aware that cotton growing accounts for ~ 25% of the world's insecticide use (see Rowledge et al. 1999: Case 4). Another generally unseen and unrecognized part of the problem is that some chemicals that have been phased out for decades, such as dichlorodiphenyl-trichloroethane (DDT), still pose significant risks.[1] Indeed, the risks from synthetic chemicals are so widespread and so substantial that human health suffers due to exposure as people perform their daily work and organize their households. To wit, a number of recent studies show that occupational exposure to agrochemicals has implications for reproductive, respiratory and neurological health and can have long-term carcinogenic effects (Arcury et al. 2001; Greenlee et al. 2004; Lu 2005). And, data are now emerging on the injurious effects of low-dose concentrations of pesticides in residential use (Greenlee et al. 2004).

Perverse Politics

In what follows, we continue with the case of toxic chemicals (the source of a multitude of seemingly intractable environmental disputes) to illustrate the perverse politics underpinning the environmental crisis. It is important to understand that the environmental crisis results in part from toxic chemicals, pollution and other agents that threaten, degrade and destabilize biospheric processes but also in part from, organizational and institutional failure in dealing with the biophysical problems. In his prescient book, *Risk Society*, German sociologist Beck (1992) identified toxic chemicals as emblematic of contemporary environmental problems because they highlight the inability of existing institutions and political processes to prevent threats to the ecosystem. To Beck, toxic chemicals create new forms of risk and are one major element in the 'risk society'. They generate consequences that can be irreversible, incalculable, uninsurable and unlimited in time and space (Beck 1992). Moreover, current systems of assessment and regulation of toxic chemicals support Beck's analysis of the 'organized irresponsibility' built into the institutional structure of the risk society whereby elite groups fail to acknowledge the seriousness of the problems they have collectively caused and delay efforts (intentionally or unintentionally) to solve the problems (Beck 1995: 24). For instance, in 1989, the Congress of the US finally moved against leaded gasoline. However, by that time, over 60 years since the first calls for precaution in its use by the Surgeon General of the US, seven million metric tons of toxic lead dust had been distributed into the environment (Montague 1999).

Governmental systems are currently faced with at least 1700 new chemicals each year. In the US, for example, testing procedures for carcinogeneity can cost more than half a million dollars and take up to 3 years to complete (Kellow 1999; Thornton 2000; US Office of Management and Budget 2004).[2] Over the next decade and a half, the global production of chemicals is expected to increase by 85% (Toepfer 2005). Despite two decades of scientific recommendations, there are still no real attempts to test the synergistic effects of chemicals (Nichols and

Crawford 1983; Kiesecker et al. 2004). They still are assessed as single entities, despite the almost incalculable numbers of mixtures possible from the 70 000 known chemicals in existence.

The history of the chemical industry illuminates the clear path that has led to this current state. Before the 1960s, the production, use and regulation of chemicals went undisputed (Hough 1998). Their value to society was taken as given. They were seen as an essential component in a mixture of technological optimism, development and growth that defined the post-war economy and restricted wider debate (Hoffman 2001). In the case of pesticides in the US, for example, a 'subgovernment'[3] of manufacturers, government officials and users deployed the discourse of 'agriculture' and 'progress' to establish hegemony over issue definition and celebrate the wonders of the avalanche of new chemical technologies (Bosso 1987).

The publication of Carson's (1962) pioneering book *Silent Spring* first raised political attention to ecosystem problems and is often credited with spawning the contemporary environmental movement (Briggs 1997; Waddell 2000). *Silent Spring* was significant because it challenged the values and norms of the chemical industry and began raising awareness of possible problems (Bosso 1987; Hoffman and Ocasio 2001). It politicized the production of toxic chemicals by highlighting contradictory perceptions from inside and outside the industry. To the clientele of the industry and other insiders, chemicals increased industrial productivity and helped manage disease; to outsiders, chemicals were now linked to new problems of frighteningly unknown dimensions. Carson confronted the subgovernmental forces and challenged science on its own grounds. She identified the residual, persistent effects of chemicals and the error of basing scientific, corporate and administrative decision-making on assimilative capacity (O'Riordan and Cameron 1994).

The immediate source of dispute after the publication of *Silent Spring* was the effect of pesticides on wildlife. However, it was not until the 1970s that institutional deficiencies in the production and regulation of chemicals became recognized (Jasanoff 1990; Montague 2004a). The Vietnam War highlighted the effects of defoliants, prestigious scientific journals published data showing higher rates of illness in children living near Love Canal in New York, and many thousands of deaths occurred after a leak of methyl isocyanate at the Union Carbide plant in Bhopal, India. In short, it took the broadening of the discourse to encompass human health for toxic chemicals to emerge as a specific policy issue (Hough 1998).

In the last two decades, there has been a rapid expansion and diversification of social movements concerned with toxins and other intractable industrial problems. In the US, for example, the pesticide subgovernment has shifted to a more pluralistic approach as the scope of issue conflict has widened to include a range of environmental and public interest groups. Yet one important lesson from this is that the multiplication of formal environmental organizations has not enabled much wider participation in decision-making. As a matter of their own survival, mainstream environmental groups prioritized gaining access to power, rather than broadening the debate to include local communities and the wider public (see Schlosberg 1999). These nationally-based organizations, embedded in systems of liberal, pluralist politics, are structurally unable to deal with the vast number of 'chemical wars' (Montague 2004a,b) waged at hundreds of thousands of toxic sites, across Europe, the US, Australia and now multiplying across the South.[4] Each is associated with their own 'risk community', each with its own set of diverse actors struggling for voice (Benn 2004). These local war zones are emblematic in that they are playing out the major failings of liberal pluralist nation-states and institutions in dealing with disputes over toxins and other environmental issues. A flawed assumption is that all interest groups have access to highly technical and interdisciplinary areas of knowledge *and* the resources to deal with high degrees of uncertainty (Eckersley 2004). This discourse, steeped in administrative 'rationalism' that demands proof with certain and impartial knowledge, obviously presents a major problem (Torgerson 1990; Dryzek 1997). As Montague (2004b: 1) puts it: 'Risk assessment serves corporate purposes because it involves large quantities of scientific data, all of it subject to limitations and uncertainties that can be disputed forever without resolution. Where data are lacking or disputed, assumptions and judgements can be substituted for fact'.

Accompanying the spread of environmentalism by means of more formal organizational developments during the late 1970s and 1980s, the grassroots environmental justice network emerged in the US as an eclectic response to local toxic sites (Szasz 1994; Rhodes 2003). Lois Gibbs, founder of the Love Canal Homeowners' Association, describes how the movement offers an alternative to the national environmental groups: '… the primary goal of grassroots groups that we work with is prevention. The mainstream, natural environmental groups are really about management and control' (Livesey 2003: 499).

The movement was lent support by a landmark 1987 study finding that 'race was the most significant variable in determining the location of risk-producing facilities' (Gauna and Foster 2003: 2). It has since snowballed, networking myriad social critiques and localized concerns at the unjust distribution of other forms of environmental degradation. Despite developing into a potent discourse in the public realm (Kurtz 2005), the environmental justice movement is confronted by serious challenges in the political administrative sphere. It has been criticized for flaws in its empirical data and for being more about irrational fear and traditional class-based politics than about 'rational mechanisms' for managing the issue (Bowen and Wells 2002: 689).

Lois Gibbs portrays the obstacles in dealing with the gulf between local understandings of risk and 'administrative rationality':

> … one time (New York State) Governor Carey came to Love Canal and made what we believed was a promise to evacuate us. But we didn't know how to read political gobbledegoo. What he actually said was that *if* you are sick, and *if* your home is found to be contaminated, and those two things are *linked*, we will relocate you. Not knowing there was no way to link this stuff, we celebrated (Livesey 2003: 492, emphasis in original).

As Gauna and Foster (2003: 4) put it: 'The highly technical arena of environmental regulation is a pervasively unequal playing field'. In a movement spearheaded by women, the forces of administrative rationality are traditionally skewed in opposition. Gibbs again: 'They call me the mother of the Superfund. I don't know if I am the mother or not. But when Superfund comes up for re-authorization, they ask the boys to talk about the details, the technical stuff' (Livesey 2003: 497).

Globalization promises both to ease and to further confound the environmental problems generated by toxic chemicals. The Stockholm Convention on Persistent Organic Pollutants (POPs), an international agreement designed to outlaw the 'dirty dozen' is evidence of recent progress. However, externalization of risk from the North to the South continues. There are numerous reports of illegal Southeast Asian workshops where villagers work long hours recycling computers from Europe and the US, unprotected from toxic fumes and other hazards (Bouman 2002; Hill and Dhanda 2004). A related problem that is also a contested terrain is the marginalizing of local practices and needs, made possible in the first instance through an elitist and trivialized concept of sustainable development (cf. Yearley 1996; Newton 2002; Banerjee 2003). While chemical companies patent alternatives to pesticides banned by the North, the South is blamed for its hesitancy in banning older versions (Hough 1998). As Shiva (1993: 152) put it: '"Global" concerns thus create the moral base for green imperialism'.

As the emblematic case of toxic chemicals illustrates, environmental problems can be severe, far-reaching and easy to underestimate. They pose serious challenges to the biosphere and to local, national and international political administrative systems, which tend to not be organized to address root causes. Subpolitical regimes distract attention from and perversely perpetuate the problem. And, toxic chemicals are only one part of the environmental crisis. From chemical contamination to reductions in biodiversity and species extinction, from deforestation and desertification to degradation of the soil, from aquifer diminution and marine pollution to water and food shortages, from the depletion of sources of energy and other natural resources to air pollution, waste and global warming, the facets of the environmental problem are deeply interwoven and its contour is indeed global. This case also illustrates the importance of taking a critical perspective in analysing and solving environmental problems as it highlights the existing institutionalization of perverse forms of politics and the current inadequacy of both nationally based environmental organizations and local forms of environmental activism.

Responding to the Global Environmental Crisis: Meta-Theory and Contemporary Forms of Green Politics

Meta-theory and the New Ecological Paradigm

Despite the magnitude of the complex environmental problems facing humanity and the powerful forces that tend to hamper effective responses, a broad range of formal and informal activism exists and there is reason to believe that forms of activism are spreading globally (Radcliffe 2000; Clapp and Dauvergne 2005). To set the stage for a richer interpretation of the NCE, we now turn to a brief overview of forms of contemporary environmentalism and their paradigmatic roots.

Politics in relation to the natural environment could be traced back centuries, as there is a long history of the impact of human civilization on the earth. While sensitive observers in previous eras recognized that human need and greed would eventually come into conflict with the welfare of other elements of nature and even with the physical limits of the biosphere (e.g. see John Muir in Bade 1924), the notion of environmental politics as a response to escalating environmental problems did not become prominent until the last third of the 20th century. During that period, a large wave of public activism culminated in legislative and regulatory activity institutionalizing concern in many nation-states about environmental degradation and destruction.

The notion of green politics first began gaining widespread attention in the early 1980s when green parties emerged in Germany and elsewhere. Meta-theoretically, green politics can mean many different things even though it is often associated colloquially with uncompromising environmental thought and activism. When it is associated with various forms of radical ecological thought, many of which emerged during this time, including the new ecological paradigm (NEP), the inherent political nature of environmentalism becomes clear (see Catton and Dunlap 1978; Egri and Pinfield 1996; Buttel and Humphrey 2002; Clapp and Dauvergne 2005). The NEP provides a coherent counterpoint to the dominant social paradigm (DSP) and sharpens the distinction between reform and radical green politics. For example, the relationship between humans and the rest of nature from the philosophical base of the DSP is grounded in very strong anthropocentrism, which accepts human domination of the rest of nature. From reform environmentalism and its modified anthropocentrism, the emphasis is on human stewardship of nature. From the NEP, the relationship is grounded in the philosophy of ecocentrism, which tends to value all species relatively equally and is opposed to human privilege and domination. Whereas the DSP advocates human progress in terms of unlimited economic expansion and material growth, and reform environmentalism construes progress in terms of sustainable development, the philosophy of the NEP emphasizes a broader concept of progress, one that emphasizes holistic balance among the elements of nature, careful protection of the non-human environment due to its fragility and irreplaceability, and comprehensive environmental and social justice (cf. Egri and Pinfield 1996; Buttel and Humphrey 2002; Clapp and Daugvergne 2005).

Contemporary Forms of Green Politics

Diversity in ecophilosophical assumptions manifests in radically different underlying paradigms and the paradigms produce different forms of green politics. Some are relatively conservative, some favour incremental reformism and some endorse more radical approaches. What is referred to as the green movement is actually highly diverse and might be better described as a collection of movements. It includes segments that tend to express concern for the environment through work in institutions and those that operate more through activism and direct action. The most visible activists in the green political movement in North America and Western Europe tend to be members of Greenpeace, Friends of the Earth, Earth First!, the Earth Liberation Front, the Animal Liberation Front and other autonomous, non-profit, political organizations that take a more uncompromising position in opposition to environmental degradation. Some members of these organizations are convinced that environmental problems are so severe and institutional constraints are so binding that legislative and other traditional methods of social change are ineffective. They practice civil disobedience and even engage in violent direct action, including ecotage (radical acts in defense of the environment) and other guerilla warfare tactics (see Foreman 1985; CBS *Sixty Minutes* 2001; Carmen and Balser 2002; Best and Nocella 2004). For instance, 35 Greenpeace protesters, dressed as workers, recently made international media headlines by chaining themselves to an assembly line in a plant in the UK that produces the Range Rover sports utility vehicle. They wanted the Ford Motor Company, parent of Range Rover's producer Land Rover, to stop manufacturing and marketing the vehicles for urban consumers because of their extremely low gas mileage and effects on global warming through greenhouse-gas emissions

(Associated Press, 'Greenpeace protesters arrested at UK Land Rover plant', 16 May 2005). Analysts contend that, despite their small numbers, militant environmentalists have a disproportionately large impact on the mass media and on public consciousness (e.g. Zimmerman 1994; Hay 2002).

It would be mistaken, however, to associate contemporary green politics exclusively with militant environmental activism. Highly visible leaders like Jonathan Porritt (former director of Friends of the Earth, founder of Forum of the Future, and – as current Chair of the UK's Sustainable Development Commission – key advisor on environmental issues to the British Prime Minister Tony Blair) have great sympathy for the concerns and ideals of those advocating a fundamental shift in values and patterns of production and consumption. Like many other contemporary environmentalists, though, Porritt has distanced himself from militant forms of direct action and continues to believe that being 'green' is fully compatible with a '*non-violent* ... overthrow of [the] whole polluting, plundering and materialistic industrial society' (quoted in Dobson 1990: 7, emphasis added). Conservationist organizations such as the Sierra Club add a politically conservative voice (Radcliffe 2000).

Another level of contemporary green politics has emerged in the form of international institutions and governance structures (e.g., The United Nations Conference on Environment and Development, Rio de Janeiro, 1992; Kyoto Protocol to the United Nations Framework Convention on Climate Change, 1997 (in effect 2005); The United Nations Commission for Sustainable Development Conference, Toronto, 1999; The Stockholm Convention on Persistent Organic Pollutants, 2001 (in effect 2004)), giving rise to a new global environmental politics (see Paterson 2000; selections in Barry and Eckersley 2005). Given the scale of many environmental problems, it makes sense that co-operative international arrangements would be launched but their development is often problematic. For example, the recent refusal of the US under the George W. Bush administration to cut its greenhouse gas emissions by the 7% required by the Kyoto Protocol temporarily disabled ratification of the accord until Russia's recent ratification. This has been very controversial because the US, an original signatory on the accord, accounts for ~ 5% of the world's population and ~ 25% of the earth's greenhouse gas emissions. Another illustration of the perverse nature of the global politics of the environment is that the World Bank, the agency that wrote the recent Millenium Development Goals advocating sustainable development, has since 1992 funded more than $25 billion worth of fossil fuel exploration and development (Juniper and Brown 2005). One-third of current World Bank funding is dedicated to providing supports for indebted governments which, in exchange, agree to follow the pro-growth advice of the World Bank in 'reforming' their economic policies (Clapp and Dauvergne 2005).

Contemporary green politics also operates in official parties within nation-states. While green political parties have captured only a small percentage of the formal vote count in nation-state electoral politics and face an up-hill battle when it comes to seating legislators, their presence in Europe, Australia, Japan, North America and elsewhere appears to be relatively secure and their influence on policy-making, while usually indirect through the traditional parties, should not be under-estimated (cf. Rootes 1997; Carter 2005; Clapp and Dauvergne 2005). What is significant about the green parties is that the philosophy underwriting their agendas is very comprehensive. By focusing on economic and environmental sustainability, social justice and equal opportunity and democratic participation (among other core concerns), they can be seen to parallel some of the most radical forms of ecological thought (cf. Hay 2002; Clapp and Dauvergne 2005). They also appear to have the potential to overlap and share energy with other social movements. Thus, despite the legislative orientation and reformist rather than radical tendencies, green party politics has not yet been co-opted and is difficult to dismiss as merely a reinforcement of the status quo (cf. Malzahn 2005; Global Green Charter at www.europeangreens.org/info/globalgreencharter.html).

A criticism of green politics has been that it is elitist, appealing more to middle and upper income people who have the privileges that make grass-roots activism less demanding and lifestyle re-orientation more feasible. The emergence and recent expansion of the voluntary simplicity movement (see http://www.poppyware.com/pna/vsres.html) in North America and Western Europe provides an interesting illustration of this point. Voluntary simplicity refers to a lifestyle decision to limit consumption without being coerced to do so by poverty, imprisonment or other constraint. It also involves cultivation of non-materialist sources of meaning and gratification (Etzioni 1998; Schor 1998; Maniates 2002). It is not surprising that this movement (also referred to as 'ecological living' because of its intended positive impact on the natural environment, (Elgin 1993; www.ecological-living.info)) emerged in one of the most affluent regions of the world.

In our illustration of subpolitics and the chemical economy, we drew attention to another grassroots movement that has emerged but that tends to be more rooted in poor and minority communities and focused on environmental justice concerns (see Rhodes 2003). These individuals and groups use legal and ancillary means to challenge corporate and other powerful interests who continue the long-time practice of situating hazardous technologies and toxic emissions in impoverished and minority areas. For example, in April 2001, a group of ~ 1500 plaintiffs from the rural southern area of Sweet Valley/Cobb Town, Alabama in the US won a toxic exposure lawsuit against Solutia (a chemical company spin-off of the Monsanto Corporation) worth nearly 43 million dollars. Residents of the community formed a coalition because they believed contamination of their area with polychlorinated biphenyls (PCBs) was the result of discrimination and violated federal law. As is typical in environmental justice actions, the coalition was strengthened with attorneys from public interest organizations (e.g. The African-American Environmental Justice Action Network and the Southern Organizing Committee for Economic and Social Justice). PCBs became illegal in 1978 but there was evidence reported in the case that Monsanto held high-level corporate meetings in which they demonstrated knowledge of the hazards posed by PCBs but decided not to inform the community and not to discontinue technologies that entailed PCBs ('Monsanto Litigation Settlement in Alabama', Associated Press, 29 April 2001).

As can be seen from this overview, the idea that there is only one form of green politics, a distinctly radical and uncompromising project aimed at producing fundamental change, lacks validity. There are many varieties of green politics and the range is instructive for interpreting what it means to be green in the world of corporations and other organizations. In the chapter's next section, we map streams of academic research that help us understand manifestations of the NCE and zoom in on some of the more promising areas of study. The purpose of this section is to elaborate the concept of the NCE, as an organizational phenomenon and as a scholarly accomplishment, placing it in the broader context of green politics and opening it up for further evaluation and critique.

The New Corporate Environmentalism as Green Politics

Basic Concepts

We defined the NCE as *rhetoric* concerning the central role of business in achieving economic growth and ecological rationality and as a *guide* for management that emphasizes voluntary, proactive control of environmental impacts in ways that exceed or go beyond environmental laws and regulatory compliance. The NCE typically involves promoting continued economic growth through open and competitive trade, advocacy of industry self-regulation as the best form of environmental protection, appropriate communication with stakeholders and striving for cleaner production and eco-efficiency through technological innovation, structural design and/or culture change motivated by deep learning (cf. Schmidheiny 1992; Wasik 1996; Morelli 1999; Gordon 2001; Holliday et al. 2002; Lyon and Maxwell 2004; also see Karliner 1997).

We refer to the NCE as *rhetoric* because it is a relatively coherent set of ideas that is advanced with oratorical and literary skill to influence the political discourse on the environment. The NCE is, first and foremost, about control. It is focused on who should control the impact of production on the environment. It contends that business should regulate itself, whether it assumes and advocates this at the level of the corporation, the industry, the sector or other levels of commerce. This theme is illustrated well by one influential spokesperson for the NCE, Swiss Industrialist Stephen Schmidheiny, founder of the Business Council for Sustainable Development and principle author of the NCE manifesto *Changing Course* (1992). He was quoted in Volume 1 of *Tomorrow – The Magazine for Business and the Environment* (1999: 8) as follows: 'I think that industry needs to do many things which government now regulates. [For example], if you talk about introducing better, more environmentally friendly technologies, who else would develop them

if not industry?' Statements like this are typical in the NCE rhetoric and reflect an underlying assumption that business must play the key leadership role in environmentalism while government's role is minimized. Schmidheiny and others in the World Business Council for Sustainable Development also argue that economic 'gains for business do not necessarily have to be losses for the environment and ... vice versa' (Holliday et al. 2002: 16), setting up an appealing win-win scenario that is a central belief in this rhetoric (also see Hawken 1993; Hawken et al. 1999). In a keynote speech on sustainable forestry to the Yale University School of Forestry and Environmental Studies in 2000, Schmidheiny provided a glimpse into the NCE vision of how business should reform itself while avoiding direct action by militant NGOs: 'the challenge is reforming the poor performers in industry, and in keeping fringe NGOs from counterproductive actions' (http://www.avina.net/ImagesAvina/sts_speech%20 forests.pdf).

We refer to the NCE as a *guide* for management because it is a set of ideas with practical significance for directive leadership, both in organizations and in the broader society. It seeks to direct thinking and action and specify courses to be pursued in corporations and in other organizations. It provides models and examples of best practice and criteria for excellence and rationality. It instructs visionary leaders to break their vision down into 'bite sized chunks of objectives, action plans and measurable results' (Holliday et al. 2002: 139) and gauges the worth of a vision based on the simplicity and clarity of the message and the 'reality of ... activity and performance measures' (Holliday et al. 2002: 129). The practical centre-piece of the NCE is environmental management and the core of environmental management at the turn of the 21st century to the present involves a variety of voluntary approaches to environmental protection that go *beyond compliance* with existing legal requirements (see Carraro and Leveque 1999; Morelli 1999; Reinhardt 2000; Lyon and Maxwell 2004). Some approaches are extremely well structured, such as the systems of formal environmental management. Others rely more on experimental organizational learning, change and development activities that seek to transform the cultures of organizations and industries with the expectation that eco-sensitive mission statements, codes of conduct, stories and rituals, material symbols and other cultural elements will enhance eco-efficiency. Technological innovation aimed at enhancing environmental performance through reducing waste and implementing cleaner production systems is also a central component of the NCE and is illustrated through numerous examples in the guidebooks (e.g. Holliday et al. 2002: Chapters 3 and 8).

We refer to contemporary corporate environmentalism as 'new' because it is only within the last decade or so that a relatively coherent and widely circulated set of ideas emerged specifying a new set of leadership responsibilities for business in relation to the natural environment and identifying a variety of techniques for enhancing corporate environmental performance. Thus, the NCE combines a specific voluntary leadership role for the corporate sector in environmental policy-making with the powerful symbolism of using comprehensive, 'rational' management approaches to address the environment. During this period, *macro* corporate environmentalism has shifted, at least at the level of rhetoric, towards a voluntary environmental leadership role. The NCE opened up a domain of corporate leadership and influence on environmental policy-making that had previously received only limited attention. This manifested in more proactive and strategic industry associations that promised ambitious self-regulation and business consortia and diplomatic alliances that sought to influence international treaties and conventions and redefine how the natural environment fit with economic growth and unfettered trade (Karliner 1997; Bruno and Karliner 2002). During this period, *micro* corporate environmentalism has also shifted from acts of compliance with environmental laws and regulations (through limited organizational means) to more comprehensive new systems of organizing that respond to the 'second generation' of regulatory dynamics. These systems emphasize voluntarism and advocate imaginative corporate environmental management (Gunningham et al. 2003). Indeed, micro corporate environmentalism is characterized by a new awareness, one that promotes recognition and integration of environmental concerns into the centre of the firm's strategic decision-making process (cf. Banerjee 2002a). The NCE takes protecting the natural environment from a fringe issue to a core strategic business issue that can, according to the rhetoric, establish sustainable advantage and reap concrete financial benefits for the corporation if performed well.

Academic Research on the NCE

Rapid Expansion of the Field

The history of academic research on corporate environmentalism is relatively brief. Starik and Marcus (2000), in their discussion of the literature on organizations and the natural environment, suggest that the field of study began in the late 1980s with scholarship primarily in the form of case studies, dissertations and dissertation-based articles, textbooks and textbook supplements. Early review pieces, including Egri and Pinfield's (1996) chapter in the first edition of the *Handbook*, focused mostly on conference papers and proceedings, discussion and working papers and a few select book chapters because there were very few theoretical and empirical studies that could be found in the research literature (see also Gladwin 1993; Starik 1995). In a cogently argued statement that both marked the limited state of research in this area in a memorable way and that has become something of a manifesto, Shrivastava (1994) pointed out that organizational studies and management researchers had developed concepts of organizational environments that severed organizations from nature. Based on a reversal of figure and ground and a misrepresentation of the ontological status of nature, these concepts prevented scholars from engaging seriously with the natural environment as an area of inquiry. He called for a more nature-centred (green) approach to the field and for a fundamental re-theorization of organizations that pays genuine attention to organization-nature relationships. Gladwin et al. (1995) commented on the paucity of attention to the natural environment in the literatures of strategic management, stakeholder theory, business ethics and management studies in general, noting that phrases such as biosphere, environmental quality, ecosystem and sustainable development were virtually absent from the scholarship. According to Gladwin et al., for the period January 1990 to January 1994 less than one-third of 1% of the abstracts of articles contained in the Abstracted Business Information/INFORM Database (ABI/Inform) made mention of these phrases.

It is widely held that there has been a vast expansion of academic research on corporate environmentalism over the past decade, an expansion that coincided with the emergence of the NCE as a domain of corporate leadership in the environmental policy-making arena and as a set of organizational innovations and practices (cf. Starik and Marcus 2000; Banerjee 2002b; Kallio and Markkanen 2006). To track the extent of the expansion and to update earlier assessments of the state of the art of research, we conducted our own analysis of trends represented by scholarly texts contained in the ABI/Inform (ProQuest) Global Database. ABI/ Inform Global, which contains over two million documents, is the standard on-line database for electronic search and retrieval of business, management and organizational literature (see Ojala 2002). Using the keywords and search criteria selected by Gladwin et al. (1995), we were able to closely replicate their findings for the period 1990–1994. For those 5 years, a total of 218 769 documents were found (an average of 43 754 per year), of which 484 (an average of 97 per year) met the keywords and search criteria. In contrast, for the most recent 5 years available (2000–2004), a total of 287 097 documents were found (an average of 57 419 per year), of which 2536 (an average of 507 per year) met the keywords and search criteria. Thus, while total scholarly documents increased by ~ 31% comparing the two periods (1990–1994 and 2000–2004), research on environment-related topics, as estimated by keywords matched in titles and abstracts, increased by over 500%. For the years 2003 and 2004 this constitutes ~ 1% of total scholarly documents listed for all topics.

Using more liberal search criteria, with keywords that encompass Gladwin et al.'s (1995) terms and terms added that provide a somewhat different interpretation of the language of corporate environmental scholars (environmentalism, natural environment, greening, environmental management, biosphere, natural resources, sustainable development), we found a similar but less extreme pattern. For the period 1990–1994, an average of 217 documents per year met the search criteria while for the period 2000–2004, an average of 723 documents per year met the search criteria. This pattern shows an increase of over 300% in environment-related studies and an increase of over 250% in environment-related studies relative to the total scholarly documents listed for all topics.

For the period 1990–2004, using either Gladwin et al.'s (1995) search criteria or our more extensive criteria, it is accurate to state both (1) that there has been a sizable expansion of published research on environment-related topics that increased in absolute numbers nearly every year and (2) that the percentage of scholarly research devoted to environment-related topics (relative to total articles listed) increased nearly every year and increased dramatically as a total over the 15 years. While these increases are impressive in some ways, it should be pointed out that the results showed *rapid increases in the absolute numbers* of scholarly articles published on environment-related topics but still *very small percentages of articles* on environment-related topics relative to what was listed for all topics (typically ~ 1%). This pattern held whether we used search criteria developed by Gladwin et al. (1995) or our own search criteria (even including other keywords such as pollution). This means that for every study on an environment-related topic in the organizations, management and business literature, there are 99 others that do not significantly address environmental issues.[5]

One of the positive things that has distinguished research on corporate environmentalism (and its researchers) is that on a regular basis, scholars have been willing to be introspective and to take stock of the field. Kallio and Markkannen (2006) identified over two dozen sources that have made a contribution to discussions of the development and status of research on corporate environmentalism. It would be impossible for any single review to be comprehensive enough to catalogue all the research on corporate environmentalism that has been published since Egri and Pinfield (1996) mapped the domain. Their task was relatively simple because most of the relevant research up to that point focused on comparing and contrasting the dominant paradigm with its reformist and radical alternatives. Therefore, we do not attempt to capture all the specific trends and angles that have developed in the field during the past 10 years. Especially given the broader purposes of our chapter and space limitations, our contribution to mapping the specific contours of the field is accomplished primarily by focusing on the three integrative questions that researchers have most frequently addressed. We base some of our mapping on key review studies that have already taken an accounting and on the critical perspective we think is particularly needed in this area of study.

Theoretical Pluralism and Core Research Questions

A good place to begin to provide a sense of what has been accomplished with the expansion of research on corporate environmentalism discussed above is with Sharma's (2002) summary of the academic disciplines and theories that have guided scholars. Sharma (2002) and Starik (2002) interviewed 24 active scholars on the state of the research on corporate environmentalism and summarized their opinions. What is most striking about Sharma's (2002) recounting of the disciplines and theories that researchers believe have guided scholarly work is the sheer number involved. He lists nearly 20 theories and all the major business and social science disciplines, suggesting that green issues are now relevant to at least some small part of every major discipline and numerous established theoretical streams. Interestingly, one of the major questions scholars have debated remains unanswered: should environment-related researchers develop their own theories or does the value of this type of work lie in advancing a unique and important problem context that has been neglected or ignored (Sharma 2002: 3)? Research that applies or illustrates existing theories continues to proliferate and there is no apparent sense of urgency with respect to or movement toward developing theories that are unique to the environment. In as much as the natural environment is the broadest of conceivable contexts, encompassing everything human and non-human within its domain, it seems likely that it will be some time before scholars agree upon the best way to theorize and study it.

In light of the wide diversity in theoretical streams and academic disciplines that are involved in environment-related research, perhaps one of the most integrative approaches to mapping contours and identifying trends in the field involves looking at the main research questions that have been posed. Gladwin (1993: 44–5) took this approach in his classic essay when he challenged researchers to determine how organizational greening really works: 'What is it? Why does it happen? Who does it happen to? When does it happen? Where does it happen? How does it happen? And what are the consequences of it happening?' It appears that much research has been conducted that is in line with these basic questions raised by Gladwin (1993). In our view, there are three abstract questions that capture much of the scope of the research conducted over the past decade. We will turn our attention to these questions and their associated research streams before beginning an overall assessment of the current state of the field.

The question that is most fundamental in this area of research is: *What is corporate greening?* The concept of corporate greening is potentially very powerful, but it has nearly as many definitions as there are scholars who use the term. Rasanen et al. (1995) remarked that it remains unclear what greening actually has amounted to in organizational systems as opposed to what it could be. They pointed out that greening is a new 'catch phrase', covering a diverse set of organizational activities. Indeed, over the past several years, virtually every organizational component, process, product and by-product has been related in theory (or more casually) to the process of greening (Jermier and Forbes 2003). For example, Shrivastava's (1996) framework for the greening of business is centred on green production, but it also emphasizes green resource use (from procurement to recycling), green energy conservation, green transportation, green facilities, green products and green employees. Along with environmentally-sensitive manufacturing, Buchholz's (1998) framework includes environmental marketing, strategy and communication. Kolk (2000) discusses process-oriented and product-oriented environmental management and broadens notions of greening to include environmental management systems and standards, environmental reporting and environmental accounting. Other frameworks include more macro phenomena, such as green partnerships that involve ecolabelling and certification programmes, alliances with NGOs and voluntary agreements implemented by industry associations (e.g. Wasik 1996; Gordon 2001; see selections in Utting 2002). At the most macro level, greening can be understood to include business coalitions (e.g. World Business Council for Sustainable Development, International Chamber of Commerce), consortia composed of businesses, governmental and non-governmental organizations (e.g. Global Reporting Initiative, Coalition for Environmentally Responsible Economies, United Nations Global Compact) and even global forums and regulatory mechanisms such as conferences, conventions, trusteeship councils and treaties, whether sponsored by the United Nations or not (cf. Deere and Esty 2002; Kolk and Mauser 2002; Utting 2002; Barnett 2004; Klee and Coles 2004; Clapp and Dauvergne 2005; selections in Barry and Eckersley 2005).

While researchers have not made constructing a precise definition of corporate greening a priority, most endorse the idea that it has to do with showing increasing concern for preserving, protecting and restoring the natural environment through the voluntary actions of individuals, subgroups in organizations, organizations themselves or sets of organizations (cf. Starik and Marcus 2000). At the micro level of the firm and beyond, they tend to rely on Hoffman's (2001: 14) notion that: '... there is no such thing as a "green company". The best one can do is describe the progression of how companies are "going green"'.

One integrative theoretical approach to describing how companies are going green has taken the form of building stage models. Beginning with Hunt and Auster's (1990) classic framework, which specifies a five-stage development continuum ranging from organizations that address environmental concerns with band-aid solutions ('beginners') to organizations that implement fully integrative systems ('proactivists'), scholars have proposed over 50 frameworks that compare and contrast the varieties of corporate and organizational greening (see Kolk and Mauser 2002 for review). The frameworks differ considerably in what they use to identify facets of greening and in how rigidly they specify progression through the stages. Some frameworks focus on technological change and other relatively narrow facets while others attempt to use more comprehensive criteria, such as implementation of an environmental management system (often considered as the 'hard core' of corporate greening (Eisner 2004: 148)), the degree of environmental sensitivity in corporate strategy, or even infusion of an organization's culture. One of the more interesting assertions advanced by several scholars in this literature is the idea that developing a green organizational culture is the *essential ingredient* in generating successful environmental performance (e.g. Callenbach et al. 1993; Halme 1996; Petts et al. 1999). Emphasis is placed on the role of learning processes in heightening the environmental awareness of employees, inculcating eco-sensitive values and in recognizing and acting on opportunities for making environmental improvements, all of which are necessary for evolutionary cultural development (also see Halme 2002; Cramer 2005). At this point, it is not clear that greening organizations monolithically, through system-wide culture change, is possible or even desirable. Researchers have found that extreme external pressure (e.g. consumer boycott) is necessary for firms to rethink their cultural assumptions (e.g. Neale 1997), that during cultural greening the environment can lose moral significance for employees and inhibit the critical, personal reflection necessary for solving environmental problems (cf. Sinclair 1993; Crane 2000), and that actual organizations are described better with subculture theory and perform better with subculture diversity (see Jermier and Forbes 2003). Similarly, some critics have challenged the popular view of organizational greening as a linear, one-dimensional progression toward heightened environmental sensitivity and ecocentric management by arguing that this approach oversimplifies developmental processes (e.g. Schaefer and Harvey 1998). Kolk and Mauser (2002) echo this concern, suggesting that most stage models cannot be meaningfully operationalized and provide a poor fit, even in case study research, to actual corporate development and environmental performance.

Although there are no clear and consensual answers to the question about what corporate greening is, some progress has been made in eliminating oversimplified frameworks. What has emerged are 'second generation' stage models that differentiate better between indicators of environmental performance and environmental management (outcome vs process measures), between forms of environmental management, and among indicators appropriate for reporting to internal operators, regulatory agencies, other stakeholders and the broader public (Kolk and Mauser 2002; also see Gilley et al. 2000). What has also been clarified is that corporate greening involves exceeding in some way (in the form of appearances or in actual measured processes and outcomes) regulatory compliance. It is based on how voluntary and proactive various agents and agencies are in their orientation toward and/or their implementation of comprehensive approaches to environmental protection and/or their ability to limit natural resource use and reduce pollution (cf. Kolk and Mauser 2002; Gunningham et al. 2003; Lyon and Maxwell 2004). While most theorists have conceptualized these phenomena at the level of the organization or at the level of industry and trade associations, some illuminating research on macro corporate greening also can be found (e.g. Susskind 1992; Levy 1997; Beamish 2001; Utting 2002; Alkon 2004; Foster and York 2004; Orsato and Clegg 2005; York and Foster 2005).

Another fundamental question in this area of research that is closely related to the first is: *What are the determinants (or drivers) of corporate greening?* The traditional answer is that the key driver corporations respond to is mandatory government regulation; the more exacting and vigilant the enforcement of regulations, the more concern businesses and other organizations show for the environment. Some scholars contend that environmental protection has been one of the more successful regulatory domains of the past several decades (Eisner 2004). It is not clear, however, how that success has been achieved and to what degree traditional (command and control) environmental regulation can be credited. Traditional regulation, more prevalent in the US than elsewhere (Gunningham et al. 2003), has been highly contentious and has been ambitiously resisted (see Hoffman 2001). It is also widely held that traditional regulation has significant limitations when it comes to greening organizations. For example, Minz (1995) showed that the US Environmental Protection Agency's effectiveness in enforcement varied considerably depending on presidential regimes and larger political processes and Gunningham et al. (2003: 80–1) reported data that suggest that US regulatory enforcement varies a good deal notwithstanding a general tendency toward 'enforcement frenzy'. In some revealing research on 'mandatory' environmental regulation in the UK, Fineman (2000: 62) found that regulators exercised considerable discretion in interpreting the law and used a 'technicist, shallow green perspective' as they satisfied in their enforcement decisions and attempted to make deals with industry officials. In Fineman's (2000: 71) view, 'mandatory regulation is far less substantial, and far less green, than it appears'. May and Winter's (1999) study of inspectors' enforcement styles in Denmark also suggests a certain unevenness in effort, stringency and vigilance across regulators. In a recent study of boatyards in the western US, May (2005) found that, while traditional mandatory regulation is more effective than a voluntary approach that allows regulators to call attention to potential hazards and facilitate addressing them, the voluntary approach did add incremental value.

Studies such as these cast doubt on the idea that advanced corporate greening can be coerced strictly through mandatory environmental regulation and enforcement (also see selections in Helfand and Berck 2003). While traditional regulation certainly has a role to play in promoting corporate greening, even its supporters acknowledge inefficiencies and recognize how difficult it is to harmonize enforcement across time and place (cf. Lyon and Maxwell 2004).

Scholars have hypothesized several other major determinants of corporate greening that lie outside the purview of traditional regulation. These factors reflect a greater degree of voluntarism in meeting or exceeding environmental standards and stem from a variety of motivations. What opened the door for experimentation with voluntary approaches was the ideological push towards deregulation and smaller government in many nation-states (Sinclair 1997) and sweeping attempts to reform environmental regulation in Western Europe, Japan, the US and elsewhere. The main theme in all these reform initiatives has been to afford greater flexibility in how and when companies meet or exceed standards (Eisner 2004). Some research shows that regulations vary greatly and that those designed with more flexibility in mind provide opportunities for companies to learn and innovate, producing better results (cf. Majumdar and Marcus 2001; Sharma 2001).

Recent overviews of the literature on voluntary environmental initiatives point to a range of forces that have received concerted attention (e.g. Starik and Marcus 2000; Forbes and Jermier 2002; Sharma 2002; Fernandez et al. 2003; Gunningham et al. 2003; Jermier and Forbes 2003; Rivera and Delmas 2004; Kallio and Markkanen 2006). One line of research focuses on factors such as managerial values or orientations and charismatic and other forms of leadership (e.g. Andersson and Bateman 2000; Cordano and Frieze 2000; Egri and Herman 2000; Sharma 2000). It seems clear that some elite, formal leaders and business representatives now understand the devastating environmental impacts of their organizations and industries. Some seem highly motivated to make changes and to adopt a new leadership role. Their heartfelt testimonials and credible speeches demonstrate that they are attempting to be active environmental stewards with their own companies and in the broader world of business. Effective environmental leadership, however, is as difficult to conceptualize (without over-psychologizing and romanticizing) as is leadership in any area. When Anderson (2005), for example, recounts his epiphany concerning the environment, and identifies the precise moment when he first realized that 'compliance is not a vision', it is tempting to use the expression of his charisma as the ideal form of environmental leadership. Researchers focusing on environmental leadership seem to be avoiding the tendency toward reductionism. For example, sophisticated models of collective leadership, idea champions from the informal organization, and extra-organizational partnering liaisons have been developed. However, there are many questions still without answers when it comes to leading corporate environmental change.

A complementary wave of research emphasizes organizational and inter-organizational forces that both constrain and open up new domains for the strategic management of interdependencies. For example, researchers have studied organizational fields and institutional contexts (e.g. Hoffman and Ventresca 2002), political ecologies (e.g. Orsato et al. 2002), industry sets (e.g. King and Lenox 2000), interorganizational networks, such as supply chains and alliances with NGOs (e.g. Green et al. 2000; Stafford et al. 2000; Argenti 2004) and environmental stakeholders (e.g. Berry 2003), all of which may be seen as both drivers of corporate greening and as opportunities for firms to negotiate their own environmental stance. Another substantial wave of research focuses on competitive greening and the idea that there are traditional, calculative business motivations that drive corporate environmentalism (see Jermier and Forbes 2003). Porter and van der Linde's (1995a) article provided an accessible and persuasive statement of the 'green-green hypothesis' and other scholars produced several studies that elaborated the theme. The possible benefits derived from investments in corporate environmentalism were articulated in terms of competitive advantage, increased productivity and heightened quality of goods and services, savings in energy expenditures and regulatory costs, recruitment and retention of talented employees, green market segmentation, reputation effects and other factors (see Lyon and Maxwell 1999; Sharma 2002; Gunningham et al. 2003; Rivera and Delmas 2004).

Although some studies found that traditional business motivations, such as those represented in the 'green-green hypothesis', were the primary drivers of greening activities (e.g. Madu 1996; Bansal and Roth 2000), it is too early to draw conclusions about which factors are the most important antecedents of corporate greening. Without more comprehensive theoretical models, and research designs and statistical methods that enable and facilitate drawing causal inferences, we are inclined to agree with critics who assert that adequate empirical evidence is not yet available to identify the key causes (e.g. Fuchs and Mazmanian 1998; Kagan et al. 2003;

Lyon and Maxwell 2004). At this point, the most promising approach to understanding the determinants of micro corporate greening involves formulating models that can estimate the relative importance of several different factors (and their interaction effects) in various contexts. It is worth noting, however, that theory and research on the antecedents of forms of macro corporate environmentalism is very limited (see Karliner 1997; Welford 1997).

The third fundamental question in this area of research that we wish to address is: *What are the consequences of corporate greening?* Depending on what is meant by corporate greening, a case can be made for a large number of possible consequences. However, most researchers have concentrated on whether it pays financially to engage in greening and whether greening actually improves environmental performance. Sharma (2002) suggests that the question about whether it pays financially to be green has been so central to intellectual efforts in this field that it would be the leading contender if scholars sought to agree on a common research paradigm. Rivera and Delmas (2004: 230, emphasis added) asserted that during the 1990s, 'research on business and environmental protection focused *for the most part* on identifying a positive link between corporate environmental performance and profitability'.

Early work on the theme of competitive greening appealed widely. It emphasized that, while there are obvious costs associated with environmental regulatory compliance, smarter regulation that is incentive-based can lead to innovations in technology, product, process and customer service that offset or, even more dramatically, that far exceed the costs of regulatory compliance (Porter and van der Linde 1995a, b). Of course the win-win spirit of this approach did not persuade everyone. As one team of critics noted, this perspective on environmental protection, properly pursued, improves on the proverbial free lunch with a 'paid lunch' (Palmer et al. 1995: 120). They contended that Porter and van der Linde grossly underestimate the costs of environmental programmes and argued that such programmes should be justified based on the societal benefits of a cleaner environment and not on the hope that they can pay for themselves (also see Walley and Whitehead 1994). This debate grew into a broader discussion about the new 'business case' for corporate environmentalism and advanced the so-called 'double dividend' hypothesis – the idea that, at a minimum, investments in environmental management programmes would both better protect the environment and generate new sources of corporate profit. King and Lenox (2002: 289) incisively summarize the theme of the research that ensued: 'The dispute over whether and where it "pays to be green" is more than simply a debate over the private cost of pollution: It is a debate about whether managers systematically miss profit opportunities'. Influential theoretical work by Hart (1995), Russo and Fouts (1997) and others, and a few early empirical studies that showed support for the hypothesis (e.g. Hamilton 1995; Hart and Ahuja 1996; Klassen and McLaughlin 1996; Nehrt 1996; Russo and Fouts 1997; Khanna et al. 1998), established this area of study. From the beginning, however, it was clear that there would be no simple answers in this area. Researchers identified fundamental contingency factors that needed to be considered in specifying models, such as type of programme (e.g. pollution prevention, waste management, sustainable management systems), timing and intensity of investments, and characteristics of the industry. By the end of the decade, the debate had not generated any convincing answers and Reinhardt (1999a, b) pointed out the reason: the profitability of environmental investments, programmes and performance is affected by specific circumstances. Continuing improvements in theory and method have marked recent research (e.g. Gilley et al. 2000; King and Lenox 2002; Aragon-Correa and Sharma 2003; Filbeck and Gorman 2004; Toffel and Marshall 2004) and some scholars contend that it shows that voluntary environmental protection appears to make good business sense (Lyon and Maxwell 2004; Mengue and Ozanne 2004). Others researchers are less sanguine, pointing to conflicting and inconclusive evidence and significant problems in both theory and method (e.g. Rivera and Delmas 2004; Salzmann et al. 2005). It appears that once the immediate return from harvesting 'low-hanging fruit' with environmental investments is realized, further financial benefits and sustainable advantages are possible but cannot be guaranteed in all situations. And, when such benefits do occur, they may be realized only in the longer run, after negative short-run impacts have been absorbed. Porter and van der Linde's thesis is abstract enough to apply at all levels of corporate greening, but the research on macro economic outcomes is still at an early stage of theory development (see Esty and Geradin 1998; Esty and Porter 2002; Hilliard 2004).

Another consequence of corporate greening that has received considerable attention is environmental performance, understood as the degree to which pollution and other negative outcomes are minimized or reduced. This is a criterion of strong interest to all with environmental concerns. Much of this research has focused on the impact of environmental management systems, particularly the International Organization for Standardization's ISO 14001 approach. Since the release of ISO 14001 in 1996 it has become the centrepiece of most environmental management systems and, as alluded to above, the hard core of corporate greening (Eisner 2004). Its visibility was elevated in 1999 when General Motors and the Ford Motor Company announced that they were requiring all their worldwide suppliers with manufacturing facilities to achieve ISO 14001 certification within 3 years ('Ford and GM demand ISO 14000 compliance', *Quality*, 38, 1999, pp. 12–13). By 2001, over 36 000 facilities worldwide were registered with ISO 14001, a growth rate of 50% per year since 1996 (Potoski and Prakash 2005a) and by December 2003, a total of 66 070 facilities received the ISO 14001 certification, distributed in 113 countries (http://www.iso.org/iso/en/iso9000-14000/pdf/survey2003.pdf (25 July 2005)). As Hortensius and Barthel (1997: 35) indicated around the time the standard was elaborated: 'The newly industrialized and developing countries from South-East Asia, Africa and South America are concerned about possible trade restrictions arising from the use of the standards in contractual specifications'. Such concern possibly explains the active participation of these countries in the preparatory ISO meetings (Technical Committee 207 on Environmental Management) and, later, the relatively high rates of ISO 14001 certification of firms operating in countries such as China, in the third position (after Japan and the UK) with 5064 certifications, Korea, with 1495 (10th position), and Brazil with 1008 certifications.[6]

ISO 14001 is sometimes mistaken for environmental performance, but unlike the Eco-Management and Audit Scheme (EMAS) – a European initiative with similar characteristics in which environmental auditing is first and foremost intended as an internal management tool to monitor performance – ISO certification does not entail high performance. ISO 14001 was set forth as a 'tool to guide managers' (Melnyk et al. 2003: 330) in their voluntary quests to meet or exceed regulatory standards and, in this respect, serves as a good indicator of the diffusion of one core component of the NCE. Some scholars have observed both positive and negative outcomes in assessing the effects of ISO 14001 and other systems of environmental management (e.g. Hillary 2000; Steger 2000; Mendel 2002). Others make a more negative interpretation. For example, Yap (2000) expresses the sentiment that ISO 14001 has far more to do with conformance than with actual performance, and Switzer et al. (2000: 3) state: '... because the standard lacks minimum environmental performance requirements and does not [even] require full legal compliance as a condition of registration, some companies may use it to garner "an easy A", while continuing to operate in illegal or irresponsible ways'. Indeed, researchers have been diligent in demystifying ISO 14001 (Hillary 2000) and in putting it to rigorous tests. In a quasi-experimental study of over 3700 regulated US facilities, Potoski and Prakash (2005a) found support for the ISO 14001 programme as certified facilities in their study spent ~ 11.4% of the time out of compliance with air pollution regulations compared with 12.5% for non-certified facilities. This equated to a difference of ~ 25 days out of a year. In subsequent research, Potoski and Prakash (2005b) found that ISO 14001 certified facilities reduced pollution emissions more than non-certified facilities. However, in their study of electronics plants, Russo and Harrison (2005) found that (a) ISO 14001 certification was associated with higher emissions and (b) it was more likely that poor past emission performance led to adoption of ISO 14001 than that the adoption of ISO 14001 led to superior environmental performance. This led Russo and Harrison (2005: 588) to wonder if ISO 14001 certification, which does not mandate emission reductions, was adopted merely to 'provide cover for poor emissions performance'.

Potoski and Prakash (2005b) developed a useful framework for conceptualizing and comparing voluntary programmes, including ISO 14001. They used the metaphor of the covenant and the sword (weak sword as monitoring only; medium sword as monitoring and public disclosure; strong sword as monitoring, public disclosure and sanctioning) to differentiate among programmes based on the method used to cajole members to honour programme obligations. They described the chemical industry's Responsible Care initiative as a 'no swords' programme, ISO 14001 as a 'weak swords' programme, and EMAS and the US E.P.A. 'Performance Track' as medium and strong swords programmes, respectively. Following King and

Lenox (2000), their contention is that voluntary programmes without effective monitoring, third-party audits and the power to sanction members are far less likely to provide environmental protection. While they see some positive results in ISO 14001 and the weak swords programmes, their framework does underscore the importance of research that cuts through rhetoric and that makes distinctions among the voluntary programmes based on the ability of the programme to enforce covenants and produce higher environmental performance. There is another important line of empirical research on corporate greening that is relevant to the analysis of empty rhetoric. This research makes a distinction between commitment to and implementation of environmental policies. It reports numerous instances of 'commitment' but lack of implementation (e.g. Haas (1996) with Norwegian firms in the printing and food industries, Winn and Angell (2000) with German manufacturing firms, and Ramus and Montiel (2006) with US firms in the chemical, oil, manufacturing and services sectors).

Critical Perspectives on the NCE

It is perhaps in the research on corporate environmentalism, more than in any other area, that we see how the study of ecology inevitably raises questions disturbing to and even subversive of business as usual. Some voluntary NCE programmes are best seen as watchdogs with rubber teeth (cf. Watson and Emery 2004) that should be exposed as such. In part, this is a task for investigative journalists (e.g. see Landrigan 2001; *Multinational Monitor Online*, http://multinationalmonitor.org/monitor.html, *CorpWatch Online,* www.corpwatch.org/) and muckraking filmmakers (see Hill and Dhanda 2004, for review) who believe that informing and entertaining the public should go hand-in-hand. However, as seen above, traditional research can also play an important role in making distinctions and establishing facts about corporate environmentalism. Organizational studies scholars have begun to make progress in distinguishing among voluntary programmes based on environmental impacts and other outcomes. While they have developed some skepticism about what type of contribution corporations really want to make to protect the natural environment, there is also a realization that the NCE cannot be dismissed. Yet, because the stakes are so high when it comes to environmental problems, there is a pressing need for scholarship that takes a more critical perspective on corporate voluntarism and NCE activities and that provides a more systematic and trenchant analysis. Here is where we believe organizational studies scholars could benefit from examining the critical literature on greenwashing more closely. It too raises questions about what corporations really want to contribute to solving environmental problems and does this through theoretical lenses that challenge superficial and weak reformist approaches in this vital area (e.g. Athanasiou 1996; Greer and Bruno 1996; Karliner 1997; Tokar 1997; Welford 1998; Beder 2002; Bruno and Karliner 2002; Utting 2002; Jermier and Forbes 2003; Laufer 2003; Clapp and Dauvergne 2005).

Critical analysis of the NCE does not need to be limited to the literature on greenwashing. There are numerous sources that would be helpful in addressing limitations in the field's present understanding of the NCE, especially from the angle of understanding this phenomenon meta-theoretically and as a form of green politics. Examples include: Seager's (1993) ecofeminist explanation of business as usual; Welford's (1997) thesis about corporate hijacking of the environmental movement; Karliner's (1997) critique of the ideology of corporate environmentalism and of the limitations of business coalitions, consortia, treaties and other macro phenomena; Newton and Harte's (1997) critical analysis of the NCE's evangelical rhetoric and de-politicizing of environmental management; Levy's (1997) reading of environmental management as an ideological production that distracts from and derails more radical initiatives; Korten's (1998) assessment of the power of the global financial system and organizational instruments that conspire to destroy the wealth of natural resources; Crane's (2000) study of how corporate greening programmes can lose their ethical significance for employees; Bruno and Karliner's (2002) evaluation of the corporate capture of global governance; Checker's (2002) illustration of how racial minority activists manage to adapt corporate-centred environmental discourse to their organizing needs; Banerjee's (2002b) development of a research agenda emphasizing non-corporatist approaches to sustainability; Forbes and Jermier's (2002) theorization of green ceremonial facades in organizational change; Starkey and Crane's (2003) replacement of the Enlightenment narrative (of progress and growth through domination of the environment)

with a postmodern green narrative, and Castro's (2004) fundamental redirection of the concept of sustainable development.

The NCE can appear apolitical and its consequences can be misconstrued as serving the broader public interest. Yet, to fully understand the NCE, it is important to appreciate it as a segment of green politics. It can then be assessed in relation to crosscurrents in green political thought and interpreted more completely as a response to environmental problems that is as much a partisan maneouvre as it is a technical project. One primary contribution that can result from developing critical perspectives on the NCE is re-situating this phenomenon (and the literature devoted to understanding it) in the paradigm of reform environmentalism and in the meta-theoretical political space of incremental change (cf. Egri and Pinfield 1996). However, what type of reformist politics characterizes the NCE? In his analysis of the ecological modernization approach to reforming policy and politics, Christoff (1996) found it helpful to differentiate between programmes that produce weak outcomes (weak reformism) and those that produce strong outcomes (strong reformism; also see York and Rosa 2003). At the level of rhetoric, the NCE has elements in common with strong reformism. At the level of practice, however, with few exceptions, it appears to be consistent with weak reformism – surface change that is far from the ideals of committed environmentalists and, in the visions of European scenario planners (see Global Scenario Group, www.gsg.org; Foster 2005), much closer to the doomsday forms of Conventional Worlds than it is to the modest utopia of the 'New Sustainability Paradigm'. Nearly 10 years ago, Karliner (1997: 39) characterized the corporate environmental response to the period's ecological and social crises as similar to bringing a band-aid to cover a gaping wound. The NCE is maturing in many ways and the scope of its influence has increased markedly. Nevertheless, its role in ensuring environmental protection and in alleviating ecological degradation has not yet been clarified. Journalists, filmmakers, traditional academic researchers and critical theorists all raise concerns about the misleading or weak reformist tendencies in NCE practice and issue warnings about the slippery slope back to full compatibility with the dominant social paradigm. Green political theorists such as Torgerson (1999) question whether the traditional labels of reform and radical environmentalism adequately represent the paradigms and strategies available to environmental actors and theorists. He introduced the concept of *incremental radicalism* to explore the possibility of a linkage between reformist incrementalism (accommodating, compromising) and transformative radicalism (confrontational, refusing). In our view, debate on the NCE should include similar hybrid, paradigmatic positions and should be enriched by drawing on broader discussions in green political thought.[7]

The other primary contribution that can result from developing critical perspectives on the NCE is exploration of a wider range of possible futures. The NCE can be criticized for advancing a form of environmentalism that is elitist and for advocating steering mechanisms that tend to exclude citizens. In the chapter's next section, we extend the discussion of the NCE and forms of green politics using neo-Habermasian studies of the natural environment. We think it is especially important that organizational studies scholars turn their attention toward developing new models of greening corporations and other organizations, models that can guide thinking and practice beyond reformist NCE toward more democratic environmentalism.

Developing Critical Reflective Organizational Systems and Green Politics (Democratic Environmentalism)

'I came as a representative of business; I left as a citizen of the earth'. Rob Koeppel, Textile Laminator and Supplier to Patagonia, commenting on his reaction to a Patagonia supplier conference on the use of organic cotton (Rowledge et al. 1999: 103).

In an era when it is often stated that schools of all kinds should be run more like businesses, we would like to advance the notion that corporations and other businesses should be run more like schools – schools offering a liberal arts curriculum and relatively democratic learning environments. Business, like all institutions, plays an educative role, teaching lessons through its formal training programmes and, equally importantly, through the hidden curriculum of everyday practice. Several factors distinguish the type of business we are envisioning in this section but, first and foremost, it is a business that encourages *life-long learning*, a process that involves

continuous change, growth and development through knowledge acquisition and sharing. It also prioritizes the development of *critical thinking skills* (which include critical reflection on the status quo and visualization of alternative futures) and *citizenship capabilities* (which means fostering a sense of civic duty and an ethic of democratic participation). Finally, this type of business emphasizes *environmental literacy* (knowledge about specific environmental problems, their causes and their consequences as well as knowledge about how the specific problems interact to create larger problems) and *ecological wisdom* (eco-centred understanding of the web of life, concern about the destabilizing role of human production and consumption, facility with the precautionary principle, and a keen sense of just and ethical conduct in business and society). This type of business also provides basic education in requisite technical skills and legal procedures.

We believe the analogy of 'business as school' is helpful in introducing the notion of a critical reflective organizational system (CROS). In this section, we propose an orienting framework for the CROS that draws on themes in green political thought and that has the potential to enhance organizational theory and practice. We extend the discussion of the NCE and forms of green politics to the idea of a CROS because we agree with scholars who are calling for profound changes. For example, York and Rosa (2003: 274) are skeptical about superindustrialization, an approach they label 'the greening of business-as-usual'. They caution against an uncritical commitment to weak ecological modernization and advocate the exploration of approaches that radically transform social structures and that have greater potential to bring about ecological sustainability.

An overarching question is how to shift systems into more critically reflective patterns so that all decision-makers at every level are confronted with the current inability of our existing institutions to forestall or manage ecological decline (Eckersley 2004). Involving decision-makers at all levels in building democratic environmentalism requires *active citizenship*, but a central theme in classical critical theory is the weakened and deplorable state of citizenship. Modern citizens are *de-activated* through non-participative and stultifying work environments, consumerism, the sway of mass media propaganda, misplaced faith in techno-administrative rationality, and other forms of domination. Contemporary green political scholars, however, have developed another theme in critical theory and have advanced theoretical concepts helpful in overcoming citizen de-activation and in reinvigorating democratic processes. Moreover, they argue that there is evidence indicating some promising developments in that direction (Dryzek 1990; 1997; Torgerson 1999). From contemporary green political thought, and particularly from neo-Habermasian critical environmental theory (CET), we bring together three concepts: *the public sphere*; *communicative rationality*; and *discursive design*. These three concepts are only sketched below. They are advanced as a bridge, however, to extensive resources that have a noteworthy presence in other interdisciplinary fields, such as communication, planning, risk assessment and policy science. We believe organizational studies scholars can benefit from examining them.

Expanding on Habermas' (1989) depiction of the *public sphere* (a site governed neither by the intimacy of the family, the authority of the state, nor the exchange of the market, but by the 'public reason of private citizens' (Peters 1993: 542)), CETs argue for bolstering an active *green public sphere* – one amongst many possible public spheres emanating from civil society. In the shared discursive space of the green public sphere, citizens focus on important green issues, engaging in teaching and learning, and in ethical and political discourse. They discuss issues not as industrialists, employees, consumers or members of formal political parties but as rational citizens voicing public concerns about ecological issues. The emerging green public sphere is now more feasible than ever because the 'language of environment' (Torgerson 2000: 6) has diffused throughout the citizenry. This language provides a way to reframe and debate the dominant and uncritical discourse of industrialism and even distinctions between reform and radical environmentalism. Torgerson (1999; 2000) argues that debate is a crucial task of green politics and we think it can be understood as one fundamental process involved in idealized learning environments that characterize citizenship-centred politics. Public sphere activities are open to all interested citizens and since there are multiple public spheres (contextualized by issue and location), involvement and contributions depend on imperatives of citizenship. To enrich these learning environments, however, it is important to move away from tendencies present in subpolitical regimes, such as 'gentlemen's agreements', and bring in voices from the margins (Dryzek 2000: 168).

From the perspective of CET, the effectiveness of public sphere activities begins with assembling diverse, concerned citizens but hangs on approximating ideal speech conditions and engendering mutual understanding through the exercise of higher forms of reasoning. Following Habermas, CETs employ the concept of *communicative rationality* and use it as an ideal type, recognizing that it can support a range of communicative actions and practices. It refers to the extent to which communication is supported with a collective commitment to free and open inquiry and discussion, and is characterized by *reflective understanding* of competent actors (cf. Dryzek 1990). It involves reciprocal listening, civility and full transparency, which are all necessary to produce conviction and commitment to a learning relationship. CETs recognize that human communication processes are always fraught with difficulties and distortions but they are particularly interested in eradicating the systematic distortion that is present in the instrumental form of reasoning. Instrumental reasoning is a process that reduces rationality to debating the best means to achieve taken-for-granted ends. They deliver a strong critique of the dominating tendencies in this form of discourse and point out that discussions about means do not substitute for debates about ends. They are especially critical of instrumental reasoning that circumvents ethical discourse while relying on elite presentations of non-contextualized, technically and scientifically determined alternatives. They also follow Habermas in insisting that only self-reflective individuals can be considered rational and in advocating the principle that the 'force of the better argument should rule'. They contend that less faith should be placed in the formal knowledge of technocratic experts and that openness to local, indigenous forms of knowledge should be indicated (cf. Fischer 2000; King 2000; Eckersley 2004). They expect debate and discussion under these conditions to lead to learning and mutual understanding among participants.

A related theoretical question centres on how these processes unfold. For Dryzek (1997; 2000) and others, the ideals of the authentic public sphere and the principles of communicative rationality are best realized by rejecting scientism and enacting radical participatory democracy. Dryzek (1990) developed the concept of a *discursive design* to specify the factors that must be in place for meaningful participatory democracy to flourish. All discursive spaces have design features, but Dryzek is interested in special institutionalized settings where the 'expectations of a number of actors converge', where they are consciously aware of the institution as a 'site for recurrent communicative interaction', where they participate exclusively as concerned citizens and where they are supported in developing competent participation with educational and other resources (p. 43). When successful, this process 'breaks the shackles' of the disadvantaged and begins to equalize participants (Dryzek 1997: 199). The concept of a discursive design might give the impression that hierarchy or formal regulations bind it, but it is a self-organizing process. Through their own reflection and discursive practices, participants create or override emergent rules and procedures (see Dryzek 1990: 43). It has radical potential because it assembles committed citizens who are driven by the goals of collective learning, growth, and mutual understanding in a space offering increasing levels of freedom, equality and influence on policy.[8]

Although to date much of the CET research focuses on the state and governmental systems, we believe it provides a valuable resource for exploring more *radical ideas* on the modification of social structures and the development of CROS thinking for the business sector. Unlike Habermas, who thought the public sphere could thrive only outside the scope of the state and the economy, some neo-Habermasians see broader applicability. For example, Dryzek (1992: 41) asserted that '… [business] organization should fall under discursively democratic control', although he also admitted that '[e]xactly how that might be accomplished without the heavy hand of the administrative state is a major unresolved issue'.[9] Torgerson (1999: 10–11) entertains the possibility that even the 'administrative sphere' (government and the complex of private and public organizations shaping advanced industrial societies) might be open to discursive designs.

CET concepts set a high standard for corporate conduct, but there are reasons to believe that possibilities for change are emerging. We can look to advances in participatory planning projects (Fischer 2000), ground rules for dialogue in public deliberation organizations (Ryfe 2002) and learning-centred approaches to government regulation (Kelly 2004; Neves-Graca 2004). If we look to the world of commerce, it is more difficult to find positive examples, but Shell Oil Company's stakeholder dialogue programme is interesting in its experimentation with

the internet (Unerman and Bennett 2004). More vividly, some business organizations appear to be on the brink of developing a type of learning environment consistent with CROS. For example, the statement above from Rob Koeppel, voiced at the conclusion of a 3-day Patagonia supplier conference on conventionally versus organically grown cotton, shows the transformative effect on citizenship that can result from ecological learning (Rowledge et al. 1999: 103).

Perspective

[W]e are in the midst of a global environmental crisis of such enormity that the web of life of the entire planet is threatened and with it the future of civilization (Foster 2005: 1).

Modern Environmentalism and Overcoming Perverse Politics

Not all readers will agree with the dire assessment above made by one prominent environmental thinker but for those open to critical reflection about environmental problems, evidence that is difficult to dismiss continues to mount. While the general public in most nation-states consistently registers concern about environmental deterioration and some percentage even endorse increased public spending for protecting the environment (e.g. Dunlap 2002; 2006; Gallup International 2002; European Commission 2005), expedient political solutions to these problems do not appear to be on the horizon. In a widely circulated on-line document, Shellenberger and Nordhaus (2005) claim that the traditional institutional guardians – the major environmental organizations and the appropriate government legislators and agencies – have failed to convert public concern about the environment into stronger protection, have lost political credibility and have faded from the picture. They contend that neo-conservative politicians are winning the culture war over core values, and are persuading the public that environmentalism is a special interest. This has enabled the gutting of some of the environmental protection infrastructure that was decades in the making and has led to a strong sense among some activists that modern environmentalism now must die so that something more effective can take its place.[10] If modern environmentalism must fade away, what will replace it? *Can* a more effective green politics be reconstituted around the highly fashionable NCE? *Should* green politics be reconstituted around the NCE? Our argument in the chapter is that these are important questions for all organizational studies scholars to contemplate, both because they are central to developing a richer theoretical understanding of organizations, and because they present an urgent practical matter. Our view is that corporate leaders, despite the best intentions of many, and meaningful incremental progress through dematerialization and eco-efficiency of innovative production initiatives, cannot act as the vanguard of the environmental movement. The economic growth imperative, capital accumulation exigencies, reproducing patterns of environmental injustice, and subpolitical regimes that organize key sectors of economies and key industries (as we illustrated with the analysis of the chemical economy) are the structural realities governing the world. The strong tendencies in these forces are more likely to shape the future than are exhortations to change values and lifestyles and they are more likely to shape the future than are weak reformist NCE programmes that cannot keep pace and that fade or disappear during economic downturns (cf. Foster 2005). Thus, we see a continuing important role for vigilant government regulation, adversarial environmental organizations and a more inclusive green public sphere. We also think strong reformist NCE programmes can play a role but favour radical approaches that attempt to modify social structures significantly, that establish cultures open to learning about ecology from a variety of sources and that practice higher forms of citizenship.

Improving the NCE Discourse

The NCE discourse, including the academic research on this phenomenon, needs more attention from organizational specialists and other business scholars. In this chapter, we invited consideration of the NCE as a potent form of green politics and provided a bridge to intellectual resources useful in critically analysing it. The academic literature on the NCE has expanded rapidly over the past decade and a half, but even for the five most current years (2000–2004), it still adds up to a very small percentage of the total articles published on business, management and organizational studies topics (no more

than 1%). A similar pattern of ~ 1% is observed when considering only highly rated organizational studies journals.

In the short history of research on the NCE, scholars have provided extensive evidence that green issues matter in theory development work and in practical situations. The research in this field has matured quickly but scholars face *several key challenges*. Since Egri and Pinfield (1996) made their assessment, the central intellectual priority in the field has changed from clarifying differences in paradigmatic underpinnings of the various environmentalisms to describing corporate greening at multiple levels of analysis and theorizing its antecedents and consequences. One key challenge facing scholars in theory development work is to *broaden the methods used in empirical studies*. Researchers continue to design case studies, a preferred method of inquiry for the early development of fields and useful in illustrating phenomena, but also have applied methods more appropriate for developing theoretical understanding. In the next few years, we expect to see even more emphasis placed on rigorous methods, including more time series and experimental designs, more reliance on validated survey measures and long interviews to complement secondary databases, and more extended, in depth, participant observation studies. Another key challenge facing scholars is to *integrate corporate environmentalism more fully with concepts of corporate sustainability*. Relationships between the environmental and economic dimensions of sustainability have been solidly specified but relatively little attention has been given to the social dimension, which could include factors such as eliminating poverty and hunger, ensuring safety and health, enhancing literacy and protecting the rights of present and future generations (see Sharma and Rudd 2003; Obach 2004; Starke 2005; Waddock 2006). This merely requires that we understand that humans are included in the notion of 'the environment'. The main challenge we centred on in this chapter is also worth underscoring: *developing a fuller appreciation of the political content and meaning of the NCE* and avoiding reduction of it to technical issues. This appreciation can flow initially from the research that has documented a gulf between 'commitment' to and implementation of environmental policies in organizations and the empirical observation that there are weak forms of the NCE that are masked in the strong reformist rhetoric. It can also flow as a discussion of the role of the NCE in the broader context of green politics, one that might encourage the development of new models of corporate greening that go beyond weak reformism, such as the critical reflective organizational system we began to imagine through the neo-Habermasian environmental literature.

There is one final challenge we would like to identify. To do so we turn to Starik's (2002) piece that *takes stock of the field* and his use of the phrase 'Childhood's End' (an allusion to Arthur C. Clarke's science fiction classic). Starik used this phrase to metaphorically represent the stage of development of NCE literature and the rise of the field of organizations and the natural environment. With it, he suggests growth beyond childhood and movement into adolescence or even early adulthood. Clarke's story is replete with symbolism and can be read at many levels.[11] The fate of the children in the dystopian world Clarke depicts, however, is not uplifting. When the children are sufficiently 'developed' (colonized) by alien 'Benevolent Overlords' (who are technologically prodigious but lacking in creative potential) they are 'harvested' and assimilated into the supreme 'Overmind'. It is at this point that the earth disintegrates. Fortunately, the intellectual community that has produced the literature on corporate environmentalism currently has few things in common with the children in the *Brave New World*-like civilization depicted in *Childhood's End*. There has been an understanding among many that environment-related research is unique and that it should not be assimilated into the managerialist mainstream. Starik's call to expand the research agenda raises the related question about what criteria to use when reflecting on the development of the discipline and possible trade-offs stemming from premature paradigmatic closure (cf. Pfeffer 1993; Van Maanen 1995). *Childhood's End* might serve as a cautionary tale and as one metaphorical touchstone in discussions about where the field should be heading.

Notes

1. Through legislative and regulatory actions, many toxic chemicals have been banned in most parts of the world. From this, it might be assumed that the harmful effects of chemicals have mostly been abated. As plausible as that assumption seems, it does not hold up well in the light of recent information. For example, take the widely known chemical DDT. It was first introduced in

insecticides in the early 1940s but has been banned in the US since 1972. DDT was just one of a wide range of technologies developed during World War II that fostered national priorities of agricultural productivity and 'progress'. In 1951 sales of DDT alone in the US were more than $110 million (Bosso 1987: 31). DDT is one chemical in a group of synthetic compounds known as persistent organic pollutants. POPs are truly insidious and share four common properties: 'they are toxic; they accumulate in the food chain; they persist in the environment; and they have a high potential to travel long distances from their source' (McGinn 2000: 80, see also McGinn 2002). The effects of DDT are both serious and fairly well understood and it has been categorized as one of the so-called 'dirty dozen' POPs which include 10 pesticides plus dioxins and furans (McGinn 2000; 2002).

While DDT is banned in the US and most regions of the world, a few countries still produce it and it is sometimes applied illegally in agricultural and other applications in an unknown number of countries (McGinn 2000). DDT is still legally in use in some parts of the world to combat malaria, which is spread by mosquitoes (McGinn 2000). Ironically, some strains of mosquitoes, the original target of DDT, are resistant to it. DDTs effects are extraordinarily destructive on other species, however, including the highly durable American alligator. Alligators are rarely seen as endearing animals. However, as a species, they do have extraordinary survival capability and they play a crucial role in balancing and sustaining the wetlands ecosystems they inhabit. It is estimated that they have inhabited the earth for $\sim 300\,000\,000$ years, making them living dinosaurs of sorts. Amazingly, according to a report detailing the plight of alligators in Lake Apopka, Florida, USA, this venerable species is no match for even minute amounts of DDT (see Semenza et al. 1997; Guillette Jr. et al. 2000). For years it has been known that exposure to DDT can cause cancer, but some of its truly insidious and extinguishing indirect effects have only recently been uncovered, as are illustrated in the story of Lake Apopka's alligators. DDT and its related byproducts, discharged by Tower Chemical Company into a marsh that drains into Lake Apopka, remain in the bottom of the Lake in quantities that are virtually undetectable and seemingly harmless. In their normal activities, however, alligators in the lake ingested and absorbed DDT and it built up in their systems. Their livers cannot process the substance. Astonishingly, DDT acted as an oestrogen substitute in Lake Apopka's female alligators, accelerating sexual development to the point that menopause began before they were old enough to mate. Males exposed to the substance had a lowered sex drive and smaller sex organs. The effects, produced with minute amounts of DDT (one part per billion), were subtle initially but became dramatic in the next generation. In a single generation, the lake's alligator population fell from 4000 to 400.

Of course DDT is not the only chemical that can mimic sexual hormones or that has other deleterious effects on living organisms, including humans (Shrader-Frechette 1999; McGinn 2002; Koger et al. 2005). There are hundreds, perhaps thousands with their own toxic trail that may or may not be known. Hazards such as DDT have been limited in their usage, but chemicals are pervasive in daily life (see Costner et al. 2005) and integral to contemporary production systems. Harm to workers occurs far beyond the manufacturing stage. An illustration could be made with a high-profile expose that was turned into a film, *A Civil Action,* involving the W.R. Grace and Beatrice food corporations and the impact of one of their subsidiaries, a leather tanning factory in the community of Woburn, MA, USA (see Harr 1995; Domagalski 1999). In a federal lawsuit, these companies were held liable for the high incidence of leukaemia, cancer and other physical abnormalities in the community because their employees dumped and buried toxic chemicals, contaminating the local drinking water. Corporate officials had knowledge of the problem but chose not to discontinue their practice.

2. Thornton (2000) argues that 33 million experiments would be required just to learn something about the effects of 25 different chemicals on a single species over a short period of time (13 weeks).

3. 'Subgovernment' is a semi-technical term in political science (see Bosso 1987: 6):

Such gaps in the pluralist response to elitism have generated a series of classic studies of policymaking in agricultural, water and public works programmes that constitute the 'subgovernment' approach. This approach presents an image of sectoral politics, where policy dominance is said to be vested in an informal but enduring series of iron triangles linking executive bureaus, congressional committees and interest group clienteles with a stake in particular programmes.

4. In 1989, an official Committee of the US Congress estimated that the total number of sites contaminated with toxic chemicals in the US might approximate 439 000 (Committee on Environmental Epidemiology 1991). They included local sites varying from mine wastes, leaking underground storage tanks, pesticide-contaminated lands, contaminated non-military federal properties, underground injection wells, abandoned municipal gas manufacturing facilities and wood-preserving plants, each with their local risk community as well as more widespread effects.

5. Readers may wonder if a different pattern holds when considering core organizational studies journals rather than the broader scholarly business literature. Coopey (2003) conducted an analysis of nine top journals for the years 1995–1999 and reported that of the 3137 total articles published during that period, 35 were on topics of sustainability and environmental management (1.1%). In our own analysis of the top 15 organizational studies journals (selected as 'top' based on their citation impact quotient in the *Social Sciences Citation Index* for the

year 2004), we found a similar pattern. For the years 1996–2004, of the 9232 articles published, 97 (1.1%) were on topics keyed with the seven environment-related terms used for the search of the general literature. The journals selected included: *Academy of Management Executive*; *Academy of Management Journal*; *Academy of Management Review*; *Administrative Science Quarterly*; *British Journal of Management*; *California Management Review*; *Harvard Business Review*; *Human Relations*; *Journal of Management*; *Journal of Management Studies*; *Leadership Quarterly*; *Organization*; *Organization Science*; *Organization Studies*; and *Strategic Management Journal*.

6. http://www.iso.org/iso/en/iso9000-14000/pdf/survey 2003.pdf (accessed 25 July 2005).

7. The debate on the NCE can also be enriched by more comparison with the strong reformist varieties of ecological modernization theory (EMT), a social theory with a prescriptive political agenda. EMT draws on the emergence of a social consensus around progressive environmental policies in countries such as Denmark, Sweden and Germany (Lundqvist 2000; Binder et al. 2001).

8. Habermas is a strong proponent of discourse in the public sphere but recognizes the limitations of communicative action outside the state and economy. His (Habermas 1992: 452) position is that 'Discourses do not govern'.

9. In a personal communication (25 August 2005), Dryzek stated that he has not written much about business organizations since the statement quoted above but that his general view is that the issue of how an economic organization can fall under democratic control is still unresolved.

10. Shellenberger and Nordhaus's thesis is directed at the environmental movement in the US and is meant to provoke discussion, which it has done. Its applicability outside the US is probably greatest where neo-conservative economic ideology tends to hold sway and impact environmental regulation (cf. Sinclair 1997).

11.Through personal communication, we know that in his 2002 piece, Mark Starik was not intentionally trying to provoke the interpretation we make. We take responsibility for this extension of his trope.

References

Alkon, A.H. (2004) 'Places, stories, and consequences: Heritage narratives and the control of erosion on Lake County, California vineyards', *Organization & Environment*, 17: 145–69.

Alvesson, M. and Deetz, S. (1996) 'Critical theory and postmodern approaches to organizational studies', in S.R. Clegg, C. Hardy and W. Nord (eds), *Handbook of Organization Studies*. London: Sage. pp. 191–217.

Alvesson, M. and Willmott, H. (2003) 'Introduction', in M. Alvesson and H. Willmott (eds), *Studying Management Critically*. London: Sage Publications. pp. 1–22.

Anderson, R. (2003) 'Envisioning the prototypical company of the 21st century', in S. Waage (ed.), *Ants, Galileo, & Gandhi: Designing the Future of Business through Nature, Genius and Compassion.* Sheffield, UK: Greenleaf Publishers. pp. 17–30.

Anderson, R. (2005) 'Corporate social responsibility and its implications for management research and education'. Presentation at the Annual Meetings of the Academy of Management, Honolulu, Hawaii, 9 August.

Andersson, L.M. and Bateman, T.S. (2000) 'Individual environmental initiative: Championing natural environmental issues in U.S. business organizations', *Academy of Management Journal*, 43: 548–70.

Annan, K. (2002) 'Foreward', in *Global Environment Outlook 3: Past, Present, and Future Perspectives.* Nairobi: United Nations Environment Programme.

Aragon-Correa, J.A. and Sharma, S. (2003) 'A contingent resource-based view of proactive corporate environmental strategy', *Academy of Management Review*, 28: 71–88.

Arcury, T., Quandt, S. and Dearry, A. (2001) 'Farmworker pesticide exposure and community-based participatory research: Rationale and practical applications', *Environmental Health Perspectives*, 109: 429–34.

Argenti, P.A. (2004) 'Collaborating with activists: How Starbucks works with NGOs', *California Management Review*, 47: 91–116.

Athanasiou, T. (1996) 'The age of greenwashing', *Capitalism, Nature, Socialism*, 7: 1–36.

Bade, W.F. (1924) *The Life and Letters of John Muir.* Boston: Houghton Mifflin.

Banerjee, B. (2002a) 'Corporate environmentalism: The construct and its measurement', *Journal of Business Research*, 55: 177–91.

Banerjee, B. (2002b) 'Organizational strategies for sustainable development: Development of a research agenda for the new millennium', *Australian Journal of Management*, 27: 105–17.

Banerjee, B. (2003) 'Who sustains whose development? Sustainable development and the reinvention of nature', *Organization Studies*, 24: 143–80.

Bansal, P. and Roth, K. (2000) 'Why companies go green: A model of ecological responsiveness', *Academy of Management Journal*, 43: 717–36.

Barnett, M. (2004) 'Are globalization and sustainability compatible? Review of the debate between the World Business Council for Sustainable Development and the International Forum on Globalization', *Organization & Environment*, 17: 523–32.

Barry, J. and Eckersley, R. (eds) (2005) *The State and the Global Ecological Crisis.* Cambridge: MIT Press.

Beamish, T. (2001) 'Environmental hazard and institutional betrayal: Lay-public perceptions of risk in the San Luis Obispo County oil spill', *Organization & Environment*, 14: 5–33.

Beck, U. (1992) *Risk Society: Towards a New Modernity.* London: Sage.

Beck, U. (1995) *Ecological Enlightenment.* New Jersey: Humanities Press.

Beder, S. (2002) *Global Spin: The Corporate Assault on Environmentalism, Revised Edition.* White River Junction, VT: Green Chelsea.

Benn, S, (2004) 'Managing toxic chemicals in Australia: a regional analysis of the risk society', *Journal of Risk Research*, 7: 399–412.

Berry, G.R. (2003) 'Organizing against multinational corporate power in Cancer Alley: The activist community as primary stakeholder', *Organization & Environment*, 16: 3–33.

Best, S. and Nocella, A.J. (2004) *Terrorists or Freedom Fighters? Reflections on the Liberation of Animals.* New York: Lantern Books.

Binder, M., Janicke, M. and Petscholow, U. (2001) *Green Industrial Restructuring: International Case Studies and Theoretical Interpretation.* Berlin: Springer-Verlag.

Bosso, C. (1987) *Pesticides and Politics: The Life Cycle of a Policy Issue.* Pittsburgh: University of Pittsburgh Press.

Bouman, J. (2002) 'Recycling poison: Inside China's e-waste workshops'. Available online at: http://news.bbc.co.uk/hi/english/static/in_depth/world/2002/disposable_planet/waste/chinese_workshop/4.stm, accessed 2 July 2005.

Bowen, W. and Wells, M. (2002) 'The politics and reality of environmental justice: A history and considerations for public administrators and policy makers', *Public Administration Review*, 62: 688–98.

Briggs, S.A. (1997) 'Thirty-five years with *Silent Spring*', *Organization & Environment*, 10: 73–84.

Bright, C. (2000) 'Anticipating environmental "surprise"', in L. Starke (ed.), *State of the World 2000: A Worldwatch Institute Report on Progress Toward a Sustainable Society.* New York/London: W.W. Norton. pp. 22–38.

Brown, L.R. (2003) *Plan B: Rescuing a Planet under Stress and a Civilization in Trouble.* New York: W.W. Norton.

Bruno, K. and Karliner, J. (2002) *earthsummit.biz: The Corporate Takeover of Sustainable Development.* Oakland, CA: Food First Books.

Buchholz, R.A. (1998) *Principles of Environmental Management: The Greening of Business.* Upper Saddle River, New Jersey: Prentice-Hall.

Buttel, F.H. and Humphrey, C.R. (2002) 'Sociological theory and the natural environment', in R.E. Dunlap and W. Michelson (eds), *Handbook of Environmental Sociology.* Westport, Connecticut: Greenwood Press. pp. 33–69.

Calas, M.B. and Smircich, L. (eds) (2002) 'Symposium: On Critical Management Studies', *Organization*, 9: 363–457.

Callenbach, E., Capra, F., Goldman, L., Lutz, R. and Marburg, S. (1993) *Ecomanagement.* San Francisco: Berrett Koehler.

Carmen, J. and Balser, D.B. (2002) 'Selecting repertoires of action in environmental movement organizations', *Organization & Environment*, 15: 365–88.

Carrraro, C. and Leveque, F. (eds) (1999) *Voluntary Approaches in Environmental Policy*. Dordrecht: Kluwer Publishers.

Carson, R. (1962) *Silent Spring*. Boston: Houghton Mifflin.

Carter, N. (2005) 'Mixed fortunes: The greens in the 2004 European Parliament Election', *Environmental Politics*, 14: 103–11.

Castro, C.J. (2004) 'Sustainable development: Mainstream and critical perspectives', *Organization & Environment*, 17: 195–225.

Catton, W.R, Jr. and Dunlap, R.E. (1978) 'Environmental sociology: A new paradigm', *The American Sociologist*, 13: 41–9.

CBS News, Sixty Minutes Television Program (2001) 'The Earth Liberation Front', 14 January.

Checker, M.A. (2002) "It's in the air': Redefining the environment as a new metaphor for old social justice struggles', *Human Organization*, 61: 94–105.

Christoff, P. (1996) 'Ecological modernization, ecological modernities', *Environmental Politics*, 5: 476–500.

Clapp, J. and Dauvergne, P. (2005) *Paths to a Green World: The Political Economy of the Global Environment*. Cambridge, MA: MIT Press.

Committee on Environmental Epidemiology (1991) *Environmental Epidemiology, Volume 1: Public Health and Hazardous Wastes*. Washington, DC: National Research Council.

Connor, S. (2005) 'The state of the world: Is it on the brink of disaster?', *The Independent UK*, 30 March. Available online at: http://www.commondreams.org/headlines 05/0330-04.htm, accessed 12 June 2005.

Coopey, J. (2003) 'Sustainable development and environmental management: The performance of UK business schools', *Management Learning*, 34: 5–26.

Cordano, M. and Frieze, I.H. (2000) 'Pollution reduction preferences of U.S. environmental managers: Applying Ajzen's theory of planned behavior', *Academy of Management Journal*, 43: 627–41.

Costner, P. Thorpe, B. and McPherson, A. (2005) 'Sick of dust: chemicals in common products – a needless health risk in our homes', *Clean Production Action, Health Care Without Harm*. Available online at: www.noharm.org, accessed 4 August 2005.

Cramer, J. (2005) 'Company learning about corporate social responsibility', *Business Strategy and the Environment*, 14: 255–66.

Crane, A. (2000) 'Corporate greening as amoralization', *Organization Studies*, 21: 673–96.

Deere, C.L. and Esty, D.C. (eds) (2002) *Greening the Americas: NAFTA's Lessons for Hemispheric Trade*. Cambridge: MIT Press.

Dobson, A. (1990) *Green Political Thought*. London: Unwin Hyman.

Domagalski, T.A. (1999) 'Contaminated water and leukemia in Woburn, MA: The failings of civil action', *Organization & Environment*, 12: 332–8.

Dryzek, J.S. (1990) *Discursive Democracy: Politics, Policy, and Political Science*. Cambridge: Cambridge University Press.

Dryzek, J.S. (1992) 'Ecology and discursive democracy: Beyond liberal capitalism and the administrative state', *Capitalism, Nature, Socialism*, 3(2): 18–42.

Dryzek, J.S. (1997) *The Politics of the Earth: Environmental Discourses*. Oxford: Oxford University Press.

Dryzek, J. (2000) *Deliberative democracy and beyond*. Oxford: Oxford University Press.

Dunlap, R.E. (2002) 'An enduring concern: Light stays green for environmental protection', *Public Perspective*, 13(September–October): 10–14.

Dunlap, R.E. (2006) 'Show us the data: The questionable empirical foundations of the "Death of Environmentalism" thesis', *Organization & Environment*, 19: in press.

Eckersley, R. (2004) *The Green State: Rethinking Democracy and Sovereignty*. Cambridge, MA & London: MIT Press.

Egri, C.P. and Herman, S. (2000) 'Leadership in the North American environmental sector: Values, leadership styles, and contexts of environmental leaders and their organizations', *Academy of Management Journal*, 43: 571–604.

Egri, C.P. and Pinfield, L.T. (1996) 'Organizations and the biosphere: Ecologies and environments', in S.R. Clegg, C. Hardy and W.R. Nord (eds), *Handbook of Organization Studies*. London: Sage Publications. pp. 459–83.

Eisner, M.A. (2004) 'Corporate environmentalism, regulatory reform, and industry self-regulation: Toward genuine regulatory reinvention in the United States', *Governance*, 17: 145–67.

Elgin, D. (1993) *Voluntary Simplicity*. New York: William Morrow.

Esty, D.C. and Geradin, D. (1998) 'Environmental protection and international competitiveness: A conceptual framework', *Journal of World Trade*, 32: 5–46.

Esty, D.C. and Porter, M. (2002) 'Ranking national environmental regulation and performance: A leading indicator of future competitiveness?'. Available online at: http://www.isc.hbs.edu/GCR_20012002_Environment.pdf, accessed 11 August 2005.

Etzioni, A. (1998) 'Voluntary simplicity: Characterization, select psychological implications, and societal consequences', *Journal of Economic Psychology*, 19: 619–43.

European Commission (2005) 'The attitudes of European citizens towards environment'. Available online at: http://europa.eu.int/comm/public_opinion/archives/ebs/ebs_217_en.pdf, accessed 7 September 2005.

Fernandez, E., Junquera, B. and Ordiz, M. (2003) 'Organizational culture and human resources in the environmental issue: A review of the literature', *International Journal of Human Resource Management*, 14: 634–56.

Filbeck, G. and Gorman, R.F. (2004) 'The relationship between the environmental and financial performance of public utilities', *Environmental and Resource Economics*, 29: 137–57.

Fineman, S. (2000) 'Enforcing the environment: Regulatory realities', *Business Strategy and the Environment*, 9: 62–72.

Fineman, S. (2001) 'Fashioning the environment', *Organization*, 8: 17–31.

Fischer, F. (2000) *Citizens, Experts, and the Environment: The Politics of Local Knowledge*. Durham: Duke University Press.

Forbes, L.C. and Jermier, J.M. (2002) 'The institutionalization of voluntary organizational greening and the ideals of environmentalism: Lessons about official culture from symbolic organization theory', in A. Hoffman and M. Ventresca (eds), *Organizations, Policy and the Natural Environment: Institutional and Strategic Perspectives*. Stanford: Stanford University Press. pp. 194–213.

Foreman, D. (ed.) (1985) *Ecodefense: A Field Guide to Monkey Wrenching*. Tucson: Earth First! Books.

Foster, J.B. (2005) 'Organizing ecological revolution', *Monthly Review*, 57: 1–10.

Foster, J.B. and York, R. (2004) 'Political economy and environmental crisis: Introduction to the special issue', *Organization & Environment*, 17: 293–5.

Fournier, V. and Grey, C. (2000) 'At the critical moment: Conditions and prospects for critical management studies', *Human Relations*, 53: 7–32.

Fuchs, D.A. and Mazmanian, D.A. (1998) 'The greening of industry: Needs of the field', *Business Strategy and the Environment*, 7: 193–203.

Gallup International (2002) 'Giving the world's people a voice at the World Summit on Sustainable Development'. Available online at: http://www.voice-of-the-people.net/ContentFiles/docs%5CVOP_Environmental_Results.pdf, accessed 5 September 2005.

Gauna, E. and Foster, S. (2003) 'Environmental justice: Stakes, stakeholders, strategies', *Human Rights*, 30(4): 2–4.

Gilley, K.M., Worrell, D.L., Davidson, W.N. and El-Jelly, A. (2000) 'Corporate environmental initiatives and anticipated firm performance: The differential effects of process-driven versus product-driven greening initiatives', *Journal of Management*, 26: 1199–216.

Gladwin, T.N. (1993) 'The meaning of greening: A plea for organizational theory', in. K. Fischer and J. Schot (eds), *Environmental Strategies for Industry*. Washington, D.C.: Island Press. pp. 37–61.

Gladwin, T.N., Kennelly, J.J. and Krause, T.-S. (1995) 'Shifting paradigms for sustainable development: Implications for management theory and research', *Academy of Management Review*, 20: 874–907.

Gordon, P.J. (2001) *Lean and Green: Profit for Your Workplace and the Environment*. San Francisco, CA: Berrett-Koehler.

Green, K., Morton, B. and New, S. (2000) 'Greening organizations: Purchasing, consumption and innovation', *Organization & Environment*, 13: 206–25.

Greenlee, A., Ellis, T. and Berg, R. (2004) 'Low-dose agrochemicals and lawn-care pesticides induce developmental toxicity in marine preimplantation embryos', *Environmental Health Perspectives*, 112: 703–9.

Greer, J. and Bruno, K. (1996) *Greenwash: The Reality Behind Corporate Environmentalism*. New York: Apex Press.

Grey, C. (2004) 'Reinventing business schools: The contribution of critical management education', *Academy of Management Learning and Education*, 3: 178–86.

Guillette, L.J. Jr., Crain, D.A., Gunderson, M.P., et al. (2000) 'Alligators and endocrine disrupting contaminants: A current perspective', *American Zoologist*, 40: 438–52.

Gunningham, N., Kagan, R.A. and Thornton, D. (2003) *Shades of Green: Business, Regulation, and Environment*. Stanford: Stanford University Press.

Haas, J. (1996) 'Environmental ('green') management typologies: An evaluation, operationalization and empirical development', *Business Strategy and Environment*, 5: 59–68.

Habermas, J. (1989) *The Structural Transformation of the Public Sphere*. Cambridge, MA: MIT Press.

Habermas, J. (1992) 'Further reflections on the public sphere', in C. Calhoun (ed.), *Habermas and the Public Sphere*. Cambridge: MIT Press. pp. 421–61.

Halme, M. (1996) 'Shifting environmental management paradigms in two Finnish paper facilities: A broader view of institutional theory', *Business Strategy and the Environment*, 5: 94–105.

Halme, M. (2002) 'Corporate environmental paradigms in shift: Learning during the course of action at UPM-Kymmene', *Journal of Management Studies*, 39: 1087–109.

Hamilton, J.T. (1995) 'Pollution as news: Media and stock market reactions to the toxics release inventory data', *Journal of Environmental Economics and Management*, 28: 98–113.

Hancock, P. and Tyler, M. (2004) "MOT your life': Critical management studies and the management of everyday life', *Human Relations*, 57: 619–45.

Harr, J. (1995) *A Civil Action*. New York: Vintage Books.

Hart, S.L. (1995) 'A natural-resource-based view of the firm', *Academy of Management Review*, 20: 986–1014.

Hart, S.L. and Ahuja, G. (1996) 'Does it pay to be green? An empirical examination of the relationship between emission reduction and firm performance', *Business Strategy and the Environment*, 5: 30–7.

Hawken, P. (1993) *The Ecology of Commerce: A Declaration of Sustainability*. New York: Harper Collins.

Hawken, P., Lovins, A. and Lovins, L.H. (1999) *Natural Capitalism: Creating the Next Industrial Revolution*. Boston: Little Brown and Company.

Hay, P. (2002) *Main Currents in Western Environmental Thought*. Bloomington: Indiana University Press.

Helfand, G.E. and Berck, P. (eds) (2003) *The Theory and Practice of Command and Control in Environmental Policy*. Aldershot, England: Ashgate Publishing.

Hill, R.P. and Dhanda, K.K. (2004) 'Confronting the environmental consequences of the high technology revolution: beyond the guise of recycling', *Organization & Environment*, 17: 254–9.

Hillary, R. (ed.) (2000) *ISO 14001: Case Studies and Practical Experiences*. Sheffield, England: Greenleaf Publishers.

Hilliard, R. (2004) 'Conflicting views: Neoclassical, Porterian, and evolutionary approaches to the analysis of the environmental regulation of industrial activity', *Journal of Economic Issues*, 38: 509–17.

Hoffman, A.J. (2001) *From Heresy to Dogma: An Institutional History of Corporate Environmentalism*, expanded edn. Stanford: Stanford University Press.

Hoffman, A.J. and Ocasio, W. (2001) 'Not all events are attended equally: Toward a middle-range theory of industry attention to external events', *Organization Science*, 12: 414–35.

Hoffman, A.J. and Ventresca, M.J. (eds) (2002) *Organizations, Policy and the Natural Environment: Institutional and Strategic Perspectives*. Stanford: Stanford University Press.

Holliday, C.O., Jr., Schmidheiny, S. and Watts, P. (2002) *Walking the Talk: The Business Case for Sustainable Development*. San Francisco, CA: Greenleaf Publishers.

Hortensius, D. and Barthel, M. (1997) 'Beyond 14001: An introduction to the ISO 14001 Series', in C. Sheldon (ed.), *ISO 14001 and Beyond*. Sheffield, England: Greenleaf Publishing. pp. 19–44.

Hough, P. (1998) *The Global Politics of Pesticides*. London: Earthscan Publications.

Hunt, C.B. and Auster, E.R. (1990) 'Proactive environmental management: avoiding the toxic trap', *Sloan Management Review*, 31: 7–18.

Jasanoff, S. (1990) *Fifth branch: Science advisers as policy makers*. Harvard: Harvard University Press.

Jermier, J.M. (1998) 'Critical perspectives on organizational control', *Administrative Science Quarterly*, 43: 235–256.

Jermier, J.M. and Forbes, L.C. (2003) 'Greening organizations: Critical issues', in M. Alvesson and H. Willmott (eds), *Studying Management Critically*. London: Sage Publications. pp. 157–76.

Juniper, T. and Brown, P. (2005) 'What on earth is happening?', *The Guardian Weekly*, 16–22 September: 7.

Kagan, R.A., Gunningham, N. and Thornton, D. (2003) 'Explaining corporate environmental performance: How does regulation matter?', *Law & Society Review*, 37: 51–90.

Kallio, T.J. and Markkanen, P. (2006) 'The evolution of organizations and the natural environment discourse: Some critical remarks'. Unpublished paper, Department of Management, Turku School of Economics and Business, Finland.

Karliner, J. (1997) *The Corporate Planet: Ecology and Politics in the Age of Globalization*. San Francisco: Sierra Club Books.

Kellow, A. (1999) *International Toxic Risk Management*. Cambridge: Cambridge University Press.

Kelly, T. (2004) 'Unlocking the iron cage: Public administration in the deliberative democratic theory of Jurgen Habermas', *Administration & Society*, 36: 38–61.

Khanna, M., Quimio, W.R.H. and Bojilova, D. (1998) 'Toxic release information: A policy tool for environmental protection', *Journal of Environmental Economics and Management*, 36: 243–66.

Kiesecker, L.K., Bleden, K.S. and Rubbo, M.J. (2004) 'Amphibian decline and emerging disease: what can sick frogs teach us about new and resurgent diseases in human populations and other species of wildlife?', *American Scientist*, 92: 138–47.

King, A. and Lenox, M. (2002) 'Exploring the locus of profitable pollution reduction', *Management Science*, 48: 289–99.

King, A.A. and Lenox, M.J. (2000) 'Industry self-regulation without sanctions: The chemical industry's Responsible Care program', *Academy of Management Journal*, 43: 698–716.

King, C.S. (2000) 'Talking beyond the rational', *American Review of Public Administration*, 30: 271–91.

Klassen, R.D. and McLaughlin, C.P. (1996) 'The impact of environmental management on firm performance', *Management Science*, 42: 1199–214.

Klee, H. and Coles, E. (2004) 'The cement sustainability initiative: Implementing change across a global industry', *Corporate Social Responsibility and Environmental Management*, 11: 114–20.

Koger, S.M., Schettler, T. and Weiss, B. (2005) 'Environmental toxicants and developmental disabilities: a challenge for psychologists', *American Psychologist*, 60: 243–55.

Kolk, A. (2000) *Economics of Environmental Management*. Harlow, England: Prentice Hall.

Kolk, A. and Mauser, A. (2002) 'The evolution of environmental management: From stage models to performance evaluation', *Business Strategy and the Environment*, 11: 14–31.

Korten, D.C. (1998) 'Do corporations rule the world? And does it matter?', *Organization & Environment*, 11: 389–98.

Kurtz, H. (2005) 'Reflections on the iconography of environmental justice activism', *Area*, 37: 79–88.

Landrigan, P. (2001) *Trade Secrets: A Moyers Report*. Public Broadcasting Video. Transcript available online at: http//www.pbs.org/tradesecrets/transcript.html

Laufer, W.S. (2003) 'Social accountability and corporate greenwashing', *Journal of Business Ethics*, 43: 253–61.

Levy, D. (1997) 'Environmental management as political sustainability', *Organization & Environment*, 10: 126–47.

Livesey, S. (2003) 'Organizing and leading the grassroots: An interview with Lois Gibbs, Love Canal Homeowners' Association activist, founder of Citizens Clearinghouse for Hazardous Waste, and Executive

Director of the Center for Health, Environment and Justice', *Organization & Environment*, 16: 488–503.

Lu, J. (2005) 'Risk factors to pesticide exposure and associated health symptoms among cut-flower farmers', *International Journal of Environmental Health Research*, 15: 161–9.

Lundqvist, L. (2000) 'Capacity-building or social construction? Explaining Sweden's shift towards ecological modernization', *Geoforum*, 31: 21–32.

Lyon, T.P. and Maxwell, J.W. (1999) 'Corporate environmental strategies as tools to influence regulation', *Business Strategy and the Environment*, 8: 189–96.

Lyon, T.P. and Maxwell, J.W. (2004) *Corporate Environmentalism and Public Policy*. Cambridge: Cambridge University Press.

Madu, C.N. (1996) *Managing Green Technologies for Global Competitiveness*. Westport, CT: Quorum.

Majumdar, S.K. and Marcus, A.A. (2001) 'Rules versus discretion: The productivity consequences of flexible regulation', *Academy of Management Journal*, 44: 170–9.

Malzahn, C.C. (2005) 'Happy 25th birthday greens', *Spiegel Online*, 13 January.

Maniates, M. (2002) 'In search of consumptive resistance: The voluntary simplicity movement', in T. Princen, M. Maniates and K. Conca (eds), *Confronting Consumption*. Cambridge: MIT Press. pp. 199–235.

May, P.J. (2005) 'Regulation and compliance motivations: Examining different approaches', *Public Administration Review*, 65: 31–44.

May, P.J. and Winter, S. (1999) 'Regulatory enforcement and compliance: Examining Danish-agro-environmental policy', *Journal of Policy Analysis and Management*, 18: 625–51.

McGinn, A.P. (2000) 'Phasing out persistent organic pollutants', in L. Starke (ed.), *State of the World 2000: A Worldwatch Institute Report on Progress Toward a Sustainable Society*. New York/London: W.W. Norton. pp. 79–100.

McGinn, A.P. (2002) 'Reducing our toxic burden', in L. Starke (ed.), *State of the World 2002: A Worldwatch Institute Report on Progress Toward a Sustainable Society*. New York/London: W.W. Norton. pp. 75–100.

Melnyk, S.A., Sroufe, R.P. and Calantone, R.J. (2003) 'A model of site-specific antecedents of ISO 14001 certification', *Production and Operations Management*, 12: 369–85.

Mendel, P.J. (2002) 'International standardization and global governance: The spread of quality and environmental standards', in A.J. Hoffman and M.J. Ventresca (eds), *Organizations, Policy, and the Natural Environment: Institutional and Strategic Perspectives*. Stanford: Stanford University Press. pp. 407–24.

Mengus, B. and Ozanne, L.K. (2004) 'Challenges of the 'green imperative': A natural resource-based approach to the environmental orientation-business performance relationship', *Journal of Business Research*, 58: 430–8.

Millennium Ecosystem Assessment (2005) *Ecosystems and Human Well-Being: Current State and Trends, Volume 1*. Geneva: World Health Organization.

Minz, J.A. (1995) *Enforcement at the E.P.A.* Austin: University of Texas Press.

Montague, P. (1999) 'Precautionary action not taken: Corporate structure and the case study of tetraethyl lead in the United States', in C. Raffensperger and J. Tickner (eds), *Protecting Public Health and the Environment*. Washington: Island Press. pp. 294–308.

Montague, P. (2004a) 'The chemical wars, part 1', *Rachel's Environment and Health News*. #798. Available online at: http://www.rachel.org, accessed 25 June 2005.

Montague, P. (2004b) 'The chemical wars, part 3', *Rachel's Democracy and Health News*. #800, 16 September 2004. Available online at: http://www.rachel.org/search/index.cfm?St=1, accessed 16 February 2006.

Montague, P. (2005) 'Isn't it time we regulated chemicals?', *Rachel's Environment & Health News*, #820. Available online at: http://www.rachel.org, accessed 23 June 2005.

Morelli, J. (1999) *Voluntary Environmental Management: The Inevitable Future*. Boca Raton, FL: Lewis Publishers.

Neale, A. (1997) 'Organizational learning in contested environments: Lessons from Brent Spar', *Business Strategy and the Environment*, 6: 93–103.

Nehrt, C. (1996) 'Timing and intensity effects of environmental investments', *Strategic Management Journal*, 17: 535–47.

Neves-Graca, K. (2004) 'Revisiting the tragedy of the commons: Ecological dilemmas of whale watching in the Azores', *Human Organization*, 63: 289–300.

Newton, T. (2002) 'Creating the new ecological order? Elias and actor-network theory', *Academy of Management Review*, 27: 523–40.

Newton, T. and Harte, G. (1997) 'Green business: Technicist kitsch?', *Journal of Management Studies*, 34: 75–98.

Nichols, J. and Crawford, P. (1983) *Managing Chemicals in the 1980s*. Paris: OECD.

Obach, B.K. (2004) *Labor and the Environmental Movement: The Quest for Common Ground*. Cambridge: MIT Press.

Ojala, M. (2002) 'ABI/Inform: History lesson', *Online*, 26(January–February). Available online at: www.onlinemag.net/jan02/ojala.htm, accessed 6 September 2005.

O'Riordan, T. and Cameron, J. (1994) 'The history and contemporary significance of the precautionary principle', in T. O'Riordan and J. Cameron (eds), *Interpreting the Precautionary Principle*. London: Earthscan Publications Ltd. pp. 12–30.

Orsato, R.J and Clegg. S.R. (2005) 'Radical reformism: Towards a critical ecological modernization', *International Journal of Sustainable Development*, 8: 253–67.

Orsato, R.J., den Hond, F. and Clegg, S.R. (2002) 'The political ecology of automobile recycling in Europe', *Organization Studies*, 23: 639–65.

Palmer, K., Oates, W.E. and Portney, P.R. (1995) 'Tightening environmental standards: The benefit-cost or the no-cost paradigm?', *Journal of Economic Perspectives*, 9: 119–32.

Paterson, M. (2000) *Understanding Global Environmental Politics*. New York: St. Martin's Press.

Peters, J.D. (1993) 'Distrust of representation: Habermas on the public sphere', *Media, Culture, and Society*, 15: 541–71.

Petts, J., Herd, A., Gerrard, S. and Horne, C. (1999) 'The climate and culture of environmental compliance within SMEs', *Business Strategy and the Environment*, 8: 14–30.

Pfeffer, J. (1993) 'Barriers to the advance of organization science: Paradigm development as a dependent variable', *Academy of Management Review*, 18: 599–620.

Porter, M. and van der Linde, C. (1995a) 'Green and competitive', *Harvard Business Review*, 73: 120–34.

Porter, M. and van der Linde, C. (1995b) 'Toward a new conception of the environment-competitiveness relationship', *Journal of Economic Perspectives*, 9: 97–118.

Potoski, M. and Prakash, A. (2005a) 'Green clubs and voluntary governance: ISO 14001 and firms' regulatory compliance', *American Journal of Political Science*, 49: 235–48.

Potoski, M. and Prakash, A. (2005b) 'Covenants with weak swords: ISO 14001 and facilities' environmental performance', *Journal of Policy Analysis and Management*, 25: 745–69.

Radcliffe, J. (2000) *Green Politics*. New York: St. Martin's Press.

Ramus, C.A. and Montiel, I. (2006) 'When are corporate environmental policies a form of 'greenwashing?'', *Business & Society*, 45: in press.

Rasanen, K., Merilaninen, S. and Lovio, R. (1995) 'Pioneering descriptions of corporate greening: notes and doubts about the emerging discussion', *Business Strategy and the Environment*, 3: 9–16.

Reinhardt, F. (1999a) 'Market failure and the environmental policies of firms: Economic rationales for 'beyond compliance' behavior', *Journal of Industrial Ecology*, 3: 9–21.

Reinhardt, F. (1999b) 'Bringing the environment down to earth', *Harvard Business Review*, 77(July–August): 149–57.

Reinhardt, F. (2000) *Down to Earth: Applying Business Principles to Environmental Management*. Boston: Harvard Business School.

Rhee, S-K. and Lee, S-Y. (2003) 'Dynamic change of corporate environmental strategy: Rhetoric and reality', *Business Strategy and the Environment*, 12: 175–90.

Rhodes, E.L. (2003) *Environmental Justice in America: A New Paradigm*. Bloomington: Indiana University Press.

Rivera, J. and Delmas, M. (2004) 'Business and environmental protection', *Human Ecology Review*, 11: 230–4.

Rootes, C.A. (1997) 'Environmental movements and green parties in western and eastern Europe', in M. Redclift and G. Woodgate (eds), *The International Handbook of Environmental Sociology*. Cheltenham, UK: Edward Elgar. pp. 319–48.

Rowledge, L.R., Barton, R.S. and Brady, K.S. (1999) *Mapping the Journey: Case Studies in Strategy and Action toward Sustainable Development*. Sheffield, UK: Greenleaf.

Russo, M.V. and Fouts, P.A. (1997) 'A resource-based perspective on corporate environmental performance and profitability', *Academy of Management Journal*, 40: 534–59.

Russo, M.V. and Harrison, N.S. (2005) 'Organizational design and environmental performance: Clues from the electronics industry', *Academy of Management Journal*, 48: 582–93.

Ryfe, D.M. (2002) 'The practice of deliberative democracy: A study of 16 deliberative organizations', *Political Communication*, 19: 359–77.

Salzmann, O., Ionescu-Somers, A. and Steger, U. (2005) 'The business case for corporate sustainability: Literature review and research options', *European Management Journal*, 23: 27–36.

Schaefer, A. and Harvey, B. (1998) 'Stage models of corporate 'greening': A critical evaluation', *Business Strategy and the Environment*, 7: 109–23.

Schlosberg, D (1999) *Environmental Justice and the New Pluralism*. Oxford: Oxford University Press.

Schmidheiny, S. (1992) *Changing Course: A Global Perspective on Development and the Environment*. Cambridge, MA: MIT Press.

Schor, J. (1998) *The Overspent American: Upscaling, Downshifting, and the New Consumer*. New York: Basic Books.

Seager, J. (1993) *Earth Follies: Coming to Feminist Terms with the Global Environmental Crisis*. New York: Routledge.

Semenza, J.C., Tolbert, P.E., Rubin, C.H., Guillette, L. J. Jr. and Jackson, R.J. (1997) 'Reproductive toxins and alligator abnormalities at Lake Apopka, Florida', *Environmental Health Perspectives*, 105: 1030–2.

Shrader-Frechette, K. (1999) 'Low-level chemical exposures and high-level risks', *Organization & Environment*, 2: 117–22.

Sharma, S. (2000) 'Managerial interpretations and organizational context as predictors of corporate choice of environmental strategy', *Academy of Management Journal*, 43: 681–97.

Sharma, S. (2001) 'Different strokes: Regulatory styles and environmental strategy in the North American oil and gas industry', *Business Strategy and the Environment*, 10: 344–64.

Sharma, S. (2002) 'Research in corporate sustainability: What really matters?', in S. Sharma and M. Starik (eds), *Research in Corporate Sustainability: The Evolving Practice of Organizations in the Natural Environment*. Cheltenham, UK: Edward Elgar. pp. 1–29.

Sharma, S. and Rudd, A. (2003) 'On the path to sustainability: Integrating social dimensions into the research and practice of environmental management', *Business Strategy and the Environment*, 12: 205–14.

Shellenberger, M. and Nordhaus, T. (2005) *The Death of Environmentalism*. Available online at: http://thebreakthrough.org/images/Death_of_Environmentalism.pdf, accessed 13 June 2005.

Shepard, P. (1969) 'Introduction: Ecology and man—A viewpoint', in P. Shepard and D. McKinley (eds), *The Subversive Science: Essays Toward an Ecology of Man*. New York: Houghton Mifflin. pp. 1–10.

Shiva, V. (1993) 'The greening of the global reach', in W. Sachs (ed.), *Global Ecology*. London: Zed Books. pp. 149–56.

Shrivastava, P. (1994) 'Castrated environment: Greening organizational studies', *Organization Studies*, 15: 705–26.

Shrivastava, P. (1995) 'The role of corporations in achieving ecological sustainability', *Academy of Management Review*, 20: 936–60.

Shrivastava, P. (1996) *Greening Business*. Cincinnati, OH: Thompson Executive Press.

Sinclair, A. (1993) 'Approaches to organizational culture and ethics', *Journal of Business Ethics*, 12: 63–73.

Sinclair, D. (1997) 'Self-regulation versus command and control? Beyond false dichotomies', *Law & Policy*, 19: 529–59.

Stafford, E.R., Polonsky, M.J. and Hartman, C.L. (2000) 'Environmental NGO-business collaboration and strategic bridging: A case analysis of the Greenpeace-Foron alliance', *Business Strategy and the Environment*, 9: 122–35.

Starik, M. (1995) 'Research on organizations and the natural environment: Some paths we have traveled, the "field" ahead', in D. Collins and M. Starik (eds), *Research in Corporate Social Performance and Policy: Sustaining the Natural Environment*. Greenwich, CT: JAI Press. pp. 1–41.

Starik, M. (2002) 'Childhood's end? Sustaining and developing the evolving field of organizations and the natural environment', in S. Sharma and M. Starik (eds), *Research in Corporate Sustainability: The Evolving Practice of Organizations in the Natural Environment*. Cheltenham, UK: Edward Elgar. pp. 319–37.

Starik, M. and Marcus, A.A. (2000) 'Special research forum on the management of organizations in the natural environment: A field emerging from multiple paths, with many challenges ahead', *Academy of Management Journal*, 43: 539–47.

Starke, L. (ed.) (2005) *State of the World 2005: Redefining Global Security*. New York: WW Norton.

Starkey, K. and Crane, A. (2003) 'Toward green narrative: Management and the evolutionary epic', *Academy of Management Review*, 28: 220–37.

Steger, U. (2000) 'Environmental management systems: Empirical evidence and further perspectives', *European Management Journal*, 18: 23–37.

Susskind, L.E. (1992) 'New corporate roles in global environmental treaty-making', *Columbia Journal of World Business*, 27(Fall and Winter): 62–73.

Switzer, J., Ehrenfeld, J. and Milledge, V. (2000) 'ISO 14001 and environmental performance: The management goal link', in R. Hillary (ed.), *ISO 14001: Case studies and practical experiences*. Sheffield, UK: Greenleaf Publishing. pp. 262–72.

Szasz, A. (1994) *Ecopopulism: Toxic Waste and the Movement for Environmental Justice*. Minneapolis: University of Minnesota Press.

Therborn, G. (1970) 'The Frankfurt school', *New Left Review*, 63: 65–96.

Thornton, J. (2000) 'Beyond risk: An ecological paradigm to prevent global chemical pollution', *International Journal of Occupational and Environmental Health*, 6: 318–30.

Toepfer, K. (2005) 'Global crusade against toxic chemicals'. Available online at: http://www.tierramerica.net/2004/0522/igrandesplumas.shtml, accessed 20 June 2005.

Toffel, M.W. and Marshall, J.D. (2004) 'Improving environmental performance assessment—A comparative analysis of weighting methods used to evaluate chemical release inventories', *Journal of Industrial Ecology*, 8: 143–72.

Tokar, B. (1997) *Earth for Sale: Reclaiming Ecology in the Age of Corporate Greenwash*. Boston, MA: South End Press.

Torgerson, D. (1990) 'Limits of the administrative mind: The problem of defining environmental problems', in R. Paehkle and D. Torgerson (eds), *Managing Leviathan: Environmental Politics and the Administrative State*. Peterborough, Ontario: Broadview. pp. 115–61.

Torgerson, D. (1999) *The Promise of Green Politics: Environmentalism and the Public Sphere*. Durham: Duke University Press.

Torgerson, D. (2000) 'Farewell to the green movement? Political action and the green public sphere', *Environmental Politics*, 9: 1–19.

Unerman, J. and Bennett, M. (2004) 'Increased stakeholder dialogue and the internet: Towards greater corporate accountability or reinforcing capitalist hegemony?', *Accounting, Organizations and Society*, 29: 685–707.

United States Office of Management and Budget (2004) 'Executive Office of the President of the United States'. Available online at: http://www.whitehouse.gov/omb/budget/fy2004/pma/newchemicals.xls, accessed 27 June 2004.

Utting, P. (ed.) (2002) *The Greening of Business in Developing Countries*. London: Zed Books.

Van Maanen, J. (1995) 'Style as theory', *Organization Science*, 6: 132–43.

Waddell, C. (ed.) (2000) *And No Birds Sing: Rhetorical Analyses of Rachel Carson's Silent Spring*. Carbondale, IL: Southern Illinois University Press.

Waddock, S. (2006) *Leading Corporate Citizens: Vision, Values, Value Added*. Boston: McGraw-Hill Irwin.

Walley, N. and Whitehead, B. (1994) 'It's not easy being green', *Harvard Business Review*, 72: 46–52.

Wallis, V. (1997) 'Lester Brown, the Worldwatch Institute, and the dilemmas of technocratic revolution', *Organization & Environment*, 10: 109–25.

Wasik, J.F. (1996) *Green Marketing and Management.* Cambridge, MA: Blackwell Publishers.

Watson, M. and Emery, A.R.T. (2004) 'Environmental management and auditing systems: The reality of environmental self-regulation', *Managerial Auditing Journal*, 19: 916–28.

Welford, R. (1997) *Hijacking Environmentalism: Corporate Responses to Sustainable Development.* London: Earthscan Publications.

Welford, R. (1998) 'Corporate environmental management, technology and sustainable development: Postmodern perspectives and the need for a critical research agenda', *Business Strategy and the Environment*, 7: 1–12.

Winn, M. and Angell, L. (2000) 'Toward a process model of corporate greening', *Organization Studies*, 21: 1119–47.

World Scientists (1996) 'World scientists warning to humanity', in P.R. Ehrlich and A.H. Ehrlich (eds), *Betrayal of Science and Reason.* Washington, DC: Island. pp. 241–50.

Yap, N.T. (2000) 'Performance based ISO 14001: Case studies from Taiwan', in R. Hillary (ed.), *ISO 14001: Case studies and practical experiences.* Sheffield, UK: Greenleaf Publishing. pp. 138–47.

Yearley, S. (1996) *Sociology, Environmentalism and Globalization.* London: Sage.

York, R. and Foster, J.B. (2005) 'The treadmill of production: Extension, refinement, and critique: Introduction to the special issue, Part II', *Organization & Environment*, 18: 5–6.

York, R. and Rosa, E.A. (2003) 'Key challenges to ecological modernization theory', *Organization & Environment*, 16: 273–88.

Zimmerman, M.E. (1994) *Contesting Earth's Future: Radical Ecology and Postmodernity.* Berkeley: University of California Press.

2.9 Globalization

BARBARA PARKER AND STEWART CLEGG

Introduction

In the 1990s some influential academics had a growing sense that the world was moving toward a single, highly integrated system. Although economic integration tended to attract greatest academic and popular attention, a backward look shows that interconnections and integration were occurring in many spheres of activity. At the organizational level, businesses faced fewer barriers to trade between nations (Ohmae 1995) and profound shifts in traditional patterns of international production, investment, and trade (Dicken 1992) stimulated worldwide opportunities for firms from many nations (Bartlett and Ghoshal 2000; Nolan and Zhang 2003) and of all sizes (Hordes et al. 1995; Simon 1996; Madsen and Servais 1997). Growing numbers of IGOs or intergovernmental global organizations (Simai 1994; Shanks et al. 1996) and NGOs or nongovernmental organizations (Clark 1995; Boli and Thomas 1997; Brown et al. 2000; Doh and Teegen 2002; Kaldor et al. 2002) also pursued their interests on a global scale. Together, these organizations contributed to, and were increasingly affected by, global shifts in political activities, industries, culture, technology, the natural environment, and economies.

Greater organizational propensity to 'go global' was followed by increased scholarly interest in global phenomena. For example, the word 'global' appeared in 12 times as many article titles in 2002 as in 1995. And as Table 2.9.1 shows, the construct had traction. In 2004, 693 scholarly articles used the word 'global' in the title, and it was a descriptor for another 3348 articles.

Research on globalization tackles disparate topics, such as, for instance, weighing the merits of globalization, tracing its sources, or anticipating its outcomes. Research that tends to focus on prime movers analyses singular sources shaping globalization, such as economics (Ohmae 1995; Sideri 1997; van Bergeijk

and Mensink 1997; Govindarajan and Gupta 2000), and communications or transportation technologies (Naisbitt 1994; Ostry and Nelson 1995; Friedman 1999; Can there be 2000; The case for globalization 2000). Other nominated sources of globalization include increasing numbers of joint ventures and the sharing of assets (Reich 1991; O'Neill 1997; Bannock et al. 1998), while other authors stress cultural factors that are lodged in western market societies (Barber 1992; Huntington 1993).

Growing evidence of global interconnections in all these spheres has been addressed through three main approaches. First is the approach exemplified by Stiglitz (2003) and Bhagwati (2004) who analyse a particular global sphere, e.g. economics, while acknowledging global interconnections between markets and other spheres such as government ones. A second, more sociological approach simultaneously examines interconnections among two or more global spheres (Castells 1998; Giddens 1999), while a third scrutinizes global issues such as environmental preservation or women's rights to demonstrate that even seemingly singular issues increasingly cross disciplinary and organizational boundaries (Osland 2003).

Variously referred to as *mondialisation, globalisierung* and *quan qui hua* in the mid-1990s (Scholte 1996), news articles, television, and even textbooks often use the word 'globalization' to mean different things. More recently, verb use has converged around the same stem to produce *globalizar, globalisieren, globalisera*. As might be expected in a new field, authors define and describe globalization in very different ways both between disciplines (Pieterse 1995; Scholte 2000) and within them. An example is management scholars who sometimes use 'global' and 'international' as synonyms when others use the terms to describe different scenarios (Sera 1992; Parker 1996; Kanter and Dretler 1998; Ricks 2003). According to some authorities, globalization is a process – and an unprecedented one at

Table 2.9.1   Growth in globalization (based on electronic searches of peer-reviewed academic journals (3 February 2003; 3 January 2005) abstracted by Academic Source Premier and Business Source Premier)

Scholarly journals abstracted	All defaults for word 'global'	Title contained the word 'global'
1995	252	65
1996	335	90
1997	576	176
1998	886	285
1999	1249	353
2000	1862	665
2001	2219	719
2002	2441	646
2003	3833	690
2004	3348	693

that (Held et al. 1999; Parker 2005) – characterized by growing worldwide interconnections. These interconnections blur traditional boundaries of time, space, nations, and academic disciplines. Although some global interconnections foster integration (Parker 1996), others are divisive. For example, 'super terrorism' (Freedman 2003) creates interconnections but also illustrates growing ideological disconnections. Other factors such as proximity to vibrant markets, a transportation infrastructure, and abundant natural resources shape global opportunities (Dollar and Kraay 2002), interconnecting nations and organizations on different schedules and terms (Sobel 2003).

In addition to fostering worldwide interconnections, globalization is also characterized by rapid and discontinuous change. The economic peaks and troughs of the early 2000s as well as the very different pace of global integration in financial and labour markets is evidence of this characteristic (Husted 2003; Buckley and Ghauri 2004). There is increasing diversity in business forms that are spearheading globalization, something that challenges both practice and research traditions. For example, firms described as 'born global' (Knight and Cavusgil 1996; 2004; Madsen and Servais 1997), as global start-ups (Jolly et al. 1992; Oviatt and McDougall 1995), and as international new ventures (McDougall et al. 1994) tend to internationalize in different ways than larger firms (Coviello and McAuley 1999; Jones 2001), involving radical increases in managerial complexity and decision making (Buckley and Ghauri 2004). Network

theories capture SME expansion more appropriately than the life cycle theories usually applied to larger firms (Coviello and Munro 1995; Holmlund and Kock 1998). Similarly, when firms go global, they demonstrate that businesses can be managed in many ways other than those traditional to single nations. For example, strategic management approaches for successful overseas Chinese businesses differ from those of most Western firms (Haley et al. 1998). Western businesses are enjoined to develop new mindsets (Prahalad and Lieberthal 1998), but firms from other nations also adopt new practices. Examples include non-Japanese CEOs at Japanese firms, erosion of social contracts in South Korea, and a more 'hard-nosed' approach to business in Latin America.

Research on Globalization: From IB to Sociology

Research on globalization is located in many academic disciplines, including international business (IB). Yet while international business began centuries ago (Lacouture 1995; Flynn and Giraldez 2002), international business (IB) research as a separate field emerged only in 1965 (Wright and Ricks 1994). Then IB research specifically did *not* include studies of economic development, foreign trade, or the international monetary system (because they 'belonged' to academic fields in development and international economics); or foreign legal, political, economic and social environments (because they fell under the purview of disciplines like law, political science, economics and behavioural science). Until recently (Lu 2003) most IB research came from English-speaking economists in economically developed nations (Parker 1996). Yet IB research seems not to have transcended the 'critical point in its development' that it faced in 1997 (Toyne and Nigh 1997; Shenkar 2004). Debate still centres on relationships between IB and other disciplines, appropriate IB theory, and to a lesser extent the role IB researchers can or should play in studies of globalization.

Much IB teaching and research is derivative, borrowing theories from marketing, strategy, human resources, or economics to examine IB activities. Because it often uses economic theories to examine international firm behaviour, such as transaction cost analysis (Caves 1998), it is often assumed, erroneously, that IB is a subset of economics or that IB tends to reduce globalization to an economic issue only (Clark and Knowles 2003). More recently, strategy research has laid claim on IB as a subset of its own field (Shenkar 2004), perhaps reflective of a general shift in international strategy research to multidisciplinary approaches (Lu 2003). More recently, IB has extended disciplinary roots to include 'anthropology, sociology, political science, modernization or area studies' (Shenkar 2004: 162–3), shifting its focus from functional areas alone (Masaaki and Aulakh 2002) to become something broader than the economic study of the entities that a given (developed) society creates (Toyne and Nigh 1997). However, repeated calls for interdisciplinarity (Dunning 1989; Toyne 1989; Inkpen and Beamish 1994; Toyne and Nigh 1998; Toyne et al. 2001; Shenkar 2004;) have produced scant results. While a limited range of political science topics, such as political risk and MNE-government relationships (Shenkar 2004), have been well-aired, a great deal of interdisciplinary potential remains fallow. In some cases interdisciplinarity has been viewed as superficial (Shenkar 2004), misapplied (Toyne and Nigh 1998), or resulting in only modest amounts of cross fertilization between disciplines (Buckley and Chapman 1996).

Buckley and Pervez (2004) believe the IB research agenda may be stalled due to its failure to examine 'big questions' (p. 81). Another possibility is that IB scholars spend too much time and energy examining the same questions, such as whether IB is the same or different from economics. Many scholars believe research should narrow the focus of its attention to the enterprise (Buckley and Chapman 1996; Peng 2004; Wilkins 1997), while others believe focus should expand to examine the changing, and increasingly global, context of business (Toyne and Nigh 1997). Toyne and Nigh's 1997 question 'whether we are dealing with a single phenomenon, the firm, as Wilkins and others argue (1997), or with a phenomenon that spans a number of different levels of society that somehow interact and influence one another' (Toyne and Nigh 1997: 676) – still finds no definitive answer among IB researchers. In later work, Toyne and Nigh (1998; 2001) called for an evolving or emerging interaction paradigm to view IB research as a 'multilevel, hierarchical process that evolves (or emerges) over time as a consequence of the interaction of two or more socially embedded, multilevel business processes' (2001: 9). The latter authors argue that the consequences of 'cultural, economic, social, and political interactions are important' to businesses (Toyne and Nig 1997). Shenkar (2004) believes that IB research can develop a 'superior ability to incorporate and interpret international issues, including political events, social processes and historical legacies, which is where economics and strategy fail'. On this basis, the global context belongs best to IB, he argues. Given the emphasis on multiple levels of analysis, time, and processes, the evolving interaction paradigm for IB research appears to be particularly useful for research on the globalization process. But it is not clear if it is one of the 'big questions' for IB (Buckley and Ghauri 2004) or merely an important but not central topic for IB research (Peng 2004).

From sociology, as one might expect, the focus is broader. Therborn (2000a: 154), for instance, defines contemporary globalization as 'tendencies to a worldwide reach, impact, or connectedness of social phenomena or to a world-encompassing awareness among social actors' and argues that 'the current overriding interest in globalization means two things. First of all, a substitution of the global for the universal; second, a substitution of space for time' (Therborn 2000b: 149).

Often the focus on globalization echoes that of political administrations such as the current US Bush government, where history is viewed as a process that is increasingly institutionalizing democratic concepts of 'rights'. Notably, in the late eighteenth century, the 'rights of man' (at least for men of property) were declared and, after bloody struggles, installed in variable degree, in many advanced societies. The relativities were always national: as late as the 1960s there was the necessity for a struggle over the meaning of Civil Rights in the US because it was clear that the 'inalienable truths' of the American Constitution, that all men were born free and had a right to the pursuit of happiness, did not include black men. Later, women, of all colours, were to conclude that they didn't include them either. Now, increasingly, we measure our rights and the rights of others in faraway places against the notion of universal human rights, institutionalized in charters in the United Nations. Rights have been relativized from what nations can choose to implement to what humanity demands. Linking national societies to humankind is the relativization of citizenship: what rights do particular citizenships bestow and how can you choose to improve your lot? For many people the only answer to these questions is to escape the weighted dice of being in an economically backward society and seeking, through either legally sanctioned or illegal means, to enter one of the more privileged parts of the world, such as Europe, the USA, or Australasia. Globalization, rather than foreclosing issues of individual or organizational identity on convergence on one form, opens them all up in a number of significant ways.

From an organizational and management perspective, a number of features develop from the 1970s onwards. These include the emergence of an increasing separation of the 'real' economy of production and its simulacra in the 'symbol economy' of financial flows and transactions. A new international division of labour and a new international financial system emerged, the latter centered on London or Hamburg, New York and Tokyo. The new international division of labour became truly global, compressing and fragmenting both space and distance in such a way that both production but various business-service industries were distributed in unlikely places (Krugman 1998). These new divisions restructure geographic space and introduce relativism and tensions to nation states. More complex notions of personal identity emerge, attendant upon revolutions in gender, sexual, ethnic and racial mores that occur elsewhere. The interpenetration of culture and economy produces new micro-markets increasingly premised on the differentiation of identities within increasingly sophisticated societies conceived as market niches by global corporations.

After the demise of the Cold War the globalization of problems of 'rights' occurred in a world that was no longer politically bipolar: Russians want the same rights as consumers in the West. But equally, as the same Russians abandoned their futile campaign to rule Afghanistan, the Taliban, repulsed by what they saw as the decadence of capitalist market society as much as they were by the communist state, gave shelter to those who, in the name of God, wished to wage war on Crusaders, whether from the East or the West. Old questions of identity re-emerge, partially as a consequence of the break-up of State Socialist hegemony, principally in the former USSR and the Balkans, but also through the assertion of religious identities founded in Islam, Orthodox Christianity and, sometimes, as in East Timor, Catholicism. Thus, even our inter-subjective experience of terrorism is globalized today through exposure to international media reporting – is there anyone who has not seen the images of the planes ripping into the World Trade Center? The consequences of this global exposure have been profound: states wage war pre-emptively in a doctrine that seemed to have died with the First World War but fight it against targets, such as 'Terror', that are hard to locate in a world where states are not the only other players, and often seem to identify it with gestures that seem as imperially pointless as the battleship shelling the African jungle in Joseph Conrad's (1970) *Heart of Darkness*. Meanwhile atrocities are visited on civilians who had no idea that they were about to become casualties in wars in which they were only dimly aware, if at all, that they were engaged. And we are informed in ceaseless detail about the latest 'victories' and 'advances' in this war from Al-Jahzeera and CNN – although the detail of what is a victory or a defeat may vary with what you watch and where you watch it. Nonetheless, there is an increase in global institutions, organizations and initiatives, and the emergence of global communication through e-mail, satellite TV, CCN etc. These help to give rise to global consciousness, perhaps most manifest in phenomena such as the Rio Earth Summit and the appreciation of the global warming threat posed by a thinning ozone layer. These issues, which go to the survival of the species and the ways of life we know, are perhaps not as televisually compelling as the 'War against Terror' but probably of longer term importance. Kyoto rather than Kabul may well mean more in the long term.

Today, however, rather than the existential issues highlighted, when globalization is referred to as a process by management writers it tends to be focused mostly on European, North American, and Japanese trade, investment and financial flows (Rugman 2005). For proponents of the globalization thesis it is the design, production, distribution and consumption of processes, products and services on a world scale, using patents, databases, advanced information, communication and transport technologies and infrastructures, to control them, which characterizes globalization.

Global Interconnections

Globalization of the Natural Environment

The natural environment is globally assessed first in terms of preserving global commons (Cleveland 1990; Buck 1998), broadly defined to include 'the oceans, the sea beds, the atmosphere, space, Antarctica, the planet's biodiversity (in forest and natural ecosystems), as well as the Earth's electromagnetic spectrum' (Henderson 1999: 24), i.e. the Internet. In addition, degradation of natural resources and consumption of finite raw materials such as wood, rubber, minerals, ores, or oil generate political and economic strife based on increased competition and shrinking supplies (Goodstein 2004; Roberts 2004). It is also evident that species biodiversity important to survival is threatened around the world. Global interdependence between human and ecological health is both causing and spreading global diseases such as HIV/AIDS (Garrett 1994; French 2003; Walters 2003), creating adverse effects on long-term growth in developing economies (Barro and Sala-I-Martin 1995: Bloom et al. 2001; Haacker 2002). Finally, as evidenced by the 2004 tsunami, natural disasters also have global impact. Increasingly, we live in 'risk societies' where state boundaries cannot insulate us from man-made or natural disasters generated elsewhere (Beck 2002). Economic growth and population growth place simultaneous demands on the natural environment by depleting resources, eliminating species, and spreading disease.

There are two opposed perspectives on environmental preservation. Some envision a future 'boom' leading to unprecedented prosperity; others cite global warming, species reduction, and global disease as harbingers of 'doom' in an environmentally impoverished future. In general, supporters of the 'boom' perspective argue that rapid economic growth will generate technologies to address environmental problems (Simon 1981; 1998; Easterbrook 1995; Von Weizsacker et al. 1998; Greening industry 1999; Lomborg 2001; Huber and Mills 2005). Supporters of the 'doom' perspective believe technology is part of the environmental problem rather than its solution (Ehrlich 1969; Hawken 1993; Daly 1996; Ehrlich and Ehrlich 2004; Diamond 2005). Wilson (2002) argues that boom and doom perspectives also differ in terms of forecasting techniques, how far proponents look in the future, and value placed on nonhuman life. The resulting 'growth vs. environment' debate may lead to win/lose thinking (Porter and van der Linde 1995) when what may be needed are new perspectives in which 'economic success and ecosystem survival are both worthy and necessary goals for individuals, organizations, society and Nature' (Stead and Stead 1996: 131). Futurist Henderson (1996) believes win/win solutions are not only possible but imperative to human and business survival. Such a win/win approach is supposed to move the debate to the common ground of 'sustainable development', or development that ensures a viable world for future generations. Sustainable development is reflected in 'cradle to cradle' thinking (McDonough and Braungart 2002), represented by global organizations such as Natural Step.

Global Economics

Trade, foreign direct investment, and capital all contribute to economic globalization. For the first time since 1980 the 55 leading economies grew in 2004 (Dancing in step 2004), demonstrating world economic synchronicity. Presumably, anticipated downturns also will be simultaneous. By 2003 world trade was $7.3 trillion in tangible goods and $1.8 trillion in commercial services, but growth was discontinuous at 4% in 1999 and 12% in 2000 (*International trade statistics* 2004). Real growth of trade is extremely strong and persistent (van Bergeijk and Mensink 1997); and together world trade in goods and services have grown to about 25% of world GDP as compared to 10% about 30 years ago (Govindarajan and Gupta 2000). FDI once moved mostly between advanced economies but now it increasingly moves between developing economies (Mathews 2002; Aykut et al. 2003) and from them to advanced economies.

The global economy creates a worldwide market for capital that moves freely, and sometimes disrupts when 'hot' money rapidly flees or floods markets (Kwan 1995). Globalization of the economy has reshaped some roles for central banks and led to restructuring in both private and more public financial institutions like the World Bank and the IMF. Evidence to date shows advanced nations benefit most from economic globalization (Shigehara 2002; Bradford et al. 2005), with fewer benefits to losses for developing economies (Rigged trade 2001; Wolf 2004; Sachs 2005).

In the mid-1990s, economic growth involving export stimulation and FDI and entailing regulatory liberalization were central concerns, but by 2000 global poverty had moved to center stage on the agenda of world economic leaders. Evident disparities between rich and poor economies highlighted challenges posed by unfettered market systems vs managed ones, reviving Chicago school/Keynsian debates. Developing economies which are open to FDI and foreign trade generally have faster growth rates which translate into higher incomes for the poor (Dollar and Kraay 2002), providing an argument for more open economies, although the emergence of China as a behemoth of world trade is hardly an argument for unfettered liberalism – it has been a highly managed economy. Alternative liberal approaches have included import substitution stimulated by microenterprise loans to the poor, and supply side opportunities that make the poor more central to a consumption society (Gabel 2004; Prahalad 2005). Other poverty alleviation proposals have included more aid (Sachs 2005), and enhanced property rights (De Soto 2000; Olson 2000) to stimulate economic growth in underdeveloped economies (*World Development Report* 2001).

Perspectives on economic globalization tend to be dominated by either/or thinking that frames globalization in fairly simple terms of good vs bad. For example, although Stiglitz (2003) argues that globalization – defined in economic terms as 'the removal of barriers to free trade and the closer integration of national economies' (p. ix) – has the potential for good, he believes that policies pursued throughout the 1990s created financial and economic turmoil in most developing economies. His conclusion is that for most of the world's poor, globalization has produced bad results. By contrast Bhagwati's (2004) view of economic globalization is

that it has received an unduly bad rap from anti-globalists. Accordingly, he argues that globalization has produced positive results for the poor. Opposing debates like these stimulate efforts to find some middle ground that balances government interventions with market activities that differ from prevailing theories of economic development by arguing that government interventions can help some countries be better off without causing others to be worse off, and emphasizing simultaneous need to improve national government performance and activities of global financial institutions (*Emerging issues in development economics* 1997).

Labour also contributes to wealth creation. Korten (1995) argues that global competition for jobs is a 'race to the bottom' replacing low-wage jobs with even lower-wage ones. A second theme in the race to the bottom argument is that labour competition puts downward pressure on labour standards. A third concern is that hiring cheap labour worldwide disrupts social contracts within economies. For example, child labour prohibitions in one country are subverted when companies from that nation substitute child labour abroad (Rodrik 1997). A contrary argument is that all workers benefit by job migration. There is some evidence of upward international wage convergence for workers in similar skill groups (Wood 1994), and manufacturing jobs previously monopolized by Western firms now provide growth in many developing economies (Krugman 1998). Despite considerable rhetoric, there is little empirical evidence for either position (Lee 1997).

Labour globalization occurs in both manufacturing and service industries, unfolding in three stages. First, low-skilled manufacturing jobs went global, followed by middle-skill jobs providing 'back office' functions such as call centres, tax preparation, or reading X-rays. More recently, professional labour and knowledge work has globalized.

From Reich's (1991) perspective, the research scientists, new professional engineers, public relations executives, investment bankers, lawyers, real estate developers, and many other professionals – including even a few global university professors – form a new global elite labour market of symbolic analysts. Symbolic analysis involves manipulating symbols to solve, identify, and broker problems. It simplifies reality into abstract images by rearranging, juggling, experimenting, communicating, and transforming these images, using analytic tools, such as mathematical algorithms, legal arguments, financial analysis, scientific principles, or psychological insights that persuade, amuse, induce, deduce, or somehow or other address conceptual puzzles (Reich 1991).

To what degree are these symbolic analysts or knowledge workers different from what has gone before? What marks out their professional identity? Management analysts, such as Alvesson (1993; Alvesson and Karreman 2001), have argued that what marks such work as different are its linguistic and symbolic accomplishment in circumstances of high ambiguity and uncertainty. In such circumstances where there are multiple and competing 'answers' to problems, the persuasive abilities of the knowledge worker come to the fore, comprising both their image intensity (the suit they wear, the briefcase they carry, the sleekness of their PowerPoint presentation) and the persuasiveness of their rhetoric (the robustness of their argument, their vocabulary, their accent). These workers are global, working for Big 4 firms or their small boutique equivalents; they regularly move between the great commercial capitals of the world, creating genuinely international corporate elites. Such transience, perhaps, fosters networking skills and alters sensibilities around risk, two other important characteristics of the symbolic analysts. In summary, they are the stressed-out but well-remunerated shifters and shapers of money, meanings and markets, doing deals, making business, moving from project to project (Garrick and Clegg 2001). Where once these road warriors came principally from advanced economies, they increasingly come from developing ones as well.

The evidence of these jobs suggests that, despite attention to the issues of wages and associated cost of taxes raised by journalists and politicians, transnational companies do not, by and large, invest their main facilities where wages and taxes are the lowest. If they did the theory of comparative costs would work far better than it does. The reasons are self-evident: wages are often a minor cost-factor; greater transaction costs are associated with the presence or absence of densely embedded networks for business in particular locales, such as the world cities of New York, London, Paris and Tokyo, which are likely to remain so. Additionally, domestic linkages institutionally frame businesses in embedded relationships with universities, financial institutions, government institutions, and so on. Government-business relations typically have an exclusive rather than open character and can be an important component in building national competitive advantage (Porter 1990), which then attracts globally skilled knowledge-workers who relocate for jobs.

The international flow of expert migrant professional and knowledge workers helps create a global labour market in a growing number of occupations, not only those that are glamorous. Supporting these wealthy symbolic analysts are household help and lower-level service workers. In global cities such as Hong Kong and Singapore you can see street level globalization in the form of the mainly Filipina and Sri Lankan female domestic workers who congregate in the public spaces of the Central Business District on their day of rest, Sunday. The rest of the week it is more likely to be thronged with global business people while the maids, chauffeurs and other domestic servants make global households run smoothly.

Additionally, there is a shadow-labour force of workers in the symbolic sphere – but workers who are tightly scripted, operating in unambiguous and simple environments, unlike their symbolic analyst counterpoints. Outside of the confines of the corporate glitterati and the symbolic analyst elite there is a category of disaggregated work quintessentially associated with globalization, and mostly associated with 'back office' functions. An example is call centres ushered into existence in the 1990s because they allow corporations to downsize internal functions by outsourcing jobs to locations where wage rates were lower and the workforce more pliable. The growth of information technology allows for the increasing codification of knowledge reducing the need for physical contact between producers and consumers, of which call centres are the perfect example – they can be located anywhere. Work is cheapened by routinization of existing tasks; re-engineered tasks can then be moved to places where wages are cheaper. The transaction costs associated are not great: satellites and computers can ensure virtual linkage. The blueprint is clear: rationalize parts of the organization; introduce jobs at just over minimum wage in deprived, post-industrial parts of the country; institute a system of surveillance aimed at maximizing efficiency.

By 2002, 3% of the US workforce and 1.3% of the European workforce were making a living from working in call centres, otherwise termed 'factories of the future'. To be more concrete about the data, currently, 2.99% of UK jobs are in contact centres; over 1 million people will be directly employed in contact centres by 2007. A good deal was written about the repetitive nature of work, the exacting management controls and the sheer amount operatives were expected to do. The last few years have seen call centres go global, as it were, moving out of relatively poor areas of advanced economies into developing ones. For instance, BT, the telecoms corporation, is cutting back its UK call centres, in favour of opening up operations in Delhi and Bangalore. Once call centres are established, they are estimated to be considerably cheaper to run in India than in the UK. For instance, in 2003, a British call center worker will typically earn £13,000–14,000 a year: in India a worker doing a similar job will make £1,200. The move to India is continuing apace, to the extent that a recent report in *The Guardian* (Tran 2003) suggests that by 2008 there will be around 100,000 call center jobs created by British companies alone. The Philippines, the Czech Republic and South Africa are also among the nations attempting to make in roads into the call center industry, to a sufficient extent that they form an important pillar of each nation's economic policy. In response to backlash from advanced economies, Indian outsourcing firms such as Wipro and Tata have introduced call centres in US communities to bring some of these jobs full circle.

In terms of globalization, there are also 'grunge jobs' (Jones 2003: 256). Jones sees grunge jobs as essentially bifurcated: first there are the semiskilled workers who work in the lower reaches of the supply chains established by the global giants, which Castells (2000) estimated at about 35% of the jobs in the US economy. It is a contingent, easily dismissible and re-employable mass of people who can be hired and fired to absorb transaction costs and cushion demand for the core companies globally. When these global companies react to signs of economic distress then it is these subcontract workers in the supply chain who bear the pain first, buffering the core company employees. These workers are low skill, add little value, and are easily disposable but at least they may have social insurance and do work in the formal economy.

The second element in the composition of the grunge economy comprises an underclass of workers who are often illegal immigrants working sporadically in extreme conditions outside of the formally regulated labour market (Castells and Portes 1989). An estimated 65% of legitimate labour is performed in the informal sector in developing economies (Henderson 1999). Home-based workers and street vendors are two of the largest sub-groups of the informal workforce (Women and men in the informal economy 2002). These workers are part of an estimated $9 trillion annual shadow economy which as a percentage of national output grew in every OECD country from 1989–1999. As Jones (2003) reports, Deloitte and Touche research (1998) suggests that informal sector activity ranges from 40% in the Greek economy, through to 8–10% of the British economy. In Latin America, the informal labour market is estimated at 20–30% of the non-agricultural labour force (Gomez-Buendia 1995). States often encourage the informal sector as an arena from which 'street level' and taxable entrepreneurs might develop in enterprises other than the marketing of drugs, prostitutes, and the proceeds of crime (Deloitte and Touche 1998; Sassen 1998).

Some 60 000 transnational or global businesses employed about 40.5 million people in 1999, an increase from 23.6 million in 1990 (*World Investment Report* 2000). This is a relatively small persentage of three billion estimated workers worldwide, but many of these global organizations have attracted significant public attention in the last decade because jobs they create are new formal sector ones in developing economies where labour standards and wages can be low. They often generate significant income in nations where they operate, and as a group these organizations often are viewed as the only powerful forces for change (Hawken 1993). According to an OECD study, global businesses pay their workers more than the national average, spend more on R&D in countries where they invest than do domestic counterparts, export more than domestic firms, and their activities have a bigger effect on poorer economies than on richer ones (Foreign friends 2000).

Transnationals also create jobs when they employ people indirectly through global supply chains, but they often attract bad press for their sub-contracting practices. For instance, writers such as Klein (2001) are extremely critical of the role that transnationals play in the developing world. Her argument is that transnationals behave irresponsibly by employing sub-contractors who pay low wages, have poor working conditions and potentially abusive environments. She singles out famous companies whose brands are known the world over. In a campaign by Oxfam – the non-governmental organization – Nike was taken to task over these issues. One thing that such campaigning activity has delivered is assurance from Nike that such concerns have been addressed, which for many is a contestable point. Yet by 2005,

Nike had not only raised standards among world-wide suppliers, but also was the first business to publish a list of its suppliers. On balance it is fair to say that they may be positive agents of change. It is clear that transnationals have the potential to create stable, long-term jobs with decent pay and conditions. Those that do not will be subject to campaigns throughout the Western World. Thus, potentially they deliver better jobs and better wages in many economies: additionally, they set standards that local industry has to aspire to in both labour and industry practice. If there really were 'no logos' it would be much harder to police these standards as there would be no brand differentia offering opportunities for discrimination between the choice of one T-shirt or another. One would expect that in such a situation that price signals would be even more sovereign and would exercise still stronger downward pressure on local wages and conditions in the Third World. Fair logos rather than no logos might be better policy. Sub-contract manufacturing jobs also create higher export earnings domestically, which can potentially enhance the tax base of national governments unless companies use sophisticated methods to move tax losses around their global operations or transfer prices of internally traded goods to minimize tax liabilities.

The employees in the sweatshops of the Third World are in some respects fortunate: it all depends on the point of comparison (Cawthorne and Kitching 2001). They have jobs: they are not hustling on the street, selling gum to standing motorists, shoe-shines to seated customers in restaurants on the street, or their bodies to whosoever wants to buy their services. In the cities of the Third World and in the ghettoes of the First World, many people on the mean streets of the barrios and *favelas*, desperate and poor, are in this underclass position. For them any organizational employment would be a step up the ladder of opportunity. It seems perverse, in these circumstances, for Western liberals to oppose the opportunities that they actually get on the basis of standards never applied to life lived on the streets.

Globalization of Political/Legal Environments

The world is organized chiefly into nation-states whose political infrastructures differ, but with globalization comes growing need for global governance systems to agree on weights and measures, provide a systematic financial system, develop guidelines for sustainable development, ensure equity, and provide unified responses to development needs, disaster relief (Commission on 1995) and security. On a worldwide scale, creating a common and global 'good' society involves many more than governmental actors in the political/legal environment. Intergovernmental organizations, nongovernmental organizations, businesses, and members of global gangs, pirates, and terrorist organizations also shape global political/legal environments.

The nation-state is a 'robust' form of political organization (Sobel 2003: 422), and political science research shows variations in outcomes depend on national factors more than global ones (Sobel 2003). Yet old rivalries persist and new ones emerge as national policies also are shaped by occurrences outside nations (Hoffman 2002). National political systems increasingly interconnect due to privatization, deregulation, and national efforts to simulate business activities such as industrial policy, trade missions, and tax breaks for foreign direct investors. Government leaders link their political destiny to that of other nations via trade agreements that are bilateral, regional, multinational, and global in scope. Trade agreements can include special arrangements like foreign economic zones and city-states within nations; industry alliances such as OPEC; regional economic agreements such as the EU, ASEAN, or the African Union; or global trade agreements such as the World Trade Organization. Despite benefits of collective power, global trade alliances often require new national definitions of what constitutes self-interest (Prestowitz et al. 1991). Sometimes these redefinitions result from citizen action such as occurred at the 1999 Seattle World Trade Organization. Established to shape worldwide commercial relationships, protestors at this and other meetings convinced WTO nations that commercial activities cannot readily be separated from labour rights and environmental concerns.

At the global level, common defense is partially served by the North American Treaty Organization; the UN also has global peacekeeping forces. But there is no common and global defense system to manage armed conflict, even as there is growing need for it. This need calls for enhanced forms of global governance that can reduce the gap between rich and poor, especially in the poorest economies where most conflict occurs (Pastor 2000). Common security also is needed to manage increased cross-border criminal activity on land and sea that includes drug and human trafficking, money laundering, and terrorism on a global scale (Dangerous waters 2001; Freedman 2003).

Examples of armed conflict, global crime, and global terrorism show that while effects are global, defense and security mechanisms are not. Their absence is due to cultural roots within nations linked to security and defense mechanisms, and to coordination and ethical problems for integrating police records into a single world database. In the absence of more global mechanisms, business investments are few in the poorest economies where conflict, corruption, crime, and terrorism are high. According to Robinson (2000), the twenty-first century will belong to transnational criminals until the world revises its notion of policing to become global as well as national.

Global Technologies

Global technological development often focuses on processes and products with greatest global impact, but there is a propensity to examine products more than processes. Certainly one of the most profound technological changes has been introduction of telecommunications to link the world, and computers that facilitate those links. According to Makridakis (1989), today's technological revolution began in the 1940s with mathematical demonstrations of computer concepts. Computerization to follow occurred in phases of processing, microcomputers, and networks (Bradley et al. 1993) that expanded to digital networks that merge telephone, Internet, television, and other media. In addition to very visible products and services, this same time period has witnessed breakthrough process technologies including just-in-time inventory management, total quality management, and organizational learning.

The rate of technological innovation has increased markedly during the last 200 years. Schumpeter's waves of creative destruction decreased from 60 years for innovations in water power, textiles, and iron to only 30 years for digital networks, software, and new media innovations. Technical innovations move quickly within and between organizations and nations (Petrella 1992), often spread by global businesses that locate R&D labs in different nations (Chiesa 1995) and via mergers and acquisition activities (von Zadtwitz et al. 2004). The basic research system is open and accessible (Castells 2000), but there is some evidence that

management higher education is moving toward an 'Americanized' model (see *Journal of Management Inquiry* 2004: 13(2) for examples). Almost 96% of national R&D traditionally is conducted by industrialized nations such as Japan, the US, Switzerland, Sweden and other Western European nations. Other countries such as Singapore are not themselves high in innovation, but rapidly import new technologies. In general, the most innovative nations also tend to be those that create an infrastructure that encourages business start-ups. Many newly Asian economies nations have become more innovative with investments that upgrade the technological base. This includes approaches such as increased expenditures on R&D, improved education, FDI incentives, and making the home country more attractive to home-country engineers and scientists. Countries that spend little on R&D often introduce technologically improved products at a low rate. As a result, they are less competitive and show lower rates of prosperity. McRae (1994) concludes that nations have been increasingly able to imitate one another because innovations can cross national borders within days and weeks. Accordingly, he believes that the best predictor of a nation's economic success will be national creativity and social responsibility more than technological achievement *per se*.

Information technologies sometimes stimulate equal opportunities due to increased interconnections for some two billion subscribers to global telecommunications services that keep them informed and connected. The original Silicon Valley has worldwide counterparts in Scotland's Silicon Glen, China's Silicon Alleys, and similar tech centres in Singapore, Taiwan, Argentina, Malaysia, and Brazil. Ability to connect with others also makes it possible for small firms to compete globally (Castells 1998; Naisbitt 1994). Israeli scientists and entrepreneurs, for example, contribute to breakthroughs in advanced computer design, electric auto fuel, data networking, medical imaging, and electronic cash transfer. Information access permits human rights groups to gather information that governments have long been able to suppress, and information sharing has enhanced knowledge transfer among women's groups worldwide. Instant on-line translators foster equality by reducing the English-language bias in the Internet. Interestingly, reasons to provide translations from English to non-English are business ones: in many countries there are not enough English-readers to support English-only Internet services. According to Global Reach (2004), the number of non-English web users grew from 10 million in 1996 to 540 million in 2003 or 69% of users, illustrating that early bias toward English-language use has abated on the Internet.

The rapid speed of information transfer also alters many traditional assumptions about knowledge. For example, in the past technological breakthroughs were once the province of advanced economies, and knowledge was power in the hands of top managers. Today any person anywhere can provide and consume information. Within organizations, knowledge has become more central to organizational success and everyone is encouraged to leverage their knowledge to benefit the company. Because knowledge management is more central to organizational success, this former staff function now is located at the top of many organizational hierarchies. Additionally, in knowledge intensive companies, there is greater reliance on and rewards for younger employees who can best leverage information breakthroughs. Changes like these alter sources of organizational power, they increase the speed of change, and they create additional demands for knowledge as an organizational input. On the output side, telecommunication connections also force business owners worldwide to answer and send emails an average 1.5 hours per day (Thornton 2005).

Breakthroughs in many process and product technologies generate questions about justice that often focus on the digital divide among rich and poor economies (Green and Ruhleder 1996). Other topics concern privacy, and the organization's ability to stimulate creativity at arms-length or in virtual teams. Knoke (1996) argues that in the face of technological change, particularly the 'fourth dimension' of computerization, nation-states will lose sovereignty, and physical place will become almost irrelevant. Cyberspace governance is difficult to achieve because the Internet supercedes national or regional rules and regulations (Kobrin 2001). Accordingly, governments have found it difficult to keep out unwanted cyber visitors or to limit Internet use to legal, moral, or ethical ends. Others argue that technological breakthroughs challenge traditions when organizations become virtual (Davidow and Malone 1992), when big businesses 'capture' smaller ones in supply chain relationships, when jobs are lost in an information-driven world (Rifkin 1995).

Globalization of Culture

Like globalization, culture is variously defined (Hofstede 1980; Terpstra and David 1991; Schein 1992). Cultural globalization represents disputed terrain. Some argue there neither is nor could there be a global culture (Smith 1990). Others present worldwide availability of branded products and accompanying consumption-based values (Bannerjee and Linstead 2001), services such as the Internet and television media that reduce communication boundaries and use of English as a common business language (Crystal 1997) as evidence of cultural globalization. This global culture may exist for a relatively small group of people such as the educated and connected (Bird and Stevens 2003), members of demographic groups such as the global elite or global teens (Hassan and Katsanis 1994; Moses 2000), or adherents to particular ideals such as a Davos culture of the global and economic elite and wanna-bes (Huntington 1993; Berger 1997).

Globalization of culture frequently explores tensions between existing cultures and emerging global culture(s). At least initially, many cultural influences moved from the Western world to developing ones (Giddens 1999; Clark and Knowles 2003), spawning concerns that Western cultural imperialism was arising to produce culture clash (Barber 1996) or destructive conflict (Huntington 1993). Said (1998) criticized the latter view of the contemporary world, arguing that thinking in terms of civilizations oversimplifies complex, diverse, and often contradictory aspects of cultures.

Others suggest 'creolization', 'mestizaje', or 'orientalization' will enhance but not necessarily redefine culture (Pieterse 1995; Husted 2003). 'Glocalization' or loose connections between what is local and what is global may instead be forged (Robertson 1995), leading to multiplication of cultural differences (Kahn 1995). The result may be hybridization or 'cross vergence in values' (Ricks et al. 1990) counterbalanced by strong local influences (Husted 2003). Scholte (2000) believes global exposure to media and improved connectivity with contacts beyond local ones helps people reconfigure their own social space. Tomlinson (2003) argues that one result can be amplified significance and greater understanding of local identity. An example is English-language use which in some quarters has become the common business language, but its use often is localized such that it becomes many forms of English (Crystal 1997). Further, English-language does not displace local languages, suggesting that cultural practice is not the same as adopting a culture (Husted 2003). A broad definition of culture is that it is the learned, shared, interrelated set of symbols and patterned assumptions that helps any group – global, national, organizational, family, etc – externally adapt and internally integrate. People typically belong to many communities simultaneously of which global culture is merely one (Sobel 2003).

Among converging global values in the last quarter century are increased emphasis on environmental protection, women's rights, participation in decision-making in economic and political life, and national cultural shifts toward secular-rational values (Ingelhart and Baker 2000). For example, 17,000 middle managers in 62 cultures expressed common belief that gender egalitarianism and humane orientation 'should be' work values (House et al. 2004).

Among paradoxes of global culturalization are growing pressures for within-culture homogeneity set against a backdrop of increased worldwide heterogeneity. As time and space compression bring us to a realization of one world, they also expose us to the infinite variety and diversity of the world. These tensions create opportunities and they exact costs for nations, and for organizations. Businesses often are the crucible to balance tensions of cultural homogeneity and heterogeneity, but other types of organizations, e.g. international NGOs also contribute to development of world culture. Among principles the latter espouse worldwide are individualism, universalism, rational voluntarist authority that encourages people to act collectively to determine equitable cultural rules, human purposes of rationalizing progress, and world citizenship that is strongly egalitarian (Boli and Thomas 1997). INGO principles such as these can challenge traditional national culture norms.

The images of globalization are so powerful that they are often presented as dissolving national cultures, national economies and national borders. It is not surprising that, in the view of some theorists of globalization, the world has apparently become one without any boundaries, despite the continued existence of borders between states and all the administrative devices that maintain them. However, to the extent the world is becoming economically global it is largely confined to Japan and the newly industrialized countries of South East Asia, Western Europe,

and North America. Technological, economic and cultural integration is developing within and between these three regions and is evident in the pattern of international trade and investment flows. Inter-firm strategic alliances are heavily concentrated among companies from these countries. It is here that scientific power, technological supremacy, economic dominance and cultural hegemony are concentrated and, thus, the ability to govern the world into the future (Petrella 1996: 77). Overwhelmingly, however, cultural dominance of these economic products is expressed in English language: thus it remains Hollywood rather than Bollywood or Shaw Studios that dominates global cinema; hip-hop rather than bangra that dominates global music. Yet, for many people globally, neither hip hop nor Hollywood will be the dominant media through which they find contemporary cultural expression.

Global Business Activities and Industries

Many examine global business by looking at tens of thousands of transnational corporations whose activities are reported in annual *World Investment Reports*. These firms directly control hundreds of thousands of subsidiaries worldwide and the trillions their combined assets represent make them important to worldwide growth and development. The biggest 1,000 of these companies generate four-fifths of world industrial output; in 2003 the Global 500 generated revenues of $13.7 trillion against a global GDP of about $40 trillion. Greatest interest often revolves around the relatively small group of global businesses that produce highly visible branded goods or services like Sony, Sanro (Hello Kitty), Nestlé, Coca-Cola, PepsiCo, and Benetton. But focusing only on firms in consumer products and services tends to obscure the fact that many other businesses operate globally. Any list of the largest among these organizations – *Fortune's* Global 500, *Business Week's* Global 1000, or the *Financial Times* 100 – provides names of global firms that are not well know such as Cemex, Mittal, Tata, Haier, and Saint Gobain. The global landscape also is populated by a wide array of organizations, including businesses that are small and large, publicly held, family owned or sponsored by 'overseas' or 'nonresident' groups. The latter retain or develop business ties with their nations of origin, for example the overseas Chinese or overseas Indians. Many business opportunities are pursued by smaller firms: Jinwoong is based in South Korea but controls 35% of the world market for tents; Hongjin Crown makes motorcycle helmets that command a 40% share of the US market alone; and Hong Kong-based Boto International is the world's largest manufacturer of artificial Christmas trees. These firms provide reasons to study smaller, less well-known, and privately owned firms as they too operate globally.

Porter defined a global industry as one 'in which a firm's competitive position in one country is significantly affected by its position in other countries or vice versa' (1990: 18). He suggested that those with a high industry trade ratio (Porter 1980) are more global, and can be assessed according to the amount of industry influence that comes from outside domestic markets. Other suggested measures of industry globalization include intrafirm flows of resources (Kobrin 1991); cross-border investment as a ratio of total industry capital invested, proportion of industry revenues generated by players competing in all the major regions of the world, and cross-border trade within the industry as a ratio of total worldwide production (Govindarajan and Gupta 2000); national border transcendence measured by cross-border mergers and acquisitions (*World Investment Report* 2000); and low to high industry globalization where low globalization is represented by high domestic focus coupled with few external linkages, and high globalization is found in industries where companies integrate most or all value-added activities with similar industries in other countries (Makhija et al. 1997). The latter authors believe a systematic analysis of industry globalization should explain the combined effects of all firms within the industry, be able to distinguish industries with significant international linkages in other countries, and should measure functional integration within the firm of value-added activities the firm conducts across national boundaries.

Industry convergence occurs when autonomous industries begin to overlap. Examples are the 'edutainment' industry that combines software with books or 'cosmeceuticals' which occupies new industry space around converging interests of pharmaceutical and cosmetics companies. Disintermediation (Hamel and Prahalad 1994) that reduces and sometimes eliminates intermediary roles also reshapes industries. Industry integration includes consolidation, alliance building (Drucker 1999), and value (Porter 1986) and supply chain management.

Industries also contract due to shifting consumer interest and demands, or availability of desirable substitutes such as file sharing instead of music CDs. Finally, some industries dissolve.

A recurring debate around businesses and industries centres on relationships between nations and businesses. Clougherty (2001) suggests researchers who believe global business mobility compromises national autonomy fall into the 'globalist' camp whose proponents argue that nations must be involved with businesses to keep or develop important ones (Porter 1999; Anholt 2000). 'Institutionalists' believe national autonomy is not compromised by global businesses (Krugman 1994; Turner 2001). The US debate was well expressed by former Labour Secretary Robert Reich who described 'American' companies as those from any nations providing high-skill jobs for Americans in America, and chief White House economist Laura Tyson who at the same time asserted that the economic fate of nations remains tied to the success of domestically-based organizations.

Perspectives on Outcomes from Globalization

Differing perspectives on globalization also lead to different projected outcomes. According to Held et al. (1999), these can be organized around three broad schools of thought defined as skeptical, hyperglobalist, and tranformationalist. The following section outlines some of the support for each perspective.

The Skeptical Thesis

A skeptical thesis argues that globalization is simply internationalization by another name (Scholte 2000). Its main pillar is that there were earlier historical periods also punctuated by interconnections similar to those of today (Sampson 1995; Williamson 1996; Friedman 1999; O'Rourke and Williamson 2000; Flynn and Giraldez 2002). Hirst and Thompson (1996: 74, 2–3) have argued that the present highly internationalized economy is not unprecedented and, in some respects, is less open and generalized than that which existed in the previous high-water mark of the global economy of 1870–1914. Despite there being significant regional players emerging in Latin America, East Asia and elsewhere, Hirst and Thompson (1996) assert that trade, investment and financial flows remain concentrated in the Triad of Europe, Japan and North America, and this dominance is likely to continue. These major G3 economic powers have the capacity if they co-ordinate policy, to exert powerful governance pressures over financial markets and other economic activities. Thus, what is distinctive about the concept of globalization that has burst into prominence in the last decade of the twentieth century is its economic magnitude and pace. But globalization itself is simply 'continuation of an old process' (Scholte 2000; Husted 2003: 432).

Supporters of the skeptical thesis pursue two themes. Some provide empirical data and closely define terms. Examples are Lipsey et al. (2000) who show that large corporations account for about the same amount of the world's output in 1990 (22%) as they did in 1980. Having defined a global business as one that both produces and sells in global pools, Veseth (1998) also asserts there are few global businesses. A second theme is that nations rather than businesses remain the key global actors (Veseth 1998). Most organizations are subject to political machinations in home countries (Gilpin 2000), causing businesses to respond to the political, economic, and cultural constraints of their home nations (Doremus et al. 1999). Thus, few businesses are ungoverned actors on the global stage. For most firms operating on a global scale, the bulk of their assets and employees are found in home countries where ownership is located and to whom the company turns for political or diplomatic protection (Hu 1992). Others believe multinationals are primarily located within national or regional geographies (Yip et al. 1997), suggesting they are at best regional actors (Rugman 2000; 2005).

These arguments underscore the skeptic's point of view which is that business is and remains international. If globalization is nothing new, then globalization of business is simply business as usual, and businesses can be guided by theories of internationalization such as internationalization processes, product life cycles, or portfolio theories when operating abroad.

Critics of the skeptical thesis believe the issue is less one of historical comparisons *per se*, but rather the scale of current interconnections. For example, the Silk Road may have provided economic and cultural links between distant nations, but these were 'thin' connections that had little direct impact on consumers along the road. Conversely, the 'thick' characteristics of 'globalization involve many relationships that are intensive as well as extensive: long-distance flows that are large and continuous, affecting the lives of many people' (Keohane and Nye 2000: 7).

The Hyperglobalist Thesis of Globalization

A 'thick' view of globalization is 'hyperglobalism' and its argument that globalization is a new stage of human history through which the power of nation-states is supplanted by business activities (Ohmae 1995), making businesses more than nation-states the 'primary economic and political units of world society' (Held et al. 1999: 3).

The hyperglobalist thesis has two variations. First, there is a self-interest perspective that views organizations as dispassionate actors on a global scale working pragmatically in pursuit of economic ends. Luttwak (1999) believes that 'turbo-charged' capitalism among competitors forces all to act rapidly. Under these conditions, businesses are little more than isolated actors in a global market where rules of profitability and survival are governed by powerful market forces. This more liberal perspective on globalization facilitates views of organizational actors and markets as part of a benign and even beneficial process (Scholte 1996). In a global world, self-interest could mean linking with suppliers and buyers or even with competitors to satisfy self-interest. It almost certainly means relocating jobs to low-wage economies because to do otherwise is to lose out to competitors. It can then be argued that linked worldwide production chains simply help businesses operate efficiently and survive in a competitive world. This type of hyperglobalist might simply claim: the market made me do it!

A second more malevolent form of hyperglobalism also is described. First given voice by Mikael Gorbachev in a 1988 speech, the concept of a New World Order was popularized by US President George H.W. Bush during the 1989 Gulf War. Since then, the term New World Order has most often described consolidation of power among already-powerful business and governmental interests. This perspective on hyperglobalism argues that global business primacy is coming about by design and it is not indifferent. Falk (1993) characterizes business roles in this New World Order as 'globalization-from-above', arguing that nations and organizations with economic and political power pool their clout to advance common interests. Worldwide proliferation of branded products like Coca-Cola or Hello Kitty and growing distribution of information and entertainment media are but two ways consumerism spreads, leading to purchases and profits that further consolidate power among global businesses and the governments that back them (Barnett and Cavanagh 1994; Korten 1995; Klein 2000). Global businesses may also concentrate power via industry consolidation; encourage trade liberalization to enhance their own wealth and positions; create wage inequalities; and hasten cultural homogeneity. Others believe globalization is simply a new name for imperialism when stronger economic entities use their economic clout to exact concessions from workers, other companies, or even nations. Overall, these concerns often are the basis of calls for global business accountability enacted by national governments, enabled by global entities such as the Global Compact, and often via engagements with nongovernmental organizations.

Steingard and Fitzgibbons (1995) believe that management literature may be partly to blame for the New World Order backlash to globalization. They argue that academic publications promote myths like 'Globalization leads to one healthy world culture', 'Globalization brings prosperity to person and planet', or 'Global markets spread naturally'. Berger (1997) suggests these ideals are shared by a faculty club international culture that promotes Western ideals such as feminism or environmentalism through existing systems such as education, think tanks and mass media.

Managers who adopt a hyperglobalist view recognize that globalization is not business as usual. If globalization is perceived to be 'survival of the fittest' on a global scale, managers are likely to scan the world for pragmatic opportunities. This might lead to dispassionate decisions when relocating jobs or shifting investments. Although managers may recognize that their actions create unpleasant consequences for others, they may believe that relentless competitive markets limit their options. Firms that conspire to subvert government authority or gain an unfair advantage over nations, employees, or competitors may be those that view hyperglobalism as an opportunity to improve their own advantages at the expense of others. Rather than respond to markets, these firms seek to shape them and may be more inclined to write the rules than to follow them.

The rubric for globalization as a 'New World Order' strikes many people as very scary indeed. It is also incomplete: it does not tell all we need to know about globalization or the role businesses can or should play in this process. Defining globalization as a New World Order may over-generalize and cause people to overlook other options. For example, although large firms have the potential to abuse their economic power, not all do and some work to enhance worldwide opportunities. Ironically, the more extreme anti-globalization protestors share a belief with some defenders of business that the relationship between business and society is a zero-sum game where one can gain only when the other loses. Ellis (2001) notes that this is a false dichotomy, because the same forces that drive business globalization can also facilitate social progress.

The Transformational Thesis of Globalization

In contrast to the hyperglobalist thesis, a transformational thesis of globalization argues that the endpoint of the globalization process is not yet decided, although some believe that disciplinary training may encourage scholars to think about globalization as 'prefiguring a singular condition or end-state' (Held et al. 1999: 11). Transformationalists argue that interconnections and interdependence will forge new links and dissolve some existing ones. Relationships among nations and people will be reconfigured and power relationships restructured (Held et al. 1999). These transformations are in process, and it is yet to be seen whether they produce positive or negative results in the longer term.

Many proponents of transformation come from the voluntary sector and work through transnational organizations 'animated by environmental concerns, human rights, hostility to patriarchy, and a vision of human community based on the unity of diverse cultures...' (Falk 1993: 39). For example, Jubilee 2000 encouraged debt relief for highly indebted nations, others encouraged an antipersonnel-mines treaty, and still others work on a vast array of human and environmental issues. Because many global voluntary organizations pursue singular issues worldwide, they face growing backlash and stakeholder demands – especially in developing economies – to demonstrate accountability (Brown et al. 2000; Marquardt 2000). Celebrities such as Bono, the singer from U2 (debt-relief) or the late Princess Diana (landmines) often attach themselves to these single-issue causes to lift the profile of them.

Business activities also can lead to transformative global outcomes (Gutpa 2004). Ellis (2001) notes that businesses have 'always had a long-term commonality of interest with wider society…business has constantly evolved to meet society's goals and fuses them into its own interests' (p. 16). The 68% of large companies in Western Europe and 41% in the US reporting on 'triple bottom line' objectives (profits, people, and the planet) suggest they are integrating social and profit goals (Buck 1998; Management barometer 2003).

Some businesses promote social justice as part of ordinary activities. For example, Benetton's advertisements highlight social issues like peace, caring, and hunger prevention. The Body Shop endorses Amnesty International; DuPont became a champion for sustainable development; British Petroleum promotes alternatives for fossil fuel. Other businesses contribute funds or underwrite volunteer time for employees to pursue social objectives. Numerous business foundations contribute to social goals such as the Global Alliance for Vaccines and Immunization, a $1.01 billion aid project launched in the late 1990s with major funding from Microsoft Corporation and the Bill and Melinda Gates Foundation.

Businesses that view globalization through a transformational filter also find it important to generate wealth. They may do this (as the hyperglobalists do) by forging links with suppliers and customers. Unlike the hyperglobalists, the manager who adopts this perspective would more likely weigh the longer run ramifications of these linkages. For example, a central concern expressed by the board of British Petroleum is the economic and social health of places where BP does business. Wealth may be broadly defined as embracing both financial and social goals, e.g. to enhance quality of life and financial wealth. Further, the transformationalist firm may alter its activities to ensure that human and other species survive. Others may collaborate to improve local communities.

Reconfiguration of existing links sometimes comes about through interconnections among businesses, governments and members of civil society. Voluntary and governmental organizations may take on business roles just as businesses can play social as well as profit-generating roles. In these ways they transform their own organizations. Thus the transformationalist view of globalization suggests that businesses and voluntary organizations do not divide neatly into opposing camps for good and evil, but that they cross boundaries and borders to interconnect their activities and initiatives.

In the last decade, strongest research emphasis was on how organizations managed global expansion with internal networks (Prahalad and Doz 1987; Bartlett and Ghoshal 1989; Ghoshal and Bartlett 1990; Hedlund 1994). These networks have expanded to link organizations externally with other businesses in supply chains (Borrus and Zysman 1998; Dicken 1998; Castells 1998) and strategic alliances that can include competitors or cross industries (Gomes–Casseres 1994; Shenkar and Li 1999). More recently, organizations seek voluntary external networks with consumers (Prahalad and Ramaswamy 2002), even as other consumers force networks via Internet 'hate sites' to harass targeted companies. Nongovernmental organizations (Bendell 2000), and both governmental and intergovernmental organizations (Waddell 2001–2002) also increasingly are part of global networks linking businesses externally. Criminal gangs and terrorist groups become part of these networks to the extent that they impact organizations and institutions. For example, the estimated $400 billion in annual sales of illegal drugs (Revenue from 1997), is partially financed by global gangs that use the global banking system and computer technology in turn to launder revenue that then is invested in legitimate assets.

Global nongovernmental or civil society organizations network with businesses through opposition and proposition. Opposition such as Global Exchange's threatened 'roast Starbucks' campaign increasingly occur on a global scale to include boycotts, demonstrations, and disruptions in business activities. These approaches may occur at arm's length, but NGOs nevertheless become influential stakeholders on key issues. Many NGOs increasingly use a propositional approach that links them organizationally with global businesses. For example, insurance companies and Human Rights Watch jointly track weather patterns and consumption of global commons like air and water. Propositional approaches vary to include dialogue, interlinked board memberships, and cross-sector partnerships that may be 'transactional' ventures – short term, constrained and largely self-interest oriented – or 'integrative' (Austin 2000) and 'developmental' (Googins and Rochlin 2000) engagements – organized around longer term collaborative efforts that serve both self and social interests. In general, businesses are more attracted to direct-impact partnerships, such as education, environmental sustainability, or job development, than to those that have indirect impacts, such as social mobilization, advocacy, good governance, or poverty reduction (Ashman 2001). Often governments play a key role in linking businesses with NGOs by 'establishing the appropriate enabling environment' (Waddell 2001: 59).

Links between business and governmental and intergovernmental organizations occur when governments transfer work or authority to the business sector and when intergovernmental authorities develop codes and standards for global business. Global NGOs also complete some amount of work previously conducted by governments, and this can locate them in the center of a business/government framework (Doh 2003). Government/business interfaces also occur in a variety of different ways. Following the September 11, 2001 attack, the US government invited Disney to help ease travel delays, Nike provided brand advice to the Secret Service, and Marriott International and FedEx suggested ways to measure security screeners' performance.

Members of all three sectors increasingly participate in tri-sector networks. CARE, GlaxoSmithKline, and the Bangladeshi government collaborated to improve hygiene and medically treat parasites, and many national governments collaborate with businesses and nongovernmental organizations to create and deliver quality education. In some cases, tri-sectoral partnerships arise; examples include the Global Compact, the Prince of Wales International Business Leaders Forum, and Bill Clinton's 2005 Global Initiative. Integrative activities between governments, businesses, and NGOs have the potential to change the essential nature of each.

If globalization is not an extension of internationalization, then firms relying exclusively on traditions of practice and theory may not be well served by them. At worst, this approach can fragment rather than strengthen boundary-spanning activities. If globalization is something new, then both transformations and hyperglobalists must find new ways to operate. There are no rulebooks to guide them through the globalization process. This means that many will experiment, and it probably means that mistakes will be made. For example, donations of second-hand clothing to Zambia have all but destroyed textile production there. This suggests that all organizations, both profit and not-for-profit, have reason to consider the second and third order global consequences of their activities.

Conclusion

Having examined globalization from many perspectives, we observe a strong tendency toward oversimplification that often dichotomizes: rich against poor; unfettered markets against managed ones; nations vs. businesses; positive against negative outcomes. Globalization is a complex and confusing process oversimplified by considering 'winners' and 'losers' at a single point in time. At the business level, these dichotomies also are evident: businesses are encouraged to be local or global, centralized or decentralized, standardized or responsive (Buckley and Ghauri 2004). The definitive specification of what globalization *is* will be likely to come from many sources, including the business sector whose leaders face conflicting demands for profitability and response to a growing array of what many used to think of as social objectives better pursued by government and the voluntary sector. Businesses will be shaped by globalization, and they also can play an active role in shaping the agenda of globalization and its consequences. Accordingly, it becomes important for business leaders to make explicit and clear choices when interpreting what growing worldwide interconnections mean for their organizations. Whether they appreciate it or not, they will have to deal with other non-business organizations, such as civil, government, union or international organizations.

Globalization challenges the increasing isolation of organization studies as a stand-alone specialism within Business Schools and their disciplines, and it challenges their dependence on a limited range of disciplines, such as IB. The failure to integrate across social science disciplines in IB research creates deficits for individual scholars and the discipline. Organization studies researchers who draw only on IB scholarship are unlikely to reach their full potential unless they combine knowledge of disciplinary scholarship with insights provided by other disciplines (Dunning 1989: 31); at the very least, international relations, political economy, anthropology, sociology, cultural studies, economic geography, and economic history. Expanding on the limited functional knowledge of IB entails opportunity costs in learning about new disciplines and/or investments in team dynamics within an interdisciplinary research group. Because the values associated with international research vary by institution, colleagues and peers (Toyne et al. 2001), some may have little motivation to learn or engage in team activities. However, the enrichment of research driven by the multiple complexities of the phenomena of globalization rather than the relative simplicities of the disciplines that deal with it provides a great opportunity for organization studies researchers. These opportunities would include an enhanced sophistication concerning the multi-layered relational qualities of globalization, necessitating research foci that ranged from the effects of globalization on the individual to its effects at a world systemic level. It would entail abandonment of single-discipline emphases, especially those entrenched in economics, which see business processes as somehow separate from society. A loosening of the hegemonic bonds of most academic views of globalization from those germinated in the rather privileged and specific fields of North America and Europe would be required. It might even mean that scholars would have to get out a bit more: out of their countries, cities and faculties, to other places, other realities, and other disciplines. Globalization, as a phenomenon, spans disciplines, making it more difficult for singular academic specialists to tackle it (Clark and Knowles 2003). While most of us are fortunate to learn our own field well, few acquire breath and depth in five or six more disciplines. Academic specialization becomes problematic when the subject of study is a topic like globalization whose domain spans disciplines rather than resides in one or a few.

Finally in a more global world of interrelatedness and interdependence, it is important to recognize that organizational activities result from human decisions. The more broadly informed these are by interdisciplinary perspectives, the less likely the biases of any one area, such as economics, strategy or IB, will exercise a disproportionate sway over problem definitions, analyses and interpretations. As individuals, as organizational participants, and as citizens of nations in an interconnected world, we should strive not to become victims of globalization seen only through a singular lens, generated in one discipline, place or time. Only by realizing that our perspective, even at its best, is our perspective, can we engage the phenomena of globalization – globally.

References

Alvesson, M. (1993) *Cultural perspectives on organizations.* Cambridge: Cambridge University Press.
Alvesson, M. and Karreman, D. (2001) 'Odd couple: Making sense of the curious concept of knowledge management', *Journal of Management Studies*, 38(7): 995–1018.
Anholt, S. (2000) 'The nation as brand', *Across the Board*, November/December: 22–27.
Ashman, D. (2001) 'Civil society collaboration with business: Bringing empowerment back in', *World Development*, 29: 1097–113.
Austin, J. (2000) 'Strategic collaboration between nonprofits and businesses', *Nonprofit and Voluntary Sector Quarterly*, 29: 69–97.
Aykut, D., Kalsi, H. and Ratha, D. (2003) 'Sustaining and promoting equity-related finance for developing countries' in World Bank (eds), *Global Development Finance*. Washington, DC: World Bank. pp. 85–106.
Bannerjee, S.B. and Linstead, S. (2001) 'Globalization', *Organization*, 8(4): 683–722.
Bannock, G., Baxter, R.E. and Davis, E. (1998) *Dictionary of Economics.* New York: Wiley.
Barber, B. (1992) 'Jihad vs. McWorld', *The Atlantic Monthly*, 269: 53–61. (See also 1996, *Jihad vs. Mcworld.* New York: Ballantine Books.)
Barber, B. (1996) *Jihad vs. McWorld: Terrorism's Challenge to Democracy.* New York: Ballantine Books.
Barnet, R.J. and Cavanagh, J. (1994) *Global dreams.* New York: Simon and Schuster.Barro, R. and Sala-I-Martin, X. (1995) *Economic growth.* New York: McGraw-Hill.
Bartlett, C.A. and Ghoshal, S. (1989) *Managing Across Borders: The transnational solution.* Boston, MA: Harvard Business School Press.
Bartlett, C. and Ghoshal, S. (2000) 'Going global: Lessons from late movers', *Harvard Business Review*, 72: 132–42.
Beck, U. (2002) *Risk society: towards a new modernity*, translated by Mark Ritter. London: Sage.
Bell, J., McNaughton, R. and Young, S. (2001) '"Born-again global" firms: An extension of the "born global" phenomenon', *Journal of International Management*, 7: 173–89.
Bendell, J. (ed.) (2000) *Terms for endearment.* Sheffield: Greenleaf.
Berger, P.L. (1997) 'Four faces of global culture', *The National Interest*, 49: 23–30.
Bhagwati, J. (2004) *In defense of globalization.* New York: Oxford University Press.
Bird, A. and Stevens, M.J. (2003) 'Toward an emergent global culture and effects of globalization on obsolescing national cultures', *Journal of International Management*, 9: 395–407.
Bloom, D.E., Canning, D. and Sevilla, J. (2001) 'The effect of health on economic growth: Theory and evidence', NBER Working Paper 8587.

Boli, J. and Thomas, G. (1997) 'World culture in the world polity: A century of international non-governmental organization', *American Sociological Review*, 62: 171–91.

Borrus, M. and Zysman, J. (1998) 'Wintelism and the changing terms of global competition: Prototype of the future', BRIEF Working Paper 96B.

Bradford, S.C., Greico, P.L.E. and Husbauer, G.C. (2005) 'The payoff to America from global integration', in F. Bergstren (ed.), *The United States and the world economy: Foreign economic policy for the next decade*. Washington DC: Institute for International Economics. pp. 65–109.

Bradley, S.P., Hausman, J.A. and Nolan, R.L. (1993) *Globalization, technology, and competition*. Boston: Harvard Business School Press.

Brown, L.D., Khagram, S., Moore, M.H., and Frumkin, P. (2000) 'Globalization, NGOs, and multisectoral relations', in J.S. Nye Jr. and J.D. Donahue (eds), *Governance in a Globalizing World*. Washington, DC: Brookings Institution Press. pp. 271–98.

Buck, S.J. (1998) *The global commons: An introduction*. Washington, D.C.: Island Press.

Buckley, P.J. and Chapman, M. (1996) 'Theory and method in international business research', *International Business Review*, 5: 233–45.

Buckley, P.J. and Ghauri, P.N. (2002) *International mergers and acquisitions: A reader*. London: Thomson.

Buckley, P.J. and Ghauri, P.N. (2004) 'Globalisation, economic geography and the strategy of multinational enterprises', *Journal of International Business Studies*, 35: 81–98.

Castells, M. (1998) *The information age: Economy, society and culture*. Malden, MA and Oxford: Blackwell.

Castells, M. (2000) *Rise of the network society*. London: Blackwell.

Castells, M. and Portes, A. (1989) 'World underneath: The origins, dynamics, and effects of the informal economy', in A. Portes, M. Castells and L. Benton (eds), *The informal economy: Studies in advanced and less developed countries*. Baltimore, MD: Johns Hopkins University Press. pp. 11–37.

Caves, R.E. (1998) 'Research on international business: Problems and prospects', *Journal of International Business Studies*, 29: 5–19.

Cawthorne, P. and Kitching, G. (2001) 'Moral dilemmas and factual claims: Some comments on Paul Krugman's defense of cheap labor', *Review of Social Economy*, 59: 455–66.

Chiesa, V. (1995) 'Globalizing R&D around centres of excellence', *Long Range Planning*, 28: 19–28.

Clark, A.M. (1995) 'Non-governmental organizations and their influence on international society', *Journal of International Affairs*, 48: 507–25.

Clark, T. and Knowles, L. (2003) 'Global myopia: Globalization theory in international business', *Journal of International Management*, 9: 361–72.

Cleveland, H. (1990) *The global commons*. Lanham, MD: University Press of America.

Clougherty, J.A. (2001) 'Globalization and the autonomy of domestic competition policy: An empirical test on the world airline industry', *Journal of International Business Studies*, 32: 459–78.

Commission on Global Governance (1995) *Our global neighborhood*. New York: Oxford University Press.

ContactBabel (2002) *UK Contact Centre Report*, www. contactbabel.com/ContactBabel%20product%20broch ure%20Sept%202004.pdf, accessed 2 February 2006.

Coviello, N.E. and McAuley, A. (1999) 'Internationalisation and the smaller firm: A review of contemporary empirical research 1', *Management International Review*, 39: 223–56.

Coviello, N.E. and Munro, H.J. (1995) 'Growing the entrepreneurial firm: Networking for international market development', *European Journal of Marketing*, 29: 49–61.

Crystal, D. (1997) *English as a global language*. Cambridge: Cambridge University Press.

Daly, H. (1996) *Beyond growth: The economics of sustainable development*. Boston: Beacon Press.

Davidow, W. and Malone, M. (1992) *The virtual corporation: Structuring and revitalizing the corporation for the 21st century*. Burlingame, NY: Harper.

Deloitte and Touche (1998) *Informal economic activities in the EU*. Brussels: European Commission.

De Soto, H. (2000) *The mystery of capitalism: Why capitalism triumphs in the West and fails everywhere else*. New York: Basic Books.

Diamond, J. (2005) *Collapse*. New York: Viking.

Dicken, P. (1992) *Global shift*, 2nd edn. London: Guilford Press.

Dicken, P. (1998) *Global shift*, 3rd edn. New York and London: Guilford Press.

Doh, J.P. (2003) 'Nongovernmental organizations, corporate strategy, and public policy: NGOs as agents of change', in J.P. Doh and H. Teegen (eds), *Globalization and NGOs*. Westport, CT: Praeger. pp. 1–18.

Doh, J.P. and Teegen, H. (2002) 'Nongovernmental organizations as institutional actors in international business: Theory and implications', *International Business Review*, 11: 665–84.

Dollar, D. and Kraay, A. (2002) 'Spreading the wealth', *Foreign Affairs*, 81: 120–33.

Doremus, P.N., Keller, W.W., Pauly, L.W. and Reich, S. (1999) *The myth of the global corporation*. Princeton, NJ: Princeton University Press.

Drucker, P.F. (1999) *Management challenges for the 21st century*. New York: HarperBusiness.

Dunning, J.H. (1989) 'The study of international business: A plea for a more interdisciplinary approach', *Journal of International Business Studies*, 20: 411–436.

Easterbrook, G. (1995) *A moment on the earth*. New York: Viking.

Ellis, V. (2001) 'Can global business be a force for good?' *Business Strategy Review*, 12: 15–20.

Emerging issues in development economics (1997) *World Bank Policy and Research Bulletin*, 1–4.

Ehrlich, P.R. (1969) *The population bomb*. Binghamton, NY: Vail-Ballou.

Ehrlich, P.R. and Ehrlich, A. (2004) *One with Nineveh*. Washington, DC: Shearwater Books.

Falk, R. (1993) 'The making of global citizenship', in J. Brecher, J.B. Childs, and J. Cutler (eds), *Global visions*. Boston, MA: South End Press. pp. 39–50.

Flynn, D. and Giraldez, A. (2002) 'Cycles Of silver: Global economic unity though the mid-18th century', *Journal Of World History*, 13: 391–427.

Foreign friends (2000) *The Economist*, 8 January. pp. 71–4.

Freedman, L. (2003) *Superterrorism: Policy responses*. London: Blackwell.

French, H. (2003) *Vanishing borders: Protecting the environment in the age of globalization*. New York: Norton Paperbacks.

Friedman, T.L. (1999) *The lexus and the olive tree*. New York: Farrar Strous and Giroux.

Gabel, M. (2004) 'Where to find 4 billion new customers', *The Futurist*, 38(4): 28–31.

Garrett, L. (1994) *The Coming Plague: Newly emerging diseases in a world out of balance*. New York: Farrar Straus Giroux.

Garrick, J. and Clegg, S.R. (2001) 'Stressed-out knowledge workers in performative times: A postmodern take on project-based learning', *Management Learning* 32: 119–34.

Ghoshal, S. and Bartlett, C.A. (1990) 'The multinational corporation as an interorganizational network', *Academy of Management Review*, 15: 603–25.

Giddens, A. (1999) *Runaway world: How globalization is reshaping our lives*. London: Profile Books.

Gilpin, R. (2000) *The Challenge of Global Capitalism*. Princeton: Princeton University Press.

Global Economic Prospects (2000) Washington, DC: World Bank.

Global Reach (2004) Available online at: http://global-reach.biz/globstats/refs.php3, accessed 25 May 2005.

Gomes-Casseres, B. (1994) 'Group vs. group: How alliance networks compete', reprinted in J.E. Garten (ed.), *World View*. Boston: Harvard Business Review Book. pp. 127–41.

Gomez-Buendia, H. (1995) 'The politics of global employment: A perspective from Latin America', in M. Simai (ed.), *Global employment: An international investigation into the future of work*. London and New Jersey: Zed Books. pp. 65–93.

Goodstein, D. (2004) *Out of gas: The end of the age of oil*. New York: W.W. Norton.

Googins, B. and Rochlin, S. (2000) 'Creating the partnership society: Understanding the rhetoric and reality of cross-sectoral partnerships', *Business and Society Review*, 105: 127–44.

Govindarajan, V. and Gupta, A.K. (2000) 'Analysis of the emerging global arena', *European Management Journal*, 18: 274–84.

Green, C. and Ruhleder, K. (1996) 'Globalization, borderless worlds, and the Tower of Babel', *Journal of Organizational Change*, 8: 55–68.

Gutpa, V. (2004) *Transformative organizations: A global perspective*. Thousand Oaks, CA: Sage.

Haacker, M. (2002) 'The Economic Consequences of HIV/AIDS in South Africa', IMF Working Paper, WP/02/38.

Haley, G.T., Tan, C.T. and Haley, U.C.V. (1998) *New Asian Emperors: The Overseas Chinese, their Strategies and Competitive Advantage*. London: Butterworth-Heinemann.

Hamel, G. and Prahalad, C.K. (1994) *Competing for the future*. Boston, MA: Harvard Business School Press.

Hassan, S.S. and Katsanis, L.P. (1994) 'Global market segment strategies and trends', in S.S. Hassan and E. Kaynak (eds.), *Globalization of consumer markets: Structures and strategies*, Binghamton, NY: International Business Press/Haworth. p. 58.

Hawken, P. (1993) *The ecology of commerce*. New York: Harper Business.

Hedlund, G. (1994) 'A model of knowledge management and the N-form corporation', *Strategic Management Journal*, 15: 73–90.

Held, D., McGrew, A., Goldblatt, D. and Perraton, J. (1999) *Global Transformations*. Stanford, CA: Stanford University Press.

Henderson, H. (1996) *Building a Win/Win World*. San Francisco: Berrett-Koehler.

Henderson, H. (1999) *Beyond globalization: Shaping a sustainable global economy*. West Hartford, CT: Kumarian Press.

Hirst, P. and Thompson, G. (1996) *Globalization in Question: The International Economy and the Possibilities of Governance*. Cambridge, UK: Polity.

Hoffman, S. (2002) 'Clash of globalization', *Foreign Affairs*, 81: 104–15.

Hofstede, G. (1980) *Culture's Consequences*. Beverly Hills, CA: Sage.

Holmlund, M. and Kock, S. (1998) Relationships and the internationalisation of Finnish small and medium sized companies. *International Small Business Journal*, 16: 46–63.

Hordes, M.W., Clancy, J.A. and Baddaley, J. (1995) 'A primer for global start-ups', *Academy of Management Executive*, 9: 7–11.

House, R.J., Hanges, P.J., Javidan, M., Dorfman, P.W. and Gupta, V. (2004) *Culture, leadership, and organizations*. Thousand Oaks, CA: Sage Publications.

Hu, Y.-S. (1992) 'Global or stateless corporations are national firms with international operations', *California Management Review*, 34: 107–26.

Huber, P.W. and Mills, M.P. (2005) *The bottomless well*. New York: Basic Books.

Huntington, S. (1993) 'The clash of civilizations', *Foreign Affairs*, 72: 22–49.

Husted, B.W. (2003) 'Globalization and cultural change in international business research', *Journal of International Management*, 9: 427–33.

Inglehart, R. and Baker, W.E. (2000) 'Modernization, cultural change, and the persistence of traditional values', *American Sociological Review*, 65: 19–33.

Inkpen, A. and Beamish, P. (1994) 'An analysis of twenty-five years of business in the *Journal of International Business Studies*', *Journal of International Business Studies*, 25: 703–13.

Jolly, V., Alahuhta, M. and Jeannet, J. (1992) 'Challenging the incumbents: How high technology start-ups compete globally', *Journal of Strategic Change*, 1: 71–82.

Jones, M.T. (2003) 'Globalization and the organization(s) of exclusion in advanced capitalism', in R. Westwood and S. Clegg (eds.), *Debating organization*. Malden, MA: Blackwell Publishing. pp. 252–70.

Jones, M.V. (2001) 'First steps in internationalization – Concepts and evidence from a sample of small high-technology firms', *Journal of International Management* 7: 191–210.

Kahn, J.S. (1995) *Culture, multiculture, and postculture*. Beverly Hills, CA: Sage.

Kaldor, M., Anheier, H. and Glasius, M. (2002) 'Global civil society in an era of regressive globalization', in M. Glasius, M. Kaldor and H. Anheier (eds), *Global civil society 2002*. Oxford: Oxford University Press. pp. 1–33.

Kanter, R.M. and Dretler, T.D. (1998) '"Global strategy" and its impact on local operations: Lessons from Gillette Singapore', *Academy of Management Executive*, 12: 60–8.

Keohane, R. and Nye, J. (2000) *Power and interdependence*. New York: Addison Wesley and Longman.

Klein, N. (2000) *No logo*. New York: St. Martin's Press.

Knight, G.A. and Cavusgil, S.T. (2004) 'Innovation, organizational capabilities, and the born-global firm', *Journal of International Business Studies*, 35: 124–41.

Knight, G.A. and Cavusgil, S.T. (1996) 'The born global firm: A challenge to traditional internationalization theory', *Advances in International Marketing*. 8: 11–26.

Knoke, W. (1996) *Bold New World: The Essential Road Map to The Twenty-First Century*. Cambridge, MA: Harvard Capital Group Kodansha America.

Kobrin, S. (1991) 'An empirical analysis of the determinants of global integration', *Strategic Management Journal*, 12: 17–31.

Kobrin, S. (2001) 'Territoriality and the governance of cyberspace', *Journal of International Business Studies*, 32: 687–704.

Korten, D. (1995) *When corporations rule the world*. San Francisco: Berrett-Koehler.

Krugman, P. (1994) 'Competitiveness: A dangerous obsession', *Foreign Affairs*, 73: 28–44.

Krugman, P. (1998) *The accidental theorist and other dispatches from the dismal science*. New York and London: W.W. Norton.

Kwan, R. (1995) 'Footloose and country free', in M. Brewlos, D. Levy, B. Redi and the Dollars and Sense Collective (eds.), *Real World International*, 2nd edn. Somerville, MA: Dollars and Sense. pp. 18–22.

Lacouture, J. (1995) *Jesuits a multibiography*. Washington, DC: Counterpoint.

Lee, E. (1997) 'Globalization and labor standards: A review of issues', *International Labor Review*, 36(2): 173–89.

Lipsey, R.E., Blomstrom, M. and Ramstetter, E.D. (2000) 'Internationalized production in world output', working paper. Washington, D.C.: National Bureau of Economic Research.

Lomborg, B. (2001) *The skeptical environmentalist: Measuring the real state of the world*. London: Cambridge University Press.

Lu, J. (2003) 'The evolving contributions in international strategic management research', *Journal of International Business Management*, 9: 193–213.

Luttwak, E. (1999) *Turbo-capitalism: Winners and losers in the global economy*. New York: HarperCollins.

Madsen, T.K. and Servais, P. (1997) 'The internationalization of born globals: An evolutionary process?' *International Business Review*, 6: 561–83.

Makhija, M.V., Kim, K. and Williamson, S.D. (1997) 'Measuring globalization of industries using a national industry approach: Empirical evidence across five countries and over time', *Journal of International Business Studies*, 28: 679–710.

Makridakis, S. (1989) 'Management in the 21st century', *Long Range Planning*, 22: 37–53.

Marquardt, R. (2000) 'Engaged or entangled? NGO and the private sector on an agenda to end poverty. Summary Report of Canada's Coalition to End Global Poverty Learning Circle', available at www.ccic.ca, accessed 22 February 2006.

Masaaki, K. and Aulakh, P.S. (2002) *Emerging issues in international business research*. Cheltenham, England: Elgar.

Mathews, J.A. (2002) *Dragon multinational*. Oxford, New York: Oxford University Press.

McDonough, W. and Braungart, M. (2002) *Cradle to cradle*. New York: North Point Press.

McDougall, P., Phillips, S.S. and Oviatt, B. (1994) 'Explaining the formation of international new ventures: the limits of theories from international business research', *Journal of Business Venturing*, 9: 469–87.

McRae, H. (1994) *The World in 2020: Power, Culture and Prosperity: a Vision of the Future*. London: HarperCollins.

Moses, E. (2000) *The $100 Billion Allowance: Accessing the Global Teen Market*. New York: John Wiley & Sons.

Naisbitt, J. (1994) *Global paradox*. New York: Easton Press.

Nolan, P. and Zhang, J. (2003) 'Globalization challenge for large firms from China's oil and aerospace industries', *European Management Journal*, 21: 285–99.

O'Brien, R., Goetz, A.M., Scholte, J.A. and Williams, M. (2002) *Contesting global governance: Multilateral* economic institutions and global social movements. London: Cambridge University Press.

O'Neill, H. (1997) 'Globalisation, competitiveness and human security: Challenges for development policy and institutional change', in K. Cristobal (ed.), *Globalisation, Competitiveness and Human Security.* London: Frank Cass. pp. 20–1.

O'Rourke, K. and Williamson, J. (2000) *Globalization and history: The Evolution of a nineteenth-century Atlantic economy.* Boston, MA: MIT Press.

Ohmae, K. (1995) *The end of the nation state.* Cambridge, MA: Free Press.

Olson, M. (2000) *Power and prosperity: Outgrowing communist and capitalist dictatorships.* New York: Basic Books.

Osland, J. (2003) 'Broadening the debate: The pros and cons of globalization', *Journal of Management Inquiry,* 12: 137–54.

Ostry, S. and Nelson, R. (1995) *Technonationalism and Technoglobalism: Conflict and Cooperation.* Washington: Brookings Institution.

Oviatt, B. and Phillips McDougall, P. (1995) 'Global start-ups: Entrepreneurs on a worldwide stage', *Academy of Management Executive,* 9: 30–43.

Oxfam (2001) 'Rigged trade and not much aid: How rich countries help to keep the least developed countries poor' Oxfam. Available online at: http://www.oxfam. org.uk/what_we_do/issues/trade/downloads/rigged_ trade.pdf, accessed 19 May 2005.

Parker, B. (1996) 'Evolution and revolution: From international business to globalization', in S. Clegg, C. Hardy and W. Nord (eds), *Handbook of Organization Studies.* London: Sage. pp. 484–506.

Parker, B. (2005) *Introduction to globalization and business.* London: Sage.

Pastor, R.A. (2000) *A century's journey: How the great powers shape the world.* New York: Basic Books.

Peng, M. (2004) 'Identifying the big question in international business research', *Journal of International Business Studies,* 35: 99–108.

Petrella, R. (1992) 'Internationalization, multinationalization and globalization of R&D: Toward a new division', *Knowledge & Policy,* 5: 3–26.

Petrella, R. (1996) 'Globalization and internationalization: The dynamics of the emerging world order', in R. Boyer and D. Drache (eds), *States Against Markets: The Limits of Globalization.* London: Routledge. pp. 62–83.

Pieterse, J.N. (1995) 'Globalization as hybridization', in M. Featherstone, S. Lash and R. Robertson (eds), *Global Modernities.* London: Sage. pp. 45–68.

Porter, M.E. (1980) *Competitive strategy.* New York: The Free Press.

Porter, M.E. (ed.) (1986) *Competition in global industries.* Boston, MA: Harvard Business School Press.

Porter, M. (1990) *The competitive advantage of nations.* Boston: Free Press.

Porter, M.E. and van der Linde, C. (1995) 'Green and competitive: Ending the stalemate', *Harvard Business Review,* 73: 120–34.

Prahalad, C.K. (2005) *The fortune at the bottom of the pyramid.* Upper Saddle River, NJ: Wharton School Publishing.

Prahalad, C.K. and Doz, Y. (1987) *The multinational mission: Balancing local demands and global vision.* New York: Free Press.

Prahalad, C.K. and Lieberthal, K. (1998) 'The end of corporate imperialism', *Harvard Business Review,* 76: 68–79.

Prahalad, C.K. and Ramaswamy, V. (2002) 'The co-creation connection', *Strategy and Business,* 27: 50–61.

Prestowitz, Jr., C.V., Tonelson, A. and Jerome, R.W. (1991) 'The last gasp of GATTism', *Harvard Business Review,* 12: 130–8.

PriceWaterhouseCoopers Management barometer (2003) *Quarterly survey in US and Western European findings reported from 14 different countries.* New York: Price WaterhouseCoopers/BS/Global Research Inc.

Reich, R. (1991) *The work of nations: Preparing ourselves for 21st Century capitalism.* New York: Alfred A. Knopf.

Ricks, D.A. (2003) 'Globalization and the role of the global corporation', *Journal of International Management,* 9: 355–9.

Ricks, D.A., Toyne, B. and Martinez, Z. (1990) 'Recent developments in international management research', *Journal of Management,* 16(2): 219–53.

Rifkin, J. (1995) *The end of work.* New York: G.P. Putnam.

Roberts, P. (2004) *The end of oil: On the edge of a perilous new world.* New York: Houghton Mifflin.

Robertson, R. (1995) 'Globalization: Time-space and homogeneity-heterogeneity', in M. Featherstone, S. Lash, and R. Robertson (eds.), *Global modernities.* London: Sage. pp. 25–44.

Robinson, J. (2000) *The merger.* Woodstock, NY: Overlook Press.

Rodrik, D. (1997) *Has Globalization Gone Too Far?* New York: Institute for International Economics.

Rugman, A.M. (2000) *The end of globalization.* London: Random House.

Rugman, A.M. (2005) *The regional multinationals.* New York: Cambridge University Press.

Sachs, J.D. (2005) *The end of poverty: Economic possibilities for our time.* New York: Penquin.

Saïd, E. (1979) *Orientalism.* New York: Vintage.

Said, E. (1998) *The myth of the 'Clash of Civilizations'* (video). Boston: Media Education Foundation.

Sampson, A. (1995) *Company man.* New York: Times Business.

Sassen, S. (1998) *Globalization and its Discontents.* New York: New Press.

Schein, E.H. (1992) *Organizational culture and leadership.* San Francisco: Jossey-Bass.

Scholte, J.A. (1996) 'Toward a critical theory of globalization', in E. Hoffman and G. Young (eds), *Globalization: Theory and practice.* London: Pinter. pp. 43–57.

Scholte, J.A. (2000) 'What is global about globalization?', in J.A. Scholte (ed.), *Globalization—A critical introduction*. New York: St. Martin's Press. pp. 41–61.

Sera, K. (1992) 'Corporate globalization: A new trend', *Academy of Management Executive*, 6: 89–96.

Shanks, C., Jacobson, H.K. and Kaplan, J.H. (1996) 'Inertia and change in the constellation of international governmental organizations, 1981–1992', *International Organization*, 50: 593–627.

Shenkar, O. (2004) 'One more time: International business in a global economy', *Journal of International Business Studies*, 35: 161–71.

Shenkar, O., and Li, J. (1999) 'Knowledge search in international cooperative ventures', *Organization Science*, 10: 134–43.

Shigerhara, K. (2002) 'Looking for models in pursuit of prosperity', *OECD Observer*, March: 235.

Sideri, S. (1997) 'Globalisation and regional integration', *European Journal of Development Research*, 9: 38–81.

Simai, M. (1994) *The future of global governance*. Washington, DC: US Institute of Peace.

Simon, H. (1996) *Hidden champions: Lessons from 500 of the world's best unknown companies*. Boston, MA: Harvard Business School Press.

Simon, J. (1981) *The ultimate resource*. Oxford: Martin Robinson.

Simon, J. (1998) *The ultimate resource 2*. Princeton, NJ: Princeton University Press.

Smith, A.D. (1990) 'Towards a global culture?' *Theory, Culture and Society*, 7: 171–91.

Sobel, A. (2003) 'Comments on globalization, interdisciplinary research, myopia and parochialism, government, convergence, and culture', *Journal of Interrnational Management*, 9: 419–25.

Stead, W.E. and Stead, J.G. (1996) *Management for a small planet*, 2nd edn. Thousand Oaks, CA: Sage.

Steingard, D.S. and Fitzgibbons, D.E. (1995) 'Challenging the juggernaut of globalization: A manifesto for academic praxis', *Journal of Organizational Change Management*, 8(4): 30–54.

Stiglitz, J. (2003) *Globalization and its discontents*. New York: W.W. Norton.

Terpstra, V. and David, K. (1991) *The cultural environment of international business*. Cincinnati, OH: South-Western Publishing.

The Economist (2000) 'The case for globalisation', *The Economist*, 23 September. pp. 19–20.

The Economist (2001) 'Dangerous waters', *The Economist*, 21 July. pp. 35–6.

The Economist (2004) 'Dancing in step', *The Economist*, 13 November. p. 83.

Therborn, G. (2000a) 'Globalizations: Dimensions, historical Waves, Regional Effects, Normative Governance', *International Sociology*, 15: 151–79.

Therborn, G. (2000b) 'Introduction: From the universal to the global', *International Sociology*, 15: 149–50.

Thornton, G. (2005) *International Business Owner's Survey 2005*. Available online at: http://www.grantthornton.com.sg/Article/IBOS/2005%20Report.pdf, accessed 25 May 2005.

Tomlinson, J. (2003) 'Globalization and cultural identity', in D. Held and A. McGrew (eds), *The global transformations reader*, 2nd edn. Cambridge, UK: Polity Press. pp. 269–77.

Toyne, B. (1989) 'International exchange: A foundation for theory building in international business', *Journal of International Business Studies*, 20: 1–17.

Toyne, B. and Nigh, D. (1997) 'The future development of international business inquiry', in B. Toyne and D. Nigh (eds), *International business: An emerging vision*. Columbia, SC: University of South Carolina Press. pp. 673–83.

Toyne, B. and Nigh, D. (1998) 'A more expansive view of international business', *Journal of International Business Studies*, 29: 863–76.

Toyne, B., Martinez, Z. and Menger, R. (2001) 'The international business scholarship challenge', in B. Toyne, Z. Martinez, and R. Menger (eds), *International business scholarship*. Westport, CT: Quorum Books. pp. 1–19.

Tran, M. (2003) 'BT confirms plans for Indian call centres', *The Guardian*, 7 March.

Turner, A. (2001) *Just capital*. London: Macmillan.

van Bergeijk, P.A.G. and Mensink, N.W. (1997) 'Measuring globalization', *Journal of World Trade*, 31: 159–68.

Velde te, D.W. and Morrissey, O. (2000) *Can there be a global standard for social policy? The 'Social Policy Principles' as a test case*, Overseas Development Institute Briefing Paper, www.odi.org.uk/briefing/2_00.html, accessed May.

Veseth, M. (1998) *Selling globalization: The myth of the global economy*. Boulder, CO and London: Lynne Rienner Publishers.

von Weizsacker, E., Lovins, A. and Lovins, H. (1998) *Factor four: Doubling wealth, halving resource use*. Snowmass, CO: Rocky Mountain Institute.

von Zedtwitz, M., Gassman, O. and Boutellier, R. (2004) 'Organizing global R&D: Challenges and dilemmas', *Journal of International Management*, 10: 21–49.

Waddell, S. (2001) 'The role of civil society in business strategy', *The Corporate Ethics Monitor*, July–August: 57–9.

Waddell, S. (2001/2002) 'Societal learning: Creating big-systems change', *The Systems Thinker*, 12: 1–5.

Walters, M.J. (2003) *Six modern plagues and how we are causing them*. Washington, D.C.: Island Press.

Wilkins, M. (1997) 'The conceptual domain of international business', in B. Toyne and D. Nigh (eds), *International business: An emerging vision*. Columbia, SC: University of South Carolina Press. pp. 31–50.

Williamson, J.G. (1996) 'Globalization and inequality: Then and now', Working Paper 5491. Cambridge, MA: National Bureau of Economic Research.

Wilson, E.O. (2002) 'The bottleneck', *Scientific American*, 82–92.

Wolf, M. (2004) *Why globalization works.* New Haven, CT: Yale University Press.

Women and men in the informal economy: A statistical picture (2002) Geneva: International Labour Office.

Wood, A. (1994) *North–South trade, employment and inequality: Changing fortunes in a skill-driven world.* Oxford: Oxford University Press.

World Bank (1999) *Greening industry: New roles for communities, markets, and governments.* New York: Oxford University Press.

World Development Report (2001) New York: World Bank.

World Drug Report (1997) 'Revenue from illicit drugs: $400 billion', *World Drug Report.* Geneva: United Nations, 24 June.

World Investment Report (2000) New York: UN, UNCTAD.

World Trade Organization (2004) *International trade statistics.* Available online at: http://www.wto.org/english/res_e/statis_e/its2004_e/its04_toc_e.htm, accessed 26 May 2005.

Wright, R.W. and Ricks, D.A. (1994) 'Trends in international business research: Twenty-Five years later', *Journal of International Business Studies,* 25: 687–701.

Yip, G.S., Johansson, J.K. and Roos, J. (1997) 'Effects of nationality on global strategy', *Management International Review,* 37: 365–85.

2.10 Emotion and Organizing

STEPHEN FINEMAN

Ten years ago I opened this chapter with an assertion: 'Writers on organizations have been slow to incorporate emotions into their thinking…'. Today, I can state confidently that things have changed. The last decade has witnessed a considerable growth, in some areas an explosion, of organizational-emotion research (e.g. see Gabriel 1999; Mann 1999; Fineman 2000b; 2003b; Ashkanasy et al. 2002; Frost 2003). But this should not been regarded as a stand-alone activity. Organizational researchers have become attuned to emotion from a range of influences, especially developments in psychology, sociology, social psychology, anthropology, philosophy and the brain sciences (see Oakley 1993; Game and Metcalfe 1996; Oatley and Jenkins 1996; Miller 1997; Nicholson 1997; Planap 1999; Damasio 2000; Williams 2001; Moldoveanu and Nohria 2002).

Emotion has now become almost respectable as a management subject in its own right. Its early stigma – as peripheral to organizational conduct, of marginal interest to serious practitioners and researchers – has faded. While the field is far from controversy-free, we now find emotion included in mainstream introductory textbooks on organizational behaviour (such as Watson 2002; Robbins 2003; Buchanan and Huczynski 2004; Fineman et al. 2005). Emotion is to be seen as the lifeblood of organizing, entwined with, rather than separate from, various meaning-making and cognitive processes (Barry 1999; Forgas 2000; Isen 2000). Emotionalising organizations has given fresh insight into many key issues and processes, such as decision making, leadership, conflict, organizational change, social/gender differences, aesthetics, learning, resistance, harassment and bullying (Fineman 2003b).

Such has been the influence of emotional theorising, some are concerned that emotion cake may now be over-egged; that the 'core rational logic' of organization has now been lost (e.g. Bolton 2000).

This is a misreading. Rationality, as a dominant rhetoric of organizational purpose, remains intact. Emotions may be 'everywhere', but organizational attempts to contain and sustain them in the service of predictable means and ends have certainty not disappeared. Indeed, on the fateful 11 September 2001, while some employers dealt openly and empathetically with the trauma (Dutton et al. 2002), others withheld news of the disaster; the event was not to disrupt the normal flow of production (Driver 2003). Managing the tensions between managerial purpose and the desires of those charged with executing the purposes are, as ever, part of the dynamic and fragile order of organization. What emotion research has exposed is the hitherto uncharted, or silenced, emotions and emotional structures that sustain and shape them (Albrow 1992; Fineman 2000c). 'Pure' rationality may be illusory, but it is both a stubborn and functional one in which we all conspire.

How such issues have been explored does, however, continue to reveal some traditional disciplinary alignments. Much of the sociologically inspired research attests to socially constructive perspectives on emotion. Emotion, accordingly, is strongly shaped by social learning, cultural protocols and societal structures, and is often politicised (e.g. Hochschild 1983; Jaggar 1989; Ratner 1989; Stearns 1993; Barbalet 1995; Harre and Parrott 1996; Lupton 1998; Gergen 1999; Frijda et al. 2000; Sturdy and Fineman 2001; Solomon 2002; Fineman 2003a). Feeling 'rules' and emotion-display conventions mark the way in and beyond organizations.

Contrastingly, psychological, psychodynamic and biological approaches tend to locate emotion 'in' an individual's makeup and personal history; they seek to link specific emotional factors or perturbations with behavioural and organizational effects (LeDoux 1988; Lazarus 1991; Gabriel 1998;

Ashkanasy et al. 2000; Frijda et al. 2000; Isen 2000; Payne and Cooper 2001). In this vein some writers subscribe to a recent, controversial, turn towards evolutionary explanations of human conduct. Building upon Darwin's classic insights, emotions are seen as expressions of ancient neurological programming ('hard wiring') that have served the changing demands of human survival. The instinctive patterns are said to be present in recurring organizational patterns, such of male dominance in organizations, the way alliances and different kinds of bonding occur, and universal patterns of emotional expression (Trivers 1985; Badcock 2000; Nicholson 2000; Ekman 2003).

An integrative reading of the field would suggest that:

- Our capacity to feel and express feeling are crucial features of our communicative and adaptive processes, laid down in brain and related structures that have evolved over many millennia.
- But these capacities are made tangible through a lifetime of accumulated experiences and social learning, including injury and trauma. They give substance and form to our sense of self and identity. They shape private feeling and public emotional display, as well as lend moral edge to our emotions.
- Emotion is both a personal and organizational resource, through which different 'rationalities' and relationships are interpreted, contested and formed. The emotional architecture of organizations features in the way all work meanings are constructed and experienced, and is especially susceptible to managerial interventions. Yet there are invariably circumstances where employee resistance and non-conformity creates emotional spaces for organizational members, free from direct, hierarchical, control.

Against this backcloth, several emotion themes have gained prominence. In this chapter some are explored. Firstly, at the individual level: how emotions in the workplace are expressed and harnessed as emotional labour and emotional intelligence. Secondly, at the organizational level: the ramifications of emotions as seen through organizational change. Thirdly, some 'globalized', cross boundary developments: the virtualisation of emotion through networks, and a new expressiveness symbolized by events such as the untimely death of Diana Princess of Wales. Finally, the chapter reviews some recent ways of appreciating emotion: methodologically through discourse, and conceptually in a 'positive turn' in emotion theorising.

Working Individually With Emotion

Emotional Labour

In 1983, Hochschild's book, *The Managed Heart: the Commercialization of Human Feeling*, cogently articulated a growing trend – the corporate capture of emotions. In the service sector, such as airlines, the employer is in effect purchasing the employee's emotional labour as much, if not more than, their physical labour. The ready smile, the unruffled composure, the 'have a nice day', is part of the labour contract. It has exchange value for the corporation seeking competitive advantage. Emotional labour is hot, exploitable, capital. Training, as Hochschild shows, is axiomatic to this process; the potent inculcation of corporate emotion scripts with display-rules on how employees are to 'appear natural' to the customer, whatever they feel 'inside'. The art of artifice requires, at the very least, skills of 'surface acting' – putting on convincing show.

Particularly worrying for Hochschild is corporate pressure to 'deep act', to *identify* with the customer and take to heart the company's pro-customer messages. It can be oppressive and confusing. Hochschild's 'theology of emotions', as Smith (1999) describes it, evokes a 'sacred' notion of self, corrupted in a capitalist culture that has a detached, instrumental, view of emotions.

Emotional Hypocrisy and its (Dis)contents

Hochschild's work has stimulated much interest and debate. One conceptual strand concerns the way emotions are subject to what we might call 'normal hypocrisy' (Fineman 2003b). The terminology reflects the non-disparaging spirit of the Greek derivation, *hypokrisi*: 'playing a part on stage'. Emotion *work*, the effort of crafting and negotiating our appearance on different social stages, sustains the emotional hypocrisy that makes social order possible. Explicit and tacit rules of feeling and emotional display in a culture will steer us from having to show what we feel, or feel what we show. Skills at masking and dissembling are a necessary civilising process, crucial to social communication and order. In these terms, the everyday hypocrisies of emotion work, such as with partners, friends and neighbours, can be as instrumental, corrosive, or rewarding as those of commercially-contrived exchanges (Price 2001). Such a viewpoint chimes with a postmodern reading of the 'self'. There is no inviolate, 'true', self that is immune from the vagaries of social construction and reconstruction. We may have multiple selves, defined variously by temporally-bound emotion narratives (Elster 1986; Rose 1989; Sande 1990; Fairclough 1992).

Hochschild's insightful, but rather bleak, view of emotional labour, has been deconstructed and developed in different ways (Leidner 1999; Zapf 2002). For example, flight attendants, a focal population for Hochschild, have been placed under the gender microscope (Taylor and Tyler 2000; Williams 2003). Williams' study reveals a Janus-faced picture of their work, where sexualised marketing and cabin/flight-deck homophobia prevail. Many flight attendants felt unsupported by management ('the customer is always right'), and laboured to construct appropriate, gendered, cultural performances. As 'silent servants' they had to cope alone with the 'monstrous' behaviour of some male customers (abusive, lewd, drunk physical contact), unappeased by whatever the flight attendant said or did. But not all felt this way. The contrived smile made some feel more cheerful, especially when they felt valued by their employer.

The emotion management exemplified in these settings is revealing, but analytically restrictive. Bolton (2000) is helpful in this respect. She proposes three types of emotion management: *presentational* (the following of general social rules), *philanthropic* (a spontaneous gift), and *pecuniary* (emotion management for specific commercial gain). The interplay of these forms will be subculturally shaped. For example, public health and social service sectors in the UK were once known for their philanthropic styles of emotion management – spontaneous acts of care, concern and compassion. However, successive governmentally-inspired 'quality' reforms have promoted competency-based, measured, 'inputs' to 'customers' (Phillips 1996). As a consequence, a more perfunctory, pecuniary style, of emotion management has evolved.

Pursuing Emotional Labour – and Safe Zones

The desegregation of emotional labour suggests that, akin to the endorphin effect of physical exercise (feelings of wellbeing and a 'high'), some forms of emotional labour can be self-enhancing and stimulating for the worker. For example Shuler and Sypher (2000) provide a vivid portrait of US call operators on the 911 emergency-line. The operator is required to maintain a 'neutral', controlled, authoritative demeanour when dealing with calls that range from ongoing, major, crises, to the bizarre ('This guy wants to know if oral sex is illegal in this state …'). Meeting the demands of expressive neutrality can be tough, but rewarding. Some operators eagerly anticipated the excitement of 'when bad things happen', or the challenge of helping a caller to feel good – a gift response. One operator recalls: a student rang in panic because she was faced, alone, with a spider. Instead of chastising her for inappropriate use of 911, the operator responded calmly:

> I said, 'Do you have a textbook, since you are a student?'. 'Well, yeah, I do'. 'So okay, hold the textbook in the corner where the spider is and drop it and that will kill the spider'.'Oh thank you'. She called me back later and said, 'Thanks, thanks. You know it worked, I killed that spider'. She was saying, 'I feel so dumb because I called 911 for that and, but I was terrified and didn't know what to do' (p. 76).

A key feature of this, and similar settings, is the opportunity for the workers to shape emotional zones to express different modes of emotional labour, but without compromising the core act. Moreover, where co-workers are present, the drama may be augmented by sharing. In the 911 centre, retelling tales of 'stupid' people and 'regulars' provided comic relief and bonding. For Korczynski (2003) such 'communities of coping' are a collective form of emotional labour – with their own regulations and emotion rules. While 911 operators would share some reactions, others were not revealed – such as feelings of distress or sorrow following a traumatic call. Confiding openly to colleagues breached the 'rule' that extreme anxieties were to be handled privately, so as not to destabilize the work team.

The negotiation of zones and boundaries of emotional labour suggests a dynamic, multi-toned, picture of emotional labour – even in highly regimented settings, such as bank call-centres. Here, typically, much executive effort goes into prescribing how employees should manage their own and customers' feelings – in order to sustain customer loyalty and maintain maximum throughput. 'Smiling down the phone', 'faking it 'til you make it' and 'striving to meet the customers' individual needs' are common ingredients (Peccei and Rosenthal 2000; Sturdy et al. 2001). Employees so attuned can struggle when faced with irate or abusive customers, where management tends to defer to the customer. The informal creation of receptive 'spaces' or zones with colleagues can be an important fallback for the aggrieved operator, and a way of resisting oppressive managerial expectations:

> Sometimes the customer is rude; they will say 'fuck off' if you've given them a high quote. These comments are rare but they stick. They affect us all; they rebound round the whole team. One person will tell the person next to them, and the word soon goes round the whole team… I once had three in a day, and I was like 'put me back on the phone and I'll kill' (Korczynski 2003: 66).

Such collectively-regulated zones can also facilitate expressions of philanthropic emotional labour. Callaghan and Thomson (2002) portray bank call-centre operators ever wary of managerial surveillance, yet sneaking odd, 'illegal', moments of pleasure with callers – by just 'being there' for them:

> At the weekend, on a Saturday, you get old women or men phoning and they just want to talk. It's great. I love getting these calls (p. 250).
>
> We have our regular callers … And they'll call once or twice in the night and talk for a wee while, they just want a bit of company. I just feel you can't cut them off. You know they just want to blether (p. 250).

Professionals Do Emotional Labour Too

An emphasis on low-skill, front-line, service work can create the impression that emotional labour is confined to highly-scripted, hierarchically controlled, occupations. The scene, however, is much broader. It includes people in 'status' professions (e.g. legal, theological, medical, teaching) and 'occupational/managerial' ones (e.g. engineering, accountancy, real estate, hairdressing, police, nursing, social work). Professionals in these areas undertake face-to-face work and have responsibility for managing their own, as well as others', emotions. They mainly call upon *implicit* emotion-display rules, rooted in norms of professional conduct, but with a potential for emotional dissonance – tension between what is displayed and what is felt (Morris and Feldman 1996; 1997; Brown 1997; Pierce 1999). In this vein, for example, nurses often have to deal

daily with issues of death, dying and bereavement, while managing their own and the patients' emotions (Phillips 1996; Kelly et al. 2000). Social workers may struggle to sustain meaningful affective relationships with clients in a culture of 'new managerialism', with its efficiency targets and quotas (Gorman 2000; Chamberlayne and Sudbery 2001). Union officials can be consumed by the 'greed' of the union movement demanding exclusive and undivided loyalty to their members (Coser 1974; Franzway 2000).

Two contrasting professions – law, and hair and beauty – reveal some of the finer details of these processes.

The Legal Profession

The legal profession includes judges, barristers, attorneys, solicitors and paralegals – clerks and assistants, often serving their apprenticeship. Emotional labour is interactive amongst them and with their clients, reflecting, and sometimes challenging, pecking orders. Harris (2002) describes how contrasting audiences, as well structural factors (insecurity of income, the increasing power of solicitors, the need to win in court), shape the emotional labour of English barristers. Sweet talking and wooing/seducing solicitors may secure assignments: 'You've got to pretend to be interested in solicitors' squalid little lives'. They 'perform' in court – the mouthpiece for an angry or upset client; showing gravitas before clerks and solicitors and clients. They surface act with clients for whom they feel little sympathy or affection. Some labour hard at suppressing their 'loathing' of 'depraved' clients. Emotional labour was often exhausting and stressful, steered by emotion rules ('not the done thing to admit stress'; 'the need to pretend to know everything'; 'having to appear cool, calm, and rational'). However it was often rationalised on instrumental grounds: 'We don't act angry or sad or aggressive for nothing. It works: if it didn't we wouldn't do it!' (p. 574).

Lively (2002) adds to this picture, exposing a complex, gendered, portrait of US paralegals as emotion managers. Paralegals are mostly female and act as buffers and nurturers for other professionals in the system. They have to learn to accept attorney anger or rudeness; to be continually interrupted or treated as invisible. They screen attorneys' phone calls – but they cannot give legal advice. Attorneys 'give' much of the emotionally draining, time-consuming, client work to their less expensive legal assistants, who often engage in deep acting in the face of client distress: '... the unending sadness ... I find the hardest things ... just the unrelenting sadness ... they are all in difficult situations – that's the nature of this kind of practice' (p. 209).

Hair and Beauty Professions

Hair and beauty professionals are dominantly (but not exclusively) female, serving female clients.[1] They are deeply implicated in the social construction and transformation of feelings about, and appearance of, the body (Shilling 1993). Hair stylists and beauty therapists are both producers and mediators in the female body-image industry, confronting clients' desires, fantasies and anxieties (Furman 1997). The beauty therapist's remit is wider than the hair stylist's, typically including services such as make-up, nail extensions, eye-brow shaping and tinting, reflexology, massage, Reiki, and hair removal (Sharma and Black 2001).

A study of UK hair stylists by Shortt (2003) suggests that the depth of exposure to, and intimacy with, clients are crucial factors in stylists' emotional labour. In the salon, familiarity is limited to relatively brief, staged, encounters. The stylists are able to detach themselves and surface act: 'You just smile and pretend to be interested, but as soon as they go you forget it all and don't care ... that's it!' (p. 32). Their proficiency at feigning determines repeat business: 'You may be the most average hairdresser, but if you listen well and act the part, you'll always be fully booked'. Skilful emotion management is also a matter of deflecting the customer's surveillance when 'they are just staring in the mirror at you ... I just try to start a conversation and get the focus away from me' (p. 47).

The stylists felt differently about home visits, where more intimate, sustained, relationships required deeper acting. Regular clients could 'pick it up when your faking it', 'It's a heavier load on emotions – they need cuddles and hugs and advice ... they value your opinion' (p. 31). Emotional labour was tested in such settings, and could be stressful – such as when entering a tense atmosphere following a domestic argument, or feeling uncomfortable in 'posh' homes. Their business also took them into homes that they 'hated', such as where they felt obliged to do the 'dirty work' for some elderly clients, '...you can end up a bit like a cleaner in their homes'(p. 32).

Stylists share with beauty therapists a requirement for *aesthetic labour* (Nickson et al. 2001). They embody the product of their service. Shortt's stylists did gendered work; conscious about being on display and, literally, mirrored before their clients. They were particular about their own hair style and colour, use of make up and choice of clothes. Beauticians researched by Sharma and Black's (2001) were similarly concerned, seeing it as disrespectful to clients not to look smart in a conventional, feminine, way. Beyond this, however, it was the client's *emotional* transformation that was axiomatic to the beautician's sense of purpose. Clients often brought problematic feelings about their bodies, so 'We pamper and we treat'; 'We try to make them feel better ... giving people confidence'. Sensitivity to the intimacies of physical contact and to client confessions personalised the work. But few were formally prepared for this on entering the profession:

> I think there's a great gap in the training, that they don't prepare you. I mean when I went to college I was 20 and I was quite naïve and I had women confiding in me their innermost secrets that they wouldn't tell their best friends about ... I was never prepared for that. But I would listen. A lot of teenagers I see, they just haven't got what it takes (p. 922).

Those who work in salons, or undertake individual home visits, are positioned at one end of an industry dedicated to aesthetic transformations of self and/or image. The other end embraces organizational image-consultants, specialist in dress, grooming and deportment for corporate clients seeking competitive advantage (Wellington and Bryson 2001; Witz et al. 2003). All exploit or mould prevailing stereotypes of gender, social class and professionalism.

In sum, emotional labour has come a long way since Hochchild's original formulations, and it continues to generate empirical work and debate. It straddles the interests of both critical and non-critical researchers – on management, organizations and human resources. It has raised the profile of the oppressiveness of the 'sincerity' industry, but also exposed key facets of the interpersonal and 'body' work of professional and skilled workers. Given this knowledge, should emotional labour be formally acknowledged in the employment contract and the costs, where they occur, compensated for? Some human resource scholars argue that emotional labour should be put on a par with any other labour, and be included in job evaluations (Arthurs 2003). Where emotional labour is patently of a pecuniary sort, this makes sense. It is harder, however, to apply to situations where emotional labour is spontaneous and emergent.

Emotional Intelligence

If number of websites is an indicator of the popularity of a topic, then emotional intelligence does rather well. At the time of writing it scored over 600,000 hits, while some 30,000 entries were dedicated to emotional intelligence consultants. Emotional intelligence, it seems, is big business.

To the critical eye, the meteoric rise of emotional intelligence over the last decade represents an uneasy fusion of conceptual ambiguity and marketing verve. Its roots can be found in the backlash to American works such as *The Bell Curve* (Herrnstein 1994), which claimed that social position in life is indelibly marked by one's IQ: cognitive ability is all. Others, however, began to argue that such a view of intelligence and its effects is too restrictive. We can have 'multiple intelligences', some of which are emotionally based and crucial to what and how we do and how we do it (Gardner 1993). Moreover, findings from the brain sciences suggest that different kinds of performance and decisions *require* emotions for their direction, form and efficacy (Bechara et al. 2000). In other words, emotions and intellect are not polar opposites; they work in concert (see Fineman 1996; Fineman 2003b). We can be rational *because* we have emotions, and emotions can themselves be particularly rational in their direction and ends.

Mayer and his associates have applied these insights to 'emotional intelligence', which they define as the ability to perceive and express emotions, to understand and use them, and to manage them to foster personal growth (Mayer et al. 1999). 'Personal growth' in this formulation is a signal that emotional intelligence is a worthy construct because it leads to personally and socially desirable outcomes … 'the difference between a conventional decision and a daring one, between a stilted speech and one that soars' (Paul 1999: 9). Nevertheless, Mayer and other emotion academics have been wary about the claims that can be made for emotional intelligence, urging caution over what it can predict and whether it is sufficiently coherent to meet formal criteria of psychological robustness. Yet, as if in a parallel universe, the 'selling' of emotional

intelligence has proceeded apace. Mayer et al. capture the discourse tensions:

> The scientist says, 'Here is what I've been working on recently …'. The journalist replies, 'This is really important,' and then jazzes up the story in a way that seems close to lunacy: 'EI is twice as important as IQ!' This often-made, often-repeated, claim cannot be substantiated …' (Mayer et al. 2001: xiii).

The 'journalist' in this declaration is a thinly disguised allusion to Goleman and those who have capitalized on his work. In 1996 Goleman, a science journalist, wrote a bestselling book, *Emotional Intelligence*, based on a liberal interpretation and of academic studies on intelligence and emotion, including those of Mayer et al. (Goleman 1996). In it he claimed that emotionally intelligent people have abilities in five main domains:

- they know their emotions,
- they manage their emotions,
- they motivate themselves,
- they recognize emotions in others, and
- they can handle relationships.

Goleman asserts that this helps them to be 'stars' in their occupation or calling. Elsewhere he claims that '25 years' worth of empirical studies tell us 'with a previously unknown precision just how much emotional intelligence matters for success' (Goleman 1988: 6). Goleman talks of a 'tipping point', when emotional intelligence takes performance beyond one's usual knowledge and intellect. Goleman creates an aura of precision for emotional intelligence in promoting a measurable 'emotional quotient' – EQ. High EQ managers are described as enthusiastic, hopeful and persistent; they also radiate empathy, self-assurance and composure.

Goleman's claims for emotional intelligence have been widely reported in the popular press, while also stimulating academics, academic practitioners and consultants to explore the topic (Fineman 2000a). There are now many different definitions offered (Davies et al. 1998; Schutte et al. 1998; Abraham 1999; Huy 1999; Sternberg 2001; Becker 2003). There are also competing claims for the best, or definitive, measure (Salovey et al. 1995; Bar-On and Parker 2000; Boyatzis et al. 2000; Ciarrochi et al. 2001). An extensive review by Matthews et al. (2002) fails to find evidence of convergent validity amongst available measures.

The appropriation of emotional intelligence by management consultants has been one of the most ubiquitous trends, where the promise of emotional intelligence for business success is highlighted (Ralston 1995; Childre and Cryer 1998; Weisinger 1998). For example:

> Modern science is proving everyday that it is emotional intelligence, not IQ or raw brain power alone that underpins the best decisions, the most dynamic organizations and the most satisfying and successful lives (Cooper and Sawaf 1988; xii).

> I was lucky enough to have access to competence models for 181 positions drawn from 121 companies and organizations worldwide, with their combined workforce numbering millions... I found that 67% – two out of three – of the abilities deemed essential for effective performance were emotional competencies (Goleman 1998: 31).

The putative mutability of emotional intelligence has sharpened its applicability and sell. While some researchers argue that emotional intelligence is a trait, formed in early-life experiences and reasonably fixed by adulthood (see Jones 1997; Salovey et al. 2000; Furnham and Petrides 2003), others are convinced that it is a competence or set of competencies, susceptible to new learning or training regimes (Dulewicz and Higgs 1988; Boyatzis 2001; Caruso and Wolfe 2001; Cherniss and Caplan 2001; Goleman 2001).

Privileging the Emotionally Intelligent?

A charitable reading of emotional intelligence suggests a nascent concept, under some strain from pressures to grow-up too quickly. It has clearly caught the mood of the times, offering a vision of emotions that can be controlled in an instrumental, 'productive' way. It is the 'intelligent' directions of feelings that are seen to count; a picture of us firmly in control of our feelings, not victims of them. As Cooper and Sawaf claim, 'you can consciously guide your intuitive feelings ... towards seeking solutions ... into being more attentive and perceptive' (1997: 59).

For the student of emotion, emotional intelligence raises some important issues. The awareness and self-direction of feelings advocated by emotional intelligence theorists are, to an extent, what automatically occurs in many everyday social interactions. But, as the long history of psychoanalytic thought demonstrates, they are also patently what

we are often unable to do. Defensive and displacement processes, mostly beyond our awareness, act on feelings in ways that defy conscious control (Gabriel 1999). The ability of the emotionally intelligent actor (either naturally or through training) to identify and prioritize their feelings, is overplayed in current formulations. The interpenetration of thinking and feeling is, as earlier suggested, a mutually informative, mobile process, where thoughts and decisions are never 'pure' cognitions (Fineman 2000c).

Goleman, and other purveyors of emotional intelligence, operate a particular discourse technology to promote a set of 'nice' emotions (Fairclough 1992). They are emotions that typically reflect an Americanized 'positive mental attitude' – described by Matthews et al. as 'a dating-agency of desirable quantities' (2002: 531). Presenting emotional intelligence as an unproblematic virtue obscures the fact that it can be deployed to various ends, 'good' or 'ill', and that what constitutes emotional intelligent action in one cultural or sub-cultural setting may not be seen so in another. For example, leaders of a destructive cult or a manipulative manager are able 'successfully' to deploy their 'emotional intelligence'. Indeed, in tough business climates it can be emotionally intelligent to be envious, angry, pessimistic or even vengeful. The prosperous paths of Henry Ford, Jack 'Neutron' Welch and Sam Goldwin attest to the productivity of the 'less nice' sentiments. At present, emotional intelligence's cultural straightjacket provides little room for manoeuvre. We require a more relativistic picture that embraces different performatory values, and their cultural, ethnic and gender dimensions (Heelas 1986; Parkin 1993; Markus and Kitayama 1994).

Emotions and Organizational Change

It has become a much-repeated cliché that, nowadays, the only constant is change. But of course, change has always been with us, large-scale and small. As French (2001: 480) wryly notes: 'Merely to alter the arrangement of the furniture in a room or to appoint just one new member of staff can be enough to set the cats of anxiety and selfishness among the pigeons of stability and cooperation'. In other words, any action that alters perceptions of the organizational status quo is likely to be an emotionalized one too. Its 'rational' purpose can be interpreted in different ways: as a threat, an opportunity, a surprise, a loss, superficial or spectacular. And just as interpretations vary, so can attendant feelings, such of anger, despair, suspicion, ambivalence, hope, glee, anxiety, resignation, or joy (Antonacopoulou and Gabriel 2001; Carr 2001). Such feelings are likely to operate interactively as the meanings of change unfold and their implications reflected upon and negotiated.

Little Changes, Big Changes

There are typically everyday variations workplace demands. They include the vagaries of working patterns, equipment reliability, office arrangements, support-staff availability, supplies of raw material, customer requirements, deadlines, travel requirements, in-house catering, absenteeism, sickness and so forth. Together they constitute much of daily ebb and flow, the minutiae of changes that confront organizational actors. For some, such variabilities are a constant and expected part of their work life and hardly merit the label 'change'. Nevertheless, we have little insight into the emotionalities and emotional shaping of such essential workaday adjustments, beyond a small number of ethnographic and narrative-style reports (e.g. Terkel 1975; Frost et al. 1992; Fineman and Gabriel 1996; Gabriel 2000). Moreover, many such changes can be far from insignificant in the eye of the beholder and are often fundamental to the political and emotional climate of workgroups or department (Vince 2002).

Shifting our attention to the emotionalities of 'big', organizational wide, changes, rather more is known. Over the past two decades radical organizational change has been a common response of corporations and public enterprises wanting to cut costs and improve efficiency. Approaches include downsizing, different forms of 'structural engineering' (Hamel and Pralahad 1994) and wholesale attempts to move an organization's culture towards a more 'flexible', 'customer-oriented', style (Deal and Kennedy 1999; Sturdy et al. 2001). Such endeavours are revealing in terms of (a) how emotion is used to mobilize or manufacture change, and (b) the intended and unintended emotional consequences of a change process.

Mobilizing Emotions

People change what they do less because they are given an analysis that shifts their *thinking* than

because they are shown a truth that influences their *feelings* ... The heart of change is in the emotions... The flow of see-feel change is more powerful than that of analysis-think-change (Kotter and Cohen 2002: 1–2).

Kotter and Cohen here advocate emotions as key to persuading people to change. In effect, they are revisiting a long-known dynamic of organizational (and other) leaders who have charisma attributed to them. Such people are able effectively to voice the concerns and feelings of their followers and provide a seductive vision, an image of hope and optimism (Bryman 1992; Heifetz 1994; Gardner and Avolio 1998; Fiol et al. 1999). Once the bond is established then change can proceed along a pathway desired by the leader.

Eye and ear-catching events are part of the dramaturgical armory of the emotion change manager. Convincing theatricality is fundamental to the rhetoric of change, and theatre invariably involves emotion. In this respect, the skilled mood manager is an archetypal emotional labourer, capitalizing on intuitive, or meticulously scripted, mannerisms, cadences of speech, as well a carefully arranged physical props (Bensman and Givant 1975; Hamburger 2000; Jackson 2002). The normative agenda of such efforts is typically aimed at eclipsing feelings that are 'known' impediments to organizational change, while exciting feelings that supposedly support change. In the former category, according to Kotter and Cohen, we have false pride, pessimism, arrogance, cynicism, panic, insecurity and anxiety, while the latter includes faith, trust, optimism, passion, hope and enthusiasm – as both targets and the medium of change (see also Fox and Hamburger 2001; Seijts and O'Farrell 2003).

The ethos of a 'positive mental attitude' underpins such aspirations, echoing the values espoused by promoters of emotional intelligence. A less deterministic perspective suggests that the good/bad emotions of change are not so easily delineated or divided. Willingness to engage in change can be a function of fluctuating emotions, co-produced by strategic leaders and their followers. As Brundin (2002) observes, this frequently reshuffles the balance of power, as well as perceptions legitimacy. 'Bad' leader emotions in these contexts, such as frustration and impatience, can be taken by subordinates as appropriate and motivating. It is proper, therefore, to regard complex organizational changes as varying in meaning and emotional complexion, where 'tough' change agents are sometime welcome and energizing (Mossholder et al. 2000; Turnbull 2002; Garrety et al. 2003).

The Emotional Detritus

> No one feels safe in their job ... The general attitude is: I don't owe them anything because they could easily, and with no hesitation, fire me tomorrow – as they have done to hundreds around me (Turnley and Feldman 1999: 914).

Major organizational restructuring and downsizing can sometimes produce particularly corrosive emotional effects. They are evident in the way some people actively oppose change; of wary, cynical, survivors of change; hurt and resentful job-losers; shocked change managers; and executives frustrated at the slow recovery of their changed organization. In such circumstances the emotional fallout can neutralize, even reverse, expected economic benefits (Burke and Cooper 2000; Guiniven 2001).

From a managerial standpoint, resistance to change is a barrier to be overcome, and much of the prescriptive literature is aimed at ways of softening resistance (Bovey 2001). Through an emotion optic, though, resistance is more subtly understood. It can be regarded as a normal and natural part of the change process, focussed on recovering meaning or preserving what was valuable in the past (Antonacopoulou and Gabriel 2001; Fineman 2003a). It feeds on nostalgia and anxiety. The past and familiar routines become especially warm and attractive in the face of anxieties about one's competence and new learning, and in challenges to one's security – material and/or existential. Cool executive explanations and prescriptions for change can be felt as identity threatening. Continuity and consistency feel safer, more rewarding, than a future which is uncertain and/or unwelcome (Fiol and O'Connor 2002). When that destiny is imposed, opposition is likely to be radicalized. Fear, anger and mistrust can mobilize individual and collective power to resist (Young 2000; Burke and Leiter 2000). It can be especially sharp when the moral implications of change are contested – such as about who is to be made redundant, surveillance procedures, discriminatory pay rates, dangerous work, and the like. In these circumstances resistance is a 'hot' activity, intrinsically passionate and feeling-defined, often expressed as aggression, rule breaking, arguing, undermining, ignoring or sabotage

(Cascio 1993; LaNuez and Jermier 1994; Kets de Vries and Balazs 1997; Sturdy and Fineman 2001). It follows that change carries less potential for resistance when it is self-initiated, participatively shaped, incremental and enhances one's feelings of self worth (Mossholder et al. 2000; Bovey 2001).

Surviving and Organizational Holes

'Survivor syndrome' or 'survivor sicknesses' are labels used to describe the emotional reactions that temper or reverse any feelings of relief or gratitude at having *not* lost one's job. They include: fear of further downsizing and more radical changes; increased feelings of insecurity; guilt at having retained one's job while other colleagues have not; stress from having to absorb the work of those who have had to leave; wariness and anger towards top management; and a decline in commitment and risk-taking – one bitten, twice shy (Brockner 1998; Cascio 1998; Appelbaum et al. 1999; Robbins 1999; Burke and Cooper 2000; Burke and Leiter 2000; Allen et al. 2001). Survivor syndrome is especially poignant amongst those whose identity is enmeshed in their organization (Noer 1993). The front-line executioners of downsizing, managers who themselves have been protected from the shake out, are not necessarily protected from the emotional consequences of their actions. There are reports of their guilt at delivering the 'death blow' to colleagues, especially in work cultures that had, hitherto, made a virtue of their retention policies (Gooding 1978; Kets de Vries et al. 1997; Lamsa and Takla 2000). Some are shunned for their efforts:

> It's very difficult to walk through the halls, I walk through and I break up conversations. You know, oh, here comes X, and there's the disappearance of six or seven people. People don't say 'Hi' to me in the hallway. They've got their heads down. That's tough (Wright 1998: 347).

We can view the downsized organization as a punctured structure; there are holes where people, relationships and knowledge once were (Burt 1992; Susskind and Miller 1998; Shah 2000). Dispersed and fractured working patterns, empty desks, lost expertise and uncertain resources can leave people feeling adrift and powerless. Adapting to such changes can be akin to grieving, classically portrayed as beginning with shock, numbness and denial; then a nostalgic phase of pining for what is lost; to a sense of disorganization and despair; and finally towards acceptance and recovery (Kubler-Ross 1973; Parkes 1986; Freeman 1997). These stages may not follow a neat order, but an image of grieving is incompatible with that of executive impatience to 'hurry normal service along'. Short-circuiting grieving simply prolongs, or complicates, it. Paradoxically, then, the 'lean, mean' organization offers no motivational advantages until it can muster sufficient social-emotional resources to perform optimally (Brockner 1998; Spreitzer and Mishra 2000). According to Huy (2002), the challenge for managers is to balance the need for familiarity and continuity in the organization, with that of newness and change. This means managers attending to their own feelings of dislocation while also addressing subordinates' feelings of loss, anger and uncertainty. Some managers will act as 'toxin handlers'. They 'take the heat' on behalf of those they manage, filtering out fear and pain, sometimes at considerable emotional costs to themselves (Frost 2003). Toxin handling, however, is an 'end of pipe', solution. Better that organizational policies are designed to prevent survivor shock from the outset, such as through open communication, employee participation, fair selection processes, outplacement services, good redundancy packages and overt appreciation of the stayers (see Baruch and Hind 2000; Cameron 2003). And, in the light of the evidence on the uncertain economic benefits of downsizing, even better to try to avoid the process altogether.

Emotion at Large

Shifts in organizational forms have expanded our horizons of emotion – both literally and metaphorically. A 'big picture' on emotion reveals two recent trends. The first is the growth of virtual organizations, where working relationships are no longer defined by co-location or geographical limits. The second, especially in many Western settings, is an apparent movement towards a greater public expression of emotion, both positive and negative.

Virtually Emotion

Virtuality has become something of a hallmark of new work arrangements. It is now common for individuals, teams and organizations to operate without direct, face-to-face contact – with one another, or with their clients or customers. Network organizations, dot.coms, telecommuting, telecottages, homeworking, hotelling, boundaryless, and modular are amongst the various descriptions of virtualized work arrangements (Carr 1999; Black and Edwards 2000; Helms and Raiszadeh 2002). These organizational forms mark a radical move from the traditional, co-located, enterprise. Instead, people and teams can be dispersed, sometimes over vast distances and different time zones, linked through information technologies, such as e-mail, the Internet, intranets, web cameras, mobile telephony, groupware, teleconferences and Electronic Data Interchange.

Organizations that exist primarily as electronic phantoms press our emotion thinking into uncharted waters. How can people bond and trust when the usual verbal and non-verbal cues of feeling and physical presence are missing? Where are the emotional rewards of daily, workplace banter, of being with people? How can control be exercised and reinforced without the social glue of face-to-face exchange? How can we talk meaningfully about team building, when the emotional dynamics – fears, insecurities, posturing, conflicts – are left untouched, or truncated in their passage through an electronic portal?

Our current researches into virtual organizing offer a few clues to such questions. A key divide is between what might be termed a *nostalgic* perspective and a *revisionist* one. The nostalgic (and predominant) view asserts that virtual working loses much of what is good and essential in face-to-face relationships and social intercourse, therefore our task is to recreate virtually as much of the non-virtual environment as possible (e.g. see Handy 1995; Sheehy and Gallager 1996; Daniels et al. 2001b; Helms and Raiszadeh 2002). The revisionist perspective argues that our understanding of processes that constitute community and collaboration have been derived from a pre-computer era, one that privileged orality and physicality (e.g. Parks and Floyd 1996; Jorge 2001). We would do better to shed this legacy and appreciate virtual communication in its own right, celebrating its unique properties. Such as, for instance, how people can communicate on the Internet and e-mail, unencumbered by personal handicaps and social stereotyping. Or how participants can create strong, multiple, ties through the instant ease of virtual exchanges.

Virtual Trust

For many commentators on virtual working, the 'trust and control question' is writ large (Handy 1995; De Sanctis and Monge 1999; Jarvenpaa and Leidner 1999; Daniels et al. 2000). Without face-to-face interaction and the traditional managerial props of status and power, how can control be exercised and trust be cultivated? How can one manage people one cannot see? How will co-workers maintain cohesion and identity without the range of emotion cues necessary for 'feeling each other out'?

Trust is commonly portrayed as a belief in the reliability, truth and ability of another person or party to do or deliver what they have promised (Luhmann 1979; Lewis and Weigert 1985). Interpersonally, trust is accrued in different ways, especially from knowledge about the dependability of the other party from prior transactions and from 'acquaintance knowledge' based on a person's appearance, mannerisms and speech (Bruner and Taguiri 1954; Gallivan 2001). But to engage *trustingly* is more than just belief and knowledge; it is emotionally located and morally loaded. This is most evident in the anger and outrage felt when expectations of trust are not met or reciprocated. The bonds of trust are united by feelings of liking, confidence, commitment, fondness or love, a platform requiring regular reinforcement.

Given this background, we are faced with a paradox. Virtual working seems a poor candidate for the development of trust, as we know it; yet virtual work appears to hinge upon trust for its very viability. In practice, virtual workers appear to create surrogates or substitutes for trust, such as exchanging virtual 'chat' and intimate confessions, and by mixing virtual methods with face-to-face meetings (Grabowski and Roberts 1999; Jarvenpaa and Leidner 1999; Daniels et al. 2000; Morris et al. 2000; Daniels et al. 2001a; Sharifi and Pawar 2002). Jarvenpaa and Leidner (1999) found that high trust teams exchanged messages frequently and optimistically, expressing (on screen) their excitement and positive feelings about project goals. Low trust teams were typified by infrequent, non-committal, communications. The very early indicators of intent, the first few keystrokes of communication, were crucial; what Meyerson et al. (1966) term 'swift trust'. In such circumstances it seems that if 'interpersonal' trust is not developed speedily, it may not develop at all. It is replaced by a less-substantive 'cool' trust where the trustworthiness of the technical system, not its operators, sustains the operation (Wilson 1999).

Virtual Emotions and the Emotions of Virtuality

Working in virtual settings may appear emotionally compromised or thin, but communication technologies have spawned their own expressive vocabularies and protocols. For example, mobile telephones have challenged traditional emotion boundaries between the private and public (Fineman 1996). It is now common to be in full earshot of 'confidential' business conversations in trains, buses, shops or restaurants, as the mobile telephoner converses as if in a secure, private, space. Early resentment or irritation of bystanders has been replaced by a collusive 'pretending not to hear'. The emotion display-rules and zones have been recast (Scherer 2001). Likewise, e-mail communications have been emotionalized with 'emoticons' to indicate the mood of the sender, as well as conventions about the emotional significance of certain fonts and formats.

An E Dark Side

Electronic mail is an attractive medium for confidences and virtual chat, but it also creates illusory privacy. It is reported that up to 14 million US workers, in some 80% of major companies, have their e-mail (and Internet) covertly monitored (American Management Association 2001; Keller 2001). Other less-savory consequences include 'flaming' and pestering, where e-mail's disinhibitions and textual ambiguities can transform a sober exchange of views into an explosion of insults and vitriol (Gackenbach 1998). Some use e-mail to harass others, as one victim explains:

> I was sent pornographic e-mails by my boss. I now have a lawyer and he says I have a case. After being told that this was offensive and unwelcomed, my boss just laughed and said 'I think it is funny, I send this type of stuff to my kids' (Anonymous 2004).

The separation of virtual communicators can produce a sense of depersonalization and immunity. The Accident Group in the UK is a notorious example. In 2003, without warning, the company text-messaged all their employees that they were redundant, forthwith: 'Sorry to inform you that you will not be paid today. Don't bother ringing the office'; 'sorry folks im gutted 4 u good luck in ur future careers. Mike' (Jones 2003). Employees were shocked at the message, and angered at what was perceived as an abuse of the virtual medium. Some converted their anger into 'justified' theft, 'relieving' the company of some of its computer equipment.

Telework's Mixed Emotions

Telework creates virtual workspaces adaptable to different physical settings. Some are relatively fixed, such as at home or part of a conventional office or a call centre. Others are flexible – hotel rooms, cafes, cars and different forms of public transport. Working from different, self-selected, places can feel liberating, an exciting uncoupling from the drudgeries of daily commuting and stressful office politics; an opportunity to combine work with recreational travel. It provides a solution to some of the dilemmas of work/life balance (Henson 1997; Panteli 2001; Rich 2001; Crooker et al. 2002). An 'extreme' telecommuter explains:

> Welcome to the office odyssey! Jack in, wire up, drop out! The Internet is all about freedom – freedom from soft-walled cubicles, freedom from bad coffee, freedom from rules that just don't apply anymore. Why do you need to be in a corporate business park when there's a whole wide, wired world out there? (Heaton, 2000).

Virtual working from home has its rewards – such as the prospect of re-bonding with loved ones and more time to devote to important domestic affairs (Musson and Tietze 2004). Yet sustaining these benefits can be challenging. Home teleworking can put a strain on household relationships, as different family members compete for the teleworker's attention (Perrons 2003). Time-zone differences can mean virtual clients are ever present while, during the 'normal' working day, the teleworker can feel lonely and isolated without the support of workplace colleagues. Indeed loneliness, as well as loss of important career networks, are concerns shared by teleworkers of various sorts (Mann and Holdsworth 2003). Colleague relationships 'on line' do not always fill the social void (Bredin 1996; Fineman 2003b). Fraser (2001), one of telework's severest critics, observes exhausted and stressed corporate teleworkers facing an ever-open virtual window. As

virtual time supplants the traditional 9 to 5, it becomes impossible to meet an employer's expectations without constant access to one's mobile phone and e-mail. It creates communication anxiety, especially when a screen goes blank or there is a less-than-immediate response to an e-mail request (Sczesny and Stahlberg 2000; Hughes et al. 2001; Panteli and Fineman 2005).

In sum, virtual working is currently poised between two eras. One is of the traditional organization where emotions have been located within the boundaries of reasonable stable enterprises, and where work is performed and managed in the physical presence of others. The other is a globalized network of faceless customers and colleagues, where many of the old emotion scripts and protocols no longer apply. In unpacking the emotional implications of this new era we may need to discard some of our cherished beliefs about the nature and necessity of the 'human moment' in the way we bond, manage, trust, like and love.

Spectacular Emotion

Following the sudden, violent, death of Diana Princess of Wales in August 1997, there was an unprecedented display of public grief. It occurred across the world, but centred especially on London where some two million people gathered to share their sorrow before the world's media. Many openly wept. The congregation was densest around Kensington Palace, London home of the British Royal family, where many thousands of flowers and personal messages were deposited. Parrott and Harre (2001) liken the event to a pilgrimage where the pilgrim undertakes an arduous journey to a place that symbolizes an important feature of a mythical figure's life. On arrival, and after commune, there is sense of personal salvation. Thus the Diana gathering bears similarities to the emotional meanings of other pilgrimages, such as to Lourdes in France, or to Graceland in the USA.

The event's significance for us is in questions it raises about a culture's emotionology. For the UK, such mass displays of emotion run against the image of 'stiff upper-lipped Brits', restrained in open displays of sentimentality. Accordingly, some have explained the phenomenon as a temporary, collective, madness (Coward 2002). Others have focused on the influence of a mawkish press, keen to extract maxim sentimentality from the event. In that journalists are inevitably implicated in the social construction of the meaning of news, this interpretation cannot be lightly dismissed. As Czarniawska (2004) shows, the emotiveness of a news event is shaped by the different ways language and metaphor are deployed by journalists.

However, there is force in the argument that media influences are realized on the back of preexisting historical and cultural patterns (Stearns and Stearns 1988). In other words, the social and psychological seeds of a new emotional expressiveness were already in place in the UK on the day that Diana died. Indeed, subsequent tragedies in the UK and beyond have brought mass grieving to the streets, such as the calamitous destruction of the New York World Trade Centre on 11 September 2001; the murder of children in Soham, UK, in 2002; and the summary execution of kidnapped Ken Bigley in Iraq in 2004, a British civilian worker who was engaged in the reconstruction process. Indeed, such were British feelings of distress at Bigley's fate that one high-profile journalist's dissenting comments ('they're wallowing in victim status') provoked a sharp public backlash. He was subjected to ritual humiliation in the British media and in Government, culminating in his public apology – in person, in Bigley's home town (Carter and Wintour 2004).

How might these reactions be understood? There are both psychodynamic and social constructionist explanations. Of the former, there is the shared despair and guilt at an unfair world where we are unable to protect the innocent, and where our most powerful institutions fail to guarantee our safety. Grieving the death of Diana can be seen as the loss of a contemporary icon of rectitude and beauty; of someone who struggled against the malevolent forces of royal adultery and an uncaring family (Richards et al. 1999; Taylor 2000).

A social constructionist perspective focuses on changes in emotion display rules. As mentioned, emotion display rules reflect cultural norms about what is, or is not, perceived as emotionally acceptable to reveal in public. While there are micro shifts within a culture, the above examples suggest macro changes. British stoicism and emotional restraint can be seen to have softened following the popular endorsement of the New Labour Government of Tony Blair in 1997, with its youthful, informal, image (Parrott and Harre 2001). It heralded a new lack of ceremony in public affairs, where more openness about feelings was celebrated. Pop stars,

sports professionals and 'trendy' business people were recruited to the New Labour persona. The British Royal family did not reflect this development, with the exception of Diana – whose death symbolized a victim of a monarchy emotionally out-of-touch, wedded to reticence and reserve.

The seduction of emotion spectacle is evident well beyond the UK's shores. It is there in the 'instant' and intimate emotional reactions to the disasters and good fortune that constitutes news, creating a voyeuristic quality (Walter et al. 1995). 'Reality' TV, 'confessional' programmes and camera diaries have crossed traditional public/private boundaries and taboos. Programme makers, hosts, invited participants, studio audiences and remote viewers collude in a virtualized expose of all manner of 'vices' (e.g. jealousies, betrayals, polygamy, incest) and personal or family crises (e.g. depression, incurable disease, suicide). The emotions stirred and shown – hate, anger, loathing, excitement, despair, pain – are axiomatic to the programme's appeal and viewer ratings (Fineman 2000a). Similarly, the spectacle of despair, exasperation or joy of the winners and losers on competitive TV shows such as 'Who wants to be a millionaire?' Orchestrated tele-emotions are at once real and contrived; they can rouse the viewer through empathy and/or emotional contagion (Rime et al. 1991; Hatfield et al. 1994), and in doing so they contribute to the norms of a culture's emotional expressiveness.

Emotion as spectacle has long been an instrument of political movements where the collective display, 'for show', of anger, indignation and rousing chants reinforces the solidarity and cause of a movement (Aminzade and McAdam 2001; Goodwin et al. 2001). Such high-profile emotional architecture has been elaborated over recent years to include groups such as environmental activists and gay campaigners. In these settings, emotion has been a vehicle for defining the movement's meaning and aims. For example, in June 1995 Greenpeace succeeded in preventing Shell dispose of a redundant oil rig in the Atlantic. Their campaign was spectacular in the extreme, involving a carefully planned sea adventure of successive, dangerous, boardings of the oil rig, in close collaboration with the world's media. Greenpeace's emotionality – moral indignation and anger at Shell's plans, appeal to public sympathy, suspicion of industrial and governmental calculation of risk – contrasted to Shell's cool, rational and narrow framing of the issue (Rose 1998; Huxham and Sumner 1999). While

Greenpeace's own science turned out to be questionable, their emotiveness gave their cause a symbolic value and ethical edge that transcended technical considerations

In the different circumstances of AIDS, the work of Gould (2000) is illuminating. She notes how the early (mid-1980s) response towards AIDS amongst America's gays and lesbians failed to cohere into a challenging project. It was entangled in their own mixed emotions about themselves – confusion, fear, loss and uncertainty. There was also ambivalence about demanding attention from a society of which they did feel fully a part. From the late 1980s, however, Gould charts a shift towards angry street-activism amongst gay and lesbian groups: outraged protests, disruptions, civil disobedience. All were aimed at politicizing their frustration at lack of attention to AIDS by government, pharmaceutical corporations and the media. The challenge, however, was also to legitimize the public expression of anger to mainstream society, where such acts were commonly viewed as irrational and immature. The movement, argues Gould, succeeded well into the mid-1990s when, amongst other things, angry confrontation became less relevant in a new political climate that 'mainstreamed' gay and lesbian movements. The significance of this, and the Shell example, lies in the way that collective, *organized*, displays of emotion can begin to redefine for others the meaning and importance of an issue or cause, where a dispassionate statement of the 'facts' fail. In doing so, societal emotion taboos or ambivalences are confronted, contributing to a shift in a society's emotionology.

Appreciating Emotion

How do we appreciate emotion? In this final section we consider the impact of two recent 'turns' in emotion theorizing. The first relates to developments in portraying and assessing emotion – through narrative. The second is positive scholarship, a move amongst some organizational scholars towards appreciating 'positiveness' as a special value.

Emotion Knowledge

How do we know emotion? Typically, social scientists of emotion have turned to the familiar tools of their trade. Work psychologists, for example, favour metrication and more recently, experience sampling; the transformation of qualities and experiences into psychometric formats (Diener et al. 1999; Ashkanasy et al. 2000; Payne 2001; Weiss and Brief 2001; Ashkanasy et al. 2002). The inchoate is made tangible through calibration and numbers. However, if we take emotion to be shaped through social/relational practices of all sorts, then we have many possible 'voices' to represent feeling and emotion. The researcher's predefined categories on scaled items can be limited at representing the *qualia*, or intrinsic texture, of feeling – such as 'being' happy, hateful, hopeful or unsure and conflicted in feeling (Pratt and Doucet 2000). They can do but modest justice to the way emotion is socially constructed as a process, in shifting, politicised, organizational relationships (Abu-Lughod and Lutz 1990; Clark 1990; Hochschild 1990; Lutz 1990; Waldron 2000; Fineman 2004).

A broad unravelling of the methodological canvass reveals emotion susceptible to exploration in many different ways, such as contextualised observations, ethnographies, free-form diaries, memory work, action research and phenomenological analysis (Crawford et al. 1992; Fineman 1993; Domagalski 1999; Fineman 2000c; 2004; Sturdy 2003). Clearly, the way we conceptualise emotion – as 'in' the body and its biography or 'of' the body and its expressive positioning within social and power structures – provide different vantage points on knowing emotion (Fineman 2003b). Narrative approaches begin to bridge these perspectives.

Emotion's Narratives and Texts

Narrative concerns the ways we recount and connect our experiences in plots, stories, myths and legends. Emotion is expressed and made sense of in narrated metaphors, phrases and verbal images (Robinson and Hawpe 1986; Sarbin 1989; Boje 1991; Sarbin 1995; Boyce 1996; Gabriel 2000). Narrative departs from the question/answer routine of interview research, or 'how do you feel' inquiries. It takes emotion as embedded in the voices and texts of lived experience, as it is told, constructed and reconstructed. Through the sharing of spoken and written words people make 'sense' and 'meaning' of their feelings, in common language. Emotions are given a communicative role – to the actor and to an audience. In this manner, emotions get worked, performed and developed in social transmission. Thus fear, love, disgust, envy, hurt, joy and so forth are not static states, once and for all, but interactively produced and reproduced, embedded and reframed with the telling. Narrative is at once intensely individual and social, tying-in the reader/audience. It is one strand of a broader interest of organizational studies in texts and discourse; the various media through which social realties are expressed and contested (Fairclough 1992; Czarniawska 1998; Grant et al. 1998).

Looking Inwards

Emotion narratives and texts can be read in two directions: 'inwards' to its emotional structure and representations, and 'outwards' to its connections with competing or complementary texts. The inward approach can be seen, for example, in Gabriel's (1999; 2000) and Fineman and Gabriel's (1996) search for the different emotional tones of workplace stories and their psychoanalytic significance; in Sandelands and Bouden's (2000) explorations of the plots and emotional tensions in people's accounts of their work; and in Frost et al.'s (2000) analysis of compassion in first-hand organizational narratives (see also Chapter 2.17, this volume). Such interpretive approaches rely on the descriptive and analytic skills of the researcher. Arguably, they also require a degree of researcher reflexivity.[2] To illustrate, take the following evocative narrative on grief from Terkel's book, *Will the Circle be Unbroken* (Terkel 2002). Reverend Barrow, age 75, speaks to Terkel of her feelings of loss:

> My middle brother is dead. My baby brother is dead. Nobody's living but me and my older sister – she's living in San Antonio. But the worst in all the deaths was the death of my son. It's a strange hurt. It's a hurt that you can't scratch, it's a pain that you can't grunt it out…. You can't scratch it, you can't rub it. But I'm finding out how grief works. I've never done a lot of crying. Only after I leave my house, get into my car, it comes down on me. I think about my husband. My husband just had presence, that's what grieves me now. But the real grief all coming together affects me to the point that I don't want to do nothing. Like some of the goals and aims that I have in life, I'm sluggish. That's what I'm trying to cope with right now (p. 126).

The challenge for the interpretive emotion researcher is to understand, interpret, the meanings and feelings of grief; but to do so in a way that preserves the core tensions of the narrative, especially at its interstices – the intervening spaces where emotion intensity and meaning lie. There are emotion words – such as 'hurt', 'grief' and 'pain'. As emotive signs they convey something of the speaker's experiences. However, 'a strange hurt, a real grief all coming together' and 'a pain that you can't grunt it out… can't scratch' create a deep texture to the meaning of her feelings of grief. The staccato of the first three sentences presents a note finality and gloom, while her despair and paralysis is poignant in 'I don't want to do nothing'. Yet in offering such interpretations the reader/researcher is no blank slate. It is the reader's constructions that impute the *kind* of emotionality to the narrator's signs and signals. We become 'active', empathic, readers and interpreters, especially if we, ourselves, have experienced some of feelings implied in the text. Our own identities matter; to factor them out is a lob-sided version of the dialectics of emotion inquiry. The researcher's emotion work is part of the appreciation and validation process.

Looking Outwards

An outward perspective addresses rather different questions. How do emotion narratives and texts become politicised and contested to shape particular actions and outcomes? Who are the stakeholders, or guardians, of particular emotion discourses? The approach resonates with critical discourse analysis. It emphasizes a qualitative appreciation of emotion, but accentuates the competing emotion discourses that shape the way individuals, groups and organizations are judged, and come to judge themselves.

Commonplace examples can be found in the moral significance attached to the display, or otherwise, of certain emotions. Such as the doctor who 'expressed little compassion'; the nurse who 'got irritated with her patient'; the 'strained looking' president; the 'dispassionate' chief executive announcing redundancies along with a pay rise for his directors; the police officer who 'laughed' at the scene of a serious crime; the 'bored' judge who 'nodded off' during a long trial. A key point in these examples is how particular emotion events or 'outbursts' are construed and presented by different, interested, parties. These may be newspaper or television journalists; public statements from professional bodies; rumours and gossip amongst colleagues. Emotion narratives in these instances are social and moral currency. They are public tender, traded the political flow of stories within and across organizations. The analyst's task is to track these narratives and their texts, explore their rhetorical forms and deduce how they gain more or less ascendance in the hands of different actors. What are the emotion labels that 'stick' in defining and escalating what happens (Mechanic 1978; Goffman 1990)? How are different media deployed to impute significance to certain emotions?

Remorse is a case in point. Remorse is a restorative emotion. 'Genuine' displays of remorse can mitigate interpersonal injuries and begin to heal wounds (Cox 1998). Yet remorse is readily politicised, according to the status of the remorseful, the intensity and history of the issue, and the injured party's feelings, such as of anger, envy, outrage or despair. In national politics there is often considerable significance attached to a politician's remorse (or lack of) for their actions. Some narratives of remorse have become institutionalised, such as in the criminal justice system (Duff 1986; Bagarik and Amarasekara 2001). Portrayals of the accused or defendants who 'broke down in court', indicted criminals who 'showed no remorse' or who 'sneered at the judge', stir both the passions and outcomes of justice. Similarly, appeals for parole can become ensnared in competing depictions of whether 'he has really repented for what he's done', 'just too evil to ever forgive or trust' (see, for example Marchbanks 1966; Ritchie 1993; Stanford 2002). Narratives of remorse are cast against those of forgiveness, anger, revulsion and retribution. The emotion researcher can call on contemporary texts, such as legal proceedings, journalists' accounts, interviews and web-based pressure groups, to track, interpret and model emotion in the construction of justice. A similar approach can be applied in other organizational settings, such as unravelling the way participants in harassment, bulling and discrimination are judged and treated.

A Positive Turn

There have been recent voices in psychology arguing that their discipline has been too long preoccupied with studying what is wrong, or pathological, in life. It should turn its attention to what is good and positive, the best in individual intentions, emotions and production (Seligman 2002a; b). Positive psychology celebrates qualities and outcomes such as wellbeing, happiness, satisfaction, joy, pleasure, optimism, hope, faith and love. It honours civic 'virtues' of forgiveness, nurturance, wisdom and the work ethic (Snyder and Lopez 2002). Some organizational behaviour researchers have rallied to the positive cry to promote 'positive organizational scholarship' (Bernstein 2003; Cameron et al. 2003b). Positive organizational scholarship is concerned with positive emotions in organizations, such as vitality, compassion, meaningfulness, exhilaration and fulfilment. Its interests embrace positive features of organizational development, Appreciative Inquiry (Cooperrider and Whitney 1999) and prosocial behaviour (Batson 1991; 1994; Cameron et al. 2003a).

Positive organizational scholarship wears its heart on its sleeve. It speaks of what is 'life giving', 'generative', 'excellent', 'virtuous', 'ennobling', 'meaningful', 'transformative', and 'high-quality connective'. Its (pre-defined) good workplaces aspire to 'excellence', are 'just', 'honest' and 'humane', but 'of course need to be profitable' (Park and Peterson 2003: 41). Positive organizational scholars have explored a number of specific themes, including:

- The way expressions of gratitude and compassion can act as softeners and antidotes to the corrosive effects of anger, envy and greed in organizations (Frost et al. 2000; Emmons 2003).
- Principled dissent, the courage to overcome fear and speak out in defence of a strong moral right (Worline and Quinn 2003).
- How positive emotions, such as pride, joy and contentment, can produce a self reinforcing, 'upward spiral', of wellbeing and 'optimal' organizational functioning (Fredericksen 2003).
- The authentic leader as true to themselves, a person who is confident, hopeful, optimistic, transparent, resilient and ethical (Luthans and Avolio 2003).
- The fusing of personal identity with one's work in creating meaningfulness (Nakamura and Csikszentmihalyi 2002; Pratt and Ashforth 2003).

The impressive verve of positive organizational scholarship contributes a seductive strand to the emotions of organizing. Yet nailing one's flag to 'the best' carries its own moral burden. The strong flavour, even fervour, of North American positiveness is present in much of the writings where individualism, optimism and self-confidence are celebrated. The positive thesis could be strengthened by addressing cultural variations; contexts where self-effacement, humility and de-individualisation are centrally valued, as in parts of Asia and Europe (Markus and Kitayama 1994; Russell and Yik 1996; Levenson 1997). Another questionable feature concerns the potential of positiveness to camouflage alienating work. This is particularly evident in routine customer-service jobs where employers, mindful of the positiveness that sells, exhort employees to smile and/or engage in corporate fun programmes to boost worker commitment and positiveness (Isen and Baron 1991; Verbeke 1997; Deal et al. 1999; Collinson 2002). A positive gloss, however, can oppressively colonise a worker's emotional labour. There is, for example, an international growth in a low paid, low power, workforce that is recruited into the fast food and food preparation industries (Gill et al. 2001). In it, Talwar (2002) reports, we find managers in McDonald's and Burger King frequently directing their employees to 'leave your problems at home' and to report to work in a 'good mood'. In sum, a discourse of positivity can encapsulate the worker in a positive bubble, deflecting managerial attention from impoverished conditions of work and important features of the workers' biographies.

Axiomatic to positive scholars' approach is the separation out of positive from negative emotions (Seligman and Pawelski 2003; Peterson 2004). Happiness, hope, love and joy are to be welcomed, while the negative emotions, such as fear, anxiety, sadness and envy are not part of the positive project. Appreciative Inquiry, asking people to focus on the good and positive sentiments of organizational life, thus gains positive scholarship's particular approval (Cameron et al. 2003a; Cooperrider and Sekerka 2003). But bracketing the positive in this way is not unproblematic. It fails to allow for the way that any emotion can, potentially, be felt and appraised positively, negatively, or a mix of both (see Campos 2003; Ryff 2003). Some anxiety and fear can be exciting. A degree of pessimism can improve one's judgement and moderate risk-taking (Peterson 2000; Held 2002). Despair can combine with hope; happiness can be shadowed by fear that it will not last; love can mix with hate. Of pride and envy, Bagozzi comments thus:

Too little pride, for example, can make a person unmotivated insensitive to incentives; too much pride can make a person haughty, unresponsive to constructive criticism, and difficult to get on with.

Envy can be motivating in moderation, disruptive and debilitating to get along with. In sum, emotional extremes are often evaluated 'negatively' as excesses or deficits, but the same emotion may be positively regarded at intermediate levels (Bagozzi 2003: 178).

The meanings attributed to positive and negative emotions can be regarded as mutually constitutive (Lazarus 2003; Tennen and Affleck 2003). We learn what is good and positive from our experiences of the negative, and vice versa. 'Healthy' identity formation, moreover, is not a matter of avoiding or denying the negative. As psychoanalytic writers point out, moral character and strength lie in incorporating both positive and negative experiences of self and others (e.g. Klein 1981; Craib 1994). For effective learning in organizations, therefore, techniques such as Appreciative Inquiry are missing a core source of data: appreciating the negative (see Barge and Oliver 2003). This is forcefully illustrated by Weeks (2004) in an ethnography of a major British bank. Staff had been exposed to successive culture-change programmes aimed at reversing their 'dominate negativity'. The programmes sought to build a sense confidence, teamwork and empathy. The attempts failed. At all levels, discourses of negativity were a strong as ever. Weeks comments: 'No one, from the chief executive down to the junior clerks, has a good word to say about the organization's culture… Never once… did I hear it mentioned in a positive context' (p. 2). Yet, paradoxically, loyalty to the bank was high and its financial performance was excellent. An internal culture of self-deprecation was core to the organization's being. There was much that was positive in the negative.

The positive turn has raised our appreciation of emotion in organizations. It points to the fact that work experiences need not be bleak or soul destroying. Its thesis, though, requires critical development. Subjectivities in the workplace are formed and reformed through the interplay of positive and negative power effects, which are individually and culturally moderated. A positive turn that is erected on a wider contextual and ontological basis would offer a promising way forward (see Fineman 2006).

In Conclusion

The themes explored in this chapter indicate that emotion has now emerged solidly from the shadows, to contribute centrally to our understanding of organizations. This is beyond simply adding a new variable to existing paradigms. It is taking emotion-life seriously as core to the vitality and consequences of what we blithely call organizational rationality. The fascination of emotion starts with its intuitive resonance, in that few would deny that thriving, coping or simply surviving in organizations impacts or implicates one's feelings. Legitimating this discourse for the development of theory and practice is one major achievement of our recent studies.

There is more to do, as this chapter indicates, on the burgeoning trend in appropriating and packaging emotion for commercial gain and quick-fix solutions. Moreover, we should be restless in our scrutiny of tempting emotional utopias and new structures of working. Indeed, it is the critical edge of emotion inquiries that can begin to shed new light on the way different emotional 'orders' in organizations are sustained and challenged, and the outcomes they produce. Challenging, and some would argue risky, styles of research, are just the ones urgently required at the current stage of development of the field. Narrative explorations, of the sort discussed, are exciting ways of unhinging emotion from the constraints of instrumentation. But so are some more traditional ones – such as ethnographies, participant observations and depth case studies.

Notes

1. I do not include men's hairdressers in this discussion.
2. See Frost (2003) and Garrety et al. (2003) for examples of reflexivity. Some postmodern researchers would deny the appropriateness of this process, arguing the text is no more than the words themselves, and the imputed intentions of the author or researcher are irrelevant to the inquiry process.

References

Abraham, R. (1999) 'Emotional intelligence in organizations: a conceptualization', *Genetic Social and General Psychology Monographs*, 125: 209–24.

Abu-Lughod, L. and Lutz, C. (1990) 'Emotion, discourse and the politics of everyday life', in C.A. Lutz and L. Abu-Lughod (eds), *Language and the Politics of Emotion*. Cambridge: Cambridge University Press. pp. 1–23.

Albrow, M. (1992) 'Sine ira et studio – or do organizations have feelings', *Organization Studies*, 13: 313–29.

Allen, T.D, Freeman, D.M. and Russell, J.E.A. (2001) 'Survivor reaction to organizational downsizing: does time ease the pain?', *Journal of Occupational and Organizational Psychology*, 74: 145–64.

Aminzade, R. and McAdam, D. (2001) 'Emotions and contentious politics', In R. Aminzade, A.J. Goldstone, D. McAdam, E.J. Perry, W.H. Sewell Jr., S. Tarrow and C. Tilly (eds), *Silence and Voice in the Study of Contentious Politics*. New York: Cambridge University Press. pp. 14–50.

Anonymous (2004) E-mail Sexual Harassment. Available online at: http://www.now.org/issues/wfw/speakout/msg00649.html, accessed 16 December 2005.

Antonacopoulou, E.P. and Gabriel, Y. (2001) 'Emotion, learning and organizational change', *Journal of Organizational Change Management*, 14: 435–51.

Appelbaum, S.H., Close, T.G. and Klasa, S. (1999) 'Downsizing: an examination of some successes and more failures', *Management Decision*, 37: 424–36.

Arthurs, A. (2003) *Recognising emotional labour – is it a route to equal pay?* Paper presented at the ESRC Seminar Day on the Regulation of Service Work, Loughborough University, 29 October.

Ashkanasy, N.M., Hartel, C.E.J. and Zerbe, W. (eds) (2000) *Emotions in the Workplace: Research, Theory and Practice*. Westport, CT: Quorum.

Ashkanasy, N.M., Zerbe, W. and Hartel, C.E.J. (eds) (2002) *Managing Emotions in the Workplace*. Armonk, NY: M. E. Sharpe.

Association, A.M. (2001) *More Companies Watching Employees: American Management Association Annual Survey Reports*. Available online at: http://www.amanet.org/press/amanews/ems2001.html, accessed 18 April 2005.

Badcock, C. (2000) *Evolutionary Psychology*. Cambridge: Polity Press.

Bagarik, M. and Amarasekara, K. (2001) 'Feeling sorry? – tell someone who cares: the irrelevance of remorse in sentencing', *The Howard Journal*, 40: 364–76.

Bagozzi, R.P. (2003) 'Positive and negative emotions in organizations', in R.E. Quinn (ed.), *Positive Organizational Scholarship: Foundations of a New Discipline*. San Francisco: Berrett–Koehler. pp. 176–93.

Barbalet, J.M. (1995) 'Climates of fear and socio-political change', *Journal for the Theory of Social Behaviour*, 25: 15–33.

Barge, J.K., and Oliver, C. (2003) 'Working with appreciation in managerial practice', *Academy of Management Review*, 28: 124–42.

Bar-On, R. and Parker, J.D.A. (eds) (2000) *The Handbook of Emotional Intelligence*. San Francisco: Jossey-Bass.

Barry, B. (1999) 'The tactical use of emotion in negotiation', in R.J. Bies, R.J. Lewicki and B.H Sheppard (eds), *Research on Negotiation in Organizations*. Stamford, Connecticut: JAI Press. Vol. 7, pp. 93–121.

Baruch, Y. and Hind, P. (2000) '"Survivor syndrome" – a management myth?', *Journal of Management Psychology*, 15: 29–45.

Batson, C.D. (1991) *The Altruism Question: Toward a Social-Psychological Answer.* New Jersey: Lawrence Erlbaum.

Batson, C.D. (1994) 'Why act for the good: 4 answers', *Personality and Social Psychology Bulletin*, 20: 603–10.

Bechara, A., Damasio, H. and Damasio, A.R. (2000) 'Emotion, decision making and the orbitofrontal cortex', *Cerebral Cortex*, 10: 295–307.

Becker, T. (2003) 'Is emotional intelligence a viable concept?', *Academy of Management Review*, 28: 192–5.

Bensman, J. and Givant, M. (1975) 'Charisma and modernity: the use and abuse of a concept', *Social Research*, 42: 570–614.

Bernstein, S.D. (2003) 'Positive Organizational Scholarship: Meet the Movement', *Journal of Management Inquiry*, 12: 266–71.

Black, J.A. and Edwards, S. (2000) 'Emergence of virtual network organizations: fad or feature', *Journal of Organizational Change Management*, 13: 567–75.

Boje, D.M. (1991) 'The storytelling organization: A study of story performance in an office-supply firm', *Administrative Science Quarterly*, 36: 106–26.

Bolton, S. (2000) 'Emotion here, emotion there, emotional organisations everywhere', *Critical Perspectives on Accounting*, 11: 155–71.

Bovey, W.H. (2001) 'Resistance to organizational change: the role of cognitive and affective processes', *Leadership and Organization Development Journal*, 22: 372–82.

Boyatzis, R.E. (2001) 'How and why individuals are able to develop emotional intelligence', in C. Cherniss and D. Goleman (eds), *The Emotionally Intelligent Workplace.* San Francisco: Jossey Bass. pp. 234–53

Boyatzis, R.E., Goleman, D. and Rhee, K.S. (2000) 'Clustering competence in emotional intelligence', in R. Bar-On and J.D.A. Parker (eds), *The Handbook of Emotional Intelligence.* San Francisco: Jossey-Bass. pp. 343–62.

Boyce, M.E. (1996) 'Organizational story and storytelling: A critical review', *Journal of Organizational Change Management*, 9: 5–26.

Bredin, A. (1996) *The Virtual Office Survival Handbook.* New York: Wiley.

Brockner, J. (1998) 'The effects of work layoffs on survivors: research, theory and practice', in B.M. Staw, and L.L. Cummings (eds), *Research in Organizational Behavior.* Greenwich, CT: JAI Press. Vol. 10. pp. 213–55.

Brown, R. (1997) 'Emotion in organizations: the case of English University Business School Academics', *Journal of Applied Behavioral Science*, 33: 247–62.

Brundin, E. (2002) *Emotions in Motion – The Strategic Leader in a Radical Change Process.* Jonkoping: Jonkoping International Business School.

Bruner, J. and Taguiri, R. (1954) 'Person Perception', in G. Lindzey (ed.), *Handbook of Social Psychology.* Reading, MA: Addison Wesley. Vol. 2. pp. 634–54.

Bryman, A. (1992) *Charisma and Leadership in Organizations.* London: Sage.

Buchanan, D.A. and Huczynski, A.A. (2004) *Organizational Behaviour.* London: Financial Times/Prentice Hall.

Burke, R.J. and Cooper, C. (2000) 'The new organizational reality: transition and renewal', in R.J. Burke and C. Cooper (eds), *The Organization in Crisis.* Oxford: Blackwell. pp. 3–19.

Burke, R.J. and Leiter, M.P. (2000) 'Contemporary organizational realities and professional efficacy: downsizing, reorganization, and transition', in P. Dewe, M.P. Leiter, and T. Cox (eds), *Stress, Coping and Health in Organizations.* London: Taylor and Francis. pp. 237–58.

Burt, R. (1992) *Structural holes: The social structure of competition.* Cambridge, Mass.: Harvard University Press.

Callaghan, G. and Thomson, P. (2002) 'We recruit attitude': the selection and shaping of routine call centre labour', *Journal of Management Studies*, 39: 233–54.

Cameron, K.S. (2003) 'Organizational virtuousness and performance', in R.E. Quinn (ed.), *Positive Organizational Scholarship: Foundations of a New Discipline.* San Francisco: Berrett–Koehler. pp. 48–65.

Cameron, K.S., Dutton, J.E. and Quinn, R.E. (2003a) 'Foundations of positive organizational scholarship', in R.E. Quinn (ed.), *Positive Organizational Scholarship: Foundations of a New Discipline.* San Francisco: Berrett–Koehler. pp. 1–19.

Cameron, K.S., Dutton, J.E. and Quinn, R.E. (eds) (2003b) *Positive Organizational Scholarship.* San Francisco: Berrett–Koehler.

Campos, J.J. (2003) 'When the negative becomes the positive and the reverse: comments on Lazarus's critique of positive psychology', *Psychological Inquiry*, 14: 110–3.

Carr, A. (2001) 'Understanding emotion and emotionality in a process of change', *Journal of Organizational Change Management*, 14: 421–34.

Carr, N.G. (1999) 'Being virtual: character of the new economy', *Harvard Business Review*, May–June: 3–7.

Carter, H. and Wintour, P. (2004) 'Johnson apologises after article claims Liverpool overdid mourning', *The Guardian*, 16 October: 1.

Caruso, D.R and Wolfe, C.J. (2001) 'Emotional intelligence in the workplace', in J. Ciarrochi, J. Forgas and J.D. Mayer (eds), *Emotional Intelligence in Everyday Life.* Philadelphia: Psychology Press. pp. 150–67.

Cascio, W.F. (1993) 'Downsizing: what do we know? What have we learnt?', *Academy of Management Executive*, 17: 95–104.

Cascio, W.F. (1998) 'Learning from outcomes: financial experiences of 311 firms. that have downsized', in M.K. Gowing, J.D. Kraft and J.C. Quick (eds), *The New Organizational Reality: Downsizing, Restructuring and Revitalization.* Washington, D.C: American Psychological Association. pp. 55–70.

Chamberlayne, P. and Sudbery, J. (2001) 'Editorial', *Journal of Social Work Practice*, 15: 125–9.

Cherniss, C. and Caplan, R.D. (2001) 'Implementing emotional intelligence programs in organizations', in

C. Cherniss, and D. Goleman (eds), *The Emotionally Intelligent Workplace*. San Francisco: Jossey-Bass. pp. 286–7.

Childre, D. and Cryer, B. (1998) *From Chaos to Coherence: Advancing Emotional and Organizational Intelligence Through Inner Quality Management*. Boston: Butterworth Heinemann.

Ciarrochi, J., Chan, A., Caputi, P. and Roberts, R. (2001) 'Measuring Emotional Intelligence', in J. Ciarrochi, J.P. Forgas and J.D. Mayer (eds), *Emotional Intelligence in Everyday Life*. Philadelphia: Psychology Press. pp. 25–45.

Clark, C. (1990) 'Emotions and micropolitics in everday life: some patterns and paradoxes of 'place'', in T.D. Kemper (ed.), *Research Agendas in the Sociology of Emotions*. Chicago: University of Chicago Press. pp. 305–33.

Collinson, D. (2002) 'Managing humour', *Human Relations*, 39: 269–88.

Cooper, R. and Sawaf, A. (1997) *Executive EQ*. London: Orion Business.

Cooperrider, D.L. and Sekerka, L.E. (2003) 'Toward a theory of positive organizational change' in R. E. Quinn (ed.), *Positive Organizational Scholarship: Foundations of a New Discipline*. San Francisco: Berrett–Koehle. pp. 225–40.

Cooperrider, D.L., and Whitney, D. (1999) *Appreciative Inquiry*. San Francisco: Berret–Koehler.

Coser, L. (1974) *Greedy Institutions: Patterns of Undivided Commitment*. New York: Free Press.

Coward, R. (2002) 'Reasons to be tearful', *Guardian*. Available online at: http://www.buzzle.com/editorials/text8-30-2002-25501.asp, accessed 16/ December 2005.

Cox, M. (1998) *Remorse and reparation*. London: Jessica Kingsley.

Craib, I. (1994) *The Importance of Disappointment*. London: Routledge.

Crawford, J., Kippax, S., Onyx, J., Gault, U. and Benton, P. (1992) *Emotion and Gender: Constructing Meaning from Memory*. London: Sage Publications.

Crooker, K., Smith, F. and Tabak, F. (2002) 'Creating work-life balance: a model of pluralism across domains', *Human Resource Development Review*, 1: 387–419.

Czarniawska, B. (1998) *A Narrative Approach to Organization Studies*. Thousand Oaks, CA: Sage.

Czarniawska, B. (2004) 'Metaphors as enemies of organizing, or the advantages of a flat discourse', *International Journal of the Sociology of Language*, 166: 45–65.

Damasio, A.R. (2000) *The Feeling of What Happens*. London: Heinemann.

Daniels, K., Lamond, D.A. and Standen, P. (eds) (2000) *Managing Telework: Perspective from Human Resource Management and Work Psychology*. London: Business Press.

Daniels, K., Lamond, D.A. and Standen, P. (2001a) 'Teleworking: framework for organizational research', *Journal of Management Studies*, 38: 1152–85.

Daniels, K., Lamond, D.A. and Standen, P. (2001b) 'Teleworking: framework for organizational research', *Journal of Management Studies*, 38: 1151–85.

Davies, M., Stankov, L. and Roberts, R.D. (1998) 'Emotional intelligence: in search of an elusive construct', *Journal of Personality and Social Psychology*, 75: 989–1015.

De Sanctis, G. and Monge, P. (1999) 'Introduction to the special issue: communication processes for virtual organizations', *Organization Science*, 10: 693–703.

Deal, T., and Kennedy, A. (1999) *The New Corporate Cultures*. London: Textere.

Diener, E., Suh, E.M. and Smith, H.L. (1999) 'Subjective wellbeing: three decades of progress', *Psychological Bulletin*, 125: 276.

Domagalski, T.A. (1999) 'Emotion in organizations: Main currents', *Human Relations*, 52: 833–47.

Driver, M. (2003) 'United we stand, or else? Exploring organizational attempts to control emotional expression by employees on September 11 (2001)', *Journal of Organizational Change Management*, 16: 534–46.

Duff, R.A. (1986) *Trials and Punishment*. Cambridge: Cambridge University Press.

Dulewicz, V. and Higgs, M. (1988) 'Emotional intelligence: Can it be measured reliably and validly using competency data?', *Competency*, 6: 28–37.

Dutton, J., Frost, P., Worline, M.C. and Kanov, J.M. (2002) 'Leading in times of trauma', *Harvard Business Review*, 55: 55.

Ekman, P. (2003) *Emotions Revealed*. New York: Times Books.

Elster, J. (ed.) (1986) *The Multiple Self*. Cambridge: Cambridge University Press.

Emmons, R.A. (2003) 'Acts of gratitude in organizations', in R. E. Quinn (ed.), *Positive Organizational Scholarship: Foundations of a New Discipline*. San Francisco: Berrett–Koehler. pp. 81–93.

Fairclough, M. (1992) *Discourse and Social Change*. Cambridge: Polity Press.

Fineman, S. (1993) 'Organizations as emotional arenas', in S. Fineman (ed.), *Emotion in Organizations*. London: Sage. pp. 9–35.

Fineman, S. (1996) 'Emotion and organizing', in S. Clegg, C. Hardy and W. Nord (eds), *Handbook of Organization Studies*. London: Sage. pp. 543–64.

Fineman, S. (2000a) 'Commodifying the emotionally intelligent', in S. Fineman (ed.), *Emotion in Organizations*, 2nd edn. London: Sage. pp. 101–15.

Fineman, S. (ed.) (2000b) *Emotion in Organizations*, 2nd edn. London: Sage.

Fineman, S. (2000c) 'Emotional arenas revisited', in S. Fineman (ed.), *Emotion in Organizations*, 2nd edn. London: Sage. pp. 1–24.

Fineman, S. (2003a) 'Emotionalizing organizational learning', in M. Easterby-Smith and M. Lyles (eds), *The Blackwell Handbook of Organizational Learning and Knowledge Management*. Oxford: Blackwell. pp. 557–74.

Fineman, S. (2003b) *Understanding Emotion at Work*. London: Sage.

Fineman, S. (2004) 'Getting the measure of emotion – and the cautionary tale of emotional intelligence', *Human Relations*, 57: 719–40.

Fineman, S. (2006) 'On being positive: concerns and counterpoints', *Academy of Management Review*, 31: in press.

Fineman, S. and Gabriel, Y. (1996) *Experiencing Organizations*. London: Sage.

Fineman, S., Gabriel, Y. and Sims, D. (2005) *Organizing and Organizations*, 3rd edn. London: Sage.

Fiol, C.M. and O'Connor, E.J. (2002) 'When hot and cold collide in radical change processes: lessons from community development', *Organization Science*, 13: 532–46.

Fiol, C.M., Harris, D. and House, R. (1999) 'Charismatic leaders: strategies for effecting social change', *Leadership Quarterly*, 10: 449–82.

Forgas, J.P. (ed.). (2000) *Feeling and Thinking: The Role of Affect in Social Cognition*. Cambridge: Cambridge University Press.

Fox, S. and Hamburger, Y.-A. (2001) 'The power of emotional appeals in promoting organizational change programs', *Academy of Management Executive*, 15: 84–94.

Franzway, S. (2000) 'Women working in a greedy institution: Commitment and emotional labour in the union movement', *Gender, Work and Organization*, 7: 258–68.

Fraser, J.A. (2001) *White Collar Sweatshop: The Deterioration of Work and Its Rewards in Corporate America*. New York: Norton.

Fredericksen, B.L. (2003) 'Positive emotions and upward spirals in organizations', in R. E. Quinn (ed.), *Positive Organizational Scholarship: Foundations of a New Discipline*. San Francisco: Berrett–Koehler. pp. 163–75.

Freeman, S. (1997) 'Organizational loss', in B. Keys and L. N. Dosier (eds), *Academy of Management Best Papers 1997*. Madison, WI: Omnipress. pp. 264–268.

French, R. (2001) '"Negative capability": managing the confusing uncertainties of change', *Journal of Organizational Change Management*, 14: 480–92.

Frijda, N.H., Manstead, S.R. and Bem, S. (eds) (2000) *Emotions and Beliefs*. Cambridge: Cambridge University Press.

Frost, P.J. (2003) *Toxic Emotions at Work*. Harvard: Harvard Business School Press.

Frost, P.J., Dutton, J.E., Worline, M.C. and Wilson, A. (2000) 'Narratives of compassion in organizations', in S. Fineman (ed.), *Emotion in Organizations*, 2nd edn. London: Sage. pp. 25–45.

Frost, P.J., Mitchell, V.F. and Nord, W.R. (1992) *Organizational Reality: Reports from the Firing Line*, 4th edn. London: Sage.

Furman, F.K. (1997) *Facing the Mirror: Older Women and Beauty Shop Culture*. London: Routledge.

Furnham, A. and Petrides, K.V. (2003) 'Trait emotional intelligence and happiness', *Social Behavior and Personality*, 31(8): 815–824.

Gabriel, Y. (1998) Psychoanalytic contributions to the study of the emotional life of organizations. *Administration and Society*, 30: 291–314.

Gabriel, Y. (1999) Organizations in Depth. London: Sage.

Gabriel, Y. (2000) *Storytelling in Organizations*. Oxford: Oxford University Press.

Gackenbach, J. (ed.) (1998) *Psychology and the Internet*. San Diego: Academic Press.

Gallivan, M.J. (2001) 'Striking a balance between trust and control in a virtual organization: a content analysis of open source software case studies', *Information Systems Journal*, 11: 277–304.

Game, A. and Metcalfe, A. (1996) *Passionate Sociology*. London: Sage.

Gardner, H. (1993) *Multiple Intelligences*. New York: Basic Books.

Gardner, W.L and Avolio, B.J. (1998) 'The charismatic relationship: a dramaturgical perspective', *Academy of Management Review*, 23: 32–59.

Garrety, K., Badham, R., Morrigan, V., Rifkin, W. and Zanko, M. (2003) 'The use of personality typing in organizational change: Discourse, emotions and the reflexive subject', *Human Relations*, 56: 211–35.

Gergen, K. (1999) *An Invitation to Social Construction*. London: Sage.

Gill, M., Fisher, B. and Bowie, V. (eds) (2001) *Violence at Work*. Cullompton: Willan.

Goffman, E. (1990) *Stigma*. Harmondsworth: Penguin.

Goleman, D. (1988) *Working With Emotional Intelligence*. London: Bloomsbury.

Goleman, D. (1996) *Emotional Intelligence*. London: Bloomsbury.

Goleman, D. (2001) 'An EI-based theory of performance', in C. Cherniss and D. Goleman (eds), *The Emotionally Intelligent Workplace*. San Francisco: Jossey-Bass. pp. 27–44.

Gooding, J. (1978) 'The art of firing an executive', in P. J. Frost, V. F. Mitchell, and W. Nord (eds), *Organizational Reality: Reports from the Firing Line*. Santa Monica, Calif: Goodyear. pp. 58–65.

Goodwin, J., Jasper, M. and Polletta, F. (eds) (2001) *Passionate Politics: Emotions and Social Movements*. Chicago: University of Chicago Press.

Gorman, H. (2000) 'Winning hearts and minds? – Emotional labour and learning for care management work' *Journal of Social Work Practice*, 14: 150–8.

Gould, D.B. (2000) 'Rock the boat, don't rock the boat baby: ambivalence and the emergence of militant AIDS activism', in F. Polletta (ed.), *Passionate Politics: Emotions and Social Movements*. Chicago: University of Chicago Press. pp. 135–57.

Grabowski, M. and Roberts, K.H. (1999) 'Risk mitigation in virtual organizations' *Organization Science*, 19: 704–21.

Grant, D., Keenoy, T. and Oswick, C. (eds) (1998) *Discourse and organizations*. London: Sage.

Guiniven, J.E. (2001) 'The lessons of survivor literature in communicating decisions to downsize', *Journal of Business and Technical Communication*, 15: 53–71.

Hamburger, Y.-A. (2000) 'Mathematical leadership vision', *The Journal of Psychology*, 134: 601–11.

Hamel, G. and Pralahad, C.K. (1994) *Competing for the Future*. Harvard: Harvard Business School Press.

Handy, C.B. (1995) 'Trust and the virtual organization', *Harvard Business Review*, 73: 40–50.

Harre, R. and Parrott, G.W (eds) (1996) *The Emotions*. London: Sage.

Harris, L.C. (2002) 'The emotional labour of barristers: an exploration of emotional labour by status professionals', *Journal of Management Studies*, 39: 553–84.

Hatfield, E., Cacioppo, J.T. and Rapson, R.L. (1994) *Emotional Contagion*. Cambridge: Cambridge University Press.

Heaton, S. (2000) Extreme telecommuting – and office odyssey with Sid and Kristine: http://www.officeodyssey.com/index.htm, accessed 19 November 2005.

Heelas, P. (1986) 'Emotion talk across cultures', in R. Harre (ed.), *The Social Construction of Emotion*. Oxford: Basil Blackwell. pp. 234–66.

Heifetz, R.A. (1994) *Leadership Without Easy Answers*. Cambridge, Massachusetts: Belknap Press.

Held, B.S. (2002) 'The tyranny of positive attitude in America: observation and speculation', *Journal of Clinical Psychology*, 58: 965–92.

Helms, M.M. and Raiszadeh, F.M.E. (2002) 'Virtual offices: understanding what you cannot see', *Work Study*, 51: 240–7.

Henson, B. (1997) 'Remote working: marvellous, perilous or both?', Colorado: University Corporation for Atmospheric Research. Available online at: http://www.ucar.edu/communications/staffnotes/9704/telecommuting.html, accessed 19 November 2005.

Herrnstein, R.J. (1994) *The Bell Curve: Intelligence and Class Structure in American Life*. New York: Free Press.

Hochschild, A. (1983) *The Managed Heart*. Berkeley: University of California.

Hochschild, A. (1990) 'Ideology and emotion management: a perspective and path for future research', in T.D. Kemper (ed.), *Research Agendas in the Sociology of Emotions*. Albany: State University of New York Press. pp. 117–42.

Hughes, J.A, O'Brien, J., Randall, D., Rouncefield, M. and Peter, T. (2001) 'Some 'real' problems of 'virtual' organization', *New Technology, Work and Employment*, 16: 49–64.

Huxham, M. and Sumner, D. (1999) 'Emotion, science and rationality: the case of the Brent Spar', *Environmental Values*, 8: 349–68.

Huy, Q.N. (1999) 'Emotional capability, emotional intelligence, and radical change', *Academy of Management Review*, 24: 325–45.

Huy, Q.N. (2002) 'Emotional balancing of organizational continuity and radical change: the contribution of middle managers', *Administrative Science Quarterly*, 47: 31–70.

Isen, A.M. (2000) 'Positive affect and decision making', in M. Lewis and J. Haviland-Jones (eds), *Handbook of Emotions*. New York: The Guildford Press. pp. 417–35.

Isen, A.M. and Baron, R.A. (1991) 'Positive affect as a factor in organizational behaviour', in B.M. Staw (ed.), *Research in Organizational Behaviour*. Greenwich, CT: JAI Press. Vol. 13, pp. 1–53.

Jackson, B. (2002) 'A fantasy theme analysis of three guru-led management fashions', in T. Clark and R. Fincham (eds), *Critical Consulting*. Oxford: Blackwell. pp. 172–88.

Jaggar, A.M. (1989) 'Love and knowledge: Emotion in feminist epistemology', In A.M. Jaggar and S.R. Bordo (eds), *Gender/Body/Knowledge*. New Brunswick, NJ: Rutgers University Press. pp. 145–71.

Jarvenpaa, S.L. and Leidner, D.E. (1999) 'Communication and trust in global virtual teams', *Organization Science*, 10: 791–815.

Jones, M.M. (1997) 'Unconventional wisdom: a report from the ninth annual convention of the American Psychological Society', *Psychology Today*, Sep/Oct: 34–6.

Jones, R. (2003) 'Firm adds insult to personal injury as it sacks its workers by text message', *The Guardian*, 31 May.

Jorge, A.D.L. (2001) 'Social networks in education', paper presented at the *Social Geographies of Educational Change: Contexts, Networks and Generalizability*, Barcelona, 11–14 March.

Keller, L. (2001) 'Monitoring employees: Eyes in the workplace: CNN.com'. Available online at: http://www.cnn.com/2001/CAREER/trends/01/02/surveillence, accessed 2 January 2005.

Kelly, D., Ross, S., Gray, B. and Smith, P. (2000) 'Death, dying and emotional labour: problematic dimensions of the bone marrow transplant nursing role?' *Journal of Advanced Nursing*, 32: 952–60.

Kets de Vries, M.F.R. and Balazs, K. (1997) 'The downside of downsizing', *Human Relations*, 50: 11–50.

Klein, M. (1981) *Love, Guilt and Reparation and Other Works*. London: Hogarth Press.

Korczynski, M. (2003) 'Communities of coping: collective emotional labour in service work', *Organization*, 10: 55–79.

Kotter, J.P. and Cohen, D.S. (2002) *The Heart of Change*. Boston, Massachusetts: Harvard Business School Press.

Kubler-Ross, E. (1973) *On Death and Dying*. London: Penguin.

Lamsa, A.–M. and Takla, T. (2000) 'Downsizing and ethics of personnel dismissals – the case of Finnish managers', *Journal of Business Ethics*, 23: 389–99.

LaNuez, D. and Jermier, J.M. (1994) 'Sabotage by Managers and Technocrats: Neglected Patterns of Resistance at Work', in J.M. Jermier, W.R. Nord and D. Knights (eds), *Resistance and Power in Organizations*. London: Routledge. pp. 219–51.

Lazarus, R.S. (1991) *Emotion and Adaptation*. New York; Toronto: Oxford University Press.

Lazarus, R.S. (2003) 'Does the positive psychology movement have legs?', *Psychological Inquiry*, 14: 93–109.

LeDoux, J.E. (1988) *The Emotional Brain*. London: Weidenfeld and Nicolson.

Leidner, R. (1999) 'Emotional labor in service work', *The Annals of the American Academy of Political and Social Science*, 561: 81–95.

Levenson, T. (1997) 'Cultural influences on emotional responding', *Journal of Cross-Cultural Psychology*, 28: 600–25.

Lewis, J.D. and Weigert, A. (1985) 'Trust as a social reality', *Social Forces*, 43: 967–85.

Lively, K.J. (2002) 'Client contact and emotional labor: upsetting the balance and evening the field', *Work and Occupations*, 29: 198–225.

Lloyd Smith, S. (1999) Theology of emotion. *Soundings*(11): 152–158.

Luhmann, N. (1979) *Trust and Power*. Chichester: Wiley.

Lupton, D. (1998) *The Emotional Self*. London: Sage.

Luthans, F. and Avolio, B.J. (2003) 'Authentic leadership development', In R.E. Quinn (ed.), *Positive Organizational Scholarship: Foundations of a New Discipline*. San Francisco: Berrett–Koehler. pp. 241–58.

Lutz, C.A. (1990) 'Engendered emotion: gender, power and the rhetoric of emotional control in American discourse', In C.A. Lutz, and L. Abu-Lughod (eds), *Language and the Politics of Emotion*. Cambridge: Cambridge University Press. pp. 69–91.

Mann, S. (1999) *Hiding What We Feel, Faking What We Don't*. Shaftesbury: Element Books.

Mann, S. and Holdsworth, L. (2003) 'The psychological impact of teleworking: stress, emotions and health', *New Technology, Work and Employment*, 18: 196–211.

Marchbanks, D.A. (1966) *The Moors Murders*. London: Frewin.

Markus, H. and Kitayama, S. (1994) *Emotion and culture: empirical studies of mutual influence*. Washington, DC: American Psychological Association.

Matthews, G., Zeider, M. and Roberts, R.D. (2002) *Emotional Intelligence: Science and Myth*. Cambridge, Mass.: The MIT Press.

Mayer, J.D., Caruso, D. and Salovey, P. (1999) 'Emotional intelligence meets traditional standards for an intelligence', *Intelligence*, 27: 267–98.

Mayer, J.D., Ciarrochi, J. and Forgas, J.P. (2001) 'Emotional intelligence in everyday life: an introduction', in J. Ciarrochi, J. Forgas, P, and J. Mayer (eds), *Emotional Intelligence in Everyday Life*. Philadelphia: Psychology Press. pp. 11–18.

Mechanic, D. (1978) *Medical Sociology*, 2nd edn. New York: Free Press.

Meyerson, D., Weick, K.E. and Kramer, R. (1966) 'Swift trust and temporary groups', in R. M. Kramer and T. R. Tyler (eds), *Trust in Organizations: Frontiers of Theory and Research*. Thousand Oaks, California: Sage. pp. 166–95.

Miller, W.I. (1997) *The Anatomy of Disgust*. Cambridge, Massachusetts: Harvard University Press.

Moldoveanu, M. and Nohria, N. (2002) *Master Passions: Emotions, Narrative and the Development of Culture*. Cambridge, Mass.: MIT.

Morris, J.A. and Feldman, D.C. (1996) 'The dimensions, antecedents, and consequences of emotional labor', *Academy of Management Review*, 21: 986–1010.

Morris, J.A. and Feldman, D.C. (1997) 'Managing emotions in the workplace', *Journal of Managerial Issues*, 9: 252–74.

Morris, M., Nadler, J., Kurtzberg, T. and Thompson, L. (2000) *Schmooze or lose: social friction in e-mail negotiations*. Stanford: Graduate School of Business, Stanford University.

Mossholder, K.W., Settoon, R.P., Armenakis, A.A. and Harris, S.G. (2000) 'Emotion during organizational transformations', *Group and Organization Management*, 25: 220–3.

Musson, G. and Tietze, S. (2004) 'Feelin' groovy: appropriating time in home-based telework', *Culture and Organization*, 10: 251–64.

Nakamura, J. and Csikszentmihalyi, M. (2002) 'The concept of flow', in C.R. Snyder and S. Lopez (eds), *Handbook of Positive Psychology*. Oxford: Oxford University Press. pp. 89–105.

Nicholson, N. (1997) 'Evolutionary psychology: towards a new view of human nature and organisational society', *Human Relations*, 50: 1053–78.

Nicholson, N. (2000) *Executive Instinct*. New York: Crown Business.

Nickson, D., Warhurst, C., Witz, A. and Cullen, A.-M. (2001) 'The importance of being aesthetic: work, employment and the service organization', in A. Sturdy, I. Grugulis and H. Willmott (eds), *Customer Service: Empowerment and Entrapment*. Basingstoke: Palgrave. pp. 170–90.

Noer, D. (1993) *Healing the Wounds: Overcoming the Trauma of Layoffs and Revitalizing Downsized Organizations*. San Francisco: Jossey–Bass.

Oakley, J. (1993) *Morality and the Emotions*. London: Routledge.

Oatley, K. and Jenkins, J.M. (1996) *Understanding Emotions*. Cambridge MA: Blackwell.

Panteli, N. (2001) 'Impressions and boundaries within virtual work spaces', paper presented at *The 17th EGOS Colloquium, The Odyssey of Organizing*, Lyon, France, 5–7 July.

Panteli, N. and Fineman, S. (2005) 'The sound of silence: the case of virtual team organising', *Behaviour & Information Technology*, 24: 347–52.

Park, N. and Peterson, C. M. (2003) 'Virtues and organizations', in R. E. Quinn (ed.), *Positive Organizational Scholarship: Foundations of a New Discipline*. San Francisco: Berrett–Koehler. pp. 33–47.

Parkes, C.M. (1986) *Bereavement: Studies of Grief in Adult Life*. London: Penguin.

Parkin, W. (1993) 'The public and the private: gender, sexuality and emotion', in S. Fineman (ed.), *Emotion in Organizations*. London: Sage. pp. 167–89.

Parks, M.R. and Floyd, K. (1996) 'Making friends in cyberspace', *Journal of Communication*, 46: 80–97.

Parrott, G.W. and Harre, R. (2001) 'Princess Diana and the emotionology of contemporary Britain', *International Journal of Group Tensions*, 30: 29–38.

Paul, A.M. (1999) Promotional intelligence. *Salon.com*. Available online at: http://archive.salon.com/book/it/

1999/06/28/emotional/print.html, accessed 19 November 2005.

Payne, R. (2001) 'Measuring emotions at work', in R.L. Payne, and C. Cooper (eds), *Emotions at Work*. Chichester: Wiley. pp. 107–33.

Payne, R.L. and Cooper, C.L. (eds) (2001) *Emotions at Work*. Chichester: Wiley.

Peccei, R. and Rosenthal, P. (2000) 'Front-line responses to customer orientation programmes: a theoretical and empirical analysis', *International Journal of Human Resource Management*, 11: 563–90.

Perrons, D. (2003) 'The new work economy and the work-life balance: conceptual explorations and a case study of new media', *Gender, Work and Organization*, 10: 65–93.

Peterson, C. (2000) 'The future of optimism', *American Psychologist*, 55: 44–55.

Peterson, C. (2004) 'Preface', *Annals of the American Academy of Political and Social Science*, 591: 6–11.

Phillips, S. (1996) 'Labouring the emotions: expanding the remit of nursing work', *Journal of Advanced Nursing*, 24: 139–43.

Pierce, J.L. (1999) 'Emotional labor among paralegals', *The Annals of the American Academy of Political and Social Science*, 561: 127–42.

Planap, S. (1999) *Communicating Emotion*. Cambridge: Cambridge University Press.

Pratt, M.G. and Ashforth, B.E. (2003) 'Fostering meaningfulness in work', in R.E. Quinn (ed.), *Positive Organizational Scholarship: Foundations of a New Discipline*. San Francisco: Berrett–Koehler. pp. 309–27.

Pratt, M.G. and Doucet, L. (2000) 'Ambivalent feelings in organizational relationships', in S. Fineman (ed.), *Emotion in Organizations*, 2nd edn. London: Sage. pp. 204–26.

Price, H. (2001) 'Emotional labour in the classroom: a psychoanalytic perspective', *Journal of Social Work Practice*, 15: 162–80.

Ralston, F. (1995) *Hidden Dynamics: How Emotions Affect Business Performance and How You can Harness their Power for Positive Results*. New York: American Management Association.

Ratner, C. (1989) 'A social constructionist critique of the naturalistic theory of emotion', *The Journal of Mind and Behaviour*, 10: 211–30.

Rich, M. (2001) 'Firms, employees look to home offices again – across the nation, interest in telecommuting rises following the attacks', *Wall Street Journal*, 3 October, Eastern edition, New York. p B8.

Richards, J., Wilson, S. and Woodhead, L. (eds) (1999) *Diana, The Making of a Media Saint*. London: I.B. Taurius.

Rime, B., Mesquita, B., Phillipott, P. and Boca, S. (1991) 'Beyond the emotional event: six studies on the social sharing of emotion', *Journal of Cognition and Emotion*, 5: 435–65.

Ritchie, J. (1993) *Myra Hindley: Inside the Mind of a Murderess*. London: Harper Collins.

Robbins, S.P. (1999) 'Layoff-survivor sickness: a missing topic in organization behaviour', *Journal of Management Education*, 23: 31–4.

Robbins, S.P. (2003) *Organizational Behavior*, 10th edn. New Jersey: Pearson.

Robinson, J.A. and Hawpe, L. (1986) 'Narrative thinking as a heuristic process', in T.R. Sarbin (ed.), *Narrative Psychology: The Storied Nature of Human Conduct*. New York: Praeger. pp. 111–25.

Rose, C. (1998) *The Turning of the Spar*. London: Greenpeace.

Rose, N. (1989) *Governing the Soul: The Shaping of the Private Self*. London: Routledge.

Russell, J.A. and Yik, S. M. (1996) 'Emotion among the Chinese', in M.H. Bond (ed.), *The Handbook of Chinese Psychology*. Hong Kong: Oxford University Press. pp. 166–88.

Ryff, C.D. (2003) 'Corners of myopia in the positive psychology parade', *Psychological Inquiry*, 14: 153–9.

Salovey, P., Bedell, B.T., Detweiler, J.B. and Mayer, J.D. (2000) 'Current directions in emotional intelligence research', in M. Lewis and J.M. Haviland-Jones (eds), *Handbook of Emotions*. New York: The Guilford Press. pp. 504–20.

Salovey, P., Mayer, J.D., Goldman, S.L., Turvey, C. and Palfai, T.P. (1995) 'Emotional attention, clarity, and repair: exploring emotional intelligence using the Trait Meta-Mood Scale', in J.W. Pennebaker (ed.), *Emotion, Disclosure and Health*. Washington, DC: American Psychological Association. pp. 125–54.

Sande, G.N. (1990) 'The multifaceted self', in J.M. Olson and M.P. Zanna (eds), *Social Inference processes: the Ontario Symposium*. Hillsdale, NJ: Lawrence Erlbaum. pp. 1–16.

Sandelands, L.E. and Boudens, C.J. (2000) 'Feeling at work', in S. Fineman (ed.), *Emotion in Organizations*, 2nd edn. London: Sage. pp. 46–63.

Sarbin, T.R. (1989) 'Emotions as narrative emplotments', in M.J. Packer and R.B. Addison (eds), *Entering the Circle: Hermeneutic Investigation in Psychology*. Albany, NY: Suny Press. pp. 185–201.

Sarbin, T.R. (1995) 'Emotional life, rhetoric and roles', *Journal of Narrative and Life History*, 5: 213–20.

Scherer, K.R. (2001) 'Emotional experience is subject to social and technological change: extrapolating to the future', *Social Science Information*, 40: 125–51.

Schutte, N.S., Malouff, J.M., Hall, L.E., Haggerty, D.J., Cooper, J.T., Golden, C.J. and Dornheim, L. (1998) 'Development and validation of a measure of emotional intelligence', *Personality and Individual Differences*, 25: 167–77.

Sczesny, S. and Stahlberg, D. (2000) 'Sexual harassment over the telephone: occupational risk at call centres', *Work and Stress*, 14: 121–36.

Seijts, G.H. and O'Farrell, G. (2003) 'Engage the heart: appealing to the emotions facilates change', *Ivey Business Journal*, January/February: 1–5.

Seligman, M.E.P. (2002a) *Authentic Happiness: Using the New Positive Psychology to Realize Your Potential for Lasting Fulfilment.* New York: Free Press.

Seligman, M.E.P. (2002b) 'Positive psychology, positive prevention, and positive therapy', in C.R. Snyder, and S.J. Lopez (eds), *Handbook of Positive Psychology.* Oxford: Oxford University Press. pp. 3–7.

Seligman, M.E.P. and Pawelski, J.O. (2003) 'Positive Psychology: FAQs', *Psychological Inquiry,* 14: 159–69.

Shah, P.P. (2000) 'Network destruction: the structural implications of downsizing', *Academy of Management Journal,* 43: 101–12.

Sharifi, S. and Pawar, K.S. (2002) 'Virtually co-located teams. Sharing teaming after the event?', *International Journal of Operations and Production Management,* 6: 656–79.

Sharma, U. and Black, P. (2001) 'Look good, feel better: beauty therapy as emotional labour', *Sociology,* 35: 913–31.

Sheehy, N. and Gallager, T. (1996) 'Can virtual organizations be made real', *The Psychologist,* April: 159–62.

Shilling, C. (1993) *The Body and Social Theory.* London: Sage.

Shortt, H.L. (2003) *'Because they're worth it',* MSc dissertation, University of Bath, Bath.

Shuler, S. and Sypher, B.D. (2000) 'Seeking emotional labor, when managing the heart enhances the work experience', *Management Communication Quarterly,* 14: 50–89.

Snyder, C.R. and Lopez, S.J. (eds) (2002) *Handbook of Positive Psychology.* Oxford: Oxford University Press.

Solomon, R.C. (2002) 'Back to basics: on the very idea of 'basic emotions'', *Journal for the Theory of Social Behavior,* 23: 115–43.

Spreitzer, G.M. and Mishra, A.M. (2000) 'An empirical examination of a stress-based framework of survivor response to downsizing', in R. Burke and C. Cooper (eds), *The Organization in Crisis.* Oxford: Blackwell. pp. 97–118.

Stanford, P. (2002) 'Obitury: Myra Hindley', *The Guardian,* 15 November.

Stearns, C.Z. and Stearns, P.N. (1988) *Emotion and Social Change: Toward a New Psychohistory.* New York: Holmes and Meier.

Stearns, P.N. (1993) 'Girls, boys and emotions: redefinitions and historical change', *Journal of American History,* 80: 36–74.

Sturdy, A. (2003) 'Knowing the unknowable? – Discussion of methodological and theoretical issues in emotion research and Organizational Studies', *Organization,* 10: 81–105.

Sturdy, A. and Fineman, S. (2001a) 'Struggles for the control of affect – resistance as politics and emotion', in A. Sturdy, I. Grugulis and H. Willmott (eds), *Customer Service: Empowerment and Entrapment.* Basingstoke: Palgrave. pp. 135–56.

Sturdy, A., Grugulis, I. and Willmott, H. (eds) (2001b) *Customer Service: Empowerment and Entrapment.* Basingstoke: Palgrave.

Susskind, A.M. and Miller, V.D. (1998) 'Downsizing and structural holes', *Communication Research,* 25: 30–6.

Talwar, J.T. (2002) *Fast Food, Fast Track.* Boulder, Colorado: Westview Press.

Taylor, J.A. (2000) *Diana, Self-Interest and British National Identity.* London: Praeger.

Taylor, S. and Tyler, M. (2000) 'Emotional labour and sexual difference in the airline industry', *Work, Employment and Society,* 14: 77–95.

Tennen, H. and Affleck, G. (2003) 'While accentuating the positive, don't eliminate the negative or Mr. In-Between', *Psychological Inquiry,* 14: 110–72, 163–9.

Terkel, S. (1975) *Working.* Harmondsworth: Penguin.

Terkel, S. (2002) *Will the Circle be Unbroken: Reflections on Death and Dignity.* London: Granta Books.

Trivers, R.L. (1985) *Social Evolution.* Menlo Park, California: Lexington Books.

Turnbull, S. (2002) 'The planned and unintended emotions generated by a corporate change programme', *Advances in Developing Human Resources,* 4: 22–38.

Turnley, W.H. and Feldman, D.C. (1999) 'The impact of psychological contract violations on exit, voice, loyalty, and neglect', *Human Relations,* 52: 895–922.

Verbeke, W. (1997) 'Individual differences in emotional contagion of salespersons: its effects on performance and burnout', *Psychology and Marketing,* 14: 617–36.

Vince, R. (2002) 'The politics of imagined stability: A psychodynamic understanding of change at Hyder plc.', *Human Relations,* 55: 1189–208.

Waldron, V.R. (2000) 'Relational experiences and emotion at work', in S. Fineman (ed.), *Emotion in Organizations,* 2nd edn. London: Sage.

Walter, T., Littlewood, J. and Pickering, M. (1995) 'Death in the news: the public invigilation oration of private emotion', *Sociology,* 29: 579–96.

Watson, T. J. (2002) *Organising and Managing Work.* Harlow: Pearson Education Ltd.

Weeks, J. (2004) *Unpopular Culture.* Chicago: University of Chicago Press.

Weisinger, H. (1998) *Emotional Intelligence at Work.* San Francisco: Jossey Bass.

Weiss, H.M. and Brief, A.P. (2001) 'Affect at work: a historical perspective', in R L. Payne, and C.L. Cooper (ed.), *Emotions at Work.* Chichester: Wiley. pp. 133–71.

Wellington, C.A. and Bryson, J.R. (2001) 'At face value? Image consultancy, emotional labour and professional work', *Sociology,* 35: 933–46.

Williams, C. (2003) 'Sky service: the demands of emotional labour in the airline industry', *Gender, Work and Organization,* 10: 513–550.

Williams, S.J. (2001) *Emotion and Social Theory: Corporeal Reflections on the (Ir)rational.* London: Sage.

Wilson, F. (1999) 'Cultural control within the virtual organization', *Sociological Review*, 47: 672–94.

Witz, A., Warhurst, C. and Nickson, D. (2003) 'The labour of aesthetics and the aesthetics of labour', *Organization*, 10: 33–54.

Worline, M.C. and Quinn, R.E. (2003) 'Courageous principled action', in R.E. Quinn (ed.), *Positive Organizational Scholarship: Foundations of a New Discipline*. San Francisco: Berrett–Koehler. pp. 138–58.

Wright, B. (1998) '"The executioners' song": listening to downsizers reflect on their experiences', *Canadian Journal of Administrative Sciences*, 15: 339–57.

Young, A.P. (2000) '"I'm just me". A study of managerial resistance', *Journal of Organizational Change Management*, 13: 375–88.

Zapf, D. (2002) 'Emotion work and psychological wellbeing. A review of the literature and some conceptual considerations', *Human Resource Management Review*, 12: 237–68.

2.11 Exploring the Aesthetic Side of Organizational Life

PASQUALE GAGLIARDI

The Tangible Organization

'... I was brought up not just by my mother but also by the colours registered by my eyes, by the noises that prompted reactions of alertness or of calm, by the smell of fragrance and danger, by the habit of distinguishing good and bad more through sampling than through opinions, through the variants of touch born out of wishes or prompted by desires' (Crovi 1993: 1).[1]

Students of organizations usually conceive, describe and interpret them as (utilitarian) forms of social aggregation. We have become accustomed to associating the idea of organization with the image of people who make decisions, by acting and interacting, each performing different tasks, more or less specialized, and more or less oriented to a collective task or purpose. If you ask a manager to describe the company for which he or she works he or she will probably draw you an organization chart, that is, nothing other than a graphic and summary representation of a set of socio-professional roles and of relations between these roles.

At one time I used to view organizations in a similar corporate way. My perspective changed as a result of some field work during which I asked a workman assigned to an old lathe to describe his company to me. In reply he said:

For me, this company is that damned gate I come through every morning, running if I'm late, my grey locker in the changing-room, this acrid smell of iron filings and grease – can't you smell it yourself? – the smooth surface of the pieces I've milled – I instinctively rub my fingers over them before putting them aside – and ... yes! that bit of glass up there, in front, where sometimes – there you are – I spot a passing cloud.

Maybe my respondent had a poetic soul and felt things that the majority of corporate actors do not feel, though I don't believe that this was the case. I think he was merely more aware than most that our experience of the real is first and foremost sensory experience of a physical reality, while he was less concerned to supply an intellectualized version of his firm. For him it was obviously above all a *place*, a physical and *tangible* reality.

He had grasped the elementary truth that the physical setting is not a naked container for organizational action (Strati 1990), but a context that *selectively* solicits – and hence, so to speak, 'cultivates' – all our senses. This context refines some of our perceptive capacities (perhaps at the expense of others), enabling us to grasp minimal gradations in the intensity of a stimulus, and accustoms us to certain sensations until we become 'fond' of them, even if those same sensations may well be unpleasant in other contexts and for other people.

The physical setting can be natural (as the rectangle of sky of my informant) but in contemporary organizations – generally receptive towards any technical expedient that may improve efficiency – it is in large measure strewn with *artifacts*. An artifact may be defined as '(a) a *product* of human action which exists independently of its creator, (b) *intentional*, it aims, that is, at solving a problem or satisfying a need, (c) *perceived by the senses*, in that it is endowed with its own corporality or physicality' (Gagliardi 1990a: 3).

The study of corporate artifacts and space has emerged in recent years as one of the more interesting new currents in the general approach whereby organizations are studied as cultures.[2] The object of this type of study is what, in the tradition of anthropological research, is defined as the material culture of a social group. In that tradition, though, material culture has been generally considered *an* element (although secondary and accessory) of the cultural system, and the objects through which the material culture is expressed have often been considered worthy only of scrupulous classification. Even the study of the artistic production of traditional societies, which, as Forge (1973) observes, was an object of particular interest on the part of pioneers of anthropology such as Haddon and Boas, has vanished from the agenda of anthropologists with the spread and development of field-work techniques.

The choice of specific researchers of organizational culture to devote themselves to the study of artifacts sprang not from the desire to become specialists in a secondary or superficial 'aspect' or 'element' of the cultural system – however fascinating it may be – but from the awareness that the study of artifacts and of physical reality enables one to approach a basic human experience: the aesthetic.

The term 'aesthetic' (from the Greek *aisthànomai* 'perceive, feel with the senses') is used here in the general sense, to refer to all types of sense experience and not simply to experience of what is socially described as 'beautiful' or defined as 'art'. In the general sense in which I employ it, aesthetic experience includes a form of:

1. *Knowledge: sensory* knowledge[3] (different from *intellectual* knowledge), often unconscious or tacit and ineffable, i.e. not translatable into speech.
2. *Action: expressive*, disinterested action shaped by impulse and by a mode of feeling rather than by the object (the opposite of *impressive* action aimed at practical ends) (Witkin 1974).
3. *Communication* (different from *speech*) which can take place to the extent that expressive actions – or the artifacts which these produce – become the object of sensory knowledge and hence a way of passing on and sharing particular ways of feeling or ineffable knowledge.

When I call the aesthetic experience 'basic', I intend the adjective also in the literal sense of the term, to indicate that the aesthetic experience is *the basis* of other experiences and forms of cognition which constitute the usual object of organizational studies, and that it therefore implies that aesthetic experiences have a profound influence on the life and performance of the organization.

Despite the basic grounds that aesthetic experience provides for the sense of organization life, until recent years it has been an aspect generally ignored in organizational literature. When this chapter was first written – in 1995 – for the first edition of this *Handbook*, there had been only some isolated attempts to explore this dimension (Jones et al. 1988; Sandelands and Buchner 1989; Strati 1990; 1992; Ramirez 1991). I intended the chapter mainly to be mould-breaking, future-oriented and agenda-setting; today the mould seems to have been broken. There is a growing body of literature on aesthetic themes, one in which systematic reflection is conducted on the relationships between these and organization (Dean et al. 1997; Strati 1999) and between art and management, (Guillet de Montoux 2004); there are research anthologies as well as special journal issues (Organization 3/2 1996; Linstead and Höpfl 2000; Human Relations 55/7 2002), which have resulted from seminars and conferences expressly devoted to analysis of the methodological implications of taking an aesthetic approach to the study of organizations. The aesthetics of organization is therefore taking shape as a distinct field of inquiry within organizational studies, and it is interesting to ask what has led to the affirmation of this analytical perspective in the space of only a few years.

I have already pointed out that interest in the aesthetic dimension first arose within the intellectual movement usually referred to as the 'cultural turn' in organizational studies, or other times referred to as 'organizational symbolism' (Turner 1990). Yet the study of organizations as 'cultures' or as 'symbolic fields' which was born in the early 1980s as a marginal and non-conformist movement is today a widespread current of thought with ample academic legitimacy. Not surprisingly, therefore, specialized interests have arisen and prospered within this broader movement. In this regard, it should be noted that – although the emphasis on the aesthetic dimension and the 'style' of organization has characterized organizational symbolism since its beginnings – the two categories of the symbolic and the aesthetic can and must be kept sharply distinct. As Hancock and Tyler (2000: 110) have pointed out:

> … While the symbolic may well require an aesthetic component for it to be effective, it continues to demand an interpretative and cognitive reception on behalf of the receiver. Symbols must represent or 'signify' something other than themselves, and as such, exist within the domain of rational understanding and articulation. Aesthetic communication, on the other hand, transcends the merely symbolic. It constitutes meaning in its own right as a sensate quality.

In other words, the aesthetic perspective seems to have found a solid grounding in the 'cultural' movement that generated it. But it has developed as a distinct strand within that movement precisely because it does not share its predominant cognitivist stance, the origins and reasons for which will be discussed in detail in the next section.

Other research approaches and intellectual interests – which have arisen in organizational studies, in sociology, geography and anthropology – have probably created a cultural climate favourable for the institutionalization of organizational aesthetics as a distinct field of inquiry. These include the following:

1. The parallel development of strands of research such as the narrative approach (Czarniawska 1997; Czarniawska and Gagliardi 2003) and the study of emotions (Fineman 1993), which differ from the aesthetic approach in their subject-matter, method and reference disciplines – although they spring historically from the same stock – but have helped legitimate and spread their shared epistemological premise: namely, the tendency to question the rational and to explore the spaces lying 'between the organization as regulatory (the Law) and as experience (the Body)' (Linstead and Höpfl 2000: 1).
2. The conception of society as a network of practices situated in time and space, in which objects are active presences, and the conviction that social theory must necessarily examine the reciprocal relations among persons, places and things (Thrift 1996).
3. An increasing awareness of the aestheticization of the economy and of social life (Lash and Urry 1994), which has prompted Welsch (1996: 4) to call the aesthetic 'the main currency of society'.
4. The interest of postmodern and feminist thinkers in the human body, viewed not as a natural given but as a social construct and the vehicle of tacit knowledge – the site and outcome of power relations – and recognition of the body as containing and revealing cognitive and motivational dispositions (Bourdieu 1990).
5. Finally, the most recent developments in epistemological reflection on the practice of ethnography; these have broken the monopoly of traditional fieldwork techniques, highlighting sensate life as a worthwhile object of analysis, and the researcher's 'sensuality' as an epistemological disposition and a prime tool with which to understand reality (Fine 1996; Stoller 1997).

Although the changes in the cultural climate just described have helped break down the rigorous distinction between art and science, and although the study of organizational aesthetics has acquired its own space and visibility, it remains a marginal rather than mainstream research phenomenon. This is because it contests fundamental epistemological assumptions of the modern social culture which academic communities and institutions continue to reproduce in the sphere of social and organizational research. From this culture derives the inveterate reluctance of social scientists to deal with things, with the body, and with aesthetics. Hence, if full account is to be given to the nature and implications of an 'aesthetics of organizations', it is indispensable to begin with critical analysis of some of the implicit assumptions dominant in the world of social and organizational research.

As I conduct this critical analysis, I shall seek simultaneously and symmetrically to construct a different conceptual framework, and to identify the language and categories appropriate to analysis and interpretation of the sensate life of organizations. Where can this language and these categories be found? Aesthetics, conceived as a single discipline in the terms of philosophy, does not prove adequate for the task: it is intrinsically ambiguous, because philosophical reflection on the 'sensible' concerns itself with multiple and overlapping objects (the senses, desires, art, illusions, poetry, virtuality, play) and attention oscillates between the cognitive dimension of sensible experience – perception – and its emotional dimension – assessment of the sensible on a scale ranging from aversion to desire, up to the highest forms of desire and pleasure, represented by artistic experience in the proper sense of the term (Gagliardi 1990a; Welsch 1996). As Wittgenstein (1958, quoted in Welsch 1996:8) put it, '... anything – and nothing – is right ... this is the position you are in if you look for definitions ... in aesthetics'.

If aesthetics alone does not prove adequate, one must, as ever if one is to engage in interesting organization studies, be catholic in one's use of sources. Points of view and analytic categories drawn from such diverse disciplines as the theory of knowledge, cultural anthropology, the psychology of perception, neuro-psychology, the sociology of art, the history of art, and others, turn out to be necessary. A glance at the references to this chapter will give the reader some idea of the wide range of disciplines invoked in the efforts so far made to grasp the hidden regularities of phenomena that remain, in many ways, ungraspable. For this reason, readers should not expect a thoroughly systematic treatment, but should instead let themselves be led along a path consisting of deferments, attempts and allusions. As Strati (2000: 16) has written, we do not have '… the presumption that the aesthetic approach can provide either a more authentic or a more complete interpretation of organizational life. Rather, the organizational knowledge thus obtained is partial, fragmented and modest. It bears no resemblance to the generalizable, universal and objective knowledge yielded by approaches that use analytical methods'.

The Reasons for Neglect: Dominant Views of Social and Organizational Knowledge

Every culture habituates those who share in it. Habituation takes the form of fundamental polarities that express oppositions or complementarities between extremes that shape the perception, analysis and structure of experience. A series of paired terms, close and partly overlapping, well rooted in modern Western culture, are of particular importance for my proposed analysis: art/science, intuitive knowledge/logico-scientific knowledge, play(or leisure)/work, beauty/utility, expressivity/instrumentality, contemplation/activity. These distinctions do not reflect – as many believe – an order inherent to reality. On the contrary, such distinctions are culturally determined and derive from visions and conceptions inspired by the utilitarian rationalism which became rooted and widespread in the West from the second half of the eighteenth century. These conceptions are, at the same time, cause and effect, reflection and justification of the industrial revolution. More generally they are grounded in that profound cultural transformation which we usually identify with the advent of 'modernity' and which Weber defined as the disenchantment of the world.

The scientific revolution and the perfecting of the cognitive framework of the natural sciences achieved by Newton divided the study of the *primary qualities* of the physical world – objective, universal and subject to the language of mathematics – from its *secondary qualities*, which are the object of subjective experiences, sensory and inexact. 'Special aesthetics',[4] meaning the study of beauty, arises at the moment when the *beautiful* is definitively split off and distinguished from the *useful* and practical, when the moment of *activity*, connected with the

exercise of the *cognitive faculties* of the intellect and its productions (science and technology), is conceptually and socially split off from the moment of *contemplation* and of the *imagination* linked to the fruition of the beautiful and of art (Carmagnola 1994). These oppositions/divisions did not exist – or did not have the same force and the same consequence – before the eighteenth century: in the Renaissance, (as in the Greco–Hellenistic civilization which inspired humanism), art and technique, functionality and beauty were hardly separable, either conceptually or in the organization of social life, and, as Hamilton (1942) suggests, the extraordinary level reached by those civilizations was the outcome of this integration.

With the advent of modernity the aforementioned distinctions hardened. New hierarchies took unequivocal shape among the values referred to by such polarities. Work and production became more important than leisure and play,[5] activity over contemplation, utility rather than beauty. Above all – for what interests us here – logico-scientific (objective) knowledge established itself definitively as a superior form of knowledge over aesthetico-intuitive (subjective) knowledge. The aesthetic was demoted to the 'secondary sphere of consumption, of spare time, of the useless'[6] (Carmagnola 1994: 129).

In the old scholastic treatises logic was considered the art of demonstration, while eloquence (or rhetoric) was held to be the art of persuasion. In the first the capacity to convince the hearer depends on objective features of the discourse, in the second on subjective qualities of the speaker and on his style, that is to say, on the formal properties – i.e. sensorially and emotionally perceptible – of his speech, which in their turn appeal to subjective characteristics and perceptual attitudes in the hearer. Rhetoric was often represented in treatises by the image of an open hand and logic by that of a fist (Howell, cited in Mamiani 1992, see Figure 2.11.1). This symbolization gave clear expression to the idea that the progress of knowledge is the fruit of an oscillation between two diverse forms of knowledge and communication of equal worth and dignity. But, starting with Newton, the sage became more and more identified with the scientist whose reports *had to be* the outcome of cold observation, stripped of any stylistic stratagem and divested of the charm of imagination. Modernity has thus inherited from the eighteenth century scientific revolution a closed fist – or at least

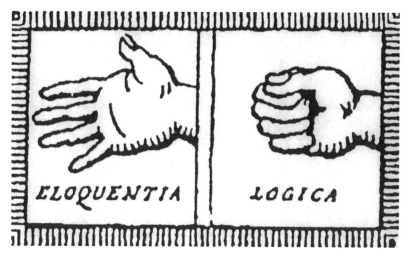

Figure 2.11.1 Two forms of knowledge and communication

the idea of the superiority of the closed fist over the open hand – and hence a conception of science 'clenched in its processes of demonstration'[7] (Mamiani 1992: 225). Such a conception is still dominant in the social sciences also, despite the fact that efforts – among which those of Polanyi (1966) and of Brown (1977) are outstanding – to establish an aesthetic view of social knowledge, combining the rigorous outlook of scientific realism with the creative potentiality of Romantic idealism, have found more than a handful of enthusiastic supporters. The war against aesthetics continues to be waged in the name of 'truth': actually, 'the sciences would be threatened with being undermined should rhetorical brilliance become more important than the justification of assertions' (Fine 1996: 12).

Recently, Guillet de Montoux (2004) has brilliantly shown that the capacity to combine art and science, imagination and technique, mind and body, expressiveness and pragmatism, passion and reason was not a prerogative of ancient Greece or of the Renaissance alone. The cultural stereotypes expressed by modernist dichotomies and hierarchies prevent us from seeing these syntheses when they are produced in practice, and they discourage those who seek to accomplish them by labelling them 'Utopian'. By means of analysis of a series of 'art firms' – from the Bayreuth Wagner Festival to Stanislavski's Artistic Theatre, to contemporary experiences like the Performance Art of Robert Wilson and the 'Cittadellarte' created by Michelangelo Pistoletto in Biella – Guillet de Montoux demonstrates that producing a work of art (when this requires a collective effort) involves the use of managerial techniques to a greater extent than might initially appear to be the case, and that, conversely, managing an industrial enterprise is more of an artistic undertaking than is commonly believed. For Guillet de Montoux, the combined use of rational and aesthetic capacities extraordinarily enriches both our ability to understand organizations and our ability to manage them. Aesthetic education consists in the development of the capacity to enhance and convey the creative energy generated in the endeavour to restore unity between nature and morality, form and substance. It is only this energy – which Guillet, following Kant, Schiller and Nietzsche, calls 'dionysiac' – that can restrict the production of the 'impoverished artifacts' (Kuhn 1996: 219) that are the organizational theories which inhabit our intellectual world, or the companies that populate the social landscape.

If Guillet de Montoux's thesis is considered by some to be the provocation of an 'artist', being thus automatically relegated to the sphere of the amusing but pointless, this is because of the cultural stereotypes that I mentioned earlier, and it demonstrates their persistence. If formal organizations are the social artifacts which best embody the rationalistic and utilitarian ideal of modernity, we can only expect those who deal with organizations – be they practitioners or academics – to continue to be irresistibly attracted to the rationalist half of the paired terms mentioned above. However open-minded organizational scholars may be, the fact remains that the knowledge that they produce is most frequently aimed at practitioners. Their epistemology, implicit or explicit, will thereby tend to reflect the worldview and theory of knowledge of those in whose eyes they strive to be credible: it is a question, so to speak, of cognitive and cultural attunement (Barley et al. 1988). It is this which explains, in my view, why even among students of organizational cultures, interest in the study of artifacts and of the aesthetic dimension is comparatively limited, despite the fact that the founding principles of this line of study included from the start the legitimacy of a form of understanding of corporate life different from and alternative to that of rational cognition, one which Ebers (1985) specifically defined as 'the poetic mode'.

When one moves from the *forms* of knowledge to the *objects* of social knowledge (that is to say, if we pass from the question of epistemology to the question of ontology), we come up against the idiosyncratic tendency of social scientists, and organizational ones in particular, to shuttle between people – as subjects of relationships – and their mental products, between the 'thinker' and the 'thought', excluding from their visual field and interests material things (the 'product', so to speak) (Ammassari 1985). Here, too, we can see, on the one hand, the influence of Descartes's idea of the self as the subject of thought capable of self-consciousness, and on the other the influence of the rooted distinction between mind and body, with the evident assumption of the superiority of the former over the latter. However, as Latour (1992a) has brilliantly observed, material things are the missing masses knocking insistently at the doors of sociology. To neglect to analyse them and observe only human action is like limiting one's gaze to half of the court during a tennis match: the observed movements seem to have no meaning. For Latour (1992a; 1992b), in fact, the development of technology in modern society makes it possible to delegate a growing number of action programmes to non-human subjects, to things which while being often stationary and lacking any trace of 'machinery' – as for example an indicator board – are machines in the more general sense of the term. They, in fact, incorporate activity that could be – or

that was previously – performed by human beings, they condition human beings, they interact with them and are conditioned by them, in a chain of delegations and transfers – or translations, as Latour calls them – which have conscious human beings at one extreme, efficient and tenacious machines at the other, and the power of symbols and signals halfway between.

From a different standpoint, but one close to that of Latour, we can also say that ideas and things, thought and action, spirit and matter do not belong to separate and non-communicating worlds. On the contrary, things can represent the *materialization of ideas* (Czarniawska-Joerges and Joerges 1995) and thus can generate in their turn ideas that tend to materialize themselves, in a process that only when it is captured in its entirety makes possible an understanding of the *nature* and the *forms* of social and organizational change.

The Relevance of Artifacts for the Study of Organizational Cultures

The need for the study of artifacts is particularly striking for those embarking on the exploration of organizations as cultures – that is to say, as symbolic systems of meaning – for at least two reasons.

In the first place, we can reasonably conjecture, as I have elsewhere claimed (Gagliardi 1990a), that artifacts do not constitute secondary and superficial manifestations of deeper cultural phenomena (Schein 1984), but are themselves – so to speak – primary cultural phenomena which influence corporate life from two distinct points of view: (a) artifacts make materially possible, help, hinder, or even prescribe organizational *action*; (b) more generally, artifacts influence our *perception* of reality, to the point of subtly shaping beliefs, norms and cultural values.

In the second place, if one is concerned with organizational symbolism, one must not forget that symbols are *concretions of sense*, for which things constitute their more usual and natural abode. To the extent to which, as I said at the beginning, material reality is the vehicle through which ineffable or tacit knowledge – which generally escapes the control of the mind – is communicated, the study of things enables us to aim directly at the heart of a culture, or at what the subjects do not wish – and above all *cannot* – communicate, at least in words.

Various authors (Whyte 1961; Van Maanen 1979; Meyerson 1991) have stated that the things most interesting to know about people are those which they take for granted or find difficulty in expressing and discussing openly: that about which the actors lie, or do not manage to be sincere even when they want, is in fact very often what is most central to them and can thus explain important aspects of their behaviour and social relations. So, corporate artifacts can function as 'clues' to ways of seeing and 'feeling' very distant from the rationalizations offered by the actors, sometimes entirely in good faith, when faced with a questionnaire or an interviewer, or during participant observation itself.

In other words, artifacts make it possible to rescue *the sense beyond the action* (Monaci 1991). Without wanting to resuscitate Dilthey and German historicism – and the stress on 'understanding' (*verstehen*) rather than on 'explanation' (*erklären*) – but taking over Weber's filtered version, one may say that as social scientists we are interested in grasping the uniformities in action and in the reasons behind it, taking as our starting-point the socially elaborated meanings of the actors. Up to now the study of action – that is to say of manifest behaviour – and of conscious intentions has been the principal mode of access to systems of meaning. Such an emphasis on behaviour has been judged a form of short-sightedness in the social sciences (Laughlin and Stephens 1980), and for some time now the necessity of providing a more rigorous reformulation of the whole problem of meaning, with the hope that new ways of exploring it will emerge, has been stressed (Foster 1980). The study of artifacts can constitute an answer to this need. It is therefore time to turn our attention to things and to the experience that the actors have of them in society and in organizations.

This experience can be analysed on two different levels, as subjective experience and as social fact. In the first case the aim is to explore the psychological dynamics entailed by our relationship with things; in the second case it is a matter of reconstructing the meaning and the impact of artifacts and of physical reality on the life of an organization and, in general, of a social group.

The Meaning of Things

The things of the world have the function of stabilizing human life, and their objectivity lies in the fact that … men, their ever-changing nature notwithstanding, can retrieve their sameness, that is, their identity, by being related to the same chair and the same table (Arendt 1958: 137).

The most careful study of transactions between people and things is that by Csikszentmihalyi and Rochberg-Halton (1981), which puts together a series of reflections deriving from psychological theories, with empirical data gathered during some ethnographic research conducted in the tradition of the Chicago School of urban sociology. Two observations – central to the authors' argument – deserve to be looked at here since they provide a convincing psychological reason for some of the regularities observable in organizational life and can serve as important elements in the conceptual framework that I am trying to construct. The first observation concerns the relationship between things and the development of the self, the second the interactive nature of our relationships with objects.

If it is easy to concede that the things we *create*, which we *use* and with which we *surround* ourselves 'reflect' our personality, it is more difficult to acknowledge, as Csikszentmihalyi and Rochberg-Halton observe, that often they are *part of* or an *extension of the self*, not in a metaphorical or mystical sense but in a factual and concrete sense. Depth psychology has from time past shown the importance of the 'object' and of 'objectual' investment in the construction of personal identity, referring generally, however, to relationships with other people and not to relationships with inanimate objects. But people invest psychic energy both in other people and in ideas or things. Things – as compared to people and ideas – have the singular property of restituting to the self a feedback that is steadily and immediately perceptible to the senses. Even the feedback from our investment in ideas or people comes to us unquestionably through material signs and things: if, for example, we seek confirmation of our identity as thinkers through the working out of ideas, it is only the *written page* in front of us – it is only the *materialized* idea – which reassures us about our capacity to pursue such aims. Only the sight, the feel, even the smell from the newly published book unequivocally tell us that we are capable of exercising those particular forms of control of external reality with which our identity as writers is bound up.

Things thus incorporate our intentions of control, and the self develops out of feedback to acts of control. In things reside the traces and memories of our past, the witness to our present experiences, our desires and our dreams for the future. Things tell us constantly who we are, what it is that differentiates us from others and what it is that we have in common with others. And in many cases it is difficult to trace out the boundary between our bodily identity and external physical reality: a judge is not a judge, does not feel himself such and is not perceived as such without his robes, a woman feels herself beautiful because she has an elegant dress, and for all of us the possibility of driving nonchalantly down a narrow street depends on the fact that we have learned to 'feel' the car as an extension of our bodily schema.

Inanimate objects that on first view seem often to be only the outcome of our projects, or the ground of our dominion, have in reality an 'active' role which has been brought out by various writers and analysed from various points of view. Scarry states that 'the object is only a fulcrum or lever across which the force of creation moves back onto the human site and remakes the makers' (1985: 307). It has been said that artifacts are pathways of action (Gagliardi 1990a) in the sense that they structure sensory experience and enlarge or narrow the range of behaviour that is materially *possible*. But they can even embody – as Latour (1992a) has shown in his analysis of, for example, the impact of an automated door-closer on human behaviour – a programme of action which prescribes a *specific* piece of behaviour. Finally, given that in all objects, even the most practical, it is difficult to separate function from symbolic meaning, the 'power' of the object derives from its capacity – as a symbol – of *awakening* sensations, feelings and reasons for acting. The stimulating and creative role of an inanimate symbol shows itself in a special way when it stands not for something else that *exists*, but for something else that *might exist*, in which case it is not a symbol *of* reality but a symbol *for* reality. This meaning of things, Csikszentmihalyi and Rochberg-Halton note, is not exclusively the outcome of a projection of categories of thought by the knowing subject. In other words the meaning of things does not depend only on the structure of the mind: it is equally determined by the intrinsic and sensible properties that things have (which make them fitted to convey specific meanings) and by the experience which the circumstances foster of them, even beyond (in the case of artifacts) the intentions of their creator.

The interactive nature of our relationship with things has also been described by Witkin (1974) – with particular regard to artistic creation – as a reverberative process, a continual shuttling between the impulse which shapes the expressive action and the material means through which the impulse expresses itself, until one becomes the echo of the other. Alluding to the same dynamics, Fabbri (1992: 38) has even spoken of a 'malignity' in objects, which constitute in their irreducible materiality and otherness 'a radical challenge to subjectivity which wearies itself, fades in the attempt to interpret their dumbness'.[8]

The Corporate Landscape

Men must feed themselves, wrest from nature the conditions for their survival; and can do so only by taking account of the environment that characterizes their habitat. History shows us, however, that their productive practices are not necessarily in functional accord with this environment, but are equally determined by rites, symbols, ideas – in brief, by a worldview. A pure productive practice does not exist; every productive practice is immediately a symbolic practice of appropriation of the world; every productive practice is a way of responding, fitted to a determined environment, to the basic biological requirement, but in so far as that is already culturally formulated. And the signature through which an environment testifies to this *cultural requirement of survival* is called landscape (Duby 1986: 29).[9]

Material reality, which performs such an important role in the construction and development of the individual self, is equally decisive, perhaps more so, for the collective identity of an organization. If, in fact, the existence of a consciousness of self which does not seek confirmation in the external world is theoretically admissible – in extreme and pathological forms of solipsism – the existence of a social self which is not *publicly* objectivized in forms which survive the coming and going of individual people and generations, and which embody a *sharable* vision of reality, is conceptually unthinkable (Arendt 1958).

In an organization, ends are pursued, energies invested and ideas are made concrete in machines, products and places. All this is done through productive practices which – as Duby says in the passage just cited – are never pure productive practices but are always also symbolic practices, combinations of expressive disinterested (aesthetic) actions and of impressive actions aimed at practical results. As Fine (1996: 230) noticed, 'work is a minuet between expressive form and instrumental function'. Actions, like thoughts and speeches, are contingent signs, destined to vanish if they are not reified. Only things last. A brilliant idea left out of the minutes of a meeting can be irretrievably lost. And students of strategic management learned long ago to identify the real strategy of an organization by the choices irreversibly incorporated in its concrete investments or disinvestments, in the renovated building, in the plant that is set up or dismantled.

In order to think and act, especially when they must reciprocally co-ordinate, organizational actors need an intelligible world. Things are the visible counterparts of this intelligibility, they indicate rational categories and hierarchies of values, and in this sense they collectively constitute an important system of communication, alternative to language, as we shall see more clearly below. Above all, things make it possible to pin down meanings, and contain their fluctuations. As Douglas and Isherwood (1979) have observed, verbal rituals, spoken and not recorded, vanish into the air, and hardly contribute to the demarcation of the field of interpretation. For this reason rituals make use of things, and the more costly the ritual accoutrements the stronger and more striking is the intention to fix the meaning for the future.

The instantaneous perception of things is linked with our idea of *space*. Just as new things are being incessantly created, others are multiplying and spreading, while still others are discarded. They reveal patterns of invention, repetition, and selection, cycles of stability and change, chaos and order: from things emerges the form which the collective identity has taken on over *time* (Kubler 1962). The physical setting of an organization (with its formal qualities, i.e. sensorially perceptible qualities) is thus the most faithful portrayal of its cultural identity, and artifacts – to the extent that they adumbrate a view of the world (and of the self in the world), in the dual sense of how one believes *it is* and of how one *would like it to be* – constitute a vital force for the evolution of the organization as culture.

The worldview that the physical setting offers daily and uninterruptedly to the unconscious perception of members constitutes at the same time

indelible testimony about the past and a guide for the future. Thus, it contains an implicit promise of immortality for the collective self, a public declaration that the organization will survive as a super-individual and impersonal reality (Sievers 1990). The concern of French presidents to link the construction of grandiose monuments to their time in office unequivocally expresses their desire to contribute and define the *form over time* of 'Frenchness'. On a smaller scale, the president of an industrial association – whose mandate was only three years – told me that all his predecessors (and he himself was following their example) had been concerned to leave behind some indelible trace of their brief occupation of the post by physically changing the shape of the presidential floor: thus waiting rooms, meeting rooms and offices changed form and aspect, shrinking and growing alternately, every time offering subtly different conceptions of a microcosm of roles and relations.

In light of the considerations set out so far, we can state that the supreme manifestation of a culture is the landscape, that is to say, a *natural* reality which has inscribed within itself a *cultural* code. This code is in the first place an aesthetic code. The argument for this latter affirmation requires some reflection on the relations existing between *ideas/concepts* and *images/forms*, identity and *style*, systems of *meanings* and systems of *sensations*.

To translate an idea into an image (or vice versa) entails passing from conceptual abstract order to formal concrete order, expressing, that is, a logical relationship between representations of the *mind* in terms of relations between formal elements perceptible to the *senses*. In a visual image these relations are spatial and chromatic, in an auditory perception they are temporal relations between sonic stimuli of different pitch and intensity, and so on. Every cultural system seems to have structural correspondences between its ontological or deontological codes and its aesthetic codes, that is to say, between systems of beliefs and of values, on the one hand, and specific patterns of relation/combination between formal elements on the other. Hauser (1952), for example, studied the connection between the geometric style, the stability of institutions and the autocracy of forms of government in the cultures of neolithic peasantry, while Vernant (1969) studied the relationship between the structuring of space and political organization in ancient Greece, and Panofsky (1974) studied the relationship between

Gothic architecture and scholastic philosophy. Coming to artistic movements closer to our time, considerable interest has been shown in the relation between Italian Futurism and fascism (De Maria 1973). Croce (1924), for example, claims that the conceptual source of fascism is to be found in Futurism and its trumpeted values of determination, aggressiveness, and thirst for the new, rejection of tradition, exaltation of force, youth and modernity. Like Croce, the leaders of the movement themselves (Marinetti 1924) stressed the links between Futurist ideology – the Futurist notion of the function of art in society – and fascist ideology, especially in its original revolutionary elements. But it is also possible to set out detailed structural correspondences between these ideologies and the Futurist aesthetic codes. For example, the exaltation of dynamism finds its correspondence in the paradoxical efforts of Boccioni (1912) to represent movement in sculpture, despite the fixity of the material. Again, the idea that Futurist art (and fascism) had to destroy society and recreate it on new foundations has its counterpart in the tendency of the Futurist painters to burst the boundaries of their traditional space through the materiality of their pigments, the stridency of their colours, and the striving to make the canvas three-dimensional (Fael 1993).

In the field of organizational studies itself, Guillén (1997) has convincingly shown that there is a structural correspondence between scientific management – as a system of concepts – and the rationalist architecture of the twentieth century. According to Guillén, scientific management contained a latent aesthetic message, an idea of beauty that could guide not only the organization of work in factories but also the architecture of those factories, and, in general, the design of cities. This idea of beauty – inspired by the metaphor of the machine – exalted regularity, continuity, simplicity, functionality, and precision. The aesthetic 'potential' of scientific management escaped the attention of both architects and organizational scholars in the United States, but it was grasped and made explicit in the first quarter of the twentieth century by 'modernist' European architects, who translated it into sensorially perceivable volumes and shapes in the buildings that characterized the new urban landscape of the main European countries. Guillén's analysis confirms, firstly, the idea that a scientific theory can assert itself because of its aesthetic qualities (Geertz 1988; Gagliardi 1999), and that these qualities are assessed according to codes which

are culturally and historically determined. Secondly, it raises a series of intriguing questions which warrant empirical investigation.

What is the 'hidden' aesthetic of the organizational theories dominant today? What is the aesthetic ideal of emergent organizational forms like 'heterarchies' (Hedlund 1986), networks, virtual communities or temporary organizations? To the extent that the organization of work and artistic production can today rely on revolutionary technologies serving both productive ends in the sphere of economic organizations, and expressive ends in the sphere of art, there may emerge, in more evident manner than in the past, correspondences and affinities between art and organization. And it may be that the metaphors used to denote some of these emergent organizational forms – the 'net', the 'platform' (Ciborra 1996), the 'virtual world', the 'moebius strip' (Sabel 1991) – also possess (like the metaphor of the machine which inspired Taylorism) an 'aesthetic potential' to be discovered or developed, which is perhaps already unconsciously experienced and 'enjoyed' in organizational practice.

Analogous to the relation between abstract sets of 'thinkable' beliefs and sensorially 'perceivable' concrete forms is the relation between identity and style. Translating a particular conception of ourselves into concrete behaviour entails passing from an abstract definition of our *identity* to the adoption of a *style,* a word which we usually associate with an aesthetic – in the broad sense – experience. This problem is well known to those who are concerned with corporate identity, and who seek to translate particular conceptions of the collective self into subtle formal variants of elements – graphic, spatial, chromatic – that are sensorially perceptible.

There is a widely held opinion, even among anthropologists and historians of art (Firth 1973), that artifacts are the illustration of a *pre-existing* worldview, and that therefore the translations of which I have been speaking are always one-directional: from abstract thought to concrete manufactured object. Indeed, the study by Guillén discussed above suggests that the nexus invariably runs from the former to the latter. But it is difficult to say whether it is ideas which produce forms or forms which generate ideas. I have from the start expressed my leaning towards considering aesthetic experience *basic,* if for no other reason than that it takes place *before* (and often *without*) the intellect's conferring of unity on the data of sensory experience through concepts

(Gagliardi 1990a). Artifacts, according to Goldwater's (1973) thesis as taken over by Geertz (1983), convey their own messages, often untranslatable into ideas, at least to the same extent as they demonstrate existing conceptions. In this sense, the relation between systems of meanings and systems of sensations is probably circular in nature.

Students of organizational cultures who have a cognitivist bias (that is, students who are primarily interested in mental representations of cultures) often use the expression 'vision of reality' metaphorically to indicate a 'conception' of reality. I am suggesting that we use the expression literally, to look at the corporate landscape as a materialization of a worldview, and strive to interpret the aesthetic code written into the landscape as a privileged pathway to the quiddity of a culture.

A land becomes landscape – it is aestheticized, so to speak – in two different ways, working, that is *in situ* (in the physical place) and also *in visu* (into the eye) (Roger 1991). The first way consists of writing the aesthetic code directly onto the physicality of the place, populating it with artifacts; the second consists in educating the eye, in furnishing it with schemata of perception and taste, models of vision, 'lenses' through which to look at reality. The two modalities described are equally important in the processes of socialization. The first – the writing of the aesthetic code into the physicality of place – is easily observed by those who do not belong to the culture in question, even if it is not always easy to interpret. Every landscape has a scenographic element, meaning that it is 'constructed to be seen'. This setting displays and hides, provides backgrounds and close-ups, sequences and articulations. Often the setting constitutes a real visual metaphor (just as a caricature does): it prompts one to interpret a factory as a cathedral, a pathway as a labyrinth, and a ministry as a monastery (Larsen and Schultz 1990).

The second mode of aestheticization of a physical place – the writing of the aesthetic code into the eye – is very much more difficult to grasp: it is a matter, in fact, of managing to see things materially 'through the eyes' of the natives. The importance of the education of the eye in a culture has been stressed by Worth (Worth and Adair 1972; Worth 1981), who speaks of the anthropology of visual communications and distinguishes it from visual anthropology, indicating by the former the study of *a way of seeing* – and hence a way of photographing, filming, portraying, putting on show – as a culturally determined phenomenon, and by the latter the ethnographer's use of film or photographs to record cultural phenomena in images which replace or fill out the written report (Dabbs 1982; Van Maanen 1982). For Worth, a way of seeing is a way of choosing and combining in images aspects and fragments of the real, expressing in this way one's conception of the world and of one's role in world. In contrast to Arnheim's (1969) objectivist standpoint, Worth denies that the natural world presents an intrinsic order to the eye: it is the eye which projects onto the world an image of order. Visual communication thus presupposes the sharing of conventions between those who transmit and those who receive a message, a shared education of the eye: looking from close to and not from a distance, looking at the details and not the whole, the form more than the colour, and so on. Even a setting which selects and combines elements for the specific purpose of exhibiting them can hence be looked at from many points of view, and it is this which often makes interpretation difficult for the outsider.

Of course, the 'aestheticization' of the corporate stage is not achieved solely by creating and acting on its visible characteristics: a landscape can be physically constructed to furnish sensory experiences which involve the other senses as well, even if not all the senses – or not all to the same extent – are solicited by the diverse artifacts which populate the different organizations. It is also true that in the human species not all the senses are equally developed or have the same completeness, the same perceptive potential, as sight. Nevertheless, the dynamics described with reference to vision are very likely common to all the forms of sense experience: every organizational culture educates the sense of taste, of smell, of touch, of hearing, as well as of sight.

It has also been rightly observed (Hancock and Tyler 2000; Witz et al. 2003) that the corporate stage is constituted not solely by inanimate material artifacts but by human beings as well: 'bodies' are a vital – in the twofold sense of essential and alive – component of the landscape. They too, like material artifacts or inert nature, can be 'aestheticized', thereby giving material form to a particular conception of an organization's identity and strategy. Thus emphatically highlighted is the character of landscaping as 'technology of control' and the relationship between aesthetics and power – a topic which I shall discuss in the next paragraph.

The idea that particular conceptions of the order which are in force in a culture are the reflection of sense experiences that are either inevitable or possible in that culture (and, conversely, the idea that every landscape is the materialization of specific, often competing conceptions of the order of things) seems well worth exploring in the world of organizations, which base their social legitimacy on their instrumentality as regards specific ends and which *should* consequently tend to be *ordered* on the basis of criteria of instrumental rationality. How do pragmatic exigencies, aesthetic codes and politically-driven logics of action combine to determine the organizational order? What relationship is there between aesthetic codes and idealized images of the collective identity? What relationship is there between the structure of the physical setting – the form of the corporate landscape – and the corporate structure – the form of the social organization? Can the form of the social organization reflect a conscious ideal of beauty (Ramirez 1991)? These questions indicate fascinating areas for research to which it would be worthwhile devoting far greater resources and energies than those that have so far been invested.

Aesthetic Experiences and Organizational Control

> Beauty is a ray of light that from the first good derives and into appearances then divides …
> Into the senses it comes and then the wits,
> and shows in one forms scattered and split apart:
> it feeds and does not sate, and creates from part
> to part desire for itself and hope of bliss (Galeazzo di Tarsia, Canzoniere).[10]

The wealth of associative and reactive capacities that people accumulate through living in a specific physical-cultural setting forms a set of patterns of classification, interpretation and reaction to perceptual stimuli that I propose to call 'sensory maps' (Gagliardi l990a), distinguishing them from 'cognitive maps' (Weick 1979). Cognitive maps can be conscious or unconscious but are 'knowable'; sensory maps are learned instinctively through intuitive and imitative processes over which the mind exercises no control, and integrated automatically into life daily.

A corporate culture, then, is recognizable not only by the specificity of its beliefs – the 'logos' that

pertains to *cognitive* experience – and of its values – the 'ethos' that pertains to *moral* experience – but also by the specificity of its 'pathos' – the particular way of perceiving and 'feeling' reality – that belongs to aesthetic experience. A concept analogous to that of 'pathos' was formulated by Kubler (1962), in his claim that cultural artifacts are bearers of a central *pattern of sensibility*. Works of art, as things made to be contemplated and admired, reveal this pattern in a special way since action is guided in them only by the expressive impulse, by the way of 'feeling', and therefore need take no account of practical exigencies, as happens instead with other cultural artifacts.

In organizations whose purpose is profit the central pattern of sensibility is difficult to recognize precisely because expressive disinterested action, and the disinterested enjoyment of it, in its ongoing process or in its outcome, has no legitimate place in them: anything gratuitous can't help but be considered waste or play in a social group which demands to be judged on its efficiency and which strives to *appear* efficient, if not to *be* so. It is the reverse in not-for-profit (e.g. voluntary) organizations in which, without renouncing instrumental rationality, the 'disinterested' action of members, central to the definition of the collective identity, is set higher on the scale of values: it is more likely that expressivity is permitted or fostered, and the pattern of sensibility is more immediately and easily recognizable. But in the majority of economically oriented organizations the pattern of sensibility lodges in the folds of impressive actions, corrects the formal scansion of objects and space dictated by practical purposes. Sometimes it stands out clearly, like a lapse in the collective unconscious, in a detail or an object, apparently insignificant and useless, but which instead synthesizes the aesthetic code of a culture, the distinctive 'way of feeling' of its members.

At the opposite extreme, in organizations in which the specific result of the coordinated action of the members is an artistic product, the socialization of a new member is essentially and expressly education to the group pattern of sensibility. The expression of the pattern is not only legitimate but indispensable for organizational action and communication between the members comes about almost exclusively on the aesthetic level. The most obvious example of such a situation is that of a chamber orchestra which – like the Orpheus Chamber Orchestra – plays without a conductor. Our admiration and astonishment in cases of the kind express our recognition of the power and mystery of ineffable communication. Yet, at levels certainly less refined and where the outcome is less startling, one may presume that there can be no organization which does not make recourse to it, given that the aesthetic is a fundamental component of every human experience: the more the pathos is distinctive and idiosyncratic, the more it constitutes a special bond between members and can turn into an extraordinary resource for coordination.

These latter observations introduce a topic I have already alluded to here and there in the preceding pages – in particular when discussing the relationships between systems of meanings and systems of sensations – but one which merits systematic treatment of its own: the essential characteristics of sensory knowledge and aesthetic communication that differentiate them from intellectual knowledge and communication through the language of words. Various commonplaces and assumptions – related to the dominant views of knowledge discussed in the second section – here invite critical scrutiny.

In first place, as Langer (1967; 1969) has cogently demonstrated, words constitute merely one of the systems that we employ in symbolizing, a system which owes its supremacy to the natural availability of words, to their cheapness and their readiness to be combined. But it is untrue that the language of words is the expression of knowledge and that other systems of symbolization are mere expression of emotions and of feelings: there is an infinity of things that we *know* and that we cannot say in words, and in the very moment that the mind confers unity on experience through concepts formulable in words, it *reduces* it irremediably. The language of words, in its literal and merely denotative function, is the most excellent of tools for exact reasoning, but its weakness lies in *discursiveness,* in the linear order of words, strung one after the other like beads on a rosary. By contrast, aesthetic communication – based on purely sensory contact with the forms – makes use of a system of symbolization that Langer calls *presentational:* the object is presented directly and holistically, in such a way that its elements – which do not have a fixed and independent meaning like words in a dictionary – are grasped in a single act of perception and understood simultaneously by virtue of their reciprocal relations and of their relation with the global structure of the object.[11]

Discursive language is the vehicle of knowledge *by description:* it permits us to say one thing at a time. Presentational language is the vehicle of knowledge *by acquaintance:* it permits us to say more – even contradictory – things simultaneously and without the filter of abstraction. But precisely in this intimacy without mediations, so to speak, lies the richness and ambiguity of aesthetic communication, its capacity to break the schemata and penetrate ineffable reality, its surprising, stunning, moving character, its being – as Bruner (1962: 108) says – 'a play of impulses at the fringe of awareness'. In this sense, aesthetic knowledge is an intuitive knowledge of the *possible,* rather and more than of the *true,* and aesthetic communication is not so much the account of that which has happened as the prompting of that which might happen or might be (Bottiroli 1993).

The *cognitive* potential of the aesthetic experience – bound up with its character of ambiguity, globality, unresolved tension – has been explored by Rochberg-Halton (1979a; 1979b). The approach of this author is based on Dewey's (1934) distinction between 'recognition' – the interpretation of the object based on pre-existent schemes and stereotypes – and 'perception' – the capacity to embrace the object while letting its qualities modify previously formed mental schemes and habits. Perception thus understood is constitutive of aesthetic experience and the source of psychological development and learning. The conclusion, seemingly paradoxical, is that: 'Aesthetic experiences, which are often considered subjective and hence inessential by social scientists, thus actually may be one of the essential ways we learn to become *objective,* in the sense of coming to recognize the pervasive qualities of the environment in their own terms' (Csikszentmihalyi and Rochberg-Halton 1981: 178). The idea of the 'superiority' of aesthetic knowledge is implicit in the approach of Dewey and Rochberg-Halton, as it is, for that matter, in the vision of a neo-positivist philosopher such as Polanyi (1966), for whom to know intellectually is to discover what one already knew unconsciously and tacitly at the subliminal level of perception of the body.

I said at the start that I would be using the term 'aesthetic experience' to include every type of sense experience and not only experiences that are socially defined as 'beautiful' or as 'art'. But it is clear that not every form of sense experience presents the above-mentioned features with the same intensity. The pleasure linked to perceptual surprise, the emotion, the learning; all these depend on at least three factors. The first is the capacity of the object perceived – be it a work of nature or a work of art – to surprise by the novelty of its form. The second is the specific 'pathos' – or pattern of sensibility – that the subject has learned by living in a particular physical-cultural setting and which he/she shares with the other members of that culture: in relation to features of this pattern an event or an object may leave us indifferent or it may reawaken our senses, it may cause pleasure or disgust, it may attract or repulse us. The third is the subjective and contingent willingness to embrace the quality of the object: a natural spectacle already seen more than once will move and surprise us as if we were seeing it for the first time only when we find the time to contemplate it and are willing to perceive it in a new way. From what I have said it follows that the feeling for beauty is a cultural product – like artifacts – and that any event or object has the potential to provide intense aesthetic emotion.

In short, one may agree with Vickers (1982) that we have two different modes of knowledge open to us, both of which we use in our efforts to understand the world in which we live. One mode relies largely on analysis, calculation, and logic, entails abstraction and the manipulation of elements – without concern for the form in which they are combined – and is completely describable. The other mode relies more on synthesis and recognition of the global context, entails recognition or creation of the form – without concern for the elements which constitute it – and is not completely describable. As we know, logico-rational knowledge and aesthetico-intuitive knowledge are both aspects of the neo-cortical development that distinguish the human species from other mammals and appear to be linked with the specialization of the hemispheres of the brain. The right hemisphere appears to synthesize the perceptual input into holistic images (visual, olfactory, tactile, and auditory) maintaining the interrelations between the elements in perception, while the left hemisphere codifies verbal information, processing it serially through hierarchical categories (Dimond and Beaumont 1974).

I have referred already to the importance of aesthetic experiences in relation to certain major organizational issues: in particular, I pointed to the role of artifacts in the formation of a concrete collective identity and in fostering the identification of members. We have also seen how the concept of

corporate pathos enables us to considerably expand both our notion of communication media and our understanding of the mechanisms of coordination among interdependent activities. The argument just put forward on the differential features of sensory knowledge *vis-à-vis* intellectual knowledge, in my view, enables us to see in a new light another crucial organizational question: that of control. Organization theory has for some time been stressing the influence of *informative premises* – logical and ideological – in determining the nature of decisions and hence organizational action. If the force of sensory knowledge and communication is in part due to the fact that it escapes the control of the mind, the importance taken on by the characteristics of the context and of *perceptual premises* in determining the effective course of events in corporate life becomes evident. For this reason I proposed (Gagliardi 1990a) adding to the three levels of control identified by Perrow (1972) – (1) direct orders, (2) programmes and procedures, (3) influence of the ideological premises of the action – a fourth level corresponding to the possibility of influencing the sensory premises of choices and behaviour. I shall look briefly at some studies that validate this suggestion and, at the same time, exemplify lines of research that could fruitfully be taken further.

Sassoon (1990) has analysed the links existing between colour codes and the formation of ideological thought, showing how shades of colour can express with extraordinary immediateness and efficacy variations in ideological vectors and in the social meaning of artifacts. It would be interesting to investigate empirically how these semantic correspondences, which seem at least in part to be cross-cultural in so far as they are bound up with universal bio-psychological experiences, translate themselves into the specific cultural codes of a society, and what use individual organizations make of these codes (to what extent they embrace them, invert them or adapt them) in relation to their own 'character' and to their own distinctive ideology (Selznick 1957).

In a study of a telecommunications company (Gagliardi 1991) the presence of a 'decompositional-sequential' archetype was identified that perhaps constituted an analogical extension of the procedure used in telegraphic transmission, the original concern of the company. The archetype was primarily recognizable in the structuring of space: the building, laid out only horizontally, had been expanded with successive additions of parts which tended to be single elements themselves, without the pre-existing or the whole ever being questioned. This formal pattern led one to interpret – or expressed the tendency to interpret – the interdependence between the parts exclusively in terms of a unilateral sequentiality, and influenced the division of tasks, the structure of internal communications, the articulation of plans and projects: tasks were extremely fragmented, communications flowed exclusively one way, plans for action tended to be broken down into successive phases minutely specified without any appeal to forms of parallel planning and mechanisms of mutual adjustment. The most obvious use of this archetype was the way in which a global plan for corporate restructuring was conducted: the areas into which the company was divided were restructured *one after another,* and no move was made to pass to the subsequent one until the previous one had been defined in detail.

In another case (Gagliardi 1989) it was possible to interpret the failure of an expensive and massive programme aimed at sensitizing the staff of a bank – the purpose was to instil the value of 'service to the customer' – through an analysis of the perceptual conditioning exerted daily on employees by physical objects and structures: the thickness of the walls, the monumental character of the entrance – extremely lofty, but largely blocked by a steel grill – the luxurious carpets and tapestry in the management offices, and so on. Each of these elements – and all as a set – solicited feelings of solidity, comfort, safety on the one hand, and feelings of independence and superiority over the world outside on the other, rendering in fact barely credible the ambition to invert the image of dominance that the artifacts embodied. Similarly to the previous example, this suggests a need to re-examine the way in which corporate planning and planned corporate change have so far been conceptualized, concentrating more attention on the interplay of physical, symbolic and social structures (Gagliardi 1992).

The subtle relationship between the stylistic qualities of artifacts and the sensuous experience of members of an organization was explored in a particularly careful fashion by Witkin (1990). He showed how the design of artifacts can be an instrument of control in bureaucratic organizations. Through an analysis of the formal characteristics of a corporate micro-setting – the boardroom of a large company – he shows how a physical place can foster certain sensations and hinder others, induce a two-dimensional rather than three-dimensional vision of reality, even deliberately suppress 'sensuous values that are centred in the being of the individual as a living subject' (1990: 334). Rosen et al. instead analysed from the macro point of view the dialectical relation between the organization of labour and the structuring of space on the one hand, and the way in which bureaucratic ideology concretely shapes social life on the other.

Various authors (Carter and Jackson 2000; Hofbauer 2000; Hancock and Tyler 2000; Cairns 2002; Witz et al. 2003) have recently explored from a critical and emancipatory standpoint the way in which the corporate stage is conceived, constructed, and invested with meaning, and they have highlighted the relation between aesthetics and power. To the extent that artifacts are 'pathways of organizational life' (Gagliardi 1990a) and shape social actions and interactions, spatial organization is in fact political organization, not just a matter of practicality or aesthetics. Office landscaping is therefore contested terrain, the form and meaning of which are subject to divergent claims and controversial, paradoxical and contradictory interpretations by diverse actors (designers, managers and users) (Cairns 2002).

Carter and Jackson have visited the landscapes created by an organization which deliberately sets out to create an 'aesthetic' – the Commonwealth War Graves Commission – and learnt that in every organization 'the aesthetic which is produced…, the evocation of a positive emotional response, appeals to the perceived threat which disorder represents to individuals and, at the same time, acts to repress the emancipatory potential of disorder' (2000: 194). Hancock and Tyler (2000) developed a critical account of the 'managerial colonization' of aesthetics, describing how the bodies of female flight attendants are constituted as organizational artifacts, and required to embody the desired aesthetic of the airline by which they are employed, thus becoming the materialized expression of a corporate strategy and ideal. In the same perspective, Witz et al. studied a rapidly expanding hotel chain – Elba Hotels – showing how labourers are corporately designed and produced as stylized component of the organizational aesthetics; through processes of recruitment, selection and training their embodied dispositions are mobilized, commodified and transformed into '…skills which are geared toward providing a 'style' of service encounter that appeals to the senses of the customer' (2003: 37). I believe that, all together, these more recent studies have contributed significantly to enhancing the analytical thrust of the 'landscaping' metaphor, and to demonstrating its hermeneutic value in analysis of the aestheticization of organizational settings and its effects in concrete situations.

Emerging Landscapes

I have repeatedly stressed that every corporate landscape tends to be unique in so far as it gives concrete form to a particular organizational culture, an idiosyncratic system of meanings. But it is also true that corporate landscapes may resemble each other – at least superficially – by virtue of isomorphism processes of various origins and kinds (Di Maggio and Powell 1983). The above-discussed study by Guillén shows, for example, how local codes are homogenized by the advent of a general aesthetic code which influences extensive and heterogeneous organizational fields. In a certain sense, therefore – and especially in an age of globalization like the present one – corporate landscapes may display marked stylistic affinities. Hence, the aspiration to 'individuation' – that is, the endeavour to construct a specific corporate identity also by means of landscaping – may engender even radical differences. These differences, however, are not apparent at first sight and can only be grasped by careful interpretation of the details.

The great social, economic and technological changes that distinguish the present age foster the birth of organizations which not only have organizational structures different from traditional bureaucracies but are physical and spatial settings radically at odds with those to which we have been accustomed for so long. The traditional organizational landscape – as outlined in previous sections – is primarily a unitary physical space, partly natural and partly artificial, in which it is generally possible to regulate (facilitate or impede) flows of information and relationality both within the organization and between the organization and the environment. But what landscape characterizes the organizations unconstrained by a territory, virtual communities or temporary organizations which are going to be the organizational forms of the future?

It is difficult to apply the idea of 'landscape', as something unitary which everyone – members or customers – are able to perceive, to deterritorialized organizations, or at any rate to organizations whose members spend increasingly more time outside formal work areas. Actors perceive only the fragment of landscape in which they are located or with which they are in contact. They can 'imagine' (or know through media-transmitted images or sounds), the work settings of the persons with which they must coordinate themselves, but they cannot perceive them sensorially and directly. Even the landscape of a small office – organizationally conceived as a unitary system of roles and relations but whose members are physically scattered – becomes a virtual landscape in which social interactions based on sensory contact (and therefore which may be regulated in their proxemic features by means of gestures and the reciprocal positioning of the actors in space) are annulled, or at least significantly reduced. In the new physical workplaces, moreover, the fragments of the 'corporate' landscape experienced by each actor may be confused with the domestic landscape and with other organizational ones: in situations like telecommuting, e-mail at home or day-care at work, the walls that separate work from the family and the other institutions to which the worker may belong, even temporarily, weaken or disappear.

If the language of things and space is – as we have seen – both a means with which individuals are able to define their personal identities, and a means with which an organization can assimilate people and control them, the new work settings will probably prompt the invention and diffusion of new corporate artifacts and new semiotic conventions. Pratt and Rafaeli (2001) have pointed out that both of these processes – identifying and assimilating – will presumably be based to an ever greater extent on 'portable' symbols: company T-shirts or corporate ties can be expected to replace architecture, and business cards to replace diplomas and awards hanging on office walls or other 'office-bound' symbols. In a certain sense, the only alternative to a virtual corporate landscape might be a miniaturized and – so to speak – pocket-size landscape.

Whilst some commentators maintain that in these circumstances it will be more difficult for managers to use landscaping to condition the workers' aesthetic experiences, and that there will be more space for individual freedom and empowerment (Duffy 1997), others argue that it is impossible to determine '...on whether the new workplace aesthetic is representative of democracy or dictator-ship, of employee empowerment or managerial control – or of all, at one and the same time' (Cairns 2002: 817). What is certain, though, is that the tried and tested systems of socialization, communication and control will become largely obsolete, and that the central role played in the new learning environ-ments by computer-mediated communication is laying the basis for new kinds of aesthetic experi-ences, while rendering others unlikely. The com-puter screen separates the user from a real world of multiple perceptions which engage all the senses and ushers him or her into a virtual world of infinite potential – made up of images, sounds and infor-mation – which requires and refines some senses but dulls others. From this point of view, the new corporate landscapes will probably require the use – and at the same time foster the development – of new 'sensory maps': that is, new patterns of classifi-cation, interpretation and reaction to perceptive stimuli. It is also likely that of the two modalities of aestheticization illustrated earlier – 'in situ' and 'in visu': the direct writing of the aesthetic code onto the physicality of the place, and education into per-ceiving in a particular way – the latter will assume more importance. If it is not possible to structure the setting so that it furnishes the sensory stimuli desired, the only alternative is to educate people to select stimuli by filtering them through the corpo-rate aesthetic code. It is to be hoped in this regard, too, that the not too distant future will see empirical data which shed clearer light on these new sensory maps, and on the 'emotional climate' (Barbalet 1998) that supports or is generated by them.

Exploring the Corporate Pathos

'… the resources of science are far from being exhausted. I think that an evening in that study would help me much.'
  'An evening alone!'
  'I propose to go up there presently … I shall seat in that room and see if its atmosphere brings me inspiration. I am a believer in the genius loci. You smile, friend Watson. Well, we shall see' (Conan Doyle, The Valley of Fear).

The reader, who has followed to this point, if he/she has become persuaded of the importance of aes-thetic knowledge, action and communication in organizational life, will be asking now how it is

possible to investigate this particular form of human and social experience. One of the first ques-tions he/she will probably come up with is whether this new object can be known using the logico-analytical methods traditionally used in the practice of organizational studies or whether the choice of aesthetic experience as object necessarily implies the recourse by the enquirer to aesthetico-intuitive forms of understanding (Strati 1992). One might ask, in other words: can we study the products of the right cerebral hemisphere with the left hemisphere, or is only the right hemisphere capable of really knowing what it produces itself?

Put in these terms, the dilemma is not easily solved. Firstly, the vocabulary available to us for description of aesthetic experiences – and to achieve shared understanding of them – is limited and uneven among the five senses. Fine (1996) has pointed out that Western cultures possess a relatively ample denotative vocabulary for visual sensations, a less ample one for tactile and auditory sensations, and a very restricted one for taste and smell. Secondly, if everything I have said about the incom-mensurability of the two realms, about the richness of the aesthetic experience and about its ineffability, is plausible, the deployment of analytical methods and of discursive language will be intrinsically reduc-tive, and we will not even be certain that our speeches even partially reflect tacit knowledge. Whether we ask corporate actors to tell us of their aesthetic experi-ences, or whether it is we ourselves as researchers who interpret them, we will always be dealing with 'espoused' theories which may not in any way coin-cide with the secret regularities of expressive action. If, on the other hand, we strive to 'feel' as the natives feel, we shall have understood more but we will be unable to transfer to other this 'knowledge by acquaintance' without ourselves employing forms of aesthetic communication. But perhaps this is to ask too much of intellectuals by profession: it is probable that those who have artistic gifts and vocation do not take up organizational studies. At all the international conferences organized over the last 15 years on orga-nizational culture, the call for papers has prompted out-of-the-way, unorthodox, creative forms of com-munication, but – with some rare, often disconcert-ing, exceptions – these have never gone beyond the use of slides that more often contained words than images.

An interesting exception – but which nevertheless proves the rule – is the attempt by Steyaert and

Hjorth to radically innovate forms of communication in the scientific community by switching from the traditional presentation and publication of a paper to other forms of 'public-action'. During a workshop on 'Organizing Aesthetics', in order to highlight the political and ethical implications of an aesthetic approach to organizing and how this can influence scholarly work, Steyaert and Hjorth staged a theatrical performance which led the audience through the history of speech genres. Their intention was to induce the spectators to imagine '… possible ways of "performing oneself" as an academic citizen in society' (Steyaert and Hjorth 2002: 767). Those attending the workshop probably benefited greatly from this strictly aesthetic experience. But when it came to involving a broader public in the experiment all that could be done was publish the script, which was only an impoverished remnant of the original performance.

The dilemma that I have posed is as old as the criticism of art: either one describes the work of art, pointing to its analytically observable formal canons – rhythm, sequences, proportions, correspondences – which usually in no way help 'to feel' the work, or one deploys an evocative, allusive, poetic language intended to transfer to the listener the aesthetic emotion experienced by the critic. It is this that leads many people to claim that the great critics are great artists in their turn. Our problem, however, is how to realistically develop in researchers the ability and the bent which will enable them to investigate aesthetic experiences through modalities appropriate to their nature without having to renounce the transference, and hence the accumulation, of their acquired knowledge, and without requiring them to have innate and marked artistic gifts.

As Bateson and Mead stated in their introduction to *Balinese Character: A Photographic Analysis* (the most comprehensive and ambitious visual ethnography ever carried out), our effort should be 'to translate aspects of culture never successfully recorded by the scientist, although often caught by the artist, into some form of communication sufficiently clear and sufficiently unequivocal to satisfy the requirements of scientific enquiry' (1942: XI). The work of Bateson and Mead is an interesting example of how pictures can be used to illustrate patterns of culture analytically described in the text: the authors used the pictures as records *about* culture rather than records *of* culture, as research tools rather than research material (Worth 1981).

However, their more or less implicit assumption that the camera can tell us the 'aesthetic truth' about the social system studied is seriously undermined by the postmodernist critique of traditional 'realist' ethnography and documentary photography: pictures are created social artifacts, to be interpreted by learning the system of conventions used by their makers to imply meanings; as such, they tell us more about the picture-makers than about what is pictured (Harper 1994).

In my view, even in exploring the pathos of an organization it is not a matter of the sole and unconditional employment of a particular form of knowledge and communication. As the scholastic philosophers claimed, knowledge progresses through a systematic shuttling between intuition and rationalization, between tacit and conscious knowledge, between the hand open and the hand closed, alternatively, with the regularity of breathing. It is a matter, therefore, of employing one or the other form of knowledge and of communication, one or the other cerebral hemisphere, according to the relevance that each may assume in the diverse phases of the research process, and according to the heuristic value of one method *vis-à-vis* the other (that is, according to how much we win or lose in terms of understanding).

There is no doubt that the sole way of *coming to grips with* the pathos of an organization without the filter of the actors' rationalizations and without the ethnocentric danger of attributing to the organization studied the pattern of sensibility we have assimilated in our own culture (Iwanska 1971), is that of *sharing in the aesthetic experiences* of the natives by immersing ourselves in their perceptual context and allowing ourselves to be imbued by sense experience (Gagliardi 1990a). The nature of this immersion has been very well described by Stoller (1997: 23): 'For ethnographers embodiment is … the realization that … we too are consumed by the sensual world, that ethnographic things capture us through our bodies, that profound lessons are learned when sharp pain streak-up our legs in the middle of night'.

If we split the process whereby a phenomenon is studied into three main phases – observation, interpretation, report – it is essential in the first phase to abandon oneself to what Kant calls 'passive intuition', and it is not difficult to do so. I have cited the Kantian expression in order to emphasize the importance of abandoning oneself unreservedly to the aesthetic experience, living it as authentically as possible. But the expression should not be taken to mean that the aesthetic experience is a passive experience metaphorically comparable to inert contemplation. Strati (2000) has rightly pointed out that, on the contrary, aesthetic experience presupposes the subject's ability to respond actively to stimuli. If stimuli were undergone without any reaction, the experience would not be aesthetic but – in the literal sense of the term – 'anaesthetic'. This capacity to live experience without intellectual filters is in general exercised spontaneously and effortlessly by those who – venturing into a physical and symbolic terrain – are prepared to stay, as the newcomers. If we are interested in exploring the pathos of an organization, we must thus initially act 'as if we are there to stay'. As I have more than once remarked, artifacts constitute the main empirical correlate of pathos. It is to them we shall mostly devote our attention, and faced with any object – even those which appear to have an exclusively practical function – we shall ask not what purpose they serve but what sensations they rouse in us, and record these sensations in the roughest and most immediate possible form in a new column of the field notes that we are inured to keeping as ethnographers.

The best illustration to date of the heuristic value of the aesthetic approach to the study of organizations, and of the methodological implications of the exploration of corporate pathos, has been provided by Martin (2002). Twenty years previously, Martin had conducted an empirical study on residential organizations for the elderly, which offered an extraordinary variety of aesthetic experiences – generally disgusting – in terms of sights, sounds and above all smells. Her research was based on a rigorously positivist paradigm which required the researcher to be as detached as possible from the situation studied. After taking part in a workshop on organizational aesthetics at the Villa Certosa di Pontignano near Siena (Italy) in May 2000, Martin realized with hindsight that she had written a 'poor' account of a 'rich' aesthetic experience, because she had left herself, her aesthetic judgements and bodily sensations out of the story. Fortunately, she had taken detailed field notes on her sensations. She returned to those notes and 'discovered' that the residential homes for the elderly could be landscaped to create – the context and the 'disgust potential' remaining equal – different ('homey' or 'institutional') realities. These different realities aroused in residents and visitors distinct sets of sensations, and therefore of emotions

and feelings, which served to shape and maintain political and social identities. The two landscapes, in fact, reflected different conceptions of the elderly: as people able to act and take care of themselves, and as people incapable of autonomy. Repugnance, like beauty, is socially and physically constructed. These intuitions were only possible because Martin had intensely and personally 'relived' the aesthetic experience that those places produced.

An alternative way of getting at ineffable knowledge is suggested by Worth and Adair (1972). They propose to ask natives to film for us, thus concretely showing their 'way of seeing' the world. Close to their idea is Meyer's (1991) notion of asking informants to answer questions with images, figure, diagrams and other visual displays. These proposals, of great interest in my opinion, aim at enriching our field of observation by adding to artifacts already *existing* artifacts produced *on the spot* at the request of the ethnographer. If on the one hand what is produced is certainly influenced by the informant's relationship with the researcher and from his/her eventual desire to lie about himself/herself and the organization to which he/she belongs, on the other hand the possibility of observing the expressive action as it takes place can offer new and diverse opportunities for intuition.

Whether it is a matter of existing artifacts or ones produced on the spot, it is important to resist the structuralist temptation to interpret them as if they had an intrinsic semiotic status, as if they were a system of signs interpretable on the basis of a self-evident grammar accessible to all (Hodder 1994). Just as for verbal language a more complex linguistic model is required to explain poetry, so visual language requires a model more complex than one that can account for an unequivocal system of signs (Forge 1973). Objects, let us remember, are mainly vectors of symbols: they can say many, even contradictory, things, simultaneously, and their meaning oscillates in an ambiguous range, an interweaving of the intentions that motivated their *production* and the conditions of their *reception,* i.e. the sensory and emotive experiences that the artifacts awaken in a specific spatial and temporal context (Semprini 1992). It is a question, true enough, of grasping a code, a syntactic principle, a pattern, a vocabulary: whatever one wants to call it, it is irremediably local.

Through detailed investigations of three US museums, Yanow (1998) vividly showed how built spaces tell stories, and how we can grasp the meaning that these stories convey. What built spaces tell depends not only on the 'authored' texts of designers (founders and architects) but also on the texts that readers (visitors, clients, and other outlookers) 'construct' on the basis of their expectations and sensory experience of the built space. The case of the Oakland Museum, in particular, shows that the position of the museum in the environment can be perceived alternatively as 'the accessible anti-monument' or 'the walled oasis'. Moreover, the three physically distinct museum levels – devoted to natural history, historical and ethnological collections and Californian art – (evoking the order of humanly bodily experience: feet, hands, brain) were alternatively felt as narrating the heroic story of humankind's triumph over nature or as a story of desecration of the earth and ecological degradation.

Gaining an awareness of the local pattern of sensibility is the most difficult part of the task, not only because it can be ambiguous and contradictory. Especially if we mainly rely on our own sensations, it must be done *in good time*. We must in fact manage to 'give a name' to our sensations before we become too inured to the aesthetic climate of the setting and while we are still capable of appreciating the specificity of the stimuli to which we are exposed. There is, in other words, a magical moment, short-lived I believe, in which one can hope to lead out the 'play of impulses at the fringe of awareness' of which Bruner (1962: 108) speaks *beyond* that fringe, translating one's sensations into thoughts without too much betraying them. In the interpretative phase it is then essential to solicit and keep in tension *both* forms of knowledge, achieving that balancing of emotion and reflection, empathy and analytic detachment that is perhaps in general – even when the focus of research is not the pathos of the organization – the essence of ethnographic work. As Whyte (1955: 357) has said of his Cornerville study,

> The parts of the study that interest me most depended upon an intimate familiarity with people and situations… This familiarity gave rise to the basic ideas in this book. I did not develop these ideas by any strictly logical processes. They dawned on me out of what I was seeing, hearing, doing – and feeling. They grew out of an effort to organize a confusing welter of experience… I had to balance familiarity with detachment, or else no insights would have come. There were fallow periods when I seemed to be just marking time. Whenever life

flowed so smoothly that I was taking it for granted, I had to try to get outside of my participating self and struggle again to explain the things that seemed obvious.

How may it be possible to develop this ability in the researcher? In the first place, we must admit that to some extent it requires a capacity for self-reflection that cannot be acquired if one does not have a minimum of talent and natural bent. For the rest, the best training is to 'try one's hand' under the guidance of able people. There are no recipes or handbooks, and the only really useful literatures, in my opinion, are autobiographical reports on ethnographic research, such as the splendid appendix to *Street Corner Society*, from which the quotation above is taken.

Finally, the drafting of the report will rigorously follow logico-analytical methods, but it will be useful if at least in part – and without any pretence to the production of literary artifacts aimed at communicating only or mainly on the aesthetic plane – 'eloquence' goes along with the 'logic' and visual reporting with the verbal reporting: we shall be more certain of not having lost too much along the road, the long journey whereby knowledge is generated and passed on. And perhaps we shall learn, little by little, to share a richer, more unitary and decidedly more attractive conception of organizational knowledge.

Notes

1. The translation is my own.
2. The Standing Conference on Organizational Symbolism – an independent work group within the European Group for Organizational Studies (EGOS) – devoted its Third International Conference (Milan 1987) to 'The Symbolics of Corporate Artifacts'. A selection of those papers which concentrated on all the elements that go to make up the physical setting of corporate life – buildings, objects, images, forms – has been published in an edited book (Gagliardi 1990b).
3. In Baumgarten's definition, aesthetics are the *scientia cognitionis sensitivae*, the science of sensory cognition, as distinct from rational cognition. Giambattista Vico (1725), who waged a deliberate assault on Cartesian philosophy, distinguished and opposed rational cognition to aesthetic cognition, which he viewed as a higher form of knowledge transmitted by myth and poetry.
4. The birth of 'special aesthetics', as a sub-discipline of philosophy which speculates on the nature and forms of

beauty, was, according to Eagleton (1990), an attempt by Enlightenment man to colonize sensible experience in the name of and through reason and to bend it to the logic of intentional action.

5. Huizinga (1964) has claimed that the eighteenth century is that which took itself and the whole of creation most seriously.

6. My translation.

7. My translation.

8. My translation.

9. My translation.

10. Translated by Michael Sullivan.

11. Langer's distinction between discursive and presentational language corresponds to that of Goodman (1976) between *articulated* language – in which the characters, as the letters of the alphabet, are separate and differentiated without ambiguity, with a univocal correspondence between syntactic and semantic unity – and the *dense/exemplificatory* language – in which the inverse procedure to notation is followed, i.e. one goes not from the label to the object but from the object to the label.

References

Ammassari, P. (1985) 'I fondamentali problemi di metodologia della ricerca sociale', *Studi di Sociologia*, 23: 176–93.

Arendt, H. (1958) *The Human Condition*. Chicago: University of Chicago Press.

Arnheim, R. (1969) *Visual Thinking*. Los Angeles: University of California Press.

Barbalet, J.M. (1998) *Emotion, social theory, and social structure: A macrosociological approach*. Cambridge: Cambridge University Press.

Barley, S.R., Meyer, G.W. and Gash, D. (1988) 'Cultures of culture: academics, practitioners, and the pragmatics of normative control', *Administrative Science Quarterly*, 33(1): 24–60.

Bateson, G. and Mead, M. (1942) *Balinese Character: a Photographic Analysis*. New York: New York Academy of Science.

Boccioni, U. (1912) *Manifesto tecnico della scultura futurista*, 11 april, poster.

Bottiroli, G. (1993) *Retorica. L'intelligenza figurale nell'arte e nella filosofia*. Torino: Bollati Boringhieri.

Bourdieu, P. (1990) *The Logic of Practice*. Cambridge: Polity.

Brown, R.H. (1977) *A Poetic for Sociology*. Cambridge: Cambridge University Press.

Bruner, J. (1962) *Essays for the Left Hand*. Cambridge, MA: Harvard University Press.

Cairns, G. (2002) 'Aesthetics, morality and power: Design as espoused freedom and implicit control', *Human Relations*, 55(7): 799–820.

Carmagnola, F. (1994) 'Non sapere di sapere', unpublished manuscript.

Carter, P. and Jackson, N. (2000) 'An-aesthetics', in S. Linstead and H. Höpfl (eds), *The Aesthetics of Organizations*. London: Sage. pp. 180–196.

Ciborra, C. (1996) 'The Platform Organization: Recombining Strategies, Structures and Surprises', *Organization Science*, 7(2): 103–18.

Croce, B. (1924) 'Fatti politici e interpretazioni storiche', *La Stampa*, 15 maggio.

Crovi, R. (1993) *La valle dei cavalieri*. Milano: Arnoldo Mondadori Editore.

Csikszentmihalyi, M. and Rochberg-Halton, E. (1981) *The Meaning of Things*. Cambridge: Cambridge University Press.

Czarniawska, B. (1997) *Narrating the Organization. Dramas of Institutional Identity*. Chicago: University of Chicago Press.

Czarniawska, B. and Gagliardi, P. (eds) (2003) *Narratives We Organize By*. Amsterdam: John Benjamins Publishing Company.

Czarniawska-Joerges, B. and Joerges, B. (1995) 'Winds of organizational change', in S. Bacharach, P. Gagliardi and B. Mundell (eds), *Studies of Organizations in the European Tradition*. Greenwich, CT: JAI Press. pp. 171-209.

Dabbs, J.M. (1982) 'Making things visible', in J. Van Maanen, J.M. Dabbs and R.R. Faulkner (eds), *Varieties of Qualitative Research*. Beverly Hills, CA: Sage. pp. 31–64.

Dean, J.W. Jr, Ottensmeyer, E. and Ramirez, R. (1997) 'An aesthetic perspective on organizations', in C. Cooper and S. Jackson (eds), *Creating tomorrow's organizations: A handbook for future research in organizational behaviour*. Chichester: Wiley. pp. 419–37.

De Maria, L. (ed.) (1973) *Per conoscere Marinetti e il futurismo*. Milano: Mondadori.

Dewey, J. (1934) *Art as Experience*. New York: Minton, Balch.

Di Maggio, P.J. and Powell, W.W. (1983) 'The iron cage revisited: institutional isomorphism and collective rationality in organizational fields', *American Sociological Review*, 35: 147–60.

Dimond, S.J. and Beaumont, J.G. (1974) 'Experimental studies of hemisphere function in the human brain', in S.J. Dimond and J.G. Beaumont (eds), *Hemisphere Function in the Human Brain*. New York: Wiley.

Douglas, M. and Isherwood, B. (1979) *The World of Goods*. New York: Basic Books.

Duby, G. (1986) *Il sogno della storia*. Milano: Garzanti.

Duffy, F. (1997) *The new office*. London: Conran Octopus.

Ebers, M. (1985) 'Understanding organizations: the poetic mode', *Journal of Management*, 11(2): 51–62.

Eagleton, T. (1990) *The Ideology of the Aesthetics*. Oxford: Blackwell.

Fabbri, P. (1992) 'Dalla parte del maligno', interview by M. Ciampa, *Leggere*, 40.

Fael, A. (1993) 'Le arti visive e il futurismo (manifesti, cinema, teatro)', unpublished dissertation, University of Milan.

Fine, G.A. (1996) *Kitchens. The Culture of Restaurant Work.* Berkeley: University of California Press.

Fineman, S. (ed.) (1993) *Emotions in organizations.* London: Sage.

Firth, R. (1973) 'Tikopia art and society', in A. Forge (ed.), *Primitive Art and Society.* London and New York: Oxford University Press. pp. 25–48.

Forge, A. (1973) 'Introduction', in A. Forge (ed.), *Primitive Art and Society.* London and New York: Oxford University Press. pp. xiii–xxii.

Foster, M.L. (1980) 'The growth of symbolism in culture', in M.L. Foster and S.H. Brandes (eds), *Symbol as Sense: New Approaches to the Analysis of Meaning.* New York: Academic Press.

Gagliardi, P. (1989) 'Instillare il valore del servizio al cliente: problemi di coerenza tra comunicazioni esplicite e implicite', unpublished research report.

Gagliardi, P. (1990a) 'Artifacts as pathways and remains of organizational life', in P. Gagliardi (ed.), *Symbols and Artifacts: Views of the Corporate Landscape.* Berlin and New York: de Gruyter. pp. 3–38.

Gagliardi, P. (ed.) (1990b) *Symbols and Artifacts: Views of the Corporate Landscape.* Berlin and New York: de Gruyter.

Gagliardi, P. (1991) 'Archetipi culturali e sviluppo organizzativo', unpublished research report.

Gagliardi, P. (1992) 'Designing organizational settings: the interplay between physical, symbolic and social structures', in R. Eisendle and E. Miklautz (eds), *Produktkulturen: Dynamik und Bedeutungswandel des Konsums.* Frankfurt/New York: Campus. pp. 67–77.

Gagliardi, P. (1999) 'Theories empowering for action', *Journal of Management Inquiry*, 8(2): 143–7.

Geertz, C. (1983) *Local Knowledge: Further Essays in Interpretive Anthropology.* New York: Basic Books.

Geertz, C. (1988) *Works and Lives. The Anthropologist as Author.* Cambridge: Polity Press.

Goldwater, R. (1973) 'Art history and anthropology: some comparisons of methodology', in A. Forge (ed.), *Primitive Art and Society.* London and New York: Oxford University Press. pp. 1–10.

Goodman, N. (1976) *Languages of Art: an Approach to a Theory of Symbols.* Cambridge: Hackett.

Guillet de Montoux, P. (2004) *The Art Firm. Aesthetic Management and Metaphysical Marketing.* Palo Alto, CA: Stanford University Press.

Guillén, M.F. (1997) 'Scientific management's lost aesthetic: Architecture, organization, and the Taylorized beauty of the mechanical', *Administrative Science Quarterly*, 42: 682–715.

Hamilton, E. (1942) *The Greek Way.* New York: Norton.

Hancock, P. and Tyler, M. (2000) 'The look of love: Gender and the organization of aesthetics', in J. Hassard, R. Holliday and H. Wilmott (eds), *Body and Organization.* London: Sage. pp. 108–29.

Harper, D. (1994) 'On the authority of the image. Visual methods at the crossroads', in N.K. Denzin and Y.S. Lincoln (eds), *Handbook of Qualitative Research.* Thousand Oaks, CA: Sage. pp. 403–12.

Hauser, A. (1952) *The Social History of Art.* New York: Knopf.

Hedlund, G. (1986) 'The hypermodern MNC. A heterarchy?', *Human Resource Management*, 25(1): 9–35.

Hodder, I. (1994) 'The interpretation of documents and material culture', in N.K. Denzin and Y.S. Lincoln (eds), *Handbook of Qualitative Research.* Thousand Oaks, CA: Sage. pp. 393–402.

Hofbauer, J. (2000) 'Bodies in a Landscape: On Office Design and Organization', in J. Hassard, R. Holliday and H. Wilmott (eds), *Body and Organization.* London: Sage. pp. 108–29.

Huizinga, J. (1964) *Homo ludens.* Milano: Il Saggiatore.

Human Relations (2002) 55(7).

Iwanska, A. (1971) 'Without art', *British Journal of Aesthetics*, 11(4): 402–11.

Jones, M.O., Moore, M.D. and Snyder, R.C. (eds) (1988) *Inside Organizations: Understanding the Human Dimension.* Newbury Park, CA: Sage.

Kubler, G. (1962) *The Shape of Time.* New Haven and London: Yale University Press.

Kuhn, J.W. (1996) 'The Misfit between Organization Theory and Processional Art: A Comment on White and Strati', *Organization*, 3(2): 219–24.

Langer, S.K. (1967) *Mind: an Essay on Human Feeling.* Baltimore, Johns Hopkins University Press.

Langer, S.K. (1969) *Philosophy in a New Key. A Study in the Symbolism of Reason, Rite, and Art.* Cambridge, MA: Harvard University Press.

Larsen, J. and Schultz, M. (1990) 'Artifacts in a bureaucratic monastery', in P. Gagliardi (ed.), *Symbols and Artifacts: Views of the Corporate Landscape.* Berlin and New York: de Gruyter. pp. 281–302.

Lash, S. and Urry, J. (1994) *Economies of Signs and Space.* London: Sage.

Latour, B. (1992a) 'Where are the missing masses? Sociology of a few mundane artifacts', in W. Bijker and J. Law (eds), *Shaping Technology-Building Society: Studies in Sociotechnical Change.* Cambridge, MA: MIT Press. pp. 225–59.

Latour, B. (1992b) 'Technology is society made durable', in J. Law (ed.), *A Sociology of Monsters: Essays on Power, Technology and Domination.* London: Routledge. pp. 103–31.

Laughlin, C.D. and Stephens, C.D. (1980) 'Symbolism, canalization, and structure', in M.L. Foster and S.H. Brandes (eds), *Symbol as Sense: New Approaches to the Analysis of Meaning.* New York: Academic Press. pp. 323–63.

Linstead, S. and Höpfl, H. (eds) (2000) *The Aesthetics of Organizations.* London: Sage.

Mamiani, M. (1992) 'La retorica della certezza: il metodo scientifico di Newton e l'interpretazione dell'Apocalisse', in M. Pera and W.R. Shea (eds), *L'arte della persuasione scientifica*. Milano: Guerini e Associati. pp. 207–26.

Marinetti, F.T. (1924) *Futurismo e fascismo*. Foligno: Campitelli.

Martin, P.Y. (2002) 'Sensations, bodies, and the spirit of a place: Aesthetics in residential organizations for elderly', *Human Relations*, 55(7): 861–85.

Meyer, A.D. (1991) 'Visual data in organizational research', *Organization Science*, 2(2): 218–36.

Meyerson, D.E. (1991) 'Acknowledging and uncovering ambiguities in cultures', in P.J. Frost, L.F. Moore, M.R. Louis, C.C. Lundberg and J. Martin (eds), *Reframing Organizational Culture*. Newbury Park, CA: Sage. pp. 254–70.

Monaci, M. (1991) 'Il valore euristico dello studio degli artefatti', unpublished manuscript.

Organization (1996) 3(2).

Panofsky, E. (1974) *Architecture gothique et pensée scolastique*. Paris: Editions de Minuit.

Perrow, C. (1972) *Complex Organizations: a Critical Essay*. Glenview, IL: Scott, Foresman.

Polanyi, M. (1966) *The Tacit Dimension*. Garden City, NY: Doubleday.

Pratt, M.G. and Rafaeli, A. (2001) 'Symbols as a Language of Organizational Relationships', *Research in Organizational Behaviour*, 23: 93–132.

Ramirez, R. (1991) *The Beauty of Social Organization*. Munich: ACCEDO.

Rochberg-Halton, E. (1979a) 'The meaning of personal art objects', in J. Zuzanek (ed.), *Social Research and Cultural Policy*. Waterloo, Ontario: Otium.

Rochberg-Halton, E. (1979b) 'Cultural signs and urban adaptation: the meaning of cherished household possessions', unpublished PhD dissertation, University of Chicago.

Roger, A. (1991) 'Il paesaggio occidentale', *Lettera internazionale*, 30: 38–43.

Rosen, M., Orlikowski, W.J. and Schmahmann, K.S. (1990) 'Building buildings and living lives: a critique of bureucracy, ideology and concrete artifacts', in P. Gagliardi (ed.), *Symbols and Artifacts: Views of the Corporate Landscape*. Berlin and New York: de Gruyter. pp. 69–84.

Sabel, C. (1991) 'Moebius-strip organizations and open labor markets: Some consequences of the reintegration of conception and execution in a volatile economy', in P. Bourdieu and J. Coleman (eds), *Social Theory for a Changing Society*. Boulder: Westview Press. pp. 23–54.

Sandelands, L.E. and Buchner, G.C. (1989), 'Of art and work: aesthetic experience and the psychology of work feelings', in L.L. Cummings and B.M. Staw (eds), *Research in Organizational Behaviour*. Greenwich, CT: JAI Press. Volume 11, pp. 105–31.

Sassoon, J. (1990) 'Colors, artifacts, and ideologies', in P. Gagliardi (ed.), *Symbols and Artifacts: Views of the Corporate Landscape*. Berlin and New York: de Gruyter. pp. 169–84.

Scarry, E. (1985) *The Body in Pain*. Oxford: Oxford University Press.

Schein, E.H. (1984) 'Coming to a new awareness of organizational culture', *Sloan Management Review*, 25(4): 3–16.

Selznick, P. (1957) *Leadership in Administration*. Evanston, IL: Harper and Row.

Semprini, A. (1992) 'Oggetti, soggetti, testi. Aspetti semiotici della relazione oggettuale', in A. Borsari (ed.), *L'esperienza delle cose*. Genova: Marietti. pp. 61–79.

Sievers, B. (1990) 'The diabolization of death: some thoughts on the obsolescence of mortality in organization theory and practice', in J. Hassard and D. Pym (eds), *The Theory and Philosophy of Organizations: Critical Issues and New Perspectives*. London: Routledge. pp. 125–36.

Steyaert, C. and Hjorth, D. (2002) 'Thou art a scholar, speak to it… – on spaces of speech: A script', *Human Relations*, 55(7): 767–96.

Stoller, P. (1997) *Sensuous scholarship*. Philadelphia: University of Pennsylvania Press.

Strati, A. (1990) 'Aesthetics and organizational skill', in B. A. Turner (ed.), *Organizational Symbolism*. Berlin: de Gruyter. pp. 207–22.

Strati, A. (1992) 'Aesthetic understanding of organizational life', *Academy of Management Review*, 17(3): 568–81.

Strati, A. (1999) *Organization and Aesthetic*. London: Sage.

Strati, A. (2000) 'The Aesthetic Approach in Organization Studies', in S. Linstead and H. Höpfl (eds), *The Aesthetics of Organizations*. London: Sage. pp. 13–32.

Thrift, N. (1996) *Spatial Formations*. London: Sage.

Turner, B.A. (1990) 'The rise of organizational symbolism', in J. Hassard and D. Pym (eds), *The Theory and Philosophy of Organizations: Critical Issues and New Perspectives*. London: Routledge.

Van Maanen, J. (1979) 'The fact of fiction in organizational ethnography', *Administrative Science Quarterly*, 24: 539–50.

Van Maanen, J. (1982) 'Fieldwork on the beat', in J. Van Maanen, J.M. Dabbs and R.R. Faulkner (eds), *Varieties of Qualitative Research*. Beverly Hills, CA: Sage. pp. 103–51.

Vernant, J.P. (1969) *Mythe et pensée chez les Grecs*. Paris: Maspero.

Vickers, G. (1982) 'Razionalità e intuizione', in J. Wechsler (ed.), *L'estetica nella scienza*. Roma: Editori Riuniti. pp. 173–99.

Vico, G. (1725) *Principi di una scienza nuova*. Napoli: Mosca. 3rd edn. 1744. (English translation: *The New Science of Giambattista Vico* (1968) ed. T. G. Bergin and M. H. Fisch. Ithaca, N.Y.: Cornell University Press).

Weick, K. (1979) 'Cognitive processes in organizations', in L.L. Cummings and B.M. Staw (eds), *Research in*

Organizational Behaviour. Greenwich, CT: JAI Press. Volume 1, pp. 41–74.

Welsch, W. (1996) 'Aestheticization Process: Phenomena, Distinctions and Prospects', *Theory, Culture & Society*, 13: 1–24.

Whyte, W.F. (1955) *Street Corner Society*. Chicago: University of Chicago Press.

Whyte, W.F. (1961) *Men at Work*. Homewood, IL: Dorsey Press.

Witkin, R.W. (1974) *The Intelligence of Feeling*. London: Heinemann.

Witkin, R.W. (1990) 'The aesthetic imperative of a rational-technical machinery: a study in organizational control through the design of artifacts', in P. Gagliardi (ed.), *Symbols and Artifacts: Views of the Corporate Landscape*. Berlin and New York: de Gruyter. pp. 325–38.

Witz, A., Warhurst, C. and Nickson, D. (2003) 'The Labour of Aesthetics and the Aesthetics of Organization', *Organization*, 10(1): 33–54.

Worth, S. (1981) *Studying Visual Communication*. Philadelphia: University of Pennsylvania Press.

Worth, S. and Adair, J. (1972) *Through Navajo Eyes: an Exploration in Film Communication and Anthropology*. Bloomington, IN: Indiana University Press.

Yanow, D. (1998) 'Space stories: Studying museums buildings as organizational spaces while reflecting on interpretive methods and their narration', *Journal of Management Inquiry*, 7(3): 215–25.

2.12 Organizational Culture: Beyond Struggles for Intellectual Dominance

JOANNE MARTIN, PETER J. FROST AND OLIVIA A. O'NEILL

This review is not structured in the usual way – a departure from tradition that merits an explanation. Literature reviews generally have a linear, often chronological structure, with attention to 'who was first?' The tone is apparently objective and decisively authoritative: 'this study demonstrated that …'. The goal is to present the objective truth about what we've learned. The result is an enlightenment tale of cumulative progress, as one 'original' contribution after another builds a deeper and broader understanding than was available before. In a traditionally structured review, intellectual differences of opinion are usually handled with indirection and tact, an approach that helps scholars co-exist in a close-knit field while continuing to have cordial intellectual exchanges. Most often an author focuses predominantly on one point of view, relegating competing perspectives to brief summaries or the margins of a text (for example, in a parenthetical aside, a separate chapter in a book or a footnote) or simply not citing them at all. This popular strategy permits full exploration and delineation of a favoured point of view, while not creating a need to criticize, or even draw attention to, conflicting perspectives. Whether silence, marginalization or tactful understatement is used, these commonly utilized strategies mask intellectual disagreements. The reader is forced to attend to silences and 'read between the lines' of what is published in order to decipher what fundamental issues are disputed.

In the last few decades, the assumptions underlying the traditionally structured literature review have been profoundly challenged. A brief review of these critiques will explain the unusual structure of this paper and provide an introduction to some controversies that have affected the cultural literature. Some of these critiques have argued that purportedly objective knowledge is deeply limited by the historical context in which the research was produced

(e.g. Grant et al. 2004). Other scholars have argued that knowledge 'development' takes a cyclical rather than linear form. For example, Barley and Kunda (1992) described an alternation between rational and normative discourses of control in organizational studies, while Perrow (1979) framed a 'short and glorious' history of the field as a struggle between the forces of light (human relations) and darkness (technical efficiency). Some postmodernists (e.g. Derrida 1976) have argued that 'original' contributions to knowledge are impossible because any text is unavoidably an unwitting assemblage of ideas and quotations, often uncited, from other texts; the same themes reappear, clothed as new insights (Calas and Smircich 1990; Jeffcutt et al. 1995). Of particular relevance to this chapter, Kuhn (1970) portrays the history of science as a political struggle for the dominance of one intellectual view over another.

Because a subjective point of view underlies an author's apparently objective account (e.g. Clifford and Marcus 1986; Van Maanen 1988; Czarniawska 1999), even the most ostensibly 'scientific' writing contains rhetorical strategies that enhance authorial authority by making the author's subjective judgements invisible (for example, by the use of passive voice or avoidance of the pronouns 'I' or 'we'). Any review chapter requires a constant stream of tacit value judgements about which studies were most important, which contributions were derivative or minor, and why one point of view gained ascendancy while another was ignored. Chronologies are disturbed by publication lags, and it is often not clear who deserves credit for a given idea. Any shared consensus that emerges is a value judgement; the objective truth about what has been learned and who was the first to learn it, is to some extent a judgement call. For all these reasons, many scholars have become increasingly worried about the uncertainties inherent in the social scientific enterprise and the inevitable exigencies of writing social scientific prose. In writing this chapter, we wanted to find a way to take these difficulties into account. We therefore decided to experiment with the conventional structure and tone of a review paper, to see if we could find another way to depict the accumulation of research on the topic of organizational culture.

A less conventional structure is particularly appropriate for a review of culture research. Norms of silencing, marginalizing and minimizing intellectual disagreements have sometimes been broken in the organizational culture literature in a way that makes these disagreements more visible than usual. Cultural scholars have fundamental disagreements about epistemology, methodology, political ideology and theory. Rather than handling these differences of opinion only in 'subterranean' outlets such as blind reviews and private conversations, a number of cultural publications argue openly for one point of view in preference to explicitly elaborated alternatives (e.g. Meyerson 1991a; Schein 1991; Putnam et al. 1993; Martin 2002; Alvesson 2004). We therefore have a textual record of overt conflict that challenges taken-for-granted certainties and inspires new ideas. Because cultural research is characterized by deep disagreements about fundamental issues, however, there is little sense of cumulative advances in knowledge in this topic area. Any full review of organizational culture research must respond to the existence of these disagreements.

Rather than telling a conventional, chronological tale of linear progress toward greater knowledge, we have decided to experiment with the conventional tone and structure of a review. In the first part of this chapter, we portray research in this domain as a struggle for intellectual dominance among the proponents of various cultural theories, methodological preferences, epistemologies and political orientations. We use a 'king of the mountain' game metaphor to structure the first part of this paper:

The childhood war game of king of the mountain is preferably played on a sandy beach so no one will get hurt. One king or queen's temporary triumph at the top of a sand pile is rapidly superseded by the reign of another would-be monarch, until a succession of short-lived victories and a plethora of defeats leave the pile flattened. Sometimes the tide washes away the traces of the struggle and sometimes children regroup (often with new playmates and reconfigured alliances), rebuild the sand pile, and start the game anew.

The game of king of the mountain has several attributes that make it a useful metaphor for our purposes. First, some players choose not to play the game, preferring as individuals or groups to build their own castles in the sand, as if saying 'make pluralism, not war' (Reed 1985). In king of the mountain games, coalitions usually evolve spontaneously, without much conscious co-ordination. Once the current monarch is deposed, the coalition often dissolves, only to reconstitute itself in a somewhat different form when a new king or queen takes over. A victory often involves a solo player climbing to the top of the sand pile, without anyone deliberately and aggressively pulling rivals down. Finally, it is important to say that we, as authors of this review, do not see ourselves as innocent, distant or dispassionate adult observers of this game. We have, for better or worse, been fully involved players in the game, sometimes consciously, sometimes not.

One reviewer aptly described our militarized use of this metaphor in a 1996 version of this chapter as tracing aggressive moves in the culture wars '... out the rise of the partisan camps, battles fought and the damage done in the back alleys of the editorial and tenure processes', aiming to offer a 'painfully accurate overview of the games academics play' (Zammuto 1998: 731). Times have changed since the first version of this chapter, and many cultural researchers are no longer so textually open about competitiveness. The authors of this chapter believe that conflict and the struggle for intellectual dominance have not disappeared. They have simply gone underground. Rather than openly discussing conflicts, some authors simply refrain from citing cultural research written from differing intellectual positions, playing the king of the mountain game by tacitly assuming they have won. Others engage in the struggle for dominance in less visible quarters, behind the closed doors and confidentiality norms of the tenure and review processes. It is a mistake to presume that less visible conflict is more benign; hidden conflicts are destructive and can escalate rapidly (Kolb and Bartunek 1992).

However, the authors of this chapter are concerned about the deleterious effects of a struggle for dominance and we therefore worry about helping to perpetuate conflict through use of the king of the mountain metaphor. Any metaphor brings some issues into focus while obscuring others (Pinder and Bourgeois 1982; Morgan 1983a). The king of the mountain game metaphor can leave the impression of intentional co-ordination when coincidence or independent simultaneity would be more accurate descriptions. What was intended to be a non-aggressive description of an intellectual position can be interpreted as a competitive move. Therefore, in the concluding part of the chapter, we offer an alternative metaphor that highlights aspects of cultural theory and research that are obscured or ignored when competitive metaphors are used and when issues that generate conflict are the main focus of attention.

Getting Started: Value Engineering and The Integration View

Space restrictions narrow the scope of this review to *organizational* culture research. We unfortunately cannot survey the burgeoning and important literature that studies culture at the national or international levels of analysis.[1] And, although we have made an effort to cite non-US literature, we are restricted by our own limits to English language publications. Finally, we cannot offer an extensive historical introduction to cultural research, although a brief context-setting may prove useful. Organizational studies experienced a renaissance of interest in culture in the late 1970s. Most accounts cite the successes of Japanese management and the perceived failures of traditional organizational analysis as catalysts for a re-awakening interest in corporate culture among practitioners (e.g. Peters and Waterman 1982: 4–5; Turner 1990: 85–6). There was also a less practitioner-oriented origin of the cultural renaissance. In the late 1970s, many academics were highly critical of mainstream organizational research, which, at that time, emphasized quantitative, neo-positivist science. Some academics and many practitioners felt that this approach was arid and fruitless because it was overly reliant on a rational model of human behaviour, a structural approach to questions of corporate strategy, and a love of numerical analysis. Business education based on such research, these critics argued, would create generations of managers who knew more about spreadsheets and models than people.

Researchers who participated in the cultural renaissance, whether or not they advocated the use of qualitative methods, shared a conviction that a cultural framework would permit them to broaden

organizational research and theory. Many of us were originally drawn to culture as an emancipatory way of approaching organizational phenomena, and as a metaphor for revitalizing organizational theory. Culture seemed to allow us to move away from the constricting 'boxes' of our theories and methods at a time when this change seemed to be needed, helpful, empowering and energizing. In these first stages of the cultural renaissance, hope was in the air, and new insights seemed likely. The possibility of a broader and more useful organizational theory was a heady tonic for many cultural researchers.

At this point, the game of king of the mountain had not yet begun. It was as if children drifted to the beach and began to play in the sand, at first without much interaction or co-ordination. Although publication dates can be misleading, and (as will be the case throughout this chapter) it is difficult to choose which of many exemplars to cite, this renaissance of interest in culture began with publications that were managerially oriented and written primarily for executive and MBA audiences (e.g. Ouchi 1981; Deal and Kennedy 1982; Peters and Waterman 1982). These authors argued that effective top managers could build a strongly unified culture by articulating a set of 'corporate' values, perhaps in a vision or mission statement. If those values were reinforced consistently through formal policies, informal norms, stories, rituals and jargon, in time almost all employees would allegedly share those values. This would supposedly set up a domino effect: higher commitment, greater productivity, and ultimately, more profits. These seductive promises were popularized in the media, complete with advice about how to create a 'strong' (meaning unitary) culture. Saffold (1988) draws a useful distinction between two aspects of a 'strong' or integrated culture: a 'positive' culture refers to the attractive content of manifestations such as norms or values and a 'cohesive' culture refers to uniformity, that is a high degree of organization-wide consensus among cultural members. Not surprisingly, when culture was defined this way, it quickly became the hottest product on the consulting market, and it continues to be an enduring concern for managerial audiences, primarily because of the attractiveness of its claim that culture can be a tool for managers to improve organizational effectiveness (e.g. Wilderom et al. 2000; Sparrow 2001). For example, Kotter and Heskett (1992: 16) report, 'The most elegant of the culture/performance perspectives, and the one most widely reported, associates "strong" cultures with excellent performance. In a strong corporate culture, almost all managers share a set of relatively consistent values and methods of doing business'. Some have labelled this cultural approach 'value engineering' as most such research offers prescriptions and techniques for generating value consensus, potentially manipulating the personal values of employees (cf. Hochschild 1983; Van Maanen and Kunda 1989).

Value engineering studies are a subset of cultural studies written from an integration perspective. Integration studies are characterized by a pattern of consistency of interpretations across types of cultural manifestations, organization-wide consensus and clarity (Martin 1992). In integration studies, culture is 'an area of meaning carved out of a vast mass of meaninglessness, a small clearing of lucidity in a formless, dark, always ominous jungle' (Berger 1967: 23, quoted in Wuthnow et al. 1984: 26). Within the domain that is considered the culture, there is virtually no ambiguity reported; Schein (1991) even argues that that which is ambiguous is not part of culture. Reviews which include a description of some of the historical roots of the integration perspective on culture are: Ott (1989); Ouchi and Wilkins (1985); and Schultz (1994). (It is noteworthy that these historical reviews do not discuss or cite cultural studies that challenge the integration view of culture.)

The integration approach to studying culture touched a responsive chord in many researchers. Taken as a whole, early integration studies (e.g. Ouchi and Jaeger 1978; Pondy et al. 1983; Schein 1985; Pennings and Gresov 1986; Enz 1988; Ott 1989) showed that organizational culture has many manifestations: espoused values (sometimes called content themes when enacted values are inferred from behaviour); formal practices (written policies that govern organizational structures and rules); informal practices (such as unwritten norms about appropriate behaviour or proper decision-making procedures), stories about employees, rituals such as Christmas parties and retirement dinners, organization-specific jargon, humour and the effects of decor, dress norms, interior design and architecture. Many researchers find it useful to define culture as the patterns of interpretation underlying these various manifestations. As Helms Mills and Mills (2000: 57) explain, cultures are not just a list of various manifestations, but are 'an explanation of what causes them to cohere in the first place'. The

question is, of course, whether that coherence takes the form advocated or tacitly assumed in integrationist studies.

The integration perspective conceptualizes cultural change as an organization-wide cultural transformation, whereby an old unity is replaced by a new one; conflict and ambiguity may occur in the interim, but these are interpreted as evidence of the deterioration of a 'strong' (meaning integrated) culture before a new 'strong' unity with different content is established (e.g. Clark 1972; Jonsson and Lundin 1977; Greenwood and Hinings 1988). When dissent appears or ambiguities emerge, integration research describes these 'anomalies' as evidence of individual deviance, insufficiently homogeneous employee selection procedures, poor socialization of new employees, a 'weak' culture, a temporary period of confusion during a time of cultural realignment, or a domain of organizational life that is not part of the culture. In these integration studies of cultural change, the bottom line is that homogeneity, harmony and a unified culture are desirable and achievable, even though regrettable deviations from this idea may temporarily occur (e.g. Schein 1991; Kotter and Heskett 1992).

Examples of integration studies include both qualitative (e.g. Schein 1985; McDonald 1991) and quantitative studies. For example, O'Reilly et al. (1991) created a Q-sort measure based on content analysis of managerially oriented qualitative literature, consisting of 54 values said to characterize 'strong', that is integrated corporate cultures. Managerial and professional employees of large accounting firms were asked which of these values characterized their companies; values not chosen by a majority were excluded as not descriptive of the firm's culture. O'Reilly et al. found that when new professional and managerial employees personally approved of the same subset of values that were endorsed by current professional and managerial employees of a company, the job satisfaction of those new employees was higher and intent to quit (turnover) was lower, in comparison with new employees with dissenting opinions. Denison (1990) used questionnaire items (originally developed to measure organizational climate) to measure culture. Respondent samples consisting mostly of managerial and professional respondents used Likert scales to describe the behavioural norms of their companies. Behavioural norms endorsed by a majority of respondents were used to define their firm's culture. Items that did not generate wide consensus were excluded, as not descriptive of the organization's culture. These results were positively correlated with various measures of firm financial performance. Other quantitative integration studies include Cooke and Szumal (2000).

Many *but not all* integration studies have value engineering overtones, claiming that culture can be managed or that 'strong' cultures can lead to increased commitment, improved productivity and performance (e.g. Brown 1990; Kotter and Heskett 1992; Denison and Mishra 1995; Beyer et al. 2000; Sparrow 2001; Collins and Porras 2002; Schrodt 2002). In contrast to such functionalist research, other integration studies take a more symbolic approach (Schultz and Hatch 1996; Rafaeli and Worline 2000). For example, Barley (1983) describes how funeral directors use a series of practices and rituals (e.g. changing the sheets on a death bed, washing and putting make-up on a corpse, closing the corpse's eyes) to create the illusion that death is life-like. Whether an integrationist study asserts a link to effectiveness, or refrains from doing so, whether it focuses on functional or symbolic aspects of culture, an integration study tacitly defines culture in terms of consistency, organization-wide consensus and clarity.

Integration studies differ, however, in their choice of which cultural manifestations to study. Many integration studies, particularly those utilizing qualitative methods, are generalist, in that they examine interpretations of a variety of cultural manifestations. For example, Pettigrew (1979) described how headmasters used rituals, stories and jargon to generate commitment to their schools. McDonald (1991) explained how uniforms, slogans, posters, a charismatic leader, well-defined rituals and a strong work ethic combined to create a sense of excitement and a commitment to excellence among volunteers and employees of a temporary organization, the Los Angeles Olympic Organizing Committee. Quantitative integration studies can also be generalist (e.g. Siehl and Martin's (1988) quantitative examination of interpretations of stories, jargon and other linguistic manifestations), but this is rare.

In contrast, specialist integration studies focus on only one (or at most two) types of cultural manifestations, usually values (e.g. Ashkanasy et al. 2000a; Zammuto et al. 2000) or self-reported behavioural norms (e.g. Cooke and Szumal 2000).[2] Other specialist integration studies focus on a single kind of symbolic manifestation, such as ceremonies (e.g. Dandridge 1986), organizational stories (e.g. Martin et al. 1983; Brown 1990; Feldman 1990) or rituals (e.g. Knuf 1993). Specialist integration studies sometimes generalize from a single type of manifestation to conclusions about the culture as a whole. The problem with this is that meanings associated with one type of manifestation may not be consistent with meanings associated with a full range of cultural manifestations. For example, values and attitudes are often inconsistent with behaviour, and formal policies are often inconsistent with informal practices (e.g. Martin 1992).

There are additional conceptual and measurement problems in integrationist value engineering studies that claim a link to organizational effectiveness (see Wilderom et al. 2000; Sparrow 2001). Many 'non-cultural' variables (such as a company's product mix, economic conditions, competitors' choices) affect firm performance, and therefore must be controlled in such a study. High performance at time one, or a particular cultural configuration at time one, may not be present at a later date. For these reasons, the oft-repeated claims of a link between a 'strong' integrated culture and organizational performance must be regarded as, at best, unproven, until longitudinal, well controlled studies, with in-depth generalist measures of culture across time, can be conducted (e.g. Siehl and Martin 1990).

In spite of these difficulties, the production of integration studies, sometimes with claims of links to organizational effectiveness, continues unabated. One reason may be that executives and managers understandably would like to believe that culture can be a tool, that their personal values are shared by most employees and reflected in consistent behavioural norms, and that these supposedly shared values and behavioural norms can be useful for generating loyalty, commitment, productivity and financial efficiency. These are seductive promises, and their appeal is unlikely to deteriorate, whatever the weaknesses of the empirical record. And as we shall see, the action implications of cultural research conducted from other points of view are often less clear.

The Opposition Gathers: The Differentiation Perspective

Roughly at the same time as the flood of integration research began to appear, another group of scholars, mostly working independently, were drawn to the study of organizational culture. They too thought that mainstream organizational theory and research needed revitalization. They too thought that a renaissance of interest in organizational culture would bring an interdisciplinary creativity into the field, expanding the types of issues being studied and the kinds of methods considered valid. Like many of the advocates of the integration viewpoint, some of this second group of scholars were qualitative researchers, who were excited because now ('at last' in the US), ethnographic research would have a home in mainstream organizational studies. They hoped that, rather than being dismissed as 'a nice story about an *N* of one', qualitative case studies would be appreciated for their richly detailed, context-specific insights.

This collection of qualitative and quantitative scholars soon generated an impressive body of work, labelled here and elsewhere (e.g. Martin and Meyerson 1988; Young 1989) as the differentiation perspective.[3] Differentiation studies find: (1) interpretations of manifestations are inconsistent; (2) consensus occurs only within subcultural boundaries; and (3) clarity exists only within subcultures, although ambiguities appear in the interstices between subcultures. In this way, subcultures are like islands of clarity in a sea of ambiguity. Differentiation studies developed these three, empirically based commonalties without much intentional co-ordination. In the terms of the king of the mountain game, it was as if some of the children playing independently on the beach (doing differentiation research) began to notice each other, eventually moving together to play in a parallel fashion, not yet noticing that the integrationist studies had already claimed dominance.

A good differentiation study has to have depth, to 'penetrate the front' that cultural members present to strangers (e.g. Schein 1985)[4], thus attempting to overcome impression management and social desirability biases. Such an approach will often reveal aspects of organizational life that do not conform to managerial ideals. In addition, many differentiation scholars stress the importance of including more than just cognitive and symbolic aspects of culture. Studies should also include the material aspects of working life such as pay inequalities, the dirt and noise of an assembly line, etc. These emphases on depth of understanding and material manifestations of culture produce differentiation studies that are

sensitive to inconsistencies between stated attitudes and actual behaviour, between formal practices and informal norms, between one story and another, and – most important – between the interpretations of one group and another (e.g. Barley 1986; Van Maanen and Kunda 1989; see also Cameron and Quinn 1998).

Rosen (1991) draws a useful distinction between horizontal and vertical subcultures. Horizontal subcultural differences delineate functions, occupations or jobs, usually of roughly equivalent status (e.g. Helmer 1993; Trice and Beyer 1993). Vertical subcultures delineate differences between groups of high and low status employees (e.g. Jaques 1951; Rosen 1985; Alvesson 1993). Just as integration research tends to focus attention on integration studies to the exclusion of all others, so too some researchers soon began to play the king of the mountain game, claiming that differentiation studies were the new dominant mode of cultural research. For example: 'Generally, the idea of a single organizational level corporate culture, frequently accompanied by the assumption of management being able to shape it, was very popular earlier ... Today most scholars emphasize the presence of subcultures in organizations' (Alvesson 2002: 157).

Examples highlight the texture of differentiation research. Bartunek and Moch (1991) show how five subcultures in a food production firm reacted differently to management's imposition of a Quality of Working Life intervention. Top management was primarily concerned with control. In-house consulting staff members were co-operative. The management of the local plants where the programme was implemented was paternalistic, using imagery of employees as 'children' in relation to managerial 'parents'. Line employees exhibited a conformist reaction, following management's preferences. Machinists, historically an active, independent and comparatively well-paid group, actively resisted the intervention. As this example illustrates, to the extent that consensus exists in differentiation studies, it exists within subcultural boundaries.

A hierarchical or vertical alignment of subcultures is evident in Van Maanen's (1991) study of ride operators at Disneyland. At the bottom of the status ranking were food vendors ('pancake ladies' and 'coke blokes'), while the male operators of yellow submarines and jungle boats held high status positions. Tension among ride operators, customers and supervisors was evident, as ride operators arranged for obnoxious customers to be soaked with water when submarine hatches opened. Supervisors were consistently foiled in their attempts to catch operators breaking rules. Similarly, in Young's (1989) study of 'bag ladies' in a British manufacturing plant, tensions between management and labour were evident, and the younger and older workers fissioned into different subcultures. As these examples indicate, subcultures often appear along lines of functional, occupational and hierarchical differentiation, often coalescing into overlapping, nested groups that coexist in harmony, conflict or independence from each other (Louis 1985; Bastien 1992).

Interpretations of manifestations are not assumed to be consistent in differentiation studies. For example, in the food production firm studied by Bartunek and Moch, top management said one thing to employees and did something different. At Disneyland, ride operators appeared to conform to management's rules, while in fact doing whatever they pleased. In a particularly detailed examination of the effects of such inconsistencies on individuals, Kunda (1992) studied engineers' reactions as they conformed to a company ritual designed to exhibit commitment to supposedly shared company values. During moments of ease while 'off stage', the engineers used humour and sarcastic side remarks to express their disapproval, skepticism or ambivalence. As these examples indicate, espoused values, behaviour mandated by formal policies and informal norms are often observed to be inconsistent (see also Coopman and Meidlinger's (2000) study of tensions in a Catholic parish and Trujillo's (1992) analysis of multiple interpretations of major league baseball ballpark culture).

In contrast to the self-contained approach of integration studies, differentiation research tends to be more sensitive to environmental influences on cultures in organizations. Differentiation research has shown that the subcultures within an organization can reflect, and be partially determined by, cultural groupings in the larger society. For example, functional subcultures within a firm can reflect occupational subcultures that span firm boundaries, as when accountants or programmers appear to create the same kinds of subcultures, no matter where they work (e.g. Gregory 1983). From the differentiation perspective, cultural change is localized within one or more subcultures, alterations tend to be incremental, and innovations are triggered

primarily by pressures from an organization's environment (e.g. Meyerson and Martin 1987). The environment is likely to be segmented, so different subcultures within the same organization experience different kinds and rates of change. Thus, from a differentiation viewpoint, an organizational culture is not unitary; it is a *nexus* where environmental influences intersect, creating a nested, overlapping set of subcultures within a permeable organizational boundary (Martin 1992: 111–4).[5]

Differentiation studies offer a bold, empirically well-supported challenge to the integration assumption that organizational culture can be a unitary monolith composed of clear values and interpretations that are perceived, enacted and shared by all or most employees, in the same ways (e.g. Turner 1986; Alvesson 2002). What differentiation studies have in common is a willingness to acknowledge inconsistencies (i.e. attitudes vs behaviour, formal policies vs actual practices, etc.). They see consensus as occurring only within subcultural boundaries. These studies describe whatever inconsistencies and subcultural differences they find in clear terms; there is little ambiguity here, except in the interstices between subcultures. Thus, differentiation studies define culture in terms of inconsistency, consensus and clarity – only within subcultural boundaries.

By the mid 1980s, the conceptual distinctions between the integration and differentiation perspectives were clearly drawn, and both teams began to gather and consolidate empirical evidence of the superior veracity of their particular point of view. The game of king of the mountain was underway. Studies of subcultural differentiation are more plentiful than ever and differentiation critiques of the integration view are being articulated clearly and with cogency (for reviews, see Alvesson 2002; Martin 2002). In spite of these efforts, integration theories of culture have some of the qualities of Lazarus; just when one thinks they are dead, they pop up, full of life. As these overt conflicts between the integration and differentiation perspectives continue to proliferate, they create openings for other parties to enter the king of the mountain game.

The New Players: Advocates of Fragmentation

A new point of view, labelled the fragmentation perspective (Meyerson and Martin 1987; Martin 1992), entered the king of the mountain game. This perspective is logically positioned on the same three dimensions that are the focus of the integration vs differentiation struggle (degrees of consistency, consensus and clarity). According to advocates of the fragmentation view, interpretations of the manifestations of a culture are multiple – neither clearly consistent nor clearly inconsistent; instead, the relationship among interpretations is complex, containing elements of contradiction and confusion. Similarly, consensus is not organization-wide nor is it specific to a given subculture. Instead, consensus among individuals is transient and issue-specific, producing short-lived affinities that are quickly replaced by a different pattern of affinities, as a new issue draws the attention of a different subset of cultural members (e.g. Feldman 1989; Kreiner and Schultz 1993). According to the fragmentation point of view, the essence of any culture is pervasive ambiguity (e.g. Feldman 1991; Meyerson 1991a). Clarity, then, is a dogma of meaningfulness and order propagated by management and researchers of a particular persuasion to create an illusion of clarity where there is none (e.g. Levitt and Nass 1989). In such an ephemeral environment, culture is no longer a clearing in a jungle of meaninglessness. Now, culture is the jungle itself.

Lack of consistency, lack of consensus and ambiguity are the hallmarks of a fragmentation view of culture. Ambiguity is defined to include irony, paradox and irreconcilable contradictions, as well as multiple meanings. In a fragmentation account, power is diffused broadly at all levels of the hierarchy and throughout the organization's environment. Change is a constant flux, rather than an intermittent interruption in an otherwise stable state. Because they portray change as largely triggered by the environment or other forces beyond an individual's control, fragmentation studies can portray alienation and apathy, as well as confusion and satisfaction, but they offer few guidelines for those who would actively control the change process. Organizational precursors of the fragmentation view include, for example, Brunsson's (1985) observations about organizational irrationality and hypocrisy, as well as March and his colleagues' studies of ambiguity in decision-making (Cohen and March 1974; March and Olsen 1976), and Weick's (1995) observations about sense-making. Most fragmentation studies put ambiguities on centre stage, so that the certainties of the integration view and the clearly defined differences of the

differentiation view seem like oversimplified, wishful thinking.

In an early example of fragmentation research, Feldman (1989) studied policy analysts in a large government bureaucracy. They spent their days writing policy reports that might never be read and, in any case, were unlikely to influence the formation of a policy. In such a context, ambiguities prevented a clear analysis of the meaningfulness or the meaninglessness of the analysts' work – a fog of contradiction and irony that permitted the analysts to keep on working, involved in the process while unsure of the ultimate outcome or utility of their work. In Meyerson's (1991b) studies of social workers, ambiguity pervaded an occupation where the objectives were unclear, the means to those goals were not specified, and where sometimes it wasn't even clear when an intervention had been successful or even what success in this context might have meant. Analyses of the humour and irony of the social workers provide the deepest insights of this unsettling case study. Meyerson concluded that to study this occupational subculture – while excluding ambiguity from the realm of what is defined as cultural – would have been dramatically incomplete, even misleading. Weick (1991) offered a fragmentation view of a foggy airport in Tenerife, as pilots, controllers and cockpit crews struggled to make themselves understood across barriers of status, language and task assignment. In this context, pervasive ambiguity was not benign; hundreds of lives were lost as two jumbo jets collided in the fog. Robertson and Swan (2003) studied highly educated consultants working within a knowledge-intensive firm where project work was inherently fluid, complex and uncertain, making acceptance of ambiguities unavoidable. These studies illustrate the main point of fragmentation research: that an understanding of ambiguities must be a central component of any cultural study that claims to capture the most important aspects of people's working lives. Such ambiguity need not only lie in structural arrangements, policies or organizational practices. It can also lie in the interpretations people make about more obviously symbolic manifestations, such as stories or rituals.

There are strong opponents to the fragmentation view of culture. As noted earlier, Schein (1991) dismisses the idea that ambiguity is part of culture. Alvesson (2002: 163–4) has challenged the need for a fragmentation approach to studying culture, arguing that a closer look at organizational conditions leads unavoidably to the discovery of at least some elements of uncertainty, confusion and contradiction. This discovery is of course a result of adopting an ambiguity perspective, but also – and this is my point here – of careful and detailed observation.

Alvesson (2002: 163) concludes, 'This is to some degree inherent in cultural phenomena and not something most researchers are concerned with on the level of the collective'. In contrast, advocates of the fragmentation perspective would concur with Alvesson's observations of the prevalence of ambiguity, acknowledge its being inherent in cultural phenomena, and argue that it is therefore an essential part of any examination of culture (e.g. Meyerson 1991a). Fragmentation research alerts organizational members and scholars to be wary of the assumption that culture (or subculture) is defined by strongly shared values, singular clear interpretations and a coherent, predictable set of norms and behaviours. If researchers miss this point they can overlook important aspects of culture and introduce more certainty and predictability into the depiction of organizational culture than is warranted. Without acknowledging ambiguity, fully, cultural research runs the risk of offering an over-simplified, clearly outlined, cartoonish portrait of a culture that fails to capture the complexity, flux and contradictions that characterize life in contemporary organizations.

Single-perspective cultural studies (consistent with only one of the three theoretical perspectives) continue to be published in increasing numbers; there is no doubt the cultural renaissance is in full bloom. With this proliferation of interest comes an intensification of the struggle for intellectual dominance – albeit one that is more complex and more superficially cordial than the rough and tumble first decades of research in this arena. Some fragmentation and differentiation studies continue to find data that challenges the integration view directly, while many others simply ignore cultural research not consistent with their view. Other cultural studies, apparently weary of this dispute among these three approaches to studying culture, turned their attention to two related sets of issues that were of growing importance in the field of organizational studies, broadly defined. These two issues are political interests (whether or not a given cultural study facilitated or was critical of a managerial point of view) and

methodological preferences (regarding the superiority of quantitative or qualitative methods). When these issues were surfaced, the configuration of cultural studies began to change, cross-cutting the integration vs differentiation vs dragmentation disputes, and creating realignments in the king of the mountain game.

Managerialists and Critical Theorists

Traditionally, much social science research claims to be objective, that is uninfluenced by the political interests and ideology of its authors, offering an accurate and unbiased picture of a context. Many contemporary researchers, including critical theorists, have argued that such neutrality is impossible. For example, Deetz, working from a quite different epistemology, posits that, 'Every story comes from a point of view that represents particular interests. The reader has a right to know what those interests are' (Putnam et al. 1993: 228). Mumby claims that in organizational studies, claims of neutrality often mask a managerial bias:

> The study of organizational behaviour is replete with research that claims such neutrality but that actually privileges managerial rationality. Such research is not overtly pro-management. However, because it tends to operate within particular institutional parameters and belief systems, it incorporates a managerial worldview (Putnam et al. 1993: 225).

Many organizational researchers continue to believe that both qualitative and quantitative work can be objective and neutral, while others argue that managerial interests are appropriate if one wishes to 'help business'. Still others advocate the deliberate use of critical perspectives (i.e. for critical ethnography, see Clifford and Marcus (1986) and Thomas (1992)). These politicized viewpoints are fervently held, in part because they often reflect differing epistemologies.

Consideration of managerial vs critical political interests is a vector that cross-cuts the three perspectives discussed in the first part of this chapter. Each perspective has produced exemplars of managerial and critical research, as well as work that claims neutrality. While some disputes between managerial and critical researchers were surfaced behind the confidentiality screens of the tenure process and blind review of journal articles, others had the courage to take these important differences of opinion into the public arena. Integration studies were an early target of critical theorists, in part because of their sheer numbers. Hundreds of integration studies have been published in the decades since the cultural renaissance began, particularly in US journals and books written for executive and MBA audiences. Systematic coding of the content of the cultural studies published in US organizational journals revealed that most were clearly integrationist and shared an explicit managerial emphasis (Barley et al. 1988; Jeffcutt et al. 1995). 'Strong' (that is, integrated) cultures continued to be pitched as the answer to managers' desires for greater control over their employees and greater profitability for their firms. Most of these integration studies were literally managerial, in that they relied primarily on data from managerial and professional employees.

Critical theorists have pointed to the managerial biases of studies that tacitly or overtly serve the needs of management at the expense of other employees (i.e. Reed 1985; Knights and Willmott 1987; Mumby 1988). Some critical researchers observed with contempt that integration studies had 'sold out' to the managerial perspective that dominated mainstream organizational research (e.g. Turner 1986; Calas and Smircich 1987; Van Maanen and Kunda 1989: 92). Stablein and Nord (1985) reviewed organizational culture research, classifying studies according to the extent to which they represent a critical point of view, and Alvesson (2002) has done so for more recent work. In spite of this effort, and perhaps because many cultural researchers are employed by business schools, most integration studies today continue to adopt an unquestioned managerial point of view (e.g. Schein 1985; Kotter and Heskett 1992). In response to this critical theory critique, some more managerially-oriented culture researchers have made their resistance clear. For example, Gagliardi (2003: 135) notes the 'blinding effect of this anti-managerial stance' in an *Administrative Sciences Quarterly* review of Alvesson's (2002) book, and further criticizes (p. 136) him for assuming that '… sharing of values opposed to his own will inevitably be accompanied by scientific work of poor quality'.

What then is the alternative to a managerial version of integration? Is there such a thing as a critical version of an integration study? Critical theorists

call for a focus on the views of all members of a culture, not just those at the top of a hierarchy. A critical integration study 'reveals the management-oriented bias that arbitrarily privileges certain meaning constructions', uncovering 'the processes through which social actors are systematically denied access to the expression of their own interests', producing a sense of closure that results in accepting the status quo as natural and immutable (Mumby, quoted in Putnam et al. 1993: 226). Critical integration accounts describe workers as unable or only partially able to see how managerial controls force them into attitudes and behaviour contrary to their own political interests. From a critical point of view, a strongly unified culture is an oppressive hegemony that successfully controls employees, in some cases even giving them a false consciousness that approves of their own oppression. Jermier (1985) describes two versions of a day in the life of a blue collar worker. In the integration version, the worker gladly embraces an oppressive, environmentally polluting workplace in exchange for the joys of consumption of products he doesn't really need. (In the other version, the façade of false consciousness cracks, and the worker has glimpses of his own oppression and the possibility of a better life.) Goffman (1961) describes life in an asylum, where the architecture of the hospital and its formal rules and practices permit hegemonic control of the behaviour of mentally disturbed patients who can be observed 24 hours a day. Other critical integration studies have offered hegemonic descriptions of work in large corporations (e.g. O'Reilly 1989; Van Maanen and Kunda 1989), total institutions such as prisons (Foucault 1976), and the shop floors of manufacturing firms (Sewall and Wilkinson 1992; 1998).

The dispute between managerial and critical approaches to culture has been evident within the differentiation perspective as well. Alvesson (2002) has argued strongly that there are two kinds of differentiation studies. The first kind simply describes subcultural differences, often representing them as based on functional or occupational assignments. In these managerial differentiation accounts, subcultures co-exist in a complementary, harmonious or orthogonally independent fashion. For example, at OZCO (a pseudonym for a high tech company) members of the Marketing division often felt that Engineering 'threw products over the wall' dividing the two subcultures of the company, expecting the marketing professionals to find ways to sell an unfamiliar product that might not even have a market

(Martin 1992; see also Martin and Siehl 1983). Although this subcultural difference produced friction, the differentiation between these groups was horizontal and complementary, and both subcultures were clearly essential to the functioning of the company. This kind of subcultural differentiation is congruent with a managerial point of view (see also Helmer (1993) and Trice and Beyer (1993) on occupational subcultures).

In contrast, a second kind of differentiation study focuses on vertical differentiation between advantaged and disadvantaged subcultures, drawing attention to the organizational life of non-managerial employees. This focus on labour vs management highlights conflicts of interest (as well as other subcultural differences associated with demographic markers such as sex or race), and is easily congruent with critical theory. For example, such conflicts of interest can be seen in two of the differentiation studies described above: in Bartunek and Moch's description of the subcultures that opposed and supported a change intervention in a food company, and in Van Maanen's tales of tension between supervisors, customers, and workers at a highly stratified Disneyland. Rosen (1985) offers a critical description of a corporate ritual, where dress norms and conversation reveal differentiated subcultures and their skeptical and hostile reactions to management's attempt to create an atmosphere of shared contentment (see also Burawoy 1979; Alvesson 1993). Studies such as these are congruent with a critical approach to differentiation research.

Clues to where differentiation studies stand on the managerial vs critical dimension can be most easily found in theoretical introductions, rather than in the content of descriptions of particular subcultures. Studies that take a more critical approach tend to cite some common intellectual predecessors to legitimate their theoretical orientation and anti-management tone. These include organizational scholars open to the insights of Marxist/critical theory, occupational research in the tradition of the Chicago school of sociology, and some early qualitative studies of organizations that included a focus on lower level employees (e.g. Selznick 1949; Jaques 1951; Crozier 1964). These intellectual predecessors share a concern with the everyday working lives of lower status people. This focus challenges the top management's views and delineates the negative consequences of the status quo on those who are relatively disadvantaged. Most

critical theorists join Mumby (quoted in Putnam et al. 1993: 226) in stressing the importance of critical work's link to action and change: 'The ultimate goal of critical theory is thus praxis – that is, the attainment of insight and the enactment of practical action informed by this insight'. It is therefore disappointing to note how few differentiation studies, even those written explicitly from a critical theory viewpoint, go beyond the delineation of subcultural differences and friction or resistance to examine processes of organizational change that might benefit those who are at the bottom of an organizational hierarchy, for example in a grass roots collective action. Although several literatures are relevant to these questions of change (for example, research on social movements, unions and sabotage), these issues have received relatively little attention to date from differentiation researchers.

Fragmentation studies can also be classified as managerial or critical. For example, managerially oriented fragmentation studies describe ambiguity as a tool that management can use to take advantage of differences in the interpretation of organizational events or 'corporate values' (see Kreiner and Schultz' (1993) study of cross-organizational organizing, Cohen and March's (1974) description of ambiguity in decision-making, and Eisenberg (1984) or McCaskey (1988) on executive's deliberate use of ambiguity). Some critically-oriented fragmentation studies show how executives deny the existence of ambiguity and offer a false claim of clarity in a complex arena, as in Perrow's (1984) study of the Three Mile Island nuclear reactor disaster and Sabrosky et al.'s (1982) examination of ambiguity in high levels of the US military command structure (see also Wilmott 1993; Grafton-Small and Linstead 1995; van Marrewijk 1996; van Reine 1996).

Thus, the struggle between managerial and critical viewpoints has intensified, highlighting differences in orientation towards power and control. This difference of opinion cross cuts the lines drawn between the integration, differentiation and fragmentation perspectives; advocates of managerial and critical approaches find their homes within each of these perspectives. Other cultural researchers did not play this round of the King of the Mountain game, clinging to the notion that it was still possible to conduct politically neutral objective research, free from bias and ideological influences. Meanwhile, down at the other end of the beach, a second King of the Mountain game was gathering players, with quantitative and qualitative researchers each struggling to articulate the strengths and even the superiority of their preferred methodologies. In time, methodological disputes became the second vector to cut across the three perspectives.

My Methodology is Better Than Yours

Disagreements about methodology permeate organizational research; they are not unique to cultural studies. These struggles continue with intensity because ontological and epistemological differences underlie qualitative and quantitative methods choices, affecting fundamental ideas about the nature of an organization – how it is constituted and how knowledge can contribute to understanding it. Because these convictions are deeply held, it is rare and difficult for most researchers to embrace both qualitative and quantitative methods. Especially in the US, many scholars adhere to traditional neo-positivist assumptions about knowledge building, which lead some to advocate hypothesis testing and quantitative methods. In Europe and elsewhere, a broader variety of ontologies, epistemologies and methods (often qualitative) are preferred. Such generalizations, however, are misleading. There are variations within geographical areas. Relationships among ontology, epistemology and methodology are not simple, constant or easily summarized in a paragraph or two, in part because organizational scholars differ among themselves about what these relationships are or should be (e.g. Burrell and Morgan 1979; Chia 2000). Given the cultural focus of this chapter, and space limitations, we will focus here simply on methods preferences, but it is important to note that the intensity of conflicts about methodology occurs because of these underlying, fundamental differences in assumptions.

In the cultural arena, some statements about methods preferences, and sometimes underlying epistemological or ontological positions, do take place out in the open (Hassard and Pym 1990; Tsoukas and Knudsen 2003). For example, quantitative methods are carefully justified in some recent edited books that focus on the relationship between organizational culture and the concept of climate, which has traditionally been measured with questionnaires (e.g. Ashkanasy et al. 2000b; Cooper et al.

2001). Qualitative methods for studying culture have been carefully justified as well (e.g. Putnam 1983; Van Maanen 1988). Researchers sometimes take umbrage at such methodological preferences. For example, Ashkanasy (2003) in a review of Martin (2002), refers to Martin's 'dismissive language reserved … for quantitative methods'. Quantitative researchers have been equally dismissive of qualitative research. For example, Denison (2003: 121) observes that Ashkanasy et al. (2000a) 'begin by acknowledging the value of qualitative methods but characterize them as complex, expensive and time-consuming. With this simple and persuasive rationale, the authors then review 18 quantitative measures of organizational culture …'.

These methodological preferences are expressed even more intensely in private or confidential settings (as in 'for example is no proof' and 'this is journalism, not science'). Such differences of opinion about methods are sometimes invoked, for example, in an editor's choice of journal reviewers for a culture article, a 'blind' reviewer's verdict about the merits of a particular manuscript, assumptions about how doctoral students should be trained, and even the content of letters from external reviewers in tenure cases. Such out-of-sight maneouvres leave few published traces that can be quoted here without breaking norms of confidentiality and blind review. Nevertheless, these non-public differences of opinion are deeply felt and consequential. Below, we summarize some of the key elements of these methods disputes, beginning with an examination of quantitative cultural research.

Most quantitative culture researchers use questionnaires to measure culture, drawing primarily on techniques used in organizational climate research (Schneider 1990). Such questionnaires are generally 'specialist' in that they focus on only one kind of cultural manifestation – usually a measure of agreement with a series of espoused (rather than enacted) values or a self-report of group behavioural norms (e.g. 'People in my work group are generally more co-operative than competitive'). Although such measures generally use Likert scales (Denison 1990), other studies have used more innovative techniques, such as adjective sorting tasks (e.g. O'Reilly et al. 1991). There are several problems with these kinds of quantitative measures of culture. Here the distinction between specialist (one or at most two manifestations of culture) and generalist (multiple manifestations) becomes relevant again.

Specialist studies tacitly assume that one kind of manifestation is consistent with or representative of the culture as a whole, disregarding the numerous differentiation studies that show evidence of inconsistency across manifestations. Additionally, there are problems of bias. Fearing that researchers' promises of anonymity will not be kept, respondents may give misleading answers that are reflective of top management's expressed preferences, rather than their own actual beliefs or behaviours. In this way, respondents create a false impression, usually one of organizational consensus. Additional bias occurs when respondents give answers that seem socially desirable or that reflect their current levels of job satisfaction (high or low), rather than answers that reveal a more enduring quality of their experience. Responses that contradict the assumptions of the researcher's theoretical perspective, and respondents who are likely to dissent from the researcher's assumptions, may be excluded from discussion and analysis – as not part of the culture (cf. Kilmann 1985; Rousseau 1990).

These kinds of quantitative measures may give a misleading representation of a culture because the researcher has generated the alternatives that the respondents are evaluating. Several innovative quantitative measures of culture avoid this problem. For example, Kilduff and Corley (2000) have developed non-reactive network measures of the three theoretical perspectives. Kolb and Shepherd (1997) created a novel measure of concept mapping. Siehl and Martin (1984) studied cultural learning with a company-specific jargon vocabulary test and a 'tacit knowledge test' (randomly selected words in a memo from the organization's president were blacked out, employees were asked to 'fill in the blanks', and responses were coded for degree of similarity to the CEO's own word choices). Even these relatively innovative quantitative methods have been criticized by qualitative researchers, primarily due to concerns about depth and breadth of cultural understanding.

Advocates of ethnographic methods generally prefer broad, generalist studies that offer richly detailed descriptions of a wide range of cultural manifestations (e.g. Smircich and Morgan 1982; Van Maanen et al. 1982; Smircich 1983; Schein 1987; Kunda 1992), especially if longitudinal data have been collected (e.g. Pettigrew 1985a, b). Many ethnographers disapprove when specialist studies focus on espoused values or self-reported behavioural norms

because such a 'superficial' focus cannot 'penetrate the front' of people's desires to present themselves in a favourable light. For all these reasons, ethnographers often consider quantitative studies far inferior to the depth of understanding made possible by long-term participant-observation and the researcher's context-specific insights (Schein 1985). This concern is particularly relevant in organizational contexts, where behaviour is often constrained by managerial preferences or employees' career ambitions and thus cannot be assumed to reflect an employee's true attitudes. According to this point of view, the long-term involvement of the ethnographic researcher (as a participant-observer or observer, not a directive interviewer) would make the researcher's presence be less disruptive of normal interaction, permitting the collection of less biased data.

Qualitative culture researchers disagree among themselves about the importance of in-depth understanding. Some ethnographers criticize short-term and/or interview-based qualitative studies as being 'smash and grab' ethnographies. A researcher would have to spend months or even years as a participant before he or she could truly 'penetrate the front' of cultural members and see things from an insider's 'emic' perspective. Anything less, according to these critics, is worthy of being classified as exploratory pilot testing – in short, probably not worth mentioning in print (see Sutton (1994) for a frank discussion of these issues). Recently, innovative qualitative methods that avoid some of these shortcomings have been introduced. For example, Witmer (1997) applied Gidden's theory of structuration to the analysis of ethnographic data, using an interpretive, interactionist methodology. Wilson (2000) combined a 'repertory grid method' of repeated interviewing, supplemented by group discussions, analysis of company documents, and observation and reflection by the author.

Many ethnographers had thought that the cultural movement would provide respect, particularly in the US where qualitative methods had been so disparaged. Some were disappointed, therefore, when the cultural domain of organizational research, like so many of the others, was in danger of being taken over by the number crunchers (Calas and Smircich 1987; Barley et al. 1988). This reaction was also expressed in public forums and reviews by the usual strategies of silence and marginalization. In more private arenas, such as 'blind reviews', the negative reaction to qualitative methods was more pronounced and many researchers felt it was difficult to get their work published due to methods preferences of reviewers and editors. When asked to evaluate research utilizing non-preferred methods, some reviewers were openly dismissive (see discussions of the reviewing process in cultural research by Martin (2002) and Rousseau (1994)). Others responded to resistance to qualitative methods constructively, by citing texts justifying their methods choices and outlining the fundamentals of good qualitative research methodology (some helpful texts include Blau 1965; Glaser and Strauss 1967; Agar 1986; Schein 1987; Golden-Biddle and Locke 1997; Nord and Connell 1998). In a promising recent development, some major journal editors have acted as peacekeepers, opening their pages to qualitative work, thereby adding some balance to the debate.

The result was, at first, an open and informative debate over the merits of qualitative and quantitative methods for studying culture. In recent years, this competition has eased a bit, and gone underground, but the issues remain unresolved in many quarters (see the edited volumes by Hassard and Pym (1990) and Tsoukas and Knudsen (2003)). There are fewer openly combative exchanges in public, and more studies use both qualitative and quantitative methods (e.g. Denison 1990). Nevertheless, the more private and less visible forms of battle continue as doctoral students are advised to avoid one method or another. Given the deep differences of epistemology and the training investments that underlie these disputes, agreement is unlikely. Although it can convincingly be argued that cultural research has, as some hoped, opened new doors to qualitative methods, it is not clear what studies or arguments could convincingly resolve these differences of opinion.

A Meta-Theoretical Move

The game of King of the Mountain was now being played in earnest, as shifting coalitions of players argued for the intellectual dominance of their own points of view. Initially there was a struggle among the integration, differentiation and fragmentation perspectives. Critical theorists and managerially oriented researchers created variants of each of the three perspectives, adding consideration of political interests to the mix of concerns. Other researchers stayed apart from this particular part of the fray, preferring to view research as objective, rather than swayed by political interests. Next, advocates of qualitative and quantitative methods entered the game, each claiming their method preference produced superior insight into cultures in organizations. The next move in the game was obvious: to bring some (but not all) of these differences under the rubric of a single framework. The methods differences outlined above were not easily reconciled (due in large part by underlying differences in ontological and epistemological assumptions). The three perspectives, however, and their critical and managerial variants, could be reconceptualized – not as competing alternatives – but as complementary parts of a meta-theory. Such a theoretical synthesis, it could be argued, was merited because each of the three perspectives, and their critical and managerial variants, had been supported by empirical evidence. If none could be rejected out of hand, perhaps each might represent a piece of a larger puzzle.

How could advocates of each of the single perspectives come up with supporting evidence, when the premises of those three perspectives were contradictory? Martin (1992) observed that integration, differentiation and fragmentation researchers defined culture in a particular way, then designed studies that made it more likely to find what they were looking for. For example, integration studies exclude, or label as undesirable, any issue that generates multiple interpretations rather than organization-wide consensus. In addition, most integration studies rely on data from managerial and professional employees, rather than all members of an organization. Such integration studies collect data from a small and unrepresentative sample of employees and then generalize to the culture of the organization as a whole. This presents a problem because it cannot be assumed that all or even most employees share the views of this minority of powerful individuals, particularly given the likelihood of differences of opinion across levels of a hierarchy (e.g. Young 1989; Alvesson 1993). Specialist integration studies make a similar part–whole error when they generalize from the study of a single kind of manifestation to the culture as a whole, assuming interpretations of all kinds of manifestations are consistent. Such part–whole errors concerning consistency, consensus and subject samples create a kind of tautology, whereby culture is defined and then measured in integration terms; evidence that is not congruent with this conceptual and empirical focus is ignored or dismissed as not part of the culture, or not part of a 'strong' culture.

Tautologies of this sort are not unique to integration research. In most differentiation studies no evidence of organization-wide consensus is sought and ambiguity is acknowledged only when it occurs outside subcultural borders (Martin and Meyerson 1988; Martin 1992). Differentiation studies define culture in terms of inconsistency, subcultural consensus and subcultural clarity, and that is what they find. Similarly, fragmentation studies often tend to focus on occupations (i.e. social worker, policy analyst) and contexts where ambiguity is easily seen (i.e. multi-lingual communication, literally in the fog, or rapidly changing industries that must cope with a turbulent environment). Such choices make it easier for fragmentation studies to conclude that ambiguity (including irony, contradictions, paradoxes, etc.) is a highly visible feature of the cultures studied. As noted regarding research conducted from the other two perspectives, fragmentation studies exhibit a kind of methodological tautology: these studies define culture in a particular way, and then find what they are looking for (Martin 2002).

This problem of tautology explains, to some extent, why evidence congruent with each perspective had been found. (Indeed, some have argued that similar tautological problems characterize all of organizational research; see Morgan 1983b). Rather than arguing that some cultures are more accurately conceptualized in terms of one perspective rather than another, Martin (1992; 2002) draws on empirical evidence to argue that *any* organizational culture contains elements congruent with all three perspectives. If any organization is studied in enough depth, some issues, values and objectives will been seen to generate organization-wide consensus, consistency and clarity (an integration view). At the same time, other aspects of an organization's culture will coalesce into subcultures that hold conflicting opinions about what is important, what should happen and why (a differentiation view). Finally, some problems and issues will be ambiguous, in a state of constant flux, generating multiple, plausible interpretations (a fragmentation view).

Studies of a wide range of organizational contexts have provided empirical support for the three-perspective framework. These include studies of a temporary educational organization for unemployed women in England, a newly privatized bank in

Turkey, truants from an urban high school in the US, changing organizational culture in the Peace Corps/Africa, a university provost search, and professional subcultures in an Australian home care service (Meyerson and Martin 1987; Enomoto 1993; Baburoglu and Gocer 1994; Bloor and Dawson 1994; Eisenberg et al. 1998; Kilduff and Corley 2000). Implicit in the three-perspective framework is the assumption that these social scientific viewpoints are subjectively imposed on the process of collecting and interpreting cultural data. Often one perspective, labelled the 'home' viewpoint, is easy for cultural members and researchers to acknowledge, while the other two perspectives can be more difficult to access. It is therefore a misunderstanding to conclude that a particular organization has a culture that is best characterized by one of the three perspectives. Rather, any culture at any point in time will have some aspects congruent with all three perspectives.

According to the three-perspective framework, when a cultural context is viewed from all three perspectives, a more complex understanding will emerge. This understanding will be broader than a single-perspective study (because data consistent with more than one perspective will be examined) and deeper (because the analysis will not stop at the easy-to-see home perspective, but will explore the two less accessible perspectives as well). The three-perspective framework is a meta-theory because the theory encompasses all three perspectives, moving to a higher level of abstraction to do so. Such a meta-theoretical move can be interpreted appreciatively or critically. Appreciatively, it can be seen as an acknowledgement of the careful research that has generated support for each of the three perspectives, in both their managerial and critical instantiations. Rather than ignoring these findings, the three-perspective framework is an attempt to signal the importance of each, as a lens for seeing cultures in their complexity.

More critically, the three-perspective framework can be viewed as an attempt to dominate other approaches to understanding cultures in organizations – a classic attempt to become King of the Mountain. Postmodern critiques of such meta-theories (e.g. Lyotard 1984; Gagliardi 1991) label meta-theories as 'narratives of transcendence' because each claims to be better than its predecessors – more abstract and yet also closer to 'the' empirical 'truth'. Such meta-theories have been viewed as totalitarian attempts, by those who are or wish to become dominant, to provide all-encompassing world views that silence diversity of opinion.

This criticism has some merit (Martin 1992). The three-perspective meta-theory is based on a series of undeconstructed categories that position the three perspectives in opposition to one another. It ignores aspects of theories and studies that straddle boundaries among the perspectives (see especially, rich ethnographies such as Kunda (1992) and Pettigrew (1985b)), omits unclassifiable research or relegates it to marginalized places in the text, and only addresses issues that transcend these categories in places (such as footnotes and parenthetical remarks) separated from the main bodies of texts. Most importantly, use of these tripartite categories to classify studies reifies the perspectives and pigeonholes individual studies into boxes, thereby diminishing the uniqueness of their contributions (cf. Schultz and Hatch 1996). While such a use of categories is not unique to this particular attempt to build a meta-theory, it can be seen to have harmful effects on knowledge creation and the ways scholarly work is and is not evaluated (e.g. Turner 1989; Gagliardi 1990). Thus, the three-perspective framework can be seen as a conventional competitive move in the King of the Mountain game. A less critical reading of postmodernists such as Lyotard might conclude that his references to master narratives, such as Marxism and Freudian thought, are more all-inclusive than the three-perspective meta-theory. From this viewpoint, some postmodernists might approve of a three-perspective approach as using multiple lenses to view a phenomenon.

Switching Metaphors

And so it goes; cultural researchers do not agree about theory, method, epistemology or the conclusions to be drawn from the empirical record to date. In spite of (or perhaps because of) this lack of consensus, the last decade of cultural research has produced a variety of insightful, innovative studies that might not have been conducted within the narrower orthodoxies of theory and method that have constrained other kinds of organizational inquiry. Cultural studies have brought epistemological and methodological variety to the field and introduced ideas from other disciplines. Qualitative generalist culture research has offered richly detailed, context-specific descriptions of organizational life, while quantitative culture studies and comparisons of qualitative case studies (see Blau 1965) have offered cross-organizational comparisons that would otherwise have been difficult to make. Postmodern thought, however, challenges the worth of these accomplishments. Postmodern scholars argue that attempts to create meta-theories, or to establish any form of intellectual dominance, are futile because multiplicity will always find a way to flourish. If taken seriously, this postmodern critique challenges the premises of the competitive game. Although this postmodern position can be configured as the ultimate move in a game of intellectual dominance, it also can be interpreted as a call to stop participating in struggles for intellectual dominance.

There are other reasons to abandon the king of the mountain metaphor at this point. In the last decade, many have come to believe that the strident conflicts of the early days of culture research have been muted. For example, Denison (2003: 123) concludes that 'The divisive paradigm wars of the past seem to have given way to healthy underlying tensions and reflect some of the critical issues in organizational studies itself'. To some extent we would concur, but it is also the case, as noted in the introduction to this paper, that some of this apparent harmony and 'healthy tension' is simply a symptom of conflict having gone underground, where its destructive potential can escalate because it is less visible (Kolb and Bartunek 1992). Because the tone of the discussion today is less strident than it was a decade ago, we removed the military metaphors (such as 'culture wars' and 'attacks') found in the earlier (1996) version of this chapter. However, believing that conflict that is hidden is still conflict, in the first part of this paper we have retained the competitive King of the Mountain metaphor, to emphasize the struggle for intellectual dominance that has characterized cultural studies of organizations. We understand that 'outing' such competitiveness, in a field that prides itself on cordial norms of discourse, is discomforting. Nonetheless, we believe it accurately highlights some aspects of what has been going on, both in print, at public talks and in private conversations.

Still, the less strident tone of today's discussion (e.g. 'healthy tensions'), and the prompting of postmodern views, suggests a second metaphor may be useful at this point in the text. The relationships between critical theory and postmodernism, and across the three perspectives, are more fluid and complex than so far acknowledged. The King of the

Mountain metaphor reads aggression, intentionality and coalition building into acts that may have not had any of these characteristics. Competitive metaphors emphasize hierarchy, restrict flexibility because they dwell on constraints rather than opportunities, and force choices among a fixed set of solutions. In this way, the King of the Mountain metaphor may tacitly legitimate and even encourage competitive behaviour, thereby becoming a self-fulfilling prophecy (Burrell et al. 1992; Wilson 1992).[6] Even if back-stabbing, selfish or nasty behaviour has occurred on the academic playing fields (and we think it still does), we believe invoking such pain and destruction as a rhetorical device may not help the problem. We decided to examine what other aspects of the cultural domain would be emphasized if we approached the field with a different metaphor.[7] We sought a rhetorical strategy that would enable us to promote an open and open-minded, constructive discussion of differences of opinion about cultural theories, political interests and research methods. We chose the metaphor of a conversation because it is more multi-vocal than a dialogue and less combative than a debate.[8] Conversation offers an opportunity for discussion conducive to transformative conflict (Burrell et al. 1992) that can deepen understanding for all. Such a metaphor is particularly appropriate for discussing postmodernism, as so many cultural researchers (including especially some critical theorists) have found postmodern ideas to be useful and insightful.

Postmodernism: Questioning the Terms of Scientific Discussion

Although it is beyond the mandate of this chapter to discuss postmodernism at length (readers should consult the chapter by Alvesson and Deetz), it is important to discuss its implications for and contributions to the work on organizational culture (see Calas and Smircich 1988; Czarniawska-Joerges 1992; Linstead and Grafton-Small 1992; Jeffcutt et al. 1995). A mini-introduction may be helpful for those who have not yet tackled the admittedly esoteric, convoluted writings of postmodernists. There is not just one postmodernism. It is not a unified theory, in part because it has attracted such a diverse group of advocates, including architects, philosophers and literary critics. In all its varieties,

postmodernism challenges ideas that constitute the foundation of modern science: rationality, order, clarity, realism, truth and intellectual progress (e.g. Derrida 1976; Foucault 1976; Baudrillard 1983; Lyotard 1984; Marcus and Fischer 1999). Post-modernism argues that any point of view carries the seeds of its own destruction. Some find this conclusion dangerous because it gives postmodernism the capacity to undermine the ideological certainties that facilitate collective political action. Other activists argue that postmodern critical analysis is useful for challenging the ideologies of opponents (e.g. Calas and Smircich 1990; Martin 1990). In its relevance to cultural studies, perhaps postmodernism will offer more as an ideological and theoretical critique than as a theory of political action.

When contrasted to postmodern ideas, modern cultural studies attempt to provide coherent accounts and to order the disorder that is organizational life. Carrying this emphasis one step further, Integration studies offer a portrait of unity, harmony and, in many instances, the promise of cultural control. In contrast, postmodern accounts draw attention to disorder and offer a multiplicity of irreconcilable interpretations, making Integration studies particularly suspect from a postmodern viewpoint. Post-modernists argue that the relationship between the signifier and the signified, between an image and the original experience it was once produced to represent, is attenuated, complex and, in part, arbitrary. This arbitrariness should not be confused with the more tepid, manageable ambiguities, irrationalities and randomness that are the focus of fragmentation research. The key difference is that, while ambiguity implies a surplus of meaning attached to a particular object – a somewhat unclear, fuzzy, vague, obscure or enigmatic relation – arbitrariness implies a capricious or willful relationship that cannot be determined by any rule or principle. While an ambiguous relationship means that there is a way of understanding and capturing the way in which a signifier represents the signified, an arbitrary relationship makes no such assumptions (Alvesson and Berg 1992: 220). Thus, while the fragmentation perspective has some affinities with postmodernism, not all fragmentation studies have a postmodern flavour (Martin 2002).

Modern (as opposed to postmodern) cultural studies, particularly 'realistic' ethnographies, attempt to cut through superficial cultural manifestations and interpretations to uncover a deeper reality, revealing knowledge that is closer to the truth.

Modern scholarship is careful to draw distinctions among the objective truth about reality, the subjectivity of a researcher-author and a text. These distinctions, however, are not inviolable. For example, modernist studies sometimes claim the flaws of an imperfect relationship between reality and data can be improved by more rigorous methods. Modern scholars also sometimes acknowledge a flawed relationship between presumably objective data and its imperfect representation in a text, but argue it can be improved by clearer, more 'transparent' writing. More rarely, a modernist author may engage in self-reflexivity concerning the effects of his or her individualized subjectivity on a text (e.g. Van Maanen 1988; Kunda 1992; Lundberg 2001). Such introspection is usually confined to the margins of a text (an introduction, an anecdote or an appendix, i.e. Kunda 1992). Marginalization enables the modern author to maintain the impersonal, supposedly objective style and language that sustains scientific credibility by making the individualized subjectivity of the author invisible in the main body of the text (e.g. Clifford and Marcus 1986).

In contrast, from a postmodern point of view, reality is a series of fictions and illusions (Clifford and Marcus 1986; Alvesson and Berg 1992). A text is not a closed system; rather, it reflects the subjective views of its author, other texts, those who read and those whose views are quoted, included, suppressed or excluded (e.g. Linstead and Grafton-Small 1992; Hassard and Parker 1993). This focus on representational issues, such as the ways impersonal language reinforces the authority of an author, undermines any claim that a text can represent the objective truth about a reality that is 'out there' – separable from the text (e.g. Cooper and Burrell 1988; Jeffcutt et al. 1995; Smircich 1995). Truth therefore becomes 'a matter of credibility rather than an objective condition' (Alvesson and Berg 1992: 223). Whereas modern scholars argue about what the truth is or what methods or modes of engagement would bring research closer to truth, postmodernists use analytic techniques such as deconstruction to reveal strategies used to establish the illusion of truth in a text. Deconstruction shows how: an author establishes his or her credibility; particular data are selected and interpreted (to the exclusion of other, equally valid data and interpretations); uncertainties are hidden; opposing meanings are suppressed or omitted; and unintended and suppressed viewpoints emerge in the margins of a text (such as footnotes, asides,

metaphors, etc.). (For examples of deconstruction of theories and speech relevant to organizational culture, see Calas and Smircich (1991), Czarniawska-Joerges (1992) and Martin (1990).) Postmodernist cultural scholars use textual analysis to interrogate, disrupt and overturn claims to truth or theoretical superiority (e.g. Gagliardi 1991; Jeffcutt et al. 1995). Their goal is not to establish a better theory of culture (this would perpetuate the struggle for intellectual dominance of the field), but rather to show why the truth claims of modern cultural scholarship merit challenge and reinterpretation (Smircich and Calas 1987; Alvesson and Berg 1992; Willmott 1993).

Many would not want to engage with postmodernism, asking, 'What positive contribution does it make?' In the 1990s, many dismissed it on grounds that it is esoteric, reactionary, a-political, too relativistic or nihilistic (e.g. Reed 1990). This reaction has been particularly strong among some empirical, relatively positivistic culture researchers, perhaps because postmodernism represents a deep challenge to basic tenets of the scientific method. Rather than seeing only the threat that the burgeoning postmodern literature represents, many contemporary organizational researchers (especially those of a critical persuasion) have learned from and used some aspects of postmodern thinking (e.g. Grant et al. 2004), as our counterparts in anthropology have done. Postmodern analysis is useful to organizational culture researchers because it reveals false claims of certainty. It offers a textual approach to greater intellectual honesty, or at least humility, in research. It uncovers insights hidden from view by accepted theories and methods. A postmodern approach could most certainly offer insight into the representational strategies that make cultural accounts more like fiction than like science (e.g. Calas 1987; Van Maanen 1988; Jermier 1992). Our cultural texts could become more self-reflexive and we could seek, as anthropologists are now doing, new ways of writing about culture that allow multiple voices to be heard and deconstructed, without transforming the researcher into a transcriber who has given informants total control of and responsibility for the text (Clifford and Marcus 1986; Van Maanen 1988; Martin 2002). Reflexivity is encouraged, researchers' and study participants' views can be contrasted, and multi-vocal texts can represent a variety of points of view. It is important to acknowledge, however, that adoption of such insights would not represent a major change in modern cultural research strategies, nor would it fully acknowledge the depth of the challenge to the scientific method that would follow from a full acceptance of postmodern ideas (Alvesson and Berg 1992).

In the first sections of this chapter, we describe the various moves in the King of the Mountain game as if these modernist culture scholars were saying 'My approach is deeper, more complex, or more inclusive than yours' (ethnography, a longitudinal approach or the three-perspective framework) or 'Look what you have been ignoring' (the fragmentation perspective). Such claims have in common the implication that each view is, somehow, closer to the truth about a culture. All are attempts to impose order and meaning. A postmodern critique would deconstruct these attempts to establish intellectual dominance. For example, such a critique would show how all these modern studies refrain from fully exploring the inherent and inescapable limitations of textual representation. Rather than perpetuating the King of the Mountain game, where each new theory or meta-theory attempts to dominate other current contenders, postmodernism is an attempt to change the terms of engagement. No longer are we discussing ways to 'penetrate the front' of cultural members and get closer to some truth; now truth is impossible to represent. Rather than labelling this ironically, as the ultimate competitive move, postmodernism could be seen as offering opening remarks in a conversation that has the capacity to change how organizational culture researchers think, talk and write.

When Cultural Research is Seen as a Conversation

When the metaphor of conversation is used, different topics of cultural study become salient. For example, consider the question: 'Where are the boundaries of a culture?' Swidler (1986) observed that cultures become most visible at their edges, where cultural work is being done to define what is and what is not characteristic of the culture. Others have noted that cultural boundaries are moveable, as when norm-loosening rituals (such as drinking together) are held off-site (e.g. Douglas 1975; Van Maanen 1986). Pettigrew (1985b) and Czarniawska-Joerges (1992) have observed that cultural boundaries fluctuate, alternately expanding and collapsing inward, as if a person were breathing. Cultural boundaries are also seen as permeable, like the

membranes of a cell that permit osmosis (e.g. Marcus and Fischer 1986/1999; Swidler 1986; Kreiner and Schultz 1993). Finally, cultural boundaries are blurred, at times in a self-conscious negotiation, and other times in a thoughtless evolution (e.g. Clifford 1997; Gupta and Ferguson 1997). Anthropologists now critique earlier studies that portrayed cultures as if societies existed in a mosaic, with each firmly bordered culture co-existing, but not overlapping with its neighbours (Keesing 1981: 111–3). Sahlins (1985) uses a similar metaphor, decrying studies that described cultures as a-historical 'islands of history'. These are arguments for the longitudinal study of external cultural influences. Such ideas are extensions of the 'nexus' approach to describing external cultural influences on subculturally differentiated organizations. They are congruent with a call to reconceptualize cultural boundaries as moveable, fluctuating, permeable and blurred (Batteau 2001; Martin 2002) – a conceptual move that would push us to re-evaluate much prior organizational culture research.[9]

These approaches to defining boundaries may even help us understand the cultures of global, wired organizations of individuals and teams who meet on line, rarely face-to-face (e.g. Dunbar and Garud 2001; Hedberg and Maravelias 2001; Barley and Kunda 2004). For example, The Well was arguably the first strongly committed community of people that 'lived' and worked together on the internet (e.g. Hafner 1997), one that evolved an odd but deeply involving on-line culture (one member literally chose to die while on line to supportive community members). Garsten (1999) studied the transient and episodic imagined cultures of US and Swedish temporary employees of flexible organizations. Consider the even greater difficulties of capturing the culture of an international cable company that consists of temporary teams of international workers, who speak different languages and gather only to perform a labourious task, like laying cable in Thailand or across the Indian ocean, and then disperse, only to reconfigure themselves in other teams in other places (Stephenson 1996). These examples show how it is increasingly difficult to separate the study of cultures across levels of analysis. The internet, air travel and an international economy have indelibly blurred and in some case erased these boundaries.

Other scholars use cultural language to describe what they do, but are involved in issues that transcend the concerns of the three perspective framework and break through boundaries of cultural research. For example, Strati (1992) and Gagliardi (1990) focus on the aesthetic aspects of cultures in organizations, especially on interpretations and effects of cultural manifestations that can been seen, felt or heard, like furniture, noise, dirt, music and architecture. Aaltio and Mills (2002); Kanter (1977) and Mills (1995; 1997) have pioneered research on the gendered aspects of organizational cultures, for example studying airlines that have had strict occupational sex segregation between pilots and flight attendants. Other gendered culture studies focus on the ways ostensibly gender-neutral 'equal opportunity' initiatives recreate traditionally gendered practices (e.g. Rubin 1997; Woodall et al. 1997). Some of these studies explore differences in gendered practices across organizational boundaries (e.g. Poggio 2000). Other studies of gendered cultures seem to have more in common with fragmentation research, for example, those that examine ambivalence among male and female secretaries (e.g. Pringle 1989; Sotirin and Gottfried 1999), the complexity of changing approaches to gender research in an organizational journal (Townsley 2003), and the ambiguities inherent in gendered organizations (Gherardi 1995; Hearn 1998), such as a transnational academic feminist organization (Mendez and Wolf 2001). Each of these kinds of research enters a conversation with cultural studies, and then moves on to address broader issues.

As a result of these kinds of cross-topic conversations, the boundary around cultural research has become permeable and sometimes disputed. Perhaps the most explicit boundary negotiations have occurred between organizational climate and organizational culture researchers, some of whom have devoted considerable energy to articulating how their respective approaches differ and overlap (e.g. Schneider 1990; Denison 1996; Ashkanasy et al. 2000b; Schein 2000; Ostroff et al. 2003).[10] When specialist integration studies of climate and culture use quantitative methods, the overlap and synergy between these traditions is evident. Generalist studies from other perspectives, using qualitative methods, have less evident commonality, which may explain why some cultural studies have failed to acknowledge the contributions of climate research.

Other areas of inquiry have evolved in a clear attempt to differentiate their area of inquiry from cultural studies. It is unclear, in some cases, whether this is cultural research under another label, or whether these are conceptually distinct areas of inquiry. For example, Albert and Whetton (1985) introduced the topic of organizational identity, defining identity as that which is central, enduring and distinctive to an organization, directly echoing the concerns of the integration perspective of cultural research. Hatch and Schultz (1997) convincingly distinguish the territory of culture from that of organizational identity, going on to define various aspects of perceived identity, distinguishing it from an organization's external image. Subsequent work on identity and image has added complexities, some of which echo aspects of the three perspective framework (e.g. Parker 2000) and others which do not (e.g. Dutton and Dukerich 1991). Finally, discourse analysis is another related area of inquiry that has the capacity to deeply inform cultural studies, especially in so far as it draws attention to ideational influences from outside the highly permeable boundaries of any particular 'culture' (e.g. Chia 2000; Alvesson 2004; Grant et al. 2004). The permeability and moveability of the boundaries around culture and related topics are evident here, in a manner more congruent with the idea of an open conversation rather than a struggle for intellectual dominance.

Then and Next

Like others, we originally came to the cultural arena excited about the ways it would open organizational studies to new kinds of thinking. It was astonishing to us, however, to see how quickly this apparently open conceptual terrain became cluttered (in part, by ourselves) with competing theories, boxes, categorizations and so forth. Many of these became reified in the emerging struggles for intellectual dominance. During the last decade, many of the most playful, inquiring, irreverent and inventing voices have left the cultural field or played less frequently on it. Culture has become a part of the hegemony within organizational theory and practice. This quixotic victory had the paradoxical effect of 'deaden-ing' culture's effect on open inquiry, a point made most eloquently by Smircich and Calas as long ago as 1987. Perhaps this is the fate of all innovative endeavours. They either die out or, if success strikes, they become co-opted and routinized so they can be used in organizations (Frost and Egri

1991). Such developments are not all negative since we must have ways to preserve creative and useful ideas and practices. However, we believe that efforts are needed to balance or even unbalance competitive mindsets, thereby counteracting the tendency for theories and methods to become constraining boxes that impede open-minded inquiry.

We seek some mechanisms to foster freer thinking that has the capacity to learn from and about the King of the Mountain games, but that can also be used to negotiate peaceful, open-minded conversation. Regarding organizational culture studies as a conversation expands the scope of ideas, cultural contexts and bodies of data that become relevant. Ostensibly non-cultural research becomes relevant. The types of organizations able to be examined as cultures grow to include even wired communities of people who meet only online, but nevertheless may have a discernible cultural identity. Such an expanded view will encourage us to ask not just what a culture is, but also what an organization is. These developments may well prompt some to seek again to define that which is unique to cultural theory (e.g. Willmott 2000), albeit from a more empirically sophisticated and epistemologically well informed position than was prevalent at the start of the cultural renaissance in organizational studies. Nevertheless, we believe it is at the edges of cultural theory where the most fundamental and interesting questions arise. The game of King of the Mountain will always be a part of cultural studies, whether the struggle for intellectual dominance is played out in the open, in the more secretive back alleys of academic life, or, less consciously, being implicit in the ways cultural research is conducted, reported and published. Competitive games don't typically end: as soon as a winner is declared another tournament begins. We expect this to continue in the culture arena. We suspect, however, that regarding cultural studies as a conversation will be far more generative and perhaps, more fun.

Acknowledgements

We wish to express our thanks to Cynthia Hardy, Mats Alvesson and Linda Putnam. All three gave us the kind of constructive, appreciative critique that could serve as the norm for discourse in a more collaborative intellectual environment. We note with great sadness the death of our colleague Peter Frost.

Notes

1. The scope of this chapter is limited in several other ways. We regret we cannot include the extensive socio-cultural work done by discipline-based sociologists and anthropologists. We begin our account in the 1970s, as if organizational culture research began then, without antecedents. However, we do cite some intellectual predecessors of particular points of view, as contributors of the history of the ideas and as totems invoked to legitimate certain points of view, drawing attention to the exclusion of other viewpoints with equally venerable intellectual lineage. We chose to constrain the historical depth of this review because of space limitations and because extensive historical treatments of organizational culture research already exist (e.g. Ouchi and Wilkins 1985; Smircich and Calas 1987; Turner 1990; Alvesson and Berg 1992; Jeffcutt et al. 1995).

2. Most international culture researchers argue that values should be the focus of cross-national studies (e.g. House et al. 1999; Sagiv and Schwartz 2000). Hofstede and Peterson (2000) also take a specialist integration perspective, arguing that values should be the focus of international culture research and behaviour should be the focus of cultural research at the organizational level of analysis.

3. See Lawrence and Lorsch (1967) for the seminal articulation of the tensions between integration and differentiation in organizational structures.

4. Although Schein (1985; 1987) is one of the best known advocates of an integration approach to culture, his emphasis on the importance of depth of understanding has been echoed and utilized by a wide range of cultural researchers, particularly those who use ethnographic methods to study cultures from a differentiation or fragmentation viewpoint. Whereas Schein, in the integration tradition, finds evidence of deeply held assumptions that are shared on an organization-wide basis, the differentiation researchers cited here use depth to reveal long-standing inter-group differences.

5. This nexus approach can be used to conceptualize overlap and nesting among national cultures as well, see Sackmann (1997).

6. In addition, some scholars have argued that competitive metaphors are gendered because such characteristics as aggression, war and competition are more frequently associated with masculine rather than feminine stereotypes (e.g. Burrell et al. 1992; Wilson 1992). We are a team of co-authors with feminist convictions, and yet we have painted a portrait of cultural research that emphasizes power, competition, conflict and domination, perhaps creating a self-fulfilling prophecy, or at least over-emphasizing these aspects of the research process.

7. We have been urged, by several readers of the earlier version of this chapter, to use the metaphor of a dance to describe relationships among differing points of view in cultural studies, as they 'embrace', 'take turns leading'

and become 'intertwined'. It is true that some attributes of this metaphor are apt, for example as partners in a dance must learn how close or how far to move, how to create something graceful, etc. However, the dance metaphor romanticizes struggles for intellectual dominance, ignores their destructive properties, and makes their import seem less serious.

8. Gherardi, Marshall and Mills faced a similar difficulty when they were asked to contribute to an edited volume (Westwood and Clegg 2003: 327) which was described as a debate, a 'text constructed around dyads of point and counterpoint, thesis to antithesis, paradigm against paradigm'. This trio of authors objected to this competitive structure and decided to reframe their task so they could build 'on each others' contributions rather than arguing competing positions (p. 325).

9. Such a discussion of boundaries mandates a brief excursion outside the scope of this chapter, into the burgeoning international culture literature. Early research on industrial and national culture in organizational studies usually assumed a mosaic approach and described culture in integration terms, each culture a clearly bounded unity. Some studies of national cultures are specialist (single manifestation) studies, using researcher-generated Likert measures of agreement with researcher-generated questions about values or self-reported behavioural norms to make cross-national comparisons (see Ashkanasy et al. 2000b; Cooper et al. 2001, for reviews). These integrationist studies assume national cultural homogeneity and downplay or ignore within-culture differences (e.g. Bryman et al. 1996; House et al. 1999; Sagiv and Schwartz 2000, cf. Hofstede 2001). Once boundaries are redefined as permeable, fluctuating, moveable and blurred, relationships among organizational, industry, national and cross-national levels of cultural analysis become more difficult to conceptualize. Other kinds of national studies focus on the complexities of cultures given by internal differences – across organizations, across age groups, classes and ethnicities, and between urban and rural locations (e.g. Koot 1997; Sackmann 1997). For example, Weiss and Delbecq (1987) examine regional cultural differences in the high technology industry. Kondo (1990) reflexively deconstructs the effects of age, gender and family background in a small family owned business in Japan, focusing on problems of individual cultural identity. Yanagisako (2002) studies the textile industry in Northern Italy, where family-owned businesses grapple with inheritance laws that enable and sometimes require that businesses pass into the control of daughters as well as sons. These latter studies are generalist (multiple manifestations). They blur boundaries as they cross levels of analysis, acknowledging simultaneously, complexity within nations, industries and organizations. Some cross-national work (e.g. Dahler-Larsen 1997; Koot 1997; Sackmann 1997) has taken the study of cultural complexity even further, both clearly echoing all three

perspectives and going beyond the three perspective framework to wrestle with the difficulties of what a nexus is and how it requires that organizational and national culture be reconceptualized. This more complex theory is better suited to illuminate the cultural complexities of transnational organizations, collections of globally distributed subsidiaries, the amalgamated products of complex mergers, and well organized collections of cottage industries or franchises.

10. One major difference between the two is that while quantitative studies of cultures measure self-reports of behavioural norms (e.g. O'Reilly et al. 1991), climate is a measure of the psychological meaning of situations as perceived by individuals. For these reasons, the content, meaning and validity of the climate construct is believed to be isomorphic at multiple levels of analysis (Ostroff et al. 2003).

References

Aaltio, I. and Mills, A. (2002) *Organizational Culture and Gendered Identities in Context*. London: Routledge.

Agar, M. (1986) *Speaking of Ethnography*. Beverly Hills, CA: Sage.

Albert, S. and Whetton, D. (1985) 'Organizational identity', in L. Cummings and R. Staw (eds), *Research in Organizational Behavior*, Vol. 7. Greenwich, CT: JAI Press. pp. 263–95.

Alvesson, M. (1993) *Cultural Perspectives on Organizations*. Cambridge, UK: Cambridge University Press.

Alvesson, M. (2002) *Understanding Organizational Culture*. London: Sage.

Alvesson, M. (2004) 'Organizational culture and discourse', in D. Grant, C. Hardy, C. Oswick and L. Putnam (eds), *Handbook of Organizational Discourse*. Thousand Oaks, CA: Sage. pp. 317–36.

Alvesson, M. and Berg, P. (1992) *Corporate Culture and Organizational Symbolism*. Berlin: Walter de Gruyter.

Ashkanasy, N. (2003) 'Book review: Joanne Martin. 'Organizational Culture: Mapping the Terrain'', *Personnel Psychology*, 56: 254–7.

Ashkanasy, N., Broadfoot, L. and Falkus, S. (2000a) 'Questionnaire measures of organizational culture', in N. Ashkanasy, C. Wilderom and M. Peterson (eds), *Handbook of Organizational Culture and Climate*. Thousand Oaks, CA: Sage. pp. 131–46.

Ashkanasy, N., Wilderom, C. and Peterson, M. (2000b) *Handbook of Organizational Culture and Climate*. Thousand Oaks, CA: Sage.

Baburoglu, O. and Gocer, A. (1994) 'Whither organizational culture? Privatization of the oldest state-owned enterprise in Turkey', *Industrial & Environmental Crisis Quarterly*, 8: 41–54.

Barley, S. (1983) 'Semiotics and the study of occupational and organizational cultures', *Administrative Science Quarterly*, 28: 393–414.

Barley, S. (1986) 'Technology as an occasion for structuring: evidence from observations of CT scanners and the social order of radiology departments', *Administrative Science Quarterly*, 31: 78–108.

Barley, S. and Kunda, G. (1992) 'Design and devotion: surges of rational and normative ideologies of control in managerial discourse', *Administrative Science Quarterly*, 37: 363–99.

Barley, S. and Kunda, G. (2004) *Gurus, Hired Guns and Warm Bodies: Itinerant Experts in a Knowledge Economy*. Princeton, NJ: Princeton University Press.

Barley, S., Meyer, G. and Gash, D. (1988) 'Cultures of culture: academics, practitioners and the pragmatics of normative control', *Administrative Science Quarterly*, 33: 24–59.

Bartunek, J. and Moch, M. (1991) 'Multiple constituencies and the quality of working life intervention at FoodCom', in P. Frost, L. Moore, M. Louis, C. Lundberg and J. Martin (eds), *Reframing Organizational Culture*. Newbury Park, CA: Sage. pp. 104–14.

Bastien, D. (1992) 'Change in organizational culture: the use of linguistic methods in corporate acquisition', *Management Communication Quarterly*, 5: 403–42.

Batteau, A. (2001) 'Negotiations and ambiguities in the cultures of organizations', *American Anthropologist*, 102: 726–40.

Baudrillard, J. (1983) *Simulations*. New York: Semiotext(e).

Berger, P. (1967) *The Sacred Canopy*. Garden City, NY: Doubleday.

Beyer, J., Hannah, D. and Milton, L. (2000) 'Ties that bind: culture and attachments in organizations', in N. Ashkanasy, C. Wilderom and M. Peterson (eds), *Handbook of Organizational Culture and Climate*. Thousand Oaks, CA: Sage. pp. 323–38.

Blau, P. (1965) 'The comparative study of organizations', *Industrial and Labour Relations Review*, 28: 323–38.

Bloor, G. and Dawson, P. (1994) 'Understanding professional culture in organizational context', *Organization Studies*, 15: 275–95.

Brown, M. (1990) 'Defining stories in organizations: characteristics and functions', *Communication Yearbook*, 13: 162–90.

Brunsson, N. (1985) *The Irrational Organization*. New York: Wiley.

Bryman, A., Gillingwater, D. and McGuiness, I. (1996) 'Industry culture and strategic response: the case of the British bus industry', *Studies in Cultures, Organizations, and Societies*, 2: 191–208.

Burawoy, M. (1979) *Manufacturing Consent*. Chicago, IL: University of Chicago.

Burrell, G. and Morgan, G. (1979) *Sociological Paradigms and Organizational Analysis*. London: Heinemann.

Burrell, N., Buzzanell, P. and McMillan, J. (1992) 'Feminine tensions in conflict situations as revealed by metaphoric analyses', *Management Communication Quarterly*, 6: 115–49.

Calás, M. (1987) 'Organizational Science/Fiction: The Post-Modern in the Management Discipline. University Microfilms, Ann Arbor, MI'. Unpublished doctoral dissertation, University of Massachusetts, Amherst, MA.

Calás, M. and Smircich, L. (1988) 'Reading leadership as a form of cultural analysis', in J. Hunt, B. Baliga, H. Dachler and A. Schriesheim (eds), *Emerging Leadership Vistas*. Lexington, MA: Lexington Books. pp. 201–26.

Calás, M. and Smircich, L. (1990) 'Thrusting towards more of the same', *Academy of Management Review*, 15: 698–705.

Calás, M. and Smircich, L. (1991) 'Voicing seduction to silence leadership', *Organizational Studies*, 12: 567–601.

Cameron, K. and Quinn, R. (1998) *Diagnosing and Changing Organizational Culture Based on The Competing Values Framework*. Boston, MA: Addison Wesley.

Chia, R. (2000) 'Discourse analysis as organizational analysis', *Organization*, 7: 513–8.

Clark, B. (1972) 'The organizational saga in higher education', *Administrative Science Quarterly*, 17: 178–84.

Clifford, J. (1997) 'Spatial practices: fieldwork, travel, and the disciplining of anthropology', in A. Gupta and J. Ferguson (eds), *Anthropological locations*. Berkeley, CA: University of California Press. pp. 185–222.

Clifford, J. and Marcus, G. (eds) (1986) *Writing Culture: The Poetics and Politics of Ethnography*. Berkeley, CA: University of California Press.

Cohen, M. and March, J. (1974) *Leadership and Ambiguity: The American College President*. New York: McGraw-Hill.

Collins, C. and Porras, J. (2002) *Built to Last: Successful Habits of Visionary Companies*. New York: HarperCollins.

Cooke, R. and Szumal, J. (2000) 'Using the organizational culture inventory to understand the operating cultures of organizations', in N. Ashkanasy, C. Wilderom and M. Peterson (eds), *Handbook of Organizational Culture and Climate*. Thousand Oaks, CA: Sage. pp. 147–62.

Cooper, C., Cartwright, S. and Earley, C. (2001) *The International Handbook of Organizational Culture and Climate*. New York: Wiley.

Cooper, R. and Burrell, G. (1988) 'Modernism, postmodernism, and organizational analysis', *Organization Studies*, 9: 91–112.

Coopman, S. and Meidlinger, K. (2000) 'Power, hierarchy, and change: the stories of a Catholic parish staff', *Management Communication Quarterly*, 13: 567–625.

Crozier, M. (1964) *The Bureaucratic Phenomenon*. Chicago, IL: University of Chicago Press.

Czarniawska, B. (1999) *Writing Management: Organization Theory as a Literary Genre*. Oxford: Oxford University Press.

Czarniawska-Joerges, B. (1992) *Exploring Complex Organizations: A Cultural Perspective*. Newbury Park, CA: Sage.

Dahler-Larsen, P. (1997) 'Organizational identity as a 'crowded category': a case of multiple shifting 'we' typifications', in S. Sackmann (ed.), *Cultural Complexity in Organizations*. Thousand Oaks, CA: Sage. pp. 367–89.

Dandridge, T. (1986) 'Ceremony as an integration of work and play', *Organization Studies*, 7: 159–70.

Deal, T. and Kennedy, A. (1982) *Corporate Cultures: The Rites and Rituals of Corporate Life*. Reading, MA: Addison-Wesley.

Denison, D. (1990) *Corporate Culture and Organizational Effectiveness*. New York: Wiley.

Denison, D. (1996) 'What IS the difference between organizational culture and organizational climate? A native's point of view on a decade of paradigm wars', *Academy of Management Review*, 21: 619–54.

Denison, D. (2003) 'Reviews on organizational culture: Ashkanasy, Wilderom, and Peterson (eds) *The Handbook of Organizational Culture and Climate* and Cooper, Cartwright, and Earley (eds) *The International Handbook of Organizational Culture and Climate*', *Administrative Sciences Quarterly*, 48: 119–26.

Denison, D. and Mishra, A. (1995) 'Toward a theory of organizational culture and effectiveness', *Organizational Science*, 6: 204–23.

Derrida, J. (1976) *Speech and Phenomenon*. Evanston, IL: Northwestern University Press.

Douglas, M. (1975) *Implicit Meanings*. Boston, MA: Routledge & Kegan Paul.

Dunbar, R. and Garud, R. (2001) 'Culture-in-the-making in telework settings', in C. Cooper, S. Cartwright and C. Earley (eds), *The International Handbook of Organizational Culture and Climate*. New York: Wiley. pp. 573–86.

Dutton, J. and Dukerich, J. (1991) 'Keeping an eye on the mirror: image and identity in organizational adaptation', *Academy of Management Review*, 34: 517–54.

Eisenberg, E. (1984) 'Ambiguity as strategy in organizational communication', *Communication Monographs*, 51: 227–42.

Eisenberg E., Murphy, A. and Andrews, L. (1998) 'Openness and decision making in the search for a university provost', *Communication Monographs*, 65: 1–23.

Enomoto, E. (1993) 'In-school truancy in a multiethnic urban high school examined through organizational culture lenses'. PhD dissertation, University of Michigan.

Enz, C. (1988) 'The role of value congruity in intraorganizational power', *Administrative Science Quarterly*, 33: 284–304.

Feldman, M. (1989) *Order Without Design: Information Processing and Policy Making*. Stanford, CA: Stanford University Press.

Feldman, M. (1991) 'The meanings of ambiguity: learning from stories and metaphors', in P. Frost, L. Moore, M. Louis, C. Lundberg and J. Martin (eds), *Reframing Organizational Culture*. Newbury Park, CA: Sage. pp. 145–56.

Feldman, S. (1990) 'Stories as cultural creativity: on the relation between symbolism and politics in organizational change', *Human Relations*, 43: 809–28.

Foucault, M. (1976) In E. Smith (trans.) *The Archeology of Knowledge*. New York, NY: Harper and Row.

Frost, P. and Egri, C. (1991) 'The political process of innovation', in L. Cummings and B. Staw (eds), *Research in Organizational Behavior*. Greenwich, CT: JAI Press. pp. 229–95.

Gagliardi, P. (ed.) (1990) *Symbols and Artifacts: Views of the Corporate Landscape*. Hawthorne, NY: Walter de Gruyter.

Gagliardi, P. (1991) 'Reflections on reframing organizational culture', Paper presented at the *International Conference on Organizational Symbolism and Corporate Culture*, Copenhagen.

Gagliardi, P. (2003) 'Review: Mats Alvesson. *Understanding Organizational Culture*', *Administrative Sciences Quarterly*, 48: 133–7.

Garsten, C. (1999) 'Betwixt and between: temporary employees as liminal subjects in flexible organizations', *Organization Studies*, 20: 601–17.

Gherardi, S. (1995) *Gender, Symbolism, and Organizational Culture*. London: Sage.

Glaser, B. and Strauss, A. (1967) *The Discovery of Grounded Theory*. Chicago, IL: Aldine Publishing.

Goffman, E. (1961) *Asylums*. Garden City, NY: Doubleday Anchor.

Golden-Biddle, K. and Locke, K. (1997) *Composing Qualitative Research*. Thousand Oaks, CA: Sage.

Grafton-Small, R. and Linstead, S. (1995) 'Bricks and bricolage: deconstructing corporate images in stone and story', Paper presented at the *Antibes Conference Workshop on Organizational Symbolism and Corporate Culture*, Antibes, France.

Grant, D., Hardy, C., Oswick, C. and Putnam, L. (eds) (2004) *Handbook of Organizational Discourse*. Thousand Oaks, CA: Sage.

Greenwood, R. and Hinings, C. (1988) 'Organizational design types, tracks and the dynamics of strategic change', *Organization Studies*, 9: 293–316.

Gregory, K. (1983) 'Native-view paradigms: multiple cultures and culture conflicts in organizations', *Administrative Science Quarterly*, 28: 359–76.

Gupta, A. and Ferguson, J. (eds) (1997) *Anthropological locations*. Berkeley: University of California Press.

Hafner, K. (1997) 'The epic saga of The Well: the world's most influential online community', *Wired*, May: 98–142.

Hassard, J. and Parker, M. (eds) (1993) *Postmodernism and Organizations*. London: Sage.

Hassard, J. and Pym, D. (eds) (1990) *The Theory and Philosophy of Organizations: Critical Issues and New Perspectives*. London: Routledge.

Hatch, M. and Schultz, M. (1997) 'Relations between organizational culture, identity, and image', *European Journal of Marketing*, 31: 356–65.

Hearn, J. (1998) 'On ambiguity, contradiction and paradox in gendered organizations', *Gender, Work and Organization*, 5: 1–4.

Hedberg, B. and Maravelias, C. (2001) 'Organizational culture and imaginary organizations', in C. Cooper, S. Cartwright and C. Earley (eds), *The International Handbook of Organizational Culture and Climate*. New York: Wiley. pp. 587–600.

Helmer, J. (1993) 'Storytelling in the creation and maintenance of organizational tension and stratification', *Southern Communication Journal*, 59: 34–44.

Helms Mills, J. and Mills, A. (2000) 'Rules, sensemaking, formative contexts, and discourses in the gendering of organizational culture', in N. Ashkanasy, C. Wilderom and M. Peterson (eds), *Handbook of Organizational Culture & Climate*. Thousand Oaks, CA: Sage. pp. 55–70.

Hochschild, A. (1983) *The Managed Heart: The Commercialization of Human Feeling*. Berkeley, CA: University of California.

Hofstede, G. (2001) *Culture's Consequences: Comparing Values, Behaviors, Institutions, and Organizations Across Nations*. Thousand Oaks, CA: Sage.

Hofstede, G. and Peterson, M. (2000) 'Culture: national values and organizational practices', in N. Ashkanasy, C. Wilderom and M. Peterson (eds), *Handbook of Organizational Culture & Climate*. Thousand Oaks, CA: Sage. pp. 401–16.

House, R., Hanges, P., Ruiz-Quintanilla, S., Dorfman, P., Javidan, M., Dickson, M., Gupta, V. and GLOBE (1999) 'Cultural influences on leadership: project GLOBE', *Advances in Global Leadership*, 1: 171–233.

Jaques, E. (1951) *The Changing Culture of a Factory: A Study of Authority and Participation in an Industrial Setting*. London: Tavistock. New York: Dryden Press.

Jeffcutt, P., Grafton-Small, R. and Linstead, S. (eds) (1995) *Understanding Management: Culture, Critique and Change*. London: Sage.

Jermier, J. (1985) 'When the sleeper wakes', *Journal of Management*, 11(2): 67–80.

Jonsson, S. and Lundin, R. (1977) 'Myths and wishful thinking as management tools', in P. Nystrom and W. Starbuck (eds), *Studies in Management Sciences: Prescriptive Models of Organizations, Vol. 5*. Amsterdam: North Holland. pp. 157–70.

Kanter, R. (1977) *Men and Women of the Corporation*. New York: Anchor Press.

Keesing, R. (1981) *Cultural Anthropology: A Contempory Perspective*. New York: Holt, Rinehart, and Winston.

Kilduff, M. and Corley, K. (2000) 'Organizational culture from a network perspective', in N. Ashkanasy, C. Wilderom and M. Peterson (eds), *Handbook of Organizational Culture & Climate*. Thousand Oaks, CA: Sage. pp. 211–21.

Kilmann, R. (1985) *Beyond the Quick Fix: Managing Five Tracks to Organizational Success*. San Francisco: Jossey-Bass.

Knights, D. and Willmott, H. (1987) 'Organizational culture as management strategy: a critique and illustration', *International Studies of Management and Organization*, 13: 40–63.

Knuf, J. (1993) 'Ritual in organizational culture theory: Some theoretical reflections and a plea for greater terminological rigor', in S. Deetz (ed.), *Communication Yearbook*, 16. Newbury Park, CA: Sage. pp. 61–103.

Kolb, D. and Bartunek, J. (1992) *Hidden Conflict in Organizations: Uncovering Behind-the-Scenes Disputes*. Newbury Park, CA: Sage.

Kolb, D. and Shepherd, D. (1997) 'Concept mapping organizational cultures', *Journal of Management Inquiry*, 6: 282–95.

Kondo, D. (1990) *Crafting Selves: Power, Gender, and Discourses of Identity in a Japanese Workplace*. Chicago, IL: University of Chicago Press.

Koot, W. (1997) 'Strategic utilization of ethnicity in contemporary organizations', in S. Sackmann (ed.), *Cultural Complexity in Organizations*. Thousand Oaks, CA: Sage. pp. 315–40.

Kotter, J. and Heskett, J. (1992) *Corporate Culture and Performance*. New York: Free Press.

Kreiner, K. and Schultz, M. (1993) 'Informal collaboration in R & D: the formation of networks across organizations', *Organization Studies*, 14: 189–209.

Kuhn, T. (1970) *The Structure of Scientific Revolutions*, 2nd edn (1st edn 1962). Chicago, IL: University of Chicago Press.

Kunda, G. (1992) *Engineering Culture: Control and Commitment in a High-Tech Corporation*. Philadelphia, PA: Temple University Press.

Lawrence, P. and Lorsch, J. (1967) *Organization and Environment: Managing Differentiation and Integration*. Cambridge, MA: Harvard Business School Press.

Levitt, B. and Nass, C. (1989) 'The lid on the garbage can: institutional constraints on decision making in the technical core of college-text publishers', *Administrative Science Quarterly*, 34: 190–207.

Linstead, S. and Grafton-Small, R. (1992) 'On reading organizational culture', *Organization Studies*, 13: 331–55.

Louis, M. (1985) 'An investigator's guide to workplace culture', in P. Frost, L. Moore, M. Louis, C. Lundberg and J. Martin (eds), *Organizational Culture*. Beverly Hills, CA: Sage. pp. 73–94.

Lundberg, C. (2001) 'Working with cultures: social rules perspective', in C. Cooper, S. Cartwright and C. Earley (eds), *The International Handbook of Organizational Culture and Climate*. New York: Wiley. pp. 325–46.

Lyotard, J. (1984) *The Postmodern Condition*. Minneapolis, MN: University of Minnesota Press.

March, J. and Olsen, J. (eds) (1976) *Ambiguity and Choice in Organizations*. Bergen, Norway: Universitetsforlaget.

Marcus, G. and Fischer, M. (1986/1999) *Anthropology as Cultural Critique: An Experimental Moment in the Human Sciences.* Chicago, IL: University of Chicago Press.

Martin, J. (1990) 'Deconstructing organizational taboos: the suppression of gender conflict in organizations', *Organizational Science,* 1: 339–59.

Martin, J. (1992) *Cultures in Organizations: Three Perspectives.* New York: Oxford University Press.

Martin, J. (2002) *Organizational Culture: Mapping the Terrain.* Thousand Oaks, CA: Sage.

Martin, J. and Meyerson, D. (1988) 'Organizational cultures and the denial, channeling, and acknowledgment of ambiguity', in L. Pondy, R. Boland and H. Thomas (eds), *Managing Ambiguity and Change.* New York: Wiley. pp. 93–125.

Martin, J. and Siehl, C. (1983) 'Organizational culture and counter culture: an uneasy symbiosis', *Organizational Dynamics,* 12: 52–64.

Martin, J., Feldman, M., Hatch, M. and Sitkin, S. (1983) 'The uniqueness paradox in organizational stories', *Administrative Science Quarterly,* 28: 438–53.

McCaskey, M. (1988) 'The challenge of managing ambiguity and change', in L. Pondy, R. Boland, Jr. and M. Thomas (eds), *Managing Ambiguity and Change.* New York: Wiley. pp. 1–16.

McDonald, P. (1991) 'The Los Angeles Olympic Organizing Committee: developing organizational culture in the short run', in P. Frost, L. Moore, M. Louis, C. Lundberg and J. Martin (eds), *Reframing Organizational Culture.* Newbury Park, CA: Sage. pp. 26–38.

Mendez, J. and Wolf, D. (2001) 'Where feminist theory meets feminist practice: border-crossing in a transnational academic feminist organization', *Organization,* 8: 723–50.

Meyerson, D. (1991a) 'Acknowledging and uncovering ambiguities in cultures', in P. Frost, L. Moore, M. Louis, C. Lundberg and J. Martin (eds), *Reframing Organizational Culture.* Newbury Park, CA: Sage. pp. 254–70.

Meyerson, D. (1991b) "Normal' ambiguity?: a glimpse of an occupational culture', in P. Frost, L. Moore, M. Louis, C. Lundberg and J. Martin (eds), *Reframing Organizational Culture.* Newbury Park, CA: Sage. pp. 131–44.

Meyerson, D. and Martin, J. (1987) 'Cultural change: an integration of three different views', *Journal of Management Studies,* 24: 623–47.

Mills, A. (1995) 'Man/aging subjectivity, silencing diversity: organizational imagery in the airline industry – the case of British Airways', *Organization,* 2: 243–69.

Mills, A. (1997) 'Gender, bureaucracy and the business curriculum', *Journal of Management Education,* 21: 325–42.

Morgan, G. (1983a) 'More on metaphor: why we cannot control tropes in administrative science', *Administrative Science Quarterly,* 28: 601–7.

Morgan, G. (ed.) (1983b) *Beyond Method: Strategies for Social Research.* Beverly Hills, CA: Sage.

Mumby, D. (1988) *Communication and Power in Organizations: Discourse, Ideology and Domination.* Norwood, MJ: Ablex.

Nord, W. and Connell, A. (1998) 'Criteria for Good Theory in Organization Studies 2000 A.D.'. Unpublished manuscript, University of South Florida, Tampa.

O'Reilly, C. (1989) 'Corporations, culture, and commitment: motivation and social control in organizations', in M. Tushman, C. O'Reilly and D. Nadler (eds), *Management of Organizations: Strategies, Tactics, and Analyses.* Cambridge, MA: Ballinger. pp. 285–303.

O'Reilly, C., Chatman, J. and Caldwell, D. (1991) 'People and organizational culture: a Q-sort approach to assessing person-organization fit', *Academy of Management Journal,* 34: 487–516.

Ostroff, C., Kinicki, A. and Tamkins, M. (2003) 'Organizational culture and climate', *Handbook of Psychology: Industrial and Organizational Psychology,* 12: 565–93.

Ott, J. (1989) *The Organizational Culture Perspective.* Pacific Grove, CA: Brooks & Cole.

Ouchi, W. (1981) *Theory Z: How American Business Can Meet the Japanese Challenge.* Reading, MA: Addison-Wesley.

Ouchi, W. and Jaeger, A. (1978) 'Type Z organization: Stability in the midst of mobility', *Academy of Management Review,* 3: 305–14.

Ouchi, W. and Wilkins, A. (1985) 'Organizational culture', *Annual Review of Sociology,* 11: 457–83.

Parker, M. (2000) *Organizational Culture and Identity: Unity and Division at Work.* London: Sage.

Pennings, J. and Gresov, C. (1986) 'Technoeconomic and structural correlates of organizational culture: an integrative framework', *Organization Studies,* 7: 317–34.

Perrow, C. (1979) *Complex Organizations: A Critical Essay.* Glenview, IL: Scott Foresman & Co.

Perrow, C. (1984) *Normal Accidents: Living with High-Risk Technologies.* New York: Basic Books.

Peters, T. and Waterman, R. (1982) *In Search of Excellence: Lessons from America's Best-Run Companies.* New York: Harper & Row.

Pettigrew, A. (1979) 'On studying organizational cultures', *Administrative Science Quarterly,* 24: 570–81.

Pettigrew, A. (1985a) 'Examining change in the long-term context of culture and politics', in J. Pennings (ed.), *Organizational Strategy and Change.* San Francisco: Jossey-Bass. pp. 269–318.

Pettigrew, A. (1985b) *The Awakening Giant: Continuity and Change in ICI.* Oxford: Blackwell Publishing.

Pinder, C. and Bourgeois, V. (1982) 'Controlling tropes in administrative science', *Administrative Science Quarterly,* 27: 641–52.

Poggio, B. (2000) 'Between bytes and bricks: gender cultures in work contexts', *Economic and Industrial Democracy,* 21: 381–402.

Pondy, L., Frost, P., Morgan, G. and Dandridge, T. (eds) (1983) *Organizational Symbolism*. Greenwich, CT: JAI Press.

Pringle, R. (1989) *Secretaries Talk: Sexuality, Power and Work*. St Leonards, Australia: Allen and Unwin.

Putnam, L. (1983) 'The interpretive perspective: an alternative to functionalism', in L. Putman and M. Pacanowsky (eds), *Communication and Organizations: An Interpretive Approach*. Newbury Park, CA: Sage. pp. 31–54.

Putnam, L., Bantz, C., Deetz, S., Mumby, D. and Van Maanen, J. (1993) 'Ethnography versus critical theory: debating organizational research', *Journal of Management Inquiry*, 2: 221–35.

Rafaeli, A. and Worline, M. (2000) 'Symbols in organizational culture', in N. Ashkanasy, C. Wilderon and M. Peterson (eds), *Handbook of Organizational Culture and Climate*. Thousand Oaks, CA: Sage. pp. 71–84.

Reed, M. (1985) *Redirections in Organizational Analysis*. London: Tavistock.

Reed, M. (1990) 'From paradigms to images: the paradigm warrior turns postmodernist guru', *Personnel Review*, 19: 35–40.

Robertson, M. and Swan, J. (2003) '"Control – what control?" Culture and ambiguity within a knowledge intensive firm', *Journal of Management Studies*, 40: 831–58.

Rosen, M. (1985) 'Breakfast at Spiro's: dramaturgy and dominance', *Journal of Management*, 11: 31–48.

Rosen, M. (1991) 'Coming to terms with the field: understanding and doing organizational ethnography', *Journal of Management Studies*, 28: 1–24.

Rousseau, D. (1990) 'Assessing organizational culture: the case for multiple methods', in B. Schneider (ed.), *Organizational Climate and Culture*. San Francisco: Jossey-Bass. pp. 153–92.

Rousseau, D. (1994) 'A fresh start for organizational culture research', *Contemporary Psychology*, 39: 194–5.

Rubin, J. (1997) 'Gender, equality and the culture of organizational assessment', *Gender, Work and Organization*, 4: 24–34.

Sabrosky, A., Thompson, J. and McPherson, K. (1982) 'Organizational anarchies: military bureaucracy in the 1980s', *Journal of Applied Behavioral Science*, 18: 137–53.

Sackmann, S. (ed.) (1997) *Cultural Complexity in Organizations*. Thousand Oaks, CA: Sage.

Saffold, G. (1988) 'Culture traits, strength, and organizational performance: moving beyond the 'strong' culture', *Academy of Management Review*, 13: 546–58.

Sagiv, L. and Schwartz, S. (2000) 'A new look at national culture: illustrative applications to role stress and managerial behavior', in N. Ashkanasy, C. Wilderon and M. Peterson (eds), *Handbook of Organizational Culture and Climate*. Thousand Oaks, CA: Sage. pp. 417–36.

Sahlins, M. (1985) *Islands of History*. Chicago, IL: University of Chicago Press.

Schein, E. (1985) *Organizational Culture and Leadership*. San Francisco: Jossey-Bass.

Schein, E. (1987) *The Clinical Perspective in Field Work*. Newbury Park, CA: Sage.

Schein, E. (1991) 'What is culture?', in P. Frost, L. Moore, M. Louis, C. Lundberg and J. Martin (eds), *Reframing Organizational Culture*. Newbury Park, CA: Sage. pp. 243–53.

Schein, E. (2000) 'Sense and nonsense about culture and climate', in N. Ashkanasy, C. Wilderon and M. Peterson (eds), *Handbook of Organizational Culture and Climate*. Thousand Oaks, CA: Sage. pp. xxiii–xxx.

Schneider, B. (ed.) (1990) *Organizational Climate and Culture*. San Francisco: Jossey-Bass.

Schrodt, P. (2002) 'The relationship between organizational identification and organizational culture: employee perceptions of culture and identification in a retail sales organization', *Communication Studies*, 53: 189–202.

Schultz, M. (1994) *On Studying Organizational Cultures: Diagnosis and Understanding*. Berlin: DeGruyter.

Schultz, M. and Hatch, M. (1996) 'Living with multiple paradigms: the case of paradigm interplay in organizational culture studies', *Academy of Management Review*, 21: 529–57.

Selznick, P. (1949) *TVA and the Grass Roots*. Berkeley, CA: University of California Press.

Sewall, G. and Wilkinson, B. (1992) 'Someone to watch over me: surveillance, discipline, and the just-in-time labour process', *Sociology*, 26: 271–89.

Sewall, G. and Wilkinson, B. (1998) 'Empowerment or emasculinization: shop floor surveillance in a total quality control organisation', in P. Blyton and P. Turnbull (eds), *Reassessing Human Resource Management*. London: Sage. pp. 97–115.

Siehl, C. and Martin, J. (1984) 'The role of symbolic management: how can managers effectively transmit organizational culture?', in J. Hunt, D. Hosking, C. Schriesheim and R. Stewart (eds), *Leaders and Managers: International Perspectives on Managerial Behaviour and Leadership*. Elmsford, NY: Pergamon. pp. 227–39.

Siehl, C. and Martin, J. (1988) 'Measuring organizational culture: mixing qualitative and quantitative methods', in M. Jones, M. Moore and R. Snyder (eds), *Inside Organizations: Understanding the Human Dimension*. Newbury Park, CA: Sage. pp. 79–103.

Siehl, C. and Martin, J. (1990) 'Organizational culture: a key to financial performance?', in B. Schneider (ed.), *Organizational Climate and Culture*. San Francisco: Jossey-Bass. pp. 241–81.

Smircich, L. (1983) 'Concepts of culture and organizational analysis', *Administrative Science Quarterly*, 28: 339–58.

Smircich, L. (1995) 'Writing organizational tales: reflections on three books on organizational culture', *Organizational Science*, 6: 232–7.

Smircich, L. and Calas, M. (1987) 'Organizational culture: a critical assessment', in F. Jablin, L. Putnam, K. Roberts and L. Porter (eds), *Handbook of Organizational Communication*. Beverly Hills, CA: Sage. pp. 228–63.

Smircich, L. and Morgan, G. (1982) 'Leadership: the management of meaning', *Journal of Applied Behavioral Science*, 18: 257–73.

Sotirin, P. and Gottfired, H. (1999) 'The ambivalent dynamics of secretarial 'bitching': control, resistance, and the construction of identity', *Organization*, 6: 57–80.

Sparrow, P. (2001) 'Developing diagnostics for high performance organization cultures', in C. Cooper, S. Cartwright and C. Earley (eds), *The International Handbook of Organizational Culture and Climate*. New York: Wiley. pp. 85–106.

Stablein, R. and Nord, W. (1985) 'Practical and emancipatory interests in organizational symbolism: a review and evaluation', *Journal of Management*, 11: 13–28.

Stephenson, N. (1996) 'The epic story of wiring the planet', *Wired*, December: 97–160.

Strati, A. (1992) *Organization and aesthetics*. London: Sage.

Sutton, R. (1994) 'The virtues of closet qualitative research'. Unpublished manuscript, Stanford University.

Swidler, A. (1986) 'A culture in action: symbols and strategies', *American Sociological Review*, 51: 237–86.

Thomas, J. (1992) *Doing Critical Ethnography*. Newbury Park, CA: Sage.

Townsley, N. (2003) 'Review article: looking back, looking forward. Mapping the gendered theories, voices, and politics of *Organization*', *Organization*, 10: 617–39.

Trice, H. and Beyer, J. (1993) *The Cultures of Work Organizations*. Englewood Cliffs, NJ: Prentice Hall.

Trujillo, N. (1992) 'Interpreting the work and talk of baseball: perspectives on baseball park culture', *Western Journal of Communication*, 56: 219–50.

Tsoukas, H. and Knudsen, C. (eds) (2003) *The Oxford Handbook of Organizational Theory: Meta-Theoretical Perspectives*. Oxford: Oxford University Press.

Turner, B. (1986) 'Sociological aspects of organizational symbolism', *Organizational Studies*, 7: 101–15.

Turner, B. (ed.) (1989) *Organizational Symbolism*. Hawthorne, NY: Walter de Gruyter.

Turner, B. (1990) 'The rise of organizational symbolism', in J. Hassard and D. Pym (eds), *The Theory and Philosophy of Organizations: Critical Issues and New Perspectives*. London: Routledge. pp. 83–96.

Van Maanen, J. (1986) 'Power in the bottle: drinking patterns and social relations in a British police agency', in S. Srivasta (ed.), *Executive Power*. San Francisco: Jossey-Bass. pp. 204–39.

Van Maanen, J. (1988) *Tales of the Field*. Chicago, IL: University of Chicago Press.

Van Maanen, J. (1991) 'The smile factory: work at Disneyland', in P. Frost, L. Moore, M. Louis, C. Lundberg and J. Martin (eds), *Reframing Organizational Culture*. Newbury Park, CA: Sage. pp. 58–76.

Van Maanen, J. and Kunda, G. (1989) '"Real feelings': emotional expression and organizational culture', in L. Cummings and B. Staw (eds), *Research in Organizational Behavior*, Vol. 11. Greenwich, CT: JAI Press. pp. 43–103.

Van Maanen, J., Dabbs, J. and Faulkner, R. (1982) *Varieties of Qualitative Research*. Newbury Park, CA: Sage.

van Marrewijk, A. (1996) 'The paradox of dependency: cross-cultural relations of three Dutch development organizations and their Bolivian counterparts', in W. Koot, I. Sabelis and S. Ymeba (eds), *Contradictions in Context*. Amsterdam: VU University Press. pp. 113–31.

van Reine, P. (1996) 'Globalization and the local development of models for management and organization: the periphery talks back', in W. Koot, I. Sabelis and S. Ymeba (eds), *Contradictions in Context*. Amsterdam: VU University Press. pp. 87–111.

Weick, K. (1991) 'The vulnerable system: an analysis of the Tenerife air disaster', in P. Frost, L. Moore, M. Louis, C. Lundberg and J. Martin (eds), *Reframing Organizational Culture*. Newbury Park, CA: Sage. pp. 117–30.

Weick, K. (1995) *Sensemaking in Organizations*. Thousand Oaks, CA: Sage.

Weiss, J. and Delbecq, A. (1987) 'High-technology cultures and management: Silicon Valley and route 128', *Group and Organization Studies*, 12: 39–54.

Westwood, R. and Clegg, S. (eds) (2003) *Debating Organization: Point-Counterpoint in Organization Studies*. Oxford: Blackwell Publishing.

Wilderom, C., Glunk, U. and Maslowski, R. (2000) 'Organizational culture as a predictor of organizational performance', in N. Ashkanasy, C. Wilderom and M. Peterson (eds), *Handbook of Organizational Culture and Climate*. Thousand Oaks, CA: Sage. pp. 193–210.

Willmott, H. (1993) 'Strength is ignorance; slavery is freedom: managing culture in modern organizations', *Journal of Management Studies*, 30: 515–52.

Willmott, R. (2000) 'The place of culture in organization theory: introducing the morphogenetic approach', *Organization*, 7: 95–128.

Wilson, F. (1992) 'Language, technology, gender, and power', *Human Relations*, 45: 883–904.

Wilson, F. (2000) 'Inclusion, exclusion, and ambiguity: the role of organisational culture', *Personnel Review*, 29: 274–303.

Witmer, D. (1997) 'Communication and recovery: structuration as an ontological approach to organizational culture', *Communication Monographs*, 64: 324–49.

Woodall, J., Edwards, C. and Welchman, R. (1997) 'Organizational restructuring and the achievement of an equal opportunity culture', *Gender, Work and Organization*, 4: 2–12.

Wuthnow, R., Hunter, J., Bergesen, A. and Kurzweil, E. (1984) *Cultural Analysis*. Boston: Routledge & Kegan Paul.

Yanagisako, S. (2002) *Producing Culture and Capital: Family Firms in Italy*. Princeton: Princeton University Press.

Young, E. (1989) 'On the naming of the rose: interests and multiple meanings as elements of organizational culture', *Organization Studies*, 10: 187–206.

Zammuto, R. (1998) 'Book review: Clegg, Hardy and Nord (eds): *Handbook of Organizational Studies*', *Administrative Science Quarterly*, 43: 732–6.

Zammuto, R. Gifford, B. and Goodman, E. (2000) 'Managerial ideologies, organizational culture, and the outcomes of innovation: a competing values perspective', in N. Ashkanasy, C. Wilderom and M. Peterson (eds), *Handbook of Organizational Culture and Climate*. Thousand Oaks, CA: Sage. pp. 261–78.

2.13   Some Dare Call it Power

CYNTHIA HARDY AND STEWART CLEGG

Introduction

Power has typically been seen as the ability to get others to do what you want them to, if necessary, against their will (Weber 1978). This seemingly simple definition, which presents the negative, rather than the positive, aspects of power has been challenged, amended, critiqued, extended and rebuffed over the years but it, nonetheless, remains the starting point for a remarkably diverse body of literature. Behind it lies a series of important struggles, not just concerning different conceptualizations of power, and different traditions of social science, but also in the interplay between critical and managerialist thought as well as between academic and practitioner discourses. There are, then, a multitude of different voices that speak to and of power and a variety of contradictory conceptualizations result. The two dominant voices – the functionalist and the critical (to use simple categorizations) – rarely communicate with each other and refer to quite different lineages of earlier work. The former has adopted a managerialist orientation whose underlying assumptions are rarely articulated, much less critiqued. The result has been an apparently pragmatic concept, easy to use but also easy to abuse. The latter has confronted issues of domination and exploitation head on but, some would argue, in ways that appear to be increasingly less relevant.

The aim of this chapter is to explore these different voices and to reflect on the changes that have occurred since the last incarnation of this chapter, 10 years ago. The first section explores the historical development of functionalist and critical voices. It discusses the broader heritage of Marx and Weber concerning power, followed by early management work on power. The second section shows how subsequent developments built on these respective approaches, in many respects, pulling them further

apart. An analysis of this work shows how the different voices have continued to follow divergent trajectories. The third section focuses on the insights provided by Foucault, and the supposed end of sovereignty, which had such an impact on this field of study in the late 1980s and early 1990s, radically changing our understanding of power. The fourth section revisits power and resistance in the light of Foucault's influence to discuss some of the developments in this area over the last 10 years, as well as to connect with some previously neglected streams around Goffman's ideas concerning 'total institutions', which we believe are particularly relevant for making sense of some of the events that have shaped our lives in recent years.

The Founding Voices

This section examines some of the key work that provided the foundations for the current work on power and politics in organizations. Broadly speaking, the impetus came from two, quite different directions. One tradition stems from the work of Marx and Weber. Obviously, with such a parentage, this body of work has focused on the existence of conflicting interests and has examined power as domination. As a result, it has addressed how power becomes embedded in organizational structures in a way that serves certain, but not all, interest groups. We then examine Goffman's work on total institutions. Finally, we examine the work developed more centrally within the field of management. Less interested in how power might be used to dominate and to serve specific interests, this body of work takes for granted the ways in which power is distributed in formal, hierarchical organizational structures and, instead, examines how groups acquire and wield power that has not been granted to them under official bureaucratic arrangements.

Power and Interests

One approach to the way in which power is structured into organization design has derived from work on class structures (see Clegg and Dunkerley 1980: 463–82, for a discussion of the key literature). In-as-much as conceptions of interests depict the arena of organizational life in terms of the leitmotif of 'class' and its social relations, they will be attuned to the general conditions of economic domination and subordination in organizations, as theorists of the left from Marx onwards have defined them (see, for instance, Carchedi (1987: 100) for an identification of these conditions).

Marx (1976) argued that class interests are structurally predetermined, irrespective of other bases of identity. They follow from relations of production: these define classes through their ownership and control of the means of production or through the absence of that ownership and control. In the view of Marx, and much subsequent theory, only collective class-based action presents an appropriate opportunity for strategic agency. Economic conditions regulate the context in which labour is sold and capital raised and, at the outset, two classes are defined: those who possess capital and those who do not. The latter have creative, differentially trained and disciplined capacities, but the fact that they are obliged to offer these on the labour market in order to be employed renders them, necessarily, as sellers, rather than buyers, of labour power and thus as members of the working class. While relations concerning production, property, ownership and control are inscribed as the key social relations of capitalist modernity (Clegg and Dunkerley 1980; Clegg et al. 1986), few scholars would be restricted to this deterministic view today.

Not long after Marx's death, Max Weber rendered Marx's view more complex by considering relations *in* production as well as relations *of* production, questioning the dichotomous representation. While Weber acknowledged that power did derive from owning and controlling the means of production, he argued that it was not reducible exclusively to these dichotomous categories of ownership and non-ownership, as proposed by Marx. From Weber's perspective, power derived from the knowledge of operations as much as from ownership. Organizations could be differentiated in terms of people's ability to control the methods of production, as embedded in diverse occupational identities

and technical relations at work. It is from these identities and relations that the subjective life-world of the organization grows. In this way, Weber emphasized the forms of identification and representation that organizational members actually used. He questioned the simple assumption that views of the world that did not correspond to Marxist theory must, by definition, be merely a 'false' consciousness.

From Weber's perspective all organizational members, in principle, have some creativity, discretion and agency to use power (although some more than others). Once their labour is sold to bureaucratic organizations (Clegg 1990), employees have the opportunity to use their capacities creatively in 'certain social relationships or carry out forms of social action within the order governing the organization' (Weber 1978: 217). So, by factoring in the differential possibilities for creativity, it becomes clear that organizational members have some control over their disposition to exercise power, both to challenge and reproduce the formal organization structure in which differential powers are vested, legitimated and reproduced. Thus, organizational 'structures of dominancy' do not depend solely on economic power for their foundation and maintenance (Weber 1978: 942).

In this way, labour power represents a capacity embodied in a person who retains discretion over the application of that capacity. From the employer's point of view, the employee represents a capacity to labour that must be realized. Standing in the way of realization is the embodiment of potential power in the capacities of the people hired, who may be more or less willing to work as subjects ruled by managerial discretion and control. Always, because of embodiment, the people hired as labour will retain an ultimate discretion over what they do and how they do it. Consequently, a potential source of resistance resides in this irreducible embodiment of labour power.

The gap between the capacity to labour and its effective realization implies power and the organization of control. The depiction of this gap is the mainstay of some Marxian traditions of analysis, particularly of alienation (Schacht 1971; Gamble and Walton 1972). Management is forever seeking new strategies and tactics through which to deflect discretion. The most effective and economical are thought to be those that substitute self-discipline for the discipline of an external manager. Less effective but historically more prolific, however, have been the attempts of organizations to close the discretionary gap through the use of rule systems, the mainstay of Weberian analyses of organizations as bureaucracies. Such rule systems seek to regulate meaning to control relations in organizations through the structure of formal organization design. Thus, a hierarchy is prescribed within which legitimate power is circumscribed.

Total Institutions

If hierarchy constrains power: how was it possible that some hierarchies claimed more total dominion than others? Why do people, much of the time, *not* resist. Obedience, in fact, is often a more perplexing question than resistance. Erving Goffman conducted one stream of research that sought to examine why some hierarchies claimed more total dominion than others.

A Canadian sociologist, Goffman (1961) used anthropological research to investigate how authority was configured in extreme contexts, in his term 'total institutions'. He chose extremes because the everyday mechanisms of authority and power were much more evident there than in the world of the corporate 'organization man' (Whyte 1960). Total institutions are organizations that contain the totality of the lives of those who are their members. As such, people within them are cut-off from any wider society for a relatively long time, leading an enclosed and formally administered existence. In such contexts, the organization has more or less monopoly control over its members' everyday life. Goffman's argument is that total institutions demonstrate in heightened and condensed form the underlying organizational processes that can be found, albeit in much less extreme cases, in more normal organizations.

Total institutions are often parts of a broader apparatus, such as a prison or detention centre, where inmates are held against their will. They also include organizations founded on voluntary membership, for instance a professional army, a boarding school, a residential college or a religious retreat, such as a monastery or nunnery. What do these very different types of organizations have in common that make them total institutions? Each member's daily life is carried out in the immediate presence of a large number of others. The members are very visible; there is no place to hide from the surveillance of others; and they tend to be strictly regimented. Life in a total institution is governed by strict, formal rational planning of time. (Think of school

bells for lesson endings and beginnings, factory whistles, timetables, schedules and so on.) People are not free to choose how they spend their time; instead, it is strictly prescribed for them. Members lose a degree of autonomy because of an all-encompassing demand for conformity to the authoritative interpretation of rules. Goffman's analysis thus shows that the essential core of organization is power. These extreme forms of power, intensified by spatial concentration, isolation and surveillance left little room in which agency could be exerted – ideas that were to reappear and gain renewed interest in later years, with the influence of Foucault.

In summary, this founding research focused on the way in which power derived from owning and controlling means of production, a power that was reinforced by organizational rules and structures, which in extreme circumstances could remove virtually all scope for agency. Weber's work provided more room for strategic manoeuvre than either Goffman's or Marxian views: workers had options and possibilities to challenge the power that controlled them. Although, as we shall see, these options proved to be far from easy to exercise due to more sophisticated strategies on the part of dominant groups.

Power and Hierarchy

As the section above demonstrates, power in organizations necessarily concerns the hierarchical structure of offices and their relation to each other. Particularly (but not exclusively) the field of management has tended to label such power as 'legitimate' power. One consequence of the widespread, if implicit, acceptance of the hierarchical nature of power has been that social scientists have rarely felt it necessary to explain why power should be hierarchical. In other words, in this stream of research, power embedded in hierarchy has been viewed as 'normal' and 'inevitable' following from the formal design of the organization. As such, it has been largely excluded from many analyses, which have instead focused on 'illegitimate' power: power exercised outside formal hierarchical structures and the channels that they sanction.

One of the earliest management studies of such power was that of Thompson (1956), who researched two USAF Bomber wings. The work of the USAF personnel was characterized by highly developed technical requirements in the operational sphere, for both aircrew and ground crew. While the aircrew possessed greater formal authority than the ground crew, the latter were in a highly central position within the workflow of the USAF base, relevant to the more autonomous aircrew. The aircrew depended upon the ground crew for their survival and safety, which conferred a degree of power of the latter not derived from the formal design of the base relations. Thompson attributed the power of the ground crew to their technical competency vis-à-vis the flight security of the planes and the strategic position it accorded them because of the centrality of concerns for the aircrew's safety. Other writers confirmed Thompson's (1956) view that the technical design of tasks and their interdependencies best explain the operational distribution of power, rather than the formal prescriptions of the organization design (e.g. Mechanic 1962). In this way, researchers began to differentiate between formally prescribed power and 'actual' power, which was also regarded as illegitimate. Researchers 'seldom regarded actual power' but instead 'stressed the rational aspects of organization to the neglect of unauthorized or illegitimate power' (Thompson 1956: 290).

Also important was Crozier's (1964) study of maintenance workers in a French state-owned tobacco monopoly whose job was to fix machine breakdowns referred to them by production workers and who had a high degree of power over the other workers in the bureaucracy because they controlled the remaining source of uncertainty. Crozier's study was a landmark. He had taken an under-explicated concept – power – and had attached it to the central concept of the emergent theory of the firm – uncertainty. As organizations attempted to behave as if they were systems (Cyert and March 1963), they did so in an uncertain environment. The ability to control that uncertainty thus represented a potential source of power (Crozier and Friedberg 1980). A theory emerged, called the 'strategic contingencies theory of intra-organizational power' (Hickson et al. 1971), central to which was the idea that power was related to uncertainty, or at least to its control. In this theory, the organization was conceptualized as comprising functional, interdependent sub-units, connected by the major task of the organization i.e. 'coping with uncertainty'. The model ascribed the balance of power among the sub-units to imbalances in terms of how they coped with this uncertainty and, in so doing, how they used 'differential power to function within the system rather than to destroy it' (Hickson et al. 1971: 217).[1]

Similar to the strategic contingencies view of power is the resource dependency view (e.g. Pfeffer and Salancik 1974). It derives from the social psychological literature that Emerson (1962) developed and which was implicit in Mechanic's (1962) study of the power of lower level participants. Sources of power include information, uncertainty, expertise, credibility, position, access and contacts with higher echelon members and the control of money, rewards, sanctions, etc. (e.g. French and Raven 1968; Pettigrew 1973; Benfari et al. 1986). Such lists of resources are infinite; however, since different phenomena become resources in different contexts. Without a total theory of contexts, which is impossible, one can never achieve closure on what the bases of power are. They might be anything, under the appropriate circumstances.

Possessing scare resources is not enough in itself, however, to confer power. Actors have to be aware of their contextual pertinence and control and use them accordingly (Pettigrew 1973). This process of mobilizing power is known as politics (Pettigrew 1973; Hickson et al. 1986), a term whose negative connotations have helped to reinforce the managerial view that power used outside formal authoritative arrangements was illegitimate and dysfunctional. It was the dichotomous nature of power and authority that created the theoretical space for the contingency and dependency approaches. The concept of power was thus reserved primarily for exercises of discretion by organization members, which were not sanctioned by their position in the formal structure. Such exercises are premised on an illegitimate or informal use of resources; while the legitimate system of authority, on the other hand, is taken for granted and rendered non-problematic.

Studies conducted in social psychology supported the idea that the legitimate system of authority is an extraordinarily powerful apparatus in its own right. Given authority, ordinary people do extraordinary things. For example, in Milgram's (1971) research subjects were instructed to administer increasing levels of electric shocks to participants in a behavioural learning programme, when they gave incorrect answers to test questions, each shock to be higher than the one before. (No shock was actually administered – the participants were actors who performed the appropriate physiological reaction.) When the subjects were face-to-face with the participants, only 30% administered shocks when told to; but when the participants were moved out of sight and earshot, over 60% did so In other words, obedience flows more easily when the subjects of action are at a distance – when they can be transformed into objects. Incremental increases also made obedience more likely – once committed, people felt obliged to obey, regardless of the moral principles that they might hold. In organizational terms, complex divisions of labour, and the resulting sequential action may make us complicit with – and obedient to – other organizational members in our many, sequential interactions with them, In contrast, what inhibited obedience was plurality – by introducing another expert and instructed them to disagree about the command being given – compliance declined (Milgram 1971). Thus, the presence of competing and conflicting voices increases the probability that people will think for themselves rather than just do what they are told. Thus, we might conclude that strong organizational cultures that suppress value difference are more likely to produce unreflective and sometimes inappropriate organizational action than more democratic and pluralistic settings.

Returning to total institutions, it is clear that these are organizational forms where we would least expect to find pluralism and difference:

> the readiness to act against one's own better judgement and against the voice of one's conscience is not just the function of authoritative command, but the result of exposure to a single-minded, unequivocal and monopolistic source of authority … The voice of individual moral conscience is best heard in the tumult of political and social discord (Bauman 1989: 165–6).

Total institutions – organizations that presume to exercise strong cultural control over their members to the extent that they diminish pluralism – squeeze the space in which civility, reflection and responsibility can thrive. For example, Haney et al. (1973) designed an experiment to create a mock prison. They divided the 21 male undergraduate volunteer subjects into two groups – prisoners and guards – and dressed them accordingly. Guards were charged with supervising prisoners. The experiment had to be aborted after less than 1 week as an escalatory chain of events occurred; the construed authority of the guards was enforced by the submissiveness of the prisoners, tempting the guards to exercise increasingly illegitimate displays of power that led to further humiliation of the prisoners (Bauman

1989: 167). Bear in mind that the subjects were all normal, well-adjusted people before the experiment began; yet after 1 week they were playing their roles with such conviction that the experiment had to be abandoned because of the real possibility of harm to the 'prisoners'. The revelations of extreme prisoner abuse during the 2004 occupation of Iraq by the 'Coalition of the willing', led by the US, demonstrate, yet again, the ease with which authority in total institutions can lead to the abuse of power.

In summary, the comparison of this early work on power reveals three diverging streams of research. The first, developed and sustained by the work of Marx and Weber, adopted a critical look at the processes whereby power was legitimated in the form of organizational structures. For these researchers, power was domination, and actions taken to challenge it constituted resistance to domination (see Barbalet 1985). Secondly, Goffman initiated a concern with extreme cases of power and authority condensed in total institutions, which finds direct echoes in later experimental work by Milgram and Zimbardo and his colleagues, work whose findings prefigure the Iraq prison scandals. Thirdly, the work that was more directly located in management tended to view power quite differently: existing organizational arrangements were not structures of domination but formal, legitimate, functional authority. Power was effectively resistance, but of an illegitimate, dysfunctional kind. In other words, in studying 'power', the early work speaks to different phenomena, and from quite different value positions. The Marxist/Weberian tradition equated power with the structures by which certain interests were dominated; Goffman's total institutions perspective saw authority leading seamlessly to illegitimate dysfunctional power, while the management theorists defined power as those actions that fell outside the legitimated structures, threatened organizational goals, and preserved a moral gulf between legitimate authority and illegitimate power.

Variations on Three Themes

Subsequent work in both these areas was designed to enhance and extend these foundational ideas as researchers directed their work principally at their own constituencies.

Strategies of Domination: Manufacturing Consent

The various constituent parts of the critical literature began to probe the means of domination in more detail. The heritage left by Weber provided a theoretical basis for reflecting on resistance by subordinate groups. However, if resistance was to be expected, why did subordinate groups so often consent to their own subjugation? Equally puzzling was the prevalence of passivity, which was so much more marked than revolutionary fervour. Marx had predicted that individual acts of resistance to exploitation would meld into a revolutionary challenge to existing power structures by the proletariat, those who peopled the base of most large, complex organizations. Yet, such dreams of a proletarian class-consciousness had failed to materialize.

One writer who addressed this issue, through a somewhat circuitous route, was Lukes (1974). He maintained that power could be used to prevent conflict by shaping peoples' perceptions, cognitions and preferences to the extent that:

> they accept their role in the existing order of things, either because they can see or imagine no alternative to it, or because they view it as natural and unchangeable, or because they value it as divinely ordained and beneficial (Lukes 1974: 24).

The study of power could not, therefore, be confined to observable conflict, the outcomes of decisions or even suppressed issues. It must also consider the question of political quiescence: why grievances do not exist; why demands are not made; and why conflict does not arise. In the 'third dimension' of power, Lukes focused attention on the societal and class mechanisms that perpetuated the status quo. They relate to Gramsci's concept of ideological hegemony (Clegg 1989a) – where 'a structure of power relations is fully legitimized by an integrated system of cultural and normative assumptions' (Hyman and Brough 1975: 199). According to this view, the ability to define reality is used by dominant classes to support and justify their material domination, thus preventing challenges to their position.[2]

Marxist theory spawned another stream of research on this issue, known as labour process theory (e.g. Braverman 1974; Burawoy 1979; Edwards 1979), which examined the day-to-day minutiae of power and resistance built around the 'games' that characterize the rhythms of organizational life (Burawoy 1979). Studies also examined the historical patterns that structure the overall context of power, from simple, direct control premised on surveillance; through technical control based on the dominance of the employee by the machine, and particularly the assembly line; to fully fledged bureaucratic control – Weber's rule by rules. In this tradition the focus is on the dialectics of power and resistance in relation to phenomena such as gender, technology, ethnicity, managerial work and other aspects of the structuration of work and its organizational context (Knights and Willmott 1985; 1989; Knights and Morgan 1991; Kerfoot and Knights 1993).

Elsewhere, in general historical sociology, the notion of 'organizational outflanking' (Mann 1986: 7) provided another answer to the question of why the dominated so frequently consent to their subordination. Outflanking works against certain groups either because they do not know enough to resist; or they know rather too much concerning the futility of such action. In the former case, the powerless remain so because they are ignorant of the ways of power. It is not that they do not know the rules of the game so much as that they do not recognize the game itself. Here resistance remains an isolated occurrence, and easily outflanked. In the second situation, the organizationally outflanked know only too well that the costs of resistance outweigh the chances of success or the benefits of succeeding. The necessity of dull compulsion in order to earn one's living, the nature of busy work, arduous exertion and ceaseless activity – such techniques of power may easily discipline the blithest of theoretically free spirits.

Strategies of Total Institutions: Denying Morality

Arendt (1994) wrote an account of the trial of Adolf Eichmann, one of Hitler's deputies, the Head of the Department for Jewish Affairs. He led the Reich's effort for the Final Solution, efficiently organizing the roundup and transportation of millions of Jews to their deaths at infamous camps such as Auschwitz, Treblinka and Bergen-Belsen. It was Arendt who coined the memorable phrase 'the banality of evil' to register her interpretation of the events reported in the trial. Eichmann's defence was important because it posed the question of the extent to which a person who is obedient to organizationally legitimate authority can be held accountable as an individual for his or her actions.

The renowned sociologist, Bauman (1989) has continued to confront these questions: essentially, he notes how central aspects of organizations contribute to the ease with which organizational malfeasance can occur. At the heart is a moral question concerning the interpenetration of power and ethics: Why do ordinary people in organizations do morally bad things when asked to do so? What aspects of an organization make unquestioning obedience feasible? It has been suggested that three organizational attributes make this phenomenon more probable (Kelman 1973): first, sanction from higher authority – when a strong leader tells you to do things, you might feel there is a good reason to actually do them; secondly, when the actions that enact the organizational action in question are routinized and you cannot see where and how your task fits into the big picture, nor can you see its consequences; thirdly, when those who are the victims of the action are dehumanized.

Bauman (1989: 101) regards moral standards as being irrelevant 'for the technical success of the bureaucratic operation'. When we master a technique, our skill has its own charm, aesthetics and beauty, and we can take sheer delight in using it, irrespective of its moral effects. Technical responsibility differs from moral responsibility in that it forgets that the action is a means to something other than itself. For instance, as a master of logistics, Eichmann was enormously proud of his achievements in the complex scheduling of trains, camps and death. Organizational power expressed in terms of technical accountability and responsibility for results expressed in a purely quantitative form has two profound effects. First, it makes action utterly transparent – the targets are achieved or they are not. Secondly, one's actions are relieved of moral indeterminacy – if one is authorized to do something and given targets to achieve by superordinates guiding strategies and plans, obedience surely is appropriate, and authority should be served.[3]

This view draws attention to organization work as a ceaseless round of activity. Most organizational members are in the middle of organizational chains whose links are not always clear. People are not always aware of the consequences of what they do and do not do – after all, most of the time, they are just doing what they are told (shred those files, write those cheques, dispatch those troops, maintain those train schedules). Divisions of labour in the complex chains enable us to keep a distance from effects; we can represent them in terms of intermediary forms of data (kill rates, efficiency statistics and so on). Our labour moves minute cogs in a bureaucratic machine necessarily intermeshed with so many others. We don't even have to try to understand the totality. The system of which we are a part is responsible, not us. When these actions are also performed at a distance on people defined as administrative categories, as less than human, the easier becomes the application of pure technique. When whatever is being worked on can be represented quantitatively, as a bottom-line calculation, it is so much easier to make rational decisions (cut costs, trim fat, speed throughput, increase efficiency, defeat the competition) without concern for the human, environmental or social effects of these decisions.

Strategies of Management: Defeating Conflict

The management literature took a different approach – instead of concerning itself with the use of power to prevent conflict, it focused almost exclusively on the use of power to defeat conflict. Definitions explicitly linked power to situations of conflict that arise when actors try to preserve their vested interests (e.g. Pettigrew 1973; 1985; Pfeffer 1981; 1992; Schwenk 1989).

> From the definition of power, it is clear that political activity is activity that is undertaken to overcome some resistance or opposition. Without opposition or contest within the organization, there is neither the need nor the expectation that one would observe political activity (Pfeffer 1981: 7).

Such definitions evoke the idea of an (almost) 'fair' fight, where one group (usually senior management) is forced to use power to overcome the opposition of another (perhaps intransigent unions or dissident employees). It is a view reinforced by a common definition of politics in the management literature as the unsanctioned or illegitimate use of power to achieve unsanctioned or illegitimate ends (e.g. Mayes and Allen 1977; Gandz and Murray 1980). More recent lamentations concerning the extent of resistance of employees to change programmes bolster this view (see Hardy and Clegg

2004). Such approaches clearly imply that the use of power, especially by employees, is dysfunctional, and usually aimed at thwarting managerial initiatives intended to benefit the organization for the sake of individual self-interest.

If power is equated with overcoming conflict, it raises a question concerning what happens when there is no conflict: does power simply cease to exist or does it turn into something else? If so, what does it become? It appears as if only the 'bad guys' use power while, given the discredited nature of the term 'political', the 'good guys' must use something else, even if the literature is not clear exactly what it is. Good guy/bad guy views are also problematic in so far as they ignore questions concerning in whose eyes is it that power is deemed illegitimate, unsanctioned or dysfunctional? Legitimacy is usually defined in terms of the 'organization', when writers really mean organizational elites: that is, senior management or top management teams. Thus, managerial interests are equated with organizational needs and the possibility that managers, like any other group, might seek to serve their own vested interests is largely ignored (Watson 1982). However, organizational structures and systems are not neutral or apolitical – they are structurally sedimented phenomena that result, in part, from a history of victories and losses already embedded in the organization. The organization is a collective life-world in which traces of the past are vested, recur, shift and take on new meanings. In Weber's terms organizations already incorporate a 'structure of dominancy' in their functioning: authority, structure, ideology, culture and expertise are invariably saturated and imbued with power.

The management tradition has taken the structures of power vested in formal organization design very much for granted (Clegg et al. 2005). One important exception was the earlier work of Follett. Central to Follett's (1918; 1924) worldview was that organizations organize and create power. She was concerned to democratize power, distinguishing between power-over and power-with (or co-active power rather than coercive power): the former needs developing, while the latter needs diminishing. In this way, organizations can be developed democratically as places where people learn to co-operate in power-with others, especially managers and workers. In a democracy, people can exercise power at the grassroots level through participation, pluralism, empowerment and education. According

to Follett, democratic diversity had great advantages over more authoritarian homogeneity: it feeds and enriches society, rather than feeding *on* society and eventually corrupting it.

Follett's concerns with democracy and power were not, however, widely shared by later management theorists, who were more inclined to focus on the exercise of power not as an act of democracy, but as an aberration within a given structure of dominancy (Perrow 1979). Such an approach focuses only on surface politics and misrepresents the balance of power. It attributes far too much power to subordinate groups who are chastised for using it; while the hidden ways in which senior managers use power behind the scenes to further their position by shaping legitimacy, values, technology and information are conveniently excluded from analysis. Using such a narrow definition (see Frost 1987) also obscures the true workings of power and depoliticizes organizational life (Clegg 1989a). It paints an ideologically conservative picture that implicitly advocates the status quo and hides the processes whereby organizational elites maintain their dominance (Alvesson 1984) as mechanisms of domination such as leadership, culture and structure are treated as neutral, inevitable or objective and, hence, unproblematic (Clegg 1989a, b; also see Ranson et al. 1980; Deetz 1985; Knights and Willmott 1992; Willmott 1993).

Managing Meaning: The Creation of Legitimacy

Some management researchers did start to question these assumptions as they became interested in power as legitimation (Astley and Sachdeva 1984). In the manner described by Lukes' (1974) third dimension of power, the process of legitimation prevents opposition from arising.

> Political analysis must then proceed on two levels simultaneously. It must examine how political actions get some groups the tangible things they want from government and at the same time it must explore what these same actions mean to the mass public and how it is placated or aroused by them. In Himmelstrand's terms, political actions are both instrumental and expressive (Edelman 1964: 12).

One writer who attempted to draw legitimation processes into the management fold was Pettigrew

(1977: 85), who explicitly addressed how power was used to create legitimacy.

> Politics concerns the creation of legitimacy for certain ideas, values and demands – not just action performed as a result of previously acquired legitimacy. The management of meaning refers to a process of symbol construction and value use designed both to create legitimacy for one's own demands and to 'de-legitimize' the demands of others.

This work acknowledges that political actors do not always define success in terms of winning in the face of confrontation where there is always a risk of losing, but in terms of their ability to section off spheres of influence where their domination is perceived as legitimate and thus unchallenged (Ranson et al. 1980; Frost 1989). In this way, power is mobilized to influence behaviour indirectly by giving outcomes and decisions certain meanings; by legitimizing and justifying them.

Pfeffer (1981) considered a similar use of power when he distinguished sentiment (attitudinal) from substantive (behavioural) outcomes of power. The latter depend largely on resource dependency considerations, while the former refer to the way people feel about the outcomes and are mainly influenced by the symbolic aspects of power, such as the use of political language, symbols and rituals. Pfeffer (1981) argued there is only a weak relationship between symbolic power and substantive outcomes: that symbolic power is only used post-hoc to legitimize outcomes already achieved by resource dependencies. In this way, Pfeffer stops short of acknowledging that power can be used to prevent conflict and opposition. There is, however, an inconsistency in Pfeffer's arguments: if symbolic power is effective enough to 'quiet' opposition *ex post*, why not use it *ex ante* to prevent opposition from arising in the first place? The only factor preventing Pfeffer from reaching this conclusion appears to be his refusal to acknowledge the existence of power in situations other than those characterized by conflict and opposition (Pfeffer 1981: 7).

The management 'school' thus remained distant from the more critical work on domination. The majority of writers continued to focus on dependency and to define power in terms of conflict and illegitimacy. Rather than delve into the power hidden in and mobilized through apparently neutral structures, cultures and technologies, the vast majority of researchers preferred to continue to view organizations from a far more comfortable and familiar position – as apolitical management tools.

The End of Sovereignty

Neither critical nor managerial conceptualizations of power remained fixed. In fact, important changes were about to occur as postmodern thinking started to infiltrate organization and management theory. In particular, the arrival of Foucault on the power scene posed a fundamental challenge by sounding the death-knell of sovereignty. The idea that power could be exercised strategically and successfully against intended targets was deeply embedded in the views of critical and management theorists alike. In disposing of sovereignty, Foucault's work transformed the study of power through the way it introduced the idea of disciplinary power, de-centred the subject and laid the foundations for new notions of resistance (see, for example, Deetz 1992a, b; Alvesson and Deetz 1996; Hardy and Leiba-O'Sullivan 1998; Mumby 2001).

Power and Discipline

Foucault's (1977) understanding of 'disciplinary practices' led to an interest in the 'micro-techniques' of power. Unlike Weber's rule systems, these techniques are not ordinarily thought of in terms of the causal concept of power (the notion of someone getting someone else to do something that they would not otherwise do). Instead, they represent ways in which both individual and collectively organized bodies become socially inscribed and normalized through routine aspects of organizations – much closer to Weber's emphasis on the importance of discipline in phenomena such as Taylorism, than to his more theoretical accounts of power as a social action.

Through discipline, power is embedded in the fibre and fabric of everyday life. At the core of Foucault's work were practices of 'surveillance', which may be more or less mediated by instrumentation. Historically, the tendency is for a greater instrumentation to develop as surveillance moves from a literal supervisory gaze to more complex forms of observation, reckoning and comparison. Surveillance, whether personal, technical, bureaucratic or legal, ranges through forms of supervision, routinization, formalization, mechanization, legislation and design that result in increasing control of employee behaviour, dispositions and embodiment. Surveillance is not only accomplished through direct control. It may happen as a result of cultural practices of moral endorsement, enablement and persuasion, or as a result of more formalized technical knowledge, such as the computer monitoring of keyboard output or low cost drug-testing systems.

The effectiveness of disciplinary power in the 19th century was linked to the emergence of new techniques of discipline appropriate for more impersonal, large scale settings in which the *gemeinschaft* conditions, whereby each person knew their place, no longer prevailed (see Foucault 1977; Bauman 1982). Previous localized, moral regulation, premised on the transparency of the person to the gaze of the community, was no longer viable. New forms of state institution emerged in which new forms of control were adopted, and later copied by the factory masters. However, as Foucault was at pains to point out, no grand plan caused these institutions to adopt similar forms of disciplinary technique. Rather, people copied what was already available, creating their own world in isomorphic likeness of key features they already knew. Disciplinary techniques had been readily available in the monastic milieu of religious vocation, the military, institutional forms of schooling, poor houses, etc. and their effectiveness had been established during the past two centuries. At a more general level, the 'disciplinary gaze' of surveillance shaped the development of disciplines of knowledge 19th century in such areas as branches of social welfare, statistics and administration (Foucault 1977).

Organizationally, the 20th century development of the personnel function under the 'human relations' guidance of Mayo (1975) may be seen to have had a similar tutelary role (see Clegg 1979; Ray 1986; Townley 1993). Such mechanisms are often local, diverse and unco-ordinated. They form no grand strategy. Yet, abstract properties of people, goods and services can be produced that are measurable, gradeable and assessable in an overall anonymous strategy of discipline. In this way, Foucault challenged sovereign notions of power: power was no longer a deterministic resource, able to be conveniently manipulated by legitimate managers against recalcitrant, illegitimate resistance by lower orders. Instead, all actors operated within an existing structure of dominancy – a prevailing web of power

relations – from which the prospects of escape were limited for dominant and subordinate groups alike.

Power and Identity

The work of Foucault and other postmodern theorists was also important in showing:

> the contemporary vanity of humankind in placing the 'individual', a relatively recent and culturally specific category, at the centre of the social, psychological, economic, and moral universe. The subject, decentred, relative, is acknowledged not as a stable constellation of essential characteristics, but as a socially constituted, socially recognized, category of analysis. For example, no necessarily essential attributes characterize 'men' or 'women'. Instead the subjectivity of those labelled as such is culturally and historically variable and specific (Clegg and Hardy 1996: 3).

Not surprisingly, Foucauldian insights played an important role in the work on gender. While early contributions (e.g. Kanter 1977) had already noted the way in which women were systematically subjected to power inside organizations in ways that were inseparable from their broader social role, Foucault's work provided an added impetus for work on gender, as well new ways of conceptualizing gender (Mumby 2001).

Scholars became increasingly aware not only of the gender blindness of organizations, but also of organization studies itself (see Mills and Tancred (1992) for a brief overview). Major texts were reassessed in terms of how their contribution to the literature was often premised on unspoken assumptions about gender or unobserved and unremarked sampling decisions or anomalies, in gender terms. For example, Crozier's (1964) maintenance workers were all men while the production workers were all women. As Hearn and Parkin (1983) were to demonstrate, this blindness was symptomatic of the field as a whole, not any specific paradigm within it. So, while gender and sexuality are pervasive aspects of organizational life and organizational identity is regularly defined through gender and the projection of forms of emotionality and sexuality implicated in it, the gender bias inherent in the study of organization helped to preserve the status quo, rather than challenge it (e.g. Pringle 1989). How else could the vantage point and privileges of white, usually Anglo Saxon, normally American, males have been taken for granted for so long (Calás and Smircich 1992)? See the chapter by Calás and Smircich in this volume for a more recent discussion of these issues.

People's identities are not tied up only in their gender or sexuality, any more than in the type of labour power that they sell to an organization. People in organizations are subject to regimes of specific organizational signification, at the same time as they are interpellated by extra-organizational issues such as ethnicity, gender, class, age and other phenomena. Embodied identities are salient only in as much as they are socially recognized and organizationally consequent. Forms of embodiment such as age, gender, sexuality, ethnicity, religiosity and handicap are particularly recognizable as bases that serve to locate practices for stratifying organization members, as evidenced by, for example, their being the precise target of various anti-discrimination laws. Accordingly, organizations can be constituted as structures of patriarchal domination, ethnic domination, age domination and so on. Such matters are clearly contingent: most organizations may have aspects of one or more of these forms of dominancy, but it is not necessarily so.

The issues of identity and subjectivity continue to interest researchers. Complaints about 'the missing subject' (Thompson 1990) have led to an emphasis on the construction of identity from a nexus of power relations, existential concerns and prevailing discourses, such as capitalism, patriarchy and sovereignty (Holmer-Nadesan 1996; Phillips and Hardy 1997). Categories of self have been seen as being constructed in 'historically specific modes of production and contingent networks of social relations' (O'Doherty and Willmott 2001: 472). Identity is complex: it is embedded in the webs of power that permeate social practices. Identity is also contingent; constantly (re)emerging out of the discourses in which it is positioned, even those identities which seek to oppose, resist or transgress the discourse. Cynical detachment, surface acting and impression management do not defend some self already there or maintain distance between the inner self and the outer world but, instead, are a key part of identity formation processes, framing it as much as do relations of production, strategies of control and disciplinary mechanisms (Fleming 2003). Consequently, there is no genuine ego, inner self or *a priori* subject to defend against incursions of power – the self is as much a product of power as something to be protected from it (Knights and Willmott 1989).

Organizations are an important site in which such identity formation occurs (Mumby and Stohl 1991; Deetz 1992a; Tretheway 1997). In fact, all organization practices, such as team-working, empowerment and TQM, confer opportunities for self-construction to those grappling with the identities they frame, constitute and change (e.g. Hardy and Leiba-O'Sullivan 1998; Knights and McCabe 2000; 2002). At the same time, it is important to remember that identity-work is only ever achieved against a lifetime of identity construction (despite some views of organization culture that seem to assume it can occur wholly within organizational space). Consequently, it is clear that 'public' organization must be interpellated by relations of power/knowledge which emanate from 'private' life (e.g. Tretheway 1997). Organizations are merely one of many arenas within which opportunities for the presentation of the self are available (Goffman 1959).

Power and Resistance Revisited

The discussion above shows the extent to which Foucault's work has influenced the study of power and resistance. It highlights the multi-faceted nature of organizational locales and shows how complex identities are subject to multivalent powers. Approaches inspired by his work seemed particularly well positioned to appreciate these struggles of power and resistance. Not because they were predisposed to know in advance who the victorious and vanquished dramatis personae should be, but because of their emphasis on the play of meaning, signification and action through which all organization actors seek to script, direct and position all others.

One of Foucault's most telling blows on modernist assumptions was his observation that knowledge and power are inseparable. He regarded the concept of ideology – which helped to explain why individuals did not act on their 'real' interests – as a 'falsehood' whose relational opposition to 'truth' can never be too far away. By demonstrating how the 'truths' and 'falsehoods' of particular discourses had been constituted historically, Foucault showed that language cannot mask anything; it simply represents possibilities. No assumption of reality exists as anything more than its representation in language and, consequently, no situation is ever free from power. Moreover, with knowledge only comes more power.

> [T]ruth isn't the reward of free spirits, the child of protracted solitude, nor the privilege of those who have succeeded in liberating themselves. Truth is a thing of this world: it is produced only by virtue of multiple forms of constraint. And it induces regular effects of power. Each society has its regime of truth, it's 'general' politics of truth: that is, the type of discourse which it accepts and makes function as true; the mechanisms and instances which enable one to distinguish true and false statements, the means by which each is sanctioned; and the techniques and procedures accorded value in the acquisition of truth; the status of those who are charged with saying what counts as true (Foucault 1980: 131).

Foucault demonstrated that bodies of knowledge – discourses – 'are practices that systematically form the objects of which they speak' (Foucault 1972: 49). In other words, discourses bring the social world into being through the way in which they constitute particular types of categories (Fairclough 1992; Fairclough and Wodak 1997; Hardy and Phillips 1999), which both make sense of and construct social 'reality.' In this way, discourse lays down the 'conditions of possibility' that determine what can be said, by whom and when (Hall 2001).

According to Foucault, power represents a complex web of relations determined by systems of knowledge constituted in discourse.

> Power is everywhere; not because it embraces everything, but because it comes from everywhere ... power is not an institution, and not a structure; neither is it a certain strength we are endowed with; it is the name that one attributes to a complex strategical situation in a particular society (Foucault 1979: 93).

Advantaged and disadvantaged alike are captured in this web (Deetz 1992a).

> To the extent that meanings become fixed or reified in certain forms, which then articulate particular practices, agents and relations, this fixity is power. Power is the apparent order of taken-for-granted categories of existence, as they are fixed and represented in a myriad of discursive forms and practices (Clegg 1989a: 183).

The frame had shifted greatly: where once were managers and employees, legitimate hierarchies and

dependencies, as well as strategic (if illegitimate contingencies) in the use of power, after Foucault (1979) the idea of power as a possession, as a thing held by the person, was untenable (Clegg 1989a). Some took this to mean as the end of agency (Reed 1998); others saw it as ushering in a fatalistic view of power in which nothing could be changed (Burman and Parker 1993). Either way, if sovereignty is dead, how can managers exercise power over organizational members?

Had managerial researchers followed these debates with much interest (which they did not appear to – although, as we shall see, it did not stop some of them appropriating some ideas at a later date), they would have had to pose the question of how is managerial power possible? For critical researchers, there would be an equally pressing question: if managers were not in sovereign positions of control, but were relays in an overall apparatus of power, what was the sense of resistance?

Power and Discourse: The Matter of Agency

Foucault's work has been critiqued for ignoring both structure and agency – for refusing to recognize that discourses and the practices and structures that they constitute are 'the direct expression of strategies of control and domination pursued by identifiable individuals, social groups, classes and movements' that occur 'within a wider historical and institutional context' (Reed 1998: 197). Reed argues that Foucault, by rejecting any distinction between constraint and action, can explain neither how certain discourses come to be as powerful as they do, nor how change occurs (Reed 1998; also see O'Doherty and Willmott 2001). However, some researchers have shown that, by bringing structure back into the picture, it is possible to find a place for agency.

Critical discourse analysts build on Foucault's work by acknowledging that discursive practices are 'constrained by the fact that they inevitably take place within a constituted material reality, with pre-constituted objects and pre-constituted social subjects' (Fairclough 1992: 60). Discourse as social action is thus engaged 'within a framework of understanding, communication and interaction which is in turn part of broader socio-cultural structures and processes' (Van Dijk 1997: 21).

> Discourse is not produced without context and cannot be understood without taking context into

consideration. … Discourses are always connected to other discourses which were produced earlier, as well as those which are produced synchronically and subsequently (Fairclough and Wodak 1997: 277).

By conceptualizing context as the previously constructed meanings that have, over time, become sedimented into the prevailing discourses that shape how we make sense and act upon the world, we tap into the constraints that Foucault emphasized and, indeed, the structure for which Reed (1998) searches. Within such a conception of context, however, is some room for manoeuvre (Hardy and Phillips 2004), since discourses are never totally fixed (Clegg 1989a). Consequently, power relations that appear insurmountable and unchangeable are nonetheless subject to some form of ongoing discursive negotiation and material support, which hold them in place (Mumby and Stohl 1991; Parker 1992; Fairclough and Wodak 1997). Moreover, situations are rarely hostage to a single discourse – multiplicities of discourse are usually at play from which 'reality' is constituted (e.g. Keenoy et al. 1997; Alvesson and Kärreman 2000a, b; Grant and Hardy 2004; Grant et al. 2004).

[D]iscourses are never completely cohesive and devoid of internal tensions, and are therefore never able to totally determine social reality. They are always partial, often crosscut by inconsistencies and contradiction, and almost always contested to some degree. Second … actors are commonly embedded in multiple discourses. The tensions between these discourses produces a discursive space in which the agent can play one discourse against another, draw on multiple discourses to create new forms of interdiscursivity, and otherwise move between and across multiple discourses (Hardy and Phillips 2004: 304).

Within these gaps, contractions and tensions that reside within and among discourses lays the potential for people to exercise their agency. For instance, actors often try to use discursive latitude to shape understandings of a social situation within the constraints afforded by the previously constituted context or, in discursive terms, prevailing discourses and previous texts (Fairclough 1995). As a result, as Reed (2004) argues, the 'structure' of discursive context and the agency of discursive innovation must be analysed dialectically. For example, while the ability to produce texts and draw on broader

discourses affords some actors opportunities for agency, only certain texts will have organizational consequences, and only some organizational consequences will become institutionalized to the extent that they can be said to constitute structure (e.g. Taylor et al. 1996; Iedema 1998; Taylor and Van Every 2000; Putnam and Cooren 2004). Thus, institutions are particular forms of practice constituted through discourse (Clegg 1975; Parker 1992; Phillips et al. 2004) and power (Clegg 1989a; Lawrence et al. 2001).

A social institution is an apparatus of verbal interaction or an 'order of discourse' … Each institution has its own set of speech events, its own differentiated settings and scenes, its cast of participants, and its own norms for their combination … a frame for action, without which they could not act (Fairclough 1995: 38).

One way to examine the structure of power in organizations is therefore to see it as a discursive product (Clegg 1975; Phillips et al. 2004) wherein certain social relations become 'ossifed and regimented' in ways that sustain and realize 'order and organization' (O'Doherty and Willmott 2001: 465).

Particular discourses produce structure and institutions through the exercise of an agency that is, in turn, constrained by existing structure and institutions. The movement is forever dialectical, never arrested, merely framed and sometimes re-framed in certain ways at certain times. In this way we can combine a realist-based discourse analysis – which accepts the sovereignties framed in the conjuncture – with a social constructionist approach, which sees them as forever contingent on the play of the actors in creatively assembling and using the discourses (also see O'Doherty and Willmott 2001). With such an approach one can provide 'historical accounts of the ways in which discursive change and innovation enter into and reshape ongoing power struggles to make and remake the institutional status quo and the configuration of power relations that it reproduces' (Reed 2004: 418).

In this way, critical researchers can still explore and expose the ways in which some actors prevail over others, within the confines of larger discursive settings. Discursive and extra-discursive realms can also be integrated. For example, as O'Doherty and Willmott (2001: 464) note, while powerful discourses constitute, to use a catch-all phrase, 'capitalism',

capitalism exists 'outside of language and text'. It is enacted through and reinforced by practices, behaviours and material entities – factories, products, machines, houses, money, poverty, unemployment, etc. – that are clearly 'out there'. While this materiality derives meaning from language and interpretation, it undoubtedly also contributes to the discourses that surround and sustain it, through the ways in which experience shapes language and interpretation.[4] In other words, critical researchers' incorporation of Foucauldian and other postmodern insights has enriched – rather than stymied – their work (Phillips and Hardy 2002).

Most managerial researchers, on the other hand, appear to ignore Foucault altogether, although in some cases, for example work on change management, Foucauldian ideas do appear (e.g. Grant et al. 2002; Szachowicz-Sempruch 2003;[5] Bradshaw and Boonstra 2004). In many respects, however, writers appear to have been highly selective in how they have interpreted his work.

> Thus, the inability to pull the strings of power … is reinterpreted as a system of power that is 'inherently diffused and shared among individuals' that allows individuals 'to become potentially active agents' … The net [of power] is appropriated; the problem of strategic agency is ignored. Similarly, to counter the disciplinary gaze individuals are exhorted to be 'authentic' by 'acting in congruence with one's own values and beliefs' and to stand 'outside dominant discourses'. Foucault's gaze is acknowledged; his disavowals of the authentic self and the possibility of standing outside discourse are rejected (Hardy and Clegg 2004: 359).

In other words, the inconvenient aspects of Foucault's work have been largely ignored, while those that offer potential for change management have been colonized and cultivated.

Change programmes have homed in on one aspect of Foucauldian-inspired work in particular – the notion of identity. If power is productive of identity, then identity becomes a target of change programmes – 'it is no longer enough for employees to believe that change is good; now they *must* feel it' (Hardy and Clegg 2004: 359). In other words, the subjectivities of employees are now the target of change programmes and must be made consistent with and supportive of them (e.g. French and Delahaye 1996; Vince and Broussine 1996). Thus, managers have secured change through cultural

engineering (e.g. Kunda 1992; Casey 1995; du Gay 1996), emotional labour (see Sturdy and Fineman 2001; Fineman, this volume), managerial techniques associated with 'Japanization' (Delbridge 1995), team work (Sewell and Wilkinson 1992; Barker 1993) and electronic monitoring (Fernie and Metcalf 1999) to target identity in what some critics have described as a prison of totalizing, panoptic control (Willmott 1993; Reed 1998). This, in turn, raises important consequences for resistance, to which we now turn.

Power and Resistance

Managerial change programmes, such as those described above, exert powerful normative controls through emotional dependence and organizational identification (see Gabriel 1999), leading some researchers to ask how employee resistance is possible when 'corporate relations of power target the hearts and minds of workers' (Fleming and Spicer 2002: 65)? When panoptic controls are added to these normative controls, through a variety of spatial and temporal monitoring arrangements (Gabriel 1999),[6] resistance seems to face even greater hurdles. It now has to overcome 'control over exterior spaces' as well as control of an 'interior world' that was 'colonized by hegemonic norms and values' (Pile 1997: 4). Nor is much reassurance to be derived from the theoretical literature. Foucault's work had already pointed out that resistance does not lead to a transformation of prevailing power relations, but merely reinforces them (Clegg 1979; Knights and Willmott 1989; Knights and Morgan 1991). In addition, researchers noted that the production of identity that emanates from power/ knowledge relations confers a positive experience on the individual (Knights and Willmott 1989). As a result, resistance exacts a heavy price from would-be dissenters who have to repudiate their sense of self, estranging 'the individual from the tradition that has formed his or her subjectivity' (Alvesson and Willmott 1992: 447). In other words, both empirically and theoretically, disciplinary control appears to be so complete that the space for, never mind the outcome of resistance, is severely constrained. Whether managers are running the show – as the empirical literature has seemed to suggest – or whether they are equally constrained by disciplinary power – as the theoretical work indicated – hardly matters: the opportunities for employee resistance do not look promising. And, if the prospects for resistance are poor, what are the prospects for the *study* of resistance?

Thompson and Ackroyd (1995: 629) went on the offensive – challenging the idea that the prospects of resistance were limited. Instead, they argued that researchers would surely find resistance if only they had 'the time and inclination to look for it'. It would appear that researchers had plenty of both, as a flurry of articles on workplace resistance appeared, apparently written by researchers intent on finding resistance even in places where none was supposed to exist (e.g. Webb and Palmer 1998; Bain and Taylor 2000; Taylor et al. 2002). It took persistence and ingenuity to identify some of these practices as resistance, now that it was no longer simply collective, organized action. Today, resistance has been so transformed that it is now inconspicuous, subtle and unorganized (Fleming and Sewell 2003), as well as indirect, unplanned and mundane (Prasad and Prasad 2000). It includes humour (Collinson 1992), irony (Tretheway 1997), cyncism (Fleming and Spicer 2003), scepticism (Knights and McCabe 2002), parody (Tretheway 1997), hidden transcripts (Murphy 1998), bitching (Sotirin and Gottfried 1999) and fiddles (Webb and Palmer 1998) amongst its myriad practices. Resistance used to stand in 'implacable opposition' to power exercised by an elite through 'oppressive, injurious and contemptible means to secure their control' as people fought back 'in defence of freedom, democracy and humanity' (Pile 1997: 1). Now resistance is more akin to 'švejkism' where, as in Hašek's (1973) novel, Josef Švejk 'resists the discipline of the Austro-Hundarian Imperiam Army through subtle forms of subversion that are "invisible" to his superiors (and often to peers too)', but which nonetheless undermine organizational power relationship in disruptive if not openly rebellious ways (Fleming and Sewell 2003: 859).[7]

[It is no longer] sufficient to assume that resistance arises from innate political subjectivities which are opposed to, or marginalized by oppressive practices, whereby those who benefit from relations of domination act to reproduce them, while the oppressed have a natural interest in over-turning the situation. Instead, resistant political subjectivities are constituted through positions taken up not only in relation to authority – which may well leave people in awkward, ambivalent, down-right contradictory and dangerous places – but also through

experiences which are not so quickly labelled 'power' such as desire and anger, capacity and ability, happiness and fear, dreaming and forgetting (Pile 1997: 3).

Resistance, it would seem, is no longer what it was, although it would appear that there is a lot more of it about.

Although there may be more resistance about, how effective is it? In what ways do irony, fiddles, cynicism, etc, overcome the power of organizations? In an era of hypocritical organizations (Brunsson 1989), organizations are increasingly characterized by discursive 'spin' on the part of their ever more sophisticated managers, who produce homes within which so-called resistances can flourish and without which real discontent might ensue. Custodians of organizational hypocrisy would be disappointed if they did not generate some resistance by whingeing. However, as long as resistance can be contained and 'spin' applied to it, then organizational power is not affected. Perhaps this is why there remain graphic forms of organized resistance – 9/11, the Bali bombing, the Battle in Seattle to name but a few – albeit utilizing new global, networked forms of organization. So formal indicators of resistance, such as strike rates, associated with some classical conceptions of identity such as social class, may be declining in some societies but less institutionalized forms of resistance that cleave around classical issues of identity, such as terrorist bombs and insurrectionary warfare, are on the rise in others. Nor is it clear that more nuanced forms of resistance are so new, for example, wasn't Švejk resisting discipline in the 1920s? Maybe, it is not the practice of resistance that has changed so much as the study and definition of it, which is only now catching up with its diversity and complexity.

Power and Reflexivity

Foucault's idea that power/knowledge could not be decoupled dealt another blow to researchers – it meant that salvation was no longer to be found in privileged academic understandings.

No longer a disinterested observer, acutely aware of the social and historical positioning of all subjects and the particular intellectual frameworks through which they are rendered visible, the researcher can only produce knowledge already embedded in the power of those very frameworks. No privileged position exists from which analysis might arbitrate (Clegg and Hardy 1996: 3).

Claims to know the real interests of any group, other than through the techniques of representation used to assert them, could not survive this re-conceptualization of power, and researchers were forced to turn to an explicit consideration of a range of reflexive techniques to view their phenomenon of choice afresh and to consider their role in its analysis. Ten years ago, we emphasized the importance of reflexivity, which we defined as conducting research in a way that turns back upon and takes account of itself (Clegg and Hardy 1996). Since then, researchers whose theoretical convictions range from realism to postmodernism have taken up the case of reflexivity (Brewer 2000; Johnson and Duberley 2003). Weick (1999: 803) has argued that, recently, theory construction has become largely an 'exercise in disciplined reflexivity'. Foucault's influence and the concomitant growth in the analysis of discourse, while creating challenges for researchers, has been profound, providing opportunities to reflect on the ambiguous and constructed nature of data and innovative ways of engaging with it (Alvesson and Kärreman 2000b). We have become more aware of the knowledge making enterprise (Weick 1999), the institutional, social and political processes that shape it (Calás and Smircich 1999) and our role as individual researchers within it (Hardy et al. 2001; Phillips and Hardy 2002).

Reflexivity can be a double-edged sword – it is occupying an increasingly glorified and privileged position (Alvesson and Sköldberg 2000), as well as leading to some narcissistic (O'Doherty and Willmott 2001), self-indulgent and circular (Weick 1999) practices. There are costs of reflexivity – it takes time, brain power and text space (Harley et al. 2004). It may be used as a rhetorical device – cynical or otherwise – designed to demonstrate researcher credentials in critical or postmodern circles (Alvesson and Sköldberg 2000; Grant and Hardy 2004). Moreover, despite different ways or techniques that help the researcher to introduce reflexivity into a text, all are riven with contradictions, tensions and paradoxes (Harley et al. 2004). None are perfect. As Foucault (1980) pointed out, every social setting has its own politics of truth – discourses that makes it possible to distinguish true and false statements – and reflexivity is rapidly becoming one of ours.

Conclusions

Many management researchers would see power as somewhat irrelevant and marginal to central concerns of current organization theory, an argument that has been put recently by Hinings and Greenwood (2002: 411) in asking what is the point of organization theory today? When organization theory was conceived as the sociology of organizations, the point was clear; it was to address the question, 'what are the *consequences* of the existence of organizations?' The question has two elements: 'First, how organizations affect the pattern of privilege and disadvantage in society; second, how privilege and disadvantage are distributed within organizations' (Hinings and Greenwood 2002: 411). Both refer to central issues of power in relation to organizations. The authors argue that the former question has all but disappeared from discussion in the 1980s and 1990s, while the latter receives only scant treatment as the field has increasingly adopted a business perspective. When these questions are asked from a sociological perspective, the focus is on control and its consequences, i.e. power; but when asked from a business perspective, the focus is on the organizational design of efficient and effective solutions to the problems of business owners. Ignoring the sociological does have, however, significant business implications. One consequence of this shift in emphasis is the effective marginalization of a capacity to address questions such as the corporate collapses of Enron, WorldCom and Arthur Andersen, among many others, as well as the ability to address the widespread disclosure of corporate malfeasance.

As we write this chapter, we cannot be oblivious to other framing factors, of course, such as the US-led coalition's occupation of Iraq and the 'War on Terrorism'. In the wake of the scandals around the abuse of power by prison guards and others in the various goals and detention centres, it would be surprising if Goffman, Milligram and Zimbardo do not enjoy a citation surge. Similarly, one might expect the Foucauldian legacy, with its emphasis on surveillance and new forms of governmentality, to see continued interest. As power operates through knowledge, through everyday ways of sensemaking that are more or less institutionalized in disciplinary knowledge, the normalcy of the normal becomes constructed as such. New forms of panoptic surveillance continue to be relevant (e.g. Sewell 1998), but also the way in which morality and obedience implicate each other. Similarly, the rhetoric of the War on Terrorism invites studies on the power of discourse, and further study of how discourses exploit and are exploited through the identities they create, the understandings they shape, and the actions they promote (e.g. Hardy and Phillips 2004; Mumby 2004) Other new directions, such as a concern with 'circular' and 'soft' power have also emerged (Munro 1999; Romme 1999; Courpasson 2000a, b).

There are, then, important business and social reasons that indicate the need for the continued study of power in organizations, and recent theoretical work, including – but not restricted to – that informed by Foucault offers important insights into some recent organizational practices. Still, we must remark, on the whole, however, that few North American theorists seem to find Foucault of much interest. For instance, when Üsdiken and Pasadeos (1995) made a comparison of co-citation networks in European and North American organization studies, they identified Foucault as the seventh-most-cited researcher in *Organization Studies*, just behind Weber, who was fifth. Neither Weber nor Foucault, nor many others influential in the European list, made the top ten in the comparable *ASQ*-based lists – Weber just snuck in at the bottom of the 'hot 100', while Foucault didn't rate a mention. Only 16 articles have appeared with power in the title in the top three US journals[8] in the last 10 years, and none made any reference to Foucault at all.

The times are right for a renewed emphasis on power: while the end of the Cold War and the collapse of communism deflated many earlier Marxist critiques, in the ensuing decade the unbridled exercise of power in organizations has become evident as something ethically repugnant, through collapses such as World Com and Enron, such that even the mainstream has to concede that there was something rotten in the existing state of power that allowed a small cadre of senior executives illegitimately to loot and plunder. In addition, the analysis of power has become more sophisticated in an era which, amongst all the other 'posts' it has been reported as being, is indubitably post-Foucauldian. And as we have remarked, the total institutions aspects of Foucault's work resonate with contemporary abuses of power in organizations as well as with classical concerns in its sociology. Additionally, the recent formal integration of the critical management

studies interest group into the Academy of Management, and the growing interest in critical work among American scholars suggests an optimistic scenario for the study of power. Similarly in Europe, Canada and other countries around the world where organizational researchers have traditionally been less reluctant to engage with the nuances of power, scholars continue to engage with concepts such as power, control and resistance. It is, then, far too soon to write off the centrality of power for the analysis of organizations simply because of its relative neglect in some quarters (Clegg 2002; Hinings and Greenwood 2002).

Acknowledgement

The authors would like to acknowledge Peter Fleming and thank him for sharing his ideas on recent developments in the work on power and resistance.

Notes

1. For more details, see Clegg and Hardy (1996).
2. For more details, see Hardy and Clegg (1996).
3. As this chapter is being written, IBM is being sued in connection for its technical contribution to the Holocaust.
4. This issue of discursive and non-discursive relates to a complex debate about what constitutes a text. For the purposes of this discussion, however, we simply wish to make the point that it can be helpful to distinguish the material from the linguistic and that this is not necessarily at odds with organizational discourse theory (e.g. Phillips and Hardy 1997; Hardy and Phillips 1999).
5. In this paper, in the *Organizational Development Journal*, one will find that it starts with the quote: power is everywhere not because it embraces everything, but because it comes from everywhere (Foucault 1979: 93).
6. Gabriel (1999) makes a conceptual distinction between normative and panoptic controls although empirical evidence seems to suggest that they are often combined through a combination of the management of culture and electronic surveillance (e.g. Fleming 2003).
7. One issue that arises is how to study resistance that is invisible to peers and superiors but not, apparently, researchers given the legitimation and representation crises posed by postmodernism (Denzin and Lincoln 1994).
8. *Administrative Science Quarterly, Academy of Management Review* and *Academy of Management Journal*.

References

Alvesson, M. (1984) 'Questioning rationality and ideology: on critical organization theory', *International Studies of Management and Organizations*, 14: 61–79.

Alvesson, M. and Deetz, S. (1996) 'Critical theory and postmodernism approaches to organizational studies', in S.R. Clegg, C. Hardy and W. Nord (eds), *Handbook of Organization Studies*. London: Sage. pp. 191–217.

Alvesson, M. and Kärreman, D. (2000a) 'Varieties of discourse: on the study of organizations through discourse analysis', *Human Relations*, 53: 1125–49.

Alvesson, M. and Kärreman, D. (2000b) 'Taking the linguistic turn in organizational research: challenges, responses, consequences', *Journal of Applied Behavioral Science*, 36: 136–58.

Alvesson, M. and Sköldberg, K. (2000) *Reflexive methodology: New vistas for qualitative research*. London: Sage.

Alvesson, M. and Willmott, H. (1992) 'On the idea of emancipation in management and organization studies', *Academy of Management Review*, 17: 432–64.

Arendt, H. (1994) *Eichmann in Jerusalem: A report on the banality of evil*. New York: Penguin Books.

Astley, W.G. and Sachdeva, P. (1984) 'Structural sources of intraorganizational power: a theoretical synthesis', *Academy of Management Review*, 9: 104–13.

Bain, P. and Taylor, P. (2000) 'Entrapped by the 'electronic panopticon'? Worker resistance in the call centre', *New Technology, Work and Employment*, 15: 2–18.

Barbalet, J.M. (1985) 'Power and resistance', *British Journal of Sociology*, 36: 531–48.

Barker, J. (1993) 'Tightening the iron cage: concertive control in self-managing teams', *Administrative Science Quarterly*, 38: 408–37.

Bauman, Z. (1982) *Memories of class: The pre-history and after-life of class*. London: Routledge & Kegan Paul.

Bauman, Z. (1989) *Modernity and the Holocaust*. Cambridge: Polity Press.

Benfari, R., Wilkinson, H. and Orth, C. (1986) The effective use of power. *Business Horizons*, 29: 12–16.

Bradshaw, P. and Boonstra, J. (2004) 'Power dynamics in organizational change: a multi-perspective approach', in J. Boonstra (ed.), *Dynamics of organizational change and learning*. London: John Wiley & Sons Ltd. pp. 279–300.

Braverman, H. (1974) *Labor and monopoly capital*. New York: Monthly Review Press.

Brewer, J. (2000) *Ethnography*. Buckingham: Open University Press.

Brunsson, N. (1989) *The organization of hypocrisy*. Chichester: John Wiley.

Burawoy, M. (1979) *Manufacturing consent*. Chicago: Chicago University Press.

Burman, E. and Parker, I. (1993) 'Introduction – discourse analysis: the turn to the text', in E. Burman and I. Parker (eds), *Discourse analytic research: Repertoires and readings of texts in action*. London: Routledge. pp. 5–13.

Calás, M. and Smircich, L. (1992) 'Using the 'F' word: feminist theories and the social consequences of organizational research', in A. Mills and P. Tancred (eds), *Gendering organization analysis*. London: Sage. pp. 222–34.

Calás, M. and Smircich, L. (1999) 'Past postmodernism. Reflections and tentative directions', *Academy of Management Review*, 24: 649–71.

Carchedi, G. (1987) *Class analysis and social research*. Oxford: Blackwell.

Casey, C. (1995) *Work, self and society: After industrialism*. London: Sage.

Clegg, S.R. (1975) *Power, rule and domination*. London: Routledge.

Clegg, S.R. (1979) *The theory of power and organization*. London: Routledge & Kegan Paul.

Clegg, S.R. (1989a) *Frameworks of power*. London: Sage.

Clegg, S.R. (1989b) 'Radical revisions: power, discipline and organizations', *Organization Studies*, 10: 97–115.

Clegg, S.R. (1990) *Modern organizations: Organization studies for the postmodern world*. London: Sage.

Clegg, S.R. (2002) "Lives in the balance'. A comment on Professor Hinings and Greenwoods' 'disconnects and consequences in organization theory?', *Administrative Science Quarterly*, 47(3): 428–41.

Clegg, S.R. and Dunkerley, D. (1980) *Organization, class and control*. London: Routledge & Kegan Paul.

Clegg, S.R. and Hardy, C. (1996) 'Introduction', in S.R. Clegg, C. Hardy and W. Nord (eds), *Handbook of organization studies*. London: Sage. pp. 1–28.

Clegg, S.R., Boreham, P. and Dow, G. (1986) *Class, politics and the economy*. London: Routledge & Kegan Paul.

Clegg, S.R., Kornberger, M. and Pitsis, T. (2005) *Managing and organizations: An introduction to theory and practice*. London: Sage.

Collinson, D. (1992) *Managing the shopfloor: Subjectivity, masculinity and workplace culture*. Berlin: Walter de Gruyter.

Courpasson, D. (2000a) 'Managerial strategies of domination: power in soft bureaucracies', *Organization Studies*, 21: 141–61.

Courpasson, D. (2000b) *L'action contrainte*. Paris: Presses Universitaires de France.

Crozier, M. (1964) *The bureaucratic phenomenon*. Chicago: University of Chicago Press.

Crozier, M. and Friedberg, E. (1980) *Actors and systems: The politics of collective action*, Arthur Goldhammer (trans.). Chicago: University of Chicago Press.

Cyert, R.M. and March, J.G. (1963) *A behavioral theory of the firm*. Englewood Cliffs, NJ: Prentice-Hall.

Deetz, S. (1985) 'Critical-cultural research: new sensibilities and old realities', *Journal of Management*, 11: 121–36.

Deetz, S. (1992a) *Democracy in an age of corporate colonization: Developments in communication and the politics of everyday life*. Albany, NY: State University of New York.

Deetz, S. (1992b) 'Disciplinary power in the modern corporation', in M. Alvesson and H. Willmott (eds), *Critical Management Studies.* London: Sage. pp. 21–45.

Delbridge, R. (1995) 'Surviving JIT: control and resistance in Japanese transplant', *Journal of Management Studies*, 32: 803–17.

Denzin, N.K. and Lincoln, Y.S. (1994) *Handbook of qualitative research.* Thousand Oaks, CA: Sage Publications.

du Gay, P. (1996) *Consumption and identity at work.* London: Sage.

Edelman, M. (1964) The symbolic uses of politics. Champaign, IL: University of Illinois Press.

Edwards, R. (1979) *Contested terrain.* New York: Basic Books.

Emerson, R.M. (1962) 'Power-dependence relations', *American Sociological Review*, 27: 31–41.

Fairclough, N. (1992) *Discourse and social change.* Cambridge: Polity Press.

Fairclough, N. (1995) *Critical discourse analysis: The critical study of language.* London: Longman.

Fairclough, N. and Wodak R. (1997) *Critical discourse analysis. Discourse as social interaction.* London: Sage.

Fernie, S. and Metcalf, D. (1999) '(Not) hanging on the telephone: Payment systems in the new sweatshops', in D. Lewin and B. Kaufmann (eds) *Advances in Industrial and Labour Relations 9.* Greenwich, CT: JAI Press. pp. 23–67.

Fleming, P. (2003) 'Diogenes goes to work: culture, cynicism and resistance in the contemporary workplace'. PhD thesis, University of Melbourne.

Fleming, P. and Sewell, G. (2003) 'Looking for the good soldier, Svejk: alternative modalities of resistance in the contemporary workplace', *Sociology*, 36: 857–73.

Fleming, P. and Spicer, A. (2002) 'Workers playtime? Unravelling the paradox of covert resistance in the contemporary workplace', in S.R. Clegg (ed.), *Paradoxical new directions in management and organization theory.* Amsterdam: Benjamin. pp. 65–85.

Fleming, P. and Spicer, A. (2003) 'Working at a cynical distance: implications for subjectivity, power and resistance', *Organization*, 10: 157–79.

Follett, M.P. (1918) *The new state: Group organization, the solution for popular government.* New York: Longman, Green and Co.

Follett, M.P. (1924) *Creative experience.* New York: Peter Smith, 1951 reprint with permission by Longmans, Green and Co.

Foucault, M. (1972) *The archaeology of knowledge.* New York: Pantheon Books.

Foucault, M. (1977) *Discipline and punish: The birth of the prison.* Harmondsworth: Penguin.

Foucault, M. (1979) *History of sexuality, Volume 1: An introduction.* Harmondsworth: Penguin.

Foucault, M. (1980) *Power/knowledge: Selected interviews and other writings 1972–1977.* Brighton: Harvester Press.

French, E. and Delahaye, B. (1996) 'Individual change transition: moving in circles can be good for you', *Leadership and Organization Development*, 17: 22–32.

French, J.R.P. and Raven, B. (1968) 'The bases of social power', in D. Cartwright and A. Zander (eds), *Group Dynamics.* New York: Harper & Row. pp. 259–69.

Frost, P.J. (1987) 'Power, politics and influence', in F.M. Tablin, L.L. Putnam, K.H. Roberts and L.W. Porter (eds), *Handbook of organizational communications: An interdisciplinary perspective.* London: Sage. pp. 503–48.

Frost, P.J. (1989) 'The role of organizational power and politics in human resource management', in G.R. Ferris and K.M. Rowland (eds), *International Human Resources Management.* Greenwich, CT: JAI Press. pp. 1–21.

Gabriel, Y. (1999) 'Beyond happy families: a critical reevaluation of the control-resistance-identity triangle', *Human Relations*, 52: 179–203.

Gamble A. and Walton, P. (1972) *From alienation to surplus value.* London: Croom Helm.

Gandz, J. and Murray, V.V. (1980) 'The experience of workplace politics', *Academy of Management Journal*, 23: 237–51.

Goffman, E. (1959) *The presentation of self in everyday life.* New Jersey: Anchor Books.

Goffman, E. (1961) *Asylums.* Harmondsworth: Penguin.

Grant, D. and Hardy, C. (2004) 'Struggles with organizational discourse', *Organization Studies*, 25: 5–14.

Grant, D., Hardy, C., Oswick, C. and Putnam, L. (2004) *Handbook of organizational discourse.* London: Sage.

Hall, S. (2001) 'Foucault: power, knowledge and discourse', in M. Wetherell, S. Taylor and S.J. Yates (eds), *Discourse theory and practice: A reader.* London, Thousand Oaks, CA, New Delhi: Sage in association with the Open University. pp. 72–81.

Haney, C., Banks, C. and Zimbardo, P. (1973) 'Interpersonal dynamics in a simulated prison', *International Journal of Criminology and Psychology*, 1: 69–97.

Hardy, C. and Clegg, S.R. (1996) 'Some dare call it power', in S.R. Clegg, C. Hardy and W.R. Nord (eds), *Handbook of organization studies.* London and Thousand Oaks: Sage Publications. pp. 622–41.

Hardy, C. and Clegg, S.R. (2004) 'Power and change: a critical reflection', in J. Boonstra (ed.), *Dynamics of organizational change and learning.* London: John Wiley & Sons Ltd. pp. 343–56.

Hardy, C. and Leiba-O'Sullivan, S. (1998) 'The power behind empowerment: implications for research and practice', *Human Relations*, 51: 451–83.

Hardy, C. and Phillips, N. (1999) 'No joking matter: discursive struggle in the Canadian refugee system', *Organization Studies*, 20: 1–24.

Hardy, C. and Phillips, N. (2004) 'Discourse and power', in S.R. Clegg, C. Hardy and W.R. Nord (eds), *Handbook of organization studies.* London and Thousand Oaks: Sage Publications. pp. 299–316.

Hardy, C., Phillips, N. and Clegg, S.R. (2001) 'Reflexivity in organization and management studies: a study of the production of the research 'subject'', *Human Relations*, 54: 3–32.

Harley, B., Hardy, C. and Alvesson, M. (2004) 'Reflecting on reflexivity', *Proceedings of the Academy of Management*, New Orleans, USA, 8–11 August.

Hasek, J. (1973) *The good solider Svejk*. Cecil Parrott (trans.). London: Heinemann.

Hearn, J. and Parkin, P.W. (1983) 'Gender and organizations: a selective review and a critique of a neglected area', *Organization Studies*, 4: 219–42.

Hickson, D.J., Butler, R.J., Cray, D., Mallory, G.R. and Wilson, D.C. (1986) *Top decisions: Strategic decision-making in organizations*. San Francisco, CA: Jossey-Bass.

Hickson, D.J., Hinings, C.R., Lee, C.A., Schneck, R.E. and Pennings, J.M. (1971) 'A strategic contingencies theory of intraorganizational power', *Administrative Science Quarterly*, 16: 216–29.

Hinings, C.R. and Greenwood, R. (2002) 'Disconnects and consequences in organization theory?', *Administrative Science Quarterly*, 47: 411–21.

Holmer-Nadesan, M. (1996) 'Organizational identity and space of action', *Organization Studies*, 17: 49–81.

Hyman, R. and Brough, I. (1975) *Social values and industrial relations*. Oxford: Basil Blackwell.

Iedema, R.A.M. (1998) 'Institutional responsibility and hidden meanings', *Discourse and Society*, 9: 481–500.

Johnson, P. and Duberley, J. (2003) 'Reflexivity in management research', *Journal of Management Studies*, 40: 1279–303.

Kanter, R.M. (1977) *Men and women of the corporation*. New York: Basic Books.

Keenoy, T., Oswick, C. and Grant, D. (1997) 'Organizational discourses: text and context', *Organization*, 4: 147–57.

Kelman, H.C. (1973) 'Violence without moral restraint', *Journal of Social Issues*, 29: 25–61.

Kerfoot, D. and Knights, D. (1993) 'Management, masculinity and manipulation: from paternalism to corporate strategy in financial services in Britain', *Journal of Management Studies*, 30: 659–77.

Knights, D. and McCabe, D. (2000) 'Ain't misbehaving? Opportunities for resistance under new forms of 'quality' management', *Sociology*, 34: 421–36.

Knights, D. and McCabe, D. (2002) 'A road less travelled: beyond managerialist, critical and processual approaches to total quality management', *Journal of Organisational Change Management*, 15: 235–54.

Knights, D. and Morgan, G. (1991) 'Strategic discourse and subjectivity: towards a critical analysis of corporate strategy in organisations', *Organization Studies*, 12: 251–73.

Knights, D. and Willmott, H. (1985) 'Power and identity in theory and practice', *Sociological Review*, 33: 22–46.

Knights, D. and Willmott, H. (1989) 'Power and subjectivity at work: from degradation to subjugation in social relations', *Sociology*, 23: 535–58.

Knights, D. and Willmott, H. (1992) 'Conceputalizing leadership processes: a study of senior managers in a financial services company', *Journal of Management Studies*, 29: 761–82.

Kunda, G. (1992) *Engineering culture: Control and commitment in a high-tech corporation*. Philadelphia: Temple University Press.

Lawrence, T.B., Winn, M. and Jennings, P.D. (2001) 'The temporal dynamics of institutionalization', *Academy of Management Review*, 26: 626–44.

Lukes, S. (1974) *Power: A radical view*. London: Macmillan.

Mann, M. (1986) *The sources of social power, Volume 1: A history of power from the beginning to A.D. 1760*. Cambridge: Cambridge University Press.

Marx, K. (1976) *Capital*. Harmondsworth: Penguin.

Mayes, B.T. and Allen, R.W. (1977) 'Toward a definition of organizational politics', *Academy of Management Review*, 2: 674–8.

Mayo, E. (1975) *The social problems of an industrial civilization*. London: Routledge & Kegan Paul.

Mechanic, D. (1962) 'Sources of power of lower participants in complex organizations', *Administrative Science Quarterly*, 7: 349–64.

Milgram, S. (1971) *The individual in a social world*. Reading, MA: Addison and Wesley.

Mills, A. and Tancred, P. (1992) *Gendering organization analysis*. London: Sage.

Mumby, D. (2001) 'Power and politics', in F. Jablin and L.L. Putnam (eds), *The new handbook of organizational communication*. Thousand Oaks, CA: Sage. pp. 585–623.

Mumby, D. (2004) 'Discourse, power and ideology: unpacking the critical approach', in D. Grant, C. Hardy, C. Oswick and L. Putnam (eds), *Handbook of organizational discourse*. London: Sage. pp. 237–58.

Mumby, D.K. and Stohl, C. (1991) 'Power and discourse in organizational studies: absence and the dialectic of control', *Discourse and Society*, 2: 313–32.

Munro, R. (1999) 'Power and discretion: membership work in the time of technology', *Organization*, 6: 439–50.

Murphy, A.G. (1998) 'Hidden transcripts of flight attendant resistance', *Management Communication Quarterly*, 11: 499–535.

O'Doherty, D. and Willmott, H. (2001) 'Debating labour process theory: the issue of subjectivity and the relevance of poststructuralism', *Sociology*, 35: 457–76.

Parker, I. (1992) *Discourse dynamics*. London: Routledge.

Perrow, C. (1979) *Complex organizations: A critical essay*. Glenview, IL: Scott Foresman.

Pettigrew, A.M. (1973) *The politics of organizational decision making*. London: Tavistock.

Pettigrew, A.M. (1977) 'Strategy formulation as a political process', *International Studies of Management and Organizations*, 7: 78–87.

Pettigrew, A.M. (1985) *The awakening giant: Continuity and change in imperial chemical industries*. Oxford: Basil Blackwell.

Pfeffer, J. (1981) *Power in organizations*. Marshfield, MA: Pitman.

Pfeffer, J. (1992) 'Understanding power in organizations', *California Management Review*, 35: 29–50.

Pfeffer, J. and Salancik, G. (1974) 'Organizational decision making as a political process', *Administrative Science Quarterly*, 19: 135–51.

Phillips, N. and Hardy, C. (1997) 'Managing multiple identities: discourse, legitimacy and resources in the UK refugee system', *Organization*, 4: 159–85.

Phillips, N. and Hardy, C. (2002) *Discourse analysis: Investigating processes of social construction*. Thousand Oaks, CA: Sage.

Phillips, N., Lawrence, T. and Hardy, C. (2004) 'Discourse and institutions', *Academy of Management Review*, 29(4): 635–52.

Pile, S. (1997) 'Introduction: opposition, political identities and spaces of resistance', in S. Pile and M. Keith (eds), *Geographies of resistance*. London and New York: Routledge. pp. 1–32.

Prasad, P. and Prasad, A. (2000) 'Stretching the iron cage: the constitution and implications of routine workplace resistance', *Organization Science*, 11: 387–403.

Pringle, R. (1989) 'Bureaucracy, rationality, and sexuality: the case of secretaries', in J.D. Hearn, D.L. Sheppard, P. Tancred-Sherriff and G. Burrell (eds), *The sexuality of organizations*. London: Sage. pp. 158–77.

Putnam, L.L. and Cooren, F. (2004) 'Alternative perspectives on the role of text and agency in constituting organizations', *Organization*, 11: 323–34.

Ranson, S., Hinings, R. and Greenwood, R. (1980) 'The structuring of organizational structure', *Administrative Science Quarterly*, 25: 1–14.

Ray, C. (1986) 'Social innovation at work: the humanization of workers in twentieth century America'. PhD thesis, University of California, Santa Cruz.

Reed, M. (1998) 'Organizational analysis as discourse analysis: a critique', in D. Grant and C. Oswick (eds), *Discourse and Organization*3. London, Sage. pp. 193–213.

Reed, M. (2004) 'Getting real about organizational discourse', in D. Grant, C. Hardy, C. Oswick and L. Putnam (eds), *Handbook of organizational discourse*. London: Sage. pp. 413–20.

Romme, A.G.L. (1999) 'Domination, self-determination and circular organizing', *Organization Studies*, 20: 801–31.

Schacht, R. (1971) *Alienation*. London: Allen & Unwin.

Schwenk, C.R. (1989) 'Linking cognitive, organizational and political factors in explaining strategic change', *Journal of Management Studies*, 26: 177–88.

Sewell, G. (1998) 'The discipline of teams: the control of team-based industrial work through electronic and peer surveillance', *Administrative Science Quarterly*, 43: 397–428.

Sewell, G. and Wilkinson, B. (1992) 'Someone to watch over me: surveillance, discipline, and the justintime labour process', *Sociology*, 29: 25–61.

Sotirin, P.J. and Gottfried, H. (1999) 'The ambivalent dynamics of secretarial 'bitching': control, resistance, and the construction of identity', *Organization*, 6: 57–80.

Sturdy, A. and Fineman, S. (2001) 'Struggles for the control of affect – resistance as politics and emotion', in A. Sturdy, I. Grugulis and H. Willmott (eds), *Customer service: Empowerment and entrapment*. London: Palgrave. pp. 135–56.

Szachowicz-Sempruch, J. (2003) 'Faking it. Notes on the margins of power theory: fortune-telling, deconstruction and organization development', *Organization Development Journal*, 21: 70–85.

Taylor, J.R. and Van Every, E.J. (2000) *The emergent organization: Communication as its site and service*. Mahwah, NJ: Lawrence Erlbaum and Associates.

Taylor, J.R., Cooren, F., Giroux, N. and Robichaud, D. (1996) 'The communicational basis of organization: between the conversation and the text', *Communication Theory*, 6: 1–39.

Taylor, P., Hyman, J., Mulvey, G. and Bain, P. (2002) 'Work organization, control and the experience of work in call centres', *Work, Employment and Society*, 16: 133–50.

Thompson, J.D. (1956) 'Authority and power in identical organizations', *American Journal of Sociology*, 62: 290–301.

Thompson, P. (1990) 'Crawling from the wreckage: the labour process and the politics of production', in D. Knights and H. Willmott (eds), *Labour Process Theory*. London: Macmillan. pp. 95–124.

Thompson, P. and Ackroyd, S. (1995) 'All quiet on the workplace front? A critique of recent trends in British industrial sociology', *Sociology*, 29: 615–33.

Townley, B. (1993) 'Foucault, power/knowledge and its relevance for human resource management', *Academy of Management Review*, 18: 518–45.

Tretheway, A. (1997) 'Resistance, identity and empowerment: a postmodern feminist analysis of clients in a human service organization', *Communication Monographs*, 64: 281–301.

Üsdiken, B. and Pasadeos, Y. (1995) 'Organizational analysis in North America and Europe: a comparison of co-citation networks', *Organization Studies*, 16: 503–26.

Van Dijk, T.A. (1997) 'Discourse as interaction in society', in T.A. Van Dijk (ed.), *Discourse as structure and process*. London: Sage. pp. 1–37.

Vince, R. and Broussine, M. (1996) 'Paradox, defense and attachment: accessing and working with emotions and relations underlying organizational change', *Organization Studies*, 17: 1–21.

Watson, T.J. (1982) 'Group ideologies and organizational change', *Journal of Management Studies*, 19: 259–75.

Webb, M. and Palmer, G. (1998) 'Evading surveillance and making time: an ethnographic view of the Japanese factory floor in Britain', *British Journal of Industrial Relations*, 36: 611–27.

Weber, M. (1978) *Economy and society: An outline of interpretive sociology*, 2 volumes, G. Roth and C. Wittich (eds). Berkeley: University of California Press.

Weick, K. (1999) 'Theory construction as disciplined reflexivity: Tradeoffs in the 90s', *Academy of Management Review*, 24: 797–806.

Whyte, W. (1960) *The organization man*. Harmondsworth: Penguin.

Willmott, H. (1993) 'Strength is ignorance, slavery is freedom: managing culture in modern organizations', *Journal of Management Studies*, 30: 515–52.

2.14 Networks and Organizations

KELLEY A. PORTER AND WALTER W. POWELL

Introduction

Networks provide three broad categories of benefits: access, timeliness and referrals (Burt 1992). They are a ubiquitous and critical feature of organizational life. Organizations have never been isolated, self-sustaining operations; thus all organizations, as well as the individuals within them, are enmeshed in networks at varied, multiple levels. More recently, however, the decline of the vertically integrated firm in favour of outsourcing, the rapid growth of the global economy, the pressing need to access knowledge and resources outside the boundaries of an organization, and the increased co-ordination efforts resulting from spreading an organization's operations to multiple locations around the world, have amplified the salience and variety of networks. This growth has triggered increased scholarly attention both to internal networks within organizations and external linkages across organizations. Over the past two decades, a steady stream of research on networks has exploded into a rich and prolific line of inquiry. Special issues of social science and management journals devoted to the topic have appeared in droves, and the term 'networking' now even takes on an instrumental, rather sketchy, connotation in business speech.

We begin with a brief overview of the leading approaches to the study of networks.[1] We suggest that much of the extensive literature can be classified in one of two ways: those that use networks as a tool to trace relationships; and those that view networks as a form of governance. We then look at the stages of an organization's life cycle and highlight periods during which networks of various forms play a crucial role. We group our discussion around key stages of organizational evolution, including founding, growth and maturity. This life cycle approach provides a fresh and complementary alternative to other recent reviews of the literature that have emphasized a division into levels of analysis. We not only highlight the current literature, but when appropriate suggest areas where additional work would be beneficial.

Networks as a Tool to Trace Relationships

A long line of work in sociology and social psychology employs networks as an analytical device for illuminating social relations, whether among individuals or groups inside an organization, in the inter-organizational ties that link organizations, or in the environments of organizations. We briefly review below some of the key studies that have shaped how social scientists view networks. The concepts are presented in a roughly chronological order, based on their first introduction. Examples of subsequent work relating to each concept are featured. Nearly all the core concepts originated at the individual level, but today they are used not only to describe relationships between people, but also between organizations, and in some cases nation-states.

Webs of Affiliation

Even before Moreno (1934) devised the familiar nodes and lines of sociograms in the 1930s, Simmel (1955 [1922]) was thinking in network terms when he argued that people's webs of affiliation – the multiple and sometimes overlapping group affiliations that humans have with family members, social organizations and/or occupational groups – were fundamental in defining the social identity of individuals. Simmel's ideas were developed further by a number of researchers. Most notably, Merton (1957) used social circles and role-set theory to emphasize the challenges posed from having multiple roles called upon at the same time (e.g. parent and employee), but also the benefit of autonomy that could result from publicly identifying the demands attached to different roles. Kadushin (1966; 1968) refined the definition of social circles, viewing them as entities without formal membership, rules or leadership that provide a rich environment for forming interpersonal connections. He showed how the presence of influential social circles could be inferred from the behavioural similarities among collections of individuals. More recently, studies of friendship networks (Marsden 1987; Moody 2001) as well as corporate elites (Useem 1984; Kadushin 1995) point out the cultural underpinnings of network ties.

Balance Theory

In the 1940s, Heider (1946) developed balance theory, which stressed the importance of maintaining an equilibrium of relations. Specifically, in any set of triads, if person A was positively linked to person B and vice-versa, their opinion of person C needed to agree in order for the triad to be balanced. In the same way, a mutually negative relationship between A and B would be balanced only if they disagreed in their opinion of C. Heider's work was quickly expanded from triads to the structural balance of entire groups and eventually led to the first substantive empirical and model-based clustering methods for social network data (Wasserman and Faust 1994). In the 1970s, both Holland and Leinhardt (1977; 1979) and Killworth and Bernard (1976; 1979) actively pursued lines of research focused on triadic analysis. More recently, Krackhardt and Kilduff (1999) use data from four small organizations to study transitive triplets, that is situations where two friends of a person are themselves friends. They demonstrate that people tend to perceive relations close to them (e.g. two of their closest friends) and far from them (e.g. two of their acquaintances) to be more balanced than relations in-between (e.g. two of their co-workers whom they interact with on a regular basis at work, but not outside of work).

Small Worlds

Milgram (1967) developed his idea of small worlds through the now famous experiment where he tracked the passage of correspondence among strangers. Specifically, he sent letters to individuals in a small town in Middle America and asked them to return the letter to a person in New York by sending the letter to someone they personally knew and whom they thought might know the targeted person. It took an average of six mailings to reach the targeted person in New York. Popularized in John Guare's play *Six Degrees of Separation* and the *Kevin Bacon Game*, Milgram's ideas provided the foundation for recent work on small worlds (Watts and Strogatz 1998; Watts 1999; 2003; Walker and Kogut 2001; Baum et al. 2004; Uzzi and Spiro 2005). The core insight is that adding only a handful of remote links to a large network when local clustering (e.g. friends of friends) is high is sufficient to create a small world network. Even a very small number of randomly distributed ties can knit together diverse clusters of nodes to produce small world phenomena.

Strength of Weak Ties

In the 1970s, through path-breaking work on job searches, Granovetter (1973; 1974) studied the process of searching for a job, and found that novel information was more likely to come from people with whom an individual was acquainted rather than close connections, because strong friends typically shared common information. This phenomenon, referred to as 'the strength of weak ties', has become a standard tool in many network studies and served as the impetus for work on social or network embeddedness. Building on Granovetter's insight about the bridging aspects of networks, Burt (1992) asked what kinds of gains were derived from brokerage activity. The answer was that individuals who serve as bridges, that is being the sole link that holds otherwise unconnected parts of the network together, are afforded considerable advantages, including higher compensation, faster promotion and access to good ideas (Burt 2000; 2002). For example, consider the propitious role of a manager who can funnel information from his group of supervisees to higher levels of the organization and similarly pass information from above down the line. Podolny (1993; 2001) amplified ideas about structural holes, suggesting they are most beneficial when the focal individual or organization is unsure about the uses of resources. On the other hand, when alters are unsure about the quality of ego's products, they often rely on the status of key affiliates to infer quality. Put differently, 'one [concept of a network in a market] is a conduit or pipe for information and resources. The second is as a lens or prism through which the qualities of actors are inferred by potential exchange partners' (Podolny 2001: 58).

Network as Governance Structures

A more multidisciplinary and prescriptive literature treats networks as a particular logic, or form of organizing, that governs relations among individuals and/or organizations. The classic differentiation here involves the organization of economic activities into markets, hierarchies or networks (Powell 1990). Markets are governed by contract or property rights. Goods are exchanged on the basis of price and participants typically seek the lowest cost supplier regardless of past relations. Conflict tends to be resolved through bargaining and, if need be, the law. In contrast, hierarchies are defined by an employment relationship. For the most part, employees are committed to their employer and subject to supervision or administrative fiat. Daily routines are conducted in the context of a mostly formal or bureaucratic system. Networks, both within and across organizations, are based on neither transactions nor rules, but on ongoing relationships, embedded in friendship, obligation, reputation and possibly trust. The interdependent and committed parties develop norms of reciprocity that lead to open-ended relationships and mutual benefits. A network form of organizing can allow organizations to simultaneously enjoy the benefits of being small (e.g. responding quickly), while at the same time gaining economies of scale that are typically reserved for much larger organizations (Scott 1998).

Powell and Smith-Doerr (1994), as well as Harrison (1994), suggest that four diverse forms of organizing typify the network form. First, within craft industries such as construction (Stinchcombe 1959) and film production (Faulkner and Anderson 1987), work is organized around specific projects, and firms are linked through joint involvement in those projects. Networks are embedded in technical communities, and formal organizations are often more temporary and less durable than long-term relationships among members of the community.

Second, small firm-led industrial districts, such as those found in machine tools, leather, furniture, clothing and foodstuffs in the Third Italy (Brusco 1982; Becattini 1990), as well as in the Taiwanese system of organization (Hamilton and Biggart 1988), lead to a model of decentralized production (Piore and Sabel 1984). Third, in some heavy production industries, networks of suppliers will often geographically cluster around a central core firm (or firms) such as automobile companies or aircraft manufacturers in a hub and spoke network (Dyer and Nobeoka 2000). Fourth, large organizations are increasingly disaggregating production, either through outsourcing, strategic alliances or efforts to access new knowledge. Such trends are particularly notable in knowledge-based industries, such as information technology, semiconductors and biotechnology (Chesbrough 2003; Powell and Snellman 2004).

We see these two approaches to networks as largely complimentary. Thus, our review incorporates studies that use networks as an analytical device, as well as studies that feature networks as a form of organization or governance. The instrumental use of networks to gain resources is profiled heavily in the early sections of the review where money and advice are essential to an organization's survival. When an organization moves beyond its initial, rapid stage of expansion, we often observe that an organization is enmeshed in a web of affiliations, and the structure of this network, and its mode of organizing, plays an important role in shaping organizational outcomes.

Networks and Organizational Life Cycles

A life cycle model is a useful framework for tracking the birth, growth and maturation (or transformation) of organizations. By grouping studies based roughly on stage of development, we underscore the differing type (e.g. formal vs informal) and level (e.g. intra- vs inter-organizational) of networks that facilitate the acquisition of resources such as advice, money, technical knowledge, customers and suppliers. This approach also allows us to highlight the differing role of several recurring themes, including informal networks, which are particularly prevalent in early and growth stages and embeddedness. While embeddedness can be seen as a position that emerges overtime and thus is associated with more developed organizations, research suggests that some organizations begin their lives already embedded in a rich network of relations. The term 'embeddedness' was first introduced by Polanyi (1944), although much of the research in the last 20 or so years has been in response to the work of Granovetter (1985), who argued that behaviour is greatly influenced by interpersonal and interorganizational relations, and that these relationships condition the extent to which individuals and organizations pursue either self-interested or other-regarding behaviour. Granovetter (1990) subsequently distinguished two types of embeddedness: relational embeddedness, which emphasizes the role of direct cohesive ties as a means to acquire fine-grained information; and structural embeddedness, which attends to the value of information derived from occupying different structural positions in a network. Embeddedness can be a double-edged sword, as access to information is enhanced by both close as well as diverse ties; however, the ties that bind can become ties that blind, restricting the flow of information as well as the capacity to adapt.

We begin with organizational foundings, emphasizing the interplay between social networks – both informal and formal – and reputation, as well as how these factors are crucial to getting an organization started, particularly through the acquisition of resources. At the outset, entrepreneurs call on who they know, as well as form new connections, to find the financial resources and organizational know-how that they need to start their organizations. Those who are successful in their initial search for resources and partnerships will find that their organizations grow. As organizations mature, access to information remains critical, but the types of networks that organizations are involved in shift from identity-based to more purposive ties. In particular, organizations transition from primarily socially embedded ties to a balance of embedded and arm's-length relations (Hite and Hesterly 2001). Thus, in our second section we focus on the search for resources as an organization grows, and the critical choice of opting for internal or external sources. We first look at how expansion shapes the ways in which organizations may utilize networks to learn effectively. We then consider how organizations collaborate, for various purposes, through different types of partnerships. As organizations grow and interact with their environments they become more

aware of their boundaries, and consciously monitor their relationships and their networks of affiliations. Thus, we consider what happens to organizations once they become embedded in their environments, and whether such close linkages entail constraints as well as benefits. We conclude with a discussion of maturity, when organizations reach a plateau after going through a period of growth, and are faced with the challenge of renewing their affiliations or facing ossification.

Before proceeding, two caveats are important. First, we do not suggest that these stages are discrete or mutually exclusive. Organizations do not stop acquiring resources and only then begin to learn how to use them. Clearly, the boundaries between stages of growth are blurry and many activities remain critical throughout an organization's lifetime. Nevertheless, each of the activities that we focus on tends to be more prevalent at certain points in an organization's history. Secondly, much of the empirical work we have included spans multiple topic areas. For example, Larson's (1992) work on the formation and control of networks by young firms analyses both the process of acquiring resources and the subsequent learning gained throughout the lifespan of an alliance.

The Role of Networks in New Ventures

Stinchcombe (1965) famously argued that people need access to sufficient resources of wealth, power and legitimacy in order to build organizations. Access to these resources often comes through social networks, which consist of relational ties that foster the flow of a wide variety of resources among individuals. These networks enable individuals to engage in activities that would be much more difficult (if not impossible) if they were not socially connected to the person with whom they were interacting (Lin 2001). Since an organization does not start with its own network, during the initial formation stages the social network of the founding team is analogous to the firm's network (Aldrich and Zimmer 1986; Bhide 2000; Hite and Hesterly 2001). Accessing ties wisely by connecting with influential partners may have substantial economic benefits for organizations, as measured by rates of growth, profitability and/or survival. Baum and Oliver (1992) showed that daycare centres in the metropolitan Toronto area were more likely to survive if they had direct connections to municipal government and community agencies, in contrast to centres that lacked such connections. Similarly, access to a diverse portfolio of highly central organizations has proven to be valuable for science-based firms in the fast-developing field of biotechnology (Powell et al. 2005). Florin et al. (2003) demonstrate that among 275 high growth firms that went public in the US in 1996, those with extensive social resources, as measured by the companies' business networks, personal networks and numbers of underwriters subscribed to the IPO, were more successful in accumulating financial capital in their pre-IPO years as compared to those with fewer social resources.

Founders do not need to wait until an organization is officially born to search for resources such as capital and initial employees. For many entrepreneurs, this process begins well before incorporation (Reynolds 1994). Reynolds and Miller (1992) suggested that the start-up process began with any of four key events – commitment, first financing, first hire or first sale – and finished when all four milestones had been reached. Commitment, through actions such as gathering information and resources and identifying potential customers and suppliers, was the first of the four events to occur in 85% of the more than 3000 organizations the authors surveyed. In the remaining 15%, the start-up process began with one of first financing, hire or sale; all 24 combinations of events were present in the full sample of firms they studied. During this start-up process, personal networks can be aggregated into extended networks that entrepreneurs then call upon for much-needed resources (Dubini and Aldrich 1991). How entrepreneurs use these social networks, however, shifts throughout the period of formation. In this section we summarize studies that highlight the role of informal and formal networks in soliciting advice and financial resources.

Advice

The primary reason entrepreneurs contact others is to gain support and test business ideas (Kamm and Nurick 1993). Some of the first people that they turn to are family and friends. Birley (1985; 1989) found that entrepreneurs in Indiana cited friends, family and colleagues as critical sources of information. Individuals starting export clothing businesses

in Turkey also said they received key information from family and friends (Bruderl and Preisendorfer 1998). In Germany, a study of 1700 new organizations revealed that those that survived longer than 5 years had founders who were more likely to cite spouses, family and friends as the most important sources of information (Riddle and Gillespie 2003).

Greve and Salaff (2003) use Wilken's (1979) three-stage model of motivation, planning and establishment of a new venture to dig deeper and investigate how entrepreneurs in four countries developed and maintained social contacts during these three phases of organizational development. Focusing exclusively on where entrepreneurs go for advice and information, the authors find that the pattern of activity is similar in the four countries, although the size of networks is not. Entrepreneurs in all countries limit the size of their discussion networks when they are initially deciding whether they should pursue a new venture. They then expand the size of their networks, as well as the time they spent connecting to others, during the planning phase. Subsequently, during the establishment stage, they reduce both the size of their networks, as well as the time spent connecting to others. Across all stages, founders in the US had the largest networks, followed by the Swedish and Italians, while entrepreneurs in Norway had the sparest discussion networks. Another study finds that Norwegian entrepreneurs also gain important information from strong ties, but finance tends to come through weak ties (Jenssen and Koenig 2002). In the US, Hansen (2000) tracked a small group of individuals enrolled in an entrepreneurship certificate course and finds that in the early and final stages of the start-up process there is a focus on strengthening existing ties and processing available information; in-between these entrepreneurs focus on building the breadth rather than depth of their networks.

Some founders look beyond their circles of informal relations for more formal role models and sources of financial capital. When thinking about whether to found an organization, nascent entrepreneurs who have more heterogeneous networks and/or a lower proportion of family members in their networks are more likely to start an organization than those with more homogenous and/or family dominated networks (Renzulli et al. 2000). Angel investors and other mentors become valuable references because they link a nascent entrepreneur to a larger community of potential resource providers, as well as teach the founders how to be more effective entrepreneurs (Malecki 1997; Leonard and Swap 2000; Thornton and Flynn 2003). Ardichvili et al. (2000) conducted in-depth interviews with 27 angel investors in the US and found that 60% of the investors provide one or more type of support in addition to financial capital. Of those who provide additional support, 52% are involved in creating or reshaping the business concept, 38% help recruit additional managers or members of the management team, and 38% find additional sources of financial capital. Surprisingly, only 20% of the angel investors who provide non-financial support work with founding teams to expand their networks of either personal and professional advisors, and/or prospective customers and suppliers.

Perhaps when making investment decisions angel investors and venture capitalists (VCs) feel that it is easier to help shape the team than it is the underlying product. Baum and Silverman (2004) sampled the population of Canadian biotechnology start-ups operating in the 1990s to analyse the companies' intellectual and human capital, as well as characteristics of the alliances they had formed. They find that VCs tend to finance start-ups with strong technology but weaker management expertise. Similarly, Hellman and Puri (2002) find that VC-backed Silicon Valley electronics start-ups move to outside management faster than non-VC-backed firms, suggesting that the venture capitalists play an important role in 'professionalizing' the organization. In addition to investors, links to other formal mentors may also shape an organization's behaviour. A handful of prominent Silicon Valley law firms have made routine the legal side of the start-up process and become the carriers of institutional practices and norms. By partnering with one of these law firms, new organizations learn the most effective methods for starting a company (Suchman et al. 2001).

Money

To supplement their own savings, many founders rely on others for additional sources of funding. Only a very small portion of firms receive this funding from venture capitalists (Bruno and Tyebjee 1985; Harrison et al. 2004), a topic to which we return below. Many more, however, rely on family and friends for not only information and emotional support as described above, but also for financial resources (Zimmer and Aldrich 1987; Staber and

Aldrich 1995). Surveys received from 160 new business owners in Indiana reported that a little over half received financial support through informal sources such as family and friends, while a third successfully obtained financial support from formal institutions such as banks (Birley 1985). More recently, in-depth interviews with 48 nascent entrepreneurs who were searching for funding and were from a range of industries in Silicon Valley reveal that a little more than a third received seed stage investments from friends and family, about a quarter received investments from professional investors, 21% received investments from both sources and the remaining nearly 20% did not obtain any outside financial support (Ferraro 2003).

Immigrant Entrepreneurs

While many entrepreneurs make a conscious choice to forgo formal channels of investments, either because they do not need or desire the money, others, such as immigrant populations, are often discriminated against by regular financial institutions (Gerber 1982). For these groups, semi-formal sources of funding such as revolving credit associations, which operate on the basis of obligations, accountability and frugality, are an important basis of entrepreneurial activity (Ardener 1964; Woodrum 1981; Biggart 2001). Specifically, these types of associations enabled many Asian immigrant entrepreneurs to start their small businesses in the US (Light 1972; Light and Bonacich 1988). In 1960s Miami, early Cuban immigrants who had been bankers in Cuba were employed first as clerks and subsequently as loan officers in Miami banks. Once established, they began offering small 'character' loans to new penniless Cuban immigrants based on their reputations back in Cuba and the knowledge that they would be ostracized in both Cuba and Miami if they did not repay their loans. The result was that not a single loan was defaulted. The policy was discontinued when the bankers could no longer verify the individuals' social reputations in their native country (Portes and Stepnick 1993). Similarly, putting one's reputation on the line, coupled with swift retribution to those who defaulted, are primary mechanisms undergirding informal loans in New York City's Dominican community, where businessmen frequently lend money to one another with little or no paperwork (Portes and Guarnizo 1991).

In contrast to these findings, however, Min (1988) found that personal savings coupled with family money financed the great majority of ethnic entrepreneurs' businesses; and Russell (1984) argued that ethnic entrepreneurs were creative in their search for financial capital and used many vehicles other than rotating credit associations to raise funds. Similarly, Bates (1997) uses US Census data to demonstrate that the majority of start-up capital comes from equity and debt, regardless of whether the individuals starting the businesses are immigrant Koreans and Chinese, non-immigrant Asian-Americans or non-minorities. Entrepreneurs may choose to forgo informal ethnic lending programmes because of constraints associated with such lending. Portes and Sensenbrenner (1993) observed that individuals who became successful were limited in their ability to grow because they were expected to support others in the community. In addition, the very solidarity that successfully enabled informal lending policies also restricted individual freedom to try things differently. Finally, individual mobility was limited by the community's 'fear that a solidarity born out of common adversity would be undermined by the departure of the more successful members' (Portes and Sensenbrenner 1993: 1342). Bates (1994) also suggested that the advantages of tight social networks among immigrant entrepreneurs were not always beneficial. In his research on the success and survival patterns of Asian immigrant firms, he found that it was large investments of financial capital and impressive educational credentials of the business owners that typified the more successful firms. In contrast, the less profitable and more failure-prone small businesses were those that depended heavily on social support networks. This latter group was also more likely to use sources other than banks to borrow funds (Bates 1997).

Reputation

For those who are able to access more formal and traditional sources of capital, reputation and/or the social capital of the people and organizations with whom they are affiliated is often a critical determinant of who will or will not receive financial capital. Unlike human capital, which is carried by an individual, social capital is a function of one's general location in a social structure and therefore can only be assessed with reference to the structure of relations in question (Burt 1992; Granovetter 1994).

Signalling social capital or reputation in the field by demonstrating valuable experience and relying on endorsements of others is important in helping entrepreneurs overcome any scepticism that outsiders may have (Schoonhoven and Eisenhardt 1996; Burton et al. 2002). For example, Canadian biotechnology firms that early in their lifecycles establish alliances with universities and other research institutions and/or with pharmaceutical, chemical or marketing companies, exhibit significantly higher early performance growth (Baum et al. 2000). Endorsement from prominent others, however, does not come without a cost. Using a sample of ventures that received multiple offers for funding, Hsu (2004) finds that reputable venture capital firms were selected most often despite offering funds that on average totalled 10–14% less than other financing offers that the new ventures received. What is lost in money, we suspect, is made up for in mentorship and increased access to important contacts for additional alliances.

Shane and colleagues (Shane and Khurana 2001; Shane and Cable 2002; Shane and Stuart 2002) draw on a database of MIT patent applications to look at the process of resource acquisition from both the entrepreneur's, as well as the investor's, point-of-view. They demonstrate the combined importance of crucial linkages, reputation and technical ability. Together, these studies show that investors will use social ties to gather information about the new ventures, including the founders' reputations in the industry, but fund the venture only if they feel it has potential. The more uncertain the technology, the more dependent the team is on its status and social relations. Thus, not only do social networks direct entrepreneurs to potential sources of capital, they also serve as conduits for background checks on the credibility of those involved. In turn, the single most important determinant of whether the firm goes public is whether it has successfully received venture funding.

Reputation looms large at the time of initial public offering. Firms with reputable venture capitalists and partners receive more funding at IPO and have a larger network of alliances (Chang 2004). At the time of IPO in American markets, endorsement by prominent affiliates such as investment bankers correlate to higher market valuations of private firms, as do management teams and board members with prominent upstream and downstream affiliations (Stuart et al. 1999; Higgins and Gulati 2003).

In addition, investments by higher status venture capital firms signal lower risks to other investors (Podolny 2001). At the same time, however, the importance of various affiliations may differ depending on the state of the equity market. For example, in the biotechnology industry, ties to prestigious venture capitalists are more beneficial during cold markets, while ties to prominent investment banks are particularly advantageous during hot markets (Gulati and Higgins 2003).

Similar results have been found outside of the biotech industry. Fischer and Pollock (2004) use a sample of all firms that went public in 1992 to demonstrate that increased network embeddedness, venture capital ownership, CEO ownership and the interaction between founder-CEO presence at the time of IPO and CEO ownership all decreased the likelihood of firm failure within 5 years of going public. Analysing a sample of Italian IPOs, Ravasi and Marchisio (2003) suggest that not only does reputation correlate with positive outcomes, the IPO itself may increase a firm's reputation by increasing its visibility, prestige and perceived trustworthiness. These factors in turn strengthen and expand a firm's network of access to important external resources.

Favoured at Birth?

Nevertheless, although some founders do establish links to influential strangers, Aldrich (1999) finds that most entrepreneurs tend to maintain an existing set of affiliations rather than strategically constructing new networks when they form an organization. One benefit of partnering with known individuals and successful past partners is reduced search costs and risks of opportunism (Gulati 1993; Gulati and Gargiulo 1999). Furthermore, people tend to start companies in geographical areas and industries in which they have previously worked and often in response to a challenge they faced (Stinchcombe 1965; Freeman 1986; Phillips 2001). Thus, they are likely to have a relevant set of potential customers and suppliers on which to draw. Hite's (2003) typology of relational embeddedness in emerging entrepreneurial firms captures some of this aforementioned variability. She suggests that, rather than thinking of ties as simply embedded or not embedded, relationships between an entrepreneur and others may be classified based on the presence of one or more of three social components. She terms these

components: personal embeddedness, characterized by a relationship based on a social rather than work connection; competency embeddedness, based on prior experience with a person with whom one has reliably done business in the past; and hollow embeddedness, based on reputation and/or a third party, rather than a direct prior tie.

Future Work: Networks or Networking?

Research on entrepreneurs and organizational foundings has excelled at incorporating both formal and informal ties into studies. This combination is much less frequent in studies of more developed organizations. The individualist focus of early stage studies on a single founder or a founding team affords easy access to a set of informal relations. Moreover, there are comparatively few formal contracts at this stage of an organization's life cycle. The result of such a focus, however, is that most empirical work has coded the relationships between nodes as the independent variables (e.g. how many financiers?) and organizational or individual outcomes (e.g. how fast does the organization grow?) as the dependent variables. We know little, if anything, about the structural placement of a founder within his or her networks, or the relations between those to whom the founder is tied. The aforementioned studies on immigrant entrepreneurs, reputation and/or multiple foundings within an industry begin to tackle these questions to varying degrees, but much more could be done to understand the networks, rather than networking activities, of entrepreneurs.

The Role of Networks in Growing Ventures

Organizations that make extensive use of external resources grow much faster than their competitors that lack connections to external resources. George et al. (2001) find that boards of directors of community banks that actively pursue external linkages outperform those that do not actively develop such networks. Similarly, Jarillo (1989) tracked the growth of nearly 2000 public American firms and found that the fastest growing companies were those that made heavy use of resources that were outside of their direct control (e.g. partnering with an original equipment manufacturer instead of investing in the manufacturing equipment themselves). Over a 10 year period, those that relied most heavily on external resources grew at a yearly rate that was on average 10% greater than their competitors. Moreover, as these firms grew, they begin to exploit their power as a critical link in a network of relationships instead of exclusively emphasizing cohesion (Uzzi 1997). They also turn inward to work out their own growing pains. Communication with, and knowledge of, the rest of the organization is much simpler when there are two or even 20 employees as compared to 50, 100 or more. Thus, organizations turn to a variety of different sources to access new information. A first avenue may be to look internally and see what information resides there. If the desired information cannot be found internally, organizations may attempt to acquire the knowledge through internal expansion and/or by forming external alliances. We consider the role of networks in the implementation of each of these strategies.

Internal Networks

Seeking information from another person is a function of knowing and valuing what the other individual knows, as well as being able to gain timely and affordable access to that person's thinking (Borgatti and Cross 2003). The structure of networks within an organization, that is how individuals and/or operating units are connected, influences the flow of information. Specific structural components, such as having a loosely connected group vs tightly formed clusters, as well as certain positions within the structure, such as a central vs peripheral location, are more beneficial. In this section, we highlight studies that consider the relationship between network structures and organization-level outcomes.

Organizations typically strive to reduce uncertainty. Hence, employees often use internal networks to gather information. The amount of discussion between buyers and sellers on a major securities exchange floor influenced both the direction and magnitude of option price volatility, a useful indicator of uncertainty. Baker (1984) found that a smaller trading group was more competitive than a large group because the clustered group shared ample information across all members, which resulted in less price volatility. In contrast, the larger group formed multiple sub-groups, each of which primarily traded amongst itself and therefore did not benefit from access to full information. Similarly, Mizruchi and Stearns (2001) studied how relationship managers in a commercial bank utilized their networks to close deals that required the approval of three bank officers. They find that while deals are more likely to be accepted when managers seek approval from individuals with whom they do not have close connections, managers instinctively go to their most trusted social connections. By using weak rather than strong ties some managers were able to craft deals that better met both the bank and customer's criteria. In a similar vein, Oh et al. (2004) examine the relationships of 60 work teams in 11 Korean organizations and find that informal social ties that bridge to other areas within the organization provide greater levels of group effectiveness when compared to more cohesive internal social ties. They suggest that moderate levels of internal socializing among group members is optimal, noting that these results counter much of the literature on team building that argues for highly cohesive teams. These studies illustrate the importance of networks in providing access to information, and suggest that structures that offer divergent points of view are quite useful.

Networks Across Divisions

As organizations grow, so does the likelihood of having multiple operating units and thus the need to transfer information across divisions increases. In general, organizational units with a dense network structure are more productive than those with a sparse network (Reagans and Zuckerman 2001). Those with both high internal density as well as numerous connections to other operating units also finish projects more quickly (Reagans et al. 2004). Moreover, the more knowledge that units contain, the more likely they are to communicate and form ties with others (Tsai 2000; Schultz 2001).

Tsai and Ghoshal (1998) found that informal social relations and tacit social arrangements in a large electronics firm encouraged productive exchange and combination of resources across units, which in turn had a positive influence on the level of product innovation. Hansen (1999) offered a more complex portrait of networks in a large computer company. He showed that weak inter-unit ties helped the search for knowledge, but not its effective transfer. When knowledge is simple, weak inter-unit ties speed up the projects, but slow them down when the knowledge that needs to be transferred is highly complex. Rulke and Galaskiewicz (2000) find similar results in experimental tests that demonstrate the impact of group structure and knowledge distribution on group performance. In most cases, teams of MBA students who have general or broadly distributed information outperform those teams that have specialized knowledge or a mix of specialized and general knowledge. When the network structure is decentralized, however, the advantage afforded to the generalist disappears. Finally, Hansen and Lovas (2004) use data on nearly 5000 dyads between product development teams and subsidiaries with relevant knowledge to explore the relationship between formal organization structure, informal relations, geographic distance and the relatedness of competencies across subsidiaries. Similar to the aforementioned study on banking, teams prefer to approach individuals they know rather than those who understand the related technologies well. In addition, even if they are expert with a relevant technology, geographically distant subsidiaries are avoided, unless informal relations have been established.

Understanding an organization's structure is also important to the successful implementation of new policies or procedures. In Krackhardt and Hanson's (1993) case study of the attempt to unionize a group of high-tech system installers, the vote ultimately failed despite a high level of initial interest. A careful look at the network structure revealed that the union organizers had focused all their attention on the individual at the centre of the formal, rather than informal, network. The authors speculated that the union may have had more success if they had targeted the person at the centre of the informal network. Gargiulo and Benassi (2000) demonstrate that when a major change occurs in an individual's task environment, the composition of his network can influence the extent to which he is able to successfully adjust to his new role. A group of European managers in a large multinational computer firm, which had traditionally worked within units, was charged with designing and co-ordinating cross-functional project teams. The results show that managers with cohesive networks (i.e. primarily based in their prior operating unit) experience greater difficulty in reshaping their networks to match the broader network that is required to pull together appropriate team members from multiple

divisions. These results suggest that when selecting an individual for a new role, or to persuade her to adopt a new initiative, both her structural position within the organization as well as her individual qualifications should be considered.

Unique Ways of Capturing Knowledge Through Networks

The study of organizational networks has traditionally focused on either intra- or inter-organizational relationships. We highlight studies related to the former above and return to the latter below. Before we do so, however, two less traditional means of tapping into diverse networks of needed information deserve mention. The first method is to hire an individual for his expertise and connections. The second is to expand geographically by setting up a foreign subsidiary or acquiring a foreign corporation. By establishing a presence in the foreign country and hiring locals, organizations often gain access to country-relevant information and networks that are unavailable to outsiders. In addition, we highlight the use of informal networks to share knowledge, which occurs often but is rarely studied due to its inherent measurement difficulties.

Hiring

If an organization concludes that relevant information is not available in-house, an effective means of acquiring it may be to hire an individual with that knowledge. By studying the patenting activities of engineers who moved from US firms to non-US firms, Song et al. (2003) find that knowledge transfer is most likely to be successful when the individuals hired are used to explore technologically distant knowledge and therefore have non-redundant information. In addition, these new hires bring with them their own set of informal contacts, thus extending the hiring firm's geographic reach. Using data on the semiconductor industry, Rosenkopf and Almeida (2003) show that firms can use individual inventors to bridge distant contexts and therefore overcome the constraints of contextually localized search.

Foreign Expansion

A second way in which organizations may learn new information is by locating their foreign R&D

activities in information-rich regions. Almeida and Phene (2004) use patent citation data to demonstrate that the technological richness of the multinational firm, the subsidiary's knowledge linkages to host country firms, and the technological diversity within the host country all have a positive influence on innovation. In a survey of nearly 300 managers in 98 foreign subsidiaries of Swedish multinational corporations in diverse industries, Andersson et al. (2001) found that the extent to which the subsidiary is technologically embedded in its local environment has a positive direct relationship to the subsidiary's performance in its local market and a positive, but indirect relationship with the subsidiary's ability to secure resources from headquarters. Technological embeddedness was measured as the extent to which the subsidiary's suppliers and/or customers directly influenced changes to its products and/or processes. Feinberg and Gupta (2004) analyse 7 years of data on foreign subsidiaries of 361 R&D-intensive US multinational corporations to determine what features of the industry and host country predict the likelihood of the multinational selecting a pre-established subsidiary for R&D activity. As the number of other US-controlled same industry subsidiaries in the host country increases, so too does the likelihood of the focal company establishing R&D activities in that country. The same effect is not observed with an increase in non-US controlled foreign subsidiaries. These results suggest that potential knowledge spillovers from US-, but not foreign-controlled, subsidiaries are salient to US multinationals. Similar results emerged for Korean multinationals investing in China. Chang and Park (2005) demonstrate that network externalities were stronger among firms within the same business groups, from the same countries and within the same industries.

Acquisitions are another way in which an organization can gain entry into a new area, although a host of post-implementation challenges often limits the benefits to the acquiring firm (Anand and Singh 1997; Larsson and Finkelstein 1999; Ranft and Lord 2002). Nevertheless, looking specifically at overseas acquisitions, Vermeulen and Barkema (2001) find that, despite initial problems with performance and implementation, acquisitions, when compared to setting up foreign subsidiaries, are more likely to broaden a company's knowledge base and decrease inertia, enhancing the viability of its later ventures. Thus, in lieu of forming partnerships with foreign

corporations, organizations will sometimes set up foreign subsidiaries either from scratch or through the process of acquisition. The result is that organizations have the potential to integrate knowledge from the parent company with local external knowledge at a deeper level than a partnership might provide. Moreover, when the outpost is established through acquisition, those networks are already in place.

Informal Networks

Informal networks can be found everywhere in organizations. The core contributions of organizational sociology in the 1950s, most notably work by Gouldner (1950), Roy (1954) and Dalton (1959), stressed the critical role of informal networks, cliques and social ties to generating solidarity, conflict and shared perceptions. This rich vein of research has not been carried forward, however, and work on informal networks as the glue that binds organizations together or as avenues for power and mobility has declined. In part, this lack of attention is a consequence of methodological predisposition. All of these superb studies were detailed ethnographies, based on lengthy periods of observation. Contemporary work on informal networks is much more likely to be based on surveys and/or interviews, rather than extensive qualitative field work.

One line of current work on informal networks focuses on the important role that they play in the transfer of knowledge. Bouty (2000) uses in-depth interviews with 38 scientists from 13 firms in multiple industries to understand the process of informal knowledge sharing. She finds that scientists frequently do share information and resources (e.g. samples) across organization boundaries, but they only share with those whom they know and trust and only when they judge that sharing will not have a negative consequence for their own companies. Saxenian (1994) showed that informal meetings and the free-flow of individuals from one organization to another were some of the driving forces behind the vitality of Silicon Valley. Schrader (1991) demonstrated that the participation of US specialty steel and mini-mill employees in informal information-transfer networks was correlated with positive economic performance. Such participation also enhanced the reputation of engineers in industry-wide professional networks. Although informal networks are commonly linked to specific individuals, organizations also utilize informal networks, as illustrated by the use of handshakes rather than formal contracts between two parties (Macaulay 1963; Larson 1992).

Creating Inter-Firm Networks as a Source of Knowledge

As organizations grow, their need for information and resources, reduced uncertainty, enhanced legitimacy and/or attainment of collective goals may lead to formal partnerships with external parties rather than in-house development (Galaskiewicz 1985). The first step in forming a collaboration with an outside party is often deciding with whom to partner. Just as entrepreneurs turn to family and colleagues for resources and support, growing organizations will often turn to those with whom they had successfully worked in the past (Gulati 1993).

Using nine years of data on alliances formed in three industries, Gulati and Garguilo (1999) find that prior mutual alliances, common third parties, increased interdependence and joint centrality in the alliance network all influence the likelihood of two organizations forming an alliance. Chung et al. (2000) use data on US investment banking houses' syndication chains in underwriting corporate stock offerings during the 1980s to show that there is an inverted U-shaped relationship between the probability that a lead bank will invite the potential partner to form an alliance and the number of deals they have jointly completed in the past. These results were stronger under more uncertain situations (i.e. a primary vs secondary offering). Similarly, Beckman et al. (2004) find that large service and industrial firms draw more heavily on former alliances and interlocks when experiencing greater market uncertainty.

Barley et al. (1992) examined strategic alliances in the early years of the US biotechnology industry and found that young, small biotechnology companies often had to exchange knowledge for money. They would partner with larger multinational corporations that would fund their research in return for equity investments or the lion's share of the profits from the product which was developed as a result of the research. These relationships reflected a fundamental asymmetry between large and small start-ups, one that younger, smaller firms overcame through time by developing a more diverse portfolio of relations, thus reducing their dependence on the large

multinational pharmaceutical corporations (Powell et al. 2005). Using data on the Canadian biotechnology industry, Baum et al. (2000) find that as organizations grow they can enhance their early performance by actively establishing alliances and configuring their networks. Those that are successful reduce redundancy, conflict and complexity, increase information diversity and partner with potential rivals before they become competitors. In a similar study of the challenges young organizations face in forming partnerships, Almeida et al. (2003) observe that as a semiconductor start-up grows, so too does its ability for external learning from both formal and informal connections. They find that smaller start-ups, despite being more limited in their breadth of formal connections, do a better job than larger firms of gaining knowledge from informal sources. These results are consistent with earlier work that demonstrated that small companies are tied into regional knowledge networks to a greater extent than large firms (Almeida and Kogut 1997).

Alliances are often formed to assist in developing new products. Ahuja (2000) developed a longitudinal dataset of the linkages and patenting activities of 97 leading chemical firms to demonstrate that both direct and indirect ties have a positive relationship with innovation, but that the number of direct ties moderates the influence of indirect ties. At the same time, as the number of structural holes increases, innovation decreases. Ahuja attributes this finding to the increased bureaucratization and operational controls that are required to maintain a diverse set of ties. He posits that time spent on maintaining relationships may detract from time spent on innovative activities. Stuart (1998) also uses a longitudinal dataset to develop a network-based mapping of the technological positions of semiconductor companies and then studies the formation of alliances among them. He finds that organizations that participate in actively innovating technological segments, as well as those firms with a track record of developing prestigious inventions, form alliances at the highest rates. Position in the overall network predicts which organizations establish the greatest number of alliances as well as which ones choose to collaborate with one another.

Beyond Dyads

Our attention has primarily focused on dyadic relationships, or partnerships between two entities, which are the most common forms of collaboration. Multiple organizations do sometimes come together to share knowledge, however. Toyota has not only developed deep relations with its suppliers to increase knowledge sharing and learning capabilities, but has also facilitated the formation of these same types of relations among suppliers themselves. Dyer and Nobeoka (2000) use interviews, archival documents and surveys to assess the influence that Toyota has on its suppliers. They find that: (1) the sharing of best practices between suppliers directly (as opposed to Toyota acting as a gatekeeper in the passing of knowledge), (2) the mandate to share information freely among all members of the supplier network, and (3) matching the correct type of knowledge with the appropriate routines, help improve the efficiency and value of knowledge shared among members of the supplier network. Ingram and Baum (1997) track the fate of 558 transient hotels operated in Manhattan between 1898 and 1980 to find that participating in a chain network provides greater advantages of knowledge transfer, which in turn increases the chance of survival. In industries that rely on common standards, employees from different organizations will often sit together on technical committees. Rosenkopf et al. (2001) determine that joint participation in technical committees helps cellular service providers and equipment manufactures to identify potential alliance partners, but that this effect erodes over time.

Two or more organizations will sometimes form R&D consortia, a legal entity that has registered with the US Justice Department under the National Cooperative Research Act of 1984. Members that are competitors outside of the consortia come together to pool resources and share decision-making for co-operative R&D. Using surveys to understand the process of consortia formation, Doz et al. (2000) identify two dominant paths to formation. They term the first path emergent because the network is characterized by competitive collaboration that is open to parties that share similar interests and a strong environmental interdependence. The consortium is formed to define boundaries and there is tight coupling among members to constrain opportunism. Learning among members is contingent on the emergent collaborative context. The second path is engineered, whereby the network is characterized by exploring options among organizations with weaker environmental interdependence and less similar interests. Usually one organization is at the centre as the

driving force, targeting diverse entities to create a hub and spoke system. In these engineered consortia, sharing and learning among members is likely to be lower. In the public sector, Mintrom and Vergari (1998) find that the likelihood of US policy-makers achieving their goals is increased by their engagement in policy networks. Greater involvement in external networks of individuals and non-profits enhances agenda setting; while greater involvement in state government networks facilitates both agenda setting as well as the likelihood that the policy innovation is approved.

Location, Location, Location

Some organizations are fortunate to be located in regions with dense overlapping ties, strong local norms of behaviour and abundant resources. In such settings, to echo Marshall's (1920) evocative phrase, the secrets of industry are really in the air. In this section, we focus on the advantages and challenges that organizations face in such locales. Organizations tend to take time to establish routines and repeat relationships that embed them in their networks. Having said that, as we noted earlier, most entrepreneurs begin their organizations by relying in large part on pre-established relationships. Moreover, certain regions afford more entrepreneurial opportunities than others. Of course, Stuart and Sorenson (2003) find that once such fertile regions become crowded, new opportunities become less financially rewarding. Thus, in this section we highlight studies that focus not only on the dyadic relationships between an ego and its alter, but also, to varying degrees, account for the influence of ties among alters.

Saxenian's (1994) comparison of high technology industries in Silicon Valley and Route 128 (located on the outskirts of Boston) emphasized how local institutions and culture, industrial structure and corporate organization led to different patterns of success in the 1980s in the two regions. In her analysis, high technology firms along Route 128 displayed a more hierarchical and less open culture than those in Silicon Valley, where conversation, resources and employees moved with relative freedom among organizations. Saxenian argued that the Valley's open environment encouraged innovation and led to growth. In analysing the co-authorship networks of all patents filed in Silicon Valley and the Boston area between 1975 and 2002, Fleming et al. (2003) demonstrate a significant correlation between level of connection or agglomeration of the network and subsequent inventive search within a region. These results extend earlier research that demonstrates that the local transfer of knowledge is influenced by the inter-firm mobility of engineers and thus highly embedded in regional labour networks (Almeida and Kogut 1999).

Even though Boston and Silicon Valley regions are regarded as canonical high-tech clusters, these are by no means the only two locales where information flows across multiple organizations, either through formal alliances or through informal means, such as movement of employees from one employer to another, special interest groups or ethnic-specific industry groups. Other emerging regional clusters of entrepreneurship and innovation include Ireland, Israel, Taiwan and the Bangalore region in India (Bresnahan et al. 2001). Universities also play a special role in the diffusion of knowledge to surrounding clusters of high technology R&D activity (Owen-Smith and Powell 2004). Largely through informal connections, novel ideas are transferred from university labs to industry personnel, often as scientists develop dual affiliations with companies and universities. Moreover, universities supply a region with an employment pool rich in human capital (Acs et al. 1999).

At the same time, however, entrepreneurs should be cautioned against assuming that establishing a start-up in a region that is dense with similar companies will guarantee success. Sorensen and Sorenson (2003) find that nascent entrepreneurs systematically misperceive opportunities for foundings in overcrowded regions. Similarly, Stuart and Sorenson (2003) show that the local conditions that promoted the creation of biotechnology company foundings in Silicon Valley changed over time, and that later entrants encountered much less propitious circumstances.

Dense connections occur not only spatially, but through communities of practice. Indeed, the contingent effects of region and common technological area can be especially powerful. The general agglomeration economies of support services, labour supply and favourable business environment can be amplified among organizations working on a common technological frontier, whether in autos, IT, semiconductors or biotech. In fields, such as biotech, where information is widely dispersed and developing rapidly, learning occurs across networks, key information is accessed externally, and firms

located in denser regions of the overall network are more likely to form alliances (Powell et al. 1996; Walker et al. 1997).

Research on the semiconductor and steel industries underscores the importance of network structure. Kogut et al. (1995) found that firms in the semiconductor industry that wanted to establish a dominant technology standard needed to secure a central position in a co-operative network. Using network centrality as a measure of technological dominance of a standard, they also observed that start-ups were more likely to enter the industry when a dominant technology had been established. Madhaven et al. (1998) examine the dual effects of the regulatory shock of 1984 and the technology shock in 1987 on the evolution of network structure of 130 companies in the steel industry. The first event, which they term a 'structure-reinforcing event', led to an overall tightening of the network and a significant correlation between one's level of centrality pre- and post-event; centrality before and after the second 'structure-loosening event' was not correlated. They suggest that a good time for a central firm to consolidate its position is following a structure-reinforcing event, while the opportunity for a peripheral firm to move to the core follows a structure-loosening event. In one of few comparative studies, Rowley et al. (2000) study the interaction between relational and structural embeddedness in both the semiconductor and steel industries. They find that very tightly interconnected strategic alliance networks dampen firm performance, especially in the semiconductor industry where there is a high level of uncertainty. In this field, strong ties produce lock-in and lack of search. In contrast, strong ties are positively related to performance in the steel industry, while more diverse weak ties positively enhance firm performance in the semiconductor industry.

Limits to Knowledge Sharing

While much research has focused on the increased benefits that stem from transferring technologically distant knowledge across organizations and/or individuals, such activities do not happen seamlessly. Nor are organizations or individuals equally capable of accessing, transferring and processing information. Cohen and Levinthal (1990: 128) suggested that there are limits on the extent to which organizations are able 'to recognize the value of new, external information, assimilate it, and apply it to commercial ends'. They argued that the degree to which firms are able to absorb and integrate new information is largely based on an organization's level of prior related knowledge. For individuals, knowledge is more easily transferred when there is social cohesion (i.e. a willingness to invest the time and energy in sharing information with someone else) and when the person sharing the information has connections to different knowledge pools (Reagans and McEvily 2003). At the business unit level, Tsai (2001) illustrates that the network position of operating units in petrochemical and foods-manufacturing companies significantly influences absorptive capacity and dictates a unit's innovation and performance. At the organizational level, Stuart and Podolny (1999) show that the technological positions of firms enhance the learning benefits derived from alliances among companies in the US semiconductor industry. Thus, at multiple levels of analysis, access to knowledge is conditioned by both structural position and prior level of knowledge.

As organizations begin to interact more with their environments, they assess both how and when to engage with competing or complementary organizations, as well as what value those relationships provide. In dynamic environments, short-term maximizing behaviour that focuses on gaining the most efficient transfer of information from existing contacts can underperform the less immediately purposive or focused strategy of learning from many diverse contacts (Allen 1988). Echoing Allen's idea, Hagedoorn and Duysters (2002: 530–1), using network data on the computer industry, suggest that 'in a dynamic environment characterized by technological change and "openness" of markets, continuous learning, even through seemingly redundant network contacts, is preferable to efficiency-based behaviour'.

Future Directions: Network Analyses of Organizational Communities

In our discussion of young organizations we noted much of the research has focused on founders and the number and types of ties they initiated. Similarly, much work on growing organizations is focused at the dyadic level, examining the nature of formal contractual connections between two parties, and the sum of such linkages. The opportunity is present to push further and move from dyadic analyses to studies of communities, and assess the

patterns of interaction among multiple participants, and how particular patterns shape the opportunity structure of affiliation.

For example, Silverman and Baum (2002) analyse the Canadian biotechnology industry, and gauge how a rival's alliances affect the competitive intensity experienced by a focal organization. They demonstrate that the extent to which the horizontal and vertical alliances of rivals influence a focal firm is determined by overall industry growth and whether such moves block or foreclose opportunities. Similarly, Gimeno (2004) analyses the global airline industry and shows that strategy in the mid-1990s was shaped by alliance exclusivity. Both studies emphasize how competitive strategy is influenced through the rivalry of network affiliations. Moreover, Bae and Gargiulo (2004: 843) argue that

> the joint consideration of the resources of a firm's alliance partners and the network structure in which those resources are exchanged can shed light on how firms may leverage the structure of their alliance network to mitigate the costs that might result from associating with resource-rich – and hence powerful – partners.

They find that firms within the US telecommunications industry use the structure of their alliance network to dampen the influence of powerful partners. They also find, however, that when a company is a broker between two powerful or non-substitutable organizations, there is little benefit to the brokerage role.

Owen-Smith and Powell (2004) broaden the idea of community, focusing on the array of diverse institutional forms – public, private and non-profit – that constitute the biotechnology community in Boston, Massachusetts from the 1980s to 1999. They show that public research organizations provided the backbone out of which a commercial biotech sector evolved and prospered, and that linkages to elite universities and research hospitals shaped the evolution of that network. Research in this vein highlights the value of a focus on the network structure of organizational communities.

Network Dynamics: Maturity, Dissolution, Ossification and Renewal

One of the most welcome developments in network studies is the creation of longitudinal databases that afford the opportunity to study both emergence and dynamics. This focus permits analysis of how changes over time in network structure can influence both markets and politics. Studies of the dynamics of networks and the maturation of network structures offer insight into how the survival chances of organizations are conditioned by the vitality of networks.

In one of the most detailed historical analyses to date, Padgett (2001) traces the evolution of banking in Renaissance Florence over three centuries, suggesting that enterprises have 'logics-of-identity' at founding. This logic-of-identity consists of the set of ideas, practices and social relations of the founder. He traces the reproduction of economic partnerships among Renaissance Florence bankers from the family banking era through the guild era (pre-Ciompi-revolt, 1349–1378) and the Popolani social-class era (post-Ciompi-revolt, 1380–1433) to the patronage era of the Medici family (1434–1494). In tracking network reproduction through time, he maps the network structure of the different eras. He notes that successful families that survived the often contentious and bloody transitions were 'multivocal', that is they were positioned at the confluence of multiple networks and able to invoke perceptions of themselves as engaged in multiple practices and followers of different logics of identity.

Powell et al. (2005) plot the network dynamics of the biotechnology field over a 13 year period and find that different rules for affiliation shape network evolution at different phases in the industry's development. Early corporate entrants who pursued commercialization strategies were supplanted by universities, research institutes, venture capitalists and small firms working together on collaborative activities. As the number and diversity of partnerships grew, cohesive sub-networks formed that were characterized by multiple, independent pathways. Consequently, the combination of scientific acumen and access to deep financial pockets became the earmark of success, at least with respect to the introduction of novel new medicines. Whether such diversified networks that provide ample access to scientific news and money prove to be robust over the course of decades remains to be seen. Nonetheless, this dual analysis of network and institutional evolution provides an explanation for this science-based field's decentralized structure.

Tie Dissolution

One important aspect of research on later stage firms is a focus on the dissolution of ties. Most extant work attends to the formation of networks, with scant attention to the breaking of relations. One reason for this inattention is methodological. Short of one partner dying or adversely failing to hold up their end of the bargain, organizations do not announce the end of a partnership with anything comparable to the fanfare that accompanies formation. Perhaps one exception to this is in the world of advertising where the informal rules of exchange include exclusivity and loyalty. Thus, the announcement of a new advertising agency typically signifies a switch from one partner to another. Under these circumstances, Baker et al. (1998) find that competition, power and institutional forces support or undermine the informal rules of exchange. Institutional forces work to reduce the risk of dissolution, while competitive pressures provide the opposite effect. Powerful advertising agencies use resources to increase tie stability, but powerful clients may use their resources to either increase or decrease stability. Another rare look at network dissolution is provided by Rowley et al.'s (2005) work on investment banks. They analyse the forces that sustain dense clique sub-structures in an inter-firm network, and show the social and instrumental factors that lead certain banks to exit cliques. They suggest that (1) exchanges built on social attraction, (2) identifying complementary skills to accomplish collaborative tasks, and (3) distributing value created among its clique members are three processes that promote clique stability.

Future Research: Network Atrophy

Networks require renewal or rejuvenation in order to maintain diversity and access to fresh ideas and news. As organizations age, their set of affiliations matures, hence concerted effort is required to refresh the portfolio of linkages. In an ethnography that focused on decision-making at a distinguished scholarly publishing house, Powell (1985) showed how the networks of editors – their links to authors and reviewers – calcified as the editors grew older, and no younger editors were hired. Moreover, the very success the press had with mainstream social science research from the 1950s to the 1970s left it poorly positioned to build contacts with new lines of research in areas such as social history, feminism and quantitative research. Consequently, the ossification of the editorial networks led to an eventual decline in the quality of the publishing house's list.

More broadly, over-embeddedness or too dense a portfolio of affiliations that deter access to new information can greatly hinder established organizations. Sorenson and Audia (2000), in their study of footwear production in the US, found that information sharing among spatially concentrated companies lead to costly conformity. Similarly, Glasmeier (1991) attributed the inability of the Swiss watch industry to adapt to the new quartz technology to its closed, tight knit circle of affiliations. In the Ruhr region of Germany, long known for its important manufacturing cluster, cognitive lock-in among homogeneous and tightly knit organizations led to the decline of steel-making (Grabher 1993). This general pattern in which networks turn inward looking, access to new information atrophies, and the diversity of contacts erodes is a powerful challenge for organizations.

Abundant research suggests that established, mature organizations have difficulty maintaining their technological edge (Tushman and Anderson 1986; Christensen 1997). Insufficient attention has focused on the role of network evolution in contributing to this decline. Two recent analyses do, however, suggest that selective organizations have the ability to transform the structure and composition of their networks. In his analysis of IBM's renewal, Chesbrough (2003) argues that policies of open innovation, including building access to external sources of R&D and linkages to smaller firms, were critical. Similarly, Powell et al. (2005) observe that a small number of global pharmaceutical corporations survived a decade of mergers and made the technological transition from organic chemistry to the new molecular biology by recalibrating their affiliations to include more R&D ties with younger companies and research institutes.

Conclusion and Discussion

This survey suggests that organizations utilize networks throughout the life cycle of their development, but the nature of that usage and degree of sophistication varies at different stages. Consider, for example, the difference in the reliance on internal networks by small, start-up organizations and large,

multi-divisional corporations. Or contrast the divergence between smaller entities that are in a largely dependent role vis-à-vis external parties from whom they seek resources or support and large powerful organizations that are actively sought out by many, either as partners or supporters. While such issues of power and dependence loom large in earlier treatments of inter-organizational relations, they have been less salient of late. In part, this shift in perspective reflects that very large organizations may, in fact, have considerable difficulty in making efficacious use of all their internal resources. This limitation is captured in the oft-repeated phrase if only the left hand and the right hand of the organization knew what each other were doing.

A life cycle perspective also directs attention to the changing locus of networks, and how organizational growth and development not only alters structural position but the character and composition of an organization's portfolio of relations. As a simple illustration, consider Genentech, today one of the bellwether companies in the biotechnology industry, with numerous innovative medicines on the market. The company was established in the mid-1970s in a context of great excitement, uncertainty and contestation over the promises of the new biotechnology and genetic engineering. Formal relations with venture capital firms, pharmaceutical companies and universities were essential for its early survival. Genentech had a very successful IPO in 1980, and released a genetically engineered version of human insulin in the early 1980s. However, it had to turn to a large corporate partner, Eli Lilly, to develop and market insulin, so Genentech's gains from its pathbreaking research were shared with its more powerful partner. By the late 1980s, difficulties and questions cropped up during the Food and Drug Administration's regulatory review process, and delayed the release of a much-anticipated new medicine for heart attacks, leaving Genentech vulnerable. The giant Swiss firm Roche became the majority stockholder in Genentech. However, rather than control the company, Roche operated with a light hand and afforded Genentech considerable autonomy, and eventually allowed the company to reassert its independence. This light touch rewarded both Roche and Genentech financially and medically, as a series of new medicines for cystic fibrosis, cancer and blindness were developed. Throughout the 1990s, Genentech grew rapidly, all the while becoming more and more central in the biotechnology industry. In particular,

Genentech became a preferred partner of smaller, young biotech companies that were developing new medicines. Perhaps Genentech was simply modelling its earlier experiences with corporate giants Lilly and Roche, or possibly it was developing new ideas about how to orchestrate a portfolio of collaborations. Either way, this extended example suggests the shifting strategies that organizations pursue as they grow and age, and how position in a network shapes the content of relations.

We also observe that the nature of embeddedness evolves as organizations age. At the founding stage, entrepreneurs are highly leveraged to family and friends, and possibly former colleagues as well, who serve as sources of financial capital, advice and possibly collaborators. Thus, organizations begin their evolution differentially positioned in a web of relations. Consider the contrast between a nascent entrepreneur in a closely connected ethnic enclave and an experienced technologist with diverse contacts to the world of venture capital. The former may experience such strong ties as constraints that bind her and preclude her from trying novel things, while the latter entrepreneur may be able to use connections to foster support for novel ideas. Both founders have a strong set of connections, but the nature of their affiliations may serve to either bind or mobilize them.

Fluidity across levels – from personal to organizational, from organizational to interorganizational – is an exciting and important topic for further inquiry. Our life cycle perspective highlights this aspect by illustrating how individual-level relations evolve into organizational-level connections as enterprises grow. Note how the measures and variables change in the course of research: studies of startups focus on connections to family, friends and angel investors; analyses of IPOs attend to linkages to investment banks and VCs, and research on multinationals examines inter-divisional transfer of knowledge and resources. The real flowering of network studies on organizations will come when research designs capture multilevel influences, attend to both formal and informal networks and chart the evolution of networks.

Note

1. There are numerous extensive reviews of the network literature (Marsden 1990; 2004; Scott 1991; Wasserman and Faust 1994; Portes 1998; Burt 2000; Smith-Doerr and Powell 2005), thus we are intentionally brief here.

References

Acs, Z., Fitzroy, F. and Smith, I. (1999) 'High technology employment, wages and R&D spillover: evidence from U.S. cities', *Economic Innovation and New Technology*, 8: 57–78.

Ahuja, G. (2000) 'Collaboration networks, structural holes, and innovation: a longitudinal study', *Administrative Science Quarterly*, 45: 425–55.

Aldrich, H.E. (1999) *Organizations evolving*. Thousand Oaks, CA: Sage.

Aldrich, H.E. and Zimmer, C. (1986) 'Entrepreneurship through social networks', in D.L. Sexton and R.W. Smilor (eds), *The art and science of entrepreneurship*. Cambridge, MA: Ballinger Publishing Company. pp. 3–23.

Allen, P. (1988) 'Evolution, innovation and economics', in G. Dosi, C. Freeman, R. Nelson, G. Silverberg and L. Soete (eds), *Technical change and economic theory*. London, UK: Pinter. pp. 95–120.

Almeida, P. and Kogut, B. (1997) 'The exploration of technological diversity and the geographic localization of innovation', *Small Business Economics*, 9: 21–31.

Almeida, P. and Kogut, B. (1999) 'Localization and the mobility of engineers in regional networks', *Management Science*, 45: 905–17.

Almeida, P. and Phene, A. (2004) 'Subsidiaries and knowledge creation: the influence of the MNC and host country on innovation', *Strategic Management Journal*, 25: 847–64.

Almeida P., Dokko, G. and Rosenkopf, L. (2003) Start-up size and the mechanisms of external learning: increasing opportunity and decreasing ability? *Research Policy*, 32: 301–15.

Anand, J and Singh, H. (1997) 'Asset redeployment, acquisitions and corporate strategy in declining industries', *Strategic Management Journal*, 18: 99–118.

Andersson, U., Holm U. and Pedersen T. (2001) 'Subsidiary performance in multinational corporations: the importance of technological embeddedness', *International Business Review*, 10: 3–23.

Ardener, S.A. (1964) 'The comparative study of rotating credit associations', *The Journal of the Royal Anthropological Institute of Great Britain and Ireland*, 94: 201–29.

Ardichvili, A., Cardozo, R.N., Tune, K. and Reinach, J. (2000) 'The role of angel investors in the assembly of non-financial resources of new ventures', in R.D. Reynolds, E. Autio, C. Brush, W. Bygrave, S. Manigart, H.J. Sapienza and K.G. Shaver (eds), *Frontiers of entrepreneurship research*, vol. 20. Wellesley, MA: Babson College. pp. 244–57.

Bae, J. and Gargiulo, M. (2004) 'Partner substitutability, alliance network structure, and firm profitability in the telecommunications industry', *Academy of Management Journal*, 47: 843–59.

Baker, W.E. (1984) 'The social structure of a national securities market', *American Journal of Sociology*, 89: 775–811.

Baker, W.E., Faulkner, R.R. and Fisher, G.A. (1998) 'Hazards of the market: the continuity and dissolution of interorganizational market relationships', *American Sociological Review*, 63: 147–77.

Barley, S.R., Freeman, J. and Hybels, R.C. (1992) 'Strategic alliances in commercial biotechnology', in N. Nohria and R.G. Eccles (eds), *Networks and organizations: Structure, form, and action*. Boston, MA: Harvard Business School Press. pp. 311–47.

Bates, T. (1994) 'Social resources generated by group support networks may not be beneficial to Asian immigrant-owned small businesses', *Social Forces*, 72: 671–89.

Bates, T. (1997) 'Financing small business creation: the case of Chinese and Korean immigrant entrepreneurs', *Journal of Business Venturing*, 12: 109–24.

Baum, J.A.C. and Oliver, C. (1992) 'Institutional embeddedness and the dynamics of organizational populations', *American Sociological Review*, 57: 540–59.

Baum, J.A.C. and Silverman, B.S. (2004) 'Picking winners or building them? Alliance, intellectual, and human capital as selection criteria in venture financing and performance of biotechnology start-ups', *Journal of Business Venturing*, 19: 411–36.

Baum, J.A.C., Calabrese, T. and Silverman, B.S. (2000) 'Don't go it alone: alliance network composition and start-ups' performance in Canadian biotechnology', *Strategic Management Journal*, 21: 267–94.

Baum, J.A.C., Rowley, T.J. and Shipilov, A.V. (2004) 'The small world of Canadian capital markets: statistical mechanics of investment bank syndicate networks, 1952–1990', *Canadian Journal of Administrative Sciences*, 21: 307–25.

Becattini, G. (1990) 'The Marshallian industrial district as a socio-economic notion', in G. Becattini, F. Pyke and W. Sengenberger (eds), *Industrial districts and inter-firm co-operation in Italy*. Geneva: International Institute for Labour Studies. pp. 37–52.

Beckman, C.M., Haunschild, P.R. and Phillips D.J. (2004) 'Friends or strangers? Firm-specific uncertainty, market uncertainty, and network partner selection', *Organization Science*, 15: 259–75.

Bhide, A. (2000) *The origin and evolution of new business*. Oxford: Oxford University Press.

Biggart, N.W. (2001) 'Banking on each other: the situational logic of rotating savings and credit associations', *Advances in Qualitative Organization Research*, 3: 129–53.

Birley, S. (1985) 'The role of networks in the entrepreneurial process', *Journal of Business Venturing*, 1: 107–17.

Birley, S. (1989) 'Female entrepreneurs: are they really any different?', *Journal of Small Business Management*, 27: 32–7.

Borgatti, S.P. and Cross, R. (2003) 'A relational view of information seeking and learning in social networks', *Management Science*, 49: 432–46.

Bouty, I. (2000) 'Interpersonal and interaction influences on informal resource exchanges between R&D researches across organizational boundaries', *Academy of Management Journal*, 43: 50–65.

Bresnahan, T., Gambardella, A. and Saxenian, A. (2001) "Old economy' inputs for 'new economy' outcomes: cluster formation in the new Silicon Valley', *Industrial and Corporate Change*, 10: 835–60.

Bruderl, J. and Preisendorfer, P. (1998) 'Network support and the success of newly founded businesses', *Small Business Economics*, 10: 213–25.

Bruno, A.V. and Tyebjee, T.T. (1985) 'The entrepreneur's search for capital', *Journal of Business Venturing*, 1: 61–74.

Brusco, S. (1982) 'The Emilian model: productive decentralization and social integration', *Cambridge Journal of Economics*, 6: 167–84.

Burt, R.S. (1992) *Structural holes*. Cambridge, MA: Harvard University Press.

Burt, R.S. (2000) 'The network structure of social capital', in R.I. Sutton and B.M. Staw (eds), *Research in organizational behaviour*, vol. 22. Greenwich, CT: JAI Press. pp. 345–423.

Burt, R.S. (2002) 'The social capital of structural holes', in M.F. Guillen, R. Collins, P. England and M. Meyer (eds), *The new economic sociology: Developments in an emerging field*. New York: Russell Sage Foundation. pp. 148–92.

Burton, M.D., Sorensen, J.B. and Beckman, C. (2002) 'Coming from good stock: career histories and new venture formation', in M. Lounsbury and M.J. Ventresca (eds), *Research in the sociology of organizations*, vol. 19. Oxford, UK: JAI Press. pp. 231–64.

Chang, S.J. (2004) 'Venture capital financing, strategic alliances, and the initial public offerings of Internet startups', *Journal of Business Venturing*, 19: 721–41.

Chang, S. and Park, S. (2005) 'Types of firms generating network externalities and MNC's co-location decisions', *Strategic Management Journal*, 26: 595–615.

Chesbrough, H.W. (2003) *Open innovation: The new imperative for creating and profiting from technology*. Boston, MA: Harvard Business School Press.

Christensen, C. (1997) *The innovator's dilemma: When new technologies cause great firms to fail*. Boston, MA: Harvard Business School Press.

Chung, S., Singh, H. and Lee, K. (2000) 'Complementarity, status similarity, and social capital as drivers of alliance formation', *Strategic Management Journal*, 21: 1–22.

Cohen, W.M. and Levinthal, D.A. (1990) 'Absorptive capacity: a new perspective on learning and innovation', *Administrative Science Quarterly*, Special Issue: Technology, Organizations, and Innovation 35: 128–52.

Dalton, M. (1959) *Men who manage: Fusions of feeling and theory in administration*. New York: John Wiley & Sons.

Doz, Y.L., Olk, P.M. and Ring, P.S. (2000) 'Formation processes of R&D consortia: which path to take? Where does it lead?', *Strategic Management Journal*, 21: 239–66.

Dubini, P. and Aldrich, H. (1991) 'Personal and extended networks are central to the entrepreneurial process', *Journal of Business Venturing*, 6: 305–14.

Dyer, J.H. and Nobeoka, K. (2000) 'Creating and managing a high-performance knowledge-sharing network: the Toyota case', *Strategic Management Journal*, 21: 345–67.

Faulkner, R.R. and Anderson, A. (1987) 'Short-term projects and emergent careers: evidence from Hollywood', *American Journal of Sociology*, 92: 879–909.

Feinberg, S.E. and Gupta, A.K. (2004) 'Knowledge spillovers and the assignment of R&D responsibilities to foreign subsidiaries', *Strategic Management Journal*, 25: 823–45.

Ferraro, F. (2003) 'Raising capital: relational practices and social capital in Silicon Valley entrepreneurship. Unpublished doctoral dissertation. Stanford University, Stanford, CA.

Fischer, H.M. and Pollock T.G. (2004) 'Effects of social capital and power on surviving transformational change: the case of initial public offerings', *Academy of Management Journal*, 47: 463–81.

Fleming, L., Juda, A. and King, C. (2003) *Small worlds and regional advantage*. Working paper no. 04-008, Harvard Business School, Boston, MA.

Florin, J., Lubatkin, M. and Schulze, W.A. (2003) 'Social capital model of high-growth ventures', *Academy Of Management Journal*, 46: 374–84.

Freeman, J. (1986) 'Entrepreneurs as organizational products: semiconductor firms and venture capital firms', in G. Libecap (ed.), *Advances in entrepreneurship, innovation and economic growth*, vol. 1. Greenwich, CT: JAI Press. pp. 33–52.

Galaskiewicz, J. (1985) 'Interorganizational relations', *Annual Review of Sociology*, 11: 281–304.

Gargiulo, M. and Benassi, M. (2000) 'Trapped in your own net? Network cohesion, structural holes, and the adaptation of social capital', *Organization Science*, 11: 183–96.

George G., Wood, D.R. and Khan, R. (2001) 'Networking strategy of boards: implications for small and medium-sized enterprises', *Entrepreneurship and Regional Development*, 13: 269–85.

Gerber, D. (1982) 'Cutting out Shylock: elite anti-semitism and the quest for moral order in the mid-nineteenth century American market place', *Journal of American History*, 9(615): 37.

Gimeno, J. (2004) 'Competition within and between networks: the contingent effect of competitive embeddedness on alliance formation', *Academy of Management Journal*, 47: 820–42.

Glasmeier, A. (1991) 'Technological discontinuities and flexible production: the case of Switzerland and the world watch industry', *Research Policy*, 20: 469–85.

Gouldner, A. (1950) *Patterns of Industrial Bureaucracy*. Glencoe, IL: Free Press.

Grabher, G. (1993) 'The weakness of strong ties: the lock-in of regional development in the Ruhr area', in G. Grabner

(ed.), *The embedded firm*. London, UK: Routledge. pp. 255–77.

Granovetter, M.S. (1973) 'The strength of weak ties', *American Journal of Sociology*, 78: 1360–80.

Granovetter, M.S. (1974) *Getting a job: A study of contacts and careers*. Cambridge, MA: Harvard University Press.

Granovetter, M.S. (1985) 'Economic action and social structure: the problem of embeddedness', *American Journal of Sociology*, 91: 481–510.

Granovetter, M.S. (1990) 'The old and the new economic sociology: a history and an agenda,' in R. Friedland and A. Robertson (eds), *Beyond the marketplace: rethinking economy and society*. New York: Aldine de Gruyter. pp. 89–112.

Granovetter, M.S. (1994) 'Business groups', in N.J. Smelser and R. Swedberg (eds), *The handbook of economic sociology*. Princeton, NJ: Princeton University Press and Russell Sage Foundation. pp. 435–75.

Greve, A. and Salaff, J.W. (2003) 'Social networks and entrepreneurship', *Entrepreneurship Theory and Practice*, 28: 1–22.

Gulati, R. (1993) 'The dynamics of alliance formation'. Unpublished doctoral dissertation, Harvard University, Cambridge, MA.

Gulati, R. and Garguilo, M. (1999) 'Where do interorganizational networks come from?', *American Journal of Sociology*, 104: 1439–93.

Gulati, R. and Higgins, M.C. (2003) 'Which ties matter when? The contingent effects of interorganizational partnerships on IPO success', *Strategic Management Journal*, 24: 127–44.

Hagedoorn, J. and Duysters, G. (2002) 'Learning in dynamic inter-firm networks: the efficacy of multiple contacts', *Organization Studies*, 23: 525–49.

Hamilton, G. and Biggart, N.W. (1988) 'Market, culture and authority: a comparative analysis of management and organization in the Far East', *American Journal of Sociology*, 94: 552–95.

Hansen, E.L. (2000) 'Resource acquisition as a startup process: initial stocks of social capital and organizational foundings', in R.D. Reynolds, E. Autio, C. Brush, W. Bygrave, S. Manigart, H.J. Sapienza and K.G. Shaver (eds), *Frontiers of entrepreneurship research*, vol. 20. Wellesley, MA: Babson College.

Hansen, M.T. (1999) 'The search-transfer problem: the role of weak ties in sharing knowledge across organization subunits', *Administrative Science Quarterly*, 44: 82–111.

Hansen, M.T. and Lovas, B. (2004) 'How do multinational companies leverage technological competencies? Moving from single to interdependent explanations', *Strategic Management Journal*, 25: 801–22.

Harrison, B. (1994) *Lean and mean: The changing landscape of corporate power in an age of flexibility*. New York: Basic Books.

Harrison, R.T., Mason, C.M. and Girling, P. (2004) 'Financial bootstrapping and venture development in the software industry', *Entrepreneurship and Regional Development*, 16: 307–33.

Heider, F. (1946) 'Attitudes and cognitive orientation', *Journal of Psychology*, 21: 107–12.

Hellmann, T. and Puri, M. (2002) 'Venture capital and the professionalization of start-up firms: empirical evidence', *Journal of Finance*, 57: 169–97.

Higgins, M.C. and Gulati, R. (2003) 'Getting off to a good start: the effects of upper echelon affiliations on underwriter prestige', *Organization Science*, 14: 244–64.

Hite, J.M. (2003) 'Patterns of multidimensionality among embedded network ties: a typology of relational embeddedness in emerging entrepreneurial firms', *Strategic Organization*, 1: 9–49.

Hite, J.M. and Hesterly, W.S. (2001) 'The evolution of firm networks: from emergence to early growth of the firm', *Strategic Management Journal*, 22: 275–86.

Holland, P. and Leinhardt, S. (1977) 'A dynamic model for social networks', *Journal of Mathematical Sociology*, 5: 5–20.

Holland, P. and Leinhardt, S. (eds) (1979) *Perspectives on social network research*. New York: Academic Press.

Hsu, D.H. (2004) 'What do entrepreneurs pay for venture capital affiliation?', *Journal of Finance*, 59: 1805–44.

Ingram, P. and Baum, J.A.C. (1997) 'Chain affiliation and the failure of Manhattan hotels, 1898–1980', *Administrative Science Quarterly*, 42: 68–102.

Jarillo, J.C. (1989) 'Entrepreneurship and growth: the strategic use of external resources', *Journal of Business Venturing*, 4: 133–47.

Jenssen, J.I. and Koenig, H.F. (2002) 'The effect of social networks on resource access and business start-ups', *European Planning Studies*, 10: 1039–46.

Kadushin, C. (1966) 'The friends and supports of psychotherapy', *American Sociological Review*, 31: 786–802.

Kadushin, C. (1968) 'Power, influence and social circles: a new methodology for studying opinion makers', *American Sociological Review*, 33: 685–99.

Kadushin, C. (1995) 'Friendship among the French Financial elite', *American Sociological Review*, 60: 202–21.

Kamm, J.B. and Nurick, A.J. (1993) 'The stages of team venture formation: a decision making model', *Entrepreneurship: Theory & Practice*, 17: 1727.

Killworth, P.D. and Bernard, H.R. (1976) 'A model of human group dynamics', *Social Science Research*, 5: 173–224.

Killworth, P.D. and Bernard, H.R. (1979) 'Informant accuracy in social network data III', *Social Networks*, 2: 19–46.

Kogut, B., Walker, G. and Kim, D. (1995) 'Cooperation and entry induction as an extension of technological rivalry', *Research Policy*, 24: 77–95.

Krackhardt, D.J. and Hanson, J.R. (1993) 'Informal networks: the company behind the chart', *Harvard Business Review*, 71: 104–11.

Krackhardt, D. and Kilduff, M. (1999) 'Whether close or far: perceptions of balance in friendship networks in organizations', *Journal of Personality and Social Psychology*, 76: 770–82.

Larson, A. (1992) 'Network dyads in entrepreneurial settings: a study of the governance of exchange relationships', *Administrative Science Quarterly*, 37: 76–104.

Larsson, R. and Finkelstein, S. (1999) 'Integrating strategic, organizational, and human resource perspectives on mergers and acquisitions: a case survey of synergy realization', *Organization Science*, 10: 1–26.

Leonard, D. and Swap, W. (2000) 'Gurus in the garage', *Harvard Business Review*, 78: 71–3, 76–80, 82.

Light, I.H. (1972) *Ethnic enterprise in America: Business and welfare among Chinese, Japanese and Blacks*. Berkeley, CA: University of California Press.

Light, I.H. and Bonacich, E. (1988) *Immigrant entrepreneurs: Koreans in Los Angeles*. Los Angeles, CA: University of California Press.

Lin, N. (2001) *Social capital: A theory of social structure and action*. Cambridge, UK: Cambridge University Press.

Macaulay, S. (1963) 'Non-contractual relations in business: a preliminary study', *American Sociological Review*, 28: 55–67.

Madhavan, R., Koka, B.R. and Prescott, J.E. (1998) 'Networks in transition: how industry events (re)shape interfirm relationships', *Strategic Management Journal*, 19: 439–59.

Malecki, E.J. (1997) 'Entrepreneurs, networks, and economic development: a review of recent research', in G. Libecap (ed.), *Advances in entrepreneurship, innovation and economic growth*, vol. 3. Greenwich, CT: JAI Press. pp. 57–118.

Marsden, P.V. (1987) 'Core discussion networks of Americans', *American Sociological Review*, 52: 122–31.

Marsden, P.V. (1990) 'Network data and measurement', *Annual Review of Sociology*, 16: 435–63.

Marsden, P.V. (2004) 'Network analysis', in K. Kempf-Leonard (ed.), *Encyclopaedia of social measurement*. San Diego, CA: Academic Press. pp. 819–25.

Marshall, A. (1920) *Principles of economics*, 8th edn. London: Macmillan and Co., Ltd.

Merton, R.K. (1957) 'Continuities in the theory of reference groups and social structure', in R.K. Merton (ed.), *Social theory and social structure*. New York: Free Press. pp. 335–440.

Milgram, S. (1967) 'The small world problem', *Psychology Today*, 1: 61–7.

Min, P.G. (1988) *Ethnic business enterprise: Korean small business in Atlanta*. New York: CMS.

Mintrom, M. and Vergari, S. (1998) 'Policy networks and innovation diffusion: the case of state education reforms', *The Journal of Politics*, 60: 126–48.

Mizruchi, M.S. and Stearns, L.B. (2001) 'Getting deals done: the use of social networks in bank decision-making', *American Sociological Review*, 66: 647–71.

Moody, J. (2001) 'Race, school integration, and friendship segregation in America', *American Journal of Sociology*, 107: 679–716.

Moreno, J.L. (1934) *Who shall survive?* Washington, DC: Nervous and Mental Diseases Publishing Co.

Oh, H., Chung, M. and Labianca, G. (2004) 'Group social capital and group effectiveness: the role of informal socializing ties', *Academy of Management Journal*, 47: 860–75.

Owen-Smith, J. and Powell, W.W. (2004) 'Knowledge networks as channels and conduits: the effects of spillovers in the Boston biotechnology community', *Organization Science*, 15: 5–21.

Padgett, J.F. (2001) 'Organizational genesis, identity and control: the transformation of banking in Renaissance Florence', in A. Cassella and J. Rauch (eds), *Markets and networks*. New York: Russell Sage Foundation. pp. 211–57.

Phillips, D. (2001) 'A genealogical approach to organizational life chances: the parent-progeny transfer and Silicon Valley law firms 1946–1956', Paper presented at the *Annual Meeting of the American Sociological Association*, Anaheim, CA.

Piore, M. and Sabel, C. (1984) *The second industrial divide*. New York: Basic Books.

Podolny, J.M. (1993) 'A status-based model of market competition', *American Journal of Sociology*, 98: 829–72.

Podolny, J.M. (2001) 'Networks as pipes and prisms of the market', *American Journal of Sociology*, 107: 33–60.

Polanyi, K. (1944) *The great transformation: The political and economic origins of our time*. Boston, MA: Beacon Press.

Portes, A. (1998) 'Social capital: its origins and applications in modern sociology', *Annual Review of Sociology*, 24: 1–24.

Portes, A. and Guarnizo, L.E. (1991) 'Tropical capitalists: US-bound immigration and small enterprise development in the Dominican Republic', in S. Diaz-Briquets and S. Weintraub (eds), *Migration, remittances, and small business development: Mexico and Caribbean basin countries*. Boulder, CO: Westview. pp. 103–27.

Portes, A. and Sensenbrenner, J. (1993) 'Embeddedness and immigration: notes on the social determinants of economic action', *American Journal of Sociology*, 98: 1320–50.

Portes, A. and Stepnick, A. (1993) *City on the edge: The transformation of Miami*. Berkeley, CA: University of California Press.

Powell, W.W. (1985) *Getting into print: The decision-making process in scholarly publishing*. Chicago, IL: University of Chicago Press.

Powell, W.W. (1990) 'Neither market nor hierarchy: network forms of organization', *Research in Organizational Behavior*, 12: 295–336.

Powell, W.W. and Smith-Doerr, L. (1994) 'Networks and economic life', in N.J. Smelser and R. Swedberg (eds), *The handbook of economic sociology*. Princeton, NJ: Princeton University Press. pp. 368–402.

Powell, W.W. and Snellman, K. (2004) 'The knowledge economy', *Annual Review of Sociology*, 30: 199–220.

Powell, W.W., Koput, K.W. and Smith-Doerr, L. (1996) 'Interorganizational collaboration and the locus of innovation: networks of learning in biotechnology', *Administrative Science Quarterly*, 41: 116–45.

Powell, W.W., White, D.R., Koput, K.K. and Owen-Smith, J. (2005) 'Network dynamics and field evolution: the growth of inter-organizational collaboration in the life sciences', *American Journal of Sociology*, 110: 1132–205.

Ranft, A.L. and Lord, M.D. (2002) 'Acquiring new technologies and capabilities: a grounded model of acquisition implementation', *Organization Science*, 13: 420–41.

Ravasi, D. and Marchisio, G. (2003) 'Going public and the enrichment of a supportive network', *Small Business Economics*, 21: 381–95.

Reagans, R. and McEvily, B. (2003) 'Network structure and knowledge transfer: the effects of cohesion and range', *Administrative Science Quarterly*, 48: 240–67.

Reagans, R. and Zuckerman, E.Z. (2001) 'Networks, diversity, and productivity: the social capital of corporate R&D teams', *Organization Science*, 12: 502–17.

Reagans, R., Zuckerman, E.Z. and McEvily, B. (2004) 'How to make the team: social networks vs demography as criteria for designing effective teams', *Administrative Science Quarterly*, 49: 101–33.

Renzulli, L.A., Aldrich, H. and Moody, J. (2000) 'Family matters: gender, networks, and entrepreneurial outcomes', *Social Forces*, 79: 523–46.

Reynolds, P.D. (1994) 'Reducing barriers to understanding new firm gestation: Prevalence and success of nascent entrepreneurs', Paper presented at the *Annual Meeting of the Academy of Management*, Dallas, TX.

Reynolds, P. and Miller, B. (1992) 'New firm gestation: conception, birth, and implications for research', *Journal of Business Venturing*, 7: 405–17.

Riddle L.A. and Gillespie, K. (2003) 'Information sources for new ventures in the Turkish clothing export industry', *Small Business Economics*, 20: 105–20.

Rosenkopf L. and Almeida, P. (2003) 'Overcoming local search through alliances and mobility', *Management Science*, 49: 751–66.

Rosenkopf, L, Metiu, A. and George, V.P. (2001) 'From the bottom up? Technical committee activity and alliance formation', *Administrative Science Quarterly*, 46: 748–72.

Rowley, T.J., Behrens, D. and Krackhardt, D. (2000) 'Redundant governance structures: an analysis of structural and relational embeddedness in the steel and semiconductor industries', *Strategic Management Journal*, 21: 369–86.

Rowley, T.J., Greve, H.R., Rao, H., Baum, J.A.C. and Shipilov, A.V. (2005) 'Time to break up: social and instrumental antecedents of firm exits from exchange cliques', *Academy of Management Journal*, 48: 499–520.

Roy, D. (1954) 'Efficiency and 'the fix': informal intergroup relations in a piecework machine shop', *American Journal of Sociology*, 60: 255–67.

Rulke, D.L. and Galaskiewicz, J. (2000) 'Distribution of knowledge, group network structure, and group performance', *Management Science*, 46: 612–25.

Russell, R. (1984) 'The role of culture and ethnicity in the degeneration of democratic firms', *Economic and Industrial Democracy*, 5: 73–96.

Saxenian, A. (1994) *Regional advantage: culture and competition in Silicon Valley and Route 128*. Cambridge, MA: Harvard University Press.

Schoonhoven, C.B. and Eisenhardt, K.M. (1996) 'Effects of founding conditions on the creation of manufacturing alliances in semiconductor ventures', in H. Thomas and D. O'Neal (eds), *Strategic Integration*. New York: John Wiley & Sons Ltd. pp. 365–400.

Schrader, S. (1991) 'Informal technology transfer between firms: cooperation through information trading', *Research Policy*, 20: 153–70.

Schultz, M. (2001) 'The uncertain relevance of newness: organizational learning and knowledge flows', *Academy of Management Journal*, 44: 661–81.

Scott, J. (1991) *Social network analysis: a handbook*. London: Sage.

Scott, W.R. (1998) *Organizations: rational, natural and open systems*, 4th edn. Upper Saddle River, NJ: Prentice Hall.

Shane, S. and Cable, D. (2002) 'Network ties, reputation, and the financing of new ventures', *Management Science*, 48: 364–81.

Shane, S. and Khurana, R. (2001) 'Bringing individuals back in: the effects of career experience on new firm founding', *Academy of Management Proceedings*, F1–7.

Shane, S. and Stuart, T. (2002) 'Organizational endowments and the performance of university start-ups', *Management Science*, 48: 154–70.

Silverman, B.S. and Baum, J.A.C. (2002) 'Alliance-based competitive dynamics', *Academy of Management Journal*, 45: 791–806.

Simmel, G. (1955 [1908, 1922]) *Conflict and the web of group affiliations*. Glencoe, IL: The Free Press.

Smith-Doerr, L. and Powell, W.W. (2005) 'Networks and economic life', in N.J. Smelser and R. Swedberg (eds), *Handbook of economic sociology*. 2nd edn. Princeton, NJ: Russell Sage Foundation/Princeton University Press. pp. 379–402.

Song, J., Almeida, P. and Wu, G. (2003) 'Learning-by-hiring: when is mobility more likely to facilitate interfirm knowledge transfer?', *Management Science*, 49: 351–65.

Sorensen, J.B. and Sorenson, O. (2003) 'From conception to birth: opportunity perception and resource mobilization in entrepreneurship', in J.A.C. Baum and O. Sorenson (eds), *Geography and strategy: Advances in strategic management*, vol. 20. Greenwich, CT: JAI Press. pp. 89–117.

Sorenson, O. and Audia, P.G. (2000) 'The social structure of entrepreneurial opportunity: geographic concentration of footwear production in the United States, 1940–1989', *American Journal of Sociology*, 106: 424–62.

Staber, U. and Aldrich, H.E. (1995) 'Cross-national similarities in the personal networks of small business owners: a comparison of two regions in North America', *Canadian Journal of Sociology-Cahiers Canadiens de Sociologie*, 20: 441–67.

Stinchcombe, A.L. (1959) 'Bureaucratic and craft administration of production', *Administrative Science Quarterly*, 4: 194–208.

Stinchcombe, A.L. (1965) 'Social structure and organizations', in J.G. March (ed.), *Handbook of organizations*. Chicago, IL: Rand McNally & Company. pp. 142–93.

Stuart, T.E. (1998) 'Network positions and propensities to collaborate: an investigation of strategic alliance formation in a high-technology industry', *Administrative Science Quarterly*, 43: 668–98.

Stuart, T.E. and Podolny, J.M. (1999) 'Positional consequences of strategic alliances in the semiconductor industry', in S.B. Andrews and D. Knoke (eds), *Research in the sociology of organizations*, vol. 16. Greenwich, CT: JAI Press. pp. 161–82.

Stuart, T.E. and Sorenson, O. (2003) 'The geography of opportunity: spatial heterogeneity in founding rates and the performance of biotechnology firms', *Research Policy*, 32: 229–53.

Stuart, T.E., Hoang, H. and Hybels, R.C. (1999) 'Interorganizational endorsements and the performance of entrepreneurial ventures', *Administrative Science Quarterly*, 44: 315–49.

Suchman, M.C., Steward, D.J. and Westfall, C.A. (2001) 'The legal environment of entrepreneurship: observations on the legitimation of venture finance in Silicon Valley', in C.B. Schoonhoven and E. Romanelli (eds), *The entrepreneurship dynamic: Origins of entrepreneurship and the evolution of industries*. Stanford, CA: Stanford University Press. pp. 349–82.

Thornton, P.H. and Flynn, K.H. (2003) 'Entrepreneurship, networks, and geographies', in Z.J. Acs and D.B. Audretsch (eds), *Handbook of entrepreneurship research*. Manchester, UK: Kluwer Law International. pp. 401–33.

Tsai, W. (2000) 'Social capital, strategic relatedness, and the formation of intra-organizational linkages', *Strategic Management Journal*, 21: 925–39.

Tsai, W. (2001) 'Knowledge transfer in intraorganizational networks: effects of network position and absorptive capacity on business unit innovation and performance', *Academy of Management Journal*, 44: 996–1004.

Tsai, W. and Ghoshal, S. (1998) 'Social capital and value creation: the role of intrafirm networks', *Academy of Management Journal*, 41: 464–76.

Tushman, M. and Anderson, P.C. (1986) 'Technological discontinuities and organizational environments', *Administrative Science Quarterly*, 31: 439–65.

Useem, M. (1984) *The inner circle: Large corporations and the rise of business political activity in the US and UK Oxford*. Oxford, UK: Oxford University Press.

Uzzi, B. (1997) 'Social structure and competition in interfirm networks: the paradox of embeddedness', *Administrative Science Quarterly*, 42: 37–70.

Uzzi, B. and Spiro, J. (2005) 'Collaboration and creativity: the small world problem', *American Journal of Sociology*, 111: 447–504.

Vermeulen, F. and Barkema, H. (2001) 'Learning through acquisitions', *Academy of Management Journal*, 44: 457–76.

Walker, G. and Kogut, B. (2001) 'The small world of Germany and the durability of national ownership networks', *American Sociological Review*, 66: 317–35.

Walker, G., Kogut, B. and Shan, W. (1997) 'Social capital, structural holes and the formation of an industry network', *Organization Science*, 8: 109–25.

Wasserman, S. and Faust, K. (1994) *Social network analysis: Methods and applications*. Cambridge, UK: Cambridge University Press.

Watts, D.J. (1999) 'Networks, dynamics, and the small-world phenomenon', *American Journal of Sociology*, 105: 493–527.

Watts, D.J. (2003) *Small worlds: The dynamics of networks between order and randomness*. Princeton, NJ: Princeton University Press.

Watts, D.J. and Strogatz, S.H. (1998) 'Collective dynamics of 'small-world' networks', *Nature*, 393: 440–2.

Wilken, P.H. (1979) *Entrepreneurship: A comparative and historical study*. Norwood, NJ: Ablex.

Woodrum, E. (1981) 'An assessment of Japanese American assimilation, pluralism, and subordination', *American Journal of Sociology*, 87: 157–69.

Zimmer, C. and Aldrich, H. (1987) 'Resource mobilization through ethnic networks: kinship and friendship ties of shopkeepers in England', *Sociological Perspectives*, 30: 422–55.

2.15   The Effect of Rhetoric on Competitive Advantage: Knowledge, Rhetoric and Resource-Based Theory

JOHN A.A. SILLINCE

Introduction

Knowledge management assumes the strategic value of knowledge within the firm and sets out ways of achieving that value such as knowledge transfer and information sharing. It is this assumption of knowledge having a strategic value which I would like to focus on as a means of investigating the role of rhetoric. Resource-based theory serves my purpose for this task, because it provides a framework for understanding the strategic value of knowledge as a key resource. My aim will be primarily to show that the strategic value of knowledge as a source of competitive advantage is increased by careful design of rhetorics. Rhetoric about knowledge has impacts on the elements that, according to resource-based theory, create competitive advantage. Also I have a secondary aim to establish that resource-based theory treats knowledge as a thing or asset, which is combined with other knowledge, whereas much writing about knowledge in organizations treats it much more appropriately as a process. This is a problem for the theory. I will suggest that this problem can be reduced by considering that knowledge has a substantial part, and that it also has a rhetoric part constituted by the processes of amplification, focusing, establishing relevance and justifying.

According to resource-based theory, a firm's competitive advantage is determined by the value, rarity, non-imitability and non-substitutability of its resources or capabilities. I shall concentrate upon these four sources of competitive advantage according to resource-based theory, i.e. the value, rarity, imitability and substitutability of resources (Rumelt 1984; Wernerfelt 1984; Barney 1986; 1991; Dierickx and Cool 1989) and one extra one (control of resources) which I add. Each of these sources of

advantage has a substantial part and a rhetorical part. The substantial part exists independent of social construction despite it being intrinsically difficult to define and value knowledge. For example, IBM's clients readily appreciate its knowledge of solutions to their problems. However, there is also a rhetorical part where rhetoric about knowledge has a substantial impact on competitive advantage. I will largely ignore the first part because I take it as true that firms do possess substantial knowledge resources that add value and produce something that customers are willing to pay a certain price for. Although competitive advantage is assisted through rhetorical means it actually requires substance, particularly if it is to be sustainable. I focus on the second, rhetorical part because it has previously not been emphasized in the literature.

The Rhetorical Construction of the Value of Knowledge

Organizations clearly do possess capabilities based on their members' knowledge and this does have strategic value which is independent of rhetoric. I will restrict my argument to saying that rhetoric adds significantly to that value.

The value of resources is defined by resource-based theory in terms of its ability to increase competitive advantage (Barney 1991). Unfortunately, this definition is circular (Priem and Butler 2001: 27) and gives rise to difficulties when specifying resources.

Knowledge as a crucial resource is intrinsically difficult to define and value. Although there are instances of seemingly objective knowledge such as product and process innovations (Verona 1999: 139), in reality the value of these can be manipulated by the rhetoric of marketing and management fads. For example, establishing relevance of total quality management in particular organizations occurs by means of selection of success stories and ignoring of failures (Zbaracki 1998). Another seemingly objective aspect of knowledge is awareness of a firm's market position, for example the resource value associated with cost leadership (Barney 2001: 43). Although this may seem objective and soundly based on economic theory and measurement, it is also based on actions in the market which benefit from rhetoric. For example, consumer knowledge can easily be amplified by publicity. And lost leaders and dumping arise from policy choices to cross-subsidize or recoup profits later when market share has increased sufficiently for the firm to exert its market power. One of the ways of achieving first mover advantage is to increase buyer switching costs. Buyer switching costs may depend on objective knowledge such as sunk cost, but may also be partly socially constructed – for example, the seller amplifies the familiarity of his product because familiarity increases the cost of switching.

Resource-based theory can be used to legitimate strategy rhetoric which makes the following argument: (1) We have valuable resources; (2) Therefore, our products are good or we deserve the support of investors; and (3) Therefore, buy our products. In this argument the aim is not to use resources for creating good products. Rather, the argument aims to use resources for creating market demand. This is how 'globalization strategy' is presented on the websites of large consultancy organizations: the rhetoric focuses on the capability (a resource) to provide a common appearance to the client no matter where they are. This is also the rationale for including 'properties' (headquarters, showrooms, delivery trucks) as one of the elements of organizational image (Schmitt and Simonson 1995). An analogous process is where value is created through advertising. For example, film studios acquire rights to unknown actors and scripts and then amplify the value of those resources by using publicity.

Reputation is knowledge about value which is perceived by the firm's competitors and customers. Of course reputation and social identity are built on objective and impartial assessments of the product. However, they can also be amplified and justified by rhetoric. Rao (1994: 31) showed in a longitudinal study of certification contests in the early years of the car industry how speed and reliability tests were focused on by industry participants as measurable criteria for the winning of contests. Contests dramatized the credibility of these two criteria. This enabled the public, formerly confused as to what constituted a 'good' car, to choose between rival products and to abandon previous modes of transport for the automobile. Contests, then, serve as rhetorical devices.

When we come to look at knowledge which cannot be imitated or substituted, it becomes even more difficult to identify the value of any piece of knowledge. Skills which Reich (1991) has called 'symbolic analytic', such as problem-solving (research, product design and engineering), problem identification (marketing and consulting) and brokerage (financing, searching and contracting) are not easy to imitate or substitute. However, these activities are also less easy to analyse as objective, observable or abstract entities than as situated and motivated activities (Blackler 1995). Problem-solving causes knowledge to be constructed and transformed as it is used (Lave 1993). When knowledge is situated and motivated, its significance can only be established after rhetoric has established relevance to the listener's problem. Establishing relevance occurs interactively within relationships between service firms and their clients. Problem identification and brokerage rely on these relationships, which involves the management of trust and shared understandings. All these forms of activity are situated because the skills they require are only relevant for dealing with the practical problem at hand (Suchman 1987). Such activities are motivated by justifying who we think we are or want to be – a matter of identity. For example, relationships with clients involve identity-relevant and unique social capital and, thus, are non-imitable. Moreover, applying specialized knowledge to service the client is socially complex. It involves establishing relevance of a solution to knowledge of a client's problem. Putting the two together produces a more situated or client-specific 'bundle' which is of greater competitive advantage than either resource on its own (Hitt et al. 2001: 16).

Alvesson (2001: 867) has suggested that 'knowledge – in the sense of a body of information, theories, methodologies broadly considered to have passed some tests of validity, being broadly shared by members of a profession or organization claimed to be based on a specific type of knowledge – is … not necessarily that significant in work'. He refers to professionals such as psychologists and architects who are experts in particular types of knowledge, and yet their daily work is actually characterized not by rationality but by uncertainty and instability. And computer consultants are often assigned to jobs for which they have no specialized knowledge and are expected by their managers to be able to cope flexibly with this. Yet, managers expect that specialists find such flexibility easier to deal with than non-specialists (Alvesson 2001: 866).

Although knowledge work seems to deal with problems about which definite and justifiable propositions are possible, it is very difficult, especially for the non-expert, to evaluate. Professional work is usually only evaluated in detail after a disaster as, for example, when auditing frauds are uncovered. Yet, the rhetorical justifying of such work is of crucial importance because the recognition that a firm possesses a particular esoteric skill is so difficult for it to acquire and so easy for it to lose. This is one reason why social skills and client relationships are so important to the exercising of such skills and to the building of reputation (Starbuck 1992).

Alvesson (2001: 869) has, therefore, argued that this 'encourages an alternative understanding of why experts are frequently used, compared to what functionalists claim. Rather than being employed for their problem-solving capacity, they may be used because institutionalized "truths" (myths) say that one should do so ... Experts imply legitimacy'. Work often involves the negotiation of meaning and the social construction of truth claims. This is a process of contestation of claims which is likely to involve the furthering of the interests of those who claim to be knowledgeable (Knights et al. 1993). Claiming to be knowledgeable, appropriate or legitimate involves rhetorically justifying the claim by making clear an identity as an expert, with sufficient authority and reputation.

Many sources of value also exist outside of the boundaries of the firm. Suppliers and customers and relationships and networks external to the firm (Uzzi 1996), together with the legitimacy and reputation which they create (Gray and Wood 1991; Westley and Vredenburg 1991) are all resources which give competitive advantage. The way in which legitimacy and reputation are created causes conflicts between managers and their constituents – managers prefer symbols whereas their constituents prefer tangible results such as profits (Ashforth and Gibbs 1990). Legitimacy increases the comprehensibility and stability of organizational actions and is

used as a strategic resource in competing with other organizations (Suchman 1995: 574).

It may be that under some circumstances competitive strategy may have to be changed to enable co-operative action with external stakeholders in order to increase social legitimacy (Bilamoria et al. 1995). Such co-operative action is causally ambiguous and socially complex. For example, pollution prevention involves internal action which is causally ambiguous, such as total quality environmental management, yet its opening up to public scrutiny in the interest of external social legitimacy involves making the process of how to avoid pollution and waste more transparent. Also product stewardship involves internal action such as design for environment which is socially complex, yet integrating stakeholders to gain legitimacy involves simplification by demonstrating real impact of such external advice even when it is inappropriate (Hart 1995: 999). Transparency will involve a rhetoric which amplifies clarity and visibility and which minimizes boundaries. Demonstrating commitment to external stakeholders will require a rhetoric which amplifies participation and which establishes relevance to stakeholders' interests.

Both the rhetoric of transparency and of demonstrating commitment to stakeholders reduce the clarity of organizational boundaries. The ability to use these collaborative relationships is a capability which is as yet imperfectly specified by resource-based theory. For example, external integration regarding customer voice and empowerment of product managers are under specified in terms of their expected competitive effect (Verona 1999: 138). Moreover, collaboration may sometimes damage long-term competitiveness because it involves risks. It is these external networks, such as those with a firm's leading clients, which are sources of demands for firms to increase integration. This leads to less flexible capabilities ('core rigidities': Leonard-Barton 1996) and less innovation (Christensen and Bower 1996).

For all these reasons, the value of a firm's resources is problematic, contestable and socially constructed. A firm whose knowledge is demonstrated in a visible product such as a car has fewer problems in this regard than one which does not, such as a consultancy. However, product visibility then increases problems of imitability. It also renders the product into a commodity which is easily compared with competitors' products. The rhetoric used in marketing and in the development of brand presence involve going beyond the product as a comparable commodity by justifying and amplifying unique expertise. Even when knowledge can be demonstrated, rhetoric can add substantially to its value. In order to add value, acquire reputation, build social capital and charge higher premiums the firm needs to convince customers that its resources are valuable. The appropriate managerial response is to use social skills and client relationships and to use rhetoric to claim legitimacy through expertise and collaboration in social networks.

The Rhetorical Construction of the Rarity of Knowledge

Some part of rarity is substantial. Rarity exists in reality because physical, financial and human resources are finite. For example, certain types of expert are objectively scarce.

However, rarity also has a rhetorical part. An example of the social construction of rarity is the autobiographies by successful business leaders, which often portray those leaders as fearless, lonely and powerful. Although such implied beliefs are usually false, they point to an underlying assumption by the users and audiences of such rhetoric that these qualities are special aspects of individual identity which are firm specific (they benefit the CEO's firm) but that they are difficult to learn (they cannot benefit other firms) (Clegg and Palmer 1996: 40). This establishes relevance of the individual identity to the firm and amplifies their implied rarity and, therefore, increases their claim as adding to competitive advantage.

There is, thus, a self-fulfilling aspect to resource-based theory. The theory states that competitive advantage follows from valuable, rare, non-imitable and non-substitutable resources. Rationalizations constructed after the alleged success has happened look for self-serving instances of this. These then persuade observers that the success was real. Success is socially constructed in this way. However, just because a CEO led a successful firm may not imply that the CEO did everything right. And short-term success may be at the expense of long-term decline. Resource-based theory's appropriation into self-serving rhetorics of leadership, therefore, provides interesting material for students of self-confirming communication. When resource-based theory is used in prospective arguments, the fact that the firm has rare resources provides grounds for an argument about why success will occur and why stakeholders should support the firm.

The Rhetorical Construction of the Non-Imitability of Knowledge

Resource-based theory suggests that sustainable competitive advantage comes from unique sets of resources or capabilities that cannot be imitated by competitors. One of the resources which is least imitable is unique, mysterious and specialized knowledge (Lado and Wilson 1994). This knowledge may be protected by its practitioners from imitation by competitors using rhetorics of obfuscation, e.g. legal language, or by definitional complexity, e.g. definitions embedded within case law. Nevertheless, much knowledge of this nature is explicit because it is contained in professional discourse and, thus, is transferable between firms.

A firm's knowledge is to some degree protected against imitation. This can occur in two ways. First, knowledge is a source of sustainable competitive advantage because of its largely tacit and socially complex nature which renders it difficult to imitate. Social complexity arises from the collective, socially embedded and relational nature of knowledge (McEvily et al. 2000). Such resources are 'uncertainly imitable' due to knowledge barriers (Lippman and Rumelt 1982).

Secondly, knowledge in the form of competences is causally ambiguous because it is impossible to say exactly how and in what degree a specific competence contributes to competitive advantage. Causal ambiguity is the uncertainty about how competences contribute to success (Lippman and Rumelt 1982; Barney 1991). Therefore, causal ambiguity also protects the firm against imitation of its competences by competitors.

The appropriate managerial response for a firm wishing to protect itself from imitation is to use rhetoric to amplify tacitness, social complexity and causal ambiguity. The aim of rhetoric here is to convince competitors that copying is pointless because of these barriers.

The Rhetorical Construction of the Non-Substitutability of Knowledge

Charismatic leadership and a formal planning system are substitute resources for achieving co-ordination. Other examples include mass customization vs after-sales-service as substitute means of tailoring products to customer needs and centralized vs decentralized control systems (McEvily et al. 2000: 296). The risk of competence substitution arises because competitors can acquire alternative resources of their own which do the same task using different resources.

To combat competence substitution by competitors, a firm may use any of three coping strategies (McEvily et al. 2000). Firstly, it may seek to continuously improve its workers' competences and to increase its commitment to its workers, thus convincing potential competitors that better performance is unlikely. Improving workers' competences involves encouraging ways of communicating collective wisdom, such as Xerox maintenance technicians' stories, which made their diagnostic and problem-solving activities widely known within the organization (Orr 1990). This uses the firm's built-in advantage of superior prior knowledge. However, continuous improvement requires variable compensation schemes, and these depend on the acquisition of information about how knowledge practices affect performance. Such information can only be derived from information sharing between firms. Managers of knowledge-intensive companies can also secure greater commitment of their workers by creating a 'strong' company culture or ideology and a sense of community and by the cultivation of a buoyant atmosphere (Alvesson 1993). Continuous improvement requires the firm to discover the sources of capabilities in order to replicate them within the firm more widely (Peteraf 1993).

Secondly, it may lock customers in by involving them co-operatively in knowledge development. This is exemplified by the consulting firm McKinsey's, which shared reports, ideas and informal, ad hoc advice with its clients (Peters 1992). Thirdly, it may publicize its business model of how it develops and utilises new knowledge in order to deter competitors from entering its market.

Combating competence substitution by competitors, therefore, requires the acquisition by the firm of explicit knowledge about the factors that affect its performance. This explicit knowledge, which reduces causal ambiguity, is intended to convince competitors that market entry is not worthwhile. However, as a firm acquires explicit knowledge it reduces the level of causal ambiguity which protects it from imitation (McEvily et al. 2000).

Rhetoric can be used in the following ways by management. First, management can increase its commitment to its workers, by focusing on employee issues. Management can encourage continuous improvement by establishing relevance of such programmes to specific groups of workers and justifying the value of worker co-operation by reference to compensation. Secondly, management can use rhetoric to lock customers in by focusing on switching costs. Thirdly, management can deter competitors entering the market by amplifying its own strong market position.

The Rhetorical Construction of the Ability to Control Knowledge

I shall define control as the organizational capability to get the maximum value from resources. This is broader than the ability to control and direct workers, because value may be maximized by enabling them to organize themselves as individuals and as groups. It is an exaggeration to say that some organization members 'control' others, because in practice politeness, politics, ambiguous language and the power of individual expertise mean that any too-heavy attempt at control can back-fire. However, it is also true that organizations hire and fire, and that they contain hierarchies. I will use control to have this more qualified meaning.

I shall argue that control of resources is another important determinant of competitive advantage. For example, knowledge is only advantageous to the firm if management can secure control over it. Not only should a resource be valuable, rare, non-imitable and non-substitutable, but it also must be controllable by the firm. However there is a risk that internal control is reduced because of causal ambiguity, social complexity and industry specificity (Coff 1997).

Causal ambiguity means that newly-hired workers often have different sets of competences compared to the workers they replace (Coff 1997). Causal ambiguity, therefore, increases the risk that labour turnover may lead to hiring of lower quality replacements.

When knowledge-based resources are systemic, they take the form of co-ordinative and integrative skills required for multidisciplinary teamwork (Miller and Shamsie 1996: 527). How such co-ordination, flexibility, adaptability and collaboration are achieved is difficult to assess given the number of individual, group and organizational variables involved. For example, these variables include integrative capabilities, semi-structures and transitional mechanisms (Brown and Eisenhardt 1997). It has been argued that the systemic nature of these skills causes the individuals' value to become attached to the firm rather than its competitors (Dierickx and Cool 1989: 1505) although it may be argued, conversely, that individuals with such experience and adaptability are made more attractive to competitors. The slow nature of this human capital accumulation means that there is an element of 'investment' in the future as collective behavioural 'assets' are built up over time, although causal ambiguity makes this process an imprecise one. Loss of motivation and forgetting lead to 'asset erosion'; development of mutually supporting routines means that there are 'asset mass efficiencies'; late starters cannot easily catch up leading to 'time compression diseconomies'; inter-personal learning in diverse groups means there is 'interconnection of asset stocks' (Dierickx and Cool 1989).

I shall argue as before that the ability to control resources has a substantial part and a rhetorical part. The substantial part exists because all these asset accumulation advantages occur objectively. This is because knowledge and learning can be likened to assets. However, there is also a rhetorical part. Asset accumulation advantages are available as rhetorical material for the firm to focus on or amplify if it wishes to impress consumers, partners or potential grantors of monopoly rights. For example, the firm may offer 'one stop shopping' for its services once its knowledge accumulation reaches a critical mass (Hitt et al. 2001: 17). Also, after a certain point a specialized service firm (law, accountancy, etc.) will justify its claim that it offers greater value for non-routine problems even where specialized knowledge exists within the client organization (Pennings et al. 1998: 426). Also, technology leaders will claim an 'experience curve' effect using the justification that they enjoy an advantage as they becomes more experienced (Porter 1985).

Social complexity partly arises due to the need to ensure workers are committed to their work. This is where my topic converges most closely to traditional concepts of managerial control. However, much tacit knowledge is individualized to the extent that workers can decide either to refuse to co-operate with management's attempts to externalize knowledge or else can leave the organization and pass the

knowledge on to their new employer. This risk is greater when such knowledge is industry-specific and of value to competitors. Tacit knowledge is often held by only a few workers, and these may leave the organization.

Individualized knowledge is, therefore, a reason why knowledge as a resource-based source of competitive advantage undermines attempts by top managers at controlling workers. Moreover, managers cannot avoid the problem of control by outsourcing to markets or by using networks of co-operative alliances. Nahapiet and Ghoshal (1998: 259) argue that social capital (networks, trust, commitment) and knowledge interact within organizations to create competitive advantage, and that this advantage would not be forthcoming outside organizations. There are several reasons why organizations provide a hospitable environment for the accumulation of social capital and knowledge. Shared knowledge creates a sense of order and of social system. Knowledge and social context are reciprocally related. Workers seek out and cultivate social connections within the organization and use these to socially construct a shared understanding of their work. The organization functions as an interpretation system within which social interaction enables retrospective sensemaking to occur (Daft and Weick 1984; Weick 1995). In this way, workers create a shared identity of the individual worker and of the work group. Management controls can monitor and enforce agreements and this increases the expectation that altruistic behaviours such as knowledge sharing will be rewarded. When the general level of co-operativeness and helpfulness is raised in this way, it is easy to trust co-workers so that the effort needed for monitoring or negotiating are reduced.

Although social capital and knowledge interact with the greatest advantage within organizations rather than outside them, the process cannot be completely controlled by top managers. For example, Wrzesniewski and Dutton (2001: 179–80) have suggested that 'employees craft their jobs by changing cognitive, task, and/or relational boundaries to shape interactions and relationships with others at work'. For example, hairdressers make personal disclosures about themselves, ask their clients personal questions, and punish clients who refuse to disclose, thus rhetorically positioning themselves as providing personal and empathic services beyond their formal role. Similarly, nurses expand their role to include getting information relevant to patient care from relatives, thus rhetorically positioning themselves as interested in patient care that extends beyond the simply medical (Wrzesniewski and Dutton 2001). Therefore, socially complex knowledge such as that which is localized in routines and cultures gives those who know them the ability to resist management's attempts to control work. Typically, individuals amplify their roles to make them appear more positive. These actions redefine 'work identity' and establish relevance to the audience.

Moreover, reduced internal control can lead to greater vulnerability to catastrophic fraud (Andersens, Barings), to a haemorrhage of departing workers, and to moonlighting, information hoarding, misinformation, sabotaging and other anti-social practices. In response, it has been argued that the risk of poor internal control can be reduced by four coping strategies (Coff 1997). Retention can be increased by demonstrating commitment to workers. Motivation can be increased by sharing profits with workers through performance-related pay or with other firms through collaborative alliances. Motivation can also be increased by rhetoric which amplifies rewards for good performance and which focuses on specific behaviour changes prescribed. The organizational design can be made more appropriate – for example by introducing an organic or flatter structure. Communication problems can be reduced by greater management transparency and information sharing by top managers. These structural and information changes, however, can be undermined by inappropriate rhetoric, e.g. authoritarian rhetoric accompanying flatter structures. Therefore, rhetoric is an important part of these coping strategies.

Under some circumstances, situated and motivated knowledge may be easier for management to control. Localization of knowledge in routines enables management to capture and inscribe work and in this way make it more visible and governable (Townley 1993: 521). Because specialized knowledge relies on few individuals, these individuals acquire a special sense of their own unique importance in the organization, not only as experts but as ethically responsible agents. Localization of knowledge in individuals' brains, therefore, means that workers become their own controllers so that self-censorship acts as a disciplinary frame. Localization of knowledge in cultures means that knowledge becomes synonymous with cultural beliefs. As long

as management can manipulate these cultural beliefs, the individual identity of workers – for example of themselves as insufficiently efficient or as superfluous – is created as a power effect of management control (Townley 1993: 522).

One reaction to the concern that the knowledge worker is mobile has been to increase the plausibility of the suggestion of raising the level of analysis away from the human resource management level of individual competences to the strategic accumulation and deployment of organizational capabilities. One argument that could be made here is that there are, therefore, great advantages for managers to emphasize organizational capabilities and de-emphasize individual competences in their rhetorics. Whereas individual actors are mobile and likely to undermine competitive advantage, capabilities are tied the firm (Henderson and Cockburn 1994) and are, thus, more easily brought under the control of strategy. This suggests that strategy should concern itself with the strategic relevance of the capability base and the degree to which it can be extended to new business areas or industries (Nordhaug 1994: 105). However, there is some evidence that this contradicts firms' actual behaviour, at least in those cases where demand for individuals exceeds their supply – firms place great stress on their ability to attract staff and use this in their recruitment rhetoric to attract other employees (Florida 2003).

Indeed, it could be argued that resource-based theory reflects a positive attitude and an ideology of managerial trust towards workers. Instead of considering the individual labour transaction as the decision point about whether to make-employ or buy-outsource, the theory suggests that management should consider the strategic benefits of building capabilities. This represents strategic thinking in that it is long-term and organizational, but also it represents a view of labour as a valuable asset rather than a disposable factor of production (Lepak and Snell 1999: 34).

The Ambiguous Role of Knowledge

Various factors conspire to render the definition of knowledge and, therefore, its role in competitive advantage, ambiguous and confusing. I have suggested above that knowledge has substantial and rhetorical parts, making estimations of its effect on competitive advantage difficult. I will now suggest that what knowledge is considered important will depend upon the organization's identity. Also, I will argue that organizational boundaries are becoming more invisible, so that it becomes difficult to know whether to take an insider's or an outsider's view of which knowledge is important. All these issues require attention when members seek to understand the role of knowledge in their organization.

What knowledge is considered important will depend upon the organization's identity. Alvesson (2001: 883) has argued that 'knowledge-intensive work tends to be ambiguity-intensive, which makes abilities to deal with rhetoric, regulate images and manage relationships with clients central. All these circumstances put some strain on, as well as lead to the centrality of, the securing and regulating of identity'. The three defining characteristics of organizational identity ('who we are as an organization') are uniqueness, centrality and enduringness (Albert and Whetten 1985). Stimpert et al. (1998) suggest that, due to its uniqueness, organizational identity is a resource which is difficult to imitate and which, therefore, provides competitive advantage. When central aspects of identity affect the ability to co-ordinate diverse production skills and integrate multiple streams of technology, the result is a set of capabilities or core competences (Pralahad and Hamel 1990; Whetten and Godfrey 1998: 119). In a stable environment, one enduring organizational identity can be a source of competitive advantage because of its easy comprehensibility and freedom from conflict (Whetten and Godfrey 1998: 121). However, in contradiction to this, an important development in the field of organizational rhetoric has been the expansion of the marketing perspective, which respects and engages with the consumer and his or her preferences (Cheney and Christensen 2001: 235). Because of the implied need to adapt to changing consumer tastes, flexibility has been foregrounded and identity-as-enduring has been backgrounded in much marketing and public relations rhetoric (Christensen 1995).

When ambiguity and uncertainty are high, multiple and shifting identities are likely to give more competitive advantage (Whetten and Godfrey 1998: 121). An example of multiple identities is when a firm holds an organizational identity as an innovative company, as a profitable company and as a company that cares for its employees. Organizations

where multiple identities are likely include knowledge-intensive organizations where there is no visible product, such as IBM, a hospital or university. The possible advantages of multiple identities for an organization include increasing requisite variety; enhancing capacity for learning; maintaining potential for future deployment; increasing response flexibility; and meeting external stakeholders' multiple expectations (Whetten and Godfrey 1998: 121; Pratt and Foreman 2000: 22–3).

An interpretive historical survey by Cheney and Vibbert (1987) suggests that organizational rhetoric has shifted from a reactive or accommodative activity to one involving proactive shaping of the premises of later, more specific claims and of the grounds of social and political issues in which organizations become implicated. A discrete area of organizational activity, called issue management, has emerged separate from public relations, for the reading and rhetorical shaping of crises or debates. This rhetoric is identity-related because each organization works to establish its unique 'self' while linking itself to the cultural crowd. Large organizations fashion not only their own selves but the identity of their industry. For example, Ford associates itself and its visible products with generic concepts of 'world car', whereas a small component supplier associates itself and its visible products with a large customer such as Ford.

Identity-related rhetoric is also political in attempting to exert influence without appearing to do so. Proactive shaping takes place, for example, when 'crises' emerge through being declared, defined and interpreted by organizational spokespersons (Vibbert and Bostdorff 1993). The rhetoric is not only for the purpose of managing the impressions of external audiences, but also 'as auto-communicative ritual that helps constitute the rhetor itself and its identity in an emergent environment' which 'tends to establish a relatively closed universe of mutual understanding not easily accessible to other publics' (Cheney and Christensen 2001: 255, 257).

The various organizational identities held will influence what type of knowledge is considered important. An identity as an innovative company will privilege knowledge about research validated via the scientific method or about product development validated via engineering principles. An identity as a profitable company will privilege financial knowledge validated via accounting methodology. An identity as a caring company will privilege human resource knowledge validated via theories and methods of organizational behaviour. Directors of an organization may hold one favourite identity. For example, the Human Resources director will hold one as a caring company, or one where workers are able to perform to their utmost. However, the board needs to reach some collective understanding which reconciles these multiple and conflicting identities. This involves development of a rhetoric which focuses on the synergies between identities and minimizes conflicts between identities. For example, an identity as an innovative company may conflict with one as a profitable company if rhetoric does not justify a link between innovation and value-creating products.

Multiple identities are difficult to deal with because they are so often in conflict. For example, Intel employees believed that technological leadership was incompatible with excellent customer service (Whetten and Godfrey 1998: 125). Being a car manufacturer which has the best technology often means forgetting about what that technology costs. This is why it is easier to allow one identity to become dominant. If one identity is too dominant – say an engineering identity in a car manufacturer, this may subvert attempts to deal with escalating costs and wasteful designs or practices. At the other extreme, too many or too incompatible multiple identities may result in confusion. For example, in the mid-1990s Digital customers thought that DEC, Digital and Digital Equipment Corporation were three separate companies (Schmitt and Simonson 1997: 74). Multiple identities, therefore, have costs as well as benefits.

Identity 'implies a moral order' in the sense that 'the determination of a firm's coherence arises out of the demand for a moral and notional consistency in the "categorization" of its activities' (Kogut and Zander 1996: 502). One way to make a moral order, bridge differences and achieve coherence in an identity is to use rhetorics establishing relevance to integrating myths (Selznik 1957; Fiol 2002: 662) or to hierarchies of values (Perelman and Olbrechts-Tyteca 1969: 80) that justify multiple identities as part of an ordered relationship. Although organizational identity may be expressed in industry terms – e.g. car manufacturer, software house – it is possible for it to be expressed in a more general and rhetorical way. The most general identities establish relevance to universal symbolic worlds (and their associated values) such as fertility (e.g. a cow – Borden Ice Cream or

Elmer's Glue), culture (e.g. Celtic heritage with Guinness), economics (efficiency), politics (e.g. leadership, power, loyalty in MGM's lion), religion (divine presence, enlightenment in Texaco's star) and technology (reliability, fun, original, innovative in IBM) (Schmitt and Simonson 1997).

Organizational boundaries are becoming more invisible, so that it becomes difficult to know whether to take an insider's or an outsider's view of which knowledge within an organization is important. Developments in the nature of organizational rhetoric have created a situation where communication now addresses both external and internal audiences. There are several reasons for this. First, marketing discourse disrupts the traditional container metaphor of the organization because the consumer is placed at the centre, inside the organizational activity. A second, reinforcing trend is that, because of high worker mobility, organizations are beginning to view employees as consumers, to which the organization must adapt and whose needs it must satisfy (Cheney and Christensen 2001: 248). Thirdly, issue management discourse also disrupts the container metaphor, because the organization proactively empathizes with the role of external constituents. Therefore, marketing and issue management discourses have eroded the importance and clarity of organizational boundaries as a construct in analysing organizational discourse.

Therefore, it is understandable that many organizations are consolidating their internal and external communications in a single function. Messages seek to link both external consumers and internal stakeholders to the same concern, identity. Organizations, therefore, are communicating with themselves. The external audience acts as a mirror in which the organization examines itself and its identity, and also seeks confirmation of that identity through various closed, self-confirming 'auto-communications' with external actors such as market research and consultancy organizations (Cheney and Christensen 2001: 245–50).

A compelling example of this is the reaction of members to poor organizational image. Under such circumstances, externally derived communications penetrate to the internal heart of the organization – the sense of individual identity of its members. When the New York Port Authority was the centre of negative publicity over its treatment of the homeless, thus problematizing the organization's identity, organization members reacted as if their *own individual* identities were being criticized (Dutton and Dukerich 1991).

Yet, while the 'container' metaphor has become problematic, and while new communication practices involve messages intended for external and internal audiences together, the metaphor remains a comforting illusion (Cheney and Christensen 2001: 240). For example, the external audience is often referred to in managerial discourse, thus becoming a social construct and a useful reference point. It is for these reasons that I will argue that externally and internally directed rhetoric about knowledge as a resource must be combined within a single message.

Establishing a Coherent View of the Role of Knowledge

I shall argue that coherence can be achieved between substantial and rhetorical parts, multiple identities and internal and external communication by means of the use of a single message. This is shown in Table 2.15.1 as an example of a knowledge-intensive service firm which delivers integrated solutions to business. To create and protect competitive advantage, rhetoric must be used to establish relevance of resources to organizational identity. For each source of competitive advantage this requires focusing internal and external audiences on a single message.

Table 2.15.1 shows that a number of sources of competitive advantage need to be simultaneously addressed, both internally and externally, in order to protect the firm.

The way in which value as a source of competitive advantage can be established is through linking capabilities (dramatised as power to do something) to identity (made positive by linkage to master myths and social values). Value is most easily constructed as a single, unifying message by means of establishing legitimacy through individual expertise or organizational capability and through demonstrating access to and ability to activate social networks.

Rarity is semantically close to uniqueness. Rhetoric directed internally will link the specialness of stakeholders to the uniqueness of organizational identity. Externally directed rhetoric will link the rarity of the resource to the uniqueness of organizational identity to convince the competitor that the resource is not available or appropriable. Therefore, rarity as a source of competitive advantage can

be established by linking rarity to unique identity and by making uniqueness claims, e.g. originality claims in patents, systems developed for solely in-house use, and rare talents, i.e. specialized and well qualified workers. These rhetorics can be combined in a single message that says that rare resources are tied to the firm as firm-specific capabilities or resource bundles which cannot be unravelled as single resources such as individual competences.

Non-imitability can be protected by convincing competitors that they cannot copy identity. Identity may be claimed in terms of externally accredited criteria of recognition. Or it may be claimed by referring to qualities such as being caring, being intellectually respected or delivering good service. These qualities must refer to tacitness or social complexity or causal ambiguity in order for identity to be non-imitable. For example, holding an organizational identity as a 'client relationship-focused consultancy' implies many of the skills are implicitly understood in consultant-client interactions, where instances of added value are difficult to make more tangible than can be expressed by words like 'confidence' or 'trust'. Internally directed rhetoric convinces stakeholders that tacitness, social complexity and causal ambiguity are important parts of identity. Externally-directed rhetoric uses tacitness, social complexity and causal ambiguity as grounds for convincing competitors that identity cannot be copied. This can be combined in a single message showing how the organization's identity is the result of processes which are tacit, socially complex and causally ambiguous.

Non-substitutability can be protected by raising the expected performance which competitors think is necessary for substitution to be profitable. This can be done for example by publicising demoralizingly superior continuous improvement programmes or by publicising lock-in arrangements of mutual investment by suppliers or customers and by publicising the business model to demonstrate the impossibility of low cost market entry. When rhetoric is used to deter competitors, it is more convincing when it links organizational identity to one or more of these three capabilities. For example, 'we are a company which keeps close relationships with its suppliers' adds the weight of identity to a lock-in strategy. Internally-directed rhetoric makes the contribution of identity transparent in order to get stakeholders' commitment. Externally-directed rhetoric makes the reasons for high performance

Table 2.15.1 Example of a knowledge-intensive service firm which delivers integrated solutions to business

Source of competitive advantage	Rhetoric to link resources to identity	Intended rhetorical effect	Single message
Value	*Internally directed* – Link valuable expertise to identity as knowledge-based work *Externally directed* – Establish legitimacy. Link resources (capabilities) to identity (master myths and social values).	Motivate workers (increase identification) Impress shareholders (raise valuation by financial markets) Impress customer (increase demand)	*Explicit* – We are involved with our large corporate clients in long-term advisory relationships *Implicit* – The use of teams and good management adds an organizational plus to high social skills of individuals
Rarity	*Internally directed* – Link the special-ness of stakeholders to the uniqueness of identity to convince them they are special *Externally directed* – Link the rarity of the resource to the uniqueness of identity to convince competitor that resource is not appropriable	Motivate workers (increase identification) Deter competitors (from acquiring resource)	*Explicit* – we are able to attract uniquely good individuals *Implicit* – We can tie rare resources to the firm, e.g. firm-specific capabilities
Imitation	*Internally directed* – Claim tacitness, social complexity or causal ambiguity as central part of identity to convince stakeholders that these three elements are important *Externally directed* – Claim tacitness, social complexity or causal ambiguity as central part of identity to convince competitor that they cannot copy identity	High identification by stakeholders Deter competitors (high identification by stakeholders keeps performance high and cannot be copied)	*Explicit* – clients have tacit knowledge of their problems. We capture it in multiple, social settings; there is no simple solution process *Implicit* – Our work involves tacitness, social complexity and causal ambiguity
Substitution	*Internally directed* – Claim these factors as central part of identity to convince stakeholders that they should give their support *Externally directed* – Claim these factors as central part of identity to convince competitor that market entry not worthwhile	High identification by stakeholders Deter/demoralize competitors (reasons for performance are visible)	*Explicit* – We have a cost model of how we solve client problems *Implicit* – We can reduce causal ambiguity by making explicit factors that affect performance
Control	*Internally directed* – Ideological, unobtrusive control and self-censorship based on identification *Externally directed* – Foreground capabilities and background individual knowledge	Shift focus from individual to organization (loss of self-based individual identity and gain in organization-based individual identity) Provide a coherent story	*Explicit* – Working in teams in a trusted company with large client base makes our capability more than the sum of individual competences *Implicit* – Strategic relevance of capability base and extent to which it can be extended to new areas of business

visible to deter market entry. These audiences can be addressed by a single message which makes explicit the organization's reasons for high performance.

Control can be maintained by means of holding an identity as an organization which is committed to its stakeholders. This involves a shift in the attention of managers away from human resource management (individual competences) and towards strategy (organizational capabilities). For example, an identity as 'an organization which lets workers develop to their full potential' is focused on individual competences and encourages an instrumentalist orientation of 'what can I get out of being here?' Alternatively, an identity as 'world class research laboratory' is focused on organizational capability as a strategic matter rather than merely the individual's competences as a human resource management matter. The internal effect of this rhetoric is to increase identification, because the effect is a loss of the sense of individual self as a self set apart from the organization, and an increase in a sense of self as part of an organization. Internally-directed rhetoric aims at shifting attention from individual competence to organizational capability. Externally-directed rhetoric uses capability as a coherence device. Both audiences are addressed by a single message that states the strategic relevance of the firm's capability base and the extent to which it can be expanded to new areas of business.

Conclusion

I have used a two part model of knowledge. Resources and capabilities have an existence which is real and independent of social construction. However, they also can be significantly affected by rhetoric. I have focused on this rhetorical part of knowledge. I have discussed a resource-based view of knowledge in order to show the rhetorical nature of knowledge as a source of competitive advantage. I did this to show that rhetoric is a useful step to protecting and increasing competitive advantage. For each of the five sources of competitive advantage (value, rarity, non-imitability, non-substitutability and control), I argued that rhetoric can increase competitive advantage. To create and protect competitive advantage, rhetoric must be used to link resources to organizational identity. For each source of competitive advantage this is directed simultaneously at the internal and external audiences in the form of a single message.

References

Albert, S. and Whetten, D. (1985) 'Organizational identity', in L.L. Cummings and B.M. Staw (eds), *Research in organizational behaviour*, Vol 7. Greenwich, CT: JAI Press. pp. 263–95.

Alvesson, M. (1993) 'Cultural-ideological modes of management control: a theory and a case study of a professional service company', in S. Deetz (ed.), *Communication Yearbook 16*. London: Sage. pp. 3–42.

Alvesson, M. (2001) 'Identity work: ambiguity, image and identity', *Human Relations*, 54(7): 863–86.

Ashforth, B.E. and Gibbs, B.W. (1990) 'The double edge of organizational legitimation', *Organization Science*, 1: 177–94.

Barney, J.B. (1986) 'Organizational culture: can it be a source of sustained competitive advantage?', *Academy of Management Review*, 11: 656–65.

Barney, J.B. (1991) 'Firm resources and sustained competitive advantage', *Journal of Management*, 17: 99–120.

Barney, J.B. (2001) 'Is the resource-based view a useful perspective for strategic management research?', *Academy of Management Review*, 26(1): 41–56.

Bilamoria, D., Cooperrider, D., Kaczmarski, K., Khalsa, G., Srivistva, S. and Upadhayaya, P. (1995) 'The organizational dimensions of global change: no limits to cooperation', *Journal of Management Inquiry*, 4(1): 71–90.

Blackler, F. (1995) 'Knowledge, knowledge work and organizations: an overview and interpretation', *Organization Studies*, 16(6): 1021–46.

Brown, S.L. and Eisenhardt, K.M. (1997) 'The art of continuous change: linking complexity theory and time-paced evolution in relentlessly shifting organizations', *Administrative Science Quarterly*, 42: 1–34.

Cheney, G. and Christensen, L.T. (2001) 'Organizational identity', in F.M. Jablin and L.L. Putnam (eds), *Handbook of organizational communication: advances in theory, research and methods*. Thousand Oaks, CA: Sage. pp. 231–69.

Cheney, G. and Vibbert, S.L. (1987) 'Corporate discourse: public relations and issue management', in F.M. Jablin, L.L. Putnam, K.H. Roberts and L.H. Porter (eds), *Handbook of organizational communication: an interdisciplinary perspective*. Newbury Park, CA: Sage. pp. 165–94.

Christensen, C.M. and Bower, J.L. (1996) 'Customer power, strategic investment, and the failure of leading firms', *Strategic Management Journal*, 17: 197–218.

Christensen, L.T. (1995) 'Buffering organisational identity in the marketing culture', *Organisation Studies*, 16(4): 651–72.

Clegg, S. and Palmer, G. (1996) *The politics of management knowledge*. London: Sage.

Coff, R.W. (1997) 'Human assets and management dilemmas: coping with hazards on the road to resource-based theory', *Academy of Management Review*, 22(2): 374–402.

Daft, R. and Weick, K. (1984) 'Toward a model of organizations as interpretation systems', *Academy of Management Review*, 9: 284–95.

Dierickx, I. and Cool, K. (1989) 'Asset stock accumulation and the sustainability of competitive advantage', *Management Science*, 35: 1504–13.

Dutton, J.E. and Dukerich, J.M. (1991) 'Keeping an eye on the mirror: the role of image and identity in organizational adaptation', *Academy of Management Journal*, 34: 517–54.

Fiol, C.M. (2002) 'Capitalizing on paradox: the role of language in transforming organizational identities', *Organization Science*, 13(6): 653–66.

Florida, R. (2003) *The rise of the creative class: and how it's transforming work, leisure, community and everyday life.* New York: Basic Books.

Gray, B. and Wood, D. (1991) 'Collaborative alliances: moving from practice to theory', *Journal of Applied Behavioral Science*, 27: 3–22.

Hart, S.L. (1995) 'A natural resource-based view of the firm', *Academy of Management Review*, 20(4): 996–1014.

Hendserson, H. and Cockburn, I. (1994) 'Measuring competence? Exploring firm effects in pharmaceutical research', *Strategic Management Journal*, 15: 63–94.

Hitt, M.A., Bierman, L., Shimazu, K. and Kochhar, R. (2001) 'Direct and moderating effects of human capital on strategin professional service firms: a resource-based perspective', *Academy of Management Journal*, 44(1): 13–28.

Knights, D., Murray, F. and Willmott, H. (1993) 'Networking as knowledge work: a study of interorganizational development in the financial services sector', *Journal of Management Studies*, 30: 975–96.

Kogut, B. and Zander, O. (1996) 'What forms do? Coordination, identity and learning', *Organization Science*, 7(5): 502–18.

Lado, A.A. and Wilson, M.C. (1994) 'Human resource systems and sustained competitive advantage: a competency-based perspective', *Academy of Management Review*, 19: 699–727.

Lave, J. (1993) 'The practice of learning', in S. Chaiklin and J. Lave (eds), *Understanding practice: perspectives on activity and context.* Cambridge: Cambridge University Press. pp. 3–32.

Leonard-Barton, D. (1996) *Wellsprings of knowledge: building and sustaining the sources of innovation.* Boston, MA: Boston Business School Press.

Lepak, D.P. and Snell, S.A. (1999) 'The human resource architecture: toward a theory of human capital allocation and development', *Academy of Management Review*, 24(1): 31–48.

Lippman, S.A. and Rumelt, R. (1982) 'Uncertain imitability: an anlysis of interfirm differences in efficiency under competition', *Bell Journal of Economics*, 13: 418–38.

McEvily, S.K., Das, S. and McCabe, K. (2000) 'Avoiding competence-substitution through knowledge-sharing', *Academy of Management Review*, 25(2): 294–311.

Miller, D. and Shamsie, J. (1996) 'The resource-based view of the firm in two environments: the Hollywood film studios from 1936 to 1965', *Academy of Management Journal*, 39(3): 519–43.

Nahapiet, J. and Ghoshal, S. (1998) 'Social capital, intellectual capital, and the organizational advantage', *Academy of Management Review*, 23(2): 242–66.

Nordhaug, O. (1994) *Human capital in organizations: competence, training and learning.* New York: Oxford University Press.

Orr, J. (1990) 'Sharing knowledge, celebrating identity: community memory in a service culture', in D. Middleton and D. Edwards (eds), *Collective remembering.* London: Sage. pp. 169–89.

Pennings, J.M. Lee, K. and van Witteloostuijn, A. (1998) 'Human capital, social capital, and firm dissolution', *Academy of Management Journal*, 41(4): 425–40.

Perelman, Ch. and Olbrechts-Tyteca, M.L. (1969) *The new rhetoric: a treatise on argumentation.* Notre Dame, IN: University of Notre Dame.

Peteraf, M.A. (1993) 'The cornerstones of competitive advantage: a resource-based view', *Strategic Management Journal*, 14: 179–91.

Peters, T.J. (1992) *Liberation management: necessary disorganization for the nanosecond nineties.* New York: Alfred Knopf.

Porter, M.E. (1985) *Competitive advantage: creating and sustaining superior performance.* New York: Free Press.

Pralahad, C.K. and Hamel, G. (1990) 'The core competence of the corporation', *Harvard Business Review*, 68(3): 79–92.

Pratt, M.G. and Foreman, P.O. (2000) 'Classifying managerial responses to multiple organizational identities', *Academy of Management Review*, 25(1): 18–42.

Priem, R.L. and Butler, J.E. (2001) 'Is the resource-based 'view' a useful perspective for strategic management research?', *Academy of Management Review*, 26(1): 22–40.

Rao, H. (1994) 'The social construction of reputation: certification contests, legitimation, and the survival of organizations in the American automobile industry 1895–1912', *Strategic Management Journal*, 15: 29–44.

Reich, R. (1991) *The work of nations: preparing ourselves for 21st-century capitalism.* London: Simon and Schuster.

Rumelt, R. (1984) 'Towards a strategic theory of the firm', in R. Lamb (ed.), *Competitive strategic management.* Englewood Cliffs, NJ: Prentice Hall. pp. 556–70.

Schmitt, B. and Simonson, A. (1995) 'Managing corporate image and identity', *Long Range Planning*, 28(5): 82–92.

Schmitt, B. and Simonson, A. (1997) *Marketing aesthetics: the strategic management of brands, identity and image.* New York: Free Press.

Selznik, P. (1957) *Leadership and administration.* New York: Harper & Row.

Starbuck, W. (1992) 'Learning by knowledge intensive forms', *Journal of Management Studies*, 29, 713–40.

Stimpert, L., Gustafsson, L. and Sarason, Y. (1998) 'What does identity imply for strategy?', in D. Whetten and P.C. Godfrey (eds), *Identity in organizations: building identity through conversations*. Thousand Oaks CA: Sage. pp. 83–170.

Suchman, L. (1987) *Plans and situated actions*. Cambridge: Cambridge University Press.

Suchman, M.C. (1995) 'Managing legitimacy: strategic and institutional approaches', *Academy of Management Review*, 20(3): 571–610.

Townley, B. (1993) 'Foucault, power/knowledge, and its relevance for human resource management', *Academy of Management Review*, 18(3): 518–45.

Uzzi, B. (1996) 'The sources and consequences of embeddedness for the economic performance of organizations: the network effect', *American Sociological Review*, 61: 674–98.

Verona, G. (1999) 'A resource-based view of product development', *Academy of Management Review*, 24(1): 132–42.

Vibbert, S.L. and Bostdorff, D.M. (1993) 'Issue management in the 'lawsuit crisis'', in C. Conrad (ed.), *The ethical nexus*. Norwood, NJ: Ablex. pp. 103–20.

Weick, K. (1995) *Sensemaking in organizations*. Thousand Oaks, CA: Sage.

Wernerfelt, B. (1984) 'The resource-based view of the firm', *Strategic Management Journal*, 16: 171–4.

Westley, F. and Vredenburg, H. (1991) 'Strategic bridging: the collaboration between environmentalists and business in the making of green products', *Journal of Applied Behavioral Science*, 27: 65–90.

Whetten, D. and Godfrey, P. (eds) (1998) *Identity in organizations: developing theory through conversations*. Thousand Oaks, CA: Sage.

Wrzesniewski, A. and Dutton, J.E. (2001) 'Crafting a job: revisioning employees as active crafters of their work', *Academy of Management Review*, 26(2): 179–202.

Zbaracki, M.J. (1998) 'The rhetoric and reality of total quality management', *Administrative Science Quarterly*, 43(3): 602–36.

2.16 Radical Organizational Change

ROYSTON GREENWOOD AND C.R. (BOB) HININGS

Introduction

Understanding organization change is, today, a central question within organization theory. It was not always so. Prior to the 1970s, change was rarely an explicit concern. Instead, most perspectives on organizations assumed change *per se* to be of modest importance and not particularly difficult to accomplish. Partly, lack of concern with change was because organizational contexts and strategies were relatively stable, making change unnecessary.

Today, it is commonplace to note that the volatility of changes confronting organizations has dramatically increased. Consequently, greater attention is given to understanding two kinds of change. First, there is the traditional concern with how organizations can remain flexible and adaptive, constantly adjusting to shifts in market opportunities. The second concern is variously labelled 'radical', 'archetypal', 'divergent' or 'quantum' change and focuses upon whether, and how, an organization can move from one organizational form to another. This chapter is concerned with radical change.

Prior to the mid-1980s, theories of radical organizational change were rare, if non-existent, with the exception of the organization life-cycle model (Greiner 1972; Kimberly and Miles 1980; Quinn and Cameron 1983). Most theories of change were about organizational development or organizational adaptation. Organizational development is about improving an existing organizational form and focuses upon processes inside the organization, emphasizing team building, inter-personal communication and facilitative management (cf, Burke 2002). It fits more comfortably with change portrayed as flexibility.

Despite the absence of formal theories, we still learned about change, but from within the basic perspectives of organization theory. Structural-contingency theory, resource-dependence theory, institutional theory, population ecology theory and so forth each said something about change. Section II reviews these theories and their contribution to our understanding of change. The intention is to outline the theory, not provide a detailed and comprehensive review. One organization theory – network theory – does not neatly fit this historical ordering because it did not really develop until *after* our pivotal date of the mid-1980s even though its origins were earlier. Nevertheless, we include it in Section II because it more closely resembles the stance of the basic theoretical perspectives in that it is not *per se* a theory of change.

We note two shifts in emphasis from the 1960s through the 1970s. The 1960s imagined change as non-problematical. Structural-contingency theory and strategic choice theory, the early dominant approaches, hardly discussed change and assumed it would happen when necessary. The behavioural theory of the firm took a less sanguine stance, but still emphasized organizational adaptation. Towards the late 1970s, change became seen as problematical. Resource-dependency theory, configuration theory, institutional theory and ecological theory, each highlighted obstacles hindering change. There was also a shift in focus from the organization to populations or networks of organizations. These later theories outlined how the embeddedness of organizations in their contexts ('fields') seriously impeded organizational change. From about 1977 onwards, then, organizational theories portrayed change as problematical and adopted an inter-organizational level of analysis. In an important way, however, the theories differed. Structural-contingency theory, institutional theory and ecological theory saw organizations responding to contextual dynamics. Organizations were reactive, environments determinant. Resource-dependence and strategic choice theories emphasized how organizations could shape, even dominate, their environments.

The shift in level of analysis from the organization to the field raised a very different question about change. Most studies of change frame the question as whether and why *an* organization can change organizational forms. However, there is another question: what determines the choice-set of organizational forms?

From the mid-1980s, freestanding theories of organizational change appeared. Some, such as punctuated-equilibrium theory, began with an overall framework, albeit in skeletal form. Later work then filled in the framework, elaborating its component stages and dynamics. Other theories, such as neo-institutional theory, were constructed retrospectively from studies that aggregate into a theory of change. Section III looks at three theories of change, roughly in the order in which they appeared: punctuated-equilibrium theory, continuity and change theory and neo-institutional theory. All three show debts to the theories reviewed in Section II.

Theories of Organizations: 1960–1985

Structural-Contingency Theory

Structural-contingency theory (S/C theory) evolved from two sets of studies, each a response to Weber's analysis of bureaucracy. One set explored whether bureaucracy was the universal, rationally efficient model. These studies showed the bureaucracy to be 'contingent' upon task uncertainty and organizational size (e.g. Burns and Stalker 1961; Woodward 1965). The second set (e.g. Pugh et al. 1969) questioned whether the component dimensions of bureaucracy are characteristic of all formal organizations, or whether multiple configurations exist. Both sets of studies concluded that there are multiple organizational forms and that their effectiveness depends upon their 'fit' with their context (see Drazin and Van de Ven 1985; Doty et al. 1993; Gresov and Drazin 1997).

The 'contingencies' that determine the appropriateness of organizational form include the extent of environmental uncertainty, organizational size, extent of diversification and the routineness of the tasks performed. The importance of 'fit' between an organization and its market context was the dominant perspective from the 1960s until the mid-1970s (Pennings 1992) and still engages research into

organizations (e.g. Gooderham et al. 1999; Donaldson 2001; Siggelkow 2002).

S/C Theory and Change

Structural contingency theory has an implicit theory of change. Organizations out of alignment with their context will move to gain to a better fit. Otherwise, the organization will perform poorly. In this sense:

> Contingencies determine structure. Organizations change their structures to fit the existing level of their contingency factors, such as size or diversification, in order to avoid performance loss from misfit (Donaldson 2001: 136).

Note that, according to this approach, change can be triggered by exogenous (environmental uncertainty) or endogenous (size: task uncertainty) factors. However, organizations do respond. As an organization increases in size it will 'become' more formalized. If the environment becomes more uncertain, an organization will 'become' more flexible. As such, S/C theory assumes decisive action by leaders, but the CEO has minimal discretion over choice of organizational form. CEOs are switching agents, aligning organizations to their contexts.

Further, change is non-problematical:

> Because the fit of organizational characteristics to contingencies leads to high performance, organizations seek to obtain fit. For this reason, organizations are motivated to avoid the misfit that results after contingencies change, and do so by adopting new organizational characteristics that fit the new levels of the contingencies (Donaldson 2001: 2).

The assumption that change is non-problematical is inconsistent with several works that Donaldson uses as theoretical building blocks. Burns and Stalker (1961), for example, describe 'pathological systems' which prevent realignment because of the political activities of groups within an organization and because managerial understanding is constrained by their cognitive belief systems.

Strategic Choice

S/C theory developed in two directions. First, Child (1972) developed strategic choice theory, challenging the idea that organizations are determined by their contingencies and that executives have minimal discretion in designing their organizations. Child drove home the point that organizations could choose not to adapt. Donaldson (2001: 135; see also 1997) disagrees: 'the best evidence to date disconfirms strategic choice and argues that it is mostly false, so that the extent of choice over structure is, at most, limited'. The logic of Donaldson's critique is consistent with influential studies by Chandler (1962) who traced the evolution of the M-form structure (see also Whittington et al. 1999).

Configuration Theory

The second development of S/C theory was 'configuration theory' (see Miller and Friesen 1980; 1982; 1984; Miller 1981; 1982). This theory builds upon the taxonomic approaches of Pugh et al. (1969) and was a response to the simplicity of S/C theory (e.g. its inability to explain how organizations might respond to inconsistent contingencies or the possibility of 'equifinality' (Drazin and Van de Ven 1985). The central idea is that strategies, structures and processes should be considered holistically, rather than variable-by-variable. Strategies and structures are underpinned by 'orchestrating themes' that provide 'the driving character of an enterprise' (Miller 1996: 506–7). Organizations with closely aligned structures and processes gain advantages that are difficult to imitate (Miller 1996: 510). Examples of configuration theory include Mintzberg (1979; 1983) and Miles and Snow (1978).

Configuration Theory and Change

Miller's later work identifies 'momentum' and 'simplicity' as dynamics that work against change. 'Momentum', the tendency of organizations to sustain prevailing arrangements, is based upon two ideas: that configurations are held in place by their interdependent 'mutually supportive' parts (Miller and Friesen 1984: 204); and that change is very disruptive and costly. 'Simplicity' is the process by which organizations develop an 'overwhelming preoccupation with a single goal, strategic activity, department, or world view' (Miller 1993: 117). We interpret this to mean that the 'orchestrating theme' of a configuration becomes amplified to the point where the organization becomes imbalanced and unable to function effectively.

Simplicity and momentum converge upon the same point. Configurations are dynamic, constantly amplifying their orchestrating theme. Siggelkow

(2001; 2002) provides case studies of these processes, tracing how organizations *reinforce* core elements by adding new 'core' and 'elaborating' elements. There is, thus, an active reproduction of an organization's current trajectory: 'configurations seem to act as *vortex-like force fields* that progressively specialize and align values and behaviour' (Miller 1993: 130, emphasis added). Although these are general processes, the intensity of momentum and simplicity varies. Highly successful organizations are prone to their effect. The 'march towards simplicity' is 'especially prevalent' in stable settings (Miller et al. 1996). For us, the key point is that simplicity and momentum are theoretical *dynamics* militating against radical change.

Configuration theory 'remains undeveloped' (Miller 1996: 506). Nevertheless, it contributed three important insights. First, organizational forms are not assemblages of structures and processes that can be easily discarded or rearranged. On the contrary, changes constitute 'reversals in *the thrust* of organizational evolution' (Miller and Chen 1994: 1, emphasis added). This depiction contrasts with the static imagery of S/C theory. Secondly, multiple 'factors' contribute to the dynamics of momentum and simplicity and collectively work against change. These factors operate at the levels of the individual, organization and industry. In this sense, configuration theory cautions against seeing the difficulties of change as simply the need to overcome disaffected individuals or the cognitive blindness of executives. Thirdly, Miller and Friesen provide an early expression of the *periodicity* of the change process, foreshadowing the punctuated-equilibrium model. Organizational histories 'demonstrate two extremes: periods of momentum in which no, or almost no trend is reversed; and dramatic periods of reversal, in which very many trends are reversed' (Miller and Friesen 1984: 206). As becomes evident later, configuration theory was also adopted by neo-institutional approaches to change.

The Behavioural Theory of the Firm

Unlike structural-contingency theorists, who sought to understand which organizational forms matched which contingent situations, Cyert and March (1963) were concerned with *how* organizations adapt to their environments. They explored the behavioural routines by which alignment is achieved. They conceptualized organizations as information processing systems and identified the routines that decision-makers use to cope with ambiguous streams of information. One routine is that decisions are activated by performance problems ('problemistic search'). Executives act only when performance falls below historical or socially defined aspirations. Solutions to performance shortfalls are generated through other routines. For example, complex problems are split into sub-problems and assigned to sub-units, such as marketing or production departments, which apply their understanding ('local rationality') to the sub-problem. Consequently, solutions may be sub-optimal from the perspective of the organization as a whole. Further, solutions are sought 'in the neighbourhood of the current alternatives' (Cyert and March 1963: 121), implying that current approaches are usually retained. These decision rules highlight how decisions are dependent on organizational histories.

Cyert and March also emphasize that attention to problems is *sequential*, focusing upon one issue at a time, depending upon the current urgency of any given problem. The direction of change, moreover, is driven by the 'dominant coalition's' *interpretation* of goals and performance. Consequently, 'bias' arises from the 'special training or experience' and the 'hopes and expectations' of influential executives (Cyert and March 1963: 122).

The Behavioural Theory and Change

As initially expressed, the behavioural theory of the firm shared features with structural-contingency theory and strategic-choice theory. The focus was upon the organization's alignment with its context and performance depended upon achieving that alignment. CEOs and senior management are pivotal in shaping an organizational response. And, whilst recognizing the politics of decision-making and thus the likelihood of resistance, adaptation to shifting circumstances is normal:

> Organizations change. Although they often appear resistant to change, they are *frequently* transformed into forms remarkably different from the original (March 1981: 563, emphasis added).

Moreover, the process of change is evolutionary rather than dramatic:

> Most change in organizations results neither from extraordinary processes nor forces, nor from uncommon imagination, persistence or skill, but from relatively stable, routine processes that relate organizations to their environments (March 1991: 78).

The theory, in other words, emphasizes experiential learning and much subsequent work confirmed these learning processes (e.g. Lant and Mezias 1990; Lant 1992). Nevertheless, much of March's work emphasizes the *difficulties* of organizational learning (e.g. Levinthal and March 1993). As Denrell and March (2001: 527) observe, 'a behavioural model of organizational learning produces a bias against risky and new alternatives'. Lant et al. (1992) and Gordon et al. (2000) found radical change is much rarer than convergent adaptation.

Greve (1995; 1996; 1998) examined whether change is driven by performance feedback. He proposes that change is a function of three factors: *motivation* (driven by performance feedback); *capability* (i.e. whether the organization has experience of changing); and *opportunity* (i.e. whether decision-makers can find attractive alternatives to current arrangements). Later, Greve (2003) added the interesting idea that managers avoid organizationally risky solutions, such as mergers that involve organizational restructuring, in favour of strategies that involve financial risk without organizational upheaval.

A different set of recent studies is revisiting the role of organizational routines (e.g. Pentland and Rueter 1994; Pentland 1995; Feldman and Rafaeli 2002; Feldman 2003). These studies are notable because they portray routines not as mechanisms of constraint and thus inertia, but of experimentation that enable learning and adaptation. Feldman and Pentland (2003), in a formal expression of this theory, distinguish 'ostensive' (the abstract idea) and performative aspects (implementation) of routines. Ostensive structures shape how a routine is to be implemented, but actors necessarily 'fill-in' its details. Routines thus constrain actions, but actions may modify the routine. Whether such 'improvisations' (Weick 1995; Moorman and Miner 1998) can add up to radical change is not yet clear. Indeed, Feldman (2003) elaborates the stabilizing effect of routines, showing how they enable 'understandings' of existing organizational purposes. Nevertheless, the focus upon how day-to-day human actions invoke reflexity and change is an important correction to the dominant imagery in organization theory of change as extraordinary. As Tsoukas and Chia (2002: 576) put it, 'Change is all there is'.

Behavioural/learning theory provides several insights. First, it emphasizes that the firm's history, encoded in its routines, shapes and reproduce its responses. As such, it connects to Pettigrew's theory of continuity and change. Secondly, it elaborates the routines used by organizations as they seek alignment with their context and explains why radical change occurs less frequently than convergent change. Thirdly, it gives greater precision to *why* change happens, identifying the importance of aspiration defined performance feedback. Finally, the theory underlines that organizational adaptation is *dynamic*, an ongoing consequence of organizational learning.

Resource Dependency Theory

Resource dependence (R/D) theory (Pfeffer and Salancik 1978; Aldrich 1979) emphasizes three features of organizational life. Firstly, a focus upon *resources*: raw materials, capital, information, authority or other inputs needed for organizational operations. Secondly, an emphasis upon context as *a network of other organizations*:

> The major factors that organizations must take account of in their environments are other organizations. Organizations control the flow of capital, personnel, information, and other essential resources through a social system and they represent concentrations of resources that administrators cannot ignore (Aldrich 1979: 265).

Thirdly, organizations seek to *avoid* becoming overdependent on other organizations whilst *exploiting* situations where other organizations are dependent upon them. Organizations seek to influence and *dominate* their resource environment, not simply *adapt* to it. Thus, the composition of boards of directors, the choice of alliance partners or acquisition targets are responses to resource dependencies. Noticeably, these decisions are about connections with other organizations. As Pfeffer (2003: xii) later pointed out: 'the (1978) book is filled with network and relationship imagery', which, at the time of the initial theoretical statement, was much less prevalent than it is today.

Despite outlining the possibility of adaptation, the R/D model directs attention to how organizations influence their context, partly in response to the (then) prevailing S/C theory, which emphasized adaptation. However, Aldrich pointed out that large corporations can engage in environmental domination but most organizations are too small to do so (Aldrich 1979: 112). Managers make choices within constraints and may seek to 'manage' those constraints, but for the most part, says Aldrich, they adapt to them. Pfeffer (2003: xii), in contrast, is clear that a central assumption of the R/D model, as initially formulated, was that:

> Organizations possessed both the desire and, occasionally, the ability to negotiate their positions within those constraints using a variety of tactics. In other words, Salancik and I argued that strategic choice was both possible (Child 1972) and sometimes, although not inevitably, efficacious …".

Resource Dependence and Change

The R/D theory of change is that misalignment between an organization and its environment produces performance decline. Misalignment is usually the result of an exogenous shift. As a consequence, there is pressure to replace incumbent CEOs, whose functional backgrounds ill-equip them to handle the new dependencies, and the board of directors. That is, performance failure allows the ascendance of executives better able to cope with changed circumstances. Pfeffer and Salancik's theory thus builds upon the 'strategic contingencies' theory of power (Hickson et al. 1971), which asserts that power within an organization will be held by the group best able to manage the critical external challenge ('dependency') confronting the organization. The logic is that as the critical dependency changes, so, too, will the distribution of *intra*-organizational power. These changes, if made, trigger change in organizational form.

There are three insights provided by the R/D model. Firstly, it recognizes that organizations attempt to control their contexts. This is perhaps the central contribution of the theory. It is surprising, therefore, that 'much of the empirical work has focused on the relationship between resource dependence and organizational decisions that might be construed as being made in response to dependence, such as efforts to absorb or co-opt constraint' (Pfeffer 2003: xvi–xvii). Particular empirical attention has been given to board interlocks, exploring how far organizations co-opt representatives from organizations on which they are dependent (e.g. Boeker and Goodstein 1991; Hillman et al. 2000). Other studies show how changes in personnel lead to shifts in organizational form (e.g. Kraatz and Moore 2002; Rao and Drazin 2002). Ocasio and Kim (1999) found support for this circulation of power thesis, suggesting that performance failures *do* lead to executive succession. However, they also show that replacing the CEO may *not* lead to change in organizational form.

Although R/D theory explicitly acknowledges that organizations can act individually or collectively, studies of organizations acting *collectively* are rare (e.g. Baum and Ingram 1998). Pfeffer (2003) is especially disappointed that attempts to intervene in the public policy process have not been studied. Notable exceptions include Dobbin and Dowd (1997; 2000) and Perrow (2002).

Secondly, the R/D model connects exogenous shifts to two intra-organizational dynamics: the cognitive frames of senior executives; and the distribution of power between functional groups. The importance of cognitive frames as constraints on sensemaking and issue diagnosis is only hinted at in the R/D model but later became a central theme within organization theory. Pfeffer and Salancik thus anticipated the importance of cognitive frames both in deterring change and in shaping the direction that change might take. The distribution of power explains why only *some* organizations respond to exogenous shifts and why organizations might shift in one direction rather than another.

Thirdly, although R/D theory focuses upon the economic context, it introduces the importance of regulatory structures. It is important not to overly credit R/D as fully recognizing the institutional context, and it is probably fair to conclude that Pfeffer and Salancik were particularly cognizant of *formal* rules and regulations, much as specified by North (1990). Nevertheless, and unlike S/C theory, which assumes the market context as 'out there', R/D theory acknowledges the interaction of market and regulatory structures.

Neoinstitutional Theory

1977 was a good year for organization theory. It heralded two new perspectives, neoinstitutional theory and population ecology, that opened novel ways of understanding organizations. Both perspectives made important and explicit statements about organizational change. Both, moreover, operate at the field or industry level of analysis, which has remained the dominant approach in organization theory.

Neoinstitutional theory (see Lawrence and Suddaby, this volume) began with Meyer and Rowan's (1977) observation that, within any given sector or industry, organizations use similar organizational forms. Meyer and Rowan explain this observation by pointing to the influence of the social context within which organizations are embedded. That context contains 'powerful institutional rules' that define appropriate and acceptable forms of organizing.

> That is, organizations are driven to incorporate the practices and procedures defined by prevailing rationalized concepts of organizational work and institutionalized in society. Organizations that do so increase their legitimacy and their survival prospects, independent of the immediate efficacy of the acquired practices and procedures (Meyer and Rowan 1977: 41).

In effect, Meyer and Rowan alerted theorists to the fact that organizations are not simply production systems, functioning in an environment comprised of suppliers, consumers and competitors, but social and cultural systems embedded within an 'institutional' context, comprising the state, professions, interest groups and public opinion.

Typically, institutional accounts describe *field-level* processes. Fields are 'a community of organizations that partakes of a common meaning system and whose participants interact more frequently and fatefully with one another than with actors outside the field' (Scott 1995: 56). Organizational fields are ordered through 'institutional logics' (Friedland and Alford 1991), i.e. socially constructed rules, norms and beliefs constituting field membership, role identities and patterns of appropriate conduct. Logics, conveyed through regulatory, normative and cognitive processes, shape how actors interpret reality and define the scope of socially legitimate conduct.

Thus, organizations are embedded within an institutional context that defines a choice-set of appropriate organizational forms (Granovetter 1985). Adoption of these organizational forms reinforces a hegemony of ideas that connect to distributions of power and privilege within society.

Neoinstitutional Theory and Change

Contained within institutional theory is a process model of change, first explicated by Tolbert and Zucker (1983; for a later articulation, see Tolbert and Zucker 1996). Tolbert and Zucker examined the diffusion of personnel reforms across municipalities in the US and suggested that institutionalization follows three stages: pre-institutionalization (habitualization), semi-institutionalization (objectification) and institutionalization (sedimentation). Habitualization is the emergence of behaviours specific to a problem. Although some imitation between organizations may occur, there is no sense of obligation to do so; on the contrary, behaviours are appraised for their pragmatic functionality (i.e. whether they work). Knowledge of a new organizational form, moreover, is restricted to small numbers of neighbouring organizations. Eventually, a social consensus emerges (objectification) over the value of a particular form, followed by increasing rates of adoption. In this semi-institutionalization stage, diffusion occurs because organizations mimic those perceived to be successful, but eventually the motivation to adopt shifts to a 'more normative base' (Tolbert and Zucker 1996: 183). That is, the more that a new form is adopted, the more it becomes regarded as an appropriate response and acquires cognitive legitimacy. Full institutionalization occurs when diffusion is almost universal and an organizational form has become taken-for-granted. Change may still occur, but would 'likely … require a major shift in the environment (e.g. long-lasting alterations in markets, radical change in technologies) which may then allow a set of social actors whose interests are in opposition to the structure to self-consciously oppose it or to exploit its liabilities' (Tolbert and Zucker 1996: 184). Hence, the model primarily explains convergent change, but hints at the possibility of radical change.

The advantage of focusing upon the organizational field, rather than the individual organization, which is the emphasis of S/C and R/D, is that doing so draws attention to the influence of social *and* technical influences upon communities of organizations. Another advantage is that institutional accounts of field-level processes encourage us to pay attention to the role of structuration. That is, organizations within a field are not only constrained by institutional structures, but, in their behaviours, act out and thus reproduce those structures, albeit sometimes imperfectly. The imagery then is of organizations dynamically responding to institutionalized expectations and, in so doing, amplifying and elaborating them. As fields mature, therefore, organizations get progressively locked into prevailing

practices. In some ways, these structuration processes mirror, at the field level, the intra-organizational dynamics of momentum and simplicity of configuration theory.

There are four insights from neo-institutionalized theory that we highlight. First, organizations are embedded in webs of social and cultural relationships that prescribe and proscribe appropriate organizational forms. Organizations are not free-floating islands of rationality nor units of political expediency; instead, they are seriously constrained by social expectations and the properties of legitimacy. Attempts to understand the emergence and adoption of organizational forms and/or the ability of organizations to move between forms has to take account of how institutionalized norms and values affect the choice-set available *and* choice processes. Secondly, neoinstitutional theory turns attention to the organizational field because it is at that level that institutional mechanisms are salient. In examining how or why individual organizations adapt to changing circumstances, it is necessary to understand how organizations are connected to and influenced by higher-level social structures. Thirdly, as already noted, neoinstitutional theory contains a process model of convergent change, which, as we show later, can become part of a broader model of radical *and* convergent change. Finally, there is recognition that institutionalized structures embody patterns of power and privilege. Underlying an apparently stable set of social relations are subjugated interests that can surface under appropriate circumstances. Neoinstitutional theory, in other words, has a paradoxical blend of processes converging towards equilibrium and internal contradictions that hint at radical possibilities.

Ecological Theories

Population ecology appeared at the same time as neoinstitutional theory and rapidly developed into one of the most rigorous approaches within organization theory (Baum and Shipolov, this volume). As initially developed (Hannan and Freeman 1977; Aldrich 1979) it was in the lineage of S/C theory. Thus, it was concerned with the multiplicity of organizational forms and regarded organizational survival as the product of fit between form and, primarily, market forces. However, the theory is distinctive in two ways: it focuses upon populations of organizations; and it challenges the view that organizations can adapt by changing from one organizational form to another.

The basic idea of ecological theory runs as follows. There are many populations of organizations, each distinguished by a particular organizational form. In early formulations of population ecology, organizational form was defined *theoretically* as:

> … A blueprint for organizational action, for transforming input. The blueprint can usually be inferred … by examining any of the following: (1) the structure of the organization in the narrow sense – tables of organization, written rules of operation, etc.; (2) the patterns of activity within the organization – what actually gets done by whom; or (3) the normative order – the ways of organizing that are defined as right and proper by both members and relative sectors of the environment (Hannan and Freeman 1977: 935).

This definition is not dissimilar to the definition of an organizational configuration. Later, a more elaborate definition distinguished *core* and *peripheral* elements of form. Core elements are:

> (1) its stated goals – the basis on which legitimacy and other resources are mobilized; (2) *forms of authority* within the organization and the basis of exchange between members and the organization; (3) *core technology*, especially as encoded in capital investment, infrastructure, and the skills of members; and (4) marketing strategy in a broad sense – the kind of clients (or customers) to which the organization orients its production and the way it attracts resources from the environment (Hannan and Freeman 1984: 156).

Research into ecological processes has taken two directions (Baum and Shipolov, this volume). One examines *demographic* factors, especially organizational age and size and their association with survival chances. For example, older, larger organizations are hypothesized to have better survival prospects because size often acts as a signal to stakeholders, including resource suppliers, of reliability and accountability. Larger organizations may also have greater resources with which to weather short-term market fluctuations. The second direction examines *ecological* factors, such as niche width and density dependency effects, emphasizing again how contextual factors determine the appropriateness or otherwise of alternative organizational forms.

Ecology and Change

A key theme within ecological approaches is *structural inertia theory*, which holds that timely organizational adaptation is extremely difficult to achieve. Organizations succeed to the extent that they develop reliability of performance and can 'account rationally for their actions' (Hannan and Freeman 1984: 153). Reliability and accountability are achieved through use of formal structures and standardized routines. These routines, however, make organizations 'highly resistant to structural change' (Hannan and Freeman 1984: 155), for many of the reasons observed by configuration theory. Changes in an organization's context thus pose survival challenges because managers are unable to change strategies, structures and processes *quickly enough*. That is, attempted movement between organizational forms is problematical and is unlikely to succeed. Instead, organizations survive or cease to exist as a consequence of environmental shifts that render their organizational form more or less appropriate:

> Most writing and research on organizations emphasize transformation and imitation as the motors of change in the world of organizations. That is, such analysis assumes, usually tacitly, that the most prevalent and most important fraction of the mix involves adaptive actions by existing organizations. Organizational ecology argues the opposite case: that few organizations succeed at transformation and imitation and that selection serves as the driving force of long-term change. This position is only tenable if organizations exhibit great inertia in their structures over time (Hannan and Carroll 1995: 23).

In this sense, ecologists highlight the *difficulties* of achieving change and are at the opposite extreme to structural-contingency theory and strategic choice theory and distant from resource-dependence. However, in a way, ecological theories echo S/Cs basic assumption that forms that survive are those that match the economic context.

Ecological theory offers several key insights. First, it reminds us that macro-contextual factors interact with organizational actions to constantly produce novel organizational forms. The theory does not, however, readily explain why or how *particular* forms emerge (but see Ruef 2000). Secondly, it specifies the exogenous variables that affect organizational alignment and which shape organizational performance. As Baum and Shipolov (this volume) state: 'Ecological approaches to organizational founding and failure … emphasize contextual or environmental causes – social, economic and political – that produce variations in organizational founding and failure rates over time'. Thirdly, the theory emphasizes that the ability of organizations to achieve adaptive change is not evenly distributed. Although ecologists believe radical change is *not* the norm, they acknowledge that some organizations exhibit adaptive behaviour and, to a limited extent, the theory suggests *which* organizations will do so (e.g. large or small).

Network Theories

Almost a decade ago, Salancik (1995) surveyed research on organizational networks and remarked upon the absence of a theory of networks as a form of organizing. Borgatti and Foster (2003: 1005) countered that, even if Salancik's comment was appropriate at the time, 'it certainly is not today'. We suggest that research and theorizing about networks may be arranged into three distinct streams.

Networks as Structures of Opportunities

One approach to networks focuses upon the structure or topography of links ('ties') connecting organizations (e.g. Christensen and Bower 1996; Burt 2000; Stuart 2000). In this approach the network is portrayed as a structure of resource flows which organizations differentially access through their connections and positions within the network. According to Burt, a critical feature of an organization's network position is its relationship to *structural holes*. Clusters consist of organizations densely tied to each other but only loosely connected to organizations in other clusters. Clusters are sometimes portrayed as competing sub-groups (e.g. Gulati and Gargiulo 1999; Baum and Ingram 2002). Gaps between the clusters constitute structural holes bridged by *few* organizations, to whom advantages flow because they can broker connections between otherwise disconnected groups.

An organization with an advantageous brokerage position is said to have *social capital*:

Social capital is the contextual complement to human capital. The social capital metaphor is that the people who do better are somehow better connected. Certain people or certain groups are connected to certain others, trusting certain others, obligated to support certain others, dependent on exchange with certain others. Holding a certain position in the structure of these exchanges can be an asset in its own right. That asset is social capital, in essence, a concept of location effects in differentiated markets (Burt 2000: 347).

We find this use of social capital very consistent with the resource-dependence approach, except that it makes explicit that dependencies have a social as well as an economic character. Social capital arises from '… the accumulation of "chits" based on previous good deeds to others, backed by the norm of reciprocity' (Portes and Sensenbrenner 1993: 1324). A defining feature of Burt's approach, however, is the imagery of an actor (organization) *using* the network. Madhaven et al. (1998: 440) elaborate this theme, emphasizing not only that organizations draw resources from their network but 'can potentially shape networks so as to provide a favourable context for future action'.

Hargadon (2002) has extended this approach to networks as structures of opportunities, by elaborating a model of the knowledge-brokering process. 'Knowledge-brokering' organizations straddle multiple domains and thus have access to disparate bases of knowledge. These organizations have the capability to learn and recombine knowledge bases, 'moving ideas from where they are known to where they are not' (Hargadon 2002: 44).

Networks as Structures of Constraints

A second approach to networks is closer to the logic of neoinstitutional theory. This approach sees organizations not as taking advantage of a network, but as being shaped by it. Researchers in this tradition are especially interested in how ideas and practices disseminate through networks (e.g. Fligstein 1985; Davis 1991; Burns and Wholey 1993; Haveman 1993; Palmer et al. 1993; Haunschild and Miner 1997). Much attention has been given to the role of direct ties between organizations (e.g. director interlocks).

A sub-theme within this approach refers to the difference between a network's 'centre' and 'periphery'. The idea of centrality has two connotations. The first, explicit within network theory, is defined by the density of ties between organizations and the 'distance' of an organization from others in the network. Centrality, in this sense, is a function of the density of ties. Another connotation of centrality distinguishes between elites and non-elites. Networks become characterized by increasing hierarchical stratification, in which, typically, a small sub-community of elite firms is distinguished by reputation (e.g. Stuart 1988; Podolny 1993; Phillips and Zuckerman 2001) and economic scale (e.g. Malerba and Orsenigo 1996).

Networks as Embedded Relationships

Conceptualizing ties between organizations as embedded relationships directs attention to the relational nature of ties. For example, Uzzi (1997) highlights the ethnic embeddedness of women's apparel firms in New York. He shows how networks help actors co-ordinate interdependencies and overcome challenges of co-operation and collective effort in a way superior to integrated, hierarchical organizations. Similar examples are provided in studies of regional clusters, e.g. Silicon Valley (Saxenian 1994).

Studies of the relational nature of organizational ties are interested in the consequences of networks (e.g. Uzzi shows how embeddedness affects the ability of a network as a whole to innovate and of individual firms to survive), but also in their antecedents, i.e. in how networks are constructed. Key explanations appear to be history, status and technological proximity. Podolny (1993), for example, shows that under conditions of uncertainty organizations favour links to organizations with whom they have previously partnered and/or that have appropriate status. In effect, the network *structure* is a function of social stratification and status (see also, Stuart 2000; Phillips and Zuckerman 2001).

The difference between networks as relationships and networks as opportunities is significant. The former sees the benefits of networks arising from social norms that enable co-ordination and co-operation by removing the fear of opportunism and malfeasance. An actor's social capital is a function of the normative strength of the network, i.e. its 'social closure' (Coleman 1988). On the other hand, those who see networks as structures of opportunities, see the benefits of networks arising from the social capital provided by diversity of ties. The underlying imagery is a combination of economics and political skill, reflecting R/D theory. The relational approach, in contrast, emphasizes how networks arise from concerns to identify trustworthy partners. Here, the underlying imagery is sociological, reflecting institutional theory. The relational approach to networks is thus very different to R/D theory because it treats the topology of the network as a function of social factors, such as status and history, and not simply as the consequence of resource dependencies (Pfeffer 2003: xxiii). Resource dependencies are a motivation for seeking interactions with others, but status determines choice of partners.

Networks and Change

The link between networks and organizational change depends upon whether the network is regarded as a constraint or an opportunity structure. Portes and Sensenbrenner's (1993) show how entrepreneurs can become caught by the web of obligations and expectations of their networks. Gargiulo and Benassi (2000: 195–6) refer to 'amplified reciprocity' and 'cognitive lock-in' as underlying mechanisms in this 'dark side' of networks. On the other hand, the network can facilitate change. Burt (2000), for example, emphasizes that 'brokerage' promotes change. Networks describe 'a world of change – a world of discovering and developing opportunities to add value by changing social structure with bridges across holes in the structure. The argument … is a story about the social order of disequilibrium' (Burt 2000: 357).

Some studies explore networks as constraint *and* opportunity. Uzzi (1997), for example, finds a *curvilinear* relationship between embeddedness and survival, suggesting that change and sustainable success requires a balance between network closure and openness. The need to secure such a balance is the 'paradox of embeddedness' (Uzzi 1997: 35). Gargiulo and Benassi (2000) also suggest that ties that are too cohesive result in *network closure*, making change difficult.

There are two points that we would emphasize. Firstly, network analysis reinforces that organizational change cannot be understood without giving proper attention to the interorganizational network level of analysis. The ability of organizations to change is affected by their embeddedness within a network of organizations and the nature of that network will affect the speed and content of change. Secondly, network analysis provides a strong clue as to *where* new organizational forms are more likely to arise, namely from the periphery but not the centre of a field, because central organizations are more fully caught within the reproductive network of exchanges.

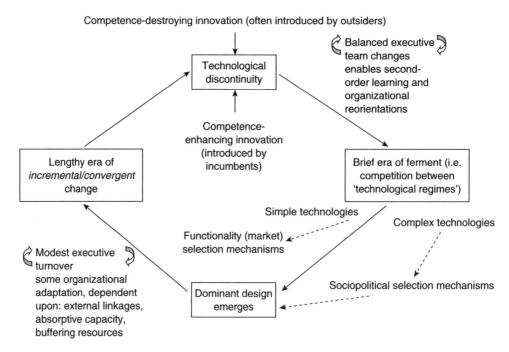

Figure 2.16.1 The punctuated-equilibrium model of change (based upon Tushman and Rosenkopf 1992)

Three Theories of Change

By the mid 1980s, organization theory was acknowledging the significance and difficulty of change (e.g. Goodman 1982; Astley and Van de Ven 1983; Kimberly 1984; Kimberly and Quinn 1984; Pennings 1985). Detailed case studies of change appeared (e.g. Kanter 1983; Pettigrew 1985; Johnson 1987; Hinings and Greenwood 1988) along with several explicit theories of change. We review three of these theories. The first looks at the determinants and locus of change and how, if at all, organizations manage change. The second looks at how changes occur in the choice-set of available forms. The third looks explicitly at change at the organizational level.

Punctuated Equilibrium

Tushman, in collaboration with several colleagues (Tushman and Romanelli 1985; Tushman and Anderson 1986; Tushman and Rosenkopf 1992; Tushman and Murmann 1998) has contributed a 'punctuated equilibrium' theory of change.

Although the focus shifts according to the question posed in different papers, there is constant emphasis on technology as an industry level variable that demands an organizational response. Tushman's work may be considered a sophisticated form of structural-contingency theory but it also embraces themes from resource-dependence and network theories. The theory addresses three important issues: the periodicity of change, the dynamics of change (*why* does change occur and *where*) and whether organizations can adapt (and, if so, the enabling factors).

The Periodicity of Change

The basic model consists of four stages (see Figure 2.16.1). For convenience, we treat the first stage as occurring when *technological discontinuities* punctuate and destabilize prevailing market practices, precipitating an *era of ferment* (stage two) where competing expressions of the new technology struggle for adoption. In the third stage, a *dominant design* emerges, heralding the fourth stage of relative equilibrium during which *incremental changes* improve the dominant design.

The model is a rare attempt to identify the temporal sequence of change. It suggests that eras of ferment are relatively brief. Comprehensive changes to strategies and structures happen quickly rather than incrementally. Convergent change, in contrast, following the emergence of a technological standard, is slower in pace and longer in duration. Romanelli and Tushman (1994) confirm that most organizational transformations are accomplished through rapid and discontinuous change to structures and strategies. They also found that incremental changes do not accumulate to produce organizational transformations. As previously noted, Miller and Friesen (1980) found similar results, as does much institutional work, suggesting that the periodicity of the punctuated-equilibrium theory is a reasonably robust observation.

However, there are important dissenting voices. Eisenhardt and Tabrizi (1995) and Brown and Eisenhardt (1997) directly challenge the model. They assert that 'while the punctuated equilibrium model is in the foreground of academic interest, it is in the background of the experience of many firms' (Brown and Eisenhardt 1997: 1). Brown and Eisenhardt looked at six high technology firms operating in fast changing, 'high velocity', environments and concluded that 'change is not the rare, episodic phenomenon described by the punctuated equilibrium model but, rather, it is endemic to the way these organizations compete' (Brown and Eisenhardt 1997: 1). They insist that the scope of change examined in their study is not restricted to product innovation but 'intimately related to broader organization change' (p. 2). However, as with Tushman's work, the description provided is of technological change; organizational changes, though assumed to happen, are less documented.

The other dissenting voice is Van de Ven and Garud (1994: 426), who sought to understand the 'origins of novelty itself to explain how a new organizational form or technological discontinuity emerges'. In their view, the punctuated equilibrium model has little to say about *how* punctuations arise other than appeals to random events or individual genius. Microanalysis of the cochlear implant technology led them to question 'the widely held assumption that novelty is produced by a discrete exogenous event of random chance or blind variation' (Van de Van and Garud 1994: 441). Instead, 'the generative process in which novelty emerges is not instantaneous; instead it entails numerous events involving many public and private sector actors over a long duration of time' (p. 441).

Dynamics of Change

Tushman and Anderson (1986) examined in detail the initial stage of technological discontinuity; and the process through which a dominant design is selected. Technological discontinuities are classified by whether they 'destroy or enhance the competence of existing firms' (Tushman and Anderson 1986: 442). Anderson and Tushman proposed that competence-enhancing technologies are more likely to originate from incumbents, whereas competence-destroying technologies are promoted by new start-ups. Incumbents, 'burdened by the consequences of prior success' (Tushman and Anderson 1986: 461) are less able or unwilling to destroy established investments. As predicted, Anderson and Tushman (1990) found competence-enhancing technologies typically come from incumbents (by a 3-to-1 ratio) but did not confirm that competence-destroying technologies arise mainly from newcomers. These technologies 'are initiated by a mixture of newcomers and incumbents' (Anderson and Tushman 1990: 625). Later studies suggest that competence-destroying technologies emerge from non-incumbents (e.g. Sorensen and Stuart 2000).

Mechanisms by which dominant designs are selected depend upon the complexity of the technology (Tushman and Rosenkopf 1992). Simple technologies are adopted because of superior performance; i.e. the selection mechanism is the market. Complex technologies, in contrast, rarely yield a clearly superior design. Technological options offer alternative combinations of performance attributes and selection arises from sociopolitical processes: 'enlivened by actors with interests in competing technical regimes … dominant designs are driven by the visible hand of organizations interacting with other organizations and practitioner communities to shape dimensions of merit and industry standards to maximize local needs' (Tushman and Rosenkopf 1992: 322). Here, Tushman is focusing on the process whereby new technologies prevail, not from where they arise. The imagery echoes that of resource-dependency theory.

By emphasizing how communities of organizations develop around particular technologies, Tushman and Rosenkopf (1992) explicate why incumbent firms are often resistant to new technologies. It is not simply because of cognitive shortfalls: incumbents are embedded in networks of suppliers and vendors, (e.g. Teece and Pisano 1994; Christensen and Bower 1996; Malerba and Orsenigo 1996; 1997). Contractual commitments and mutual obligations within a network of firms make it difficult for a firm to reorient itself, whilst, at the same time, reinforcing cognitive logics. Christensen and Bower (1996: 198), for example, found that firms in the disc drive industry 'listen(ed) too carefully to their customers – and customers place stringent limits on the strategies firms can and cannot pursue'. Technological communities also act politically to resist new technologies (e.g. Frost and Egri 1990). Van de Ven and Garud's (1989; 1994) account of the emergence of the cochlear implant device is a superb illustration of these community level processes and shows that change involves the co-evolution of institutional, market and technological forces.

Can Organizations Adapt?

The evidence, as summarized by Tushman and Murmann (1998), is that competence-destroying innovation is more likely to arise from new entrants to an industry and that incumbents find it difficult to adapt them. Cooper and Smith (1992) found 21 of 27 incumbents recognized the need for change, belying the view that managers fail to *see* the need for change, but that only seven successfully did so (underlining the critical difficulty of *implementation*).

However, some firms do adapt. Competence-*enhancing* innovations are *still* revolutionary; therefore, incumbents deploying these breakthrough technologies *are* adapting. Further, there are documented instances of incumbents successfully developing competence-destroying technologies (e.g. Methé et al. 1996; Sull et al. 1997), even though the process might sometimes be tortuous and drawn over several decades. The question, therefore, is not *whether* organizations can adapt, but the circumstances that enable or constrain them from doing so. As Tripsas (1997: 344) bluntly puts it, the interesting question is: 'Although incumbents on average may fail relative to new entrants, what explains the differential success of incumbents?'

Early work addressing this question focused upon *the role of senior management* and assumed that the key barrier was weak organizational learning

(a form of cognitive lock-in) combined with intra-organizational resistance. The basic thesis is that dramatic change is beyond the capability of existing executives because they are constrained by their cognitive frames *and* their sunk political investments in the prevailing order (see Anderson and Tushman 1990; Virany et al. 1992; Tushman and Rosenkopf 1996). Therefore, changes in senior personnel are required to enable the organization to learn of the need for change; however, retention of some existing senior managers provides understanding of how to implement change (O'Reilly and Tushman 2004). That is, it helps to open the organization to new ideas and competencies whilst building upon incumbent political skills and experiences, especially when the crisis originates from outside the organization: 'the success of an organization, as defined by its longevity, occurs when firms … combine the benefits of newness in heterogeneous teams with the benefits of longevity embodied in seasoned teams' (Keck and Tushman 1993: 1338).

However, executive leadership is not a sufficient explanation. Some organizational forms better enable adaptation. O'Reilly and Tushman (2004) refer to these forms as the 'ambidextrous organization', which concurrently use separate structures for exploiting current technologies and for facilitating breakthrough technologies. Each set of structures has 'its own processes, structures, and cultures … integrated into the existing senior management hierarchy' (O'Reilly and Tushman 2004: 74). The idea is that successful organizations are comprised of multiple organizational forms and that, as a technology matures, one part of the parent organization shifts to exploit that technology whilst another part assumes the entrepreneurial role.

A rather different, though complementary, account of how change is accomplished by incumbent firms is offered by Tripsas (1997; Tripsas and Gavetti 2000). Tripsas analysed the typesetter industry in which an incumbent leader, Mergenthaler Linotype, survived three eras of ferment. Mergenthaler's success is attributed an external integrative capability, combined with geographically distributed research sites. External integrative capability is the ability to identify and synthesize knowledge from outside the firm, an ability nurtured by investing in R&D and by developing a strong set of external links, both formal and informal. Geographically distributed research spurs competition between research teams and allows different generations of technology to be developed at separate locations.

The importance of external networks is also recognized by Rosenbloom and Christensen (1994) and Christensen and Rosenbloom (1995). These authors refer to the 'value network', i.e. the dense network of commercial exchanges within which firms are embedded. Firms develop new technologies if they solve needs within *their* network. Otherwise, the network obstructs change:

> As they become increasingly well-adapted to a given environment, and it to them, incumbents may therefore become progressively less well suited to compete in other networks. Their abilities and incentives to create new markets for their technology ... may atrophy (Rosenbloom and Christensen 1994: 655).

Two attributes of an external network appear important: being *connected* to sources of emerging ideas (as emphasized by Tripsas); and *political skill* at exploiting emerging opportunities. McGrath et al. (1992), for example, describe how executive teams can promote adoption of new technologies *and* secure that their firm's technology becomes the new dominant design (see also, Cusumano et al. 1992).

A third explanation for the adaptability of an incumbent organization are its 'complementary assets', such as marketing and distribution systems, or service networks (Teece 1986). Where complementary assets retain value during an era of ferment, incumbents are able to 'buy time' for adaptation. The ongoing value of specialized assets 'buffer' firms that might otherwise fail (Tripsas 1997). Kraatz and Zajac (2001) are unsupportive of this view.

Conclusion

The punctuated equilibrium model is an elaborate and well-researched account of organizational change under circumstances of technological disruption. We emphasize five points. Firstly, the periodicity of change involves lengthy periods of convergent change punctuated by rapid and extensive eras of discontinuity. Secondly, only some organizations are able to adapt to technological disruptions. Thirdly, turnover of personnel provides for organizational learning and sensitivity to the need for change. Retention of personnel provides

the political skills and organizational capability necessary for change implementation. Fourthly, adaptation is more likely to occur in organizations with distinctive structural features and where they have complementary assets that shield them through eras of ferment. Finally, the theory points to the *co-evolution* of institutions, organizational forms and technologies. An unresolved question is whether the punctuated model applies to settings *not* characterized by technological discontinuities, such as low capital-intensive industries (e.g. professional services).

A Neo-Institutional Approach to Change

There is no neoinstitutional theory of change in the way that there is *a* punctuated equilibrium theory (Dacin et al. 2002). Instead, we describe a composite constructed from work conducted at the University of Alberta (Hinings and Greenwood 1988; Greenwood and Hinings 1993; 1996; Greenwood et al. 2002; Reay and Hinings 2005; Suddaby and Greenwood 2005; Greenwood and Suddaby 2006; Reay et al. 2006), elaborated by complementary research. The model, summarized in Figure 2.16.2, contains similar stages to the punctuated-equilibrium model but the language and focus are different.

Earlier, we noted that institutional accounts emphasize the influence of social expectations. Applied to institutional change, such accounts focus upon organizational fields and the institutional logics that prescribe appropriate behaviour, including 'templates for organizing' (Powell and DiMaggio 1991) or 'archetypes' (Greenwood and Hinings 1993). Archetypes are similar to configurations except that they emphasize the importance of achieving institutional legitimacy. The starting question, therefore, for this model, is not whether organizations can or cannot move between archetypal forms, but with the social processes that construct the *choice-set* of acceptable templates. That is, radical change means, first, change to the choice-set of organizational forms. Exploring the processes by which this occurs gives attention to values, meanings and language and to the role of the professions, regulators and the state. A second and consequential question is how and why organizations in the same organizational field respond differently to institutional processes.

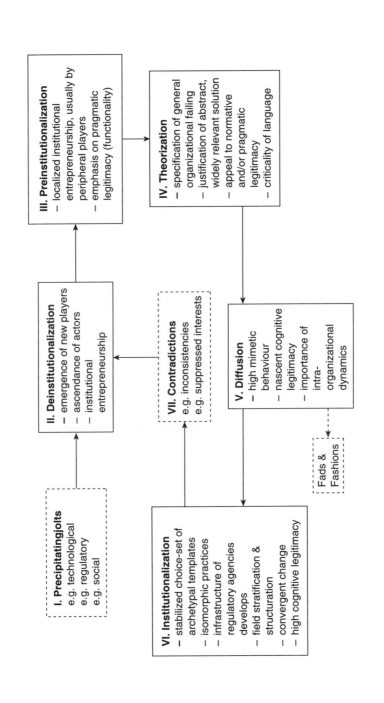

Figure 2.16.2   A neo-institutional model of change (based upon Tolbert and Zucker 1996; Greenwood et al. 2002)

Stages of Change

Institutionalization. Figure 2.16.2 builds upon Tolbert and Zucker's (1996) three-stage model of institutionalization. Progress through these three stages is marked by a narrowing of the choice-set of socially approved organizational forms and increasing convergence around them. A mature, institutionalized field (stage VI in Figure 2.16.2) has stable, routinized interactions between its participants and increasing stratification as elite firms are differentiated by reputation and influence. Critically, mature settings are characterized by an infrastructure of regulatory agencies that disseminate and monitor compliance with approved practices and of supporting firms such as professional advisors (Saxenian 1994). Universities and professional training institutions generate and disseminate knowledge relevant to the field (Li and Greenwood 2004: 1138). Representative associations develop. Consequently, the field exhibits a sustaining momentum as its internal dynamics both constrain its members and is reproduced by their actions.

The imagery of dynamic stability raises a central question: How and where does change occur where there are elaborate reproductive dynamics at work and where organizational forms are taken-for-granted? In other words, how does *de*-institutionalization occur?

Deinstitutionalization. The dynamics that precipitate change may arise from outside the field, as destabilizing 'jolts' (Meyer 1982; Meyer et al. 1990). These can take the form of social upheaval, technological disruptions, competitive discontinuities or regulatory change (Fox-Wolfgramm et al. 1998; Lounsbury 1999). These events precipitate the entry of new players (Thornton 1995; Thornton and Ocasio 1999; Kraatz and Moore 2002), enable the ascendance of existing actors (Scott et al. 2000), encourage local entrepreneurship (DiMaggio 1988; Leblebici et al. 1991; Lawrence 1999; Suddaby and Greenwood 1999) and change the intellectual climate of ideas (e.g. Davis et al. 1994). Their effect is to disturb the socially constructed field-level consensus by introducing new ideas.

Change can also arise from *endogenous* sources. Seo and Creed (2002) point to 'contradictions' within organizational fields, such as mutually inconsistent values (e.g. equality versus affirmative action). Where contradictions become amplified by shifting circumstances they set the stage for 'praxis', i.e. reflection by actors who, 'on the basis of reasoned analysis', reconstruct institutional arrangements. Seo and Creed's model is consistent with Hoffman's (1999) description of fields as populations of organizations that, though connected and influenced by overarching logics, nevertheless subscribe to different values and beliefs. Consequently, at any moment, fields contain tensions between dominant and latent logics 'that may lie within the individual populations (or constituencies) that inhabit the field' (Hoffman 1999: 365; see also Reay and Hinings 2005). Change, thus, occurs 'in the wake of triggering events that cause a reconfiguration of field membership and/or interaction patterns' (Hoffman 1999: 351). A key point is that as fields mature, internal contradictions become amplified and thus more potent precipitators of change.

Pre-institutionalization. So which organizations are more likely to innovate and why? Initially, most researchers focused upon exogenous sources of disruption because of the imagery of institutions as enduring and hegemonic. Hence, change was expected to arise from entrants 'transposing' ideas from one field to another (Sewell 1992). A later explanation portrays logics not as hegemonic, but as imperfectly diffused. Drawing upon network theory's distinction between central and peripheral players, this explanation suggests peripheral organizations are more likely to innovate because they are less embedded and less privileged. Organizations at the field's centre, on the other hand, are more socialized, better advantaged and, thus, more resistant to change. Several studies support this basic proposition (e.g. Hirsch 1986; Galaskiewicz and Wasserman 1989; Davis 1991; Leblebici et al. 1991; Kraatz and Zajac 1996; Haveman and Rao 1997; Westphal et al. 1997; Kraatz 1998; D'Aunno et al. 2000; Palmer and Barber 2001). However, the proposition that change originates from the periphery of a field is not absolute (e.g. Podolny 1993; Greenwood et al. 2002; Sherer and Lee 2002; Rao et al. 2003). Greenwood and Suddaby (2006) examined the introduction of a new organizational form by the Big 5 accounting firms in the 1990s and concluded that markets and institutional forces unfold at different rates enabling larger, central organizations to outgrow their 'institutional moorings', allowing strategic choice.

A key point is that fields are never static. They are vulnerable to ideas entering from neighbouring fields and to the entrepreneurial motivations of imperfectly embedded organizations (Lawrence et al. 2002). Even mature fields contain tensions that can trigger change. Nevertheless, the likelihood of change will vary across fields. Not all fields are equally open to new ideas. Instead, they vary in the extent to which their boundaries are 'permeable' (Greenwood and Hinings 1996). Fields also vary in the degree to which they have clearly legitimated organizational templates combined with 'highly articulated mechanisms (the state, professional associations, regulatory agencies ...) for transmitting those templates to organizations ...' (Greenwood and Hinings 1996: 1029). The more elaborated these templates and the stronger the mechanisms for their deployment, the more resistant the field will be to change.

Theorization. Theorization is the rendering of ideas into compelling formats (Strang and Meyer 1993) and is critical for the ascription of legitimacy. Theorization is the process whereby new organizational forms gain legitimacy and how 'renegotiations of meaning take place' (Aldrich and Fiol 1994: 649). Tolbert and Zucker (1996) propose that theorization involves two major tasks: specification of a general organizational failing, in order to challenge the adequacy of existing arrangements; and justification of the new organizational form as a widely appropriate solution.

Research into theorization is taking several complementary directions. One stream of research examines the roles of theorizing agents, such as management consultants (e.g. Abrahamson 1991; Sahlin-Anderson and Engwall 2002), the media (Davis et al. 1994; Rao et al. 2003) and professional associations (Greenwood et al. 2002). A second focuses upon the use of cultural symbols and (especially) language as proponents and opponents contest the appropriateness of existing and nascent templates (Greenwood et al. 2002; Covaleski et al. 2003; MacGuire et al. 2004; Suddaby and Greenwood 2005). Several theorists draw on social movement theory (Rao 1998; Hoffman and Ventresca 1999; Ruef 2000; Lounsbury 2001; Rao et al. 2003), which has long recognized 'framing' as critical for mobilizing change. Other researchers have examined 'transorganizational structures' that increase mutual awareness and contribute towards legitimation, such as 'rituals' (Anand and Watson 2004), certification contests (Rao 1994) and the activities of professional associations (Greenwood et al. 2002).

Theorization resembles the era of ferment of the punctuated-equilibrium model. It is the stage where competing versions struggle for superiority. However, the contribution of institutional theory is the attention it gives to socio-cultural processes and, increasingly, the rhetoric of language as means by which novelty is rendered acceptable and preferable. These processes attach social approval to novelty. Importantly, there are differences across fields. In commercial settings, the rhetoric of theorization is grounded in appeals to efficiency. For example, Japanese management practices were urged upon US corporations for their superior efficiency and quality. In professional settings, theorization has to incorporate a normative justification. Thus, the Big Five accounting firms sought to legitimate the multi-disciplinary practice (which deviated from the then archetypal model) by appealing to norms of progress and service. The rhetoric of these claims sought moral acceptability for the new form, irrespective of other benefits (Suddaby and Greenwood 2005).

Diffusion. Diffusion follows successful theorization. Meyer and Rowan's (1977) pioneering work and the conceptual framework of DiMaggio and Powell (1983) generated a flurry of papers demonstrating the role of mimetic, coercive and normative mechanisms, and the occurrence of isomorphism. Nevertheless, as Oliver (1991) pointed out, organizations do not blindly follow institutional prescriptions, raising an interesting question: Why do organizations make different selections from the available choice-set of archetypal forms?

Various explanations have been offered. Lounsbury (2001) suggests organizations of similar status respond in similar fashion. Kraatz and Zajac (1996) and D'Aunno et al. (2000) point to the influence of local market forces. Others emphasize the sense-making processes of senior managers (Dutton and Duncan 1987; Gioia and Thomas 1996; Fox-Wolfgramm et al. 1998; Johnson et al. 2000). Hinings and Greenwood (1988; see also Greenwood and Hinings 1996) point to the internal complexity of organizations. Building upon resource-dependence theory, they see organizations as coalitions of structurally differentiated groups. Inevitably, groups dissatisfied with how their interests are accommodated will favour change. Organizations also experience contested values. For example, Greenwood and Hinings (1996) found that, as accounting firms grew they hired marketing and human resource professionals who favoured more corporate organizational forms. This led to contested values because accountants traditionally favoured the professional partnership form (Greenwood and Hinings 1990). The inference here is that institutional values 'enter' organizations filtered through the value-sets of occupational groups. Thornton (2004) provides a very similar analysis of the same tension in the publishing industry.

Interests and values are pressures for change, to manage the change process *and* the new organizational form.

The distribution of power within an organization is not fixed, but, as presented in resource-dependence theory can shift with external conditions. However, the institutional model emphasizes the role of the institutional context, which also confers power and status upon groups and not necessarily in a manner consistent with market forces. For example, market conditions promoted the revenue-generating contribution of consultants within accounting firms but power remained with accountants because of regulations prohibiting non-accountants from controlling accounting firms (Greenwood et al. 2002). The resolution of contested values depends upon how well groups can successfully appeal to, and draw upon, wider institutional and market forces.

The paradox of the institutional model of change is that institutional theory began as an explanation of the similarity and stability of organizational forms in a given population of organizations. Yet, implicit in the theory was that organizations *can* and *will* change, if institutional forces shift the choice-set of templates. Diffusion studies repeatedly show organizations adopting new organizational strategies and structures. Studies of attempted shifts between archetypes, however, indicate that less than one in four are successful (Hinings and Greenwood 1988; Kikulis et al. 1995a, b; Morris and Pinnington 1999; Amis et al. 2004).

Conclusion

For us, neoinstitutional theory provides four key insights. First, it stresses the social processes whereby the choice-set of archetypal forms is constructed and sustained. That is, the theory approaches radical change, first, as change in the range of socially legitimated forms. Secondly, the theory notes the differential embeddedness of organizations within fields, which provides clues to the likely locus of institutional entrepreneurship. Thirdly, the theory articulates the role of theorization in the legitimation of new forms, giving explicit attention to how language is used 'to persuade constituencies of the desirability and appropriateness of institutional deviance' (Suddaby and Greenwood 2005: 37). Fourthly, it addresses why some organizations change whereas others do not, pointing to intraorganizational dynamics that link organizations to their context and direct their responses to it.

Continuity and Change

Pettigrew and colleagues have developed a perspective on change that emphasizes continuity as well as change, a focus on the processual approach to the study of change, and the interaction of organizational and contextual elements to produce change. This approach emphasizes that organizations find it difficult to change because they are embedded in their history and their context. The central concern for this theory, unlike the previous two, is its concern with how organizations manage the change from one form to another. A recurrent theme explores 'the potency of leaders in changing circumstances' (Pettigrew et al. 1992: 649).

Key components

For Pettigrew, a central problem with the literature on change is the consideration of events disconnected from the wider context that produces and supports them, and a lack of consistent attention to the processes and mechanisms through which changes are created. A further problem is that changes are treated as though they have discrete beginnings and endings. For these authors, emphasis should be less on *a change* and more on *changing*. Therefore, they suggest that change be understood through the unfolding interaction of three constructs: content, context and process. The theoretical challenge is to establish the relationships between these constructs.

The *content of change* speaks to the 'what' of change. Content could be examined concretely, as in the introduction of a divisional structure, a major technological innovation, or a new strategic positioning. However, the content of change can also be classified more abstractly as radical or incremental, technological or organizational. The point is that the organizational response to a change will be shaped by the characteristics of the change.

A distinction is drawn between the *'outer' and 'inner' context*, which constitute the 'why' of change. Outer context refers to the economic, political and social environment, together with their histories, in which an organization operates. To a certain extent, this way of thinking draws on contingency theory (Donaldson 2001) in that notions of environment are important in explanations of organizational form. However, this formulation goes much further with an emphasis on the evolution of environments. Outer context has to be perceived and interpreted by organizations which themselves are evolving, historical entities. This leads to the notion of inner context. Inner context refers to the ongoing strategy and structure, management and intraorganizational political arrangements within which a change is introduced. Inner context essentially points to the capacity of an organization to recognize the need for change, and to formulate and then implement that response. The way an organization is structured, the values and beliefs under which it operates, and the distribution of power between organizational groups influence how the outer context will be interpreted and delimit the nature and scale of change that those dominant in the organization will be able to formulate and implement.

Process 'refers to the actions, reactions and interactions of the various interested parties as they negotiate around proposals for change' (Pettigrew et al. 1992: 7). It is the 'how' of change. Emphasis here is on organizations as political and cultural systems. Organizational processes are shaped by dominating beliefs that direct and give coherence to internal activities, but which also provide schemas for understanding organizational environments. Cultural beliefs and processes produce power relationships and ground rules that structure political processes. They provide assumptions used by powerful groups working either for or against change. Cultural and political processes are intimately related to the management of meaning: 'a process of symbol construction and value use designed to create legitimacy for one's ideas, actions, and demands, and to delegitimate the demands of one's opponents' (Pettigrew 1987: 659).

The Developing Framework

The basic conceptual framework and several core themes were established early in a meticulous study of ICI (Pettigrew 1985; 1987). Subsequently, the framework and themes were elaborated in a sustained programme of ambitious research investigations of a variety of settings.

The study of ICI examined five change initiatives. The genesis for change is 'in the advocacy by a small group of people of a performance gap arising from some perception of an incipient or actual environmental change and the internal structure and organizational culture of the firm' (Pettigrew 1985: 439). The challenge is to persuade the rest of the organization that change is needed (the 'why' of change) and to provide a compelling solution (i.e. the 'what' of change). Overcoming the challenge is difficult because complex organizations (*all* of Pettigrew's studies are of large, complex, mature organizations) have core rationalities (cultures) that are entrenched both in the cognitive frames of organizational members and in the organization's routines and processes that serve their interests. Consequently, the 'forces of bureaucratic momentum' are for continuity not change (Pettigrew 1987: 659). Notably, of the five change initiatives, only two resulted in stabilized change, two achieved radical change but then regressed and one failed to change.

Breaking down existing inertia in an organization is a long-term 'conditioning' process 'through which strategies and changes are legitimated and delegitimated' (Pettigrew 1985: 443). This process requires generation of a perceived crisis, because without it executives 'do not have sufficient leverage to break through the pattern of inertia' (Pettigrew 1987: 665). Substantial changes in ICI were only possible in the face of severe economic difficulties and relative decline. However, Pettigrew emphasizes that change is not simply a matter of adaptation and subsequent alignment. At ICI, managers actively built a climate receptive to change and *used* contextual (both inner and outer) events. Critical in ICI was the ability of those promoting change to take advantage of 'the massive enabling opportunity created by changes in outer context' (Pettigrew 1987: 661) by demonstrating that proposed changes represented continuity with past values, strategies and practices.

How was this achieved? Pettigrew (1987: 66) describes the important role of the CEO, not as taking 'apocalyptic' actions, but in 'articulation of an imprecise vision of a better future … clarified through additive implementation'. 'Additive implementation' refers to the seizing of small opportunities as they occur:

… activities were rarely part of some grand process design. Instead opportunities were taken as they presented themselves to break any emerging global vision of a better future into manageable bits; of finding small steps on the way to larger breaks; of using any political momentum created by a number of complementary moves to bind a critical mass of powerful people around a set of principles which eventually would allow a series of pieces in the jigsaw to be moved simultaneously (Pettigrew 1985: 458).

Additive implementation requires patience and perseverance, waiting for people to retire, advancing known sympathizers as replacements for known skeptics, using executive succession as opportunities to introduce structural change, and 'backing off' and moving the change effort to less contentious areas. Change, therefore, is not an easy linear progression. Instead, the ICI study showed the lengthy and uneven process of change. Change began in the 1960s and continued into the 1990s. Bursts of radical change, associated with changes in senior leadership and power, were 'interspersed with eras of learning and incremental adjustment' (Pettigrew 1983: 442). Pettigrew (1983: 447) sees this cycle as confirming the P/E model at the level of the organization: 'changes tend to occur in radical packages interspersed with longish periods of both absorbing the impact of revolutionary action, and then coming to terms with the fact that further changes are eventually necessary'. (This same pattern was observed by Amis et al. 2004.)

Pettigrew and Whipp's (1991) studies of the automobile, merchant banking, insurance and book publishing sectors built on these ideas by comparing superior performing firms with those that do less well in managing change for competitive success. Throughout, there is emphasis upon the importance of the assessment and interpretation of the outer context and its interaction with inner context and process. Environmental assessment in underperforming organizations was the preserve of a single functional unit and not built into the political and technical processes of the organization. Successful organizations, in comparison, enabled actors at various levels to acquire, interpret and process information about the environment and sense the need for change. In these organizations, moreover, the inner context enabled a variety of views to be in play in formulating the content and process of change. Similarly, leadership was not located in particular, specified actors but was context-sensitive. Leadership involved activating people at all levels and across all functions, as part of building an appropriate climate for change. And, importantly, there was a coherence and alignment in managing the interpretation of context, the development of change content and the design of change processes. Given the wide scope of necessary actions, the ability to manage multiple, interrelated actions and, importantly, emergent changes proved critical. (For a recent extension of this theme, see Ethiraj and Levinthal 2004.)

Pettigrew et al. (1992) examined several change projects in the NHS in the UK. Again, there is an emphasis on how contexts and processes link together. Thus, the role of the outer context was elaborated by observing that excessive pressure 'can deflect or drain energy out of the system' (Pettigrew et al. 1992: 280). In terms of the inner context, the NHS study highlighted factors shaping the differential receptivity of organizations for change. One factor is the availability of key people: too much personnel rotation leads to loss of momentum and frustration. Another important aspect is a supportive organizational culture, such as use of flexible, cross-boundary working based on skill not status; an openness to innovation and evaluation; and a focus on achievement. Subsequently, Pettigrew described receptive organizational contexts using Kanter's (1983) distinction between 'segmentalist' and 'integrative' structures. Integrative structures are more receptive and contexts for change.

The content of change has two important analytical aspects. First, there has to be clear fit between the change agenda and local circumstances. Relevance has to be demonstrated. Secondly, the change proposal must, at the same time, provide a broad, imprecise vision of what the change is, but, paradoxically, substantiate the case for change. Further, the new direction has to be disaggregated so that the implementation path can be clearly seen.

What processes support successful change? In the NHS situation, one contributing process was the ability to generate effective managerial-clinical relations. This observation points to the importance of change processes linking those responsible for designing change with those at the 'sharp end' of changing behaviours and attitudes. Such a process goes hand-in-hand with building co-operative networks inside and outside the organization. Boundary spanners are also important. They are directly involved in trust-building, bargaining and deal-making as emergent aspects of content and context develop. A further process supporting change in the NHS was *simplifying* and clarifying goals and priorities. Major change generates uncertainty and the success of a change effort is assisted if managers can focus the agenda of change upon key priorities, especially in the face of constantly shifting pressures, such as the 'culture of panics' characteristic of the NHS (Pettigrew et al. 1992: 288).

The third project was the largest and most ambitious. The *Innovative Forms of Organizing* (INN-FORMS) project examined organizational innovation in almost 800 firms in Europe, Japan and the USA, at two time points, 1992 and 1996. It involved a large-scale survey and 18 detailed case studies. The survey showed variation between countries, indicating the influence of national institutions. The survey showed that less than 5% of firms were simultaneously changing their boundaries, structures and processes *despite* 'a performance premium of more than 60%' for those that did (Pettigrew and Fenton 2000: 281). This surprising observation led the authors to the role of 'complementarities' and the J-curve.

Complementarity theory has a clear affinity with configuration theory and the notion of archetypes. It shares with configuration theory a focus upon 'holism, the importance of mutual reinforcement and the problem of change' (Whittington and Pettigrew 2003: 127). The basic idea is that doing more of one thing increases returns from doing more of another by providing an internal synergy. This idea has several implications for change. It is only when initiatives 'are cumulated into complementary packages' (Whittington and Pettigrew 2003: 129) that they show performance benefits. Hence, complementarities require 'strong central leadership, capable of imposing and maintaining coherence between complementary elements' (Whittington and Pettigrew 2003: 129). However, change cannot be accomplished in an instant:

> The challenge for managers, therefore, is to manage the steps between untangling one complementary system and bedding down the new complementary system. With no new system in place, and with some of its building blocks potentially dysfunctional as they await their complements, organizations in transition are likely to suffer severe performance penalties, possibly worse than the original status quo (Whittington and Pettigrew 2003: 129).

In short, things get worse before they get better. Therefore, 'leadership must be strong, not just to assemble comprehensive programmes, but to survive the long gap before the positive effects of completed systems kick in' (Whittington and Pettigrew 2003: 131). Strong leadership requires the ability to orchestrate the multiple, additive processes and the simplifying processes identified in earlier work. Simplifying processes included the provision of 'clear, simple and evocative messages', periodic pruning of 'burgeoning' network complexity and use of IT to facilitate intraorganizational communication.

Conclusion

A central purpose of this research programme is to show how a contextual, historical and processual approach to understanding change produces intimations, suggestions and understandings rather than definitive causes and irreversible relationships. Because organizations are different in their specific contexts and histories, Pettigrew is repeatedly cautious of offering a singular theory of change. Nevertheless, from the work conducted by Pettigrew and colleagues, several key insights about the *management* of change can be highlighted.

First, change is problematical because of cognitive frames that blind most organizational members to the need for change. These frames are embedded in organizational routines that privilege the interests of certain stakeholders. Change is also problematical because modern organizational forms are more complex than predecessor forms. Finally, change is problematical because of the holistic nature of organizational systems: multiple parts of the organization have to move before performance benefits begin to be realized. Politically, moving an organization though the J-curve requires considerable leadership skill and power, to move the organization beyond the bottom of the curve.

Secondly, change will not occur without sustained market or (as in the case of the NHS study) institutional pressures. These pressures have to be recognized by skillful leaders who prepare organizations for change by delegitimating existing frames and legitimating new ones. Using the language of neo-institutional theory, the need for change has to be *theorized* within the organization. There is a potential tension between the dynamics of change legitimation and of complementarities. On the one hand, underlying legitimation is the need to persuade rather than coerce members into not only accepting that change is preferable, but that the proposed direction of change is worthy of commitment. Change will not occur until this lengthy, after incremental process is accomplished. Yet, the transitional performance decline implied by the J-curve points to the benefit of speed. Reconciling these two dynamics requires sustained and skillful leadership.

Thirdly, the processes of leadership occur not as dramatic interventions, but in the form of additive, often opportunistic, skillfully timed interventions that aggregate into a direction of change. The challenge of sustaining the momentum required for change is considerable. Some organizational contexts, however, are more receptive than others to change, i.e. those that are integrative in their structures and information processes. Finally, effective processes include simplifying mechanisms that guide and *stabilize* progress towards change. In the midst of the buzzing array of initiatives and performance uncertainties, leadership has to recurrently simplify the purpose of change (the 'why') and the processes of achieving it (the 'how').

Conclusions

Change is one of the grand themes in the social sciences and today is a central theme in organization theory. From the mid-1980s, change has been a point of intellectual debate and theoretical consideration. This chapter has traced the development of ideas about change, from early considerations within the major perspectives of organization theory, to more explicit theorizing about change from the mid-1980s onwards. We emphasized that this progression was associated with increasing recognition of the difficulty of change and of the importance of field-level processes. We used three theories to illustrate the range of questions currently being addressed: What are the dynamics that precipitate change? Where do new organizational forms arise and how is the choice-set of socially approved organizational templates extended or revised? What are the temporal and organizational processes by which change unfolds? *Can* change be successfully managed and, if so, how?

The literature on change cannot be summarized as a neat package of agreed-upon conclusions. There is broad agreement on the difficulties of achieving organizational change and on some of the key processes that are involved in the emergence of new organizational forms and the complexities of adopting them. We certainly know more today than in the late 1960s. The theories summarized in this chapter testify to the progress made. Yet, there is clearly much that is not known.

We especially need to know more about the co-evolution of field level and organizational arrangements. In this sense, we concur with Pettigrew's call for more historical and multi-levelled analysis, in order to tease out the ways that institutional and market structures interact with each other, shaping organizational responses and, in turn, being shaped by them. There are clear exemplars of this approach, but too few.

However, perhaps the most glaring weakness in current studies is the absence of concern for the consequences of change. Studies of organizational change basically concerned how the choice-sets of organizational templates changes our time, and with the responses of organizations to them. Where and how do new organizational forms arise? And, to what extent and by which means can organizations exercise choice between that choice-set? Rarely do we ask about the effect of these macro and micro processes. Perrow (2002) has gone furthest in exploring the relationship between organizational form (especially the large corporation) and class interests within society. The focus links the choice-set of organizational forms to the material consequences for groups within society. We need to know about these sorts of consequences. We also need to know more about the consequences of organizations moving within that choice-set. Does the shift from a vertically integrated M-Form to a geographically dispersed organizational network affect the material and other interests of different stakeholders and in different locations? Our presumption is that it does, but theory is silent on this question. Does the empirically documented shift in the organizational forms of accounting firms, from the relatively modest-sized professional partnership to a more corporatist and managerial transnational form, have implications for the practice of professional work, relationships between professions and clients and the workings of financial and capital markets? Almost certainly: but we know little about such consequences.

We know much more today than in the 1960s. However, there are few absolutes. In reality, we profess to know more than we do and there is a worrying disjunct between our research observations and our claims to practitioners (Miller et al. 1997). We suspect that, a decade from now, the study of radical organization change will still be a high priority within organization theory, both because of its relevance to the experiences of organizations and because of the multiplicity of important themes within it. We also suspect that we will especially know much more about how and why individual organizations can *manage* radical change. We are less optimistic that we will know much about its broader societal consequences.

References

Abrahamson, E. (1991) 'Managerial fads and fashions: the diffusion and rejection of innovations', *Academy of Management Review*, 16(3): 586–612.

Aldrich, H. (1979) *Organizations and Environments*. Englewood Cliffs, NJ: Prentice-Hall.

Aldrich, H.E. and Fiol, C.M. (1994) 'Fools rush in? The institutional context of industry creation', *Academy of Management Review*, 19: 645–70.

Amis, J., Slack, T. and Hinings, C.R. (2004) 'The pace, sequence and linearity of radical change', *Academy of Management Journal*, 47(1): 15–39.

Anand, N. and Watson, M.R. (2004) 'Tournament rituals in the evolution of fields: the case of the Grammy Awards', *Academy of Management Journal*, 47(1): 59–80.

Anderson, P. and Tushman, M. (1990) 'Technological discontinuities and dominant designs: a cyclical model of technological change', *Administrative Science Quarterly*, 35: 604–33.

Astley, W.G. and Van de Ven, A.H. (1983) 'Central perspectives and debates in organizational theory', *Administrative Science Quarterly*, 28: 245–73.

Baum, J.A.C. and Ingram, P. (1998) 'Survival enhancing learning in the Manhattan hotel industry, 1898–1980', *Management Science*, 44(7): 996–1017.

Baum, J.A.C. and Ingram, P. (2002) 'Interorganizational learning and network organizations: toward a behavioral theory of the 'interfirm'', in M. Augier and J.G. March (eds), *The Economics of Change, Choice, and Structure: Essays in the memory of Richard M. Cyert*. Cheltenham, UK: Edward Elgar. pp. 191–218.

Boeker, W. and Goodstein, J. (1991) 'Organizational performance and adaptation: effects of environment and performance on changes in board composition', *Academy of Management Journal*, 34(4): 805–26.

Borgatti, S.P. and Foster, P.C. (2003) 'The network paradigm in organizational research: a review of typology', *Journal of Management*, 29(6): 991.

Brown, S.L. and Eisenhardt, K.M. (1997) 'The art of continuous change: linking complexity theory and time-paced evolution in relentlessly shifting organizations', *Administrative Science Quarterly*, 42(1): 1–34.

Burke, W.W. (2002) *Organization Change: Theory and Practice*. Thousand Oaks, CA: Sage Publications.

Burns, L.R. and Wholey, D.R. (1993) 'Adoption and abandonment of matrix management programs: effects of organizational characteristics and interorganizational networks', *Academy of Management Journal*, 36(1): 106–38.

Burns, T. and Stalker, G.M. (1961) *The Management of Innovation*. London: Tavistock.

Burt, R.S. (2000) 'The network structure of social capital', *Research in Organizational Behaviour*, 22: 345–423.

Chandler, A.D. (1962) *Strategy & Structure*. Cambridge, MA: MIT Press

Child, A.J.E. (1972) 'Viewpoint: Social responsibility of the businessman: the success of his company and little else', *Business Quarterly*, 27(3): 15–20.

Christensen, C.M. and Bower, J.L. (1996) 'Customer power, strategic investment, and the failure of leading firms', *Strategic Management Journal*, 17(3): 197–219.

Christensen, C.M. and Rosenbloom, R.S. (1995) 'Explaining the attacker's advantage: technological paradigms, organizational dynamics, and the value network', *Research Policy*, 24(2): 233–58.

Coleman, J.S. (1988) 'Social capital in the creation of human capital', *American Journal of Sociology*, 94: S95–S120.

Cooper, A.C. and Smith, C.G. (1992) 'How established firms respond to threatening technologies', *The Executive*, 6(2): 55–71.

Covaleski, M., Dirsmith, M.W. and Rittenberg, L. (2003) 'Jurisdictional disputes over professional work: the institutionalization of the global knowledge expert', *Accounting Organizations and Society*, 28(4): 325–55.

Cusumano, M., Mylonadis, Y. and Rosenbloom, R. (1992) 'Strategic maneuvering and mass market dynamics: the triumph of VHS over Beta', *Business History Review*, 66(1): 51–93.

Cyert, R.M. and March, J.G. (1963) *The Behavioral Theory of the Firm*. Englewood Cliffs, NJ: Prentice-Hall.

D'Aunno, T., Succi, M. and Alexander, J.A. (2000) 'The role of institutional and market forces in divergent organizational change', *Administrative Science Quarterly*, 45(4): 679–703.

Dacin, M.T., Goodstein, J. and Scott, W.R. (2002) 'Institutional theory and institutional change: introduction to the special research forum', *Academy of Management Journal*, 45(1): 45–7.

Davis, G.F., Diekmann, K.A. and Tinsley, C.H. (1994) 'The decline and fall of the conglomerate firm in the 1980s: the deinstitutionalization of an organizational form', *American Sociological Review*, 59(4): 547–70.

Davis, G.R. (1991) 'Agents without principle? The spread of the poison pill through the intercorporate network', *Administrative Science Quarterly*, 36: 583–613.

Denrell, J. and March, J.G. (2001) 'Adaptation as information restriction: the hot stove effect', *Organization Science*, 12(5): 523–38.

DiMaggio, P.J. (1988) 'Interest and agency in institutional theory', in L.G. Zucker (ed.), *Institutional Patterns and Organizations: Culture and Environment*. Cambridge, MA: Ballinger. pp. 3–22.

DiMaggio, P.J. and Powell, W.W. (1983) 'The iron cage revisited: Institutional isomorphism and collective rationality in organizational fields', *American Sociological Review*, 48: 147–60.

Dobbin, F. and Dowd, T.J. (1997) 'How policy shapes competition: early railroad foundings in Massachusetts', *Administrative Science Quarterly*, 42: 501–29.

Dobbin, F. and Dowd, T.J. (2000) 'The market that antitrust built: public policy, private coercion, and railroad acquisitions, 1825–1922', *American Sociological Review*, 65: 631–57.

Donaldson, L. (1997) 'A positive alternative to the structure-action approach', *Organization Studies*, 18(1): 77–92.

Donaldson, L. (2001) *The Contingency Theory of Organizations*. Thousand Oaks, CA: Sage Publications.

Doty, D.H., Glick, W.H. and Huber, G.P. (1993) 'Fit, equifinality, and organizational effectiveness: a test of two configurational theories', *Academy of Management Journal*, 36(6): 1196–250.

Drazin, R. and Van de Ven, A.H. (1985) 'Alternative forms of fit in contingency theory', *Administrative Science Quarterly*, 30(4): 514–40.

Dutton, J.E. and Duncan, R.B. (1987) 'The creation of momentum for change through the process of strategic issue diagnosis', *Strategic Management Journal*, 8(3): 279–95.

Eisenhardt, K. and Tabrizi, B. (1995) 'Acceleration adaptive processes', *Administrative Science Quarterly*, 40: 84–110.

Ethiraj, S.K. and Levinthal, D. (2004) 'Bounded rationality and the search for organizational architecture: an evolutionary perspective on the design of organizations and their evolvability', *Administrative Science Quarterly*, 49: 404–37.

Feldman, M.S. (2003) 'A performative perspective on stability and change in organizational routines', *Industrial and Corporate Change*, 12(4): 727.

Feldman, M.S. and Pentland, B.T. (2003) 'Reconceptualizing organizational routines as a source of flexibility and change', *Administrative Science Quarterly*, 48(1): 94.

Feldman, M.S. and Rafaeli, A. (2002) 'Organizational routines as sources of connections and understandings', *Journal of Management Studies*, 39(3): 309.

Fligstein, N. (1985) 'The spread of the multidivisional form among large firms, 1919–1979', *American Sociological Review*, 50: 377–91.

Fox-Wolfgramm, S.J., Boal, K. and Hunt, J.G. (1998) 'Organizational adaptation to institutional change: a comparative study of first-order change in prospector and defender banks', *Administrative Science Quarterly*, 43: 87–126.

Friedland, R. and Alford, R.R. (1991) 'Bringing society back in: symbols, practices and institutional contradictions', in W.W. Powell and P.J. DiMaggio (eds), *The New Institutionalism in Organizational Analysis*. Chicago, IL: University of Chicago Press. pp. 232–63.

Frost, P.J. and Egri, C.P. (1991) 'The political process of innovation', in L.L. Cummings and B.M. Staw (eds), *Research in Organizational Behavior*, Vol. 13. London: JAI Press. pp. 229–95.

Galaskiewicz, J. and Wasserman, S. (1989) 'Mimetic processes within an interorganizational field', *Administrative Science Quarterly*, 34(3): 454–80.

Gargiulo, M. and Benassi, M. (2000) 'Trapped in your own net? Network cohesion, structural holes, and the adaptation of social capital', *Organization Science*, 11(2): 183–96.

Gioia, D.A. and Thomas, J.B. (1996) 'Identity, image, and issue interpretation: sensemaking during strategic change in academia', *Administrative Science Quarterly*, 41(3): 370–404.

Gooderham, P.N., Nordhaug, O. and Ringdal, K. (1999) 'Institutional and rational determinants of organizational practices: Human resource management in European firms', *Administrative Science Quarterly*, 44(3): 507–32.

Goodman, P.S. (1982) *Change in Organizations*. San Francisco, CA: Jossey-Bass Inc.

Gordon, S.S., Stewart, W.H. Jr., Sweo, R. and Luker, W.A. (2000) 'Convergence versus strategic reorientation: the antecedents of fast-paced organizational change', *Journal of Management*, 26(5): 911–45.

Granovetter, M. (1985) 'Economic actions and social structure: the problem of embeddedness', *American Journal of Sociology*, 91: 481–510.

Greenwood, R. and Hinings, C.R. (1990) '"P2 Form" strategic management: corporate practices in professional partnerships', *Academy of Management Journal*, 33(4): 725–55.

Greenwood, R. and Hinings, C.R. (1993) 'Understanding strategic change: the contribution of archetypes', *Academy of Management Journal*, 36(5): 1052–82.

Greenwood, R. and Hinings, C.R. (1996) 'Understanding radical organizational change: bringing together the old and the new institutionalism', *Academy of Management Review*, 21(4): 1022–55.

Greenwood, R. and Suddaby, R. (2006) 'Institutional entrepreneurship in mature fields: the Big Five accounting firms', *Academy of Management Journal*, 49(1).

Greenwood, R., Suddaby, R., Hinings, C.R. (2002) 'Theorizing change: the role of professional associations in the transformation of institutional fields', *Academy of Management Journal*, 45(1): 58–80.

Greiner, L.E. (1972) 'Evolution and revolution as organizations grow', *Harvard Business Review*, 50(4): 37.

Gresov, C. and Drazin, R. (1997) 'Equifinality, functional equivalence in organization design', *Academy of Management Review*, 22: 403–28.

Greve, H.R. (1995) 'Jumping ship: The diffusion of strategy abandonment', *Administrative Science Quarterly*, 40(3): 444–73.

Greve, H.R. (1996) 'Patterns of competition: the diffusion of a market position in radio broadcasting', *Administrative Science Quarterly*, 41: 29–60.

Greve, H.R. (1998) 'Performance, aspirations and risky organizational change', *Administrative Science Quarterly*, 43: 58–86.

Greve, H.R. (2003) *Organizational Learning from Performance Feedback*. Cambridge: Cambridge University Press.

Gulati, R. and Gargiulo, M. (1999) 'Where do interorganizational networks come from?', *American Journal of Sociology*, 104: 1439–93.

Hannan, M.T. and Carroll, G. (eds) (1995) *Organizations in Industry*. Oxford, UK: Oxford University Press.

Hannan, M.T. and Freeman, J. (1977) 'The population ecology of organizations', *American Journal of Sociology*, 82(5): 929–64.

Hannan, M.T. and Freeman, J. (1984) 'Structural inertia and organizational change', *American Sociological Review*, 49: 149–64.

Hargadon, A.B. (2002) 'Brokering knowledge: linking learning and innovation', *Research in Organizational Behavior*, 24: 41–85.

Haunschild, P. and Miner, A.S. (1997) Models of interorganizational imitation. *Administrative Science Quarterly*, 42: 472-500.

Haveman, H.A. (1993) 'Follow the leader', *Administrative Science Quarterly*, 38: 564–92.

Haveman, H.A. and Rao, H. (1997) 'Structuring a theory of moral sentiments: institutional and organizational coevolution in the early thrift industry', *American Journal of Sociology*, 102: 1606–51.

Hickson, D.J., Hinings, C.R., Lee, C.A., Schneck, R.E. and Pennings, J.M. (1971) 'Strategic contingencies theory of intraorganizational power', *Administrative Science Quarterly*, 16(2): 216–29.

Hillman, A.J., Cannella, A.A. and Paetzold, R.L. (2000) 'The resource dependence role of corporate directors: strategic adaptation of board composition in response to environmental change', *Journal of Management Studies*, 37(2): 235–55.

Hinings, C.R. and Greenwood, R. (1988) *The Dynamics of Strategic Change*. Oxford, UK: Basil Blackwell.

Hirsch, P.M. (1986) 'From ambushes to golden parachutes: corporate takeovers as an instance of cultural framing and institutional integration', *American Journal of Sociology*, 91(4): 800–37.

Hoffman, A.J. (1999) 'Institutional evolution and change: environmentalism and the US chemical industry', *Academy of Management Journal*, 42(4): 351–71.

Hoffman, A.J. and Ventresca, M.J. (1999) 'The institutional framing of policy debates', *American Behavioral Scientist*, 42(8): 1368–92.

Johnson, G. (1987) *Strategic Change and the Management Process*. Oxford, UK: Basil Blackwell.

Johnson, G., Smith, S. and Codling, B. (2000) 'Microprocesses of institutional change in the context of privatization', *Academy of Management Review*, 25(3): 572–80.

Kanter, R.M. (1983) *The Change Masters*. New York: Simon and Schuster.

Keck, S.L. and Tushman, M.L. (1993) 'Environmental and organizational context and executive team structure', *Academy of Management Journal*, 36(6): 1314–44.

Kikulis, L., Slack, T. and Hinings, C.R. (1995a) 'Sector-specific patterns of organizational design change', *Journal of Management Studies*, 32: 67–100.

Kikulis, L., Slack, T. and Hinings, C.R. (1995b) 'Towards an understanding of the role of agency and choice in the changing structure of Canada's national sport organizations', *Journal of Sport Management*, 9: 135–52.

Kimberly, J.R. (1984) 'Anatomy of organizational design', *Journal of Management*, 10: 109–26.

Kimberly, J.R. and Miles, R.H. (1980) *The Organizational Life Cycle*. San Francisco, CA: Jossey-Bass Inc.

Kimberly, J.R. and Quinn, R.E. (1984) *New Futures: The Challenge of Managing Corporate Transitions*. Homewood, IL: Dow Jones-Irwin.

Kraatz, M.S. (1998) 'Learning by association? Interorganizational networks and adaptation to environmental change', *Academy of Management Journal*, 41(6): 621–43.

Kraatz, M.S. and Moore, J.H. (2002) 'Executive migration and institutional change', *Academy of Management Journal*, 45(1): 120–43.

Kraatz, M.S. and Zajac, E.J. (1996) 'Exploring the limits of the new institutionalism: the causes and consequences of illegitimate organizational change', *American Sociological Review*, 61(5): 812–36.

Kraatz, M.S. and Zajac, E.J. (2001) 'How organizational resources affect strategic change and performance in turbulent environments: theory and evidence', *Organization Science*, 12(5): 632–57.

Lant, T.K. (1992) 'Aspiration level adaptation: an empirical exploration', *Management Science*, 38(5): 623–44.

Lant, T.K. and Mezias, S.J. (1990) 'Managing discontinuous change: a simulation study of organizational learning and entrepreneurship', *Strategic Management Journal*, 11: 147–79.

Lant, T.K., Milliken, F.J. and Batra, B. (1992) 'The role of managerial learning and interpretation in strategic persistence and reorientation: an empirical exploration', *Strategic Management Journal*, 13(8): 585–608.

Lawrence, T. (1999) 'Institutional strategy', *Journal of Management*, 25(2): 161–88.

Lawrence, T., Hardy, C. and Phillips, N. (2002) 'Institutional effects of interorganizational collaboration: the emergence of proto-institutions', *Academy of Management Journal*, 45: 281–91.

Leblebici, H., Salancik, G., Copay, A. and King, T. (1991) 'Institutional change and the transformation of the US radio broadcasting industry', *Administrative Science Quarterly*, 36: 333–63.

Levinthal, D.A. and March, J.G. (1993) 'The myopia of learning', *Strategic Management Journal*, 14(Special Issue): 95–112.

Li, S.X. and Greenwood, R. (2004) 'The effect of within-industry diversification on firm performance: synergy creation, multi-market contact and market structuration', *Strategic Management Journal*, 25(12): 1131–53.

Lounsbury, M. (1999) 'From heresy to dogma: an institutional history of corporate environmentalism', *Administrative Science Quarterly*, 44(1): 193–6.

Lounsbury, M. (2001) 'Institutional sources of practice variation: staffing college and university recycling programs', *Administrative Science Quarterly*, 46(1): 29–56.

Madhavan, R., Koka, B.R. and Prescott, J.E. (1998) 'Networks in transition: how industry events (re)shape interfirm relationships', *Strategic Management Journal*, 19: 439–59.

Maguire, S., Hardy, C. and Lawrence, T.G. (2004) 'Institutional entrepreneurship in emerging fields: HIV/AIDS treatment advocacy in Canada', *Academy of Management Journal*, 47(5): 657–79.

Malerba, F. and Orsenigo, L. (1996) 'The dynamics and evolution of industries', *Industrial and Corporate Change*, 5(1): 51–88.

Malerba, F. and Orsenigo, L. (1997) 'Technological regimes and sectoral patterns of innovative activities', *Industrial and Corporate Change*, 6(1): 83–118.

March, J.G. (1981) 'Footnotes to organizational change', *Administrative Science Quarterly*, 26: 563–77.

March, J.G. (1991) 'Exploration and exploitation in organizational learning', *Organization Science*, 2: 71–87.

McGrath, R.M., MacMillan, I.C. and Tushman, M.L. (1992) 'The role of executive team actions in shaping dominant designs: towards the strategic shaping of technological progress', *Strategic Management Journal*, 13(Special Issue, Winter): 137–61.

Methé, D., Swaminathan, A. and Mitchell, W. (1996) 'The underemphasized role of established firms as the sources of major innovations', *Industrial and Corporate Change*, 5(4): 1181–204.

Meyer, A.D. (1982) 'Adapting to environmental jolts', *Administrative Science Quarterly*, 27(4): 515–37.

Meyer, A.D., Brooks, G.R. and Goes, J.B. (1990) 'Environmental jolts and industry revolutions: organizational responses to discontinuous change', *Strategic Management Journal*, 11(Special Issue): 93–110.

Meyer, J.W. and Rowan, B. (1977) 'Institutionalized organizations: formal structure as myth and ceremony', *American Journal of Sociology*, 83(2): 440–63.

Miles, R.E. and Snow, C.C. (1978) *Organizational Strategy, Structure, and Process*. McGraw-Hill Series in Management. New York: McGraw-Hill.

Miller, D. (1981) 'Toward a new contingency approach: the search for organizational gestalts', *Journal of Management Studies*, 18: 1–27.

Miller, D. (1982) 'Evolution and revolution: a quantum view of structural change in organizations', *Journal of Management Studies*, 9: 131–51.

Miller, D. (1993) 'The architecture of simplicity', *Academy of Management Review*, 18(1): 116–38.

Miller, D. (1996) 'Configurations revisited', *Strategic Management Journal*, 17: 505–12.

Miller, D. and Chen, M-J. (1994) 'Sources and consequences of competitive inertia: a study of the US airline industry', *Administrative Science Quarterly*, 39(1): 1–23.

Miller, D. and Friesen, P. (1980) 'Momentum and revolution in organization adaptation', *Academy of Management Journal*, 23(4): 591–614.

Miller, D. and Friesen, P. (1982) 'Structural change and performance: quantum vs piecemeal-incremental approaches', *Academy of Management Journal*, 25: 867–92.

Miller, D. and Friesen, P.H. (1984) *Organizations: A Quantum View*. Englewood Cliffs, NJ: Prentice Hall.

Miller, D., Greenwood, R. and Hinings, C.R. (1997) 'Creative chaos on munificent momentum: academic and practitioner view of organizational change', *Journal of Management Inquiry*, 6: 71–8.

Miller, D., Lant, T.K., Milliken, F.J. and Korn, H.J. (1996) 'The evolution of strategic simplicity: exploring two models of organizational adaptation', *Journal of Management*, 22(6): 863–87.

Mintzberg, H. (1979) *The Structuring of Organizations*. Englewood Cliffs, NJ: Prentice Hall.

Mintzberg, H. (1983) *Power in and Around Organizations*. Englewood Cliffs, NJ: Prentice Hall.

Moorman, C. and Miner, A.S. (1998) 'Organizational improvisation and organizational memory', *Academy of Management Review*, 23(4): 698–723.

Morris, T. and Pinnington, A. (1999) 'Continuity and change in professional organizations: the evidence from law firms', in D. Brock, M. Powell and C.R. Hinings (eds), *Restructuring the Professional Organization: Accounting, Health Care and Law*. London: Routledge. pp. 200–14.

North, D.C. (1990) *Institutions, Institutional Change and Economic Performance*. Cambridge: Cambridge University Press.

O'Reilly III, C.A. and Tushman, M.L. (2004) 'The ambidextrous organization', *Harvard Business Review*, 82(4): 74.

Ocasio, W. and Kim, H. (1999) 'The circulation of corporate control: selection of functional backgrounds of new CEOs in large US manufacturing firms, 1981–1992', *Administrative Science Quarterly*, 44: 532–62.

Oliver, C. (1991) 'The antecedents of deinstitutionalization', *Organization Studies*, 13(4): 563–88.

Palmer, D. and Barber, M. (2001) 'Challengers, elites and owning families: a social class theory of corporate acquisitions in the 1960s', *Administrative Science Quarterly*, 46: 87–120.

Palmer, D., Jennings, P.D. and Zhou, X. (1993) 'Late adoption of the multidivisional form by large US corporations: institutional, political and economic accounts', *Administrative Science Quarterly*, 38(1): 100–32.

Pennings, J.M. (1985) *Organizational Strategy and Change*. San Francisco, CA: Jossey-Bass Inc.

Pennings, J.M. (1992) 'Structural contingency theory: a reappraisal', *Research in Organizational Behavior*, 14: 267–309.

Pentland, B.T. (1995) 'Grammatical models of organizational processes', *Organization Science*, 6(5): 541–57.

Pentland. B.T. and Rueter, H.H. (1994) 'Organizational routines as grammars of action. *Administrative Science Quarterly*, 39(3): 484–511.

Perrow, C. (2002) *Organizing America Wealth, Power and the Origins of Corporate Capitalism*. Princeton: Princeton University Press.

Pettigrew, A.M. (1983) 'Patterns of managerial response as organizations move from rich to poor environments', *Educational Management Administration*, 2: 104–14.

Pettigrew, A.M. (1985) *The Awakening Giant: Continuity and Change in Imperial Chemical Industries*. Oxford, UK: Blackwell.

Pettigrew, A.M. (1987) 'Context and action in the transformation of the firm', *Journal of Management Studies*, 24(6): 649–70.

Pettigrew, A.M. and Fenton, E.M. (2000) 'Complexities and dualities in innovative forms of organizing', in A.M. Pettigrew and E.M. Fenton (eds), *The Innovating Organization*. London, UK: Sage Publications. pp. 279–300.

Pettigrew, A.M. and Whipp, R. (1991) *Managing Change for Competitive Success*. Oxford: Blackwell.

Pettigrew, A., Ferlie, E. and McKee, L. (1992) *Shaping Strategic Change*. London: Sage.

Pfeffer, J. (2003) 'Preface', in J. Pfeffer and G.R. Salancik (eds), *The External Control of Organizations*, 2nd edn. Stanford, CA: Stanford Business Classics. pp. xxxi–iii.

Pfeffer, J. and Salancik, G.R. (1978) *The External Control of Organizations*. New York: Harper and Row.

Phillips, D.J. and Zuckerman, E.W. (2001) 'Middle-status conformity: theoretical restatement and empirical demonstration in two markets', *American Journal of Sociology*, 107(2): 379–429.

Podolny, J.M. (1993) 'A status-based model of market competition', *American Journal of Sociology*, 98: 829–72.

Portes, A. and Sensenbrenner, J. (1993) 'Embeddedness and immigration: notes on the social determinants of economic action', *American Journal of Sociology*, 98: 1320–50.

Powell, W.W. and DiMaggio, P.J. (1991) *The New Institutionalism in Organizational Analysis*. Chicago, IL: University of Chicago Press.

Pugh, D.S., Hickson, D.J. and Hinings, C.R. (1969) 'The context of organization structures', *Administrative Science Quarterly*, 14: 91–114.

Quinn, R.E. and Cameron, K.S. (1983) 'Organizational life cycles and shifting criteria of effectiveness: some preliminary evidence', *Management Science*, 29: 33–51.

Rao, H. (1994) 'The social construction of reputation: certification contests, legitimation and the survival of organizations in the American automobile company', *Strategic Management Journal*, 15(Special Issue): 29–44.

Rao, H. (1998) 'Caveat emptor: the construction of non-profit consumer watchdog organizations', *American Journal of Sociology*, 103: 912–61.

Rao, H. and Drazin, R. (2002) 'Overcoming resource constraints on product innovation by recruiting talent from rivals: a study of the mutual fund industry, 1986–94', *Academy of Management Journal*, 45(3): 491–507.

Rao, H., Monin, P. and Durand, R. (2003) 'Institutional change in Toque Ville: nouvelle cuisine as an identity movement in French gastronomy', *American Journal of Sociology*, 108(4): 795–843.

Reay, T. and Hinings, C.R. (2005) 'The recomposition of an organizational field: health care in Alberta', *Organization Studies*, 26(3): 351–84.

Reay, T., Golden-Biddle, K. and GermAnn, K. (2006) 'Legitimizing a new role: small wins and microprocesses of change', *Academy of Management Journal*, in press.

Romanelli, E. and Tushman, M.L. (1994) 'Organizational transition as punctuated equilibrium: an empirical test', *Academy of Management Journal*, 37(5): 1141–66.

Rosenbloom, R.S. and Christensen, C.M. (1994) 'Technological discontinuities, organizational capabilities, and strategic commitments', *Industrial and Corporate Change*, 3(3): 655–85.

Ruef, M. (2000) 'The emergence of organizational forms: a community ecology approach', *American Journal of Sociology*, 106(3): 658–714.

Sahlin-Anderson, K. and Engwall, L. (eds) (2002) *The Expansion of Management Knowledge: Carriers, Flows, and Sources*. Stanford, CA: Stanford Business Books.

Salancik, G.R. (1995) 'Wanted: a good network theory of organization', *Administrative Science Quarterly*, 40: 345–9.

Saxenian, A. (1994) *Regional Advantage: Culture and Competition in Silicon Valley and Route 128*. Cambridge, MA: Harvard University Press.

Scott, W.R. (1995) *Institutions and Organizations*. Thousand Oaks, CA: Sage.

Scott, W.R., Ruef, M., Mendel, P.J. and Caronna, C.A. (2000) *Institutional Change and Healthcare Organizations: From Professional Dominance to Managed Care*. Chicago, IL: University of Chicago Press.

Seo, M-G. and Creed, W.E.D. (2002) 'Institutional contradictions, praxis, and institutional change: a dialectic perspective', *Academy of Management Review*, 27(2): 222–47.

Sewell, W.H. Jr. (1992) 'A theory of structure: duality, agency, and transformation', *American Journal of Sociology*, 98: 1–29.

Sherer, P.D. and Lee, K. (2002) 'Institutional change in large law firms: a resource dependency and institutional perspective', *Academy of Management Journal*, 45: 102–19.

Siggelkow, N. (2001) 'Change in the presence of fit: the rise, the fall and the renaissance of Liz Clairborne', *Academy of Management Journal*, 44(4): 838–57.

Siggelkow, N. (2002) 'Evolution toward fit', *Administrative Science Quarterly*, 47: 125–59.

Sorensen, J.B. and Stuart, T.E. (2000) 'Aging, obsolescence, and organizational innovation', *Administrative Science Quarterly*, 45: 81–112.

Strang, D. and Meyer, J.W. (1993) 'Institutional conditions for diffusion', *Theory and Society*, 22: 487–511.

Stuart, T.E. (1988) 'Network positions and propensities to collaborate: an investigation of strategic alliance formation in a high-technology industry', *Administrative Science Quarterly*, 43: 668–98.

Stuart, T.E. (2000) 'Interorganizational alliances and the performance of firms: a study of growth and innovation rates in a high-technology industry', *Strategic Management Journal*, 21(8): 791–811.

Suddaby, R. and Greenwood, R. (2005) 'Rhetorical strategies of legitimacy', *Administrative Science Quarterly*, 50: 35–67.

Sull, D.N., Tedlow, R.S. and Rosenbloom, R.S. (1997) 'Managerial commitments and technological change in the US tire industry', *Industrial and Corporate Change*, 6(2): 461–501.

Teece, D.J. (1986) 'Profiting from technological innovation: Implications for integration, collaboration, licensing and public policy', *Research Policy*, 15(6): 285–305.

Teece, D. and Pisano, G. (1994) 'The dynamic capabilities of firms: an introduction', *Industrial and Corporate Change*, 3(3): 537–56.

Thornton, P.H. (1995) 'Accounting for acquisition waves: evidence from the US college publishing industry', in W.R. Scott and S. Christensen (eds), *The Institutional Construction of Organizations: International and Longitudinal Studies*. Thousand Oaks, CA: Sage. pp. 199–225.

Thornton, P.H. (2004) *Markets from Culture*. Stanford, CA: Stanford University Press.

Thornton, P.H. and Ocasio, W. (1999) 'Institutional logics and the historical contingency of power in organizations: executive succession in the higher education publishing industry, 1958–1990', *American Journal of Sociology*, 105(3): 801–43.

Tolbert, P.S. and Zucker, L.G. (1983) 'Institutional sources of change in the formal structure of organizations: the diffusion of civil service reform, 1880–1935', *Administrative Science Quarterly*, 30: 22–39.

Tolbert, P.S. and Zucker, L.G. (1996) 'The institutionalization of institutional theory', in S.R. Clegg, C. Hardy and W.R. Nord (eds), *Handbook of Organizational Studies*. Thousand Oaks, CA: Sage. pp. 148–74.

Tripsas, M. (1997) 'Unraveling the process of creative destruction: complementary assets and incumbent survival in the typesetter industry', *Strategic Management Journal*, 18(Special Issue): 119–42.

Tripsas, M. and Gavetti, G. (2000) 'Capabilities, cognition, and inertia: evidence from digital imaging', *Strategic Management Journal*, 21: 1147–61.

Tsoukas, H. and Chia, R. (2002) 'On organizational becoming: rethinking organizational change', *Organization Science*, 13(5): 567–82.

Tushman, M. and Anderson, P. (1986) 'Technological discontinuities and organizational environments', *Administrative Science Quarterly*, 31: 439–65.

Tushman, M.L. and Murmann, J.P. (1998) 'Dominant designs, technology cycles, and organizational outcomes', *Research in Organizational Behavior*, 20: 231–66.

Tushman, M.L. and Romanelli, E. (1985) 'Organizational evolution: a metamorphosis model of convergence and reorientation', *Research in Organizational Behavior*, 7: 171–222.

Tushman, M.L. and Rosenkopf, L. (1992) 'Organizational determinants of technological change: toward a sociology of technological evolution', *Research in Organizational Behavior*, 14: 311–47.

Tushman, M.L. and Rosenkopf, L. (1996) 'Executive succession, strategic reorientation and performance growth: a longitudinal study in the US cement industry', *Management Science*, 42(7): 939–53.

Uzzi, B. (1997) 'Social structure and competition in interfirm networks: the paradox of embeddedness', *Administrative Science Quarterly*, 42(1): 35–67.

Van de Ven, A.H. and Garud, R. (1989) 'A framework for understanding the emergence of new industries', in R.S. Rosenbloom (ed.), *Research on Technological Innovation, Management, and Policy*. Greenwich, CT: JAI Press. pp. 295–325.

Van de Ven, A. and Garud, R. (1994) 'The co-evolution of technical and institutional events in the development of an innovation', in J. Baum and J. Singh (eds), *Evolutionary Dynamics of Organizations*. New York: Oxford University Press. pp. 425–43.

Virany, B., Tushman, M.L. and Romanelli, E. (1992) 'Executive succession and organization outcomes in turbulent environments: an organization learning approach', *Organization Science*, 3(1): 72–91.

Weick, K.E. (1995) *Sensemaking in Organizations*. Thousand Oaks, CA: Sage Publications.

Westphal, J.D., Gulati, R. and Shortell, S. (1997) 'Customization or conformity? An institutional and network perspective on the content and consequences of TQM adoption', *Administrative Science Quarterly*, 42: 366–94.

Whittington, R. and Pettigrew, A.M. (2003) 'Complementarities thinking', in A.M. Pettigrew, R. Whittington, L. Melin, C. Sánchez-Runde, F.A.J. Van den Bosch, W. Ruigrok and T. Numagami (eds), *Innovative Forms of Organizing*. London: Sage Publications. pp. 125–32.

Whittington, R., Mayer, M. and Curto, F. (1999) 'Chanderlism in post-war Europe: strategic and structural change in France, Germany and the UK, 1950–1993', *Industrial and Corporate Change*, 8(3): 519–51.

Woodward, J. (1965) *Industrial Organization, Theory and Practice*. London: Oxford University Press.

2.17 Seeing Organizations Differently: Three Lenses on Compassion

PETER J. FROST[1], JANE E. DUTTON, SALLY MAITLIS, JACOBA M. LILIUS, JASON M. KANOV AND MONICA C. WORLINE

One of the unspoken realities of life in organizations is that people suffer. Someone who has just been told that she has breast cancer confronts a jolt to her confidence and her sense of mortality that play out at work as well as in other spheres of her life. Someone who is dealing with dashed hopes of promotion or is feeling marginalized at work may experience sadness and deflation. Someone who is dealing with the breakdown of a personal relationship, or is struggling with difficult financial issues, or is working overtime to care for an ageing parent may feel a loss of control and a growing sense of hopelessness that affects his work, despite the expectation in many organizations that such emotions be checked at the door. People with these burdens carry them wherever they go, regardless of expectations that suffering should not affect work. While organizational rules and policies can sometimes lessen or alleviate pain, compassion can help to make a heavy burden of suffering more bearable. This chapter is founded on the assumption that compassion is a healing force that is indispensable in organizations.

The desire to see organizations as purely rational and calculated systems is not only a managerial one, but also one that has a long history in organizational studies (see Taylor 1911; Mastenbroek 2000). For this reason, a chapter on compassion in organizations may seem somehow out of place in a handbook for organizational scholars. Many theorists have challenged the desire to simplify workplaces, to dilute their emotional and relational qualities, and to quantify the terms of organizational life in tidy units (see for example, Salovey and Mayer 1990; Ashforth and Humphrey 1995; Fineman 1996, 2000; Fletcher 1999; Rafaeli and Worline 2001; Dutton 2003; Frost 2003). This chapter is a response to those challenges. The value of seeing compassion in organizations is that it brings the organic, the moving and heartfelt, the emotional, and the relational elements of life into sharp relief. A chapter on compassion shows us that we cannot fully see organizations until we allow people to speak the unspoken reality of suffering and reveal the human response to suffering that is compassion.

Feeding the Wolf of Compassion

He said to them, 'A fight is going on inside me ... it is a terrible fight and it is between two wolves. One wolf represents fear, anger, envy, sorrow, regret, greed, arrogance, self-pity, guilt, resentment, inferiority, lies, false pride, superiority and ego. The other wolf stands for joy, peace, love, hope, sharing, serenity, humility, kindness, benevolence, friendship, empathy, generosity, truth, compassion and faith. The same fight is going on inside you, and inside every other person, too.' They thought about it for a minute and then one child asked his grandfather, 'Which wolf will win?' The old Cherokee simply replied ... 'The one you feed' (Cherokee Proverb [www.snowowl.com]).

The two wolves in this old Cherokee proverb can also be found fighting it out in organization studies. The first we regard as the wolf of ego, characterized by self-interest and negativity; the second as the wolf of compassion, characterized by humanity and virtue. While both wolves get fed in practice, organizational scholars spend a disproportionate amount of time attending to the wolf of ego in their theories and research. Historically, scholarship demonstrates a strong bias, apparent in psychological and organizational research, toward understanding negative or detrimental conditions rather than positive or virtuous ones (Seligman and Csikszentmihalyi 2000;

Cameron et al. 2003; Cameron and Caza 2004). The emphasis on scientific management and what has become known as Taylorism (Taylor 1911) provided a strong foundation for stripping away a focus on humanity in the workplace, a tendency that has continued with organizational scholars demonstrating greater concern for society's economic ends rather than its social ones (Walsh et al. 2003). Organizational research has thus tended to feed the wolf of ego at the expense of the wolf of compassion.

Because of the field's emphasis on scientific management and economic outcomes, emotion was long construed as illegitimate in organizational research (Fineman 1993; 2000). However, as Fineman (2003) observes, work organizations are sites of pain, and the ignorance about emotional aspects of organizing is costly. According to the Grief Recovery Institute, the hidden cost of workplace grief exceeds $75 million per year (www.grief-recovery.com). Many scholars have challenged our ignorance about the emotion at work. For example, the last decade has seen a growing interest in the emotional toll of change (Kotter 2002), control mechanisms (Fineman and Sturdy 1999), decision-making (Maitlis and Ozceilk 2004) and downsizing (Cameron et al. 1993; Cameron 1998). This increasing attention to emotional pain in organizations is also evident in research and commentary on workplace incivility (e.g. Pearson et al. 2001), abusive bosses (Tepper 2000), corrosive politics (e.g. Williams and Dutton 1999) and work-family conflict (Rice et al. 1992). We now have an increasingly clear picture of how various sources of pain contribute to a toxic workplace, one in which employees feel their confidence weakened, their self-esteem undermined, and their hope diminished or destroyed (Frost 2003). In the meantime, the wolf of compassion grows ever hungrier.

Two harbingers of change in the field offer hope. Both an increased concern with the public goods created by organizations, and a focus on images of organizations that are more organic than mechanistic suggest that there are organizational research perspectives compatible with feeding the wolf of compassion. For example, researchers have recently issued a renewed call to consider organizations as contexts that produce outcomes important to society and the public good, apart from economic concerns (Walsh et al. 2003). This call hearkens back to the roots of the humanistic response to Taylor's ideas (e.g. Mayo 1946; McGregor 1960; Herzberg 1966). It also reminds us of management scholars

such as Follet (1918), who re-visioned the study of organizations as systems that either promoted or depleted the public good. Similarly in organizational psychology, Likert (1967) and Katz and Kahn (1978) urged scholars to develop an understanding of organizations as systems with enormous impact on members' psychological health and thriving. At the same time, the Tavistock school (e.g. Whitehead 1938) showed that human responses to workplace phenomena are not necessarily predictable with economic models, validating that human psychology is essential in understanding basic organizational processes. More recently, researchers have suggested that organizations can be studied as caregiving systems (Kahn 1993), sources of social support (House 1981), and sources of healing and health (Dutton et al. 2003; Frost 2003). These works, in honoring the humane and virtuous aspects of organizational life, open the door for the perspective that we offer in this chapter, a perspective intended to feed the wolf of compassion.

In this chapter, we first discuss the definitional issues that surround the idea of compassion. We then situate compassion at the crossroads of three different and independent theoretical perspectives or lenses – interpersonal work, narrative and organizing – as a way of offering three distinctive viewpoints from which to see the phenomenon of compassion. By invoking the notion of 'lenses', we mean to suggest that scholars may see compassion differently depending upon the theoretical tradition and empirical conversation from which they approach the topic (Allison 1971; Morgan 1997). Each of the lenses offers a view of compassion that is unique, and each is situated in a broader, ongoing perspective within organization studies. We conclude the chapter by looking across these three lenses to see how the study of compassion elaborates and enriches our view of life in organizations. Ultimately, focusing on the human response to suffering in organizations enables scholars' understanding of the proactive, creative, and generative potential that lies unstudied in organizations and that is a wellspring of nourishment for the wolf of compassion.

Defining Compassion

While attention to compassion in organizations is relatively recent (e.g. Frost 1999), discussions of the concept span both time and discipline. Meditations on compassion are found in conversations across religion, philosophy, psychology, sociology, and medicine dating back two thousand years. In building a working definition of compassion, we provide a brief overview of the intellectual history of the idea. Central to this history is the role of compassion in religious ideology and theology. Despite their fundamental philosophical differences, all of the great world religions have compassion as their overarching ideal (Armstrong 1994). For example, the Biblical tradition teaches compassion as 'a duty to divine law, as a response to divine love, and a sign of commitment to the Judeo-Christian ethic' (Wuthnow 1991, p. 50), and mandates humanity to emulate God in his attribute of compassion (Sears 1998). Islam is based in the same emulation of compassion between God and humanity, with the Prophet declaring in the Qu'ran, 'O people, be compassionate to others so that you may be granted compassion by God.' Compassion has also been equated with humanity across traditions, from Buddhist philosophy that considers the basic nature of human beings to be compassionate (e.g. Dalai Lama 1995) to the Christian perspective on compassion as 'full immersion in the condition of being human' (Nouwen et al. 1983, p. 4). Gupta (2000) suggests an additional similarity with Hindu philosophy, which teaches that everything in the world is God, and therefore that we are all the same and that should extend ourselves to help others.

Early philosophical discussions of compassion through to more contemporary accounts demonstrate a similar consistency. Aristotle saw compassion as an emotion directed at another's misfortune or suffering, and described three elements necessary for the experience: one must see the suffering of another as serious; one must believe that the suffering is not deserved; and one must acknowledge that he or she has vulnerabilities similar to those of the sufferer (Aristotle 1939). The same elements are found in the work of later philosophers (e.g. Smith 1976; Rousseau 1979; Schopenhauer 1995) and in contemporary moral philosophy (Mead 1962; Blum 1980; Reich 1989; Wuthnow 1991; Nussbaum, 1996, 2001; Solomon 1998; Harrington 2002; Post 2003). Across time, compassion has been framed both as innate (Smith 1976; Wuthnow 1991; Himmelfarb 2001) and as contributing to the well-being of communities and individuals (Rousseau 1979; Blum 1980; Wuthnow 1991; Nussbaum 2001; Post 2003).

Contemporary work in social science offers further insight into the nature of compassion, and builds on theology and philosophy in demonstrating that compassion is an innate human instinct (Keltner 2004). First, investigating the biological basis of compassion, neuroscientists suggest a link between feelings of compassion and activity in particular regions of the brain (Nitschke 2001; Davidson 2002, 2003) that are also activated when people contemplate harm to others (Greene et al. 2001). Other biopsychological findings indicate that helping others triggers brain activity in portions of the brain also activated by the experience of pleasure (Rilling et al. 2002). Taken together, this research suggests that the brain may be adapted to respond to the suffering of others, thus supporting the religious and philosophical claims for compassion as innate. Second, social psychologists (Davis 1983; Batson 1991) and sociologists (Mead 1962; Shott 1979; Clark 1997; Nussbaum, 2001) have expanded on Aristotle's third requirement for compassion – seeing oneself as similarly vulnerable to the sufferer – in ways that have clarified the construct. For instance, sociologists identify empathy as an important element of compassion and regard empathy as a product not only of perceiving another person as being in need, but also of adopting the other's perspective (Clark 1997; Nussbaum 2001). Social psychologists provide empirical evidence of a link between felt empathy and the likelihood of engaging in helping behaviour (Davis 1983; Batson 1991).

Finally, interest in compassion as a moral imperative appears in the medical (e.g. Barber 1976; Brody 1992; Dougherty and Purtillo 1995; Cassell 2002) and nursing literatures (Benner et al. 1996; von Deitze and Orb 2000). Here, compassion is seen as an essential component of patient care that is 'directly related to the recognition and treatment of patient suffering' (Cassell 2002, p. 442). Medical scholars suggest that compassion enables physicians to fulfill their central duties to their patients (to put the patient's interests first, to deliver proper care, and to maintain confidentiality) (Dougherty and Purtillo 1995), and brings medical practitioners closer to their patients to achieve a deeper level of healing (Brody 1992; Benner et al. 1996; von Dietze and Orb 2000).

In our working definition of compassion, we pull from each of these disciplines. Drawing from Clark's (1997) discussion of sympathy as a three part process, we identify compassion as comprised of three interrelated elements: noticing another's suffering, feeling empathy for the other's pain, and responding to the suffering in some way. Noticing involves a process of becoming aware of another's emotional state, and typically requires being open and attentive to emotional cues and to what is happening in one's context (Frost 2003). Feeling for the other's pain involves empathic concern (Davis 1983; Batson 1994) or 'taking the attitude' of the other person (Mead 1962, p. 366; Shott 1979). In this way, compassion resembles empathy (Davis 1983; Batson 1994), but goes beyond this to involve a response to suffering. Responding indicates action in which one attempts to alleviate or overcome the other's condition in some way (Reich 1989; von Dietz and Orb 2000; Nussbaum 2001). Compassion defined in this manner, as a three-part human experience, does not require a successful outcome. The necessary link is between one's noticing of suffering, feelings of concern, and attempts to help alleviate that suffering.

Three Ways of Seeing Compassion in Organizations

We have introduced compassion as a subject in organizational studies by situating it within important historical traditions and by linking it to current scholarly research interests. Next, we offer three distinct theoretical lenses through which to view compassion. These lenses are tied to three well-established, independent perspectives on organizations and each identifies a different research agenda. Seeing compassion as a topic of research from each of these three perspectives provides a wide vista of possibilities for the study of compassion. Together, all three lenses help us see how organizational research may feed the wolf of compassion.

The three lenses we bring to compassion are: (1) interpersonal work; (2) narrative; and (3) organizing. In the discussion of each lens, we first highlight important defining features of the lens that anchor compassion in the theoretical perspective. After discussing compassion through the particular lens, we examine the core insights it offers, opening up different ways of seeing individual, unit, and organizational functioning. Finally, we offer new and interesting research questions evoked by each lens. Table 2.17.1 presents a comparative summary of the three lenses. While very different from one another,

each of these lenses offers an appreciative perspective, highlighting what is positive and generative in compassion as it occurs in organizations. We acknowledge, however, that there are other, potentially darker sides to compassion as it relates to concepts such as power and gender, which we examine later in the paper.

Lens 1: Interpersonal Work

Interpersonal work is the work that happens in the space between two people (Josselson 1992). While such work has often been 'disappeared' in organizations (Fletcher 1998), this type of skill in crafting connections and managing the relational space between people is increasingly recognized as essential to the core work of occupations such as nursing (Benner et al. 1986), social work and health care (Kahn 1993; von Deitze and Orb 2000), teaching occupations (Noddings 1984), and in work organizations more generally (Jacques 1993; Fletcher 1998). The activity that we term 'interpersonal work' is the effortful handling of interpersonal interactions. The success or failure of interpersonal work is a product of the joint qualities and behaviours of the people involved in a work interaction; and is an activity that consumes both cognitive effort and emotional energy (Miller and Stiver 1997). We assume that interpersonal work is productive in the sense of creating consequences for the individuals engaged in it. For example, the skilled work of a toxin handler who helps a colleague who has been berated by a boss is a form of interpersonal work that can help that colleague carry on and is productive in that it allows both of them to complete their work (Frost 2003).

Interpersonal work often involves some kind of helping behaviour, and a variety of forms of everyday interpersonal work have been well documented, such as organizational citizenship behaviour (see Podsakoff et al. 2000, for a review) and prosocial organizational behaviour (Brief and Motowildo 1986). Kahn (1993; 1998), Fletcher (1998) and others have emphasized more relational and person-focused forms of interpersonal work and have highlighted both the existence and consequential nature of relationship-centered interpersonal work. These lines of research demonstrate that relational work is not just 'nice' or 'soft', but is crucial in order to accomplish the work of the organization.

Table 2.17.1 Three ways of seeing compassion in organizations

	Compassion as interpersonal work	Compassion as narrative	Compassion as organizing
Main idea	Compassion is a form of everyday interpersonal interactions that takes place in organizations	Compassion is carried in language and stories in ways that help people make sense of pain and make meaning of their experiences at work	Compassion becomes a collective accomplishment through processes that create, maintain, and dissolve social units
Core assumptions of this lens	• Interpersonal work requires skill and competence • Interpersonal work is consequential and productive	• Compassion narratives reflect the hidden reality of pain in organizations • Compassion narratives help constitute the human response to pain • Narratives are powerful windows into the construction of individual and collective identities	• Different processes in organizations enable people to notice, feel, and respond to pain • Features of the organizational context facilitate or hinder noticing, feeling, and responding to pain • Agentic activity by proactive individuals can amplify collective response to pain
Central ideas about compassion as seen through this lens	Compassion involves a three-part human experience of noticing, feeling, and responding. Several types of well-known interpersonal interactions help to facilitate elements of this experience	Compassion narratives reveal important shared values and beliefs that are the heart of organizations. Compassion narratives also help constitute organizational members' identities and realign them with organizational identity	Compassion becomes an effective collective accomplishment when individual agentic actions are legitimated, when attention and information about pain is propagated, and when systems are in place that allow for easy coordination of effort.
Key insights developed through this lens	• Compassion is effortful work that involves expenditure of cognitive and emotional energy • Compassion depends on skilled interpersonal interactions • Compassion as interpersonal work may be gendered and rendered less visible than other forms of interpersonal work • Small acts of compassion may have large consequences	• Compassion narratives show the emotional tendencies of a collective • Exposure to compassion narratives in organizations affects people in consequential ways, often having a developmental effect • Compassion narratives reveal a process by which members re-align their sense of the organizational identity with their perceptions of organizational action • Compassion narratives allow access to the multiple voices of an organization, revealing different experiences of compassion at work	• Compassion as organizing relies on interdependent observations, feelings, and actions • Compassion as organizing is subject to nonlinear dynamics and feedback loops that influence the shape of the response • Organizing processes are embedded in time and may feed into expectations for compassionate response in the future • Organizing compassion has secondary effects such as raising the level of efficacy to meet challenges in a system

Compassion as Interpersonal Work

Compassion as interpersonal work can show up in all kinds of situations in which employees experience pain. The interpersonal work of noticing pain, feeling empathetic concern, and responding to pain in some manner takes effort and often has important consequences. Researchers have associated the interpersonal work of compassion with negotiation performance (Alfred et al. 1997), and our own work suggests that experiencing compassion (either as a direct recipient or as a witness) changes how people see themselves, their colleagues, and their organizations (Lilius et al. 2004). Compassion as interpersonal work, while often invisible and sometimes associated with the enactment of power differences, is nevertheless associated with important outcomes that may have significance beyond the immediate feelings and acts of compassion. Below, we offer an example which we use both to elaborate how compassion as interpersonal work looks, and to begin the discussion of how different forms of interpersonal work illustrate the skill involved in noticing, feeling and responding to suffering.

At an offsite meeting of three hundred of Cisco's managers, Janet Skadden, a new manager in human resources, wanted to try something different. She had come to Cisco from Tandem, a company whose relaxed, interpersonal culture encouraged employees to participate in activities like trust-building games. Skadden hoped such games might help the Cisco engineers loosen up a little, especially given the beachfront atmosphere of the meeting. But, to put it mildly, Skadden's exercises didn't go over well. When the attendees returned to the office, they were still talking about Skadden's 'beach games'. Skadden was despondent. But CEO John Chambers, who'd witnessed Skadden's efforts at the beach, came to her office and told her what a great job she'd done in pulling the offsite together. When Skadden pointed out that her exercises had bombed, Chambers said: 'The minute you stop trying to do things like that, I'm going to be really disappointed. If you're not taking risks and trying new things, you're not trying hard enough. I loved the fact that we tried something different (Kruger 1997, p. 152).'

In this story, Chambers does not sugarcoat Skadden's failure. As Skadden told us in an interview, it was clear to both of them that her exercise did not work. What he does, however, is the essence of compassion as interpersonal work. First, he notices, feels,

and responds to her experienced pain in failing at her first challenge as a new organizational member. Skadden described to us her surprise that Chambers, as CEO, noticed how she was feeling. Further, he responded to her pain in a way that frames her efforts as a worthy attempt at innovation. His comment, 'I loved the fact that we tried something different', expresses empathetic concern that will help to raise her spirits and to ease her pain, particularly as he talks about it as a shared effort ('we'), linking himself to the event. The often unstated and easily overlooked elements of interpersonal work are implicit in Chambers' compassion, including noticing what had happened in terms of Skadden's role in the outcome and her body language at the end of the session, feeling empathetic concern that she likely would be upset and somewhat deflated by the experience, and taking action through words to give her an emotional lift and a vote of confidence. In this example, Chambers' actions, which are barely noticeable to others but deeply meaningful to Skadden, demonstrate the skilled performative elements of compassion as interpersonal work. In doing the work of compassion, the space between the two people is shaped, through the timing, the content, the focus and the whole interaction sequence, to leave the person in pain better off. And, while this is a story of a CEO and a vice president, in the simplicity of its plot line, this story illustrates the commonality of compassion as interpersonal work in organizations. Disappointments, failed attempts, and unexpected setbacks are natural and frequent experiences of work, and others in the workplace often perform similar interpersonal work of compassion when they notice the pain caused by these events and respond to it in some manner.

While thinking about compassion as a form of interpersonal work is relatively new to the field of organizational studies, research on some of the skills involved in this type of work is not new. Researchers have identified a number of interpersonal behaviours that are involved in the performance of compassion as interpersonal work. We elaborate two of these behavioural forms here – open listening and holding space – to illustrate ways that compassion as interpersonal work may appear in organizations.

Open Listening

Listening in ways that convey an openness to the experience of the other is an illustration of one behavioural form that is involved in compassion but may not be recognized as such in organizational research. Listening in this way can help the three aspects of compassion: noticing, feeling and responding. Since the focus of listening is on the 'other', open listening steers attention to both verbal and non-verbal aspects of messages and facilitates noticing that a person is in pain. Listening also draws the listener into the emotional space of another, enhancing the possibility for empathy. The information gathering aspects of listening help guide appropriate responses to the needs of the sufferer (Kahn 1993). Listening is a process for gaining a cognitive and emotional understanding of the state of others as well as providing a means for sensing and feeling the pain of another person. The centrality of open listening in responding to another person's pain explains why listening is such a key interpersonal practice for physicians and others whose work routinely involves dealing with the suffering of other people (Candib 1995). Open listening is an important practice in other work contexts as well, as people who listen in this way are receptive to ways in which pain is expressed, and are therefore more likely to notice a broader range of pain triggers.

Kahn (1998: 44), for instance, describes the case of an office manager in a department store who is upset at her own ineffectiveness at supervising one of her staff. When she brings her problem to the business owner, the owner openly listens then asks a few questions, without prejudging her situation or jumping to quick answers. He tells the manager how impressed he is that she is trying to learn how to be more effective, and shares a similar situation that he faced in the past. Finally, the owner offers feedback about how to reframe the situation in a less constraining way. This example illustrates how listening increases the likelihood that someone like the office manager will be heard rather than ignored, rebuffed, or admonished for her behaviour. By listening and withholding judgment, the business owner was more likely to pick up cues about the nature of the manager's situation, the pain in her sense of inadequacy, and her needs for the future. The owner's expressions of support include sharing an experience that signals the congruence of his feelings with hers. His praise and his suggestions can help to restore the manager's confidence. A close look at listening as an element of compassion shows that compassion takes work, often skilled work, that is built on perspective and experience and developed over time.

Creating a Holding Space for Pain

Another form that compassion as interpersonal work may take involves creating conditions in which conversations, reflections, and steps toward growth and connection can be addressed (Benner et al. 1996). One way to describe the establishment of these conditions is captured in the idea of creating a 'holding space', a psychological space that provides an environment in which people have an opportunity to grieve and to regroup (Heifetz 1994; Kahn 2001; Frost 2003). The term holding environment (Winnicott 1960) was first used in psychoanalysis to capture the relationship between a therapist and a patient in which 'the therapist "holds" the patient in a process of developmental learning in a way that has some similarities to the way a mother or a father hold their newborn or maturing children' (Heifetz 1994: 104). In organizations, Heifetz (1994), Kahn (2001) and Frost (2003) suggest that the idea of a holding environment works as a means of helping employees manage pain, debilitating stress, or anxiety. Creating a holding space can sometimes involve changing the physical conditions, such as providing a private office where problems can be discussed, or it can involve changing the emotional conditions, such as making the time to be present with the person in pain (Hallowell 1999; Frost 2003). The practice of holding space entails finding ways to create and sustain an emotional and physical zone that will provide the sufferer with respite. Respite may differ across people. For example, creating holding space for one person may mean granting a day off; for another, quiet time in an office; or for someone else, a release from work responsibilities for a few weeks. Giving careful attention to the form of the holding space created in each particular situation becomes part of doing the work of compassion.

The Value of Seeing Compassion as Interpersonal Work

Viewing compassion in organizations through the lens of interpersonal work highlights the emotional and connective features of such work in ways that help scholars grasp what people do when they are being compassionate. We elaborate four key insights that come from this lens on compassion.

Firstly, seeing compassion as interpersonal work emphasizes the work of compassion. Having defined compassion as a three-part human experience that involves noticing pain, feeling empathetic concern for another, and responding to alleviate pain, we imply that compassion is effortful. This lens expands on that implication. The interpersonal work of compassion encompasses a wide range of activities, such as open listening and creating a holding space for pain.

Secondly, seeing compassion as interpersonal work highlights the competence or skillful action involved in doing compassion. This competence comes not only from skillful execution of interpersonal behaviours, but also from emotional attunement. To be successfully implemented, interpersonal work such as open listening and creating holding space places emotional demands on those engaged. For instance, open listening requires cognitive attention toward others while remaining non-judgmental and it demands emotional energy to be empathetic (Miller and Stiver 1997). This lens suggests that skill in offering compassion can be built over time, as people become better at listening, attunement and communication. In addition, this lens suggests that the experience of receiving compassion depends on the shared competence of the recipient and the person offering support, who jointly create a situation that alleviates suffering. For instance, pain in organizations can often be overlooked or misinterpreted unless the listener actively engages empathically and commits to listen for emotions in the messages that those in pain allow themselves to send.

Thirdly, this view facilitates seeing that the work of compassion, like other forms of relational work, is often gendered through its association with the work of women in the private sphere. Compassion as a form of interpersonal work is often rendered invisible because it is an expertise that is not domain specific (such as medical expertise or engineering expertise), but is a form of expertise that travels across domains (Jacques 1993). In addition, where compassion as work is seen as 'soft' and not 'tough enough', it may reduce a person's perceived potential for leadership or other roles with power and prestige (Acker 1990; Mumby and Putnam 1992; Kanter 1977). As a consequence, the skilled work of compassion may also be associated with the enactment of power differences, which often renders the work of compassion invisible or 'disappeared' (Fletcher 1999). Consideration of the gendering of compassion as interpersonal work inside many organizations raises questions about whether this form of work is recognized and valued. For instance, as

women come to be associated with a given job or role, its status diminishes (Pfeffer and Davis-Blake 1987) and therefore when the interpersonal work of compassion is acknowledged in organizations it may quickly become devalued.

Fourthly, seeing compassion as interpersonal work demonstrates the potential impact of small moves. Small actions in an organization can make big differences. Even seemingly simple things, such as taking a few minutes to visit someone who is suffering or offering a card with a few words of comfort to someone who has experienced a loss can renew a sense of hope in the recipient (Frost et al. 2000; Frost 2003). In the story from Cisco, the few words from CEO Chambers to Janet Skadden helped transform her experience of failure. Hallowell (1999) has called these 'human moments' at work, when someone is physically and psychologically present for another person. Hallowell suggests that compassion can help the sufferer reconnect to his or her workplace and feel valued. Other research indicates that a few hours permitted off from work, a hug, a note of caring, sharing a story of vulnerability, and other small acts can help transform people's sense of themselves, change the way they relate to their colleagues, and shape the way they view their organizations (Lilius et al. 2004).

Research Possibilities for Compassion as Interpersonal Work

Seeing compassion as interpersonal work highlights several possibilities for research on the concept. We elaborate only two of the many possible avenues for generative future research on compassion as interpersonal work:

(1) *The shape of compassion as interpersonal work*: We have argued here that compassion is a type of interpersonal work, and that as such it is effortful. Generative future research in this domain would involve investigating the microdynamics that comprise 'the work of compassion'. Such research would address questions such as: How is compassion expressed in particular kinds of work organizations? How are noticing, feeling and responding to pain shaped by the culture and routines that distinguish particular organizational units? How does the expression of compassion vary across organizations, across units within organizations, across task groupings, and so forth? Do people vary in their ability and willingness to offer compassion at work, and what accounts for that variation?

(2) *Consequences of the interpersonal work of compassion*: We have argued that small moves in organizations have the potential for large impact through their effect on suffering and also through their effect on people's sense of self, sense of others, and sense of the organization We have assumed that there are positive consequences for a sufferer who receives compassion from other members of their organization. We have suggested that there also are organizational benefits from such acts of compassion. Generative future research along these lines would explore short-term vs. long-term effects of compassion. It would show empirically the effects of such expressions of care, for the recipient, for the provider, and for the organization.

Lens 2: Narrative

While the first lens focuses on compassion as a form of interpersonal work, a narrative perspective highlights that lived experience is captured, stored, and told in storied ways (Bruner 1986), and that people express what they know and how they feel in organizations through stories (O'Connor 1998). For purposes of this chapter, we define narratives very simply as 'verbal acts consisting of someone telling someone else that something happened' (Smith 1981, p. 182). People understand their actions as being temporally organized (McAdams 1993), lending power to a view of stories as a representation of experience. People use stories and narrative to make sense of their organizations (Weick 1995). As ways of creating meaning and making sense of organizations, narratives provide a window into many aspects of organizational life. People tell stories for a reason – 'to complain, to boast, to inform, to alert, to tease, to explain or excuse or justify…' (Schegloff 1997, p. 97). This implies that where a story begins and ends, what it includes and excludes, what it highlights or suppresses are all choices that a narrator makes, choices that help reveal something about organizational and personal reality.

Besides having a reflective quality, stories also constitute organizational reality. Stories are often collected, categorized, and analysed for insights into organizational life (Boje 1991). Narratives have a 'restorying' quality (Connelly and Clandidnin 1990), in that they 'give birth to many different meanings, generating "children" of meaning in their own image' (McAdams 1993, p. 30). In this way narratives are social products that both reflect and constitute life inside organizations; that is, stories reflect ideas about 'what happened' at the same time that they construct

identities of individuals and of collectives (Gergen and Gergen 1998). In this view, stories shape and animate life in particular directions, rather than serving as static reflections of activity. Thus we connect compassion narratives to the general body of theory in organization studies that focuses on how people make meaning of their experiences and what those meanings, in turn, allow people to do.

Compassion as Narrative

A narrative view of compassion provides a storied view of responses to pain, helping to reveal the rich detail that comprises compassion. This lens brings alive the ways in which people understand and experience compassion at work by highlighting the key symbols and plot-lines that organization members use to describe their experience (Martin et al.1983). Compassion narratives capture the micro-moves that happen as people 'work the context' to create a compassionate response (Dutton et al. 2006). Another aspect of the narrative view is that it allows researchers to move between compassion as an individual experience and compassion as a collective experience. Through employees' and outside observers' stories of collective responses to pain, we come to see elements of organizations, such as value systems, belief systems, and cultural systems that support a compassionate response to pain. Finally, narratives are powerful windows into the construction of identities, both individual and collective (Gergen and Gergen 1998). We draw specifically upon notions of self-identity and organizational identity (Whetten and Godfrey 1998) in our discussion of the ways that compassion as narrative illuminates identity in organizations.

In discussing compassion as narrative, we focus on three key ideas that stand out when we look through this lens. The first is that compassion as narrative reveals a hidden side of organizations, showing us the feeling tone of organizations evidenced by how they handle pain and suffering. The second idea is that narratives show us how organizational identity is constituted and reconstituted, as people see the organization anew in its response to pain. The third idea is that a narrative lens informs us about the construction of self-identities of those within organizations.

Compassion Narratives Reveal the Feeling Tone of an Organization

Painful events calling for compassion are often unexpected and can draw attention away from other key organizational issues. Under these conditions, people's shared beliefs and values in the organization emerge from where they are typically hidden, revealing how people in the organization handle suffering. Unexpected moments provide windows into the organization that are captured in the stories that are shared among members. For instance, Reuters is an organization whose caring actions immediately following the crisis of 9/11 2001 were depicted in stories that affirmed important organizational values. In their efforts to track the whereabouts of missing staff members, Reuters staff learned that several employees had perished. Reuters' handling of this sad outcome was reflected in its response to Nelly Braginsky whose son, Alex, had died in the attack. Phil Lynch, the CEO of Reuters America, had called her on a Tuesday night and the next day she met with Lynch and HR manager Sharon Greenholt (Dutton et al. 2002b). Greenholt's narrative follows:

> She (Braginsky) refused to believe that anything had happened. This was understandable. Reuters did everything they could to help her with this. Phil Lynch called her in the mornings to make sure she had eaten breakfast. We got her a car to take her around New York. We got her sandwiches to keep her fed on her visits to the hospitals. She shared stories of her son. We were very conscious that we would not challenge what she thought. The family drove the process. It was heart wrenching, as the families would call with possible scenarios that might eliminate the possibility that their sons were in the WTC. We kept saying we will do everything we can, and we did (Dutton et al. 2002b: 7).

The theme of compassionate responsiveness revealed in this story was echoed in several other stories circulating in the organization about how Reuters dealt with the families of deceased employees and of managers' and employees' efforts to get the company back serving its customers. These narratives of compassion are told and retold, ultimately contributing to a shared recognition of the value placed by the company on its employees. One employee commented, 'Watching Phil Lynch get so involved with the families – so quickly – with their personal lives, bringing them in, comforting them, involved with their personal pain – I saw the heart – not just the company, not just technology and lines – I saw the heart of the company in him responding to the families' (Dutton et al. 2002b, p. 7). Narratives

like these expose the hidden values regarding responsiveness to human pain in Reuters and reveal an organization's feeling tone, or what the story teller calls 'the heart' of the organization.

Compassion narratives shape organizational identity. A second key idea that comes from seeing compassion as narrative is its connection to organizational identity. Narratives not only reflect organizational values, but also shape organizational identities. Organizational identity is typically construed as what members take to be central, distinctive, and enduring about their organization (Albert and Whetten 1985). Compassion narratives, as they circulate through the organization, may build upon or contradict existing ideas of 'what the organization is'. As stories of compassion are shared, they shape employees' understandings of their organization in new ways, building an appreciation of their workplace as caring and responsive (or lacking in care and responsiveness). Such narratives are thus constitutive of the collective organizational identity. The story below provides an illustration:

> Recently (on a Monday) I was told my stepbrother had been killed in an auto accident. I called my manager at home to find out what to do about my schedule as I would have to travel from Michigan to Tennessee for the funeral and to be with my family. My manager was very sympathetic, told me not to worry about coming in the rest of the week and not to worry about any paperwork – she would fill out what was needed so I would not lose any pay. When I returned home from Tennessee I had already received cards from my manager and coworkers and a plant with a sympathy card from the organization itself. I am proud to work for an organization that is large enough to have the technology and facilities that we do, but small enough to still know that people are the important part (Employee, Midwest Hospital).

Here, the narrator tells of the sudden loss of a family member and of how her colleagues' responses shaped her sense of the organization as both competent and humane. Looking closely at this narrative in the wake of this painful event, we can see the narrator's construction of her manager as sympathetic, her coworkers as responsive and caring, and the organization at large as people-focused and humane. A narrative lens on compassion thus reveals how individuals come to construct the identity of their organization and its members through the compassionate responses that they witness and share. Moreover, the organizational identity in turn has a powerful influence on employees' behaviour (Dutton et al. 1994), shaping their expectations of how to respond to painful events and the suffering of others. In this way, compassion narratives are not only constitutive of organizational identity, but also of an organization's responses to future tragedies.

Compassion Narratives Constitute Members' Identities

In addition to shaping the identity of an organization, narratives are also used by individuals to construct their own identities (Gergen and Gergen 1998). As Reissman (1993) explains, 'in telling about an experience, I am also creating a self – how I want to be known by others' (p. 11). Through compassion narratives, organizational members make sense of who they are. A third key idea that comes from seeing compassion as narrative, then, is that members' identities are constructed in part through their stories of encounters with pain and compassion in their organizations (White and Epston 1990; Maitlis 2004). Viewed in this way, narratives of compassion help to constitute organizational members' identities.

We see compassion narratives as helping to construct individual identities in a story from research at a Canadian not-for-profit organization where a manager described what it was like to be part of a workplace in which compassion was shown to members experiencing pain. She spoke of a time when she found herself in a role that was too large for her and that she did not feel competent to perform. She explained, 'when I was finding things just too overwhelming and felt that I had just too many balls in the air that I didn't feel capable of managing, I felt awful for that, and ashamed and inadequate and all that stuff'. She went on to describe how her colleagues responded to her plight, saying, 'I was very nurtured and supported by the organization in a lot of ways.' Through her story of compassion at work, she began to construct herself more positively, as capable and energized by her job ('It's fun and it feeds me and I learn a lot and that's always really critical for me') and also as someone who gives to others ('I feel nurturing') (Maitlis 2004). In this narrative of compassion, we see a woman's identity shifting from someone who is failing and inadequate to someone who is a capable, engaged, passionate and nurturing colleague.

The Value of Seeing Compassion as Narrative

In general, the narrative lens helps us form a richer picture of compassion as it takes place in organizational contexts. Hearing stories of compassionate responses to pain brings compassion to life in vivid detail, demonstrating the phenomenon in ways that are compelling and different from numerical displays or statistical tests. In addition, examining compassion through the lens of narrative yields four distinct and important insights about the nature of compassion in organizations.

Firstly, seeing compassion as narrative reveals hidden elements of an organization's culture, where culture is defined as shared beliefs or values that shape, in part, people's emotional experience at work. It has been argued that narrative is one way to tap into latent values and beliefs at work in an organization (Schein 1996; Czarniawska 1998). Compassion narratives help organizational members (as well as organizational researchers) to identify latent beliefs about appropriate responses to pain. As scholars collect and examine stories of compassion in a workplace, they begin to uncover these shared beliefs and values and to see how they inform the collective emotional tendencies in an organization.

Secondly, seeing compassion as narrative reveals how exposure to stories affects people in important ways. As compassion stories are shared in organizations, they help people make sense of who they are within that context. Because stories help to constitute members' identities, they have dramatic effects on the possibilities for growth and development in the organization. Exposure to stories of compassion – hearing them, telling them, and re-telling them – may also influence how people are able to construct their identities outside of work (Somers 1994; Gergen and Gergen 1998). Given the permeability of the boundaries between work and home (Hochschild 1997), narratives of compassion in organizations may help people grow into more caring and confident people across life domains. For example, in a study of the physician billing department at Midwest hospital, the majority of interviewees in the 30-person unit told how the stories of compassion that reflected their own and others' experiences helped them to see new possibilities of how to care for loved ones at home (Worline et al. 2004).

Thirdly, seeing compassion as narrative helps organizational researchers see the construction and re-construction of organizational identity in ways that make plain how members align and re-align their understanding of the organization with their perceptions of its actions. Organizational scholars have suggested that organizational identity is not a static feature of organizations (Gioia et al. 2000). Seeing compassion as narrative helps make clear how an organization's response to an unexpected painful event can serve as a prompt for members to align their sense of the organization with how they perceive it responding to incidents of pain and suffering over time. In this way, compassion as narrative is constitutive not only of individual members' identities, but of organizational identity as well.

Finally, seeing compassion as narrative provides an opportunity to hear multiple voices in an organization. Compassion narratives, as told by organizational members, uncover whether the surface stated values that reside in the organizational mission statement have teeth in capturing the reality of lived experience inside the organization. Organizational members as narrators make choices in telling a story such as where the story begins and ends, what details it includes and excludes, and what aspects are emphasized or suppressed. In this way, organizational members may use compassion narratives to produce and reproduce an organization's power structure. Narratives can therefore become a window into the 'workings of power' in a situation (Mumby 1987; 1988). Narratives can reveal the legitimacy accorded to certain forms of pain in an organization: for example, that losing a loved one is regarded as a more legitimate source of pain than experiencing sexual harassment. Less legitimate forms of pain are more likely to go unnoticed and be left unattended, which is particularly problematic where these forms of pain are specific to members of marginalized groups (e.g. women are more likely than men to experience the pain of sexual harassment). By examining the content, structure, and narrative choices within compassion stories, we enhance the richness that emanates from the compassion narrative and widen the lens of understanding about the organization and its members.

Research Possibilities

Seeing compassion through a narrative lens raises many research possibilities. Below, we highlight three areas that we see as generative for further research:

(1) *How narratives of compassion shape interpretation and action over time*: When people hear and talk about compassion in relation to one major incident, they may compartmentalize this and keep it separate from their everyday work. Generative future research could examine when and how compassion narratives circulate, and when and how they take on different interpretations over time. For instance, when are compassion narratives taken to be reflective of the organization as a whole and when are they simply taken to be indicative of one compartmentalized response?

(2) *The construction of individual and organizational identity*: Because narratives are constitutive of identity, generative future research could investigate the micro-processes through which individual and organizational identities are constructed. For example, what is the nature of the processes through which people's understandings of themselves and their organizations are shaped following a compassionate response to suffering? How do these processes differ when a person witnesses, rather than personally experiences, such a response? And what is the nature of these micro-processes in the context of a failure to experience or witness compassion in response to pain?

(3) *The discursive construction of compassion*: Also in line with our suggestion of narratives as a window into a critical perspective on organizations, generative future research could examine several elements of the construction of compassion through stories and narrative. For instance, such research might look at the ways in which different groups in an organization construct compassion narratives. How do the tropes used by men and women differ? How does the structure of compassion narratives vary in different social, cultural and institutional contexts?

Lens 3: Organizing

The third lens, compassion as organizing, looks at compassion specifically as a process that unfolds collectively across individuals. This lens regards compassion as a social accomplishment that requires active co-ordination across actors that gives rise to complex, nonlinear processes in the organization. As actions unfold through time, the organizing lens focuses scholars on various aspects of the organization, such as routines or networks of contact, that give shape to complex processes.

Reconceptualizing 'organizations' into processes of organizing is one of the core insights of Weick's (1979) work, which proposed a way of looking at organizations that combined a natural systems and an open systems perspective. Weick (1979), and more recently Heath and Sitkin (2001), encourage scholars to examine the processes that create, maintain, and dissolve social collectives, and the processes by which people co-ordinate goal-directed activities. An organizing lens shifts the emphasis of inquiry from a structural and top-down view to one that emphasizes proactive human actors and emergent social processes. In viewing compassion as organizing, we adopt this shift in focus and look toward the ways in which compassion becomes a collective accomplishment of multiple actors in combination with processes of legitimation, propagation, and co-ordination.

Compassion as Organizing

This lens on compassion highlights the different processes that enable a group of people to organize around pain, highlighting the path dependence and time dependence of the social accomplishment of compassion. An organizing lens reveals the ebbs and flows of activities involved in accomplishing compassion as a collective process. This lens also invites consideration of how features of the organizational context (e.g. routines, networks) facilitate or hinder compassion through their shaping of three key social processes: legitimating, propagating and co-ordinating. An organizing lens on compassion suggests that the proactive behaviours of individuals who notice and respond to pain in organizations will give rise to complex processes that unfold in nonlinear ways.

In this section we consider three processes that facilitate compassion in organizations: legitimation, propagation and co-ordination. Each process is known to be important in organizational studies; here we describe the potency of each process in helping to explain how compassion unfolds as a collective process (Kanov et al. 2004).

Legitimating

Legitimating is a process that ensures that actions of an entity are desirable, proper and/or appropriate (Suchman 1995). Legitimation happens through multiple means in organizations, but its natural

effect is to grant individuals freedom to feel and act in particular ways. Where the noticing of pain is legitimate, where the expression of feelings is legitimate, and where acting toward others ways that facilitate healing is legitimate, the organizing of compassion is more likely to take place and to be enacted with competence. We define competence here in terms of the speed, scope, scale and customization of the response to the needs of the person in pain (Dutton et al. 2002b; 2006). For example, some organizations have created policies and procedures that allow employees to donate vacation time to a type of collective bank, and then developed procedures that allow employees to use this donated time if they need it to care for a sick spouse or family member (e.g. Dutton et al. 2002b). While this process directly facilitates the co-ordination of care, it also bestows the practice of giving time to others with acceptability as a type of 'proper' investment in another person's welfare at a time of need. These policies often have names that imbue them with an appropriate and desirable formality (e.g. Employee Vacation Investment programmes). By turning this voluntary action into a form of routine, the management (or whomever institutionalizes the practice) imbues the process with legitimacy (Feldman and Pentland 2003), that in turn fuels further noticing of pain, and eases the co-ordination of individual responses.

Legitimating can also facilitate compassion organizing by granting people the freedom to display feelings, which in turn facilitates co-ordination of responding. In particular, actions of leaders offer important symbolic endorsement of what is appropriate or inappropriate feeling (Pfeffer 1981). Leaders' actions can quickly make illegitimate the expression of grief and shock, which so often accompany pain, ultimately stifling collective responding. For example, in one organization that we studied, the unexpected death of a visitor was never acknowledged publicly by top management despite personal requests by employees to acknowledge the tragedy. Employees who witnessed or heard about the death were demoralized by this lack of response and felt uneasy about their own grief and disconnected from the feelings of their co-workers. No organizational guidance or permission was available to them (Dutton et al. 2002b). In contrast, the former dean of Big Ten business school interrupted his well-scripted annual 'State of the School' address to alumni in order to tell the audience of the plight of three business school students who lost all their belongings in a fire early that morning. He assured the students publicly that the school would support them, expressed feelings of concern for their well-being, and in a powerful symbolic demonstration of the legitimacy of responding to pain, he took action by writing a personal check while in front of the audience. The impact of his words and actions drew the attention of many people to the students' suffering and gave momentum to widespread efforts within the business school community to offer assistance to the students (Frost 2003; Dutton et al. 2006). In this example, the dean facilitated the collective noticing, feeling and responding to pain through his use of power and his actions legitimated empathetic feelings and desirable responding for others associated with the organization.

Propagating

Propagating refers to the spreading of ideas, feelings, and information between people. Propagating is critical for compassion organizing in that it facilitates collective noticing, collective feeling, and collective responding to organizational member's pain. For instance, propagating with respect to noticing another's pain might occur as follows: A person notices that a fellow organizational member is in pain and she communicates this to some of her co-workers. This promotes collective noticing by spreading the information about what she noticed to others in her organization so that they too become of aware of the person's pain. Similarly, expressing or communicating her feelings to others facilitates the development of collective feeling. Propagating facilitates collective responding in that the spreading of ideas about how to respond to a person's pain allows individuals to see their own responses relative to others, enabling responses to be co-ordinated.

Propagating can be facilitated by established systems in the organization (e.g. e-mail networks within the organization, video conferencing facilities, town hall meetings). Following the terrorist attacks on New York in September 2001, Reuters' management adapted its systems for tracking information and clients and its virtual town hall meeting technology to communicate information and concern about the well-being of its employees (Dutton et al. 2002a). Cisco Systems' Serious Health

Notification System is another example of a propagating mechanism. It involves organizational members working together in a systematized way to quickly communicate information about suffering employees to the CEO so that a response may be initiated (Kanov et al. 2004). Leaders can also serve as propagators of information within the organization, by initiating a flow of information that is shared by others or by extending and sustaining an information flow over time. In the 1990's, *Newsweek* Chairman and editor-in-chief Richard Smith informed his staff that one of the magazine's veteran editors, Maynard Parker had been diagnosed with leukemia. He used his daily briefings to staff to update them on Parker's condition and to provide sustained communication about the situation (Dutton et al. 2002b). The dean's State of the School address described above not only served as a legitimating mechanism for shared noticing and feeling among his audience, it also served as a propagating mechanism to spread the word about suffering to a wider audience (Dutton et al. 2006).

The above discussion of legitimation and propagation reveals a recursive relationship between them. When ideas and emotions are spread about someone who is suffering it helps to legitimate the situation, which in turn can widen the scope of shared responses to the situation. What has been noticed and shared as a legitimate observation by organizational members makes it more probable that it will be spread in the system.

Co-ordinating

Co-ordinating refers to the process by which people arrange interdependent actions in ways that they believe will enable them to accomplish their goals (Weick 1979). Co-ordination is often essential to compassion organizing as it facilitates the transformation of collective noticing and feeling into collective responding to suffering. Without structures and systems in place that co-ordinate member responses, joint efforts to offer compassion may fail as good intentions dissipate for lack of means to turn efforts into tangible help. Co-ordinating can be done institutionally, as is the case with many organizations where employees are automatically notified if an organizational member suffers from a serious illness or death. Many organizations have designated policies and practices for helping members facing these circumstances. Co-ordinating can also be done spontaneously, as people improvise about how to respond and take on emergent roles. These spontaneous actions often allow resources to be directed effectively and efficiently to persons in need (Dutton et al. 2006). For example, in the school fire example, several MBA students crafted roles for themselves (e.g. resource collector, emotional buffer) that allowed the offerings of help to be more efficiently organized without overwhelming the fire victims. In the example of Maynard Parker's fight with his leukemia, several secretaries volunteered to manage blood donations, which immediately flooded in upon notification of his condition. As his care extended in time, these secretaries took on new responsibilities and altered their roles to make the adjustments necessary to ensure the organization was getting him the help that he needed.

The Value of Seeing Compassion as Organizing

Seeing compassion as organizing reveals that compassion is often a collective accomplishment in organizations. It focuses attention on how groups of people are able or unable to notice and respond to a person in pain in a co-ordinated way. Instead of attending only to the efforts and competencies of individual compassion-givers, as was the case with the first two lenses, through this lens we are able to see mechanisms of legitimating, propagating, and co-ordinating make up compassion organizing. This lens augments our understanding of compassion in work organizations in at least four ways.

Firstly, compassion as organizing makes salient the organizational interdependencies inherent in an organizational response to pain. Compassion as organizing requires interlinked observations, feelings, and actions, and these interlinked elements of compassion are directly and indirectly enabled by properties of the organization. For example, co-ordinated responses to situations of suffering may act on pooled, sequential or reciprocal interdependence (Thompson 1967). When a group of coworkers get together to decide how best to help a suffering colleague, they pool their observations, feelings and ideas for assistance to respond compassionately to the situation. This may be the most common form of interdependency enacted between a sufferer and those providing care. However, the relationship becomes reciprocal when expressions of compassion are modified in response to the

reactions of the person in pain. The sufferer thus plays a critical role by communicating his or her emotional state, while those providing care must be receptive to this communication and let it guide their response. For example, the students who lost all their possessions in a fire, as described earlier, eventually signaled that they were feeling embarrassed and overwhelmed by all of the attention and material goods they had received (Dutton et al. 2006). Compassion organizing in this case involved stopping or adjusting the flow of assistance in light of what was learned from the sufferers.

Secondly, an organizing lens highlights that compassion is a dynamic process and reveals the influence of feedback loops on the nature and direction of compassionate acts. People who share how they feel may find the level of their emotions amplified or dampened by what they learn from others. Access to one another's feelings and thoughts facilitated by organizational practices and systems will likely influence how the compassion process unfolds. A tug of concern for a sufferer may grow into a swell of empathy as coworkers learn how others feel about the situation. On the other hand, initial empathy for a sufferer may be drained when an employee reads or hears from others in the organization that they don't see the situation or the person as worthy of concern. An audience of emotionally neutral people may change into one of sympathetic concern for someone when a leader announces an emotionally painful event and frames the condition as worthy of compassion (e.g. the 'state of the school' address by the former business school dean). Sometimes these dynamics can create a process of collective compassion that takes on a life of its own, as was the case with the response of the staff at Newsweek to a colleague stricken with leukaemia. The dynamic nature of organizing alerts us to the temporality in collective compassion (episodes of helping that come to an end), of punctuation (e.g. the Dean's intervention at the state of the school address), and of nonlinearity (members enter the process at different times and in different ways and their inputs can change the direction and nature of responses).

Thirdly, an organizing lens illustrates the historical embeddedness of compassion. A shared delivery of compassion in an organization may draw on the cultural memory of how collective responses were made to suffering in the past in an organization. In the example used above of responses to a fire, the organized response to students affected by the fire provided the backdrop for a later episode of emergent compassion organizing in response to an earthquake in India that touched the lives of several students' families (Dutton et al. 2006). The effects of collective compassion may also feed forward to inform what is expected of organizational members in subsequent moments of suffering. A coworker who knows that help was previously provided when someone was in pain may expect to receive assistance when she is hurting. The institutionalized effects of collective compassion organizing may support or constrain the actions of subsequent members of the organization when facing new instances of employee pain and suffering.

Fourthly, the organizing lens illustrates the secondary effects of collective compassion. The delivery of collective compassion through existing practices and routines in organizations increases members' confidence in rising to painful challenges. It may also improve the quality and robustness of existing routines and practices that help members accomplish other goals and objectives. For example, the *Newsweek* staff not only co-ordinated their efforts to respond to their colleague's leukaemia, but several junior editors took on additional responsibilities in the newsroom, including the sensitive task of breaking the Clinton-Lewinsky scandal. The magazine subsequently won an award for their reporting of this event (Dutton et al. 2002b; Frost 2003). Whitaker, a *Newsweek* editor, observed: 'Everyone rallied around in a very impressive and moving way' (Frost 2003, p. 171). Smith noted, 'The efforts of everyone involved were aimed at putting out the best possible magazine each week' (Frost 2003, p. 171).

Research Possibilities

As with the previous lenses, this lens offers several unique research possibilities that explore different facets of compassion in work organizations:

(1) *Examining the costs and benefits of organizing for compassion*: Allocating organizing mechanisms to address the need for compassionate responses to suffering likely shifts resources (e.g. time, energy and money) from other organizational initiatives and requirements. Is this a cost or a benefit to the organization and to its members? Does the cost of institutionalizing practices (e.g. Cisco's Serious Health Notification System or a mechanism for delivering medical care to employees away from their home country) outweigh the benefits that

flow from such initiatives? What are the benefits, to individuals, to the organization of sharing feelings and of taking time and using the organization to deliver care and compassion? We might also ask what particular characteristics of legitimation, propagation and co-ordination are most critical to competence in compassion organizing?

(2) *Pressures to routinize compassion*: Non-routine or non-programmed activities in organizations tend over time to become routinized yet it seems important that compassion be tailored to the particular needs of a person in pain and to their context. Relevant questions here might be: Is customization of response a necessary condition of compassion in a work organization? Can compassion be delivered from a standardized program? Is there a tipping point beyond which institutionalized responses to compassion fail to achieve their objective? How can the personalization of compassion be preserved when it is institutionalized?

(3) *Distinguishing collective from individual compassion*: What characteristics and processes influence the value of collective compassion over individual efforts to be compassionate? Is there a 'critical mass' of effort or other variables that provide advantage to collective compassion? What are the necessary organizational characteristics that influence this outcome?

Implications

This chapter provides some nourishment for the wolf of compassion. We have explored the historical, religious, and interdisciplinary roots of compassion, and we have discussed three distinct lenses on compassion in organizations. Each of these lenses takes a particular focus in organizational studies and applies that focus to the issue of human pain, illuminating how suffering is addressed in organizational contexts. As Morgan (1997) discusses, any one theoretical perspective centre-stages certain interpretations while obscuring others. Part of the power of seeing compassion through these three different theoretical lenses is that we are able to provide a more complete view of compassion in work organizations by generating both complementary and competing insights (Allison 1971; Morgan 1997).

Comparative Perspectives on Compassion

While each lens provides its own important view of compassion, an additional power that comes from presenting compassion through three different lenses is the capacity to compare ideas across theoretical frameworks. Table 2.17.1 suggests the power of a comparative perspective by showing the key assumptions and insights of each lens alongside one another. For the sake of illustration, here we take one example from our data and look at it through each of the three lenses:

> I work in the Finance Dept at Midwest Hospital. We have a programme that allows employees to donate their unused vacation time to a fellow employee that is experiencing undue financial hardships, due to unusual circumstances such as illness, fire, accident, or death. I have witnessed an incredible amount of compassion among the staff at Midwest while administering this programme. The employees' caring and willingness to give up their benefits to help a co-worker in need is extraordinary. Time and again Midwest's staff recognizes a need, takes the steps to get the cause approved and campaigns to get others to help. It's this genuine caring for those we work with that makes me glad I work at Midwest. I have also witnessed the profound impact this program has on the co-worker receiving their help. It's great! (Employee, Midwest Hospital).

In looking across the three lenses on compassion, we see different aspects of this story as important and informative. For example, if we were to understand compassion as interpersonal work, we could pay attention to the strands of evidence from relational practice to understand the work that people in this context are doing that is seen as compassion (e.g. 'time and again Midwest's staff recognizes a need, takes the steps to get the cause approved, and campaigns to get others to help'). If we were to understand compassion as narrative, we could also look at how the person telling this story constructs others' identities through suggesting that part of the identity of the organization is its caring competency (e.g. '… makes me glad I work at Midwest'). And finally, if we were to understand compassion as organizing, we could attend to the vacation donation programme, which provides a set of routines for institutionalizing compassion in such a way that it becomes legitimated and easily co-ordinated within the organization.

Compassion as a Window into Organization Studies

Not only is there value in considering the differences highlighted by the three lenses, but their commonalities

also have important implications for organization studies. At the core of each lens lies the assumption that compassion is worthwhile in its own right. In this chapter, we have argued that compassion is central to and expressive of the very essence of being human. As such, our examination of compassion draws our attention to the human side of organizations and organizing, one that is often overlooked in traditional organization studies. None of the lenses has focused on outcomes such as organizational performance or efficiency, for while these are often the concern of mainstream organizational research, they all too often trump or overshadow the humanity of organizational life. Along with Cameron and colleagues (Cameron 2003; Cameron et al. 2003), we argue that although compassion may contribute to high performance and financial success, such outcomes are peripheral to the meaning and impact of compassion. Compassion connects us with the aliveness of organizational life, putting us in touch with the human condition and reminding us that work organizations are fundamentally human institutions capable of caring for, healing, and enlivening people (Frost et al. 2000; Cameron et al. 2003). Organizations that adopt compassionate practices as strategic means to an end may weaken or destroy the integrity of such practices. As such, compassion is currently in a precarious position as it sits on the fringe of organization studies. If we attempt to understand the nature and significance of compassion in work organizations in ways typical of our field (e.g. aiming to identify the competitive edge associated with compassion or questioning the value of compassion in terms of the bottom line) we will likely end up with only a shell of a construct that is a far cry from the rich and timeless images of compassion throughout history. If instead we recognize that the study of phenomena like compassion begs for a different approach to organizational inquiry – one that emphasizes human experience and social life – then we will allow ourselves to enter into a dimension of organizational life that is often invisible and unappreciated (Sandelands 2003).

A Critical Lens on Compassion

While the lenses we have used in this chapter highlight the good that can come from individual and collective acts of compassion in organizations and the generative power of compassion narratives, we also see value in bringing more critical perspectives to the study of compassion. Doing so raises different sets of questions that merit serious attention.

For example, looking critically at compassion as interpersonal work brings to the forefront the possibilities of 'compassion work' and 'compassion labour'. In parallel with Hochschild's (1983) notion of 'emotion work', compassion work can be seen as the effort put into 'feeling compassionate' and 'doing compassion' in day-to-day living. This can be demanding and difficult for individuals who feel they 'ought' to engage in emotions and perform actions that may be at odds with how they are actually feeling towards a given person, project, or priority. Similarly, organizational researchers' interest in emotional labour and bounded emotionality (e.g. Mumby and Putnam 1992; Ashforth and Humphrey 1993; Martin et al. 1998; Grandey 2003) leads us to consider the notion of 'compassion labour', as the organizational appropriation of compassion work. This is common in jobs in which being compassionate is part of the role requirement, such as counsellors, social workers, physicians, and nurses, where incumbents are paid, in part, to notice, feel and respond compassionately to those in pain. It is likely that these individuals experience some of the costs of compassion as a form of labour, especially if, as is often the case, they work in organizations that lack compassion for their own employees. Those who do not adequately 'do compassion' may suffer reproof from their managers, while those who do may experience 'compassion burnout'. Compassion burnout has been discussed as the physical, mental, and emotional exhaustion that comes from spending too much time engaged in the work of providing care and compassion to others, and this form of burnout is all too commonly found in the helping professions (Figley 1995; Meyerson 1998; Rainer 2000; Collins and Long 2003). In addition to burnout, because it often means interacting directly with toxins, compassion workers can be toxin handlers of sorts, with attendant risks to their emotional and physical health (Frost 2003). These aspects of compassion in organizations are worthy of more investigation and attention.

Another critical lens demands an appreciation of the role of power in compassion as interpersonal work. Anyone may feel compassion for another, but not all individuals are equally free to engage in compassionate behaviour; nor is compassion always wanted from those who wish to give it. For example,

we might expect to see more 'upward' (enacted from a junior employee toward a senior one) than 'downward' compassion in organizations, as those in junior positions are more attentive to the conditions of those above them (Fiske and Depret 1996). Power plays a role in the enactment of compassion, and those at lower levels may find it required 'deference work' to offer help to someone senior. At the same time, research suggests that people higher up in the hierarchy are less attentive to the conditions of those below them, making it less likely that senior managers will even notice pain among lower level employees (Fiske and Depret 1996). Alternatively, it could be argued that employees at higher levels will be less comfortable revealing their pain to those junior to themselves. Whichever of these dynamics plays out in a given organization or situation, we argue that any examination of compassion at work must acknowledge the role of power in its enactment.

Looking at compassion as interpersonal work also raises questions about the meanings and displays of compassion in other than North American contexts. Since there is considerable cross-cultural variation in the meaning and expression of emotions such as grief and despair (Armon-Jones 1986; Heelas 1996), we should also expect differences in the extent to which and ways in which compassion is expressed in, for example, North American, European, and Asian societies. While compassion may be regarded as innate and instinctual (Keltner 2004), its form and its appropriateness and acceptability will vary with the context in which it is enacted. Indeed, seen as a component of cultural life, successfully carrying out the work of compassion is contingent upon having learned to interpret suffering and a response to that suffering according to the values, norms, and expectations of the culture in which one is participating.

With its roots in social constructionism and connections to critical perspectives, the narrative lens raises particularly pertinent questions about compassion stories as strategic products of self-interested actors. One aspect of this critical perspective concerns attention to whose voices are heard in narratives of compassion, and whose are marginalized or silenced. Returning to the story about the vacation donation program, we see, on one hand, an organization in which compassionate responding is enabled by a powerful institutional mechanism. Endorsed by employees, it leads to compassionate acts that leave the narrator enthusing about his colleagues and workplace. At the same time, it raises questions about what is not told: Are there negative consequences for members who choose not to donate to the programme? What happens to employees who do not want to be helped – are they treated differently because they refuse to 'get with the programme'? Moreover, no attention is drawn in this story to the fact that the compassionate programme costs the organization little beyond expenses to administer. Has the compassion of many members of the organization been co-opted by the organization through this distribution of costs? Every narrative offers only a partial story; applying a critical lens to narratives of compassion helps reveal those storylines that may not be immediately visible.

Another set of critical issues relating to narratives as strategic resources concerns the relationship between narrator and narrative and what this reveals about the story that is told. The vacation donation story is also revealing about the narrator himself and his relationship to the compassionate acts he describes. From a critical perspective, we might ask: Why does he tell this particular story? Is it to enhance his standing as a compassionate person? Is he a champion of a caring workplace and the story helps promote the practices that sustain this care? Does he seek to highlight the importance of his role at Midwest? He is, after all, the administrator of the programme he so strongly endorses. Does the story celebrate a truly compassionate workplace, or is it a vehicle to reinforce organizational rhetoric about Midwest as a place to work or that might help the organization to secure external resources for its goals? The narrative taken at face value gives a sense of a caring organization in which employees share in the commitment to help suffering colleagues. By critically examining the content, structure, and the narrative position of the story, however, we widen the lens of inquiry about the organization, its members, and the compassionate acts described.

A critical perspective is also valuable to the lens of compassion as organizing, or compassion as a collective accomplishment. Having highlighted the processes that produce compassion at the collective level, we should also ask: When and where are these processes not likely to be found in an organization? What are their costs to an organization? Who are the beneficiaries of compassion organizing and who is overlooked? What happens when these processes

become merely instrumental means to non-compassionate ends? While compassion as organizing may occur in any kind of organization, it may be especially likely in high performing organizations, where adequate slack in the system allows room for collective responses to pain. Would we expect to find compassion in an organization struggling to stay afloat during a major financial crisis? As is often the case after natural disasters (Sanchez et al. 1995), some of the companies showing greatest compassion during the 9/11 crisis were unable to maintain this stance in the hardship of the months that followed (SHRM/eePulse 2002). Perhaps only certain organizations can 'afford' compassion at certain points in time. Similarly, compassion may be more common in jobs that endow incumbents with sufficient autonomy to be able to help a co-worker who is overloaded. While compassion is still possible in highly controlled and standardized or 'McDonaldized' (Ritzer 1998) jobs, we should acknowledge that it is less likely to proliferate where workers have minimal latitude over what they do and how they do it (cf. Fineman 2003; this volume).

It is also important to note that even in places where collective compassion is widely expressed, there will still be individuals who continue to suffer, unaided by those around them. Whether their suffering is ignored or simply goes unnoticed, whether they belong to a group that is marginalized in the organization, or whether the oversight is more circumstantial, these individuals may feel envious and resentful about the attention that their co-workers receive, adding to their pain. Compassion can thus be divisive in organizations, with the potential to be seen as favouritism by those going without. This may be endemic to a company's compassion organizing processes, but is especially likely, for example, in a restructuring or downsizing situation where many suffering individuals do not receive equally compassionate treatment.

Finally, we should be aware that compassion organizing can be motivated less by a desire to alleviate suffering than by instrumental goals, such as good public relations or increased productivity. While a leader may engage in a variety of actions that legitimate and help propagate compassionate responses, these actions may be driven by his or her wish to appear to be a caring person, for the hope of winning a 'best employer' award, or by a belief that employees will be more efficient and effective if organizational systems and policies are in place to support them in times of need. The genuine expression of suffering and response to it are likely to be inhibited or abused in organizations in which compassion organizing is co-ordinated to accomplish only instrumental goals (Fineman 2003; this volume). Although the focus of this chapter has been appreciative, examining compassion through a critical lens is one key to a fuller understanding of the phenomenon in organizations.

Conclusions

The study of compassion in work organizations has a short history, but a promising future. In this chapter we have sought to illuminate the possibilities that different lenses in organizational studies create for the study of compassion. We have demonstrated that the use of these lenses will help identify fruitful topics for future research and can lead to the creation of a systematic body of knowledge about compassion in organizations. We have also raised possibilities from the application of critical lenses on compassion that provide additional invitations to inquiry for those who are interested in studying compassion in organizations. Something perhaps less obvious, but equally important, is that we have tried throughout the chapter to evoke the emotional tone of compassion and to underscore that its role is to make a contribution of healing to those who are suffering. We attempt to treat compassion as a gift, not a commodity (Hyde 1979).

His holiness the 14th Dalai Lama says in his lecture 'Living the Compassionate Life' (Shambhala Sun Online 2004), that, 'Whether people are beautiful or plain, friendly or cruel, ultimately they are human beings, just like oneself. Like oneself, they want happiness and do not want suffering.' Our focus on compassion in organizations grows from this fundamental observation about our common humanity. Within every organizational system are human beings, like ourselves, who want happiness and who do not want suffering – human beings who suffer and who respond to one another's suffering with compassion. An emphasis on understanding compassion in organizations helps us see the proactive and responsive actions that coworkers take toward one another, and, however small those actions may be, their true significance in human terms. Ultimately, an emphasis on compassion in organizations is highly consequential, as the Dalai Lama writes in the same lecture:

I believe that at every level of society – familial, national and international – the key to a happier and more successful world is the growth of compassion. We do not need to become religious, nor do we need to believe in a particular ideology. All that is necessary is for each of us to develop our good human qualities. I believe that the cultivation of individual happiness can contribute in a profound and effective way to the overall improvement of the entire human community.

A focus on compassion in organizations shows us the potential for cultivating more positive and healthy organizations. Like the Dalai Lama, we believe an emphasis on compassion may improve the condition of the human community at large.

With such a vision for the potential of studying compassion in organizations, we look forward with enthusiasm to the time, a few years hence, when perhaps this chapter will be revised for a new edition of the *Handbook of Organization Studies* and the depth and range of understanding of compassion in organizations will be significantly greater than it is today. We believe that such a future will serve to build the field of organizational studies and will contribute to the experience of more healthy organizations and organizational members. As we expand our knowledge of organizations to encompass topics like compassion, and also thriving, resilience, vitality and social life, then the wolf of compassion, hope and generosity is truly well fed.

Note

1. Peter Frost had just completed the first draft of this chapter when he was diagnosed with the melanoma cancer that soon after took his life. The chapter, which would never have come into being without him, is dedicated to Peter, our wonderful colleague and friend.

Acknowledgements

We thank Tom Lawrence, Jean Bartunek, Steve Fineman, Joyce Fletcher, and Bill Kahn for their helpful comments on an earlier draft of this chapter.

References

Acker, J. (1990) 'Hierarchies, jobs, bodies: A theory of gendered organizations', *Gender & Society*, 4: 139–58.

Albert, S. and Whetton, D. A. (1985) 'Organizational identity', in L.L. Cummings and B.M. Staw (eds), *Research in Organizational Behaviour*, 7. Greenwich, CT: JAI Press. pp. 263–95.

Alfred, K.G., Mallozi, J.S., Matsui, F. and Raja, C.P. (1997) 'The influence of anger and compassion on negotiation performance', *Organizational Behaviour and Human Decision Performance*, 3: 175–87.

Allison, G.T. (1971) *Essence of Decision: Explaining the Cuban Missile Crisis.* Boston: Little and Brown.

Aristotle (1939) *The Art of Rhetoric,* J.H. Freese (trans.), Cambridge, MA: Harvard University Press.

Armon-Jones, C. (1986) 'The thesis of constructionism', in R. Harré (ed.), *The Social Construction of Emotions,* Oxford: Basil Blackwell. pp. 32–56.

Armstrong, K. (1994) *A History of God: The 4,000-Year Quest of Judaism, Christianity, and Islam,* New York: Ballantine Books.

Ashforth B.E. and Humphrey, R.H.(1993) 'Emotional labor in service roles: The influence of identity', *Academy of Management Review,* 18: 88–115.

Ashforth, B.E. and Humphrey, R.H. (1995) 'Emotion in the workplace: A reappraisal', *Human Relations,* 48: 97–125.

Barber, B. (1976) 'Compassion in medicine: Toward new definitions and new institutions', *New England Journal of Medicine,* 295: 939–43.

Batson, C.D. (1991) *The Altruism Question: Toward a Social Psychological Answer.* Hillsdale, NJ: Lawrence Erlbaum Associates.

Batson, C.D. (1994) 'Why act for the public good? Four answers', *Personality & Social Psychology Bulletin: Special Issue: The self and the collective,* 20: 603–10.

Benner, P.A., Tanner, C. and Chesla, C. (1996) *Expertise in Nursing Practice: Care, Clinical Judgement, and Ethics.* New York: Springer.

Blum, L. (1980) 'Compassion', in A.O. Rorty (ed.), *Explaining Emotions.* Berkeley, CA: University of California Press. pp. 507–17.

Boje, D.M. (1991) 'The storytelling organization: a study of story performance in an office-supply firm', *Administrative Science Quarterly,* 36: 106–26.

Brief, A.P. and Motowidlo, S.J. (1986) 'Prosocial organizational behaviours', *Academy of Management Review,* 11: 710–25.

Brody, H. (1992) *The Healer's Power.* New Haven, CT: Yale University Press.

Bruner, J.S. (1986) *Actual Minds, Possible Worlds.* Cambridge, MA: Harvard University Press.

Cameron, K.S. (1998) 'Strategic organizational downsizing: An extreme case', in B. Staw and L.L. Cummings (eds), *Research in Organizational Behaviour,* 20. Greenwich, CT: JAI Press. pp. 185–229.

Cameron, K.S. (2003) 'Organizational virtuousness and performance', in K. Cameron, J. Dutton and R. Quinn (eds), *Positive Organizational Scholarship.* San Francisco: Berrett-Koehler. pp. 48–65.

Cameron, K.S. and Caza, A. (2004) 'Contributions to the discipline of positive organizational scholarship', *American Behavioural Scientist,* 47: 731–9.

Cameron, K.S., Bright, D. and Caza, A. (2003a) 'Exploring the relationships between organizational virtuousness and performance', *American Behavioural Scientist: A Special Issue on Positive Organizational Scholarship,* 47: 766–90.

Cameron, K.S., Dutton, J.E. and Quinn, R. (2003b) *Positive Organizational Scholarship.* San Francisco: Berrett-Koehler.

Cameron, K.S., Freeman, S.J. and Mishra, A.K. (1993) 'Downsizing and redesigning organizations', in G.P. Huber and W.H. Glick (eds), Organizational Change and Redesign. New York: Oxford University Press. pp. 19–65.

Candib, L. (1995) *Medicine and the Family.* New York: Basic Books.

Cassell, E.J. (2002) 'Compassion', in C.R. Snyder and S.J. Lopez (eds), *Handbook of Positive Psychology.* London: Oxford University Press. pp. 434–45.

Clark, C. (1997) *Misery and Company: Sympathy in Everyday Life.* Chicago: The University of Chicago Press.

Collins, S. and Long, A. (2003) 'Too tired to care? The psychological effects of working with trauma', *Journal of Psychiatric & Mental Health Nursing,* 10: 17–27.

Connelly, F.M. and Clandinin, D.J. (1990) 'Stories of experience and narrative inquiry', *Educational Researcher,* 19: 2–14.

Czarniawska, B. (1998) *A Narrative Approach to Organization Studies.* Thousand Oaks, CA: Sage.

Dalai Lama (1995) *The Power of Compassion.* London: Thorsons.

Dalai Lama (2001) *Living the Compassionate Life.* Available online at: http://www.shambhalasun.com/revolving_themes/HHDL/compassion.htm, accessed 19 December 2005.

Davidson, R. (2002) Toward a biology of positive affect and compassion, in R. J. Davidson and A. Harrington (eds), *Visions of Compassion: Western Scientists and Tibetan Buddhists Examine Human Nature.* Oxford, NY: Oxford University Press. pp. 107–30.

Davidson, R.J. (2003) 'The neuroscience of emotion', in D. Goleman (ed.), *Destructive Emotions: How Can we Overcome Them? A Scientific Dialogue with the Dalai Lama.* New York: Bantam Books. pp. 179–205.

Davis, M.H. (1983) 'Measuring individual difference in empathy: Evidence for a multidimensional approach', *Journal of Personality & Social Psychology,* 44: 113–26.

Dougherty, C. J. and Purtillo, R. (1995) 'Physician's duty of compassion', *Cambridge Quarterly of Healthcare Ethics,* 4: 426–33.

Dutton, J.E. (2003) 'Breathing life into organizational studies', *Journal of Management Inquiry,* 12: 1–19.

Dutton, J.E., Dukerich, J.E. and Harquail, C.V. (1994) 'Organizational images and member identification', *Administrative Science Quarterly,* 39: 239–62.

Dutton, J.E., Lilius, J.M. and Kanov, J. (in press) 'The transformative potential of compassion at work', to appear in D. Cooperrider, R. Fry and S. Pederit (eds), *New Designs for Transformative Cooperation*. Palo Alto, CA: Stanford University Press.

Dutton, J.E., Quinn, R. and Pasick, R. (2002a) *The Heart of Reuters (A) and (B)*. Ann Arbor, MI: Center for Positive Organizational Scholarship, University of Michigan Business School.

Dutton, J.E., Worline, M.C., Frost, P.J. and Lilius, J.M. (2006) 'Explaining compassion organizing.' *Administrative Science Quarterly*, forthcoming.

Dutton, J., Frost, P., Worline, M., Lilius, J. and Kanov, J. (2002b) 'Leading in times of trauma', *Harvard Business Review*, Jan, 54–61.

Feldman, M.S. and Pentland, B. T. (2003) 'Reconceptualizing organizational routines as a source of flexibility and change', *Administrative Science Quarterly*, 48: 94–118.

Figley, C.R. (1995) 'Compassion fatigue: Toward a new understanding of the costs of caring', in B.H. Stamm (ed.), *Secondary Traumatic Stress: Self-care Issues for Clinicians, Researchers, and Eeducators*. Baltimore, MD: Sidran Press. pp. 3–28.

Fineman, S. (1993) *Emotion in Organizations*, first edition. London: Sage.

Fineman, S. (1996) Emotion and organizing, in C. Hardy, S. Clegg and W. Nord (eds), *Handbook of Organization Studies*. London: Sage. pp. 543–64.

Fineman, S. (2000) *Emotion in Organizations*, second edition. London: Sage.

Fineman, S. (2003) *Understanding Emotion in Organizations*. London: Sage.

Fineman, S. and Sturdy, A. (1999) 'The emotions of control: A qualitative exploration of environmental control', *Human Relations*, 52: 631–63.

Fiske, S.T. and Depret, E. (1996) 'Control, interdependence and power: Understanding social cognition in its social context', in W, Stroebe and N. Hewstone (eds), *European Review of Social Psychology*. pp. 31–61.

Fletcher, J.K. (1998) 'Relational practice: A feminist reconstruction of work', *Journal of Management Inquiry*, 7: 163–87.

Fletcher, J.K. (1999) *Disappearing Acts: Gender, Power and Relational Practice at Work*. Cambridge, MA: MIT Press.

Follett, M.P. (1918) *The New State*. New York: Longman's Green.

Frost, P.J. (1999) 'Why compassion counts!', *Journal of Management Inquiry*, 8: 127–33.

Frost, P.J. (2003) *Toxic Emotions at Work: How Compassionate Managers Handle Pain and Conflict*. Boston, MA: Harvard Business School Press.

Frost, P.J., Dutton, J.E., Worline, M.C. and Wilson, A. (2000) 'Narratives of compassion in organizations, in S. Fineman (ed.), *Emotion in Organizations*. Thousand Oaks, CA: Sage Publications, pp. 25–45.

Gergen, K.J. and Gergen, M.M. (1998) 'Narrative and the self as relationship, in L. Berkowitz (ed.), *Advances in Experimental Social Psychology*, 21. New York: Academic. pp. 17–56.

Gioia, D.A., Schultz, M and Corley, KG. (2000) 'Organizational identity, image, and adaptive instability', *Academy of Management Review*, 25: 63–82.

Grandey, A.A. (2003) 'When "The show must go on": Surface acting and deep acting as determinants of emotional exhaustion and peer-rated service delivery', *Academy of Management Journal*, 46: 86–96.

Greene, J.D., Sommerville, R., Nystrom, L.E., Darley, J.M. and Cohen, J.D. (2001) 'An fMRI investigation of emotional engagement in moral judgement', *Science*, 293: 2105–08.

Gupta, V.B. (2000) 'Social justice in Hindu tradition', *The Record*, 10 Feb. Bergen, NY: Bergen Record Corporation. Consolidation for Social Awareness and Responsibility. Available online at: http://www3.sympatico.ca/truegrowth/society5.html, accessed 19 August 2004.

Hallowell, E.M. (1999) 'The human moment at work', *Harvard Business Review*, 77: 58–66.

Harrington, A. (2002) 'Is compassion an emotion? A crosscultural exploration of mental typologies', in R.J. Davidson and A. Harrington (eds), *Visions of Compassion: Western Scientists and Tibetan Buddhists Examine Human Nature*. Oxford, NY: Oxford University Press. pp. 18–30.

Heath, C. and Sitkin, S.B. (2001) 'Big-B versus Big-O: What is organizational about organizational behaviour?', *Journal of Organizational Behaviour*, 22: 43–58.

Heelas, P. (1996) 'Emotion talk across cultures', in R. Harré and W.G. Parrott (eds), *The Emotions: Social, Cultural, and Biological Dimensions*. Thousand Oaks, CA: Sage. pp. 171–199.

Heifetz, R.A. (1994) *Leadership Without Easy Answers*. Cambridge, MA: Belknap Press of Harvard University Press.

Herzberg, F. (1966) *Work and the Nature of Man*. Cleveland, OH: World.

Himmelfarb, G. (2001) 'The idea of compassion: The British vs. the French enlightenment', *Public Interest*, 145: 3–24.

Hochschild, A.R. (1983) *The Managed Heart: Commercialization of Human Feeling*. Berkeley, CA: University of California Press.

Hochschild, A.R. (1997) *The Time Bind: When Work Becomes Home and Home Becomes Work*. New York: Metropolitan Books.

House, J.S. (1981) *Work Stress and Social Support*. Reading, MA: Addison Wesley.

Hyde, L. (1979) *The Gift: Imagination and the Erotic Life of Property*. New York: Vintage Books.

Jacques, R. (1993) 'Untheorized dimensions of caring work: Caring as structural practice and caring as a way of seeing', *Nursing Administration Quarterly*, 17: 1–10.

Josselson, R. (1992) *The Space Between Us: Exploring the Dimensions of Human Relationships*. San Francisco: Jossey-Bass.

Kahn, W.A. (1993) 'Caring for the caregivers: Patterns of organizational caregiving', *Administrative Science Quarterly*, 38: 539–63.

Kahn, W.A. (1998) 'Relational systems at work', in B.M. Staw and L.L. Cummings (eds), *Research in Organizational Behaviour*, 20. Greenwich, CT: JAI Press. pp. 39–76.

Kahn, W.A. (2001) 'Holding environments at work', *Journal of Applied Behavioural Science*, 37: 260–79.

Kanov, J., Maitlis, S., Worline, M.C., Dutton, J.E., Frost, P.J. and Lilius, J. (2004) 'Compassion in organizational life', *American Behavioural Scientist*, 47: 808–27.

Kanter, R.M. (1977) *Men and Women of the Corporation*. New York: Anchor Press.

Katz, D. and Kahn, R. (1978) *The Social Psychology of Organizations*. New York: Wiley.

Keltner, D. (2004) 'The compassion instinct', *Greater Good*, 1: 6–10. Availablobe online at: http://peacecenter.berkeley.edu, accessed 2 January 2005.

Kotter, J. (2002) *The Heart of Change: Real Life Stories of How People Change their Organizations*. Boston, MA: Harvard Business School Press.

Kruger, P. (1997) 'Make smarter mistakes', *Fast Company*, 11 October: 152.

Likert, R. (1967) The Human Organization: Its Management and Value. New York: McGraw Hill.

Lilius, J.M., Worline, M.C., Dutton, J.E., Kanov, J.M., Frost, P.J. and Maitlis, S. (2004) 'Exploring the contours of compassion at work', paper under review.

Maitlis, S. (2006) 'Meeting emotion: The role of emotion in top management team politics', working paper, University of British Columbia.

Maitlis, S. and Ozcelik, H. (2004) 'Toxic decision processes: A study of emotion and organizational decision making', *Organization Science*, 15: 375–93.

Martin, J., Feldman, M. Hatch, M.J. and Sitkin, S.B. (1983) 'The uniqueness paradox in organizational stories', *Administrative Science Quarterly*, 28: 438–53.

Martin, J., Knopoff, K. and Beckman, C. (1998) 'An alternative to bureaucratic impersonality and emotional labor: Bounded emotionality at The Body Shop', *Administrative Science Quarterly*, 43: 429–69.

Mastenbroek, W. (2000) 'Behaviour in organizations as emotion management: Past and present', in N.M. Ashkenasy, C.E.J. Hartel, and W.J. Zerbe (eds), *Emotions in the Workplace: Theory, Research, and Practice*. Westport, CT: Quorum. pp. 60–74.

Mayo, E. (1946) *The Human Problems of an Industrial Civilization*. Boston: Harvard University.

McAdams, D.P. (1993) *The Stories We Live by: Personal Myths and the Making of the Self*. New York: W. Morrow.

McGregor, D. (1960) *The Human Side of Enterprise*. New York: McGraw-Hill.

Mead, G.H. (1962) *Mind, Self, and Society: From the Standpoint of a Social Behaviourist*. Chicago: The University of Chicago Press.

Meyerson, D. (1998) 'Feeling stressed and burned out: A feminist reading and re-visioning of stress-based emotions within medicine and organization science', *Organization Science*, 9: 103–18.

Miller, J.P. and Stiver, I.P. (1997) *The Healing Connection*. Boston: Beacon Press.

Morgan, G. (1997) *Images of Organization*. Thousand Oaks, CA: Sage.

Mumby, D.K. (1987) 'The political function of narrative in organizations', *Communication Monographs*, 54: 115–27.

Mumby, D.K. (1988) *Communication and Power in Organizations: Discourse, Ideology, and Domination*. Norwood, NJ: Ablex.

Mumby, D. and Putnam, L. (1992) 'The politics of emotion: A feminist reading of bounded rationality', *Academy of Management Review.* 17: 465–85.

Nitschke, J.B. (2001) 'Neural circuitry of positive emotion: An fMRI study of mothers viewing pictures of their infants', paper session presented at the 2001 Positive Psychology Summer Institute, Sea Ranch, CA.

Noddings, N. (1984) *Caring: A Feminine Approach to Ethics and Moral Education*. Berkeley, CA: University of California Press.

Nouwen, H.J.M., McNeil, D.P. and Morrison, D.A. (1983) *Compassion: A Reflection on the Christian Life*. New York: Doubleday.

Nussbaum, M.C. (1996) 'Compassion: The basic social emotion', *Social Philosophy and Policy*, 13: 27–58.

Nussbaum, M.C. (2001) *Upheavals of Thought: The Intelligence of Emotions*. Cambridge: Cambridge University Press.

O'Connor, E.S. (1998) 'The plot thickens: Past developments and future possibilities for narrative studies of organizations', paper presented at SCANCOR (Samples of the Future: A Conference on Organizations Research), Stanford, CA.

Pearson, C., Andersson, L. and Wegner, J.W. (2001) 'When workers flout convention: A study of workplace incivility', *Human Relations*, 54: 1387–419.

Pfeffer, J. (1981) 'Management as symbolic action: The creation and maintenance of organizational paradigms', in L.L. Cummings and B.M. Staw (eds), *Advances in Organizational Behaviour*, 3. Greenwich, CT: JAI Press. pp. 1–52.

Pfeffer, J. and Davis-Blake, A. (1987) 'The effect of the proportion of women on salaries: The case of college administrators', *Administrative Science Quarterly*, 32: 1–24.

Podsakoff, P.M., MacKenzie, S.B., Paine, J.B. and Bachrach, D.G. (2000) 'Organizational citizenship behaviours: A critical review of the theoretical and empirical literature and suggestions for future research', *Journal of Management*, 26: 513–63.

Post, S.G. (2003) *Unlimited Love, Altruism, Compassion and Service*. Philadelphia, PA: Templeton Foundation Press.

Rafaeli, A. and Worline, M.C. (2001) *Individual Emotion in Work Organizations*. Social Science Information, 40: 95–123.

Rainer, J.P. (2000) 'Compassion fatigue: When caregiving begins to hurt, in L.Vandecreek and T. Jackson (eds), *Clinical Practice: A Source Book*, 18. Sarasota, FL: Professional Resource Press. pp. 441–53.

Reich, W.T. (1989) ,Speaking of suffering: A moral account of compassion', *Soundings*, 72: 83–108.

Reissman, C.K. (1993) *Narrative Analysis*. Newbury Park, CA: Sage Publications.

Rice, R.W., Frone, M.R. and McFarlin, D.B. (1992) 'Work-nonwork conflict and the perceived quality of life', *Journal of Organizational Behaviour*, 13: 155–68.

Rilling, J.K., Gutman, D.A., Zeh, T.R., Pagnoni, G., Berns, G.S. and Kilts, C.D. (2002) 'A neural basis for social cooperation', *Neuron*, 35: 395–405.

Ritzer, G. (1998) *The McDonaldization Thesis*. London: Sage.

Rousseau, J.J. (1979) *Emile*, in A. Bloom (trans.). New York: Basic Books.

Salovey, P. and Mayer, J.D. (1990) 'Emotional intelligence', *Imagination, Cognition, and Personality*, 9: 185–211.

Sanchez, J.I., Korbin, W.P. and Viscarra, D.M. (1995) 'Corporate support in the aftermath of natural disasters: Effects on employee strains', *Academy of Management Journal*, 38: 504–21.

Sandelands, L. (2003) *Thinking About Social Life*. Lanham, MD: University Press of America.

Schegloff, E.A. (1997) 'Narrative analysis thirty years later', *Journal of Narrative and Life History*, 7: 97–106.

Schein, E.H. (1996) 'Culture: The missing concept in organization studies', *Administrative Science Quarterly*, 41: 229–40.

Schopenhauer, A. (1995) *On the Basis of Morality*, in E.F.J. Payne (trans.). Providence and Oxford: Berghahn Books.

Sears, D. (1998) *Compassion for Humanity in the Jewish Tradition*. New Jersey: Jason Aronson.

Seligman, M.E.P. and Csikszentmihalyi, M. (2000) 'Positive psychology: An introduction', *American Psychologist*, 55: 51–83.

Shott, S. (1979) 'Emotion and social life: Symbolic interactionist analysis', *American Journal of Sociology*, 84: 1317–34.

SHRM/eePulse. (2002) *SHRM/eePulse Survey on the HR Implications of the Attack on America: One Year Later*. Alexandria, VA: Society for Human Resource Management. Available online at: http://www.shrm.org, accessed 21 July 2004.

Smith, A. (1976) *The Theory of Moral Sentiments*, D.D. Raphael and A.L. Macfie (eds). Oxford: Clarendon Press.

Smith. B.H. (1981) 'Narrative versions, narrative theories', in I. Konigsberg (ed.), *American Criticism in the Postructural Age*. Ann Arbor, MI: University of Michigan Press. pp. 162–86.

Solomon, R.C. (1998) 'The moral psychology of business: Care and compassion in the corporation', *Business Ethics Quarterly*, 8: 515–33.

Somers, M.R. (1994) 'The narrative constitution of identity: A relational and network approach', *Theory and Society*, 23: 605–49.

Suchman, M. (1995) 'Managing legitimacy: Strategic and institutional approaches', *Academy of Management Review*, 20: 571–610.

Taylor, F.W. (1911) *The Principles of Scientific Management*. New York: Harper & Brothers.

Tepper, B.J. (2000) 'Consequences of abusive supervision', *Academy of Management Journal*, 42: 178–90.

Thompson, J.D. (1967) *Organizations in Action: Social Science Bases of Administrative Theory*. New York: McGraw-Hill.

von Dietze, E. and Orb, A. (2000) 'Compassionate care: A moral dimension of nursing', *Nursing Inquiry*, 7: 166–74.

Walsh, J.P., Weber, K. and Margolis, J.D. (2003) 'Social issues and management: Our lost cause found', *Journal of Management*, 29: 859–81.

Weick, K.E. (1979) *The Social Psychology of Organizing*, second edition. Reading, MA: Addison Wesley.

Weick, K.E. (1995) *Sensemaking in Organizations*. Thousand Oaks, CA: Sage Publications.

Whetten, D. and Godfrey, P. (1998) *Identity in Organizations: Building Theory Through Conversations*. Thousand Oaks, CA: Sage Publications.

White, M. and Epston, D. (1990) *Narrative Means to Therapeutic Ends*. New York: Norton.

Whitehead, T. N. (1938). The industrial worker. Cambridge, MA: Harvard University Press.

Williams, M. and Dutton, J.E. (1999) 'Corrosive political climates: The heavy toll of negative political behaviour in organizations', in R.E. Quinn, R.M. O'Neill and L. St. Clair (eds), The Pressing Problems of Modern Organizations: Transforming the Agenda for Research and Practice. New York: American Management Association. pp. 3–30.

Winnicott, D.W. (1960) 'The theory of the parent-infant relationship', *International Journal of Psychoanalysis*, 41: 585–95.

Worline, M.C., Dutton, J.E., Frost, P.J., Kanov, J.M., Lilius, J.M. and Maitlis, S. (2004) 'Creating fertile soil: The organizing dynamics of resilience', paper under review .

Wuthnow, R. (1991) *Acts of Compassion: Caring for Others and Helping Ourselves*. Princeton, NJ: Princeton University Press.

Index

social networks, 779
  research, 293
social order, naturalization, 261
social reality, meta-theoretical debate, 40
social relationships, in economic
    transactions, 119–20
social responsibility, discourses of, 557
social science
  philosophy of see philosophy, of social sciences
  as public philosophy, 373
social skills, 218
social support networks, 547
social systems, equilibrating, 26
social welfare, implications of SCP paradigm, 131
socialist feminist theory, 301–6
  dual-systems theory, 304
  and gendering of organizing, 306–8
  on gendering, 302–3
  research methods, 305–6
  unified-systems theory, 304
society, as organism, 409
sociograms, 776
sociology, 152–3
  of knowledge, 418–19
  meso thinking, 153
  micro–macro distinction, 152–3
  of practice, 218–19
  view of globalization, 653–4
socio-technical thinking, 389–90
Socrates, 371
sovereignty, end of, 762–4
space, idea, 709
specialists, 81
specialization, 579
  flexible, 32
specification processes, 522–3
speech, 702
speech act theory, 312, 549, 550
'spin', 768
spirituality, discourses of, 557
stability
  change vs, 561
  dynamic, 829
standardization, 579
standards, 410
standpoint theory, 304
stereotyping, 490–2
stock price, 'managing', 587–8
stockholders, as monitor of monitors, 113
stories, 553–4, 851
  see also narrative(s)
storytelling, 554–5
strange attractor, 169
strategic alliances, 548, 666, 787
  cheating in, 139–40
  and co-operation, 136–40
    incentives to co-operate, 137–9

strategic alliances, cont.
  innovation and, 787
  institutional context, 138–9
  types, 136–7
strategic articulation, integration by, 606, 609–10, 614
strategic choice theory, 815–16
strategic contingencies theory, 472, 757, 818
strategic essentialism, 319
strategic groups, 95, 129–30
strategic management, 579–80, 709
  fallacies, 481
  role of strategist, 580–1
  and SCP paradigm, 128–30
strategic uncertainty, management in alliances, 138
strategizing, 481–2
strategy
  complexity science perspective, 203
  definition, 481
  formulation, 504
  strategic decisions and, 480–2
strategy-as-practice, 482
strategy research, 653
strength of weak ties, 777–8
stress, 449
structural artifacts, 584
structural-contingency theory (S/C theory), 815–16
  and change, 815
structural facilitation, 477
structural functionalism, 26–7
structural holes, 777, 822
structural inertia theory, 56, 59, 68, 69, 821
  effects of core changes, 74–5
  structure in, 68
structural linguistics, 309
structuralism, 266
structuralist language theory, 257
structuration, 549, 550, 820
structuration theory, 612, 737
structure(s)
  actors and, 380–1
  agency vs, 41–2
  boundary conditions, 592
  circular, 197
  definition, 578
  disruptive, 172
  dissipative, 167, 172, 189, 199
  of dominancy, 755
  of domination, 30, 612
  integrative, 833
  mechanistic, 578
  organic, 578
  process themes, 591
  quasi-natural, 197
  regulatory, disruption, 236
  segmentalist, 833
  see also organizational design
structure-conduct-performance see SCP paradigm

The Sage handbook of
organization studies